WHITE'S CONSPECTUS

OF

AMERICAN BIOGRAPHY

A Tabulated Record of American History and Biography

Second Edition

A revised and enlarged edition of
A CONSPECTUS OF AMERICAN BIOGRAPHY

Compiled by the Editorial Staff of
THE NATIONAL CYCLOPÆDIA OF
AMERICAN BIOGRAPHY

JAMES T. WHITE & COMPANY, *Publishers* — NEW YORK
1937
Republished 1972
Scholarly Press, Inc., 22929 Industrial Drive East
St. Clair Shores, Michigan 48080

Library of Congress Cataloging in Publication Data

Main entry under title:

White's conspectus of American biography.

"A revised and enlarged edition of A conspectus of American biography."

1. United States--Biography. I. National cyclopaedia of American biography.

E176.W588 1972 920'.073 75-145366

ISBN 0-403-01271-6

PREFACE

WHITE'S CONSPECTUS OF AMERICAN BIOGRAPHY is a tabulated record of Americans who have achieved distinction in every field of endeavor. It consists largely of lists of the leaders in government, both national and state, the church, education, the arts and sciences, and the professional fields, from Colonial times to the present day. The book is a revised and modernized edition of A CONSPECTUS OF AMERICAN BIOGRAPHY which was published in 1906 in combination with the indexes to THE NATIONAL CYCLOPÆDIA OF AMERICAN BIOGRAPHY. The first Conspectus so thoroughly proved its worth independently of the Cyclopædia that the publishers decided to issue an up-to-date edition, augmented by new compilations, to extend its usefulness to the research worker and student of American history and biography. While the references given are to the biographies in THE NATIONAL CYCLOPÆDIA OF AMERICAN BIOGRAPHY, the lists and compilations in this work are in themselves so comprehensive and informative that WHITE'S CONSPECTUS will be a valuable reference tool even in those libraries not equipped with the Cyclopædia.

This new Conspectus includes a collection of tabulated records which hitherto could be gleaned only from widely scattered sources. Beginning with the Colonial period, from the signing of the Mayflower Compact to the signing of the Declaration of Independence, WHITE'S CONSPECTUS OF AMERICAN BIOGRAPHY continues with its reference outline of American history down to the present day presenting, among other groups, lists of the

Presidents and Vice Presidents of the United States.
Cabinet Officers in each administration.
Justices of the Supreme Court of the United States and other federal courts, and the highest state courts.
Administrators of the more important government bureaus and agencies.
Ambassadors and ministers to foreign countries.
United States senators and congressmen.
Governors of all the states.
Presidents of 150 leading colleges and universities.
Presidents of national associations and societies identified with the learned professions, commerce, finance and industry.
American recipients of nationally and internationally known medals and awards.
Museum and observatory directors.
Bishops of the principal church denominations.
Commanders of both the army and navy in times of war.

Thus, WHITE'S CONSPECTUS OF AMERICAN BIOGRAPHY will answer such questions as:

Who were the delegates to the Second Colonial Congress?
Who were the Roman Catholic bishops of the Diocese of Louisville?
Who were the presidents of the American Bar Association?
What Americans received the John Fritz Medal?
Who were the directors of the United States Naval Observatory?

An interesting and valuable feature of this volume is the listing of American leaders in eighty-one professions. Each group, in conjunction with the biographies of the men listed, represents a history of the profession itself.

It will be observed that in the tabulation of the lists, a chronological rather than an alphabetical arrangement has been used in order that the contemporary celebrities of any given period may be ascertained and a consecutive history of any institution or movement readily traced. This arrangement makes it possible, for example, to discover with a minimum of effort answers to such questions as:

Who were America's famous physicians of the 18th Century?
Who was the American minister to France in 1843?
What authors and poets were the contemporaries of John Howard Payne?
Who were the United States senators from Connecticut when Oliver Wolcott was its governor?
Who succeeded Jonathan Edwards as president of Princeton University?
Who was secretary of the treasury in Rutherford B. Hayes' cabinet?

Other unique and valuable features of this Conspectus are a list of the treaties negotiated between the United States and foreign countries, together with the names of the American signers; a long list of distinguished Americans who appear as characters in fiction, poetry, or the drama; a directory of public statues of famous men, with the names of the sculptors; a collection of pseudonyms and sobriquets, and a calendar of birthdays and noteworthy events in American history.

WHITE'S CONSPECTUS OF AMERICAN BIOGRAPHY has been carefully prepared by the editorial staff of THE NATIONAL CYCLOPÆDIA OF AMERICAN BIOGRAPHY. Its compilations have been taken from original and authentic sources and their verification has involved consultations and extensive correspondence with officials of public institutions and organizations, government bureaus, state, county and municipal officials and private individuals. The publication, therefore, besides being an uniquely comprehensive work, because of the painstaking care expended upon it, possesses the additional merit of authority.

JAMES T. WHITE & COMPANY,
Publishers.

December 1, 1937.

CONTENTS

EXPLANATORY NOTES

1. The numeral before the name indicates the year in which the subject entered office, received an award, etc. The numerals after the name refer to the volume and page of *The National Cyclopædia of American Biography* where the biography will be found. The volumes covered are I to XXVI and Current Volumes "A" to "D," inclusive.

   Example:

   1893..Tucker, William J. 24: 242

   This indicates that Tucker began his term of office in 1893 and that his biography appears in Volume XXIV on page 242.

2. If no numerals follow the name, the biography has not been published in the Cyclopædia but is being compiled for inclusion in one of the forthcoming volumes. This procedure is in accordance with our editorial policy of preserving in the Cyclopædia records of all Americans who, by virtue of office or exceptional achievement, have gained national recognition.

3. A detailed index to *White's Conspectus of American Biography* begins on page 445.

White's
Conspectus of American Biography

Delegates to the First Colonial Congress, New York, May 1, 1690

Delancey, Etienne (N. Y.) 4:550
Gold, Nathan (Conn.) 12:311
Leisler, Jacob (N. Y.) 13:448
Pitkin, William (Conn.) 10:327
Sewall, Samuel (Mass.) 5:339
Stoughton, William (Mass.) 7:373
Wolley, John (Plymouth) ......

Delegates to the Second Colonial Congress, Albany, N. Y., June 19, 1754

Atkinson, Theodore (N. H.) ...11:486
Barnes, Abraham (Md.) 13:586
Chambers, John (N. Y.) 13:557
Chandler, John (Mass.) 13:557
De Lancey, James (N. Y.) 4:550
Franklin, Benjamin (Pa.) 1:328
Hopkins, Stephen (R. I.) 10: 13
Howard, Martin, Jr. (R. I.) ... 9:535
Johnson, Sir William (N. Y.) . 5:101
Murray, Joseph (N. Y.) 13:577
Norris, Isaac (Pa.) 5: 88
Partridge, Oliver (Mass.) 13:459
Penn, John (Pa.) 2:276
Peters, Richard (Pa.) 13:577
Pitkin, William (Conn.) 10:327
Sherburne, Henry, Jr. (N. H.)..13:567
Smith, William (N. Y.) 11: 20
Tasker, Benjamin (Md.) 9:188
Weare, Meshech (N. H.) 13:344
Welles, Samuel (Mass.) ....
Wibird, Richard (N. H.) 5:258
Williams, Elisha (Conn.) 1:165
Wolcott, Roger (Conn.) 10:326
Worthington, John (Mass.) 5:258

Delegates to the Stamp Act Congress, New York, Oct. 7, 1765

Bayard, William (N. Y.) 1:498
Borden, Joseph (N. J.) 13:428
Bowler, Metcalf (R. I.) 4:556
Bryan, George (Pa.) 2:280
Cruger, John (N. Y.) 1:495
Dickinson, John (Pa.) 2:281
Dyer, Eliphalet (Conn.) 11:172
Fisher, Hendrick (N. J.) 13:324
Gadsden, Christopher (S. C.) ... 1: 76
Johnson, William S. (Conn.) ... 6:342
Lispenard, Leonard (N. Y.) ... 5:534
Livingston, Philip (N. Y.) 3:306
Livingston, Robert R. (N. Y.).. 2:396
Lynch, Thomas (S. C.) 5:544
McKean, Thomas (Del.) 2:284
Morton, John (Pa.) 10:127
Murdock, William (Md.) 13:459
Ogden, Robert (N. J.) ....
Otis, James (Mass.) 1: 17
Partridge, Oliver (Mass.) 13:459
Ringgold, Thomas (Md.) ....
Rodney, Cæsar (Del.) 5:173
Rowland, David (Conn.) ....
Ruggles, Timothy (Mass.) 2: 57
Rutledge, John (S. C.) 1: 21
Tilghman, Edward (Md.) 13:421
Ward, Henry (R. I.) 11:517

Delegates to the First Continental Congress at Carpenters' Hall, Philadelphia, Pa., Sept. 5, 1774

Adams, John (Mass.) 2: 1
Adams, Samuel (Mass.) 1:104
Biddle, Edward (Pa.) 13:586
Bland, Richard (Va.) 7:133
Chase, Samuel (Md.) 1: 24
Crane, Stephen (N. J.) 5:386
Cushing, Thomas (Mass.) 7:113
Deane, Silas (Conn.) 12:357
De Hart, John (N. J.) 5:538
Duane, James (N. Y.) 2:489
Dyer, Eliphalet (Conn.) 11:172
Floyd, William (N. Y.) 4: 75
Folsom, Nathaniel (N. H.) 11: 39
Gadsden, Christopher (S. C.) ... 1: 76
Galloway, Joseph (Pa.) 1:383
Goldsborough, Robert (Md.) 4:180
Harrison, Benjamin (Va.) 10:153
Henry, Patrick (Va.) 1:337
Hopkins, Stephen (R. I.) 10: 13
Humphreys, Charles (Pa.) 3:359
Jay, John (N. Y.) 1: 20
Kinsey, James (N. J.) 12:257
Lee, Richard Henry (Va.) 3:159
Livingston, Philip (N. Y.) 3:306
Livingston, William (N. J.) ... 5:201
Low, Isaac (N. Y.) 1:496
Lynch, Thomas (S. C.) 5:544
McKean, Thomas (Newcastle, Kent and Sussex) 2:284
Middleton, Henry (S. C.) 5:367
Mifflin, Thomas (Pa.) 2:283
Morton, John (Pa.) 10:127
Paca, William (Md.) 9:291
Paine, Robert Treat (Mass.) ... 5:429
Pendleton, Edmund (Va.) 10:240
Randolph, Peyton (Va.) 2:114
Read, George (Newcastle, Kent and Sussex) 3:297
Rhoads, Samuel (Pa.) 13:582
Rodney, Cæsar (Newcastle, Kent and Sussex) 5:173
Rutledge, Edward (S. C.) 12:162
Rutledge, John (S. C.) 1: 21
Sherman, Roger (Conn.) 2:352
Smith, Richard (N. J.) 13:582
Sullivan, John (N. H.) 1: 56
Ward, Samuel (R. I.) 10: 14
Washington, George (Va.) 1: 1

Signers of the Declaration of Independence, Adopted by Congress July 4, 1776

Adams, John (Mass.) 2: 1
Adams, Samuel (Mass.) 1:104
Bartlett, Josiah (N. H.) 11:121
Braxton, Carter (Va.) 7:302
Carroll, Charles, of Carollton (Md.) 7:441
Chase, Samuel (Md.) 1: 24
Clark, Abraham (N. J.) 3:302
Clymer, George (Pa.) 3:272
Ellery, William (R. I.) 8: 59
Floyd, William (N. Y.) 4: 75
Franklin, Benjamin (Pa.) 1:328
Gerry, Elbridge (Mass.) 5:371
Gwinnett, Button (Ga.) 1:493
Hall, Lyman (Ga.) 2: 12
Hancock, John (Mass.) 1:103
Harrison, Benjamin (Va.) 10:153
Hart, John (N. J.) 5:538
Hewes, Joseph (N. C.) 10:189
Heyward, Thomas, Jr. (S. C.) .. 1:441
Hooper, William (N. C.) 5:457
Hopkins, Stephen (R. I.) 10: 13
Hopkinson, Francis (N. J.) ... 5:460
Huntington, Samuel (Conn.) ...10:329
Jefferson, Thomas (Va.) 3: 1
Lee, Francis Lightfoot (Va.) .. 5:252
Lee, Richard Henry (Va.) 3:159
Lewis, Francis (N. J.) 5:314
Livingston, Philip (N. Y.) 3:306
Lynch, Thomas, Jr. (S. C.) 10:135
McKean, Thomas (Del.) 2:284
Middleton, Arthur (S. C.) 5:197
Morris, Lewis (N. Y.) 3:351
Morris, Robert (Pa.) 2:411
Morton, John (Pa.) 10:127
Nelson, Thomas, Jr. (Va.) 7:253
Paca, William (Pa.) 9:291
Paine, Robert Treat (Mass.) ... 5:429
Penn, John (N. C.) 7: 58
Read, George (Del.) 3:297
Rodney, Cæsar (Del.) 5:173
Ross, George (Pa.) 10:119
Rush, Benjamin (Pa.) 3:333
Rutledge, Edward (S. C.) 12:162

References are to THE NATIONAL CYCLOPEDIA OF AMERICAN BIOGRAPHY

Sherman, Roger (Conn.) 2:352
Smith, James (Pa.) 2:343
Stockton, Richard (N. J.) 12:218
Stone, Thomas (Md.) 8:169
Taylor, George (Pa.) 5:431
Thornton, Matthew (N. H.) ...11:540
Walton, George (Ga.) 1:219
Whipple, William (N. H.) 4:437
Williams, William (Conn.) 10:392
Wilson, James (Md.) 1: 22
Witherspoon, John (N. J.) 5:466
Wolcott, Oliver (Conn.) 10:330
Wythe, George (Va.) 3:308

Committee That Prepared the Articles of Confederation

Adams, Samuel (Mass.) 1:104
Bartlett, Josiah (N. H.) 11:121
Dickinson, John, [Chairman] (Pa.) 2:281
Gwinnett, Button (Ga.) 1:493
Hewes, Joseph (N. C.) 10:139
Hopkins, Stephen (R. I.) 10: 13
Hopkinson, Francis (N. J.) 5:460
Livingston, Robert R. (N. Y.) .. 2:396
McKean, Thomas (Del.) 2:284
Nelson, Thomas, Jr. (Va.) 7:253
Rutledge, Edward (S. C.) 12:162
Sherman, Roger (Conn.) 2:352
Stone, Thomas (Md.) 8:169

Signers of the Articles of Confederation, Adopted by Congress Nov. 15, 1777

Adams, Andrew (Conn.) 11:184
Adams, Samuel (Mass.) 1:104
Adams, Thomas (Va.) 7:499
Banister, John (Va.) 7:504
Bartlett, Josiah (N. H.) 11:121
Carroll, Daniel (Md.) 2:389
Clingan, William (Pa.) 7:494
Collins, John (R. I.) 9:392
Dana, Francis (Mass.) 3:240
Dickinson, John (Del.) 2:281
Drayton, William Henry (S. C.) 7:419
Duane, James (N. Y.) 2:489
Duer, William (N. Y.) 7:508
Ellery, William (R. I.) 8: 59
Gerry, Elbridge (Mass.) 5:371
Hancock, John (Mass.) 1:103
Hanson, John (Md.) 10:312
Harnett, Cornelius (N. C.) 7:403
Harvie, John (Va.) 7:500
Heyward, Thomas, Jr. (S. C.) .. 1:441
Holten, Samuel (Mass.) 13:154
Hosmer, Titus (Conn.) 4:172
Huntington, Samuel (Conn.) ...10:329
Hutson, Richard (S. C.) 7:504
Langworthy, Edward (Ga.) 7:500
Laurens, Henry (S. C.) 3:426
Lee, Francis Lightfoot (Va.)... 5:252
Lee, Richard Henry (Va.) 3:159
Lewis, Francis (N. Y.) 5:314
Lovell, James (Mass.) 12:428
McKean, Thomas (Del.) 2:284
Marchant, Henry (R. I.) 9:366
Mathews, John (S. C.) 12:160
Morris, Gouverneur (N. Y.) 2:526
Morris, Robert (Pa.) 2:411
Penn, John (N. C.) 7: 58
Reed, Joseph (Pa.) 1: 74
Roberdeau, Daniel (Pa.) 2: 14
Scudder, Nathaniel (N. J.) 4:152
Sherman, Roger (Conn.) 2:352
Smith, Jonathan Bayard (Pa.).. 4:346
Telfair, Edward (Ga.) 1:219
Van Dyke, Nicholas (Del.) 4:398
Walton, George (Ga.) 1:219
Wentworth, John (N. H.) 4:350
Williams, John (N. C.) 1:181
Witherspoon, John (N. J.) 5:466
Wolcott, Oliver (Conn.) 10:330

Delegates to the Federal Convention That Prepared the National Constitution, Philadelphia, Pa., May 24, 1787

Baldwin, Abraham (Ga.) 9:178
Bassett, Richard (Del.) 11:530
Bedford, Gunning, Jr. (Del.) ... 2:391
Blair, John (Va.) 1: 23
Blount, William (N. C.) 7:206
Brearley, David (N. J.) 2: 38
Broom, Jacob (Del.) 3: 85
Butler, Pierce (S. C.) 2:162
Carroll, Daniel (Md.) 2:389
Clark, Abraham (N. J.) 3:302
Clymer, George (Pa.) 3:272
Dana, Francis (Mass.) 3:240
Davie, William R. (N. C.) 1: 77
Dayton, Jonathan (N. J.) 1:306
Dickinson, John (Del.) 2:281
Ellsworth, Oliver (Conn.) 1: 22
Few, William (Ga.) 2:346
Fitzsimmons, Thomas (Pa.) ... 6:533
Franklin, Benjamin (Pa.) 1:328
Gerry, Elbridge (Mass.) 5:371
Gorham, Nathaniel (Mass.) 2:525
Hamilton, Alexander (N. Y.) .. 1: 9
Houston, William (Ga.) 3:223
Houston, William C. (N. J.) ... 3:261
Ingersoll, Jared (Pa.) 2:439
Jenifer, Daniel (Md.) 2:362
Johnson, William S. (Conn.) .. 6:342
King, Rufus (Mass.) 6:301
Langdon, John (N. H.) 11:123
Lansing, John, Jr. (N. Y.) 4:254
Livingston, William (N. J.) 5:201
McHenry, James (Md.) 1: 13
Madison, James, Jr. (Va.) 5:369
Martin, Alexander (N. C.) 4:420
Martin, Luther (Md.) 3:431
Mason, George (Va.) 3:337
Mercer, John Francis (Md.) ... 9:295
Mifflin, Thomas (Pa.) 2:283
Morris, Gouverneur (Pa.) 2:526
Morris, Robert (Pa.) 2:411
Neilson, John (N. J.) 3:476
Paterson, William (N. J.) 1: 24
Pendleton, Nathaniel (Ga.) 3:273
Pickering, John (N. H.) 3:224
Pierce, William (Ga.) 7: 96
Pinckney, Charles (S. C.) 12:161
Pinckney, Charles C. (S. C.) ... 2:302
Randolph, Edmund (Va.) 1: 12
Read, George (Del.) 3:297
Rutledge, John (S. C.) 1: 21
Sherman, Roger (Conn.) 2:352
Spaight, Richard Dobbs (N. C.) 4:420
Strong, Caleb (Mass.) 1:110
Walton, George (Ga.) 1:219
Washington, George (Va.) 1: 1
Williamson, Hugh (N. C.) 2:492
Wilson, James (Pa.) 1: 22
Wythe, George (Va.) 3:308
Yates, Robert (N. Y.) 5:260

Presidents of the Continental Congress

ELECTED

Sept. 5, 1774 Randolph, Peyton... 2:114
Oct. 2, 1774 Middleton, Henry... 5:367
May 10, 1775 Randolph, Peyton... 2:114
May 24, 1775 Hancock, John.... 1:103
Nov. 1, 1777 Laurens, Henry... 3:426
Dec. 10, 1778 Jay, John 1: 20
Sept. 28, 1779 Huntington, Samuel 10:329
July 10, 1781 McKean, Thomas.. 2:284
Nov. 5, 1781 Hanson, John.....10:312
Nov. 4, 1782 Boudinot, Elias.... 2:296
Nov. 3, 1783 Mifflin, Thomas.... 2:283
Nov. 30, 1784 Lee, Richard Henry 3:159
June 6, 1786 Gorham, Nathaniel 2:525
Feb. 2, 1787 St. Clair, Arthur.. 1: 94
Jan. 22, 1788 Griffin, Cyrus 5:228

Presidents of the United States

	President	Born	Residence	Profession	Religion	Politics	Year Inaugurated	Bills Vetoed	Died	Where Buried	Biography
1	Washington, George	1732	Va.	Soldier	Episcopalian	Fed.	1789	2	1799	Mt. Vernon, Va.	1: 1
2	Adams, John	1735	Mass.	Lawyer	Unitarian	Fed.	1797	0	1826	Quincy, Mass.	2: 1
3	Jefferson, Thomas	1743	Va.	Lawyer	Liberal	Rep.	1801	0	1826	Charlottesville, Va.	3: 1
4	Madison, James	1751	Va.	Lawyer	Episcopalian	Rep.	1809	6	1836	Montpelier, Va.	5:369
5	Monroe, James	1758	Va.	Politician	Episcopalian	Rep.	1817	1	1831	Richmond, Va.	6: 81
6	Adams, John Quincy	1767	Mass.	Lawyer	Unitarian	Rep.	1825	0	1848	Quincy, Mass.	5: 73
7	Jackson, Andrew	1767	Tenn.	Lawyer	Presbyterian	Dem.	1829	12	1845	Nashville, Tenn.	5:289
8	Van Buren, Martin	1782	N. Y.	Lawyer	Dutch Ref'm'd	Dem.	1837	0	1862	Kinderhook, N. Y.	6:433
9	Harrison, William H.	1773	Ohio	Soldier	Episcopalian	Whig	1841	0	1841	North Bend, Ind.	3: 33
10	Tyler, John	1790	Va.	Lawyer	Episcopalian	Dem.	1841	9	1862	Richmond, Va.	6: 1
11	Polk, James K.	1795	Tenn.	Lawyer	Presbyterian	Dem.	1845	3	1849	Nashville, Tenn.	6:265
12	Taylor, Zachary	1784	La.	Soldier	Episcopalian	Whig	1849	0	1850	Louisville, Ky.	4:367
13	Fillmore, Millard	1800	N. Y.	Lawyer	Episcopalian	Whig	1850	0	1874	Buffalo, N. Y.	6:177
14	Pierce, Franklin	1804	N. H.	Lawyer	Episcopalian	Dem.	1853	9	1869	Concord, N. H.	4:145
15	Buchanan, James	1791	Pa.	Lawyer	Presbyterian	Dem.	1857	7	1868	Lancaster, Pa.	5: 1
16	Lincoln, Abraham	1809	Ill.	Lawyer	Liberal	Rep.	1861	3	1865	Springfield, Ill.	2: 65
17	Johnson, Andrew	1808	Tenn.	Politician	Liberal	Rep.	1865	21	1875	Greenville, Tenn.	2:454
18	Grant, Ulysses S.	1822	D. C.	Soldier	Methodist	Rep.	1869	43	1885	New York, N. Y.	4: 1
19	Hayes, Rutherford B.	1822	Ohio	Lawyer	Methodist	Rep.	1877	12	1893	Fremont, Ohio	3:191
20	Garfield, James A.	1831	Ohio	Lawyer	Disciples	Rep.	1881	0	1881	Cleveland, Ohio	4:238
21	Arthur, Chester A.	1830	N. Y.	Lawyer	Episcopalian	Rep.	1881	4	1886	Albany, N. Y.	4:247
22	Cleveland, Grover	1837	N. Y.	Lawyer	Presbyterian	Dem.	1885	301	1908	Princeton, N. J.	2:400
23	Harrison, Benjamin	1833	Ind.	Lawyer	Presbyterian	Rep.	1889	19	1901	Indianapolis, Ind.	1:133
24	Cleveland, Grover	1837	N. Y.	Lawyer	Presbyterian	Dem.	1893	44	1908	Princeton, N. J.	2:400
25	McKinley, William	1843	Ohio	Lawyer	Methodist	Rep.	1897	6	1901	Canton, Ohio	11: 1
26	Roosevelt, Theodore	1858	N. Y.	Politician	Dutch Ref'm'd	Rep.	1901	40	1919	Oyster Bay, N. Y.	14: 1
27	Taft, William H.	1857	Ohio	Jurist	Unitarian	Rep.	1909	29	1930	Arlington, Va.	23: 1
28	Wilson, Woodrow	1856	N. J.	Educator	Presbyterian	Dem.	1913	32	1924	Washington, D. C.	19: 1
29	Harding, Warren G.	1865	Ohio	Journalist	Presbyterian	Rep.	1921	2	1923	Marion, Ohio	19:268
30	Coolidge, Calvin	1872	Mass.	Lawyer	Congrega'list	Rep.	1923	37	1933	Plymouth, Vt.	24: 1
31	Hoover, Herbert C.	1874	Calif.	Engineer	Soc. of Friends	Rep.	1929	21	—	—	C: 1
32	Roosevelt, Franklin D.	1882	N. Y.	Lawyer	Episcopalian	Dem.	1933	—	—	—	D: 1

References are to THE NATIONAL CYCLOPEDIA OF AMERICAN BIOGRAPHY

Vice Presidents of the United States

	Vice President	Born	Paternal Ancestry	Residence	Qualified	Politics	Place of Death	Year	Age	Biography
1	Adams, John	1735	English	Mass.	1789	Fed.	Quincy, Mass.	1826	90	2: 1
2	Jefferson, Thomas	1743	Welsh	Va.	1797	Rep.	Monticello, Va.	1826	83	3: 1
3	Burr, Aaron	1756	English	N. Y.	1801	Rep.	Staten Island, N. Y.	1836	80	3: 5
4	Clinton, George	1739	English	N. Y.	1805	Rep.	Washington, D. C.	1812	73	3: 41
5	Gerry, Elbridge	1744	English	Mass.	1813	Rep.	Washington, D. C.	1814	70	5:371
6	Tompkins, Daniel D.	1774	English	N. Y.	1817	Rep.	Staten Island, N. Y.	1825	51	6: 83
7	Calhoun, John C.	1782	Scotch-Irish	S. C.	1825	Rep.	Washington, D. C.	1850	68	6: 83
8	Van Buren, Martin	1782	Dutch	N. Y.	1833	Dem.	Kinderhook, N. Y.	1862	79	6:433
9	Johnson, Richard M.	1780	English	Ky.	1837	Dem.	Frankfort, Ky.	1850	70	6:434
10	Tyler, John	1790	English	Va.	1841	Dem.	Richmond, Va.	1862	72	6: 1
11	Dallas, George M.	1792	English	Pa.	1845	Dem.	Philadelphia, Pa.	1864	72	6:268
12	Fillmore, Millard	1800	English	N. Y.	1849	Whig	Buffalo, N. Y.	1874	74	6:177
13	King, William R.	1786	English	Ala.	1853	Dem.	Dallas County, Ala.	1853	67	4:147
14	Breckinridge, John C.	1821	Scotch	Ky.	1857	Dem.	Lexington, Ky.	1875	54	5: 3
15	Hamlin, Hannibal	1809	English	Maine	1861	Rep.	Bangor, Maine	1891	81	2: 76
16	Johnson, Andrew	1808	English	Tenn.	1865	Rep.	Carter County, Tenn.	1875	66	2:454
17	Colfax, Schuyler	1823	English	Ind.	1869	Rep.	Mankato, Minn.	1885	62	4: 12
18	Wilson, Henry	1812	English	Mass.	1873	Rep.	Washington, D. C.	1875	63	4: 13
19	Wheeler, William A.	1819	English	N. Y.	1877	Rep.	Malone, N. Y.	1887	67	3:196
20	Arthur, Chester A.	1830	Scotch-Irish	N. Y.	1881	Rep.	New York, N. Y.	1886	56	4:247
21	Hendricks, Thomas A.	1819	Scotch-Irish	Ind.	1885	Dem.	Indianapolis, Ind.	1885	66	2:403
22	Morton, Levi P.	1824	Scotch	N. Y.	1889	Rep.	Rhinecliff, N. Y.	1920	96	1:136
23	Stevenson, Adlai E.	1835	Scotch-Irish	Ill.	1893	Dem.	Chicago, Ill.	1914	78	2:487
24	Hobart, Garret A.	1844	English	N. J.	1897	Rep.	Paterson, N. J.	1899	55	11: 10
25	Roosevelt, Theodore	1858	Dutch	N. Y.	1901	Rep.	Oyster Bay, N. Y.	1919	61	14: 1
26	Fairbanks, Charles W.	1852	English	Ind.	1905	Rep.	Indianapolis, Ind.	1918	66	14: 10
27	Sherman, James S.	1855	English	N. Y.	1909	Rep.	Utica, N. Y.	1912	57	14:406
28	Marshall, Thomas R.	1854	English	Ind.	1913	Dem.	Washington, D. C.	1925	71	19:137
29	Coolidge, Calvin	1872	English	Mass.	1921	Rep.	Northampton, Mass.	1933	60	24: 1
30	Dawes, Charles G.	1865	English	Ill.	1925	Rep.	——	——	—	A:508
31	Curtis, Charles	1860	English	Kans.	1929	Rep.	Washington, D. C.	1936	76	C: 7
32	Garner, John N.	1868	English	Tex.	1933	Dem.	——	——	—	D: 9

References are to THE NATIONAL CYCLOPEDIA OF AMERICAN BIOGRAPHY

Members of the Cabinet

SECRETARIES OF STATE

President	Secretary of State	Residence	Date of Appointment	Biography
Washington, George	Jefferson, Thomas	Virginia	1789	3: 1
"	Randolph, Edmund	"	1794	1: 12
"	Pickering, Timothy	Massachusetts	1795	1: 12
Adams, John	"	"	1797	1: 12
"	Marshall, John	Virginia	1800	1: 25
Jefferson, Thomas	Madison, James	"	1801	5:369
Madison, James	Smith, Robert	Maryland	1809	3: 11
"	Monroe, James	Virginia	1811	6: 81
Monroe, James	Adams, John Quincy	Massachusetts	1817	5: 73
Adams, John Quincy	Clay, Henry	Kentucky	1825	5: 77
Jackson, Andrew	Van Buren, Martin	New York	1829	6:433
"	Livingston, Edward	Louisiana	1831	5:293
"	McLane, Louis	Delaware	1833	5:293
"	Forsyth, John	Georgia	1834	6:435
Van Buren, Martin	"	"	1837	6:435
Harrison, William H.	Webster, Daniel	Massachusetts	1841	3: 36
Tyler, John	"	"	1841	3: 36
"	Legaré, Hugh S.	South Carolina	1843	6: 5
"	Upshur, Abel P.	Virginia	1843	6: 8
"	Calhoun, John C.	South Carolina	1844	6: 83
Polk, James K.	Buchanan, James	Pennsylvania	1845	5: 1
Taylor, Zachary	Clayton, John M.	Delaware	1849	6:179
Fillmore, Millard	Webster, Daniel	Massachusetts	1850	3: 36
"	Everett, Edward	"	1852	6:179
Pierce, Franklin	Marcy, William L.	New York	1853	6:269
Buchanan, James	Cass, Lewis	Michigan	1857	5: 3
"	Black, Jeremiah S.	Pennsylvania	1860	5: 5
Lincoln, Abraham	Seward, William H.	New York	1861	2: 77
Johnson, Andrew	"	"	1865	2: 77
Grant, Ulysses S.	Washburne, Elihu B.	Illinois	1869	4: 14
"	Fish, Hamilton	New York	1869	4: 15
Hayes, Rutherford B.	Evarts, William M.	"	1877	3:197
Garfield, James A.	Blaine, James G.	Maine	1881	1:137
Arthur, Chester A.	Frelinghuysen, Frederick T.	New Jersey	1881	4:250
Cleveland, Grover	Bayard, Thomas F.	Delaware	1885	2:404
Harrison, Benjamin	Blaine, James G.	Maine	1889	1:137
"	Foster, John W.	Indiana	1892	3:268
Cleveland, Grover	Gresham, Walter Q.	Illinois	1893	24:330
"	Olney, Richard	Massachusetts	1895	7:143
McKinley, William	Sherman, John	Ohio	1897	3:198
"	Day, William R.	"	1898	11: 11
"	Hay, John	"	1898	11: 12
Roosevelt, Theodore	"	"	1901	11: 12
"	Root, Elihu	New York	1905	26: 1
"	Bacon, Robert	"	1909	14: 16
Taft, William H.	Knox, Philander C.	Pennsylvania	1909	24: 7
Wilson, Woodrow	Bryan, William J.	Nebraska	1913	19:453
"	Lansing, Robert	Washington, D. C.	1915	20: 1
"	Colby, Bainbridge	New York	1920	A: 32
Harding, Warren G.	Hughes, Charles E.	"	1921	A: 6
Coolidge, Calvin	"	"	1923	A: 6
"	Kellogg, Frank B.	Minnesota	1925	A: 8
Hoover, Herbert C.	Stimson, Henry L.	New York	1929	C: 8
Roosevelt, Franklin D.	Hull, Cordell	Tennessee	1933	D: 10

References are to THE NATIONAL CYCLOPEDIA OF AMERICAN BIOGRAPHY

SECRETARIES OF THE TREASURY

President	Secretary of the Treasury	Residence	Date of Appointment	Biography
Washington, George	Hamilton, Alexander	New York	1789	1: 9
"	Wolcott, Oliver	Connecticut	1795	10:333
Adams, John	"	"	1797	10:333
"	Dexter, Samuel	Massachusetts	1801	2: 6
Jefferson, Thomas	"	"	1801	2: 6
"	Gallatin, Albert	Pennsylvania	1801	3: 9
Madison, James	"	"	1809	3: 9
"	Campbell, George W.	Tennessee	1814	5:372
"	Dallas, Alexander J.	Pennsylvania	1814	5:372
"	Crawford, William H.	Georgia	1816	5: 82
Monroe, James	"	"	1817	5: 82
Adams, John Quincy	Rush, Richard	Pennsylvania	1825	5: 80
Jackson, Andrew	Ingham, Samuel D.	"	1829	5:294
"	McLane, Louis	Delaware	1831	5:293
"	Duane, William J.	Pennsylvania	1833	5:294
"	Taney, Roger B.	Maryland	1833	1: 27
"	Woodbury, Levi	New Hampshire	1834	2:471
Van Buren, Martin	"	"	1837	2:471
Harrison, William H.	Ewing, Thomas	Ohio	1841	25: 14
Tyler, John	"	"	1841	25: 14
"	Forward, Walter	Pennsylvania	1841	6: 5
"	Spencer, John C.	New York	1843	6: 6
"	Bibb, George M.	Kentucky	1844	6: 6
Polk, James K.	Walker, Robert J.	Mississippi	1845	6:269
Taylor, Zachary	Meredith, William M.	Pennsylvania	1849	4:370
Fillmore, Millard	Corwin, Thomas	Ohio	1850	6:180
Pierce, Franklin	Guthrie, James	Kentucky	1853	4:147
Buchanan, James	Cobb, Howell	Georgia	1857	1:226
"	Thomas, Philip F.	Maryland	1860	5: 6
"	Dix, John A.	New York	1861	5: 6
Lincoln, Abraham	Chase, Salmon P.	Ohio	1861	1: 28
"	Fessenden, William P.	Maine	1864	2: 90
"	McCulloch, Hugh	Indiana	1865	4:251
Johnson, Andrew	"	"	1865	4:251
Grant, Ulysses S.	Boutwell, George S.	Massachusetts	1869	4:382
"	Richardson, William A.	"	1873	4: 17
"	Bristow, Benjamin H.	Kentucky	1874	4: 23
"	Morrill, Lot M.	Maine	1876	6:313
Hayes, Rutherford B.	Sherman, John	Ohio	1877	3:198
Garfield, James A.	Windom, William	Minnesota	1881	1:148
Arthur, Chester A.	Folger, Charles J.	New York	1881	4:250
"	Gresham, Walter Q.	Indiana	1884	24:330
"	McCulloch, Hugh	"	1884	4:251
Cleveland, Grover	Manning, Daniel	New York	1885	2:405
"	Fairchild, Charles S.	"	1887	2:406
Harrison, Benjamin	Windom, William	Minnesota	1889	1:148
"	Foster, Charles	Ohio	1891	1:139
Cleveland, Grover	Carlisle, John G.	Kentucky	1893	1:461
McKinley, William	Gage, Lyman J.	Illinois	1897	26:444
Roosevelt, Theodore	"	"	1901	26:444
"	Shaw, Leslie M.	Iowa	1902	23:118
"	Cortelyou, George B.	New York	1907	14: 18
Taft, William H.	MacVeagh, Franklin	Illinois	1909	14:409
Wilson, Woodrow	McAdoo, William G.	New York	1913	A: 34
"	Glass, Carter	Virginia	1918	A: 36
"	Houston, David F.	New York	1920	A: 38
Harding, Warren G.	Mellon, Andrew W.	Pennsylvania	1921	A: 16
Coolidge, Calvin	"	"	1923	A: 16
Hoover, Herbert C.	"	"	1929	A: 16
"	Mills, Ogden L.	New York	1932	D: 77
Roosevelt, Franklin D.	Woodin, William H.	"	1933	25: 4
"	Morgenthau, Henry, Jr.	"	1933	D: 11

References are to The National Cyclopedia of American Biography

SECRETARIES OF WAR

President	Secretary of War	Residence	Date of Appointment	Biography
Washington, George	Knox, Henry	Massachusetts	1789	1: 14
"	Pickering, Timothy	"	1795	1: 12
"	McHenry, James	Maryland	1796	1: 13
Adams, John	"	"	1797	1: 13
"	Dexter, Samuel	Massachusetts	1800	2: 6
"	Griswold, Roger	Connecticut	1801	10:331
Jefferson, Thomas	Dearborn, Henry	Massachusetts	1801	1: 93
Madison, James	Eustis, William	"	1809	5:372
"	Armstrong, John, 2d	New York	1813	1: 48
"	Monroe, James	Virginia	1814	6: 81
"	Crawford, William Harris	Georgia	1815	5: 82
Monroe, James	Calhoun, John C.	South Carolina	1817	6: 83
Adams, John Quincy	Barbour, James	Virginia	1825	5: 82
"	Porter, Peter B.	New York	1828	5: 81
Jackson, Andrew	Eaton, John H.	Tennessee	1829	5:295
"	Cass, Lewis	Ohio	1831	5: 3
"	Butler, Benjamin F.	New York	1836	5:297
Van Buren, Martin	Poinsett, Joel R.	South Carolina	1837	6:435
Harrison, William H.	Bell, John	Tennessee	1841	3: 39
Tyler, John	"	"	1841	3: 39
"	Spencer, John C.	New York	1841	6: 6
"	Porter, James M.	Pennsylvania	1843	6: 9
"	Wilkins, William	"	1844	6: 9
Polk, James K.	Marcy, William L.	New York	1845	6:269
Taylor, Zachary	Crawford, George W.	Georgia	1849	4:370
Fillmore, Millard	Conrad, Charles M.	Louisiana	1850	6:181
Pierce, Franklin	Davis, Jefferson	Mississippi	1853	4:148
Buchanan, James	Floyd, John B.	Virginia	1857	5: 7
"	Holt, Joseph	Kentucky	1861	1:354
Lincoln, Abraham	Cameron, Simon	Pennsylvania	1861	2: 79
"	Stanton, Edwin McM.	Ohio	1862	2: 83
Johnson, Andrew	"	"	1865	2: 83
"	Grant, Ulysses S. (*ad. in.*)	Illinois	1867	4: 1
"	Thomas, Lorenzo (*ad. in.*)	Delaware	1868	11:352
"	Schofield, John M.	New York	1868	4:259
Grant, Ulysses S.	Rawlins, John A.	Illinois	1869	4:218
"	Belknap, William W.	Iowa	1869	4: 23
"	Taft, Alphonso	Ohio	1876	4: 24
"	Cameron, James D.	Pennsylvania	1876	4: 25
Hayes, Rutherford B.	McCrary, George W.	Iowa	1877	3:201
"	Ramsey, Alexander	Minnesota	1879	10: 62
Garfield, James A.	Lincoln, Robert T.	Illinois	1881	21: 59
Arthur, Chester A.	"	"	1881	21: 59
Cleveland, Grover	Endicott, William C.	Massachusetts	1885	2:406
Harrison, Benjamin	Proctor, Redfield	Vermont	1889	1:141
"	Elkins, Stephen B.	West Virginia	1891	1:142
Cleveland, Grover	Lamont, Daniel S.	New York	1893	3: 58
McKinley, William	Alger, Russell A.	Michigan	1897	5:276
"	Root, Elihu	New York	1899	26: 1
Roosevelt, Theodore	"	"	1901	26: 1
"	Taft, William H.	Ohio	1904	23: 1
"	Wright, Luke E.	Tennessee	1908	14: 20
Taft, William H.	Dickinson, Jacob M.	"	1909	14:410
"	Stimson, Henry L.	New York	1911	C: 8
Wilson, Woodrow	Garrison, Lindley M.	New Jersey	1913	A: 39
"	Baker, Newton D.	Ohio	1916	A: 40
Harding, Warren G.	Weeks, John W.	Massachusetts	1921	20: 4
Coolidge, Calvin	"	"	1923	20: 4
"	Davis, Dwight F.	Missouri	1925	A: 10
Hoover, Herbert C.	Good, James W.	Iowa	1929	21: 94
"	Hurley, Patrick J.	Oklahoma	1929	C: 9
Roosevelt, Franklin D.	Dern, George H.	Utah	1933	26: 9

ATTORNEYS-GENERAL

President	Attorney-General	Residence	Date of Appointment	Biography
Washington, George	Randolph, Edmund	Virginia	1789	1: 12
“	Bradford, William	Pennsylvania	1794	1: 14
“	Lee, Charles	Virginia	1795	1: 14
Adams, John	“	“	1797	1: 14
Jefferson, Thomas	Lincoln, Levi	“	1801	1:111
“	Smith, Robert	Maryland	1805	3: 11
“	Breckenridge, John	Kentucky	1805	3: 9
“	Rodney, Cæsar A.	Delaware	1807	3: 11
Madison, James	“	“	1809	3: 11
“	Pinkney, William	Maryland	1811	5:373
“	Rush, Richard	Pennsylvania	1814	5: 80
Monroe, James	“	“	1817	5: 80
“	Wirt, William	Virginia	1817	6: 86
Adams, John Quincy	“	“	1825	6: 86
Jackson, Andrew	Berrien, John M.	Georgia	1829	5:298
“	Taney, Roger B.	Maryland	1831	1: 27
“	Butler, Benjamin F.	New York	1833	5:297
Van Buren, Martin	“	“	1837	5:297
“	Grundy, Felix	Tennessee	1838	6:436
“	Gilpin, Henry D.	Pennsylvania	1840	6:437
Harrison, William H.	Crittenden, John J.	Kentucky	1841	13: 6
Tyler, John	“	“	1841	13: 6
“	Legaré, Hugh S.	South Carolina	1841	6: 5
“	Nelson, John	Maryland	1843	6: 8
Polk, James K.	Mason, John Y.	Virginia	1845	6: 7
“	Clifford, Nathan	Maine	1846	2:473
“	Toucey, Isaac	Connecticut	1848	5: 7
Taylor, Zachary	Johnson, Reverdy	Maryland	1849	4:371
Fillmore, Millard	Crittenden, John J.	Kentucky	1850	13: 6
Pierce, Franklin	Cushing, Caleb	Massachusetts	1853	4:151
Buchanan, James	Black, Jeremiah S.	Pennsylvania	1857	5: 5
“	Stanton, Edwin M.	Ohio	1860	2: 83
Lincoln, Abraham	Bates, Edward	Missouri	1861	2: 89
“	Coffey, Titian J. (*ad. in.*)	Pennsylvania	1863	5:135
“	Speed, James	Kentucky	1864	2: 89
Johnson, Andrew	“	“	1865	2: 89
“	Stanbery, Henry	Ohio	1866	2:458
“	Evarts, William M.	New York	1868	3:197
Grant, Ulysses S.	Hoar, Ebenezer R.	Massachusetts	1869	4: 20
“	Akerman, Amos T.	Georgia	1870	9:209
“	Williams, George H.	Oregon	1871	4: 21
“	Pierrepont, Edwards	New York	1875	4: 21
“	Taft, Alphonso	Ohio	1876	4: 24
Hayes, Rutherford B.	Devens, Charles	Massachusetts	1877	3:203
Garfield, James A.	MacVeagh, Wayne	Pennsylvania	1881	4:246
Arthur, Chester A.	Brewster, Benjamin H.	“	1881	4:253
Cleveland, Grover	Garland, Augustus H.	Arkansas	1885	2:409
Harrison, Benjamin	Miller, William H. H.	Indiana	1889	18:189
Cleveland, Grover	Olney, Richard	Massachusetts	1893	7:143
“	Harmon, Judson	Ohio	1895	13:279
McKinley, William	McKenna, Joseph	California	1897	11: 18
“	Griggs, John W.	New Jersey	1898	11: 19
“	Knox, Philander C.	Pennsylvania	1901	24: 7
Roosevelt, Theodore	“	“	1901	24: 7
“	Moody, William H.	Massachusetts	1904	14: 21
“	Bonaparte, Charles J.	Maryland	1906	14: 22
Taft, William H.	Wickersham, George W.	New York	1909	C: 16
Wilson, Woodrow	McReynolds, James C.	“	1913	A: 42
“	Gregory, Thomas W.	Texas	1914	A: 43
“	Palmer, A. Mitchell	Pennsylvania	1919	A: 44
Harding, Warren G.	Daugherty, Harry M.	Ohio	1921	A: 27
Coolidge, Calvin	“	“	1923	A: 27
“	Stone, Harlan F.	New York	1924	A: 11
“	Sargent, John G.	Vermont	1925	A: 12
Hoover, Herbert C.	Mitchell, William D.	Minnesota	1929	C: 10
Roosevelt, Franklin D.	Cummings, Homer S.	Connecticut	1933	D: 13

POSTMASTERS-GENERAL*

President	Postmaster-General	Residence	Date of Appointment	Biography
Washington, George	Osgood, Samuel	Massachusetts	1789	1: 18
"	Pickering, Timothy	"	1791	1: 12
"	Habersham, Joseph	Georgia	1795	1: 18
Adams, John	"	"	1797	1: 18
Jefferson, Thomas	"	"	1801	1: 18
"	Granger, Gideon	Connecticut	1801	5:391
Madison, James	"	"	1809	5:391
"	Meigs, Return J.	Ohio	1814	3:137
Monroe, James	"	"	1817	3:137
"	McLean, John	"	1823	2:469
Adams, John Quincy	"	"	1825	2:469
Jackson, Andrew	Barry, William T.	Kentucky	1829	5:296
"	Kendall, Amos	"	1835	5:296
Van Buren, Martin	"	"	1837	5:296
"	Niles, John M.	Connecticut	1840	6:436
Harrison, William H.	Granger, Francis	New York	1841	6: 7
Tyler, John	"	"	1841	6: 7
"	Wickliffe, Charles A.	Kentucky	1841	6: 8
Polk, James K.	Johnson, Cave	Tennessee	1845	6:270
Taylor, Zachary	Collamer, Jacob	Vermont	1849	4:371
Fillmore, Millard	Hall, Nathan K.	New York	1850	6:183
"	Hubbard, Samuel D.	Connecticut	1852	6:183
Pierce, Franklin	Campbell, James	Pennsylvania	1853	4:152
Buchanan, James	Brown, Aaron V.	Tennessee	1857	5: 8
"	Holt, Joseph	Kentucky	1859	1:354
"	King, Horatio	Maine	1861	5: 8
Lincoln, Abraham	Blair, Montgomery	Maryland	1861	2: 88
"	Dennison, William	Ohio	1864	3:141
Johnson, Andrew	"	"	1865	3:141
"	Randall, Alexander W.	Wisconsin	1866	2:458
Grant, Ulysses S.	Creswell, John A. J.	Maryland	1869	4: 19
"	Marshall, James W.	Virginia	1874	4: 19
"	Jewell, Marshall	Connecticut	1874	4: 20
"	Tyner, James N.	Indiana	1876	4: 20
Hayes, Rutherford B.	Key, David McK.	Tennessee	1877	3:203
"	Maynard, Horace	"	1880	9:286
Garfield, James A.	James, Thomas L.	New York	1881	4:245
Arthur, Chester A.	Howe, Timothy O.	Wisconsin	1881	4:252
"	Gresham, Walter Q.	Indiana	1883	24:330
"	Hatton, Frank	Iowa	1884	4:252
Cleveland, Grover	Vilas, William F.	Wisconsin	1885	2:409
"	Dickinson, Don M.	Michigan	1888	2:410
Harrison, Benjamin	Wanamaker, John	Pennsylvania	1889	1:143
Cleveland, Grover	Bissell, Wilson S.	New York	1893	13:117
"	Wilson, William L.	West Virginia	1895	8:162
McKinley, William	Gary, James A.	Maryland	1897	11: 16
"	Smith, Charles E.	Pennsylvania	1898	11: 17
Roosevelt, Theodore	"	"	1901	11: 17
"	Payne, Henry C.	Wisconsin	1902	14: 23
"	Wynne, Robert J.	Washington, D. C.	1904	14: 24
"	Cortelyou, George B.	New York	1905	14: 18
"	Meyer, George von L.	Massachusetts	1907	14:413
Taft, William H.	Hitchcock, Frank H.	Washington, D. C.	1909	14:412
Wilson, Woodrow	Burleson, Albert S.	Texas	1913	A: 45
Harding, Warren G.	Hays, Will H.	Indiana	1921	A:354
"	Work, Hubert	Colorado	1922	A: 14
"	New, Harry S.	Indiana	1923	A: 13
Coolidge, Calvin	"	"	1923	A: 13
Hoover, Herbert C.	Brown, Walter F.	Ohio	1929	C: 10
Roosevelt, Franklin D.	Farley, James A.	New York	1933	D: 14

* The Postmaster-General was not considered a Cabinet Officer until 1829.

SECRETARIES OF THE NAVY

President	Secretary of the Navy	Residence	Date of Appointment	Biography
Adams, John	Stoddert, Benjamin	Maryland	1798	2: 5
Jefferson, Thomas	“	“	1801	2: 5
“	Smith, Robert	“	1801	3: 11
“	Crowninshield, Jacob	Massachusetts	1805	3: 7
Madison, James	Hamilton, Paul	South Carolina	1809	5:373
“	Jones, William	Pennsylvania	1813	5:373
“	Crowninshield, Benjamin W.	Massachusetts	1814	5:373
Monroe, James	“	“	1817	5:373
“	Thompson, Smith	New York	1818	6: 86
“	Southard, Samuel L.	New Jersey	1823	6: 85
Adams, John Quincy	“	“	1825	6: 85
Jackson, Andrew	Branch, John	North Carolina	1829	5:295
“	Woodbury, Levi	New Hampshire	1831	2:471
“	Dickerson, Mahlon	New Jersey	1834	5:295
Van Buren, Martin	“	“	1837	5:295
“	Paulding, James K.	New York	1838	7:193
Harrison, William H.	Badger, George E.	North Carolina	1841	3:305
Tyler, John	“	“	1841	3:305
“	Upshur, Abel P.	Virginia	1841	6: 8
“	Henshaw, David	Massachusetts	1843	6: 7
“	Gilmer, Thomas W.	Virginia	1844	5:449
“	Mason, John Y.	“	1844	6: 7
Polk, James K.	Bancroft, George	Massachusetts	1845	3:160
“	Mason, John Y.	Virginia	1846	6: 7
Taylor, Zachary	Preston, William B.	“	1849	4:371
Fillmore, Millard	Graham, William A.	North Carolina	1850	4:426
“	Kennedy, John P.	Maryland	1852	6:181
Pierce, Franklin	Dobbin, James C.	North Carolina	1853	4:150
Buchanan, James	Toucey, Isaac	Connecticut	1857	5: 7
Lincoln, Abraham	Welles, Gideon	“	1861	2: 86
Johnson, Andrew	“	“	1865	2: 86
Grant, Ulysses S.	Borie, Adolph E.	Pennsylvania	1869	4: 25
“	Robeson, George M.	New Jersey	1869	4: 25
Hayes, Rutherford B.	Thompson, Richard W.	Indiana	1877	3:202
“	Goff, Nathan, Jr.	West Virginia	1881	3:202
Garfield, James A.	Hunt, William H.	Louisiana	1881	4:244
Arthur, Chester A.	Chandler, William E.	New Hampshire	1882	4:252
Cleveland, Grover	Whitney, William C.	New York	1885	2:407
Harrison, Benjamin	Tracy, Benjamin F.	“	1889	1:145
Cleveland, Grover	Herbert, Hilary A.	Alabama	1893	7:544
McKinley, William	Long, John D.	Massachusetts	1897	11: 15
Roosevelt, Theodore	“	“	1901	11: 15
“	Moody, William H.	“	1902	14: 21
“	Morton, Paul	New York	1904	14: 24
“	Bonaparte, Charles J.	Maryland	1905	14: 22
“	Metcalf, Victor H.	California	1906	14: 25
“	Newberry, Truman H.	Michigan	1908	14: 26
Taft, William H.	Meyer, George von L.	Massachusetts	1909	14:413
Wilson, Woodrow	Daniels, Josephus	North Carolina	1913	A: 46
Harding, Warren G.	Denby, Edwin	Michigan	1921	21:486
Coolidge, Calvin	“	“	1923	21:486
“	Wilbur, Curtis D.	California	1924	A: 13
Hoover, Herbert C.	Adams, Charles F.	Massachusetts	1929	C: 11
Roosevelt, Franklin D.	Swanson, Claude A.	Virginia	1933	D: 15

SECRETARIES OF THE INTERIOR

President	Secretary of the Interior	Residence	Date of Appointment	Biography
Taylor, Zachary	Ewing, Thomas	Ohio	1849	25: 14
Fillmore, Millard	McKennan, Thomas M. T.	Pennsylvania	1850	
"	Stuart, Alexander H. H.	Virginia	1850	6:182
Pierce, Franklin	McClelland, Robert	Michigan	1853	4:150
Buchanan, James	Thompson, Jacob	Mississippi	1857	5: 8
Lincoln, Abraham	Smith, Caleb B.	Indiana	1861	2: 88
"	Usher, John P.	"	1863	2: 88
Johnson, Andrew	"	"	1865	2: 88
"	Harlan, James	Iowa	1865	2:457
"	Browning, Orville H.	Illinois	1866	2:457
Grant, Ulysses S.	Cox, Jacob D.	Ohio	1869	22:231
"	Delano, Columbus	"	1870	4: 18
"	Chandler, Zachariah	Michigan	1875	4: 18
Hayes, Rutherford B.	Schurz, Carl	Missouri	1877	3:202
Garfield, James A.	Kirkwood, Samuel J.	Iowa	1881	4:245
Arthur, Chester A.	Teller, Henry M.	Colorado	1882	15:228
Cleveland, Grover	Lamar, Lucius Q. C.	Mississippi	1885	1: 37
"	Vilas, William F.	Wisconsin	1888	2:409
Harrison, Benjamin	Noble, John W.	Missouri	1889	1:146
Cleveland, Grover	Smith, Hoke	Georgia	1893	1:183
"	Francis, David R.	Missouri	1896	12: 9
McKinley, William	Bliss, Cornelius N.	New York	1897	11: 15
"	Hitchcock, Ethan A.	Missouri	1898	11: 16
Roosevelt, Theodore	"	"	1901	11: 16
"	Garfield, James R.	Ohio	1907	14: 27
Taft, William H.	Ballinger, Richard A.	Washington	1909	14:413
"	Fisher, Walter L.	Illinois	1911	17:406
Wilson, Woodrow	Lane, Franklin K.	California	1913	19:101
"	Payne, John B.	Illinois	1920	D:348
Harding, Warren G.	Fall, Albert B.	New Mexico	1921	A:355
"	Work, Hubert	Colorado	1923	A: 14
Coolidge, Calvin	"	"	1923	A: 14
"	West, Roy O.	Illinois	1928	
Hoover, Herbert C.	Wilbur, Ray L.	California	1929	C: 12
Roosevelt, Franklin D.	Ickes, Harold L.	Illinois	1933	D: 16

SECRETARIES OF AGRICULTURE

President	Secretary of Agriculture	Residence	Date of Appointment	Biography
Cleveland, Grover	Colman, Norman J.	Missouri	1889	16: 69
Harrison, Benjamin	Rusk, Jeremiah McL.	Wisconsin	1889	1:147
Cleveland, Grover	Morton, J. Sterling	Nebraska	1893	6:487
McKinley, William	Wilson, James	Iowa	1897	14: 27
Roosevelt, Theodore	"	"	1901	14: 27
Taft, William H.	"	"	1909	14: 27
Wilson, Woodrow	Houston, David F.	Missouri	1913	A: 38
"	Meredith, Edwin T.	Iowa	1920	21: 32
Harding, Warren G.	Wallace, Henry C.	"	1921	19: 14
Coolidge, Calvin	"	"	1923	19: 14
"	Gore, Howard M.	West Virginia	1924	B: 45
"	Jardine, William M.	Kansas	1925	A: 14
Hoover, Herbert C.	Hyde, Arthur M.	Missouri	1929	C: 13
Roosevelt, Franklin D.	Wallace, Henry A.	Iowa	1933	D: 17

SECRETARIES OF COMMERCE AND LABOR*

President	Secretary of Commerce and Labor	Residence	Date of Appointment	Biography
Roosevelt, Theodore	Cortelyou, George B.	New York	1903	14: 18
"	Metcalf, Victor H.	California	1904	14: 25
"	Straus, Oscar S.	New York	1906	10: 42
Taft, William H.	Nagel, Charles	Missouri	1909	D:266

*By act of Congress, effective March 3, 1913, the Department of Commerce and Labor was replaced by two departments, the Department of Commerce and the Department of Labor.

SECRETARIES OF COMMERCE

President	Secretary of Commerce	Residence	Date of Appointment	Biography
Wilson, Woodrow	Redfield, William C.	New York	1913	A: 50
"	Alexander, Joshua W.	Missouri	1919	A: 51
Harding, Warren G.	Hoover, Herbert C.	California	1921	C: 1
Coolidge, Calvin	"	"	1923	C: 1
"	Whiting, William F.	Massachusetts	1928	D:380
Hoover, Herbert C.	Lamont, Robert P.	Michigan	1929	C: 13
"	Chapin, Roy D.	"	1932	D:400
Roosevelt, Franklin D.	Roper, Daniel C.	North Carolina	1933	D: 18

SECRETARIES OF LABOR

President	Secretary of Labor	Residence	Date of Appointment	Biography
Wilson, Woodrow	Wilson, William B.	Pennsylvania	1913	A: 52
Harding, Warren G.	Davis, James J.	"	1921	A: 17
Coolidge, Calvin	"	"	1923	A: 17
Hoover, Herbert C.	"	"	1929	A: 17
"	Doak, William N.	Virginia	1930	25: 29
Roosevelt, Franklin D.	Perkins, Frances	New York	1933	D: 19

Electoral Votes for President and Vice President

From March 4, 1789 to March 4, 1933

Candidates	Electoral Votes	Biography	Candidates	Electoral Votes	Biography
FIRST TERM (1789-1793)			**THIRD TERM (1797-1801)**		
Washington, George	69	1: 1	Adams, John	71	2: 1
Adams, John	34	2: 1	Jefferson, Thomas	68	3: 1
Jay, John	9	1: 20	Pinckney, Thomas	59	12:160
Harrison, Robert H.	6	1:316	Burr, Aaron	30	3: 5
Rutledge, John	6	1: 21	Adams, Samuel	15	1:104
Hancock, John	4	1:103	Ellsworth, Oliver	11	1: 22
Clinton, George	3	3: 41	Clinton, George	7	3: 41
Huntington, Samuel	2	10:329	Jay, John	5	1: 20
Milton, John	2	4:305	Iredell, James	3	1: 23
Armstrong, John	1	14:125	Henry, John	2	9:294
Lincoln, Benjamin	1	1: 62	Johnston, Samuel	2	4:420
Telfair, Edward	1	1:219	Washington, George	2	1: 1
			Pinckney, Charles C.	1	2:302
SECOND TERM (1793-1797)			**FOURTH TERM (1801-1805)**		
Washington, George	132	1: 1	Jefferson, Thomas	73	3: 1
Adams, John	77	2: 1	Burr, Aaron	73	3: 5
Clinton, George	50	3: 41	Adams, John	65	2: 1
Jefferson, Thomas	4	3: 1	Pinckney, Charles C.	64	2:302
Burr, Aaron	1	3: 5	Jay, John	1	1: 20

Until 1804 each elector voted for two candidates for President. The one who received the largest number of votes was declared President, and the one who received the next largest number of votes was declared Vice President.

Presidential Candidates	Electoral Votes	Biography	Vice Presidential Candidates	Electoral Votes	Biography
FIFTH TERM (1805-1809)					
Jefferson, Thomas	162	3: 1	Clinton, George	162	3: 41
Pinckney, Charles C.	14	2:302	King, Rufus	14	6:301
SIXTH TERM (1809-1813)					
Madison, James	122	5:369	Clinton, George	113	3: 41
Pinckney, Charles C.	47	2:302	King, Rufus	47	6:301
Clinton, George	6	3: 41	Langdon, John	9	11:123
			Madison, James	3	5:369
			Monroe, James	3	6: 81
SEVENTH TERM (1813-1817)					
Madison, James	128	5:369	Gerry, Elbridge	131	5:371
Clinton, De Witt	89	3: 43	Ingersoll, Jared	86	2:439
EIGHTH TERM (1817-1821)					
Monroe, James	183	6: 81	Tompkins, Daniel D.	183	6: 83
King, Rufus	34	6:301	Howard, John E.	22	9:292
			Ross, James	5	5:438
			Marshall, John	4	1: 25
			Harper, Robert G.	3	5:374

Presidential Candidates	Electoral Votes	Biography	Vice Presidential Candidates	Electoral Votes	Biography
NINTH TERM (1821-1825)					
Monroe, James	231	6: 81	Tompkins, Daniel D.	218	6: 83
Adams, John Quincy	1	5: 73	Stockton, Richard	8	2: 7
			Rodney, Daniel	4	11:531
			Harper, Robert G.	1	5:374
			Rush, Richard	1	5: 80
TENTH TERM (1825-1829)					
Jackson, Andrew	99	5:289	Calhoun, John C.	182	6: 83
Adams, John Quincy	84	5: 73	Sanford, Nathan	30	3:383
Crawford, William H.	41	5: 82	Macon, Nathaniel	24	5:176
Clay, Henry	37	5: 77	Jackson, Andrew	13	5:289
			Van Buren, Martin	9	6:433
			Clay, Henry	2	5: 77

No choice for President having been made by the people, the election devolved upon the House of Representatives, and John Quincy Adams was elected, receiving the votes of thirteen states to seven for Andrew Jackson and four for William H. Crawford.

Presidential Candidates	Electoral Votes	Biography	Vice Presidential Candidates	Electoral Votes	Biography
ELEVENTH TERM (1829-1833)					
Jackson, Andrew	178	5:289	Calhoun, John C.	171	6: 83
Adams, John Quincy	83	5: 73	Rush, Richard	83	5: 80
			Smith, William	7	2:481
TWELFTH TERM (1833-1837)					
Jackson, Andrew	219	5:289	Van Buren, Martin	189	6:433
Clay, Henry	49	5: 77	Sergeant, John	49	2:229
Floyd, John	11	5:448	Wilkins, William	30	6: 9
Wirt, William	7	6: 86	Lee, Henry	11	13:585
			Ellmaker, Amos	7	7:537
THIRTEENTH TERM (1837-1841)					
Van Buren, Martin	170	6:433	Johnson, Richard M.	147	6:434
Harrison, William H.	73	3: 33	Granger, Francis	77	6: 7
White, Hugh L.	26	11:395	Tyler, John	47	6: 1
Webster, Daniel	14	3: 36	Smith, William	23	2:481
Mangum, Willie P.	11	4: 47			

There being no choice for Vice President by the people, the election devolved upon the Senate of the United States. Richard M. Johnson received thirty-three votes and Francis Granger sixteen votes. Richard M. Johnson was thereupon declared Vice President.

Presidential Candidates	Electoral Votes	Biography	Vice Presidential Candidates	Electoral Votes	Biography
FOURTEENTH TERM (1841-1845)					
Harrison, William H.	234	3: 33	Tyler, John	234	6: 1
Van Buren, Martin	60	6:433	Johnson, Richard M.	48	6:434
			Tazewell, Littleton W.	11	5:448
			Polk, James K.	1	6:265

William Henry Harrison, ninth President of the United States, died at Washington, April 4, 1841. The duties of the Presidential office devolving in this event, upon the Vice President, John Tyler, he accordingly took the oath of office, April 6, 1841.

Presidential Candidates	Electoral Votes	Biography	Vice Presidential Candidates	Electoral Votes	Biography
FIFTEENTH TERM (1845-1849)					
Polk, James K.	170	6:265	Dallas, George M.	170	6:268
Clay, Henry	105	5: 77	Frelinghuysen, Theodore	105	3:401
SIXTEENTH TERM (1849-1853)					
Taylor, Zachary	163	4:367	Fillmore, Millard	163	6:177
Cass, Lewis	127	5: 3	Butler, William O.	127	6:183

Zachary Taylor, twelfth President of the United States, died at Washington, July 9, 1850. The duties of the Presidential office devolving, in this event, upon the Vice President, Millard Fillmore, he accordingly took the oath of office, July 10, 1850.

Presidential Candidates	Electoral Votes	Biography	Vice Presidential Candidates	Electoral Votes	Biography

SEVENTEENTH TERM (1853-1857)

Presidential Candidates	Electoral Votes	Biography	Vice Presidential Candidates	Electoral Votes	Biography
Pierce, Franklin	254	4:145	King, William R.	254	4:147
Scott, Winfield	42	3:502	Graham, William A.	42	4:426

EIGHTEENTH TERM (1857-1861)

Presidential Candidates	Electoral Votes	Biography	Vice Presidential Candidates	Electoral Votes	Biography
Buchanan, James	174	5: 1	Breckinridge, John C.	174	5: 3
Fremont, John C.	114	4:270	Dayton, William L.	114	4:325
Fillmore, Millard	8	6:177	Donelson, Andrew J.	8	7:489

NINETEENTH TERM (1861-1865)

Presidential Candidates	Electoral Votes	Biography	Vice Presidential Candidates	Electoral Votes	Biography
Lincoln, Abraham	180	2: 65	Hamlin, Hannibal	180	2: 76
Breckinridge, John C.	72	5: 3	Lane, Joseph	72	8: 2
Bell, John	39	3: 39	Everett, Edward	39	6:179
Douglas, Stephen A.	12	2:428	Johnson, Herschel V.	12	1:226

TWENTIETH TERM (1865-1869)

Presidential Candidates	Electoral Votes	Biography	Vice Presidential Candidates	Electoral Votes	Biography
Lincoln, Abraham	212	2: 65	Johnson, Andrew	212	2:454
McClellan, George B.	21	4:140	Pendleton, George H.	21	3:278

Abraham Lincoln, sixteenth President of the United States, was shot by an assassin on the night of April 14, 1865, and died the following morning. The duties of the Presidential office devolving, in this event, upon the Vice President, Andrew Johnson, he accordingly took the oath of office, April 15, 1865.

TWENTY-FIRST TERM (1869-1873)

Presidential Candidates	Electoral Votes	Biography	Vice Presidential Candidates	Electoral Votes	Biography
Grant, Ulysses S.	214	4: 1	Colfax, Schuyler	214	4: 12
Seymour, Horatio	80	3: 48	Blair, Francis P., Jr.	80	4:223

TWENTY-SECOND TERM (1873-1877)

Presidential Candidates	Electoral Votes	Biography	Vice Presidential Candidates	Electoral Votes	Biography
Grant, Ulysses S.	286	4: 1	Wilson, Henry	286	4: 13
Greeley, Horace	*	3:448	Brown, B. Gratz	47	20:318
Hendricks, Thomas A.	42	2:403	Julian, George W.	5	5:502
Brown, B. Gratz	18	20:318	Colquitt, Alfred H.	5	1:291
Jenkins, Charles J.	2	1:228	Palmer, John M.	3	11: 49
Davis, David	1	2:474	Bramlette, Thomas E.	3	13: 9
			Banks, Nathaniel P.	1	4:222
			Groesbeck, William S.	1	13:150
			Machen, Willis B.	1	12:395

*Greeley died after election and the Democratic electors scattered their vote.

TWENTY-THIRD TERM (1877-1881)

Presidential Candidates	Electoral Votes	Biography	Vice Presidential Candidates	Electoral Votes	Biography
Hayes, Rutherford B.	185	3:191	Wheeler, William A.	185	3:190
Tilden, Samuel J.	184	3: 53	Hendricks, Thomas A.	184	2:403

TWENTY-FOURTH TERM (1881-1885)

Presidential Candidates	Electoral Votes	Biography	Vice Presidential Candidates	Electoral Votes	Biography
Garfield, James A.	214	4:238	Arthur, Chester A.	214	4:247
Hancock, Winfield S.	155	4:134	English, William H.	155	9:376

James A. Garfield, the twentieth President of the United States, was shot by an assassin, July 2, 1881, and died from the effects of his wounds, September 19, 1881. The duties of the Presidential office devolving, in this event, upon the Vice President, Chester A. Arthur, he accordingly took the oath of office in New York city, September 20, 1881, and again formally took the oath of office at Washington, September 22, 1881.

TWENTY-FIFTH TERM (1885-1889)

Presidential Candidates	Electoral Votes	Biography	Vice Presidential Candidates	Electoral Votes	Biography
Cleveland, Grover	219	2:400	Hendricks, Thomas A.	219	2:403
Blaine, James G.	182	1:137	Logan, John A.	182	4:298

TWENTY-SIXTH TERM (1889-1893)

Presidential Candidates	Electoral Votes	Biography	Vice Presidential Candidates	Electoral Votes	Biography
Harrison, Benjamin	233	1:133	Morton, Levi P.	233	1:136
Cleveland, Grover	168	2:400	Thurman, Allen G.	168	3:144

Presidential Candidates	Electoral Votes	Biography	Vice Presidential Candidates	Electoral Votes	Biography
TWENTY-SEVENTH TERM (1893-1897)					
Cleveland, Grover	277	2:400	Stevenson, Adlai E.	277	2:487
Harrison, Benjamin	145	1:133	Reid, Whitelaw	145	22: 1
Weaver, James B.	22	16:146	Field, James G.	22	12:485
TWENTY-EIGHTH TERM (1897-1901)					
McKinley, William	271	11: 1	Hobart, Garret A.	271	11: 10
Bryan, William J.	176	19:453	Sewall, Arthur	149	10:502
			Watson, Thomas E.	27	3:373
TWENTY-NINTH TERM (1901-1905)					
McKinley, William	292	11: 1	Roosevelt, Theodore	292	14: 1
Bryan, William J.	155	19:453	Stevenson, Adlai E.	155	2:487
THIRTIETH TERM (1905-1909)					
Roosevelt, Theodore	336	14: 1	Fairbanks, Charles W.	336	14: 10
Parker, Alton B.	140	10:122	Davis, Henry G.	140	10:468
THIRTY-FIRST TERM (1909-1913)					
Taft, William H.	321	23: 1	Sherman, James S.	321	14:406
Bryan, William J.	162	19:453	Kern, John W.	162	14:137
THIRTY-SECOND TERM (1913-1917)					
Wilson, Woodrow	435	19: 1	Marshall, Thomas R.	435	19:137
Roosevelt, Theodore	88	14: 1	Johnson, Hiram W.	88	15:133
Taft, William H.	8	23: 1	Butler, Nicholas Murray	8	B:186
THIRTY-THIRD TERM (1917-1921)					
Wilson, Woodrow	277	19: 1	Marshall, Thomas R.	277	19:137
Hughes, Charles E.	254	A: 6	Fairbanks, Charles W.	254	14: 10
THIRTY-FOURTH TERM (1921-1925)					
Harding, Warren G.	404	19:268	Coolidge, Calvin	404	24: 1
Cox, James M.	127	D:269	Roosevelt, Franklin D.	127	D: 1

Warren G. Harding, twenty-ninth President of the United States, died at San Francisco, Calif., August 2, 1923. The duties of the Presidential office devolving, in this event, upon the Vice President, Calvin Coolidge, he accordingly took the oath of office, August 3, 1923.

Presidential Candidates	Electoral Votes	Biography	Vice Presidential Candidates	Electoral Votes	Biography
THIRTY-FIFTH TERM (1925-1929)					
Coolidge, Calvin	382	24: 1	Dawes, Charles G.	382	A:508
Davis, John W.	136	A: 25	Bryan, Charles W.	136	A:520
La Follette, Robert	13	19:425	Wheeler, Burton K.	13	A:153
THIRTY-SIXTH TERM (1929-1933)					
Hoover, Herbert	444	C: 1	Curtis, Charles	444	C: 7
Smith, Alfred E.	87	A:404	Robinson, Joseph T.	87	B:193
THIRTY-SEVENTH TERM (1933-1937)					
Roosevelt, Franklin D.	472	D: 1	Garner, John N.	472	D: 9
Hoover, Herbert	59	C: 1	Curtis, Charles	59	C: 7

References are to THE NATIONAL CYCLOPEDIA OF AMERICAN BIOGRAPHY

Heads of Federal Services and Bureaus

Department of the Treasury

Comptrollers of the Currency

1863..McCulloch, Hugh 4:251
1865..Clarke, Freeman ....
1867..Hulburd, Hiland R. ......
1872..Knox, John Jay 3: 15
1884..Cannon, Henry W. 1:158
1886..Trenholm, William L. ....
1889..Lacey, Edward S. 17:427
1892..Hepburn, Alonzo B. 23:100
1893..Eckels, James H. 21:355
1898..Dawes, Charles G. A:508
1901..Ridgely, William B. ......
1908..Murray, Lawrence O. ....
1914..Williams, John S. ....
1921..Crissinger, Daniel R. C:244
1923..Dawes, Henry M. ....
1924..McIntosh, Joseph W. .....
1928..Pole, John W. ....
1933..O'Connor, James F. T. ...

Treasurers of the United States

1775..Hillegas, Michael 11:229
1789..Meredith, Samuel ....
1801..Tucker, Thomas T. 9:534
1828..Clark, William ....
1829..Campbell, John ....
1839..Selden, William ....
1850..Sloan, John ....
1853..Casey, Samuel ....
1860..Price, William C. ....
1861..Spinner, Francis E. 12:388
1875..New, John C. 13:439
1876..Wyman, Albert U. ....
1877..Gilfillan, James ....
1883..Wyman, Albert U. ....
1885..Jordan, Conrad N. ....
1887..Hyatt, James W. ....
1889..Huston, James N. ....
1891..Nebecker, Enos H. ....
1893..Morgan, Daniel N. ....
1897..Roberts, Ellis H. 11:507
1905..Treat, Charles H. ....
1909..McClung, Lee 20:382
1912..Thompson, Carmi A. .....
1913..Burke, John 14:449
1921..White, Frank 13:519
1928..Tate, H. Theodore ....
1929..Woods, Walter O. ....
1933..Julian, William A. ...... D: 37

Commissioners of Internal Revenue

1862..Boutwell, George S. 4:382
1863..Lewis, Joseph J. ....
1865..Orton, William 7:502
1865..Rollins, Edward A. ......
1869..Delano, Columbus 4: 18
1871..Pleasonton, Alfred 4:164
1871..Douglass, John W. ....
1875..Pratt, Daniel D. 11:187
1876..Raum, Green B. 13:588
1883..Evans, Walter 17:112
1885..Miller, Joseph S. ....
1889..Mason, John W. ....
1893..Miller, Joseph S. ....
1896..Forman, William St. J. ..
1898..Scott, Nathan B. 19: 59
1899..Wilson, George W. 8:297
1900..Yerkes, John W. ....
1907..Capers, John G. ....
1909..Cabell, Royal E. ....
1913..Osborn, William H. 19:243
1917..Roper, Daniel C. .... D: 18
1920..Williams, William M. ....
1921..Blair, David H. ....
1929..Lucas, Robert H. ....
1930..Burnet, David ....
1933..Helvering, Guy T. ....

Directors of the Mint

1792..Rittenhouse, David 1:346
1795..Desaussure, Henry W. 13:154
1795..Boudinot, Elias 2:296
1806..Patterson, Robert 26: 59
1824..Moore, Samuel 12:421
1835..Patterson, Robert M. 26: 59
1851..Eckert, George N. ....
1853..Pettit, Thomas McK. 12:129
1853..Snowden, James R. 13:464
1861..Pollock, James 2:289
1867..Linderman, Henry R. 4:120
1869..Pollock, James 2:289
1873..Linderman, Henry R. 4:120
1879..Burchard, Horatio C. 13:183
1885..Kimball, James P. 11: 91
1889..Leech, Edward O. 13: 87
1893..Preston, Robert E. ....
1898..Roberts, George E. 12:365
1907..Leach, Frank A. 14:333
1909..Andrew, A. Piatt 15:326
1910..Roberts, George E. 12:365
1915..Wooley, Robert W. ......
1916..VonEngelken, Friedrich J. H. ....
1917..Baker, Raymond T. ......
1922..Scobey, Frank E. ....
1923..Grant, Robert J. ....
1933..Ross, Nellie Tayloe B:454

Surgeons General of the Public Health Service

1871..Woodworth, John M. ....
1879..Hamilton, John B. 23:245
1891..Wyman, Walter 12:508
1912..Blue, Rupert 15:129
1920..Cumming, Hugh S. ......

Directors of the Bureau of the Budget

1921..Dawes, Charles G. A:508
1922..Lord, Herbert M. 21: 29
1929..Roop, J. Clawson ....
1933..Douglas, Lewis W. .... D: 22
1934..Bell, Daniel W. (acting)..

Department of War

Commanders of the U. S. Army Since 1775

1775..Washington, George 1: 1
1783..Knox, Henry 1: 14
1784..Doughty, John 7:517
1784..Harmar, Josiah 5:430
1791..St. Clair, Arthur 1: 94
1792..Wayne, Anthony 1: 55
1796..Wilkinson, James 1: 56
1798..Washington, George 1: 1
1799..Hamilton, Alexander 1: 9
1800..Wilkinson, James 1: 56
1812..Dearborn, Henry 1: 93
1815..Brown, Jacob 5:400
1828..Macomb, Alexander 2:241
1841..Scott, Winfield 3:502
1861..McClellan, George B. 4:140
1862..Halleck, Henry W. 4:257
1864..Grant, Ulysses S. 4: 1
1869..Sherman, William T. 4: 32
1883..Sheridan, Philip H. 4: 63
1888..Schofield, John M. 4:259
1895..Miles, Nelson A. 9: 26
1903..Young, Samuel B. M. 13:313

NOTE:—*Gen. Young was the last Commanding General of the Army. The general staff law went into effect Aug. 15, 1903, and Gen. Young became the first Chief of Staff.*

Chiefs of Staff

1903..Young, Samuel B. M. 13:313
1904..Chaffee, Adna R. 10:493
1906..Bell, James F. 22:276
1910..Wood, Leonard 9: 20
1914..Scott, Hugh L. 14:494
1917..Bliss, Tasker H. 21: 86
1918..March, Peyton C. A:541
1921..Pershing, John J. A:434
1924..Hines, John L. ....
1926..Summerall, Charles P. ... A:150
1930..MacArthur, Douglas C:407
1935..Craig, Malin ....

Judge Advocate Generals

1775..Tudor, William 7:217
1777..Laurence, John 2: 8
1782..Edwards, Thomas ....
1801..Smith, Campbell ....
1849..Lee, John F. ....
1862..Holt, Joseph 1:354
1875..Dunn, William McK. 4:224
1881..Swaim, Davis G. ....
1895..Lieber, G. Norman ....
1901..Barr, Thomas F. ....
1901..Clous, John W. ....
1901..Davis, George B. 22:397
1911..Crowder, Enoch H. A:455
1923..Bethel, Walter A. ....
1924..Hull, John A. ....
1928..Kreger, Edward A. ......
1931..Winship, Blanton ....
1933..Brown, Arthur W. ....

Quartermaster Generals

1775..Mifflin, Thomas 2.233
1776..Moylan, Stephen 1: 56
1778..Greene, Nathaniel 1: 39
1780..Pickering, Timothy 1: 12
1791..Hodgdon, Samuel ....
1792..O'Hara, James 17: 169
1796..Wilkins, John, Jr. ....
1812..Lewis, Morgan 3: 43
1813..Swartwout, Robert 7: 535
1816..Mullany, James R. ....
1816..Gibson, George ....
1818..Cumming, William ....
1818..Jesup, Thomas S. 12: 65
1860..Johnston, Joseph E. 5: 328
1861..Meigs, Montgomery C. ... 4: 69
1882..Rucker, Daniel H. ....
1882..Ingalls, Rufus 12: 240
1883..Holabird, Samuel B. 10: 122
1890..Batchelder, Richard N. ..
1896..Sawtelle, Charles G. ......
1897..Weeks, George H. ....
1898..Ludington, Marshall I. ...18: 284
1903..Humphrey, Charles F. ...
1907..Aleshire, James B. ......
1916..Sharpe, Henry G. .... B: 133
1918..Rogers, Harry L. 24: 411
1922..Hart, William H. ....
1926..Cheatham, Benjamin F. ..11: 90
1930..DeWitt, John L. ....
1934..Bash, Louis H. ....

Surgeons General

1775..Church, Benjamin 7: 167
1775..Morgan, John 10: 267
1777..Shippen, William 10: 384
1781..Cochran, John 8: 410
1798..Craik, James 7: 494
1813..Tilton, James 3: 515
1818..Lovell, Joseph 4: 181
1836..Lawson, Thomas 4: 186
1861..Finley, Clement A. 4: 180
1862..Hammond, William A. ... 9: 338
1864..Barnes, Joseph K. 4: 359
1882..Crane, Charles H. 4: 174
1883..Murray, Robert 13: 443
1886..Moore, John 12: 209
1890..Baxter, Jedediah H. 4: 180
1890..Sutherland, Charles 4: 473
1893..Sternberg, George M. 4: 388
1902..O'Reilly, Robert M. 18: 261
1909..Torney, George H. ....
1914..Gorgas, William C. 14: 528
1918..Vacant
1919..Ireland, Merritte W. ..... A: 220
1931..Patterson, Robert U. .....
1935..Reynolds, Charles R. .....

Chiefs of Engineering

1802..Williams, Jonathan 3: 239
1812..Swift, Joseph Gardner ...10: 17
1818..Armistead, Walter K. 5: 507
1821..Macomb, Alexander 2: 241
1828..Gratiot, Charles 12: 323
1838..Totten, Joseph G. 4: 164
1864..Delafield, Richard 11: 29
1866..Humphreys, Andrew A. .. 7: 34
1879..Wright, Horatio G. 4: 273
1884..Newton, John 4: 312
1886..Duane, James C. 10: 85
1888..Casey, Thomas L. 4: 279
1895. Craighill, William P. 12: 223
1897 Wilson, John M. 4: 538
1901..Robert, Henry M. 10: 142
1901..Gillespie, George L. 12: 184
1904..Mackenzie, Alexander 14: 250
1908..Marshall, William L. 11: 467
1910..Bixby, William H. 21: 337
1913..Kingman, Dan C. ....
1916..Black, William M. .... A: 489
1920..Beach, Lansing H. ....
1924..Taylor, Harry 23: 141
1926..Jadwin, Edgar .... A: 521
1929..Brown, Lytle ....
1933..Markham, Edward M. ...

Chiefs of Ordnance

1815..Wadsworth, Decius ......
1821..Bomford, George 7: 495
1848..Talcott, George ....
1851..Craig, H. K. ....
1861..Ripley, James W. 3: 347
1863..Ramsey, George D. ....
1864..Dyer, Alexander B. 4: 338
1874..Benet, Stephen V. ....
1891..Flagler, Daniel W. 9: 249
1899..Buffington, Adelbert R. ... 5: 329
1901..Crozier, William 12: 267
1917..Wheeler, Charles B. (acting) ....
1918..Peirce, William S. (acting) 19: 239
1918..Williams, Clarence C. ....
1930..Hof, Samuel ....
1934..Tschappat, William H. ...

Chief Signal Officers

1860..Myer, Albert J. 24: 196
1880..Hazen, William B. 3: 408
1887..Greely, Adolphus W. 3: 285
1906..Allen, James ....
1913..Scriven, George P. 8: 496
1917..Squier, George O. 24: 320
1924..Saltzman, Charles McK. ..
1928..Gibbs, George S. ....
1931..Carr, Irving J. ....
1935..Allison, James B. ....

Chiefs of the Air Corps
(Known as Director of Air Service until 1921)

1918..Ryan, John D. 23: 248
1918..Menoher, Charles T. .....
1921..Patrick, Mason M. .... C: 276
1927..Fechet, James E. ....
1931..Foulois, Benjamin D. ....
1935..Westover, Oscar ....

Chiefs of the Chemical Warfare Service

1920..Fries, Amos A. .... B: 363
1929..Gilchrist, Harry L. ...... A: 464
1933..Brigham, Claude E. ......

Department of Justice

Solicitors-General of the United States

1870..Bristow, Benjamin H. 4: 23
1872..Philips, Samuel F. 5: 538
1885..Goode, John 11: 370
1886..Jenks, George A. 13: 190
1889..Chapman, Orlow W. 5: 530
1890..Taft, William H. 23: 1
1892..Aldrich, Charles H. 13: 163
1893..Maxwell, Lawrence 23: 204
1895..Conrad, Holmes 16: 399
1897..Richards, John K. 13: 227
1903..Hoyt, Henry M., Jr. 9: 548
1909..Bowers, Lloyd W. 22: 148
1910..Lehmann, Frederick W. ..12: 30
1912..Bullitt, William M. ...... D: 58
1913..Davis, John W. .... A: 25
1918..King, Alexander C. 22: 431
1920..Frierson, William L. .....
1921..Beck, James M. .... B: 463
1925..Mitchell, William D. ..... C: 10
1929..Hughes, Charles E., Jr. .. C: 61
1930..Thacher, Thomas D. ..... D: 252
1933..Biggs, James C. .... D: 24
1935..Reed, Stanley ....

Department of the Navy

Admirals of the U. S. Navy

1866..Farragut, David G. 2: 45
1870..Porter, David D. 2: 97
1899..Dewey, George 9: 3

Chiefs of Naval Operations

1915..Benson, William S. 23: 388
1919..Coontz, Robert E. 25: 333
1923..Eberle, Edward W. 21: 328
1927..Hughes, Charles F. ......
1930..Pratt, William V. .... C: 513
1933..Standley, William H. .....

Chiefs of the Bureau of Ordnance

1842..Crane, William M. 12: 422
1846..Warrington, Lewis 6: 232
1851..Morris, Charles 9: 118
1856..Ingraham, Duncan N. 8: 336
1860..Magruder, George A. .....
1861..Harwood, Andrew A. 4: 418
1862..Dahlgren, John A. 9: 377
1863..Wise, Henry A. 13: 589
1868..Dahlgren, John A. 9: 377
1869..Case, Augustus L. ....
1873..Jeffers, William N. 4: 281
1881..Sicard, Montgomery 10: 485
1890..Folger, William M. ......
1893..Sampson, William T. 9: 9
1897..O'Neil, Charles 24: 313
1904..Converse, George A. .....
1904..Mason, Newton E. ....
1911..Twining, Nathan C. .....
1913..Strauss, Joseph .... A: 225
1916..Earle, Ralph ....
1920..McVay, Charles B., Jr. ...
1923..Bloch, Claude C. ....
1927..Leahy, William D. ....
1931..Larimer, Edgar B. ....
1934..Stark, Harold R. ....

Chiefs of the Bureau of Construction and Repair

1853..Hartt, Samuel ....
1853..Lenthall, John ....
1871..Hanscom, Isaiah ....
1877..Easby, John W. ....

1882..Wilson, Theodore D. 7: 508
1892..Hichborn, Philip ....
1901..Bowles, Francis T. 20: 39
1903..Capps, Washington L. ...26: 42
1910..Watt, Richard M. ....
1914..Taylor, David W. 15: 87
1922..Beuret, John D. ....
1929..Rock, George H. ....
1932..Land, Emory S. ....

Chiefs of the Bureau of Engineering

1844..Haswell, Charles H. 9: 486
1850..Stuart, Charles B. ....
1853..Martin, Daniel B. ....
1857..Archbold, Samuel ....
1861..Isherwood, Benjamin F. ..12: 199
1869..King, James W. 13: 186
1873..Wood, William W. W. ...12: 198
1877..Shock, William H. 6: 200
1884..Loring, Charles H. 12: 502
1887..Melville, George W. 3: 283
1903..Rae, Charles W. 15: 355
1908..Barton, John K. ....
1909..Cone, Hutch I. ....
1913..Griffin, Robert S. ....
1921..Robinson, John K. ....
1925..Halligen, John ....
1928..Yarnell, Harry E. ....
1931..Robinson, Samuel M. ....
1935..Bowen, Harold G. ....

Chiefs of the Bureau of Medicine and Surgery

1842..Barton, William P. C. ...13: 279
1844..Harris, Thomas ....
1853..Whelan, William ....
1865..Horwitz, Phineas J. 11: 525
1869..Wood, William M. ....
1871..Foltz, Jonathan M. 5: 150
1872..Palmer, James C. 8: 222
1873..Beale, Joseph ....
1877..Grier, William ....
1878..Taylor, J. Winthrop .....
1879..Wales, Philip S. 11: 261
1884..Gunnell, Francis M. ......
1888..Browne, John M. 14: 233
1893..Tryon, J. Rufus ....
1897..Bates, Newton L. ....
1897..Van Reypen, William K. ..13: 215
1902..Rixey, Presley M. 21: 315
1910..Stokes, Charles F. ....
1914..Braisted, William C. ...... A: 76
1920..Stitt, Edward R. ....
1928..Riggs, Charles E. ....
1933..Rossiter, Perceval S. .....

Judge Advocate Generals

1880..Remey, William B. ......
1892..Lemly, Samuel C. ....
1904..Diehl, Samuel W. B. .....
1907..Campbell, Edward H. ....
1909..Russell, Robert L. ....
1913..McLean, Ridley 25: 277
1917..Watts, William C. ....
1918..Clark, George C. ....
1921..Latimer, Julian L. ....
1925..Campbell, Edward H. ....
1929..Sellers, David F. ....
1931..Murfin, Orin G. ....
1934..Bloch, Claude C. ....

Commandants of the United States Marine Corps

1775..Nicholas, Samuel ....
1798..Burrows, William W. .....
1804..Wharton, Franklin ......
1819..Gale, Anthony ....
1820..Henderson, Archibald 4: 193
1859..Harris, John ....
1864..Zeilin, Jacob 11: 349
1876..McCawley, Charles G. ....
1891..Heywood, Charles ....
1903..Elliott, George F. ....
1911..Biddle, William P. ....
1914..Barnett, George ....
1920..Lejeune, John A. .... A: 375
1929..Neville, Wendell C. 22: 277
1930..Fuller, Ben H. ....
1934..Russell, John H. ....

Department of the Interior

Commissioners of Education

1867..Barnard, Henry 1: 505
1870..Eaton, John 8: 390
1886..Dawson, Nathaniel H. R. . 9: 544
1889..Harris, William T. 15: 1
1906..Brown, Elmer E. 14: 252
1911..Claxton, Philander P. 15: 270
1921..Tigert, John J. .... D: 428
1929..Cooper, William J. ....
1933..Zook, George F. ....
1934..Studebaker, John W. .....

Pension Commissioners

1861..Barrett, Joseph H. 13: 167
1868..Cox, Christopher C. 10: 497
1869..VanAernam, Henry 5: 524
1871..Baker, James H. 4: 412
1875..Atkinson, Henry M. 12: 9
1876..Gill, Charles R. 9: 558
1876..Bentley, John A. 13: 412
1881..Dudley, William W. 2: 222
1884..Clarke, Otis P. G. 12: 397
1885..Black, John C. 12: 101
1889..Tanner, James 1: 287
1889..Raum, Green B. 13: 588
1893..Lochren, William 12: 385
1896..Murphy, Dominic I. 13: 599
1897..Evans, Henry C. 13: 220
1902..Ware, Eugene F. 9: 202
1905..Warner, Vespasian 21: 362
1909..Davenport, James L. 20: 112
1913..Saltzgaber, Gaylord M. ...
1921..Gardner, Washington 5: 475
1925..Scott, Winfield ....
1929..Church, Earl D. 22: 149

(Under an act of July 3, 1930, the duties of this office were absorbed into the newly created Veterans' Administration.)

Directors of the U. S. Geological Survey

1879..King, Clarence 13: 248
1881..Powell, John W. 3: 340
1894..Walcott, Charles D. 22: 135
1907..Smith, George O. 14: 130
1931..Mendenhall, Walter C. ...

Commissioners of Reclamation

1907..Newell, Frederick H. 23: 162
1914..Davis, Arthur P. 24: 116
1923..Davis, David W. ....
1924..Mead, Elwood .... A: 528

Directors of the Bureau of Mines

1910..Holmes, Joseph A. 23: 104
1915..Manning, Vannoy H. .... A: 316
1920..Cottrell, Frederick G. ....
1921..Bain, H. Foster ....
1925..Turner, Scott ....
1934..Finch, John W. ....

Department of Agriculture

Chiefs of the Weather Bureau

1870..Myer, Albert J. 24: 196
1880..Drum, Richard C. 12: 359
1880..Hazen, William B. 3: 408
1886..Greely, Adolphus W. 3: 285
1891..Harrington, Mark W. 10: 448
1895..Moore, Willis L. 21: 84
1913..Marvin, Charles F. 16: 47
1934..Gregg, Willis R. ....

Chiefs of the Bureau of Plant Industry

1901..Galloway, Beverly T. 12: 504
1913..Taylor, William A. ....
1934..Ryerson, Knowles A. .....
1934..Richey, Frederick D. .....

Chiefs of the Forest Service

1876..Hough, Franklin B. 13: 340
1883..Egleston, Nathaniel H. ..13: 340
1886..Fernow, Bernhard E. 19: 166
1898..Pinchot, Gifford 14: 30
1910..Graves, Henry S. .... A: 479
1920..Greeley, William B. ......
1928..Stuart, Robert Y. 25: 156
1933..Silcox, Ferdinand A. .....

Chiefs of the Bureau of Entomology

1863..Glover, Townend 23: 209
1878..Riley, Charles V. 9: 443
1879..Comstock, John H. 22: 10
1881..Riley, Charles V. 9: 443
1894..Howard, Leland O. 12: 356
1927..Marlatt, Charles L. 13: 186
1933..Strong, Lee A. ....

Chiefs of the Bureau of Plant Quarantine

(Known as the Federal Horticultural Board until 1929; as the Plant Quarantine and Control Administration until 1932)

1912..Marlatt, Charles L. 13: 186
1930..Strong, Lee A. ....
1933..Hoyt, Avery S. (acting)..

Chiefs of the Bureau of Entomology and Plant Quarantine

1934..Strong, Lee A. ....

Department of Commerce

Census Officials

1790..President of United States 1: 1
1800..Secretary of State (John Marshall) 1: 25
1810..Secretary of State (Robert Smith) 3: 11
1820..Secretary of State (John Quincy Adams) 5: 73
1830..Secretary of State (Martin Van Buren) 6: 433
1840..Secretary of State (John Forsyth) 6: 435

Superintendents

1850..Kennedy, Joseph C. G. ...16: 444
1853..DeBow, James D. B. 8: 161
1860..Kennedy, Joseph C. G. ...16: 444
1870..Walker, Francis A. 5: 401
1881..Seaton, Charles W. 12: 217
1889..Porter, Robert P. 12: 216

Directors

1899..Merriam, William R. 10: 68
1903..North, Simeon N. D. 13: 62
1909..Durand, Edward D. ...... C: 450
1913..Harris, William J. 24: 266
1915..Rogers, Samuel L. .... A: 471
1921..Steuart, William M. ..... A: 19
1933..Austin, William L. ....

Directors of the Bureau of Foreign and Domestic Commerce

1912..Baldwin, Albertus H. .....
1914..Pratt, Edward E. ....
1917..Cutler, Burwell S. ....
1919..Kennedy, Philip B. ....
1920..MacElwee, Roy S. .... D: 315
1921..Klein, Julius .... C: 23
1929..Cooper, William L. ......
1931..Feiker, Frederick M. .....
1933..Thorp, Willard L. ....
1934..Murchison, Claudius T. ...

Directors of the Bureau of Standards

1901..Stratton, Samuel W. 13: 142
1923..Burgess, George K. 24: 312
1933..Briggs, Lyman J. ....

Superintendents of the Coast and Geodetic Survey

1816..Hassler, Ferdinand R. 3: 413
1843..Bache, Alexander D. 3: 348
1867..Peirce, Benjamin 8: 152
1874..Patterson, Carlile P. 4: 304
1881..Hilgard, Julius E. 10: 118
1885..Thorn, Frank M. 13: 198
1889..Mendenhall, Thomas C. ..10: 117
1894..Duffield, William W. .....
1897..Pritchett, Henry S. 10: 508
1900..Tittmann, Otto H. 13: 412
1915..Jones, E. Lester 26: 24
1929..Patton, Raymond S. ......

Commissioners of Patents

1836..Ellsworth, Henry L. 7: 516
1845..Burke, Edmund 7: 553
1849..Ewbank, Thomas 7: 559
1852..Hodges, Silas H. 5: 391
1853..Mason, Charles 3: 504
1857..Holt, Joseph 1: 354
1859..Bishop, William D. 11: 451
1860..Thomas, Philip F. 5: 6
1861..Holloway, David P. 7: 499
1865..Theaker, Thomas C. 7: 487
1868..Foote, Elisha 21: 339
1869..Fisher, Samuel S. 7: 499
1871..Leggett, Mortimer D. 2: 350
1874..Thacher, John M. 3: 530
1875..Duell, Rodolphus H. 12: 285
1877..Spear, Ellis 13: 364
1878..Paine, Halbert E. 10: 54
1880..Marble, Edgar M. 13: 310
1883..Butterworth, Benjamin ..13: 363
1885..Montgomery, Martin VanB. 5: 505
1887..Hall, Benton J. 12: 447
1889..Mitchell, Charles E. 1: 366
1891..Simonds, William E. 1: 363
1893..Seymour, John S. 12: 373
1897..Butterworth, Benjamin ...13: 363
1898..Duell, Charles H. 12: 285
1901..Allen, Frederick I. 5: 516
1907..Moore, Edward B. ....
1913..Ewing, Thomas, Jr. 14: 101
1917..Newton, James T. .... A: 453
1920..Whitehead, Robert F. ....
1921..Robertson, Thomas E. ....
1934..Conway, P. Coe ....

Department of Labor

Chiefs of the Children's Bureau

1912..Lathrop, Julia C. 24: 298
1921..Abbott, Grace .... C: 25
1934..Lenroot, Katharine F. ...

Independent Offices and Establishments

Chairmen of the Interstate Commerce Commission

1887..Cooley, Thomas McI. 9: 522
1891..Morrison, William R. 13: 132
1898..Knapp, Martin A. 4: 287
1911..Clements, Judson C. 22: 178
1912..Prouty, Charles A. ....
1913..Clark, Edgar E. .... A: 452
1914..Harlan, James S. ....
1915..McChord, Charles C. .....
1916..Meyer, Balthasar H. .....
1917..Hall, Henry C. ....
1918..Daniels, Winthrop M. ....
1919..Aitchison, Clyde B. ......
1920..Clark, Edgar E. .... A: 452
1921..McChord, Charles C. .....
1923..Meyer, Balthasar H. .....
1924..Hall, Henry C. ....
1925..Aitchison, Clyde B. ....
1926..Eastman, Joseph B. ..... D: 259
1927..Esch, John J. .... A: 530
1928..Campbell, Johnston B. ...
1929..Lewis, Ernest I. .... D: 110
1930..McManamy, Frank ....
1931..Brainerd, Ezra, Jr. ......
1932..Porter, Claude R. ....
1933..Farrell, Patrick J. ....
1934..Lee, William E. ....
1935..Tate, Hugh McCall .... D: 201

Chairmen of the Board of Governors Federal Reserve System

1914..Hamlin, Charles S. 15: 265
1916..Harding, Warren P. G. ..
1923..Crissinger, Daniel R. ..... C: 244
1927..Young, Roy A. ....
1930..Meyer, Eugene .... B: 271
1933..Black, Eugene R. ....
1934..Eccles, Marriner S. ......

Chairmen of the Federal Trade Commission

1915..Davies, Joseph E. .... C: 456
1916..Hurley, Edward N. ...... A: 60
1917..Harris, William J. 24: 266
1918..Colver, William B. ....
1919..Fort, John F. 14: 123
1919..Murdock, Victor ....
1920..Thompson, Huston ....
1921..Gaskill, Nelson B. ....
1922..Murdock, Victor ....
1923..Thompson, Huston ....
1924..Van Fleet, Vernon W. ...24: 253
1925..Nugent, John F. .... A: 425
1926..Hunt, Charles W. ....
1927..Humphrey, William E. ...
1928..Myers, Abram F. ....
1929..McCulloch, Edgar A. 15: 360
1930..Ferguson, Garland S., Jr.
1931..Hunt, Charles W. ....
1932..Humphrey, William E. ...
1933..March, Charles H. ....
1934..Ferguson, Garland S., Jr.
1935..Davis, Ewin L. ....

Chairmen of the Tariff Commission

1917..Taussig, Frank W. ...... A: 457
1920..Page, Thomas W. ....
1922..Marvin, Thomas O. ......
1930..Brossard, Edgar B. ......
1930..Fletcher, Henry P. .... D: 428
1931..O'Brien, Robert L. .... B: 435

Chairmen of the Federal Power Commission

1920..Baker, Newton D. .... A: 40
1921..Weeks, John W. 20: 4
1925..Davis, Dwight F. .... A: 10
1929..Good, James W. 21: 94
1929..Wilbur, Ray Lyman (acting) .... C: 12
1930..Smith, George O. ....
1933..McNinch, Frank R. ......

Chairmen of the Commission of Fine Arts

1910..Burnham, Daniel H. 9: 335
1912..French, Daniel C. .... A: 460
1915..Moore, Charles ....

Librarians of Congress

(*The Clerk of the House of Representatives was Librarian until 1815*)

1815..Watterston, George 7: 501
1829..Meehan, John S. 13: 170
1860..Stephenson, John G. .....
1864..Spofford, Ainsworth R. ... 6: 477
1897..Young, John R. 2: 214
1899..Putnam, Herbert .... D: 52

Judiciary of the United States

The Supreme Court of the United States

Chief Justices

1789-1795	Jay, John	1: 20
1795	Rutledge, John	1: 21
1796-1800	Ellsworth, Oliver	1: 22
1801-1835	Marshall, John	1: 25
1836-1864	Taney, Roger B.	1: 27
1864-1873	Chase, Salmon P.	1: 28
1874-1888	Waite, Morrison R.	1: 30
1888-1910	Fuller, Melville W.	1: 31
1910-1921	White, Edward D.	21: 3
1921-1930	Taft, William H.	23: 1
1930-	Hughes, Charles E.	A: 6

Associate Justices

1789-1791	Rutledge, John	1: 21
1789-1810	Cushing, William	12:548
1789-1798	Wilson, James	1: 22
1789-1796	Blair, John	1: 23
1790-1799	Iredell, James	1: 23
1791-1793	Johnson, Thomas	9:289
1793-1806	Paterson, William	1: 24
1796-1811	Chase, Samuel	1: 24
1798-1829	Washington, Bushrod	2:231
1799-1804	Moore, Alfred	2:467
1804-1834	Johnson, William	2:467
1806-1823	Livingston, Henry B.	2:467
1807-1826	Todd, Thomas	2:467
1811-1836	Duval, Gabriel	2:468
1811-1845	Story, Joseph	2:468
1823-1843	Thompson, Smith	6: 86
1826-1828	Trimble, Robert	2:469
1829-1861	McLean, John	2:469
1830-1844	Baldwin, Henry	2:257
1835-1867	Wayne, James M.	2:176
1836-1841	Barbour, Philip P.	2:259
1837-1865	Catron, John	2:261
1837-1852	McKinley, John	2:470
1841-1860	Daniel, Peter V.	2:174
1845-1872	Nelson, Samuel	2:470
1845-1851	Woodbury, Levi	2:471
1846-1870	Grier, Robert C.	2:472
1851-1857	Curtis, Benjamin R.	2:472
1853-1861	Campbell, John A.	2:472
1858-1881	Clifford, Nathan	2:473
1862-1881	Swayne, Noah H.	4:156
1862-1890	Miller, Samuel F.	2:473
1862-1877	Davis, David	2:474
1863-1897	Field, Stephen J.	1: 32
1870-1880	Strong, William	21: 4
1870-1892	Bradley, Joseph P.	1: 33
1872-1882	Hunt, Ward	2:475
1877-1911	Harlan, John M.	1: 34
1880-1887	Woods, William B.	2:476
1881-1889	Matthews, Stanley	2:476
1881-1902	Gray, Horace	1: 35
1882-1893	Blatchford, Samuel	1: 36
1888-1893	Lamar, Lucius Q. C.	1: 37
1889-1910	Brewer, David J.	1: 37
1890-1906	Brown, Henry B.	1: 38
1892-1903	Shiras, George, Jr.	2:477
1893-1895	Jackson, Howell E.	8:243
1894-1910	White, Edward D.	21: 3
1895-1909	Peckham, Rufus William	11:410
1898-1925	McKenna, Joseph	11: 18
1902-1932	Holmes, Oliver W.	12:349
1903-1922	Day, William R.	11: 11
1906-1910	Moody, William H.	14: 21
1910-1914	Lurton, Horace H.	8:235
1910-1916	Hughes, Charles E.	A: 6
1910-	VanDevanter, Willis	D: 82
1910-1916	Lamar, Joseph R.	15:414
1912-1922	Pitney, Mahlon	15: 61
1914-	McReynolds, James C.	A: 42
1916-	Brandeis, Louis D.	C:432
1916-1922	Clarke, John H.	A:248
1922-	Sutherland, George	13:413
1922-	Butler, Pierce	A:135
1923-1930	Sanford, Edward T.	21: 92
1925-	Stone, Harlan F.	A: 11
1930-	Roberts, Owen J.	A: 88
1932-	Cardozo, Benjamin N.	D: 50

Circuit Court of Appeals of the United States

(Abolished by Act of Congress in 1802; reëstablished in 1869)

First Circuit

1801-1802	Lowell, John	7: 62
1801-1802	Bourne, Benjamin	12:345
1801-1802	Smith, Jeremiah	11:123
1869-1878	Shepley, George F.	10: 78
1878-1884	Lowell, John	11:550
1884-1913	Colt, LeBaron B.	15:408
1892-1917	Putnam, William LeB.	19:278
1905-1911	Lowell, Francis C.	21:320
1911-1912	Schofield, William	15:138
1912-1918	Dodge, Frederic	22:413
1913-	Bingham, George H.	C:424
1917-1930	Johnson, Charles F.	21:193
1918-1931	Anderson, George W.	A:412
1929-	Wilson, Scott	
1932-	Morton, James M., Jr.	

Second Circuit

1801-1802	Wolcott, Oliver	10:333
1801-1802	Hitchcock, Samuel	11:195
1801-1802	Benson, Egbert	3:461
1869-1875	Woodruff, Lewis B.	
1875-1878	Johnson, Alexander S.	5:507
1878-1882	Blatchford, Samuel	1: 36
1882-1907	Wallace, William J.	17:316
1887-1916	Lacombe, Emile H.	
1892-1902	Shipman, Nathaniel	19:234
1902-1907	Townsend, William K.	20:239
1902-1917	Coxe, Alfred C.	
1907-1924	Ward, Henry G.	23: 25
1907-1913	Noyes, Walter C.	20:318
1911-	Mack, Julian W.	
1913-1926	Rogers, Henry W.	13:351
1916-1927	Hough, Charles M.	20:190
1918-	Manton, Martin T.	
1921-1924	Mayer, Julius M.	20:371
1924-	Hand, Learned	
1926-	Swan, Thomas W.	
1927-	Hand, Augustus N.	
1929-	Chase, Harrie B.	

CIRCUIT COURT OF APPEALS (*Continued*)

Third Circuit

1801-1802	Griffith, William	
1801-1802	Bassett, Richard	11:530
1801-1802	Tilghman, William	6:194
1869-1891	McKennan, William	9:553
1891-1906	Acheson, Marcus W.	10:119
1892-1909	Dallas, George M.	6:268
1899-1914	Gray, George	6: 70
1906-	Buffington, Joseph	
1909-1912	Lanning, William M.	
1911-1913	Archbold, Robert W. (*impeached*)	
1912-1919	McPherson, John B.	
1914-	Woolley, Victor B.	
1919-1920	Haight, Thomas G.	
1920-	Davis, J. Warren	
1931-	Thompson, J. Whitaker	

Fourth Circuit

1801-1802	Key, Philip B.	11:488
1801-1802	Taylor, George K.	
1801-1802	Magill, Charles	
1870-1893	Bond, Hugh L.	11:408
1892-1913	Goff, Nathan, Jr.	3:202
1893-1904	Simonton, Charles H.	12:436
1904-1921	Pritchard, Jeter C.	19:223
1910-1923	Knapp, Martin A.	4:287
1913-1925	Woods, Charles A.	
1921-1931	Waddill, Edmund, Jr.	
1922-1927	Rose, John C.	
1925-	Parker, John J.	
1927-	Northcott, Elliott	14:495
1931-	Soper, Morris A.	

Fifth Circuit

1801-1802	Clay, Joseph	
1801-1802	Potter, Henry	11:259
1801-1802	Hall, Dominick A.	13:465
1802-	Harris, Edward	
1869-1880	Woods, William B.	2:476
1881-1919	Pardee, Don Albert	18:253
1892-1916	McCormick, Andrew P.	19:259
1899-1914	Shelby, David D.	21:351
1914-1936	Walker, Richard W.	
1917-1919	Batts, Robert L.	
1920-1935	Bryan, Nathan P.	C:391
1920-1925	King, Alexander C.	22:431
1925-	Foster, Rufus E.	18:257
1931-	Sibley, Samuel H.	
1931-	Hutcheson, Joseph C., Jr.	
1936-	Holmes, Edwin R.	

Sixth Circuit

1801-1802	McClung, William	
1870-1877	Emmons, Halmor H.	
1877-1886	Baxter, John	11: 98
1886-1893	Jackson, Howell E.	8:243
1892-1900	Taft, William H.	23: 1
1893-1909	Lurton, Horace H.	8:235
1899-1903	Day, William R.	11: 11
1900-1911	Severens, Henry F.	19:354
1903-1909	Richards, John K.	13:227
1909-1919	Warrington, John W.	
1910-1930	Knappen, Loyal E.	
1911-1931	Denison, Arthur C.	C:518
1919-1928	Donahue, Maurice H.	
1925-	Moorman, Charles H.	
1928-	Hicks, Xenophon	
1928-1933	Hickenlooper, Smith	
1932-	Simons, Charles C.	
1934-	Allen, Florence E.	C:111

Seventh Circuit

1869-1884	Drummond, Thomas	20:111
1884-1893	Gresham, Walter Q.	4:251
1892-1901	Woods, William A.	18:303
1893-1905	Jenkins, James G.	19:188
1895-1898	Showalter, John W.	
1899-1911	Grosscup, Peter S.	15:253
1902-1924	Baker, Francis E.	22: 50
1905-1915	Seaman, William H.	20:297
1905-1918	Kohlsaat, Christian C.	
1915-1936	Alschuler, Samuel	
1916-	Evans, Evan A.	
1919-1930	Page, George T.	A:366
1925-1929	Anderson, Albert B.	
1929-	Sparks, William M.	
1933-	FitzHenry, Louis	

Eighth Circuit

1869-1879	Dillon, John F.	1:268
1879-1884	McCrary, George W.	3:201
1884-1890	Brewer, David J.	1: 37
1890-1903	Caldwell, Henry C.	11:478
1892-1928	Sanborn, Walter H.	12:526
1894-1905	Thayer, Amos M.	10:504
1903-1910	VanDevanter, Willis	D: 82
1903-1921	Hook, William C.	
1905-1916	Adams, Elmer B.	5:385
1911-1922	Smith, Walter I.	
1911-1922	Carland, John E.	
1916-	Stone, Kimbrough	
1922-1933	Kenyon, William S.	24: 60
1923-	Woodrough, Joseph W.	
1925-1933	VanValkenburgh, Arba S.	
1925-1931	Booth, Wilbur F.	
1928-1933	Cotteral, John H.	
1929-	Gardner, Archibald K.	
1932-	Sanborn, John B.	
1935-1936	Faris, Charles B.	
1935-	Thomas, Seth	

Ninth Circuit

1870-1891	Sawyer, Lorenzo	13:195
1892-1897	McKenna, Joseph	11: 18
1892-1931	Gilbert, William B.	23: 48
1895-1929	Ross, Erskine M.	
1897-1929	Morrow, William W.	B:308
1911-1928	Hunt, William H.	
1923-1931	Rudkin, Frank H.	18:400
1925-1926	McComant, Wallace	
1927-1930	Dietrich, Frank S.	
1929-	Wilbur, Curtis D.	A: 13
1931-1934	Sawtelle, William H.	
1933-	Garrecht, Francis A.	
1933-1934	Norcross, Frank N.	
1935-	Denman, William	
1935-	Mathews, Clifton	
1935-	Haney, Bert E.	

*Tenth Circuit**

1855-1862	McAllister, Matthew H.	11:474
1921-	Lewis, Robert E.	
1929-	Phillips, Orie L.	
1929-	McDermott, George T.	
1933-	Bratton, Sam G.	B:488

*California Circuit organized by Act of March 2, 1855; abolished by Act of March 3, 1863, creating the Tenth Circuit. However, no judges were appointed to this Circuit until 1921.

United States Court of Customs and Patent Appeals

(Known as the United States Court of Customs Appeals from 1910 to 1929, and thereafter under its present title)

Presiding Judges

1910-1920	Montgomery, Robert M.	12:113
1921-1922	DeVries, Marion	
1923-1924	Martin, George E.	
1924-	Graham, William J.	

Associate Judges

1910-1911	Hunt, William H.	
1910-1928	Smith, James F.	
1910-1928	Barber, Orion M.	
1910-1921	DeVries, Marion	
1911-1923	Martin, George E.	
1923-	Bland, Oscar E.	
1923-	Hatfield, Charles S.	
1929-	Garrett, Finis J.	
1929-	Lenroot, Irvine L.	B:184

Court of Claims of the United States

Chief Justices*

1863-1870	Casey, Joseph	
1870-1885	Drake, Charles D.	3:427
1885-1896	Richardson, William A.	4: 17
1896-1906	Nott, Charles C.	12:357
1906-1913	Peelle, Stanton J.	14: 96
1913-1928	Campbell, Edward K.	
1928-	Booth, Fenton W.	

*Before the act of March 3, 1863, there was no chief justice. Judge Gilchrist was chosen as presiding judge upon the organization of the court in 1855; after his death in 1858 the senior judge presided.

Associate Judges

1855-1858	Gilchrist, John J.	7:508
1855-1859	Blackford, Isaac N.	11:490
1855-1861	Scarburgh, George P.	
1858-1877	Loring, Edward G.	
1860-1865	Hughes, James	23:157
1861-1863	Casey, Joseph	
1863-1868	Wilmot, David	3:419
1863-1878	Peck, Ebenezer	
1865-1896	Nott, Charles C.	12:357
1868-1874	Milligan, Samuel	5:193
1874-1885	Richardson, William A.	4: 17
1877-1881	Davis, J. C. Bancroft	11:115
1878-1881	Hunt, William H.	4:244
1881-1892	Scofield, Glenni W.	11:511
1882-1883	Davis, J. C. Bancroft	11:115
1883-1905	Weldon, Lawrence	
1885-1902	Davis, John	22:349
1892-1906	Peelle, Stanton J.	14: 96
1897-1915	Howry, Charles B.	22: 55
1903-1905	Wright, Francis M.	
1905-1928	Booth, Fenton W.	
1905-1916	Atkinson, George W.	12:432
1906-1919	Barney, Samuel S.	
1915-1926	Downey, George E.	
1916-1928	Hay, James	23:241
1919-1930	Graham, Samuel J.	
1926-1929	Moss, McKenzie	
1928-	Green, William R.	
1928-1929	Sinnott, Nicholas J.	
1929-	Williams, Thomas S.	
1929-	Littleton, Benjamin H.	
1930-	Whaley, Richard S.	

Permanent Court of International Justice The Hague

1922-1928	Moore, John Bassett	A: 72
1928-1930	Hughes, Charles Evans	A: 6
1930-	Kellogg, Frank B.	A: 8

Mixed Courts of Egypt

Justices of the Court of Appeals at Alexandria

1875-1894	Barringer, Victor C.	13:351
1894-1902	Keiley, Anthony M.	13:433
1902-1908	Batcheller, George S.	4:464
1908-1920	Tuck, Somerville P.	12:369
1921-	Brinton, Jasper Y.	

Judges of the District Courts

1875-1885	Batcheller, George S.	4:464
1877-1880	Morgan, Philip H.	13:596
1884-1889	Kinsman, J. B.	
1885-1889	Farman, Elbert E.	6:508
1886-1894	Keiley, Anthony M.	13:433
1889-1894	Crosby, Ernest H.	10: 61
1894-1897	Fearn, Walker	
1894-1908	Tuck, Somerville P.	12:369
1897-1902	Batcheller, George S.	4:464
1902-1924	VanHorne, William G.	
1908-1911	Berry, Walter VanR.	22: 71
1911-	Crabites, Pierre	
1924-	Henry, Robert L.	
1930-	Wright, Julian M.	

United States Ambassadors, Envoys Extraordinary, and Ministers Plenipotentiary

AFGHANISTAN

1935..Hornibrook, William H. .. B: 47

ALBANIA

1922..Grant-Smith, Ulysses .....
1925..Hart, Charles C. ....
1930..Bernstein, Herman ...... C: 116
1933..Wheeler, Post ....
1935..Grant, Hugh G. ....

ALGIERS

1793..Humphreys, David 1: 71
1815..Shaler, William 4: 532
1815..Bainbridge, William 8: 93
1815..Decatur, Stephen 4: 56
1816..Chauncey, Isaac 8: 95

ARGENTINA

1823..Rodney, Cæsar A. 3: 11
1825..Forbes, John M. (Chargés d'Affaires) 13: 374
1832..Baylies, Francis (Chargés d'Affaires) 11: 372
1843..Watterson, Harvey M. ... 1: 403
1844..Brent, William, Jr. (Chargés d'Affaires) ... 5: 528
1846..Harris, William A. (Chargés d'Affaires) ..12: 529
1851..Pendleton, John S. (Chargés d'Affaires) ..12: 323
1854..Peden, James A. ....
1858..Yancey, Benjamin C. 13: 560
1859..Cushman, John F. 5: 528
1861..Palmer, Robert M. 13: 29
1862..Kirk, Robert C. 12: 440
1866..Asboth, Alexander S. 4: 413
1868..Worthington, Henry G. ..12: 436
1869..Kirk, Robert C. 12: 440
1871..Clapp, Dexter E. 5: 526
1872..White, Julius 4: 335
1874..Osborn, Thomas O. 10: 146
1885..Hanna, Bayliss W. 12: 118
1888..Pitkin, John R. G. 11: 553
1894..Buchanan, William I. 2: 271
1900..Lord, William P. 8: 7
1903..Barrett, John .... D: 450
1904..Beaupré, Arthur M. 14: 338
1908..Eddy, Spencer 14: 395
1909..Sherrill, Charles H. 14: 523
1911..Garrett, John W. .... A: 335
1914..Stimson, Frederic J. 10: 361
1921..Riddle, John W. 14: 53
1925..Jay, Peter A. .... C: 400
1927..Bliss, Robert W. .... A: 514
1933..Weddell, Alexander W. .. D: 234

AUSTRIA

1838..Muhlenberg, Henry A. ..
1841..Jenifer, Daniel 13: 324
1845..Stiles, William H. (Chargés d'Affaires) 12: 558
1849..Webb, J. Watson (Chargés d'Affaires) 3: 30
1850..McCurdy, Charles J. (Chargés d'Affaires) ... 4: 376
1852..Foote, Thomas M. (Chargés d'Affaires) 7: 533
1853..Jackson, Henry R. (Chargés d'Affaires) 3: 369
1858..Jones, Jehu G. 7: 532
1861..Burlingame, Anson 8: 55
1861..Motley, J. Lothrop 5: 213
1867..Hay, John (Chargés d'Affaires) 11: 12

AUSTRIA-HUNGARY

1868..Watts, Henry M. 4: 305
1869..Jay, John 7: 347
1875..Orth, Godlove S. 5: 128
1876..Beale, Edward F. 11: 364
1877..Kasson, John A. 4: 379
1881..Phelps, William W. 7: 451
1882..Taft, Alphonso 4: 24
1884..Francis, John M. 1: 242
1887..Lawton, Alexander R. 2: 148
1889..Grant, Frederick D. 15: 93
1893..Tripp, Bartlett 8: 100
1897..Tower, Charlemagne 26: 124
1899..Harris, Addison C. 17: 191
1901..McCormick, Robert S. ...13: 375
1902..Storer, Bellamy 11: 338
1906..Francis, Charles S. 12: 117
1909..Kerens, Richard C. 14: 106
1913..Penfield, Frederic C. 15: 311

AUSTRIA

1919..Halstead, Albert (commissioner) ....
1920..Frazier, Arthur H. (commissioner) ....
1921..Frazier, Arthur H. (Chargés d'Affaires) ..
1922..Washburn, Albert H. 26: 234
1930..Stockton, Gilchrist B. ... D: 173
1933..Earle, George H., 3rd ....
1934..Messersmith, George S. ..

BELGIUM

1832..Legaré, Hugh S. (Chargés d'Affaires) 6: 5
1837..Maxcy, Virgil (Chargés d'Affaires) 4: 88
1842..Hilliard, Henry W. (Chargés d'Affaires) .. 2: 114
1844..Clemson, Thomas G. (Chargés d'Affaires) ..13: 43
1850..Bayard, Richard H. (Chargés d'Affaires) ... 4: 351
1853..Seibels, John J. (Chargés d'Affaires) 12: 310
1858..Fair, Elisha Y. 12: 101
1861..Sanford, Henry S. 7: 140
1870..Jones, Joseph R. 1: 534
1876..Merrill, Ayers P. 12: 314
1878..Goodloe, William G. 7: 540
1880..Putnam, James O. 10: 40
1882..Fish, Nicholas 11: 27
1885..Tree, Lambert 6: 161
1888..Parkhurst, John G. 7: 482
1889..Terrell, Edwin H. 1: 387
1893..Ewing, James S. 8: 179
1897..Storer, Bellamy 11: 338
1899..Townsend, Lawrence 12: 54
1905..Wilson, Henry L. 12: 126
1909..Bryan, Charles P. 12: 452
1911..Anderson, Larz 15: 349
1912..Marburg, Theodore 15: 45
1913..Whitlock, Brand .... A: 544
1922..Fletcher, Henry P. ...... D: 428
1924..Phillips, William .... B: 56
1927..Gibson, Hugh .... A: 419
1933..Morris, Dave H. .... D: 107

BOLIVIA

1848..Appleton, John (Chargés d'Affaires) 12: 275
1849..McClung, Alexander K. (Chargés d'Affaires) .. 3: 212
1852..Miller, Horace H. (Chargés d'Affaires) ...
1853..Dana, John W. 6: 310
1858..Smith, John C. 10: 332
1861..Carter, David K. ....
1863..Hall, Allen A. 7: 535
1868..Caldwell, John W. ....
1869..Markbreit, Leopold 12: 467
1872..Croxton, John T. 7: 534
1874..Reynolds, Robert M. 12: 150
1878..Pettis, S. Newton 11: 193
1880..Adams, Charles 13: 247
1881..Trescot, William H. 13: 206
1882..Maney, George 5: 196
1883..Gibbs, Richard 12: 131
1885..Seay, William A. 7: 555
1887..Carlisle, S. S. ....
1889..Anderson, Thomas H. 12: 324
1892..Grant, Frederic J. 9: 549
1894..Moonlight, Thomas 12: 312
1897..Bridgman, George H. 13: 191
1902..Sorsby, William B. 13: 535
1908..Stutesman, James F. 19: 19
1910..Knowles, Horace G. 14: 487
1913..O'Rear, John D. 19: 56
1919..Maginnis, Samuel A. .... B: 52
1921..Cottrell, Jesse S. ....
1928..Kaufman, David E. ......
1930..Feely, Edward F. ....
1933..DesPortes, Fay A. ......

BRAZIL

1825..Raquet, Condy (Chargés d'Affaires) 11: 519
1827..Tudor, William (Chargés d'Affaires) 8: 351

1830..Brown, Ethan A. (Chargés d'Affaires) 3:138
1834..Hunter, William 9:269
1843..Proffit, George H. ....
1844..Wise, Henry A. 5:452
1847..Tod, David 3:141
1851..Schenck, Robert C. 3:206
1853..Trousdale, William 7:209
1857..Meade, Richard K. 10:151
1861..Webb, J. Watson 3: 30
1869..Blow, Henry T. 4:291
1871..Partridge, James R. 7:519
1877..Hilliard, Henry W. 2:114
1881..Osborn, Thomas A. 8:345
1885..Jarvis, Thomas J. 4:429
1889..Adams, Robert 12:219
1890..Conger, Edwin H. 8:176
1893..Thompson, Thomas L. ... 8:178
1897..Conger, Edwin H. 8:176
1898..Bryan, Charles P. 12:452
1902..Thompson, David E. 14:166
1906..Griscom, Lloyd C. 12:196
1906..Dudley, Irving B. 13:296
1912..Morgan, Edwin V. 14:432
1933..Gibson, Hugh A:419

BULGARIA

1901..Dickinson, Charles M. (Agent) 11: 91
1903..Jackson, John B. (Diplomatic Agent) 12:250
1907..Knowles, Horace G. (Diplomatic Agent) 14:487
1909..Eddy, Spencer (Diplomatic Agent) 14:395
1909..Carter, John R. (Agent) .14:199
1911..Jackson, John B. 12:250
1913..Vopicka, Charles J. 25:374
1921..Wilson, Charles S. ....
1928..Schoenfeld, Hans F. A:129
1929..Vacant
1930..Shoemaker, Henry W. .. D:303
1933..Sterling, Frederick A. ....

CANADA

1927..Phillips, William .... B: 56
1930..MacNider, Hanford A:527
1932..MacChesney, Nathan W...
1933..Robbins, Warren D. .....
1935..Armour, Norman ....

CHILE

1823..Allen, Heman 11:158
1828..Larned, Samuel (Chargés d'Affaires) 12:476
1830..Hamm, John (Chargés d'Affaires) ....
1834..Pollard, Richard (Chargés d'Affaires) 12:109
1841..Pendleton, John S. (Chargés d'Affaires) ...12:323
1844..Crump, William (Chargés d'Affaires) ....
1847..Barton, Seth (Chargés d'Affaires) 13:137
1849..Peyton, Balie 7:176
1854..Starkweather, David A. .. 7:529
1857..Bigler, John 4:106
1861..Nelson, Thomas H. 11:550
1865..Kilpatrick, Hugh J. 4:273
1870..Root, Joseph P. 13:309
1873..Logan, Cornelius A. 5:531
1877..Osborn, Thomas A. 8:345
1881..Kilpatrick, Hugh J. 4:273
1881..Trescot, William H. 13:206
1882..Logan, Cornelius A. 5:531
1885..Roberts, William R. 8:123
1889..Egan, Patrick 5:399
1893..Porter, James D. 7:211
1894..Strobel, Edward H. 12:324
1897..Wilson, Henry L. 12:126
1905..Hicks, John 12:141
1909..Dawson, Thomas C. 13:512
1909..Fletcher, Henry P. D:428
1916..Shea, Joseph H. 22: 31
1921..Collier, William M. 13:547
1928..Culbertson, William S. ... D:321
1933..Sevier, Henry H. ....
1935..Philip, Hoffman B:348

CHINA

1843..Cushing, Caleb 4:151
1845..Everett, Alexander H. ... 9:256
1848..Davis, John W. 8: 3
1851..Nelson, Thomas A. R. ....
1852..Marshall, Humphrey 6: 65
1853..McLane, Robert M. 9:311
1855..Parker, Peter 10:284
1857..Reed, William B. 7:533
1858..Ward, John E. 1:373
1861..Burlingame, Anson 8: 55
1868..Browne, John R. 8:117
1869..Low, Frederick F. 4:109
1874..Avery, Benjamin P. 1:319
1876..Seward, George F. 7: 91
1880..Angell, James B. 1:251
1882..Young, John R. 2:214
1885..Denby, Charles 8:276
1897..Bryan, Charles P. 12:452
1898..Conger, Edwin H. 8:176
1900..Rockhill, William W. 8:129
1909..Crane, Charles R. ....
1909..Calhoun, William J. 14:429
1913..Reinsch, Paul S. 19:285
1919..Vacant
1920..Crane, Charles R. ....
1921..Schurman, Jacob G. 4:478
1925..MacMurray, John Van A.
1929..Johnson, Nelson T. ......

COLUMBIA

1823..Anderson, Richard C. 6:115
1827..Beaufort, T. Watts (Chargés d'Affaires) ...
1828..Harrison, William H. 3: 33
1829..Moore, Thomas P. 5:526
1833..McAfee, Robert B. (Chargés d'Affaires) 5:508
1837..Semple, James (Chargés d'Affaires) 4:361
1842..Blackford, William M. (Chargés d'Affaires) ..
1845..Bidlack, Benjamin A. (Chargés d'Affaires) ...13:415
1849..Foote, Thomas M. (Chargés d'Affaires) 7:533
1851..King, Yelverton P. (Chargés d'Affaires) 5:530
1853..Green, James S. 7:535
1854..Bowlin, James B. 5:528
1859..Jones, George W. 3:433
1861..Burton, Allen A. 5:534
1867..Sullivan, Peter J. 5:526
1869..Hurlbut, Stephen A. 4:218
1873..Scruggs, William L. 2:165
1878..Dickman, Ernst 5:339
1881..Maney, George 5:196
1882..Scruggs, William L. 2:165
1885..Jacob, Charles D. 7:357
1886..Maury, Dabney H. 4: 35
1889..Abbott, John T. 13: 47
1893..McKinney, Luther F. 12:143
1897..Hart, Charles B. 13:470
1903..Beaupré, Arthur M. 14:338
1904..Russell, William W. 15: 58
1905..Barrett, John D:450
1906..Vacant
1907..Dawson, Thomas C. 13:512
1909..Northcott, Elliott 14:495
1911..DuBois, James T. 18:363
1913..Thomson, Thaddeus A. ...
1916..Vacant
1917..Philip, Hoffman B:348
1922..Piles, Samuel H. 14:389
1928..Caffery, Jefferson ....
1933..Whitehouse, Sheldon D:188
1935..Dawson, William ....

COSTA RICA

1853..Borland, Solon 4:386
1858..Lamar, Mirabeau B. 9: 66
1859..Dimitry, Alexander 10:176
1861..Riotte, Charles N. ....
1866..Lawrence, Albert G. 11:447
1868..Blair, Jacob B. 12:275
1873..Williamson, George McW. 12: 52
1879..Logan, Cornelius A. 5:531
1882..Hall, Henry C. 5:551
1889..Mizner, Lansing B. 5:556
1890..Pacheco, Romnaldo 4:110
1891..Shannon, Richard C. 12:361
1893..Baker, Lewis 1:246
1897..Merry, William L. 12:310
1911..Einstein, Lewis ....
1913..Hale, Edward J. 19:200
1919..Vacant
1922..Davis, Roy T. ....
1931..Eberhardt, Charles C. ....
1933..Sack, Leo R. ....

CUBA

1902..Squires, Herbert G. 12:333
1905..Morgan, Edwin V. 14:432
1909..Jackson, John B. 12:250
1911..Beaupré, Arthur M. 14:338
1913..Gonzales, William E. ....
1919..Long, Boaz W. ....
1923..Crowder, Enoch H. A:455
1927..Judah, Noble B. ....
1929..Guggenheim, Harry F. ... C: 48
1933..Welles, Sumner ....
1934..Caffery, Jefferson ....

CZECHOSLOVAKIA

1919..Crane, Richard ....
1921..Einstein, Lewis ....
1930..Ratshesky, Abraham C. ..
1932..Vacant
1933..White, Francis ....
1934..Wright, J. Butler ....

DENMARK

1811..Erving, George W. 12: 275
1827..Wheaton, Henry (Chargés d'Affaires) 1: 274
1835..Woodside, Jonathan F. (Chargés d'Affaires) ...
1841..Jackson, Isaac R. (Chargés d'Affaires) ....
1843..Irwin, William W. (Chargés d'Affaires) 7: 534
1847..Flenniken, Robert P. (Chargés d'Affaires) ...
1849..Forward, Walter (Chargés d'Affaires) 6: 5
1852..Grieve, Miller (Chargés d'Affaires) 13: 92
1853..Bedinger, Henry 11: 261
1858..Buchanan, James M. 7: 536
1861..Wood, Bradford R. 12: 504
1865..Yeaman, George H. 9: 187
1870..Cramer, Michael J. 12: 310
1881..Payson, Charles (Chargés d'Affaires) ....
1882..Wickersham, James P. ...12: 239
1883..Hoffman, Wickham 12: 71
1885..Anderson, Rasmus B. 9: 320
1889..Carr, Clark E. 12: 99
1893..Risley, John E. 12: 284
1897..Swenson, Laurits S. 12: 108
1905..O'Brien, Thomas J. ...... B: 225
1907..Egan, Maurice F. 11: 111
1918..Vacant
1919..Hapgood, Norman ....
1920..Grew, Joseph C. .... A: 412
1921..Prince, John D. .... C: 43
1926..Dodge, Henry P. 14: 428
1930..Booth, Ralph H. .... C: 188
1931..Coleman, Frederick W. B.. C: 500
1933..Owen, Ruth Bryan ...... A: 368

DOMINICAN REPUBLIC

1883..Langston, John M. (Chargés d'Affaires) ... 3: 328
1885..Thompson, John E. W. (Chargés d'Affaires) ...13: 477
1889..Douglass, Frederick (Chargés d'Affaires) ... 2: 309
1892..Durham, John S. (Chargés d'Affaires) 4: 408
1897..Powell, William F. (Chargés d'Affaires) 12: 195
1904..Dawson, Thomas C. 13: 512
1907..McCreery, Fenton R. 14: 118
1909..Knowles, Horace G. 14: 487
1910..Russell, William W. 15: 58
1913..Sullivan, James M. ......
1915..Russell, William W. 15: 58
1925..Young, Evan E. ....
1929..Curtis, Charles B. ....
1931..Schoenfeld, Hans F. ..... A: 129

ECUADOR

1848..Livingston, Van Brugh ..13: 177
1849..VanAlen, John T. ....
1850..Cushing, Courtland 12: 274
1853..White, Philo 5: 536
1858..Buckalew, Charles R. 11: 190
1861..Hassaurek, Friedrich 11: 279
1866..Coggeshall, William T. ...12: 57
1869..Wing, Edward R. 5: 537
1875..Biddle, Thomas 12: 145
1875..Wullweber, Christian F. W. J. 5: 556
1892..Mahany, Rowland B. 9: 419
1894..Strobel, Edward H. 12: 324
1895..Tillman, James D. 12: 316
1897..Sampson, Archibald J. ... 3: 359
1905..Lee, Joseph W. J. 14: 428
1907..Fox, Williams C. 14: 114
1911..Young, Evan E. ....
1913..Schuyler, Montgomery ... B: 449
1913..Hartman, Charles S. 21: 43
1922..Bading, Gerhard A. ......
1930..Dawson, William ....
1935..Gonzales, Antonio C. .....

EGYPT

1876..Farman, Elbert E. (Consul General) 6: 508
1881..Wolf, Simon (Consul General) ....
1882..Pomeroy, George P. (Consul General) ....
1885..Cardwell, John (Consul General) ....
1889..Schuyler, Eugene (Consul General) 8: 339
1891..Anderson, John A. (Consul General) 8: 458
1892..Little, Edward C. (Consul General) ....
1893..Penfield, Frederic C. (Consul General) 15: 311
1897..Harrison, Thomas S. (Consul General) ......
1899..Long, John G. (Consul General) ....
1903..Riddle, John W. (Consul General) 14: 53
1905..Iddings, Lewis M. (Consul General) ....
1909..Jay, Peter A. (Consul General) .... C: 400
1913..Arnold, Olney (Consul General) ....
1917..Gary, Hampson (Consul General) .... A: 432
1920..Sprigg, Carroll (Consul General) ....
1921..Howell, Joseph M. .... B: 240
1928..Gunther, Franklin M. ....
1930..Jardine, William M. ..... A: 14
1933..Fish, Bert ....

EL SALVADOR

1853..Borland, Solon 4: 386
1863..Partridge, James R. 7: 519
1866..Williams, Alpheus S. 4: 365
1869..Torbert, Alfred T. A. ... 4: 537
1871..Biddle, Thomas 12: 145
1873..Williamson, George McW..12: 52
1879..Logan, Cornelius A. 5: 531
1882..Hall, Henry C. 5: 551
1889..Mizner, Lansing B. 5: 556
1890..Pacheco, Romnaldó 4: 110
1891..Shannon, Richard C. 12: 361
1893..Baker, Lewis 1: 246
1897..Merry, William L. 12: 310
1907..Dodge, Henry P. 14: 428
1909..Heimke, William ....
1914..Long, Boaz W. ....
1920..Jay, Peter A. .... C: 400
1921..Schuyler, Montgomery ... B: 449
1926..Caffery, Jefferson ....
1928..Robbins, Warren D. .....
1931..Curtis, Charles B. ....
1934..Corrigan, Frank P. ......

ESTONIA

1922..Coleman, Frederick W. B.. C: 500
1931..Skinner, Robert P. .... B: 356
1933..MacMurray, John Van A.

FINLAND

1919..Haynes, Thornwell (Commissioner) ....
1920..Magruder, Alexander R. (Chargés d'Affaires) ...
1921..Kagey, Charles L. .... C: 316
1925..Pearson, Alfred J. ...... A: 188
1930..Brodie, Edward E. .... D: 119
1933..Albright, Edward ....

FRANCE

1785..Jefferson, Thomas 3: 1
1790..Short, William (Chargés d'Affaires) 4: 530
1792..Morris, Gouverneur 2: 526
1794..Monroe, James 6: 81
1796 Pinckney, Charles C. 2: 302
1797 Gerry, Elbridge 5: 371
1797 Marshall, John 1: 25
Ellsworth, Oliver 1: 22
1799 Murray, William V. 11: 360
Davie, William R. 1: 77
1801 Livingston, Robert R. 2: 396
1803 Monroe, James 6: 81
1803 Livingston, Robert R. 2: 396
1804..Armstrong, John, 2d 1: 48
1810..Russell, Jonathan (Chargés d'Affaires) 8: 57
1811..Barlow, Joel 3: 186
1813..Crawford, William H. ... 5: 82
1815..Gallatin, Albert 3: 9
1823..Brown, James 4: 376
1829..Rives, William C. 6: 486
1832..Niles, Nathaniel 5: 374
1833..Harris, Leavitt (Chargés d'Affaires) ....
1833..Livingston, Edward 5: 293
1835..Barton, Thomas P. 14: 365
1836..Cass, Lewis 5: 3
1842..Ledyard, Henry (Chargés d'Affaires) 22: 27
1844..King, William R. 4: 147
1847..Rush, Richard 5: 80
1849..Rives, William C. 6: 486
1853..Sanford, Henry S. 7: 140
1853..Mason, John Y. 6: 7
1860..Faulkner, Charles J., Sr. . 2: 392
1861..Dayton, William L. 4: 325
1865..Bigelow, John 26: 25
1866..Dix, John A. 5: 6
1869..Washburne, Elihu B. 4: 14
1877..Noyes, Edward F. 3: 142
1881..Morton, Levi P. 1: 136
1885..McLane, Robert M. 9: 311
1889..Reid, Whitelaw 22: 1
1892..Coolidge, T. Jefferson 12: 58
1893..Eustis, James B. 1: 462

1897..Porter, Horace 4: 310
1905..McCormick, Robert S. 13: 375
1906..White, Henry 14: 171
1909..Bacon, Robert 14: 16
1912..Herrick, Myron T. 13: 68
1914..Sharp, William G. 19: 299
1919..Wallace, Hugh C. ....
1921..Herrick, Myron T. 13: 68
1929..Edge, Walter E. .... B: 279
1933..Straus, Jesse I. .... D: 33

GERMANY
(Prussia to 1871)

1797..Adams, John Quincy 5: 73
1835..Wheaton, Henry (Chargés d'Affaires) 1: 274
1846..Donelson, Andrew J. 7: 489
1849..Hannegan, Edward A. ...11: 372
1850..Barnard, Daniel D. 10: 70
1853..Vroom, Peter D. 5: 205
1857..Wright, Joseph A. 13: 269
1861..Judd, Norman B. 11: 273
1865..Wright, Joseph A. 13: 269
1867..Bancroft, George 3: 160
1874..Davis, John C. B. 11: 115
1877..Everett, Henry S. (Chargés d'Affaires) 9: 186
1878..Taylor, Bayard 3: 454
1878..Everett, Henry S. (Chargés d'Affaires) 9: 186
1879..White, Andrew D. 4: 476
1881..Everett, Henry S. (Chargés d'Affaires) 9: 186
1882..Sargent, Aaron A. 13: 475
1884..Kasson, John A. 4: 379
1885..Pendleton, George H. 3: 278
1889..Phelps, William W. 7: 451
1893..Runyon, Theodore 7: 255
1896..Uhl, Edwin F. 15: 100
1897..White, Andrew D. 4: 476
1902..Tower, Charlemagne 5: 190
1908..Hill, David J. 12: 244
1911..Leishman, John G. A. ...13: 598
1913..Gerard, James W. .... A: 168
1917..Relations severed
1919..Dresel, Ellis L. (Commissioner, Chargés d'Affaires)
1922..Houghton, Alanson B. ... B: 7
1925..Schurman, Jacob G. 4: 478
1930..Sackett, Frederic M., Jr... B: 421
1933..Dodd, William E. .... D: 34

GREAT BRITAIN

1792..Pinckney, Thomas 12: 160
1794..Jay, John 1: 20
1796..King, Rufus 6: 301
1803..Monroe, James 6: 81
1806..Pinkney, William 5: 373
1811..Smith, John S. (Chargés d'Affaires) 12: 188
1811..Russell, Jonathan (Chargés d'Affaires) 8: 57
1815..Adams, John Quincy 5: 73
1817..Rush, Richard 5: 80
1825..King, Rufus 6: 301
1826..King, John A. (Chargés d'Affaires) 3: 50
1826..Gallatin, Albert 3: 9
1827..Laurence, William Beach (Chargés d'Affaires) .. 9: 399
1828..Barbour, James 5: 82
1829..McLane, Louis 5: 293
1831..VanBuren, Martin 6: 433
1832..Vail, Aaron 5: 555
1836..Stevenson, Andrew 5: 298
1841..Everett, Edward 6: 179
1845..McLane, Louis 5: 293
1846..Bancroft, George 3: 160
1849..Davis, John C. B. 11: 115
1849..Lawrence, Abbott 3: 62
1852..Ingersoll, Joseph R. 7: 530
1853..Buchanan, James 5: 1
1856..Dallas, George M. 6: 268
1861..Adams, Charles F. 8: 351
1868..Johnson, Reverdy 4: 371
1869..Motley, John L. 5: 213
1870..Schenck, Robert C. 3: 206
1876..Pierrepont, Edwards 4: 21
1877..Welsh, John 3: 412
1879..Hoppin, William J. (Chargés d'Affaires) ... 5: 186
1880..Lowell, James R. 2: 32
1885..Phelps, Edward J. 5: 411
1889..Lincoln, Robert T. 21: 59
1893..Bayard, Thomas F. 2: 404
1897..Hay, John 11: 12
1899..Choate, Joseph H. 9: 159
1905..Reid, Whitelaw 22: 1
1913..Page, Walter H. 19: 13
1918..Davis, John W. .... A: 25
1921..Harvey, George 13: 604
1923..Kellogg, Frank B. .... A: 8
1925..Houghton, Alanson B. .... B: 7
1929..Dawes, Charles G. .... A: 508
1932..Mellon, Andrew W. ...... A: 16
1933..Bingham, Robert W. ..... D: 32

GREECE

1868..Tuckerman, Charles K. ...14: 426
1871..Francis, John M. 1: 242
1873..Read, John M. 2: 223
1882..Schuyler, Eugene 8: 339
1885..Fearn, John W. 12: 312
1889..Snowden, Archibald L. ...12: 119
1892..Beale, Truxtun 13: 77
1893..Alexander, Eben 12: 266
1897..Rockhill, William W. 8: 129
1899..Hardy, Arthur S. 2: 303
1900..Francis, Charles S. 12: 117
1902..Jackson, John B. 12: 250
1907..Pearson, Richmond 14: 131
1909..Moses, George H. .... C: 71
1912..Schurman, Jacob G. 4: 478
1913..Williams, George F. ......
1914..Droppers, Garrett 20: 16
1920..Capps, Edward .... A: 416
1921..Vacant
1924..Laughlin, Irwin B. ...... D: 164
1926..Skinner, Robert P. ...... B: 356
1931..Vacant
1933..MacVeagh, Lincoln ....

GUATEMALA

1848..Hise, Elijah (Chargés d'Affaires) 12: 54
1849..Squier, Ephraim G. (Chargés d'Affaires) ... 4: 79
1853..Borland, Solon 4: 386
1854..Marling, John L. 13: 372
1857..Venable, William E. 13: 535
1858..Clarke, Beverly L. 12: 200
1861..Crosby, Elisha O. ....
1865..Warren, Fitz Henry 12: 228
1869..Hudson, Silas A. 12: 63
1873..Williamson, George McW..12: 52
1879..Logan, Cornelius A. 5: 531
1882..Hall, Henry C. 5: 551
1889..Mizner, Lansing B. 5: 556
1890..Pacheco, Romnaldo 4: 110
1893..Young, Pierce M. B. 2: 382
1896..Coxe, Macgrane 12: 476
1897..Hunter, Whiteside G. 5: 518
1902..Combs, Leslie 13: 309
1907..Lee, Joseph W. J. 14: 428
1908..Heimke, William ....
1909..Sands, William F. 14: 495
1910..Hitt, Robert S. R. 14: 477
1913..Leavell, William H. ..... C: 332
1919..McMillin, Benton 13: 79
1921..Davis, Roy T. ....
1922..Geissler, Arthur H. ......
1929..Whitehouse, Sheldon ..... D: 188
1933..Hanna, Matthew E. ......

HAITI

1862..Whidden, Benjamin F. (Commissioner) ......
1865..Peck, Henry E. 12: 115
1868..Hollister, Gideon H. 12: 56
1869..Bassett, Ebenezer D. C. ..13: 86
1877..Langston, John M. 3: 328
1885..Thompson, John E. W. ..13: 477
1889..Douglass, Frederick 2: 309
1891..Durham, John S. 4: 408
1893..Smythe, Henry M. 13: 241
1897..Powell, William F. 12: 195
1905..Furniss, Henry W. 14: 443
1913..Smith, Madison R. 19: 349
1914..Bailly-Blanchard, Arthur..
1922..Russell, John H. (High Commissioner) ....
1925..Vacant
1930..Munro, Dana G. ....
1932..Armour, Norman ....
1935..Gordon, George A. ....

HAWAII

1841..Ten Eyck, Anthony (Commissioner) 12: 259
1843..Brown, George (Commissioner) ....
1849..Eames, Charles (Commissioner) 11: 477
1850..Severance, Luther (Commissioner) 13: 473
1853..Gregg, David L. (Commissioner) 13: 319
1858..Borden, James W. (Commissioner) 12: 292
1861..Dryer, Thomas J. (Commissioner) ....
1863..McBride, James 13: 470
1866..McCook, Edward M. 6: 448
1869..Pierce, Henry A. 5: 180
1877..Comly, James M. 12: 465
1882..Daggett, Rollin M. 12: 223
1885..Merrill, George W. 12: 273
1889..Stevens, John L. 2: 172
1893..Blount, James H. 13: 371
1894..Willis, Albert S. 12: 369
1897..Sewall, Harold M. 21: 64

HOLLAND

(See Netherlands)

HONDURAS

1853..Borland, Solon 4:386
1858..Clarke, Beverly L. 12:200
1862..Partridge, James R. 7:519
1863..Clay, Thomas H. 13: 51
1866..Rousseau, Richard H. 12:185
1869..Baxter, Henry 4:334
1873..Williamson, George McW..12: 52
1879..Logan, Cornelius A. 5:531
1882..Hall, Henry C. 5:551
1889..Mizner, Lansing B. 5:556
1890..Pacheco, Romnaldo 4:110
1893..Young, Pierce M. B. 2:382
1896..Coxe, Macgrane 12:476
1897..Hunter, Whiteside G. 5:518
1902..Combs, Leslie 13:309
1907..Lee, Joseph W. J. 14:428
1907..Dodge, Henry P. 14:428
1908..Sorsby, William B. 13:535
1908..Brown, Philip M. A:222
1909..McCreery, Fenton R. 14:118
1911..White, Charles D. ....
1913..Ewing, John 24:194
1918..Jones, T. Sambola ....
1921..Morales, Franklin E. .....
1925..Summerlin, George T. ....
1929..Lay, Julius G. A:385
1935..Keena, Leo J. ....

HUNGARY

(See also Austria-Hungary)

1919..Grant-Smith, Ulysses (Commissioner, Chargés d'Affaires) ....
1922..Brentano, Theodore C:487
1927..Wright, J. Butler ....
1930..Roosevelt, Nicholas ......
1933..Montgomery, John F. D:410

IRAN

1883..Benjamin, Samuel G. W... 7: 26
1885..Winston, Frederick H..... 4:529
1886..Pratt, E. Spencer ....
1891..Beale, Truxtun 13: 77
1892..Sperry, Watson R. 1:416
1893..McDonald, Alexander 13:357
1897..Hardy, Arthur S. 2:303
1899..Bowen, Herbert W. 20: 46
1901..Griscom, Lloyd C. 12:196
1902..Pearson, Richmond 14:131
1907..Jackson, John B. 12:250
1909..Russell, Charles W. 15:358
1914..Caldwell, John L. ....
1921..Kornfeld, Joseph S. ......
1925..Philip, Hoffman B:348
1929..Hart, Charles C. ....
1933..Hornibrook, William H. .. B: 47

IRISH FREE STATE

1927..Sterling, Frederick A. ....
1933..McDowell, W. W. ....
1934..Vacant
1935..Owsley, Alvin M. ....

ITALY

1854..Cass, Lewis, Jr. 7:528
1861..Marsh, George P. 2:380
1882..Astor, William W. 8:105
1885..Stallo, John B. 11:259
1889..Porter, Albert G. 13:274
1892..Potter, William 13:469
1893..MacVeagh, Wayne 4:246
1897..Draper, William F. 6: 98
1900..Meyer, George VonL. 14:413
1905..White, Henry 14:171
1906..Griscom, Lloyd C. 12:196
1909..Leishman, John G. A. ...13:598
1911..O'Brien, Thomas J. 25:420
1913..Page, Thomas N. 19:405
1920..Johnson, Robert U. C:519
1921..Child, Richard W. 26:478
1924..Fletcher, Henry P. D:428
1929..Garrett, John W. A:335
1933..Long, Breckenridge ......

JAPANESE EMPIRE

1852..Perry, Matthew C. 4: 42
1855..Harris, Townsend 5:493
1861..Pruyn, Robert H. 13:439
1866..VanValkenburg, Robert B. 7:529
1869..DeLong, Charles E. ......
1873..Bingham, John A. 9:375
1885..Hubbard, Richard B. 9: 72
1889..Swift, John F. 18:405
1892..Coombs, Frank L. 13: 64
1893..Dun, Edwin 12:121
1897..Buck, Alfred E. 1:386
1902..Griscom, Lloyd C. 12:196
1906..Wright, Luke E. 26: 94
1907..O'Brien, Thomas J. 25:420
1911..Bryan, Charles P. 12:452
1912..Anderson, Larz 15:349
1913..Guthrie, George W. 18: 19
1917..Morris, Roland S. ....
1921..Warren, Charles B. 26: 15
1923..Woods, Cyrus E. ....
1924..Bancroft, Edgar A. 14:373
1925..MacVeagh, Charles 23: 17
1929..Castle, William R., Jr. ... D:342
1930..Forbes, W. Cameron C:509
1932..Grew, Joseph C. A:412

KOREA

1883..Foote, Lucius H. 7:267
1886..Parker, William H. ......
1887..Dinsmore, Hugh A. 5:264
1890..Heard, Augustine ....
1894..Sill, John M. B. 10:353
1897..Allen, Horace N. ....
1905..Morgan, Edwin V. 14:432

LATVIA

1922..Coleman, Frederick W. B.. C:500
1931..Skinner, Robert P. B:356
1933..MacMurray, John VanA.

LIBERIA

1863..Henry John J. (Commissioner) ....
1863..Henson, Abraham (Commissioner) ....
1866..Seys, John ....
1870..Mason, James W. ....
1871..Turner, J. Milton ....
1878..Smyth, John H. 12:526
1881..Garnet, Henry H. 2:414
1882..Smyth, John H. 12:526
1885..Hopkins, Moses A. 12:112
1887..Taylor, Charles H. J. 5:551
1888..Smith, Ezekiel E. ....
1890..Clark, Alexander 5:530
1892..McCoy, William D. 14: 58
1895..Heard, William H. 12:212
1898..Smith, Owen L. W. 14:206
1902..Crossland, J. R. A. 14:471
1903..Lyon, Ernest 14:421
1910..Crum, William D. ....
1913..Moore, Fred R. ....
1913..Buckner, George W. .....
1915..Curtis, James L. ....
1918..Johnson, Joseph L. ......
1921..Hood, Solomon P. ....
1927..Francis, William T. ......
1930..Mitchell, Charles E. ......
1933..Vacant
1935..Walton, Lester A. ....

LITHUANIA

1922..Coleman, Frederick W. B.. C:500
1931..Skinner, Robert P. B:356
1933..MacMurray, John VanA.

LUXEMBURG

1903..Newel, Stanford 11:239
1905..Hill, David J. 12:244
1908..Beaupré, Arthur M. 14:338
1911..Bryce, Lloyd 1:252
1913..VanDyke, Henry 25: 10
1917..Garret, John W. A:335
1920..Phillips, William .... B: 56
1923..Fletcher, Henry P. D:428
1924..Phillips, William .... B: 56
1927..Gibson, Hugh A:419
1933..Morris, Dave H. D:107

MEXICO

1825..Poinsett, Joel R. 6:435
1829..Butler, Anthony ....
1836..Ellis, Powhatan 11: 53
1842..Thompson, Waddy 3:511
1844..Green, Benjamin E. (Chargés d'Affaires) ... 5:531
1844..Shannon, Wilson 8:340
1845..Slidell, John 2: 93
1848..Sevier, Ambrose H. 2:239
1848..Clifford, Nathan 2:473
1849..Letcher, Robert P. 13: 5
1852..Conkling, Alfred 11:487
1853..Gadsden, James 12: 68
1856..Forsyth, John 8:471
1859..McLane, Robert M. 9:311
1860..Weller, John B. 4:107
1861..Corwin, Thomas 6:180
1864..Corwin, W. H. ....
1866..Campbell, Lewis D. 13:278
1867..Otterbourg, Marcus ......
1868..Rosecrans, William S. ... 4:162
1869..Nelson, Thomas H. 11:550
1873..Foster, John W. 3:268
1880..Morgan, Philip H. 13:596
1885..Jackson, Henry R. 3:369
1886..Manning, Thomas C. 4:344

1888..Bragg, Edward S. 10: 16
1889..Ryan, Thomas 12:127
1893..Gray, Isaac P. 13:273
1896..Ransom, Matthew W. 10:251
1897..Clayton, Powell 16:262
1905..Conger, Edwin H. 8:176
1906..Thompson, David E. 14:166
1909..Wilson, Henry L. 12:126
1913..Vacant
1916..Fletcher, Henry P. D:428
1920..Vacant
1924..Warren, Charles B. 26: 15
1924..Sheffield, James R. B:451
1927..Morrow, Dwight W. 23: 10
1930..Clark, J. Reuben, Jr. D:290
1933..Daniels, Josephus .... A: 46

MONTENEGRO

1905..Jackson, John B. 12:250
1907..Pearson, Richmond 14:131
1909..Moses, George H. .... C: 71
1912..Schurman, Jacob G. 4:478
1913..Williams, George F. .....
1914..Droppers, Garrett 20: 16
1920..Capps, Edward A:416

NETHERLANDS

1792..Short, William 4:530
1794..Adams, John Quincy 5: 73
1797..Murray, William V. 11:360
1814..Eustis, William 5:372
1818..Everett, Alexander H. ... 9:256
1825..Hughes, Christopher 7:165
1829..Preble, William P. 13:220
1831..D'Avezac, Auguste (Chargés d'Affaires) ..13:107
1839..Bleecker, Harmanus (Chargés d'Affaires) ...11:324
1842..Hughes, Christopher (Chargés d'Affaires) ... 7:165
1845..D'Avezac, Auguste (Chargés d'Affaires) ...13:107
1850..Folsom, George (Chargés d'Affaires) 12:228
1853..Belmont, August 11:499
1857..Murphy, Henry C. 10: 33
1861..Pike, James S. 11:165
1866..Ewing, Hugh B. 5: 11
1870..Gorham, Charles T. 7:549
1875..Stockbridge, Francis B. .. 1:460
1876..Birney, James 12:224
1882..Dayton, William L. 4:175
1885..Bell, Isaac 7:536
1888..Roosevelt, Robert B. 3:415
1889..Thayer, Samuel R. 12:123
1893..Quinby, William E. 1:254
1897..Newel, Stanford 11:239
1905..Hill, David J. 12:244
1908..Beaupré, Arthur M. 14:338
1911..Bryce, Lloyd 1:252
1913..VanDyke, Henry 25: 10
1917..Garrett, John W. A:335
1920..Phillips, William .... B: 56
1923..Tobin, Richard M. ....
1929..Diekema, Gerrit J. 23:140
1931..Swenson, Laurits S. 12:108
1934..Emmett, Grenville T. ....

NICARAGUA

1851..Kerr, John B. (Chargés d'Affaires) 5:536
1853..Borland, Solon 4:386
1854..Wheeler, John H. 6:485
1858..Lamar, Mirabeau B. 9: 66
1859..Dimitry, Alexander 10:176
1861..Dickinson, Andrew B. 12:477
1862..Clay, Thomas H. 13: 51
1863..Dickinson, Andrew B. 12:477
1869..Riotte, Charles N. ....
1873..Williamson, George McW..12: 52
1879..Logan, Cornelius A. 5:531
1882..Hall, Henry C. 5:551
1889..Mizner, Lansing B. 5:556
1890..Pacheco, Romnaldo 4:110
1891..Shannon, Richard C. 12:361
1893..Baker, Lewis 1:246
1897..Merry, William L. 12:310
1908..Coolidge, John G. ....
1909..Vacant
1911..Northcott, Elliott 14:495
1911..Weitzel, George T. C:521
1913..Jefferson, Benjamin L. ...
1921..Ramer, John E. ....
1925..Eberhart, Charles C. .....
1929..Hanna, Matthew E. ......
1933..Lane, Arthur Bliss ....

NORWAY

1905..Graves, Charles H. 22:228
1906..Peirce, Herbert H. D. 9:539
1911..Swenson, Laurits S. 12:108
1913..Schmedemann, Albert G...
1921..Swenson, Laurits S. 12:108
1930..Philip, Hoffman B:348
1935..Biddle, Anthony J. D. 7:446

NORWAY and SWEDEN

1814..Russell, Jonathan 8: 57
1819..Hughes, Christopher (Chargés d'Affaires) ... 7:165
1826..Appleton, John James (Chargés d'Affaires) ...13:392
1830..Hughes, Christopher (Chargés d'Affaires) ... 7:165
1842..Lay, George W. (Chargés d'Affaires) ...12:257
1845..Ellsworth, Henry W. (Chargés d'Affaires) ... 7:516
1849..Schroeder, Francis 4:534
1857..Angel, Benjamin F. 10:478
1861..Haldeman, Jacob S. 13: 64
1862..Tefft, Benjamin F. 13:575
1864..Campbell, James H. 4:293
1867..Bartlett, Joseph J. 4:335
1869..Andrews, Christopher C..11:393
1877..Stevens, John L. 2:172
1883..Thomas, William W. 2:132
1885..Magee, Rufus 12:263
1889..Thomas, William W. 2;132
1894..Ferguson, Thomas B. 13:343
1897..Thomas, William W. 2:132

PANAMA

1903..Buchanan, William I. 2:271
1904..Barrett, John D:450
1905..Magoon, Charles E. 14: 32
1906..Squiers, Herbert G. 12:333
1909..Hitt, Robert S. R. 14:477
1910..Dawson, Thomas C. 13:512
1911..Dodge, Henry P. 14:428
1913..Price, William J. D:100
1921..South, John G. ....
1929..Davis, Roy T. ....
1933..Gonzales, Antonio C. .....
1934..Summerlin, George T. ....

PARAGUAY

1858..Bowlin, James B. (Commissioner) 5:528
1860..Johnson, Cave (Commissioner) 6:270
1861..Washburn, Charles A. ... 5:255
1868..McMahon, Martin T. 4:129
1870..Stevens, John L. 2:172
1874..Caldwell, John C. 5:248
1882..Williams, William 12:454
1885..Bacon, John E. 12:270
1889..Maney, George 5:196
1894..Stuart, Granville 12:123
1897..Finch, William R. 15:400
1905..O'Brien, Edward C. 14:492
1909..Morgan, Edwin V. 14:432
1911..Grevstad, Nicolay A. .....
1914..Mooney, Daniel F. ....
1922..O'Toole, William J. ......
1924..Vacant
1925..Kreeck, George L. ....
1929..Wheeler, Post ....
1933..Nicholson, Meredith A:512
1935..Howard, Findley B. ......

PERSIA
(See Iran)

PERU

1826..Cooley, James (Chargés d'Affaires) ....
1828..Larned, Samuel (Chargés d'Affaires) 12:476
1829..West, Emanuel J. (Chargés d'Affaires) ...
1830..Larned, Samuel (Chargés d'Affaires) 12:476
1836..Thornton, James B. (Chargés d'Affaires) ..13:483
1838..Pickett, James C. (Chargés d'Affaires) ..13:159
1844..Bryan, John A. (Chargés d'Affaires) 11:576
1845..Jewett, Albert G. (Chargés d'Affaires) 12:438
1847..Clay, John R. 12: 80
1861..Robinson, Christopher 12:117
1865..Hovey, Alvin P. 13:274
1871..Settle, Thomas 12:199
1872..Thomas, Francis 9:304
1875..Gibbs, Richard 12:131
1879..Christiancy, Isaac P. 23:348
1881..Hurlbut, Stephen A. 4:218
1882..Partridge, James R. 7:519
1883..Phelps, Seth L. 12:358
1885..Buck, Charles W. 12:225
1889..Hicks, John 12:141
1893..McKenzie, James A. 13: 38
1897..Dudley, Irving B. 13:296
1906..Combs, Leslie 13:309
1911..Howard, H. Clay ....
1913..McMillin, Benton 13: 79

1919..Gonzales, William E. .....
1923..Poindexter, Miles 15: 211
1928..Moore, Alexander P. 24: 211
1930..Dearing, Fred M. .... B: 480

POLAND

1919..Gibson, Hugh S. .... A: 419
1924..Pearson, Alfred J. .... A: 188
1925..Stetson, John B., Jr. .....
1930..Willys, John N. ....
1932..Belin, F. Lammot ....
1933..Cudahy, John ....

PORTUGAL

1791..Humphreys, David 1: 71
1797..Smith, William L. 12: 338
1809..Sumter, Thomas 1: 79
1819..Graham, John 11: 317
1822..Dearborn, Henry 1: 93
1825..Brent, Thomas L. L. (Chargés d'Affaires) ...12: 337
1835..Kavanagh, Edward (Chargés d'Affaires) ... 6: 309
1841..Barrow, Washington (Chargés d'Affaires) ...13: 329
1843..Rencher, Abraham (Chargés d'Affaires) ...12: 337
1847..Hopkins, George W. (Chargés d'Affaires) ... 4: 445
1849..Clay, James B. (Chargés d'Affaires) 13: 319
1850..Haddock, Charles B. (Chargés d'Affaires) ... 9: 96
1854..O'Sullivan, John L. 12: 337
1858..Morgan, George W. 4: 71
1861..Harvey, James E. ....
1869..Shellabarger, Samuel 2: 357
1870..Lewis, Charles Hance 12: 121
1874..Moran, Benjamin 10: 56
1882..Francis, John Morgan ... 1: 242
1884..Richmond, Lewis 12: 345
1885..Lewis, Edward P. C. 13: 596
1889..Loring, George B. 15: 349
1890..Batcheller, George S. 4: 464
1893..Pierce, Gilbert A. 1: 294
1893..Caruth, George W. 8: 176
1897..Townsend, Lawrence 12: 54
1899..Irwin, John N. 12: 477
1901..Loomis, Francis B. 12: 195
1903..Bryan, Charles P. 12: 452
1909..Gage, Henry T. 4: 114
1911..Morgan, Edwin V. 14: 432
1912..Woods, Cyrus E. ....
1913..Birch, Thomas H. 22: 390
1922..Dearing, Fred M. .... B: 480
1929..South, John G. ....
1933..Caldwell, Robert G. ......

PRUSSIA
(See Germany)

RUMANIA

1880..Schuyler, Eugene 8: 339
1885..Fearn, John W. 12: 312
1889..Snowden, Archibald L. ...12: 119
1892..Beale, Truxtun 13: 77
1893..Alexander, Eben 12: 266
1897..Rockhill, William W. 8: 129
1899..Hardy, Arthur S. 2: 303
1900..Francis, Charles S. 12: 117
1902..Jackson, John B. 12: 250
1905..Riddle, John W. 14: 53
1907..Knowles, Horace G. 14: 487
1909..Eddy, Spencer 14: 395
1909..Carter, John R. 14: 199
1911..Jackson, John B. 12: 250
1913..Vopicka, Charles J. 25: 374
1921..Jay, Peter A. .... C: 400
1925..Culbertson, William S. ... D: 321
1928..Wilson, Charles S. ....
1933..Owsley, Alvin M. ....
1935..Harrison, Leland ....

RUSSIA

1809..Adams, John Quincy 5: 73
1814..Harris, Leavitt (Chargés d'Affaires) ....
1816..Pinkney, William 5: 373
1818..Pinkney, Charles (Chargés d'Affaires) 13: 317
1818..Campbell, George W. 5: 372
1820..Middleton, Henry 12: 163
1830..Randolph, John 5: 97
1832..Buchanan, James 5: 1
1834..Wilkins, William 6: 9
1836..Clay, John R. (Chargés d'Affaires) 12: 80
1837..Dallas, George M. 6: 268
1839..Chew, William W. (Chargés d'Affaires) ... 5: 531
1840..Cambreleng, Churchill C...10: 381
1841..Todd, Charles S. 1: 409
1846..Clay, John R. (Chargés d'Affaires) 12: 80
1846..Ingersoll, Ralph I. ....
1848..Ingersoll, Colin M. (Chargés d'Affaires) ...13: 397
1848..Bagby, Arthur P. 10: 428
1850..Brown, Neil S. 7: 209
1853..Seymour, Thomas H. 10: 337
1858..Pickens, Francis W. 12: 173
1860..Appleton, John 12: 275
1861..Clay, Cassius M. 2: 311
1862..Cameron, Simon 2: 79
1863..Clay, Cassius M. 2: 311
1869..Coffey, Titian J. 5: 135
1869..Curtin, Andrew G. 24: 412
1872..Schuyler, Eugene (Chargés d'Affaires) 8: 339
1872..Orr, James L. 12: 175
1873..Jewell, Marshall 4: 20
1874..Schuyler, Eugene (Chargés d'Affaires) 8: 339
1875..Boker, George H. 6: 73
1877..Stoughton, Edwin W. 3: 533
1879..Hoffman, Wickham (Chargés d'Affaires) ...12: 71
1880..Foster, John W. 3: 268
1881..Hoffman, Wickham (Chargés d'Affaires) ...12: 71
1882..Hunt, William H. 4: 244
1884..Wurts, George W. (Chargés d'Affaires) 13: 477
1884..Taft, Alphonso 4: 24
1885..Lothrop, George VanN. .. 5: 160
1888..Wurts, George W. (Chargés d'Affaires) 13: 477
1888..Tree, Lambert 6: 161
1889..Wurts, George W. (Chargés d'Affaires) 13: 477
1890..Smith, Charles E. 11: 17
1892..White, Andrew D. 4: 476
1894..Breckinridge, Clifton R. .. 8: 191
1897..Hitchcock, Ethan A. 11: 16
1899..Tower, Charlemagne 26: 124
1902..McCormick, Robert S. ...13: 375
1905..Meyer, George VonL. 14: 413
1906..Riddle, John W. 14: 53
1909..Rockhill, William W. 8: 129
1911..Guild, Curtis, Jr. 14: 454
1914..Marye, George T. .... A: 139
1916..Francis, David R. 24: 322
1918..Vacant

UNION OF SOVIET SOCIALIST REPUBLICS

1933..Bullitt, William C. .... D: 35

SERBIA

1882..Schuyler, Eugene 8: 339
1885..Fearn, John W. 12: 312
1889..Snowden, Archibald L. ...12: 119
1892..Beale, Truxtun 13: 77
1893..Alexander, Eben 12: 266
1897..Rockhill, William W. 8: 129
1899..Hardy, Arthur S. 2: 303
1900..Francis, Charles S. 12: 117
1902..Jackson, John B. 12: 250
1905..Riddle, John W. 14: 53
1907..Knowles, Horace G. 14: 487
1909..Eddy, Spencer 14: 395
1909..Carter, John R. 14: 199
1911..Jackson, John B. 12: 250
1913..Vopicka, Charles J. 25: 374
1919..Dodge, Henry P. 14: 428
1926..Prince, John D. .... C: 43

SIAM

1882..Halderman, John A. 7: 556
1886..Child, Jacob T. ....
1890..Boyd, Sempronius H. 12: 139
1894..Barrett, John .... D: 450
1898..King, Hamilton 12: 122
1912..Carpenter, Fred W. .....
1914..Vacant
1915..Hornibrook, William H. .. B: 47
1917..Ingersoll, George P. 24: 216
1920..Hunt, George W. .... C: 40
1921..Brodie, Edward E. ...... D: 119
1925..Russell, William W. 15: 58
1927..Mackenzie, Harold O. ....
1929..Geissler, Arthur H. ......
1930..Kaufman, David E. ......
1933..Baker, James M. ....

THE TWO SICILIES

1831..Nelson, John (Chargés d'Affaires) 6: 8
1838..Throop, Enos T. (Chargés d'Affaires) 3: 46
1841..Bowlware, William (Chargés d'Affaires) ...12: 475
1845..Polk, William H. (Chargés d'Affaires) 11: 398
1848..Rowan, John (Chargés d'Affaires) 6: 95
1849..Chinn, Thomas W. (Chargés d'Affaires) ...12: 251

1850..Morris, Edward J. (Chargés d'Affaires) ...13: 25
1853..Owen, Robert D. 9: 222
1858..Chandler, Joseph R. 11: 396
(Post discontinued in 1860)

SPAIN

1790..Carmichael, William (Chargés d'Affaires) ...11: 366
1794..Short, William 4: 530
1794..Pinckney, Thomas 12: 160
1796..Humphreys, David 1: 71
1801..Pinckney, Charles 12: 161
1804..Bowdoin, James 1: 419
1805..Erving, George W. (Chargés d'Affaires) ...12: 275
1808..Vacant
1814..Erving, George W. 12: 275
1819..Forsyth, John 6: 435
1823..Nelson, Hugh 7: 540
1825..Everett, Alexander H. ... 9: 256
1829..Van Ness, Cornelius P. .. 8: 316
1835..Barry, William T. 5: 296
1836..Middleton, Arthur (Chargés d'Affaires) ...
1836..Eaton, John H. 5: 295
1840..Vail, Aaron (Chargés d'Affaires) 5: 555
1842..Irving, Washington 3: 17
1846..Saunders, Romulus M. ...13: 376
1849..Barringer, Daniel M. 11: 505
1853..Perry, Horatio J. 10: 51
1853..Soulé, Pierre 3: 117
1855..Perry, Horatio J. 10: 51
1855..Dodge, Augustus C. 12: 53
1858..Preston, William 9: 433
1861..Schurz, Carl 3: 202
1861..Perry, Horatio J. 10: 51
1862..Koerner, Gustavus 8: 180
1864..Perry, Horatio J. (Chargés d'Affaires) ...10: 51
1865..Hale, John P. 3: 120
1869..Sickles, Daniel E. 12: 450
1873..Adee, Alvey A. (Chargés d'Affaires) 12: 459
1874..Cushing, Caleb 4: 151
1877..Adee, Alvey A. (Chargés d'Affaires) 12: 459
1877..Lowell, James Russell 2: 32
1880..Fairchild, Lucius 12: 76
1881..Hamlin, Hannibal 2: 76
1883..Foster, John W. 3: 268
1885..Curry, Jabez L. M. 4: 357
1888..Belmont, Perry .... D: 349
1889..Palmer, Thomas W. 11: 362
1890..Grubb, Edward B. 3: 192
1892..Snowden, Archibald L. ...12: 119
1893..Taylor, Hannis 8: 118
1897..Woodford, Stewart L. 9: 2
1899..Storer, Bellamy 11: 338
1902..Hardy, Arthur S. 2: 303
1905..Collier, William M. 13: 547
1909..Ide, Henry C. 23: 29
1913..Willard, Joseph E. 20: 85
1921..Woods, Cyrus E. ....
1923..Moore, Alexander P. 24: 211
1925..Hammond, Ogden H. .... D: 350
1929..Laughlin, Irwin B. ...... D: 164
1933..Bowers, Claude G. ....

SWEDEN
(See Norway and Sweden)

1905..Graves, Charles H. 22: 228
1914..Morris, Ira Nelson ....
1923..Bliss, Robert W. .... A: 514
1927..Harrison, Leland ....
1930..Morehead, John M. ......
1933..Steinhardt, Laurence A. ..

SWITZERLAND

1853..Fay, Theodore S. 7: 475
1861..Fogg, George G. 4: 374
1865..Harrington, George 12: 337
1869..Rublee, Horace 1: 213
1877..Fish, Nicholas (Chargés d'Affaires) 11: 27
1881..Cramer, Michael J. 12: 310
1885..Winchester, Boyd 13: 374
1889..Washburn, John D. 12: 464
1892..Cheney, Person C. 11: 135
1893..Broadhead, James O. 5: 68
1895..Peak, John L. 13: 411
1897..Leishman, John G. A. 13: 598
1901..Hardy, Arthur S. 2: 303
1902..Bryan, Charles P. 12: 452
1903..Hill, David J. 12: 244
1905..Clay, Brutus J. 14: 442
1909..Swenson, Laurits S. 12: 108
1911..Boutell, Henry S. 21: 407
1913..Stovall, Pleasant A. 26: 307
1920..Gary, Hampson .... A: 432
1921..Grew, Joseph C. .... A: 412
1924..Gibson, Hugh .... A: 419
1927..Wilson, Hugh R. .... C: 370

TURKEY

1831..Porter, David 2: 98
1843..Carr, Dabney S. 11: 449
1849..Marsh, George P. 2: 380
1853..Spence, Carroll 12: 318
1858..Williams, James 9: 560
1861..Morris, Edward J. 13: 25
1870..MacVeagh, Wayne 4: 246
1871..Boker, George H. 6: 73
1875..Maynard, Horace 9: 286
1880..Longstreet, James 4: 263
1881..Wallace, Lew 4: 363
1885..Cox, Samuel S. 6: 363
1887..Straus, Oscar S. 10: 42
1889..Hirsch, Solomon 13: 40
1892..Thompson, David P. 7: 113
1893..Terrell, Alexander W. 5: 555
1897..Angell, James B. 1: 251
1898..Straus, Oscar S. 10: 42
1900..Leishman, John G. A. ...13: 598
1909..Straus, Oscar S. 10: 42
1911..Rockhill, William W. 8: 129
1913..Morgenthau, Henry 15: 363
1916..Elkus, Abram I. .... D: 366
1917..Vacant
1918..Heck, Lewis (Commissioner)
1919..Ravndal, Gabriel B. .....
1919..Bristol, Mark L. .... A: 63
1927..Grew, Joseph C. .... A: 412
1932..Sherrill, Charles H. 14: 523
1933..Skinner, Robert P. .... B: 356

UNION OF SOUTH AFRICA

1929..Totten, Ralph J. .... D: 317

UNION OF SOVIET SOCIALIST REPUBLICS

1933..Bullitt, William C. ...... D: 35

URUGUAY

1867..Asboth, Alexander S. 4: 413
1868..Worthington, Henry G. ..12: 436
1869..Kirk, Robert C. 12: 440
1870..Stevens, John L. 2: 172
1874..Caldwell, John C. 5: 248
1882..Williams, William (Chargés d'Affaires) ...12: 454
1885..Bacon, John E. 12: 270
1889..Maney, George 5: 196
1894..Stuart, Granville 12: 123
1897..Finch, William R. 15: 400
1905..O'Brien, Edward C. 14: 492
1909..Morgan, Edwin V. 14: 432
1911..Grevstad, Nicolay A. .....
1914..DeSaulles, John L. ....
1915..Jeffery, Robert E. ....
1921..Vacant
1922..Philip, Hoffman .... B: 348
1925..Grant-Smith, Ulysses ....
1929..Harrison, Leland ....
1930..Wright, J. Butler ....
1934..Messersmith, George S. ...
1934..Lay, Julius G. .... A: 385

VENEZUELA

1835..Williamson, John G. A. (Chargés d'Affaires) ...
1841..Hall, Allen A. (Chargés d'Affaires) 7: 535
1844..Ellis, Vespasian (Chargés d'Affaires) ....
1845..Shields, Benjamin G. (Chargés d'Affaires) ...13: 319
1849..Steele, Isaac N. (Chargés d'Affaires) 14: 77
1854..Eames, Charles 11: 477
1858..Turpin, Edwin A. ....
1861..Blow, Henry T. 4: 291
1862..Culver, Erastus D. 9: 529
1866..Wilson, James 12: 126
1867..Stilwell, Thomas N. 13: 79
1869..Partridge, James R. 7: 519
1871..Pile, William A. 11: 191
1874..Russell, Thomas 13: 446
1878..Baker, Jehu 12: 427
1881..Carter, George W. ....
1882..Baker, Jehu 12: 427
1885..Scott, Charles L. 12: 210
1889..Scruggs, William L. 2: 165
1893..Partridge, Frank C. 9: 549
1894..Haselton, Seneca 13: 319
1895..Thomas, Allen 8: 350
1897..Loomis, Francis B. 12: 195
1901..Bowen, Herbert W. 20: 46
1905..Russell, William W. 15: 58
1910..Garrett, John W. .... A: 335
1911..Northcott, Elliott 14: 495
1913..McGoodwin, Preston B. ..
1921..Cook, Willis C. ....
1929..Summerlin, George T. ....
1935..Nicholson, Meredith ...... A: 512

YUGO-SLAVIA

1919..Dodge, Henry P. 14: 428
1926..Prince, John D. .... C: 43
1933..Wilson, Charles S. ....

United States Senators

Arranged According to Congresses

First Congress (1789-91)

Adams, John, president of the senate 2: 1
Bassett, Richard (Del.) 11: 530
Butler, Pierce (S. C.) 2: 162
Carroll, Charles (Md.) 7: 441
Dalton, Tristram (Mass.) 11: 529
Dickinson, Philemon (N. J.) ... 7: 517
Ellsworth, Oliver (Conn.) 1: 22
Elmer, Jonathan (N. J.) 11: 538
Few, William (Ga.) 2: 346
Foster, Theodore (R. I.) 2: 9
Grayson, William (Va.) 12: 247
Gunn, James (Ga.) 2: 11
Hawkins, Benjamin (N. C.) ... 4: 59
Henry, John (Md.) 9: 294
Izard, Ralph (S. C.) 3: 175
Johnson, William S. (Conn.) .. 6: 342
Johnston, Samuel (N. C.) 4: 420
King, Rufus (N. Y.) 6: 301
Langdon, John (N. H.) 11: 123
Lee, Richard H. (Va.) 3: 159
Maclay, William (Pa.) 5: 143
Monroe, James (Va) 6: 81
Morris, Robert (Pa.) 2: 411
Paterson, William (N. J.) 1: 24
Read, George (Del.) 3: 297
Schuyler, Philip J. (N. Y.) ... 1: 97
Stanton, Joseph (R. I.) 5: 224
Strong, Caleb (Mass.) 1: 110
Walker, John (Va.) 11: 323
Wingate, Paine (N. H.) 12: 558

Second Congress (1791-93)

Adams, John, president of the senate 2: 1
Bassett, Richard (Del.) 11: 530
Bradley, Stephen R. (Vt.) 2: 432
Brown, John (Ky.) 6: 535
Burr, Aaron (N. Y.) 3: 5
Butler, Pierce (S. C.) 2: 162
Cabot, George (Mass.) 2: 5
Carroll, Charles (Md.) 7: 441
Dickinson, Philemon (N. J.) ... 7: 517
Edwards, John (Ky.) 4: 314
Ellsworth, Oliver (Conn.) 1: 22
Few, William (Ga.) 2: 346
Foster, Theodore (R. I.) 2: 9
Gunn, James (Ga.) 2: 11
Hawkins, Benjamin (N. C.) ... 4: 59
Henry, John (Md.) 9: 294
Izard, Ralph (S. C.) 3: 175
Johnston, Samuel (N.C.) 4: 420
King, Rufus (N. Y.) 6: 301
Langdon, John (N. H.) 11: 123
Lee, Richard H. (Va.) 3: 159
Monroe, James (Va.) 6: 81
Morris, Robert (Pa.) 2: 411
Potts, Richard (Md.) 11: 397
Read, George (Del.) 3: 297
Robinson, Moses (Vt.) 8: 313
Rutherfurd, John (N. J.) 2: 10
Sherman, Roger (Conn.) 2: 352
Stanton, Joseph (R. I.) 5: 224
Strong, Caleb (Mass.) 1: 110
Taylor, John (Va.) 9: 509
Wingate, Paine (N. H.) 12: 558

Third Congress (1793-95)

Adams, John, president of the senate 2: 1
Bradford, William (R. I.) 2: 373
Bradley, Stephen R. (Vt.) 2: 432
Brown, John (Ky.) 6: 535
Burr, Aaron (N. Y.) 3: 5
Butler, Pierce (S. C.) 2: 162
Cabot, George (Mass.) 2: 5
Edwards, John (Ky.) 4: 314
Ellsworth, Oliver (Conn.) 1: 22
Foster, Theodore (R. I.) 2: 9
Frelinghuysen, Frederick (N. J.) 7: 540
Gallatin, Albert (Pa.) 3: 9
Gunn, James (Ga.) 2: 11
Hawkins, Benjamin (N. C.) 4: 59
Henry, John (Md.) 9: 294
Izard, Ralph (S. C.) 3: 175
Jackson, James (Ga.) 1: 220
King, Rufus (N. Y.) 6: 301
Langdon, John (N. H.) 11: 123
Lattimer, Henry (Del.) 2: 10
Livermore, Samuel (N. H.) 2: 8
Martin, Alexander (N. C.) 4: 420
Mason, Stevens T. (Va.) 2: 9
Mitchell, Stephen M. (Conn.) ... 3: 509
Monroe, James (Va.) 6: 81
Morris, Robert (Pa.) 2: 411
Potts, Richard (Md.) 11: 397
Read, George (Del.) 3: 297
Robinson, Moses (Vt.) 8: 313
Ross, James (Pa.) 5: 438
Rutherfurd, John (N. J.) 2: 10
Strong, Caleb (Mass.) 1: 110
Taylor, John (Va.) 9: 509
Tazewell, Henry (Va.) 2: 215
Vining, John (Del.) 2: 6

Fourth Congress (1795-97)

Adams, John, president of the senate 2: 1
Bingham, William (Pa.) 2: 133
Bloodworth, Timothy (N. C.) ... 5: 147
Blount, William (Tenn.) 7: 206
Bradford, William (R. I.) 2: 373
Brown, John (Ky.) 6: 535
Burr, Aaron (N. Y.) 3: 5
Butler, Pierce (S. C.) 2: 162
Cabot, George (Mass.) 2: 5
Cocke, William (Tenn.) 11: 409
Ellsworth, Oliver (Conn.) 1: 22
Foster, Theodore (R. I.) 2: 9
Frelinghuysen, Frederick (N. J.) 7: 540
Goodhue, Benjamin (Mass.) 2: 10
Gunn, James (Ga.) 2: 11
Henry, John (Md.) 9: 294
Hillhouse, James (Conn.) 2: 9
Howard, John E. (Md.) 9: 292
Hunter, John (S. C.) 12: 395
Jackson, James (Ga.) 1: 220
King, Rufus (N. Y.) 6: 301
Langdon, John (N. H.) 11: 123
Lattimer, Henry (Del.) 2: 10
Laurance, John (N. Y.) 2: 8
Livermore, Samuel (N. H.) 2: 8
Marshall, Humphrey (Ky.) 2: 368
Martin, Alexander (N. C.) 4: 420
Mason, Stevens T. (Va.) 2: 9
Paine, Elijah (Vt.) 8: 174
Potts, Richard (Md.) 11: 397
Read, Jacob (S. C.) 2: 496
Robinson, Moses (Vt.) 8: 313
Ross, James (Pa.) 5: 438
Rutherfurd, John (N. J.) 2: 10
Sedgwick, Theodore (Mass.) 2: 8
Stockton, Richard (N. J.) 2: 7
Strong, Caleb (Mass.) 1: 110
Tattnall, Josiah (Ga.) 1: 221
Tazewell, Henry (Va.) 2: 215
Tichenor, Isaac (Vt.) 8: 313
Tracy, Uriah (Conn.) 2: 34
Trumbull, Jonathan (Conn.) ... 10: 331
Vining, John (Del.) 2: 6
Walton, George (Ga). 1: 219

Fifth Congress (1797-99)

Jefferson, Thomas, president of the senate 3: 1
Anderson, Joseph (Tenn.) 2: 11
Bingham, William (Pa.) 2: 133
Bloodworth, Timothy (N. C.) .. 5: 147
Blount, William (Tenn.) 7: 206
Bradford, William (R. I.) 2: 373
Brown, John (Ky.) 6: 535
Chipman, Nathaniel (Vt.) 2: 10
Clayton, Joshua (Del.) 11: 530
Cocke, William (Tenn.) 11: 409
Davenport, Franklin (N. J.) ... 2: 8
Foster, Theodore (R. I.) 2: 9
Goodhue, Benjamin (Mass.) 2: 10
Greene, Ray (R. I.) 4: 256
Gunn, James (Ga.) 2: 11
Henry, John (Md.) 9: 294
Hillhouse, James (Conn.) 2: 9
Hobart, John S. (N. Y.) 2: 35
Howard, John E. (Md.) 4: 292
Hunter, John (S. C.) 12: 395
Jackson Andrew (Tenn.) 5: 289
Langdon, John (N. H.) 11: 123
Lattimer, Henry (Del.) 2: 10
Laurance, John (N. Y.) 2: 8
Livermore, Samuel (N. H.) 2: 8
Lloyd, James (Md.) 4: 313
Marshall, Humphrey (Ky.) 2: 368
Martin, Alexander (N. C.) 4: 420
Mason, Stevens T. (Va.) 2: 9
North, William (N. Y.) 2: 7
Paine, Elijah (Vt.) 8: 174
Pinckney, Charles (S. C.) 12: 161
Read, Jacob (S. C.) 2: 496
Ross, James (Pa.) 5: 438
Rutherfurd, John (N. J.) 2: 10
Schureman, James (N. J.) 2: 11
Schuyler, Philip J. (N. Y.) 1: 97
Sedgwick, Theodore (Mass.) ... 2: 8
Smith, Daniel (Tenn) 2: 7
Stockton, Richard (N. J.) 2: 7
Tattnall, Josiah (Ga.) 1: 221
Tazewell, Henry (Va.) 2: 215
Tichenor, Isaac (Vt.) 8: 313
Tracy, Uriah (Conn.) 2: 34
Vining, John (Del.) 2: 6
Watson, James (N. Y.) 2: 347
Wells, William H. (Del.) 2: 9

Sixth Congress (1799-1801)

Jefferson, Thomas, president of the senate 3: 1
Anderson, Joseph (Tenn.) 2: 11
Armstrong, John, 2d. (N. Y.).. 1: 48
Baldwin, Abraham (Ga.) 9: 178
Bingham, William (Pa.) 2: 133
Bloodworth, Timothy (N. C.) .. 5: 147
Brown, John (Ky.) 6: 535
Chipman, Nathaniel (Vt.) 2: 10
Cocke, William (Tenn.) 11: 409
Dayton, Jonathan (N. J.) 1: 306
Dexter, Samuel (Mass.) 2: 6
Foster, Dwight (Mass.) 2: 6
Foster, Theodore (R. I.) 2: 9
Franklin, Jesse (N. C.) 4: 423
Goodhue, Benjamin (Mass.) ... 2: 10
Greene, Ray (R. I.) 4: 256
Gunn, James (Ga.) 2: 11
Hillhouse, James (Conn.) 2: 9
Hindman, William (Md) 2: 133
Howard, John E. (Md.) 4: 292
Langdon, John (N. H.) 11: 123
Lattimer, Henry (Del.) 2: 10
Laurance, John (N. Y.) 2: 8
Livermore, Samuel (N. H.) 2: 8
Lloyd, James (Md.) 4: 313
Marshall, Humphrey (Ky.) 2: 368
Mason, Jonathan (Mass.) 2: 7
Mason, Stevens T. (Va.) 2: 9
Morris, Gouverneur (N. Y.) ... 2: 526
Nicholas, Wilson C. (Va.) 5: 446
Ogden, Aaron (N. J.) 5: 203
Paine, Elijah (Vt.) 8: 174
Pinckney, Charles (S. C.) 12: 161
Read, Jacob (S. C.) 2: 496
Ross, James (Pa.) 5: 438
Schureman, James (N. J.) 2: 11

Tracy, Uriah (Conn.) 2: 34
Watson, James (N. Y.) 2: 347
Wells, William H. (Del.) 2: 9
White, Samuel (Del.) 13: 249

Seventh Congress (1801-03)

Burr, Aaron, president of the senate 3: 5
Anderson, Joseph (Tenn.)...... 2: 11
Armstrong, John, 2d (N. Y.) .. 1: 48
Baldwin, Abraham (Ga.) 9: 178
Bradley, Stephen R. (Vt.) 2: 432
Breckenridge, John (Ky.) 3: 9
Brown, John (Ky.) 6: 535
Butler, Pierce (S. C.) 2: 162
Chipman, Nathaniel (Vt.) 2: 10
Clinton, De Witt (N. Y.) 3: 43
Cocke, William (Tenn.) 11: 409
Colhoun, John E. (S. C.) 5: 552
Dayton, Jonathan (N. J.) 1: 306
Ellery, Christopher (R. I.) 5: 338
Foster, Dwight (Mass.) 2: 6
Foster, Theodore (R. I.) 2: 9
Franklin, Jesse (N. C.) 4: 423
Greene, Ray (R. I.) 4: 256
Hillhouse, James (Conn.) 2: 9
Hindman, William (Md.) 2: 133
Howard, John E. (Md.) 9: 292
Jackson, James (Ga.) 1: 220
Livermore, Samuel (N. H.) 2: 8
Logan, George (Pa.) 8: 255
Mason, Jonathan (Mass.) 2: 7
Mason, Stevens T. (Va.) 2: 9
Morris, Gouverneur (N. Y.) ... 2: 526
Muhlenberg, John P. G. (Pa.) .. 1: 149
Nicholas, Wilson C. (Va.) 5: 446
Ogden, Aaron (N. J.) 5: 203
Olcott, Simeon (N. H.) 1: 363
Pickering, Timothy (Mass.) 1: 12
Pinckney, Charles (S. C.) 12: 161
Plumer, William (N. H.) 11: 124
Ross, James (Pa.) 5: 438
Sheafe, James (N. H.) 2: 10
Stone, David (N. C.) 4: 421
Sumter, Thomas (S. C.) 1: 79
Tracy, Uriah (Conn.) 2: 34
Wells, William H. (Del.) 2: 9
White, Samuel (Del.) 13: 249
Wright, Robert (Md.) 9: 297

Eighth Congress (1803-05)

Burr, Aaron, president of the senate 3: 5
Adams, John Quincy (Mass.) .. 5: 73
Anderson, Joseph (Tenn.) 2: 11
Armstrong, John (N. Y.) 1: 48
Bailey, Theodorus (N. Y.) 13: 348
Baldwin, Abraham (Ga.) 9: 178
Bayard, James A. (Del.) 7: 300
Bradley, Stephen R. (Vt.) 2: 432
Breckenridge, John (Ky.) 3: 9
Brown, John (Ky.) 6: 535
Butler, Pierce (S. C.) 2: 162
Clinton, De Witt (N. Y.) 3: 43
Cocke, William (Tenn.) 11: 409
Condit, John (N. J.) 11: 41
Dayton, Jonathan (N. J.) 1: 306
Ellery, Christopher (R. I.) 5: 338
Franklin, Jesse (N. C.) 4: 423
Gaillard, John (S. C.) 4: 291
Giles, William B. (Va.) 5: 447
Hillhouse, James (Conn.) 2: 9
Howland, Benjamin (R. I.) 4: 70
Jackson, James (Ga.) 1: 220
Logan, George (Pa.) 8: 255
Maclay, Samuel (Pa.) 12: 211
Mason, Stevens T. (Va.) 2: 9
Mitchill, Samuel L. (N. Y.) ... 4: 409
Moore, Andrew (Va.) 5: 505
Nicholas, Wilson C. (Va.) 5: 446
Olcott, Simeon (N. H.) 1: 363
Pickering, Timothy (Mass.) 1: 12
Plumer, William (N. H.) 11: 124
Potter, Samuel J. (R. I.) 13: 159
Smith, Israel (Vt.) 8: 314
Smith, John (Ohio) 6: 224
Smith, John (N. Y.) 11: 197
Smith, Samuel (Md.) 1: 73
Stone, David (N. C.) 4: 421
Sumter, Thomas (S. C.) 1: 79
Taylor, John (Va.) 9: 509
Tracy, Uriah (Conn.) 2: 34
Venable, Abraham B. (Va.) ...11: 86
Wells, William H. (Del.) 2: 9
White, Samuel (Del.) 13: 249
Worthington, Thomas (Ohio) .. 3: 138
Wright, Robert (Md.) 9: 297

Ninth Congress (1805-07)

Clinton, George, president of the senate 3: 41
Adair, John (Ky.) 13: 3
Adams, John Quincy (Mass.) .. 5: 73
Anderson, Joseph (Tenn.) 2: 11
Baldwin, Abraham (Ga.) 9: 178
Bayard, James A. (Del.) 7: 300
Bradley, Stephen R. (Vt.) 2: 432
Breckenridge, John (Ky.) 3: 9
Clay, Henry (Ky.) 5: 77
Condit, John (N. J.) 11: 41
Fenner, James (R. I.) 9: 394
Gaillard, John (S. C.) 4: 291
Giles, William B. (Va.) 5: 447
Gilman, Nicholas (N. H.) 2: 447
Hillhouse, James (Conn.) 2: 9
Howland, Benjamin (R. I.) 4: 70
Jackson, James (Ga) 1: 220
Kitchell, Aaron (N. J.) 11: 441
Logan, George (Pa.) 8: 255
Maclay, Samuel (Pa.) 12: 211
Milledge, John (Ga.) 1: 221
Mitchill, Samuel L. (N. Y.) 4: 409
Moore, Andrew (Va.) 5: 505
Pickering, Timothy (Mass.) 1: 12
Plumer, William (N. H.) 11: 124
Reed, Philip (Md.) 7: 308
Smith, Daniel (Tenn.) 2: 7
Smith, Israel (Vt.) 8: 314
Smith, John (Ohio) 6: 224
Smith, John (N. Y.) 11: 197
Smith, Samuel (Md.) 1: 73
Stone, David (N. C.) 4: 421
Sumter, Thomas (S. C.) 1: 79
Thruston, Buckner (Ky.) 3: 515
Tracy, Uriah (Conn.) 2: 34
Turner, James (N. C.) 4: 421
White, Samuel (Del.) 13: 249
Wright, Robert (Md.) 9: 297

Tenth Congress (1807-09)

Clinton, George, president of the senate 3: 41
Adams, John Quincy (Mass.) .. 5: 73
Anderson, Joseph (Tenn.) 2: 11
Bayard, James A. (Del.) 7: 300
Bradley, Stephen R. (Vt.) 2: 432
Condit, John (N. J.) 11: 41
Crawford, William H. (Ga.) ... 5: 82
Fenner, James (R. I.) 9: 394
Franklin, Jesse (N. C.) 4: 423
Gaillard, John (S. C.) 4: 291
Giles, William B. (Va.) 5: 447
Gilman, Nicholas (N. H.) 2: 447
Goodrich, Chauncey (Conn.) ... 2: 138
Gregg, Andrew (Pa.) 4: 207
Hillhouse, James (Conn.) 2: 9
Howland, Benjamin (R. I.) 4: 70
Jones, George (Ga.) 5: 548
Kitchell, Aaron (N. J.) 11: 441
Leib, Michael (Pa.) 4: 559
Lloyd, James (Mass.) 4: 469
Maclay, Samuel (Pa.) 12: 211
Matthewson, Elisha (R. I.) 4: 174
Meigs, Return J. (Ohio) 3: 137
Milledge, John (Ga.) 1: 221
Mitchill, Samuel L. (N. Y.) ... 4: 409
Moore, Andrew (Va.) 5: 505
Parker, Nahum (N. H.) 5: 223
Pickering, Timothy (Mass.) 1: 12
Pope, John (Ky.) 10: 184
Reed, Philip (Md.) 7: 308
Robinson, Jonathan (Vt.) 2: 530
Smith, Daniel (Tenn.) 2: 7
Smith, Israel (Vt.) 8: 314
Smith, John (Ohio) 6: 224
Smith, John (N. Y.) 11: 197
Smith, Samuel (Md.) 1: 73
Sumter, Thomas (S. C.) 1: 79
Thruston, Buckner (Ky.) 3: 515
Tiffin, Edward (Ohio) 3: 137
Turner, James (N. C.) 4: 421
White, Samuel (Del.) 13: 249

Eleventh Congress (1809-11)

Clinton, George, president of the senate 3: 41
Anderson, Joseph (Tenn.) 2: 11
Bayard, James A. (Del.) 7: 300
Bradley, Stephen R. (Vt.) 2: 432
Brent, Richard (Va.) 7: 534
Campbell, Alexander (Ohio) ... 4: 314
Champlin, Christopher G. (R. I.) 7: 559
Clay, Henry (Ky.) 5: 77
Condit, John (N. J.) 11: 41
Crawford, William H. (Ga.) ... 5: 82
Cutts, Charles (N. H.) 4: 510
Dana, Samuel W. (Conn.) 2: 10
Franklin, Jesse (N. C.) 4: 423
Gaillard, John (S. C.) 4: 291
German, Obadiah (N. Y.) 12: 545
Giles, William B. (Va.) 5: 447
Gilman, Nicholas (N. H.) 2: 447
Goodrich, Chauncey (Conn.) ... 2: 138
Gregg, Andrew (Pa.) 4: 207
Griswold, Stanley (Ohio) 4: 95
Hillhouse, James (Conn.) 2: 9
Horsey, Outerbridge (Del.) 4: 70
Lambert, John (N. J.) 11: 489
Leib, Michael (Pa.) 4: 559
Lloyd, James (Mass.) 4: 469
Malbone, Francis (R. I.) 8: 192
Mathewson, Elisha (R. I.) 4: 174
Meigs, Return J. (Ohio) 3: 137
Milledge, John (Ga.) 1: 221
Parker, Nahum (N. H.) 5: 223
Pickering, Timothy (Mass.) 1: 12
Pope, John (Ky.) 10: 184
Reed, Philip (Md.) 7: 308
Robinson, Jonathan (Vt.) 2: 530
Smith, Daniel (Tenn.) 2: 7
Smith, John (N. Y.) 11: 197
Smith, Samuel (Md.) 1: 73
Sumter, Thomas (S. C.) 1: 79
Tait, Charles (Ga.) 4: 348
Taylor, John (S. C.) 12: 165
Thruston, Buckner (Ky.) 3: 515
Tiffin, Edward (Ohio) 3: 137
Turner, James (N. C.) 4: 421
White, Samuel (Del.) 13: 249
Whiteside, Jenkins (Tenn.) 11: 77
Worthington, Thomas (Ohio) .. 3: 138

Twelfth Congress (1811-13)

Clinton, George, president of the senate 3: 41
Anderson, Joseph (Tenn.) 2: 11
Bayard, James A. (Del.) 7: 300
Bibb, George M. (Ky.) 6: 6
Bradley, Stephen R. (Vt.) 2: 432
Brent, Richard (Va.) 7: 534
Brown, James (La.) 4: 376
Campbell, Alexander (Ohio) ... 4: 314
Campbell, George W. (Tenn.) .. 5: 372
Champlin, Christopher G. (R. I.) 7: 559
Condit, John (N. J.) 11: 41
Crawford, William H. (Ga.) 5: 82
Cutts, Charles (N. H.) 4: 510
Dana, Samuel W. (Conn.) 2: 10
Destrehan, Jean N. (La.) 12: 250
Franklin, Jesse (N. C.) 4: 423
Gaillard, John (S. C.) 4: 291
German, Obadiah (N. Y.) 12: 545
Giles, William B. (Va.) 5: 447
Gilman, Nicholas (N. H.) 2: 447
Goodrich, Chauncey (Conn.) ... 2: 138
Gregg, Andrew (Pa.) 4: 207
Horsey, Outerbridge (Del.) 4: 70
Howell, Jeremiah B. (R. I.) ... 9: 510
Hunter, William (R. I.) 9: 269
Lambert, John (N. J.) 11: 489
Leib, Michael (Pa.) 4: 559
Lloyd, James (Mass.) 4: 469
Magruder, Allen B. (La.) 4: 349
Pope, John (Ky.) 10: 184
Posey, Thomas (La.) 13: 265
Reed, Philip (Md.) 7: 308
Robinson, Jonathan (Vt.) 2: 530
Smith, John (N. Y.) 11: 197
Smith, Samuel (Md.) 1: 73
Tait, Charles (Ga.) 4: 348
Taylor, John (S. C.) 12: 165
Turner, James (N. C.) 4: 421
Varnum, Joseph B. (Mass.) ... 1: 70
Whiteside, Jenkins (Tenn.) 11: 77
Worthington, Thomas (Ohio) .. 3: 138

Thirteenth Congress (1813-15)

Gerry, Elbridge, president of the senate 5: 371
Anderson, Joseph (Tenn.) 2: 11
Barbour, James (Va.) 5: 446

Barry, William T. (Ky.) 5: 296
Bibb, George M. (Ky.) 6: 6
Bibb, William W. (Ga.) 10: 425
Bledsoe, Jesse (Ky.) 11: 415
Brent, Richard (Va.) 7: 534
Brown, James (La.) 4: 376
Bulloch, William B. (Ga.) 4: 153
Campbell, George W. (Tenn.) .. 5: 372
Chase, Dudley (Vt.) 8: 178
Condit, John (N. J.) 11: 41
Cutts, Charles (N. H.) 4: 510
Daggett, David (Conn.) 4: 31
Dana, Samuel W. (Conn.) 2: 10
Fromentin, Eligius (La.) 12: 552
Gaillard, John (S. C.) 4: 291
German, Obadiah (N. Y.) 12: 545
Giles, William B. (Va.) 5: 447
Gilman, Nicholas (N. H.) 2: 447
Goldsborough, Robert H. (Md.) .. 7: 215
Gore, Christopher (Mass.) 1: 112
Horsey, Outerbridge (Del.) 4: 70
Howell, Jeremiah B. (R. I.) ... 9: 510
Hunter, William (R. I.) 9: 269
Kerr, Joseph (Ohio) 12: 390
King, Rufus (N. Y.) 6: 301
Lacock, Abner (Pa.) 10: 478
Lambert, John (N. J.) 11: 489
Leib, Michael (Pa.) 4: 559
Lloyd, James (Mass.) 4: 469
Locke, Francis (N. C.) 7: 518
Mason, Jeremiah (N. H.) 2: 490
Morrow, Jeremiah (Ohio) 3: 138
Roberts, Jonathan (Pa.) 4: 508
Robinson, Jonathan (Vt.) 2: 530
Smith, Samuel (Md.) 1: 73
Stone, David (N. C.) 4: 421
Tait, Charles (Ga.) 4: 348
Talbot, Isham (Ky.) 14: 151
Taylor, John (S. C.) 12: 165
Thompson, Thomas W. (N. H.) 3: 524
Turner, James (N. C.) 4: 421
Varnum, Joseph B. (Mass.) ... 1: 70
Walker, George (Ky.) 12: 237
Wells, William H. (Del.) 2: 9
Wharton, Jesse (Tenn.) 4: 545
Worthington, Thomas (Ohio) .. 3: 138

Fourteenth Congress (1815-17)

Gaillard, John, president
pro tem. 4: 291
Ashmun, Eli P. (Mass.) 11: 285
Barbour, James (Va.) 5: 446
Barry, William T. (Ky) 5: 296
Bibb, William W. (Ga.) 10: 425
Brown, James (La.) 4: 376
Campbell, George W. (Tenn.) .. 5: 372
Chase, Dudley (Vt.) 8: 178
Condit, John (N. J.) 11: 41
Daggett, David (Conn.) 4: 31
Dana, Samuel W. (Conn.) 2: 10
Fromentin, Eligius (La.) 12: 552
Gaillard, John (S. C.) 4: 291
Giles, William B. (Va.) 5: 447
Goldsborough, Robert H. (Md.) .. 7: 215
Gore, Christopher (Mass.) 1: 112
Hanson, Alexander C., Jr. (Md.) 12: 235
Hardin, Martin D. (Ky.) 12: 146
Harper, Robert G. (Md.) 5: 374
Horsey, Outerbridge (Del.) 4: 70
Howell, Jeremiah B. (R. I.) ... 9: 510
Hunter, William (R. I.) 9: 269
King, Rufus (N. Y.) 6: 301
Lacock, Abner (Pa.) 10: 478
Macon, Nathaniel (N. C.) 5: 176
Mason, Armistead T. (Va.) 4: 550
Mason, Jeremiah (N. H.) 2: 490
Morrow, Jeremiah (Ohio) 3: 138
Noble, James (Ind.) 11: 551
Roberts, Jonathan (Pa.) 4: 508
Ruggles, Benjamin (Ohio) 13: 162
Sanford, Nathan (N. Y.) 3: 383
Smith, William (S. C.) 2: 481
Stokes, Montfort (N. C.) 4: 424
Tait, Charles (Ga.) 4: 348
Talbot, Isham (Ky.) 14: 151
Taylor, John (S. C.) 12: 165
Taylor, Waller (Ind.) 4: 531
Thompson, Thomas W. (N. H.) 3: 524
Tichenor, Isaac (Vt.) 8: 313
Troup, George M. (Ga.) 1: 223
Turner, James (N. C.) 4: 421
Varnum, Joseph B. (Mass.) 1: 70
Wells, William H. (Del.) 2: 9
Williams, John (Tenn.) 1: 272
Wilson, James J. (N. J.) 3: 530

Fifteenth Congress (1817-19)

Tompkins, Daniel D., president
of the senate 6: 83
Ashmun, Eli P. (Mass.) 11: 285
Barbour, James (Va.) 5: 446
Burrill, James (R. I.) 11: 366
Campbell, George W. (Tenn.) .. 5: 372
Chase, Dudley (Vt.) 8: 178
Claiborne, William C. C. (La.) ..10: 74
Crittenden, John J. (Ky.) 13: 6
Daggett, David (Conn.) 4: 31
Dana, Samuel W. (Conn.) 2: 10
Dickerson, Mahlon (N. J.) 5: 295
Eaton, John H. (Tenn.) 5: 295
Edwards, Ninian (Ill.) 11: 42
Eppes, John W. (Va.) 11: 41
Fisk, James (Vt.) 8: 100
Forsyth, John (Ga.) 6: 435
Fromentin, Eligius (La.) 12: 552
Gaillard, John (S. C.) 4: 291
Goldsborough, Robert H. (Md.) .. 7: 215
Hanson, Alexander C. (Md.) ...12: 235
Horsey, Outerbridge (Del.) 4: 70
Hunter, William (R. I.) 9: 269
Johnson, Henry (La.) 10: 75
King, Rufus (N. Y.) 6: 301
Lacock, Abner (Pa.) 10: 478
Leake, Walter (Miss.) 13: 486
Macon, Nathaniel (N. C.) 5: 176
Mason, Jeremiah (N. H.) 2: 490
Mellen, Prentiss (Mass.) 11: 335
Morril, David L. (N. H.) 11: 125
Morrow, Jeremiah (Ohio) 3: 138
Noble, James (Ind.) 11: 551
Otis, Harrison G. (Mass.) 7: 66
Palmer, William A. (Vt.) 8: 317
Roberts, Jonathan (Pa.) 4: 508
Ruggles, Benjamin (Ohio) 13: 162
Sanford, Nathan (N. Y.) 3: 383
Smith, William (S. C.) 2: 481
Stokes, Montfort (N. C.) 4: 424
Storer, Clement (N. H.) 7: 48
Tait, Charles (Ga.) 4: 348
Talbot, Isham (Ky.) 14: 151
Taylor, Waller (Ind.) 4: 531
Tichenor, Isaac (Vt.) 8: 313
Troup, George M. (Ga.) 1: 223
Van Dyke, Nicholas (Del.) 4: 346
Williams, John (Tenn.) 1: 272
Williams, Thomas H. (Miss.) ..11: 551
Wilson, James J. (N. J.) 3: 530

Sixteenth Congress (1819-21)

Tompkins, Daniel D., president
of the senate 6: 83
Barbour, James (Va.) 5: 446
Brown, James (La.) 4: 376
Burrill, James (R. I.) 11: 366
Chandler, John (Maine) 4: 203
Dana, Samuel W. (Conn.) 2: 10
Dickerson, Mahlon (N. J.) 5: 295
Eaton, John H. (Tenn.) 5: 295
Edwards, Ninian (Ill.) 11: 42
Elliott, John (Ga.) 4: 72
Forsyth, John (Ga.) 6: 435
Gaillard, John (S. C.) 4: 291
Holmes, David (Miss.) 13: 485
Holmes, John (Maine) 10: 296
Horsey, Outerbridge (Del.) 4: 70
Hunter, William (R. I.) 9: 269
Johnson, Henry (La.) 10: 75
Johnson, Richard M. (Ky.) 6: 434
King, Rufus (N. Y.) 6: 301
King, William R. (Ala.) 4: 147
Knight, Nehemiah R. (R. I.) .. 9: 394
Lanman, James (Conn.) 4: 71
Leake, Walter (Miss.) 13: 486
Lloyd, Edward (Md.) 9: 297
Logan, William (Ky.) 4: 526
Lowrie, Walter (Pa.) 11: 558
Macon, Nathaniel (N. C.) 5: 176
Mellen, Prentiss (Mass.) 11: 335
Mills, Elijah H. (Mass.) 10: 486
Morril, David L. (N. H.) 11: 125
Noble, James (Ind.) 11: 551
Otis, Harrison G. (Mass.) 7: 66
Parrott, John F. (N. H.) 11: 576
Palmer, William A. (Vt.) 8: 317
Pinkney, William (Md.) 5: 373
Pleasants, James (Va.) 5: 447
Roberts, Jonathan (Pa.) 4: 508
Ruggles, Benjamin (Ohio) 13: 162
Sanford, Nathan (N. Y.) 3: 383
Smith, William (S. C.) 2: 481
Southard, Samuel L. (N. J.) .. 6: 85
Stokes, Montfort (N. C.) 4: 424
Talbot, Isham (Ky.) 14: 151
Taylor, Waller (Ind.) 4: 531
Thomas, Jesse B. (Ill.) 11: 315
Tichenor, Isaac (Vt.) 8: 313
Trimble, William A. (Ohio) 10: 382
Van Dyke, Nicholas (Del.) 4: 346
Walker, Freeman (Ga.) 11: 504
Walker, John W. (Ala.) 11: 471
Williams, John (Tenn.) 1: 272
Williams, Thomas H. (Miss.) ..11: 551
Wilson, James J. (N. J.) 3: 530

Seventeenth Congress (1821-23)

Tompkins, Daniel D., president
of the senate 6: 83
Barbour, James (Va.) 5: 446
Barton, David (Mo.) 7: 532
Benton, Thomas H. (Mo.) 4: 399
Boardman, Elijah (Conn.) 4: 153
Brown, Ethan A. (Ohio) 3: 138
Brown, James (La.) 4: 376
Chandler, John (Maine) 4: 203
De Wolf, James (R. I.) 8: 61
Dickerson, Mahlon (N. J.) 5: 295
Eaton, John Henry (Tenn.) ... 5: 295
Edwards, Ninian (Ill.) 11: 42
Elliott, John (Ga.) 4: 72
Findlay, William (Pa.) 2: 285
Gaillard, John (S. C.) 4: 291
Holmes, David (Miss.) 13: 485
Holmes, John (Maine) 10: 296
Johnson, Henry (La.) 10: 75
Johnson, Richard M. (Ky.) 6: 434
Kelly, William (Ala.) 11: 553
King, Rufus (N. Y.) 6: 301
King, William R. (Ala.) 4: 147
Knight, Nehemiah R. (R. I.) .. 9: 394
Lanman, James (Conn.) 4: 71
Lloyd, Edward (Md.) 9: 297
Lloyd, James (Mass.) 4: 469
Lowrie, Walter (Pa.) 11: 558
Macon, Nathaniel (N. C.) 5: 176
Mills, Elijah H. (Mass.) 10: 486
Morril, David L. (N. H.) 11: 125
Noble, James (Ind.) 11: 551
Otis, Harrison G. (Mass.) 7: 66
Palmer, William A. (Vt.) 8: 317
Parrott, John F. (N. H.) 11: 576
Pinkney, William (Md.) 5: 373
Pleasants, James (Va.) 5: 447
Rodney, Cæsar A. (Del.) 3: 11
Ruggles, Benjamin (Ohio) 13: 162
Seymour, Horatio (Vt.) 8: 473
Smith, Samuel (Md.) 1: 73
Smith, William (S. C.) 2: 481
Southard, Samuel L. (N. J.) ... 6: 85
Stokes, Montfort (N. C.) 4: 424
Talbot, Isham (Ky.) 14: 151
Taylor, John (Va.) 9: 509
Taylor, Waller (Ind.) 4: 531
Thomas, Jesse B. (Ill.) 11: 315
Trimble, William A. (Ohio) 10: 382
Van Buren, Martin (N. Y.) ... 6: 433
Van Dyke, Nicholas (Del.) 4: 346
Walker, Freeman (Ga.) 11: 504
Walker, John W. (Ala.) 11: 471
Ware, Nicholas (Ga.) 5: 70
Williams, John (Tenn.) 1: 272
Williams, Thomas H. (Miss.) ..11: 551

Eighteenth Congress (1823-25)

Tompkins, Daniel D., president
of the senate 6: 83
Barbour, James (Va.) 5: 446
Barton, David (Mo.) 7: 532
Bell, Samuel (N. H.) 11: 125
Benton, Thomas H. (Mo.) 4: 399
Boardman, Elijah (Conn.) 4: 153
Bouligny, Dominique (La.) 11: 312
Branch, John (N. C.) 5: 295
Brown, Ethan A. (Ohio) 3: 138
Brown, James (La.) 4: 376
Chandler, John (Maine) 4: 203
Clayton, Thomas (Del.) 12: 552
Cobb, Thomas W. (Ga.) 4: 467
De Wolf, James (R. I.) 8: 61
Dickerson, Mahlon (N. J.) 5: 295
Eaton, John Henry (Tenn.) ... 5: 295
Edwards, Henry W. (Conn.) ...10: 334
Edwards, Ninian (Ill.) 11: 42
Elliott, John (Ga.) 4: 72
Findlay, William (Pa.) 2: 285
Gaillard, John (S. C.) 4: 291

Hayne, Robert Y. (S. C.) 12:166
Holmes, David (Miss.) 13:485
Holmes, John (Maine) 10:296
Jackson, Andrew (Tenn.) 5:289
Johnson, Henry (La.) 10: 75
Johnson, Richard M. (Ky.) 6:434
Johnston, Josiah S. (La.) 5: 45
Kelly, William (Ala.) 11:553
King, Rufus (N. Y.) 6:301
King, William R. (Ala.) 4:147
Knight, Nehemiah R. (R. I.) .. 9:394
Lanman, James (Conn.) 4: 71
Lloyd, Edward (Md.) 9:297
Lloyd, James (Mass.) 4:469
Lowrie, Walter (Pa.) 11:558
McIlvaine, Joseph (N. J.) 11:313
McLean, John J. (Ill.) 5:509
Macon, Nathaniel (N. C.) 5:176
Mills, Elijah H. (Mass.) 10:486
Noble, James (Ind.) 11:551
Palmer, William A. (Vt.) 8:317
Parrott, John F. (N. H.) 11:576
Rodney, Cæsar A. (Del.) 3: 11
Ruggles, Benjamin (Ohio) 13:162
Seymour, Horatio (Vt.) 8:473
Smith, Samuel (Md.) 1: 73
Southard, Samuel L. (N. J.) .. 6: 85
Talbot, Isham (Ky.) 14:151
Taylor, John (Va.) 9:509
Taylor, Waller (Ind.) 4:531
Tazewell, Littleton W. (Va.) ... 5:448
Thomas, Jesse B. (Ill.) 11:315
Van Buren, Martin (N. Y.) 6:433
Van Dyke, Nicholas (Del.) 4:346
Ware, Nicholas (Ga.) 5: 70
Williams, Thomas H. (Miss.) ..11:551

Nineteenth Congress (1825-27)

Calhoun, John C., president of the senate 6:83
Barbour, James (Va.) 5:446
Barton, David (Mo.) 7:532
Bateman, Ephraim (N. J.) 12:270
Bell, Samuel (N. H.) 11:125
Benton, Thomas H. (Mo.) 4:399
Berrien, John M. (Ga.) 5:298
Bouligny, Dominique (La.) 11:312
Branch, John (N. C.) 5:295
Chambers, Ezekiel F. (Md.) ... 7:307
Chambers, Henry (Ala.) 11:235
Chandler, John (Maine) 4:203
Chase, Dudley (Vt.) 8:178
Clayton, Thomas (Del.) 12:552
Cobb, Thomas W. (Ga.) 4:467
De Wolf, James (R. I.) 8: 61
Dickerson, Mahlon (N. J.) 5:295
Eaton, John Henry (Tenn.) ... 5:295
Edwards, Henry W. (Conn.) ..10:334
Ellis, Powhatan (Miss.) 11: 53
Findlay, William (Pa.) 2:285
Gaillard, John (S. C.) 4:291
Harper, William (S. C.) 11:420
Harrison, William H. (Ohio) .. 3: 33
Hayne, Robert Y. (S. C.) 12:166
Hendricks, William (Ind.) 13:266
Holmes, David (Miss.) 13:485
Holmes, John (Maine) 10:296
Jackson, Andrew (Tenn.) 5:289
Johnson, Richard M. (Ky.) 6:434
Johnston, Josiah S. (La.) 5: 45
Kane, Elias K. (Ill.) 11:495
King, William R. (Ala.) 4:147
Knight, Nehemiah R. (R. I.) ... 9:394
Lloyd, Edward (Md.) 9:297
Lloyd, James (Mass.) 4:469
McIlvaine, Joseph (N. J.) 11:313
McKinley, John (Ala.) 2:470
Macon, Nathaniel (N. C.) 5:176
Marks, William (Pa.) 11:558
Mills, Elijah H. (Mass.) 10:486
Noble, James (Ind.) 11:551
Pickens, Israel (Ala.) 10:426
Randolph, John (Va.) 5: 97
Reed, Thomas B. (Miss.) 4:468
Ridgely, Henry M. (Del.) 4:392
Robbins, Ashur (R. I.) 1:452
Rodney, Daniel (Del.) 11:531
Rowan, John (Ky.) 6: 95
Ruggles, Benjamin (Ohio) 13:162
Sanford, Nathan (N. Y.) 3:383
Seymour, Horatio (Vt.) 8:473
Silsbee, Nathaniel (Mass.) 12:551
Smith, Samuel (Md.) 1: 73
Smith, William (S. C.) 2:481
Tazewell, Littleton W. (Va.) .. 5:448
Thomas, Jesse B. (Ill.) 11:315

Van Buren, Martin (N. Y.) ... 6:433
Van Dyke, Nicholas (Del.) 4:346
White, Hugh L. (Tenn.) 11:395
Willey, Calvin (Conn.) 11:314
Williams, Thomas H. (Miss.) ..11:551
Woodbury, Levi (N. H.) 2:471

Twentieth Congress (1827-29)

Calhoun, John C., president of the senate 6: 83
Barnard, Isaac D. (Pa.) 7:529
Barton, David (Mo.) 7:532
Bateman, Ephraim (N. J.) 12:270
Bell, Samuel (N. H.) 11:125
Benton, Thomas H. (Mo.) 4:399
Berrien, John M. (Ga.) 5:298
Bouligny, Dominique (La.) 11:312
Branch, John (N. C.) 5:295
Burnet, Jacob (Ohio) 11:155
Chambers, Ezekiel F. (Md.) ... 7:307
Chandler, John (Maine) 4:203
Chase, Dudley (Vt.) 8:178
Cobb, Thomas W. (Ga.) 4:467
Dickerson, Mahlon (N. J.) 5:295
Dudley, Charles E. (N. Y.) 4:353
Eaton, John Henry (Tenn.) ... 5:295
Ellis, Powhatan (Miss.) 11: 53
Foote, Samuel A. (Conn.) 10:334
Harrison, William H. (Ohio) ... 3: 33
Hayne, Robert Y. (S. C.) 12:166
Hendricks, Williams (Ind.) 13:266
Holmes, John (Maine) 10:296
Iredell, James, Jr. (N. C.) 4:423
Johnson, Richard M. (Ky.) 6:434
Johnston, Josiah S. (La.) 5: 45
Kane, Elias K. (Ill.) 11:495
King, William R. (Ala.) 4:147
Knight, Nehemiah R. (R. I.) .. 9:394
McKinley, John (Ala.) 2:470
McLane, Louis (Del.) 5:293
Macon, Nathaniel (N. C.) 5:176
Marks, William (Pa.) 11:558
Noble, James (Ind.) 11:551
Parris, Albion K. (Maine) 6:306
Prince, Oliver H. (Ga.) 11:399
Ridgely, Henry M. (Del.) 4:392
Robbins, Ashur (R. I.) 1:452
Rowan, John (Ky.) 6: 95
Ruggles, Benjamin (Ohio) 13:162
Sanford, Nathan (N. Y.) 3:383
Seymour, Horatio (Vt.) 8:473
Silsbee, Nathaniel (Mass.) 12:551
Smith, Samuel (Md.) 1: 73
Smith, William (S. C.) 2: 481
Tazewell, Littleton W. (Va.) ... 5:448
Thomas, Jesse B. (Ill.) 11:315
Tyler, John (Va.) 6: 1
Van Buren, Martin (N. Y.) ... 6:433
Webster, Daniel (Mass.) 3: 36
White, Hugh L. (Tenn.) 11:395
Willey, Calvin (Conn.) 11:314
Williams, Thomas H. (Miss.) ..11:551
Woodbury, Levi (N. H.) 2:471

Twenty-first Congress (1829-31)

Calhoun, John C., president of the senate 6: 83
Adams, Robert H. (Miss.) 3:533
Baker, David J. (Ill.) ....11:5°6
Barnard, Isaac D. (Pa.) 7:529
Barton, David (Mo.) 7:532
Bell, Samuel (N. H.) 11:125
Benton, Thomas H. (Mo.) 4:399
Berrien, John McP. (Ga.) 5:298
Bibb, George M. (Ky.) 6: 6
Brown, Bedford (N. C.) 9:458
Burnet, Jacob (Ohio) 11:155
Chambers, Ezekiel F. (Md.) ... 7:307
Chase, Dudley (Vt.) 8:178
Clayton, John M. (Del.) 6:179
Dickerson, Mahlon (N. J.) 5:295
Dudley, Charles E. (N. Y.) 4:353
Eaton, John Henry (Tenn.) ... 5:295
Ellis, Powhatan (Miss.) 11: 53
Foote, Samuel A. (Conn.) 10:334
Forsyth, John (Ga.) 6:435
Frelinghuysen, Theodore (N. J.) 3:401
Grundy, Felix (Tenn.) 6:436
Hayne, Robert Y. (S. C.) 12:166
Hendricks, William (Ind.) 13:266
Holmes, John (Maine) 10:296
Iredell, James, Jr. (N. C.) 4:423
Johnston, Josiah S. (La.) 5: 45
Kane, Elias K. (Ill.) 11:495

King, William R. (Ala.) 4:147
Knight, Nehemiah R. (R. I.) ... 9:394
Livingston, Edward (La.) 5:293
McKinley, John (Ala.) 2:470
McLane, Louis (Del.) 5:293
McLean, John J. (Ill.) 5:509
Marks, William (Pa.) 11:558
Naudain, Arnold (Del.) 11:504
Noble, James (Ind.) 11:551
Poindexter, George (Miss.) 13:485
Reed, Thomas B. (Miss.) 4:468
Robbins, Ashur (R. I.) 1:452
Robinson, John M. (Ill.) 13:161
Rowan, John (Ky.) 6: 95
Ruggles, Benjamin (Ohio) 13:162
Sanford, Nathan (N. Y.) 3:383
Seymour, Horatio (Vt.) 8:473
Silsbee, Nathaniel (Mass.) 12:551
Smith, Samuel (Md.) 1: 73
Smith, William (S. C.) 2:481
Sprague, Peleg (Maine) 5:414
Tazewell, Littleton W. (Va.) ... 5:448
Troup, George M. (Ga.) 1:223
Tyler, John (Va.) 6: 1
Webster, Daniel (Mass.) 3: 36
White, Hugh L. (Tenn.) 11:395
Willey, Calvin (Conn.) 11:314
Woodbury, Levi (N. H.) 2:471

Twenty-second Congress (1831-33)

Calhoun, John C., president of the senate 6: 83
Barnard, Isaac D. (Pa.) 7:529
Bell, Samuel (N. H.) 11:125
Benton, Thomas H. (Mo.) 4:399
Bibb, George M. (Ky.) 6: 6
Black, John (Miss.) 11:164
Brown, Bedford (N. C.) 9:458
Buckner, Alexander (Mo.) 4:292
Chambers, Ezekiel F. (Md.) ... 7:307
Clay, Henry (Ky.) 5: 77
Clayton, John M. (Del.) 6:179
Dallas, George M. (Pa.) 6:268
Dickerson, Mahlon (N. J.) 5:295
Dudley, Charles E. (N. Y.) 4:353
Ellis, Powhatan (Miss.) 11: 53
Ewing, Thomas (Ohio) 25: 14
Foote, Samuel A. (Conn.) 10:334
Forsyth, John (Ga.) 6:435
Frelinghuysen, Theodore (N. J.) 3:401
Grundy, Felix (Tenn.) 6:436
Hanna, Robert (Ind.) 4:253
Hayne, Robert Y. (S. C.) 12:166
Hendricks, William (Ind.) 13:266
Hill, Isaac (N. H.) 11:127
Holmes, John (Maine) 10:296
Johnston, Josiah S. (La.) 5: 45
Kane, Elias K. (Ill.) 11:495
King, William R. (Ala.) 4:147
Knight, Nehemiah R. (R. I.) ... 9:394
Livingston, Edward (La.) 5:293
Mangum, Willie P. (N. C.) 4: 47
Marcy, William L. (N. Y.) ... 6:269
Miller, Stephen D. (S. C.) 12:166
Moore, Gabriel (Ala.) 10:426
Naudain, Arnold (Del.) 11:504
Poindexter, George (Miss.) 13:485
Prentiss, Samuel (Vt.) 8:402
Rives, William C. (Va.) 6:486
Robbins, Ashur (R. I.) 1:452
Robinson, John M. (Ill.) 13:161
Ruggles, Benjamin (Ohio) 13:162
Seymour, Horatio (Vt.) 8:473
Silsbee, Nathaniel (Mass.) 12:551
Smith, Samuel (Md.) 1: 73
Sprague, Peleg (Maine) 5:414
Tazewell, Littleton W. (Va.) ... 5:448
Tipton, John (Ind.) 11:314
Tomlinson, Gideon (Conn.) 10:334
Troup, George M. (Ga.) 1:223
Tyler, John (Va.) 6: 1
Waggamann, George A. (La.) ..11: 25
Webster, Daniel (Mass.) 3: 36
White, Hugh L. (Tenn.) 11:395
Wilkins, William (Pa.) 6: 9
Wright, Silas (N. Y.) 3: 47

Twenty-third Congress (1833-35)

Van Buren, Martin, president of the senate 6:433
Bell, Samuel (N. H.) 11:125
Benton, Thomas H. (Mo.) 4:399
Bibb, George M. (Ky.) 6: 6
Black, John (Miss.) 11:164

Brown, Bedford (N. C.) 9: 458
Buchanan, James (Pa.) 5: 1
Callhoun, John C. (S. C.) 6: 83
Chambers, Ezekiel F. (Md.) ... 7: 307
Clay, Henry (Ky.) 5: 77
Clayton, John M. (Del.) 6: 179
Ewing, Thomas (Ohio) 25: 14
Forsyth, John (Ga.) 6: 435
Frelinghuysen, Theodore (N. J.) 3: 401
Goldsborough, Robert H. (Md.).. 7: 215
Grundy, Felix (Tenn.) 6: 436
Hendricks, William (Ind.) 13: 266
Hill, Isaac (N. H.) 11: 127
Johnston, Josiah S. (La.) 5: 45
Kane, Elias K. (Ill.) 11: 495
Kent, Joseph (Md.) 9: 301
King, John P. (Ga.) 2: 178
King, William R. (Ala.) 4: 147
Knight, Nehemiah R. (R. I.) .. 9: 394
Leigh, Benjamin W. (Va.) 11: 312
Linn, Lewis F. (Mo.) 4: 551
McKean, Samuel (Pa.) 11: 322
Mangum, Willie P. (N. C.) 4: 47
Moore, Gabriel (Ala.) 10: 426
Morris, Thomas (Ohio) 11: 39
Naudain, Arnold (Del.) 11: 504
Poindexter, George (Miss.) 13: 485
Porter, Alexander J. (La.) 13: 158
Prentiss, Samuel (Vt.) 8: 402
Preston, William C. (S. C.) 11: 33
Rives, William C. (Va.) 6: 486
Robbins, Ashur (R. I.) 1: 452
Robinson, John M. (Ill.) 13: 161
Ruggles, John (Maine) 12: 230
Shepley, Ether (Maine) 2: 7
Silsbee, Nathaniel (Mass.) 12: 551
Smith, Nathan (Conn.) 5: 516
Southard, Samuel L. (N. J.) .. 6: 85
Sprague, Peleg (Maine) 5: 414
Swift, Benjamin (Vt.) 3: 517
Tallmadge, Nathaniel P. (N. Y.) 12: 73
Tipton, John (Ind.) 11: 314
Tomlinson, Gideon (Conn.) 10: 334
Troup, George M. (Ga.) 1: 223
Tyler, John (Va.) 6: 1
Waggamann, George A. (La.) ..11: 25
Webster, Daniel (Mass.) 3: 36
White, Hugh L. (Tenn.) 11: 395
Wilkins, William (Pa.) 6: 9
Wright, Silas (N. Y.) 3: 47

Twenty-fourth Congress (1835-37)

Van Buren, Martin, president of the senate 6: 433
Bayard, Richard H. (Del.) 4: 351
Benton, Thomas H. (Mo.) 4: 399
Black, John (Miss.) 11: 164
Brown, Bedford (N. C.) 9: 458
Buchanan, James (Pa.) 5: 1
Calhoun, John C. (S. C.) 6: 83
Clay, Henry (Ky.) 5: 77
Clayton, John M. (Del.) 6: 179
Clayton, Thomas (Del.) 12: 552
Crittenden, John J. (Ky.) 13: 6
Dana, Judah (Maine). 11: 38
Davis, John (Mass.) 1: 115
Ewing, Thomas (Ohio) 25: 14
Ewing, William L. D. (Ill.) ...11: 44
Forsyth, John (Ga.) 6: 435
Fulton, William S. (Ark.) 10: 184
Goldsborough, Robert H. (Md.) 7: 215
Grundy, Felix (Tenn.) 6: 436
Hendricks, William (Ind.) 13: 266
Hill, Isaac (N. H.) 11: 127
Hubbard, Henry (N. H.) 11: 128
Kane, Elias K. (Ill.) 11: 495
Kent, Joseph (Md.) 9: 301
King, John P. (Ga.) 2: 178
King, William R. (Ala.) 4: 147
Knight, Nehemiah R. (R. I.) .. 9: 394
Leigh, Benjamin W. (Va.) 11: 312
Linn, Lewis F. (Mo.) 4: 551
Lyon, Lucius, (Mich.) 11: 334
McKean, Samuel (Pa.) 11: 322
Mangum, Willie P. (N. C.) 4: 47
Moore, Gabriel (Ala.) 10: 426
Morris, Thomas (Ohio) 11: 39
Mouton, Alexandre (La.) 10: 76
Naudain, Arnold (Del.) 11: 504
Nicholas, Robert C. (La.) 5: 505
Niles, John M. (Conn.) 6: 436
Norvell, John (Mich.) 11: 500
Page, John (N. H.) 11: 128
Parker, Richard E. (Va.) 11: 335
Porter, Alexander J. (La.) 13: 158
Prentiss, Samuel (Vt.) 8: 402
Preston, William C. (S. C.) ...11: 33
Rives, William C. (Va.) 6: 486
Robbins, Ashur (R. I.) 1: 452
Robinson, John M. (Ill.) 13: 161
Ruggles, John (Maine) 12: 230
Sevier, Ambrose H. (Ark.) 2: 239
Shepley, Ether (Maine) 2: 7
Smith, Nathan (Conn.) 5: 516
Southard, Samuel L. (N. J.) ... 6: 85
Spence, John S. (Md.) 7: 288
Strange, Robert (N. C.) 7: 321
Swift, Benjamin, (Vt.) 3: 517
Tallmadge, Nathaniel P. (N. Y.) 12: 73
Tipton, John (Ind.) 11: 314
Tomlinson, Gideon (Conn.) 10: 334
Tyler, John (Va.) 6: 1
Walker, Robert J. (Miss.) 6: 269
Wall, Garret D. (N. J.) 5: 529
Webster, Daniel (Mass.) 3: 36
White, Hugh L. (Tenn.) 11: 395
Wright, Silas (N. Y.) 3: 47

Twenty-fifth Congress (1837-39)

Johnson, Richard M., president of the senate 6: 434
Allen, William (Ohio) 3: 142
Bayard, Richard H. (Del.) 4: 351
Benton, Thomas H. (Mo.) 4: 399
Black, John (Miss.) 11: 164
Brown, Bedford (N. C.) 9: 458
Buchanan, James (Pa.) 5: 1
Calhoun, John C. (S. C.) 6: 83
Clay, Clement Comer (Ala.) ...10: 427
Clay, Henry (Ky.) 5: 77
Clayton, Thomas (Del.) 12: 552
Crittenden, John J. (Ky.) 13: 6
Cuthbert, Alfred (Ga.) 11: 560
Davis, John (Mass.) 1: 115
Foster, Ephraim H. (Tenn.) ... 7: 541
Fulton, William S. (Ark.) 10: 184
Grundy, Felix (Tenn.) 6: 436
Hubbard, Henry (N. H.) 11: 128
Kent, Joseph (Md.) 9: 301
King, John P. (Ga.) 2: 178
King, William R. (Ala.) 4: 147
Knight, Nehemiah R. (R. I.) ... 9: 394
Linn, Lewis F. (Mo.) 4: 551
Lumpkin, Wilson (Ga.) 1: 224
Lyon, Lucius (Mich.) 11: 334
McKean, Samuel (Pa.) 11: 322
McKinley, John (Ala.) 2: 470
Merrick, William D. (Md.) 7: 323
Morris, Thomas (Ohio) 11: 39
Mouton, Alexander (La.) 10: 76
Nicholas, Robert C. (La.) 5: 505
Niles, John M. (Conn.) 6: 436
Norvell, John (Mich.) 11: 500
Parker, Richard E. (Va.) 11: 335
Pierce, Franklin (N. H.) 4: 145
Prentiss, Samuel (Vt.) 8: 402
Preston, William C. (S. C.) 11: 33
Rives, William C. (Va.) 6: 486
Roane, William H. (Va.) 4: 377
Robbins, Ashur (R. I.) 1: 452
Robinson, John M. (Ill.) 13: 161
Ruggles, John (Maine) 12: 230
Sevier, Ambrose H. (Ark.) 2: 239
Smith, Oliver H. (Ind.) 5: 517
Smith, Perry (Conn.) 5: 518
Southard, Samuel L. (N. J.) .. 6: 85
Spence, John S. (Md.) 7: 288
Strange, Robert (N. C.) 7: 321
Swift, Benjamin (Vt.) 3: 517
Tallmadge, Nathaniel P. (N. Y.) 12: 73
Tipton, John (Ind.) 11: 314
Trotter, James F. (Miss.) 12: 331
Walker, Robert J. (Miss.) 6: 269
Wall, Garret D. (N. J.) 5: 529
Webster, Daniel (Mass.) 3: 36
White, Hugh L. (Tenn.) 11: 395
Williams, Reuel (Maine) 10: 254
Williams, Thomas H. (Miss.) ..11: 551
Wright, Silas (N. Y.) 3: 47
Young, Richard M. (Ill.) 12: 240

Twenty-sixth Congress (1839-41)

Johnson, Richard M., president of the senate 6: 434
Allen, William (Ohio) 3: 142
Anderson, Alexander (Tenn.) ...11: 400
Bates, Isaac C. (Mass.) 3: 532
Bayard, Richard H. (Del.) 4: 351
Benton, Thomas H. (Mo.) 4: 399
Betts, Thaddeus (Conn.) 4: 350
Brown, Bedford (N. C.) 9: 458
Buchanan, James (Pa.) 5: 1
Calhoun, John C. (S. C.) 6: 83
Choate, Rufus (Mass.) 6: 17
Clay, Clement Comer (Ala.) 10: 427
Clay, Henry (Ky.) 5: 77
Clayton, Thomas (Del.) 12: 552
Crittenden, John J. (Ky.) 13: 6
Cuthbert, Alfred (Ga.) 11: 560
Davis, John (Mass.) 1: 115
Dixon, Nathan F. (R. I.) 13: 197
Fulton, William S. (Ark.) 10: 184
Graham, William A. (N. C.) .. 4: 426
Grundy, Felix (Tenn.) 6: 436
Henderson, John (Miss.) 11: 250
Hubbard, Henry (N. H.) 11: 128
Huntington, Jabez W. (Conn.) .. 4: 540
Kerr, John L. (Md.) 7: 419
King, William R. (Ala.) 4: 147
Knight, Nehemiah R. (R. I.) .. 9: 394
Linn, Lewis F. (Mo.) 4: 551
Lumpkin, Wilson (Ga.) 1: 224
Mangum, Willie P. (N. C.) 4: 47
Merrick, William D. (Md.) 7: 323
Morehead, James T. (Ky.) 13: 5
Mouton, Alexandre (La.) 10: 76
Nicholas, Robert C. (La.) 5: 505
Nicholson, Alfred O. P. (Tenn.) .11: 317
Norvell, John (Mich.) 11: 500
Phelps, Samuel S. (Vt.) 8: 400
Pierce, Franklin (N. H.) 4: 145
Porter, Augustus S. (Mich.) ...11: 551
Prentiss, Samuel (Vt.) 8: 402
Preston, William C. (S. C.) 11: 33
Rives, William C. (Va.) 6: 486
Roane, William H. (Va.) 4: 377
Robinson, John M. (Ill.) 13: 161
Ruggles, John (Maine) 12: 230
Sevier, Ambrose H. (Ark.) 2: 239
Smith, Oliver H. (Ind.) 5: 517
Smith, Perry (Conn.) 5: 518
Southard, Samuel L. (N. J.) ... 6: 85
Spence, John S. (Md.) 7: 288
Strange, Robert (N. C.) 7: 321
Sturgeon, Daniel (Pa.) 11: 83
Tallmadge, Nathaniel P. (N. Y.) 12: 73
Tappan, Benjamin (Ohio) 5: 403
Walker, Robert J. (Miss.) 6: 269
Wall, Garret D. (N. J.) 5: 529
Webster, Daniel (Mass.) 3: 36
White, Albert S. (Ind.) 3: 507
White, Hugh L. (Tenn.) 11: 395
Williams, Reuel (Maine) 10: 254
Wright, Silas (N. Y.) 3: 47
Young, Richard M. (Ill.) 12: 240

Twenty-seventh Congress (1841-43)

Tyler, John, president of the senate 6: 1
Allen, William (Ohio) 3: 142
Archer, William S. (Va.) 11: 505
Bagby, Arthur P. (Ala.) 10: 428
Barrow, Alexander (La.) 7: 528
Bates, Isaac C. (Mass.) 3: 532
Bayard, Richard H. (Del.) 4: 351
Benton, Thomas H. (Mo.) 4: 399
Berrien, John M. (Ga.) 5: 298
Buchanan, James (Pa.) 5: 1
Calhoun, John C. (S. C.) 6: 83
Choate, Rufus (Mass.) 6: 17
Clay, Clement Comer (Ala.) ...10: 427
Clay, Henry (Ky.) 5: 77
Clayton, Thomas (Del.) 12: 552
Conrad, Charles M. (La.) 6: 181
Crafts, Samuel C. (Vt.) 8: 317
Crittenden, John J. (Ky.) 13: 6
Cuthbert, Alfred (Ga.) 11: 560
Dayton, William L. (N. J.) 4: 325
Dixon, Nathan F. (R. I.) 13: 197
Evans, George (Maine) 6: 299
Fulton, William S. (Ark.) 10: 184
Graham, William A. (N. C.) ... 4: 426
Henderson, John (Miss.) 11: 250
Huger, Daniel E. (S. C.) 4: 511
Huntington, Jabez W. (Conn.) .. 4: 540
Jarnagin, Spencer (Tenn.) 11: 488
Kerr, John L. (Md.) 7: 419
King, William R. (Ala.) 4: 147
Linn, Lewis F. (Mo.) 4: 551
McDuffie, George (S. C.) 12: 167
McRoberts, Samuel (Ill.) 5: 509
Mangum, Willie P. (N. C.) 4: 47
Merrick, William D. (Md.) 7: 323
Miller, Jacob W. (N. J.) 4: 269
Morehead, James T. (Ky.) 13: 5

Mouton, Alexandre (La.) 10: 76
Nicholson, Alfred O. P. (Tenn.) 11: 317
Phelps, Samuel S. (Vt.) 8: 400
Pierce, Franklin (N. H.) 4: 145
Porter, Augustus S. (Mich.) ...11: 551
Prentiss, Samuel (Vt.) 8: 402
Preston, William C. (S. C.) ...11: 33
Rives, William C. (Va.) 6: 486
Sevier, Ambrose H. (Ark.) 2: 239
Simmons, James F. (R. I.) 9: 498
Smith, Oliver H. (Ind.) 5: 517
Smith, Perry (Conn.) 5: 518
Southard, Samuel L. (N. J.) .. 6: 85
Sprague, William (R. I.) 9: 396
Sturgeon, Daniel (Pa.) 11: 83
Tallmadge, Nathaniel P. (N. Y.) 12: 73
Tappan, Benjamin (Ohio) 5: 403
Walker, Robert J. (Miss.) 6: 269
White, Albert S. (Ind.) 3: 507
Wilcox, Leonard (N. H.) 11: 159
Williams, Reuel (Maine) 10: 254
Woodbridge, William (Mich.) .. 5: 272
Woodbury, Levi (N. H.) 2: 471
Wright, Silas (N. Y.) 3: 47
Young, Richard M. (Ill.) 12: 240

Twenty-eighth Congress (1843-45)

Mangum, Willie P., president *pro tem.* 4: 47
Allen, William (Ohio) 3: 142
Archer, William S. (Va.) 11: 505
Ashley, Chester (Ark.) 7: 48
Atchison, David R. (Mo.) 10: 223
Atherton, Charles G. (N. H.) ..10: 383
Bagby, Arthur P. (Ala.) 10: 428
Barrow, Alexander (La.) 7: 528
Bates, Isaac C. (Mass.) 3: 532
Bayard, Richard H. (Del.) 4: 351
Benton, Thomas H. (Mo.) 4: 399
Berrien, John M. (Ga.) 5: 298
Breese, Sidney (Ill.) 8: 122
Buchanan, James (Pa.) 5: 1
Choate, Rufus (Mass.) 6: 17
Clayton, Thomas (Del.) 12: 552
Colquitt, Walter T. (Ga.) 7: 560
Crittenden, John J. (Ky.) 13: 6
Dayton, William L. (N. J.) 4: 325
Dickinson, Daniel S. (N. Y.) .. 5: 388
Dix, John A. (N. Y.) 5: 6
Evans, George (Maine) 6: 299
Fairfield, John (Maine) 6: 309
Foster, Ephraim H. (Tenn.) ... 7: 541
Foster, Henry A. (N. Y.) 4: 551
Francis, John B. (R. I.) 9: 396
Fulton, William S. (Ark.) 10: 184
Hannegan, Edward A. (Ind.) ..11: 372
Haywood, William H. (N. C.) .. 4: 325
Henderson, John (Miss.) 11: 250
Huger, Daniel E. (S. C.) 4: 511
Huntington, Jabez W. (Conn.) .. 4: 540
Jarnagin, Spencer (Tenn.) 11: 488
Johnson, Henry (La.) 10: 75
King, William R. (Ala.) 4: 147
Lewis, Dixon H. (Ala.) 4: 525
Linn, Lewis F. (Mo.) 4: 551
McDuffie, George (S. C.) 12: 167
McRoberts, Samuel (Ill.) 5: 509
Merrick, William D. (Md.) 7: 323
Miller, Jacob W. (N. J.) 4: 269
Niles, John M. (Conn.) 6: 436
Pearce, James A. (Md.) 10: 249
Phelps, Samuel S. (Vt.) 8: 400
Porter, Augustus S. (Mich.) 11: 551
Rives, William C. (Va.) 6: 486
Semple, James (Ill.) 4: 361
Sevier, Ambrose H. (Ark.) 2: 239
Simmons, James F. (R. I.) 9: 498
Sprague, William (R. I.) 9: 396
Sturgeon, Daniel (Pa.) 11: 83
Tallmadge, Nathaniel P. (N. Y.) 12: 73
Tappan, Benjamin (Ohio) 5: 403
Upham, William (Vt.) 6: 505
Walker, Robert J. (Miss.) 6: 269
White, Albert S. (Ind.) 3: 507
Woodbridge, William (Mich.) .. 5: 272
Woodbury, Levi (N. H.) 2: 471
Wright, Silas (N. Y.) 3: 47

Twenty-ninth Congress (1845-47)

Dallas, George M., president of the senate 6: 268
Allen, William (Ohio) 3: 142
Archer, William S. (Va.) 11: 505
Ashley, Chester (Ark.) 7: 48
Atchinson, David R. (Mo.) 10: 223
Atherton, Charles G. (N. H.) ..10: 383
Badger, George E. (N. C.) 3: 305
Bagby, Arthur P. (Ala.) 10: 428
Barrow, Alexander (La.) 7: 528
Bates, Isaac C. (Mass.) 3: 532
Benton, Thomas H. (Mo.) 4: 399
Berrien John M. (Ga.) 5: 298
Breese, Sidney (Ill.) 8: 122
Bright, Jesse D. (Ind.) 3: 428
Butler, Andrew P. (S. C.) 3: 414
Calhoun, John C. (S. C.) 6: 83
Cameron, Simon (Pa.) 2: 79
Cass, Lewis (Mich.) 5: 3
Chalmers, Joseph W. (Miss.) .. 4: 351
Cilley, Joseph (N. H.) 10: 109
Clayton, John M. (Del.) 6: 179
Clayton, Thomas (Del.) 12: 552
Colquitt, Walter T. (Ga.) 7: 560
Corwin, Thomas (Ohio) 6: 180
Crittenden, John J. (Ky.) 13: 6
Davis, John (Mass.) 1: 115
Dayton, William L. (N. J.) 4: 325
Dickinson, Daniel S. (N. Y.) .. 5: 388
Dix, John A. (N. Y.) 5: 6
Evans, George (Maine) 6: 299
Fairfield, John (Maine) 6: 309
Greene, Albert C. (R. I.) 8: 14
Hannegan, Edward A. (Ind.) ..11: 372
Haywood, William H. (N. C.) .. 4: 325
Houston, Samuel (Tex.) 9: 63
Huntington, Jabez W. (Conn.) .. 4: 540
Jarnagin, Spencer (Tenn.) 11: 488
Jenness, Benning W. (N. H.) .. 7: 538
Johnson, Henry (La.) 10: 75
Johnson, Reverdy (Md.) 4: 371
Lewis, Dixon H. (Ala.) 4: 525
McDuffie, George (S. C.) 12: 167
Mangum, Willie P. (N. C.) 4: 47
Mason, James M. (Va.) 2: 93
Miller, Jacob W. (N. J.) 4: 269
Morehead, James T. (Ky.) 13: 5
Niles, John M. (Conn.) 6: 436
Pearce, James A. (Md.) 10: 249
Pennybacker, Isaac S. (Va.) ...11: 503
Phelps, Samuel S. (Vt.) 8: 400
Rusk, Thomas J. (Tex.) 3: 113
Semple, James (Ill.) 4: 361
Sevier, Ambrose H. (Ark.) 2: 239
Simmons, James F. (R. I.) 9: 498
Soulé, Pierre (La.) 3: 117
Speight, Jesse (Miss.) 11: 502
Sturgeon, Daniel (Pa.) 11: 83
Turney, Hopkins L. (Tenn.) ... 5: 509
Upham, William (Vt.) 6: 505
Walker, Robert J. (Miss.) 6: 269
Webster, Daniel (Mass.) 3: 36
Westcott, James D. (Fla.) 12: 464
Woodbridge, William (Mich.) .. 5: 272
Woodbury, Levi (N. H.) 2: 471
Yulee, David L. (Fla.) 11: 425

Thirtieth Congress (1847-49)

Dallas, George M., president of the senate 6: 268
Allen, William (Ohio) 3: 142
Ashley, Chester (Ark.) 7: 48
Atchison, David R. (Mo.) 10: 223
Atherton, Charles G. (N. H.) ..10: 383
Badger, George E. (N. C.) 3: 305
Bagby, Arthur P. (Ala.) 10: 428
Baldwin, Roger S. (Conn.) 10: 336
Bell, John (Tenn.) 3: 39
Benton, Thomas H. (Mo.) 4: 399
Berrien, John M. (Ga.) 5: 298
Borland, Solon (Ark.) 4: 386
Bradbury, James W. (Maine) .. 4: 323
Breese, Sidney (Ill.) 8: 122
Bright, Jesse D. (Ind.) 3: 428
Butler, Andrew P. (S. C.) 3: 414
Calhoun, John C. (S. C.) 6: 83
Cameron, Simon (Pa.) 2: 79
Cass, Lewis (Mich.) 5: 3
Clarke, John H. (R. I.) 6: 459
Clayton, John M. (Del.) 6: 179
Colquitt, Walter T. (Ga.) 7: 560
Corwin, Thomas (Ohio) 6: 180
Crittenden, John J. (Ky.) 13: 6
Davis, Jefferson (Miss.) 4: 148
Davis, John (Mass.) 1: 115
Dayton, William L. (N. J.) 4: 325
Dickinson, Daniel S. (N. Y.) .. 5: 388
Dix, John A. (N. Y.) 5: 6
Dodge, Augustus C. (Iowa) 12: 53
Dodge, Henry (Wis.) 12: 72
Douglas, Stephen A. (Ill.) 2: 428
Downs, Solomon W. (La.) 12: 373
Fairfield, John (Maine) 6: 309
Felch, Alpheus (Mich.) 3: 295
Fitzgerald, Thomas (Mich.) 7: 542
Fitzpatrick, Benjamin (Ala.) ...10: 429
Foote, Henry S. (Miss.) 13: 490
Greene, Albert C. (R. I.) 8: 14
Hale, John P. (N. H.) 3: 120
Hannegan, Edward A. (Ind.) ..11: 372
Hamlin, Hannibal (Maine) 2: 76
Houston, Samuel (Tex.) 9: 63
Hunter, Robert M. T. (Va.) ... 9: 158
Huntington, Jabez W. (Conn.) .. 4: 540
Johnson, Henry (La.) 10: 75
Johnson, Herschel V. (Ga.) 1: 226
Johnson, Reverdy (Md.) 4: 371
Jones, George W. (Iowa) 3: 433
King, William R. (Ala.) 4: 147
Lewis, Dixon H. (Ala.) 4: 525
Mangum, Willie P. (N. C.) 4: 47
Mason, James M. (Va.) 2: 93
Metcalfe, Thomas (Ky.) 13: 4
Miller, Jacob W. (N. J.) 4: 269
Moor, Wyman B. S. (Maine) ... 5: 505
Niles, John M. (Conn.) 6: 436
Pearce, James A. (Md.) 10: 249
Phelps, Samuel S. (Vt.) 8: 400
Rusk, Thomas J. (Tex.) 3: 113
Sebastian, William K. (Ark.) ... 4: 548
Sevier, Ambrose H. (Ark.) 2: 239
Speight, Jesse (Miss.) 11: 502
Spruance, Presley (Del.) 4: 351
Sturgeon, Daniel (Pa.) 11: 83
Turney, Hopkins L. (Tenn.) ... 5: 509
Underwood, Joseph R. (Ky.) .. 3: 428
Upham, William (Vt.) 6: 505
Wales, John (Del.) 11: 354
Walker, Isaac P. (Wis.) 3: 530
Webster, Daniel (Mass.) 3: 36
Westcott, James D. (Fla.) 12: 464
Yulee, David L. (Fla.) 11: 425

Thirty-first Congress (1849-51)

Fillmore, Millard, president of the senate 6: 177
Atchison, David R. (Mo.) 10: 223
Badger, George E. (N. C.) 3: 305
Baldwin, Roger S. (Conn.) 10: 336
Barnwell, Robert W. (S. C.) ...11: 32
Bell, John (Tenn.) 3: 39
Benton, Thomas H. (Mo.) 4: 399
Berrien, John M. (Ga.) 5: 298
Borland, Solon (Ark.) 4: 386
Bradbury, James W. (Maine) .. 4: 323
Bright, Jesse D. (Ind.) 3: 428
Butler, Andrew P. (S. C.) 3: 414
Calhoun, John C. (S. C.) 6: 83
Cass, Lewis (Mich.) 5: 3
Chase, Salmon P. (Ohio) 1: 28
Clarke, John H. (R. I.) 6: 459
Clay, Henry (Ky.) 5: 77
Clemens, Jeremiah (Ala.) 7: 234
Cooper, James (Pa.) 5: 498
Corwin, Thomas (Ohio) 6: 180
Davis, Jefferson (Miss.) 4: 148
Davis, John (Mass.) 1: 115
Dawson, William C. (Ga.) 11: 263
Dayton, William L. (N. J.) 4: 325
Dickinson, Daniel S. (N. Y.) .. 5: 388
Dodge, Augustus C. (Iowa) 12: 53
Dodge, Henry (Wis.) 12: 72
Douglas, Stephen A. (Ill.) 2: 428
Downs, Solomon W. (La.) 12: 373
Elmore, Franklin H. (S. C.) ...11: 335
Ewing, Thomas (Ohio) 25: 14
Felch, Alpheus (Mich.) 3: 295
Fitzpatrick, Benjamin (Ala.) ..10: 429
Foote, Henry S. (Miss.) 13: 490
Frémont, John C. (Calif.) 4: 270
Greene, Albert C. (R. I.) 8: 14
Gwin, William McK. (Calif.) ... 5: 145
Hale, John P. (N. H.) 3: 120
Hamlin, Hannibal (Maine) 2: 76
Houston, Samuel (Tex.) 9: 63
Hunter, Robert M. T. (Va.) ... 9: 158
Johnson, Reverdy (Md.) 4: 371
Jones, George W. (Iowa) 3: 433
King, William R. (Ala.) 4: 147
Mangum, Willie P. (N. C.) 4: 47
Mason, James M. (Va.) 2: 93
Miller, Jacob W. (N. J.) 4: 269
Morton, Jackson (Fla.) 5: 259
Norris, Moses (N. H.) 12: 394
Pearce, James A. (Md.) 10: 249
Phelps, Samuel S. (Vt.) 8: 400

Pratt, Thomas G. (Md.) 9: 305
Rantoul, Robert, Jr. (Mass.) 11: 232
Rhett, Robert B. (S. C.) 4: 303
Rusk, Thomas J. (Tex.) 3: 113
Sebastian, William K. (Ark.) .. 4: 548
Seward, William H. (N. Y.) ... 2: 77
Shields, James (Ill.) 8: 2
Smith, Truman (Conn.) 12: 220
Soulé, Pierre (La.) 3: 117
Spruance, Presley (Del.) 4: 351
Stewart, David (Md.) 4: 348
Sturgeon, Daniel (Pa.) 11: 83
Turney, Hopkins L. (Tenn.) ... 5: 509
Underwood, Joseph R. (Ky.) ... 3: 428
Upham, William (Vt.) 6: 505
Wales, John (Del.) 11: 354
Walker, Isaac P. (Wis.) 3: 530
Webster, Daniel (Mass.) 3: 36
Whitcomb, James (Ind.) 13: 268
Winthrop, Robert C. (Mass.) ... 6: 217
Yulee, David L. (Fla.) 11: 425

Thirty-second Congress (1851-53)

King, William R., president of the senate 4: 147
Adams, Stephen (Miss.) 3: 418
Atchison, David R. (Mo.) 10: 223
Badger, George E. (N. C.) 3: 305
Bayard, James A. (Del.) 13: 206
Bell, John (Tenn.) 3: 39
Berrien, John M. (Ga.) 5: 298
Borland, Solon (Ark.) 4: 386
Bradbury, James W. (Maine) .. 4: 323
Bright, Jesse D. (Ind.) 3: 428
Brodhead, Richard (Pa.) 4: 417
Brooke, Walker (Miss.) 11: 191
Butler, Andrew P. (S. C.) 3: 414
Cass, Lewis (Mich.) 5: 3
Cathcart ,Charles W. (Ind.) ... 4: 384
Charlton, Robert M. (Ga.) 4: 191
Chase, Salmon P. (Ohio) 1: 28
Clarke, John H. (R. I.) 6: 459
Clay, Henry (Ky.) 5: 77
Clemens, Jeremiah (Ala.) 7: 234
Cooper, James (Pa.) 5: 498
Davis, Jefferson (Miss.) 4: 148
Davis, John (Mass.) 1: 115
Dawson, William C. (Ga.) 11: 263
De Saussure, William F. (S. C.) 5: 119
Dixon, Archibald (Ky.) 3: 434
Dodge, Augustus C. (Iowa) 12: 53
Dodge, Henry (Wis.) 12: 72
Douglas, Stephen A. (Ill.) 2: 428
Downs, Solomon W. (La.) 12: 373
Felch, Alpheus (Mich.) 3: 295
Fish, Hamilton (N. Y.) 4: 15
Fitzpatrick, Benjamin (Ala.) ..10: 429
Foot, Solomon (Vt.) 2: 91
Foote, Henry S. (Miss.) 13: 490
Geyer, Henry S. (Mo.) 4: 61
Gwin, William McK. (Calif.) .. 5: 145
Hale, John P. (N. H.) 3: 120
Hamlin, Hannibal (Maine) 2: 76
Houston, Samuel (Tex.) 9: 63
Hunter, Robert M. T. (Va.) ... 9: 158
James, Charles T. (R. I.) 3: 324
Jones, George W. (Iowa) 3: 433
Jones, James C. (Tenn.) 7: 209
King, William R. (Ala.) 4: 147
McRae, John J. (Miss.) 13: 490
Mallory, Stephen R. (Fla.) 4: 364
Mangum, Willie P. (N. C.) 4: 47
Mason, James M. (Va.) 2: 93
Meriwether, David (Ky.) 12: 219
Miller, Jacob W. (N. J.) 4: 269
Morton, Jackson (Fla.) 5: 259
Norris, Moses (N. H.) 12: 394
Pearce, James A. (Md.) 10: 249
Pettit, John (Ind.) 4: 537
Phelps, Samuel S. (Vt.) 8: 400
Pratt, Thomas G. (Md.) 9: 305
Rhett, Robert B. (S. C.) 4: 303
Rusk, Thomas J. (Tex.) 3: 113
Sebastian, William K. (Ark.) .. 4: 548
Seward, William H. (N. Y.) ... 2: 77
Shields, James (Ill.) 8: 2
Smith, Truman (Conn.) 12: 220
Soulé, Pierre (La.) 3: 117
Spruance, Presley (Del.) 4: 351
Stockton, Robert F. (N. J.) ... 4: 205
Sumner, Charles (Mass.) 3: 300
Toucey, Isaac (Conn.) 5: 7
Underwood, Joseph R. (Ky.) ... 3: 428
Upham, William (Vt.) 6: 505
Wade, Benjamin F. (Ohio) 2: 94
Walker, Isaac P. (Wis.) 3: 530
Weller, John B. (Calif.) 4: 107
Whitcomb, James (Ind.) 13: 268

Thirty-third Congress (1853-55)

King, William R., president of the senate 4: 147
Adams, Stephen (Miss.) 3: 418
Allen, Philip (R. I.) 9: 399
Atchison, David R. (Mo.) 10: 223
Atherton, Charles G. (N. H.) ..10: 383
Badger, George E. (N. C.) 3: 305
Bayard, James A. (Del.) 13: 206
Bell, John (Tenn.) 3: 39
Benjamin, Judah P. (La.) 4: 285
Brainerd, Lawrence (Vt.) 8: 474
Bright, Jesse D. (Ind.) 3: 428
Brodhead, Richard (Pa.) 4: 417
Brown, Albert G. (Miss.) 13: 488
Butler, Andrew P. (S. C.) 3: 414
Cass, Lewis (Mich.) 5: 3
Chase, Salmon P. (Ohio) 1: 28
Clay, Clement Claiborne (Ala.) .. 4: 198
Clayton, John M. (Del.) 6: 179
Cooper, James (Pa.) 5: 498
Dawson, William C. (Ga.) 11: 263
Dixon, Archibald (Ky.) 3: 434
Dodge, Augustus C. (Iowa) 12: 53
Douglas, Stephen A. (Ill.) 2: 428
Evans, Josiah J. (S. C.) 7: 533
Everett, Edward (Mass.) 6: 179
Fessenden, William P. (Maine).. 2: 90
Fish, Hamilton (N. Y.) 4: 15
Fitzpatrick, Benjamin (Ala.) ..10: 429
Foot, Solomon (Vt.) 2: 91
Geyer, Henry S. (Mo.) 4: 61
Gillette, Francis (Conn.) 4: 72
Gwin, William McK. (Calif.) .. 5: 145
Hamlin, Hannibal (Maine) 2: 76
Houston, Samuel (Tex.) 9: 63
Hunter, Robert M. T. (Va.) 9: 158
James, Charles T. (R. I.) 3: 324
Johnson, Robert W. (Ark.) 5: 252
Jones, James C. (Tenn.) 7: 209
Mallory, Stephen R. (Fla.) 4: 364
Mason, James M. (Va.) 2: 93
Morton, Jackson (Fla.) 5: 259
Norris, Moses (N. H.) 12: 394
Pearce, James A. (Md.) 10: 249
Pettit, John (Ind.) 4: 537
Phelps, Samuel S. (Vt.) 8: 400
Pratt, Thomas G. (Md.) 9: 305
Reid, David S. (N. C.) 4: 427
Rockwell, Julius (Mass.) 11: 401
Rusk, Thomas J. (Tex.) 3: 113
Sebastian, William K. (Ark.)... 4: 548
Seward, William H. (N. Y.) ... 2: 77
Shields, James (Ill.) 8: 2
Slidell, John (La.) 2: 93
Smith, Truman (Conn.) 12: 220
Soulé, Pierre (La.) 3: 117
Stuart, Charles E. (Mich.) 11: 436
Sumner, Charles (Mass.) 3: 300
Thompson, John B. (Ky.) 12: 226
Thomson, John R. (N. J.) 12: 212
Toombs, Robert (Ga.) 4: 392
Toucey, Isaac (Conn.) 5: 7
Wade, Benjamin F. (Ohio) 2: 94
Walker, Isaac P. (Wis.) 3: 530
Weller, John B. (Calif.) 4: 107
Wells, John S. (N. H.) 3: 507
Williams, Jared W. (N. H.) ...11: 129
Wilson, Henry (Mass.) 4: 13
Wright, William (N. J.) 4: 548

Thirty-fourth Congress (1855-57)

Bright, Jesse D., and Mason, James M., presidents *pro tem.*
Adams, Stephen (Miss.) 3: 418
Allen, Philip (R. I.) 9: 399
Bates, Martin W. (Del.) 13: 476
Bayard, James A. (Del.) 13: 206
Bell, James (N. H.) 7: 531
Bell, John (Tenn.) 3: 39
Benjamin, Judah P. (La.) 4: 285
Biggs, Asa (N. C.) 11: 189
Bigler, William (Pa.) 2: 288
Bright, Jesse D. (Ind.) 3: 428
Brodhead, Richard (Pa.) 4: 417
Brown, Albert G. (Miss.) 13: 488
Butler, Andrew P. (S. C.) 3: 414
Cass, Lewis (Mich.) 5: 3
Clay, Clement Claiborne (Ala.) .. 4: 198
Clayton, John M. (Del.) 6: 179
Collamer, Jacob (Vt.) 4: 371
Comegys, Joseph P. (Del.) 7: 497
Crittenden, John J. (Ky.) 13: 6
Dodge, Henry (Wis.) 12: 72
Douglas, Stephen A. (Ill.) 2: 428
Durkee, Charles (Wis.) 11: 262
Evans, Josiah J. (S. C.) 7: 533
Fessenden, William P. (Maine) .. 2: 90
Fish, Hamilton (N. Y.) 4: 15
Fitch, Graham N. (Ind.) 12: 209
Fitzpatrick, Benjamin (Ala.) ..10: 429
Foot, Solomon (Vt.) 2: 91
Foster, La Fayette S. (Conn.) .. 2: 95
Geyer, Henry S. (Mo.) 4: 61
Green, James S. (Mo.) 7: 535
Gwin, William McK. (Calif.) ... 5: 145
Hale, John P. (N. H.) 3: 120
Hamlin, Hannibal (Maine) 2: 76
Harlan, James (Iowa) 2: 457
Houston, Samuel (Tex.) 9: 63
Hunter, Robert M. T. (Va.) 9: 158
Iverson, Alfred (Ga.) 4: 438
James, Charles T. (R. I.) 3: 324
Johnson, Robert W. (Ark.) 5: 252
Jones, George W. (Iowa) 3: 433
Jones, James C. (Tenn.) 7: 209
Mallory, Stephen R. (Fla.) 4: 364
Mason, James M. (Va.) 2: 93
Nourse, Amos (Maine) 11: 158
Pearce, James A. (Md.) 10: 249
Pratt, Thomas G. (Md.) 9: 305
Pugh, George E. (Ohio) 4: 547
Reid, David S. (N. C.) 4: 427
Rusk, Thomas J. (Tex.) 3: 113
Sebastian, William K. (Ark.) .. 4: 548
Seward, William H. (N. Y.) ... 2: 77
Slidell, John (La.) 2: 93
Stuart, Charles E. (Mich.) 11: 436
Sumner, Charles (Mass.) 3: 300
Thompson, John B. (Ky.) 12: 226
Thomson, John R. (N. J.) 12: 212
Toombs, Robert (Ga.) 4: 392
Toucey, Isaac (Conn.) 5: 7
Trumbull, Lyman (Ill.) 12: 342
Wade, Benjamin F. (Ohio) 2: 94
Weller, John B. (Calif.) 4: 107
Wilson, Henry (Mass.) 4: 13
Wright, William (N. J.) 4: 548
Yulee, David L. (Fla.) 11: 425

Thirty-fifth Congress (1857-59)

Breckinridge, John C., president of the senate 5: 3
Allen, Philip (R. I.) 9: 399
Bates, Martin W. (Del.) 13: 476
Bayard, James A. (Del.) 13: 206
Bell, James (N. H.) 7: 531
Bell, John (Tenn.) 3: 39
Benjamin, Judah P. (La.) 4: 285
Biggs, Asa (N. C.) 11: 189
Bigler, William (Pa.) 2: 288
Bright, Jesse D. (Ind.) 3: 428
Broderick, David C. (Calif.) 4: 185
Brown, Albert G. (Miss.) 13: 488
Butler, Andrew P. (S. C.) 3: 414
Cameron, Simon (Pa.) 2: 79
Chandler, Zachariah (Mich.) ... 4: 18
Chestnut, James, Jr. (S. C.) .. 5: 54
Clark, Daniel (N. H.) 2: 87
Clay, Clement Claiborne (Ala.) .. 4: 198
Clingman, Thomas L. (N. C.) .. 7: 199
Collamer, Jacob (Vt.) 4: 371
Crittenden, John J. (Ky) 13: 6
Davis, Jefferson (Miss.) 4: 148
Dixon, James (Conn.) 4: 447
Doolittle, James R. (Wis.) 4: 382
Douglas, Stephen A. (Ill.) 2: 428
Durkee, Charles (Wis.) 11: 262
Evans, Josiah J. (S. C.) 7: 533
Fessenden, William P. (Maine) . 2: 90
Fitch, Graham N. (Ind.) 12: 209
Fitzpatrick, Benjamin (Ala.) ..10: 429
Foot, Solomon (Vt.) 2: 91
Foster, La Fayette S. (Conn.) .. 2: 95
Green, James S. (Mo.) 7: 535
Gwin, William McK. (Calif.) .. 5: 145
Hale, John P. (N. H.) 3: 120
Hamlin, Hannibal (Maine) 2: 76
Hammond, James H. (S. C.) ...12: 169
Harlan, James (Iowa) 2: 457
Hayne, Arthur P. (S. C.) 11: 198
Henderson, James P. (Tex.).... 1: 442
Houston, Samuel (Tex.) 9: 63
Hunter, Robert M. T. (Va.) 9: 158
Iverson, Alfred (Ga.) 4: 438
Johnson, Andrew (Tenn.) 2: 454
Johnson, Robert W. (Ark.) 5: 252

Jones, George W. (Iowa) 3: 433
Kennedy, Anthony (Md.) 7: 481
King, Preston (N. Y.) 2: 93
Lane, Joseph (Oreg.) 8: 2
Mallory, Stephen R. (Fla.) 4: 364
Mason, James M. (Va.) 2: 93
Pearce, James A. (Md.) 10: 249
Polk, Trusten (Mo.) 12: 304
Pugh, George E. (Ohio) 4: 547
Reid, David S. (N. C.) 4: 427
Rice, Henry M. (Minn.) 21: 273
Rusk, Thomas J. (Tex.) 3: 113
Sebastian, William K. (Ark.) .. 4: 548
Seward, William H. (N. Y.) ... 2: 77
Shields, James (Minn.) 8: 2
Simmons, James F. (R. I.) 9: 498
Slidell, John (La.) 2: 93
Smith, Delazon (Oreg.) 11: 502
Stuart, Charles E. (Mich.) 11: 436
Sumner, Charles (Mass.) 3: 300
Thompson, John B. (Ky.) 12: 226
Thomson, John R. (N. J.) 12: 212
Toombs, Robert (Ga.) 4: 392
Trumbull, Lyman (Ill.) 12: 342
Wade, Benjamin F. (Ohio) 2: 94
Ward, Matthias (Tex.) 4: 375
Wilson, Henry (Mass.) 4: 13
Wright, William (N. J.) 4: 548
Yulee, David L. (Fla.) 11: 425

Thirty-sixth Congress (1859-61)

Breckinridge, John C., president
of the senate 5: 3
Anthony, Henry B. (R. I.) 9: 398
Baker, Edward D. (Oreg.) 2: 92
Bayard, James A. (Del.) 13: 206
Benjamin, Judah P. (La.) 4: 285
Bigler, William (Pa.) 2: 288
Bingham, Kinsley S. (Mich.) .. 5: 273
Bragg, Thomas (N. C.) 4: 427
Bright, Jesse D. (Ind.) 3: 428
Broderick, David C. (Calif.) ... 4: 185
Brown, Albert G. (Miss.) 13: 488
Cameron, Simon (Pa.) 2: 79
Chandler, Zachariah (Mich.) ... 4: 18
Chestnut, James, Jr. (S. C.) ... 5: 54
Clark, Daniel (N. H.) 2: 87
Clay, Clement Claiborne (Ala.) .. 4: 198
Clingman, Thomas L. (N. C.) .. 7: 199
Collamer, Jacob (Vt.) 4: 371
Crittenden, John J. (Ky.) 13: 6
Davis, Jefferson (Miss.) 4: 148
Dixon, James (Conn.) 4: 447
Doolittle, James R. (Wis.) 4: 382
Douglas. Stephen A. (Ill.) 2: 428
Durkee, Charles (Wis.) 11: 262
Fessenden, William P. (Maine) .. 2: 90
Fitch, Graham N. (Ind.) 12: 209
Fitzpatrick, Benjamin (Ala.) ..10: 429
Foot, Solomon (Vt.) 2: 91
Foster, La Fayette S. (Conn.) .. 2: 95
Green, James S. (Mo.) 7: 535
Grimes, James W. (Iowa) 11: 430
Gwin, William McK. (Calif.) .. 5: 145
Hale, John P. (N. H.) 3: 120
Hamlin, Hannibal (Maine) 2: 76
Hammond, James H. (S. C.) ...12: 169
Harlan, James (Iowa) 2: 457
Haun, Henry P. (Calif.) 11: 369
Hemphill, John (Tex.) 4: 501
Hunter, Robert M. T. (Va.) ... 9: 158
Iverson, Alfred (Ga.) 4: 438
Johnson, Andrew (Tenn.) 2: 454
Johnson, Robert W. (Ark.) 5: 252
Kennedy, Anthony (Md.) 7: 481
King, Preston (N. Y.) 2: 93
Lane, Joseph (Oreg.) 8: 2
Latham, Milton S. (Calif.) 4: 108
Mallory, Stephen R. (Fla.) 4: 364
Mason, James M. (Va.) 2: 93
Morrill, Lot M. (Maine) 6: 313
Nicholson Alfred O. P. (Tenn.) .11: 317
Pearce, James A. (Md.) 10: 249
Polk, Trusten (Mo.) 12: 304
Powell, Lazarus W. (Ky.) 13: 7
Pugh, George E. (Ohio) 4: 547
Rice, Henry M. (Minn.) 21: 273
Saulsbury, Willard (Del.) 11: 471
Sebastian, William K. (Ark.) .. 4: 548
Seward, William H. (N. Y.) .. 2: 77
Simmons, James F. (R. I.) 9: 498
Slidell, John (La.) 2: 93
Sumner, Charles (Mass.) 3: 300
Ten Eyck, John C. (N. J.) 2: 95
Thomson, John R. (N. J.) 12: 212
Toombs, Robert (Ga.) 4: 392
Trumbull, Lyman (Ill.) 12: 342
Wade, Benjamin F. (Ohio) 2: 94
Ward, Matthias (Tex.) 4: 375
Wigfall, Louis T. (Tex.) 5: 262
Wilkinson, Morton S. (Minn.) ..12: 207
Wilson, Henry (Mass.) 4: 13
Yulee, David L. (Fla.) 11: 425

Thirty-seventh Congress (1861-63)

Hamlin, Hannibal, president
of the senate 2: 76
Anthony, Henry B. (R. I.) 9: 398
Arnold, Samuel G. (R. I.) 13: 148
Baker, Edward D. (Oreg.) 2: 92
Bayard, James A. (Del.) 13: 206
Bingham, Kinsley S. (Mich.) ... 5: 273
Breckinridge, John C. (Ky.) ... 5: 3
Bright, Jesse D. (Ind.) 3: 428
Browning, Orville H. (Ill.) 2: 457
Cameron, Simon (Pa.) 2: 79
Carlile, John S. (Va.) 4: 347
Chase, Salmon P. (Ohio) 1: 28
Chandler, Zachariah (Mich.) ... 4: 18
Clark, Daniel (N. H.) 2: 87
Collamer, Jacob (Vt.) 4: 371
Cowan, Edgar, (Pa.) 2: 94
Davis, Garrett (Ky.) 2: 225
Dixon, James (Conn.) 4: 447
Doolittle, James R. (Wis.) 4: 382
Douglas, Stephen A. (Ill.) 2: 428
Fessenden, William P. (Maine) . 2: 90
Field, Richard S. (N. J.) 3: 216
Foot, Solomon (Vt.) 2: 91
Foster, La Fayette S. (Conn.) .. 2: 95
Grimes, James W. (Iowa) 11: 430
Hale, John P. (N. H.) 3: 120
Harding, Benjamin F. (Oreg.) ..12: 394
Harlan, James (Iowa) 2: 457
Harris, Ira (N. Y.) 2: 96
Hemphill, John (Tex.) 4: 501
Henderson, John B. (Mo.) 13: 49
Hicks, Thomas H. (Md.) 9: 306
Howard, Jacob M. (Mich.) 4: 472
Howe, Timothy O. (Wis.) 4: 252
Johnson, Andrew (Tenn.) 2: 454
Johnson, Waldo P. (Mo.) 12: 392
Kennedy, Anthony (Md.) 7: 481
King, Preston (N. Y.) 2: 93
Lane, Henry S. (Ind.) 13: 270
Lane, James H. (Kans.) 4: 278
Latham, Milton S. (Calif.) 4: 108
McDougall, James A. (Calif.) ..11: 330
Mitchell, Charles B. (Ark.) 4: 63
Morrill, Lot M. (Maine) 6: 313
Nesmith, James W. (Oreg.) ... 4: 72
Pearce, James A. (Md.) 10: 249
Polk, Trusten (Mo.) 12: 304
Pomeroy, Samuel C. (Kans.) ... 12: 69
Powell, Lazarus W. (Ky.) 13: 7
Rice, Henry M. (Minn.) 21: 273
Richardson, William A. (Ill.) ...
Saulsbury, Willard (Del.) 11: 471
Sebastian, William K. (Ark.) .. 4: 548
Sherman, John (Ohio) 3: 198
Simmons, James F. (R. I.) 9: 498
Stark, Benjamin (Oreg.) 4: 549
Sumner, Charles (Mass.) 3: 300
Ten Eyck, John C. (N. J.) 2: 95
Thomson, John R. (N. J.) 12: 212
Trumbull, Lyman (Ill.) 12: 342
Turpie, David (Ind.) 1: 218
Wade, Benjamin F. (Ohio) 2: 94
Wall, James W. (N. J.) 10: 123
Wilkinson, Morton S. (Minn.) ..12: 207
Willey, Waitman T. (Va., W.Va.) 12: 455
Wilmot, David (Pa.) 3: 419
Wilson, Henry (Mass.) 4: 13
Wilson, Robert (Mo.) 12: 335
Wright, Joseph A. (Ind.) 13: 269

Thirty-eighth Congress (1863-65)

Hamlin, Hannibal, president
of the senate 2: 76
Anthony, Henry B. (R. I.) 9: 398
Bayard, James A. (Del.) 13: 206
Bowden, Lemuel J. (Va.) 4: 377
Brown, B. Gratz (Mo.) 20: 318
Buckalew, Charles R. (Pa.) 11: 190
Carlile, John S. (Va.) 4: 347
Chandler, Zachariah (Mich.) ... 4: 18
Clark, Daniel (N. H.) 2: 87
Collamer, Jacob (Vt.) 4: 371
Conness, John (Calif.) 11: 369
Cowan, Edgar (Pa.) 2: 94
Creswell, John A. J. (Md.) 4: 19
Davis, Garrett (Ky.) 2: 225
Dixon, James (Conn.) 4: 447
Doolittle, James R. (Wis.) 4: 382
Farwell, Nathan A. (Maine) ...10: 89
Fessenden, William P. (Maine) . 2: 90
Foot, Solomon (Vt.) 2: 91
Foster, La Fayette S. (Conn.) .. 2: 95
Grimes, James W. (Iowa) 11: 430
Hale, John P. (N. H.) 3: 120
Harding, Benjamin F. (Oreg.) ..12: 394
Harlan, James (Iowa) 2: 457
Harris, Ira (N. Y.) 2: 96
Henderson, John B. (Mo.) 13: 49
Hendricks, Thomas A. (Ind.) .. 2: 403
Hicks, Thomas H. (Md.) 9: 306
Howard, Jacob M. (Mich.) 4: 472
Howe, Timothy O. (Wis.) 4: 252
Johnson, Reverdy (Md.) 4: 371
Lane, Henry S. (Ind.) 13: 270
Lane, James H. (Kans.) 4: 278
McDougall, James A. (Calif.) ..11: 330
Morgan, Edwin D. (N. Y.) ... 3: 51
Morrill, Lot M. (Maine) 6: 313
Nesmith, James W. (Oreg.) ... 4: 72
Nye, James W. (Nev.) 11: 200
Pomeroy, Samuel C. (Kans.) ...12: 69
Powell, Lazarus W. (Ky.) 13: 7
Ramsey, Alexander (Minn.) ...10: 62
Richardson, William A. (Ill.) ..
Riddle, George R. (Del.) 4: 543
Saulsbury, Willard (Del.) 11: 471
Sherman, John (Ohio) 3: 198
Sprague, William (R. I.) 9: 396
Stewart, William M. (Nev.) 1: 325
Sumner, Charles (Mass.) 3: 300
Ten Eyck, John C. (N. J.) 2: 95
Trumbull, Lyman (Ill.) 12: 342
Van Winkle, Peter G. (W. Va.) 4: 377
Wade, Benjamin F. (Ohio) ... 2: 94
Wilkinson, Morton S. (Minn.) ..12: 207
Willey, Waitman T. (Va.,W.Va.) 12: 455
Wilson, Henry (Mass.) 4: 13
Wilson, Robert (Mo.) 12: 335
Wright, William (Ind.) 4: 548

Thirty-ninth Congress (1865-67)

Johnson, Andrew, president
of the senate 2: 454
Anthony, Henry B. (R. I.) 9: 398
Brown, B. Gratz (Mo.) 20: 318
Buckalew, Charles R. (Pa.) 11: 190
Cattell, Alexander G. (N. J.) .. 2: 35
Chandler, Zachariah (Mich.) .. 4: 18
Clark, Daniel (N. H.) 2: 87
Collamer, Jacob (Vt.) 4: 371
Conness, John (Calif.) 11: 369
Cowan, Edgar (Pa.) 2: 94
Cragin, Aaron H. (N. H.) 12: 394
Creswell, John A. J. (Md.) 4: 19
Davis, Garrett (Ky.) 2: 225
Dixon, James (Conn.) 4: 447
Doolittle, James R. (Wis.) 4: 382
Edmunds, George F. (Vt.) 2: 384
Fessenden, William P. (Maine) .. 2: 90
Fogg, George G. (N. H.) 4: 374
Foot, Solomon (Vt.) 2: 91
Foster, La Fayette S. (Conn.) .. 2: 95
Fowler, Joseph S. (Tenn.) 10: 511
Frelinghuysen, Fred. T. (N. J.) 4: 250
Grimes, James W. (Iowa) 11: 430
Guthrie, James (Ky.) 4: 147
Harlan, James (Iowa) 2: 457
Harris, Ira (N. Y.) 2: 96
Henderson, John B. (Mo.) 13: 49
Hendricks, Thomas A. (Ind.) .. 2: 403
Howard, Jacob M. (Mich.) 4: 472
Howe, Timothy O. (Wis.) 4: 252
Johnson, Reverdy (Md.) 4: 371
Kirkwood, Samuel J. (Iowa) ... 4: 245
Lane, Henry S. (Ind.) 13: 270
Lane, James H. (Kans.) 4: 278
McDougall, James A. (Calif.) ..11: 330
Morgan, Edwin D. (N. Y.) ..3: 51
Morrill, Lot M. (Maine) 6: 313
Nesmith, James W. (Oreg.) ... 4: 72
Norton, Daniel S. (Minn.) 11: 396
Nye, James W. (Nev.) 11: 200
Patterson, David T. (Tenn.) ...12: 217
Poland, Luke P. (Vt.) 5: 253
Pomeroy, Samuel C. (Kans.) ..12: 69
Ramsey, Alexander (Minn.) ...10: 62
Riddle, George R. (Del.) 4: 543
Ross, Edmund G. (Kans.) 13: 232
Saulsbury, Willard (Del.) 11: 471
Sherman, John (Ohio) 3: 198

Sprague, William (R. I.) 9:396
Stewart, William M. (Nev.) 1:325
Stockton, John P. (N. J.) 13: 86
Sumner, Charles (Mass.) 3:300
Trumbull, Lyman (Ill.) 12:342
Van Winkle, Peter G. (W. Va.) 4:377
Wade, Benjamin F. (Ohio) 2: 94
Willey, Waitman T. (Va., W.Va.) 12:455
Williams, George H. (Oreg.) ... 4: 21
Wilson, Henry (Mass.) 4: 13
Wright, William (Ind.) 4:548
Yates, Richard (Ill.) 11: 48

Fortieth Congress (1867-69)

Wade, Benjamin F., president
  pro tem. 2: 94
Abbott, Joseph C. (N. C.) 5: 48
Anthony, Henry B. (R. I.) 9:398
Bayard, James A. (Del.) 13:206
Buckalew, Charles R. (Pa.) 11:190
Cameron, Simon (Pa.) 2: 79
Cattell, Alexander G. (N. J.) .. 2: 35
Chandler, Zachariah (Mich.) ... 4: 18
Cole, Cornelius (Calif.) 22: 95
Conkling, Roscoe (N. Y.) 3:220
Conness, John (Calif.) 11:396
Corbett, Henry W. (Oreg.) 6:111
Cragin, Aaron H. (N. H.) 12:394
Davis, Garrett (Ky.) 2:225
Dixon, James (Conn.) 4:447
Doolittle, James R. (Wis.) 4:382
Drake, Charles D. (Mo.) 3:427
Edmunds, George F. (Vt.) 2:384
Ferry, Orris S. (Conn.) 2: 95
Fessenden, William P. (Maine) 2: 90
Fowler, Joseph S. (Tenn.) 10:511
Frelinghuysen, Fred. T. (N. J.) 4:250
Grimes, James W. (Iowa) 11:430
Guthrie, James (Ky.) 4:147
Harlan, James (Iowa) 2:457
Harris, John S. (La.) 4:528
Henderson, John B. (Mo.) 13: 49
Hendricks, Thomas A. (Ind.) .. 2:403
Hill, Joshua (Ga.) 4:442
Howard, Jacob M. (Mich.) 4:472
Howe, Timothy O. (Wis.) 4:252
Johnson, Reverdy (Md.) 4:371
Kellogg, William P. (La.) 10: 82
McCreery, Thomas C. (Ky.) ... 4:377
McDonald, Alexander (Ark.) ...12:336
Miller, Homer V. M. (Ga.) 12:344
Morgan, Edwin D. (N. Y.) 3: 51
Morrill, Justin S. (Vt.) 1:377
Morrill, Lot M. (Maine) 6:313
Morton, Oliver H. P. T. (Ind.) ..13:271
Norton, Daniel S. (Minn.) 11:396
Nye, James W. (Nev.) 11:200
Osborn, Thomas W. (Fla.) 12:394
Patterson, David T. (Tenn.) ...12:217
Patterson, James W. (N. H.) ..11:364
Pomeroy, Samuel C. (Kans.) ...12: 69
Pool, John (N. C.) 12:399
Ramsey, Alexander (Minn.) ...10: 62
Rice, Benjamin F. (Ark.) 12:395
Riddle, George R. (Del.) 4:543
Robertson, Thomas J. (S. C.) ..12:203
Ross, Edmund G. (Kans.) 13:232
Saulsbury, Willard (Del.) 11:471
Sawyer, Frederick A. (S. C.) .. 3:522
Sherman, John (Ohio) 3:198
Spencer, George E. (Ala.) 13: 72
Sprague, William (R. I.) 9:396
Stewart, William M. (Nev.) ... 1:325
Sumner, Charles (Mass.) 3:300
Thayer, John M. (Nebr.) 12: 2
Tipton, Thomas W. (Nebr.) ...12:226
Trumbull, Lyman (Ill.) 12:342
Van Winkle, Peter G. (W. Va.) 4:377
Vickers, George (Md.) 7:221
Wade, Benjamin F. (Ohio) 2: 94
Warner, Willard (Ala.) 10:396
Welch, Adonijah S. (Fla.) 12:291
Whyte, William P. (Md.) 9:309
Willey, Waitman T. (Va., W.Va.) 12:455
Williams, George H. (Oreg.) ... 4: 21
Wilson, Henry (Mass.) 4: 13
Yates, Richard (Ill.) 11: 48

Forty-first Congress (1869-71)

Colfax, Schuyler, president
  of the senate 4: 12
Abbott, Joseph C. (N. C.) 5: 48
Ames, Adelbert (Miss.) 13:492
Anthony, Henry B. (R. I.) 9:398
Bayard, Thomas F. (Del.) 2:404
Blair, Francis P., 2d (Mo.) 4:223
Boreman, Arthur I. (W. Va.) ..12:430
Brownlow, William G. (Tenn.) .. 7:210
Buckingham, William A. (Conn.) 10:339
Cameron, Simon (Pa.) 2: 79
Carpenter, Matthew H. (Wis.) .. 4: 22
Casserly, Eugene (Calif.) 4:351
Cattell, Alexander G. (N. J.) .. 2: 35
Chandler, Zachariah (Mich.) .. 4: 18
Cole, Cornelius (Calif.) 22: 95
Conkling, Roscoe (N. Y.) 3:220
Corbett, Henry W. (Oreg.) 6:111
Cragin, Aaron H. (N. H.) 12:394
Davis, Garrett (Ky.) 2:225
Drake, Charles D. (Mo.) 3:427
Edmunds, George F. (Vt.) 2:384
Fenton, Reuben E. (N. Y.) 3: 51
Ferry, Orris S. (Conn.) 2: 95
Fessenden, William P. (Maine) .. 2: 90
Flanagan, James W. (Tex.) ...12:509
Fowler, Joseph S. (Tenn.) 10:511
Gilbert, Abijah (Fla.) 4:173
Grimes, James W. (Iowa) 11:430
Hamilton, Morgan C. (Tex.) ..12:393
Hamilton, William T. (Md.) ... 9:311
Hamlin, Hannibal (Maine) 2: 76
Harlan, James (Iowa) 2:457
Harris, John S. (La.) 4:528
Hill, Joshua (Ga.) 4:442
Howard, Jacob M. (Mich.) 4:472
Howe, Timothy O. (Wis.) 4:252
Howell, James B. (Iowa) 9:450
Jewett, Daniel T. (Mo.) 12:399
Johnston, John W. (Va.) 12:226
Kellogg, William P. (La.) 10: 82
Lewis, John F. (Va.) 13: 86
McCreery, Thomas C. (Ky.) ... 4:377
McDonald, Alexander (Ark.) ...12:336
Miller, Homer V. M. (Ga.) 12:344
Morrill, Justin S. (Vt.) 1:377
Morrill, Lot M. (Maine) 6:313
Morton, Oliver H. P. T. (Ind.) ..13:271
Norton, Daniel S. (Minn.) 11:396
Nye, James W. (Nev.) 11:200
Osborn, Thomas W. (Fla.) 12:394
Patterson, James W. (N. H.) ..11:364
Pomeroy, Samuel C. (Kans.) ...12: 69
Pool, John (N. C.) 12:399
Pratt, Daniel D. (Ind.) 11:187
Ramsey, Alexander (Minn.) ...10: 62
Revels, Hiram R. (Miss.) 11:405
Rice, Benjamin F. (Ark.) 12:395
Robertson, Thomas J. (S. C.) ..12:203
Ross, Edmund G. (Kans.) 13:232
Saulsbury, William (Del.) 11:471
Sawyer, Frederick A. (S. C.) .. 3:522
Schurz, Carl (Mo.) 3:202
Scott, John (Pa.) 24:187
Sherman, John (Ohio) 3:198
Spencer, George E. (Ala.) 13: 72
Sprague, William (R. I.) 9:396
Stearns, Ozora P. (Minn.) 10:230
Stewart, William M. (Nev.) ... 1:325
Stockton, John P. (N. J.) 13: 86
Sumner, Charles (Mass.) 3:300
Thayer, John M. (Nebr.) 12: 2
Thurman, Allen G. (Ohio) 3:144
Tipton, Thomas W. (Nebr.) ...12:226
Trumbull, Lyman (Ill.) 12:342
Vickers, George (Md.) 7:221
Warner, Willard (Ala.) 10:396
Willey, Waitman T. (Va., W.Va.) 12:455
Williams, George H. (Oreg.) ... 4: 21
Wilson, Henry (Mass.) 4: 13
Windom, William (Minn.) 1:148
Yates, Richard (Ill.) 11:48

Forty-second Congress (1871-73)

Colfax, Schuyler, president
  of the senate 4: 12
Alcorn, James L. (Miss.) 13:493
Ames, Adelbert (Miss.) 13:492
Anthony, Henry B. (R. I.) 9:398
Bayard, Thomas F. (Del.) 2:404
Blair, Francis P., 2d (Mo.) 4:223
Boreman, Arthur I. (W. Va.) ..12:430
Brownlow, William G. (Tenn.) .. 7:210
Buckingham, William A. (Conn.) 10:339
Caldwell, Alexander (Kans.) ...12:458
Cameron, Simon (Pa.) 2: 79
Carpenter, Matthew H. (Wis.) .. 4: 22
Casserly, Eugene (Calif.) 4:351
Chandler, Zachariah (Mich.) ... 4: 18
Clayton, Powell (Ark.) 16:262
Cole, Cornelius (Calif.) 22: 95
Conkling, Roscoe (N. Y.) 3:220
Cooper, Henry (Tenn.) 12:378
Corbett, Henry W. (Oreg.) 6:111
Cragin, Aaron H. (N. H.) 12:394
Davis, Garrett, (Ky.) 2:225
Davis, Henry G. (W. Va.) 10:468
Edmunds, George F. (Va.) 2:384
Fenton, Reuben E. (N. Y.) 3: 51
Ferry, Orris S. (Conn.) 2: 95
Ferry, Thomas W. (Mich.) 9:169
Flanagan, James W. (Tex.) ...12:509
Frelinghuysen, Fred. T. (N. J.) 4:250
Gilbert, Abijah (Fla.) 4:173
Goldthwaite, George (Ala.) 4:350
Hamilton, Morgan C. (Tex.) ...12:393
Hamilton, William T. (Md.) ... 9:311
Hamlin, Hannibal (Maine) 2: 76
Harlan, James (Iowa) 2:457
Hill, Joshua (Ga.) 4:442
Hitchcock, Phineas W. (Nebr.) .. 7:490
Howe, Timothy O. (Wis.) 4:252
Johnston, John W. (Va.) 12:226
Kellogg, William P. (La.) 10: 82
Kelly, James K. (Oreg.) 12:229
Lewis, John F. (Va.) 13: 86
Logan, John A. (Ill.) 4:298
Machen, Willis B. (Ky.) 12:395
Morrill, Justin S. (Vt.) 1:377
Morrill, Lot M. (Maine) 6:313
Morton, Oliver H. P. T. (Ind.) ..13:271
Norwood, Thomas M. (Ga.) 13:474
Nye, James W. (Nev.) 11:200
Osborn, Thomas W. (Fla.) 12:394
Patterson, James W. (N. H.) ..11:364
Pomeroy, Samuel C. (Kans.) ...12: 69
Pool, John (N. C.) 12:399
Pratt, Daniel D. (Ind.) 11:187
Ramsey, Alexander (Minn.) 10: 62
Ransom, Matthew W. (N. C.) ..10:251
Rice, Benjamin F. (Ark.) 12:395
Robertson, Thomas J. (S. C.) ..12:203
Saulsbury, Eli (Del.) 11:471
Sawyer, Frederick A. (S. C.) .. 3:522
Schurz, Carl (Mo.) 3:202
Scott, John (Pa.) 24:187
Sherman, John (Ohio) 3:198
Spencer, George E. (Ala.) 13: 72
Sprague, William (R. I.) 9:396
Stevenson, John W. (Ky.) 13: 9
Stewart, William M. (Nev.) 1:325
Stockton, John P. (N. J.) 13: 86
Sumner, Charles (Mass.) 3:300
Thurman, Allen G. (Ohio) 3:144
Tipton, Thomas W. (Nebr.) ...12:226
Trumbull, Lyman (Ill.) 12:342
Vickers, George (Md.) 7:221
West, Joseph R. (La.) 9:233
Wilson, Henry (Mass.) 4: 13
Windom, William (Minn.) 1:148
Wright, George C. (Iowa) 3:523

Forty-third Congress (1873-75)

Wilson, Henry, president
  of the senate 4:13
Alcorn, James L. (Miss.) 13:493
Allison, William B. (Iowa) 1:296
Ames, Adelbert (Miss.) 13:492
Anthony, Henry B. (R. I.) 9:398
Bayard, Thomas F. (Del.) 2:404
Bogy, Lewis V. (Mo.) 12:422
Boreman, Arthur I. (W. Va.) ..12:430
Boutwell, George S. (Mass.) 4:382
Brownlow, William G. (Tenn.) .. 7:210
Buckingham, William A. (Conn.) 10:339
Caldwell, Alexander (Kans.) 12:458
Cameron, Simon (Pa.) 2: 79
Carpenter, Matthew H. (Wis.) .. 4: 22
Casserly, Eugene (Calif.) 4:351
Chandler, Zachariah (Mich.) ... 4: 18
Clayton, Powell (Ark.) 16:262
Conkling, Roscoe (N. Y.) 3:220
Conover, Simon B. (Fla.) 12:389
Cooper, Henry (Tenn.) 12:378
Cragin, Aaron H. (N. H.) 12:394
Crozier, Robert (Kans.) 7:490
Davis, Henry G. (W. Va.) 10:468
Dennis, George R. (Md.) 7:283
Dorsey, Stephen W. (Ark.) 7: 22
Eaton, William W. (Conn.) 11:172
Edmunds, George F. (Vt.) 2:384
Fenton, Reuben E. (N. Y.) 3: 51
Ferry, Orris S. (Conn.) 2: 95
Ferry, Thomas W. (Mich.) 9:169
Flanagan, James W. (Tex.) 12:509
Frelinghuysen, Fred. T. (N. J.) 4:250
Gilbert, Abijah (Fla.) 4:173

Goldthwaite, George (Ala.) 4:350
Gordon, John B. (Ga.) 1:231
Hager, John S. (Calif.) 13:330
Hamilton, Morgan C. (Tex.) ...12:393
Hamilton, William T. (Md.) ... 9:311
Hamlin, Hannibal (Maine) 2: 76
Harvey, James M. (Kans.) 8:344
Hitchcock, Phineas W. (Nebr.).. 7:490
Howe, Timothy O. (Wis.) 4:252
Ingalls, John J. (Kans.) 8:415
Johnston, John W. (Va.) 12:226
Jones, John P. (Nev.) 1:300
Kelly, James K. (Oreg.) 12:229
Lewis, John F. (Va.) 13: 86
Logan, John A. (Ill.) 4:298
McCreery, Thomas C. (Ky.) 4:377
Merrimon, Augustus S. (N. C.).. 9:270
Mitchell, John H. (Oreg.) 2:301
Morrill, Justin S. (Vt.) 1:377
Morrill, Lot M. (Maine) 6:313
Morton, Oliver H. P. T. (Ind.)..13:271
Norwood, Thomas M. (Ga.) 13:474
Oglesby, Richard J. (Ill.) 11: 48
Patterson, John J. (S. C.) 12:395
Pease, Henry R. (Miss.) 12:389
Pratt, Daniel D. (Ind.) 11:187
Ramsey, Alexander (Minn.) 10: 62
Ransom, Matthew W. (N. C.) ..10:251
Robertson, Thomas J. (S. C.) ..12:203
Sargent, Aaron A. (Calif.) 13:475
Saulsbury, Eli (Del.) 11:471
Schurz, Carl (Mo.) 3:202
Scott, John (Pa.) 24:187
Sherman, John (Ohio) 3:198
Spencer, George E. (Ala.) 13: 72
Sprague, William (R. I.) 9:396
Stevenson, John W. (Ky.) 13: 9
Stewart, William M. (Nev.) 1:325
Stockton, John P. (N. J.) 13: 86
Sumner, Charles (Mass.) 3:300
Thurman, Allen G. (Ohio) 3:144
Tipton, Thomas W. (Nebr.) ...12:226
Wadleigh, Bainbridge (N. H.)..24: 27
Washburn, William B. (Mass.).. 1:120
West, Joseph R. (La.) 9:233
Windom, William (Minn.) 1:148
Wright, George C. (Iowa) 3:523

Forty-fourth Congress (1875-77)

Ferry, Thomas W., president *pro tem* 9:169
Alcorn, James L. (Miss.) 13:493
Allison, William B. (Iowa) 1:296
Anthony, Henry B. (R. I.) 9:398
Bailey, James E. (Tenn.) 12:282
Barnum, William H. (Conn.) ..12:389
Bayard, Thomas F. (Del.) 2:404
Blaine, James G. (Maine) 1:137
Bogy, Lewis V. (Mo.)..........12:422
Booth, Newton (Calif.) 4:110
Boutwell, George S. (Mass.) 4:382
Bruce, Blanche K. (Miss.) 11:394
Burnside, Ambrose E. (R. I.) .. 4: 53
Cameron, Angus (Wis.) 12: 83
Cameron, Simon (Pa.) 2: 79
Caperton, Allen T. (W. Va.) .. 7:303
Chaffee, Jerome B. (Colo.) 6:199
Christiancy, Isaac P. (Mich.) ..23:348
Clayton, Powell (Ark.) 16:262
Cockrell, Francis M. (Mo.) 3:297
Conkling, Roscoe (N. Y.) 3:220
Conover, Simon B. (Fla.) 12:389
Cooper, Henry (Tenn.) 12:378
Cragin, Aaron H. (N. H.) 12:394
Davis, Henry G. (W. Va.) 10:468
Dawes, Henry L. (Mass.) 4:321
Dennis, George R. (Md.) 7:283
Dorsey, Stephen W. (Ark.) 7: 22
Eaton, William W. (Conn.) 11:172
Edmunds, George F. (Vt.) 2:384
English, James E. (Conn.) 10:340
Eustis, James B. (La.) 1:462
Ferry, Orris S. (Conn.) 2: 95
Ferry, Thomas W. (Mich.) 9:169
Frelinghuysen, Fred. T. (N. J.) 4:250
Goldthwaite, George (Ala.) 4:350
Gordon, John B. (Ga.) 1:231
Hamilton, Morgan C. (Tex.) ...12:393
Hamlin, Hannibal (Maine) 2: 76
Harvey, James M. (Kans.) 8:344
Hereford, Frank (W. Va.) 12:252
Hitchcock, Phineas W. (Nebr.). 7:490
Howe, Timothy O. (Wis.) 4:252
Ingalls, John J. (Kans.) 8:415
Johnston, John W. (Va.) 12:226
Jones, Charles W. (Fla.) 10:383
Jones, John P. (Nev.) 1:300
Kelly, James K. (Oreg.) 12:229
Kernan, Francis (N. Y.) 8:368
Key, David McK. (Tenn.) 3:203
Logan, John A. (Ill.) 4:298
McCreery, Thomas C. (Ky.) 4:377
McDonald, Joseph E. (Ind.) ...11:504
McMillan, Samuel J. R. (Minn.) 4:469
Maxey, Samuel B. (Tex.) 4: 50
Merrimon, Augustus S. (N. C.) . 9:270
Mitchell, John H. (Oreg.) 2:301
Morrill, Justin S. (Vt.) 1:377
Morrill, Lot M. (Maine) 6:313
Morton, Oliver H. P. T. (Ind.)..13:271
Norwood, Thomas M. (Ga.) 13:474
Oglesby, Richard J. (Ill.) 11: 48
Paddock, Algernon S. (Nebr.) .. 2:247
Patterson, John J. (S. C.) 12:395
Price, Samuel (W. Va.) 5:518
Randolph, Theodore F. (N. J.).. 5:210
Ransom, Matthew W. (N. C.) ..10:251
Robertson, Thomas J. (S. C.) ..12:203
Sargent, Aaron A. (Calif.) 13:475
Saulsbury, Eli (Del.) 11:471
Sharon, William (Nev.) 5:512
Sherman, John (Ohio) 3:198
Spencer, George E. (Ala.) 13: 72
Stevenson, John W. (Ky.) 13: 9
Teller, Henry M. (Colo.) 15:228
Thurman, Allen G. (Ohio) 3:144
Wadleigh, Bainbridge (N. H.) ..24: 27
Wallace, William A. (Pa.) 10: 47
West, Joseph R. (La.) 9:233
Whyte, William P. (Md.) 9:309
Windom, William (Minn.) 1:148
Withers, Robert E. (Va.) 12:512
Wright, George C. (Iowa) 3:523

Forty-fifth Congress (1877-79)

Wheeler, William A., president of the senate 3:196
Allison, William B. (Iowa) 1:296
Anthony, Henry B. (R. I.) 9:398
Armstrong, David H. (Mo.) 5:517
Bailey, James E. (Tenn.) 12:282
Barnum, William H. (Conn.) ..12:389
Bayard, Thomas F. (Del.) 2:404
Beck, James B. (Ky.) 3:418
Blaine, James G. (Maine) 1:137
Bogy, Lewis V. (Mo.) 12:422
Booth, Newton (Calif.) 4:110
Bruce, Blanche K. (Miss.) 11:394
Burnside, Ambrose E. (R. I.) .. 4: 53
Butler, Matthew C. (S. C.) 1:298
Cameron, Angus (Wis.) 12: 83
Cameron, James D. (Pa.) 4: 25
Chaffee, Jerome B. (Colo.) 6:199
Christiancy, Isaac P. (Mich.) ..23:348
Cockrell, Francis M. (Mo.) 3:297
Coke, Richard (Tex.) 9: 72
Conkling, Roscoe (N. Y.) 3:220
Conover, Simon B. (Fla.) 12:389
Davis, David (Ill.) 2:474
Davis, Henry G. (W. Va.) 10:468
Dawes, Henry L. (Mass.) 4:321
Dennis, George R. (Md.) 7:283
Dorsey, Stephen W. (Ark.) 7: 22
Eaton, William W. (Conn.) 11:172
Edmunds, George F. (Vt.) 2:384
Eustis, James B. (La.) 1:462
Ferry, Thomas W. (Mich.) 9:169
Garland, Augustus H. (Ark.) .. 2:409
Gordon, John B. (Ga.) 1:231
Grover, La Fayette (Oreg.) 8: 5
Hamlin, Hannibal (Maine) 2: 76
Harris, Isham G. (Tenn.) 2:209
Hereford, Frank (W. Va.) 12:252
Hill, Benjamin H. (Ga.) 10:194
Hoar, George F. (Mass.) 1:453
Howe, Timothy O. (Wis.) 4:252
Ingalls, John J. (Kans.) 8:415
Johnston, John W. (Va.) 12:226
Jones, Charles W. (Fla.) 10:383
Jones, John Percival (Nev.) ... 1:300
Kellogg, William P. (La.) 10: 82
Kernan, Francis (N. Y.) 8:368
Kirkwood, Samuel J. (Iowa) ... 4:245
Lamar, Lucius Q. C. (Miss.) ... 1: 37
McCreery, Thomas C. (Ky.) ... 4:377
McDonald, Joseph E. (Ind.) ...11:504
McMillan, Samuel J. R. (Minn.) 4:469
McPherson, John R. (N. J.) ... 3: 71
Matthews, Stanley (Ohio) 2:476
Maxey, Samuel B. (Tex.) 4: 50
Merrimon, Augustus S. (N. C.) . 9:270
Mitchell, John H. (Oreg.) 2:301
Morgan, John T (Ala.) 1:295
Morrill, Justin S. (Vt.) 1:377
Morton, Oliver H. P. T. (Ind.)..13:271
Oglesby, Richard J. (Ill.) 11: 48
Paddock, Algernon S. (Nebr.) .. 2:247
Patterson, John J. (S. C.) 12:395
Plumb, Preston B. (Kans.) 2:529
Randolph, Theodore F. (N. J.).. 5:210
Ransom, Matthew W. (N. C.) ..10:251
Rollins, Edward H. (N. H.) 7:512
Sargent, Aaron A. (Calif.) 13:475
Saulsbury, Eli (Del.) 11:471
Saunders, Alvin (Nebr.) 13:221
Sharon, William (Nev.) 5:512
Sherman, John (Ohio) 3:198
Shields, James (Mo.) 8: 2
Spencer, George E. (Ala.) 13: 72
Teller, Henry M. (Colo.) 15:228
Thurman, Allen G. (Ohio) 3:144
Wadleigh, Bainbridge (N. H.)..24: 27
Wallace, William A. (Pa.) 10: 47
Whyte, William P. (Md.) 9:309
Windom, William (Minn.) 1:148
Withers, Robert E. (Va.) 12:512

Forty-sixth Congress (1879-81)

Wheeler, William A., president of the senate 3:196
Allison, William B. (Iowa) 1:296
Anthony, Henry B. (R. I.) 9:398
Bailey, James E. (Tenn.) 12:282
Baldwin, Henry P. (Mich.) 5:274
Bayard, Thomas F. (Del.) 2:404
Beck, James B. (Ky.) 3:418
Bell, Charles H. (N. H.) 11:137
Blaine, James G. (Maine) 1:137
Blair, Henry W. (N. H.) 1:458
Booth, Newton (Calif.) 4:110
Brown, Joseph E. (Ga.) 1:227
Bruce, Blanche K. (Miss.) 11:394
Burnside, Ambrose E. (R. I.) .. 4: 53
Butler, Matthew C. (S. C.) 1:298
Call, Wilkinson (Fla.) 2:525
Cameron, Angus (Wis.) 12: 83
Cameron, James D. (Pa.) 4: 25
Carpenter, Matthew H. (Wis.).. 4: 22
Chandler, Zachariah (Mich.) ... 4: 18
Cockrell, Francis M. (Mo.) ... 3:297
Coke, Richard (Tex.) 9: 72
Conkling, Roscoe (N. Y.) 3:220
Davis, David (Ill.) 2:474
Davis, Henry G. (W. Va.) 10:468
Dawes, Henry L. (Mass.) 4:321
Eaton, William W. (Conn.) 11:172
Edmunds, George F. (Vt.) 2:384
Farley, James T. (Calif.) 4:173
Ferry, Thomas W. (Mich.) 9:169
Garland, Augustus H. (Ark.) .. 2:409
Gordon, John B. (Ga.) 1:231
Groome, James B. (Md.) 9:310
Grover, La Fayette (Oreg.) 8: 5
Hamlin, Hannibal (Maine) 2: 76
Hampton, Wade, 3d (S. C.) 12:177
Harris, Isham G. (Tenn.) 2:209
Hereford, Frank (W. Va.) 12:252
Hill, Benjamin H. (Ga.) 10:194
Hill, Nathaniel P. (Colo.) 6: 38
Hoar, George F. (Mass.) 1:453
Houston, George S. (Ala.) 10:436
Ingalls, John J. (Kans.) 8:415
Johnston, John W. (Va.) 12:226
Jonas, Benjamin F. (La.) 4:544
Jones, Charles W. (Fla.) 10:383
Jones, John P. (Nev.) 1:300
Kellogg, William P. (La.) 10: 82
Kernan, Francis (N. Y.) 8:368
Kirkwood, Samuel J. (Iowa) ... 4:245
Lamar, Lucius Q. C. (Miss.) ... 1: 37
Logan, John A. (Ill.) 4:298
McDonald, Joseph E. (Ind.) 11:504
McMillan, Samuel J. R. (Minn.) 4:469
McPherson, John R. (N. J.) ... 3: 71
Maxey, Samuel B. (Tex.) 4: 50
Morgan, John T. (Ala.) 1:295
Morrill, Justin S. (Vt.) 1:377
Paddock, Algernon S. (Nebr.) . 2:247
Pendleton, George H. (Ohio) ... 3:278
Platt, Orville H. (Conn.) 2:339
Plumb, Preston B. (Kans.) 2:529
Pryor, Luke (Ala.) 12:269
Pugh, James L. (Ala.) 1:292
Randolph, Theodore F. (N. J.).. 5:210
Ransom, Matthew W. (N. C.) ..10:251
Rollins, Edward H. (N. H.) 7:512
Saulsbury, Eli (Del.) 11:471
Saunders, Alvin (Nebr.) 13:221

Sharon, William (Nev.) 5:512
Slater, James H. (Oreg.) 4:549
Teller, Henry M. (Colo.) 15:228
Thurman, Allen G. (Ohio) 3:144
Vance, Zebulon B. (N. C.) 2:384
Vest, George G. (Mo.) 2:297
Voorhees, Daniel W. (Ind.) 2:359
Walker, James D. (Ark.) 12:288
Wallace, William A. (Pa.) 10: 47
Whyte, William P. (Md.) 9:309
Williams, John Stuart (Ky.) ...12:388
Windom, William (Minn.) 1:148
Withers, Robert E. (Va.) 12:512

Forty-seventh Congress (1881-83)

Arthur, Chester A., president of the senate 4:247
Davis, David, president *pro tem.* 2:474
Aldrich, Nelson W. (R. I.) 10:206
Allison, William B. (Iowa) 1:296
Anthony, Henry B. (R. I.) 9:398
Barrow, Pope (Ga.) 9:501
Bayard, Thomas F. (Del.) 2:404
Beck, James B. (Ky.) 3:418
Blair, Henry W. (N. H.) 1:458
Brown, Joseph E. (Ga.) 1:227
Burnside, Ambrose E. (R. I.) .. 4: 53
Butler, Matthew C. (S. C.) ... 1:298
Call, Wilkinson, (Fla.) 2:525
Camden, Johnson N. (W. Va.) ..20:329
Cameron, Angus (Wis.) 12: 83
Cameron, James D. (Pa.) 4: 25
Chilcott, George M. (Colo.) 7:522
Cockrell, Francis M. (Mo.) 3:297
Coke, Richard (Tex.) 9: 72
Conger, Omar D. (Mich.) 12:394
Conkling, Roscoe (N. Y.) 3:220
Davis, David (Ill.) 2:474
Davis, Henry G. (W. Va.) 10:468
Dawes, Henry L. (Mass.) 4:321
Edgerton, Alonzo J. (Minn.)...12: 54
Edmunds, George F. (Vt.) 2:384
Fair, James G. (Nev.) 11:189
Farley, James T. (Calif.) 4:173
Ferry, Thomas W. (Mich.) 9:169
Frye, William P. (Maine) 1:290
Garland, Augustus H. (Ark.) .. 2:409
George, James Z. (Minn.) 2:358
Gorman, Arthur P. (Md.) 1:296
Groome, James B. (Md.) 9:310
Grover, La Fayette (Oreg.) 8: 5
Hale, Eugene (Maine) 20:220
Hampton, Wade, 3d (S. C.) 12:177
Harris, Isham G. (Tenn.) 2:209
Harrison, Benjamin (Ind.) 1:133
Hawley, Joseph R. (Conn.) 1:457
Hill, Benjamin H. (Ga.) 10:194
Hill, Nathaniel P. (Colo.) 6: 38
Hoar, George F. (Mass.) 1:453
Ingalls, John J. (Kans.) 8:415
Jackson, Howell E. (Tenn.) ... 8:243
Johnston, John W. (Va.) 12:226
Jonas, Benjamin F. (La.) 4:544
Jones, Charles W. (Fla.) 10:383
Jones, John P. (Nev.) 1:300
Kellogg, William P. (La.) 10: 82
Kirkwood, Samuel J. (Iowa) ... 4:245
Lamar, Lucius Q. C. (Miss.) ...1: 37
Lapham, Elbridge G. (N. Y.)...11:157
Logan, John A. (Ill.) 4:298
McDill, James W. (Iowa) 11:479
McMillan, Samuel J. R. (Minn.) 4:469
McPherson, John R. (N. J.) ... 3: 71
Mahone, William (Va.) 5: 12
Maxey, Samuel B. (Tex.) 4: 50
Miller, John F. (Calif.) 8: 91
Miller, Warner (N. Y.) 4:560
Mitchell, John I. (Pa.) 12:389
Morgan, John T. (Ala.) 1:295
Morrill, Justin S. (Vt.) 1:377
Pendleton, George H. (Ohio) ... 3:278
Platt, Orville H. (Conn.) 2:339
Platt, Thomas C. (N. Y.) 11:509
Plumb, Preston B. (Kans.) 2:529
Pugh, James L. (Ala.) 1:292
Ransom, Matthew W. (N. C.) ..10:251
Rollins, Edward H. (N. H.) ... 7:512
Saulsbury, Eli (Del.) 11:471
Saunders, Alvin (Nebr.) 13:221
Sawyer, Philetus (Wis.) 1:326
Sewell, William J. (N. J.) 12:217
Sherman, John (Ohio) 3:198
Slater, James H. (Oreg.) 4:549
Tabor, Horace A. W. (Colo.) ..11: 92
Teller, Henry M. (Colo.) 15:228
Vance, Zebulon B. (N. C.) 2:384
Van Wyck, Charles H. (Nebr.).. 5:334
Vest, George G. (Mo.) 2:297
Vorhees, Daniel W. (Ind.) 2:359
Walker, James D. (Ark.) 12:288
Williams, John S. (Ky.) 12:388
Windom, William (Minn.) 1:148

Forty-eighth Congress (1883-85)

Edmunds, George F., president *pro tem* 2:384
Aldrich, Nelson W. (R. I.) 10:206
Allison, William B. (Iowa) 1:296
Anthony, Henry B. (R. I.) 9:398
Bayard, Thomas F. (Del.) 2:404
Beck James B. (Ky.) 3:418
Blair, Henry W. (N. H.) 1:458
Bowen, Thomas M. (Colo.) 12:560
Brown, Joseph E. (Ga.) 1:227
Butler, Matthew C. (S. C.) 1:298
Call, Wilkinson (Fla.) 2:525
Camden, Johnson N. (W. Va.)..20:329
Cameron, Angus (Wis.) 12: 83
Cameron, James D. (Pa.) 4: 25
Chace, Jonathan (R. I.) 12:387
Cockrell, Francis M. (Mo.) 3:297
Coke, Richard (Tex.) 9: 72
Colquitt, Alfred H. (Ga.) 1:291
Conger, Omar D. (Mich.) 12:394
Cullom, Shelby M. (Ill.) 11: 50
Dawes, Henry L. (Mass.) 4:321
Dolph, Joseph N. (Oreg.) 1:294
Edmunds, George F. (Vt.) 2:384
Fair, James G. (Nev.) 11:189
Farley, James T. (Calif.) 4:173
Frye, William P. (Maine) 1:290
Garland, Augustus H. (Ark.) .. 2:409
George, James Z. (Minn.) 2:358
Gibson, Randall L. (La.) 1:297
Gorman, Arthur P. (Md.) 1:296
Groome, James B. (Md.) 9:310
Hale, Eugene (Maine) 20:220
Hampton, Wade, 3d (S. C.) 12:177
Harris, Isham G. (Tenn.) 2:209
Harrison, Benjamin (Ind.) 1:133
Hawley, Joseph R. (Conn.) 1:457
Hill, Nathaniel P. (Colo.) 6: 38
Hoar, George F. (Mass.) 1:453
Ingalls, John J. (Kans.) 8:415
Jackson, Howell E. (Tenn.) 8:243
Jonas, Benjamin F. (La.) 4:544
Jones, Charles W. (Fla.) 10:383
Jones, John P. (Nev.) 1:300
Kenna, John E. (W. Va.) 1:299
Lamar, Lucius Q. C. (Miss.).... 1: 37
Lapham, Elbridge G. (N. Y.) ..11:157
Logan, John A. (Ill.) 4:298
McMillan, Samuel J. R. (Minn.) 4:469
McPherson, John R. (N. J.) .. 3: 71
Mahone, William (Va.) 5: 12
Manderson, Charles F. (Nebr.).. 1:454
Maxey, Samuel B. (Tex.) 4: 50
Miller, John F. (Calif.) 8: 91
Miller, Warner (N. Y.) 4:560
Mitchell, John I. (Pa.) 12:389
Morgan, John T. (Ala.) 1:295
Morrill, Justin S. (Vt.) 1:377
Palmer, Thomas W. (Mich.) ...11:362
Pendleton, George H. (Ohio) ... 3:278
Pike, Austin F. (N. H.) 10:259
Platt, Orville H. (Conn.) 2:339
Plumb, Preston B. (Kans.) 2:529
Pugh, James L. (Ala.) 1:292
Ransom, Matthew W. (N. C.) ..10:251
Riddleberger, Harrison H. (Va.) 13:162
Sabin, Dwight M. (Minn.) 2:374
Saulsbury, Eli (Del.) 11:471
Sawyer, Philetus (Wis.) 1:326
Sewell, William J. (N. J.) 12:217
Sheffield, William P. (R. I.) 12:390
Sherman, John (Ohio) 3:198
Slater, James H. (Oreg.) 4:549
Vance, Zebulon B. (N. C.) 2:384
Van Wyck, Charles H. (Nebr.).. 5:334
Vest, George G. (Mo.) 2:297
Vorhees, Daniel W. (Ind.) 2:359
Walker, James D. (Ark.) 12:288
Williams, John S. (Ky.) 12:388
Wilson, James F. (Iowa) 1:289

Forty-ninth Congress (1885-87)

Sherman, John, president *pro tem.* 3:198
Aldrich, Nelson W. (R. I.) 10:206
Allison, William B. (Iowa) 1:296
Bayard, Thomas F. (Del.) 2:404
Beck, James B. (Ky.) 3:418
Berry, James H. (Ark.) 10:190
Blackburn, Joseph C. S. (Ky.).. 1:295
Blair, Henry W. (N. H.) 1:458
Bowen, Thomas M. (Colo.) 12:560
Brown, Joseph E. (Ga.) 1:227
Butler, Matthew C. (S. C.) 1:298
Call, Wilkinson (Fla.) 2:525
Camden, Johnson N. (W. Va.)..20:329
Cameron, James D. (Pa.) 4: 25
Chace, Jonathan (R. I.) 12:387
Cheney, Person C. (N. H.) 11:135
Cockrell, Francis M. (Mo.) ... 3:297
Coke, Richard (Tex.) 9: 72
Colquitt, Alfred H. (Ga.) 1:291
Conger, Omar D. (Mich.) 12:394
Cullom, Shelby M. (Ill.) 11: 50
Dawes, Henry L. (Mass.) 4:321
Dolph, Joseph N. (Oreg.) 1:294
Edmunds, George F. (Vt.) 2:384
Eustis, James B. (La.) 1:462
Evarts, William M. (N. Y.) 3:197
Fair, James G. (Nev.) 11:189
Farwell, Charles B. (Ill.) 6:394
Frye, William P. (Maine) 1:290
Garland, Augustus H. (Ark.) .. 2:409
George, James Z. (Minn.) 2:358
Gibson, Randall L. (La.) 1:297
Gorman, Arthur P. (Md.) 1:296
Gray, George (Del.) 26: 17
Hale, Eugene (Maine) 20:220
Hampton, Wade, 3d (S. C.) 12:177
Harris, Isham G. (Tenn.) 2:209
Harrison, Benjamin (Ind.) 1:133
Hawley, Joseph R. (Conn.) 1:457
Hearst, George F. (Calif.) 1:315
Hoar, George F. (Mass.) 1:453
Ingalls, John J. (Kans.) 8:415
Jackson, Howell E. (Tenn.) ... 8:243
Jones, Charles W. (Fla.) 10:383
Jones, James K. (Ark.) 1:293
Jones, John P. (Nev.) 1:300
Kenna, John E. (W. Va.) 1:299
Lamar, Lucius Q. C. (Miss.).... 1: 37
Logan, John A. (Ill.) 4:298
McMillan, Samuel J. R. (Minn.) 4:469
McPherson, John R. (N. J.) ... 3: 71
Mahone, William (Va.) 5: 12
Manderson, Charles F. (Nebr.).. 1:454
Maxey, Samuel B. (Tex.) 4: 50
Miller, John F. (Calif.) 8: 91
Miller, Warner (N. Y.) 4:560
Mitchell, John H. (Oreg.) 2:301
Mitchell, John I. (Pa.) 12:389
Morgan, John Tyler (Ala.) 1:295
Morrill, Justin S. (Vt.) 1:377
Palmer, Thomas W. (Mich.) ...11:362
Payne, Henry B. (Ohio) 1:427
Pike, Austin F. (N. H.) 10:259
Platt, Orville H. (Conn.) 2:339
Plumb, Preston B. (Kans.) 2:529
Pugh, James L. (Ala.) 1:292
Ransom, Matthew W. (N. C.) ..10:251
Riddleberger, Harrison H. (Va.) 13:162
Sabin, Dwight M. (Minn.) 2:374
Saulsbury, Eli (Del.) 11:471
Sawyer, Philetus (Wis.) 1:326
Sewell, William J. (N. J.) 12:217
Spooner, John C. (Wis.) 14: 33
Stanford, Leland (Calif.) 2:128
Teller, Henry M. (Colo.) 15:228
Vance, Zebulon B. (N. C.) 2:384
Van Wyck, Charles H. (Nebr.).. 5:334
Vest, George G. (Mo.) 2:297
Voorhees, Daniel W. (Ind.) 2:359
Walthall, Edward C. (Miss.) ... 1:389
Whitthorne, W. C. (Tenn.) 10:140
Williams, Abram P. (Calif.) ...13: 52
Wilson, Ephraim K. (Md.) 1:295
Wilson, James F. (Iowa) 1:289

Fiftieth Congress (1887-89)

Ingalls, John J., president *pro tem.* 8:415
Aldrich, Nelson W. (R. I.) 10:206
Allison, William B. (Iowa) 1:296
Bate, William B. (Tenn.) 7:213
Beck, James B. (Ky.) 3:418
Berry, James H. (Ark.) 10:190
Blackburn, Joseph C. S. (Ky.).. 1:295
Blair, Henry W. (N. H.) 1:458
Blodgett, Rufus (N. J.) 1:217

Bowen, Thomas M. (Colo.) 12: 560
Brown, Joseph E. (Ga.) 1: 227
Butler, Matthew C. (S. C.) 1: 298
Call, Wilkinson (Fla.) 2: 525
Cameron, James D. (Pa.) 4: 25
Chace, Jonathan (R. I.) 12: 387
Chandler, William E. (N. H.) .. 4: 252
Cheney, Person C. (N. H.) 11: 135
Cockrell, Francis M. (Mo.) 3: 297
Coke, Richard (Tex.) 9: 72
Colquitt, Alfred H. (Ga.) 1: 291
Collum, Shelby M. (Ill.) 11: 50
Daniel, John W. (Va.) 1: 218
Davis, Cushman K. (Minn.) ...10: 65
Dawes, Henry L. (Mass.) 4: 321
Dolph, Joseph N. (Oreg.) 1: 294
Edmunds, George F. (Vt.) 2: 384
Eustis, James B. (La.) 1: 462
Evarts, William M. (N. Y.) ... 3: 197
Farwell, Charles B. (Ill.) 6: 394
Faulkner, Charles J., Jr. (W.Va.) 2: 392
Frye, William P. (Maine) 1: 290
George, James Z. (Minn.)....... 2: 358
Gibson, Randall L. (La.) 1: 297
Gorman, Arthur P. (Md.) 1: 296
Gray, George (Del.) 26: 17
Hale, Eugene (Maine) 20: 220
Hampton, Wade, 3d (S. C.) 12: 177
Harris, Isham G. (Tenn.) 2: 209
Hawley, Joseph R. (Conn.) 1: 457
Hearst, George F. (Calif.) 1: 315
Hiscock, Frank (N. Y.) 12: 352
Hoar, George F. (Mass.) 1: 453
Jones, James K. (Ark.) 1: 293
Jones, John P. (Nev.) 1: 300
Kenna, John E. (W. Va.) 1: 299
McPherson, John R. (N. J.) ... 3: 71
Manderson, Charles F. (Nebr.) .. 1: 454
Mitchell, John H. (Oreg.) 2: 301
Morgan, John T. (Ala.) 1: 295
Morrill, Justin S. (Vt.) 1: 377
Paddock, Algernon S. (Nebr.) .. 2: 247
Palmer, Thomas W. (Mich.) ...11: 362
Pasco, Samuel (Fla.) 1: 293
Payne, Henry B. (Ohio) 1: 427
Platt, Orville H. (Conn.) 2: 339
Plumb, Preston B. (Kans.) 2: 529
Pugh, James L. (Ala.) 1: 292
Quay, Matthew S. (Pa.) 1: 459
Ransom, Matthew W. (N. C.) ..10: 251
Reagan, John H. (Tex.) 1: 292
Riddleberger, Harrison H. (Va.) 13: 162
Sabin, Dwight M. (Minn.) 2: 374
Saulsbury, Eli (Del.) 11: 471
Sawyer, Philetus (Wis.) 1: 326
Sherman, John (Ohio) 3: 198
Spooner, John C. (Wis.) 14: 33
Stanford, Leland (Calif.) 2: 128
Stewart, William M. (Nev.) 1: 325
Stockbridge, Francis B. (Mich.) 1: 460
Teller, Henry M. (Colo.) 15: 228
Turpie, David (Ind.) 1: 218
Vance, Zebulon B. (N. C.) 2: 384
Vest, George G. (Mo.) 2: 297
Voorhees, Daniel W. (Mo.) 2: 359
Walthall, Edward C. (Miss.) ... 1: 389
Wilson, Ephraim K. (Md.) 1: 295
Wilson, James F. (Iowa) 1: 289

Fifty-first Congress (1889-91)

Morton, Levi P., president
of the senate 1: 136
Aldrich, Nelson W. (R. I.) 10: 206
Allen, John B. (Wash.) 11: 561
Allison, William B. (Iowa) 1: 296
Barbour, John S., 2d (Va.) ...12: 59
Bate, William B. (Tenn.) 7: 213
Beck, James B. (Ky.) 3: 418
Berry, James H. (Ark.) 10: 190
Blackburn, Joseph C. S. (Ky.) .. 1: 295
Blair, Henry W. (N. H.) 1: 458
Blodgett, Rufus (N. J.) 1: 217
Brown, Joseph E. (Ga.) 1: 227
Butler, Matthew C. (S. C.) 1: 298
Call, Wilkinson (Fla.) 2: 525
Cameron, James D. (Pa.) 4: 25
Carey, Joseph M. (Wyo.) 1: 462
Carlisle, John G. (Ky.) 1: 461
Casey, Lyman R. (N. Dak.) ... 1: 291
Chace, Jonathan (R. I.) 12: 387
Chandler, William E. (N. H.) .. 4: 252
Cockrell, Francis M. (Mo.) 3: 297
Coke, Richard (Tex.) 9: 72
Colquitt, Alfred H. (Ga.) 1: 291
Collum, Shelby M. (Ill.) 11: 50
Daniel, John W. (Va.) 1: 218
Davis, Cushman K. (Minn.) ...10: 65
Dawes, Henry L. (Mass.) 4: 321
Dixon, Nathan F. (R. I.) 1: 291
Dolph, Joseph N. (Oreg.) 1: 294
Edmunds, George F. (Vt.) 2: 384
Eustis, James B. (La.) 1: 462
Evarts, William M. (N. Y.) ... 3: 197
Farwell, Charles B. (Ill.) 6: 394
Faulkner, Charles J., Jr. (W.Va.) 2: 392
Felton, Charles N. (Calif.) 12: 392
Frye, William P. (Maine) 1: 290
George, James Z. (Minn.) 2: 358
Gibson, Randall L. (La.) 1: 297
Gorman, Arthur P. (Md.) 1: 296
Gray, George (Del.) 26: 17
Hale, Eugene (Maine) 20: 220
Hampton, Wade, 3d (S. C.) 12: 177
Harris, Isham G. (Tenn.) 2: 209
Hawley, Joseph R. (Conn.) 1: 457
Hearst, George F. (Calif.) 1: 315
Higgins, Anthony (Del.) 1: 290
Hiscock, Frank (N. Y.) 12: 352
Hoar, George F. (Mass.) 1: 453
Ingalls, John J. (Kans.) 8: 415
Jones, James K. (Ark.) 1: 293
Jones, John P. (Mo.) 1: 300
Kenna, John E. (W. Va.) 1: 299
McConnell, William J. (Idaho) ..12: 492
McMillan, James (Mich.) 2: 227
McPherson, John R. (N. J.) ... 3: 71
Manderson, Charles F. (Nebr.) .. 1: 454
Marston, Gilman (N. H.) 5: 329
Mitchell, John H. (Oreg.) 2: 301
Moody, Gideon C. (S. Dak.) ... 2: 395
Morgan, John Tyler (Ala.) 1: 295
Morrill, Justin S. (Vt.) 1: 377
Paddock, Algernon S. (Nebr.) .. 2: 247
Pasco, Samuel (Fla.) 1: 293
Payne, Henry B. (Ohio) 1: 427
Pettigrew, Richard F. (S. Dak.) 2: 202
Pierce, Gilbert A. (N. Dak.) ... 1: 294
Platt, Orville H. (Conn.) 2: 339
Plumb, Preston B. (Kans.) 2: 529
Power, Thomas C. (Mont.) 19: 288
Pugh, James L. (Ala.) 1: 292
Quay, Matthew S. (Pa.) 1: 459
Ransom, Matthew W. (N. C.) ..10: 251
Reagan, John H. (Tex.) 1: 292
Sanders, Wilbur F. (Mont.) 1: 457
Sawyer, Philetus (Wis.) 1: 326
Sherman, John (Ohio) 3: 198
Shoup, George L. (Idaho) 12: 491
Spooner, John C. (Wis.) 14: 33
Squire, Watson C. (Wash.) 3: 59
Stanford, Leland (Calif.) 2: 128
Stewart, William M. (Nev.) 1: 325
Stockbridge, Francis B. (Mich.) 1: 460
Teller, Henry M. (Colo.) 15: 228
Turpie, David (Ind.) 1: 218
Vance, Zebulon B. (N. C.) 2: 384
Vest, George G. (Mo.) 2: 297
Voorhees, Daniel W. (Ind.) 2: 359
Walthall, Edward C. (Miss.) 1: 389
Warren, Francis E. (Wyo.) ...23: 220
Washburn, William D. (Minn.) ..16: 361
Wilson, Ephraim K. (Md.) 1: 295
Wilson, James F. (Iowa) 1: 289
Wolcott, Edward O. (Colo.) 8: 397

Fifty-second Congress (1891-93)

Morton, Levi P., president
of the senate 1: 136
Aldrich, Nelson W. (R. I.) 10: 206
Allen, John B. (Wash.) 11: 561
Allison, William B. (Iowa) 1: 296
Barbour, John S. (Va.) 12: 59
Bate, William B. (Tenn.) 7: 213
Berry, James H. (Ark.) 10: 190
Blackburn, Joseph C. S. (Ky.) . 1: 295
Blodgett, Rufus (N. J.) 1: 217
Brice, Calvin S. (Ohio) 2: 425
Butler, Matthew C. (S. C.) 1: 298
Caffery, Donelson (La.) 13: 63
Call, Wilkinson (Fla.) 2: 525
Camden, Johnson N. (W. Va.) ..20: 329
Cameron, James D. (Pa.) 4: 25
Carey, Joseph M. (Wyo.) 1: 462
Carlisle, John G. (Ky.) 1: 461
Casey, Lyman R. (N. Dak.) 1: 291
Chandler, William E. (N. H.) .. 4: 252
Cockrell, Francis M. (Mo.) 3: 297
Coke, Richard (Tex.) 9: 72
Colquitt, Alfred H. (Ga.) 1: 291
Cullom, Shelby M. (Ill.) 11: 50
Daniel, John W. (Va.) 1: 218
Davis, Cushman K. (Minn.) ...10: 65
Dawes, Henry L. (Mass.) 4: 321
Dixon, Nathan F. (R. I.) 1: 291
Dolph, Joseph N. (Oreg.) 1: 294
Dubois, Frederick T. (Idaho) ..12: 519
Edmunds, George F. (Vt.) 2: 384
Faulkner, Charles J., Jr. (W.Va.) 2: 392
Felton, Charles N. (Calif.) 12: 392
Frye, William P. (Maine) 1: 290
Gallinger, Jacob H. (N. H.) ... 2: 247
George, James Z. (Minn.) 2: 358
Gibson, Charles H. (Md.) 5: 495
Gibson, Randall L. (La.) 1: 297
Gordon, John B. (Ga.) 1: 231
Gorman, Arthur P. (Md.) 1: 296
Gray, George (Del.) 26: 17
Hale, Eugene (Maine) 20: 220
Hansbrough, Henry C. (N.Dak.) 4: 496
Harris, Isham G. (Tenn.) 2: 209
Hawley, Joseph R. (N. Y.) 1: 457
Higgins, Anthony (Del.) 1: 290
Hill, David B. (N. Y.) 1: 453
Hiscock, Frank (N. Y.) 12: 352
Hoar, George F. (Mass.) 1: 453
Hunton, Eppa (Va.) 13: 459
Irby, John L. M. (S. C.) 2: 251
Jones, James K. (Ark.) 1: 293
Jones, John P. (Nev.) 1: 300
Kenna, John E. (W. Va.) 1: 299
Kyle, James H. (S. Dak.) 1: 323
Lindsay, William (Ky.) 11: 485
McMillan, James (Mich.) 2: 227
McPherson, John R. (N. J.) .. 3: 71
Manderson, Charles F. (Nebr.) ..1: 454
Mills, Roger Q. (Tex.) 8: 403
Mitchell, John H. (Oreg.) 2: 301
Morgan, John Tyler (Ala.) 1: 295
Morrill, Justin S. (Vt.) 1: 377
Paddock, Algernon S. (Nebr.) .. 2: 247
Palmer, John McA. (Ill.) 11: 49
Pasco, Samuel (Fla.) 1: 293
Peffer, William A. (Kans.) 1: 299
Perkins, Bishop W. (Kans.) ... 3: 302
Pettigrew, Richard F. (S. Dak.) 2: 202
Platt, Orville H. (Conn.) 2: 339
Plumb, Preston B. (Kans.) 2: 529
Power, Thomas C. (Mont.) 19: 228
Proctor, Redfield (Vt.) 1: 141
Pugh, James L. (Ala.) 1: 292
Quay, Matthew S. (Pa.) 1: 459
Ransom, Matthew W. (N. C.) ..10: 251
Reagan, John H. (Tex.) 1: 292
Sanders, Wilbur F. (Mont.) 1: 457
Sawyer, Philetus (Wis.) 1: 326
Sherman, John (Ohio) 3: 198
Shoup, George L. (Idaho) 12: 491
Squire, Watson C. (Wash.) 3: 59
Stanford, Leland (Calif.) 2: 128
Stewart, William M. (Nev.) 1: 325
Stockbridge, Francis B. (Mich.) 1: 460
Teller, Henry M. (Colo.) 15: 228
Turpie, David (Ind.) 1: 218
Vance, Zebulon B. (N. C.) 2: 384
Vest, George G. (Mo.) 2: 297
Vilas, William F. (Wis.) 2: 409
Voorhees, Daniel W. (Ind.) 2: 359
Walthall, Edward C. (Miss.) ... 1: 389
Warren, Francis E. (Wyo.) 23: 220
Washburn, William D. (Minn.) ..16: 361
White, Edward D. (La.) 21: 3
Wilson, James F. (Iowa) 1: 289
Wolcott, Edward O. (Colo.) 8: 397

Fifty-third Congress (1893-95)

Stevenson, Adlai E., president
of the senate 2: 487
Aldrich, Nelson W. (R. I.) ...10: 206
Allen, William V. (Nebr.) 5: 217
Allison, William B. (Iowa) 1: 296
Bate, William B. (Tenn.) 7: 213
Berry, James H. (Ark.) 10: 190
Blackburn, Joseph C. S. (Ky.) .. 1: 295
Blanchard, Newton C. (La.) ... 4: 498
Brice, Calvin S. (Ohio) 2: 425
Burrows, Julius C. (Mich.) 12: 515
Butler, Matthew C. (S. C.) 1: 298
Caffery, Donelson (La.) 13: 63
Call, Wilkinson (Fla.) 2: 525

Camden, Johnson N. (W. Va.) ..20: 329
Cameron, James D. (Pa.) 4: 25
Carey, Joseph M. (Wyo.) 1: 462
Chandler, William E. (N. H.) .. 4: 252
Clark, Clarence D. (Wyo.) 13: 60
Cockrell, Francis M. (Mo.) 3: 297
Coke, Richard (Tex.) 9: 72
Colquitt, Alfred H. (Ga.) 1: 291
Cullom, Shelby M. (Ill.) 11: 50
Daniel, John W. (Va.) 1: 218
Davis, Cushman K. (Minn.) 10: 65
Dixon, Nathan F. (R. I.) 1: 291
Dolph, Joseph N. (Oreg.) 1: 294
Dubois, Frederick T. (Idaho) ..12: 519
Faulkner, Charles J., Jr. (W.Va.) 2: 392
Frye, William P. (Maine) 1: 290
Gallinger, Jacob H. (N. H.) 2: 247
George, James Z. (Minn.) 2: 358
Gibson, Charles H. (Md.) 5: 495
Gordon, John B. (Ga.) 1: 231
Gorman, Arthur P. (Md.) 1: 296
Gray, George (Del.) 26: 17
Hale, Eugene (Maine) 20: 220
Hansbrough, Henry C. (N.Dak.) 4: 496
Harris, Isham G. (Tenn.) 2: 209
Hawley, Joseph R. (Conn.) 1: 457
Higgins, Anthony (Del.) 1: 290
Hill, David B. (N. Y.) 1: 453
Hoar, George F. (Mass.) 1: 453
Hunton, Eppa (Va.) 13: 459
Irby, John L. M. (S. C.) 2: 251
Jarvis, Thomas J. (N. C.) 4: 429
Jones, James K. (Ark.) 1: 293
Jones, John P. (Nev.) 1: 300
Kyle, James H. (S. Dak.) 1: 323
Lindsay, William (Ky.) 11: 485
Lodge, Henry C. (Mass.) 19: 52
McLaurin, Anselm J. (Miss.) ..13: 494
McMillan, James (Mich.) 2: 227
McPherson, John R. (N. J.) 3: 71
Manderson, Charles F. (Nebr.) .. 1: 454
Mantle, Lee (Mont.) 11: 313
Martin, John (Kans.) 7: 20
Mills, Roger Q. (Tex.) 8: 403
Mitchell, John H. (Oreg.) 2: 301
Mitchell, John L. (Wis.) 2: 341
Morgan, John T. (Ala.) 1: 295
Morrill, Justin S. (Vt.) 1: 377
Murphy, Edward, Jr. (N. Y.) ..13: 182
Palmer, John M. (Ill.) 11: 49
Pasco, Samuel (Fla.) 1: 293
Patton, John (Mich.) 12: 391
Peffer, William A. (Kans.) 1: 299
Perkins, George C. (Calif.) 4: 111
Pettigrew, Richard F. (S. Dak.) 2: 202
Platt, Orville H. (Conn.) 2: 339
Power, Thomas C. (Mont.) 19: 288
Pritchard, Jeter C. (N. C.) 19: 223
Proctor, Redfield (Vt.) 1: 141
Pugh, James L. (Ala.) 1: 292
Quay, Matthew S. (Pa.) 1: 459
Ransom, Matthew W. (N. C.) ..10: 251
Roach, William N. (N. Dak.) .. 5: 263
Sherman, John (Ohio) 3: 198
Shoup, George L. (Idaho) 12: 491
Smith, James, Jr. (N. J.) 12: 391
Squire, Watson C. (Wash.) 3: 59
Stanford, Leland (Calif.) 2: 128
Stewart, William M. (Nev.) 1: 325
Stockbridge, Francis B. (Mich.) 1: 460
Teller, Henry M. (Colo.) 15: 228
Turpie, David (Ind.) 1: 218
Vance, Zebulon B. (N. C.) 2: 384
Vest, George G. (Mo.) 2: 297
Vilas, William F. (Wis.) 2: 409
Voorhees, Daniel W. (Ind.) 2: 359
Walsh, Patrick (Ga.) 2: 50
Walthall, Edward C. (Miss.) ... 1: 389
Washburn, William D. (Minn.) ..16: 361
White, Edward D. (La.) 21: 3
White, Stephen M. (Calif.) 12: 509
Wilson, James F. (Iowa) 1: 289
Wilson, John L. (Wash.) 12: 126
Wolcott, Edward O. (Colo.) 8: 397

Fifty-fourth Congress (1895-97)

Stevenson, Adlai E., president of the senate 2: 487
Aldrich, Nelson W. (R. I.) 10: 206
Allen, William V. (Nebr.) 5: 217
Allison, William B. (Iowa) 1: 296
Bacon, Augustus O. (Ga.) 12: 527
Baker, Lucien (Kans.) 12: 495
Bate, William B. (Tenn.) 7: 213
Berry, James H. (Ark.) 10: 190
Blackburn, Joseph C. S. (Ky.) .. 1: 295
Blanchard, Newton C. (La.) 4: 498
Brice, Calvin S. (Ohio) 2: 425
Brown, Arthur (Utah) 13: 179
Burrows, Julius C. (Mich.) 12: 515
Butler, Marion (N. C.) 13: 19
Caffery, Donelson (La.) 13: 63
Call, Wilkinson (Fla.) 2: 525
Cameron, James D. (Pa.) 4: 25
Cannon, Frank J. (Utah) 16: 442
Carter, Thomas H. (Mont.) ...13: 199
Chandler, William E. (N. H.) ... 4: 252
Chilton, Horace (Tex.) 2: 241
Clark, Clarence D. (Wyo.) 13: 60
Cockrell, Francis M. (Mo.) 3: 297
Cullom, Shelby M. (Ill.) 11: 50
Daniel, John W. (Va.) 1: 218
Davis, Cushman K. (Minn.) ...10: 65
Dubois, Frederick T. (Idaho) ..12: 519
Elkins, Stephen B. (W. Va.) ... 1: 142
Faulkner, Charles J., Jr. (W.Va.) 2: 392
Frye, William P. (Maine) 1: 290
Gallinger, Jacob H. (N. H.) ... 2: 247
Gear, John H. (Iowa) 11: 433
George, James Z. (Minn.) 2: 358
Gibson, Charles H. (Md.) 5: 495
Gordon, John B. (Ga.) 1: 231
Gorman, Arthur P. (Md.) 1: 296
Gray, George (Del.) 26: 17
Hale, Eugene (Maine) 20: 220
Hansbrough, Henry C. (N.Dak.) 4: 496
Harris, Isham G. (Tenn.) 2: 209
Hawley, Joseph R. (Conn.) 1: 457
Hill, David B. (N. Y.) 1: 453
Hoar, George F. (Mass.) 1: 453
Irby, John L. M. (S. C.) 2: 251
Jones, James K. (Ark.) 1: 293
Jones, John P. (Nev.) 1: 300
Kenney, Richard R. (Del.) 12: 538
Kyle, James H. (S. Dak.) 1: 323
Lindsay, William (Ky.) 11: 485
Lodge, Henry C. (Mass.) 19: 52
McBride, George W. (Oreg.) ...11: 234
McMillan, James (Mich.) 2: 227
Mantle, Lee (Mont.) 11: 313
Martin, Thomas S. (Va.) 11: 30
Mills, Roger Q. (Tex.) 8: 403
Mitchell, John H. (Oreg.) 2: 301
Mitchell, John L. (Wis.) 2: 341
Morgan, John T. (Ala.) 1: 295
Morrill, Justin S. (Vt.) 1: 377
Murphy, Edward, Jr. (N. Y.) ..13: 182
Nelson, Knute (Minn.) 19: 18
Palmer, John M. (Ill.) 11: 49
Pasco, Samuel (Fla.) 1: 293
Peffer, William A. (Kans.) 1: 299
Perkins, George C. (Calif.) 4: 111
Pettigrew, Richard F. (S. Dak.) 2: 202
Platt, Orville H. (Conn.) 2: 339
Pritchard, Jeter C. (N. C.) 19: 223
Proctor, Redfield (Vt.) 1: 141
Pugh, James L. (Ala.) 1: 292
Quay, Matthew S. (Pa.) 1: 459
Roach, William N. (N. Dak.) .. 5: 263
Sewell, William J. (N. J.) 12: 217
Sherman, John (Ohio) 3: 198
Shoup, George L. (Idaho) 12: 491
Smith, James, Jr. (N. J.) 12: 391
Squire, Watson C. (Wash.) 3: 59
Stewart, William M. (Nev.) ... 1: 325
Teller, Henry M. (Colo.) 15: 228
Thurston, John M. (Nebr.) 5: 105
Tillman, Benjamin R. (S. C.) ..12: 180
Turpie, David (Ind.) 1: 218
Vest, George G. (Mo.) 2: 297
Vilas, William F. (Wis.) 2: 409
Voorhees, Daniel W. (Ind.) 2: 359
Walthall, Edward C. (Miss.) ... 1: 389
Warren, Francis E. (Wyo.) 23: 220
Wetmore, George P. (R. I.) ... 9: 407
White, Stephen M. (Calif.) 12: 509
Wilson, John L. (Wash.) 12: 126
Wolcott, Edward O. (Colo.) 8: 397

Fifty-fifth Congress (1897-99)

Hobart, Garret A., president of the senate 11: 10
Aldrich, Nelson W. (R. I.) 10: 206
Allen, William V. (Nebr.) 5: 217
Allison, William B. (Iowa) 1: 296
Bacon, Augustus O. (Ga.) 12: 527
Baker, Lucien (Kans.) 12: 495
Bate, William B. (Tenn.) 7: 213
Berry, James H. (Ark.) 10: 190
Burrows, Julius C. (Mich.) 12: 515
Butler, Marion (N. C.) 13: 19
Caffery, Donelson (La.) 13: 63
Cannon, Frank J. (Utah) 16: 442
Carter, Thomas H. (Mont.) 13: 199
Chandler, William E. (N. H.) .. 4: 252
Chilton, Horace (Tex.) 2: 241
Clark, Clarence D. (Wyo.) 13: 60
Clay, Alexander S. (Ga.) 5: 548
Cockrell, Francis M. (Mo.) 3: 297
Cullom, Shelby M. (Ill.) 11: 50
Daniel, John W. (Va.) 1: 218
Davis, Cushman K. (Minn.) ...10: 65
Deboe, William J. (Ky.) 13: 23
Earle, Joseph H. (S. C.) 12: 208
Elkins, Stephen B. (W. Va.) ... 1: 142
Fairbanks, Charles W. (Ind.) ..14: 10
Faulkner, Charles J., Jr. (W.Va.) 2: 392
Foraker, Joseph B. (Ohio) 3: 144
Frye, William P. (Maine) 1: 290
Gallinger, Jacob H. (N. H.) ... 2: 247
Gear, John H. (Iowa) 11: 433
George, James Z. (Minn.) 2: 358
Gorman, Arthur P. (Md.) 1: 296
Gray, George (Del.) 26: 17
Hale, Eugene (Maine) 20: 220
Hanna, Marcus A. (Ohio) 22: 13
Hansbrough, Henry C. (N.Dak.) 4: 496
Harris, Isham G. (Tenn.) 2: 209
Harris, William A. (Kans.) 13: 21
Hawley, Joseph R. (Conn.) 1: 457
Heitfeld, Henry (Idaho) 13: 581
Hoar, George F. (Mass.) 1: 453
Jones, James K. (Ark.) 1: 293
Jones, John P. (Nev.) 1: 300
Kenney, Richard R. (Del.) 12: 538
Kyle, James H. (S. Dak.) 1: 323
Lindsay, William (Ky.) 11: 485
Lodge, Henry C. (Mass.) 19: 52
McBride, George W. (Oreg.) ...11: 234
McEnery, Samuel D. (La.) 10: 83
McLaurin, John L. (S. C.) 13: 21
McMillan, James (Mich.) 2: 227
Mallory, Stephen R. (Fla.) 12: 132
Mantle, Lee (Mont.) 11: 313
Martin, Thomas S. (Va.) 11: 30
Mason, William E. (Ill.) 12: 445
Mills, Roger Q. (Tex.) 8: 403
Mitchell, John L. (Oreg.) 2: 341
Money, Hernando D. S. (Miss.) .11: 492
Morgan, John Tyler (Ala.) 1: 295
Morrill, Justin S. (Vt.) 1: 377
Murphy, Edward, Jr. (N. Y.) ..13: 182
Nelson, Knute (Minn.) 19: 18
Pasco, Samuel (Fla.) 1: 293
Penrose, Boies (Pa.) 2: 444
Perkins, George C. (Calif.) 4: 111
Pettigrew, Richard F. (S. Dak.) 2: 202
Pettus, Edmund W. (Ala.) 12: 320
Platt, Orville H. (Conn.) 2: 339
Platt, Thomas C. (N. Y.) 11: 509
Pritchard, Jeter C. (N. C.) 19: 223
Proctor, Redfield (Vt.) 1: 141
Quay, Matthew S. (Pa.) 1: 459
Rawlins, Joseph L. (Utah) 11: 427
Roach, William N. (N. Dak.) .. 5: 263
Ross, Jonathan (Vt.) 7: 493
Sewell, William J. (N. J.) 12: 217
Sherman, John (Ohio) 3: 198
Shoup, George L. (Idaho) 12: 491
Simon, Joseph (Oreg.) 12: 329
Smith, James, Jr. (N. J.) 12: 391
Spooner, John C. (Wis.) 14: 33
Stewart, William M. (Nev.) ... 1: 325
Sullivan, William Van A. (Miss.) 12: 387
Teller, Henry M. (Colo.) 15: 228
Thurston, John M. (Nebr.) 5: 105
Tillman, Benjamin R. (S. C.) ..12: 180
Turley, Thomas B. (Tenn.) 12: 391
Turner, George (Wash.) 12: 385
Turpie, David (Ind.) 1: 218
Vest, George G. (Mo.) 2: 297
Walthall, Edward C. (Miss.) ... 1: 389
Warren, Francis E. (Wyo.) ...23: 220
Wellington, George L. (Md.) ...13: 545
Wetmore, George P. (R. I.) 9: 407
White, Stephen M. (Calif.) 12: 509
Wilson, John L. (Wash.) 12: 126
Wolcott, Edward O. (Colo.) 8: 397

Fifty-sixth Congress (1899-1901)

Frye, William P., president *pro tem.* 1:290
Aldrich, Nelson W. (R. I.) 10:206
Allen, William V. (Nebr.) 5:217
Allison, William B. (Iowa) 1:296
Bacon, Augustus O. (Ga.) 12:527
Baker, Lucien (Kans.) 12:495
Bard, Thomas R. (Calif.) 12: 57
Bate, William B. (Tenn.) 7:213
Berry, James H. (Ark.) 10:190
Beveridge, Albert J. (Ind.) 13: 26
Burrows, Julius C. (Mich.) 12:515
Butler, Marion (N. C.) 13: 19
Caffery, Donelson (La.) 13: 63
Carter, Thomas H. (Mont.) 13:199
Chandler, William E. (N. H.) .. 4:252
Chilton, Horace (Tex.) 2:241
Clark, Clarence D. (Wyo.) 13: 60
Clark, William A. (Mont.) 21: 10
Clay, Alexander S. (Ga.) 5:548
Cockrell, Francis M. (Mo.) 3:297
Culberson, Charles A. (Tex.) .. 9: 76
Cullom, Shelby M. (Ill.) 11: 50
Daniel, John W. (Va.) 1:218
Davis, Cushman K. (Minn.) 10: 65
Deboe, William J. (Ky.) 13: 23
Depew, Chauncey M. (N. Y.) ..23: 96
Dillingham, William P. (Vt.) .. 8:411
Dolliver, Jonathan P. (Iowa) ..12:392
Elkins, Stephen B. (W. Va.) ... 1:142
Fairbanks, Charles W. (Ind.) ..14: 10
Foraker, Joseph B. (Ohio) 3:144
Foster, Addison G. (Wash.) 12:390
Frye, William P. (Maine) 1:290
Gallinger, Jacob H. (N. H.) ... 2:247
Gear, John H. (Iowa) 11:433
Hale, Eugene (Maine) 20:220
Hanna, Marcus A. (Ohio) 22: 13
Hansbrough, Henry C. (N. Dak.) 4:496
Harris, William A. (Kans.) 13: 21
Hawley, Joseph R. (Conn.) 1:457
Hayward, Monroe L. (Nebr.) ..12:111
Heitfield, Henry (Idaho) 13:581
Hoar, George F. (Mass.) 1:453
Jones, James K. (Ark.) 1:293
Jones, John P. (Nev.) 1:300
Kean, John (N. J.) 18:152
Kearns, Thomas (Utah) 12:516
Kenney, Richard R. (Del.) 12:538
Kyle, James H. (S. Dak.) 1:323
Lindsay, William (Ky.) 11:485
Lodge, Henry C. (Mass.) 19: 52
McBride, George W. (Oreg.) 11:234
McComas, Louis E. (Md.) 12:488
McCumber, Porter J. (N. Dak.) 13: 62
McEnery, Samuel D. (La.) 10: 83
McLaurin, John L. (S. C.) 13: 21
McMillan, James (Mich.) 2:227
Mallory, Stephen R. (Fla.) 12:132
Martin, Thomas S. (Va.) 11: 30
Mason, William E. (Ill.) 12:445
Money, Hernando D. S. (Miss.) .11:492
Morgan, John T. (Ala.) 1:295
Nelson, Knute (Minn.) 19: 18
Penrose, Boies (Pa.) 2:444
Perkins, George C. (Calif.) 4:111
Pettigrew, Richard F. (S. Dak.) 2:202
Pettus, Edmund W. (Ala.) 12:320
Platt, Orville H. (Conn.) 2:339
Platt, Thomas C. (N. Y.) 11:509
Pritchard, Jeter C. (N. C.) 19:223
Proctor, Redfield (Vt.) 1:141
Quarles, Joseph V. (Wis.) 13: 17
Quay, Matthew S. (Pa.) 1:459
Rawlins, Joseph L. (Utah) 11:427
Ross, Jonathan (Vt.) 7:493
Scott, Nathan B. (W. Va.) 19: 59
Sewell, William J. (N. J.) 12:217
Shoup, George L. (Idaho) 12:491
Simon, Joseph (Oreg.) 13:329
Spooner, John C. (Wis.) 14: 33
Stewart, William M. (Nev.) 1:325
Sullivan, William Van A. (Miss.) 12:387
Taliaferro, James P. (Fla.) 10:175
Teller, Henry M. (Colo.) 15:228
Thurston, John M. (Nebr.) 5:105
Tillman, Benjamin R. (S. C.) ..12:180
Towne, Charles A. (Minn.) 12:258
Turley, Thomas B. (Tenn.) 12:391
Turner, George (Wash.) 12:385
Vest, George G. (Mo.) 2:297
Warren, Francis E. (Wyo.) 23:220
Wellington, George L. (Md.) ...13:545
Wetmore, George P. (R. I.) 9:407
Wolcott, Edward O. (Colo.) 8:397

Fifty-seventh Congress (1901-03)

Frye, William P., president *pro tem.* 1:290
Aldrich, Nelson W. (R. I.) 10:206
Allison, William B. (Iowa) 1:296
Bacon, Augustus O. (Ga.) 12:527
Bailey, Joseph W. (Tex.) 13:587
Bard, Thomas R. (Calif.) 12: 57
Bate, William B. (Tenn.) 7:213
Berry, James H. (Ark.) 10:190
Beveridge, Albert J. (Ind.) 13: 26
Blackburn, Joseph C. S. (Ky.) .. 1:295
Burnham, Henry E. (N. H.) ...13: 43
Burrows, Julius C. (Mich.) 12:515
Burton, Joseph R. (Kans.) 13:168
Carmack, Edward W. (Tenn.) ..13:300
Clapp, Moses E. (Minn.) 12:232
Clark, Clarence D. (Wyo.) 13: 60
Clark, William A. (Mont.) 21: 10
Clay, Alexander S. (Ga.) 5:548
Cockrell, Francis M. (Mo.) 3:297
Culberson, Charles A. (Tex.) .. 9: 76
Cullom, Shelby M. (Ill.) 11: 50
Daniel, John W. (Va.) 1:218
Deboe, William J., (Ky.) 13: 23
Depew, Chauncey M. (N. Y.) ..23: 96
Dietrich, Charles H. (Nebr.) ...12: 4
Dillingham, William P. (Vt.) .. 8:411
Dolliver, Jonathan P. (Iowa) ...12:392
Dryden, John F. (N. J.) 9:415
Dubois, Frederick T. (Idaho) ..12:519
Elkins, Stephen B. (W. Va.) .. 1:142
Fairbanks, Charles W. (Ind.) ..14: 10
Foraker, Joseph B. (Ohio) 3:144
Foster, Addison G. (Wash.) ...12:390
Foster, Murphy J. (La.) 10: 83
Frye, William P. (Maine) 1:290
Gallinger, Jacob H. (N. H.) 2:247
Gamble, Robert J. (S. Dak.) ...12:392
Gibson, Paris (Mont.) 8: 71
Hale, Eugene (Maine) 20:220
Hanna, Marcus A. (Ohio) 22: 13
Hansbrough, Henry C. (N.Dak.) 4:496
Harris, William A. (Kans.) 13: 21
Hawley, Joseph R. (Conn.) 1:457
Heitfeld, Henry (Idaho) 13:581
Hoar, George F. (Mass.) 1:453
Jones, James K. (Ark.) 1:293
Jones, John P. (Nev.) 1:300
Kean, John (N. J.) 18:152
Kearns, Thomas (Utah) 12:516
Kittredge, Alfred B. (S. Dak.) ..16:125
Lodge, Henry C. (Mass.) 19: 52
McComas, Louis E. (Md.) 12:488
McCumber, Porter J. (N. Dak.) 13: 62
McEnery, Samuel D. (La.) 10: 83
McLaurin, Anselm J. (Miss.) ..13:494
McLaurin, John L. (S. C.) 13: 21
McMillan, James (Mich.) 2:227
Mallory, Stephen R. (Fla.) 12:132
Martin, Thomas S. (Va.) 11: 30
Mason, William E. (Ill.) 12:445
Millard, Joseph H. (Nebr.) 13:367
Mitchell, John H. (Oreg.) 2:301
Money, Hernando D. S. (Miss.) 11:492
Morgan, John T. (Ala.) 1:295
Nelson, Knute (Minn.) 19: 18
Patterson, Thomas M. (Colo.) ..12:555
Penrose, Boies (Pa.) 2:444
Perkins, George C. (Calif.) 4:111
Pettus, Edmund W. (Ala.) 12:320
Platt, Orville H. (Conn.) 2:339
Platt, Thomas C. (N. Y.) 11:509
Pritchard, Jeter C. (N. C.) 19:223
Proctor, Redfield (Vt.) 1:141
Quarles, Joseph V. (Wis.) 13: 17
Quay, Matthew S. (Pa.) 1:459
Rawlins, Joseph L. (Utah) 11:427
Scott, Nathan B. (W. Va.) 19: 59
Sewell, William J. (N. J.) 12:217
Simmons, Furnifold McL. (N.C.) 12:517
Simon, Joseph (Oreg.) 13:329
Spooner, John C. (Wis.) 14: 33
Stewart, William M. (Nev.) 1:325
Taliaferro, James P. (Fla.) 10:175
Teller, Henry M. (Colo.) 15:228
Tillman, Benjamin R. (S. C.) ..12:180
Turner, George (Wash.) 12:385
Vest, George G. (Mo.) 2:297
Warren, Francis E. (Wyo.) 23:220
Wellington, George L. (Md.) ...13:545
Wetmore, George P. (R. I.) 9:407

Fifty-eighth Congress (1903-05)

Frye, William P., president *pro tem.* 1:290
Aldrich, Nelson W. (R. I.) 10:206
Alger, Russell A. (Mich.) 5:276
Allee, James F. (Del.) 13:292
Allison, William B. (Iowa) 1:296
Ankeny, Levi (Wash.) 9:558
Bacon, Augustus O. (Ga.) 12:527
Bailey, Joseph W. (Tex.) 13:587
Ball, Lewis H. (Del.) 13:546
Bard, Thomas R. (Calif.) 12: 57
Bate, William B. (Tenn.) 7:213
Berry, James H. (Ark.) 10:190
Beveridge, Albert J. (Ind.) 13: 26
Blackburn, Joseph C. S. (Ky.) .. 1:295
Burnham, Henry E. (N. H.) ...13: 43
Burrows, Julius C. (Mich.) 12:515
Burton, Joseph R. (Kans.) 13:168
Carmack, Edward W. (Tenn.) ..13:300
Clapp, Moses E. (Minn.) 12:232
Clark, Clarence D. (Wyo.) 13: 60
Clark, William A. (Mont.) 21: 10
Clarke, James P. (Ark.) 10:193
Clay, Alexander S. (Ga.) 5:548
Cockrell, Francis M. (Mo.) 3:297
Culberson, Charles A. (Tex.) .. 9: 76
Cullom, Shelby M. (Ill.) 11: 50
Daniel, John W. (Va.) 1:218
Depew, Chauncey M. (N. Y.) ..23: 96
Dick, Charles (Ohio) 13:445
Dietrich, Charles H. (Nebr.) ..12: 4
Dillingham, William P. (Vt.) .. 8:411
Dolliver, Jonathan P. (Iowa) ..12:392
Dryden, John F. (N. J.) 9:415
Dubois, Frederick T. (Idaho) ..12:519
Elkins, Stephen B. (W. Va.) .. 1:142
Fairbanks, Charles W. (Ind.) ..14: 10
Foraker, Joseph B. (Ohio) 3:144
Foster, Addison G. (Wash.) 12:390
Foster, Murphy J. (La.) 10: 83
Frye, William P. (Maine) 1:290
Fulton, Charles W. (Oreg.) 13:463
Gallinger, Jacob H. (N. H.) .. 2:247
Gamble, Robert J. (S. Dak.) ...12:392
Gibson, Paris (Mont.) 8: 71
Gorman, Arthur P. (Md.) 1:296
Hale, Eugene (Maine) 20:220
Hanna, Marcus A. (Ohio) 22: 13
Hansbrough, Henry C. (N.Dak.) 4:496
Hawley, Joseph R. (Conn.) 1:457
Heyburn, Weldon B. (Idaho) ..13:101
Hoar, George F. (Mass.) 1:453
Hopkins, Albert J. (Ill.) 11:396
Kean, John (N. J.) 18:152
Kearns, Thomas (Utah) 12:516
Kittredge, Alfred B. (S. Dak.) ..16:125
Knox, Philander C. (Pa.) 24: 7
Latimer, Asbury C. (S. C.) 12:493
Lodge, Henry C. (Mass.) 19: 52
Long, Chester I. (Kans.) ...... C: 56
McComas, Louis E. (Md.) 12:488
McCreary, James B. (Ky.) 13: 10
McCumber, Porter J. (N. Dak.) 13: 62
McEnery, Samuel D. (La.) 10: 83
McLaurin, Anselm J. (Miss.) ..13:494
Mallory, Stephen R. (Fla.) 12:132
Martin, Thomas S. (Va.) 11: 30
Millard, Joseph H. (Nebr.) 13:367
Mitchell, John H. (Oreg.) 2:301
Money, Hernando D. S. (Miss.) .11:492
Morgan, John T. (Ala.) 1:295
Nelson, Knute (Minn.) 19: 18
Newlands, Francis G. (Nev.) ...13:219
Overman, Lee S. (N. C.) 13:305
Patterson, Thomas M. (Colo.) ..12:555
Penrose, Boies, (Pa.) 2:444
Perkins, George C. (Calif.) 4:111
Pettus, Edmund W. (Ala.) 12:320
Platt, Orville H. (Conn.) 2:339
Platt, Thomas C. (N. Y.) 11:509
Proctor, Redfield (Vt.) 1:141
Quarles, Joseph V. (Wis.) 13: 17
Quay, Matthew S. (Pa.) 1:459
Scott, Nathan B. (W. Va.) 19: 59
Simmons, Furnifold McL. (N.C.) 12:517
Smoot, Reed (Utah) 13:197
Spooner, John C. (Wis.) 14: 33
Stewart, William M. (Nev.) ... 1:325
Stone, William J. (Mo.) 12:308
Taliaferro, James P. (Fla.) 10:175
Teller, Henry M. (Colo.) 15:228
Tillman, Benjamin R. (S. C.) ..12:180
Warren, Francis E. (Wyo.) 23:220
Wetmore, George P. (R. I.) 9:407

Fifty-ninth Congress (1905-07)

Fairbanks, Charles W., president.14: 10
Frye, William P., president
pro tem. 1: 290
Aldrich, Nelson W. (R. I.) 10: 206
Alger, Russell A. (Mich.) 5: 276
Allee, James F. (Del.) 13: 292
Allison, William B. (Iowa) 1: 296
Ankeny, Levi (Wash.) 9: 558
Bacon, Augustus O. (Ga.) 12: 527
Bailey, Joseph W. (Tex.) 13: 587
Berry, James H. (Ark.) 10: 190
Beveridge, Albert J. (Ind.) 13: 26
Blackburn, Joseph C. S. (Ky.).. 1: 295
Brandegee, Frank B. (Conn.) ..13: 600
Bulkeley, Morgan G. (Conn.) ...10: 345
Burkett, Elmer J. (Nebr.) 13: 582
Burnham, Henry E. (N. H.) ..13: 43
Burrows, Julius C. (Mich.) 12: 515
Burton, Joseph R. (Kans.) 13: 168
Carmack, Edward W. (Tenn.) ..13: 300
Carter, Thomas H. (Mont.) 13: 199
Clapp, Moses E. (Minn.) 12: 232
Clark, Clarence D. (Wyo.) 13: 60
Clark, William A. (Mont.) 21: 10
Clarke, James P. (Ark.) 10: 193
Clay, Alexander S. (Ga.) 5: 548
Crane, Winthrop M. (Mass.) ..13: 69
Culberson, Charles A. (Tex.) ... 9: 76
Cullom, Shelby M. (Ill.) 11: 50
Daniel, John W. (Va.) 1: 218
Depew, Chauncey M. (N. Y.) ..23: 96
Dick, Charles (Ohio) 13: 445
Dillingham, William P. (Vt.) .. 8: 411
Dolliver, Jonathan P. (Iowa) ..12: 392
Dryden, John F. (N. J.) 9: 415
Dubois, Frederick T. (Idaho) ..12: 519
Elkins, Stephen B. (W. Va.) .. 1: 142
Flint, Frank P. (Calif.) 13: 595
Foraker, Joseph B. (Ohio) 3: 144
Foster, Murphy J. (La.) 10: 83
Frazier, James B. (Tenn.) 13: 532
Fulton, Charles W. (Oreg.) 13: 463
Gallinger, Jacob H. (N. H.) ... 2: 247
Gamble, Robert J. (S. Dak.) ...12: 392
Gorman, Arthur P. (Md.)) 1: 296
Hale, Eugene (Maine) 20: 220
Hansbrough, Henry C. (N.Dak.) 4: 496
Heyburn, Weldon B. (Idaho) ..13: 101
Hopkins, Albert J. (Ill.) 11: 396
Kean, John (N. J.) 18: 152
Kittredge, Alfred B. (S. Dak.) ..16: 125
Knox, Philander C. (Pa.) 24: 7
La Follette, Robert M. (Wis.) ..19: 425
Latimer, Asbury C. (S. C.) 12: 493
Lodge, Henry C. (Mass.) 19: 52
Long, Chester I. (Kans.) ...... C: 56
McCreary, James B. (Ky.) 13: 10
McCumber, Porter J. (N. Dak.)13: 62
McEnery, Samuel D. (La.) 10: 83
McLaurin, Anselm J. (Miss.) ..13: 494
Mallory, Stephen R. (Fla.) 12: 132
Martin, Thomas S. (Va.) 11: 30
Millard, Joseph H. (Nebr.) 13: 367
Mitchell, John H. (Oreg.) 2: 301
Money, Hernando D. (Miss.) ...11: 492
Morgan, John T. (Ala.) 1: 295
Nelson, Knute (Minn.) 19: 18
Newlands, Francis G. (Nev.) ..13: 219
Nixon, George S. (Nev.) 14: 443
Overman, Lee S. (N. C.) 13: 305
Patterson, Thomas M. (Colo.) ..12: 555
Penrose, Boies (Pa.) 2: 444
Perkins, George C. (Calif.) 4: 111
Pettus, Edmund W. (Ala.) 12: 320
Piles, Samuel H. (Wash.) 14: 389
Platt, Orville H. (Conn.) 2: 339
Platt, Thomas C. (N. Y.) 11: 509
Proctor, Redfield (Vt.) 1: 141
Rayner, Isidor (Md.) 13: 544
Scott, Nathan B. (W. Va.) 19: 59
Simmons, Furnifold McL. (N.C.)12: 517
Smoot, Reed (Utah) 13: 197
Spooner, John C. (Wis.) 14: 33
Stone, William J. (Mo.) 12: 308
Sutherland, George (Utah) 13: 413
Taliaferro, James P. (Fla.) 10: 175
Teller, Henry M. (Colo.) 15: 228
Tillman, Benjamin R. (S. C.) ..12: 180
Warner, William (Mo.) 20: 161
Warren, Francis E. (Wyo.)....23: 220
Wetmore, George P. (R. I.) 9: 407

Sixtieth Congress (1907-09)

Frye, William P., president
pro tem. 1: 290
Aldrich, Nelson W. (R. I.) 10: 206
Allison, William B. (Iowa) 1: 296
Ankeny, Levi (Wash.) 9: 558
Bacon, Augustus O. (Ga.) 12: 527
Bailey, Joseph W. (Tex.) 13: 587
Bankhead, John H. (Ala.) 14: 210
Beveridge, Albert J. (Ind.) 13: 26
Borah, William E. (Idaho) .... B: 115
Bourne, Jonathan, Jr. (Oreg.).. B: 94
Brandegee, Frank B. (Conn.) ..13: 600
Briggs, Frank O. (N. J.) 14: 305
Brown, Norris (Nebr.) 14: 328
Bryan, William James (Fla.) ..14: 236
Bulkeley, Morgan G. (Conn.) ..10: 345
Burkett, Elmer J. (Nebr.) 13: 582
Burnham, Henry E. (N. H.) ...13: 43
Burrows, Julius C. (Mich.) 12: 515
Carter, Thomas H. (Mont.) 13: 199
Clapp, Moses E. (Minn.) 12: 232
Clark, Clarence D. (Wyo.) 13: 60
Clarke, James P. (Ark.) 10: 193
Clay, Alexander S. (Ga.) 5: 548
Crane, Winthrop M. (Mass.) ...13: 69
Culberson, Charles A. (Tex.) ... 9: 76
Cullom, Shelby M. (Ill.) 11: 50
Cummins, Albert B. (Iowa) 13: 176
Curtis, Charles (Kans.) .... C: 7
Daniel, John W. (Va.) 1: 218
Davis, Jefferson (Ark.) 13: 366
Depew, Chauncey M. (N. Y.) ..23: 96
Dick, Charles (Ohio) 13: 445
Dillingham, William P. (Vt.) .. 8: 411
Dixon, Joseph M. (Mont.) 14: 107
Dolliver, Jonathan P. (Iowa) ..12: 392
DuPont, Henry A. (Del.) 6: 457
Elkins, Stephen B. (W. Va.) .. 1: 142
Flint, Frank P. (Calif.) 13: 595
Foraker, Joseph B. (Ohio) 3: 144
Foster, Murphy J. (La.) 10: 83
Frazier, James B. (Tenn.) 13: 532
Fulton, Charles W. (Oreg.) 13: 463
Gallinger, Jacob H. (N. H.) ... 2: 247
Gamble, Robert J. (S. Dak.) ...12: 392
Gary, Frank B. (S. C.) 14: 123
Gore, Thomas P. (Okla.) 14: 323
Guggenheim, Simon (Colo.) .... C: 50
Hale, Eugene (Maine) 20: 220
Hansbrough, Henry C. (N.Dak.) 4: 496
Hemenway, James A. (Ind.) ...14: 187
Heyburn, Weldon B. (Idaho) ...13: 101
Hopkins, Albert J. (Ill.) 11: 396
Johnston, Joseph F. (Ala.) 10: 439
Kean, John (N. J.) 18: 152
Kittredge, Alfred B. (S. Dak.)..16: 125
Knox, Philander C. (Pa.) 24: 7
LaFollette, Robert M. (Wis.) ..19: 425
Latimer, Asbury C. (S. C.) 12: 493
Lodge, Henry C. (Mass.) 19: 52
Long, Chester I. (Kans.) .... C: 56
McCreary, James B. (Ky.) 13: 10
McCumber, Porter J. (N. Dak.) .13: 62
McEnery, Samuel D. (La.) 10: 83
McLaurin, Anselm J. (Miss.) ..13: 494
Mallory, Stephen R. (Fla.) 12: 132
Martin, Thomas S. (Va.) 11: 30
Milton, William H. (Fla.) 14: 388
Money, Hernando D. (Miss.) ...11: 492
Morgan, John T. (Ala.) 1: 295
Nelson, Knute (Minn.) 19: 18
Newlands, Francis G. (Nev.) ..13: 219
Nixon, George S. (Nev.) 14: 443
Overman, Lee S. (N. C.) 13: 305
Owen, Robert L. (Okla.) 14: 248
Page, Carroll S. (Vt.) 8: 329
Paynter, Thomas H. (Ky.) 12: 125
Penrose, Boies (Pa.) 2: 444
Perkins, George C. (Calif.) 4: 111
Pettus, Edmund W. (Ala.) 12: 320
Piles, Samuel H. (Wash.) 14: 389
Platt, Thomas C. (N. Y.) 11: 509
Proctor, Redfield (Vt.) 1: 141
Rayner, Isidor (Md.) 13: 544
Richardson, Harry A. (Del.) ...14: 310
Scott, Nathan B. (W. Va.) 19: 59
Simmons, Furnifold McL. (N.C.)12: 517
Smith, John W. (Md.) 13: 205
Smith, William A. (Mich.) 26: 53
Smoot, Reed (Utah) 13: 197
Spooner, John C. (Wis.) 14: 33
Stephenson, Isaac (Wis.) 14: 50
Stewart, John W. (Vt.) 8: 325
Stone, William J. (Mo.) 12: 308
Sutherland, George (Utah) 13: 413
Taliaferro, James P. (Fla.) ...10: 175
Taylor, Robert L. (Tenn.) 8: 365
Teller, Henry M. (Colo.) 15: 228
Tillman, Benjamin R. (S. C.) ..12: 180
Warner, William (Mo.) 20: 161
Warren, Francis E. (Wyo.) 23: 220
Wetmore, George P. (R. I.) 9: 407
Whyte, William P. (Md.) 9: 309

Sixty-first Congress (1909-11)

Frye, William P., president
pro tem. 1: 290
Aldrich, Nelson W. (R. I.) 10: 206
Bacon, Augustus O. (Ga.) 12: 527
Bailey, Joseph W. (Tex.) 13: 587
Bankhead, John H. (Ala.) 14: 210
Beveridge, Albert J. (Ind.) ...13: 26
Bourne, Jonathan, Jr. (Oreg.).. B: 94
Bradley, William O'C. (Ky.) ...13: 12
Brandegee, Frank B. (Conn.) ..13: 600
Bristow, Joseph L. (Kans.) 14: 29
Brown, Norris (Nebr.) 14: 328
Bulkeley, Morgan G. (Conn.) ..10: 345
Burkett, Elmer J. (Nebr.) 13: 582
Burnham, Henry E. (N. H.) ...13: 43
Burrows, Julius C. (Mich.) 12: 515
Burton, Theodore E. (Ohio) 21: 50
Carter, Thomas H. (Mont.) 13: 199
Chamberlain, George E. (Oreg.) 14: 135
Clapp, Moses E. (Minn.) 12: 232
Clark, Clarence D. (Wyo.) 13: 60
Clarke, James P. (Ark.) 10: 193
Crane, Winthrop M. (Mass.) ...13: 69
Crawford, Corie I. (S. Dak.) ...14: 200
Culberson, Charles A. (Tex.) ... 9: 76
Cullom, Shelby M. (Ill.) 11: 50
Cummins, Albert B. (Iowa) 13: 176
Curtis, Charles (Kans.) .... C: 7
Daniel, John W. (Va.) 1: 218
Davis, Jefferson (Ark.) 13: 366
Depew, Chauncey M. (N. Y.) ..23: 96
Dick, Charles (Ohio) 13: 445
Dillingham, William P. (Vt.) .. 8: 411
Dixon, Joseph M. (Mont.) 14: 107
Dolliver, Jonathan P. (Iowa) ..12: 392
DuPont, Henry A. (Del.) 4: 457
Elkins, Davis (Va.) .... C: 527
Elkins, Stephen B. (W. Va.) .. 1: 142
Fletcher, Duncan U. (Fla.) .....A: 330
Flint, Frank P. (Calif.) 3: 595
Foster, Murphy J. (La.) 10: 83
Frazier, James B. (Tenn.) 13: 532
Gallinger, Jacob H. (N. H.) ... 2: 247
Gamble, Robert J. (S. Dak.) ...12: 392
Gordon, James (Miss.) ....
Gore, Thomas P. (Okla.) 14: 323
Gronna, Asle J. (N. Dak.) 19: 420
Guggenheim, Simon (Colo.) .... C: 50
Hale, Eugene (Maine) 20: 220
Heyburn, Weldon B. (Idaho)....13: 101
Hughes, Charles J. (Colo.) 20: 43
Johnson, Martin N. (N. Dak.)..14: 489
Johnston, Joseph F. (Ala.) 10: 439
Jones, Wesley L. (Wash.) 14: 393
Kean, John (N. J.) 18: 152
LaFollette, Robert M. (Wis.) ...19: 425
Lodge, Henry C. (Mass.) 19: 52
Lorimer, William (Ill.) 14: 91
McCumber, Porter J. (N. Dak.) 13: 62
McEnery, Samuel D. (La.) 10: 83
McLaurin, Anselm J. (Miss.) ..13: 494
Martin, Thomas S. (Va.) 11: 30
Money, Hernando D. (Miss.) ...11: 492
Nelson, Knute (Minn.) 19: 18
Newlands, Francis G. (Nev.) ..13: 219
Nixon, George S. (Nev.) 14: 443
Oliver, George T. (Pa.) 22: 286
Overman, Lee S. (N. C.) 13: 305
Owen, Robert L. (Okla.) 14: 248
Page, Carroll S. (Vt.) 8: 329
Paynter, Thomas H. (Ky.) 12: 125
Penrose, Boies (Pa.) 2: 444
Percy, LeRoy (Miss.) 15: 107
Perkins, George C. (Calif.) 4: 111
Piles, Samuel H. (Wash.) 14: 389
Purcell, William E. (N. Dak.) ..
Rayner, Isidor (Md.) 13: 544
Richardson, Harry A. (Del.) ...14: 310
Root, Elihu (N. Y.) 26: 1
Scott, Nathan B. (W. Va.) 19: 59
Simmons, Furnifold McL. (N.C.)12: 517
Shively, Benjamin F. (Ind.) 14: 442

Smith, Ellison D. (S. C.) 14: 489
Smith, John W. (Md.) 13: 205
Smith, William A. (Mich.) 26: 53
Smoot, Reed (Utah) 13: 197
Stephenson, Isaac (Wis.) 14: 50
Stone, William J. (Mo.) 12: 308
Sutherland, George (Utah) 13: 413
Swanson, Claude A. (Va.) ..... D: 15
Taliaferro, James P. (Fla.) 10: 175
Taylor, Robert L. (Tenn.) 8: 365
Terrell, Joseph M. (Ga.) 12: 396
Thompson, Fountain L. (N.Dak.)
Thornton, John R. (La.) 18: 318
Tillman, Benjamin R. (S. C.) ..12: 180
Warner, William (Mo.) 20: 161
Warren, Francis E. (Wyo.) 23: 220
Watson, Clarence W. (W. Va.) .. C: 529
Wetmore, George P. (R. I.) 9: 407
Young, Lafayette (Iowa) ......

Sixty-second Congress (1911-13)

William P. Frye, Charles Curtis, Augustus O. Bacon, Jacob H. Gallinger, Henry Cabot Lodge and Frank B. Brandegee, presidents *pro tem.*

Ashurst, Henry F. (Ariz.) 15: 415
Bacon, Augustus O. (Ga.) 12: 527
Bailey, Joseph W. (Tex.) 13: 587
Bankhead, John H. (Ala.) 14: 210
Borah, William E. (Idaho) .... B: 115
Bourne, Jonathan, Jr. (Oreg.) .. B: 94
Bradley, William O'C. (Ky.) ...13: 12
Brady, James H. (Idaho) 15: 266
Brandegee, Frank B. (Conn.) ..13: 600
Briggs, Frank O. (N. J.) 14: 305
Bristow, Joseph L. (Kans.) 14: 29
Brown, Norris (Nebr.) 14: 328
Bryan, Nathan P. (Fla.) ...... C: 391
Burnham, Henry E. (N. H.) ...13: 43
Burton, Theodore E. (Ohio) 21: 50
Catron, Thomas B. (N. Mex.) ..
Chamberlain, George E. (Oreg.) .14: 135
Chilton, William E. (W. Va.) ..15: 343
Clapp, Moses E. (Minn.) 12: 232
Clark, Clarence D. (Wyo.) 13: 60
Clarke, James P. (Ark.) 10: 193
Crane, Winthrop M. (Mass.) ..13: 69
Crawford, Corie I. (S. Dak.) ..14: 200
Culberson, Charles A. (Tex.) .. 9: 76
Cullom, Shelby M. (Ill.) 11: 50
Cummins, Albert B. (Iowa) 13: 176
Curtis, Charles (Kans.) .... C: 7
Davis, Jefferson (Ark.) 13: 366
Dillingham, William P. (Vt.) .. 8: 411
Dixon, Joseph M. (Mont.) 14: 107
DuPont, Henry A. (Del.) 6: 457
Fall, Albert B. (N. Mex.) .....A: 355
Fletcher, Duncan U. (Fla.) .....A: 330
Foster, Murphy J. (La.) 10: 83
Frye, William P. (Maine) 1: 290
Gallinger, Jacob H. (N. H.) ... 2: 247
Gamble, Robert J. (S. Dak.) ...12: 392
Gardner, Obadiah (Maine) 15: 230
Gore, Thomas P. (Okla.) 14: 323
Gronna, Asle J. (N. Dak.) 19: 420
Guggenheim, Simon (Colo.) .... C: 50
Heiskell, John N. (Ark.) ......
Heyburn, Weldon B. (Idaho) ...13: 101
Hitchcock, Gilbert M. (Nebr.) ..25: 100
Jackson, William P. (Md.) 15: 48
Johnson, Charles F. (Maine) ..21: 193
Johnston, Joseph F. (Ala.) 10: 439
Johnston, Rienzi M. (Tex.) 21: 297
Jones, Wesley L. (Wash.) 14: 393
Kavanaugh, William M. (Ark.) .19: 419
Kenyon, William S. (Iowa) 24: 60
Kern, John W. (Ind.) 14: 137
LaFollette, Robert M. (Wis.) ..19: 425
Lea, Luke (Tenn.) 15: 26
Lippitt, Henry F. (R. I.) 25: 115
Lodge, Henry C. (Mass.) 19: 52
Lorimer, William (Ill.) 14: 91
McCumber, Porter J. (N. Dak.) .13: 62
McLean, George P. (Conn.) .... B: 395
Martin, Thomas S. (Va.) 11: 30
Martine, James E. (N. J.) 15: 145
Massey, William A. (Nev.) ....
Myers, Henry L. (Mont.) 15: 48
Nelson, Knute (Minn.) 19: 18
Newlands, Francis G. (Nev.) ...13: 219
Nixon, George S. (Nev.) 14: 443
O'Gorman, James A. (N. Y.) ..15: 13
Oliver, George T. (Pa.) 22: 286
Overman, Lee S. (N. C.) 13: 305
Owen, Robert L. (Okla.) 14: 248
Page, Carroll S. (Vt.) 8: 329
Paynter, Thomas H. (Ky.) 12: 125
Penrose, Boies (Pa.) 2: 444
Percy, LeRoy (Miss.) 15: 107
Perkins, George C. (Calif.) 4: 111
Perky, Kirtland I. (Idaho) .....
Pittman, Key (Nev.) .... B: 375
Poindexter, Miles (Wash.) 15: 211
Pomerene, Atlee (Ohio) .... C: 341
Rayner, Isidor (Md.) 13: 544
Reed, James A. (Mo.) 15: 99
Richardson, Harry A. (Del.) ...14: 310
Root, Elihu (N. Y.) 26: 1
Sanders, Newell (Tenn.) .... C: 312
Sheppard, Morris (Tex.) 15: 274
Shively, Benjamin F. (Ind.) 14: 442
Simmons, Furnifold McL. (N.C.) 12: 517
Smith, Ellison D. (S. C.) 14: 489
Smith, Hoke (Ga.) 1: 183
Smith, John W. (Md.) 13: 205
Smith, Marcus A. (Ariz.) 26: 95
Smith, William A. (Mich.) 26: 53
Smoot, Reed (Utah) 13: 197
Stephenson, Isaac (Wis.) 14: 50
Stone, William J. (Mo.) 12: 308
Sutherland, George (Utah) 13: 413
Swanson, Claude A. (Va.) ..... D: 15
Taylor, Robert L. (Tenn.) 8: 365
Terrell, Joseph M. (Ga.) 12: 396
Thomas, Charles S. (Colo.) 13: 362
Thornton, John R. (La.) 18: 318
Tillman, Benjamin R. (S. C.) ..12: 180
Townsend, Charles E. (Mich.) ..15: 220
Warren, Francis E. (Wyo.) 23: 220
Watson, Clarence W. (W. Va.) .. C: 529
Webb, William R. (Tenn.) .....
Wetmore, George P. (R. I.) 9: 407
Williams, John S. (Miss.) 13: 396
Works, John D. (Calif.) 13: 93
Young, Lafayette (Iowa) ......

Sixty-third Congress (1913-15)

Clarke, James P., president *pro tem.* 10: 193
Ashurst, Henry F. (Ariz.) 15: 415
Bacon, Augustus O. (Ga.) 12: 527
Bankhead, John H. (Ala.) 14: 210
Borah, William E. (Idaho) ..... B: 115
Bradley, William O. (Ky.) 13: 12
Brady, James H. (Idaho) 15: 266
Brandegee, Frank B. (Conn.) ..13: 600
Bristow, Joseph L. (Kans.) 14: 29
Bryan, Nathan P. (Fla.) ...... C: 391
Burleigh, Edwin C. (Maine) 1: 429
Burton, Theodore E. (Ohio) 21: 50
Camden, Johnson N. (Ky.) 20: 329
Catron, Thomas B. (N. Mex.) ..
Chamberlain, George E. (Oreg.) 14: 135
Chilton, William E. (W. Va.) ..15: 343
Clapp, Moses E. (Minn.) 12: 232
Clark, Clarence D. (Wyo.) 13: 60
Clarke, James P. (Ark.) 10: 193
Colt, LeBaron B. (R. I.) 15: 408
Crawford, Corie I. (S. Dak.) ..14: 200
Culberson, Charles A. (Tex.) .. 9: 76
Cummins, Albert B. (Iowa) 13: 176
Dillingham, William P. (Vt.) .. 8: 411
DuPont, Henry A. (Del.) 6: 457
Fall, Albert B. (N. Mex.) ......A: 355
Fletcher, Duncan U. (Fla.) ....A: 330
Gallinger, Jacob H. (N. H.) ... 2: 247
Goff, Nathan (W. Va.) ....
Gore, Thomas P. (Okla.) 14: 323
Gronna, Asle J. (N. Dak.) 19: 420
Hardwick, Thomas W. (Ga.) .. B: 296
Hitchcock, Gilbert M. (Nebr.) ..25: 100
Hollis, Henry F. (N. H.) 15: 272
Hughes, William (N. J.) 21: 307
Jackson, William P. (Md.) 15: 48
James, Ollie M. (Ky.) 15: 332
Johnson, Charles F. (Maine) ...21: 193
Johnston, Joseph F. (Ala.) 10: 439
Jones, Wesley L. (Wash.) 14: 393
Kenyon, William S. (Iowa) 24: 60
Kern, John W. (Ind.) 14: 137
LaFollette, Robert M. (Wis.) ...19: 425
Lane, Harry (Oreg.) 18: 212
Lea, Luke (Tenn.) 15: 26
Lee, Blair (Md.) .... C: 453
Lewis, J. Hamilton (Ill.) 15: 63
Lippitt, Henry F. (R. I.) 25: 115
Lodge, Henry C. (Mass.) 19: 52
McCumber, Porter J. (N. Dak.) .13: 62
McLean, George P. (Conn.) ... B: 395
Martin, Thomas S. (Va.) 11: 30
Martine, James E. (N. J.) 15: 145
Myers, Henry L. (Mont.) 15: 48
Nelson, Knute (Minn.) 19: 18
Newlands, Francis G. (Nev.) ..13: 219
Norris, George W. (Nebr.) ..... B: 171
O'Gorman, James A. (N. Y.) ..15: 13
Oliver, George T. (Pa.) 22: 286
Overman, Lee S. (N. C.) 13: 305
Owen, Robert L. (Okla.) 14: 248
Page, Carroll S. (Vt.) 8: 329
Penrose, Boies (Pa.) 2: 444
Perkins, George C. (Calif.) 4: 111
Pittman, Key (Nev.) .... B: 375
Poindexter, Miles (Wash.) 15: 211
Pomerene, Atlee (Ohio) .... C: 341
Ransdell, Joseph E. (La.) 15: 407
Reed, James A. (Mo.) 15: 99
Robinson, Joseph T. (Ark.) ... B: 193
Root, Elihu (N. Y.) 26: 1
Saulsbury, Willard (Del.) 15: 105
Shafroth, John F. (Colo.) 14: 502
Sheppard, Morris (Tex.) 15: 274
Sherman, Lawrence Y. (Ill.) ...15: 101
Shields, John K. (Tenn.) 26: 109
Shively, Benjamin F. (Ind.) ...14: 442
Simmons, Furnifold McL. (N.C.) 12: 517
Smith, Ellison D. (S. C.) 14: 489
Smith, Hoke (Ga.) 1: 183
Smith, John W. (Md.) 13: 205
Smith, Marcus A. (Ariz.) 26: 95
Smith, William A. (Mich.) 26: 53
Smoot, Reed (Utah) 13: 197
Stephenson, Isaac (Wis.) 14: 50
Sterling, Thomas (S. Dak.) 15: 287
Stone, William J. (Mo.) 12: 308
Sutherland, George (Utah) 13: 413
Swanson, Claude A. (Va.) ..... D: 15
Thomas, Charles S. (Colo.) ...13: 362
Thompson, William H. (Kans.) ..15: 57
Thornton, John R. (La.) 18: 318
Tillman, Benjamin R. (S. C.) ..12: 180
Townsend, Charles E. (Mich.) ..15: 220
Vardaman, James K. (Miss.) ...13: 495
Walsh, Thomas J. (Mont.) 24: 10
Warren, Francis E. (Wyo.) ...23: 220
Weeks, John W. (Mass.) 20: 4
West, William S. (Ga.) 18: 216
White, Frank S. (Ala.) ....
Williams, John S. (Miss.) 13: 396
Works, John D. (Calif.) 13: 93

Sixty-fourth Congress (1915-17)

Clarke, James P., and Saulsbury, Willard, presidents *pro tem.*

Ashurst, Henry F. (Ariz.) 15: 415
Bankhead, John H. (Ala.) 14: 210
Beckham, John C. W. (Ky.) ...13: 14
Borah, William E. (Idaho) ..... B: 115
Brady, James H. (Idaho) 15: 266
Brandegee, Frank B. (Conn.) ..13: 600
Broussard, Robert F. (La.) 15: 387
Bryan, Nathan P. (Fla.) .... C: 391
Burleigh, Edwin C. (Maine) 1: 429
Catron, Thomas B. (N. Mex.) ..
Chamberlain, George E. (Oreg.) 14: 135
Chilton, William E. (W. Va.) ..15: 343
Clapp, Moses E. (Minn.) 12: 232
Clark, Clarence D. (Wyo.) 13: 60
Clarke, James P. (Ark.) 10: 193
Colt, LeBaron B. (R. I.) 15: 408
Culberson, Charles A. (Tex.) ... 9: 76
Cummins, Albert B. (Iowa) 13: 176
Curtis, Charles (Kans.) .... C: 7
Dillingham, William P. (Vt.) .. 8: 411
DuPont, Henry A. (Del.) 6: 457
Fall, Albert B. (N. Mex.) ......A: 355
Fernald, Bert M. (Maine) 24: 157
Fletcher, Duncan U. (Fla.) .....A: 330
Gallinger, Jacob H. (N. H.) ... 2: 247
Goff, Nathan (W. Va.) ....
Gore, Thomas P. (Okla.) 14: 323
Gronna, Asle J. (N. Dak.) 19: 420
Harding, Warren G. (Ohio) 19: 268
Hardwick, Thomas W. (Ga.) .. B: 296
Hitchcock, Gilbert M. (Nebr.) ..25: 100
Hollis, Henry F. (N. H.) 15: 272
Hughes, William (N. J.) 21: 307
Husting, Paul O. (Wis.) 15: 332
James, Ollie M. (Ky.) 15: 332

Johnson, Charles F. (Maine) ..21: 193
Johnson, Edwin S. (S. Dak.) ...A: 365
Jones, Wesley L. (Wash.) 14: 393
Kenyon, William S. (Iowa) 24: 60
Kern, John W. (Ind.) 14: 137
Kirby, William F. (Ark.) ...... C: 191
LaFollette, Robert M. (Wis.) ...19: 425
Lane, Harry (Oreg.) 18: 212
Lea, Luke (Tenn.) 15: 26
Lee, Blair (Md.) .... C: 453
Lewis, J. Hamilton (Ill.) 15: 63
Lippitt, Henry F. (R. I.) 25: 115
Lodge, Henry C. (Mass.) 19: 52
McCumber, Porter J. (N. Dak.) 13: 62
McLean, George P. (Conn.) .... B: 395
Martin, Thomas S. (Va.) 11: 30
Martine, James E. (N. J.) 15: 145
Myers, Henry L. (Mont.) 15: 48
Nelson, Knute (Minn.) 19: 18
Newlands, Francis G. (Nev.) ..13: 219
Norris, George W. (Nebr.) .... B: 171
O'Gorman, James A. (N. Y.) ..15: 13
Oliver, George T. (Pa.) 22: 286
Overman, Lee S. (N. C.) 13: 305
Owen, Robert L. (Okla.) 14: 248
Page, Carroll S. (Vt.) 8: 329
Penrose, Boies (Pa.) 2: 444
Phelan, James D. (Calif.) 8: 478
Pittman, Key (Nev.) .... B: 375
Poindexter, Miles (Wash.) 15: 211
Pomerene, Atlee (Ohio) .... C: 341
Ransdell, Joseph E. (La.) 15: 407
Reed, James A. (Mo.) 15: 99
Robinson, Joseph T. (Ark.) .... B: 193
Saulsbury, Willard (Del.) 15: 105
Shafroth, John F. (Colo.) 14: 502
Sheppard, Morris (Tex.) 15: 274
Sherman, Lawrence Y. (Ill.) ...15: 101
Shields, John K. (Tenn.) 26: 109
Shively, Benjamin F. (Ind.) ...14: 442
Simmons, Furnifold McL. (N.C.) 12: 517
Smith, Ellison D. (S. C.) 14: 489
Smith, Hoke (Ga.) 1: 183
Smith, John W. (Md.) 13: 205
Smith, Marcus A. (Ariz.) 26: 95
Smith, William A. (Mich.) 26: 53
Smoot, Reed (Utah) 13: 197
Sterling, Thomas (S. Dak.) 15: 287
Stone, William J. (Mo.) 12: 308
Sutherland, George (Utah) 13: 413
Swanson, Claude A. (Va.) .... D: 15
Taggart, Thomas (Ind.) ....
Thomas, Charles S. (Colo.) 13: 362
Thompson, William H. (Kans.) ..15: 57
Tillman, Benjamin R. (S. C.) ..12: 180
Townsend, Charles E. (Mich.) ..15: 220
Underwood, Oscar W. (Ala.) ...21: 22
Vardaman, James K. (Miss.) ..13: 495
Wadsworth, James W.,Jr.(N.Y.) 15: 34
Walsh, Thomas J. (Mont.) 24: 10
Warren, Francis E. (Wyo.) 23: 220
Watson, James E. (Ind.) ......A: 409
Weeks, John W. (Mass.) 20: 4
Williams, John S. (Miss.) 13: 396
Works, John D. (Calif.) 13: 93

Sixty-fifth Congress (1917-19)

Saulsbury, Willard, president *pro tem.* 15: 105
Ashurst, Henry F. (Ariz.) 15: 415
Baird, David (N. J.) 20: 38
Bankhead, John H. (Ala.) 14: 210
Beckham, John C. W. (Ky.) 13: 14
Benet, Christie (S. C.) ....A: 238
Borah, William E. (Idaho) .... B: 115
Brady, James H. (Idaho) 15: 266
Brandegee, Frank B. (Conn.) ..13: 600
Broussard, Robert F. (La.) 15: 387
Calder, William M. (N. Y.) .... C: 203
Chamberlain, George E. (Oreg.) 14: 135
Colt, LeBaron B. (R. I.) 15: 408
Culberson, Charles A. (Tex.) .. 9: 76
Cummins, Albert B. (Iowa) 13: 176
Curtis, Charles (Kans.) .... C: 7
Dillingham, William P. (Vt.) .. 8: 411
Drew, Irving W. (N. H.) 21: 229
Fall, Albert B. (N. Mex.) ......A: 355
Fernald, Bert M. (Maine) 24: 157
Fletcher, Duncan U. (Fla.) ....A: 330
France, Joseph I. (Md.) .... C: 143
Frelinghuysen, Joseph S. (N. J.) C: 252
Gallinger, Jacob H. (N. H.) ... 2: 247
Gay, Edward J. (La.) ....
Gerry, Peter G. (R. I.) .... B: 508
Goff, Nathan (W. Va.) ....
Gore, Thomas P. (Okla.) 14: 323
Gronna, Asle J. (N. Dak.) 19: 420
Guion, Walter (La.) 24: 382
Hale, Frederick (Maine) .... B: 181
Harding, Warren G. (Ohio) ...19: 268
Hardwick, Thomas W. (Ga.) .. B: 296
Henderson, Charles B. (Nev.) ..A: 306
Hitchcock, Gilbert M. (Nebr.) ..25: 100
Hollis, Henry F. (N. H.) 15: 272
Husting, Paul O. (Wis.) 15: 332
James, Ollie M. (Ky.) 15: 332
Johnson, Edwin S. (S. Dak.) ...A: 365
Johnson, Hiram W. (Calif.) ...15: 133
Jones, Andrieus A. (N. Mex.) ..20: 18
Jones, Wesley L. (Wash.) 14: 393
Kellogg, Frank B. (Minn.) .....A: 8
Kendrick, John B. (Wyo.) ..... B: 459
Kenyon, William S. (Iowa) 24: 60
King, William H. (Utah) ......
Kirby, William F. (Ark.) ...... C: 191
Knox, Philander C. (Pa.) 24: 7
LaFollette, Robert M. (Wis.) ...19: 425
Lane, Harry (Oreg.) 18: 212
Lenroot, Irvine L. (Wis.) ...... B: 184
Lewis, J. Hamilton (Ill.) 15: 63
Lodge, Henry C. (Mass.) 19: 52
McCumber, Porter J. (N. Dak.) .13: 62
McKellar, Kenneth D. (Tenn.) .. C: 427
McLean, George P. (Conn.) ... B: 395
McNary, Charles L. (Oreg.) .... B: 400
Martin, George B. (Ky.) .... D: 241
Martin, Thomas S. (Va.) 11: 30
Moses, George H. (N. H.) ..... C: 71
Mulkey, Frederick W. (Oreg.) ..23: 140
Myers, Henry L. (Mont.) 15: 48
Nelson, Knute (Minn.) 19: 18
New, Harry S. (Ind.) ....A: 13
Newlands, Francis G. (Nev.) ..13: 219
Norris, George W. (Nebr.) ..... B: 171
Nugent, John F. (Idaho) ....A: 425
Overman, Lee S. (N. C.) 13: 305
Owen, Robert L. (Okla.) 14: 248
Page, Carroll S. (Vt.) 8: 329
Penrose, Boies (Pa.) 2: 444
Phelan, James D. (Calif.) 8: 478
Pittman, Key (Nev.) .... B: 375
Poindexter, Miles (Wash.) 15: 211
Pollock, William P. (S. C.) 19: 41
Pomerene, Atlee (Ohio) .... C: 341
Ransdell, Joseph E. (La.) 15: 407
Reed, James A. (Mo.) 15: 99
Robinson, Joseph T. (Ark.) .... B: 193
Saulsbury, Willard (Del.) 15: 105
Shafroth, John F. (Colo.) 14: 502
Sheppard, Morris (Tex.) 15: 274
Sherman, Lawrence Y. (Ill.) ..15: 101
Shields, John K. (Tenn.) 26: 109
Simmons, Furnifold McL. (N.C.) 12: 517
Smith, Ellison D. (S. C.) 14: 489
Smith, Hoke (Ga.) 1: 183
Smith, John W. (Md.) 13: 205
Smith, Marcus A. (Ariz.) 26: 95
Smith, William A. (Mich.) 26: 53
Smoot, Reed (Utah) 13: 197
Spencer, Selden P. (Mo.) 20: 193
Sterling, Thomas (S. Dak.) 15: 287
Stone, William J. (Mo.) 12: 308
Sutherland, Howard (W. Va.) ..A: 29
Swanson, Claude A. (Va.) ..... D: 15
Thomas, Charles S. (Colo.) 13: 362
Thompson, William H. (Kans.) .15: 57
Tillman, Benjamin R. (S. C.) ..12: 180
Townsend, Charles E. (Mich.) ..15: 220
Trammell, Park (Fla.) ....A: 180
Underwood, Oscar W. (Ala.) ...21: 22
Vardaman, James K. (Miss.) ...13: 495
Wadsworth, James W.,Jr.(N.Y.) 15: 34
Walsh, Thomas J. (Mont.) 24: 10
Warren, Francis E. (Wyo.) 23: 220
Watson, James E. (Ind.) ...... A: 409
Weeks, John W. (Mass.) 20: 4
Wilfley, Xenophon P. (Mo.) .... C: 364
Williams, John S. (Miss.) 13: 396
Wolcott, Josiah O. (Del.) ....A: 235

Sixty-sixth Congress (1919-21)

Cummins, Albert B., president *pro tem.* 13: 176
Ashurst, Henry F. (Ariz.) 15: 415
Ball, Lewis H. (Del.) 13: 546
Bankhead, John H. (Ala.) 14: 210
Beckham, John C. W. (Ky.) ...13: 14
Borah, William E. (Idaho) ..... B: 115
Brandegee, Frank B. (Conn.) ..13: 600
Calder, William M. (N. Y.) .... C: 203
Capper, Arthur (Kans.) .... C: 58
Chamberlain, George E. (Oreg.) 14: 135
Colt, LeBaron B. (R. I.) 15: 408
Comer, Braxton B. (Ala.) 14: 91
Culberson, Charles A. (Tex.) ... 9: 76
Cummins, Albert B. (Iowa) 13: 176
Curtis, Charles (Kans.) .... C: 7
Dial, Nathaniel B. (S. C.) .....A: 85
Dillingham, William P. (Vt.) .. 8: 411
Edge, Walter E. (N. J.) .... B: 279
Elkins, Davis (W. Va.) .... C: 527
Fall, Albert B. (N. Mex.) ......A: 355
Fernald, Bert M. (Maine) 24: 157
Fletcher, Duncan U. (Fla.) ....A: 330
France, Joseph I. (Md.) .... C: 143
Frelinghuysen, Joseph S. (N. J.) C: 252
Gay, Edward J. (La.) ....
Gerry, Peter G. (R. I.) .... B: 508
Glass, Carter (Va.) ....A: 36
Gooding, Frank R. (Idaho) 21: 7
Gore, Thomas P. (Okla.) 14: 323
Gronna, Asle J. (N. Dak.) 19: 420
Hale, Frederick (Maine) .... B: 181
Harding, Warren G. (Ohio) ...19: 268
Harris, William J. (Ga.) 24: 266
Harrison, Byron P. (Miss.) ... A: 173
Heflin, J. Thomas (Ala.) ...... B: 60
Henderson, Charles B. (Nev.) ...A: 306
Hitchcock, Gilbert M. (Nebr.) ..25: 100
Johnson, Edwin S. (S. Dak.) ..A: 365
Johnson, Hiram W. (Calif.) ...15: 133
Jones, Andrieus A. (N. Mex.) ..20: 18
Jones, Wesley L. (Wash.) 14: 393
Kellogg, Frank B. (Minn.) .....A: 8
Kendrick, John B. (Wyo.) ..... B: 459
Kenyon, William S. (Iowa) 24: 60
Keyes, Henry W. (N. H.) ..... C: 245
King, William H. (Utah) ......
Kirby, William F. (Ark.) ...... C: 191
Knox, Philander C. (Pa.) 24: 7
LaFollette, Robert M. (Wis.) ...19: 425
Lenroot, Irvine L. (Wis.) ...... B: 184
Lodge, Henry C. (Mass.) 19: 52
McCormick, Medill (Ill.) 19: 94
McCumber, Porter J. (N. Dak.) 13: 62
McKellar, Kenneth D. (Tenn.) .. C: 427
McLean, George P. (Conn.) ... B: 395
McNary, Charles L. (Oreg.) .... B: 400
Martin, Thomas S. (Va.) 11: 30
Moses, George H. (N. H.) ..... C: 71
Myers, Henry L. (Mont.) 15: 48
Nelson, Knute (Minn.) 19: 18
New, Harry S. (Ind.) ....A: 13
Newberry, Truman H. (Mich.)..14: 26
Norris, George W. (Nebr.) .... B: 171
Nugent, John F. (Idaho) ......A: 425
Overman, Lee S. (N. C.) 13: 305
Owen, Robert L. (Okla.) 14: 248
Page, Carroll S. (Vt.) 8: 329
Penrose, Boies (Pa.) 2: 444
Phelan, James D. (Calif.) 8: 478
Phipps, Lawrence C. (Colo.) ....A: 328
Pittman, Key (Nev.) .... B: 375
Poindexter, Miles (Wash.) 15: 211
Pomerene, Atlee (Ohio) .... C: 341
Ransdell, Joseph E. (La.) 15: 407
Reed, James A. (Mo.) 15: 99
Robinson, Joseph T. (Ark.) .... B: 193
Sheppard, Morris (Tex.) 15: 274
Sherman, Lawrence Y. (Ill.) ...15: 101
Shields, John K. (Tenn.) 26: 109
Simmons, Furnifold McL. (N.C.) 12: 517
Smith, Ellison D. (S. C.) 14: 489
Smith, Hoke (Ga.) 1: 183
Smith, John W. (Md.) 13: 205
Smith, Marcus A. (Ariz.) 26: 95
Smoot, Reed (Utah) 13: 197
Spencer, Selden P. (Mo.) 20: 193
Stanley, A. Owsley (Ky.) ......A: 422
Sterling, Thomas (S. Dak.) 15: 287
Sutherland, Howard (W. Va.) ..A: 29
Swanson, Claude A. (Va.) ..... D: 15
Thomas, Charles S. (Colo.) 13: 362
Townsend, Charles E. (Mich.) ..15: 220
Trammell, Park (Fla.) ....A: 180
Underwood, Oscar W. (Ala.) ...21: 22
Wadsworth, James W.,Jr.(N.Y.) 15: 34
Walsh, David I. (Mass.) 15: 99
Walsh, Thomas J. (Mont.) 24: 10
Warren, Francis E. (Wyo.) 23: 220
Watson, James E. (Ind.) ...... A: 409
Williams, John S. (Miss.) 13: 396
Willis, Frank B. (Ohio) 21: 445
Wolcott, Josiah O. (Del.) ....A: 235

Sixty-seventh Congress (1921-23)

Cummins, Albert B., president *pro tem.* 13:176
Ashurst, Henry F. (Ariz.) 15:415
Ball, Lewis H. (Del.) 13:546
Bayard, Thomas F. (Del.) C:152
Borah, William E. (Idaho) B:115
Brandegee, Frank B. (Conn.) ..13:600
Brookhart, Smith W. (Iowa) .. B:276
Broussard, Edwin S. (La.) C:421
Bursum, Holm O. (N. Mex.) ... C:524
Calder, William M. (N. Y.) ... C:203
Cameron, Ralph H. (Ariz.) ....
Capper, Arthur (Kans.) .... C: 58
Caraway, Thaddeus H. (Ark.) ..A:123
Colt, LeBaron B. (R. I.) 15:408
Couzens, James (Mich.) A:216
Crow, William E. (Pa.) 19:411
Culberson, Charles A. (Tex.) ... 9: 76
Cummins, Albert B. (Iowa) 13:176
Curtis, Charles (Kans.) .... C: 7
Dial, Nathaniel B. (S. C.) ....A: 85
Dillingham, William P. (Vt.) .. 8:411
DuPont, T. Coleman (Del.) A:310
Edge, Walter E. (N. J.) B:279
Elkins, Davis (W. Va.) C:527
Ernst, Richard P. (Ky.) A:333
Fall, Albert B. (N. Mex.) A:355
Felton, Mrs. Rebecca L. ....
Fernald, Bert M. (Maine) 24:157
Fletcher, Duncan U. (Fla.) A:330
France, Joseph I. (Md.) C:143
Frelinghuysen, Joseph S. (N. J.) C:252
George, Walter F. (Ga.) A:521
Gerry, Peter G. (R. I.) B:508
Glass, Carter (Va.) ....A: 36
Gooding, Frank R. (Idaho) 21: 7
Hale, Frederick (Maine) B:181
Harreld, John W. (Okla.) B:426
Harris, William J. (Ga.) 24:266
Harrison, Byron P. (Miss.) A:173
Heflin, J. Thomas (Ala.) ...... B: 60
Hitchcock, Gilbert M. (Nebr.) ..12:100
Johnson, Hiram W. (Calif.) 15:133
Jones, Andrieus A. (N. Mex.) ..20: 18
Jones, Wesley L. (Wash.) 14:393
Kellogg, Frank B. (Minn.) ....A: 8
Kendrick, John B. (Wyo.) B:459
Kenyon, William S. (Iowa) 24: 60
Keyes, Henry W. (N. H.) C:245
King, William H. (Utah) ......
Knox, Philander C. (Pa.) 24: 7
Ladd, Edwin F. (N. Dak.) 19:432
LaFollette, Robert M. (Wis.) ..19:425
Lenroot, Irvine L. (Wis.) B:184
Lodge, Henry C. (Mass.) 19: 52
McCormick, Medill (Ill.) 19: 94
McCumber, Porter J. (N. Dak.) 13: 62
McKellar, Kenneth D. (Tenn.) .. C:427
McKinley, William B. (Ill.) 15:115
McLean, George P. (Conn.) ... B:395
McNary, Charles L. (Oreg.) B:400
Moses, George H. (N. H.) ..... C: 71
Myers, Henry L. (Mont.) 15: 48
Nelson, Knute (Minn.) 19: 18
New, Harry S. (Ind.) ....A: 13
Newberry, Truman H. (Mich.) ..14: 26
Nicholson, Samuel D. (Colo.) ..23: 52
Norbeck, Peter (S. Dak.) B:479
Norris, George W. (Nebr.) B:171
Oddie, Tasker L. (Nev.) ....A: 83
Overman, Lee S. (N. C.) 13:305
Owen, Robert L. (Okla.) 14:248
Page, Carroll S. (Vt.) 8:329
Penrose, Boies (Pa.) 2:444
Pepper, George W. (Pa.) A:469
Phipps, Lawrence C. (Colo.) ...A:328
Pittman, Key (Nev.) B:375
Poindexter, Miles (Wash.) 15:211
Pomerene, Atlee (Ohio) C:341
Ransdell, Joseph E. (La.) 15:407
Rawson, Charles A. (Iowa) ....
Reed, David A. (Pa.) B:384
Reed, James A. (Mo.) 15: 99
Robinson, Joseph T. (Ark.) B:193
Sheppard, Morris (Tex.) 15:274
Shields, John K. (Tenn.) 26:109
Shortridge, Samuel M. (Calif.) B:193
Simmons, Furnifold McL. (N.C.) 12:517
Smith, Ellison D. (S. C.) 14:489
Smoot, Reed (Utah) 13:197
Spencer, Selden P. (Mo.) 20:193
Stanfield, Robert N. (Oreg.) ... C:133
Stanley, A. Owsley (Ky.) A:422
Sterling, Thomas (S. Dak.) 15:287
Sutherland, Howard (W. Va.) ..A: 29
Swanson, Claude A. (Va.) ..... D: 15
Townsend, Charles E. (Mich.) ..15:220
Trammell, Park (Fla.) A:180
Underwood, Oscar W. (Ala.) ...21: 22
Wadsworth, James W.,Jr.(N.Y.) 15: 34
Walsh, David I. (Mass.) 15: 99
Walsh, Thomas J. (Mont.) 24: 10
Warren, Francis E. (Wyo.) ...23:220
Watson, James E. (Ind.) A:409
Watson, Thomas E. (Ga.) ......
Weller, Ovington E. (Md.) ....
Williams, John S. (Miss.) 13:396
Willis, Frank B. (Ohio) 21:445
Wolcott, Josiah O. (Del.) A:235

Sixty-eighth Congress (1923-25)

Cummins, Albert B., president *pro tem.* 13:176
Adams, Alva B. (Colo.) B:162
Ashurst, Henry F. (Ariz.) 15:415
Ball, Lewis H. (Del.) 13:546
Bayard, Thomas F. (Del.) C:152
Bingham, Hiram (Conn.) ...... A: 28
Borah, William E. (Idaho) B:115
Brandegee, Frank B. (Conn.) ..13:600
Brookhart, Smith W. (Iowa) ... B:276
Broussard, Edwin S. (La.) C:421
Bruce, William C. (Md.) 18: 47
Bursum, Holm O. (N. Mex.) ... C:524
Butler, William M. (Mass.) B:192
Cameron, Ralph H. (Ariz.) ....
Capper, Arthur (Kans.) .... C: 58
Caraway, Thaddeus H. (Ark.) .. A:123
Colt, LeBaron B. (R. I.) 15:408
Copeland, Royal S. (N. Y.) 15:358
Couzens, James (Mich.) A:216
Curtis, Charles (Kans.) .... C: 7
Dale, Porter H. (Vt.) B:397
Deneen, Charles S. (Ill.) 14:364
Dial, Nathaniel B. (S. C.) ..... A: 85
Dill, Clarence C. (Wash.) B:200
Dillingham, William P. (Vt.) .. 8:411
Edge, Walter E. (N. J.) B:279
Edwards, Edward I. (N. J.) ...24:256
Elkins, Davis (W. Va.) C:527
Ernst, Richard P. (Ky.) A:333
Fernald, Bert M. (Maine) 24:157
Ferris, Woodbridge N. (Mich.) ..15:213
Fess, Simeon D. (Ohio) C:283
Fletcher, Duncan U. (Fla.) A:330
Frazier, Lynn J. (N. Dak.) B:189
George, Walter F. (Ga.) A:521
Gerry, Peter G. (R. I.) B:508
Glass, Carter (Va.) .... A: 36
Gooding, Frank R. (Idaho) 21: 7
Greene, Frank L. (Vt.) 25: 92
Hale, Frederick (Maine) B:181
Harreld, John W. (Okla.) B:426
Harris, William J. (Ga.) 24:266
Harrison, Byron P. (Miss.) A:173
Heflin, J. Thomas (Ala.) ...... B: 60
Howell, Robert B. (Nebr.) C:390
Johnson, Hiram W. (Calif.) ...15:133
Johnson, Magnus (Minn.) ......
Jones, Andrieus A. (N. Mex.) ..20: 18
Jones, Wesley L. (Wash.) 14:393
Kendrick, John B. (Wyo.) B:459
Keyes, Henry W. (N. H.) C:245
King, William H. (Utah) ......
Ladd, Edwin F. (N. Dak.) 19:432
LaFollette, Robert M. (Wis.) ..19:425
Lenroot, Irvine L. (Wis.) B:184
Lodge, Henry C. (Mass.) 19: 52
McCormick, Medill (Ill.) 19: 94
McKellar, Kenneth D. (Tenn.) .. C:427
McKinley, William B. (Ill.) 15:115
McLean, George P. (Conn.) B:395
McNary, Charles L. (Oreg.) B:400
Mayfield, Earle B. (Tex.) C:440
Means, Rice W. (Colo.) C:177
Metcalf, Jesse H. (R. I.) ....
Moses, George H. (N. H.) ..... C: 71
Neely, Matthew M. (W. Va.) ... C:104
Nelson, Knute (Minn.) 19: 18
Nicholson, Samuel D. (Colo.) ...23: 52
Norbeck, Peter (S. Dak.) B:479
Norris, George W. (Nebr.) B:171
Oddie, Tasker L. (Nev.) .... A: 83
Overman, Lee S. (N. C.) 13:305
Owen, Robert L. (Okla.) 14:248
Pepper, George W. (Pa.) A:469
Phipps, Lawrence C. (Colo.) ... A:328
Pittman, Key (Nev.) B:375
Ralston, Samuel M. (Ind.) 15:142
Ransdell, Joseph E. (La.) 15:407
Reed, David A. (Pa.) B:384
Reed, James A. (Mo.) 15: 99
Robinson, Joseph T. (Ark.) B:193
Sheppard, Morris (Tex.) 15:274
Shields, John K. (Tenn.) 26:109
Shipstead, Henrik (Minn.) B:256
Shortridge, Samuel M. (Calif.) .. B:193
Simmons, Furnifold McL. (N.C.) 12:517
Smith, Ellison D. (S. C.) 14:489
Smoot, Reed (Utah) 13:197
Spencer, Selden P. (Mo.) 20:193
Stanfield, Robert N. (Oreg.) C:133
Stanley, A. Owsley (Ky.) A:422
Stephens, Hubert D. (Miss.) C:215
Sterling, Thomas (S. Dak.) 15:287
Swanson, Claude A. (Va.) ..... D: 15
Trammell, Park (Fla.) A:180
Underwood, Oscar W. (Ala.) ...21: 22
Wadsworth, James W.,Jr.(N.Y.) 15: 34
Walsh, David I. (Mass.) 15: 99
Walsh, Thomas J. (Mont.) 24: 10
Warren, Francis E. (Wyo.) ...23:220
Watson, James E. (Ind.) A:409
Weller, Ovington E. (Md.) ....
Wheeler, Burton K. (Mont.) ... A:153
Willis, Frank B. (Ohio) 21:445

Sixty-ninth Congress (1925-27)

Cummins, Albert B., and Moses, George H., presidents *pro tem.*
Ashurst, Henry F. (Ariz.) 15:415
Bayard, Thomas F. (Del.) C:152
Bingham, Hiram (Conn.) ...... A: 28
Blease, Coleman L. (S. C.) 15:276
Borah, William E. (Idaho) B:115
Bratton, Sam G. (N. Mex.) B:488
Brookhart, Smith W. (Iowa) ... B:276
Broussard, Edwin S. (La.) C:421
Bruce, William C. (Md.) 18: 47
Butler, William M. (Mass.) B:192
Cameron, Ralph H. (Ariz.) ....
Capper, Arthur (Kans.) .... C: 58
Caraway, Thaddeus H. (Ark.) .. A:123
Copeland, Royal S. (N. Y.) 15:358
Couzens, James (Mich.) A:216
Cummins, Albert B. (Iowa) 13:176
Curtis, Charles (Kans.) .... C: 7
Dale, Porter H. (Vt.) B:397
Deneen, Charles S. (Ill.) 14:364
Dill, Clarence C. (Wash.) B:200
DuPont, T. Coleman (Del.) A:310
Edge, Walter E. (N. J.) B:279
Edwards, Edward I. (N. J.) ...24:256
Ernst, Richard P. (Ky.) A:333
Fernald, Bert M. (Maine) 24:157
Ferris, Woodbridge N. (Mich.) ..15:213
Fess, Simeon D. (Ohio) C:283
Fletcher, Duncan U. (Fla.) A:330
Frazier, Lynn J. (N. Dak.) B:189
George, Walter F. (Ga.) A:521
Gerry, Peter G. (R. I.) B:508
Gillett, Frederick H. (Mass.) ... B:198
Glass, Carter (Va.) .... A: 36
Goff, Guy D. (W. Va.) 24: 24
Gooding, Frank R. (Idaho) 21: 7
Gould, Arthur R. (Maine) C:439
Greene, Frank L. (Vt.) 25: 92
Hale, Frederick (Maine) B:181
Harreld, John W. (Okla.) B:426
Harris, William J. (Ga.) 24:266
Harrison, Byron P. (Miss.) A:173
Hawes, Harry B. (Mo.) .... C: 65
Heflin, J. Thomas (Ala.) ...... B: 60
Howell, Robert B. (Nebr.) C:390
Johnson, Hiram W. (Calif.) ...15:133
Jones, Andrieus A. (N. Mex.) ..20: 18
Kendrick, John B. (Wyo.) B:459
Keyes, Henry W. (N. H.) C:245
King, William H. (Utah) ......
Ladd, Edwin F. (N. Dak.) 19:432
LaFollette, Robert M. (Wis.) 19:425
LaFollette, Robert M., Jr. (Wis.) C:351
Lenroot, Irvine L. (Wis.) B:184
McKellar, Kenneth D. (Tenn.) .. C:427
McKinley, William B. (Ill.) 15:115
McLean, George P. (Conn.) B:395
McMaster, William H. (S. Dak.) C: 39
McNary, Charles L. (Oreg.) ... B:400

Mayfield, Earle B. (Tex.) ...... C: 440
Means, Rice W. (Colo.) .... C: 177
Metcalf, Jesse H. (R. I.) ......
Moses, George H. (N. H.) ..... C: 71
Neely, Matthew M. (W. Va.) .. C: 104
Norbeck, Peter (S. Dak.) ...... B: 479
Norris, George W. (Nebr.) .... B: 171
Nye, Gerald P. (N. Dak.) ..... C: 360
Oddie, Tasker L. (Nev.) .... A: 83
Overman, Lee S. (N. C.) 13: 305
Pepper, George W. (Pa.) ...... A: 469
Phipps, Lawrence C. (Colo.) ... A: 328
Pine, William B. (Okla.) ...... A: 484
Pittman, Key (Nev.) .... B: 375
Ralston, Samuel M. (Ind.) 15: 142
Ransdell, Joseph E. (La.) 15: 407
Reed, David A. (Pa.) .... B: 384
Reed, James A. (Mo.) 15: 99
Robinson, Arthur R. (Ind.) .... B: 366
Robinson, Joseph T. (Ark.) .... B: 193
Sackett, Frederic M. (Ky.) ..... B: 421
Schall, Thomas D. (Minn.) ..... C: 337
Sheppard, Morris (Tex.) 15: 274
Shipstead, Henrik (Minn.) .... B: 256
Shortridge, Samuel M. (Calif.) .. B: 193
Simmons, Furnifold McL. (N.C.) 12: 517
Smith, Ellison D. (S. C.) 14: 489
Smoot, Reed (Utah) 13: 197
Spencer, Selden P. (Mo.) 20: 193
Stanfield, Robert N. (Oreg.) .. C: 133
Steck, Daniel F. (Iowa) .... C: 196
Stephens, Hubert D. (Miss.) .... C: 215
Stewart, David W. (Iowa) ....
Swanson, Claude A. (Va.) ..... D: 15
Trammell, Park (Fla.) .... A: 180
Tyson, Lawrence D. (Tenn.) ...21: 487
Underwood, Oscar W. (Ala.) ...21: 22
Wadsworth, James W., Jr. (N.Y.) 15: 34
Walsh, David I. (Mass.) 15: 99
Walsh, Thomas J. (Mont.) 24: 10
Warren, Francis E. (Wyo.) ...23: 220
Watson, James E. (Ind.) ...... A: 409
Weller, Ovington E. (Md.) .....
Wheeler, Burton K. (Mont.) ... A: 153
Williams, George H. (Mo.) ....
Willis, Frank B. (Ohio) 21: 445

Seventieth Congress (1927-29)

Moses, George H. president *pro tem.* .... C: 71
Ashurst, Henry F. (Ariz.) 15: 415
Barkley, Alben W. (Ky.) ...... C: 411
Bayard, Thomas F. (Del.) ..... C: 152
Bingham, Hiram (Conn.) ...... A: 28
Black, Hugo L. (Ala.) .... C: 502
Blaine, John J. (Wis.) .... B: 110
Blease, Coleman L. (S. C.) 15: 276
Borah, William E. (Idaho) .... B: 115
Bratton, Sam G. (N. Mex.) .... B: 488
Brookhart, Smith W. (Iowa) ... B: 276
Broussard, Edwin S. (La.) ..... C: 421
Bruce, William C. (Md.) 18: 47
Capper, Arthur (Kans.) .... C: 58
Caraway, Thaddeus H. (Ark.) .. A: 123
Copeland, Royal S. (N. Y.) 15: 358
Couzens, James (Mich.) .... A: 216
Curtis, Charles (Kans.) .... C: 7
Cutting, Bronson M. (N. Mex.) 26: 443
Dale, Porter H. (Vt.) .... B: 397
Deneen, Charles S. (Ill.) 14: 364
Dill, Clarence C. (Wash.) ...... B: 200
DuPont, T. Coleman (Del.) .... A: 310
Edge, Walter E. (N. J.) ...... B: 279
Edwards, Edward I. (N. J.) 24: 256
Ferris, Woodbridge N. (Mich.) ..15: 213
Fess, Simeon D. (Ohio) .... C: 283
Fletcher, Duncan U. (Fla.) .... A: 330
Frazier, Lynn J. (N. Dak.) .... B: 189
George, Walter F. (Ga.) .... A: 521
Gerry, Peter G. (R. I.) .... B: 508
Gillett, Frederick H. (Mass.) ... B: 198
Glass, Carter (Va.) .... A: 36
Goff, Guy D. (W. Va.) 24: 24
Gooding, Frank R. (Idaho) 21: 7
Gould, Arthur R. (Maine) ..... C: 439
Greene, Frank L. (Vt.) 25: 92
Hale, Frederick (Maine) .... B: 181
Harris, William J. (Ga.) 24: 266
Harrison, Byron P. (Miss.) .... A: 173
Hastings, Daniel O. (Del.) .....
Hawes, Harry B. (Mo.) .... C: 65
Hayden, Carl T. (Ariz.) .... C: 218
Heflin, J. Thomas (Ala.) ...... B: 60
Howell, Robert B. (Nebr.) ..... C: 390
Johnson, Hiram W. (Calif.) ...15: 133
Jones, Wesley L. (Wash.) 14: 393
Kendrick, John B. (Wyo.) ..... B: 459
Keyes, Henry W. (N. H.) ..... C: 245
King, William H. (Utah) ......
LaFollette, Robert M., Jr. (Wis.) C: 351
McKellar, Kenneth D. (Tenn.) .. C: 427
McLean, George P. (Conn.) 13: 370
McMaster, William H. (S. Dak.) C: 39
McNary, Charles L. (Oreg.) .... B: 400
Mayfield, Earle B. (Tex.) ...... C: 440
Metcalf, Jesse H. (R. I.) ......
Neely, Matthew M. (W. Va.) .. C: 104
Norbeck, Peter (S. Dak.) ...... B: 479
Norris, George (Nebr.) .... B: 86
Nye, Gerald P. (N. Dak.) ...... C: 360
Oddie, Tasker L. (Nev.) .... A: 83
Overman, Lee S. (N. C.) 13: 305
Phipps, Laurence C. (Colo.) .... A: 328
Pine, William B. (Okla.) ...... A: 484
Pittman, Key (Nev.) .... B: 375
Ransdell, Joseph E. (La.) 15: 407
Reed, David A. (Pa.) .... B: 384
Reed, James A. (Mo.) 15: 99
Robinson, Arthur R. (Ind.) .... B: 366
Robinson, Joseph T. (Ark.) ... B: 193
Sackett, Frederick M. (Ky.) .... B: 421
Schall, Thomas D. (Minn.) .... C: 337
Sheppard, Morris (Tex.) 15: 274
Shipstead, Henrik (Minn.) .... B: 256
Shortridge, Samuel M. (Calif.).. B: 193
Simmons, Furnifold McL. (N.C.) 12: 517
Smith, Ellison D. (S. C.) 14: 489
Smoot, Reed (Utah) 13: 197
Steck, Daniel F. (Iowa) .... C: 196
Steiwer, Frederick (Oreg.) ....
Stephens, Hubert D. (Miss.) .... C: 215
Swanson, Claude A. (Va.) ..... D: 15
Thomas, Elmer (Okla.) .... C: 106
Thomas, John (Idaho) .... D: 139
Trammell, Park (Fla.) .... A: 180
Tydings, Millard E. (Md.) ..... C: 302
Tyson, Lawrence D. (Tenn.) ...21: 487
Vandenberg, Arthur H. (Mich.) D: 394
Wagner, Robert F. (N. Y.) .... D: 39
Walsh, David I. (Mass.) 15: 99
Walsh, Thomas J. (Mont.) 24: 10
Warren, Francis E. (Wyo.) ...23: 220
Waterman, Charles W. (Colo.) ..24: 258
Watson, James E. (Ind.) ...... A: 409
Wheeler, Burton K. (Mont.) ... A: 153
Willis, Frank B. (Ohio) 21: 445

Seventy-first Congress (1929-31)

Moses, George H., president *pro tem.* .... C: 71
Allen, Henry J. (Kans.) ......
Ashurst, Henry F. (Ariz.) 15: 415
Baird, David, Jr. ....
Barkley, Alben W. (Ky.) ...... C: 411
Bingham, Hiram (Conn.) ...... A: 28
Black, Hugo L. (Ala.) .... C: 502
Blaine, John J. (Wis.) .... B: 110
Blease, Coleman L. (S. C.) 15: 276
Borah, William E. (Idaho) ..... B: 115
Bratton, Sam G. (N. Mex.) .... B: 488
Brock, William E. (Tenn.) .....
Brookhart, Smith W. (Iowa) .. B: 276
Broussard, Edwin S. (La.) ..... C: 421
Burton, Theodore E. (Ohio) 21: 50
Capper, Arthur (Kans.) .... C: 58
Caraway, Thaddeus H. (Ark.) .. A: 123
Connally, Thomas T. (Tex.) ... C: 452
Copeland, Royal S. (N. Y.) 15: 358
Couzens, James (Mich.) .... A: 216
Cutting, Bronson M. (N. Mex.) 26: 443
Dale, Porter H. (Vt.) .... B: 397
Deneen, Charles S. (Ill.) 14: 364
Dill, Clarence C. (Wash.) ...... B: 200
Edwards, Edward I. (N. J.) ...24: 256
Fess, Simeon D. (Ohio) .... C: 283
Fletcher, Duncan U. (Fla.) .... A: 330
Frazier, Lynn J. (N. Dak.) .... B: 189
George, Walter F. (Ga.) .... A: 521
Gillett, Frederick H. (Mass.) .. B: 198
Glass, Carter (Va.) .... A: 36
Glenn, Otis F. (Ill.) .... A: 20
Goff, Guy D. (W. Va.) 24: 24
Goldsborough, Phillips L. (Md.) .15: 190
Gould, Arthur R. (Maine) ..... C: 439
Greene, Frank L. (Vt.) 25: 92
Grundy, Joseph R. (Pa.) ......
Hale, Frederick (Maine) .... B: 181
Harris, William J. (Ga.) 24: 266
Harrison, Byron P. (Miss.) .... A: 173
Hastings, Daniel O. (Del.) .....
Hatfield, Henry D. (W. Va.) ... C: 409
Hawes, Harry B. (Mo.) .... C: 65
Hayden, Carl T. (Ariz.) .... C: 218
Hebert, Felix (R. I.) ....
Heflin, J. Thomas (Ala.) ...... B: 60
Howell, Robert B. (Nebr.) ..... C: 390
Johnson, Hiram W. (Calif.) ...15: 133
Jones, Wesley L. (Wash.) 14: 393
Kean, Hamilton F. (N. J.) .... C: 173
Kendrick, John B. (Wyo.) ..... B: 459
Keyes, Henry W. (N. H.) ..... C: 245
King, William H. (Utah) ......
LaFollette, Robert M., Jr. (Wis.) C: 351
McCulloch, Roscoe C. (Ohio) ...
McGill, George (Kans.) .... D: 185
McKellar, Kenneth D. (Tenn.) .. C: 427
McMaster, William H. (S. Dak.) C: 39
McNary, Charles L. (Oreg.) .... B: 400
Metcalf, Jesse H. (R. I.) ......
Norbeck, Peter (S. Dak.) ...... B: 479
Norris, George W. (Nebr.) ..... B: 86
Nye, Gerald P. (N. Dak.) ...... C: 360
Oddie, Tasker L. (Nev.) .... A: 83
Overman, Lee S. (N. C.) 13: 305
Partridge, Frank C. (Vt.) ......
Patterson, Roscoe C. (Mo.) .... A: 396
Phipps, Laurence C. (Colo.) .... A: 328
Pine, William B. (Okla.) ...... A: 484
Pittman, Key (Nev.) .... B: 375
Ransdell, Joseph E. (La.) 15: 407
Reed, David A. (Pa.) .... B: 384
Robinson, Arthur R. (Ind.) .... B: 366
Robinson, Joseph T. (Ark.) .... B: 193
Robsion, John M. (Ky.) .... D: 351
Sackett, Frederic M. (Ky.) .... B: 421
Schall, Thomas D. (Minn.) ..... C: 337
Sheppard, Morris (Tex.) 15: 274
Shipstead, Henrik (Minn.) .... B: 256
Shortridge, Samuel M. (Calif.) .. B: 193
Simmons, Furnifold McL. (N.C.) 12: 517
Smith, Ellison D. (S. C.) 14: 489
Smoot, Reed (Utah) 13: 197
Steck, Daniel F. (Iowa) .... C: 196
Steiwer, Frederick (Oreg.) ....
Stephens, Hubert D. (Miss.) ... C: 215
Sullivan, Patrick J. (Wyo.) .. D: 116
Swanson, Claude A. (Va.) ..... D: 15
Thomas, Elmer (Okla.) .... C: 106
Thomas, John (Idaho) .... D: 139
Townsend, John G. (Del.) .....
Trammell, Park (Fla.) .... A: 180
Tydings, Millard E. (Md.) ...... C: 302
Vandenberg, Arthur H. (Mich.) D: 394
Wagner, Robert F. (N. Y.) .... D: 39
Walcott, Frederic C. (Conn.) ... C: 294
Walsh, David I. (Mass.) 15: 99
Walsh, Thomas J. (Mont.) 24: 10
Waterman, Charles W. (Colo.) ..24: 258
Watson, James E. (Ind.) ...... A: 409
Wheeler, Burton K. (Mont.) ... A: 153

Seventy-second Congress (1931-33)

Moses, George H., president *pro tem.* .... C: 71
Ashurst, Henry F. (Ariz.) 15: 415
Austin, Warren R. (Vt.) ......
Bailey, Josiah W. (N. C.) ..... D: 440
Bankhead, John H., Jr. (Ala.) ..
Barkley, Alben W. (Ky.) .... C: 411
Bingham, Hiram (Conn.) ...... A: 28
Black, Hugo L. (Ala.) .... C: 502
Blaine, John J. (Wis.) .... B: 110
Borah, William E. (Idaho) ..... B: 115
Bratton, Sam G. (N. Mex.) ..... B: 488
Broussard, Edwin S. (La.) ..... C: 421
Bulkley, Robert J. (Ohio) ..... D: 244
Bulow, William J. (S. Dak.) ... C: 63
Byrnes, James F. (S. C.) ......
Capper, Arthur (Kans.) .... C: 58
Caraway, Hattie O. W. (Ark.) . D: 148
Caraway, Thaddeus H. (Ark.) .. A: 123
Carey, Robert D. (Wyo.) ......
Cohen, John S. (Ga.) .... D: 106
Connally, Thomas T. (Tex.) ... C: 452
Coolidge, Marcus A. (Mass.) ....
Copeland, Royal S. (N. Y.) 15: 358
Costigan, Edward P. (Colo.) ... D: 255
Couzens, James (Mich.) .... A: 216
Cutting, Bronson M. (N. Mex.) 26: 443

Dale, Porter H. (Vt.) .... B: 397
Davis, James J. (Pa.) .... A: 17
Dickinson, Lester J. (Iowa) .... D: 438
Dill, Clarence C. (Wash.) ...... B: 200
Fess, Simeon D. (Ohio) .... C: 283
Fletcher, Duncan U. (Fla.) .... A: 330
Frazier, Lynn J. (N. Dak.) .... B: 189
George, Walter F. (Ga.) .... A: 521
Glass, Carter (Va.) .... A: 36
Glenn, Otis F. (Ill.) .... A: 20
Goldsborough, Phillips L. (Md.) .15: 190
Gore, Thomas P. (Okla.) 14: 323
Hale, Frederick (Maine) .... B: 181
Harris, William J. (Ga.) 24: 266
Harrison, Byron P. (Miss.) .... A: 173
Hastings, Daniel O. (Del.) .....
Hatfield, Henry D. (W. Va.) ... C: 409
Hawes, Harry B. (Mo.) .... C: 65
Hayden, Carl T. (Ariz.) .... C: 218
Hebert, Felix (R. I.) ....
Howell, Robert B. (Nebr.) ..... C: 390
Hull, Cordell (Tenn.) .... D: 10
Johnson, Hiram W. (Calif.) 15: 133
Jones, Wesley L. (Wash.) 14: 393
Kean, Hamilton F. (N. J.) .... C: 173
Kendrick, John B. (Wyo.) ..... B: 459
Keyes, Henry W. (N. H.) ..... C: 245
King, William H. (Utah) ......
LaFollette, Robert M., Jr. (Wis.) C: 351
Lewis, J. Hamilton (Ill.) 15: 63
Logan, Marvel M. (Ky.) .... D: 231
Long, Huey P. (La.) .... D: 409
McGill, George (Kans.) .... D: 185
McKellar, Kenneth D. (Tenn.) .. C: 427
McNary, Charles L. (Oreg.) ... B: 400
Metcalf, Jesse H. (R. I.) ......
Morrison, Cameron (N. C.) ....
Morrow, Dwight W. (N. J.) 23: 10
Murphy, Louis (Iowa) ....
Neely, Matthew M. (W. Va.) .. C: 104
Norbeck, Peter (S. Dak.) ...... B: 479
Norris, George W. (Nebr.) ..... B: 86
Nye, Gerald P. (N. Dak.) ...... C: 360
Oddie, Tasker L. (Nev.) .... A: 83
Overman, Lee S. (N. C.) 13: 305
Patterson, Roscoe C. (Mo.) .... A: 396
Pittman, Key (Nev.) .... B: 375
Pope, James P. (Idaho) .... D: 341
Reed, David A. (Pa.) .... B: 384
Robinson, Arthur R. (Ind.) .... B: 366
Robinson, Joseph T. (Ark.) .... B: 193
Schall, Thomas D. (Minn.) ..... C: 337
Sheppard, Morris (Tex.) 15: 274
Shipstead, Henrik (Minn.) ..... B: 256
Shortridge, Samuel M. (Calif.) .. B: 193
Smith, Ellison D. (S. C.) 14: 489
Smoot, Reed (Utah) 13: 197
Steiwer, Frederick (Oreg.) .....
Stephens, Hubert D. (Miss.) ... C: 215
Swanson, Claude A. (Va.) ..... D: 15
Thomas, Elmer (Okla.) .... C: 106
Thomas, John (Idaho) .... D: 139
Townsend, John G. (Del.) .....
Trammell, Park (Fla.) .... A: 180
Tydings, Millard E. (Md.) ..... C: 302
Vandenberg, Arthur H. (Mich.) D: 394
Wagner, Robert F. (N. Y.) .... D: 39
Walcott, Frederick C. (Conn.) .. C: 294
Walsh, David I. (Mass.) 15: 99
Walsh, Thomas J. (Mont.) 24: 10
Waterman, Charles W. (Colo.) ..24: 258
Watson, James E. (Ind.) ...... A: 409
Wheeler, Burton K. (Mont.) ... A: 153
White, Wallace H., Jr. (Maine) D: 208

Seventy-third Congress (1933-35)

Pittman, Key, president *pro tem.* B: 375
Adams, Alva B. (Colo.) .... B: 162
Ashurst, Henry F. (Ariz.) 15: 415
Austin, Warren R. (Vt.) ......
Bachman, Nathan L. (Tenn.) ..
Bailey, Josiah W. (N. C.) ..... D: 440
Bankhead, John H., Jr. (Ala.) ..
Barbour, William W. (N. J.) .. D: 256
Barkley, Alben W. (Ky.) ...... C: 411
Black, Hugo L. (Ala.) .... C: 502
Bone, Homer T. (Wash.) ......
Borah, William E. (Idaho) ..... B: 115
Brown, Fred H. (N. H.) .... C: 243
Bulkley, Robert J. (Ohio) ..... D: 244
Bulow, William J. (S. Dak.) ... C: 63
Byrd, Harry F. (Va.) .... B: 430
Byrnes, James F. (S. C.) ......
Capper, Arthur (Kans.) .... C: 58
Caraway, Hattie W. O. (Ark.) .. D: 148
Carey, Robert D. (Wyo.) ....
Clark, Bennett (Champ) (Mo.)
Connally, Thomas T. (Tex.) ... C: 452
Coolidge, Marcus A. (Mass.) ...
Copeland, Royal S. (N. Y.) ...15: 358
Costigan, Edward P. (Colo.) ... D: 255
Couzens, James (Mich.) .... A: 216
Cutting, Bronson M. (N. Mex.) 26: 443
Davis, James J. (Pa.) .... A: 17
Dickinson, Lester J. (Iowa) .... D: 438
Dietrich, William H. (Ill.) .....
Dill, Clarence C. (Wash.) ...... B: 200
Duffy, Francis R. (Wis.) ...... D: 136
Erickson, John E. (Mont.) .... D: 143
Fess, Simeon D. (Ohio) .... C: 283
Fletcher, Duncan U. (Fla.) .... A: 330
Frazier, Lynn J. (N. Dak.) .... B: 189
George, Walter F. (Ga.) ...... A: 521
Gibson, Ernest W. (Vt.) ....
Glass, Carter (Vt.) .... A: 36
Goldsborough, Phillips L. (Md.) .15: 190
Gore, Thomas P. (Okla.) 14: 323
Hale, Frederick (Maine) .... B: 181
Harrison, Byron P. (Miss.) .... A: 173
Hastings, Daniel O. (Del.) .....
Hatch, Carl A. (N. Mex.) .....
Hatfield, Henry D. (W. Va.) .. C: 409
Hayden, Carl T. (Ariz.) .... C: 218
Hebert, Felix (R. I.) ....
Hunter, Richard C. (Nebr.) ....
Johnson, Hiram W. (Calif.) 15: 133
Kean, Hamilton F. (N. J.) .... C: 173
Keyes, Henry W. (N. H.) ..... C: 245
King, William H. (Utah) ......
LaFollette, Robert M., Jr. (Wis.) C: 351
Lewis, J. Hamilton (Ill.) 15: 63
Logan, Marvel M. (Ky.) .... D: 231
Lonergan, Augustine (Conn.) .. D: 236
Long, Huey P. (La.) .... D: 409
McAdoo, William G. (Calif.) ... A: 34
McCarren, Patrick A. (Nev.) ... D: 214
McGill, George (Kans.) .... D: 185
McKellar, Kenneth D. (Tenn.) .. C: 427
McNary, Charles L. (Oreg.) .... B: 400
Metcalf, Jesse H. (R. I.) ....
Morrison, Cameron (N. C.) ....
Murphy, Louis (Iowa) ....
Murray, James E. (Mont.) ....
Neely, Matthew M. (W. Va.) ... C: 104
Norbeck, Peter (S. Dak.) ...... B: 479
Norris, George W. (Nebr.) ..... B: 86
Nye, Gerald P. (N. Dak.) ...... C: 360
O'Mahoney, Joseph C. (Wyo.) .. D: 391
Overton, John H. (La.) .... D: 285
Patterson, Roscoe C. (Mo.) .... A: 396
Pope, James P. (Idaho) .... D: 341
Reed, David A. (Pa.) .... B: 384
Robinson, Arthur R. (Ind.) .... B: 366
Robinson, Joseph T. (Ark.) .... B: 193
Russell, Richard B., Jr. (Ga.) ..
Schall, Thomas D. (Minn.) ..... C: 337
Sheppard, Morris (Tex.) 15: 274
Shipstead, Henrik (Minn.) ..... B: 256
Smith, Ellison D. (S. C.) 14: 489
Steiwer, Frederick (Oreg.) .....
Stephens, Hubert D. (Miss.) ... C: 215
Thomas, Elbert D. (Utah) ..... D: 326
Thomas, Elmer (Okla.) .... C: 106
Thompson, William H. (Nebr.) .15: 57
Townsend, John G., Jr. (Del.) ..
Trammell, Park (Fla.) .... A: 180
Tydings, Millard E. (Md.) ..... C: 302
Vandenberg, Arthur H. (Mich.) D: 394
VanNuys, Frederick (Ind.) ...
Wagner, Robert F. (N. Y.) ... D: 39
Walcott, Frederic C. (Conn.) .. C: 294
Walsh, David I. (Mass.) 15: 99
Wheeler, Burton K. (Mont.) ... A: 153
White, Wallace H., Jr. (Maine) D: 208

Seventy-fourth Congress (1935-37)

Pittman, Key, president *pro tem.* B: 375
Adams, Alva B. (Colo.) .... B: 162
Ashurst, Henry F. (Ariz.) 15: 415
Austin, Warren R. (Vt.) ....
Bachman, Nathan L. (Tenn.) ..
Bailey, Josiah W. (N. C.) ..... D: 440
Bankhead, John H., Jr. (Ala.) ..
Barbour, William W. (N. J.) ... D: 256
Barkley, Alben W. (Ky.) ...... C: 411
Bilbo, Theodore G. (Mich.) ..... A: 313
Black, Hugo L. (Ala.) .... C: 502
Bone, Homer T. (Wash.) ......
Borah, William E. (Idaho) ..... B: 115
Brown, Fred H. (N. H.) .... C: 243
Bulkley, Robert J. (Ohio) ..... D: 244
Bulow, William J. (S. Dak.) ... C: 63
Burke, Edward R. (Nebr.) .....
Byrd, Harry F. (Va.) .... B: 430
Byrnes, James F. (S. C.) ......
Capper, Arthur (Kans.) .... C: 58
Caraway, Hattie W. O. (Ark.) .. D: 148
Carey, Robert D. (Wyo.) ......
Chavez, Dennis (N. Mex.) .....
Clark, Bennett (Champ) (Mo.)
Connally, Thomas T. (Tex.) ... C: 452
Coolidge, Marcus A. (Mass.) ...
Copeland, Royal S. (N. Y.) 15: 358
Costigan, Edward P. (Colo.) ... D: 255
Couzens, James (Mich.) .... A: 216
Davis, James J. (Pa.) .... A: 17
Dickinson, Lester J. (Iowa) .... D: 438
Dietrich, William H. (Ill.) ....
Donahey, Alvin V. (Ohio) ..... B: 511
Duffy, Francis R. (Wis.) ...... D: 136
Fletcher, Duncan U. (Fla.) .... A: 330
Frazier, Lynn J. (N. Dak.) .... B: 189
George, Walter F. (Ga.) .... A: 521
Gibson, Ernest W. (Vt.) ....
Glass, Carter (Va.) .... A: 36
Gore, Thomas P. (Okla.) 14: 323
Guffey, Joseph F. (Pa.) ....
Hale, Frederick (Maine) .... B: 181
Harrison, Byron P. (Miss.) ... A: 173
Hastings, Daniel O. (Del.) .....
Hatch, Carl A. (N. Mex.) .....
Hayden, Carl T. (Ariz.) .... C: 218
Hebert, Felix (R. I.) ....
Holt, Rush D. (W. Va.) ....
Johnson, Hiram W. (Calif.) ...15: 135
Keyes, Henry W. (N. H.) ...... C: 245
King, William H. (Utah) ....
LaFollette, Robert M., Jr. (Wis.) C: 351
Lewis, J. Hamilton (Ill.) 15: 63
Logan, Marvel M. (Ky.) .... D: 231
Lonergan, Augustine (Conn.) .. D: 236
Long, Huey P. (La.) .... D: 409
McAdoo, William G. (Calif.) ... A: 34
McCarren, Patrick A. (Nev.) .. D: 214
McGill, George (Kans.) .... D: 185
McKellar, Kenneth D. (Tenn.) .. C: 427
McNary, Charles L. (Oreg.) .... B: 400
Maloney, Francis T. (Conn.) ...
Metcalf, Jesse H. (R. I.) ....
Minton, Sherman (Ind.) ....
Moore, A. Harry (N. J.) ...... B: 178
Morrison, Cameron (N. C.) ....
Murphy, Louis (Iowa) ....
Murray, James E. (Mont.) .....
Neely, Matthew M. (W. Va.) ... C: 104
Norbeck, Peter (S. Dak.) ...... B: 479
Norris, George W. (Nebr.) ..... B: 86
Nye, Gerald P. (N. Dak.) ...... C: 360
O'Mahoney, Joseph C. (Wyo.) .. D: 391
Overton, John H. (La.) .... D: 285
Pope, James P. (Idaho) .... D: 341
Radcliffe, George L. (Md.) .....
Robinson, Joseph T. (Ark.) .... B: 193
Russell, Richard B., Jr. (Ga.) ..
Schall, Thomas D. (Minn.) ..... C: 337
Schwellenbach, Lewis B. (Wash.)
Sheppard, Morris (Tex.) 15: 274
Shipstead, Henrik (Minn.) ..... B: 256
Smith, Ellison D. (S. C.) 14: 489
Steiwer, Frederick (Oreg.) ....
Thomas, Elbert D. (Utah) ..... D: 326
Thomas, Elmer (Okla.) .... C: 106
Townsend, John G., Jr. (Del.) ..
Trammell, Park (Fla.) .... A: 180
Truman, Harry S. (Mo.) ......
Tydings, Millard E. (Md.) ..... C: 302
Vandenberg, Arthur H. (Mich.) D: 394
VanNuys, Frederick (Ind.) ....
Wagner, Robert F. (N. Y.) .... D: 39
Walsh, David I. (Mass.) 15: 99
Wheeler, Burton K. (Mont.) .... A: 153
White, Wallace H., Jr. (Maine) D: 208

United States Congressmen

The First Congress (1789-91)

Muhlenberg, Frederick A. C. (Pa.), Speaker.

Ames, Fisher (Mass.)
Ashe, John B. (N. C.)
Baldwin, Abraham (Ga.)
Benson, Egbert (N. Y.)
Bland, Theodoric (Va.)
Bloodworth, Timothy (N. C.)
Boudinot, Elias (N. J.)
Bourn, Benjamin (R. I.)
Brown, John (Va.)
Burke, Ædanus (S. C.)
Cadwalader, Lambert (N. J.)
Carroll, Daniel (Md.)
Clymer, George (Pa.)
Coles, Isaac (Va.)
Contee, Benjamin (Md.)
Fitzsimons, Thomas (Pa.)
Floyd, William (N. Y.)
Foster, Abiel (N. H.)
Gale, George (Md.)
Gerry, Elbridge (Mass.)
Giles, William B. (Va.)
Gilman, Nicholas (N. H.)
Goodhue, Benjamin (Mass.)
Griffin, Samuel (Va.)
Grout, Jonathan (Mass.)
Hartley, Thomas (Pa.)
Hathorn, John (N. Y.)
Hiester, Daniel (Pa.)
Huger, Daniel (S. C.)
Huntington, Benjamin (Conn.)
Jackson James (Ga.)
Laurance, John (N. Y.)
Lee, Richard Bland (Va.)
Leonard, George (Mass.)
Livermore, Samuel (N. H.)
Madison, James (Va.)
Matthews, George (Ga.)
Moore, Andrew (Va.)
Muhlenberg, Frederick A. C. (Pa.)
Muhlenberg, John Peter G. (Pa.)
Page, John (Va.)
Parker, Josiah (Va.)
Partridge, George (Mass.)
Schureman, James (N. J.)
Scott, Thomas (Pa.)
Sedgwick, Theodore (Mass.)
Seney, Joshua (Md.)
Sevier, John (N. C.)
Sherman, Roger (Conn.)
Silvester, Peter (N. Y.)
Sinnickson, Thomas (N. J.)
Smith, William (Md.)
Smith, William L. (S. C.)
Steele, John (N. C.)
Stone, Michael Jenifer (Md.)
Sturges, Jonathan (Conn.)
Sumter, Thomas (S. C.)
Thacher, George (Mass.)
Trumbull, Jonathan, (Conn.)
Tucker, Thomas T. (S. C.)
Van Rensselaer, Jeremiah (N. Y.)
Vining, John (Del.)
Wadsworth, Jeremiah (Conn.)
White, Alexander (Va.)
Williamson, Hugh (N. C.)
Wynkoop, Henry (Pa.)

The Second Congress (1791-93)

Jonathan Trumbull (Conn.) Speaker.

Ames, Fisher (Mass.)
Ashe, John B. (N. C.)
Baldwin, Abraham (Ga.)
Barnwell, Robert (S. C.)
Benson, Egbert (N. Y.)
Boudinot, Elias (N. J.)
Bourn, Benjamin (R. I.)
Bourne, Shearjashub (Mass.)
Brown, John (Va.)
Clark, Abraham (N. J.)
Dayton, Jonathan (N. J.)
Findley, William (Pa.)
Fitzsimons, Thomas (Pa.)
Gerry, Elbridge (Mass.)
Giles, William B. (Va.)
Gilman, Nicholas (N. H.)
Goodhue, Benjamin (Mass.)
Gordon, James (N. Y.)
Greenup, Christopher (Ky.)
Gregg, Andrew (Pa.)
Griffin, Samuel (Va.)
Grove, William B. (N. C.)
Hartley, Thomas (Pa.)
Hiester, Daniel (Pa.)
Hillhouse, James (Conn.)
Hindman, William (Md.)
Huger, Daniel (S. C.)
Jacobs, Israel (Pa.)
Key, Philip (Md.)
Kitchell, Aaron (N. J.)
Kittera, John W. (Pa.)
Laurance, John (N. Y.)
Learned, Amasa (Conn.)
Lee, Richard B. (Va.)
Livermore, Samuel (N. H.)
Macon, Nathaniel (N. C.)
Madison, James (Va.)
Mercer, John F. (Md.)
Milledge, John (Ga.)
Moore Andrew (Va.)
Muhlenberg, Frederick A. C. (Pa.)
Murray, William V. (Md.)
Niles, Nathaniel (Vt.)
Orr, Alexander D. (Ky.)
Page, John (Va.)
Parker, Josiah (Va.)
Pinkney, William (Md.)
Schoonmaker, Cornelius C. (N. Y.)
Sedgwick, Theodore (Mass.)
Seney, Joshua (Md.)
Sheridine, Upton (Md.)
Silvester, Peter (N. Y.)
Smith, Israel (Vt.)
Smith, Jeremiah (N. H.)
Smith, William L. (S. C.)
Steele, John (N. C.)
Sterrett, Samuel (Md.)
Sturges, Jonathan (Conn.)
Sumter, Thomas (S. C.)
Thacher, George (Mass.)
Tredwell, Thomas (N. Y.)
Trumbull, Jonathan (Conn.)
Tucker, Thomas T. (S. C.)
Venable, Abraham B. (Va.)
Vining, John (Del.)
Wadsworth, Jeremiah (Conn.)
Ward, Artemas (Mass.)
Wayne, Anthony (Ga.)
White, Alexander (Va.)
Williamson, Hugh (N. C.)
Willis, Francis (Ga.)

The Third Congress (1793-95)

Muhlenberg, Frederick A. C. (Pa.), Speaker.

Ames, Fisher (Mass.)
Armstrong, James (Pa.)
Bailey, Theodorus (N. Y.)
Baldwin, Abraham (Ga.)
Beatty, John (N. J.)
Benton, Lemuel (S. C.)
Blount, Thomas (N. C.)
Boudinot, Elias (N. J.)
Bourn, Benjamin (R. I.)
Bourne, Shearjashub (Mass.)
Cadwallader, Lambert (N. J.)
Carnes, Thomas P. (Ga.)
Christie, Gabriel (Md.)
Claiborne, Thomas (Va.)
Clark, Abraham (N. J.)
Cobb, David (Mass.)
Coffin, Peleg, Jr. (Mass.)
Coit, Joshua (Conn.)
Coles, Isaac (Va.)
Dawson, William J. (N. C.)
Dayton, Jonathan (N. J.)
Dearborn, Henry (Mass.)
Dent, George (Md.)
Dexter, Samuel, Jr. (Mass.)
Duval, Gabriel (Md.)
Edwards, Benjamin (Md.)
Findley, William (Pa.)
Fitzsimons, Thomas (Pa.)
Forrest, Uriah (Md.)
Foster, Dwight (Mass.)
Gilbert, Ezekiel (N. Y.)
Giles, William B. (Va.)
Gillespie, James (N. C.)
Gillon, Alexander (S. C.)
Gilman, Nicholas (N. H.)
Glen, Henry (N. Y.)
Goodhue, Benjamin (Mass.)
Gordon, James (N. Y.)
Greenup, Christopher (Ky.)
Gregg, Andrew (Pa.)
Griffin, Samuel (Va.)
Grove, William B. (N. C.)
Hancock, George (Va.)
Harper, Robert G. (S. C.)
Harrison, Carter B. (Va.)
Hartley, Thomas (Pa.)
Heath, John (Va.)
Hiester, Daniel (Pa.)
Hillhouse, James (Conn.)
Hindham, William (Md.)
Holten, Samuel (Mass.)
Hunter, John (S. C.)
Irine, William (Pa.)
Kitchell, Aaron (N. J.)
Kittera, John W. (Pa.)
Latimer, Henry (Del.)
Learned, Amasa (Conn.)
Lee, Richard B. (Va.)
Locke, Matthew (N. C.)
Lyman, William (Mass.)
McDowell, Joseph (N. C.)
Macon, Nathaniel (N. C.)
Madison, James (Va.)
Malbone, Francis (R. I.)
Mebane, Alexander (N. C.)
Mercer, John F. (Md.)
Montgomery, William (Pa.)
Moore, Andrew (Va.)
Muhlenberg, Frederick A. C. (Pa.)
Muhlenberg, John Peter G. (Pa.)
Murray, William Vans (Md.)
Neville, Joseph (Va.)
New, Anthony (Va.)
Nicholas, John (Va.)
Niles, Nathaniel (Vt.)
Orr, Alexander D. (Ky.)
Page, John (Va.)
Parker, Josiah (Va.)
Patten, John (Del.)
Pickens, Andrew (S. C.)
Preston, Francis (Va.)
Rutherford, Robert (Va.)
Scott, Thomas (Pa.)
Sedgwick, Theodore (Mass.)
Sherburne, John S. (N. H.)
Smilie, John (Pa.)
Smith, Israel (Vt.)
Smith, Jeremiah (N. H.)
Smith, Samuel (Md.)
Smith, William L. (S. C.)
Sprigg, Thomas (Md.)
Swift, Zephaniah (Conn.)
Talbot, Silas (N. Y.)
Thacher, George (Mass.)
Tracy, Uriah (Conn.)
Tredwell, Thomas (N. Y.)
Trumbull, Jonathan (Conn.)
Van Alen, John E. (N. Y.)
Van Cortlandt, Philip (N. Y.)
Van Gaasbeck, Peter (N. Y.)
Venable, Abraham B. (Va.)
Wadsworth, Jeremiah (Conn.)
Wadsworth, Peleg (Mass.)
Bailey, Theodorus (N. Y.)
Walker, Francis (Va.)
Ward, Artemas (Mass.)
Watts, John (N. Y.)
Williams, Benjamin (N. C.)
Wingate, Paine (N. H.)
Winn, Richard (S. C.)
Winston, Joseph (N. C.)

The Fourth Congress (1795-97)

Dayton, Jonathan (N. J.) Speaker.

Ames, Fisher (Mass.)
Bailey, Theodorus (N. Y.)
Baldwin, Abraham (Ga.)
Bard, David (Pa.)
Benton, Lemuel (S. C.)
Blount, Thomas (N. C.)
Bourn, Benjamin (R. I.)
Bradbury, Theophilus (Mass.)
Brent, Richard (Va.)
Bryan, Nathan (N. C.)
Buck, Daniel (Vt.)
Burges, Dempsey (N. C.)
Cabell, Samuel J. (Va.)
Christie, Gabriel (Md.)
Claiborne, Thomas (Va.)
Clopton, John (Va.)
Coit, Joshua (Conn.)
Coles, Isaac (Va.)
Cooper, William (N. Y.)
Crabb, Jeremiah (Md.)
Craik, William (Md.)
Dana, Samuel W. (Conn.)
Davenport, James (Conn.)
Dayton, Jonathan (N. J.)
Dearborn, Henry (Mass.)
Dent, George (Md.)
Duvall, Gabriel (Md.)
Earle, Samuel (S. C.)
Ege, George (Pa.)
Findley, William (Pa.)
Foster, Abiel (N. H.)
Foster, Dwight (Mass.)
Franklin, Jesse (N. C.)
Freeman, Nathaniel, Jr. (Mass.)
Gallatin, Albert (Pa.)
Gilbert, Ezekiel (N. Y.)
Giles, William B. (Va.)
Gillespie, James (N. C.)
Gilman, Nicholas (N. H.)
Glen, Henry (N. Y.)
Goodhue, Benjamin (Mass.)
Goodrich, Chauncey (Conn.)
Greenup, Christopher (Ky.)
Gregg, Andrew (Pa.)
Griswold, Roger (Conn.)
Grove, William B. (N. C.)
Hampton, Wade (S. C.)
Hancock, George (Va.)
Harper, Robert G. (S. C.)
Harrison, Carter B. (Va.)
Hartley, Thomas (Pa.)
Hathorn, John (N. Y.)
Havens, Jonathan N. (N. Y.)
Heath, John (Va.)
Hiester, Daniel (Pa.)
Henderson, Thomas (N. J.)

Hillhouse, James (Conn.)
Hindman, William (Md.)
Holland, James (N. C.)
Jackson, Andrew (Tenn.)
Jackson, George (Va.)
Kitchell, Aaron (N. J.)
Kittera, John W. (Pa.)
Leonard, George (Mass.)
Livingston, Edward (N. Y.)
Locke, Matthew (N. C.)
Lyman, Samuel (Mass.)
Lyman, William (Mass.)
Maclay, Samuel (Pa.)
Macon, Nathaniel (N. C.)
Madison, James (Va.)
Malbone, Francis (R. I.)
Milledge, John (Ga.)
Moore, Andrew (Va.)
Muhlenberg, Frederick A. C. (Pa.)
Murray, William V. (Md.)
New, Anthony (Va.)
Nicholas, John (Va.)
Orr, Alexander D. (Ky.)
Page, John (Va.)
Parker, Josiah (Va.)
Patten, John (Del.)
Potter, Elisha R. (R. I.)
Preston, Francis (Va.)
Reed, John (Mass.)
Richards, John (Pa.)
Rutherford, Robert (Va.)
Sedgwick, Theodore (Mass.)
Sewall, Samuel (Mass.)
Sherburne, John S. (N. H.)
Sitgreaves, Samuel (Pa.)
Skinner, Thomson J. (Mass.)
Smith, Isaac (N. J.)
Smith, Israel (Vt.)
Smith, Jeremiah (N. H.)
Smith, Nathaniel (Conn.)
Smith, Samuel (Md.)
Smith, William L. (S. C.)
Sprigg, Richard, Jr. (Md.)
Sprigg, Thomas (Md.)
Strudwick, William F. (N. C.)
Swanwick, John (Pa.)
Swift, Zephaniah (Conn.)
Tatom, Absalom (N. C.)
Thacher, George (Mass.)
Thomas, Richard (Pa.)
Thomson, Mark (N. J.)
Tracy, Uriah (Conn.)
Van Alen, John E. (N. Y.)
Van Cortlandt, Philip (N. Y.)
Varnum, Joseph B. (Mass.)
Venable, Abraham B. (Va.)
Wadsworth, Peleg (Mass.)
Williams, John (N. Y.)
Winn, Richard (S. C.)

The Fifth Congress (1797-99)

Jonathan, Dayton (N. J.) Speaker.

Allen, John (Conn.)
Baer, George, Jr. (Md.)
Baldwin, Abraham (Ga.)
Bard, David (Pa.)
Bartlett, Bailey (Mass.)
Bayard, James A. (Del.)
Benton, Lemuel (S. C.)
Blount, Thomas (N. C.)
Brace, Jonathan (Conn.)
Bradbury, Theophilus (Mass.)
Brent, Richard (Va.)
Brooks, David (N. Y.)
Brown, Robert (Pa.)
Bryan, Nathan (N. C.)
Bullock, Stephen (Mass.)
Burges, Dempsey (N. C.)
Cabell, Samuel J. (Va.)
Champlin, Christopher G. (R. I.)
Chapman, John (Pa.)
Claiborne, William C. C. (Tenn.)
Claiborne, Thomas (Va.)
Clay, Matthew (Va.)
Clopton, John (Va.)
Cochran, James (N. Y.)
Coit, Joshua (Conn.)
Craik, William (Md.)
Dana, Samuel W. (Conn.)
Davenport, James (Conn.)
Davis, Thomas T. (Ky.)
Dawson, John (Va.)
Dayton, Jonathan (N. J.)
Dennis, John (Md.)
Dent, George (Md.)
Edmond, William (Conn.)
Ege, George (Pa.)
Eggleston, Joseph (Va.)
Evans, Thomas (Va.)
Elmendorf, Lucas D. (N. Y.)
Findley, William (Pa.)
Foster, Abiel (N. H.)
Foster, Dwight (Mass.)
Fowler, John (Ky.)
Freeman, Jonathan (N. H.)
Freeman, Nathaniel, Jr. (Mass.)
Gallatin, Albert (Pa.)
Giles, William B. (Va.)
Gillespie, James (N. C.)
Glen, Henry (N. Y.)
Goodrich, Chauncey (Conn.)
Gordon, William (N. H.)
Gregg, Andrew (Pa.)
Griswold, Roger (Conn.)
Grove, William B. (N. C.)
Hanna, John A. (Pa.)
Harper, Robert G. (S. C.)
Harrison, Carter B. (Va.)
Hartley, Thomas (Pa.)
Havens, Jonathan N. (N. Y.)
Hiester, Joseph (Pa.)
Hindman, William (Md.)
Holmes, David (Va.)
Hosmer, Hezekiah L. (N. Y.)
Imlay, James H. (N. J.)
Jones, Walter (Va.)
Kittera, John W. (Pa.)
Livingston, Edward (N. Y.)
Locke, Matthew (N. C.)
Lyman, Samuel (Mass.)
Lyon, Matthew (Vt.)
McClenachan, Blair (Pa.)
McDowell, Joseph (N. C.)
Machir, James (Va.)
Macon, Nathaniel (N. C.)
Matthews, William (Md.)
Milledge, John (Ga.)
Morgan, Daniel (Va.)
Morris, Lewis R. (Vt.)
New, Anthony (Va.)
Nicholas, John (Va.)
Otis, Harrison G. (Mass.)
Parker, Isaac (Mass.)
Parker, Josiah (Va.)
Pinckney, Thomas (S. C.)
Potter, Elisha R. (R. I.)
Reed, John (Mass.)
Rutledge, John, Jr. (S. C.)
Schureman, James (N. J.)
Sewall, Samuel (Mass.)
Shepherd, William (Mass.)
Sinnickson, Thomas (N. J.)
Sitgreaves, Samuel (Pa.)
Skinner, Thomson J. (Mass.)
Smith, Jeremiah (N. H.)
Smith, Nathaniel (Conn.)
Smith, Samuel (Md.)
Smith, William L. (Charleston District, S. C.)
Smith, William (Pinckney District, S. C.)
Spaight, Richard D. (N. C.)
Sprague, Peleg (N. H.)
Sprigg, Richard, Jr. (Md.)
Stanford, Richard (N. C.)
Sumter, Thomas (S. C.)
Swanwick, John (Pa.)
Thacher, George (Mass.)
Thomas, Richard (Pa.)
Thompson, Mark (N. J.)
Tillinghast, Thomas (R. I.)
Trigg, Abram (Va.)
Trigg, John (Va.)
Van Alen, John E. (N. Y.)
Van Cortlandt, Philip (N. Y.)
Varnum, Joseph B. (Mass.)
Venable, Abraham B. (Va.)
Wadsworth, Peleg (Mass.)
Waln, Robert (Pa.)
Williams, John (N. Y.)
Williams, Robert (N. C.)

The Sixth Congress (1799-1801)

Sedgwick, Theodore (Mass.) Speaker.
Alston, Willis, Jr. (N. C.)
Baer, George (Md.)
Bailey, Theodorus (N. Y.)
Bartlett, Bailey (Mass.)
Bayard, James A. (Del.)
Bird, John (N. Y.)
Bishop, Phanuel (Mass.)
Brace, Jonathan (Conn.)
Brown, John (R. I.)
Brown, Robert (Pa.)
Cabell, Samuel J. (Va.)
Champlin, Christopher G. (R. I.)
Christie, Gabriel (Md.)
Claiborne, William C. C. (Tenn.)
Clay, Matthew (Va.)
Condit, John (N. J.)
Cooper, William (N. Y.)
Craik, William (Md.)
Dana, Samuel W. (Conn.)
Davenport, Franklin (N. J.)
Davenport, John (Conn.)
Davis, Thomas T. (Ky.)
Dawson, John (Va.)
Dennis, John (Md.)
Dent, George (Md.)
Dickson, Joseph (N. C.)
Edmond, William (Conn.)
Eggleston, Joseph (Va.)
Elmendorf, Lucas C. (N. Y.)
Evans, Thomas (Va.)
Foster, Abiel (N. H.)
Foster, Dwight (Mass.)
Fowler, John (Ky.)
Freeman, Jonathan (N. H.)
Gallatin, Albert (Pa.)
Glen, Henry (N. Y.)
Goode, Samuel (Va.)
Goodrich, Chauncey (Conn.)
Goodrich, Elizur (Conn.)
Gordon, William (N. H.)
Gray, Edwin (Va.)
Gregg, Andrew (Pa.)
Griswold, Roger (Conn.)
Grove, William Barry (N. C.)
Hanna, John A. (Pa.)
Harper, Robert Goodloe (S. C.)
Hartley, Thomas (Pa.)
Hiester, Joseph (Pa.)
Henderson, Archibald (N. C.)
Hill, William H. (N. C.)
Holmes, David (Va.)
Huger, Benjamin (S. C.)
Imlay, James H. (N. J.)
Jackson, George (Va.)
Jones, James (Ga.)
Kitchell, Aaron (N. J.)
Kittera, John Wilkes (Pa.)
Lee, Henry (Va.)
Lee, Silas (Mass.)
Leib, Michael (Pa.)
Lincoln, Levi (Mass.)
Linn, James (N. J.)
Livingston, Edward (N. Y.)
Lyman, Samuel (Mass.)
Lyon, Matthew (Vt.)
Macon, Nathaniel (N. C.)
Marshall, John (Va.)
Mattoon, Ebenezer (Mass.)
Morris, Lewis R. (Vt.)
Muhlenberg, John Peter G. (Pa.)
New, Anthony (Va.)
Nicholas, John (Va.)
Nicholson, Joseph H. (Md.)
Nott, Abraham (S. C.)
Otis, Harrison G. (Mass.)
Page, Robert (Va.)
Parker, Josiah (Va.)
Pinckney, Thomas (S. C.)
Platt, Jonas (N. Y.)
Powell, Levin (Va.)
Randolph, John (Va.)
Rutledge, John, Jr. (S. C.)
Read, Nathan (Mass.)
Reed, John (Mass.)
Sedgwick, Theodore (Mass.)
Sewall, Samuel (Mass.)
Sheafe, James (N. H.)
Shepherd, William (Mass.)
Smilie, John (Pa.)
Smith, John (N. Y.)
Smith, John C. (Conn.)
Smith, Samuel (Md.)
Spaight, Richard D. (N. C.)
Stanford, Richard (N. C.)
Stewart, John (Pa.)
Stone, David (N. C.)
Sumter, Thomas (S. C.)
Taliaferro, Benjamin (Ga.)
Tazewell, Littleton W. (Va.)
Tenney, Samuel (N. H.)
Thacher, George (Mass.)
Thomas, John Chew (Md.)
Thomas, Richard (Pa.)
Thompson, John (N. Y.)
Trigg, Abram (Va.)
Trigg, John (Va.)
Van Cortlandt, Philip (N. Y.)
Varnum, Joseph B. (Mass.)
Wadsworth, Peleg (Mass.)
Waln, Robert (Pa.)
Williams, Lemuel (Mass.)
Williams, Robert (N. C.)
Woods, Henry (Pa.)

The Seventh Congress (1801-03)

Macon, Nathaniel (N. C.), Speaker.
Alston, Willis (N. C.)
Archer, John (Md.)
Bacon, John (Mass.)
Bailey, Theodorus (N. Y.)
Bayard, James A. (Del.)
Bishop, Phanuel (Mass.)
Boude, Thomas (Pa.)
Bowie, Walter (Md.)
Brent, Richard (Va.)
Brown, Robert (Pa.)
Butler, William (S. C.)
Cabell, Samuel (Va.)
Campbell, John (Md.)
Claiborne, Thomas (Va.)
Clay, Matthew (Va.)
Clopton, John (Va.)
Condit, John (N. J.)
Cutler, Manasseh (Mass.)
Cutts, Richard (Mass.)
Dana, Samuel W. (Conn.)
Davenport, John (Conn.)
Davis, Thomas T. (Ky.)
Dawson, John (Va.)
Dennis, John (Md.)
Dickson, William (Tenn.)
Early, Peter (Ga.)
Elmendorf, Lucas C. (N. Y.)
Elmer, Ebenezer (N. J.)
Eustis, William (Mass.)
Foster, Abiel (N. H.)
Fowler, John (Ky.)
Giles, William B. (Va.)
Goddard, Calvin (Conn.)
Gray, Edwin (Va.)
Gregg, Andrew (Pa.)
Griswold, Roger (Conn.)
Grove, William B. (N. C.)
Hanna, John A. (Pa.)
Hastings, Seth (Mass.)
Helms, William (N. J.)
Hemphill, Joseph (Pa.)
Henderson, Archibald (N. C.)
Hiester, Daniel (Md.)
Hiester, Joseph (Pa.)
Hill, William H. (N. C.)
Hoge, William (Pa.)
Holland, James (N. C.)
Holmes, David (Va.)
Huger, Benjamin (S. C.)
Hunt, Samuel (N. H.)
Jackson, George (Va.)
Johnson, Charles (N. C.)
Jones, William (Pa.)
Lee, Silas (Mass.)
Leib, Michael (Pa.)
Lowndes, Thomas (S. C.)
Macon, Nathaniel (N. C.)
Mattoon, Ebenezer (Mass.)
Meriwether, David (Ga.)
Milledge, John (Ga.)
Mitchell, Samuel L. (N. Y.)
Moore, Thomas (S. C.)
Morris, Lewis R. (Vt.)
Morris, Thomas (N. Y.)

Mott, James (N. J.)
New, Anthony (Va.)
Newton, Thomas, Jr. (Va.)
Nicholson, Joseph H. (Md.)
Peirce, Joseph (N. H.)
Perkins, Elias (Conn.)
Plater, Thomas (Md.)
Randolph, John (Va.)
Read, Nathan (Mass.)
Rutledge, John (S. C.)
Shepard, William (Mass.)
Smilie, John (Pa.)
Smith, Israel (Vt.)
Smith, John (N. Y.)
Smith, John (Va.)
Smith, John C. (Conn.)
Smith, Josiah (Mass.)
Smith, Samuel (Md.)
Southard, Henry (N. J.)
Sprigg, Richard (Md.)
Stanford, Richard (N. C.)
Stanly, John (N. C.)
Stanton, Joseph, Jr. (R. I.)
Stewart, John (Pa.)
Stratton, John (Va.)
Sumter, Thomas (S. C.)
Taliaferro, Benjamin (Ga.)
Taliaferro, John, Jr. (Va.)
Tallmadge, Benjamin (Conn.)
Tenney, Samuel (N. H.)
Thatcher, Samuel (Mass.)
Thomas, David (N. Y.)
Thompson, Philip R. (Va.)
Tillinghast, Thomas (R. I.)
Trigg, Abram (Va.)
Trigg, John (Va.)
Upham, George B. (N. H.)
Van Cortlandt, Philip (N. Y.)
Van Horne, Isaac (Pa.)
Van Ness, John P. (N. Y.)
Van Rensselaer, Killian K. (N. Y.)
Varnum, Joseph B. (Mass.)
Wadsworth, Peleg (Mass.)
Walker, Benjamin (N. Y.)
Williams, Lemuel (Mass.)
Williams, Robert (N. C.)
Winn, Richard (S. C.)
Woods, Henry (Pa.)
Wynns, Thomas (N. C.)

The Eighth Congress (1803-05)

Macon, Nathaniel (N. C.) Speaker.

Alexander, Nathaniel (N. C.)
Alston, Willis, Jr. (N. C.)
Anderson, Isaac (Pa.)
Archer, John (Md.)
Baldwin, Simeon (Conn.)
Bard, David (Pa.)
Bedinger, George M. (Ky.)
Betton, Silas (N. H.)
Bishop, Phanuel (Mass.)
Blackledge, William (N. C.)
Bowie, Walter (Md.)
Boyd, Adam (N. J.)
Boyle, John (Ky.)
Brown, Robert (Pa.)
Bruce, Phineas (Mass.)
Bryan, Joseph (Ga.)
Butler, William (S. C.)
Campbell, George W. (Tenn.)
Campbell, John (Md.)
Casey, Levi (S. C.)
Chamberlain, William (Vt.)
Chittenden, Martin (Vt.)
Clagett, Clifton (N. H.)
Claiborne, Thomas (Va.)
Clark, Christopher (Va.)
Clay, Joseph (Pa.)
Clay, Matthew (Va.)
Clinton, George, Jr. (N. Y.)
Clopton, John (Va.)
Conrad, Frederick (Pa.)
Crowninshield, Jacob (Mass.)
Cutler, Manasseh (Mass.)
Cutts, Richard (Mass.)
Dana, Samuel W. (Conn.)
Davenport, John (Conn.)
Dawson, John (Va.)
Dennis, John (Md.)
Dickson, William (Tenn.)
Dwight, Thomas (Mass.)
Earle, John B. (S. C.)
Early, Peter (Ga.)
Elliott, James (Vt.)
Elmer, Ebenezer (N. J.)
Eppes, John W. (Va.)
Eustis, William (Mass.)
Findley, William (Pa.)
Fowler, John (Ky.)
Gillespie, James (N. C.)
Goddard, Calvin (Conn.)
Goodwyn, Peterson (Va.)
Gray, Edwin (Va.)
Gregg, Andrew (Pa.)
Griffin, Thomas (Va.)
Griswold, Gaylord (N. Y.)
Griswold, Roger (Conn.)
Hammond, Samuel (Ga.)
Hampton, Wade (S. C.)
Hanna, John A. (Pa.)
Hasbrouck, Josiah (N. Y.)
Hastings, Seth (Mass.)
Helms, William (N. J.)
Hiester, Daniel (Md.)
Hiester, Joseph (Pa.)
Hoge, John (Pa.)
Hoge, William (Pa.)
Holland, James (N. C.)
Holmes, David (Va.)
Hough, David (N. H.)
Huger, Benjamin (S. C.)
Hunt, Samuel (N. H.)
Jackson, John G. (Va.)
Jones, Walter (Va.)
Kennedy, William (N. C.)
Knight, Nehemiah (R. I.)
Larned, Simon (Mass.)
Leib, Michael (Pa.)
Lewis, Joseph, Jr. (Va.)
Lewis, Thomas (Va.)
Livingston, Henry W. (N. Y.)
Lowndes, Thomas (S. C.)
Lucas, John B. C. (Pa.)
Lyon, Matthew (Ky.)
McCord, Andrew (N. Y.)
Macon, Nathaniel (N. C.)
McCreery, William (Md.)
Meriwether, David (Ga.)
Mitchell, Nahum (Mass.)
Mitchill, Samuel L. (N. Y.)
Moore, Andrew (Va.)
Moore, Nicholas R. (Md.)
Moore, Thomas (S. C.)
Morrow, Jeremiah (Ohio)
Mott, James (N. J.)
Nelson, Roger (Md.)
New, Anthony (Va.)
Newton, Thomas (Va.)
Nicholson, Joseph H. (Md.)
Olin, Gideon (Vt.)
Palmer, Beriah (N. Y.)
Patterson, John (N. Y.)
Phelps, Oliver (N. Y.)
Plater, Thomas (Md.)
Purviance, Samuel D. (N. C.)
Randolph, John, Jr. (Va.)
Randolph, Thomas M. (Va.)
Rea, John (Pa.)
Rhea, John (Tenn.)
Richards, Jacob (Pa.)
Riker, Samuel (N. Y.)
Rodney, Cæsar A. (Del.)
Root, Erastus (N. Y.)
Sammons, Thomas (N. Y.)
Sandford, Thomas (Ky.)
Sands, Joshua (N. Y.)
Seaver, Ebenezer (Mass.)
Skinner, Thomson J. (Mass.)
Sloan, James (N. J.)
Smilie, John (Pa.)
Smith, John (N. Y.)
Smith, John (Va.)
Smith, John C. (Conn.)
Southard, Henry (N. J.)
Stanford, Richard (N. C.)
Stanton, Joseph (R. I.)
Stedman, William (Mass.)
Stephenson, James (Va.)
Stewart, John (Pa.)
Taggart, Samuel (Mass.)
Tallmadge, Benjamin (Conn.)
Tenney, Samuel (N. H.)
Thatcher, Samuel (Mass.)
Thomas, David (N. Y.)
Thompson, Philip R. (Va.)
Tibbitts, George (N. Y.)
Trigg, Abram (Va.)
Trigg, John (Va.)
Van Cortlandt, Philip (N. Y.)
Van Horne, Isaac (Pa.)
Van Rensselaer, Killian K. (N. Y.)
Varnum, Joseph B. (Mass.)
Verplanck, Daniel C. (N. Y.)
Wadsworth, Peleg (Mass.)
Walton, Matthew (Ky.)
Whitehill, John (Pa.)
Williams, Lemuel (Mass.)
Williams, Marmaduke (N. C.)
Wilson, Alexander (Va.)
Winn, Richard (S. C.)
Winston, Joseph (N. C.)
Wynns, Thomas (N. C.)

The Ninth Congress (1805-07)

Macon, Nathaniel (N. C.) Speaker.

Alston, Willis, Jr. (N. C.)
Alexander, Evan S. (N. C.)
Alexander, Nathaniel (N. C.)
Anderson, Isaac (Pa.)
Archer, John (Md.)
Barker, Joseph (Mass.)
Bard, David (Pa.)
Bassett, Burwell (Va.)
Bedinger, George Michael (Ky.)
Betton, Silas (N. H.)
Bibb, William W. (Ga.)
Bidwell, Barnabas (Mass.)
Bishop, Phanuel (Mass.)
Blackledge, William (N. C.)
Blake, John, Jr. (N. Y.)
Blount, Thomas (N. C.)
Boyle, John (Ky.)
Broom, James M. (Del.)
Brown, Robert (Pa.)
Bryan, Joseph (Ga.)
Burwell, William A. (Va.)
Butler, William (S. C.)
Campbell, George W. (Tenn.)
Campbell, John (Md.)
Casey, Levi (S. C.)
Chandler, John (Mass.)
Chittenden, Martin (Vt.)
Claiborne, John (Va.)
Clark, Christopher (Va.)
Clay, Joseph (Pa.)
Clay, Matthew (Va.)
Clinton, George, Jr. (N. Y.)
Clopton, John (Va.)
Conrad, Frederick (Pa.)
Cook, Orchard (Mass.)
Covington, Leonard (Md.)
Crowninshield, Jacob (Mass.)
Cutts, Richard (Mass.)
Dana, Samuel W. (Conn.)
Darby, Ezra (N. J.)
Davenport, John, Jr. (Conn.)
Dawson, John (Va.)
Dickson, William (Tenn.)
Dwight, Theodore (Conn.)
Earle, Elias (S. C.)
Early, Peter (Ga.)
Elliott, James (Vt.)
Ellis, Caleb (N. H.)
Elmer, Ebenezer (N. J.)
Ely, William (Mass.)
Eppes, John W. (Va.)
Findley, William (Pa.)
Fisk, James (Vt.)
Fowler, John (Ky.)
Garnett, James M. (Va.)
Goldsborough, Charles (Md.)
Goodwin, Peterson (Va.)
Gray, Edwin (Va.)
Green, Isaiah L. (Mass.)
Gregg, Andrew (Pa.)
Halsey, Silas (N. Y.)
Hamilton, John (Pa.)
Hastings, Seth (Mass.)
Helms, William (N. J.)
Holland, James (N. C.)
Holmes, David (Va.)
Hough, David (N. H.)
Jackson, John G. (Va.)
Jones, Walter (Va.)
Kenan, Thomas (N. C.)
Kelly, James (Pa.)
Knight, Nehemiah (R. I.)
Lambert, John (N. J.)
Leib, Michael (Pa.)
Lewis, Joseph, Jr. (Va.)
Livingston, Henry W. (N. Y.)
Lloyd, Edward (Md.)
Lyon, Matthew (Ky.)
McCreery, William (Md.)
McFarlan, Duncan (N. C.)
Macon, Nathaniel (N. C.)
Magruder, Patrick (Md.)
Marion, Robert (S. C.)
Masters, Josiah (N. Y.)
Mead, Cowles (Ga.)
Meriwether, David (Ga.)
Moore, Nicholas R. (Md.)
Moore, Thomas (S. C.)
Morrow, Jeremiah (Ohio)
Morrow, John (Va.)
Moseley, Jonathan O. (Conn.)
Mumford, Gurdon S. (N. Y.)
Nelson, Jeremiah (Mass.)
Nelson, Roger (Md.)
Newton, Thomas, Jr. (Va.)
Nicholson, Joseph H. (Md.)
Olin, Gideon (Vt.)
Pitkin, Timothy, Jr. (Conn.)
Porter, John (Pa.)
Pugh, John (Pa.)
Quincy, Josiah (Mass.)
Randolph, John (Va.)
Randolph, Thomas M. (Va.)
Rea, John (Pa.)
Rhea, John (Tenn.)
Sammons, Thomas (N. Y.)
Richards, Jacob (Pa.)
Russell, John (N. Y.)
Sailly, Peter (N. Y.)
Sandford, Thomas (Ky.)
Seaver, Ebenezer (Mass.)
Schuneman, Martin G. (N. Y.)
Sloan, James (N. J.)
Smelt, Dennis (Ga.)
Smilie, John (Pa.)
Smith, John (Va.)
Smith, John Cotton (Conn.)
Smith, O'Brien (S. C.)
Smith, Samuel (Pa.)
Southard, Henry (N. J.)
Spalding, Thomas (Ga.)
Stanford, Richard (N. C.)
Stanton, Joseph (R. I.)
Stedman, William (Mass.)
Sturgis, Lewis B. (Conn.)
Taggart, Samuel (Mass.)
Tallmadge, Benjamin (Conn.)
Tenney, Samuel (N. H.)
Thomas, David (N. Y.)
Thompson, Philip R. (Va.)
Thompson, Thomas W. (N.H.)
Tracy, Uri (N. Y.)
Trigg, Abram (Va.)
Van Cortlandt, Philip (N. Y.)
Van Rensselaer, Killian K. (N. Y.)
Varnum, Joseph B. (Mass.)
Verplanck, Daniel C. (N. Y.)
Wadsworth, Peleg (Mass.)
Walton, Matthew (Ky.)
Whitehill, John (Pa.)
Whitehill, Robert (Pa.)
Wickes, Eliphalet (N. Y.)
Williams, David R. (S. C.)
Williams, Marmaduke (N. C.)
Williams, Nathan (N. Y.)
Wilson, Alexander (Va.)
Winston, Joseph (N. C.)
Winn, Richard (S. C.)
Wynns, Thomas (N. C.)

The Tenth Congress (1807-09)

Varnum, Joseph B. (Mass.) Speaker.

Alexander, Evan S. (N. C.)
Alston, Lemuel J. (S. C.)
Alston, Willis, Jr. (N. C.)
Bacon, Ezekiel (Mass.)
Bard, David (Pa.)
Barker, Joseph (Mass.)
Bassett, Burwell (Va.)

Bibb, William W. (Ga.)
Blake, John, Jr. (N. Y.)
Blackledge, William (N. C.)
Blount, Thomas (N. C.)
Boyd, Adam (N. J.)
Boyle, John (Ky.)
Brown, Robert (Pa.)
Burwell, William A. (Va.)
Butler, William (S. C.)
Calhoun, Joseph (S. C.)
Campbell, George W. (Tenn.)
Campbell, John (Md.)
Carleton, Peter (N. H.)
Champion, Epaphroditus (Conn.)
Chandler, John (Mass.)
Chittenden, Martin (Vt.)
Claiborne, John (Va.)
Clay, Joseph (Pa.)
Clay, Matthew (Va.)
Clinton, George, Jr. (N. Y.)
Clopton, John (Va.)
Cobb, Howell (Ga.)
Cook, Orchard (Mass.)
Crowninshield, Jacob (Mass.)
Culpepper, John (N. C.)
Cutts, Richard (Mass.)
Dana, Samuel W. (Conn.)
Darby, Ezra (N. J.)
Davenport, John, Jr. (Conn.)
Dawson, John (Va.)
Dean, Josiah (Mass.)
Desha, Joseph (Ky.)
Durell, Daniel M. (N. H.)
Elliott, James (Vt.)
Ely, William (Mass.)
Eppes, John W. (Va.)
Findley, William (Pa.)
Fisk, James (Vt.)
Franklin, Meshack (N. C.)
Gardenier, Barnet (N. Y.)
Gardner, Francis (N. H.)
Garnett, James M. (Va.)
Gholson, Thomas, Jr. (Va.)
Goldsborough, Charles (Md.)
Goodwyn, Peterson (Va.)
Gray, Edwin (Va.)
Green, Isaiah L. (Mass.)
Harris, John (N. Y.)
Helms, William (N. J.)
Hiester, John (Pa.)
Hoge, William (Pa.)
Holland, James (N. C.)
Holmes, David (Va.)
Howard, Benjamin (Ky.)
Humphrey, Reuben (N. Y.)
Ilsley, Daniel (Mass.)
Jackson, John G. (Va.)
Jackson, Richard (R. I.)
Jenkins, Robert (Pa.)
Johnson, Richard M. (Ky.)
Jones, Walter (Va.)
Kelly, James (Pa.)
Kenan, Thomas (N. C.)
Key, Philip B. (Md.)
Kirkpatrick, Wm. (N. Y.)
Knight, Nehemiah (R. I.)
Lambert, John (N. J.)
Lewis, Joseph, Jr. (Va.)
Livermore, E. St. Loe (Mass.)
Lloyd, Edward (Md.)
Love, John (Va.)
Lyon, Matthew (Ky.)
McCreery, William (Md.)
Macon, Nathaniel (N. C.)
Marion, Robert (S. C.)
Masters, Josiah (N. Y.)
Milnor, William (Pa.)
Montgomery, Daniel, Jr. (Pa.)
Montgomery, John (Md.)
Moore, Nicholas R. (Md.)
Moore, Thomas (S. C.)
Morrow, Jeremiah (Ohio)
Morrow, John (Va.)
Moseley, Jonathan O. (Conn.)
Mumford, Gurdon S. (N. Y.)
Nelson, Roger (Md.)
Newbold, Thomas (N. J.)
Newton, Thomas, Jr. (Va.)
Nicholas, Wilson C. (Va.)
Pitkin, Timothy, Jr. (Conn.)
Porter, John (Pa.)
Pugh, John (Pa.)
Quincy, Josiah (Mass.)
Randolph, John (Va.)
Rea, John (Pa.)
Rhea, John (Tenn.)
Richards, Jacob (Pa.)
Richards, Matthias (Pa.)
Riker, Samuel (N. Y.)
Rowan, John (Ky.)
Russell, John (N. Y.)
Sawyer, Lemuel (N. C.)
Say, Benjamin (Pa.)
Seaver, Ebenezer (Mass.)
Shaw, Samuel (Vt.)
Sloan, James (N. J.)
Smelt, Dennis (Ga.)
Smilie, John (Pa.)
Smith, Jedediah K. (N. H.)
Smith, John (Va.)
Smith, Samuel (Pa.)
Southard, Henry (N. J.)
Stanford, Richard (N. C.)
Stedman, William (Mass.)
Storer, Clement (N. H.)
Story, Joseph (Mass.)
Sturges, Lewis B. (Conn.)
Swart, Peter (N. Y.)
Taggart, Samuel (Mass.)
Tallmadge, Benjamin (Conn.)
Taylor, John (S. C.)
Thomas, David (N. Y.)
Thompson, John (N. Y.)
Trigg, Abram (Va.)
Troup, George M. (Ga.)
Upham, Jabez (Mass.)
Van Alen, James I. (N. Y.)
Van Cortlandt, Philip (N. Y.)
Van Dyke, Nicholas (Del.)
Van Horne, Archibald (Md.)
Van Rensselaer, Killian K. (N. Y.)
Varnum, Joseph B. (Mass.)
Verplanck, Daniel C. (N. Y.)
Wharton, Jesse (Tenn.)
Whitehill, Robert (Pa.)
Wilbour, Isaac (R. I.)
Williams, David R. (S. C.)
Williams, Marmaduke (N. C.)
Wilson, Alexander (Va.)
Wilson, Nathan (N. Y.)
Winn, Richard (S. C.)
Witherell, James (Vt.)

The Eleventh Congress (1809-11)

Varnum, Joseph B. (Mass.) Speaker.

Allen, Joseph (Mass.)
Alston, Lemuel J. (S. C.)
Alston, Willis, Jr. (N. C.)
Anderson, William (Pa.)
Bacon, Ezekiel (Mass.)
Bard, David (Pa.)
Barry, William T. (Ky.)
Bassett, Burwell (Va.)
Baylies, William (Mass.)
Bibb, William W. (Ga.)
Bigelow, Abijah (Mass.)
Blaisdell, Daniel (N. H.)
Boyd, Adam (N. J.)
Brown, John (Md.)
Brown, Robert (Pa.)
Breckinridge, James (Va.)
Burwell, William A. (Va.)
Butler, William (S. C.)
Calhoun, Joseph (S. C.)
Campbell, John (Md.)
Chamberlain, John C. (N. H.)
Chamberlain, William (Vt.)
Champion, Epaphroditus (Conn.)
Cheves, Langdon (S. C.)
Chittenden, Martin (Vt.)
Clay, Matthew (Va.)
Clopton, John (Va.)
Cobb, Howell (Ga.)
Cochran, James (N. C.)
Cook, Orchard (Mass.)
Cox, James (N. J.)
Crawford, William (Pa.)
Crist, Henry (Ky.)
Cutts, Richard (Mass.)
Dana, Samuel W. (Conn.)
Davenport, John (Conn.)
Dawson, John (Va.)
Desha, Joseph (Ky.)
Ely, William (Mass.)
Emott, James (N. Y.)
Eppes, John W. (Va.)
Fisk, Jonathan (N. Y.)
Findley, William (Pa.)
Franklin, Meshack (N. C.)
Gannett, Barzillai (Mass.)
Gardenier, Barnet (N. Y.)
Gardner, Gideon (Mass.)
Garland, David S. (Va.)
Gholson, Thomas, Jr. (Va.)
Gold, Thomas R. (N. Y.)
Goldsborough, Charles (Md.)
Goodwyn, Peterson (Va.)
Gray, Edwin (Va.)
Hale, William (N. H.)
Haven, Nathaniel A. (N. H.)
Helms, William (N. J.)
Hiester, Daniel (Pa.)
Holland, James (N. C.)
Howard, Benjamin (Ky.)
Hubbard, Jonathan H. (Vt.)
Hufty, Jacob (N. J.)
Huntington, Ebenezer (Conn.)
Jackson, John G. (Va.)
Jackson, Richard, Jr. (R. I.)
Jenkins, Robert (Pa.)
Johnson, Richard M. (Ky.)
Jones, Walter (Va.)
Kenan, Thomas (N. C.)
Kennedy, William (N. C.)
Key, Philip B. (Md.)
Knickerbocker, Herman (N. Y.)
Lewis, Joseph (Va.)
Livermore, E. St. Loe (Mass.)
Livingston, Robert Le Roy (N. Y.)
Love, John (Va.)
Lyle, Aaron (Pa.)
Lyon, Matthew (Ky.)
McBryde, Archibald (N. C.)
McKee, Samuel (Ky.)
McKim, Alexander (Md.)
McKinley, William (Va.)
Macon, Nathaniel (N. C.)
Marion, Robert (S. C.)
Mathews, Vincent (N. Y.)
Miller, Pleasant M. (Tenn.)
Milnor, William (Pa.)
Mitchill, Samuel L. (N. Y.)
Montgomery, John (Md.)
Moore, Nicholas R. (Md.)
Moore, Thomas (S. C.)
Morrow, Jeremiah (Ohio)
Moseley, Jonathan O. (Conn.)
Mumford, Gurdon S. (N. Y.)
Nelson, Roger (Md.)
Newbold, Thomas (N. J.)
Newton, Thomas (Va.)
Nicholas, Wilson C. (Va.)
Nicholson, John (N. Y).
Pearson, Joseph (N. C.)
Pickman, Benjamin (Mass.)
Pitkin, Timothy, Jr. (Conn.)
Porter, John (Pa.)
Porter, Peter B. (N. Y.)
Potter, Elisha R. (R. I.)
Quincy, Josiah (Mass.)
Randolph, John (Va.)
Rea, John (Pa.)
Rhea, John (Tenn.)
Richards, Matthias (Pa.)
Ringgold, Samuel (Md.)
Roane, John (Va.)
Root, Erastus (N. Y.)
Ross, John (Pa.)
Sage, Ebenezer (N. Y.)
Sammons, Thomas (N. Y.)
Sawyer, Lemuel (N. C.)
Say, Benjamin (Pa.)
Scudder, John A. (N. J.)
Seaver, Ebenezer (Mass.)
Seybert, Adam (Pa.)
Shaw, Samuel (Vt.)
Sheffey, Daniel (Va.)
Smelt, Dennis (Ga.)
Smilie, John (Pa.)
Smith, George (Pa.)
Smith, John (Va.)
Smith, Samuel (Pa.)
Southard, Henry (N. J.)
Stanford, Richard (N. C.)
Stanly, John (N. C.)
Stedman, William (Mass.)
Stephenson, James (Va.)
Sturges, Lewis B. (Conn.)
Swoope, Jacob (Va.)
Taggart, Samuel (Mass.)
Tallmadge, Benjamin (Conn.)
Taylor, John (S. C.)
Thompson, John (N. Y.)
Tracy, Uri (N. Y.)
Troup, George M. (Ga.)
Turner, Charles, Jr. (Mass.)
Upham, Jabez (Mass.)
Van Dyke, Nicholas (Del.)
Van Horne, Archibald (Md.)
Van Rensselaer, Killian K. (N. Y.)
Varnum, Joseph B. (Mass.)
Weakley, Robert (Tenn.)
Wheaton, Laban (Mass.)
Whitehill, Robert (Pa.)
Whitman, Ezekiel (Mass.)
Wilson, James (N. H.)
Winn, Richard (S. C.)
Witherspoon, Robert (S.C.)
Wright, Robert (Md.)

The Twelfth Congress (1811-13)

Clay, Henry (Ky.) Speaker.

Alston, Willis, Jr. (N. C.)
Anderson, William (Pa.)
Archer, Stevenson (Md.)
Avery, Daniel (N. Y.)
Bacon, Ezekiel (Mass.)
Baker, John (Va.)
Bard, David (Pa.)
Barnett, William (Ga.)
Bartlett, Josiah (N. H.)
Bassett, Burwell (Va.)
Bibb, William W. (Ga.)
Bigelow, Abijah (Mass.)
Blackledge, William (N. C.)
Bleecker, Hermanus (N. Y.)
Blount, Thomas (N. C.)
Boyd, Adam (N. J.)
Breckinridge, James (Va.)
Brigham, Elijah (Mass.)
Brown, Robert (Pa.)
Burwell, William A. (Va.)
Butler, William (S. C.)
Calhoun, John C. (S. C.)
Carr, Francis (Mass.)
Champion, Epaphroditus (Conn.)
Cheves, Langdon (S. C.)
Chittenden, Martin (Vt.)
Clay, Henry (Ky.)
Clay, Matthew (Va.)
Clopton, John (Va.)
Cobb, Howell (Ga.)
Cochran, James (N. C.)
Condict, Lewis (N. J.)
Cooke, Thomas B. (N. Y.)
Crawford, William (Pa.)
Cutts, Richard (Mass.)
Dana, Samuel W. (Conn.)
Davenport, John (Conn.)
Davis, Roger (Pa.)
Dawson, John (Va.)
Desha, Joseph (Ky.)
Dinsmore, Samuel (N. H.)
Earle, Elias (S. C.)
Ely, William (Mass.)
Emott, James (N. Y.)
Findley, William (Pa.)
Fisk, James (Vt.)
Fitch, Asa (N. Y.)
Franklin, Meshack (N. C.)
Gholson, Thomas (Va.)
Gold, Thomas R. (N. Y.)
Goldsborough, Charles (Md.)
Goodwyn, Peterson (Va.)
Gray, Edwin (Va.)
Green, Isaiah L. (Mass.)
Grosvenor, Thomas P. (N. Y.)
Grundy, Felix (Tenn.)
Hall, Bolling (Ga.)
Hall, Obed (N. H.)
Harper, John A. (N. H.)
Hawes, Aylett (Va.)
Hufty, Jacob (N. J.)
Hungerford, John P. (Va.)
Hyneman, John M. (Pa.)
Jackson, Richard, Jr. (R. I.)
Johnson, Richard M. (Ky.)
Kennedy, William (N. C.)
Kent, Joseph (Md.)

Key, Phillip B. (Md.)
King, William R. (N. C.)
Lacock, Abner (Pa.)
Law, Lyman (Conn.)
Lefever, Joseph (Pa.)
Lewis, Joseph, Jr. (Va.)
Little, Peter (Md.)
Livingston, Robert Le Roy (N. Y.)
Lowndes, William (S. C.)
Lyle, Aaron (Pa.)
McBryde, Archibald (N. C.)
McCoy, William (Va.)
McKee, Samuel (Ky.)
McKim, Alexander (Md.)
Macon, Nathaniel (N. C.)
Maxwell, George C. (N. J.)
Metcalf, Arunah (N. Y.)
Milnor, James (Pa.)
Mitchill, Samuel L. (N. Y.)
Moore, Thomas (S. C.)
Morgan, James (N. J.)
Morrow, Jeremiah (Ohio)
Moseley, Jonathan O. (Conn.)
Nelson, Hugh (Va.)
New, Anthony (Ky.)
Newbold, Thomas (N. J.)
Newton, Thomas (Va.)
Ormsby, Stephen (Ky.)
Paulding, William, Jr. (N. Y.)
Pearson, Joseph (N. C.)
Pickens, Israel (N. C.)
Piper, William (Pa.)
Pitkin, Timothy, Jr. (Conn.)
Pleasants, James, Jr. (Va.)
Pond, Benjamin (N. Y.)
Porter, Peter B. (N. Y.)
Potter, Elisha R. (R. I.)
Quincy, Josiah (Mass.)
Randolph, John (Va.)
Reed, William (Mass.)
Rhea, John (Tenn.)
Richardson, William M. (Mass.)
Ridgeley, Henry M. (Del.)
Ringgold, Samuel (Md.)
Roane, John (Va.)
Roberts, Jonathan (Pa.)
Robertson, Thomas B. (La.)
Rodman, William (Pa.)
Sage, Ebenezer (N. Y.)
Sammons, Thomas (N. Y.)
Sawyer, Lemuel (N. C.)
Seaver, Ebenezer (Mass.)
Sevier, John (Tenn.)
Seybert, Adam (Pa.)
Shaw, Samuel (Vt.)
Sheffey, Daniel (Va.)
Smilie, John (Pa.)
Smith, George (Pa.)
Smith, John (Va.)
Stanford, Richard (N. C.)
Stow, Silas (N. Y.)
Strong, William (Vt.)
Stuart, Philip (Md.)
Sturges, Lewis B. (Conn.)
Sullivan, George (N. H.)
Taggart, Samuel (Mass.)
Taliaferro, John (Va.)
Tallmadge, Benjamin (Conn.)
Tallman, Peleg (Mass.)
Tracy, Uri (N. Y.)
Troup, George M. (Ga.)
Turner, Charles, Jr. (Mass.)
Van Cortlandt, Pierre, Jr. (N. Y.)
Wheaton, Laban (Mass.)
White, Leonard (Mass.)
Whitehill, Robert (Pa.)
Widgery, William (Mass.)
Williams, David R. (S. C.)
Wilson, Thomas (Va.)
Winn, Richard (S. C.)
Wright, Robert (Md.)

The Thirteenth Congress (1813-15)

Langdon, Cheves (S. C.)
Speaker.

Anderson, William (Pa.)
Alexander, John (Ohio)
Alston, Willis (N. C.)
Archer, Stevenson (Md.)
Avery, Daniel (N. Y.)
Barbour, Philip P. (Va.)
Bard, David (Pa.)
Barnett, William (Ga.)
Baylies, William (Mass.)
Bayly, Thomas M. (Va.)
Beall, Reasin (Ohio)
Benson, Egbert (N. Y.)
Bibb, William W. (Ga.)
Bigelow, Abijah (Mass.)
Bines, Thomas (N. J.)
Bowen, John H. (Tenn.)
Bowers, John M. (N. Y.)
Boyd, Alexander (N. Y.)
Bradbury, George (Mass.)
Bradley, William C. (Vt.)
Breckinridge, James (Va.)
Brigham, Elijah (Mass.)
Brown, Robert (Pa.)
Burwell, William A. (Va.)
Butler, Ezra (Vt.)
Caldwell, James (Ohio)
Calhoun, John C. (S. C.)
Cannon, Newton (Tenn.)
Caperton, Hugh (Va.)
Champion, Epaphroditus (Conn.)
Chappell, John J. (S. C.)
Cheves, Langdon (S. C.)
Cilley, Bradbury (N. H.)
Clark, James (Ky.)
Clay, Henry (Ky.)
Clendenin, David (Ohio)
Clopton, John (Va.)
Comstock, Oliver C. (N. Y.)
Conard, John (Pa.)
Condict, Lewis (N. J.)
Cooper, Thomas (Del.)
Coxe, William (N. J.)
Crawford, William (Pa.)
Creighton, William, Jr. (Ohio)
Crouch, Edward (Pa.)
Culpepper, John (N. C.)
Cuthbert, Alfred (Ga.)
Dana, Samuel (Mass.)
Davenport, John (Conn.)
Davis, Roger (Pa.)
Davis, Samuel (Mass.)
Dawson, John (Va.)
Denoyelles, Peter (N. Y.)
Desha, Joseph (Ky.)
Dewey, Daniel (Mass.)
Duval, William P. (Ky.)
Earle, Elias (S. C.)
Ely, William (Mass.)
Eppes, John W. (Va.)
Evans, David R. (S. C.)
Farrow, Samuel (S. C.)
Findley, William (Pa.)
Fisk, James (Vt.)
Fisk, Jonathan (N. Y.)
Forney, Peter (N. C.)
Forsyth, John (Ga.)
Franklin, Meshack (N. C.)
Gaston, William (N. C.)
Geddes, James (N. Y.)
Gholson, Thomas (Va.)
Glasgow, Hugh (Pa.)
Gloninger, John (Pa.)
Goldsborough, Charles (Md.)
Goodwyn, Peterson (Va.)
Gourdin, Theodore (S. C.)
Griffin, Isaac (Pa.)
Grosvenor, Thomas P. (N. Y.)
Grundy, Felix (Tenn.)
Hale, William (N. H.)
Hall, Bolling (Ga.)
Hanson, Alexander C. (Md.)
Harris, Thomas K. (Tenn.)
Hasbrouck, Abraham J. (N.Y.)
Hawes, Aylett (Va.)
Hawkins, Joseph H. (Ky.)
Henderson, Samuel (Pa.)
Hopkins, Samuel (Ky.)
Hopkins, Samuel M. (N. Y.)
Howell, Nathaniel W. (N. Y.)
Hubbard, Levi (Mass.)
Hufty, Jacob (N. J.)
Hulbert, John W. (Mass.)
Humphreys, Parry W. (Tenn.)
Hungerford, John P. (Va.)
Hyneman, John M. (Pa.)
Ingersoll, Charles J. (Pa.)
Ingham, Samuel D. (Pa.)
Irving, William (N. Y.)
Irwin, Jared (Pa.)
Jackson, John G. (Va.)
Jackson, Richard, Jr. (R. I.)
Johnson, James (Va.)
Johnson, Richard M. (Ky.)
Kennedy, William (N. C.)
Kent, Joseph (Md.)
Kent, Moss (N. Y.)
Kerr, John (Va.)
Kershaw, John (S. C.)
Kilbourne, James (Ohio)
King, Cyrus (Mass.)
King, William R. (N. C.)
Law, Lyman (Conn.)
Lefferts, John (N. Y.)
Lewis, Joseph, Jr. (Va.)
Lovett, John (N. Y.)
Lowndes, William (S. C.)
Lyle, Aaron (Pa.)
McCoy, William (Va.)
McKee, Samuel (Ky.)
McKim, Alexander (Md.)
McLean, John (Ohio)
Macon, Nathaniel (N. C.)
Markell, Jacob (N. Y.)
Miller, Morris S. (N. Y.)
Moffitt, Hosea (N. Y.)
Moore, Nicholas R. (Md.)
Montgomery, Thomas (Ky.)
Moseley, Jonathan O. (Conn.)
Murfree, William H. (N. C.)
Nelson, Hugh (Va.)
Newton, Thomas (Va.)
Oakley, Thomas J. (N. Y.)
Ormsby, Stephen (Ky.)
Parker, James (Mass.)
Pearson, Joseph (N. C.)
Pickens, Israel (N. C.)
Pickering, Timothy (Mass.)
Piper, William (Pa.)
Pitkin, Timothy, Jr. (Conn.)
Pleasants, James, Jr. (Va.)
Post, Jotham, Jr. (N. Y.)
Potter, Elisha R. (R. I.)
Rea, John (Pa.)
Reed, John (Mass.)
Reed, William (Mass.)
Rhea, John (Tenn.)
Rich, Charles (Vt.)
Richardson, William M. (Mass.)
Ridgeley, Henry M. (Del.)
Ringgold, Samuel (Md.)
Roane, John (Va.)
Roberts, Jonathan (Pa.)
Robertson, Thomas B. (La.)
Ruggles, Nathaniel (Mass.)
Sage, Ebenezer (N. Y.)
Schureman, James (N. J.)
Sevier, John (Tenn.)
Seybert, Adam (Pa.)
Sharp, Solomon P. (Ky.)
Sheffey, Daniel (Va.)
Sherwood, Samuel (N. Y.)
Shipherd, Zebulon R. (N. Y.)
Skinner, Richard (Vt.)
Slaymaker, Amos (Pa.)
Smith, Isaac (Pa.)
Smith, John (Va.)
Smith, Samuel (N. H.)
Smith, Samuel S. (N. Y.)
Stanford, Richard (N. C.)
Stockton, Richard (N. J.)
Strong, William (Vt.)
Stuart, Philip (Md.)
Sturges, Lewis B. (Conn.)
Taggart, Samuel (Mass.)
Tallmadge, Benjamin (Conn.)
Tannehill, Adamson (Pa.)
Taylor, John W. (N. Y.)
Telfair, Thomas (Ga.)
Thompson, Joel (N. Y.)
Troup, George M. (Ga.)
Udree, Daniel (Pa.)
Vose, Roger (N. H.)
Ward, Artemas (Mass.)
Ward, Thomas (N. J.)
Webster, Daniel (N. H.)
Wheaton, Laban (Mass.)
White, Francis (Va.)
Whitehill, James (Pa.)
Wilcox, Jeduthun (N. H.)
Williams, Isaac, Jr. (N. Y.)
Winter, Elisha J. (N. Y.)
Wilson, Thomas (Pa.)
Wilson, John (Mass.)
Wood, Abiel (Mass.)
Wright, Robert (Md.)
Yancy, Bartlett (N. C.)

The Fourteenth Congress (1815-16)

Clay, Henry (Ky.)
Speaker.

Adams, Benjamin (Mass.)
Adam, John (N. Y.)
Adgate, Asa (N. Y.)
Alexander, John (Ohio)
Archer, Stevenson (Md.)
Atherton, Charles H. (N. H.)
Avery, Daniel (N. Y.)
Baer, George (Md.)
Baker, Ezra (N. J.)
Barbour, Philip P. (Va.)
Bassett, Burwell (Va.)
Bateman, Ephraim (N. J.)
Baylies, William (Mass.)
Bennet, Benjamin (N. J.)
Betts, Samuel R. (N. Y.)
Birdsall, James (N. Y.)
Birdseye, Victory (N. Y.)
Blount, William G. (Tenn.)
Boss, John L., Jr. (R. I.)
Bradbury, George (Mass.)
Breckinridge, James (Va.)
Brigham, Elijah (Mass.)
Brown, Benjamin (Mass.)
Brooks, Micah (N. Y.)
Bryan, Joseph H. (N. C.)
Burnside, Thomas (Pa.)
Burwell, William A. (Va.)
Cady, Daniel (N. Y.)
Caldwell, James (Ohio)
Calhoun, John C. (S. C.)
Cannon, Newton (Tenn.)
Carr, James (Mass.)
Champion, Epaphroditus (Conn.)
Chappell, John J. (S. C.)
Chipman, Daniel (Vt.)
Cilley, Bradbury (N. H.)
Clarke, Archibald S. (N. Y.)
Clark, James (Ky.)
Clark, James W. (N. C.)
Clay, Henry (Ky.)
Clayton, Thomas (Del.)
Clendenin, David (Ohio)
Clopton, John (Va.)
Comstock, Oliver C. (N. Y.)
Condict, Lewis (N. J.)
Connor, Samuel S. (Mass.)
Cook, Zadock (Ga.)
Cooper, Thomas (Del.)
Crawford, William (Pa.)
Creighton, William, Jr. (Ohio)
Crocheron, Henry (N. Y.)
Culpepper, John (N. C.)
Cuthbert, Alfred (Ga.)
Darlington, William (Pa.)
Davenport, John, Jr. (Conn.)
Desha, Joseph (Ky.)
Dickens, Samuel (N. C.)
Edwards, Weldon N. (N. C.)
Findley, William (Pa.)
Fletcher, Thomas (Ky.)
Forney, Daniel M. (N. C.)
Forsyth, John (Ga.)
Gaston, William (N. C.)
Gholson, Thomas (Va.)
Glasgow, Hugh (Pa.)
Gold, Thomas R. (N. Y.)
Goldsborough, Charles (Md.)
Goodwyn, Peterson (Va.)
Griffin, Isaac (Pa.)
Grosvenor, Thomas P. (N. Y.)
Hahn, John (Pa.)
Hale, William (N. H.)
Hall, Bolling (Ga.)
Hammond, Jabez D. (N. Y.)
Hanson, Alex. C. (Md.)
Hardin, Benjamin (Ky.)
Harrison, William H. (Ohio)
Hawes, Aylett (Va.)
Henderson, Bennett H. (Tenn.)
Hendricks, William (Ind.)
Herbert, John C. (Md.)
Hiester, Joseph (Pa.)
Hooks, Charles (N. C.)
Hopkinson, Joseph (Pa.)
Huger, Benjamin (S. C.)
Hulbert, John W. (Mass.)
Hungerford, John P. (Va.)
Ingham, Samuel D. (Pa.)

Irving, William (N. Y.)
Irwin, Jared (Pa.)
Jackson, John G. (Va.)
Jewett, Luther (Vt.)
Johnson, James (Va.)
Johnson, Richard M. (Ky.)
Kent, Moss (N. Y.)
Kerr, John (Va.)
Kilbourne, James (Ohio)
King, Cyrus (Mass.)
King, William R. (N. C.)
Langdon, Chauncey (Vt.)
Law, Lyman (Conn.)
Lewis, Joseph, Jr. (Va.)
Little, Peter (Md.)
Lowndes, William (S. C.)
Love, William C. (N. C.)
Lovett, John (N. Y.)
Lumpkin, Wilson (Ga.)
Lyle, Aaron (Pa.)
Lyon, Asa (Vt.)
McCoy, William (Va.)
McKee, Samuel (Ky.)
Maclay, William (Pa.)
Maclay, Wm. P. (Pa.)
McLean, Alney (Ky.)
McLean, John (Ohio)
Macon, Nathaniel (N. C.)
Marsh, Charles (Vt.)
Mason, James B. (R. I.)
Mayrant, William (S. C.)
Middleton, Henry (S. C.)
Miller, Stephen D. (S. C.)
Mills, Elijah H. (Mass.)
Milnor, William (Pa.)
Moffitt, Hosea (N. Y.)
Moore, Thomas (S. C.)
Moseley, Jonathan O. (Conn.)
Murfree, William H. (N. C.)
Nelson, Jeremiah (Mass.)
Nelson, Hugh (Va.)
Nelson, Thomas M. (Va.)
Newton, Thomas (Va.)
Noyes, John (Vt.)
Ormsby, Stephen (Ky.)
Parris, Albion K. (Mass.)
Peter, George (Md.)
Pickens, Israel (N. C.)
Pickering, Timothy (Mass.)
Pinkney, William (Md.)
Piper, William (Pa.)
Pitkin, Timothy (Conn.)
Pleasants, James (Va.)
Porter, Peter B. (N. Y.)
Powell, Samuel (Tenn.)
Randolph, John (Va.)
Reed, John (Mass.)
Reynolds, James B. (Tenn.)
Rice, Thomas (Mass.)
Roane, William H. (Va.)
Robertson, Thomas B. (La.)
Root, Erastus (N. Y.)
Ross, John (Pa.)
Ruggles, Nathaniel (Mass.)
Savage, John (N. Y.)
Schenck, Abraham H. (N. Y.)
Sergeant, John (Pa.)
Sharp, Solomon P. (Ky.)
Sheffey, Daniel (Va.)
Smith, Ballard (Va.)
Smith, Samuel (Md.)
Smith, Thomas (Pa.)
Southard, Henry (N. J.)
Stanford, Richard (N. C.)
Stearns, Asahel (Mass.)
Strong, Solomon (Mass.)
Stuart, Philip (Md.)
Sturges, Lewis B. (Conn.)
Taggart, Samuel (Mass.)
Tallmadge, Benjamin (Conn.)
Tate, Magnus (Va.)
Taul, Micah (Ky.)
Taylor, John (S. C.)
Taylor, John W. (N. Y.)
Telfair, Thomas (Ga.)
Thomas, Isaac (Tenn.)
Throop, Enos T. (N. Y.)
Townsend, George (N. Y.)
Tucker, Henry St. George (Va.)
Tyler, John (Va.)
Vose, Roger (N. H.)
Wallace, James M. (Pa.)
Ward, Artemas (Mass.)
Ward, Jonathan (N. Y.)
Ward, Thomas (N. J.)
Webster, Daniel (N. H.)
Wendover, Peter H. (N. Y.)
Wheaton, Laban (Mass.)
Whiteside, John (Pa.)
Wilcox, Jeduthun (N. H.)
Wilde, Richard Henry (Ga.)
Wilkin, James W. (N. Y.)
Williams, Lewis (N. C.)
Willoughby, Westel, Jr. (N. Y.)
Wilson, Thomas (Pa.)
Wilson, William (Pa.)
Woodward, William (S. C.)
Wright, Robert (Md.)
Yancey, Bartlett (N. C.)
Yates, John B. (N. Y.)

The Fifteenth Congress (1815-17)

Clay, Henry (Ky.) Speaker.

Abbot, Joel (Ga.)
Adams, Benjamin (Mass.)
Allen, Heman (Vt.)
Allen, Samuel C. (Mass.)
Anderson, Richard C., Jr. (Ky.)
Anderson, William (Pa.)
Austin, Archibald (Va.)
Baldwin, Henry (Pa.)
Ball, William Lee (Vt.)
Barber, Levi (Ohio)
Barbour, Philip P. (Va.)
Bassett, Burwell (Va.)
Bateman, Ephraim (N. J.)
Bayly, Thomas (Md.)
Beecher, Philemon (Ohio)
Bellinger, Joseph (S. C.)
Bennett, Benjamin (N. J.)
Bloomfield, Joseph (N. J.)
Blount, William G. (Tenn.)
Boden, Andrew (Pa.)
Boss, John L., Jr. (R. I.)
Bryan, Joseph H. (N. C.)
Butler, Josiah (N. H.)
Butler, Thomas (La.)
Burwell, William A. (Va.)
Campbell, John W. (Ohio)
Clagett, Clifton (N. H.)
Claiborne, Thomas (Tenn.)
Clay, Henry (Ky.)
Cobb, Thomas W. (Ga.)
Colston, Edward (Va.)
Comstock, Oliver C. (N. Y.)
Cook, Zadock (Ga.)
Crafts, Samuel C. (Vt.)
Crawford, Joel (Ga.)
Cruger, Daniel (N. Y.)
Culbreth, Thomas (Md.)
Cushman, John P. (N. Y.)
Darlington, Isaac (Pa.)
Davidson, William (N. C.)
Desha, Joseph (Ky.)
Drake, John R. (N. Y.)
Earle, Elias (S. C.)
Edwards, Weldon N. (N. C.)
Ellicott, Benjamin (N. Y.)
Ervin, James (S. C.)
Fisher, Charles (N. C.)
Floyd, John (Va.)
Folger, Walter, Jr. (Mass.)
Forney, Daniel M. (N. C.)
Forsyth, John (Ga.)
Fuller, Timothy (Mass.)
Gage, Joshua (Mass.)
Garnett, Robert S. (Va.)
Gilbert, Sylvester (Conn.)
Goodwyn, Peterson (Va.)
Hale, Salma (N. H.)
Hall, Thomas H. (N. C.)
Hall, Willard (Del.)
Hasbrouck, Josiah (N. Y.)
Harrison, William H. (Ohio)
Hiester, Joseph (Pa.)
Hendricks, William (Ind.)
Herbert, John C. (Md.)
Herkimer, John (N. Y.)
Herrick, Samuel (Ohio)
Hitchcock, Peter (Ohio)
Hogg, Samuel (Tenn.)
Holmes, John (Mass)
Holmes, Uriel (Conn.)
Hopkinson, Joseph (Pa.)
Hostetter, Jacob (Va.)
Hubbard, Thomas H. (N. Y.)
Hunter, William (Vt.)
Huntington, Ebenezer (Conn.)
Ingham, Samuel D. (Pa.)
Irving, William (N. Y.)
Johnson, James (Va.)
Johnson, Richard M. (Ky.)
Jones, Francis (Tenn.)
Kinsey, Charles (N. J.)
Kirtland, Dorrance (N. Y.)
Lawyer, Thomas (N. Y.)
Lewis, William J. (Va.)
Lincoln, Enoch (Mass.)
Linn, John (N. J.)
Little, Peter (Md.)
Livermore, Arthur (N. H.)
Lowndes, William (S. C.)
McCoy, William (Va.)
McLane, Louis (Del.)
Maclay, William (Pa.)
Maclay, William P. (Pa.)
McLean, John (Ill.)
Marchand, David (Pa.)
Marr, George W. L. (Tenn.)
Mason, James B. (R. I.)
Mason, Jonathan (Mass.)
Mercer, Charles F. (Va.)
Merrill, Orsamus C. (Vt.)
Middleton, Henry (S. C.)
Miller, Stephen D. (S. C.)
Mills, Elijah H. (Mass.)
Moore, Robert (Pa.)
Moore, Samuel (Pa.)
Morton, Marcus (Mass.)
Moseley, Jonathan O. (Conn.)
Mumford, George (N. C.)
Murray, John (Pa.)
Nelson, Hugh (Va.)
Nelson, Jeremiah (Mass.)
Nelson, Thomas M. (Va.)
Nesbitt, Wilson (S. C.)
New, Anthony (Ky.)
Newton, Thomas (Va.)
Ogden, David A. (N. Y.)
Ogle, Alexander (Pa.)
Orr, Benjamin (Mass.)
Owen, James (N. C.)
Palmer, John (N. Y.)
Parris, Albion K. (Mass.)
Parrott, John F. (N. H.)
Patterson, Thomas (Pa.)
Pawling, Levi (Pa.)
Pegram, John (Va.)
Peter, George (Md.)
Pindall, James (Va.)
Pitkin, Timothy (Conn.)
Pleasants, James (Va.)
Poindexter, George (Miss.)
Porter, James (N. Y.)
Quarles, Tunstall, Jr. (Ky.)
Reed, Philip (Md.)
Reid, Robert R. (Ga.)
Rhea, John (Tenn.)
Rice, Thomas (Mass.)
Rich, Charles (Vt.)
Richards, Mark (Vt.)
Ringgold, Samuel (Md.)
Robertson, George (Ky.)
Robertson, Thomas B. (La.)
Rogers, Thomas J. (Pa.)
Ross, John (Pa.)
Ruggles, Nathaniel (Mass.)
Savage, John (N. Y.)
Sampson, Zabdiel (Mass.)
Sawyer, Lemuel (N. C.)
Schuyler, Philip J. (N. Y.)
Scudder, Treadwell (N. Y.)
Sergeant, John (Pa.)
Settle, Thomas (N. C.)
Seybert, Adam (Pa.)
Shaw, Henry (Mass.)
Sherwood, Samuel B. (Conn.)
Silsbee, Nathaniel (Mass.)
Simkins, Eldred (S. C.)
Slocumb, Jesse (N. C.)
Smith, Ballard (Va.)
Smith, James S. (N. C.)
Smith, Samuel (Md.)
Smyth, Alexander (Va.)
Southard, Henry (N. J.)
Spangler, Jacob (Pa.)
Speed, Thomas (Ky.)
Spencer, John C. (N. Y.)
Stewart, James (N. C.)
Stuart, Philip (Md.)
Storrs, Henry R. (N. Y.)
Strong, Solomon (Mass.)
Strother, George F. (Va.)
Tallmadge, James, Jr. (N. Y.)
Tarr, Christian (Pa.)
Taylor, John W. (N. Y.)
Terrell, William (Ga.)
Terry, Nathaniel (Conn.)
Tompkins, Caleb (N. Y.)
Townsend, George (N. Y.
Trimble, David (Ky.)
Tucker, Henry St. George (Va.)
Tucker, Starling, (S. C.)
Tyler, John (Va.)
Upham, Nathaniel (N. H.)
Walker, David (Ky.)
Walker, Felix (N. C.)
Wallace, James M. (Pa.)
Wendover, Peter H. (N. Y.)
Westerlo, Rensselaer (N. Y.)
Whiteside, John (Pa.)
Whitman, Ezekiel (Mass.)
Wilkin, James W. (N. Y.)
Williams, Isaac (N. Y.)
Williams, Lewis (N. C.)
Williams, Thomas S. (Conn.)
Wilson, John (Mass.)
Wilson, William (Pa.)

The Sixteenth Congress (1819-21)

Clay, Henry (Ky.) and Taylor, John W. (N. Y.) Speakers.

Abbot, Joel (Ga.)
Adams, Benjamin (Mass.)
Allen, Nathaniel (N. Y.)
Allen, Robert (Tenn.)
Allen, Samuel C. (Mass.)
Alexander, Mark (Va.)
Anderson, Richard C., Jr. (Ky.)
Archer, Stevenson (Md.)
Archer, William S. (Va.)
Baker, Caleb (N. Y.)
Baldwin, Henry (Pa.)
Ball, William Lee (Va.)
Barbour, Philip P. (Va.)
Bateman, Ephraim (N. J.)
Bayly, Thomas (Md.)
Beecher, Philemon (Ohio)
Blackledge, William S. (N. C.)
Bloomfield, Joseph (N. J.)
Boden, Andrew (Pa.)
Brevard, Joseph (S. C.)
Brown, William (Ky.)
Brush, Henry (Ohio)
Bryan, Henry H. (Tenn.)
Buffum, Joseph, Jr. (N. H.)
Burton, Hutchins G. (N. C.)
Burwell, William A. (Va.)
Butler, Josiah (N. H.)
Butler, Thomas (La.)
Campbell, John W. (Ohio)
Cannon, Newton (Tenn.)
Case, Walter (N. Y.)
Clagett, Clifton (N. H.)
Clark, Robert (N. Y.)
Clay, Henry (Ky.)
Cobb, Thomas W. (Ga.)
Cocke, John (Tenn.)
Cook, Daniel P. (Ill.)
Crafts, Samuel C. (Vt.)
Crawford, Joel (Ga.)
Crowell, John (Ala.)
Culbreth, Thomas (Md.)
Culpepper, John (N. C.)
Cushman, Joshua (Mass.)
Cuthbert, John A. (Ga.)
Dane, Joseph (Maine)
Darlington, William (Pa.)
Davidson, William (N. C.)
Denison, George (Pa.)
De Witt, Jacob H. (N. Y.)
Dickinson, John D. (N. Y.)
Dowse, Edward (Mass.)
Earle, Elias (S. C.)
Eddy, Samuel (R. I.)
Edwards, Henry W. (Conn.)
Edwards, Samuel (Pa.)
Edwards, Weldon N. (N. C.)
Ervin, James (S. C.)
Eustis, William (Mass.)
Fay, John (N. Y.)
Fisher, Charles (N. C.)

Floyd, John (Va.)
Folger, Walter, Jr. (Mass.)
Foote, Samuel A. (Conn.)
Ford, William D. (N. Y.)
Forrest, Thomas (Pa.)
Fuller, Timothy (Mass.)
Fullerton, David (Pa.)
Garnett, Robert S. (Va.)
Gorham, Benjamin (Mass.)
Gray, John C. (Va.)
Gross, Ezra C. (N. Y.)
Gross, Samuel (Pa.)
Guyon, James, Jr. (N. Y.)
Hackley, Aaron, Jr. (N. Y.)
Hall, George (N. Y.)
Hall, Thomas H. (N. C.)
Hall, Willard (Del.)
Hardin, Benjamin (Ky.)
Hazard, Nathaniel (R. I.)
Hemphill, Joseph (Pa.)
Hendricks, William (Ind.)
Herrick, Samuel (Ohio)
Hibschman, Jacob (Pa.)
Hiester, Joseph (Pa.)
Hill, Mark L. (Mass.)
Hobart, Aaron (Mass.)
Holmes, John (Mass.)
Hooks, Charles (N. C.)
Hostetter, Jacob (Pa.)
Jackson, Edward B. (Va.)
Johnson, Francis (Ky.)
Johnson, James (Va.)
Jones, Francis (Tenn.)
Jones, James (Va.)
Kendall, Jonas (Mass.)
Kent, Joseph (Md.)
Kinsey, Charles (N. J.)
Kinsley, Martin (Mass.)
Lathrop, Samuel (Mass.)
Lincoln, Enoch (Mass.)
Linn, John (N. J.)
Little, Peter (Md.)
Livermore, Arthur (N. H.)
Lowndes, William (S. C.)
Lyman, Joseph S. (N. Y.)
McCoy, William (Va.)
McCreary, John (S. C.)
McCullough, Thomas G. (Pa.)
McLane, Louis (Del.)
Maclay, William P. (Pa.)
McLean, Alney (Ky.)
Mallary, Rollin C. (Vt.)
Marchand, David (Pa.)
Mason, Jonathan (Mass.)
Meech, Ezra (Vt.)
Meigs, Henry (N. Y.)
Mercer, Charles F. (Va.)
Merrill, Orasmus C. (Vt.)
Metcalfe, Thomas (Ky.)
Monell, Robert (N. Y.)
Montgomery, Thomas (Ky.)
Moore, Robert (Pa.)
Moore, Samuel (Pa.)
Moore, Thomas L. (Va.)
Morton, Marcus (Mass.)
Moseley, Jonathan O. (Conn.)
Murray, John (Pa.)
Neale, Raphael (Md.)
Nelson, Hugh (Va.)
Nelson, Jeremiah (Mass.)
Newton, Thomas (Va.)
Overstreet, James (S. C.)
Parker, James (Mass.)
Parker, Severn E. (Va.)
Patterson, Thomas (Pa.)
Peek, Hermanus (N. Y.)
Phelps, Elisha (Conn.)
Philson, Robert (Pa.)
Pinckney, Charles (S. C.)
Pindall, James (Va.)
Pitcher, Nathaniel (N. Y.)
Pleasants, James (Va.)
Plumer, William, Jr. (N. H.)
Quarles, Tunstall, Jr. (Ky.)
Randolph, John (Va.)
Rankin, Christopher (Miss.)
Reid, Robert R. (Ga.)
Rhea, John (Tenn.)
Rich, Charles (Vt.)
Richards, Mark (Vt.)
Richmond, Jonathan (N. Y.)
Ringgold, Samuel (Md.)
Robertson, George (Ky.)
Rogers, Thomas J. (Pa.)
Ross, Thomas R. (Ohio)
Russ, John (Conn.)
Sampson, Zabdiel (Mass.)
Sawyer, Lemuel (N. C.)
Sergeant, John (Pa.)
Settle, Thomas (N. C.)
Shaw, Henry (Mass.)
Silsbee, Nathaniel (Mass.)
Simkins, Eldred (S. C.)
Sloane, John (Ohio)
Slocumb, Jesse (N. C.)
Smith, Ballard (Va.)
Smith, Bernard (N. J.)
Smith, James S. (N. C.)
Smith, Samuel (Md.)
Smyth, Alexander (Va.)
Southard, Henry (N. J.)
Stevens, James (Conn.)
Storrs, Henry R. (N. Y.)
Street, Randall S. (N. Y.)
Strong, James (N. Y.)
Strong, William (Vt.)
Strother, George F. (Va.)
Swearingen, Thomas (Va.)
Tarr, Christian (Pa.)
Taylor, John W. (N. Y.)
Terrell, William (Ga.)
Tomlinson, Gideon (Conn.)
Tompkins, Caleb (N. Y.)
Tracey, Albert H. (N. Y.)
Trimble, David (Ky.)
Tucker, George (Va.)
Tucker, Starling (S. C.)
Tyler, John (Va.)
Udree, Daniel (Pa.)
Upham, Nathaniel (N. H.)
Van Rensselaer, Solomon (N. Y.)
Walker, David (Ky.)
Walker, Felix (N. C.)
Wallace, James M. (Pa.)
Warfield, Henry R. (Md.)
Wendover, Peter H. (N. Y.)
Whitman, Ezekiel (Mass.)
Williams, Jared (Va.)
Williams, Lewis (N. C.)
Wood, Silas (N. Y.)

The Seventeenth Congress (1821-23)

Barbour, Philip P. (Va.) Speaker.

Abbot, Joel (Ga.)
Alexander, Mark (Va.)
Allen, Robert (Tenn.)
Allen, Samuel C. (Mass.)
Archer, William S. (Va.)
Ball, William Lee (Va.)
Baldwin, Henry (Pa.)
Barber, Noyes (Conn.)
Barber, Levi (Ohio)
Barbour, Philip P. (Va.)
Bassett, Burwell (Va.)
Barstow, Gideon (Mass.)
Bateman, Ephraim (N. J.)
Baylies, Francis (Mass.)
Bayly, Thomas (Md.)
Bigelow, Lewis (Mass.)
Blackledge, William S. (N. C.)
Blair, James (S. C.)
Borland, Charles (N. Y.)
Breckinridge, James D. (Ky.)
Brown, John (Pa.)
Buchanan, James (Pa.)
Burton, Hutchins G. (N. C.)
Burrows, Daniel (Conn.)
Butler, Josiah (N. H.)
Cambreleng, Churchill C. (N. Y.)
Campbell, John W. (Ohio)
Campbell, Samuel (N. Y.)
Cannon, Newton (Tenn.)
Carter, John (S. C.)
Cassedy, George (N. J.)
Chambers, David (Ohio)
Cocke, John (Tenn.)
Colden, Cadwallader D. (N.Y.)
Condict, Lewis (N. J.)
Conkling, Alfred (N. Y.)
Connor, Henry W. (N. C.)
Cook, Daniel P. (Ill.)
Cosden, Jeremiah (Md.)
Crafts, Samuel C. (Vt.)
Crudup, Josiah (N. C.)
Cushman, Joshua (Maine)
Cuthbert, Alfred (Ga.)
Dane, Joseph (Maine)
Darlington, William (Pa.)
Denison, George (Pa.)
Dickinson, John D. (N. Y.)
Durfee, Job (R. I.)
Dwight, Henry W. (Mass.)
Eddy, Samuel (R. I.)
Edwards, Henry W. (Conn.)
Edwards, Samuel (Pa.)
Edwards, Weldon N. (N. C.)
Eustis, William (Mass.)
Farrelly, Patrick (Pa.)
Findley, John (Pa.)
Floyd, John (Va.)
Forrest, Thomas (Pa.)
Forward, Walter (Pa.)
Fuller, Timothy (Mass.)
Garnett, Robert S. (Va.)
Gebhard, John (N. Y.)
Gilmer, George R. (Ga.)
Gist, Joseph (S. C.)
Gorham, Benjamin (Mass.)
Govan, Andrew R. (S. C.)
Gross, Samuel (Pa.)
Hall, Thomas H. (N. C.)
Hamilton, James (S. C.)
Hardin, Benjamin (Ky.)
Harris, Mark (Maine)
Harvey, Matthew (N. H.)
Hawkes, James (N. Y.)
Hemphill, Joseph (Pa.)
Hendricks, William (Ind.)
Herrick, Ebenezer (Maine)
Hill, Mark L. (Maine)
Hobart, Aaron (Mass.)
Holcombe, George (N. J.)
Hooks, Charles (N. C.)
Hubbard, Thomas H. (N. Y.)
Ingham, Samuel D. (Pa.)
Jackson, Edward B. (Va.)
Jennings, Jonathan (Ind.)
Johnson, Francis (Ky.)
Johnson, John T. (Ky.)
Johnston, Josiah S. (La.)
Jones, Francis (Tenn.)
Jones, James (Va.)
Kent, Joseph (Md.)
Keyes, Elias (Vt.)
Kirkland, Joseph (N. Y.)
Lathrop, Samuel (Mass.)
Leftwich, Jabez (Va.)
Lincoln, Enoch (Maine)
Litchfield, Elisha (N. Y.)
Little, Peter (Md.)
Long, John (N. C.)
Lowndes, William (S. C.)
McCarty, Richard (N. Y.)
McCoy, William (Va.)
McDuffie, George (S. C.)
McLane, Louis (Del.)
McKim, Isaac (Md.)
McNeill, Archibald (N. C.)
McSherry, James (Pa.)
Mallary, Rollin C. (Vt.)
Matlack, James (N. J.)
Matson, Aaron (N. H.)
Mattocks, John (Vt.)
Mercer, Charles F. (Va.)
Metcalfe, Thomas (Ky.)
Milnor, William (Pa.)
Mitchell, James S. (Pa.)
Mitchell, Thomas R. (S. C.)
Montgomery, Thomas (Ky.)
Moore, Gabriel (Ala.)
Moore, Samuel (Pa.)
Moore, Thomas L. (Va.)
Morgan, John J. (N. Y.)
Murray, Thomas, Jr. (Pa.)
Neale, Raphael (Md.)
Nelson, Hugh (Va.)
Nelson, Jeremiah (Mass.)
Nelson, John (Md.)
New, Anthony (Ky.)
Newton, Thomas (Va.)
Overstreet, James (S. C.)
Patterson, Thomas (Pa.)
Patterson, Walter (N. Y.)
Phillips, John (Pa.)
Pierson, Jeremiah H. (N. Y.)
Pitcher, Nathaniel (N. Y.)
Plumer, George (Pa.)
Plumer, William, Jr. (N. H.)
Poinsett, Joel R. (S. C.)
Randolph, John (Va.)
Rankin, Christopher (Miss.)
Reed, John (Mass.)
Reed, Philip (Md.)
Reid, Robert R. (Ga.)
Rhea, John (Tenn.)
Rich, Charles (Vt.)
Rochester, William B. (N. Y.)
Rodney, Cæsar A. (Del.)
Rodney, Daniel (Del.)
Rogers, Thomas J. (Pa.)
Ross, Thomas R. (Ohio)
Ruggles, Charles H. (N. Y.)
Russ, John (Conn.)
Russell, Jonathan (Mass.)
Saunders, Romulus M. (N. C.)
Sawyer, Lemuel (N. C.)
Scott, John (Mo.)
Sergeant, John (Pa.)
Sloane, John (Ohio)
Smith, Arthur (Va.)
Smith, John S. (Ky.)
Smith, Samuel (Md.)
Smith, William (Va.)
Smyth, Alexander (Va.)
Spencer, Elijah (N. Y.)
Stephenson, James (Va.)
Sterling, Ansel (Conn.)
Sterling, Micah (N. Y.)
Stevenson, Andrew (Va.)
Stewart, Andrew (Pa.)
Stoddard, Ebenezer (Conn.)
Swan, Samuel (N. J.)
Tatnall, Edward F. (Ga.)
Taylor, John W. (N. Y.)
Thompson, Wiley (Ga.)
Tod, John (Pa.)
Tomlinson, Gideon (Conn.)
Tracy, Albert H. (N. Y.)
Trimble, David (Ky.)
Tucker, George (Va.)
Tucker, Starling (S. C.)
Udree, Daniel (Pa.)
Upham, Nathaniel (N. H.)
Vance, Joseph (Ohio)
Van Rensselaer, Solomon (N. Y.)
Van Rensselaer, Stephen (N. Y.)
Van Swearingen, Thomas (Va.)
Van Wyck, William W. (N.Y.)
Walker, Felix (N. C.)
Walworth, Reuben H. (N. Y.)
Warfield, Henry R. (Md.)
Whipple, Thomas, Jr. (N. H.)
White, Phineas (Vt.)
Whitman, Ezekiel (Maine)
Williams, Jared (Va.)
Williams, Lewis (N. C.)
Williamson, William D. (Maine)
Wilson, John (S. C.)
Wood, Silas (N. Y.)
Woodcock, David (N. Y.)
Woodson, Samuel H. (Ky.)
Worman, Ludwig (Pa.)
Wright, Robert (Md.)

The Eighteenth Congres (1823-25)

Clay, Henry (Ky.) Speaker.

Abbott, Joel (Ga.)
Adams, Parmenio (N. Y.)
Alexander, Adam R. (Tenn.)
Alexander, Mark (Va.)
Allen, Robert (Tenn.)
Allen, Samuel C. (Mass.)
Allison, James (Pa.)
Archer, William S. (Va.)
Bailey, John (Mass.)
Ball, William L. (Va.)
Barber, Noyes (Conn.)
Barbour, John S. (Va.)
Barbour, Philip P. (Va.)
Bartlett, Ichabod (N. H.)
Bartley, Mordecai (Ohio)
Bassett, Burwell (Va.)
Baylies, Francis (Mass.)
Beecher, Philemon (Ohio)
Blair, John (Tenn.)
Bradley, William C. (Vt.)
Breck, Samuel (Pa.)
Brent, William L. (La.)
Brown, John (Pa.)
Buchanan, James (Pa.)

Buck, Daniel A. A. (Vt.)
Buckner, Richard A. (Ky.)
Burleigh, William (Maine)
Burton, Hutchins G. (N. C.)
Cady, John W. (N. Y.)
Call, Jacob (Ind.)
Cambreleng, Churchill C. (N. Y.)
Campbell, John W. (Ohio)
Campbell, Robert B. (S. C.)
Carter, John (S. C.)
Cary, George (Ga.)
Cassedy, George (N. J.)
Clark, Lot (N. Y.)
Clay, Henry (Ky.)
Cobb, Thomas W. (Ga.)
Cocke, John (Tenn.)
Collins, Ela (N. Y.)
Condict, Lewis (N. J.)
Connor, Henry W. (N. C.)
Connor,, Henry W. (N. C.)
Cook, Daniel P. (Ill.)
Crafts, Samuel C. (Vt.)
Craig, Hector (N. Y.)
Crowninshield, Benjamin W. (Mass.)
Culpepper, John (N. C.)
Cushman, Joshua (Maine)
Cuthbert, Alfred (Ga.)
Day, Roland (N. Y.)
Durfee, Job (R. I.)
Dwight, Henry W. (Mass.)
Dwinell, Justin (N. Y.)
Eaton, Lewis (N. Y.)
Eddy, Samuel (R. I.)
Edwards, Samuel (Pa.)
Edwards, Weldon N. (N. C.)
Ellis, William Cox (Pa.)
Farrelly, Patrick (Pa.)
Findlay, John (Pa.)
Floyd, John (Va.)
Foote, Samuel A. (Conn.)
Foote, Charles A. (N. Y.)
Forsyth, John (Ga.)
Forward, Walter (Pa.)
Frost, Joel (N. Y.)
Fuller, Timothy (Mass.)
Garnett, Robert S. (Va.)
Garrison, Daniel (N. J.)
Gatlin, Alfred M. (N. C.)
Gazlay, John W. (Ohio)
Gist, Joseph (S. C.)
Govan, Andrew R. (S. C.)
Gurley, Henry H. (La.)
Hall, Thomas H. (N. C.)
Hamilton, James, Jr. (S. C.)
Harris, Robert (Pa.)
Harvey, Matthew (N. H.)
Hayden, Moses (N. Y.)
Hemphill, Joseph (Pa.)
Henry, Robert P. (Ky.)
Herkimer, John (N. Y.)
Herrick, Ebenezer (Maine)
Heyward, William, Jr. (Md.)
Hobart, Aaron (Mass.)
Hogeboom, James L. (N. Y.)
Holcombe, George (N. J.)
Hooks, Charles (N. C.)
Houston, Samuel (Tenn.)
Ingham, Samuel D. (Pa.)
Isacks, Jacob C. (Tenn.)
Jenkins, Lemuel (N. Y.)
Jennings, Jonathan (Ind.)
Johnson, Francis (Ky.)
Johnson, John T. (Ky.)
Johnson, Joseph (Va.)
Kent, Joseph (Md.)
Kidder, David (Maine)
Kremer, George (Pa.)
Lathrop, Samuel (Mass.)
Lawrence, Samuel (N. Y.)
Lee, John (Md.)
Leftwich, Jabez (Va.)
Letcher, Robert P. (Ky.)
Lincoln, Enoch (Maine)
Litchfield, Elisha (N. Y.)
Little, Peter (Md.)
Livermore, Arthur (N. H.)
Livingston, Edward (La.)
Locke, John (Mass.)
Long, John (N. C.)
Longfellow, Stephen (Maine)
McArthur, Duncan (Ohio)
McCoy, William (Va.)
McDuffie, George (S. C.)
McKean, Samuel (Pa.)
McKee, John (Ala.)
McKim, Isaac (Md.)
McLane, Louis (Del.)
McLean, William (Ohio)
Mallary, Rollin C. (Vt.)
Mangum, Willie P. (N. C.)
Markley, Philip S. (Pa.)
Martindale, Henry C. (N. Y.)
Marvin, Dudley (N. Y.)
Matlack, James (N. J.)
Matson, Aaron (N. H.)
Mercer, Charles F. (Va.)
Metcalfe, Thomas (Ky.)
Miller, Daniel H. (Pa.)
Mitchell, George E. (Md.)
Mitchell, James S. (Pa.)
Moore, Gabriel (Ala.)
Moore, Thomas P. (Ky.)
Morgan, John J. (N. Y.)
Neale, Raphael (Md.)
Nelson, Jeremiah (Mass.)
Newton, Thomas (Va.)
O'Brien, Jeremiah (Maine)
Olin, Henry (Vt.)
Outlaw, George (N. C.)
Owen, George W. (Ala.)
Patterson, John (Ohio)
Patterson, Thomas (Pa.)
Plumer, George (Pa.)
Plumer, William, Jr. (N. H.)
Poinsett, Joel R. (S. C.)
Prince, William (Ind.)
Randolph, John (Va.)
Rankin, Christopher (Miss.)
Reed, John (Mass.)
Reynolds, James B. (Tenn.)
Rich, Charles (Vt.)
Richards, John (N. Y.)
Rives, William C. (Va.)
Rogers, Thomas J. (Pa.)
Rose, Robert S. (N. Y.)
Ross, Thomas R. (Ohio)
Sandford, James T. (Tenn.)
Saunders, Romulus M. (N. C.)
Scott, John (Mo.)
Sharpe, Peter (N. Y.)
Sibley, Jonas (Mass.)
Sloane, John (Ohio)
Smith, Arthur (Va.)
Smith, William (Va.)
Smyth, Alexander (Va.)
Spaight, Richard D. (N. C.)
Spence, John S. (Md.)
Standifer, James (Tenn.)
Stephenson, James (Va.)
Sterling, Ansel (Conn.)
Stevenson, Andrew (Va.)
Stewart, Andrew (Pa.)
Stoddard, Ebenezer (Conn.)
Storrs, Henry R. (N. Y.)
Strong, James (N. Y.)
Swan, Samuel (N. J.)
Taliaferro, John (Va.)
Tattnall, Edward T. (Ga.)
Taylor, John W. (N. Y.)
Ten Eyck, Egbert (N. Y.)
Test, John (Ind.)
Thompson, Philip (Ky.)
Thompson, Wiley (Ga.)
Thomson, Alexander (Pa.)
Tod, John (Pa.)
Tomlinson, Gideon (Conn.)
Tracy, Albert H. (N. Y.)
Trimble, David (Ky.)
Tucker, George (Va.)
Tucker, Starling (S. C.)
Tyson, Jacob (N. Y.)
Udree, Daniel (Pa.)
Vance, Joseph (Ohio)
Vance, Robert B. (N. C.)
Van Rensselaer, Stephen (N. Y.)
Van Wyck, William W. (N.Y.)
Vinton, Samuel F. (Ohio)
Warfield, Henry R. (Md.)
Wayne, Isaac (Pa.)
Webster, Daniel (Mass.)
Whipple, Thomas (N. H.)
White, David (Ky.)
Whitman, Lemuel (Conn.)
Whittlesey, Elisha (Ohio)
Wickliffe, Charles A. (Ky.)
Wilde, Richard Henry (Ga.)
Williams, Isaac (N. Y.)
Williams, Jared (Va.)
Williams, Lewis (N. C.)
Wilson, Henry (Pa.)
Wilson, Isaac (N. Y.)
Wilson, James (Pa.)
Wilson, John (S. C.)
Wilson, William (Ohio)
Wolf, George (Pa.)
Wood, Silas (N. Y.)
Woods, William (N. Y.)
Wright, John C. (Ohio)

The Nineteenth Congress (1825-27)

Taylor, John W. (N. Y.) Speaker.

Adams, Parmenio (N. Y.)
Addams, William (Pa.)
Alexander, Adam R. (Tenn.)
Alexander, Mark (Va.)
Allen, Robert (Tenn.)
Allen, Samuel C. (Mass.)
Alston, Willis (N. C.)
Anderson, John (Maine)
Angel, William G. (N. Y.)
Archer, William S. (Va.)
Armstrong, William (Va.)
Ashley, Henry (N. Y.)
Badger, Luther (N. Y.)
Bailey, John (Mass.)
Baldwin, John (Conn.)
Barber, Noyes (Conn.)
Barbour, John S. (Va.)
Barney, John (Md.)
Barringer, Daniel L. (N. C.)
Bartlett, Ichabod (N. H.)
Bartley, Mordecai (Ohio)
Bassett, Burwell (Va.)
Baylies, Francis (Mass.)
Beecher, Philemon (Ohio)
Blair, John (Tenn.)
Boon, Ratliffe (Ind.)
Bradley, William C. (Vt.)
Brent, William L. (La.)
Brown, Titus (N. H.)
Bryan, John H. (N. C.)
Buchanan, James (Pa.)
Buckner, Richard A. (Ky.)
Burges, Tristam (R. I.)
Burleigh, William (Maine)
Cambreleng, Churchill C. (N. Y.)
Campbell, John W. (Ohio)
Carson, Samuel P. (N. C.)
Carter, John (S. C.)
Cary, George (Ga.)
Cassedy, George (N. J.)
Claiborne, Nathaniel H. (Va.)
Clark, James (Ky.)
Cocke, John (Tenn.)
Condict, Lewis (N. J.)
Connor, Henry W. (N. C.)
Cook, Daniel P. (Ill.)
Crowninshield, Benjamin W. (Mass.)
Crump, George W. (Va.)
Cuthbert, Alfred (Ga.)
Davenport, Thomas (Va.)
Davis, John (Mass.)
Dietz, William (N. Y.)
Dorsey, Clement (Md.)
Drayton, William (S. C.)
Dwight, Henry W. (Mass.)
Eastman, Nehemiah (N. H.)
Edwards, Samuel (Pa.)
Edwards, Weldon N. (N. C.)
Estil, Benjamin (Va.)
Everett, Edward (Mass.)
Farrelly, Patrick (Pa.)
Findlay, James (Ohio)
Findlay, John (Pa.)
Floyd, John (Va.)
Forsyth, John (Ga.)
Forward, Chauncey (Pa.)
Fosdick, Nicoll (N. Y.)
Garnett, Robert S. (Va.)
Garnsey, Daniel G. (N. Y.)
Garrison, Daniel (N. J.)
Gist, Joseph (S. C.)
Govan, Andrew R. (S. C.)
Gurley, Henry H. (La.)
Haile, William (Miss.)
Hallock, John (N. Y.)
Hamilton, James (S. C.)
Harris, Robert (Pa.)
Harvey, Jonathan (N. H.)
Hasbrouck, Abraham B. (N. Y.)
Hayden, Moses (N. Y.)
Haynes, Charles E. (Ga.)
Healy, Joseph (N. H.)
Hemphill, Joseph (Pa.)
Henry, John F. (Ky.)
Henry, Robert P. (Ky.)
Herrick, Ebenezer (Maine)
Hines, Richard (N. C.)
Hobart, Aaron (Mass.)
Hoffman, Michael (N. Y.)
Holcombe, George (N. J.)
Holmes, Gabriel (N. C.)
Houston, Samuel (Tenn.)
Hugunin, Daniel, Jr. (N. Y.)
Humphrey, Charles (N. Y.)
Ingersoll, Ralph I. (Conn.)
Ingham, Samuel D. (Pa.)
Isacks, Jacob C. (Tenn.)
Jennings, David (Ohio)
Jennings, Jonathan (Ind.)
Johnson, Francis (Ky.)
Johnson, James (Ky.)
Johnson, Jeromus (N. Y.)
Johnson, Joseph (Va.)
Kellogg, Charles (N. Y.)
Kent, Joseph (Md.)
Kerr, John Leeds (Md.)
Kidder, David (Maine)
Kittera, Thomas (Pa.)
Krebs, Jacob (Pa.)
Kremer, George (Pa.)
Lathrop, Samuel (Mass.)
Lawrence, Joseph (Pa.)
Lecompte, Joseph (Ky.)
Letcher, Robert P. (Ky.)
Lincoln, Enoch (Maine)
Little, Peter (Md.)
Livingston, Edward (La.)
Lloyd, James (Mass.)
Long, John (N. C.)
McCoy, William (Va.)
McDuffie, George (S. C.)
McHatton, Robert (Ky.)
McKean, Samuel (Pa.)
McKee, John (Ala.)
McLane, Louis (Del.)
McLean, William (Ohio)
McManus, William (N. Y.)
McNeill, Archibald (N. C.)
Mallary, Rollin C. (Vt.)
Mangum, Willie P. (N. C.)
Marable, John H. (Tenn.)
Markell, Henry (N. Y.)
Markley, Philip S. (Pa.)
Martin, Robert N. (Md.)
Martindale, Henry C. (N. Y.)
Marvin, Dudley (N. Y.)
Mattocks, John (Vt.)
Meech, Ezra (Vt.)
Mercer, Charles F. (Va.)
Meriwether, James (Ga.)
Merwin, Orange (Conn.)
Metcalfe, Thomas (Ky.)
Miller, Daniel H. (Pa.)
Miller, John (N. Y.)
Miner, Charles (Pa.)
Mitchell, George E. (Md.)
Mitchell, James C. (Tenn.)
Mitchell, James S. (Pa.)
Mitchell, John (Pa.)
Mitchell, Thomas R. (S. C.)
Moore, Gabriel (Ala.)
Moore, Thomas P. (Ky.)
Newton, Thomas (Va.)
O'Brien, Jeremiah (Maine)
Orr, Robert (Pa.)
Owen, George W. (Ala.)
Pearce, Dutee J. (R. I.)
Peter, George (Md.)
Phelps, Elisha (Conn.)
Plumer, George (Pa.)
Polk, James K. (Tenn.)
Porter, Timothy H. (N. Y.)
Powell, Alfred H. (Va.)
Rankin, Christopher (Miss.)
Reed, John (Mass.)
Ripley, James W. (Maine)
Rives, William C. (Va.)
Rose, Robert S. (N. Y.)
Ross, Henry H. (N. Y.)
Sands, Joshua (N. Y.)
Saunders, Romulus M. (N. C.)
Sawyer, Lemuel (N. C.)
Scott, John (Mo.)
Shannon, Thomas (Ohio)
Sill, Thomas H. (Pa.)
Sloane, John (Ohio)
Smith, William (Va.)

Sprague, Peleg (Maine)
Stevenson, Andrew (Va.)
Stevenson, James S. (Pa.)
Stewart, Andrew (Pa.)
Storrs, Henry R. (N. Y.)
Strong, James (N. Y.)
Swan, Samuel (N. J.)
Taliaferro, John (Va.)
Tattnall, Edward F. (Ga.)
Ten Eyck, Egbert (N. Y.)
Taylor, John W. (N. Y.)
Taylor, Robert (Va.)
Test, John (Ind.)
Thomson, John (Ohio)
Thompson, Wiley (Ga.)
Thomson, Alexander (Pa.)
Tomlinson, Gideon (Conn.)
Trezvant, James (Va.)
Trimble, David (Ky.)
Tucker, Ebenezer (N. J.)
Tucker, Starling (S. C.)
Vance, Joseph (Ohio)
Van Horne, Espy (Pa.)
Van Rensselaer, Stephen (N. Y.)
Varnum, John (Mass.)
Verplanck, Gulian C. (N. Y.)
Vinton, Samuel F. (Ohio)
Wales, George E. (Vt.)
Ward, Aaron (N. Y.)
Webster, Daniel (Mass.)
Weems, John C. (Md.)
Whipple, Thomas, Jr. (N. H.)
White, Bartow (N. Y.)
Whitmore, Elias (N. Y.)
Whittlesey, Elisha (Ohio)
Wickliffe, Charles A. (Ky.)
Williams, Lewis (N. C.)
Wilson, Henry (Pa.)
Wilson, James (Pa.)
Wilson, John (S. C.)
Wilson, William (Ohio)
Wolf, George (Pa.)
Wood, Silas (N. Y.)
Woods, John (Ohio)
Worthington, Thomas C. (Md.)
Wright, John C. (Ohio)
Wurts, John (Pa.)
Young, William S. (Ky.)

The Twentieth Congress (1827-29)

Stevenson, Andrew (Va.) Speaker.

Addams, William (Pa.)
Alexander, Mark (Va.)
Allen, Robert (Va.)
Allen, Samuel C. (Mass.)
Alston, Willis (N. C.)
Anderson, John (Maine)
Anderson, Samuel (Pa.)
Archer, William S. (Va.)
Armstrong, William (Va.)
Bailey, John (Mass.)
Baldwin, John (Conn.)
Barber, Noyes (Conn.)
Barbour, John S. (Va.)
Barbour, Philip P. (Va.)
Barker, David, Jr. (N. H.)
Barlow, Stephen (Pa.)
Barnard, Daniel D. (N. Y.)
Barney, John (Md.)
Barringer, Daniel L. (N. C.)
Bartlett, Ichabod (N. H.)
Bartley, Mordecai (Ohio)
Bassett, Burwell (Va.)
Bates, Edward (Mo.)
Bates, Isaac C. (Mass.)
Beecher, Philemon (Ohio)
Belden, George O. (N. Y.)
Bell, John (Tenn.)
Blair, John (Tenn.)
Blake, Thomas H. (Ind.)
Brown, Titus (N. H.)
Brent, William L. (La.)
Bryan, John H. (N. C.)
Buchanan, James (Pa.)
Buck, Daniel A. A. (Vt.)
Buckner, Richard A. (Ky.)
Bunner, Rudolph (N. Y.)
Burges, Tristam (R. I.)
Butman, Samuel (Maine)
Cambreleng, Churchill C. (N. Y.)
Carson, Samuel P. (N. C.)
Carter, John (S. C.)
Chambers, John (Ky.)
Chase, Samuel (N. Y.)
Chilton, Thomas (Ky.)
Claiborne, Nathaniel H. (Va.)
Clark, James (Ky.)
Clark, John C. (N. Y.)
Condict, Lewis (N. J.)
Connor, Henry W. (N. C.)
Coulter, Richard (Pa.)
Creighton, William, Jr. (Ohio)
Crockett, David (Tenn.)
Crowninshield, Benjamin W. (Mass.)
Culpepper, John (N. C.)
Daniel, Henry (Ky.)
Davenport, John (Ohio)
Davenport, Thomas (Va.)
Davis, John (Mass.)
Davis, Warren R. (S. C.)
De Graff, John I. (N. Y.)
Desha, Robert (Tenn.)
Dickinson, John D. (N. Y.)
Dorsey, Clement (Md.)
Drayton, William (S. C.)
Duncan, Joseph (Ill.)
Dwight, Henry W. (Mass.)
Earll, Jonas (N. Y.)
Everett, Edward (Mass.)
Findlay, James (Ohio)
Floyd, John (Ga.)
Floyd, John (Va.)
Fort, Tomlinson (Ga.)
Forward, Chauncey (Pa.)
Fry, Joseph, Jr. (Pa.)
Gale, Levin (Md.)
Garnsey, Daniel G. (N. Y.)
Garrow, Nathaniel (N. Y.)
Gilmer, George R. (Ga.)
Gorham, Benjamin (Mass.)
Green, Innis (Pa.)
Gurley, Henry H. (La.)
Haile, William (Miss.)
Hall, Thomas H. (N. C.)
Hallock, John (N. Y.)
Hamilton, James, Jr. (S. C.)
Harvey, Jonathan (N. H.)
Haynes, Charles E. (Ga.)
Healy, Joseph (N. H.)
Hinds, Thomas (Miss.)
Hobbie, Selah R. (N. Y.)
Hodges, James L. (Mass.)
Hoffman, Michael (N. Y.)
Holcombe, George (N. J.)
Holmes, Gabriel (N. C.)
Hunt, Jonathan (Vt.)
Ingham, Samuel D. (Pa.)
Ingersoll, Ralph I. (Conn.)
Isacks, Jacob C. (Tenn.)
Jennings, Jonathan (Ind.)
Johns, Kensey, Jr. (Del.)
Johnson, Jeromus (N. Y.)
Keese, Richard (N. Y.)
Kerr, John Leeds (Md.)
King, Adam (Pa.)
Kremer, George (Pa.)
Lawrence, Joseph (Pa.)
Lea, Pryor (Tenn.)
Lecompte, Joseph (Ky.)
Leffler, Isaac (Va.)
Letcher, Robert P. (Ky.)
Little, Peter (Md.)
Livingston, Edward (La.)
Locke, John (Mass.)
Long, John (N. C.)
Lumpkin, Wilson (Ga.)
Lyon, Chittenden (Ky.)
McCoy, William (Va.)
McDuffie, George (S. C.)
McHatton, Robert (Ky.)
McIntire, Rufus (Maine)
McKean, Samuel (Pa.)
McKee, John (Ala.)
McLean, William (Ohio)
Magee, John (N. Y.)
Mallary, Rollin C. (Vt.)
Marable, John H. (Tenn.)
Markell, Henry (N. Y.)
Martin, William D. (S. C.)
Martindale, Henry C. (N. Y.)
Marvin, Dudley, (N. Y.)
Maxwell, Lewis (Va.)
Maynard, John (N. Y.)
Mercer, Charles F. (Va.)
Merwin, Orange (Conn.)
Metcalfe, Thomas (Ky.)
Miller, Daniel H. (Pa.)
Miner, Charles (Pa.)
Mitchell, James C. (Tenn.)
Mitchell, John (Pa.)
Mitchell, Thomas R. (S. C.)
Moore, Gabriel (Ala.)
Moore, Thomas P. (Ky.)
Muhlenberg, Francis S. (Ohio)
Newton, Thomas (Va.)
Nuckolls, William T. (S. C.)
Oakley, Thomas J. (N. Y.)
O'Brien, Jeremiah (Maine)
Orr, Robert, Jr. (Pa.)
Owen, George W. (Ala.)
Pearce, Dutee J. (R. I.)
Phelps, Elisha (Conn.)
Pierson, Isaac (N. J.)
Plant, David (Conn.)
Polk, James K. (Tenn.)
Ramsey, William (Pa.)
Randolph, James F. (N. J.)
Randolph, John (Va.)
Reed, John (Mass.)
Richardson, Joseph (Mass.)
Ripley, James W. (Maine)
Rives, William C. (Va.)
Roane, John (Va.)
Russell, William (Ohio)
Sawyer, Lemuel (N. C.)
Sergeant, John (Pa.)
Shepperd, Augustine H. (N. C.)
Sinnickson, Thomas (N. J.)
Sloane, John (Ohio)
Stower, John G. (N. Y.)
Smith, Oliver H. (Ind.)
Smyth, Alexander (Va.)
Sprague, Peleg (Maine)
Sprigg, Michael C. (Md.)
Stanbery, William (Ohio)
Sterigere, John B. (Pa.)
Stevenson, Andrew (Va.)
Stevenson, James S. (Pa.)
Stewart, Andrew (Pa.)
Storrs, Henry R. (N. Y.)
Stower, John G. (N. Y.)
Strong, James (N. Y.)
Sutherland, Joel B. (Pa.)
Swan, Samuel (N. J.)
Swift, Benjamin (Vt.)
Taber, Thomas, 2d (N. Y.)
Taliaferro, John (Va.)
Taylor, John W. (N. Y.)
Thompson, Hedge (N. J.)
Thompson, Wiley, (Ga.)
Tracy, Phineas L. (N. Y.)
Trezvant, James (Va.)
Tucker, Ebenezer (N. J.)
Tucker, Starling (S. C.)
Turner, Daniel (N. C.)
Vance, Joseph (Ohio)
Van Horne, Espy (Pa.)
Van Rensselaer, Stephen (N. Y.)
Varnum, John (Mass.)
Verplanck, Gulian C. (N. Y.)
Vinton, Samuel F. (Ohio)
Wales, George E. (Vt.)
Ward, Aaron (N. Y.)
Washington, George C. (Md.)
Weems, John C. (Md.)
Whipple, Thomas, Jr. (N. H.)
Whittlesey, Elisha (Ohio)
Wickliffe, Charles A. (Ky.)
Wilde, Richard Henry (Ga.)
Williams, Lewis (N. C.)
Wilson, Ephraim K. (Md.)
Wilson, James (Pa.)
Wingate, Joseph F. (Maine)
Wolf, George (Pa.)
Wood, John J. (N. Y.)
Wood, Silas (N. Y.)
Woodcock, David (N. Y.)
Woods, John (Ohio)
Wright, John C. (Ohio)
Wright, Silas (N. Y.)
Yancey, Joel (Ky.)

The Twenty-first Congress (1829-31)

Stevenson, Andrew (Va.) Speaker.

Alexander, Mark (Va.)
Allen, Robert (Va.)
Alston, Willis (N. C.)
Anderson, John (Maine)
Angel, William G. (N. Y.)
Archer, William S. (Va.)
Armstrong, William (Va.)
Arnold, Benedict (N. Y.)
Bailey, John (Mass.)
Barber, Noyes (Conn.)
Barbour, John S. (Va.)
Barbour, Philip P. (Va.)
Barnwell, Robert W. (S. C.)
Barringer, Daniel L. (N. C.)
Bartley, Mordecai (Ohio)
Bates, Isaac C. (Mass.)
Baylor, Robert E. B. (Ala.)
Beekman, Thomas (N. Y.)
Bell, John (Tenn.)
Blair, James (S. C.)
Blair, John (Tenn.)
Bockee, Abraham (N. Y.)
Boon, Ratcliffe (Ind.)
Borst, Peter I. (N. Y.)
Bouldin, Thomas T. (Va.)
Brodhead, John (N. H.)
Brown, Elias (Md.)
Buchanan, James (Pa.)
Burges, Tristam (R. I.)
Butman, Samuel (Maine)
Cahoon, William (Vt.)
Cambreleng, Churchill C. (N. Y.)
Campbell, John (S. C.)
Carson, Samuel P. (N. C.)
Chandler, Thomas (N. H.)
Childs, Timothy (N. Y.)
Chilton, Thomas (Ky.)
Claiborne, Nathaniel H. (Va.)
Clark, James (Ky.)
Clay, Clement C. (Ala.)
Coke, Richard (Va.)
Coleman, Nicholas D. (Ky.)
Condict, Lewis (N. J.)
Connor, Henry W. (N. C.)
Cooper, Richard M. (N. J.)
Coulter, Richard (Pa.)
Cowles, Henry B. (N. Y.)
Craig, Hector (N. Y.)
Craig, Robert (Va.)
Crane, Joseph H. (Ohio)
Crawford, Thomas H. (Pa.)
Creighton, William (Ohio)
Crocheron, Jacob (N. Y.)
Crockett, David (Tenn.)
Crowninshield, Benjamin W. (Mass.)
Daniel, Henry (Ky.)
Davenport, Thomas (Va.)
Davis, John (Mass.)
Davis, Warren R. (S. C.)
Deberry, Edmund (N. C.)
Denny, Harmar (Pa.)
Desha, Robert (Tenn.)
DeWitt, Charles G. (N. Y.)
Dickinson, John D. (N. Y.)
Doddridge, Philip (Va.)
Dorsey, Clement (Md.)
Draper, Joseph (Va.)
Drayton, William (S. C.)
Dudley, Edward B. (N. C.)
Duncan, Joseph (Ill.)
Dwight, Henry W. (Mass.)
Eager, Samuel W. (N. Y.)
Earll, Jonas, Jr. (N. Y.)
Evans, George (Maine)
Evans, Joshua (Pa.)
Ellsworth, William W. (Conn.)
Everett, Edward (Mass.)
Everett, Horace (Vt.)
Finch, Isaac (N. Y.)
Findlay, James (Ohio)
Fisher, George (N. Y.)
Ford, James (Pa.)
Forward, Chauncey (Pa.)
Foster, Thomas F. (Ga.)
Fry, Joseph, Jr. (Pa.)
Gaither, Nathan (Ky.)
Gilmore, John (Pa.)
Gorham, Benjamin (Mass.)
Gordon, William F. (Va.)
Green, Innis (Pa.)
Grennell, George, Jr. (Mass.)
Gurley, Henry H. (La.)
Hall, Thomas H. (N. C.)
Halsey, Jehiel H. (N. Y.)
Hammons, Joseph (N. H.)
Harvey, Jonathan (N. H.)
Haynes, Charles E. (Ga.)
Hawkins, Joseph (N. Y.)
Hemphill, Joseph (Pa.)
Hinds, Thomas (Miss.)
Hodges, James L. (Mass.)
Hoffman, Michael (N. Y.)
Holland, Cornelius (Maine)
Howard, Benjamin C. (Md.)

Hubbard, Henry (N. H.)
Hughes, Thomas H. (N. J.)
Hunt, Jonathan (Vt.)
Huntington, Jabez W. (Conn.)
Ihrie, Peter (Pa.)
Ingersoll, Ralph I. (Conn.)
Irvin, William W. (Ohio)
Irwin, Thomas (Pa.)
Isacks, Jacob C. (Tenn.)
Jarvis, Leonard (Maine)
Jennings, Jonathan (Ind.)
Johns, Kensey, Jr. (Del.)
Johnson, Cave (Tenn.)
Johnson, Richard M. (Ky.)
Kendall, Joseph G. (Mass.)
Kennon, William (Ohio)
Kincaid, John (Ky.)
King, Adam (Pa.)
King, Perkins (N. Y.)
Lamar, Henry G. (Ga.)
Lea, Pryor (Tenn.)
Leavitt, Humphrey H. (Ohio)
Lecompte, Joseph (Ky.)
Leiper, George C. (Pa.)
Lent, James (N. Y.)
Letcher, Robert P. (Ky.)
Lewis, Dixon H. (Ala.)
Loyall, George (Va.)
Lumpkin, Wilson (Ga.)
Lyon, Chittenden (Ky.)
McCoy, William (Va.)
McCreery, William (Pa.)
McDuffie, George (S. C.)
McIntire, Rufus (Maine)
Magee, John (N. Y.)
Mallary, Rollin C. (Vt.)
Marr, Alem (Pa.)
Martin, William D. (S. C.)
Martindale, Henry C. (N. Y.)
Maxwell, Lewis (Va.)
Maxwell, Thomas (N. Y.)
Mercer, Charles F. (Va.)
Miller, Daniel H. (Pa.)
Mitchell, George E. (Md.)
Monell, Robert (N. Y.)
Muhlenberg, Henry A. P. (Pa.)
Newton, Thomas (Va.)
Norton, Ebenezer F. (N. Y.)
Nuckolls, William T. (S. C.)
Overton, Walter H. (La.)
Patton, John M. (Va.)
Pearce, Dutee J. (R. I.)
Pettis, Spencer S. (Mo.)
Pierson, Isaac (N. J.)
Polk, James K. (Tenn.)
Potter, Robert (N. C.)
Powers, Gershom (N. Y.)
Ramsey, William (Pa.)
Randolph, James F. (N. J.)
Reed, John (Mass.)
Rencher, Abraham (N. C.)
Richardson, Joseph (Mass.)
Ripley, James W. (Maine)
Roane, John (Va.)
Rose, Robert S. (N. Y.)
Russell, William (Ohio)
Sanford, Jonah (N. Y.)
Scott, John (Pa.)
Semmes, Benedict J. (Md.)
Shepard, William B. (N. C.)
Shepperd, Augustine H. (N.C.)
Shields, James (Ohio)
Sill, Thomas H. (Pa.)
Smith, Samuel A. (Pa.)
Smyth, Alexander (Va.)
Speight, Jesse (N. C.)
Spencer, Ambrose (N. Y.)
Spencer, Richard (Md.)
Sprigg, Michael C. (Md.)
Stanbery, William (Ohio)
Standifer, James (Tenn.)
Stephens, Philander (Pa.)
Sterigere, John B. (Pa.)
Stevenson, Andrew (Va.)
Storrs, Henry R. (N. Y.)
Storrs, William L. (Conn.)
Strong, James (N. Y.)
Sutherland, Joel B. (Pa.)
Swan, Samuel (N. J.)
Swift, Benjamin (Vt.)
Taliaferro, John (Va.)
Taylor, John W. (N. Y.)
Test, John (Ind.)
Thompson, Wiley (Ga.)
Thomson, John (Ohio)
Tracy, Phineas L. (N. Y.)
Trezvant, James (Va.)
Tucker, Starling (S. C.)
Vance, Joseph (Ohio)
Varnum, John (Mass.)
Verplanck, Gulian C. (N. Y.)
Vinton, Samuel F. (Ohio)
Washington, George C. (Md.)
Wayne, James M. (Ga.)
Weeks, John W. (N. H.)
White, Campbell P. (N. Y.)
White, Edward D. (La.)
Whittlesey, Elisha (Ohio)
Wickliffe, Charles A. (Ky.)
Wilde, Richard H. (Ga.)
Williams, Lewis (N. C.)
Wilson, Ephraim K. (Md.)
Wingate, Joseph F. (Maine)
Wright, Silas (N. Y.)
Yancey, Joel (Ky.)
Young, Ebenezer (Conn.)

The Twenty-second Congress (1831-33)

Stevenson, Andrew (Va.) Speaker.

Adair, John (Ky.)
Adams, John Q. (Mass.)
Alexander, Mark (Va.)
Allen, Chilton (Ky.)
Allen, Heman (Vt.)
Allen, Robert (Va.)
Allison, Robert (Pa.)
Anderson, John (Maine)
Angel, William G. (N. Y.)
Appleton, Nathan (Mass.)
Archer, William S. (Va.)
Armstrong, William (Va.)
Arnold, Thomas D. (Tenn.)
Ashley, William H. (Mo.)
Babcock, William (N. Y.)
Banks, John (Pa.)
Barber, Noyes (Conn.)
Barbour, John S. (Va.)
Barnwell, Robert W. (S. C.)
Barringer, Daniel L. (N. C.)
Barstow, Gamaliel H. (N. Y.)
Bates, Isaac C. (Mass.)
Bates, James (Maine)
Beardsley, Samuel (N. Y.)
Bell, John (Tenn.)
Bergen, John T. (N. Y.)
Bethune, Lauchlin (N. C.)
Blair, James (S. C.)
Blair, John (Tenn.)
Boon, Ratliff (Ind.)
Bouck, Joseph (N. Y.)
Bouldin, Thomas T. (Va.)
Branch, John (N. C.)
Briggs, George N. (Mass.)
Brodhead, John (N. H.)
Brodhead, John C. (N. Y.)
Bucher, John C. (Pa.)
Bullard, Henry A. (La.)
Burd, George (Pa.)
Burges, Tristam (R. I.)
Cahoon, William (Vt.)
Cambreleng, Churchill C. (N. Y.)
Carr, John (Ind.)
Carson, Samuel P. (N. C.)
Chandler, Thomas (N. H.)
Chinn, Joseph W. (Va.)
Choate, Rufus (Mass.)
Claiborne, Nathaniel H. (Va.)
Clay, Clement C. (Ala.)
Clayton, Augustine S. (Ga.)
Coke, Richard, Jr. (Va.)
Collier, John A. (N. Y.)
Condict, Lewis (N. J.)
Condit, Silas (N. J.)
Connor, Henry W. (N. C.)
Cooke, Bates (N. Y.)
Cooke, Eleutheros (Ohio)
Cooper, Richard M. (N. J.)
Corwin, Thomas (Ohio)
Coulter, Richard (Pa.)
Craig, Robert (Va.)
Crane, Joseph H. (Ohio)
Crawford, Thomas H. (Pa.)
Creighton, William (Ohio)
Daniel, Henry (Ky.)
Davenport, Thomas (Va.)
Davis, John (Mass.)
Davis, Warren R. (S. C.)
Dayan, Charles (N. Y.)
Dearborn, Henry A. S. (Mass.)
Denny, Harmar (Pa.)
Dewart, Lewis (Pa.)
Dickson, John (N. Y.)
Doddridge, Philip (Va.)
Doubleday, Ulysses F. (N. Y.)
Draper, Joseph (Va.)
Drayton, William (S. C.)
Duncan, Joseph (Ill.)
Ellsworth, William W. (Conn.)
Evans, George (Maine)
Evans, Joshua (Pa.)
Everett, Edward (Mass.)
Everett, Horace (Vt.)
Felder, John M. (S. C.)
Findlay, James (Ohio)
Fitzgerald, William (Tenn.)
Ford, James (Pa.)
Foster, Thomas F. (Ga.)
Gaither, Nathan (Ky.)
Gilmore, John (Pa.)
Gordon, William F. (Va.)
Grennell, George, Jr. (Mass.)
Griffin, John K. (S. C.)
Hall, Hiland (Vt.)
Hall, Thomas H. (N. C.)
Hall, William (Tenn.)
Hammons, Joseph (N. H.)
Harper, Joseph M. (N. H.)
Hawes, Albert G. (Ky.)
Hawkins, Micajah T. (N. C.)
Hiester, William (Pa.)
Hodges, James L. (Mass.)
Hoffman, Michael (N. Y.)
Hogan, William (N. Y.)
Holland, Cornelius (Maine)
Horn, Henry (Pa.)
Howard, Benjamin C. (Md.)
Hubbard, Henry (N. H.)
Hughes, Thomas H. (N. J.)
Hunt, Jonathan (Vt.)
Huntington, Jabez W. (Conn.)
Ihrie, Peter, Jr. (Pa.)
Ingersoll, Ralph I. (Conn.)
Irvin, William W. (Ohio)
Isacks, Jacob C. (Tenn.)
Jarvis, Leonard (Maine)
Jenifer, Daniel (Md.)
Jewett, Freeborn G. (N. Y.)
Johnson, Cave (Tenn.)
Johnson, Joseph (Va.)
Johnson, Richard M. (Ky.)
Johnston, Charles C. (Va.)
Kavanagh, Edward (Maine)
Kendall, Joseph G. (Mass.)
Kennon, William (Ohio)
Kerr, John L. (Md.)
King, Adam (Pa.)
King, Henry (Pa.)
King, John (N. Y.)
Lamar, Henry G. (Ga.)
Lansing, Gerrit Y. (N. Y.)
Leavitt, Humphrey H. (Ohio)
Lecompte, Joseph (Ky.)
Lent, James (N. Y.)
Letcher, Robert P. (Ky.)
Lewis, Dixon H. (Ala.)
Lyon, Chittenden (Ky.)
McCarty, Jonathan (Ind.)
McCoy, Robert (Pa.)
McCoy, William (Va.)
McDuffie, George (S. C.)
McIntire, Rufus (Maine)
McKay, James I. (N. C.)
McKennan, Thomas M. T. (Pa.)
Mann, Joel K. (Pa.)
Mardis, Samuel W. (Ala.)
Marshall, Thomas A. (Ky.)
Mason, John Y. (Va.)
Maxwell, Lewis (Va.)
Mercer, Charles F. (Va.)
Milligan, John J. (Del.)
Mitchell, George E. (Md.)
Mitchell, Thomas R. (S. C.)
Muhlenberg, Henry A. P. (Pa.)
Nelson, Jeremiah (Mass.)
Newnan, Daniel (Ga.)
Newton, Thomas (Va.)
Nuckolls, William T. (S. C.)
Patton, John M. (Va.)
Pearce, Dutee J. (R. I.)
Pendleton, Edmund H. (N. Y.)
Pierson, Job (N. Y.)
Pitcher, Nathaniel (N. Y.)
Plummer, Franklin E. (Miss.)
Polk, James K. (Tenn.)
Potts, David, Jr. (Pa.)
Randolph, James F. (N. J.)
Reed, Edward C. (N. Y.)
Reed, John (Mass.)
Rencher, Abraham (N. C.)
Roane, John J. (Va.)
Root, Erastus (N. Y.)
Russell, William (Ohio)
Semmes, Benedict J. (Md.)
Sewall, Charles S. (Md.)
Shepard, William B. (N. C.)
Shepperd, Augustine H. (N.C.)
Slade, William (Vt.)
Smith, Samuel A. (Pa.)
Soule, Nathan (N. Y.)
Southard, Isaac (N. J.)
Speight, Jesse (N. C.)
Spence, John S. (Md.)
Stanbery, William (Ohio)
Standifer, James (Tenn.)
Stephens, Philander (Pa.)
Stevenson, Andrew (Va.)
Stewart, Andrew (Pa.)
Storrs, William L. (Conn.)
Sutherland, Joel B. (Pa.)
Taylor, John W. (N. Y.)
Thomas, Francis (Md.)
Thomas, Philemon (La.)
Tompkins, Christopher (Ky.)
Thompson, Wiley (Ga.)
Thomson, John (Ohio)
Tracy, Phineas L. (N. Y.)
Vance, Joseph (Ohio)
Verplanck, Gulian C. (N. Y.)
Vinton, Samuel F. (Ohio)
Ward, Aaron (N. Y.)
Wardwell, Daniel (N. Y.)
Washington, George C. (Md.)
Watmough, John G. (Pa.)
Wayne, James M. (Ga.)
Weeks, John W. (N. H.)
Wheeler, Grattan H. (N. Y.)
White, Campbell P. (N. Y.)
White, Edward D. (La.)
Whittlesey, Elisha (Ohio)
Whittlesey, Frederick (N. Y.)
Wickliffe, Charles A. (Ky.)
Wilde, Richard H. (Ga.)
Wilkin, Samuel J. (N. Y.)
Williams, Lewis (N. C.)
Worthington, John T. H. (Md.)
Young, Ebenezer (Conn.)

The Twenty-third Congress (1833-35)

Stevenson, Andrew (Va.) Speaker.

Adams, John (N. Y.)
Adams, John Q. (Mass.)
Allan, Chilton (Ky.)
Allen, Heman (Vt.)
Allen, John J. (Va.)
Allen, William (Ohio)
Anthony, Joseph B. (Pa.)
Archer, William S. (Va.)
Ashley, William H. (Mo.)
Banks, John (Pa.)
Barber, Noyes (Conn.)
Barnitz, Charles A. (Pa.)
Barringer, Daniel L. (N. C.)
Bates, Isaac C. (Mass.)
Baylies, William (Mass.)
Beale, James M. H. (Va.)
Bean, Benning M. (N. H.)
Beardsley, Samuel (N. Y.)
Beaty, Martin (Ky.)
Beaumont, Andrew (Pa.)
Bell, James M. (Ohio)
Bell, John (Tenn.)
Binney, Horace (Pa.)
Blair, James (S. C.)
Blair, John (Tenn.)
Bockee, Abraham (N. Y.)
Bodle, Charles (N. Y.)
Boon, Ratliff (Ind.)
Bouldin, James W. (Va.)
Bouldin, Thomas T. (Va.)
Briggs, George N. (Mass.)
Brown, John W. (N. Y.)
Bullard, Henry A. (La.)
Bull, John (Mo.)
Bunch, Samuel (Tenn.)
Burd, George (Pa.)
Burges, Tristam (R. I.)
Burns, Robert (N. H.)
Bynum, Jesse A. (N. C.)
Cage, Harry (Miss.)
Cambreleng, Churchill C. (N. Y.)
Campbell, Robert B. (S. C.)

Carmichael, Richard B. (Md.)
Carr, John (Ind.)
Casey, Zadoc (Ill.)
Chambers, George (Pa.)
Chaney, John (Ohio)
Chilton, Thomas (Ky.)
Chinn, Joseph W. (Va.)
Choate, Rufus (Mass.)
Claiborne, Nathaniel H. (Va.)
Clark, Samuel (N. Y.)
Clark, William (Pa.)
Clay, Clement C. (Ala.)
Clayton, Augustin S. (Ga.)
Clowny, William K. (S. C.)
Coffee, John (Ga.)
Connor, Henry W. (N. C.)
Corwin, Thomas (Ohio)
Coulter, Richard (Pa.)
Cramer, John (N. Y.)
Crane, Joseph H. (Ohio)
Crockett, David (Tenn.)
Darlington, Edward (Pa.)
Davenport, Thomas (Va.)
Davis, Amos (Ky.)
Davis, John (Mass.)
Davis, Warren R. (S. C.)
Day, Rowland (N. Y.)
Deberry, Edmund (N. C.)
Deming, Benjamin F. (Vt.)
Denny, Harmar (Pa.)
Dickerson, Philemon (N. J.)
Dickinson, David W. (Tenn.)
Dickson, John (N. Y.)
Dennis, Littleton P. (Md.)
Dunlap, William C. (Tenn.)
Duncan, Joseph (Ill.)
Ellsworth, William W. (Conn.)
Evans, George (Maine)
Everett, Edward (Mass.)
Everett, Horace (Vt.)
Ewing, John (Ind.)
Felder, John M. (S. C.)
Ferris, Charles G. (N. Y.)
Fillmore, Millard (N. Y.)
Foote, Samuel A. (Conn.)
Forester, John B. (Tenn.)
Foster, Thomas F. (Ga.)
Fowler, Samuel (N. J.)
Fuller, Philo C. (N. Y.)
Fuller, William K. (N. Y.)
Fulton, John H. (Va.)
Galbraith, John (Pa.)
Gamble, Roger L. (Ga.)
Garland, Rice (La.)
Gholson, James H. (Va.)
Gillet, Ransom H. (N. Y.)
Gilmer, George R. (Ga.)
Gordon, William F. (Va.)
Gorham, Benjamin (Mass.)
Graham, James (N. C.)
Grayson, William J. (S. C.)
Grennell, George, Jr. (Mass.)
Griffin, John K. (S. C.)
Hall, Hiland (Vt.)
Hall, Joseph (Maine)
Hall, Thomas H. (N. C.)
Halsey, Nicoll (N. Y.)
Hamer, Thomas L. (Ohio)
Hannegan, Edward A. (Ind.)
Hard, Gideon (N. Y.)
Hardin, Benjamin (Ky.)
Harper, James (Pa.)
Harper, Joseph M. (N. H.)
Harrison, Samuel S. (Pa.)
Hathaway, Samuel G. (N. Y.)
Hawes, Albert G. (Ky.)
Hawkins, Micajah T. (N. C.)
Hazeltine, Abner (N. Y.)
Heath, James P. (Md.)
Henderson, Joseph (Pa.)
Hiester, William (Pa.)
Howell, Edward (N. Y.)
Hubbard, Henry (N. H.)
Huntington, Abel (N. Y.)
Huntington, Jabez W. (Conn.)
Inge, William M. (Tenn.)
Jackson, Ebenezer (Conn.)
Jackson, William (Mass.)
Janes, Henry F. (Vt.)
Jarvis, Leonard (Maine)
Johnson, Cave (Tenn.)
Johnson, Henry (La.)
Johnson, Noadiah (N. Y.)
Johnson, Richard M. (Ky.)
Johnson, William Cost (Md.)
Jones, Benjamin (Ohio)
Jones, Seaborn (Ga.)
Kavanagh, Edward (Maine)
Kilgore, Daniel (Ohio)
King, Henry (Pa.)
Kinnard, George L. (Ind.)
Lane, Amos (Ind.)
Lansing, Gerrit Y. (N. Y.)
Laporte, John (Pa.)
Lawrence, Cornelius W. (N. Y.)
Lay, George W. (N. Y.)
Lea, Luke (Tenn.)
Leavitt, Humphrey H. (Ohio)
Lee, Thomas (N. J.)
Letcher, Robert P. (Ky.)
Lewis, Dixon H. (Ala.)
Lincoln, Levi (Mass.)
Love, James (Ky.)
Loyall, George (Va.)
Lucas, Edward (Va.)
Lyon, Chittenden (Ky.)
Lytle, Robert T. (Ohio)
McCarty, Jonathan (Ind.)
McComas, William (Va.)
McDuffie, George (S. C.)
McIntire, Rufus (Maine)
McKay, James I. (N. C.)
McKennan, Thomas M. T. (Pa.)
McKim, Isaac (Md.)
McKinley, John (Ala.)
McLene, Jeremiah (Ohio)
McVean, Charles (N. Y.)
Mann, Abijah, Jr. (N. Y.)
Mann, Joel K. (Pa.)
Manning, Richard I. (S. C.)
Mardis, Samuel W. (Ala.)
Marshall, Thomas A. (Ky.)
Martindale, Henry C. (N. Y.)
Mason, John Y. (Va.)
Mason, Moses, Jr. (Maine)
May, William L. (Ill.)
Mercer, Charles F. (Va.)
Miller, Jesse (Pa.)
Milligan, John J. (Del.)
Miner, Phineas (Conn.)
Mitchell, Henry (N. Y.)
Mitchell, Robert (Ohio)
Moore, Samuel McDowell (Va.)
Morgan, John J. (N. Y.)
Muhlenberg, Henry A. P. (Pa.)
Murphy, John (Ala.)
Osgood, Gayton P. (Mass.)
Page, Sherman (N. Y.)
Parker, James (N. J.)
Parks, Gorham (Maine)
Patterson, William (Ohio)
Patton, John M. (Va.)
Pearce, Dutee J. (R. I.)
Peyton, Balie (Tenn.)
Phillips, Stephen C. (Mass.)
Pickens, Francis W. (S. C.)
Pierce, Franklin (N. H.)
Pierson, Job (N. Y.)
Pinckney, Henry L. (S. C.)
Plummer, Franklin E. (Miss.)
Polk, James K. (Tenn.)
Pope, Patrick H. (Ky.)
Potts, David, Jr. (Pa.)
Ramsay, Robert (Pa.)
Reed, John (Mass.)
Rencher, Abraham (N. C.)
Reynolds, John (Ill.)
Robertson, John (Va.)
Schenck, Ferdinand S. (N. J.)
Schley, William (Ga.)
Selden, Dudley (N. Y.)
Shepard, William B. (N. C.)
Shepperd, Augustine H. (N. C.)
Shinn, William N. (N. J.)
Slade, Charles (Ill.)
Slade, William (Vt.)
Sloane, Jonathan (Ohio)
Smith, Francis O. J. (Maine)
Spangler, David (Ohio)
Speight, Jesse (N. C.)
Standifer, James (Tenn.)
Steele, John N. (Md.)
Stevenson, Andrew (Va.)
Stewart, Andrew (Pa.)
Stoddert, John T. (Md.)
Sutherland, Joel B. (Pa.)
Taylor, William (N. Y.)
Taylor, William P. (Va.)
Thomas, Francis (Md.)
Thomas, Philemon (La.)
Thomson, John (Ohio)
Tompkins, Christopher (Ky.)
Trumbull, Joseph (Conn.)
Turner, James (Md.)
Turrill, Joel (N. Y.)
Tweedy, Samuel (Conn.)
Vance, Joseph (Ohio)
Vanderpoel Aaron (N. Y.)
Van Houten, Isaac B. (N. Y.)
Vinton, Samuel F. (Ohio)
Wagener, David D. (Pa.)
Ward, Aaron (N. Y.)
Wardwell, Daniel (N. Y.)
Watmough, John G. (Pa.)
Wayne, James M. (Ga.)
Webster, Taylor (Ohio)
Whallon, Reuben (N. Y.)
White, Campbell P. (N. Y.)
White, Edward D. (La.)
Whittlesey, Elisha (Ohio)
Whittlesey, Frederick (N. Y.)
Wilde, Richard Henry (Ga.)
Williams, Lewis (N. C.)
Wilson, Edgar C. (Va.)
Wise, Henry A. (Va.)
Young, Ebenezer (Conn.)

The Twenty-fourth Congress (1835-37)

Polk, James K. (Tenn.) Speaker.
Adams, John Q. (Mass.)
Alford, Julius C. (Ga.)
Allan, Chilton (Ky.)
Allen, Heman (Vt.)
Anthony, Joseph B. (Pa.)
Ash, Michael W. (Pa.)
Ashley, William H. (Mo.)
Bailey, Jeremiah (Maine)
Banks, John (Pa.)
Barton, Samuel (N. Y.)
Beale, James M. H. (Va.)
Bean, Benning M. (N. H.)
Beardsley, Samuel (N. Y.)
Beaumont, Andrew (Pa.)
Bell, John (Tenn.)
Black, James (Pa.)
Bockee, Abraham (N. Y.)
Bond, William K. (Ohio)
Boon, Ratliff (Ind.)
Borden, Nathaniel B. (Mass.)
Bouldin, James W. (Va.)
Bovee, Matthias J. (N. Y.)
Boyd, Linn (Ky.)
Briggs, George N. (Mass.)
Brown, John W. (N. Y.)
Buchanan, Andrew (Pa.)
Bunch, Samuel (Tenn.)
Burns, Robert (N. H.)
Bynum, Jesse A. (N. C.)
Calhoon, John (Ky.)
Calhoun, William B. (Mass.)
Cambreleng, Churchill C. (N. Y.)
Campbell, Robert B. (S. C.)
Carr, John (Ind.)
Carter, William B. (Tenn.)
Casey, Zadoc (Ill.)
Chambers, George (Pa.)
Chambers, John (Ky.)
Chaney, John (Ohio)
Chapin, Graham H. (N. Y.)
Chapman, Reuben (Ala.)
Chetwood, William (N. J.)
Childs, Timothy (N. Y.)
Claiborne, John F. H. (Miss.)
Claiborne, Nathaniel H. (Va.)
Clark, William (Pa.)
Cleveland, Jesse F. (Ga.)
Coffee, John (Ga.)
Coles, Walter (Va.)
Connor, Henry W. (N. C.)
Corwin, Thomas (Ohio)
Craig, Robert (Va.)
Cramer, John (N. Y.)
Crane, Joseph H. (Ohio)
Crary, Isaac E. (Mich.)
Cushing, Caleb (Mass.)
Cushman, Samuel (N. H.)
Darlington, Edward (Pa.)
Davis, John W. (Ind.)
Dawson, Wm. C. (Ga.)
Deberry, Edmund (N. C.)
Denny, Harmer (Pa.)
Dickerson, Philemon (N. J.)
Dickson, David (Miss.)
Doubleday, Ulysses F. (N. Y.)
Dromgoole, George C. (Va.)
Dunlap, William C. (Tenn.)
Efner, Valentine (N. Y.)
Elmore, Franklin H. (S. C.)
Evans, George (Maine)
Everett, Horace (Vt.)
Fairfield, John (Maine)
Farlin, Dudley (N. Y.)
Forester, John B. (Tenn.)
Fowler, Samuel (N. J.)
French, Richard (Ky.)
Fry, Jacob, Jr. (Pa.)
Fuller, Philo C. (N. Y.)
Fuller, William K. (N. Y.)
Galbraith, John (Pa.)
Garland, James (Va.)
Garland, Rice (La.)
Gholson, Samuel J. (Miss.)
Gillet, Ransom H. (N. Y.)
Glascock, Thomas (Ga.)
Graham, James (N. C.)
Granger, Francis (N. Y.)
Grantland, Seaton (Ga.)
Graves, William J. (Ky.)
Grayson, William J. (S. C.)
Grennell, George, Jr. (Mass.)
Griffin, John K. (S. C.)
Haley, Elisha (Conn.)
Hall, Hiland (Vt.)
Hall, Joseph (Maine)
Hamer, Thomas L. (Ohio)
Hammond, James H. (S. C.)
Hannegan, Edward A. (Ind.)
Hard, Gideon (N. Y.)
Hardin, Benjamin (Ky.)
Harlan, James (Ky.)
Harper, James (Pa.)
Harrison, Albert G. (Mo.)
Harrison, Samuel S. (Pa.)
Hawes, Albert G. (Ky.)
Hawkins, Micajah T. (N. C.)
Haynes, Charles E. (Ga.)
Hazeltine, Abner (N. Y.)
Henderson, Joseph (Pa.)
Herod, William (Ind.)
Hiester, William (Pa.)
Hoar, Samuel (Mass.)
Holsey, Hopkins (Ga.)
Holt, Orrin (Conn.)
Hopkins, George W. (Va.)
Howard, Benjamin C. (Md.)
Howell, Elias (Ohio)
Hubley, Edward B. (Pa.)
Hunt, Hiram P. (N. Y.)
Huntington, Abel (N. Y.)
Huntsman, Adam (Tenn.)
Ingersoll, Joseph R. (Pa.)
Ingham, Samuel (Conn.)
Jackson, Jabez (Ga.)
Jackson, William (Mass.)
Jarvis, Leonard (Maine)
Janes, Henry F. (Va.)
Jenifer, Daniel (Md.)
Johnson, Cave (Tenn.)
Johnson, Henry (La.)
Johnson, Joseph (Va.)
Johnson, Richard M. (Ky.)
Jones, Benjamin (Ohio)
Jones, John W. (Va.)
Judson, Andrew T. (Conn.)
Kennon, William (Ohio)
Kilgore, Daniel (Ohio)
Kinnard, George L. (Ind.)
Klingensmith, John (Pa.)
Lane, Amos (Ind.)
Lansing, Gerrit Y. (N. Y.)
Laporte, John (Pa.)
Lawler, Joab (Ala.)
Lawrence, Abbott (Mass.)
Lay, George W. (N. Y.)
Lea, Luke (Tenn.)
Lee, Gideon (N. Y.)
Lee, Joshua (N. Y.)
Lee, Thomas (N. J.)
Leonard, Stephen B. (N. Y.)
Lewis, Dixon H. (Ala.)
Lincoln, Levi (Mass.)
Logan, Henry (Pa.)
Love, Thomas C. (N. Y.)
Loyall, George (Va.)
Lucas, Edward, Jr. (Va.)
Lyon, Francis S. (Ala.)
McCarty, Jonathan (Ind.)
McComas, William (Va.)
McKay, James I. (N. C.)
McKeon, John (N. Y.)
McKennan, Thomas M. T. (Pa.)
McKim, Isaac (Md.)
McLene, Jeremiah (Ohio)
Mann, Abijah, Jr. (N. Y.)
Mann, Job (Pa.)
Manning, Richard I. (S. C.)
Martin, Joshua L. (Ala.)
Mason, John Y. (Va.)
Mason, Moses, Jr. (Maine)

Mason, Samson (Ohio)
Mason, William (N. Y.)
Maury, Abram P. (Tenn.)
May, William L. (Ill.)
Mercer, Charles F. (Va.)
Miller, Jesse (Pa.)
Miller, Rutger B. (N. Y.)
Milligan, John J. (Del.)
Montgomery, William (N. C.)
Moore, Ely (N. Y.)
Morgan, William S. (Va.)
Morris, Mathias (Pa.)
Muhlenberg, Henry A. P. (Pa.)
Owens, George W. (Ga.)
Page, Sherman (N. Y.)
Parker, James (N. J.)
Parks, Gorham (Maine)
Patterson, William (Ohio)
Patton, John M. (Va.)
Pearce, Dutee J. (R. I.)
Pearce, James A. (Md.)
Pearson, John J. (Pa.)
Pettigrew, Ebenezer (N. C.)
Peyton, Balie (Tenn.)
Phelps, Lancelot (Conn.)
Phillips, Stephen C. (Mass.)
Pickens, Francis W. (S. C.)
Pierce, Franklin (N. H.)
Pinckney, Henry L. (S. C.)
Polk, James K. (Tenn.)
Potts, David, Jr. (Pa.)
Reed, John (Mass.)
Rencher, Abraham (N. C.)
Reynolds, John (Ill.)
Reynolds, Joseph (N. Y.)
Richardson, John P. (S. C.)
Ripley, Eleazar W. (La.)
Roane, John (Va.)
Robertson, John (Va.)
Rogers, James (S. C.)
Russell, David (N. Y.)
Schenck, Ferdinand S. (N. J.)
Seymour, William (N. Y.)
Shepard, William B. (N. C.)
Shepperd, Augustine H. (N. C.)
Shields, Ebenezer J. (Tenn.)
Shinn, William N. (N. J.)
Sickles, Nicholas (N. Y.)
Slade, William (Vt.)
Sloane, Jonathan (Ohio)
Smith, Francis O. J. (Maine)
Spangler, David (Ohio)
Speight, Jesse (N. C.)
Sprague, William, Jr. (R. I.)
Standifer, James (Tenn.)
Steele, John N. (Md.)
Storer, Bellamy (Ohio)
Sutherland, Joel B. (Pa.)
Taliaferro, John (Va.)
Taylor, William (N. Y.)
Thomas, Francis (Md.)
Thompson, Waddy, Jr. (S. C.)
Thomson, John (Ohio)
Toucey, Isaac (Conn.)
Towns, George W. B. (Ga.)
Turner, James (Md.)
Turrill, Joel (N. Y.)
Underwood, Joseph R. (Ky.)
Vanderpoel, Aaron (N. Y.)
Vinton, Samuel F. (Ohio)
Wagener, David D. (Pa.)
Ward, Aaron (N. Y.)
Wardwell, Daniel (N. Y.)
Washington, George C. (Md.)
Webster, Taylor (Ohio)
Weeks, Joseph (N. H.)
White, John (Ky.)
Whittlesey, Elisha (Ohio)
Whittlesey, Thomas T. (Conn.)
Wildman, Zalmon (Conn.)
Williams, Sherrod (Ky.)
Williams, Lewis (N. C.)
Wise, Henry A. (Va.)
Yell, Archibald (Ark.)
Young, John (N. Y.)

The Twenty-fifth Congress (1837-39)

Polk, James K. (Tenn.) Speaker.

Adams, John Q. (Mass.)
Alexander, James (Ohio)
Allen, Heman (Vt.)
Allen, John W. (Ohio)
Anderson, Hugh J. (Maine)
Andrews, John T. (N. Y.)
Atherton, Charles G. (N. H.)
Aycrigg, John B. (N. J.)
Banks, Linn (Va.)
Beatty, William (Pa.)
Beers, Cyrus (N. Y.)
Beirne, Andrew (Va.)
Bell, John (Tenn.)
Bicknell, Bennet (N. Y.)
Biddle, Richard (Pa.)
Birdsall, Samuel (N. Y.)
Bond, William K. (Ohio)
Boon, Ratliff (Ind.)
Borden, Nathaniel B. (Mass.)
Bouldin, James W. (Va.)
Briggs, George N. (Mass.)
Brodhead, John C. (N. Y.)
Bronson, Isaac H. (N. Y.)
Bruyn, Andrew D. W. (N. Y.)
Buchanan, Andrew (Pa.)
Bynum, Jesse A. (N. C.)
Calhoon, John (Ky.)
Calhoun, William B. (Mass.)
Cambreleng, Churchill C. (N. Y.)
Campbell, John (S. C.)
Campbell, William B. (Tenn.)
Carter, Timothy J. (Maine)
Carter, William B. (Tenn.)
Casey, Zadoc (Ill.)
Chambers, John (Ky.)
Chaney, John (Ohio)
Chapman, Reuben (Ala.)
Cheatham, Richard (Tenn.)
Childs, Timothy (N. Y.)
Cilley, Jonathan (Maine)
Claiborne, John F. H. (Miss.)
Clark, John C. (N. Y.)
Cleveland, Jesse F. (Ga.)
Clowney, William K. (S. C.)
Coffin, Charles D. (Ohio)
Coles, Walter (Va.)
Connor, Henry W. (N. C.)
Corwin, Thomas (Ohio)
Crabb, George W. (Ala.)
Craig, Robert (Va.)
Cranston, Robert B. (R. I.)
Crary, Isaac E. (Mich.)
Crockett, John W. (Tenn.)
Curtis, Edward (N. Y.)
Cushing, Caleb (Mass.)
Cushman, Samuel (N. H.)
Darlington, Edward (Pa.)
Davee, Thomas (Maine)
Davies, Edward (Pa.)
Dawson, William C. (Ga.)
Deberry, Edmund (N. C.)
De Graff, John I. (N. Y.)
Dennis, John (Md.)
Dromgoole, George C. (Va.)
Duncan, Alexander (Ohio)
Dunn, George H. (Ind.)
Edwards, John (N. Y.)
Elmore, Franklin H. (S. C.)
Evans, George (Maine)
Everett, Horace (Vt.)
Ewing, John (Ind.)
Fairfield, John (Maine)
Farrington, James (N. H.)
Fillmore, Millard (N. Y.)
Fletcher, Isaac (Vt.)
Fletcher, Richard (Mass.)
Foster, Henry A. (N. Y.)
Fry, Jacob, Jr. (Pa.)
Gallup, Albert (N. Y.)
Garland, James (Va.)
Garland, Rice (La.)
Gholson, Samuel J. (Miss.)
Giddings, Joshua R. (Ohio)
Glascock, Thomas (Ga.)
Goode, Patrick G. (Ohio)
Graham, James (N. C.)
Graham, William (Ind.)
Grant, Abraham P. (N. Y.)
Grantland, Seaton (Ga.)
Graves, William J. (Ky.)
Gray, Hiram (N. Y.)
Grennell, George, Jr. (Mass.)
Griffin, John K. (S. C.)
Haley, Elisha (Conn.)
Hall, Hiland (Vt.)
Halstead, William (N. J.)
Hamer, Thomas L. (Ohio)
Hammond, Robert H. (Pa.)
Harlan, James (Ky.)
Harper, Alexander (Ohio)
Harrison, Albert G. (Mo.)
Hastings, William S. (Mass.)
Hawes, Richard (Ky.)
Hawkins, Micajah T. (N. C.)
Haynes, Charles E. (Ga.)
Henry, Thomas (Pa.)
Herod, William (Ind.)
Hoffman, J. Ogden (N. Y.)
Holsey, Hopkins (Ga.)
Holt, Orrin (Conn.)
Hopkins, George W. (Va.)
Howard, Benjamin C. (Md.)
Hubley, Edward B. (Pa.)
Hunter, Robert M. T. (Va.)
Hunter, William H. (Ohio)
Ingham, Samuel (Conn.)
Jackson, Jabez (Ga.)
Jackson, Thomas B. (N. Y.)
Jenifer, Daniel (Md.)
Johnson, Henry (La.)
Johnson, Joseph (Va.)
Johnson, William C. (Md.)
Jones, John W. (Va.)
Jones, Nathaniel (N. Y.)
Keim, George M. (Pa.)
Kemble, Gouverneur (N. Y.)
Kennedy, John P. (Md.)
Kilgore, Daniel (Ohio)
Klingensmith, John (Pa.)
Lawler, Joab (Ala.)
Leadbetter, Daniel P. (Ohio)
Legare, Hugh S. (S. C.)
Lewis, Dixon H. (Ala.)
Lincoln, Levi (Mass.)
Logan, Henry (Pa.)
Loomis, Andrew W. (Ohio)
Loomis, Arphaxed (N. Y.)
Lyon, Francis S. (Ala.)
McClellan, Abraham (Tenn.)
McClellan, Robert (N. Y.)
McClure, Charles (Pa.)
McKay, James I. (N. C.)
McKennan, Thomas M. T. (Pa.)
McKim, Isaac (Md.)
Mallory, Francis (Va.)
Martin, Joshua L. (Ala.)
Marvin, Richard P. (N. Y.)
Mason, James M. (Va.)
Mason, Samson (Ohio)
Maury, Abram P. (Tenn.)
Maxwell, John P. B. (N. J.)
May, William L. (Ill.)
Menifee, Richard H. (Ky.)
Mercer, Charles F. (Va.)
Miller, John (Mo.)
Milligan, John J. (Del.)
Mitchell, Charles F. (N. Y.)
Montgomery, William (N. C.)
Moore, Ely (N. Y.)
Morgan, William S. (Va.)
Morris, Calvary (Ohio)
Morris, Mathias (Pa.)
Morris, Samuel W. (Pa.)
Muhlenberg, Henry A. P. (Pa.)
Murry, John L. (Ky.)
Naylor, Charles (Pa.)
Noble, William H. (N. Y.)
Noyes, Joseph C. (Maine)
Ogle, Charles (Pa.)
Owens, George W. (Ga.)
Palmer, John (N. Y.)
Parker, Amasa J. (N. Y.)
Parmenter, William (Mass.)
Parris, Virgil D. (Maine)
Patterson, William (N. Y.)
Patton, John M. (Va.)
Paynter, Lemuel (Pa.)
Pearce, James A. (Md.)
Peck, Luther C. (N. Y.)
Pennybacker, Isaac S. (Va.)
Petrikin, David (Pa.)
Phelps, Launcelot (Conn.)
Phillips, Stephen C. (Mass.)
Pickens, Francis W. (S. C.)
Plumer, Arnold (Pa.)
Polk, James K. (Tenn.)
Pope, John (Ky.)
Potter, William W. (Pa.)
Potts, David (Pa.)
Pratt, Zadoc (N. Y.)
Prentiss, John H. (N. Y.)
Prentiss, Sergeant S. (Miss.)
Putnam, Harvey (N. Y.)
Randolph, Joseph F. (N. J.)
Rariden, James (Ind.)
Reed, John (Mass.)
Reily, Luther (Pa.)
Rencher, Abraham (N. C.)
Rhett, Robert B. (S. C.)
Richardson, John P. (S. C.)
Ridgway, Joseph (Ohio)
Rives, Francis E. (Va.)
Robertson, John (Va.)
Robinson, Edward (Maine)
Rumsey, Edward (Ky.)
Russell, David A. (N. Y.)
Saltonstall, Leverett (Mass.)
Sawyer, Samuel T. (N. C.)
Sergeant, John (Pa.)
Sheffer, Daniel (Pa.)
Shepard, Charles B. (N. C.)
Shepperd, Augustine H. (N. C.)
Shepler, Matthias (Ohio)
Shields, Ebenezer J. (Tenn.)
Sibley, Mark H. (N. Y.)
Slade, William (Vt.)
Smith, Francis O. J. (Maine)
Snyder, Adam W. (Ill.)
Southgate, William W. (Ky.)
Spencer, James B. (N. Y.)
Stanley, Edward (N. C.)
Stone, William (Tenn.)
Stratton, Charles C. (N. J.)
Stuart, Archibald (Va.)
Swearingen, Henry (Ohio)
Taliaferro, John (Va.)
Taylor, William (N. Y.)
Thomas, Francis (Md.)
Thompson, Waddy (S. C.)
Tillinghast, Joseph L. (R. I.)
Titus, Obadiah (N. Y.)
Toland, George W. (Pa.)
Toucey, Isaac (Conn.)
Towns, George W. B. (Ga.)
Turney, Hopkins L. (Tenn.)
Underwood, Joseph R. (Ky.)
Vail, Henry (N. Y.)
Vanderveer, Abraham (N. Y.)
Wagener, David D. (Pa.)
Word, Thomas J. (Miss.)
Weeks, Joseph (N. H.)
Webster, Taylor (Ohio)
White, Albert S. (Ind.)
White, John (Ky.)
Whittlesey, Elisha (Ohio)
Whittlesey, Thomas T. (Conn.)
Williams, Christopher H. (Tenn.)
Williams, Jared W. (N. H.)
Williams, Joseph L. (Tenn.)
Williams, Lewis (N. C.)
Williams, Sherrod (Ky.)
Wise, Henry A. (Va.)
Worthington, John T. H. (Md.)
Yell, Archibald (Ark.)
Yorke, Thomas J. (N. J.)

The Twenty-Sixth Congress (1839-41)

Hunter, Robert M. T. (Va.) Speaker.

Adams, John Q. (Mass.)
Alford, Julius C. (Ga.)
Allen, John W. (Ohio)
Allen, Judson (N. Y.)
Anderson, Hugh J. (Maine)
Anderson, Simeon H. (Ky.)
Andrews, Landaff W. (Ky.)
Atherton, Charles G. (N. H.)
Baker, Osmyn (Mass.)
Banks, Linn (Va.)
Barnard, Daniel D. (N. Y.)
Beatty, William (Pa.)
Beirne, Andrew (Va.)
Bell, John (Tenn.)
Biddle, Richard (Pa.)
Black, Edward J. (Ga.)
Blackwell, Julius W. (Tenn.)
Boardman, William W. (Conn.)
Bond, William K. (Ohio)
Botts, John M. (Va.)
Boyd, Linn (Ky.)
Brackenridge, Henry M. (Pa.)
Brewster, David P. (N. Y.)
Briggs, George N. (Mass.)
Brockway, John H (Conn.)
Brown, Aaron V. (Tenn.)
Brown, Albert G. (Miss.)
Brown, Anson (N. Y.)
Burke, Edmund (N. H.)
Butler, Sampson H. (S. C.)
Butler, William O. (Ky.)
Bynum, Jesse A. (N. C.)
Calhoun, William B. (Mass.)

Campbell, John (S. C.)
Campbell, William B. (Tenn.)
Carr, John (Ind.)
Carroll, James (Md.)
Carter, William B. (Tenn.)
Casey, Zadoc (Ill.)
Chapman, Reuben (Ala.)
Chinn, Thomas W. (La.)
Chittenden, Thomas C. (N. Y.)
Clark, John C. (N. Y.)
Clifford, Nathan (Maine)
Coles, Walter (Va.)
Colquitt, Walter T. (Ga.)
Connor, Henry W. (N. C.)
Cooper, James (Pa.)
Cooper, Mark A. (Ga.)
Cooper, William R. (N. J.)
Corwin, Thomas (Ohio)
Crabb, George W. (Ala.)
Craig, Robert (Va.)
Cranston, Robert B. (R. I.)
Crary, Isaac E. (Mich.)
Crockett, John W. (Tenn.)
Cross, Edward (Ark.)
Curtis, Edward (N. Y.)
Cushing, Caleb (Mass.)
Dana, Amasa (N. Y.)
Davee, Thomas (Maine)
Davies, Edward (Pa.)
Davis, Garrett (Ky.)
Davis, John (Pa.)
Davis, John W. (Ind.)
Dawson, William C. (Ga.)
Deberry, Edmund (N. C.)
Dennis, John (Md.)
Dickerson, Philemon (N. J.)
Dellett, James (Ala.)
Doan, William (Ohio)
Doe, Nicholas B. (N. Y.)
Doig, Andrew W. (N. Y.)
Dromgoole, George C. (Va.)
Duncan, Alexander (Ohio)
Earll, Nehemiah H. (N. Y.)
Eastman, Ira A. (N. H.)
Edwards, John (Pa.)
Ely, John (N. Y.)
Evans, George (Maine)
Everett, Horace (Vt.)
Fillmore, Millard (N. Y.)
Fine, John (N. Y.)
Fisher, Charles (N. C.)
Fletcher, Isaac (Vt.)
Floyd, John G. (N. Y.)
Fornance, Joseph (Pa.)
Galbraith, John (Pa.)
Garland, James (Va.)
Garland, Rice (La.)
Gates, Seth M. (N. Y.)
Gentry, Meredith P. (Tenn.)
Gerry, James (Pa.)
Giddings, Joshua R. (Ohio)
Goggin, William L. (Va.)
Goode, Patrick G. (Ohio)
Graham, James (N. C.)
Granger, Francis (N. Y.)
Graves, William J. (Ky.)
Green, Willis (Ky.)
Griffin, John K. (S. C.)
Grinnell, Moses H. (N. Y.)
Habersham, Richard W. (Ga.)
Hall, Hiland (Vt.)
Hand, Augustus C. (N. Y.)
Hammond, Robert H. (Pa.)
Hastings, John (Ohio)
Hastings, William S. (Mass.)
Hawes, Richard (Ky.)
Hawkins, Micajah T. (N. C.)
Henry, Thomas (Pa.)
Hill, John (N. C.)
Hill, John (Va.)
Hillen, Solomon (Md.)
Hoffman, Ogden (N. Y.)
Holleman, Joel (Va.)
Holmes, Isaac E. (S. C.)
Holt, Hines (Ga.)
Hook, Enos (Pa.)
Hopkins, George W. (Va.)
Howard, Tilghman A. (Ind.)
Hubbard, David (Ala.)
Hunt, Hiram P. (N. Y.)
Hunter, Robert M. T. (Va.)
Jackson, Thomas B. (N. Y.)
James, Francis (Pa.)
Jameson, John (Mo.)
Jenifer, Daniel (Md.)
Johnson, Cave (Tenn.)
Johnson, Charles (N. Y.)
Johnson, Joseph (Va.)
Johnson, William C. (Md.)
Jones, John W. (Va.)
Jones, Nathaniel (N. Y.)
Keim, George M. (Pa.)
Kemble, Gouverneur (N. Y.)
Kempshall, Thomas (N. Y.)
Kille, Joseph (N. J.)
King, Thomas B. (Ga.)
Lane, Henry S. (Ind.)
Lawrence, Abbott (Mass.)
Leadbetter, Daniel P. (Ohio)
Leet, Isaac (Pa.)
Leonard, Stephen B. (N. Y.)
Lewis, Dixon H. (Ala.)
Lincoln, Levi (Mass.)
Lowell, Joshua A. (Maine)
Lucas, William (Va.)
McCarty, William M. (Va.)
McClellan, Abraham (Tenn.)
McClure, Charles (Pa.)
McCulloch, George (Pa.)
McKay, James I. (N. C.)
Mallory, Francis (Va.)
Mallory, Meredith (N. Y.)
Marchand, Albert G. (Pa.)
Marvin, Richard P. (N. Y.)
Mason, Samson (Ohio)
Medill, William (Ohio)
Mercer, Charles F. (Va.)
Miller, John (Mo.)
Mitchell, Charles F. (N. Y.)
Monroe, James (N. Y.)
Montanya, James DeLa. (N. Y.)
Montgomery, William (N. C.)
Moore, John (La.)
Morgan, Christopher (N. Y.)
Morris, Calvary (Ohio)
Morris, Samuel W. (Pa.)
Morrow, Jeremiah (Ohio)
Naylor, Charles (Pa.)
Newhard, Peter (Pa.)
Nisbet, Eugenius A. (Ga.)
Ogle, Charles (Pa.)
Osborne, Thomas B. (Conn.)
Palen, Rufus (N. Y.)
Parmenter, William (Mass.)
Parris, Virgil D. (Maine)
Parrish, Isaac (Ohio)
Paynter, Lemuel (Pa.)
Peck, Luther C. (N. Y.)
Petrikin, David (Pa.)
Pickens, Francis W. (S. C.)
Pope, John (Ky.)
Prentiss, John H. (N. Y.)
Proffit, George H. (Ind.)
Ramsey, William S. (Pa.)
Randall, Benjamin (Maine)
Randolph Joseph F. (N. J.)
Rariden, James (Ind.)
Rayner, Kenneth (N. C.)
Reed, Josh (Mass.)
Reynolds, John (Ill.)
Rhett, R. Barnwell (S. C.)
Ridgway, Joseph (Ohio)
Rives, Francis E. (Va.)
Robinson, Thomas, Jr. (Del.)
Rogers, Edward (N. Y.)
Rogers, James (S. C.)
Russell, David A. (N. Y.)
Ryall, Daniel B. (N. J.)
Saltonstall, Leverett (Mass.)
Samuel, Green B. (Va.)
Sergeant, John (Pa.)
Shaw, Tristram (N. H.)
Shepard, Charles B. (N. C.)
Simonton, William (Pa.)
Slade, William (Vt.)
Smith, Albert (Maine)
Smith, John (Vt.)
Smith, Thomas (Ind.)
Smith, Truman (Conn.)
Stanly, Edward (N. C.)
Starkweather, David A. (Ohio)
Steenrod, Lewis (Va.)
Storrs, William L. (Conn.)
Strong, Theron R. (N. Y.)
Stuart, John T. (Ill.)
Sumter, Thomas D. (S. C.)
Swearingen, Henry (Ohio)
Sweeny, George (Ohio)
Taliaferro, John (Va.)
Taylor, Jonathan (Ohio)
Thomas, Francis (Md.)
Thomas, Philip F. (Md.)
Thompson, Jacob (Miss.)
Thompson, John B. (Ky.)
Thompson, Waddy, Jr. (S. C.)
Tillinghast, Joseph L. (R. I.)
Toland, George W. (Pa.)
Triplett, Philip (Ky.)
Trumbull, Joseph (Conn.)
Turney, Hopkins L. (Tenn.)
Underwood, Joseph R. (Ky.)
Vanderpoel, Aaron (N. Y.)
Vroom, Peter D. (N. J.)
Wagener, David D. (Pa.)
Wagner, Peter J. (N. Y.)
Warren, Lott (Ga.)
Watterson, Harvey M. (Tenn.)
Weller, John B. (Ohio)
White, Edward D. (La.)
White, John (Ky.)
Williams, Christopher H. (Tenn.)
Williams, Henry (Mass.)
Williams, Jared W. (N. H.)
Williams, Joseph L. (Tenn.)
Williams, Lewis (N. C.)
Williams, Sherrod (Ky.)
Williams, Thomas W. (Conn.)
Wick, William W. (Ind.)
Winthrop, Robert C. (Mass.)
Wise, Henry A. (Va.)
Worthington, John T. H. (Md.)

The Twenty-seventh Congress (1841-43)

White, John (Ky.)
Speaker.

Adams, John Q. (Mass.)
Alford, Julius C. (Ga.)
Allen, Elisha H. (Maine)
Andrews, Landaff W. (Ky.)
Andrews, Sherlock J. (Ohio)
Appleton, Nathan (Mass.)
Arnold, Thomas D. (Tenn.)
Arrington, Archibald H. (N. C.)
Atherton, Charles G. (N. H.)
Aycrigg, John B. (N. J.)
Babcock, Alfred (N. Y.)
Baker, Osmyn (Mass.)
Banks, Linn (Va.)
Barnard, Daniel D. (N. Y.)
Barton, Richard W. (Va.)
Beeson, Henry W. (Pa.)
Bidlack, Benjamin A. (Pa.)
Birdseye, Victory (N. Y.)
Black, Edward J. (Ga.)
Black, Henry (Pa.)
Blair, Barnard (N. Y.)
Boardman, William W. (Conn.)
Borden, Nathaniel B. (Mass.)
Botts, John M. (Va.)
Bowne, Samuel S. (N. Y.)
Boyd, Linn (Ky.)
Brewster, David P. (N. Y.)
Briggs, George N. (Mass.)
Brockway, John H. (Conn.)
Bronson, David (Maine)
Brown, Aaron V. (Tenn.)
Brown, Charles (Pa.)
Brown, Jeremiah (Pa.)
Brown, Milton (Tenn.)
Burke, Edmund (N. H.)
Burnell, Barker (Mass.)
Butler, Sampson H. (S. C.)
Butler, William (S. C.)
Butler, William O. (Ky.)
Caldwell, Greene W. (N. C.)
Caldwell, Patrick C. (S. C.)
Calhoun, William B. (Mass.)
Campell, John (S. C.)
Campbell, Thomas J. (Tenn.)
Campbell, William B. (Tenn.)
Caruthers, Robert L. (Tenn.)
Cary, George B. (Va.)
Casey, Zadoc (Ill.)
Chapman, Reuben (Ala.)
Childs, Timothy (N. Y.)
Chittenden, Thomas C. (N. Y.)
Clark, John C. (N. Y.)
Clarke, Staley N. (N. Y.)
Clifford, Nathan (Maine)
Clinton, James G. (N. Y.)
Colquitt, Walter T. (Ga.)
Coles, Walter (Va.)
Cooper, James (Pa.)
Cooper, Mark A. (Ga.)
Cowen, Benjamin S. (Ohio)
Cranston, Robert B. (R. I.)
Cross, Edward (Ark.)
Cravens, James H. (Ind.)
Crawford, George W. (Ga.)
Cushing, Caleb (Mass.)
Daniel, John R. J. (N. C.)
Davis, Garrett (Ky.)
Davis, Richard D. (N. Y.)
Dawson, John B. (La.)
Dawson, William C. (Ga.)
Dean, Ezra (Ohio)
Deberry, Edmund (N. C.)
Dimock, Davis, Jr. (Pa.)
Doan, William (Ohio)
Doig, Andrew W. (N. Y.)
Eastman, Ira A. (N. H.)
Edwards, John (Pa.)
Edwards, John C. (Mo.)
Egbert, Joseph (N. Y.)
Everett, Horace (Vt.)
Ferris, Charles G. (N. Y.)
Fessenden, William P. (Maine)
Fillmore, Millard (N. Y.)
Floyd, Charles A. (N. Y.)
Floyd, John G. (N. Y.)
Foster, A. Lawrence (N. Y.)
Foster, Thomas F. (Ga.)
Fornance, Joseph (Pa.)
Gamble, Roger L. (Ga.)
Gates, Seth M. (N. Y.)
Gentry, Meredith P. (Tenn.)
Gerry, James (Pa.)
Giddings, Joshua R. (Ohio)
Gilmer, Thomas W. (Va.)
Goggin, William L. (Va.)
Goode, Patrick G. (Ohio)
Goode, William O. (Va.)
Gordon, Samuel (N. Y.)
Graham, James (N. C.)
Granger, Francis (N. Y.)
Green, Willis (Ky.)
Greig, John (N. Y.)
Gustine, Amos (Pa.)
Gwin, William M. (Miss.)
Habersham, Richard W. (Ga.)
Hall, Hiland (Vt.)
Halstead, William (N. J.)
Harris, William A. (Va.)
Hastings, John (Ohio)
Hastings, William S. (Mass.)
Hays, Samuel L. (Va.)
Henry, Thomas (Pa.)
Holmes, Isaac E. (S. C.)
Hook, Enos (Pa.)
Hopkins, George W. (Va.)
Houck, Jacob, Jr. (N. Y.)
Houston, George S. (Ala.)
Howard, Jacob M. (Mich.)
Hubard, Edmund W. (Va.)
Hudson, Charles (Mass.)
Hunt, Hiram P. (N. Y.)
Hunter, Robert M. T. (Va.)
Ingersoll, Charles J. (Pa.)
Ingersoll, Joseph R. (Pa.)
Irvin, James (Pa.)
Irwin, William W. (Pa.)
Jack, William (Pa.)
James, Francis (Pa.)
Johnson, Cave (Tenn.)
Johnson, William C. (Md.)
Jones, Isaac D. (Md.)
Jones, John W. (Va.)
Keim, George M. (Pa.)
Kennedy, Andrew (Ind.)
Kennedy, John P. (Md.)
King, Thomas B (Ga.)
Lane, Henry S. (Ind.)
Lawrence, Joseph (Pa.)
Lewis, Dixon H. (Ala.)
Linn, Archibald L. (N. Y.)
Littlefield, Nathaniel S. (Maine)
Lowell, Joshua A. (Maine)
McClellan, Abraham (Tenn.)
McClellan, Robert (N. Y.)
McKay, James I. (N. C.)
McKennan, Thomas M. T. (Pa.)
McKeon, John (N. Y.)
Mallory, Francis (Va.)
Marchand, Albert G. (Pa.)
Marshall, Alfred (Maine)
Marshall, Thomas F. (Ky.)
Mason, John T. (Md.)
Mason, Samson (Ohio)
Mathews, James (Ohio)
Mathiot, Joshua (Ohio)
Mattocks, John (Vt.)
Maxwell, John P. B. (N. J.)
Maynard, John (N. Y.)
Medill, William (Ohio)
Meriwether, James A. (Ga.)
Miller, John (Mo.)
Mitchell, Anderson (N. C.)
Moore, John (La.)
Morgan, Christopher (N. Y.)

Morris, Calvary (Ohio)
Morrow, Jeremiah (Ohio)
Newhard, Peter (Pa.)
Nisbet, Eugenius A. (Ga.)
Oliver, William M. (N. Y.)
Osborne, Thomas B. (Conn.)
Owsley, Bryan Y. (Ky.)
Parmenter, William (Mass.)
Partridge, Samuel (N. Y.)
Payne, William W. (Ala.)
Pearce, James A. (Md.)
Pendleton, Nathaniel G. (Ohio)
Pickens, Francis W. (S. C.)
Plumer, Arnold (Pa.)
Pope, John (Ky.)
Powell, Cuthbert (Va.)
Proffit, George H. (Ind.)
Ramsey, Robert (Pa.)
Randall, Alexander (Md.)
Randall, Benjamin (Maine)
Randolph, Joseph F. (N. J.)
Rayner, Kenneth (N. C.)
Read, Alman H. (Pa.)
Reding, John R. (N. H.)
Rencher, Abraham (N. C.)
Reynolds, John (Ill.)
Rhett, R. Barnwell (S. C.)
Ridgway, Joseph (Ohio)
Riggs, Lewis (N. Y.)
Rodney, George B. (Del.)
Rogers, James (S. C.)
Roosevelt, James I. (N. Y.)
Russell, Joseph M. (Pa.)
Russell, William (Ohio)
Saltonstall, Leverett (Mass.)
Sanford, John (N. Y.)
Saunders, Romulus M. (N. C.)
Sergeant, John (Pa.)
Sewall, Charles S. (Md.)
Shaw, Tristram (N. H.)
Shepperd, Augustine H. (N. C.)
Shields, Benjamin G. (Ala.)
Simonton, William (Pa.)
Slade, William (Vt.)
Smith, Truman (Conn.)
Smith, William (Va.)
Snyder, John (Pa.)
Sollers, Augustus R. (Md.)
Sprigg, James C. (Ky.)
Stanly, Edward (N. C.)
Steenrod, Lewis (Va.)
Stokely, Samuel (Ohio)
Stratton, Charles C. (N. J.)
Stuart, Alexander H. H. (Va.)
Stuart, John T. (Ill.)
Summers, George W. (Va.)
Sumter, Thomas D. (S. C.)
Sweeny, George (Ohio)
Taliaferro, John (Va.)
Thompson, Jacob (Miss.)
Thompson, John B. (Ky.)
Thompson, Richard W. (Ind.)
Tillinghast, Joseph L. (R. I.)
Toland, George W. (Pa.)
Tomlinson, Thomas A. (N. Y.)
Triplett, Philip (Ky.)
Trotti, Samuel W. (S. C.)
Trumbull, Joseph (Conn.)
Turney, Hopkins L. (Tenn.)
Underwood, Joseph R. (Ky.)
Van Buren, John (N. Y.)
Van Rensselaer, Henry (N. Y.)
Wallace, David (Ind.)
Ward, Aaron (N. Y.)
Warren, Lott (Ga.)
Washington, William H. (N. C.)
Watterson, Harvey M. (Tenn.)
Weller, John B. (Ohio)
Westbrook, John (Pa.)
White, Edward D. (La.)
White, John (Ky.)
White, Joseph L. (Ind.)
Williams, Christopher H. (Tenn.)
Williams, James W. (Md.)
Williams, Joseph L. (Tenn.)
Williams, Lewis (N. C.)
Williams, Thomas W. (Conn.)
Winthrop, Robert C. (Mass.)
Wise, Henry A. (Va.)
Wood, Fernando (N. Y.)
Yorke, Thomas J. (N. J.)
Young, Augustus (Vt.)
Young, John (N. Y.)

The Twenty-eighth Congress (1843-45)

Jones, John W. (Va.)
Speaker.

Abbott, Amos (Mass.)
Adams, John Q. (Mass.)
Anderson, Joseph H. (N. Y.)
Arrington, Archibald H. (N. C.)
Ashe, John B. (Tenn.)
Atkinson, Archibald (Va.)
Baker, Osmyn (Mass.)
Barnard, Daniel D. (N. Y.)
Barringer, Daniel M. (N. C.)
Bayly, Thomas H. (Va.)
Beardsley, Samuel (N. Y.)
Belser, James E. (Ala.)
Benton, Charles S. (N. Y.)
Bidlack, Benjamin A. (Pa.)
Black, Edward J. (Ga.)
Black, James (Pa.)
Black, James A. (S. C.)
Blackwell, Julius W. (Tenn.)
Bossier, Pierre E. J. B. (La.)
Bower, Gustavus M. (Mo.)
Bowlin, James B. (Mo.)
Boyd, Linn (Ky.)
Brengle, Francis (Md.)
Brinkerhoff, Jacob (Ohio)
Brodhead, Richard (Pa.)
Brown, Aaron V. (Tenn.)
Brown, Jeremiah (Pa.)
Brown, Milton (Tenn.)
Brown, William J. (Ind.)
Buffington, Joseph (Pa.)
Burke, Edmund (N. H.)
Burt, Armistead (S. C.)
Caldwell, George A. (Ky.)
Campbell, John (S. C.)
Carpenter, Levi D. (N. Y.)
Carroll, Charles H. (N. Y.)
Cary, Jeremiah E. (N. Y.)
Cary, Shepard (Maine)
Catlin, George S. (Conn.)
Causin, John M. S. (Md.)
Chapman, Augustus A. (Va.)
Chapman, Reuben (Ala.)
Chappell, Absalom H. (Ga.)
Chilton, Samuel (Va.)
Clinch, Duncan L. (Ga.)
Clingman, Thomas L. (N. C.)
Clinton, James G. (N. Y.)
Cobb, Howell (Ga.)
Coles, Walter (Va.)
Collamer, Jacob (Vt.)
Cranston, Henry Y. (R. I.)
Cross, Edward (Ark.)
Cullom, Alvan (Tenn.)
Dana, Amasa (N. Y.)
Daniel John R. J. (N. C.)
Darragh, Cornelius (Pa.)
Davis, Garrett (Ky.)
Davis, John W. (Ind.)
Davis, Richard D. (N. Y.)
Dawson, John B. (La.)
Dean, Ezra (Ohio)
Deberry, Edmund (N. C.)
Dellett, James (Ala.)
Dickey, John (Pa.)
Dickinson, David W. (Tenn.)
Dillingham, Paul, Jr. (Vt.)
Douglas, Stephen A. (Ill.)
Dromgoole, George C. (Va.)
Duncan, Alexander (Ohio)
Dunlap, Robert P. (Maine)
Ellis, Chesselden (N. Y.)
Elmer, Lucius Q. C. (N. J.)
Farlee, Isaac G. (N. J.)
Ficklin, Orlando B. (Ill.)
Fish, Hamilton (N. Y.)
Florence, Elias (Ohio)
Foot, Solomon (Vt.)
Foster, Henry D. (Pa.)
French, Richard (Ky.)
Frick, Henry (Pa.)
Fuller, George (Pa.)
Giddings, Joshua R. (Ohio)
Gilmer, Thomas W. (Va.)
Goggin, William L. (Va.)
Green, Byram (N. Y.)
Green, Willis (Ky.)
Grider, Henry (Ky.)
Grinnell, Joseph (Mass.)
Hale, John P. (N. H.)
Hamlin, Edward S. (Ohio)
Hamlin, Hannibal (Maine)
Hammett, William H. (Miss.)
Haralson, Hugh A. (Ga.)
Hardin, John J. (Ill.)
Harper, Alexander (Ohio)
Hays, Samuel (Pa.)
Henley, Thomas J. (Ind.)
Herrick, Joshua (Maine)
Hoge, Joseph P. (Ill.)
Holmes, Isaac E. (S. C.)
Hopkins, George W. (Va.)
Houston, George S. (Ala.)
Hubard, Edmund W. (Va.)
Hubbell, William S. (N. Y.)
Hudson, Charles (Mass.)
Hughes, James M. (Mo.)
Hungerford, Orville (N. Y.)
Hunt, James B. (Mich.)
Hunt, Washington (N. Y.)
Ingersoll, Charles J. (Pa.)
Ingersoll, Joseph R. (Pa.)
Irvin, James (Pa.)
Jameson, John (Mo.)
Jenks, Michael H. (Pa.)
Johnson, Andrew (Tenn.)
Johnson, Cave (Tenn.)
Johnson, Perley B. (Ohio)
Jones, George W. (Tenn.)
Jones, John W. (Va.)
Kennedy, Andrew (Ind.)
Kennedy, John P. (Md.)
King, Daniel P. (Mass.)
King, Preston (N. Y.)
Kirkpatrick, Littleton (N. J.)
Labranche, Alcee L. (La.)
Leonard, Moses G. (N. Y.)
Lewis, Dixon H. (Ala.)
Lucas, William (Va.)
Lumpkin, John H. (Ga.)
Lyon, Lucius (Mich.)
McCauslen, William C. (Ohio)
McClelland, Robert (Mich.)
McClernand, John A. (Ill.)
McConnell, Felix G. (Ala.)
McDowell, Joseph J. (Ohio)
McIlvaine, Abraham R. (Pa.)
McKay, James I. (N. C.)
Maclay, William B. (N. Y.)
Marsh, George P. (Vt.)
Mathews, James (Ohio)
Moore, Heman A. (Ohio)
Morris, Edward Joy (Pa.)
Morris, Joseph (Ohio)
Morse, Freeman H. (Maine)
Morse, Isaac E. (La.)
Moseley, William A. (N. Y.)
Murphy, Henry C. (N. Y.)
Nes, Henry (Pa.)
Newton, Willoughby (Va.)
Norris, Moses, Jr. (N. H.)
Owen, Robert Dale (Ind.)
Parmenter, William (Mass.)
Patterson, Thomas J. (N. Y.)
Payne, William W. (Ala.)
Pettit, John (Ind.)
Peyton, Joseph H. (Tenn.)
Phoenix, J. Phillips (N. Y.)
Pollock, James (Pa.)
Potter, Elisha R. (R. I.)
Potter, Emery D. (Ohio)
Pratt, Zadock (N. Y.)
Preston, Jacob A. (Md.)
Purdy, Smith M. (N. Y.)
Ramsey, Alexander (Pa.)
Rathbun, George (N. Y.)
Rayner, Kenneth (N. C.)
Read, Almon H. (Pa.)
Reed, Charles M. (Pa.)
Reding, John R. (N. H.)
Reid, David S. (N. C.)
Relfe, James H. (Mo.)
Rhett, R. Barnwell (S. C.)
Ritter, John (Pa.)
Roberts, Robert W. (Miss.)
Robinson, Orville (N. Y.)
Rockwell, Julius (Mass.)
Rodney, George B. (Del.)
Rogers, Charles (N. Y.)
Russell, Jeremiah (N. Y.)
St. John, Henry (Ohio)
Sample, Samuel C. (Ind.)
Saunders, Romulus M. (N. C.)
Schenck, Robert C. (Ohio)
Senter, William T. (Tenn.)
Severance, Luther (Maine)
Seymour, David L. (N. Y.)
Seymour, Thomas H. (Conn.)
Simons, Samuel (Conn.)
Simpson, Richard F. (S. C.)
Slidell, John (La.)
Smith, Albert (N. Y.)
Smith, Caleb B. (Ind.)
Smith, John T. (Pa.)
Smith, Robert (Ill.)
Smith, Thomas (Ind.)
Spence, Thomas A. (Md.)
Steenrod, Lewis (Va.)
Stephens, Alexander H. (Ga.)
Stetson, Lemuel (N. Y.)
Stewart, Andrew (Pa.)
Stewart, John (Conn.)
Stiles, William H. (Ga.)
Stone, Alfred P. (Ohio)
Stone, James W. (Ky.)
Strong, Selah B. (N. Y.)
Summers, George W. (Va.)
Sykes, George (N. J.)
Taylor, William (Va.)
Thomasson, William P. (Ky.)
Thompson, Jacob (Miss.)
Tibbatts, John W. (Ky.)
Tilden, Daniel R. (Ohio)
Tucker, Tilghman M. (Miss.)
Tyler, Asher (N. Y.)
Vance, Joseph (Ohio)
Vanmeter, John I. (Ohio)
Vinton, Samuel F. (Ohio)
Weller, John B. (Ohio)
Wentworth, John (Ill.)
Wethered, John (Md.)
Wheaton, Horace (N. Y.)
White, Benjamin (Maine)
White, John (Ky.)
Wilkins, William (Pa.)
Williams, Henry (Mass.)
Winthrop, Robert C. (Mass.)
Wise, Henry A. (Va.)
Woodward, Joseph A. (S. C.)
Wright, Joseph A. (Ind.)
Wright, William (N. J.)
Yancey, William L. (Ala.)
Yost, Jacob S. (Pa.)

The Twenty-ninth Congress (1845-47)

Davis, John W. (Ind.)
Speaker.

Abbott, Amos (Mass.)
Adams, John Q. (Mass.)
Adams, Stephen (Miss.)
Anderson, Joseph H. (N. Y.)
Arnold, Lemuel H. (R. I.)
Ashmun, George (Mass.)
Atkinson, Archibald (Va.)
Baker, Edward D. (Ill.)
Barringer, Daniel M. (N. C.)
Bayly, Thomas H. (Va.)
Bedinger, Henry (Va.)
Bell, Joshua F. (Ky.)
Benton, Charles S. (N. Y.)
Biggs, Asa (N. C.)
Black, James (Pa.)
Black, James A. (S. C.)
Blanchard, John (Pa.)
Bowdon, Franklin W. (Ala.)
Bowlin, James B. (Mo.)
Boyd, Linn (Ky.)
Brinkerhoff, Jacob (Ohio)
Brockenbrough, William H. (Fla.)
Brodhead, Richard (Pa.)
Brown, Milton (Tenn.)
Brown, William G. (Va.)
Buffington, Joseph (Pa.)
Burt, Armistead (S. C.)
Cabell, Edward C. (Fla.)
Campbell, John H. (Pa.)
Campbell, William W. (N. Y.)
Carroll, Charles H. (N. Y.)
Cathcart, Charles W. (Ind.)
Chapman, Augustus A. (Va.)
Chapman, John G. (Md.)
Chapman, Reuben (Ala.)
Chase, Lucien B. (Tenn.)
Chipman, John S. (Mich.)
Clark, Henry S. (N. C.)
Cobb, Howell (Ga.)
Cocke, William M. (Tenn.)
Collamer, Jacob (Vt.)
Collin, John F. (N. Y.)
Constable, Albert (Md.)
Cottrell, James L. F. (Ala.)
Cranston, Henry Y. (R. I.)
Crozier, John H. (Tenn.)
Cullum, Alvan (Tenn.)
Culver, Erastus D. (N. Y.)
Cummins, John D. (Ohio)
Cunningham, Francis A. (Ohio)

Daniel, John R. J. (N. C.)
Dargan, Edmund S. (Ala.)
Darragh, Cornelius (Pa.)
Davis, Garrett (Ky.)
Davis, Jefferson (Miss.)
Davis, John W. (Ind.)
Delano, Columbus (Ohio)
De Mott, John (N. Y.)
Dillingham, Paul, Jr. (Vt.)
Dixon, James (Conn.)
Dobbin, James C. (N. C.)
Dockery, Alfred (N. C.)
Douglas, Stephen A. (Ill.)
Dromgoole, George C. (Va.)
Dunlap, Robert P. (Maine)
Edsall, Joseph E. (N. J.)
Ellett, Henry T. (Miss.)
Ellsworth, Samuel S. (N. Y.)
Erdman, Jacob (Pa.)
Ewing, Edwin H. (Tenn.)
Ewing, John H. (Pa.)
Faran, James J. (Ohio)
Ficklin, Orlando B. (Ill.)
Foot, Solomon (Vt.)
Foster, Henry D. (Pa.)
Fries, George (Ohio)
Garvin, William S. (Pa.)
Gentry, Meredith P. (Tenn.)
Giddings, Joshua R. (Ohio)
Giles, William F. (Md.)
Gordon, Samuel (N. Y.)
Goodyear, Charles (N. Y.)
Graham, James (N. C.)
Grider, Henry (Ky.)
Grinnell, Joseph (Mass.)
Grover, Martin (N. Y.)
Hale, Artemas (Mass.)
Hamlin, Hannibal (Maine)
Hampton, James G. (N. J.)
Haralson, Hugh A. (Ga.)
Harmanson, John H. (La.)
Harper, Alexander (Ohio)
Hastings, S. Clinton (Iowa)
Henley, Thomas J. (Ind.)
Henry, John (Ill.)
Herrick, Richard P. (N. Y.)
Hilliard, Henry W. (Ala.)
Hoge, Joseph P. (Ill.)
Holmes, Elias B. (N. Y.)
Holmes, Isaac E. (S. C.)
Hopkins, George W. (Va.)
Hough, William J. (N. Y.)
Houston, George S. (Ala.)
Houston, John W. (Del.)
Hubard, Edmund W. (Va.)
Hubbard, Samuel D. (Conn.)
Hudson, Charles (Mass.)
Hungerford, Orville (N. Y.)
Hunt, James B. (Mich.)
Hunt, Washington (N. Y.)
Hunter, Robert M. T. (Va.)
Ingersoll, Charles J. (Pa.)
Ingersoll, Joseph R. (Pa.)
Jenkins, Timothy (N. Y.)
Johnson, Andrew (Tenn.)
Johnson, James H. (N. H.)
Johnson, Joseph (Va.)
Jones, George W. (Tenn.)
Jones, Seaborn (Ga.)
Kaufman, David S. (Tex.)
Kennedy, Andrew (Ind.)
King, Daniel P. (Mass.)
King, Preston (N. Y.)
King, Thomas B. (Ga.)
La Sere, Emile (La.)
Lawrence, John W. (N. Y.)
Leake, Shelton F. (Va.)
Leffler, Shepherd (Iowa)
Leib, Owen D. (Pa.)
Levin, Lewis C. (Pa.)
Lewis, Abner (N. Y.)
Ligon, Thomas W. (Md.)
Long, Edward H. C. (Md.)
Lumpkin, John H. (Ga.)
McClean, Moses (Pa.)
McClelland, Robert (Mich.)
McClernand, John A. (Ill.)
McConnell, Felix G. (Ala.)
McCrate, John D. (Maine)
McDaniel, William (Mo.)
McDowell, James (Va.)
McDowell, Joseph J. (Ohio)
McGaughey, Edward W. (Ind.)
McHenry, John H. (Ky.)
McIlvaine, Abraham R. (Pa.)
McKay, James I. (N. C.)
Maclay, William B. (N. Y.)
Marsh, George P. (Vt.)
Martin, Barclay (Tenn.)
Martin, John P. (Ky.)

Miller, William S. (N. Y.)
Morris, Joseph (Ohio)
Morse, Isaac E. (La.)
Moseley, William A. (N. Y.)
Moulton, Mace (N. H.)
Newton, Thomas W. (Ark.)
Niven, Archibald C. (N. Y.)
Norris, Moses, Jr. (N. H.)
Owen, Robert D. (Ind.)
Parrish, Isaac (Ohio)
Payne, William W. (Ala.)
Pendleton, John S. (Va.)
Perrill, Augustus L. (Ohio)
Perry, Thomas J. (Md.)
Pettit, John (Ind.)
Phelps, John S. (Mo.)
Pillsbury, Timothy (Tex.)
Pollock, James (Pa.)
Price, Sterling (Mo.)
Ramsey, Alexander (Pa.)
Rathbun, George (N. Y.)
Reid, David S. (N. C.)
Relfe, James H. (Mo.)
Rhett, R. Barnwell (S. C.)
Ripley, Thomas C. (N. Y.)
Ritter, John (Pa.)
Roberts, Robert W. (Miss.)
Rockwell, John A. (Conn.)
Rockwell, Julius (Mass.)
Root, Joseph M. (Ohio)
Runk, John (N. J.)
Russell, Joseph (N. Y.)
St. John, Henry (Ohio)
Sawtelle, Cullen (Maine)
Sawyer, William (Ohio)
Scammon, John F. (Maine)
Schenck, Robert C. (Ohio)
Seaman, Henry I. (N. Y.)
Seddon, James A. (Va.)
Severance, Luther (Maine)
Simpson, Richard F. (S. C.)
Sims, Alexander D. (S. C.)
Sims, Leonard H. (Mo.)
Slidell, John (La.)
Smith, Albert (N. Y.)
Smith, Caleb B. (Ind)
Smith, Robert (Ill.)
Smith, Thomas (Ind.)
Smith, Truman (Conn.)
Stanton, Frederick P. (Tenn.)
Starkweather, David A. (Ohio)
Stephens, Alexander H. (Ga.)
Stewart, Andrew (Pa.)
Strohm, John (Pa.)
Strong, Stephen (N. Y.)
Sykes, George (N. J.)
Taylor, William (Va.)
Thibodeaux, Bannon G. (La.)
Thomasson, William P. (Ky.)
Thompson, Benjamin (Mass.)
Thompson, Jacob (Miss.)
Thompson, James (Pa.)
Thurman, Allen G. (Ohio)
Tibbatts, John W. (Ky.)
Tilden, Daniel R. (Ohio)
Toombs, Robert (Ga.)
Towns, George W. B. (Ga.)
Tredway, William M. (Va.)
Trumbo, Andrew (Ky.)
Vance, Joseph (Ohio)
Vinton, Samuel F. (Ohio)
Wentworth, John (Ill.)
Wheaton, Horace (N. Y.)
White, Hugh (N. Y.)
Wick, William W. (Ind.)
Williams, Hezekiah (Maine)
Wilmot, David (Pa.)
Winthrop, Robert C. (Mass.)
Wood, Bradford R. (N. Y.)
Woodruff, Thomas M. (N. Y.)
Woodward, Joseph A. (S. C.)
Woodworth, William W. (N.Y).
Wright, William (N. J.)
Yancey, William L. (Ala.)
Yell, Archibald (Ark.)
Yost, Jacob S. (Pa.)
Young, Bryan R. (Ky.)

The Thirtieth Congress (1847-49)

Winthrop, Robert C. (Mass.) Speaker.
Abbott, Amos (Mass.)
Adams, Green (Ky.)
Adams, John Q. (Mass.)
Ashmun, George (Mass.)
Atkinson, Archibald (Va.)
Barringer, Daniel M. (N. C.)
Barrow, Washington (Tenn.)
Bayly, Thomas H. (Va.)
Beale, Richard L. T. (Va.)
Bedinger, Henry (Va.)
Belcher, Hiram (Maine)
Bingham, Kinsley S. (Mich.)
Birdsall, Ausburn (N. Y.)
Black, James A. (S. C.)
Blackmar, Esbon (N. Y.)
Blanchard, John (Pa.)
Bocock, Thomas S. (Va.)
Botts, John M. (Va.)
Bowdon, Franklin W. (Ala.)
Bowlin, James B. (Mo.)
Boyd, Linn (Ky.)
Boyden, Nathaniel (N. C.)
Brady, Jasper E. (Pa.)
Bridges, Samuel A. (Pa.)
Brodhead, Richard (Pa.)
Brown, Albert G. (Miss.)
Brown, Charles (Pa.)
Brown, William G. (Va.)
Buckner, Aylett (Ky.)
Burt, Armistead (S. C.)
Butler, Chester P. (Pa.)
Cabell, Edward C. (Fla.)
Canby, Richard S. (Ohio)
Cathcart, Charles W. (Ind.)
Chapman, John G. (Md.)
Chase, Lucien B. (Tenn.)
Clapp, Asa W. H. (Maine)
Clark, Franklin (Maine)
Clarke, Beverly L. (Ky.)
Clingman, Thomas L. (N. C.)
Cobb, Howell (Ga.)
Cobb, Williamson R. W. (Ala.)
Cocke, William M. (Tenn.)
Collamer, Jacob (Vt.)
Collins, William (N. Y.)
Conger, Harmon S. (N. Y.)
Cranston, Robert B. (R. I.)
Crisfield, John W. (Md.)
Crowell, John (Ohio)
Crozier, John H. (Tenn.)
Cummins, John D. (Ohio)
Daniel, John R. J. (N. C.)
Darling, Mason C. (Wis.)
Dickey, John (Pa.)
Dickinson, Rudolphus (Ohio)
Dixon, James (Conn.)
Donnell, Richard S. (N. C.)
Duer, William (N. Y.)
Duncan, W. Garnett (Ky.)
Duncan, Daniel (Ohio)
Dunn, George G. (Ind.)
Eckert, George N. (Pa.)
Edsall, Joseph E. (N. J.)
Edwards, Thomas O. (Ohio)
Embree, Elisha (Ind.)
Evans, Alexander (Md.)
Evans, Nathan (Ohio)
Faran, James J. (Ohio)
Farrelly, John W. (Pa.)
Featherston, Winfield S. (Miss.)
Ficklin, Orlando B. (Ill.)
Fisher, David (Ohio)
Flournoy, Thomas S. (Va.)
Freedley, John (Pa.)
French, Richard (Ky.)
Fries, George (Ohio)
Fulton, Andrew S. (Va.)
Gaines, John P. (Ky.)
Gayle, John (Ala.)
Gentry, Meredith P. (Tenn.)
Giddings, Joshua R. (Ohio)
Goggin, William L. (Va.)
Gott, Daniel (N. Y.)
Greeley, Horace (N. Y.)
Green, James S. (Mo.)
Gregory, Dudley S. (N. J.)
Grinnell, Joseph (Mass.)
Hale, Artemas (Mass.)
Hall, Nathan K. (N. Y.)
Hall, Willard P. (Mo.)
Hammons, David (Maine)
Hampton, James G. (N. J.)
Hampton, Moses (Pa.)
Haralson, Hugh A. (Ga.)
Harmanson, John H. (La.)
Harris, Sampson W. (Ala.)
Haskell, William T. (Tenn.)
Henley, Thomas J. (Ind.)
Henry, William (Vt.)
Hill, Hugh L. W. (Tenn.)
Hillard, Henry W. (Ala.)

Holley, John M. (N. Y.)
Holmes, Elias B. (N. Y.)
Holmes, Isaac E. (S. C.)
Hornbeck, John W. (Pa.)
Houston, George S. (Ala.)
Houston, John W. (Del.)
Hubbard, Samuel D. (Conn.)
Hudson, Charles (Mass.)
Hunt, Washington (N. Y.)
Inge, Samuel W. (Ala.)
Ingersoll, Charles J. (Pa.)
Ingersoll, Joseph R. (Pa.)
Iverson, Alfred (Ga.)
Irvin, Alexander (Pa.)
Jackson, David S. (N. Y.)
Jameson, John (Mo.)
Jenkins, Timothy (N. Y.)
Johnson, Andrew (Tenn.)
Johnson, James H. (N. H.)
Johnson, Robert W. (Ark.)
Jones, George W. (Tenn.)
Jones, John W. (Ga.)
Kaufman, David S. (Tex.)
Kellogg, Orlando (N. Y.)
Kennon, William, Jr. (Ohio)
King, Daniel P. (Mass.)
King, Thomas B. (Ga.)
Lahm, Samuel (Ohio)
La Sere, Emile (La.)
Lawrence, Sidney (N. Y.)
Lawrence, William T. (N. Y.)
Leffler, Shepherd (Iowa)
Levin, Lewis C. (Pa.)
Ligon, Thomas W. (Md.)
Lincoln, Abraham (Ill.)
Lord, Frederick W. (N. Y.)
Lumpkin, John H. (Ga.)
Lynde, William P. (Wis.)
McClelland, Robert (Mich.)
McClernand, John A. (Ill.)
McDowell, James (Va.)
McIlvaine, Abraham R. (Pa.)
McKay, James I. (N. C.)
McLane, Robert M. (Md.)
Maclay, William B. (N. Y.)
McQueen, John (S. C.)
Mann, Horace (Mass.)
Mann, Job (Pa.)
Marsh, George P. (Vt.)
Marvin, Dudley (N. Y.)
Meade, Richard K. (Va.)
Miller, John K. (Ohio)
Morehead, Charles S. (Ky.)
Morris, Jonathan D. (Ohio)
Morse, Isaac E. (La.)
Mullin, Joseph (N. Y.)
Murphy, Henry C. (N. Y.)
Nelson, William (N. Y.)
Nes, Henry (Pa.)
Newell, William A. (N. J.)
Nicoll, Henry (N. Y.)
Outlaw, David (N. C.)
Palfrey, John G. (Mass.)
Peaslee, Charles H. (N. H.)
Peck, Lucius B. (Vt.)
Pendleton, John S. (Va.)
Petrie, George (N. Y.)
Pettit, John (Ind.)
Peyton, Samuel O. (Ky.)
Phelps, John S. (Mo.)
Pillsbury, Timothy (Tex.)
Pollock, James (Pa.)
Preston, William B. (Va.)
Putnam, Harvey (N. Y.)
Reynolds, Gideon (N. Y.)
Rhett, R. Barnwell (S. C.)
Richardson, William A. (Ill.)
Ritchey, Thomas (Ohio)
Robinson, John L. (Ind.)
Rockhill, William (Ind.)
Rockwell, John A. (Conn.)
Rockwell, Julius (Mass.)
Roman, J. Dixon (Md.)
Root, Joseph M. (Ohio)
Rose, Robert L. (N. Y.)
Rumsey, David, Jr. (N. Y.)
St. John, Daniel B. (N. Y.)
Sawyer, William (Ohio)
Schenck, Robert C. (Ohio)
Shepperd, Augustine H. (N. C).
Sherrill, Eliakim (N. Y.)
Simpson, Richard F. (S. C.)
Sims, Alexander D. (S. C.)
Slingerland, John I. (N. Y.)
Smart, Ephraim K. (Maine)
Smith, Caleb B. (Ind.)
Smith, Robert (Ill.)
Smith, Truman (Conn.)

Stanton, Frederick P. (Tenn.)
Starkweather, George A. (N. Y.)
Stephens, Alexander H. (Ga.)
Stewart, Andrew (Pa.)
Strohm, John (Pa.)
Strong, William (Pa.)
Stuart, Charles E. (Mich.)
Sylvester, Peter H. (N. Y.)
Tallmadge, Frederick A. (N. Y.)
Taylor, John L. (Ohio)
Thibodeaux, Bannon G. (La.)
Thomas, James H. (Tenn.)
Thompson, Jacob (Miss.)
Thompson, James (Pa.)
Thompson, John B. (Ky.)
Thompson, Richard W. (Ind.)
Thompson, Robert A. (Va.)
Thompson, William (Iowa)
Thurston, Benjamin B. (R. I.)
Tompkins, Patrick W. (Miss.)
Toombs, Robert (Ga.)
Tuck, Amos (N. H.)
Turner, Thomas J. (Ill.)
Van Dyke, John (N. J.)
Venable, Abraham W. (N. C.)
Vinton, Samuel F. (Ohio)
Wallace, Daniel (S. C.)
Warren, Cornelius (N. Y.)
Wentworth, John (Ill.)
White, Hugh (N. Y.)
Wick, William W. (Ind.)
Wiley, James S. (Maine)
Williams, Hezekiah (Maine)
Wilmot, David (Pa.)
Wilson, James (N. H.)
Winthrop, Robert C. (Mass.)
Woodward, Joseph A. (S. C.)

The Thirty-first Congress (1849-51)

Cobb, Howell (Ga.)
Speaker.

Albertson, Nathaniel (Ind.)
Alexander, Henry P. (N. Y.)
Allen, Charles (Mass.)
Alston, William J. (Ala.)
Anderson, Josiah M. (Tenn.)
Andrews, George R. (N. Y.)
Ashe, William S. (N. C.)
Ashmun, George (Mass.)
Averett, Thomas H. (Va.)
Baker, Edward D. (Ill.)
Bay, William V. N. (Mo.)
Bayly, Thomas H. (Va.)
Beale, James M. H. (Va.)
Bell, John (Ohio)
Bennett, Henry (N. Y.)
Bingham, Kingsley S. (Mich.)
Bissell, William H. (Ill.)
Bocock, Thomas S. (Va.)
Bokee, David A. (N. Y.)
Booth, Walter (Conn.)
Bowdon, Franklin W. (Ala.)
Bowie, Richard J. (Md.)
Bowlin, James B. (Mo.)
Boyd, Linn (Ky.)
Breck, Daniel (Ky.)
Briggs, George (N. Y.)
Brisbin, John (Pa.)
Brooks, James (N. Y.)
Brown, Albert G. (Miss.)
Brown, William J. (Ind.)
Buel, Alexander W. (Mich.)
Bullard, Henry A. (La.)
Burrows, Lorenzo (N. Y.)
Burt, Armistead (S. C.)
Butler, Chester P. (Pa.)
Butler, Thomas B. (Conn.)
Cabell, Edward C. (Fla.)
Cable, Joseph (Ohio)
Caldwell, George A. (Ky.)
Caldwell, Joseph P. (N. C.)
Calvin, Samuel (Pa.)
Campbell, Lewis D. (Ohio)
Cartter, David K. (Ohio)
Casey, Joseph (Pa.)
Chandler, Joseph R. (Pa.)
Clarke, Charles E. (N. Y.)
Cleveland, Chauncey F. (Conn.)
Clingman, Thomas L. (N. C.)
Cobb, Howell (Ga.)
Cobb, Williamson R. W. (Ala.)
Colcock, William F. (S. C.)
Cole, Orsamus (Wis.)
Conger, Harmon S. (N. Y.)
Conrad, Charles M. (La.)
Corwin, Moses B. (Ohio)
Crowell, John (Ohio)
Daniel, John R. J. (N. C.)
Danner, Joel B. (Pa.)
Deberry, Edmund (N. C.)
Dickey, Jesse C. (Pa.)
Dickinson, Rudolphus (Ohio)
Dimmick, Milo M. (Pa.)
Disney, David T. (Ohio)
Dixon, Nathan F. (R. I.)
Doty, James Duane (Wis.)
Duer, William (N. Y.)
Duncan, James H. (Mass.)
Dunham, Cyrus L. (Ind.)
Durkee, Charles (Wis.)
Edmundson, Henry A. (Va.)
Eliot, Samuel A. (Mass.)
Evans, Alexander (Md.)
Evans, Nathan (Ohio)
Ewing, Andrew (Tenn.)
Featherston, Winfield S. (Miss.)
Fitch, Graham N. (Ind.)
Fowler, Orin (Mass.)
Freedley, John (Pa.)
Fuller, Thomas J. D. (Maine)
Gentry, Meredith P. (Tenn.)
Gerry, Elbridge (Maine)
Giddings, Joshua R. (Ohio)
Gilbert, Edward (Calif.)
Gilmore, Alfred (Pa.)
Goodenow, Rufus K. (Maine)
Gorman, Willis A. (Ind.)
Gott, Daniel (N. Y.)
Gould, Herman D. (N. Y.)
Green, James S. (Mo.)
Grinnell, Joseph (Mass.)
Hackett, Thomas C. (Ga.)
Hall, Willard P. (Mo.)
Halloway, Ransom (N. Y.)
Hamilton, William T. (Md.)
Hammond, Edward (Md.)
Hampton, Moses (Pa.)
Haralson, Hugh A. (Ga.)
Harlan, Andrew J. (Ind.)
Harmanson, John H. (La.)
Harris, Isham G. (Tenn.)
Harris, Sampson W. (Ala.)
Harris, Thomas L. (Ill.)
Hay, Andrew K. (N. J.)
Haymond, Thomas S. (Va.)
Hebard, William (Vt.)
Henry, William (Vt.)
Hibbard, Harry (N. H.)
Hilliard, Henry W. (Ala.)
Hoagland, Moses (Ohio)
Holladay, Alexander R. (Va.)
Holmes, Isaac E. (S. C.)
Houston, John W. (Del.)
Howard, Volney E. (Tex.)
Howe, John W. (Pa.)
Hubbard, David (Ala.)
Hunter, William F. (Ohio)
Inge, Samuel W. (Ala.)
Jackson, Joseph W. (Ga.)
Jackson, William T. (N. Y.)
Johnson, Andrew (Tenn.)
Johnson, James L. (Ky.)
Johnson, Robert W. (Ark.)
Jones, George W. (Tenn.)
Julian, George W. (Ind.)
Kaufman, David S. (Tex.)
Kerr, John B. (Md.)
King, Daniel P. (Mass.)
King, George W. (R. I.)
King, James G. (N .J.)
King, John A. (N. Y.)
King, Preston (N. Y.)
King, Thomas Butler (Ga.)
La Sere, Emile (La.)
Leffler, Shepherd (Iowa)
Levin, Lewis C. (Pa.)
Littlefield, Nathaniel S. (Maine)
McClernand, John A. (Ill.)
McDonald, Joseph E. (Ind.)
McDowell, James (Va.)
McGaughey, Edward W. (Ind.)
McKissock, Thomas (N. Y.)
McLanahan, James X. (Pa.)
McLane, Robert M. (Md.)
McLean, Finis E. (Ky.)
McMullen, Fayette (Va.)
McQueen, John (S. C.)
McWillie, William (Miss.)
Mann, Horace (Mass.)
Mann, Job (Pa.)
Marshall, Humphrey (Ky.)
Mason, John C. (Ky.)
Matteson, Orsamus B. (N. Y.)
Meacham, James (Vt.)
Meade, Richard K. (Va.)
Miller, Daniel F. (Iowa)
Miller, John K. (Ohio)
Millson, John S. (Va.)
Moore, Henry D. (Pa.)
Moorehead, Charles S. (Ky.)
Morris, Jonathan D. (Ohio)
Morrison, George W. (N. H.)
Morse, Isaac E. (La.)
Morton, Jeremiah (Va.)
Nelson, William (N. Y.)
Nes, Henry (Pa.)
Newell, William A. (N. J.)
Ogle, Andrew J. (Pa.)
Olds, Edson B. (Ohio)
Orr, James L. (S. C.)
Otis, John (Maine)
Outlaw, David (N. C.)
Owen, Allen F. (Ga.)
Parker, Richard (Va.)
Peaslee, Charles H. (N. H.)
Peck, Lucius B. (Vt.)
Penn, Alexander G. (La.)
Phelps, John S. (Mo.)
Phoenix, J. Phillips (N. Y.)
Pitman, Charles W. (Pa.)
Potter, Emery D. (Ohio)
Powell, Paulus (Va.)
Putnam, Harvey (N. Y.)
Reed, Robert R. (Pa.)
Reynolds, Gideon (N. Y.)
Richardson, William A. (Ill.)
Risley, Elijah (N. Y.)
Robbins, John, Jr. (Pa.)
Robinson, John L. (Ind.)
Rockwell, Julius (Mass.)
Root, Joseph M. (Ohio)
Rose, Robert L. (N. Y.)
Ross, Thomas (Pa.)
Rumsey, David, Jr. (N. Y.)
Sackett, William A. (N. Y.)
Sawtelle, Cullen (Maine)
Savage, John H. (Tenn.)
Schenck, Robert C. (Ohio)
Schermerhorn, Abraham M. (N. Y.)
Schoolcraft, John L. (N. Y.)
Seddon, James A. (Va.)
Shepperd, Augustine H. (N. C.)
Silvester, Peter H. (N. Y.)
Spaulding, Elbridge G. (N. Y.)
Sprague, William (Mich.)
Stanly, Edward (N. C.)
Stanton, Frederick P. (Tenn.)
Stanton, Richard H. (Ky.)
Stephens, Alexander H. (Ga.)
Stetson, Charles (Maine)
Stevens, Thaddeus (Pa.)
Strong, William (Pa.)
Sweetser, Charles (Ohio)
Taylor, John L. (Ohio)
Thomas, James H. (Tenn.)
Thompson, Jacob (Miss.)
Thompson, James (Pa.)
Thompson, John B. (Ky.)
Thompson, William (Iowa)
Thurman, John R. (N. Y.)
Toombs, Robert (Ga.)
Tuck, Amos (N. H.)
Underhill, Walter (N. Y.)
Van Dyke, John (N. J.)
Venable, Abraham W. (N. C.)
Vinton, Samuel F. (Ohio)
Walden, Hiram (N. Y.)
Waldo, Loren P. (Conn.)
Wallace, Daniel (S. C.)
Watkins, Albert G. (Tenn.)
Wellborn, Marshall J. (Ga.)
Wentworth, John (Ill.)
White, Hugh (N. Y.)
Whittlesey, William A. (Ohio)
Wildrick, Isaac (N. J.)
Williams, Christopher H. (Tenn.)
Wilmot, David (Pa.)
Wilson, James (N. H.)
Winthrop, Robert C. (Mass.)
Wood, Amos E. (Ohio)
Woodward, Joseph A. (S. C.)
Wright, George W. (Calif.)
Young Timothy R. (Ill.)

The Thirty-second Congress (1851-53)

Boyd, Linn (Ky.)
Speaker.

Abercrombie, James (Ala.)
Aiken, William (S. C.)
Allen, Charles (Mass.)
Allen, Willis (Ill.)
Allison, John (Pa.)
Andrews, Charles (Maine)
Appleton, John (Maine)
Appleton, William (Mass.)
Ashe, William S. (N. C.)
Averett, Thomas H. (Va.)
Babcock, Leander (N. Y.)
Bailey, David J. (Ga.)
Barrere, Nelson (Ohio)
Bartlett, Thomas, Jr. (Vt.)
Bayly, Thomas H. (Va.)
Beale, James M. H. (Va.)
Bell, Hiram (Ohio)
Bennett, Henry (N. Y.)
Bibighaus, Thomas M. (Pa.)
Bissell, William H. (Ill.)
Bocock, Thomas S. (Va.)
Bowie, Richard J. (Md.)
Bowne, Obediah (N. Y.)
Boyd, John H. (N. Y.)
Bragg, John (Ala.)
Breckinridge, John C. (Ky.)
Brenton, Samuel (Ind.)
Briggs, George (N. Y.)
Brooks, James (N. Y.)
Brown, Albert G. (Miss.)
Brown, George H. (N. J.)
Buell, Alexander H. (N. Y.)
Burrows, Lorenzo (N. Y.)
Burt, Armistead (S. C.)
Busby, George H. (Ohio)
Cabell, Edward C. (Fla.)
Cable, Joseph (Ohio)
Caldwell, Joseph P. (N. C.)
Campbell, Lewis D. (Ohio)
Campbell, Thompson (Ill.)
Cartter, David K. (Ohio)
Caskie, John S. (Va.)
Chandler, Joseph R. (Pa.)
Chapman, Charles (Conn.)
Chastain, Elijah W. (Ga.)
Churchwell, William M. (Tenn.)
Clark, Lincoln (Iowa)
Clemens, Sherrard (Va.)
Cleveland, Chauncey F. (Conn.)
Clingman, Thomas L. (N. C.)
Cobb, Williamson R. W. (Ala.)
Colcock, William F. (S. C.)
Conger, James L. (Mich.)
Cottman, Joseph S. (Md.)
Cullom, William (Tenn.)
Curtis, Carlton B. (Pa.)
Daniel, John R. J. (N. C.)
Darby, John F. (Mo.)
Davis, George T. (Mass.)
Davis, John G. (Ind.)
Dawson, John L. (Pa.)
Dean, Gilbert (N. Y.)
Dimmick, Milo M. (Pa.)
Disney, David T. (Ohio)
Dockery, Alfred (N. C.)
Doty, James D. (Wis.)
Duncan, James H. (Mass.)
Dunham, Cyrus L. (Ind.)
Durkee, Charles (Wis.)
Eastman, Benjamin C. (Wis.)
Edgerton, Alfred P. (Ohio)
Edmundson, Henry A. (Va.)
Evans, Alexander (Md.)
Ewing, Presley U. (Ky.)
Faulkner, Charles J. (Va.)
Fay, Francis B. (Mass.)
Ficklin, Orlando B. (Ill.)
Fitch, Graham N. (Ind.)
Florence, Thomas B. (Pa.)
Floyd, John G. (N. Y.)
Fowler, Orin (Mass.)
Freeman, John D. (Miss.)
Fuller, Henry M. (Pa.)
Fuller, Thomas J. D. (Maine)
Gamble, James (Pa.)
Gaylord, James M. (Ohio)
Gentry, Meredith P. (Tenn.)
Giddings, Joshua R. (Ohio)
Gilmore, Alfred (Pa.)
Goodenow, Robert (Maine)
Goodrich, John Z. (Mass.)

Gorman, Willis A. (Ind.)
Green, Frederick W. (Ohio)
Grey, Benjamin E. (Ky.)
Grow, Galusha A. (Pa.)
Hall, Willard P. (Mo.)
Hamilton, William T. (Md.)
Hammond, Edward (Md.)
Harper, Alexander (Ohio)
Harris, Isham G. (Tenn.)
Harris, Sampson W. (Ala.)
Hart, Emanuel B. (N. Y.)
Hascall, Augustus P. (N. Y.)
Haven, Solomon G. (N. Y.)
Haws, J. H. Hobart (N. Y.)
Hebard, William (Vt.)
Hendricks, Thomas A. (Ind.)
Henn, Bernhart, (Iowa)
Hibbard, Harry (N. H.)
Hillyer, Junius (Ga.)
Holladay, Alexander R. (Va.)
Horsford, Jerediah (N. Y.)
Houston, George S. (Ala.)
Howard, Volney E. (Tex.)
Howe, John W. (Pa.)
Howe, Thomas M. (Pa.)
Howe, Thomas Y. (N. Y.)
Hunter, William F. (Ohio)
Ingersoll, Colin M. (Conn.)
Ives, William (N. Y.)
Jackson, Joseph W. (Ga.)
Jenkins, Timothy (N. Y.)
Johnson, Andrew (Tenn.)
Johnson, James (Ga.)
Johnson, John (Ohio)
Johnson, Robert W. (Ark.)
Jones, Daniel T. (N. Y.)
Jones, George W. (Tenn.)
Jones, J. Glancy (Pa.)
King, George G. (R. I.)
King, Preston (N. Y.)
Kuhns, Joseph H. (Pa.)
Kurtz, William H. (Pa.)
Landry, J. Aristide (La.)
Letcher, John (Va.)
Little, Edward P. (Mass.)
Lockhart, James (Ind.)
McCorkle, Joseph W. (Calif.)
Macdonald, Moses (Maine)
Mace, Daniel (Ind.)
McLanahan, James X. (Pa.)
McMullen, Fayette (Va.)
McNair, John (Pa.)
McQueen, John (S. C.)
Mann, Horace (Mass.)
Marshall, Edward C. (Calif.)
Marshall, Humphrey (Ky.)
Martin, Frederick S. (N. Y.)
Mason, John C. (Ky.)
Meacham, James (Vt.)
Meade, Richard K. (Va.)
Miller, John G. (Mo.)
Millson, John S. (Va.)
Miner, Ahiman L. (Vt.)
Molony, Richard S. (Ill.)
Moore, Henry D. (Pa.)
Moore, John (La.)
Morehead, James T. (N. C.)
Morrison, John A. (Pa.)
Murphey, Charles (Ga.)
Murray, William (N. Y.)
Nabers, Benjamin D. (Miss.)
Newton, Eben (Ohio)
Olds, Edson B. (Ohio)
Orr, James L. (S. C.)
Outlaw, David (N. C.)
Parker, Andrew (Pa.)
Parker, Samuel W. (Ind.)
Peaslee, Charles H. (N. H.)
Penn, Alexander G. (La.)
Penniman, Ebenezer J. (Mich.)
Perkins, Jared (N. H.)
Phelps, John S. (Mo.)
Polk, William H. (Tenn.)
Porter, Gilchrist (Mo.)
Powell, Paulus (Va.)
Preston, William (Ky.)
Price, Rodman M. (N. J.)
Rantoul, Robert, Jr. (Mass.)
Reed, Isaac (Maine)
Richardson, William A. (Ill.)
Riddle, George R. (Del.)
Robbins, John, Jr. (Pa.)
Robie, Reuben (N. Y.)
Robinson, John L. (Ind.)
Ross, Thomas (Pa.)
Russell, Joseph (N. Y.)
Sabine, Lorenzo (Mass.)
Sackett, William A. (N. Y.)
St. Martin, Louis (La.)
Savage, John H. (Tenn.)
Schermerhorn, Abraham M. (N. Y.)
Schoolcraft, John L. (N. Y.)
Schoonmaker, Marius (N. Y.)
Scudder, Zeno (Mass.)
Scurry, Richardson (Tex.)
Seymour, David L. (N. Y.)
Seymour, Origen S. (Conn.)
Skelton, Charles (N. J.)
Smart, Ephraim K. (Maine)
Smart, Ephraim K. (Me.)
Smith, William R. (Ala.)
Snow, William W. (N. Y.)
Stanly, Edward (N. C.)
Stanton, Benjamin (Ohio)
Stanton, Frederick P. (Tenn.)
Stanton, Richard H. (Ky.)
Stephens, Abraham P. (N. Y.)
Stephens, Alexander H. (Ga.)
Stevens, Thaddeus (Pa.)
Stone, James W. (Ky.)
Stratton, Nathan T. (N. J.)
Strother, James F. (Va.)
Stuart, Charles E. (Mich.)
Sutherland, Josiah (N. Y.)
Sweetser, Charles (Ohio)
Taylor, John L. (Ohio)
Thompson, Benjamin (Mass.)
Thompson, George W. (Va.)
Thurston, Benjamin B. (R. I.)
Toombs, Robert (Ga.)
Townshend, Norton S. (Ohio)
Tuck, Amos (N. H.)
Venable, Abraham W. (N. C.)
Walbridge, Henry S. (N. Y.)
Wallace, Daniel (S. C.)
Walsh, Thomas Y. (Md.)
Ward, William T. (Ky.)
Washburn, Israel, Jr. (Maine)
Watkins, Albert G. (Tenn.)
Wells, John (N. Y.)
Welsh, John (Ohio)
White, Addison (Ky.)
White, Alexander (Ala.)
Wilcox, John A. (Miss.)
Wildrick, Isaac (N. J.)
Williams, Christopher H. (Tenn.)
Woodward, Joseph A. (S. C.)
Yates, Richard (Ill.)

The Thirty-third Congress (1853-55)

Boyd, Linn (Ky.)
Speaker.

Abercrombie, James (Ala.)
Aiken, William (S. C.)
Allen, James C. (Ill.)
Allen, Willis (Ill.)
Appleton, William (Mass.)
Ashe, William S. (N. C.)
Bailey, David J. (Ga.)
Ball, Edward (Ohio)
Banks, Nathaniel P. (Mass.)
Barksdale, William (Miss.)
Barry, William T. S. (Miss.)
Bayly, Thomas H. (Va.)
Belcher, Nathan (Conn.)
Bell, Peter H. (Tex.)
Bennett, Henry (N. Y.)
Benson, Samuel P. (Maine)
Benton, Thomas H. (Mo.)
Bissell, William H. (Ill.)
Bliss, George (Ohio)
Bocock, Thomas S. (Va.)
Boyce, William W. (S. C.)
Breckenridge, John C. (Ky.)
Bridges, Samuel A. (Pa.)
Bristow, Francis M. (Ky.)
Brooks, Preston S. (S. C.)
Bugg, Robert M. (Tenn.)
Campbell, Lewis D. (Ohio)
Carpenter, Davis (N. Y.)
Caruthers, Samuel (Mo.)
Caskie, John S. (Va.)
Chamberlain, Ebenezer M. (Ind.)
Chandler, Joseph R. (Pa.)
Chase, George W. (N. Y.)
Chastain, Elijah W. (Ga.)
Chrisman, James S. (Ky.)
Churchwell, William M. (Tenn.)
Clark, Samuel (Mich.)
Clingman, Thomas L. (N. C.)
Cobb, Williamson R. W. (Ala.)
Colquitt, Alfred H. (Ga.)
Cook, John P. (Iowa)
Corwin, Moses B. (Ohio)
Cox, Leander M. (Ky.)
Craige, E. Burton (N. C.)
Crocker, Samuel L. (Mass.)
Cullom, William (Tenn.)
Cumming, Thomas W. (N. Y.)
Curtis, Carlton B. (Pa.)
Cutting, Francis B. (N. Y.)
Davis, John G. (Ind.)
Davis, Thomas (R. I.)
Dawson, John L. (Pa.)
Dean, Gilbert (N. Y.)
Dent, William B. W. (Ga.)
De Witt, Alexander (Mass.)
Dick, John (Pa.)
Dickinson, Edward (Mass.)
Disney, David T. (Ohio)
Dowdell, James F. (Ala.)
Drum, Augustus (Pa.)
Dunbar, William (La.)
Dunham, Cyrus L. (Ind.)
Eastman, Benjamin C. (Wis.)
Eddy, Norman (Ind.)
Edgerton, Alfred P. (Ohio)
Edmonds, J. Wiley (Mass.)
Edmundson, Henry A. (Ohio)
Eliot, Thomas D. (Mass.)
Elliott, John M. (Ky.)
Ellison, Andrew (Ohio)
English, William H. (Ind.)
Etheridge, Emerson (Tenn.)
Everhart, William (Pa.)
Ewing, Presley U. (Ky.)
Farley, E. Wilder (Maine)
Faulkner, Charles J. (Va.)
Fenton, Reuben E. (N. Y.)
Flagler, Thomas T. (N. Y.)
Florence, Thomas B. (Pa.)
Franklin, John R. (Md.)
Fuller, Thomas J. D. (Maine)
Gamble, James (Pa.)
Giddings, Joshua R. (Ohio)
Goode, William O. (Va.)
Goodrich, John Z. (Mass.)
Goodwin, Henry C. (N. Y.)
Green, Frederick W. (Ohio)
Greenwood, Alfred B. (Ark.)
Grey, Benjamin E. (Ky.)
Grow, Galusha A. (Pa.)
Hamilton, William T. (Md.)
Harlan, Aaron (Ohio)
Harlan, Andrew J. (Ind.)
Harris, Sampson W. (Ala.)
Harris, Wiley P. (Miss.)
Harrison, John S. (Ohio)
Hastings, George (N. Y.)
Haven, Solomon G. (N. Y.)
Hendricks, Thomas A. (Ind.)
Henn, Bernhart (Iowa)
Hibbard, Harry (N. H.)
Hiester, Isaac E. (Pa.)
Hill, Clement S. (Ky.)
Hillyer, Junius (Ga.)
Houston, George S. (Ala.)
Howe, Thomas M. (Pa.)
Hughes, Charles (N. Y.)
Hunt, Theodore G. (La.)
Ingersoll, Colin M. (Conn.)
Johnson, Harvey H. (Ohio)
Jones, Daniel T. (N. Y.)
Jones, George W. (Tenn.)
Jones, J. Glancy (Pa.)
Jones, Roland (La.)
Keitt, Laurence M. (S. C.)
Kerr, John, Jr. (N. C.)
Kidwell, Zedekiah (Va.)
Kittredge, George W. (N. H.)
Knox, James (Ill.)
Kurtz, William H. (Pa.)
Lamb, Alfred W. (Mo.)
Lane, James H. (Ind.)
Latham, Milton S. (Calif.)
Letcher, John (Va.)
Lewis, Charles S. (Va.)
Lilly, Samuel (N. J.)
Lindley, James J. (Mo.)
Lindsley, William D. (Ohio)
Lyon, Caleb (N. Y.)
McCullough, John (Pa.)
Macdonald, Moses (Maine)
McDougall, James A. (Calif.)
Mace, Daniel (Ind.)
McMullen, Fayette (Va.)
McNair, John (Pa.)
McQueen, John (S. C.)
Macy, John B. (Wis.)
Matteson, Orasmus B. (N. Y.)
Maurice, James (N. Y.)
Maxwell, Augustus E. (Fla.)
May, Henry (Md.)
Mayall, Samuel (Maine)
Meacham, James (Vt.)
Middleswarth, Ner (Pa.)
Miller, John G. (Mo.)
Miller, Smith (Ind.)
Millson, John S. (Va.)
Morgan, Edwin B. (N. Y.)
Morrison, George W. (N. H.)
Muhlenberg, Henry A. (Pa.)
Murray, William (N. Y.)
Nichols, Matthias H. (Ohio)
Noble, David A. (Mich.)
Norton, Jesse O. (Ill.)
Olds, Edson B. (Ohio)
Oliver, Andrew (N. Y.)
Oliver, Mordecai (Mo.)
Orr, James L. (S. C.)
Packer, Asa (Pa.)
Parker, Samuel W. (Ind.)
Peck, Jared V. (N. Y.)
Peckham, Rufus W. (N. Y.)
Pennington, Alexander C. M. (N. J.)
Perkins, Bishop (N Y.)
Perkins, John, Jr. (La.)
Phelps, John S. (Mo.)
Phillips, Philip (Ala.)
Powell, Paulus (Va.)
Pratt, James T. (Conn.)
Preston, William (Ky.)
Pringle, Benjamin (N. Y.)
Puryear, Richard C. (N. C.)
Ready, Charles (Tenn.)
Reese, David A. (Ga.)
Richardson, William A. (Ill.)
Riddle, George R. (Del.)
Ritchey, Thomas (Ohio)
Ritchie, David (Pa.)
Robbins, John, Jr. (Pa.)
Rogers, Sion H. (N. C.)
Rowe, Peter (N. Y.)
Ruffin, Thomas (N. C.)
Russell, Samuel L. (Pa.)
Sabin, Alvah (Vt.)
Sage, Russell (N. Y.)
Sapp, William R. (Ohio)
Scudder, Zeno (Mass.)
Seward, James L. (Ga.)
Seymour, Origen S. (Conn.)
Shannon, Wilson (Ohio)
Shaw, Henry M. (N. C.)
Shower, Jacob (Md.)
Simmons, George A. (N. Y.)
Singleton, Otho R. (Miss.)
Skelton, Charles (N. J.)
Smith, Gerrit (N. Y.)
Smith, Samuel A. (Tenn.)
Smith, William (Va.)
Smith, William R. (Ala.)
Smyth, George W. (Tex.)
Snodgrass, John F. (Va.)
Sollers, Augustus R. (Md.)
Stanton, Frederick P. (Tenn.)
Stanton, Richard H. (Ky.)
Stephens, Alexander H. (Ga.)
Stevens, Hestor L. (Mich.)
Stratton, Nathan T. (N. J.)
Straub, Christian M. (Pa.)
Stuart, Andrew (Ohio)
Stuart, David (Mich.)
Taylor, John J. (N. Y.)
Taylor, John L. (Ohio)
Taylor, Nathaniel G. (Tenn.)
Teller, Isaac (N. Y.)
Thurston, Benjamin B. (R. I.)
Tracy, Andrew (Vt.)
Trout, Michael C. (Pa.)
Tweed, William M. (N. Y.)
Upham, Charles W. (Mass.)
Vail, George (N. J.)
Vansant, Joshua (Md.)
Wade, Edward (Ohio)
Walbridge, Hiram (N. Y.)
Walker, William A. (N. Y.)
Walley, Samuel H. (Mass.)
Walsh, Mike (N. Y.)
Warren, Edward A. (Ark.)
Washburn, Israel, Jr. (Maine)
Washburne, Elihu B. (Ill.)
Wells, Daniel, Jr. (Wis.)
Wentworth, John (Ill.)
Wentworth, Tappan (Mass.)
Westbrook, Theodore R. (N. Y.)
Wheeler, John (N. Y.)
Witte, William H. (Pa.)

Wright, Daniel B. (Miss.)
Wright, Hendrick B. (Pa.)
Yates, Richard (Ill.)
Zollicoffer, Felix K. (Tenn.)

The Thirty-fourth Congress (1855-57)

Branch, Lawrence O'B. (N.C.) Speaker.

Aiken, William (S. C.)
Akers, Thomas P. (Mo.)
Albright, Charles J. (Ohio)
Allen, James C. (Ill.)
Allison, John (Pa.)
Ball, Edward (Ohio)
Banks, Nathaniel P. (Mass.)
Barbour, Lucien (Ind.)
Barclay, David (Pa.)
Barksdale, William (Miss.)
Bayly, Thomas H. (Va.)
Bell, Peter H. (Tex.)
Bennett, Hendley S. (Miss.)
Bennett, Henry (N. Y.)
Benson, Samuel P. (Maine.)
Billinghurst, Charles (Wis.)
Bingham, John A. (Ohio)
Bishop, James (N. J.)
Bliss, Philemon (Ohio)
Bocock, Thomas S. (Va.)
Bowie, Thomas F. (Md.)
Boyce, William W. (S. C.)
Bradshaw, Samuel C. (Pa.)
Brenton, Samuel (Ind.)
Brodhead, Samuel C. (Pa.)
Brooks, Preston S. (S. C.)
Broom, Jacob (Pa.)
Buffinton, James (Mass.)
Burlingame, Anson (Mass.)
Burnett, Henry C. (Ky.)
Cadwalader, John (Pa.)
Campbell, James H. (Pa.)
Campbell, John P. (Ky.)
Campbell, Lewis D. (Ohio)
Carlile, John S. (Va.)
Caruthers, Samuel (Mo.)
Caskie, John S. (Va.)
Chaffee, Calvin C. (Mass.)
Child, Thomas, Jr. (N. Y.)
Clark, Ezra, Jr. (Conn.)
Clarke, Bayard (N. Y.)
Clawson, Isaiah D. (N. J.)
Clingman, Thomas L. (N. C.)
Cobb, Howell (Ga.)
Cobb, Williamson R. W. (Ala.)
Colfax, Schuyler (Ind.)
Comins, Linus B. (Mass.)
Covode, John (Pa.)
Cox, Leander M. (Ky.)
Cragin, Aaron H. (N. H.)
Craige, F. Burton (N. C.)
Crawford, Martin J. (Ga.)
Cullen, Elisha D. (Del.)
Cumback, William (Ind.)
Damrell, William S. (Mass.)
Davidson, Thomas G. (La.)
Davis, H. Winter (Md.)
Davis, Jacob C. (Ill.)
Davis, Timothy (Mass.)
Day, Timothy C. (Ohio)
Dean, Sidney (Conn.)
Denver, James W. (Calif.)
DeWitt, Alexander (Mass.)
Dick, John (Pa.)
Dickson, Samuel (N. Y.)
Dodd, Edward (N. Y.)
Dowdell, James F. (Ala.)
Dunn, George G. (Ind.)
Durfee, Nathaniel B. (R. I.)
Edie, John R. (Pa.)
Edmundson, Henry A. (Va.)
Edwards, Francis F. (N. Y.)
Elliott, John M. (Ky.)
Emrie, Joseph R. (Ohio)
English, William H. (Ind.)
Etheridge, Emerson (Tenn.)
Eustis, George, Jr. (La.)
Evans, Lemuel D. (Tex.)
Faulkner, Charles J. (Va.)
Flagler, Thomas T. (N. Y.)
Florence, Thomas B. (Pa.)
Foster, Nathaniel G. (Ga.)
Fuller, Henry M. (Pa.)
Fuller, Thomas J. D. (Maine)
Galloway, Samuel (Ohio)
Garnett, Muscoe R. H. (Va.)
Giddings, Joshua R. (Ohio)
Gilbert, William A. (N. Y.)
Goode, William O. (Va.)
Granger, Amos P. (N. Y.)
Greenwood, Alfred B. (Ark.)
Grow, Galusha A. (Pa.)
Hall, Augustus (Iowa)
Hall, Robert B. (Mass.)
Harlan, Aaron (Ohio)
Harris, J. Morrison, (Md.)
Harris, Sampson W. (Ala.)
Harris, Thomas L. (Ill.)
Harrison, John S. (Ohio)
Haven, Solomon G. (N. Y.)
Herbert, Philemon T. (Calif.)
Hickman, John (Pa)
Hodges, George T (Vt.)
Hoffman, Henry W. (Md.)
Holloway, David P. (Ind.)
Horton, Thomas R. (N. Y.)
Horton, Valentine B. (Ohio)
Houston, George S. (Ala.)
Howard, William A. (Mich.)
Hughston, Jonas A. (N. Y.)
Jewett, Joshua H. (Ky.)
Jones, George W. (Tenn.)
Jones, J. Glancy (Pa.)
Keitt, Laurence M. (S. C.)
Kelly, John (N. Y.)
Kelsey, William H. (N. Y.)
Kennett, Luther M. (Mo.)
Kidwell, Zedekiah (Va.)
King, Rufus H. (N. Y.)
Knapp, Chauncey L. (Mass.)
Knight, Jonathan (Pa.)
Knowlton, Ebenezer (Maine)
Knox, James (Ill.)
Kunkel, John C. (Pa.)
Lake, William A. (Miss.)
Leiter, Benjamin F. (Ohio)
Letcher, John (Va.)
Lindley, James J. (Mo.)
Lumpkin, John H. (Ga.)
McCarty, Andrew Z. (N. Y.)
Mace, Daniel (Ind.)
McMullen, Fayette (Va.)
McQueen, John (S. C.)
Marshall, Alexander K. (Ky.)
Marshall, Humphrey (Ky.)
Marshall, Samuel S. (Ill.)
Matteson, Orsamus B. (N. Y.)
Maxwell, Augustus E. (Fla.)
Meacham, James (Vt.)
Miller, John G. (Mo.)
Miller, Killian (N. Y.)
Miller, Smith (Ind.)
Millson, John S. (Va.)
Millward, William (Pa.)
Moore, Oscar F. (Ohio)
Morgan, Edwin B. (N. Y.)
Morrill, Justin S. (Vt.)
Morrison, James L. D. (Ill.)
Mott, Richard (Ohio)
Murray, Ambrose S. (N. Y.)
Nichols, Matthias H. (Ohio)
Norton, Jesse O. (Ill.)
Oliver, Andrew (N. Y.)
Oliver, Mordecai (Mo.)
Orr, James L. (S. C.)
Packer, Asa (Pa.)
Paine, Robert T. (N. C.)
Parker, John M. (N. Y.)
Pearce, John J. (Pa.)
Peck, George W. (Mich.)
Pelton, Guy R. (N. Y.)
Pennington, Alexander C. M. (N. J.)
Perry, John J. (Maine)
Pettit, John U. (Ind.)
Phelps, John S. (Mo.)
Pike, James (N. H.)
Porter, Gilchrist (Mo.)
Powell, Paulus (Va.)
Pringle, Benjamin (N. Y.)
Purviance, Samuel A. (Pa.)
Puryear, Richard C. (N. C.)
Quitman, John A. (Miss.)
Reade, Edwin G. (N. C.)
Ready, Charles (Tenn.)
Ricaud, James B. (Md.)
Richardson, William A. (Ill.)
Ritchie, David (Pa.)
Rivers, Thomas (Tenn.)
Robbins, George R. (N. J.)
Roberts, Anthony E. (Pa.)
Robison, David F. (Pa.)
Ruffin, Thomas (N. C.)
Rust, Albert (Ark.)
Sabin, Alvah (Vt.)
Sage, Russell (N. Y.)
Sandidge, John M. (La.)
Sapp, William R. (Ohio)
Savage, John H. (Tenn.)
Scott, Harvey D. (Ind.)
Seward, James L. (Ga.)
Sherman, John (Ohio)
Shorter, Eli S. (Ala.)
Simmons, George A. (N. Y.)
Smith, Samuel A. (Tenn.)
Smith, William (Va.)
Smith, William R. (Ala.)
Sneed, William H. (Tenn.)
Spinner, Francis E. (N. Y.)
Stanton, Benjamin (Ohio)
Stephens, Alexander H. (Ga.)
Stewart, James A. (Md.)
Stranahan, James S. T. (N. Y.)
Swope, Samuel F. (Ky.)
Talbott, Albert G. (Ky.)
Tappan, Mason W. (N. H.)
Taylor, Miles (La.)
Thorington, James (La.)
Thurston, Benjamin B. (R. I.)
Todd, Lemuel (Pa.)
Trafton, Mark (Mass.)
Trippe, Robert P. (Ga.)
Tyson, Job R. (Pa.)
Underwood, Warner L. (Ky.)
Vail, George (N. J.)
Valk, William W. (N. Y.)
Wade, Edward (Ohio)
Wakeman, Abram (N. Y.)
Walbridge, David S. (Mich.)
Waldron, Henry (Mich.)
Walker, Percy (Ala.)
Warner, Hiram (Ga.)
Washburn, Cadwallader C. (Wis.)
Washburn, Israel, Jr. (Maine)
Washburne, Elihu B. (Ill.)
Watkins, Albert G. (Tenn.)
Watson, Cooper K. (Ohio)
Welch, William W. (Conn.)
Wells, Daniel, Jr. (Wis.)
Wheeler, John (N. Y.)
Whitney, Thomas R. (N. Y.)
Williams, John (N. Y.)
Winslow, Warren (N. C.)
Wood, John M. (Maine)
Woodruff, John (Conn.)
Woodworth, James H. (Ill.)
Wright, Daniel B. (Mass.)
Wright, John V. (Tenn.)
Zollicoffer, Felix K. (Tenn.)

The Thirty-fifth Congress (1857-59)

Orr, James L. (S. C.) Speaker.

Abbott, Nehemiah (Maine)
Adrain, Carnett B. (N. J.)
Ahl, John A. (Pa.)
Anderson, Thomas L. (Mo.)
Andrews, Samuel G. (N. Y.)
Arnold, Samuel (Conn.)
Atkins, John D. C. (Tenn.)
Avery, William T. (Tenn.)
Banks, Nathaniel P. (Mass.)
Barksdale, William (Miss.)
Barr, Thomas J. (N. Y.)
Bennett, Henry (N. Y.)
Billinghurst, Charles (Wis.)
Bingham, John A. (Ohio)
Bishop, William D. (Conn.)
Blair, Francis P., Jr. (Mo.)
Bliss, Philemon (Ohio)
Bocock, Thomas S. (Va.)
Bonham, Milledge L. (S. C.)
Bowie, Thomas F. (Md.)
Boyce, William W. (S. C.)
Branch, Lawrence O'B. (N.C.)
Brayton, William D. (R. I.)
Brenton, Samuel (Ind.)
Bryan, Guy M. (Tex.)
Buffinton, James (Mass.)
Burlingame, Anson (Mass.)
Burnett, Henry C. (Ky.)
Burns, Joseph (Ohio)
Burroughs, Silas M. (N. Y.)
Campbell, Lewis D. (Ohio)
Caruthers, Samuel (Mo.)
Case, Charles (Ind.)
Caskie, John S. (Va.)
Cavanaugh, James M. (Minn.)
Chaffee, Calvin C. (Mass.)
Chapman, Henry (Pa.)
Clark, Ezra, Jr. (Conn.)
Clark, Horace F. (N. Y.)
Clark, John B. (Mo.)
Clawson, Isaiah D. (N. J.)
Clay, James B. (Ky.)
Clemens, Sherrard (Va.)
Clingman, Thomas L. (N. C.)
Cobb, Williamson R. W. (Ala.)
Cochrane, Clark B. (N. Y.)
Cochrane, John (N. Y.)
Cockerill, Joseph R. (Ohio)
Colfax, Schuyler (Ind.)
Comins, Linus B. (Mass.)
Corning, Erastus (N. Y.)
Covode, John (Pa.)
Cox, Samuel S. (Ohio)
Cragin, Aaron H. (N. H.)
Craig, James (Mo.)
Craige, E. Burton (N. C.)
Crawford, Martin J. (Ga.)
Curry, Jabez L. M. (Ala.)
Curtis, Samuel R. (Iowa)
Damrell, William S. (Mass.)
Davidson, Thomas G. (La.)
Davis, H. Winter (Md.)
Davis, John G. (Ind.)
Davis, Reuben (Miss.)
Davis, Timothy (Iowa)
Davis, Timothy (Mass.)
Dawes, Henry L. (Mass.)
Dean, Sidney (Conn.)
Dewart, William L. (Pa.)
Dick, John (Pa.)
Dimmick, William H. (Pa.)
Dodd, Edward (N. Y.)
Dowdell, James F. (Ala.)
Durfee, Nathaniel B. (R. I.)
Edie, John R. (Pa.)
Edmundson, Henry A. (Va.)
Elliott, John M. (Ky.)
English, William H. (Ind.)
Eustis, George, Jr. (La.)
Farnsworth, John F. (Ill.)
Faulkner, Charles J. (Va.)
Fenton, Reuben E. (N. Y.)
Florence, Thomas B. (Pa.)
Foley, James B. (Ind.)
Foster, Stephen C. (Maine)
Garnett, Muscoe R. H. (Va.)
Gartrell, Lucius J. (Ga.)
Giddings, Joshua R. (Ohio)
Gillis, James L. (Pa.)
Gilman, Charles J. (Maine)
Gilmer, John A. (N. C.)
Gooch, Daniel W. (Mass.)
Goode, William O. (Va.)
Goodwin, Henry C. (N. Y.)
Granger, Amos P. (N. Y.)
Greenwood, Alfred B. (Ark.)
Gregg, James M. (Ind.)
Groesbeck, William S. (Ohio)
Grover, La Fayette (Oreg.)
Grow, Galusha A. (Pa.)
Hall, Lawrence W. (Ohio)
Hall, Robert B. (Mass.)
Harlan, Aaron (Ohio)
Harris, J. Morrison (Md.)
Harris, Thomas L. (Ill.)
Haskin, John B. (N. Y.)
Hatch, Israel T. (N. Y.)
Hawkins, George S. (Fla.)
Hickman, John (Pa.)
Hill, Joshua (Ga.)
Hoard, Charles B. (N. Y.)
Hodges, Charles D. (Ill.)
Hopkins, George W. (Va.)
Horton, Valentine B. (Ohio)
Houston, George S. (Ala.)
Howard, William A. (Mich.)
Hughes, James (Ind.)
Huyler, John (N. J.)
Jackson, James (Ga.)
Jenkins, Albert G. (Va.)
Jewett, Joshua H. (Ky.)
Jones, George W. (Tenn.)
Jones, J. Glancy (Pa.)
Jones, Owen (Pa.)
Keim, William H. (Pa.)
Keitt, Laurence M. (S. C.)
Kellogg, William (Ill.)
Kelly, John (N. Y.)
Kelsey, William H. (N. Y.)
Kilgore, David (Ind.)
Knapp, Chauncey L. (Mass.)
Kunkel, Jacob M. (Md.)

Kunkel, John C. (Pa.)
Lamar, Lucius Q. C. (Miss.)
Landy, James (Pa.)
Lawrence, William (Ohio)
Leach, DeWitt C. (Mich.)
Leidy, Paul (Pa.)
Leiter, Benjamin F. (Ohio)
Letcher, John (Va.)
Lockhart, James (Ind.)
Lovejoy, Owen (Ill.)
McKibbin, Joseph C. (Calif.)
Maclay, William B. (N. Y.)
McQueen, John (S. C.)
McRea, John J. (Miss.)
Marshall, Humphrey (Ky.)
Marshall, Samuel S. (Ill.)
Mason, John C. (Ky.)
Matteson, Orsamus B. (N. Y.)
Maynard, Horace (Tenn.)
Miles, William P. (S. C.)
Miller, Joseph (Ohio)
Millson, John S. (Va.)
Montgomery, William (Pa.)
Moore, Sydenham (Ala.)
Morgan, Edwin B. (N. Y.)
Morrill, Justin S. (Vt.)
Morris, Edward Joy (Pa.)
Morris, Isaac N. (Ill.)
Morse, Freeman H. (Maine)
Morse, Oliver A. (N. Y.)
Mott, Richard (Ohio)
Murray, Ambrose S. (N. Y.)
Niblack, William E. (Ind.)
Nichols, Matthias H. (Ohio)
Olin, Abram B. (N. Y.)
Palmer, George W. (N. Y.)
Parker, John M. (N. Y.)
Pendleton, George H. (Ohio)
Pettit, John U. (Ind.)
Peyton, Samuel O. (Ky.)
Phelps, John S. (Mo.)
Phelps, William W. (Minn.)
Phillips, Henry M. (Pa.)
Pike, James (N. H.)
Potter, John F. (Wis.)
Pottle, Emory B. (N. Y.)
Powell, Paulus (Va.)
Purviance, Samuel A. (Pa.)
Quitman, John A. (Miss.)
Ready, Charles (Tenn.)
Reagan, John H. (Tex.)
Reilly, Wilson (Pa.)
Ricaud, James B. (Md.)
Ritchie, David (Pa.)
Robbins, George R. (N. J.)
Roberts, Anthony E. (Pa.)
Royce, Homer E. (Vt.)
Ruffin, Thomas (N. C.)
Russell, William F. (N. Y.)
Sandidge, John M. (La.)
Savage, John H. (Tenn.)
Scales, Alfred M. (N. C.)
Scott, Charles L. (Calif.)
Searing, John A. (N. Y.)
Seward, James L. (Ga.)
Shaw, Aaron (Ill.)
Shaw, Henry M. (N. C.)
Sherman, John (Ohio).
Sherman, Judson W. (N. Y.)
Shorter, Eli S. (Ala.)
Sickles, Daniel E. (N. Y.)
Singleton, Otho R. (Miss.)
Smith, Robert (Ill.)
Smith, Samuel A. (Tenn.)
Smith, William (Va.)
Spinner, Francis E. (N. Y.)
Stallworth, James A. (Ala.)
Stanton, Benjamin (Ohio)
Stephens, Alexander H. (Ga.)
Stevenson, John W. (Ky.)
Stewart, James A. (Md.)
Stewart, William (Pa.)
Talbot, Albert G. (Ky.)
Tappan, Mason W. (N. H.)
Taylor, George (N. Y.)
Taylor, Miles (La.)
Thayer, Eli (Mass.)
Thompson, John (N. Y.)
Tompkins, Cydnor B. (Ohio)
Trippe, Robert P. (Ga.)
Underwood, Warner L. (Ky.)
Vallandigham, Clement L. (Ohio)
Vance, Zebulon B. (N. C.)
Wade, Edward (Ohio)
Walbridge, David S. (Mich.)
Waldron, Henry (Mich.)
Walton, Eliakim P. (Vt.)
Ward, Elijah (N. Y.)
Warren, Edward A. (Ark.)
Washburn, Cadwallader C. (Wis.)
Washburn, Israel, Jr. (Maine)
Washburne, Elihu B. (Ill.)
Watkins, Albert G. (Tenn.)
White, Allison (Pa.)
Whiteley, William G. (Del.)
Wilson, James (Ind.)
Winslow, Warren (N. C.)
Wood, John M. (Maine)
Woodson, Samuel H. (Mo.)
Wortendyke, Jacob R. (N. J.)
Wright, Augustus R. (Ga.)
Wright, John V. (Tenn.)
Zollicoffer, Felix K. (Tenn.)

The Thirty-sixth Congress (1859-61)

Pennington, William (N. J.) Speaker.

Adams, Charles F. (Mass.)
Adams, Green (Ky.)
Adrain, Garnett B. (N. J.)
Aldrich, Cyrus (Minn.)
Allen, William (Ohio)
Alley, John B. (Mass.)
Anderson, Thomas L. (Mo.)
Anderson, William C. (Ky.)
Ashley, James M. (Ohio)
Ashmore, John D. (S. C.)
Avery, William T. (Tenn.)
Babbitt, Elijah (Pa.)
Barksdale, William (Miss.)
Barr, Thomas J. (N. Y.)
Barret, John R. (Mo.)
Beale, Charles L. (N. Y.)
Bingham, John A. (Ohio)
Blair, Francis P., Jr. (Mo.)
Blair, Samuel S. (Pa.)
Blake, Harrison G. O. (Ohio)
Bocock, Thomas S. (Va.)
Bonham, Milledge L. (S. C.)
Boteler, Alexander R. (Va.)
Bouligny, John E. (La.)
Boyce, William W. (S. C.)
Brabson, Reese B. (Tenn.)
Branch, Lawrence O'B. (N. C.)
Brayton, William D. (R. I.)
Briggs, George (N. Y.)
Bristow, Francis M. (Ky.)
Brown, John Y. (Ky.)
Buffinton, James (Mass.)
Burch, John C. (Calif.)
Burlingame, Anson (Mass.)
Burnett, Henry C. (Ky.)
Burnham, Alfred A. (Conn.)
Burroughs, Silas M. (N. Y.)
Butterfield, Martin (N. Y.)
Campbell, James H. (Pa.)
Carey, John (Ohio)
Carter, Luther C. (N. Y.)
Case, Charles (Ind.)
Clark, Horace F. (N. Y.)
Clark, John B. (Mo.)
Clemens, Sherrard (Va.)
Clopton, David (Ala.)
Cobb, Williamson R. W. (Ala.)
Coburn, Stephen (Maine)
Cochrane, Clark B. (N. Y.)
Cochrane, John (N. Y.)
Colfax, Schuyler (Ind.)
Conkling, Roscoe (N. Y.)
Conway, Martin F. (Kans.)
Cooper, George B. (Mich.)
Corwin, Thomas (Ohio)
Covode, John (Pa.)
Cox, Samuel S. (Ohio)
Craig, James (Mo.)
Craige, F. Burton (N. C.)
Crawford, Martin J. (Ga.)
Curry, Jabez L. M. (Ala.)
Curtis, Samuel R. (Iowa)
Davidson, Thomas G. (La.)
Davis, H. Winter (Md.)
Davis, John G. (Ind.)
Davis, Reuben (Miss.)
Dawes, Henry L. (Mass.)
De Jarnette, Daniel C. (Va.)
Delano, Charles (Mass.)
Dimmick, William H. (Pa.)
Duell, R. Holland (N. Y.)
Dunn, William McK. (Ind.)
Edgerton, Sidney (Ohio)
Edmundson, Henry A. (Va.)
Edwards, Thomas M. (N. H.)
Eliot, Thomas D. (Mass.)
Ely, Alfred (N. Y.)
English, William H. (Ind.)
Etheridge, Emerson (Tenn.)
Farnsworth, John F. (Ill.)
Fenton, Reuben E. (N. Y.)
Ferry, Orris F. (Conn.)
Florence, Thomas B. (Pa.)
Foster, Stephen C. (Maine)
Fouke, Philip B. (Ill.)
Frank, Augustus (N. Y.)
French, Ezra B. (Maine)
Garnett, Muscoe R. H. (Va.)
Gartrell, Lucius J. (Ga.)
Gilmer, John A. (N. C.)
Gooch, Daniel W. (Mass.)
Graham, James H. (N. Y.)
Grow, Galusha A. (Pa.)
Gurley, John A. (Ohio)
Hale, James T. (Pa.)
Hall, Chapin (Pa.)
Hamilton, Andrew J. (Tex.)
Hardeman, Thomas, Jr. (Ga.)
Harris, J. Morrison (Md.)
Harris, John T. (Va.)
Haskin, John B. (N. Y.)
Hatton, Robert H. (Tenn.)
Hawkins, George S. (Fla.)
Helmick, William (Ohio)
Hickman, John (Pa.)
Hill, Joshua (Ga.)
Hindman, Thomas C. (Ark.)
Hoard, Charles B. (N. Y.)
Holman, William S. (Ind.)
Houston, George S. (Ala.)
Howard, William (Ohio)
Howard, William A. (Mich.)
Hughes, George W. (Md.)
Humphrey, James (N. Y.)
Hutchins, John (Ohio)
Irvine, William (N. Y.)
Jackson, James (Ga.)
Jenkins, Albert G. (Va.)
Jones, John J. (Ga.)
Junkin, Benjamin F. (Pa.)
Keitt, Laurence M. (S. C.)
Kellogg, Francis W. (Mich.)
Kellogg, William (Ill.)
Kenyon, William S. (N. Y.)
Kilgore, David (Ind.)
Killinger, John W. (Pa.)
Kunkel, Jacob M. (Md.)
Lamar, Lucius Q. C. (Miss.)
Landrum, John M. (La.)
Larrabee, Charles H. (Wis.)
Leach, De Witt C. (Mich.)
Leach, James M. (N. C.)
Leake, Shelton F. (Va.)
Lee, M. Lindley (N. Y.)
Logan, John A. (Ill.)
Longnecker, Henry C. (Pa.)
Loomis, Dwight (Conn.)
Love, Peter E. (Ga.)
Lovejoy, Owen (Ill.)
McClernand, John A. (Ill.)
McKean, James B. (N. Y.)
McKenty, Jacob K. (Pa.)
McKnight, Robert (Pa.)
Maclay, William B. (N. Y.)
McPherson, Edward (Pa.)
McQueen, John (S. C.)
McRae, John J. (Miss.)
Mallory, Robert (Ky.)
Marston, Gilman (N. H.)
Martin, Charles D. (Ohio)
Martin, Elbert S. (Va.)
Maynard, Horace (Tenn.)
Miles, William P. (S. C.)
Millson, John S. (Va.)
Millward, William (Pa.)
Montgomery, William (Pa.)
Moore, Laban T. (Ky.)
Moore, Sydenham (Ala.)
Moorhead, James K. (Pa.)
Morrill, Justin S. (Vt.)
Morris, Edward J. (Pa.)
Morris, Isaac N. (Ill.)
Morse, Freeman H. (Maine)
Nelson, Thomas A. R. (Tenn.)
Niblack, William E. (Ind.)
Nixon, John T. (N. J.)
Noell, John W. (Mo.)
Olin, Abram B. (N. Y.)
Palmer, George W. (N. Y.)
Pendleton, George H. (Ohio)
Perry, John J. (Maine)
Pettit, John U. (Ind.)
Peyton, Samuel O. (Ky.)
Phelps, John S. (Mo.)
Porter, Albert G. (Ind.)
Potter, John F. (Wis.)
Pottle, Emory B. (N. Y.)
Pryor, Roger A. (Va.)
Pugh, James L. (Ala.)
Quarles, James M. (Tenn.)
Reagan, John H. (Tex.)
Reynolds, Edwin R. (N. Y.)
Reynolds, John H. (N. Y.)
Rice, Alexander H. (Mass.)
Riggs, Jetur R. (N. J.)
Robinson, Christopher (R. I.)
Robinson, James C. (Ill.)
Royce, Homer E. (Vt.)
Ruffin, Thomas (N. C.)
Rust, Albert (Ark.)
Schwartz, John (Pa.)
Scott, Charles L. (Calif.)
Scranton, George W. (Pa.)
Sedgwick, Charles B. (N. Y.)
Sherman, John (Ohio)
Sickles, Daniel E. (N. Y.)
Simms, William E. (Ky.)
Singleton, Otho R. (Miss.)
Smith, William (Va.)
Smith, William N. H. (N. C.)
Somes, Daniel E. (Maine)
Spaulding, Elbridge G. (N. Y.)
Spinner, Francis E. (N. Y.)
Stallworth, James A. (Ala.)
Stanton, Benjamin (Ohio)
Stevens, Thaddeus (Pa.)
Stevenson, John W. (Ky.)
Stewart, James A. (Md.)
Stewart, William (Pa.)
Stokes, William B. (Tenn.)
Stout, Lansing (Oreg.)
Stratton, John L. N. (N. J.)
Tappan, Mason W. (N. H.)
Taylor, Miles (La.)
Thayer, Eli (Mass.)
Theaker, Thomas C. (Ohio)
Thomas, James H. (Tenn.)
Tompkins, Cydnor B. (Ohio)
Train, Charles R. (Mass.)
Trimble, Carey A. (Ohio)
Underwood, John W. H. (Ga.)
Vallandigham, Clement L. (Ohio)
Vance, Zebulon B. (N. C.)
Vandever, William (Iowa)
Van Wyck, Charles H. (N. Y.)
Verree, John P. (Pa.)
Wade, Edward (Ohio)
Waldron, Henry (Mich.)
Walton, Eliakim P. (Vt.)
Washburn, Cadwallader C. (Wis.)
Washburn, Israel, Jr. (Maine)
Washburne, Elihu B. (Ill.)
Webster, Edwin H. (Md.)
Wells, Alfred (N. Y.)
Whiteley, William G. (Del.)
Wilson, James (Ind.)
Windom, William (Minn.)
Winslow, Warren (N. C.)
Wood, John (Pa.)
Woodruff, John (Conn.)
Woodson, Samuel H. (Mo.)
Wright, John V. (Tenn.)

The Thirty-seventh Congress (1861-63)

Grow, Galusha A. (Pa.) Speaker.

Aldrich, Cyrus (Minn.)
Allen, William (Ohio)
Allen, William J. (Ill.)
Alley, John B. (Mass.)
Ancona, Sydenham E. (Pa.)
Appleton, William (Mass.)
Arnold, Isaac N. (Ill.)
Ashley, James M. (Ohio)
Babbitt, Elijah (Pa.)
Bailey, Goldsmith F. (Mass.)
Bailey, Joseph (Pa.)
Baker, Stephen (N. Y.)
Baxter, Portus (Vt.)
Beaman, Fernando C. (Mich.)
Biddle, Charles J. (Pa.)
Bingham, John A. (Ohio)
Blair, Francis P., Jr. (Mo.)
Blair, Jacob B. (Va.)

Blair, Samuel S. (Pa.)
Blake, Harrison G. O. (Ohio)
Bridges, George W. (Tenn.)
Brown, William G. (Va.)
Browne, George H. (R. I.)
Buffinton, James (Mass.)
Burnett, Henry C. (Ky.)
Burnham, Alfred A. (Conn.)
Calvert, Charles B. (Md.)
Campbell, James H. (Pa.)
Carlile, John S. (Va.)
Casey, Samuel L. (Ky.)
Chamberlain, Jacob P. (N. Y.)
Clark, Ambrose W. (N. Y.)
Clements, Andrew J. (Tenn.)
Cobb, George T. (N. J.)
Colfax, Schuyler (Ind.)
Conklin, Frederick A. (N. Y.)
Conklin, Roscoe (N. Y.)
Conway, Martin F. (Kans.)
Cooper, Thomas B. (Pa.)
Corning, Erastus (N. Y.)
Covode, John (Pa.)
Cox, Samuel S. (Ohio)
Cravens, James A. (Ind.)
Crisfield, John W. (Md.)
Crittenden, John J. (Ky.)
Curtis, Samuel R. (Iowa)
Cutler, William P. (Ohio)
Davis, William M. (Pa.)
Dawes, Henry L. (Mass.)
Delano, Charles (Mass.)
Delaplaine, Isaac C. (N. Y.)
Diven, Alexander S. (N. Y.)
Duell, R. Holland (N. Y.)
Dunlap, George W. (Ky.)
Dunn, William McKee (Ind.)
Edgerton, Sidney (Ohio)
Edwards, Thomas M. (N. H.)
Eliot, Thomas D. (Mass.)
Ely, Alfred (N. Y.)
English, James E. (Conn.)
Fenton, Reuben E. (N. Y.)
Fessenden, Samuel C. (Maine)
Fessenden, Thomas A. D. (Maine)
Fisher, George P. (Del.)
Flanders, Benjamin F. (La.)
Fouke, Philip B. (Ill.)
Franchot, Richard (N. Y.)
Frank, Augustus (N. Y.)
Gooch, Daniel W. (Mass.)
Goodwin, John N. (Maine)
Granger, Bradley F. (Mich.)
Grider, Henry (Ky.)
Gurley, John A. (Ohio)
Hahn, Michael (La.)
Haight, Edward (N. Y.)
Hale, James T. (Pa.)
Hall, William A. (Mo.)
Hanchett, Luther (Wis.)
Harding, Aaron (Ky.)
Harrison, Richard A. (Ohio)
Hickman, John (Pa.)
Holman, William S. (Ind.)
Hooper, Samuel (Mass.)
Horton, Valentine B. (Ohio)
Hutchins, John (Ohio)
Jackson, James S. (Ky.)
Johnson, Philip (Pa.)
Julian, George W. (Ind.)
Kelley, William D. (Pa.)
Kellogg, Francis W. (Mich.)
Kellogg, William (Ill.)
Kerrigan, James E. (N. Y.)
Killinger, John W. (Pa.)
Knapp, Anthony L. (Ill.)
Lansing, William E. (N. Y.)
Law, John (Ind.)
Lazer, Jesse (Pa.)
Leary, Cornelius L. L. (Md.)
Lehman, William E. (Pa.)
Logan, John A. (Ill.)
Loomis, Dwight (Conn.)
Lovejoy, Owen (Ill.)
Low, Frederick F. (Calif.)
McClernand, John A. (Ill.)
McIndoe, Walter D. (Wis.)
McKean, James B. (N. Y.)
McKenzie, Lewis (Va.)
McKnight, Robert (Pa.)
McPherson, Edward (Pa.)
Mallory, Robert (Ky.)
Marston, Gilman (N. H.)
May, Henry (Md.)
Maynard, Horace (Tenn.)
Menzies, John W. (Ky.)
Mitchell, William (Ind.)
Moorhead, James K. (Pa.)
Morrill, Anson P. (Maine)
Morrill, Justin S. (Vt.)
Morris, James R. (Ohio)
Nixon, John T. (N. J.)
Noble, Warren P. (Ohio)
Noell, John W. (Mo.)
Norton, Elijah H. (Mo.)
Nugen, Robert H. (Ohio)
Odell, Moses F. (N. Y.)
Olin, Abram B. (N. Y.)
Patton, John (Pa.)
Pendleton, George H. (Ohio)
Perry, Nehemiah (N. J.)
Phelps, John S. (Mo.)
Phelps, Timothy G. (Calif.)
Pike, Frederick A. (Maine)
Pomeroy, Theodore M. (N. Y.)
Porter, Albert G. (Ind.)
Potter, John F. (Wis.)
Price, Thomas L. (Mo.)
Reid, John W. (Mo.)
Rice, Alexander H. (Mass.)
Rice, John H. (Maine)
Richardson, William A. (Ill.)
Riddle, Albert G. (Ohio)
Robinson, James C. (Ill.)
Rollins, Edward H. (N. H.)
Rollins, James S. (Mo.)
Sargent, Aaron A. (Calif.)
Sedgwick, Charles B. (N. Y.)
Segar, Joseph E. (Va.)
Shanks, John P. C. (Ind.)
Sheffield, William P. (R. I.)
Shellabarger, Samuel (Ohio)
Sherman, Socrates N. (N. Y.)
Shiel, George K. (Oreg.)
Sloan, A. Scott (Wis.)
Smith, Edward H. (N. Y.)
Spaulding, Elbridge G. (N. Y.)
Steele, John B. (N. Y.)
Steele, William G. (N. J.)
Stevens, Thaddeus (Pa.)
Stiles, John D. (Pa.)
Stratton, John L. N. (N. J.)
Thayer, Andrew J. (Oreg.)
Thomas, Benjamin F. (Mass.)
Thomas, Francis (Md.)
Train, Charles R. (Mass.)
Trimble, Carey A. (Ohio)
Trowbridge, Rowland E. (Mich.)
Upton, Charles H. (Va.)
Vallandigham, Clement C. (Ohio)
Vandever, William (Iowa)
Van Horn, Burt (N. Y.)
Van Valkenburg, Robert B. (N. Y.)
Van Wyck, Charles H. (N. Y.)
Verree, John P. (Pa.)
Vibbard, Chauncey (N. Y.)
Voorhees, Daniel W. (Ind.)
Wadsworth, William H. (Ky.)
Walker, Amasa (Mass.)
Wall, William (N. Y.)
Wallace, John W. (Pa.)
Walton, Charles W. (Maine)
Walton, Eliakim P. (Vt.)
Ward, Elijah (N. Y.)
Washburne, Elihu B. (Ill.)
Webster, Edwin H. (Md.)
Whaley, Killian V. (Va.)
Wheeler, William A. (N. Y.)
White, Albert S. (Ind.)
White, Chilton A. (Ohio)
Wickliffe, Charles A. (Ky.)
Wilson, James F. (Iowa)
Windom, William (Minn.)
Wood, Benjamin (N. Y.)
Woodruff, George C. (Conn.)
Worcester, Samuel T. (Ohio)
Wright, Hendrick B. (Pa.)
Yeaman, George H. (Ky.)

The Thirty-eighth Congress (1863-65)

Colfax, Schuyler (Ind.) Speaker.

Allen, James C. (Ill.)
Allen, William J. (Ill.)
Alley, John B. (Mass.)
Allison, William B. (Iowa)
Ames, Oakes (Mass.)
Ancona, Sydenham E. (Pa.)
Anderson, Lucien (Ky.)
Arnold, Isaac N. (Ill.)
Ashley, James M. (Ohio)
Bailey, Joseph (Pa.)
Baldwin, Augustus C. (Mich.)
Baldwin, John D. (Mass.)
Baxter, Portus (Vt.)
Beaman, Fernando C. (Mich.)
Blaine, James G. (Maine)
Blair, Francis P., Jr. (Mo.)
Blair, Jacob B. (W. Va.)
Bliss, George (Ohio)
Blow, Henry T. (Mo.)
Boutwell, George S. (Mass.)
Boyd, Sempronius H. (Mo.)
Brandegee, Augustus (Conn.)
Brooks, James (N. Y.)
Broomall, John M. (Pa.)
Brown, James S. (Wis.)
Brown, William G. (W. Va.)
Chanler, John W. (N. Y.)
Clark, Ambrose W. (N. Y.)
Clarke, Freeman (N. Y.)
Clay, Brutus J. (Ky.)
Cobb, Amasa (Wis.)
Coffroth, Alexander H. (Pa.)
Cole, Cornelius (Calif.)
Cox, Samuel S. (Ohio)
Cravens, James A. (Ind.)
Creswell, John A. J. (Md.)
Davis, Henry Winter (Md.)
Davis, Thomas T. (N. Y.)
Dawes, Henry L. (Mass.)
Dawson, John L. (Pa.)
Deming, Henry C. (Conn.)
Denison, Charles (Pa.)
Dixon, Nathan F. (R. I.)
Donnelly, Ignatius (Minn.)
Driggs, John F. (Mich.)
Dumont, Ebenezer (Ind.)
Eckley, Ephraim R. (Ohio)
Eden, John R. (Ill.)
Edgerton, Joseph K. (Ind.)
Eldridge, Charles A. (Wis.)
Eliot, Thomas D. (Mass.)
English, James E. (Conn.)
Farnsworth, John F. (Ill.)
Fenton, Reuben E. (N. Y.)
Finck, William E. (Ohio)
Frank, Augustus (N. Y.)
Ganson, John (N. Y.)
Garfield, James A. (Ohio)
Gooch, Daniel W. (Mass.)
Grider, Henry (Ky.)
Grinnell, Josiah B. (Iowa)
Griswold, John A. (N. Y.)
Hale, James T. (Pa.)
Hall, William A. (Mo.)
Harding, Aaron (Ky.)
Harrington, Henry W. (Ind.)
Harris, Benjamin G. (Md.)
Harris, Charles M. (Ill.)
Herrick, Anson (N. Y.)
Higby, William (Calif.)
Holman, William S. (Ind.)
Hooper, Samuel (Mass.)
Hotchkiss, Giles W. (N. Y.)
Hubbard, Asahel W. (Iowa)
Hubbard, John H. (Conn.)
Hulburd, Calvin T. (N. Y.)
Hutchins, Wells A. (Ohio)
Ingersoll, Ebon C. (Ill.)
Jenckes, Thomas A. (R. I.)
Johnson, Philip (Pa.)
Johnston, William (Ohio)
Julian, George W. (Ind.)
Kalbfleisch, Martin (N. Y.)
Kasson, John A. (Iowa)
Kelley, William D. (Pa.)
Kellogg, Francis W. (Mich.)
Kellogg, Orlando (N. Y.)
Kernan, Francis (N. Y.)
King, Austin A. (Mo.)
Knapp, Anthony L. (Ill.)
Knox, Samuel (Mo.)
Law, John (Ind.)
Lazear, Jesse (Pa.)
Le Blond, Francis C. (Ohio)
Littlejohn, De Witt C. (N. Y.)
Loan, Benjamin F. (Mo.)
Long, Alexander (Ohio)
Longyear, John W. (Mich.)
Lovejoy, Owen (Ill.)
McAllister, Archibald (Pa.)
McBride, John B. (Oreg.)
McClurg, Joseph W. (Mo.)
McDowell, James F. (Ind.)
McIndoe, Walter D. (Wis.)
McKinney, John F. (Ohio)
Mallory, Robert (Ky.)
Marcy, Daniel (N. H.)
Marvin, James M. (N. Y.)
Middleton, George (N. J.)
Miller, Samuel F. (N. Y.)
Miller, William H. (Pa.)
Moorhead, James K. (Pa.)
Morrill, Justin S. (Vt.)
Morris, Daniel (N. Y.)
Morris, James R. (Ohio)
Morrison, William R. (Ill.)
Myers, Amos (Pa.)
Myers, Leonard (Pa.)
Nelson, Homer A. (N. Y.)
Noble, Warren P. (Ohio)
Norton, Jesse O. (Ill.)
Odell, Moses F. (N. Y.)
O'Neill, Charles (Pa.)
O'Neill, John (Ohio)
Orth, Godlove S. (Ind.)
Patterson, James W. (N. H.)
Pendleton, George H. (Ohio)
Perham, Sidney (Maine)
Perry, Nehemiah (N. J.)
Pike, Frederick A. (Maine)
Pomeroy, Theodore M. (N. Y.)
Price, Hiram (Iowa)
Pruyn, John V. L. (N. Y.)
Radford, William (N. Y.)
Randall, Samuel J. (Pa.)
Randall, William H. (Ky.)
Rice, Alexander H. (Mass.)
Rice, John H. (Maine)
Robinson, James C. (Ill.)
Rogers, Andrew J. (N. J.)
Rollins, Edward H. (N. H.)
Rollins, James S. (Mo.)
Ross, Lewis W. (Ill.)
Schenck, Robert C. (Ohio)
Scofield, Glenni W. (Pa.)
Scott, John G. (Mo.)
Shannon, Thomas B. (Calif.)
Sloan, Ithamar C. (Wis.)
Smith, Green C. (Ky.)
Smithers, Nathaniel B. (Del.)
Spalding, Rufus P. (Ohio)
Starr, John F. (N. J.)
Stebbins, Henry G. (N. Y.)
Steele, John B. (N. Y.)
Steele, William G. (N. J.)
Stevens, Thaddeus (Pa.)
Stiles, John D. (Pa.)
Strouse, Myer (Pa.)
Stuart, John T. (Ill.)
Sweat, Lorenzo D. M. (Maine)
Thayer, M. Russell (Pa.)
Thomas, Francis (Md.)
Townsend, Dwight (N. Y.)
Tracy, Henry W. (Pa.)
Upson, Charles (Mich.)
Van Valkenburg, Robert B. (N. Y.)
Voorhees, Daniel W. (Ind.)
Wadsworth, William H. (Ky.)
Ward, Elijah (N. Y.)
Washburn, William B. (Mass.)
Washburne, Elihu B. (Ill.)
Webster, Edwin H. (Md.)
Whaley, Kellian V. (W. Va.)
Wheeler, Ezra (Wis.)
White, Chilton A. (Ohio)
White, Joseph W. (Ohio)
Wilder, A. Carter (Kans.)
Williams, Thomas (Pa.)
Wilson, James F. (Iowa)
Windom, William (Minn.)
Winfield, Charles H. (N. Y.)
Wood, Benjamin (N. Y.)
Wood, Fernando (N. Y.)
Woodbridge, Frederick E. (Vt.)
Worthington, Henry G. (Nev.)
Yeaman, George H. (Ky.)

The Thirty-ninth Congress (1865-67)

Colfax, Schuyler (Ind.) Speaker.

Alley, John B. (Mass.)
Allison, William B. (Iowa)
Ames, Oakes (Mass.)
Ancona, Sydenham E. (Pa.)
Anderson, George W. (Mo.)
Arnell, Samuel M. (Tenn.)
Ashley, Delos R. (Nev.)
Ashley, James M. (Ohio)

Baker, Jehu (Ill.)
Baldwin, John D. (Mass.)
Banks, Nathaniel P. (Mass.)
Barker, Abraham A. (Pa.)
Baxter, Portus (Vt.)
Beaman, Fernando C. (Mich.)
Benjamin, John F. (Mo.)
Bergen, Teunis G. (N. Y.)
Bidwell, John (Calif.)
Bingham, John A. (Ohio)
Blaine, James G. (Maine)
Blow, Henry T. (Mo.)
Boutwell, George S. (Mass.)
Boyer, Benjamin M. (Pa.)
Brandegee, Augustus (Conn.)
Bromwell, Henry P. H. (Ill.)
Brooks, James (N. Y.)
Broomall, John M. (Pa.)
Buckland, Ralph P. (Ohio)
Bundy, Hezekiah S. (Ohio)
Campbell, William B. (Tenn.)
Chanler, John W. (N. Y.)
Clarke, Reader W. (Ohio)
Clarke, Sidney (Kans.)
Cobb, Amasa (Wis.)
Coffroth, Alexander H. (Pa.)
Conkling, Roscoe (N. Y.)
Cook, Burton C. (Ill.)
Cooper, Edmund (Tenn.)
Cullom, Shelby M. (Ill.)
Culver, Charles G. (Pa.)
Darling, William A. (N. Y.)
Davis, Thomas T. (N. Y.)
Dawes, Henry L. (Mass.)
Dawson, John L. (Pa.)
Defrees, Joseph H. (Ind.)
Delano, Columbus (Ohio)
Deming, Henry C. (Conn.)
Denison, Charles (Pa.)
Dixon, Nathan F. (R. I.)
Dodge, William E. (N. Y.)
Donnelly, Ignatius (Minn.)
Driggs, John F. (Mich.)
Dumont, Ebenezer (Ind.)
Eckley, Ephraim R. (Ohio)
Eggleston, Benjamin (Ohio)
Eldridge, Charles A. (Wis.)
Eliot, Thomas D. (Mass.)
Farnsworth, John F. (Ill.)
Farquhar, John H. (Ind.)
Ferry, Thomas W. (Mich.)
Finck, William E. (Ohio)
Garfield, James A. (Ohio)
Glossbrenner, Adam J. (Pa.)
Goodyear, Charles (N. Y.)
Grider, Henry (Ky.)
Grinnell, Josiah B. (Iowa)
Griswold, John A. (N. Y.)
Hale, Robert S. (N. Y.)
Harding, Aaron (Ky.)
Harding, Abner C. (Ill.)
Harris, Benjamin G. (Md.)
Hart, Roswell (N. Y.)
Hawkins, Isaac R. (Tenn.)
Hayes, Rutherford B. (Ohio)
Henderson, James H. D. (Oreg.)
Higby, William (Calif.)
Hill, Ralph (Ind.)
Hise, Elijah (Ky.)
Hogan, John (Mo.)
Holmes, Sidney T. (N. Y.)
Hooper, Samuel (Mass.)
Hotchkiss, Giles W. (N. Y.)
Hubbard, Asahel W. (Iowa)
Hubbard, Chester D. (W. Va.)
Hubbard, Demas, Jr. (N. Y.)
Hubbard, John H. (Conn.)
Hubbell, Edwin N. (N. Y.)
Hubbell, James R. (Ohio)
Hulburd, Calvin T. (N. Y.)
Humphrey, James (N. Y.)
Humphrey, James M. (N. Y.)
Hunter, John W. (N. Y.)
Ingersoll, Ebon C. (Ill.)
Jenckes, Thomas A. (R. I.)
Johnson, Philip (Pa.)
Jones, Morgan (N. Y.)
Julian, George W. (Ind.)
Kasson, John A. (Iowa)
Kelley, William D. (Pa.)
Kelso, John R. (Mo.)
Kerr, Michael C. (Ind.)
Ketcham, John H. (N. Y.)
Koontz, William H. (Pa.)
Kuykendall, Andrew J. (Ill.)
Laflin, Addison H. (N. Y.)
Latham, George R. (W. Va.)
Lawrence, George V. (Pa.)
Lawrence, William (Ohio)
Le Blond, Francis C. (Ohio)
Leftwitch, John W. (Tenn.)
Loan, Benjamin F. (Mo.)
Longyear, John W. (Mich.)
Lynch, John (Maine)
McClurg, Joseph W. (Mo.)
McCullough, Hiram (Md.)
McIndoe, Walter D. (Wis.)
McKee, Samuel (Ky.)
McRuer, Donald C. (Calif.)
Marquette, Turner M. (Nebr.)
Marshall, Samuel S. (Ill.)
Marston, Gilman (N. H.)
Marvin, James M. (N. Y.)
Maynard, Horace (Tenn.)
Mercur, Ulysses (Pa.)
Miller, George F. (Pa.)
Moorhead, James K. (Pa.)
Morrill, Justin S. (Vt.)
Morris, Daniel (N. Y.)
Moulton, Samuel W. (Ill.)
Myers, Leonard (Pa.)
Newell, William A. (N. J.)
Niblack, William E. (Ind.)
Nicholson, John A. (Del.)
Noell, Thomas E. (Mo.)
O'Neill, Charles (Pa.)
Orth, Godlove S. (Ind.)
Paine, Halbert E. (Wis.)
Patterson, James W. (N. H.)
Perham, Sidney (Maine)
Phelps, Charles E. (Md.)
Pike, Frederick A. (Maine)
Plants, Tobias A. (Ohio)
Pomeroy, Theodore M. (N. Y.)
Price, Hiram (Iowa)
Radford, William (N. Y.)
Randall, Samuel J. (Pa.)
Randall, William H. (Ky.)
Raymond, Henry J. (N. Y.)
Rice, Alexander H. (Mass.)
Rice, John H. (Maine)
Ritter, Burwell C. (Ky.)
Rogers, Andrew J. (N. J.)
Rollins, Edward H. (N. H.)
Ross, Lewis W. (Ill.)
Rousseau, Lovell H. (Ky.)
Sawyer, Philetus (Wis.)
Schenck, Robert C. (Ohio)
Scofield, Glenni W. (Pa.)
Shanklin, George S. (Ky.)
Shellabarger, Samuel (Ohio)
Sitgreaves, Charles (N. J.)
Sloan, Ithamar C. (Wis.)
Smith, Green C. (Ky.)
Spalding, Rufus P. (Ohio)
Starr, John F. (N. J.)
Stevens, Thaddeus (Pa.)
Stillwell, Thomas N. (Ind.)
Stokes, William B. (Tenn.)
Strouse, Myer (Pa.)
Taber, Stephen (N. Y.)
Taylor, Nathaniel G. (Tenn.)
Taylor, Nelson (N. Y.)
Thayer, M. Russell (Pa.)
Thomas, Francis (Md.)
Thomas, John L., Jr. (Md.)
Thornton, Anthony (Ill.)
Trimble, Lawrence S. (Ky.)
Trowbridge, Rowland E. (Mich.)
Upson, Charles (Mich.)
Van Aernam, Henry (N. Y.)
Van Horn, Burt (N. Y.)
Van Horn, Robert T. (Mo.)
Voorhees, Daniel W. (Ind.)
Ward, Andrew H. (Ky.)
Ward, Hamilton (N. Y.)
Warner, Samuel L. (Conn.)
Washburn, Henry D. (Ind.)
Washburn, William B. (Mass.)
Washburne, Elihu B. (Ill.)
Welker, Martin (Ohio)
Wentworth, John (Ill.)
Whaley, Kellian V. (W. Va.)
Williams, Thomas (Pa.)
Wilson, James F. (Iowa)
Wilson, Stephen F. (Pa.)
Windom, William (Minn.)
Winfield, Charles H. (N. Y.)
Woodbridge, Frederick E. (Vt.)
Wright, Edwin R. V. (N. J.)

The Fortieth Congress (1867-69)

Colfax, Schuyler (Ind.) Speaker.

Adams, George M. (Ky.)
Allison, William B. (Iowa)
Ames, Oakes (Mass.)
Anderson, George W. (Mo.)
Archer, Stevenson (Md.)
Arnell, Samuel M. (Tenn.)
Ashley, Delos R. (Nev.)
Ashley, James M. (Ohio)
Axtell, Samuel B. (Calif.)
Bailey, Alexander H. (N. Y.)
Baker, Jehu (Ill.)
Baldwin, John D. (Mass.)
Banks, Nathaniel P. (Mass.)
Barnes, Demas (N. Y.)
Barnum, William H. (Conn.)
Beaman, Fernando C. (Mich.)
Beatty, John (Ohio)
Beck, James B. (Ky.)
Benjamin, John F. (Mo.)
Benton, Jacob (N. H.)
Bingham, John A. (Ohio)
Blackburn, W. Jasper (La.)
Blaine, James G. (Maine)
Blair, Austin (Mich.)
Boles, Thomas (Ark.)
Boutwell, George S. (Mass.)
Bowen, Christopher C. (S. C.)
Boyden, Nathaniel (N. C.)
Boyer, Benjamin M. (Pa.)
Bromwell, Henry P. H. (Ill.)
Brooks, James (N. Y.)
Broomall, John M. (Pa.)
Buckland, Ralph P. (Ohio)
Buckley, Charles W. (Ala.)
Burr, Albert G. (Ill.)
Butler, Benjamin F. (Mass.)
Butler, Roderick R. (Tenn.)
Cake, Henry L. (Pa.)
Callis, John B. (Ala.)
Cary, Samuel F. (Ohio)
Chanler, John W. (N. Y.)
Churchill, John C. (N. Y.)
Clarke, Reader W. (Ohio)
Clarke, Sidney (Kans.)
Clift, Joseph W. (Ga.)
Cobb, Amasa (Wis.)
Coburn, John (Ind.)
Cook, Burton C. (Ill.)
Corley, M. Simeon (S. C.)
Cornell, Thomas (N. Y.)
Covode, John (Pa.)
Cullom, Shelby M. (Ill.)
Dawes, Henry L. (Mass.)
Delano, Columbus (Ohio)
Denison, Charles (Pa.)
Deweese, John T. (N. C.)
Dickey, Oliver J. (Pa.)
Dixon, Nathan F. (R. I.)
Dockery, Oliver H. (N. C.)
Dodge, Grenville M. (Iowa)
Donnelly, Ignatius (Minn.)
Driggs, John F. (Mich.)
Eckley, Ephraim R. (Ohio)
Edwards, William P. (Ga.)
Eggleston, Benjamin (Ohio)
Ela, Jacob H. (N. H.)
Eldridge, Charles A. (Wis.)
Eliot, Thomas D. (Mass.)
Elliott, James T. (Ark.)
Farnsworth, John F. (Ill.)
Ferriss, Orange (N. Y.)
Ferry, Thomas W. (Mich.)
Fields, William C. (N. Y.)
Finney, Darwin A. (Pa.)
Fox, John (N. Y.)
French, John R. (N. C.)
Garfield, James A. (Ohio)
Getz, J. Lawrence (Pa.)
Glossbrenner, Adam J. (Pa.)
Golladay, Jacob S. (Ky.)
Goss, James H. (S. C.)
Gove, Samuel F. (Ga.)
Gravely, Joseph J. (Mo.)
Griswold, John A. (N. Y.)
Grover, Asa P. (Ky.)
Haight, Charles (N. J.)
Halsey, George A. (N. J.)
Hamilton, Charles M. (Fla.)
Hamilton, Cornelius S. (Ohio)
Harding, Abner C. (Ill.)
Haughey, Thomas (Ala.)
Hawkins, Isaac R. (Tenn.)
Hayes, Rutherford B. (Ohio)
Heaton, David (N. C.)
Higby, William (Calif.)
Hill, John (N. J.)
Hinds, James (Ark.)
Hise, Elijah (Ky.)
Holman, William S. (Ind.)
Hopkins, Benjamin F. (Wis.)
Hotchkiss, Julius (Conn.)
Hooper, Samuel (Mass.)
Hubbard, Asahel W. (Iowa)
Hubbard, Chester D. (W. Va.)
Hubbard, Richard D. (Conn.)
Hulburd, Calvin T. (N. Y.)
Humphrey, James M. (N. Y.)
Hunter, Morton C. (Ind.)
Ingersoll, Ebon C. (Ill.)
Jenckes, Thomas A. (R. I.)
Johnson, James A. (Calif.)
Jones, Alexander H. (N. C.)
Jones, Thomas L. (Ky.)
Judd, Norman B. (Ill.)
Julian, George W. (Ind.)
Kelley, William D. (Pa.)
Kellogg, Francis W. (Ala.)
Kelsey, William H. (N. Y.)
Kerr, Michael C. (Ind.)
Ketcham, John H. (N. Y.)
Kitchen, Bethuel M. (W. Va.)
Knott, J. Proctor (Ky.)
Koontz, William H. (Pa.)
Laflin, Addison H. (N. Y.)
Lash, Israel G. (N. C.)
Lawrence, George V. (Pa.)
Lawrence, William (Ohio)
Lincoln, William S. (N. Y.)
Loan, Benjamin F. (Mo.)
Logan, John A. (Ill.)
Loughridge, William (Iowa)
Lynch, John (Maine)
McCarthy, Dennis (N. Y.)
McClurg, Joseph W. (Mo.)
McCormick, James R. (Mo.)
McCullough, Hiram (Md.)
McKee, Samuel (Ky.)
Mallory, Rufus (Oreg.)
Mann, James (La.)
Marshall, Samuel S. (Ill.)
Marvin, James M. (N. Y.)
Maynard, Horace (Tenn.)
Mercur, Ulysses (Pa.)
Miller, George F. (Pa.)
Moore, William (N. J.)
Moorehead, James K. (Pa.)
Morgan, George W. (Ohio)
Morrell, Daniel J. (Pa.)
Morrissey, John (N. Y.)
Mullins, James (Tenn.)
Mungen, William (Ohio)
Myers, Leonard (Pa.)
Newcomb, Carman A. (Mo.)
Newsham, Joseph P. (La.)
Niblack, William E. (Ind.)
Nicholson, John A. (Del.)
Noell, Thomas E. (Mo.)
Norris, Benjamin W. (Ala.)
Nunn, David A. (Tenn.)
O'Neill, Charles (Pa.)
Orth, Godlove S. (Ind.)
Paine, Halbert E. (Wis.)
Perham, Sidney (Maine)
Peters, John A. (Maine)
Pettis, S. Newton (Pa.)
Phelps, Charles E. (Md.)
Pierce, Charles W. (Ala.)
Pike, Frederick A. (Maine)
Pile, William A. (Mo.)
Plants, Tobias A. (Ohio)
Poland, Luke P. (Vt.)
Polsley, Daniel (W. Va.)
Pomeroy, Theodore M. (N. Y.)
Price, Hiram (Iowa)
Prince, Charles H. (Ga.)
Pruyn, John V. L. (N. Y.)
Randall, Samuel J. (Pa.)
Raum, Green B. (Ill.)
Robertson, William H. (N. Y.)
Robinson, William E. (N. Y.)
Roots, Logan H. (Ark.)
Ross, Lewis W. (Ill.)
Sawyer, Philetus (Wis.)
Schenck, Robert C. (Ohio)
Scofield, Glenni W. (Pa.)
Selye, Lewis (N. Y.)
Shanks, John P. C. (Ind.)
Shellabarger, Samuel (Ohio)
Sitgreaves, Charles (N. J.)
Smith, Worthington C. (Vt.)
Spalding, Rufus P. (Ohio)

Starkweather, Henry H. (Conn.)
Stevens, Aaron F. (N. H.)
Stevens, Thaddeus (Pa.)
Stewart, Thomas E. (N. Y.)
Stokes, William B. (Tenn.)
Stone, Frederick (Md.)
Stover, John H. (Mo.)
Sypher, J. Hale (La.)
Taber, Stephen (N. Y.)
Taffe, John (Nebr.)
Taylor, Caleb N. (Pa.)
Thomas, Francis (Md.)
Tift, Nelson (Ga.)
Trimble, John (Tenn.)
Trimble, Lawrence S. (Ky.)
Trowbridge, Rowland E. (Mich.)
Twichell, Ginery (Mass.)
Upson, Charles (Mich.)
Van Aernam, Henry (N. Y.)
Van Auken, Daniel M. (Pa.)
Van Horn, Burt (N. Y.)
Van Horn, Robert T. (Mo.)
Van Trump, Philadelph (Ohio)
Van Wyck, Charles H. (N. Y.)
Vidal, Michel (La.)
Ward, Hamilton (N. Y.)
Washburn, Cadwallader C. (Wis.)
Washburn, Henry D. (Ind.)
Washburn, William B. (Mass.)
Washburne, Elihu B. (Ill.)
Welker, Martin (Ohio)
Whittemore, B. Frank (S. C.)
Williams, Thomas (Pa.)
Williams, William (Ind.)
Wilson, James F. (Iowa)
Wilson, John T. (Ohio)
Wilson, Stephen F. (Pa.)
Windom, William (Minn.)
Wood, Fernando (N. Y.)
Woodbridge, Frederick E. (Vt.)
Woodward, George W. (Pa.)
Young, Pierce M. B. (Ga.)

The Forty-first Congress (1869-71)

Blaine, James G. (Maine) Speaker.

Adams, George M. (Ky.)
Allison, William B. (Iowa)
Ambler, Jacob A. (Ohio)
Ames, Oakes (Mass.)
Archer, Stevenson (Md.)
Armstrong, William H. (Pa.)
Arnell, Samuel M. (Tenn.)
Asper, Joel F. (Mo.)
Atwood, David (Wis.)
Axtell, Samuel B. (Calif.)
Ayer, Richard S. (Va.)
Bailey, Alexander H. (N. Y.)
Banks, Nathaniel P. (Mass.)
Barnum, William H. (Conn.)
Barry, Henry W. (Miss.)
Beaman, Fernando C. (Mich.)
Beatty, John (Ohio)
Beck, James B. (Ky.)
Benjamin, John F. (Mo.)
Bennett, David S. (N. Y.)
Benton, Jacob (N. H.)
Bethune, Marion (Ga.)
Biggs, Benjamin T. (Del.)
Bingham, John A. (Ohio)
Bird, John T. (N. J.)
Blair, Austin (Mich.)
Boles, Thomas (Ark.)
Booker, George W. (Va.)
Boutwell, George S. (Mass.)
Bowen, Christopher C. (S. C.)
Boyd, Sempronius H. (Mo.)
Brooks, George M. (Mass.)
Brooks, James (N. Y.)
Buck, Alfred E. (Ala.)
Buckley, Charles W. (Ala.)
Buffinton, James (Mass.)
Burchard, Horatio C. (Ill.)
Burdett, Samuel S. (Mo.)
Burr, Albert G. (Ill.)
Butler, Benjamin F. (Mass.)
Butler, Roderick R. (Tenn.)
Cake, Henry L. (Pa.)
Calkin, Hervey C. (N. Y.)
Cessna, John (Pa.)
Churchill, John C. (N. Y.)
Clark, William T. (Tex.)
Clarke, Sidney (Kans.)
Cleveland, Orestes (N. J.)
Cobb, Amasa (Wis.)
Cobb, Clinton L. (N. C.)
Coburn, John (Ind.)
Conger, Omar D. (Mich.)
Connor, John C. (Tex.)
Cook, Burton C. (Ill.)
Cook, Stephen A. (Ga.)
Corker, Stephen A. (Ga.)
Covode, John (Pa.)
Cowles, George W. (N. Y.)
Cox, Samuel S. (N. Y.)
Crebs, John M. (Ill.)
Cullom, Shelby M. (Ill.)
Darrall, Chester B. (La.)
Davis, Noah (N. Y.)
Dawes, Henry L. (Mass.)
Degener, Edward (Tex.)
Deweese, John T. (N. C.)
Dickey, Oliver J. (Pa.)
Dickinson, Edward F. (Ohio)
Dixon, Joseph (N. C.)
Dixon, Nathan F. (R. I.)
Dockery, Oliver H. (N. C.)
Donley, Joseph B. (Pa.)
Dox, Peter M. (Ala.)
Duke, Richard T. W. (Va.)
Duval, Isaac H. (W. Va.)
Dyer, David P. (Mo.)
Ela, Jacob H. (N. H.)
Eldridge, Charles A. (Wis.)
Farnsworth, John F. (Ill.)
Ferriss, Orange (N. Y.)
Ferry, Thomas W. (Mich.)
Finkelnburg, Gustavus A. (Mo.)
Fisher, John (N. Y.)
Fitch, Thomas (Nev.)
Fox, John (N. Y.)
Garfield, James A. (Ohio)
Getz, J. Lawrence (Pa.)
Gibson, James K. (Va.)
Gilfillan, Calvin W. (Pa.)
Golladay, Jacob S. (Ky.)
Greene, George W. (N. Y.)
Griswold, John A. (N. Y.)
Haight, Charles (N. J.)
Haldeman, Richard J. (Pa.)
Hale, Eugene (Maine)
Hambleton, Samuel (Md.)
Hamill, Patrick (Md.)
Hamilton, Charles M. (Fla.)
Harris, George E. (Miss.)
Hawkins, Isaac R. (Tenn.)
Hawley, John B. (Ill.)
Hay, John B. (Ill.)
Hays, Charles (Ala.)
Heaton, David (N. C.)
Heflin, Robert S. (Ala.)
Hill, John (N. J.)
Hoag, Truman H. (Ohio)
Hoar, George F. (Mass.)
Hoge, Solomon L. (S. C.)
Holman, William S. (Ind.)
Holmes, Charles H. (N. Y.)
Hooper, Samuel (Mass.)
Hopkins, Benjamin F. (Wis.)
Hotchkiss, Giles W. (N. Y.)
Ingersoll, Ebon C. (Ill.)
Jenckes, Thomas A. (R. I.)
Johnson, James A. (Calif.)
Jones, Alexander H. (N. C.)
Jones, Thomas L. (Ky.)
Judd, Norman B. (Ill.)
Julian, George W. (Ind.)
Kellogg, Stephen W. (Conn.)
Kelley, William D. (Pa.)
Kelsey, William H. (N. Y.)
Kerr, Michael C. (Ind.)
Ketcham, John H. (N. Y.)
Knapp, Charles (N. Y.)
Knott, J. Proctor (Ky.)
Laflin, Addison H. (N. Y.)
Lash, Israel G. (N. C.)
Lawrence, William (Ohio)
Lewis, Joseph H. (Ky.)
Logan, John A. (Ill.)
Long, Jefferson F. (Ga.)
Loughridge, William (Iowa)
Lynch, John (Maine)
McCarthy, Dennis (N. Y.)
McCormick, James R. (Mo.)
McCrary, George W. (Iowa)
McGrew, James C. (W. Va.)
McKee, George C. (Miss.)
McKenzie, Lewis (Va.)
McNeely, Thompson W. (Ill.)
Manning, John, Jr. (N. C.)
Marshall, Samuel S. (Ill.)
Mayham, Stephen L. (N. Y.)
Maynard, Horace (Tenn.)
Mercur, Ulysses (Pa.)
Milnes, William, Jr. (Va.)
Moffet, John (Pa.)
Moore, Eliakim H. (Ohio)
Moore, Jesse H. (Ill.)
Moore, William (N. J.)
Morey, Frank (La.)
Morgan, George W. (Ohio)
Morphis, Joseph L. (Miss.)
Morrell, Daniel J. (Pa.)
Morrill, Samuel P. (Maine)
Morrissey, John (N. Y.)
Mungen, William (Ohio)
Myers, Leonard (Pa.)
Negley, James S. (Pa.)
Newsham, Joseph P. (La.)
Niblack, William E. (Ind.)
O'Neill, Charles (Pa.)
Orth, Godlove S. (Ind.)
Packard, Jasper (Ind.)
Packer, John B. (Pa.)
Paine, Halbert E. (Wis.)
Paine, William W. (Ga.)
Palmer, Frank W. (Iowa)
Peck, Erasmus D. (Ohio)
Perce, Legrand W. (Miss.)
Peters, John A. (Maine)
Phelps, Darwin (Pa.)
Platt, James H., Jr. (Va.)
Poland, Luke P. (Vt.)
Pomeroy, Charles (Iowa)
Porter, Charles H. (Va.)
Potter, Clarkson N. (N. Y.)
Price, William P. (Ga.)
Prosser, William F. (Tenn.)
Rainey, Joseph H. (S. C.)
Randall, Samuel J. (Pa.)
Reading, John R. (Pa.)
Reeves, Henry A. (N. Y.)
Rice, John M. (Ky.)
Ridgway, Robert (Va.)
Rogers, Anthony A. C. (Ark.)
Roots, Logan H. (Ark.)
Sanford, Stephen (N. Y.)
Sargent, Aaron A. (Calif.)
Sawyer, Philetus (Wis.)
Schenck, Robert C. (Ohio)
Schumaker, John G. (N. Y.)
Scofield, Glenni W. (Pa.)
Shanks, John P. C. (Ind.)
Sheldon, Lionel A. (La.)
Sheldon, Porter (N. Y.)
Sherrod, William C. (Ala.)
Shober, Francis E. (N. C.)
Slocum, Henry W. (N. Y.)
Smith, John A. (Ohio)
Smith, Joseph S. (Oreg.)
Smith, William J. (Tenn.)
Smith, Worthington C. (Vt.)
Smyth, William (Iowa)
Starkweather, Henry H. (Conn.)
Stevens, Aaron F. (N. H.)
Stevenson, Job E. (Ohio)
Stiles, John D. (Pa.)
Stokes, William B. (Tenn.)
Stone, Frederick (Md.)
Stoughton, William L. (Mich.)
Strader, Peter W. (Ohio)
Strickland, Randolph (Mich.)
Strong, Julius L. (Conn.)
Swann, Thomas (Md.)
Sweeney, William N. (Ky.)
Sypher, J. Hale (La.)
Taffe, John (Nebr.)
Tanner, Adolphus H. (N. Y.)
Taylor, Caleb N. (Pa.)
Tillman, Lewis (Tenn.)
Townsend, Washington (Pa.)
Trimble, Lawrence S. (Ky.)
Twichell, Ginery (Mass.)
Tyner, James N. (Ind.)
Upson, William H. (Ohio)
Van Auken, Daniel M. (Pa.)
Van Horn, Robert T. (Mo.)
Van Trump, Philadelph (Ohio)
Van Wyck, Charles H. (N. Y.)
Voorhees, Daniel W. (Ind.)
Wallace, Alexander S. (S. C.)
Ward, Hamilton (N. Y.)
Washburn, Cadwallader C. (Wis.)
Washburn, William B. (Mass.)
Washburne, Elihu B. (Ill.)
Welker, Martin (Ohio)
Wells, Erastus (Mo.)
Wheeler, William A. (N. Y.)
Whiteley, Richard H. (Ga.)
Whitmore, George W. (Tex.)
Whittemore, B. Frank (S. C.)
Wilkinson, Morton S. (Minn.)
Willard, Charles W. (Vt.)
Williams, William (Ind.)
Wilson, Eugene M. (Minn.)
Wilson, John T. (Ohio)
Winans, James J. (Ohio)
Winchester, Boyd (Ky.)
Witcher, John S. (W. Va.)
Wolf, William P. (Iowa)
Wood, Fernando (N. Y.)
Woodward, George W. (Pa.)
Young, Pierce M. B. (Ga.)

The Forty-second Congress (1871-73)

Blaine, James G. (Maine) Speaker.

Acker, Ephraim L. (Pa.)
Adams, George M. (Ky.)
Ambler, Jacob A. (Ohio)
Ames, Oakes (Mass.)
Archer, Stevenson (Md.)
Arthur, William E. (Ky.)
Averill, John T. (Minn.)
Banks, Nathaniel P. (Mass.)
Barber, J. Allen (Wis.)
Barnum, William H. (Conn.)
Barry, Henry W. (Miss.)
Beatty, John (Ohio)
Beck, Erasmus W. (Ga.)
Beck, James B. (Ky.)
Bell, Samuel N. (N. H.)
Beveridge, John L. (Ill.)
Bigby, John S. (Ga.)
Biggs, Benjamin T. (Del.)
Bingham, John A. (Ohio)
Bird, John T. (N. J.)
Blair, Austin (Mich.)
Blair, James G. (Mo.)
Boarman, Aleck (La.)
Boles, Thomas (Ark.)
Braxton, Elliott M. (Va.)
Bright, John M. (Tenn.)
Brooks, George M. (Mass.)
Brooks, James (N. Y.)
Buckley, Charles W. (Ala.)
Buffinton, James (Mass.)
Bunnell, Frank C. (Pa.)
Burchard, Horatio C. (Ill.)
Burdett, Samuel S. (Mo.)
Butler, Benjamin F. (Mass.)
Butler, Roderick R. (Tenn.)
Caldwell, Robert P. (Tenn.)
Campbell, Lewis D. (Ohio)
Carroll, John M. (N. Y.)
Clark, William T. (Tex.)
Clarke, Freeman (N. Y.)
Cobb, Clinton L. (N. C.)
Coburn, John (Ind.)
Coghlan, John M. (Calif.)
Comingo, Abram (Mo.)
Conger, Omar D. (Mich.)
Conner, John C. (Tex.)
Cook, Burton C. (Ill.)
Cotton, Aylett R. (Iowa)
Cox, Samuel S. (N. Y.)
Crebs, John M. (Ill.)
Creely, John V. (Pa.)
Critcher, John (Va.)
Crocker, Alvah (Mass.)
Crossland, Edward (Ky.)
Darrell, Chester B. (La.)
Davis, John J. (W. Va.)
Dawes, Henry L. (Mass.)
De Large, Robert C. (S. C.)
Dickey, Oliver J. (Pa.)
Dodds, Ozro J. (Ohio)
Donnan, William G. (Iowa)
Dox, Peter M. (Ala.)
DuBose, Dudley M. (Ga.)
Duell, R. Holland (N. Y.)
Duke, Richard T. W. (Va.)
Dunnell, Mark H. (Minn.)
Eames, Benjamin T. (R. I.)
Edwards, John (Ark.)
Eldridge, Charles A. (Wis.)
Elliott, Robert B. (S. C.)
Ely, Smith, Jr. (N. Y.)
Esty, Constantine C. (Mass.)

Farnsworth, John F. (Ill.)
Farwell, Charles B. (Ill.)
Finkelnburg, Gustavus A. (Mo.)
Forker, Samuel C. (N. J.)
Foster, Charles (Ohio)
Foster, Henry D. (Pa.)
Foster, Wilder D. (Mich.)
Frye, William P. (Maine)
Garfield, James A. (Ohio)
Garrett, Abraham E. (Tenn.)
Getz, J. Lawrence (Pa.)
Giddings, De Witt C. (Tex.)
Golladay, Edward I. (Tenn.)
Goodrich, Milo (N. Y.)
Griffith, Samuel (Pa.)
Haldeman, Richard J. (Pa.)
Hale, Eugene (Maine)
Halsey, George A. (N. J.)
Hambleton, Samuel (Md.)
Hancock, John (Tex.)
Handley, William A. (Ala.)
Hanks, James M. (Ark.)
Harmer, Alfred C. (Pa.)
Harper, James C. (N. C.)
Harris, George E. (Miss.)
Harris, John T. (Va.)
Havens, Harrison E. (Mo.)
Hawley, John B. (Ill.)
Hawley, Joseph R. (Conn.)
Hay, John B. (Ill.)
Hays, Charles (Ala.)
Hazelton, Gerry W. (Wis.)
Hazelton, John W. (N. J.)
Hereford, Frank (W. Va.)
Herndon, William S. (Tex.)
Hibbard, Ellery A. (N. H.)
Hill, John (N. J.)
Hoar, George F. (Mass.)
Holman, William S. (Ind.)
Hooper, Samuel (Mass.)
Houghton, Sherman O. (Calif.)
Kelley, William D. (Pa.)
Kellogg, Stephen W. (Conn.)
Kendall, Charles W. (Nev.)
Kerr, Michael C. (Ind.)
Ketcham, John H. (N. Y.)
Killinger, John W. (Pa.)
King, Andrew (Mo.)
Kinsella, Thomas (N. Y.)
Lamison, Charles N. (Ohio)
Lamport, William H. (N. Y.)
Lansing, William E. (N. Y.)
Leach, James M. (N. C.)
Lewis, Joseph H. (Ky.)
Lowe, David P. (Kans.)
Lynch, John (Maine)
McClelland, William (Pa.)
McCormick, James R. (Mo.)
McCrary, George W. (Iowa)
McGrew, James C. (W. Va.).
McHenry, Henry D. (Ky.)
MacIntyre, Archibald T. (Ga.)
McJunkin, Ebenezer (Pa.)
McKee, George C. (Miss.)
McKinney, John F. (Ohio)
McNeely, Thompson, T. W. (Ill.)
Manson, Mahlon D. (Ind.)
Marshall, Samuel S. (Ill.)
Maynard, Horace (Tenn.)
Mercur, Ulysses (Pa.)
Merriam, Clinton L. (N. Y.)
Merrick, William M. (Md.)
Meyers, Benjamin F. (Pa.)
Mitchell, Alexander (Wis.)
Monroe, James (Ohio)
Moore, Jesse H. (Ill.)
Morey, Frank (La.)
Morgan, George W. (Ohio)
Morphis, Joseph L. (Miss.)
Myers, Leonard (Pa.)
Negley, James S. (Pa.)
Niblack, Silas L. (Fla.)
Niblack, William E. (Ind.)
Orr, Jackson (Iowa)
Packard, Jasper (Ind.)
Packer, John B. (Pa.)
Palmer, Frank W. (Iowa)
Parker, Hosea W. (N. H.)
Parker, Isaac C. (Mo.)
Peck, Erasmus D. (Ohio)
Pendleton, James M. (R. I.)
Perce, Legrand W. (Miss.)
Perry, Aaron F. (Ohio)
Perry, Eli (N. Y.)
Peters, John A. (Maine)
Platt, James H., Jr. (Va.)
Poland, Luke P. (Vt.)
Porter, Charles H. (Va.)
Potter, Clarkson N. (N. Y.)
Price, William P. (Ga.)
Prindle, Elizur H. (N. Y.)
Rainey, Joseph H. (S. C.)
Randall, Samuel J. (Pa.)
Read, William B. (Ky.)
Rice, Edward Y. (Ill.)
Rice, John M. (Ky.)
Ritchie, John (Md.)
Roberts, Ellis H. (N. Y.)
Roberts, William R. (N. Y.)
Robinson, James C. (Ill.)
Rogers, John (N. Y.)
Rogers, Sion H. (N. C.)
Roosevelt, Robert B. (N. Y.)
Rusk, Jeremiah M. (Wis.)
St. John, Charles (N. Y.)
Sargent, Aaron A. (Calif.)
Sawyer, Philetus (Wis.)
Scofield, Glenni W. (Pa.)
Seeley, John E. (N. Y.)
Sessions, Walter L. (N. Y.)
Shanks, John P. C. (Ind.)
Sheldon, Lionel A. (La.)
Shellabarger, Samuel (Ohio)
Sherwood, Henry (Pa.)
Shober, Francis E. (N. C.)
Shoemaker, Lazarus D. (Pa.)
Slater, James H. (Oreg.)
Slocum, Henry W. (N. Y.)
Sloss, Joseph H. (Ala.)
Smith, H. Boardman (N. Y.)
Smith, John A. (Ohio)
Smith, Worthington C. (Vt.)
Snapp, Henry (Ill.)
Snyder, Oliver P. (Ark.)
Speer, R. Milton (Pa.)
Speer, Thomas J. (Ga.)
Sprague, William P. (Ohio)
Starkweather, Henry H. (Conn.)
Stevens, Bradford N. (Ill.)
Stevenson, Job E. (Ohio)
Storm, John B. (Pa.)
Stoughton, William L. (Mich.)
Stowell, William H. H. (Va.)
Strong, Julius L. (Conn.)
Sutherland, Jabez G. (Mich.)
Swann, Thomas (Md.)
Sypher, J. Hale (La.)
Taffe, John (Nebr.)
Terry, William (Va.)
Thomas, Charles R. (N. C.)
Townsend, Dwight (N. Y.)
Townsend, Washington (Pa.)
Turner, Benjamin S. (Ala.)
Tuthill, Joseph H. (N. Y.)
Twichell, Ginery (Mass.)
Tyner, James N. (Ind.)
Upson, William H. (Ohio)
Van Trump, Philadelph (Ohio)
Vaughn, William W. (Tenn.)
Voorhees, Daniel W. (Ind.)
Waddell, Alfred M. (N. C.)
Wakeman, Seth (N. Y.)
Walden, Madison M. (Iowa)
Waldron, Henry (Mich.)
Wallace, Alexander S. (S. C.)
Walls, Josiah T. (Fla.)
Warren, Joseph M. (N. Y.)
Washburn, William B. (Mass.)
Wells, Erastus (Mo.)
Wheeler, William A. (N. Y.)
Whiteley, Richard H. (Ga.)
Whitthorne, Washington C. (Tenn.)
Willard, Charles W. (Vt.)
Williams, William (Ind.)
Williams, William (N. Y.)
Wilson, Jeremiah M. (Ind.)
Wilson, John T. (Ohio)
Winchester, Boyd (Ky.)
Wood, Fernando (N. Y.)
Young, Pierce M. B. (Ga.)

The Forty-third Congress (1873-75)

Blaine, James G. (Maine) Speaker.

Adams, George M. (Ky.)
Albert, William J. (Md.)
Albright, Charles (Pa.)
Archer, Stevenson (Md.)
Arthur, William E. (Ky.)
Ashe, Thomas S. (N. C.)
Atkins, John D. C. (Tenn.)
Averill, John T. (Minn.)
Banning, Henry B. (Ohio)
Barber, J. Allen (Wis.)
Barnum, William H. (Conn.)
Barrere, Granville (Ill.)
Barry, Henry W. (Miss.)
Bass, Lyman K. (N. Y.)
Beck, James B. (Ky.)
Begole, Josiah W. (Mich.)
Bell, Hiram P. (Ga.)
Berry, John (Ohio)
Biery, James S. (Pa.)
Bland, Richard P. (Mo.)
Blount, James H. (Ga.)
Bowen, Rees T. (Va.)
Bradley, Nathan B. (Mich.)
Bright, John M. (Tenn.)
Bromberg, Frederick G. (Ala.)
Brown, John Y. (Ky.)
Buckner, Aylett H. (Mo.)
Buffinton, James (Mass.)
Bundy, Hezekiah S. (Ohio)
Burchard, Horatio C. (Ill.)
Burleigh, John H. (Maine)
Burrows, Julius C. (Mich.)
Butler, Benjamin F. (Mass.)
Butler, Roderick R. (Tenn.)
Cain, Richard H. (S. C.)
Caldwell, John H. (Ala.)
Cannon, Joseph G. (Ill.)
Carpenter, Lewis C. (S. C.)
Cason, Thomas J. (Ind.)
Caulfield, Bernard G. (Ill.)
Cessna, John (Pa.)
Chittenden, Simeon B. (N. Y.)
Clark, Amos, Jr. (N. J.)
Clark, John B., Jr. (Mo.)
Clarke, Freeman (N. Y.)
Clayton, Charles (Calif.)
Clements, Isaac (Ill.)
Clymer, Hiester (Pa.)
Cobb, Clinton L. (N. C.)
Cobb, Stephen A. (Kans.)
Coburn, John (Ind.)
Comingo, Abram (Mo.)
Conger, Omar D. (Mich.)
Cook, Philip (Ga.)
Corwin, Franklin (Ill.)
Cotton, Aylett R. (Iowa)
Cox, Samuel S. (N. Y.)
Creamer, Thomas J. (N. Y.)
Crittenden, Thomas T. (Mo.)
Crocker, Alvah (Mass.)
Crooke, Philip S. (N. Y.)
Crossland, Edward (Ky.)
Crounse, Lorenzo (Nebr.)
Crutchfield, William (Tenn.)
Curtis, Carlton B. (Pa.)
Danford, Lorenzo (Ohio)
Darrall, Chester B. (La.)
Davis, Alexander M. (Va.)
Davis, John J. (W. Va.)
Dawes, Henry L. (Mass.)
De Witt, David M. (N. Y.)
Dobbins, Samuel A. (N. J.)
Donnan, William G. (Iowa)
Duell, R. Holland (N. Y.)
Dunnell, Mark H. (Minn.)
Durham, Milton J. (Ky.)
Eames, Benjamin T. (R. I.)
Eden, John R. (Ill.)
Eldridge, Charles A. (Wis.)
Elliott, Robert B. (S. C.)
Farwell, Charles B. (Ill.)
Field, Moses W. (Mich.)
Finck, William E. (Ohio)
Fort, Greenbury L. (Ill.)
Foster, Charles (Ohio)
Freeman, James C. (Ga.)
Frye, William P. (Maine)
Garfield, James A. (Ohio)
Giddings, De Witt C. (Tex.)
Glover, John M. (Mo.)
Gooch, Daniel W. (Mass.)
Gunckel, Lewis B. (Ohio)
Gunter, Thomas M. (Ark.)
Hagans, John M. (W. Va.)
Hale, Eugene (Maine)
Hale, Robert S. (N. Y.)
Hamilton, Robert (N. J.)
Hancock, John (Tex.)
Harmer, Alfred C. (Pa.)
Harris, Benjamin W. (Mass.)
Harris, Henry R. (Ga.)
Harris, John T. (Va.)
Harrison, Horace H. (Tenn.)
Hatcher, Robert A. (Mo.)
Hathorn, Henry H. (N. Y.)
Havens, Harrison E. (Mo.)
Hawley, John B. (Ill.)
Hawley, Joseph R. (Conn.)
Hays, Charles (Ala.)
Hazelton, Gerry W. (Wis.)
Hazelton, John W. (N. J.)
Hendee, George W. (Vt.)
Hereford, Frank (W. Va.)
Herndon, William S. (Tex.)
Hersey, Samuel (Maine)
Hoar, Ebenezer R. (Mass.)
Hoar, George F. (Mass.)
Hodges, Asa (Ark.)
Holman, William S. (Ind.)
Hooper, Samuel (Mass.)
Hoskins, George G. (N. Y.)
Houghton, Sherman O. (Calif.)
Howe, Albert R. (Miss.)
Hubbell, Jay A. (Mich.)
Hunter, Morton C. (Ind.)
Hunton, Eppa (Va.)
Hurlbut, Stephen A. (Ill.)
Hyde, Ira B. (Mo.)
Hynes, William J. (Ark.)
Jewett, Hugh J. (Ohio)
Kasson, John A. (Iowa)
Kelley, William D. (Pa.)
Kellogg, Stephen W. (Conn.)
Kendall, Charles W. (Nev.)
Killinger, John W. (Pa.)
Knapp, Robert M. (Ill.)
Lamar, Lucius Q. C. (Miss.)
Lamison, Charles N. (Ohio)
Lamport, William H. (N. Y.)
Lansing, William E. (N. Y.)
Lawrence, Effingham (La.)
Lawrence, William (Ohio)
Lawson, John D. (N. Y.)
Leach, James M. (N. C.)
Lewis, Barbour (Tenn.)
Lofland, James R. (Del.)
Loughridge, William (Iowa)
Lowe, David P. (Kans.)
Lowndes, Lloyd, Jr. (Md.)
Luttrell, John K. (Calif.)
Lynch, John R. (Miss.)
McCrary, George W. (Iowa)
McDill, Alexander S. (Wis.)
McDill, James W. (Iowa)
MacDougall, Clinton D. (N.Y.)
McJunkin, Ebenezer (Pa.)
McKee, George C. (Miss.)
McLean, William P. (Tex.)
McNulta, John (Ill.)
Magee, John A. (Pa.)
Marshall, Samuel S. (Ill.)
Martin, James S. (Ill.)
Maynard, Horace (Tenn.)
Mellish, David B. (N. Y.)
Merriam, Clinton L. (N. Y.)
Milliken, Charles W. (Ky.)
Mills, Roger Q. (Tex.)
Mitchell, Alexander (Wis.)
Monroe, James (Ohio)
Moore, William S. (Pa.)
Morey, Frank (La.)
Morrison, William R. (Ill.)
Myers, Leonard (Pa.)
Neal, Lawrence T. (Ohio)
Negley, James S. (Pa.)
Nesmith, James W. (Oreg.)
Niblack, William E. (Ind.)
Niles, Jason (Miss.)
Nunn, David A. (Tenn.)
O'Brien, William J. (Md.)
O'Neill, Charles (Pa.)
Orr, Jackson (Iowa)
Orth, Godlove S. (Ind.)
Packard, Jasper (Ind.)
Packer, John B. (Pa.)
Page, Horace F. (Calif.)
Parker, Hosea W. (N. H.)
Parker, Isaac C. (Mo.)
Parsons, Richard C. (Ohio)
Pelham, Charles (Ala.)
Pendleton, James M. (R. I.)
Perry, Eli (N. Y.)
Phelps, William W. (N. J.)
Phillips, William A. (Kans.)
Pierce, Henry L. (Mass.)
Pike, Austin F. (N. H.)
Platt, James H., Jr. (Va.)
Platt, Thomas C. (N. Y.)
Poland, Luke P. (Vt.)
Potter, Clarkson N. (N. Y.)

Pratt, Henry O. (Iowa)
Purman, William J. (Fla.)
Rainey, Joseph H. (S. C.)
Randall, Samuel J. (Pa.)
Ransier, Alonzo J. (S. C.)
Rapier, James T. (Ala.)
Rawls, Morgan (Ga.)
Ray, William H. (Ill.)
Read, William B. (Ky.)
Rice, John B. (Ill.)
Richmond, Hiram L. (Pa.)
Robbins, William M. (N. C.)
Roberts, Ellis H. (N. Y.)
Roberts, William R. (N. Y.)
Robinson, James C. (Ill.)
Robinson, James W. (Ohio)
Ross, Sobieski (Pa.)
Rusk, Jeremiah M. (Wis.)
St. John, Charles (N. Y.)
Sawyer, Philetus (Wis.)
Sayler, Henry B. (Ind.)
Sayler, Milton (Ohio)
Schell, Richard (N. Y.)
Schumaker, John G. (N. Y.)
Scofield, Glenni W. (Pa.)
Scudder, Henry J. (N. Y.)
Scudder, Isaac W. (N. J.)
Sener, James B. (Va.)
Sessions, Walter L. (N. Y.)
Shanks, John P. C. (Ind.)
Sheats, Charles C. (Ala.)
Sheldon, Lionel A. (La.)
Sheridan, George A. (La.)
Sherwood, Isaac R. (Ohio)
Shoemaker, Lazarus D. (Pa.)
Sloan, Andrew (Ga.)
Sloss, Joseph H. (Ala.)
Small, William B. (N. H.)
Smart, James S. (N. Y.)
Smith, A. Herr (Pa.)
Smith, George L. (La.)
Smith, H. Boardman (N. Y.)
Smith, J. Ambler (Va.)
Smith, John Q. (Ohio)
Smith, William A. (N. C.)
Snyder, Oliver P. (Ark.)
Southard, Milton I. (Ohio)
Speer, R. Milton (Pa.)
Sprague, William P. (Ohio)
Stanard, Edwin O. (Mo.)
Staniford, Elisha D. (Ky.)
Starkweather, Henry H. (Conn.)
Stephens, Alexander H. (Ga.)
Stevens, Charles A. (Mass.)
Stone, William H. (Mo.)
Storm, John B. (Pa.)
Stowell, William H. H. (Va.)
Strait, Horace B. (Minn.)
Strawbridge, James D. (Pa.)
Swann, Thomas (Md.)
Sypher, J. Hale (La.)
Taylor, Alexander W. (Pa.)
Thomas, Charles R. (N. C.)
Thomas, Christopher Y. (Va.)
Thompson, John M. (Pa.)
Thornburgh, Jacob M. (Tenn.)
Todd, Lemuel (Pa.)
Townsend, Washington (Pa.)
Tremain, Lyman (N. Y.)
Tyner, James N. (Ind.)
Vance, Robert V. (N. C.)
Waddell, Alfred M. (N. C.)
Waldron, Henry (Mich.)
Wallace, Alexander S. (S. C.)
Walls, Josiah T. (Fla.)
Ward, Jasper D. (Ill.)
Ward, Marcus L. (N. J.)
Wells, Erastus (Mo.)
Wheeler, William A. (N. Y.)
White, Alexander (Ala.)
Whitehead, Thomas (Va.)
Whitehouse, John O. (N. Y.)
Whiteley, Richard H. (Ga.)
Whitthorne, Washington C. (Tenn.)
Wilber, David (N. Y.)
Willard, Charles W. (Vt.)
Willard, George (Mich.)
Williams, Charles G. (Wis.)
Williams, John M. S. (Mass.)
Williams, William (Ind.)
Williams, William B. (Mich.)
Willie, Asa H. (Tex.)
Wilson, Ephraim K. (Md.)
Wilson, James (Iowa)
Wilson, Jeremiah M. (Ind.)
Wilshire, William W. (Ark.)
Wolfe, Simeon K. (Ind.)
Wood, Fernando (N. Y.)
Woodworth, Laurin D. (Ohio)
Young, John D. (Ky.)
Young, Pierce M. B. (Ga.)

The Forty-fourth Congress (1875-77)

Kerr, Michael C. (Ind.)
Randall, Samuel J. (Pa.)
Speakers.

Abbott, Josiah G. (Mass.)
Adams, Charles H. (N. Y.)
Ainsworth, Lucien L. (Iowa)
Anderson, William B. (Ill.)
Ashe, Thomas S. (N. C.)
Atkins, John D. C. (Tenn.)
Bagby, John C. (Ill.)
Bagley, George A. (N. Y.)
Bagley, John H., Jr. (N. Y.)
Baker, John H. (Ind.)
Baker, William H. (N. Y.)
Ballou, Latimer W. (R. I.)
Banks, Nathaniel P. (Mass.)
Banning, Henry B. (Ohio)
Barnum, William H. (Conn.)
Bass, Lyman K. (N. Y.)
Beebe, George M. (N. Y.)
Belford, James B. (Colo.)
Bell, Samuel N. (N. H.)
Blackburn, Joseph C. S. (Ky.)
Blaine, James G. (Maine)
Blair, Henry W. (N. H.)
Bland, Richard P. (Mo.)
Bliss, Archibald M. (N. Y.)
Blount, James H. (Ga.)
Boone, Andrew R. (Ky.)
Bradford, Taul (Ala.)
Bradley, Nathan B. (Mich.)
Bright, John M. (Tenn.)
Brown, John Y. (Ky.)
Brown, William R. (Kans.)
Buckner, Aylett H. (Mo.)
Burchard, Horatio C. (Ill.)
Burchard, Samuel D. (Wis.)
Burleigh, John H. (Maine)
Buttz, Charles W. (S. C.)
Cabell, George C. (Va.)
Caldwell, John H. (Ala.)
Caldwell William P. (Tenn.)
Campbell, Alexander (Ill.)
Candler, Milton A. (Ga.)
Cannon, Joseph G. (Ill.)
Carr, Nathan T. (Ind.)
Cason, Thomas J. (Ind.)
Caswell, Lucien B. (Wis.)
Cate, George W. (Wis.)
Caulfield, Bernard G. (Ill.)
Chapin, Chester W. (Mass.)
Chittenden, Simeon B. (N. Y.)
Clark, John B., Jr. (Mo.)
Clarke, John B. (Ky.)
Clymer, Hiester (Pa.)
Cochrane, Alexander G. (Pa.)
Collins, Francis D. (Pa.)
Conger, Omar D. (Mich.)
Cook, Philip (Ga.)
Cowan, Jacob P. (Ohio)
Cox, Samuel S. (N. Y.)
Crapo, William W. (Mass.)
Crounse, Lorenzo (Nebr.)
Culberson, David R. (Tex.)
Cutler, Augustus W. (N. J.)
Danford, Lorenzo (Ohio)
Darrall, Chester B. (La.)
Davis, Joseph J. (N. C.)
Davy, John M. (N. Y.)
De Bolt, Rezin A. (Mo.)
Denison, Dudley C. (Vt.)
Dibrell, George G. (Tenn.)
Dobbins, Samuel A. (N. J.)
Douglas, Beverly B. (Va.)
Dunnell, Mark H. (Minn.)
Durand, George H. (Mich.)
Durham, Milton J. (Ky.)
Eames, Benjamin T. (R. I.)
Eden, John R. (Ill.)
Egbert, Albert G. (Pa.)
Ellis, E. John (La.)
Ely, Smith, Jr. (N. Y.)
Evans, James L. (Ind.)
Farwell, Charles B. (Ill.)
Faulkner, Charles J. (W. Va.)
Felton, William H. (Ga.)
Field, David D. (N. Y.)
Finley, Jesse J. (Fla.)
Flye, Edwin (Maine)
Forney, William H. (Ala.)
Fort, Greenbury L. (Ill.)
Foster, Charles (Ohio)
Franklin, Benjamin J. (Mo.)
Freeman, Chapman (Pa.)
Frost, Rufus S. (Mass.)
Frye, William P. (Maine)
Fuller, Benoni S. (Ind.)
Garfield, James A. (Ohio)
Gause, Lucien C. (Ark.)
Gibson, Randall L. (La.)
Glover, John M. (Mo.)
Goode, John, Jr. (Va.)
Goodin, John R. (Kans.)
Gunter, Thomas M. (Ark.)
Hale, Eugene (Maine)
Hamilton, Andrew H. (Ind.)
Hamilton, Robert (N. J.)
Hancock, John (Tex.)
Haralson, Jeremiah (Ala.)
Hardenbergh, Augustus A. (N. J.)
Harris, Benjamin W. (Mass.)
Harris, Henry R. (Ga.)
Harris, John T. (Va.)
Harrison, Carter H. (Ill.)
Hartridge, Julian (Ga.)
Hartzell, William (Ill.)
Hatcher, Robert A. (Mo.)
Hathorn, Henry H. (N. Y.)
Hayes, Charles (Ala.)
Haymond, William S. (Ind.)
Hendee, George W. (Vt.)
Henderson, Thomas J. (Ill.)
Henkle, Eli J. (Md.)
Hereford, Frank (W. Va.)
Hewitt, Abram S. (N. Y.)
Hewitt, Goldsmith W. (Ala.)
Hill, Benjamin H. (Ga.)
Hoar, George F. (Mass.)
Hoge, Solomon L. (S. C.)
Holman, William S. (Ind.)
Hooker, Charles E. (Miss.)
Hopkins, James H. (Pa.)
Hoskins, George G. (N. Y.)
House, John F. (Tenn.)
Hubbell, Jay A. (Mich.)
Humphreys, Andrew (Ind.)
Hunter, Morton C. (Ind.)
Hunton, Eppa (Va.)
Hurd, Frank H. (Ohio)
Hurlbut, Stephen A. (Ill.)
Hyman, John A. (N. C.)
Jenks, George A. (Pa.)
Jones, Frank (N. H.)
Jones, Thomas L. (Ky.)
Joyce, Charles H. (Vt.)
Kasson, John A. (Iowa)
Kehr, Edward C. (Mo.)
Kelley, William D. (Pa.)
Ketchum, Winthrop W. (Pa.)
Kimball, Alanson M. (Wis.)
King, William S. (Minn.)
Knott, J. Proctor (Ky.)
Lamar, Lucius Q. C. (Miss.)
Landers, Franklin (Ind.)
Landers, George M. (Conn.)
Lane, La Fayette (Oreg.)
Lapham, Elbridge G. (N. Y.)
Lawrence, William (Ohio)
Leavenworth, Elias W. (N.Y.)
Le Moyne, John V. (Ill.)
Levy, William M. (La.)
Lewis, B. B. (Ala.)
Lord, Scott (N. Y.)
Luttrell, John K. (Calif.)
Lynch, John R. (Miss.)
Lynde, William P. (Wis.)
McCrary, George W. (Iowa)
McDill, James W. (Iowa)
MacDougall, Clinton D. (N.Y.)
McFarland, William (Tenn.)
Mackey, Edmund W. M. (S.C.)
Mackey, Levi A. (Pa.)
McMahon, John A. (Ohio)
Magoon, Henry S. (Wis.)
Maish, Levi (Pa.)
Meade, Edwin R. (N. Y.)
Metcalf, Henry B. (N. Y.)
Miller, Samuel F. (N. Y.)
Milliken, Charles W. (Ky.)
Mills, Roger Q. (Tex.)
Money, Hernando D. (Miss.)
Monroe, James (Ohio)
Morey, Frank (La.)
Morgan, Charles H. (Mo.)
Morrison, William R. (Ill.)
Mutchler, William (Pa.)
Nash, Charles E. (La.)
Neal, Lawrence T. (Ohio)
New, Jeptha D. (Ind.)
Norton, Nelson I. (N. Y.)
O'Brien, William J. (Md.)
Odell, N. Holmes (N. Y.)
Oliver, S. Addison (Iowa)
O'Neill, Charles (Pa.)
Packer, John B. (Pa.)
Page, Horace F. (Calif.)
Parsons, Edward Y. (Ky.)
Payne, Henry B. (Ohio)
Phelps, James (Conn.)
Philips, John F. (Mo.)
Phillips, William A. (Kans.)
Pierce, Henry L. (Mass.)
Piper, William A. (Calif.)
Plaisted, Harris M. (Maine)
Platt, Thomas C. (N. Y.)
Poppleton, Earley F. (Ohio)
Potter, Allen (Mich.)
Powell, Joseph (Pa.)
Pratt, Henry O. (Iowa)
Purman, William J. (Fla.)
Rainey, Joseph H. (S. C.)
Rea, David (Mo.)
Reagan, John H. (Tex.)
Reilly, James B. (Pa.)
Reilly, John (Pa.)
Rice, Americus V. (Ohio)
Riddle, Haywood Y. (Tenn.)
Robbins, John (Pa.)
Robbins, William M. (N. C.)
Roberts, Charles B. (Md.)
Robinson, Milton S. (Ind.)
Ross, Miles (N. J.)
Ross, Sobieski (Pa.)
Rusk, Jeremiah M. (Wis.)
Sampson, Ezekiel S. (Iowa)
Savage, John S. (Ohio)
Sayler, Milton (Ohio)
Scales, Alfred M. (N. C.)
Schleicher, Gustave (Tex.)
Schumaker, John G. (N. Y.)
Seelye, Julius H. (Mass.)
Sheakley, James (Pa.)
Singleton, Otho R. (Miss.)
Sinnickson, Clement H. (N.J.)
Slemons, William F. (Ark.)
Smalls, Robert (S. C.)
Smith, A. Herr (Pa.)
Smith, William E. (Ga.)
Southard, Milton I. (Ohio)
Sparks, William A. J. (Ill.)
Spencer, William B. (La.)
Springer, William M. (Ill.)
Stanton, William H. (Pa.)
Starkweather, Henry H. (Conn.)
Stenger, William S. (Pa.)
Stephens, Alexander H. (Ga.)
Stevenson, Adlai E. (Ill.)
Stone, William H. (Mo.)
Stowell, William H. H. (Va.)
Strait, Horace B. (Minn.)
Swann, Thomas (Md.)
Tarbox, John K. (Mass.)
Teese, Frederick H. (N. J.)
Terry, William (Va.)
Thomas, Philip F. (Md.)
Thompson, Charles P. (Mass.)
Thornburgh, Jacob M. (Tenn.)
Throckmorton, James W. (Tex.)
Townsend, Martin I. (N. Y.)
Townsend, Washington (Pa.)
Tucker, John R. (Va.)
Tufts, John Q. (Iowa)
Turney, Jacob (Pa.)
Vance, John L. (Ohio)
Vance, Robert B. (N. C.)
Van Vorhes, Nelson H. (Ohio)
Waddell, Alfred M. (N. C.)
Wait, John T. (Conn.)
Waldron, Henry (Mich.)
Walker, Charles C. B. (N. Y.)
Walker, Gilbert C. (Va.)
Wallace, Alexander S. (S. C.)
Wallace, John W. (Pa.)
Walling, Ansel T. (Ohio)
Walls, Josiah T. (Fla.)
Walsh, William (Md.)
Ward, Elijah (N. Y.)
Warner, Levi (Conn.)
Warren, William W. (Mass.)
Watterson, Henry (Ky.)
Wells, Erastus (Mo.)
Wells, G. Wiley (Miss.)
Wheeler, William A. (N. Y.)
White, John D. (Ky.)
Whitehouse, John O. (N. Y.)
Whiting, Richard H. (Ill.)

Whitthorne, Washington C. (Tenn.)
Wigginton, Peter D. (Calif.)
Wike, Scott (Ill.)
Willard, George (Mich.)
Williams, Alpheus S. (Mich.)
Williams, Andrew (N. Y.)
Williams, Charles G. (Wis.)
Williams, James (Del.)
Williams, James D. (Ind.)
Williams, Jeremiah N. (Ala.)
Williams, William B. (Mich.)
Willis, Benjamin A. (N. Y.)
Wilshire, William W. (Ark.)
Wilson, Benjamin (W. Va.)
Wilson, James (Iowa)
Wood, Alan, Jr. (Pa.)
Wood, Fernando (N. Y.)
Woodburn, William (Nev.)
Woodworth, Laurin D. (Ohio)
Yeates, Jesse J. (N. C.)
Young, H. Casey (Tenn.)

The Forty-fifth Congress (1877-79)

Randall, Samuel J. (Pa.) Speaker.

Acklen, Joseph H. (La.)
Aiken, D. Wyatt (S. C.)
Aldrich, William (Ill.)
Atkins, John D. C. (Tenn.)
Bacon, William J. (N. Y.)
Bagley, George A. (N. Y.)
Bailey, John M. (N. Y.)
Baker, John H. (Ind.)
Baker, William H. (N. Y.)
Ballou, Latimer W. (R. I.)
Banks, Nathaniel P. (Mass.)
Banning, Henry B. (Ohio)
Bayne, Thomas M. (Pa.)
Beale, Richard L. T. (Va.)
Beebe, George M. (N. Y.)
Belford, James B. (Colo.)
Bell, Hiram P. (Ga.)
Benedict, Charles B. (N. Y.)
Bicknell, George A. (Ind.)
Bisbee, Horatio, Jr. (Fla.)
Blackburn, Joseph C. S. (Ky.)
Blair, Henry W. (N. H.)
Bland, Richard P. (Mo.)
Bliss, Archibald M. (N. Y.)
Blount, James H. (Ga.)
Boone, Andrew R. (Ky.)
Bouck, Gabriel (Wis.)
Boyd, Thomas A. (Ill.)
Bragg, Edward S. (Wis.)
Brentano, Lorenzo (Ill.)
Brewer, Mark S. (Mich.)
Bridges, Samuel A. (Pa.)
Briggs, James F. (N. H.)
Bright, John M. (Tenn.)
Brogden, Curtis H. (N. C.)
Browne, Thomas M. (Ind.)
Buckner, Aylett H. (Mo.)
Bundy, Solomon (N. Y.)
Burchard, Horatio C. (Ill.)
Burdick, Theodore W. (Iowa)
Butler, Benjamin F. (Mass.)
Cabell, George C. (Va.)
Cain, Richard H. (S. C.)
Caldwell, John W. (Ky.)
Caldwell, William P. (Tenn.)
Calkins, William H. (Ind.)
Camp, John H. (N. Y.)
Campbell, Jacob M. (Pa.)
Candler, Milton A. (Ga.)
Cannon, Joseph G. (Ill.)
Carlisle, John G. (Ky.)
Caswell, Lucien B. (Wis.)
Chalmers, James R. (Miss.)
Chittenden, Simeon B. (N. Y.)
Claflin, William (Mass.)
Clark, Alvah A. (N. J.)
Clark, John B., Jr. (Mo.)
Clark, Rush (Iowa)
Clarke, John B. (Ky.)
Clymer, Hiester (Pa.)
Cobb, Thomas R. (Ind.)
Cole, Nathan (Mo.)
Collins, Francis D. (Pa.)
Conger, Omar D. (Mich.)
Cook, Philip (Ga.)
Covert, James W. (N. Y.)
Cox, Jacob D. (Ohio)
Cox, Samuel S. (N. Y.)
Crapo, William W. (Mass.)
Cravens, Jordan E. (Ark.)
Crittenden, Thomas T. (Mo.)
Culberson, David B. (Tex.)
Cummings, Henry J. B. (Iowa)
Cutler, Augustus W. (N. J.)
Danford, Lorenzo (Ohio)
Darrall, Chester B. (La.)
Davidson, Robert H. M. (Fla.)
Davis, Horace (Calif.)
Davis, Joseph J. (N. C.)
Dean, Benjamin (Mass.)
Deering, Nathaniel C. (Iowa)
Denison, Dudley C. (Vt.)
Dibrell, George G. (Tenn.)
Dickey, Henry L. (Ohio)
Douglas, Beverly B. (Va.)
Dunnell, Mark H. (Minn.)
Durham, Milton J. (Ky.)
Dwight, Jeremiah W. (N. Y.)
Eames, Benjamin T. (R. I.)
Eden, John R. (Ill.)
Eickhoff, Anthony (N. Y.)
Elam, Joseph B. (La.)
Ellis, E. John (La.)
Ellsworth, Charles C. (Mich.)
Errett, Russell (Pa.)
Evans, I. Newton (Pa.)
Evans, James L. (Ind.)
Evins, John H. (S. C.)
Ewing, Thomas (Ohio)
Felton, William H. (Ga.)
Field, Walbridge A. (Mass.)
Finley, Ebenezer B. (Ohio)
Finley, Jesse J. (Fla.)
Fleming, William B. (Ga.)
Forney, William H. (Ala.)
Fort, Greenbury L. (Ill.)
Foster, Charles (Ohio)
Franklin, Benjamin J. (Mo.)
Freeman, Chapman (Pa.)
Frye, William P. (Maine)
Fuller, Benoni S. (Ind.)
Gardner, Mills (Ohio)
Garfield, James A. (Ohio)
Garth, William W. (Ala.)
Gause, Lucien C. (Ark.)
Gibson, Randall L. (La.)
Giddings, De Witt C. (Tex.)
Glover, John M. (Mo.)
Goode, John, Jr. (Va.)
Gunter, Thomas M. (Ark.)
Hale, Eugene (Maine)
Hamilton, Andrew H. (Ind.)
Hanna, John (Ind.)
Hardenbergh, Augustus A. (N. J.)
Harmer, Alfred C. (Pa.)
Harris, Benjamin W. (Mass.)
Harris, Henry R. (Ga.)
Harris, John T. (Va.)
Harrison, Carter H. (Ill.)
Hart, E. Kirke (N. Y.)
Hartridge, Julian (Ga.)
Hartzell, William (Ill.)
Haskell, Dudley C. (Kans.)
Hatcher, Robert A. (Mo.)
Hayes, Philip C. (Ill.)
Hazelton, George C. (Wis.)
Hendee, George W. (Vt.)
Henderson, Thomas J. (Ill.)
Henkle, Eli J. (Md.)
Henry, Daniel M. (Md.)
Herbert, Hilary A. (Ala.)
Hewitt, Abram S. (N. Y.)
Hewitt, Goldsmith W. (Ala.)
Hiscock, Frank (N. Y.)
Hooker, Charles E. (Miss.)
House, John F. (Tenn.)
Hubbell, Jay A. (Mich.)
Humphrey, Herman L. (Wis.)
Hungerford, John N. (N. Y.)
Hunter, Morton C. (Ind.)
Hunton, Eppa (Va.)
Ittner, Anthony (Mo.)
James, Amaziah B. (N. Y.)
Jones, Frank (N. H.)
Jones, James T. (Ala.)
Jones, John S. (Ohio)
Jorgensen, Joseph (Va.)
Joyce, Charles H. (Vt.)
Keifer, J. Warren (Ohio)
Keightley, Edwin W. (Mich.)
Kelley, William D. (Pa.)
Kenna, John E. (W. Va.)
Ketcham, John H. (N. Y.)
Killinger, John W. (Pa.)
Kimmel, William (Md.)
Knapp, Robert M. (Ill.)
Knott, J. Proctor (Ky.)
Landers, George M. (Conn.)
Lapham, Elbridge G. (N. Y.)
Lathrop, William (Ill.)
Leonard, John E. (La.)
Ligon, Robert F. (Ala.)
Lindsey, Stephen D. (Maine)
Lockwood, Daniel N. (N. Y.)
Loring, George B. (Mass.)
Luttrell, John K. (Calif.)
Lynde, William P. (Wis.)
McCook, Anson G. (N. Y.)
McGowan, Jonas H. (Mich.)
McKenzie, James A. (Ky.)
Mackey, Levi A. (Pa.)
McKinley, William, Jr. (Ohio)
McMahon, John A. (Ohio)
Maish, Levi (Pa.)
Majors, Thomas J. (Nebr.)
Manning, Vannoy H. (Miss.)
Marsh, Benjamin F. (Ill.)
Martin, Benjamin F. (W. Va.)
Mayham, Stephen L. (N. Y.)
Metcalfe, Lyne S. (Mo.)
Mills, Roger Q. (Tex.)
Mitchell, John I. (Pa.)
Money, Hernando D. (Miss.)
Monroe, James (Ohio)
Morgan, Charles H. (Mo.)
Morrison, William R. (Ill.)
Morse, Leopold (Mass.)
Muldrow, Henry L. (Miss.)
Muller, Nicholas (N. Y.)
Neal, Henry S. (Ohio)
Norcross, Amasa (Mass.)
Oliver, S. Addison (Iowa)
O'Neill, Charles (Pa.)
Overton, Edward, Jr. (Pa.)
Pacheco, Romualdo (Calif.)
Page, Horace F. (Calif.)
Patterson, George W. (N. Y.)
Patterson, Thomas M. (Colo.)
Peddie, Thomas B. (N. J.)
Phelps, James (Conn.)
Phillips, William A. (Kans.)
Pollard, Henry M. (Mo.)
Potter, Clarkson N. (N. Y.)
Pound, Thaddeus C. (Wis.)
Powers, Llewellyn (Maine)
Price, Hiram (Iowa)
Pridemore, Auburn L. (Va.)
Pugh, John H. (N. J.)
Quinn, Terence J. (N. Y.)
Rainey, Joseph H. (S. C.)
Randolph, James H. (Tenn.)
Rea, David (Mo.)
Reagan, John H. (Tex.)
Reed, Thomas B. (Maine)
Reilly, James B. (Pa.)
Rice, Americus V. (Ohio)
Rice, William W. (Mass.)
Riddle, Haywood Y. (Tenn.)
Robbins, William M. (N. C.)
Roberts, Charles B. (Md.)
Robertson, Edward W. (La.)
Robinson, George D. (Mass.)
Robinson, Milton S. (Ind.)
Ross, Miles (N. J.)
Ryan, Thomas (Kans.)
Sampson, Ezekiel S. (Iowa)
Sapp, William F. (Iowa)
Sayler, Milton (Ohio)
Scales, Alfred M. (N. C.)
Schleicher, Gustave (Tex.)
Sexton, Leonidas (Ind.)
Shallenberger, William S. (Pa.)
Shelley, Charles M. (Ala.)
Singleton, Otho R. (Miss.)
Sinnickson, Clement H. (N. J.)
Slemons, William F. (Ark.)
Smalls, Robert (S. C.)
Smith, A. Herr (Pa.)
Smith, William E. (Ga.)
Southard, Milton I. (Ohio)
Sparks, William A. J. (Ill.)
Springer, William M. (Ill.)
Starin, John H. (N. Y.)
Steele, Walter L. (N. C.)
Stenger, William S. (Pa.)
Stephens, Alexander H. (Ga.)
Stewart, Jacob H. (Minn.)
Stone, John W. (Mich.)
Stone, Joseph C. (Iowa)
Strait, Horace B. (Minn.)
Swann, Thomas (Md.)
Thompson, John M. (Pa.)
Thornburgh, Jacob M. (Tenn.)
Throckmorton, James W. (Tenn.)
Tipton, Thomas F. (Ill.)
Townsend, Amos (Ohio)
Townsend, Martin I. (N. Y.)
Townshend, Richard W. (Ill.)
Tucker, John R. (Va.)
Turner, Thomas (Ky.)
Turney, Jacob (Pa.)
Vance, Robert V. (N. C.)
Van Vorhes, Nelson H. (Ohio)
Veeder, William D. (N. Y.)
Waddell, Alfred M. (N. C.)
Wait, John T. (Conn.)
Walker, Gilbert C. (Va.)
Walsh, William (Md.)
Ward, William (Pa.)
Warner, Levi (Conn.)
Watson, Lewis F. (Pa.)
Welch, Frank (Nebr.)
White, Harry (Pa.)
White, Michael D. (Ind.)
Whitthorne, Washington C. (Tenn.)
Wigginton, Peter D. (Calif.)
Williams, Alpheus S. (Mich.)
Williams, Andrew (N. Y.)
Williams, Charles G. (Wis.)
Williams, James (Del.)
Williams, Jeremiah N. (Ala.)
Williams, Richard (Oreg.)
Willis, Albert S. (Ky.)
Willis, Benjamin A. (N. Y.)
Willits, Edwin (Mich.)
Wilson, Benjamin (W. Va.)
Wood, Fernando (N. Y.)
Wren, Thomas (Nev.)
Wright, Hendrick B. (Pa.)
Yeates, Jesse J. (N. C.)
Young, H. Casey (Tenn.)
Young, John S. (La.)

The Forty-sixth Congress (1879-81)

Randall, Samuel J. (Pa.) Speaker.

Acklen, Joseph H. (La.)
Aiken, D. Wyatt (S. C.)
Aldrich, Nelson W. (R. I.)
Aldrich, William (Ill.)
Anderson, John A. (Kans.)
Armfield, Robert F. (N. C.)
Atherton, Gibson (Ohio)
Atkins, John D. C. (Tenn.)
Bachman, Reuben K. (Pa.)
Bailey, John M. (N. Y.)
Baker, John H. (Ind.)
Ballou, Latimer W. (R. I.)
Barber, Hiram, Jr. (Ill.)
Barlow, Bradley (Vt.)
Bayne, Thomas M. (Pa.)
Beale, Richard L. T. (Va.)
Belford, James B. (Colo.)
Beltzhoover, Frank E. (Pa.)
Berry, Campbell P. (Calif.)
Bisbee, Horatio, Jr. (Fla.)
Bicknell, George A. (Ind.)
Bingham, Henry H. (Pa.)
Blackburn, Joseph C. S. (Ky.)
Blake, John L. (N. J.)
Bland, Richard P. (Mo.)
Bliss, Archibald M. (N. Y.)
Blount, James H. (Ga.)
Bouck, Gabriel (Wis.)
Bowman, Selwyn Z. (Mass.)
Boyd, Thomas A. (Ill.)
Bragg, Edward S. (Wis.)
Brewer, Mark S. (Mich.)
Briggs, James F. (N. H.)
Brigham, Lewis A. (N. J.)
Bright, John M. (Tenn.)
Browne, Thomas M. (Ind.)
Buckner, Aylett H. (Mo.)
Burrows, Julius C. (Mich.)
Butterworth, Benjamin (Ohio)
Cabell, George C. (Va.)
Caldwell, John W. (Ky.)
Calkins, William H. (Ind.)
Camp, John H. (N. Y.)
Cannon, Joseph G. (Ill.)
Carlisle, John G. (Ky.)
Carpenter, Cyrus C. (Iowa)
Caswell, Lucien B. (Wis.)
Chalmers, James R. (Miss.)
Chittenden, Simon B. (N. Y.)

Claflin, William (Mass.)
Clardy, Martin L. (Mo.)
Clark, Alvah A. (N. J.)
Clark, John B., Jr. (Mo.)
Clark, Rush (Iowa)
Clements, Newton N. (Ala.)
Clymer, Hiester (Pa.)
Cobb, Thomas R. (Ind.)
Coffroth, Alexander H. (Pa.)
Colerick, Walpole G. (Ind.)
Conger, Omar D. (Mich.)
Converse, George L. (Ohio)
Cook, Philip (Ga.)
Covert, James W. (N. Y.)
Cowgill, Calvin (Ind.)
Cox, Samuel S. (N. Y.)
Crapo, William W. (Mass.)
Cravens, Jordan E. (Ark.)
Crowley, Richard (N. Y.)
Culberson, David B. (Tex.)
Daggett, Rollin M. (Nev.)
Davidson, Robert H. M. (Fla.)
Davis, George R. (Ill.)
Davis, Horace (Calif.)
Davis, Joseph J. (N. C.)
Davis, Lowndes H. (Mo.)
Deering, Nathaniel C. (Iowa)
De La Matyr, Gilbert (Ind.)
Deuster, Peter V. (Wis.)
Dibrell, George G. (Tenn.)
Dick, Samuel B. (Pa.)
Dickey, Henry L. (Ohio)
Dunn, Poindexter (Ark.)
Dunnell, Mark H. (Minn.)
Dwight, Jeremiah W. (N. Y.)
Einstein, Edwin (N. Y.)
Elam, Joseph B. (La.)
Ellis, E. John (La.)
Errett, Russell (Pa.)
Evins, John H. (S. C.)
Ewing, Thomas (Ohio)
Farr, Evarts W. (N. H.)
Felton, William H. (Ga.)
Ferdon, John W. (N. Y.)
Field, Walbridge A. (Mass.)
Finley, Ebenezer B. (Ohio)
Fisher, Horatio G. (Pa.)
Ford, Nicholas (Mo.)
Forney, William H. (Ala.)
Forsythe, Albert P. (Ill.)
Fort, Greenbury L. (Ill.)
Frost, Richard G. (Mo.)
Frye, William P. (Maine)
Garfield, James A. (Ohio)
Geddes, George W. (Ohio)
Gibson, Randall L. (La.)
Gillette, Edward H. (Iowa)
Godshalk, William (Pa.)
Goode, John, Jr. (Va.)
Gunter, Thomas M. (Ark.)
Hall, Joshua G. (N. H.)
Hammond, John (N. Y.)
Hammond, Nathaniel J. (Ga.)
Harmer, Alfred C. (Pa.)
Harris, Benjamin W. (Mass.)
Harris, John T. (Va.)
Haskell, Dudley C. (Kans.)
Hatch, William H. (Mo.)
Hawk, Robert M. A. (Ill.)
Hawley, Joseph R. (Conn.)
Hayes, Philip C. (Ill.)
Hazelton, George C. (Wis.)
Heilman, William (Ind.)
Henderson, Thomas J. (Ill.)
Henkle, Eli J. (Md.)
Henry, Daniel M. (Md.)
Herbert, Hilary A. (Ala.)
Herndon, Thomas H. (Ala.)
Hill, William D. (Ohio)
Hiscock, Frank (N. Y.)
Hooker, Charles E. (Miss.)
Horr, Roswell G. (Mich.)
Hostetler, Abraham J. (Ind.)
Houk, Leonidas C. (Tenn.)
House, John F. (Tenn.)
Hubbell, Jay A. (Mich.)
Hull, Noble A. (Fla.)
Humphrey, Herman L. (Wis.)
Hunton, Eppa (Va.)
Hurd, Frank H. (Ohio)
Hutchins, Waldo (N. Y.)
James, Amaziah B. (N. Y.)
Johnston, Joseph E. (Va.)
Jones, George W. (Tex.)
Jorgensen, Joseph (Va.)
Joyce, Charles H. (Vt.)
Keifer, J. Warren (Ohio)
Kelley, William D. (Pa.)
Kenna, John E. (W. Va.)
Ketcham, John H. (N. Y.)
Killinger, John W. (Pa.)
Kimmel, William (Md.)
King, J. Floyd (La.)
Kitchin, William H. (N. C.)
Klotz, Robert (Pa.)
Knott, J. Proctor (Ky.)
Ladd, George W. (Maine)
Lapham, Elbridge G. (N. Y.)
Lay, Alfred M. (Mo.)
Le Fevre, Benjamin (Ohio)
Lewis, Burwell B. (Ala.)
Lindsey, Stephen D. (Maine)
Loring, George B. (Mass.)
Lounsbery, William (N. Y.)
Lowe, William M. (Ala.)
McCoid, Moses A. (Iowa)
McCook, Anson G. (N. Y.)
McGowan, Jonas H. (Mich.)
McKenzie, James A. (Ky.)
McKinley, William, Jr. (Ohio)
McLane, Robert M. (Md.)
McMahon, John A. (Ohio)
McMillin, Benton (Tenn.)
Manning, Vannoy H. (Miss.)
Marsh, Benjamin F. (Ill.)
Martin, Benjamin F. (W. Va.)
Martin, Edward L. (Del.)
Martin, Joseph J. (N. C.)
Mason, Joseph (N. Y.)
Miles, Frederick (Conn.)
Miller, Warner (N. Y.)
Mills, Roger Q. (Tex.)
Mitchell, John I. (Pa.)
Money, Hernando D. (Miss.)
Monroe, James (Ohio)
Morrison, William R. (Ill.)
Morse, Leopold (Mass.)
Morton, Levi P. (N. Y.)
Muldrow, Henry I. (Miss.)
Muller, Nicholas (N. Y.)
Murch, Thompson H. (Maine)
Myers, William R. (Ind.)
Neal, Henry S. (Ohio)
New, Jeptha D. (Ind.)
Newberry, John S. (Mich.)
Nicholls, John C. (Ga.)
Norcross, Amasa (Mass.)
O'Brien, James (N. Y.)
O'Connor, Michael P. (S. C.)
O'Neill, Charles (Pa.)
O'Rielly, Daniel (N. Y.)
Orth, Godlove S. (Ind.)
Osmer, James H. (Pa.)
Overton, Edward, Jr. (Pa.)
Pacheco, Romualdo (Calif.)
Page, Horace F. (Calif.)
Persons, Henry (Ga.)
Phelps, James (Conn.)
Philips, John F. (Mo.)
Phister, Elijah C. (Ky.)
Pierce, Ray V. (N. Y.)
Poehler, Henry (Minn.)
Pound, Thaddeus C. (Wis.)
Prescott, Cyrus D. (N. Y.)
Price, Hiram (Iowa)
Ray, Ossian (N. H.)
Reagan, John H. (Tex.)
Reed, Thomas B. (Maine)
Rice, William W. (Mass.)
Richardson, David P. (N. Y.)
Richardson, John S. (S. C.)
Richmond, James B. (Va.)
Robertson, Edward W. ((La.)
Robeson, George M. (N. J.)
Robinson, George D. (Mass.)
Ross, Miles (N. J.)
Rothwell, Gideon F. (Mo.)
Russell, Daniel L. (N. C.)
Russell, William A. (Mass.)
Ryan, Thomas (Kans.)
Ryon, John W. (Pa.)
Samford, William J. (Ala.)
Sapp, William F. (Iowa)
Sawyer, Samuel L. (Mo.)
Scales, Alfred M. (N. C.)
Scoville, Jonathan (N. Y.)
Shallenberger, William S. (Pa.)
Shelley, Charles M. (Ala.)
Sherwin, John C. (Ill.)
Simonton, Charles B. (Tenn.)
Singleton, James W. (Ill.)
Singleton, Otho R. (Miss.)
Slemons, William F. (Ark.)
Smith, A. Herr (Pa.)
Smith, Hezekiah B. (N. J.)
Smith, William E. (Ga.)
Sparks, William A. J. (Ill.)
Speer, Emory (Ga.)
Springer, William M. (Ill.)
Starin, John H. (N. Y.)
Steele, Walter L. (N. C.)
Stephens, Alexander H. (Ga.)
Stevenson, Adlai E. (Ill.)
Stone, John W. (Mich.)
Talbott, J. Frederick C. (Md.)
Taylor, Ezra B. (Ohio)
Taylor, Robert L. (Tenn.)
Thomas, John R. (Ill.)
Thompson, Philip B., Jr. (Ky.)
Thompson, William G. (Iowa)
Tillman, George D. (S. C.)
Townsend, Amos (Ohio)
Townshend, Richard W. (Ill.)
Tucker, John R. (Va.)
Turner, Oscar (Ky.)
Turner, Thomas (Ky.)
Tyler, James M. (Vt.)
Updegraff, Jonathan T. (Ohio)
Updegraff, Thomas (Iowa)
Upson, Christopher C. (Tex.)
Urner, Milton G. (Md.)
Valentine, Edward K. (Nebr.)
Van Aernam, Henry (N. Y.)
Vance, Robert B. (N. C.)
Van Voorhis, John (N. Y.)
Voorhis, Charles H. (N. J.)
Waddill, James R. (Mo.)
Wait, John T. (Conn.)
Ward, William (Pa.)
Warner, Adoniram J. (Ohio)
Washburn, William D. (Minn.)
Weaver, James B. (Iowa)
Wellborn, Olin (Tex.)
Wells, Erastus (Mo.)
White, Harry (Pa.)
Whiteaker, John (Oreg.)
Whitthorne, Washington C. (Tenn.)
Wilber, David (N. Y.)
Williams, Charles G. (Wis.)
Williams, Thomas (Ala.)
Willis, Albert S. (Ky.)
Willits, Edwin (Mich.)
Wilson, Benjamin (W. Va.)
Wise, Morgan R. (Pa.)
Wood, Fernando (N. Y.)
Wood, Walter A. (N. Y.)
Wright, Hendrick B. (Pa.)
Yeates, Jesse J. (N. C.)
Yocum, Seth H. (Pa.)
Young, H. Casey (Tenn.)
Young, Thomas L. (Ohio)

The Forty-seventh Congress (1881-83)

Keifer, J. Warren (Ohio)
Speaker.

Aiken, D. Wyatt (S. C.)
Aldrich, William (Ill.)
Allen, Thomas (Mo.)
Anderson, John A. (Kans.)
Armfield, Robert F. (N. C.)
Atherton, Gibson (Ohio)
Atkins, John D. C. (Tenn.)
Barbour, John S. (Va.)
Barr, Samuel F. (Pa.)
Bayne, Thomas M. (Pa.)
Beach, Lewis (N. Y.)
Belford, James B. (Colo.)
Belmont, Perry (N. Y.)
Beltzhoover, Frank E. (Pa.)
Berry, Campbell P. (Calif.)
Bingham, Henry H. (Pa.)
Bisbee, Horatio, Jr. (Fla.)
Black, George R. (Ga.)
Blackburn, Joseph C. S. (Ky.)
Blanchard, Newton C. (La.)
Bland, Richard P. (Mo.)
Bliss, Archibald M. (N. Y.)
Blount, James H. (Ga.)
Bowman, Selwyn Z. (Mass.)
Bragg, Edward S. (Wis.)
Brewer, J. Hart (N. J.)
Briggs, James F. (N. H.)
Browne, Thomas M. (Ind.)
Brumm, Charles N. (Pa.)
Buchanan, Hugh (Ga.)
Buck, John R. (Conn.)
Buckner, Aylett H. (Mo.)
Burrows, Julius C. (Mich.)
Burrows, Joseph H. (Mo.)
Butterworth, Benjamin (Ohio)
Cabell, George C. (Va.)
Caldwell, John W. (Ky.)
Calkins, William H. (Ind.)
Camp, John H. (N. Y.)
Campbell, Jacob M. (Pa.)
Candler, John W. (Mass.)
Cannon, Joseph G. (Ill.)
Carlisle, John G. (Ky.)
Carpenter, Cyrus C. (Iowa)
Cassidy, George W. (Nev.)
Caswell, Lucien B. (Wis.)
Chace, Jonathan (R. I.)
Chalmers, James R. (Miss.)
Chapman, Andrew G. (Md.)
Clardy, Martin L. (Mo.)
Clark, John B., Jr. (Mo.)
Clements, Judson C. (Ga.)
Cobb, Thomas R. (Ind.)
Colerick, Walpole G. (Ind.)
Converse, George L. (Ohio)
Cook, John C. (Iowa)
Cook, Philip (Ga.)
Cornell, Thomas (N. Y.)
Covington, George W. (Md.)
Cox, Samuel S. (N. Y.)
Cox, William R. (N. C.)
Crapo, William W. (Mass.)
Cravens, Jordan E. (Ark.)
Crowley, Richard (N. Y.)
Culberson, David B. (Tex.)
Cullen, William (Ill.)
Curtin, Andrew G. (Pa.)
Cutts, Marsena E. (Iowa)
Darrall, Chester B. (La.)
Davidson, Robert H. M. (Fla.)
Davis, George R. (Ill.)
Davis, Lowndes H. (Mo.)
Dawes, Rufus R. (Ohio)
Deering, Nathaniel C. (Iowa)
De Motte, Mark L. (Ind.)
Deuster, Peter V. (Wis.)
Dezendorf, John F. (Va.)
Dibble, Samuel (S. C.)
Dibrell, George C. (Tenn.)
Dingley, Nelson, Jr. (Maine)
Dowd, Clement (N. C.)
Doxey, Charles T. (Ind.)
Dugro, P. Henry (N. Y.)
Dunn, Poindexter (Ark.)
Dunnell, Mark H. (Minn.)
Dwight, Jeremiah W. (N. Y.)
Ellis, E. John (La.)
Ermentrout, Daniel (Pa.)
Errett, Russell (Pa.)
Evins, John H. (S. C.)
Farwell, Charles B. (Ill.)
Farwell, Sewall S. (Iowa)
Finley, Jesse J. (Fla.)
Fisher, Horatio G. (Pa.)
Flower, Roswell P. (N. Y.)
Ford, Nicholas (Mo.)
Forney, William H. (Ala.)
Frost, Richard G. (Mo.)
Frye, William P. (Maine)
Fulkerson, Abram (Va.)
Garrison, George T. (Va.)
Geddes, George W. (Ohio)
George, Melvin C. (Oreg.)
Gibson, Randall L. (La.)
Godshalk, William (Pa.)
Grout, William W. (Vt.)
Guenther, Richard W. (Wis.)
Gunter, Thomas M. (Ark.)
Hall, Joshua G. (N. H.)
Hammond, John (N. Y.)
Hammond, Nathaniel J. (Ga.)
Hardenbergh, Augustus A. (N. J.)
Hardy, John (N. Y.)
Harmer, Alfred C. (Pa.)
Harris, Benjamin W. (Mass.)
Harris, Henry S. (N. J.)
Haskell, Dudley C. (Kans.)
Hatch, William H. (Mo.)
Hawk, Robert M. A. (Ill.)
Hazeltine, Ira S. (Mo.)
Hazelton, George C. (Wis.)
Heilman, William (Ind.)
Henderson, Thomas J. (Ill.)
Hepburn, William P. (Iowa)
Herbert, Hilary A. (Ala.)
Herndon, Thomas H. (Ala.)
Hewitt, Abram S. (N. Y.)
Hewitt, Goldsmith W. (Ala.)
Hill, John (N. J.)
Hiscock, Frank (N. Y.)
Hitt, Robert R. (Ill.)
Hoblitzell, Fetter S. (Md.)

Hoge, John B. (W. Va.)
Holman, William S. (Ind.)
Hooker, Charles E. (Miss.)
Horr, Roswell G. (Mich.)
Houk, Leonidas C. (Tenn.)
House, John F. (Tenn.)
Hubbell, Jay A. (Mich.)
Hubbs, Orlando (N. C.)
Humphrey, Herman L. (Wis.)
Hutchins, Waldo (N. Y.)
Jacobs, Ferris, Jr. (N. Y.)
Jadwin, Cornelius C. (Pa.)
Jones, George W. (Tex.)
Jones, James K. (Ark.)
Jones, Phineas (N. J.)
Jorgensen, Joseph (Va.)
Joyce, Charles H. (Vt.)
Kasson, John A. (Iowa)
Kelley, William D. (Pa.)
Kenna, John E. (W. Va.)
Ketcham, John H. (N. Y.)
King, J. Floyd (La.)
Klotz, Robert (Pa.)
Knott, J. Proctor (Ky.)
Lacey, Edward S. (Mich.)
Ladd, George W. (Maine)
Latham, Louis C. (N. C.)
Leedom, John P. (Ohio)
Le Fevre, Benjamin (Ohio)
Lewis, John H. (Ill.)
Lindsey, Stephen D. (Maine)
Lord, Henry W. (Mich.)
Lowe, William M. (Ala.)
Lynch, John R. (Miss.)
McClure, Addison S. (Ohio)
McCoid, Moses A. (Iowa)
McCook, Anson G. (N. Y.)
McKenzie, James A. (Ky.)
Mackey, Edmund W. M. (S.C.)
McKinley, William, Jr. (Ohio)
McLane, Robert M. (Md.)
McLean, James H. (Mo.)
McMillin, Benton (Tenn.)
Manning, Vannoy H. (Miss.)
Marsh, Benjamin F. (Ill.)
Martin, Edward L. (Del.)
Mason, Joseph (N. Y.)
Matson, Courtland C. (Ind.)
Miles, Frederick (Conn.)
Miller, Samuel H. (Pa.)
Mills, Roger Q. (Tex.)
Money, Hernando D. (Miss.)
Moore, William R. (Tenn.)
Morey, Henry L. (Ohio)
Morrison, William R. (Ill.)
Morse, Leopold (Mass.)
Mosgrove, James (Pa.)
Moulton, Samuel W. (Ill.)
Muldrow, Henry L. (Miss.)
Murch, Thompson H. (Maine)
Mutchler, William (Pa.)
Neal, Henry S. (Ohio)
Nolan, Michael N. (N. Y.)
Norcross, Amasa (Mass.)
Oates, William C. (Ala.)
O'Neill, Charles (Pa.)
Orth, Godlove S. (Ind.)
Pacheco, Romualdo (Calif.)
Page, Horace F. (Calif.)
Parker, Abraham X. (N. Y.)
Paul, John (Va.)
Payson, Lewis E. (Ill.)
Peelle, Stanton J. (Ind.)
Pettibone, Augustus H. (Tenn.)
Phelps, James (Conn.)
Phister, Elijah C. (Ky.)
Pierce, Robert B. F. (Ind.)
Pound, Thaddeus C. (Wis.)
Prescott, Cyrus D. (N. Y.)
Randall, Samuel J. (Pa.)
Ranney, Ambrose A. (Mass.)
Ray, Ossian (N. H.)
Reagan, John H. (Tex.)
Reed, Thomas B. (Maine)
Reese, Seaborn (Ga.)
Rice, John B. (Ohio)
Rice, Theron M. (Mo.)
Rice, William W. (Mass.)
Rich, John T. (Mich.)
Richardson, David P. (N. Y.)
Richardson, John S. (S. C.)
Ritchie, James M. (Ohio)
Robertson, Edward W. (La.)
Robeson, George M. (N. J.)
Robinson, George D. (Mass.)
Robinson, James S. (Ohio)
Robinson, William E. (N. Y.)
Rosecrans, William S. (Calif.)
Ross, Miles (N. J.)
Russell, William A. (Mass.)
Ryan, Thomas (Kans.)
Scales, Alfred M. (N. C.)
Scoville, Jonathan (N. Y.)
Scranton, Joseph A. (Pa.)
Sessinghaus, Gustavus (Mo.)
Shackelford, John W. (N. C.)
Shallenberger, William S. (Pa.)
Shelley, Charles M. (Ala.)
Sherwin, John C. (Ill.)
Shultz, Emanuel (Ohio)
Simonton, Charles B. (Tenn.)
Singleton, James W. (Ill.)
Singleton, Otho R. (Miss.)
Skinner, Charles R. (N. Y.)
Smalls, Robert (S. C.)
Smith, A. Herr (Pa.)
Smith, Dietrich C. (Ill.)
Smith, J. Hyatt (N. Y.)
Smith, James Q. (Ala.)
Sparks, William A. J. (Ill.)
Spaulding, Oliver L. (Mich.)
Speer, Emory (Ga.)
Spooner, Henry J. (R. I.)
Springer, William M. (Ill.)
Steele, George W. (Ind.)
Stephens, Alexander H. (Ga.)
Stockslager, Strother M. (Ind.)
Stone, Eben F. (Mass.)
Strait, Horace B. (Minn.)
Talbot, J. Frederick C. (Md.)
Taylor, Ezra B. (Ohio)
Taylor, Joseph D. (Ohio)
Thomas, John R. (Ill.)
Thompson, Philip B., Jr. (Ky.)
Thompson, William G. (Iowa)
Tillman, George D. (S. C.)
Townsend, Amos (Ohio)
Townshend, Richard W. (Ill.)
Tucker, John R. (Va.)
Turner, Henry G. (Ga.)
Turner, Oscar (Ky.)
Tyler, James M. (Vt.)
Upson, Christopher C. (Tex.)
Updegraff, Jonathan T. (Ohio)
Updegraff, Thomas (Iowa)
Urner, Milton G. (Md.)
Valentine, Edward K. (Nebr.)
Van Aernam, Henry (N. Y.)
Vance, Robert B. (N. C.)
Van Horn, Robert T. (Mo.)
Van Voorhis, John (N. Y.)
Wadsworth, James W. (N. Y.)
Wait, John T. (Conn.)
Walker, Robert J. C. (Pa.)
Ward, William (Pa.)
Warner, Richard (Tenn.)
Washburn, William D. (Minn.)
Watson, Lewis F. (Pa.)
Webber, George W. (Mich.)
Wellborn, Olin (Tex.)
West, George (N. Y.)
Wheeler, Joseph (Ala.)
White, John D. (Ky.)
Whitthorne, Washington C. (Tenn.)
Williams, Charles G. (Wis.)
Williams, Thomas (Ala.)
Willis, Albert S. (Ky.)
Willits, Edwin (Mich.)
Wilson, Benjamin (W. Va.)
Wise, George D. (Va.)
Wise, Morgan R. (Pa.)
Wood, Benjamin (N. Y.)
Wood, Walter A. (N. Y.)
Young, Thomas L. (Ohio)

The Forty-eighth Congress (1883-85)

Carlisle, John G. (Ky.)
Speaker.

Adams, George E. (Ill.)
Adams, John J. (N. Y.)
Aiken, D. Wyatt (S. C.)
Alexander, Armstead M. (Mo.)
Anderson, John A. (Kans.)
Arnot, John, Jr. (N. Y.)
Atkinson, Louis E. (Pa.)
Bagley, John H., Jr. (N. Y.)
Ballentine, John G. (Tenn.)
Barbour, John S. (Va.)
Barksdale, Ethelbert (Miss.)
Barr, Samuel F. (Pa.)
Bayne, Thomas M. (Pa.)
Beach, Lewis (N. Y.)
Belford, James B. (Colo.)
Belmont, Perry (N. Y.)
Bennett, Risden T. (N. C.)
Bingham, Henry H. (Pa.)
Bisbee, Horatio, Jr. (Fla.)
Blackburn, Joseph C. S. (Ky.)
Blanchard, Newton C. (La.)
Bland, Richard P. (Mo.)
Blount, James H. (Ga.)
Boutelle, Charles A. (Maine)
Bowen, Henry (Va.)
Boyle, Charles E. (Pa.)
Brainerd, Samuel M. (Pa.)
Bratton, John (S. C.)
Breckinridge, Clifton R. (Ark.)
Breitung, Edward (Mich.)
Brewer, Francis B. (N. Y.)
Brewer, J. Hart (N. J.)
Broadhead, James O. (Mo.)
Brown, William W. (Pa.)
Browne, Thomas M. (Ind.)
Brumm, Charles N. (Pa.)
Buchanan, Hugh (Ga.)
Buckner, Aylett H. (Mo.)
Budd, James H. (Calif.)
Burleigh, Henry G. (N. Y.)
Burnes, James N. (Mo.)
Cabell, George C. (Va.)
Caldwell, Andrew J. (Tenn.)
Calkins, William H. (Ind.)
Campbell, Felix (N. Y.)
Campbell, Jacob M. (Pa.)
Campbell, James E. (Ohio)
Candler, Allen D. (Ga.)
Cannon, Joseph G. (Ill.)
Carleton, Ezra C. (Mich.)
Cassidy, George W. (Nev.)
Chace, Jonathan (R. I.)
Chalmers, James R. (Miss.)
Clardy, Martin L. (Mo.)
Clay, James F. (Ky.)
Clements, Judson C. (Ga.)
Cobb, Thomas R. (Ind.)
Collins, Patrick A. (Mass.)
Connolly, Daniel W. (Pa.)
Converse, George L. (Ohio)
Cook, John C. (Iowa)
Cosgrove, John (Mo.)
Covington, George W. (Md.)
Cox, Samuel S. (N. Y.)
Cox, William R. (N. C.)
Craig, George H. (Ala.)
Crisp, Charles F. (Ga.)
Culberson, David B. (Tex.)
Culbertson, William W. (Ky.)
Cullen, William (Ill.)
Curtin, Andrew G. (Pa.)
Cutcheon, Byron M. (Mich.)
Dargan, George W. (S. C.)
Davidson, Robert H. M. (Fla.)
Davis, George R. (Ill.)
Davis, Lowndes H. (Mo.)
Davis, Robert T. (Mass.)
Deuster, Peter V. (Wis.)
Dibble, Samuel (S. C.)
Dibrell, George G. (Tenn.)
Dingley, Nelson, Jr. (Maine)
Dixon, Nathan F. (R. I.)
Dockery, Alexander M. (Mo.)
Dorsheimer, William (N. Y.)
Dowd, Clement (N. C.)
Duncan, William A. (Pa.)
Dunham, Ransom W. (Ill.)
Dunn, Poindexter (Ark.)
Eaton, William W. (Conn.)
Eldredge, Nathaniel B. (Mich.)
Elliott, Mortimer F. (Pa.)
Ellis, E. John (La.)
Ellwood, Reuben (Ill.)
English, William E. (Ind.)
Ermentrout, Daniel (Pa.)
Evans, I. Newton (Pa.)
Everhart, James B. (Pa.)
Evins, John H. (S. C.)
Ferrell, Thomas M. (N. J.)
Fiedler, William H. F. (N. J.)
Findlay, John V. L. (Md.)
Finerty, John F. (Ill.)
Follett, John F. (Ohio)
Foran, Martin A. (Ohio)
Forney, William H. (Ala.)
Frederick, Benjamin T. (Iowa)
Funston, Edward H. (Kans.)
Fyan, Robert W. (Mo.)
Garrison, George T. (Va.)
Geddes, George W. (Ohio)
George, Melvin C. (Oreg.)
Gibson, Eustace (Va.)
Glascock, John R. (Calif.)
Goff, Nathan, Jr. (W. Va.)
Graves, Alexander (Mo.)
Green, Wharton J. (N. C.)
Greenleaf, Halbert S. (N. Y.)
Guenther, Richard W. (Wis.)
Halsell, John E. (Ky.)
Hammond, Nathaniel J. (Ga.)
Hanback, Lewis (Kans.)
Hancock, John (Tex.)
Hardeman, Thomas (Ga.)
Hardy, John (N. Y.)
Harmer, Alfred C. (Pa.)
Hart, Alphonso (Ohio)
Haskell, Dudley C. (Kans.)
Hatch, Herschel H. (Mich.)
Hatch, William H. (Mo.)
Haynes, Martin A. (N. H.)
Hemphill, John J. (S. C.)
Henderson, David B. (Iowa)
Henderson, Thomas J. (Ill.)
Henley, Barclay (Calif.)
Hepburn, William P. (Iowa)
Herbert, Hilary A. (Ala.)
Hewitt, Abram S. (N. Y.)
Hewitt, Goldsmith W. (Ala.)
Hill, William D. (Ohio)
Hiscock, Frank (N. Y.)
Hitt, Robert R. (Ill.)
Hoblitzell, Fetter S. (Md.)
Holman, William S. (Ind.)
Holmes, Adoniram J. (Iowa)
Holton, Hart B. (Md.)
Hooper, Benjamin S. (Va.)
Hopkins, James H. (Pa.)
Horr, Roswell G. (Mich.)
Houk, Leonidas C. (Tenn.)
Houseman, Julius (Mich.)
Howey, Benjamin F. (N. J.)
Hunt, Carleton (La.)
Hurd, Frank H. (Ohio)
Hutchins, Waldo (N. Y.)
James, Darwin R. (N. Y.)
Jeffords, Elza (Miss.)
Johnson, Frederick A. (N. Y.)
Jones, Burr W. (Wis.)
Jones, James H. (Tex.)
Jones, James K. (Ark.)
Jones, James T. (Ala.)
Jordan, Isaac M. (Ohio)
Kasson, John A. (Iowa)
Kean, John (N. J.)
Keifer, J. Warren (Ohio)
Kelley, William D. (Pa.)
Kellogg, William P. (La.)
Ketcham, John H. (N. Y.)
King, J. Floyd (La.)
Kleiner, John J. (Ind.)
Lacey, Edward S. (Mich.)
Laird, James (Nebr.)
Lamb, John E. (Ind.)
Lanham, Samuel W. T. (Tex.)
Lawrence, George V. (Pa.)
Le Fevre, Benjamin (Ohio)
Lewis, Edward T. (La.)
Libbey, Harry (Va.)
Long, John D. (Mass.)
Lore, Charles B. (Del.)
Lovering, Henry B. (Mass.)
Lowry, Robert (Ind.)
Lyman, Theodore (Mass.)
McAdoo, William (N. J.)
McCoid, Moses A. (Iowa)
McComas, Louis E. (Md.)
McCormick, John W. (Ohio)
Mackey, Edmund W. M. (S.C.)
McKinley, William, Jr. (Ohio)
McMillin, Benton (Tenn.)
Matson, Courtland C. (Ind.)
Maybury, William C. (Mich.)
Mayo, Robert M. (Va.)
Millard, Stephen C. (N. Y.)
Miller, James F. (Tex.)
Miller, Samuel H. (Pa.)
Milliken, Seth L. (Maine)
Mills, Roger Q. (Tex.)
Mitchell, Charles L. (Conn.)
Money, Hernando D. (Miss.)
Morey, Henry L. (Ohio)
Morgan, Charles H. (Mo.)
Morrill, Edmund N. (Kans.)
Morrison, William R. (Ill.)
Morse, Leopold (Mass.)
Moulton, Samuel W. (Ill.)
Muldrow, Henry L. (Miss.)
Muller, Nicholas (N. Y.)
Murphy, Jeremiah H. (Iowa)

Murray, Robert M. (Ohio)
Mutchler, William (Pa.)
Neece, William H. (Ill.)
Nelson, Knute, Minn.)
Nicholls, John C. (Ga.)
Nutting, Newton W. (N. Y.)
Oates, William C. (Ala.)
Ochiltree, Thomas P. (Tex.)
O'Ferrall, Charles T. (Va.)
O'Hara, James E. (N. C.)
O'Neill, Charles (Pa.)
O'Neill, John J. (Mo.)
Paige, David R. (Ohio)
Parker, Abraham X. (N. Y.)
Patton, John D. (Pa.)
Payne, Sereno E. (N. Y.)
Payson, Lewis E. (Ill.)
Peel, Samuel W. (Ark.)
Peelle, Stanton J. (Ind.)
Perkins, Bishop W. (Kans.)
Peters, Samuel R. (Kans.)
Pettibone, Augustus H. (Tenn.)
Phelps, William W. (N. J.)
Pierce, Rice A. (Tenn.)
Poland, Luke P. (Vt.)
Post, George A. (Pa.)
Potter, Orlando B. (N. Y.)
Price, William T. (Wis.)
Pryor, Luke (Ala.)
Pusey, William H. M. (Iowa)
Randall, Samuel J. (Pa.)
Rankin, Joseph (Wis.)
Ranney, Ambrose A. (Mass.)
Ray, George W. (N. Y.)
Ray, Ossian (N. H.)
Reagan, John H. (Tex.)
Reed, Thomas B. (Maine)
Reese, Seaborn (Ga.)
Reid, James W. (N. C.)
Rice, William W. (Mass.)
Riggs, James M. (Ill.)
Robertson, Thomas A. (Ky.)
Robinson, George D. (Mass.)
Robinson, James S. (Ohio)
Robinson, William E. (N. Y.)
Rockwell, Francis W. (Mass.)
Rogers, John H. (Ark.)
Rogers, William F. (N. Y.)
Rosecrans, William S. (Calif.)
Rowell, Jonathan H. (Ill.)
Russell, William A. (Mass.)
Ryan, Thomas (Kans.)
Scales, Alfred M. (N. C.)
Seney, George E. (Ohio)
Seymour, Edward W. (Conn.)
Shaw, Aaron (Ill.)
Shelley, Charles M. (Ala.)
Shively, Benjamin F. (Ind.)
Singleton, Otho R. (Miss.)
Skinner, Charles R. (N. Y.)
Skinner, Thomas G. (N. C.)
Slocum, Henry W. (N. Y.)
Smalls, Robert (S. C.)
Smith, A. Herr (Pa.)
Smith, Hiram Y. (Iowa)
Snyder, Charles P. (W. Va.)
Spooner, Henry J. (R. I.)
Spriggs, John T. (N. Y.)
Springer, William M. (Ill.)
Steele, George W. (Ind.)
Stephenson, Isaac (Wis.)
Stevens, Robert S. (N. Y.)
Stewart, Charles (Tex.)
Stewart, John W. (Vt.)
Stockslager, Strother M. (Ind.)
Stone, Eben F. (Mass.)
Storm, John B. (Pa.)
Strait, Horace B. (Minn.)
Struble, Isaac S. (Iowa)
Sumner, Charles A. (Calif.)
Sumner, Daniel H. (Wis.)
Swope, John A. (Pa.)
Talbott, J. Frederick C. (Md.)
Taylor, Ezra B. (Ohio)
Taylor, John M. (Tenn.)
Taylor, Joseph D. (Ohio)
Thomas, John R. (Ill.)
Thompson, Philip B., Jr. (Ky.)
Throckmorton, James W. (Tex.)
Tillman, George D. (S. C.)
Townshend, Richard W. (Ill.)
Tucker, John R. (Va.)
Tulley, Pleasant B. (Calif.)
Turner, Henry G. (Ga.)
Turner, Oscar (Ky.)
Valentine, Edward K. (Nebr.)
Van Alstyne, Thomas J. (N. Y.)
Vance, Robert B. (N. C.)
Van Eaton, Henry S. (Miss.)
Wadsworth, James W. (N. Y.)
Wait, John T. (Conn.)
Wakefield, James B. (Minn.)
Wallace, Jonathan H. (Ohio)
Ward, Thomas B. (Ind.)
Warner, Adoniram J. (Ohio)
Warner, Richard (Tenn.)
Washburn, William D. (Minn.)
Weaver, Archibald J. (Nebr.)
Wellborn, Olin (Tex.)
Weller, Luman H. (Iowa)
Wemple, Edward (N. Y.)
White, John D. (Ky.)
White, Milo (Minn.)
Whiting, William (Mass.)
Wilkins, Beriah (Ohio)
Williams, Thomas (Ala.)
Willis, Albert S. (Ky.)
Wilson, James (Iowa)
Wilson, William L. (W. Va.)
Winans, Edwin B. (Mich.)
Winans, John (Wis.)
Wise, George D. (Va.)
Wise, John S. (Va.)
Wolford, Frank L. (Ky.)
Wood, Thomas J. (Ind.)
Woodward, Gilbert M. (Wis.)
Worthington, Nicholas E. (Ill.)
Yaple, George L. (Mich.)
York, Tyre (N. C.)
Young, H. Casey (Tenn.)

The Forty-ninth Congress (1885-87)

Carlisle, John G. (Ky.) Speaker.

Adams, George E. (Ill.)
Adams, John J. (N. Y.)
Aiken, D. Wyatt (S. C.)
Allen, Charles H. (Mass.)
Allen, John M. (Miss.)
Anderson, Charles M. (Ohio)
Anderson, John A. (Kans.)
Arnot, John, Jr. (N. Y.)
Atkinson, Louis E. (Pa.)
Bacon, Henry (N. Y.)
Baker, Charles S. (N. Y.)
Ballentine, John G. (Tenn.)
Barbour, John S. (Va.)
Barksdale, Ethelbert (Miss.)
Barnes, George T. (Ga.)
Barry, Frederick G. (Miss.)
Bayne, Thomas M. (Pa.)
Beach, Lewis (N. Y.)
Belmont, Perry (N. Y.)
Bennett, Risden T. (N. C.)
Bingham, Henry H. (Pa.)
Blanchard, Newton C. (La.)
Bland, Richard P. (Mo.)
Bliss, Archibald M. (N. Y.)
Blount, James H. (Ga.)
Bound, Franklin (Pa.)
Boutelle, Charles A. (Maine)
Boyle, Charles E. (Pa.)
Brady, James D. (Va.)
Bragg, Edward S. (Wis.)
Breckenridge, Clifton R. (Ark.)
Breckenridge, William C. P. (Ky.)
Brown, Charles E. (Ohio)
Brown, William W. (Pa.)
Browne, Thomas M. (Ind.)
Brumm, Charles N. (Pa.)
Buchanan, James (N. J.)
Buck, John R. (Conn.)
Bunnell, Frank C. (Pa.)
Burleigh, Henry G. (N. Y.)
Burnes, James N. (Mo.)
Burrows, Julius C. (Mich.)
Butterworth, Benjamin (Ohio)
Bynum, William D. (Ind.)
Cabell, George C. (Va.)
Caldwell, Andrew J. (Tenn.)
Campbell, Felix (N. Y.)
Campbell, Jacob M. (Pa.)
Campbell, James E. (Ohio)
Campbell, Timothy J. (N. Y.)
Candler, Allen D. (Ga.)
Cannon, Joseph G. (Ill.)
Carleton, Ezra C. (Mich.)
Caswell, Lucien B. (Wis.)
Catchings, Thomas C. (Miss.)
Clardy, Martin L. (Mo.)
Clements, Judson C. (Ga.)
Cobb, Thomas R. (Ind.)
Cole, William H. (Md.)
Collins, Patrick A. (Mass.)
Compton, Barnes (Md.)
Comstock, Charles C. (Mich.)
Conger, Edwin H. (Iowa)
Cooper, William C. (Ohio)
Cowles, William H. H. (N. C.)
Cox, Samuel S. (N. Y.)
Cox, William R. (N. C.)
Crain, William H. (Tex.)
Crisp, Charles F. (Ga.)
Croxton, Thomas (Va.)
Culberson, David B. (Tex.)
Curtin, Andrew G. (Pa.)
Cutcheon, Byron M. (Mich.)
Daniel, John W. (Va.)
Dargan, George W. (S. C.)
Davenport, Ira (N. Y.)
Davidson, Alexander C. (Ala.)
Davidson, Robert H. M. (Fla.)
Davis, Robert T. (Mass.)
Dawson, William (Mo.)
Dibble, Samuel (S. C.)
Dingley, Nelson, Jr. (Maine)
Dockery, Alexander M. (Mo.)
Dorsey, George W. E. (Nebr.)
Dougherty, Charles (Fla.)
Dowdney, Abraham (N. Y.)
Dunham, Ransom W. (Ill.)
Dunn, Poindexter (Ark.)
Eden, John R. (Ill.)
Eldredge, Nathaniel B. (Mich.)
Ellsberry, William W. (Ohio)
Ely, Frederick D. (Mass.)
Ermentrout, Daniel (Pa.)
Evans, I. Newton (Pa.)
Everhart, James B. (Pa.)
Farquhar, John M. (N. Y.)
Felton, Charles N. (Calif.)
Findlay, John V. L. (Md.)
Fisher, Spencer O. (Mich.)
Fleeger, George W. (Pa.)
Foran, Martin A. (Ohio)
Ford, George (Ind.)
Forney, William H. (Ala.)
Frederick, Benjamin T. (Iowa)
Fuller, William E. (Iowa)
Funston, Edward H. (Kans.)
Gallinger, Jacob H. (N. H.)
Gay, Edward J. (La.)
Geddes, George W. (Ohio)
Gibson, Charles H. (Md.)
Gibson, Eustace (W. Va.)
Gilfillan, John B. (Minn.)
Glass, Presley T. (Tenn.)
Glover, John M. (Mo.)
Goff, Nathan, Jr. (W. V.)
Green, Robert S. (N. J.)
Green, Wharton J. (N. C.)
Grosvenor, Charles H. (Ohio)
Grout, William W. (Vt.)
Guenther, Richard W. (Wis.)
Hale, John B. (Mo.)
Hahn, Michael (La.)
Hall, Benton J. (Iowa)
Halsell, John E. (Ky.)
Hammond, Nathaniel J. (Ga.)
Hanback, Lewis (Kans.)
Harmer, Alfred C. (Pa.)
Harris, Henry R. (Ga.)
Hatch, William H. (Mo.)
Hayden, Edward D. (Mass.)
Haynes, Martin A. (N. H.)
Heard, John T. (Mo.)
Hemphill, John J. (S. C.)
Henderson, David B. (Iowa)
Henderson, John S. (N. C.)
Henderson, Thomas J. (Ill.)
Henley, Barclay (Calif.)
Hepburn, William P. (Iowa)
Herbert, Hilary A. (Ala.)
Hermann, Binger (Oreg.)
Hewitt, Abram S. (N. Y.)
Hiestand, John A. (Pa.)
Hill, William D. (Ohio)
Hires, George (N. J.)
Hiscock, Frank (N. Y.)
Hitt, Robert R. (Ill.)
Holman, William S. (Ind.)
Holmes, Adoniram J. (Iowa)
Hopkins, Albert J. (Ill.)
Houk, Leonidas C. (Tenn.)
Howard, Jonas G. (Ind.)
Hudd, Thomas R. (Wis.)
Hutton, John E. (Mo.)
Irion, Alfred B. (La.)
Jackson, Oscar L. (Pa.)
James, Darwin R. (N. Y.)
Johnson, Frederick A. (N. Y.)
Johnston, James T. (Ind.)
Johnston, Thomas D. (N. C.)
Jones, James H. (Tex.)
Jones, James T. (Ala.)
Kelley, William D. (Pa.)
Ketcham, John H. (N. Y.)
King, J. Floyd (La.)
Kleiner, John J. (Ind.)
Laffoon, Polk (Ky.)
LaFollette, Robert M. (Wis.)
Laird, James (Nebr.)
Landes, Silas Z. (Ill.)
Lanham, Samuel W. T. (Tex.)
Lawler, Frank (Ill.)
Le Fevre, Benjamin (Ohio)
Lehlbach, Herman (N. J.)
Libbey, Harry (Va.)
Lindsley, James G. (N. Y.)
Little, John (Ohio)
Long, John D. (Mass.)
Lore, Charles B. (Del.)
Louttit, James A. (Calif.)
Lovering, Henry B. (Mass.)
Lowry, Robert (Ind.)
Lyman, Joseph (Iowa)
McAdoo, William (N. J.)
McComas, Louis E. (Md.)
McCreary, James B. (Ky.)
McKenna, Joseph (Calif.)
McKinley, William, Jr. (Ohio)
McMillin, Benton (Tenn.)
McRae, Thomas C. (Ark.)
Mahoney, Peter P. (N. Y.)
Markham, Henry H. (Calif.)
Martin, John M. (Ala.)
Matson, Courtland C. (Ind.)
Maybury, William C. (Mich.)
Merriman, Truman A. (N. Y.)
Millard, Stephen C. (N. Y.)
Miller, James F. (Tex.)
Milliken, Seth L. (Maine)
Mills, Roger Q. (Tex.)
Mitchell, Charles L. (Conn.)
Moffatt, Seth C. (Mich.)
Morgan, James B. (Miss.)
Morrill, Edmund N. (Kans.)
Morrison, William R. (Ill.)
Morrow, William W. (Calif.)
Muller, Nicholas (N. Y.)
Murphy, Jeremiah H. (Iowa)
Neal, John R. (Tenn.)
Neece, William H. (Ill.)
Negley, James S. (Pa.)
Nelson, Knute (Minn.)
Norwood, Thomas M. (Ga.)
Oates, William C. (Ala.)
O'Donnell, James (Mich.)
O'Ferrall, Charles T. (Va.)
O'Hara, James E. (N. C.)
O'Neill, Charles (Pa.)
O'Neill, John J. (Mo.)
Osborne, Edwin S. (Pa.)
Outhwaite, Joseph H. (Ohio)
Owen, William D. (Ind.)
Page, Charles H. (R. I.)
Parker, Abraham X. (N. Y.)
Payne, Sereno E. (N. Y.)
Payson, Lewis E. (Ill.)
Peel, Samuel W. (Ark.)
Perkins, Bishop W. (Kans.)
Perry, William H. (S. C.)
Peters, Samuel R. (Kans.)
Pettibone, Augustus H. (Tenn.)
Phelps, William W. (N. J.)
Pidcock, James N. (N. J.)
Pindar, John S. (N. Y.)
Pirce, William A. (R. I.)
Plumb, Ralph (Ill.)
Price, Hugh H. (Wis.)
Price, William T. (Wis.)
Pulitzer, Joseph (N. Y.)
Randall, Samuel J. (Pa.)
Rankin, Joseph (Wis.)
Ranney, Ambrose A. (Mass.)
Reagan, John H. (Tex.)
Reed, Thomas B. (Maine)
Reese, Seaborn (Ga.)
Reid, James W. (N. C.)
Rice, William W. (Mass.)
Richardson, James D. (Tenn.)
Riggs, James M. (Ill.)
Robertson, Thomas A. (Ky.)
Rockwell, Francis W. (Mass.)

Rogers, John H. (Ark.)
Romeis, Jacob (Ohio)
Rowell, Jonathan H. (Ill.)
Rusk, Harry W. (Md.)
Ryan, Thomas (Kans.)
Sadler, Thomas W. (Ala.)
St. Martin, Louis (La.)
Sawyer, John G. (N. Y.)
Sayers, Joseph D. (Tex.)
Scott, William L. (Pa.)
Scranton, Joseph A. (Pa.)
Seney, George E. (Ohio)
Sessions, Walter L. (N. Y.)
Seymour, Edward W. (Conn.)
Shaw, Frank T. (Md.)
Singleton, Otho R. (Miss.)
Skinner, Thomas G. (N. C.)
Smalls, Robert (S. C.)
Snyder, Charles P. (W. Va.)
Sowden, William H. (Pa.)
Spooner, Henry J. (R. I.)
Spriggs, John T. (N. Y.)
Springer, William M. (Ill.)
Stahlnecker, William G. (N. Y.)
Steele, George W. (Ind.)
Stephenson, Isaac (Wis.)
Stewart, Charles (Tex.)
Stewart, John W. (Vt.)
Stone, Eben F. (Mass.)
Stone, William J. (Ky.)
Stone, William J. (Mo.)
Storm, John B. (Pa.)
Strait, Horace B. (Minn.)
Struble, Isaac S. (Iowa)
Swinburne, John (N. Y.)
Swope, John A. (Pa.)
Symes, George G. (Colo.)
Tarsney, Timothy E. (Mich.)
Taulbee, William P. (Ky.)
Taylor, Ezra B. (Ohio)
Taylor, Isaac H. (Ohio)
Taylor, John M. (Tenn.)
Taylor, Zachary (Tenn.)
Thomas, John R. (Ill.)
Thomas, Ormsby B. (Wis.)
Thompson, Albert C. (Ohio)
Throckmorton, James W. (Tex.)
Tillman, George D. (S. C.)
Townshend, Richard W. (Ill.)
Trigg, Connally F. (Va.)
Tucker, John R. (Va.)
Turner, Henry G. (Ga.)
Van Eaton, Henry S. (Miss.)
Van Schaick, Isaac W. (Wis.)
Viele, Egbert L. (N. Y.)
Wade, William H. (Mo.)
Wadsworth, William H. (Ky.)
Wait, John T. (Conn.)
Wakefield, James B. (Minn.)
Wallace, Nathaniel D. (La.)
Ward, James H. (Ill.)
Ward, Thomas B. (Ind.)
Warner, Adoniram J. (Ohio)
Warner, William (Mo.)
Weaver, Archibald J. (Nebr.)
Weaver, James B. (Iowa)
Weber, John B. (N. Y.)
Wellborn, Olin (Tex.)
West, George (N. Y.)
Wheeler, Joseph (Ala.)
White, Alexander C. (Pa.)
White, Milo (Minn.)
Whiting, William (Mass.)
Wilkins, Beriah (Ohio)
Willis, Albert S. (Ky.)
Wilson, William L. (W. Va.)
Winans, Edwin B. (Mich.)
Wise, George D. (Va.)
Wolford, Frank L. (Ky.)
Woodburn, William (Nev.)
Worthington, Nicholas E. (Ill.)

The Fiftieth Congress (1887-89)

Carlisle, John G. (Ky.) Speaker.
Abbott, Jo (Tex.)
Adams, George E. (Ill.)
Allen, Charles H. (Mass.)
Allen, Edward P. (Mich.)
Allen, John M. (Miss.)
Anderson, Albert R. (Iowa)
Anderson, Chapman L. (Miss.)
Anderson, George A. (Ill.)
Anderson, John A. (Kans.)
Arnold, Warren O. (R. I.)
Atkinson, Louis E. (Pa.)
Bacon, Henry (N. Y.)
Baker, Charles S. (N. Y.)
Baker, Jehu (Ill.)
Bankhead, John H. (Ala.)
Barnes, George T. (Ga.)
Barry, Frederick G. (Miss.)
Bayne, Thomas M. (Pa.)
Belden, James J. (N. Y.)
Belmont, Perry (N. Y.)
Biggs, Marion (Calif.)
Bingham, Henry H. (Pa.)
Blanchard, Newton C. (La.)
Bland, Richard P. (Mo.)
Bliss, Archibald M. (N. Y.)
Blount, James H. (Ga.)
Booher, Charles F. (Mo.)
Boothman, Melvin M. (Ohio)
Bound, Franklin (Pa.)
Boutelle, Charles A. (Maine)
Bowden, George E. (Va.)
Bowen, Henry (Va.)
Breckinridge, Clifton R. (Ark.)
Breckinridge, William C. P. (Ky.)
Brewer, Mark S. (Mich.)
Brower, John M. (N. C.)
Brown, Charles E. (Ohio)
Brown, John R. (Va.)
Browne, Thomas H. B. (Va.)
Browne, Thomas M. (Ind.)
Brumm, Charles N. (Pa.)
Bryce, Lloyd S. (N. Y.)
Buchanan, James (N. J.)
Buckalew, Charles R. (Pa.)
Bunnell, Frank C. (Pa.)
Burnes, James M. (Mo.)
Burnett, Edward (Mass.)
Burrows, Julius C. (Mich.)
Butler, Roderick R. (Tenn.)
Butterworth, Benjamin (Ohio)
Bynum, William D. (Ind.)
Campbell, Felix (N. Y.)
Campbell, James E. (Ohio)
Campbell, Timothy J. (N. Y.)
Candler, Allen D. (Ga.)
Cannon, Joseph G. (Ill.)
Carlton, Henry H. (Ga.)
Caruth, Asher G. (Ky.)
Caswell, Lucien B. (Wis.)
Catchings, Thomas C. (Miss.)
Cheadle, Joseph B. (Ind.)
Chipman, J. Logan (Mich.)
Clardy, Martin L. (Mo.)
Clark, Charles B. (Wis.)
Clements, Judson C. (Ga.)
Cobb, James E. (Ala.)
Cockran, W. Bourke (N. Y.)
Cogswell, William (Mass.)
Collins, Patrick A. (Mass.)
Compton, Barnes (Md.)
Conger, Edwin H. (Iowa)
Cooper, William C. (Ohio)
Cothran, James S. (S. C.)
Cowles, William H. H. (N. C.)
Cox, Samuel S. (N. Y.)
Crain, William H. (Tex.)
Crisp, Charles F. (Ga.)
Crouse, George W. (Ohio)
Culberson, David B. (Tex.)
Cummings, Amos J. (N. Y.)
Cutcheon, Byron M. (Mich.)
Dalzell, John (Pa.)
Dargan, George W. (S. C.)
Darlington, Smedley (Pa.)
Davenport, Ira (N. Y.)
Davidson, Alexander C. (Ala.)
Davidson, Robert H. M. (Fla.)
Davis, Robert T. (Mass.)
De Lano, Milton (N. Y.)
Dibble, Samuel (S. C.)
Dingley, Nelson, Jr. (Maine)
Dockery, Alexander M. (Mo.)
Dorsey, George W. E. (Nebr.)
Dougherty, Charles (Fla.)
Dunham, Ransom W. (Ill.)
Dunn, Poindexter (Ark.)
Elliott, William (S. C.)
Enloe, Benjamin A. (Tenn.)
Ermentrout, Daniel (Pa.)
Farquhar, John M. (N. Y.)
Felton, Charles N. (Calif.)
Finley, Hugh F. (Ky.)
Fisher, Spencer O. (Mich.)
Fitch, Ashbel P. (N. Y.)
Flood, Thomas S. (N. Y.)
Foran, Martin A. (Ohio)
Ford, Melbourne H. (Mich.)
Forney, William H. (Ala.)
French, Carlos (Conn.)
Fuller, William E. (Iowa)
Funston, Edward H. (Kans.)
Gaines, William E. (Va.)
Gallinger, Jacob H. (N. H.)
Gay, Edward J. (La.)
Gear, John H. (Iowa)
Gest, William H. (Ill.)
Gibson, Charles H. (Md.)
Glass, Presley T. (Tenn.)
Glover, John M. (Mo.)
Goff, Nathan, Jr. (W. Va.)
Granger, Miles T. (Conn.)
Greenman, Edward W. (N.Y.)
Grimes, Thomas W. (Ga.)
Grosvenor, Charles H. (Ohio)
Grout, William W. (Vt.)
Guenther, Richard W. (Wis.)
Hall, Norman (Pa.)
Hare, Silas (Tex.)
Harmer, Alfred C. (Pa.)
Hatch, William H. (Mo.)
Haugen, Nils P. (Wis.)
Hayden, Edward D. (Mass.)
Hayes, Walter I. (Iowa)
Heard, John T. (Mo.)
Hemphill, John J. (S. C.)
Henderson, David B. (Iowa)
Henderson, John S. (N. C.)
Henderson, Thomas J. (Ill.)
Herbert, Hilary A. (Ala.)
Hermann, Binger (Oreg.)
Hiestand, John A. (Pa.)
Hires, George (N. J.)
Hitt, Robert R. (Ill.)
Hogg, Charles E. (W. Va.)
Holman, William S. (Ind.)
Holmes, Adoniram J. (Iowa)
Hooker, Charles E. (Miss.)
Hopkins, Arthur J. (Ill.)
Hopkins, Samuel I. (Va.)
Hopkins, Stephen T. (N. Y.)
Houk, Leonidas C. (Tenn.)
Hovey, Alvin P. (Ind.)
Howard, Jonas G. (Ind.)
Hudd, Thomas R. (Wis.)
Hunter, W. Godfrey (Ky.)
Hutton, John E. (Mo.)
Jackson, Oscar L. (Pa.)
Johnston, James T. (Ind.)
Johnston, Thomas D. (N. C.)
Jones, James T. (Ala.)
Kean, John (N. J.)
Kelley, William D. (Pa.)
Kennedy, Robert P. (Ohio)
Kerr, Daniel (Iowa)
Ketcham, John H. (N. Y.)
Kilgore, Constantine B. (Tex.)
Laffoon, Polk (Ky.)
LaFollette, Robert M. (Wis.)
Lagan, Matthew D. (La.)
Laidlaw, William G. (N. Y.)
Laird, James (Nebr.)
Landes, Silas Z. (Ill.)
Lane, Edward (Ill.)
Lanham, Samuel W. T. (Tex.)
Latham, Louis C. (N. C.)
Lawler, Frank (Ill.)
Lee, William H. F. (Va.)
Lehlbach, Herman (N. J.)
Lind, John (Minn.)
Lodge, Henry C. (Mass.)
Long, John D. (Mass.)
Lyman, Joseph (Iowa)
Lynch, John (Pa.)
McAdoo, William (N. J.)
McClammy, Charles W. (N.C.)
McComas, Louis E. (Md.)
McCormick, Henry C. (Pa.)
McCreary, James B. (Ky.)
McCullogh, Welty (Pa.)
MacDonald, John L. (Minn.)
McKenna, Joseph (Calif.)
McKinley, William, Jr. (Ohio)
McKinney, Luther F. (N. H.)
McMillin, Benton (Tenn.)
McRae, Thomas C. (Ark.)
McShane, John A. (Nebr.)
Maffett, James T. (Pa.)
Mahoney, Peter P. (N. Y.)
Maish, Levi (Pa.)
Mansur, Charles H. (Mo.)
Martin, William H. (Tex.)
Mason, William E. (Ill.)
Matson, Courtland C. (Ind.)
Merriman, Truman A. (N. Y.)
Milliken, Seth L. (Maine)
Mills, Roger Q. (Tex.)
Moffitt, John H. (N. Y.)
Montgomery, Alexander B. (Ky.)
Moore, Littleton W. (Tex.)
Morgan, James B. (Miss.)
Morrill, Edmund N. (Kans.)
Morrow, William W. (Calif.)
Morse, Leopold, (Mass.)
Neal, John R. (Tenn.)
Nelson, Knute (Minn.)
Newton, Cherubusco (La.)
Nichols, John (N. C.)
Norwood, Thomas M. (Ga.)
Nutting, Newton W. (N. Y.)
Oates, William C. (Ala.)
O'Donnell, James (Mich.)
O'Ferrall, Charles T. (Va.)
O'Neall, John H. (Ind.)
O'Neill, Charles (Pa.)
O'Neill, John J. (Mo.)
Osborne, Edwin S. (Pa.)
Outhwaite, Joseph H. (Ohio)
Owen, William D. (Ind.)
Parker, Abraham X. (N. Y.)
Patton, John (Pa.)
Payson, Lewis E. (Ill.)
Peel, Samuel W. (Ark.)
Penington, John B. (Del.)
Perkins, Bishop W. (Kans.)
Perry, William H. (S. C.)
Peters, Samuel R. (Kans.)
Phelan, James (Tenn.)
Phelps, William W. (N. J.)
Pidcock, James N. (N. J.)
Plumb, Ralph (Ill.)
Posey, Francis B. (Ind.)
Post, Philip S. (Ill.)
Pugsley, Jacob J. (Ohio)
Randall, Samuel J. (Pa.)
Rayner, Isidor (Md.)
Reed, Thomas B. (Maine)
Rice, Edmund (Minn.)
Richardson, James D. (Tenn.)
Robertson, Samuel M. (La.)
Rockwell, Francis W. (Mass.)
Rogers, John H. (Ark.)
Romeis, Jacob (Ohio)
Rowell, Jonathan H. (Ill.)
Rowland, Alfred (N. C.)
Rusk, Harry W. (Md.)
Russell, Charles A. (Conn.)
Russell, John E. (Mass.)
Ryan, Thomas (Kans.)
Sawyer, John G. (N. Y.)
Sayers, Joseph D. (Tex.)
Scott, William L. (Pa.)
Scull, Edward (Pa.)
Seney, George E. (Ohio)
Seymour, Henry W. (Mich.)
Shaw, Frank T. (Md.)
Sherman, James S. (N. Y.)
Shively, Benjamin F. (Ind.)
Simmons, Furnifold McL. (N. C.)
Smith, Henry (Wis.)
Snyder, Charles P. (W. Va.)
Sowden, William H. (Pa.)
Spinola, Francis B. (N. Y.)
Spooner, Henry J. (R. I.)
Springer, William M. (Ill.)
Stahlnecker, William G. (N. Y.)
Steele, George W. (Ind.)
Stephenson, Isaac (Wis.)
Stewart, Charles (Tex.)
Stewart, John D. (Ga.)
Stewart, John W. (Vt.)
Stockdale, Thomas R. (Miss.)
Stone, William J. (Ky.)
Struble, Isaac S. (Iowa)
Symes, George G. (Colo.)
Tarsney, Timothy E. (Mich.)
Taulbee, William P. (Ky.)
Taylor, Ezra B. (Ohio)
Taylor, Joseph D. (Ohio)
Thomas, George M. (Ky.)
Thomas, John R. (Ill.)
Thomas, Ormsby B. (Wis.)
Thompson, Albert C. (Ohio)
Tillman, George D. (S. C.)
Tompson, Thomas L. (Calif.)
Townshend, Richard W. (Ill.)
Turner, Erastus J. (Kans.)
Tracey, Charles (N. Y.)
Turner, Henry G. (Ga.)
Vance, Robert J. (Conn.)
Vandever, William (Calif.)
Wade, William H. (Mo.)

Walker, James P. (Mo.)
Warner, William (Mo.)
Washington, Joseph E. (Tenn.)
Weaver, James B. (Iowa)
Weber, John B. (N. Y.)
West, George (N. Y.)
Wheeler, Joseph (Ala.)
White, Jacob B. (Ind.)
White, Stephen V. (N. Y.)
Whiting, Justin R. (Mich.)
Whiting, William (Mass.)
Whitthorne, Washington C. (Tenn.)
Wickham, Charles P. (Ohio)
Wilber, David (N. Y.)
Wilkins, Beriah (Ohio)
Wilkinson, Theodore S. (La.)
Williams, Elihu S. (Ohio)
Wilson, Thomas (Minn.)
Wilson, William L. (W. Va.)
Wise, George D. (Va.)
Woodburn, William (Nev.)
Yardley, Robert M. (Pa.)
Yoder, Samuel S. (Ohio)
Yost, Jacob (Va.)

The Fifty-first Congress (1889-91)

Reed, Thomas B. (Maine) Speaker.

Abbott, Jo (Tex.)
Adams, George E. (Ill.)
Alderson, John D. (W. Va.)
Allen, Edward P. (Mich.)
Allen, John M. (Miss.)
Anderson, Chapman L. (Miss.)
Anderson, John A. (Kans.)
Andrew, John F. (Mass.)
Arnold, Warren O. (R. I.)
Atkinson, George W. (W. Va.)
Atkinson, Louis E. (Pa.)
Baker, Charles S. (N. Y.)
Bankhead, John H. (Ala.)
Banks, Nathaniel P. (Mass.)
Barnes, George T. (Ga.)
Bartine, Horace F. (Nev.)
Barwig, Charles (Wis.)
Bayne, Thomas M. (Pa.)
Beckwith, Charles D. (N. J.)
Belden, James J. (N. Y.)
Belknap, Charles E. (Mich.)
Bergen, Christopher A. (N. J.)
Biggs, Marion (Calif.)
Bingham, Henry H. (Pa.)
Blanchard, Newton C. (La.)
Bland, Richard P. (Mo.)
Bliss, Aaron T. (Mich.)
Blount, James H. (Ga.)
Boatner, Charles J. (La.)
Boothman, Melvin M. (Ohio)
Boutelle, Charles A. (Maine)
Bowden, George E. (Va.)
Breckinridge, Clifton R. (Ark.)
Breckinridge, William C. P. (Ky.)
Brewer, Mark S. (Mich.)
Brickner, George H. (Wis.)
Brookshire, Elijah V. (Ind.)
Brosius, Marriott (Pa.)
Brower, John M. (N. C.)
Brown, Jason B. (Ind.)
Browne, Thomas H. B. (Va.)
Browne, Thomas M. (Ind.)
Brunner, David B. (Pa.)
Buchanan, James (N. J.)
Buchanan, John A. (Va.)
Buckalew, Charles R. (Pa.)
Bullock, Robert (Fla.)
Bunn, Benjamin H. (N. C.)
Burrows, Julius C. (Mich.)
Burton, Theodore E. (Ohio)
Butterworth, Benjamin (Ohio)
Bynum, William D. (Ind.)
Caldwell, John A. (Ohio)
Campbell, Felix (N. Y.)
Candler, Allen D. (Ga.)
Candler, John W. (Mass.)
Cannon, Joseph G. (Ill.)
Carlisle, John G. (Ky.)
Carlton, Henry H. (Ga.)
Carter, Thomas H. (Mont.)
Caruth, Asher G. (Ky.)
Caswell, Lucien B. (Wis.)
Cate, William H. (Ark.)
Cathings, Thomas C. (Miss.)
Cheadle, Joseph B. (Ind.)
Cheatham, Henry P. (N. C.)
Chipman, J. Logan (Mich.)
Clancy, John M. (N. Y.)
Clark, Charles B. (Wis.)
Clark, Clarence D. (Wyo.)
Clarke, Richard H. (Ala.)
Clements, Judson C. (Ga.)
Clunie, Thomas J. (Calif.)
Cobb, James E. (Ala.)
Cogswell, William (Mass.)
Coleman, Hamilton D. (La.)
Compton, Barnes (Md.)
Comstock, Solomon G. (Minn.)
Conger, Edwin H. (Iowa)
Connell, William J. (Nebr.)
Cooper, George W. (Ind.)
Cooper, William C. (Ohio)
Cothran, James S. (S. C.)
Covert, James W. (N. Y.)
Cowles, William H. H. (N. C.)
Craig, Samuel A. (Pa.)
Crain, William H. (Tex.)
Crisp, Charles F. (Ga.)
Culberson, David B. (Tex.)
Culbertson, William C. (Pa.)
Cummings, Amos J. (N. Y.)
Cutcheon, Byron M. (Mich.)
Dalzell, John (Pa.)
Dargan, George W. (S. C.)
Darlington, Smedley (Pa.)
Davidson, Robert H. M. (Fla.)
De Haven, John J. (Calif.)
De Lano, Milton (N. Y.)
Dibble, Samuel (S. C.)
Dickerson, William W. (Ky.)
Dingley, Nelson, Jr. (Maine)
Dockery, Alexander M. (Mo.)
Dolliver, Jonathan P. (Iowa)
Dorsey, George W. E. (Nebr.)
Dunnell, Mark H. (Minn.)
Dunphy, Edward J. (N. Y.)
Edmunds, Paul C. (Va.)
Elliott, William (S. C.)
Ellis, William T. (Ky.)
Enloe, Benjamin A. (Tenn.)
Evans, H. Clay (Tenn.)
Ewart, Hamilton G. (N. C.)
Farquhar, John M. (N. Y.)
Featherston, Lewis P. (Ark.)
Finley, Hugh F. (Ky.)
Fitch, Ashbel P. (N. Y.)
Fithian, George W. (Ill.)
Flick, James P. (Iowa)
Flood, Thomas S. (N. Y.)
Flower, Roswell P. (N. Y.)
Forman, William S. (Ill.)
Forney, William H. (Ala.)
Fowler, Samuel (N. J.)
Frank, Nathan (Mo.)
Funston, Edward H. (Kans.)
Gear, John H. (Iowa)
Geary, Thomas J. (Calif.)
Geissenhainer, Jacob A. (N.J.)
Gest, William H. (Ill.)
Gibson, Charles H. (Md.)
Gifford, Oscar S. (S. Dak.)
Goodnight, Isaac H. (Ky.)
Greenhalge, Frederic T. (Mass.)
Grimes, Thomas W. (Ga.)
Grosvenor, Charles H. (Ohio)
Grout, William W. (Vt.)
Hall, Darwin S. (Minn.)
Hansbrough, Henry C. (N. Dak.)
Hare, Silas (Tex.)
Harmer, Alfred C. (Pa.)
Hatch, William H. (Mo.)
Haugen, Nils P. (Wis.)
Hayes, Walter I. (Iowa)
Haynes, William E. (Ohio)
Hays, Edward R. (Iowa)
Heard, John T. (Mo.)
Hemphill, John J. (S. C.)
Henderson, David B. (Iowa)
Henderson, John S. (N. C.)
Henderson, Thomas J. (Ill.)
Herbert, Hilary A. (Ala.)
Hermann, Binger (Oreg.)
Hill, Charles A. (Ill.)
Hitt, Robert R. (Ill.)
Holman, William S. (Ind.)
Hooker, Charles E. (Miss.)
Hopkins, Albert J. (Ill.)
Houk, Leonidas C. (Tenn.)
Jackson, J. Monroe (W. Va.)
Kelley, Harrison (Kans.)
Kelley, William D. (Pa.)
Kennedy, Robert P. (Ohio)
Kerr, Daniel (Iowa)
Kerr, James (Pa.)
Ketcham, John H. (N. Y.)
Kilgore, Constantine B. (Tex.)
Kinsey, William M. (Mo.)
Knapp, Charles J. (N. Y.)
Lacey, John F. (Iowa)
LaFollette, Robert M. (Wis.)
Laidlaw, William G. (N. Y.)
Lane, Edward (Ill.)
Langston, John M. (Va.)
Lanham, Samuel W. T. (Tex.)
Lansing, Frederick (N. Y.)
Lawler, Frank (Ill.)
Laws, Gilbert L. (Nebr.)
Lee, William H. F. (Va.)
Lehlbach, Herman (N. J.)
Lester, Posey G. (Va.)
Lester, Rufus E. (Ga.)
Lewis, Clarke (Miss.)
Lind, John (Minn.)
Lodge, Henry C. (Mass.)
McAdoo, William (N. J.)
McCarthy, John H. (N. Y.)
McClammy, Charles W. (N.C.)
McClellan, Charles A. O. (Ind.)
McComas, Louis E. (Md.)
McCord, Myron H. (Wis.)
McCormick, Henry C. (Pa.)
McCreary, James B. (Ky.)
McDuffie, John V. (Ala.)
McKenna, Joseph (Calif.)
McKinley, William, Jr. (Ohio)
McMillin, Benton (Tenn.)
McRae, Thomas C. (Ark.)
Magner, Thomas F. (N. Y.)
Maish, Levi (Pa.)
Mansur, Charles H. (Mo.)
Martin, Augustus N. (Ind.)
Martin, William H. (Tex.)
Mason, William E. (Ill.)
Miles, Frederick (Conn.)
Miller, Thomas E. (S. C.)
Milliken, Seth L. (Maine)
Mills, Robert Q. (Tex.)
Moffitt, John H. (N. Y.)
Montgomery, Alexander B. (Ky.)
Moore, Littleton W. (Tex.)
Moore, Orren C. (N. H.)
Morey, Henry L. (Ohio)
Morgan, James B. (Miss.)
Morrill, Edmund N. (Kans.)
Morrow, William W. (Calif.)
Morse, Elijah A. (Mass.)
Mudd, Sydney E. (Md.)
Mutchler, William (Pa.)
Niedringhaus, Frederick G. (Mo.)
Norton, Richard H. (Mo.)
Nute, Alonzo (N. H.)
Oates, William C. (Ala.)
O'Donnell, James (Mich.)
O'Ferrall, Charles T. (Va.)
O'Neall, John H. (Ind.)
O'Neil, Joseph H. (Mass.)
O'Neill, Charles (Pa.)
Osborne, Edwin S. (Pa.)
Outhwaite, Joseph H. (Ohio)
Owen, William D. (Ind.)
Owens, James W. (Ohio)
Parrett, William F. (Ind.)
Payne, Sereno E. (N. Y.)
Paynter, Thomas H. (Ky.)
Payson, Lewis E. (Ill.)
Peel, Samuel W. (Ark.)
Pendleton, John O. (W. Va.)
Penington, John B. (Del.)
Perkins, Bishop W. (Kans.)
Perry, William H. (S. C.)
Peters, Samuel R. (Kans.)
Phelan, James (Tenn.)
Pickler, John A. (S. Dak.)
Pierce, Rice A. (Tenn.)
Pindar, John S. (N. Y.)
Post, Philip S. (Ill.)
Price, Andrew (La.)
Pugsley, Jacob J. (Ohio)
Quackenbush, John A. (N. Y.)
Quinn, John (N. Y.)
Raines, John (N. Y.)
Randall, Charles S. (Mass.)
Randall, Samuel J. (Pa.)
Ray, Joseph W. (Pa.)
Reed, Joseph R. (Iowa)
Reilly, James B. (Pa.)
Reyburn, John E. (Pa.)
Richardson, James D. (Tenn.)
Rife, John W. (Pa.)
Robertson, Samuel M. (La.)
Rockwell, Francis W. (Mass.)
Rogers, John H. (Ark.)
Rowell, Jonathan H. (Ill.)
Rowland, Alfred (N. C.)
Rusk, Harry W. (Md.)
Russell, Charles A. (Conn.)
Sanford, John (N. Y.)
Sawyer, John G. (N. Y.)
Sayers, Joseph D. (Tex.)
Scranton, Joseph A. (Pa.)
Scull, Edward (Pa.)
Seney, George E. (Ohio)
Sherman, James S. (N. Y.)
Shively, Benjamin F. (Ind.)
Simonds, William E. (Conn.)
Skinner, Thomas G. (N. C.)
Smith, Charles B. (W. Va.)
Smith, George W. (Ill.)
Smyser, Martin L. (Ohio)
Snider, Samuel P. (Minn.)
Spinola, Francis B. (N. Y.)
Spooner, Henry J. (R. I.)
Springer, William M. (Ill.)
Stahlnecker, William G. (N. Y.)
Stephenson, Samuel M. (Mich.)
Stewart, Charles (Tex.)
Stewart, John D. (Ga.)
Stewart, John W. (Vt.)
Stivers, Moses D. (N. Y.)
Stockbridge, Henry, Jr. (Md.)
Stockdale, Thomas R. (Miss.)
Stone, Charles W. (Pa.)
Stone, William J. (Ky.)
Stone, William J. (Mo.)
Struble, Isaac S. (Iowa)
Stump, Herman (Md.)
Sweet, Willis (Idaho)
Sweney, Joseph H. (Iowa)
Tarsney, John C. (Mo.)
Taylor, Abner (Ill.)
Taylor, Alfred A. (Tenn.)
Taylor, Ezra B. (Ohio)
Taylor, Joseph D. (Ohio)
Thomas, Ormsby B. (Wis.)
Thompson, Albert C. (Ohio)
Tillman, George D. (S. C.)
Townsend, Charles C. (Pa.)
Townsend, Hosea (Colo.)
Tracey, Charles (N. Y.)
Tucker, Henry St. G. (Va.)
Turner, Charles H. (N. Y.)
Turner, Erastus J. (Kans.)
Turner, Henry G. (Ga.)
Turpin, Louis W. (Ala.)
Vandever, William (Calif.)
Van Schaick, Isaac W. (Wis.)
Vaux, Richard (Pa.)
Venable, Edward C. (Va.)
Wade, William H. (Mo.)
Wadill, Edmund, Jr. (Va.)
Walker, James P. (Mo.)
Walker, Joseph H. (Mass.)
Wallace, Rodney (Mass.)
Wallace, William C. (N. Y.)
Washington, Joseph E. (Tenn.)
Watson, Lewis F. (Pa.)
Wheeler, Frank W. (Mich.)
Wheeler, Joseph (Ala.)
Whitelaw, Robert H. (Mo.)
Whiting, Justin R. (Mich.)
Whitthorne, Washington C. (Tenn.)
Wickham, Charles P. (Ohio)
Wike, Scott, (Ill.)
Wilber, David (N. Y.)
Wiley, John McC. (N. Y.)
Wilkinson, Theodore S. (La.)
Willcox, Washington F. (Conn.)
Williams, Elihu S. (Ohio)
Williams, James R. (Ill.)
Wilson, John H. (Ky.)
Wilson, John L. (Wash.)
Wilson, Robert P. C. (Mo.)
Wilson, William L. (W. Va.)
Wise, George D. (Va.)
Wright, Myron B. (Pa.)
Yardley, Robert M. (Pa.)
Yoder, Samuel S. (Ohio)

The Fifty-second Congress (1891-93)

Crisp, Charles F. (Ga.)
Speaker.

Abbott, Jo (Tex.)
Alderson, John D. (W. Va.)
Alexander, Sydenham B. (N. C.)
Allen, John M. (Miss.)
Amerman, Lemuel (Pa.)
Andrew, John F. (Mass.)
Antony, Edwin LeR. (Tex.)
Arnold, Marshall (Mo.)
Atkinson, Louis E. (Pa.)
Babbitt, Clinton (Wis.)
Bacon, Henry (N. Y.)
Bailey, Joseph W. (Tex.)
Baker, William (Kans.)
Bankhead, John H. (Ala.)
Bartine, Horace F. (Nev.)
Barwig, Charles (Wis.)
Beeman, Joseph H. (Miss.)
Belden, James J. (N. Y.)
Belknap, Charles E. (Mich.)
Beltzhoover, Frank E. (Pa.)
Bentley, Henry W. (N. Y.)
Bergen, Christopher A. (N. J.)
Bingham, Henry H. (Pa.)
Blanchard, Newton C. (La.)
Bland, Richard P. (Mo.)
Blount, James H. (Ga.)
Boatner, Charles J. (La.)
Boutelle, Charles A. (Maine)
Bowers, William W. (Calif.)
Bowman, Thomas (Iowa)
Branch, William A. B. (N. C.)
Brawley, William H. (S. C.)
Breckinridge, Clifton R. (Ark.)
Breckinridge, William C. P. (Ky.)
Bretz, John L. (Ind.)
Brickner, George H. (Wis.)
Broderick, Case (Kans.)
Brookshire, Elijah V. (Ind.)
Brosius, Marriott (Pa.)
Brown, Jason B. (Ind.)
Brown, John B. (Md.)
Brunner, David B. (Pa.)
Bryan, William J. (Nebr.)
Buchanan, James (N. J.)
Buchanan, John A. (Va.)
Bullock, Robert (Fla.)
Bunn, Benjamin H. (N. C.)
Bunting, Thomas L. (N. Y.)
Burrows, Julius C. (Mich.)
Busey, Samuel T. (Ill.)
Bushnell, Allen R. (Wis.)
Butler, Walter H. (Iowa)
Bynum, William D. (Ind.)
Byrns, Samuel (Mo.)
Cable, Benjamin T. (Ill.)
Cadmus, Cornelius A. (N. J.)
Caldwell, John A. (Ohio)
Caminetti, Anthony (Calif.)
Campbell, Timothy J. (N. Y.)
Capehart, James (W. Va.)
Caruth, Asher G. (Ky.)
Castle, James N. (Minn.)
Catchings, Thomas C. (Miss.)
Cate, William H. (Ark.)
Causey, John W. (Del.)
Chapin, Alfred C. (N. Y.)
Cheatham, Henry P. (N. C.)
Chipman, J. Logan (Mich.)
Clancy, John M. (N. Y.)
Clark, Clarence D. (Wyo.)
Clarke, Richard H. (Ala.)
Clover, Benjamin H. (Kans.)
Cobb, James E. (Ala.)
Cobb, Seth W. (Mo.)
Coburn, Frank P. (Wis.)
Cockran, W. Bourke (N. Y.)
Cogswell, William (Mass.)
Compton, Barnes (Md.)
Coolidge, Frederick S. (Mass.)
Coombs, William J. (N. Y.)
Cooper, George W. (Ind.)
Covert, James W. (N. Y.)
Cowles, William H. H. (N. C.)
Cox, Isaac N. (N. Y.)
Cox, Nicholas N. (Tenn.)
Craig, Alexander K. (Pa.)
Crain, William H. (Tex.)
Crawford, William T. (N. C.)
Crisp, Charles F. (Ga.)
Crosby, John C. (Mass.)
Culberson, David B. (Tex.)
Cummings, Amos J. (N. Y.)
Curtis, Newton M. (N. Y.)
Cutting, John T. (Calif.)
Dalzell, John (Pa.)
Daniell, Warren F. (N. H.)
Davis, John (Kans.)
De Armond, David A. (Mo.)
De Forest, Robert E. (Conn.)
Dickerson, William W. (Ky.)
Dingley, Nelson, Jr. (Maine)
Dixon, William W. (Mont.)
Doan, Robert E. (Ohio)
Dockery, Alexander M. (Mo.)
Dolliver, Jonathan P. (Iowa)
Donovan, Dennis D. (Ohio)
Dungan, Irvine (Ohio)
Dunphy, Edward J. (N. Y.)
Durborow, Allan C., Jr. (Ill.)
Edmunds, Paul C. (Va.)
Elliott, William (S. C.)
Ellis, William T. (Ky.)
English, Thomas D. (N. J.)
Enloe, Benjamin A. (Tenn.)
Enochs, William H. (Ohio)
Epes, James F. (Va.)
Everett, Robert W. (Ga.)
Fellows, John R. (N. Y.)
Fitch, Ashbel P. (N. Y.)
Fithian, George W. (Ill.)
Flick, James P. (Iowa)
Forman, William S. (Ill.)
Forney, William H. (Ala.)
Fowler, Samuel (N. J.)
Funston, Edward H. (Kans.)
Fyan, Robert W. (Mo.)
Gantz, Martin K. (Ohio)
Geary, Thomas J. (Calif.)
Geissenhainer, Jacob A. (N. J.)
Gillespie, Eugene P. (Pa.)
Goodnight, Isaac H. (Ky.)
Gorman, James S. (Mich.)
Grady, Benjamin F. (N. C.)
Greenleaf, Halbert S. (N. Y.)
Griswold, Matthew (Pa.)
Grout, William W. (Vt.)
Hall, Osee M. (Minn.)
Hallowell, Edwin (Pa.)
Halvorson, Kittel (Minn.)
Hamilton, John T. (Iowa)
Hare, Darius D. (Ohio)
Harmer, Alfred C. (Pa.)
Harries, William H. (Minn.)
Harter, Michael D. (Ohio)
Hatch, William H. (Mo.)
Haugen, Nils P. (Wis.)
Hayes, Walter I. (Iowa)
Haynes, William E. (Ohio)
Heard, John T. (Mo.)
Hemphill, John J. (S. C.)
Henderson, David B. (Iowa)
Henderson, John S. (N. C.)
Henderson, Thomas J. (Ill.)
Herbert, Hilary A. (Ala.)
Hermann, Binger (Oreg.)
Hilborn, Samuel G. (Calif.)
Hitt, Robert R. (Ill.)
Hoar, Sherman (Mass.)
Holman, William S. (Ind.)
Hooker, Charles E. (Miss.)
Hooker, Warren B. (N. Y.)
Hopkins, Albert C. (Pa.)
Hopkins, Albert J. (Ill.)
Houk, George W. (Ohio)
Houk, John C. (Tenn.)
Huff, George F. (Pa.)
Hull, John A. T. (Iowa)
Johnson, Henry U. (Ind.)
Johnson, Martin N. (N. Dak.)
Johnson, Tom L. (Ohio)
Johnstone, George (S. C.)
Jolley, John L. (S. Dak.)
Jones, William A. (Va.)
Kem, Omer M. (Nebr.)
Kendall, John W. (Ky.)
Kendall, Joseph M. (Ky.)
Ketcham, John H. (N. Y.)
Kilgore, Constantine B. (Tex.)
Kribbs, George F. (Pa.)
Kyle, John C. (Miss.)
Lagan, Matthew D. (La.)
Lane, Edward (Ill.)
Lanham, Samuel W. T. (Tex.)
Lapham, Oscar (R. I.)
Lawson, John W. (Va.)
Lawson, Thomas G. (Ga.)
Layton, Fernando C. (Ohio)
Lester, Posey G. (Va.)
Lester, Rufus E. (Ga.)
Lewis, Clarke (Miss.)
Lind, John (Minn.)
Little, Joseph J. (N. Y.)
Livingston, Leonidas F. (Ga.)
Lockwood, Daniel N. (N. Y.)
Lodge, Henry C. (Mass.)
Long, John B. (Tex.)
Loud, Eugene F. (Calif.)
Lynch, Thomas (Wis.)
McAleer, William (Pa.)
McClellan, Charles A. O. (Ind.)
McCreary, James B. (Ky.)
McDonald, Edward F. (N. J.)
McGann, Lawrence E. (Ill.)
McKaig, William M. (Md.)
McKeighan, William A. (Nebr.)
McKenna, Joseph (Calif.)
McKinney, Luther F. (N. H.)
McLaurin, John L. (S. C.)
McMillin, Benton (Tenn.)
McRae, Thomas C. (Ark.)
Magner, Thomas F. (N. Y.)
Mallory, Stephen R. (Fla.)
Mansur, Charles H. (Mo.)
Martin, Augustus N. (Ind.)
Meredith, Elisha E. (Va.)
Meyer, Adolph (La.)
Miller, Lucas M. (Wis.)
Milliken, Seth L. (Maine)
Mills, Roger Q. (Tex.)
Mitchell, John L. (Wis.)
Montgomery, Alexander B. (Ky.)
Moore, Littleton W. (Tex.)
Morse, Elijah A. (Mass.)
Moses, Charles L. (Ga.)
Mutchler, William (Pa.)
Newberry, Walter C. (Ill.)
Norton, Richard H. (Mo.)
Oates, William C. (Ala.)
O'Donnell, James (Mich.)
O'Ferrall, Charles T. (Va.)
Ohliger, Lewis P. (Ohio)
O'Neil, Joseph H. (Mass.)
O'Neill, Charles (Pa.)
O'Neill, John J. (Mo.)
Otis, John G. (Kans.)
Outhwaite, Joseph H. (Ohio)
Owens, James W. (Ohio)
Page, Charles H. (R. I.)
Page, Henry (Md.)
Parrett, William F. (Ind.)
Patterson, Josiah (Tenn.)
Pattison, John M. (Ohio)
Patton, David H. (Ind.)
Payne, Sereno E. (N. Y.)
Paynter, Thomas H. (Ky.)
Pearson, Albert J. (Ohio)
Peel, Samuel W. (Ark.)
Pendleton, John O. (W. Va.)
Perkins, George D. (Iowa)
Pickler, John A. (S. Dak.)
Pierce, Rice A. (Tenn.)
Post, Philip S. (Ill.)
Powers, H. Henry (Vt.)
Price, Andrew (La.)
Quackenbush, John A. (N. Y.)
Raines, John (N. Y.)
Randall, Charles S. (Mass.)
Ray, George W. (N. Y.)
Rayner, Isidor (Md.)
Reed, Thomas B. (Maine)
Reilly, James B. (Pa.)
Reyburn, John E. (Pa.)
Richardson, James D. (Tenn.)
Rife, John W. (Pa.)
Robertson, Samuel M. (La.)
Robinson, John B. (Pa.)
Rockwell, Hosea H. (N. Y.)
Rusk, H. W. (Md.)
Russell, Charles A. (Conn.)
Sanford, John (N. Y.)
Sayers, Joseph D. (Tex.)
Scott, Owen (Ill.)
Scull, Edward (Pa.)
Seerley, John J. (Iowa)
Shell, George W. (S. C.)
Shively, Benjamin F. (Ind.)
Shonk, George W. (Pa.)
Simpson, Jeremiah (Kans.)
Sipe, William A. (Pa.)
Smith, George W. (Ill.)
Snodgrass, Henry C. (Tenn.)
Snow, Herman W. (Ill.)
Sperry, Lewis (Conn.)
Springer, William M. (Ill.)
Stackhouse, Eli T. (S. C.)
Stahlnecker, William G. (N.Y.)
Stephenson, Samuel M. (Mich.)
Stevens, Moses T. (Mass.)
Steward, Lewis (Ill.)
Stewart, Andrew (Pa.)
Stewart, Charles (Tex.)
Stockdale, Thomas R. (Miss.)
Stone, Charles W. (Pa.)
Stone, William A. (Pa.)
Stone, William J. (Ky.)
Storer, Bellamy (Ohio)
Stout, Byron G. (Mich.)
Stump, Herman (Md.)
Sweet, Willis (Idaho)
Tarsney, John C. (Mo.)
Taylor, Abner (Ill.)
Taylor, Alfred A. (Tenn.)
Taylor, Ezra B. (Ohio)
Taylor, Joseph D. (Ohio)
Taylor, Vincent A. (Ohio)
Terry, William L. (Ark.)
Tillman, George D. (S. C.)
Townsend, Hosea (Colo.)
Tracey, Charles (N. Y.)
Tucker, Henry St. G. (Va.)
Turner, Henry G. (Ga.)
Turpin, Louis W. (Ala.)
Van Horn, George (N. Y.)
Wadsworth, James W. (N. Y.)
Walker, Joseph H. (Mass.)
Warner, J. DeWitt (N. Y.)
Warwick, John G. (Ohio)
Washington, Joseph E. (Tenn.)
Watson, Thomas E. (Ga.)
Waugh, Daniel W. (Ind.)
Weadock, Thomas A. E. (Mich.)
Wever, John M. (N. Y.)
Wheeler, Harrison H. (Mich.)
Wheeler, Joseph (Ala.)
White, Frederick E. (Iowa)
Whiting, Justin R. (Mich.)
Wike, Scott (Ill.)
Willcox, Washington F. (Conn.)
Williams, Archibald H. A. (N. C.)
Williams, George F. (Mass.)
Williams, James R. (Ill.)
Wilson, John H. (Ky.)
Wilson, John L. (Wash.)
Wilson, Robert P. C. (Mo.)
Wilson, William L. (W. Va.)
Winn, Thomas E. (Ga.)
Wise, George D. (Va.)
Wolverton, Simon P. (Pa.)
Wright, Myron B. (Pa.)
Youmans, Henry M. (Mich.)

The Fifty-third Congress (1893-95)

Crisp, Charles F. (Ga.)
Speaker.

Abbott, Jo (Tex.)
Adams, Robert, Jr. (Pa.)
Adams, Silas (Ky.)
Aitken, David D. (Mich.)
Alderson, John D. (W. Va.)
Aldrich, J. Frank (Ill.)
Alexander, Sydenham B. (N. C.)
Allen, John M. (Miss.)
Apsley, Lewis D. (Mass.)
Arnold, Marshall (Mo.)
Avery, John (Mich.)
Babcock, Joseph W. (Wis.)
Bailey, Joseph W. (Tex.)
Baker, Henry M. (N. H.)
Baker, William (Kans.)
Baldwin, Melvin R. (Minn.)
Bankhead, John H. (Ala.)
Barnes, Lyman E. (Wis.)
Bartholdt, Richard (Mo.)
Bartlett, Franklin (N. Y.)
Barwig, Charles (Wis.)
Beckner, William M. (Ky.)
Belden, James J. (N. Y.)
Bell, Charles K. (Tex.)
Bell, John C. (Colo.)
Beltzhoover, Frank E. (Pa.)
Berry, Albert S. (Ky.)
Bingham, Henry H. (Pa.)
Black, James C. C. (Ga.)
Black, John C. (Ill.)

Blair, Henry W. (N. H.)
Bland, Richard P. (Mo.)
Blanchard, Newton C. (La.)
Boatner, Charles J. (La.)
Boen, Haldor E. (Minn.)
Boutelle, Charles A. (Maine)
Bower, William H. (N. C.)
Bowers, William W. (Calif.)
Branch, William A. B. (N. C.)
Bratton, Robert F. (Md.)
Brawley, William H. (S. C.)
Breckinridge, Clifton R. (Ark.)
Breckinridge, William C. P. (Ky.)
Bretz, John L. (Ind.)
Brickner, George H. (Wis.)
Broderick, Case (Kans.)
Bromwell, Jacob H. (Ohio)
Brookshire, Elijah V. (Ind.)
Brosius, Marriott (Pa.)
Brown, Jason B. (Ind.)
Bryan, William J. (Nebr.)
Bundy, Hezekiah S. (Ohio)
Bunn, Benjamin H. (N. C.)
Burnes, Daniel D. (Mo.)
Burrows, Julius C. (Mich.)
Bynum, William D. (Ind.)
Cabaniss, Thomas B. (Ga.)
Cadmus, Cornelius A. (N. J.)
Caldwell, John A. (Ohio)
Caminetti, Anthony (Calif.)
Campbell, Timothy J. (N. Y.)
Cannon, Joseph G. (Ill.)
Cannon, Marion (Calif.)
Capehart, James (W. Va.)
Caruth, Asher G. (Ky.)
Catchings, Thomas C. (Miss.)
Causey, John W. (Del.)
Chickering, Charles A. (N. Y.)
Childs, Robert A. (Ill.)
Clancy, John M. (N. Y.)
Clark, Champ (Mo.)
Clarke, Richard H. (Ala.)
Cobb, James E. (Ala.)
Cobb, Seth W. (Mo.)
Cockran, W. Bourke (N. Y.)
Cockrell, Jeremiah V. (Tex.)
Coffeen, Henry A. (Wyo.)
Coffin, Charles E. (Md.)
Cogswell, William (Mass.)
Compton, Barnes (Md.)
Conn, Charles G. (Ind.)
Coombs, William J. (N. Y.)
Cooper, Charles M. (Fla.)
Cooper, George W. (Ind.)
Cooper, Henry A. (Wis.)
Cooper, Samuel B. (Tex.)
Cornish, Johnston (N. J.)
Cousins, Robert G. (Iowa)
Covert, James W. (N. Y.)
Cox, Nicholas N. (Tenn.)
Crain, William H. (Tex.)
Crawford, William T. (N. C.)
Crisp, Charles F. (Ga.)
Culberson, David B. (Tex.)
Cummings, Amos J. (N. Y.)
Curtis, Charles (Kans.)
Curtis, Newton M. (N. Y.)
Dalzell, John (Pa.)
Daniels, Charles (N. Y.)
Davey, Robert C. (La.)
Davis, John (Kans.)
De Armond, David A. (Mo.)
De Forest, Robert E. (Conn.)
Denson, William H. (Ala.)
Dingley, Nelson, Jr. (Maine)
Dinsmore, Hugh A. (Ark.)
Dockery, Alexander M. (Mo.)
Dolliver, Jonathan P. (Iowa)
Donovan, Dennis D. (Ohio)
Doolittle, William H. (Wash.)
Draper, William F. (Mass.)
Dunn, John T. (N. J.)
Dunphy, Edward J. (N. Y.)
Durborow, Allan C., Jr. (Ill.)
Edmunds, Paul C. (Va.)
Ellis, William R. (Oreg.)
Ellis, William T. (Ky.)
English, Thomas D. (N. J.)
English, Warren B. (Calif.)
Enloe, Benjamin A. (Tenn.)
Epes, James F. (Va.)
Erdman, Constantine J. (Pa.)
Everett, William (Mass.)
Fellows, John R. (N. Y.)
Fielder, George B. (N. J.)
Fitch, Ashbel P. (N. Y.)
Fithian, George W. (Ill.)
Fletcher, Loren (Minn.)
Forman, William S. (Ill.)
Funk, Benjamin F. (Ill.)
Funston, Edward H. (Kans.)
Fyan, Robert W. (Mo.)
Gardner, John J. (N. J.)
Gear, John H. (Iowa)
Geary, Thomas J. (Calif.)
Geissenhainer, Jacob A. (N.J.)
Gillet, Charles W. (N. Y.)
Gillett, Frederick H. (Mass.)
Goldzier, Julius (Ill.)
Goodnight, Isaac H. (Ky.)
Gorman, James S. (Mich.)
Grady, Benjamin F. (N. C.)
Graham, John H. (N. Y.)
Gresham, Walter (Tex.)
Griffin, Levi T. (Mich.)
Griffin, Michael (Wis.)
Grosvenor, Charles H. (Ohio)
Grout, William W. (Vt.)
Grow, Galusha A. (Pa.)
Hager, Alva L. (Iowa)
Hainer, Eugene J. (Nebr.)
Haines, Charles D. (N. Y.)
Hall, Osee M. (Minn.)
Hall, Uriel S. (Mo.)
Hammond, Thomas (Ind.)
Hare, Darius D. (Ohio)
Harmer, Alfred C. (Pa.)
Harris, William A. (Kans.)
Harrison, George P. (Ala.)
Harter, Michael D. (Ohio)
Hartman, Charles S. (Mont.)
Hatch, William H. (Mo.)
Haugen, Nils P. (Wis.)
Hayes, Walter I. (Iowa)
Heard, John T. (Mo.)
Heiner, Daniel B. (Pa.)
Henderson, David B. (Iowa)
Henderson, John S. (N. C.)
Henderson, Thomas J. (Ill.)
Hendrix, Joseph C. (N. Y.)
Henry, W. Laird (Md.)
Hepburn, William P. (Iowa)
Hermann, Binger (Oreg.)
Hicks, Josiah D. (Pa.)
Hilborn, Samuel G. (Calif.)
Hines, William H. (Pa.)
Hitt, Robert R. (Ill.)
Holman, William S. (Ind.)
Hooker, Charles E. (Miss.)
Hooker, Warren B. (N. Y.)
Hopkins, Albert C. (Pa.)
Hopkins, Albert J. (Ill.)
Houk, George W. (Ohio)
Hudson, Thomas J. (Kans.)
Hulick, George W. (Ohio)
Hull, John A. T. (Iowa)
Hunter, Andrew J. (Ill.)
Hutcheson, Joseph C. (Tex.)
Ikirt, George P. (Ohio)
Izlar, James F. (S. C.)
Johnson, Henry U. (Ind.)
Johnson, Martin N. (N. Dak.)
Johnson, Tom L. (Ohio)
Jones, William A. (Va.)
Jorden, Edwin J. (Pa.)
Joy, Charles F. (Mo.)
Kem, Omer M. (Nebr.)
Kiefer, Andrew R. (Minn.)
Kilgore, Constantine B. (Tex.)
Kribbs, George F. (Pa.)
Kyle, John C. (Miss.)
Lacey, John F. (Iowa)
Lane, Edward (Ill.)
Lapham, Oscar (R. I.)
Latimer, Asbury C. (S. C.)
Lawson, Thomas G. (Ga.)
Layton, Fernando C. (Ohio)
Le Fever, Jacob (N. Y.)
Lester, Rufus E. (Ga.)
Lilly, William (Pa.)
Linton, William S. (Mich.)
Lisle, Marcus C. (Ky.)
Little, John S. (Ark.)
Livingston, Leonidas F. (Ga.)
Lockwood, Daniel N. (N. Y.)
Loud, Eugene F. (Calif.)
Loudenslager, Henry C. (N.J.)
Lucas, William V. (S. Dak.)
Lynch, Thomas (Wis.)
McAleer, William (Pa.)
McCall, Samuel W. (Mass.)
McCleary, James T. (Minn.)
McCreary, James B. (Ky.)
McCulloch, Philip D., Jr. (Ark.)
McDannold, John J. (Ill.)
McDearmon, James C. (Tenn.)
McDowell, Alexander (Pa.)
McEttrick, Michael J. (Mass.)
McGann, Lawrence E. (Ill.)
McKaig, William M. (Md.)
McKeighan, William A. (Nebr.)
McLaurin, John L. (S. C.)
McMillin, Benton (Tenn.)
McNagny, William F. (Ind.)
McRae, Thomas C. (Ark.)
Maddox, John W. (Ga.)
Magner, Thomas F. (N. Y.)
Maguire, James G. (Calif.)
Mahon, Thaddeus M. (Pa.)
Mallory, Stephen R. (Fla.)
Marsh, Benjamin F. (Ill.)
Marshall, James W. (Va.)
Martin, Augustus N. (Ind.)
Marvin, Francis (N. Y.)
Meiklejohn, George D. (Nebr.)
Mercer, David H. (Nebr.)
Meredith, Elisha E. (Va.)
Meyer, Adolph (La.)
Milliken, Seth L. (Maine)
Money, Hernando D. (Miss.)
Montgomery, Alexander B. (Ky.)
Moon, John W. (Mich.)
Moore, Horace L. (Kans.)
Morgan, Charles H. (Mo.)
Morse, Elijah A. (Mass.)
Moses, Charles L. (Ga.)
Murray, George W. (S. C.)
Mutchler, Howard (Pa.)
Neill, Robert (Ark.)
Newlands, Francis G. (Nev.)
Northway, Stephen A. (Ohio)
Oates, William C. (Ala.)
O'Ferrall, Charles T. (Va.)
Ogden, Henry W. (La.)
O'Neil, Joseph H. (Mass.)
O'Neill, Charles (Pa.)
O'Neill, John J. (Mo.)
Outhwaite, Joseph H. (Ohio)
Page, Charles H. (R. I.)
Paschal, Thomas M. (Tex.)
Patterson, Josiah (Tenn.)
Payne, Sereno E. (N. Y.)
Paynter, Thomas H. (Ky.)
Pearson, Albert J. (Ohio)
Pence, Lafayette (Colo.)
Pendleton, George C. (Tex.)
Pendleton, John O. (W. Va.)
Perkins, George D. (Iowa)
Phillips, Thomas W. (Pa.)
Pickler, John A. (S. Dak.)
Pigott, James P. (Conn.)
Post, Philip S. (Ill.)
Powers, H. Henry (Vt.)
Price, Andrew (La.)
Quigg, Lemuel E. (N. Y.)
Randall, Charles S. (Mass.)
Ray, George W. (N. Y.)
Rayner, Isidor (Md.)
Reed, Thomas B. (Maine)
Reilly, James B. (Pa.)
Reyburn, John E. (Pa.)
Richards, James A. D. (Ohio)
Richardson, George F. (Mich.)
Richardson, James D. (Tenn.)
Ritchie, Byron F. (Ohio)
Robbins, Gaston A. (Ala.)
Robertson, Samuel M. (La.)
Robinson, John B. (Pa.)
Rusk, Harry W. (Md.)
Russell, Benjamin E. (Ga.)
Russell, Charles A. (Conn.)
Ryan, William (N. Y.)
Sayers, Joseph D. (Tex.)
Schermerhorn, Simon J. (N.Y.)
Scranton, Joseph A. (Pa.)
Settle, Thomas (N. C.)
Shaw, George B. (Wis.)
Shell, George W. (S. C.)
Sherman, James S. (N. Y.)
Sibley, Joseph C. (Pa.)
Sickles, Daniel E. (N. Y.)
Simpson, Jeremiah (Kans.)
Sipe, William A. (Pa.)
Smith, George W. (Ill.)
Snodgrass, Henry C. (Tenn.)
Somers, Peter J. (Wis.)
Sorg, Paul J. (Ohio)
Sperry, Lewis (Conn.)
Springer, William M. (Ill.)
Stallings, Jesse F. (Ala.)
Stephenson, Samuel M. (Mich.)
Stevens, Moses T. (Mass.)
Stockdale, Thomas R. (Miss.)
Stone, Charles W. (Pa.)
Stone, William A. (Pa.)
Stone, William J. (Ky.)
Storer, Bellamy (Ohio)
Strait, Thomas J. (S. C.)
Straus, Isidor (N. Y.)
Strong, Luther M. (Ohio)
Swanson, Claude A. (Va.)
Sweet, Willis (Idaho)
Talbert, W. Jasper (S. C.)
Talbott, J. Fred C. (Md.)
Tarsney, John C. (Mo.)
Tate, Farish C. (Ga.)
Tawney, James A. (Minn.)
Taylor, Alfred A. (Tenn.)
Taylor, Arthur H. (Ind.)
Terry, William L. (Ark.)
Thomas, Henry F. (Mich.)
Tracey, Charles (N. Y.)
Tucker, Henry St. G. (Va.)
Turner, Henry G. (Ga.)
Turner, Smith S. (Va.)
Turpin, Louis W. (Ala.)
Tyler, D. Gardiner (Va.)
Updegraff, Thomas (Iowa)
Van Voorhis, Henry C. (Ohio)
Van Voorhis, John (N. Y.)
Wadsworth, James W. (N. Y.)
Walker, Joseph H. (Mass.)
Wanger, Irving P. (Pa.)
Warner, John De W. (N. Y.)
Washington, Joseph E. (Tenn.)
Waugh, Daniel W. (Ind.)
Weadock, Thomas A. E. (Mich.)
Wells, Owen A. (Wis.)
Wever, John M. (N. Y.)
Wheeler, Hamilton K. (Ill.)
Wheeler, Joseph (Ala.)
White, William J. (Ohio)
Whiting, Justin R. (Mich.)
Williams, James R. (Ill.)
Williams, John S. (Miss.)
Wilson, George W. (Ohio)
Wilson, John L. (Wash.)
Wilson, William L. (W. Va.)
Wise, George D. (Va.)
Wolverton, Simon P. (Pa.)
Woodard, Frederick A. (N. C.)
Woomer, Ephraim M. (Pa.)
Wright, Ashley B. (Mass.)
Wright, Myron B. (Pa.)

The Fifty-fourth Congress (1895-97)

Reed, Thomas B. (Maine) Speaker.

Abbott, Jo (Tex.)
Acheson, Ernest F. (Pa.)
Adams, Robert, Jr. (Pa.)
Aitken, David D. (Mich.)
Aldrich, J. Frank (Ill.)
Aldrich, Truman H. (Ala.)
Aldrich, William F. (Ala.)
Allen, Clarence E. (Utah)
Allen, John M. (Miss.)
Anderson, William C. (Tenn.)
Andrews, William E. (Nebr.)
Apsley, Lewis D. (Mass.)
Arnold, Warren O. (R. I.)
Arnold, William C. (Pa.)
Atwood, Harrison H. (Mass.)
Avery, John (Mich.)
Babcock, Joseph W. (Wis.)
Bailey, Joseph W. (Tex.)
Baker, Henry M. (N. H.)
Baker, William (Kans.)
Baker, William B. (Md.)
Bankhead, John H. (Ala.)
Barham, John A. (Calif.)
Barney, Samuel S. (Wis.)
Barrett, William E. (Mass.)
Bartholdt, Richard (Mo.)
Bartlett, Charles L. (Ga.)
Bartlett, Franklin (N. Y.)
Beach, Clifton B. (Ohio)
Belknap, Hugh R. (Ill.)
Bell, Charles K. (Tex.)
Bell, John C. (Colo.)
Bennett, Charles G. (N. Y.)

Berry, Albert S. (Ky.)
Bingham, Henry H. (Pa.)
Bishop, Roswell P. (Mich.)
Black, Frank S. (N. Y.)
Black, James C. C. (Ga.)
Blue, Richard W. (Kans.)
Boatner, Charles J. (La.)
Boutelle, Charles A. (Maine)
Bowers, William W. (Calif.)
Brewster, Henry C. (N. Y.)
Broderick, Case (Kans.)
Bromwell, Jacob H. (Ohio)
Brosius, Marriott (Pa.)
Brown, Foster V. (Tenn.)
Brumm, Charles N. (Pa.)
Buck, Charles F. (La.)
Bull, Melville (R. I.)
Burrell, Orlando (Ill.)
Burton, Charles G. (Mo.)
Burton, Theodore E. (Ohio)
Calderhead, William A. (Kans.)
Cannon, Joseph G. (Ill.)
Catchings, Thomas C. (Miss.)
Chickering, Charles A. (N. Y.)
Clardy, John D. (Ky.)
Clark, Charles N. (Mo.)
Clark, Samuel M. (Iowa)
Clarke, Richard H. (Ala.)
Cobb, James E. (Ala.)
Cobb, Seth W. (Mo.)
Cockrell, Jeremiah V. (Tex.)
Codding, James H. (Pa.)
Coffin, Charles E. (Md.)
Colson, David G. (Ky.)
Connolly, James A. (Ill.)
Cook, Samuel A. (Wis.)
Cooke, Edward D. (Ill.)
Cooper, Charles M. (Fla.)
Cooper, Henry A. (Wis.)
Cooper, Samuel B. (Tex.)
Corliss, John B. (Mich.)
Cousins, Robert G. (Iowa)
Cowen, John K. (Md.)
Cox, Nicholas N. (Tenn.)
Crain, William H. (Tex.)
Crisp, Charles F. (Ga.)
Crisp, Charles R. (Ga.)
Crowley, Miles (Tex.)
Crowther, George C. (Mo.)
Crump, Rousseau O. (Mich.)
Culberson, David B. (Tex.)
Cummings, Amos J. (N. Y.)
Curtis, Charles (Kans.)
Curtis, George M. (Iowa)
Curtis, Newton M. (N. Y.)
Dalzell, John (Pa.)
Danford, Lorenzo (Ohio)
Daniels, Charles (N. Y.)
Dayton, Alston G. (W. Va.)
De Armond, David A. (Mo.)
Denny, Walter McK. (Miss.)
De Witt, Francis B. (Ohio)
Dingley, Nelson, Jr. (Maine)
Dinsmore, Hugh A. (Ark.)
Dockery, Alexander M. (Mo.)
Dolliver, Jonathan P. (Iowa)
Doolittle, William H. (Wash.)
Dovener, Blackburn B. (W.Va.)
Downing, Finis E. (Ill.)
Draper, William F. (Mass.)
Eddy, Frank M. (Minn.)
Ellett, Tazewell (Va.)
Elliott, William (S. C.)
Ellis, William R. (Oreg.)
Erdman, Constantine J. (Pa.)
Evans, Walter (Ky.)
Fairchild, Benjamin L. (N.Y.)
Faris, George W. (Ind.)
Fenton, Lucien J. (Ohio)
Fischer, Israel F. (N. Y.)
Fitzgerald, John F. (Mass.)
Fletcher, Loren (Minn.)
Foote, Wallace T., Jr. (N. Y.)
Foss, George E. (Ill.)
Fowler, Charles N. (N. J.)
Gamble, Robert J. (S. Dak.)
Gardner, John J. (N. J.)
Gibson, Henry R. (Tenn.)
Gillet, Charles W. (N. Y.)
Gillett, Frederick H. (Mass.)
Goodwyn, Albert T. (Ala.)
Graff, Joseph V. (Ill.)
Griffin, Michael (Wis.)
Griswold, Matthew (Pa.)
Grosvenor, Charles H. (Ohio)
Grout, William W. (Vt.)
Grow, Galusha A. (Pa.)
Hadley, William F. L. (Ill.)
Hager, Alva L. (Iowa)
Hainer, Eugene J. (Nebr.)
Hall, Uriel S. (Mo.)
Halterman, Frederick (Pa.)
Hanly, J. Frank (Ind.)
Hardy, Alexander M. (Ind.)
Harmer, Alfred C. (Pa.)
Harris, Stephen R. (Ohio)
Harrison, George P. (Ala.)
Hart, Joseph J. (Pa.)
Hartman, Charles S. (Mont.)
Hatch, Jethro A. (Ind.)
Heatwole, Joel P. (Minn.)
Heiner, Daniel B. (Pa.)
Hemenway, James A. (Ind.)
Henderson, David B. (Iowa)
Hendrick, John K. (Ky.)
Henry, Charles L. (Ind.)
Henry, E. Stevens (Conn.)
Hepburn, William P. (Iowa)
Hermann, Binger (Oreg.)
Hicks, Josiah D. (Pa.)
Hilborn, Samuel G. (Calif.)
Hill, Ebenezer J. (Conn.)
Hitt, Robert R. (Ill.)
Hooker, Warren B. (N. Y.)
Hopkins, Albert J. (Ill.)
Hopkins, Nathan T. (Ky.)
Howard, Milford W. (Ala.)
Howe, James R. (N. Y.)
Howell, Benjamin F. (N. J.)
Hubbard, Joel D. (Mo.)
Huff, George F. (Pa.)
Hulick, George W. (Ohio)
Huling, James H. (W. Va.)
Hull, John A. T. (Iowa)
Hunter, W. Godfrey (Ky.)
Hurley, Denis M. (N. Y.)
Hutcheson, Joseph C. (Tex.)
Hyde, Samuel C. (Wash.)
Jenkins, John J. (Wis.)
Johnson, Grove L. (Calif.)
Johnson, Henry U. (Ind.)
Johnson, Martin N. (N. Dak.)
Jones, William A. (Va.)
Joy, Charles F. (Mo.)
Keifer, Andrew R. (Minn.)
Kem, Omer M. (Nebr.)
Kendall, Joseph M. (Ky.)
Kerr, Winfield S. (Ohio)
Kirkpatrick, Snyder S. (Kans.)
Kleberg, Rudolph (Tex.)
Knox, William S. (Mass.)
Kulp, Monroe H. (Pa.)
Kyle, John C. (Miss.)
Lacey, John F. (Iowa)
Latimer, Asbury C. (S. C.)
Lawson, Thomas G. (Ga.)
Layton, Fernando C. (Ohio)
Le Fever, Jacob (N. Y.)
Leighty, Jacob D. (Ind.)
Leisenring, John (Pa.)
Leonard, Fred C. (Pa.)
Lester, Rufus E. (Ga.)
Lewis, John W. (Ky.)
Linney, Romulus Z. (N. C.)
Linton, William S. (Mich.)
Little, John S. (Ark.)
Livingston, Leonidas F. (Ga.)
Lockhart, James A. (N. C.)
Long, Chester I. (Kans.)
Lorimer, William (Ill.)
Loud, Eugene F. (Calif.)
Loudenslager, Henry C. (N.J.)
Low, Philip B. (N. Y.)
McCall, John E. (Tenn.)
McCall, Samuel W. (Mass.)
McCleary, James T. (Minn.)
McClellan, George B. (N. Y.)
McClure, Addison S. (Ohio)
McCormick, Richard C. (N.Y.)
McCreary, James B. (Ky.)
McCulloch, Philip D. (Ark.)
McDearmon, James C. (Tenn.)
McEwan, Thomas, Jr. (N. J.)
McKenney, William R. (Va.)
McLachlan, James (Calif.)
McLaurin, John L. (S. C.)
McMillin, Benton (Tenn.)
McRae, Thomas C. (Ark.)
Maddox, John W. (Ga.)
Maguire, James G. (Calif.)
Mahany, Rowland B. (N. Y.)
Mahon, Thaddeus M. (Pa.)
Marsh, Benjamin F. (Ill.)
Martin, Charles H. (N. C.)
Meiklejohn, George D. (Nebr.)
Mercer, David H. (Nebr.)
Meredith, Elisha E. (Va.)
Meyer, Adolph (La.)
Miles, Joshua W. (Md.)
Miller, Orrin L. (Kans.)
Miller, Warren (W. Va.)
Milliken, Seth L. (Maine)
Milnes, Alfred (Mich.)
Miner, Henry C. (N. Y.)
Minor, Edward S. (Wis.)
Mitchell, John M. (N. Y.)
Mondell, Frank W. (Wyo.)
Money, Hernando D. (Miss.)
Moody, William H. (Mass.)
Morse, Elijah A. (Mass.)
Moses, Charles L. (Ga.)
Mozley, Norman A. (Mo.)
Murphy, Everett J. (Ill.)
Murray, George W. (S. C.)
Neill, Robert (Ark.)
Newlands, Francis G. (Nev.)
Noonan, George H. (Tex.)
Northway, Stephen A. (Ohio)
Odell, Benjamin B., Jr. (N.Y.)
Ogden, Henry W. (La.)
Otey, Peter J. (Va.)
Otjen, Theobald (Wis.)
Overstreet, Jesse (Ind.)
Owens, William C. (Ky.)
Parker, Richard W. (N. J.)
Patterson, Josiah (Tenn.)
Payne, Sereno E. (N. Y.)
Pearson, Richmond (N. C.)
Pendleton, George C. (Tex.)
Perkins, George D. (Iowa)
Phillips, Thomas W. (Pa.)
Pickler, John A. (S. Dak.)
Pitney, Mahlon (N. J.)
Poole, Theodore L. (N. Y.)
Powers, H. Henry (Vt.)
Price, Andrew (La.)
Prince, George W. (Ill.)
Pugh, Samuel J. (Ky.)
Quigg, Lemuel E. (N. Y.)
Raney, John H. (Mo.)
Ray, George W. (N. Y.)
Reed, Thomas B. (Maine)
Reeves, Walter (Ill.)
Reyburn, John E. (Pa.)
Richardson, James D. (Tenn.)
Rinaker, John I. (Ill.)
Robbins, Gaston A. (Ala.)
Robertson, Samuel M. (La.)
Robinson, John B. (Pa.)
Royse, Lemuel W. (Ind.)
Rusk, Harry W. (Md.)
Russell, Benjamin E. (Ga.)
Russell, Charles A. (Conn.)
Sauerhering, Edward (Wis.)
Sayers, Joseph D. (Tex.)
Scranton, Joseph A. (Pa.)
Settle, Thomas (N. C.)
Shafroth, John F. (Colo.)
Shannon, Richard C. (N. Y.)
Shaw, John G. (N. C.)
Sherman, James S. (N. Y.)
Shuford, Alonzo C. (N. C.)
Simpkins, John (Mass.)
Skinner, Harry (N. C.)
Smith, George W. (Ill.)
Smith, William A. (Mich.)
Snover, Horace G. (Mich.)
Sorg, Paul J. (Ohio)
Southard, James H. (Ohio)
Southwick, George N. (N. Y.)
Spalding, George (Mich.)
Sparkman, Stephen M. (Fla.)
Spencer, James G. (Miss.)
Sperry, Nehemiah D. (Conn.)
Stahle, James A. (Pa.)
Stallings, Jesse F. (Ala.)
Steele, George W. (Ind.)
Stephenson, Samuel M. (Mich.)
Stewart, Alexander (Wis.)
Stewart, James F. (N. J.)
Stokes, J. William (S. C.)
Stone, Charles W. (Pa.)
Stone, William A. (Pa.)
Strait, Thomas J. (S. C.)
Strode, Jesse B. (Nebr.)
Strong, Luther M. (Ohio)
Strowd, William F. (N. C.)
Sulloway, Cyrus A. (N. H.)
Sulzer, William (N. Y.)
Swanson, Claude A. (Va.)
Taft, Charles P. (Ohio)
Talbert, W. Jasper (S. C.)
Tarsney, John C. (Mo.)
Tate, Farish C. (Ga.)
Tawney, James A. (Minn.)
Tayler, Robert W. (Ohio)
Terry, William L. (Ark.)
Thomas, Henry F. (Mich.)
Thorp, Robert T. (Va.)
Towne, Charles A. (Minn.)
Tracewell, Robert J. (Ind.)
Tracey, John P. (Mo.)
Treloar, William M. (Mo.)
Tucker, Henry St. G. (Va.)
Turner, Henry G. (Ga.)
Turner, Smith S. (Va.)
Tyler, D. Gardiner (Va.)
Underwood, Oscar W. (Ala.)
Updegraff, Thomas (Iowa)
Van Horn, Robert T. (Mo.)
Van Voorhis, Henry C. (Ohio)
Wadsworth, James W. (N. Y.)
Walker, James A. (Va.)
Walker, Joseph H. (Mass.)
Walsh, James J. (N. Y.)
Wanger, Irving P. (Pa.)
Warner, Vespasian (Ill.)
Washington, Joseph E. (Tenn.)
Watson, David K. (Ohio)
Watson, James E. (Ind.)
Wellington, George L. (Md.)
Wheeler, Joseph (Ala.)
White, George E. (Ill.)
Wilber, David F. (N. Y.)
Williams, John S. (Miss.)
Willis, Jonathan S. (Del.)
Wilson, Edgar (Idaho)
Wilson, Francis H. (N. Y.)
Wilson, George W. (Ohio)
Wilson, Stanyarne (S. C.)
Wood, Benson (Ill.)
Woodard, Frederick A. (N. C.)
Woodman, Charles W. (Ill.)
Woomer, Ephraim M. (Pa.)
Wright, Ashley B. (Mass.)
Yoakum, Charles H. (Tex.)

The Fifty-fifth Congress (1897-99)

Reed, Thomas B. (Maine)
Speaker.

Acheson, Ernest F. (Pa.)
Adams, Robert, Jr. (Pa.)
Adamson, William C. (Ga.)
Aldrich, William F. (Ala.)
Alexander, De Alva S. (N. Y.)
Allen, John M. (Miss.)
Arnold, William C. (Pa.)
Babcock, Joseph W. (Wis.)
Bailey, Joseph W. (Tex.)
Baird, Samuel T. (La.)
Baker, Jehu (Ill.)
Baker, William B. (Md.)
Ball, Thomas H. (Tex.)
Bankhead, John H. (Ala.)
Barber, Isaac A. (Md.)
Barham, John A. (Calif.)
Barlow, Charles A. (Calif.)
Barney, Samuel S. (Wis.)
Barrett, William E. (Mass.)
Barrows, Samuel J. (Mass.)
Bartholdt, Richard (Mo.)
Bartlett, Charles L. (Ga.)
Beach, Clifton B. (Ohio)
Belden, James J. (N. Y.)
Belford, Joseph M. (N. Y.)
Belknap, Hugh R. (Ill.)
Bell, John C. (Colo.)
Benner, George J. (Pa.)
Bennett, Charles G. (N. Y.)
Benton, Maecenas E. (Mo.)
Berry, Albert S. (Ky.)
Bingham, Henry H. (Pa.)
Bishop, Roswell P. (Mich.)
Bland, Richard P. (Mo.)
Bodine, Robert N. (Mo.)
Booze, William S. (Md.)
Botkin, Jeremiah D. (Kans.)
Boutell, Henry S. (Ill.)
Boutelle, Charles A. (Maine)
Bradley, Thomas J. (N. Y.)
Brantley, William G. (Ga.)
Brenner, John L. (Ohio)
Brewer, Willis (Ala.)
Brewster, Henry C. (N. Y.)
Broderick, Case (Kans.)
Bromwell, Jacob H. (Ohio)
Brosius, Marriott (Pa.)
Broussard, Robert F. (La.)
Brown, Seth W. (Ohio)
Brownlow, Walter P. (Tenn.)

Brucker, Ferdinand (Mich.)
Brumm, Charles N. (Pa.)
Brundidge, Stephen, Jr. (Ark.)
Bull, Melville (R. I.)
Burke, Robert E. (Tex.)
Burleigh, Edwin C. (Maine)
Burton, Theodore E. (Ohio)
Butler, Thomas S. (Pa.)
Campbell, James R. (Ill.)
Cannon, Joseph G. (Ill.)
Capron, Adin B. (R. I.)
Carmack, Edward W. (Tenn.)
Castle, Curtis H. (Calif.)
Catchings, Thomas C. (Miss.)
Chickering, Charles A. (N. Y.)
Clardy, John D. (Ky.)
Clark, Champ (Mo.)
Clark, Samuel M. (Iowa)
Clarke, Frank G. (N. H.)
Clayton, Henry D. (Ala.)
Cochran, Charles F. (Mo.)
Cochrane, Aaron V. S. (N.Y.)
Codding, James H. (Pa.)
Colson, David G. (Ky.)
Connell, William (Pa.)
Connolly, James A. (Ill.)
Cooke, Edward D. (Ill.)
Cooney, James (Mo.)
Cooper, Henry A. (Wis.)
Cooper, Samuel B. (Tex.)
Corliss, John B. (Mich.)
Cousins, Robert G. (Iowa)
Cowherd, William S. (Mo.)
Cox, Nicholas N. (Tenn.)
Cranford, John W. (Tex.)
Crump, Rousseau O. (Mich.)
Crumpacker, Edgar D. (Ind.)
Cummings, Amos J. (N. Y.)
Curtis, Charles (Kans.)
Curtis, George M. (Iowa)
Dalzell, John (Pa.)
Danford, Lorenzo (Ohio)
Davenport, Samuel A. (Pa.)
Davey, Robert C. (La.)
Davidson, James H. (Wis.)
Davis, Robert W. (Fla.)
Davison, George M. (Ky.)
Dayton, Alston G. (W. Va.)
De Armond, David A. (Mo.)
De Graffenreid, Reese C. (Tex.)
De Vries, Marion (Calif.)
Dick, Charles W. F. (Ohio)
Dingley, Nelson (Maine)
Dinsmore, Hugh A. (Ark.)
Dockery, Alexander M. (Mo.)
Dolliver, Jonathan P. (Iowa)
Dorr, Charles P. (W. Va.)
Dovener, Blackburn B. (W. Va.)
Driggs, Edmund H. (N. Y.)
Eddy, Frank M. (Minn.)
Elliott, William (S. C.)
Ellis, William R. (Oreg.)
Epes, Sydney P. (Va.)
Ermentrout, Daniel (Pa.)
Evans, Walter (Ky.)
Faris, George W. (Ind.)
Fenton, Lucien J. (Ohio)
Fischer, Israel F. (N. Y.)
Fitzgerald, John F. (Mass.)
Fitzpatrick, Thomas Y. (Ky.)
Fleming, William H. (Ga.)
Fletcher, Loren (Minn.)
Foote, Wallace T., Jr. (N. Y.)
Foss, George E. (Ill.)
Fowler, Charles N. (N. J.)
Fowler, John E. (N. C.)
Fox, Andrew F. (Miss.)
Gaines, John W. (Tenn.)
Gardner, John J. (N. J.)
Gibson, Henry R. (Tenn.)
Gillet, Charles W. (N. Y.)
Gillett, Frederick H. (Mass.)
Graff, Joseph V. (Ill.)
Graham, William H. (Pa.)
Greene, William L. (Nebr.)
Greene, William S. (Mass.)
Griffin, Michael (Wis.)
Griffith, Francis M. (Ind.)
Griggs, James M. (Ga.)
Grosvenor, Charles H. (Ohio)
Grout, William W. (Vt.)
Grow, Galusha A. (Pa.)
Gunn, James (Idaho)
Hager, Alva L. (Iowa)
Hamilton, Edward L. (Mich.)
Handy, Levin I. (Del.)
Harmer, Alfred C. (Pa.)
Hartman, Charles S. (Mont.)
Hawley, Robert B. (Tex.)
Hay, James (Va.)
Heatwole, Joel P. (Minn.)
Hemenway, James A. (Ind.)
Henderson, David B. (Iowa)
Henry, Charles L. (Ind.)
Henry, E. Stevens (Conn.)
Henry, Patrick (Miss.)
Henry, Robert L. (Tex.)
Hepburn, William P. (Iowa)
Hicks, Josiah D. (Pa.)
Hilborn, Samuel G. (Calif.)
Hill, Ebenezer J. (Conn.)
Hinrichsen, William H. (Ill.)
Hitt, Robert R. (Ill.)
Holman, William S. (Ind.)
Hooker, Warren B. (N. Y.)
Hopkins, Albert J. (Ill.)
Howard, Milford W. (Ala.)
Howard, William M. (Ga.)
Howe, James R. (N. Y.)
Howell, Benjamin F. (N. J.)
Hull, John A. T. (Iowa)
Hunter, Andrew J. (Ill.)
Hurley, Denis M. (N. Y.)
Jenkins, John J. (Wis.)
Jett, Thomas M. (Ill.)
Johnson, Henry U. (Ind.)
Johnson, Martin N. (N. Dak.)
Jones, William A. (Va.)
Jones, William C. (Wash.)
Joy, Charles F. (Mo.)
Kelley, John E. (S. Dak.)
Kerr, Winfield S. (Ohio)
Ketcham, John H. (N. Y.)
King, William H. (Utah)
Kirkpatrick, William S. (Pa.)
Kitchin, William W. (N. C.)
Kleberg, Rudolph (Tex.)
Knowles, Freeman (S. Dak.)
Knox, William S. (Mass.)
Kulp, Monroe H. (Pa.)
Lacey, John F. (Iowa)
Lamb, John (Va.)
Landis, Charles B. (Ind.)
Lanham, Samuel W. T. (Tex.)
Latimer, Asbury C. (S. C.)
Lawrence, George P. (Mass.)
Lentz, John J. (Ohio)
Lester, Rufus E. (Ga.)
Lewis, Elijah B. (Ga.)
Lewis, James H. (Wash.)
Linney, Romulus Z. (N. C.)
Littauer, Lucius N. (N. Y.)
Little, John S. (Ark.)
Livingston, Leonidas F. (Ga.)
Lloyd, James T. (Mo.)
Lorimer, William (Ill.)
Loud, Eugene F. (Calif.)
Loudenslager, Henry C. (N.J.)
Love, William F. (Miss.)
Lovering, William C. (Mass.)
Low, Philip B. (N. Y.)
Lybrand, Archibald (Ohio)
McAleer, William (Pa.)
McCall, Samuel W. (Mass.)
McCleary, James T. (Minn.)
McClellan, George B. (N. Y.)
McCormick, Nelson B. (Kans.)
McCulloch, Philip D. (Ark.)
McDonald, John (Md.)
McDowell, John A. (Ohio)
McEwan, Thomas, Jr. (N. J.)
McIntire, William W. (Md.)
McLain, Frank A. (Miss.)
McLaurin, John L. (S. C.)
McMillin, Benton (Tenn.)
McRae, Thomas C. (Ark.)
Maddox, John W. (Ga.)
Maguire, James G. (Calif.)
Mahany, Rowland B. (N. Y.)
Mahon, Thaddeus M. (Pa.)
Mann, James R. (Ill.)
Marsh, Benjamin F. (Ill.)
Marshall, George A. (Ohio)
Martin, Charles H. (N. C.)
Maxwell, Samuel (Nebr.)
Meekison, David (Ohio)
Mercer, David H. (Nebr.)
Mesick, William S. (Mich.)
Meyer, Adolph (La.)
Miers, Robert W. (Ind.)
Miller, Warren (W. Va.)
Milliken, Seth L. (Maine)
Mills, Daniel W. (Ill.)
Minor, Edward S. (Wis.)
Mitchell, John M. (N. Y.)
Moody, William H. (Mass.)
Moon, John A. (Tenn.)
Morris, R. Page W. (Minn.)
Mudd, Sydney E. (Md.)
Newlands, Francis G. (Nev.)
Northway, Stephen A. (Ohio)
Norton, James (S. C.)
Norton, James A. (Ohio)
Odell, Benjamin B., Jr. (N.Y.)
Ogden, Henry W. (La.)
Olmsted, Marlin E. (Pa.)
Osborne, John E. (Wyo.)
Otey, Peter J. (Va.)
Otjen, Theobold (Wis.)
Overstreet, Jesse (Ind.)
Packer, Horace B. (Pa.)
Parker, Richard W. (N. J.)
Payne, Sereno E. (N. Y.)
Pearce, Charles E. (Mo.)
Pearson, Richmond (N. C.)
Perkins, George D. (Iowa)
Peters, Mason S. (Kans.)
Pierce, Rice A. (Tenn.)
Pitney, Mahlon (N. J.)
Plowman, Thomas S. (Ala.)
Powers, H. Henry (Vt.)
Prince, George W. (Ill.)
Pugh, Samuel J. (Ky.)
Quigg, Lemuel E. (N. Y.)
Ray, George W. (N. Y.)
Reed, Thomas B. (Maine)
Reeves, Walter (Ill.)
Rhea, John S. (Ky.)
Richardson, James D. (Tenn.)
Ridgely, Edwin R. (Kans.)
Rixey, John F. (Va.)
Robb, Edward (Mo.)
Robbins, Edward E. (Pa.)
Robertson, Samuel M. (La.)
Robinson, James M. (Ind.)
Royse, Lemuel W. (Ind.)
Russell, Charles A. (Conn.)
Sauerhering, Edward (Wis.)
Sayers, Joseph D. (Tex.)
Settle, Evan E. (Ky.)
Shafroth, John F. (Colo.)
Shannon, Richard C. (N. Y.)
Shattuc, William B. (Ohio)
Shelden, Carlos D. (Mich.)
Sherman, James S. (N. Y.)
Showalter, Joseph B. (Pa.)
Shuford, Alonzo C. (N. C.)
Simpkins, John (Mass.)
Simpson, Jeremiah (Kans.)
Sims, Thetus W. (Tenn.)
Skinner, Harry (N. C.)
Slayden, James L. (Tex.)
Smith, David H. (Ky.)
Smith, George W. (Ill.)
Smith, Samuel W. (Mich.)
Smith, William A. (Mich.)
Snover, Horace G. (Mich.)
Southard, James H. (Ohio)
Southwick, George N. (N. Y.)
Spalding, George (Mich.)
Sparkman, Stephen M. (Fla.)
Sperry, Nehemiah D. (Conn.)
Spight, Thomas (Miss.)
Sprague, Charles F. (Mass.)
Stallings, Jesse F. (Ala.)
Stark, William L. (Nebr.)
Steele, George W. (Ind.)
Stephens, John H. (Tex.)
Stevens, Frederick C. (Minn.)
Stewart, Alexander (Wis.)
Stewart, James F. (N. J.)
Stokes, J. William (S. C.)
Stone, Charles W. (Pa.)
Stone, William A. (Pa.)
Strait, Thomas J. (S C..)
Strode, Jesse B. (Nebr.)
Strowd, William F. (N. C.)
Sturtevant, John C. (Pa.)
Sullivan, William V. (Miss.)
Sulloway, Cyrus A. (N. H.)
Sulzer, William (N. Y.)
Sutherland, Roderick D. (Nebr.)
Swanson, Claude A. (Va.)
Talbert, W. Jasper (S. C.)
Tate, Farish C. (Ga.)
Tawney, James A. (Minn.)
Tayler, Robert W. (Ohio)
Taylor, George W. (Ala.)
Terry, William L. (Ark.)
Thorp, Robert T. (Va.)
Todd, Albert M. (Mich.)
Tongue, Thomas H. (Oreg.)
Underwood, Oscar W. (Ala.)
Updegraff, Thomas (Iowa)
Vandiver, Willard D. (Mo.)
Van Voorhis, Henry C. (Ohio)
Vehslage, John H. G. (N. Y.)
Vincent, William D. (Kans.)
Wadsworth, James W. (N. Y.)
Walker, James A. (Va.)
Walker, Joseph H. (Mass.)
Wanger, Irving P. (Pa.)
Ward, William L. (N. Y.)
Warner, Vespasian (Ill.)
Weaver, Walter L. (Ohio)
Weymouth, George W. (Mass.)
Wheeler, Charles K. (Ky.)
Wheeler, Joseph (Ala.)
White, George E. (Ill.)
White, George H. (N. C.)
Wilber, David F. (N. Y.)
Williams, John S. (Miss.)
Williams, Morgan B. (Pa.)
Wilson, Francis H. (N. Y.)
Wilson, Stanyarne (S. C.)
Wise, Richard A. (Va.)
Wright, Ashley B. (Mass.)
Yost, Jacob (Va.)
Young, James R. (Pa.)
Young, William A. (Va.)
Zenor, William T. (Ind.)

The Fifty-sixth Congress (1899-1901)

Henderson, David B. (Iowa) Speaker.

Acheson, Ernest F. (Pa.)
Adams, Robert, Jr. (Pa.)
Adamson, William C. (Ga.)
Aldrich, William F. (Ala.)
Alexander, De Alva S. (N. Y.)
Allen, Amos L. (Maine)
Allen, Henry D. (Ky.)
Allen, John M. (Miss.)
Atwater, John W. (N. C.)
Babcock, Joseph W. (Wis.)
Bailey, Joseph W. (Tex.)
Bailey, Willis J. (Kans.)
Baker, William B. (Md.)
Ball, Thomas H. (Tex.)
Bankhead, John H. (Ala.)
Barber, Laird H. (Pa.)
Barham, John A. (Calif.)
Barney, Samuel S. (Wis.)
Bartholdt, Richard (Mo.)
Bartlett, Charles L. (Ga.)
Bell, John C. (Colo.)
Bellamy, John D. (N. C.)
Benton, Maecenas E. (Mo.)
Berry, Albert S. (Ky.)
Bingham, Henry H. (Pa.)
Bishop, Roswell P. (Mich.)
Boreing, Vincent S. (Ky.)
Boutell, Henry S. (Ill.)
Boutelle, Charles A. (Maine)
Bowersock, Justin D. (Kans.)
Bradley, Thomas J. (N. Y.)
Brantley, William G. (Ga.)
Breazeale, Phanor (La.)
Brenner, John L. (Ohio)
Brewer, Willis (Ala.)
Brick, Abraham L. (Ind.)
Bromwell, Jacob H. (Ohio)
Brosius, Marriott (Pa.)
Broussard, Robert F. (La.)
Brown, Seth W. (Ohio)
Brownlow, Walter P. (Tenn.)
Brundidge, Stephen, Jr. (Ark.)
Bull, Melville (R. I.)
Burke, Charles H. (S. Dak.)
Burke, Robert E. (Tex.)
Burkett, Elmer J. (Nebr.)
Burleigh, Edwin C. (Maine)
Burleson, Albert S. (Tex.)
Burnett, John L. (Ala.)
Burton, Theodore E. (Ohio)
Butler, Thomas S. (Pa.)
Calderhead, William A. (Kans.)
Caldwell, Ben F. (Ill.)
Campbell, Albert J. (Mont.)
Cannon, Joseph G. (Ill.)
Capron, Adin B. (R. I.)
Carmack, Edward W. (Tenn.)
Catchings, Thomas C. (Miss.)
Chanler, William A. (N. Y.)
Chickering, Charles A. (N. Y.)
Clark, Champ (Mo.)
Clarke, Frank G. (N. H.)
Clayton, Bertram T. (N. Y.)
Clayton, Henry D. (Ala.)

Cochran, Charles F. (Mo.)
Cochrane, Aaron V. S. (N.Y.)
Connell, William (Pa.)
Conner, James P. (Iowa)
Cooney, James (Mo.)
Cooper, Henry A. (Wis.)
Cooper, Samuel B. (Tex.)
Corliss, John B. (Mich.)
Cousins, Robert G. (Iowa)
Cowherd, William S. (Mo.)
Cox, Nicholas N. (Tenn.)
Crawford, William T. (N. C.)
Cromer, George W. (Ind.)
Crowley, Joseph B. (Ill.)
Crump, Rousseau O. (Mich.)
Crumpacker, Edgar D. (Ind.)
Cummings, Amos J. (N. Y.)
Curtis, Charles (Kans.)
Cusack, Thomas (Ill.)
Cushman, Francis W. (Wash.)
Dahle, Herman B. (Wis.)
Daly, William D. (N. J.)
Dalzell, John (Pa.)
Davenport, Samuel A. (Pa.)
Davenport, Stanley W. (Pa.)
Davey, Robert C. (La.)
Davidson, James H. (Wis.)
Davis, Robert W. (Fla.)
Dayton, Alston G. (W. Va.)
De Armond, David A. (Mo.)
De Graffenreid, Reese C. (Tex.)
De Vries, Marion (Calif.)
Denny, James W. (Md.)
Dick, Charles W. F. (Ohio)
Dinsmore, Hugh A. (Ark.)
Dolliver, Jonathan P. (Iowa)
Dougherty, John (Mo.)
Dovener, Blackburn B. (W. Va.)
Driggs, Edmund H. (N. Y.)
Driscoll, Michael E. (N. Y.)
Eddy, Frank M. (Minn.)
Elliott, William (S. C.)
Emerson, Louis W. (N. Y.)
Epes, Sydney P. (Va.)
Esch, John J. (Wis.)
Faris, George W. (Ind.)
Finley, David E. (S. C.)
Fitzgerald, John F. (Mass.)
Fitzgerald, John J. (N. Y.)
Fitzpatrick, Thomas Y. (Ky.)
Fleming, William H. (Ga.)
Fletcher, Loren (Minn.)
Fordney, Joseph W. (Mich.)
Foss, George E. (Ill.)
Foster, George P. (Ill.)
Fowler, Charles N. (N. J.)
Fox, Andrew F. (Miss.)
Freer, Romeo H. (W. Va.)
Gaines, John W. (Tenn.)
Gamble, Robert J. (S. Dak.)
Gardner, John J. (N. J.)
Gardner, Washington (Mich.)
Gaston, Athelston (Pa.)
Gayle, June W. (Ky.)
Gibson, Henry R. (Tenn.)
Gilbert, George G. (Ky.)
Gill, Joseph J. (Ohio)
Gillet, Charles W. (N. Y.)
Gillett, Frederick H. (Mass.)
Glynn, Martin H. (N. Y.)
Gordon, Robert B. (Ohio)
Graff, Joseph V. (Ill.)
Graham, William H. (Pa.)
Green, Henry D. (Pa.)
Greene, William S. (Mass.)
Griffith, Francis M. (Ind.)
Griggs, James M. (Ga.)
Grosvenor, Charles H. (Ohio)
Grout, William W. (Vt.)
Grow, Galusha A. (Pa.)
Hall, James K. P. (Pa.)
Hamilton, Edward L. (Mich.)
Harmer, Alfred C. (Pa.)
Haugen, Gilbert N. (Iowa)
Hawley, Robert B. (Tex.)
Hay, James (Va.)
Heatwole, Joel P. (Minn.)
Hedge, Thomas (Iowa)
Hemenway, James A. (Ind.)
Henderson, David B. (Iowa)
Henry, E. Stevens (Conn.)
Henry, Patrick (Miss.)
Henry, Robert L. (Tex.)
Hepburn, William P. (Iowa)
Hill, Ebenezer J. (Conn.)
Hitt, Robert R. (Ill.)
Hoffecker, John H. (Del.)
Hoffecker, Walter O. (Del.)
Hopkins, Albert J. (Ill.)
Howard, William M. (Ga.)
Howell, Benjamin F. (N. J.)
Hull, John A. T. (Iowa)
Jack, Summers M. (Pa.)
Jenkins, John J. (Wis.)
Jett, Thomas M. (Ill.)
Johnston, David E. (W. Va.)
Jones, Wesley L. (Wash.)
Jones, William A. (Va.)
Joy, Charles F. (Mo.)
Kahn, Julius (Calif.)
Kerr, Josiah L. (Md.)
Kerr, Winfield S. (Ohio)
Ketcham, John H. (N. Y.)
King, William H. (Utah)
Kitchin, William W. (N. C.)
Kleberg, Rudolph (Tex.)
Kluttz, Theodore F. (N. C.)
Knox, William S. (Mass.)
Lacey, John F. (Iowa)
Lamb, John (Va.)
Landis, Charles B. (Ind.)
Lane, Joseph R. (Iowa)
Lanham, Samuel W. T. (Tex.)
Lassiter, Francis R. (Va.)
Latimer, Asbury C. (S. C.)
Lawrence, George P. (Mass.)
Lentz, John J. (Ohio)
Lester, Rufus E. (Ga.)
Levy, Jefferson M. (N. Y.)
Lewis, Elijah B. (Ga.)
Linney, Romulus Z. (N. C.)
Littauer, Lucius N. (N. Y.)
Little, John S. (Ark.)
Littlefield, Charles E. (Maine)
Livingston, Leonidas F. (Ga.)
Lloyd, James T. (Mo.)
Long, Chester I. (Kans.)
Lorimer, William (Ill.)
Loud, Eugene F. (Calif.)
Loudenslager, Henry C. (N.J.)
Lovering, William C. (Mass.)
Lybrand, Archibald (Ohio)
McAleer, William (Pa.)
McCall, Samuel W. (Mass.)
McCleary, James T. (Minn.)
McClellan, George B. (N. Y.)
McCulloch, Philip D. (Ark.)
McDermott, Allen L. (N. J.)
McDowell, John A. (Ohio)
McLain, Frank A. (Miss.)
McPherson, Smith (Iowa)
McRae, Thomas C. (Ark.)
Maddox, John W. (Ga.)
Mahon, Thaddeus M. (Pa.)
Mann, James R. (Ill.)
Marsh, Benjamin F. (Ill.)
May, Mitchell (N. Y.)
Meekison, David (Ohio)
Mercer, David H. (Nebr.)
Mesick, William S. (Mich.)
Metcalf, Victor H. (Calif.)
Meyer, Adolph (La.)
Miers, Robert W. (Ind.)
Miller, James M. (Kans.)
Minor, Edward S. (Wis.)
Mondell, Frank W. (Wyo.)
Moody, Malcolm A. (Oreg.)
Moody, William H. (Mass.)
Moon, John A. (Tenn.)
Morgan, Stephen (Ohio)
Morrell, Edward De V. (Pa.)
Morris, R. Page W. (Minn.)
Mudd, Sydney E. (Md.)
Muller, Nicholas (N. Y.)
Naphen, Henry F. (Mass.)
Needham, James C. (Calif.)
Neville, William (Nebr.)
Newlands, Francis G. (Nev.)
Noonan, Edward T. (Ill.)
Norton, James (S. C.)
Norton, James A. (Ohio)
O'Grady, James M. E. (N. Y.)
Olmsted, Marlin E. (Pa.)
Otey, Peter J. (Va.)
Otjen, Theobald (Wis.)
Overstreet, Jesse (Ind.)
Packer, Horace B. (Pa.)
Parker, Richard W. (N. J.)
Payne, Sereno E. (N. Y.)
Pearce, Charles E. (Mo.)
Pearre, George A. (Md.)
Pearson, Richmond (N. C.)
Phillips, Fremont O. (Ohio)
Pierce, Rice A. (Tenn.)
Polk, Rufus K. (Pa.)
Powers, H. Henry (Vt.)
Prince, George W. (Ill.)
Pugh, Samuel J. (Ky.)
Quarles, Julian M. (Va.)
Ransdell, Joseph E. (La.)
Ray, George W. (N. Y.)
Reeder, William A. (Kans.)
Reeves, Walter (Ill.)
Rhea, John S. (Ky.)
Rhea, William F. (Va.)
Richardson, James D. (Tenn.)
Richardson, William (Ala.)
Ridgely, Edwin R. (Kans.)
Riordan, Daniel J. (N. Y.)
Rixey, John F. (Va.)
Robb, Edward (Mo.)
Robbins, Gaston A. (Ala.)
Roberts, Ernest W. (Mass.)
Robertson, Samuel M. (La.)
Robinson, James M. (Ind.)
Robinson, John S. (Nebr.)
Rodenberg, William A. (Ill.)
Rucker, William W. (Mo.)
Ruppert, Jacob, Jr. (N. Y.)
Russell, Charles A. (Conn.)
Ryan, James W. (Pa.)
Ryan, William H. (N. Y.)
Salmon, Joshua S. (N. J.)
Scudder, Townsend (N. Y.)
Shackleford, Dorsey W. (Mo.)
Shafroth, John F. (Colo.)
Shattuc, William B. (Ohio)
Shaw, Albert D. (N. Y.)
Shelden, Carlos D. (Mich.)
Sheppard, John L. (Tex.)
Sherman, James S. (N. Y.)
Showalter, Joseph B. (Pa.)
Sibley, Joseph C. (Pa.)
Sims, Thetus W. (Tenn.)
Slayden, James L. (Tex.)
Small, John H. (N. C.)
Smith, David H. (Ky.)
Smith, George W. (Ill.)
Smith, Henry C. (Mich.)
Smith, John W. (Md.)
Smith, Samuel W. (Mich.)
Smith, Walter I. (Iowa)
Smith, William A. (Mich.)
Snodgrass, Charles E. (Tenn.)
Southard, James H. (Ohio)
Spalding, Burleigh F. (N. Dak.)
Sparkman, Stephen M. (Fla.)
Sperry, Nehemiah D. (Conn.)
Spight, Thomas (Miss.)
Sprague, Charles F. (Mass.)
Stallings, Jesse F. (Ala.)
Stark, William L. (Nebr.)
Steele, George W. (Ind.)
Stephens, John H. (Tex.)
Stevens, Frederick C. (Minn.)
Stewart, Alexander (Wis.)
Stewart, James F. (N. J.)
Stewart, John K. (N. Y.)
Stokes, J. William (S. C.)
Sulloway, Cyrus A. (N. H.)
Sulzer, William (N. Y.)
Sutherland, Roderick D. (Nebr.)
Swanson, Claude A. (Va.)
Talbert, W. Jasper (S. C.)
Tate, Farish C. (Ga.)
Tawney, James A. (Minn.)
Tayler, Robert W. (Ohio)
Taylor, George W. (Ala.)
Terry, William L. (Ark.)
Thayer, John R. (Mass.)
Thomas, Charles R. (N. C.)
Thomas, Lot (Iowa)
Thropp, Joseph E. (Pa.)
Tompkins, Arthur S. (N. Y.)
Tongue, Thomas H. (Oreg.)
Turner, Oscar (Ky.)
Underhill, John Q. (N. Y.)
Underwood, Oscar W. (Ala.)
Vandiver, Willard D. (Mo.)
Van Voorhis, Henry C. (Ohio)
Vreeland, Edward B. (N. Y.)
Wachter, Frank C. (Md.)
Wadsworth, James W. (N. Y.)
Wanger, Irving P. (Pa.)
Warner, Vespasian (Ill.)
Waters, Russell J. (Calif.)
Watson, James E. (Ind.)
Weaver, Walter L. (Ohio)
Weeks, Edgar (Mich.)
Weymouth, George W. (Mass.)
Wheeler, Charles K. (Ky.)
Wheeler, Joseph (Ala.)
White, George H. (N. C.)
Williams, James R. (Ill.)
Williams, John S. (Miss.)
Williams, William E. (Ill.)
Wilson, Edgar (Idaho)
Wilson, Frank E. (N. Y.)
Wilson, Stanyarne (S. C.)
Wise, Richard A. (Va.)
Woods, Samuel D. (Calif.)
Wright, Charles F. (Pa.)
Young, James R. (Pa.)
Young, William A. (Va.)
Zenor, William T. (Ind.)
Ziegler, Edward D. (Pa.)

The Fifty-seventh Congress (1901-03)

Henderson, David B. (Iowa)
Speaker.

Acheson, Ernest F. (Pa.)
Adams, Robert, Jr. (Pa.)
Adamson, William C. (Ga.)
Alexander, De Alva S. (N. Y.)
Allen, Amos L. (Maine)
Allen, Henry D. (Ky.)
Aplin, Henry H. (Mich.)
Babcock, Joseph W. (Wis.)
Ball, L. Heisler (Del.)
Ball, Thomas H. (Tex.)
Bankhead, John H. (Ala.)
Barney, Samuel S. (Wis.)
Bartholdt, Richard (Mo.)
Bartlett, Charles L. (Ga.)
Bates, Arthur L. (Pa.)
Beidler, Jacob A. (Ohio)
Bell, John C. (Colo.)
Bellamy, John D. (N. C.)
Belmont, Oliver H. P. (N. Y.)
Benton, Maecenas E. (Mo.)
Billmeyer, Alexander (Pa.)
Bingham, Henry H. (Pa.)
Bishop, Roswell P. (Mich.)
Blackburn, Edmund S. (N. C.)
Blakeney, Albert A. (Md.)
Boreing, Vincent (Ky.)
Boutell, Henry S. (Ill.)
Bowersock, Justin D. (Kans.)
Bowie, Sydney J. (Ala.)
Brandegee, Frank B. (Conn.)
Brantley, William G. (Ga.)
Breazeale, Phanor (La.)
Brick, Abraham L. (Ind.)
Bristow, Henry (N. Y.)
Bromwell, Jacob H. (Ohio)
Broussard, Robert F. (La.)
Brown, Webster E. (Wis.)
Brownlow, Walter P. (Tenn.)
Brundidge, Stephen, Jr. (Ark.)
Bull, Melville (R. I.)
Burgess, George F. (Tex.)
Burk, Henry (Pa.)
Burke, Charles H. (S. Dak.)
Burkett, Elmer J. (Nebr.)
Burleigh, Edwin C. (Maine)
Burleson, Albert S. (Tex.)
Burnett, John L. (Ala.)
Burton, Theodore E. (Ohio)
Butler, James J. (Mo.)
Butler, Thomas S. (Pa.)
Calderhead, William A. (Kans.)
Caldwell, Ben F. (Ill.)
Candler, Ezekiel S., Jr. (Miss.)
Cannon, Joseph G. (Ill.)
Capron, Adin B. (R. I.)
Cassel, Henry B. (Pa.)
Cassingham, John W. (Ohio)
Clark, Champ (Mo.)
Clayton, Henry D. (Ala.)
Cochran, Charles F. (Mo.)
Coombs, Frank L. (Calif.)
Connell, William (Pa.)
Conner, James P. (Iowa)
Conry, Joseph A. (Mass.)
Corliss, John B. (Mich.)
Cousins, Robert G. (Iowa)
Cooney, James (Mo.)
Cooper, Henry A. (Wis.)
Cooper, Samuel B. (Tex.)
Cowherd, William S. (Mo.)
Creamer, Thomas J. (N. Y.)
Cromer, George W. (Ind.)
Crowley, Joseph B. (Ill.)
Crumpacker, Edgar D. (Ind.)
Cummings, Amos J. (N. Y.)
Currier, Frank D. (N. H.)

Curtis, Charles (Kans.)
Cushman, Francis W. (Wash.)
Dahle, Herman B. (Wis.)
Dalzell, John (Pa.)
Darragh, Archibald B. (Mich.)
Davey, Robert C. (La.)
Davidson, James H. (Wis.)
Davis, Robert W. (Fla.)
Dayton, Alston G. (W. Va.)
De Armond, David A. (Mo.)
Deemer, Elias (Pa.)
De Graffenreid, Reese C. (Tex.)
Dick, Charles W. F. (Ohio)
Dinsmore, Hugh A. (Ark.)
Dougherty, John (Mo.)
Douglas, William H. (N. Y.)
Dovener, Blackburn B. (W. Va).
Draper, William H. (N. Y.)
Driscoll, Michael E. (N. Y.)
Dwight, John W. (N. Y.)
Eddy, Frank M. (Minn.)
Edwards, Caldwell (Mont.)
Elliott, William (S. C.)
Emerson, Louis W. (N. Y.)
Esch, John J. (Wis.)
Evans, Alvin (Pa.)
Feely, John J. (Ill.)
Finley, David E. (S. C.)
Fitzgerald, John J. (N. Y.)
Flanagan, De Witt C. (N. J.)
Fleming, William H. (Ga.)
Fletcher, Loren (Minn.)
Flood, Henry D. (Va.)
Foerderer, Robert H. (Pa.)
Fordney, Joseph W. (Mich.)
Foss, George E. (Ill.)
Foster, David J. (Vt.)
Foster, George P. (Ill.)
Fowler, Charles N. (N. J.)
Fox, Andrew F. (Miss.)
Gaines, John W. (Tenn.)
Gaines, Joseph H. (W. Va.)
Gardner, Augustus P. (Mass.)
Gardner, John J. (N. J.)
Gardner, Washington (Mich.)
Gibson, Henry R. (Tenn.)
Gilbert, George G. (Ky.)
Gill, Joseph J. (Ohio)
Gillet, Charles W. (N. Y.)
Gillett, Frederick H. (Mass.)
Glass, Carter (Va.)
Glenn, Thomas L. (Idaho)
Goldfogle, Henry M. (N. Y.)
Gooch, Daniel L. (Ky.)
Gordon, Robert B. (Ohio)
Graff, Joseph V. (Ill.)
Graham, William H. (Pa.)
Green, Henry D. (Pa.)
Greene, William S. (Mass.)
Griffith, Francis M. (Ind.)
Griggs, James M. (Ga.)
Grosvenor, Charles H. (Ohio)
Grow, Galusha A. (Pa.)
Hall, James K. P. (Pa.)
Hamilton, Edward L. (Mich.)
Hanbury, Harry A. (N. Y.)
Haskins, Kittredge (Vt.)
Haugen, Gilbert N. (Iowa)
Hay, James (Va.)
Heatwole, Joel P. (Minn.)
Hedge, Thomas (Iowa)
Hemenway, James A. (Ind.)
Henderson, David B. (Iowa)
Henry, E. Stevens (Conn.)
Henry, Patrick (Miss.)
Henry, Robert L. (Tex.)
Hepburn, William P. (Iowa)
Hildebrant, Charles Q. (Ohio)
Hill, Ebenezer J. (Conn.)
Hitt, Robert R. (Ill.)
Holliday, Elias S. (Ind.)
Hooker, Charles E. (Miss.)
Hopkins, Albert J. (Ill.)
Howard, William M. (Ga.)
Howell, Benjamin F. (N. J.)
Hughes, James A. (W. Va.)
Hull, John A. T. (Iowa)
Irwin, Harvey S. (Ky.)
Jack, Summers M. (Pa.)
Jackson, Alfred M. (Kans.)
Jackson, William H. (Md.)
Jenkins, John J. (Wis.)
Jett, Thomas M. (Ill.)
Johnson, Joseph T. (S. C.)
Jones, Wesley L. (Wash.)
Jones, William A. (Va.)
Joy, Charles F. (Mo.)
Kahn, Julius (Calif.)

Kehoe, James N. (Ky.)
Kern, Frederick J. (Ill.)
Ketcham, John H. (N. Y.)
Kitchin, Claude (N. C.)
Kitchin, William W. (N. C.)
Kleberg, Rudolph (Tex.)
Kluttz, Theodore F. (N. C.)
Knapp, Charles L. (N. Y.)
Knox, William S. (Mass.)
Kyle, Thomas B. (Ohio)
Lacey, John F. (Iowa)
Lamb, John (Va.)
Landis, Charles B. (Ind.)
Lanham, Samuel W. T. (Tex.)
Lassiter, Francis R. (Va.)
Latimer, Asbury C. (S. C.)
Lawrence, George P. (Mass.)
Lessler, Montague (N. Y.)
Lester, Rufus E. (Ga.)
Lever, Asbury F. (S. C.)
Lewis, Elijah B. (Ga.)
Lewis, Robert J. (Pa.)
Lindsay, George H. (N. Y.)
Littauer, Lucius N. (N. Y.)
Little, John S. (Ark.)
Littlefield, Charles E. (Maine)
Livingston, Leonidas F. (Ga.)
Lloyd, James T. (Mo.)
Long, Chester I. (Kans.)
Loud, Eugene F. (Calif.)
Loudenslager, Henry C. (N.J.)
Lovering, William C. (Mass.)
McAndrews, James (Ill.)
McCall, Samuel W. (Mass.)
McCleary, James T. (Minn.)
McClellan, George B. (N. Y.)
McCulloch, Philip D. (Ark.)
McDermott, Allan L. (N. J.)
McLachlan, James (Calif.)
McLain, Frank A. (Miss.)
McRae, Thomas C. (Ark.)
Maddox, John W. (Ga.)
Mahon, Thaddeus M. (Pa.)
Mahoney, William F. (Ill.)
Mann, James R. (Ill.)
Marshall, Thomas F. (N.Dak.)
Martin, Eben W. (S. Dak.)
Maynard, Harry L. (Va.)
Mercer, David H. (Nebr.)
Metcalf, Victor H. (Calif.)
Meyer, Adolph (La.)
Mickey, J. Ross (Ill.)
Miers, Robert W. (Ind.)
Miller, James M. (Kans.)
Minor, Edward S. (Wis.)
Mondell, Frank W. (Wyo.)
Moody, James M. (N. C.)
Moody, Malcom A. (Oreg.)
Moody, William H. (Mass.)
Moon, John A. (Tenn.)
Morgan, Stephen (Ohio)
Morrell, Edward DeV. (Pa.)
Morris, R. Page W. (Minn.)
Moss, J. McKenzie (Ky.)
Mudd, Sydney E. (Md.)
Muller, Nicholas (N. Y.)
Mutchler, Howard (Pa.)
Naphen, Henry F. (Mass.)
Needham, James C. (Calif.)
Neville, William (Nebr.)
Nevin, Robert M. (Ohio)
Newlands, Francis G. (Nev.)
Norton, James A. (Ohio)
Olmsted, Marlin E. (Pa.)
Otey, Peter J. (Va.)
Otjen, Theobald (Wis.)
Overstreet, Jesse (Ind.)
Padgett, Lemuel P. (Tenn.)
Palmer, Henry W. (Pa.)
Parker, Richard W. (N. J.)
Patterson, George R. (Pa.)
Patterson, Malcolm R. (Tenn.)
Payne, Sereno E. (N. Y.)
Pearre, George A. (Md.)
Perkins, James B. (N. Y.)
Pierce, Rice A. (Tenn.)
Polk, Rufus K. (Pa.)
Pou, Edward W. (N. C.)
Powers, Llewellyn (Maine)
Powers, Samuel L. (Mass.)
Prince, George W. (Ill.)
Pugsley, Cornelius A. (N. Y.)
Randell, Choice B. (Tex.)
Ransdell, Joseph E. (La.)
Ray, George W. (N. Y.)
Reeder, William A. (Kans.)
Reeves, Walter (Ill.)
Reid, Charles C. (Ark.)
Rhea, John S. (Ky.)

Rhea, William F. (Va.)
Richardson, James D. (Tenn.)
Richardson, William (Ala.)
Rixey, John F. (Va.)
Robb, Edward (Mo.)
Roberts, Ernest W. (Mass.)
Robertson, Samuel M. (La.)
Robinson, James M. (Ind.)
Robinson, John S. (Nebr.)
Rucker, William W. (Mo.)
Rumple, John N. W. (Iowa)
Ruppert, Jacob, Jr. (N. Y.)
Russell, Charles A. (Conn.)
Russell, Gordon J. (Tex.)
Ryan, William H. (N. Y.)
Salmon, Joshua S. (N. J.)
Scarborough, Robert B. (Tenn.)
Schirm, Charles R. (Md.)
Scott, Charles F. (Kans.)
Selby, Thomas J. (Ill.)
Shackleford, Dorsey W. (Mo.)
Shafroth, John F. (Colo.)
Shallenberger, Ashton C. (Nebr.)
Shattuc, William B. (Ohio)
Shelden, Carlos D. (Mich.)
Sheppard, John L. (Tex.)
Sheppard, Morris (Tex.)
Sherman, James S. (N. Y.)
Showalter, Joseph B. (Pa.)
Sibley, Joseph C. (Pa.)
Sims, Thetus W. (Tenn.)
Skiles, William W. (Ohio)
Slayden, James L. (Tex.)
Small, John H. (N. C.)
Smith, David H. (Ky.)
Smith, George W. (Ill.)
Smith, Henry C. (Mich.)
Smith, Samuel W. (Mich.)
Smith, Walter I. (Iowa)
Smith, William A. (Mich.)
Snodgrass, Charles E. (Tenn.)
Snook, John S. (Ohio)
Southard, James H. (Ohio)
Southwick, George N. (N. Y.)
Sparkman, Stephen M. (Fla.)
Sperry, Nehemiah D. (Conn.)
Spight, Thomas (Miss.)
Stark, William L. (Nebr.)
Steele, George W. (Ind.)
Stephens, John H. (Tex.)
Stevens, Frederick C. (Minn.)
Stewart, James F. (N. J.)
Stewart, John K. (N. Y.)
Storm, Frederic (N. Y.)
Sulloway, Cyrus A. (N. H.)
Sulzer, William (N. Y.)
Sutherland, George (Utah)
Swann, Edward (N. Y.)
Swanson, Claude A. (Va.)
Talbert, William J. (S. C.)
Tate, Farish C. (Ga.)
Tawney, James A. (Minn.)
Tayler, Robert W. (Ohio)
Taylor, George W. (Ala.)
Thayer, John R. (Mass.)
Thomas, Charles R. (N. C.)
Thomas, Lot (Iowa)
Thompson, Charles W. (Ala.)
Tirrell, Charles Q. (Mass.)
Tompkins, Arthur S. (N. Y.)
Tompkins, Emmett (Ohio)
Tongue, Thomas H. (Oreg.)
Trimble, South (Ky.)
Underwood, Oscar W. (Ala.)
Vandiver, Willard D. (Mo.)
Van Voorhis, Henry C. (Ohio)
Vreeland, Edward B. (N. Y.)
Wachter, Frank C. (Md.)
Wadsworth, James W. (N. Y.)
Wagoner, George C. R. (Mo.)
Wanger, Irving P. (Pa.)
Warner, Vespasian (Ill.)
Warnock, William R. (Ohio)
Watson, James E. (Ind.)
Weeks, Edgar, (Mich.)
Wheeler, Charles K. (Ky.)
White, James B. (Ky.)
Wiley, Ariosto A. (Ala.)
Williams, James R. (Ill.)
Williams, John S. (Miss.)
Wilson, Frank E. (N. Y.)
Woods, Samuel D. (Calif.)
Wooten, Dudley G. (Tex.)
Wright, Charles F. (Pa.)
Young, James R. (Pa.)
Zenor, William T. (Ind.)

The Fifty-eighth Congress (1903-05)

Cannon, Joseph G. (Ill.)
Speaker.

Acheson, Ernest F. (Pa.)
Adams, Henry C. (Wis.)
Adams, Robert, Jr. (Pa.)
Adamson, William C. (Ga.)
Aiken, Wyatt (S. C.)
Alexander, De Alva S. (N. Y.)
Allen, Amos L. (Maine)
Ames, Butler (Mass.)
Babcock, Joseph W. (Wis.)
Badger, De Witt C. (Ohio)
Baker, Robert (N. Y.)
Ball, Thomas H. (Tex.)
Bankhead, John H. (Ala.)
Bartholdt, Richard (Mo.)
Bartlett, Charles L. (Ga.)
Bassett, Edward M. (N. Y.)
Bates, Arthur L. (Pa.)
Beall, Jack (Tex.)
Bede, J. Adam (Minn.)
Beidler, Jacob A. (Ohio)
Bell, Theodore A. (Calif.)
Benny, Allan (N. J.)
Benton, Maecenas E. (Mo.)
Bingham, Henry H. (Pa.)
Birdsall, Benjamin P. (Iowa)
Bishop, Roswell P. (Mich.)
Bonynge, Robert W. (Colo.)
Boutell, Henry S. (Ill.)
Bowers, Eaton J. (Miss.)
Bowersock, Justin D. (Kans.)
Bowie, Sydney J. (Ala.)
Bradley, Thomas W. (N. Y.)
Brandegee, Frank B. (Conn.)
Brantley, William G. (Ga.)
Breazeale, Phanor (La.)
Brick, Abraham L. (Ind.)
Brooks, Franklin E. (Colo.)
Broussard, Robert F. (La.)
Brown, James W. (Pa.)
Brown, Webster E. (Wis.)
Brownlow, Walter P. (Tenn.)
Brundidge, Stephen, Jr. (Ark.)
Buckman, Clarence B. (Minn.)
Burgess, George F. (Tex.)
Burk, Henry (Pa.)
Burke, Charles H. (S. Dak.)
Burkett, Elmer J. (Nebr.)
Burleigh, Edwin C. (Maine)
Burleson, Albert S. (Tex.)
Burnett, John L. (Ala.)
Burton, Theodore E. (Ohio)
Butler, James J. (Mo.)
Butler, Thomas S. (Pa.)
Byrd, Adam M. (Miss.)
Calderhead, William A. (Kans.)
Caldwell, Ben F. (Ill.)
Campbell, Philip P. (Kans.)
Candler, Ezekiel S., Jr. (Miss.)
Cannon, Joseph G. (Ill.)
Capron, Adin B. (R. I.)
Cassel, Henry B. (Pa.)
Cassingham, John W. (Ohio)
Castor, George A. (Pa.)
Clark, Champ (Mo.)
Clayton, Henry D. (Ala.)
Cochran, Charles F. (Mo.)
Cochran, W. Bourke (N. Y.)
Connell, William (Pa.)
Conner, James P. (Iowa)
Cooper, Allen F. (Pa.)
Cooper, Henry A. (Wis.)
Cooper, Samuel B. (Tex.)
Cousins, Robert G. (Iowa)
Cowherd, William S. (Mo.)
Croft, George W. (S. C.)
Croft, Theodore G. (S. C.)
Cromer, George W. (Ind.)
Crowley, Joseph B. (Ill.)
Crumpacker, Edgar D. (Ind.)
Currier, Frank D. (N. H.)
Curtis, Charles (Kans.)
Cushman, Francis W. (Wash.)
Dalzell, John (Pa.)
Daniels, Milton J. (Calif.)
Darragh, Archibald B. (Mich.)
Davey, Robert C. (La.)
Davidson, James H. (Wis.)
Davis, Charles R. (Minn.)
Davis, Robert W. (Fla.)

Dayton, Alston G. (W. Va.)
De Armond, David A. (Mo.)
Deemer, Elias (Pa.)
Denny, James W. (Md.)
Dick, Charles W. F. (Ohio)
Dickerman, Charles H. (Pa.)
Dinsmore, Hugh A. (Ark.)
Dixon, Joseph M. (Mont.)
Dougherty, John (Mo.)
Douglas, William H. (N. Y.)
Dovener, Blackburn B. (W. Va.)
Draper, William H. (N. Y.)
Dresser, Solomon R. (Pa.)
Driscoll, Michael E. (N. Y.)
Dunwell, Charles T. (N. Y.)
Dwight, John W. (N. Y.)
Emerich, Martin (Ill.)
Esch, John J. (Wis.)
Evans, Alvin (Pa.)
Field, Scott (Tex.)
Finley, David E. (S. C.)
Fitzgerald, John J. (N. Y.)
Fitzpatrick, Morgan C. (Tenn.)
Flack, William H. (N. Y.)
Flood, Henry D. (Va.)
Fordney, Joseph W. (Mich.)
Foss, George E. (Ill.)
Foster, David J. (Vt.)
Foster, George P. (Ill.)
Fowler, Charles N. (N. J.)
French, Burton L. (Idaho)
Fuller, Charles E. (Ill.)
Gaines, John W. (Tenn.)
Gaines, Joseph H. (W. Va.)
Garber, Harvey C. (Ohio)
Gardner, Augustus P. (Mass.)
Gardner, John J. (N. J.)
Gardner, Washington (Mich.)
Garner, John N. (Tex.)
Gibson, Henry R. (Tenn.)
Gilbert, George G. (Ky.)
Gillespie, Oscar W. (Tex.)
Gillet, Charles W. (N. Y.)
Gillett, Frederick H. (Mass.)
Gillett, James N. (Calif.)
Glass, Carter (Va.)
Goebel, Herman P. (Ohio)
Goldfogle, Henry M. (N. Y.)
Gooch, D. Linn (Ky.)
Goulden, Joseph A. (N. Y.)
Graff, Joseph V. (Ill.)
Granger, Daniel L. D. (R. I.)
Greene, William S. (Mass.)
Gregg, Alexander W. (Tex.)
Griffith, Francis M. (Ind.)
Griggs, James M. (Ga.)
Grosvenor, Charles H. (Ohio)
Gudger, James M., Jr. (N.C.)
Hamilton, Edward L. (Mich.)
Hamlin, Courtney W. (Mo.)
Hardwick, Thomas W. (Ga.)
Harrison, Francis B. (N. Y.)
Haskins, Kittredge (Vt.)
Haugen, Gilbert N. (Iowa)
Hay, James (Va.)
Hearst, William R. (N. Y.)
Hedge, Thomas (Iowa)
Heflin, J. Thomas (Ala.)
Hemenway, James A. (Ind.)
Henry, E. Stevens (Conn.)
Henry, Robert L. (Tex.)
Hepburn, William P. (Iowa)
Hermann, Binger (Oreg.)
Hildebrant, Charles Q. (Ohio)
Hill, Ebenezer J. (Conn.)
Hill, Wilson S. (Miss.)
Hinshaw, Edmund H. (Nebr.)
Hitchcock, Gilbert M. (Nebr.)
Hitt, Robert R. (Ill.)
Hogg, Herschel M. (Colo.)
Holliday, Elias S. (Ind.)
Hopkins, Frank A. (Ky.)
Houston, Henry A. (Del.)
Howard, William M. (Ga.)
Howell, Benjamin F. (N. J.)
Howell, George (Pa.)
Howell, Joseph (Utah)
Huff, George F. (Pa.)
Hughes, James A. (W. Va.)
Hughes, William (N. J.)
Hull, John A. T. (Iowa)
Humphrey, William E. (Wash.)
Humphreys, Benjamin G. (Miss.)
Hunt, John T. (Mo.)
Hunter, W. Godfrey (Ky.)
Jackson, Amos H. (Ohio)
Jackson, William H. (Md.)
James, Ollie M. (Ky.)
Jenkins, John J. (Wis.)
Johnson, Joseph T. (S. C.)
Jones, Wesley L. (Wash.)
Jones, William A. (Va.)
Kehoe, James N. (Ky.)
Keliher, John A. (Mass.)
Kennedy, James (Ohio)
Ketcham, John H. (N. Y.)
Kinkaid, Moses P. (Nebr.)
Kitchin, Claude (N. C.)
Kitchin, William W. (N. C.)
Kline, Marcus C. L. (Pa.)
Kluttz, Theodore F. (N. C.)
Knapp, Charles L. (N. Y.)
Knopf, Philip (Ill.)
Knowland, Joseph R. (Calif.)
Kyle, Thomas B. (Ohio)
Lacey, John F. (Iowa)
Lafean, Daniel F. (Pa.)
Lamar, J. Robert (Mo.)
Lamar, William B. (Fla.)
Lamb, John (Va.)
Landis, Charles B. (Ind.)
Landis, Frederick (Ind.)
Lanning, William M. (N. J.)
Lawrence, George P. (Mass.)
Legaré, George S. (S. C.)
Lester, Rufus E. (Ga.)
Lever, Asbury F. (S. C.)
Lewis, Elijah B. (Ga.)
Lilley, George L. (Conn.)
Lind, John (Minn.)
Lindsay, George H. (N. Y.)
Littauer, Lucius N. (N. Y.)
Little, John S. (Ark.)
Littlefield, Charles E. (Maine)
Livernash, Edward J. (Calif.)
Livingston, Leonidas F. (Ga.)
Lloyd, James T. (Mo.)
Longworth, Nicholas (Ohio)
Lorimer, William (Ill.)
Loud, George A. (Mich.)
Loudenslager, Henry C. (N.J.)
Lovering, William C. (Mass.)
Lucking, Alfred (Mich.)
McAndrews, James (Ill.)
McCall, Samuel W. (Mass.)
McCarthy, John J. (Nebr.)
McCleary, James T. (Minn.)
McClellan, George B. (N. Y.)
McCreary, George D. (Pa.)
McDermott, Allen L. (N. J.)
McLachlan, James (Calif.)
McLain, Frank A. (Miss.)
McMorran, Henry (Mich.)
McNary, William S. (Mass.)
Macon, Robert B. (Ark.)
Maddox, John W. (Ga.)
Mahon, Thaddeus M. (Pa.)
Mahoney, William F. (Ill.)
Mann, James R. (Ill.)
Marsh, Benjamin F. (Ill.)
Marshall, Thomas F. (N.Dak.)
Martin, Eben W. (S. Dak.)
Maynard, Harry L. (Va.)
Metcalf, Victor H. (Calif.)
Meyer, Adolph (La.)
Miers, Robert W. (Ind.)
Miller, James M. (Kans.)
Minor, Edward S. (Wis.)
Mondell, Frank W. (Wyo.)
Moon, John A (Tenn.)
Moon, Reuben O. (Pa.)
Morgan, Stephen (Ohio)
Morrell, Edward de V. (Pa.)
Mudd, Sydney E. (Md.)
Murdock, Victor (Kans.)
Needham, James C. (Calif.)
Nevin, Robert M. (Ohio)
Norris, George W. (Nebr.)
Olmsted, Marlin E. (Pa.)
Otis, Norton P. (N. Y.)
Otjen, Theobald (Wis.)
Overstreet, Jesse (Ind.)
Padgett, Lemuel P. (Tenn.)
Page, Robert N. (N. C.)
Palmer, Henry W. (Pa.)
Parker, Richard W. (N. J.)
Patterson, George R. (Pa.)
Patterson, Gilbert B. (N. C.)
Patterson, Malcolm R. (Tenn.)
Payne, Sereno E. (N. Y.)
Pearre, George A. (Md.)
Perkins, James B. (N. Y.)
Pierce, Rice A. (Tenn.)
Pinckney, John M. (Tex.)
Porter, Henry K. (Pa.)
Pou, Edward W. (N. C.)
Powers, Llewellyn (Maine)
Powers, Samuel L. (Mass.)
Prince, George W. (Ill.)
Pujo, Arsène P. (La.)
Rainey, Henry T. (Ill.)
Randell, Choice B. (Tex.)
Ransdell, Joseph E. (La.)
Reeder, William A. (Kans.)
Reid, Charles C. (Ark.)
Rhea, John S. (Ky.)
Richardson, James D. (Tenn.)
Richardson, William (Ala.)
Rider, Ira E. (N. Y.)
Rixey, John F. (Va.)
Robb, Edward (Mo.)
Roberts, Ernest W. (Mass.)
Robertson, Samuel M. (La.)
Robinson, James M. (Ind.)
Robinson, Joseph T. (Ark.)
Rodenberg, William A. (Ill.)
Rucker, William W. (Mo.)
Ruppert, Jacob, Jr. (N. Y.)
Russell, Gordon J. (Tex.)
Ryan, William H. (N. Y.)
Scarborough, Robert B. (S. C.)
Scott, Charles F. (Kans.)
Scudder, Townsend (N. Y.)
Shackleford, Dorsey W. (Mo.)
Shafroth, John F. (Colo.)
Sheppard, Morris (Tex.)
Sherley, J. Swagar (Ky.)
Sherman, James S. (N. Y.)
Shiras, George, 3d (Pa.)
Shober, Francis E. (N. Y.)
Shull, Joseph H. (Pa.)
Sibley, Joseph C. (Pa.)
Sims, Thetus W. (Tenn.)
Skiles, William W. (Ohio)
Slayden, James L. (Tex.)
Slemp, Campbell (Va.)
Small, John H. (N. C.)
Smith, David H. (Ky.)
Smith, George J. (N. Y.)
Smith, George W. (Ill.)
Smith, Samuel W. (Mich.)
Smith, Walter I. (Iowa)
Smith, William Alden (Mich.)
Smith, William O. (Pa.)
Smith, William R. (Tex.)
Snapp, Howard M. (Ill.)
Snook, John S. (Ohio)
Southall, Robert G. (Va.)
Southard, James H. (Ohio)
Southwick, George N. (N. Y.)
Spalding, Burleigh F. (N. Dak.)
Sparkman, Stephen M. (Fla.)
Sperry, Nehemiah D. (Conn.)
Spight, Thomas (Miss.)
Stafford, William H. (Wis.)
Stanley, Augustus O. (Ky.)
Steenerson, Halvor (Minn.)
Stephens, John H. (Tex.)
Sterling, John A. (Ill.)
Stevens, Frederick C. (Minn.)
Sullivan, John A. (Mass.)
Sullivan, Timothy D. (N. Y.)
Sulloway, Cyrus A. (N. H.)
Sulzer, William (N. Y.)
Swanson, Claude A. (Va.)
Talbott, J. Frederick C. (Md.)
Tate, Farish C. (Ga.)
Tawney, James A. (Minn.)
Taylor, George W. (Ala.)
Thayer, John R. (Mass.)
Thomas, Charles R. (N. C.)
Thomas, Lot (Iowa)
Thomas, William A. (Ohio)
Thompson, Charles W. (Ala.)
Tirrell, Charles Q. (Mass.)
Townsend, Charles E. (Mich.)
Trimble, South (Ky.)
Underwood, Oscar W. (Ala.)
Vandiver, Willard D. (Mo.)
Van Duzer, Clarence D. (Nev.)
Van Voorhis, Henry C. (Ohio)
Volstead, Andrew J. (Minn.)
Vreeland, Edward B. (N. Y.)
Wachter, Frank C. (Md.)
Wade, Martin J. (Iowa)
Wadsworth, James W. (N.Y.)
Wallace, Robert M. (Ark.)
Wanger, Irving P. (Pa.)
Warner, Vespasian (Ill.)
Warnock, William R. (Ohio)
Watson, James E. (Ind.)
Webb, Edwin Y. (N. C.)
Webber, Amos R. (Ohio)
Weems, Capell L. (Ohio)
Weisse, Charles H. (Wis.)
Wiley, Ariosto A. (Ala.)
Wiley, William H. (N. J.)
Williams, James R. (Ill.)
Williams, John S. (Miss.)
Williamson, John N. (Oreg.)
Wilson, Frank E. (N. Y.)
Wilson, William W. (Ill.)
Wood, Ira W. (N. J.)
Woodyard Harry C. (W. Va.)
Wright, Charles F. (Pa.)
Wynn, William J. (Calif.)
Young, H. Olin (Mich.)
Zenor, William T. (Ind.)

The Fifty-ninth Congress (1905-07)

Cannon, Joseph G. (Ill.) Speaker.

Acheson, Ernest F. (Pa.)
Adams, Henry C. (Wis.)
Adams, Robert, Jr. (Pa.)
Adamson, William C. (Ga.)
Aiken, Wyatt (S. C.)
Alexander, De Alva S. (N. Y.)
Allen, Amos L. (Maine)
Allen, Henry C. (N. J.)
Ames, Butler (Mass.)
Andrews, William H. (N. Mex.)
Andrus, John E. (N. Y.)
Backcock, Joseph W. (Wis.)
Bankhead, John H. (Ala.)
Bannon, Henry T. (Ohio)
Barchfeld, Andrew J. (Pa.)
Bartholdt, Richard (Mo.)
Bartlett, Charles L. (Ga.)
Bates, Arthur L. (Pa.)
Beall, Jack (Tex.)
Bede, J. Adam (Minn.)
Beidler, Jacob A. (Ohio)
Bell, Thomas M. (Ga.)
Bennet, William S. (N. Y.)
Bennett, Joseph B. (Ky.)
Bingham, Henry H. (Pa.)
Birdsall, Benjamin P. (Iowa)
Bishop, Roswell P. (Mich.)
Blackburn, E. Spencer (N. C.)
Bonynge, Robert W. (Colo.)
Boutell, Henry S. (Ill.)
Bowers, Eaton J. (Miss.)
Bowersock, Justin D. (Kans.)
Bowie, Sydney J. (Ala.)
Bradley, Thomas W. (N. Y.)
Brantley, William G. (Ga.)
Brick, Abraham L. (Ind.)
Broocks, Moses L. (Tex.)
Brooks, Franklin E. (Colo.)
Broussard, Robert F. (La.)
Brown, Webster E. (Wis.)
Brownlow, Walter P. (Tenn.)
Brumm, Charles N. (Pa.)
Brundidge, Stephen, Jr. (Ark.)
Buckman, Clarence B. (Minn.)
Burgess, George F. (Tex.)
Burke, Charles H. (S. Dak.)
Burke, James F. (Pa.)
Burleigh, Edwin C. (Maine)
Burleson, Albert S. (Tex.)
Burnett, John L. (Ala.)
Burton, Hiram R. (Del.)
Burton, Theodore E. (Ohio)
Butler, Mounce G. (Tenn.)
Butler, Thomas S. (Pa.)
Byrd, Adam M. (Miss.)
Calder, William M. (N. Y.)
Calderhead, William A. (Kans.)
Campbell, Philip P. (Kans.)
Campbell, William W. (Ohio)
Candler, Ezekiel S., Jr. (Miss.)
Cannon, Joseph G. (Ill.)
Capron, Adin B. (R. I.)
Cassel, Henry B. (Pa.)
Castor, George A. (Pa.)
Chaney, John C. (Ind.)

Chapman, Pleasant T. (Ill.)
Clark, Champ (Mo.)
Clark, Frank (Fla.)
Clayton, Henry D. (Ala.)
Cockran, W. Bourke (N. Y.)
Cocks, William W. (N. Y.)
Cole, Ralph D. (Ohio)
Conner, James P. (Iowa)
Cooper, Allen F. (Pa.)
Cooper, Henry A. (Wis.)
Coudrey, Harry M. (Mo.)
Cousins, Robert G. (Iowa)
Cromer, George W. (Ind.)
Crumpacker, Edgar D. (Ind.)
Currier, Frank D. (N. H.)
Curtis, Charles (Kans.)
Cushman, Francis W. (Wash.)
Dale, Thomas H. (Pa.)
Dalzell, John (Pa.)
Darragh, Archibald B. (Mich.)
Davey, Robert C. (La.)
Davidson, James H. (Wis.)
Davis, Charles R. (Minn.)
Davis, Thomas B. (W. Va.)
Dawes, Beman G. (Ohio)
Dawson, Albert F. (Iowa)
De Armond, David A. (Mo.)
Deemer, Elias (Pa.)
Denby, Edwin (Mich.)
Dickson, Frank S. (Ill.)
Dixon, Joseph M. (Mont.)
Dixon, Lincoln (Ind.)
Dovener, Blackburn B. (W. Va.)
Draper, William H. (N. Y.)
Dresser, Solomon R. (Pa.)
Driscoll, Michael E. (N. Y.)
Dunwell, Charles T. (N. Y.)
Dwight, John W. (N. Y.)
Edwards, Don C. (Ky.)
Ellerbe, J. Edwin (S. C.)
Ellis, Edgar C. (Mo.)
Englebright, William F. (Calif.)
Esch, John J. (Wis.)
Fassett, J. Sloat (N. Y.)
Field, Scott (Tex.)
Finley, David E. (S. C.)
Fitzgerald, John J. (N. Y.)
Flack, William H. (N. Y.)
Fletcher, Loren (Minn.)
Flood, Henry D. (Va.)
Floyd, John C. (Ark.)
Fordney, Joseph W. (Mich.)
Foss, George E. (Ill.)
Foster, David J. (Vt.)
Foster, John H. (Ind.)
Fowler, Charles N. (N. J.)
French, Burton L. (Idaho)
Fulkerson, Frank B. (Mo.)
Fuller, Charles E. (Ill.)
Gaines, John W. (Tenn.)
Gaines, Joseph H. (W. Va.)
Garber, Harvey C. (Ohio)
Gardner, Augustus P. (Mass.)
Gardner, John J. (N. J.)
Gardner, Washington (Mich.)
Garner, John N. (Tex.)
Garrett, Finis J. (Tenn.)
Gilbert, George G. (Ky.)
Gilbert, Newton W. (Ind.)
Gilhams, Clarence C. (Ind.)
Gill, John, Jr. (Md.)
Gillespie, Oscar W. (Tex.)
Gillett, Frederick H. (Mass.)
Gillett, James N. (Calif.)
Glass, Carter (Va.)
Goebel, Herman P. (Ohio)
Goldfogle, Henry M. (N. Y.)
Goulden, Joseph A. (N. Y.)
Graff, Joseph V. (Ill.)
Graham, William H. (Pa.)
Granger, Daniel L. D. (R. I.)
Greene, William S. (Mass.)
Gregg, Alexander W. (Tex.)
Griggs, James M. (Ga.)
Gronna, Asle J. (N. Dak.)
Grosvenor, Charles H. (Ohio)
Gudger, James M., Jr. (N. C.)
Hale, Nathan W. (Tenn.)
Hamilton, Edward L. (Mich.)
Hardwick, Thomas W. (Ga.)
Haskins, Kittredge (Vt.)
Haugen, Gilbert N. (Iowa)
Hay, James (Va.)
Hayes, Everis A. (Calif.)
Hearst, William R. (N. Y.)
Hedge, Thomas (Iowa)
Heflin, J. Thomas (Ala.)
Henry, E. Stevens (Conn.)
Henry, Robert L. (Tex.)
Hepburn, William P. (Iowa)
Hermann, Binger (Oreg.)
Higgins, Edwin W. (Conn.)
Hill, Ebenezer J. (Conn.)
Hill, Wilson S. (Miss.)
Hinshaw, Edmund H. (Nebr.)
Hitt, Robert R. (Ill.)
Hoar, Rockwood (Mass.)
Hogg, Herschel M. (Colo.)
Holliday, Elias S. (Ind.)
Hopkins, Frank A. (Ky.)
Houston, William C. (Tenn.)
Howard, William M. (Ga.)
Howell, Benjamin F. (N. J.)
Howell, Joseph (Utah)
Hubbard, Elbert H. (Iowa)
Huff, George F. (Pa.)
Hughes, James A. (W. Va.)
Hull, John A. T. (Iowa)
Humphrey, William E. (Wash.)
Humphreys, Benjamin G. (Miss.)
Hunt, John T. (Mo.)
James, Ollie M. (Ky.)
Jenkins, John J. (Wis.)
Johnson, Joseph T. (S. C.)
Jones, Wesley L. (Wash.)
Jones, William A. (Va.)
Kahn, Julius (Calif.)
Keifer, J. Warren (Ohio)
Keliher, John A. (Mass.)
Kennedy, James (Ohio)
Kennedy, John L. (Nebr.)
Ketcham, John H. (N. Y.)
Kinkaid, Moses P. (Nebr.)
Kitchin, Claude (N. C.)
Kitchin, William W. (N. C.)
Klepper, Frank B. (Mo.)
Kline, Marcus C. L. (Pa.)
Knapp, Charles L. (N. Y.)
Knopf, Philip (Ill.)
Knowland, Joseph R. (Calif.)
Lacey, John F. (Iowa)
Lafean, Daniel F. (Pa.)
Lamar, William B. (Fla.)
Lamb, John (Va.)
Landis, Charles B. (Ind.)
Landis, Frederick (Ind.)
Law, Charles B. (N. Y.)
Lawrence, George P. (Mass.)
Lee, Gordon (Ga.)
Le Fevre, Frank J. (N. Y.)
Legaré, George S. (S. C.)
Lester, Rufus E. (Ga.)
Lever, Asbury F. (S. C.)
Lewis, Elijah B. (Ga.)
Lilley, George L. (Conn.)
Lilley, Mial E. (Pa.)
Lindsay, George H. (N. Y.)
Littauer, Lucius N. (N. Y.)
Little, John S. (Ark.)
Littlefield, Charles E. (Maine)
Livingston, Leonidas F. (Ga.)
Lloyd, James T. (Mo.)
Longworth, Nicholas (Ohio)
Lorimer, William (Ill.)
Loud, George A. (Mich.)
Loudenslager, Henry C. (N. J.)
Lovering, William C. (Mass.)
Lowden, Frank O. (Ill.)
McCall, Samuel W. (Mass.)
McCarthy, John J. (Nebr.)
McCleary, James T. (Minn.)
McCreary, George D. (Pa.)
McDermott, Allan L. (N. J.)
McGavin, Charles (Ill.)
McKinlay, Duncan E. (Calif.)
McKinley, William B. (Ill.)
McKinney, James (Ill.)
McLachlan, James (Calif.)
McLain, Frank A. (Miss.)
McMorran, Henry (Mich.)
McNary, William S. (Mass.)
Macon, Robert B. (Ark.)
Madden, Martin B. (Ill.)
Mahon, Thaddeus M. (Pa.)
Mann, James R. (Ill.)
Marshall, Thomas F. (N.Dak.)
Martin, Eben W. (S. Dak.)
Maynard, Harry L. (Va.)
Meyer, Adolph (La.)
Michalek, Anthony (Ill.)
Miller, James M. (Kans.)
Minor, Edward S. (Wis.)
Mondell, Frank W. (Wyo.)
Moon, John A. (Tenn.)
Moon, Reuben O. (Pa.)
Moore, J. Hampton (Pa.)
Moore, John M. (Tex.)
Morrell, Edward De V. (Pa.)
Mouser, Grant E. (Ohio)
Mudd, Sydney E. (Md.)
Murdock, Victor (Kans.)
Murphy, Arthur P. (Mo.)
Needham, James C. (Calif.)
Nelson, John M. (Wis.)
Nevin, Robert M. (Ohio)
Norris, George W. (Nebr.)
Olcott, J. Van Vechten (N. Y.)
Olmsted, Marlin E. (Pa.)
Otjen, Theobald (Wis.)
Overstreet, James W. (Ga.)
Overstreet, Jesse (Ind.)
Padgett, Lemuel P. (Tenn.)
Page, Robert N. (N. C.)
Palmer, Henry W. (Pa.)
Parker, Richard W. (N. J.)
Parsons, Herbert (N. Y.)
Patterson, George R. (Pa.)
Patterson, Gilbert B. (N. C.)
Patterson, James O'H. (S. C.)
Patterson, Malcolm R. (Tenn.)
Payne, Sereno E. (N. Y.)
Pearre, George A. (Md.)
Perkins, James B. (N. Y.)
Pollard, Ernest M. (Nebr.)
Pou, Edward W. (N. C.)
Powers, Llewellyn (Maine)
Prince, George W. (Ill.)
Pujo, Arsene P. (La.)
Rainey, Henry T. (Ill.)
Randell, Choice B. (Tex.)
Ransdell, Joseph E. (La.)
Reeder, William A. (Kans.)
Reid, Charles C. (Ark.)
Reyburn, John E. (Pa.)
Reynolds, John M. (Pa.)
Rhinock, Joseph L. (Ky.)
Rhodes, Marion E. (Mo.)
Richardson, James M. (Ky.)
Richardson, William (Ala.)
Riordan, Daniel J. (N. Y.)
Rives, Zeno J. (Ill.)
Rixey, John F. (Va.)
Roberts, Ernest W. (Mass.)
Robertson, Samuel M. (La.)
Robinson, Joseph T. (Ark.)
Rodenberg, William A. (Ill.)
Rucker, William W. (Mo.)
Ruppert, Jacob, Jr. (N. Y.)
Russell, Gordon J. (Tex.)
Ryan, William H. (N. Y.)
Samuel, Edmund W. (Pa.)
Saunders, Edward W. (Va.)
Schneebeli, Gustav A. (Pa.)
Scott, Charles F. (Kans.)
Scroggy, Thomas E. (Ohio)
Shackleford, Dorsey W. (Mo.)
Shartel, Cassius M. (Mo.)
Sheppard, Morris (Tex.)
Sherley, J. Swagar (Ky.)
Sherman, James S. (N. Y.)
Sibley, Joseph C. (Pa.)
Sims, Thetus W. (Tenn.)
Slayden, James L. (Tex.)
Slemp, Campbell (Va.)
Small, John H. (N. C.)
Smith, David H. (Ky.)
Smith, George W. (Ill.)
Smith, Marcus A. (Ariz.)
Smith, Samuel W. (Mich.)
Smith, Sylvester C. (Calif.)
Smith, Thomas A. (Md.)
Smith, Walter I. (Iowa)
Smith, William Alden (Mich.)
Smith, William O. (Pa.)
Smith, William R. (Tex.)
Smyser, Martin L. (Ohio)
Snapp, Howard M. (Ill.)
Southall, Robert G. (Va.)
Southard, James H. (Ohio)
Southwick, George N. (N. Y.)
Sparkman, Stephen M. (Fla.)
Sperry, Nehemiah D. (Conn.)
Spight, Thomas (Miss.)
Stafford, William H. (Wis.)
Stanley, Augustus O. (Ky.)
Steenerson, Halvor (Minn.)
Stephens, John H. (Tex.)
Sterling, John A. (Ill.)
Stevens, Frederick C. (Minn.)
Sullivan, John A. (Mass.)
Sullivan, Timothy D. (N. Y.)
Sulloway, Cyrus A. (N. H.)
Sulzer, William (N. Y.)
Swanson, Claude A. (Va.)
Talbott, J. Frederick C. (Md.)
Tawney, James A. (Minn.)
Taylor, Edward L., Jr. (Ohio)
Taylor, George W. (Ala.)
Thomas, Charles R. (N. C.)
Thomas, W. Aubrey (Ohio)
Tirrell, Charles Q. (Mass.)
Towne, Charles A. (N. Y.)
Townsend, Charles E. (Mich.)
Trimble, South (Ky.)
Tyndall, William T. (Mo.)
Underwood, Oscar W. (Ala.)
Van Duzer, Clarence D. (Nev.)
Van Winkle, Marshall (N. J.)
Volstead, Andrew J. (Minn.)
Vreeland, Edward B. (N. Y.)
Wachter, Frank C. (Md.)
Wadsworth, James W. (N. Y.)
Waldo, George E. (N. Y.)
Wallace, Robert M. (Ark.)
Wanger, Irving P. (Pa.)
Washburn, Charles G. (Mass.)
Watkins, John T. (La.)
Watson, James E. (Ind.)
Webb, Edwin Y. (N. C.)
Webber, Amos R. (Ohio)
Weeks, John W. (Mass.)
Weems, Capell L. (Ohio)
Weisse, Charles H. (Wis.)
Welborn, John (Mo.)
Wharton, Charles S. (Ill.)
Wiley, Ariosto A. (Ala.)
Wiley, William H. (N. J.)
Williams, John S. (Miss.)
Wilson, William W. (Ill.)
Wood, Ernest E. (Mo.)
Wood, Ira W. (N. J.)
Woodyard, Harry C. (W. Va.)
Young, H. Olin (Mich.)
Zenor, William T. (Ind.)

The Sixtieth Congress (1907-09)

Cannon, Joseph G. (Ill.) Speaker.

Acheson, Ernest F. (Pa.)
Adair, John A. M. (Ind.)
Adamson, William C. (Ga.)
Aiken, Wyatt (S. C.)
Alexander, De Alva S. (N. Y.)
Alexander, Joshua W. (Mo.)
Allen, Amos L. (Maine)
Ames, Butler (Mass.)
Andrus, John E. (N. Y.)
Ansberry, Timothy T. (Ohio)
Anthony, Daniel R. (Kans.)
Ashbrook, William A. (Ohio)
Bannon, Henry T. (Ohio)
Barchfeld, Andrew J. (Pa.)
Barclay, Charles F. (Pa.)
Barnhart, Henry A. (Ind.)
Bartholdt, Richard (Mo.)
Bartlett, Charles L. (Ga.)
Bartlett, George A. (Nev.)
Bates, Arthur L. (Pa.)
Beale, Joseph G. (Pa.)
Beall, Jack (Tex.)
Bede, J. Adam (Minn.)
Bell, Thomas M. (Ga.)
Bennet, William S. (N. Y.)
Bennett, Joseph B. (Ky.)
Bingham, Henry H. (Pa.)
Birdsall, Benjamin P. (Iowa)
Bonynge, Robert W. (Colo.)
Booher, Charles F. (Mo.)
Boutell, Henry S. (Ill.)
Bowers, Eaton J. (Miss.)
Boyd, John F. (Nebr.)
Bradley, Thomas W. (N. Y.)
Brantley, William G. (Ga.)
Brick, Abraham L. (Ind.)
Brodhead, J. Davis (Pa.)
Broussard, Robert F. (La.)
Brownlow, Walter P. (Tenn.)
Brumm, Charles N. (Pa.)
Brundidge, Stephen, Jr. (Ark.)

Burgess, George F. (Tex.)
Burke, James F. (Pa.)
Burleigh, Edwin C. (Maine)
Burleson, Albert S. (Tex.)
Burnett, John L. (Ala.)
Burton, Hiram R. (Del.)
Burton, Theodore E. (Ohio)
Butler, Thomas S. (Pa.)
Byrd, Adam M. (Miss.)
Calder, William M. (N. Y.)
Calderhead, William A. (Kans.)
Caldwell, Benjamin F. (Ill.)
Campbell, Philip P. (Kans.)
Candler, Ezekiel S., Jr. (Miss.)
Cannon, Joseph G. (Ill.)
Capron, Adin B. (R. I.)
Carlin, Charles C. (Va.)
Carter, Charles D. (Okla.)
Cary, William J. (Wis.)
Cassel, Henry B. (Pa.)
Caulfield, Henry S. (Mo.)
Chaney, John C. (Ind.)
Chapman, Pleasant T. (Ill.)
Clark, Champ (Mo.)
Clark, Frank (Fla.)
Clayton, Henry D. (Ala.)
Cockran, W. Bourke (N. Y.)
Cocks, William W. (N. Y.)
Cole, Ralph D. (Ohio)
Conner, James P. (Iowa)
Cook, George W. (Colo.)
Cook, Joel (Pa.)
Cooper, Allen F. (Pa.)
Cooper, Henry A. (Wis.)
Cooper, Samuel B. (Tex.)
Coudrey, Harry M. (Mo.)
Cousins, Robert G. (Iowa)
Cox, William E. (Ind.)
Craig, William B. (Ala.)
Cravens, William B. (Ark.)
Crawford, William T. (N. C.)
Crumpacker, Edgar D. (Ind.)
Currier, Frank D. (N. H.)
Cushman, Francis W. (Wash.)
Dalzell, John (Pa.)
Darragh, Archibald B. (Mich.)
Davenport, James S. (Okla.)
Davey, Robert C. (La.)
Davidson, James H. (Wis.)
Davis, Charles R. (Minn.)
Dawes, Beman G. (Ohio)
Dawson, Albert F. (Iowa)
DeArmond, David A. (Mo.)
Denby, Edwin (Mich.)
Denver, Matthew R. (Ohio)
Diekema, Gerrit J. (Mich.)
Dixon, Lincoln (Ind.)
Douglas, Albert (Ohio)
Draper, William H. (N. Y.)
Driscoll, Michael E. (N. Y.)
Dunwell, Charles T. (N. Y.)
Durey, Cyrus (N. Y.)
Dwight, John W. (N. Y.)
Edwards, Charles G. (Ga.)
Edwards, Don C. (Ky.)
Ellerbe, J. Edwin (S. C.)
Ellis, Edgar C. (Mo.)
Ellis, William R. (Oreg.)
Englebright, William F. (Calif.)
Esch, John J. (Wis.)
Estopinal, Albert (La.)
Fairchild, George W. (N. Y.)
Fassett, J. Sloat (N. Y.)
Favrot, George K. (La.)
Ferris, Scott (Okla.)
Finley, David E. (S. C.)
Fitzgerald, John J. (N. Y.)
Flood, Henry D. (Va.)
Floyd, John C. (Ark.)
Focht, Benjamin K. (Pa.)
Foelker, Otto G. (N. Y.)
Fordney, Joseph W. (Mich.)
Fornes, Charles V. (N. Y.)
Foss, George E. (Ill.)
Foster, David J. (Vt.)
Foster, John H. (Ind.)
Foster, Martin D. (Ill.)
Foulkrod, William W. (Pa.)
Fowler, Charles N. (N. J.)
French, Burton L. (Idaho)
Fuller, Charles E. (Ill.)
Fulton, Elmer L. (Okla.)
Gaines, John W. (Tenn.)
Gaines, Joseph H. (W. Va.)
Gardner, Augustus P. (Mass.)
Gardner, John J. (N. J.)
Gardner, Washington (Mich.)
Garner, John N. (Tex.)
Garrett, Finis J. (Tenn.)
Gilhams, Clarence C. (Ind.)
Gill, John, Jr. (Md.)
Gillespie, Oscar W. (Tex.)
Gillett, Frederick H. (Mass.)
Glass, Carter (Va.)
Godwin, Hannibal L. (N. C.)
Goebel, Herman P. (Ohio)
Goldfogle, Henry M. (N. Y.)
Gordon, George W. (Tenn.)
Goulden, Joseph A. (N. Y.)
Graff, Joseph V. (Ill.)
Graham, William H. (Pa.)
Granger, Daniel L. D. (R. I.)
Greene, William S. (Mass.)
Gregg, Alexander W. (Tex.)
Griggs, James M. (Ga.)
Gronna, Asle J. (N. Dak.)
Guernsey, Frank E. (Maine)
Hackett, Richard N. (N. C.)
Hackney, Thomas (Mo.)
Haggott, Warren A. (Colo.)
Hale, Nathan W. (Tenn.)
Hall, Philo (S. Dak.)
Hamill, James A. (N. J.)
Hamilton, Daniel W. (Iowa)
Hamilton, Edward L. (Mich.)
Hamlin, Courtney W. (Mo.)
Hammond, Winfield S. (Minn.)
Harding, J. Eugene (Ohio)
Hardwick, Thomas W. (Ga.)
Hardy, Rufus (Tex.)
Harrison, Francis B. (N. Y.)
Haskins, Kittredge (Vt.)
Haugen, Gilbert N. (Iowa)
Hawley, Willis C. (Oreg.)
Hay, James (Va.)
Hayes, Everis A. (Calif.)
Heflin, J. Thomas (Ala.)
Helm, Harvey (Ky.)
Henry, E. Stevens (Conn.)
Henry, Robert L. (Tex.)
Hepburn, William P. (Iowa)
Higgins, Edwin W. (Conn.)
Hill, Ebenezer J. (Conn.)
Hill, Wilson S. (Miss.)
Hinshaw, Edmund H. (Nebr.)
Hitchcock, Gilbert M. (Nebr.)
Hobson, Richmond P. (Ala.)
Holliday, Elias S. (Ind.)
Houston, William C. (Tenn.)
Howard, William M. (Ga.)
Howell, Benjamin F. (N. J.)
Howell, Joseph (Utah)
Howland, L. Paul (Ohio)
Hubbard, Elbert H. (Iowa)
Hubbard, William P. (W. Va.)
Huff, George F. (Pa.)
Hughes, James A. (W. Va.)
Hughes, William (N. J.)
Hull, Cordell (Tenn.)
Hull, John A. T. (Iowa)
Humphrey, William E. (Wash.)
Humphreys, Benjamin G. (Miss.)
Jackson, William H. (Md.)
James, Addison D. (Ky.)
James, Ollie M. (Ky.)
Jenkins, John J. (Wis.)
Johnson, Ben (Ky.)
Johnson, Joseph T. (S. C.)
Jones, Wesley L. (Wash.)
Jones, William A. (Va.)
Kahn, Julius (Calif.)
Keifer, J. Warren (Ohio)
Keliher, John A. (Mass.)
Kennedy, Charles A. (Iowa)
Kennedy, James (Ohio)
Kinkaid, Moses P. (Nebr.)
Kipp, George W. (Pa.)
Kitchin, Claude (N. C.)
Kitchin, William W. (N. C.)
Kimball, William P. (Ky.)
Knapp, Charles L. (N. Y.)
Knopf, Philip (Ill.)
Knowland, Joseph R. (Calif.)
Kustermann, Gustav (Wis.)
Lafean, Daniel F. (Pa.)
Lamar, J. Robert (Mo.)
Lamar, William B. (Fla.)
Lamb, John (Va.)
Landis, Charles B. (Ind.)
Langley, John W. (Ky.)
Laning, J. Ford (Ohio)
Lassiter, Francis R. (Va.)
Law, Charles B. (N. Y.)
Lawrence, George P. (Mass.)
Leake, Eugene W. (N. J.)
Lee, Gordon (Ga.)
Legaré, George S. (S. C.)
Lenahan, John T. (Pa.)
Lever, Asbury F. (S. C.)
Lewis, Elijah B. (Ga.)
Lilley, George L. (Conn.)
Lindbergh, Charles A. (Minn.)
Lindsay, George H. (N. Y.)
Littlefield, Charles E. (Maine)
Livingston, Leonidas F. (Ga.)
Lloyd, James T. (Mo.)
Longworth, Nicholas (Ohio)
Lorimer, William (Ill.)
Loud, George A. (Mich.)
Loudenslager, Henry C. (N. J.)
Lovering, William C. (Mass.)
Lowden, Frank O. (Ill.)
McCall, Samuel W. (Mass.)
McCreary, George D. (Pa.)
McDermott, James T. (Ill.)
McGavin, Charles (Ill.)
McGuire, Bird S. (Okla.)
McHenry, John G. (Pa.)
McKinlay, Duncan E. (Calif.)
McKinley, William B. (Ill.)
McKinney, James (Ill.)
McLachlan, James (Calif.)
McLain, Frank A. (Miss.)
McLaughlin, James C. (Mich.)
McMillan, Samuel (N. Y.)
McMorran, Henry (Mich.)
Macon, Robert B. (Ark.)
Madden, Martin B. (Ill.)
Madison, Edmond H. (Kans.)
Malby, George R. (N. Y.)
Mann, James R. (Ill.)
Marshall, Thomas F. (N.Dak.)
Martin, Eben W. (S. Dak.)
Maynard, Harry L. (Va.)
Meyer, Adolph (La.)
Miller, James M. (Kans.)
Mondell, Frank W. (Wyo.)
Moon, John A. (Tenn.)
Moon, Reuben O. (Pa.)
Moore, J. Hampton (Pa.)
Moore, John M. (Tex.)
Morse, Elmer A. (Wis.)
Mouser, Grant E. (Ohio)
Mudd, Sydney E. (Md.)
Murdock, Victor (Kans.)
Murphy, James W. (Wis.)
Needham, James C. (Calif.)
Nelson, John M. (Wis.)
Nicholls, Thomas D. (Pa.)
Norris, George W. (Nebr.)
Nye, Frank M. (Minn.)
O'Connell, Joseph F. (Mass.)
Olcott, J. Van Vechten (N. Y.)
Olmsted, Marlin E. (Pa.)
Overstreet, Jesse (Ind.)
Padgett, Lemuel P. (Tenn.)
Page, Robert N. (N. C.)
Parker, Richard W. (N. J.)
Parker, William H. (S. Dak.)
Parsons, Herbert (N. Y.)
Patterson, James O'H. (S.C.)
Payne, Sereno E. (N. Y.)
Pearre, George A. (Md.)
Perkins, James B. (N. Y.)
Peters, Andrew J. (Mass.)
Pollard, Ernest M. (Nebr.)
Porter, Peter A. (N. Y.)
Pou, Edward W. (N. C.)
Powers, Llewellyn (Maine)
Pratt, LeGage (N. J.)
Pray, Charles N. (Mont.)
Prince, George W. (Ill.)
Pujo, Arsene P. (La.)
Rainey, Henry T. (Ill.)
Randell, Choice B. (Tex.)
Ransdell, Joseph E. (La.)
Rauch, George W. (Ind.)
Reeder, William A. (Kans.)
Reid, Charles C. (Ark.)
Reynolds, John M. (Pa.)
Rhinock, Joseph L. (Ky.)
Richardson, William (Ala.)
Riordan, Daniel J. (N. Y.)
Roberts, Ernest W. (Mass.)
Robinson, Joseph T. (Ark.)
Rodenberg, William A. (Ill.)
Rothermel, John H. (Pa.)
Rucker, William W. (Mo.)
Russell, Gordon J. (Tex.)
Russell, Joseph J. (Mo.)
Ryan, William H. (N. Y.)
Sabath, Adolph J. (Ill.)
Saunders, Edward W. (Va.)
Scott, Charles F. (Kans.)
Shackleford, Dorsey W. (Mo.)
Sheppard, Morris (Tex.)
Sherley, J. Swagar (Ky.)
Sherman, James S. (N. Y.)
Sherwood, Isaac R. (Ohio)
Sims, Thetus W. (Tenn.)
Slayden, James L. (Tex.)
Small, John H. (N. C.)
Smith, Madison R. (Mo.)
Smith, Samuel W. (Mich.)
Smith, Sylvester C. (Calif.)
Smith, Walter I. (Iowa)
Smith, William R. (Tex.)
Snapp, Howard M. (Ill.)
Southwick, George N. (N. Y.)
Sparkman, Stephen M. (Fla.)
Sperry, Nehemiah D. (Conn.)
Spight, Thomas (Miss.)
Stafford, William H. (Wis.)
Stanley, Augustus O. (Ky.)
Steenerson, Halvor (Minn.)
Stephens, John H. (Tex.)
Sterling, John A. (Ill.)
Stevens, Frederick C. (Minn.)
Sturgiss, George C. (W. Va.)
Sulloway, Cyrus A. (N. H.)
Sulzer, William (N. Y.)
Swasey, John P. (Maine)
Talbott, J. Frederick C. (Md.)
Tawney, James A. (Minn.)
Taylor, Edward L., Jr. (Ohio)
Taylor, George W. (Ala.)
Thistlewood, Napoleon B. (Ill.)
Thomas, Charles R. (N. C.)
Thomas, W. Aubrey (Ohio)
Tirrell, Charles Q. (Mass.)
Tou Velle, William E. (Ohio)
Townsend, Charles E. (Mich.)
Underwood, Oscar W. (Ala.)
Volstead, Andrew J. (Minn.)
Vreeland, Edward B. (N. Y.)
Waldo, George E. (N. Y.)
Wallace, Robert M. (Ark.)
Wanger, Irving P. (Pa.)
Washburn, Charles G. (Mass.)
Watkins, John T. (La.)
Watson, James E. (Ind.)
Webb, Edwin Y. (N. C.)
Weeks, John W. (Mass.)
Weems, Capell L. (Ohio)
Weisse, Charles H. (Wis.)
Wheeler, Nelson P. (Pa.)
Wiley, Ariosto A. (Ala.)
Wiley, Oliver C. (Ala.)
Willett, William, Jr. (N. Y.)
Williams, John S. (Miss.)
Wilson, William B. (Pa.)
Wilson, William W. (Ill.)
Wolf, Harry B. (Md.)
Wood, Ira W. (N. J.)
Woodyard, Harry C. (W. Va.)
Young, H. Olin (Mich.)

The Sixty-first Congress (1909-11)

Cannon, Joseph G. (Ill.) Speaker.

Adair, John A. M. (Ind.)
Adamson, William C. (Ga.)
Aiken, Wyatt (S. C.)
Alexander, De Alva S. (N. Y.)
Alexander, Joshua W. (Mo.)
Allen, Amos L. (Maine)
Ames, Butler (Mass.)
Anderson, Carl C. (Ohio)
Andrus, John E. (N. Y.)
Ansberry, Timothy T. (Ohio)
Anthony, Daniel R., Jr. (Kans.)
Ashbrook, William A. (Ohio)
Austin, Richard W. (Tenn.)
Barchfeld, Andrew J. (Pa.)
Barclay, Charles F. (Pa.)

Barnard, William O. (Ind.)
Barnhart, Henry A. (Ind.)
Bartholdt, Richard (Mo.)
Bartlett, Charles L. (Ga.)
Bartlett, George A. (Nev.)
Bates, Arthur L. (Pa.)
Borland, William P. (Mo.)
Beall, Jack (Tex.)
Bell, Thomas M. (Ga.)
Bennet, William S. (N. Y.)
Bennett, Joseph B. (Ky.)
Bingham, Henry H. (Pa.)
Boehne, John W. (Ind.)
Booher, Charles F. (Mo.)
Boutell, Henry S. (Ill.)
Bowers, Eaton J. (Miss.)
Bradley, Thomas W. (N. Y.)
Brantley, William G. (Ga.)
Broussard, Robert F. (La.)
Brownlow, Walter P. (Tenn.)
Burgess, George F. (Tex.)
Burke, Charles H. (S. Dak.)
Burke, James F. (Pa.)
Burleigh, Edwin C. (Maine)
Burleson, Albert S. (Tex.)
Burnett, John L. (Ala.)
Butler, Thomas S. (Pa.)
Byrd, Adam M. (Miss.)
Byrns, Joseph W. (Tenn.)
Calder, William M. (N. Y.)
Calderhead, William A. (Kans.)
Campbell, Philip P. (Kans.)
Candler, Ezekiel S., Jr. (Miss.)
Cannon, Joseph G. (Ill.)
Cantrill, James C. (Ky.)
Capron, Adin B. (R. I.)
Carlin, Charles C. (Va.)
Carter, Charles D. (Okla.)
Cary, William J. (Wis.)
Cassidy, James H. (Ohio)
Chapman, Pleasant T. (Ill.)
Clark, Champ (Mo.)
Clark, Frank (Fla.)
Clayton, Henry D. (Ala.)
Cline, Cyrus (Ind.)
Cocks, William W. (N. Y.)
Cole, Ralph D. (Ohio)
Collier, James W. (Miss.)
Conry, Michael F. (N. Y.)
Cook, Joel (Pa.)
Cooper, Allen F. (Pa.)
Cooper, Henry A. (Wis.)
Coudrey, Harry M. (Mo.)
Covington, J. Harry (Md.)
Cowles, Charles H. (N. C.)
Cox, James M. (Ohio)
Cox, William E. (Ind.)
Craig, William B. (Ala.)
Cravens, William B. (Ark.)
Creager, Charles E. (Okla.)
Crow, Charles A. (Mo.)
Crumpacker, Edgar D. (Ind.)
Cullop, William A. (Ind.)
Currier, Frank D. (N. H.)
Cushman, Francis W. (Wash.)
Dalzell, John (Pa.)
Danby, Edwin (Mich.)
Davidson, James H. (Wis.)
Davis, Charles R. (Minn.)
Dawson, Albert F. (Iowa)
DeArmond, David A. (Mo.)
Denby, Edwin (Mich.)
Dent, S. Hubert, Jr. (Ala.)
Denver, Matthew R. (Ohio)
Dickinson, Clement C. (Mo.)
Dickson, William A. (Miss.)
Diekema, Gerrit J. (Mich.)
Dies, Martin (Tex.)
Dixon, Lincoln (Ind.)
Dobbs, Francis H. (Mich.)
Douglas, Albert (Ohio)
Draper, William H. (N. Y.)
Driscoll, Daniel A. (N. Y.)
Driscoll, Michael E. (N. Y.)
Dupre, H. Garland (La.)
Durey, Cyrus (N. Y.)
Dwight, John W. (N. Y.)
Edwards, Charles G. (Ga.)
Edwards, Don C. (Ky.)
Ellerbe, J. Edwin (S. C.)
Ellis, William R. (Oreg.)
Elvins, Politte (Mo.)
Englebright, William F. (Calif.)
Esch, John J. (Wis.)
Estopinal, Albert (La.)
Fairchild, George W. (N. Y.)
Fassett, J. Sloat (N. Y.)
Ferris, Scott (Okla.)
Finley, David E. (S. C.)
Fish, Hamilton (N. Y.)
Fitzgerald, John J. (N. Y.)
Flood, Henry D. (Va.)
Floyd, John C. (Ark.)
Focht, Benjamin K. (Pa.)
Foelker, Otto G. (N. Y.)
Fordney, Joseph W. (Mich.)
Fornes, Charles V. (N. Y.)
Foss, Eugene N. (Mass.)
Foss, George E. (Ill.)
Foster, David J. (Vt.)
Foster, Martin D. (Ill.)
Foulkrod, William W. (Pa.)
Fowler, Charles N. (N. J.)
Fuller, Charles E. (Ill.)
Gaines, Joseph H. (W. Va.)
Gallagher, Thomas (Ill.)
Gardner, Augustus P. (Mass.)
Gardner, John J. (N. J.)
Gardner, Washington (Mich.)
Garner, Alfred B. (Pa.)
Garner, John N. (Tex.)
Garrett, Finis J. (Tenn.)
Gill, John, Jr. (Md.)
Gill, Patrick F. (Mo.)
Gillespie, Oscar W. (Tex.)
Gillett, Frederick H. (Mass.)
Gilmore, Samuel L. (La.)
Glass, Carter (Va.)
Godwin, Hannibal L. (N. C.)
Goebel, Herman P. (Ohio)
Goldfogle, Henry M. (N. Y.)
Good, James W. (Iowa)
Gordon, George W. (Tenn.)
Goulden, Joseph A. (N. Y.)
Graff, Joseph V. (Ill.)
Graham, James M. (Ill.)
Graham, William H. (Pa.)
Grant, John G. (N. C.)
Greene, William S. (Mass.)
Gregg, Alexander W. (Tex.)
Griest, William W. (Pa.)
Griggs, James M. (Ga.)
Gronna, Asle J. (N. Dak.)
Guernsey, Frank E. (Maine)
Hamer, Thomas R. (Idaho)
Hamill, James A. (N. J.)
Hamilton, Edward L. (Mich.)
Hamlin, Courtney W. (Mo.)
Hammond, Winfield S. (Minn.)
Hanna, Louis B. (N. Dak.)
Hardwick, Thomas W. (Ga.)
Hardy, Rufus (Tex.)
Harrison, Francis B. (N. Y.)
Haugen, Gilbert N. (Iowa)
Havens, James S. (N. Y.)
Hawley, Willis C. (Oreg.)
Hay, James (Va.)
Hayes, Everis A. (Calif.)
Heald, William H. (Del.)
Heflin, J. Thomas (Ala.)
Helm, Harvey (Ky.)
Henry, E. Stevens (Conn.)
Henry, Robert L. (Tex.)
Higgins, Edwin W. (Conn.)
Hill, Ebenezer J. (Conn.)
Hinshaw, Edmund H. (Nebr.)
Hitchcock, Gilbert M. (Nebr.)
Hobson, Richmond P. (Ala.)
Hollingsworth, David A. (Ohio)
Houston, William C. (Tenn.)
Howard, William M. (Ga.)
Howell, Benjamin F. (N. J.)
Howell, Joseph (Utah)
Howland, L. Paul (Ohio)
Hubbard, Elbert H. (Iowa)
Hubbard, William P. (W. Va.)
Huff, George F. (Pa.)
Hughes, Dudley M. (Ga.)
Hughes, James A. (W. Va.)
Hughes, William (N. J.)
Hull, Cordell (Tenn.)
Hull, John A. T. (Iowa)
Humphrey, William E. (Wash.)
Humphreys, Benjamin G. (Miss.)
James, Ollie M. (Ky.)
Jamieson, William D. (Iowa)
Johnson, Adna R. (Ohio)
Johnson, Ben (Ky.)
Johnson, Joseph T. (S. C.)
Jones, William A. (Va.)
Joyce, James (Ohio)
Kahn, Julius (Calif.)
Keifer, J. Warren (Ohio)
Keliher, John A. (Mass.)
Kendall, Nathan E. (Iowa)
Kennedy, Charles A. (Iowa)
Kennedy, James (Ohio)
Kinkaid, Moses P. (Nebr.)
Kinkead, Eugene F. (N. J.)
Kitchin, Claude (N. C.)
Knapp, Charles L. (N. Y.)
Kopp, Arthur W. (Wis.)
Knowland, Joseph R. (Calif.)
Korbly, Charles A. (Ind.)
Kronmiller, John (Md.)
Kustermann, Gustav (Wis.)
Lafean, Daniel F. (Pa.)
Lamb, John (Va.)
Langham, Jonathan N. (Pa.)
Langley, John W. (Ky.)
Lassiter, Francis R. (Va.)
Latta, James P. (Nebr.)
Law, Charles B. (N. Y.)
Lawrence, George P. (Mass.)
Lee, Gordon (Ga.)
Legaré, George S. (S. C.)
Lenroot, Irvine L. (Wis.)
Lever, Asbury F. (S. C.)
Lindbergh, Charles A. (Minn.)
Lindsay, George H. (N. Y.)
Lively, Robert M. (Tex.)
Livingston, Leonidas F. (Ga.)
Lloyd, James T. (Mo.)
Longworth, Nicholas (Ohio)
Lorimer, William (Ill.)
Loud, George A. (Mich.)
Loudenslager, Henry C. (N.J.)
Lovering, William C. (Mass.)
Lowden, Frank O. (Ill.)
Lundin, Frederick (Ill.)
McCall, Samuel W. (Mass.)
McCreary, George D. (Pa.)
McCredie, William W. (Wash.)
McDermott, James T. (Ill.)
McGuire, Bird S. (Okla.)
McHenry, John G. (Pa.)
McKinlay, Duncan E. (Calif.)
McKinley, William B. (Ill.)
McKinney, James (Ill.)
McLachlan, James (Calif.)
McLaughlin, James C. (Mich.)
McMorran, Henry (Mich.)
Macon, Robert B. (Ark.)
Madden, Martin B. (Ill.)
Madison, Edmund H. (Kans.)
Maguire, John A. (Nebr.)
Malby, George R. (N. Y.)
Mann, James R. (Ill.)
Martin, Eben W. (S. Dak.)
Martin, John A. (Colo.)
Massey, Zachary D. (Tenn.)
Maynard, Harry L. (Va.)
Mays, Dannitte H. (Fla.)
Miller, Clarence B. (Minn.)
Miller, James M. (Kans.)
Millington, Charles S. (N. Y.)
Mitchell, John J. (Mass.)
Mondell, Frank W. (Wyo.)
Moon, John A. (Tenn.)
Moon, Reuben O. (Pa.)
Moore, J. Hampton (Pa.)
Moore, John M. (Tex.)
Morehead, John M. (N. C.)
Morgan, Charles H. (Mo.)
Morgan, Dick T. (Okla.)
Morrison, Martin A. (Ind.)
Morse, Elmer A. (Wis.)
Moss, Ralph W. (Ind.)
Moxley, William J. (Ill.)
Mudd, Sydney E. (Md.)
Murdock, Victor (Kans.)
Murphy, Arthur P. (Mo.)
Needham, James C. (Calif.)
Nelson, John M. (Wis.)
Nicholls, Thomas D. (Pa.)
Norris, George W. (Nebr.)
Nye, Frank M. (Minn.)
O'Connell, Joseph F. (Mass.)
Olcott, J. Van Vechten (N.Y.)
Oldfield, William A. (Ark.)
Olmsted, Marlin E. (Pa.)
Padgett, Lemuel P. (Tenn.)
Page, Robert N. (N. C.)
Palmer, A. Mitchell (Pa.)
Palmer, Henry W. (Pa.)
Parker, Richard W. (N. J.)
Parsons, Herbert (N. Y.)
Patterson, James O'H. (S. C.)
Payne, Sereno E. (N. Y.)
Pearre, George A. (Md.)
Perkins, James B. (N. Y.)
Peters, Andrew J. (Mass.)
Pickett, Charles E. (Iowa)
Plumley, Frank (Vt.)
Poindexter, Miles (Wash.)
Pou, Edward W. (N. C.)
Pratt, Charles C. (Pa.)
Pray, Charles N. (Mont.)
Prince, George W. (Ill.)
Pujo, Arsene P. (La.)
Rainey, Henry T. (Ill.)
Randell, Choice B. (Tex.)
Ransdell, Joseph E. (La.)
Rauch, George W. (Ind.)
Reeder, William A. (Kans.)
Reid, Charles C. (Ark.)
Reynolds, John M. (Pa.)
Rhinock, Joseph L. (Ky.)
Richardson, William (Ala.)
Riordan, Daniel J. (N. Y.)
Roberts, Ernest W. (Mass.)
Robinson, Joseph T. (Ark.)
Roddenbery, Seaborn A. (Ga.)
Rodenberg, William A. (Ill.)
Rothermel, John H. (Pa.)
Rucker, Atterson W. (Colo.)
Rucker, William W. (Mo.)
Russell, Gordon J. (Tex.)
Sabath, Adolph J. (Ill.)
Saunders, Edward W. (Va.)
Scott, Charles F. (Kans.)
Shackleford, Dorsey W. (Mo.)
Sharp, William G. (Ohio)
Sheffield, William P. (R. I.)
Sheppard, Morris (Tex.)
Sherley, J. Swagar (Ky.)
Sherwood, Isaac R. (Ohio)
Simmons, James S. (N. Y.)
Sims, Thetus W. (Tenn.)
Sisson, Thomas U. (Miss.)
Slayden, James L. (Tex.)
Slemp, C. Bascom (Va.)
Small, John H. (N. C.)
Smith, Samuel W. (Mich.)
Smith, Sylvester C. (Calif.)
Smith, Walter I. (Iowa)
Smith, William R. (Tex.)
Snapp, Howard M. (Ill.)
Southwick, George N. (N. Y.)
Sparkman, Stephen M. (Fla.)
Sperry, Nehemiah D. (Conn.)
Spight, Thomas (Miss.)
Stafford, William H. (Wis.)
Stanley, Augustus O. (Ky.)
Steenerson, Halvor (Minn.)
Stephens, John H. (Tex.)
Sterling, John A. (Ill.)
Stevens, Frederick C. (Minn.)
Sturgiss, George C. (W. Va.)
Sulloway, Cyrus A. (N. H.)
Sulzer, William (N. Y.)
Swasey, John P. (Maine)
Talbott, J. Frederick C. (Md.)
Tawney, James A. (Minn.)
Taylor, Edward L., Jr. (Ohio)
Taylor, Edward T. (Colo.)
Taylor, George W. (Ala.)
Tener, John K. (Pa.)
Thistlewood, Napoleon B. (Ill.)
Thomas, Charles R. (N. C.)
Thomas, Robert Y., Jr. (Ky.)
Thomas, William A. (Ohio)
Tilson, John Q. (Conn.)
Tirrell, Charles Q. (Mass.)
Tou Velle, William E. (Ohio)
Townsend, Charles E. (Mich.)
Turnbull, Robert (Va.)
Underwood, Oscar W. (Ala.)
Volstead, Andrew J. (Minn.)
Vreeland, Edward B. (N. Y.)
Wallace, Robert M. (Ark.)
Wanger, Irving P. (Pa.)
Washburn, Charles G. (Mass.)
Watkins, John T. (La.)
Webb, Edwin Y. (N. C.)
Weeks, John W. (Mass.)
Weisse, Charles H. (Wis.)
Wheeler, Nelson P. (Pa.)
Wickliffe, Robert C. (La.)
Wiley, William H. (N. J.)
Willett, William, Jr. (N. Y.)

Wilson, William B. (Pa.)
Wilson, William W. (Ill.)
Wood, Ira W. (N. J.)
Woods, Frank P. (Iowa)
Woodyard, Harry C. (W. Va.)
Young, H. Olin (Mich.)
Young, Richard (N. Y.)

The Sixty-second Congress (1911-13)

Clark, Champ (Mo.)
Speaker.
Adair, John A. M. (Ind.)
Adamson, William C. (Ga.)
Aiken, Wyatt (S. C.)
Ainey, William D. B. (Pa.)
Akin, Theron (N. Y.)
Alexander, Joshua W. (Mo.)
Allen, Alfred G. (Ohio)
Ames, Butler (Mass.)
Anderson, Carl C. (Ohio)
Anderson, Sydney (Minn.)
Andrus, John E. (N. Y.)
Ansberry, Timothy T. (Ohio)
Anthony, Daniel R., Jr. (Kans.)
Ashbrook, William A. (Ohio)
Austin, Richard W. (Tenn.)
Ayres, Steven B. (N. Y.)
Barchfeld, Andrew J. (Pa.)
Barnhardt, Henry A. (Ind.)
Bartholdt, Richard (Mo.)
Bartlett, Charles L. (Ga.)
Bates, Arthur L. (Pa.)
Bathrick, Ellsworth R. (Ohio)
Beall, Jack (Tex.)
Bell, Thomas M. (Ga.)
Berger, Victor L. (Wis.)
Bingham, Henry H. (Pa.)
Blackmon, Fred L. (Ala.)
Boehne, John W. (Ind.)
Booher, Charles F. (Mo.)
Borland, William P. (Mo.)
Bowman, Charles C. (Pa.)
Bradley, Thomas W. (N. Y.)
Brantley, William G. (Ga.)
Broussard, Robert F. (La.)
Brown, William G., Jr. (W. Va.)
Browning, William J. (N. J.)
Buchanan, Frank (Ill.)
Bulkley, Robert J. (Ohio)
Burgess, George F. (Tex.)
Burke, Charles H. (S. Dak.)
Burke, James F. (Pa.)
Burke, Michael E. (Wis.)
Burleson, Albert S. (Tex.)
Burnett, John L. (Ala.)
Butler, Thomas S. (Pa.)
Byrnes, James F. (S. C.)
Byrns, Joseph W. (Tenn.)
Calder, William M. (N. Y.)
Callaway, Oscar (Tex.)
Campbell, Philip P. (Kans.)
Candler, Ezekiel S. (Miss.)
Cannon, Joseph G. (Ill.)
Cantrill, James C. (Ky.)
Carlin, Charles C. (Va.)
Carter, Charles D. (Okla.)
Cary, William J. (Wis.)
Catlin, Theron E. (Mo.)
Clark, Champ (Mo.)
Clark, Frank (Fla.)
Claypool, Horatio C. (Ohio)
Clayton, Henry D. (Ala.)
Cline, Cyrus (Ind.)
Collier, James W. (Miss.)
Connell, Richard E. (N. Y.)
Conry, Michael F. (N. Y.)
Cooper, Henry A. (Wis.)
Copley, Ira C. (Ill.)
Covington, J. Harry (Md.)
Cox, James M. (Ohio)
Cox, William E. (Ind.)
Crago, Thomas S. (Pa.)
Cravens, William B. (Ark.)
Crumpacker, Edgar D. (Ind.)
Cullop, William A. (Ind.)
Curley, James M. (Mass.)
Currier, Frank D. (N. H.)
Curry, George (N. Mex.)
Dalzell, John (Pa.)
Danforth, Henry G. (N. Y.)
Daugherty, James A. (Mo.)
Davenport, James S. (Okla.)
Davidson, James H. (Wis.)
Davis, Charles R. (Minn.)
Davis, John W. (W. Va.)
De Forest, Henry S. (N. Y.)
Dent, S. Hubert, Jr. (Ala.)
Denver, Matthew R. (Ohio)
Dickinson, Clement C. (Mo.)
Dickson, William A. (Miss.)
Dies, Martin (Tex.)
Difenderfer, Robert E. (Pa.)
Dixon, Lincoln (Ind.)
Dodds, Francis H. (Mich.)
Donohoe, Michael (Pa.)
Doremus, Frank E. (Mich.)
Doughton, Robert L. (N. C.)
Draper, William H. (N. Y.)
Driscoll, Daniel A. (N. Y.)
Driscoll, Michael E. (N. Y.)
Dupre, H. Garland (La.)
Dwight, John W. (N. Y.)
Dyer, Leonidas C. (Mo.)
Edwards, Charles G. (Ga.)
Ellerbe, J. Edwin (S. C.)
Esch, John J. (Wis.)
Estopinal, Albert (La.)
Evans, Lynden (Ill.)
Fairchild, George W. (N. Y.)
Faison, John M. (N. C.)
Farr, John R (Pa.)
Fergusson, Harvey B. (N. Mex.)
Ferris, Scott (Okla)
Fields, William J. (Ky.)
Finley, David E. (S. C.)
Fitzgerald, John J. (N. Y.)
Flood, Henry D. (Va.)
Floyd, John C. (Ark.)
Focht, Benjamin K. (Pa.)
Fordney, Joseph W. (Mich.)
Fornes, Charles V. (N. Y.)
Foss, George E. (Ill.)
Foster, David J. (Vt.)
Foster, Martin D. (Ill.)
Fowler, H. Robert (Ill.)
Francis, William B. (Ohio)
French, Burton L. (Idaho)
Fuller, Charles E. (Ill.)
Gallagher, Thomas (Ill.)
Gardner, Augustus P. (Mass.)
Gardner, John J. (N. J.)
Garner, John N. (Tex.)
Garrett, Finis J. (Tenn.)
George, Henry, Jr. (N. Y.)
Gill, Patrick F. (Mo.)
Gillett, Frederick H. (Mass.)
Glass, Carter (Va.)
Godwin, Hannibal L. (N. C.)
Goeke, J. Henry (Ohio)
Goldfogle, Henry M. (N. Y.)
Good, James W. (Iowa)
Goodwin, William S. (Ark.)
Gordon, George W. (Tenn.)
Gould, Samuel W. (Maine)
Graham, James M. (Ill.)
Gray, Finly H. (Ind.)
Green, William R. (Iowa)
Greene, Frank L. (Vt.)
Greene, William S. (Mass.)
Gregg, Alexander W. (Tex.)
Gregg, Curtis H. (Pa.)
Griest, William W. (Pa.)
Gudger, James M., Jr. (N. C.)
Guernsey, Frank E. (Maine)
Hamill, James A. (N. J.)
Hamilton, Edward L. (Mich.)
Hamilton, John M. (W. Va.)
Hamlin, Courtney W. (Mo.)
Hammond, Winfield S. (Minn.)
Hanna, Louis B. (N. Dak.)
Hardwick, Thomas W. (Ga.)
Hardy, Rufus (Tex.)
Harris, Robert O. (Mass.)
Harrison, Francis B. (N. Y.)
Harrison, Pat (Miss.)
Hart, Archibald C. (N. J.)
Hartman, Jesse L. (Pa.)
Haugen, Gilbert N. (Iowa)
Hawley, Willis C. (Oreg.)
Hay, James (Va.)
Hayden, Carl (Ariz.)
Hayes, Everis A. (Calif.)
Heald, William H. (Del.)
Heflin, J. Thomas (Ala.)
Helgesen, Henry T. (N. Dak.)
Helm, Harvey (Ky.)
Henry, E. Stevens (Conn.)
Henry, Robert L. (Tex.)
Hensley, Walter L. (Mo.)
Higgins, Edwin W. (Conn.)
Hill, Ebenezer J. (Conn.)
Hinds, Asher C. (Maine)
Hobson, Richmond P. (Ala.)
Holland, Edward E. (Va.)
Houston, William C. (Tenn.)
Howard, William S. (Ga.)
Howell, Joseph (Utah)
Howland, L. Paul (Ohio)
Hubbard, Elbert H. (Iowa)
Hughes, Dudley M. (Ga.)
Hughes, James A. (W. Va.)
Hughes, William (N. J.)
Humphrey, William E. (Wash.)
Humphreys, Benjamin G. (Miss.)
Hull, Cordell, (Tenn.)
Jackson, Fred S. (Kans.)
Jacoway, Henderson M. (Ark.)
James, Ollie M. (Ky.)
Johnson, Ben (Ky.)
Johnson, Joseph T. (S. C.)
Jones, William A. (Va.)
Kahn, Julius (Calif.)
Kendall, Nathan E. (Iowa)
Kennedy, Charles A. (Iowa)
Kent, William (Calif.)
Kindred, John J. (N. Y.)
Kinkaid, Moses P. (Nebr.)
Kinkead, Eugene F. (N. J.)
Kipp, George W. (Pa.)
Kitchin, Claude (N. C.)
Knowland, Joseph R. (Calif.)
Konig, George (Md.)
Konop, Thomas F. (Wis.)
Kopp, Arthur W. (Wis.)
Korbly, Charles A. (Ind.)
Lafean, Daniel F. (Pa.)
Lafferty, Abraham W. (Oreg.)
LaFollette, William L. (Wash.)
Lamb, John (Va.)
Langham, Jonathan N. (Pa.)
Langley, John W. (Ky.)
Latta, James P. (Nebr.)
Lawrence, George P. (Mass.)
Lee, Gordon (Ga.)
Lee, Robert E. (Pa.)
Legare, George S. (S. C.)
Lenroot, Irvine L. (Wis.)
Lever, Asbury F. (S. C.)
Levy, Jefferson M. (N. Y.)
Lewis, David J. (Md.)
Lindbergh, Charles A. (Minn.)
Lindsey, George H. (N. Y.)
Linthicum, J. Charles (Md.)
Littlepage, Adam B. (W. Va.)
Littleton, Martin W. (N. Y.)
Lloyd, James T. (Mo.)
Lobeck, Charles O. (Nebr.)
Longworth, Nicholas (Ohio)
Loud, George A. (Mich.)
Loudenslager, Henry C. (N.J.)
McCall, Samuel W. (Mass.)
McCoy, Walter I. (N. J.)
McCreary, George D. (Pa.)
McDermott, James T. (Ill.)
McGillicuddy, Daniel J. (Maine)
McGuire, Bird S. (Okla.)
McHenry, John G. (Pa.)
McKellar, Kenneth D. (Tenn.)
McKenzie, John C. (Ill.)
McKinley, William B. (Ill.)
McKinney, James (Ill.)
McLaughlin, James C. (Mich.)
McMorran, Henry (Mich.)
Macon, Robert B. (Ark.)
Madden, Martin B. (Ill.)
Madison, Edmond H. (Kans.)
Maguire, John A. (Nebr.)
Maher, James P. (N. Y.)
Malby, George R. (N. Y.)
Mann, James R. (Ill.)
Martin, Eben W. (S. Dak.)
Martin, John A. (Colo.)
Matthews, Charles (Pa.)
Mays, Dannitte H. (Fla.)
Merritt, Edwin A., Jr. (N.Y.)
Miller, Clarence B. (Minn.)
Mitchell, Alexander C. (Kans.)
Mondell, Frank W. (Wyo.)
Moon, John A. (Tenn.)
Moon, Reuben O. (Pa.)
Moore, J. Hampton (Pa.)
Moore, John M. (Tex.)
Morgan, Dick T. (Okla.)
Morgan, Lewis L. (La.)
Morrison, Martin A. (Ind.)
Morse, Elmer A. (Wis.)
Moss, Ralph W. (Ind.)
Mott, Luther W. (N. Y.)
Murdock, Victor (Kans.)
Murray, William F. (Mass.)
Needham, James C. (Calif.)
Neeley, George A. (Kans.)
Nelson, John M. (Wis.)
Norris, George W. (Nebr.)
Nye, Frank M. (Minn.)
Oldfield, William A. (Ark.)
Olmsted, Marlin E. (Pa.)
O'Shaunessy, George F. (R. I.)
Padgett, Lemuel P. (Tenn.)
Page, Robert N. (N. C.)
Palmer, A. Mitchell (Pa.)
Parran, Thomas (Md.)
Patten, Thomas G. (N. Y.)
Patton, Charles E. (Pa.)
Payne, Sereno E. (N. Y.)
Pepper, Irvin S. (Iowa)
Peters, Andrew J. (Mass.)
Pickett, Charles E. (Iowa)
Plumley, Frank (Vt.)
Porter, Stephen G. (Pa.)
Post, James D. (Ohio)
Pou, Edward W. (N. C.)
Powers, Caleb (Ky.)
Pray, Charles N. (Mont.)
Prince, George W. (Ill.)
Prouty, Solomon F. (Iowa)
Pujo, Arsene P. (La.)
Rainey, Henry T. (Ill.)
Raker, John E. (Calif.)
Randell, Choice B. (Tex.)
Ransdell, Joseph E. (La.)
Rauch, George W. (Ind.)
Redfield, William C. (N. Y.)
Rees, Rollin R. (Kans.)
Reilly, Thomas L. (Conn.)
Reyburn, William S. (Pa.)
Richardson, William (Ala.)
Riordan, Daniel J. (N. Y.)
Roberts, Edwin E. (Nev.)
Roberts, Ernest W. (Mass.)
Robinson, Joseph T. (Ark.)
Roddenbery, Seaborn A. (Ga.)
Rodenberg, William A. (Ill.)
Rothermel, John H. (Pa.)
Rouse, Arthur B. (Ky.)
Rubey, Thomas L. (Mo.)
Rucker, Atterson W. (Colo.)
Rucker, William W. (Mo.)
Russell, Joseph J. (Mo.)
Sabath, Adolph J. (Ill.)
Saunders, Edward W. (Va.)
Scott, George C. (Iowa)
Scully, Thomas J. (N. J.)
Sells, Samuel R. (Tenn.)
Shackleford, Dorsey W. (Mo.)
Sharp, William G. (Ohio)
Sheppard, Morris (Tex.)
Sherley, J. Swagar (Ky.)
Sherwood, Isaac R. (Ohio)
Simmons, James S. (N. Y.)
Sims, Thetus W. (Tenn.)
Sisson, Thomas U. (Miss.)
Slayden, James L. (Tex.)
Slemp, C. Bascom (Va.)
Sloan, Charles H. (Nebr.)
Small, John H. (N. C.)
Smith, Charles B. (N. Y.)
Smith, John M. C. (Mich.)
Smith, Samuel W. (Mich.)
Smith, Sylvester C. (Calif.)
Smith, William R. (Tex.)
Sparkman, Stephen M. (Fla.)
Speer, Peter M. (Pa.)
Stack, Edmund J. (Ill.)
Stanley, Augustus O. (Ky.)
Stedman, Charles M. (N. C.)
Steenerson, Halvor (Minn.)
Stephens, Daniel V. (Nebr.)
Stephens, Hubert D. (Miss.)
Stephens, John H. (Tex.)
Stephens, William D. (Calif.)
Sterling, John A. (Ill.)
Stevens, Frederick C. (Minn.)
Stone, Claudius U. (Ill.)
Sulloway, Cyrus A. (N. H.)
Sulzer, William (N. Y.)
Sweet, Edwin F. (Mich.)
Switzer, Robert M. (Ohio)
Taggart, Joseph (Kans.)
Talbott, J. Frederick C. (Md.)
Talcott, Charles A. (N. Y.)

Taylor, Edward L., Jr. (Ohio)
Taylor, Edward T. (Colo.)
Taylor, George W. (Ala.)
Taylor, Samuel M. (Ark.)
Thayer, John A. (Mass.)
Thistlewood, Napoleon B. (Ill.)
Thomas, Robert Y., Jr. (Ky.)
Tilson, John Q. (Conn.)
Towner, Horace M. (Iowa)
Townsend, Edward W. (N. J.)
Tribble, Samuel J. (Ga.)
Turnbull, Robert (Va.)
Tuttle, William E., Jr. (N.J.)
Underhill, Edwin S. (N. Y.)
Underwood, Oscar W. (Ala.)
Utter, George H. (R. I.)
Vare, William S. (Pa.)
Volstead, Andrew J. (Minn.)
Vreeland, Edward B. (N. Y.)
Warburton, Stanton (Wash.)
Watkins, John T. (La.)
Webb, Edwin Y. (N. C.)
Wedemeyer, William W. (Mich).
Weeks, John W. (Mass.)
Whitacre, John J. (Ohio)
White, George (Ohio)
Wickliffe, Robert C. (La.)
Wilder, William H. (Mass.)
Willis, Frank B. (Ohio)
Wilson, Frank E. (N. Y.)
Wilson, William B. (Pa.)
Wilson, William W. (Ill.)
Witherspoon, Samuel A. (Miss.)
Wood, Ira W. (N. J.)
Woods, Frank P. (Iowa)
Young, H. Olin (Mich.)
Young, Isaac D. (Kans.)
Young, James (Tex.)

The Sixty-third Congress (1913-15)

Clark, Champ (Mo.) Speaker.

Abercrombie, John W. (Ala.)
Adair, John A. M. (Ind.)
Adamson, William C. (Ga.)
Aiken, Wyatt (S. C.)
Ainey, William D. B. (Pa.)
Alexander, Joshua W. (Mo.)
Allen, Alfred G. (Ohio)
Anderson, Sydney (Minn.)
Ansberry, Timothy T. (Ohio)
Anthony, Daniel R., Jr. (Kans.)
Ashbrook, William A. (Ohio)
Aswell, James B. (La.)
Austin, Richard W. (Tenn.)
Avis, Samuel B. (W. Va.)
Bailey, Warren W. (Pa.)
Baker, J. Thompson (N. J.)
Baltz, William N. (Ill.)
Barchfeld, Andrew J. (Pa.)
Barkley, Alben W. (Ky.)
Barnhart, Henry A. (Ind.)
Bartholdt, Richard (Mo.)
Bartlett, Charles L. (Ga.)
Barton, Silas R. (Nebr.)
Bathrick, Ellsworth R. (Ohio)
Beakes, Samuel W. (Mich.)
Beall, Jack (Tex.)
Bell, Charles W. (Calif.)
Bell, Thomas M. (Ga.)
Blackmon, Fred L. (Ala.)
Booher, Charles F. (Mo.)
Borchers, Charles M. (Ill.)
Borland, William P. (Mo.)
Bowdle, Stanley E. (Ohio)
Bremner, Robert G. (N. J.)
Britten, Fred A. (Ill.)
Brockson, Franklin (Del.)
Brodbeck, Andrew R. (Pa.)
Broussard, Robert F. (La.)
Brown, Lathrop (N. Y.)
Brown, William G., Jr. (W. Va.)
Browning, William J. (N. J.)
Browne, Edward E. (Wis.)
Bruckner, Henry (N. Y.)
Brumbaugh, Clement L. (Ohio)
Bryan, James W. (Wash.)
Buchanan, Frank (Ill.)
Buchanan, James P. (Tex.)
Bulkley, Robert J. (Ohio)
Burgess, George F. (Tex.)
Burke, Charles H. (S. Dak.)
Burke, James F. (Pa.)
Burke, Michael E. (Wis.)
Burnett, John L. (Ala.)
Butler, Thomas S. (Pa.)
Byrnes, James F. (S. C.)
Byrns, Joseph W. (Tenn.)
Calder, William M. (N. Y.)
Callaway, Oscar (Tex.)
Campbell, Philip P. (Kans.)
Candler, Ezekiel S., Jr. (Miss.)
Cantor, Jacob A. (N. Y.)
Cantrill, James C. (Ky.)
Caraway, Thaddeus H. (Ark.)
Carew, John F. (N. Y.)
Carlin, Charles C. (Va.)
Carr, Wooda N. (Pa.)
Carter, Charles D. (Okla.)
Cary, William J. (Wis.)
Casey, John J. (Pa.)
Chandler, Walter M. (N. Y.)
Church, Denver S. (Calif.)
Clancy, John R. (N. Y.)
Clark, Champ, (Mo.)
Clark, Frank (Fla.)
Claypool, Horatio C. (Ohio)
Clayton, Henry D. (Ala.)
Cline, Cyrus (Ind.)
Coady, Charles P. (Md.)
Collier, James W. (Miss.)
Connelly, John R. (Kans.)
Connolly, Maurice (Iowa)
Conry, Michael F. (N. Y.)
Cooper, Henry A. (Wis.)
Copley, Ira C. (Ill.)
Covington, J. Harry (Md.)
Cox, William E. (Ind.)
Cramton, Louis C. (Mich.)
Crisp, Charles R. (Ga.)
Crosser, Robert (Ohio)
Cullop, William A. (Ind.)
Curley, James M. (Mass.)
Curry, Charles F. (Calif.)
Dale, Harry H. (N. Y.)
Danforth, Henry G. (N. Y.)
Davenport, James S. (Okla.)
Davis, Charles R. (Minn.)
Davis, John W. (W. Va.)
Decker, Perl D. (Mo.)
Deitrick, Frederick S. (Mass.)
Dent, S. Hubert, Jr. (Ala.)
Dershem, Frank L. (Pa.)
Dickinson, Clement C. (Mo.)
Dies, Martin (Tex.)
Difenderfer, Robert E. (Pa.)
Dillon, Charles H. (S. Dak.)
Dixon, Lincoln (Ind.)
Donohoe, Michael (Pa.)
Donovan, Jeremiah (Conn.)
Dooling, Peter J. (N. Y.)
Doolittle, Dudley (Kans.)
Doremus, Frank E. (Mich.)
Doughton, Robert L. (N. C.)
Driscoll, Daniel A. (N. Y.)
Drukker, Dow H. (N. J.)
Dunn, Thomas B. (N. Y.)
Dupre, H. Garland (La.)
Dyer, Leonidas C. (Mo.)
Eagan, John J. (N. J.)
Eagle, Joe H. (Tex.)
Edmonds, George W. (Pa.)
Edwards, Charles G. (Ga.)
Elder, J. Walter (La.)
Esch, John J. (Wis.)
Estopinal, Albert (La.)
Evans, John M. (Mont.)
Fairchild, George W. (N. Y.)
Faison, John M. (N. C.)
Falconer, Jacob A. (Wash.)
Farr, John R. (Pa.)
Fergusson, Harvey B. (N. Mex.)
Ferris, Scott (Okla.)
Fess, Simeon D. (Ohio)
Fields, William J. (Ky.)
Finley, David E. (S. C.)
Fitzgerald, John J. (N. Y.)
FitzHenry, Louis (Ill.)
Flood, Henry D. (Va.)
Floyd, John C. (Ark.)
Fordney, Joseph W. (Mich.)
Foster, Martin D. (Ill.)
Fowler, H. Robert (Ill.)
Francis, William B. (Ohio)
Frear, James A. (Wis.)
French, Burton L. (Idaho)
Gallagher, Thomas (Ill.)
Gallivan, James A. (Mass.)
Gard, Warren (Ohio)
Gardner, Augustus P. (Mass.)
Garner, John N. (Tex.)
Garrett, Daniel E. (Tex.)
Garrett, Finis J. (Tenn.)
George, Henry, Jr. (N. Y.)
Gerry, Peter G. (R. I.)
Gill, Michael J. (Mo.)
Gillett, Frederick H. (Mass.)
Gilmore, Edward (Mass.)
Gittins, Robert H. (N. Y.)
Glass, Carter (Va.)
Godwin, Hannibal L. (N. C.)
Goeke, J. Henry (Ohio)
Goldfogle, Henry M. (N. Y.)
Good, James W. (Iowa)
Goodwin, Forrest (Maine)
Goodwin, William S. (Ark.)
Gordon, William (Ohio)
Gorman, George E. (Ill.)
Goulden, Joseph A. (N. Y.)
Graham, George S. (Pa.)
Graham, James M. (Ill.)
Gray, Finly H. (Ind.)
Green, William R. (Iowa)
Greene, Frank L. (Vt.)
Greene, William S. (Mass.)
Gregg, Alexander W. (Tex.)
Griest, William W. (Pa.)
Griffin, Daniel J. (N. Y.)
Gudger, James M., Jr. (N.C.)
Guernsey, Frank E. (Maine)
Hamill, James A. (N. J.)
Hamlin, Courtney W. (Mo.)
Hamilton, Charles M. (N. Y.)
Hamilton, Edward L. (Mich.)
Hammond, Winfield S. (Minn.)
Hardwick, Thomas W. (Ga.)
Hardy, Rufus (Tex.)
Harris, Christopher C. (Ala.)
Harrison, Francis B. (N. Y.)
Harrison, Pat (Miss.)
Hart, Archibald C. (N. J.)
Haugen, Gilbert N. (Iowa)
Hay, James (Va.)
Hayden, Carl (Ariz.)
Hayes, Everis A. (Calif.)
Haugen, Gilbert N. (Iowa)
Hawley, Willis C. (Oreg.)
Heflin, J. Thomas (Ala.)
Helgesen, Henry T. (N. Dak.)
Helm, Harvey (Ky.)
Helvering, Guy T. (Kans.)
Henry, Robert L. (Tex.)
Hensley, Walter L. (Mo.)
Hill, Robert P. (Ill.)
Hinds, Asher C. (Maine)
Hinebaugh, William H. (Ill.)
Hobson, Richmond P. (Ala.)
Holland, Edward E. (Va.)
Houston, William C. (Tenn.)
Howard, William S. (Ga.)
Howell, Joseph (Utah)
Hoxworth, Stephen A. (Ill.)
Hughes, Dudley M. (Ga.)
Hughes, James A. (W. Va.)
Hulings, Willis J. (Pa.)
Hull, Cordell (Tenn.)
Humphrey, William E. (Wash.)
Humphreys, Benjamin G. (Miss.)
Igoe, William L. (Mo.)
Jacoway, Henderson M. (Ark.)
Johnson, Albert (Wash.)
Johnson, Ben (Ky.)
Johnson, Jacob (Utah)
Johnson, Joseph T. (S. C.)
Jones, William A. (Va.)
Kahn, Julius (Calif.)
Keating, Edward (Colo.)
Keister, Abraham L. (Pa.)
Kelly, M. Clyde (Pa.)
Kelly, Patrick H. (Mich.)
Kennedy, Ambrose (R. I.)
Kennedy, Charles A. (Iowa)
Kennedy, William (Conn.)
Kent, William (Calif.)
Kettner, William (Calif.)
Key, John A. (Ohio)
Kiess, Edgar R. (Pa.)
Kindel, George J. (Colo.)
Kinkaid, Moses P. (Nebr.)
Kinkead, Eugene F. (N. J.)
Kirkpatrick, Sanford (Iowa)
Kitchin, Claude (N. C.)
Knowland, Joseph R. (Calif.)
Konig, George (Md.)
Konop, Thomas F. (Wis.)
Korbly, Charles A. (Ind.)
Kreider, Aaron S. (Pa.)
Lafferty, Abraham W. (Oreg.)
La Follette, William L. (Wash.)
Langham, Jonathan N. (Pa.)
Langley, John W. (Ky.)
Lazaro, Ladislas (La.)
Lee, Gordon (Ga.)
Lee, Robert E. (Pa.)
L'Engle, Claude (Fla.)
Lenroot, Irvine L. (Wis.)
Lesher, John V. (Pa.)
Lever, Asbury F. (S. C.)
Levy, Jefferson M. (N. Y.)
Lewis, David J. (Md.)
Lewis, Fred E. (Pa.)
Lieb, Charles (Ind.)
Lindbergh, Charles A. (Minn.)
Lindquist, Francis O. (Mich.)
Linthicum, J. Charles (Md.)
Lloyd, James T. (Mo.)
Lobeck, Charles O. (Nebr.)
Loft, George W. (N. Y.)
Logue, J. Washington (Pa.)
Lonergan, Augustine (Conn.)
McAndrews, James (Ill.)
MacDonald, William J. (Mich.)
McClellan, George (N. Y.)
McCoy, Walter I. (N. J.)
McDermott, James T. (Ill.)
McGillicuddy, Daniel J. (Maine)
McGuire, Bird S. (Okla.)
McKellar, Kenneth D. (Tenn.)
McKenzie, John C. (Ill.)
McLaughlin, James C. (Mich.)
Madden, Martin B. (Ill.)
Maguire, John A. (Nebr.)
Mahan, Bryan F. (Conn.)
Maher, James P. (N. Y.)
Manahan, James (Minn.)
Mann, James R. (Ill.)
Mapes, Carl E. (Mich.)
Martin, Eben W. (S. Dak.)
Martin, Lewis J. (N. J.)
Merritt, Edwin A., Jr. (N.Y.)
Metz, Herman A. (N. Y.)
Miller, Clarence B. (Minn.)
Mitchell, John J. (Mass.)
Mondell, Frank W. (Wyo.)
Montague, Andrew J. (Va.)
Moon, John A. (Tenn.)
Moore, J. Hampton (Pa.)
Morgan, Dick T. (Okla.)
Morgan, Lewis L. (La.)
Morin, John M. (Pa.)
Morrison, Martin A. (Ind.)
Moss, Hunter H., Jr. (W.Va.)
Moss, Ralph W. (Ind.)
Mott, Luther W. (N. Y.)
Mulkey, William O. (Ala.)
Murdock, Victor (Kans.)
Murray, William F. (Mass.)
Murray, William H. (Okla.)
Neeley, George A. (Kans.)
Neely, Matthew M. (W. Va.)
Nelson, John M. (Wis.)
Nolan, John I. (Calif.)
Norton, Patrick D. (N. Dak.)
O'Brien, James H. (N. Y.)
Oglesby, Woodson R. (N. Y.)
O'Hair, Frank T. (Ill.)
Oldfield, William A. (Ark.)
O'Leary, Denis (N. Y.)
O'Shaunessy, George F. (R. I.)
Padgett, Lemuel P. (Tenn.)
Page, Robert N. (N. C.)
Paige, Calvin D. (Mass.)
Palmer, A. Mitchell (Pa.)
Park, Frank (Ga.)
Parker, James S. (N. Y.)
Parker, Richard W. (N. J.)
Patten, Thomas G. (N. Y.)
Patton, Charles E. (Pa.)
Payne, Sereno E. (N. Y.)
Pepper, Irvin S. (Iowa)
Peters, Andrew J. (Mass.)
Peters, John A. (Maine)
Peterson, John B. (Ind.)
Phelan, Michael F. (Mass.)
Platt, Edmund (N. Y.)

Plumley, Frank (Vt.)
Porter, Stephen G. (Pa.)
Post, James D. (Ohio)
Pou, Edward W. (N. C.)
Powers, Caleb (Ky.)
Price, Jesse D. (Md.)
Prouty, Solomon F. (Iowa)
Quin, Percy E. (Miss.)
Ragsdale, J. Willard (S. C.)
Rainey, Henry T. (Ill.)
Raker, John E. (Calif.)
Rauch, George W. (Ind.)
Rayburn, Samuel T. (Tex.)
Reed, Eugene E. (N. H.)
Reilly, Michael K. (Wis.)
Reilly, Thomas L. (Conn.)
Richardson, William (Ala.)
Riordan, Daniel J. (N. Y.)
Roberts, Edwin E. (Nev.)
Roberts, Ernest W. (Mass.)
Roddenbery, Seaborn A. (Ga.)
Rogers, John Jacob (Mass.)
Rothermel, John H. (Pa.)
Rouse, Arthur B. (Ky.)
Rubey, Thomas L. (Mo.)
Rucker, William W. (Mo.)
Rupley, Arthur R. (Pa.)
Russell, Joseph J. (Mo.)
Sabath, Adolph J. (Ill.)
Saunders, Edward W. (Va.)
Scott, George C. (Iowa)
Scully, Thomas J. (N. J.)
Seldomridge, Harry H. (Colo.)
Sells, Samuel R. (Tenn.)
Shackleford, Dorsey W. (Mo.)
Sharp, William G. (Ohio)
Sherley, J. Swagar (Ky.)
Sherwood, Isaac R. (Ohio)
Shreve, Milton W. (Pa.)
Sims, Thetus W. (Tenn.)
Sinnott, Nicholas J. (Oreg.)
Sisson, Thomas U. (Miss.)
Slayden, James L. (Tex.)
Slemp, C. Bascom (Va.)
Sloan, Charles H. (Nebr.)
Small, John H. (N. C.)
Smith, Addison T. (Idaho)
Smith, Charles B. (N. Y.)
Smith, Frank O. (Md.)
Smith, George R. (Minn.)
Smith, John M. C. (Mich.)
Smith, Samuel W. (Mich.)
Smith, William R. (Tex.)
Sparkman, Stephen M. (Fla.)
Stafford, William H. (Wis.)
Stanley, Augustus O. (Ky.)
Stedman, Charles M. (N. C.)
Steenerson, Halvor (Minn.)
Stephens, Daniel V. (Nebr.)
Stephens, Hubert D. (Miss.)
Stephens, John H. (Tex.)
Stephens, William D. (Calif.)
Stevens, Frederick C. (Minn.)
Stevens, Raymond B. (N. H.)
Stone, Claudius U. (Ill.)
Stout, Tom (Mont.)
Stringer, Lawrence B. (Ill.)
Sullivan, Timothy D. (N. Y.)
Sumners, Hatton W. (Tex.)
Sutherland, Howard (W. Va.)
Switzer, Robert M. (Ohio)
Taggart, Joseph (Kans.)
Talbott, J. Frederick C. (Md.)
Talcott, Charles A. (N. Y.)
Tavender, Clyde H. (Ill.)
Taylor, Benjamin I. (N. Y.)
Taylor, Edward T. (Colo.)
Taylor, George W. (Ala.)
Taylor, Samuel M. (Ark.)
Temple, Henry W. (Pa.)
TenEyck, Peter G. (N. Y.)
Thacher, Thomas C. (Mass.)
Thomas, Robert Y., Jr. (Ky.)
Thompson, Joseph B. (Okla.)
Thomson, Charles M. (Ill.)
Towner, Horace M. (Iowa)
Townsend, Edward W. (N.J.)
Treadway, Allen T. (Mass.)
Tribble, Samuel J. (Ga.)
Tuttle, William E., Jr. (N. J.)
Underhill, Edwin S. (N. Y.)
Underwood, Oscar W. (Ala.)
Vare, William S. (Pa.)
Vaughan, Horace W. (Tex.)
Vinson, Carl (Ga.)
Vollmer, Henry (Iowa)
Volstead, Andrew J. (Minn.)
Walker, John R. (Ga.)
Wallin, Samuel (N. Y.)
Walsh, Allan B. (N. J.)
Walters, Anderson H. (Pa.)
Watkins, John T. (La.)
Watson, Walter A. (Va.)
Weaver, Claude (Okla.)
Webb, Edwin Y. (N. C.)
Whaley, Richard S. (S. C.)
Whitacre, John J. (Ohio)
White, George (Ohio)
Wilder, William H. (Mass.)
Williams, William E. (Ill.)
Willis, Frank B. (Ohio)
Wilson, Emmett (Fla.)
Wilson, Frank E. (N. Y.)
Wingo, Otis (Ark.)
Winslow, Samuel E. (Mass.)
Witherspoon, Samuel A. (Miss.)
Woodruff, Roy O. (Mich.)
Woods, Frank P. (Iowa)
Young, George M. (N. Dak.)
Young, H. Olin (Mich.)
Young, James (Tex.)

The Sixty-fourth Congress (1915-17)

Clark, Champ (Mo.)
Speaker.

Abercrombie, John W. (Ala.)
Adair, John A. M. (Ind.)
Adamson, William C. (Ga.)
Aiken, Wyatt (S. C.)
Alexander, Joshua W. (Mo.)
Allen, Alfred G. (Ohio)
Almon, Edward B. (Ala.)
Anderson, Sydney (Minn.)
Anthony, Daniel R., Jr. (Kans.)
Ashbrook, William A. (Ohio)
Aswell, James B. (La.)
Austin, Richard W. (Tenn.)
Ayres, William A. (Kans.)
Bacharach, Isaac (N. J.)
Bailey, Warren W. (Pa.)
Barchfeld, Andrew J. (Pa.)
Barkley, Alben W. (Ky.)
Barnhart, Henry A. (Ind.)
Beakes, Samuel W. (Mich.)
Beales, C. William (Pa.)
Bell, Thomas M. (Ga.)
Benedict, H. Stanley (Calif.)
Bennet, William S. (N. Y.)
Black, Eugene (Tex.)
Blackmon, Fred L. (Ala.)
Booher, Charles F. (Mo.)
Borland, William P. (Mo.)
Bowers, George M. (W. Va.)
Britt, James J. (N. C.)
Britten, Fred A. (Ill.)
Brown, William G., Jr. (W. Va.)
Browne, Edward E. (Wis.)
Browning, William J. (N. J.)
Bruckner, Henry (N. Y.)
Brumbaugh, Clement L. (Ohio)
Buchanan, Frank (Ill.)
Buchanan, James P. (Tex.)
Burgess, George F. (Tex.)
Burke, Michael E. (Wis.)
Burnett, John L. (Ala.)
Butler, Thomas S. (Pa.)
Byrnes, James F. (S. C.)
Byrns, Joseph W. (Tenn.)
Caldwell, Charles P. (N. Y.)
Callaway, Oscar (Tex.)
Campbell, Philip P. (Kans.)
Candler, Ezekiel S., Jr. (Miss.)
Cannon, Joseph G. (Ill.)
Cantrill, James C. (Ky.)
Capstick, John H. (N. J.)
Caraway, Thaddeus H. (Ark.)
Carew, John F. (N. Y.)
Carlin, Charles C. (Va.)
Carter, Charles D. (Okla.)
Carter, William H. (Mass.)
Cary, William J. (Wis.)
Casey, John J. (Pa.)
Chandler, Walter M. (N. Y.)
Charles, William B. (N. Y.)
Chiperfield, Burnett M. (Ill.)
Church, Denver S. (Calif.)
Clark, Champ (Mo.)
Clark, Frank (Fla.)
Cline, Cyrus (Ind.)
Coady, Charles P. (Md.)
Coleman, William H. (Pa.)
Collier, James W. (Miss.)
Connelly, John R. (Kans.)
Conry, Michael F. (N. Y.)
Cooper, Edward (W. Va.)
Cooper, Henry A. (Wis.)
Cooper, John G. (Ohio)
Copley, Ira C. (Ill.)
Costello, Peter E. (Pa.)
Cox, William E. (Ind.)
Crago, Thomas S. (Pa.)
Cramton, Louis C. (Mich.)
Crisp, Charles R. (Ga.)
Crosser, Robert (Ohio)
Cullop, William A. (Ind.)
Curry, Charles F. (Calif.)
Dale, Harry H. (N. Y.)
Dale, Porter H. (Vt.)
Dallinger, Frederick W. (Mass.)
Danforth, Henry G. (N. Y.)
Darrow, George P. (Pa.)
Davenport, James S. (Okla.)
Davis, Charles R. (Minn.)
Davis, James H. (Tex.)
Decker, Perl D. (Mo.)
Dempsey, S. Wallace (N. Y.)
Denison, Edward E. (Ill.)
Dent, S. Hubert, Jr. (Ala.)
Dewalt, Arthur G. (Pa.)
Dickinson, Clement C. (Mo.)
Dies, Martin (Tex.)
Dill, Clarence C. (Wash.)
Dillon, Charles H. (S. Dak.)
Dixon, Lincoln (Ind.)
Dooling, Peter J. (N. Y.)
Doolittle, Dudley (Kans.)
Doremus, Frank E. (Mich.)
Doughton, Robert L. (N. C.)
Dowell, Cassius C. (Iowa)
Driscoll, Daniel A. (N. Y.)
Drukker, Dow H. (N. J.)
Dunn, Thomas B. (N. Y.)
Dupre, H. Garland (La.)
Dyer, Leonidas C. (Mo.)
Eagan, John J. (N. J.)
Eagle, Joe H (Tex.)
Edmonds, George W. (Pa.)
Edwards, Charles G. (Ga.)
Ellsworth, Franklin F. (Minn.)
Elston, John A. (Calif.)
Emerson, Henry I. (Ohio)
Esch, John J. (Wis.)
Estopinal, Albert (La.)
Evans, John M. (Mont.)
Fairchild, George W. (N. Y.)
Farley, Michael F. (N. Y.)
Farr, John R. (Pa.)
Ferris, Scott (Okla.)
Fess, Simeon D. (Ohio)
Fields, William J. (Ky.)
Finley, David E. (S. C.)
Fitzgerald, John J. (N. Y.)
Flood, Henry D. (Va.)
Flynn, Joseph V. (N . Y.)
Focht, Benjamin K. (Pa.)
Fordney, Joseph W. (Mich.)
Foss, George E. (Ill.)
Foster, Martin D. (Ill.)
Frear, James A. (Wis.)
Freeman, Richard P. (Conn.)
Fuller, Charles E. (Ill.)
Gallagher, Thomas (Ill.)
Gallivan, James A. (Mass.)
Gandy, Harry L. (S. Dak.)
Gard, Warren (Ohio)
Gardner, Augustus P. (Mass.)
Garland, Mahlon M. (Pa.)
Garner, John N. (Tex.)
Garrett, Finis J. (Tenn.)
Gillett, Frederick H. (Mass.)
Glass, Carter (Va.)
Glynn, James P. (Conn.)
Godwin, Hannibal L. (N. C.)
Good, James W. (Iowa)
Goodwin, William S. (Ark.)
Gordon, William (Ohio)
Gould, Norman J. (N. Y.)
Graham, George S. (Pa.)
Gray, Edward W. (N. J.)
Gray, Finly H. (Ind.)
Gray, Oscar L. (Ala.)
Green, William R. (Iowa)
Greene, Frank L. (Vt.)
Greene, William S. (Mass.)
Gregg, Alexander W. (Tex.)
Griest, William W. (Pa.)
Griffin, Daniel J. (N. Y.)
Guernsey, Frank E. (Maine)
Hadley, Lindley H. (Wash.)
Hamill, James A. (N. J.)
Hamilton, Charles M. (N. Y.)
Hamilton, Edward L. (Mich.)
Hamlin, Courtney W. (Mo.)
Hardy, Rufus (Tex.)
Harrison, Pat (Miss.)
Harrison, Thomas W. (Va.)
Hart, Archibald C. (N. J.)
Haskell, Reuben L. (N. Y.)
Hastings, William W. (Okla.)
Haugen, Gilbert N. (Iowa)
Hawley, Willis C. (Oreg.)
Hay, James (Va.)
Hayden, Carl (Ariz.)
Hayes, Everis A. (Calif.)
Heaton, Robert D. (Pa.)
Heflin, J. Thomas (Ala.)
Helgesen, Henry T. (N. Dak.)
Helm, Harvey (Ky.)
Helvering, Guy T. (Kans.)
Henry, Robert L. (Tex.)
Hensley, Walter L. (Mo.)
Hernandez, Benigno C. (N. Mex.)
Hicks, Frederick C. (N. Y.)
Hill, Ebenezer J. (Conn.)
Hilliard, Benjamin C. (Colo.)
Hinds, Asher C. (Maine)
Holland, Edward E. (Va.)
Hollingsworth, David A. (Ohio)
Hood, George E. (N. C.)
Hopwood, Robert F. (Pa.)
Houston, William C. (Tenn.)
Howard, William S. (Ga.)
Howell, Joseph (Utah)
Huddleston, George (Ala.)
Hughes, Dudley M. (Ga.)
Hulbert, G. Murray (N. Y.)
Hull, Cordell (Tenn.)
Hull, Harry E. (Iowa)
Humphrey, William E. (Wash.)
Humphreys, Benjamin G. (Miss.)
Husted, James W. (N. Y.)
Hutchinson, Elijah C. (N. J.)
Igoe, William L. (Mo.)
Jacoway, Henderson M. (Ark.)
James, W. Frank (Mich.)
Johnson, Albert (Wash.)
Johnson, Ben (Ky.)
Johnson, Royal C. (S. Dak.)
Jones, William A. (Va.)
Kahn, Julius (Calif.)
Kearns, Charles C. (Ohio)
Keating, Edward (Colo.)
Keister, Abraham L. (Pa.)
Kelley, Patrick H. (Mich.)
Kennedy, Ambrose (R. I.)
Kennedy, Charles A. (Iowa)
Kent, William (Calif.)
Kettner, William (Calif.)
Key, John A. (Ohio)
Kiess, Edgar R. (Pa.)
Kincheloe, David H. (Ky.)
King, Edward J. (Ill.)
Kinkaid, Moses P. (Nebr.)
Kitchin, Claude (N. C.)
Konop, Thomas F. (Wis.)
Kreider, Aaron S. (Pa.)
Lafean, Daniel F. (Pa.)
LaFollette, William L. (Wash.)
Langley, John W. (Ky.)
Lazaro, Ladislas (La.)
Lee, Gordon (Ga.)
Lehlbach, Frederick R. (N. J.)
Lenroot, Irvine L. (Wis.)
Lesher, John V. (Pa.)
Lever, Asbury F. (S. C.)
Lewis, David J. (Md.)
Lieb, Charles (Ind.)
Liebel, Michael, Jr. (Pa.)
Lindbergh, Charles A. (Minn.)
Linthicum, J. Charles (Md.)
Littlepage, Adam B. (W. Va.)
Lloyd, James T. (Mo.)
Lobeck, Charles O. (Nebr.)
Loft, George W. (N. Y.)
London, Meyer (N. Y.)
Longworth, Nicholas (Ohio)
Loud, George A. (Mich.)
McAndrews, James (Ill.)
McArthur, Clifton N. (Oreg.)
McClintic, James V. (Okla.)

McCorkle, Paul G. (S. C.)
McCracken, Robert M. (Idaho)
McCulloch, Roscoe C. (Ohio)
McDermott, James T. (Ill.)
McFadden, Louis T. (Pa.)
McGillicuddy, Daniel J. (Maine)
McKellar, Kenneth D. (Tenn.)
McKenzie, John C. (Ill.)
McKinley, William B. (Ill.)
McLaughlin, James C. (Mich.)
McLemore, A. Jeff (Tex.)
Madden, Martin B. (Ill.)
Magee, Walter W. (N. Y.)
Maher, James P. (N. Y.)
Mann, James R. (Ill.)
Mapes, Carl E. (Mich.)
Martin, Whitmell P. (La.)
Matthews, Nelson E. (Ohio)
Mays, James H. (Utah)
Meeker, Jacob E. (Mo.)
Miller, Clarence B. (Minn.)
Miller, Samuel H. (Pa.)
Miller, Thomas W. (Del.)
Mondell, Frank W. (Wyo.)
Montague, Andrew J. (Va.)
Moon, John A. (Tenn.)
Mooney, William C. (Ohio)
Moore, J. Hampton (Pa.)
Moores, Merrill (Ind.)
Morgan, Dick T. (Okla.)
Morgan, Lewis L. (La.)
Morin, John M. (Pa.)
Morrison, Martin A. (Ind.)
Moss, Hunter H., Jr. (W.Va.)
Moss, Ralph W. (Ind.)
Mott, Luther W. (N. Y.)
Mudd, Sydney E. (Md.)
Murray, William H. (Okla.)
Neely, Matthew M. (W. Va.)
Nelson, John M. (Wis.)
Nichols, Charles A. (Mich.)
Nicholls, Samuel J. (S. C.)
Nolan, John I. (Calif.)
North, S. Taylor (Pa.)
Norton, Patrick D. (N. Dak.)
Oakey, P. Davis (Conn.)
Oglesby, Woodson R. (N. Y.)
Oldfield, William A. (Ark.)
Oliver, William B. (Ala.)
Olney, Richard (Mass.)
O'Shaunessy, George F. (R.I.)
Overmyer, Arthur W. (Ohio)
Padgett, Lemuel P. (Tenn.)
Page, Robert N. (N. C.)
Paige, Calvin D. (Mass.)
Park, Frank (Ga.)
Parker, James S. (N. Y.)
Parker, Richard W. (N. J.)
Patten, Thomas G. (N. Y.)
Peters, John A. (Maine)
Phelan, Michael F. (Mass.)
Platt, Edmund (N. Y.)
Porter, Stephen G. (Pa.)
Pou, Edward W. (N. C.)
Powers, Caleb (Ky.)
Pratt, Harry H. (N. Y.)
Price, Jesse D. (Md.)
Quin, Percy E. (Miss.)
Ragsdale, J. Willard (S. C.)
Rainey, Henry T. (Ill.)
Raker, John E. (Calif.)
Ramseyer, C. William (Iowa.)
Randall, Charles H. (Calif.)
Rauch, George W. (Ind.)
Rayburn, Samuel T. (Tex.)
Reavis, C. Frank (Nebr.)
Reilly, Michael K. (Wis.)
Ricketts, Edwin D. (Ohio)
Riordan, Daniel J. (N. Y.)
Roberts, Edwin E. (Nev.)
Roberts, Ernest W. (Mass.)
Rodenberg, William A. (Ill.)
Rogers, John J. (Mass.)
Rouse, Arthur B. (Ky.)
Rowe, Frederick W. (N. Y.)
Rowland, Charles H. (Pa.)
Rubey, Thomas L. (Mo.)
Rucker, Tinsley W. (Ga.)
Rucker, William W. (Mo.)
Russell, J. Edward (Ohio)
Russell, Joseph J. (Mo.)
Sabath, Adolph J. (Ill.)
Sanford, Rollin B. (N. Y.)
Saunders, Edward W. (Va.)
Schall, Thomas D. (Minn.)
Scott, Frank D. (Mich.)
Scott, John R. K. (Pa.)
Scully, Thomas J. (N. J.)
Sears, William J. (Fla.)
Sells, Samuel R. (Tenn.)
Shackleford, Dorsey W. (Mo.)
Shallenberger, Ashton C. (Nebr.)
Sherley, J. Swagar (Ky.)
Sherwood, Isaac R. (Ohio)
Shouse, Jouett (Kans.)
Siegel, Isaac (N. Y.)
Sims, Thetus W. (Tenn.)
Sinnott, Nicholas J. (Oreg.)
Sisson, Thomas U. (Miss.)
Slayden, James L. (Tex.)
Slemp, C. Bascom (Va.)
Sloan, Charles H. (Nebr.)
Small, John H. (N. C.)
Smith, Addison T. (Idaho)
Smith, Charles B. (N. Y.)
Smith, George R. (Minn.)
Smith, John M. C. (Mich.)
Smith, William R. (Tex.)
Snell, Bertrand H. (N. Y.)
Snyder, Homer P. (N. Y.)
Sparkman, Stephen M. (Fla.)
Stafford, William H. (Wis.)
Steagall, Henry B. (Ala.)
Stedman, Charles M. (N. C.)
Steele, Henry J. (Pa.)
Steele, Thomas J. (Iowa)
Steenerson, Halvor (Minn.)
Stephens, Daniel V. (Nebr.)
Stephens, Hubert D. (Miss.)
Stephens, John H. (Tex.)
Stephens, William D. (Calif.)
Sterling, John A. (Ill.)
Stiness, Walter R. (R. I.)
Stone, Claudius U. (Ill.)
Stout, Tom (Mont.)
Sulloway, Cyrus A. (N. H.)
Sumners, Hatton W. (Tex.)
Sutherland, Howard (W. Va.)
Sweet, Burton E. (Iowa)
Swift, Oscar W. (N. Y.)
Switzer, Robert M. (Ohio)
Taggart, Joseph (Kans.)
Tague, Peter F. (Mass.)
Talbott, J. Frederick C. (Md.)
Tavenner, Clyde H. (Ill.)
Taylor, Edward T. (Colo.)
Taylor, Samuel M. (Ark.)
Temple, Henry W. (Pa.)
Thomas, Robert Y., Jr. (Ky.)
Thompson, Joseph B. (Okla.)
Tillman, John N. (Ark.)
Tilson, John Q. (Conn.)
Timberlake, Charles B. (Colo.)
Tinkham, George H. (Mass.)
Towner, Horace M. (Iowa)
Treadway, Allen T. (Mass.)
Tribble, Samuel J. (Ga.)
Van Dyke, Carl C. (Minn.)
Vare, William S. (Pa.)
Venable, William W. (Miss.)
Vinson, Carl (Ga.)
Volstead, Andrew J. (Minn.)
Walker, John R. (Ga.)
Walsh, Joseph (Mass.)
Ward, Charles B. (N. Y.)
Wason, Edward H. (N. H.)
Watkins, John T. (La.)
Watson, Henry W. (Pa.)
Watson, Walter A. (Va.)
Webb, Edwin Y. (N. C.)
Whaley, Richard S. (S. C.)
Wheeler, Loren E. (Ill.)
Williams, Seward H. (Ohio)
Williams, Thomas S. (Ill.)
Williams, William E. (Ill.)
Wilson, Emmett (Fla.)
Wilson, Riley J. (La.)
Wilson, William W. (Ill.)
Wingo, Otis (Ark.)
Winslow, Samuel E. (Mass.)
Wise, James W. (Ga.)
Wood, William R. (Ind.)
Woods, Frank P. (Iowa)
Woodyard, Harry C. (W. Va.)
Young, George M. (N. Dak.)
Young, James (Tex.)

The Sixty-fifth Congress (1917-19)

Clark, Champ (Mo.)
Speaker.

Adamson, William C. (Ga.)
Alexander, Joshua W. (Mo.)
Almon, Edward B. (Ala.)
Anderson, Sydney (Minn.)
Anthony, Daniel R., Jr. (Kans.)
Ashbrook, William A. (Ohio)
Aswell, James B. (La.)
Austin, Richard W. (Tenn.)
Ayres, William A. (Kans.)
Bacharach, Isaac (N. J.)
Bacon, Mark R. (Mich.)
Baer, John M. (N. Dak.)
Bankhead, William B. (Ala.)
Barkley, Alben W. (Ky.)
Barnhart, Henry A. (Ind.)
Bathrick, Ellsworth R. (Ohio)
Beakes, Samuel W. (Mich.)
Bell, Thomas M. (Ga.)
Benson, Carville D. (Md.)
Beshlin, Earl H. (Pa.)
Birch, William F. (N. J.)
Black, Eugene (Tex.)
Blackmon, Fred L. (Ala.)
Bland, Oscar E. (Ind.)
Bland, Schuyler O. (Va.)
Blanton, Thomas L. (Tex.)
Booher, Charles F. (Mo.)
Borland, William P. (Mo.)
Bowers, George M. (W. Va.)
Brand, Charles H. (Ga.)
Britt, James J. (N. C.)
Britten, Fred A. (Ill.)
Brodbeck, Andrew R. (Pa.)
Browne, Edward E. (Wis.)
Browning, William J. (N. J.)
Bruckner, Henry (N. Y.)
Brumbaugh, Clement L. (Ohio)
Buchanan, James P. (Tex.)
Burnett, John L. (Ala.)
Burroughs, Sherman E. (N. H.)
Butler, Thomas S. (Pa.)
Byrnes, James F. (S. C.)
Byrns, Joseph W. (Tenn.)
Caldwell, Charles P. (N. Y.)
Campbell, Guy E. (Pa.)
Campbell, Philip P. (Kans.)
Candler, Ezekiel S. (Miss.)
Cannon, Joseph G. (Ill.)
Cantrill, James C. (Ky.)
Capstick, John H. (N. J.)
Caraway, Thaddeus H. (Ark.)
Carew, John F. (N. Y.)
Carlin, Charles C. (Va.)
Carter, Charles D. (Okla.)
Carter, William H. (Mass.)
Cary, William J. (Wis.)
Chandler, Thomas A. (Okla.)
Chandler, Walter M. (N. Y.)
Church, Denver S. (Calif.)
Clark, Champ (Mo.)
Clark, Frank (Fla.)
Clark, Henry A. (Pa.)
Classon, David G. (Wis.)
Claypool, Horatio C. (Ohio)
Cleary, William E. (N. Y.)
Coady, Charles P. (Md.)
Collier, James W. (Miss.)
Comstock, Daniel W. (Ind.)
Connally, Tom T. (Tex.)
Connelly, John R. (Kans.)
Cooper, Edward (W. Va.)
Cooper, Henry A. (Wis.)
Cooper, John G. (Ohio)
Copley, Ira C. (Ill.)
Costello, Peter E. (Pa.)
Cox, William E. (Ind.)
Crago, Thomas S. (Pa.)
Cramton, Louis C. (Mich.)
Crisp, Charles R. (Ga.)
Crosser, Robert (Ohio)
Currie, Gilbert A. (Mich.)
Curry, Charles F. (Calif.)
Dale, Harry H. (N. Y.)
Dale, Porter H. (Vt.)
Dallinger, Frederick W. (Mass.)
Darrow, George P. (Pa.)
Davey, Martin L. (Ohio)
Davidson, James H. (Wis.)
Davis, Charles R. (Minn.)
Decker, Perl D. (Mo.)
Delaney, John J. (N. Y.)
Dempsey, S. Wallace (N. Y.)
Denison, Edward E. (Ill.)
Dent, S. Hubert, Jr. (Ala.)
Denton, George K. (Ind.)
Dewalt, Arthur G. (Pa.)
Dickinson, Clement C. (Mo.)
Dies, Martin (Tex.)
Dill, Clarence C. (Wash.)
Dillon, Charles H. (S. Dak.)
Dixon, Lincoln (Ind.)
Dominick, Fred H. (S. C.)
Donovan, Jerome F. (N. Y.)
Dooling, Peter J. (N. Y.)
Doolittle, Dudley (Kans.)
Doremus, Frank E. (Mich.)
Doughton, Robert L. (N. C.)
Dowell, Cassius C. (Iowa)
Drane, Herbert J. (Fla.)
Drukker, Dow H. (N. J.)
Dunn, Thomas B. (N. Y.)
Dupre, H. Garland (La.)
Dyer, Leonidas C. (Mo.)
Eagan, John J. (N. J.)
Eagle, Joe H. (Tex.)
Edmonds, George W. (Pa.)
Elliott, Richard N. (Ind.)
Ellsworth, Franklin F. (Minn.)
Elston, John A. (Calif.)
Emerson, Henry I. (Ohio)
Esch, John J. (Wis.)
Essen, Frederick (Mo.)
Estopinal, Albert (La.)
Evans, John M. (Mont.)
Fairchild, Benjamin L. (N.Y.)
Fairchild, George W. (N. Y.)
Fairfield, Louis W. (Ind.)
Farr, John R. (Pa.)
Ferris, Scott (Okla.)
Fess, Simeon D. (Ohio)
Fields, William J. (Ky.)
Fisher, Hubert F. (Tenn.)
Fitzgerald, John J. (N. Y.)
Flood, Henry D. (Va.)
Flynn, Joseph V. (N. Y.)
Focht, Benjamin K. (Pa.)
Fordney, Joseph W. (Mich.)
Foss, George E. (Ill.)
Foster, Martin D. (Ill.)
Francis, George B. (N. Y.)
Frear, James A. (Wis.)
Freeman, Richard P. (Conn.)
French, Burton L. (Idaho)
Fuller, Alvan T. (Mass.)
Fuller, Charles E. (Ill.)
Gallagher, Thomas (Ill.)
Gallivan, James A. (Mass.)
Gandy, Harry L. (S. Dak.)
Gard, Warren (Ohio)
Gardner, Augustus P. (Mass.)
Garland, Mahlon M. (Pa.)
Garner, John N. (Tex.)
Garrett, Daniel E. (Tex.)
Garrett, Finis J. (Tenn.)
Gillett, Frederick H. (Mass.)
Glass, Carter (Va.)
Glynn, James P. (Conn.)
Godwin, Hannibal L. (N. C.)
Good, James W. (Iowa)
Goodall, Louis B. (Maine)
Goodwin, William S. (Ark.)
Gordon, William (Ohio)
Gould, Norman J. (N. Y.)
Graham, George S. (Pa.)
Graham, William J. (Ill.)
Gray, Edward W. (N. J.)
Gray, Oscar L. (Ala.)
Green, William R. (Iowa)
Greene, Frank L. (Vt.)
Greene, William S. (Mass.)
Gregg, Alexander W. (Tex.)
Griest, William W. (Pa.)
Griffin, Anthony J. (N. Y.)
Griffin, Daniel J. (N. Y.)
Hadley, Lindley H. (Wash.)
Hamill, James A. (N. J.)
Hamilton, Charles M. (N. Y.)
Hamilton, Edward L. (Mich.)
Hamlin, Courtney W. (Mo.)
Hardy, Rufus (Tex.)
Harrison, Pat (Miss.)
Harrison, Thomas W. (Va.)
Haskell, Reuben L. (N. Y.)
Hastings, William W. (Okla.)
Haugen, Gilbert N. (Iowa)
Hawley, Willis C. (Oreg.)
Hayden, Carl (Ariz.)
Hayes, Everis A. (Calif.)
Heaton, Robert D. (Pa.)
Heflin, J. Thomas (Ala.)
Heintz, Victor (Ohio)
Helgesen, Henry T. (N. Dak.)
Helm, Harvey (Ky.)
Helvering, Guy T. (Kans.)
Hensley, Walter L. (Mo.)
Hersey, Ira G. (Maine)
Hicks, Frederick C. (N. Y.)
Hill, Ebenezer J. (Conn.)

Hilliard, Benjamin C. (Colo.)
Holland, Edward E. (Va.)
Hollingsworth, David A. (Ohio)
Hood, George E. (N. C.)
Houston, William C. (Tenn.)
Howard, William S. (Ga.)
Huddleston, George (Ala.)
Hulbert, G. Murray (N. Y.)
Hull, Cordell (Tenn.)
Hull, Harry E. (Iowa)
Humphreys, Benjamin G. (Miss.)
Husted, James W. (N. Y.)
Hutchinson, Elijah C. (N. J.)
Igoe, William L. (Mo.)
Ireland, Clifford (Ill.)
Jacoway, Henderson M. (Ark.)
James, W. Frank (Mich.)
Johnson, Albert (Wash.)
Johnson, Ben (Ky.)
Johnson, Royal C. (S. Dak.)
Jones, Marvin (Tex.)
Jones, William A. (Va.)
Juul, Niels (Ill.)
Kahn, Julius (Calif.)
Kearns, Charles C. (Ohio)
Keating, Edward (Colo.)
Kehoe, J. Walter (Fla.)
Kelley, Patrick H. (Mich.)
Kelly, M. Clyde (Pa.)
Kennedy, Ambrose (R. I.)
Kennedy, Charles A. (Iowa)
Kettner, William (Calif.)
Key, John A. (Ohio)
Kiess, Edgar R. (Pa.)
Kincheloe, David H. (Ky.)
King, Edward J. (Ill.)
Kinkaid, Moses P. (Nebr.)
Kitchin, Claude (N. C.)
Knutson, Harold (Minn.)
Kraus, Milton (Ind.)
Kreider, Aaron S. (Pa.)
LaFollette, William L. (Wash.)
LaGuardia, Fiorello H. (N.Y.)
Lampert, Florian (Wis.)
Langley, John W. (Ky.)
Larsen, William W. (Ga.)
Lazaro, Ladislas (La.)
Lea, Clarence F. (Calif.)
Lee, Gordon (Ga.)
Lehlbach, Frederick R. (N. J.)
Lenroot, Irvine L. (Wis.)
Lesher, John V. (Pa.)
Lever, Asbury F. (S. C.)
Linthicum, J. Charles (Md.)
Little, Edward C. (Kans.)
Littlepage, Adam B. (W. Va.)
Lobeck, Charles O. (Nebr.)
London, Meyer (N. Y.)
Lonergan, Augustine (Conn.)
Longworth, Nicholas (Ohio)
Lufkin, Willfred W. (Mass.)
Lundeen, Ernest (Minn.)
Lunn, George R. (N. Y.)
McAndrews, James (Ill.)
McArthur, Clifton N. (Oreg.)
McClintic, James V. (Okla.)
McCormick, Medill, (Ill.)
McCulloch, Roscoe C. (Ohio)
McFadden, Louis T. (Pa.)
McKenzie, John C. (Ill.)
McKeown, Thomas D. (Okla.)
McKinley, William B. (Ill.)
McLaughlin, James C. (Mich.)
McLaughlin, Joseph (Pa.)
McLemore, A. Jeff (Tex.)
Madden, Martin B. (Ill.)
Magee, Walter W. (N. Y.)
Maher, James P. (N. Y.)
Mann, James R. (Ill.)
Mansfield, Joseph J. (Tex.)
Mapes, Carl E. (Mich.)
Martin, Charles (Ill.)
Martin, Whitmell P. (La.)
Mason, William E. (Ill.)
Mays, James H. (Utah)
Meeker, Jacob E. (Mo.)
Merritt, Schuyler (Conn.)
Miller, Clarence B. (Minn.)
Miller, John F. (Wash.)
Mondell, Frank W. (Wyo.)
Montague, Andrew J. (Va.)
Moon, John A. (Tenn.)
Moore, J. Hampton (Pa.)
Moores, Merrill (Ind.)
Morgan, Dick T. (Okla.)
Morin, John M. (Pa.)
Mott, Luther W. (N. Y.)
Mudd, Sydney E. (Md.)
Neely, Matthew M. (W. Va.)
Nelson, Adolphus P. (Wis.)
Nelson, John M. (Wis.)
Nicholls, Samuel J. (S. C.)
Nichols, Charles A. (Mich.)
Nolan, John I. (Calif.)
Norton, Patrick D. (N. Dak.)
Oldfield, William A. (Ark.)
Oliver, Daniel C. (N. Y.)
Oliver, William B. (Ala.)
Olney, Richard (Mass.)
Osborne, Henry Z. (Calif.)
O'Shaunessy, George F. (R. I.)
Overmyer, Arthur W. (Ohio)
Overstreet, James W. (Ga.)
Padgett, Lemuel P. (Tenn.)
Paige, Calvin D. (Mass.)
Park, Frank (Ga.)
Parker, James S. (N. Y.)
Parker, Richard W. (N. J.)
Peters, John A. (Maine)
Phelan, Michael F. (Mass.)
Platt, Edmund (N. Y.)
Polk, Albert F. (Del.)
Porter, Stephen G. (Pa.)
Pou, Edward W. (N. C.)
Powers, Caleb (Ky.)
Pratt, Harry H. (N. Y.)
Price, Jesse D. (Md.)
Purnell, Fred S. (Ind.)
Quin, Percy E. (Miss.)
Ragsdale, J. Willard (S. C.)
Rainey, Henry T. (Ill.)
Rainey, John W. (Ill.)
Raker, John E. (Calif.)
Ramsey, John R. (N. J.)
Ramseyer, C. William (Iowa)
Randall, Charles H. (Calif.)
Rankin, Jeannette (Mont.)
Rayburn, Samuel T. (Tex.)
Reavis, C. Frank (Nebr.)
Reed, Stuart F. (W. Va.)
Riordan, Daniel J. (N. Y.)
Robbins, Edward E. (Pa.)
Roberts, Edwin E. (Nev.)
Robinson, Leonidas D. (N. C.)
Rodenberg, William A. (Ill.)
Rogers, John Jacob (Mass.)
Romjue, Milton A. (Mo.)
Rose, John M. (Pa.)
Rouse, Arthur B. (Ky.)
Rowe, Frederick W. (N. Y.)
Rowland, Charles H. (Pa.)
Rubey, Thomas L. (Mo.)
Rucker, William W. (Mo.)
Russell, Joseph J. (Mo.)
Sabath, Adolph J. (Ill.)
Sanders, Archie D. (N. Y.)
Sanders, Everett (Ind.)
Sanders, Jared Y. (La.)
Sanford, Rollin B. (N. Y.)
Saunders, Edward W. (Va.)
Schall, Thomas D. (Minn.)
Scott, Frank D. (Mich.)
Scott, George C. (Iowa)
Scott, John R. K. (Pa.)
Scully, Thomas J. (N. J.)
Sears, William J. (Fla.)
Sells, Samuel R. (Tenn.)
Shackleford, Dorsey W. (Mo.)
Shallenberger, Ashton C. (Nebr.)
Sherley, J. Swagar (Ky.)
Sherwood, Isaac R. (Ohio)
Shouse, Jouett (Kans.)
Siegel, Isaac (N. Y.)
Sims, Thetus W. (Tenn.)
Sinnott, Nicholas J. (Oreg.)
Sisson, Thomas U. (Miss.)
Slayden, James L. (Tex.)
Slemp, C. Bascom (Va.)
Sloan, Charles H. (Nebr.)
Small, John H. (N. C.)
Smith, Addison T. (Idaho)
Smith, Charles B. (N .Y.)
Smith, John M. C. (Mich.)
Smith, Thomas F. (N. Y.)
Snell, Bertrand H. (N. Y.)
Snook, John S. (Ohio)
Snyder, Homer P. (N. Y.)
Stafford, William H. (Wis.)
Steagall, Henry B. (Ala.)
Stedman, Charles M. (N. C.)
Steele, Henry J. (Pa.)
Steenerson, Halvor (Minn.)
Stephens, Daniel V. (Nebr.)
Stephens, Hubert D. (Miss.)
Sterling, Bruce F. (Pa.)
Sterling, John A. (Ill.)
Stevenson, William F. (S. C.)
Stiness, Walter R. (R. I.)
Strong, Nathan L. (Pa.)
Sullivan, Christopher D. (N. Y.)
Sumners, Hatton W. (Tex.)
Sweet, Burton E. (Iowa)
Swift, Oscar W. (N. Y.)
Switzer, Robert M. (Ohio)
Tague, Peter F. (Mass.)
Talbott, J. Frederick C. (Md.)
Taylor, Edward T. (Colo.)
Taylor, Samuel M. (Ark.)
Temple, Henry W. (Pa.)
Templeton, Thomas W. (Pa.)
Thomas, Robert Y., Jr. (Ky.)
Thompson, Joseph B. (Okla.)
Tillman, John N. (Ark.)
Tilson, John Q. (Conn.)
Timberlake, Charles B. (Colo.)
Tinkham, George H. (Mass.)
Towner, Horace M. (Iowa)
Treadway, Allen T. (Mass.)
Van Dyke, Carl C. (Minn.)
Vare, William S. (Pa.)
Venable, William W. (Miss.)
Vestal, Albert H. (Ind.)
Vinson, Carl (Ga.)
Voigt, Edward (Wis.)
Volstead, Andrew J. (Minn.)
Waldow, William F. (N. Y.)
Walker, John R. (Ga.)
Walsh, Joseph (Mass.)
Walton, William B. (N. Mex.)
Ward, Charles B. (N. Y.)
Wason, Edward H. (N. H.)
Watkins, John T. (La.)
Watson, Henry W. (Pa.)
Watson, Walter A. (Va.)
Weaver, Zebulon (N. C.)
Webb, Edwin Y. (N. C.)
Welling, Milton H. (Utah)
Welty, Benjamin F. (Ohio)
Whaley, Richard S. (S. C.)
Wheeler, Loren E. (Ill.)
White, George (Ohio)
White, Wallace H., Jr. (Maine)
Williams, Thomas S. (Ill.)
Wilson, James C. (Tex.)
Wilson, Riley J. (La.)
Wilson, William W. (Ill.)
Wingo, Otis (Ark.)
Winslow, Samuel E. (Mass.)
Wise, James W. (Ga.)
Wood, William R. (Ind.)
Woods, Frank P. (Iowa)
Woods, James P. (Va.)
Woodyard, Harry C. (W. Va.)
Wright, William C. (Ga.)
Young, George M. (N. Dak.)
Young, James (Tex.)
Zihlman, Frederick N. (Md.)

The Sixty-sixth Congress (1919-21)

Gillett, Frederick H. (Mass.) Speaker.

Ackerman, Ernest R. (N. J.)
Alexander, Joshua W. (Mo.)
Almon, Edward B. (Ala.)
Anderson, Sydney (Minn.)
Andrews, William E. (Nebr.)
Andrews, William N. (Md.)
Anthony, Daniel R., Jr. (Kans.)
Ashbrook, William A. (Ohio)
Aswell, James B. (La.)
Ayres, William A. (Kans.)
Babka, John J. (Ohio)
Bacharach, Isaac (N. J.)
Baer, John M. (N. Dak.)
Bankhead, William B. (Ala.)
Barbour, Henry E. (Calif.)
Barkley, Alben W. (Ky.)
Bee, Carlos (Tex.)
Begg, James T. (Ohio)
Bell, Thomas M. (Ga.)
Benham, John S. (Ind.)
Benson, Carville D. (Md.)
Berger, Victor L. (Wis.)
Black, Eugene (Tex.)
Blackmon, Fred L. (Ala.)
Bland, Oscar E. (Ind.)
Bland, Schuyler O. (Va.)
Bland, William T. (Mo.)
Blanton, Thomas L. (Tex.)
Boies, William D. (Iowa)
Booher, Charles F. (Mo.)
Bowers, George M. (W. Va.)
Bowling, William B. (Ala.)
Box, John C. (Tex.)
Brand, Charles H. (Ga.)
Briggs, Clay Stone (Tex.)
Brinson, Samuel M. (N. C.)
Britten, Fred A. (Ill.)
Brooks, Edward S. (Pa.)
Brooks, Edwin B. (Ill.)
Browne, Edward E. (Wis.)
Browning, William J. (N. J.)
Brumbaugh, Clement L. (Ohio)
Buchanan, James P. (Tex.)
Burdick, Clark (R. I.)
Burke, William J. (Pa.)
Burnett, John L. (Ala.)
Burroughs, Sherman E. (N. H.)
Butler, Thomas S. (Pa.)
Byrnes, James F. (S. C.)
Byrns, Joseph W. (Tenn.)
Caldwell, Charles P. (N. Y.)
Campbell, Guy E. (Pa.)
Campbell, Philip P. (Kans.)
Candler, Ezekiel S. (Miss.)
Cannon, Joseph G. (Ill.)
Cantrill, James C. (Ky.)
Caraway, Thaddeus H. (Ark.)
Carew, John F. (N. Y.)
Carss, William L. (Minn.)
Carter, Charles D. (Okla.)
Casey, John J. (Pa.)
Chindblom, Carl R. (Ill.)
Christopherson, Charles A. (S. Dak.)
Clark, Champ (Mo.)
Clark, Frank (Fla.)
Classon, David G. (Wis.)
Cleary, William E. (N. Y.)
Coady, Charles P. (Md.)
Cole, R. Clint (Ohio)
Collier, James W. (Miss.)
Connally, Tom T. (Tex.)
Cooper, John G. (Ohio)
Copley, Ira C. (Ill.)
Costello, Peter E. (Pa.)
Crago, Thomas S. (Pa.)
Cramton, Louis C. (Mich.)
Crisp, Charles R. (Ga.)
Crowther, Frank (N. Y.)
Cullen, Thomas H. (N. Y.)
Currie, Gilbert A. (Mich.)
Curry, Charles F. (Calif.)
Dale, Porter H. (Vt.)
Dallinger, Frederick W. (Mass.)
Darrow, George P. (Pa.)
Davey, Martin L. (Ohio)
Davis, Charles R. (Minn.)
Davis, Ewin L. (Tenn.)
Dempsey, S. Wallace (N. Y.)
Denison, Edward E. (Ill.)
Dent, S. Hubert, Jr. (Ala.)
Dewalt, Arthur G. (Pa.)
Dickinson, Clement C. (Mo.)
Dickinson, Lester J. (Iowa)
Dominick, Fred H. (S. C.)
Donovan, Jerome F. (N. Y.)
Dooling, Peter J. (N. Y.)
Doremus, Frank E. (Mich.)
Doughton, Robert L. (N. C.)
Dowell, Cassius C. (Iowa)
Drane, Herbert J. (Fla.)
Drewry, Patrick Henry (Va.)
Dunbar, James W. (Ind.)
Dunn, Thomas B. (N. Y.)
Dupre, H. Garland (La.)
Dyer, Leonidas C. (Mo.)
Eagan, John J. (N. J.)
Eagle, Joe H. (Tex.)
Echols, Leonard S. (W. Va.)
Edmonds, George W. (Pa.)
Elliott, Richard N. (Ind.)
Ellsworth, Franklin F. (Minn.)
Elston, John A. (Calif.)
Emerson, Henry I. (Ohio)
Esch, John J. (Wis.)
Estopinal, Albert (La.)
Evans, Charles R. (Nev.)
Evans, John M. (Mont.)
Evans, Robert E. (Nebr.)

Fairfield, Louis W. (Ind.)
Farr, John R. (Pa.)
Ferris, Scott (Okla.)
Fess, Simeon D. (Ohio)
Fields, William J. (Ky.)
Fish, Hamilton, Jr. (N. Y.)
Fisher, Hubert F. (Tenn.)
Fitzgerald, John F. (Mass.)
Flood, Henry D. (Va.)
Focht, Benjamin K. (Pa.)
Fordney, Joseph W. (Mich.)
Foster, Israel M. (Ohio)
Frear, James A. (Wis.)
Freeman, Richard P. (Conn.)
French, Burton L. (Idaho)
Fuller, Alvan T. (Mass.)
Fuller, Charles E. (Ill.)
Gallagher, Thomas (Ill.)
Gallivan, James A. (Mass.)
Gandy, Harry L. (S. Dak.)
Ganly, James V. (N. Y.)
Gard, Warren (Ohio)
Garland, Mahlon M. (Pa.)
Garner, John N. (Tex.)
Garrett, Finis J. (Tenn.)
Glynn, James P. (Conn.)
Godwin, Hannibal L. (N. C.)
Goldfogle, Henry M. (N. Y.)
Good, James W. (Iowa)
Goodall, Louis B. (Maine)
Goodwin, William S. (Ark.)
Goodykoontz, Wells (W. Va.)
Gould, Norman J. (N. Y.)
Graham, George S. (Pa.)
Graham, William J. (Ill.)
Green, William R. (Iowa)
Greene, Frank L. (Vt.)
Greene, William S. (Mass.)
Griest, William W. (Pa.)
Griffin, Anthony J. (N. Y.)
Hadley, Lindley H. (Wash.)
Hamill, James A. (N. J.)
Hamilton, Edward L. (Mich.)
Hardy, Guy U. (Colo.)
Hardy, Rufus (Tex.)
Harreld, John W. (Okla.)
Harrison, Thomas W. (Va.)
Haskell, Reuben L. (N. Y.)
Hastings, William W. (Okla.)
Haugen, Gilbert N. (Iowa)
Hawley, Willis C. (Oreg.)
Hayden, Carl (Ariz.)
Hays, Edward D. (Mo.)
Heflin, J. Thomas (Ala.)
Hernandez, Benigno C. (N. Mex.)
Hersey, Ira G. (Maine)
Hersman, Hugh S. (Calif.)
Hickey, Andrew J. (Ind.)
Hicks, Frederick C. (N. Y.)
Hill, William H. (N. Y.)
Hoch, Homer (Kans.)
Hoey, Clyde R. (N. C.)
Holland, Edward E. (Va.)
Houghton, Alanson B. (N. Y.)
Howard, Everette B. (Okla.)
Huddleston, George (Ala.)
Hudspeth Claude B. (Tex.)
Hulings, Willis J. (Pa.)
Hull, Cordell (Tenn.)
Hull, Harry E. (Iowa)
Humphreys, Benjamin G. (Miss.)
Husted, James W. (N. Y.)
Hutchinson, Elijah C. (N. J.)
Igoe, William L. (Mo.)
Ireland, Clifford (Ill.)
Jacoway, Henderson M. (Ark.)
James, Rorer A. (Va.)
James, W. Frank (Mich.)
Jefferis, Albert W. (Nebr.)
Johnson, Albert (Wash.)
Johnson, Ben (Ky.)
Johnson Paul B. (Miss.)
Johnson, Royal C. (S. Dak.)
Johnston, John B. (N. Y.)
Jones, Evan J. (Pa.)
Jones, Marvin (Tex.)
Juul, Niels (Ill.)
Kahn, Julius (Calif.)
Kearns, Charles C. (Ohio)
Keller, Oscar E. (Minn.)
Kelley, Patrick H. (Mich.)
Kelly, M. Clyde (Pa.)
Kendall, Samuel A. (Pa.)
Kennedy, Ambrose (R. I.)
Kennedy, Charles A. (Iowa)
Kettner, William (Calif.)

Kiess, Edgar R. (Pa.)
Kincheloe, David H. (Ky.)
King, Edward J. (Ill.)
Kinkaid, Moses P. (Nebr.)
Kitchin, Claude (N. C.)
Kleczka, John C. (Wis.)
Knutson, Harold (Minn.)
Kraus, Milton (Ind.)
Kreider, Aaron S. (Pa.)
LaGuardia, Fiorella H. (N.Y.)
Lampert, Florian (Wis.)
Langley, John W. (Ky.)
Lanham, Fritz G. (Tex.)
Lankford, William C. (Ga.)
Larsen, William W. (Ga.)
Layton, Caleb R. (Del.)
Lazaro, Ladislas (La.)
Lea, Clarence F. (Calif.)
Lee, Gordon (Ga.)
Lehlbach, Frederick R. (N.J.)
Lesher, John V. (Pa.)
Lever, Asbury F. (S. C.)
Linthicum, J. Charles (Md.)
Little, Edward C. (Kans.)
Lonergan, Augustine (Conn.)
Longworth, Nicholas (Ohio)
Luce, Robert (Mass.)
Lufkin, Willfred W. (Mass.)
Luhring, Oscar R. (Ind.)
McAndrews. James (Ill.)
McArthur, Clifton N. (Oreg.)
McClintic, James V. (Okla.)
MacCrate, John (N. Y.)
McCulloch, Roscoe C. (Ohio)
McDuffie, John (Ala.)
McFadden, Louis T. (Pa.)
McGlennon, Cornelius A. (N. J.)
MacGregor, Clarence (N. Y.)
McKenzie, John C. (Ill.)
McKeown, Thomas D. (Okla.)
McKiniry, Richard F. (N. Y.)
McKinley, William B. (Ill.)
McLane, Patrick (Pa.)
McLaughlin, James C. (Mich.)
McLaughlin, Melvin O. (Nebr.)
McLeod, Clarence J. (Mich.)
McPherson, Isaac V. (Mo.)
Madden, Martin B. (Ill.)
Magee, Walter W. (N. Y.)
Maher, James P. (N. Y.)
Major, Samuel C. (Mo.)
Mann, Edward C. (S. C.)
Mann, James R. (Ill.)
Mansfield, Joseph J. (Tex.)
Mapes, Carl E. (Mich.)
Martin, Whitmell P. (La.)
Mays, James H. (Utah)
Mead, James M. (N. Y.)
Merritt, Schuyler (Conn.)
Michener, Earl C. (Mich.)
Miller, John F. (Wash.)
Milligan, Jacob L. (Mo.)
Minahan, Daniel F. (N. J.)
Monahan, James G. (Wis.)
Mondell, Frank W. (Wyo.)
Montague, Andrew J. (Va.)
Moon, John A. (Tenn.)
Mooney, Charles A. (Ohio)
Moore, C. Ellis (Ohio)
Moore, J. Hampton (Pa.)
Moore, R. Walton (Va.)
Moores, Merrill (Ind.)
Morgan, Dick T. (Okla.)
Morin, John M. (Pa.)
Mott, Luther W. (N. Y.)
Mudd, Sydney E. (Md.)
Murphy, B. Frank (Ohio)
Neely, Matthew M. (W. Va.)
Nelson, Adolphus P. (Wis.)
Nelson, William L. (Mo.)
Newton, Cleveland A. (Mo.)
Newton, Walter H. (Minn.)
Nicholls, Samuel J. (S. C.)
Nichols, Charles A. (Mich.)
Nolan, John I. (Calif.)
O'Connell, David J. (N. Y.)
O'Connor, James (La.)
Ogden, Charles F. (Ky.)
Oldfield, William A. (Ark.)
Oliver, William B. (Ala.)
Olney, Richard (Mass.)
Osborne, Henry Z. (Calif.)
Overstreet, James W. (Ga.)
Padgett, Lemuel P. (Tenn.)
Paige, Calvin D. (Mass.)
Park, Frank (Ga.)
Parker, James S. (N. Y.)

Parrish, Lucian W. (Tex.)
Patterson, Francis F., Jr. (N. J.)
Pell, Herbert C., Jr. (N. Y.)
Perlman, Nathan D. (N. Y.)
Peters, John A. (Maine)
Phelan, Michael F. (Mass.)
Platt, Edmond (N. Y.)
Porter, Stephen G. (Pa.)
Pou, Edward W. (N. C.)
Purnell, Fred S. (Ind.)
Quin, Percy E. (Miss.)
Radcliffe, Amos H. (N. J.)
Ragsdale, J. Willard (S. C.)
Rainey, Henry T. (Ill.)
Rainey, John W. (Ill.)
Rainey, Lilius B. (Ala.)
Raker, John E. (Calif.)
Ramsey, John R. (N. J.)
Ramseyer, C. William (Iowa)
Randall, Charles H. (Calif.)
Randall, Clifford E. (Wis.)
Ransley, Harry C. (Pa.)
Rayburn, Sam T. (Tex.)
Reavis, C. Frank (Nebr.)
Reber, John (Pa.)
Reed, Daniel A. (N. Y.)
Reed, Stuart F. (W. Va.)
Rhodes, Marion E. (Mo.)
Ricketts, Edwin D. (Ohio)
Riddick, Carl W. (Mont.)
Riordan, Daniel J. (N. Y.)
Robinson, Leonidas D. (N. C.)
Robsion, John M. (Ky.)
Rodenberg, William A. (Ill.)
Rogers, John Jacob (Mass.)
Romjue, Milton A. (Mo.)
Rose, John M. (Pa.)
Rouse, Arthur B. (Ky.)
Rowan, Joseph (N. Y.)
Rowe, Frederick W. (N. Y.)
Rubey, Thomas L. (Mo.)
Rucker, William W. (Mo.)
Sabath, Adolph J. (Ill.)
Sanders, Archie D. (N. Y.)
Sanders, Everett (Ind.)
Sanders, Jared Y. (La.)
Sanford, Rollin B. (N. Y.)
Saunders, Edward W. (Va.)
Schall, Thomas D. (Minn.)
Scott, Frank D. (Mich.)
Scully, Thomas J. (N. J.)
Sears, William J. (Fla.)
Sells, Samuel R. (Tenn.)
Sherwood, Isaac R. (Ohio)
Shreve, Milton W. (Pa.)
Siegel, Isaac (N. Y.)
Sims, Thetus W. (Tenn.)
Sinclair, James H. (N. Dak.)
Sinnott, Nicholas J. (Oreg.)
Sisson, Thomas U. (Miss.)
Slemp, C. Bascom (Va.)
Small, John H. (N. C.)
Smith, Addison T. (Idaho)
Smith, Frank L. (Ill.)
Smith, John M. C. (Mich.)
Smith, Thomas F. (N. Y.)
Smithwick, John H. (Fla.)
Snell, Bertrand H. (N. Y.)
Snyder, Homer P. (N. Y.)
Steagall, Henry B. (Ala.)
Steele, Henry J. (Pa.)
Stedman, Charles M. (N. C.)
Steenerson, Halvor (Minn.)
Stephens, Ambrose E. B. (Ohio)
Stephens, Hubert D. (Miss.)
Stevenson, William F. (S. C.)
Stiness, Walter R. (R. I.)
Stoll, Philip H. (S. C.)
Strong, James G. (Kans.)
Strong, Nathan L. (Pa.)
Sullivan, Christopher D. (N. Y.)
Summers, John W. (Wash.)
Sumners, Hatton W. (Tex.)
Sweet, Burton E. (Iowa)
Swindall, Charles (Okla.)
Swope, King (Ky.)
Tague, Peter F. (Mass.)
Taylor, Edward T. (Colo.)
Taylor, J. Will (Tenn.)
Taylor, Samuel M. (Ark.)
Temple, Henry W. (Pa.)
Thomas, Robert Y., Jr. (Ky.)
Thompson, Charles J. (Ohio)
Thompson, Joseph B. (Okla.)
Tillman, John N. (Ark.)

Tilson, John Q. (Conn.)
Timberlake, Charles B. (Colo.)
Tincher, Jasper N. (Kans.)
Tinkham, George H. (Mass.)
Towner, Horace M. (Iowa)
Treadway, Allen T. (Mass.)
Upshaw, William D. (Ga.)
Vaile, William N. (Colo.)
VanDyke, Carl C. (Minn.)
Vare, William S. (Pa.)
Venable, William W. (Miss.)
Vestal, Albert H. (Ind.)
Vinson, Carl (Ga.)
Voigt, Edward (Wis.)
Volk, Lester D. (N. Y.)
Volstead, Andrew J. (Minn.)
Walsh, Joseph (Mass.)
Walters, Anderson H. (Pa.)
Ward, Charles B. (N. Y.)
Wason, Edward H. (N. H.)
Watkins, John T. (La.)
Watson, Henry W. (Pa.)
Watson, Walter A. (Va.)
Weaver, Zebulon (N. C.)
Webb, Edwin Y. (N. C.)
Webster, J. Stanley (Wash.)
Welling, Milton H. (Utah.)
Welty, Benjamin F. (Ohio)
Whaley, Richard S. (S. C.)
Wheeler, Loren E. (Ill.)
White, Hays B. (Kans.)
White, Wallace H., Jr. (Maine)
Williams, Thomas S. (Ill.)
Wilson, James C. (Tex.)
Wilson, John H. (Pa.)
Wilson, Riley J. (La.)
Wilson, William W. (Ill.)
Wingo, Otis (Ark.)
Winslow, Samuel E. (Mass.)
Wise, James W. (Ga.)
Wood, William R. (Ind.)
Woods, James P. (Va.)
Woodyard, Harry C. (W. Va.)
Wright, William C. (Ga.)
Young, George M. (N. Dak.)
Young, James (Tex.)
Zihlman, Frederick N. (Md.)

The Sixty-seventh Congress (1921-23)

Gillett, Frederick H. (Mass.) Speaker.

Abernethy, Charles L. (N. C.)
Ackerman, Ernest R. (N. J.)
Almon, Edward B. (Ala.)
Anderson, Sydney (Minn.)
Andrew, A. Piatt, Jr. (Mass.)
Andrews, William E. (Nebr.)
Ansorge, Martin C. (N. Y.)
Anthony, Daniel R. (Kans.)
Appleby, T. Frank (N. J.)
Arentz, Samuel S. (Nev.)
Aswell, James B. (La.)
Atkeson, William O. (Mo.)
Bacharach, Isaac (N. J.)
Bankhead, William B. (Ala.)
Barbour, Henry E. (Calif.)
Barkley, Alben W. (Ky.)
Beck, Joseph D. (Wis.)
Beedy, Carroll L. (Maine)
Begg, James T. (Ohio)
Bell, Thomas M. (Ga.)
Benham, John S. (Ind.)
Bird, Richard E. (Kans.)
Bixler, Harris J. (Pa.)
Black, Eugene (Tex.)
Blakeney, Albert A. (Md.)
Bland, Oscar E. (Ind.)
Bland, Schuyler Otis (Va.)
Blanton, Thomas L. (Tex.)
Boies, William D. (Iowa)
Bond, Charles G. (N. Y.)
Bowers, George M. (W. Va.)
Bowling, William B. (Ala.)
Box, John C. (Tex.)
Brand, Charles H. (Ga.)
Brennan, Vincent M. (Mich.)
Briggs, Clay Stone (Tex.)
Brinson, Samuel M. (N. C.)
Britten, Fred A. (Ill.)
Brooks, Edward S. (Pa.)
Brooks, Edwin B. (Ill.)

Brown, Joseph (Tenn.)
Browne, Edward E. (Wis.)
Buchanan, James P. (Tex.)
Bulwinkle, Alfred L. (N. C.)
Burdick, Clark (R. I.)
Burke, William J. (Pa.)
Burroughs, Sherman E. (N. H.)
Burtness, Olger B. (N. Dak.)
Burton, Theodore E. (Ohio)
Butler, Thomas S. (Pa.)
Byrnes, James F. (S. C.)
Byrns, Joseph W. (Tenn.)
Cable, John L. (Ohio)
Campbell, Guy E. (Pa.)
Campbell, Philip P. (Kans.)
Cannon, Joseph G. (Ill.)
Cantrill, James C. (Ky.)
Carew, John F. (N. Y.)
Carter, Charles D. (Okla.)
Chalmers, William W. (Ohio)
Chandler, Thomas A. (Okla.)
Chandler, Walter M. (N. Y.)
Chindblom, Carl R. (Ill.)
Christopherson, Charles A. (S. Dak.)
Clague, Frank (Minn.)
Clark, Frank (Fla.)
Clarke, John D. (N. Y.)
Classon, David G. (Wis.)
Clouse, Wynne F. (Tenn.)
Cockran, W. Bourke (N. Y.)
Codd, George P. (Mich.)
Cole, Cyrenus (Iowa)
Cole, R. Clinton (Ohio)
Collier, James W. (Miss.)
Collins, Ross A. (Miss.)
Colton, Don B. (Utah)
Connally, Tom T. (Tex.)
Connell, Charles R. (Pa.)
Connolly, James J. (Pa.)
Cooper, Henry A. (Wis.)
Cooper, John G. (Ohio)
Copley, Ira C. (Ill.)
Coughlin, Clarence D. (Pa.)
Crago, Thomas S. (Pa.)
Cramton, Louis C. (Mich.)
Crisp, Charles R. (Ga.)
Crowther, Frank (N. Y.)
Cullen, Thomas H. (N. Y.)
Curry, Charles F. (Calif.)
Dale, Porter H. (Vt.)
Dallinger, Frederick W. (Mass.)
Darrow, George P. (Pa.)
Davis, Charles R. (Minn.)
Davis, Ewin L. (Tenn.)
Deal, Joseph T. (Va.)
Dempsey, S. Wallace (N. Y.)
Denison, Edward E. (Ill.)
Dickinson, Lester J. (Iowa)
Dominick, Fred H. (S. C.)
Doughton, Robert L. (N. C.)
Dowell, Cassius C. (Iowa)
Drane, Herbert J. (Fla.)
Drewry, Patrick Henry (Va.)
Driver, William J. (Ark.)
Dunbar, James W. (Ind.)
Dunn, Thomas B. (N. Y.)
Dupre, H. Garland (La.)
Dyer, Leonidas C. (Mo.)
Echols, Leonard S. (W. Va.)
Edmonds, George W. (Pa.)
Elliott, Richard N. (Ind.)
Ellis, Edgar C. (Mo.)
Elston, John A. (Calif.)
Evans, Robert E. (Nebr.)
Fairchild, Benjamin L. (N.Y.)
Fairfield, Louis W. (Ind.)
Faust, Charles L. (Mo.)
Favrot, George K. (La.)
Fenn, E. Hart (Conn.)
Fess, Simeon D. (Ohio)
Fields, William J. (Ky.)
Fish, Hamilton, Jr. (N. Y.)
Fisher, Hubert F. (Tenn.)
Fitzgerald, Roy G. (Ohio)
Flood, Henry D. (Va.)
Focht, Benjamin K. (Pa.)
Fordney, Joseph W. (Mich.)
Foster, Israel M. (Ohio)
Frear, James A. (Wis.)
Free, Arthur M. (Calif.)
Freeman, Richard P. (Conn.)
French, Burton L. (Idaho)
Frothingham, Louis A. (Mass.)
Fuller, Charles E. (Ill.)
Fulmer, Hampton P. (S. C.)
Funk, Frank H. (Ill.)

Gahn, Harry C. (Ohio)
Gallivan, James A. (Mass.)
Garner, John N. (Tex.)
Garrett, Daniel E. (Tex.)
Garrett, Finis J. (Tenn.)
Gensman, Lorraine M. (Okla.)
Gernerd, Fred B. (Pa.)
Gifford, Charles L. (Mass.)
Gilbert, Ralph (Ky.)
Gillett, Frederick H. (Mass.)
Glynn, James P. (Conn.)
Goldsborough, T. Alan (Md.)
Good, James W. (Iowa)
Goodykoontz, Wells (W. Va.)
Gorman, John J. (Ill.)
Gould, Norman J. (N. Y.)
Graham, George S. (Pa.)
Graham, William J. (Ill.)
Green, William R. (Iowa)
Greene, Frank L. (Vt.)
Greene, William S. (Mass.)
Griest, William W. (Pa.)
Griffin, Anthony J. (N. Y.)
Hadley, Lindley H. (Wash.)
Hammer, William C. (N. C.)
Hardy, Guy U. (Colo.)
Hardy, Rufus (Tex.)
Harrison, Thomas W. (Va.)
Haugen, Gilbert N. (Iowa)
Hawes, Harry B. (Mo.)
Hawley, Willis C. (Oreg.)
Hayden, Carl (Ariz.)
Hays, Edward D. (Mo.)
Henry, Lewis (N. Y.)
Herrick, Manuel (Okla.)
Hersey, Ira G. (Maine)
Hickey, Andrew J. (Ind.)
Hicks, Frederick C. (N. Y.)
Hill, John Philip (Md.)
Himes, Joseph H. (Ohio)
Hoch, Homer (Kans.)
Hogan, Michael J. (N. Y.)
Hooker, James M. (Va.)
Houghton, Alanson B. (N. Y.)
Huck, Mrs. Winnifred S. M. (Ill.)
Huddleston, George (Ala.)
Hudspeth, Claude B. (Tex.)
Hukriede, Theodore W. (Mo.)
Hull, Harry E. (Iowa)
Humphrey, Augustin R. (Nebr.)
Humphreys, Benjamin G. (Miss.)
Husted, James W. (N. Y.)
Hutchinson, Elijah C. (N. J.)
Ireland, Clifford (Ill.)
Jacoway, Henderson M. (Ark.)
James, Rorer A. (Va.)
James, W. Frank (Mich.)
Jefferis, Albert W. (Nebr.)
Jeffers, Lamar (Ala.)
Johnson, Albert (Wash.)
Johnson, Ben (Ky.)
Johnson, Paul B. (Miss.)
Johnson, Royal C. (S. Dak.)
Jones, Evan J. (Pa.)
Jones, Marvin (Tex.)
Kahn, Julius (Calif.)
Kearns, Charles C. (Ohio)
Keller, Oscar E. (Minn.)
Kelley, Patrick H. (Mich.)
Kelly, M. Clyde (Pa.)
Kendall, Samuel A. (Pa.)
Kennedy, Ambrose (R. I.)
Ketcham, John C. (Mich.)
Kiess, Edgar R. (Pa.)
Kincheloe, David H. (Ky.)
Kindred, John J. (N. Y.)
King, Edward J. (Ill.)
Kinkaid, Moses P. (Nebr.)
Kirkpatrick, William H. (Pa.)
Kissel, John (N. Y.)
Kitchin, Claude (N. C.)
Kleczka, John C. (Wis.)
Kline, Ardolph L. (N. Y.)
Kline, I. Clinton (Pa.)
Knight, Charles L. (Ohio)
Knutson, Harold (Minn.)
Kopp, William F. (Iowa)
Kraus, Milton (Ind.)
Kreider, Aaron S. (Pa.)
Kunz, Stanley H. (Ill.)
Lampert, Florian (Wis.)
Langley, John W. (Ky.)
Lanham, Fritz G. (Tex.)
Lankford, William C. (Ga.)
Larsen, William W. (Ga.)

Larson, Oscar J. (Minn.)
Lawrence, Henry F. (Mo.)
Layton, Caleb R. (Del.)
Lazaro, Ladislas (La.)
Lea, Clarence F. (Calif.)
Leatherwood, Elmer O. (Utah)
Lee, Gordon (Ga.)
Lee, Warren I. (N. Y.)
Lehlbach, Frederick R. (N. J.)
Lineberger, Walter F. (Calif.)
Linthicum, J. Charles (Md.)
Little, Edward C. (Kans.)
Logan, W. Turner (S. C.)
London, Meyer (N. Y.)
Longworth, Nicholas (Ohio)
Lowrey, Bill G. (Miss.)
Luce, Robert (Mass.)
Lufkin, Willfred W. (Mass.)
Luhring, Oscar R. (Ind.)
Lyon, Homer L. (N. C.)
McArthur, Clinton N. (Oreg.)
McClintic, James V. (Okla.)
McCormick, Washington J. (Mont.)
McDuffie, John (Ala.)
McFadden, Louis T. (Pa.)
MacGregor, Clarence (N. Y.)
McKenzie, John C. (Ill.)
MacLafferty, James H. (Calif.)
McLaughlin, James C. (Mich.)
McLaughlin, Joseph (Pa.)
McLaughlin, Melvin O. (Nebr.)
McPherson, Isaac V. (Mo.)
McSwain, John J. (S. C.)
Madden, Martin B. (Ill.)
Magee, Walter W. (N. Y.)
Maloney, Robert S. (Mass.)
Mann, James R. (Ill.)
Mansfield, Joseph J. (Tex.)
Mapes, Carl E. (Mich.)
Martin, Whitmell P. (La.)
Mason, William E. (Ill.)
Mead, James M. (N. Y.)
Merritt, Schuyler (Conn.)
Michaelson, M. Alfred (Ill.)
Michener, Earl C. (Mich.)
Miller, John F. (Wash.)
Mills, Ogden L. (N. Y.)
Millspaugh, Frank C. (Mo.)
Mondell, Frank W. (Wyo.)
Montague, Andrew J. (Va.)
Montoya, Nestor (N. Mex.)
Moore, Allen F. (Ill.)
Moore, C. Ellis (Ohio)
Moore, R. Walton (Va.)
Moores, Merrill (Ind.)
Morgan, William M. (Ohio)
Morin, John M. (Pa.)
Mott, Luther W. (N. Y.)
Mudd, Sydney E. (Md.)
Murphy, B. Frank (Ohio)
Nelson, Adolphus P. (Wis.)
Nelson, John E. (Maine)
Nelson, John M. (Wis.)
Newton, Cleveland A. (Mo.)
Newton, Walter H. (Minn.)
Nolan, John I. (Calif.)
Nolan, Mrs. Mae E. (Calif.)
Norton, Miner G. (Ohio)
O'Brien, Charles F. X. (N. J.)
O'Connor, James (La.)
Ogden, Charles F. (Ky.)
Oldfield, William A. (Ark.)
Oliver, William B. (Ala.)
Olpp, Archibald E. (N. J.)
Osborne, Henry Z. (Calif.)
Overstreet, James W. (Ga.)
Padgett, Lemuel P. (Tenn.)
Paige, Calvin D. (Mass.)
Park, Frank (Ga.)
Parker, James S. (N. Y.)
Parker, Richard W. (N. J.)
Parks, Tilman B. (Ark.)
Parrish, Lucian W. (Tex.)
Patterson, Francis F., Jr. (N. J.)
Patterson, Roscoe C. (Mo.)
Paul, John (Va.)
Perkins, Randolph (N. J.)
Perlman, Nathan D. (N. Y.)
Peters, John A. (Maine)
Petersen, Andrew N. (N. Y.)
Porter, Stephen G. (Pa.)
Pou, Edward W. (N. C.)
Pringey, Joseph C. (Okla.)
Purnell, Fred S. (Ind.)
Quin, Percy E. (Miss.)

Radcliffe, Amos H. (N. J.)
Rainey, John W. (Ill.)
Rainey, Lilius B. (Ala.)
Raker, John E. (Calif.)
Ramseyer, C. William (Iowa)
Rankin, John E. (Miss.)
Ransley, Harry C. (Pa.)
Rayburn, Sam T. (Tex.)
Reavis, C. Frank (Nebr.)
Reber, John (Pa.)
Reece, B. Carroll (Tenn.)
Reed, Daniel A. (N. Y.)
Reed, Stuart F. (W. Va.)
Rhodes, Marion E. (Mo.)
Ricketts, Edwin D. (Ohio)
Riddick, Carl W. (Mont.)
Riordan, Daniel J. (N. Y.)
Roach, Sidney C. (Mo.)
Robertson, Alice M. (Okla.)
Robsion, John M. (Ky.)
Rodenberg, William A. (Ill.)
Rogers, John Jacob (Mass.)
Rose, John M. (Pa.)
Rosenbloom, Benjamin L. (W. Va.)
Rossdale, Albert B. (N. Y.)
Rouse, Arthur B. (Ky.)
Rucker, William W. (Mo.)
Ryan, Thomas J. (N. Y.)
Sabath, Adolph J. (Ill.)
Sanders, Archie D. (N. Y.)
Sanders, Everett (Ind.)
Sanders, Morgan G. (Tex.)
Sandlin, John N. (La.)
Schall, Thomas D. (Minn.)
Scott, Frank D. (Mich.)
Scott, Lon A. (Tenn.)
Sears, William J. (Fla.)
Shaw, Guy L. (Ill.)
Shelton, Samuel A. (Mo.)
Shreve, Milton W. (Pa.)
Siegel, Isaac (N. Y.)
Sinclair, James H. (N. Dak.)
Sinnott, Nicholas J. (Oreg.)
Sisson, Thomas U. (Miss.)
Slemp, C. Bascom (Va.)
Smith, Addison T. (Idaho)
Smith, John M. C. (Mich.)
Smithwick, John H. (Fla.)
Snell, Bertrand H. (N. Y.)
Snyder, Homer P. (N. Y.)
Speaks, John C. (Ohio)
Sproul, Elliott W. (Ill.)
Stafford, William H. (Wis.)
Steagall, Henry B. (Ala.)
Stedman, Charles M. (N. C.)
Steenerson, Halvor (Minn.)
Stephens, Ambrose E. B. (Ohio)
Stevenson, William F. (S. C.)
Stiness, Walter R. (R. I.)
Stoll, Philip H. (S. C.)
Strong, James G. (Kans.)
Strong, Nathan L. (Pa.)
Sullivan, Christopher D. (N. Y.)
Summers, John W. (Wash.)
Sumners, Hatton W. (Tex.)
Swank, Fletcher B. (Okla.)
Sweet, Burton E. (Iowa)
Swing, Philip D. (Calif.)
Tague, Peter F. (Mass.)
Taylor, Chester W. (Ark.)
Taylor, Edward T. (Colo.)
Taylor, Herbert W. (N. J.)
Taylor, J. Will (Tenn.)
Taylor, Samuel M. (Ark.)
Temple, Henry W. (Pa.)
Ten Eyck, Peter G. (N. Y.)
Thomas, Robert Y., Jr. (Ky.)
Thompson, Charles J. (Ohio)
Thorpe, Roy H. (Nebr.)
Tillman, John N. (Ark.)
Tilson, John Q. (Conn.)
Timberlake, Charles B. (Colo.)
Tincher, Jasper N. (Kans.)
Tinkham, George H. (Mass.)
Towner, Horace M. (Iowa)
Treadway, Allen T. (Mass.)
Tucker, Henry St. G. (Va.)
Turner, Clarence W. (Tenn.)
Tyson, John R. (Ala.)
Underhill, Charles L. (Mass.)
Upshaw, William D. (Ga.)
Vaile, William N. (Colo.)
Vare, William S. (Pa.)
Vestal, Albert H. (Ind.)
Vinson, Carl (Ga.)
Voigt, Edward (Wis.)

Volk, Lester D. (N. Y.)
Volstead, Andrew J. (Minn.)
Walsh, Joseph (Mass.)
Walters, Anderson H. (Pa.)
Ward, Charles B. (N. Y.)
Ward, Hallett S. (N. C.)
Wason, Edward H. (N. H.)
Watson, Henry W. (Pa.)
Weaver, Zebulon (N. C.)
Webster, J. Stanley (Wash.)
Wheeler, Loren E. (Ill.)
White, Hays B. (Kans.)
White, Wallace H., Jr. (Maine)
Williams, Guinn (Tex.)
Williams, Thomas S. (Ill.)
Williamson, William (S. Dak.)
Wilson, Riley J. (La.)
Wingo, Otis (Ark.)
Winslow, Samuel E. (Mass.)
Wise, James W. (Ga.)
Wood, William R. (Ind.)
Woodruff, Roy O. (Mich.)
Woods, James P. (Va.)
Woodyard, Harry C. (W. Va.)
Wright, William C. (Ga.)
Wurzbach, Harry M. (Tex.)
Wyant, Adam M. (Pa.)
Yates, Richard (Ill.)
Young, George M. (N. Dak.)
Zihlman, Frederick N. (Md.)

The Sixty-eighth Congress (1923-25)

Gillett, Frederick H. (Mass.) Speaker.

Abernethy, Charles L. (N. C.)
Ackerman, Ernest R. (N. J.)
Aldrich, Richard S. (R. I.)
Allen, Robert E. L. (W. Va.)
Allgood, Miles C. (Ala.)
Almon, Edward B. (Ala.)
Anderson, Sydney (Minn.)
Andrew, A. Piatt, Jr. (Mass.)
Anthony, Daniel R., Jr. (Kans.)
Arnold, William W. (Ill.)
Aswell, James B. (La.)
Ayres, William A. (Kans.)
Bacharach, Isaac (N. J.)
Bacon, Robert L. (N. Y.)
Bankhead, William B. (Ala.)
Barbour, Henry E. (Calif.)
Barkley, Alben W. (Ky.)
Beck, Joseph D. (Wis.)
Beedy, Carroll L. (Maine)
Beers, Edward M. (Pa.)
Begg, James T. (Ohio)
Bell, Thomas M. (Ga.)
Berger, Victor L. (Wis.)
Bixler, Harris J. (Pa.)
Black, Eugene (Tex.)
Black, Loring M., Jr. (N. Y.)
Bland, Schuyler Otis (Va.)
Blanton, Thomas L. (Tex.)
Bloom, Sol (N. Y.)
Boies, William D. (Iowa)
Bowling, William B. (Ala.)
Box, John C. (Tex.)
Boyce, William H. (Del.)
Boylan, John J. (N. Y.)
Brand, Charles (Ohio)
Brand, Charles H. (Ga.)
Briggs, Clay Stone (Tex.)
Britten, Fred A. (Ill.)
Browne, Charles (N. J.)
Browne, Edward E. (Wis.)
Browning, Gordon (Tenn.)
Brumm, George F. (Pa.)
Buchanan, James P. (Tex.)
Buckley, James R. (Ill.)
Bulwinkle, Alfred L. (N. C.)
Burdick, Clark (R. I.)
Burtness, Olger B. (N. Dak.)
Burton, Theodore E. (Ohio)
Busby, T. Jeff. (Miss.)
Butler, Thomas S. (Pa.)
Byrnes, James F. (S. C.)
Byrns, Joseph W. (Tenn.)
Cable, John L. (Ohio)
Campbell, Guy E. (Pa.)
Canfield, Harry C. (Ind.)
Cannon, Clarence (Mo.)
Carew, John F. (N. Y.)
Carter, Charles D. (Okla.)
Casey, John J. (Pa.)
Celler, Emanuel (N. Y.)
Chindblom, Carl R. (Ill.)
Christopherson, Charles A. (S. Dak.)
Clague, Frank (Minn.)
Clancy, Robert H. (Mich.)
Clark, Frank (Fla.)
Clarke, John D. (N. Y.)
Cleary, William E. (N. Y.)
Cole, Cyrenus (Iowa)
Cole, R. Clinton (Ohio)
Collier, James W. (Miss.)
Collins, Ross A. (Miss.)
Colton, Don B. (Utah)
Connally, Tom T. (Tex.)
Connery, William P., Jr. (Mass.)
Connolly, James J. (Pa.)
Cook, Samuel E. (Ind.)
Cooper, Henry A. (Wis.)
Cooper, John G. (Ohio)
Corning, Parker (N. Y.)
Cramton, Louis C. (Mich.)
Crisp, Charles R. (Ga.)
Croll, William M. (Pa.)
Crosser, Robert (Ohio)
Crowther, Frank (N. Y.)
Cullen, Thomas H. (N. Y.)
Cummings, Herbert W. (Pa.)
Curry, Charles F. (Calif.)
Dallinger, Frederick W. (Mass.)
Darrow, George P. (Pa.)
Davey, Martin L. (Ohio)
Davis, Charles R. (Minn.)
Davis, Ewin L. (Tenn.)
Deal, Joseph T. (Va.)
Dempsey, S. Wallace (N. Y.)
Denison, Edward E. (Ill.)
Dickinson, Clement C. (Mo.)
Dickinson, Lester J. (Iowa)
Dickstein, Samuel (N. Y.)
Dominick, Frederick H. (S. C.)
Doughton, Robert L. (N. C.)
Dowell, Cassius C. (Iowa)
Doyle, Thomas A. (Ill.)
Drane, Herbert J. (Fla.)
Drewry, Patrick Henry (Va.)
Driver, William J. (Ark.)
Dupre, H. Garland (La.)
Dyer, Leonidas C. (Mo.)
Eagan, John J. (N. J.)
Edmonds, George W. (Pa.)
Elliott, Richard N. (Ind.)
Evans, Hiram K. (Iowa)
Evans, John M. (Mont.)
Fairchild, Benjamin L. (N.Y.)
Fairfield, Louis W. (Ind.)
Faust, Charles L. (Mo.)
Favrot, George K. (La.)
Fenn, E. Hart (Conn.)
Fields, William J. (Ky.)
Fish, Hamilton, Jr. (N. Y.)
Fisher, Hubert F. (Tenn.)
Fitzgerald, Roy G. (Ohio)
Fleetwood, Frederick G. (Vt.)
Foster, Israel M. (Ohio)
Frear, James A. (Wis.)
Fredericks, John D. (Calif.)
Free, Arthur M. (Calif.)
Freeman, Richard P. (Conn.)
French, Burton L. (Idaho)
Frothingham, Louis A. (Mass.)
Fulbright, James F. (Mo.)
Fuller, Charles E. (Ill.)
Fulmer, Hampton P. (S. C.)
Funk, Frank H. (Ill.)
Gallivan, James A. (Mass.)
Gambrill, Stephen W. (Md.)
Garber, Milton C. (Okla.)
Gardner, Frank (Ind.)
Garner, John N. (Tex.)
Garrett, Daniel E. (Tex.)
Garrett, Finis J. (Tenn.)
Gasque, Allard H. (S. C.)
Geran, Elmer H. (N. J.)
Gibson, Ernest W. (Vt.)
Gifford, Charles L. (Mass.)
Gilbert, Ralph (Ky.)
Gillett, Frederick H. (Mass.)
Glatfelter, Samuel F. (Pa.)
Goldsborough, T. Alan (Md.)
Graham, George S. (Pa.)
Graham, William J. (Ill.)
Green, William R. (Iowa)
Greene, William S. (Mass.)
Greenwood, Arthur H. (Ind.)
Griest, William W. (Pa.)
Griffin, Anthony J. (N. Y.)
Guyer, Ulysses S. (Kans.)
Hadley, Lindley H. (Wash.)
Hall, Thomas (N. Dak.)
Hammer, William C. (N. C.)
Hardy, Guy U. (Colo.)
Harrison, Thomas W. (Va.)
Hastings, William W. (Okla.)
Haugen, Gilbert N. (Iowa)
Hawes, Harry B. (Mo.)
Hawley, Willis C. (Oreg.)
Hayden, Carl (Ariz.)
Hersey, Ira G. (Maine)
Hickey, Andrew J. (Ind.)
Hill, John P. (Md.)
Hill, Lister (Ala.)
Hill, Samuel B. (Wash.)
Hoch, Homer (Kans.)
Holaday, William P. (Ill.)
Hooker, James M. (Va.)
Howard, Edgar (Nebr.)
Howard, Everett B. (Okla.)
Huddleston, George (Ala.)
Hudson, Grant M. (Mich.)
Hudspeth, Claude B. (Tex.)
Hull, Cordell (Tenn.)
Hull, Harry E. (Iowa)
Hull, Morton D. (Ill.)
Hull, William E. (Ill.)
Humphreys, William Y. (Miss.)
Jacobstein, Meyer (N. Y.)
James, W. Frank (Mich.)
Jeffers, Lamar (Ala.)
Johnson, Albert (Wash.)
Johnson, Ben (Ky.)
Johnson, George W. (W. Va.)
Johnson, Luther A. (Tex.)
Johnson, Royal C. (S. Dak.)
Jones, Marvin (Tex.)
Jost, Henry L. (Mo.)
Kahn, Julius (Calif.)
Kearns, Charles C. (Ohio)
Keller, Oscar E. (Minn.)
Kelly, M. Clyde (Pa.)
Kendall, Samuel A. (Pa.)
Kent, Everett (Pa.)
Kerr, John H. (N. C.)
Ketcham, John C. (Mich.)
Kiess, Edgar R. (Pa.)
Kincheloe, David H. (Ky.)
Kindred, John J. (N. Y.)
King, Edward J. (Ill.)
Knutson, Harold (Minn.)
Kopp, William F. (Iowa)
Kunz, Stanley H. (Ill.)
Kurtz, J. Banks (Pa.)
Kvale, O. J. (Minn.)
LaGuardia, Fiorello H. (N.Y.)
Lampert, Florian (Wis.)
Langley, John W. (Ky.)
Lanham, Fritz G. (Tex.)
Lankford, William C. (Ga.)
Larsen, William W. (Ga.)
Larson, Oscar J. (Minn.)
Lazaro, Ladislas (La.)
Lea, Clarence F. (Calif.)
Leach, Robert M. (Mass.)
Leatherwood, Elmer O. (Utah)
Leavitt, Scott (Mont.)
Lee, Gordon (Ga.)
Lehlbach, Frederick R. (N.J.)
Lilly, Thomas J. (W. Va.)
Lindsay, George W. (N. Y.)
Lineberger, Walter F. (Calif.)
Linthicum, J. Charles (Md.)
Little, Edward C. (Kans.)
Logan, W. Turner (S. C.)
Longworth, Nicholas (Ohio)
Lowrey, Bill G. (Miss.)
Lozier, Ralph F. (Mo.)
Luce, Robert (Mass.)
Lyon, Homer L. (N. C.)
McClintic, James V. (Okla.)
McDuffie, John (Ala.)
McFadden, Louis T. (Pa.)
MacGregor, Clarence (N. Y.)
McKenzie, John C. (Ill.)
McKeown, Thomas D. (Okla.)
MacLafferty, James H. (Calif.)
McLaughlin, James C. (Mich.)
McLaughlin, Melvin O. (Nebr.)
McLeod, Clarence J. (Mich.)
McNulty, Frank J. (N. J.)
McReynolds, Samuel D. (Tenn.)
McSwain, John J. (S. C.)
McSweeney, John (Ohio)
Madden, Martin B. (Ill.)
Magee, James M. (Pa.)
Magee, Walter W. (N. Y.)
Major, J. Earl (Ill.)
Major, Samuel C. (Mo.)
Manlove, Joe J. (Mo.)
Mansfield, Joseph J. (Tex.)
Mapes, Carl E. (Mich.)
Martin, Whitmell P. (La.)
Mead, James M. (N. Y.)
Merritt, Schuyler (Conn.)
Michaelson, M. Alfred (Ill.)
Michener, Earl C. (Mich.)
Miller, Edward E. (Ill.)
Miller, John F. (Wash.)
Milligan, Jacob L. (Mo.)
Mills, Ogden L. (N. Y.)
Minahan, Daniel F. (N. J.)
Montague, Andrew J. (Va.)
Mooney, Charles A. (Ohio)
Moore, Allen F. (Ill.)
Moore, C. Ellis (Ohio)
Moore, R. Lee (Ga.)
Moore, R. Walton (Va.)
Moores, Merrill (Ind.)
Morehead, John H. (Nebr.)
Morgan, William M. (Ohio)
Morin, John M. (Pa.)
Morris, Joseph W. (Ky.)
Morrow, John (N. Mex.)
Mudd, Sydney E. (Md.)
Murphy, B. Frank (Ohio)
Nelson, John E. (Maine)
Nelson, John M. (Wis.)
Newton, Cleveland A. (Mo.)
Newton, Walter H. (Minn.)
Nolan, Mrs. Mae E. (Calif.)
O'Brien, Charles F. X. (N. J.)
O'Connell, David J. (N. Y.)
O'Connell, Jeremiah E. (R. I.)
O'Connor, James (La.)
O'Connor, John J. (N. Y.)
Oldfield, William A. (Ark.)
Oliver, Frank (N. Y.)
Oliver, William B. (Ala.)
O'Sullivan, Patrick B. (Conn.)
Paige, Calvin D. (Mass.)
Park, Frank (Ga.)
Parker, James S. (N. Y.)
Parks, Tilman B. (Ark.)
Patterson, Francis F., Jr. (N. J.)
Peavey, Hubert H. (Wis.)
Peery, George C. (Va.)
Perkins, Randolph (N. J.)
Perlman, Nathan D. (N. Y.)
Phillips, Thomas W., Jr. (Pa.)
Porter, Stephen G. (Pa.)
Pou, Edward W. (N. C.)
Prall, Anning S. (N. Y.)
Purnell, Fred S. (Ind.)
Quayle, John F. (N. Y.)
Quin, Percy E. (Miss.)
Ragon, Heartsill (Ark.)
Rainey, Henry T. (Ill.)
Raker, John E. (Calif.)
Ramseyer, C. William (Iowa)
Rankin, John E. (Miss.)
Ransley, Harry C. (Pa.)
Rathbone, Henry R. (Ill.)
Rayburn, Sam T. (Tex.)
Reece, B. Carroll (Tenn.)
Reed, Daniel A. (N. Y.)
Reed, James B. (Ark.)
Reed, Stuart F. (W. Va.)
Reid, Frank R. (Ill.)
Richards, Charles L. (Nev.)
Roach, Sidney C. (Mo.)
Robinson, Thomas J. B. (Iowa)
Robsion, John M. (Ky.)
Rogers, John Jacob (Mass.)
Rogers, William N. (N. H.)
Romjue, Milton A. (Mo.)
Rosenbloom, Benjamin L. (W. Va.)
Rouse, Arthur B. (Ky.)
Rubey, Thomas L. (Mo.)
Sabath, Adolph J. (Ill.)
Salmon, William C. (Tenn.)
Sanders, Archie D. (N. Y.)
Sanders, Everett (Ind.)
Sanders, Morgan G. (Tex.)
Sandlin, John N. (La.)
Schafer, John C. (Wis.)
Schall, Thomas D. (Minn.)
Schneider, George J. (Wis.)
Scott, Frank D. (Mich.)
Sears, William J. (Fla.)
Sears, Willis G. (Nebr.)

Seger, George N. (N. J.)
Shallenberger, Ashton C. (Nebr.)
Sherwood, Isaac R. (Ohio)
Shreve, Milton W. (Pa.)
Simmons, Robert G. (Nebr.)
Sinclair, James H. (N. Dak.)
Sinnott, Nicholas J. (Oreg.)
Sites, Frank C. (Pa.)
Smith, Addison T. (Idaho)
Smithwick, John H. (Fla.)
Snell, Bertrand H. (N. Y.)
Snyder, Homer P. (N. Y.)
Speaks, John C. (Ohio)
Spearing, J. Zacharie (La.)
Sproul, Elliott W. (Ill.)
Sproul, William H. (Kans.)
Stalker, Gale H. (N. Y.)
Steagall, Henry B. (Ala.)
Stedman, Charles M. (N. C.)
Stengle, Charles I. (N. Y.)
Stephens, Ambrose E. B. (Ohio)
Stevenson, William F. (S. C.)
Strong, James G. (Kans.)
Strong, Nathan L. (Pa.)
Sullivan, Christopher D. (N. Y.)
Summers, John W. (Wash.)
Sumners, Hatton W. (Tex.)
Swank, Fletcher B. (Okla.)
Sweet, Thaddeus C. (N. Y.)
Swing, Philip D. (Calif.)
Swoope, William I. (Pa.)
Taber, John (N. Y.)
Tague, Peter F. (Mass.)
Taylor, Edward T. (Colo.)
Taylor, J. Alfred (W. Va.)
Taylor, J. Will (Tenn.)
Temple, Henry W. (Pa.)
Thatcher, Maurice H. (Ky.)
Thomas, J. W. Elmer (Okla.)
Thomas, Robert Y., Jr. (Ky.)
Thompson, Charles J. (Ohio)
Tillman, John N. (Ark.)
Tilson, John Q. (Conn.)
Timberlake, Charles B. (Colo.)
Tincher, Jasper N. (Kans.)
Tinkham, George H. (Mass.)
Treadway, Allen T. (Mass.)
Tucker, Henry St. G. (Va.)
Tydings, Millard E. (Md.)
Underhill, Charles L. (Mass.)
Underwood, Mell G. (Ohio)
Upshaw, William D. (Ga.)
Vaile, William N. (Colo.)
Vare, William S. (Pa.)
Vestal, Albert H. (Ind.)
Vincent, Bird J. (Mich.)
Vinson, Carl (Ga.)
Vinson, Frederick M. (Ky.)
Voigt, Edward (Wis.)
Wainwright, J. Mayhew (N. Y.)
Ward, Charles B. (N. Y.)
Ward, Hallett S. (N. C.)
Wason, Edward H. (N. H.)
Watkins, Elton (Oreg.)
Watres, Laurence H. (Pa.)
Watson, Henry W. (Pa.)
Weaver, Zebulin (N. C.)
Wefald, Knud (Minn.)
Weller, Royal H. (N. Y.)
Welsh, George A. (Pa.)
Wertz, George M. (Pa.)
White, Hays B. (Kans.)
White, Wallace H., Jr. (Maine)
Williams, Arthur B. (Mich.)
Williams, Guinn (Tex.)
Williams, Thomas S. (Ill.)
Williamson, William (S. Dak.)
Wilson, Riley J. (La.)
Wilson, T. Webber (Miss.)
Wilson, William E. (Ind.)
Wingo, Otis (Ark.)
Winslow, Samuel E. (Mass.)
Winter, Charles E. (Wyo.)
Wolff, J. Scott (Mo.)
Wood, William R. (Ind.)
Woodruff, Roy O. (Mich.)
Woodrum, Clifton A. (Va.)
Wright, William C. (Ga.)
Wurzbach, Harry M. (Tex.)
Wyant, Adam M. (Pa.)
Yates, Richard (Ill.)
Young George M. (N. Dak.)
Zihlman, Frederick N. (Md.)

The Sixty-ninth Congress (1925-27)

Longworth, Nicholas (Ohio) Speaker.

Abernethy, Charles L. (N. C.)
Ackerman, Ernest R. (N. J.)
Adkins, Charles (Ill.)
Aldrich, Richard S. (R. I.)
Allen, John C. (Ill.)
Allgood, Miles C. (Ala.)
Almon, Edward B. (Ala.)
Andresen, August H. (Minn.)
Andrew, A. Piatt, Jr. (Mass.)
Anthony, Daniel R., Jr. (Kans.)
Appleby, Stewart H. (N. J.)
Arentz, Samuel S. (Nev.)
Arnold, William W. (Ill.)
Aswell, James B. (La.)
Auf der Heide, Oscar L. (N. J.)
Ayres, William A. (Kans.)
Bacharach, Isaac (N. J.)
Bachmann, Carl G. (W. Va.)
Bacon, Robert L. (N. Y.)
Bailey, Ralph E. (Mo.)
Bankhead, William B. (Ala.)
Barbour, Henry E. (Calif.)
Barkley, Alben W. (Ky.)
Beck, Joseph D. (Wis.)
Beedy, Carroll L. (Maine)
Beers, Edward M. (Pa.)
Begg, James T. (Ohio)
Bell, Thomas M. (Ga.)
Berger, Victor L. (Wis.)
Bixler, Harris J. (Pa.)
Black, Eugene (Tex.)
Black, Loring M., Jr. (N. Y.)
Bland, Schuyler O. (Va.)
Blanton, Thomas L. (Tex.)
Bloom, Sol (N. Y.)
Boies, William D. (Iowa)
Bowles, Henry L. (Mass.)
Bowling, William B. (Ala.)
Bowman, Frank L. (W. Va.)
Box, John C. (Tex.)
Boylan, John J. (N. Y.)
Brand, Charles (Ohio)
Brand, Charles H. (Ga.)
Briggs, Clay Stone (Tex.)
Brigham, Elbert S. (Vt.)
Britten, Fred A. (Ill.)
Browne, Edward E. (Wis.)
Browning, Gordon (Tenn.)
Brumm, George F. (Pa.)
Buchanan, James P. (Tex.)
Bulwinkle, Alfred L. (N. C.)
Burdick, Clark (R. I.)
Burtness, Olger B. (N. Dak.)
Burton, Theodore E. (Ohio)
Busby, T. Jefferson (Miss.)
Butler, Thomas S. (Pa.)
Byrns, Joseph W. (Tenn.)
Campbell, Guy E. (Pa.)
Canfield, Harry C. (Ind.)
Cannon, Clarence (Mo.)
Carew, John F. (N. Y.)
Carpenter, Edmund N. (Pa.)
Carss, William L. (Minn.)
Carter, Albert E. (Calif.)
Carter, Charles D. (Okla.)
Celler, Emanuel (N. Y.)
Chalmers, William W. (Ohio)
Chapman, Virgil M. (Ky.)
Chindblom, Carl R. (Ill.)
Christopherson, Charles A. (S. Dak.)
Clague, Frank (Minn.)
Cleary, William E. (N. Y.)
Cochran, John J. (Mo.)
Cole, Cyrenus (Iowa)
Collier, James W. (Miss.)
Collins, Ross A. (Miss.)
Colton, Don B. (Utah)
Connally, Tom T. (Tex.)
Connery, William P., Jr. (Mass.)
Connolly, James J. (Pa.)
Cooper, Henry A. (Wis.)
Cooper, John G. (Ohio)
Corning, Parker (N. Y.)
Cox, Edward E. (Ga.)
Coyle, William R. (Pa.)
Cramton, Louis C. (Mich.)
Crisp, Charles R. (Ga.)
Crosser, Robert (Ohio)
Crowther, Frank (N. Y.)
Crumpacker, Maurice E. (Oreg.)
Cullen, Thomas H. (N. Y.)
Curry, Charles F. (Calif.)
Dallinger, Frederick W. (Mass.)
Darrow, George P. (Pa.)
Davenport, Frederick M. (N. Y.)
Davey, Martin L. (Ohio)
Davis, Ewin L. (Tenn.)
Deal, Joseph T. (Va.)
Dempsey, S. Wallace (N. Y.)
Denison, Edward E. (Ill.)
Dickinson, Clement C. (Mo.)
Dickinson, Lester J. (Iowa)
Dickstein, Samuel (N. Y.)
Dominick, Fred H. (S. C.)
Doughton, Robert L. (N. C.)
Douglass, John J. (Mass.)
Dowell, Cassius C. (Iowa)
Doyle, Thomas A. (Ill.)
Drane, Herbert J. (Fla.)
Drewry, Patrick Henry (Va.)
Driver, William J. (Ark.)
Dyer, Leonidas C. (Mo.)
Eaton, Charles A. (N. J.)
Edwards, Charles G. (Ga.)
Elliott, Richard N. (Ind.)
Ellis, Edgar C. (Mo.)
Englebright, Harry L. (Calif.)
Eslick, Edward E. (Tenn.)
Esterly, Charles J. (Pa.)
Evans, John M. (Mont.)
Fairchild, Benjamin L. (N.Y.)
Faust, Charles L. (Mo.)
Fenn, E. Hart (Conn.)
Fish, Hamilton, Jr. (N. Y.)
Fisher, Hubert F. (Tenn.)
Fitzgerald, Roy G. (Ohio)
Fitzgerald, William T. (Ohio)
Flaherty, Lawrence J. (Calif.)
Fletcher, Brooks (Ohio)
Fort, Franklin W. (N. J.)
Foss, Frank H. (Mass.)
Frear, James A. (Wis.)
Fredericks, John D. (Calif.)
Free, Arthur M. (Calif.)
Freeman, Richard P. (Conn.)
French, Burton L. (Idaho)
Frothingham, Louis A. (Mass.)
Fuller, Charles E. (Ill.)
Fulmer, Hampton P. (S. C.)
Funk, Frank H. (Ill.)
Furlow, Allen J. (Minn.)
Gallivan, James A. (Mass.)
Gambrill, Stephen W. (Md.)
Garber, Milton C. (Okla.)
Gardner, Frank (Ind.)
Garner, John N. (Tex.)
Garrett, Daniel E. (Tex.)
Garrett, Finis J. (Tenn.)
Gasque, Allard H. (S. C.)
Gibson, Ernest W. (Vt.)
Gifford, Charles L. (Mass.)
Gilbert, Ralph (Ky.)
Glynn, James P. (Conn.)
Golder, Benjamin M. (Pa.)
Goldsborough, T. Alan (Md.)
Goodwin, Godfrey G. (Minn.)
Gorman, John J. (Ill.)
Graham, George S. (Pa.)
Green, Robert A. (Fla.)
Green, William R. (Iowa)
Greenwood, Arthur H. (Ind.)
Griest, William W. (Pa.)
Griffin, Anthony J. (N. Y.)
Hadley, Lindley H. (Wash.)
Hale, Fletcher (N. H.)
Hall, Albert R. (Ind.)
Hall, Thomas (N. Dak.)
Hammer, William C. (N. C.)
Hardy, Guy U. (Colo.)
Hare, Butler B. (S. C.)
Harrison, Thomas W. (Va.)
Hastings, William W. (Okla.)
Haugen, Gilbert N. (Iowa)
Hawes, Harry B. (Mo.)
Hawley, Willis C. (Oreg.)
Hayden, Carl (Ariz.)
Hersey, Ira G. (Maine)
Hickey, Andrew J. (Ind.)
Hill, John Philip (Md.)
Hill, Lister (Ala.)
Hill, Samuel B. (Wash.)
Hoch, Homer (Kans.)
Hogg, David (Ind.)
Holaday, William P. (Ill.)
Hooper, Joseph L. (Mich.)
Houston, Robert G. (Del.)
Howard, Edgar (Nebr.)
Huddleston, George (Ala.)
Hudson, Grant M. (Mich.)
Hudspeth, Claude B. (Tex.)
Hull, Cordell (Tenn.)
Hull, Morton D. (Ill.)
Hull, William E. (Ill.)
Irwin, Edward M. (Ill.)
Jacobstein, Meyer (N. Y.)
James, W. Frank (Mich.)
Jeffers, Lamar (Ala.)
Jenkins, Thomas A. (Ohio)
Johnson, Albert (Wash.)
Johnson, Ben (Ky.)
Johnson, Luther A. (Tex.)
Johnson, Noble J. (Ind.)
Johnson, Royal C. (S. Dak.)
Johnson, William R. (Ill.)
Jones, Marvin (Tex.)
Kahn, Florence P. (Calif.)
Kearns, Charles C. (Ohio)
Keller, Oscar E. (Minn.)
Kelly, M. Clyde (Pa.)
Kemp, Bolivar E. (La.)
Kendall, Samuel A. (Pa.)
Kerr, John H. (N. C.)
Ketcham, John C. (Mich.)
Kiefner, Charles E. (Mo.)
Kiess, Edgar R. (Pa.)
Kincheloe, David H. (Ky.)
Kindred, John J. (N. Y.)
King, Edward J. (Ill.)
Kirk, Andrew J. (Ky.)
Knutson, Harold (Minn.)
Kopp, William F. (Iowa)
Kunz, Stanley H. (Ill.)
Kurtz, J. Banks (Pa.)
Kvale, O. J. (Minn.)
LaGuardia, Fiorello H. (N.Y.)
Lampert, Florian (Wis.)
Lanham, Fritz G. (Tex.)
Lankford, William C. (Ga.)
Larsen, William W. (Ga.)
Lazaro, Ladislas (La.)
Lea, Clarence F. (Calif.)
Leatherwood, Elmer O. (Utah)
Leavitt, Scott (Mont.)
Lee, Gordon (Ga.)
Lehlbach, Frederick R. (N.J.)
Letts, F. Dickinson (Iowa)
Lindsay, George W. (N. Y.)
Lineberger, Walter F. (Calif.)
Linthicum, J. Charles (Md.)
Little, Chauncey B. (Kans.)
Longworth, Nicholas (Ohio)
Lowrey, Bill G. (Miss.)
Lozier, Ralph F. (Mo.)
Luce, Robert (Mass.)
Lyon, Homer L. (N. C.)
McClintic, James V. (Okla.)
McDuffie, John (Ala.)
McFadden, Louis T. (Pa.)
MacGregor, Clarence (N. Y.)
McKeown, Thomas D. (Okla.)
McLaughlin, James C. (Mich.)
McLaughlin, Melvin O. (Nebr.)
McLeod, Clarence J. (Mich.)
McMillan, Thomas S. (S. C.)
McReynolds, Samuel D. (Tenn.)
McSwain, John J. (S. C.)
McSweeney, John (Ohio)
Madden, Martin B. (Ill.)
Magee, James M. (Pa.)
Magee, Walter W. (N. Y.)
Magrady, Frederick W. (Pa.)
Major, Samuel C. (Mo.)
Manlove, Joe J. (Mo.)
Mansfield, Joseph J. (Tex.)
Mapes, Carl E. (Mich.)
Martin, Joseph W., Jr. (Mass.)
Martin, Whitmell P. (La.)
Mead, James M. (N. Y.)
Menges, Franklin (Pa.)
Merritt, Schuyler (Conn.)
Michaelson, M. Alfred (Ill.)
Michener, Earl C. (Mich.)
Miller, John F. (Wash.)
Milligan, Jacob L. (Mo.)
Mills, Ogden L. (N. Y.)
Montague, Andrew J. (Va.)
Montgomery, Samuel J. (Okla.)
Mooney, Charles A. (Ohio)
Moore, C. Ellis (Ohio)
Moore, John W. (Ky.)

Moore, R. Walton (Va.)
Morehead, John H. (Nebr.)
Morgan, William M. (Ohio)
Morin, John M. (Pa.)
Morrow, John (N. Mex.)
Murphy, B. Frank (Ohio)
Nelson, John E. (Maine)
Nelson, John M. (Wis.)
Nelson, William L. (Mo.)
Newton, Cleveland A. (Mo.)
Newton, Walter H. (Minn.)
Norton, Mary T. (N. J.)
O'Connell, David J. (N. Y.)
O'Connell, Jeremiah E. (R.I.)
O'Connor, James (La.)
O'Connor, John J. (N. Y.)
Oldfield, William A. (Ark.)
Oliver, Frank (N. Y.)
Oliver, William B. (Ala.)
Parker, James S. (N. Y.)
Parks, Tilman B. (Ark.)
Patterson, Francis F., Jr. (N. J.)
Peavey, Hubert H. (Wis.)
Peery, George C. (Va.)
Perkins, Randolph (N. J.)
Perlman, Nathan D. (N. Y.)
Phillips, Thomas W., Jr. (Pa.)
Porter, Stephen G. (Pa.)
Pou, Edward W. (N. C.)
Prall, Anning S. (N. Y.)
Pratt, Harcourt J. (N. Y.)
Purnell, Fred S. (Ind.)
Quayle, John F. (N. Y.)
Quin, Percy E. (Miss.)
Ragon, Heartsill (Ark.)
Rainey, Henry T. (Ill.)
Raker, John E. (Calif.)
Ramseyer, C. William (Iowa)
Rankin, John E. (Miss.)
Ransley, Harry C. (Pa.)
Rathbone, Henry R. (Ill.)
Rayburn, Sam (Tex.)
Reece, B. Carroll (Tenn.)
Reed, Daniel A. (N. Y.)
Reed, James B. (Ark.)
Reid, Frank R. (Ill.)
Robinson, Thomas J. B. (Iowa)
Robsion, John M. (Ky.)
Rogers, Edith Nourse (Mass.)
Romjue, Milton A. (Mo.)
Rouse, Arthur B. (Ky.)
Rowbottom, Harry E. (Ind.)
Rubey, Thomas L. (Mo.)
Rutherford, Samuel (Ga.)
Sabath, Adolph J. (Ill.)
Sanders, Archie D. (N. Y.)
Sanders, Morgan G. (Tex.)
Sandlin, John N. (La.)
Schafer, John C. (Wis.)
Schneider, George J. (Wis.)
Scott, Frank D. (Mich.)
Sears, William J. (Fla.)
Sears, Willis G. (Nebr.)
Seger, George N. (N. J.)
Shallenberger, Ashton C. (Nebr.)
Shreve, Milton W. (Pa.)
Simmons, Robert G. (Nebr.)
Sinclair, James H. (N. Dak.)
Sinnott, Nicholas J. (Oreg.)
Smith, Addison T. (Idaho)
Smithwick, John H. (Fla.)
Snell, Bertrand H. (N. Y.)
Somers, Andrew L. (N. Y.)
Sosnowski, John B. (Mich.)
Speaks, John C. (Ohio)
Spearing, J. Zacharie (La.)
Sproul, Elliott W. (Ill.)
Sproul, William H. (Kans.)
Stalker, Gale H. (N. Y.)
Steagall, Henry B. (Ala.)
Stedman, Charles M. (N. C.)
Stephens, Ambrose E. B. (Ohio)
Stevenson, William F. (S. C.)
Stobbs, George R. (Mass.)
Strong, James G. (Kans.)
Strong, Nathan L. (Pa.)
Strother, James French (W. Va.)
Sullivan, Christopher D. (N. Y.)
Summers, John W. (Wash.)
Sumners, Hatton W. (Tex.)
Swank, Fletcher B. (Okla.)
Swartz, Joshua W. (Pa.)
Sweet, Thaddeus C. (N. Y.)
Swing, Philip D. (Calif.)
Swoope, William I. (Pa.)
Taber, John (N. Y.)
Taylor, Edward T. (Colo.)
Taylor, Herbert W. (N. J.)
Taylor, J. Alfred (W. Va.)
Taylor, J. Will (Tenn.)
Temple, Henry W. (Pa.)
Thatcher, Maurice H. (Ky.)
Thayer, Harry I. (Mass.)
Thomas, J. W. Elmer (Okla.)
Thompson, Charles J. (Ohio)
Thurston, Lloyd (Iowa)
Tillman, John N. (Ark.)
Tilson, John Q. (Conn.)
Timberlake, Charles B. (Colo.)
Tincher, Jasper N. (Kans.)
Tinkham, George H. (Mass.)
Tolley, Harold S. (N. Y.)
Treadway, Allen T. (Mass.)
Tucker, Henry St. G. (Va.)
Tydings, Millard E. (Md.)
Underhill, Charles L. (Mass.)
Underwood, Mell G. (Ohio)
Updike, Ralph E., Sr. (Ind.)
Upshaw, William D. (Ga.)
Vaile, William N. (Colo.)
Vare, William S. (Pa.)
Vestal, Albert H. (Ind.)
Vincent, Bird J. (Mich.)
Vinson, Carl (Ga.)
Vinson, Frederick M. (Ky.)
Voigt, Edward (Wis.)
Wainwright, J. Mayhew (N. Y).
Walters, Anderson H. (Pa.)
Warren, Lindsay C. (N. C.)
Wason, Edward H. (N. H.)
Watres, Laurence H. (Pa.)
Watson, Henry W. (Pa.)
Weaver, Zebulon (N. C.)
Wefald, Knud (Minn.)
Welch, Richard J. (Calif.)
Weller, Royal H. (N. Y.)
Welsh, George A. (Pa.)
Wheeler, Loren E. (Ill.)
White, Hays B. (Kans.)
White, Wallace H., Jr. (Maine)
Whitehead, Joseph (Va.)
Whittington, William M. (Miss.)
Williams, Guinn (Tex.)
Williams, Thomas S. (Ill.)
Williamson, William (S. Dak.)
Wilson, Riley J. (La.)
Wilson, T. Webber (Miss.)
Wingo, Otis (Ark.)
Winter, Charles E. (Wyo.)
Wolverton, John M. (W. Va.)
Wood, William R. (Ind.)
Woodruff, Roy O. (Mich.)
Woodrum, Clifton A. (Va.)
Woodyard, Harry C. (W. Va.)
Wright, William C. (Ga.)
Wurzbach, Harry M. (Tex.)
Wyant, Adam M. (Pa.)
Yates, Richard (Ill.)
Zihlman, Frederick N. (Md.)

The Seventieth Congress (1927-29)

Longworth, Nicholas (Ohio) Speaker.

Abernethy, Charles L. (N. C.)
Ackerman, Ernest R. (N. J.)
Adkins, Charles (Ill.)
Aldrich, Richard S. (R. I.)
Allen, John C. (Ill.)
Allgood, Miles C. (Ala.)
Almon, Edward B. (Ala.)
Andresen, August H. (Minn.)
Andrew, A. Piatt (Mass.)
Anthony, Daniel R., Jr. (Kans.)
Arentz, Samuel S. (Nev.)
Arnold, William W. (Ill.)
Aswell, James B. (La.)
Auf der Heide, Oscar L. (N. J.)
Ayres, William A. (Kans.)
Bacharach, Isaac (N. J.)
Bachmann, Carl G. (W. Va.)
Bacon, Robert L. (N. Y.)
Bankhead, William B. (Ala.)
Barbour, Henry E. (Calif.)
Beck, James M. (Pa.)
Beck, Joseph D. (Wis.)
Beedy, Carroll L. (Maine)
Beers, Edward M. (Pa.)
Begg, James T. (Ohio)
Bell, Thomas M. (Ga.)
Berger, Victor L. (Wis.)
Black, Eugene (Tex.)
Black, Loring M., Jr. (N. Y.)
Bland, Schuyler Otis (Va.)
Blanton, Thomas L. (Tex.)
Bloom, Sol (N. Y.)
Bohn, Frank P. (Mich.)
Boies, William D. (Iowa.)
Bowles, Henry L. (Mass.)
Bowling, William B. (Ala.)
Bowman, Frank L. (W. Va.)
Box, John C. (Tex.)
Boylan, John J. (N. Y.)
Brand, Charles (Ohio)
Brand, Charles H. (Ga.)
Briggs, Clay Stone (Tex.)
Brigham, Elbert S. (Vt.)
Britten, Fred A. (Ill.)
Browne, Edward E. (Wis.)
Browning, Gordon (Tenn.)
Buchanan, James P. (Tex.)
Buckbee, John T. (Ill.)
Bulwinkle, Alfred L. (N. C.)
Burdick, Clark (R. I.)
Burtness, Olger B. (N. Dak.)
Burton, Theodore E. (Ohio)
Busby, Jeff (Miss.)
Bushong, Robert G. (Pa.)
Butler, Robert R. (Oreg.)
Butler, Thomas S. (Pa.)
Byrns, Joseph W. (Tenn.)
Campbell, Guy E. (Pa.)
Canfield, Harry C. (Ind.)
Cannon, Clarence (Mo.)
Carew, John F. (N. Y.)
Carley, Patrick J. (N. Y.)
Carss, William L. (Minn.)
Carter, Albert E. (Calif.)
Cartwright, Wilbur (Okla.)
Casey, John J. (Pa.)
Celler, Emanuel (N. Y.)
Chalmers, William W. (Ohio)
Chapman, Virgil (Ky.)
Chase, J. Mitchell (Pa.)
Chindblom, Carl R. (Ill.)
Christopherson, Charles A. (S. Dak.)
Clague, Frank (Minn.)
Clancy, Robert H. (Mich.)
Clarke, John D. (N. Y.)
Cochran, John J. (Mo.)
Cochran, Thomas C. (Pa.)
Cohen, William W. (N. Y.)
Cole, Cyrenus (Iowa)
Cole, William P., Jr. (Md.)
Collier, James W. (Miss.)
Collins, Ross A. (Miss.)
Colton, Don B. (Utah)
Combs, George H., Jr. (Mo.)
Connally, Tom (Tex.)
Connery, William P., Jr. (Mass.)
Connolly, James J. (Pa.)
Cooper, Henry Allen (Wis.)
Cooper, John G. (Ohio)
Corning, Parker (N. Y.)
Cox, Edward E. (Ga.)
Crail, Joe (Calif.)
Cramton, Louis C. (Mich.)
Crisp, Charles R. (Ga.)
Crosser, Robert (Ohio)
Crowther, Frank (N. Y.)
Culkin, Francis D. (N. Y.)
Cullen, Thomas H. (N. Y.)
Curry, Charles F. (Calif.)
Dallinger, Frederick W. (Mass.)
Darrow, George P. (Pa.)
Davenport, Frederick M. (N. Y.)
Davey, Martin L. (Ohio)
Davis, Ewin L. (Tenn.)
Deal, Joseph T. (Va.)
Dempsey, S. Wallace (N. Y.)
Denison, Edward E. (Ill.)
DeRouen, Rene L. (La.)
Dickinson, Clement C. (Mo.)
Dickinson, Lester J. (Iowa)
Dickstein, Samuel (N. Y.)
Dominick, Fred H. (S. C.)
Doughton, Robert L. (N. C.)
Douglas, Louis W. (Ariz.)
Douglass, John J. (Mass.)
Doutrich, Isaac H. (Pa.)
Dowell, Cassius C. (Iowa)
Doyle, Thomas A. (Ill.)
Drane, Herbert J. (Fla.)
Drewry, Patrick H. (Va.)
Driver, William J. (Ark.)
Dyer, Leonidas C. (Mo.)
Eaton, Charles A. (N. J.)
Edwards, Charles G. (Ga.)
Elliott, Richard N. (Ind.)
England, Edward T. (W. Va.)
Englebright, Harry L. (Calif.)
Eslick, Edward E. (Tenn.)
Estep, Harry A. (Pa.)
Evans, John M. (Mont.)
Evans, William E. (Calif.)
Faust, Charles L. (Mo)
Fenn, E. Hart (Conn.)
Fish, Hamilton, Jr. (N. Y.)
Fisher, Hubert F. (Tenn.)
Fitzgerald, Roy G. (Ohio)
Fitzgerald, W. Thomas (Ohio)
Fitzpatrick, James M. (N. Y.)
Fletcher, Brooks (Ohio)
Fort, Franklin W. (N. J.)
Foss, Frank H. (Mass.)
Frear, James A. (Wis.)
Free, Arthur M. (Calif.)
Freeman, Richard P. (Conn.)
French, Burton L. (Idaho)
Frothingham, Louis A. (Mass.)
Fulbright, James F. (Mo.)
Fulmer, Hampton P. (S. C.)
Furlow, Allen J. (Minn.)
Gallivan, James A. (Mass.)
Gambrill, Stephen W. (Md.)
Garber, Milton C. (Okla.)
Gardner, Frank (Ind.)
Garner, John N. (Tex.)
Garrett, Daniel E. (Tex.)
Garrett, Finis J. (Tenn.)
Gasque, Allard H. (S. C.)
Gibson, Ernest W. (Vt.)
Gifford, Charles L. (Mass.)
Gilbert, Ralph (Ky.)
Glynn, James P. (Conn.)
Golder, Benjamin M. (Pa.)
Goldsborough T. Alan (Md.)
Goodwin, Godfrey G. (Minn.)
Graham, George S. (Pa.)
Green, Robert A. (Fla.)
Green, William R. (Iowa)
Greenwood, Arthur H. (Ind.)
Gregory, William V. (Ky.)
Griest, William W. (Pa.)
Griffin, Anthony J. (N. Y.)
Guyer, Ulysses S. (Kans.)
Hadley, Lindley H. (Wash.)
Hale, Fletcher (N. H.)
Hall, Albert R. (Ind.)
Hall, Homer W. (Ill.)
Hall, Thomas (N. Dak.)
Hammer, William C. (N. C.)
Hancock, Clarence E. (N. Y.)
Hardy, Guy U. (Colo.)
Hare, Butler B. (S. C.)
Harrison, Thomas W. (Va.)
Hastings, William W. (Okla.)
Haugen, Gilbert N. (Iowa)
Hawley, Willis C. (Oreg.)
Hersey, Ira G. (Maine)
Hickey, Andrew J. (Ind.)
Hill, Lister (Ala.)
Hill, Samuel B. (Wash.)
Hoch, Homer (Kans.)
Hoffman, Harold G. (N. J.)
Hogg, David (Ind.)
Holaday, William P. (Ill.)
Hooper, Joseph L. (Mich.)
Hope, Clifford R. (Kans.)
Houston, Robert G. (Del.)
Howard, Edgar (Nebr.)
Howard, Everette B. (Okla.)
Huddleston, George (Ala.)
Hudson, Grant M. (Mich.)
Hudspeth, C. B. (Tex.)
Hughes, James A. (W. Va.)
Hull, Cordell (Tenn.)
Hull, Morton D. (Ill.)
Hull, William (Ill.)
Igoe, James T. (Ill.)
Irwin, Edward M. (Ill.)
Jacobstein, Meyer (N. Y.)
James, W. Frank (Mich.)
Jeffers, Lamar (Ala.)
Jenkins, Thomas A. (Ohio)
Johnson, Albert (Wash.)
Johnson, Jed (Okla.)

Johnson, Luther A. (Tex.)
Johnson, Noble J. (Ind.)
Johnson, Royal C. (S. Dak.)
Johnson, William R. (Ill.)
Jones, Marvin (Tex.)
Kading, Charles A. (Wis.)
Kahn, Florence P. (Calif.)
Kearns, Charles C. (Ohio)
Kelly, M. Clyde (Pa.)
Kemp, Bolivar E. (La.)
Kendall, Samuel A. (Pa.)
Kent, Everett (Pa.)
Kerr, John H. (N. C.)
Ketcham, John C. (Mich.)
Kiess, Edgar R. (Pa.)
Kincheloe, David H. (Ky.)
Kindred, John J. (N. Y.)
King, Edward J. (Ill.)
Knutson, Harold (Minn.)
Kopp, William F. (Iowa)
Korell, Franklin F. (Oreg.)
Kunz, Stanley H. (Ill.)
Kurtz, J. Banks (Pa.)
Kvale, O. J. (Minn.)
LaGuardia, Fiorello H. (N.Y.)
Lampert, Florian (Wis.)
Langley, Katherine (Ky.)
Lanham, Fritz G. (Tex.)
Lankford, William C. (Ga.)
Larsen, William W. (Ga.)
Lea, Clarence F. (Calif.)
Leatherwood, Elmer O. (Utah)
Leavitt, Scott (Mont.)
Leech, J. Russell (Pa.)
Lehlbach, Frederick R. (N.J.)
Letts, F. Dickinson (Iowa)
Lindsay, George W. (N. Y.)
Linthicum, J. Charles (Md.)
Longworth, Nicholas (Ohio)
Lowrey, Bill G. (Miss.)
Lozier, Ralph F. (Mo.)
Luce, Robert (Mass.)
Lyon, Homer L. (N. C.)
McClintic, James V. (Okla.)
McCormack, John W. (Mass.)
McDuffie, John (Ala.)
McFadden, Louis T. (Pa.)
MacGregor, Clarence (N. Y.)
McKeown, Tom D. (Okla.)
McLaughlin, James C. (Mich.)
McLeod, Clarence J. (Mich.)
McMillan, Thomas S. (S. C.)
McReynolds, Samuel D. (Tenn.)
McSwain, John J. (S. C.)
McSweeney, John (Ohio)
Maas, Melvin J. (Minn.)
Madden, Martin B. (Ill.)
Magrady, Frederick W. (Pa.)
Major, J. Earl (Ill.)
Major, Samuel C. (Mo.)
Manlove, Joe J. (Mo.)
Mansfield, Joseph J. (Tex.)
Mapes, Carl E. (Mich.)
Martin, Joseph W., Jr. (Mass.)
Martin, Whitmell P. (La.)
Mead, James M. (N. Y.)
Menges, Franklin (Pa.)
Merritt, Schuyler (Conn.)
Michaelson, M. Alfred (Ill.)
Michener, Earl C. (Mich.)
Miller, John F. (Wash.)
Milligan, Jacob L. (Mo.)
Monast, Louis (R. I.)
Montague, Andrew J. (Va.)
Mooney, Charles A. (Ohio)
Moore, C. Ellis (Ohio)
Moore, John W. (Ky.)
Moore, Paul J. (N. J.)
Moore, R. Walton (Va.)
Moorman, Henry D. (Ky.)
Morehead, John H. (Nebr.)
Morgan, William M. (Ohio)
Morin, John M. (Pa.)
Morrow, John (N. Mex.)
Murphy, Frank (Ohio)
Nelson, John E. (Maine)
Nelson, John M. (Wis.)
Nelson, William L. (Mo.)
Newton, Walter H. (Minn.)
Niedringhaus, Henry F. (Mo.)
Norton, John N. (Nebr.)
Norton, Mary T. (N. J.)
O'Brien, William S. (W. Va.)
O'Connell, David J. (N. Y.)
O'Connor, James (La.)
O'Connor, John J. (N. Y.)
Oldfield, William A. (Ark.)
Oliver, Frank (N. Y.)
Oliver, William B. (Ala.)
Palmer, Cyrus M. (Pa.)
Palmisano, Vincent L. (Md.)
Parker, James S. (N. Y.)
Parks, Tilman B. (Ark.)
Paterson, Lafayette L. (Ala.)
Peavey, Hubert H. (Wis.)
Peery, George C. (Va.)
Perkins, Randolph (N. J.)
Porter, Stephen G. (Pa.)
Pou, Edward W. (N. C.)
Prall, Anning S. (N. Y.)
Pratt, Harcourt J. (N. Y.)
Purnell, Fred S. (Ind.)
Quayle, John F. (N. Y.)
Quin, Percy E. (Miss.)
Ragon, Heartsill (Ark.)
Rainey, Henry T. (Ill.)
Ramseyer, C. William (Iowa)
Rankin, John E. (Miss.)
Ransley, Harry C. (Pa.)
Rathbone, Henry R. (Ill.)
Rayburn, Sam (Tex.)
Reece, B. Carroll (Tenn.)
Reed, Daniel A. (N. Y.)
Reed, James B. (Ark.)
Reid, Frank R. (Ill.)
Robinson, Thomas J. B. (Iowa)
Robsion, John M. (Ky.)
Rogers, Edith Nourse (Mass.)
Romjue, Milton A. (Mo.)
Rowbottom, Harry E. (Ind.)
Rubey, Thomas L. (Mo.)
Rutherford, Samuel (Ga.)
Sabath, Adolph J. (Ill.)
Sanders, Archie D. (N. Y.)
Sanders, Morgan G. (Tex.)
Sandlin, John N. (La.)
Schafer, John C. (Wis.)
Schneider, George J. (Wis.)
Sears, William J. (Fla.)
Sears, Willis G. (Nebr.)
Seger, George N. (N. J.)
Selvig, Conrad G. (Minn.)
Shallenberger, Ashton C. (Nebr.)
Shreve, Milton W. (Pa.)
Simmons, Robert G. (Nebr.)
Sinclair, James H. (N. Dak.)
Sinnott, Nicholas J. (Oreg.)
Sirovich, William I. (N. Y.)
Smith, Addison T. (Idaho)
Snell, Bertrand H. (N. Y.)
Somers, Andrew L. (N. Y.)
Speaks, John C. (Ohio)
Spearing, J. Zacharie (La.)
Sproul, Elliott W. (Ill.)
Sproul, William H. (Kans.)
Stalker, Gale H. (N. Y.)
Steagall, Henry B. (Ala.)
Stedman, Charles M. (N. C.)
Steele, Leslie J. (Ga.)
Stevenson, William F. (S. C.)
Stobbs, George R. (Mass.)
Strong, James G. (Kans.)
Strong, Nathan L. (Pa.)
Strother, James French (W. Va.)
Sullivan, Christopher D. (N. Y.)
Summers, John W. (Wash.)
Sumners, Hatton W. (Tex.)
Swank, Fletcher B. (Okla.)
Sweet, Thaddeus C. (N. Y.)
Swick, J. Howard (Pa.)
Swing, Philip D. (Calif.)
Taber, John (N. Y.)
Tarver, Malcolm C. (Ga.)
Tatgenhorst, Charles, Jr. (Ohio)
Taylor, Edward T. (Colo.)
Taylor, J. Will (Tenn.)
Temple, Henry W. (Pa.)
Thatcher, Maurice H. (Ky.)
Thompson, Charles J. (Ohio)
Thurston, Lloyd (Iowa)
Tillman, John N. (Ark.)
Tilson, John Q. (Conn.)
Timberlake, Charles B. (Colo.)
Tinkham, George Holden (Mass.)
Treadway, Allen T. (Mass.)
Tucker, Henry St. G. (Va.)
Underhill, Charles L. (Mass.)
Underwood, Mell G. (Ohio)
Updike, Ralph E., Sr. (Ind.)
Vestal, Albert H. (Ind.)
Vincent, Bird J. (Mich.)
Vincent, Earle W. (Iowa)
Vinson, Carl (Ga.)
Vinson, Frederick M. (Ky.)
Wainwright, J. Mayhew (N. Y.)
Ware, Orie S. (Ky.)
Warren, Lindsay (N. C.)
Wason, Edward H. (N. H.)
Watres, Laurence H. (Pa.)
Watson, Henry W. (Pa.)
Weaver, Zebulon (N. C.)
Welch, Richard J. (Calif.)
Weller, Royal H. (N. Y.)
Welsh, George A. (Pa.)
White, Hays B. (Kans.)
White, S. Harrison (Colo.)
White, Wallace H., Jr. (Maine)
Whitehead, Joseph (Va.)
Whittington, William M. (Miss.)
Wigglesworth, Richard B. (Mass.)
Williams, Clyde (Mo.)
Williams, Guinn (Tex.)
Williams, Thomas S. (Ill.)
Williamson, William (S. Dak.)
Wilson, Riley J. (La.)
Wilson, T. Webber (Miss.)
Wingo, Otis (Ark.)
Winter, Charles E. (Wyo.)
Wolfenden, James (Pa.)
Wolverton, Charles A. (N. J.)
Wood, William R. (Ind.)
Woodruff, Roy O. (Mich.)
Woodrum, Clifton A. (Va.)
Wright, William C. (Ga.)
Wurzbach, Harry M. (Tex.)
Wyant, Adam M. (Pa.)
Yates, Richard (Ill.)
Yon, Tom A. (Fla.)
Zihlman, Frederick N. (Md.)

The Seventy-first Congress (1929-31)

Longworth, Nicholas (Ohio) Speaker.

Abernethy, Charles L. (N. C.)
Ackerman, Ernest R. (N. J.)
Adkins, Charles (Ill.)
Aldrich, Richard S. (R. I.)
Allen, John C. (Ill.)
Allgood, Miles C. (Ala.)
Almon, Edward B. (Ala.)
Andresen, August H. (Minn.)
Andrew, A. Piatt (Mass.)
Arentz, Samuel S. (Nev.)
Arnold, William W. (Ill.)
Aswell, James B. (La.)
Auf der Heide, Oscar L. (N. J.)
Ayres, William A. (Kans.)
Bacharach, Isaac (N. J.)
Bachmann, Carl G. (W. Va.)
Bacon, Robert L. (N. Y.)
Baird, Joe E. (Ohio)
Bankhead, William B. (Ala.)
Barbour, Henry E. (Calif.)
Beck, James M. (Pa.)
Beedy, Carroll L. (Maine)
Beers, Edward M. (Pa.)
Bell, Thomas M. (Ga.)
Black, Loring M., Jr. (N.Y.)
Blackburn, Robert (Ky.)
Bland, Schuyler Otis (Va.)
Bloom, Sol (N. Y.)
Bohn, Frank P. (Mich.)
Bolton, Chester C. (Ohio)
Bowman, Frank L. (W. Va.)
Box, John C. (Tex.)
Boylan, John J. (N. Y.)
Brand, Charles (Ohio)
Brand, Charles H. (Ga.)
Briggs, Clay Stone (Tex.)
Brigham, Elbert S. (Vt.)
Britten, Fred A. (Ill.)
Browne, Edward E. (Wis.)
Browning, Gordon (Tenn.)
Brumm, George F. (Pa.)
Brunner, William F. (N. Y.)
Buchanan, James P. (Tex.)
Buckbee, John T. (Ill.)
Burdick, Clark (R. I.)
Burtness, Olger B. (N. Dak.)
Busby, Jeff (Miss.)
Butler, Robert R. (Oreg.)
Byrns, Joseph W. (Tenn.)
Cable, John L. (Ohio)
Campbell, Ed H. (Iowa)
Campbell, Guy E. (Pa.)
Canfield, Harry C. (Ind.)
Cannon, Clarence (Mo.)
Carew, John P. (N. Y.)
Carley, Patrick J. (N. Y.)
Carter, Albert E. (Calif.)
Carter, Vincent (Wyo.)
Cartwright, Wilburn (Okla.)
Celler Emanuel (N. Y.)
Chalmers, William W. (Ohio)
Chase, J. Mitchell (Pa.)
Chrindblom, Carl R. (Ill.)
Christgau, Victor (Minn.)
Christopherson, Charles A. (S. Dak.)
Clague, Frank (Minn.)
Clancy, Robert H. (Mich.)
Clark, J. Bayard (N. C.)
Clark, Linwood (Md.)
Clarke, John D. (N. Y.)
Cochran, John J. (Mo.)
Cochran, Thomas C. (Pa.)
Cole, Cyrenus (Iowa)
Collier, James W. (Miss.)
Collins, Ross A. (Miss.)
Colton, Don B. (Utah)
Connery, William P., Jr. (Mass.)
Connolly, James J. (Pa.)
Cooke, Edmund F. (N. Y.)
Cooper, Henry Allen (Wis.)
Cooper, Jere (Tenn.)
Cooper, John G. (Ohio)
Corning, Parker (N. Y.)
Cox, Edward E. (Ga.)
Coyle, William R. (Pa.)
Craddock, John D. (Ky.)
Crail, Joe (Calif.)
Crampton, Louis C. (Mich.)
Crisp, Charles R. (Ga.)
Cross, Oliver H. (Tex.)
Crosser, Robert (Ohio)
Crowther, Frank (N. Y.)
Culkin, Francis D. (N. Y.)
Cullen, Thomas H. (N. Y.)
Curry, Charles F. (Calif.)
Dallinger, Frederick W. (Mass.)
Darrow, George P. (Pa.)
Davenport, Frederick M. (N. Y.)
Davis, Ewin L. (Tenn.)
Dempsey, S. Wallace (N. Y.)
Denison, Edward E. (Ill.)
DePriest, Oscar (Ill.)
De Rouen, Rene L. (La.)
Dickinson, Lester J. (Iowa)
Dickstein, Samuel (N. Y.)
Dominick, Fred H. (S. C.)
Doughton, Robert L. (N. C.)
Douglas, Lewis W. (Ariz.)
Douglass, John J. (Mass.)
Doutrich, Isaac H. (Pa.)
Dowell, Cassius C. (Iowa)
Doxey, Wall (Miss.)
Doyle, Thomas A. (Ill.)
Drane, Herbert J. (Fla.)
Drewry, Patrick H. (Va.)
Driver, William J. (Ark.)
Dunbar, James W. (Ind.)
Dyer, Leonidas C. (Mo.)
Eaton, Charles A. (N. J.)
Eaton, William R. (Colo.)
Edwards, Charles G. (Ga.)
Elliott, Richard N. (Ind.)
Ellis, Edgar C. (Mo.)
Englebright, Harry L. (Calif.)
Eslick, Edward E. (Tenn.)
Estep, Harry A. (Pa.)
Esterly, Charles J. (Pa.)
Evans, John M. (Mont.)
Evans, William E. (Calif.)
Fenn, E. Hart (Conn.)
Fish, Hamilton, Jr. (N. Y.)
Fisher, Hubert F. (Tenn.)
Fitzgerald, Roy G. (Ohio)
Fitzpatrick, James M. (N. Y.)
Fort, Franklin W. (N. J.)
Foss, Frank H. (Mass.)
Frear, James A. (Wis.)
Free, Arthur M. (Calif.)
Freeman, Richard P. (Conn.)
French, Burton L. (Idaho)
Fuller, Claude A. (Ark.)
Fulmer, Hampton P. (S. C.)

Gambrill, Stephen W. (Md.)
Garber, Jacob A. (Va.)
Garber, Milton C. (Okla.)
Garner, John N. (Tex.)
Garrett, Daniel E. (Tex.)
Gasque, Allard H. (S. C.)
Gavagan, Joseph A. (N. Y.)
Gibson, Ernest W. (Vt.)
Gifford, Charles L. (Mass.)
Glover, D. D. (Ark.)
Glynn, James P. (Conn.)
Golder, Benjamin M. (Pa.)
Goldsborough, T. Alan (Md.)
Goodwin, Godfrey G. (Minn.)
Graham, George S. (Pa.)
Green, Robert A. (Fla.)
Greenwood, Arthur H. (Ind.)
Gregory, William V. (Ky.)
Griffin, Anthony J. (N. Y.)
Guyer, Ulysses S. (Kans.)
Hadley, Lindley H. (Wash.)
Hale, Fletcher (N. H.)
Hall, Albert R. (Ind.)
Hall, Homer W. (Ill.)
Hall, Robert S. (Miss.)
Hall, Thomas (N. Dak.)
Halsey, Thomas J. (Mo.)
Hammer, William C. (N. C.)
Hancock, Clarence E. (N. Y.)
Hardy, Guy U. (Colo.)
Hare, Butler B. (S. C.)
Hartley, Fred A., Jr. (N. J.)
Hastings, William W. (Okla.)
Haugen, Gilbert N. (Iowa)
Hawley, Willis C. (Oreg.)
Hess, William E. (Ohio)
Hickey, Andrew J. (Ind.)
Hill, Lister (Ala.)
Hill, Samuel B. (Wash.)
Hoch, Homer (Kans.)
Hoffman, Harold G. (N. J.)
Hogg, David (Ind.)
Holaday, William P. (Ill.)
Hooper, Joseph L. (Mich.)
Hope, Clifford R. (Kans.)
Hopkins, David (Mo.)
Houston, Robert G. (Del.)
Howard, Edgar (Nebr.)
Huddleston, George (Ala.)
Hudson, Grant M. (Mich.)
Hudspeth, C. B. (Tex.)
Hughes, James A. (W. Va.)
Hull, Cordell (Tenn.)
Hull, Merlin (Wis.)
Hull, Morton D. (Ill.)
Hull, William (Ill.)
Igoe, James T. (Ill.)
Irwin, Edward M. (Ill.)
James, W. Frank (Mich.)
Jeffers, Lamar (Ala.)
Jenkins, Thomas A. (Ohio)
Johnson, Albert (Wash.)
Johnson, Fred G. (Nebr.)
Johnson, Jed (Okla.)
Johnson, Luther A. (Tex.)
Johnson, Noble J. (Ind.)
Johnson, Royal C. (S. Dak.)
Johnson, William R. (Ill.)
Johnston, Rowland L. (Mo.)
Jonas, Charles A. (N. C.)
Jones, Marvin (Tex.)
Kading, Charles A. (Wis.)
Kahn, Florence P. (Calif.)
Kaynor, William K. (Mass.)
Kearns, Charles C. (Ohio)
Kelly, M. Clyde (Pa.)
Kemp, Bolivar E. (La.)
Kendall, Elva R. (Ky.)
Kendall, Samuel A. (Pa.)
Kerr, John H. (N. C.)
Ketcham, John C. (Mich.)
Kiefner, Charles E. (Mo.)
Kiess, Edgar R. (Pa.)
Kincheloe, David H. (Ky.)
Knutson, Harold (Minn.)
Kopp, William F. (Iowa)
Korell Franklin F. (Oreg.)
Kunz, Stanley H. (Ill.)
Kurtz, J. Banks (Pa.)
Kvale, Paul J. (Minn.)
LaGuardia, Fiorello H. (N.Y.)
Lambertson, William P. (Kans.)
Lampert, Florian (Wis.)
Langley, Katherine (Ky.)
Lanham, Fritz G. (Tenn.)
Lankford, Menalus (Va.)
Lankford, William C. (Ga.)
Larsen, William W. (Ga.)
Lea, Clarence F. (Calif.)
Leatherwood, Elmer O. (Utah)
Leavitt, Scott (Mont.)
Lee, R. Q. (Tex.)
Leech, J. Russell (Pa.)
Lehlbach, Frederick R. (N. J.)
Letts, F. Dickinson (Iowa)
Lindsay, George W. (N. Y.)
Linthicum, J. Charles (Md.)
Longworth, Nicholas (Ohio)
Lozier, Ralph F. (Mo.)
Luce, Robert (Mass.)
Ludlow, Louis (Ind.)
McClintic, James V. (Okla.)
McClintock, Charles B. (Ohio)
McCloskey, Augustus (Tex.)
McCormack, John W. (Mass.)
McCormick, Ruth H. (Ill.)
McDuffie, John (Ala.)
McFadden, Louis T. (Pa.)
McKeown, Tom D. (Okla.)
McLaughlin, James C. (Mich.)
McLeod, Clarence J. (Mich.)
McMillan, Thomas S. (S. C.)
McReynolds, Samuel D. (Tenn.)
McSwain, John J. (S. C.)
Maas, Melvin J. (Minn.)
Magrady, Frederick W. (Pa.)
Manlove, Joe J. (Mo.)
Mansfield, Joseph J. (Tex.)
Mapes, Carl E. (Mich.)
Martin, Joseph W., Jr. (Mass.)
Mead, James M. (N. Y.)
Menges, Franklin (Pa.)
Merritt, Schuyler (Conn.)
Michaelson, M. Alfred (Ill.)
Michener, Earl C. (Mich.)
Miller, John F. (Wash.)
Milligan, Jacob L. (Mo.)
Montague, Andrew J. (Va.)
Montet, Numa F. (La.)
Mooney, Charles A. (Ohio)
Moore, C. Ellis (Ohio)
Moore, John W. (Ky.)
Moore, Paul J. (N. J.)
Moore, R. Walton (Va.)
Morehead, John H. (Nebr.)
Morgan, William M. (Ohio)
Mouser, Grant E. (Ohio)
Murphy, Frank (Ohio)
Nelson, John E. (Maine)
Nelson, John M. (Wis.)
Nelson, William L. (Mo.)
Newhall, J. Lincoln (Ky.)
Niedringhaus, Henry F. (Mo.)
Nolan, William I. (Minn.)
Norton, Mary T. (N. J.)
O'Connell, David J. (N. Y.)
O'Connell, Jeremiah E. (R. I.)
O'Connor, Charles (Okla.)
O'Connor, James (La.)
O'Connor, John J. (N. Y.)
Oldfield, Pearl P. (Ark.)
Oliver, Frank (N. Y.)
Oliver, William B. (Ala.)
Owen, Ruth Bryan (Fla.)
Palmer, John W. (Mo.)
Palmisano, Vincent L. (Md.)
Parker, James S. (N. Y.)
Parks, Tilman B. (Ark.)
Patman, Wright (Tex.)
Patterson, LaFayette L. (Ala.)
Peavey, Hubert H. (Wis.)
Perkins, Randolph (N. J.)
Pittenger, William A. (Minn.)
Porter, Stephen G. (Pa.)
Pou, Edward W. (N. C.)
Prall, Anning S. (N. Y.)
Pratt, Harcourt J. (N. Y.)
Pratt, Ruth (N. Y.)
Pritchard, George M. (N. C.)
Purnell, Fred S. (Ind.)
Quayle, John F. (N. Y.)
Quin, Percy E. (Miss.)
Ragon, Heartsill (Ark.)
Rainey, Henry T. (Ill.)
Ramey, Frank M. (Ill.)
Ramseyer, C. William (Iowa)
Ramspeck, Robert (Ga.)
Rankin, John E. (Miss.)
Ransley, Harry C. (Pa.)
Rayburn, Sam (Tex.)
Reece, B. Carroll (Tenn.)
Reed, Daniel A. (N. Y.)
Reid, Frank R. (Ill.)
Robinson, Thomas J. B. (Iowa)
Robsion, John M. (Ky.)
Rogers, Edith Nourse (Mass.)
Romjue, Milton A. (Mo.)
Rowbottom, Harry E. (Ind.)
Rutherford, Samuel (Ga.)
Sabath, Adolph J. (Ill.)
Sanders, Archie D. (N. Y.)
Sanders, Morgan G. (Tex.)
Sandlin, John N. (La.)
Shafer, John C. (Wis.)
Schneider, George J. (Wis.)
Sears, Willis G. (Nebr.)
Seger, George N. (N. J.)
Seiberling, Francis (Ohio)
Selvig, Conrad G. (Minn.)
Shaffer, Joseph C. (Va.)
Short, Dewey (Mo.)
Shott, Hugh Ike (W. Va.)
Shreve, Milton W. (Pa.)
Simmons, Robert G. (Nebr.)
Sims, Albert G. (N. Mex.)
Sinclair, James H. (N. Dak.)
Sirovich, William I. (N. Y.)
Sloan, Charles H. (Nebr.)
Smith, Addison T. (Idaho)
Smith, Joe L. (W. Va.)
Snell, Bertrand H. (N. Y.)
Snow, Donald F. (Maine)
Somers, Andrew L. (N. Y.)
Sparks, Charles I. (Kans.)
Speaks, John C. (Ohio)
Spearing, J. Zacharie (La.)
Sproul, Elliott W. (Ill.)
Sproul, William H. (Kans.)
Stafford, William H. (Wis.)
Stalker, Gale H. (N. Y.)
Steagall, Henry B. (Ala.)
Stedman, Charles M. (N. C.)
Stevenson, William F. (S. C.)
Stobbs, George R. (Mass.)
Stone, Ulysses S. (Okla.)
Strong, James G. (Kans.)
Strong, Nathan L. (Pa.)
Sullivan, Christopher D. (N. Y.)
Sullivan, Patrick J. (Pa.)
Summers, John W. (Wash.)
Sumners, Hatton W. (Tex.)
Swanson, Charles E. (Iowa)
Swick, J. Howard (Pa.)
Swing, Philip D. (Calif.)
Taber, John (N. Y.)
Tarver, Malcolm C. (Ga.)
Taylor, Edward T. (Colo.)
Taylor, J. Will (Tenn.)
Temple, Henry W. (Pa.)
Thatcher, Maurice H. (Ky.)
Thompson, Charles J. (Ohio)
Thurston, Lloyd (Iowa)
Tilson, John Q. (Conn.)
Timberlake, Charles B. (Colo.)
Tinkham, George H. (Mass.)
Treadway, Allen T. (Mass.)
Tucker, Henry St. G. (Va.)
Turpin, C. Murray (Pa.)
Underhill, Charles L. (Mass.)
Underwood, Mell G. (Ohio)
Vestal, Albert H. (Ind.)
Vincent, Bird J. (Mich.)
Vinson, Carl (Ga.)
Wainwright, J. Mayhew (N. Y.)
Walker, Lewis L. (Ky.)
Warren, Lindsay C. (N. C.)
Wason, Edward H. (N. H.)
Watres, Laurence H. (Pa.)
Watson, Henry W. (Pa.)
Welch, Richard J. (Calif.)
Welsh, George A. (Pa.)
White, Wallace H., Jr. (Maine)
Whitehead, Joseph (Va.)
Whitley, James L. (N. Y.)
Whittington, William M. (Miss.)
Wigglesworth, Richard B. (Mass.)
Williams, Guinn (Tex.)
Williamson, William (S. Dak.)
Wilson, Riley J. (La.)
Wingo, Effiegene (Ark.)
Wingo, Otis (Ark.)
Wolfenden, James (Pa.)
Wolverton, Charles A. (N. J.)
Wolverton, John M. (W. Va.)
Wood, William R. (Ind.)
Woodruff, Roy O. (Mich.)
Woodrum, Clifton A. (Va.)
Wright, William C. (Ga.)
Wyant, Adam M. (Pa.)
Yates, Richard (Ill.)
Yon, Thomas A. (Fla.)
Zihlman, Frederick N. (Md.)

The Seventy-second Congress (1931-33)

Garner, John N. (Tex.)
Speaker.

Abernethy, Charles L. (N. C.)
Adkins, Charles (Ill.)
Aldrich, Richard S. (R. I.)
Allen, John C. (Ill.)
Allgood, Miles C. (Ala.)
Almon, Edward B. (Ala.)
Amlie, Thomas R. (Wis.)
Andresen, August H. (Minn.)
Andrew, A. Piatt (Mass.)
Andrews, Walter G. (N. Y.)
Arentz, Samuel S. (Nev.)
Arnold, William W. (Ill.)
Auf der Heide, Oscar L. (N. J.)
Ayres, William A. (Kans.)
Bacharach, Isaac (N. J.)
Bachmann, Carl G. (W. Va.)
Bacon, Robert L. (N. Y.)
Baldrige, Malcolm B. (Nebr.)
Bankhead, William B. (Ala.)
Barbour, Henry E. (Calif.)
Barton, William E. (Mo.)
Beam, Harry P. (Ill.)
Beck, James M. (Pa.)
Beedy, Carroll L. (Maine)
Beers, Edward M. (Pa.)
Black, Loring M., Jr. (N. Y.)
Bland, Schuyler O. (Va.)
Blanton, Thomas L. (Tex.)
Bloom, Sol (N. Y.)
Boehne, John W., Jr. (Ind.)
Bohn, Frank P. (Mich.)
Boileau, Gerald J. (Wis.)
Boland, Patrick J. (Pa.)
Bolton, Chester C. (Ohio)
Bowman, Frank L. (W. Va.)
Boylan, John J. (N. Y.)
Brand, Charles (Ohio)
Brand, Charles H. (Ga.)
Briggs, Clay Stone (Tex.)
Britten, Fred A. (Ill.)
Browning, Gordon (Tenn.)
Brumm, George F. (Pa.)
Brunner, William F. (N. Y.)
Buchanan, James P. (Tex.)
Buckbee, John T. (Ill.)
Bulwinkle, Alfred L. (N. C.)
Burch, Thomas G. (Va.)
Burdick, Clark (R. I.)
Burtness, Olger B. (N. Dak.)
Busby, Jeff (Miss.)
Butler, Robert R. (Oreg.)
Byrns, Joseph W. (Tenn.)
Cable, John L. (Ohio)
Campbell, Ed H. (Iowa)
Campbell, Guy E. (Pa.)
Canfield, Harry C. (Ind.)
Cannon, Clarence (Mo.)
Carden, Cap R. (Ky.)
Carley, Patrick J. (N. Y.)
Carter, Albert E. (Calif.)
Carter, Vincent (Wyo.)
Cartwright, Wilburn (Okla.)
Cary, Glover H. (Ky.)
Cavicchia, Peter A. (N. J.)
Celler, Emanuel (N. Y.)
Chapman, Virgil (Ky.)
Chase, J. Mitchell (Pa.)
Chavez, Dennis (N. Mex.)
Chindblom, Carl R. (Ill.)
Chiperfield, Burnett M. (Ill.)
Christgau, Victor (Minn.)
Christopherson, C. A. (S.Dak.)
Clague, Frank (Minn.)
Clancy, Robert H. (Mich.)
Clark, J. Bayard (N. C.)
Clarke, John D. (N. Y.)
Cochran, John J. (Mo.)
Cochran, Thomas C. (Pa.)
Cole, Cyrenus (Iowa)
Cole, William P., Jr. (Md.)
Collier, James W. (Miss.)
Collins, Ross A. (Miss.)
Colton, Don B. (Utah)
Condon, Francis B. (R. I.)
Connery, William P., Jr. (Mass.)
Connelly, James J. (Pa.)
Cooke, Edmund F. (N. Y.)
Cooper, Jere (Tenn.)
Cooper, John G. (Ohio)
Corning, Parker (N. Y.)

Cox, Edward E. (Ga.)
Coyle, William R. (Pa.)
Crail, Joe (Calif.)
Crisp, Charles R. (Ga.)
Cross, Oliver H. (Tex.)
Crosser, Robert (Ohio)
Crowe, Eugene B. (Ind.)
Crowther, Frank (N. Y.)
Crump, Edward H. (Tenn.)
Culkin, Francis D. (N. Y.)
Cullen, Thomas H. (N. Y.)
Curry, Charles F. (Calif.)
Dallinger, Fred W. (Mass.)
Darrow, George P. (Pa.)
Davenport, Fred M. (N. Y.)
Davis, Ewin L. (Tenn.)
Delaney, John J. (N. Y.)
DePriest, Oscar (Ill.)
DeRouen, Rene L. (La.)
Dickinson, Clement C. (Mo.)
Dickstein, Samuel (N. Y.)
Dies, Martin, Jr. (Tex.)
Dieterich, William H. (Ill.)
Disney, Wesley E. (Okla.)
Dominick, Fred H. (S. C.)
Doughton, Robert L. (N. C.)
Douglas, Lewis W. (Ariz.)
Douglass, John J. (Mass.)
Doutrich, Isaac H. (Pa.)
Dowell, Cassius C. (Iowa)
Doxey, Wall (Miss.)
Drane, Herbert J. (Fla.)
Drewry, Patrick H. (Va.)
Driver, William J. (Ark.)
Dyer, Leonidas C. (Mo.)
Eaton, Charles A. (N. J.)
Eaton, William R. (Colo.)
Englebright, Harry L. (Calif.)
Erk, Edmund F. (Pa.)
Eslick, Edward E. (Tenn.)
Estep, Harry A. (Pa.)
Evans, John M. (Mont.)
Evans, William E. (Calif.)
Fernandez, Joachim O. (La.)
Fiesinger, William L. (Ohio)
Finley, Charles (Ky.)
Fish, Hamilton, Jr. (N. Y.)
Fishburne, John W. (Va.)
Fitzpatrick, James M. (N. Y.)
Flannagan, John W., Jr. (Va.)
Foss, Frank H. (Mass.)
Frear, James A. (Wis.)
Free, Arthur M. (Calif.)
Freeman, Richard P. (Conn.)
French, Burton L. (Idaho)
Fulbright, James F. (Mo.)
Fuller, Claude A. (Ark.)
Fulmer, Hampton R. (S. C.)
Gambrill, Stephen W. (Md.)
Garber, Milton C. (Okla.)
Garner, John N. (Tex.)
Garrett, Daniel E. (Tex.)
Gasque, Allard H. (S. C.)
Gavagan, Joseph A. (N. Y.)
Gibson, Ernest W. (Vt.)
Gifford, Charles L. (Mass.)
Gilbert, Ralph (Ky.)
Gilchrist, Fred C. (Iowa)
Gillen, Courtland C. (Ind.)
Glover, D. D. (Ark.)
Golder, Benjamin M. (Pa.)
Goldsborough, T. Alan (Md.)
Goodwin, Godfrey G. (Minn.)
Goss, Edward W. (Conn.)
Granata, Peter C. (Ill.)
Granfield, William J. (Mass.)
Green, Robert A. (Fla.)
Greenwood, Arthur H. (Ind.)
Gregory, William V. (Ky.)
Griffin, Anthony J. (N. Y.)
Griswold, Glenn (Ind.)
Guyer, Ulysses S. (Kans.)
Hadley, Lindley H. (Wash.)
Haines, Harry L. (Pa.)
Hall, Homer W. (Ill.)
Hall, Robert S. (Miss.)
Hall, Thomas (N. Dak.)
Hancock, Clarence E. (N. Y.)
Hancock, Frank W. (N. C.)
Hardy, Guy U. (Colo.)
Hare, Butler B. (S. C.)
Harlan, Byron B. (Ohio)
Hart, Michael J. (Mich.)
Hartley, Fred A., Jr. (N. J.)
Hastings, William W. (Okla.)
Haugen, Gilbert N. (Iowa)
Hawley, Willis C. (Oreg.)
Hess, William E. (Ohio)
Hill, Lister (Ala.)
Hill, Samuel B. (Wash.)
Hoch, Homer (Kans.)
Hogg, David (Ind.)
Hogg, Robert L. (W. Va.)
Holaday, William P. (Ill.)
Hollister, John B. (Ohio)
Holmes, Pehr G. (Mass.)
Hooper, Joseph L. (Mich.)
Hope, Clifford R. (Kans.)
Hopkins, David (Mo.)
Horner, Lynn S. (W. Va.)
Horr, Ralph A. (Wash.)
Houston, Robert G. (Del.)
Howard, Edgar (Nebr.)
Huddleston, George (Ala.)
Hull, Morton D. (Ill.)
Hull, William E. (Ill.)
Igoe, James T. (Ill.)
Jacobsen, Bernhard M. (Iowa)
James, W. Frank (Mich.)
Jeffers, Lamar (Ala.)
Jenkins, Thomas A. (Ohio)
Johnson, Albert (Wash.)
Johnson, Jed (Okla.)
Johnson, Luther A. (Tex.)
Johnson, Robert D. (Mo.)
Johnson, Royal C. (S. Dak.)
Johnson, William R. (Ill.)
Jones, Marvin (Tex.)
Kading, Charles A. (Wis.)
Kahn, Florence P. (Calif.)
Kapp, W. F. (Iowa)
Karch, Charles A. (Ill.)
Keller, Kent E. (Ill.)
Kelly, Clyde (Pa.)
Kelly, Edward A. (Ill.)
Kemp, Bolivar E. (La.)
Kendall, Samuel A. (Pa.)
Kennedy, Martin J. (N. Y.)
Kerr, John H. (N. C.)
Ketcham, John C. (Mich.)
Kinzer, J. Roland (Pa.)
Kleberg, Richard M. (Tex.)
Kniffin, Frank C. (Ohio)
Knutson, Harold (Minn.)
Kurtz, J. Banks (Pa.)
Kvale, Paul J. (Minn.)
LaGuardia, Fiorello H. (N.Y.)
Lambertson, William P. (Kans.)
Lambeth, J. Walter (N. C.)
Lamneck, Arthur P. (Ohio)
Lanham, Fritz G. (Tex.)
Lankford, Menalcus (Va.)
Lankford, William C. (Ga.)
Larrabee, William H. (Ind.)
Larsen, William W. (Ga.)
Lea, Clarence F. (Calif.)
Leavitt, Scott (Mont.)
Leech, J. Russell (Pa.)
Lehlbach, Frederick R. (N. J.)
Lewis, David J. (Md.)
Lichtenwalner, Norton (Pa.)
Lindsay, George W. (N. Y.)
Linthicum, J. Charles (Md.)
Lonergan, Augustine (Conn.)
Loofbourow, Fred C. (Utah)
Lovette, O. B. (Tenn.)
Lozier, Ralph F. (Mo.)
Luce, Robert (Mass.)
Ludlow, Louis (Ind.)
McClintic, James V. (Okla.)
McClintock, Charles B. (Ohio)
McCormack, John W. (Mass.)
McDuffie, John (Ala.)
McFadden, Louis T. (Pa.)
McGugin, Harold (Kans.)
McKeown, Tom D. (Okla.)
McLaughlin, James C. (Mich.)
McLeod, Clarence J. (Mich.)
McMillan, Thomas S. (S. C.)
McReynolds, Samuel D. (Tenn.)
McSwain, John J. (S. C.)
Magrady, Fred W. (Pa.)
Major, J. Earl (Ill.)
Maloney, Paul H. (La.)
Manlove, Joe J. (Mo.)
Mansfield, Joseph J. (Tex.)
Mapes, Carl E. (Mich.)
Martin, Charles H. (Oreg.)
Martin, Joseph W., Jr. (Mass.)
Mass, Melvin J. (Minn.)
May, Andrew J. (Ky.)
Mead, James M. (N. Y.)
Michener, Earl C. (Mich.)
Millard, Charles D. (N. Y.)
Miller, John E. (Ark.)
Milligan, Jacob L. (Mo.)
Mitchell, John R. (Tenn.)
Montague, Andrew J. (Va.)
Montet, Numa F. (La.)
Moore, C. Ellis (Ohio)
Moore, John W. (Ky.)
Morehead, John H. (Nebr.)
Mouser, Grant E., Jr. (Ohio)
Murphy, Frank (Ohio)
Nelson, John E. (Maine)
Nelson, John M. (Wis.)
Nelson, William L. (Mo.)
Niedringhaus, Henry F. (Mo.)
Nolan, William I. (Minn.)
Norton, John N. (Nebr.)
Norton, Mary T. (N. J.)
O'Connor, John J. (N. Y.)
Oliver, Frank (N. Y.)
Oliver, William B. (Ala.)
Overton, John H. (La.)
Owen, Ruth Bryan (Fla.)
Palmisano, Vincent L. (Md.)
Parker, Homer C. (Ga.)
Parker, James S. (N. Y.)
Parks, Tilman B. (Ark.)
Parsons, Claude V. (Ill.)
Partridge, Donald B. (Maine)
Patman, Wright (Tex.)
Patterson, L. L. (Ala.)
Peavey, Hubert H. (Wis.)
Perkins, Randolph (N. J.)
Person, Seymour H. (Mich.)
Pettengill, Samuel B. (Ind.)
Pittenger, William A. (Minn.)
Polk, James G. (Ohio)
Pou, Edward W. (N. C.)
Prall, Anning S. (N. Y.)
Pratt, Harcourt J. (N. Y.)
Pratt, Ruth (N. Y.)
Purnell, Fred S. (Ind.)
Quin, Percy E. (Miss.)
Ragon, Heartsill (Ark.)
Rainey, Henry T. (Ill.)
Ramseyer, C. William (Iowa)
Ramspeck, Robert (Ga.)
Rankin, John E. (Miss.)
Ransley, Harry C. (Pa.)
Rayburn, Sam (Tex.)
Reed, Daniel A. (N. Y.)
Reid, Frank R. (Ill.)
Reilly, Michael K. (Wis.)
Rich, Robert F. (Pa.)
Robinson, Thomas J. B. (Iowa)
Rogers, Edith Nourse (Mass.)
Romjue, Milton A. (Mo.)
Rudd, Stephen A. (N. Y.)
Rutherford, Samuel (Ga.)
Sabath, Adolph J. (Ill.)
Sanders, Archie D. (N. Y.)
Sanders, Morgan G. (Tex.)
Sandlin, John N. (La.)
Schafer, John C. (Wis.)
Schneider, George J. (Wis.)
Schuetz, Leonard W. (Ill.)
Seger, George N. (N. J.)
Seiberling, Francis (Ohio)
Selvig, Conrad G. (Minn.)
Shallenberger, Ashton C. (Nebr.)
Shannon, Joseph B. (Mo.)
Shott, Hugh Ike (W. Va.)
Shreve, Milton W. (Pa.)
Simmons, Robert G. (Nebr.)
Sinclair, James H. (N. Dak.)
Sirovich, William I. (N. Y.)
Smith, Addison T. (Idaho)
Smith, Howard W. (Va.)
Smith, Joe L. (W. Va.)
Snell, Bertrand H. (N. Y.)
Snow, Donald F. (Maine)
Somers, Andrew L. (N. Y.)
Sparks, Charles I. (Kans.)
Spence, Brent (Ky.)
Stafford, William H. (Wis.)
Stalker, Gale H. (N. Y.)
Steagall, Henry B. (Ala.)
Stevenson, William F. (S. C.)
Stewart, Percy H. (N. J.)
Stokes, Edward L. (Pa.)
Strong, James G. (Kans.)
Strong, Nathan L. (Pa.)
Sullivan, Christopher D. (N. Y.)
Sullivan, Patrick J. (Pa.)
Summners, John W. (Wash.)
Sumners, Hatton W. (Tex.)
Sutphin, William H. (N. J.)
Swank, Fletcher B. (Okla.)
Swanson, Charles E. (Iowa)
Sweeney, Martin L. (Ohio)
Swick, J. Howard (Pa.)
Swing, Phil D. (Calif.)
Taber, John (N. Y.)
Tarver, Malcolm C. (Ga.)
Taylor, Edward T. (Colo.)
Taylor, J. Will (Tenn.)
Temple, Henry W. (Pa.)
Thatcher, Maurice H. (Ky.)
Thomason, R. Ewing (Tex.)
Thurston, Lloyd (Iowa)
Tierney, William L. (Conn.)
Tilson, John Q. (Conn.)
Timberlake, Charles B. (Colo.)
Tinkham, George H. (Mass.)
Treadway, Allen T. (Mass.)
Tucker, Henry St. G. (Va.)
Turpin, C. Murray (Pa.)
Underhill, Charles L. (Mass.)
Underwood, Mell G. (Ohio)
Vestal, Albert H. (Ind.)
Vinson, Carl (Ga.)
Vinson, Frederick M. (Ky.)
Warren, Lindsay C. (N. C.)
Wason, Edward H. (N. H.)
Watson, Henry W. (Pa.)
Weaver, Zebulon (N. C.)
Weeks, John E. (Vt.)
Welch, Richard J. (Calif.)
Welsh, George A. (Pa.)
West, Charles (Ohio)
White, Wilbur M. (Ohio)
Whitley, James L. (N. Y.)
Whittington, William M. (Miss.)
Wigglesworth, Richard B. (Mass.)
Williams, Clyde (Mo.)
Williams, Guinn (Tex.)
Williamson, William (S. Dak.)
Wilson, Riley J. (La.)
Wingo, Effiegene (Ark.)
Withrow, Gardner R. (Wis.)
Wolcott, Jesse P. (Mich.)
Wolfenden, James (Pa.)
Wolverton, Charles A. (N. J.)
Wood, John S. (Ga.)
Wood, William R. (Ind.)
Woodruff, Roy O. (Mich.)
Woodrum, Clifton A. (Va.)
Wright, William C. (Ga.)
Wyant, Adam M. (Pa.)
Yates, Richard (Ill.)
Yon, Tom A. (Fla.)

The Seventy-third Congress (1933-35)

Rainey, Henry T. (Ill.) Speaker.

Abernethy, Charles L. (N. C.)
Adair, J. LeRoy (Ill.)
Adams, Wilbur L. (Del.)
Allen, Leo E. (Ill.)
Allgood, Miles C. (Ala.)
Almon, Edward B. (Ala.)
Andrew, A. Piatt (Mass.)
Andrews, Walter G. (N. Y.)
Arens, Henry (Minn.)
Arnold, William W. (Ill.)
Auf der Heide, Oscar L. (N. J.)
Ayers, Roy E. (Mont.)
Ayres, William A. (Kans.)
Bacharach, Isaac (N. J.)
Bacon, Robert L. (N. Y.)
Bailey, Joseph W. (Tex.)
Bakewell, Charles M. (Conn.)
Bankhead, William B. (Ala.)
Beam, Harry P. (Ill.)
Beck, James M. (Pa.)
Beedy, Carroll L. (Maine)
Beiter, Alfred F. (N. Y.)
Berlin, William M. (Pa.)
Biermann, Fred (Iowa)
Black, Loring M., Jr. (N. Y.)
Blanchard, George W. (Wis.)
Bland, Schuyler Otis (Va.)
Blanton, Thomas L. (Tex.)
Bloom, Sol (N. Y.)
Boehne, John W., Jr. (Ind.)
Boileau, Gerald J. (Wis.)
Boland, Patrick J. (Pa.)
Bolton, Chester C. (Ohio)
Boylan, John J. (N. Y.)
Brennan, Martin A. (Ill.)
Britten, Fred A. (Ill.)

Brooks, J. Twing (Pa.)
Brown, John Young (Ky.)
Brown, Paul (Ga.)
Brown, Prentiss M. (Mich.)
Browning, Gordon (Tenn.)
Brumm, George F. (Pa.)
Brunner, William F. (N. Y.)
Buchanan, James P. (Tex.)
Buck, Frank H. (Calif.)
Buckbee, John T. (Ill.)
Bulwinkle, Alfred L. (N. C.)
Burch, Thomas G. (Va.)
Burke, Edward R. (Nebr.)
Burke, John H. (Calif.)
Burnham, George (Calif.)
Busby, Jeff (Miss.)
Byrns, Joseph W. (Tenn.)
Cady, Claude E. (Mich.)
Caldwell, Millard F. (Fla.)
Cannon, Clarence (Mo.)
Cannon, Raymond J. (Wis.)
Carden, Cap R. (Ky.)
Carley, Patrick J. (N. Y.)
Carmichael, Archibald H. (Ala.)
Carpenter, Randolph (Kans.)
Carpenter, Terry M. (Nebr.)
Carter, Albert E. (Calif.)
Carter, Vincent (Wyo.)
Cartwright, Wilburn (Okla.)
Cary, Glover H. (Ky.)
Castellow, Bryant T. (Ga.)
Cavicchia, Peter A. (N. J.)
Celler, Emanuel (N. Y.)
Chapman, Virgil (Ky.)
Chase, Ray P. (Minn.)
Chaves, Dennis (N. Mex.)
Christianson, Theodore (Minn.)
Church, Denver S. (Calif.)
Claiborne, James R. (Mo.)
Clark, J. Bayard (N. C.)
Clarke, John D. (N. Y.)
Cochran, John J. (Mo.)
Cochran, Thomas C. (Pa.)
Coffin, Thomas C. (Idaho)
Colden, Charles J. (Calif.)
Cole, William P., Jr. (Md.)
Collins, Ross A. (Miss.)
Collins, Samuel (Calif.)
Colmer, William M. (Miss.)
Condon, Francis B. (R. I.)
Connery, William P. (Mass.)
Connolly, James J. (Pa.)
Cooper, Jere (Tenn.)
Cooper, John G. (Ohio)
Corning, Parker (N. Y.)
Cox, Edward E. (Ga.)
Cravens, Ben (Ark.)
Crosby, Charles N. (Pa.)
Cross, Oliver H. (Tex.)
Crosser, Robert (Ohio)
Crowe, Eugene B. (Ind.)
Crowther, Frank (N. Y.)
Crump, Edward H. (Tenn.)
Culkin, Francis D. (N. Y.)
Cullen, Thomas H. (N. Y.)
Cummings, Fred (Colo.)
Darden, Colgate W., Jr. (Va.)
Darrow, George P. (Pa.)
Dear, Cleveland (La.)
Deen, Braswell (Ga.)
Delaney, John J. (N. Y.)
DePriest, Oscar (Ill.)
DeRouen, Rene L. (La.)
Dickinson, Clement C. (Mo.)
Dickstein, Samuel (N. Y.)
Dies, Martin (Tex.)
Dingell, John D. (Mich.)
Dirksen, Everett M. (Ill.)
Disney, Wesley E. (Okla.)
Ditter, J. William (Pa.)
Dobbins, Donald C. (Ill.)
Dockweiler, John F. (Calif.)
Dondero, George A. (Mich.)
Doughton, Robert L. (N. C.)
Douglass, John J. (Mass.)
Doutrich, Isaac H. (Pa.)
Dowell, Cassius C. (Iowa)
Doxey, Wall (Miss.)
Drewry, Patrick H. (Va.)
Driver, William J. (Ark.)
Duffey, Warren J. (Ohio)
Duncan, Richard M. (Mo.)
Dunn, Matthew A. (Pa.)
Durgan, George R. (Ind.)
Eagle, Joe H. (Tex.)
Eaton, Charles A. (N. J.)
Edmiston, Andrew, Jr. (W. Va.)
Edmonds, George W. (Pa.)
Eicher, Edward C. (Iowa)
Ellenbogen, Henry (Pa.)
Ellzey, Russell (Miss.)
Eltse, Ralph R. (Calif.)
Englebright, Harry L. (Calif.)
Evans, William E. (Calif.)
Faddis, Charles I. (Pa.)
Farley, James I. (Ind.)
Fernandez, Joachim O. (La.)
Fiesinger, William L. (Ohio)
Fish, Hamilton, Jr. (N. Y.)
Fitzgibbons, John (N. Y.)
Fitzpatrick, James M. (N. Y.)
Flannagan, John W., Jr. (Va.)
Fletcher, Brooks (Ohio)
Focht, Benjamin K. (Pa.)
Ford, Thomas F. (Calif.
Foss, Frank H. (Mass.)
Foulkes, George (Mich.)
Frear, James A. (Wis.)
Frey, Oliver W. (Pa.)
Fuller, Claude A. (Ark.)
Fulmer, Hampton P. (S. C.)
Gambrill, Stephen W. (Md.)
Gasque, Allard H. (S. C.)
Gavagan, Joseph A. (N. Y.)
Gibson, Ernest W. (Vt.)
Gifford, Charles L. (Mass.)
Gilchrist, Fred C. (Iowa)
Gillespie, Frank (Ill.)
Gillette, Guy M. (Iowa)
Glover, D. D. (Ark.)
Goldsborough, T. Alan (Md.)
Goodwin, Philip A. (N. Y.)
Goss, Edward W. (Conn.)
Granfield, William J. (Mass.)
Gray, Finly H. (Ind.)
Green, Robert A. (Fla.)
Greenway, Isabella (Ariz.)
Greenwood, Arthur H. (Ind.)
Gregory, William V. (Ky.)
Griffin, Anthony J. (N. Y.)
Griswold, Glenn (Ind.)
Guyer, Ulysses S. (Kans.)
Haines, Harry L. (Pa.)
Hamilton, Finley (Ky.))
Hancock, Clarence E. (N. Y.)
Hancock, Frank (N. C.)
Harlan, Byron B. (Ohio)
Hart, Michael J. (Mich.)
Harter, Dow W. (Ohio)
Hartley, Fred A., Jr. (N. J.)
Hastings, William W. (Okla.)
Healey, Arthur D. (Mass.)
Henney, Charles W. (Wis.)
Hess, William E. (Ohio)
Higgins, William L. (Conn.)
Hildebrandt, Fred H. (S.Dak.)
Hill, Knute (Wash.)
Hill, Lister (Ala.)
Hill, Samuel B. (Wash.)
Hoeppel, John H. (Calif.)
Hoidale, Einar (Minn.)
Hollister, John B. (Ohio)
Holmes, Pehr G. (Mass.)
Hooper, Joseph L. (Mich.)
Hope, Clifford R. (Kans.)
Hornor, Lynn S. (W. Va.)
Howard, Edgar (Nebr.)
Huddleston, George (Ala.)
Hughes, James (Wis.)
Imhoff, Lawrence E. (Ohio)
Jacobsen, Bernard M. (Iowa)
James, W. Frank (Mich.)
Jeffers, Lamar (Ala.)
Jenckes, Virginia E. (Ind.)
Jenkins, Thomas A. (Ohio)
Johnson, George W. (W. Va.)
Johnson, Jed (Okla.)
Johnson, Luther A. (Tex.)
Johnson, Magnus (Minn.)
Jones, Marvin (Tex.)
Kahn, Florence P. (Calif.)
Kee, John (W. Va.)
Keller, Kent E. (Ill.)
Kelly, Clyde (Pa.)
Kelly, Edward A. (Ill.)
Kemp, Bolivar E. (La.)
Kennedy, Ambrose J. (Md.)
Kennedy, Martin J. (N. Y.)
Kenney, Edward A. (N. J.)
Kerr, John H. (N. C.)
Kinzer, J. Roland (Pa.)
Kleberg, Richard M. (Tex.)
Kloeb, Frank L. (Ohio)
Kniffin, Frank C. (Ohio)
Knutson, Harold (Minn.)
Kocialkowski, Leo (Ill.)
Koppleman, Herman P. (Conn.)
Kramer, Charles (Calif.)
Kurtz, J. Banks (Pa.)
Kvale, Paul J. (Minn.)
Lambertson, William P. (Kans.)
Lambeth, J. Walter (N. C.)
Lamneck, Arthur P. (Ohio)
Lanham, Fritz G. (Tex.)
Lanzetta, James J. (N. Y.)
Larrabee, William H. (Ind.)
Lea, Clarence F. (Calif.)
Lee, Frank H. (Mo.)
Lehlbach, Frederick R. (N. J.)
Lehr, John C. (Mich.)
Lemke, William (N. Dak.)
Lesinski, John (Mich.)
Lewis, David J. (Md.)
Lewis, Lawrence (Colo.)
Lindsay, George W. (N. Y.)
Lloyd, Wesley (Wash.)
Lozier, Ralph F. (Mo.)
Luce, Robert (Mass.)
Ludlow, Louis (Ind.)
Lundeen, Ernest (Minn.)
McCarthy, Kathryn O'L. (Kans.)
McClintic, James V. (Okla.)
McCormack, John W. (Mass.)
McDuffie, John (Ala.)
McFadden, Louis T. (Pa.)
McFarlane, William D. (Tex.)
McGrath, John J. (Calif.)
McGugin, Harold (Kans.)
McKeown, Tom D. (Okla.)
McLean, Donald H. (N. J.)
McLeod, Clarence J. (Mich.)
McMillan, Thomas S. (S. C.)
McReynolds, Samuel D. (Tenn.)
McSwain, John J. (S. C.)
Major, J. Earl (Ill.)
Maloney, Francis T. (Conn.)
Maloney, Paul H. ((La.)
Mansfield, Joseph J. (Tex.)
Mapes, Carl E. (Mich.)
Marland, Ernest W. (Okla.)
Marshall, Leroy T. (Ohio)
Martin, Charles H. (Oreg.)
Martin, John A. (Colo.)
Martin, Joseph W. (Mass.)
May, Andrew J. (Ky.)
Mead, James M. (N. Y.)
Meeks, James A. (Ill.)
Merritt, Schuyler (Conn.)
Millard, Charles D. (N. Y.)
Miller, John E. (Ark.)
Milligan, Jacob L. (Mo.)
Mitchell, John R. (Tenn.)
Monaghan, Joseph P. (Mont.)
Montague, Andrew J. (Va.)
Montet, Numa F. (La.)
Moran, Edward C. (Maine)
Morehead, John H. (Nebr.)
Mott, James W. (Oreg.)
Moynihan, P. H. (Ill.)
Muldowney, Michael J. (Pa.)
Murdock, Abe (Utah)
Musselwhite, Harry W. (Mich.)
Nesbit, Walter (Ill.)
Norton, Mary T. (N. J.)
O'Brien, Thomas J. (Ill.)
O'Connell, John M. (R. I.)
O'Connor, John J. (N. Y.)
Oliver, Frank (N. Y.)
Oliver, William B. (Ala.)
O'Malley, Thomas (Wis.)
Owen, Emmett M. (Ga.)
Palmisano, Vincent L. (Md.)
Parker, Homer C. (Ga.)
Parker, James S. (N. Y.)
Parks, Tilman B. (Ark.)
Parsons, Claude V. (Ill.)
Patman, Wright (Tex.)
Peavey, Hubert H. (Wis.)
Perkins, Randolph (N. J.)
Peterson, J. Hardin (Fla.)
Pettengill, Samuel B. (Ind.)
Peyser, Theodore A. (N. Y.)
Pierce, Walter M. (Oreg.)
Plumley, Charles A. (Vt.)
Polk, James G. (Ohio)
Pou, Edward W. (N. C.)
Powers, D. Lane (N. J.)
Prall, Anning S. (N. Y.)
Ragon, Heartsill (Ark.)
Rainey, Henry T. (Ill.)
Ramsay, Robert L. (W. Va.)
Ramspeck, Robert (Ga.)
Randolph, Jennings (W. Va.)
Rankin, John E. (Miss.)
Ransley, Harry C. (Pa.)
Rayburn, Sam (Tex.)
Reece, B. Carroll (Tenn.)
Reed, Daniel A. (N. Y.)
Reid, Frank R. (Ill.)
Reilly, Michael K. (Wis.)
Rich, Robert F. (Pa.)
Richards, James P. (S. C.)
Richardson, William E. (Pa.)
Robertson, A. Willis (Va.)
Robinson, J. Will (Utah)
Rogers, Edith Nourse (Mass.)
Rogers, Will (Okla.)
Rogers, William N. (N. H.)
Romjue, Milton A. (Mo.)
Rudd, Stephen A. (N. Y.)
Ruffin, James E. (Mo.)
Sabath, Adolph J. (Ill.)
Sadowsky, George G. (Mich.)
Sanders, Jared Y., Jr. (La.)
Sanders, Morgan G. (Tex.)
Sandlin, John N. (La.)
Schaefer, Edwin M. (Ill.)
Schuetz, Leonard W. (Ill.)
Schulte, William T. (Ind.)
Scrugham, James G. (Nev.)
Sears, William J. (Fla.)
Secrest, Robert T. (Ohio)
Seger, George N. (N. J.)
Shallenberger, Ashton C. (Nebr.)
Shannon, Joseph B. (Mo.)
Shoemaker, Francis H. (Minn.)
Simpson, James, Jr. (Ill.)
Sinclair, James H. (N. Dak.)
Sirovich, William I. (N. Y.)
Sisson, Fred J. (N. Y.)
Smith, Howard W. (Va.)
Smith, Joe L. (W. Va.)
Smith, Martin F. (Wash.)
Snell, Bertrand H. (N. Y.)
Snyder, J. Buell (Pa.)
Somers, Andrew L. (N. Y.)
Spence, Brent (Ky.)
Stalker, Gale H. (N. Y.)
Steagall, Henry B. (Ala.)
Stokes, Edward L. (Pa.)
Strong, Nathan L. (Pa.)
Strong, Sterling P. (Tex.)
Stubbs, Henry E. (Calif.)
Studley, Elmer E. (N. Y.)
Sullivan, Christopher D. (N. Y.)
Sumners, Hatton W. (Tex.)
Sutphin, William H. (N. J.)
Swank, Fletcher B. (Okla.)
Sweeney, Martin L. (Ohio)
Swick, J. Howard (Pa.)
Taber, John (N. Y.)
Tarver, Malcolm C. (La.)
Taylor, Edward T. (Colo.)
Taylor, J. Will (Tenn.)
Taylor, John C. (S. C.)
Terrall, George B. (Tex.)
Terry, David D. (Ark.)
Thom, William R. (Ohio)
Thomas, William D. (N. Y.)
Thomason, R. Ewing (Tex.)
Thompson, Chester (Ill.)
Thompson, Clark W. (Tex.)
Thurston, Lloyd (Iowa)
Tinkham, George H. (Mass.)
Tobey, Charles W. (N. H.)
Traeger, William I. (Calif.)
Treadway, Allen T. (Mass.)
Truax, Charles V. (Ohio)
Turner, Clarence W. (Tenn.)
Turpin, C. Murray (Pa.)
Umstead, William B. (N. C.)
Underwood, Mell G. (Ohio)
Utterback, John G. (Maine)
Vinson, Carl (Ga.)
Vinson, Fred M. (Ky.)
Wadsworth, James W. (N. Y.)
Waldron, Alfred M. (Pa.)
Wallgren, Monrad C. (Wash.)
Walter, Francis E. (Pa.)
Warren, Lindsay C. (N. C.)
Watson, Henry W. (Pa.)
Wearin, Otha D. (Iowa)
Weaver, Zebulon (N. C.)

Weideman, Carl M. (Mich.)
Welch, Richard J. (Calif.)
Werner, Theo. B. (S. Dak.)
West, Charles (Ohio)
West, Milton H. (Tex.)
White, Compton I. (Idaho)
Whitley, James L. (N. Y.)
Whittington, William M. (Miss.)
Wigglesworth, Richard B. (Mass.)
Wilcox, J. Mark (Fla.)
Willford, Albert C. (Iowa)
Williams, Clyde (Mo.)
Wilson, Riley J. (La.)
Withrow, Gardner R. (Wis.)
Wolcott, Jesse P. (Mich.)
Wolfenden, James (Pa.)
Wolverton, Charles A. (N. J.)
Wood, John S. (Ga.)
Wood, Reuben T. (Mo.)
Woodruff, Roy O. (Mich.)
Woodrum, Clifton A. (Va.)
Young, Stephen M. (Ohio)
Zioncheck, Marion A. (Wash.)

The Seventy-fourth Congress (1935-37)

Byrns, Joseph W. (Tenn.) Speaker.

Adair, J. Leroy (Ill.)
Allen, Leo E. (Ill.)
Amlie, Thomas R. (Wis.)
Andresen, August H. (Minn.)
Andrew, A. Piatt (Mass.)
Andrews, Walter G. (N. Y.)
Arends, Leslie C. (Ill.)
Arnold, William W. (Ill.)
Ashbrook, William A. (Ohio)
Ayers, Roy E. (Mont.)
Bacharach, Isaac (N. J.)
Bacon, Robert L. (N. Y.)
Bankhead, William B. (Ala.)
Barden, Graham A. (N. C.)
Barry, William B. (N. Y.)
Beam, Harry P. (Ill.)
Beiter, Alfred F. (N. Y.)
Bell, C. Jasper (Mo.)
Berlin, William M. (Pa.)
Biermann, Fred (Iowa)
Binderup, Charles G. (Nebr.)
Blackney, William W. (Mich.)
Bland, Schuyler Otis (Va.)
Blanton, Thomas L. (Tex.)
Bloom, Sol (N. Y.)
Boehne, John W., Jr. (Ind.)
Boileau, Gerald J. (Wis.)
Boland, Patrick J. (Pa.)
Bolton, Chester C. (Ohio)
Boykin, Frank W. (Ala.)
Boylan, John J. (N. Y.)
Brennan, Martin A. (Ill.)
Brewster, Ralph O. (Maine)
Brooks, J. Twing (Pa.)
Brown, Paul (Ga.)
Brown, Prentiss M. (Mich.)
Brunner, William F. (N. Y.)
Buchanan, James P. (Tex.)
Buck, Frank H. (Calif.)
Buckbee, John T. (Ill.)
Buckler, Richard T. (Minn.)
Buckley, Charles A. (N. Y.)
Bulwinkle, Alfred L. (N. C.)
Burch, Thomas G. (Va.)
Burdick, Usher L. (N. Dak.)
Burnham, George (Calif.)
Byrns, Joseph W. (Tenn.)
Caldwell, Millard F. (Fla.)
Cannon, Clarence (Mo.)
Cannon, Raymond J. (Wis.)
Carden, Cap R. (Ky.)
Carlson, Frank (Kans.)
Carmichael, Archibald H. (Ala.)
Carmichael, A. H. (Ala.)
Carpenter, Randolph (Kans.)
Carter, Albert E. (Calif.)
Cartwright, Wilburn (Okla.)
Cary, Glover H. (Ky.)
Casey, Joseph E. (Mass.)
Castellow, Bryant T. (Ga.)
Cavicchia, Peter A. (N. J.)
Celler, Emanuel (N. Y.)
Chandler, Walter (Tenn.)
Chapman, Virgil (Ky.)
Christianson, Theodore (Minn.)
Church, Ralph E. (Ill.)
Citron, William M. (Conn.)
Claiborne, James R. (Mo.)
Clark, D. Worth (Idaho)
Clark, J. Bayard (N. C.)
Cochran, John J. (Mo.)
Coffee, Harry B. (Nebr.)
Colden, Charles J. (Calif.)
Cole, W. Sterling (N. Y.)
Cole, William P., Jr. (Md.)
Collins, Samuel (Calif.)
Colmer, William M. (Miss.)
Condon, Francis B. (R. I.)
Connery, William P., Jr. (Mass.)
Cooley, Harold D. (N. C.)
Cooper, Jere (Tenn.)
Cooper, John G. (Ohio)
Corning, Parker (N. Y.)
Costello, John M. (Calif.)
Cox, Edward E. (Ga.)
Cravens, Ben (Ark.)
Crawford, Fred L. (Mich.)
Creal, Edward W. (Ky.)
Crosby, Charles N. (Pa.)
Cross, Oliver H. (Tex.)
Crosser, Robert (Ohio)
Crowe, Eugene B. (Ind.)
Crowther, Frank (N. Y.)
Culkin, Francis D. (N. Y.)
Cullen, Thomas H. (N. Y.)
Cummings, Fred (Colo.)
Curley, Edward W. (N. Y.)
Daly, J. Burrwood (Pa.)
Darden, Colgate W., Jr. (Va.)
Darrow, George P. (Pa.)
Dear, Cleveland (La.)
Deen, Braswell (Ga.)
Delaney, John J. (N. Y.)
Dempsey, John J. (N. Mex.)
De Rouen, Rene L. (La.)
Dickstein, Samuel (N. Y.)
Dies, Martin (Tex.)
Dietrich, C. Elmer (Pa.)
Dingell, John D. (Mich.)
Dirksen, Everett M. (Ill.)
Disney, Wesley E. (Okla.)
Ditter, J. William (Pa.)
Dobbins, Donald C. (Ill.)
Dockweiler, John F. (Calif.)
Dondero, George A. (Mich.)
Dorsey, Frank J. G. (Pa.)
Doughton, Robert L. (N. C.)
Doutrich, Isaac H. (Pa.)
Doxey, Wall (Miss.)
Drewry, Patrick H. (Va.)
Driscoll, Denis J. (Pa.)
Driver, William J. (Ark.)
Duffey, Warren J. (Ohio)
Duffy, James P. B. (N. Y.)
Duncan, Richard M. (Mo.)
Dunn, Aubert C. (Miss.)
Dunn, Matthew A. (Pa.)
Eagle, Joe H. (Tex.)
Eaton, Charles A. (N. J.)
Eckert, Charles R. (Pa.)
Edmiston, Andrew (W. Va.)
Eicher, Edward C. (Iowa)
Ekwall, William A. (Oreg.)
Ellenbogen, Henry (Pa.)
Engel, Albert J. (Mich.)
Englebright, Harry L. (Calif.)
Evans, Marcellus H. (N. Y.)
Faddis, Charles I. (Pa.)
Farley, James I. (Ind.)
Fenerty, Clare G. (Pa.)
Ferguson, Phil (Okla.)
Fernandez, Joachim O. (La.)
Fiesinger, William L. (Ohio)
Fish, Hamilton, Jr. (N. Y.)
Fitzpatrick, James M. (N. Y.)
Flannagan, John W., Jr. (Va.)
Fletcher, Brooks (Ohio)
Focht, Benjamin K. (Pa.)
Ford, Aaron L. (Miss.)
Ford, Thomas F. (Calif.)
Frey, Oliver W. (Pa.)
Fuller, Claude A. (Ark.)
Fulmer, Hampton P. (S. C.)
Gambrill, Stephen W. (Md.)
Gasque, Allard H. (S. C.)
Gassaway, Percy L. (Okla.)
Gavagan, Joseph A. (N. Y.)
Gearhart, Bertrand W. (Calif.)
Gehrmann, Bernard J. (Wis.)
Gifford, Charles L. (Mass.)
Gilchrist, Fred C. (Iowa)
Gildea, James H. (Pa.)
Gillette, Guy M. (Iowa)
Gingery, Don (Pa.)
Goldsborough, T. Alan (Md.)
Goodwin, Philip A. (N. Y.)
Granfield, William J. (Mass.)
Gray, Finly H. (Ind.)
Gray, Joseph (Pa.)
Green, Robert A. (Fla.)
Greenway, Isabella (Ariz.)
Greenwood, Arthur H. (Ind.)
Greever, Paul R. (Wyo.)
Gregory, William V. (Ky.)
Griffin, Anthony J. (N. Y.)
Griswold, Glenn (Ind.)
Guyer, Ulysses S. (Kans.)
Gwynne, John W. (Iowa)
Haines, Harry L. (Pa.)
Halleck, Charles A. (Ind.)
Hamlin, Simon M. (Maine)
Hancock, Clarence E. (N. Y.)
Hancock, Frank (N. C.)
Harlan, Byron B. (Ohio)
Hart, Edward J. (N. J.)
Harter, Dow W. (Ohio)
Hartley, Fred A., Jr. (N. J.)
Healey, Arthur D. (Mass.)
Hennings, Thomas C., Jr. (Mo.)
Hess, William E. (Ohio)
Higgins, John P. (Mass.)
Higgins, William L. (Conn.)
Hildebrandt, Fred H. (S. Dak.)
Hill, Knute (Wash.)
Hill, Lister (Ala.)
Hill, Samuel B. (Wash.)
Hobbs, Sam (Ala.)
Hoeppel, John H. (Calif.)
Hoffman, Clare E. (Mich.)
Hollister, John B. (Ohio)
Holmes, Pehr G. (Mass.)
Hook, Frank E. (Mich.)
Hope, Clifford R. (Kans.)
Houston, John M. (Kans.)
Huddleston, George (Ala.)
Hull, Merlin (Wis.)
Igoe, Michael L. (Ill.)
Imoff, Lawrence E. (Ohio)
Jacobsen, Bernhard M. (Iowa)
Jenckes, Virginia E. (Ind.)
Jenkins, Thomas A. (Ohio)
Johnson, George W. (W. Va.)
Johnson, Jed (Okla.)
Johnson, Luther A. (Tex.)
Jones, Marvin (Tex.)
Kahn, Florence P. (Calif.)
Kee, John (W. Va.)
Keller, Kent E. (Ill.)
Kelly, Edward A. (Ill.)
Kennedy, Ambrose J. (Md.)
Kennedy, Martin J. (N. Y.)
Kenney, Edward A. (N. J.)
Kerr, John H. (N. C.)
Kimball, Henry M. (Mich.)
Kinzer, J. Roland (Pa.)
Kleberg, Richard M. (Tex.)
Kloeb, Frank L. (Ohio)
Kniffin, Frank C. (Ohio)
Knutson, Harold (Minn.)
Kocialkowski, Leo (Ill.)
Koppleman, Herman P. (Conn.)
Kramer, Charles (Calif.)
Kvale, Paul J. (Minn.)
Lambertson, William P. (Kans.)
Lambeth, J. Walter (N. C.)
Lamneck, Arthur P. (Ohio)
Lanham, Fritz G. (Tex.)
Larrabee, William H. (Ind.)
Lea, Clarence F. (Calif.)
Lee, Josh (Okla.)
Lehlbach, Frederick R. (N. J.)
Lemke, William (N. Dak.)
Lesinski, John (Mich.)
Lewis, David J. (Md.)
Lewis, Lawrence (Colo.)
Lloyd, Wesley (Wash.)
Lord, Bert (N. Y.)
Lucas, Scott W. (Ill.)
Luckey, Henry C. (Nebr.)
Ludlow, Louis (Ind.)
Lundeen, Ernest M. (Minn.)
McAndrews, James (Ill.)
McClellan, John L. (Ark.)
McCormack, John W. (Mass.)
McDuffie, John (Ala.)
McFarlane, William D. (Tex.)
McGehee, Dan R. (Miss.)
McGrath, John J. (Calif.)
McGroarty, John S. (Calif.)
McKeough, Raymond S. (Ill.)
McLaughlin, Charles F. (Nebr.)
McLean, Donald H. (N. J.)
McLeod, Clarence J. (Mich.)
McMillan, Thomas S. (S. C.)
McReynolds, Samuel D. (Tenn.)
McSwain, John J. (S. C.)
Maas, Melvin J. (Minn.)
Mahon, George H. (Tex.)
Maloney, Paul H. (La.)
Mansfield, Joseph J. (Tex.)
Mapes, Carl E.. (Mich.)
Marcantonio, Vito (N. Y.)
Marshall, Leroy T. (Ohio)
Martin, John A. (Colo.)
Martin, Joseph W., Jr. (Mass.)
Mason, Harry H. (Ill.)
Massingale, Samuel C. (Okla.)
Maverick, Maury (Tex.)
May, Andrew J. (Ky.)
Mead, James M. (N. Y.)
Meeks, James A. (Ill.)
Merritt, Mathew J. (N. Y.)
Merritt, Schuyler (Conn.)
Michener, Earl C. (Mich.)
Millard, Charles D. (N. Y.)
Miller, John E. (Ark.)
Mitchell, Arthur W. (Ill.)
Mitchell, John R. (Tenn.)
Monaghan, Joseph P. (Mont.)
Montague, Andrew J. (Va.)
Montet, Numa F. (La.)
Moran, Edward C. (Maine)
Moritz, Theodore L. (Pa.)
Mott, James W. (Oreg.)
Murdock, Abe (Utah)
Nelson, William L. (Mo.)
Nichols, Jack (Okla.)
Norton, Mary T. (N. J.)
O'Brien, Thomas J. (Ill.)
O'Connell, John M. (R. I.)
O'Connor, John J. (N. Y.)
O'Day, Caroline (N. Y.)
O'Leary, James A. (N. Y.)
Oliver, William B. (Ala.)
O'Malley, Thomas (Wis.)
O'Neal, Emmet (Ky.)
Owen, Emmett M. (Ga.)
Palmisano, Vincent L. (Md.)
Parks, Tilman B. (Ark.)
Parsons, Claude V. (Ill.)
Patman, Wright (Tex.)
Patterson, Edward W. (Kans.)
Patton, Nat (Tex.)
Pearson, Herron (Tenn.)
Perkins, Randolph (N. J.)
Peterson, Hugh, Jr. (Ga.)
Peterson, J. Hardon (Fla.)
Pettengill, Samuel B. (Ind.)
Peyser, Theodore A. (N. Y.)
Pfeifer, Joseph L. (N. Y.)
Pierce, Walter M. (Oreg.)
Pittenger, William A. (Minn.)
Plumley, Charles A. (Vt.)
Polk, James G. (Ohio)
Powers, D. Lane (N. J.)
Quinn, James L. (Pa.)
Rabaut, Louis C. (Mich.)
Ramsay, Robert L. (W. Va.)
Ramspeck, Robert (Ga.)
Randolph, Jennings (W. Va.)
Rankin, John E. (Miss.)
Ransley, Harry C. (Pa.)
Rayburn, Sam (Tex.)
Reece, B. Carroll (Tenn.)
Reed, Chauncey W. (Ill.)
Reed, Daniel A. (N. Y.)
Reilly, Michael K. (Wis.)
Rich, Robert F. (Pa.)
Richards, James P. (S. C.)
Richardson, William E. (Pa.)
Robertson, A. Willis (Va.)
Robinson, J. Will (Utah)
Robsion, John M. (Ky.)
Rogers, Edith Nourse (Mass.)
Rogers, Will (Okla.)
Rogers, William N. (N. H.)
Romjue, Milton A. (Mo.)
Rudd, Stephen A. (N. Y.)
Russell, Richard M. (Mass.)
Ryan, Elmer J. (Minn.)
Sabath, Adolph J. (Ill.)
Sadowski, George G. (Mich.)
Sanders, Jared Y., Jr. (La.)
Sanders, Morgan G. (Tex.)

Sandlin, John N. (La.)
Sauthoff, Harry (Wis.)
Schaefer, Edwin M. (Ill.)
Schneider, George J. (Wis.)
Schuetz, Leonard W. (Ill.)
Schulte, William T. (Ind.)
Scott, Byron N. (Calif.)
Scrugham, James G. (Nev.)
Sears, William J. (Fla.)
Secrest, Robert T. (Ohio)
Seger, George N. (N. J.)
Shanley, James A. (Conn.)
Shannon, Joseph B. (Mo.)
Short, Dewey (Mo.)
Sirovich, William I. (N. Y.)
Sisson, Fred J. (N. Y.)
Smith, Howard W. (Va.)
Smith, J. Joseph (Conn.)
Smith, Joe L. (W. Va.)
Smith, Martin F. (Wash.)
Snell, Bertrand H. (N. Y.)
Snyder, J. Buell (Pa.)
Somers, Andrew L. (N. Y.)
South, Charles L. (Tex.)
Spence, Brent (Ky.)
Stack, Michael J. (Pa.)
Starnes, Joe (Ala.)
Steagall, Henry B. (Ala.)
Stefan, Karl (Nebr.)
Stewart, J. George (Del.)
Stubbs, Henry E. (Calif.)
Sullivan, Christopher D. (N.Y.)
Sumners, Hatton W. (Tex.)
Sutphin, William H. (N. J.)
Sweeney, Martin L. (Ohio)
Taber, John (N. Y.)
Tarver, Malcolm C. (Ga.)
Taylor, Edward T. (Colo.)
Taylor, J. Will (Tenn.)
Taylor, John C. (S. C.)
Terry, David D. (Ark.)
Thom, William R. (Ohio)
Thomas, William D. (N. Y.)
Thomason, R. Ewing (Tex.)
Thompson, Chester (Ill.)
Thurston, Lloyd (Iowa)
Tinkham, George H. (Mass.)
Tobey, Charles W. (N. H.)
Tolan, John H. (Calif.)
Tonry, Richard J. (N. Y.)
Treadway, Allen T. (Mass.)
Truax, Charles V. (Ohio)
Turner, Clarence W. (Tenn.)
Turpin, C. Murray (Pa.)
Umstead, William B. (N. C.)
Underwood, Mell G. (Ohio)
Utterback, Hubert (Iowa)
Vinson, Carl (Ga.)
Vinson, Fred M. (Ky.)
Wadsworth, James W. (N.Y.)
Wallgren, Monrad C. (Wash.)
Walter, Francis E. (Pa.)
Warren, Lindsay C. (N. C.)
Wearin, Otha D. (Iowa)
Weaver, Zebulon (N. C.)
Welch, Richard J. (Calif.)
Werner, Theo. B. (S. Dak.)
West, Milton H. (Tex.)
Whelchel, B. Frank (Ga.)
White, Compton I. (Idaho)
Whittington, William M. (Miss.)
Wigglesworth, Richard B. (Mass.)
Wilcox, J. Mark (Fla.)
Williams, Clyde (Mo.)
Wilson, Riley J. (La.)
Wilson, William H. (Pa.)
Withrow, Gardner R. (Wis.)
Wolcott, Jesse P. (Mich.)
Wolfenden, James (Pa.)
Wolverton, Charles A. (N. J.)
Wood, Reuben T. (Mo.)
Woodruff, Roy O. (Mich.)
Woodrum, Clifton A. (Va.)
Young, Stephen M. (Ohio)
Zimmerman, Orville (Mo.)
Zioncheck, Marion A. (Wash.)

The

Governors, United States Senators And Chief Justices

Arranged Chronologically

ALABAMA

Date	Governors	Biography	U. S. Senators		Biography	Chief Justices	Biography
1819	Bibb, William W.	10:425	King, William Rufus		4:147		
1819	"		"	Walker, John W.	11:471		
1820	Bibb, Thomas	10:425	"	"		Clay, Clement C.	10:427
1821	Pickens, Israel	10:426	"	"		"	
1823	"		"	Kelly, William	11:553	Lipscomb, Abner S.	5:165
1825	Murphy, John	10:426	"	Chambers, Henry	11:235	"	
1826	"		"	Pickens, Israel	10:426	"	
1826	"		"	McKinley, John	2:470	"	
1829	Moore, Gabriel	10:426	"	"		"	
1831	Moore, Samuel B.	10:426	"	Moore, Gabriel	10:426	"	
1831	Gayle, John	10:427	"	"		"	
1835	Clay, Clement C.	10:427	"	"		Saffold, Reuben	4:359
1836	"		"	"		Hitchcock, Henry	11:196
1837	Bagby, Arthur P.	10:428	"	McKinley, John	2:470	Hopkins, Arthur F.	4:356
1837	"		"	Clay, Clement C.	10:427	Collier, Henry W.	10:430
1841	Fitzpatrick, Benjamin	10:429	"	Bagby, Arthur P.	10:428	"	
1844	"		Lewis, Dixon H.	"	4:525	"	
1845	Martin, Joshua L.	10:429	"	"		"	
1847	Chapman, Reuben	10:430	"	"		"	
1848	"		"	King, William R.	4:147	"	
1848	"		Fitzpatrick, Benjamin	"	10:429	"	
1849	Collier, Henry W.	10:430	Clemens, Jeremiah	"	7:234	Dargan, Edmund S.	4:214
1852	"		"	"		Chilton, William P.	4:153
1853	Winston, John A.	10:431	Clay, Clement C.		10:427	"	
1853	"		"	Fitzpatrick, Benjamin	10:429		
1856	"		"	"		Goldthwaite, George	4:350
1857	Moore, Andrew B.	10:431	"	"		Rice, Samuel F.	4:353
1859	"		"	"		Walker, Abram J.	4:207
1861	Shorter, John G.	10:432	Vacant	Vacant		"	
1863	Watts, Thomas H.	10:432	"	"		"	
1865	Parsons, Lewis E.	10:433	"	"		Peck, Elijah W.	8: 52
1865	Patton, Robert M.	10:434	Warner, Willard	"	10:396	"	
1868	Smith, William H.	10:434	"	Spencer, George E.	13: 72	"	
1870	Lindsay, Robert B.	10:435	"	"		"	
1872	Lewis, David P.	10:435	Goldthwaite, George	"	4:350	"	
1873	"		"	"		Peters, Thomas M.	7:495
1874	Houston, George S.	10:436	"	"		Brickell, Robert C.	7:507
1877	"		Morgan, John Tyler	"	1:295	"	
1878	Cobb, Rufus W.	10:436	"	"		"	
1879	"		"	Houston, George S.	10:436	"	
1880	"		"	Pryor, Luke	12:269	"	
1880	"		"	Pugh, James L.	1:292	"	
1882	O'Neal, Edward A.	10:437	"	"		"	
1884	"		"	"		Stone, George W.	4:344
1886	Seay, Thomas	10:437	"	"		"	
1890	Jones, Thomas G.	10:437	"	"		"	
1894	Oates, William C.	2:243	"	"		Brickell, Robert C.	7:507
1896	Johnston, Joseph F.	10:439	"	"		"	
1897	"		"	Pettus, Edmund W.	12:320	"	
1898	"		"	"		McClellan, Thomas N.	12:549
1900	Samford, William J.	19: 55	"	"		"	
1903	Jelks, William D.	13:172	"	"		"	
1906	"		"	"		Weakley, Samuel D.	19:280
1907	Comer, Braxton B.	14: 91	Bankhead, John H.		14:210	Tyson, John R.	12:130
1907	"		"	Johnston, Joseph F.	10:439	"	
1909	"		"	"		Dowdell, James R.	20:285
1911	O'Neal, Emmet	15:273	"	"		"	
1914	"		"	White, Francis S.		Anderson, John C.	18:392
1915	Henderson, Charles	B:254	"	Underwood, Oscar W.	21: 22	"	
1919	Kilby, Thomas E.	A: 99	"	"		"	
1920	"		Comer, Braxton B.	"	14: 91	"	
1920	"		Heflin, J. Thomas	"	B: 60	"	
1923	Brandon, William W.	C:295	"	"		"	
1927	Graves, David Bibb	A:353	"	Black, Hugo L.	C:502	"	
1931	Miller, Benjamin M.		Bankhead, John H., Jr.	"		"	
1935	Graves, David Bibb	A:353	"	"		"	

ARIZONA

Date	Governors	Biography	U. S. Senators	Biography	Chief Justices	Biography
1912	Hunt, George W. P.	C: 40	Smith, Marcus A.	26: 95	Franklin, Alfred	D:159
1912	“		“ Ashurst, Henry F.	15:415	“	
1915	“		“ “		Ross, Henry D.	17:342
1917	“		“ “		Franklin, Alfred	D:159
1918	“		“ “		Cunningham, Donnell L.	D:325
1919	Campbell, Thomas E.	B:404	“ “		“	
1921	“		Cameron, Ralph H. “		Ross, Henry D.	17:342
1923	Hunt, George W. P.	C: 40	“ “		McAlister, Archibald G.	B:370
1927	“		Hayden, Carl T. “	C:218	“	
1928	“		“ “		Ross, Henry D.	17:342
1929	Phillips, John C.	D:359	“ “		Lockwood, Alfred C.	
1931	Hunt, George W. P.	C: 40	“ “		McAlister, Archibald G.	B:370
1932	“		“ “		Lockwood, Alfred C.	
1933	Moeur, Benjamin B.		“ “		Ross, Henry D.	17:342
1935	“		“ “		Lockwood, Alfred C.	

ARKANSAS

Date	Governors	Biography	U. S. Senators	Biography	Chief Justices	Biography
1836	Conway, James S.	10:184	Fulton, William S.	10:184		
1836	“		“ Sevier, Ambrose H.	2:239	Ringo, Daniel	13:199
1840	Yell, Archibald	10:185	“ “		“	
1844	Adams, Samuel	10:185	“ “		“	
1844	Drew, Thomas S.	10:186	Ashley, Chester “	7: 48	Johnson, Thomas	5:519
1848	“		“ Borland, Solon	4:386	“	
1848	Roane, John S.	10:186	Sebastian, William K. “	4:548	“	
1852	Conway, Elias N.	10:186	“ “		Watkins, George C.	13:144
1853	“		“ Johnson, Robert W.	5:252	“	
1854	“		“ “		English, Elbert H.	12:507
1860	Rector, Henry M.	10:187	“ “		“	
1861	“		“ Mitchell, Charles B.	4: 63	“	
1862	Flanagin, Harris	10:189	“		“	
1864	Murphy, Isaac	10:187	“ “		Baxter, Elisha	10:189
1866	“		“ “		Walker, David	13:145
1868	Clayton, Powell	16:262	“ Rice, Benjamin F.	12:395	Wilshire, William W.	13:483
1868	“		McDonald, Alexander “	12:336	“	
1871	Hadley, Ozro A.	10:188	Clayton, Powell “	16:262	McClure, John	19:224
1873	Baxter, Elisha	10:189	“ Dorsey, Stephen W.	7: 22	“	
1874	Garland, Augustus H.	2:409	“ “		English, Elbert H.	12:507
1877	Miller, William R.	10:189	Garland, Augustus H.	2:409	“	
1879	“		“ Walker, James D.	12:288	“	
1881	Churchill, Thomas J.	10:190	“ “		“	
1883	Berry, James H.	10:190	“ “		“	
1884	“		“ “		Cockrill, Sterling R.	12:448
1885	Hughes, Simon P.	10:191	Berry, James H.	10:190	“	
1885	“		“ Jones, James K.	1:293	“	
1889	Eagle, James P.	10:191	“ “		“	
1893	Fishback, William M.	10:192	“ “		Bunn, Henry G.	9:446
1895	Clarke, James P.	10:193	“ “		“	
1897	Jones, Daniel W.	10:193	“ “		“	
1901	Davis, Jefferson	13:366	“ “		“	
1903	“		“ Clarke, James P.	10:193	“	
1904	“		“ “		Hill, Joseph M.	13:297
1907	Little, John S.	23:307	Davis, Jefferson “	13:366	“	
1907	Pindall, Xenophon O.	C:413	“ “		“	
1909	Donaghey, George W.	C:414	“ “		McCulloch, Edgar A.	15:360
1913	Robinson, Joseph T.	B:193	Heiskell, John N. “		“	
1913	“		Kavanaugh, Williams M. “	19:419	“	
1913	Hays, George W.	20: 32	Robinson, Joseph T. “	B:193	“	
1916	“		“ Kirby, William F.	C:191	“	
1917	Brough, Charles H.	C:414	“ “		“	
1921	McRae, Thomas C.	17:261	“ Caraway, Thadeus H.	A:123	“	
1925	Terrel, Thomas J.		“ “		“	
1927	Martineau, John E.	C:535	“ “		Hart, Jesse C.	
1929	Parnell, Harvey	26:104	“ “		“	
1932	“		“ Caraway, Hattie O. W.	D:148	Johnson, C. E.	
1933	Futrell, J. Marion		“ “		“	

References are to The National Cyclopedia of American Biography

CALIFORNIA

Date	Governors	Biography	U. S. Senators	Biography	Chief Justices	Biography
1849	Burnett, Peter H.	4:105	Fremont, John C.	4:270	Hastings, Clinton	3:510
1849	"		" Gwin, William M.	5:145	"	
1851	McDougall, John	4:106	Weller, John B. "	4:107	"	
1852	Bigler, John	4:106	" "		Lyons, Henry A.	12:331
1853	"		" "		Murray, Hugh C.	12:330
1856	Johnson, James N.	4:107	" "		"	
1857	"		Broderick, David C. "	4:185	Terry, David S.	12:104
1858	Weller, John B.	4:107	" "		"	
1859	"		Haun, Henry P. "	11:369	Field, Stephen	1: 32
1860	Latham, Milton S.	4:108	" "		"	
1860	Downey, John G.	4:108	Latham, Milton S. "	4:108	"	
1861	"		" McDougall, James A.	11:330	"	
1862	Stanford, Leland	2:128	" "		"	
1863	"		Conness, John "	11:369	Cope, Warren W.	12: 99
1864	Low, Frederick F.	4:109	" "		"	
1864	"		" "		Sanderson, Silas W.	12: 46
1866	"		" "		Currey, John	12:418
1867	"		" Cole, Cornelius	22: 95	"	
1868	Haight, Henry H.	4:109	" "		Sawyer, Lorenzo	13:195
1869	"		Casserly, Eugene "	4:351	"	
1870	"		" "		Rhodes, Augustus L.	12: 97
1872	Booth, Newton	4:110	" "		Sprague, Royal T.	5:524
1872	"		" "		Wallace, William T.	13:261
1873	"		Hager, John S. "	13:330	"	
1873	"		" Sargent, Aaron A.	13:475	"	
1874	Pacheco, Romualdo	4:110	" "		"	
1875	"		Booth, Newton "	4:110	"	
1876	Irwin, William	4:110	" "		"	
1879	"		" Farley, James J.	4:173	"	
1880	Perkins, George C.	4:111	" "		Morrison, Robert F.	12:125
1881	"		Miller, John F. "	8: 91	"	
1883	Stoneman, George	4:112	" "		"	
1885	"		" Stanford, Leland	2:128	"	
1886	"		Hearst, George "	1:315	"	
1886	"		Williams, Abram P. "	13: 52	"	
1887	Bartlett, Washington	4:113	Hearst, George "	1:315	Searls, Niles	13:419
1887	Waterman, Robert W.	4:113	" "		"	
1889	"		" "		Beatty, William H.	12:268
1891	Markham, Henry H.	4:114	Felton, Cornelius N. "		"	
1893	"		White, Stephen M. "	12:509	"	
1893	"		" Perkins, George C.	4:111	"	
1895	Budd, James H.	4:114	" "		"	
1899	Gage, Henry T.	4:114	" "		"	
1900	"		Bard, Thomas R. "	12: 57	"	
1903	Pardee, George C.	13:175	" "		"	
1905	"		Flint, Frank P. "	13:595	"	
1911	Johnson, Hiram W.	15:133	Works, John D. "	13: 93	"	
1914	"		" "		Sullivan, Matt I.	
1915	"		" Phelan, James D.	8:478	Angellotti, Frank M.	23:412
1917	Stephens, William D.		Johnson, Hiram W. "	15:133	"	
1921	"		" Shortridge, Samuel M.	B:193	Shaw, Lucien	
1923	Richardson, Friend W.	C:410	" "		Wilbur, Curtis D.	A: 13
1924	"		" "		Myers, Louis W.	B:134
1926	"		" "		Waste, William H.	D:161
1927	Young, Clement C.		" "		"	
1931	Rolph, James, Jr.	25:228	" McAdoo, William G.	A: 34	"	
1934	Merriam, Frank F.		" "		"	

COLORADO

Date	Governors	Biography	U. S. Senators		Biography	Chief Justices	Biography
1876	Routt, John L.	6:449	Teller, Henry M.		15:228	Hallett, Moses	12:339
1876	"		"	Chaffee, Jerome B.	6:199	"	
1877	"		"	"		Thatcher, Henry C.	12:513
1879	Pitkin, Frederick W.	6:450	"	Hill, Nathaniel P.	6: 38	"	
1880	"		"	"		Elbert, Samuel H.	6:449
1882	"		Chilcott, George M.	"	7:522	"	
1883	Grant, James B.	6:450	Tabor, Horace A. W.	"	11: 92	Beck, William E.	5:516
1883	"		Bowen, Thomas M.	"	12:560		
1885	Eaton, Benjamin H.	6:451	"	Teller, Henry M.	15:228	"	
1887	Adams, Alva	6:451	"	"		"	
1889	Cooper, Job A.	6:451	Wolcott, Edward O.	"	8:397	Helm, Joseph C.	13: 58
1891	Routt, John L.	6:449	"	"		"	
1893	Waite, Davis H.	6:452	"	"		Hayt, Charles D.	12:197
1895	McIntire, Albert W.	6:453	"	"		"	
1897	Adams, Alva	6:451	"	"		"	
1898	"		"	"		Campbell, John	12:324
1899	Thomas, Charles S.	13:362	"	"		"	
1901	Orman, James B.	3:245	Patterson, Thomas M.	"	12:555	"	
1903	Peabody, James H.	1:316	"	"		"	
1904	"		"	"		Gabbert, William H.	13:230
1905	Adams, Alva	6:451	"	"		"	
1905	Peabody, James H.	1:316	"	"		"	
1905	McDonald, Jesse F.	14:114	"	"		"	
1907	Buchtel, Henry A.	14:502	Guggenheim, Simon	"	C: 50	Steele, Robert W.	20:370
1909	Shafroth, John F.	14:502	"	Hughes, Charles J., Jr.	20: 43	"	
1910	"		"	"		Campbell, John	12:324
1911	"		"	Vacant		"	
1913	Ammons, Elias M.	15:405	"	Thomas, Charles S.	13:362	Musser, George W.	19:235
1913	"		Shafroth, John F.	"	14:502	"	
1915	Carlson, George A.	15:405	"	"		Gabbert, William H.	13:230
1916	"		"	"		White, S. Harrison	
1917	Gunter, Julius C.	C:422	"	"		"	
1918	"		"	"		Hill, William A.	26:343
1919	Shoup, Oliver H.	A:339	Phipps, Lawrence C.	"	A:328	Garrigues, James E.	A:134
1921	"		"	Nicholson, Samuel D.	23: 52	Scott, Tully	23:121
1923	Sweet, William E.	C:498	"	Adams, Alva B.	B:162	Teller, James H.	B:212
1924	"		"	Means, Rice W.	C:177	"	
1925	Morley, Clarence J.	B:321	"	"		Allen, George W.	24:325
1927	"		"	Waterman, Charles W.	24:258	Burke, Haslett P.	D:109
1928	"		"	"		Dennison, John H.	
1929	Adams, William H.	C: 74	"	"		Whitford, Greeley W.	
1931	"		Costigan, Edward P.	"	D:255	Adams, John T.	
1933	Johnson, Edwin C.		"	Adams, Alva B.	B:162	"	
1935	"		"	"		Butler, Charles C.	C:227

CONNECTICUT

Date	Governors	Biography	U. S. Senators	Biography	Chief Justices	Biography
1639	Haynes, John	7:371				
1640	Hopkins, Edward	10:319				
1641	Haynes, John	7:371				
1642	Wyllys, George	10:320				
1643	Haynes, John	7:371				
1644	Hopkins, Edward	10:319				
1645	Haynes, John	7:371				
1646	Hopkins, Edward	10:319				
1647	Haynes, John	7:371				
1648	Hopkins, Edward	10:319				
1649	Haynes, John	7:371				
1650	Hopkins, Edward	10:319				
1651	Haynes, John	7:371				
1652	Hopkins, Edward	10:319				
1653	Haynes, John	7:371				
1654	Hopkins, Edward	10:319				
1655	Welles, Thomas	10:320				
1656	Webster, John	10:321				
1657	Winthrop, John, Jr.	10:321				
1658	Welles, Thomas	10:320				
1659	Winthrop, John, Jr.	10:321				
1675	Leete, William	10:322				
1683	Treat, Robert	10:323				
1687	Andros, Edmund	6: 90				
1689	Treat, Robert	10:323				
1698	Winthrop, Fitz-John	10:324				
1707	Saltonstall, Gurdon	1:163				
1711	"				Saltonstall, Gurdon	1:163
1712	"				Gold, Nathan	12:311
1713	"				Pitkin, William	10:327
1714	"				Gold, Nathan	12:311
1723	"				Burr, Peter	
1724	Talcott, Joseph	10:325			"	
1725	"				Law, Jonathan	10:325
1741	Law, Jonathan	10:325			Wolcott, Roger	10:326
1750	Wolcott, Roger	10:326			Fitch, Thomas	10:327
1754	Fitch, Thomas	10:327			Pitkin, William	10:327
1766	Pitkin, William	10:327			Trumbull, Jonathan	10:328
1769	Trumbull, Jonathan	10:328			Griswold, Matthew	10:329
1784	Griswold, Matthew	10:329			Huntington, Samuel	10:329
1785	"				Law, Richard	4:545
1786	Huntington, Samuel	10:329			"	
1789	"		Ellsworth, Oliver	1: 22	Dyer, Eliphalet	11:172
1789	"		" Johnson, William S.	6:342	"	
1791	"		" Sherman, Roger	2:352	"	
1793	"		" Mitchell, Stephen M.	3:509	Adams, Andrew	11:184
1795	"		" Trumbull, Jonathan	10:331	"	
1796	Wolcott, Oliver	10:330	Hillhouse, James	2: 9	"	
1819	"		" Tracy, Uriah	2: 34	"	
1798	Trumbull, Jonathan	10:331	" "		Root, Jesse	4:375
1807	"		" Goodrich, Chauncey	2:138	Mitchell, Stephen M.	3:509
1809	Treadwell, John	10:331	" "		"	
1810	"		Dana, Samuel W. "	2: 10	"	
1811	Griswold, Roger	10:331	" "		"	
1813	Smith, John C.	10:332	" Daggett, David	4: 31	"	
1814	"		" "		Reeve, Tapping	6:175
1815	"		" "		Swift, Zephaniah	3:511
1817	Wolcott, Oliver	10:333	" "		"	
1819	"		" Lanman, James	4: 71	Hosmer, Stephen T.	7:490
1821	"		Boardman, Elijah "	4:153	"	
1823	"		Edwards, Henry W.	10:334	"	
1825	"		" Willey, Calvin	11:314	"	
1827	Tomlinson, Gideon	10:334	Foot, Samuel A. "	7:236	"	
1831	Peters, John S.	10:334	" Tomlinson, Gideon	10:334	"	
1833	Edwards, Henry W.	10:334	Smith, Nathan "	5:516	Daggett, David	4: 31
1834	"		" "		Williams, Thomas S.	4: 61
1834	Foote, Samuel A.	10:334	" "		"	
1835	Edwards, Henry W.	10:334	Niles, John M. "	6:436	"	
1837	"		" Smith, Perry	5:518	"	

CONNECTICUT (*Continued*)

Date	Governors	Biography	U. S. Senators		Biography	Chief Justices	Biography
1838	Ellsworth, William W.	10:335	Niles, John M.		6:436	Williams, Thomas S.	4: 61
1838	"		"	Smith, Perry	5:518	"	
1839	"		Betts, Thaddeus	"	4:350	"	
1840	"		Huntington, Jabez W.	"	4:540	"	
1842	Cleveland, Chauncey F.	10:335	"	"		"	
1843	"		"	Niles, John M.	6:436	"	
1844	Baldwin, Roger S.	10:336	"	"		"	
1846	Toucey, Isaac	5: 7	"	"		"	
1847	Bissell, Clark	10:336	Baldwin, Roger S.	"	10:336	Church, Samuel	7:534
1849	Trumbull, Joseph	10:337	"	Smith, Truman	12:220	"	
1850	Seymour, Thomas H.	10:337	"	"		"	
1852	"		Toucey, Isaac	"	5: 7	"	
1854	Dutton, Henry	10:338	"	Gillette, Francis	4: 72	Waite, Henry M.	
1855	Minor, William T.	10:338	"	Foster, LaFayette S.	2: 95	"	
1857	Holley, Alexander H.	10:338	Dixon, James	"	4:447	Storrs, William L.	7:501
1858	Buckingham, William A.	10:339	"	"		"	
1861	"		"	"		Hinman, Joel	11:357
1866	Hawley, Joseph R.	1:457	"	"		"	
1867	English, James E.	10:340	"	Ferry, Orris S.	2: 95	"	
1869	Jewell, Marshall	4: 20	Buckingham, W. A.	"	10:339	"	
1870	English, James E.	10:340	"	"		Butler, Thomas B.	12:224
1871	Jewell, Marshall	4: 20	"	"		"	
1873	Ingersoll, Charles R.	10:341	"	"		Seymour, Origen S.	10:258
1874	"		"	"		Park, John D.	12:311
1875	"		Eaton, William W.	"	11:172	"	
1875	"		"	English, James	10:340	"	
1876	"		"	Barnum, William H.	12:389	"	
1877	Hubbard, Richard D.	10:342	"	"		"	
1879	Andrews, Charles B.	10:342	"	Platt, Orville H.	2:339	"	
1881	Bigelow, Hobart B.	10:342	Hawley, Joseph R.	"	1:457	"	
1883	Waller, Thomas M.	10:343	"	"		"	
1885	Harrison, Henry B.	10:343	"	"		"	
1887	Lounsbury, Phineas C.	10:344	"	"		"	
1889	Bulkeley, Morgan G.	10:345	"	"		Andrews, Charles B.	10:342
1893	Morris, Luzon B.	10:345	"	"		"	
1895	Coffin, Owen V.	10:346	"	"		"	
1897	Cooke, Lorrin A.	10:346	"	"		"	
1899	Lounsbury, George E.	12:283	"	"		"	
1901	McLean, George P.	13:370	"	"		"	
1902	"		"	"		Torrance, David	12:339
1903	Chamberlain, Abiram	13:370	"	"		"	
1905	Roberts, Henry	13:124	Bulkeley, Morgan G.		10:345	"	
1905	"		"	Brandegee, Frank B.	13:600	"	
1907	Woodruff, Rollin S.	14:524	"	"		Baldwin, Simeon E.	21: 86
1909	Lilley, George L.	14:474	"	"		"	
1909	Weeks, Frank B.	C:495	"	"		"	
1910	"		"	"		Hall, Frederick B.	22:339
1911	Baldwin, Simeon E.	21: 86	McLean, George P.	"	13:370	"	
1913	"		"	"		Prentice, Samuel O.	16:182
1915	Holcomb, Marcus H.	23:381	"	"		"	
1920	"		"	"		Wheeler, George W.	24:136
1921	Lake, Everett J.	C: 66	"	"		"	
1923	Templeton, Charles A.		"	"		"	
1924	"		"	Bingham, Hiram	A: 28	"	
1925	Trumbull, John H.		"	"		"	
1929	"		Walcott, Frederick C.	"	C:294	"	
1930	"		"	"		Maltbie, William M.	D:212
1931	Cross, Wilbur L.	C:451	"	"		"	
1933	"		"	Lonergan, Augustine	D:236	"	
1935	"		Maloney, Francis T.	"			

DELAWARE

Date	Governors	Biography	U. S. Senators		Biography	Chief Justices	Biography
1776	McKinley, John	5:543					
1777	"					Killen, William	**4:173**
1778	Rodney, Cæsar	5:173				"	
1782	Dickinson, John	2:281				"	
1783	Van Dyke, Nicholas	4:398				"	
1786	Collins, Thomas	5:554				"	
1789	Clayton, Joshua	11:530	Read, George		3:297	"	
1789	"		"	Bassett, Richard	11:530	"	
1793	"		"	Vining, John	2: 6	Bassett, Richard	11:550
1793	"		Johns, Kersey	"	5:196	Read, George	3:297
1795	"		Lattimer, Henry	"	2: 10	"	
1796	Bedford, Gunning	11:530	"	"		"	
1797	Rogers, D. (*acting*)		"	"		"	
1798	"		"	Clayton, Joshua	11:530	"	
1799	Bassett, Richard	11:530	"	Wells, William H.	2: 9	Johns, Kersey	5:196
1799	"		"	"		Booth, James	4: 72
1801	Sykes, James (*acting*)	11:530	White, Samuel	"	13:249	"	
1802	Hall, David	11:531	"	"		"	
1804	"		"	Bayard, James A.	7:300	"	
1805	Mitchell, Nathaniel	11:531	"	"		"	
1808	Truitt, George	11:531	"	"		"	
1810	"		Horsey, Outerbridge	"	4: 70	"	
1811	Haslet, Joseph	11:531	"	"		"	
1813	"		"	Wells, William H.	2: 9	"	
1814	Rodney, Daniel	11:531	"	"		"	
1817	Clark, John	11:531	"	Van Dyke, Nicholas	4:346	"	
1820	Collins, John	11:532	"	"		"	
1822	Rodney, Cæsar (*acting*)	11:532	Rodney, Cæsar A.	"	3: 11	"	
1823	Haslet, Joseph	11:531	"	"		"	
1823	Thomas, Charles (*acting*)	11:531	"	"		"	
1824	Paynter, Samuel	11:532	Clayton, Thomas	"	12:552	"	
1826	"		"	Rodney, Daniel	11:531	"	
1827	Polk, Charles	11:532	McLane, Louis	"	5:293	"	
1827	"		"	Ridgely, Henry M.	4:392	"	
1828	"		"	"		Clayton, Thomas	12:552
1829	"		"	Clayton, John M.	6:179		
1830	Hazzard, David	11:532	Naudain, Arnold	"	11:504	Vacant	
1832	"		"	"		Clayton, Thomas	12:552
1833	Bennett, Caleb P.	11:533	"	"		"	
1836	"		Bayard, Richard H.	"	4:351	"	
1837	Comegys, Cornelius P.	11:533	"	Clayton, Thomas	12:552	Clayton, John M.	6:179
1839	"		"	"		Bayard, Richard H.	4:351
1841	Cooper, William B.	11:533	"	"		Booth, James	4: 72
1845	Stockton, Thomas	11:533	Clayton, John M.	"	6:179	"	
1847	Tharp, William	11:534	"	Spruance, Presley	4:351	"	
1849	"		Wales, John	"	11:354	"	
1851	Ross, William H. H.	11:534	Bayard, James A.	"	13:206	"	
1853	"		"	Clayton, John M.	6:179	"	
1855	Causey, Peter F.	11:534	"	"		Harrington, Samuel M.	13:473
1856	"		"	Comegys, Joseph P.	7:497	"	
1857	"		"	Bates, Martin W.	13:476	Gilpin, Edward W.	7:497
1859	Burton, William	11:534	"	Saulsbury, Willard	11:471	"	
1863	Cannon, William	11:535	"	"		"	
1864	"		Riddle, George R.	"	4:543	"	
1865	Saulsbury, Gove	11:535	"	"		"	
1867	"		Bayard, James A.	"	13:206	"	
1869	"		Bayard, Thomas F.	"	2:404	"	
1871	Ponder, James	11:535	"	Saulsbury, Eli	11:471	"	
1875	Cochran, John P.	11:536	"	"		"	
1876	"		"	"		Comegys, Joseph P.	7:497
1879	Hall, John W.	11:536	"	"		"	
1883	Stockley, Charles C.	11:536	"	"		"	
1885	"		Gray, George	"	26: 17	"	
1887	Biggs, Benjamin T.	11:536	"	"		"	
1889	"		"	Higgins, Anthony	1:290	"	
1891	Reynolds, Robert J.	11:537	"	"		"	
1893	"		"	"		Lore, Charles B.	7:553
1895	Marvil, Joshua H.	11:537	"	"		"	
1895	Watson, Wm. T. (*act.*)	11:537	"	"		"	

References are to THE NATIONAL CYCLOPEDIA OF AMERICAN BIOGRAPHY

DELAWARE (*Continued*)

Date	Governors	Biography	U. S. Senators		Biography	Chief Justices	Biography
1897	Tunnell, Ebe W.	11:537	Gray, George		26: 17	Lore, Charles B.	7:553
1897	"		"	Kenney, Richard R.	12:538	"	
1899	"		Vacant	"		"	
1901	Hunn, John	11:538	"	Vacant		"	
1903	"		Ball, Lewis H.		13:546	"	
1903	"		"	Alee, James Frank	13:292	"	
1905	Lea, Preston	13:586	Vacant	"		"	
1906	"		Du Pont, Henry A.	"	6:457	"	
1907	"		"	Richardson, Harry A.	14:310	"	
1909	Pennewill, Simeon S.		"	"		Pennewill, James	18:391
1913	Miller, Charles R.	20: 32	"	Saulsbury, Willard	15:105	"	
1917	Townsend, John G., Jr.		Wolcott, Josiah O.	"	A:235	"	
1919	"		"	Ball, Lewis H.	13:546	"	
1921	Denney, William duH.		Du Pont, T. Coleman	"	A:310	"	
1922	"		Bayard, Thomas F.	"	C:152	"	
1925	Robinson, Robert P.		"	Du Pont, T. Coleman	A:310	"	
1928	"		"	Hastings, Daniel O.		"	
1929	Buck, C. Douglass		Townsend, John G., Jr.	"		"	
1933	"		"	"		Layton, Daniel W.	

FLORIDA

Date	Governors	Biography	U. S. Senators		Biography	Chief Justices	Biography
1845	Moseley, William D.	11:377	Yulee, David L.		11:425		
1845	"		"	Westcott, James D., Jr.	12:464		
1846	"		"	"		Douglas, Thomas	12:275
1849	Brown, Thomas	11:378	"	Morton, Jackson	5:259	"	
1851	"		Mallory, Stephen R.	"	4:364	Anderson, Walker	12: 59
1853	Broome, James E.	11:378	"	"		Wright, Benjamin D.	12:436
1854	"		"	"		Baltzell, Thomas	12:332
1855	"		"	Yulee, David L.	11:425	"	
1857	Perry, Madison S.	11:378	"	"		"	
1860	"		"	"		DuPont, Charles H.	12:255
1861	Milton, John	11:378	"	Vacant		"	
1861	"		Vacant	"		"	
1865	Marvin, William	11:379	"	"		"	
1865	Walker, David S.	11:379	"	"		"	
1868	Reed, Harrison	11:380	Welch, Adonijah S.		12:291	Randall, Edwin M.	12:215
1868	"		"	Osborn, Thomas W.	12:394	"	
1869	"		Gilbert, Abijah	"	4:173	"	
1873	Hart, Ossian B.	11:380	"	Conover, Simon B.	12:389	"	
1874	Stearns, Marcellus L.	11:381	"	"		"	
1875	"		Jones, Charles W.	"	10:383	"	
1877	Drew, George F.	11:381	"	"		"	
1879	"		"	Call, Wilkinson	2:525	"	
1881	Bloxham, William D.	11:382	"	"		"	
1885	Perry, Edward A.	11:382	"	"		McWhorter, George G.	12:210
1887	"		Pasco, Samuel	"	1:293	Maxwell, Augustus E.	7:487
1889	Fleming, Francis P.	11:382	"	"		Raney, George P.	12:215
1893	Mitchell, Henry L.	11:383	"	"		"	
1894	"		"	"		Liddon, Benjamin S.	12:462
1895	"		"	"		Mabry, Milton H.	5:397
1897	Bloxham, William D.	11:382	"	Mallory, Stephen R.	12:132	Taylor, R. Fenwick	12:213
1899	"		Taliaferro, James P.	"	10:175	"	
1901	Jennings, William S.	11:383	"	"		"	
1905	Broward, Napoleon B.		"	"		Shackelford, Thomas M.	10:489
1907	"		"	Bryan, William J.	14:236	"	
1908	"		"	Milton, William H.	14:388	"	
1909	Gilchrist, Albert W.	14: 59	"	Fletcher, Duncan U.	A:330	Whitfield, James B.	18:158
1911	"		Bryan, Nathan P.	"	C:391	"	
1913	Trammell, Park	A:180	"	"		Shackelford, Thomas M.	10:489
1915	"		"	"		Taylor, Robert F.	12:213
1917	Catts, Sidney J.	B:400	Trammell, Park	"	A:180	Browne, Jefferson B.	
1921	Hardee, Carey A.		"	"		"	
1923	"		"	"		Taylor, Robert F.	12:213
1925	Martin, John W.	D:206	"	"		West, Thomas F.	23:363
1926	"		"	"		Ellis, William H.	
1929	Carlton, Doyle E.	D:160	"	"		"	
1930	"		"	"		Terrell, Glenn	
1931	"		"	"		Buford, Rivers	
1933	Sholtz, Dave		"	"		Davis, Fred H.	
1935	"		"	"		Whitfield, James B.	18:158

GEORGIA

Date	Governors	Biography	U. S. Senators		Biography	Chief Justices	Biography
1733	Oglethorpe, James E.	1:490					
1743	Stephens, William	1:490					
1750	Parker, Henry	1:491					
1754	Reynolds, John	1:491					
1757	Ellis, Henry	1:491					
1760	Wright, James	1:491					
1776	Bulloch, Archibald	1:492					
1777	Gwinnet, Button	1:493					
1777	Treutlen, John A.	1:493					
1778	Houston, John	1:493					
1779	Walton, George	1:219					
1779	Wright, James	1:491					
1782	Martin, John	2: 12					
1783	Hall, Lyman	2: 12					
1784	Houston, John	1:493					
1785	Elbert, Samuel	2: 13					
1786	Telfair, Edward	1:219					
1787	Matthews, George	1:219					
1788	Handley, George	2: 13					
1789	Walton, George	1:219	Few, William		2:346		
1789	“		“	Gunn, James	2: 11		
1791	Telfair, Edward	1:219	“	“			
1793	“		Jackson, James	“	1:220		
1794	Mathews, George	1:219	“	“			
1795	“		Walton, George	“	1:219		
1796	Irwin, Jared	1:220	Tatnall, Josiah	“	1:221		
1798	Jackson, James	1:220	“	“			
1799	“		Baldwin, Abraham	“	9:178		
1801	Emanuel, David	1:221	“	Jackson, James	1:220		
1802	Tattnall, Josiah	1:221	“	“			
1803	Milledge, John	1:221	“	“			
1806	Irwin, Jared	1:220	“	Milledge, John	1:221		
1807	“		Jones, George	“	5:548		
1807	“		Crawford, William H.	“	5: 82		
1809	Mitchell, David B.	1:222	“	Tait, Charles	4:348		
1813	Early, Peter	1:222	Bulloch, William B.	“	4:153		
1813	“		Bibb, William W.	“	10:425		
1815	Mitchell, David B.	1:222	“	“			
1816	“		Troup, George M.	“	1:223		
1817	Rabun, William	1:222	“	“			
1818	“		Forsyth, John	“	6:435		
1819	Talbot, Matthew (*ex off.*)	1:223	Walker, Freeman		11:504		
1819	Clarke, John		“	Elliott, John	4: 72		
1821	“		Ware, Nicholas	“	5: 70		
1823	Troup, George M.	1:223	“	“			
1824	“		Cobb, Thomas W.	“	4:467		
1825	“		“	Berrien, John M.	5:298		
1827	Forsyth, John	6:435	“	“			
1828	“		Prince, Oliver H.	“	11:399		
1829	Gilmer, George R.	1:224	Troup, George M.	“	1:223		
1829	“		“	Forsyth, John	6:435		
1831	Lumpkin, Wilson	1:224	“	“			
1833	“		King, John P.	“	2:178		
1835	Schley, William	1:225	“	“			
1837	“		Lumpkin, Wilson	“	1:224		
1837	Gilmer, George R.	1:224	“	Cuthbert, Alfred	11:560		
1839	McDonald, Charles J.	1:225	“	“			
1841	“		Berrien, John M.	“	5:298		
1843	Crawford, George W.	4:370	“	Colquitt, Walter T.	7:560		
1845	“		“	“		Lumpkin, Joseph H.	10:23
1847	Towns, George W.	1:225	“	“		“	
1848	“		“	Johnson, Herschel V.	1:226	“	
1849	“		“	Dawson, William C.	11:263	“	
1851	Cobb, Howell	1:226	“	“		“	
1852	“		Charlton, Robert M.	“	4:191	“	
1853	Johnson, Herschel V.	1:226	Toombs, Robert	“	4:392	“	
1855	“		“	Iverson, Alfred	4:438	“	
1857	Brown, Joseph E.	1:227	“	“		“	
1861	“		Vacant			“	

GEORGIA (*Continued*)

Date	Governors	Biography	U. S. Senators		Biography	Chief Justices	Biography
1861	Brown, Joseph E.	1:227	Vacant	Vacant		Lumpkin, Joseph H.	10: 23
1865	Johnson, James	1:227	"	"		"	
1865	Jenkins, Charles J.	1:228	"	"		"	
1867	"		"	"		Warner, Hiram	7:502
1868	Ruger, Thomas H.	1:229	Miller, Homer V. M.		12:344	Brown, Joseph E.	1:227
1868	Bullock, Rufus B.	1:229	"	Hill, Joshua	4:442	"	
1870	"		"	"		Lochrane, Osborne A.	1:508
1871	Conley, Benjamin	1:229	Norwood, Thomas M.	"	13:474	"	
1872	Smith, Joseph M.		"	"		Warner, Hiram	7:502
1873	"		"	Gordon, John B.	1:231	"	
1876	Colquitt, Alfred H.	1:291	"	"		"	
1877	"		Hill, Benjamin H.	"	10:194	"	
1880	"		"	Brown, Joseph E.	1:227	Jackson, James	2:515
1882	Stephens, Alexander H.	3:420	Barrow, Pope	"	9:501	"	
1883	Boynton, James S. (*act.*)	1:230	Colquitt, Alfred H.	"	1:291	"	
1883	McDaniel, Henry D.	26:368	"	"		"	
1886	Gordon, John B.	1:231	"	"		"	
1887	"		"	"		Bleckley, Logan E.	2:195
1890	Northern, William J.	1:232	"	"		"	
1891	"		"	Gordon, John B.	1:231	"	
1894	"		Walsh, Patrick	"	2: 50	Simmons, Thomas J.	2:212
1895	Atkinson, William Y.	13:139	Bacon, Augustus O.	"	12:527	"	
1897	"		"	Clay, Alexander S.	5:548	"	
1899	Candler, Allen D.	2:121	"	"		"	
1903	Terrell, Joseph M.	12:393	"	"		"	
1905	"		"	"		Fish, William H.	18:394
1907	Smith, Hoke	1:183	"	"		"	
1909	Brown, Joseph M.	B:505	"	"		"	
1910	"		"	Terrell, Joseph M.	12:396	"	
1911	Smith, Hoke	1:183	"	"		"	
1911	Brown, Joseph M.	B:505	"	Smith, Hoke	1:183	"	
1913	Slaton, John M.	A:497	"	"		"	
1914	"		West, William S.	"	18:216	"	
1914	"		Hardwick, Thomas W.	"	B:296	"	
1915	Harris, Nathaniel E.	23:400	"	"		"	
1917	Dorsey, Hugh M.	18:356	"	"		"	
1919	"		Harris, William J.	"	24:266	"	
1921	Hardwick, Thomas W.	B:296	"	Watson, Thomas E.		"	
1922	"		"	Felton, Rebecca L.		"	
1922	"		"	George, Walter F.	A:521	"	
1923	Walker, Clifford	D:210	"	"		Russell, Richard B.	
1927	Hardman, Lamartine G.	A:399	"	"		"	
1931	Russell, Richard B., Jr.		"	"		"	
1932	"		Cohen, John S.	"	D:106	"	
1933	Talmadge, Eugene		Russel, Richard B., Jr.	"		"	

IDAHO

Date	Governors	Biography	U. S. Senators	Biography	Chief Justices	Biography
1889	Shoup, George L.	12:491				
1890	Willey, Norman B.	12:492	Shoup, George L.	12:491	Sullivan, Isaac N.	13:230
1890	"		" McConnell, William J.	12:492	"	
1891	"		" Dubois, Frederick T.	12:519	Huston, Joseph W.	5:510
1893	McConnell, William J.	12:492	" "		"	
1895	"		" "		Morgan, John T.	1:295
1896	Steunenberg, Frank	12:492	" "		"	
1897	"		" Heitfield, Henry	13:581	Sullivan, Isaac N.	13:230
1899	"		" "		Huston, Joseph W.	5:510
1901	Hunt, Frank W.	12:492	Dubois, Frederick T. "	12:519	Quarles, Ralph P.	13:231
1903	Morrison, John T.	12:493	" Heyburn, Weldon B.	13:101	"	
1904	"		" "		Sullivan, Isaac N.	13:230
1905	Gooding, Frank R.	21: 7	" "		Stocklager, Charles O.	14:200
1907	"		Borah, William E. "	B:115	Ailshie, James F.	18:310
1909	Brady, James H.	15:266	" "		Sullivan, Isaac N.	13:230
1911	Hawley, James H.	15:297	" "		Stewart, George H.	20:472
1912	"		" Perky, Kirtland I.		"	
1913	Haines, John M.	15: 8	" Brady, James H.	15:266	Ailshie, James F.	18:310
1915	Alexander, Moses	23:200	" "		Sullivan, Isaac N.	13:230
1917	"		" "		Budge, Alfred	D:185
1918	"		" Nugent, John F.	A:425	"	
1919	Davis, David W.		" "		Morgan, William M.	C:526
1921	"		" Gooding, Frank R.	21: 7	Rice, John C.	
1923	Moore, Charles C.	B:152	" "		Budge, Alfred	D:185
1924	"		" "		McCarthy, Charles P.	D:289
1925	"		" "		Dunn, Robert N.	
1925	"		" "		Lee, William A.	20:276
1927	Baldridge, H. Clarence	D:415	" "		"	
1928	"		" Thomas, John	D:139	"	
1929	"		" "		Budge, Alfred	D:185
1931	Ross, C. Ben		" "		"	
1932	"		" Pope, James P.	D:341	"	
1935	"		" "		Givens, Raymond L.	

ILLINOIS

Date	Governors	Biography	U. S. Senators	Biography	Chief Justices	Biography
1818	Bond, Shadrach	11: 43	Thomas, Jesse B.	11:315	Phillips, Joseph	12:184
1818	"		" Edwards, Ninian	11: 42	"	
1822	Coles, Edward	11: 43	" "		Reynolds, Thomas	12:303
1824	"		" McLean, John J.	5:509	"	
1825	"		" Kane, Elias K.	11:495	Wilson, William	5:514
1826	Edwards, Ninian	11: 42	" "		"	
1829	"		McLean, John J. "	5:509	"	
1830	Reynolds, John	11: 44	Baker, David J. "	11:506	"	
1830	"		Robinson, John M. "	13:161	"	
1834	Ewing, Wm. L. D. (*act.*)	11: 44	" "		"	
1834	Duncan, Joseph	11: 45	" "		"	
1835	"		" Ewing, William L. D.	11: 44	"	
1837	"		" Young, Richard M.	12:240	"	
1838	Carlin, Thomas	11: 45	" "		"	
1841	"		McRoberts, Samuel "	5:509	"	
1842	Ford, Thomas	11: 46	" "		"	
1843	"		Semple, James	4:361	"	
1843	"		" Breese, Sidney	8:122	"	
1846	French, Augustus C.	11: 46	" "		"	
1847	"		Douglas, Stephen A. "	2:428	"	
1848	"		" "		Treat, Samuel H.	12:374
1849	"		" Shields, James	8: 2	"	
1853	Matteson, Joel A.	11: 47	" "		"	
1855	"		" Trumbull, Lyman	12:342	Skinner, Onias C.	5:515
1856	"		" "		Scates, Walter B.	12:209
1857	Bissell, William H.	11: 47	" "		Breese, Sidney	8:122
1858	"		" "		Caton, John D.	4:510
1860	Wood, John (*acting*)	11: 47	" "		"	
1861	Yates, Richard	11: 48	Browning, Orville H. "	2:457	"	

ILLINOIS (*Continued*)

Date	Governors	Biography	U. S. Senators	Biography
1863	Yates, Richard	11: 48	Richardson, William A.	
1863	"		" Trumbull, Lyman	12:342
1864	"		" "	
1865	Oglesby, Richard	11: 48	Yates, Richard "	11: 48
1867	"		" "	
1869	Palmer, John M.	11: 49	" "	
1870	"		" "	
1871	"		Logan, John A. "	4:298
1873	Oglesby, Richard	11: 48	" "	
1873	Beveridge, John L.	11: 50	" Oglesby, Richard	11: 48
1874	"		" "	
1875	"		" "	
1876	"		" "	
1877	Cullom, Shelby M.	11: 50	Davis, David "	2:474
1878	"		" "	
1879	"		" Logan, John A.	4:298
1880	"		" "	
1881	"		" "	
1882	"		" "	
1883	Hamilton, John M.	11: 50	Cullom, Shelby M. "	11: 50
1884	"		" "	
1885	Oglesby, Richard	11: 48	" "	
1886	"		" "	
1887	"		" Farwell, Charles B.	6:394
1888	"		" "	
1889	Fifer, Joseph W.	11: 51	" "	
1890	"		" "	
1891	"		" Palmer, John M.	11: 49
1892	"		" "	
1893	Altgeld, John P.	11: 51	" "	
1894	"		" "	
1895	"		" "	
1896	"		" "	
1897	Tanner, John R.	11: 52	" Mason, William E.	12:445
1898	"		" "	
1899	"		" "	
1900	"		" "	
1901	Yates, Richard	11: 52	" "	
1902	"		" "	
1903	"		" Hopkins, Albert J.	11:396
1904	"		" "	
1905	Deneen, Charles S.	14:364	" "	
1905	"		" "	
1906	"		" "	
1907	"		" "	
1908	"		" "	
1909	"		" Lorimer, William	14: 91
1910	"		" "	
1911	"		" "	
1912	"		" "	
1913	Dunne, Edward F.	16:122	" Sherman, Lawrence Y.	15:101
1913	"		Lewis, J. Hamilton "	15: 63
1914	"		" "	
1915	"		" "	
1916	"		" "	
1917	Lowden, Frank O.	B: 35	" "	
1918	"		" "	
1919	"		McCormick, Medill "	19: 94
1920	"		" "	
1921	Small, Len	D:192	" McKinley, William B.	15:115
1922	"		" "	
1923	"		" "	
1924	"		" "	
1925	"		Deneen, Charles S. "	14:364
1926	"		" "	
1927	"		" Vacancy	
1929	Emmerson, Louis L.	D:337	" Glenn, Otis F.	A: 20
1930	"		" "	
1931	"		Lewis J. Hamilton "	15: 63
1933	Horner, Henry		" Dietrich, William H.	
1935	"		" "	

Chief Justices	Biography
Caton, John D.	4:510
"	
Walker, Pinkney H.	5:513
"	
Breese, Sidney	8:122
"	
Lawrence, Charles B.	5:437
"	
Breese, Sidney	8:122
"	
Walker, Pinkney H.	5:513
Scott, John M.	12:123
Sheldon, Benjamin R.	13:345
Scholfield, John	13:176
Craig, Alfred M.	13:481
Walker, Pinkney H.	5:513
Dickey, Theodore L.	12:223
Craig, Alfred M.	13:481
Scott, John M.	12:123
Sheldon, Benjamin R.	13:345
Scholfield, John	13:176
Mulkey, John H.	6:506
Scott, John M.	12:123
Sheldon, Benjamin R.	13:345
Craig, Alfred M.	13:481
Shope, Simeon	12: 69
Scholfield, John	13:176
Magruder, Benjamin D.	12:263
Bailey, Joseph M.	13:240
Baker, David J.	12:351
Wilkin, Jacob W.	13:223
Craig, Alfred M.	13:481
Magruder, Benjamin D.	12:263
Phillips, Jesse J.	12:184
Carter, Joseph N.	5:512
Cartwright, James H.	5:512
Boggs, Carroll C.	12:465
Wilkin, Jacob W.	13:223
Hand, John P.	13:307
Magruder, Benjamin D.	12:263
Hand, John P.	13:307
Ricks, James B.	17:171
Cartwright, James H.	5:512
Scott, Guy C.	
Hand, John P.	13:307
Cartwright, James H.	5:512
Farmer, William M.	17:293
Vickers, Alonzo K.	
Carter, Orrin N.	24:335
Dunn, Frank K.	D:431
Cooke, George A.	B:298
"	
Cartwright, James H.	5:512
Farmer, William M.	17:293
Craig, Charles C.	D:241
Carter, Orrin N.	24:335
Duncan, Warren W.	
Dunn, Frank K.	D:431
Cartwright, James H.	5:512
Stone, Clyde E.	
Thompson, Floyd E.	
Farmer, William M.	17:293
Duncan, Warren W.	
Dunn, Frank K.	D:431
Stone, Clyde E.	
Heard, Oscar E.	
Farmer, William M.	17:293
Dunn, Frank K.	D:431
Stone, Clyde E.	
Orr, Warren H.	
Stone, Clyde E.	

References are to THE NATIONAL CYCLOPEDIA OF AMERICAN BIOGRAPHY

INDIANA

Date	Governors	Biography	U. S. Senators		Biography	Chief Justices	Biography
1816	Jennings, Jonathan	13:266	Noble, James		11:551		
1816	"		"	Taylor, Waller	4:531		
1822	Boon, Ratliff	13:266	"	"			
1822	Hendricks, William	13:266	"	"			
1825	Ray, James B.	13:267	"	Hendricks, William	13:266		
1831	Noble, Noah	13:267	Hanna, Robert	"	4:253		
1831	"		Tipton, John	"	11:314		
1837	Wallace, David	13:267	"	Smith, Oliver H.	5:517		
1839	"		White, Albert S.	"	3:507		
1840	Bigger, Samuel	13:268	"	"			
1843	Whitcomb, James	13:268	"	Hannegan, Edward A.	11:372		
1845	"		Bright, Jesse D.	"	3:428		
1848	Dunning, Paris C.	13:269	"	"			
1849	Wright, Joseph A.	13:269	"	Whitcomb, James	13:268		
1852	"		"	Cathcart, Charles W.	4:384		
1853	"		"	Pettit, John	4:537		
1857	Willard, Ashbel P.	13:270	"	Fitch, Graham N.	12:209		
1860	Hammond, Abram A.	13:270	"	"			
1861	Lane, Henry S.	13:270	"	"			
1861	Morton, Oliver H. P. T.	13:271	"	Lane, Henry S.	13:270		
1862	"		Wright, Joseph A.	"	13:269		
1863	"		Turpie, David	"	1:218		
1863	"		Hendricks, Thomas A.	"	2:403		
1867	Baker, Conrad	13:272	"	Morton, Oliver H. P. T.	12:271		
1869	"		Pratt, Daniel D.	"	11:187		
1873	Hendricks, Thomas A.	2:403	"	"			
1875	"		McDonald, Joseph E.	"	11:504		
1877	Williams, James D.	13:272	"	Voorhees, Daniel W.	2:359		
1880	Gray, Isaac P.	13:273	"	"			
1881	Porter, Albert G.	13:274	Harrison, Benjamin	"	1:133		
1885	Gray, Isaac P.	13:273	"	"			
1887	"		Turpie, David	"	1:218		
1889	Hovey, Alvin P.	13:274	"	"			
1891	Chase, Ira J.	13:275	"	"			
1893	Matthews, Claude	13:275	"	"			
1897	Mount, James A.	13:276	"	Fairbanks, Charles W.	14: 10		
1899	"		Beveridge, Albert J.	"	13: 26		
1901	Durbin, Winfield T.	21: 40	"	"			
1905	Hanly, J. Frank	19:219	"	Hemenway, James A.	14:187		
1909	Marshall, Thomas R.	19:137	"	Shively, Benjamin F.	14:442		
1911	"		Kern, John W.	"	14:137		
1913	Ralston, Samuel M.	15:142	"	"			
1916	"		"	Taggart, Thomas	22:430		
1916	"		"	Watson, James E.	A:409		
1917	Goodrich, James P.		New, Harry S.	"	A: 13		
1921	McCray, Warren T.	B:218	"	"			
1923	"		Ralston, Samuel M.	"	15:142		
1925	Jackson, Ed	D:216	Robinson, Arthur R.	"	B:366		
1929	Leslie, Harry G.		"	"			
1933	McNutt, Paul V.	D:378	"	VanNuys, Frederick			
1935	"		Minton, Sherman	"			

NOTE: *The chief justices of Indiana are not elected, but the office rotates among the members of the Supreme Court, a different member being selected at each term.*

IOWA

Date	Governors	Biography	U. S. Senators		Biography	Chief Justices	Biography
1846	Briggs, Ansel	11:429				Mason, Charles	3:504
1847	"					Williams, Joseph	12:342
1848	"		Jones, George W.		3:433	Hastings, S. Clinton	3:510
1848	"		"	Dodge, Augustus A. C.	12: 53	"	
1849	"		"	"		Williams, Joseph	12:342
1850	Hempstead, Stephen	11:430	"	"		"	
1854	Grimes, James W.	11:430	"	"		"	
1855	"		"	Harlan, James	2:457	Wright, George G.	3:523
1858	Lowe, Ralph P.	11:431	"	"		"	
1859	"		Grimes, James W.	"	11:430	"	
1860	Kirkwood, Samuel J.	4:245	"	"		Lowe, Ralph P.	11:431
1862	"		"	"		Baldwin, Caleb	13:253
1864	Stone, William M.	11:431	"	"		Wright, George G.	3:523
1865	"		"	Kirkwood, Samuel J.	4:245	"	
1866	"		"	"		Lowe, Ralph P.	11:431
1867	"		"	Harlan, James	2:457	"	
1868	Merrill, Samuel	11:432	"	"		Dillon, John F.	1:268
1870	"		Howell, James B.	"	9:450	Cole, Chester C.	13:278
1871	"		Wright, George G.	"	3:523	Day, James G.	12:518
1872	Carpenter, Cyrus C.	11:432	"	"		Beck, Joseph M.	12:533
1873	"		"	Allison, William B.	1:296	"	
1874	"		"	"		Miller, William E.	12: 70
1876	Kirkwood, Samuel J.	4:245	"	"		Cole, Chester C.	13:278
1876	"		"	"		Seevers, William H.	12: 70
1877	Newbold, Joshua G.	11:433	Kirkwood, Samuel J.	"	4:245	Day, James G.	12:518
1878	Gear, John H.	11:433	"	"		Rothrock, James H.	12:336
1879	"		"	"		Beck, Joseph M.	12:533
1880	"		"	"		Adams, Austin	12:393
1881	"		McDill, James W.	"	11:479	"	
1882	Sherman, Buren R.	11:433	"	"		Seevers, William H.	12: 70
1883	"		Wilson, James F.	"	1:289	Day, James G.	12:518
1884	"		"	"		Rothrock, James H.	12:336
1885	"		"	"		Beck, Joseph M.	12:533
1886	Larrabee, William	11:433	"	"		Adams, Austin	12:393
1888	"		"	"		Seevers, William H.	12: 70
1889	"		"	"		Reed, Joseph R.	21:104
1889	"		"	"		Given, Josiah	12:511
1890	Boies, Horace	11:433	"	"		Rothrock, James H.	12:336
1891	"		"	"		Beck, Joseph M.	12:533
1892	"		"	"		Robinson, Gifford S.	12:373
1894	Jackson, Frank D.	11:434	"	"		Granger, Charles T.	12: 69
1895	"		Gear, John H.	"	11:433	Given, Josiah	12:511
1896	Drake, Francis M.	11:434	"	"		Rothrock, James H.	12:336
1897	"		"	"		Kinne, Lavega G.	12:446
1898	Shaw, Leslie M.	23:118	"	"		Deemer, Horace E.	18:145
1899	"		"	"		Robinson, Gifford S.	12:373
1900	"		Dolliver, Jonathan P.	"	12:392	Granger, Charles T.	12: 69
1901	"		"	"		Given, Josiah	12:511
1902	Cummins, Albert B.	13:176	"	"		Ladd, Scott M.	12:373
1903	"		"	"		Bishop, Charles A.	12:378
1904	"		"	"		Deemer, Horace E.	18:145
1905	"		"	"		Sherwin, John C.	
1906	"		"	"		McClain, Emlin	16:253
1907	"		"	"		Weaver, Silas M.	22:203
1908	"		"	Cummins, Albert B.	13:176	Ladd, Scott M.	12:373
1909	Carroll, Beryl F.	C:427	"	"		Evans, William D.	18: 91
1910	"		Young, Lafayette	"		Deemer, Horace E.	18:145
1911	"		Kenyon, William S.	"	24: 60	Sherwin, John C.	
1912	"		"	"		McClain, Emlin	16:253
1913	Clarke, George W.	15:257	"	"		Weaver, Silas M.	22:203
1914	"		"	"		Ladd, Scott M.	12:373
1915	"		"	"		Deemer, Horace E.	18:145
1916	"		"	"		Evans, William D.	18: 91
1917	Harding, William L.	B: 98	"	"		Gaynor, Francis R.	22:182
1918	"		"	"		Preston, Byron W.	D:124
1919	"		"	"		Ladd, Scott M.	12:373
1920	"		"	"		Weaver, Silas M.	22:203
1921	Kendall, Nathan E.		"	"		Evans, William D.	18: 91
1922	"		Rawson, Charles A.	"		"	

IOWA (*Continued*)

Date	Governors	Biography	U. S. Senators	Biography	Chief Justices	Biography
1922	Kendall, Nathan E.		Cummins, Albert B.	13:176	Stevens, Truman S.	
1922	"		Brookhart, Smith W. "	B:276	"	
1923	"		" "		Preston, Byron W.	D:124
1924	"		" "		Arthur, Thomas	
1925	Hammill, John	26:360	" "		Faville, Frederick F.	D: 79
1926	"		Steck, Daniel F. "	C:196	DeGraff, Lawrence	
1926	"		" Stewart, David W.		"	
1927	"		" Brookhart, Smith W.	B:276	Evans, William D.	18: 91
1928	"		" "		Stevens, Truman S.	
1929	"		" "		Albert, Elma G.	
1930	"		" "		Morling, Edgar A.	
1931	Turner, Dan W.		Dickinson, Lester J. "	D:438	Faville, Frederick F.	D: 79
1931	"		" Murphy, Louis		"	
1932	"		" "		Stevens, Truman S.	
1932	"		" "		Wagner, Henry F.	
1933	Herring, Clyde L.		" "		Albert, Elma G.	
1933	"		" "		Kindig, James W.	
1934	"		" "		Claussen, George	
1934	"		" "		Mitchell, Richard F.	
1935	"		" "		Anderson, John W.	
1935	"		" "		Kintzinger, John W.	

KANSAS

Date	Governors	Biography	U. S. Senators	Biography	Chief Justices	Biography
1861	Robinson, Charles	8:342	Lane, James H.	4:278	Ewing, Thomas	25: 15
1861	"		" Pomeroy, Samuel C.	12: 69	"	
1862	"		" "		Cobb, Nelson	5:519
1863	Carney, Thomas	8:343	" "		"	
1864	"		" "		Crozier, Robert	7:490
1865	Crawford, Samuel J.	8:344	" "		"	
1866	"		Ross, Edmund G. "	13:232	"	
1867	"		" "		Kingman, Samuel A.	13: 76
1869	Harvey, James M.	8:344	" "		"	
1871	"		Caldwell, Alexander "	12:458	"	
1873	Osborn, Thomas A.	8:345	Crozier, Robert	7:490	"	
1873	"		" Ingalls, John J.	8:415	"	
1874	"		Harvey, James M. "	8:344	"	
1877	Anthony, George T.	8:345	Plumb, Preston B. "	2:529	Horton, Albert H.	6:129
1879	St. John, John P.	8:346	" "		"	
1883	Glick, George W.	8:346	" "		"	
1885	Martin, John A.	8:347	" "		"	
1889	Humphrey, Lyman U.	1:456	" "		"	
1891	"		" Peffer, William A.	1:299	"	
1892	"		Perkins, Bishop W. "	3:302	"	
1893	Lewelling, Lorenzo D.	8:347	Martin, John "	7: 20	"	
1895	Morill, Edmund N.	8:348	Baker, Lucien "	12:495	Martin, David	12: 63
1897	Leedy, John W.	8:348	" Harris, William A.	13: 21	Doster, Frank	12:125
1899	Stanley, William E.	13:394	" "		"	
1901	"		Burton, Joseph R. "	13:168	"	
1903	Bailey, Willis J.	13:395	" Long, Chester I.	C: 56	Johnston, William A.	5:519
1905	Hoch, Edward W.	14:426	" "		"	
1906	"		Benson, Alfred W. "	21:363	"	
1907	"		Curtis, Charles "	C: 7	"	
1909	Stubbs, Walter R.		" Bristow, Joseph L.	14: 29	"	
1913	Hodges, George H.	15:292	Thompson, William H. "	15: 57	"	
1915	Capper, Arthur	C: 58	" Curtis, Charles	C: 7	"	
1919	Allen, Henry J.		Capper, Arthur "	C: 58	"	
1923	Davis, Jonathan M.	B: 43	" "		"	
1925	Paulen, Ben S.		" "		"	
1929	Reed, Clyde M.	D:152	" Allen, Henry J.		"	
1930	"		" McGill, George	D:185	"	
1931	Woodring, Harry H.		" "		"	
1933	Landon, Alfred M.		" "		"	
1935	"		" "		Burch, Rousseau A.	

KENTUCKY

Date	Governors	Biography	U. S. Senators	Biography	Chief Justices	Biography
1792	Shelby, Isaac	13: 1	Brown, John	6:535	Innes, Harry	10:409
1792	"		" Edwards, John	4:314	Muter, George	12:249
1795	"		" Marshall, Humphrey	2:368	"	
1796	Garrard, James	13: 2	" "		"	
1801	"		" Breckenridge, John	3: 9	"	
1804	Greenup, Christopher	13: 2	" "		"	
1805	"		Thruston, Buckner	3:515	"	
1805	"		" Adair, John	13: 3	"	
1806	"		" Clay, Henry	5: 77	Todd, Thomas	2:467
1807	"		" Pope, John	10:184	Grundy, Felix	6:436
1808	Scott, Charles	13: 3	" "		Edwards, Ninian	11: 42
1809	"		" "		Bibb, George M.	6: 6
1810	"		Clay, Henry "	5: 77	Boyle, John	11:191
1811	"		Bibb, George M. "	6: 6	"	
1812	Shelby, Isaac	13: 3	" "		"	
1813	"		" Bledsoe, Jesse	11:415	"	
1814	"		Walker, George "	12:237	"	
1814	"		Barry, William T. "	5:296	"	
1815	"		" Talbot, Isham	14:151	"	
1816	Madison, George	13: 3	" "		"	
1816	Slaughter, Gabriel	13: 3	Hardin, Martin D. "	12:146	"	
1817	"		Crittenden, John J."	13: 6	"	
1819	"		Johnson, Richard M.	6:434	"	
1819	"		" Logan, William	4:526	"	
1820	Adair, John	13: 3	" Talbot, Isham	14:151	"	
1824	Desha, Joseph	13: 4	" "		"	
1825	"		" Rowan, John	6: 95	Bibb, George M.	6: 6
1828	Metcalfe, Thomas	13: 4	" "		"	
1829	"		Bibb, George M. "	6: 6	Robertson, George	1:363
1831	"		" Clay, Henry	5: 77	"	
1832	Breathitt, John	13: 5	" "		"	
1834	Morehead, James T.	13: 5	" "		"	
1835	"		Crittenden, John J. "	13: 6	"	
1836	Clark, James	13: 5	" "		"	
1839	Wickliffe, Charles A.	6: 8	" "		"	
1840	Letcher, Robert P.	13: 5	" "		"	
1841	"		Morehead, James T. "	13: 5	"	
1842	"		" Crittenden, John J.	13: 6	"	
1843	"		" "		Ewing, Ephraim M.	12:364
1844	Owsley, William	13: 6	" "		"	
1847	"		Underwood, Joseph R.	3:428	"	
1847	"		" Crittenden, John J.	13: 6	Marshall, Thomas A.	4:517
1848	Crittenden, John J.	13: 6	" Metcalfe, Thomas	13: 4	"	
1849	"		" Clay, Henry	5: 77	"	
1850	Helm, John L.	13: 7	" "		"	
1851	Powell, Lazarus W.	13: 7	" "		"	
1852	"		" Meriwether, David	12:219	Simpson, James	12: 48
1852	"		" Dixon, Archibald	3:434	"	
1853	"		Thompson, John B. "	12:226	"	
1854	"		" "		Hise, Elijah	12: 54
1855	Morehead, Charles S.	13: 8	" Crittenden, John J.	13: 6	"	
1856	"		" "		Marshall, Thomas A.	4:517
1857	"		" "		Crenshaw, Ben Mills	12:277
1859	Magoffin, Beriah	13: 8	Powell, Lazarus W. "	13: 7	"	
1860	"		" "		Simpson, James	12: 48
1861	"		" Breckinridge, John C.	5: 3	"	
1861	"		" Davis, Garrett	2:225	"	
1862	Robinson, James F.	13: 9	" "		Stites, Henry J.	12:110
1863	Bramlette, Thomas E.	13: 9	" "		"	
1864	"		" "		Duvall, Alvin	6:509
1865	"		Guthrie, James "	4:147	Bullitt, Joshua F.	13: 19
1866	"		" "		Sampson, William	12:101
1866	"		" "		Marshall, Thomas A.	4:517
1867	Helm, John L.	13: 7	" "		"	
1867	Stevenson, John W.	13: 9	" "		"	
1868	"		McCreery, Thomas C. "	4:377	Peters, Belvart J.	12:140
1871	Leslie, Preston H.	11: 81	Stevenson, John W. "	13: 9	Robertson, George	1:363
1872	"		" Machen, Willis B.	12:395	Pryor, William S.	12:100
1873	"		" McCreery, Thomas C.	4:377	"	
1874	"		" "		Hardin, Mordecai R.	12:443
1875	McCreary, James B.	13: 10	" "		"	

KENTUCKY (*Continued*)

Date	Governors	Biography	U. S. Senators	Biography	Chief Justices	Biography
1876	McCreary, James B.	13: 10	Stevenson, John W.	13: 9	Peters, Belvart J.	12:140
1876	“		“ McCreery, Thomas C.	4:377	“	
1877	“		Beck, James B. “	3:418	“	
1878	“		“ “		Lindsay, William	11:485
1879	Blackburn, Luke P.	13: 10	“ Williams, John S.	12:388	“	
1880	“		“ “		Pryor, William S.	12:100
1881	“		“ “		Cofer, Martin H.	12: 63
1882	“		“ “		Lewis, Joseph H.	12: 92
1883	Knott, J. Proctor	13: 11	“ “		“	
1884	“		“ “		Hargis, Thomas F.	12:137
1885	“		“ Blackburn, Joseph C. S.	1:295	Hines, Thomas H.	12:453
1886	“		Beck, James B. “	3:418	Pryor, William S.	12:100
1887	Buckner, Simon B.	16:341	“ “		Lewis, Joseph H.	12: 92
1888	“		“ “		Holt, William H.	13:496
1890	“		Carlisle, John G. “	1:461		
1891	Brown, John Y.	13: 12	“ “		“	
1893	“		Lindsay, William “	11:485	Bennett, Caswell	12:442
1894	“		“ “		Pryor, William S.	12:100
1894	“		“ “		Quigley, Isaac M.	12:321
1895	Bradley, William O.	13: 12	“ “		Pryor, William S.	12:100
1897	“		“ Deboe, William J.	13: 23	Lewis, Joseph H.	12: 92
1899	“		“ “		Hazelrigg, James H.	12:400
1900	Taylor, William S.		“ “		“	
1900	Goebel, William	13: 13	“ “		“	
1900	Beckham, John C. W.	13: 14	“ “		“	
1901	“		Blackburn, Joseph C. S. “	1:295	Paynter, Thomas H.	12:125
1902	“		“ “		Guffy, Bayless L. D.	12:454
1903	“		“ McCreary, James B.	13: 10	Burnam, Anthony R.	12:322
1906	“		Paynter, Thomas H. “	12:125	“	
1906	“		Blackburn, Joseph C. S. “	1:295	Hobson, John P.	13:540
1907	Willson, Augustus E.	14:266	Paynter, Thomas H. “	12:125	O'Rear, Edward C.	18:391
1908	“		“ “		Settle, Warner E.	23:182
1909	“		“ Bradley, William O'C.	13: 12	Nunn, Thomas J.	
1910	“		“ “		Barker, Henry S.	
1911	McCreary, James B.	13: 10	“ “		“	
1912	“		“ “		Hobson, John P.	13:540
1913	“		James, Ollie M. “	15:332	“	
1914	“		“ Camden, Johnson N.	20:329	“	
1915	Stanley, A. Owsley	A:422	“ Beckham, John C. W.	13: 14	Miller, Shackelford	16:386
1917	“		“ “		Settle, Warner E.	23:182
1918	“		Martin, George B. “	D:241	“	
1919	Black, James D.	D:273	Stanley, A. Owsley “	A:422	Carroll, John D.	24:265
1919	Morrow, Edwin P.	A:472	“ “		“	
1921	“		“ Ernst, Richard P.	A:333	Hurt, Rollin	
1923	“		“ “		Sampson, Flem D.	A:326
1924	Fields, William J.	C:399	“ “		“	
1925	“		“ “		Settle, Warner E.	23:182
1925	“		Sackett, Frederic M. “	B:421	Clarke, Ernest S.	
1926	“		“ “		Clay, William R.	
1927	“		“ Barkley, Alben W.	C:411	“	
1928	Sampson, Flem D.	A:326	“ “		“	
1929	“		“ “		Thomas, Gus	
1930	“		Robsion, John M. “	D:351	“	
1931	“		Logan, Marvel M. “	D:231	Deitzman, Richard P.	
1932	Laffoon, Ruby		“ “		“	
1933	“		“ “		Reese, William H.	
1935	“		“ “		Clay, William R.	

LOUISIANA

Date	Governors	Biography	U. S. Senators	Biography	Chief Justices	Biography
1812	Claiborne, William C.	10: 74	Destréhan, Jean N.	12:250		
1812	“		“ Magruder, Allan B.	4:349		
1812	“		Posey, Thomas “	13:265		
1812	“		Brown, James “	4:376		
1813	“		“ Fromentin, Eligius	12:552	Mathews, George	5:505
1816	Villeré, Jacques P.	10: 74	“ “		“	
1817	“		Claiborne, Wm. C. C. “	10: 74	“	
1818	“		Johnson, Henry “	10: 75	“	
1819	“		“ Brown, James	4:376	“	

LOUISIANA (*Continued*)

Date	Governors	Biography	U. S. Senators		Biography	Chief Justices	Biography
1820	Robertson, Thomas B.	10: 74	Johnson, Henry	Brown, James	4:376	Mathews, George	5:505
1824	Thibodaux, H. S. (*act.*)	10: 75	Bouligny, Dominique		11:312	"	
1824	Johnson, Henry	10: 75	"	Johnston, Josiah S.	5: 45	"	
1828	Derbigny, Pierre A. C. B.	10: 75	"	"		"	
1829	Beauvais, Armand (*act.*)	10: 75	Livingston, Edward	"	5:293	"	
1830	Dupré, Jacques	10: 75	"	"		"	
1831	Roman, André B.	10: 76	Waggaman, George A.	"	11: 25	"	
1833	"		"	Porter, Alexander J.	13:158	"	
1835	White, Edward D.	10: 76	Nicholas, Robert C.	"	5:505	"	
1836	"		"	"		Martin, Francois X.	5:436
1837	"		"	Mouton, Alexandre	10: 76	"	
1839	Roman, André B.	10: 76	"	"		"	
1841	"		Barrow, Alexander	"	7:528	"	
1842	"		"	Conrad, Charles M.	6:181	"	
1843	Mouton, Alexandre	10: 76	"	Johnson, Henry	10: 75	"	
1846	Johnson, Isaac	10: 77	"	"		Eustis, George	7:509
1847	"		Soulé, Pierre	"	3:117	"	
1847	"		Downs, Solomon W.	"	12:373	"	
1849	"		"	Soulé, Pierre	3:117	"	
1850	Walker, Joseph M.	10: 77	"	"		"	
1853	Hebert, Paul O.	10: 77	Benjamin, Judah P.		4:285	Slidell, Thomas	7:496
1853	"		"	Slidell, John	2: 93	"	
1855	"		"	"		Merrick, Edwin T.	10:147
1856	Wickliffe, Robert C.	10: 77	"	"		"	
1860	Moore, Thomas O.	10: 78	"	"		"	
1861	"		Vacant	Vacant		"	
1862	Shepley, George F.	10: 78	"	"		"	
1864	Allen, Henry W.	10: 78	"	"		"	
1864	Hahn, Michael	10: 79	"	"		"	
1865	Wells, James M.	10: 79	"	"		Hyman, William B.	12:253
1867	Flanders, Benjamin F.	10: 80	"	"		"	
1867	Baker, Joshua	10: 80	"	"		"	
1868	Warmoth, Henry C.	23:307	Harris, John S.		4:528	Ludeling, John T.	13:592
1868	"		"	Kellogg, William P.	10: 82	"	
1871	"		West, Joseph Rodman	"	9:233	"	
1873	McEnery, John	10: 81	"	"		"	
1873	Kellogg, William P.	10: 82	"	"		"	
1877	Nicholls, Francis T.	10: 82	Kellogg, William P.	"	10: 82	Manning, Thomas C.	4:344
1877	"		"	Eustis, James B.	1:462	"	
1879	"		"	Jonas, Benjamin F.	4:544	"	
1880	Wiltz, Louis A.	10: 83	"	"		Bermudez, Edward E.	5:507
1881	McEnery, Samuel D.	10: 83	"	"		"	
1883	"		Gibson, Randall L.	"	1:297	"	
1885	"		"	Eustis, James B.	1:462	"	
1888	Nicholls, Francis T.	10: 82	"	"		"	
1891	"		"	White, Edward D.	11:368	"	
1892	Foster, Murphy J.	10: 83	Caffery, Donelson	"	13: 63	Nicholls, Francis T.	10: 82
1894	"		"	Blanchard, Newton C.	4:498	"	
1897	"		"	McEnery, Samuel D.	10: 83	"	
1900	Heard, William W.	13:437	"	"		"	
1901	"		Foster, Murphy J.	"	10: 83	"	
1904	Blanchard, Newton C.	4:498	"	"		Breaux, Joseph A.	13:526
1908	Sanders, Jared Y.	14:104	"	"		"	
1910	"		"	Thornton, John R.	18:318	"	
1912	Hall, Luther E.	15:135	"	"		"	
1913	"		Ransdell, Joseph E.	"	15:407	"	
1914	"		"	"		Monroe, Frank A.	12:103
1915	"		"	Broussard, Robert F.	15:387	"	
1916	Pleasant, Ruffin G.	C:405	"	"		"	
1918	"		"	Guion, Walter	24:382	"	
1918	"		"	Gay, Edward J.		"	
1920	Parker, John M.		"	"		"	
1921	"		"	Broussard, Edwin S.	C:421	"	
1922	"		"	"		Provosty, Olivier O.	20:309
1922	"		"	"		O'Neill, Charles A.	
1924	Fuqua, Henry L.	22:180	"	"		"	
1926	Simpson, Oramel H.	25:259	"	"		"	
1928	Long, Huey P.	D:409	"	"		"	
1931	"		Long, Huey P.	"	D:409	"	
1932	Allen, Oscar K.		"	"		"	
1933	"		"	Overton, John H.	D:285	"	

References are to The National Cyclopedia of American Biography

MAINE

Date	Governors	Biography	U. S. Senators	Biography	Chief Justices	Biography
1820	King, William	6:305	Holmes, John	10:296	Mellen, Prentis	11:335
1820	"		" Chandler, John	4:203	"	
1821	Williamson, W. D. (*act.*)	6:305	" "		"	
1822	Parris, Albion K.	6:306	" "		"	
1827	Lincoln, Enoch	6:306	Parris, Albion K. "	6:306	"	
1829	Cutler, Nathan	6:307	Holmes, John	10:296	"	
1829	"		" Sprague, Peleg	5:414	"	
1830	Hunton, Jonathan G.	6:307	" "		"	
1831	Smith, Samuel E.	6:307	" "		"	
1833	"		Shepley, Ether "	2: 7	Weston, Nathan	7:503
1834	Dunlap, Robert P.	6:308	" "		"	
1835	"		" Ruggles, John	12:230	"	
1836	"		Dana, Judah "	11: 38	"	
1837	"		Williams, Reuel "	10:254	"	
1838	Kent, Edward	6:308	" "		"	
1839	Fairfield, John	6:309	" "		"	
1840	Kent, Edward	6:308	" "		"	
1841	Fairfield, John	6:309	" Evans, George	6:299	Whitman, Ezekiel	11:542
1843	Kavanagh, Edward	6:309	Fairfield, John "	6:309	"	
1844	Anderson, Hugh J.	6:310	" "		"	
1847	Dana, John W.	6:310	" Bradbury, James W.	4:323	"	
1848	"		Moor, Wyman B. S. "	5:505	Shepley, Ether	2: 7
1848	"		Hamlin, Hannibal "	2: 76	"	
1850	Hubbard, John	6:311	" "		"	
1853	Crosby, William G.	6:311	" Fessenden, William P.	2: 90	"	
1855	Morrill, Anson P.	6:312	" "		Tenney, John S.	10:163
1856	Wells, Samuel	6:312	" "		"	
1857	Hamlin, Hannibal	2: 76	Nourse, Amos "	11:158	"	
1857	Williams, Joseph H. (*act.*)	6:312	Hamlin, Hannibal "	2: 76	"	
1858	Morrill, Lot M.	6:313	" "		"	
1861	Washburn, Israel J.	5:400	Morrill, Lot M. "	6:313	"	
1862	"		" "		Appleton, John	11:462
1863	Coburn, Abner	6:313	" "		"	
1864	Cony, Samuel	6:314	" Farwell, Nathan A.	10: 89	"	
1865	"		" Fessenden, William P.	2: 90	"	
1867	Chamberlain, Joshua L.	1:419	" "		"	
1869	"		Hamlin, Hannibal	2: 76	"	
1869	"		" Morrill, Lot M.	6:313	"	
1871	Perham, Sidney	6:315	" "		"	
1874	Dingley, Nelson, Jr.	6:315	" "		"	
1876	Connor, Selden	6:316	" Blaine, James G.	1:137	"	
1879	Garcelon, Alonzo	6:316	" "		"	
1880	Davis, Daniel F.	6:317	" "		"	
1881	Plaisted, Harris M.	6:317	Hale, Eugene	20:220	"	
1881	"		" Frye, William P.	1:290	"	
1883	Robie, Frederick	6:318	" "		Peters, John A.	9:463
1887	Bodwell, Joseph R.	6:318	" "		"	
1887	Marble, Sebastian S.	5:555	" "		"	
1889	Burleigh, Edwin C.	1:429	" "		"	
1893	Cleaves, Henry B.	6:319	" "		"	
1897	Powers, Llewellyn	13:314	" "		"	
1900	"		" "		Wiswell, Andrew P.	13:321
1901	Hill, John F.	13:314	" "		"	
1905	Cobb, William T.	14:378	" "		"	
1906	"		" "		Emery, Lucilius A.	14:510
1909	Fernald, Bert M.	24:157	" "		"	
1911	Plaisted, Frederick W.	B:455	Johnson, Charles F. "	21:193	Whitehouse, William P.	10: 20
1911	"		" Gardner, Obadiah	15:230	"	
1913	Haines, William T.	19:66	" Burleigh, Edwin C.	1:429	Savage, Albert R.	20:24
1915	Curtis, Oakley C.	22:205	" "		"	
1916	"		" Fernald, Bert M.	24:157	"	
1917	"		Hale, Frederick "	B:181	Cornish, Leslie C.	22:342
1921	Parkhurst, Frederick H.	26: 60	" "		"	
1921	Baxter, Percival P.	B:210	" "		"	
1925	Brewster, Ralph O.	B: 24	" "		Wilson, Scott	
1926	"		" Gould, Arthur R.	C:439	"	
1929	Gardiner, William T.	D:112	" "		Deasy, Luere B.	D:414
1931	"		" White, Wallace H., Jr.	D:208	Pattangall, William R.	D:121
1933	Brann, Louis J.		" "		"	
1935	"		" "		Dunn, Charles J.	

References are to The National Cyclopedia of American Biography

MARYLAND

Date	Governors	Biography	U. S. Senators		Biography	Chief Justices	Biography
1634	Calvert, Leonard	7:332					
1647	Green, Thomas	7:333					
1649	Stone, William	7:333					
1654	Governed by Commissioners						
1657	Fendall, Josias	7:333					
1660	Calvert, Philip	7:334					
1661	Calvert, Charles	7:334					
1676	Notley, Thomas	7:334					
1680	Calvert, Charles	7:334					
1684	Joseph, William	7:334					
1688	Governed by Protestant Associators						
1691	Copley, Lionel	7:335					
1694	Nicholson, Francis	7:335					
1699	Blackistone, Nathaniel	7:335					
1701	Tench, Thomas	9:320					
1703	Seymour, John	7:335					
1709	Lloyd, Edward	9:474					
1714	Hart, John	7:336					
1720	Calvert, Charles	7:336					
1727	Calvert, Benedict L.	7:336					
1731	Ogle, Samuel	7:336					
1732	Calvert, Charles	7:336					
1733	Ogle, Samuel	7:336					
1742	Bladen, Thomas	7:336					
1747	Ogle, Samuel	7:336					
1752	Tasker, Benjamin	9:188					
1753	Sharpe, Horatio	7:337					
1769	Eden, Robert	7:337					
1776	Governed by The Convention and Council of Safety						
1777	Johnson, Thomas	9:289					
1778	"					Rumsey, Benjamin	7:491
1779	Lee, Thomas Sim	9:290				"	
1782	Paca, William	9:291				"	
1785	Smallwood, William	9:292				"	
1788	Howard, John E.	9:292				"	
1789	"		Carroll, Charles (of Carrollton)		7:441	"	
1789	"		"	Henry, John	9:294	"	
1791	Plater, George	9:293	"	"		"	
1792	Lee, Thomas S.	9:290	"	"		"	
1793	"		Potts, Richard	"	11:397	"	
1794	Stone, John H.	9:294	"	"		"	
1796	"		Howard, John E.	"	9:292	"	
1797	Henry, John	9:294	"	Lloyd, James	4:313	"	
1798	Ogle, Benjamin	9:295	"	"		"	
1800	"		"	Hindman, William	2:133	"	
1801	Mercer, John F.	9:295	"	Wright, Robert	9:297	"	
1803	Bowie, Robert	9:296	Smith, Samuel	"	1: 73	"	
1806	Wright, Robert	9:297	"	Reed, Philip	7:308	Chase, Jeremiah T.	13:496
1809	Lloyd, Edward	9:297	"	"		"	
1811	Bowie, Robert	9:296	"	"		"	
1812	Winder, Levin	9:298	"	"		"	
1813	"		"	Goldsborough, Robert H.	7:215	"	
1815	Ridgely, Charles C.	9:299	"	"		"	
1816	"		Harper, Robert G.	"	5:374	"	
1816	"		Hanson, Alexander C.	"	12:235	"	
1818	Goldsborough, Charles	9:299	"	"		"	
1819	Sprigg, Samuel	9:300	Pinkney, William	"	5:373	"	
1819	"		"	Lloyd, Edward	9:297	"	
1822	Stevens, Samuel, Jr.	9:300	Smith, Samuel	"	1: 73	"	
1825	"		"	"		Buchanan, John	10:120
1826	Kent, Joseph	9:301	"	Chambers, Ezekiel F.	7:307	"	
1828	Martin, Daniel	9:301	"	"		"	
1829	Carroll, Thomas K.	9:302	"	"		"	
1830	Martin, Daniel	9:301	"	"		"	
1831	Howard, George	9:302	"	"		"	
1833	Thomas, James	9:303	Kent, Joseph	"	9:301	"	

MARYLAND (*Continued*)

Date	Governors	Biography	U. S. Senators		Biography	Chief Justices	Biography
1835	Veazey, Thomas W.	9:303	Kent, Joseph		9:301	Buchanan, John	10:120
1835	"		"	Goldsborough, Robert H.	7:215	"	
1836	"		"	Spence, John S.	7:288	"	
1838	Grason, William	9:304	Merrick, William D.	"	7:323	"	
1841	Thomas, Francis	9:304	"	Kerr, John L.	7:419	"	
1843	"		"	Pearce, James A.	10:249	"	
1844	Pratt, Thomas G.	9:305	"	"		Archer, Stevenson	7:492
1845	"		Johnson, Reverdy	"	4:371	"	
1847	Thomas, Philip F.	5: 6	"	"		"	
1848	"		"	"		Dorsey, Thomas B.	12:268
1849	"		Stewart, David	"	4:348	"	
1850	Lowe, Enoch L.	9:305	Pratt, Thomas G.	"	9:305	"	
1851	"		"	"		LeGrand, John C.	12:262
1854	Ligon, Thomas W.	9:306	Kennedy, Anthony	"	7:481	"	
1858	Hicks, Thomas H.	9:306	"	"		"	
1861	"		"	"		Bowie, Richard J.	13:152
1862	Bradford, Augustus W.	9:307	"	Hicks, Thomas H.	9:306	"	
1863	"		Johnson, Reverdy	"	4:371	"	
1865	Swann, Thomas	9:308	"	Creswell, John A. J.	4: 19	"	
1867	"		"	Vickers, George	7:221	Bartol, James L.	7:557
1868	"		Whyte, William P.	"	9:309	"	
1869	Bowie, Oden	3:260	"	"		"	
1872	Whyte, William P.	9:309	"	"		"	
1873	"		"	Dennis, George R.	7:283	"	
1874	Groome, James B.	9:310	"	"		"	
1876	Carroll, John L.	9:310	"	"		"	
1879	"		"	Groome, James B.	9:310	"	
1880	Hamilton, William T.	9:311	"	"		"	
1881	"		Gorman, Arthur P.	"	1:296	"	
1883	"		"	"		Alvey, Richard H.	12:231
1884	McLane, Robert M.	9:311	"	"		"	
1885	Lloyd, Henry	9:312	"	Wilson, Ephraim K.	1:295	"	
1888	Jackson, Elihu E.	9:313	"	"		"	
1891	"		"	Gibson, Charles H.	5:495	"	
1892	Brown, Frank	9:313	"	"		"	
1893	"		"	"		Robinson, John M.	7:491
1896	Lowndes, Lloyd	9:313	"	"		McSherry, James	13:312
1897	"		"	Wellington, George L.	13:545	"	
1899	"		McComas, Louis E.	"	12:488	"	
1900	Smith, John W.	13:205	"	"		"	
1903	"		"	Gorman, Arthur P.	1:296	"	
1904	Warfield, Edwin	13:205	"	"		"	
1905	"		Rayner, Isidor	"	13:544	"	
1906	"		"	Whyte, William P.	9:309	"	
1907	"		"	"		Boyd, A. Hunter	15: 86
1908	Crothers, Austin L.	14:180	"	Smith, John W.	13:205	"	
1912	Goldsborough, Phillips L.	15:190	Jackson, William P.	"	15: 48	"	
1914	"		Lee, Blair	"	C:453	"	
1916	Harrington, Emerson C.	15:135	"	"		"	
1917	"		France, Joseph I.	"	C:143	"	
1920	Ritchie, Albert C.	A: 75	"	"		"	
1921	"		"	Weller, Ovington E.		"	
1923	"		Bruce, William C.	"	18: 47	"	
1924	"		"	"		Bond, Carroll T.	B:198
1927	"		"	Tydings, Millard E.	C:302	"	
1929	"		Goldsborough, Phillips L.	"	15:190	"	
1935	Nice, Harry W.		Radcliffe, George L.	"			

MASSACHUSETTS

Date	Governors	Biography	U. S. Senators	Biography	Chief Justices	Biography
	PLYMOUTH COLONY					
1620	Carver, John	7:367				
1621	Bradford, William	7:368				
1633	Winslow, Edward	7:369				
1634	Prince, Thomas	7:370				
1635	Bradford, William	7:368				
1636	Winslow, Edward	7:369				
1637	Bradford, William	7:368				
1638	Prince, Thomas	7:370				
1639	Bradford, William	7:369				
1644	Winslow, Edward	7:369				
1645	Bradford, William	7:369				
1657	Prince, Thomas	7:370				
1673	Winslow, Josiah	5:389				
1681	Hinckley, Thomas	7:370				
1686	Andros, Edmund	6: 90				
1689	Hinckley, Thomas	7:370				
	MASSACHUSETTS BAY COLONY					
1629	Endicott, John	5:113				
1630	Winthrop, John	6:201				
1634	Dudley, Thomas	7:370				
1635	Haynes, John	7:371				
1636	Vane, Henry	7:371				
1637	Winthrop, John	6:201				
1640	Dudley, Thomas	7:370				
1641	Bellingham, Richard	5:421				
1642	Winthrop, John	6:201				
1644	Endicott, John	5:113				
1645	Dudley, Thomas	7:370				
1646	Winthrop, John	6:201				
1649	Endicott, John	5:113				
1650	Dudley, Thomas	7:370				
1651	Endicott, John	5:113				
1654	Bellingham, Richard	5:421				
1655	Endicott, John	5:113				
1665	Bellingham, Richard	5:421				
1673	Leverett, John	3:177				
1679	Bradstreet, Simon	7:372				
1686	Dudley, Joseph	7:372				
1687	Andros, Edmund	6: 90				
1689	Bradstreet, Simon	7:372				
1692	Phips, William	6: 97			Stoughton, William	7:373
1694	Stoughton, William	7:373			“ (*acting*) ..	
1699	Coote, Richard	7:373			“	
1700	Stoughton, William	7:373			“ (*acting*) ..	
1701	The Council				Winthrop, Waitstill	4:500
1702	Dudley, Joseph	7:372			Addington, Isaac	4:485
1708	“				Winthrop, Waitstill	4:500
1715	Tailer, William (*acting*)				“	
1716	Shute, Samuel	7:374			“	
1718	“				Sewall, Samuel	5:339
1723	Dummer, William (*acting*)				“	
1728	Burnet, William	7:374			“	
1729	Dummer, William (*acting*)				Lynde, Benjamin	4:345
1730	Tailer, William				“	
1730	Belcher, Jonathan	6:301			“	
1741	Shirley, William	7:375			“	
1745	“				Dudley, Paul	7:175
1749	Phipps, Spencer				“	
1753	Shirley, William	7:375			Sewall, Stephen	8: 54
1756	Phipps, Spencer				“	
1757	Pownall, Thomas	7:375			“	
1760	Bernard, Francis	5:432			“	
1761	“				Hutchinson, Thomas	7:376
1769	Hutchinson, Thomas	7:376			Lynde, Benjamin	4:345
1772	“				Oliver, Peter	4:344
1774	Gage, Thomas	7:377			“	
1775	The Council				Adams, John	2: 1
1777	“				Cushing, William	12:548

MASSACHUSETTS *(Continued)*

Date	Governors	Biography	U. S. Senators	Biography	Chief Justices	Biography
	THE COMMONWEALTH					
1780	Hancock, John	1:103			Cushing, William	12:548
1785	Bowdoin, James	2:488			“	
1787	Hancock, John	1:103			“	
1789	“		Dalton, Tristram	11:529	“	
1789	“		“ Strong, Caleb	1:110	Sargeant, Nathaniel P.	4:534
1791	“		Cabot, George “	2: 5	Dana, Francis	3:240
1793	Adams, Samuel	1:104	“ “		“	
1796	“		Goodhue, Benjamin	2: 10	“	
1796	“		“ Sedgwick, Theodore	2: 8	“	
1797	Sumner, Increase	1:109	“ “		“	
1799	“		“ Dexter, Samuel	2: 6	“	
1800	Strong, Caleb	1:110	Mason, Jonathan “	2: 7	“	
1800	“		“ Foster, Dwight	2: 6	“	
1803	“		Adams, John A. “	5: 73	“	
1803	“		“ Pickering, Timothy	1: 12	“	
1806	“		“ “		Parsons, Theophilus	5:441
1807	Sullivan, James	1:110	“ “		“	
1808	“		Lloyd, James, Jr. “	4:469	“	
1809	Lincoln, Levi *(acting)*	1:111	“ “		“	
1809	Gore, Christopher	1:112	“ “		“	
1810	Gerry, Elbridge	5:371	“ “		“	
1811	“		“ Varnum, Joseph B.	1: 70	“	
1812	Strong, Caleb	1:110	“ “		“	
1813	“		Gore, Christopher “	1:112	Sewall, Samuel	6:189
1814	“		“ “		Parker, Isaac	2:152
1816	Brooks, John	1:112	Ashmun, Eli P. “	11:285	“	
1817	“		“ Otis, Harrison G.	7: 66	“	
1818	“		Mellen, Prentiss “	11:335	“	
1820	“		Mills, Elijah H. “	10:486	“	
1822	“		“ Lloyd, James	4:469	“	
1823	Eustis, William	5:372	“ “		“	
1825	Morton, Marcus *(acting)*		“ “		“	
1825	Lincoln, Levi	1:111	“ “		“	
1826	“		“ Silsbee, Nathaniel	12:551	“	
1827	“		Webster, Daniel “	3: 36	“	
1830	“		“ “		Shaw, Lemuel	5:415
1834	Davis, John	1:115	“ “		“	
1835	Armstrong, Samuel *(act.)*	6:515	“ Davis, John	1:115	“	
1836	Everett, Edward	6:179	“ “		“	
1840	Morton, Marcus	1:115	“ “		“	
1841	Davis, John	1:115	Choate, Rufus	6: 17	“	
1841	“		“ Bates, Isaac C.	3:532	“	
1843	Morton, Marcus	1:115	“ “		“	
1844	Briggs, George N.	1:115	“ “		“	
1845	“		Webster, Daniel “	3: 36	“	
1845	“		“ Davis, John	1:115	“	
1850	“		Winthrop, Robert C. “	6:217	“	
1851	Boutwell, George S.	4:382	Rantoul, Robert “	11:232	“	
1851	“		Sumner, Charles “	3:300	“	
1853	Clifford, John H.	1:116	“ Everett, Edward	6:179	“	
1854	Washburn, Emory	1:116	“ Rockwell, Julius	11:401	“	
1855	Gardner, Henry J.	1:117	“ Wilson, Henry	4: 13	“	
1858	Banks, Nathaniel P.	4:222	“ “		“	
1860	“		“ “		Bigelow, George T.	7:537
1861	Andrew, John A.	1:118	“ “		“	
1866	Bullock, Alexander H.	1:118	“ “		“	
1868	“		“ “		Chapman, Reuben A.	7:507
1869	Claflin, William	1:119	“ “		“	
1872	Washburn, William B.	1:120	“ “		“	
1873	“		“ Boutwell, George S.	4:382	Gray, Horace	1: 35
1874	Talbott, Thomas *(act.)*	1:121	Washburn, William B. “	1:120	“	
1875	Gaston, William	1:120	Dawes, Henry L. “	4:321	“	
1876	Rice, Alexander H.	1:120	“ “		“	
1877	“		“ Hoar, George F.	1:453	“	
1879	Talbot, Thomas	1:121	“ “		“	
1880	Long, John D.	11: 15	“ “		“	
1882	“		“ “		Morton, Marcus	2:111
1883	Butler, Benjamin F.	1:121	“ “		“	

MASSACHUSETTS *(Continued)*

Date	Governors	Biography	U. S. Senators		Biography	Chief Justices	Biography
1884	Robinson, George D.	1:124	Dawes, Henry L.		4:321	Morton, Marcus	2:111
1884	"		"	Hoar, George F.	1:453	"	
1887	Ames, Oliver	1:124	"	"		"	
1890	Brackett, John Q. A.	1:125	"	"		Field, Walbridge A.	13:209
1891	Russell, William E.	1:125	"	"		"	
1893	"		Lodge, Henry C.	"	19: 52	"	
1894	Greenhalge, Frederic T.	1:126	"	"		"	
1896	Wolcott, Roger	1:127	"	"		"	
1899	"		"	"		Holmes, Oliver W.	12:349
1900	Crane, Winthrop M.	13: 69	"	"		"	
1903	Bates, John L.	10:133	"	"		Knowlton, Marcus P.	13:400
1905	Douglas, William L.	13:436	"	Crane, Winthrop M.	13: 69	"	
1906	Guild, Curtis, Jr.	14:454	"	"		"	
1909	Draper, Eben S.	23: 55	"	"		"	
1911	Foss, Eugene N.	C:345	"	"		Rugg, Arthur P.	17:243
1913	"		"	Weeks, John W.	20: 4	"	
1914	Walsh, David I.	15: 99	"	"		"	
1916	McCall, Samuel W.	20:303	"	"		"	
1919	Coolidge, Calvin	24: 1	"	Walsh, David I.	15: 99	"	
1921	Cox, Channing H.	D:283	"	"		"	
1924	"		Butler, William M.	"	B:192	"	
1925	Fuller, Alvan T.	B: 30	"	Gillett, Frederick H.	B:198	"	
1926	"		Walsh, David I.	"	15: 99	"	
1929	Allen, Frank G.	D:336	"	"		"	
1931	Ely, Joseph B.	D:323	"	Coolidge, Marcus A.		"	
1935	Curley, James M.	A:431	"	"		"	

MICHICAN

Date	Governors	Biography	U. S. Senators		Biography	Chief Justices	Biography
1837	Mason, Stevens T.	5:271	Lyon, Lucius		11:334		
1837	"		"	Norvell, John	11:500	Fletcher, William A.	3:531
1839	"		Porter, Augustus S.	"	11:551	"	
1840	Woodbridge, William	5:272	"	"		"	
1841	Gordon, James W.	5:272	"	Woodbridge, William	5:272	"	
1842	Barry, John S.	5:272	"	"		"	
1844	"		"	"		Ransom, Epaphroditus	1:509
1845	"		Cass, Lewis	"	5: 3	"	
1846	Felch, Alpheus	3:295	"	"		"	
1847	Greenly, William L.	5:272	"	Felch, Alpheus	3:295	"	
1848	Ransom, Epaphroditus	1:509	Fitzgerald, Thomas	"	7:542	Whipple, Charles W.	5:508
1849	"		Cass, Lewis	"	5: 3	"	
1850	Barry, John S.	5:272	"	"		"	
1852	McClelland, Robert	4:150	"	"		"	
1853	Parsons, Andrew	5:273	"	Stuart, Charles E.	11:436	*During 1852-58 a presiding justice was chosen for each term of the court.*	
1855	Bingham, Kinsley S.	5:273	"	"			
1857	"		Chandler, Zachariah	"	4: 18		
1858	"		"	"		Martin, George	12:334
1859	Wisner, Moses	5:273	"	Bingham, Kinsley S.	5:273	"	
1861	Blair, Austin	5:273	"	Howard, Jacob M.	4:472	"	
1865	Crapo, Henry H.	5:274	"	"		"	
1868	"		"	"		Cooley, Thomas M.	9:522
1869	Baldwin, Henry P.	5:274	"	"		"	
1870	"		"	"		Campbell, James V.	9:145
1871	"		"	Ferry, Thomas W.	9:169	"	
1872	"		"	"		Christiancy, Isaac P.	23:348
1873	Bagley, John J.	5:274	"	"		"	
1874	"		"	"		Graves, Benjamin F.	12:211
1875	"		Christiancy, Isaac P.	"	23:348	"	
1876	"		"	"		Cooley, Thomas M.	9:522
1877	Croswell, Charles M.	5:275	"	"		"	
1878	"		"	"		Campbell, James V.	9:145
1879	"		Chandler, Zachariah	"	4: 18	"	
1879	"		Baldwin, Henry P.	"	5:274	"	
1880	"		"	"		Marston, Isaac	4:155
1881	Jerome, David H.	5:275	Conger, Omar D.	"	12:394	"	

MICHIGAN *(Continued)*

Date	Governors	Biography	U. S. Senators	Biography	Chief Justices	Biography
1882	Jerome, David H.	5:275	Conger, Omar D.	12:394	Graves, Benjamin F.	12:211
1882	"		" Ferry, Thomas W.	9:169	"	
1883	Begole, Josiah W.	5:275	" Palmer, Thomas W.	11:362	"	
1884	"		" "		Cooley, Thomas M.	9:522
1885	Alger, Russell A.	5:276	" "		"	
1886	"		" "		Campbell, James V.	9:145
1887	Luce, Cyrus G.	5:277	Stockbridge, Francis B. "	1:460	"	
1888	"		" "		Sherwood, Thomas R.	12:251
1889	"		" McMillan, James	2:227	"	
1890	"		" "		Champlin, John W.	4:351
1891	Winans, Edwin B.	2:452	" "		"	
1892	"		" "		Morse, Allen B.	12:429
1893	Rich, John T.	5:277	" "		"	
1894	"		Patton, John, Jr. "	12:391	McGrath, John W.	5:456
1895	"		Burrows, Julius C. "	12:515	"	
1896	"		" "		Long, Charles D.	5:521
1897	Pingree, Hazen S.	7:119	" "		"	
1898	"		" "		Grant, Claudius B.	18: 50
1900	"		" "		Montgomery, Robert M.	12:113
1901	Bliss, Aaron T.	13:361	" "		"	
1902	"		" Alger, Russell A.	5:276	Hooker, Frank A.	12:490
1904	"		" "		Moore, Joseph B.	7:102
1905	Warner, Frederick M.	13:293	" "		"	
1906	"		" "		Carpenter, William L.	14:364
1907	"		" Smith, William A.	26: 53	McAlvay, Aaron V.	20:142
1908	"		" "		Grant, Claudius B.	18: 50
1909	"		" "		Blair, Charles A.	15: 48
1910	"		" "		Montgomery, Robert M.	12:113
1911	Osborn, Chase S.	17:420	Townsend, Charles E. "	15:220	Ostrander, Russell C.	17:360
1912	"		" "		Moore, Joseph B.	7:102
1913	Ferris, Woodbridge N.	15:213	" "		Steere, Joseph H.	
1914	"		" "		McAlvay, Aaron V.	20:142
1915	"		" "		Brooke, Flavius L.	17:244
1916	"		" "		Stone, John W.	22:456
1917	Sleeper, Albert E.	24:433	" "		Kuhn, Franz C.	
1918	"		" "		Ostrander, Russell C.	17:360
1919	"		" Newberry, Truman H.	14: 26	Bird, John E.	22:202
1920	"		" "		Moore, Joseph B.	7:102
1921	Groesbeck, Alexander J.		" "		Steere, Joseph H.	
1922	"		" Couzens, James	A:216	Fellows, Grant	
1923	"		Ferris, Woodbridge N. "	15:213	Wiest, Howard	D:304
1924	"		" "		Clark, George M.	
1925	"		" "		McDonald, John S.	
1927	Green, Fred W.	D: 60	" "		Sharpe, Nelson	26: 26
1928	"		Vandenberg, Arthur H. "		"	
1929	"		" "		Wiest, Howard	D:304
1931	Brucker, Wilber M.	D:126	" "		Butzel, Henry M.	
1933	Comstock, William A.		" "		McDonald, John S.	
1935	Fitzgerald, Frank D.		" "		Potter, William W.	

MINNESOTA

Date	Governors	Biography	U. S. Senators	Biography	Chief Justices	Biography
1858	Sibley, Henry H.	10: 63	Rice, Henry M.	21:273	Emmett, Lafayette	13: 71
1858	“		“ Shields, James	8: 2	“	
1859	“		“ Wilkinson, Morton S.	12:207	“	
1860	Ramsey, Alexander	10: 62	“ “		“	
1863	Swift, H. A. (*pro. tem.*)		Ramsey, Alexander “	10: 62	“	
1864	Miller, Stephen	10: 63	“ “		“	
1865	“		“ Norton, Daniel S.	11:396	Wilson, Thomas	1:271
1866	Marshall, William R.	10: 64	“ “		“	
1869	“		“ “		Gilfillan, James	16:311
1870	Austin, Horace	10: 64	“ Windom, William	1:148	Ripley, Christopher G.	12: 43
1871	“		“ Stearns, Ozora P.	10:230	“	
1871	“		“ Windom, William	1:148	“	
1874	Davis, Cushman K.	10: 65	“ “		McMillan, Samuel J. R.	4:469
1875	“		McMillan, Samuel J. R. “	4:469	Gilfillan, James	16:311
1876	Pillsbury, John S.	10: 65	“ “		“	
1881	“		“ Edgerton, Alonzo J.	12: 54	“	
1881	“		“ Windom, William	1:148	“	
1882	Hubbard, Lucius F.	10: 66	“ “		“	
1883	“		“ Sabin, Dwight M.	2:374	“	
1887	McGill, Andrew R.	10: 67	Davis, Cushman K. “	10: 65	“	
1889	Merriam, William R.	10: 68	“ Washburn, William D.	16:361	“	
1893	Nelson, Knute	19: 18	“ “		“	
1895	Clough, David M.	10: 69	“ Nelson, Knute	19: 18	Start, Charles M.	13:141
1899	Lind, John	10: 69	“ “		“	
1900	“		Towne, Charles A. “	12:258	“	
1901	Van Sant, Samuel R.	13:325	Clapp, Moses E. “	12:232	“	
1905	Johnson, John A.	14:164	“ “		“	
1909	Eberhart, Adolph O.	B:298	“ “		“	
1913	“		“ “		Brown, Calvin L.	18:217
1915	Hammond, Winfield S.	16: 99	“ “		“	
1915	Burnquist, Joseph A. A.	D:199	“ “		“	
1917	“		Kellogg, Frank B. “	A: 8	“	
1921	Preus, Jacob A. O.	C: 67	“ “		“	
1923	“		Shipstead, Henrik “	B:256	Wilson, Samuel B.	B:492
1923	“		“ Johnson, Magnus		“	
1925	Christianson, Theodore	B:170	“ Schall, Thomas D.	C:337	“	
1931	Olson, Floyd B.	D:176	“ “		“	
1933	“		“ “		Devaney, John P.	

MISSISSIPPI

Date	Governors	Biography	U. S. Senators	Biography	Chief Justices	Biography
1817	Holmes, David	13:485	Leake, Walter	13:486		
1817	"		" Williams, Thomas H.	11:551		
1820	Poindexter, George	13:485	" "			
1820	"		Holmes, David "	13:485		
1822	Leake, Walter	13:486	" "			
1825	Brandon, Gerard (*act.*)	13:486	Ellis, Powhatan "	11: 53		
1826	Holmes, David	13:485	Reed, Thomas B. "	4:468		
1827	Brandon, Gerard C.	13:486	Ellis, Powhatan "	11: 53		
1829	"		" Reed, Thomas B.	4:468		
1830	"		" Adams, Robert H.	3:533		
1830	"		" Poindexter, George	13:485		
1832	Scott, Abram M.	13:487	Black, John "	11:164	Sharkey, William L.	13:491
1833	Lynch, Charles (*ad. int.*)	13:487	" "		"	
1833	Runnels, Hiram G.	13:487	" "		"	
1835	Quitman, John A. (*act.*)	13:489	" Walker, Robert J.	6:269	"	
1836	Lynch, Charles	13:487	" "		"	
1838	McNutt, Alexander G.	13:487	Trotter, James F. "	12:331	"	
1838	"		Williams, Thomas H. "	11:551	"	
1839	"		Henderson, John "	11:250	"	
1842	Tucker, Tilghman M.	13:488	" "		"	
1844	Brown, Albert G.	13:488	Speight, Jesse "	11:502	"	
1845	"		" Chalmers, Joseph W.	4:351	"	
1845	"		Davis, Jefferson "	4:148	"	
1847	"		" Foote, Henry S.	13:490	"	
1848	Matthews, Joseph W.	13:488	" "		"	
1850	Quitman, John A.	13:489	" "		"	
1851	Guion, John I.	13:489	McRae, John J. "	13:490	Smith, Cotesworth P.	5:506
1851	Whitfield, James	13:489	" "		"	
1852	Foote, Henry S.	13:490	Adams, Stephen	3:418	"	
1852	"		" Brooke, Walker	11:191	"	
1853	"		" Brown, Albert G.	13:488	"	
1854	McRae, John J.	13:490	" "		"	
1857	"		Davis, Jefferson "	4:148	"	
1858	McWillie, William	13:490	" "		"	
1860	Pettus, John J.	13:491	" "		"	
1861	"		Vacant Vacant		"	
1862	Thompson, Jacob	5: 8	" "		"	
1864	Clark, Charles	13:491	" "		Handy, Alexander H.	13:150
1865	Sharkey, William L. (*provisional*)	13:491	" "		"	
1865	Humphreys, Benjamin G.	13:492	" "		"	
1868	Ames, Adelbert (*military*)	13:492	" "		Shackleford, Thomas G.	5:511
1870	Alcorn, James L.	13:493	Ames, Adelbert	13:492	Peyton, Ephraim G.	7:294
1870	"		" Revels, Hiram R.	11:405	"	
1871	Powers, Ridgley C. (*act.*)	13:493	" Alcorn, James L.	13:493	"	
1874	Ames, Adelbert	13:492	Pease, Henry R. "	12:389	"	
1875	"		Bruce, Blanche K. "	11:394	"	
1876	Stone, John M. (*acting*)	13:493	" "		Simrall, Horatio F.	5:456
1877	"		" Lamar, Lucius Q. C.	1: 37	"	
1879	"		" "		George, James Z.	2:358
1881	"		George, James Z. "	2:358	Chalmers, Hamilton H.	5:534
1882	Lowry, Robert	13:494	" "		Campbell, Josiah A. P.	7:531
1885	"		" Walthall, Edward C.	1:389	Cooper, Tim E.	5:538
1888	"		" "		Arnold, James M.	5:535
1889	"		" "		Woods, Thomas H.	12:453
1890	Stone, John M.	13:493	" "		"	
1894	"		" McLaurin, Anselm J.	13:494	Cooper, Tim E.	5:538
1895	"		" Walthall, Edward C.	1:389	"	
1896	McLaurin, Anselm J.	13:494	" "		Woods, Thomas H.	12:453
1897	"		Money, Hernando D. S. "	11:492	"	
1898	"		" Sullivan, William V. A.	12:387	"	
1900	Longino, Andrew H.	13:495	" "		Whitfield, Albert H.	13: 55
1901	"		" McLaurin, Anselm J.	13:494	"	
1904	Vardaman, James K.	13:495	" "		"	
1908	Noel, Edmund F.	14:518	" "		"	
1910	"		" Gordon, James		"	
1910	"		" Percy, LeRoy	15:107	Mayes, Robert B.	17:293
1911	"		Williams, John S. "	13:396	"	

MISSISSIPPI *(Continued)*

Date	Governors	Biography	U. S. Senators	Biography	Chief Justices	Biography
1912	Brewer, Earl L.	15:333	Williams, John S.	13:396	Smith, Sydney	
1912	"		" Percy, LeRoy	15:107	"	
1913	"		" Vardaman, James K.	13:495	"	
1916	Bilbo, Theodore G.	A:313	" "		"	
1919	"		" Harrison, Byron (Pat)	A:173	"	
1920	Russell, Lee M.	B:149	" "		"	
1923	"		Stephens, Hubert D. "	C:215	"	
1924	Whitfield, Henry L.	21:481	" "		"	
1927	Murphree, Dennis		" "		"	
1928	Bilbo, Theodore G.	A:313	" "		"	
1932	Conner, Sennet		" "		"	
1935	"		Bilbo, Theodore G. "	A:313	"	

MISSOURI

Date	Governors	Biography	U. S. Senators	Biography	Chief Justices	Biography
1821	McNair, Alexander	12:302	Benton, Thomas H.	4:399	McGirk, Matthias	12:227
1821	"		" Barton, David	7:532	"	
1824	Bates, Frederick	12:302	" "		"	
1825	Williams, Abraham J. (*acting*)		" "		"	
1826	Miller, John	12:302	" "		"	
1831	"		" Buckner, Alexander	4:292	"	
1832	Dunklin, Daniel	12:303	" "		"	
1833	"		" Linn, Lewis F.	4:551	"	
1836	Boggs, Lilburn W.	12:303	" "		"	
1840	Reynolds, Thomas	12:303	" "			
1841	"		" "		Tompkins, George	3:509
1843	"		" Atchison, David R.	10:223	"	
1844	Marmaduke, Meredith M. (*acting*)	12:303	" "		"	
1844	Edwards, John C.	12:303	" "		"	
1845	"		" "		Napton, William B.	12:201
1848	King, Austin A.	12:304	" "		"	
1851	"		Geyer, Henry S. "	4: 61	Gamble, Hamilton R.	12:305
1853	Price, Sterling	12:304	" "		"	
1854	"		" "		Scott, William	12:188
1857	Polk, Trusten	12:304	" Green, James S.	7:535	"	
1857	Jackson, Hancock		" "		"	
1857	Stewart, Robert M.	12:305	Polk, Trusten "	12:304	"	
1861	Jackson, Claiborne F.	12:305	" Johnson, Waldo P.	12:392	"	
1861	Gamble, Hamilton R. (*Provisional*)	12:305	" "		"	
1862	"		Henderson, John B.	13: 49	Bates, Barton	12: 93
1862	"		" Wilson, Robert	12:335	"	
1863	"		" Brown, B. Gratz	20:318	"	
1864	Hall, Willard P. (*act.*)	22:237	" "		"	
1865	Fletcher, Thomas C.	12:306	" "		Wagner, David	12:457
1867	"		" Drake, Charles D.	3:427	"	
1869	McClurg, Joseph W.	12:306	Schurz, Carl "	3:202	"	
1870	"		" Jewett, Daniel T.	12:399	"	
1871	Brown, B. Gratz	20:318	" Blair, Francis P., Jr.	4:223	"	
1873	Woodson, Silas	12:307	" Bogy, Lewis V.	12:422	"	
1875	Hardin, Charles H.	12:307	Cockrell, Francis M. "	3:297	"	
1876	"		" "		Sherwood, Thomas A.	7: 53
1877	Phelps, John S.	12:307	" Armstrong, David H.	5:517	"	
1879	"		" Shields, James	8: 2	"	
1879	"		" Vest, George G.	2:397	"	
1881	Crittenden, Thomas T.	12:307	" "		"	
1883	"		" "		Hough, Warwick	7:149
1885	Marmaduke, John S.	12:308	" "		Henry, John W.	12: 45
1887	Morehouse, Allen P.	12:308	" "		Norton, Elijah H.	5:508
1889	Francis, David R.	12: 9	" "		Ray, Robert D.	13:320
1891	"		" "		Sherwood, Thomas A.	7: 53
1893	Stone, William J.	12:308	" "		Black, Francis M.	13:558
1895	"		" "		Brace, Theodore	13:309

MISSOURI *(Continued)*

Date	Governors	Biography	U. S. Senators	Biography	Chief Justices	Biography
1897	Stephens, Lon V.	12:309	Cockrell, Francis M.	3:297	Barclay, Shepard	12:455
1898	"		" Vest, George G.	2:397	Gantt, James B.	12:132
1901	Dockery, Alexander M.	20: 44	" "		Burgess, Gavon D.	12:193
1903	"		" Stone, William J.	12:308	Robinson, Waltour M.	25:114
1905	Folk, Joseph W.	22:171	Warner, William "	20:161	"	
1905	"		" "		Brace, Theodore	13:309
1907	"		" "		Gantt, James B.	12:132
1909	Hadley, Herbert S.	14:475	" "		Palliant, Leroy B.	
1911	"		Reed, James A. "	15: 99	"	
1913	Major, Elliott W.	15:121	" "		Lamm, Henry	21:470
1915	"		" "		Woodson, Archelaus M.	20: 33
1916	"		" "		Graves, Waller W.	26:324
1918	"		" Wilfley, Xenophon P.	C:364	"	
1918	"		" Spencer, Selden R.	20:193	Bond, Henry W.	
1919	"		" "		Walker, Robert F.	26:107
1921	Hyde, Arthur M.	C: 13	" "		"	
1922	"		" "		Blair, James T.	B:159
1922	"		" "		Woodson, Archelaus M.	20: 33
1924	"		" "		Graves, Waller W.	26:324
1925	Baker, Sam A.	B:216	" Williams, George H.		Blair, David E.	B:169
1926	"		" Hawes, Harry B.	C: 65	"	
1927	"		" "		Walker, Robert F.	26:107
1928	"		" "		White, John T.	
1929	Caulfield, Henry S.		Patterson, Roscoe C. "	A:396	"	
1930	"		" "		Ragland, William T.	
1931	"		" "		Atwood, Frank E.	
1932	"		" "		Gantt, Ernest S.	
1933	Park, Guy B.		" Clark, Bennett		"	
1934	"		" "		Frank, William F.	
1935	"		Truman, Harry S. "		Ellison, George R.	

MONTANA

Date	Governors	Biography	U. S. Senators	Biography	Chief Justices	Biography
1889	Toole, Joseph K.	11: 82			Blake, Henry N.	13:178
1890	"		Sanders, Wilbur F.	1:457	"	
1890	"		" Power, Thomas C.	19:288	"	
1893	Rickards, John E.	11: 82	Vacant "		Pemberton, William Y.	12:453
1895	"		Mantle, Lee "	11:313	"	
1895	"		" Carter, Thomas H.	13:199	"	
1897	Smith, Robert B.	11: 82	" "			
1898	"		" "		Brantly, Theodore	12:190
1899	"		Clark, William A. "	21: 10	"	
1901	Toole, Joseph K.	11: 82	Gibson, Paris "	8: 71	"	
1901	"		" Clark, William A.	21: 10	"	
1905	"		Carter, Thomas H. "	13:199	"	
1907	"		" Dixon, Joseph M.	14:107	"	
1909	Norris, Edwin L.	14:431	" "		"	
1911	"		Myers, Henry L. "	15: 48	"	
1913	Stewart, Samuel V.	15:241	" Walsh, Thomas J.	15:409	"	
1921	Dixon, Joseph M.	14:107	" "		"	
1922	"		" "		Callaway, Llewellyn L.	
1923	"		Wheeler, Burton K. "	A:153	"	
1925	Erickson, John E.	D:143	" "		"	
1933	Cooney, Frank H.	26:302	" Erickson, John E.	D:143	"	
1934	"		" Murray, James E.		"	
1935	"		" "		Sands, W. B.	

NEBRASKA

Date	Governors	Biography	U. S. Senators	Biography	Chief Justices	Biography
1867	Butler, David	12: 1	Tipton, Thomas W.	12:226	Mason, Oliver P.	5:511
1867	“		“ Thayer, John M.	12: 2	“	
1871	James, William H. (*act.*)	12: 1	“ Hitchcock, Phineas W.	7:490	“	
1873	Furnas, Robert W.	12: 1	“ “		Lake, George B.	5:456
1875	Garber, Silas	12: 2	Paddock, Algernon S.	2:247	“	
1877	“		“ Saunders, Alvin	13:221	“	
1878	“		“ “		Gantt, Daniel	13:483
1878	“		“ “		Maxwell, Samuel	12:338
1879	Nance, Albinus	12: 2	“ “		“	
1881	“		VanWyck, Charles H. “	5:334	“	
1882	“		“ “		Lake, George B.	10:456
1883	Dawes, James W.	12: 2	“ Manderson, Charles F.	1:454	“	
1884	“		“ “		Cobb, Amasa	6:191
1886	“		“ “		Maxwell, Samuel	12:338
1887	Thayer, John M.	12: 2	Paddock, Algernon S.	2:247	“	
1888	“		“ “		Reese, Manoah B.	8:364
1890	“		“ “		Cobb, Amasa	6:191
1891	Boyd, James E.	12: 3	“ “		“	
1891	Thayer, John M.	12: 2	“ “		“	
1892	Boyd, James E.	12: 3	“ “		Maxwell, Samuel	12:338
1893	Crounse, Lorenzo	12: 3	Allen, William V. “	5:217	“	
1894	“		“ “		Norval, Theophilus L.	13:302
1895	Holcomb, Silas A.	12: 4	“ Thurston, John M.	5:105	“	
1896	“		“ “		Post, A. M.	
1898	“		“ “		Harrison, T. O. C.	
1899	Poynter, William A.	12: 4	“ “		“	
1900	“		“ “		Norval, Theophilus L.	13:302
1901	Dietrich, Charles H.	12: 4	“ Millard, Joseph H.	13:367	“	
1901	Savage, Ezra P.	12: 4	Dietrich, Charles H. “	12: 4	“	
1902	“		“ “		Sullivan, John J.	22:194
1903	Mickey, John H.	12: 5	“ “		“	
1904	“		“ “		Holcomb, Silas A.	12: 4
1905	“		Burkett, Elmer J. “	13:582	“	
1906	“		“ “		Sedgwick, Samuel H.	14:319
1907	Sheldon, George L.		“ Brown, Norris	14:328	“	
1908	“		“ “		Barnes, John B.	18:382
1908	“		“ “		Reese, Manoah B.	8:364
1909	Shallenberger, Ashton C.	A:100	“ “		“	
1911	Aldrich, Chester H.	25: 42	Hitchcock, Gilbert M. “	25:100	“	
1913	Morehead, John H.	15:230	“ Norris, George W.	B:171	“	
1915	“		“ “		Hollenbeck, Conrad	20:283
1915	“		“ “		Fawcett, Jacob	
1915	“		“ “		Morrissey, Andrew M.	17:260
1917	Neville, Keith		“ “		“	
1919	McKelvie, Samuel R.		“ “		“	
1923	Bryan, Charles W.	A:520	Howell, Robert B. “	C:390	“	
1925	McMullen, Adam	C:406	“ “		“	
1927	“		“ “		Goss, Charles A.	
1929	Weaver, Arthur J.		“ “		“	
1931	Bryan, Charles W.	A:520	“ “		“	
1933	“		Thompson, William H. “	15: 57	“	
1934	“		Hunter, Richard C. “		“	
1935	Cochran, Robert L.		Burke, Edward R. “		“	

NEVADA

Date	Governors	Biography	U. S. Senators		Biography	Chief Justices	Biography
1864	Blasdel, Henry G.	11:200	Stewart, William M.		1:325	Lewis, John F.	13: 86
1864	"		"	Nye, James W.	11:200	"	
1867	"		"	"		Beatty, Henry O.	12:268
1868	"		"	"		Lewis, John F.	13: 86
1871	Bradley, Lewis R.	11:200	"	"		"	
1873	"		"	Jones, John P.	1:300	Whitman, Bernard C.	12:188
1875	"		Sharon, William	"	6:512	Hawley, Thomas P.	12:191
1879	Kinkead, John H.	11:201	"	"		Beatty, William H.	12:268
1881	"		Fair, James G.	"	11:189	Leonard, Orville R.	12:458
1883	Adams, Jewett W.	11:201	"	"		Hawley, Thomas P.	12:191
1885	"		"	"		Belknap, Charles H.	12:476
1887	Stevenson, Charles C.	12:369	Stewart, William M.	"	1:325	Leonard, Orville R.	12:458
1889	"		"	"		Hawley, Thomas P.	12:191
1890	Bell, Frank (*acting*)		"	"		Belknap, Charles H.	12:476
1891	Colcord, Roswell K.	11:201	"	"		"	
1893	"		"	"		Murphy, Michael A.	12:458
1895	Jones, John E.	11:201	"	"		Biglow, R. R.	
1896	Sadler, Reinhold	11:202	"	"		"	
1897	"		"	"		Belknap, Charles H.	12:476
1899	"		"	"		Bonnifield, M. S.	12:145
1901	"		"	"		Massey, W. A.	
1902	"		"	"		Belknap, Charles H.	12:476
1903	Sparks, John		"	Newlands, Francis G.	13:219	"	
1904	"		Nixon, George S.	"	14:443	"	
1905	"		"	"		Fitzgerald, Adolphus L.	18:413
1907	"		"	"		Talbot, George F.	
1908	Dickerson, Denver S.	20:219	"	"		"	
1909	"		"	"		Norcross, Frank H.	18: 53
1910	Oddie, Tasker L.	A: 83	"	"		"	
1911	"		"	"		Sweeney, James G.	
1912	"		Massey, William A.	"		"	
1913	"		Pittman, Key	"	B:375	Talbot, George F.	
1915	Boyle, Emmet D.	21:234	"	"		Norcross, Frank H.	18: 53
1917	"		"	"		McCarren, Patrick A.	D:214
1918	"		"	Henderson, Charles B.	A:306	"	
1919	"		"	"		Coleman, Benjamin W.	
1921	"		"	Oddie, Tasker L.	A: 83	Sanders, John A.	
1923	Scrugham, James G.		"	"		Ducker, Edward A.	
1925	"		"	"		Coleman, Benjamin W.	
1927	Balzar, Frederick B.		"	"		Sanders, John A.	
1929	"		"	"		Ducker, Edward A.	
1931	"		"	"		Coleman, Benjamin W.	
1933	"		"	McCarren, Patrick A.	D:214	Sanders, John A.	
1934	Griswold, Morley		"	"		"	
1935	Kirman, Richard, Sr.		"	"		Ducker, Edward A.	

NEW HAMPSHIRE

Date	Governors	Biography	U. S. Senators	Biography	Chief Justices	Biography
1679	Cutts, John	13:434				
1681	Waldron, Richard	13:434				
1682	Cranfield, Edward	13:435				
1686	Barefoot, Walter					
1686	Dudley, Joseph	7:372				
1686	Andros, Edmund	6: 90				
1690	Bradstreet, Simon	7:372				
1692	Allen, Samuel	13:454				
1699	Coote, Richard					
1702	Dudley, Joseph	7:373				
1716	Shute, Samuel	7:374				
1728	Burnet, William	7:374				
1729	Belcher, Jonathan	6:301				
1741	Wentworth, Benning	6:303				
1767	Wentworth, John	5:194				
1775	Thornton, Matthew	11:540				
1776	Weare, Mesech	13:344				
1785	Langdon, John	11:123				
1786	Sullivan, John	1: 56				
1788	Langdon, John	11:123				
1789	Sullivan, John	1: 56	Wingate, Paine	12:558	Bartlett, Josiah	11:121
1789	"		" Langdon, John	11:123	"	
1790	Bartlett, Josiah	11:121	" "		Pickering, John	3:224
1793	"		Livermore, Samuel "	2: 8	"	
1794	Gilman, John T.	11:122	" "		"	
1795	"		" "		Olcott, Simeon	1:363
1801	"		Olcott, Simeon	1:363	"	
1801	"		" Sheafe, James	2: 10	"	
1802	"		" Plumer, William	11:124	Smith, Jeremiah	11:123
1805	Langdon, John	11:123	Gilman, Nicholas "	2:447	"	
1807	"		" Parker, Nahum	5:223	"	
1809	Smith, Jeremiah	11:123	" "		Livermore, Arthur	12:436
1810	Langdon, John	11:123	" Cutts, Charles	4:510	"	
1812	Plumer, William	11:124	" "		"	
1813	Gilman, John T.	11:122	" Mason, Jeremiah	2:490	Smith, Jeremiah	11:123
1814	"		Thompson, Thomas W. "	3:524	"	
1816	Plumer, William	11:124	" "		Richardson, William M.	4:155
1817	"		Morril, David L.	11:125	"	
1817	"		" Storer, Clement	7: 48	"	
1819	Bell, Samuel	11:125	" Parrott, John F.	11:576	"	
1823	Woodbury, Levi	2:471	Bell, Samuel "	11:125	"	
1824	Morril, David L.	11:125	" "		"	
1825	"		" Woodbury, Levi	2:471	"	
1827	Pierce, Benjamin	11:125	" "		"	
1828	Bell, John	11:126	" "		"	
1829	Pierce, Benjamin	11:125	" "		"	
1830	Harvey, Matthew	11:126	" "		"	
1831	Harper, Joseph M. (*act.*)	11:126	" Hill, Isaac	11:127	"	
1831	Dinsmoor, Samuel	11:127	" "		"	
1834	Badger, William	11:127	" "		"	
1835	"		Hubbard, Henry "	11:128	"	
1836	Hill, Isaac	11:127	" Page, John	11:128	"	
1837	"		" Pierce, Franklin	4:145	Parker, Joel	12:113
1839	Page, John	11:128	" "		"	
1841	"		Woodbury, Levi "	2:471	"	
1842	Hubbard, Henry	11:128	" Wilcox, Leonard	11:159	"	
1843	"		" Atherton, Charles G.	10:383	"	
1844	Steele, John H.	11:128	" "		"	
1845	"		Jenness, Benning W. "	7:538	"	
1846	Colby, Anthony	11:129	" "		"	
1846	"		Cilley, Joseph "	10:109	"	
1847	Williams, Jared W.	11:129	Hale, John P. "	3:120	"	
1848	"		" "		Gilchrist, John J.	7:508
1849	Dinsmoor, Samuel	11:129	" Norris, Moses, Jr.	12:394	"	
1852	Martin, Noah	11:130	" "		"	
1853	"		Atherton, Charles G. "	10:383	"	
1853	"		Williams, Jared W. "	11:129	"	
1854	Baker, Nathaniel B.	11:130	" "		"	

NEW HAMPSHIRE *(Continued)*

Date	Governors	Biography	U. S. Senators	Biography	Chief Justices	Biography
1855	Metcalf, Ralph	11:130	Hale, John P.	3:120	Woods, Andrew S.	12:435
1855	“		“ Wells, John S.	3:507	Perley, Ira	12:435
1855	“		“ Bell, James	7:531	“	
1857	Haile, William	11:131	“ Clark, Daniel	2: 87	“	
1859	Goodwin, Ichabod	11:131	“ “		Bell, Samuel D.	12:145
1861	Berry, Nathaniel S.	11:132	“ “		“	
1863	Gilmore, Joseph A.	11:132	“ “		“	
1864	“		“ “		Perley, Ira	12:435
1865	Smyth, Frederick	11:133	Cragin, Aaron H. “	12:394	“	
1866	“		“ Fogg, George G.	4:374	“	
1867	Harriman, Walter	11:133	“ Patterson, James W.	11:364	“	
1869	Stearns, Onslow	11:134	“ “		Bellows, Henry A.	12:435
1871	Weston, James A.	11:134	“ “		“	
1872	Straw, Ezekiel A.	11:135	“ “		“	
1873	“		“ Wadleigh, Bainbridge	7:439	Sargent, Jonathan E.	12:145
1874	Weston, James A.	11:134	“ “		Cushing, Edmund L.	12:435
1875	Cheney, Person C.	11:135	“ “		“	
1876	“		“ “		Doe, Charles	12:436
1877	Prescott, Benjamin F.	11:136	Rollins, Edward H. “	7:512	“	
1879	Head, Natt	11:136	“ Bell, Charles H.	11:137	“	
1879	“		“ Blair, Henry W.	1:458	“	
1881	Bell, Charles H.	11:137	“ “		“	
1883	Hale, Samuel W.	11:137	Pike, Austin F. “	10:259	“	
1885	Currier, Moody	11:138	“ “		“	
1886	“		Cheney, Person C. “	11:135	“	
1887	Sawyer, Charles H.	11:139	Chandler, William E. “	4:252	“	
1889	Goodell, David H.	11:139	Marston, Gilman E. “	5:329	“	
1889	“		Chandler, William E. “	4:252	“	
1891	Tuttle, Hiram A.	11:139	“ Gallinger, Jacob H.	2:247	“	
1893	Smith, John B.	11:140	“ “		“	
1895	Busiel, Charles A.	11:140	“ “		“	
1896	“		“ “		Carpenter, Alonzo P.	12:326
1897	Ramsdell, George A.	11:141	“ “		“	
1898	“		“ “		Clark, Lewis W.	13:364
1898	“		“ “		Blodgett, Isaac N.	12:377
1899	Rollins, Frank W.	11:141	“ “		“	
1901	Jordan, Chester B.	11:141	Burnham, Henry E. “	13: 43	“	
1902	“		“ “		Parsons, Frank N.	13:325
1903	Bachelder, Nahum J.	13:169	“ “		“	
1905	McLane, John	14:100	“ “		“	
1907	Floyd, Charles M.	20: 58	“ “		“	
1909	Quinby, Henry B.	14:498	“ “		“	
1911	Bass, Robert P.	B:284	“ “		“	
1913	Felker, Samuel D.	A:113	Hollis, Henry F. “	15:272	“	
1915	Spaulding, Rolland H.	18:418	“ “		“	
1917	Keyes, Henry W.	C:245	“ “		“	
1918	“		“ Drew, Irving W.	21:229	“	
1918	“		“ Moses, George H.	C: 71	“	
1919	Bartlett, John H.	B:119	Keyes, Henry W. “	C:245	“	
1921	Brown, Albert O.	A: 50	“ “		“	
1923	Brown, Fred H.	C:243	“ “		“	
1924	“		“ “		Peaslee, Robert J.	C:109
1925	Winant, John G.	B:471	“ “		“	
1927	Spaulding, Huntley N.	B:494	“ “		“	
1929	Tobey, Charles W.		“ “		“	
1931	Winant, John G.	B:471	“ “		“	
1933	“		“ Brown, Fred H.	C:243	“	
1934	“		“ “		Allen, John E.	
1935	Bridges, H. Styles		“ “		“	

NEW JERSEY

Date	Governors	Biography	U. S. Senators	Biography	Chief Justices	Biography
1702	Hyde, Edward	5:407				
1704	"				Mompesson, Roger	13:155
1708	Lovelace, John	13:448			"	
1709	"				Gordon, Thomas	12:256
1710	Hunter, Robert	7:155			Jamison, David	12:335
1720	Burnet, William	7:374			"	
1723	"				Trent, William	12:150
1724	"				Hooper, Robert L.	12:262
1728	Montgomerie, John	13:453			Farmer, Thomas	12:458
1731	Morris, Lewis	3:113			"	
1732	Crosby, William	12: 5			"	
1736	Hamilton, John	5:543			"	
1738	Morris, Lewis	3:113			Morris, Robert Hunter	12:483
1746	Hamilton, John	5:543			"	
1746	Reading, John				"	
1747	Belcher, Jonathan	6:301			"	
1757	Reading, John				"	
1758	Bernard, Francis	5:432			Aynsley, William	12:263
1760	Boone, Thomas	12:158			"	
1761	Hardy, Josiah	13:102			"	
1763	Franklin, William	13:102			"	
1764	"				Read, Charles	12:263
1764	"				Smyth, Frederick	12:377
1776	Livingston, William	5:201			"	
1777	"				Morris, Robert	12:484
1779	"				Brearley, David	2: 38
1789	"		Elmer, Jonathan	11:538	Kinsey, James	12:257
1789	"		" Paterson, William	1: 24	"	
1790	Paterson, William	1: 24	" Dickinson, Philemon	7:517	"	
1791	"		Rutherfurd, John "	2: 10	"	
1793	Howell, Richard	5:202	" Frelinghuysen, Fred'k	7:540	"	
1796	"		" Stockton, Richard	12:218	"	
1799	"		Schureman, James	2: 11	"	
1799	"		" Dayton, Jonathan	1:306	"	
1801	Bloomfield, Joseph	5:202	Ogden, Aaron "	5:203	"	
1802	Lambert, John (*acting*)	11:489	" "		"	
1803	Bloomfield, Joseph	5:202	Condit, John "	11: 41	Kirkpatrick, Andrew	12:241
1805	"		" Kitchell, Aaron	11:441	"	
1809	"		Lambert, John	11:489	"	
1809	"		" Condit, John	11: 41	"	
1812	Ogden, Aaron	5:203	" "		"	
1813	Pennington, William S.	5:204	" "		"	
1815	Dickerson, Mahlon	5:295	Wilson, James J. "	3:530	"	
1817	Williamson, Isaac H.	5:204	" Dickerson, Mahlon	5:295	"	
1821	"		Southard, Samuel L. "	6: 85	"	
1823	"		McIlvaine, Joseph "	11:313	"	
1824	"		" "		Ewing, Charles	7:535
1826	"		Bateman, Ephraim "	12:270	"	
1829	Vroom, Peter D.	5:205	Dickerson, Mahlon "	5:295	"	
1829	"		" Frelinghuysen, Theodore	3:401	"	
1832	Southard, Samuel L.	6: 85	" "		Hornblower, Joseph C.	13:155
1833	Seeley, Elias P.	5:205	Southard, Samuel L. "	6: 85	"	
1833	Vroom, Peter D.	5:205	" "		"	
1835	"		" Wall, Garret D.	5:529	"	
1836	Dickerson, Philemon	5:205	" "		"	
1837	Pennington, William	5:206	" "		"	
1841	"		" Miller, Jacob W.	4:269	"	
1842	"		Dayton, William L. "	4:325	"	
1843	Haines, Daniel	5:207	" "		"	
1844	Stratton, Charles C.	5:207	" "		"	
1846	"		" "		Green, Henry W.	7:495
1848	Haines, Daniel	5:207	" "		"	
1851	Fort, George F.	5:207	Stockton, Robert F. "	4:205	"	
1853	"		Thompson, John R.	12:212	Vroom, Peter D.	5:205
1853	"		" Wright, William	4:548	"	
1854	Price, Rodman M.	5:207	" "		"	
1857	Newell, William A.	5:208	" "		"	
1859	"		" Ten Eyck, John C.	2: 95	"	
1860	Olden, Charles S.	5:209	" "		"	

NEW JERSEY *(Continued)*

Date	Governors	Biography	U. S. Senators	Biography	Chief Justices	Biography
1861	Olden, Charles S.	5:209	Thompson, John R.	12:112	Whelpley, Edward W.	7:495
1861	"		" Ten Eyck, John C.	2: 95	"	
1862	"		Field, Richard S. "	3:216	"	
1863	Parker, Joel	5:209	Wall, James W. "	10:123	"	
1863	"		Wright, William "	4:548	"	
1864	"		" "		Beasley, Mercer	13:261
1865	"		" Stockton, John P.	13: 86	"	
1866	Ward, Marcus L.	5:209	Frelinghuysen, Frederick T.	4:250	"	
1866	"		" Cattell, Alexander	2: 35	"	
1869	Randolph, Theodore F.	5:210	Stockton, John P. "	13: 86	"	
1871	"		" Frelinghuysen, Fred'k T.	4:250	"	
1872	Parker, Joel	5:209	" "		"	
1875	Bedle, Joseph D.	5:210	Randolph, Theodore F. "	5:210	"	
1877	"		" McPherson, John R.	3: 71	"	
1878	McClellan, George B.	4:140	" "		"	
1881	Ludlow, George C.	5:211	Sewell, William J. "	12:217	"	
1884	Abbett, Leon	1:458	" "		"	
1887	Green, Robert S.	5:212	Blodgett, Rufus "	1:217	"	
1890	Abbett, Leon	1:458	" "		"	
1893	Werts, George T.	5:212	Smith, John, Jr. "	12:391	"	
1895	"		" Sewell, William J.	12:217	"	
1896	Griggs, John W.	11: 19	" "		Magie, William J.	12:424
1898	Voorhees, Foster M.	14:399	" "		"	
1899	"		Kean, John "	18:152	Depue, David A.	5:532
1900	"		" "		Gummere, William S.	13:521
1902	Murphy, Franklin	13:570	" Dryden, John F.	9:415	"	
1905	Stokes, Edward C.	13:455	" "		"	
1907	"		" Briggs, Frank O.	14:305	"	
1908	Fort, John F.	14:123	" "		"	
1911	Wilson, Woodrow	19: 1	Martine, James E. "	15:145	"	
1913	"		" Hughes, William	21:307	"	
1914	Fielder, James F.	15:114	" "		"	
1917	Edge, Walter E.	B:279	Frelinghuysen, Joseph S."	C:252	"	
1918	"		" Baird, David	20: 38	"	
1919	"		" Edge, Walter E.	B:279	"	
1920	Edwards, Edward I.	24:256	" "		"	
1923	Silzer, George S.		Edwards, Edward I. "	24:256	"	
1926	Moore, A. Harry	B:178	" "		"	
1929	Larson, Morgan F.		" Baird, David, Jr.		"	
1929	"		Kean, Hamilton F. "	C:173	"	
1931	"		" Morrow, Dwight W.	23: 10	"	
1932	Moore, A. Harry	B:178	" "		"	
1933	"		" Barbour, William W.	D:256	Brogan, Thomas J.	
1935	Hoffman, Harold G.		Moore, A. Harry "	B:178	"	

NEW MEXICO

Date	Governors	Biography	U. S. Senators	Biography	Chief Justices	Biography
1912	McDonald, William C.	17:447	Catron, Thomas B.		Roberts, Clarence J.	18:400
1912	"		" Fall, Albert B.	A:355	"	
1917	DeBaca, Ezequiel C.	19:278	Jones, Andrieus A."	20: 18	Hanna, Richard H.	
1917	Lindsey, Washington E.	23:115	" "		"	
1919	Larrazolo, Octaviano A.	C:416	" "		Parker, Frank W.	
1921	Mechem, Merritt C.		" Bursum, Holm O.	C:524	Roberts, Clarence J.	18:400
1921	"		" "		Raynolds, Herbert F.	
1922	"		" "		Parker, Frank W.	
1923	Hinkle, James F.		" "		"	
1925	Hannett, Arthur T.	C:424	" Bratton, Sam G.	B:488	"	
1927	Dillon, Richard C.		Cutting, Bronson "	26:443	"	
1929	"		" "		Bickley, Howard L.	
1931	Seligman, Arthur	26:319	" "		"	
1933	Hockenhull, Andy W.		" Hatch, Carl A.		Watson, John C.	
1935	Tingley, Clyde		Chavez, Dennis "		Sadler, Daniel K.	

NEW YORK

Date	Governors	Biography	U. S. Senators	Biography	Chief Justices	Biography
1624	Mey, Cornelius J.	12:208				
1625	Verhulst, William	12:208				
1626	Minuit, Peter	12:208				
1633	VanTwiller, Wouter	13:171				
1638	Kieft, William	6: 91				
1647	Stuyvesant, Peter	5:138				
1664	Nicolls, Richard	13:447				
1668	Lovelace, Francis	13:448				
1673	Colve, Anthony					
1674	Andros, Edmund	6: 90				
1683	Dongan, Thomas	10:241				
1688	Nicholson, Francis	7:335				
1689	Leisler, Jacob	13:448				
1691	Sloughter, Henry	13:448			Dudley, Joseph	7:372
1691	Ingoldsby, Richard	13:449			"	
1692	Fletcher, Benjamin	13:449			Smith, William	12:252
1698	Coote, Richard	8:373			"	
1700	"				VanCortlandt, Stephanus	5:532
1701	"				DePeyster, Abraham	2: 43
1701	"				Attwood, William	12:271
1702	Hyde, Edward	5:407			Smith, William	12:252
1703	"				Bridges, John	
1704	"				Mompesson, Roger	13:155
1708	Lovelace, John	13:448			"	
1709	Ingoldsby, Richard (*acting*)				"	
1710	Beekman, Gerardus	10:461			"	
1710	Hunter, Robert	7:155			"	
1715	"				Morris, Lewis	3:113
1719	Schuyler, Peter (*acting*)				"	
1720	Burnet, William	7:374			"	
1728	Montgomerie, John	13:453			"	
1731	Van Dam, Rip	13:454			"	
1732	Crosby, William	12: 5			"	
1733	"				Delancey, James	4:550
1736	Clarke, George				"	
1743	Clinton, George	5:541			"	
1753	Osborne, Danvers				"	
1753	Delancey, James	4:550			"	
1755	Hardy, Charles				"	
1757	Delancey, James	4:550			"	
1760	Colden, Cadwallader	2:270			"	
1761	Monckton, Robert	13:117			Pratt, Benjamin	7:147
1761	Colden, Cadwallader	2:270			"	
1763	"				Horsmanden, Daniel	7:560
1765	Moore, Henry	5:540			"	
1769	Colden, Cadwallader	2:270			"	
1770	Murray, John	13:391			"	
1771	Tryon, William	7:514			"	
1777	Clinton, George	3: 41			Jay, John	1: 20
1789	"				Morris, Richard	12:508
1789	"		Schuyler, Philip J.	1: 97	"	
1789	"		" King, Rufus	6:301	"	
1790	"		" "		Yates, Robert	5:260
1791	"		Burr, Aaron "	3: 5	"	
1795	Jay, John	1: 20	" "		"	
1796	"		" Laurance, John	2: 8	"	
1797	"		Schuyler, Philip J. "	1: 97	"	
1798	"		Hobart, John S. "	2: 35	Lansing, John, Jr.	4:254
1798	"		North, William "	2: 7	"	
1798	"		Watson, James "	2:347	"	
1800	"		Morris, Gouverneur	2:526	"	
1800	"		" Armstrong John	1: 48	"	
1801	Clinton, George	3: 41	" "		Lewis, Morgan	3: 43
1802	"		" Clinton, DeWitt	3: 43	"	
1803	"		Bailey, Theodorus	13:348	"	
1803	"		" Armstrong, John	1: 48	"	
1804	Lewis, Morgan	3: 43	Armstrong, John	1: 48	Kent, James	3: 55
1804	"		" Smith, John	11:197	"	
1804	"		Mitchill, Samuel L. "	4:409	"	

NEW YORK *(Continued)*

Date	Governors	Biography	U. S. Senators		Biography	Chief Justices	Biography
1807	Tompkins, Daniel D.	6: 83	Mitchill, Samuel L.		4:409	Kent, James	3: 55
1807	"		"	Smith, John	11:197	"	
1809	"		German, Obadiah	"	12:545	"	
1813	"		"	King, Rufus	6:301	"	
1814	"		"	"		Thompson, Smith	6: 86
1815	"		Sanford, Nathan	"	3:383	"	
1817	Clinton, De Witt	3: 43	"	"		"	
1819	"		"	"		Spencer, Ambrose	3:423
1821	"		Van Buren, Martin	"	6:533	"	
1823	Yates, Joseph C.	3: 45	"	"		Savage, John	11:509
1825	Clinton, DeWitt	3: 43	"	Sanford, Nathan	3:383	"	
1828	Pitcher, Nathaniel	3: 45	"	"		"	
1829	VanBuren, Martin	6:433	Dudley, Charles E.		4:353	"	
1829	Throop, Enos T.	3: 46	"	"		Nelson, Samuel	2:470
1831	"		"	Marcy, William L.	6:269	"	
1833	Marcy, William L.	6:260	"	Wright, Silas, Jr.	3: 47	"	
1833	"		Tallmadge, Nathaniel P.	"	12: 73	"	
1839	Seward, William H.	2: 77	"	"		"	
1843	Bouck, William C.	3: 46	"	"		"	
1844	"		Dickinson, Daniel S.		5:388	"	
1844	"		"	Foster, Henry A.	4:551	"	
1845	Wright, Silas, Jr.	3: 47	"	Dix, John A.	5: 6	Bronson, Greene C.	3:387
1847	Young, John	3: 48	"	"		Beardsley, Samuel	4:485
1847	"		"	"		Jewett, Freeborn G.	12: 65
1849	Fish, Hamilton	4: 15	"	Seward, William H.	2: 77	"	
1850	"		"	"		Bronson, Greene C.	3:387
1851	Hunt, Washington	3: 48	Fish, Hamilton	"	4: 15	Ruggles, Charles H.	11:335
1853	Seymour, Horatio	3: 48	"	"		"	
1854	"		"	"		Gardiner, Addison	13:181
1855	Clark, Myron H.	3: 50	"	"		"	
1856	"		"	"		Denio, Hiram	4:359
1857	King, John A.	3: 50	King, Preston	"	2: 93	"	
1858	"		"	"		Johnson, Alexander S.	6:507
1859	Morgan, Edwin D.	3: 51	"	"		"	
1860	"		"	"		Comstock, George F.	13:151
1861	"		"	Harris, Ira	2: 96	"	
1862	"		"	"		Selden, Samuel L.	4:154
1862	"		"	"		Denio, Hiram	4:359
1863	Seymour, Horatio	3: 48	Morgan, Edwin D.	"	3: 51	"	
1865	Fenton, Reuben E.	3: 51	"	"		"	
1866	"		"	"		Davies, Henry E.	3: 26
1867	"		"	Conkling, Roscoe	3:220	"	
1868	"		"	"		Hunt, Ward	2:475
1869	Hoffman, John T.	3: 52	Fenton, Reuben E.	"	3: 51	"	
1870	"		"	"		Earl, Robert	12: 59
1870	"		"	"		Church, Sanford E.	11:267
1873	Dix, John A.	5: 6	"	"		"	
1875	Tilden, Samuel J.	3: 53	Kernan, Francis	"	8:368	"	
1877	Robinson, Lucius	3: 54	"	"		"	
1880	Cornell, Alonzo B.	3: 54	"	"		Folger, Charles J.	4:250
1881	"		Platt, Thomas C.	"	11:509	Andrews, Charles	12: 56
1881	"		Miller, Warner	"	4:560	"	
1881	"		"	Lapham, Elbridge G.	11:157	"	
1882	"		"	Evarts, William M.	3:197	Ruger, William C.	5:219
1883	Cleveland, Grover	2:400	"	"		"	
1884	Hill, David B.	1:453	"	"		"	
1885	"		"	"		"	
1891	"		"	Hill, David B.	1:453	"	
1892	Flower, Roswell P.	2:344	"	"		Earl, Robert	12: 59
1893	"		Murphy, Edward, Jr.	"	13:182	"	
1895	Morton, Levi P.	1:136	"	"		"	
1897	Black, Frank S.	16:255	"	Platt, Thomas C.	11:509	Parker, Alton B.	10:122
1899	Roosevelt, Theodore	14: 1	Depew, Chauncey M.	"	23: 96	"	27:166
1901	Odell, Benjamin B., Jr.	14:436	"	"		"	
1904	"		"	"		Cullen, Edgar M.	13:444
1905	Higgins, Frank W.	13:551	"	"		"	
1907	Hughes, Charles E.	A: 6	"	"		"	
1909	"		"	Root, Elihu	26: 1	"	
1910	White, Horace	16:110	"	"		"	
1911	Dix, John Alden	23:226	O'Gorman, James A.	"	15: 13	"	
1913	Sulzer, William	3:369	"	"		"	

References are to THE NATIONAL CYCLOPEDIA OF AMERICAN BIOGRAPHY

NEW YORK *(Continued)*

Date	Governors	Biography	U. S. Senators	Biography	Chief Justices	Biography
1914	Sulzer, William	3:369	O'Gorman, James A.	15: 13	Bartlett, Willard	15:412
1914	"		" Root, Elihu	26: 1	"	
1915	Whitman, Charles S.	15:207	" Wadsworth, James W., Jr.	15: 34	"	
1917	"		Calder, William M. "	C:203	Hiscock, Frank H.	A: 10
1919	Smith, Alfred E.	A:404	" "		"	
1921	Miller, Nathan L.	8: 47	" "		"	
1923	Smith, Alfred E.	A:404	Copeland, Royal S. "	15:358	"	
1927	"		" Wagner, Robert F.	D: 39	Cardozo, Benjamin N.	D: 50
1929	Roosevelt, Franklin D.	D: 1	" "		"	
1932	"		" "		Pound, Cuthbert W.	25: 5
1933	Lehman, Herbert H.	B:456	" "		"	
1935	"		" "		Crane, Frederick E.	

NORTH CAROLINA

Date	Governors	Biography	U. S. Senators	Biography	Chief Justices	Biography
1663	Drummond, William	10:395				
1667	Stephens, Samuel	10:395				
1670	Carteret, Peter					
1673	Jenkins, John					
1676	Eastchurch, Thomas					
1677	Miller, Thomas					
1677	Culpepper, John	12:223				
1678	Sothell, Seth	12:152				
1679	Harvey, John	13:383				
1679	Jenkins, John					
1682	Sothell, Seth	12:152				
1689	Ludwell, Philip	12:153				
1691	Jarvis, Thomas	4:429				
1694	Archdale, John	12:153				
1694	Harvey, John	13:383				
1699	Walker, Henderson					
1704	Daniel, Robert	12:155				
1705	Cary, Thomas					
1706	Glover, William					
1708	Cary, Thomas					
1710	Hyde, Edward	5:407				
1712	Pollock, Thomas					
1714	Eden, Charles					
1722	Pollock, Thomas					
1722	Reed, William					
1724	Burrington, George	11:282				
1725	Everard, Richard	9:464				
1731	Burrington, George	11:282				
1734	Johnston, Gabriel	5:554				
1752	Rice, Nathaniel					
1752	Rowan, Matthew					
1754	Dobbs, Arthur	5:543				
1765	Tryon, William	7:514				
1771	Martin, Josiah	13:439				
1776	Caswell, Richard	4:419				
1779	Nash, Abner	4:419				
1781	Burke, Thomas	7:264				
1782	Martin, Alexander	4:420				
1784	Caswell, Richard	4:419				
1787	Johnston, Samuel	4:420				
1789	Martin, Alexander	5:420	Johnston, Samuel	4:420		
1789	"		" Hawkins, Benjamin	4: 59		
1792	Spaight, Richard D.	4:420	" "			
1793	"		Martin, Alexander "	4:420		
1795	Ashe, Samuel	4:421	" Bloodworth, Timothy	5:147		
1798	Davie, William R.	1: 77	" "			
1799	Williams, Benjamin	4:421	Franklin, Jesse "	4:423		
1801	"		" Stone, David	4:421		
1802	Turner, James	4:421	" "			
1805	Alexander, Nathaniel	4:421	Turner, James "	4:421		
1807	Williams, Benjamin	4:421	" Franklin, Jesse	4:423		

NORTH CAROLINA *(Continued)*

Date	Governors	Biography	U. S. Senators	Biography	Chief Justices	Biography
1808	Stone, David	4:421	Turner, James	4:421		
1808	“		“ Franklin, Jesse	4:423		
1810	Smith, Benjamin	4:422	“ “			
1811	Hawkins, William	4:422	“ “			
1813	“		“ Stone, David	4:421		
1814	Miller, William	4:423	“ “			
1815	“		“ Macon, Nathaniel	5:176		
1816	“		Stokes, Montfort “	4:424		
1817	Branch, John	5:295	“ “		Taylor, John L.	9:285
1820	Franklin, Jesse	4:423	“ “		“	
1821	Holmes, Gabriel	4:423	“ “		“	
1823	“		Branch, John “	5:295	“	
1824	Burton, Hutchings G.	4:423	“ “		“	
1827	Iredell, James, Jr.	4:423	“ “		“	
1828	Owen, John	4:423	“ Iredell, James	4:423	“	
1829	“		Brown, Bedford “	9:458	Henderson, Leonard	4:161
1830	Stokes, Montfort	4:424	“ “		“	
1831	“		“ Mangum, Willie P.	4: 47	“	
1832	Swain, David L.	4:424	“ “		Ruffin, Thomas	6:289
1835	Spaight, Richard D., 2d		“ “		“	
1836	“		“ Strange, Robert	7:321	“	
1837	Dudley, Edward B.	4:425	“ “		“	
1840	“		Mangum, Willie P.	4: 47	“	
1840	“		“ Graham, William A.	4:426	“	
1841	Morehead, John M.	4:425	“ “		Ruffin, Thomas	6:289
1843	“		“ Haywood, William H.	4:325	“	
1845	Graham, William A.	4:426	“ “		“	
1846	“		“ Badger, George E.	3:305	“	
1849	Manly, Charles	4:426	“ “		“	
1851	Reid, David S.	4:427	“ “		“	
1852	“		“ “		Nash, Frederick	7:200
1853	“		Vacant “		“	
1854	Winslow, Warren (*act.*)	3:510	Reid, David S. “	4:427	“	
1855	Bragg, Thomas	4:427	“ Biggs, Asa	11:189	“	
1858	“		“ Clingman, Thomas L.	7:199	Pearson, Richmond M.	11: 89
1859	Ellis, John W.	4:427	Bragg, Thomas “	4:427	“	
1861	Clark, Henry T.	4:427	Vacant Vacant		“	
1862	Vance, Zebulon B.	2:384	“ “		“	
1865	Holden, Wm. W. (*prov.*)	4:427	“ “		“	
1865	Worth, Jonathan	4:428	“ “		“	
1868	Holden, William W.	4:427	Abbott, Joseph C.	5: 48	“	
1868	“		“ Pool, Joseph	10:226	“	
1871	Caldwell, Tod R.	4:428	“ “		“	
1872	“		Ransom, Matthew W. “	10:251	“	
1873	“		“ Merrimon, Augustus S.	9:270	“	
1874	Brogden, Curtis H.	4:428	“ “		“	
1877	Vance, Zebulon B.	2:384	“ “		“	
1878	“		“ “		Smith, William N. H.	13:164
1879	Jarvis, Thomas J.	4:429	“ Vance, Zebulon B.	2:384	“	
1885	Scales, Alfred M.	4:429	“ “		“	
1889	Fowle, Daniel G.	4:429	“ “		Merrimon, Augustus S.	9:270
1891	Holt, Thomas M.	4:430	“ “		“	
1892	“		“ “		Shepherd, James E.	12:423
1893	Carr, Elias	4:430	“ “		“	
1894	“		“ Jarvis, Thomas J.	4:429	“	
1895	“		Butler, Marion	13: 19	Faircloth, William T.	12:227
1895	“		“ Pritchard, Jeter C.	19:223	“	
1897	Russell, Daniel L.	13:356	“ “		“	
1901	Aycock, Charles B.	13:356	Simmons, Furnifold M. “	12:517	Furches, David M.	12:457
1903	“		“ Overman, Lee S.	13:305	Clark, Walter	8: 63
1905	Glenn, Robert B.	19:317	“ “		“	
1909	Kitchin, William W.	14:461	“ “		“	
1913	Craig, Locke	20:358	“ “		“	
1917	Bickett, Thomas W.		“ “		“	
1921	Morrison, Cameron		“ “		“	
1924	“		“ “		Hoke, William A.	24:345
1925	McLean, Angus W.	26:469	“ “		Stacy, Walter P.	B:466
1929	Gardner, Max C.		“ “		“	
1931	“		Bailey, Josiah W. “	D:440	“	
1932	“		“ Morrison, Cameron		“	
1933	Ehringhaus, John C. B.		“ “		“	

References are to THE NATIONAL CYCLOPEDIA OF AMERICAN BIOGRAPHY

NORTH DAKOTA

Date	Governors	Biography	U. S. Senators	Biography	Chief Justices	Biography
1889	Miller, John	13:518	Casey, Lyman R.	1:291	Corliss, Guy C. H.	13:175
1889	"		" Pierce, Gilbert A.	1:294	"	
1891	Burke, Andrew H.	1:320	" Hansbrough, Henry C.	4:496	"	
1892	"		" "		Bartholomew, Joseph M.	13:376
1893	Shortridge, Edward C.D.	13:518	Roach, William N. "	5:263	"	
1894	"		" "		Wallin, Alfred	5:242
1895	Allin, Roger	13:518	" "		"	
1896	"		" "		Corliss, Guy C. H.	13:175
1897	Briggs, Frank A.	13:518	" "		"	
1899	Fancher, Frederick B.	13:519	McCumber, Porter J. "	13: 62	Bartholomew, Joseph M.	13:376
1901	White, Frank	13:519	" "		Wallin, Alfred	5:242
1903	"		" "		Young, Newton C.	5:552
1905	Sarles, Elmore Y.	13:519	Hansbrough, Henry C. "	4:496	"	
1906	"		" McCumber, Porter J.	13: 62	Morgan, David E.	14:499
1907	Burke, John	14:449	" "		"	
1909	"		Johnson, Martin N. "	14:489	"	
1909	"		Thompson, Fountain L. "		"	
1910	"		Purcell, William E. "		"	
1911	"		Gronna, Asle J. "	19:420	Spalding, Burleigh F.	18: 70
1913	Hanna, Louis B.	15:382	" "		"	
1915	"		" "		Fisk, Charles J.	
1917	Frazier, Lynn J.	B:189	" "		Bruce, Andrew A.	
1918	"		" "		Christianson, Adolph M.	
1921	Nestos, Ragnvald A.	C: 64	Ladd, Edwin F. "	19:432	Robinson, James E.	
1921	"		" "		Grace, Richard H.	
1922	"		" "		Birdzell, Luther E.	
1923	"		" Frazier, Lynn J.	B:189	Bronson, Harrison A.	
1925	Sorlie, Arthur G.		" "		Christianson, Adolph M.	
1926	"		Nye, Gerald P. "	C:360	"	
1927	"		" "		Birdzell, Luther E.	
1928	Maddock, Walter		" "		Nuessle, William L.	
1929	Shafer, George F.		" "		Burke, John	14:449
1931	"		" "		Christianson, Adolph M.	
1933	Langer, William		" "		Nuessle, William L.	
1933	"		" "		Birdzell, Luther E.	
1933	"		" "		Burr, Alexander G.	
1935	Welford, Walter		" "		Burke, John	14:449

OHIO

Date	Governors	Biography	U. S. Senators	Biography	Chief Justices	Biography
1803	Tiffin, Edward	3:137	Smith, John	6:224	Huntington, Samuel	3:137
1803	“		“ Worthington, Thomas	3:138	“	
1807	“		“ Tiffin, Edward	3:137	“	
1807	Kirker, Thomas		“ “		“	
1808	Huntington, Samuel	3:137	Meigs, Return J., Jr.	3:137	Sprigg, William	5:512
1809	“		“ Griswold, Stanley	4: 95	“	
1809	“		“ Campbell, Alexander	4:314	“	
1810	Meigs, Return J., Jr.	3:137	Worthington, Thomas “	3:138	Scott, Thomas	5:512
1813	“		“ Morrow, Jeremiah	3:138	“	
1814	Looker, Othniel (*act.*)		“ “		“	
1814	Worthington, Thomas	3:138	Kerr, Joseph “	12:390	“	
1815	“		Ruggles, Benjamin “	13:162	Brown, Ethan A.	3:138
1819	Brown, Ethan A.	3:138	“ Trimble, William	10:382	Couch, Jessup N.	7:557
1821	“		“ “		Pease, Calvin	7:557
1822	Trimble, Allen (*acting*)	3:138	“ “		“	
1822	Morrow, Jeremiah	3:138	“ Brown, Ethan A.	3:138	“	
1825	“		“ Harrison, William H.	3: 33	“	
1826	Trimble, Allen	3:138	“ “		“	
1828	“		“ Burnet, Jacob	11:155	“	
1829	“		“ “		Hitchcock, Peter	1:370
1830	McArthur, Duncan	3:139	“ “		Hitchcock, Peter	1:370
1831	“		“ Ewing, Thomas	25: 14	“	
1832	Lucas, Robert	3:139	“ “		“	
1833	“		Morris, Thomas “	11: 39	Collett, Joshua	12:342
1835	“		“ “		Zane, Ebenezer	11: 90
1836	Vance, Joseph	3:139	“ “		“	
1837	“		“ Allen, William	3:142	“	
1838	Shannon, Wilson	8:340	“ “		“	
1839	“		Tappan, Benjamin “	5:403	“	
1840	Corwin, Thomas	6:180	“ “		“	
1842	Shannon, Wilson	8:340	“ “		“	
1844	Bartley, Mordecai	3:140	“ “		“	
1845	“		Corwin, Thomas “	6:180	Wood, Reuben	3:140
1846	Bebb, William	3:140	“ “		“	
1847	“		“ “		Birchard, Matthew	15: 53
1848	Ford, Seabury	3:140	“ “		“	
1849	“		“ Chase, Salmon P.	1: 28	Hitchcock, Peter	1:370
1850	Wood, Reuben	3:140	Ewing, Thomas “	25: 14	“	
1851	“		Wade, Benjamin F. “	2: 94	“	
1852	“		“ “		Caldwell, William B.	7:545
1853	Medill, William	3:141	“ “		“	
1855	“		“ Pugh, George E.	4:547	Ranney, Rufus P.	13:161
1856	Chase, Salmon P.	1: 28	“ “		“	
1857	“		“ “		Bartley, Thomas W.	7:519
1858	“		“ “		Swan, Joseph R.	5:183
1859	“		“ “		Brinkerhoff, Jacob	13:152
1860	Dennison, William	3:141	“ “		“	
1861	“		“ Salmon P. Chase	1: 28	“	
1861	“		“ Sherman, John	3:198	“	
1862	Tod, David	3:141	“ “		“	
1864	Brough, John	3:142	“ “		“	
1866	Cox, Jacob D.	22:231	“ “		“	
1868	Hayes, Rutherford B.	3:191	“ “		“	
1869	“		Thurman, Allen G. “	3:144	“	
1871	“		“ “		Scott, Josiah	12:222
1872	Noyes, Edward F.	3:142	“ “		Welch, John	11:437
1873	“		“ “		White, William	4:354
1874	Allen, William	3:142	“ “		Day, Luther	4:553
1875	“		“ “		Rex, George	12: 65
1876	Hayes, Rutherford B.	3:193	“ “		“	
1877	Young, Thomas L.	3:143	“ Matthews, Stanley	2:476	Welch, John	11:437
1878	Bishop, Richard M.	3:143	“ “		White, William	4:354
1879	“		“ Pendleton, George H.	3:278	Gilmore, William J.	12:212
1880	Foster, Charles	1:139	“ “		McIlvaine, George W.	12:210
1881	“		Sherman, John “	3:198	Boynton, Washington W.	12:485
1882	“		“ “		Okey, John W.	12:201
1883	“		“ “		White, William	4:354
1884	Hoadley, George	3:143	“ “		Owen, Selwyn N.	4:557
1885	“		“ Payne, Henry B.	1:427	McIlvaine, George W.	12:210

OHIO *(Continued)*

Date	Governors	Biography	U. S. Senators	Biography	Chief Justices	Biography
1886	Foraker, Joseph B.	3:144	Sherman, John	3:198	Owen, Selwyn N.	4:557
1886	"		" Payne, Henry B.	1:427	"	
1889	"		" "		Minshall, Thaddeus A.	12:273
1890	Campbell, James E.	1:470	" "		"	
1891	"		" Brice, Calvin S.	2:425	Williams, Marshall J.	12:119
1892	McKinley, William J.	11: 1	Sherman, John "	3:198	Spear, William T.	18:403
1893	"		" "		Bradbury, Joseph P.	5:560
1894	"		" "		Dickman, Franklin	7:517
1895	"		" "		Minshall, Thaddeus A.	12:273
1896	Bushnell, Asa S.	8: 43	" "		Williams, Marshall	12:119
1897	"		Hanna, Marcus A.	22: 13	Burket, Jacob	4:550
1897	"		" Foraker, Joseph B.	3:144	"	
1898	"		" "		Spear, William T.	18:403
1899	"		" "		Bradbury, Joseph P.	5:560
1900	Nash, George K.	5:337	" "		Shauck, John A.	12:134
1901	"		" "		Minshall, Thaddeus A.	12:273
1902	"		" "		Burket, Jacob	4:550
1904	Herrick, Myron T.	13: 68	" "		"	
1905	"		Dick, Charles "	13:445	Davis, William Z.	9:551
1906	Pattison, John M.	14:444	" "		Shauck, John A.	12:134
1906	Harris, Andrew L.	14:226	" "		"	
1908	"		" "		Price, James L.	20:383
1909	Harmon, Judson	13:279	Burton, Theodore E. "	21: 50	Crew, William B.	21:113
1910	"		" "		Summers, Augustus N.	
1911	"		" Pomerene, Atlee	C:341	Spear, William T.	18:403
1912	"		" "		Davis, William Z.	9:551
1913	Cox, James M.	D:269	" "		Shauck, John A.	12:134
1913	"		" "		Nichols, Hugh L.	
1915	Willis, Frank B.	21:445	Harding, Warren G. "	19:268	"	
1917	Cox, James M.	D:269	" "		"	
1921	Davis, Harry L.		Willis, Frank B. "	21:445	Marshall, Carrington T.	C:335
1923	Donahey, A. Victor	B:511	" Fess, Simeon D.	C:283; 27:340	"	
1929	Cooper, Myers Y.	C:385	Burton, Theodore E. "	21: 50	"	
1929	"		McCulloch, Roscoe C. "		"	
1931	White, George	D:187	Bulkley, Robert J. "	D:244	"	
1933	"		" "		Weygandt, Carl V.	
1935	Davey, Martin L.		" Donahey, A. Victor	B:511	"	

OKLAHOMA

Date	Governors	Biography	U. S. Senators	Biography	Chief Justices	Biography
1907	Haskell, Charles N.	14:465	Owen, Robert L.	14:248	Williams, Robert L.	14:496
1907	"		" Gore, Thomas P.	14:323	"	
1909	"		" "		Kane, Matthew J.	18:110
1910	"		" "		Dunn, Jesse J.	
1911	Cruce, Lee	16: 96	" "		Turner, John B.	
1913	"		" "		Hayes, Samuel W.	
1914	"		" "		Kane, Matthew J.	18:110
1915	Williams, Robert L.	14:496	" "		"	
1917	"		" "		Sharp, John F.	
1919	"		" "		Hardy, Summers	
1919	Robertson, James B. A.		" "		Owen, Thomas H.	
1920	"		" "		Rainey, Robert M.	
1921	"		" Harreld, John W.	B:426	Harrison, John B.	
1923	Walton, James C.		" "		Pitchford, John H.	20:129
1923	Trapp, Martin E.	B:196	" "		Johnson, John T.	
1924	"		" "		McNeill, Neal E.	B:238
1925	"		Pine, William B. "	A:484	Nicholson, George M.	
1927	Johnston, Henry S.		" Thomas, Elmer	C:106	Branson, Fred P.	
1929	Holloway, William J.		" "		Mason, Charles W.	
1931	Murray, William H.		Gore, Thomas P. "	14:323	Lester, E. F.	
1933	"		" "		Riley, Fletcher	
1935	Marland, Ernest W.		" "		McNeill, Edwin R.	

OREGON

Date	Governors	Biography	U. S. Senators	Biography	Chief Justices	Biography
1859	Whiteaker, John	8: 4	Smith, Delazon	11:502	Williams, George H.	4: 21
1859	"		" Lane, Joseph	8: 2	Wait, Aaron E.	5:242
1860	"		Baker, Edward D. "	2: 92	"	
1861	"		Stark, Benjamin "	4:549	"	
1861	"		" Nesmith, James W.	4: 72	"	
1862	Gibbs, Addison C.	8: 4	Harding, Benjamin F. "	12:394	"	
1864	"		" "		Boise, Reuben P.	5:517
1865	"		Williams, George H. "	4: 21	Prim, Payne P.	13:580
1866	Woods, George L.	8: 5	" "		"	
1867	"		" Corbett, Henry W.	6:111	Shattuck, Erasmus D.	
1868	"		" "		Boise, Reuben	6:517
1870	Grover, LaFayette	8: 5	" "		Prim, Payne P.	13:580
1871	"		Kelly, James K. "	12:229	"	
1872	"		" "		Upton, William W.	12: 44
1873	"		" Mitchell, John H.	2:301	"	
1874	"		" "		Bonham, B. F.	5:470
1876	"		" "		Prim, Payne P.	13:580
1877	Chadwick, Stephen F.	8: 6	Grover, La Fayette "	8: 5	"	
1878	Thayer, William W.	8: 6	" "		Kelly, James K.	12:229
1879	"		" Slater, James H.	4:549	"	
1880	"		" "		Lord, William P.	8: 7
1882	Moody, Zenas F.	8: 6	" "		Watson, Edward B.	9:552
1883	"		Dolph, Joseph N. "	1:294	"	
1884	"		" "		Waldo, John B.	5:524
1885	"		" Mitchell, John H.	2:301	"	
1886	"		" "		Lord, William P.	8: 7
1887	Pennoyer, Sylvester	8: 7	" "		"	
1888	"		" "		Thayer, William W.	8: 6
1890	"		" "		Strahan, R. S.	13:531
1892	"		" "		Lord, William P.	8: 7
1894	"		" "		Bean, Robert S.	22: 68
1895	Lord, William P.	8: 7	McBride, George W. "	11:234	"	
1896	"		" "		Moore, Frank A.	9:555
1898	"		" Simon, Joseph	13:329	Wolverton, Charles E.	13:366
1899	Geer, Theodore T.	13:166	" "		"	
1900	"		" "		Bean, Robert S.	22: 68
1901	"		Mitchell, John H. "	2:301	"	
1902	"		" "		Moore, Frank A.	9:555
1903	Chamberlain, George E.	14:135	" Fulton, Charles W.	13:463	"	
1905	"		Gearin, Joseph M. "	14:475	Bean, Robert S.	22: 68
1907	"		Mulkey, Frederick W. "	23:140	"	
1907	"		Bourne, Jonathan, Jr. "	B: 94	"	
1909	Benson, Frank W.	14:439	" Chamberlain, George E.	14:135	Moore, Frank A.	9:555
1911	West, Oswald	16:365	" "		Eakin, Robert	19:416
1913	"		Lane, Harry "	18:212	McBride, Thomas A.	B:325
1915	Withycombe, James	20: 87	" "		Moore, Frank A.	9:555
1917	"		McNary, Charles L. "	B:400	McBride, Thomas A.	B:325
1918	"		Mulkey, Frederick W. "	23:140	"	
1918	"		McNary, Charles L. "	B:400	"	
1919	Olcott, Ben W.	B:442	" "		"	
1921	"		" Stanfield, Robert N.	C:133	Burnett, George H.	
1923	Pierce, Walter M.	D:226	" "		McBride, Thomas A.	B:325
1927	Patterson, Isaac L.	25:262	" Steiwer, Frederick		Burnett, George H.	
1927	"		" "		Rand, John L.	B:178
1929	Norblad, Albin W.	D:295	" "		Coshow, Oliver P.	17:147
1931	Meier, Julius		" "		Bean, Henry J.	
1933	"		" "		Rand, John L.	B:178
1935	Martin, Charles H.		" "		Campbell, James U.	

PENNSYLVANIA

Date	Governors	Biography	U. S. Senators		Biography	Chief Justices	Biography
1681	Markham, William	5:545					
1682	Penn, William	2:274					
1684	Lloyd, Thomas	5:544					
1688	Five Commissioners						
1688	Blackwell, John						
1690	Lloyd, Thomas						
1691	"						
1691	Markham, William (lower counties)						
1693	Fletcher, Benjamin						
1695	Markham, William						
1699	Penn, William						
1701	Hamilton, Andrew	5:545					
1703	Shippen, Edward	18: 86					
1704	Evans, John	5:545					
1709	Gookin, Charles	5:546					
1717	Keith, William	2:277					
1726	Gordon, Patrick	2:278					
1736	Logan, James	2:278					
1738	Thomas, George	2:279					
1747	Palmer, Anthony	13:239					
1748	Hamilton, James	5:537					
1754	Morris, Robert H.	12:483					
1756	Denny, William	9:546					
1759	Hamilton, James	5:537					
1763	Penn, John	2:276					
1771	Penn, Richard	2:276					
1773	Penn, John	2:276					
1776	Wharton, Thomas	2:280					
1778	Ryan, George	2:280				McKean, Thomas	2:284
1778	Reed, Joseph	2:280				"	
1781	Moore, William	2:281				"	
1782	Dickinson, John	2:281				"	
1785	Franklin, Benjamin	1:328				"	
1788	Mifflin, Thomas	2:283				"	
1789	"		Maclay, William		5:143	"	
1789	"		"	Morris, Robert	2:411	"	
1793	"		Gallatin, Albert	"	3: 9	"	
1794	"		Ross, James	"	5:438	"	
1795	"		"	Bingham, William	2:133	"	
1799	McKean, Thomas	2:284	"	"		Shippen, Edward	10:385
1801	"		"	Muhlenberg, John P. G.	1:149	"	
1801	"		"	Logan, George	8:255	"	
1803	"		Maclay, Samuel	"	12:211	"	
1806	"		"	"		Tilghman, William	6:194
1807	"		"	Gregg, Andrew	4:207	"	
1808	Snyder, Simon	2:284	Leib, Michael	"	4:559	"	
1813	"		"	Lacock, Abner	10:478	"	
1815	"		Roberts, Jonathan	"	4:508	"	
1817	Findlay, William	2:285	"	"		"	
1819	"		"	Lowrie, Walter	11:558	"	
1820	Hiester, Joseph	2:285	"	"		"	
1821	"		Findlay, William	"	2:285	"	
1823	Shulze, John A.	2:286	"	"		"	
1825	"		"	Marks, William	11:558	"	
1827	"		Barnard, Isaac D.	"	7:529	Gibson, John B.	14:338
1829	Wolf, George	2:286	"	"		"	
1831	"		Dallas, George M.	"	6:268	"	
1831	"		"	Wilkins, William	6: 9	"	
1833	"		McKean, Samuel	"	11:322	"	
1834	"		"	Buchanan, James	6: 1	"	
1835	Ritner, Joseph	2:286	"	"		"	
1839	Porter, David R.	2:287	Sturgeon, Daniel	"	11: 83	"	
1845	Shunk, Francis R.	2:288	"	Cameron, Simon	2: 79	"	
1848	Johnston, William F.	2:288	"	"		"	
1849	"		"	Cooper, James	5:498	"	
1851	"		Brodhead, Richard	"	4:417	Black, Jeremiah S.	5: 5
1852	Bigler, William	2:288	"	"		"	
1854	"		"	"		Lewis, Ellis	10:484

References are to THE NATIONAL CYCLOPEDIA OF AMERICAN BIOGRAPHY

PENNSYLVANIA *(Continued)*

Date	Governors	Biography	U. S. Senators	Biography	Chief Justices	Biography
1855	Pollock, James	2:289	Brodhead, Richard	4:417	Lewis, Ellis	10:484
1855	"		" Bigler, William	2:288	"	
1857	"		Cameron, Simon "	2: 79	Lowrie, Walter H.	13:157
1858	Packer, William F.	2:289	" "		"	
1861	Curtin, Andrew G.	2:290	Wilmot, David "	3:419	"	
1861	"		" Cowan, Edgar	2: 94	"	
1863	"		Buckalew, Chas. R. "	11:190	Woodward, George W.	11:517
1867	Geary, John W.	2:291	" Cameron, Simon	2: 79	Thompson, James	4:412
1869	"		Scott, John "	12:389	"	
1872	"		" "		Read, John M.	4:500
1873	Hartranft, John F.	2:291	" "		Agnew, Daniel	4: 28
1875	"		Wallace, Wm. A. "	10: 47	"	
1877	"		" Cameron, James	4: 25	"	
1879	Hoyt, Henry M.	2:292	" "		Sharswood, George	2:168
1881	"		Mitchell, John I. "	12:389	"	
1883	Pattison, Robert E.	1:278	" "		Mercur, Ulysses	13:203
1887	Beaver, James A.	2:293	Quay, Matthew S. "	1:459	Gordon, Isaac G.	13:138
1889	"		" "		Paxson, Edward M.	5:382
1891	Pattison, Robert E.	1:278	" "		"	
1893	"		" "		Sterett, James P.	13:551
1895	Hastings, Daniel H.	5: 27	" "		"	
1897	"		" Penrose, Boies	2:444	"	
1899	Stone, William A.	13:341	" "		Green, Henry	12:465
1900	"		" "		McCollum, J. Brewster	12:366
1903	Pennypacker, Samuel W.	9:487	" "		Mitchell, James T.	11:336
1905	"		Knox, Philander C."	24: 7	"	
1907	Stuart, Edwin S.	14:443	" "		"	
1909	"		Oliver, George T. "	22:286	"	
1910	"		" "		Fell, D. Newlin	17:124
1911	Tener, John K.		" "		"	
1915	Brumbaugh, Martin G.	15:409	" "		Brown, J. Hay	
1917	"		Knox, Philander C. "	24: 7	"	
1919	Sproul, William C.	21: 49	" "		"	
1921	"		Crow, William E. "	19:411	Von Moschzisker, Robert	A: 54
1922	"		Reed, David A. "	B:384	"	
1922	"		" Pepper, George W.	A:469	"	
1923	Pinchot, Gifford	14: 30	" "		"	
1927	Fisher, John S.		" Vacant		"	
1929	"		" Grundy, Joseph R.		"	
1930	"		" "		Frazer, Robert S.	
1931	Pinchot, Gifford	14: 30	" Davis, James J.	A: 17	"	
1935	Earle, George H.		Guffey, Joseph F. "		"	

RHODE ISLAND

Date	Governors	Biography	U. S. Senators	Biography	Chief Justices	Biography
1640	Coddington, William	10: 1				
1647	Coggeshall, John	10: 2				
1648	Clarke, Jeremy	10: 2				
1649	Williams, Roger *(act.)*	10: 4				
1649	Smith, John	10: 3				
1650	Easton, Nicholas	10: 3				
1651	Coddington, William	10: 1				
1652	Smith, John	10: 3				
1653	Dexter, Gregory	10: 3				
1654	Easton, Nicholas	10: 3				
1654	Williams, Roger	10: 4				
1657	Arnold, Benedict	10: 6				
1660	Brenton, William	10: 6				
1662	Arnold, Benedict	10: 6				
1666	Brenton, William	10: 6				
1669	Arnold, Benedict	10: 6				
1672	Easton, Nicholas	10: 3				
1674	Coddington, William	10: 1				

RHODE ISLAND (*Continued*)

Date	Governors	Biography	U. S. Senators	Biography	Chief Justices	Biography
1676	Clarke, Walter	10: 7				
1677	Arnold, Benedict	10: 6				
1678	Coddington, William	10: 1				
1678	Cranston, John	10: 7				
1680	Sanford, Peleg	10: 8				
1683	Coddington, William, Jr.	10: 8				
1685	Bull, Henry	10: 8				
1686	Clarke, Walter	10: 7				
1686	Charter Suspended					
1689	Coggeshall, John, Jr.	10: 9				
1690	Bull, Henry	10: 8				
1690	Easton, John	10: 9				
1695	Carr, Caleb	10: 10				
1696	Clarke, Walter	10: 7				
1698	Cranston, Samuel	10: 10				
1727	Jenckes, Joseph	10: 10				
1732	Wanton, William	10: 10				
1733	Wanton, John	10: 12				
1740	Ward, Richard	10: 12				
1743	Greene, William	10: 12				
1745	Wanton, Gideon	10: 13				
1746	Greene, William	10: 12				
1747	Wanton, Gideon	10: 13			Cornell, Gideon	4:356
1748	Greene, William	10: 12			"	
1749	"				Babcock, Joshua	4:356
1751	"				Hopkins, Stephen	10: 13
1755	Hopkins, Stephen	10: 13			Willett, Francis	4:235
1755	"				Hopkins, Stephen	10: 13
1756	"				Gardner, John	8: 41
1757	Greene, William	10: 12			"	
1758	Hopkins, Stephen	10: 13			"	
1761	"				Ward, Samuel	10: 14
1762	Ward, Samuel	10: 14			Niles, Jeremiah	4:356
1763	Hopkins, Stephen	10: 13			Babcock, Joshua	4:356
1764	"				Cole, John	4:519
1765	Ward, Samuel	10: 14			Russell, Joseph	13:162
1767	Hopkins, Stephen	10: 13			Helm, James	13:162
1768	Lyndon, Josias	10: 15			Russell, Joseph	13:162
1769	Wanton, Joseph	10: 15			Helm, James	13:162
1770	"				Hopkins, Stephen	10: 13
1775	Cooke, Nicholas	9:391			"	
1776	"				Bowler, Metcalf	4:556
1777	"				Greene, William	9:392
1778	Greene, William	9:392			Bourne, Shearjashub	12:345
1781	"				Bowen, Jabez	8: 29
1781	"				Mumford, Paul	9:393
1785	"				Ellery, William	8: 59
1786	Collins, John	9:392			Mumford, Paul	9:393
1788	"				Gorton, Othniel	13:137
1790	Fenner, Arthur	9:393	Foster, Theodore	2: 9	"	
1790	"		" Stanton, Joseph	5:224	Owen, Daniel	7:530
1793	"		" Bradford, William	2:373	Arnold, Peleg	4:519
1797	"		" Greene, Ray	4:256	"	
1801	"		" Ellery, Christopher	5:338	"	
1803	"		Potter, Samuel J. "	13:159	"	
1804	"		Howland, Benjamin "	4: 70	"	
1805	Mumford, Paul	9:393	" Fenner, James	9:394	"	
1805	Smith, Henry (*acting*)	9:393	" "		"	
1806	Wilbour, Isaac (*act.*)	9:393	" "		"	
1807	Fenner, James	9:394	" Mathewson, Elisha	4:174	Arnold, Thomas	
1809	"		Malbone, Francis "	8:192	"	
1809	"		Champlin, Chris. G. "	7:559	Arnold, Peleg	4:519
1811	Jones, William	9:394	Hunter, William	9:510	"	
1811	"		" Howell, Jeremiah B.	9:510	Lyman, Daniel	10:119
1812	"		" "		Burrill, James, Jr.	11:366
1816	"		" "		Burges, Tristam	8: 32
1817	Knight, Nehemiah R.	9:394	" Burrill, James, Jr.	11:366	Fenner, James	9:394
1818	"		" "		Wilbour, Isaac	9:393
1821	Gibbs, William C.	9:395	DeWolf, James	8: 61	"	

RHODE ISLAND (*Continued*)

Date	Governors	Biography	U. S. Senators	Biography	Chief Justices	Biography
1821	Gibbs, William C.	9:395	DeWolf, James	8: 61	Wilbour, Isaac	9:393
1821	“		“ Knight, Nehemiah R.	9:394	“	
1824	Fenner, James	9:394	“ “		“	
1825	“		Robbins, Ashur “	1:452	Eddy, Samuel	8:230
1831	Arnold, Lemuel H.	9:395	“ “		“	
1833	Francis, John B.	9:396	“ “		Durfee, Job	7:414
1838	Sprague, William	9:396	“ “		“	
1839	King, Samuel W.	9:396	Dixon, Nathan F. “	13:197	“	
1841	“		“ Simmons, James F.	9:498	“	
1842	“		Sprague, William “	9:396	“	
1843	Fenner, James	9:394	“ “		“	
1844	“		Francis, John B. “	9:396	“	
1845	Jackson, Charles	9:397	Greene, Albert C. “	8: 14	“	
1846	Diman, Byron	9:397	“ “		“	
1847	Harris, Elisha	9:398	“ Clarke, John H.	6:459	Greene, Richard W.	4:460
1849	Anthony, Henry B.	9:398	“ “		“	
1851	Allen, Philip	9:399	James, Charles T. “	3:324	“	
1852	Laurence, William B.	9:399	“ “		“	
1853	Allen, Philip	9:399	“ “		“	
1853	Dimond, Francis M. (*act.*)	9:400	“ Allen, Philip	9:399	“	
1854	Hoppin, William W.	9:400	“ “		Staples, William R.	8: 63
1856	“		“ “		Ames, Samuel	10:304
1857	Dyer, Elisha	9:400	Simmons, James F. “	9:498	“	
1859	Turner, Thomas G.	9:401	“ Anthony, Henry B.	9:398	“	
1860	Sprague, William	9:402	“ “		“	
1861	Bartlett, John R. (*act.*)	9:402	“ “		“	
1863	Cozzens, Wm. C. (*act.*)	9:403	Sprague, William “	9:402	“	
1863	Smith, James Y.	9:403	“ “		“	
1866	Burnside, Ambrose E.	4: 53	“ “		Bradley, Charles S.	13:508
1868	“		“ “		Brayton, George A.	5:526
1869	Padelford, Seth	9:404	“ “		“	
1873	Howard, Henry	9:404	“ “		“	
1875	Lippitt, Henry	9:405	Burnside, Ambrose E. “	4: 53	Durfee, Thomas	12:251
1877	Van Zandt, Charles C.	9:405	“ “		“	
1880	Littlefield, Alfred H.	9:406	“ “		“	
1881	“		Aldrich, Nelson W. “	25: 20	“	
1883	Bourn, Augustus O.	9:406	“ “		“	
1884	“		“ Sheffield, William P.	12:390	“	
1885	Wetmore, George P.	9:407	“ Chace, Jonathan	12:387	“	
1887	Davis, John W.	9:407	“ “		“	
1888	Taft, Royal C.	9:408	“ “		“	
1889	Ladd, Herbert W.	9:408	“ Dixon, Nathan F.	1:291	“	
1890	Davis, John W.	9:407	“ “		“	
1891	Ladd, Herbert W.	9:408	“ “		Matteson, Charles	12:202
1892	Brown, Daniel R.	9:409	“ “		“	
1895	Lippitt, Charles W.	9:409	“ Wetmore, George P.	9:407	“	
1897	Dyer, Elisha	9:410	“ “		“	
1900	Gregory, William	13:361	“ “		Stiness, John H.	12:248
1901	Kimball, Charles D.	25:162	“ “		“	
1903	Garvin, Lucius F. C.	26:109	“ “		“	
1904	“		“ “		Tillinghast, Pardon E.	13:517
1905	Utter, George H.	13:333	“ “		Douglas, William W.	14:241
1907	Higgins, James H.	14:402	“ “		“	
1909	Pothier, Aram J.	15:114	“ “		Dubois, Edward C.	14:524
1911	“		Lippitt, Henry F. “	25:115	“	
1913	“		“ Colt, Le Baron B.	15:408	Johnson, Clarke H.	18:216
1915	Beeckman, R. Livingston	B:403	“ “		“	
1917	“		Gerry, Peter G. “	B:508	Parkhurst, Christopher F.	24:272
1920	“		“ “		Sweetland, William H.	B:249
1921	San Souci, Emery J.		“ “		“	
1923	Flynn, William S.		“ “		“	
1924	“		“ Metcalf, Jesse H.		“	
1925	Pothier, Aram J.	15:114	“ “		“	
1928	Case, Norman S.		“ “		“	
1929	“		Hebert, Felix “		Stearns, Charles F.	
1933	Green, Theodore F.	18:211	“ “		“	
1935	“		“ “		Flynn, Edmund W.	

SOUTH CAROLINA

Date	Governors	Biography	U. S. Senators	Biography	Chief Justices	Biography
1669	Sayle, William	12:151				
1672	Yeamans, John	12:151				
1674	West, Joseph	12:151				
1682	Morton, Joseph	12:152				
1684	Kyrle, Richard					
1684	Quarry, Robert					
1685	West, Joseph	12:151				
1685	Morton, Joseph	12:152				
1686	Colleton, James	12:152				
1689	Smith, Thomas					
1690	Sothell, John	12:152				
1691	Ludwell, Philip	12:153				
1693	Smith, Thomas					
1694	Blake, Joseph	12:153				
1695	Archdale, John	12:153				
1696	Blake, Joseph	12:153				
1700	Moore, James	12:154				
1703	Johnson, Nathaniel	12:154				
1708	Tynte, Edward					
1709	Gibbes, Robert	12:155				
1712	Craven, Charles	12:155				
1716	Daniel, Robert	12:155				
1717	Johnson, Robert	12:155				
1719	Moore, James	12:156				
1721	Nicholson, Francis	12:156				
1725	Middleton, Arthur	12:156				
1731	Johnson, Robert	12:155				
1735	Broughton, Thomas	12:157				
1737	Bull, William	12:157				
1743	Glen, James	12:157				
1756	Lyttleton, William H.	12:157				
1760	Bull, William	12:158				
1761	Boone, Thomas	12:158				
1764	Bull, William	12:158				
1766	Montagu, Charles G.	12:158				
1768	Bull, William	12:158				
1768	Montagu, Charles G.	12:158				
1769	Bull, William	12:158				
1771	Montagu, Charles G.	12:158				
1773	Bull, William	12:158				
1775	Campbell, William	12:159				
1776	Rutledge, John	1: 21				
1778	Lowndes, Rawlins	12:159				
1779	Rutledge, John	1: 21			Drayton, William H.	7:419
1782	Mathews, John	12:160			"	
1783	Guerard, Benjamin	12:160			"	
1785	Moultrie, William	1: 96			"	
1787	Pinckney, Thomas	12:160			"	
1789	Pinckney, Charles	12:161	Butler, Pierce	2:162	"	
1789	"		" Izard, Ralph	3:175	"	
1791	"		" "		Rutledge, John	1: 21
1792	Vanderhorst, Arnoldus	12:162	" "		"	
1794	Moultrie, William	1: 96	" "		"	
1795	"		" Read, Jacob	2:496	"	
1796	Pinckney, Charles	12:161	Hunter, John "	12:395		
1798	Rutledge, Edward	12:162	Pinckney, Charles "	12:161		
1800	Drayton, John	12:162	" "			
1801	"		Sumter, Thomas	1: 79		
1801	"		" Calhoun, John E.		*There were no chief justices of South Carolina from 1795 to 1860.*	
1802	Richardson, James B.	12:163	" Butler, Pierce	2:162		
1804	Hamilton, Paul	5:373	" Gaillard, John	4:291		
1806	Pinckney, Charles	12:161	" "			
1808	Drayton, John	12:162	" "			
1810	Middleton, Henry	12:163	Taylor, John "	12:165		
1812	Alston, Joseph	12:163	" "			
1814	Williams, David R.	12:164	" "			
1816	Pickens, Andrew	12:164	Smith, William "	2:481		
1818	Geddes, John	12:164	" "			
1820	Bennett, Thomas	12:164	" "			

SOUTH CAROLINA *(Continued)*

Date	Governors	Biography	U. S. Senators	Biography	Chief Justices	Biography
1822	Wilson, John L.	12:164	Smith, William	2:481		
1822	"		" Gaillard, John	4:291		
1823	"		Hayne, Robert Y. "	12:166		
1824	Manning, Richard I.	12:165	" "			
1826	Taylor, John	12:165	" Harper, William	11:420		
1826	"		" Smith, William	2:481		
1828	Miller, Stephen D.	12:166	" "			
1830	Hamilton, James	12:166	" "			
1831	"		" Miller, Stephen D.	12:166		
1832	Hayne, Robert Y.	12:166	Calhoun, John C. "	6: 83		
1833	"		" Preston, William C.	11: 33		
1834	McDuffie, George	12:167	" "			
1836	Butler, Pierce M.	12:168	" "			
1838	Noble, Patrick	12:168	" "			
1840	Richardson, John P.	12:168	" "			
1842	Hammond, James H.	12:169	Huger, Daniel E. "	4:511		
1842	"		" McDuffie, George	12:167		
1844	Aiken, William	12:170	" "			
1845	"		Calhoun, John C. "	6: 83		
1846	Johnson, David	12:170	" "			
1846	"		" Butler, Andrew P.	3:414		
1848	Seabrook, Whitemarsh B.	12:170	" "			
1850	Means, John H.	12:171	Elmore, Franklin H. "	11:335		
1850	"		Barnwell, Robert "	11: 32		
1850	"		Rhett, R. Barnwell "	4:303		
1852	Manning, John L.	12:171	DeSaussure, Wm. F. "	5:119		
1853	"		Evans, Josiah "	7:533		
1854	Adams, James H.	12:172	" "			
1856	Allston, Robert F. W.	12:172	" "			
1857	"		" Hammond, James H.	12:169		
1858	Gist, William H.	12:172	Hayne, Arthur P. "	11:198		
1858	"		Chestnut, James, Jr. "	5: 54		
1860	Pickens, Francis W.	12:173	" "		O'Neall, John B.	6:170
1862	Bonham, Milledge L.	12:173	Vacant Vacant		"	
1864	Magrath, Andrew G.	12:174	" "		"	
1865	Perry, Benjamin F.	12:174	" "		Dunkin, Benjamin F.	5:503
1866	Orr, James L.	12:175	" "		"	
1868	Scott, Robert K.	12:175	Robertson, Thomas J.	12:203	"	
1868	"		" Sawyer, Frederick A.	3:522	"	
1872	Moses, Franklin J.	12:176	" "		"	
1873	"		" Patterson, John J.	12:395	"	
1874	Chamberlain, Daniel H.	12:176	" "		"	
1876	Hampton, Wade	12:177	" "		"	
1877	"		Butler, Matthew C. "	1:298	Willard, Ammiel J.	
1878	Simpson, William D.	12:178	" "		"	
1879	"		" Hampton, Wade	12:177	Simpson, William D.	12:178
1880	Jeter, Thomas B.	12:178	" "		"	
1880	Hagood, Johnson	12:178	" "		"	
1882	Thompson, Hugh S.	12:179	" "		"	
1886	Sheppard, John C.	12:180	" "		"	
1886	Richardson, John P.	12:180	" "		"	
1890	Tillman, Benjamin R.	12:180	" "		"	
1891	"		" Irby, John L. M.	2:251	"	
1894	Evans, John G.	12:181	" "		"	
1895	"		Tillman, Benjamin R. "	12:180	"	
1896	Ellerbe, William H.	12:182	" "		"	
1897	"		" Earle, Joseph H.	12:208	"	
1897	"		" McLaurin, John L.	13: 21	"	
1899	McSweeney, Miles B.	12:182	" "		McIver, Henry	7: 56
1903	Heyward, Duncan C.	15:284	" Latimer, Asbury C.	12:493	Pope, Young J.	13:399
1907	Ansel, Martin F.	14:373	" "		"	
1908	"		" Gary, Frank B.	14:123	"	
1909	"		" Smith, Ellison D.	14:489	Jones, Ira B.	21:257
1911	Blease, Coleman L.	15:276	" "		"	
1912	"		" "		Gary, Eugene B.	20:185
1915	Manning, Richard I.	23:114	" "		"	
1918	"		Benet, Christie "	A:238	"	
1918	"		Pollock, William P. "	19: 41	"	
1919	Cooper, Robert A.		Dial, Nathaniel B. "	A: 85	"	

SOUTH CAROLINA *(Continued)*

Date	Governors	Biography	U. S. Senators	Biography	Chief Justices	Biography
1923	McLeod, Thomas G.	B:499	Dial, Nathaniel B.	A: 85	Gary, Eugene B.	20:185
1923	"		" Smith, Ellison D.	14:489	"	
1925	"		Blease, Coleman L. "	15:276	"	
1926	"		" "		Watts, Richard C.	
1927	Richards, John G.		" "		"	
1931	Blackwood, Ibra C.		Byrnes, James F. "		Blease, Eugene S.	
1935	Johnston, Olin D.		" "		Stabler, John G.	

SOUTH DAKOTA

Date	Governors	Biography	U. S. Senators	Biography	Chief Justices	Biography
1889	Mellette, Arthur C.	2:295	Pettigrew, Richard F.	2:202		
1889	"		" Moody, Gideon C.	2:395		
1891	"		" Kyle, James H.	1:323		
1893	Sheldon, Charles H.	13:558	" "			
1897	Lee, Andrew E.	13:558	" "			
1901	Herreid, Charles N.	13:558	Gamble, Robert J. "	12:392		
1901	"		" Kittredge, Alfred B.	16:125	*There are no chief justices of South Dakota. The members of the Supreme Court select one of their members to act as presiding judge.*	
1905	Elrod, Samuel H.	13:559	" "			
1907	Crawford, Corie I.	14:200	" "			
1909	Vessey, Robert S.	14:200	" Crawford, Corie I.	14:200		
1913	"		Sterling, Thomas "	15:287		
1915	Byrne, Frank M.	21:471	" Johnson, Edwin S.	A:365		
1917	Norbeck, Peter	B:479	" "			
1921	McMaster, William H.	C: 39	" Norbeck, Peter	B:479		
1925	Gunderson, Carl	24:144	McMaster, Wm. H."	C: 39		
1927	Bulow, William J.	C:63	" "			
1931	Green, Warren E.		Bulow, William J. "	C: 63		
1933	Berry, Tom		" "			

TENNESSEE

Date	Governors	Biography	U. S. Senators	Biography	Chief Justices	Biography
1796	Sevier, John	3:430	Cocke, William	11:409		
1796	"		" Blount, Willie	7:207		
1797	"		Jackson, Andrew	5:289		
1797	"		" Anderson, Joseph	2: 11		
1798	"		Smith, Daniel "	2: 7		
1798	"		Anderson, Joseph Vacant	2: 11		
1799	"		" Cocke, William	11:409		
1801	Roane, Archibald	7:207	" "			
1803	Sevier, John	3:430	" "			
1805	"		" Smith, Daniel	2: 9		
1809	Blount, Willie	7:207	" Whiteside, Jenkins	11: 77		
1811	"		" Campbell, George W.	5:372		
1814	"		" Wharton, Jesse	4:545		
1815	McMinn, Joseph	7:207	Campbell, George W.	5:372		
1815	"		" Williams, John	1:272		
1818	"		Eaton, John H. "	5:295		
1821	Carroll, William	7:208	" "			
1823	"		" Jackson, Andrew	5:289		
1825	"		" White, Hugh L.	11:395		
1827	Houston, Samuel	9: 63	" "			
1829	Hall, William	7:208	Grundy, Felix "	6:436		
1829	Carroll, William	7:208	" "			
1831	"		" "		Catron, John	2:261
1835	Cannon, Newton	7:208	" "		"	

TENNESSEE *(Continued)*

Date	Governors	Biography	U. S. Senators	Biography	Chief Justices	Biography
1838	Cannon, Newton	7:208	White, Hugh L.	11:395		
1838	"		Foster, Ephraim H. "	7:541		
1839	Polk, James K.	6:265	Grundy, Felix "	6:436		
1840	"		Nicholson, Alfred O. P.	11:317		
1840	"		" Anderson, Alexander	11:400		
1841	Jones, James C.	7:209	" Jarnagin, Spencer	11:488		
1843	"		Foster, Ephraim H. "	7:541		
1845	Brown, Aaron V.	5: 8	Turney, Hopkins L."	5:509		
1847	Brown, Neal S.	7:209	" Bell, John	3: 39	*There were no chief justices of Tennessee between 1835 and 1870.*	
1849	Trousdale, William	7:209	" "			
1851	Campbell, William B.	7:209	Jones, James C. "	7:209		
1853	Johnson, Andrew	2:454	" "			
1857	Harris, Isham G.	2:209	Johnson, Andrew "	2:454		
1859	"		" Nicholson, Alfred O. P.	11:317		
1862	Johnson, Andrew	2:454	Vacant Vacant			
1865	Brownlow, William G.	7:210	Patterson, David T.	12:217		
1865	"		" Fowler, Joseph S.	10:511		
1869	Senter, DeWitt C.	7:211	Brownlow, William G. "	7:210		
1870	"		" "		Nicholson, Alfred O. P.	11:317
1871	Brown, John C.	7:211	" Cooper, Henry	12:378	"	
1875	Porter, James D.	7:211	" "		"	
1875	"		Johnson, Andrew "	2:454	"	
1876	"		Key, David M. "	3:203	Deaderick, James W.	5:532
1877	"		Bailey, James E. "	12:282	"	
1879	Marks, Albert S.	7:212	" Harris, Isham G.	2:209	"	
1881	Hawkins, Alvin	7:213	" "		"	
1883	Bate, William B.	7:213	Jackson, Howell E. "	8:243	"	
1886	"		" "		Turney, Peter	7:213
1887	Taylor, Robert L.	8:365	Whitthorne, Washington C. "	10:140	"	
1891	Buchanan, John P.	7:213	Bate, William B. "	7:213	"	
1893	Turney, Peter	7:213	" "		Lurton, Horace H.	8:235
1893	"		" "		Lea, Benjamin J.	13:320
1894	"		" "		Snodgrass, David L.	12:331
1897	Taylor, Robert L.	8:365	" "		"	
1899	McMillin, Benton	13: 79	" Turley, Thomas B.	12:391	"	
1902	"		" Carmack, Edward W.	13:300	Beard, William D.	13:398
1903	Frazier, James B.	13:532	" "		"	
1905	Cox, John I.	13:532	Frazier, James B. "	13:532	"	
1907	Patterson, Malcolm R.	14:484	" Taylor, Robert L.	8:365	"	
1910	"		" "		Shields, John K.	26:109
1911	Hooper, Ben W.		Lea, Luke "	15: 26	"	
1912	"		" Sanders, Newell	C:312	"	
1913	"		" Webb, William R.		"	
1913	"		" Shields, John K.	26:109	Webb, William R.	
1915	Rye, Thomas C.		" "		"	
1917	"		McKellar, Kenneth D. "	C:427	"	
1918	"		" "		Lansden, Dick L.	
1919	Roberts, Albert H.		" "		"	
1921	Taylor, Alfred A.	11:405	" "		"	
1923	Peay, Austin		" "		Green, Grafton	
1925	"		" Tyson, Lawrence D.	21:487	"	
1927	Horton, Henry H.	25:286	" "		"	
1929	"		" Brock, William E.		"	
1931	"		" Hull, Cordell	D: 10	"	
1933	McAlister, Hill		" Bachman, Nathan L.		"	

TEXAS

Date	Governors	Biography	U. S. Senators	Biography	Chief Justices	Biography
1846	Henderson, James P.	1:442	Rusk, Thomas J.	3:113	Hemphill, John	4:501
1846	“		“ Houston, Samuel	9: 63	“	
1847	Wood, George T.	9: 67	“ “		“	
1849	Bell, Peter H.	9: 67	“ “		“	
1853	Henderson, J. W. (*act.*)	9: 68	“ “		“	
1853	Pease, Elisha M.	9: 68	“ “		“	
1857	Runnels, Hardin R.	9: 69	Henderson, James P. “	1:442	“	
1858	“		Ward, Matthias “	4:375	Wheeler, Royal T.	7:489
1859	Houston, Samuel	9: 63	Wigfall, Louis T. “	5:262	“	
1859	“		“ Hemphill, John	4:501	“	
1861	Clark, Edward (*acting*)	9: 69	Vacant Vacant		“	
1861	Lubbock, Francis R.	9: 69	“ “		“	
1863	Murrah, Pendleton	9: 70	“ “		“	
1864	“		“ “		Roberts, Oran Milo	9: 73
1865	Hamilton, Andrew J.	9: 70	“ “		“	
1866	Throckmorton, James W.	9: 71	“ “		Moore, George F.	5:512
1867	Pease, Elisha M.	9: 68	“ “		Morrill, Amos	13:145
1870	Davis, Edmund J.	9: 71	Flanagan, James W.	12:509	Evans, Lemuel D.	4:200
1870	“		“ Hamilton, Morgan C.	12:393	“	
1873	“		“ “		Ogden, Wesley	
1874	Coke, Richard	9: 72	“ “		Roberts, Oran M.	9: 73
1875	“		Maxey, Samuel B. “	4: 50	“	
1877	Hubbard, Richard B.	9: 72	“ Coke, Richard	9: 72	“	
1878	“		“ “		Moore, George F.	5:512
1879	Roberts, Oran Milo	9: 73	“ “		“	
1881	“		“ “		Gould, Robert S.	4:470
1882	“		“ “		Willie, Asa H.	11:453
1883	Ireland, John	9: 74	“ “		“	
1887	Ross, Lawrence S.	9: 75	Reagan, John H. “	1:292	“	
1888	“		“ “		Stayton, John W.	4:237
1891	Hogg, James S.	9: 75	Chilton, Horace “	2:241	“	
1892	“		Mills, Roger Q. “	8:403	“	
1894	“		“ “		Gaines, Reuben R.	10: 458
1895	Culberson, Charles A.	9: 76	“ Chilton, Horace	2:241	“	
1899	Sayers, Joseph D.	9: 76	Culberson, Charles A. “	9: 76	“	
1901	“		“ Bailey, Joseph W.	13:587	“	
1903	Lanham, Samuel W. T.	13:418	“ “		“	
1907	Campbell, Thomas M.	14: 43	“ “		“	
1911	Colquitt, Oscar B.		“ “		Brown, Thomas J.	18:381
1913	“		“ Johnston, Rienzi M.	21:297	“	
1913	“		“ Sheppard, Morris	15:274	“	
1915	Ferguson, James E.	15: 9	“ “		Phillips, Nelson	17:366
1917	Hobby, William P.		“ “		“	
1921	Neff, Pat M.		“ “		Cureton, Calvin M.	
1923	“		Mayfield, Earle B. “	C:440	“	
1925	Ferguson, Miriam A.	A:428	“ “		“	
1927	Moody, Dan		“ “		“	
1929	“		Connally, Tom “	C:452	“	
1931	Sterling, Ross S.		“ “		“	
1933	Ferguson, Miriam A.	A:428	“ “		“	
1935	Allred, James V.		“ “		“	

UTAH

Date	Governors	Biography	U. S. Senators	Biography	Chief Justices	Biography
1896	Wells, Heber M.	7:552	Cannon, Frank J.	12:511	Zane, Charles S.	12:128
1896	"		" Brown, Arthur	13:179	"	
1897	"		" Rawlins, Joseph L.	11:427	"	
1899	"		" "		Bartch, George W.	20:199
1901	"		Kearns, Thomas "	12:516	Miner, James A.	13:477
1902	"		" "		Baskin, Robert N.	13:477
1903	"		" Smoot, Reed	13:197	"	
1905	Cutler, John C.	13:598	Sutherland, George "	13:413	Bartch, George W.	20:199
1906	"		" "		McCarty, William M.	19:301
1909	Spry, William	15:383	" "		Straup, Daniel N.	
1911	"		" "		Frick, Joseph E.	22:250
1913	"		" "		McCarty, William M.	19:301
1915	"		" "		Straup, Daniel N.	
1917	Bamberger, Simon	20: 49	King, William H. "		Frick, Joseph E.	22:250
1919	"		" "		Corfman, Elmer E.	
1921	Mabey, Charles R.		" "		"	
1923	"		" "		Weber, Albert J.	
1925	Dern, George H.	26: 9	" "		Gideon, Valentine	
1927	"		" "		Thurman, Samuel R.	
1929	"		" "		Cherry, James W.	
1933	Blood, Henry H.		" Thomas, Elbert D.	D:326	Straup, Daniel N.	
1935	"		" "		Hansen, Elias	

VERMONT

Date	Governors	Biography	U. S. Senators	Biography	Chief Justices	Biography
1778	Chittenden, Thomas	8:312			Robinson, Moses	8:313
1782	"				Spooner, Paul	4:235
1784	"				Robinson, Moses	8:313
1785	"				Chipman, Nathaniel	2: 10
1789	Robinson, Moses	8:313			"	
1790	Chittenden, Thomas	8:312			"	
1791	"		Robinson, Moses	8:313	Knight, Samuel	4: 83
1791	"		" Bradley, Stephen R.	2:432	"	
1794	"		" "		Tichenor, Isaac	8:313
1795	"		" Paine, Elijah	8:174	"	
1796	"		Tichenor, Isaac "	8:313	Chipman, Nathaniel	2: 10
1797	Brigham, Paul	8:313	Chipman, Nathaniel "	2: 10	Smith, Israel	8:314
1797	Tichenor, Isaac	8:313	" "		"	
1798	"		" "		Woodbridge, Enoch	6: 82
1801	"		" Bradley, Stephen R.	2:432	Robinson, Jonathan	2:530
1803	"		Smith, Israel "	8:314	"	
1807	Smith, Israel	8:314	Robinson, Jonathan "	2:530	Tyler, Royall	7: 39
1809	Galusha, Jonas	8:314	" "		"	
1813	Chittenden, Martin	8:315	" Chase, Dudley	8:178	Chipman, Nathaniel	2: 10
1815	Galusha, Jonas	8:314	Tichenor, Isaac "	8:313	Aldis, Asa	4:152
1817	"		" Fisk, James	8:100	Chase, Dudley	8:178
1818	"		" Palmer, William A.	8:317	"	
1820	Skinner, Richard	8:315	" "		"	
1821	"		Seymour, Horatio "	8:473	VanNess, Cornelius P.	8:316
1823	VanNess, Cornelius	8:316	" "		Skinner, Richard	8:315
1825	"		" Chase, Dudley	8:178	"	
1826	Butler, Ezra	8:316	" "		"	
1828	Crafts, Samuel C.	8:317	" "		"	
1829	"		" "		Prentiss, Samuel	8:402
1830	"		" "		Hutchinson, Titus	4:442
1831	Palmer, William A.	8:317	" Prentiss, Samuel	8:402	"	
1833	"		Swift, Benjamin "	3:517	Williams, Charles K.	8:320
1835	Jenison, Silas H.	8:318	" "		"	
1839	"		Phelps, Samuel S. "	8:400	"	
1841	Paine, Charles	8:318	" "		"	
1842	"		" Crafts, Samuel C.	8:317	"	
1843	Mattocks, John	8:318	" Upham, William	6:505	"	
1844	Slade, William	8:319	" "		"	
1846	Eaton, Horace	8:319	" "		Royce, Stephen	8:321

VERMONT *(Continued)*

Date	Governors	Biography	U. S. Senators		Biography	Chief Justices	Biography
1849	Coolidge, Carlos	8:320	Phelps, Samuel S.		8:400	Royce, Stephen	8:321
1849	"		"	Upham, William	6:505	"	
1850	Williams, Charles K.	8:320	"	"		"	
1851	"		Foot, Solomon	"	2: 91	"	
1852	Fairbanks, Erastus	8:320	"	"		Redfield, Isaac F.	7: 77
1853	Robinson, John S.	8:321	"	Phelps, Samuel S.	8:400	"	
1854	Royce, Stephen	8:321	Brainerd, Lawrence	"	8:474	"	
1855	"		"	Collamar, Jacob	4:371	"	
1856	Fletcher, Ryland	8:322	"	"		"	
1858	Hall, Hiland	8:322	"	"		"	
1860	Fairbanks, Erastus	8:320	"	"		"	
1860	Hall, Hiland	8:322	"	"		Poland, Luke P.	5:253
1861	Holbrook, Frederick	8:323	"	"		"	
1863	Smith, John G.	8:323	"	"		"	
1865	Dillingham, Paul	8:324	"	Poland, Luke P.	5:253	Pierpont, John	4:466
1866	"		Edmunds, George F.	"	2:384	"	
1867	Page, John B.	8:324	"	Morrill, Justin S.	1:377	"	
1869	Washburn, Peter T.	8:325	"	"		"	
1870	Hendee, George W.	8:325	"	"		"	
1870	Stewart, John W.	8:325	"	"		"	
1872	Converse, Julius	8:326	"	"		"	
1874	Peck, Asahel	8:326	"	"		"	
1876	Fairbanks, Horace	8:327	"	"		"	
1878	Proctor, Redfield	1:141	"	"		"	
1880	Farnham, Roswell	8:327	"	"		"	
1882	Barstow, John L.	8:328	"	"		Royce, Homer E.	4:200
1884	Pingree, Samuel E.	8:328	"	"		"	
1886	Ormsbee, Ebenezer J.	8:329	"	"		"	
1888	Dillingham, William P.	8:411	"	"		"	
1890	Page, Carroll S.	8:329	"	"		Ross, Jonathan	7:493
1891	"		Proctor, Redfield	"	1:141	"	
1892	Fuller, Levi K.	8:330	"	"		"	
1894	Woodbury, Urban A.	8:330	"	"		"	
1896	Grout, Josiah	8:331	"	"		"	
1898	Smith, Edward C.	26:346	"	Ross, Jonathan	7:493	Taft, Russell S.	4: 83
1900	Stickney, William W.	25:337	"	Dillingham, William P.	8:411	"	
1902	McCullough, John G.	14:322	"	"		Rowell, John W.	5:407
1904	Bell, Charles J.	13:296	"	"		"	
1906	Proctor, Fletcher D.	25:252	"	"		"	
1908	"		Stewart, John W.	"	8:325	"	
1908	Prouty, George H.	14:448	Page, Carroll S.	"	8:329	"	
1910	Mead, John A.	19: 61	"	"		"	
1912	Fletcher, Allen M.	19: 89	"	"		"	
1913	"		"	"		Powers, George McC.	17:334
1915	Gates, Charles W.	15:104	"	"		Munson, Loveland	17:322
1917	Graham, Horace F.		"	"		Watson, John H.	21:409
1919	Clement, Percival W.	21:108	"	"		"	
1921	Hartness, James	15:294	"	"		"	
1923	Proctor, Redfield	B:432	Greene, Frank L.	"	25: 92	"	
1923	"		"	Dale, Porter H.	B:397	"	
1925	Billings, Franklin S.	B:463	"	"		"	
1927	Weeks, John E.		"	"		"	
1929	"		"	"		Powers, George McC.	17:334
1930	"		Partridge, Frank C.	"	9:549	"	
1931	Wilson, Stanley C.		Austin, Warren R.	"		"	
1933	"		"	Gibson, Ernest W.		"	
1935	Smith, Charles M.		"	"		"	

VIRGINIA

Date	Governors	Biography	U. S. Senators	Biography	Chief Justices	Biography
1607	Wingfield, Edward M.	13:377				
1607	Ratcliffe, John	13:377				
1608	Smith, John	13:378				
1609	Percy, George	13:379				
1610	Gates, Thomas	13:379				
1610	West, Thomas	13:380				
1611	Percy, George	13:379				
1611	Dale, Thomas	13:381				
1611	Gates, Thomas	13:379				
1614	Dale, Thomas	13:381				
1616	Yeardley, George	13:381				
1617	Argall, Samuel	13:381				
1619	Yeardley, George	13:381				
1621	Wyatt, Francis	13:382				
1626	Yeardley, George	13:381				
1627	West, Francis	13:382				
1629	Pott, John	13:383				
1630	Harvey, John	13:383				
1635	West, John	13:383				
1636	Harvey, John	13:383				
1639	Wyatt, Francis	13:382				
1642	Berkeley, William	13:383				
1644	Kemp, Richard	13:384				
1645	Berkeley, William	13:383				
1652	Bennett, Richard	7:333				
1655	Digges, Edward	13:384				
1657	Matthews, Samuel	13:384				
1660	Berkeley, William	13:383				
1661	Moryson, Francis	13:385				
1662	Berkeley, William	13:383				
1677	Jeffreys, Herbert	13:385				
1678	Chichley, Henry	13:385				
1680	Colepepper, Thomas	13:385				
1683	Spencer, Nicholas	13:386				
1684	Howard, Francis	13:386				
1688	Bacon, Nathaniel	13:386				
1690	Nicholson, Francis	13:386				
1693	Andros, Edmund	6:90				
1698	Nicholson, Francis	13:386				
1705	Nott, Edward	13:387				
1706	Jenings, Edmund	13:387				
1710	Spotswood, Alexander	13:387				
1722	Drysdale, Hugh	13:388				
1726	Carter, Robert	13:388				
1727	Gooch, William	13:388				
1740	Blair, James	13:388				
1741	Gooch, William	13:388				
1749	Robinson, John	13:388				
1749	Lee, Thomas	13:389				
1750	Burwell, Lewis	13:389				
1751	Dinwiddie, Robert	13:389				
1758	Blair, John	13:390				
1758	Fauquier, Francis	13:390				
1768	Blair, John	13:390				
1768	Berkeley, Norborne	13:390				
1770	Nelson, William	13:390				
1771	Murray, John	13:391				
1776	Henry, Patrick	1:337				
1779	Jefferson, Thomas	3: 1			Pendleton, Edmund	10:240
1781	Nelson, Thomas	7:253			"	
1782	Harrison, Benjamin	10:153			"	
1784	Henry, Patrick	1:337			"	
1786	Randolph, Edmund	1: 12			"	
1788	Randolph, Beverly	5:443			"	
1789	"		Grayson, William	12:247	"	
1789	"		" Lee, Richard H.	3:159	"	
1790	"		Walker, John "	11:323	"	
1790	"		Monroe, James "	6: 81	"	
1791	Lee, Henry	3: 25	" "		"	

References are to THE NATIONAL CYCLOPEDIA OF AMERICAN BIOGRAPHY

VIRGINIA *(Continued)*

Date	Governors	Biography	U. S. Senators	Biography	Chief Justices	Biography
1792	Lee, Henry	3: 25	Monroe, James	6: 81	Pendleton, Edmund	10:240
1792	“		“ Taylor, John	9:509	“	
1794	Brooke, Robert	5:443	Mason, Stevens T.	2: 9	“	
1794	“		“ Tazewell, Henry	2:215	“	
1796	Wood, James	5:443	“ “		“	
1799	Monroe, James	6: 81	“ Nicholas, Wilson C.	5:446	“	
1802	Page, John	3:219	“ “		“	
1803	“		Taylor, John “	9:509	Tucker, St. George	7:136
1803	“		Venable, Abraham B. “	11: 86	“	
1804	“		Giles, William B.	5:447	“	
1804	“		“ Moore, Andrew	5:505	“	
1804	“		Moore, Andrew	5:505	“	
1804	“		“ Giles, William B.	5:447	“	
1805	Cabell, William H.	5:444	“ “		“	
1808	Tyler, John	5:444	“ “		“	
1809	“		Brent, Richard “	7:534	“	
1810	“		“ “		Fleming, William F.	12:541
1811	Monroe, James	6: 81	“ “		“	
1811	Smith, George W.	5:445	“ “		“	
1812	Barbour, James	5: 82	“ “		“	
1814	Nicholas, Wilson C.	5:446	“ “		“	
1815	“		Barbour, James “	5: 82	“	
1816	Preston, James P.	5:446	“ Mason, Armistead T.	4:550	“	
1817	“		“ Eppes, John W.	11: 41	“	
1819	Randolph, Thomas M.	5:446	“ Pleasants, James, Jr.	5:447	“	
1822	Pleasants, James, Jr.	5:447	“ Taylor, John	12:165	“	
1824	“		“ Tazewell, Littleton W.	5:448	Brooke, Francis T.	7:542
1825	Tyler, John	5:444	Randolph, John “	5: 97	“	
1827	Giles, William B.	5:447	Tyler, John “	6: 1	“	
1830	Floyd, John	5:448	“ “		“	
1831	“		“ “		“	
1832	“		“ Rives, William C.	6:486	Tucker, Henry St. George	7:520
1834	Tazewell, Littleton W.	5:448	“ Leigh, Benjamin W.	11:312	“	
1836	Robertson, Wyndham	5:449	Rives, William C.	6:486	“	
1836	“		“ Parker, Richard E.	11:335	“	
1837	Campbell, David	5:449	“ Roane, William H.	4:377	“	
1840	Gilmer, Thomas W.	5:449	“ “		“	
1841	Rutherfoord, John	5:450	“ Archer, William S.	11:505	“	
1842	Gregory, John M.	5:450	“ “		Cabell, William H.	5:444
1843	McDowell, James	5:450	“ “		“	
1845	“		Pennybacker, Isaac S. “	11:503	“	
1846	Smith, William	5:451	“ “		“	
1847	“		Mason, James M.	2: 93	“	
1847	“		“ Hunter, Robert M. T.	9:158	“	
1849	Floyd, John B.	5: 7	“ “		“	
1851	“		“ “		Allen, John J.	7:552
1852	Johnson, Joseph	5:451	“ “		“	
1856	Wise, Henry A.	5:452	“ “		“	
1860	Letcher, John	5:452	“ “		“	
1861	“		Willey, Waitman T.	12:455	“	
1861	“		“ Carlile, John S.	4:347	“	
1863	“		Bowden, Lemuel J. “	4:377	“	
1864	Pierrepont, Francis H.	5:453	Vacant “		“	
1865	“		“ Vacant		“	
1868	Wells, Henry H.	5:453	“ “		“	
1869	Walker, Gilbert C.	5:453	“ “		“	
1870	Wells, Henry H.	5:453	Lewis, John F.	13: 86	Moncure, Richard C. L.	7:542
1870	“		“ Johnston, John W.	12:226	“	
1874	Kemper, James L.	5:454	“ “		“	
1875	“		Withers, Robert E. “	12:512	“	
1878	Holliday, Frederick W.M.	5:454	“ “		“	
1881	“		Mahone, William “	5: 12	“	
1882	Cameron, William E.	5:455	“ “		Lewis, Lunsford L.	12: 96
1883	“		“ Riddleberger, Harrison H.	13:162	“	
1886	Lee, Fitzhugh	9: 1	“ “		“	
1887	“		Daniel, John W. “	1:218	“	
1889	“		“ Barbour, John S.	12: 59	“	
1890	McKinney, Philip W.	2:393	“ “		“	
1892	“		“ Hunton, Eppa	13:459	“	

VIRGINIA *(Continued)*

Date	Governors	Biography	U. S. Senators	Biography	Chief Justices	Biography
1894	O'Ferrall, Charles T.	5:455	Daniel, John W.	1:218	Keith, James	13:322
1894	"		" Hunton, Eppa	13:459	"	
1895	"		" Martin, Thomas S.	11: 30	"	
1898	Tyler, J. Hoge	13:358	" "		"	
1902	Montague, Andrew J.	13:358	" "		"	
1906	Swanson, Claude A.	D: 15	" "		"	
1910	Mann, William H.	14:104	Swanson, Claude A. "	D: 15	"	
1914	Stuart, Henry C.	15:333	" "		"	
1916	"		" "		Cardwell, Richard H.	
1916	"		" "		Harrison, George M.	20:415
1917	"		" "		Whittle, Stafford G.	
1918	Davis, Westmoreland	C:100	" "		"	
1920	"		" Glass, Carter	A: 36	Kelly, Joseph L.	20: 84
1922	Trinkle, E. Lee		" "		"	
1924	"		" "		Sime, Frederick W.	
1925	"		" "		Prentis, Robert R.	24:352
1926	Byrd, Harry F.	B:430	" "		"	
1930	Pollard, John G.		" "		"	
1931	"		" "		Campbell, Preston W.	
1933	"		Byrd, Harry F. "	B:430	"	
1934	Peery, George C.		" "		"	

WASHINGTON

Date	Governors	Biography	U. S. Senators	Biography	Chief Justices	Biography
1889	Ferry, Elisha P.	1:454	Allen, John B.	11:561	Anders, Thomas J.	13:312
1889	"		" Squire, Watson C.	3: 59	"	
1893	McGraw, John H.	12:207	" "		Dunbar, Ralph O.	5:441
1895	"		Wilson, John L. "	12:126	Hoyt, John P.	11:556
1897	Rogers, John R.	12:104	" Turner, George	12:335	Scott, Elmon	12:203
1899	"		Foster, Addison G. "	12:390	Gordon, Merritt J.	25:326
1901	McBride, Henry	14:447	" "		Reavis, James B.	5:407
1903	"		" Ankeny, Levi	9:558	Fullerton, Mark A.	13:161
1905	Mead, Albert E.	14:447	Piles, Samuel H. "	14:389	Mount, Wallace	14:505
1907	"		" "		Hadley, Hiram E.	24:269
1909	Cosgrove, Samuel G.	14:447	" Jones, Wesley L.	14:393	Rudkin, Frank H.	18:400
1909	Hay, Marion E.	14:448	" "		"	
1911	"		Poindexter, Miles "	15:211	Dunbar, Ralph O.	5:441
1913	Lister, Ernest	15:341	" "		"	
1914	"		" "		Crow, Herman D.	
1915	"		" "		Morris, George E.	
1917	"		" "		Ellis, Overton G.	
1919	"		" "		Chadwick, Stephen J.	
1921	"		" "		Parker, Emmett N.	
1923	"		Dill, Clarence C. "	B:200	Main, John F.	B:139
1925	Hartley, Roland H.		" "		Tolman, Warren W.	
1926	"		" "		Main, John F.	B:139
1927	"		" "		Mackintosh, Kenneth	C: 79
1929	"		" "		Mitchell, John R.	
1931	"		" "		Tolman, Warren W.	
1933	Martin, Clarence D.		" Bone, Homer T.		Beals, Walter B.	
1935	"		Schwellenbach, Lewis B. "		Millard, William J.	

WEST VIRGINIA

Date	Governors	Biography	U. S. Senators	Biography	Chief Justices	Biography
1863	Boreman, Arthur I.	12:430	VanWinkle, Peter G.	4:377		
1863	“		“ Willey, Waitman T.	12:455		
1869	Farnsworth, Daniel D. T.	12:430	Boreman, Arthur I. “	12:430		
1869	Stevenson, William E.	12:430	“ “			
1871	Jacob, John J.	12:430	“ Davis, Henry G.	10:468		
1875	“		Caperton, Allen T. “	7:303		
1876	“		Price, Samuel “	5:518		
1877	Mathews, Henry M.	12:431	Hereford, Frank “	12:252		
1881	Jackson, Jacob B.	12:431	Camden, Johnson N. “	20:329		
1883	“		“ Kenna, John E.	1:299		
1885	Wilson, Emanuel W.	12:432	“ “			
1887	“		Faulkner, Charles J. “	2:392	*There are no chief justices of West Virginia. At the beginning of the January term each year, the members of the Supreme Court of Appeals designate one of their number to act as president during that year.*	
1890	Fleming, Aretas B.	12:432	“ “			
1893	MacCorkle, William A.	12:432	“ Camden, Johnson N.	20:329		
1895	“		“ Elkins, Stephen B.	1:142		
1897	Atkinson, George W.	12:432	“ “			
1899	“		Scott, Nathan B. “	19: 59		
1901	White, Albert B.	12:433	“ “			
1905	Dawson, William M. O.	13:576	“ “			
1909	Classcock, William E.	23:265	“ “			
1911	“		“ Elkins, Davis	C:527		
1911	“		“ Watson, Clarence W.	C:529		
1911	“		Chilton, William E. “	15:343		
1913	Hatfield, Henry D.	C:409	“ Goff, Nathan			
1917	Cornwell, John J.	17: 54	Sutherland, Howard “	A: 29		
1919	“		“ Elkins, Davis	C:527		
1921	Morgan, Ephraim F.		“ “			
1923	“		Neely, Matthew M. “	C:104		
1925	Gore, Howard M.	B: 45	“ Goff, Guy D.	24: 24		
1929	Conley, William G.	C:453	Hatfield, Henry D. “	C:409		
1931	“		“ Neely, Matthew M.	C:104		
1933	Kump, Herman G.		“ “			
1935	“		Holt, Rush D. “			

WISCONSIN

Date	Governors	Biography	U. S. Senators	Biography	Chief Justices	Biography
1848	Dewey, Nelson	12: 73	Dodge, Henry	12: 72	Stow, Alexander W.	12:513
1848	“		“ Walker, Isaac P.	3:530	“	
1852	Farwell, Leonard J.	12: 73	“ “		“	
1853	“		“ “		Whiton, Edward V.	12:515
1854	Barstow, William A.	12: 74	“ “		“	
1855	“		“ Durkee, Charles	11:262	“	
1856	MacArthur, Arthur	13:477	“ “		“	
1856	Bashford, Coles	12: 74	“ “		“	
1857	“		Doolittle, James R. “	4:382	“	
1858	Randall, Alexander W.	2:458	“ “		“	
1859	“		“ “		Dixon, Luther S.	12:513
1861	“		“ Howe, Timothy O.	4:252	“	
1862	Harvey, Louis P.	12: 74	“ “		“	
1862	Salomon, Edward	12: 75	“ “		“	
1864	Lewis, James T.	12: 75	“ “		“	
1866	Fairchild, Lucius	12: 76	“ “		“	
1869	“		Carpenter, Matthew H. “	4: 22	“	
1872	Washburn, Cadwallader	12: 77	“ “		“	
1874	Taylor, William R.	12: 77	“ “		Ryan, Edward G.	12:230
1875	“		Cameron, Angus “	12: 83	“	
1876	Ludington, Harrison	12: 78	“ “		“	
1878	Smith, William E.	12: 78	“ “		“	
1879	“		“ Carpenter, Matthew H.	12: 22	“	
1880	“		“ “		Cole, Orsamus	12:251
1881	“		Sawyer, Philetus	1:326	“	
1881	“		“ Cameron, Angus	12: 83	“	
1882	Rusk, Jeremiah M.	1:147	“ “		“	
1885	“		“ Spooner, John C.	14: 33	“	

WISCONSIN *(Continued)*

Date	Governors	Biography	U. S. Senators	Biography	Chief Justices	Biography
1889	Hoard, William D.	16:398	Sawyer, Philetus	1:326	Cole, Orsamus	12:251
1889	“		“ Spooner, John C.	14: 38	“	
1891	Peck, George W.	12: 79	“ Vilas, William F.	2:400	“	
1892	“		“ “		Lyon, William P.	13: 98
1893	“		Mitchell, John L. “	2:341	“	
1894	“		“ “		Orton, Harlow S.	13:170
1895	Upham, William H.	12: 79	“ “		Cassoday, John B.	13:309
1897	Scofield, Edward	12: 80	“ Spooner, John C.	14: 33	“	
1899	“		Quarles, Joseph V. “	13: 17		
1901	LaFollette, Robert M.	19:425	“ “		“	
1905	Davidson, James O.	14:109	LaFollette, Robert M. “	19:425	“	
1907	“		“ Stephenson, Isaac	14: 50	Winslow, John B.	14:469
1911	McGovern, Francis E.	17:151	“ “		“	
1915	Philipp, Emanuel L.	19:427	“ Husting, Paul O.	15:332	“	
1918	“		“ Lenroot, Irvine L.	B:184	“	
1920	“		“ “		Siebecker, Robert G.	19:400
1921	Blaine, John J.	26:280	“ “		“	
1922	“		“ “		Vinje, Aad J.	
1925	“ .		LaFollette, Robert M., Jr. “	C:351	“	
1927	Zimmerman, Fred R.		“ Blaine, John J.	B:110	“	
1929	Kohler, Walter J.		“ “		Rosenberry, Marvin B.	
1931	LaFollette, Philip F.		“ “		“	
1933	Schmedeman, Albert G.		“ Duffy, Francis R.	D:136	“	
1935	LaFollette, Philip F.		“ “		“	

WYOMING

Date	Governors	Biography	U. S. Senators	Biography	Chief Justices	Biography
1890	Warren, Francis E.	23:220	Carey, Joseph M.	1:462	Devanter, William Van	12: 47
1890	Barber, Amos W.	11:482	Warren, Francis E. “	23:220	Groesbeck, Herman V. S.	13:425
1893	Osborne, John E.	11:482	Vacant “		“	
1895	Richards, William A.	11:483	Clark, Clarence D. “	12: 60	“	
1895	“		“ Warren, Francis E.	23:220	“	
1897	“		“ “		Potter, Charles N.	3:528
1899	Richards, DeForest	11:483	“ “		“	
1903	Chatterton, Fennimore		“ “		Corn, Samuel T.	5:513
1905	Brooks, Bryant B.	13:294	“ “		Knight, Jesse	14:213
1905	“		“ “		Potter, Charles N.	3:528
1911	Carey, Joseph M.	1:462	“ “		Beard, Cyrus	17:243
1913	“		“ “		Scott, Richard H.	20:334
1915	Kendrick, John B.	25:108	“ “		Potter, Charles N.	3:528
1917	Houx, Frank L.		Kendrick, John B. “	25:108	“	
1919	Carey, Robert D.		“ “		Beard, Cyrus	17:243
1920	“		“ “		Potter, Charles N.	3:528
1923	Ross, William B.	20:272	“ “		“	
1925	Ross, Nellie T.	B:454	“ “		“	
1927	Emerson, Frank C.	25:423	“ “		Blume, Fred H.	
1929	“		“ Sullivan, Patrick J.	D:116	“	
1931	Clark, Alonzo M.		“ Carey, Robert D.		Kimball, Ralph	
1933	Miller, Leslie A.	D:237	O'Mahoney, Joseph C. “	D:391	“	

References are to THE NATIONAL CYCLOPEDIA OF AMERICAN BIOGRAPHY

Directors of Astronomical Observatories in the United States

Allegheny Observatory
PITTSBURGH, Pa.

1867..Langley, Samuel P. 15: 7
1891..Keeler, James E. 10: 498
1898..Brashear, John A. *(acting)* 4: 552
1899..Wadsworth, Frank L. O. .26: 376
1905..Schlesinger, Frank .... C: 497
1920..Curtis, Heber D. ....
1930..Jordan, Frank C. ....

Amherst College Observatory
AMHERST, MASS.

1881..Todd, David P. 7: 203
1921..Green, Warren K. ....

Cincinnati Observatory
CINCINNATI, OHIO

1843..Mitchel, Ormsby M. 3: 440
1868..Abbe, Cleveland 8: 264
1875..Stone, Ormond 6: 194
1884..Porter, Jermain G. 13: 73
1930..Yowell, Everett I. ....

Columbia University Observatory
NEW YORK, N. Y.

1882..Rees, John K. 11: 513
1906..Jacoby, Harold 23: 132
1932..Schilt, Jan ....

Dearborn Observatory
EVANSTON, ILL.

1865..Safford, Truman H. 13: 359
1879..Hough, George W. 8: 337
1909..Fox, Philip .... C: 528
1929..Lee, Oliver J. ....

Flower Astronomical Observatory
PHILADELPHIA, PA.

1895..Doolittle, Charles L. 20: 340
1919..Doolittle, Eric 19: 300
1920..Barton, Samuel G. *(acting)*
1928..Olivier, Charles P. ....

Harvard Observatory
CAMBRIDGE, MASS.

1840..Bond, William C. 8: 381
1859..Bond, George P. 5: 503
1866..Winlock, Joseph 9: 266
1875..Searle, Arthur *(acting)* ..19: 34
1877..Pickering, Edward C. 6: 424
1919..Bailey, Solon I. *(acting)*..
1921..Shapley, Harlow .... C: 95

University of Illinois Observatory
URBANA, ILL.

1906..Stebbins, Joel .... B: 342
1923..Baker, Robert H. ....

Leander McCormick Observatory
UNIVERSITY, PA.

1883..Stone, Ormond 6: 194
1913..Mitchell, Samuel A. .....

Lick Observatory
MT. HAMILTON, CALIF.

1888..Holden, Edward S. 7: 229
1898..Keeler, James E. 10: 498
1901..Campbell, William W. 11: 278
1930..Aitken, Robert G. ....

Lowell Observatory
FLAGSTAFF, ARIZ.

1894..Lowell, Percival 8: 309
1916..Slipher, Vesto M. ....

McDonald Observatory
FT. DAVIS, TEX.

1932..Struve, Otto ....

The Observatory of the University of Michigan
ANN ARBOR, MICH.

1854..Brunnow, Franz F. E. ...13: 78
1863..Watson, James C. 7: 70
1879..Harrington, Mark W. 10: 448
1892..Hall, Asaph, Jr. ....
1905..Hussey, William J. 21: 95
1926..Curtiss, Ralph H. 21: 259
1929..Rufus, Will C. *(acting)* ..
1930..Curtis, Heber D. ....

Mt. Wilson Observatory
PASADENA, CALIF.

1904..Hale, George E. .... C: 45
1923..Adams, Walter S. .... B: 171

Perkins Observatory
DELAWARE, OHIO

1923..Crump, Clifford C. ....
1929..Stetson, Harlan T. ....
1934..Bobrovnikoff, N. T. *(acting)* ....

Princeton University Observatory
PRINCETON, N. J.

1882..Young, Charles A. 6: 325
1905..Lovett, Edgar O. *(acting)*
1912..Russell, Henry N. .... A: 346

Smithsonian Institution Astrophysical Observatory
WASHINGTON, D. C.

1890..Langley, Samuel P. 15: 7
1906..Abbot, Charles G. .... A: 366

Sproul Observatory
SWARTHMORE, PA.

1911..Miller, John A. ....

United States Naval Observatory
WASHINGTON, D. C.

Superintendents

1845..Maury, Matthew F. 6: 35
1861..Gilliss, James M. 9: 230
1865..Davis, Charles H. 4: 166
1867..Sands, Benjamin F. 4: 295
1874..Davis, Charles H. 4: 166
1877..Rodgers, John 25: 188
1882..Sampson, William T. 9: 9
1882..Rowan, Stephen C. 2: 101
1883..Shufeldt, Robert W. 4: 293
1884..Franklin, Samuel R. 4: 391
1885..Belknap, George E. 4: 206
1886..Phythian, Robert L. 13: 180
1890..McNair, Frederick V. 10: 255
1894..Phythian, Robert L. 13: 180
1897..Davis, Charles H., 2d 4: 120
1898..Phythian, Robert L. 13: 180
1898..Davis, Charles H., 2d 4: 120
1902..Chester, Colby M. ....
1906..Walker, Asa ....
1907..Barnette, William J. .....
1909..Veeder, TenEyck DeW. ..
1911..Jayne, Joseph L. ....
1914..Hoogewerff, John A. 25: 266
1917..Howard, Thomas B. 15: 27
1919..Hoogewerff, John A. 25: 266
1921..MacDougall, William D. ..
1923..Pollock, Edwin T. ....
1927..Freeman, Charles S. .....
1930..Hellweg, Julius F. ....

Van Vleck Observatory
MIDDLETOWN, CONN.

1914..Slocum, Frederick ....
1918..Vacant
1920..Slocum, Frederick ....

Washburn Observatory
MADISON, WIS.

1878..Watson, James C. 7: 70
1881..Holden, Edward S. 7: 229
1887..Hall, Asaph 22: 287
1889..Comstock, George C. 12: 454
1922..Stebbins, Joel .... B: 342

Yale Observatory
NEW HAVEN, CONN.

1882..Newton, Hubert A. 9: 219
1896..Elkin, William L. 24: 117
1910..Vacant ....
1917..Brown, Ernest W. 15: 24
1920..Schlesinger, Frank .... C: 497

Yerkes Observatory
WILLIAMS BAY, WIS.

1895..Hale, George E. .... C: 45
1905..Frost, Edwin B. 25: 316
1932..Struve, Otto ....

Presidents of Colleges and Universities

ADELPHI COLLEGE
GARDEN CITY, N. Y.

1896..Levermore, Charles H. ... 5:192
1912..Cadman, S. Parkes B:121
1915..Blodgett, Frank D. D:252

UNIVERSITY OF ALABAMA
UNIVERSITY, ALA.

1831..Woods, Alva 12:293
1837..Manly, Basil 25:122
1855..Garland, Landon C. 8:226
1865..Vacant
1870..Smith, William R. 12:294
1871..Lupton, Nathaniel T. 12:294
1874..Smith, Carlos G. 12:295
1878..Gorgas, Josiah 12:295
1879..Lewis, Burwell B. 12:295
1886..Clayton, Henry DeL. 12:296
1890..Jones, Richard C. 12:296
1897..Powers, James K. 15:362
1901..Wyman, William S. 12:297
1902..Abercrombie, John W. ...12:297
1911..Denny, George H. 13:101

ALBION COLLEGE
(Albion Wesleyan Seminary until 1861)
ALBION, MICH.

1843..Stockwell, Charles F. 5:471
1846..Hinman, Clark T. 5:471
1853..Mayhew, Ira 5:471
1854..Sinex, Thomas H. 5:472
1864..Jocelyn, George B. 5:472
1870..Silber, William B 5:473
1871..McKeown, J. L. G. ......
1871..Jocelyn, George B. 5:472
1877..Fiske, Lewis R. 5:473
1898..Ashley, John P. 13:173
1902..Dickie, Samuel 21: 55
1921..Laird, John W. ....
1924..Seaton John L. ....

AMERICAN UNIVERSITY
WASHINGTON, D.C.

1891..Hurst, John F. 9:122
1902..McCabe Charles C. 13: 76
1922..Clark, Lucius C. ....
1933..Gray, Joseph M. M. ......

AMHERST COLLEGE
AMHERST, MASS.

1821..Moore, Zephaniah S. 5:307
1823..Humphrey, Heman 5:308
1844..Hitchcock, Edward 5:308
1854..Stearns, William A. 5:309
1876..Seelye, Julius H. 6:157
1890..Gates, Merrill E. 5:309
1899..Harris, George 10:101
1912..Meiklejohn, Alexander ... A:406
1923..Olds, George D. 24:384
1927..Pease, Arthur S. A:463
1933..King, Stanley A:447

ANDOVER THEOLOGICAL SEMINARY
ANDOVER, MASS.

1827..Porter, Ebenezer 10: 99
1836..Edwards, Justin 10:100
1842..Woods, Leonard 9:121
1846..Emerson, Ralph 10:101
1853..Park, Edwards A. 9:202
1868..Taylor, John L. 26:441
1877..Smyth, Egbert C. 10:101
1896..Harris, George 10:101
1899..Moore, George F. 10:101
1901..Day, Charles O. 13:434

Removed to Cambridge, Mass., in 1907 and affiliated with Harvard University

1909..Fitch, Albert P. ....
1917..Platner, John W. 19:352
1922..Sperry, Willard L. ....

Court dissolved affiliation with Harvard in 1925 and seminary did not operate again until 1931 when it became affiliated with Newton Theological Seminary under name of

ANDOVER NEWTON THEOLOGICAL SCHOOL
NEWTON CENTRE, MASS.

1931..Herrick, Everett C. ......

ANTIOCH COLLEGE
YELLOW SPRINGS, OHIO

1853..Mann, Horace 3: 78
1859..Hill, Thomas 6:420
1862..Weston, John B. 6:535
1865..Craig, Austin 13: 91
1866..Hosmer, George W. 7:292
1873..Orton, Edward 24:106
1873..Derby, Samuel C. 7:418
1876..Weston, John B. 6:535
1877..Derby, Samuel C. 7:418
1881..Wait, Oren J. 12:311
1884..Long, Daniel A. 12:184
1899..Bell, William A. 12:183
1902..Weston, Stephen F. ......
1906..Fess, Simeon D. C:283
1917..Black, George D. ....
1919..Dawson, William M. .....
1920..Morgan, Arthur E. ...... B: 15
1935..Henderson, Algo D. ......

UNIVERSITY OF ARIZONA
TUCSON, ARIZ.

1893..Comstock, Theodore B. ...13:450
1895..Billman, Howard 24:174
1897..Parker, Millard M. ......
1901..Adams, Frank Y. ....
1903..Babcock, Kendric C. 25:201
1911..Wilde, Arthur H. ....
1914..Kleinsmid, Rufus B. .....
1922..Marvin, Cloyd H. D:377
1927..Shantz, Homer L. ....

ATLANTA UNIVERSITY
ATLANTA, GA.

1867..Ware, Edmund Asa 5:380
1885..Bumstead, Horace 5:381
1907..Ware, Edward T. 22:192
1923..Adams, Myron W. B:371
1929..Hope, John ....

BATES COLLEGE
LEWISTON, MAINE

1863..Cheney, Oren B. 8:394
1894..Chase, George C. 8:395
1920..Gray, Clifton D. A:527

BELOIT COLLEGE
BELOIT, WIS.

1850..Chapin, Aaron L. 3:184
1886..Eaton, Edward D. 3:185
1917..Brannon, Melvin A. .....
1923..Hamilton, William A. ...24:134
1924..Maurer, Irving ....

BEREA COLLEGE
BEREA, KY.

1855..Fee, John G. 24:301
1869..Fairchild, Edward H. 24:263
1892..Frost, William G. ....
1920..Hutchins, William J. D:368

BOSTON UNIVERSITY
BOSTON, MASS.

1873..Warren, William F. 11:177
1903..Huntington, William E. .11:179
1911..Murlin, Lemuel H. 26:285
1925..Anderson, William F. 14:486
1926..Marsh, Daniel L. A:133

BOWDOIN COLLEGE
BRUNSWICK, MAINE

1802..McKeen, Joseph 1:417
1807..Appleton, Jesse 1:417
1819..Allen, William 1:418
1839..Woods, Leonard 1:418

BOWDOIN COLLEGE (*continued*)

1867..Harris, Samuel 1:418
1871..Chamberlain, Joshua L. .. 1:419
1885..Hyde, William DeW. 1:419
1918..Sills, Kenneth C. M. .....

BROWN UNIVERSITY
PROVIDENCE, R. I.

1764..Manning, James 8: 20
1792..Maxcy, Jonathan 8: 21
1802..Messer, Asa 8: 21
1827..Wayland, Francis 8: 22
1855..Sears, Barnas 8: 24
1867..Chace, George Ide (*pro tem*) 8: 25
1868..Caswell, Alexis 8: 25
1872..Robinson, Ezekiel G. 8: 26
1889..Andrews, Elisha B. 8: 26
1899..Faunce, William H. P. ...10: 306
1929..Barbour, Clarence A. .....A: 283

BRYN MAWR COLLEGE
BRYN MAWR, PA.

1883..Rhoads, James E. 13: 84
1894..Thomas, M. Carey 13: 84
1922..Park, Marion E. ....A: 224

BUCKNELL UNIVERSITY
LEWISBURG, PA.

1851..Malcolm, Howard 12: 300
1857..Loomis, Justin 12: 300
1879..Hill, David J. 12: 244
1889..Harris, John H. 22: 134
1919..Hunt, Emory W. 13: 234
1931..Rainey, Homer P. ....

UNIVERSITY OF BUFFALO
BUFFALO, N. Y.

1846..Fillmore, Millard 6: 177
1874..Marshall, Orsamus H. ....
1884..Sprague, E. Carleton ....
1895..Putnam, James O. 10: 40
1902..Bissell, Wilson S. 13: 117
1903..Gorham, George (*acting*)
1905..Norton, Charles P. ....
1920..Cooke, Walter P. (*acting*) 23: 143
1922..Capen, Samuel P. ....

UNIVERSITY OF CALIFORNIA
BERKELEY, CALIF.

1870..Durant, Henry 7: 228
1871..Gilman, Daniel C. 5: 170
1876..LeConte, John 7: 228
1881..Reid, William T. 2: 258
1886..Holden, Edward S. 7: 229
1888..Davis, Horace 7: 230
1890..Kellogg, Martin 7: 230
1899..Wheeler, Benjamin Ide ... 4: 480
1919..Barrows, David P. .... B: 157
1924..Campbell, William W. 11: 278
1930..Sproul, Robert G. .... C: 387

CARNEGIE INSTITUTE OF TECHNOLOGY
PITTSBURG, PA.

1912..Hamerschlag, Arthur A. ..23: 52
1923..Baker, Thomas S. .... C: 507
1935..Watkins, Charles (*acting*)

CASE SCHOOL OF APPLIED SCIENCE
CLEVELAND, OHIO

Founded in 1880 and governed by board of trustees until 1886

1886..Staley, Cady 11: 154
1902..Howe, Charles S. 15: 259
1929..Wickenden, William E. ..

CATHOLIC UNIVERSITY OF AMERICA
WASHINGTON, D. C.

1886..Keane, John J. 6: 285
1896..Conaty, Thomas J. 12: 407
1903..O'Connell, Dennis J. 15: 65
1909..Shahan, Thomas J. 5: 531
1928..Ryan, James H. ....

UNIVERSITY OF CHICAGO
CHICAGO, ILL.

1858..Burroughs, John C. 11: 65
1874..Moss, Lemuel 11: 65
1875..Abernethy, Alonzo (*pro tem*) ....
1878..Anderson, Galusha 11: 65
1885..Vacant
1891..Harper, William R. 11: 65
1907..Judson, Harry P. 20: 24
1923..Burton, Ernest DeW. 11: 68
1925..Mason, Max .... B: 485
1929..Hutchins, Robert M. ..... C: 54

UNIVERSITY OF CINCINNATI
CINCINNATI, OHIO

University founded in 1870; governed by board of trustees until 1875 when Henry T. Eddy was appointed dean.

1877..Vickers, Thomas (*Rector*)
1884..Eddy, Henry T. (*Rector pro tempore*) 15: 331
1885..Cox, Jacob D. 22: 281
1890..Eddy, Henry T. (*acting*)..15: 331

University under administration of deans from June 1890 to July 1899

1899..Ayres, Howard 18: 398
1904..Dabney, Charles W. ...... B: 239
1920..Hicks, Frederick C. ......
1929..Schneider, Herman ......
1932..Walters, Raymond ....

CLARK UNIVERSITY
WORCESTER, MASS.

1888..Hall, Granville S. 9: 203
1920..Atwood, Wallace W. .....

COLBY COLLEGE
WATERVILLE, MAINE

1820..Chaplin, Jeremiah 8: 404
1833..Babcock, Rufus 8: 405
1836..Pattison, Robert E. 8: 405
1839..Suspended
1841..Fay, Eliphaz 8: 406
1843..Sheldon, David N. 8: 406
1854..Pattison, Robert E. 8: 405
1857..Champlin, James T. 8: 406
1873..Robins, Henry E 17: 356
1882..Pepper, George D. B. 8: 407
1889..Small, Albion W. 25: 242
1892..Whitman, Benaiah L. 8: 408
1896..Butler, Nathaniel 8: 409
1901..White, Charles L. 13: 109
1908..Roberts, Arthur J. 21: 329
1929..Johnson, Franklin W. .... D: 200

COLGATE UNIVERSITY
(Madison University until 1890)
HAMILTON, N. Y.

1836..Kendrick, Nathaniel (*act.*) 5: 427
1848..Vacant
1851..Taylor, Stephen W. 5: 427
1856..Eaton, George W. 5: 428
1868..Dodge, Ebenezer 5: 428
1890..Andrews, Newton L. (*act.*) 5: 429
1895..Smith, George W. 13: 226
1899..Merrill, George E. 13: 226
1909..Bryan, Elmer B. 14: 496
1922..Cutten, George B. .... D: 263

COLLEGE OF NEW JERSEY
See Princeton University

COLORADO COLLEGE
COLORADO SPRINGS, COLO.

1874..Edwards, Jonathan ......
1874..Dougherty, James G. ....
1876..Tenney, Edward P. 7: 530
1888..Slocum, William F. 13: 194
1917..Duniway, Clyde A. 13: 525
1923..Mierow, Charles C. ...... D: 442
1934..Davies, Thurston J. ......

UNIVERSITY OF COLORADO
BOULDER, COLO.

1877..Sewall, Joseph A. 6: 492
1887..Hale, Horace M. 6: 492
1892..Baker, James H. 6: 493
1914..Farrand, Livingston ..... A: 117
1919..Norlin, George .... A: 320

COLUMBIA UNIVERSITY
NEW YORK, N. Y.

1754..Johnson, Samuel 6: 341
1763..Cooper, Myles 6: 341
1792..Johnson, William S. 6: 342
1801..Moore, Benjamin 1: 514
1811..Harris, William 6: 344
1829..Duer, William A. 6: 344
1842..Moore, Nathaniel F. 6: 345
1849..King, Charles 6: 345
1864..Barnard, Frederick A. P. 6: 347
1890..Low, Seth 6: 348
1901..Butler, Nicholas Murray .. B: 186

COLUMBIAN UNIVERSITY
See George Washington University

COOPER UNION FOR ADVANCEMENT OF SCIENCE AND ART
NEW YORK, N. Y.

1859..Cooper, Peter 3: 114
1884..Cooper, Edward 3: 115
1905..Parsons, John E. ....
1915..Cutting, R. Fulton 15: 183
1935..Dunn, Gano S. 18: 105

CORNELL COLLEGE
MT. VERNON, IOWA

1856..Keeler, Richard W. 7: 79
1859..Fellows, Samuel M. 7: 79
1863..King, William F. 7: 79
1908..Harlan, James E. ....
1915..Flint, Charles W. .... B: 421
1923..Updergraff, Harlan ......
1927..Burgsthaler, Herbert J. ..

CORNELL UNIVERSITY
ITHACA, N. Y.

1867..White, Andrew D. 4: 476
1885..Adams, Charles K. 4: 477
1892..Schurman, Jacob G. 4: 478
1921..Farrand, Livingston ..... A: 117

DARTMOUTH COLLEGE
HANOVER, N. H.

1770..Wheelock, Eleazer 9: 85
1779..Wheelock, John 9: 86
1815..Brown, Francis 9: 86
1820..Dana, Daniel 9: 87
1822..Tyler, Bennett 9: 87
1828..Lord, Nathan 9: 88
1863..Smith, Asa Dodge 9: 89
1877..Bartlett, Samuel C. 9: 89
1893..Tucker, William J. 24: 242
1909..Nichols, Ernest F. 21: 68
1916..Hopkins, Ernest M. ...... A: 119

DENISON UNIVERSITY
GRANVILLE, OHIO

1831..Pratt John 1: 301
1837..Going, Jonathan 1: 301
1844..Bailey, Silas 1: 302
1853..Hall, Jeremiah 1: 302
1863..Talbot, Samson 1: 302
1873..Marsh, F. O. *(acting)* ....
1875..Andrews, Elisha B. 8: 26
1879..Owen, Alfred 1: 303
1887..Anderson, Galusha 1: 303
1890..Purinton, Daniel B. 1: 304
1901..Hunt, Emory W. 13: 234
1913..Chamberlain, Clark W. ..
1925..Spencer, Bunyan ....
1927..Shaw, Avery A. ....

DE PAUW UNIVERSITY
GREENCASTLE, IND.

1839..Simpson, Matthew 7: 381
1849..Berry, Lucien W. 7: 382
1855..Curry, Daniel 7: 382
1859..Bowman, Thomas 7: 383
1872..Andrus, Reuben 7: 383
1875..Martin, Alexander 7: 383
1889..John, John P. D. 7: 384
1896..Gobin, Hillary A. 7: 384
1903..Hughes, Edwin H. 13: 417
1909..McConnell, Francis J. 15: 215
1912..Grose, George R. 15: 332
1924..Murlin, Lemuel H. 26: 285
1928..Oxnam, G. Bromley ...... A: 452

DICKINSON COLLEGE
CARLISLE, PA.

1785..Nisbet, Charles 6: 462
1804..Davidson, Robert 6: 462
1809..Atwater, Jeremiah 12: 105
1821..Mason, John M. 6: 462
1824..Neill, William 6: 463
1830..How, Samuel B. 6: 463
1833..Durbin, John P. 6: 463
1845..Emory, Robert ....
1848..Peck, Jesse T. 6: 464
1852..Collins, Charles 6: 464
1860..Johnson, Herman M. 6: 464
1868..Dashiell, Robert L. ......
1872..McCauley, James A. 6: 464
1889..Reed, George E. 6: 465
1911..Noble, Eugene A. 18: 297
1914..Morgan, James H. .... B: 355
1928..Filler, Mervin G. 25: 42
1931..Morgan, James H. *(act.)* . B: 355
1932..Waugh, Karl T. ....
1933..Morgan, James H. *(act.)* . B: 355
1934..Corson, Fred P. ....

DRAKE UNIVERSITY
DES MOINES, IOWA

1881..Carpenter, George T. ....
1894..Aylesworth, Barton O. ...11: 520
1897..Craig, William B. 21: 314
1902..Bell, H. McClelland 20: 277
1918..Holmes, Arthur ....
1923..Morehouse, Daniel W. ...

DREW UNIVERSITY
(Drew Theological Seminary until 1928)
MADISON, N. J.

1867..McClintock, John 6: 466
1870..Foster, Randolph S. 13: 62
1872..Hurst, John F. 9: 122
1880..Buttz, Henry A. 13: 110
1912..Tipple, Ezra S. 15: 414
1929..Brown, Arlo A. .... B: 402

DREXEL INSTITUTE
PHILADELPHIA, PA.

1892..MacAlister, James 13: 79
1913..Godfrey, Hollis .... A: 283
1922..Matheson, Kenneth G. ...23: 23
1932..Kolbe, Parke R. ....

DRURY COLLEGE
SPRINGFIELD, MO.

1873..Morrison, Nathan J. 13: 509
1887..Ingalls, Francis T. 13: 510
1894..Fuller, Homer T. 13: 510
1917..Nadal, Thomas W. ......

DUKE UNIVERSITY
(Trinity College until 1924)
DURHAM, N. C.

1842..Craven, Braxton 3: 445
1883..Wood, Marquis L. 3: 447
1885..Heitman, John F.
(chairman of faculty) .. 3: 447
1887..Crowell, John F. 3: 447
1894..Kilgo, John C. 13: 97
1910..Few, William P. 15: 196

EMORY UNIVERSITY
(Emory College until 1915)
EMORY UNIVERSITY, GA.

1837..Few, Ignatius A. 1: 517
1839..Longstreet, Augustus B. . 1: 517
1848..Pierce, George F. 1: 518
1854..Means, Alexander 1: 518
1855..Thomas, James R. 1: 519
1867..Smith, Luther M. 1: 519
1872..Smith, Osborn L. 1: 519
1876..Haygood, Atticus G. 1: 520
1885..Hopkins, Isaac S. 1: 520
1889..Candler, Warren A. 1: 521
1898..Dowman, Charles E. 16: 249
1902..Dickey, James E. 13: 94
1915..Candler, Warren A.
(chancellor) 1: 521
1920..Cox, Harvey W. 18: 436

FLORIDA STATE COLLEGE FOR WOMEN
TALLAHASSEE, FLA.

1905..Murphree, Albert A. ..... C: 144
1909..Conradi, Edward ....

UNIVERSITY OF FLORIDA
GAINESVILLE, FLA.

1904..Sledd, Andrew ....
1909..Murphree, Albert A. ..... C: 144
1928..Tigert, John J. .... D: 428

FORDHAM UNIVERSITY
(St. John's College until 1905)
NEW YORK, N. Y.

1841..McCloskey, John 1: 195
1844..Harley, John B. 2: 265
1844..Bayley, James R. 1: 487
1846..Thebaud, Augustus 2: 265
1851..Larkin, John 2: 265
1854..Tellier, Remigius 2: 266
1860..Thebaud, Augustus 2: 265
1863..Doucet, Edward 2: 266
1865..Moylan, William 2: 267
1868..Shea, Joseph 2: 267
1874..Gockeln, Fred W. 2: 267
1882..Dealy, Patrick F. 2: 267
1885..Campbell, Thomas J. 2: 268
1888..Scully, John 2: 268
1891..Gannon, Thomas J. 2: 269
1896..Campbell, Thomas J. 2: 268
1900..Pettit, George A. J. 14: 487
1904..Collins, J. J. ....
1906..Quinn, Daniel J. ....
1911..McCluskey, Thomas J. 14: 438
1915..Mulry, Joseph A. 25: 32
1919..Tivnan, Edward P. ......
1924..Duane, William J. ......
1930..Hogan, Aloysius J. ......

FRANKLIN AND MARSHALL COLLEGE
LANCASTER, PA.

1854..Gerhart, Emanuel V. 12: 443
1866..Nevin, John W. 5: 256
1877..Appel, Thomas G. 12: 444
1889..Stahr, John S. 12: 444
1909..Apple, Henry H. 14: 345

FURMAN UNIVERSITY
GREENVILLE, S. C.

1859..Furman, James C. ....
1881..Manly, Charles 25: 123
1897..Montague, Andrew P. 25: 232
1903..Poteat, Edwin McN. 14: 523
1919..McGlothlin, William J. ... A: 349
1933..Geer, Bennett E. ....

GEORGE WASHINGTON UNIVERSITY
(Columbian University until 1904)
WASHINGTON, D. C.

1821..Staughton, William 3: 151
1827..Chapin, Stephen 3: 152
1841..Bacon, Joel Smith 3: 152
1854..Binney, Joseph G. 3: 152
1859..Samson, George W. 3: 152
1871..Welling, James Clarke ... 1: 505
1894..Greene, Samuel H. 2: 424
1895..Whitman, Benaiah L. 8: 408
1900..Greene, Samuel H. 2: 424
1902..Needham, Charles W. 14: 515
1910..Stockton, Charles H. 25: 214
1918..Collier, William M. 13: 547
1921..Hodgkins, Howard L. 23: 29
1923..Lewis, William M. ....
1927..Marvin, Cloyd H. .... D: 377

GEORGIA SCHOOL OF TECHNOLOGY
ATLANTA, GA.

1886..Hopkins, Isaac S. 1: 520
1896..Hall, Lyman ....
1905..Matheson, Kenneth G. 23: 23
1922..Pratt, Nathaniel P. *(act.)* B: 123
1922..Brittain, Marion L. ...... B: 126

UNIVERSITY OF GEORGIA
ATHENS, GA.

1786..Baldwin, Abraham 9: 178
1801..Meigs, Josiah 9: 178
1811..Brown, John 9: 179
1817..Finley, Robert 9: 179
1819..Waddell, Moses 9: 179
1829..Church, Alonzo 9: 180
1860..Lipscomb, Andrew A. 6: 217
1874..Tucker, Henry H. 6: 498
1878..Mell, Patrick H. 9: 181
1888..Boggs, William E. 26: 153
1899..Hill, Walter B. 19: 93
1906..Barrow, David C. 15: 138
1925..Snelling, Charles M. .....
1932..Sanford, Steadman V. ...

GIRARD COLLEGE
PHILADELPHIA, PA.

1847..Jones, Joel 7: 13
1850..Allen, William H. 7: 13
1863..Smith, Richard S. 7: 14
1867..Allen, William H. 7: 13
1882..Fetterolf, Adam H. 7: 14
1910..Herrick, Cheesman A. ...

GOUCHER COLLEGE
BALTIMORE, MD.

1886..Hopkins, William H. 1: 507
1890..Goucher, John F. 24: 174
1908..Noble, Eugene A. 18: 297
1911..Van Meter, John B. *(act.)* 26: 70
1913..Guth, William W. 23: 92
1929..Froelicher, Hans *(acting)*.
1930..Stimson, Dorothy *(acting)*
1930..Robertson, David A. .....

HAMILTON COLLEGE
CLINTON, N. Y.

1812..Backus, Azel 7: 405
1817..Davis, Henry 7: 405
1833..Dwight, Sereno E. 7: 406
1835..Penney, Joseph 7: 406
1839..North, Simeon 7: 407
1858..Fisher, Samuel W. 7: 407
1867..Brown, Samuel G. 7: 408
1881..Darling, Henry 7: 408
1892..Stryker, M. Woolsey 26: 142
1917..Ferry, Frederick C. ......

HAMPDEN-SIDNEY COLLEGE
HAMPDEN-SIDNEY, VA.

1775..Smith, Samuel S. 2: 21
1779..Smith, John Blair 2: 21
1789..Lacy, Drury 2: 22
1796..Alexander, Archibald 2: 22
1806..Reid, William S. 2: 22
1807..Hoge, Moses 2: 23
1820..Cushing, Jonathan P. 2: 23
1835..Baxter, George A. 2: 24
1835..Carroll, David L. 2: 24
1838..Maxwell, William 2: 24
1844..Sparrow, Patrick J. 2: 25
1847..Wilson, Samuel B. 2: 25
1848..Green, Lewis W. 2: 25
1856..Dabney, Robert L. 2: 26
1856..Holladay, Albert L. 2: 26
1857..Atkinson, John M. P. ... 2: 26
1883..McIlwaine, Richard 2: 26
1889..Holladay, Lewis L. 2: 27
1891..McIlwaine, Richard 2: 26
1905..McAllister, James G. 14: 471
1908..Graham, H. Tucker 14: 471
1917..McWorter, Ashton ....
1919..Eggleston, Joseph D. ..... B: 293

HAMPTON INSTITUTE
(Hampton Normal and Agricultural Institute until 1930)
HAMPTON, VA.

1868..Armstrong, Samuel C. ... 1: 436
1893..Frissell, Hollis B. 18: 387
1919..Gregg, James E. .... A: 285
1929..Phenix, George P. ....
1931..Howe, Arthur ....

HARVARD UNIVERSITY
CAMBRIDGE, MASS.

1640..Eaton, Nathaniel 6: 409
1640..Dunster, Henry 6: 409
1654..Chauncy, Charles 6: 410
1672..Hoar, Leonard 6: 411
1675..Oakes, Urian 6: 411
1682..Rogers, John 6: 411
1685..Mather, Increase 6: 412
1701..Willard, Samuel 6: 413
1707..Leverett, John 6: 413
1725..Wadsworth, Benjamin ... 6: 414
1737..Holyoke, Edward 6: 415
1770..Locke, Samuel 6: 416
1774..Langdon, Samuel 6: 416
1781..Willard, Joseph 6: 416
1805..Vacant
1806..Webber, Samuel 6: 417
1810..Kirkland, John T. 6: 417
1829..Quincy, Josiah 6: 417
1846..Everett, Edward 6: 179
1849..Sparks, Jared 5: 433
1853..Walker, James 6: 419
1860..Felton, Cornelius C. 6: 419
1862..Hill, Thomas 6: 420
1869..Eliot, Charles W. 6: 421
1909..Lowell, A. Lawrence ..... D: 46
1933..Conant, James B. .... D: 48

HEBREW UNION COLLEGE
CINCINNATI, OHIO

1875..Wise, Isaac M. 10: 116
1900..Mielziner, Moses *(acting)*. 7: 215
1903..Deutsch, Gottehard *(act.)*.
1903..Kohler, Kaufman 13: 396
1921..Morgenstern, Julian .....

HOBART COLLEGE
GENEVA, N. Y.

1826..Adams, Jasper 12: 520
1828..Mason, Richard S. 12: 516
1836..Hale, Benjamin 13: 39
1858..Jackson, Abner 3: 497
1867..Wilson, William D. 12: 510
1868..Stone, James K. 7: 7
1869..Rankine, James 12: 551
1871..VanRensselaer, Maunsell . 2: 51
1876..Perry, William S. 3: 469
1876..Hinsdale, Robert G. ......
1883..Smith, Hamilton L. 12: 466
1884..Potter, Eliphalet N. 7: 171
1897..Jones, Robert E. 13: 367
1903..Stewardson, Langdon C. ..15: 311
1913..Powell, Lyman P. 15: 312
1919..Bartlett, Murray ....

HOWARD UNIVERSITY
WASHINGTON, D. C.

1867..Boynton, Charles B. .....
1868..Howard, Oliver O. 4: 103
1874..Smith, Edward P. ....
1876..Patton, William W. 10: 165
1889..Rankin, Jeremiah E. 5: 482
1903..Hamlin, Teunis S. 6: 165
1906..Thirkield, Wilbur P. .....
1912..Newman, Stephen M. ....
1918..Durkee, J. Stanlee ....
1926..Johnson, Mordecai W. ....

HUNTER COLLEGE
NEW YORK, N. Y.

1870..Hunter, Thomas 22: 244
1906..Gillet, Joseph A. *(acting)*.23: 300
1908..Davis, George S. ....
1929..Kieran, James M. 26: 14
1933..Colligan, Eugene A. .....

UNIVERSITY OF ILLINOIS
URBANA, ILL.

1867..Gregory, John M. 12: 497
1880..Peabody, Selim H. 1: 271
1891..Burrill, Thomas J. 18: 187
1894..Draper, Andrew S. 12: 498
1904..James, Edmund J. 11: 67
1920..Kinley, David .... B: 76
1930..Chase, Harry W. .... A: 298
1934..Willard, Arthur C. ......

INDIANA UNIVERSITY
BLOOMINGTON, IND.

1829..Wylie, Andrew 13: 116
1852..Ryors, Alfred 4: 444
1853..Daily, William M. 13: 101
1859..Lathrop, John H. 5: 178
1860..Nutt, Cyrus 13: 424
1875..Moss, Lemuel 11: 65
1884..Jordan, David S. 22: 68
1891..Coulter, John M. 11: 68
1893..Swain, Joseph 6: 355
1902..Bryan, William L. 13: 464

IOWA STATE AGRIGULTURAL COLLEGE
AMES, IOWA

1869..Welch, Adonijah S. 12: 291
1883..Knapp, S. A. ....
1885..Hunt, Leigh 24: 13
1886..Chamberlain, W. I. ......
1891..Beardshear, William M. ..12: 291
1903..Storms, Albert B. 13: 219
1912..Pearson, Raymond A. 15: 299
1927..Hughes, Raymond M. ....

STATE UNIVERSITY OF IOWA
IOWA CITY, IOWA

1855..Dean, Amos 22: 116
1859..Totten, Silas 3: 496
1862..Spencer, Oliver M. ......
1866..Leonard, Nathan R. *(act.)* 25: 227
1868..Black, James ....
1870..Leonard, Nathan R. *(act.)* 25: 227
1871..Thacher, George ....
1877..Slagle, Christian W. 21: 186
1878..Pickard, Josiah L. 12: 512
1887..Schaeffer, Charles A. 26: 426
1898..Currier, Amos N. *(acting)* 20: 158
1899..MacLean, George E. 8: 362
1912..Bowman, John G. ....
1914..MacBride, Thomas H. ...11: 473
1916..Jessup, Walter A. ....
1934..Gilmore, Eugene A. ......

JEFFERSON COLLEGE
(Merged with Washington College to form Washington and Jefferson College in 1866)
CANONSBURG, PA.

1802..Watson, John ....
1803..Dunlap, James 5: 525
1812..Wylie, Andrew 13: 116
1817..McMillan, William ....
1822..Brown, Matthew 4: 539
1845..Breckenridge, Robert J. .. 9: 242
1847..Brown, Alexander B. ....
1857..Alden, Joseph 5: 406
1862..Riddle, David H. 24: 82

JEWISH THEOLOGICAL SEMINARY OF AMERICA
NEW YORK, N. Y.

1886..Morais, Sabato 10: 170
1902..Schechter, Solomon 13: 414
1915..Adler, Cyrus 11: 371

JOHN B. STETSON UNIVERSITY
DE LAND, FLA.

1885..Forbes, John F. 22: 360
1904..Hulley, Lincoln 24: 35
1934..Allen, William S. ....

JOHNS HOPKINS UNIVERSITY
BALTIMORE, MD.

1875..Gilman, Daniel C. 5: 170
1901..Remsen, Ira 9: 240
1913..Welch, William H. 10: 24
1915..Goodnow, Frank J. ...... C: 19
1929..Ames, Joseph S. .... A: 342
1935..Bowman, Isaiah ....

UNIVERSITY OF KANSAS
LAWRENCE, KANS.

1865..Oliver, Robert W. ....
1868..Fraser, John 9: 493
1874..Marvin, James 9: 493
1883..Lippincott, Joshua A. ... 9: 494
1890..Snow, Francis H. 9: 494
1901..Spangler, W. C. *(acting)*..
1902..Strong, Frank .... B: 217
1921..Lindley, Ernest H. .... B: 345

UNIVERSITY OF KENTUCKY
(Kentucky A & M College until 1908; State University until 1916)
LEXINGTON, KY.

1866..Williams, John A. ....
1867..Pickett, James D. ....
1869..Patterson, James K. 11: 422
1910..White, James G. *(acting)* .15: 313
1910..Barker, Henry S. ....
1917..Boyd, Paul P. *(acting)* ...
1917..McVey, Frank LeR. 13: 316

KENYON COLLEGE
GAMBIER, OHIO

1826..Chase, Philander 7: 1
1833..McIlvaine, Charles P. 7: 2
1841..Douglass, David B. 7: 3
1845..Bronson, Sherlock A. 7: 5
1850..Smith, Thomas M. 7: 6
1854..Andrews, Lorin 7: 6
1861..Vacant
1863..Short, Charles 7: 7
1867..Stone, James K. 7: 7
1868..Tappan, Eli Todd 7: 7
1876..Bodine, William Budd 23: 28
1891..Sterling, Theodore *(acting)* 7: 9
1896..Peirce, William F. 8: 138

KNOX COLLEGE
GALESBURG, ILL.

1839..Kellogg, Hiram H. ....
1845..Blanchard, Jonathan 21: 447
1858..Curtis, Harvey 21: 169
1863..Curtis, William S. 21: 170
1868..Gulliver, John P. 20: 375
1874..Bateman, Newton 27: 260
1892..Finley, John H. 13: 503
1900..McClelland, Thomas 20: 432
1918..McConaughy, James L. ... B: 424
1925..McKinley, Charles E. .....
1925..Britt, Albert ....

LAFAYETTE COLLEGE
EASTON, PA.

1832..Junkin, George 11: 240
1841..Yeomans, John W. 11: 241
1844..Junkin, George 11: 240
1848..Nassau, Charles W. 11: 241
1850..McLean, Daniel V. 11: 241
1857..McPhail, George W. 11: 242
1863..Cattell, William C. 11: 242
1883..Knox, James H. M. 11: 243
1890..Green, Traill 11: 243
1891..Warfield, Ethelbert D. ...11: 243
1915..MacCracken, John H. ...15: 205
1927..Lewis, William M. ....

LEHIGH UNIVERSITY
BETHLEHEM, PA.

1866..Coppee, Henry 7: 111
1875..Leavitt, John McD. 1: 507
1880..Lamberton, Robert A. ... 7: 111
1893..Coppee, Henry 7: 111
1895..Drown, Thomas M. 7: 112
1905..Drinker, Henry S. 15: 114
1922..Richards, Charles R. ..... B: 393
1935..Williams, Clarence C. ....

LELAND STANFORD JUNIOR UNIVERSITY
See Stanford University

LOUISIANA STATE UNIVERSITY
BATON ROUGE, LA.

1860..Sherman, William T. 4: 32
1865..Boyd, David F. 13: 235
1880..Johnston, William P. 9: 130
1883..Nicholson, James W. *(acting)* 13: 236
1884..Boyd, David F. 13: 235
1886..Nicholson, James W. 13: 236
1896..Boyd, Thomas D. 13: 236
1927..Atkinson, Thomas W. 24: 40
1930..Smith, James M. ....

UNIVERSITY OF MAINE
ORONO, MAINE

1871..Allen, Charles F. 14: 138
1879..Fernald, Merritt C. 14: 138
1893..Harris, Abram W. 14: 138
1901..Fellows, George E. 14: 139
1910..Aley, Robert J. 15: 13
1922..Little, Clarence C. .... B: 205
1926..Boardman, Harold S. .... D: 242
1935..Hauck, Arthur A. ....

UNIVERSITY OF MARYLAND
BALTIMORE, MD.

Administrator known as provost until 1920 when title was changed to president.

1813..Smith, Robert 3: 11
1815..Kemp, James 6:224
1826..Taney, Roger B. 1: 27
1839..Alexander, Ashton ......
1850..Kennedy, John P. 6:181
1870..Wallis, Severn T. 9:136
1894..Carter, Bernard ....
1912..Stockbridge, Henry (*pro tem*) ....
1913..Fell, Thomas 1:507
1920..Woods, Albert F. B:467
1926..Pearson, Raymond A. 15:299
1935..Byrd, Harry C. ....

MASSACHUSETTS INSTITUTE OF TECHNOLOGY
BOSTON, MASS.

1862..Rogers, William B. 7:410
1870..Runkle, John D. 6:350
1878..Rogers, William B. 7:410
1881..Walker, Francis A. 5:401
1897..Crafts, James M. 13:474
1900..Pritchett, Henry S. C:498
1909..Maclaurin, Richard C. ...14:483
1921..Nichols, Ernest F. 21: 68
1923..Stratton, Samuel W. 13:142
1930..Compton, Karl T. .... C: 81

MASSACHUSETTS STATE COLLEGE
(*Massachusetts Agricultural College until 1931*)
AMHERST, MASS.

1864..French, Henry F. 25:217
1866..Chadbourne, Paul A. 6:238
1867..Clark, William S. 5:310
1879..Flint, Charles L. (*ad int.*).25:338
1880..Stockbridge, Levi 5:508
1882..Chadbourne, Paul A. 6:238
1883..Greenough, James C. 27:348
1886..Goodell, Henry H. 8:116
1906..Butterfield, Kenyon L. ... B: 27
1924..Lewis, Edward M. ....
1927..Thatcher, Roscoe W. .....
1933..Baker, Hugh P. ....

MERCER UNIVERSITY
MACON, GA.

1833..Sanders, Billington M. ... 6:497
1839..Smith, Otis 26:262
1844..Dagg, John L. 6:497
1854..Crawford, Nathaniel M. .. 6:497
1866..Tucker, Henry H. 6:498
1871..Battle, Archibald J. 6:498
1890..Nunnally, Gustavus A. ... 6:498
1893..Gambrell, James B. 6:499
1896..Pollock, Pinckney D. 13:541
1905..Smith, Charles L. 14:459
1906..Jameson, Samuel Y. 25:282
1914..Pickard, William L. B:415
1918..Weaver, Rufus W. A:453
1928..Dowell, Spright ....

UNIVERSITY OF MICHIGAN
ANN ARBOR, MICH.

1855..Tappan, Henry P. 1:249
1863..Haven, Erastus O. 1:250
1869..Frieze, Henry S. 1:250
1871..Angell, James B. 1:251
1910..Hutchins, Harry B. 16:371
1920..Burton, Marion L. 14:113
1925..Little, Clarence C. B:205
1929..Ruthven, Alexander G. ... C: 95

MIDDLEBURY COLLEGE
MIDDLEBURY, VT.

1800..Atwater, Jeremiah 12:105
1809..Davis, Henry 7:405
1818..Bates, Joshua 12:106
1840..Labaree, Benjamin 12:106
1866..Kitchel, Harvey D. 12:106
1875..Hulbert, Calvin B. 12:106
1880..Hamlin, Cyrus 10:491
1885..Brainerd, Ezra 12:107
1908..Thomas, John M. 14:509
1921..Moody, Paul D. B:420

UNIVERSITY OF MINNESOTA
MINNEAPOLIS, MINN.

1869..Folwell, William W. 13:328
1884..Northrop, Cyrus 13:328
1911..Vincent, George E. ...... B: 6
1917..Burton, Marion L. 14:113
1921..Coffman, Lotus D. C:241

UNIVERSITY OF MISSISSIPPI
UNIVERSITY, MISS.

1848..Holmes, George F. 13:209
1849..Longstreet, Augustus B. .. 1:517
1856..Barnard, Frederick A. P. . 6:347
1865..Waddel, John N. 13:136
1874..Stewart, Alexander P. ... 4:502
1886..Mayes, Edward 13:480
1892..Fulton, Robert B. 13:547
1907..Kincannon, Andrew A. ..15:326
1914..Powers, Joseph N. ....
1924..Hume, Alfred ....
1935..Butts, Alfred B. ....

UNIVERSITY OF MISSOURI
COLUMBIA, MO.

1841..Lathrop, John H. 5:178
1849..Hudson, William W. 8:183
1850..Shannon, James 8:183
1856..Hudson, William W. 8:183
1860..Matthews, George H. 8:184
1860..Minor, Benjamin B. 8:184
1865..Lathrop, John H 5:178
1866..Read, Daniel 8:185
1876..Laws, Samuel S. 8:186
1889..Fisher, Michael M. 8:187
1891..Blackwell, James S. 8:187
1891..Jesse, Richard H. 8:188
1908..Hill, Albert R. 14:428
1922..Jones, John C. ....
1923..Brooks, Stratton D. 18:277
1930..Williams, Walter C:522

STATE UNIVERSITY OF MONTANA
MISSOULA, MONT.

1895..Craig, Oscar J. 25:218
1908..Duniway, Clyde A. 13:525
1912..Craighead, Edwin B. 14:143
1915..Scheuch, Frederick C. (*acting*) ....
1917..Sisson, Edward O. ....
1921..Clapp, Charles H. ....
1935..Scheuch, Frederick C. (*acting*) ....

MOUNT HOLYOKE COLLEGE
SOUTH HADLEY, MASS.

1837..Lyon, Mary 4:462
1849..Whitman, Mary C. ....
1850..Chapin, Mary W. ....
1865..Stoddard, Sophia H. (*act.*)
1867..French, Helen M. ....
1872..Ward, Julia E. ....
1883..Blanchard, Elizabeth .....
1889..Cowles, Louise F. ....
1890..Mead, Elizabeth S. 4:462
1900..Woolley, Mary E. .... D: 58

MUHLENBERG COLLEGE
ALLENTOWN, PA.

1867..Muhlenberg, Fred. A. 5:499
1877..Sadtler, Benjamin 5:500
1885..Seip, Theodore L. 5:500
1904..Haas, John A. W. 5:193

NATIONAL UNIVERSITY
WASHINGTON, D. C.

1869..Grant, Ulysses S. 4: 1
1877..Hayes, Rutherford B. 3:191
1881..Garfield, James A. 4:238
1881..Arthur, Chester A. 4:247
1885..Cleveland, Grover 2:400
1889..Miller, Samuel F. 2:473
1891..Hurst, John F. 9:122
1891..MacArthur, Arthur 13:477
1896..Alvey, Richard H. 12:231
1906..Carusi, Eugene 22:288
1925..Carusi, Charles F. 22:288
1931..Johnson, Hayden ....

NAVAL WAR COLLEGE
NEWPORT, R. I.

1884..Luce, Stephen B. 4:410
1886..Mahan, Alfred T. 10:440
1889..Goodrich, Caspar F. 13: 76
1889..Jewell, Theodore F. 13:194
1892..Mahan, Alfred T. 10:440
1893..Stockton, Charles H. 25:214
1893..Taylor, Henry C. 9: 15
1896..Goodrich, Caspar F. 13: 76
1898..Stockton, Charles H. 25:214
1900..Chadwick, French E. 9: 16
1902..Sperry, Charles S. 21: 51
1906..Merrell, John P. 6:108
1909..Rogers, Raymond P. .....
1911..Rogers, William L. ....
1913..Knight, Austin M. 24:324
1917..Parker, James P. ....
1919..Sims, William S. A:192
1922..Williams, Clarence S. ....
1925..Pratt, William V. C:513

UNIVERSITY OF NEBRASKA

LINCOLN, NEBR.

1871..Benton, Allen R. 8:360
1876..Fairfield, Edmund B. 8:360
1882..Hitchcock, Henry E. 8:361
1884..Manatt, James I. 8:361
1889..Bessey, Charles E. 8:361
1891..Canfield, James H. 7:417
1895..MacLean, George E. 8:362
1900..Andrews, Elisha B. 8: 26
1908..Avery, Samuel 14:473
1927..Burnett, Edgar A. ....

UNIVERSITY OF NEVADA

RENO, NEV.

1887..Brown, Le Roy D. 24:257
1889..Jones, Stephen A. 25:341
1894..Stubbs, Joseph E. 16: 42
1914..Hendrick, Archie W. .....
1917..Clark, Walter E. ....

UNIVERSITY OF NEW HAMPSHIRE

(New Hampshire College of Agriculture and Mechanic Arts until 1923)

DURHAM, N. H.

1866..Smith, Asa D. 9: 89
1877..Bartlett, Samuel C. 9: 89
1891..Stevens, Lyman D. *(act.)* .
1893..Murkland, Charles S. .....
1903..Gibbs, William D. ....
1912..Fairchild, Edward T. 19: 38
1917..Hetzel, Ralph D. B:349
1927..Lewis, Edward M. ....

COLLEGE OF THE CITY OF NEW YORK

NEW YORK, N. Y.

1848..Webster, Horace 19:320
1869..Webb, Alexander S. 3: 31
1903..Finley, John H. 13:503
1913..Werner, Adolph *(acting)*..
1914..Mezes, Sidney E. 15:206
1927..Robinson, Frederick B. .. C:115

NEW YORK UNIVERSITY

NEW YORK, N. Y.

1831..Mathews, James M. 6:323
1839..Frelinghuysen, Theodore .. 3:401
1852..Ferris, Isaac 6:323
1870..Crosby, Howard 4:193
1881..Hall, John 6:323
1891..MacCracken, Henry M. ... 6:324
1911..Brown, Elmer E. 14:252
1933..Chase, Harry W. A:298

UNIVERSITY OF NORTH CAROLINA

CHAPEL HILL, N. C.

1804..Caldwell, Joseph 13:241
1812..Chapman, Robert H. 13:242
1817..Caldwell, Joseph 13:241
1835..Swain, David L. 4:424
1869..Pool, Solomon 13:243
1876..Battle, Kemp P. 13:243
1891..Winston, George T. 13:243
1896..Alderman, Edwin A. 23: 38
1900..Venable, Francis P. 13:245
1914..Graham, Edward K. 19:147
1919..Chase, Harry W. A:298
1930..Graham, Frank P. D:409

UNIVERSITY OF NORTH DAKOTA

UNIVERSITY, N. DAK.

1884..Blackburn, William M. ... 9:441
1885..Montgomery, Henry *(acting)* .... Canadian
1887..Sprague, Homer B. 24: 65
1891..Merrifield, Webster 17:278
1909..McVey, Frank LeR. 13:316
1917..Babcock, Earle J. *(acting)* 25: 55
1918..Kane, Thomas F. ....
1933..West, John C. ....

NORTHWESTERN UNIVERSITY

EVANSTON, ILL.

1853..Hinman, Clark T. 5:471
1856..Foster, Randolph S. 13: 62
1867..Marcy, Oliver 13:536
1867..Wheeler, David H. *(act.)*..25:129
1869..Haven, Erastus O. 1:250
1872..Fowler, Charles H. 7:310
1876..Marcy, Oliver *(acting)* ...13:536
1881..Cummings, Joseph 9:430
1890..Marcy, Oliver 13:536
1890..Rogers, Henry W. 26: 50
1900..Bonbright, Daniel 25:420
1902..James, Edmund J. 11: 67
1906..Harris, Abram W. 14:138
1916..Holgate, Thomas F. B:184
1920..Scott, Walter D. ....

UNIVERSITY OF NOTRE DAME

NOTRE DAME, IND.

1842..Sorin, Edward ....
1865..Dillon, Patrick ....
1866..Corby, William ....
1872..Lemonnier, Augustus ....
1874..Colovin, Patrick J. ....
1877..Corby, William ....
1881..Walsh, Thomas E. ....
1893..Morrissey, Andrew 13:327
1905..Cavanaugh, John W. 14:473
1919..Burns, James A. ....
1922..Walsh, Matthew J. ......
1928..O'Donnell, Charles L. 25: 86
1934..O'Hara, John F. ....

OBERLIN COLLEGE

OBERLIN, OHIO

1835..Mahan, Asa 2:461
1851..Finney, Charles G. 2:462
1866..Fairchild, James H. 2:464
1891..Ballantine, William G. ... 2:465
1898..Barrows, John H. 8:116
1902..King, Henry C. 13:296
1927..Wilkins, Ernest H. ......

OHIO STATE UNIVERSITY

COLUMBUS, OHIO

1873..Orton, Edward 24:106
1881..Scott, Walter Q. 10:106
1883..Scott, William H. 7:417
1895..Canfield, James H. 7:417
1899..Thompson, William O. ...24:262
1926..Rightmire, George W. ...

OHIO UNIVERSITY

ATHENS, OHIO

1822..Irvine, James 4:443
1824..Wilson, Robert G. 4:443
1839..McGuffey, William H. 4:443
1848..Ryors, Alfred 4:444
1852..Howard, Solomon 4:444
1873..Scott, William H. 7:417
1884..Super, Charles W. 4:444
1896..Crook, Isaac 13:300
1898..Super, Charles W. 4:444
1901..Ellis, Alston 26:352
1920..Chubb, Edwin W. *(acting)*
1921..Bryan, Elmer B. 14:496
1934..Chubb, Edwin W. *(acting)*

OHIO WESLEYAN UNIVERSITY

DELAWARE, OHIO

1848..Thomson, Edward 4:159
1860..Merrick, Frederick 4:159
1875..Payne, Charles H. 4:159
1889..Bashford, James W. 4:160
1905..Welch, Herbert 14: 42
1916..Hoffman, John W. B:215
1928..Soper, Edmund D. ....

UNIVERSITY OF OREGON

EUGENE, OREG.

1876..Johnson, John W. ....
1893..Chapman, Charles H. ....
1899..Strong, Frank B:217
1902..Campbell, Prince L. 21:231
1926..Hall, Arnold B. ....
1932..Vacant
1934..Boyer, C. Valentine ......

PENNSYLVANIA STATE COLLEGE

STATE COLLEGE, PA.

1860..Pugh, Evan 11:320
1864..Allen, William H. 7: 13
1867..Fraser, John 9:493
1868..Burrowes, Thomas H. 25:439
1871..Calder, James 20:178
1880..Shortlidge, Joseph ....
1882..Atherton, George W. 20:486
1908..Sparks, Edwin E. 20:350
1921..Thomas, John M. 14:509
1926..Hetzel, Ralph D. B:349

UNIVERSITY OF PENNSYLVANIA
PHILADELPHIA, PA.

1754..Smith, William 1:340
1779..Ewing, John 1:341
1806..McDowell, John 1:342
1810..Andrews, John 1:342
1813..Beasley, Frederic 1:342
1828..Delancey, William H. 1:342
1834..Ludlow, John 1:343
1854..Vethake, Henry 1:344
1860..Goodwin, Daniel R. 1:344
1868..Stille, Charles J. 1:344
1881..Pepper, William 1:345
1895..Harrison, Charles C. 13:393
1911..Smith, Edgar F. 21: 53
1921..Penniman, Josiah H. D:104
1930..Gates, Thomas S. ....

PHILLIPS ACADEMY
ANDOVER, MASS.

1778..Pearson, Eliphalet 10: 94
1786..Pemberton, Ebenezer 10: 95
1795..Newman, Mark 10: 95
1810..Adams, John 10: 95
1833..Johnson, Osgood 10: 96
1838..Taylor, Samuel H. 10: 96
1871..Tilton, Frederic W. 10: 97
1873..Bancroft, Cecil F. P. 24:311
1903..Stearns, Alfred E. 13: 63
1933..Fuess, Claude M. ....

PHILLIPS EXETER ACADEMY
EXETER, N. H.

1783..Woodbridge, William 10:104
1788..Abbot, Benjamin 10:104
1838..Soule, Gideon L. 10:105
1873..Perkins, Albert C. 10:106
1884..Scott, Walter Q. 10:106
1890..Fish, Charles E. 10:107
1895..Amen, Harlan P. 10:107
1914..Perry, Lewis .... D: 41

PRINCETON UNIVERSITY
PRINCETON, N. J.

1746..Dickinson, Jonathan 5:463
1748..Burr, Aaron 5:463
1758..Edwards, Jonathan 5:464
1759..Davies, Samuel 5:465
1761..Finley, Samuel 5:465
1768..Witherspoon, John 5:466
1794..Smith, Samuel S. 2: 21
1812..Green, Ashbel 5:467
1823..Carnahan, James 5:467
1853..Maclean, John 5:467
1868..McCosh, James 5:468
1888..Patton, Francis L. 5:468
1902..Wilson, Woodrow 19: 1
1912..Hibben, John G. 15:199
1932..Dodds, Harold W. .... D: 59

PURDUE UNIVERSITY
LAFAYETTE, IND.

1872..Owen, Richard ....
1874..Shortridge, A. C. ....
1876..White, Emerson E. 13: 40
1883..Smart, James H. 6:106
1900..Stone, Winthrop E. 21:451
1921..Marshall, Henry W. ......
1922..Elliott, Edward C. B:361

RADCLIFFE COLLEGE
CAMBRIDGE, MASS.

1882..Agassiz, Elizabeth C. 12: 46
1903..Briggs, LeBaron R. 7: 81
1923..Comstock, Ada L. .... C: 21

RENSSELAER POLYTECHNIC INSTITUTE
TROY, N. Y.

1824..Blatchford, Samuel 20:394
1828..Chester, John 20:358
1829..Nott, Eliphalet 7:170
1845..Beman, Nathan S. S. 5:550
1865..Winslow, John F. 4:181
1867..Brinsmade, Thomas C. ...20:463
1868..Forsyth, James ....
1888..Peck, John H. 3:251
1901..Ricketts, Palmer C. 26:236

UNIVERSITY OF RICHMOND
(Richmond College until 1920)
RICHMOND, VA.

1832..Ryland, Robert 11:354
1866..Jones, Tiberius G. ....
1869..Puryear, Bennett *(chairman of faculty)* 11:354
1885..Harris, H. H. *(chairman of faculty)* ....
1889..Puryear, Bennett 11:354
1895..Boatwright, Frederick W. 11:353

ROANOKE COLLEGE
SALEM, VA.

1853..Bittle, David F. 10: 58
1876..Dosh, Thomas W. ....
1878..Dreher, Julius D. 10: 58
1903..Morehead, John A. 13:544
1920..Smith, Charles J. ....

ROBERT COLLEGE
ISTANBUL, TURKEY

1863..Hamlin, Cyrus 10:491
1878..Washburn, George 26:102
1903..Gates, Caleb F. C:167
1932..Monroe, Paul B:206

UNIVERSITY OF ROCHESTER
ROCHESTER, N. Y.

1850..Harris, Ira *(chancellor)* .. 2: 96
1853..Anderson, Martin B. 12:243
1889..Hill, David J. 12:244
1896..Lattimore, Samuel A. *(acting)* 12:244
1898..Burton, Henry F. *(acting)* 12:245
1900..Rhees, Rush 12:245
1908..Burton, Henry F. *(acting)* 12:245
1909..Rhees, Rush 12:245

RUTGERS COLLEGE
NEW BRUNSWICK, N. J.

1785..Hardenbergh, Jacob R. .. 3:399
1791..Linn, William 3:399
1794..Condict, Ira 3:400
1810..Livingston, John H. 3:400
1825..Milledoler, Philip 3:401
1840..Hasbrouck, Abraham B. .. 3:401
1850..Frelinghuysen, Theodore .. 3:401
1863..Campbell, William H. 3:402
1882..Gates, Merrill E. 5:309
1890..Doolittle, Theodore S. 3:403
1891..Scott, Austin 3:403
1906..Demarest, William H. S. .15: 35
1925..Thomas, John M. 14:509
1932..Clothier, Robert C. D:427

ST. LAWRENCE UNIVERSITY
CANTON, NEW YORK

1859..Lee, John S. 10:199
1868..Fisk, Richmond 10:199
1872..Gaines, Absalom G. 10:199
1889..Hervey, Alpheus B. 10:200
1896..Lee, John C. 10:200
1900..Gunnison, Almon 10:200
1916..Gallup, Frank A. ....
1919..Sykes, Richard E. A:250

SMITH COLLEGE
NORTHAMPTON, MASS.

1873..Seelye, Laurenus C. 7:121
1910..Burton, Marion L. 14:113
1917..Neilson, William A. A:286

UNIVERSITY OF SOUTH CAROLINA
COLUMBIA, S. C.

1804..Maxcy, Jonathan 8: 21
1820..Cooper, Thomas 11: 31
1834..Barnwell, Robert W. 11: 32
1841..Henry, Robert 11: 32
1845..Preston, William C. 11: 33
1851..Lieber, Francis 5:116
1851..Thornwell, James H. 11: 33
1855..McCay, Charles F. 11: 34
1857..LaBorde, Maximilian 11: 34
1857..Longstreet, Augustus B. .. 1:517
1863..Suspended
1866..Barnwell, Robert W. 11: 32
1880..Miles, William P. 11: 35
1883..McBryde, John McL. ...11: 35
1891..Woodrow, James 11: 35
1897..Woodward, Franklin C. ..11: 36
1902..Sloan, Benjamin 13:116
1908..Mitchell, Samuel C. 14: 88
1914..Currell, William S. 18:348
1922..Melton, William D. ......
1927..Douglas, Davison McD. ...26:186
1931..Baker, Leonard T. ....

UNIVERSITY OF SOUTH DAKOTA
VERMILLION, S. DAK.

1882..Epstein, Ephriam M. ....
1883..Simonds, John W. ....
1885..Herrick, John R. ....
1887..Olson, Edward ....
1890..Grose, Howard B. ....
1892..Mauck, Joseph W. ....
1897..Todd, James E. *(acting)* .10:117
1898..Droppers, Garrett 20: 16
1906..Gault, Franklin B. 18:200
1914..Slagle, Robert L. 25:411
1929..James, Herman G. D:287

STANFORD UNIVERSITY
PALO ALTO, CALIF.

1891..Jordan, David S. 22: 68
1913..Branner, John C. 24: 278
1916..Wilbur, Ray L. .... C: 12

STEVENS INSTITUTE OF TECHNOLOGY
HOBOKEN, N. J.

1870..Morton, Henry 24: 374
1902..Humphreys, Alexander C. 13: 203
1928..Davis, Harvey N. .... A: 348

SWARTHMORE COLLEGE
SWARTHMORE, PA.

1869..Parrish, Edward 5: 348
1872..Magill, Edward H. 6: 354
1889..Appleton, William H. ....
1891..DeGarmo, Charles 6: 354
1898..Birdsall, William W. 13: 113
1902..Swain, Joseph 6: 355
1921..Aldelotte, Frank ....

SYRACUSE UNIVERSITY
SYRACUSE, N. Y.

1871..Steele, Daniel 12: 490
1873..Winchell, Alexander 16: 119
1874..Haven, Erastus O. 1: 250
1881..Sims, Charles N. 13: 206
1893..French, John R. 2: 367
1894..Day, James R. 12: 418
1922..Flint, Charles W. .... B: 421

TEMPLE UNIVERSITY
PHILADELPHIA, PA.

1884..Conwell, Russell H. 3: 29
1926..Beury, Charles E. ....

UNIVERSITY OF TEXAS
AUSTIN, TEXAS

1884..Mallet, John W. 13: 55
1885..Waggener, Leslie 5: 280
1894..Miller, Thomas S. ....
1895..Waggener, Leslie 5: 280
1896..Winston, George T. 13: 243
1899..Prather, William L. ......
1905..Houston, David F. .... A: 38
1908..Mezes, Sidney E. 15: 206
1916..Vinson, Robert E. .... D: 370
1924..Sutton, William S. 21: 436
1925..Splawn, Walter M. W. ... B: 365
1927..Benedict, Harry Y. ...... D: 389

TRANSYLVANIA COLLEGE
(Transylvania Seminary until 1798; Kentucky University 1865-1908)
LEXINGTON, KY.

1785..Mitchell, James ....
1789..Wilson, Isaac ....
1791..Moore, James 4: 513
1794..Toulmin, Harry 4: 512
1796..Moore, James 4: 513
1804..Blythe, James 2: 123
1818..Holley, Horace 4: 513
1828..Woods, Alva 4: 514
1833..Peers, Benjamin O. 4: 514
1835..Coit, Thomas W. 4: 514
1837..Marshall, Louis 3: 164
1840..Davidson, Robert 4: 515
1842..Bascom, Henry B. 4: 515
1849..Dodd, James B. 4: 515
1856..Green, Lewis W. 2: 25
1859..Milligan, Robert 4: 515
1865..Bowman, John B. 4: 516
1878..White, Henry H. ....
1880..Loos, Charles L. 4: 516
1897..Cave, Reuben L. 4: 516
1901..Jenkins, Burris A. 13: 25
1908..Crossfield, Richard H. 14: 416
1922..Harmon, Andrew D. .....
1930..Braden, Arthur ....

TRINITY COLLEGE
HARTFORD, CONN.

1824..Brownell, Thomas C. 3: 495
1831..Wheaton, Nathaniel S. ... 3: 495
1837..Totten, Silas 3: 496
1848..Williams, John 3: 496
1853..Goodwin, Daniel R. 1: 344
1860..Eliot, Samuel 3: 496
1864..Kerfoot, John B. 3: 497
1867..Jackson, Abner 3: 497
1874..Pynchon, Thomas R. 3: 497
1883..Smith, George W. 3: 498
1904..Luther, Flavel S. 13: 126
1920..Ogilby, Remsen B. .... A: 94

TUFTS COLLEGE
MEDFORD, MASS.

1852..Ballou, Hosea, 2d 6: 241
1862..Miner, Alonzo A. 1: 315
1875..Capen, Elmer H. 6: 241
1905..Hamilton, Frederick W. ..14: 436
1914..Bumpus, Hermon C. 13: 110
1919..Cousens, John A. .... B: 360

TULANE UNIVERSITY OF LOUISIANA
(Medical College of Louisiana until 1847; University of Louisiana until 1884)
NEW ORLEANS, LA.

1834..Hunt, Thomas *(dean)* ....
1847..Hawks, Francis L. 7: 90
1850..McCaleb, Theodore H. 26: 390
1862..Suspended
1866..Hunt, Thomas ....
1867..Hunt, Randell ....
1884..Johnston, William P. 9: 130
1900..Alderman, Edward A. 23: 38
1905..Craighead, Edwin B. 14: 143
1912..Sharp, Robert 24: 141
1918..Dinwiddie, Albert B. .... D: 268

TUSKEGEE NORMAL AND INDUSTRIAL INSTITUTE
TUSKEGEE, ALA.

1881..Washington, Booker T. ... 7: 363
1916..Moton, Robert R. .... B: 75

UNION COLLEGE
SCHENECTADY, N. Y.

1791..Smith, John B. 2: 21
1799..Edwards, Jonathan, Jr. .. 7: 169
1802..Maxcy, Jonathan 8: 21
1804..Nott, Eliphalet 7: 170
1866..Hickok, Laurens P. 7: 171
1869..Aiken, Charles A. 7: 171
1872..Potter, Eliphalet N. 7: 171
1888..Webster, Harrison E. 7: 172
1894..Raymond, Andrew VanV. 7: 173
1907..Alexander, George 23: 227
1909..Richmond, Charles A. 14: 187
1928..Day, Frank P. .... C: 37
1933..Ellery, Edward *(acting)* ..
1934..Fox, Dixon R. ....

UNION THEOLOGICAL SEMINARY
NEW YORK, N. Y.

1836..McAuley, Thomas 7: 316
1840..Parker, Joel 7: 316
1842..Vacant
1873..Adams, William 7: 317
1880..Hitchcock, Roswell D. 2: 256
1888..Hastings, Thomas S. 7: 317
1897..Hall, Charles C. 6: 186
1908..Brown, Francis 14: 220
1916..McGiffert, Arthur C. 24: 120
1926..Coffin, Henry S. .... B: 36

UNITED STATES MILITARY ACADEMY
WEST POINT, N. Y.

1802..Williams, Jonathan 3: 239
1803..Vacant
1805..Williams, Jonathan 3: 239
1812..Swift, Joseph G. 10: 17
1817..Thayer, Sylvanus 7: 37
1833..DeRussy, Rene E. 4: 555
1838..Delafield, Richard 11: 29
1845..Brewerton, Henry 5: 503
1852..Lee, Robert E. 4: 95
1855..Barnard, John G. 4: 183
1856..Delafield, Richard 11: 29
1861..Beauregard, Pierre G. T. . 4: 178
1861..Delafield, Richard 11: 29
1861..Bowman, Alexander H. .. 5: 522
1864..Tower, Zealous B. 4: 225
1864..Cullum, George W. 4: 258
1866..Pitcher, Thomas G. 13: 420
1871..Ruger, Thomas H. 1: 229
1876..Schofield, John M. 4: 259
1881..Howard, Oliver O. 4: 103
1882..Merritt, Wesley 9: 28
1887..Parke, John G. 12: 242
1889..Wilson, John M. 4: 538
1893..Ernst, Oswald H. 4: 36
1898..Mills, Albert L. 11: 555
1906..Scott, Hugh L. 14: 494
1906..Biddle, John 26: 301
1910..Barry, Thomas H. 21: 116
1912..Townsley, Clarence P. 18: 113
1917..Tillman, Samuel E. ......
1919..MacArthur, Douglas ..... C: 407
1922..Sladen, Fred W. .... C: 210
1926..Stewart, Merch B. 26: 103
1927..Winans, Edwin B. ......
1928..Smith, William R. .... A: 54
1932..Connor, William D. ......

UNITED STATES NAVAL ACADEMY
ANNAPOLIS, MD.

1845..Buchanan, Franklin 4: 38
1847..Upshur, George P. 4:198
1850..Stribling, Cornelius K. ... 4:335
1853..Goldsborough, Louis M. .. 2:107
1857..Blake, George S. 13:422
1865..Porter, David D. 2: 97
1869..Worden, John L. 4:284
1874..Rodgers, Christopher R. P. 4:222
1878..Parker, Foxhall A. 5:368
1879..Balch, George B. 5: 30
1881..Rodgers, Christopher R. P. 4:222
1881..Ramsay, Francis M. 15:122
1886..Sampson, William T. 9: 9
1890..Phythian, Robert L. 13:180
1894..Cooper, Philip H. 16:235
1898..McNair, Frederick V. 10:255
1900..Wainwright, Richard 9: 17
1902..Brownson, Willard H. 25: 56
1905..Sands, James H. 20:321
1907..Badger, Charles J. .... B: 85
1909..Bowyer, John M. ....
1911..Gibbons, John H. ....
1914..Fullam, William F. 20:478
1915..Eberle, Edward W. 21:328
1919..Scales, Archibald H. .....
1921..Wilson, Henry B. B:350
1925..Nulton, Louis M. ....
1928..Robinson, Samuel S. .....
1931..Hart, Thomas C. ....

UNIVERSITY OF UTAH
SALT LAKE CITY, UTAH

1869..Park, John R. 22: 82
1894..Talmage, James E. 16: 19
1897..Kingsbury, Joseph T. ....
1916..Widtsoe, John A. ....
1921..Thomas, George ....

VANDERBILT UNIVERSITY
NASHVILLE, TENN.

1875..Garland, Landon C. 8:226
1893..Kirkland, James H. 8:227

VASSAR COLLEGE
POUGHKEEPSIE, N. Y.

1862..Jewett, Milo P. 5:234
1865..Raymond, John H. 5:234
1878..Caldwell, Samuel L. 5:235
1885..Kendrick, James R. 5:235
1886..Taylor, James M. 5:235
1915..MacCracken, Henry N. ... D:238

UNIVERSITY OF VERMONT
BURLINGTON, VT.

1800..Sanders, Daniel C. 2: 39
1815..Austin, Samuel 2: 39
1821..Haskel, Daniel 2: 40
1825..Preston, Willard 2: 40
1826..Marsh, James 2: 40
1833..Wheeler, John 2: 41
1849..Smith, Worthington 2: 41
1855..Pease, Calvin 2: 42
1862..Torrey, Joseph 2: 42
1866..Angell, James B. 1:251
1871..Buckham, Matthew H. ... 2: 42
1911..Benton, Guy P. 15:171
1920..Bailey, Guy W. B:427

VIRGINIA POLYTECHNIC INSTITUTE
BLACKSBURG, VA.

1872..Minor, C. L. C. ....
1879..Vacant
1880..Buchanan, John L. ......
1881..Conrad, Thomas M. ......
1886..Lomax, Lunsford L. 6: 16
1891..McBryde, John McL. 11: 35
1907..Barringer, Paul B. 13:512
1915..Eggleston, Joseph D. B:293
1919..Burruss, Julian A. ....

UNIVERSITY OF VIRGINIA
UNIVERSITY, VA.

(Administrator known as chairman of faculty until 1904, when title became president)

1825..Tucker, George 7:521
1826..Dunglison, Robley 10:270
1827..Lomax, John T. 5:531
1828..Tucker, George 7:521
1828..Dunglison, Robley 10:270
1830..Patterson, Robert M. 1:347
1832..Tucker, George 7:521
1833..Bonnycastle, Charles 13:180
1835..Davis, John A. G. 5:519
1837..Harrison, Gessner ....
1839..Davis, John A. G. 5:519
1840..Harrison, Gessner ....
1842..Tucker, Henry St. G. 7:520
1844..Rogers, William B. 7:410
1845..Courteney, Edward H. ... 5:519
1846..Cabell, James L. 12:452
1847..Harrison, Gessner ....
1854..Maupin, Socrates 13:134
1870..Venable, Charles S. 10:386
1873..Harrison, James F. .....
1886..Venable, Charles S. 10:386
1888..Thornton, William M. ....
1896..Barringer, Paul B. 13:512
1904..Alderman, Edwin A. 23: 38
1931..Newcomb, John L. ....

WASHINGTON COLLEGE
WASHINGTON COLLEGE, TENN.

1795..Doak, Samuel 7:340
1818..Doak, John W. 7:340
1821..Bovell, John V. 7:341
1829..McLin, James ....
1838..Doak, Samuel W. 7:341
1840..Foote, Joseph I. ....
1840..Doak, Archibald A. 7:341
1850..Baird, E. Thompson 7:342
1853..Doak, Archibald A. 7:341
1857..Hodge, Samuel 7:342
1866 {Telford, Eva A. ....
1866 {Telford, G. Ada ....
1868..Rankin, William B. 7:342
1877..Alexander, John E. 7:342
1883..Willoughby, John W. C. .. 7:342
1891..Cooter, James T. 7:342
1923..Lyle, Hubert S. ....
1932..Webb, Aquilla ....

WASHINGTON COLLEGE
(Merged with Jefferson College to form Washington and Jefferson College in 1866)
WASHINGTON, PA.

1806..Brown, Matthew 4:539
1817..Wylie, Andrew 13:116
1830..Elliot, David ....
1831..McConaulghy, David .....
1850..Clark, James ....
1852..Brownson, James I. .....
1853..Scott, John W. 20:460

WASHINGTON AND JEFFERSON COLLEGE
(See also Washington and Jefferson colleges)
WASHINGTON, PA.

1866..Edwards, Jonathan 2:124
1869..Wilson, Samuel J. ....
1870..Brownson, James I. ......
1870..Hays, George P. 2:302
1881..Moffat, James D. 21:179
1914..Hinitt, Fred W. 22:237
1918..Slemmons, William E. ...
1919..Black, S. Charles 23:153
1921..Baker, Simon S. 24:228
1931..Hutchinson, Ralph C. ....

WASHINGTON AND LEE UNIVERSITY
LEXINGTON, VA.

1775..Graham, William 3:163
1798..Campbell, Samuel L. 3:164
1799..Baxter, George A. 2: 24
1830..Marshall, Louis 3:164
1835..Vethake, Henry 3:164
1836..Ruffner, Henry 3:164
1848..Junkin, George 3:165
1865..Lee, Robert E. 3:165
1871..Lee, George W. C. 3:166
1897..Wilson, William L. 8:162
1900..Tucker, Henry St. G. 7:520
1902..Denny, George H. 13:101
1912..Smith, Henry L. 15:141
1930..Gaines, Francis P. D:302

WASHINGTON UNIVERSITY
ST. LOUIS, MO.

1858..Hoyt, Joseph G. 11:209
1862..Chauvenet, William 11:210
1869..Eliot, William G. 11:210
1887..Snow, Marshall S. 11:211
1891..Chaplin, Winfield S. 11:211
1908..Houston, David F. .... A: 38
1917..Hall, Frederic A. 20:187
1923..Hadley, Herbert S. ......
1928..Throop, George R. ....

WELLESLEY COLLEGE
WELLESLEY, MASS.

1875..Howard, Ada L. 7:328
1882..Palmer, Alice E. F. 7:328
1888..Shafter, Helen A. 7:328
1895..Irvine, Julia J. T. 12:221
1899..Hazard, Caroline C:501
1911..Pendleton, Ellen F. A:190

WESLEYAN UNIVERSITY
MIDDLETOWN, CONN.

1831..Fisk, Wilbur 3:177
1839..Olin, Stephen 9:429
1841..Bangs, Nathan 9:429
1842..Olin, Stephen 9:429
1852..Smith, Augustus W. 9:430
1857..Cummings, Joseph 9:430
1875..Foss, Cyrus D. 9:430
1880..Beach, John W. 9:431
1889..Raymond, Bradford P. ... 9:431
1909..Shanklin, William A. 14:292
1925..McConaughy, James L. ... B:424

WEST VIRGINIA UNIVERSITY
MORGANTOWN, W. VA.

1867..Martin, Alexander 7:383
1875..Scott, John W. 20:460
1877..Thompson, John R. 22:123
1881..Purinton, Daniel B. 1:304
1882..Wilson, William L. 8:162
1883..Berkley, Robert C. *(chairman of faculty)* ....
1885..Turner, Eli M. ....
1895..Goodnight, James L. .....
1897..Raymond, Jerome H. 25:401
1901..Purinton, Daniel B. 1:304
1911..Hodges, Thomas E. ....
1914..Trotter, Frank B. A:234
1928..Turner, John R. ....
1935..Boucher, Chauncey S. ....

WESTERN RESERVE UNIVERSITY
CLEVELAND, OHIO

1831..Storrs, Charles B. 2:326
1834..Pierce, George E. 7:224
1855..Hitchcock, Henry L. 7:224
1871..Cutler, Carroll 7:224
1888..Haydn, Hiram C. 7:225
1891..Thwing, Charles F. 7:226
1923..Vinson, Robert E. D:370

WILLIAM AND MARY COLLEGE
WILLIAMSBURG, VA.

1693..Blair, James 3:231
1743..Dawson, William 3:232
1752..Stith, William 3:232
1755..Dawson, Thomas 3:232
1761..Yates, William 3:233
1764..Horrocks, James 3:233
1772..Camm, John 3:233
1777..Madison, James 3:234
1812..Bracken, John 3:234
1814..Smith, John A. 3:234
1826..Wilmer, William H. 3:235
1827..Empie, Adam 3:235
1836..Dew, Thomas R. 3:235
1847..Saunders, Robert 3:236
1849..Johns, John 3:236
1854..Ewell, Benjamin S. 3:236
1888..Tyler, Lyon G. 3:237
1919..Chandler, Julian A. C. ..24: 73
1934..Bryan, John S. D:380

WILLIAMS COLLEGE
WILLIAMSTOWN, MASS.

1793..Fitch, Ebenezer 6:237
1815..Moore, Zephaniah S. 5:307
1821..Griffin, Edward D. 6:237
1836..Hopkins, Mark 6:237
1872..Chadbourne, Paul A. 6:238
1881..Carter, Franklin 6:239
1902..Hopkins, Henry 13: 96
1908..Garfield, Harry A. A:102
1934..Dennett, Tyler D:429

UNIVERSITY OF WISCONSIN
MADISON, WIS.

1848..Lathrop, John H. 5:178
1859..Barnard, Henry 1:505
1867..Chadbourne, Paul A. 6:238
1871..Twombly, John H. 12:147
1874..Bascom, John 8:196
1887..Chamberlin, Thomas C. ..19: 25
1892..Adams, Charles K. 4:477
1900..Birge, Edward A. 12:290
1903..VanHise, Charles R. 19: 19
1918..Birge, Edward A. 12:290
1925..Frank, Glenn C:454

UNIVERSITY OF WYOMING
LARAMIE, WYO.

1887..Hoyt, John W. 13:158
1891..Johnson, Albinus A. .....
1896..Graves, Frank P. A:277
1898..Smiley, Elmer E. ....
1903..Lewis, Charles W. ....
1904..Tisdel, Frederick M. .....
1908..Merica, Charles O. 17:334
1912..Duniway, Clyde A. 13:525
1917..Nelson, Aven ....
1922..Crane, Arthur G. ....

YALE UNIVERSITY
NEW HAVEN, CONN.

1701..Pierson, Abraham 1:164
1707..Andrew, Samuel 1:164
1719..Cutley, Timothy 1:165
1725..Williams, Elisha 1:165
1740..Clap, Thomas 1:166
1766..Daggett, Naphtali 1:166
1778..Stiles, Ezra 1:167
1795..Dwight, Timothy 1:168
1817..Day, Jeremiah 1:169
1846..Woolsey, Theodore D. 1:170
1871..Porter, Noah 1:171
1887..Dwight, Timothy 1:173
1899..Hadley, Arthur T. 9:267
1903..Gates, Caleb F. C:167
1921..Angell, James R. .... B: 5

Presidents of National Learned, Scientific and Technical Societies

Academy of Natural Sciences of Philadelphia

1812..Troost, Gerard 7: 349
1817..Maclure, William 13: 368
1840..Hembel, William 11: 187
1849..Morton, Samuel G. 10: 265
1851..Ord, George 13: 356
1858..Lea, Isaac 6: 23
1863..Wilson, Thomas B. 13: 165
1864..Bridges, Robert 5: 346
1865..Hays, Isaac 11: 256
1869..Ruschenberger, William S. W. 13: 369
1881..Leidy, Joseph 5: 220
1891..Wistar, Isaac J. 12: 359
1895..Dixon, Samuel G. 13: 562
1918..Cadwalader, John 15: 305
1922..Penrose, Richard A. F. .. 2: 443
1926..Palmer, T. Chalkley ......
1928..Morris, Effingham B. ...... A: 132

Actuarial Society of America

1889..Homans, Sheppard 6: 539
1891..Fackler, David P. 12: 446
1893..St. John, Howell W. 13: 58
1895..McClintock, Emory 12: 202
1897..Miller, Bloomfield J. 12: 95
1899..Macaulay, Thomas B. .. Canadian
1901..Ireland, Oscar B. 12: 520
1903..Pierson, Israel C. 25: 293
1905..Weeks, Rufus W. 14: 508
1906..Wells, Daniel H. 14: 167
1908..Gore, J. Kinsey 14: 112
1910..Welch, Archibald A. 25: 64
1912..MacDonald, William C. ...
1914..Craig, James M. 6: 197
1916..Hunter, Arthur ....
1918..Moir, Henry ....
1920..Hutcheson, William A. ...
1922..Henderson, Robert ....
1924..Wood, Arthur B. ....
1926..Rhodes, Edward E. ......
1928..Craig, James D. ....
1930..Strong, Wendell M. ......
1932..Thompson, John S. ......
1934..Parker, John G. ....

Agassiz Association

1875..Ballard, Harlan H. 9: 488
1907..Bigelow, Edward F. ......

American Academy of Arts and Letters

1908..Howells, William D. 1: 281
1920..Sloane, William M. 21: 95
1928..Butler, Nicholas Murray .. B: 186

American Academy of Arts and Sciences

1780..Bowdoin, James 2: 488
1791..Adams, John 2: 1
1814..Holyoke, Edward A. 7: 488
1820..Adams, John Q. 5: 73
1829..Bowditch, Nathaniel 6: 377
1838..Jackson, James 5: 401
1839..Pickering, John 7: 294
1846..Bigelow, Jacob 4: 526
1863..Gray, Asa 3: 407
1873..Adams, Charles F. 8: 351
1880..Lovering, Joseph 6: 425
1892..Cooke, Josiah P. 6: 12
1894..Agassiz, Alexander 3: 98
1903..Goodwin, William W. 6: 428
1908..Trowbridge, John 23: 53
1915..Walcott, Henry P. 12: 445
1917..Bowditch, Charles P. 20: 290
1919..Richards, Theodore W. ...12: 362
1921..Moore, George F. ....
1924..Lyman, Theodore 24: 347
1927..Wilson, Edwin B. .... D: 271
1931..Ford, Jeremiah D. M. ....
1933..Parker, George H. ....
1935..Pound, Roscoe .... B: 51

American Academy of Political and Social Science

1890..James, Edmund J. 11: 67
1901..Lindsay, Samuel McC. ...12: 374
1902..Rowe, Leo S. 18: 316
1930..Patterson, Ernest M. ..... D: 298

American Anthropological Association

1902..McGee, W J 10: 349
1905..Putnam, Frederic W. 23: 257
1907..Boas, Franz 12: 509
1909..Holmes, William H. 16: 441
1911..Fewkes, Jesse W. 15: 32
1913..Dixon, Roland B. 14: 353
1915..Hodge, Frederick W. 10: 51
1917..Kroeber, Alfred L. 14: 120
1919..Wissler, Clark .... B: 257
1921..Farabee, William C. 24: 207
1923..Hough, Walter 25: 277
1925..Hrdlicka, Ales .... C: 90
1927..Saville, Marshall H. .....
1929..Tozzer, Alfred M. ....
1931..MacCurdy, George G. ..... C: 98
1932..Swanton, John R. .... A: 26
1933..Cole, Fay-Cooper ....
1935..Lowie, Robert H. ....

American Antiquarian Society

1812..Thomas, Isaiah 6: 264
1831..Winthrop, Thomas L. 7: 504
1841..Everett, Edward 6: 179
1853..Davis, John 1: 115
1854..Salisbury, Stephen ....
1884..Hoar, George F. 1: 453
1887..Salisbury, Stephen, Jr. ... 7: 554
1905..Hale, Edward Everett 1: 199
1907..Lincoln, Waldo 14: 101
1927..Nichols, Charles L. 24: 423
1929..Coolidge, Calvin 24: 1
1934..Rugg, Arthur P. 17: 243

American Association for the Advancement of Science

1848..Rogers, William B. 11: 186
1848..Redfield, William C. 7: 354
1849..Henry, Joseph 3: 405
1850..Bache, Alexander D. 3: 348
1851..Agassiz, Louis 2: 360
1853..Pierce, Benjamin 8: 152
1854..Dana, James D. 6: 206
1855..Torrey, John 6: 361
1856..Hall, James 3: 280
1857..Bailey, Jacob W. 10: 157
1858..Wyman, Jeffries 2: 254
1859..Alexander, Stephen 11: 422
1860..Lea, Isaac 6: 23
1866..Barnard, Frederick A. P. 6: 347
1867..Newberry, John S. 9: 235
1868..Gould, Benjamin Apthorp 5: 108
1869..Foster, John W. 10: 169
1870..Chauvenet, William 11: 210
1871..Gray, Asa 3: 407
1872..Smith, J. Lawrence 6: 54
1873..Lovering, Joseph 6: 425
1874..LeConte, John L. 11: 106
1875..Hilgard, Julius E. 10: 118
1876..Rogers, William B. 7: 410
1877..Newcomb, Simon 7: 17
1878..Marsh, Othniel C. 9: 317
1879..Barker, George F. 4: 532
1880..Morgan, Lewis H. 6: 192
1881..Brush, George J. 10: 298
1882..Dawson, J. W. .... Canadian
1883..Young, Charles A. 6: 325
1884..Lesley, J. Peter 8: 79
1885..Newton, Hubert A. 9: 219
1886..Morse, Edward S. 24: 407
1887..Langley, Samuel P. 15: 7
1888..Powell, John W. 3: 340
1889..Mendenhall, Thomas C. ...10: 117
1890..Goodale, George L. 6: 427
1891..Prescott, Albert B. 13: 53
1892..LeConte, Joseph 7: 231
1893..Harkness, William 8: 395
1894..Brinton, Daniel G. 9: 265
1895..Morley, Edward W. 4: 520

1896..Cope, Edward D. 7:474
1897..Gibbs, Wolcott 10:469
1898..Putman, Frederic W. 23:257
1899..Orton, Edward 24:106
1899..Gilbert, Grove K. 13: 46
1900..Woodward, Robert S. 13:108
1901..Minot, Charles S. 6:112
1902..Hall, Asaph 22:287
1903..Remsen, Ira 9:240
1904..Wright, Carroll D. 19:421
1905..Farlow, William G. 22:207
1906..Woodward, Calvin M. 9:469
1907..Welch, William H. 26: 6
1908..Nicholas, Edward L. 4:482
1909..Chamberlin, Thomas C. ...19: 25
1910..Jordan, David Starr 22: 68
1911..Michelson, Albert A. ..... C: 42
1912..Bessey, Charles E. 8:361
1913..Pickering, Edward C. 6:424
1914..Wilson, Edmund B. 13: 59
1915..Eliot, Charles W. 6:421
1916..Campbell, William W. ...11:278
1917..VanHise, Charles R. 19: 19
1918..Richards, Theodore W. ...12:362
1919..Coulter, John Merle 11: 68
1920..Flexner, Simon .... B: 19
1921..Howard, Leland O. 12:356
1922..Moore, Eliakim H. 12:477
1923..McMurrich, J. Playfair ..14: 49
1924..Walcott, Charles D. 22:135
1925..Cattell, J. McKeen .... D: 94
1926..Pupin, Michael I. 26: 5
1927..Bailey, Liberty H. 10:145
1928..Noyes, Arthur A. 13:284
1929..Osborn, Henry Fairfield ..26: 18
1930..Millikan, Robert A. A:268
1931..Morgan, Thomas H. ..... D: 44
1932..Boas, Franz 12:509
1933..Abel, John J. A:392
1934..Compton, Karl T. .... C: 81
1935..Conklin, Edwin G. 12:351

American Association of Anatomists

1888..Leidy, Joseph 5:220
1891..Allen, Harrison 9:359
1893..Dwight, Thomas 12:101
1895..Baker, Frank 19:260
1897..Wilder, Burt G. 4:481
1900..Huntington, George S. ...12:236
1904..Minot, Charles S. 6:112
1906..Mall, Franklin P. 14:309
1908..McMurrich, James P. 14: 49
1910..Piersol, George A. ....
1912..Harrison, Ross G. 15:172
1914..Huber, G. Carl D:274
1918..Bensley, Robert R. ....
1920..McClure, Charles F. W. ..15:227
1922..Jackson, Clarence M. B:209
1924..Sabin, Florence R. C:288
1926..Streeter, George L. D:124
1928..Stockard, Charles R. .....
1930..Evans, Herbert M. ......
1932..Coghill, George E. ....
1934..Lewis, Warren H. ....

American Association of Economic Entomologists

1889..Riley, Charles V. 9:443
1891..Fletcher, James .... Canadian
1892..Lintner, Joseph A. 5:260
1893..Forbes, Stephen A. 22:291
1894..Howard, Leland O. 12:356
1895..Smith, John B. 13:201
1896..Fernald, Charles H. 9:232
1897..Webster, Francis M. 13:603
1898..Osborn, Herbert 13:202
1899..Marlatt, Charles L. 13:186
1900..Bruner, Lawrence 13:232
1901..Gillette, Clarence P. 13:407
1902..Felt, Ephraim P. 12:330
1903..Slingerland, Mark V. 13:315
1904..Quaintance, Altus L. .....
1906..Garman, Harrison 14:460
1906..Kirkland, Archie H. 14:433
1907..Morgan, John H. A. 14:439
1908..Forbes, Stephen A. 22:291
1909..Britton, Wilton E. A:260
1910..Sanderson, Dwight A:251
1911..Washburn, Frederick L. ..18: 74
1913..Hunter, Walter D. 21:155
1913..Parrott, Percival J. A:309
1914..Fernald, Henry T. 18:362
1915..Herrick, Glenn W. 18:259
1916..Hewitt, C. Gordon .... Canadian
1917..Cooley, Robert A. ....
1918..Ball, Elmer D. 18:263
1919..O'Kane, Walter C. ....
1920..Newell, Wilmon ....
1921..Dean, George A. ....
1922..Sanders, James G. ....
1923..Ruggles, Arthur G. ......
1924..Burgess, Albert F. ....
1926..Gibson, Arthur ....
1927..Harned, Robey W. ....
1928..Herms, William B. ....
1929..Headlee, Thomas J. ......
1930..Sherman, Franklin ....
1931..Houser, John S. ....
1932..Flint, Wesley P. ....
1933..Hinds, Warren E. ....
1934..Phillips, Everett F. ......
1935..Strong, Lee A. ....

American Association of Immunologists

1913..Webb, Gerald B. ....
1915..Jobling, James W. ....
1916..Weil, Richard ....
1917..Kolmer, John A. ....
1918..Park, William H. C:314
1919..Zinsser, Hans ....
1920..Cole, Rufus I. ....
1921..Gay, Frederick P. B:268
1922..McCoy, George W. .... C: 87
1923..Wells, H. Gideon ....
1924..Novy, Frederick G. 16: 93
1925..Manwaring, Wilfred H. .. C:110
1926..Hektoen, Ludwig 18:146
1927..Landsteiner, Karl D:403
1928..Opie, Eugene L D:242
1929..Avery, Oswald T. ....
1930..Bayne-Jones, Stanhope ... D:276
1931..Dochez, Alphonse R. .....
1932..Wadsworth, Augustus B. ..
1933..Rivers, Thomas M. ....
1934..Blake, Francis G. ....
1935..Longcope, Warfield T. ....
1936..Hooper, Sanford B. ......
1937..TenBroeck, Carl ....

American Association of University Professors

1915..Dewey, John A:547
1916..Wigmore, John H. .... A: 79
1917..Thilly, Frank ....
1918..Coulter, John Merle 11: 68
1919..Lovejoy, Arthur O. ......
1920..Capps, Edward A:416
1920..Kellogg, Vernon A:203
1921..Seligman, Edwin R. A. ...10: 49
1922..Denney, Joseph V. ....
1924..Leuschner, Armin O. .....
1926..Semple, William T. ......
1928..Crew, Henry 15: 60
1930..Munro, William B. D:404
1932..Cook, Walter W. ....
1934..Mitchell, Samuel A. ......

American Astronomical Society

1899..Newcomb, Simon 7: 17
1905..Pickering, Edward C. 6:424
1919..Schlesinger, Frank C:497
1922..Campbell, William W. 11:278
1925..Comstock, George C. 12:454
1928..Brown, Ernest W. 15: 24
1931..Adams, Walter S. B:171
1934..Russell, Henry N. A:346

American Bankers Association

1875..Hall, Charles B. 13: 39
1878..Mitchell, Alexander 1:362
1881..Coe, George S. 7:488
1883..Gage, Lyman J. 11: 14
1886..Murray, Logan C. 12:227
1888..Parsons, Charles 12:424
1890..McMichael, Morton, Jr. ..14:189
1892..Rhawn, William H. 12:532
1893..White, Mordecai M. 22:238
1894..Odell, John J. P. 13: 16
1895..Pullen, Eugene H. 4:560
1896..Lowry, Robert J. 12:234
1897..Hendrix, Joseph C. 12:235
1898..Russell, George H. 12:212
1899..Hill, Walker 12: 31
1900..Trowbridge, Alvah 12:448
1901..Herrick, Myron T. 13: 68
1902..Hardy, Caldwell 13:423
1904..Swinney, Edward F. 13: 91
1905..Hamilton, John L. 20:158
1906..Whitson, Gilson S. ....
1907..Powers, Joshua D. 25:431
1908..Reynolds, George M. .....
1909..Pierson, Lewis E. 15: 65
1910..Watts, Frank O. ....
1911..Livingstone, William 25:239
1912..Huttig, Charles H. 25:219
1913..Reynolds, Arthur ....
1914..Law, William A. ....
1915..Lynch, James K. ....
1916..Goebel, Peter W. ....
1917..Hinsch, Charles A. 24:226
1918..Maddox, Robert F. ....
1919..Hawes, Richard S. ....
1920..Drum, John S. ....
1921..McAdams, Thomas B. ....
1922..Puelicher, John H. A:155
1923..Head, Walter W. A:485
1924..Knox, William E. 26:185

1925..Wells, Oscar ....
1926..Traylor, Melvin A. .... C: 275
1927..Preston, Thomas R. ...... C: 333
1928..Hazlewood, Craig B. .....
1929..Lonsdale, John G. 13: 475
1930..Stephenson, Rome C. .....
1931..Haas, Harry J. ....
1932..Sisson, Francis H. 24: 400
1933..Law, Francis M. ....
1934..Hecht, Rudolph S. ....
1935..Fleming, Robert V. ...... D: 161

American Bar Association

1878..Broadhead, James O. 5: 68
1879..Bristow, Benjamin H. 4: 23
1880..Phelps, Edward J. 5: 411
1881..Potter, Clarkson N. 3: 60
1882..Lawton, Alexander R. ... 2: 148
1883..Parker, Cortlandt 12: 268
1884..Stevenson, John W. 13: 19
1885..Butler, William A. 7: 315
1886..Semmes, Thomas J. 10: 86
1887..Wright, George C. 3: 523
1888..Field, David D. 4: 236
1889..Hitchcock, Henry 11: 196
1890..Baldwin, Simeon E. 21: 86
1891..Dillon, John F. 1: 268
1892..Tucker, John R. 7: 487
1893..Cooley, Thomas McI. 9: 522
1894..Carter, James C. 22: 26
1895..Storey, Moorfield 12: 218
1896..Woolworth, James M. 11: 566
1897..Howe, William W. 13: 161
1898..Choate, Joseph H. 9: 159
1899..Manderson, Charles F. ... 1: 454
1900..Wetmore, Edmund 13: 376
1901..Rose, U. M. 7: 126
1902..Rawle, Francis 17: 388
1903..Hagerman, James 16: 169
1904..Tucker, Henry St. G. 7: 520
1905..Peck, George R. 10: 317
1906..Parker, Alton B. 10: 122
1907..Dickinson, Jacob M. 14: 410
1908..Lehmann, Frederick W. ..12: 30
1909..Libby, Charles F. 14: 332
1910..Farrar, Edgar H. 19: 346
1911..Gregory, Stephen S. 18: 273
1912..Kellogg, Frank B. .... A: 8
1913..Taft, William H. 23: 1
1914..Meldrim, Peter W. 24: 9
1915..Root, Elihu 26: 1
1916..Sutherland, George 13: 413
1917..Smith, Walter G. 21: 43
1918..Page, George T. .... A: 366
1919..Carson, Hampton L. 3: 264
1920..Blount, William A. 9: 492
1921..Severance, Cordenio A. ...19: 143
1922..Davis, John W. .... A: 25
1923..Saner, Robert E. L. ...... B: 152
1924..Hughes, Charles E. ...... A: 6
1925..Long, Chester I. .... C: 56
1926..Whiteman, Charles S. 15: 207
1927..Strawn, Silas H. .... C: 44
1928..Newlin, Guerney E. ......
1929..Sims, Henry U. .... A: 192
1930..Marvel, Josiah 18: 201
1930..Boston, Charles A. 16: 108
1931..Thompson, Guy A. ....
1932..Martin, Clarence E. ..... D: 278
1933..Evans, Earle W. ....
1934..Lottin, Scott M. ....
1935..Ransom, William L. .....

American Bible Society

1816..Boudinot, Elias 2: 296
1821..Jay, John 1: 20
1828..Varick, Richard 13: 471
1831..Smith, John C. 8: 120
1846..Frelinghuysen, Theodore .. 3: 402
1862..Bradish, Luther 3: 463
1864..Lenox, James 3: 413
1872..Allen, William Henry 7: 13
1881..Williams, Samuel Wells .. 1: 422
1884..Frelinghuysen, Theodore .. 3: 402
1885..Fancher, Enoch L. 7: 505
1903..Gilman, Daniel C. 5: 170
1909..Brouwer, Theophilus A. ..
1911..Wood, James 25: 266
1919..Cutting, Churchill H. ....
1924..Hyde, E. Francis 24: 124
1931..Talcott, J. Frederick ..... D: 438
1934..Manson, John T. .... D: 314

American Chemical Society

1876..Draper, John W. 3: 406
1877..Smith, J. Lawrence 6: 54
1878..Johnson, Samuel W. 6: 262
1879..Hunt, T. Sterry 3: 254
1880..Genth, Frederick A. 7: 493
1881..Chandler, Charles F. 23: 46
1882..Mallet, John W. 13: 55
1883..Booth, James C. 13: 245
1886..Prescott, Albert B. 13: 53
1887..Goessmann, Charles A. ...11: 350
1888..Hunt, T. Sterry 3: 254
1889..Chandler, Charles F. 23: 46
1890..Nason, Henry B. 2: 157
1891..Barker, George F. 4: 532
1892..Caldwell, George C. 4: 482
1893..Wiley, Harvey W. 21: 72
1895..Smith, Edgar F. 21: 53
1896..Dudley, Charles B. 12: 348
1898..Munroe, Charles E. 9: 234
1899..Morley, Edward W. 4: 520
1900..McMurtrie, William 12: 206
1901..Clarke, Frank W. 3: 525
1902..Remsen, Ira 9: 240
1903..Long, John H. 19: 31
1904..Noyes, Arthur A. 13: 284
1905..Venable, Francis P. 13: 245
1906..Hillebrand, William F. ...14: 132
1907..Bogert, Marston T. 14: 207
1909..Whitney, Willis R. 15: 393
1910..Bancroft, Wilder D. 14: 206
1911..Smith, Alexander 20: 421
1912..Little, Arthur D. 15: 64
1914..Richards, Theodore W. ...12: 362
1915..Herty, Charles H. 18: 85
1917..Stieglitz, Julius .... C: 401
1918..Nichols, William H. 24: 285
1920..Noyes, William A. .... B: 314
1921..Smith, Edgar F. 21: 53
1923..Franklin, Edward C. ..... A: 411
1924..Baekeland, Leo H. 15: 330
1925..Norris, James F. .... A: 190
1927..Rosengarten, George D. ..
1928..Parr, Samuel W. .... C: 153
1929..Langmuir, Irving .... C: 29
1930..McPherson, William ......
1931..Gomberg, Moses 16: 109
1932..Redman, Lawrence V. .... D: 148
1933..Lamb, Arthur B. ....
1934..Reese, Charles L. ....
1935..Adams, Roger ....

American College of Surgeons

1913..Finney, John M. T. .....
1916..Crile, George W. .... C: 72
1918..Mayo, William J. .... A: 330
1920..Armstrong, George E...Canadian
1921..Deaver, John B. 22: 7
1922..Cushing, Harvey .... C: 36
1923..Ochsner, Albert J. 20: 439
1924..Mayo, Charles H. .... A: 331
1925..Matas, Rudolph .... D: 399
1926..Chipman, Walter W. .. Canadian
1927..Stewart, George D. 23: 30
1928..Martin, Franklin H. ..... C: 372
1929..Ireland, Merritte W. ..... A: 220
1930..Miller, C. Jeff ....
1931..Kanavel, Allen B. ....
1932..Squier, J. Bentley ....
1933..Haggard, William D. .....
1934..Greenough, Robert B. 26: 379
1935..Pool, Eugene H. ....

American Dialect Society

1889..Child, Francis J. 8: 256
1891..Hart, James M. 9: 263
1893..Garnett, James M. 1: 506
1894..Sheldon, Edward S. 6: 189
1896..Grandgent, Charles H. ...13: 539
1897..Kittredge, George L. 13: 96
1898..Emerson, Oliver F. 13: 188
1899..Mott, Lewis F. 13: 583
1901..Hempl, George 13: 365
1906..Emerson, Oliver F. 13: 188
1910..Weeks, Raymond 18: 428
1911..Thomas, Calvin 16: 220
1913..Mead, William E. 16: 292
1916..Bright, James W. 20: 189
1922..Neilson, William A. ...... A: 286

American Economic Association

1886..Walker, Francis A. 5: 401
1892..Dunbar, Charles F. 9: 209
1894..Clark, John B. 13: 48
1896..Adams, Henry C. 12: 219
1898..Hadley, Arthur T. 9: 267
1900..Ely, Richard T. .... B: 201
1902..Seligman, Edwin R. A. ..10: 49
1904..Taussig, Frank W. ...... A: 457
1906..Jenks, Jeremiah W. ...... B: 140
1908..Patten, Simon N. 11: 230
1909..Dewey, Davis R. 13: 371
1910..James, Edmund J. 11: 67
1911..Farnam, Henry W. 24: 254
1912..Fetter, Frank A. .... B: 339
1913..Kinley, David .... B: 76
1914..Gray, John H. 15: 29
1915..Willcox, Walter F. .... A: 345
1916..Carver, Thomas N. ...... A: 349
1917..Commons, John R... ..... A: 423
1918..Fisher, Irving .... C: 51
1919..Gardner, Henry B. ....
1920..Davenport, Herbert J. ...26: 232
1921..Hollander, Jacob H. 13: 372
1922..Seager, Henry R. 22: 180
1923..Plehn, Carl C. .... A: 314
1924..Mitchell, Wesley C. ...... C: 511
1925..Young, Allyn A. ....
1926..Kemmerer, Edwin W. .... B: 126
1927..Adams, Thomas S. 25: 269

1928..Taylor, Fred M. 25: 37
1929..Gay, Edwin F. ....
1930..Hammond, Matthew B. ...
1931..Bogart, Ernest L. ....
1932..Barnett, George E. ....
1933..Ripley, William Z. ....
1934..Millis, Harry A. ....
1935..Clark, John M. ....

American Engineering Council

1920..Hoover, Herbert .... C: 1
1921..Cooley, Mortimer E. ..... A: 511
1923..Hartness, James 15: 294
1925..Kimball, Dexter S. .... D: 343
1927..Berresford, Arthur W. ... A: 378
1929..Grunsky, Carl E. 13: 224
1931..Lee, William S. 24: 155
1934..Coleman, John F. ....

American Entomological Society

1859..LeConte, John L. 11: 106
1861..Newman, George ....
1863..Bland, James H. B. ......
1866..Frazier, Robert ....
1867..Horn, George H. 7: 502
1869..Robinson, Coleman T. 21: 189
1870..LeConte, John L. 11: 106
1884..Horn, George H. 7: 502
1898..McCook, Henry C. 4: 131
1901..Calvert, Philip P. 12: 335
1916..Skinner, Henry 21: 139
1926..Williams, Roswell C., Jr. .
1935..Schmieder, Rudolph G. ...

American Fine Arts Society

1889..Butler, Howard R. .... B: 60
1906..Faxon, William B. ....
1921..Coffin, William A. 6: 368
1925..Dunsmore, John W. 10: 366

American Folk-Lore Society

1888..Child, Francis J. 8: 256
1890..Brinton, Daniel G. 9: 265
1891..Mason, Otis T. 10: 174
1892..Putnam, Frederic W. 23: 257
1893..Hale, Horatio 3: 358
1894..Fortier, Alcée 9: 135
1895..Matthews, Washington ...13: 54
1896..Bourke, John G. 13: 67
1897..Culin, Stewart 13: 216
1898..Wood, Henry 13: 585
1899..Edwards, Charles L. 13: 440
1900..Boas, Franz 12: 509
1901..Russell, Frank 12: 457
1902..Dorsey, George A. 22: 200
1903..Farrand, Livingston ..... A: 117
1904..Kittredge, George L. 13: 96
1905..Fletcher, Alice C. 5: 182
1906..Kroeber, Alfred L. 14: 120
1907..Dixon, Roland B. 14: 353
1909..Swanton, John R. .... A: 26
1910..Belden, Henry M. .... A: 297
1912..Lomax, John A. ....
1914..Goddard, Pliny E. 17: 419
1916..Lowie, Robert H. ....
1918..Barbeau, C. Marius ......
1919..Parsons, Elsie C. ....
1921..Speck, Frank G. ....
1923..Espinosa, Aurelio M. .....
1925..Pound, Louise .... B: 51
1927..Tozzer, Alfred M. ....
1929..Sapir, Edward ....
1931..Boas, Franz 12: 509
1932..Beckwith, Martha W. ....
1934..Boas, Franz 12: 509
1935..Taylor, Archer ....

American Forestry Association

1875..Warder, John A. 4: 536
1883..Loring, George B. 15: 349
1885..Higley, Warren 3: 504
1887..Minier, George W. 12: 186
1888..Pringle, Coleman R. 4: 309
1889..Beaver, James A. 2: 293
1891..Alvord, William 12: 326
1893..Morton, J. Sterling 6: 487
1897..Appleton, Francis H. 12: 231
1899..Wilson, James 14: 27
1909..Guild, Curtis 9: 502
1910..Bass, Robert P. .... B: 284
1913..Drinker, Henry S. 15: 114
1916..Pack, Charles L. .... A: 408
1923..Graves, Henry S. .... A: 479
1924..Pratt, George D. .... C: 384
1934..Graves, Henry S. .... A: 479

American Genetic Association

1903..Wilson, James 14: 27
1913..Fairchild, David .... C: 253

American Geographical Society

1852..Bancroft, George 3: 160
1855..Hawks, Francis L. 7: 90
1861..Grinnell, Henry 3: 281
1864..Daly, Charles P. 3: 158
1900..Low, Seth 6: 348
1903..Peary, Robert E. 14: 60
1907..Huntington, Archer M. ..15: 19
1916..Greenough, John ....
1925..Finley, John H. 13: 503
1934..Redmond, Roland L. .....

American Gynecological Society

1876..Barker, Fordyce 4: 157
1878..Peaslee, Edmund R. 10: 289
1879..Thomas, T. Gaillard 26: 49
1880..Sims, J. Marion 2: 356
1881..Byford, William H. 2: 13
1882..Emmet, Thomas A. 10: 286
1883..Kimball, Gilman 5: 200
1884..Smith, Albert H. 12: 421
1885..Howard, William T. 12: 316
1886..Reamy, Thaddeus A. 12: 474
1887..Skene, Alexander J. C. ... 5: 436
1888..Battey, Robert 9: 349
1889..Wilson, Henry P. C. 6: 340
1890..Reynolds, John P. 12: 216
1891..Jackson, Abraham R. 7: 510
1892..Byrne, John 9: 336
1893..Parvin, Theophilus 4: 305
1894..Lusk, William T. 9: 337
1895..Mann, Matthew D. 10: 84
1896..Polk, William M. 2: 109
1897..Chadwick, James R. 12: 368
1898..Mundé, Paul F. 12: 272
1899..Johnson, Joseph Tabor ...12: 143
1900..Engelmann, George J. 11: 157
1901..Van De Warker, Ely 12: 187
1902..Gordon, Seth C. 12: 66
1903..Janvrin, Joseph E. ......
1904..Reynolds, Edward 9: 556
1905..Dudley, Emilius C. 13: 109
1906..Maury, Richard B. 14: 240
1907..Cleveland, Clement 14: 426
1908..Baldy, J. Montgomery 14: 144
1909..Goffe, J. Riddle 25: 83
1910..Davis, Edward P. .... A: 440
1911..Peterson, Reuben .... B: 190
1912..Kelly, Howard A. 15: 210
1913..Coe, Henry C. ....
1914..Williams, J. Whitridge ...25: 187
1915..Watkins, Thomas J. ......
1916..Bovee, J. Wesley 22: 257
1917..Simpson, Frank F. ....
1918..Clark, John G. 21: 63
1919..Martin, Franklin H. ..... C: 372
1920..Dickinson, Robert L. .....
1921..Chipman, Walter W. .. Canadian
1922..Ward, George G. ....
1923..Simpson, John A. ....
1924..Hirst, Barton C. ....
1925..Taylor, Howard C. ....
1926..Newell, Franklin S. ......
1927..Curtis, Arthur H. .... D: 244
1928..Brettauer, Joseph ....
1929..Miller, C. Jeff ....
1930..Norris, Charles C. ....
1931..Graves, William P. ...... A: 141
1932..Gellhorn, George ....
1933..Keene, Floyd E. ....
1934..Lynch, Frank W. ....
1935..Anspach, Brooke M. .....

American Historical Association

1884..White, Andrew D. 4: 476
1885..Bancroft, George 3: 160
1886..Winsor, Justin 1: 150
1887..Poole, William F. 6: 479
1888..Adams, Charles K. 4: 477
1889..Jay, John 7: 347
1890..Henry, William W. 9: 272
1891..Angell, James B. 1: 251
1893..Adams, Henry 11: 475
1895..Hoar, George F. 1: 453
1896..Storrs, Richard S. 8: 110
1897..Schouler, James 11: 181
1898..Fisher, George P. 10: 424
1899..Rhodes, James F. 7: 92
1900..Eggleston, Edward 6: 57
1901..Adams, Charles F. 8: 353
1902..Mahan, Alfred T. 10: 440
1903..Lea, Henry C. 23: 17
1904..Smith, Goldwin ....
1905..McMaster, John B. 11: 445
1906..Baldwin, Simeon E. 21: 86
1907..Jameson, John F. 10: 442
1908..Adams, George B. 14: 253
1909..Hart, Albert B. 11: 394
1910..Turner, Frederick J. 13: 174
1911..Sloane, William M. 21: 95
1912..Roosevelt, Theodore 14: 1
1913..Dunning, William A. 19: 27

1914..McLaughlin, Andrew C. ..13: 217
1915..Stephens, H. Morse 13: 463
1916..Burr, George L. 4: 479
1917..Ford, Worthington C. 13: 105
1918..Thayer, William R. 12: 530
1920..Channing, Edward 13: 432
1921..Jusserand, Jean J. ....
1922..Haskins, Charles H. ..... C: 378
1923..Cheyney, Edward P. .....
1924..Wilson, Woodrow 19: 1
1925..Andrews, Charles McL. ..13: 160
1926..Munro, Dana C. 23: 81
1927..Taylor, Henry O. ....
1928..Breasted, James H. ...... B: 377
1929..Robinson, James Harvey . C: 28
1930..Greene, Evarts B. .... C: 278
1931..Becker, Carl L. ....
1932..Bolton, Herbert E. .... A: 204
1933..Beard, Charles A. .... D: 231
1934..Dodd, William E. .... D: 34
1935..Rostovtzeff, Michael .....

American Institute of Architects

1857..Upjohn, Richard 2: 182
1877..Walter, Thomas U. 9: 333
1888..Hunt, Richard M. 6: 430
1892..Kendall, Edward H. 12: 247
1894..Burnham, Daniel H. 9: 335
1896..Post, George B. 15: 250
1899..Van Brunt, Henry 11: 324
1900..Peabody, Robert S. 12: 200
1902..McKim, Charles F. 23: 89
1904..Eames, William S. 13: 216
1906..Day, Frank M. 14: 311
1908..Gilbert, Cass .... C: 464
1910..Pond, Irving K. .... C: 127
1912..Cook, Walter 14: 344
1913..Sturgis, R. Clipston ...... A: 368
1915..Mauran, John L. ....
1918..Kimball, Thomas R. 25: 364
1920..Kendall, Henry H. ......
1922..Faville, William B. ......
1924..Waid, D. Everett .... B: 28
1926..Medary, Milton B. 24: 424
1928..Hammond, C. Herrick ....
1930..Kohn, Robert D. ....
1932..Russell, Ernest J. ....
1935..Voorhees, Stephen F. ....

American Institute of Consulting Engineers

1910..Boller, Alfred P. 9: 43
1912..Noble, Alfred 9: 44
1914..Sprague, Frank J. 24: 15
1915..Corthell, Elmer L. 9: 42
1916..Gibbs, George ....
1918..Stillwell, Lewis B. 14: 520
1920..Humphreys, Alexander C...13: 203
1923..Leavitt, Charles W. 24: 37
1924..Kinnear, Wilson S. ...... D: 393
1926..Parsons, Harry deB. .....
1927..Fay, Frederic H. .... C: 292
1928..Coleman, John F. ....
1929..Main, Charles T. 15: 327
1930..Molitor, Frederick A. ....
1932..Perin, Charles P. ....
1934..Burpee, George W. .... C: 178

American Institute of Electrical Engineers

1884..Green, Norvin 11: 550
1886..Pope, Franklin L. 7: 414
1887..Martin, T. Commeford ...13: 582
1888..Weston, Edward 5: 176
1889..Thomson, Elihu .... B: 106
1890..Anthony, William A. 11: 389
1891..Bell, Alexander Graham .. 6: 220
1892..Sprague, Frank J. 24: 15
1893..Houston, Edwin J. 13: 359
1895..Duncan, Louis 14: 145
1897..Crocker, Francis B. 12: 424
1898..Kennelly, Arthur E. 13: 452
1900..Hering, Carl 12: 349
1901..Steinmetz, Charles P. 23: 94
1902..Scott, Charles F. 13: 207
1903..Arnold, Bion J. .... B: 456
1904..Lieb, John W. 13: 606
1905..Wheeler, Schuyler S. 10: 162
1906..Sheldon, Samuel 14: 208
1907..Stott, Henry G. 14: 240
1908..Ferguson, Louis A. 14: 526
1909..Stillwell, Lewis B. 14: 520
1910..Jackson, Dugald C. ...... B: 357
1911..Dunn, Gano S. 18: 105
1912..Mershon, Ralph D. 15: 225
1913..Mailloux, Cyprien O. 26: 428
1914..Lincoln, Paul M. .... B: 280
1915..Carty, John J. 23: 36
1916..Buck, Harold W. ....
1917..Rice, E. Wilbur 26: 10
1918..Adams, Comfort A. ...... A: 421
1919..Townley, Calvert 24: 340
1920..Berresford, Arthur W. ... A: 378
1921..McClellin, William ....
1922..Jewett, Frank B. .... C: 272
1923..Ryan, Harris J. ....
1924..Osgood, Farley ....
1925..Pupin, Michael I. 26: 5
1926..Chesney, Cummings C. ...
1927..Gherardi, Bancroft 12: 489
1928..Schuchardt, Rudolph F. ..
1929..Smith, Harold B. ....
1930..Lee, William S. 24: 155
1931..Skinner, Charles E. ......
1932..Charlesworth, Harry P. ..
1933..Whitehead, John B. ......
1934..Johnson, J. Allen ....
1935..Meyer, Edward B. ....

American Institute of Mining and Metallurgical Engineers

1871..Thomas, David 3: 360
1872..Raymond, Rossiter W. ... 8: 44
1875..Holley, Alexander L. 11: 508
1876..Hewitt, Abram S. 3: 294
1877..Hunt, T. Sterry 3: 254
1878..Coxe, Eckley B. 11: 559
1880..Shinn, William P. 11: 344
1881..Metcalf, William 12: 232
1882..Rothwell, Richard P. 10: 229
1883..Hunt, Robert W. 19: 17
1884..Bayles, James C. 13: 437
1886..Richards, Robert H. 12: 347
1887..Egleston, Thomas 3: 244
1888..Potter, William B. 13: 21
1889..Pearce, Richard ....
1890..Hewitt, Abram S. 3: 294
1891..Birkinbine, John 12: 199
1893..Howe, Henry M. 13: 78
1894..Fritz, John 13: 74
1895..Weeks, Joseph D. 13: 27
1896..Spilsbury, Edmund G. 13: 546
1897..Drown, Thomas M. 7: 112
1898..Kirchhoff, Charles 10: 227
1899..Douglas, James 23: 22
1901..Olcott, Eben E. 5: 265
1903..Ledoux, Albert R. 12: 449
1904..Gayley, James 14: 70
1906..Hunt, Robert W. 19: 17
1907..Hammond, John Hays ...26: 45
1909..Brunton, David W. 23: 99
1911..Gayley, James 14: 70
1912..Kemp, James F. 21: 5
1913..Rand, Charles F. 21: 333
1914..Thayer, Benjamin B. 15: 66
1915..Saunders, William L. 26: 81
1916..Ricketts, Louis D. ....
1917..Moore, Philip N. ....
1918..Jennings, Sidney J. 26: 326
1919..Winchell, Horace V. 20: 200
1920..Hoover, Herbert .... C: 1
1921..Ludlow, Edwin 23: 151
1922..Dwight, Arthur S. .... C: 228
1923..Mathewson, Edward P. ... C: 41
1924..Kelly, William .... D: 300
1925..Reynders, John V. ....
1926..Taylor, Samuel A. ....
1927..DeGolyer, Everette L. .... D: 356
1928..Smith, George O. 14: 130
1929..Bradley, Frederick W. ....
1930..Bassett, William H. 26: 156
1931..Tally, Robert E. ....
1932..Turner, Scott ....
1933..Becket, Frederick M. ..... B: 163
1934..Eavenson, Howard N. ... A: 364
1935..Buehler, Henry A. ....

American Iron and Steel Institute

1908..Gary, Elbert H. 14: 69
1927..Schwab, Charles M. ...... A: 238
1932..Lamont, Robert P. .... C: 13
1934..Grace, Eugene G. ....

American Library Association

1876..Winsor, Justin 1: 150
1885..Poole, William F. 6: 478
1887..Cutter, Charles A. 13: 180
1889..Crunden, Frederick M. ... 6: 480
1890..Dewey, Melvil 23: 14
1891..Green, Samuel S. 6: 484
1891..Fletcher, William I. 12: 379
1892..Dewey, Melvil 23: 14
1893..Larned, Josephus N. 16: 344
1894..Utley, Henry M. 17: 213
1895..Dana, John Cotton 22: 321
1896..Brett, William H. 6: 480
1897..Winsor, Justin 1: 150
1898..Putnam, Herbert .... D: 52
1898..Lane, William Coolidge ...12: 261
1899..Thwaites, Reuben G. 10: 35
1900..Carr, Henry J. 12: 368
1901..Billings, John S. 4: 78
1902..Hosmer, James K. 6: 481
1903..Putnam, Herbert .... D: 52
1904..Richardson, Ernest C. ...13: 461
1905..Hill, Frank P. 2: 149
1906..Andrews, Clement W. 14: 340

1907..Bostwick, Arthur E. 14: 339
1908..Gould, Charles H. ..... Canadian
1909..Hodges, Nathaniel D. C. ..12: 262
1910..Wyer, James I. .... D: 44
1911..Elmendorf, Theresa H. W. 23: 28
1912..Legler, Henry E. 24: 296
1913..Anderson, Edwin H. ..... D: 56
1914..Wellman, Hiller C. .... A: 293
1915..Plummer, Mary W. 21: 107
1916..Brown, Walter L. 24: 107
1917..Montgomery, Thomas L. .24: 396
1918..Bishop, William W. ..... D: 312
1919..Hadley, Chalmers .... A: 258
1920..Tyler, Alice S. ....
1921..Root, Azariah S. 22: 113
1922..Utley, George B. .... A: 481
1923..Jennings, Judson T. ..... D: 282
1924..Meyer, Herman H. B. .... D: 92
1925..Belden, Charles F. D. 23: 53
1926..Locke, George H. ..... Canadian
1927..Roden, Carl B. .... C: 479
1928..Eastman, Linda A. ...... C: 465
1929..Keogh, Andrew .... D: 267
1930..Strohm, Adam ....
1931..Rathbone, Josephine A. .. D: 411
1932..Lydenberg, Harry M. ....
1933..Countryman, Gratia A. ..
1934..Compton, Charles H. .....
1935..Wilson, Louis R. ....

American Mathematical Society

1889..VanAmringe, John H. ...13: 241
1891..McClintock, Emory 12: 202
1895..Hill, George W. 13: 442
1897..Newcomb, Simon 7: 17
1899..Woodward, Robert S. 13: 108
1901..Moore, Eliakim H. 12: 447
1903..Fiske, Thomas S. 12: 489
1905..Osgood, William F. 13: 524
1907..White, Henry S. 14: 382
1909..Bocher, Maxim 18: 302
1911..Fine, Henry B. 14: 499
1913..VanVleck, Edward B. .... A: 338
1915..Brown, Ernest W. 15: 24
1917..Dickson, Leonard E. 18: 411
1919..Morley, Frank 15: 147
1921..Bliss, Gilbert A. .... A: 371
1923..Veblen, Oswald ....
1925..Birkhoff, George D. ......
1927..Snyder, Virgil ....
1929..Hedrick, Earle R. ....
1931..Eisenhart, Luther P. .....
1933..Coble, Arthur B. ....
1935..Lepchetz, Solomon ....

American Medical Association

1847..Chapman, Nathaniel 3: 294
1848..Stevens, Alexander H. 9: 355
1849..Warren, John C. 6: 426
1850..Mussey, Reuben D. 9: 91
1851..Moultrie, James 12: 229
1852..Wellford, Beverly R. 12: 201
1853..Knight, Jonathan 12: 228
1854..Pope, Charles A. 12: 217
1855..Wood, George B. 5: 346
1856..Pitcher, Zina 12: 214
1857..Eve, Paul F. 10: 30
1858..Lindsley, Harvey 12: 205
1859..Miller, Henry 12: 229
1860..Ives, Eli 12: 253
1863..March, Alden 2: 445
1864..Davis, Nathan S. 10: 266
1866..Storer, D. Humphreys ...11: 336
1867..Askew, Henry F. ....
1868..Gross, Samuel D. 8: 216
1869..Baldwin, William O. 12: 473
1870..Mendenhall, George 12: 230
1871..Stillé, Alfred 9: 358
1872..Yandell, David W. 12: 219
1873..Logan, Thomas M. 12: 235
1874..Toner, Joseph M. 7: 539
1875..Bowling, William K. 12: 225
1876..Sims, J. Marion 2: 356
1877..Bowditch, Henry I. 8: 214
1878..Richardson, Tobias G. 9: 554
1879..Parvin, Theophilus 4: 305
1880..Sayre, Lewis A. 2: 31
1881..Hodgen, John T. 8: 204
1882..Woodward, Joseph J. 11: 518
1883..Atlee, John L. 11: 25
1884..Flint, Austin 8: 311
1885..Campbell, Henry F. 12: 68
1886..Brodie, William 12: 224
1887..Gregory, Elisha H. 10: 504
1888..Garnett, Alexander Y. P...12: 230
1889..Dawson, William W. 12: 250
1890..Moore, Edward M. 12: 55
1891..Briggs, William T. 12: 56
1892..Marcy, Henry O. 6: 510
1893..McGuire, Hunter 5: 163
1894..Hibberd, James F. 12: 236
1895..Maclean, Donald 5: 536
1896..Cole, Richard B. 7: 288
1897..Senn, Nicholas 6: 371
1898..Sternberg, George M. 4: 388
1899..Mathews, Joseph McD. ..13: 18
1900..Keen, William W. 11: 367
1901..Reed, Charles A. L. 24: 325
1902..Wyeth, John A. 6: 74
1903..Billings, Frank 23: 315
1904..Musser, John H. 13: 545
1905..McMurtry, Lewis S. 13: 280
1906..Mayo, William J. .... A: 330
1907..Bryant, Joseph D. 23: 31
1908..Burrell, Herbert L. 14: 506
1909..Gorgas, William C. 14: 528
1910..Welch, William H. 26: 6
1911..Murphy, John B. 13: 602
1912..Jacobi, Abraham 9: 345
1913..Witherspoon, John A. ....
1914..Vaughan, Victor C. 12: 207
1915..Rodman, William L. 27: 228
1915..Vander Veer, Albert 16: 359
1916..Blue, Rupert 15: 129
1917..Mayo, Charles H. .... A: 331
1918..Bevan, Arthur D. .... D: 90
1919..Lambert, Alexander ..... D: 219
1920..Braisted, William C. ..... A: 76
1921..Work, Hubert .... A: 14
1922..DeSchweinitz, George E. . C: 144
1923..Wilbur, Ray Lyman ...... C: 12
1924..Pusey, William A. ....
1925..Haggard, William D. .....
1926..Phillips, Wendell C. 25: 186
1927..Jackson, Jabez N. ....
1928..Thayer, William S. 24: 409
1929..Harris, Malcolm LaS. 26: 99
1930..Morgan, William G. ..... C: 94
1931..Judd, E. Starr ....
1932..Cary, Edward H. ....
1933..Lewis, Dean D. ....
1934..Bierring, Walter L. ......
1935..McLester, James S. ......

American Meteorological Society

1920..Ward, Robert DeC. 24: 190
1922..Stupart, Frederic .... English
1924..Milham, Willis I. 14: 430
1926..Marvin, Charles F. 16: 47
1928..Humphreys, William J. ..
1930..Patterson, John ....
1932..Kimball, Herbert H. .....
1934..Cline, Isaac M. 16: 126

American Microscopical Society

1878..Ward, Richard H. 13: 149
1879..Smith, Hamilton L. 12: 466
1880..Hyatt, Jonathan D. 13: 566
1881..Blackham, George E. 13: 15
1882..McCalla, Albert 13: 313
1883..Cox, Jacob D. 22: 231
1884..Smith, Hamilton L. 12: 466
1885..Burrill, Thomas J. 18: 187
1886..Rogers, William A. 9: 530
1887..Kellicott, David S. 13: 299
1888..Lewis, William J. 13: 17
1889..Fell, George E. 12: 340
1890..James, Frank L. 12: 226
1891..Ewell, Marshall D. 12: 375
1892..Cox, Jacob D. 22: 231
1893..Curtis, Lester 24: 51
1894..Gage, Simon H. 4: 483
1895..Mercer, A. Clifford 12: 211
1896..Claypole, Edward W. 13: 259
1897..Kellicott, David S. 13: 299
1898..Krauss, William C. 12: 210
1899..Bleile, Albert M. 24: 78
1900..Eigenmann, Carl H. 21: 47
1901..Bessey, Charles E. 8: 361
1902..Birge, Edward A. 12: 290
1903..Burrill, Thomas J. 18: 187
1904..Ward, Henry B. 13: 150
1905..Gage, Simon H. 4: 483
1906..Ewell, Marshall D. 12: 375
1909..Osborn, Herbert 13: 202
1911..Hertzler, Arthur E. ...... C: 189
1912..Heald, Frederick DeF. .... B: 175
1913..Wellman, Creighton ...... D: 302
1914..Brookover, Charles 20: 69
1915..Kofoid, Charles A. .... A: 280
1916..Guyer, Michael F. .... A: 357
1918..Griffin, Laurence E. ......
1920..Galloway, Thomas W. 22: 63
1921..Smith, Frank .... D: 93
1922..Cobb, Nathan A. 23: 87
1923..Juday, Chancey ....
1924..Ransom, Brayton H. .....
1925..Esterly, Calvin O. ....
1926..LaRue, George R. ... ...
1927..Metcalf, Zeno P. ....
1928..Welch, Paul S. ....
1929..Smith, Gilbert M. ....
1930..Wenrich, David H. ......
1931..VanCleave, Harley J. ....
1932..Gilbert, Edward M. ......
1933..Elrod, Morton J. ....
1934..Tiffany, Lewis H. ....
1935..Guberlet, John E. ....

American Museum of Natural History

1869..Wolfe, John D. ....
1872..Stuart, Robert L. 10: 24
1881..Jesup, Morris K. 11: 93
1908..Osborn, Henry Fairfield ..26: 18
1933..Davison, Frederick T. ....

American Neurological Association

1875..Mitchell, S. Weir 9: 346
1876..Jewell, James S. ....
1880..Miles, Francis T. 20: 437
1881..Bartholow, Roberts 22: 212
1882..Hammond, William A. ... 9: 338
1883..Edes, Robert T. 8: 212
1884..Ott, Isaac 20: 188
1885..Wilder, Burt G. 4: 481
1886..Mills, Charles K. .... B: 331
1887..Gray, Landon C. 5: 380
1888..Putnam, James J. ....
1889..Seguin, Edouard C. 15: 151
1890..Spitzka, Edward C. 19: 450
1891..Sinkler, Wharton ....
1892..Dana, Charles L. 13: 528
1893..Lyman, Henry M. 12: 298
1894..Sachs, Bernard ....
1896..Dercum, Francis X. 22: 143
1897..Starr, Moses A. 16: 102
1898..Hammond, Graeme M. ...15: 199
1899..Lloyd, James H. ....
1900..Fisher, Edward D. ....
1901..Wharton, George L. ......
1902..Collins, Joseph ....
1903..Putnam, James W. ....
1904..Fray, Frank R. ....
1905..Spiller, William G. ....
1906..Stedman, Henry R. ......
1907..Patrick, Hugh T. .... D: 453
1908..Burr, Charles W. ....
1909..Mitchell, S. Weir 9: 346
1910..Prince, Morton H. 25: 313
1911..Thomas, Henry M. 20: 163
1912..Bullard, William N. ......
1913..Bailey, Pearce 24: 192
1914..Hun, Henry 19: 285
1915..Jacoby, George W. ....
1916..Barker, Llewellys F. ..... A: 265
1917..Taylor, Edward W. 25: 157
1918..Weisenburg, Theodore H. .
1919..McBride, James ....
1920..Hunt, J. Ramsay ....
1921..Schwab, Sidney I. ....
1922..Meyer, Adolf ....
1923..Cushing, Harvey .... C: 36
1924..Mills, Charles K. .... B: 331
1925..Peterson, Frederick 16: 175
1926..Tilney, Frederick ....
1927..Bascoe, Peter ....
1928..Dana, Charles L. ....
1929..Frazier, Charles H. ......
1930..Jelliffe, Smith E. ....
1931..Ayer, James B. ....
1932..Sachs, Bernard ....
1933..McCarthy, Daniel J. ......
1934..Strauss, Israel ....
1935..Russell, Colin K. ...... Canadian
1936..Barrett, Albert M. ....
1937..Donaldson, Henry H. ....

American Ophthalmological Society

1864..Delafield, Edward 10: 278
1869..Williams, Henry W. 3: 223
1874..Agnew, Cornelius R. 8: 205
1879..Noyes, Henry D. ....
1885..Norris, William F. 18: 175
1890..Derby, Hasket 17: 422
1894..Harlan, George C. 24: 129
1899..Wadsworth, Oliver F. 20: 389
1903..Bull, Charles S. 9: 336
1906..Mathewson, Arthur ......
1907..Kipp, Charles J. ....
1908..Risley, Samuel D. 7: 513
1909..St. John, Samuel B. .....
1910..Theobald, Samuel 24: 74
1911..Gruening, Emil 19: 47
1912..Jackson, Edward 12: 446
1913..Standish, Myles 23: 168
1914..Sattler, Robert ....
1915..Post, Martin H. 19: 31
1916..DeSchweinitz, George E. . C: 144
1917..Callan, Peter A. 25: 203
1918..Wilder, William H. ......
1919..Howe, Lucien 23: 218
1920..Woods, Hiram ....
1921..Weeks, John E. ....
1922..Sweet, William M. ....
1923..Wilmer, William H. ..... C: 78
1924..Duane, Alexander 26: 306
1925..Westcott, Cassius D. ...... C: 226
1926..Harrower, David ....
1927..Zentmayer, William ......
1928..Lambert, Walter E. 24: 389
1929..Parker, Walter R. ....
1930..Posey, William C. ....
1931..Knapp, Arnold ....
1932..Ellett, Edward C. ....
1933..Holloway, Thomas B. ....
1934..Byers, W. Gordon M. ....

American Oriental Society

1842..Pickering, John 7: 294
1846..Robinson, Edward 2: 242
1863..Salisbury, Edward E. 11: 448
1866..Woolsey, Theodore D. 1: 170
1871..Hadley, James 1: 175
1873..Salisbury, Edward E. 11: 448
1881..Williams, Samuel Wells .. 1: 422
1884..Whitney, William D. 2: 340
1890..Ward, William H. 8: 147
1893..Gilman, Daniel C. 5: 170
1906..Toy, Crawford H. 6: 94
1907..Lanman, Charles R. 11: 96
1908..Hopkins, Edward W. 14: 476
1909..Ward, William H. 8: 147
1910..Bloomfield, Maurice 10: 400
1911..Moore, George F. 10: 101
1913..Haupt, Paul 22: 157
1914..Jastrow, Morris 11: 372
1915..Jackson, Abraham V. W..13: 550
1916..Barton, George A. .... D: 441
1917..Torrey, Charles C. ....
1918..Breasted, James H. ...... B: 377
1919..Lanman, Charles R. 11: 96
1920..Williams, Talcott 15: 306
1921..Nies, James B. 20: 256
1922..Hopkins, Edward W. 14: 476
1923..Adler, Cyrus 11: 371
1925..Clark, Walter E. ....
1926..Montgomery, James A. ...
1927..Morgenstern, Julian ......
1928..Edgerton, Franklin ......
1929..Jackson, Abraham V. W. .13: 550
1930..Laufer, Berthold ....
1931..Schmidt, Nathaniel ......
1932..Olmstead, Albert T. ......
1933..Gottheil, Richard J. H. ...14: 276
1934..Burrows, Millar ....
1935..Albright, William F. .....

American Ornithologists' Union

1883..Allen, Joel A. 3: 100
1890..Elliot, Daniel G. 16: 196
1892..Coues, Elliott 5: 240
1895..Brewster, William 22: 140
1898..Ridgway, Robert 8: 460
1900..Merriam, C. Hart 13: 264
1903..Cory, Charles B. 13: 225
1905..Batchelder, Charles F. ....
1908..Nelson, Edward W. 26: 434
1911..Chapman, Frank M. ..... C: 188
1914..Fisher, Albert K. .... A: 377
1917..Sage, John H. 21: 177
1920..Stone, Witmer ....
1923..Dwight, Jonathan 22: 353
1926..Wetmore, Alexander .....
1929..Grinnell, Joseph ....
1934..Fleming, James H. ....

American Orthopædic Association

1887..Gibney, Virgil P. 21: 46
1888..Shaffer, Newton M. 3: 392
1889..Bradford, Edward H. ....
1890..Willard, DeForest 15: 86
1891..Judson, Adoniram B. 20: 384
1892..Lee, Benjamin 11: 99
1893..Steele, Aaron J. 20: 298
1894..Phelps, Abel M. 12: 233
1895..Ridlon, John 17: 368
1896..Whitman, Royal ....
1897..Ketch, Samuel 22: 387
1898..Lovett, Robert W. 20: 398
1899..Townsend, Wisner R. 20: 475
1900..Sherman, Harry M. 21: 334
1901..Gillette, Arthur J. 19: 227
1902..Wilson, Hugh A. ....
1903..Weigle, Luther A. ....
1904..Sayre, Reginald H. 21: 161
1905..Brackett, Elliott G. ......
1906..McKenzie, B. E. ...... Canadian
1907..Goldthwait, Joel E. ......
1908..Taylor, Henry L. 24: 296
1909..Cook, Ansel G. 24: 413
1910..Thorndike, Augustus .....
1911..Freiberg, Albert H. ...... D: 294
1912..Gibney, Virgil P. 21: 46
1913..Shands, Aurelius R. ......
1914..Davis, Gwilym G. ....
1915..Packard, George B. ......
1916..Painter, Charles F. ......
1917..Silver, David ....
1918..Porter, John L. ....
1919..Galloway, Herbert B. H...
1920..Starr, Clarence L. ....
1921..Osgood, Robert B. .... D: 60
1922..Allison, Nathaniel 26: 200
1923..Fitch, Ralph R. ....
1924..Baer, William S. ....

1925..Ryerson, Edwin W. ......
1926..Hoke, Michael ....
1927..Watkins, James T. 24: 83
1928..Forbes, A. Mackenzie ....
1929..Albee, Fred H. .... C: 129
1930..Adams, Zabdiel B. ....
1931..Campbell, Willis C. ......
1932..Gallie, William E. ....
1933..Steindler, Arthur ....
1934..Henderson, Melvin S. ....
1935..Willard, DeForest P., Jr...

American Peace Society

1828..Ladd, William 13: 187
1841..Coues, Samuel E. 14: 185
1846..Frelinghuysen, Theodore .. 3: 401
1847..Phelps, Anson G. 12: 491
1848..Jay, William 8: 74
1859..Wayland, Francis ....
1861..Malcolm, Howard 12: 300
1873..Tobey, Edward S. 13: 416
1891..Paine, Robert Treat 26: 13
1911..Burton, Theodore E. 21: 50
1916..Kirchwey, George W. .... B: 466
1917..Slayden, James L. 19: 355
1920..Montague, Andrew J. 13: 358
1924..Burton, Theodore E. 21: 50
1928..Fortune, William .... B: 278
1930..Esch, John J. .... A: 305

American Pharmaceutical Association

1852..Smith, Daniel B. 5: 343
1853..Brewer, William A. ......
1854..Chapman, William B. ....
1855..Meakim, John ....
1856..Andrews, George W. .....
1857..Ellis, Charles 5: 344
1858..Kidwell, John I. ....
1859..Colcord, Samuel M. ......
1860..Kiersted, Henry T. ....
1862..Proctor, William, Jr. .....
1863..Moore, J. Faris ....
1864..Gordon, William J. M. ...
1865..Lincoln, Henry W. ....
1866..Stearnes, Frederick ......
1867..Milhau, John 2: 225
1868..Parrish, Edward 5: 348
1869..Sargent, Ezekiel H. ......
1870..Stabler, Richard S. ......
1871..Sander, Enno 13: 306
1872..Ebert, Albert E. ....
1873..Hancock, John F. ....
1874..Diehl, C. Lewis ....
1875..Markoe, George F. H. ....
1876..Bullock, Charles 5: 344
1877..Saunders, William ....
1878..Luhn, Gustavus J. ....
1879..Sloan, George W. ....
1880..Shinn, James T. 25: 231
1881..Bedford, P. Wendover ....
1882..Heinitch, Charles A. .....
1883..Thompson, William S. ....
1884..Ingalls, John ....
1885..Roberts, Joseph ....
1886..Tufts, Charles A. ....
1887..Lloyd, John Uri .... D: 106
1888..Alexander, Maurice W. ...
1889..Painter, Emlen ....
1890..Taylor, A. B. ....
1891..Finlay, A. K. ....
1892..Remington, Joseph P. 5: 349
1893..Patch, Edgar L. 25: 339
1894..Simpson, William 24: 167
1895..Good, James M. ....
1896..Morrison, Joseph E. ......
1897..Whitney, Henry M. ......
1898..Dohme, Charles E. 23: 191
1899..Prescott, Albert B. 13: 53
1900..Patton, John F. ....
1901..Whelpley, Henry M. 20: 488
1902..Payne, George F. 20: 169
1903..Hopp, Lewis C. ....
1904..Beal, James H. ....
1905..Lemberger, Joseph L. ....
1906..Eliel, Leo ....
1907..Searby, William M. 20: 51
1908..Oldberg, Oscar 20: 429
1909..Rusby, Henry H. .... A: 172
1910..Eberle, Eugene G. ....
1911..Godding, John G. 22: 425
1912..Day, William B. ....
1913..Beringer, George M. ......
1914..Mayo, Caswell A. 22: 52
1915..Alpers, William C. 22: 76
1916..Wulling, Frederick J. .... B: 498
1917..Holzhauer, Charles ....
1918..LaWall, Charles H. ......
1919..Sayre, Lucius E. 22: 100
1920..Packard, C. Herbert .....
1921..Hilton, Samuel L. ....
1922..Koch, Julius A. ....
1923..Arny, Henry V. .... B: 206
1924..Holton, Charles W. ....
1925..Walton, Lucius L. ....
1926..Bradley, Theodore J. .....
1927..Johnson, Charles W. .....
1928..Jones, David F. ....
1929..Dunning, Henry A. B. ...
1930..Christensen, Henry C. ...
1931..Adams, Walter D. ....
1932..Philip, W. Bruce ....
1933..Fischelis, Robert P. ......
1934..Costello, Patrick H. ......

American Philological Association

1869..Whitney, William D. 2: 340
1870..Crosby, Howard 4: 193
1871..Goodwin, William W. 6: 428
1872..Kendrick, Asahel C. 12: 245
1873..March, Francis A. 11: 244
1874..Trumbull, James H. 9: 422
1875..Harkness, Albert 6: 23
1876..Haldeman, Samuel S. 9: 246
1877..Gildersleeve, Basil L. 10: 469
1878..Sewall, Jotham B. 12: 259
1879..Toy, Crawford H. 6: 94
1880..Packard, Lewis R. 4: 550
1881..Allen, Frederick deF. 12: 225
1882..Humphreys, Milton W. ... B: 53
1883..D'Ooge, Martin L. 12: 207
1884..Goodwin, William W. 6: 428
1885..Peck, Tracy 12: 214
1886..Merriam, Augustus C. 8: 397
1887..Hall, Isaac H. 12: 143
1888..Seymour, Thomas D. 12: 365
1889..Lanman, Charles R. 11: 96
1890..Sachs, Julius 13: 560
1891..Hart, Samuel 13: 48
1892..Hale, William G. 23: 80
1893..Garnett, James M. 1: 506
1894..Wright, John H. 8: 48
1895..March, Francis A. 11: 244
1896..Perrin, Bernadotte 12: 248
1897..Warren, Minton 12: 443
1898..Smith, Clement L. 7: 163
1899..Leach, Abby 12: 257
1900..Platner, Samuel B. 12: 214
1901..West, Andrew F. 12: 209
1902..Smith, Charles F. 12: 368
1903..Hempl, George 13: 365
1904..Smyth, Herbert W. 13: 539
1905..Merrill, Elmer T. 14: 312
1906..Kelsey, Francis W. 26: 461
1907..Bennett, Charles E. .....
1908..Gildersleeve, Basil L. 10: 469
1909..Shorey, Paul .... C: 36
1910..Rolfe, John C. .... A: 341
1911..Goodell, Thomas D. 19: 146
1912..Fowler, Harold N. .... A: 494
1913..Capps, Edward .... A: 416
1914..Morris, Edward P. .... A: 223
1915..Buck, Carl D. .... A: 278
1916..Moore, Frank G. ....
1917..Abbott, Frank F. 19: 430
1918..Scott, John A. ....
1919..Moore, Clifford H. 24: 102
1920..McDaniel, Walton B. ....
1921..Allinson, Francis G. 23: 192
1922..Rand, Edward K. ....
1923..Bassett, Samuel E. ....
1924..Laing, Gordon J. ....
1925..Fairclough, Henry R. .... C: 59
1926..Babbitt, Frank C. 25: 400
1927..Bill, Clarence P. ....
1928..Frank, Tenney 19: 236
1929..Gulick, Charles B. ....
1930..Prescott, Henry W. ......
1931..Linforth, Ivan M. ....
1932..Bonner, Campbell ....
1933..Shorey, Paul .... C: 36
1934..Haight, Elizabeth H. .....
1935..Ullman, Berthold L. ....

American Philosophical Society

The Original Members

Bond, Thomas, as Physician ...13: 431
Bartram, John, as Botanist 7: 153
Godfrey, Thomas, as Mathematician 23: 368
Rhoads, Samuel, as Mechanician 13: 582
Parsons, William, as Geographer 1: 330
Bond, Phineas, as Natural Philosopher 13: 431
Hopkinson, Thomas, President .. 7: 249
Coleman, William, Treasurer ...17: 166
Franklin, Benjamin, Secretary .. 1: 328

The Presidents

1769..Franklin, Benjamin 1: 328
1791..Rittenhouse, David 1: 346
1797..Jefferson, Thomas 3: 1
1815..Wistar, Caspar 1: 273
1819..Patterson, Robert 1: 347
1825..Tilghman, William 6: 194
1828..Duponceau, Peter S. 7: 510
1845..Patterson, Robert M. 1: 347
1846..Chapman, Nathaniel 3: 294
1849..Patterson, Robert M. 1: 347
1853..Bache, Franklin 5: 346
1855..Bache, Alexander D. 3: 348

1857..Kane, John K. 11:190
1859..Wood, George B. 5:346
1880..Fraley, Frederic 7:513
1902..Wistar, Isaac J. 12:359
1903..Smith, Edgar F. 21: 53
1907..Keen, William W. 11:367
1918..Scott, William B. 13:214
1925..Walcott, Charles D. 22:135
1927..Dercum, Francis X. 22:143
1931..Russell, Henry N. A:346
1932..Morris, Roland S. ....

American Physical Society

1899..Rowland, Henry A. 11: 25
1901..Michelson, Albert A. ..... C: 42
1903..Webster, Arthur G. 13:532
1905..Barus, Carl 26: 8
1907..Nichols, Edward L. 4:482
1909..Crew, Henry 15: 60
1911..Magie, William F. 12:425
1913..Peirce, Benjamin O. 20:366
1914..Merritt, Ernest G. 15:195
1916..Millikan, Robert A. A:268
1918..Bumstead, Henry A. 21: 77
1919..Ames, Joseph S. A:342
1921..Lyman, Theodore ....
1923..Mendenhall, Charles E. ...
1925..Miller, Dayton C. C:515
1927..Compton, Karl T. .... C: 81
1929..Gale, Henry G. ....
1931..Swann, William F. G. ....
1933..Foote, Paul D. ....
1935..Compton, Arthur H. ..... C: 34

American Planning and Civic Association

1914..McFarland, J. Horace A:196
1925..Delano, Frederic A. A:410
1937..Albright, Horace M. .....

American Political Science Association

1905..Goodnow, Frank J. ...... C: 19
1906..Shaw, Albert 9:469
1907..Judson, Frederick N. 7:284
1908..Bryce, James .... British
1909..Lowell, A. Lawrence ..... D: 46
1910..Wilson, Woodrow 19: 1
1911..Baldwin, Simeon E. 21: 86
1912..Hart, Albert B. 11:394
1913..Willoughby, Westel W. ...13:435
1914..Moore, John Bassett ..... A: 72
1915..Freund, Ernest 26: 98
1916..Macy, Jesse 21: 18
1917..Smith, Munroe 11:100
1918..Ford, Henry J. 21: 14
1920..Reinsch, Paul S. 19:285
1921..Rowe, Leo S. 18:316
1922..Dunning, William A. 19: 27
1923..Garfield, Harry A. A:102
1924..Garner, James W. ....
1925..Merriam, Charles E. D:435
1926..Beard, Charles A. D:231
1927..Munro, William B. D:404
1928..Reeves, Jesse S. ....
1929..Fairlie, John A. ....
1930..Shambaugh, Benjamin F.
1931..Corwin, Edward S. ......
1932..Willoughby, William F. .. A:212
1933..Loeb, Isidor ....
1934..Shepard, Walter J. ......
1935..Coker, Francis W. ....

American Psychiatric Association

1844..Woodward, Samuel B. ....
1848..Awl, William M. 22:133
1851..Bell, Luther V. 22:160
1855..Ray, Isaac ....
1859..McFarland, Andrew .....
1862..Kirkbride, Thomas S. 6:388
1870..Butler, John S. ....
1873..Nichols, Charles H. ......
1879..Walker, Clement A. ......
1882..Callender, John H. 8:135
1883..Gray, John P. 7:273
1884..Earle, Pliny 11:146
1885..Everts, Orpheus ....
1886..Buttolph, H. A. ....
1887..Grissom, Eugene 22: 98
1888..Chapin, John B. ....
1889..Godding, William W. 23:247
1890..Stearns, Henry P. 22: 87
1891..Clark, Daniel ....
1892..Andrews, Judson B. ......
1893..Curwen, John ....
1894..Cowles, Edward 19:250
1895..Dewey, Richard ....
1896..Powell, Theophilus O. 2:484
1897..Bucke, Richard M. ....
1898..Hurd, Henry M. 12:112
1899..Rogers, Joseph G. ....
1900..Wise, Peter M. ....
1901..Preston, Robert J. ....
1902..Blumer, G. Adler D:322
1903..Macdonald, Alexander E. .
1904..Burgess, Thomas J. W. ...
1905..Burr, Colonel B. B:311
1906..Hill, Charles G. 20:372
1907..Bancroft, Charles P. .....
1908..Kilbourne, Arthur F. .....
1909..Drewry, William F. ......
1910..Pilgrim, Charles W. 25:391
1911..Work, Hubert .... A: 14
1912..Searcy, James T. ....
1913..MacDonald, Carlos F. 20: 7
1914..Smith, Samuel E. ....
1915..Brush, Edward N. 24:297
1916..Wagner, Charles G. 24:143
1917..Anglin, James V. ....
1918..Southard, Elmer E. 19:113
1919..Eyman, Henry C. 21:186
1920..Copp, Owen ....
1921..Barrett, Albert M. ....
1922..Mitchell, Harry W. ......
1923..Salmon, Thomas W. 21: 39
1924..White, William A. ....
1925..Haviland, Clarence F. 24: 31
1926..Kline, George M. ....
1927..Meyer, Adolf ....
1928..Orton, Samuel T. D:117
1929..Bond, Earl D. ....
1930..English, Walter M. ......
1931..Russell, William L. ....
1932..May, James V. ....
1933..Kirby, George H. 26: 35
1934..Williams, Charles F. .....
1935..Cheney, Clarence O. ......

American Psychological Association

1892..Hall, G. Stanley 9:203
1893..Ladd, George T. 13: 81
1894..James, William 18: 31
1895..Cattell, J. McKeen .... D: 94
1896..Fullerton, George S. 12: 57
1897..Baldwin, J. Mark 25: 89
1898..Münsterberg, Hugo 13: 85
1899..Dewey, John A:547
1900..Jastrow, Joseph 11:373
1901..Royce, Josiah 25:356
1902..Sanford, Edmund C. 12:272
1903..Bryan, William L. 13:464
1904..James, William 18: 31
1905..Calkins, Mary W. 13: 75
1906..Angell, James R. .... B: 5
1907..Marshall, Henry R. 11:328
1908..Stratton, George M. 13:551
1909..Judd, Charles H. A:251
1910..Pillsbury, Walter B. 15:416
1911..Seashore, Carl E. A:227
1912..Thorndike, Edward L. 15:205
1913..Warren, Howard C. 25:344
1914..Woodworth, Robert S. .... A: 24
1915..Watson, John B. .... A: 86
1916..Dodge, Raymond B:324
1917..Yerkes, Robert M. A:109
1918..Baird, John W. 22:213
1919..Scott, Walter D. ....
1920..Franz, Shepard I. A:477
1921..Washburn, Margaret F. ..
1922..Dunlap, Knight ....
1923..Terman, Lewis M. ....
1924..Hall, G. Stanley 9:203
1925..Bentley, Madison ....
1926..Carr, Harvey A. ....
1927..Hollingworth, Harry L. ..
1928..Boring, Edwin G. ....
1929..Lashley, Karl S. ....
1930..Langfeld, Herbert S. .....
1931..Hunter, Walter S. ....
1932..Miles, Walter R. D:146
1933..Thurstone, Louis L. .....
1934..Peterson, Joseph ....
1935..Poffenberger, Albert T. ..

American Public Health Association

1872..Smith, Stephen 2:207
1875..Toner, Joseph M. 7:539
1876..Snow, Edwin M. 13:285
1877..Rauch, John H. 12:452
1878..Harris, Elisha 9:352
1879..Cabell, James L. 12:452
1880..Billings, John S. 4: 78
1881..White, Charles B. 13: 50
1882..Kedzie, Robert C. 8:488
1883..Hunt, Ezra M. 12:129
1884..Gihon, Albert L. 9:154
1885..Reeves, James E. ....
1886..Walcott, Henry P. 12:445
1887..Sternberg, George M. 4:388
1888..Hewitt, Charles N. 13: 57
1889..Johnson, Hosmer A. 12:490
1890..Baker, Henry B. 12:136
1891..Montizambert, Frederick .
1892..Formento, Felix 12:228
1893..Durgin, Samuel H. 13:574
1894..Lachapelle, Emmanuel P..

1895..Bailey, William 13: 45
1896..Liceaga, Eduardo ....
1897..Horlbeck, Henry B. ......
1898..Lindsey, Charles A. ......
1899..Rohe, George H. 7: 275
1899..Mitchell, Henry 13: 585
1900..Bryce, Peter H. ....
1901..Lee, Benjamin 11: 99
1902..Holton, Henry P. ....
1903..Wyman, Walter 12: 508
1904..Finlay, Carlos J. ....
1905..Westbrook, Frank F. 14: 472
1906..Robinson, Franklin C. ...14: 181
1907..Orvananos, Domingo .....
1908..Lewis, Richard H. .... A: 467
1909..Swarts, Gardner T. 20: 346
1910..Probst, Charles O. ....
1911..Simpson, R. M. ....
1912..Hurty, John N. 22: 370
1913..Hering, Rudolph 10: 226
1914..Woodward, William C. ...
1915..Sedgwick, William T. 13: 290
1916..Anderson, John F. .... B: 102
1917..Evans, William A. ....
1918..Hastings, C. J. ....
1919..Frankel, Lee K. 23: 208
1920..Rankin, Watson S. ....
1921..Ravenel, Mazyck P. ......
1922..McLaughlin, Allan J. ....
1923..Levy, Ernest C. ....
1924..Park, William H. .... C: 314
1925..Vaughan, Henry F. ......
1926..Winslow, Charles-
Edward A. .... D: 443
1927..Chapin, Charles V. ....
1928..Bundesen, Herman N. ....
1929..Fuller, George W. ....
1930..Chesley, Albert J. ....
1931..Cumming, Hugh S. ......
1932..Dublin, Louis I. .... D: 101
1933..Ferrell, John A. .... B: 346
1934..Emerson, Haven ....
1935..Brown, Walter H. ....

The American Red Cross

1881..Barton, Clara 15: 314
1904..VanReypen, William K. ..13: 215
1905..Taft, William H. 23: 1
1913..Wilson, Woodrow 19: 1
1921..Harding, Warren G. 19: 268
1923..Coolidge, Calvin 24: 1
1929..Hoover, Herbert .... C: 1
1933..Roosevelt, Franklin D. ... D: 1

American Social Hygiene Association

1914..Eliot, Charles W. 6: 421
1915..Harris, Abram W. 14: 138
1917..Welch, William H. 26: 6
1919..Biggs, Hermann M. 19: 219
1923..Keyes, Edward L. 9: 343

American Society of Biological Chemists

1907..Chittenden, Russell H. ...10: 181
1908..Abel, John J. .... A: 392
1909..Folin, Otto K. O. 25: 197
1910..Osborne, Thomas B. 21: 356
1911..Mendel, Lafayette B. 26: 424
1912..Macallum, Archibald B. ..
1914..Lusk, Graham 15: 88
1915..Jones, Walter ....
1917..Alsberg, Carl L. ....
1919..Benedict, Stanley R. .....
1921..Van Slyke, Donald D. ....
1923..Shaffer, Philip A. ....
1925..Sherman, Henry C. ...... D: 65
1926..Kendall, Edward C. ......
1927..McCollum, Elmer V. ..... C: 477
1929..Bloor, Walter R. ....
1931..Bradley, Harold C. ....
1933..Clark, W. Mansfield ......
1935..Lewis, Howard B. ....

American Society of Civil Engineers

1852..Laurie, James 9: 38
1867..Kirkwood, James P. 9: 36
1868..McAlpine, William J. 10: 507
1869..Craven, Alfred W. 9: 37
1871..Allen, Horatio 8: 233
1873..Adams, Julius W. 9: 33
1875..Greene, George S. 1: 320
1877..Chesbrough, Ellis S. 9: 35
1878..Roberts, W. Milnor 13: 254
1879..Fink, Albert 9: 489
1880..Francis, James B. 9; 46
1882..Welch, Ashbel 9: 36
1883..Paine, Charles 12: 269
1884..Whittemore, Don Juan ...13: 248
1885..Graff, Frederic 25: 383
1886..Flad, Henry 12: 290
1887..Worthen, William Ezra ..12: 206
1888..Keefer, Thomas C. 12: 227
1889..Becker, Max J. 12: 231
1890..Shinn, William P. 11: 344
1891..Chanute, Octave 10: 212
1892..Cohen, Mendes 13: 136
1893..Metcalf, William 12: 232
1894..Craighill, William P. 12: 223
1895..Morison, George S. 10: 129
1896..Clarke, Thomas C. 7: 500
1897..Harrod, Benjamin M. 12: 328
1898..Fteley, Alphonse 13: 561
1899..Fitzgerald, Desmond 9: 44
1900..Wallace, John F. 10: 168
1901..Croes, John James R. 6: 46
1902..Moore, Robert 12: 202
1903..Noble, Alfred 9: 44
1904..Hermany, Charles 13: 299
1905..Schneider, Charles C. 18: 91
1906..Stearns, Frederick P. 14: 306
1907..Benzenberg, George H. ...14: 205
1908..MacDonald, Charles 11: 475
1909..Bates, Onward 15: 208
1910..Bensel, John A. 11: 239
1911..Endicott, Mordecai T. 15: 237
1912..Ockerson, John A. 25: 381
1913..Swain, George F. 12: 276
1914..McDonald, Hunter .... C: 185
1915..Marx, Charles D. ....
1916..Corthell, Elmer L. 9: 42
1916..Herschel, Clemens 22: 342
1917..Pegram, George H. 9: 40
1918..Talbot, Arthur N. ....
1919..Curtis, Fayette S. 23: 120
1920..Davis, Arthur P. 24: 116
1921..Webster, George S. 25: 382
1922..Freeman, John R. .... C: 397
1923..Loweth, Charles F. ......
1924..Grunsky, Carl E. 13: 224
1925..Ridgway, Robert ....
1926..Davison, George S. ......
1927..Stevens, John F. .... D: 213
1928..Bush, Lincoln ....
1929..Marston, Anson ....
1930..Coleman, John F. ....
1931..Stuart, Francis L. 27: 334
1932..Crocker, Herbert S. .....
1933..Hammond, Alonzo J. ..... D: 199
1934..Eddy, Harrison P. ....
1935..Tuttle, Arthur S. ....

American Society of International Law

1907..Root, Elihu 26: 1
1924..Hughes, Charles E. ...... A: 6
1929..Scott, James B. .... C: 69

American Society of Landscape Architects

1899..Olmsted, John C. 13: 460
1902..Parsons, Samuel 26: 308
1903..Barrett, Nathan F. ......
1904..Olmsted, John C. 13: 460
1906..Parsons, Samuel 26: 308
1908..Olmsted, Frederick L. 2: 298
1910..Lowrie, Charles N. ......
1912..Caparn, Harold A. .... D: 340
1913..Simonds, Ossian C. 22: 91
1914..Manning, Warren H. ..... B: 291
1915..Pray, James S. 27: 377
1920..Olmsted, Frederick L. 2: 298
1923..Greenleaf, James L. ......
1927..Shurcliff, Arthur A. .....
1931..Hubbard, Henry V. ...... C: 504

American Society of Mechanical Engineers

1880..Thurston, Robert H. 4: 479
1883..Leavitt, Erasmus D. 24: 324
1884..Sweet, John E. 13: 54
1885..Holloway, Josephus F. ...12: 116
1886..Sellers, Coleman 11: 53
1887..Babcock, George Herman . 5: 304
1888..See, Horace 2: 220
1889..Towne, Henry R. 21: 384
1890..Smith, Oberlin 12: 461
1891..Hunt, Robert W. 19: 17
1892..Loring, Charles H. 12: 502
1893..Coxe, Eckley B. 11: 559
1895..Davis, Ezekiel F. C. 12: 323
1895..Billings, Charles E. 5: 408
1896..Fritz, John 13: 74
1897..Warner, Worcester R. 21: 70
1898..Hunt, Charles W. 13: 455
1899..Melville, George W. 3: 283
1900..Morgan, Charles H. 23: 197
1901..Wellman, Samuel T. 13: 37
1902..Reynolds, Edwin 2: 524
1903..Dodge, James M. 12: 490
1904..Swasey, Ambrose .... B: 274
1905..Freeman, John R. .... C: 397
1906..Taylor, Frederick W. 23: 47
1907..Hutton, Frederick R. 16: 439
1908..Holman, Minard L. 14: 419
1909..Smith, Jesse M. 22: 165
1910..Westinghouse, George 15: 41

1911..Meier, Edward D. 23: 103
1912..Humphreys, Alexander C..13: 203
1913..Goss, William F. M. 20: 16
1914..Hartness, James 15: 294
1915..Brashear, John A. 4: 552
1916..Jacobus, David S. .... C: 112
1917..Hollis, Ira N. 22: 21
1918..Main, Charles T. 15: 327
1919..Cooley, Mortimer E. ..... A: 511
1920..Miller, Fred J. ....
1921..Carman, Edwin S. .... C: 406
1922..Kimball, Dexter S. .... D: 343
1923..Harrington, John L. ..... A: 459
1924..Low, Frederick R. .... C: 337
1925..Durand, William F. ...... D: 260
1926..Abbott, William L. ......
1927..Schwab, Charles M. ...... A: 238
1928..Dow, Alexander ....
1929..Sperry, Elmer A. 23: 78
1930..Piez, Charles 24: 17
1931..Wright, Roy V. .... D: 296
1932..Lauer, Conrad N. ....
1933..Potter, Andrey A. ....
1934..Doty, Paul 16: 95
1935..Flanders, Ralph E. ....

American Society of Naturalists

1883..Hyatt, Alpheus 23: 362
1885..Gilbert, Grove K. 13: 46
1887..Harrison, Allen ....
1889..Goodale, George L. 6: 427
1890..Martin, Henry Newell 12: 113
1891..Rice, William N. 12: 264
1892..Osborn, Henry Fairfield ..26: 18
1893..Chittenden, Russell H. 10: 181
1894..Minot, Charles S. 6: 112
1895..Cope, Edward D. 7: 474
1896..Scott, William B. 13: 214
1897..Whitman, Charles O. 11: 73
1898..Bowditch, Henry P. 12: 252
1899..Farlow, William G. 22: 207
1900..Wilson, Edmund B. 13: 59
1901..Sedgwick, William T. 13: 290
1902..Cattell, J. McKeen .... D: 94
1903..Trelease, William 11: 212
1904..Mark, Edward L. 9: 271
1906..Davenport, Charles B. ...15: 397
1907..McMurrich, James P. 14: 49
1908..Penhallow, David P. 20: 216
1909..Morgan, Thomas H. ..... D: 44
1910..MacDougal, Daniel T. 13: 125
1911..Jennings, Herbert S. ..... A: 278
1913..Conklin, Edwin G. 12: 351
1913..Harrison, Ross G. 15: 172
1914..Clarke, Samuel F. 21: 151
1915..Lillie, Frank R. 14: 479
1916..Pearl, Raymond 15: 382
1918..Shull, George H. .... A: 126
1918..Castle, William E. 16: 297
1919..East, Edward M. .... D: 196
1920..Loeb, Jacques 11: 72
1921..Davis, Bradley M. .... C: 167
1922..Wheeler, William M. .....
1923..Emerson, Rollins A. ...... D: 361
1924..Howell, William H. ......
1925..Merriam, C. Hart 13: 264
1926..Harris, J. Arthur 22: 32
1927..McClung, Clarence E. ....
1928..Donaldson, Henry H. 11: 56
1929..Parker, George H. ....
1930..Blakeslee, Albert F. ......
1931..Holmes, Samuel J. ....
1932..Gortner, Ross A. ....
1933..Livingston, Burton E. ....
1934..Shell, A. Franklin ....
1935..Merriam, John C. .... A: 485

American Society of Zoologists

(Formerly the American Morphological Society)

1890..Wilson, Edmund B. 13: 59
1891..Whitman, Charles O. 11: 73
1895..Wilson, Edmund B. 13: 59
1896..Mark, Edward L. 9: 271
1897..Minot, Charles S. 6: 112
1898..Osborn, Henry Fairfield ..26: 18
1899..Conklin, Edwin G. 12: 351
1900..Morgan, Thomas H. ..... D: 44
1901..Kingsley, John S. 12: 119
1902..Bumpus, Hermon C. 13: 110
1903..Parker, George H. ....
1904..Andrews, Ethan A. ...... B: 226
1905..Castle, William E. 16: 297
1907..Davenport, Charles B. ...15: 397
1908..Wheeler, William M. .....
1909..Jennings, Herbert S. .... A: 278
1910..Montgomery, Thomas H. .15: 216
1911..Wilson, Henry V. ....
1912..Mayer, Alfred G. ....
1913..Pearl, Raymond 15: 382
1914..McClung, Clarence E. ....
1915..Locy, William A. 18: 192
1916..Tennent, David H. ......
1917..Metcalf, Maynard M. .... B: 20
1918..Lefevre, George 20: 268
1919..Child, Charles M. ....
1920..Drew, Gilman A. ....
1921..Kofoid, Charles A. ...... A: 280
1922..Wilder, Harris H. .... B: 360
1923..Guyer, Michael F. .... A: 357
1924..Harrison, Ross G. 15: 172
1925..Stockard, Charles R. .....
1926..Mast, Samuel O. ....
1927..Holmes, Samuel J. ....
1928..Grave, Caswell ....
1929..Davenport, Charles B. ...15: 397
1930..Neal, Herbert V. ....
1931..Payne, Fernandus ....
1932..Curtis, Winterton C. .....
1933..Zeleny, Charles ....
1934..Sturtevant, Alfred H. ...
1935..Hegner, Robert W. ......

American Statistical Association

1839..Fletcher, Richard 12: 92
1846..Shattuck, George C. 12: 197
1852..Jarvis, Edward 12: 116
1883..Walker, Francis A. 5: 401
1897..Wright, Carroll D. 19: 421
1910..North, Simon N. D. 13: 62
1911..Hoffman, Frederick L. ...
1912..Willcox, Walter F. ...... A: 345
1913..Koren, John 19: 397
1915..Durand, Edward Dana ... C: 450
1916..Neill, Charles P. ....
1917..Young, Allyn A. ....
1918..Mitchell, Wesley C. ...... C: 511
1919..Hill, Joseph A. ....
1920..Roberts, George E. ......
1921..Doten, Carroll W. ....
1922..Rossiter, William S. 23: 333
1923..Persons, Warren M. ......
1924..Dublin, Louis I. .... D: 101
1925..Chaddock, Robert E. .....
1926..Ayres, Leonard P. .... A: 148
1927..Day, Edmund E. ....
1928..Snyder, Carl ....
1929..Wilson, Edwin B. .... D: 271
1930..Rorty, Malcolm C. ....
1931..Ogburn, William F. ......
1932..Fisher, Irving .... C: 51
1933..Rice, Stuart A. ....
1934..Fisher, Irving .... C: 51
1935..King, Willford I. ....

American Surgical Association

1880..Gross, Samuel D. 8: 216
1883..Moore, Edward M. 12: 55
1884..Briggs, William T. 12: 56
1885..Gunn, Moses 12: 423
1886..McGuire, Hunter 5: 163
1887..Agnew, D. Hayes 8: 203
1888..Cheever, David W. 13: 515
1889..Yandell, David W. 12: 219
1890..Mastin, Claudius H. 10: 279
1891..Conner, Phineas S. 12: 68
1892..Senn, Nicholas 6: 371
1893..Mears, James E. ....
1894..Dennis, Frederic S. 13: 601
1895..Tiffany, Louis McL. 24: 358
1896..Warren, John C. ....
1897..Prewitt, Theodore F. 9: 560
1898..Keen, William W. 11: 367
1899..Weir, Robert F. 12: 377
1900..Park, Roswell 8: 220
1901..Willard, DeForest 15: 86
1902..Richardson, Maurice H. .18: 425
1903..Dandridge, Nathaniel P. .13: 567
1904..Johnson, George Ben .....
1905..VanderVeer, Albert 16: 359
1906..Allen, Dudley P. 16: 165
1907..Carmalt, William H. 14: 207
1908..DeNancrede, Charles B. G. 14: 370
1909..Matas, Rudolph .... D: 399
1910..Harte, Richard H. 22: 441
1911..Gerster, Arpad G. C. 26: 427
1912..Powers, Charles A. 20: 60
1913..Mayo, William J. .... A: 330
1914..Armstrong, George E. ...
1915..LeConte, Robert G. 20: 162
1916..Mixter, Samuel J. ....
1917..Huntington, Thomas W. .22: 292
1918..Pilcher, Lewis S. ....
1919..Brewer, George E. ....
1920..Roberts, John B. 13: 290
1921..Finney, John M. T. .....
1922..McArthur, Lewis L. .....
1923..Crile, George W. .... C: 72
1924..Ochsner, Albert J. 20: 439
1925..Gibbon, John H. ....
1926..Cushing, Harvey .... C: 36
1927..Rixford, Emmet ....
1928..Eliot, Ellsworth ....
1929..Lund, Fred B. ....
1930..Primrose, Alexander .....
1931..Mayo, Charles H. .... A: 331
1932..Bevan, Arthur D. .... D: 90
1933..Jones, Daniel F. ....
1934..Archibald, Edward W. ...

Archæological Institute of America

1879..Norton, Charles E. 6:425
1890..Low, Seth 6:348
1897..White, John W. 12:352
1904..Seymour, Thomas D. 12:365
1908..Kelsey, Francis W. 26:461
1913..Wilson, Harry L. ....
1913..Shipley, Frederick W. ...17:410
1918..Egbert, James C. ....
1922..Magoffin, Ralph VanD. ..
1932..Lord, Louis E. ....

Association of American Geographers

1904..Davis, William M. 24: 32
1906..Adams, Cyrus C. D:288
1907..Heilprin, Angelo 12:381
1908..Gilbert, Grove K. 13: 46
1909..Davis, William M. 24: 32
1910..Cowles, Henry C. ....
1911..Tarr, Ralph S. 10:311
1912..Salisbury, Rollin D. 11: 73
1913..Bryant, Henry G. 25:359
1914..Brigham, Albert P. 24:281
1915..Dodge, Richard E. 13:549
1916..Jefferson, Mark ....
1917..Ward, Robert DeC. 24:190
1918..Fenneman, Nevin M. D:304
1919..Dryer, Charles R. 23:107
1920..Gregory, Herbert E. A:395
1921..Semple, Ellen C. A:389
1922..Barrows, Harlan H. ......
1923..Huntington, Ellsworth ... A:510
1924..Marbut, Curtis F. ....
1925..Whitbeck, Ray H. ....
1926..Goode, John P. 23:386
1927..Campbell, Marius R. .....
1928..Johnson, Douglas W. D:177
1929..Martin, Lawrence ....
1930..Parkins, Almon E. ......
1931..Bowman, Isaiah ....
1932..Baker, Oliver E. ....
1933..Matthes, Francois ....
1934..Atwood, Wallace W. .....
1935..Colby, Charles C. ....

Association of American Physicians

1886..Delafield, Francis 10:278
1887..Mitchell, S. Weir 9:346
1888..Draper, William H. 7:490
1889..Minot, Francis 12:211
1890..Busey, Samuel C. ....
1891..Pepper, William 1:345
1892..Lyman, Henry M. 12:298
1893..Loomis, Alfred L. 8:223
1894..Fitz, Reginald H. 10:456
1895..Osler, William 12:201
1896..Jacobi, Abraham 9:345
1897..DaCosta, Jacob M. 9:342
1898..Shattuck, Frederick C. ...12:272
1899..Baumgarten, Gustav 12:253
1900..Janeway, Edward G. 13:499
1901..Welch, William H. 26: 6
1902..Wilson, James C. 25:365
1903..Stewart, James ...... Canadian
1904..Councilman, William T. .. 5:550
1905..Trudeau, Edward L. 13:564
1906..Billings, Frank 23:315
1907..Kinnicutt, Francis P. 15:255
1908..Tyson, James 9:356
1909..Vaughan, Victor C. 12:207
1910..Hun, Henry 19:285
1911..Forchheimer, Frederick ..16:388
1912..Adami, J. George ...... English
1913..Barker, Lewellys F. A:265
1914..Flexner, Simon .... B: 19
1915..Meltzer, Samuel J. 15:354
1916..Sewall, Henry 26:323
1917..Dock, George C:360
1918..Williams, Francis H. ....
1919..McPhedran, Alexander..Canadian
1920..Biggs, Hermann M. 19:219
1921..Thayer, William S. 24:409
1922..Moffitt, Herbert C. ....
1923..Herrick, James B. ....
1924..Martin, Charles F. ......
1925..Conner, Lewis A. ....
1926..Strong, Richard P. ...... A: 93
1927..Hoover, Charles F. ......
1928..Warthin, Aldred S. 25:367
1929..Howard, Campbell P. ....
1930..McCrae, Thomas ....
1931..Cole, Rufus ....
1932..Futcher, Thomas B. .....
1933..Robinson, G. Canby .....
1934..Capps, Joseph A. ....
1935..Woodyatt, Rollin T. ......

Authors' League of America

1912..Churchill, Winston 10:178
1917..Beach, Rex 14: 58
1922..Williams, Jesse L. 21: 26
1923..Butler, Ellis P. 14:179
1925..McCutcheon, George B. ...14:264
1926..Davis, Owen ....
1928..Train, Arthur 14:427
1929..Richman, Arthur ....
1931..Irwin, Inez Haynes ......
1933..Connelly, Marc ....

Automobile Manufacturers Association

1914..Clifton, Charles 21:186
1925..Chapin, Roy D. D:400
1927..Macauley, Alvan ....

Bibliographical Society of America

1904..Lane, William C. 12:261
1909..Root, Azariah S. 22:112
1910..Johnston, W. Dawson ...
1911..Gould, C. H. ....
1912..Keogh, Andrew D:267
1914..Roden, Carl B. C:479
1916..Cole, George W. .... D: 42
1921..Bishop, William W. D:312
1923..Root, Azariah S. 22:112
1926..Meyer, Herman H. B. ... D: 92
1929..Lydenberg, Harry M. ....
1931..Wroth, Lawrence C. .....
1933..Shearer, Augustus H. D:347

Botanical Society of America

1894..Trelease, William 11:212
1895..Bessey, Charles E. 8:361
1896..Coulter, John Merle 11: 68
1897..Britton, Nathaniel L. 25: 88
1898..Underwood, Lucien M. ...12:238
1899..Robinson, Benjamin L. ..12:138
1900..Halsted, Byron D. 10:123
1901..Arthur, Joseph C. 12:350
1902..Galloway, Beverly T. 12:504
1903..Barnes, Charles R. 13:118
1904..Coville, Frederick V. 12:349
1905..Harper, Robert A. A:401
1907..Atkinson, George F. 13:478
1908..Ganong, William F. 14:483
1909..Thaxter, Roland ....
1910..Smith, Edwin F. ....
1911..Farlow, William G. 22:207
1912..Jones, Lewis R. A:456
1913..Campbell, Douglas H. A:284
1914..Hitchcock, Albert S. 26: 41
1915..Coulter, John Merle 11: 68
1916..Harper, Robert A. A:401
1917..Newcombe, Frederick C. .
1918..Trelease, William 11:212
1919..Arthur, Joseph C. 12:350
1920..Britton, Nathaniel L. 25: 88
1921..Allen, Charles E. ....
1922..Cowles, Henry C. ....
1923..Duggar, Benjamin M. ...
1924..Crocker, William D:330
1925..Schramm, Jacob R. ......
1926..Bailey, Liberty H. 10:145
1927..Bartlett, Harley H. ......
1928..Buller, A. H. Reginald..Canadian
1929..Ferguson, Margaret C. ...
1930..Sharp, Lester W. ....
1931..Chamberlain, Charles J. ..
1932..Peirce, George J. ....
1933..Kraus, Ezra J. ....
1934..Merrill, Elmer D. ....
1935..Nelson, Aven ....

Chamber of Commerce of the United States of America

1912..Wheeler, Harry A. B:281
1914..Fahey, John H. ....
1916..Rhett, Robert G. 11:225
1918..Wheeler, Harry A. B:281
1919..Ferguson, Homer L. 17:166
1920..Defrees, Joseph H. 25: 26
1922..Barnes, Julius H. C:530
1924..Grant, Richard F. ....
1925..O'Leary, John W. A:504
1927..Pierson, Lewis E. 15: 65
1928..Butterworth, William ....
1931..Strawn, Silas H. .... C: 44
1932..Harriman, Henry I. .....
1935..Sibley, Harper ....

Congress of American Physicians and Surgeons

1888..Billings, John S. 4: 78
1891..Mitchell, S. Weir 9:346
1894..Loomis, Alfred L. 8:223
1897..Welch, William H. 26: 6
1900..Bowditch, Henry P. 12:252
1903..Keen, William W. 11:367
1907..Fitz, Reginald H. 10:456
1910..Trudeau, Edward L. 13:564
1913..Gorgas, William C. 14:528
1916..Thayer, William S. 24:409
1919..Flexner, Simon .... B: 19

1922..Billings, Frank 23: 315
1925..Mayo, William J. .... A: 330
1928..Smith, Theobald .... D: 133
1933..Cushing, Harvey .... C: 36

Electrochemical Society, Inc.

1902..Richards, Joseph W. 13: 509
1904..Carhart, Henry S. 4: 455
1905..Bancroft, Wilder D. 14: 206
1906..Hering, Carl 12: 349
1907..Burgess, Charles F. ...... C: 420
1908..Acheson, Edward G. 23: 136
1909..Baekeland, Leo H. 15: 330
1910..Walker, William H. ...... A: 167
1911..Whitney, Willis R. 15: 393
1912..Miller, W. Lash ...... Canadian
1913..Roeber, Eugene F. 17: 317
1914..Lidbury, Frank A. ....
1915..Addicks, Lawrence ......
1916..Fitzgerald, Francis A. J.
1917..Fink, Colin G. .... B: 79
1918..Tone, Frank J. .... D: 420
1919..Landis, Walter S. ....
1920..Smith, Acheson 24: 112
1921..Schluederberg, Carl G. ... A: 552
1922..Hinckley, Arthur T. ......
1924..Parmelee, Howard C. ....
1925..Becket, Frederick M. .... B: 163
1926..Blum, William ....
1927..Lind, Samuel C. ....
1928..Kruesi, Paul J. .... B: 465
1929..Frary, Francis C. ....
1930..Kahlenberg, Louis ....
1931..Stoughton, Bradley 14: 265
1932..Witherspoon, R. A. ... Canadian
1933..Johnston, John ....
1934..Lukens, Hiram S. ....
1935..Critchett, James H. .....

Entomological Society of America

1907..Comstock, John H. 22: 10
1908..Wheeler, William M. ....
1909..Skinner, Henry 21: 139
1910..Smith, John B. 15: 71
1911..Osborn, Herbert 13: 202
1912..Forbes, Stephen A. 22: 291
1913..Bethune, Charles J. S. Canadian
1914..Calvert, Philip P. 12: 335
1915..Kellogg, Vernon L. ...... A: 203
1916..Webster, Francis M. 13: 603
1917..Bruner, Lawrence 13: 232
1918..Banks, Nathan ....
1919..Needham, James G. ..... B: 289
1920..Howard, Leland O. 12: 356
1921..Aldrich, John M. .... A: 254
1922..Gibson, Arthur ....
1923..Cockerell, Theodore D. A..
1924..Johnson, Charles W. .....
1925..Dean, George A. ....
1926..Riley, William A. ....
1927..Lutz, Frank E. ....
1928..Essig, Edward O. ....
1929..Brues, Charles T. ....
1930..Patch, Edith M. 18: 408
1931..Folsom, Justus W. ....
1932..Davis, John J. ....
1933..Snodgrass, Robert E. ....
1934..Metcalf, Clell L. ....
1935..Kennedy, Clarence H. ....

Eugenics Research Association

1913..Davenport, Charles B. 15: 397
1914..Cattell, J. McKeen .... D: 94
1916..Meyer, Adolf 16: 64
1917..Crampton, Henry E. .....
1918..Grant, Madison ....
1919..Paton, Stewart ....
1920..Fisher, Irving .... C: 51
1921..Barker, Lewellys F. ...... A: 265
1922..Olson, Harry .... B: 118
1923..Johnson, Albert ....
1924..Burr, Charles W. ....
1925..Estabrook, Arthur H. ....
1926..Babbott, Frank L. 25: 273
1927..Howe, Lucien 23: 218
1928..Campbell, Clarence G. ....
1935..Goethe, C. M. ....

The Franklin Institute

1824..Ronaldson, James 12: 507
1842..Merrick, Samuel V. 13: 333
1855..Cresson, John C. 12: 466
1864..Sellers, William 7: 185
1867..Merrick, J. Vaughan ....
1870..Sellers, Coleman 11: 53
1875..Rogers, Robert E. 7: 518
1879..Tatham, William P. 13: 250
1886..Banes, Charles H. 4: 434
1887..Wilson, Joseph M. 7: 492
1897..Birkinbine, John 12: 199
1907..Clark, Walton ....
1924..Eglin, William C. L. ....
1929..Hayward, Nathan ....

Geological Society of America

1889..Hall, James 3: 280
1890..Dana, James D. 6: 206
1891..Winchell, Alexander 16: 119
1892..Gilbert, Grove K. 13: 46
1893..Dawson, Sir J. W. .... Canadian
1894..Chamberlin, Thomas C. ..19: 25
1895..Shaler, Nathaniel S. 9: 315
1896..LeConte, Joseph 7: 231
1897..Orton, Edward 24: 106
1898..Stevenson, John J. 7: 137
1899..Emerson, Benjamin K. ...12: 316
1900..Dawson, George M. ... Canadian
1901..Walcott, Charles D. 22: 135
1902..Winchell, Newton H. 7: 451
1903..Emmons, Samuel F. 10: 448
1904..Branner, John C. 13: 599
1905..Pumpelly, Raphael 6: 359
1906..Russell, Israel C. 10: 306
1907..Van Hise, Charles R. 19: 19
1908..Calvin, Samuel 13: 182
1909..Gilbert, Grove K. 13: 46
1910..Hague, Arnold 3: 225
1911..Davis, William M. 24: 32
1912..Fairchild, Herman LeR...13: 527
1913..Smith, Eugene A. 6: 185
1914..Becker, George F. 20: 272
1915..Coleman, Arthur P. ... Canadian
1916..Clarke, John M. 19: 456
1917..Adams, Frank D. ..... Canadian
1918..Cross, Whitman 15: 214
1919..Merriam, John C. .... A: 485
1920..White, Israel C. 18: 164
1921..Kemp, James F. 21: 5
1922..Schuchert, Charles 15: 122
1923..White, David 18: 60
1924..Lindgren, Waldemar .....
1925..Scott, William S. ....
1926..Lawson, Andrew C. .....
1927..Keith, Arthur .... C: 475
1928..Lane, Alfred C. 13: 395
1929..Ries, Heinrich ....
1930..Penrose, Richard A. F. ...26: 378
1931..Lane, Alfred C. 13: 395
1932..Daly, Reginald F. ....
1933..Leith, Charles K. ....
1934..Collins, William H. ... Canadian
1935..Fenneman, Nevin M. .... D: 304

Modern Language Association of America

1884..Carter, Franklin 6: 239
1887..Lowell, James R. 2: 32
1892..March, Francis A. 11: 244
1894..Elliott, A. Marshall 14: 229
1895..Hart, James M. 9: 263
1896..Thomas, Calvin 16: 220
1897..Cook, Albert S. 9: 167
1898..Fortier, Alcée 9: 135
1899..VonJagemann, Hans C. G. 20: 50
1900..Price, Thomas R. 12: 248
1901..Sheldon, Edward S. 6: 189
1902..Bright, James W. 20: 189
1903..Hempl, George 13: 365
1904..Kittredge, George L. 13: 96
1905..Gummere, Francis B. 18: 9
1906..Todd, Henry A. 24: 33
1907..Scott, Fred N. 14: 399
1908..Warren, Frederick M. ...14: 230
1909..Learned, Marion D. 4: 538
1910..Matthews, Brander 26: 16
1911..Mott, Lewis F. 13: 583
1912..Grandgent, Charles H. ...13: 539
1913..Hohlfeld, Rudolph A. ..... A: 302
1914..Schelling, Felix E. ...... A: 426
1915..Fletcher, Jefferson B. ....
1916..Bruce, J. Douglas 21: 115
1917..Francke, Kuno 10: 512
1918..Armstrong, Edward C. .. B: 274
1920..Manly, John W. ....
1921..Howard, William G. .....
1922..Weeks, Raymond 18: 428
1923..Emerson, Oliver F. 24: 35
1924..Neilson, William A. ..... A: 286
1925..Collitz, Hermann .... D: 284
1926..Jenkins, T. Atkinson ....
1927..Thorndike, Ashley ....
1928..Schilling, Hugo K. 23: 353
1929..Nitze, William A. ....
1930..Tupper, Frederick ....
1931..Curme, George O. .... D: 53
1932..Marden, Carroll C. ......
1932..Buchanan, Milton A. ..Canadian
1933..Lowes, John L. .... D: 96
1934..Hatfield, James T. .... A: 226
1935..Searles, Colbert ....

National Academy of Design

1826..Morse, Samuel F. B. 4: 449
1845..Durand, Asher B. 4: 408
1861..Morse, Samuel F. B. 4: 449
1862..Huntington, Daniel 5: 323
1870..Gray, Henry P. 5: 32
1871..Page, William 11: 289
1873..Ward, John Q. A. 2: 364
1874..Whittredge, Worthington . 7: 458
1877..Huntington, Daniel 5: 323

1890..Wood, Thomas W. 3: 345
1899..Dielman, Frederick 7: 471
1909..Alexander, John W. 11: 297
1915..Weir, J. Alden 22: 296
1917..Adams, Herbert 13: 510
1920..Blashfield, Edwin H. .... D: 80
1926..Gilbert, Cass 26: 20
1934..Lie, Jonas .... D: 248

National Academy of Sciences

1863..Bache, Alexander D. 3: 348
1866..Henry, Joseph 3: 405
1878..Marsh, Othniel C. 9: 317
1879..Rogers, William B. 7: 410
1882..Marsh, Othniel C. 9: 317
1895..Gibbs, Wolcott 10: 469
1900..Hall, Asaph 22: 287
1901..Agassiz, Alexander 3: 98
1907..Remsen, Ira 9: 240
1913..Welch, William H. 26: 6
1917..Walcott, Charles D. 22: 135
1923..Michelson, Albert A. ..... C: 42
1927..Morgan, Thomas H. ..... D: 44
1931..Campbell, William W. ...11: 278
1935..Lillie, Frank R. 14: 479

National Aëronautic Association

1922..Coffin, Howard E. 16: 53
1923..Patterson, Frederick B. .. B: 429
1924..Cabot, Godfrey L. .... B: 380
1926..Adams, Porter ....
1928..Bingham, Hiram .... A: 28
1934..McAdoo, William G. ...... A: 34

National Association of Manufacturers

1895..Dolan, Thomas 2: 158
1896..Search, Theodore C. 12: 393
1902..Parry, David McL. 12: 462
1906..Van Cleave, James W. ...14: 372
1909..Kirby, John, Jr. 18: 401
1913..Pope, George 18: 227
1918..Mason, Stephen C. ......
1921..Edgerton, John E. ....
1932..Lund, Robert L. ....
1934..Bardo, Clinton L. ....

National Education Association

(Known as the National Teachers Association 1857-1870; National Educational Association 1871-1907.)

1857..Enos, James L. ....
1858..Richards, Zalmon 13: 578
1859..Rickoff, Andrew J. 4: 556
1860..Buckley, J. W. ....
1863..Philbrick, John D. 12: 242
1864..Wells, William H. 9: 558
1865..Greene, Samuel S. 8: 349
1866..Wickersham, James P. ...12: 239
1868..Gregory, John M. 12: 497
1869..Van Bokkelen, Libertus .. 3: 213
1870..Hagar, Daniel B. 13: 578
1871..Pickard, Josiah L. 12: 512
1872..White, Emerson E. 13: 40
1873..Northrop, Birdsey G. 10: 225
1874..White, Samuel H. 13: 101
1875..Harris, William T. 15: 1
1876..Phelps, William F. 12: 480
1877..Newell, McFadden A. 12: 512
1879..Hancock, John 5: 553
1880..Wilson, J. Ormond 13: 58
1881..Smart, James H. 6: 106
1882..Orr, Gustavus J. 9: 55
1883..Tappan, Eli T. 7: 7
1884..Bicknell, Thomas W. 1: 421
1885..Soldan, Frank L. 12: 516
1886..Calkins, Norman A. 10: 86
1887..Sheldon, William E. 5: 542
1888..Gove, Aaron 12: 531
1889..Marble, Albert P. 13: 581
1890..Canfield, James H. 7: 417
1891..Garrett, William R. 12: 560
1892..Cook, Ezekiel H. 13: 579
1893..Lane, Albert G. 12: 510
1895..Butler, Nicholas Murray .. B: 186
1896..Dougherty, Newton C. ...13: 532
1897..Skinner, Charles R. 10: 388
1898..Greenwood, James M. 13: 62
1899..Lyte, E. Oram 5: 227
1900..Corson, Oscar T. 12: 510
1901..Green, James M. 13: 516
1902..Beardshear, William M. ..12: 291
1903..Eliot, Charles W. 6: 421
1904..Cook, John W. 27: 428
1905..Maxwell, William H. 13: 218
1907..Schaeffer, Nathan C. 22: 454
1908..Cooley, Edwin G. 14: 136
1909..Harvey, Lorenzo D. 14: 87
1910..Joyner, James Y. .... A: 307
1911..Young, Ella Flagg 19: 26
1912..Pearse, Carroll G. ....
1913..Fairchild, Edward T. 19: 38
1914..Swain, Joseph 6: 355
1915..Jordan, David Starr 22: 68
1916..Johnson, David B. 3: 123
1917..Aley, Robert J. 15: 13
1918..Bradford, Mary C. C. .... B: 207
1919..Strayer, George D. .... A: 337
1920..Preston, Josephine C. ....
1921..Hunter, Fred M. ....
1922..Williams, Charl O. ....
1923..Owen, William B. 23: 66
1924..Jones, Olive M. ....
1925..Newlon, Jesse H. ....
1926..McSkimmon, Mary ....
1927..Blair, Francis G. ....
1928..Adair, Cornelia S. ....
1929..Lamkin, Uel W. ....
1930..Pyrtle, E. Ruth ....
1931..Sutton, Willis A. ....
1932..Hale, Florence ....
1933..Rosier, Joseph ....
1934..Gray, Jessie ....
1935..Smith, Henry L. 15: 141

National Geographic Society

1888..Hubbard, Gardiner G. 5: 162
1898..Bell, Alexander G. 6: 220
1904..McGee, W J 10: 349
1904..Gilbert, Grove K. 13: 46
1905..Moore, Willis L. 21: 84
1910..Gannett, Henry 19: 207
1915..Tittmann, Otto H. 13: 412
1919..Pillsbury, John E. 20: 287
1920..Grosvenor, Gilbert H. .... A: 309

National Health Council

1921..Farrand, Livingston ..... A: 117
1923..Frankel, Lee K. 23: 208
1927..Snow, William F. ....
1934..Roosevelt, Theodore ...... D: 64

National Institute of Arts and Letters

1898..Warner, Charles Dudley .. 2: 116
1901..Howells, William D. 1: 281
1904..Stedman, Edmund C. 3: 136
1906..Sloane, William M. 21: 95
1910..Van Dyke, Henry 25: 10
1911..Alexander, John W. 11: 297
1912..Matthews, Brander 26: 16
1914..Blashfield, Edwin H. .... D: 80
1916..Thomas, Augustus .... C: 438
1918..Gilbert, Cass 26: 20
1920..Grant, Robert .... C: 431
1923..Egan, Maurice F. 11: 111
1924..Van Dyke, John C. ...... C: 489
1925..Hadley, Arthur T. 9: 267
1927..Damrosch, Walter .... C: 57
1929..Phelps, William Lyon .... A: 375
1931..Cross, Wilbur L. .... C: 451

National Institute of Social Sciences

(Known as the American Social Science Association prior to 1912)

1865..Rogers, William B. 7: 410
1869..Eliot, Samuel 3: 496
1873..Curtis, George W. 3: 96
1876..Wells, David A. 10: 363
1878..Gilman, Daniel C. 5: 170
1880..Wayland, Francis 12: 221
1883..Eaton, John 8: 390
1885..Wright, Carroll D. 19: 421
1889..White, Andrew D. 4: 476
1891..Wayland, Heman L. 10: 494
1894..Kingsbury, Frederick J. ..12: 208
1896..Angell, James B. 1: 251
1897..Baldwin, Simeon E. 21: 86
1899..Warner, Charles Dudley .. 2: 116
1900..Straus, Oscar S. 10: 42
1904..Brooks, John G. 13: 534
1906..Finley, John H. 13: 503
1912..Mabie, Hamilton W. 10: 43
1916..Butler, Nicholas Murray... B: 186
1917..Fisher, Irving .... C: 51
1918..Johnson, Emory R. ......
1922..Fletcher, Austin B. 1: 524
1923..Jenkins, Helen H. ....
1924..Lord, Chester S. 25: 11
1926..Redfield, William C. ...... A: 50
1932..Gager, C. Stuart ....
1935..Fletcher, Henry ....

National Research Council

1916..Hale, George E. .... C: 45
1919..Merriam, John C. .... A: 485
1919..Angell, James R. .... B: 5
1920..Bumstead, Henry A. 21: 77
1923..Dunn, Gano S. 18: 105
1928..Burgess, George K. 24: 312
1932..Howell, William H. ......
1933..Bowman, Isaiah ....
1935..Lillie, Frank R. 14: 479

National Sculpture Society

1893..Ward, John Q. A. 2: 364
1904..French, Daniel C. .... A: 460
1906..Bitter, Karl 24: 385
1908..Adams, Herbert 13: 510
1910..MacNeil, Hermon A. 13: 480
1912..Adams, Herbert 13: 510
1914..Bitter, Karl 24: 385

1916..Adams, Herbert 13: 510
1917..Bartlett, Paul W. 12: 553
1919..Roth, Frederick G. R. ....
1920..Aitken, Robert I. 15: 215
1922..MacNeil, Hermon A. 13: 480
1924..Fraser, James E. .... C: 468
1927..Beach, Chester ....
1928..Weinman, Adolph A. .....
1931..Keck, Charles .... D: 179
1934..Gregory, John ....

National Temperance Society and Publication House

1865..Dodge, William E. 3: 174
1883..Hopkins, Mark 6: 237
1885..Cuyler, Theodore L. 5: 246
1892..Howard, Oliver O. 4: 103
1895..Baily, Joshua L. ....
1903..Dodge, David S. 9: 553
1922..Scanlon, Charles 20: 17
1928..Durkee, J. Stanley ....

National Tuberculosis Association

1904..Trudeau, Edward L. 13: 564
1905..Biggs, Hermann M. 19: 219
1907..Billings, Frank 23: 315
1908..Bowditch, Vincent Y. ....
1909..Janeway, Edward G. 13: 499
1910..Welch, William H. 26: 6
1911..Ravenel, Mazyck P. ......
1912..Folks, Homer .... A: 459
1913..Lowman, John H. ....
1914..Kober, George M. ....
1915..Sachs, Theodore B. ......
1916..Baldwin, Edward R. ...... B: 99
1917..Minor, Charles L. 24: 343
1918..Lyman, David R. ....
1919..Vaughan, Victor C. 12: 207
1920..Webb, Gerald B. ....
1921..Miller, James A. ....
1922..Brown, Lawrason .... A: 399
1923..Farrand, Livingston ..... A: 117
1924..Hatfield, Charles J. .....
1925..Smith, Theobald .... D: 133
1926..Sewall, Henry 26: 323
1927..Taylor, H. Longstreet ...
1928..Opie, Eugene L. .... D: 242
1929..Williams, Linsly R. ......
1930..Boswell, Henry ....
1931..Henry, Alfred ....
1932..Peck, John H. ....
1933..Pritchard, Stuart ....
1934..Kennon, Dunham ....
1935..Waring, James J. ....

Optical Society of America

1916..Nutting, Perley G. ...... D: 218
1918..Wright, Frederick E. .... A: 550
1920..Richtmyer, Floyd K. .... B: 174
1921..Southall, James P. C. ....
1922..Troland, Leonard T. .....
1924..Ives, Herbert E. .... C: 39
1926..Forsythe, William E. ....
1928..Priest, Irwin G. ....
1930..Jones, Loyd A. ....
1932..Crittenden, Eugene C. ...
1934..Rayton, Wilbur B. ....

The Players

1888..Booth, Edwin 3: 180
1893..Jefferson, Joseph 1: 522
1905..Drew, John 3: 531
1927..Hampden, Walter .... B: 12

Seismological Society of America

1911..Branner, John C. 24: 278
1912..Reid, Harry F. ....
1914..Louderback, George D. ...17: 426
1915..McAdie, Alexander G. ...
1916..Woodworth, Jay B. 20: 232
1918..Marvin, Charles F. 16: 47
1920..Klotz, Otto .... Canadian
1921..Willis, Bailey ....
1927..Macelwane, James B. ....
1929..Louderback, George D. ...17: 426
1935..Townley, Sidney D. ......

Smithsonian Institution

Secretaries

1846..Henry, Joseph 3: 405
1878..Baird, Spencer F. 3: 405
1887..Langley, Samuel P. 15: 7
1907..Walcott, Charles D. 22: 135
1928..Abbot, Charles G. .... A: 366

Society of American Bacteriologists

1900..Sedgwick, William T. 13: 290
1901..Welch, William H. 26: 6
1902..Conn, Herbert W. 20: 409
1903..Smith, Theobald .... D: 133
1904..Novy, Frederick G. 16: 93
1905..Jordan, Edwin O. ....
1906..Smith, Erwin F. 20: 273
1907..Carroll, James ....
1908..Russell, Henry L. 16: 417
1909..Kinyoun, Joseph J. 23: 360
1910..Moore, Veranus A. 22: 366
1911..Gorham, Frederic P. 23: 168
1912..Park, William H. .... C: 314
1913..Winslow, Charles-Edward A. .... D: 443
1914..Marshall, Charles E. 23: 191
1915..Bergey, David H. ....
1916..Burrill, Thomas J. 18: 187
1917..Rettger, Leo F. ....
1918..Buchanan, Robert E. ....
1919..Prescott, Samuel C. ...... C: 389
1920..Krumwiede, Charles .....
1921..Harrison, Francis C. ...Canadian
1922..Rogers, Lore A. ....
1923..Hastings, Edwin G. ......
1924..Hitchens, A. Parker .....
1925..Harris, Norman MacL. ..
1926..Zinsser, Hans ....
1927..Breed, Robert S. .... A: 288
1928..Evans, Alice C. ....
1929..Hektoen, Ludvig 18: 146
1930..Bayne-Jones, Stanhope .. D: 276
1931..Brown, J. Howard ....
1932..Fred, Erwin B. ....
1933..Clark, W. Mansfield .....
1934..Rosenau, Milton J. ......
1935..Meyer, Karl F. ....

Society of Naval Architects and Marine Engineers

1893..Griscom, Clement A. 4: 186
1904..Bowles, Francis T. 20: 39
1910..Taylor, Stevenson 23: 316
1913..Thompson, Robert M. 15: 202
1916..Taylor, Stevenson 23: 316
1919..Capps, Washington L. ...26: 42
1922..McFarland, Walter M. ...
1925..Taylor, David W. 15: 87
1928..Ferguson, Homer L. 17: 166
1931..Gardner, J. Howland ....
1934..Rock, George H. ....

Society for the Promotion of Engineering Education

1893..Wood, De Volson 13: 351
1894..Swain, George F. 12: 276
1895..Merriman, Mansfield 23: 70
1896..Eddy, Henry T. 15: 331
1897..Johnson, John B. 11: 217
1898..Mendenhall, Thomas C. ..10: 117
1899..Baker, Ira O. ....
1900..Marvin, Frank O. ....
1901..Fletcher, Robert 26: 464
1902..Woodward, Calvin M. ... 9: 469
1903..Allen, C. Frank ....
1904..McNair, Fred W. ....
1905..Crandall, Charles L. 4: 481
1906..Jackson, Dugald C. ...... B: 357
1907..Howe, Charles S. 15: 259
1908..Turneaure, Frederick E. .. A: 215
1909..Munroe, Henry S. ....
1910..Talbot, Arthur N. ....
1911..Raymond, William G. 17: 427
1912..Magruder, William T. ...
1913..Anthony, Gardner C. ....
1914..Marston, Anson ....
1915..Jacoby, Henry S. .... D: 108
1916..Chatburn, George R. .....
1917..Ketchum, Milo S. ....
1918..Hayford, John F. 14: 371
1919..Greene, Arthur M., Jr. ...
1920..Cooley, Mortimer E. ..... A: 511
1921..Scott, Charles F. 13: 207
1923..Walker, Perley F. ....
1924..Potter, Andrey A. ....
1925..Pegram, George B. ......
1926..Leland, Ora M. ....
1927..Sackett, Robert L. ....
1928..Kimball, Dexter S. ...... D: 343
1929..Rees, Robert I. .... A: 300
1930..Boardman, Harold S. .... D: 242
1931..Evans, Herbert S. ....
1932..Seaton, Roy A. ....
1933..Wickenden, William E. ..

United Engineering Trustees, Inc.

1904..Ledoux, Albert R. 12: 449
1906..Olcott, Eben E. 5: 265
1908..Hunt, Charles W. 13: 144
1910..Stott, Henry G. 14: 240
1911..Olcott, Eben E. 5: 265
1912..Humphreys, Alexander C. 13: 203
1913..Dunn, Gano S. 18: 105
1916..Rand, Charles F. 21: 333
1920..Davies, J. Vipond 14: 209
1924..Saunders, William L. 26: 81
1927..Gherardi, Bancroft 12: 489
1928..Wright, Roy V. .... D: 296
1930..Stuart, Francis Lee ......
1931..Dorr, John V. N. ....
1932..Kidder, H. A. ....
1933..Coes, Harold V. ....
1935..Knight, George L. ....

Recipients of Awards, Medals and Honors

Edward Goodrich Acheson Medal

Established in 1928 by Dr. Acheson and awarded every second year by the Electrochemical Society, Inc., to anyone who has made a distinguished contribution to any of the branches fostered by the Society.

1929 Acheson, Edward G. 23:136
1931 Northrup, Edwin F. ....
1933 Fink, Colin G. .... B: 79
1935 Tone, Frank J. D:420

Agassiz Medal for Oceanography

Established in 1911 by Sir John Murray as a memorial to Alexander Agassiz, and awarded by the National Academy of Sciences for contributions to oceanography.

American Recipients

1920 Sigsbee, Charles D. 9: 2
1931 Bigelow, Henry B. ....
1935 Vaughan, T. Wayland ....

Altman Prize of $1000

Awarded by the National Academy of Design for a figure or genre painted by an American-born citizen.

1915 Hawthorne, Charles W. 22:452
1916 Parker, Lawton ....
1917 Garber, Daniel C:442
1918 Higgins, Victor ....
1919 Curran, Charles C. 13:364
1921 Ufer, Walter ....
1921 Blumenschein, Ernest L. ....
1922 Kroll, Leon ....
1923 Betts, Louis ....
1924 Hassam, Childe 10:374
1926 Anderson, Karl ....
1926 Adams, Wayman .... B: 37
1927 Hale, Lilian W. ....
1928 Schlaikjer, Jes ....
1929 Watrous, Harry W. 13:369
1930 Beal, Gifford R. ....
1931 Higgins, Eugene ....
1932 Kroll, Leon ....
1935 MacLane, Jean ....
1936 Dickinson, Sidney E. ....

Altman First Prize

Awarded by the National Academy of Design for a landscape painted by an American-born citizen.

1916 Rosen, Charles ....
1917 Davis, Charles H. 8:431
1918 Dougherty, Paul ....
1919 Redfield, Edward W. ....
1920 Schofield, W. Elmer D:166
1921 Lawson, Ernest ....
1922 Garber, Daniel C:442
1923 King, Paul B. D:380
1924 Lathrop, William L. ....
1925 Nichols, Hobart ....
1926 Hassam, Childe 10:374
1927 Garber, Daniel C:442
1928 Lawson, Ernest ....
1929 Robinson, William S. ....
1930 Van Soelen, Theodore ....
1931 Hibbard, Aldro T. ....
1932 Higgins, Victor ....
1933 Granville-Smith, Walter ....
1934 Nichols, Hobart ....
1935 Kroll, Leon ....
1936 Carlson, John F. ....

American Academy of Arts and Letters Gold Medal

Awarded in recognition of special distinction in literature, art, or music, and for the entire work of the recipient, who must be a native or citizen of the United States and not a member of the Academy.

1915 Eliot, Charles W. 6:421
1923 Van Rensselaer, Marianna G. 14:338
1925 Beaux, Cecilia 11:299
1929 Wharton, Edith .... B: 32
1930 Huntington, Anna H. ....

American Association for the Advancement of Science $1000 Prize

Awarded annually to the author of a noteworthy paper presented as a part of its winter meeting program.

1924 Dickson, Leonard E. 18:411
1925 Hubble, Edwin P. ....
1925 Cleveland, Lemuel R. ....
1926 Miller, Dayton C. C:515
1927 Birkhoff, George D. ....
1928 Muller, Hermann J. C:331
1929 Kamm, Oliver ....
1930 Dempster, Arthur J. ....
1931 Tuve, Merle A. ....
1931 Hafstad, Lawrence R. ....
1931 Dahl, Otto G. C. ....
1932 Speidel, Carl C. ....
1933 Eyring, Henry ....
1934 Kahn, Reuben L. ....
1935 Knudsen, Vern O. ....
1936 Zimmerman, Percy W. .... D: 91
1936 Hitchcock, Albert S. 26: 41

American Bar Association Medal

Awarded to a member of the Bar in the United States who shall have rendered conspicuous service to the cause of American jurisprudence.

1929 Williston, Samuel 5:313
1930 Root, Elihu 26: 1
1931 Holmes, Oliver W. 12:349
1932 Wigmore, John H. .... A: 79
1934 Wickersham, George W. .... C: 16

American Institute of Architects Gold Medal

Awarded as occasion may arise for distinguished work in architecture.

American Recipients

1909 McKim, Charles F. 23: 89
1911 Post, George B. 15:250
1922 Bacon, Henry 20:339
1925 Goodhue, Bertram G. 19:402
1927 Shaw, Howard V. 20:159
1929 Medary, Milton B. 24:424

American Iron and Steel Institute Gold Medal

Awarded for outstanding achievement in the iron and steel industry.

1929 Farrell, James A. .... D: 66
1930 Schwab, Charles M. A:238
1931 Filbert, William J. ....
1932 Kennedy, Julian 24:135
1933 King, Willis L. ....
1934 Grace, Eugene G. ....
1935 Tytus, John B. ....

American Society of Mechanical Engineers Medal

Established in 1920 to be awarded for distinguished service in engineering and science. May be presented for service in science having possible application in engineering.

1921 Carlson, Hjalmar G. ....
1923 Halsey, Frederick A. 26:451
1923 Freeman, John R. C:397
1926 Millikan, Robert A. A:268
1927 Lewis, Wilfred ....
1928 Kennedy, Julian 24:135
1929 Emmet, William L. D:413
1931 Kingsbury, Albert ....
1933 Swasey, Ambrose B:274
1934 Carrier, Willis H. ....
1935 Main, Charles T. 15:327

Architectural League of New York

Medal of Honor in Architecture

1916 Gilbert, Cass 26: 20
1917 Pope, John Russell ....
1918 Morris, Benjamin W. ....
1920 Delano & Aldrich ....
1921 Klauder, Charles Z. ....
1922 Walker & Gillette ....
1923 Baum, Dwight J. C:162
1925 Harmon, Arthur L. ....
1925 Mellor, Meigs & Howe ....
1926 Howells, John M. } *jointly*
Hood, Raymond M. }
1927 McKenzie, Voorhees & Gmelin } *jointly*
Walker, Ralph T. .... } B:496
1928 Cret, Paul P. ....
1929 Barney, William P. } *jointly*
Davis, Dunlap & Barney }
1930 Holabird & Root ....
1931 Saarinen, Eliel ....
1931 Lamb, William F. } *jointly*
Shreve, Lamb & Harmon }
1933 Shepley, Henry R. C:518
1933 Ellett, Thomas H. ....

Medal of Honor in Painting

1909 LaFarge, John 9: 59
1910 Cox, Kenyon 5:321
1911 Blashfield, Edwin H. .... D: 80
1912 Turner, Charles Y. 6:469
1914 Faulkner, Barry ....
1916 Oakley, Violet ....
1917 Parrish, Maxfield 12:487
1920 Crisp, Arthur ....
1921 Savage, Eugene F. ....
1922 Winter, Ezra A. .... D: 97
1923 Simmons, Edward E. 13:601
1925 Covey, Arthur ....
1926 Davidson, George ....
1927 Hewlett, James M. 11:330
1928 Meiere, Hildreth D:337
1929 Savage, Eugene F. ....
1930 Robinson, Boardman ....
1931 Norton, John ....
1932 Brinley, D. Putnam ....
1933 Benton, Thomas H. ....

Medal of Honor in Sculpture

1909 Ward, John Q. A. 2:364
1911 Proctor, A. Phimister ....
1912 French, Daniel C. A:460
1913 Weinman, Adolph A. ....
1914 Bitter, Karl T. F. 24:385
1915 Aitken, Robert I. 15:215
1916 Adams, Herbert 13:510
1917 MacNeil, Hermon A. 13:480
1918 Bartlett, Paul W. 12:553
1921 Gregory, John ....
1922 Lentelli, Leo ....
1923 McCartan, Edward ....
1924 Beach, Chester ....
1925 Fraser, James E. C:468
1926 Keck, Charles D:179
1927 Jennewein, C. Paul ....
1929 Ellerhusen, Ulric ....
1931 Lawrie, Lee .... D: 49
1932 Calder, A. Stirling ....
1933 Friedlander, Leo ....

Barnard Gold Medal

Awarded every five years by the National Academy of Sciences for meritorious services to science, discoveries in physical or astronomical science or novel application of science to purposes beneficial to the human race.

American Recipient

1935 Hubble, Edwin P. ....

Bessemer Gold Medal

Awarded by the Iron and Steel Institute of London (1) to the inventor or introducer of any important or remarkable invention, either in the mechanical or chemical processes employed in the manufacture of iron or steel; (2) for a paper read before the Institute and having special merit and importance in connection with iron and steel manufacture; (3) for a contribution to the Journal of the Institute, being an original investigation bearing on the iron and steel manufacture and capable of being productive of valuable practical results.

American Recipients

1879 Cooper, Peter 3:114
1882 Holley, Alexander L. 11:508
1890 Hewitt, Abram S. 3:294
1893 Fritz, John 13: 74
1895 Howe, Henry M. 13: 78
1904 Carnegie, Andrew 9:151
1924 Sauveur, Albert D:104
1928 Schwab, Charles M. A:238

Bigelow Medal

Established in 1915 by Dr. William Sturgis Bigelow and awarded by the Boston Surgical Society for contributions to the advancement of surgery.

1921 Mayo, William J. A:330
1922 Keen, William W. 11:367
1926 Matas, Rudolph D:399
1928 Jackson, Chevalier ....
1932 Finney, John M. T. ....
1933 Cushing, Harvey .... C: 36

Bigsby Medal

Awarded by the Geological Society of London as "An acknowledgment of eminent services in any department of geology, irrespective of the receiver's country; but he must not be older than forty-five years at his last birthday, thus probably not too old for further work, and not too young to have done much."

American Recipients

1877 Marsh, Othniel C. 9:317
1891 Dawson, George M. ....
1895 Walcott, Charles D. 22:135

Bocher Prize

Awarded by the American Mathematical Society for a notable research memoir in analysis published during the preceding five years in some journal on the editorial board of which the society is represented; the recipient must be a member of the society and not more than fifty years old at the time of publication of his memoir.

1923 Birkhoff, George D. ....
1924 Bell, Elexious T. ....
1924 Lefschetz, Solomon ....
1928 Alexander, James W. ....
1932 Morse, Marston ....
1932 Wiener, Norbert ....

Brewster Medal

Awarded biennially by the American Ornithologists' Union to the author of the most important work relating to the birds of the western hemisphere published during the preceding six years.

1921 Ridgway, Robert 8:460
1923 Bent, Arthur C. ....
1925 Todd, W. E. Clyde / Carriker, Melbourne A. } *jointly*
1927 Phillips, John C. ....
1931 Bailey, Florence M. A:257
1933 Chapman, Frank M. C:188
1935 Stoddard, Herbert L. ....

Bruce Gold Medal

Awarded by the Astronomical Society of the Pacific for distinguished services to astronomy.

American Recipients

1898 Newcomb, Simon 7: 17
1908 Pickering, Edward C. 6:424
1909 Hill, George W. 13:442
1915 Campbell, William W. 11:278
1916 Hale, George E. .... C: 45
1917 Barnard, Edward E. 7: 44
1920 Brown, Ernest W. 15: 24
1925 Russell, Henry N. A:346
1926 Aitken, Robert G. ....
1928 Adams, Walter A. B:171
1929 Schlesinger, Frank C:497
1935 Slipher, Vesto M. ....
1936 Leuschner, Armin O. ....

John Burroughs Memorial Association Medal

Awarded by the American Museum of Natural History for the best piece of nature writing, either poetry or prose, published within recent years.

1926 Beebe, William B:337
1927 Seton, Ernest T. C:392
1928 McCarthy, John R. ....
1929 Chapman, Frank M. C:188
1930 Rutledge, Archibald ....
1932 Dellenbaugh, Frederick S. ....
1933 Medsger, Oliver P. ....
1934 Christman, William W. ....

Butler Gold Medal

Awarded by Columbia University every five years for the most distinguished contribution to philosophy or to educational theory, practice or administration during the preceding five-year period.

American Recipients

1925 Thorndike, Edward L. 15:205
1930 Whithead, Alfred N. ....
1935 Dewey, John A:547

Butler Silver Medal

Awarded by Columbia University annually to the graduate of Columbia who in the preceding year has shown the most competence in philosophy or in educational theory, practice or administration.

1915 Cubberly, Ellwood P. ....
1917 Alexander, Hartley B. A:174
1918 Woodworth, Robert S. .... A: 24
1919 Erskine, John .... B: 59
1920 Marshall, Henry R. 11:328
1921 Hollingworth, Harry L. ....
1923 Strayer, George D. A:337
1924 Franz, Shepherd I. A:477
1925 Newlon, Jesse H. ....
1926 Wood, Benjamin DeK. ....
1927 Graves, Frank P. A:277
1928 Russell, William F. ....
1929 Schneider, Herbert W. ....
1930 Kandel, Isaac L. ....
1931 Peterson, Houston ....
1932 Murphy, Gardner ....
1933 Mort, Paul R. ....
1934 Lamprecht, Sterling P. ....

Carnegie Institute International Exhibition Honors Awarded

American Recipients

First Prize

1898 Tryon, Dwight W. 8:423
1899 Beaux, Cecilia 11:299
1901 Maurer, Alfred H. 25:153
1903 Benson, Frank W. 13:413
1904 Schofield, W. Elmer D:166
1908 Dewing, Thomas W. 9:545
1909 Tarbell, Edmund C. B:151
1911 Alexander, John W. 11:297
1914 Redfield, Edward W. ....
1920 Thayer, Abbott H. 6:471
1921 Lawson, Ernest ....
1922 Bellows, George W. 20: 77
1923 Davies, Arthur B. 14:453
1931 Watkins, Franklin C. ....
1934 Blume, Peter ....

Second Prize

1898 Hassam, Childe 10:374
1899 Benson, Frank W. 13:413
1900 Foster, Ben 11:303
1901 Ahrens, Ellen W. ....
1903 Burroughs, Bryson A:131
1904 Tarbell, Edmund C. B:151
1905 Redfield, Edward W. ....
1907 Eakins, Thomas 5:421
1910 Anderson, Karl ....
1912 Dougherty, Paul ....
1921 Giles, Howard ....
1923 Speicher, Eugene B:453
1929 Glackens, William J. ....
1930 Brook, Alexander ....
1933 Curry, John S. ....
1935 Burchfield, Charles ....

Third Prize

1896	Beaux, Cecilia	11:299
1897	Weir, J. Alden	22:296
1900	Kendall, William S.	13:208
1901	Tarbell, Edmund C.	B:151
1903	Lathrop, William L.	
1904	Cushing, Howard G.	24:165
1905	Hassam, Childe	10:374
1908	Carlsen, Emil	24:277
1909	Crane, Bruce	11:310
1910	Rook, Edward F.	
1913	Beal, Gifford R.	
1914	Bellows, George W.	20: 77
1920	Ufer, Walter	
1921	Speicher, Eugene	B:453
1924	Garber, Daniel	C:442
1925	Hawthorne, Charles W.	22:452
1926	Spencer, Robert	
1927	Dasburg, Andrew	
1928	Coleman, Glenn O.	
1933	Poor, Henry V.	
1934	Laufman, Sidney	
1935	Mattson, Henry E.	

John J. Carty Medal

Awarded by the National Academy of Sciences not oftener than once every two years to an individual for noteworthy and distinguished accomplishment in any field of science coming within the scope of the charter of the Academy.

1932	Carty, John J.	23: 36
1936	Wilson, Edmund B.	13: 59

Chandler Medal

Awarded annually by Columbia University to the person appointed Chandler Lecturer on the Charles Frederick Chandler Foundation established by the alumni and former students of Professor Chandler.

American Recipients

1914	Baekeland, Leo H.	15:330
1916	Hillebrand, William F.	14:132
1920	Whitney, Willis R.	15:393
1922	Smith, Edgar F.	21: 53
1923	Swain, Robert E.	
1925	Kendall, Edward C.	
1926	Parr, Samuel W.	C:153
1927	Gomberg, Moses	16:109
1928	Wilson, John A.	C:207
1929	Langmuir, Irving	C: 29
1931	Conant, James B.	D: 48
1933	Curme, George O., Jr.	D: 53

Chemical Industry Medal

This medal has replaced the Grasselli Medal since 1933. It is awarded annually by the Society of Chemical Industry, American section, to the person making valuable application of chemical research to industry, primary consideration given to applications in the public interest.

1920	Rogers, Allen	D:281
1922	Fulweiler, Walter H.	
1924	Saklatvala, Phirozshaw D.	
1925	Berry, Edward R.	26:385
1926	Downs, Charles R.	
1928	Rose, Harold J.	
1929	Stoughton, Bradley	14:265
1930	Frolich, Per K.	
1931	Redman, Lawrence V.	D:148
1932	Clark, George L.	
1933	Vail, James G.	
1934	Metzger, Floyd J.	
1936	Landis, Walter S.	

Chemists Medal

Awarded by the American Institute of Chemists for noteworthy and outstanding service to the science of chemistry or the profession of chemist in America.

1926	Blum, William	
1927	Mendel, Lafayette B.	26:424
1929	Garvan, Mr. and Mrs. Francis P.	C:156
1930	Eastman, George	26: 32
1931	Mellon, Richard B. } jointly	24: 56
	Mellon, Andrew W. } jointly	A: 16
1932	Herty, Charles H.	18: 85
1933	Sherman, Henry C.	D: 65
1934	Conant, James B.	D: 48
1936	Bogert, Marston T.	14:207

W. A. Clark Prizes

Awarded by the Corcoran Gallery of Art, Washington, D. C.

First Prize

Accompanied by Corcoran Gold Medal

1907	Metcalf, Willard L.	13:603
1909	Redfield, Edward W.	
1911	Tarbell, Edmund C.	B:151
1913	Hassam, Childe	10:374
1915	Weir, J. Alden	22:296
1917	Davies, Arthur B.	14:453
1920	Benson, Frank W.	13:413
1922	Garber, Daniel	C:442
1924	Bellows, George W.	20: 77
1926	Hawthorne, Charles W.	22:452
1928	Karfiol, Bernard	
1931	Sterne, Maurice	
1933	Luks, George	
1935	Speicher, Eugene	B:453

Second Prize

Accompanied by the Corcoran Silver Medal

1907	Benson, Frank W.	13:413
1909	De Camp, Joseph	13:216
1911	Melchers, Gari	B:120
1913	Garber, Daniel	C:442
1915	Woodbury, Charles H.	
1917	Lawson, Ernest	
1920	Davis, Charles H.	8:431
1922	Baker, Burtis	B:373
1924	Hawthorne, Charles W.	22:452
1926	Schofield, W. Elmer	D:166
1928	Speicher, Eugene	B:453
1931	Beal, Gifford R.	
1933	Grabach, John R.	B:165
1935	Frieseke, Frederick C.	

Thomas B. Clarke Prize

Awarded by the National Academy of Design for the best American figure composition painted in the United States by an American citizen, without limitation of age.

1884	Ulrich, Charles F.	1:202
1885	Jones, Francis C.	13:126
1886	Satterlee, Walter	13:557
1887	Dewing, Thomas W.	9:545
1888	Mowbray, H. Siddons	23:188
1889	Wiles, Irving R.	6:468
1890	Tarbell, Edmund C.	B:151
1891	Benson, Frank W.	13:413
1892	Harper, William St. J.	13:533
1893	Curran, Charles C.	13:364
1894	Watrous, Harry W.	13:369
1895	Walker, Henry O.	22:401
1896	Reid, Robert	6:476
1898	Thayer, Abbott H.	6:471

1899	Potthast, Edward H.	22:339
1900	Schreyvogel, Charles	13:411
1901	Kline, William F.	13:511
1902	Daingerfield, Elliott	13:111
1903	Sewell, Lydia A.	13:565
1904	Walcott, Harry M.	
1905	Hassam, Childe	10:374
1906	Ballin, Hugo	
1907	Prellwitz, Henry	
1908	Gauley, Robert D.	
1909	Emmet, Lydia F.	15:340
1910	Waugh, Frederick J.	
1911	Hawthorne, Charles W.	22:452
1912	Bittinger, Charles	
1913	Beal, Gifford R.	
1914	Olinsky, Ivan G.	B:159
1915	Miller, Richard E.	A:270
1916	Church, Frederic E.	20: 33
1917	Bohm, Max	21:156
1918	Ufer, Walter	
1919	Myers, Jerome	
1920	Hopkins, James R.	
1921	Kroll, Leon	
1922	Fiske, Gertrude H.	B:286
1923	Savage, Eugene F.	
1924	Addams, Clifford	
1925	Fiske, Gertrude H.	B:286
1926	Foster, Will	
1927	Costigan, John E.	B:304
1928	Stoddard, Alice K.	
1929	Caser, Ettore	
1930	Trubach, Ernest	
1931	Samstag, Gordon	
1932	Brackman, Robert	
1933	Farnsworth, Jerry	
1934	Leaky, Gerald	
1935	Sterne, Maurice	

Collier Trophy

Established by Robert J. Collier and first awarded in 1911. Presented annually by the National Aëronautic Association for the greatest achievement in aviation in America, the value of which has been thoroughly demonstrated by actual use during the preceding year.

1911	Curtiss, Glenn H.	22:195
1912	Curtiss, Glenn H.	22:195
1913	Wright, Orville	14: 57
1914	Sperry, Elmer A.	23: 78
1915	Burgess, W. Starling	
1916	Sperry, Elmer A.	23: 78
1917 to 1920	No award made because of the war	
1921	Loening, Grover	B:283
1922	Personnel of the U. S. Air Mail Service	
1923	Pilots and other personnel of the U. S. Air Mail Service	
1924	U. S. Army Air Service	
1925	Reed, S. Albert	
1926	Hoffman, Edward L.	
1927	Lawrance, Charles L.	D:194
1928	Aëronautics Branch, Department of Commerce	
1929	National Advisory Committee for Aëronautics	
1930	Pitcairn, Harold F.	
1931	Packard Motor Car Co.	
1932	Martin, Glenn L.	A:324
1933	Hamilton Standard Propeller Co., with particular credit to Frank W. Caldwell	
1934	Hegenberger, Albert F.	
1935	Douglas, Donald W.	

Cyrus B. Comstock Prize

Awarded by the National Academy of Sciences every five years for the most important discovery or investigation in electricity, magnetism, and radiant energy, or to aid worthy investigations in those subjects.

1913	Millikan, Robert A.	A:268
1918	Barnett, Samuel J.	
1923	Duane, William	A:345
1928	Davisson, Clinton J.	C:233
1933	Bridgman, Percy W.	

Congressional Gold Medal

Granted by special act or resolution of congress.

1776	Washington, George	1: 1
	Capture of Boston	
1777	Gates, Horatio	1: 47
	Surrender of Burgoyne	
1779	Wayne, Anthony	1: 55
	Capture of Stony Point	
1779	Lee, Henry	3: 25
	Surprise of Pawlus Hook	
1781	Morgan, Daniel	1: 84
	Victory of Cowpens	
1781	Greene, Nathanael	1: 39
	Victory of Eutaw Springs	
1787	Jones, John Paul	2: 14
	Capture of the "Serapis"	
1800	Truxton, Thomas	2:431
	Action with the "Vengeance"	
1805	Preble, Edward	8: 92
	Naval operations against Tripoli	
1813	Hull, Isaac	13:426
	Capture of the "Guerriere"	
1813	Decatur, Stephen	4: 56
	Capture of the "Macedonian"	
1813	Jones, Jacob	2:233
	Capture of the "Frolic"	
1813	Bainbridge, William	8: 93
	Capture of the "Java"	
1814	Perry, Oliver H.	4:288
	Elliott, Jesse D.	7: 39
	Conduct in the battle of Lake Erie	
1814	Burrows, William	7: 71
	McCall, Edward R.	12:497
	Capture of the "Boxer"	
1814	Lawrence, James	8: 92
	Capture of the "Peacock"	
1814	Macdonough, Thomas	7: 28
	Henley, Robert	13: 52
	Cassin, Stephen	13:263
	Conduct in the battle of Lake Champlain	
1814	Warrington, Lewis	6:232
	Capture of the "Epervier"	
1814	Blakely, Johnston	5:440
	Capture of the "Reindeer"	
1814	Brown, Jacob	5:400
	Scott, Winfield	3:502
	Gaines, Edmund P.	9:372
	Macomb, Alexander	2:241
	Porter, Peter B.	5: 81
	Ripley, Eleazar W.	3:263
	Miller, James	10:183
	Conduct in the victories of Chippewa, Niagara and Erie	
1815	Jackson, Andrew	5:289
	Conduct in the battle of New Orleans	
1816	Stewart, Charles	8:156
	Capture of the "Cyane" and the "Levant"	
1816	Biddle, James	6: 55
	Capture of the "Penguin"	
1818	Harrison, William Henry	3: 33
	Shelby, Isaac	13: 1
	Conduct in the victory of the Thames	
1835	Croghan, George	4:256
	Defense of Ft. Stephenson	

1846 Taylor, Zachary ... 4:397
Conduct in operations on the Rio Grande
1847 Taylor, Zachary ... 4:367
Taking of Monterey
1848 Scott, Winfield ... 3:502
Conduct in the Mexican campaign of 1847
1848 Taylor, Zachary ... 4:367
Conduct in the battle of Buena Vista
1854 Ingraham, Duncan N. ... 8:336
Rescue of Martin Koszta from Austrian brig "Hussar"
1858 Rose, Fred A. ... British
Services in the care of yellow-fever patients on U. S. S. "Susquehanna"
1863 Grant, Ulysses S. ... 4: 1
Conduct in various battles
1864 Vanderbilt, Cornelius ... 6:208
Gift of a steamship to the United States during the Civil war
1867 Field, Cyrus W. ... 4:451
Laying of the Atlantic cable
1867 Peabody, George ... 5:335
Gift for education in southern and southwestern states
1871 Robinson, George F. ...
Saving the life of Secretary Seward
1874 Horn, John ... 13:463
Life-saving on Detroit river
1883 Slater, John F. ... 12:148
Gift for education of negroes in southern states
1888 Francis, Joseph ... 10: 83
Perfection of life-saving appliances
1890 Members of "Jeanette" arctic expedition ...
For services in said expedition
1900 Newcomb, Frank H. ... 25:312
and command
Rescue of torpedo boat "Winslow"
1902 { Jarvis, David N. ... 13:190
Bertholf, Ellsworth P. ... 18:348
Call, Samuel J. ... }
Overland expedition for relief of whaling fleet in arctic regions, 1897-98
1909 { Wright, Orville ... 14: 57
Wright, Wilbur ... 14: 56 }
Services to science of aërial navigation
1912 Rostron, Arthur, captain of the "Carpathia"
"Titanic" relief
1914 Officers and crew of the "Kroonland" ...
Relief of the "Volturno"
1915 Senors de Gama, Naón and Suáres ...
Mediation between the United States and warring parties in Mexico
1928 Lindbergh, Charles A. ... B: 34
In recognition of achievements
1928 Edison, Thomas A. ... 25: 1
In recognition of achievements
1928 { Ellsworth, Lincoln ... B: 38
Amundsen, Roald ...
Nobile, Umberto ... }
Transpolar flight of 1926
1929 { Reed, Walter ... 13:284
Carroll, James, and twenty others ... }
Services in yellow fever investigation in Cuba
1930 Byrd, Richard E. ... B:431
and officers and men of his expedition
Antarctic explorations
1932 { Boardman, Russell N. ...
Polando, John L. ...
Post, Wiley ...
Gatty, Harold ... }
Trans-Atlantic and round-the-world flights

Philip A. Conne Medal

Awarded by The Chemists' Club to an individual responsible for a discovery in chemistry which has proven of value in the treatment of human disease.

1932 Abel, John J. ... A:392
1933 Dakin, Henry D. ...
1934 Mendel, Lafayette B. ... 26:424
1935 Doisy, Edward A. ...
1936 Van Slyke, Donald D. ...

Elliot Cresson Medal

Awarded by the Franklin Institute of the State of Pennsylvania for discoveries in the arts or sciences, or for the invention or improvement of some useful machine, or for some new process or combination of materials in manufacture, or for ingenuity, skill or perfection in workmanship.

American Recipients

1871 Tilghman, Benjamin C. ... 15:263
1874 Zentmayer, Joseph ... 13:215
1874 Chambers Bros. & Co. ...
1874 Powers & Weightman ...
1875 Bullock, William A. ... 9:538
1876 Bonwill, William G. A. ... 5:177
1876 Dudley, Plimmon H. ... 19:281
1878 Bower, Henry ...
1880 Goddwin, William F. ...
1881 Griscom, William W. ...
1886 Delany, Patrick B. ... 13:590
1886 Ramsey, Robert H. ...
1886 Lowe, Thaddeus S. C. ... 9:542
1886 Pratt & Whitney Co. ...
1887 Cowles, Alfred H. } *jointly* ... 22: 44
Cowles, Eugene H. } ... 23: 51
1887 Albert, Charles F. ...
1889 Simonds, George F. ...
1889 Cowper, Edward A. } *jointly*
Robertson, J. Hart }
1890 Hayes, Mayer & Co. ...
1890 Mergenthaler, Ottmar ... 9:490
1891 Hammond, James B. ... 3:321
1891 Bates, Stockton } *jointly*
Shaw, Edwin F.
Von Culen, G. M. }
1892 Bevington, James H. ...
1892 Holmes, Philip H. ...
1893 Fiske, Bradley A. ... B: 57
1893 Marks, George E. ...
1893 Ives, Frederic E. ... 15: 77
1893 Tesla, Nikola ... 6:500
1893 Batchellor, Clifford H. ...
1895 Pelton, Lester A. ... 13:602
1895 Peckover, James ... 13:413
1895 Howe, Henry M. ... 13: 78
1896 Lanston, Tolbert ... 13:573
1896 Herschel, Clemens ... 22:342
1896 Gray, Elisha ... 4:453
1896 Delany, Patrick B. ... 13:590
1897 Jenkins, Charles F. ... B:246
1897 Corscaden, Thomas ...
1900 Atwater, Wilbur O. ... 6:262
1900 Rosa, Edward B. ... 26:312
1900 Levy, Louis E. ... 13:589
1900 U. S. Geological Survey ...
1900 American Cotton Co. ...
1901 Haupt, Lewis M. ... 13:233
1901 Forbes Co. ...
1901 Mason & Hamlin Co. ... 13:437
1902 White, Munsel } *jointly*
Taylor, Frederick W. } ... 23: 47
1902 Acker, Charles E. ... 13:573
1903 Sprague, Frank J. ... 24: 15
1903 Ferrell, Joseph L. ...
1903 Gill, Wilson L. ... 4: 90
1904 Outerbridge, Alexander E. ... 13:118
1904 Parker, John C. ... C:429
1904 Dodge, James M. ... 12:490
1904 Levy, Louis E. ... 13:589
1904 Clamer, Guilliam H. ...
1905 Pupin, Michael I. ... 26: 5

1906	Hammer, William J.	15:218
1907	Taylor, Edward R.	
1907	Phillips, Ferdinand	
1907	Heany, J. Allen	
1908	Hough, Romeyn B.	20:170
1908	Delany, Patrick B.	13:590
1909	Gayley, James	14: 70
1909	Wood, Henry A. Wise	14:270
1909	Turner, Walter V.	18:310
1910	Hewitt, Peter C.	14:470
1910	Sauveur, Albert	D:104
1910	Brashear, John A.	4:552
1910	Fritz, John	13: 74
1910	Weston, Edward	5:176
1910	Wiley, Harvey W.	21: 72
1912	Thomson, Elihu	B:106
1912	Squier, George O.	24:320
1912	Morley, Edward W.	4:520
1912	Stratton, Samuel W.	13:142
1912	Michelson, Albert A.	C: 42
1912	Bell, Alexander G.	6:220
1913	Fischer, Emil	
1913	Randolph, Isham	19:385
1913	Steinmetz, Charles P.	23: 94
1913	Berliner, Emile	21: 6
1914	Smith, Edgar F.	21: 53
1914	Linde, Karl P. G.	
1914	Wright, Orville	14: 57
1915	Owens, Michael J.	13:504
1916	American Telephone & Telegraph Co.	
1917	Northrup, Edwin F.	
1918	Lewis, Isaac N.	16:213
1920	Emmet, William L.	D:413
1921	Eldred, Byron E.	
1922	DeForest, Lee	A: 18
1923	Johnson, Raymond D.	
1923	Kingsbury, Albert	
1925	Hodgkinson, Francis	B: 18
1926	Miller, Dayton C.	C:515
1926	Hale, George E.	C: 45
1926	Hastings, Charles S.	
1927	Elmen, Gustaf W.	
1927	Karapetoff, Vladimir N.	D:176
1927	Nichols, Edward L.	4:482
1928	Ford, Henry	B: 1
1929	Jackson, Chevalier	
1929	Sperry, Elmer A.	23: 78
1930	Gibson, Norman R.	
1930	Moultrop, Irving E.	
1930	Lyman, Theodore	24:347
1931	Davisson, Clinton J.	C:233
1931	Germer, Lester H.	
1931	Lyman, Theodore	24:347
1932	Fortescue, Charles L.	
1932	Bridgman, Percy W.	
1932	Whitehead, John B.	
1934	Ballantine, Stuart	
1934	Union Switch & Signal Co.	

Cullum Geographical Medal

Awarded by vote of the Council of the American Geographical Society to those who distinguish themselves by geographical discoveries, or in the advancement of geographical science.

American Recipients

1896	Peary, Robert E.	14: 60
1901	Mendenhall, Thomas C.	10:117
1902	Smith, A. Donaldson	13:608
1906	Bell, Robert	
1908	Davis, William M.	24: 32
1914	Semple, Ellen C.	A:389
1917	Goethals, George W.	24: 6
1918	Newell, Frederick H.	23:162
1919	Osborn, Henry Fairfield	26: 18
1930	Marbut, Curtis F.	
1931	Jefferson, Mark	
1935	Johnson, Douglas	D:177

Helen Culver Gold Medal

Awarded by the Geographic Society of Chicago in recognition of valuable contributions to the science of geography.

American Recipients

1910	Chamberlin, Thomas C.	19: 25
1910	Peary, Robert E.	14: 60
1913	Davis, William M.	24: 32
1917	Salisbury, Rollin D.	11: 73
1918	Bartholomew, John G.	
1918	Chisholm, George G.	
1919	Stefansson, Vilhjalmur	A:230
1922	Goode, John P.	23:386
1925	Romer, Eugene	
1926	Byrd, Richard E.	B:431
1927	Grosvenor, Gilbert H.	A:309
1931	Semple, Ellen C.	A:389
1932	Jefferson, Mark	

Charles P. Daly Medal

Established in 1900 by Charles P. Daly and awarded by the American Geographical Society to explorers, writers and men of science who have contributed to the advancement of geographical knowledge.

American Recipients

1902	Peary, Robert E.	14: 60
1908	Davidson, George	7:227
1909	Rockhill, William W.	8:129
1909	Chaille-Long, Charles	10: 28
1910	Gilbert, Grove K.	13: 46
1912	Amundsen, Roald	
1913	Brooks, Alfred H.	22:298
1918	Stefansson, Vilhjalmur	A:230
1920	Smith, George O.	14:130
1922	Greely, Adolphus W.	3:285
1923	Leffingwell, Ernest deK.	A:401
1924	Birdseye, Claude H.	
1925	Bartlett, Robert A.	
1925	Brainard, David L.	3:286
1930	Darton, Nelson H.	
1935	Andrews, Roy Chapman	A:302

Leslie Dana Medal

Awarded by the St. Louis Society for the Blind for outstanding achievement in the prevention of blindness and the conservation of vision.

American Recipients

1925	Jackson, Edward	12:446
1926	Schuyler, Louisa L.	20: 19
1927	Howe, Lucien	23:218
1930	DeSchweinitz, George E.	C:144
1933	Luedde, William H.	
1935	Wilder, William H.	

Diction Medal

Awarded by the American Academy of Arts and Letters for good diction on the stage.

1924	Hampden, Walter	B: 12
1927	Matthison, Edith W.	
1928	Skinner, Otis	11:220
1929	Marlowe, Julia	13:217
1930	Arliss, George	
1932	Carlisle, Alexandra	
1933	Tibbett, Lawrence	
1935	Fontanne, Lynn	D:317

James Douglas Medal

Established in 1922 in memory of James Douglas, and awarded by the American Institute of Mining and Metallurgical Engineers for distinguished achievement in non-ferrous metallurgy.

American Recipients

1923	Laist, Frederick	
1924	Merrill, Charles W.	15:102
1925	Bassett, William H.	26:156
1926	Callow, John M.	
1927	Jeffries, Zay	A:155
1929	Merica, Paul D.	
1930	Dorr, John Van N.	
1931	Peirce, William H.	
1932	Mathewson, Champion H.	
1933	Elton, James O.	

Henry Draper Medal

Established in 1883 by Mrs. Mary Anna Palmer Draper and awarded by the National Academy of Sciences for original discovery in astronomical physics, preference given to a citizen of the United States in the case of discoveries of equal importance.

American Recipients

1886	Langley, Samuel P.	15: 7
1888	Pickering, Edward C.	6:424
1890	Rowland, Henry A.	11: 25
1899	Keeler, James E.	10:498
1904	Hale, George E.	C: 45
1906	Campbell, William W.	11:278
1910	Abbot, Charles G.	A:366
1915	Stebbins, Joel	B:342
1916	Michelson, Albert A.	C: 42
1918	Adams, Walter S.	B:171
1922	Russell, Henry N.	A:346
1926	Shapley, Harlow	C: 95
1928	Wright, William H.	
1931	Cannon, Annie J.	B:482
1932	Slipher, Vesto M.	
1934	Plaskett, John S.	
1936	Mees, C. E. Kenneth	

Lucy Wharton Drexel Medal

Established by Mrs. Drexel in 1902 and awarded by the Museum of Science and Art of the University of Pennsylvania for the best archæological excavations or for the best publication based on such excavations by an English scholar during the previous five years.

American Recipients

1903	Putnam, Frederic W.	23:257
1903	Hilprecht, Hermann V.	10:380
1910	Butler, Howard C.	20: 56

Edison Medal

Awarded by the American Institute of Electrical Engineers for meritorious achievement in electrical science or electrical engineering or the electrical arts.

1909	Thomson, Elihu	B:106
1910	Sprague, Frank J.	24: 15
1911	Westinghouse, George	15: 41
1912	Stanley, William	24:394
1913	Brush, Charles F.	21: 1
1914	Bell, Alexander Graham	6:220
1916	Tesla, Nikola	6:500
1917	Carty, John J.	23: 36
1918	Lamme, Benjamin G.	20: 36
1919	Emmet, William L.	D:413
1920	Pupin, Michael I.	26: 5
1921	Chesney, Cummings C.	
1922	Millikan, Robert A.	A:268
1923	Lieb, John W.	13:606
1924	Howell, John W.	B:503
1925	Ryan, Harris J.	
1927	Coolidge, William D.	
1928	Jewett, Frank B.	C:272
1929	Scott, Charles F.	13:207
1930	Conrad, Frank	
1931	Rice, E. Wilbur, Jr.	26: 10
1932	Gherardi, Bancroft	
1933	Kennelly, Arthur E.	13:452
1934	Whitney, Willis R.	15:393
1935	Stillwell, Lewis B.	14:520

Daniel Giraud Elliot Medal

Awarded by the National Academy of Sciences for most meritorious work in zoölogy or paleontology published each year.

American Recipients

1917	Chapman, Frank M.	C:188
1918	Beebe, William	B:337
1919	Ridgway, Robert	8:460
1921	Dean, Bashford	21: 29
1922	Wheeler, William M.	
1925	Wilson, Edmund B.	13: 59
1928	Seton, Ernest T.	C:392
1929	Osborn, Henry Fairfield	26: 18
1930	Coghill, George E.	
1932	Chapin, James P.	

Fine Arts Medal

Established in 1919 and awarded by the American Institute of Architects for distinguished achievement in the fine arts, embracing painting, sculpture, music and literature.

American Recipients

1921	Manship, Paul	C:312
1922	Mathews, Arthur F.	
1925	Sargent, John S.	11:291
1926	Stokowski, Leopold	
1927	Lawrie, Lee	D: 49
1928	Mowbray, H. Siddons	23:188
1930	Weinman, Adolph A.	
1931	Olmsted, Frederick L.	2:298
1934	Breasted, James H.	B:377
1936	Jones, Robert E.	

Franklin Medal

Awarded annually by the Franklin Institute to those workers in physical science or technology, whose efforts have done most to advance a knowledge of physical science or its applications.

American Recipients

1915	Edison, Thomas A.	25: 1
1916	Carty, John J.	23: 36
1916	Richards, Theodore W.	12:362
1917	Taylor, David W.	15: 87
1918	Mendenhall, Thomas C.	10:117
1919	Squier, George O.	24:320
1921	Sprague, Frank J.	24: 15
1922	Modjeski, Ralph	15: 68
1923	Michelson, Albert A.	C: 42
1924	Weston, Edward	5:176
1925	Thomson, Elihu	B:106
1926	Rea, Samuel	15:289
1927	Hale, George E.	C: 45
1928	Brush, Charles F.	21: 1
1929	Berliner, Emile	21: 6
1930	Stevens, John F.	D:213

1931 Whitney, Willis R. 15:393
1932 Swasey, Ambrose B:274
1933 Wright, Orville 14: 57
1934 Russell, Henry N. A:346
1934 Langmuir, Irving .... C: 29
1935 Einstein, Albert ....

John Fritz Medal

Established in 1902 in honor of John Fritz. It is awarded annually by the John Fritz Medal Board of Award, composed of members of the American Society of Civil Engineers, American Society of Mining and Metallurgical Engineers, American Society of Mechanical Engineers, and American Society of Electrical Engineers, for notable scientific or industrial achievement.

American Recipients

1902 Fritz, John 13: 74
1906 Westinghouse, George 15: 41
1907 Bell, Alexander Graham 6:220
1908 Edison, Thomas A. 25: 1
1909 Porter, Charles T. 20:494
1910 Noble, Alfred 9: 44
1912 Hunt, Robert W. 19: 17
1914 Sweet, John E. 13: 54
1915 Douglas, James 23: 22
1916 Thomson, Elihu B:106
1917 Howe, Henry M. 13: 78
1918 Smith, J. Waldo 24:108
1919 Goethals, George W. 24: 6
1920 Wright, Orville 14: 57
1924 Swasey, Ambrose B:274
1925 Stevens, John F. D:213
1926 Adams, Edward D. 10:419
1927 Sperry, Elmer A. 23: 78
1928 Carty, John J. 23: 36
1929 Hoover, Herbert C. .... C: 1
1930 Modjeski, Ralph 15: 68
1931 Taylor, David W. 15: 87
1932 Pupin, Michael I. 26: 5
1933 Jackling, Daniel C. D:245
1934 Freeman, John R. C:397
1935 Sprague, Frank J. 24: 15
1936 Durand, William F. D:260

Geographic Society of Chicago Gold Medal

Awarded for valuable contributions to the science of geography.

American Recipients

1915 Goethals, George W. 24: 6
1916 Gorgas, William C. 14:528
1927 Bowman, Isaiah ....
1928 Cox, Henry J. 24:307
1929 Breasted, James H. B:377
1930 Byrd, Richard E. B:431
1930 Cole, Fay-Cooper ....
1931 Gould, Laurence M. ....
1936 Ellsworth, Lincoln .... B: 38

Willard Gibbs Medal

Awarded annually by the American Chemical Society, Chicago section, for eminent work in and original contributions to pure or applied chemistry.

American Recipients

1912 Richards, Theodore W. 12:362
1913 Baekeland, Leo H. 15:330
1914 Remsen, Ira 9:240
1915 Noyes, Arthur A. 13:284
1916 Whitney, Willis R. 15:393
1917 Morley, Edward W. 4:520
1918 Burton, William M. C:243
1919 Noyes, William A. B:314
1920 Cottrell, Frederick G. ....
1923 Stieglitz, Julius C:401
1924 Lewis, Gilbert N. ....
1925 Gomberg, Moses 16:109
1926 Irvine, James C. ....
1927 Abel, John J. A:392
1928 Harkins, William D. ....
1929 Hudson, Claude S. ....
1930 Langmuir, Irving .... C: 29
1931 Levene, Phoebus A. ....
1932 Franklin, Edward C. A:411
1934 Urey, Harold C. ....
1935 Kraus, Charles A. ....
1936 Adams, Roger ....
1937 McCoy, Herbert N. ....

Gottheil Medal

Awarded by Zeta Beta Tau College Fraternity for distinguished service to Jewry.

1925 Wise, Stephen S. .... B: 25
1926 Brown, David ....
1927 Sapiro, Aaron C:120
1928 Rosenwald, Julius .... A: 80
1929 Warburg, Felix M. ....
1930 Lehman, Herbert H. B:456
1932 Holmes, John H. C:461
1933 Clinchy, Everett R. ....
1933 Ross, J. Elliot ....
1933 Lazaron, Morris S. ....
1935 McDonald, James G. ....

Grasselli Medal

See Chemical Industry Medal

Daniel Guggenheim Medal

Established in 1927 by the Daniel Guggenheim Fund for the promotion of aëronautics and sponsored by the American Society of Mechanical Engineers and the Society of Automotive Engineers.

American Recipients

1929 Wright, Orville 14: 57
1933 Hunsaker, Jerome C. .... A: 84
1934 Boeing, William E. ....
1935 Durand, William F. D:260
1936 Lewis, George W. ....

Hall of Fame for Great Americans

Established through the generosity of Mrs. Finley J. Shepard and administered through the Senate of New York University, which appoints a body of approximately 100 persons known as The Electors. The Electors through their votes select the names to be honored by representation in the Hall of Fame. (The number before the name indicates the number of votes cast by the electors.)

Names chosen in 1900

97 Washington, George 1: 1
96 Lincoln, Abraham 2: 65
96 Webster, Daniel 3: 36
94 Franklin, Benjamin 1:328
93 Grant, Ulysses S. 4: 1
91 Marshall, John 1: 25
91 Jefferson, Thomas 3: 1
87 Emerson, Ralph Waldo 3:416
86 Fulton, Robert 3:104

85 Longfellow, Henry W. 2:160
83 Irving, Washington 3: 17
82 Edwards, Jonathan 5:464
82 Morse, Samuel F. B. 4:449
79 Farragut, David G. 2: 45
74 Clay, Henry 5: 77
74 Peabody, George 5:335
73 Hawthorne, Nathaniel 3: 64
69 Cooper, Peter 3:114
69 Whitney, Eli 4:495
68 Lee, Robert E. 4: 95
67 Mann, Horace 3: 78
67 Audubon, John J. 6: 75
65 Kent, James 3: 55
64 Beecher, Henry Ward 3:129
64 Story, Joseph 2:468
62 Adams, John 2: 1
58 Channing, William Ellery 5:458
52 Stuart, Gilbert C. 5:324
51 Gray, Asa 3:407

Names chosen in 1905

89 Lowell, James Russell 2: 32
60 Adams, John Quincy 5: 73
59 Lyon, Mary 4:462
58 Sherman, William T. 4: 32
56 Madison, James 5:369
53 Whittier, John Greenleaf 1:407
50 Willard, Emma 1:244
48 Mitchell, Maria 5:236

Names chosen in 1910

74 Stowe, Harriet Beecher 1:423
69 Poe, Edgar Allan 1:463
69 Holmes, Oliver Wendell 2:336
62 Cooper, James Fenimore 1:398
60 Brooks, Phillips 2:304
59 Bryant, William Cullen 4: 79
55 Willard, Frances E. 1:376
53 Bancroft, George 3:160
53 Jackson, Andrew 5:289
51 Motley, John L. 5:213

Names chosen in 1915

70 Hamilton, Alexander 1: 9
69 Hopkins, Mark 6:237
68 Parkman, Francis 1:431
65 Agassiz, Louis 2:360
61 Howe, Elias 4:432
56 Henry, Joseph 3:405
53 Cushman, Charlotte S. 4: 40
52 Boone, Daniel 3:110
52 Choate, Rufus 6: 17

Names chosen in 1920

72 Clemens, Samuel L. 6: 24
72 Morton, William T. G. 8:332
67 Saint-Gaudens, Augustus 8:287
66 Williams, Roger 10: 4
57 Henry, Patrick 1:337
53 Palmer, Alice E. Freeman 7:328
51 Eads, James B. 5:134

Names chosen in 1925

85 Booth, Edwin 3:180
68 Jones, John Paul 2: 14

Names chosen in 1930

74 Whistler, J. McNeill 9: 49
66 Maury, Matthew F. 6: 35
66 Monroe, James 6: 81
64 Whitman, Walt 1:255

Names chosen in 1935

83 Penn, William 2:274
78 Newcomb, Simon 7: 17
77 Cleveland, Grover 2:400

Harben Gold Medal

Awarded by the Royal Institute of Public Health of London to such persons whom the Council of the Institute should determine had rendered eminent services to public health.

American Recipients

1920 Gorgas, William C. 14:528
1931 Welch, William H. 26: 6

Marcellus Hartley Medal

See Public Welfare Medal

Hayden Memorial Geological Award

Awarded by the Academy of Natural Sciences of Philadelphia and presented for distinguished service in geological and paleontological science.

American Recipients

1890 Hall, James 3:280
1891 Cope, Edward D. 7:474
1905 Walcott, Charles D. 22:135
1908 Clarke, John M. 19:456
1911 Branner, John C. 24:278
1914 Osborn, Henry Fairfield 26: 18
1917 Davis, William M. 24: 32
1920 Chamberlin, Thomas C. 19: 25
1926 Scott, William B. 13:214
1929 Schuchert, Charles 15:122
1932 Daly, Reginald A.

Holley Medal

Instituted and endowed in 1924 by George I. Rockwood and awarded by the American Society of Mechanical Engineers for some great and unique act of genius in engineering that has accomplished a great and timely public benefit.

1928 Sperry, Elmer A. 23: 78
1934 Langmuir, Irving C: 29

Hoover Medal

Administered by a Board of Award, consisting of three representatives from each of the four founder engineering societies, to engineers for distinguished public service.

1930 Hoover, Herbert C: 1
1936 Swasey, Ambrose B:274

Howells Medal

Awarded by the American Academy of Arts and Letters "to commemorate the name of our great American novelist" every fifth year in recognition of the most distinguished work of American fiction published during that period.

1925 Freeman, Mary E. Wilkins 9:229
1930 Cather, Willa S. A:537
1935 Buck, Pearl

Hubbard Gold Medal

Awarded by the National Geographic Society for outstanding work in research and exploration.

American Recipients

1906 Peary, Robert E. 14: 60
1909 Bartlett, Robert A.

1909 Gilbert, Grove K. 13: 46
1919 Stefansson, Vilhjalmur A:230
1926 Byrd, Richard E. B:431
1927 Lindbergh, Charles A. .... B: 34
1931 Andrews, Roy Chapman A:302
1934 Lindbergh, Anne M. ....
1935 Stevens, Albert W. ....
1935 Anderson, Orvil A. ....
1936 Ellsworth, Lincoln .... B: 38

Institute of Radio Engineers Medal of Honor

Awarded to that person who has made public the greatest advance in the science or art of radio communication, regardless of the time of performance or publication of the work on which the award is based.

American Recipients

1918 Armstrong, Edwin H. ....
1919 Alexanderson, Ernst F. W. .... A: 30
1921 Fessenden, Reginald A. 15: 21
1922 DeForest, Lee .... A: 18
1923 Stone, John S. 14:106
1924 Pupin, Michael I. 26: 5
1926 Pickard, Greenleaf W. B:294
1927 Austin, Louis W. 24:118
1929 Pierce, George W. ....
1932 Kennelly, Arthur E. 13:452
1934 Hooper, Stanford C. ....

International Award

Awarded by the National Academy of Design for distinguished service to the fine arts.

1929 Root, Elihu 26: 1
1934 Morse, Samuel F. B. 4:449
1934 Blashfield, Edwin H. .... D: 80

Isidor Medal

Awarded by the National Academy of Design for the best figure composition painted by an American artist.

1907 Ballin, Hugo ....
1908 Kendall, William S. 13:208
1909 Williams, Frederick B. 17:349
1910 Cox, Kenyon 5:321
1911 Couse, E. Irving 13:539
1912 Blumenschein, Ernest L. ....
1913 Jones, Francis C. 13:126
1914 Hawthorne, Charles W. 22:452
1915 Hawthorne, Charles W. 22:452
1916 Bellows, George W. 20: 77
1917 Stoddard, Alice K. ....
1918 Blondheim, Adolphe W. ....
1919 McLellan, Ralph ....
1921 Smith, Howard E. ....
1921 Nelson, George L. ....
1923 Page, Marie D. ....
1924 Savage, Eugene F. ....
1926 Hennings, E. Martin ....
1926 Ufer, Walter ....
1927 Kendall, William S. 13:208
1928 Spencer, Robert ....
1929 Tarbell, Edmund C. B:151
1930 Benson, John W. ....
1931 Seyffert, Leopold B:388
1932 Sample, Paul ....
1935 Winter, Andrew ....
1936 Farnsworth, Jerry ....

Frederic Ives Medal

Established in 1928 by Herbert E. Ives and awarded by the Optical Society of America for distinguished work in optics.

1929 Nichols, Edward L. 4:482
1931 Lyman, Theodore ....
1933 Wood, Robert W. 14:457
1935 Hale, George E. .... C: 45

Jarvie Fellowship Medal

Awarded by the Dental Society of the State of New York to those who have accomplished an outstanding performance in the dental profession.

American Recipients

1906 Black, Greene V. 13:537
1906 Darby, Edwin T. ....
1907 Jarvie, William 12:509
1907 Brophy, Truman W. 12:374
1908 Talbot, Eugene S. 13:147
1909 Cryer, Matthew H. 17:432
1910 Jenkins, Newell S. 19:111
1911 Andrews, Robert R. ....
1912 Perry, S. G. ....
1913 Truman, James 25:299
1914 Carr, William ....
1915 Johnson, Charles N. 16:412
1916 Jackson, Victor H. 22:112
1917 Callahan, John R. ....
1918 Wilson, George H. ....
1919 Logan, William H. G. .... D: 95
1920 Burkhart, Harvey J. 12:115
1921 Brown, George Von I. ....
1922 Prinz, Hermann ....
1923 Kells, C. Edmund ....
1924 Gilmer, Thomas L. ....
1925 Grieves, Clarence J. ....
1926 Howe, Percy R. ....
1927 Jones, Alfred C. ....
1928 Kirk, Edward C. ....
1929 Noyes, Frederick B. ....
1930 Mershon, John V. ....
1931 Gillett, Henry W. ....
1933 Lyons, Chalmers ....
1934 Hyatt, Thaddeus P. ....
1935 Waugh, Leuman M. ....

Elisha Kent Kane Medal

Awarded by the Geographical Society of Philadelphia from time to time to explorers and scientists for outstanding work in the field of geography.

American Recipients

1901 Smith, A. Donaldson 13:608
1902 Peary, Robert E. 14: 60
1903 Heilprin, Angelo 12:381
1905 Scott, William B. 13:214
1911 Melville, George W. 3:283
1912 Davis, William M. 24: 32
1915 Huntington, Ellsworth A:510
1916 Farabee, William C. 24:207
1918 Stefansson, Vilhjalmur A:230
1920 Rice, A. Hamilton ....
1922 Johnson, Douglas W. D:177
1926 Byrd, Richard E. B:431
1928 Andrews, Roy Chapman A:302
1933 Lattimore, Owen ....
1936 Ellsworth, Lincoln .... B: 38

George M. Kober Medal

Established in 1923 by Dr. George M. Kober and awarded by the Association of American Physicians to a member who has contributed to the progress and achievement of the medical sciences or preventive medicine.

1925	Noguchi, Hideyo	
1926	Smith, Theobald	D:133
1927	Welch, William H.	26: 6
1928	Vaughan, Victor C.	12:207
1929	Minot, George R.	
1930	Herrick, James B.	
1931	Sewall, Henry	26:323
1932	Joslin, Elliott P.	
1933	Richards, Alfred N.	
1934	Abel, John J.	A:392
1935	Mallory, Frank B.	
1936	Baldwin, Edward R.	B: 99

Laetare Medal

Awarded by the University of Notre Dame as a recognition of services rendered by the laity in behalf of religion, education and morality.

1883	Shea, John D. G.	6:162
1884	Keeley, Patrick J.	
1885	Starr, Eliza A.	13:564
1886	Newton, John	4:312
1887	Preuss, Edward	
1888	Hickley, Patrick V.	
1889	Dorsey, Anna H.	11:361
1890	Onahan, William J.	
1891	Dougherty, Daniel	5:477
1892	Brownson, Henry F.	16:436
1893	Donahue, Patrick	
1894	Daly, Augustin	1:285
1895	Sadlier, Mrs. James	
1896	Rosecrans, William S.	4:162
1897	Emmet, Thomas A.	10:286
1898	Howard, Timothy E.	16:441
1899	Caldwell, Mary G.	
1900	Creighton, John A.	11:369
1901	Cockran, William B.	
1902	Murphy, John B.	13:602
1903	Bonaparte, Charles J.	14: 22
1904	Kerens, Richard C.	14:106
1905	Fitzpatrick, Thomas B.	14:114
1906	Quinlan, Francis	
1907	Conway, Katherine E.	
1908	Monaghan, James C.	
1909	Tiernan, Frances C. F.	20:293
1910	Egan, Maurice F.	11:111
1911	Repplier, Agnes	C:368
1912	Mulry, Thomas M.	25: 32
1913	Herbermann, Charles G.	16:326
1914	White, Edward D.	
1915	Merrick, Mary V.	
1916	Walsh, James J.	
1917	Benson, William S.	23:388
1918	Scott, Joseph	16: 32
1919	Duval, George L.	
1920	Flick, Lawrence F.	
1921	Nourse, Elizabeth	11:304
1922	Neill, Charles P.	
1923	Smith, Walter G.	21: 43
1924	Maginnis, Charles D.	
1925	Zahm, Albert F.	
1926	Hurley, Edward N.	A: 60
1927	Anglin, Margaret	
1928	Spalding, Jack J.	
1929	Smith, Alfred E.	A:404
1930	Kenkel, Fred P.	
1931	Phelan, James J.	C:234
1932	Maher, Stephen J.	D:171
1933	McCormack, John	
1934	Brady, Genevieve G.	
1935	Spearman, Francis H.	

Lamme Gold Medal

Established in 1926 and awarded by the American Institute of Electrical Engineers for meritorious achievement in the development of electrical apparatus or machinery.

1928	Field, Allan B.	
1929	Hellmund, Rudolf E.	
1930	Foster, William J.	
1931	Faccioli, Giuseppe	24: 31
1932	Weston, Edward	5:176
1933	Stillwell, Lewis B.	14:520
1934	Warren, Henry E.	
1935	Bush, Vannevar	

Langley Medal

Awarded by the Smithsonian Institution for specially meritorious investigations in connection with the science of aërodromics and its application to aviation.

1909	Wright, Wilbur } *jointly*	14: 56
	Wright, Orville }	14: 57
1913	Curtiss, Glenn H.	22:195
1913	Eiffel, Gustave	
1927	Lindbergh, Charles A.	B: 34
1929	Manly, Charles M.	21:321
1929	Byrd, Richard E.	B:431
1935	Ames, Joseph S.	A:342

Joseph Leidy Memorial Medal

Awarded tri-annually by the Academy of Natural Sciences of Philadelphia for the best publication, exploration, discovery or research in the natural sciences in such particular branches thereof as may be designated.

1925	Jennings, Herbert S.	A:278
1928	Pilsbry, Henry A.	
1931	Wheeler, William M.	
1934	Miller, Gerrit S.	

Morris Liebmann Memorial Prize

Awarded by the Institute of Radio Engineers to that member who shall have made the most important contribution to the radio art during the preceding calendar year.

American Recipients

1919	Fuller, Leonard F.	B:216
1920	Weagant, Roy A.	C:349
1921	Heising, Raymond A.	
1924	Carson, John R.	
1925	Conrad, Frank	
1926	Bown, Ralph	
1927	Taylor, A. Hoyt	
1928	Cady, Walter G.	
1930	Hull, Albert W.	
1931	Ballantine, Stuart	
1934	Zworsykin, Vladimir K.	
1935	Llewellyn, Frederick B.	

David Livingstone Centenary Medal

Awarded by the American Geographical Society for scientific achievement in the field of geography in the southern hemisphere.

American Recipients

1917	Roosevelt, Theodore	14: 1
1923	Taylor, Griffith	
1929	Byrd, Richard E.	B:431
1930	Gould, Lawrence M.	

Edward Longstreth Medal

Awarded by the Franklin Institute for inventions or for meritorious improvements and developments in machines and mechanical processes.

American Recipients

1890	Menlo Park Ceramic Works	
1891	Dodge, Wallace H.	
1891	Pitkin, Albert J.	
1891	Roby, Henry W.	
1891	Schermerhorn, W. George	
1891	White, John J.	
1892	Chenoweth, Alexander C.	12:332
1892	Jones, J. R.	
1892	Philadelphia Cremation Society	
1892	Roeder, J. R.	
1892	Stearns Manufacturing Co.	
1893	Adams, W. G.	
1893	Bradburn & Pennock	
1893	Forbes, John S.	
1893	Hill, Frederick B.	
1893	Mackay, William M.	
1893	Rosendale Belting Co.	
1894	Baush, Christian H.	
1894	Bloede, Victor G.	D:445
1894	Bristol, W. H.	
1894	Clark, William H.	
1894	Collins, Frank W.	
1894	DeVoe, W. R.	
1894	Ivins, E.	
1894	Johnston, Andrew L.	
1894	Lewis, John F.	
1894	Mattes, William F.	
1894	Schmidt, Max	
1894	Sieber, Joseph	
1894	Star Brass Manufacturing Co.	
1895	Bates, E. G.	
1895	Cheney, Walter L.	
1895	Cooper, W. S.	
1895	Goodyear, Charles	3: 86
1895	Taintor, C. C.	
1896	Armstrong, William T.	
1896	Cox, Jacob D.	
1896	Kroll, G.	
1896	Lodge, George	
1896	Pantasote Leather Co.	
1897	Heilprin, A.	
1897	Marsh, E. B.	
1897	Regan, H. C., Jr.	
1897	Richards, G. M.	
1898	Doolittle, Thomas B.	
1898	Hollingshead, W. B.	
1899	Brown, Harold P.	B:329
1899	Edison, Thomas A.	25: 1
1899	Frick, Frederick	
1899	Henning, G. C.	
1899	Lewis, W.	
1900	Caffrey, C. S., & Co.	
1900	Deshler, Charles	
1900	Hoadley, H. G.	
1900	Holman, A. J., & Co.	
1900	Laird, Schober & Co.	
1900	Lewis, Eugene C.	8:417
1900	McAllister, Edward J.	
1900	Reeves, Milton O.	
1900	Riker, C. L.	
1900	Tucker, William H.	
1900	Williams, H. D.	
1901	Bonnell, Russell	
1901	Fay, C. N.	
1901	Goldman, Henry	
1901	Hochklassen, H.	
1901	International Light, Heat & Power Co.	
1901	Kitson, A.	
1901	Schmitt, Henry J.	
1901	Sholes, Z. G.	
1901	Welsbach Light Co.	
1902	Roussell, Willis J.	
1902	Wagner Electric Manufacturing Co.	
1902	Williams, Brown & Earle	
1903	Arnold, Bion J.	B:456
1903	Cummings, Henry H.	
1903	Ives, Frederic E.	15: 77
1903	Morsell, W. F. C.	
1903	Pittler, J. W. Von	
1903	Scripture, Edward W.	10:310
1903	Shellenbach, William L.	
1903	Toerring, C. J.	
1903	Wentworth, C. C.	
1904	Draper, C. W.	
1904	Eberhardt, Henry F.	
1904	Lupton, D., Son & Co.	
1904	Ruud, Edwin	24:244
1904	Seitz, Henry J.	
1904	Shaw, H. M.	
1904	Ulrich, Frederick L.	
1904	Waterbury Tool Co.	
1904	Yawman & Erbe Mfg. Co.	
1905	Alexander, John E.	
1905	Alteneder, Theodore, & Sons	
1905	Carty, John J.	23: 36
1905	Folmer & Schwing Mfg. Co.	
1905	Miley, Henry M.	
1905	Miley, Michael	
1906	Colt's Patent Fire Arms Mfg. Co.	
1906	Follett, W. I.	
1906	Meeker, George H.	
1906	Weidlog, Charles B.	
1906	Wetherill, Henry E.	
1907	Ives, Herbert E.	C: 39
1907	Townsend, T. F.	
1908	Breed, G.	
1908	Cushman, Allerton S.	26: 86
1909	Bennett, Charles A.	
1909	Crisfield, J. A. P.	
1909	Granbery, J. H.	
1909	Karns, J. P., Co.	
1909	Roper, Charles	
1909	Teal, B. F.	
1910	Reese, B. D.	
1910	Rushton, Kenneth	
1911	Hepburn, Joseph S.	
1911	Hyde, E. P.	
1911	Lloyd, Morton G.	
1911	Turner, Walter V.	18:310
1912	Baskerville, Charles	13:300
1912	Chance, Edwin M.	
1912	Lathrop, E.	
1912	Northrup, Edwin F.	
1912	Schreiner, Oswald	B: 74
1912	Thomas, C. C.	
1913	Abbe, Cleveland	8:264
1913	Chaffee, Emory L.	B:376
1913	Jones, Harry C.	
1913	Knapp, Isaac N.	
1913	Stone, John S.	14:106
1914	Herr, Herbert T.	B: 68
1914	Hirsch, Hiram H.	
1914	Humphreys, W. J.	
1914	Kinkead Manufacturing Co.	
1914	Rusby, J. M.	
1914	Wheeler, George A.	
1915	Ives, Herbert E.	C: 39
1915	Lenker, Will G.	
1915	Tutwiler, Carrington C.	
1915	Underwood, John, & Co.	
1915	Von Recklinghausen, Max	
1915	Young, Charles D.	

1916 Abbott, Robert R.
1916 Ellis, Carleton
1916 Fuller, George W.
1916 Sharples Specialty Co.
1916 Stradling, George F. 24:439
1916 Waggner, Benjamin G.
1916 Wahl Adding Machine Co.
1917 Achard, F. H.
1917 Austin, John T. 18:129
1917 Becker, Christopher A.
1917 Ball, John D.
1917 Dana, A. S.
1917 Hooven, Owens, Rentschler Co.
1917 Kennelly, Arthur E. 13:452
1917 Levy, Max
1917 Miller, Dayton C. C:515
1917 International Money Machine Co.
1917 Rankin, George A.
1917 Ringland, Albert
1917 Schoenfuss, Frank H.
1918 Edwards, Levi T.
1918 Creighton, Henry J. M. B:227
1918 Taussig, John H.
1918 Van Aller, Tycho
1918 Whitehead, John B.
1918 Zeek, Charles F. 20:117
1919 Ives, Herbert E. C: 39
1919 Karrer, Enoch
1919 Kemp, William W.
1919 Kingsbury, Edwin F. C:119
1919 Ledoux, John W. 23: 93
1919 Moore, Richard B.
1919 Schlink, Frederick J.
1919 Skinner, Joshua J.
1919 Snook, Homer C.
1919 Van Horn, William H.
1920 Hite, Bert H.
1920 Kothny, Gottdank L.
1920 Leeds, Morris E.
1920 Luckiesh, M.
1920 Suczek, Robert
1921 Adams, Leason H.
1921 Eddison, William B. B:320
1921 Spitzglass, Jacob M.
1921 Williamson, E. D.
1922 Brandt, Edward J.
1922 Freas, Samuel T.
1922 Hartness, James 15:294
1922 Hicks, Thomas W. C:223
1922 Keller, Joseph F.
1922 Noiseless Typewriter Co.
1922 Pfund, A. Herman
1922 Tiernan, Martin F.
1922 Wallace, Charles F.
1923 Parke, Harry S.
1924 Elliott, William S.
1924 McBride, Thomas C.
1924 Nachod, Carl P.
1924 Sheen, Milton R.
1924 Zimmermann, William F.
1925 Chance, Thomas M.
1925 Hoke, William E.
1925 Meloche, Daniel H.
1925 Midgley, Thomas, Jr.
1926 Kinyon, Alonzo G.
1926 Lewis, W.
1926 Smathers, Frank W.
1927 Hardinge, Harry W.
1927 Speller, Frank N.
1928 Herbert, Edward G.
1928 Machlet, Adolph W.
1928 Valentine, Warren P.
1930 Bailey, Ervin G.
1930 Weyl, Charles
1933 Ingersoll, Howard L.
1933 McAdam, Dunlap J., Jr.
1934 Sykes, William E.
1935 Bruce, Edmond
1935 Colman, Howard D.
1935 Davey, Peter
1935 McEachron, Karl B.
1935 Peterson, Burt A.

Loubat Prize

Awarded by Columbia University for the best work printed and published in the English language on the history, geography, archæology, ethnology, philology, or numismatics of North America.

First Prize

1893 Adams, Henry 11:475
1898 Holmes, William H. 16:441
1908 Osgood, Herbert L.
1913 Beer, George L. 19:167
1918 Alvord, Clarence W.
1923 Smith, Justin H. B:471
1928 Osgood, Herbert L.
1933 Paullin, Charles O.
1933 Wright, John K.

Second Prize

1893 Bandelier, Adolphe F. A. 26:240
1898 Boas, Franz 12:509
1908 Hughes, Thomas A.
1913 Swarton, John R,
1918 Priestley, Herbert I.
1923 Holmes, William H. 16:441
1928 Spinden, Herbert J.
1933 Webb, Walter P.

Cyrus Hall McCormick Gold Medal

Awarded by the American Society of Agricultural Engineers for exceptional, meritorious engineering achievements in agriculture.

1932 Stout, Oscar Van P.
1933 Davidson, J. Brownlee
1934 Nichols, Mark L.
1935 Brown, Theodore
1936 Mead, Elwood A:528

Magellanic Premium

Established in 1786 by John Hyacinth deMagellan and awarded by the American Philosophical Society for the best discovery or invention in navigation, astronomy or natural philosophy.

1790 Hopkinson, Francis 5:460
1792 Patterson, Robert 1:347
1792 Thornton, William 13:470
1794 Collin, Nicholas 13:365
1804 Barton, Benjamin S. 8:377
1864 Chase, Pliny E. 6: 53
1869 Wood, Horatio C. 13:569
1887 Haupt, Lewis M. 13:233
1922 Heyl, Paul R.
1922 Briggs, Lyman J.

John Marshall Prize

Awarded by Johns Hopkins University to the graduate who has produced the best work during the year upon some subject in historical or political science. This prize has not been awarded since 1913.

1892 Adams, Henry C. 12:219
1892 Levermore, Charles H. 5:192
1892 Vincent, John M. 13:540

1892 Wilson, Woodrow ... 19: 1
1893 Andrews, Charles McL. ... 13:160
1894 Warner, Amos G. ... 13:446
1895 Shaw, Albert ... 9:469
1896 Willoughby, Westel W. ... 13:435
1897 Jameson, John F. ... 10:442
1898 Hazen, Charles D. ... 13:398
1899 Hollander, Jacob H. ... 13:372
1900 Callahan, James M. ... 11:546
1901 Latané, John H. ... 23:394
1902 Ballagh, James C. ...
1903 Woodburn, James A. ... 13:408
1904 Dewey, Davis R. ... 13:371
1905 Friedenwald, Herbert ...
1906 Bassett, John S. ... 16: 47
1907 Steiner, Bernard C. ... 18:334
1909 Reeves, Jesse S. ...
1910 Barnett, George E. ...
1913 Moore, Henry L. ...

Isaac N. Maynard Prize

Awarded by the National Academy of Design for the best portrait in the annual exhibition.

1913 Richardson, Margaret F. ...
1914 Bellows, George W. ... 20: 77
1915 Volk, Douglas ... C:138
1916 Smedley, William T. ... 10:378
1917 Borie, Adolphe ...
1918 Emmet, Lydia F. ... 15:340
1919 Wiles, Irving R. ... 6:468
1920 Rittenberg, Henry R. ...
1921 Bredin, R. Sloan ...
1922 Lockman, DeWitt ...
1923 MacLane, M. Jean ...
1924 Franzen, August ...
1925 Levy, William A. ...
1926 Inuka, Kyohei ...
1927 Turner, Helen M. ...
1928 MacLane, M. Jean ...
1929 Ipsen, Ernest L. ...
1931 Smith, Howard E. ...
1932 Young, Mahonri ...
1933 Dickinson, Sidney E. ...
1934 Davidson, Jo ...

Frank N. Meyer Medal

Awarded by the American Genetic Association for distinguished services in plant introduction.

American Recipients

1920 Lathrop, Barbour ...
1923 Sargent, Charles S. ... 13:398
1923 Simpson, Charles T. ... 23:255
1927 Taft, Charles P. ...
1929 Nehrling, Henry ...
1930 Rixford, Gulian P. ... B:172
1931 Armour, Allison V. ...

Mining and Metallurgical Society of America Gold Medal

Awarded for conspicuous professional or public service for the advancement of the science of mining and metallurgy, or of economic geology; for the betterment of the conditions under which these industries are carried on, for the protection of mine investors, and especially for the better protection of the health and safety of workmen in the mines and metallurgical establishments.

1914 Hoover, Herbert / Hoover, Lou } *jointly* ... C: 1
1915 Richards, Robert H. ... 12:347
1916 Kemp, James F. ... 21: 5
1917 Mathewson, Edward P. ... C: 41
1918 Yeatman, Pope ... 18:176
1919 Schneider, Charles E. ...
1920 Smith, E. A. Cappelen ...
1921 Goodale, Charles W. ...
1922 Peele, Robert ...
1924 Cottrell, Frederick G. ...
1926 Jackling, Daniel C. ... D:245
1929 Kelley, Cornelius F. ...

National Geographic Society Special Gold Medal

Awarded for outstanding work in exploration and achievement.

American Recipients

1909 Peary, Robert E. ... 14: 60
1914 Goethals, George W. ... 24: 6
1930 Byrd, Richard E. ... B:431
1932 Earhart, Amelia ... D:395

National Institute of Arts and Letters Gold Medal

Awarded annually to any citizen of the United States, whether a member of the Institute or not, for distinguished services to arts or letters in the creation of original work.

1909 Saint-Gaudens, Augustus ... 8:287
1910 Rhodes, James F. ... 7: 92
1911 Riley, James Whitcomb ... 6: 31
1912 Mead, William R. ... 23: 91
1913 Thomas, Augustus ... C:438
1914 Sargent, John S. ... 11:291
1915 Howells, William D. ... 1:281
1916 Burroughs, John ... 1:247
1917 French, Daniel C. ... A:460
1918 Thayer, William R. ... 12:530
1919 Loeffler, Charles M. ...
1921 Gilbert, Cass ... 26: 20
1922 O'Neill, Eugene G. ... A:443
1923 Blashfield, Edwin H. ... D: 80
1924 Wharton, Edith ... B: 32
1925 Brownell, William C. ... 22: 6
1926 Adams, Herbert ... 13:510
1927 Sloane, William M. ... 21: 95
1928 Chadwick, George W. ... 7:326
1929 Robinson, Edwin A. ... B: 15
1930 Platt, Charles A. ... 11:306
1931 Gillette, William ... 2:249
1932 Melchers, Gari ... B:120
1933 Tarkington, Booth ... A: 84
1935 Repplier, Agnes ... C:368
1936 Barnard, George G. G. ... A: 67
1937 Andrews, Charles McL. ... 13:160

National Institute of Social Sciences Gold Medal

Awarded to men and women who have performed distinguished service for mankind.

American Recipients

1913 Huntington, Archer M. ... 15: 19
1913 Parrish, Samuel L. ... B:371
1913 Taft, William H. ... 23: 1
1914 Eliot, Charles W. ... 6:421
1914 Goethals, George W. ... 24: 6
1914 Jacobi, Abraham ... 9:345
1914 Osborn, Henry Fairfield ... 26: 18
1915 Burbank, Luther ... 11:374

1915	Carnegie, Andrew	9:151
1916	Bacon, Robert	14: 16
1916	Jenkins, Helen Hartley	
1916	Lewisohn, Adolph	
1917	Crile, George W.	C: 72
1917	Gorgas, William C.	14:528
1917	Mitchel, John Purroy	18:289
1917	Pupin, Michael I.	26: 5
1918	Davison, Henry P.	20: 88
1918	Hoover, Herbert C.	C: 1
1918	Mayo, William J.	A:330
1919	Gompers, Samuel	11:539
1919	Welch, William H.	26: 6
1920	Carrel, Alexis	15:301
1920	Curtis, H. Holbrook	14:376
1920	Judson, Harry P.	20: 24
1921	Chandler, Charles F.	23: 46
1921	Coolidge, Calvin	24: 1
1921	Dodge, Cleveland H.	26:407
1923	Davenport, Charles B.	15:397
1923	Johnson, Emory R.	
1923	Rockefeller, John D., Sr.	11: 63
1924	Hampden, Walter	B: 12
1924	Hughes, Charles E.	A: 6
1924	Spencer, Mrs. C. Lorillard	
1925	Harriman, Mary W.	23:187
1925	Park, William H.	C:314
1925	Root, Elihu	26: 1
1925	Young, Owen D.	A: 81
1926	Cadman, S. Parkes	B:121
1926	Mackay, Clarence H.	14: 85
1926	Woolman, Mary S.	A:543
1926	Mather, Stephen T.	26:210
1927	Baker, George P.	25: 28
1927	Damrosch, Walter	C: 57
1927	Fosdick, Harry Emerson	B:194
1927	Ochs, Adolph S.	A: 76
1928	Bailey, Liberty H.	10:145
1928	DeForest, Robert W.	B: 61
1928	Whitney, Willis R.	15:393
1929	Langeloth, Valeria	
1929	Livingston, Rose	
1929	Rockefeller, John D., Jr.	B: 21
1929	Shotwell, James T.	B: 16
1929	Willard, Daniel	18: 8
1930	Gallup, Anna B.	
1930	Minot, George R.	7:133
1930	Phelps, William L.	A:375
1930	Straus, Nathan	22: 46
1931	Abbott, Grace	C: 25
1931	Cabot, Richard C.	A:223
1931	Coolidge, Grace G.	
1931	Kellogg, Frank B.	A: 8
1932	Allen, Edward E.	A:130
1932	Post, James H.	C:103
1932	Redfield, William C.	A: 50
1932	Swope, Gerard	
1933	Baker, Newton D.	A: 40
1933	Beers, Clifford W.	
1933	Booth, Evangeline C.	B:127
1934	Belmont, Eleanor R.	
1934	Cannon, Walter B.	D: 72
1934	Seabury, Samuel	D: 76
1935	Cushing, Harvey	C: 36
1935	Glass, Carter	A: 36
1935	Bliss, Cornelius N.	11: 15
1935	Vincent, George E.	B: 6
1936	Butler, Nicholas M.	B:186
1936	Morgan, J. Pierpont	C:418
1936	Eustis, Dorothy H.	
1936	Hall, William E.	

National Sculpture Society Medal of Honor

Awarded for distinguished service rendered in the advancement of American sculpture.

1927	French, Daniel C.	A:460
1929	Adams, Adeline	
1929	Huntington, Archer M.	15: 19

William H. Nichols Medal

Established in 1902 and awarded by the American Chemical Society, New York section, for stimulating original research in chemistry.

1903	Voorhees, Edward B.	13:587
1905	Parsons, Charles L.	14:280
1906	Bogert, Marston T.	14:207
1907	Bishop, M. B.	
1908	Walker, William H.	A:167
1909	Noyes, William A.	B:314
1909	Weber, Henry C. P.	
1910	Baekeland, Leo H.	15:330
1911	Rosanoff, Martin A.	C:285
1911	Easley, Charles W.	20: 44
1912	James, Charles	26: 47
1914	Gomberg, Moses	16:109
1915	Langmuir, Irving	C: 29
1916	Hudson, Claude S.	
1918	Johnson, Treat B.	
1920	Langmuir, Irving	C: 29
1921	Lewis, Gilbert N.	
1923	Midgley, Thomas, Jr.	
1924	Kraus, Charles A.	
1925	Franklin, Edward C.	A:411
1926	Lind, Samuel C.	
1927	Adams, Roger	
1928	Taylor, Hugh S.	
1929	Evans, William L.	
1930	Sheppard, Samuel E.	
1931	Wilson, John A.	C:207
1932	Conant, James B.	D: 48
1934	Sherman, Henry C.	D: 65
1935	Nieuwland, Julius A.	26:357
1936	Clark, William M.	

Alfred B. Nobel Prize

Financed by the interest on $9,000,000 bequeathed by Alfred B. Nobel, and awarded annually by various Swedish and Norwegian institutions to those who, in the previous year, made the most outstanding contributions for the benefit of mankind.

American Recipients

In Chemistry

1914	Richards, Theodore W.	12:362
1932	Langmuir, Irving	C: 29
1934	Urey, Harold C.	

In Literature

1930	Lewis, Sinclair	B:202

In Peace

1906	Roosevelt, Theodore	14: 1
1912	Root, Elihu	26: 1
1919	Wilson, Woodrow	19: 1
1925	Dawes, Charles G.	A:508
1929	Kellogg, Frank B.	A: 8
1931	Butler, Nicholas Murray	B:186
1931	Addams, Jane	C: 83

In Physics

1907	Michelson, Albert A.	C: 42
1923	Millikan, Robert A.	A:268
1927	Compton, Arthur H.	C: 34
1936	Anderson, Carl D.	

In Physiology and Medicine

1912 Carrel, Alexis 15:301
1930 Landsteiner, Karl D:403
1933 Morgan, Thomas H. .... D: 44
1934 Minot, George R. ....
1934 Whipple, George H. ....
1934 Murphy, William P. ....

Norman Medal

Awarded by the American Society of Civil Engineers for a paper which shall be judged worthy of special commendation for its merit as a contribution to engineering science.

1874 Croes, John J. R. 6: 46
1875 Ellis, Theodore G. ....
1877 Maclay, William W. 13: 75
1879 North, Edward P. ....
1880 Cooper, Theodore 19:261
1881 Buck, Leffert L. 10:115
1882 Stearns, Frederic P. 14:306
1882 Fteley, Alphonse 13:561
1883 Shinn, William P. 11:344
1884 Christie, James ....
1885 Clarke, Eliot C. ....
1886 Dorsey, Edward B. ....
1887 Fitz Gerald, Desmond 9: 44
1888 Tratman, E. E. Russell ....
1889 Cooper, Theodore 19:261
1890 Freeman, John R. C:397
1891 Freeman, John R. C:397
1892 Starling, William ....
1893 Fitz Gerald, Desmond 9: 44
1894 Hunt, Alfred E. 25: 38
1895 Hall, William H. ....
1896 Greiner, John E. D:298
1897 Baier, Julius ....
1898 Thomas, Benjamin F. 20:208
1899 Stone, E. Herbert ....
1900 Seddon, James A. ....
1902 Williams, Gardner S. ....
1902 Hubbell, Clarence W. ....
1902 Fenkell, George H. ....
1904 Low, Emile 25:242
1905 Schneider, Charles C. 18: 91
1906 Sewell, John S. ....
1907 Cox, Leonard M. ....
1908 Schneider, Charles C. 18: 91
1909 Waddell, John A. L. .... D: 86
1910 Grunsky, Carl E. 13:224
1911 Gibbs, George 12:131
1912 Kinnear, Wilson S. D:393
1913 Davies, John V. 14:209
1914 Saville, Caleb M. ....
1915 Hazen, Allen M. ....
1916 Waddell, John A. L. .... D: 86
1917 Groat, Benjamin F. ....
1918 Jorgensen, Lars R. ....
1919 Parsons, William B. 14:217
1920 Waddell, John A. L. .... D: 86
1922 Paul, Charles H. ....
1923 Steinman, David B. ....
1924 Jakobsen, Bernhard F. ....
1925 Eddy, Harrison P. ....
1926 Hinds, Julian ....
1927 Jakobsen, Bernhard F. ....
1928 Sudler, Charles E. ....
1929 Rude, Gilbert T. ....
1930 Terzaghi, Charles K. .... Austrian
1931 Davis, Albion R. ....
1931 Nagler, Floyd A. ....
1933 Cross, Hardy ....
1934 Moisseiff, Leon S. ....
1935 Henny, David C. 26: 68

Pennsylvania Academy of Fine Arts Medal of Honor

Awarded in recognition of high achievement of American painters and sculptors who may be exhibitors at the Academy or represented in the permanent collection, or who, for eminent services in the cause of art or to the academy, have merited the distinction.

1893 Knight, D. Ridgway 13:158
1894 Harrison, Alexander 11:300
1895 Chase, William M. 13: 28
1896 Homer, Winslow 11:304
1898 Abbey, Edwin A. 15:280
1898 Beaux, Cecilia 11:299
1899 Grafly, Charles 22: 40
1901 Thouron, Henry J. 13:398
1902 Whistler, J. McNeill 9: 49
1903 Sargent, John S. 11:291
1904 Alexander, John W. 11:297
1905 Richards, William T. 12:362
1905 Oakley, Violet ....
1906 Walker, Horatio ....
1907 Redfield, Edward W. ....
1908 Tarbell, Edmund C. B:151
1909 Anshutz, Thomas P. 15:279
1911 Metcalf, Willard L. 13:603
1914 Cassatt, Mary ....
1915 Coates, Edward H. 19:326
1916 Weir, J. Alden 22:296
1918 Hamilton, John McL. ....
1919 Breckenridge, Hugh H. ....
1920 Hassam, Childe 10:374
1926 Benson, Frank W. 13:413
1929 Garber, Daniel C:442

Penrose Gold Medal

Established in 1927 by Dr. Richard A. F. Penrose, Jr., and awarded by the Geological Society of America for outstanding contribution to geologic science.

American Recipients

1927 Chamberlin, Thomas C. 19: 25
1931 Davis, William M. 24: 32
1932 Ulrich, Edward O. ....
1933 Lindgren, Waldemar ....
1934 Schuchert, Charles 15:122
1935 Daly, Reginald A. ....

Perkin Medal

Established in 1906 and awarded by the Society of Chemical Industry, American section, for the most valuable work in applied chemistry.

American Recipients

1908 Herreshoff, J. B. Francis 24: 96
1909 Behr, Arno ....
1910 Acheson, Edward G. 23:136
1911 Hall, Charles M. 13: 94
1912 Frasch, Herman 19:347
1913 Gayley, James 14: 70
1914 Hyatt, John W. 12:148
1915 Weston, Edward 5:176
1916 Baekeland, Leo H. 15:330
1917 Twitchell, Ernest ....
1918 Rossi, Auguste J. ....
1919 Cottrell, Frederick G. ....
1920 Chandler, Charles F. 23: 46
1921 Whitney, Willis R. 15:393
1922 Burton, William M. C:243
1923 Whitaker, Milton C. ....
1924 Becket, Frederick M. B:163

1925	Moore, Hugh K.	
1926	Moore, Richard B.	
1927	Teeple, John E.	B:417
1928	Langmuir, Irving	C: 29
1929	Sullivan, Eugene C.	
1930	Dow, Herbert H.	24: 12
1931	Little, Arthur D.	15: 64
1932	Burgess, Charles F.	C:420
1933	Oenslager, George	
1934	Curme, George O., Jr.	D: 54
1935	Lewis, Warren K.	

John Phillips Memorial Medal

Awarded by the American College of Physicians for achievement in internal medicine.

1932	Avery, Oswold T.	
1933	Castle, William B.	
1935	Loeb, Leo	
1936	Landis, Eugene M.	

Howard N. Potts Medal

Awarded by the Franklin Institute for distinguished work in science or the arts; important development of previous basic discoveries; inventions or products of superior excellence or utilizing important principles.

American Recipients

1911	Coblentz, William W.	
1912	Bizzell, James A.	
1912	Lyon, Thomas L.	
1913	Bone, William A.	
1914	Modjeski, Ralph	15: 68
1915	Humphreys, William J.	
1917	Dahlgren, Ulric	
1918	Kennelly, Arthur E.	13:452
1918	Gray, Alexander	
1919	Janney, Reynold	
1919	Landreth, Clarence P.	
1919	Williams, Harvey D.	
1920	Bullard, Edward P., Jr.	
1920	Barker, Wendell A.	
1921	McCollum, Elmer V.	C:477
1922	Coker, E. G.	
1922	Moore, Richard B.	
1922	Weiss, John M.	
1922	Downs, Charles R.	
1923	Gaertner, William	B:235
1923	Hull, Albert W.	
1924	Anderson, John A.	
1925	Wilson, C. T. R.	
1926	Coolidge, William D.	
1926	Beggs, George E.	
1927	Eppley, Marion	
1927	Thurlow, Oscar G.	
1928	Sullivan, Eugene C.	
1928	Taylor, William E.	
1933	Sikorsky, Igor I.	
1934	Fischer, Ernst G.	

Priestley Medal

Established in 1923 and awarded every three years by the American Chemical Society for distinguished services in chemistry.

1923	Remsen, Ira	9:240
1926	Smith, Edgar F.	21: 53
1929	Garvan, Francis P.	C:156
1932	Parsons, Charles L.	14:280
1935	Noyes, William A.	B:314

Public Welfare Medal

Established in memory of Marcellus Hartley and awarded by the National Academy of Sciences for eminence in the application of science to the public welfare.

1914	Goethals, George W.	24: 6
1914	Gorgas, William C.	14:528
1916	Abbe, Cleveland	8:264
1916	Pinchot, Gifford	14: 30
1917	Stratton, Samuel W.	13:142
1920	Hoover, Herbert	C: 1
1921	Stiles, Charles W.	D: 62
1928	Chapin, Charles V.	
1930	Mather, Stephen T.	26:210
1931	Rose, Wickliffe	A:265
1932	Park, William H.	C:314
1933	Fairchild, David G.	C:253
1934	Vollmer, August	
1935	Cumming, Hugh S.	
1935	Russell, Frederick F.	

Cornelius Amory Pugsley Medal

Awarded by the American Scenic and Historic Preservation Society for park services.

Gold Medal

1928	Mather, Stephen T.	26:210
1929	Harriman, Mary W.	23:187
1930	Albright, Horace M.	
1931	Lieber, Richard	
1932	Hamlin, Chauncey J.	
1933	Niles, William W.	
1934	Welch, William A.	
1935	Bloomer, Howard B.	

Silver Medal

1928	McDuffie, Duncan	
1929	Britton, Nathaniel L.	25: 88
1930	Wirth, Theodore	
1931	Turner, Albert M.	
1932	Norbeck, Peter	B:479
1933	Wallace, Tom	
1934	Carson, William E.	
1935	MacLaren, John	

Bronze Medal

1928	Nelson, Beatrice W.	
1929	Hardison, Thomas W.	
1930	Sauers, Charles G.	
1931	Leviston, Stella M.	
1932	Frankel, Mrs. Henry	
1933	Colp, Dave E.	
1934	Ayres, Philip W.	
1935	Doolittle, Will O.	

Pulitzer Prize in Letters

Established by the late Joseph Pulitzer in a bequest to Columbia University, New York, and awarded annually by the trustees of Columbia University on recommendation of the advisory board of the School of Journalism at Columbia.

For the best volume of verse by an American author

1922	Robinson, Edwin A.	B: 15
1923	Millay, Edna St. Vincent	B:176
1924	Frost, Robert	A:540
1925	Robinson, Edwin A.	B: 15
1926	Lowell, Amy	19:407
1927	Speyer, Leonora	
1928	Robinson, Edwin A.	B: 15
1929	Benét, Stephen V.	A:215
1930	Aiken, Conrad P.	C:393
1931	Frost, Robert	A:540

1932	Dillon, George	
1933	MacLeish, Archibald	
1934	Hillyer, Robert S.	D:332
1935	Wurdemann, Audrey	
1936	Coffin, Robert P. T.	

For the best book upon the history of the United States

1918	Rhodes, James F.	7: 92
1920	Smith, Justin H.	B:471
1921	Sims, William S.	A:192
1922	Adams, James T.	D: 56
1923	Warren, Charles	
1924	McIlwain, Charles H.	
1925	Paxson, Frederick L.	
1926	Channing, Edward	13:432
1927	Bemis, Samuel F.	
1928	Parrington, Vernon L.	25:248
1929	Shannon, Fred A.	
1930	VanTyne, Claude H.	26:268
1931	Schmitt, Bernadotte E.	
1932	Pershing, John J.	A:434
1933	Turner, Frederick J.	13:174
1934	Agar, Herbert	
1935	Andrews, Charles McL.	13:160
1936	McLaughlin, Andrew C.	13:217

For the original American play, performed in New York up to April, 1934, which shall best represent the educational value and power of the stage

1918	Williams, Jesse L.	21: 26
1920	O'Neill, Eugene G.	A:443
1921	Gale, Zona	B:301
1922	O'Neill, Eugene G.	A:443
1923	Davis, Owen	
1924	Hughes, Hatcher	
1925	Howard, Sidney C.	
1926	Kelly, George	
1927	Green, Paul E.	
1928	O'Neill, Eugene G.	A:443
1929	Rice, Elmer L.	A:534
1930	Connelly, Marc	
1931	Glaspell, Susan	C:505
1932	Kaufman, George S.	
1932	Ryskind, Morrie	
1932	Gershwin, Ira	
1933	Anderson, Maxwell	
1934	Kingsley, Sidney	
1935	Akins, Zoe	
1936	Sherwood, Robert E.	

For the best American biography teaching patriotic and unselfish services to the people

1917	Richards, Laura E.	15:176
1917	Elliott, Maud H.	
1918	Bruce, William C.	18: 47
1919	Adams, Henry	11:475
1920	Beveridge, Albert J.	13: 26
1921	Bok, Edward W.	23: 41
1922	Garland, Hamlin	B: 4
1923	Hendrick, Burton J.	
1924	Pupin, Michael I.	26: 5
1925	Howe, Mark A. deW.	13:278
1926	Cushing, Harvey	C: 36
1927	Holloway, Emory	A:364
1928	Russell, Charles E.	A:106
1929	Hendrick, Burton J.	
1930	James, Marquis	
1931	James, Henry	
1932	Pringle, Henry F.	
1933	Nevins, Allan	
1934	Dennett, Tyler	D:429
1935	Freeman, Douglas S.	
1936	Perry, Ralph B.	

For the best novel published during the year by an American author

1918	Poole, Ernest	18:420
1919	Tarkington, Booth	A: 84
1921	Wharton, Edith	B: 32
1922	Tarkington, Booth	A: 84
1923	Cather, Willa S.	A:537
1924	Wilson, Margaret	
1925	Ferber, Edna	C:298
1926	Lewis, Sinclair (declined)	B:202
1927	Bromfield, Louis	C:295
1928	Wilder, Thornton N.	
1929	Peterkin, Julia	C: 75
1930	LaFarge, Oliver	
1931	Barnes, Margaret A.	
1932	Buck, Pearl	
1933	Stribling, Thomas S.	
1934	Meller, Caroline	
1935	Johnson, Josephine W.	
1936	Davis, Harold L.	

Remington Honor Medal

Awarded by the American Pharmaceutical Association to the man or woman who has done most for American pharmacy during the preceding year or during a longer period of outstanding activity or fruitful achievement.

1919	Beal, James H.	
1920	Lloyd, John Uri	D:106
1922	Arny, Henry V.	B:206
1923	Rusby, Henry H.	A:172
1924	Beringer, George M.	
1925	Whelpley, Henry M.	20:488
1926	Dunning, Henry A. B.	
1928	LaWall, Charles H.	
1929	Scoville, Wilbur L.	
1930	Kremers, Edward	
1931	Cook, Ernest F.	
1932	Eberle, Eugene G.	
1933	Kelly, Evander F.	
1934	Wellcome, Henry S.	
1935	Hilton, Samuel L.	
1936	Gathercoal, Edmund N.	

Theodore William Richards Medal

Awarded by the American Chemical Society at intervals of two to three years to scientists who have attained outstanding eminence in the field of pure chemistry.

1932	Noyes, Arthur A.	13:284
1935	Baxter, Gregory P.	

Roosevelt Medal

Awarded by the Roosevelt Memorial Association for certain fields of human endeavor, which include administration of public offices; development of public and international law; promotion of industrial peace; conservation of natural resources; promotion of social justice; the study of natural history; the promotion of outdoor life; of national defense; the leadership of youth and the development of American character; an eminent contribution to literature in the field of biography, history or the science of government.

1923	Schuyler, Louisa Lee	20: 19
1923	Osborn, Henry Fairfield	26: 18
1923	Wood, Leonard	9: 20
1924	Holmes, Oliver W.	12:349
1924	Root, Elihu	26: 1
1924	Eliot, Charles W.	6:421
1925	Pinchot, Gifford	14: 30
1925	Grinnell, George B.	B:478
1925	Berry, Martha M.	C: 49
1926	Beard, Daniel C.	5:317

1926 Sims, William S. A:192
1926 Beveridge, Albert J. 13: 26
1927 Moore, John Bassett .... A: 72
1927 Hoover, Herbert C. .... C: 1
1927 Pershing, John J. A:434
1928 Hughes, Charles E. .... A: 6
1928 Chapman, Frank M. C:188
1928 Lindbergh, Charles A. .... B: 34
1929 Putnam, Herbert .... D: 52
1929 Wister, Owen C:459
1929 Young, Owen D. .... A: 81
1930 Byrd, Richard E. B:431
1930 Green, William .... B: 45
1930 Hart, Hastings H. 23:170
1931 Garland, Hamlin .... B: 4
1931 Cardozo, Benjamin N. .... D: 50
1931 Merriam, C. Hart 13:264
1932 Millikan, Robert A. A:268
1933 Benét, Stephen V. A:215
1934 Seabury, Samuel .... D: 76
1934 White, William A. B:433
1935 Park, William H. C:314
1936 Keller, Helen A. 15:177
1936 Macy, Anne S. ....

Thomas Fitch Rowland Prize

Awarded by the American Society of Civil Engineers, but not restricted to members of the society. Preference is given to papers describing in detail accomplished works of construction, their cost, and errors in design and execution.

American Recipients

1883 Lindenthal, Gustav 16:117
1884 Smith, Hamilton, Jr. ....
1885 Wellington, Arthur M. 11:167
1886 Schneider, Charles C. 18: 91
1887 Metcalf, William 12:232
1888 Herschel, Clemens 22:342
1889 Schuyler, James D. 18:317
1890 Chanute, Octave 10:212
1890 Wallace, John F. 10:168
1891 Burr, William H. D:220
1892 Rowe, Samuel M. ....
1892 Quimby, Henry H. ....
1892 Robinson, Stillman W. 10:232
1893 Black, William M. A:489
1894 Barnes, David L. ....
1895 Hill, William R. ....
1896 Coppee, Henry St. L. ....
1897 Adams, Arthur L. ....
1898 Goldmark, Henry ....
1899 Buck, Richard S. ....
1900 Hazen, Allen ....
1902 Harts, William W. ....
1903 Fuller, George W. ....
1905 Harrison, Charles L. ....
1905 Woodard, Silas H. ....
1906 Dennis, William F. ....
1906 Francis, George B. 16:276
1907 Schuyler, James D. 18:317
1908 Wall, Edward E. ....
1909 Wilgus, William J. 11:115
1910 Gregory, John H. ....
1911 Brown, William L. ....
1912 Douglas, Walter J. ....
1912 Klapp, Eugene ....
1913 Coy, Burgis G. ....
1914 Cory, Harry T. 18:421
1915 Staniford, Charles W. ....
1916 Polk, Armour C. ....
1917 Davies, John V. 14:209
1918 Scheidenhelm, Frederick W. B:102
1919 Ammann, Othmar H. D:320
1920 Fowler, Charles E. ....
1921 Howard, Ernest E. B:433
1922 Lindenthal, Gustav 16:117
1923 Peek, Frank W., Jr. 24:289
1925 Parsons, Harry DeB. ....
1926 Hill, Nicholas S., Jr. 16: 28
1927 Stiles, Linford S. ....
1928 Young, Roderick B. ....
1929 Grove, William G. ....
1929 Steinman, David B. ....
1930 Beanfield, Rufus McC. ....
1931 Greeley, Samuel A. ....
1931 Hatfield, William D. ....
1932 Betts, Clifford A. ....
1933 Baxter, John C. 24:426
1934 Killmer, Miles I. ....
1935 Kirkbride, Walter H. ....

Royal Astronomical Society Gold Medal

Awarded for discovery or research in astronomy.

American Recipients

1904 Hale, George E. .... C: 45
1905 Boss, Lewis 13:251
1906 Campbell, William W. 11:278
1907 Brown, Ernest W. 15: 24
1917 Adams, Walter A. B:171
1921 Russell, Henry N. A:346
1923 Michelson, Albert A. .... C: 42
1927 Schlesinger, Frank C:497
1932 Aitken, Robert G. ....
1933 Slipher, Vesto M. ....
1934 Shapley, Harlow .... C: 95

Rumford Medal

Awarded by The Royal Society, London, England, biennially to the author of the most important discovery or useful improvement which shall be made and published by printing or in any way made known to the public in any part of Europe during the preceding two years on heat or on light, the preference always being given to such discoveries as in the opinion of the President and Council of the Royal Society tend most to promote the good of mankind.

American Recipients

1800 Rumford, (Count) Benjamin T. 5:410
1814 Wells, William C. 12: 60
1886 Langley, Samuel P. 15: 7

Rumford Premium

Established in conformity with the terms of the gift of Benjamin, Count Rumford, granting a certain fund to the American Academy of Arts and Sciences, and with a decree of the Supreme Judicial Court of Massachusetts for carrying into effect the general charitable intent and purpose of Count Rumford as expressed in his letter of gift, the Academy is empowered to make from the income of said fund, as it now exists, at any annual meeting, an award of a gold and a silver medal, being together of the intrinsic value of $300, as a premium to the author of any important discovery or useful improvement in light or in heat, which shall have been made and published by printing or in any way made known to the public in any part of the continent of America or any of the American islands, preference being always given to such discoveries as shall . . . tend most to promote the good of mankind; and to add to such medals as a further premium for such discovery and improvements, if the academy sees fit so to do, a sum of money not exceeding $300.

1839 Hare, Robert 5:398
1862 Ericsson, John 4: 46
1865 Treadwell, Daniel 10:165
1866 Clark, Alvan 6:440
1869 Corliss, George H. 10:394

1871 Harrison, Joseph, Jr. 12:495
1873 Rutherfurd, Lewis M. 6:376
1875 Draper, John W. 3:406
1880 Gibbs, Josiah W. 4:543
1883 Rowland, Henry A. 11: 25
1886 Langley, Samuel P. 15: 7
1888 Michelson, Albert A. .... C: 42
1891 Pickering, Edward C. 6:424
1895 Edison, Thomas A. 25: 1
1898 Keeler, James E. 10:498
1899 Brush, Charles F. 21: 1
1900 Barus, Carl 26: 8
1901 Thomson, Elihu B:106
1902 Hale, George E. .... C: 45
1904 Nichols, Ernest F. 21: 68
1907 Acheson, Edward G. 23:136
1909 Wood, Robert W. 14:457
1910 Curtis, Charles G. ....
1911 Crafts, James M. 13:474
1912 Ives, Frederic E. 15: 77
1913 Stebbins, Joel B:342
1914 Coolidge, William D. ....
1915 Abbot, Charles G. A:366
1917 Bridgman, Percy W. ....
1918 Lyman, Theodore ....
1920 Langmuir, Irving .... C: 29
1925 Russell, Henry N. A:346
1926 Compton, Arthur H. .... C: 34
1928 Nichols, Edward L. 4:482
1930 Plaskett, John S. .... Canadian
1931 Compton, Karl T. .... C: 81
1933 Shapley, Harlow .... C: 95

Saltus Medal

Awarded by the National Academy of Design for artistic merit in painting or sculpture.

1908 Tarbell, Edmund C. B:151
1909 Brush, George deF. 13:578
1910 Volk, Douglas C:138
1911 Johansen, John C. ....
1912 Crane, Bruce 11:310
1913 Symons, Gardner ....
1914 Beaux, Cecilia 11:299
1915 Thayer, Abbott H. 6:471
1916 Carlsen, Emil 24:277
1917 Chapman, Charles S. ....
1918 Pearson, Joseph T., Jr. ....
1919 Parcell, Malcolm S. ....
1920 Hyatt, Anna V. 18:163
1921 Davis, Charles H. 8:431
1922 Hyatt, Anna V. 18:163
1923 Savage, Eugene F. ....
1924 Fraser, Laura G. C:469
1925 Costigan, John E. B:304
1926 Piccirilli, Attilio ....
1927 Redfield, Edward W. ....
1928 Fraser, Laura G. C:469
1929 Rungius, Carl ....
1930 Lawson, Ernest ....
1931 Betts, Louis ....
1933 Nickerson, Ruth ....
1934 Watrous, Harry W. 13:369
1935 Hassam, Childe 10:374
1936 Lie, Jonas D:248

William Lawrence Saunders Medal

Awarded by the American Institute of Mining and Metallurgical Engineers for distinguished achievement in mining.

1927 Brunton, David W. 23: 99
1928 Hoover, Herbert C. .... C: 1
1929 Hammond, John Hays 26: 45
1930 Jackling, Daniel C. D:245
1931 MacLennan, Francis W. ....
1932 Bradley, Frederick W. ....
1933 Aldridge, Walter H. ....
1934 Yeatman, Pope 18:176
1935 MacNaughton, James ....
1936 Crane, Clinton H. 12: 96

Sedgwick Memorial Medal

Established in 1926 and awarded by the American Public Health Association for distinguished service in public health.

1929 Chapin, Charles V. ....
1930 Smith, Theobald D:133
1931 McCoy, George W. .... C: 87
1932 Park, William H. C:314
1933 Rosenau, Milton J. ....
1934 Jordan, Edwin O. ....
1935 Emerson, Haven ....

J. Lawrence Smith Medal

Established in 1884 by Mrs. Sarah J. Smith in memory of her husband, and awarded by the National Academy of Sciences for important original investigations of meteoric bodies, preference to be given, in case of equal importance, to one made by a citizen of the United States.

1888 Newton, Hubert A. 9:219
1922 Merrill, George P. 8: 35

Spingarn Medal

Established in 1914 and awarded annually by the National Association for the Advancement of Colored People for the highest or noblest achievement by an American Negro during the preceding year or years.

1915 Just, Ernest E. ....
1916 Young, Charles ....
1917 Burleigh, Harry T. ....
1918 Braithwaite, William S. ....
1919 Grimké, Archibald H. 9:543
1920 DuBois, William E. B. 13:307
1921 Gilpin, Charles S. 23:314
1922 Talbert, Mary B. ....
1923 Carver, George W. ....
1924 Hayes, Roland A:529
1925 Johnson, James W. C:488
1926 Woodson, Carter G. ....
1927 Overton, Anthony ....
1928 Chesnutt, Charles W. 12:266
1929 Johnson, Mordecai W. ....
1930 Hunt, Henry A. ....
1931 Harrison, Richard B. 26:364
1932 Moton, Robert R. .... B: 75
1933 Yergan, Max ....
1934 Williams, W. T. B. ....
1935 Bethune, Mary McLeod ....
1936 Hope, John ....

Spirit of St. Louis Medal

Awarded, at approximately three-year periods, by the American Society of Mechanical Engineers, for meritorious service in the field of aëronautical engineering. Endowed by members of the Society and citizens of St. Louis, Mo.

1929 Guggenheim, Daniel 22: 7
1932 Litchfield, Paul ....
1935 Rogers, Will .... B: 67

Temple Gold Medal

Awarded by the Pennsylvania Academy of the Fine Arts. The Temple Trust Fund, created by Joseph E. Temple, yields an annual income of $1800 for the purchase of works of American art at the discretion of the directors of the Academy and for the issue of a gold medal. From 1884 until 1890 the Temple Gold Medal was awarded by the directors to the best figure picture, and the Temple Silver Medal to the best landscape and marine. In 1891 and 1892 the medals were awarded to the best and second-best pictures, irrespective of subject.

1884 Maynard, George W. 11:287
1885 Pearce, Charles S. 11:286
1887 Grayson, Clifford P. 13:337
1888 Reinhart, Charles S. 7:465
1889 Klumpke, Anna E. ....
1890 Howe, William H. 13:430
1891 Thayer, Abbott H. 6:471
1892 Bisbing, Henry S. 5:556
1894 Whistler, J. McNeill 9: 49
1894 Sargent, John S. 11:291
1895 Tarbell, Edmund C. B:151
1895 Twachtman, John H. 13:530
1896 Melchers, Gari B:120
1896 Johnston, J. Humphreys 13:545
1897 Brush, George DeF. 13:578
1897 Alexander, John W. 11:297
1898 Rook, Edward F. ....
1898 Lockwood, Wilton 24:275
1899 DeCamp, Joseph 13:216
1899 Hassam, Childe 10:374
1900 Beaux, Cecilia 11:299
1901 Chase, William M. 13: 28
1902 Homer, Winslow 11:304
1903 Redfield, Edward W. ....
1904 Eakins, Thomas 5:421
1905 Weir, J. Alden 22:296
1906 Ullman, Eugene P. ....
1907 Metcalf, Willard L. 13:603
1908 Benson, Frank W. 13:413
1909 Vinton, Frederic P. 5:317
1910 Cushing, Howard G. 24:165
1911 Miller, Richard E. A:270
1912 Carlsen, Emil 24:277
1913 Frieske, Frederick C. ....
1914 Schofield, W. Elmer D:166
1915 Hawthorne, Charles W. 22:452
1916 Pearson, Joseph T., Jr. ....
1917 Bellows, George W. 20: 77
1918 Luks, George B. ....
1919 Garber, Daniel C:442
1920 Lawson, Ernest ....
1921 Seyffert, Leopold B:388
1922 Lathrop, William L. ....
1923 Ufer, Walter ....
1924 Glackens, William ....
1925 Addams, Clifford ....
1926 Lever, Hayley ....
1927 Kroll, Leon ....
1928 Chapin, James ....
1929 Henri, Robert 15:146
1930 Carles, Arthur B. ....
1931 Brook, Alexander ....
1932 Bartlett, Paul W. 12:553
1933 Norris, S. Walter ....
1934 Kuniyoshi, Yasuo ....
1935 Hopper, Edward ....
1936 Sample, Paul ....

Mary Clark Thompson Medal

Established in 1919 and awarded by the National Academy of Sciences for the most important services to geology and paleontology.

1921 Walcott, Charles D. 22:135
1923 Margeri, Emmanuel de ....
1925 Clarke, John M. 19:456
1928 Smith, James P. ....
1930 Scott, William B. 13:214
1930 Ulrich, Edward O. ....
1931 White, David 18: 60
1932 Bather, Francis A. ....
1934 Schuchert, Charles 15:122
1936 Grabau, Amadeus W. ....

Trudeau Medal

Established in 1925 and awarded by the National Tuberculosis Association to that individual who in the judgment of the association has made the most meritorious contributions on the cause, prevention or treatment of tuberculosis.

American Recipients

1926 Smith, Theobald D:133
1927 Baldwin, Edward R. .... B: 99
1929 Opie, Eugene L. D:242
1930 Sewall, Henry 26:323
1931 Krause, Allen K. ....
1932 Long, Esmond R. ....
1933 Brown, Lawrason A:399
1934 Miller, William S. ....
1935 Gardner, Leroy U. ....

Mark Twain Silver Medal

Awarded by the International Mark Twain Society for outstanding achievement in some cultural field.

1930 Pershing, John J. A:434
1930 Hughes, Charles E. .... A: 6
1931 Holmes, Oliver Wendell 12:349
1931 Tarkington, Booth .... A: 84
1933 Roosevelt, Franklin D. .... D: 1
1934 Cather, Willa S. A:537
1935 Robinson, Edwin Arlington .... B: 15
1936 Masters, Edgar Lee A:387

Charles Doolittle Walcott Medal

Awarded by the National Academy of Sciences to persons, the results of whose published researches, explorations and discoveries in pre-Cambrian or Cambrian life and history shall be judged by the trust fund board to be most meritorious.

1934 White, David 18: 60

James Craig Watson Medal

Awarded by The National Academy of Sciences for the promotion of astronomical research.

American Recipients

1887 Gould, Benjamin A. 5:108
1889 Schoenfeld, Ed ....
1894 Chandler, Seth C. 9:538
1915 Leuschner, Armin O. ....
1936 Brown, Ernest W. 15: 24

Washington Award

Awarded by the Western Society of Engineers.

1919 Hoover, Herbert C. .... C: 1
1922 Hunt, Robert W. 19: 17
1923 Talbot, Arthur N. ....
1925 Smith, J. Waldo 24:108
1926 Alvord, John W. 16: 48
1927 Wright, Orville 14: 57
1928 Pupin, Michael I. 26: 5
1929 Arnold, Bion J. B:456
1930 Cooley, Mortimer E. A:511

1931	Modjeski, Ralph	15: 68
1932	Coolidge, William D.	
1935	Swasey, Ambrose	B:274
1936	Kettering, Charles F.	B:260

Weldon Memorial Prize

Awarded by Oxford University, Oxford, England.

1921	Harris, J. Arthur	22: 32

John Price Wetherill Medal

Awarded by the Franklin Institute for discovery or invention in the physical sciences, or for new and important combinations of principles or methods already known.

American Recipients

1925	Twyman, Frank	
1926	Akeley, Carl E.	26:130
1927	Howell, Albert S.	D:255
1928	Mason, William H.	
1928	Ross, Frank E.	
1929	Chrisman, Charles S.	
1929	Fast, Gustave	C:351
1930	Jennings, William N.	
1931	Steele, Edwin G.	
1931	Steele, Walter L.	
1931	Wente, Edward C.	
1931	Gray, Thomas T.	24:156
1931	Mason, Arthur J.	
1931	Sutton, Harry M.	
1932	Hem, Halvor O.	
1932	Monroe Calculating Machine Co.	
1933	Hulbert, Henry S.	
1933	McMath, Francis C.	
1933	McMath, Robert E.	
1933	Industrial Brownhoist Corp.	
1933	Koppers Co.	
1934	Harvey, E. Newton	
1934	Loomis, Alfred L.	
1935	Lucas, Francis F.	
1935	Naumburg, Robert E.	C:394
1935	Shrader, James E.	
1935	Tuckerman, Louis B.	
1935	Warren, Henry E.	

George Robert White Medal of Honor

Awarded by the Massachusetts Horticultural Society for eminent service in horticulture.

1909	Sargent, Charles S.	13:398
1910	Dawson, Jackson T.	
1912	Walsh, Michael H.	
1913	Park Commission of Rochester, N. Y.	
1915	Wilson, Ernest H.	
1917	Hansen, Niels E.	
1918	VanFleet, Walter	
1921	King, Louisa Y.	
1922	Burrage, Albert C.	12:551
1923	McLaren, John	
1925	Hedrick, Ulysses P.	
1926	DuPont, Pierre S.	A: 97
1927	Bailey, Liberty H.	10:145
1928	Thompson, William B.	22:123
1930	Fairchild, David G.	C:253
1931	Coville, Frederick V.	12:349
1932	Manda, W. A.	
1933	McFarland, J. Horace	A:196
1935	Ames, Oakes	

Wollaston Medal

Awarded by the Geological Society of London to promote researches concerning the mineral structure of the earth, and to enable the council of the Geological Society to reward those individuals of any country by whom such researches may hereafter be made.

American Recipients

1836	Agassiz, Louis	2:360
1858	Hall, James	3:280
1900	Gilbert, Grove K.	13: 46
1910	Scott, William B.	13:214
1918	Walcott, Charles D.	22:135
1926	Osborn, Henry Fairfield	26: 18

Woman's Eminent Achievement Award

Awarded annually by the American Woman's Association for outstanding contributions in one or more of the following fields: commerce, education, industry, law, literature, public relations, science, social welfare or the arts.

1931	Sanger, Margaret	
1932	Perkins, Frances	D: 19
1933	Earhart, Amelia	D:395
1934	Sabin, Pauline M.	
1935	Reid, Mrs. Ogden	
1936	Gildersleeve, Virginia C.	A:181

Founders of Religious Sects, Societies and Movements In the United States

Denomination	Year Founded	Name of Founder	
Adventists (Millerites)	1831	Miller, William	6:542
African Methodist Church	1816	Allen, Richard	13:200
Allenites	1774	Allen, Henry	7:492
Amana Community	1855	Metz, Christian	13: 39
Brethren in Christ—*see Christadelphians*			
Brotherhood of the New Life	1861	Harris, Thomas L.	3:289
Campbellites—*see Disciples of Christ*			
Christadelphians (Thomasites or Brethren in Christ)	1847	Thomas, John	4: 61
Christian Catholics	1896	Dowie, John A.	13:252
Christian Scientists	1867	Eddy, Mary Baker	3: 80
Christians	1793	O'Kelly, James	13:282
Church of God (Winebrennians)	1830	Winebrenner, John	1:180
Church of Jesus Christ of Latter-day Saints (Mormons)	1830	Smith, Joseph	16: 1
Disciples of Christ (Campbellites)	1827	Campbell, Alexander	4:161
Dunkards—*see German Baptist Brethren*			
Ebenezer Community	1842	Metz, Christian	13: 39
Ethical Culture Society	1876	Adler, Felix	23: 98
Evangelical Association	1807	Albright, Jacob	11:114
First Century Christian Fellowship (Oxford Movement)	1921	Buchman, Frank N. D.	B:405
Freewill Baptists	1780	Randall, Benjamin	4:345
German Baptist Brethren (Dunkards)	1728	Beissel, Johann Conrad	7:497
Harmonists	1803	Rapp, George	4:353
Hicksites	1827	Hicks, Elias	11:464
Hopedale Community—*see Practical Christian Republic*			
Independent Christian Universalists	1779	Murray, John	13:175
Millenial Church—*see Shakers*			
Millerites—*see Adventists*			
Moravian Church in the United States	1742	Zinzendorf, Nicholas L.	2:170
Mormons—*see Church of Jesus Christ of Latter-day Saints*			
Nothingarians	1636	Gorton, Samuel	7:178
Oneida Community	1848	Noyes, John H.	11:238
Osgoodites	1812	Osgood, Jacob	4:375
Oxford Movement—*see First Century Christian Fellowship*			
Peoples Liberal Church	1917	Frank, Henry	23:196
Perfectionists	1836	Noyes, John H.	11:238
Pillar of Fire Church	1901	White, Alma B.	B:208
Practical Christian Republic (Hopedale Community)	1842	Ballou, Adin	7:558
Quakers—*see Society of Friends*			
Reformed Mennonites	1812	Herr, John	7:498
River Brethren	1776	Engel, Jacob	7:491
Sandemanians	1765	Sandeman, Robert	13:547
Separtist Society of Zoar (Zoarites)	1817	Bimeler, Joseph M.	13:147
Shakers (Millenial Church)	1774	Lee, Ann	5:132
Society of Friends (Quakers)	1647	Fox, George	7: 10
Theosophical Society	1875	Blavatsky, Helena P. H.	15:336
Thomasites—*see Christadelphians*			
Unitarian Church	1787	Freeman, James	7:447
United Brethren in Christ	1789	Otterbein, Philip W.	10:504
		Boehm, Martin	21:137
Unity Movement	1914	Fillmore, Charles	B: 58
Universal Brotherhood and Theosophical Society	1897	Tingley, Katherine W.	15:337
Universalists	1774	Murray, John	13:175
Wesleyan Methodist Church	1843	Scott, Orange	2:315
Winebrennians—*see Church of God*			
Zionists	1893	Dowie, John A.	13:252
Zoarites—*see Separtist Society of Zoar*			

The American Episcopates

The Protestant Episcopal Church in the United States of America

Succession of Bishops

Succession	Date of Consecration		Diocese	
1	Nov. 14, 1784	Seabury, Samuel	Connecticut	3:475
2	Feb. 4, 1787	White, William	Pennsylvania	3:470
3	Feb. 4, 1787	Provoost, Samuel	New York	1:513
4	Sept. 19, 1790	Madison, James	Virginia	3:234
5	Sept. 17, 1792	Claggett, John T.	Maryland	6:224
6	Sept. 13, 1795	Smith, Robert	South Carolina	12:318
7	May 7, 1797	Bass, Edward	Massachusetts; Rhode Island, 1798	6: 15
8	Sept. 18, 1797	Jarvis, Abraham	Connecticut	3:475
9	Sept. 11, 1801	Moore, Benjamin	New York, coadjutor; bishop, 1815	1:514
10	Sept. 14, 1804	Parker, Samuel	Massachusetts	6: 15
11	May 29, 1811	Hobart, John H.	New York, coadjutor; bishop, 1816	1:514
12	May 29, 1811	Griswold, Alexander V.	Eastern Diocese	4: 78
13	Oct. 15, 1812	Dehon, Theodore	South Carolina	12:318
14	May 18, 1814	Moore, Richard C.	Virginia	7:216
15	Sept. 1, 1814	Kemp, James	Maryland, suffragan; bishop, 1816	6:224
16	Nov. 19, 1815	Croes, John	New Jersey	3:472
17	Oct. 8, 1818	Bowen, Nathaniel	South Carolina	12:318
18	Feb. 11, 1819	Chase, Philander	Ohio; Illinois, 1835	7: 1
19	Oct. 27, 1819	Brownell, Thomas C.	Connecticut	3:495
20	May 22, 1823	Ravenscroft, John S.	North Carolina	6: 52
21	Oct. 25, 1827	Onderdonk, Henry U.	Pennsylvania, assistant; bishop, 1836	3:470
22	Aug. 19, 1829	Meade, William	Virginia, coadjutor; bishop, 1841	7:216
23	Oct. 21, 1830	Stone, William M.	Maryland	6:224
24	Nov. 16, 1830	Onderdonk, Benjamin T.	New York	1:515
25	Sept. 22, 1831	Ives, Levi S.	North Carolina	5:409
26	Oct. 31, 1832	Hopkins, John H.	Vermont	11:496
27	Oct. 31, 1832	Smith, Benjamin B.	Kentucky	3:466
28	Oct. 31, 1832	McIlvaine, Charles P.	Ohio	7: 2
29	Oct. 31, 1832	Doane, George W.	New Jersey	3:473
30	Jan. 14, 1834	Otey, James H.	Tennessee	5:486
31	Sept. 25, 1835	Kemper, Jackson	Missouri and Indiana; Wisconsin, 1859	11: 57
32	July 7, 1836	McCoskry, Samuel A.	Michigan	5:239
33	Dec. 9, 1838	Polk, Leonidas	Arkansas, missionary; Louisiana, 1841	11:341
34	May 9, 1839	DeLancey, William H.	Western New York	1:342
35	June 21, 1840	Gadsden, Christopher E.	South Carolina	12:319
36	Sept. 17, 1840	Whittingham, William R.	Maryland	6:225
37	Feb. 28, 1841	Elliott, Stephen	Georgia	5:425
38	Oct. 12, 1841	Lee, Alfred	Delaware	11: 99
39	Oct. 13, 1842	Johns, John	Virginia, assistant; bishop, 1862	3:236
40	Dec. 29, 1842	Eastburn, Manton	Massachusetts, coadjutor; bishop, 1843	6: 15
41	Aug. 11, 1843	Henshaw, John P. K.	Rhode Island	11:107
42	Oct. 20, 1844	Chase, Carlton	New Hampshire	11:226
43	Oct. 20, 1844	Cobbs, Nicholas H.	Alabama	3:465
44	Oct. 20, 1844	Hawks, Cicero S.	Missouri	6: 58
45	Oct. 25, 1844	Boone, William J.	Amoy (China), missionary	5: 16
46	Oct. 26, 1844	Freeman, George W.	Arkansas and the Southwest, missionary	13:452
47	Oct. 26, 1844	Southgate, Horatio	Constantinople, missionary	13:417
48	Sept. 23, 1845	Potter, Alonzo	Pennsylvania	3:470
49	Oct. 31, 1847	Burgess, George	Maine	4:380
50	Dec. 16, 1849	Upfold, George	Indiana	3:466
51	Feb. 24, 1850	Green, William M.	Mississippi	9:326
52	July 11, 1851	Payne, John	Africa, missionary	5: 21
53	Oct. 15, 1851	Rutledge, Francis H.	Florida	13:501
54	Oct. 29, 1851	Williams, John	Connecticut, coadjutor; bishop 1865	3:496
55	Nov. 20, 1851	Whitehouse, Henry J.	Illinois, coadjutor; bishop, 1852	11:331
56	Nov. 10, 1852	Wainwright, Jonathan M.	New York, provisional	1:515
57	Oct. 17, 1853	Davis, Thomas F.	South Carolina	12:319

References are to THE NATIONAL CYCLOPEDIA OF AMERICAN BIOGRAPHY

Succession	Date of Consecration		Diocese	
58	Oct. 17, 1853	Atkinson, Thomas	North Carolina	6: 52
59	Oct. 28, 1853	Kip, William I.	California, missionary; bishop, 1857	3:474
60	Jan. 8, 1854	Scott, Thomas F.	Oregon and Washington territory, missionary	5:535
61	Oct. 18, 1854	Lee, Henry W.	Iowa	3:469
62	Nov. 22, 1854	Potter, Horatio	New York, provisional; bishop, 1861	1:515
63	Dec. 6, 1854	Clark, Thomas M.	Rhode Island	1:445
64	Aug. 25, 1858	Bowman, Samuel	Pennsylvania, assistant	3:471
65	Oct. 13, 1859	Gregg, Alexander	Texas	12:315
66	Oct. 13, 1859	Odenheimer, William H.	New Jersey; Northern New Jersey, 1874	3:473
67	Oct. 13, 1859	Bedell, Gregory T.	Ohio, coadjutor; bishop, 1873	7:456
68	Oct. 13, 1859	Whipple, Henry B.	Minnesota	4: 58
69	Oct. 23, 1859	Lay, Henry C.	Southwest, missionary; Arkansas, missionary; Easton, 1869	13:425
70	Feb. 15, 1860	Talbot, Joseph C.	Northwest, missionary; Indiana, coadjutor, 1865; bishop, 1872	3:466
71	Jan. 2, 1862	Stevens, William B.	Pennsylvania, coadjutor; bishop, 1865	3:471
72	Mar. 6, 1862	Wilmer, Richard H.	Alabama	3:465
73	Dec. 15, 1864	Vail, Thomas H.	Kansas	12: 89
74	Jan. 4, 1865	Coxe, Arthur C.	Western New York, coadjutor; bishop, 1865	3:474
75	Oct. 11, 1865	Quintard, Charles T.	Tennessee	5:487
76	Nov. 15, 1865	Clarkson, Robert H.	Nebraska, missionary; bishop, 1870	12:501
77	Dec. 28, 1865	Randall, George M.	Colorado and adjacent territory, missionary	8: 44
78	Jan. 25, 1866	Kerfoot, John B.	Pittsburgh	3:497
79	Oct. 3, 1866	Williams, Channing M.	China and Japan, missionary; Yedo, 1874	5:533
80	Nov. 7, 1866	Wilmer, Joseph P. B.	Louisiana	11:342
81	Nov. 15, 1866	Cummins, George D	Kentucky, assistant	7: 57
82	Dec. 6, 1866	Armitage, William E.	Wisconsin, coadjutor; bishop, 1870	11: 58
83	Jan. 25, 1867	Neely, Henry A.	Maine	12:266
84	May 1, 1867	Tuttle, Daniel S.	Montana, Idaho and Utah, missionary; Missouri, 1886	6: 58
85	July 25, 1867	Young, John F.	Florida	13:501
86	Apr. 2, 1868	Beckwith, John W.	Georgia	6: 50
87	Apr. 30, 1868	Whittle, Francis McN.	Virginia, coadjutor; bishop, 1876	7:216
88	June 3, 1868	Bissell, William H. A.	Vermont	11:496
89	Oct. 25, 1868	Robertson, Charles F.	Missouri	6: 58
90	Dec. 3, 1868	Morris, Benjamin W.	Oregon and Washington territory; Oregon, missionary, 1880; bishop, 1889	5:535
91	Jan. 27, 1869	Littlejohn, Abram N.	Long Island	3:472
92	Feb. 2, 1869	Doane, William C.	Albany	4:489
93	Apr. 8, 1869	Huntington, Frederic D.	Central New York	3:363
94	Oct. 13, 1869	Whitaker, Ozi W.	Nevada and Arizona, missionary; Nevada, 1874; Pennsylvania, coadjutor 1886; bishop, 1887	3:471
95	Jan. 25, 1870	Pierce, Henry N.	Arkansas, missionary; bishop, 1871	5:542
96	Sept. 21, 1870	Niles, William W.	New Hampshire	5:255
97	Oct. 6, 1870	Pinkney, William	Maryland, coadjutor; bishop 1879	6:226
98	Oct. 8, 1871	Howe, William B. W.	South Carolina	12:319
99	Dec. 28, 1871	Howe, Mark A. DeW.	Central Pennsylvania	13:278
100	Jan. 9, 1873	Hare, William H.	South Dakota (Niobrara), missionary	3:468
101	Apr. 17, 1873	Auer, John G.	Cape Palmas (Africa), missionary	5:554
102	Sept. 17, 1873	Paddock, Benjamin H.	Massachusetts	6: 15
103	Dec. 11, 1873	Lyman, Theodore B.	New York, coadjutor; bishop 1881	6: 53
104	Dec. 31, 1873	Spalding, John F.	Colorado, missionary; bishop 1887	3:467
105	Oct. 25, 1874	Welles, Edward R.	Wisconsin	11: 58
106	Nov. 15, 1874	Elliott, Robert W. B.	West Texas, missionary	13:502
107	Dec. 2, 1874	Wingfield, John H. D.	Northern California, missionary	3:468
108	Dec. 20, 1874	Garrett, Alexander C.	Northern Texas, missionary; Dallas, 1895	13:501
109	Jan. 17, 1875	Adams, William F.	New Mexico and Arizona, missionary; Easton, 1887	12: 87
110	Jan. 27, 1875	Dudley, Thomas U.	Kentucky, coadjutor; bishop, 1884	3:467
111	Feb. 2, 1875	Scarborough, John	New Jersey	3:473
112	Feb. 14, 1875	Gillespie, George DeN.	Western Michigan	13:452
113	Apr. 28, 1875	Jaggar, Thomas A.	Southern Ohio	13:126
114	Dec. 8, 1875	McLaren, William E.	Illinois; Chicago, 1883	11:331
115	Dec. 15, 1875	Brown, J. H. Hobart	Fond du Lac	12: 90
116	Sept. 10, 1876	Perry, William S.	Iowa	3:469
117	Feb. 3, 1877	Penick, Charles C.	Cape Palmas, missionary	11:474
118	Oct. 31, 1877	Schereschewsky, Samuel I. J.	Shanghai, missionary	13:429
119	May 15, 1878	Burgess, Alexander	Quincy	11:468
120	May 30, 1878	Peterkin, George W.	West Virginia	12: 88
121	June 11, 1878	Seymour, George F.	Springfield	10:357
122	Sept. 17, 1879	Harris, Samuel S.	Michigan	13: 95
123	Jan. 8, 1880	Starkey, Thomas A.	Newark	3:474
124	Feb. 5, 1880	Galleher, John N.	Louisiana	11:342
125	Nov. 21, 1880	Dunlop, George K.	New Mexico and Arizona, missionary	12: 88

Succession	Date of Consecration		Diocese	
126	Dec. 8, 1880	Brewer, Leigh R.	Montana, missionary; bishop, 1904	11:192
127	Dec. 15, 1880	Paddock, John A.	Washington territory, missionary; Olympia, missionary, 1892	3:469
128	Jan. 25, 1882	Whitehead, Cortlandt	Pittsburgh	3:465
129	Feb. 24, 1883	Thompson, Hugh M.	Mississippi, coadjutor; bishop, 1887	9:326
130	Oct. 14, 1883	Knickerbacker, David B.	Indiana	3:466
131	Oct. 20, 1883	Potter, Henry C.	New York, coadjutor; bishop, 1887	14: 35
132	Oct. 21, 1883	Randolph, Alfred M.	Virginia, coadjutor; bishop, South Virginia, 1892	7:217
133	Dec. 20, 1883	Walker, William D.	North Dakota, missionary; Western New York, bishop, 1897	12: 91
134	Apr. 17, 1884	Watson, Alfred A.	East Carolina	5:534
135	Oct. 28, 1884	Boone, William J.	Shanghai, missionary	5: 16
136	Oct. 28, 1884	Rulison, Nelson S.	Central Pennsylvania, coadjutor; bishop, 1895	1:511
137	Jan. 8, 1885	Paret, William	Maryland	6:226
138	Feb. 24, 1885	Worthington, George	Nebraska	12:501
139	June 24, 1885	Ferguson, Samuel D.	Liberia, missionary	13:544
140	Aug. 11, 1886	Weed, Edwin G.	Florida	9:441
141	Oct. 17, 1886	Gilbert, Mahlon N.	Minnesota, coadjutor	2:146
142	May 4, 1887	Thomas, Elisha S.	Kansas, coadjutor; bishop, 1889	12: 89
143	May 27, 1887	Talbot, Ethelbert	Wyoming and Idaho, missionary; tranferred to Central Pennsylvania, 1897; Bethlehem, 1908	8:389
144	Jan. 6, 1888	Johnston, James S.	West Texas, missionary; bishop, 1904	13:502
145	Jan. 25, 1888	Leonard, Abiel, 3d	Nevada and Utah; Salt Lake, missionary, 1898	12: 87
146	Oct. 18, 1888	Coleman, Leighton	Delaware	11:100
147	Jan. 18, 1889	Kendrick, John M.	New Mexico and Arizona, missionary; Arizona, 1892	12: 88
148	Jan. 25, 1889	Vincent, Boyd	Southern Ohio, coadjutor; bishop, 1904	13: 21
149	Mar. 26, 1889	Knight, Cyrus F.	Milwaukee	11: 58
150	Apr. 25, 1889	Grafton, Charles C.	Fond du Lac	12: 90
151	Oct. 12, 1889	Leonard, William A.	Ohio	24:326
152	Oct. 18, 1889	Davies, Thomas F.	Michigan	5:390
153	Jan. 1, 1890	Graves, Anson R.	The Platte, missionary; Kearney, missionary, 1907	4:286
154	June 24, 1890	Nichols, William F.	California, coadjutor; bishop, 1893	12: 86
155	Oct. 14, 1890	Atwill, Edward R.	Western Missouri; Kansas City, 1904	12: 87
156	Jan. 21, 1891	Jackson, Henry M.	Alabama, coadjutor	3:465
157	June 24, 1891	Sessums, Davis	Louisiana, coadjutor; bishop, 1891	11:343
158	Oct. 14, 1891	Brooks, Phillips	Massachusetts	2:304
159	Oct. 28, 1891	Nicholson, Isaac L.	Milwaukee	11: 59
160	Feb. 24, 1892	Nelson, Cleland K.	Georgia; Atlanta, 1907	13:321
161	July 26, 1892	Hale, Charles R.	Springfield, coadjutor	7:508
162	Oct. 12, 1892	Kinsolving, George H.	Texas, coadjutor; bishop, 1893	12:315
163	Dec. 16, 1892	Wells, Lemuel H.	Spokane, missionary	12:133
164	Dec. 29, 1892	Gray, William C.	South Florida, missionary	13:502
165	Jan. 6, 1893	Brooke, Francis K.	Oklahoma, missionary	7:552
166	Jan. 25, 1893	Barker, William M.	Western Colorado, missionary; Olympia, 1894; bishop, 1894	13:316
167	June 14, 1893	McKim, John	North Tokyo, missionary	13:280
168	June 14, 1893	Graves, Frederick R.	Shanghai, missionary	13:541
169	July 20, 1893	Capers, Ellison	South Carolina, coadjutor; bishop, 1894	12:319
170	July 25, 1893	Gailor, Thomas F.	Tennessee, coadjutor; bishop, 1898	C:338
171	Oct. 5, 1893	Lawrence, William	Massachusetts	C:479
172	Oct. 15, 1893	Cheshire, Joseph B., Jr.	North Carolina, coadjutor; bishop, 1893	13:443
173	Feb. 2, 1894	Hall, Arthur C. A.	Vermont	11:496
174	May 16, 1894	Newton, John B.	Virginia, coadjutor	11:318
175	May 1, 1895	White, John H.	Indianapolis; Michigan City, 1899	26: 89
176	Sept. 19, 1895	Millspaugh, Frank R.	Kansas	12: 89
177	Nov. 30, 1895	Rowe, Peter T.	Alaska, missionary	
178	Jan. 30, 1896	Burton, Lewis W.	Lexington	13:228
179	Feb. 24, 1896	Johnson, Joseph H.	Los Angeles	12:132
180	Mar. 25, 1896	Satterlee, Henry Y.	Washington	10:408
181	May 1, 1896	Williams, Gershom M.	Marquette	12: 89
182	Feb. 2, 1897	Morrison, James D.	Duluth, missionary	11:436
183	Oct. 28, 1897	Brewster, Chauncey B.	Connecticut, coadjutor; bishop, 1899	7:496
184	Nov. 3, 1897	Gibson, Robert A.	Virginia, coadjutor; bishop, 1902	12:189
185	Jan. 27, 1898	McVickar, William N.	Rhode Island, coadjutor; bishop, 1903	11: 62
186	June 24, 1898	Brown, William M.	Arkansas, coadjutor; bishop, 1899	C:485
187	Dec. 28, 1898	Horner, Junius M.	Asheville, missionary; Western North Carolina, 1922	11:234
	Jan. 6, 1899	Kinsolving, Lucien L.	Southern Brazil, missionary, 1907	
188	Jan. 25, 1899	Moreland, William H.	Sacramento, missionary	13:221
189	Jan. 25, 1899	Edsall, Samuel C.	North Dakota, missionary; Minnesota, bishop, 1901	12: 91
190	Feb. 22, 1899	Morrison, Theodore N.	Iowa	13:257
191	July 13, 1899	Funsten, James B.	Boise, missionary; Wyoming, 1907; Idaho, 1907	26:242
192	Sept. 21, 1899	Francis, Joseph M.	Indianapolis	12: 90

References are to THE NATIONAL CYCLOPEDIA OF AMERICAN BIOGRAPHY

Succession	Date of Consecration		Diocese	
193	Oct. 18, 1899	Williams, Arthur L.	Nebraska, coadjutor; bishop, 1908	12:502
194	Nov. 10, 1899	Gravatt, William L.	West Virginia, coadjutor; bishop, 1916	13:356
195	Feb. 2, 1900	Partridge, Sidney C.	Kyoto, missionary; Western Missouri, 1911	25:353
196	Feb. 24, 1900	Codman, Robert	Maine	12:267
197	Feb. 24, 1900	Anderson, Charles P.	Chicago, coadjutor; bishop, 1905	4:519
198	July 25, 1900	Barnwell, Robert W.	Alabama	13:502
199	Nov. 8, 1900	Weller, Reginald H.	Fond du Lac, coadjutor; bishop, 1912	12: 90
200	Aug. 6, 1901	Taylor, Frederick W.	Quincy	13:228
201	Dec. 4, 1901	Mann, Cameron	North Dakota, missionary; South Florida, missionary, 1913; bishop, 1922	13:220
202	Dec. 19, 1901	Brent, Charles H.	Philippines, missionary; Western New York, bishop, 1918	26:482
203	Jan. 8, 1902	Keator, Frederick W.	Olympia, missionary	5:538
204	Jan. 15, 1902	Burgess, Frederick	Long Island	13:229
205	Feb. 24, 1902	Ingle, James A.	Hankow, missionary	5:185
206	Apr. 22, 1902	Vinton, Alexander H.	Western Massachusetts	9:543
207	May 1, 1902	Olmsted, Charles S.	Colorado	12: 88
208	May 1, 1902	Mackay-Smith, Alexander	Pennsylvania, coadjutor; bishop, 1911	
209	June 24, 1902	VanBuren, James H.	Puerto Rico, missionary	13:123
210	July 2, 1902	Restarick, Henry B.	Honolulu	13:104
211	Oct. 2, 1902	Olmsted, Charles T.	Central New York, coadjutor; bishop, 1904	13:461
212	Dec. 17, 1902	Beckwith, Charles M.	Alabama	13:503
213	Jan. 8, 1903	Griswold, Sheldon M.	Salina, missionary; Chicago, suffragan, 1917; bishop, 1930	13:530
214	Sept. 29, 1903	Bratton, Theodore DuB.	Mississippi	12: 89
215	Nov. 18, 1903	Lines, Edwin S.	Newark	13:265
216	Jan. 20, 1904	Fawcett, M. Edward	Quincy	13:531
217	Jan. 26, 1904	Greer, David H.	New York, coadjutor; bishop, 1908	8:272
218	May 19, 1904	Nelson, Richard H.	Albany, coadjutor; bishop, 1913	15: 23
219	Oct. 23, 1904	Osborne, Edward W.	Springfield, coadjutor; bishop, 1906	21:423
220	Nov. 1, 1904	Strange, Robert	East Carolina, coadjutor; bishop, 1905	16:156
221	Nov. 14, 1904	Roots, Logan H.	Hankow, missionary	13:607
222	Dec. 14, 1904	Spalding, Franklin S.	Utah, missionary (Western Colorado, 1904-07)	15:374
223	Dec. 14, 1904	Aves, Henry D.	Mexico, missionary	
224	Dec. 21, 1904	Knight, Albion W.	Cuba, missionary; New Jersey, coadjutor, 1923	16:212
225	Jan. 25, 1905	Woodcock, Charles E.	Kentucky	5:390
226	Apr. 26, 1905	Darlington, James H.	Harrisburg	15:408
227	Nov. 2, 1905	Johnson, Frederick F.	South Dakota, assistant; missionary, 1910; Missouri, coadjutor, 1911; bishop, 1923	C:405
228	Feb. 7, 1906	Williams, Charles D.	Michigan	19:457
229	Feb. 9, 1906	Parker, Edward M.	New Hampshire, coadjutor; bishop, 1914	25:351
230	Feb. 14, 1906	McCormick, John N.	Western Michigan, coadjutor; bishop, 1909	C: 55
231	Feb. 24, 1906	Webb, William W.	Milwaukee, coadjutor; bishop, 1906	16:439
232	Sept. 29, 1906	Scadding, Charles	Oregon	20:335
233	Oct. 3, 1906	Tucker, Beverly D.	Southern Virginia, coadjutor; bishop, 1918	
234	Sept. 15, 1907	Guerry, William A.	South Carolina, coadjutor; bishop, 1908	21:209
235	Dec. 18, 1907	Paddock, Robert L.	Eastern Oregon, missionary	14:499
236	Dec. 19, 1907	Knight, Edward J.	Western Colorado, missionary	14:438
237	Mar. 25, 1908	Robinson, Henry D.	Nevada, missionary	
238	May 20, 1908	Reese, Frederick F.	Georgia	14:438
239	Oct. 28, 1908	Kinsman, Frederick J.	Delaware	14:274
240	Jan. 25, 1909	Harding, Alfred	Washington	15:258
241	May 6, 1909	Thomas, Nathaniel S.	Wyoming, missionary	
242	June 17, 1909	Brewster, Benjamin	Western Colorado, missionary; Maine, bishop, 1916	D:339
243	Sept. 29, 1909	Murray, John G.	Maryland, coadjutor; bishop, 1911	25:429
244	Oct. 20, 1909	Lloyd, Arthur S.	Virginia, coadjutor; New York, suffragan, 1921	
245	Nov. 30, 1910	Beecher, George A.	Western Nebraska, missionary	
246	Dec. 15, 1910	Temple, Edward A.	North Texas, missionary	21:280
247	Jan. 6, 1911	Perry, James DeWolf	Rhode Island	A: 49
248	Jan. 18, 1911	Atwood, Julius W.	Arizona, missionary	
249	Jan. 25, 1911	Thurston, Theodore P.	Eastern Oklahoma, missionary; combined Eastern Oklahoma and Oklahoma, 1919	
250	Jan. 25, 1911	Sanford, Louis C.	San Joaquin, missionary	
251	Feb. 24, 1911	Burch, Charles S.	New York, suffragan; bishop, 1919	19:298
252	Feb. 24, 1911	Israel, Rogers	Erie	21:449
253	Sept. 29, 1911	Winchester, James R.	Arkansas, coadjutor; bishop, 1912	
254	Oct. 18, 1911	Davies, Thomas F.	Western Massachusetts	26:310
255	Oct. 28, 1911	Rhinelander, Philip M.	Pennsylvania, coadjutor; bishop, 1911	
256	Oct. 28, 1911	Garland, Thomas J.	Pennsylvania, suffragan; bishop, 1924	22:311
257	Dec. 27, 1911	Toll, William E.	Chicago, suffragan	25:252
258	Mar. 25, 1912	Tucker, Henry St. G.	Kyoto, missionary; Virginia, coadjutor, 1926; bishop, 1927	

Succession	Date of Consecration		Diocese	Ref.
259	Mar. 25, 1912	Huntington, Daniel T.	Anking, missionary	
260	Sept. 18, 1912	Biller, George, Jr.	South Dakota, missionary	20:226
261	Oct. 23, 1912	Longley, Harry S.	Iowa, suffragan; coadjutor, 1917; bishop, 1929	C: 31
262	Oct. 20, 1912	McElwain, Frank A.	Minnesota, suffragan; bishop, 1917	
263	Jan. 29, 1913	Weeks, William F.	Vermont, coadjutor	
264	Mar. 25, 1913	Reese, Theodore I.	Southern Ohio, coadjutor; bishop, 1929	C: 50
265	June 17, 1913	Babcock, Samuel G.	Massachusetts, suffragan	
266	Dec. 17, 1913	Colmore, Charles B.	Puerto Rico, missionary	
267	Jan. 6, 1914	Tyler, John P.	North Dakota, missionary	24:163
268	Jan. 8, 1914	DuMoulin, Frank	Ohio, coadjutor	
269	Jan. 14, 1914	Howden, Frederick B.	New Mexico, missionary	A:299
270	May 1, 1914	Capers, William T.	West Texas, coadjutor; bishop, 1916	
271	Oct. 28, 1914	Brown, William C.	Virginia, coadjutor; bishop, 1919	25:220
272	Nov. 10, 1914	Faber, William F.	Montana, coadjutor; bishop, 1916	C:421
273	Dec. 16, 1914	Hunting, George C.	Nevada, missionary	21:319
274	Dec. 16, 1914	Jones, Paul	Utah, missionary	B: 88
275	Jan. 6, 1915	Darst, Thomas C.	East Carolina	
276	Jan. 6, 1915	Sumner, Walter T.	Oregon	
277	Jan. 12, 1915	Hulse, Hiram R.	Cuba, missionary	C:483
278	Jan. 25, 1915	Matthews, Paul	New Jersey	
279	Jan. 28, 1915	Page, Herman	Spokane, missionary; Michigan, 1923	
280	Apr. 21, 1915	Bliss, George Y.	Vermont, coadjutor	25:335
281	Sept. 29, 1915	Fiske, Charles	Central New York, coadjutor; bishop, 1924	
282	Oct. 21, 1915	Stearly, Wilson R.	Newark, suffragan; coadjutor, 1917; bishop, 1927	
283	Nov. 4, 1915	Acheson, E. Campion	Connecticut, suffragan; coadjutor, 1926; bishop, 1928	26: 66
284	Oct. 28, 1916	Wise, James	Kansas, coadjutor; bishop, 1916	
285	Dec. 14, 1916	Burleson, Hugh L.	South Dakota, missionary	C:523
286	Jan. 1, 1917	Johnson, Irving P.	Colorado, coadjutor; bishop, 1918	C:409
287	Feb. 2, 1917	Touret, Frank H.	Western Colorado, missionary; Idaho, 1919	
288	Apr. 25, 1917	Sherwood, Granville H.	Springfield	20:114
289	Aug. 24, 1917	Saphore, Edwin W.	Arkansas, suffragan; bishop, 1935	
290	Sept. 24, 1917	Thomson, Arthur C.	Southern Virginia, suffragan; coadjutor, 1919; bishop, 1930	A: 72
291	Oct. 4, 1917	Moore, Henry T.	Dallas, coadjutor; bishop, 1924	
292	Nov. 1, 1917	Mikell, Henry J.	Atlanta	B:366
293	Jan. 10, 1918	Remington, William P.	South Dakota, suffragan; Eastern Oregon, missionary, 1922	C:457
294	Jan. 17, 1918	Sage, John C.	Salina, missionary	25:425
295	Feb. 7, 1918	Harris, Robert LeR.	Marquette, coadjutor; bishop, 1919	
296	Sept. 29, 1918	Denby, Edward T.	Arkansas and Province of the Southwest, suffragan	
297	Oct. 31, 1918	Quin, Clinton S.	Texas, coadjutor; bishop, 1928	
298	Nov. 21, 1918	Delany, Henry B.	North Carolina, suffragan	
299	May 29, 1919	Green, William M.	Mississippi, coadjutor	C:431
300	Sept. 11, 1919	Shayler, Ernest V.	Nebraska	
301	Sept. 18, 1919	Beatty, Troy	Tennessee, coadjutor	20: 54
302	Nov. 5, 1919	Parsons, Edward L.	California, coadjutor; bishop, 1924	
303	Dec. 18, 1919	Overs, Walter H.	Liberia, missionary	
304	Feb. 5, 1920	Morris, James C.	Canal Zone, missionary; Louisiana, bishop, 1930	
305	Feb. 25, 1920	Mosher, Gouverneur F.	Philippine Islands, missionary	
306	Mar. 24, 1920	Jett, Robert C.	Southwestern, Virginia	A:297
307	Apr. 29, 1920	Moulton, Arthur W.	Utah	
308	Sept. 15, 1920	Davenport, George W.	Easton	
309	Oct. 12, 1920	Stevens, William B.	Los Angeles, coadjutor; bishop, 1928	
310	Oct. 13, 1920	Ferris, David L.	Western New York, suffragan; coadjutor, 1924; bishop, 1929; Rochester, 1931	
311	Oct. 14, 1920	Cook, Philip	Delaware	D:131
312	Nov. 10, 1920	Fox, Herbert H. H.	Montana, suffragan; coadjutor, 1925; bishop, 1934	
313	Nov. 17, 1920	Bennett, Granville G.	Duluth, coadjutor; bishop, 1922	
314	Jan. 19, 1921	Mize, Robert H.	Salina, missionary	
315	Jan. 20, 1921	Finlay, Kirkman G.	South Carolina, coadjutor; Upper South Carolina, bishop, 1922	
316	May 11, 1921	Manning, William T.	New York	A:507
317	June 11, 1921	Ingley, Fred	Colorado, coadjutor	
318	June 23, 1921	Gardiner, Theophilus M.	Liberia, suffragan	
319	June 29, 1921	LaMothe, John D.	Honolulu, missionary	
320	Sept. 22, 1921	Ward, John C.	Erie	C:423
321	Nov. 30, 1921	Shipman, Herbert	New York, suffragan	18: 72
322	Oct. 15, 1922	Penick, Edwin A.	North Carolina, coadjutor; bishop, 1932	
323	Oct. 18, 1922	Maxon, James M.	Tennessee, coadjutor; bishop, 1935	
324	Oct. 20, 1922	McDowell, William G.	Alabama, coadjutor; bishop, 1928	
325	Oct. 24, 1922	Oldham, George A.	Albany, coadjutor; bishop, 1929	
326	Oct. 31, 1922	Slattery, Charles L.	Massachusetts, coadjutor; bishop, 1927	21: 38

Succession	Date of Consecration		Diocese	
327	Dec. 6, 1922	Roberts, William B.	South Dakota, suffragan; bishop, 1931	
328	Jan. 10, 1923	Carson, Harry R.	Haiti, missionary	
329	Jan. 25, 1923	Mann, Alexander	Pittsburgh	
	Mar. 15, 1923	Ferrando, Manuel	Puerto Rico, suffragan	
330	Sept. 29, 1923	Freeman, James E.	Washington, D. C.	12:327
331	Nov. 1, 1923	Strider, Robert E.	West Virginia, coadjutor	
332	Nov. 9, 1923	Sterrett, Frank W.	Bethlehem, coadjutor; bishop, 1928	C:288
333	Feb. 12, 1924	Reifsnider, Charles S.	North Tokyo, suffragan; missionary, 1935	
334	Feb. 20, 1924	Cross, Edward M.	Spokane, missionary	
335	May 14, 1924	White, John C.	Springfield	
336	Oct. 7, 1924	Coley, Edward H.	Central New York, suffragan; bishop, 1936	
337	Nov. 25, 1924	Juhan, Frank A.	Florida	
338	Jan. 18, 1925	Seaman, Eugene C.	North Texas, missionary	
339	Feb. 17, 1925	Booth, Samuel B.	Vermont, coadjutor; bishop, 1930	
340	Mar. 4, 1925	Gilman, Alfred A.	Hankow, suffragan	
341	Apr. 30, 1925	Rogers, Warren L.	Ohio, coadjutor; bishop, 1930	C:128
342	May 1, 1925	Gray, Campbell	Northern Indiana	
343	May 7, 1925	Ivins, Benjamin F. P.	Milwaukee, coadjutor; bishop, 1933	
344	May 15, 1925	Huston, Simeon A.	Olympia	
345	Sept. 29, 1925	Wing, John D.	South Florida, coadjutor; bishop, 1932	
346	Nov. 24, 1925	Stires, Ernest M.	Long Island	C: 53
347	Nov. 30, 1925	Campbell, Robert E.	Liberia, missionary	
348	Dec. 28, 1925	Thomas, William M. M.	Southern Brazil, suffragan; missionary, 1928	
349	Dec. 30, 1925	Barnwell, Middleton S.	Idaho, missionary; Georgia, coadjutor, 1935	
350	Jan. 5, 1926	Mitchell, Walter	Arizona, missionary	
351	Jan. 12, 1926	Creighton, Frank W.	Mexico, missionary; Long Island, suffragan, 1933	
352	Apr. 13, 1926	Nichols, Shirley H.	Kyoto, missionary	
353	May 4, 1926	Dallas, John T.	New Hampshire	
354	Dec. 28, 1926	Helfenstein, Edward T.	Maryland, coadjutor; bishop, 1929	
355	Oct. 2, 1927	Casady, Thomas	Oklahoma, missionary	
356	Nov. 30, 1928	Thomas, Albert S.	South Carolina	
357	Dec. 3, 1928	Binsted, Norman S.	Tohuku, missionary	
358	Jan. 25, 1929	Jenkins, Thomas	Nevada, missionary	
359	Feb. 11, 1929	Larned, John I. B.	Long Island, suffragan	
360	May 1, 1929	Wilson, Frank E.	Eau Claire	
361	May 15, 1929	Abbott, Henry P. A.	Lexington	
362	Oct. 4, 1929	Taitt, Francis M.	Pennsylvania, coadjutor; bishop, 1931	
363	Nov. 30, 1929	Sturtevant, Harwood	Fond du Lac, coadjutor; bishop, 1933	
364	Dec. 13, 1929	Schmuck, Elmer N.	Wyoming, missionary	
365	Jan. 23, 1930	Davis, Cameron J.	Western New York, coadjutor; bishop, 1931	
366	Feb. 27, 1930	Littell, Samuel H.	Honolulu, missionary	
367	Mar. 25, 1930	Ablewhite, Hayward S.	Marquette	
368	May 1, 1930	Hobson, Henry W.	Southern Ohio, coadjutor; bishop, 1931	
369	May 6, 1930	Scarlett, William	Missouri, coadjutor; bishop, 1933	
370	May 27, 1930	Gooden, Robert B.	Los Angeles, suffragan	
371	June 18, 1930	Stewart, George C.	Chicago, coadjutor; bishop, 1930	
372	Oct. 14, 1930	Sherrill, Henry K.	Massachusetts	
373	Oct. 16, 1930	Goodwin, Frederick D.	Virginia, coadjutor	
374	Oct. 28, 1930	Gilbert, Charles K.	New York, suffragan	
375	Oct. 28, 1930	Spencer, Robert M.	Western Missouri	
376	Nov. 5, 1930	Kemerer, Benjamin T.	Duluth, coadjutor; bishop, 1933	
377	May 1, 1931	Brown, Wyatt	Harrisburg	
378	June 24, 1931	Keeler, Stephen E.	Minnesota, coadjutor	
379	Sept. 29, 1931	Bentley, John B.	Alaska, suffragan	
380	Sept. 29, 1931	Salinas y Velasco, Efrain	Mexico, suffragan; missionary, 1934	
381	Dec. 16, 1931	Budlong, Frederick G.	Connecticut, coadjutor; bishop, 1934	
382	Dec. 16, 1931	Bartlett, Frederick B.	North Dakota, missionary; Idaho, missionary, 1936	
383	Oct. 14, 1932	Washburn, Benjamin M.	Newark, coadjutor; bishop, 1935	
384	Nov. 11, 1932	Urban, Ralph E.	New Jersey, suffragan	
385	May 23, 1933	Porter, A. W. Noel	Sacramento, coadjutor; bishop, 1933	
386	Jan. 25, 1934	Gribbin, Robert E.	Western North Carolina	
387	Nov. 1, 1934	Nichols, John W.	Shanghai, suffragan	
388	Jan. 25, 1936	Ludlow, Theodore R.	Newark, suffragan	
389	Feb. 12, 1936	Dagwell, Benjamin D.	Oregon	
390	Feb. 20, 1936	Kroll, Leopold	Liberia, missionary	
391	Feb. 24, 1936	VanDyck, Vedder	Vermont	
392	Mar. 4, 1936	Reinheimer, Bartel H.	Rochester, coadjutor	
393	Apr. 22, 1936	Clingman, Charles	Kentucky	
394	May 1, 1936	Whittemore, Lewis B.	Western Michigan, coadjutor	
395	June 3, 1936	Gardner, Wallace J.	New Jersey, coadjutor	
396	Sept. 29, 1936	Essex, William L.	Quincy	

Bishops by Diocese

Alabama

Inaugurated	Name	Reference
1844	Cobbs, Nicholas H.	3:465
1862	Wilmer, Richard H.	3:465
1900	Barnwell, Robert W.	13:502
1902	Beckwith, Charles M.	13:503
1928	McDowell, William G.	

Alaska

Inaugurated	Name	Reference
1895	Rowe, Peter T.	

Albany

Inaugurated	Name	Reference
1869	Doane, William C.	4:489
1913	Nelson, Richard H.	15: 23
1929	Oldham, George A.	

Anking

Inaugurated	Name	Reference
1912	Huntington, Daniel T.	

Arizona

Inaugurated	Name	Reference
1869	Whitaker, Ozi W.	3:471
1875	Adams, William F.	12: 87
1880	Dunlop, George K.	12: 88
1889	Kendrick, John M.	12: 88
1911	Atwood, Julius W.	
1926	Mitchell, Walter	

Arkansas

Inaugurated	Name	Reference
1838	Polk, Leonidas	11:341
1844	Freeman, George W.	13:452
1859	Lay, Henry C.	13:425
1870	Pierce, Henry N.	5:542
1899	Brown, William M.	C:485
1912	Winchester, James R.	
1935	Saphoré, Edwin W.	

Atlanta

Inaugurated	Name	Reference
1907	Nelson, Cleland K.	13:321
1917	Mikell, Henry J.	B:366

Bethlehem

(Diocese of Central Pennsylvania until 1908)

Inaugurated	Name	Reference
1871	Howe, Mark A. DeW.	13:278
1895	Rulison, Nelson S.	1:511
1897	Talbot, Ethelbert	8:389
1928	Sterrett, Frank W.	C:288

California

Inaugurated	Name	Reference
1853	Kip, William I.	3:474
1893	Nichols, William F.	12: 86
1924	Parsons, Edward L.	

Canal Zone

Inaugurated	Name	Reference
1920	Morris, James C.	

Chicago

(Diocese of Illinois until 1883)

Inaugurated	Name	Reference
1835	Chase, Philander	7: 1
1852	Whitehouse, Henry J.	11:331
1875	McLaren, William E.	11:331
1905	Anderson, Charles P.	4:519
1930	Griswold, Sheldon M.	13:530
1930	Stewart, George C.	

Colorado

Inaugurated	Name	Reference
1865	Randall, George M.	8: 44
1873	Spalding, John F.	3:467
1902	Olmsted, Charles S.	12: 88
1918	Johnson, Irving P.	C:409

Western Colorado

Inaugurated	Name	Reference
1893	Barker, William M.	13:316
1895	Leonard, Abiel	12: 87
1904	Spalding, Franklin S.	15:374
1907	Knight, Edward J.	14:438
1909	Brewster, Benjamin	D:339
1917	Touret, Frank H.	

Connecticut

Inaugurated	Name	Reference
1784	Seabury, Samuel	3:475
1797	Jarvis, Abraham	3:475
1819	Brownell, Thomas C.	3:495
1865	Williams, John	3:496
1899	Brewster, Chauncey B.	7:496
1928	Acheson, E. Campion	26: 66
1934	Budlong, Frederick G.	

Constantinople

(Diocese discontinued in 1850)

Inaugurated	Name	Reference
1844	Southgate, Horatio	13:417

Cuba

Inaugurated	Name	Reference
1904	Knight, Albion W.	16:212
1915	Hulse, Hiram R.	C:483

Dallas

(Diocese of Northern Texas until 1895)

Inaugurated	Name	Reference
1874	Garrett, Alexander C.	13:501
1924	Moore, Harry T.	

Delaware

Inaugurated	Name	Reference
1841	Lee, Alfred	11: 99
1888	Coleman, Leighton	11:100
1908	Kinsman, Frederick J.	14:274
1920	Cook, Philip	D:131

Duluth

Inaugurated	Name	Reference
1897	Morrison, James D.	11:436
1922	Bennett, Granville G.	
1933	Kemerer, Benjamin T.	

East Carolina

Inaugurated	Name	Reference
1884	Watson, Alfred A.	5:534
1905	Strange, Robert	16:156
1915	Darst, Thomas C.	

Eastern Diocese

(Included present states of Maine, New Hampshire, Vermont, Massachusetts and Rhode Island; discontinued in 1843)

Inaugurated	Name	Reference
1811	Griswold, Alexander V.	4: 78

Easton

Inaugurated	Name	Reference
1869	Lay, Henry C.	13:425
1887	Adams, William F.	12: 87
1920	Davenport, George W.	

Eau Claire

Inaugurated	Name	Reference
1929	Wilson, Frank E.	

Inaugurated

Erie

1911 Israel, Rogers 21:449
1921 Ward, John C. C:423

Florida

1851 Rutledge, Francis H. 13:501
1867 Young, John F. 13:501
1886 Weed, Edwin G. 9:441
1924 Juhan, Frank A. .....

South Florida

1892 Gray, William C. 13:502
1913 Mann, Cameron 13:220
1932 Wing, John D. .....

Fond du Lac

1875 Brown, J. H. Hobart 12: 90
1889 Grafton, Charles C. 12: 90
1912 Weller, Reginald H. 12: 90
1933 Sturtevant, Harwood .....

Georgia

1841 Elliott, Stephen 5:425
1868 Beckwith, John W. 6: 50
1892 Nelson, Cleland K. 13:321
1908 Reese, Frederick F. 14:438

Haiti

1923 Carson, Harry R. .....

Hankow

1902 Ingle, James A. 5:185
1904 Roots, Logan H. 13:607

Harrisburg

1905 Darlington, James H. 15:408
1931 Brown, Wyatt .....

Honolulu

1902 Restarick, Henry B. 13:104
1921 LaMothe, John D. .....
1930 Littell, Samuel H. .....

Idaho

(Diocese of Boise from 1898 to 1907)

1867 Tuttle, Daniel S. 6: 58
1887 Talbot, Ethelbert 8:389
1899 Funsten, James B. 26:242
1919 Touret, Frank H. .....
1925 Barnwell, Middleton S. .....
1936 Bartlett, Frederick B. .....

Indianapolis

(Diocese of Indiana until 1902)

1835 Kemper, Jackson 11: 57
1849 Upfold, George 3:466
1872 Talbot, Joseph C. 3:466
1883 Knickerbacker, David B. 3:466
1895 White, John H. 26: 89
1899 Francis, Joseph M. 12: 90

Northern Indiana

(Diocese of Michigan City until 1925)

1899 White, John H. 26: 89
1925 Gray, Campbell .....

Iowa

1845 Lee, Henry W. 3:469
1876 Perry, William S. 3:469
1899 Morrison, Theodore N. 13:257
1929 Longley, Harry S. ..... C: 31

Inaugurated

Kansas

1864 Vail, Thomas H. 12: 89
1889 Thomas, Elisha S. 12: 89
1895 Millspaugh, Frank R. 12: 89
1916 Wise, James .....

Kearney

(Diocese of The Platte until 1907)

1890 Graves, Anson R. 4:286

Kentucky

1832 Smith, Benjamin B. 3:466
1884 Dudley, Thomas U. 3:467
1905 Woodcock, Charles E. 5:390
1936 Clingman, Charles .....

Kyoto

1900 Partridge, Sidney C. 25:353
1912 Tucker, Henry St. G. .....
1926 Nichols, Shirley H. .....

Lexington

1896 Burton, Lewis W. 13:228
1929 Abbott, Henry P. A. .....

Liberia

(Diocese of Cape Palmas until 1885)

1851 Payne, John 5: 21
1873 Auer, John G. 5:554
1877 Penick, Charles C. 11:474
1885 Ferguson, Samuel D. 13:544
1919 Overs, Walter H. .....
1925 Campbell, Robert E. .....
1936 Kroll, Leopold .....

Long Island

1869 Littlejohn, Abram N. 3:472
1902 Burgess, Frederick 13:229
1925 Stires, Ernest M. ..... C: 53

Los Angeles

1896 Johnson, Joseph H. 12:132
1928 Stevens, William B. .....

Louisiana

1841 Polk, Leonidas 11:341
1866 Wilmer, Joseph P. B. 11:342
1880 Galleher, John N. 11:342
1891 Sessums, Davis 11:343
1930 Morris, James C. .....

Maine

1847 Burgess, George 4:380
1867 Neely, Henry A. 12:266
1900 Codman, Robert 12:267
1916 Brewster, Benjamin D:339

Marquette

1896 Williams, Gershom M. 12: 89
1919 Harris, Robert LeR. .....
1930 Ablewhite, Hayward S. .....

Maryland

1792 Claggett, John T. 6:224
1816 Kemp, James 6:224
1830 Stone, William M. 6:224
1840 Whittingham, William R. 6:225
1879 Pinkney, William 6:226
1885 Paret, William 6:226
1911 Murray, John G. 25:429
1929 Helfenstein, Edward T. .....

Massachusetts

Inaugurated		
1797	Bass, Edward	6: 15
1804	Parker, Samuel	6: 15
1811	Griswold, Alexander V.	4: 78
1843	Eastburn, Manton	6: 15
1873	Paddock, Benjamin H.	6: 15
1891	Brooks, Phillips	2:304
1893	Lawrence, William	C:479
1927	Slattery, Charles L.	21: 38
1930	Sherrill, Henry K.	

Western Massachusetts

1902	Vinton, Alexander H.	9:543
1911	Davies, Thomas F.	26:310

Mexico

1904	Aves, Henry D.	
1926	Creighton, Frank W.	
1934	Salinas y Velasco, Efrain	

Michigan

1836	McCoskry, Samuel A.	5:239
1879	Harris, Samuel S.	13: 95
1889	Davies, Thomas F.	5:390
1906	Williams, Charles D.	19:457
1923	Page, Herman	

Western Michigan

1875	Gillespie, George DeN.	13:452
1909	McCormick, John N.	C: 55

Milwaukee

(Diocese of Wisconsin until 1884)

1859	Kemper, Jackson	11: 57
1870	Armitage, William E.	11: 58
1874	Welles, Edward R.	11: 58
1889	Knight, Cyrus F.	11: 58
1891	Nicholson, Isaac L.	11: 59
1906	Webb, William W.	16:439
1933	Ivins, Benjamin F. P.	

Minnesota

1859	Whipple, Henry B.	4: 58
1901	Edsall, Samuel C.	12: 91
1917	McElwain, Frank A.	

Mississippi

1850	Green, William M.	9:326
1887	Thompson, Hugh M.	9:326
1903	Bratton, Theodore DuB.	12: 89

Missouri

1835	Kemper, Jackson	11: 57
1844	Hawks, Cicero S.	6: 58
1868	Robertson, Charles F.	6: 58
1886	Tuttle, Daniel S.	6: 58
1923	Johnson, Frederick F.	C:405
1933	Scarlett, William	

West Missouri

(Diocese of Kansas City from 1904 to 1911)

1890	Atwill, Edward R.	12: 87
1911	Partridge, Sidney C.	25:353
1930	Spencer, Robert N.	

Montana

1867	Tuttle, Daniel S.	6: 58
1880	Brewer, Leigh R.	11:192
1916	Faber, William F.	C:421
1934	Fox, Herbert H. H.	

Nebraska

Inaugurated		
1865	Clarkson, Robert H.	12:501
1885	Worthington, George	12:501
1908	Williams, Arthur L.	12:502
1919	Shayler, Ernest V.	

Western Nebraska

(Diocese of The Platt until 1907; Kearney until 1910)

1890	Graves, Anson R.	4:286
1910	Beecher, George A.	

Nevada

(Diocese divided between Sacramento and Salt Lake from 1898 to 1907)

1869	Whitaker, Ozi W.	3:471
1888	Leonard, Abiel	12: 87
1908	Robinson, Henry D.	
1914	Hunting, George C.	21:319
1929	Jenkins, Thomas	

New Hampshire

1844	Chase, Carlton	11:226
1870	Niles, William W.	5:255
1914	Parker, Edward M.	25:351
1926	Dallas, John T.	

New Jersey

1815	Croes, John	3:472
1832	Doane, George W.	3:473
1859	Odenheimer, William H.	3:473
1875	Scarborough, John	3:473
1915	Matthews, Paul	

New Mexico

1875	Adams, William F.	12: 87
1880	Dunlop, George K.	12: 88
1889	Kendrick, John M.	12: 88
1914	Howden, Frederick B.	A:299

New York

1787	Provoost, Samuel	1:513
1815	Moore, Benjamin	1:514
1816	Hobart, John H.	1:514
1830	Onderdonk, Benjamin T.	1:515
1852	Wainwright, Jonathan M.	1:515
1854	Potter, Horatio	1:515
1887	Potter, Henry C.	14: 35
1908	Greer, David H.	8:272
1919	Burch, Charles S.	19:298
1921	Manning, William T.	A:507

Central New York

1869	Huntington, Frederic D.	3:363
1904	Olmsted, Charles T.	13:461
1924	Fiske, Charles	
1936	Coley, Edward H.	

Western New York

1839	DeLancey, William H.	1:342
1865	Coxe, Arthur C.	3:474
1897	Walker, William D.	12: 91
1918	Brent, Charles H.	26:482
1929	Ferris, David L.	
1931	Davis, Cameron J.	

Newark

(Diocese of Northern New Jersey until 1886)

1874	Odenheimer, William H.	3:473
1880	Starkey, Thomas A.	3:474
1903	Lines, Edwin S.	13:265
1927	Stearly, Wilson R.	
1935	Washburn, Benjamin M.	

Inaugurated

North Carolina

1823	Ravenscroft, John S.	6: 52
1831	Ives, Levi S.	5:409
1853	Atkinson, Thomas	6: 52
1881	Lyman, Theodore B.	6: 53
1893	Cheshire, Joseph B., Jr.	13:443
1932	Penick, Edwin A.	

Western North Carolina

(Diocese of Asheville until 1922)

1898	Horner, Junius M.	11:234
1934	Gribbin, Robert E.	

North Dakota

1883	Walker, William D.	12: 91
1899	Edsall, Samuel C.	12: 91
1901	Mann, Cameron	13:220
1914	Tyler, John P.	24:163
1931	Bartlett, Frederick B.	

North Tokyo

1893	McKim, John	13:280
1935	Reifsnider, Charles S.	

Northwest

(Diocese discontinued in 1865)

1860	Talbot, Joseph C.	3:466

Ohio

1819	Chase, Philander	7: 1
1832	McIlvaine, Charles P.	7: 2
1873	Bedell, Gregory T.	7:456
1889	Leonard, William A.	24:326
1930	Rogers, Warren L.	C:128

Southern Ohio

1875	Jaggar, Thomas A.	13:126
1904	Vincent, Boyd	13: 21
1929	Reese, Theodore I.	C: 50
1931	Hobson, Henry W.	

Oklahoma

1893	Brooke, Francis K.	7:552
1919	Thurston, Theodore P.	
1927	Casady, Thomas	

Eastern Oklahoma

1911	Thurston, Theodore P.	

Olympia

(Diocese of Oregon and Washington Territory until 1880; Washington Territory until 1892)

1854	Scott, Thomas F.	5:535
1868	Morris, Benjamin W.	5:535
1880	Paddock, John A.	3:469
1894	Barker, William M.	13:316
1902	Keator, Frederick W.	5:538
1925	Huston, Simeon A.	

Oregon

(Diocese of Oregon and Washington Territory until 1880)

1854	Scott, Thomas F.	5:535
1868	Morris, Benjamin W.	5:535
1906	Scadding, Charles	20:335
1915	Sumner, Walter T.	
1936	Dagwell, Benjamin D.	

Eastern Oregon

1907	Paddock, Robert L.	14:499
1922	Remington, William P.	C:457

Inaugurated

Pennsylvania

1787	White, William	3:470
1836	Onderdonk, Henry U.	3:470
1845	Potter, Alonzo	3:470
1865	Stevens, William B.	3:471
1887	Whitaker, Ozi W.	3:471
1911	Mackay-Smith, Alexander	
1911	Rhinelander, Philip M.	
1924	Garland, Thomas J.	22:311
1931	Taitt, Francis M.	

Philippines

1901	Brent, Charles H.	26:482
1920	Mosher, Gouverneur F.	

Pittsburgh

1866	Kerfoot, John B.	3:497
1882	Whitehead, Cortlandt	3:465
1923	Mann, Alexander	

Puerto Rico

1902	VanBuren, James H.	13:123
1913	Colmore, Charles B.	

Quincy

1878	Burgess, Alexander	11:468
1901	Taylor, Frederick W.	13:228
1904	Fawcett, M. Edward	13:531
1936	Essex, William L.	

Rhode Island

1790	Seabury, Samuel	3:475
1798	Bass, Edward	6: 15
1811	Griswold, Alexander V.	4: 78
1843	Henshaw, John P. K.	11:107
1854	Clark, Thomas M.	1:445
1903	McVickar, William N.	11: 62
1911	Perry, James DeWolf	A: 49

Rochester

1931	Ferris, David L.	

Sacramento

(Diocese of Northern California until 1899)

1874	Wingfield, John H. D.	3:468
1899	Moreland, William H.	13:221
1933	Porter, A. W. Noel	

Salina

1903	Griswold, Sheldon M.	13:530
1918	Sage, John C.	25:425
1921	Mize, Robert H.	

San Joaquin

1911	Sanford, Louis C.	

Shanghai

(Diocese of Amoy until 1866; China until 1877)

1844	Boone, William J.	5: 16
1866	Williams, Channing M.	5:533
1877	Schereschewsky, Samuel I. J.	13:429
1884	Boone, William J., Jr.	5: 16
1893	Graves, Frederick R.	13:541

South Carolina

1795	Smith, Robert	12:318
1811	Dehon, Theodore	12:318
1818	Bowen, Nathaniel	12:318
1840	Gadsden, Christopher E.	12:319
1853	Davis, Thomas F.	12:319
1871	Howe, William B. W.	12:319
1894	Capers, Ellison	12:319
1908	Guerry, William A.	21:209
1928	Thomas, Albert S.	

Upper South Carolina

Inaugurated		
1922	Finlay, Kirkman G.	

South Dakota

(Diocese of Niobrara until 1883)

1873	Hare, William H.	3:468
1910	Johnson, Frederick F.	C:405
1912	Biller, George, Jr.	20:226
1916	Burleson, Hugh L.	C:523
1931	Roberts, William B.	

Southern Brazil

1907	Kinsolving, Lucien Lee	
1928	Thomas, William M. M.	

Southwest

(Included present states of Arkansas, New Mexico, Arizona and the Indian Territory; discontinued in 1865)

1859	Lay, Henry C.	13:425

Spokane

1892	Wells, Lemuel H.	12:133
1915	Page, Herman	
1924	Cross, Edward M.	

Springfield

1878	Seymour, George F.	10:357
1906	Osborne, Edward W.	21:423
1917	Sherwood, Granville H.	20:114
1924	White, John C.	

Tennessee

1834	Otey, James H.	5:486
1865	Quintard, Charles T.	5:487
1898	Gailor, Thomas F.	C:338
1935	Maxon, James M.	

Texas

1859	Gregg, Alexander	12:315
1893	Kinsolving, George H.	12:315
1928	Quin, Clinton S.	

North Texas

(See also Dallas)

1910	Temple, Edward A.	21:280
1925	Seaman, Eugene C.	

West Texas

1874	Elliott, Robert W. B.	13:502
1888	Johnston, James S.	13:502
1916	Capers, William T.	

Tohuku

1928	Binsted, Norman S.	

Utah

(Diocese of Utah from 1867 to 1868, and then apparently discontinued; Diocese of Salt Lake from 1898 to 1907)

Inaugurated		
1867	Tuttle, Daniel S.	6: 58
1888	Leonard, Abiel	12: 87
1904	Spalding, Franklin S.	15:374
1914	Jones, Paul	B: 88
1920	Moulton, Arthur W.	

Vermont

1832	Hopkins, John H.	11:496
1868	Bissell, William H. A.	11:496
1894	Hall, Arthur C. A.	11:496
1930	Booth, Samuel B.	
1936	Van Dyck, Vedder	

Virginia

1790	Madison, James	3:234
1814	Moore, Richard C.	7:216
1841	Meade, William	7:216
1862	Johns, John	3:236
1876	Whittle, Francis McN.	7:216
1902	Gibson, Robert A.	12:189
1919	Brown, William C.	25:220
1927	Tucker, Henry St. G.	

Southern Virginia

1892	Randolph, Alfred M.	7:217
1918	Tucker, Beverly D.	
1930	Thomson, Arthur C.	A: 72

Southwestern Virginia

1920	Jett, Robert C.	A:297

Washington, D. C.

1896	Satterlee, Henry Y.	10:408
1909	Harding, Alfred	15:258
1923	Freeman, James E.	12:327

West Virginia

1878	Peterkin, George W.	12: 88
1916	Gravatt, William L.	13:356

Wyoming

1887	Talbot, Ethelbert	8:389
1907	Funsten, James B.	26:242
1909	Thomas, Nathaniel S.	
1929	Schmuck, Elmer N.	

Yedo

(Diocese discontinued in 1889)

1874	Williams, Channing M.	5:533

Roman Catholic Hierarchy in the United States

CARDINALS

Created			Created		
Mar. 15, 1875	McCloskey, John	1:195	Mar. 7, 1921	Dougherty, Denis J.	16: 90
June 7, 1886	Gibbons, James	1:488	Mar. 24, 1924	Mundelein, George W.	15: 36
May 19, 1901	O'Connell, William H.	15:294	Mar. 24, 1924	Hayes, Patrick J.	C:246
Nov. 27, 1911	Farley, John M.	13:394			

ARCHDIOCESE OF BALTIMORE

(Established as a Diocese in 1789 and elevated to an Archdiocese in 1808)

Consecrated		Inaugurated in Archdiocese	
Aug. 15, 1790	Carroll, John	Bishop, 1790; archbishop, 1808	1:480
Dec. 7, 1800	Neale, Leonard	Coadjutor, 1800; archbishop, 1815	1:482
Dec. 14, 1817	Marechal, Ambrose	Archbishop, 1817	1:482
May 25, 1828	Whitfield, James	Archbishop, 1828	1:483
Sept. 14, 1834	Eccleston, Samuel	Archbishop, 1834	1:484
June 6, 1830	Kenrick, Francis P.	Archbishop, 1851	1:485
Sept. 10, 1848	Spalding, Martin J.	Archbishop, 1864	1:486
Oct. 30, 1853	Bayley, James R.	Archbishop, 1872	1:487
Aug. 18, 1868	Gibbons, James	Archbishop, 1877	1:488
June 30, 1914	Curley, Michael J.	Archbishop, 1921	16: 89
Mar. 29, 1928	McNamara, John M.	Auxiliary, 1928	

ARCHDIOCESE OF BOSTON

(Established as a Diocese in 1808 and elevated to an Archdiocese in 1875)

Nov. 1, 1810	DeCheverus, Jean L.	Bishop, 1810	6:331
Nov. 1, 1825	Fenwick, Benedict J.	Bishop, 1825	6:332
Mar. 24, 1844	Fitzpatrick, John B.	Coadjutor, 1844; bishop, 1846	6:332
Mar. 11, 1866	Williams, John J.	Bishop, 1866; archbishop, 1875	4:415
May 19, 1901	O'Connell, William H.	Coadjutor, 1906; archbishop, 1907	15:294

ARCHDIOCESE OF CHICAGO

(Established as a Diocese in 1843 and elevated to an Archdiocese in 1880)

Mar. 10, 1844	Quarter, William	Bishop, 1844	9: 78
Feb. 11, 1849	Van de Velde, James O.	Bishop, 1849	9: 78
July 25, 1854	O'Regan, Anthony	Bishop, 1854	9: 79
May 1, 1857	Duggan, James	Bishop, 1859	9: 79
Feb. 27, 1870	Foley, Thomas	Coadjutor and administrator, 1870	9: 80
Nov. 1, 1865	Feehan, Patrick A.	Archbishop, 1880	9: 80
Feb. 24, 1897	Quigley, James E.	Archbishop, 1903	12:484
Sept. 21, 1909	Mundelein, George W.	Archbishop, 1915	15: 36
May 1, 1929	Sheil, Bernard J.	Auxiliary, 1929	
Apr. 25, 1934	O'Brien, William D.	Auxiliary, 1934	

ARCHDIOCESE OF CINCINNATI

(Established as a Diocese in 1821 and elevated to an Archdiocese in 1850)

Jan. 13, 1822	Fenwick, Edward D.	Bishop, 1822	5:186
Oct. 13, 1833	Purcell, John B.	Bishop, 1833; archbishop, 1850	5:186
May 3, 1857	Elder, William H.	Coadjutor, 1880; archbishop, 1883	5:188
Aug. 25, 1900	Moeller, Henry	Coadjutor, 1903; archbishop, 1904	13:546
Sept. 8, 1918	McNicholas, John T.	Archbishop, 1925	
Dec. 27, 1929	Albers, Joseph H.	Auxiliary, 1929	

ARCHDIOCESE OF DUBUQUE

(Established as a Diocese in 1837 and elevated to an Archdiocese in 1893)

Dec. 10, 1837	Loras, Mathias	Bishop, 1837	12:408
May 3, 1857	Smyth, Clement	Bishop, 1857	12:408
Sept. 30, 1866	Hennessy, John	Bishop, 1866; archbishop, 1893	10:297
Aug. 25, 1878	Keane, John J.	Archbishop, 1900	6:285
Oct. 28, 1902	Keane, James J.	Archbishop, 1911	15:208
May 1, 1924	Beckman, Francis J.	Archbishop, 1930	

ARCHDIOCESE OF MILWAUKEE

(Established as a Diocese in 1843 and elevated to an Archdiocese in 1875)

Consecrated		Inaugurated in Archdiocese	
Mar. 19, 1844	Henni, John M.	Bishop, 1844; archbishop, 1875	7:516
Sept. 6, 1868	Heiss, Michael	Coadjutor, 1880; archbishop, 1881	12:411
Sept. 21, 1886	Katzer, Frederick X.	Archbishop, 1891	12:412
Mar. 27, 1892	Messmer, Sebastian G.	Archbishop, 1903	12:413
Nov. 30, 1921	Stritch, Samuel A.	Archbishop, 1930	

ARCHDIOCESE OF NEW ORLEANS*

(Established as a Diocese in 1793 and elevated to an Archdiocese in 1850)

1793	Cardenas, Louis P.	Bishop, 1793	5:423
Sept. 24, 1815	Dubourg, Louis G. V.	Bishop, 1815	4:435
Mar. 25, 1824	Rosati, Joseph	Coadjutor, 1824; bishop, 1826	13: 30
Aug. 4, 1829	DeNeckere, Leo R.	Bishop, 1829	5:418
Nov. 22, 1835	Blanc, Anthony	Bishop, 1835; archbishop, 1850	7:304
Mar. 6, 1842	Odin, John M.	Archbishop, 1861	7:102
Mar. 21, 1870	Perche, Napoleon J.	Coadjutor, 1870; archbishop, 1870	5:546
Apr. 22, 1877	Leray, Francis X.	Coadjutor, 1879; archbishop, 1883	5:547
May 1, 1881	Janssens, Francis	Archbishop, 1888	7:300
Nov. 1, 1881	Chappelle, Placide L.	Archbishop, 1897	7:554
Apr. 9, 1899	Rouxel, G. A.	Auxiliary, 1899	
July 2, 1899	Blenk, James H.	Archbishop, 1906	14:237
Apr. 14, 1910	Shaw, John W.	Archbishop, 1918	15:260
May 29, 1928	Rummell, Joseph F.	Archbishop, 1935	

*Diocese under administration of Archbishop of Baltimore from 1809 to 1815.

ARCHDIOCESE OF NEW YORK

(Established as a Diocese in 1808 and elevated to an Archdiocese in 1850)

Apr. 24, 1808	Concannen, Luke	Bishop, 1808	1:191
Nov. 6, 1814	Connolly, John	Bishop, 1814	1:191
Oct. 29, 1826	Dubois, John	Bishop, 1826	1:192
Jan. 7, 1838	Hughes, John	Coadjutor, 1838; bishop, 1842; archbishop, 1850	1:193
Mar. 10, 1844	McCloskey, John	Archbishop, 1864	1:195
May 4, 1873	Corrigan, Michael A.	Coadjutor, 1880; archbishop, 1885	1:196
Dec. 21, 1895	Farley, John M.	Auxiliary, 1895; archbishop, 1902	13:394
Oct. 28, 1914	Hayes, Patrick J.	Auxiliary, 1914; archbishop, 1919	C:246
May 1, 1934	Donahue, Stephen J.	Auxiliary, 1934	

ARCHDIOCESE OF PHILADELPHIA

(Established as a Diocese in 1808 and elevated to an Archdiocese in 1875)

Oct. 28, 1810	Egan, Michael	Bishop, 1810	5:269
Sept. 24, 1820	Conwell, Henry	Bishop, 1820	6:304
June 6, 1830	Kenrick, Francis P.	Bishop, 1830	1:485
Mar. 28, 1852	Neumann, John N.	Bishop, 1852	5:232
Apr. 26, 1857	Wood, James F.	Coadjutor, 1857; bishop, 1860; archbishop, 1875	7:251
Apr. 14, 1872	Ryan, Patrick J.	Archbishop, 1884	6:285
Feb. 24, 1897	Prendergast, Edmond F.	Archbishop, 1911	15:222
June 14, 1903	Dougherty, Denis J.	Archbishop, 1918	16: 90

ARCHDIOCESE OF PORTLAND IN OREGON

July 25, 1845	Blanchet, Francis H.	Archbishop, 1846	13: 32
June 29, 1873	Seghers, Charles J.	Coadjutor, 1878; archbishop, 1880	13: 32
Apr. 27, 1873	Gross, William H.	Archbishop, 1885	13: 32
June 29, 1898	Christie, Alexander	Archbishop, 1899	13: 33
Apr. 8, 1924	Howard, Edward D.	Archbishop, 1926	

ARCHDIOCESE OF ST. LOUIS

(Established as a Diocese in 1826 and elevated to an Archdiocese in 1847)

Mar. 25, 1824	Rosati, Joseph	Bishop, 1827	13: 30
Nov. 30, 1841	Kenrick, Peter R.	Bishop, 1843; archbishop, 1847	13: 30
May 23, 1875	Kain, John J.	Coadjutor, 1893; archbishop, 1895	13: 31
June 29, 1896	Glennon, John J.	Coadjutor, 1903; archbishop, 1903	13: 31
Nov. 30, 1933	Winkelmann, Christian H.	Auxiliary, 1933	

ARCHDIOCESE OF ST. PAUL

(Established as a Diocese in 1850 and elevated to an Archdiocese in 1888)

Consecrated		Inaugurated in Archdiocese	
Jan. 26, 1851	Cretin, Joseph	Bishop, 1851	9:225
July 24, 1859	Grace, Thomas L.	Bishop, 1859	9:225
Dec. 21, 1875	Ireland, John	Coadjutor, 1875; bishop, 1884; archbishop, 1888	9:226
Apr. 25, 1912	Dowling, Austin	Archbishop, 1919	15:171
Apr. 28, 1920	Murray, John G.	Archbishop, 1931	

ARCHDIOCESE OF SAN ANTONIO

(Established as a Diocese in 1874 and elevated to an Archdiocese in 1926)

Dec. 8, 1874	Pellicer, Anthony D.	Bishop, 1874	13: 85
May 8, 1881	Neraz, Jean C.	Bishop, 1881	13: 85
Oct. 28, 1895	Forest, John A.	Bishop, 1895	13: 85
Apr. 14, 1910	Shaw, John W.	Coadjutor, 1910; bishop, 1911	15:260
Dec. 8, 1918	Drossaerts, Arthur J.	Bishop, 1918; archbishop, 1926	

ARCHDIOCESE OF SAN FRANCISCO

(Established as the Diocese of both Californias in 1840 and elevated to an Archdiocese in 1853)

Oct. 4, 1840	Moreno, Francis G. D. S.	Bishop, 1840	12:405
June 30, 1850	Alemany, Joseph S.	Bishop, 1850; archbishop, 1853	12:408
Sept. 16, 1883	Riordan, Patrick W.	Coadjutor, 1883; archbishop, 1884	15:248
Apr. 8, 1894	Montgomery, George	Coadjutor, 1903	12:407
May 3, 1908	O'Connell, Denis J.	Auxiliary, 1908	15: 65
Dec. 4, 1912	Hanna, Edward J.	Auxiliary, 1912; archbishop, 1915	D:280
Sept. 8, 1926	Mitty, John J.	Coadjutor, 1932; archbishop, 1935	

ARCHDIOCESE OF SANTA FE

(Established as a Diocese in 1850 and elevated to an Archdiocese in 1875)

Nov. 24, 1850	Lamy, John B.	Bishop, 1850; archbishop, 1875	12: 49
June 20, 1869	Salpointe, Jean B.	Coadjutor, 1884; archbishop, 1885	12: 50
Nov. 1, 1891	Chapelle, Placide L.	Coadjutor, 1891; archbishop, 1894	7:554
May 1, 1885	Bourgade, Peter	Archbishop, 1899	12: 50
July 25, 1902	Pitaval, John B.	Auxiliary, 1902; archbishop, 1909	15:200
May 7, 1919	Daeger, Anthony T. (Albert)	Archbishop, 1919	25:336
Apr. 26, 1927	Gerken, Rudolph A.	Archbishop, 1933	

Diocese of Albany

Consecrated		Inaugurated	
Mar. 10, 1844	McCloskey, John	1847	1:195
Oct. 15, 1865	Conroy, John J.	1865	12:494
Apr. 21, 1872	McNierney, Francis	Adminis., 1874; bishop, 1877	3:372
July 1, 1894	Burke, Thomas M. A.	1894	12:403
Apr. 25, 1904	Cusack, Thomas F.	1915	15:411
Mar. 25, 1919	Gibbons, Edmund F.	1919	

Diocese of Alexandria, La.

(Erected as Diocese of Natchitoches in 1853; transferred to Alexandria in 1910)

Nov. 30, 1853	Martin, Augustus M.	1853	5:547
Apr. 22, 1877	Leray, Francis X.	1877	5:547
Mar. 19, 1885	Durier, Anthony	1885	5:547
Nov. 30, 1904	Van de Ven, Cornelius	1904	5:547
Jan. 5, 1933	Desmond, Daniel F.	1933	

Diocese of Altoona

Sept. 8, 1901	Garvey, Eugene A.	1901	
Sept. 17, 1912	McCort, John J.	1920	16:119

Diocese of Amarillo

Apr. 26, 1927	Gerken, Rudolph A.	1927	
May 1, 1934	Lucey, Robert E.	1934	

Diocese of Baker City

Consecrated		Inaugurated	
Aug. 25, 1903	O'Reilly, Charles J.	1903	15: 3
Mar. 25, 1919	McGrath, Joseph F.	1919	

Diocese of Belleville

Apr. 25, 1888	Janssen, John	1888	12:402
Feb. 24, 1914	Althoff, Henry	1914	15:243

Diocese of Bismarck

May 19, 1910	Wehrle, Vincent	1910	15:248

Diocese of Boise

Apr. 19, 1885	Glorieux, Alphonsus J.	1893	5:116
May 1, 1918	Gorman, Daniel M.	1918	
Mar. 6, 1928	Kelly, Edward J.	1928	

Diocese of Brooklyn

Oct. 30, 1853	Loughlin, John	1853	3:431
Apr. 25, 1892	McDonnell, Charles E.	1892	12:401
Oct. 3, 1920	Molloy, Thomas E.	1921	B:200

Diocese of Buffalo

Oct. 17, 1847	Timon, John	1847	12:484
Nov. 8, 1868	Ryan, Stephen V.	1868	12:484
Feb. 24, 1897	Quigley, James E.	1897	12:484

Diocese of Buffalo (Cont'd)

Consecrated		Inaugurated	
Aug. 24, 1903	Colton, Charles H.	1903	12:485
June 14, 1903	Dougherty, Denis J.	1915	16: 90
Mar. 30, 1919	Turner, William	1919	

Diocese of Burlington

Oct. 30, 1853	DeGoesbriand, Louis	1853	5:513
June 29, 1892	Michaud, John S.	1892	5:517
Apr. 14, 1910	Rice, Joseph J.	1910	

Diocese of Charleston

Sept. 21, 1820	England, John	1820	5: 28
Mar. 19, 1844	Reynolds, Ignatius A.	1844	12:410
Mar. 14, 1858	Lynch, Patrick N.	1858	12:410
Jan. 8, 1882	Northrop, Henry P.	1883	12:411
Mar. 15, 1917	Russell, William T.	1917	
Sept. 8, 1927	Walsh, Emmet M.	1927	

Diocese of Cheyenne

Oct. 28, 1887	Burke, Maurice F.	1887	12:404
Feb. 24, 1897	Lenihan, Thomas M.	1897	12:405
Oct. 28, 1902	Keane, James J.	1902	15:208
Apr. 11, 1912	McGovern, Patrick A.	1912	15:378

Diocese of Cleveland

Oct. 10, 1847	Rappe, Amedeus	1847	5:340
Apr. 14, 1872	Gilmour, Richard	1872	5:341
Feb. 25, 1892	Horstmann, Ignatius F.	1892	5:341
May 1, 1909	Farrelly, John P.	1909	15: 10
Feb. 22, 1911	Schrembs, Joseph	1921	15:316
Sept. 8, 1932	McFadden, James A. Auxiliary,	1932	

Diocese of Columbus

Mar. 25, 1862	Rosecrans, Sylvester H.	1868	9:412
Aug. 8, 1880	Watterson, John A.	1880	9:413
Aug. 25, 1900	Moeller, Henry	1900	13:546
Feb. 25, 1904	Hartley, James J.	1904	

Diocese of Concordia

Nov. 30, 1887	Scannell, Richard	1887	13: 33
Sept. 21, 1898	Cunningham, John F.	1898	15:250
Mar. 30, 1921	Tief, Francis J.	1921	

Diocese of Corpus Christi

May 20, 1913	Nussbaum, Paul J.	1913	15:137
June 14, 1921	Ledvina, Emmanuel B.	1921	

Diocese of Covington

Nov. 1, 1853	Carrell, George A.	1853	12: 51
Jan. 9, 1870	Toebbe, Augustus M.	1870	12: 51
Jan. 25, 1885	Maes, Camillus P.	1885	12: 51
Jan. 25, 1916	Brassart, Ferdinand	1916	
July 15, 1923	Howard, Francis W.	1923	

Diocese of Crookston

May 19, 1910	Corbett, Timothy	1910	15:247

Diocese of Dallas

Apr. 5, 1891	Brennan, Thomas F.	1891	
Nov. 30, 1893	Dunne, Edward J.	1893	13:501
July 12, 1911	Lynch, Joseph P.	1911	15:283

Diocese of Davenport

July 25, 1881	McMullen, John	1881	12:402
Sept. 14, 1884	Cosgrove, Henry	1884	12:402
Nov. 30, 1904	Davis, James	1904	16:383
July 25, 1927	Rohlman, Henry P.	1927	

Diocese of Denver

Consecrated		Inaugurated	
Aug. 16, 1868	Macheboeuf, Joseph P.	1887	12:409
Oct. 28, 1887	Chrysostom, Nicholas	1889	
July 6, 1911	Tihen, John H.	1917	16:102
June 10, 1931	Vehr, Urban J.	1931	

Diocese of Des Moines

Apr. 25, 1912	Dowling, Austin	1912	15:171
May 21, 1919	Drumm, Thomas W.	1919	
June 13, 1934	Bergan, Gerald T.	1934	

Diocese of Detroit

Oct. 6, 1833	Rese, Frederick	1833	13: 34
Nov. 22, 1841	Lefevre, Peter P. Coadjutor and Adminis.,	1841	5:327
Apr. 24, 1870	Borgess, Caspar H.	1870	13: 34
Nov. 4, 1888	Foley, John S.	1888	13: 35

Diocese of Duluth

Dec. 27, 1889	McGolrick, James	1889	19:140
Sept. 8, 1918	McNicholas, John T.	1918	
Feb. 3, 1926	Welch, Thomas A.	1926	

Diocese of El Paso

	Brown, John J. Preconized,	1915	
Oct. 28, 1915	Schuler, Anthony J.	1915	15:171

Diocese of Erie

Aug. 15, 1843	O'Connor, Michael Transferred,	1853	6:336
Apr. 23, 1854	Young, Josue M.	1854	13:460
Aug. 2, 1868	Mullen, Tobias	1868	9:545
Feb. 24, 1898	FitzMaurice, John E.	1898	
Feb. 6, 1918	Gannon, John M.	1920	

Diocese of Fall River

May 1, 1904	Stang, William	1904	15: 39
Sept. 19, 1907	Feehan, Daniel F.	1907	15: 99
May 27, 1930	Cassidy, James E. Appointed,	1934	

Diocese of Fargo

Dec. 27, 1889	Shanley, John	1889	
May 19, 1910	O'Reilly, James	1910	15:206
Oct. 15, 1935	Muench, Aloisius J.	1935	

Diocese of Fort Wayne

Jan. 10, 1858	Luers, John H.	1858	13: 29
Apr. 14, 1872	Dwenger, Joseph	1872	13: 30
June 24, 1833	Rademacher, Joseph Transferred,	1893	12:367
Nov. 30, 1900	Alerding, Herman J.	1900	13: 30
June 30, 1925	Noll, John F.	1925	

Diocese of Galveston

Mar. 6, 1842	Odin, John M. Transferred,	1847	7:102
Nov. 23, 1862	Dubuis, Claude M.	1862	12:401
Nov. 15, 1860	Dufal, P. .... Coadjutor,	1878	
Apr. 30, 1882	Gallagher, Nicholas Succeeded,	1892	12:401
Nov. 10, 1918	Byrne, Christopher E.	1918	

Diocese of Grand Island

(Erected at Kearney in 1912; see transferred to Grand Island in 1917)

Apr. 16, 1913	Duffy, James A.	1913	15:234
Feb. 25, 1932	Bona, Stanislaus V.	1932	

Diocese of Grand Rapids

Consecrated		Inaugurated	
Apr. 22, 1883	Richter, Henry J.	1883	12:403
Sept. 8, 1915	Gallagher, Michael J. Coadjutor, 1915; succeeded,	1916	
Jan. 16, 1911	Kelly, Edward D. Translated,	1919	
May 3, 1922	Pinten, Joseph G. Translated,	1926	

Diocese of Great Falls

Consecrated		Inaugurated	
Sept. 21, 1904	Lenihan, Mathias C.	1904	13:593
Oct. 28, 1930	O'Hara, Edwin V.	1930	

Diocese of Green Bay

Consecrated		Inaugurated	
July 12, 1868	Melcher, Joseph	1868	12:412
June 29, 1875	Krautbauer, Francis X.	1875	12:412
Sept. 21, 1886	Katzer, Frederick X.	1886	12:412
Mar. 27, 1892	Messmer, Sebastian G.	1892	12:413
July 25, 1904	Fox, Joseph J.	1904	15:214
July 29, 1908	Rhode, Paul P. Transferred,	1915	

Diocese of Harrisburg

Consecrated		Inaugurated	
July 12, 1868	Shanahan, Jeremiah F.	1868	13:500
Mar. 11, 1888	McGovern, Thomas	1888	13:500
May 1, 1899	Shanahan, John W.	1899	21:145
Sept. 21, 1916	McDevitt, Philip R.	1916	25: 82
Oct. 17, 1935	Leech, George L.	1935	

Diocese of Hartford

Consecrated		Inaugurated	
Mar. 17, 1844	Tyler, William	1844	10:136
Nov. 10, 1850	O'Reilly, Bernard	1850	10:136
Mar. 14, 1859	McFarland, Francis P.	1858	10:137
Mar. 19, 1876	Galberry, Thomas	1876	10:137
Aug. 10, 1879	McMahon, Laurence S.	1879	10:137
Feb. 22, 1894	Tierney, Michael	1894	10:138
Apr. 28, 1910	Nilan, John J.	1910	15:387
Apr. 28, 1926	McAuliffe, Maurice F. Auxiliary, 1926; bishop,	1934	

Diocese of Helena

Consecrated		Inaugurated	
Dec. 14, 1879	Brondel, John B.	1884	13:327
Dec. 21, 1904	Carroll, John P.	1904	15:262
Aug. 1, 1927	Finnigan, George J.	1927	
Sept. 21, 1933	Hayes, Ralph L.	1933	
Feb. 19, 1936	Gilmore, Joseph M.	1936	

Diocese of Indianapolis

(Established as the Diocese of Vincennes; title changed in 1898)

Consecrated		Inaugurated	
Oct. 28, 1834	Bruté, Simon G.	1834	12:413
Aug. 18, 1839	LeHailandiére, Celestine de	1839	
Oct. 24, 1847	Bazin, John S.	1847	12:414
Jan. 14, 1848	St. Palais, James M.	1849	12:414
May 12, 1878	Chatard, Francis S.	1878	12:415
Sept. 15, 1910	Chartrand, Joseph Coadjutor, 1910; succeeded,	1918	
Mar. 28, 1933	Ritter, Joseph E.	1933	

Diocese of Kansas City

Consecrated		Inaugurated	
Sept. 13, 1868	Hogan, John J. Transferred,	1880	12:404
Dec. 27, 1904	Lillis, Thomas F. Coadjutor, 1910; bishop,	1913	16:329

Diocese of LaCrosse

Consecrated		Inaugurated	
Sept. 6, 1868	Heiss, Michael	1868	12:411
Aug. 24, 1881	Flasch, Kilian C.	1881	12:411
Feb. 25, 1892	Schwebach, James	1892	12:412
May 1, 1899	McGavick, Alexander J. Promoted,	1921	
May 1, 1935	Griffin, William R. Auxiliary,	1935	

Diocese of Lafayette

Consecrated		Inaugurated	
Dec. 8, 1918	Jeanmard, Jules B.	1918	

Diocese of Leavenworth

Consecrated		Inaugurated	
Mar. 25, 1851	Miege, J. B.	1877	
June 11, 1871	Fink, Louis M. Transferred,	1877	9:541
Dec. 27, 1904	Lillis, Thomas F.	1904	16:329
Feb. 22, 1911	Ward, John	1911	
May 1, 1928	Johannes, Francis Coadjutor, 1928; succeeded,	1929	

Diocese of Lincoln

Consecrated		Inaugurated	
Nov. 30, 1887	Bonacum, Thomas	1887	12:141
July 6, 1911	Tihen, John H.	1911	16:102
Aug. 24, 1903	O'Reilly, Charles J. Transferred,	1918	15: 3
May 1, 1924	Beckman, Francis J. L.	1924	
Oct. 28, 1930	Kucera, Louis B.	1930	

Diocese of Little Rock

Consecrated		Inaugurated	
Mar. 10, 1844	Byrne, Andrew	1844	12:488
Feb. 3, 1867	Fitzgerald, Edward Preconized,	1866	12:488
June 11, 1906	Morris, John B.	1906	15:370

Diocese of Los Angeles and San Diego

Consecrated		Inaugurated	
Oct. 4, 1840	Moreno, Francis G. D. S.	1840	12:405
June 30, 1850	Alemany, Joseph S.	1850	12:408
Mar. 12, 1854	Amat, Thaddeus	1854	12:406
May 20, 1873	Mora, Francis Coadjutor, 1873; bishop,	1878	12:406
Apr. 8, 1894	Montgomery, George Coadjutor, 1894; succeeded,	1896	12:407
Nov. 24, 1901	Conaty, Thomas J.	1903	12:407
Dec. 5, 1917	Cantwell, John J.	1917	

Diocese of Louisville

(Established at Bardstown in 1808; transferred to Louisville in 1841)

Consecrated		Inaugurated	
Nov. 4, 1810	Flaget, Benedict J.	1810	6:333
Aug. 15, 1819	David, John B. M. Coadjutor,	1819	12:149
July 20, 1834	Chabrat, Guy I. Coadjutor,	1834	
Sept. 10, 1848	Spalding, Martin J. Coadjutor, 1848; succeeded,	1850	1:486
Sept. 24, 1865	Lavialle, Peter J.	1865	12: 92
May 24, 1868	McCloskey, William G.	1868	12: 65
Sept. 6, 1874	O'Donaghue, Denis Transferred,	1910	15:224
Apr. 8, 1923	Floersh, John A. Coadjutor, 1923; succeeded,	1924	

Diocese of Manchester

Consecrated		Inaugurated	
June 11, 1884	Bradley, Denis M.	1884	12:404
Sept. 8, 1904	Delaney, John B.	1904	13:337
Mar. 19, 1907	Guertin, George A.	1907	
Nov. 10, 1927	Peterson, John B. Transferred,	1932	

Diocese of Marquette

Nov. 1, 1853	Baraga, Frederic	1853	12:415
Feb. 7, 1869	Mrak, Ignatius	1869	12:416
Sept. 14, 1879	Vertin, John	1879	12:416
Aug. 24, 1899	Eis, Frederick	1899	
May 20, 1913	Nussbaum, Paul J. Appointed,	1922	15:137
Sept. 30, 1924	Plagens, Joseph C. Appointed,	1935	

Diocese of Mobile

Nov. 5, 1826	Portier, Michael	1826	7:256
Dec. 4, 1859	Quinlan, John	1859	13:499
Dec. 8, 1874	Manucy, Dominic Transferred,	1884	13:500
Sept. 20, 1885	O'Sullivan, Jeremiah	1885	13:541
May 16, 1897	Allen, Edward P.	1897	13:500
May 4, 1927	Toolen, Thomas J.	1927	

Diocese of Monterey-Fresno

May 10, 1910	MacGinley, John B.	1910	
June 29, 1933	Scher, Philip G.	1933	

Diocese of Nashville

Sept. 16, 1838	Miles, Richard P.	1838	12:367
May 1859	Whelan, James	1859	12:367
Nov. 1, 1865	Feehan, Patrick A.	1865	9: 80
June 24, 1883	Rademacher, Joseph	1883	12:367
July 25, 1894	Byrne, Thomas S.	1894	12:367
Mar. 25, 1924	Smith, Alphonse J.	1924	
Apr. 16, 1936	Adrian, William L.	1936	

Diocese of Natchez

Mar. 14, 1841	Chanche, John M. J.	1841	4:540
Feb. 11, 1849	Van de Velde, James O. Transferred,	1853	9: 78
May 3, 1857	Elder, William H.	1857	5:188
May 1, 1881	Janssens, Francis	1881	7:300
June 18, 1889	Heslin, Thomas	1889	13:516
Aug. 29, 1911	Gunn, John E.	1911	15:193
Oct. 15, 1924	Gerow, Richard O.	1924	

Diocese of Newark

Oct. 30, 1853	Bayley, J. Roosevelt	1853	1:487
May 4, 1873	Corrigan, Michael A.	1873	1:196
Oct. 18, 1881	Wigger, Winand M.	1881	12:402
July 25, 1901	O'Connor, John J.	1901	12:403
July 25, 1918	Walsh, Thomas J. Transferred,	1928	
July 25, 1935	McLaughlin, Thomas H. Auxiliary,	1935	

Diocese of Ogdensburg

May 5, 1872	Wadhams, Edgar P.	1872	12: 50
May 5, 1892	Gabriels, Henry	1892	4:266
May 1, 1912	Conroy, Joseph H. Auxiliary, 1912; succeeded,	1921	C:443

Diocese of Oklahoma City and Tulsa

(Diocese of Oklahoma until 1930)

Sept. 8, 1891	Meerschaert, Theophile	1905	15:346
Oct. 2, 1924	Kelley, Francis C.	1924	

Diocese of Omaha

Consecrated		Inaugurated	
Aug. 20, 1876	O'Connor, James	1885	13: 33
Nov. 30, 1887	Scannell, Richard Transferred,	1891	13: 33
Aug. 15, 1903	Harty, Jeremiah J. Transferred,	1916	15: 45
May 1, 1925	Beckman, Francis J. Administrator,	1926	
May 29, 1928	Rummell, Joseph F.	1928	
Oct. 25, 1933	Ryan, James H. Installed,	1935	

Diocese of Peoria

May 1, 1877	Spalding, John L.	1877	10: 44
Sept. 1, 1909	Dunne, Edmund M.	1909	15:325
June 17, 1930	Schlarman, Joseph H.	1930	

Diocese of Pittsburgh

Aug. 15, 1843	O'Connor, Michael	1843	6:336
Dec. 9, 1860	Domenec, Michael	1860	6:336
Mar. 19, 1876	Tuigg, John	1876	6:337
Aug. 2, 1885	Phelan, Richard Coadjutor, 1885; succeeded,	1889	6:337
Feb. 24, 1903	Canevin, John F. R. Coadjutor, 1903; succeeded,	1904	15:187
June 29, 1921	Boyle, Hugh C.	1921	

Diocese of Portland

Apr. 22, 1855	Bacon, David W.	1855	10:242
June 2, 1872	Healy, James A.	1875	10:242
May 19, 1901	O'Connell, William H.	1901	15:294
Oct. 18, 1906	Walsh, Louis S.	1906	15:252
Apr. 28, 1920	Murray, John G. Transferred,	1925	
Aug. 24, 1932	McCarthy, Joseph E.	1932	

Diocese of Providence

Apr. 28, 1872	Hendricken, Thomas F.	1872	8:165
Apr. 14, 1887	Harkins, Matthew	1887	13:120
Apr. 28, 1915	Doran, Thomas F. Auxiliary,	1915	
Oct. 23, 1917	Lowney, Dennis M. Auxiliary,	1917	
Apr. 10, 1919	Hickey, William A. Coadjutor, 1919; succeeded,	1921	
May 22, 1934	Keough, Francis P.	1934	

Diocese of Raleigh

(Established as Vicariate-Apostolic of North Carolina in 1860; established as Diocese of Raleigh in 1924)

Aug. 16, 1868	Gibbons, James	1868	1:488
Aug. 25, 1878	Keane, John J.	1878	6:285
Jan. 8, 1882	Northrop, Henry P.	1882	12:411
July 1, 1888	Haid, Leo	1888	26:217
June 24, 1925	Hafey, William J.	1925	

Diocese of Rapid City, S. Dak.

(Erected as Diocese of Lead in 1902; transferred to Rapid City in 1930)

Oct. 28, 1902	Stariha, John N.	1902	15:378
May 19, 1910	Busch, Joseph F.	1910	15:272
May 19, 1910	Lawler, John J. Transferred,	1916	15: 73

Diocese of Reno

July 22, 1931	Gorman, Thomas K.	1931	

Diocese of Richmond

Consecrated		Inaugurated	
	Kelly, Patrick	1820	6:331
Mar. 21, 1841	Whelan, Richard V.	1841	10:156
Nov. 10, 1850	McGill, John	1850	10:156
Aug. 16, 1868	Gibbons, James	Translated, 1872	1:488
Aug. 25, 1878	Keane, John J.	1878	6:285
Oct. 20, 1889	Van de Vyver, Augustine	1889	
May 3, 1908	O'Connell, Denis J.	Appointed, 1912	15: 65
Apr. 25, 1923	Brennan, Andrew J.	Transferred, 1926	
Oct. 23, 1935	Ireton, Peter L.	Coadjutor and apostolic administrator, 1935	

Diocese of Rochester

July 12, 1868	McQuaid, Bernard J.	1868	12:141
May 24, 1905	Hickey, Thomas F.	Succeeded, 1909	15: 58
Jan. 31, 1926	Mooney, Edward	Transferred, 1933	

Diocese of Rockford

July 25, 1901	Muldoon, Peter J.	Appointed, 1908	16:111
Dec. 21, 1921	Hoban, Edward F.	Appointed, 1928	

Diocese of Sacramento

Jan. 16, 1881	Manogue, Patrick	Coadjutor, 1881; bishop, 1886	9:541
June 16, 1896	Grace, Thomas L.	1896	9:225
Dec. 14, 1920	Keane, Patrick J.	Appointed, 1922	
Mar. 12, 1929	Armstrong, Robert J.	1929	

Diocese of St. Augustine

Apr. 25, 1858	Verot, Augustin	Appointed, 1870	12:535
May 13, 1877	Moore, John	1877	9:541
May 18, 1902	Kenny, William J.	1902	15:293
June 30, 1914	Curley, Michael J.	1914	16: 89
May 3, 1922	Barry, Patrick	1922	

Diocese of St. Cloud

May 30, 1875	Seidenbusch, Rupert	1875	12:409
Oct. 20, 1889	Zardetti, Otto	1889	
Feb. 1, 1880	Marty, Martin	Transferred, 1894	12:416
Sept. 21, 1897	Trobec, James	1897	12:417
May 19, 1910	Busch, Joseph F.	Translated, 1915	15:272

Diocese of St. Joseph

Sept. 13, 1868	Hogan, John J.	1868	12:404
Oct. 28, 1887	Burke, Maurice F.	Transferred, 1893	12:404
Nov. 8, 1922	Gilfillan, Francis	Coadjutor, 1922; succeeded, 1923	
Sept. 21, 1933	LeBlond, Charles H.	1933	

Diocese of Salt Lake

June 29, 1887	Scanlan, Lawrence	1891	12:144
Aug. 24, 1915	Glass, Joseph S.	1915	15:296
Sept. 8, 1926	Mitty, John J.	1926	
Oct. 28, 1932	Kearney, James E.	1932	

Diocese of Savannah

Consecrated		Inaugurated	
Nov. 10, 1850	Gartland, Francis X.	1850	12:534
Aug. 2, 1857	Barry, John	1857	12:534
Apr. 25, 1858	Verot, Augustin	Transferred, 1861	12:535
1854	Persico, Ignatius	Transferred, 1870	12:535
Apr. 27, 1873	Gross, William H.	1873	13: 32
Aug. 16, 1868	Becker, Thomas A.	Transferred, 1886	12:535
June 3, 1900	Keiley, Benjamin J.	1900	12:535
Oct. 18, 1922	Keyes, Michael J.	1922	
May 20, 1929	O'Hara, Gerald P.	Transferred, 1935	

Diocese of Scranton

July 12, 1868	O'Hara, William	1868	12: 45
Mar. 22, 1896	Hoban, Michael J.	Coadjutor, 1896; succeeded, 1899	12: 45
Feb. 16, 1928	O'Reilly, Thomas C.	1928	

Diocese of Seattle

(Name changed from Nesqually in 1907)

Sept. 27, 1846	Blanchet, Augustine M. A.	Transferred, 1850	13:229
Oct. 28, 1879	Junger, Aegidius	1879	13:229
Sept. 8, 1896	O'Dea, Edward J.	1896	14:527
Sept. 10, 1933	Shaughnessy, Gerald	1933	

Diocese of Sioux City

May 25, 1902	Garrigan, Philip J.	1902	12: 49
Apr. 8, 1919	Heelan, Edmond	Auxiliary, 1919; bishop, 1920	

Diocese of Sioux Falls

Feb. 1, 1880	Marty, Martin	1889	12:416
Apr. 19, 1896	O'Gorman, Thomas	1896	12:417
June 29, 1922	Mahoney, Bernard J.	1922	

Diocese of Spokane

July 25, 1905	Schinner, Augustine F.	Appointed, 1914	15:269
Feb. 24, 1927	White, Charles D.	1927	

Diocese of Springfield, Ill.

(Erected as Diocese of Quincy in 1853; transferred to Alton in 1857 and to Springfield in 1923)

Apr. 28, 1857	Juncker, Henry D.	1857	12:478
Jan. 23, 1870	Baltes, Peter J.	1870	12:479
May 1, 1888	Ryan, James	1888	12:479
Feb. 25, 1924	Griffin, James A.	1924	

Diocese of Springfield, Mass.

Sept. 25, 1870	O'Reilly, Patrick T.	1870	13:459
Oct. 18, 1892	Bevan, Thomas D.	1892	
Sept. 8, 1921	O'Leary, Thomas M.	1921	

Diocese of Superior

July 25, 1905	Schinner, Augustine F.	1905	15:269
Feb. 25, 1908	Koudelka, Joseph M.	Appointed, 1913	15:147
May 3, 1922	Pinten, Joseph G.	1922	
Nov. 30, 1926	Reverman, Theodore H.	1926	

Diocese of Syracuse

Consecrated		Inaugurated	
May 1, 1887	Ludden, Patrick A.	1887	13:593
May 16, 1909	Grimes, John	1909	2:447
May 1, 1923	Curley, Daniel J.	1923	22:396
June 29, 1933	Duffy, James A.	1933	15:234

Diocese of Toledo

Consecrated		Inaugurated	
Feb. 22, 1911	Schrembs, Joseph	Transferred, 1911	15:316
Nov. 30, 1921	Stritch, Samuel A.	1921	
June 17, 1931	Alter, Karl J.	1931	

Diocese of Trenton

Consecrated		Inaugurated	
Nov. 1, 1881	O'Farrell, Michael J.	1881	12:347
Oct. 18, 1894	McFaul, James A.	1894	12:347
July 25, 1918	Walsh, Thomas J.	1918	
Apr. 26, 1928	McMahon, John J.	1928	23:232
Mar. 17, 1934	Kiley, Moses E.	1934	

Diocese of Tucson

Consecrated		Inaugurated	
June 20, 1869	Salpointe, Jean B., Vicar Apostolic		12: 50
May 1, 1885	Bourgade, Peter	Appointed, 1897	12: 50
June 17, 1900	Granjon, Henry	1900	15:122
Nov. 6, 1923	Gercke, Daniel J.	1923	

Diocese of Wheeling

Consecrated		Inaugurated	
Mar. 21, 1841	Whelan, Richard V.	Transferred, 1850	10:156
May 23, 1875	Kain, John J.	1875	13: 31
Apr. 8, 1894	Donahue, Patrick J.	1894	12:400
May 11, 1922	Swint, John J.	Auxiliary, 1922; bishop, 1922	

Diocese of Wichita

Consecrated		Inaugurated	
Nov. 30, 1888	Hennessy, John J.	1888	12:405
June 8, 1921	Schwetner, Augustus J.	1921	

Diocese of Wilmington

Consecrated		Inaugurated	
Aug. 16, 1868	Becker, Thomas A.	1868	12:535
Nov. 1886	Curtis, Alfred A.	1886	9:541
May 9, 1897	Monaghan, John J.	1897	15:148
Nov. 30, 1925	Fitzmaurice, Edmond J.	1925	

Diocese of Winona

Consecrated		Inaugurated	
Dec. 27, 1889	Cotter, Joseph B.	1889	15:332
May 19, 1910	Heffron, Patrick R.	1910	15:139
June 9, 1926	Kelly, Francis M.	Transferred, 1928	

Methodist Episcopal Bishops

Consecrated		
Aug. 1784	Coke, Thomas	10: 89
Dec. 27, 1784	Asbury, Francis	6:293
May 6, 1800	Whatcoat, Richard	13:180
May 18, 1808	McKendree, William	10:224
May 17, 1816	George, Enoch	5:527
May 17, 1816	Roberts, Robert R.	9:484
May 28, 1824	Soulé, Joshua	5: 85
May 28, 1824	Hedding, Elijah	10:207
May 1832	Andrew, James O.	1:521
May 1832	Emory, John	10:353
May 2, 1836	Waugh, Beverly	11:119
May 2, 1836	Morris, Thomas Asbury	5:525
June 7, 1844	Hamline, Leonidas L.	13: 88
June 7, 1844	Janes, Edmund S.	10:458
May 1852	Scott, Levi	9:529
May 1852	Simpson, Matthew	7:381
May 1852	Baker, Osmond C.	5:548
May 1852	Ames, Edward R.	3:215
May 24, 1864	Clark, Davis W.	13:553
May 24, 1864	Thomson, Edward	4:159
May 24, 1864	Kingsley, Calvin	13:320
May 24, 1872	Bowman, Thomas	7:383
May 24, 1872	Harris, W. Logan	10:468
May 24, 1872	Foster, Randolph S.	13: 62
May 24, 1872	Wiley, Isaac W.	5:511
May 24, 1872	Merrill, Stephen M.	5:518
May 24, 1872	Andrews, Edward G.	12:130
May 24, 1872	Haven, Gilbert	13:261
May 24, 1872	Peck, Jesse T.	6:464
May 19, 1880	Warren, Henry W.	9:189
May 19, 1880	Foss, Cyrus D.	9:430
May 19, 1880	Hurst, John F.	9:122
May 19, 1880	Haven, Erastus O.	1:250
May 22, 1884	Ninde, William X.	13:177
May 22, 1884	Walden, John M.	12:496
May 22, 1884	Mallalieu, Willard F.	7:261
May 22, 1884	Fowler, Charles H.	7:310
May 29, 1888	Vincent, John H.	24:378
May 29, 1888	FitzGerald, James N.	12:379
May 29, 1888	Joyce, Isaac W.	13:165
May 29, 1888	Newman, John P.	6:431
May 29, 1888	Goodsell, Daniel A.	13:394
May 28, 1896	McCabe, Charles C.	13: 76
May 28, 1896	Cranston, Earl	12:533
May 28, 1900	Moore, David H.	19: 20
May 28, 1900	Hamilton, John W.	B:365
May 26, 1904	Berry, Joseph F.	13:573
May 26, 1904	Spellmeyer, Henry	13:311
May 26, 1904	Bashford, James W.	4:160
May 26, 1904	Burt, William	26:475
May 26, 1904	Wilson, Luther B.	13:593
May 26, 1904	Neely, Thomas B.	
May 26, 1904	McDowell, William F.	13:412
May 31, 1908	Anderson, William F.	14:486
May 31, 1908	Nuelson, John L.	
May 31, 1908	Quayle, William A.	6:506
May 31, 1908	Smith, Charles W.	13:575
May 31, 1908	Lewis, Wilson S.	
May 31, 1908	Hughes, Edwin H.	13:417
May 31, 1908	McIntyre, Robert	16: 92

Consecrated		
May 31, 1908	Bristol, Frank M.	25:406
May 26, 1912	Stuntz, Homer C.	20:117
May 26, 1912	Henderson, Theodore S.	25:302
May 26, 1912	Shepard, William O.	24:144
May 26, 1912	Luccock, Naphtali	
May 26, 1912	Cooke, Richard J.	23:201
May 26, 1912	Leete, Frederick DeL.	
May 26, 1912	McConnell, Francis J.	15:215
May 26, 1912	Thirkield, Wilbur P.	
May 28, 1916	Welch, Herbert	14: 42
May 28, 1916	Nicholson, Thomas	
May 28, 1916	Leonard, Adna W.	
May 28, 1916	Hughes, Matt Simpson	21:285
May 28, 1916	Oldham, William F.	14:336
May 28, 1916	Mitchell, Charles B.	C:256
May 28, 1916	Hamilton, Franklin E. E.	14:435
May 23, 1920	Warne, Francis W.	26: 71
May 23, 1920	Robinson, John W.	
May 23, 1920	Johnson, Eben S.	
May 23, 1920	Birney, Lauress J.	
May 23, 1920	Fisher, Fred B.	
May 23, 1920	Waldorf, Ernest L.	
May 23, 1920	Richardson, Ernest G.	C:357

Consecrated		
May 23, 1920	Burns, Charles W.	
May 23, 1920	Locke, Charles E.	
May 23, 1920	Blake, Edgar	
May 23, 1920	Bickley, George H.	
May 23, 1920	Keeney, Frederick T.	
May 23, 1920	Smith, H. Lester	
May 23, 1920	Mead, Charles L.	
May 23, 1920	Jones, Robert E.	
May 23, 1920	Clair, Matthew W.	
May 25, 1924	Miller, George A.	
May 25, 1924	Lowe, Titus	
May 25, 1924	Grose, George R.	15:332
May 25, 1924	Bradley, Brenton T.	
May 25, 1924	Brown, Wallace E.	
May 27, 1928	Wade, Raymond J.	
May 27, 1928	Baker, James C.	
May 22, 1932	Magee, Junius R.	
May 22, 1932	Cushman, Ralph S.	
May 17, 1936	Hammaker, Wilbur E.	
May 17, 1936	Flint, Charles W.	B:421
May 17, 1936	Oxnam, G. Bromley	A:452
May 17, 1936	Shaw, Alexander P.	

Directors of Museums in the United States

Adler Planetarium and Astronomical Museum
CHICAGO, ILL.

1930..Fox, Philip .... C: 528

Albright Art Gallery
BUFFALO, N. Y.

1905..Kurtz, Charles M. ....
1910..Quinton, Cornelia B. Sage A: 305
1924..Hekking, William M. ....

The American Museum of Natural History
NEW YORK, N. Y.

1869..Bickmore, Albert S. 8: 268
1884..Jesup, Morris K. 11: 93
1902..Bumpus, Hermon C. 13: 110
1910..Townsend, Charles H. *(acting)* ....
1911..Lucas, Frederic A. 13: 529
1924..Sherwood, George H. ....
1935..Andrews, Roy Chapman .. A: 302

The Art Institute of Chicago
CHICAGO, ILL.

1885..French, William M. R. ...15: 266
1914..Carpenter, Newton H. *(pro tem)* ....
1916..Eggers, George W. ......
1921..Harshe, Robert B. ....

Baltimore Museum of Art
BALTIMORE, MD.

1922..Levy, Florence N. .... B: 488
1927..Gale, Walter *(acting)* ....
1927..Rogers, Meyric R. ....
1929..McKinney, Roland J......

Boston Society of Natural History
BOSTON, MASS.

1830..Nuttall, Thomas 8: 374
1830..Greene, Benjamin D. 7: 509
1837..Emerson, George B. 11: 526
1843..Binney, Amos 7: 510
1847..Warren, John C. 6: 426
1856..Wyman, Jeffries 2: 254
1870..Bouve, Thomas T. 7: 506
1880..Scudder, Samuel H. 24: 180
1887..Putnam, Frederic W. 23: 257
1891..Goodale, George L. 6: 427
1892..Niles, William H. 12: 481
1897..Minot, Charles S. 6: 112
1914..Morse, Edward S. 24: 407
1920..Forbes, W. Cameron ..... C: 509
1925..Barbour, Thomas ....
1927..Taylor, Charles H. ....
1935..Hunnewell, Francis W. ..
1936..Wigglesworth, Edward ...

Brooklyn Museums
BROOKLYN, N. Y.

1904..Lucas, Frederic A. 13: 529
1911..Morris, Edward L. ....
1913..Fox, William H. ....
1934..Youtz, Philip N. ....

Buffalo Museum of Science
BUFFALO, N. Y.

1865..Stewart, William W. ....
1866..Linden, Charles ....
1873..Grote, Augustus R. 22: 74
1883..Pohlman, Julius ....
1890..Barrett, William C. ......
1892..Mixer, Frederick K. ......
1900..Letson, Elizabeth J. .....
1909..Bryant, William L. ......
1925..Bumpus, Hermon C. 13: 110
1926..Fish, Charles J. ....
1934..Cummings, Carlos E. .....

California Academy of Sciences
SAN FRANCISCO, CALIF.

1868..Stearns, Robert E. C. ....
1868..Bloomer, Henry G. ....
1875..Kellogg, Albert 25: 205
1876..Hartford, W. G. W. ......
1887..Cooper, J. G. ....
1892..Davis, J. Z. ....
1897..Keeler, Charles A. ....
1902..Loomis, Leverett M. .....
1913..Rixford, Gulian P. .... B: 172
1914..Evermann, Barton W. ...13: 570
1932..Grunsky, Carl E. *(acting)* 13: 224
1934..MacFarland, Frank M. *(acting)* ....

California Palace of the Legion of Honor
SAN FRANCISCO, CALIF.

1924..Quinton, Cornelia B. Sage A: 305
1930..Rollins, Lloyd LaP. ......
1933..Heil, Walter ....

Carnegie Institute, Department of Fine Arts
PITTSBURGH, PA.

1896..Beatty, John W. 14: 88
1922..Saint-Gaudens, Homer ...

Carnegie Museum
PITTSBURGH, PA.

1898..Holland, William J. 13: 141
1922..Stewart, Douglas ....
1926..Avinoff, Andrey ....

Chicago Historical Society
CHICAGO, ILL.

1856..Barry, William ....
1866..Armstrong, Thomas H. ..
1868..Olmstead, Lemuel G. .....
1869..Corkran, William ....
1870..Hoyt, John W. 13: 158
1874..Culver, Belden F. ....
1877..Hager, Albert D. 3: 224
1887..Moses, John ....
1893..Mason, Edward G. *(acting)*
1896..Evans, Charles ....
1901..Fertig, James W. ....
1907..McIlvaine, Caroline M. ...
1927..Shattuck, L. Hubbard ...

Cincinnati Art Museum
CINCINNATI, OHIO

1882..Goshorn, Alfred T. 25: 206
1902..Gest, Joseph H. ....
1929..Siple, Walter H. ....

City Art Museum of St. Louis
ST. LOUIS, MO.

1909..Ives, Halsey C. 24: 55
1911..Holland, Robert A. ....
1920..Sherer, Samuel L. 21: 309
1928..Davis, Charles P. ....
1929..Rogers, Meyric R. ....

Cleveland Museum of Art
CLEVELAND, OHIO

1913..Whiting, Frederick A. ....
1930..Milliken, William M. ....

Cleveland Museum of Natural History
CLEVELAND, OHIO

1920..Rea, Paul M. ....
1928..Madison, Harold L. ......

Colorado Museum of Natural History
DENVER, COLO.

1901..Borcherdt, Rudolph ......
1910..Figgins, Jesse D. ....
1936..Bailey, Alfred M. ....

Corcoran Gallery of Art
WASHINGTON, D. C.

1873..MacLeod, William ....
1889..Barbarin, F. Sinclair ....
1900..McGuire, Frederick B. ...
1915..Minnigerode, C. Powell ...

Denver Art Museum
DENVER, COLO.

1919..Poland, Reginald H. .....
1921..Eggers, George W. ....
1926..Ronnebeck, Arnold *(art adviser)* ....
1928..Heavenrich, Samuel ......
1929..Evans, Anne *(acting)* ...
1930..Kay-Scott, Cyril ....
1935..Bear, Donald J. ....

Detroit Institute of Arts
DETROIT, MICH.

1891..Griffith, Armond H. 15:404
1913..Burroughs, Clyde H. *(acting)* ....
1914..Moore, Charles ....
1916..Burroughs, Clyde H. .....
1924..Valentiner, Wilhelm R. ...

Field Museum of Natural History
CHICAGO, ILL.

1893..Skiff, Frederick J. V. 12: 29
1921..Davies, David C. ....
1928..Simms, Stephen C. ....
1937..Gregg, Clifford C. ....

Freer Gallery of Art
WASHINGTON, D. C.

1923..Lodge, John E. ....

Los Angeles Museum of History, Science and Art
LOS ANGELES, CALIF.

1910..Daggett, Frank S. ....
1921..Bryan, William A. ....

Metropolitan Museum of Art
NEW YORK, N. Y.

1879..DiCesnola, Luigi P. 1:422
1905..Clarke, Caspar P. .... Irish
1910..Robinson, Edward 23: 8
1932..Winlock, Herbert E. .....

Milwaukee Art Institute
MILWAUKEE, WIS.

1914..Watson, Dudley C. ......
1924..Trask, John A. D. ....
1926..Pelikan, Alfred G. ....

Minneapolis Institute of Arts
MINNEAPOLIS, MINN.

1914..Breck, Joseph 25: 47
1917..VanDerlip, John R. *(acting)* 26:372
1921..Plimpton, Russell A. .....

Museum of the American Indian Heye Foundation
NEW YORK, N. Y.

1903..Heye, George G. C:182

Museum of Fine Arts
BOSTON, MASS.

1876..Loring, Charles G. 25:301
1902..Robinson, Edward 23: 8
1907..Fairbanks, Arthur ....
1926..Holmes, Edward J. ......
1935..Edgell, George H. ....

National Gallery of Art
WASHINGTON, D. C.

1906..Holmes, William H. 16:441
1932..Tilman, Ruel P. *(acting)*..

National Museum
WASHINGTON, D. C.

1850..Baird, Spencer F. 3:405
1878..Goode, G. Brown 3:408
1898..Rathbun, Richard 13:526
1919..Ravenel, William DeC. ...
1925..Wetmore, Alexander .....

Newark Museum
NEWARK, N. J.

1909..Dana, John Cotton 22:321
1929..Winser, Beatrice ....

New York State Museum
ALBANY, N. Y.

1870..Hall, James 3:280
1894..Merrill, Frederick J. H. ..13:293
1904..Clarke, John M. 19:456
1926..VanDeLoo, James *(acting)*
1926..Adams, Charles C. A:448

Pennsylvania Museum of Art
PHILADELPHIA, PA.

1907..Barber, Edwin A. 22:267
1917..Warner, Langdon ....
1923..Woodhouse, Samuel W. *(acting)* ....
1925..Kimball, Fiske ....

Smithsonian Institution
WASHINGTON, D. C.

1846..Henry, Joseph 3:405
1878..Baird, Spencer F. 3:405
1887..Langley, Samuel P. 15: 7
1907..Walcott, Charles D. 22:135
1928..Abbot, Charles G. A:366

Toledo Museum of Art
TOLEDO, OHIO

1903..Stevens, George W. ......
1926..Godwin, Blake-More .....

Wadsworth Atheneum
HARTFORD, CONN.

1911..Gay, Frank B. 25:192
1927..Austin, Arthur E., Jr. ..

William Rockhill Nelson Gallery of Art
KANSAS CITY, MO.

1933..Gardner, Paul ....

Worcester Art Museum
WORCESTER, MASS.

1900..Heywood, John G. ....
1908..Pratt, Frederick S. ....
1909..Gentner, Philip J. ....
1918..Henniker-Heaton, Raymond
1926..Eggers, George W. ....
1931..Taylor, Francis H. ....

Principal Treaties and Conventions Negotiated Between the United States and Foreign Countries With the Names of the American Signers

Treaty of Alliance with France

Signed at Paris, February 6, 1778

Providing recognition of the independence of the United States, relinquishment of territory by France and the renunciation of claims.

Franklin, Benjamin 1:328
Deane, Silas 12:457
Lee, Arthur 8:298

Provisional Articles of Peace

Signed at Paris, November 30, 1782

Providing peace terms with Great Britain.

Adams, John 2: 1
Franklin, Benjamin 1:328
Jay, John 1: 20
Laurens, Henry 3:426

Armistice with Great Britain

Signed at Versailles, January 20, 1783

Declaring the cessation of hostilities.

Adams, John 2: 1
Franklin, Benjamin 1:328

Definitive Treaty of Peace

Signed at Paris, September 3, 1783

Treaty of peace between Great Britain and the United States, concluding the Revolutionary war.

Adams, John 2: 1
Franklin, Benjamin 1:328
Jay, John 1: 20

Jay Treaty

Signed at London, November 19, 1794

Providing for the evacuation of British troops in the Northwest and the free navigation of the Mississippi river, and for the settlement of boundary controversies, spoliation claims of American citizens, and British claims for the collection of private debts.

Jay, John 1: 20

Treaty of San Lorenzo

Signed October 27, 1795

Whereby Spain ceded the right of navigation of the Mississippi river and of entry and deposit at New Orleans, and fixed the Florida boundary at 31°.

Pinckney, Thomas 12:160

Treaty for the Cession of Louisiana

Signed at Paris, April 30, 1803

Concluding the Louisiana Purchase from France.

Livingston, Robert R. 2:396
Monroe, James 6: 81

Treaty of Ghent

Signed December 24, 1814

Concluding the War of 1812.

Adams, John Quincy 5: 73
Bayard, James A. 7:300
Clay, Henry 5: 77
Russell, Jonathan 8: 57
Gallatin, Albert 3: 9

Treaty of Peace with Algiers

Signed at Algiers, June 30 and July 3, 1815

Providing for peace and amity between Algiers and the United States; that no tribute shall ever be required by Algiers; for the immediate surrender of the American squadron; for the just and full compensation to American citizens who had been captured or forced to abandon property in Algiers; and for amity and commerce between the two nations.

Shaler, William 4:532
Decatur, Stephen 4: 56

Convention with Great Britain

Signed at London, October 20, 1818

Respecting fisheries, boundary and the restoration of slaves.

Gallatin, Albert 3: 9
Rush, Richard 5: 80

Treaty of Friendship with Spain

Signed at Washington, February 22, 1819

Providing for the cession of the Floridas and boundary settlements.

Adams, John Quincy 5: 73

Convention of 1822

Signed at St. Petersburg, July 12, 1822

For determining the indemnity of Great Britain under award of the Emperor of Russia as the true construction of the first article of the treaty of Dec. 24, 1814.

Middleton, Henry 12:163
Bagot, Charles ....

Treaty with Russia

Signed at St. Petersburg, April 17, 1824

Respecting rights in the Pacific ocean and on the northwest coast of America.

Middleton, Henry 12:163

Convention with Great Britain

Signed at London, September 29, 1827

For the submission to arbitration of the northeastern boundary question.

Gallatin, Albert 3: 9

Treaty of Limits with Mexico

Signed at Mexico City, January 12, 1828

Defining the boundary between the United States and Mexico.

Poinsett, Joel R. 6:435

Convention with Texas

Signed at Washington, April 25, 1838

For marking the boundary between the United States and the Republic of Texas.

Forsyth, John 6:435

Webster-Ashburton Treaty

Signed at Washington, August 9, 1842

Agreement with Great Britain on the northeastern boundary and for the final suppression of the African slave trade.

Webster, Daniel 3: 36

Treaty of Annexation of Texas

Signed at Washington, April 12, 1844

Calhoun, John C. 6: 83

Boundary Treaty with Great Britain

Signed at Washington, June 15, 1846

Establishing the boundary west of the Rocky mountains.

Buchanan, James 5: 1

Treaty of Guadalupe Hidalgo

Signed February 2, 1848

Declaration of peace with Mexico.

Trist, Nicholas P. 7:505

Clayton-Bulwer Treaty

Signed at Washington, April 19, 1850

Convention with Great Britain relating to a ship canal connecting the Atlantic and Pacific oceans.

Clayton, John M. 6:179

Gadsden Treaty

Signed at Mexico City, December 30, 1853

Concluded with Mexico, providing for the cession of territory and payment therefor; transit of the Isthmus of Tehuantepec, and navigation of the Gulf of California and the Colorado and Bravo rivers.

Gadsden, James 12: 68

Treaty with Japan

Signed at Yokohama, March 30, 1854

Providing for peace, treaty ports, the rights of shipwrecked sailors, commerce, most-favored-nation treatment and the residence of an American consul.

Perry, Matthew C. 4: 42

Treaty with Russia

Signed at Washington, March 30, 1867

Convention ceding Alaska to the United States.

Seward, William H. 2: 77

International Bureau of Weights and Measures Convention

Signed at Paris, May 20, 1875

For the establishment of such a bureau.

Washburne, Elihu B. 4: 14

Immigration Treaty with China

Signed at Peiping, November 17, 1880

Regulating, limiting or suspending the immigration of Chinese subjects to the United States.

Angell, James B. 1:251
Swift, John F. 18:405
Trescot, William H. 13:206

Convention for the International Exchange of Official Documents, Scientific and Literary Publications

Signed at Brussels, March 15, 1886

Tree, Lambert 6:161

General Act on the Samoan Islands

Signed at Berlin, June 14, 1889

Between the United States, Germany and Great Britain, providing for the neutrality and autonomous government of the Samoan islands.

Kasson, John A. 4:379
Phelps, William W. 7:451
Bates, George H. ....

First International American Conference

(Pan-American Congress)

Met in Washington, October 2, 1889

To consider the free navigation of American rivers; a uniform system of weights and measures, and sanitary regulations; an international banking system and the establishment of a bureau of intelligence concerning commerce and resources of the American republics.

Blaine, James G. (*president*) 1:137
Bliss, Cornelius N. 11: 15
Carnegie, Andrew 9:151

General Act for the Repression of the African Slave Trade

Signed at Brussels, July 2, 1890

Terrell, Edwin H. 1:387
Sanford, Henry S. 7:140

Convention on Customs Tariffs

Signed at Brussels, July 5, 1890

Concerning the formation of an international union for the publication of customs tariffs.

Terrell, Edwin H. 1:387

Treaty with Russia

Signed at Washington, May 4, 1894

Agreement for a modus vivendi in relation to the fur-seal fisheries in the Behring sea and the North Pacific ocean.

Gresham, Walter Q. 24:330

Treaty of Peace with Spain

Signed at Paris, December 10, 1898

Concluding the Spanish-American war.

Day, William R. 11: 11
Davis, Cushman K. 10: 65
Frye, William P. 1:290
Gray, George 6: 70
Reid, Whitelaw 22: 1

Conventions Signed July 29, 1899, at the First Universal Peace Conference Held at The Hague

Assembled upon invitation of the Czar of Russia to consider terms of universal and permanent peace

I. For the pacific adjustment of international disputes
II. Declaration as to launching of projectiles and explosives from balloons

Low, Seth 6:348
White, Andrew D. 4:476
Newel, Stanford 11:239
Crozier, William 12:267
Mahan, Alfred T. 10:440

III. With respect to the laws and usages of war on land
IV. For the adaptation of the rules of maritime warfare to the principles of the Geneva Convention of 1864 (This convention provided for the amelioration of the condition of the wounded in times of war. While the United States did not participated in the convention, the President declared adhesion on March 1, 1892).

Newel, Stanford 11:239

Final Protocol

Signed at Peiping, September 7, 1901

Entered into between the plenipotentiaries of various powers at the conclusion of the so-called "Boxer" troubles.

Rockhill, William W. 8:129

Treaty with Spain

Signed at Washington, November 7, 1900

For the cession of outlying islands of the Philippines.

Hay, John 11: 12

Protocol with Nicaragua

Signed at Washington, December 1, 1900

Providing for the arrangement of negotiations in the event that an interoceanic canal be constructed at Nicaragua.

Hay, John 11: 12

Conventions Signed at the Second Pan-American Congress Held at Mexico City in 1902

I. On literary and artistic copyrights, signed January 27, 1902.
II. Treaty for the arbitration of pecuniary claims, signed January 30, 1902.

Buchanan, William I. 2:271
Pepper, Charles M. B:148
Foster, Volney W. 13:401

Convention with Panama

Signed at Washington, November 18, 1903

Providing for recognition of the independence of Panama; for the construction of a ship canal at Panama; authority in the Canal Zone, and the acquisition of territory.

Hay, John 11: 12

International Sanitary Convention

Signed at Paris, December 3, 1903

Geddings, H. D. ....
Anderson, Frank ....

Convention for the Creation of an International Institute of Agriculture

Signed at Rome, June 7, 1905

White, Henry 14:171

Hay-Quesada Treaty

Signed at Washington, March 2, 1904

Entered into with Cuba for the adjustment of title to the ownership of the Isle of Pines.

Hay, John 11: 12

International Sanitary Convention

Signed at Washington, October 14, 1905

Wyman, Walter 12:508
Geddings, H. D. ....
Fulton, John S. ....
McCaw, Walter D. .... A: 89
Gatewood, J. D. ....
Johnson, H. L. E. ....

International Conference at Algeciras

Signed April 7, 1906

For the settlement of European differences regarding claims in Morocco.

White, Henry 14:171
Gummeré, Samuel R. 13:521

International Red Cross Convention

Signed at Geneva, July 6, 1906

For the amelioration of the condition of the wounded of the armies in the field.

Sanger, William C. 20: 84
Sperry, Charles S. 21: 51
Davis, George B. 22:397
O'Reilly, Robert M. 18:261

International Law Commission Convention

Signed at Rio de Janeiro, August 23, 1906

For the establishment of such a body.

Buchanan, William I. 2:271
Rowe, Leo S. 18:316
Montague, Andrew J. 13:358
Larrinaga, Tulio ....
Polk, Van Leer ....
Reinsch, Paul S. 19:285

International Wireless Telegraph Convention

Signed at Berlin, November 3, 1906

Tower, Charlemagne 5:190
Manney, H. N. ....
Allen, James ....
Waterbury, John I. ....

Conventions Signed October 19, 1907, at the Second International Peace Conference Held at The Hague

I. For the pacific settlement of international disputes
II. Respecting the limitation of the employment of force for recovery of contract debts
III. Relative to the opening of hostilities
IV. Respecting the laws and customs of war on land
V. Relating to the laying of automatic submarine contact mines
VI. Respecting bombardment by naval forces
VII. Adaptation to naval war of the principles of the Geneva Convention
VIII. Right of capture in naval war
IX. Prohibiting the discharge of projectiles and explosives from balloons
X. Respecting the rights and duties of neutral powers and persons in war on land.

Choate, Joseph H. 9:159
Porter, Horace 4:310
Rose, Uriah M. 7:126
Hill, David Jayne 12:244
Sperry, Charles S. 21: 51
Buchanan, William I. 2:271

International Office of Public Health Convention

Signed at Rome, December 9, 1907

For the establishment of such an organization.

Laughlin, A. M. ....
Hitt, R. S. Reynolds 14:477

Treaty with Great Britain

Signed at Washington, April 11, 1908

Concerning the Canadian international boundary.

Root, Elihu 26: 1

Convention with Great Britain

Signed at Washington, January 11, 1909

Concerning the boundary waters between the United States and Canada.

Root, Elihu 26: 1

Additional Act for the Protection of Industrial Property

Signed at Brussels, December 14, 1909

The original convention for the international protection of industrial property was signed at Paris, March 20, 1883. While the United States did not participate at this convention, the senate advised adhesion on March 2, 1887.

Townsend, Lawrence 12: 54
Forbes, Francis ....
Chamberlain, Walter H. ....

Treaty with Great Britain

Signed at Washington, May 21, 1910

Concerning the boundary line in Passamaquoddy bay.

Knox, Philander C. 24: 7

Convention with Mexico

Signed at Washington, June 24, 1910

For arbitration of the Chamizal case upon which the members of the international boundary commission failed to agree.

Knox, Philander C. 24: 7

Conventions Signed at the Fourth International Congress of American States Held at Buenos Aires in 1910

I. For the settlement of pecuniary claims, signed August 11, 1910
II. Concerning literary and artistic copyrights, signed August 11, 1910
III. Relating to inventions, patents, designs, industrial models, etc., signed August 20, 1910
IV. Relating to the protection of trade marks, signed August 20, 1910.

White, Henry 14:171
Crowder, Enoch H. A:455
Nixon, Lewis 13: 42
Moore, John Bassett .... A: 72
Moses, Bernard ....
Quintero, Lamar C. ....
Reinsch, Paul S. 19:285
Kinley, David .... B: 76

Convention for the Unification of Certain Rules of Law

Signed at Brussels, September 23, 1910

With respect to assistance salvage at sea.

Noyes, Walter C. 20:318
Burlingham, Charles C. ....
Montague, Andrew J. 13:358
Smith, Edwin W. C:426

Convention for the Protection of Industrial Property

Signed at Washington, June 2, 1911

Revising the Paris convention of March 20, 1883, as modified by the additional act signed at Brussels on December 14, 1900.

Moore, Edward Bruce ....
Fish, Frederick P. 26:202
Duell, Charles H. 12:285
Parkinson, Robert H. ....
Church, Melville ....

Convention between the United States, Great Britain and Russia

Signed at Washington, July 7, 1911

For the preservation and protection of fur seals.

Nagel, Charles D:266
Anderson, Chandler P. ....

International Sanitary Convention

Signed at Paris, January 17, 1912

Bailly-Blanchard, Arthur ....

First International Opium Conference

Signed at The Hague, January 23, 1912

Convention and final protocol for the suppression of the abuse of opium and other drugs.

Brent, Charles H. 14:433
Wright, Hamilton 22:430
Finger, H. J. ....

International Wireless Telegraph Convention

Signed at London, July 5, 1912

Edwards, John R. 6:523
Walton, John Q. ....
Moore, Willis L. 21: 84
Squier, George O. 24:320
Russell, Edgar 20: 31
Saltzman, C. McK. ....
Todd, David W. ....
Hammond, John Hays, Jr. D:391
Terrell, W. D. ....
Waterbury, John I. ....

Second International Opium Conference

Signed at The Hague, July 9, 1913

Wright, Hamilton 22:430
Bryce, Lloyd 1:252
Kollen, Gerrit J. ....

Treaty with Colombia

Signed at Bogota, April 6, 1914

For the settlement of differences arising out of the events which took place on the Isthmus of Panama in November 1903.

Thomson, Thaddeus A. ....

Nicaragua Canal Route Convention

Signed at Washington, August 5, 1914

For the perpetual grant by way of San Juan river and Lake Nicaragua and ninety-year leases of Great and Little Corn islands and of naval base rights on the Gulf of Fonesca.

Bryan, William Jennings 19:453

Third International Opium Conference

Signed at The Hague, June 25, 1914

Van Dyke, Henry 25: 10
Denby, Charles A:461

Boundary Convention

Signed at Panama, September 2, 1914

To establish permanently the boundary lines of the lands and waters owned by the United States in Panama.

Price, William Jennings D:100

Convention with Denmark

Signed at New York, August 4, 1916

For the cession to the United States of the Danish West Indies.

Lansing, Robert 20: 1

Treaty of Peace between the Allied and Associated Powers and Germany

Signed at Versailles, June 28, 1919

Wilson, Woodrow 19: 1
Lansing, Robert 20: 1
White, Henry 14:171
House, Edward M. .... A: 55
Bliss, Tasker H. 21: 86

Treaty of Peace between the Allied and Associated Powers and Austria

Signed at Saint-Germain-en-Laye, September 10,1919

Polk, Frank Lyon A:417
White, Henry 14:171
Bliss, Tasker H. 21: 86

Convention between the United States And Other Powers

Signed at Saint-Germain-en-Laye, December 10, 1919

Revising the General Act of the African Conference signed at Berlin, February 26, 1885, and the General Act, at Brussels, signed July 2, 1890.

Polk, Frank L. A:417
White, Henry 14:171
Bliss, Tasker H. 21: 86

Treaty of Peace between the Allied and Associated Powers and Hungary

Signed at Trianon, June 4, 1920

Wallace, Hugh Campbell ....

Treaty with Germany

Signed at Berlin, August 25, 1921

Restoring friendly relations, and respecting the rights and privileges of the United States under the Treaty of Versailles.

Dresel, Ellis L. ....

Convention between the United States And Other Powers

Signed at Sevres, France, October 6, 1921

Amending the convention relating to weights and measures signed May 20, 1875.

Whitehouse, Sheldon D:188
Stratton, Samuel W. 13:142

Treaties Signed February 6, 1922, at the Conference on the Limitation of Armament and Far Eastern Questions Held at Washington

Between the United States, the British Empire, France, Italy and Japan, for the limitation of naval armaments.

Hughes, Charles E. .... A: 6
Lodge, Henry C. 19: 52
Underwood, Oscar W. 21: 22
Root, Elihu 26: 1

Between the United States, the British Empire, France, Italy and Japan, relating to the use of submarines and noxious gases in warfare.

Hughes, Charles E. .... A: 6
Lodge, Henry C. 19: 52

Between the United States, the British Empire, France and Japan, relating to insular possessions and dominions in the Pacific ocean.

Hughes, Charles E. .... A: 6
Lodge, Henry C. 19: 52
Underwood, Oscar W. 21: 22
Root, Elihu 26: 1

Between the United States, Belgium, the British Empire, China, France, Italy, Japan, The Netherlands and Portugal, relating to the principles to be followed in matters concerning China.

Hughes, Charles E. .... A: 6
Lodge, Henry C. 19: 52
Underwood, Oscar W. 21: 22
Root, Elihu 26: 1

Between the United States, Belgium, the British Empire, China, France, Italy, Japan, The Netherlands and Portugal, relating to the revision of Chinese customs tariff.

Hughes, Charles E. .... A: 6
Lodge, Henry C. 19: 52
Root, Elihu 26: 1
Underwood, Oscar W. 21: 22

Treaty with Japan

Signed at Washington, February 11, 1922

Regarding rights in former German islands in the Pacific, north of the equator, and in particular the Island of Yap.

Hughes, Charles E. .... A: 6

Agreement for a Mixed Commission

Signed at Berlin, August 10, 1922

To determine the amount to be paid by Germany to the United States in satisfaction of Germany's financial obligations under the treaty concluded on August 25, 1921.

Houghton, Alanson B. .... B: 7

International Commissions Convention

Signed at Washington, February 7, 1923

For the establishment of international commissions of inquiry.

Hughes, Charles E. .... A: 6
Welles, Sumner ....

Conventions and Treaties Signed at the Fifth International Conference of American States Held at Santiago, Chile, in 1923

I. Convention for the protection of commercial, industrial and agricultural trade marks and commercial names, signed April 28, 1923
II. Pan American Treaty of Friendship to avoid or prevent conflicts between the American states, signed May 3, 1923
III. Convention providing for the publicity of customs documents, signed May 3, 1923
IV. Convention providing for uniformity of nomenclature for the classification of merchandise, signed May 3, 1923.

Fletcher, Henry P. 15:342
Kellogg, Frank B. .... A: 8
Pomerene, Atlee ....
Saulsbury, Willard 15:105
Partridge, Frank C. 9:549
Vincent, George E. .... B: 6
Fowler, William E. ....
Rowe, Leo S. 18: 316

Universal Postal Union

Signed at Stockholm, August 28, 1924

For the revision of the Universal Postal Convention concluded at Madrid November 30, 1920.

Stewart, Joseph 22:172
White, Eugene R. ....
Sands, Edwin ....

Sanitary Convention

Signed at Havana, November 14, 1924

Between the United States and other American republics.

Cumming, Hugh S. ....
Creel, Richard ....
Cronin, P. D. ....
Patterson, Francis D. ....

Convention with Great Britain

Signed at London, February 10, 1925

Relating to rights in East Africa.

Kellogg, Frank B. .... A: 8

Convention with Great Britain

Signed at London, February 10, 1925

Relating to rights in the Cameroons.

Kellogg, Frank B. .... A: 8

Boundary Treaty with Great Britain

Signed at Washington, February 24, 1925

To establish international boundary between the United States and Canada from the mouth of the Pigeon river to the northwesternmost point of Lake of the Woods, and thence to the summit of the Rocky mountains.

Hughes, Charles E. .... A: 6

Convention with Great Britain

Signed at London, December 3, 1924

Respecting rights in Palestine.

Kellogg, Frank B. .... A: 8

Treaty with the Netherlands

Signed at Washington, January 23, 1925

Agreement for the arbitration of differences respecting sovereignty over the Island of Palmas.

Hughes, Charles E. .... A: 6

Convention with Great Britain

Signed at London, February 10, 1925

Relating to rights in Togoland.

Kellogg, Frank B. .... A: 8

Convention for the Protection of Industrial Property

Signed at The Hague, November 6, 1925

Robertson, Thomas E. ....
Lane, Wallace R. C:397
Brown, Jo Baily ....

Convention between the United States And Other Powers

Signed at Paris, June 21, 1926

Revising the International Sanitary Convention of January 17, 1912.

Cumming, Hugh S. ....
Clark, Taliaferro ....
King, W. W. ....

International Radiotelegraph Convention And General Regulations

Signed at Washington, November 25, 1927

Hoover, Herbert .... C: 1
Davis, Stephen ....
Watson, James E. A:409
White, Wallace H., Jr. D:208
Castle, William R., Jr. D:342
Vallance, William R. ....
Saltzman, C. McK. ....
Smith, E. D. ....
Craven, Thomas T. ....
Terrell, W. D. ....
Young, Owen D. .... A: 81
Reber, Samuel 24:416
White, J. B. ....
Kennelly, Arthur E. 13:452

Conventions Signed February 20, 1928, at the Sixth International Conference of American States Held at Havana

I. Concerning commercial aviation
II. Concerning American maritime neutrality
III. Concerning the setting forth of the duties and rights of states in the event of civil strife.

Hughes, Charles E. .... A: 6
Judah, Noble B. ....
Fletcher, Henry P. D:428
Underwood, Oscar W. 21: 22
Morrow, Dwight W. 23: 10
O'Brien, Morgan J. D:235
Scott, James B. .... C: 69
Wilbur, Ray L. .... C: 12
Rowe, Leo S. 18:316

Pact of Paris

(*Briand-Kellogg Treaty*)

Signed at Paris, August 27, 1928

Between the United States, France, Germany, Belgium, Italy, Japan, Poland, Czechoslovakia and the British Empire, renouncing war as an instrument of national policy and pledging to settle all disputes by pacific means.

Kellogg, Frank B. .... A: 8

Inter-American Arbitration Treaty and Protocol of Progressive Arbitration

Signed at Washington, January 5, 1929

Kellogg, Frank B. .... A: 8
Hughes, Charles E. .... A: 6

Convention of Inter-American Conciliation

Signed at Washington, January 5, 1929

Between the United States and other American republics desiring to demonstrate the condemnation of war as an instrument of national policy in their mutual relations.

Kellogg, Frank B. .... A: 8
Hughes, Charles E. .... A: 6

Convention and Protocol Between the United States and other American Republics

Signed at Washington, February 20, 1929

For trade-mark and commercial protection.

White, Francis ....
Robertson, Thomas E. ....
Rogers, Edward S. ....

Treaty between the United States, the British Empire, France, Italy and Japan

Signed at London, April 22, 1930

For the limitation and reduction of naval armament.

Stimson, Henry L. .... C: 8
Dawes, Charles G. A:508
Adams, Charles F. .... C: 11
Robinson, Joseph T. B:193
Reed, David A. B:384
Gibson, Hugh A:419
Morrow, Dwight W. 23: 10

Multilateral Convention and Protocol Of Signature

Signed at Geneva, July 13, 1931

Concerning narcotic drugs.

Caldwell, John K. ....
Auslinger, Harry J. ....
Treadway, Walter L. ....
Young, Sanborn ....

International Telecommunication Convention

Signed at the International Radio Conference

Held at Madrid, December 9, 1932

General radio regulations annexed thereto, and a final radio protocol between the United States and other powers concluded.

Sykes, Eugene O. ....
Jolliffe, C. B. ....
Lichtenstein, Walter ....
Stewart, Irvin ....

Public Statues in the United States

City	Statue		Sculptor	
Adams, Massachusetts	McKinley, William	11: 1	Lukeman, Augustus	B:437
Akron, Ohio	Perkins, Simon	10: 56	Moretti, G.	
Albany, New York	Burns, Robert		Calverly, Charles	
"	Sheldon, Edward A.	7: 67	Brines, J. R.	
Alleghany City, Pennsylvania	Washington, George	1: 1	Pausch, Edward	
Amesbury, Massachusetts	Bartlett, Josiah	11:121	Gerhardt, Karl	
Anaconda, Montana	Daly, Marcus		Saint-Gaudens, Augustus	8:287
Annapolis, Maryland	De Kalb, Johann	1: 73	Keyser, Ephraim	
"	Schley, Winfield S.	9: 8	Keyser, Ernest W.	
"	Taney, Roger B.	1: 27	Rinehart, William H.	2:345
Arcata, California	McKinley, William	11: 1	Patigian, Haig	18: 44
Atlanta, Georgia	Gordon, John P.		Borglum, Solon H.	13:214
"	Grady, Henry W.	1:526	Doyle, Alexander	10:371
"	Hill, Benjamin H.	10:194	"	
Auburn, New York	Seward, William H.	2: 77	Robinson, Walter G.	
Austin, Texas	Austin, Stephen F.	6: 70	Ney, Elizabet	13:371
"	Houston, Samuel	9: 63	"	
"	Johnston, Albert S.	1:388	"	
Baltimore, Maryland	Baltimore, Lord	7:331	Pike, Charles J.	24:101
"	Howard, John E.	9:292	Fremiet, Emmanuel	
"	Lafayette	1: 63	O'Connor, Andrew	
"	Peabody, George	5:335	Story, William W.	5:417
"	Poe, Edgar Allan	1:463	Ezekiel, Moses J.	18:217
"	Taney, Roger B.	1: 27	Rinehart, William H.	2:345
"	Whyte, William Pinkney	9:309	Schuler, Hans	
Battle Creek, Michigan	Post, William		Gelert, Johannes S.	9: 58
Bellefonte, Pennsylvania	Curtin, Andrew G.	24:412	Noble, W. Clark	A:454
Berkeley, California	McKinley, William	11: 1	Aitken, Robert I.	15:215
Birmingham, Alabama	Davis, William E. B.	13:514	Moretti, G.	
Bismarck, North Dakota	Sacagawea	13:419	Crunelle, Leonard	
Boston, Massachusetts	Adams, Samuel	1:104	Whitney, Anne	7: 72
"	Agassiz, Alexander	3: 98	Bartlett, Paul W.	12:553
"	Andrew, John A.	1:118	Ball, Thomas	5:199
"	Banks, Louis A.	13:103	Kitson, Henry H.	12:398
"	Bartlett, William F.	4:358	French, Daniel C.	A:460
"	Beethoven		Crawford, Thomas	8:292
"	Brooks, Phillips	2:304	Saint-Gaudens, Augustus	8:287
"	"		Pratt, Bela L.	14:378
"	Burns, Robert		Cairns, Hugh	
"	"		Kitson, Henry H.	12:398
"	Cass, Thomas	9:528	Brooks, Richard E.	22:229
"	Channing, William Ellery	5:458	Adams, Herbert	13:510
"	Choate, Rufus	6: 17	French, Daniel C.	A:460
"	Collins, Patrick A.	11:413	Kitson, Henry H. and Kitson, A. R.	12:398
"	Columbus, Christopher	3:436	Buyens, Alois	
"	Cotton, John	7: 27	Pratt, Bela L.	14:378
"	Devens, Charles	3:203	Warner, Olin L.	8:282
"	Ericsson, Leif		Whitney, Anne	7: 72
"	Everett, Edward	6:179	Story, William W.	5:417
"	Farragut, David G.	2: 45	Kitson, Henry H.	12:398
"	Franklin, Benjamin	1:328	Greenough, Richard S.	23:252
"	Garrison, William L.	2:305	Warner, Olin L.	8:282
"	Glover, John	8:223	Milmore, Martin	8:291
"	Hale, Edward Everett	1:199	Pratt, Bela L.	14:378
"	Hamilton, Alexander	1: 9	Rimmer, William	4:375
"	Hooker, Joseph	4:176	French, Daniel C. and Potter, Edward C.	A:460 26:272
"	Hutchinson, Anne	9:148	Dallin, Cyrus E.	14:478
"	Lincoln, Abraham	2: 65	Ball, Thomas	5:199
"	Mann, Horace	3: 78	Stebbins, Emma	8:292
"	Milmore, Martin	8:291	French, Daniel C.	A:460
"	O'Reilly, John B.	1:428	"	
"	Prescott, William	1: 91	Story, William W.	5:417
"	Prescott, William H.	6: 66	Greenough, Richard S.	23:252
"	Quincy, Josiah	6:417	Ball, Thomas	5:199
"	Shaw, Robert G.	8:142	Saint-Gaudens, Augustus	8:287
"	Sumner, Charles	3:300	Ball, Thomas	5:199

References are to THE NATIONAL CYCLOPEDIA OF AMERICAN BIOGRAPHY

City	Statue		Statue	
Boston, Massachusetts	Vane, Sir Henry	7:371	MacMonnies, Frederick	8:289
"	Warren, James	5: 92	Bartlett, Paul W.	12:553
"	Washington, George (Public Garden)	1: 1	Ball, Thomas	5:199
"	Washington, George (State House)	1: 1	Chantrey, Sir Francis	
"	Webster, Daniel	3: 36	Powers, Hiram	3:421
"	Winslow, John A. (bust)	2:102	Couper, William	C:219
"	Winthrop, John	10:321	Greenough, Richard S.	23:252
"	Wolcott, Roger	10:326	French, Daniel C.	A:460
Bridgeport, Connecticut	Barnum, Phineas T.	3:258	Ball, Thomas	5:199
"	Howe, Elias	4:432	Ellis, S.	
"	Stratton, Charles S.	10:422	Unknown	
Brooklyn, Connecticut	Putnam, Israel	1: 87	Gerhardt, Karl	
Brooklyn, New York	Beecher, Henry Ward	3:129	Ward, John Q. A.	2:364
"	Beethoven		Baerer, Henry	12: 98
"	Bethune, George W.	8:166	Brown, Henry K.	1:511
"	Clinton, De Witt	3: 43	"	
"	Fowler, Edward B.	9:529	Baerer, Henry	12: 98
"	Grant, Ulysses S. (Prospect Park)	4: 1	O'Donovan, William R.	20:467
"	" (Grant Square)		Partridge, William Ordway	23: 12
"	Greeley, Horace	3:448	Calverly, Charles	
"	Grieg, Edward		Asbjornsen, Sigvard	
"	Hamilton, Alexander	1: 9	Partridge, William Ordway	23: 12
"	Howe, Elias	4:432	Calverly, Charles	
"	Irving, Washington	3: 17	Baerer, Henry	12: 98
"	Lafayette	1: 63	French, Daniel C.	A:460
"	Lincoln, Abraham (Prospect Park)	2: 65	Brown, Henry K.	1:511
"	" "		O'Donovan, William R.	20:467
"	McDonnell, Charles E.	12:401	Noble, W. Clark	A:454
"	Payne, John H.	2:347	Baerer, Henry	12: 98
"	Skene, Alexander J. C.	5:436	Rhind, J. Massey	
"	Slocum, Henry W.	24:305	MacMonnies, Frederick	8:289
"	Stranahan, James S. T.	3:433	"	
"	Turner, Peter		Noble, W. Clark	A:454
"	Warren, Gouverneur K.	4: 68	Baerer, Henry	12: 98
"	Washington, George	1: 1	Shrady, Henry M.	13:393
Brunswick, Maine	Peary, Robert	14: 60	Partridge, William Ordway	23: 12
Buffalo, New York	Mozart		Lainin, C. S.	
Burlington, Iowa	Corse, John M.	4:297	Rohl-Smith, Charles	
Burlington, Vermont	Allen, Ethan	1: 45	Stephenson, Peter	8:455
"	Lafayette	1: 63	Ward, John Q. A.	2:364
Burlington, Wisconsin	Lincoln, Abraham	2: 65	Ganiere, George E.	
Butte, Montana	Daly, Marcus		Saint-Gaudens, Augustus	8:287
Caldwell, New York	Johnson, Sir William	5:101	Weinert, Albert	10:370
Calumet, Michigan	Agassiz, Alexander	3: 98	Bartlett, Paul W.	12:553
Cambridge, Massachusetts	Adams, John	2: 1	Rogers, Randolph	8:286
"	Ballou, Hosea	5:487	Brackett, Edward A.	13:583
"	Bowditch, Nathaniel	6:377	Hughes, Ball	8:290
"	Harvard, John	6:408	French, Daniel C.	A:460
"	Otis, James	1: 17	Crawford, Thomas	8:292
"	Story, Joseph	2:468	Story, William W.	5:417
"	Winthrop, John	6:201	Greenough, Richard S.	23:252
Canton, Ohio	McKinley, William	11: 1	Niehaus, Charles H.	9: 57
Carrollton, Maryland	Shields, James	8: 2	Hibbard, Frederick C.	
Chappaqua, New York	Greeley, Horace	3:448	Partridge, William Ordway	23: 12
Charleston, South Carolina	Calhoun, John C.	6: 83	Rhind, J. Massey	
"	Jasper, William	1: 52	Viett, E. T.	
"	Pitt, William		Wilton, Henry	
"	Simms, W. Gilmore	6:204	Ward, John Q. A.	2:364
Charleston, West Virginia	Jackson, Andrew	5:289	Ezekiel, Moses J.	18:217
Charlestown, Massachusetts	Prescott, William	1: 91	Story, William W.	5:417
"	Warren, Gouverneur K.	4: 68	Dexter, Henry	8:288
"	Warren, Joseph	1: 57	"	
Charlottesville, Virginia	Clark, George Rogers	1: 82	Aitken, Robert I.	15:215
"	Jackson, Andrew	5:289	Keck, Charles	D:179
"	Jefferson, Thomas	3: 1	Bitter, Karl	24:385
"	Lee, Robert E.	4: 95	Shrady, Henry M.	13:393
"	Poe, Edgar Allan	1:463	Zolnay, George J.	
Chicago, Illinois	Altgeld, John P.	11: 51	Borglum, Gutzon	14: 80
"	Andersen, Hans Christian		Gelert, Johannes S.	9: 58

City	Statue		Sculptor	
Chicago, Illinois	Beethoven		Gelert, Johannes S.	9: 58
“	Burns, Robert		Grant-Stevenson, W.	
“	Columbus, Christopher	3:436	Ezekiel, Moses J.	18:217
“	Douglas, Stephen A.	2:428	Volk, Leonard W.	7:469
“	Drexel, Joseph W.	2:366	Mander, Henry	
“	Ericsson, Leif		Asbjornsen, Sigvard	
“	Finnerty, John F.		Mulligan, Charles J.	26:287
“	Franklin, Benjamin	1:328	Parks, R. H.	
“	Garibaldi		Gherardi, Victor	
“	Gladstone		Joy, Bruce	
“	Grant, Ulysses S.	4: 1	Rebisso, Louis T.	
“	Hamilton, Alexander	1: 9	Pratt, Bela L.	14:378
“	Harrison, Carter H.	10:144	Hibbard, Frederick K.	
“	Humboldt, Baron Alexander von		Goerling, F.	
“	Jolliet, Louis	5:121	MacNeil, Hermon A.	13:480
“	Kosciuszko, Thaddeus	1: 54	Chodzinski, Alexander	
“	La Salle, Robert	5:125	Lelaing, Jacques	
“	Lincoln, Abraham (Garfield Park)	2: 65	Mulligan, Charles J.	26:287
“	Lincoln, Abraham	2: 65	Saint-Gaudens, Augustus	8:287
“	Linneus, Carolus		Dyreman	
“	Logan, John A.	4:298	Saint-Gaudens, Augustus	8:287
“	McKinley, William	11: 1	Mulligan, Charles J.	26:287
“	Marquette, Jacques	12:220	MacNeil, Hermon A.	13:480
“	Oglesby, Richard J.	11: 48	Crunelle, Leonard	
“	Reuter, Fritz		Engelsmann	
“	Shakespeare		Partridge, William Ordway	23: 12
“	Sheridan, Philip H.	4: 63	Borglum, Gutzon	14: 80
“	Washington, George	1: 1	French, Daniel C.	A:460
Cincinnati, Ohio	Desmond, John J.		Adams, Ross C.	
“	Garfield, James A.	4:238	Niehaus, Charles H.	9: 57
“	Harrison, William H.	3: 33	Rebisso, Louis T.	
“	Lincoln, Abraham (Lyttle Park)	2: 65	Barnard, George G.	A: 67
“	“		Hastings, W. G.	
“	Schmidlapp, Jacob G.	19:315	Longman, Evelyn B.	B:313
“	Thomas, Theodore	2:139	Barnhorn, Clement J.	
“	Woodward, William	5:251	Von Kroeling	
Clermont, Iowa	Dodge, Grenville M.	16:191	Rhind, J. Massey	
“	Farragut, David G.	2: 45	Bissell, George E.	8:278
“	Grant, Ulysses S.	4: 1	Rhind, J. Massey	
“	Henderson, David B.	11:403	“	
“	Lincoln, Abraham	2: 65	Bissell, George E.	8:278
“	Sherman, William T.	4: 32	“	
Cleveland, Ohio	Cleveland, Moses	6:257	Hamilton, James G. C.	
“	“ (Public Square)		Matzen, Herman N.	
“	Garfield, James A.	4:238	Doyle, Alexander	10:371
“	Hanna, Marcus A.	22: 13	Saint-Gaudens, Augustus	8:287
“	Johnson, Tom L.	14:148	Matzen, Herman N.	
“	Kossuth, Louis		Toth, Andreas	
“	Perry, Oliver H.	4:288	Walcutt, William	13: 87
“	Rappe, Louis A.	5:340	Varney, Luella	
“	Rice, Harvey	13: 81	Hamilton, James G. C.	
“	Shakespeare		Rebeck, Stephen	
Clyde, Ohio	McPherson, James B.	4:203	Rebisso, Louis T.	
Cody, Wyoming	Cody, William F.	5:483	Whitney, Gertrude V.	B: 54
Coloma, California	Marshall, James W.	5:146	Wells, Marion	
Colorado Springs, Colorado	Pike, Zebulon M.	2:516	Pike, Charles J.	24:101
Columbia, South Carolina	Washington, George	1: 1	Houdon, Jean A.	8:292
Columbus, Indiana	Irwin, Joseph I.		Schwarz, Rudolph	
Columbus, Ohio	Chase, Salmon P.	1: 28	Scofield, Levi T.	12:321
“	Garfield, James A.	4:238	“	
“	Grant, Ulysses S.	4: 1	“	
“	Hayes, Rutherford B.	3:191	“	
“	McKinley, William	11: 1	MacNeil, Hermon A.	13:480
“	Sheridan, Philip H.	4: 63	Scofield, Levi T.	12:321
“	Sherman, William T.	4: 32	“	
“	Stanton, Edwin M.	2: 83	“	
Concord, Massachusetts	Emerson, Ralph Waldo	3:416	French, Daniel C.	A:460
Concord, New Hampshire	Coit, Henry A.	9:531	Pratt, Bela L.	14:378
“	Hale, John P.	3:120	Von Mueller, Ferdinand	
“	Perkins, George H.	26:398	French, Daniel C.	A:460
			and Bacon, Henry	20:339

City	Statue		Sculptor	
Concord, New Hampshire	Pierce, Franklin	4:145	Lukeman, Augustus	B:437
"	Stark, John	1: 80	Conrads, Carl	
"	Webster, Daniel	3: 36	Ball, Thomas	5:199
Crawfordsville, Indiana	Wallace, Lew	4:363	O'Connor, Andrew	
Dalton, Georgia	Johnson, Joseph E.		Kinney, Beel	
Denver, Colorado	Burns, Robert		Grant-Stevenson, W.	
"	Routt, John L.	6:449	Couper, William	C:219
Des Moines, Iowa	Allison, William B.	1:296	Longman, Evelyn B.	B:313
"	Corse, John M.	4:297	Rohl-Smith, Charles	
"	Crocker, Marcellus M.	4:220	"	
"	Curtis, Samuel R.	4:300	"	
"	Dodge, Grenville M.	16:191	"	
Detroit, Michigan	Cadillac, Antoine de la M.	5:172	Melchers, Julius	
"	Columbus, Christopher	3:436	Rivalta, Carlo	
"	La Salle, Robert	5:125	Melchers, Julius	
"	Macomb, Alexander	2:241	Weinman, Adolph A.	
"	Marquette, Jacques	12:220	Melchers, Julius	
"	Pingree, Hazen S.	7:119	Schwarz, Rudolph	
"	Williams, Alpheus S.	4:365	Shrady, Henry M.	13:393
Dorchester, Massachusetts	Everett, Edward	6:179	Story, William W.	5:417
Duluth, Minnesota	Cooke, Jay	1:253	Shrady, Henry M.	13:393
Durham, North Carolina	Duke, James B.	17:382	Keck, Charles	D:179
Easton, Pennsylvania	Lafayette	1: 63	French, Daniel C.	A:460
Elmira, N. Y.	Beecher, Thomas K.	3:131	Hartley, J. Scott	7:459
English, Indiana	English, William H.	9:376	Mahoney, John H.	
Fall River, Massachusetts	Lafayette	1: 63	Zaschi, Ettore and Arnold	
Ford City, Pennsylvania	Ford, John B.	13:505	Conrads, Carl	
Fordham, New York	Hughes, John	1:193	O'Donovan, William R.	20:467
Fort Wayne, Indiana	Wayne, Anthony	1: 55	Ganiere, George E.	
Fort Worth, Texas	Smith, John Peter		Bowman, George	
Frankfort, Kentucky	Goebel, William (cemetery)	13: 13	Niehaus, Charles H.	9: 57
Frederick, Maryland	Barry, John	4:188	Keyser, Ernest W.	
Fredericksburg, Virginia	Humphreys, Andrew A.	7: 34	Adams, Herbert	13:510
"	Mercer, Hugh	10:171	Valentine, Edward V.	10:377
Galena, Illinois	Grant, Ulysses S.	4: 1	Gelert, Johannes S.	9: 58
Galveston, Texas	Rosenberg, Henry	9:523	Amatus, Edmond R.	
Gettysburg, Pennsylvania	Buford, John	4:488	Kelly, James E.	25:434
"	Greene, George S.	1:320	Perry, R. Hinton	9: 54
"	Hancock, Winfield S.	4:134	Elwell, Francis E.	10:368
"	Meade, George G.	4: 66	Bush-Brown, Henry K.	10:374
"	Reynolds, John F. (Battlefield)	4:224	"	
"	"		Ward, John Q. A.	2:364
"	Slocum, Henry W.	24:305	MacMonnies, Frederick	8:289
"	"		Potter, Edward C.	26:272
"	Wadsworth, James S.	5: 13	Perry, R. Hinton	9: 54
Grand Rapids, Michigan	Longfellow, Henry Wadsworth	2:160	Couper, William	C:219
Greensboro, North Carolina	Greene, Nathanael	1: 39	Unknown	
Greenwich, Connecticut	Bolling, Raynal C.	19:242	Potter, Edward C.	26:272
Groton, Connecticut	Mason, John	4:136	Hamilton, James G. C.	
Hackensack, New Jersey	Poor, Enoch	1: 76	Piatti, E. T.	
Hannibal, Missouri	Clemens, Samuel L.	6: 24	Hibbard, Frederick K.	
Hartford, Connecticut	Brownell, Thomas C.	3:495	Ives, Chauncey B.	
"	Buckingham, William A.	10:339	Warner, Olin L.	8:282
"	Colt, Samuel	6:175	Rhind, J. Massey	
"	Davenport, John	1:161	Niehaus, Charles H.	9: 57
"	Hale, Nathan	1: 51	Gerhardt, Karl	
"	"		Woods, Enoch S.	
"	Hooker, Thomas	6:279	Niehaus, Charles H.	9: 57
"	Hubbard, Richard D.	10:342	Gerhardt, Karl	
"	Knowlton, Thomas	2:299	Woods, Enoch S.	
"	Putnam, Israel	1: 87	Ward, John Q. A.	2:364
"	Stedman, Griffin A.	5: 15	Maslen, Stephen	
"	Wells, Horace	6:438	Bartlett, T. H.	
"	Winthrop, John	10:321	Bartlett, Paul W.	12:553
"	Wooster, David	1: 82	MacNeil, Hermon A.	13:480
Haverhill, Massachusetts	Dustin, Hannah	6:102	Weeks, Calvin H.	
Harrisburg, Pennsylvania	Hartranft, John F.	2:291	Ruckstuhl, F. W.	
Helena, Montana	Meagher, Thomas F.	5:364	Burns	
"	"		Mulligan, Charles J.	26:287
"	Sanders, Wilbur F.	1:457	Asbjornsen, Sigvard	
Hingham, Massachusetts	Andrew, John A.	1:118	Gould, Thomas R.	8:281

City	Statue		Sculptor	
Hodgenville, Kentucky	Lincoln, Abraham	2: 65	Weinman, Adolph A.	
Honesdale, Pennsylvania	Meredith, Samuel		Martiny, Philip	24: 86
Houston, Texas	Houston, Samuel	9: 63	Cerracchio, Enrico F.	
"	Johnston, Albert S.	1:388	Ney, Elizabet	13:371
Indianapolis, Indiana	Clark, George Rogers	1: 82	Mahoney, John H.	
"	Colfax, Schuyler	4: 12	Taft, Lorado	A:461
"	Harrison, Benjamin	1:133	Schwarz, Rudolph	
"	Harrison, William H.	3: 33	Mahoney, John H.	
"	Hendricks, Thomas A.	2:403	Parks, R. H.	
"	Lawton, Henry W.	10:290	O'Connor, Andrew	
"	Morton, Oliver H. P. T.	13:271	Simmons, Franklin	11:316
"	Whitcomb, James	13:268	Mahoney, John H.	
Jamestown, Virginia	Pocahontas	7:102	Partridge, William Ordway	23: 12
Jamestown Island, Virginia	Smith, John	13:378	Couper, William	C:219
Jersey City, New Jersey	Stuyvesant, Peter	5:138	Rhind, J. Massey	
Johnstown, New York	Johnson, Sir William	5:101	Piatti, E. T.	
Joliet, Illinois	Jolliet, Louis	5:121	Asbjornsen, Sigvard	
Keokuk, Iowa	Curtis, Samuel R.	4:300	Rohl-Smith, Charles	
"	Keokuk	9:221	Walker, Nellie V.	
Kirksville, Missouri	Still, Andrew T.	14:451	Zolnay, George J.	10:372
Lafayette, Indiana	Lafayette	1: 63	Bartholdi, Frederic A.	
Lake George, New York	Johnson, Sir William	5:101	Weinert, Albert	10:370
Lancaster, Pennsylvania	Buchanan, James	5: 1	Grafly, Charles	22: 40
"	De Peyster, Abraham	2: 43	Bissell, George E.	8:278
Lancaster, Wisconsin	Dewey, Nelson	12: 73	Trentanove, Gaetano	
Lansing, Michigan	Blair, Austin	5:273	Potter, Edward C.	26:272
Lenox, Massachusetts	Paterson, John	3:242	Unknown	
Lexington, Kentucky	Breckinridge, John C.	5: 3	Valentine, Edward V.	10:377
Lexington, Massachusetts	Hancock, John	1:103	Gould, Thomas R.	8:281
"	Parker, John	1: 96	Kitson, Henry H.	12:398
Lexington, Virginia	Lee, Robert E.	4: 95	Valentine, Edward V.	10:377
Lincoln, Nebraska	Lincoln, Abraham	2: 65	French, Daniel C.	A:460
Los Angeles, California	"		Barnard, George G.	A: 67
"	White, Stephen M.	12:509	Tilden, Douglas	
Louisville, Kentucky	Boone, Daniel	3:110	Yandell, Enid	13:210
"	Castelman, John B.		Perry, R. Hinton	9: 54
"	Clay, Henry	5: 77	Hart, Joel T.	6:514
"	Davis, Jefferson	4:148	Ezekiel, Moses J.	18:217
"	Foster, Stephen C.	7:439	Roop, J. L.	
"	Jefferson, Thomas	3: 1	Ezekiel, Moses J.	18:217
"	Lincoln, Abraham	2: 65	Barnard, George G.	A: 67
"	Prentice, George D.	3:121	Bouly, A.	
Lowell, Massachusetts	Butler, Benjamin F.	1:121	Pratt, Bela L.	14:378
Manchester, New Hampshire	Lincoln, Abraham	2: 65	Rogers, John	8:277
Marquette, Michigan	Marquette, Jacques	12:220	Trentanove, Gaetano	
Memphis, Tennessee	Forrest, Nathan B.	10: 36	Niehaus, Charles H.	9: 57
"	Jackson, Andrew	5:289	Frazee, John	8:289
Methuen, Massachusetts	Washington, George	1: 1	Ball, Thomas	5:199
Milwaukee, Wisconsin	Bergh, Henry	3:106	Mahoney, John H.	
"	Ericsson, Leif		Whitney, Anne	7: 72
"	Juneau, Solomon	6: 18	Park, R. H.	
"	Kosciuszko, Thaddeus	1: 54	Trentanove, Gaetano	
"	Steuben, Frederick W. A.	1: 57	Schweizer, J. Otto	
"	Wahl, Christian		Trentanove, Gaetano	
"	Washington, George	1: 1	Park, R. H.	
Minneapolis, Minnesota	Bull, Ole	4:234	Fjelde, J.	
"	Pillsbury, John S.	10: 65	French, Daniel C.	A:460
Mobile, Alabama	Semmes, Raphael	4:340	Briberl, Caspar	
Monroe, Michigan	Custer, George A.	4:274	Potter, Edward C.	26:272
Montgomery, Alabama	Oates, William C.	2:243	Newman, Allen G.	
Montpelier, Vermont	Allen, Ethan	1: 45	Mead, Larkin G.	1:278
Morristown, New Jersey	Washington, George	1: 1	Roth, Frederick G. R.	
Muskegon, Michigan	Farragut, David G.	2: 45	Niehaus, Charles H.	9: 57
"	Grant, Ulysses S.	4: 1	Rhind, J. Massey	
"	Kearny, Philip	4:260	Carabelli, Joseph	
"	Lincoln, Abraham	2: 65	Niehaus, Charles H.	9: 57
"	McKinley, William	11: 1	"	
"	Sherman, William T.	4: 32	Rhind, J. Massey	
Nashville, Tennessee	Davis, Samuel	8:334	Zolnay, George J.	10:372
"	Jackson, Andrew	5:289	Mills, Clark	5:160
"	Vanderbilt, Cornelius	6:208	Moretti, G.	

City	Statue		Sculptor	
Nebraska City, Nebraska	Morton, J. Sterling	6:487	Evans, Rudolph	
Newark, New Jersey	Boyden, Seth	11: 87	Gerhardt, Karl	
"	Coles, Abraham	2:434	Ward, John Q. A.	2:364
"	Doane, George H.	8: 88	Noble, W. Clark	A:454
"	Frelinghuysen, Frederick T.	4:250	Gerhardt, Karl	
"	Kearney, Philip	4:260	Brown, Henry K.	1:511
"	Lincoln, Abraham	2: 65	Borglum, Gutzon	14: 80
New Brighton, New York	Randall, Robert R.	11:253	Saint-Gaudens, Augustus	8:287
Newburgh, New York	Clinton, George	3: 43	Brown, Henry K.	1:511
Newburyport, Massachusetts	Washington, George	1: 1	Ward, John Q. A.	2:364
New Haven, Connecticut	Bushnell, Cornelius S.	9:535	Adams, Herbert	13:510
"	Columbus, Christopher	3:436	Unknown	
"	Hale, Nathan	1: 51	Pratt, Bela L.	14:378
"	Lewis, Henry G.	5:534	Yandell, Enid	13:210
"	Pierson, Abraham	1:164	Thompson, Launt	8:283
"	Silliman, Benjamin	2:385	Weir, John F.	6:429
"	Woolsey, Theodore D.	1:170	"	
New London, Connecticut	Winthrop, John	10:321	Pratt, Bela L.	14:378
New Orleans, Louisiana	Audubon, John J.	6: 75	Valentine, Edward V.	10:377
"	Clay, Henry	5: 77	Hart, Joel T.	6:514
"	Franklin, Benjamin	1:328	Powers, Hiram	3:421
"	Gaffney, Margaret	2:373	Doyle, Alexander	10:371
"	Jackson, Andrew	5:289	Mills, Clark	5:160
"	Johnston, Albert S.	1:388	Doyle, Alexander	10:371
"	Lee, Robert E.	4: 95	"	
"	McDonough, John	9:465	Picirilli, Atillio	
"	White, Edward Douglas	10: 76	Baker, Bryant	D:109
Newport, Rhode Island	Channing, William Ellery	5:458	Noble, W. Clark	A:454
"	Perry, Mathew C.	4: 42	Ward, John Q. A.	2:364
"	Perry, Oliver H.	4:288	Turner, William G.	17:211
New York, New York	Arthur, Chester A.	4:247	Bissell, George E.	8:278
"	Bacon, Henry	20:339	Longman, Evelyn	B:313
"	Beethoven		Baerer, Henry	12: 98
"	Bellows, Henry W.	3:261	Saint-Gaudens, Augustus	8:287
"	Bolivar, Simon		Farnum, Sally James	
"	"		Turini, G.	
"	Booth, Edwin	3:180	Quinn, Edmond T.	26:163
"	Bryant, William Cullen	4: 79	Adams, Herbert	13:510
"	Burns, Robert		Steele, John	
"	Butterfield, Daniel	4:128	Borglum, Gutzon	14: 80
"	Clinton, De Witt (Chamber of Commerce)	3: 43	French, Daniel C.	A:460
"	" (Hall of Records)		Martiny, Philip	24: 86
"	" (Exchange Court)		Rhind, J. Massey	
"	Colden, Cadwallader	2:270	Martiny, Philip	24: 86
"	Columbus, Christopher (59th St.)	3:436	Russo, G.	
"	" (Central Park)		Sunol	
"	" (Custom House)		Lukeman, Augustus	B:437
"	Conkling, Roscoe	3:220	Ward, John Q. A.	2:364
"	Cooper, Peter	3:114	Saint-Gaudens, Augustus	8:287
"	Cox, Samuel S.	6:363	Lawson, Louise	
"	Daly, Charles P.	3:158	O'Donovan, William R.	20:467
"	De Peyster, Abraham	2: 43	Bissell, George E.	8:278
"	De Vries, David P.		Martiny, Philip	24: 86
"	Dodge, William E.	3:174	Ward, John Q. A.	2:364
"	Drumgoole, John C.	13:211	Cushing, Robert	
"	Duane, James	2:489	Martiny, Philip	24: 86
"	Duffy, James A.	15:234	Keck, Charles	D:179
"	Ericsson, John	4: 46	Hartley, J. Scott	7:459
"	Farragut, David G.	2: 45	Saint-Gaudens, Augustus	8:287
"	Franklin, Benjamin	1:328	Plassman, Ernest	
"	Gilbert, John G.	1:261	Hartley, J. Scott	7:459
"	Greeley, Horace (Greeley Sq.)	3:448	Doyle, Alexander	10:371
"	" (Tribune Building)		Ward, John Q. A.	2:364
"	Hale, Nathan	1: 51	MacMonnies, Frederick	8:289
"	Halleck, Fitz-Greene	3:226	MacDonald, Wilson	
"	Hamilton, Alexander	1: 9	Conrads, Carl	
"	" (Columbia University)		Partridge, William Ordway	23: 12
"	Hancock, Winfield S.	4:134	MacDonald, Wilson	
"	Heathcote, Caleb	7:515	Martiny, Philip	24: 86

City	Statue		Sculptor	
New York, N. Y.	Hewitt, Abram S.			
"	(Chamber of Commerce)	3:294	Couper, William	C:219
"	" (Hall of Records)		Martiny, Philip	24: 86
"	Holley, Alexander L.	11:508	Ward, John Q. A.	2:364
"	Hone, Philip		Martiny, Philip	24: 86
"	Hudson, Henry	9:453	Rhind, J. Massey	
"	Hughes, John	1:193	O'Donovan, William R.	20:467
"	Humboldt, Baron Alexander von		Blaeser, Gustav	
"	Hunt, Richard M.	6:430	French, Daniel C.	A:460
"	Hyde, Henry B.	4:196	Ward, John Q. A.	2:364
"	Irving, Washington	3: 17	Beer	
"	Jefferson, Thomas	3: 1	D'Angers, D.	
"	" (Columbia University		Partridge, William Ordway	23: 12
"	Jesup, Morris K.	11: 93	Couper, William	C:219
"	Kennedy, John S.	15:150	Longman, Evelyn B.	B:313
"	Lafayette (114th St.)	1: 63	Bartholdi, A.	
"	" (Union Square)		Bartholdi, G.	
"	Lincoln, Abraham (Union Sq.)	2: 65	Brown, Henry K.	1:511
"	Morse, Samuel F. B.	4:449	Pickett, Byron M.	
"	Palmer, Alice Freeman	7:328	Longman, Evelyn B.	-B:313
"	Poe, Edgar Allen	1:463	Quinn, Edmond T.	26:163
"	Porter, Josiah	5:251	Noble, W. Clark	A:454
"	Potter, Alonzo	3:470	Fraser, James E.	C:468
"	Potter, Robert B.	4:392	Noble, W. Clark	A:454
"	Schurz, Carl	3:202	Bitter, Karl	24:385
"	Scott, Sir Walter		Steele, John	
"	Seward, William H.	2: 77	Rogers, Randolph	8:286
"	Shakespeare		Ward, John Q. A.	2:364
"	Sherman, William T.	4: 32	Saint-Gaudens, Augustus	8:287
"	Sigel, Franz	4:136	Bitter, Karl	24:385
"	Sims, J. Marion	2:356	Müller, Eduard	
"	Stowe, Harriet Beecher	1:423	Putnam, Brenda	B:398
"	Stuyvesant, Peter	5:138	Martiny, Philip	24: 86
"	"		Rhind, J. Massey	
"	Tilden, Samuel J.	3: 53	Partridge, William Ordway	23: 12
"	Verdi, Guiseppe		Civiletti, Pasquale	
"	Washington, George (14th St.)	1: 1	Bartholdi	
"	" (Union Square)		Brown, Henry K.	1:511
"	" (Riverside Drive)		Houdon, Jean A.	8:292
"	" (Wall Street)		Ward, John Q. A.	2:364
"	Watts, John		Bissell, George E.	8:278
"	Webb, Alexander S.	3: 31	Rhind, J. Massey	
"	Webster, Daniel	3: 36	Ball, Thomas	5:199
"	Wolfe, James	1:102	Rhind, J. Massey	
Ogdensburg, New York	Curtis, Newton M.	4:328	Perry, R. Hinton	9: 54
Oregon, Illinois	Black Hawk	9:477	Taft, Lorado	A:461
Palo Alto, California	Stanford Family	2:129	Mead, Larkin G.	1:278
Paterson, New Jersey	Hobart, Garret A.	11: 10	Martiny, Philip	24: 86
"	Stewart, James F.	5:506	Federeci, Gaetano	
Peekskill, New York	Depew, Chauncey M.	23: 96	Neaddross, Sigurd	
Penacook, New Hampshire	Dustin, Hannah	6:102	Andrews, William	
Perth Amboy, New Jersey	Washington, George	1: 1	Alling, N.	
Philadelphia, Pennsylvania	Baldwin, Mathias W.	9:476	Adams, Herbert	13:510
"	Barry, John	4:188	Murray, Samuel	
"	Caldwell, James	5: 91	Calder, Milne	20: 97
"	Columbus, Christopher	3:436	Unknown	
"	Davies, Samuel	5:465	Calder, Milne	20: 97
"	Decatur, Stephen	4: 56	Pietz, Adam	
"	Dickens and Little Nell		Elwell, Francis E.	10:368
"	Dodge, Grenville M.	16:191	Rhind, J. Massey	
"	Drexel, Anthony J.	2:273	Ezekiel, Moses J.	18:217
"	Forrest, Edwin	5: 86	Ball, Thomas	5:199
"	Franklin, Benjamin	1:328	Battin	
"	" (Post Office Plaza)		Boyle, John J,	13: 73
"	"Youthful Franklin"	1:328	McKenaie, R. Tait	C:357
"	Garfield, James A.	4:238	Saint-Gaudens, Augustus	8:287
"	Girard, Stephen (Girard College)	7: 11	Gerelot	
"	" (City Hall Square)		Rhind, J. Massey	
"	Grant, Ulysses S.	4: 1	French, Daniel C.	A:460
"	" (Fairmount Park)		Potter, Edward C.	26:272
"	Hancock, Winfield S.	4:134	Ward, John Q. A.	2:364

City	Statue		Sculptor	
Philadelphia, Pennsylvania	Humboldt, Baron Alexander von		Drake, Friedrich	
"	Joan of Arc		Fremiet, Emmanuel	
"	Leidy, Joseph	5:220	Murray, Samuel	
"	Lincoln, Abraham	2: 65	Thorn	
"	" (Fairmount Park)		Rogers, Randolph	8:286
"	" (Union League)		Schweizer, J. Otto	
"	McClellan, George B.	4:140	Bartlett, Paul W.	12:553
"	"		Ellicott, Henry J.	12:122
"	McMichael, Morton	2:211	Mahoney, John H.	
"	McMillan, John	5:251	Calder, Milne	20: 97
"	Makemie, Francis	11:384	"	
"	Meade, George G.	4: 66	"	
"	"		French, Daniel C.	A:460
"	Morris, Robert	2:411	Bartlett, Paul W.	12:553
"	Muhlenberg, Peter	1:149	Schweizer, J. Otto	
"	Penn, William (City Hall)	2:274	Calder, Milne	20: 97
"	"		Kirn, Herman	
"	Pepper, William	1:345	Bitter, Karl	24:385
"	Porter, David D.	2: 97	Grafly, Charles	22: 40
"	Reynolds, John F. (Fairmount Park)	4:224	"	
"	" (City Hall)		Rogers, John	8:277
"	Smith, Edgar F.	21: 53	McKenzie, R. Tait	C:357
"	Smith, Richard		Adams, Herbert	13:510
"	Washington, George	1: 1	Bailly, Joseph A.	
"	" (Independence Hall)		Rush, William	8:287
"	" (State House)		Siemering	
"	Whitefield, George	5:384	McKenzie, R. Tait	C:357
"	Whitman, Marcus	11:112	Calder, Milne	20: 97
"	Witherspoon, John	5:466	"	
"	"		Rhind, J. Massey	
Pittsburgh, Pensylvania	Burns, Robert		"	
"	Hawkins, Alexander L.	9:533	Couper, William	C:219
"	Magee, Christopher L.	5:179	Saint-Gaudens, Augustus	8:287
Plattsburg, New York	Champlain		Heber, Carl A.	
Plymouth, Massachusetts	Massassoit		Dallin, Cyrus E.	14:478
Pocantico Hills, New York	Rockefeller, John D., Sr.	11: 63	Couper, William	C:219
Portland, Maine	Longfellow, Henry Wadsworth	2:160	Simmons, Franklin	11:316
"	Neely, Henry A.	12:266	Pratt, Bela L.	14:378
"	Reed, Thomas B.	2:383	Unknown	
Portland, Oregon	Roosevelt, Theodore	14: 1	Proctor, A. Phimister	
"	Sacajawea	13:419	Cooper, Alice	
"	Washington, George	1: 1	Coppini, Pompeo	
Portsmouth, New Hampshire	Porter, Fitz-John	4:261	Kelly, James E.	25:434
Princeton, New Jersey	Franklin, Benjamin	1:328	Heber, Carl A.	
"	Henry, Joseph	3:405	Lukeman, Augustus	B:437
"	McCosh, James	5:468	Saint-Gaudens, Augustus	8:287
Providence, Rhode Island	Burns, Robert		Noble, W. Clark	A:454
"	Burnside, Ambrose E.	4: 53	Thompson, Launt	8:283
"	Dexter, Ebenezer K.	8:420	Hubert, Hippolyte	
"	Hopkins, Esek	2: 18	Kitson, Mrs. Theodore A. R.	
"	Williams, Roger	10: 4	Simmons, Franklin	11:316
Puyallup, Washington	Meeker, Ezra	21:305	Noble, W. Clark	A:454
Quincy, Illinois	Clark, George Rogers	1: 82	Mulligan, Charles J.	26:287
"	Wood, John	11: 47	Volk, G. C.	
Quincy, Massachusetts	Burns, Robert		Horrigan, John and Gerald	
"	Hancock, John	1:103	Saville, Bruce W.	
Raleigh, North Carolina	Wyatt, Lawson		Borglum, Gutzon	14: 80
Reading, Pennsylvania	Evans, Charles		Ellicott, Henry J.	12:122
"	Gregg, David McM.	4:330	Lukeman, Augustus	B:437
Richmond, Missouri	Doniphan, Alexander W.	11:389	Hibbard, Frederick C.	
Richmond, Virginia	Clay, Henry	5: 77	Hart, Joel T.	6:514
"	Davis, Jefferson	4:148	Valentine, Edward V.	10:377
"	"		Zolnay, George J.	10:372
"	Henry, Patrick	1:337	Crawford, Thomas	8:292
"	Jackson, "Stonewall"	4:125	Foley, Margaret E.	9:121
"	Jefferson, Thomas	3: 1	Crawford, Thomas	8:292
"	"		Valentine, Edward V.	10:377
"	Lee, Robert E.	4: 95	Fremiet, Emmanuel	
"	"		Mercié, Antonin	
"	Lewis, Andrew	1: 75	Crawford, Thomas	8:292

City	Statue		Sculptor	
Richmond, Virginia	Lewis, Andrew	1: 75	Rogers, Randolph	8:286
"	McGuire, Hunter	5:163	Couper, William	C:219
"	Marshall, John	1: 25	Rogers, Randolph	8:286
"	Mason, George	3:337	"	
"	Nelson, Thomas	7:253	"	
"	Smith, William	5:451	Sheppard, William L.	19:291
"	Washington, George (Capitol Sq.)	1: 1	Crawford, Thomas	8:292
"	" (Capitol)		Houdon, Jean A.	8:292
"	Wickham, William C.	13:605	Valentine, Edward V.	10:377
Rochester, New York	Douglass, Frederick	2:309	Edwards, Sidney N.	
"	Lincoln, Abraham	2: 65	Volk, Leonard W.	7:469
"	Parker, Ely S.	5:330	Noble, W. Clark	A:454
Rock Island, Illinois	Black Hawk	9:477	Richards, David	
Rome, New York	Gansevoort, Peter	1:382	Platte	
Roxbury, Massachusetts	Warren, Joseph	1: 57	Bartlett, Paul W.	12:553
Sacramento, California	Columbus, Christopher	3:436	Mead, Larkin G.	1:278
St. Helena, California	McKinley, William	11: 1	Aitken, Robert I.	15:215
St. Louis, Missouri	Bates, Edward	2: 89	MacDonald, James W. A.	25:390
"	Benton, Thomas H.	4:399	Hosmer, Harriet G.	8:284
"	Blair, Francis P.	4:223	Gardner, W.	
"	Columbus, Christopher	3:436	Von Mueller, Ferdinand	
"	Grant, Ulysses S.	4: 1	Bringhurst, R. P.	
"	Humboldt, Baron Alexander von		Von Mueller, Ferdinand	
"	Jefferson, Thomas	3: 1	Bitter, Karl	24:385
"	Laclede, Pierre		Zolnay, George J.	10:372
"	Livingston, Robert	24: 57	Lukeman, Augustus	B:437
"	Lyon, Nathaniel	4:201	Bruiding, Adolphus	
"	Sigel, Franz	4:136	Cauer, Robert	
"	Washington, George (Lafayette Park)	1: 1	Houdon, Jean A.	8:292
"	"		Hubard	
St. Paul, Minnesota	Hale, Nathan	1: 51	Partridge, William Ordway	23: 12
"	King, Josias R.	14:201	Daniel, John K.	
"	Pillsbury, John S.	10: 65	French, Daniel C.	A:460
Salisbury, North Carolina	Washington, George	1: 1	Houdon, Jean A.	8:292
Salt Lake City, Utah	Young, Brigham	16: 3	Dallin, Cyrus E.	14:478
San Diego, California	Grant, Ulysses S.	4: 1	Lukeman, Augustus	B:437
San Francisco, California	Balboa, Vasco N. de	5:431	Linden	
"	Cogswell, Henry D.	8:500	Unknown	
"	Garfield, James A.	4:238	French, Daniel C.	A:460
"	"		Happerberger, F.	
"	Grant, Ulysses S.	4: 1	Schmidt, Rupert	
"	Halleck, Henry W.	4:257	Conrads, Carl	
"	"		Story, William W,	5:417
"	Key, Francis Scott	5:498	"	
"	King, Thomas Starr	4:472	French, Daniel C.	A:460
"	Lincoln, Abraham	2: 65	Mezzara, P.	
"	McKinley, William	11: 1	Aitken, Robert I.	15:215
"	Serra, Junipero	12:134	Tilden, Douglas	26:489
San Jose, California	Cogswell, Henry D.	8:500	Schmidt, Rupert	
"	McKinley, William	11: 1	"	
Saratoga, New York	Morgan, Daniel	1: 84	O'Donovan, William R.	20:467
"	Schuyler, Philip J.	1: 97	Doyle, Alexander	10:371
"	Trask, Spencer	11:444	Partridge, William Ordway	23: 12
Savannah, Georgia	Anderson, Robert H.	4:130	Doyle, Alexander	10:371
"	McLaws, Lafayette	4:317	Zolnay, George J.	10:372
"	Oglethorpe, James E.	1:490	French, Daniel C.	A:460
Saybrook, Connecticut	Gardiner, Lion	23:181	Partridge, William Ordway	23: 12
Schuylersville, New York	Gates, Horatio	1: 47	Bissell, George E.	8:278
Scottsburg, Indiana	English, William H.	9:376	Mahoney, John H.	
Scranton, Pennsylvania	Columbus, Christopher	3:436	Cottini, Albini	
"	McKinley, William	11: 1	Couper, William	C:219
"	Washington, George	1: 1	Lusi, S. A.	
Seattle, Washington	Seward, William H.	2: 77	Brooks, Richard E.	22:229
"	Washington, George	1: 1	Taft, Lorado	A:461
Somerset, Ohio	Sheridan, Philip H.	4: 63	Heber, Carl A.	
Spartansburg, South Carolina	Morgan, Daniel	1: 84	Ward, John Q. A.	2:364
Springfield, Illinois	Douglas, Stephen A.	2:428	Volk, Leonard W.	7:469
"	Lincoln, Abraham (Oak Ridge Cemetery)	2: 65	Mead, Larkin G.	1:278
"	"		O'Connor, Andrew	

City	Statue	Sculptor
Springfield, Illinois	Lincoln, Abraham 2: 65	Volk, Leonard W. 7:469
Springfield, Massachusetts	Chapin, Samuel	Saint-Gaudens, Augustus 8:287
"	McKinley, William 11: 1	Martiny, Philip 24: 86
"	Morgan, Miles 6:184	Hartley, J. Scott 7:459
Sunbury, Pennsylvania	Cameron, James 4:136	Ellicott, Henry J. 12:122
Taunton, Massachusetts	Paine, Robert T. 5:429	Brooks, Richard E. 22:229
Titusville, Pennsylvania	Drake, Edwin L. 26:458	Niehaus, Charles H. 9: 57
Toledo, Ohio	McKinley, William 11: 1	Weinert, Albert 10:370
"	Steedman, James B. 4:395	Doyle, Matthew
Topeka, Kansas	Lincoln, Abraham 2: 65	Gage, Merrill
Trenton, New Jersey	Roebling, John A. 4:404	Couper, William C:219
"	Stryker, William S. 3:424	O'Donovan, William R. 20:467
"	Washington Crossing the Delaware 1: 1	Unknown
Tuskegee, Alabama	Washington, Booker T. 7:363	Keck, Charles D:179
Urbana, Illinois	Lincoln, Abraham 2: 65	Taft, Lorado A:461
Utica, New York	Seymour, Horatio 3: 48	Richards, David
Valley Forge, Pennsylvania	Wayne, Anthony 1: 55	Bush-Brown, Henry K. 10:374
Vicksburg, Mississippi	Grant, Ulysses S. 4: 1	Hibbard, Frederick K.
Virginia City, Nevada	Mackay, John W. 4:487	Borglum, Gutzon 14: 80
Warner, New Hampshire	Harriman, Walter 11:133	Mosman, M. H.
Washington, Connecticut	Gibson, W. Hamilton 7:463	Bush-Brown, Henry K. 10:374
Washington, D. C.	Adams, Samuel 1:104	Whitney, Anne 7: 72
"	Allen, Ethan 1: 45	Mead, Larkin G. 1:278
"	Allen, William 3:142	Niehaus, Charles H. 9: 57
"	Asbury, Francis 6:293	Lukeman, Augustus B:437
"	Austin, Stephen F. 6: 70	Ney, Elizabet 13:371
"	Bacon, Joel S. 3:152	Boyle, John J. 13: 73
"	Benton, Thomas H. 4:399	Doyle, Alexander 10:371
"	Blair, Francis P. 4:223	Couper, William C:219
"	" (The Capitol)	Doyle, Alexander 10:371
"	Carroll, Charles 7:441	Brooks, Richard E. 22:229
"	Cass, Lewis 5: 3	French, Daniel C. A:460
"	Clinton, George 5:541	Brown, Henry K. 1:511
"	Collamer, Jacob 4:371	Powers, Preston
"	Columbus, Christopher 3:436	Bartlett, Paul W. 12:553
"	Daguerre, L. J. M.	Hartley, J. Scott 7:459
"	Davis, Cushman K. 10: 65	Trentanove, Gaetano
"	DuPont, Samuel F. 5: 50	Thompson, Launt 8:283
"	Ericsson, John 4: 46	Fraser, James E. C:468
"	Farragut, David G. 2: 45	Ream, Vinnie 1:442
"	Foote, Andrew H. 5: 10	Couper, William C:219
"	Franklin, Benjamin (Penn. Ave.) 1:328	Plassman and Juvenal
"	" (Senate Chamber)	Powers, Hiram 3:421
"	Fuller, Melville W. 1: 31	Partridge, William Ordway 23: 12
"	Fulton, Robert 3:104	Roberts, Howard
"	" (Library of Congress)	Potter, Edward C. 26:272
"	Gallaudet, Thomas H. 9:138	French, Daniel C. A:460
"	Garfield, James A. (Statuary Hall) 4:238	Niehaus, Charles H. 9: 57
"	" (Pennsylvania Avenue)	Ward, John Q. A. 2:364
"	Grant, Ulysses S. 4: 1	Shrady, Henry M. 13:393
"	Greene, Nathanael (Stanton Pl.) 1: 39	Brown, Henry K. 1:511
"	" (Statuary Hall)	"
"	Gross, Samuel D. 8:216	Calder, Milne 20: 97
"	Hahnemann, Christian S. F.	Niehaus, Charles H. 9: 57
"	Hale, Nathan 1: 51	Partridge, William Ordway 23: 12
"	Hamilton, Alexander (Treasury Building) 1: 9	Fraser, James E. C:468
"	"	Stone, Horatio
"	Hancock, John 1:103	"
"	Hancock, Winfield S. 4:134	Ellicott, Henry J. 12:122
"	Hanson, John 10:312	Brooks, Richard E. 22:229
"	Henry, Joseph (Library of Congress) 3:405	Adams, Herbert 13:510
"	" (Smithsonian Institution)	Story, William W. 5:417
"	Homer	Saint-Gaudens, Augustus 8:287
"	Houston, Samuel 9: 63	Ney, Elizabet 13:371
"	Ingalls, John J. 8:415	Niehaus, Charles H. 9: 57
"	Jackson, Andrew 5:289	Mills, Clark 5:160
"	Jefferson, Thomas (Statuary Hall) 3: 1	D'Angers, David
"	" (Hall of Representatives)	Powers, Hiram 3:421
"	Jones, Paul 2: 14	Niehaus, Charles H. 9: 57

City	Sculptor		Sculptor	
Washington, D. C.	Kearny, Philip	4:260	Brown, Henry K.	1:511
"	Kenna, John E.	1:299	Doyle, Alexander	10:371
"	Kent, James	3: 55	Bissell, George E.	8:278
"	King, William	6:305	Simmons, Franklin	11:316
"	Lincoln, Abraham (Statuary Hall)	2: 65	Ball, Thomas	5:199
"	" (head)		Borglum, Gutzon	14: 80
"	" (4th and D Streets)		Flannery, Lot	19:337
"	" (Lincoln Memorial)		French, Daniel C.	A:460
"	" (Capitol)		Ream, Vinnie	1:442
"	" (Lincoln Park)		Ward, John Q. A.	2:364
"	Livingston, Robert R.	2:396	Palmer, Erastus D.	5:416
"	Logan, John A.	4:298	Simmons, Franklin	11:316
"	Longfellow, Henry Wadsworth	2:160	Couper, William	C:219
"	McClellan, George B.	4:140	MacMonnies, Frederick	8:289
"	McPherson, James B.	4:203	Rebisso, Louis	
"	Marquette, Jacques	12:200	Trentanove, Gaetano	
"	Marshall, John	1: 25	Story, William W.	5:417
"	Michel, Angelo		Bartlett, Paul W.	12:553
"	Morton, Oliver P.	13:271	Niehaus, Charles H.	9: 57
"	Muhlenberg, Peter	1:149	Nevin, Blanche	
"	Newton, Sir Isaac		Dallin, Cyrus E.	14:478
"	Pike, Albert	1:527	Trentanove, Gaetano	
"	Plato		Boyle, John J.	13: 73
"	Quimby, Isaac F.		Couper, William	C:219
"	Rawlins, John A.	4:218	Bailly, Joseph A.	
"	Rochambeau, Jean B.	1: 68	Hamar, Ferdinand	
"	Rodney, Caesar	5:173	Kelly, James E.	25:434
"	Scott, Winfield	3:502	Brown, Henry K.	1:511
"	" (Soldiers' Home)		Thompson, Launt	8:283
"	Sequoyah	5:510	Zolnay, George J.	10:372
"	Serra, Junipero	12:134	Tilden, Douglas	26:489
"	Shakespeare		MacMonnies, Frederick	8:289
"	Sheridan, Philip H.	4: 63	Borglum, Gutzon	14: 80
"	Sherman, Roger	2:352	Ives, Chauncey B.	
"	Sherman, William T.	4: 32	Rohl-Smith, Charles	
"	Shields, James	8: 2	Volk, Leonard W.	7:469
"	Stark, John	1: 80	Conrads, Carl	
"	Stephenson, Benjamin F.	14:111	Unknown	
"	Stockton, Richard	2: 7	Brown, Henry K.	1:511
"	Thomas, George H.	4: 48	Ward, John Q. A.	2:364
"	Trumbull, Jonathan	10:328	Ives, Chauncey B.	
"	Von Steuben, Frederick W. A.	1: 57	Jaegers, Albert	16:179
"	Washington, George (Capitol)	1: 1	Greenough, Horatio	6:232
"	" (The Rotunda)		Houdon, Jean A.	8:292
"	" (Washington Circle)		Mills, Clark	5:160
"	Webster, Daniel (Statuary Hall)	3: 36	Conrads, Carl	
"	" (Scott Circle)		Trentanove, Gaetano	
"	Willard, Frances E.	1:376	Mears, Helen F.	
"	Williams, Roger	10: 4	Simmons, Franklin	11:316
"	Winthrop, John	10:321	Greenough, Richard S.	23:252
"	Witherspoon, John	5:466	Couper, William	C:219
Waterbury, Connecticut	Chatfield, John L.		Bissell, George E.	8:278
"	Franklin, Benjamin	1:328	Bartlett, Paul W.	12:553
Watertown, New York	Flower, Roswell P.	2:344	Saint-Gaudens, Augustus	8:287
Webster City, Iowa	Lincoln, Abraham	2: 65	Ganiere, George E.	
Wellesley, Massachusetts	Martineau, Harriet		Whitney, Anne	7: 72
Westfield, Massachusetts	Shepard, William	2: 51	Lukeman, Augustus	B:437
West Point, New York	Sedgwick, John	4:132	Thompson, Launt	8:283
"	Thayer, Sylvanus	7: 37	Milmore, Martin	8:291
West Roxbury, Massachusetts	Parker, Theodore	2:377	Kraus, Robert	
Williamsburg, Virginia	Berkeley, Norborne	13:390	Unknown	
Williamsport, Pennsylvania	Howard, John	9:292	Putnam, Brenda	B:398
Willimantic, Connecticut	Columbus, Christopher	3:436	Zeus, Mathias	
Wilmington, Delaware	Rodney, Caesar	5:173	Kelly, James E.	25:434
Winchester, Virginia	Rouss, Charles B.	8:433	Coppini, Pompeo	
Woodlawn, New York	Pulitzer, Joseph	1:375	Partridge, William Ordway	23: 12
Worcester, Massachusetts	Bigelow, Timothy	5:422	Snell, George	
"	Devens, Charles	3:203	French, Daniel C.	A:460
"	Hoar, Ebenezer R.	4: 20	"	
"	Hoar, George F.	1:453	"	
Yonkers, New York	Watts, John		Bissell, George E.	8:278

Americans in Fiction, Poetry, and the Drama

Character		Novel, Poem, or Play	Author	
Abercrombie, James	1:102	*A Soldier of Manhattan*	Altsheler, Joseph A.	11:205
"		*A Soldier of the Wilderness*	Tomlinson, Everett T.	25:435
Adams, John	2: 1	*M'Fingal* (poem)	Trumbull, John	7:351
"		*The Adulateur* (play)	Warren, Mercy	7:177
"		*The Conqueror*	Atherton, Gertrude	D:378
Adams, Nehemiah	2:318	*A Pastoral Letter* (poem)	Whittier, John G.	1:407
Adams, Samuel	1:104	*The Adulateur* (play)	Warren, Mercy	7:177
"		*The Colonials*	French, Allen	
"		*The Echo* (poem)	Dwight, Theodore	11:216
Agassiz, Louis	2:360	*Noel* (poem)	Longfellow, Henry W.	2:160
"		*Three Friends of Mine* (poem)	"	
Akers, Paul	6:132	*The Marble Faun*	Hawthorne, Nathaniel	3: 64
Alcott, A. Bronson	2:218	*A Fable for Critics* (poem)	Lowell, James Russell	2: 32
Alden, John	10:295	*Standish of Standish*	Austin, Jane G.	6: 62
"		*The Courtship of Miles Standish* (poem)	Longfellow, Henry W.	2:160
Alexander, William	1: 16	*Lord Stirling's Stand* (ballad)	Babcock, William H.	20:373
"		*The Battle of Brooklyn* (farce)	Anonymous	
Allen, Ethan	1: 45	*Hester of the Grants*	Peck, Theodora	
"		*On General Ethan Allen* (poem)	Hopkins, Lemuel	7:282
"		*The Green Mountain Boys*	Thompson, Daniel P.	6:233
Allen, Ira	4: 29	*Hester of the Grants*	Peck, Theodora	
Anderson, Robert	4:179	*A National Trio* (poem)	Anonymous	
"		*Ballad of Fort Sumter*	"	
"		*Ballad of Major Anderson*	"	
"		*December 26, 1910* (poem)	Dorr, Julia C. R.	6: 56
"		*Peter Hart* (ballad)	Anonymous	
André, John	1: 48	*A Colonial Dame*	Fessenden, Laura D.	
"		*A Great Treason*	Hoppus, Mary A. M.	
"		*André's Lament* (song)	Anonymous	
"		*Arnold and André* (poem)	Calvert, George H.	5:357
"		*Brave Paulding and the Spy* (ballad)	Anonymous	
"		*Edwin Brothertoft*	Winthrop, Theodore	1:130
"		*Hugh Wynne*	Mitchell, S. Weir	9:346
"		*Janice Meredith*	Ford, Paul Leicester	13:105
"		*The Old Continental*	Paulding, James K.	7:193
Andrew, John A.	1:118	*Andrew* (poem)	Parsons, Thomas W.	5:359
Andros, Sir Edmund	6: 90	*The Romance of the Charter Oak*	Seton, William	
Applegate, Jesse	20: 30	*The Soul of America*	Dye, Eva Emery	13:346
Appleseed, Johnny	11: 98	*Johnny Appleseed* (poem)	Child, L. Maria	2:324
"		*The Farm*	Bromfield, Louis	C:295
"		*The Quest of John Chapman*	Hillis, Newell D.	21:280
Armistead, Lewis Addison	5: 15	*High Tide at Gettysburg* (poem)	Thompson, Will H.	11:522
Arnold, Benedict	1: 53	*A Great Treason*	Hoppus, Mary A. M.	
"		*Arnold and André* (poem)	Calvert, George H.	5:357
"		*Arundel*	Roberts, Kenneth	
"		*At the Siege of Quebec*	Kaler, James Otis	13:475
"		*Betsy Ross*	Hotchkiss, Chauncey C.	
"		*Canolles*	Cooke, John E.	7:330
"		*Grace Dudley*	Peterson, Charles J.	
"		*In Blue and White*	Brooks, Elbridge S.	7:156
"		*Loyal Hearts and True*	Ide, Ruth Ogden	
"		*Margaret Moncrieffe*	Burdett, Charles	
"		*My Lady of Doubt*	Parish, Randall	
"		*Rabble in Arms*	Roberts, Kenneth	
"		*Sergeant Champe* (song)	Anonymous	
"		*Song of a Tory*	Scollard, Clinton	23:160
"		*The Death of General Montgomery* (poem)	Brackenridge, Hugh H.	8: 49
"		*The Maid-at-Arms*	Chambers, Robert W.	C:402
"		*The Patrol of the Mountain*	Curtis, Newton M.	4:328
"		*To the Traitor Arnold* (poem)	Anonymous	
"		*Under Colonial Colors*	Tomlinson, Everett T.	25:435
Arnold, George	9:432	*George Arnold* (poem)	Stedman, Edmund C.	3:136
Ashby, Turner	4:296	*Ashby* (poem)	Thompson, John R.	6: 49
"		*Surry of Eagle's Nest*	Cooke, John E.	7:330
Ashmun, Jehudi	6:195	*The Burial of Ashmun* (poem)	Sigourney, Lydia H.	1:154
Atherton, Charles G.	10:383	*The Gag* (poem)	Pierpont, John	6:155

Character		Novel, Poem, or Play	Author	
Auchmuty, Samuel	9:102	*M'Fingal* (poem)	Trumbull, John	7:351
Bacon, Nathaniel, 1st	13:386	*A Century Too Soon*	Musick, John R.	
"		*A White Guard to Satan*	Ewell, Alice M.	
"		*Hansford*	Tucker, P. St. George	
"		*The Head of a Hundred*	Goodwin, Maud W.	
"		*The Youth of the Old Dominion*	Hopkins, Samuel	7:501
"		*Vivian of Virginia*	Fuller, Hulbert	
"		*White Aprons*	Goodwin, Maude W.	
Bacon, Nathaniel, 2d	5:337	*A Century Too Soon*	Musick, John R.	
"		*A White Guard to Satan*	Ewell, Alice M.	
"		*Hansford*	Tucker, P. St. George	
"		*The Head of a Hundred*	Goodwin, Maud W.	
"		*The Youth of the Old Dominion*	Hopkins, Samuel	7:501
"		*Vivian of Virginia*	Fuller, Hulbert	
"		*White Aprons*	Goodwin, Maud W.	
Balboa, Vasco N. de	5:431	*The Damsel of Darien*	Simms, W. Gilmore	6:204
Baltimore, Lord	7:336	*Barnaby Lee*	Bennett, John	
Bancroft, George	3:160	*A Decanter of Madeira* (poem)	Mitchell, S. Weir	9:346
Bartlett, Josiah	11:121	*One of the Signers* (poem)	Whittier, John G.	1:407
Beauregard, Pierre G. T.	4:178	*Beauregard* (poem)	Anonymous	
"		*Call 'em Names, Jeff!* (ballad)	"	
"		*Peter Ashley*	Heyward, DuBose	
"		*Surry of Eagle's Nest*	Cooke, John E.	7:330
Bedel, Timothy	17:155	*Arundel*	Roberts, Kenneth	
Beecher, Henry Ward	3:129	*Henry Ward Beecher* (poem)	Phelps, Charles H.	8:197
Bellingham, Richard	5:421	*John Endicott* (poem)	Longfellow, Henry W.	2:160
"		*Penelope's Suitors*	Bynner, Edwin L.	7:486
Berkeley, Sir John		*The Old Dominion*	Johnston, Mary	C:430
Berkeley, Sir William	13:383	*Hansford*	Tucker, P. St. George	
"		*The Head of a Hundred*	Goodwin, Maud W.	
"		*The Youth of the Old Dominion*	Hopkins, Samuel	7:501
"		*White Aprons*	Goodwin, Maud W.	
Bienville, Sieur de	5:491	*The Black Wolf's Breed*	Dickson, Harris	
Bigelow, Timothy	5:422	*Arundel*	Roberts, Kenneth	
Black Hawk (Indian chief)	9:477	*The Prairie Schooner*	Barton, William E.	17:380
Blair, Montgomery	2: 88	*Forever Free*	Morrow, Honoré W.	
Blennerhassett, Harman	13:153	*Blennerhassett*	Pidgin, Charles F.	13:479
Bonaparte, Jerome N.	14: 22	*Hearts Triumphant*	Tupper, Edith Sessions	
Bonnet, Stede		*Kate Bonnet*	Stockton, Francis R.	1:396
Boone, Daniel	3:110	*The Old Pioneer* (poem)	O'Hara, Theodore	4:362
Booth, J. Wilkes	3:182	*Katy of Catoctin*	Townsend, George A.	1:154
"		*The Last Full Measure*	Morrow, Honoré W.	
Borah, William E.	B:115	*Black River*	Beals, Carleton	D:442
Bowdoin, James	2:488	*Captain Shays*	Rivers, George R. R.	
Bowie, James	4:210	*With Crockett and Bowie*	Munroe, Kirk	11:523
Braddock, Edward	2: 58	*A Soldier of Virginia*	Stevenson, Burton E.	13:143
"		*Braddock*	Musick, John R.	
"		*Braddock's Fate* (poem)	Tilden, ——	
"		*The Virginians*	Thackeray, William M.	
Bradford, Alice (Southworth)		*Barbara Standish*	Austin, Jane G.	6: 62
Bradford, William	7:368	*Standish of Standish*	"	
"		*The Knight of the Golden Melice*	Adams, John T.	
Bradford, William, Jr.		*David Alden's Daughters*	Austin, Jane G.	6: 62
Bradstreet, Simon	7:372	*The Heroine of the Strait*	Crawley, Mary C.	
Brant, Joseph	9:142	*Brant and Red Jacket*	Eggleston, Edward	6: 57
"		*Drums Along the Mohawk*	Edmonds, Walter D.	
"		*The Maid-at-Arms*	Chambers, Robert W.	C:402
Brewster, William	7: 30	*Standish of Standish*	Austin, Jane G.	6: 62
Bridger, James	13:428	*The Covered Wagon*	Hough, Emerson	19: 60
Briggs, Charles F. (Harry Franco)	9:254	*A Fable for Critics* (poem)	Lowell, James Russell	2: 32
Brown, John	2:307	*Avenged* (poem)	Newell, Richard H.	
"		*Before the Crisis*	Mott, Frederick T.	
"		*Brown of Ossawatomie* (poem)	Whittier, John G.	1:407
"		*God's Angry Man*	Ehrlich, Leonard	
"		*How Old Brown Took Harper's Ferry* (ballad)	Stedman, Edmund C.	3:136
"		*John Brown of Gettysburg* (ballad)	Harte, Bret	1:404
"		*John Brown's Body*	Benét, Stephen Vincent	A:215
"		*Katy of Catoctin*	Townsend, George A.	1:154
"		*Manassas*	Sinclair, Upton	C:114
"		*The President's Proclamation* (poem)	Proctor, Edna D.	7:250

Character		Novel, Poem, or Play	Author	
Brown, John	2:307	*The Spectre at Sumter* (poem)	Anonymous	
Brownson, Orestes A.	7:197	*A Fable for Critics* (poem)	Lowell, James Russell	2: 32
Bryant, William Cullen	4: 79	"	"	
"		*On Board the '76* (poem)	Longfellow, Henry W.	2:160
Bull, Ole	4:234	*Ole Bull* (poem)	Child, L. Maria	2:324
"		*Tales of a Wayside Inn* (poem)	Longfellow, Henry W.	2:160
Burgoyne, John		*Bunker's Hill* (dramatic poem)	Brackenridge, Hugh H.	8: 49
"		*The Fall of Burgoyne* (ballad)	Case, Wheeler	
"		*The Sun of Saratoga*	Altsheler, Joseph A.	11:205
Burnett, Vivian		*Little Lord Fauntleroy*	Burnett, Frances Hodgson	20:423
Burns, Anthony		*The Rendition* (poem)	Whittier, John G.	1:407
Burr, Aaron	3: 5	*Arundel*	Roberts, Kenneth	
"		*Blennerhassett*	Pidgin, Charles F.	13:479
"		*Golden Ladder*	Hughes, Rupert	C:314
"		*Hearts Triumphant*	Tupper, Edith Sessions	
"		*Margaret Moncrieffe*	Burdett, Charles	
"		*The Climax*	Pidgin, Charles F.	13:479
"		*The Conspirator*	Dupuy, Eliza A.	6:200
"		*The Death of General Montgomery* (poem)	Brackenridge, Hugh H.	8: 49
"		*The Minister's Wooing*	Stowe, Harriet Beecher	1:423
"		*The Stirrup Cup*	Tyson, J. Aubrey	
Burroughs, George	9:329	*Burroughs* (poem)	Cary, Alice	1:535
Butler, Benjamin F.	1:121	*With Malice Toward None*	Morrow, Honoré W.	
Butler, John		*The Maid-at-Arms*	Chambers, Robert W.	C:402
Butler, Walter		*Cardigan*	"	
"		*Drums Along the Mohawk*	Edmonds, Walter D.	
"		*Son of a Tory*	Scollard, Clinton	23:160
"		*The Death of Walter Butler* (ballad)	English, Thomas Dunn	4:322
"		*The Maid-at-Arms*	Chambers, Robert W.	C:402
"		*The Reckoning*	"	
Byles, Mather	7:145	*The Rebels*	Child, L. Maria	2:324
Byrd, Evelyn	7:247	*Audrey*	Johnston, Mary	C:430
Calef, Robert	8:164	*Calef in Boston* (poem)	Whittier, John G.	1:407
Calhoun, John C.	6: 83	*54-40 or Fight*	Hough, Emerson	19: 60
"		*Manassas*	Sinclair, Upton	C:114
Calvert, Charles	7:336	*Barnaby Lee*	Bennett, John	
Calvert, Frederick	7:337	*Richard Carvel*	Churchill, Winston	10:178
Calvert, Leonard	7:332	*Mistress Brent*	Thruston, Lucy M.	
Camp, Walter	21:293	*The Earthquake*	Train, Arthur	14:427
Canonchet (Indian chief)	10:402	*The Wept of Wish-ton-Wish*	Cooper, J. Fenimore	1:393
Carrell, Alexis	15:301	*The Earthquake*	Train, Arthur	14:427
Carson, Christopher (Kit)	3:273	*Dark Circles of Branches*	Armer, Laura Adams	
"		*Kit Carson's Ride* (poem)	Miller, Joaquin	7: 69
"		*The Wolf Song*	Ferguson, Harvey	
Carver, John	7:367	*Standish of Standish*	Austin, Jane G.	6: 62
Carver, Jonathan	1:476	*Northwest Passage*	Roberts, Kenneth	
Cary, Alice	1:535	*The Singer* (poem)	Whittier, John G.	1:407
Chalkley, Thomas	11: 92	*Chalkley Hall* (poem)	Aiken, Ednah	
Champe, John	7:162	*Sergeant Champe* (song)	Anonymous	
Chapman, John	11: 98	*The Farm*	Bromfield, Louis	C:295
Chase, Salmon P.	1: 28	*Forever Free*	Morrow, Honoré W.	
"		*With Malice Toward None*	"	
Chase, Samuel	1: 24	*The Word of Congress* (poem)	Odell, Jonathan	25:212
Child, L. Maria	2:324	*Within the Gate* (poem)	Whittier, John G.	1:407
Chittenden, Thomas	8:312	*Hester of the Grants*	Peck, Theodora	
Chouteau, Pierre	13:469	*The Rose of Old St. Louis*	Dillon, Mary	
Christmas, Lee	6:380	*Soldiers of Fortune*	Davis, Richard Harding	8:176
Church, Benjamin	7:149	*The Gallant Church* (ballad)	Anonymous	
Church, Dr. Benjamin	7:167	*The Colonists*	French, Allen	
Claiborne, William C. C.	10: 74	*Black Ivory*	Banks, Polan	
Clark, George Rogers	1: 82	*Alice of Old Vincennes*	Thompson, Maurice	11:521
"		*The Crossing*	Churchill, Winston	10:178
"		*The Rangers*	Thompson, N. P.	
Clark, William	12:301	*The Conquest*	Dye, Eva Emery	13:346
"		*The Rose of Old St. Louis*	Dillon, Mary	
Clay, Henry	5: 77	*A Herald of the West*	Altsheler, Joseph A.	11:205
"		*A Kentucky Chronicle*	Gray, J. Thompson	
Cleveland, Grover	2:400	*The Honorable Peter Sterling*	Ford, Paul Leicester	13:105
Clinton, DeWitt	3: 43	*The State Triumvirate* (poem)	Verplanck, Gulian C.	5:405
Clinton, George	3: 41	*A Colonial Dame*	Fessenden, Laura D.	
"		*Drums Along the Mohawk*	Edmonds, Walter D.	

Character	Novel, Poem, or Play	Author
Coffin, Catherine	*Uncle Tom's Cabin*	Stowe, Harriet Beecher 1:423
Coffin, Levi 12:124	*Innocents Abroad*	Twain, Mark 6: 24
"	*Manassas*	Sinclair, Upton C:114
"	*Uncle Tom's Cabin*	Stowe, Harriet Beecher 1:423
Colden, Cadwallader 2:270	*In the Valley*	Frederic, Harold 5:358
Coleman, William T. 8:336	*In the Gray Dawn*	White, Stewart Edward 13:313
Columbus, Christopher 3:436	*Columbia*	Musick, John R.
"	*Columbus Before the University of Salamanca* (poem)	Sigourney, Lydia H. 1:154
"	*Mercedes of Castile*	Cooper, J. Fenimore 1:398
"	*Out of the Sunset Sea*	Tourgee, Albion W. 7:324
"	*The Vision of Columbus* (poem)	Barlow, Joel 3:186
"	*Westward with Columbus*	Stables, Gordon
Conyngham, Gustavus 4:266	*With the Flag in the Channel*	Barnes, James 14:437
Cooper, J. Fenimore 1:398	*A Fable for Critics* (poem)	Lowell, James Russell 2: 32
Copley, Thomas Singleton 6:467	*Northwest Passage*	Roberts, Kenneth
Corey, Giles 12:506	*Giles Corey of the Salem Farms* (poem)	Longfellow, Henry W. 2:160
"	*Giles Corey, Yeoman* (play)	Freeman, Mary E. Wilkins 9:229
"	*Martha Cory*	Dubois, Constance G.
Cornbury, Lord 5:407	*Free to Serve*	Rayner, Emma
Cornwallis, Lord Charles 7:543	*The Dance* (ballad)	Anonymous
"	*The Scarlet Coat*	Ross, Clinton
"	*The Scout*	Simms, W. Gilmore 6:204
Cory, Harry T. 18:421	*The River*	Aiken, Ednah
"	*The Winning of Barbara Worth*	Wright, Harold Bell D:382
Cotton, John 7: 27	*Mistress Content Craddock*	Trumbull, Annie E.
Craven, Charles 12:155	*Yemassee*	"
Craven, Tunis A. McD. 12:371	*The Bay Fight* (poem)	Brownell, Henry H. 5:357
Crockett, David 4: 85	*Remember the Alamo!*	Barr, Amelia E. 4:485
"	*With Crocket and Bowie*	Munroe, Kirk 11:523
Crook, George 4: 70	*Red Men and White*	Wister, Owen C:459
"	*The Heritage of Unrest*	Overton, Gwendolen
Crosby, Enoch (Harvey Birch)	*The Spy*	Cooper, J. Fenimore 1:398
Curtis, Cyrus H. K. 24: 26	*A Man from Maine*	Bok, Edward W. 23: 41
Custer, George A. 4:274	*Revenge of Rain-in-the-Face* (poem)	Longfellow, Henry W. 2:160
Cutter, Bloodgood H.	*Innocents Abroad*	Twain, Mark 6: 24
Dale, Richard 2: 17	*Paul Jones*	Seawell, Molly E. 7:253
Dana, Richard Henry 7:182	*A Fable for Critics* (poem)	Lowell, James Russell 2: 32
Dare, Virginia	*John Vytal*	Payson, William F.
Davenport, Abraham	*Abraham Davenport* (poem)	Whittier, John G. 1:407
Davenport, John 1:161	*The Regicides* (poem)	Bacon, Delia S. 1:477
Davis, Jefferson 4:148	*Acrostic on Jefferson Davis*	Rice, Roswell
"	*Before the Dawn*	Altsheler, Joseph A. 11:205
"	*Davis' Address* (ballad)	Bennett, William C.
"	*England and France* (ballad)	Anonymous
"	*Manassas*	Sinclair, Upton C:114
Davis, Samuel 8:334	*Sam Davis*	Fox, Walter D.
Dearborn, Henry 1: 93	*Rabble in Arms*	Roberts, Kenneth
Debs, Eugene V. 12:340	*Regardin' Terry Hut*	Riley, James Whitcomb 6: 31
Decatur, Stephen 4: 56	*Decatur and Somers*	Seawell, Molly E. 7:253
De Leon, Daniel	*Death and Birth of David Markand*	Frank, Waldo A:398
Dennie, Joseph 7:204	*Salmagundi*	Irving, Washington 3: 17
De Soto, Fernando 5:126	*The Virgin of the Sun*	Griffith, George
"	*Vasconcelos*	Simms, W. Gilmore 6:204
Douglas, Stephen A. 2:428	*Children of the Market Place*	Masters, Edgar Lee A:387
"	*Manassas*	Sinclair, Upton C:114
Douglass, Frederick 2:309	*God's Angry Man*	Ehrlich, Leonard
"	*Manassas*	Sinclair, Upton C:114
"	*With Malice Toward None*	Morrow, Honoré W.
Drake, Sir Francis 9:284	*Drake and his Yeomen*	Barnes, James 14:437
"	*Under Drake's Flag*	Henty, George A.
Drummond, William 10:395	*White Aprons*	Goodwin, Maud W.
Dudley, Thomas 7:370	*The Knight of the Golden Melice*	Adams, John T.
Dunmore, Earl of 13:391	*Cardigan*	Chambers, Robert W. C:402
"	*Henry St. John*	Cooke, John E. 7:330
" (Lord Kidnapper)	*The Fall of British Tyranny* (play)	Leacock, John
Dwyer, Abram	*Bethel* (poem)	Duganne, Augustine J. H. 4:315
Early, Jubal A. 4:137	*Evelyn Byrd*	Eggleston, George C. 1:213
"	*Hilt to Hilt*	Cooke, John E. 7:330
Eaton, John Henry 5:295	*Gorgeous Hussy*	Adams, Samuel H. 14:166
Eaton, Peggy O'Neill 6:290	*Peggy O'Neill*	Lewis, Alfred H. 25:261

Character		Novel, Poem, or Play	Author	
Eaton, Peggy O'Neill	6:290	*The Rake and the Hussy*	Chambers, Robert W.	C:402
Eliot, John	2:419	*Eliot's Oak* (poem)	Longfellow, Henry W.	2:160
"		*Mistress Content Craddock*	Trumbull, Annie E.	
"		*The Doomed Chief*	Thompson, Daniel P.	6:233
"		*The Knight of the Golden Melice*	Adams, John T.	
Ellsworth, Elmer E.	4:166	*Colonel Ellsworth* (poem)	Stoddard, Richard H.	3:297
"		*Ellsworth* (poem)	Anonymous	
"		*Ellsworth* (poem)	Burleigh, William H.	2:378
"		*Promoted* (poem)	Phelps, Rufus K.	
"		*The Death of Colonel Ellsworth* (poem)	Townsend, George A.	1:154
Elwell, Edward H.	9:259	*The Boys of '35*	Elwell, Edward H.	9:259
Emmet, Thomas Addis	5: 63	*Thomas Addis Emmet* (poem)	Clason, Isaac S.	
Endicott, John	5:113	*John Endicott* (poem)	Longfellow, Henry W.	2:160
"		*Merry-Mount*	Motley, John L.	5:213
"		*The Fair Pilgrim*	Bacon, Delia S.	1:477
"		*The King's Missive* (poem)	Whittier, John G.	1:407
"		*The Knight of the Golden Melice*	Adams, John T.	
Enos, Roger	5:258	*Arundel*	Roberts, Kenneth	
Everett, Edward	6:179	*Governor Everett receiving the Indian Chiefs* (poem)	Fuller, Margaret	3: 28
Ewell, Richard Stoddert	4: 55	*Evelyn Byrd*	Eggleston, George C.	1:213
Farragut, David G.	2: 45	*Farragut* (poem)	Meredith, William T.	
"		*The River Fight* (ballad)	Brownell, Henry H.	5:357
Felton, Cornelius C.	6:419	*Three Friends of Mine* (poem)	Longfellow, Henry W.	2:160
Field, Cyrus W.	4:451	*How Cyrus Laid the Cable* (ballad)	Saxe, John G.	1:438
Fields, James T.	1:283	*Auf Wiedersehen* (poem)	Longfellow, Henry W.	2:160
Follen, Charles T. C.	7:289	*Follen* (poem)	Whittier, John G.	1:407
Ford, John T.	1:242	*Forever Free*	Morrow, Honoré W.	
Fox, George	7: 10	*A Gallant Quaker*	Robertson, Mrs. M. H.	
"		*Friend Olivia*	Barr, Amelia E.	4:485
Franklin, Benjamin	1:328	*Israel Potter*	Melville, Herman	4: 59
"		*Northwest Passage*	Roberts, Kenneth	
"		*The Days of Poor Richard*	Bacheller, Irving	C:411
"		*The Virginians*	Thackeray, William M.	
Frémont, John C.	4:270	*With Frémont, the Pathfinder*	Whitson, John H.	
Fritchie, Barbara	10:113	*Barbara Frietchie* (play)	Fitch, Clyde	15:192
"		*Barbara Frietchie* (poem)	Whittier, John G.	1:407
Frohman, Daniel	11:440	*Soldiers of Fortune*	Davis, Richard Harding	8:176
Fuller, George	6:475	*An Artist of the Beautiful* (poem)	Whittier, John G.	1:407
Fuller, Margaret	3: 28	*The Blithedale Romance*	Hawthorne, Nathaniel	3: 64
Gadsden, Christopher	1: 76	*An Affair of Honor* (ballad)	André, John	1: 48
Gage, Thomas	7:377	*Bunker Hill* (poem)	Cozzens, Frederick S.	6: 29
"		*Bunker's Hill* (dramatic poem)	Brackenridge, Hugh H.	8: 49
"		*Cardigan*	Chambers, Robert W.	C:402
"		*Dan Monroe*	Stoddard, William O.	8:121
"		*Gage's Proclamation* (ballad)	Anonymous	
"		*General Gage's Soliloquy* (ballad)	Freneau, Philip	6:201
"		*M'Fingal* (poem)	Trumbull, John	7:351
"		*Northwest Passage*	Roberts, Kenneth	
"		*On the Conqueror of America* (poem)	Freneau, Philip	6:201
"		*Poem Containing Remarks on the Present War*	Anonymous	
"		*The Colonials*	French, Allen	
" (Lord Boston)		*The Fall of British Tyranny* (play)	Leacock, John	
Galbraith, Victor	8: 37	*Victor Galbraith* (ballad)	Longfellow, Henry W.	2:160
Gansevoort, Peter	1:382	*In the Valley*	Frederic, Harold	5:358
Gates, Horatio	1: 47	*Rabble in Arms*	Roberts, Kenneth	
Geronimo	23:351	*Geronimo*	McGaffney, Ernest	
"		*In Those Days*	Ferguson, Harvey	
Giddings, Joshua R.	2:329	*The Portrait*	Riddle, Albert G.	2:371
Goffe, William	11:458	*Shad and Shed*	Edwards, E. J.	
"		*The Regicides*	Bacon, Delia S.	1:477
"		*The Romance of the Charter Oak*	Seton, William	
"		*The Spectre of the Forest*	McHenry, James	
Gorgas, William C.	14:528	*Yellow Jack*	Howard, Sidney	
Gorges, Sir Ferdinando	5:166	*Merry-Mount*	Motley, John L.	5:213
Gosnold, Bartholomew	12:186	*The Youth of the Old Dominion*	Hopkins, Samuel	7:501
Grant, Ulysses S.	4: 1	*Grant* (poem)	Boker, George H.	6: 73
"		*Grant at Shiloh* (poem)	Miller, Joaquin	7: 69
"		*The Battle Ground*	Glasgow, Ellen	C:348
"		*The Big Barn*	Edmonds, Walter D.	
"		*The Captain*	Williams, Francis C.	13:143

Character		Novel, Poem, or Play	Author	
Grant, Ulysses S.	4: 1	*The Claybornes*	Sage, William	
"		*The Crisis*	Churchill, Winston	10:178
"		*The Death of Grant* (poem)	Bierce, Ambrose	14:180
"		*The Iron Brigade*	King, Charles	25:148
"		*The Last Full Measure*	Morrow, Honoré W.	
"		*Trail Makers of the Middle Border*	Garland, Hamlin	B: 4
Gratz, Rebecca	10:130	*Ivanhoe*	Scott, Walter	
Greeley, Horace	3:448	*Eben Holden*	Bacheller, Irving	C:411
"		*In Those Days*	Ferguson, Harvey	
Greene, Nathanael	1: 39	*A Continental Cavalier*	Scribner, Kimball	
"		*Eutaw Springs* (poem)	Freneau, Philip	6:201
"		*Margaret Moncrieffe*	Burdett, Charles	
"		*The Scout*	Simms, W. Gilmore	6:204
Hale, Nathan	1: 51	*Nathan Hale* (ballad)	Finch, Francis M.	11:356
"		*Nathan Hale* (play)	Fitch, Clyde	15:192
Halleck, Fitz-Greene	3:226	*A Fable for Critics* (poem)	Lowell, James Russell	2: 32
"		*Fitz-Greene Halleck* (poem)	Whittier, John G.	1:407
Hamilton, Alexander	1: 9	*Mrs. Reynolds and Hamilton*	Townsend, George A.	1:154
"		*My Lady of Doubt*	Parish, Randall	
"		*The Climax*	Pidgin, Charles F.	13:479
"		*The Conqueror*	Atherton, Gertrude	D:378
Hamlin, Hannibal	2: 76	*With Malice Toward None*	Morrow, Honoré W.	
Hancock, John	1:103	*My Lady Laughter*	Tilton, Dwight	
"		*The Echo* (poem)	Dwight, Theodore	11:216
Hanford, Thomas		*White Aprons*	Goodwin, Maud W.	
Harrington, Jonathan	1:367	*Psalm of the West* (poem)	Lanier, Sidney	2:438
Hathorne, John		*Giles Corey* (poem)	Longfellow, Henry W.	2:160
Hawthorne, Nathaniel	3: 64	*A Fable for Critics* (poem)	Lowell, James Russell	2: 32
"		*Hawthorne* (poem)	Longfellow, Henry W.	2:160
" (Miles Coverdale)		*The Blithedale Romance*	Hawthorne, Nathaniel	3: 64
Hay, John	11: 12	*Forever Free*	Morrow, Honoré W.	
"		*The Last Full Measure*	"	
"		*With Malice Toward None*	"	
Hayne, Isaac	1:440	*Grosvenor*	Hale, Sarah J.	22: 39
Hazen, Moses	1: 78	*Arundel*	Roberts, Kenneth	
Henry, Patrick	1:337	*Hearts Courageous*	Rives, Hallie E.	
"		*Henry St. John*	Cooke, John E.	7:330
"		*The Virginia Comedians*	"	
Herkimer, Nicholas	1: 70	*Drums Along the Mohawk*	Edmonds, Walter D.	
"		*In the Valley*	Frederic, Harold	5:358
"		*The Maid-at-Arms*	Chambers, Robert W.	C:402
Hewes, George R. T.	5:528	*My Lady Laughter*	Tilton, Dwight	
Hibbins, Ann		*Penelope's Suitors*	Bynner, Edwin L.	7:486
Higginson, Thomas W.	1:394	*God's Angry Man*	Ehrlich, Leonard	
Hill, Ambrose P.	4:101	*Surry of Eagle's Nest*	Cooke, John E.	7:330
Hobson, Richmond Pearson	9: 10	*Seven League Boots*	Halliburton, Richard	D:407
Holmes, Oliver Wendell	2:336	*A Fable for Critics* (poem)	Lowell, James Russell	2: 32
"		*Filling an Order* (poem)	Trowbridge, John T.	3:374
"		*Our Autocrat* (poem)	Whittier, John G.	1:407
"		*The Sailing of the Autocrat* (poem)	Aldrich, Thomas Bailey	1:283
Holt, Joseph	1:354	*A National Trio* (poem)	Anonymous	
Holyoke, Edward	6:415	*Agnes Surriage*	Bynner, Edwin L.	7:486
Hooker, Joseph	4:176	*General Lee's Wooing* (ballad)	Anonymous	
"		*Hooker's Across* (ballad)	Boker, George H.	6: 73
"		*The Fight Above the Clouds* (poem)	Wallace, William R.	8:375
"		*The Gallant Fighting Joe* (ballad)	Stevenson, James	
Hoover, Herbert	C: 1	*The Earthquake*	Train, Arthur	14:427
Hopkins, Samuel	7:154	*The Minister's Wooing*	Stowe, Harriet Beecher	1:423
Houston, Sam	9: 63	*Remember the Alamo*	Barr, Amelia E.	4:485
Howard, Oliver Otis	4:103	*Howard at Atlanta* (poem)	Whittier, John G.	1:407
Howe, Robert	6: 79	*An Affair of Honor* (ballad)	André, John	1: 48
Howe, Samuel G.	8:372	*The Hero* (poem)	Whittier, John G.	1:407
Howe, William	7:151	*Rabble In Arms*	Roberts, Kenneth	
Howland, John	8: 58	*Standish of Standish*	Austin, Jane G.	6: 62
Hull, Isaac	13:426	*The Constitution and the Guerrière* (ballad)	Anonymous	
Hutchinson, Anne	9:148	*The Golden Arrow*	Hall, Ruth	
Hutchinson, Thomas (Rapatio)	7:376	*The Adulateur* (play)	Warren, Mercy	7:177
"		*The Rebels*	Child, L. Maria	2:324
Hyde, Edward	5:407	*Free to Serve*	Rayner, Emma	
Irving, Washington	3: 17	*A Fable for Critics* (poem)	Lowell, James Russell	2: 32
Jackson, Abraham R.	7:510	*Innocents Abroad*	Twain, Mark	6: 24

Character		Novel, Poem, or Play	Author	
Jackson, Andrew	5:289	*An Epic in Homespun*	Johnson, G. W.	
"		*By the Eternal*	Read, Opie P.	1:353
"		*Coniston*	Churchill, Winston	10:178
"		*Courageous Heart*	James, M. and B.	
"		*Gorgeous Hussy*	Adams, Samuel H.	14:166
"		*Out of the Cypress Swamp*	Rickert, Edith	
"		*Peggy O'Neill*	Lewis, Alfred H.	25:261
"		*Strength of the Hills*	Clark, Ellery H.	
"		*The Battle of New Orleans* (ballad)	English, Thomas Dunn	4:322
"		*The Border Captain*	James, Marquis	
"		*The Bright Land*	Faribank, Janet	
"		*The Cavalier of Tennessee*	Nicholson, Meredith	A:512
"		*The Crossing*	Churchill, Winston	10:178
"		*The Errand Boy of Andrew Jackson*	Stoddard, William O.	8:121
"		*The Patience of John Moreland*	Dillon, Mary G.	
"		*The Rake and the Hussy*	Chambers, Robert W.	C:402
Jackson, Rachel D.	5:298	*Gorgeous Hussy*	Adams, Samuel H.	14:166
Jackson, Thomas J. (Stonewall)	4:125	*Barbara Frietchie* (poem)	Whittier, John G.	1:407
"		*Dying Words of Stonewall Jackson* (poem)	Lanier, Sidney	2:438
"		*Joined the Blues* (ballad)	Rooney, John J.	
"		*Marching On*	Boyd, James	C:381
"		*Mohun*	Cooke, John E.	7:330
"		*Stonewall Jackson* (ballad)	Melville, Herman	4: 59
"		*Stonewall Jackson* (poem)	Flash, Henry L.	13:279
"		*Stonewall Jackson's Way* (ballad)	Palmer, John W.	8:222
"		*Stonewall's Scout*	Horseley, Reginald	
"		*Surry of Eagle's Nest*	Cooke, John E.	7:330
"		*Under the Shade of the Trees* (poem)	Preston, Margaret J.	7:147
Jasper, William	1: 25	*The Death of Jasper*	Charlton, Robert M.	4:191
"		*The Swamp Steed*	Eagan, Pierce	
Jay, John	1: 20	*The Word of Congress* (poem)	Odell, Jonathan	25:212
Jefferson, Thomas	3: 1	*The Rose of Old St. Louis*	Dillon, Mary	
"		*The Youth of Jefferson*	Cooke, John E.	7:330
Jewett, Father		*A Greeting* (poem)	Whittier, John G.	1:407
Jogues, Father Isaac		*The Lady of Fort St. John*	Catherwood, Mary H.	9:215
Johnson, Andrew	2:454	*Andrew Johnson of Tennessee* (ballad)	W. J. G.	
Johnson, Guy		*The Maid-at-Arms*	Chambers, Robert W.	C:402
Johnson, Sir John	8:156	*The Maid-at-Arms*	"	
Johnson, Sir William	5:101	*Cardigan*	"	
"		*In the Valley*	Frederic, Harold	5:358
"		*Northwest Passage*	Roberts, Kenneth	
"		*The Story of Old Fort Johnson*	Reid, W. M.	
Jones, John (Sheriff Jones)	5: 29	*Old-Town Folks*	Stowe, Harriet Beecher	1:423
Jones, Paul	2: 14	*Drums*	Boyd, James	C:381
"		*For Love of Country*	Brady, Cyrus T.	10:477
"		*Grip of Honor*	"	
"		*Israel Potter*	Melville, Herman	4: 59
"		*Lively Lady*	Roberts, Kenneth	
"		*Old-Town Folks*	Stowe, Harriet Beecher	1:423
"		*On the Memorable Victory* (poem)	Freneau, Philip	6:201
"		*Paul Jones*	Seawell, Molly E.	7:253
"		*Richard Carvel*	Churchill, Winston	10:178
"		*The Pilot*	Cooper, J. Fenimore	1:398
"		*The Refugee*	Melville, Herman	4: 59
"		*The Tory Lover*	Jewett, Sarah O.	1:374
"		*The Yankee Man of War* (ballad)	Anonymous	
Judd, Sylvester	9:273	*A Fable for Critics* (poem)	Lowell, James Russell	2: 32
Judson, Adoniram	3: 92	*The Burmans and their Missionary* (poem)	Sigourney, Lydia H.	1:154
Kane, Elisha K.	3:288	*Doctor Kane in Cuba* (poem)	Whittier, Elizabeth H.	8:109
Kearny, Dennis		*The Days of Her Life*	Irwin, Wallace	14:184
Kearny, Philip	4:260	*Dirge for a Soldier*	Boker, George H.	6: 73
"		*Kearny at Seven Pines* (ballad)	Stedman, Edmund C.	3:136
Kenton, Simon	3:527	*Alice of Old Vincennes*	Thompson, Maurice	11:521
Kimberly, Lewis A.	10:181	*The Bay Fight* (ballad)	Brownell, Henry H.	5:357
King, James, of William		*The Gray Dawn*	White, Stewart Edward	13:313
King, John		*Barnaby Lee*	Bennett, John	
King Philip (Indian chief)	10: 50	*Mount Hope*	Hollister, Gideon H.	12: 56
"		*The Wept of Wish-ton-Wish*	Cooper, J. Fenimore	1:398
"		*Uncrowning a King* (poem)	Eliot, E. S.	
King, Thomas Starr	4:472	*Thomas Starr King* (poem)	Whittier, John G.	1:407
Knox, Henry	1: 14	*My Lady of Doubt*	Parish, Randall	

Character		Novel, Poem, or Play	Author	
Kosciuszko, Thaddeus	1: 54	*Rabble in Arms*	Roberts, Kenneth	
“		*The Scout*	Simms, W. Gilmore	6:204
Kountz, John S.	4:332	*The Drummer Boy of Mission Ridge*	Sherwood, Katherine M. B.	2:201
Lafayette, Marquis de	1: 63	*A Continental Cavalier*	Scribner, Kimball	
“		*Hugh Wynne*	Mitchell, S. Weir	9:346
“		*In Blue and White*	Brooks, Elbridge S.	7:156
“		*My Sword for Lafayette*	Pemberton, Max	
“		*The Conqueror*	Atherton, Gertrude	D:378
“		*The Linwoods*	Sedgwick, Catharine M.	1:446
“		*The Scarlet Coat*	Ross, Clinton	
La Follette, Robert M.	19:425	*Black River*	Beals, Carleton	D:442
Lander, Frederick W.	8:127	*Lander* (poem)	Aldrich, Thomas Bailey	1:283
La Salle, Robert, Sieur de	5:125	*Robert Cavalier*	Orcutt, William D.	B:462
“		*The Black Wolf's Breed*	Dickson, Harris	
“		*The Story of Tonty*	Catherwood, Mary H.	9:215
“		*The Young Pioneers*	Greene, E. Everett	
“		*With Sword and Crucifix*	Van Zile, Edward S.	25:278
Laurens, Henry	3:426	*The Word of Congress* (poem)	Odell, Jonathan	25:212
Laurens, John	1: 67	*The Address* (poem)	Humphreys, David	1: 71
“		*The Conqueror*	Atherton, Gertrude	D:378
Le Baron, Francis		*Dr. LeBaron and His Daughters*	Austin, Jane G.	6: 62
Lee, Charles	8:238	*The Fall of British Tyranny* (play)	Leacock, John	
Lee, Henry	3: 25	*The Man Without a Home*	Hughes, Rupert	C:314
“		*The Sword of Harry Lee* (ballad)	McCabe, James D.	7:511
Lee, Robert E.	4: 95	*Before the Dawn*	Altsheler, Joseph A.	11:205
“		*General Lee's Wooing* (ballad)	Anonymous	
“		*God's Angry Man*	Ehrlich, Leonard	
“		*High Tide at Gettysburg* (poem)	Thompson, Will H.	11:522
“		*How are you, General Lee?* (ballad)	Anonymous	
“		*In Old Bellaire*	Dillon, Mary	
“		*Lee to the Rear* (ballad)	Thompson, John R.	6: 49
“		*Mohun*	Cooke, John E.	7:330
“		*With Lee in Virginia*	Henty, George A.	
Leete, William	10:322	*The Regicides*	Bacon, Delia S.	1:477
Leggett, William	6:275	*Flower of the Fort*	Hemstreet, Charles	
“		*Leggett's Monument* (poem)	Whittier, John G.	1:407
Leisler, Jacob	13:448	*Jacob Leisler*	Mathews, Cornelius	13:542
“		*Old New York, or Jacob Leisler*	Smith, Elizabeth O. P.	9:171
“		*The Begum's Daughter*	Bynner, Edwin L.	7:486
Le Moyne, Jean B.	5:491	*The Black Wolf's Breed*	Dickson, Harris	
Lewis, Meriwether	5:122	*On the Discoveries of Capt. Lewis*	Adams, John Q.	5: 73
“		*The Conquest*	Dye, Eva Emery	13:346
“		*The Rose of Old St. Louis*	Dillon, Mary	
Lincoln, Abraham	2: 65	*A Boy at Gettysburg*	Singmaster, Elsie	C:130
“		*A Fragment—Cabinet Council* (ballad)	Anonymous	
“		*A Man for the Ages*	Bacheller, Irving	C:411
“		*A Song to Abe* (ballad)	W. B.	
“		*A Word from Spain* (poem)	De Perry, Caroline C.	
“		*Commemoration Ode*	Lowell, James Russell	2: 32
“		*Abraham Lincoln* (poem)	Bryant, William Cullen	4: 79
“		“ “	Burleigh, William H.	2:378
“		“ “	Gallagher, William D.	9:250
“		“ “	Lowell, James Russell	2: 32
“		“ “	Stoddard, Richard H.	3:297
“		“ “	Taylor, Tom	
“		*Abraham Lincoln, the Mohammed of the Modern Hegira* (ballad)	Anonymous	
“		*Eben Holden*	Bacheller, Irving	C:411
“		*Father Abraham*	“	
“		*Forever Free*	Morrow, Honoré W.	
“		*Fort Sumter* (poem)	Leverett, Charles E., Jr.	
“		*God Bless Abraham Lincoln!* (poem)	Mason, Caroline A.	4:525
“		*God's Angry Man*	Ehrlich, Leonard	
“		*In Circling Camps*	Altsheler, Joseph A.	11:205
“		*Katy of Catoctin*	Townsend, George A.	1:154
“		*Lincoln's Inaugural Address* (poem)	Anonymous	
“		*Manassas*	Sinclair, Upton	C:114
“		*O Captain! My Captain* (poem)	Whitman, Walt	1:255
“		*On the Life-Mask of Abraham Lincoln* (poem)	Gilder, Richard W.	1:312
“		*On the Wings of Occasion*	Harris, Joel Chandler	1:410
“		*Song of the Southern Women* (poem)	Mildred, Julia	

Character	Novel, Poem, or Play	Author
Lincoln, Abraham 2: 65	*Spanish Peggy*	Catherwood, Mary H. 9:215
"	*Swords of Steel*	Singmaster, Elsie C:130
"	*The Ballad of Abraham Lincoln*	Taylor, Bayard 3:454
"	*The Battleground*	Glasgow, Ellen C:348
"	*The Crisis*	Churchill, Winston 10:178
"	*The Death of Lincoln* (poem)	Rice, Samuel
"	*The Emancipation Group* (poem)	Whittier, John G. 1:407
"	*The Farm*	Bromfield, Louis C:295
"	*The Graysons*	Eggleston, Edward 6: 57
"	*The Hand of Lincoln* (poem)	Stedman, Edmund C. 3:136
"	*The Hoosier Schoolmaster*	Eggleston, Edward 6: 57
"	*The Iron Brigade*	King, Charles 25:148
"	*The Last Full Measure*	Morrow, Honoré W.
"	*The McVeys*	Kirkland, Joseph 5:481
"	*The Martyr* (poem)	Cranch, Christopher P. 7:140
"	*The Pilot that Weathered the Storm* (ballad)	Coggin, Richard
"	*The Prairie Schooner*	Barton, William E. 17:380
"	*The Southerner*	Dixon, Thomas, Jr. 13:189
"	*The Toy Shop*	Gerry, Margarita S.
"	*The Washingtonians*	Mackie, Pauline Bradford
"	*Uncle Abe's Contract* (ballad)	Silsbee, Samuel
"	*When Lilacs Last in the Dooryard Bloomed* (poem)	Whitman, Walt 1:255
"	*With Malice Toward None*	Morrow, Honoré W.
"	*Ye Flyght of Ye Rayl-Splitter* (ballad)	Anonymous
Lincoln, Benjamin 1: 62	*Captain Shays*	Rivers, George R. R.
Lincoln, Mary 2: 75	*On the Wings of Occasion*	Harris, Joel Chandler 1:410
"	*The Last Full Measure*	Morrow, Honoré W.
"	*With Malice Toward None*	"
Lincoln, Robert T. 21: 59	"	"
Lind, Jenny 3:255	*Charles Auchester*	Sheppard, Elizabeth S.
Lindbergh, Charles A. B: 34	*Lindbergh*	Benét, William Rose A:214
"	*The Arrow of Acestes*	Ferril, Thomas H.
"	*The Flight*	Deutsch, Babette
"	*The Wings of Lead*	Crane, Nathalia
Livingston, Philip 3:306	*Cardigan*	Chambers, Robert W. C:402
Livingston, Robert R., Jr. 2:396	*The Rose of Old St. Louis*	Dillon, Mary
Livingston, William 5:201	*The Word of Congress* (poem)	Odell, Jonathan 25:212
Logan, John 10:204	*Logan*	Neal, John 11:346
London, Jack 13:133	*The Days of Her Life*	Irwin, Wallace 14:184
Longfellow, Henry W. 2:160	*Longfellow* (poem)	Riley, James Whitcomb 6: 31
"	*The Poet and the Children* (poem)	Whittier, John G. 1:407
Lovell, Mansfield 4:352	*The New Ballad of Lord Lovell*	Anonymous
"	*Ye Ballad of Mansfield Lovell*	"
Lovewell, John 10:398	*Lovewell's Fight* (ballad)	"
"	*Ode for the Commemoration at Fryeburg*	Longfellow, Henry W. 2:160
"	*The Battle of Lovewell's Pond* (poem)	"
Lowell, James Russell 2: 32	*A Fable for Critics* (poem)	Lowell, James Russell 2: 32
"	*A Good-by* (poem)	Holmes, Oliver Wendell 2:336
"	*A Welcome to Lowell* (poem)	Whittier, John G. 1:407
"	*Elmwood* (poem)	Aldrich, Thomas Bailey 1:283
Lyon, Nathaniel 4:201	*Lyon* (ballad)	Peterson, Henry
"	*There Let Him Sweetly Sleep* (poem)	Bungay, George W.
McClellan, George B. 4:140	*Forever Free*	Morrow, Honoré W.
"	*McClellan* (poem)	Randolph, Anson D. F. 8:460
"	*McClellan's Soliloquy* (ballad)	Anonymous
"	*Tardy George* (ballad)	"
McCosh, James 5:468	*James McCosh* (poem)	Bridges, Robert
McCrea, Jane 10: 88	*The Bride of Fort Edward*	Bacon, Delia S. 1:477
"	*The Columbiad* (poem)	Barlow, Joel 3:186
"	*The Tragical Death of Miss M'Crea* (ballad)	Case, Wheeler
McDowell, Katherine (Margaret Kent) 11:496	*The Story of Margaret Kent*	Kirk, Ellen Olney 1:373
McLoughlin, John 6:390	*The Soul of America*	Dye, Eva Emery 13:346
"	*We Must March*	Morrow, Honoré W.
Macomb, Alexander 2:241	*McComb and McDonough's Victory* (ballad)	Anonymous
Macy, Thomas	*The Exiles* (poem)	Whittier, John G. 1:407
"	*The New Puritan*	Pike, James S. 11:165
Madison, James 5:369	*A Herald of the West*	Altsheler, Joseph A. 11:205
Magoffin, Beriah 13: 8	*The Meeting on the Border* (ballad)	Anonymous
Marion, Francis 1: 59	*A Continental Cavalier*	Scribner, Kimball

Character		Novel, Poem, or Play	Author	
Marion, Francis	1: 59	*Horse-Shoe Robinson*	Kennedy, John C.	
"		*The Song of Marion's Men* (ballad)	Bryant, William Cullen	4: 79
"		*The Swamp Steed*	Eagan, Pierce	
Mason, James M.	2: 93	*A Kongrataletery Pome*	Anonymous	
"		*Ecloga* (ballad)	"	
"		*The C. S. A. Commissioners* (ballad)	"	
Mason, Jeremiah	2:490	*Black Daniel*	Morrow, Honoré W.	
Mason, Stevens T.	2: 9	*The Echo* (poem)	Dwight, Theodore	11:216
Massasoit		*Long Feather the Peace Maker*	Munroe, Kirk	11:523
Mather, Cotton	4:232	*Anne Scarlett*	Taylor, M. Imlay	
"		*Connecticut* (poem)	Halleck, Fitz-Greene	3:226
"		*Giles Corey* (poem)	Longfellow, Henry W.	2:160
"		*The Black Shilling*	Barr, Amelia E.	4:485
"		*The Coast of Freedom*	Shaw, Marie A.	
"		*Ye Lyttle Salem Maide*	Mackie, Pauline Bradford	
Mather, Increase	6:412	*The Romance of the Charter Oak*	Seton, William	
Melvill, Thomas	11:364	*The Last Leaf* (poem)	Holmes, Oliver Wendell	2:336
Mercer, George A.	2:435	*My Lady of Doubt*	Parish, Randall	
Metacom (Indian chief)	10: 60	*The Doomed Chief*	Thompson, Daniel P.	6:233
"		*The Wept of Wish-ton-Wish*	Cooper, J. Fenimore	1:398
Miantonomo (Indian chief)	10:407	" "	"	
Mifflin, Thomas	2:283	*Margaret Moncrieffe*	Burdett, Charles	
Montgomery, Richard	1:100	*Arundel*	Roberts, Kenneth	
"		*At the Siege of Quebec*	Kaler, James Otis	13:475
"		*The Death of General Montgomery* (ballad)	Brackenridge, Hugh H.	8: 49
Morgan, Daniel	1: 84	*A Continental Cavalier*	Scribner, Kimball	
"		*My Lady of Doubt*	Parish, Randall	
"		*Rabble in Arms*	Roberts, Kenneth	
"		*The Battle of the Cowpens* (ballad)	English, Thomas D.	4:322
Morris, George Upham	4:278	*On Board the Cumberland* (ballad)	Boker, George H.	6: 73
"		*The Cumberland* (ballad)	Longfellow, Henry W.	2:160
"		*The Sword Bearer* (poem)	Boker, George H.	6: 73
Morris, Gouverneur	2:526	*The Word of Congress* (poem)	Odell, Jonathan	25:212
Morris, Robert	2:411	*The Word of Congress* (poem)	"	
Morton, Thomas	7:350	*Merry-Mount*	Motley, John L.	5:213
"		*The May-Pole of Merry-Mount*	Hawthorne, Nathaniel	3: 64
Motley, John L.	5:213	*A Parting Health* (poem)	Holmes, Oliver Wendell	2:336
Mott, Valentine	6:281	*Procès Verbal of the Ceremony of Installation* (poem)	Verplanck, Gulian C.	5:405
Mudd, Samuel		*Seven League Boots*	Halliburton, Richard	D:407
Muhlenberg, Peter	1:149	*General Peter Muhlenberg*	Wollenweber, Ludwig A.	11:418
" (Berkley)		*The Wagoner of the Alleghanies* (poem)	Read, Thomas B.	6:474
Murray, John	13:391	*Cardigan*	Chambers, Robert W.	C:402
"		*Henry St. John*	Cooke, John E.	7:330
" (Lord Kidnapper)		*The Fall of British Tyranny* (play)	Leacock, John	
Neal, John	11:346	*A Fable for Critics* (poem)	Lowell, James Russell	2: 32
Nicholson, Sir Francis	13:386	*Flower of the Fort*	Hemstreet, Charles	
Nicolay, John G.	8:170	*Forever Free*	Morrow, Honoré W.	
"		*With Malice Toward None*	"	
Norton, John	7: 36	*John Endicott* (poem)	Longfellow, Henry W.	2:160
Ogden, Peter Skene		*Soil of America*	Dye, Eva Emery	13:346
Oliver, Peter (Lord Chief Justice Hazlerod)	4:344	*The Group* (play)	Warren, Mercy	7:177
O'Neill, Peggy	6:290	*Peggy O'Neill*	Lewis, Alfred H.	25:261
"		*The Rake and the Hussy*	Chambers, Robert W.	C:402
Opechancanough (Indian chief)		*The Youth of the Old Dominion*	Hopkins, Samuel	7:154
Osceola (Indian chief)	9:211	*Osceola*	Sherburne, John H.	
Otis, James (Brutus)	1: 17	*The Adulateur* (play)	Warren, Mercy	7:177
"		*The Rebels*	Child, L. Maria	2:324
Packard, Alpheus Spring	3:102	*Morituri Salutamus* (poem)	Longfellow, Henry W.	2:160
Paine, Thomas	5:412	*The Word of Congress* (poem)	Odell, Jonathan	25:212
Parker, Theodore	2:377	*A Fable For Critics* (poem)	Lowell, James Russell	2: 32
Parris, Samuel	13:166	*Dorothy the Puritan*	Watson, Augusta M.	
Parsons, Thomas W.	5:359	*Tales of a Wayside Inn* (poem)	Longfellow, Henry W.	2:160
Pastorius, Francis D.	11:352	*The Pennsylyvania Pilgrim* (poem)	Whittier, John G.	1:407
Patch, Samuel	5:521	*Monody on Samuel Patch*	Sands, Robert C.	8:354
Paulding, John	13:318	*Brave Paulding and the Spy* (ballad)	Anonymous	
Payne, John Howard	2:347	*The Man Without a Home*	Hughes, Rupert	C:314
Payson, Edward	10: 51	*Scene at the Death-bed of Edward Payson* (poem)	Sigourney, Lydia H.	1:154
Penn, William	2:274	*A Gallant Quaker*	Robertson, Mrs. M. H.	

Character		Novel, Poem, or Play	Author	
Penn, William	2:274	*Acrostic on William Penn*	Rice, Russell	
Pepperrell, Sir William (Sir Sparrow Spendall)	3:330	*The Adulateur* (play)	Warren, Mercy	7:177
Perry, Oliver H.	4:288	*D'ri and I*	Bacheller, Irving	C:411
"		*Perry's Victory on Lake Erie* (poem)	Percival, James G.	8:305
Peters, Samuel	8:339	*M'Fingal* (poem)	Trumbull, John	7:351
Pettigrew, James J.	9:511	*High Tide at Gettysburg* (poem)	Thompson, Will H.	11:522
Phelan, James D.	8:478	*The Days of Her Life*	Irwin, Wallace	14:184
Philip (Indian chief)	10: 50	*Mount Hope*	Hollister, Gideon H.	12: 56
"		*The Doomed Chief*	Thompson, Daniel P.	6:233
Phillips, Wendell	2:314	*Wendell Phillips* (poem)	Lowell, James Russell	2: 32
"		" "	O'Reilly, John B.	1:428
Phillips, William		*Canolles*	Cooke, John E.	7:330
Phips, Sir William	6: 97	*The Trail of the Sword*	Parker, Gilbert	
"		*Ye Lyttle Salem Maide*	Mackie, Pauline Bradford	
Pickett, George E.	5: 49	*High Tide at Gettysburg* (poem)	Thompson, Will H.	11:522
Pike, Zebulon M.	2:516	*As the Crow Flies*	Meigs, Cornelia	
"		*The Death of General Pike* (ballad)	Osborn, Laughton	
Pleasanton, Augustus J. (Peter Keenan)	10:480	*Keenan's Charge* (poem)	Lathrop, George P.	9:193
Pocahontas	7:102	*My Lady Pocahontas*	Cooke, John E.	7:330
"		*Pocahontas* (poem)	Sigourney, Lydia H.	1:154
"		"	Musick, John R.	
"		*Powhatan* (poem)	Smith, Elizabeth O. P.	9:171
"		*The Youth of the Old Dominion*	Hopkins, Samuel	7:154
Poe, Edgar Allan	**1:463**	*A Fable for Critics* (poem)	Lowell, James Russell	2: 32
"		*Edgar Allan Poe* (play)	Hazelton, George C.	
"		*Poe's Cottage at Fordham* (poem)	Boner, John H.	2:497
Polk, James K.	6:265	*54-40 or Fight*	Hough, Emerson	19: 60
Polk, Leonidas	11:341	*The Soldier of the Cross* (poem)	Anonymous	
Ponce De Leon, Juan	11:335	*Romance of the Fountain*	Hamilton, E. Lee	
Pontiac (Indian chief)	10:415	*At War with Pontiac*	Munroe, Kirk	11:523
"		*Pontiac or the Savages* (play)	Rogers, Robert	7:450
Porter, Noah	1:171	*Noah Porter* (poem)	Rogers, Robert C.	15:281
Pory, John	8:416	*The Head of a Hundred*	Goodwin, Maud W.	
Powhatan (Indian chief)	10:413	*Pocahontas* (poem)	Sigourney, Lydia H.	1:154
"		*Powhatan* (poem)	Smith, Elizabeth O. P.	9:171
"		*The Youth of the Old Dominion*	Hopkins, Samuel	7:154
Prescott, William	1: 91	*The Crossed Swords* (poem)	Frothingham, Nathaniel L.	5:120
Price, Sterling	12:304	*General Price's Proclamation* (ballad)	Anonymous	
Prince, Thomas	7:144	*A Ballad of the French Fleet*	Longfellow, Henry W.	2:160
"		*The Lord's Day Gale* (poem)	Stedman, Edmund C.	3:136
Putnam, Israel	1: 87	*A Yankee Volunteer*	Taylor, M. Imlay	
"		*Bunker Hill* (poem)	Cozzens, Frederick S.	6: 29
"		*Bunker's Hill* (dramatic poem)	Brackenridge, Hugh H.	8: 49
"		*Edwin Brothertoft*	Winthrop, Theodore	1:130
"		*Margaret Moncrieffe*	Burdett, Charles	
"		*The Battle of Brooklyn* (farce)	Anonymous	
"		*The Fall of British Tyranny* (play)	Leacock, John	
Rain in the Face (Indian chief)		*On the Big Horn* (poem)	Whittier, John G.	1:407
Raleigh, Sir Walter	7:221	*Raleigh in Guiana* (play)	Wendell, Barrett	9:207
"		*The White King of Manoa*	Hatton, Joseph	
"		*Westward Ho!*	Kingsley, Charles	
Randolph, John	5: 97	*Randolph of Roanoke* (poem)	Whittier, John G.	1:407
Red Cloud (Indian chief)		*Warrior Gap*	King, Charles	25:148
Red Jacket	13:422	*Brant and Red Jacket*	Eggleston, Edward	6: 57
"		*Red Jacket* (poem)	Halleck, Fitz-Greene	3:226
"		*Red Jacket, the Last of the Senecas*	Gordon, H. R.	
Reed, Walter	13:284	*Yellow Jack*	Howard, Sidney	
Renwick, Jane Jeffrey		*Blue-eyed Jeannie* (poem)	Burns, Robert	
Revere, Paul	1: 83	*Paul Revere's Ride* (poem)	Longfellow, Henry W.	2:160
Reynolds, John	11: 44	*The Prairie Schooner*	Barton, William E.	17:380
Riker, Richard	3:385	*The Recorder* (poem)	Halleck, Fitz-Greene	3:226
Ripley, Roswell Sabine	3:299	*Ripley* (poem)	Timrod, Henry	7:473
Ritner, Joseph	2:286	*Ritner* (poem)	Whittier, John G.	1:407
Rivington, James	3:227	*Rivington's Last Will and Testament* (ballad)	Freneau, Philip	6:201
Rodgers, John	5:261	*A Herald of the West*	Altsheler, Joseph A.	11:205
Rogers, Robert	7:450	*Northwest Passage*	Roberts, Kenneth	
Rolfe, John		*The Head of a Hundred*	Goodwin, Maud W.	
"		*To Have and to Hold*	Johnston, Mary	C:430
Roosevelt, Theodore	14: 1	*The Rough Riders*	Hagedorn, Hermann	A:247

Character		Novel, Poem, or Play	Author	
Roosevelt, Theodore	14: 1	*The Teddysee*	Irwin, William H.	C:256
Rose, Aquila	8: 78	*An Elegy*	Keimer, Samuel	
Ross, Betsey	12:438	*Betsey Ross*	Hotchkiss, Chauncey C.	
Royal, Anne Newport		*The Gorgeous Hussy*	Adams, Samuel H.	14:166
Rush, Benjamin	3:333	*Hugh Wynne*	Mitchell, S. Weir	9:346
Rutledge, John	1: 21	*A Carolina Cavalier*	Eggleston, George C.	1:213
Sacajawea	13:419	*The Conquest*	Dye, Eva Emery	13:346
St. Clair, Arthur	1: 94	*General St. Clair* (poem)	Sigourney, Lydia H.	1:154
"		*The Heritage*	Stevenson, Burton E.	13:143
"		*The Linwoods*	Sedgwick, Catharine M.	1:446
St. Leger, Barry		*The Patrol of the Mountain*	Curtis, Newton M.	4:328
"		*Son of a Tory*	Scollard, Clinton	23:160
Samoset (Indian chief)		*Standish of Standish*	Austin, Jane G.	6: 62
Sansome, Emma		*Emma Sansome* (poem)	Moore, John T.	13:138
Santa Anna		*Remember the Alamo!*	Barr, Amelia E.	4:485
Sassacus (Indian chief)		*Sassacus* (poem)	Green, Frances H.	
"		*The Knight of the Golden Melice*	Adams, John T.	
Scammell, Alexander	2:261	*The Address* (poem)	Humphreys, David	1: 71
Schuyler, Lady		*The Maid-at-Arms*	Chambers, Robert W.	C:402
Schuyler, Philip J.	4: 97	"	"	
"		*In the Valley*	Frederic, Harold	5:358
Schuyler Family		*The Royal Americans*	Foote, Mary Hallock	6:407
Scott, Winfield	3:502	*A National Trio* (poem)	Anonymous	
"		*Scott and the Veteran* (poem)	Taylor, Bayard	3:454
"		*Song on General Scott*	N. B. T.	
"		*Winfield Scott* (poem)	Stoddard, Richard H.	3:297
Sewall, Samuel	5:339	*The Prophecy of Samuel Sewall* (poem)	Whittier, John G.	1:407
Seward, William H.	2: 77	*Katy of Catoctin*	Townsend, George A.	1:154
Shafter, William R.	9: 18	*The Rough Riders*	Hagedorn, Hermann	A:247
Sharpe, Horatio	7:337	*Richard Carvel*	Churchill, Winston	10:178
Shaw, Robert G.	8:142	*Ode on the Unveiling of the Shaw Monument*	Aldrich, Thomas Bailey	1:283
Shays, Daniel	2:137	*Captain Shays*	Rivers, George R. R.	
"		*Raw Material*	Fisher, Dorothy Canfield	18: 63
"		*The Duke of Stockbridge*	Bellamy, Edward	1:263
Sheridan, Philip H.	4: 63	*Action at Aquila*	Allen, Hervey	
"		*Joined the Blues* (ballad)	Rooney, James J.	
"		*Shenandoah* (play)	Howard, Bronson	3: 75
"		*Sheridan's Ride* (ballad)	Read, Thomas B.	6:474
Sherman, John	3:198	*The Farm*	Bromfield, Louis	C:295
Sherman, William T.	4: 32	*Gone With the Wind*	Mitchell, Margaret	
"		*Sherman* (poem)	Gilder, Richard W.	1:312
"		*Sherman's March to the Sea* (song)	Byers, Samuel H. M.	14:150
"		*The Battleground*	Glasgow, Ellen	C:348
"		*The Crisis*	Churchill, Winston	10:178
Shirley, William	7:375	*Agnes Surriage*	Bynner, Edwin L.	7:486
Sill, Edward Rowland	7:249	*The Letter* (poem)	Aldrich, Thomas Bailey	1:283
Simms, W. Gilmore	6:204	*Peter Ashley*	Heyward, DuBose	
Sitting Bull	13:454	*The Book of the American Indian*	Garland, Hamlin	8: 37
Slidell, John	2: 93	*A Kongrataletery Pome*	Anonymous	
"		*Ecloga* (poem)	"	
"		*The C. S. A. Commissioners* (ballad)	"	
Smith, Deaf	2:108	*The Fight at San Jacinto* (poem)	Palmer, John W.	8:222
Smith, John	13:378	*John O'Jamestown*	Kester, Vaughan	25:285
"		*The Youth of the Old Dominion*	Hopkins, Samuel	7:154
Smith, Joseph	16: 1	*The Mormon Prophet*	Dougall, Lillie	
"		*The Prophet*	Riddle, Albert G.	2:371
Smybert, John	5:325	*Agnes Surriage*	Bynner, Edwin L.	7:486
Somers, Richard	8:412	*Decatur and Somers*	Seawell, Molly E.	7:253
"		*Richard Somers* (poem)	Eastman, Barrett	
Spotswood, Alexander (Blackbeard)	13:387	*Kate Bonnet*	Stockton, Francis R.	1:396
Standish, Miles	5:417	*An Interview with Miles Standish* (poem)	Longfellow, Henry W.	2:160
"		*Exploits of Myles Standish*	Johnson, Henry	
"		*Merry-Mount*	Motley, John L.	5:213
"		*Standish of Standish*	Austin, Jane G.	6: 62
"		*The Courtship of Miles Standish* (poem)	Longfellow, Henry W.	2:160
Standish, Rose		*Barbara Standish*	Austin, Jane G.	6: 62
"		*Her Picture* (poem)	Hutchinson, Ellen M.	
Stanton, Edward		*Forever Free*	Morrow, Honoré W.	
Stanton, Edwin M.	2: 83	*On the Wings of Occasion*	Harris, Joel Chandler	1:410
" (Secretary West)		*The Washingtonians*	Mackie, Pauline Bradford	

Character		Novel, Poem, or Play	Author	
Stark, John	1: 80	*Bennington* (poem)	Babcock, William H.	
"		*Connecticut* (poem)	Halleck, Fitz-Greene	3:226
"		*Hester of the Grants*	Peck, Theodora	
"		*Northwest Passage*	Roberts, Kenneth	
Stewart, Charles	8:156	*The Old Admiral* (poem)	Stedman, Edmund C.	3:136
Stirling, Lord	1: 16	*Lord Stirling's Stand* (ballad)	Babcock, William H.	20:373
Stoneman, George	4:112	*O Stoneman's Up and Away, Boys!* (ballad)	Anonymous	
Stowe, Harriet Beecher	1:423	*A Greeting* (poem)	Whittier, John G.	1:407
"		*Harriet Beecher Stowe* (poem)	Dunbar, Paul L.	9:276
Stuart, J. E. B.	4: 51	*God's Angry Man*	Ehrlich, Leonard	
"		*Katy of Catoctin*	Townsend, George A.	1:154
"		*Mohun*	Cooke, John E.	7:330
"		*Surry of Eagle's Nest*	"	
Sturgis, James Garland		*Miles Keogh's Horse* (poem)	Hay, John	11: 12
Stuyvesant, Peter	5:138	*Barnaby Lee*	Bennett, John	
"		*Peter Stuyvesant's New Year's Call* (poem)	Longfellow, Henry W.	2:160
"		*Rembrandt van Ryn*	Van Loon, Hendrik W.	B: 44
"		*The Maid of Old New York*	Barr, Amelia E.	4:485
Sullivan, John	1: 56	*Arundel*	Roberts, Kenneth	
"		*Margaret Moncrieffe*	Burdett, Charles	
"		*The Battle of Brooklyn* (farce)	Anonymous	
"		*The Word of Congress* (poem)	Odell, Jonathan	25:212
Sumner, Charles	3:300	*Charles Sumner* (poem)	Whittier, John G.	1:407
"		*Sumner* (poem)	Longfellow, Henry W.	2:160
"		*Three Friends of Mine* (poem)	"	
"		*With Malice Toward None*	Morrow, Honoré W.	
Sutter, John A.	4:191	*Gold*	White, Stewart Edward	13:313
Tabor, Horace A. W.	11: 92	*The Days of Her Life*	Irwin, Wallace	14:184
Tallmadge, Benjamin	1: 90	*A Continental Cavalier*	Scribner, Kimball	
Tammany (Indian chief)		*The Echo* (poem)	Dwight, Theodore	11:216
"		*The Fall of British Tyranny* (play)	Leacock, John	
"		*The Last of the Mohicans*	Cooper, J. Fenimore	1:398
Tarleton, Sir Banastre		*A Continental Cavalier*	Scribner, Kimball	
"		*The Battle of the Cowpens* (ballad)	English, Thomas D.	4:322
Taylor, Bayard	3:454	*Bayard Taylor* (poem)	Aldrich, Thomas Bailey	1:283
"		" "	Longfellow, Henry W.	2:160
Taylor, Zachary	4:367	*Buena Vista* (ballad)	O'Hara, Theodore	4:362
"		*The Bivouac of the Dead* (ballad)	"	
Tecumseh (Indian chief)	11:363	*Tecumseh and the Shawnee Prophet*	Eggleston, Edward	6: 57
Terry, David S.	12:104	*In the Gray Dawn*	White, Stewart Edward	13:313
Thayendanegea	9:142	*Brant and Red Jacket*	Eggleston, Edward	6: 57
"		*Drums Along the Mohawk*	Edmonds, Walter D.	
"		*The Maid-at-Arms*	Chambers, Robert W.	C:402
Thompson, John R.	6: 49	*A Grave in the Hollywood Cemetery* (poem)	Preston, Margaret J.	7:147
Thoreau, Henry D.	2:300	*God's Angry Man*	Ehrlich, Leonard	
Tichenor, Isaac	8:313	*Hester of the Grants*	Peck, Theodora	
Tilden, Samuel J.	3: 53	*Samuel J. Tilden* (poem)	Whittier, John G.	1:407
Todd, John (The Parson)	8:125	*The Birds of Killingworth* (poem)	Longfellow, Henry W.	2:160
Treadwell, Daniel	10:165	*Tales of a Wayside Inn*	"	
Trumbull, John	3:334	*The Declaration of Independence* (poem)	Drake, Joseph R.	5:420
Truxtun, Thomas	2:431	*Truxtun's Victory* (ballad)	Anonymous	
Tyler, John	6: 1	*54-40 or Fight*	Hough, Emerson	19: 60
Uncas (Indian chief)	12:461	*Last Days of Uncas* (poem)	Benjamin, Park	7:166
"		*The Wept of Wish-ton-Wish*	Cooper, J. Fenimore	1:398
Vallandigham, Clement L.	3:145	*Waits and Watches on the Border* (ballad)	Quinby, J. B.	
Van Buren, Martin	6:433	*The Partisan Leader*	Tucker, Beverley	
Vanderlip, Frank A.	15: 29	*The Earthquake*	Train, Arthur	14:427
Van Schaick, Goose	1: 78	*Drums Along the Mohawk*	Edmonds, Walter D.	
Wadsworth, Joseph		*The Romance of the Charter Oak*	Seton, William	
Wallace, Zerelda G.	5:404	*Ben Hur*	Wallace, Lew	4:363
Warner, Seth	1: 86	*Hester of the Grants*	Peck, Theodora	
Warren, Joseph	1: 57	*Bunker Hill* (poem)	Cozzens, Frederick S.	6: 29
"		*Bunker's Hill* (dramatic poem)	Brackenridge, Hugh H.	8: 49
"		*Death of Warren* (poem)	Sargent, Epes	7:243
"		*Old Boston*	Stevens, A. De Grasse	
"		*Poem Containing some Remarks on the Present War*	Anonymous	
" (Portius)		*The Adulateur* (play)	Warren, Mercy	7:177
"		*Warren's Address* (poem)	Pierpont, John	6:155
Warren, Mercy	7:177	*My Lady Laughter*	Tilton, Dwight	
Washington, George	1: 1	*A Soldier of Virginia*	Stevenson, Burton E.	13:143

Character		Novel, Poem, or Play	Author	
Washington, George	1: 1	*A Virginia Cavalier*	Seawell, Molly E.	7:253
"		*A Yankee Volunteer*	Taylor, M. Imlay	
"		*Arnold and André* (poem)	Calvert, George H.	5:357
"		*Betsy Ross*	Hotchkiss, Chauncey C.	
"		*Columbia's Glory* (poem)	Prime, Benjamin Y.	6:392
"		*Edwin Brothertoft*	Winthrop, Theodore	1:130
"		*From Kingdom to Colony*	Devereaux, Mary	
"		*George Washington* (poem)	Ingham, John H.	
"		*His Excellency, George Washington* (poem)	Wheatley, Phillis	1:259
"		*Hugh Wynne*	Mitchell, S. Weir	9:346
"		*In Blue and White*	Brooks, Elbridge S.	7:156
"		*In Hostile Red*	Altsheler, Joseph A.	11:205
"		*Janice Meredith*	Ford, Paul Leicester	13:105
"		*Master Simon's Garden*	Meigs, Cornelia	
"		*Mount Vernon, an Ode*	Humphreys, David	1: 71
"		*My Lady of Doubt*	Parish, Randall	
"		*Ode for Washington's Birthday*	Holmes, Oliver Wendell	2:336
"		*Ode to Washington*	Pierpont, John	6:155
"		*Old Boston*	Stevens, A. De Grasse	
"		*Poem Containing some Remarks on the Present War*	Anonymous	
"		*Rabble in Arms*	Roberts, Kenneth	
"		*Richard Carvel*	Churchill, Winston	10:178
"		*Song Composed for Washington's Birthday*	Timrod, Henry	7:473
"		*The Battle of Brooklyn* (farce)	Anonymous	
"		*The Battle of Bunker's Hill* (ballad)	Brackenridge, Hugh H.	8: 49
"		*The Confederate Cavalry*	Seawell, Molly E.	7:253
"		*The Days of Poor Richard*	Bacheller, Irving	C:411
"		*The Fall of British Tyranny* (play)	Leacock, John	
"		*The Foresters*	Belknap, Jeremy	7:204
"		*The Heart of Washington*	Knox, Dorothea H.	
"		*The Master of Chaos*	Bacheller, Irving	C:411
"		*The Portrait* (poem)	Pierpont, John	6:155
"		*The Spy*	Cooper, J. Fenimore	1:398
"		*The Virginians*	Thackeray, William M.	
"		*The Vow of Washington* (poem)	Whittier, John G.	1:407
"		*The Word of Congress* (poem)	Odell, Jonathan	25:212
"		*The Youth of Washington*	Mitchell, S. Weir	9:346
"		*Under Colonial Colors*	Tomlinson, Everett T.	25:435
"		*Under the Elm* (poem)	Lowell, James Russell	2: 32
"		*Verses on the Grave of Washington*	Davidson, Lucretia M.	7:476
"		*Washington* (poem)	Case, Wheeler	
"		" "	Pierpont, John	6:155
"		*Washington and His Generals*	Lippard, George	
"		*With Washington in the West*	Stratemeyer, Edward	16: 37
Washington, Martha	1: 7	*A Yankee Volunteer*	Taylor, M. Imlay	
"		*Martha Washington* (poem)	Lanier, Sidney	2:438
Wayne, Anthony	1: 55	*Canolles*	Cooke, John E.	7:330
"		*The Cow-Chase* (ballad)	André, John	1: 48
Webster, Daniel	3: 36	*A Kentucky Chronicle*	Gray, J. Thompson	
"		*Black Daniel*	Morrow, Honoré W.	
"		*54-40 or Fight*	Hough, Emerson	19: 60
"		*Ichabod* (poem)	Whittier, John G.	1:407
"		*On the Death of Webster* (poem)	Parsons, Thomas W.	5:359
"		*The Birthday of Daniel Webster* (poem)	Holmes, Oliver Wendell	2:336
"		*The Lost Occasion* (poem)	Whittier, John G.	1:407
"		*The Voice of Webster* (poem)	Johnson, Robert U.	C:519
"		*Webster: An Ode*	Wilkinson, William C.	11: 72
Welles, Gideon	2: 86	*Forever Free*	Morrow, Honoré W.	
"		*With Malice Toward None*	"	
Wentworth, Benning	6:303	*Northwest Passage*	Roberts, Kenneth	
Wentworth, Mrs. Benning		*Lady Wentworth* (poem)	Longfellow, Henry W.	2:160
Wesley, John	5: 57	*Hetty Wesley*	Quiller-Couch, A. T.	
"		*The Birthright*	Hocking, Joseph	
West, Benjamin	5:322	*Northwest Passage*	Roberts, Kenneth	
Whalley, Edward	11:458	*Shad and Shed*	Edwards, E. T.	
Wheeler, Joseph	9: 19	*The Rough Riders*	Hagedorn, Hermann	A:247
Whitefield, George	5:384	*Bernicia*	Barr, Amelia E.	4:485
"		*Diary of Mrs. Kitty Trevylyan*	Charles, Mrs. E. R.	
Whitefield, George	5:384	*The Preacher* (poem)	Whittier, John G.	1:407
"		*The Rebels*	Child, L. Maria	2:324

Character	Novel, Poem, or Play	Author
Whitman, Marcus 11:112	*We Must March*	Morrow, Honoré W.
Whitman, Walt 1:255	*Walt Whitman* (poem)	Morris, Harrison S. 10:219
"	" "	Williams, Francis H. 10: 49
Whittier, John G. 1:407	*A Fable for Critics* (poem)	Lowell, James Russell 2: 32
"	*Whittier* (poem)	Sangster, Margaret E. 6:169
Wilkinson, James 1: 56	*Arundel*	Roberts, Kenneth
Willett, Marinus 3:378	*Drums Along the Mohawk*	Edmonds, Walter D.
Williams, Eleazer 1: 68	*Lazarre*	Catherwood, Mary H. 9:215
"	*The Lost Dauphin*	Stevens, Augusta De G.
Williams, Eunice	*Great-Grandmother's Girls in New France*	Champney, Elizabeth W. 11:308
Williams, Roger 10: 4	*Mistress Content Craddock*	Trumbull, Annie E.
"	*Roger Williams* (poem)	Whitman, Sarah H. P. 8:145
"	*The Doomed Chief*	Thompson, Daniel P. 6:233
"	*What Cheer* (poem)	Durfee, Job 7:414
Willis, Nathaniel P. 3:108	*A Fable for Critics* (poem)	Lowell, James Russell 2: 32
Wilson, Henry 4: 13	*Wilson* (poem)	Whittier, John G. 1:407
Wilson, Henry L. 12:126	*The Stones Awake*	Beals, Carleton D:442
Wilson, Woodrow 19: 1	*Black River*	"
"	*Death and Birth of David Markand*	Frank, Waldo A:398
Wingfield, Edward M. 13:377	*The Youth of the Old Dominion*	Hopkins, Samuel 7:154
Winslow, Edward 1:200	*Standish of Standish*	Austin, Jane G. 6: 62
Winslow, John A. 2:102	*The Kearsage and the Alabama* (ballad)	Anonymous
Winthrop, Fitz-John 10:324	*Brief Account of the Agency of the Hon. John Winthrop* (poem)	Wolcott, Roger 10:326
Winthrop, John 6:201	*The Knight of the Golden Melice*	Adams, John T.
Winthrop, Theodore 1:130	*Bethel* (poem)	Duganne, Augustine J. H. 4:315
Wirt, William 6: 86	*Last Hours of William Wirt* (poem)	Sigourney, Lydia H. 1:154
Wolfe, James 1:102	*Heroic Poem on War*	Cockings, George
"	*The Seats of the Mighty*	Parker, Gilbert
"	*With Wolfe in Canada*	Henty, George A.
Wood, Leonard 9: 20	*The Rough Riders*	Hagedorn, Hermann A:247
Woolman, John 1:288	*John Woolman* (poem)	Chandler, Elizabeth M.
Wright, Silas 3: 47	*The Light in the Clearing*	Bacheller, Irving C:411
"	*The Lost Statesman* (poem)	Whittier, John G. 1:407
Yancey, William L. 4:319	*Manassas*	Sinclair, Upton C:114
Young, Brigham 16: 3	*The Portrait*	Riddle, Albert G. 2:371
Zane, Elizabeth	*Betty Zane*	Grey, Zane B:114
Zinzendorf, Nicholas L. 2:170	*Zinzendorf* (poem)	Sigourney, Lydia H. 1:154

Pseudonyms and Sobriquets

A.

Pseudonym / Sobriquet	Reference	Name
A. Fiske Shelley	11: 333	Gerard, Jr.
A. Lunar Wray	1: 351	Savage
A. Men Dur	9: 77	Burnham
A. T. Sechand	8: 68	Lee
A. W. Farmer	3: 475	Seabury
Abe, Honest	2: 65	Lincoln
Abolition, Father of	7: 154	Hopkins
Abraham, Father	1: 328	Franklin
Abraham, Father	2: 65	Lincoln
Abraham Page	6: 277	Holt
Accomac, Apostle of the	11: 384	Makemie
Adam, Bigliar	21: 103	Bailey
Adams, Moses	24: 102	Bagby
Addison of America	7: 204	Dennie
Addison of America	10: 121	Kingsley
Adeler, Max	14: 400	Clark
Adina	7: 413	Ingraham
Adirondack	13: 553	Chittenden
Adirondack Murray	10: 230	Murray
Admiral of New England	13: 378	Smith
Admiral, Old	3: 436	Columbus
Æsop	11: 61	Blake
Æsop, G. Washington	8: 90	Lanigan
African Astronomer	5: 36	Banneker
Afterwit, Anthony	1: 328	Franklin
Agamemnon, Old	5: 54	Carrington
Agassiz, Methodist	13: 536	Marcy
Agate	22: 1	Reid
Aglaus	7: 473	Timrod
Agnes Hampton	12: 294	Smith
Ago, Felix	9: 246	Haldeman
Agricola	13: 131	Elliott
Agricultural Moses	12: 181	Tillman
Aiken Hart	12: 471	Helmuth
Aimwell, Walter	5: 120	Simonds
Akers, Elizabeth	6: 133	Allen
Akers, Floyd	18: 332	Baum
Alabama, Talleyrand of	18: 371	McGillivray
Albani	9: 119	Gye
Albert Edwards	21: 392	Bullard
Albertine, Mlle.	9: 209	Manchester
Albin	11: 219	Lindstrand
Alcott, Ten	10: 237	Totten
Alden of the Times	6: 326	Alden
Alex	13: 495	White
Alexander, Master	9: 327	Herrmann
Alfred Ayres	9: 125	Osmun
Algernon, Sidney	5: 391	Granger
Algiers, Native of	13: 180	Markoe
Ali Bey	7: 472	Knapp
Alice Caldwell Hegan	14: 484	Rice
Alice, Cousin	5: 386	Haven
Alice Eliot	1: 374	Jewett
Alice G. Lee	5: 386	Haven
Alice Hawthorne	1: 310	Winner
Allan, Major	3: 208	Pinkerton
Allen, Earthquake	3: 142	Allen
Allen, Grahame	9: 432	Arnold
Allen, John W., Jr.	8: 79	Lesley
Almore, Caspar	1: 342	Beasley
Altamont	8: 222	Palmer
Ambrose, Paul	6: 181	Kennedy
Amelia	6: 503	Welby
Amélie Rives	B: 293	Troubetzkoy
Amen Durst	10: 107	Amen
America, Atlas of	1: 1	Washington
America, Cincinnatus of	1: 1	Washington
America, Deliverer of	1: 1	Washington
America, Father of	1: 104	Adams
America, Moses of	10: 116	Wise
America, Murat of	9: 168	Wheat
American, Native of	13: 191	Parke
America, Newman of	11: 358	Hewitt
America, Watt of	6: 66	Evans
American, An	1: 9	Hamilton
American, An	2: 526	Morris
American, An	5: 249	Watson
American, An	6: 392	Prime
American, An	9: 468	Brackenridge
American, An	13: 131	Elliott
American Addison, the	7: 204	Dennie
American Addison, the	10: 121	Kingsley
American Anthracite Industry, Father of	3: 360	Thomas
American Anthropology, Father of	6: 192	Morgan
American Ballad Poetry, Father of	11: 363	Hewitt
American Baptists, Father of	7: 346	Clarke
American Bar, Erskine of the	11: 84	Hoffman
American Bewick, the	6: 259	Anderson
American Blackstone	7: 136	Tucker
American Bridge Building, Father of	9: 35	Whipple
American Cato, the	1: 104	Adams
American Charles Lamb, the	3: 96	Curtis
American Chesterfield, the	8: 295	Riker
American Cicero, the	5: 298	Berrien
American Commerce With India, Father of	4: 545	Derby
American Cotton Industry, Father of	6: 14	Coxe
American Cruikshank, the	5: 519	Johnston
American Democracy, Father of	6: 279	Hooker
American Devil, the	13: 130	McDougal
American Diplomacy, Father of	2: 380	Marsh
American Fabius, the	1: 1	Washington
American Farmer	8: 253	Crevecoeur
American, Fiery	10: 132	Thompson
American Geography, Father of	13: 352	Morse
American Goldsmith, the	1: 434	Woodworth
American, Hemans, the	1: 154	Sigourney
American Howard, the	3: 512	Eddy
American Kipling, the	13: 133	London
American Mapmaking, Father of	19: 208	Gannett
American Mathematics, Nestor of	8: 153	Peirce
American Meissonier, the	13: 369	Watrous
American Navy, Father of	5: 110	Humphreys
American Pharmacy, Father of	5: 347	Procter
American Piano, Father of the	6: 190	Chickering
American Professor, the	6: 419	Felton
American Revolution, Day-star of	13: 298	Hamilton
American Revolution, Father of	1: 104	Adams
American Revolution, Navarre of	8: 84	Butler, J.
American Richard Savage, the	1: 463	Poe
American Romulus, the	12: 374	Stevenson
American Sappho, the	8: 370	Morton
American Shipmaster, the	13: 584	Codman
American Socrates, the	1: 328	Franklin
American Stage, Queen of the	6: 60	Duff
American Strauss	14: 518	Englander
American Stuart, the	5: 324	Stuart
American Surgery, Father of	6: 391	Physick
American Titian, the	5: 383	Allston

B.

Pseudonym	Ref.	Name
Biglow, Hosea	2: 32	Lowell
Bill Arp	3: 308	Smith
Bill Barney	18: 208	Bonner
Bill, Bloody	7: 60	Fanning
Bill, Buffalo	5: 483	Cody
Bill Nye	6: 26	Nye
Bill Snort, Col.	6: 69	Sweet
Billings, Josh	6: 28	Shaw
Billy, Extra	5: 451	Smith
Birch, Harry	6: 231	White
Bishop, Good	5: 486	Otey
Bizarre	2: 214	Young
Black Eagle	23: 74	Cobb
Black Fish	3: 111	Boone
Black Jack	4: 299	Logan
Black Patti	13: 424	Jones
Black Spurgeon of America	13: 37	Walker
Blacksmith, Learned	6: 133	Burritt
Blacksnake	1: 55	Wayne
Blackstone, American	7: 136	Tucker
Blanchan, Neltje	13: 400	DoubledayN.B.D.
Blank Etcetera	6: 217	Winthrop
Blind Boat Builder	12: 353	Herreshoff
Blind Historian	6: 57	Prescott
Blind Poet	11: 150	Heady
Blind Preacher	7: 157	Milburn
Blind Sculptor	8: 283	Mundy
Blind Senator	14: 323	Gore
Blind Tom	10: 198	Wiggins
Blizzard, Old	4: 364	Loring
Blodgett, Levi	2: 377	Parker
Bloody Bill	7: 60	Fanning
Blue Jacket	9: 377	Dahlgren
Blue-jeans Williams	13: 272	Williams
Bluff, Bachelor	2: 512	Bunce
Bluff, Harry	6: 35	Maury
Bluster	1: 17	Otis
Bly, Nellie	1: 241	Cochrane
Blythe White	3: 454	Robinson
Boat Builder, Blind	12: 353	Herreshoff
Bob Burdette	1: 235	Burdette
Bob, Fiddling	8: 366	Taylor
Bob, Fighting	9: 13	Evans
Bob Lee	3: 165	Lee
Bob Short	1: 517	Longstreet
Boersianer	17: 16	Friend
Bold Bean Hill Man	12: 234	Durkee
Bonehill, Captain Ralph	16: 37	Stratemeyer
Bonner, Sherwood	11: 496	McDowell
Boone, Benjamin F. Johnson of	6: 31	Riley
Boscawen	11: 228	Greene
Botheration Primus	5: 374	Niles
Botheration Secundus	5: 374	Niles
Boy, Benicia	3: 370	Leslie
Boy Preacher	6: 217	Lipscomb
Boy Preacher	12: 292	Furman
Boy Preacher	12: 536	Stover
Braddock Field	10: 176	Dimitry
Brains of the Confederacy	4: 285	Benjamin
Brains, Old	4: 257	Halleck
Branford, Father of	13: 472	Bogue
Brannigan, Calvin	8: 265	Roche
Bread-father	13: 346	Sower
Breakfast Table, Autocrat of the	2: 336	Holmes
Breitmann, Hans	5: 356	Leland
Bret Harte	1: 404	Harte
Brick, Pomeroy	2: 502	Pomeroy
Bridge-building, Father of American	9: 35	Whipple
Bridges, Madeline S.	8: 440	De Vere
Brigadier	4: 322	English
Briscoe, Margaret Sutton	5: 524	Hopkins
British American, A	9: 548	Mason
Britt, Bailey of	22: 103	Bailey
Brooke, Wesley	6: 536	Lunt
Brooks, Chatty	5: 540	Rice
Brother Azarias	7: 525	Mullany
Brother Jonathan	10: 328	Trumbull
Brown, Ossawatomie	2: 307	Brown
Brown, Van Dyke	13: 375	Cook
Browne, Dunn	11: 438	Fiske
Brownlow, Parson	7: 210	Brownlow
Brunswick	8: 441	Gilder
Brutus	2: 382	Ames
Brutus	5: 543	Simpson
Brutus, Junius	2: 114	Hillyard
Brutus, Lucius Junius	7: 139	Cranch
Buck, Old	5: 1	Buchanan
Buckeye	9: 226	Arnold
Buddha of the West	3: 416	Emerson
Buena Vista, Old	4: 367	Taylor
Buffalo Bill	5: 483	Cody
Buffalo Head	2: 192	Ochiltree
Bull Dog, Federal	3: 431	Martin
Bull Dog Ferguson	2: 43	De Peyster, A. S.
Bullion, Old	4: 399	Benton
Bullus, Hector	7: 193	Paulding
Buntline, Ned	13: 194	Judson
Bunyan, Modern	10: 19	Miller
Burchelle, Old	6: 133	Burritt
Burdette, Bob	1: 235	Burdette
Burgomaster, The	16: 67	Busse
Burleigh	2: 34	Smith
Burns of the Green Mountains	9: 252	Eastman
Burroughs, Ellen	12: 198	Jewett
Burton	4: 217	Habberton
Busby, Scriblerus	5: 405	Verplanck
Bushwhacker, Dr.	6: 29	Cozzens
Busy Body	1: 328	Franklin
Butler, Picayune	5: 297	Butler

C.

Pseudonym	Ref.	Name
C. Auton	9: 483	Hoppin
C. E. Raimond	10: 377	Pennell
C. Effingham, Esq.	7: 330	Cooke
C. G. David	11: 234	Croly
C. O. Nevers	8: 449	Converse
Cabinet, Old	1: 312	Gilder
Cain, Tubal	11: 508	Holley
Calcraft, Henry	5: 145	Schoolcraft
Caliban of Science	10: 62	Ramsey
Calico Charlie	1: 139	Foster
Callisthenes	1: 19	Quincy
Cambray	6: 59	Fennell
Camillo Querno	9: 123	Boucher
Camillus	1: 9	Hamilton
Camillus	2: 383	Ames
Camillus	6: 301	King
Camillus	8: 180	Duane
Candor	2: 394	Webster
Candor, Toby	5: 367	Whitman
Canfield, Dorothy	18: 62	Fisher
Cannon, Uncle Joe	22: 4	Cannon
Capelsay, John	6: 277	Holt
Captain Hugh Fitzgerald	18: 332	Baum
Captain, Puritan	5: 417	Standish
Captain Ralph Bonehill	16: 37	Stratemeyer
Captain Ringbolt	13: 584	Codman
Carl Benson	6: 366	Bristed
Carl de Muldor	8: 423	Miller
Carleton	1: 438	Coffin
Caro	4: 525	Mason
Caroline Thomas	6: 56	Dorr
Carson, Kit	3: 278	Carson
Cartaphilus	7: 129	Hoffman
Carter, King	13: 388	Carter
Carver, John, Esq.	11: 233	Dodge
Casca	6: 140	Thompson

Pseudonym	Reference	Name
Caspar Almore	1: 342	Beasley
Caspipina	4: 384	Duché
Cassio	4: 527	Gould
Cassius	7: 133	Bland, T.
Cassius	11: 156	Tibbitts
Castine	7: 57	Brooks
Catherine N. Sinclair	5: 86	Forrest
Cato	1: 10	Hamilton
Cato	2: 396	Livingston
Cato	5: 180	Higginson
Cato	11: 156	Tibbitts
Caucus, King	11: 251	Stilwell
Caustic, Christopher	7: 260	Fessenden
Cavazza, E.	8: 373	Pullen
Caxton	7: 45	Rhodes
Cecil de Groot	13: 199	Rice
Celia Single	1: 328	Franklin
Cerberus	13: 555	Dole
Cerberus of the Treasury	1: 22	Ellsworth
Chaff, Gumbo	4: 432	Howe
Champ	11: 308	Champney
Chandler, Bessie	6: 259	Anderson
Chapultepec, Old	3: 502	Scott
Charles Egbert Craddock	2: 363	Murfree
Charles Observator	4: 176	Sabin
Charles Sherry	7: 243	Sargent
Charleston, Hero of	8: 238	Lee
Charley, Silent	13: 574	Murphy
Charlie, Calico	1: 139	Foster
Chatty Brooks	5: 540	Rice
Cheeki, Tono	6: 201	Freneau
Chesney, Esther	7: 545	MacLean
Chester, John	5: 514	Mitchell
Chesterfield, American	8: 294	Riker
Chesterfield of the Navy	4: 413	Le Roy
Chevalier	1: 316	Wikoff
Chevalier, H. E.	8: 378	Sears
Chickamauga, Old	4: 395	Steedman
Chickamauga, Rock of	4: 48	Thomas
Chicot	7: 243	Sargent
Chief, Old	5: 77	Clay
Children's Friend	10: 166	Brace
Chordal	9: 506	Lee
Christian Reid	20: 293	Tiernan
Christian Statesman	3: 401	Frelinghuysen
Christopher Caustic	7: 260	Fessenden
Christopher Crowfield	1: 423	Stowe
Christy, George	23: 305	Christy
Chrysantheus	3: 289	Harris
Churton, Henry	7: 324	Tourgee
Cicero, American	5: 298	Berrien
Cicero of the Senate	1: 452	Robbins
Cider, Hard	3: 33	Harrison
Cincinnatus	11: 124	Plumer
Cincinnatus of America	1: 1	Washington
Cincinnatus of the West	3: 33	Harrison
Citizen	2: 352	Sherman
Citizen of Brooklyn, First	3: 433	Stranahan
Citizen, First	9: 234	Dulaney
Civil War, Napoleon of the	4: 1	Grant
Civil War, Thermopylæ of the	4: 103	Hill
Clarissa Packard	6: 259	Gilman
Clara Moreton	9: 473	Moore
Clarke, Nina Gray	6: 235	Clarke
Clary-Squire, Claudia	7: 545	MacLean
Claudia	7: 545	MacLean
Claudia Clary-Squire	7: 545	MacLean
Clavers, Mary	5: 356	Kirkland
Clementine	7: 487	Howarth
Clemmer, Mary	7: 233	Ames
Clergyman	3: 523	Fish
Clinton, Dangerfield	13: 312	Bryan
Clubs, Jack of	4: 63	Sheridan
Clubs, Mother of	8: 108	Severance
Cobbler, The Natick	4: 13	Wilson
Cocked Hats, Last of the	5: 516	Mease
Cockloft, Esq.	9: 383	Irving
Coin Harvey	18: 16	Harvey
Coffin, Peter	5: 393	Parsons
Coffinberry, Good Count	3: 396	Coffinberry
Cole, Father	2: 446	Cole
Coleman	8: 334	Davis
Coles, Miriam	11: 515	Harris
College Puritan	7: 75	Sherman
Collins, Percy	15: 232	Collier
Col. Bill Snort	6: 69	Sweet
Colonel, Fighting	19: 170	Galbraith
Colonial Wallis	22: 208	Wallis
Colonneh	9: 63	Houston
Colorado, Father of Prohibition in	2: 61	Fowler
Colossus of Independence	2: 1	Adams
Columbia, Patriarch of	12: 165	Taylor
Columbus	5: 73	Adams
Columbus of New England	7: 62	Lowell
Commerce with India, Father of American	4: 545	Derby
Common School Education in Connecticut, Father of	10: 331	Treadwell
Common Sense	4: 30	Stevens
Common Sense	5: 77	Clay
Common Sense	6: 181	Kennedy
Common Sense	7: 310	Fowler
Commoner, Nevada	1: 300	Jones
Commonplace, Poet of the	2: 160	Longfellow
Communipaw	5: 242	Miles
Concepcion, Hero of	4: 132	Fannin
Confederacy, Brains of the	4: 285	Benjamin
Confederacy, Mother of the	8: 415	Carnes
Confederacy, Ney of the	11: 90	Cheatham
Congregationalism, Nestor of	1: 176	Bacon
Connecticut Jurisprudence, Father of	12: 60	Ludlow
Connecticut School Fund, Father of	5: 391	Granger
Conrad Mascol	9: 133	Smith
Constituent, The	5: 447	Giles
Constitution, Expounder of the	1: 25	Marshall
Constitution, Expounder of the	3: 36	Webster
Continent, Northern	5: 249	Watson
Contributor, Fat	6: 29	Griswold
Convicts, Friend of the	B: 400	Catts
Conway, Schuyler	14: 352	Donnelly
Conyngham, Kate	7: 413	Ingraham
Coody, Abimelech	5: 405	Verplanck
Cooke, John Estes	18: 332	Baum
Coolidge, Susan	11: 352	Woolsey
Cooper, Frank	6: 204	Simms
Corinne L'Estrange	8: 202	Hartshorne
Cornelia Littlepage	1: 398	Cooper
Corrector	1: 514	Hobart
Corrine	22: 411	Dahlgren
Cosmopolite	10: 472	Dow
Cosmos	B: 187	Butler
Cotton Industry, Father of American	6: 14	Coxe
Counsellor, Poor Man's	3: 302	Clark
Count Paul Crillon	13: 279	Barton
Countryman	3: 43	Clinton
Countryman, Military	1: 68	Heath
Cousin Alice	5: 386	Haven
Cousin Virginia	13: 107	Johnson
Coventry, John	8: 222	Palmer
Covode, Honest John	23: 296	Covode
Cow-killer	13: 422	Red-Jacket
Cox, Sunset	6: 363	Cox
Craddock, Charles Egbert	2: 363	Murfree
Cramer, Julian	10: 174	Chester
Crassus, Lucius	1: 9	Hamilton
Crater, Hero of the	5: 12	Mahone
Crayon, Geoffrey	3: 17	Irving
Crayon, Porte	9: 365	Strother

D.

E.

Pseudonym	Reference	Name
Effingham, C., Esq.	7:330	Cooke
Effingham, John	1:398	Cooper
Egomet, Demens	1:183	Williams
Elberp	8: 92	Preble
Elbertus, Fra	13:571	Hubbard
Eldred Grayson	5:398	Hare
Eleanor Putnam	8: 12	Bates
Eli Perkins	6: 27	Landon
Eliot, Alice	1:374	Jewett
Eliot of the West	6:493	Baker
Elizabeth Akers	6:133	Allen
Elizabeth Wetherell	5:354	Warner
Elizapham of Parnach	7:167	Church
Ella Dietz	13: 68	Glynes
Ellen Burroughs	12:198	Jewett
Ellen Louise	3:365	Moulton
Ellen, The Late Henry, Esq.	7:241	Hope
Elmina, Aunt	7:488	Slenker
Eloquent, Old Man	5: 73	Adams
Emanuel, Morgan	A:175	Bynner
Emel Jay	2:515	Jackson
Emile Walter	4:189	Del Mar
Engineer	7:521	Tucker
Enquirer, An	7:521	Tucker
Enrique, Erratic	13:347	Lukens
Epaminondas	5:391	Granger
Ephraim Kirby	8:132	Smith
Epping Forest, Rose of	1: 1	Washington
Equity in Tennessee, Father of	5:552	Green
Erasmus	8:441	Gilder
Erie Douglas	2:425	Keith
Ernest Berthold	2:242	Robinson
Ernest Helfenstein	9:171	Smith
Ernest Leslie	12:256	Brown
Erodore	6:136	Abbott
Erratic Enrique	13:347	Lukens
Erskine of the American Bar	11: 84	Hoffman
Esek, Uncle	6: 28	Shaw
Essayists, Napoleon of	3:448	Greeley
Esther Chesney	7:545	MacLean
Ethel Lynn	8:358	Beers
Eugene Raymond	11:363	Hewitt
Eusebius	7:238	Prime, E. D. J.
Everett, Richard	4:208	Cross
Evergreen, Anthony	9:383	Irving
Evil Genius of Maryland	11:421	Claiborne
Experimental Physics, Father of	13:507	Rood
Explorer, Picturesque	3:444	Lanman
Expounder of the Constitution	1: 25	Marshall
Expounder of the Constitution	3: 36	Webster
Extra Billy	5:451	Smith

F.

Pseudonym	Reference	Name
F. G. S.	13:343	Fischer
F. J. C.	8:256	Child
F. Pylodet	7:491	Leypoldt
F. Sedley	7:475	Fay
Fabius	2:281	Dickinson
Fabius, American	1: 1	Washington
Fadette	4:377	Reeves
Fairplay, Oliver	3: 1	Jefferson
Falkland	2:382	Ames
Falkland	3:294	Chapman
Fane, Florence	13:432	Victor
Fanny, Aunt	2:321	Gage
Fanny, Aunt	4:556	Barrow
Fanny Fern	1:391	Parton
Fanny Forrester	3: 93	Judson
Fanny J. Crosby	7: 65	Van Alstyne
Far West	11:365	Munch
Farbink, Jonathan	7:289	Holbrook
Farmer, A. W.	3:475	Seabury
Farmer, American	8:253	Crevecoeur
Farmer, Orator	15:145	Martine
Farquharson, Martha	11:267	Finley
Fat Contributor	6: 29	Griswold
Father Abraham	2: 65	Lincoln
Father Abraham	1:328	Franklin
Father of America	1:104	Adams
Father of American Abolition	7:154	Hopkins
Father of American Anthropology	6:192	Morgan
Father of American Ballad Poetry	11:363	Hewitt
Father of American Baptists	7:346	Clarke
Father of American Bridge Building	9: 35	Whipple
Father of American Commerce with India	4:545	Derby
Father of American Cotton Industry	6: 14	Coxe
Father of American Democracy	6:279	Hooker
Father of American Geography	13:352	Morse
Father of American Geology	13:368	Maclure
Father of American Literature	3: 17	Irving
Father of American Map-making	19:208	Gannett
Father of the American Navy	5:110	Humphreys
Father of American Pharmacy	5:347	Procter
Father of the American Piano	6:190	Chickering
Father of the American Revolution	1:104	Adams
Father of American Surgery	6:391	Physick
Father of American Unitarianism	7:403	Gay
Father of American Wood Engraving	6:259	Anderson
Father of American Zoölogy	6:107	Say
Father of the Anthracite Iron Industry in America	3:360	Thomas
Father of the Automobile Industry	20:223	Selden
Father of Branford	13:472	Bogue
Father Cole	2:446	Cole
Father of Connecticut Jurisprudence	12: 60	Ludlow
Father of Connecticut School Fund	5:391	Granger
Father of Equity in Tennessee	5:552	Green
Father of Experimental Physics	13:507	Rood
Father of Foreign Mission Work in America	13:187	Mills
Father of Forestry	19:181	Rothrock
Father of Golf in America	22: 99	Reid
Father of Greater New York	13: 70	Green
Father of Greenbacks	6:355	Spaulding
Father of His Country	1: 1	Washington
Father of Historical Societies	3:461	Pintard
Father of Homœopathy in America	12:349	Hering
Father Keep	2:465	Keep
Father of Louisiana Jurisprudence	5:436	Martin
Father of Massachusetts	6:201	Winthrop
Father of Microscopic Research in America	10:157	Bailey
Father of the Modern Peace Movement	13:352	Dodge
Father of New England Commerce	6:105	Allerton
Father of the New York Bar	9:162	VanVechten
Father of the New York Bar	11:489	Jones
Father of Outdoor Advertising	23:131	Curran
Father of Paper Currency	3:302	Clark
Father of Physiography	B: 93	Davis
Father of Presbyterianism in the Northwest	2:126	Whitworth
Father of Presbyterianism in Virginia	5:516	Morris
Father of Prohibition in Colorado	2: 61	Fowler
Father of Reclamation	15:243	Wisner
Father of the Republican Party	2:446	Cole
Father of Rhode Island	7:346	Clarke
Father Ryan	5:111	Ryan
Father of Tacoma	8:439	Wright
Father of Tennessee	11: 90	Cheatham
Father of the Criminal Bar	22: 49	Howe
Father of the Dutch Reformed Church in America	3:400	Livingston
Father of the Flint Glass Industry in America	22:218	Bakewell

G.

George Fleming	13:458	Fletcher
George, Four-eyed	4: 66	Meade
George, Gentleman	3:278	Pendleton
George, Live Oak	3: 94	Law
George Stephens	5:424	Stephens
Georgia, Savior of	4:102	Twiggs
Geraldine Fleming	21:279	Coryell
Germanicus	1: 12	Randolph
Giant of the Law	5:441	Parsons
Gibbons, Lucy	26:415	Morse
Girard, Old	7: 11	Girard
Glance Gaylord	4:260	Bradley
Gleaner	6:377	Bowditch
Glory of her Sex	7: 10	Bradstreet
Glyndon, Howard	9:496	Searing
Golden Gate, Poet of the	11:266	Kirchhoff
Golden Gate Trinity	13:512	Coolbrith
Golden Rule Jones	10:414	Jones
Goldsmith, American	1:434	Woodworth
Goldsmith of America	11:159	Taylor
Golf in America, Father of	22: 99	Reid
Gong, The Ohio	3:142	Allen
Good Bishop	5:486	Otey
Good Count Coffinberry	3:396	Coffinberry
Good Governor	12:155	Johnson
Good Gray Poet	1:255	Whitman
Gordon, Julien	7: 85	Cruger
Gorilla, Learned	1:197	White
Governor, Good	12:155	Johnson
Cracchus	6:140	Thompson
Grace Darling of America	5:247	Lewis
Grace Greenwood	6:536	Lippincott
Graham, Allen	9:432	Arnold
Grand Old Man	6:445	Evans
Grandfather of all the Missionaries	9:484	Roberts
Grant Allan	11:412	Wilson
Gray, Barry	6:525	Coffin
Gray, Old Billy	5:337	Gray
Gray, Robertson	8: 44	Raymond
Gray-eyed Man of Destiny	11: 24	Walker
Grayson, David	C:415	Baker
Grayson, Eldred	5:398	Hare
Graystone, Sage of	3: 53	Tilden
Great American Traveler	9:423	Pratt
Great American Woodsman	6: 75	Audubon
Great Commoner	4: 30	Stevens
Great Commoner	5: 77	Clay
Great Commoner	7:310	Fowler
Great Decliner	4:163	Rosecrans
Great Father of Detroit	5: 3	Cass
Great Objector	5:457	Holman
Great Pacificator	5: 77	Clay
Great Warrior	12:236	Hendy
Great White Arrow	13:449	Fletcher
Great White Devil	5:533	Van Cortlandt
Great Wolf	7:514	Tryon
Greater New York, Father of	13: 70	Green
Greek Revolution, Lafayette of the	8:372	Howe
Green, Anna Katharine	9:257	Rohlfs
Green Mountains, Burns of the	9:252	Eastman
Greenbacks, Father of	6:355	Spaulding
Greenwood, Grace	4:536	Lippincott
Grievous, Peter, Esq.	5:460	Hopkinson
Grile, Dod	14:180	Bierce
Grimes, Old	9:501	Greene
Gringo, Harry	5:452	Wise
Groot, Cecil de	13:199	Rice
Grotius	3: 41	Clinton
Grumbler, Anthony	7:129	Hoffman
Guard, Theodore de la	7: 64	Ward
Guarnerius, Tobias	10:176	Dimitry
Guarnerius, Tobias, Jr.	10:176	Dimitry
Gumbo Chaff	4:432	Howe

H.

H. C.	3:309	Carroll
H. E. Chevalier	8:379	Hoffman
H. H.	1:433	Jackson
H. H. M.	8:202	Hartshorne
H. Trusta	9:368	Phelps
Habeas Corpus Howe	22: 49	Howe
Hal, a Dacotah	10: 63	Sibley
Halford, Dr. Henry	1:311	Holland
Hall, Holworthy	A:259	Porter
Hamden	2:394	Webster
Hamilton	8: 77	Watson
Hamilton, Gail	9:227	Dodge
Hamilton, Henry	10: 44	Spalding
Hamilton, Philip	15:361	Hubert
Hammond, Mudsill	11:170	Hammond
Hampden	5:457	Hooper
Hampden	9: 46	Jervis
Hampden, Junius	5:393	Thomas
Hampton, Agnes	12:294	Smith
Handkerchief Moody	11: 59	Farley
Hannah More of America	9:295	Mercer
Hannah Warner	13:599	Jewett
Hans Breitmann	5:356	Leland
Hans, King	1:526	Grady
Hans Pfaal	1:463	Poe
Hans Yorkel	3:389	Hall
Hard Cider	3: 33	Harrison
Hard Pan	12:246	Bonner
Hardshell Democracy	3: 52	Hoffman
Hardy, John	3:280	Hayes
Harland, Marion	2:122	Terhune
Harrington, G. F.	8:392	Baker
Harrison, Log-cabin	3: 33	Harrison
Harry Birch	6:231	White
Harry Bluff	6: 35	Maury
Harry Franco	9:254	Briggs
Harry Gringo	5:452	Wise
Harry Henderson	1:423	Stowe
Harry, Legion	3: 25	Lee
Harry, Lighthorse	3: 25	Lee
Harry of the West, Gallant	5: 77	Clay
Hart, Aiken	12:471	Helmuth
Hart, Honest John	5:538	Hart
Harte, Bret	1:404	Harte
Hartley, Samuel	7:501	Hopkins
Harvey	12:313	Mathes
Harvey, Coin	18: 16	Harvey
Harwood, John	5:525	Miner
Hattie, Aunt	14:154	Baker
Havelock of the War	4:103	Howard
Hawser Martingale	13:206	Sleeper
Hawthorne, Alice	1:310	Winner
Hayes, Henry	1:373	Kirk
Hays, Will S.	3:178	Hays
Hayword, Richard	6: 29	Cozzens
Head, Buffalo	2:192	Ochiltree
Head of Iron	12:504	Forbes
Hector Bullus	7:193	Paulding
Hedbrook, Andrew	7:249	Sill
Hegan, Alice Caldwell	14:484	Rice
Heiress of Wando	2:119	Chisolm
Helen	8:145	Whitman
Helen Berkley	3:227	Ritchie
Helen Dhu	13:111	Lester
Helen Luqueer	1:431	Bushnell
Helen Swift	C:341	Neilson
Helfenstein, Ernest	9:171	Smith
Hell-and-Maria Dawes	A:509	Dawes
Helvidius	5:369	Madison
Hemans of America	1:154	Sigourney
Henderson, Harry	1:423	Stowe
Henry, Calcraft	5:145	Schoolcraft

Pseudonym	Reference	Name
Henry Churton	7:324	Tourgee
Henry, Daniel, Jun.	23:294	Holmes
Henry Ellen, Esq.	7:241	Hope
Henry Hamilton	10: 44	Spalding
Henry Hayes	1:373	Kirk
Henry Homespun	4:304	Southwick
Henry J. Mann	11:513	Montague
Henry, O.	15:170	Porter
Henry Richards	3:297	Stoddard
Hermanus	5:412	Paine
Hermes, Paul	12:530	Thayer
Hermine	11:252	Elder
Hero Boy of '76	4: 88	Peyton
Hero of Charleston	8:238	Lee
Hero of Concepcion	4:132	Fannin
Hero of the Crater	5: 12	Mahone
Hero of Ft. McHenry	13:324	Armistead
Hero of Ft. Meigs	11:456	Christy
Hero of Ft. Mifflin	8:110	Thayer
Heteroscian	9:442	Hazard
Hewer, Rough	5:260	Yates
Hezekiah Salem	6:201	Freneau
Hibernicus	3: 41	Clinton
Hickling, William	22:355	DeCosta
Hickory, Old	5:289	Jackson
Hickory, Young	6:265	Polk
Hill, Mrs.	4:439	Wallack
Hill, Yankee	1:401	Hill
Historian, Blind	6: 7	Prescott
Historical Societies in America, Father of	3:461	Pintard
Hobbes, John Oliver	10:506	Craigie
Hock, Francis	7:243	Sargent
Hogarth, Jr.	D: 98	Kent
Hollingsworth, P. Rankin	7:429	Palmer
Holme, Saxe	1:433	Jackson
Holworthy Hall	A:259	Porter
Homespun, Henry	4:304	Southwick
Homœopathy in America, Father of	12:349	Hering
Hon. John Philip Refalo	11:360	Dunlop
Honest Abe	2: 65	Lincoln
Honest John Covode	23:296	Covode
Honest John Hart	5:538	Hart
Honest John Stephenson	7:364	Stephenson
Honest Lawyer	5:159	Ogden
Honest Old Jack	4: 18	Chandler
Honest Old Joe Vance	8:340	Shannon
Honestus	12:429	Austin
Honorius	2:394	Webster
Hooper, King	19:435	Hooper
Hoosier Orator	13:170	Orton
Hoosier Poet	6: 31	Riley
Hope, Arthur	2:203	Wilkinson
Horace	9:240	Ingersoll
Horse Marine	2:104	Carter
Hortensius	11:420	Hay
Horticulture, Wizard of	11:374	Burbank
Hosea Bigelow	2: 32	Lowell
Hotspur, Young	10:341	Ingersoll
House of Representatives, Father of the	1:434	Woodward
House of Representatives, Father of the	3:508	Williams
House of Representatives, Father of the	5:176	Macon
Howadji	3: 96	Curtis
Howard	4:213	Howard
Howard, American	3:512	Eddy
Howard, Barbara	21:280	Coryell
Howard Glyndon	9:497	Searing
Howe, Habeas Corpus	22: 49	Howe
Howitts of America, The	8:119	Smith
Hugh Fitzgerald, Captain	18:331	Baum
Hugo Dusenbury	7:303	Bunner
Hunnibee, Kate	11:366	Lyman
Hunter, Harry	4:451	Field
Hurlburt, Loammi N.	9:422	Trumbull
Hustings, Demosthenes of the	13:409	Leake
Hyperion	1: 19	Quincy

I.

Pseudonym	Reference	Name
I.	7:169	Edwards
Ianthe	9:211	Embury
Idler, The	8: 57	Gregory
Ignatius L. Robertson	7:472	Knapp
Ik Iopas	11:198	Flint
Ik Marvel	6: 97	Mitchell
Ike, Uncle	14: 51	Stephenson
Il Segretario	7:545	Pleasants
I'll Try	10:183	Miller
Immortal Thirteen	7:309	Jones
Inchiquin	7:141	Ingersoll
Inconnue	7:240	French
Independence, Colossus of	2: 1	Adams
Indian Apostle	2:419	Eliot
Indian Fighter	9: 26	Miles
Indians, Friend of the	13:141	Stuart
Indigina	11:528	Newell
Industry, Friend of	4:473	Dearborn
Inez	10:233	Mace
Iopas, Ik	11:198	Flint
Ira Zell	3:415	Roosevelt
Iranæus	7:237	Prime
Irish Nightingale	4:506	Hayes
Ironquill	9:202	Ware
Isabel	3:227	Ritchie
Isabel Leslie	6: 56	Dorr
Ivory Black	12:460	Janvier

J.

Pseudonym	Reference	Name
J. B.	13:207	Brent
J. Cypress, Jr	11:355	Hawes
J. I. D. B.	3:279	Bristol
J. O. T.	13:185	Terry
J. P. Mowbray	25:375	Wheeler
J. S. of Dale	10:361	Stimson
Jack, Black	4:298	Logan
Jack, Captain	5:333	Canby
Jack of Clubs	4: 63	Sheridan
Jack Downing	8:118	Smith
Jack Downing, Major	8:119	Smith
Jack, Mad	11:400	Percival
Jack, Old	4:125	Jackson
Jack Retort	13:102	Franklin
Jack of Spades	4:298	Logan
Jacket, Blue	9:377	Dahlgren
Jackson, Stonewall	4:125	Jackson
James, Livingston	1: 9	Hamilton
James Otis	13:475	Kaler
James S. D.	1:284	Scudder
Jane Kingsford	13: 64	Barnard
Jasper Dwight	8:180	Duane
Jay, Emel	2:515	Jackson
Jean Stanley	4:435	Hosmer
Jeff, Uncle	18:379	Rhoads
Jehu O'Cataract	11:346	Neal
Jenkins, Bawling	10:442	Jenkins
Jenks	11:363	Hewitt
Jennie Deans	2:316	Swisshelm
Jennier	15:345	Gorrie
Jenny June	6:499	Croly
Jerseys, Don Quixote of the	5:201	Livingston
Jethro	4:521	Vaill
Jim Crow Rice	11:207	Rice
Jim, Sunny	14:407	Sherman
Jimmy Jones, Lean	7:209	Jones

K.

L.

M.

Pseudonym	Reference	Name
Martlet	13:149	Davis
Martyr President	2: 65	Lincoln
Marvel, Ik	6: 97	Mitchell
Marvell, Andrew	5:197	Middleton
Mary Clavers	5:356	Kirkland
Mary Clemmer	7:233	Ames
Mary Langdon	11:165	Pike
Mary Orne	13:140	Nichols
Maryland, Evil Genius of	11:421	Claiborne
Mascol, Conrad	9:133	Smith
Mason, Mark	1:310	Winner
Massachusettensis	2: 59	Sewall
Massachusetts	4:545	Derby, 2d
Massachusetts, Citizen of	7: 62	Lowell
Massachusetts, Father of	6:201	Winthrop
Massachusetts Lawyer	11:550	Lowell
Master Alexander	9:327	Herrmann
Master Johnny	2:134	Wilson
Master of the St. Louis Bar	12:399	Jewett
Mathematical Prodigy	7: 74	Colburn
Mathematics, Nestor of American	8:153	Peirce
Mathew Marshall	17:185	Hitchcock
Matthew White, Jr.	5:108	Alden
Maumee, Drummer-boy of the	4:332	Kountz
Max	22: 52	Mayo
Max Adeler	14:400	Clark
Max Mannering	1:311	Holland
Max Vernon	A:203	Vernon
May, Edith	11:502	Drinker
May, Sophie	8:339	Clarke
Mayer, Ferdinand	12:256	Brown
Medius	1:328	Franklin
Meigs, Hero of Ft.	11:456	Christy
Meissonier, American	13:369	Watrous
Meister, Karl	5:356	Leland
Mellen, Queen	12: 8	Palmer
Melmoth	7:136	Tucker
Memander	5:429	Paine
Member of the Vermont Bar	6:233	Thompson
Men Dur, A.	9: 77	Burnham
Menlo Park, Wizard of	25: 1	Edison
Mercutio	4: 83	Winter
Merlin	9:348	Wilder
Merriam, Florence A.	13:263	Bailey
Merry, Felix	1:431	Duyckinck
Merry, Robert	6:154	Stearns
Metador	6:326	Alden
Metcalf, Susan	18:331	Baum
Meteor Smith	20: 94	Smith
Methodism, Apostle of	13:187	Lee
Methodism, Mother of	13:115	Heck
Methodist Agassiz	13:536	Marcy
Mexican Army, Marion of the	8: 2	Lane
Meyette, Minnie	8:260	Piatt
Miboy	4:322	English
Michael Strange	B:498	Barrymore
Microscopic Research in America, Father of	10:157	Bailey
Middlesex, Red Fox of	13:358	Montague
Midgets, The	12: 64	Flynn
Mignon, August	8:359	Darling
Miles O'Reilly	6: 26	Halpin
Military Countryman	1: 68	Heath
Millboy	4:322	English
Mill-boy of the Slashes	5: 77	Clay
Miller, Frank	6: 43	Hook
Miller, Joaquin	7: 69	Miller
Miller, Olive Thorne	9:208	Miller
Milton, Edmund	11:438	Holland
Milton Quarterly	21:279	Coryell
Minister's Wife	3:130	Beecher
Minnie Meyette	8:260	Piatt
Minstrel Girl	6:503	Welby
Miriam Coles	11:515	Harris
Missionaries, Grandfather of the	9:484	Roberts
Missouri, Liberator of	9:279	Pillow
Mr. Dooley	14: 53	Dunne
Mr. Penn	4:524	Colwell
Mr. Philemon Perch	1:440	Johnston
Mr. Sparrowgrass	6: 29	Cozzens
Mr. Thom. Whyte	13:465	Elliott
Mrs. Clara Morton	9:473	Moore
Mrs. George Archibald	22:127	Palmer
Mrs. Hill	4:439	Wallack
Mrs. L. L. Worth	11:492	Ellsworth
Mrs. Marion Vaughan	10:363	Gilman
Mrs. Mark Peabody	4:522	Victor
Mistress, Old	2:151	Seals
Mrs. Partington	6: 32	Shillaber
Mizpah	23: 17	Lea
Modern Bunyan	10: 19	Miller
Moina	13:149	Dinnies
Molly E. Moore	10: 21	Davis
Molly Pitcher	6:399	Corbin
Montaigne, American	3:416	Emerson
Montclair, John W.	12:327	Weidemeyer
Moody, Handkerchief	11: 59	Farley
Moore, Florence	11:161	Morris
Moore, Mollie E.	10: 21	Davis
More of America, Hannah	9:295	Mercer
Moreton, Mrs. Clara	9:473	Moore
Morgan, Emanuel	A:175	Bynner
Moria	5:411	Ryan
Morris, Robert	9: 84	Gibbons
Moses Adams	24:102	Bagby
Moses, Agricultural	12:180	Tillman
Moses of America	10:116	Wise
Mother Ann	5:132	Lee
Mother of Clubs	8:108	Severance
Mother of the Confederacy	8:415	Carnes
Mother Hancock, Old	1:103	Hancock
Mother Jones	23: 72	Jones
Mother of Methodism in the U. S.	13:115	Heck
Mother Stewart	7: 37	Stewart
Motley Manners	4:315	Duganne
Mountain, Old Man of the	2:320	Rogers
Mountains, Demosthenes of the	12:344	Miller
Mowbray, J. P.	25:375	Wheeler
Mucius Scævola	8:139	Greenleaf, J.
Mudsill Hammond	12:169	Hammond
Muldor, Carl de	8:423	Miller
Muly Malack	9:200	Noah
Munchausen of the West	4: 85	Crockett
Mungo Park	13:151	Locke
Murat of America	9:168	Wheat
Murray, Adirondack	10:230	Murray
Muse, the Tenth	7: 10	Bradstreet

N.

Pseudonym	Reference	Name
N. H.	3:409	Holmes
N. N.	10:377	Pennell
N. O. M.	11:552	Kimber
Namby Pamby Willis	3:108	Willis
Napoleon of the Civil War	4: 1	Grant
Napoleon of Essayists	3:448	Greeley
Napoleon of the North	2:150	Kellogg
Napoleon of the Stump	4:265	Polk
Nasby, Petroleum Vesuvius	6:152	Locke
Nat, Fighting	13:464	Snowden
Nathaniel Shotwell	1:314	Dodge
Natick Cobbler	4: 13	Wilson
National Poet	6: 31	Riley
Native of Algiers	13:180	Markoe
Native of America	13:191	Parke
Native of Virginia	1:206	Conway
Navarre of the American Revolution	8: 84	Butler
Navy, Chesterfield of the	4:413	LeRoy

Navy, Father of the American	5:110	Humphreys
Ned Buntline	13:194	Judson
Needham, Marchmont	1: 19	Quincy
Neighbor, A	7:501	Fiske
Neill, Beau	13:513	Neill
Nellie A. Mann	4:523	Manville
Nellie Blessing-Eyster	10:392	Eyster
Nellie Bly	1:241	Cochrane
Neltje Blanchan	13:400	Doubleday
Nemesis	13:474	Norwood
Neptune	11:360	Dunlap
Nestor of American Mathematics	8:153	Peirce
Nestor of Congregationalism	1:176	Bacon
Nestor of the St. Louis Bar	12:399	Jewett
Nevada Commoner	1:300	Jones
Nevers, C. O.	8:449	Converse
Neville, Follow-Me	22:277	Neville
New England, Admiral of	13:378	Smith
New England, Busby of	7:204	Belknap
New England, Columbus of	7: 62	Lowell
New England Commerce, Father of	6:105	Allerton
New England, Cromwell of	1:104	Adams
New England Democracy, Rock of	2:471	Woodbury
New England, Patrick Henry of	2:314	Phillips
New Jersey, Samuel Adams of	13:324	Fisher
New Netherlands Mercury	2:483	Van Rensselaer
New York Bar, Father of the	9:162	Van Vechten
New York Bar, Father of the	11:489	Jones, Sr. and Jr.
Newman of America	11:357	Hewit
Ney of the Confederacy	11: 90	Cheatham
Nightingale, Irish	4:506	Hayes
Nimblechops, Aquiline	2:467	Livingston
Nina Gray Clarke	6:235	Clarke
Nolichucky Jack	3:430	Sevier
Nonconformists, St. Paul of the	5: 57	Wesley
Norna	13:581	Brooks
North, Napoleon of the	2:150	Kellogg
Northern Continent	5:249	Watson
Notitia Literaria	5:312	Tuckerman
Novanglus	2: 1	Adams
Now or Never	7:487	Forrest
Nubibus, Tertius in	1: 19	Quincy
Nullifier, A	2:114	Hilliard
Nye, Bill	6: 25	Nye
Nym Crinkle	25:375	Wheeler

O.

O	7:169	Edwards
O. Henry	15:170	Porter
Oates, Felix	3:270	Catlin
Objector, Great	5:457	Holman
Observator, Charles	6:176	Sabin
Observer	2:369	Marshall
Observer, General	7:501	Fiske
O'Cataract, Jehu	11:346	Neal
Occidente, Maria del	8:169	Brooks
Ockside, Knight Russ	11:521	Thompson
Octave Thanet	10:163	French
Ohio Gong, The	3:142	Allen
Ola, Onkel	11:219	Lindstrand
Old Admiral	3:436	Columbus
Old Agamemnon	5: 54	Carrington
Old Aristides	8: 44	Bicknell
Old Bachelor	2:305	Garrison
Old Beaury	4:178	Beauregard
Old Beeswax	4:340	Semmes
Old Ben Wade	2: 94	Wade
Old Billy Gray	5:337	Gray
Old Blizzard	4:364	Loring
Old Boy in Specs	5:514	Davis
Old Brains	4:257	Halleck
Old Buck	5: 1	Buchanan
Old Buena Vista	4:367	Taylor
Old Bullion	4:399	Benton
Old Murchelle	6:133	Burritt
Old Cabinet	1:312	Gilder
Old Chapultepec	3:502	Scott
Old Chickamauga	4:395	Steedman
Old Chief	5: 77	Clay
Old Denmark	1: 86	Febiger
Old Double Quick	10:495	Hollingsworth
Old Fogy	1:403	Watterson
Old Girard	7: 11	Girard
Old Hays	12:354	Hays
Old Hero	5:289	Jackson
Old Hickory	5:289	Jackson
Old Jack	4:125	Jackson
Old Jack, Honest	4: 18	Chandler
Old John Robinson	3:337	Robinson
Old Jube	4:137	Early
Old Man Eloquent, The	5: 73	Adams
Old Man, Grand	6:445	Evans
Old Man of the Mountain	2:320	Rogers
Old Man of the South	12:429	Austin
Old Mistress	2:151	Seals
Old Mother Hancock	1:103	Hancock
Old Pete	4:263	Longstreet
Old Probability	4:216	Myer
Old Probability	8:264	Abbe
Old Public Functionary	5: 1	Buchanan
Old Put	1: 87	Putnam
Old Ranger	11: 44	Reynolds
Old Reliable	4: 48	Thomas
Old Rosey	4:162	Rosecrans
Old Rough and Ready	4:367	Taylor, Z.
Old Round About	1:508	Cleveland
Old Saddle Bags	11:504	McDonald
Old Sleuth	9:145	Halsey
Old South	12:429	Austin
Old Stars	3:440	Mitchel
Old Steady	4:395	Steedman
Old Stone Hammer	13: 4	Metcalfe
Old Tecumseh	4:432	Sherman
Old Thad	4: 30	Stevens
Old Three Star	4: 1	Grant
Old Tiger	3:308	Smith
Old Tiger	13:247	Anderson
Old Timer, An	7:487	Forrest
Old Tip	3: 33	Harrison
Old Un	8:237	Durivage
Old War Horse	4:182	Cook
Old Warder	1:470	Bradford
Old Wheel-horse of Democracy	8:342	Medary
Old Zach	4:367	Taylor
Oldbuck, Jonathan	11:251	Stilwell
Oldbug, Jonathan	5:512	Withington
Oldfield, Traverse	3:152	Samson
Old-School, Oliver	7:204	Dennie
Oldschool, Oliver	13:320	Sargent
Oldstyle, Jonathan	3: 17	Irving
Oldstyle, Oliver	7:193	Paulding
Olive Thorne Miller	9:208	Miller
Oliver Fairplay	3: 1	Jefferson
Oliver Goldsmith of America	11:159	Taylor
Oliver Old-School	7:204	Dennie
Oliver Oldschool	13:320	Sargent
Oliver Oldstyle	7:193	Paulding
Oliver Optic	1:203	Adams
Oliver Thurston	11:114	Flanders
Ollapod	8:454	Clark, W. G.
Onas	2:276	Penn
One of the Barclays	7: 66	Otis
One-armed Devil	4:260	Kearny
One-armed Phil	4:260	Kearny
O'Neill, Peggy	6:290	Eaton
Onkel Ola	11:219	Lindstrand
Onyx	9:368	Ward

Name	Reference	Person
Optic, Oliver	1: 203	Adams
Oracle, Town	1: 470	Bradford
Orator, Hoosier	13: 170	Orton
Orator, Silver-tongued	13: 581	Bell
Oraz	7: 429	Palmer
Oregon, Apostle of	13: 32	Blanchet
O'Reilly, Miles	6: 26	Halpine
Orlando	7: 198	Hall
Orme, Mary	13: 140	Nichols
Orphans' Friend, Margaret the	2: 373	Gaffney
Orpheus C. Kerr	11: 528	Newell
Osawatomie Brown	2: 307	Brown
Osborne, John	7: 243	Sargent
Otis, James	13: 475	Kaler
Overland Three	13: 512	Coolbrith
Owen Knox	13: 225	Cory

P.

Name	Reference	Person
P. C.	13: 279	Barton
P. D.	11: 184	James
P. Rankin Hollingsworth	7: 429	Palmer
Pa Thomas	4: 48	Thomas
Pacific, Pocahontas of the	13: 419	Sacajawea
Pacificator	11: 84	Hoffman, M.
Pacificator, Great	5: 77	Clay
Pacificus	1: 9	Hamilton
Pacificus	1: 185	Worcester
Packard, Clarissa	6: 259	Gilman
Padre of the Rains	23: 70	Ricard
Page, Abraham	6: 277	Holt
Page, Stanton	23: 406	Fuller
Paget, R. I.	18: 243	Knowles
Pai Ta-shun	16: 17	Peterson
Palestinensis	8: 15	Smith
Palmer, Lynde	4: 39	Peebles
Palmer, Pie-crust	4: 554	Palmer
Pan, Hard	12: 246	Bonner
Pang	16: 283	Pangborn
Pansy	10: 405	Alden
Pantarch	6: 442	Andrews
Paper Currency, Father of	3: 302	Clark
Paper King	11: 188	Law
Paqua	6: 257	Cleaveland
Park, Mungo	13: 151	Locke
Parker, Bentley	7: 166	Benjamin
Parley, Peter	5: 355	Goodrich
Parliamentarians, Prince of	9: 181	Mell
Parnach, Elizapham of	7: 167	Church
Parson Brownlow	7: 210	Brownlow
Parson, Fighting	5: 318	Allen
Parson, Fighting, of Bennington Fields	7: 210	Brownlow
Partington, Mrs.	6: 32	Shillaber
Pasquin, Anthony	1: 179	Williams
Pastor, Felix	8: 420	Lockhart
Pastor, Tony	9: 145	Halsey
Pat Malloy Robinson	3: 116	Robinson
Patent Office. Father of the	12: 230	Ruggles
Pathfinder, The	4: 270	Fremont
Patriarch of American Diplomacy	2: 380	Marsh
Patriarch of Columbia	12: 165	Taylor
Patrick Henry of New England	2: 314	Phillips
Patriot, A True	1: 57	Warren
Patti, Black	13: 424	Jones
Patty, Aunt	6: 261	Hentz
Patty Lee	1: 535	Cary, A.
Paul Ambrose	6: 181	Kennedy
Paul Creyton	3: 374	Trowbridge
Paul Hermes	12: 530	Thayer
Paul, John	10: 42	Webb
Paul Potiphar	3: 96	Curtis
Paul Potter	3: 458	Congdon
Paul Preston	13: 185	Picton
Paul Siegvolk	8: 50	Mathews
Paul Wright	12: 447	Moore
Paxton, Philip	22: 389	Hammett
Paymaster, Fighting	16: 229	Stanton
Peabody, Mrs. Mark	4: 522	Victor
Peace, Secretary of	23: 1	Taft
Peacock, Timothy	6: 233	Thompson
Pearl Rivers	1: 306	Nicholson
Pearlfisher	4: 184	Foote
Peggy O'Neill	6: 290	Eaton
Peleg Arkwright	8: 33	Proudfit
Pen of the Revolution	3: 1	Jefferson
Penciller Willis	3: 108	Willis
Pen-holder	6: 57	Eggleston
Penn, Mr.	4: 524	Colwell
Penn Shirley	8: 339	Clarke
Penn, William	2: 343	Evarts
Pennsylvania Farmer, A	2: 281	Dickinson
Pennsylvania Politics, Czar of	2: 79	Cameron
People, Man of the	1: 337	Henry
Pepper, Tom	9: 254	Briggs
Pepperbox, Peter	7: 260	Fessenden
Pepys, Puritan	5: 339	Sewall
Pequot	11: 268	Marsh
Perch, Mr. Philemon	1: 440	Johnston
Percy Collins	15: 232	Collier
Percy, Florence	6: 133	Allen
Peregrine Prolix	4: 346	Nicklin
Periwinkle, Peter	7: 260	Fessenden
Periwinkle, Tribulation	1: 204	Alcott
Perkins, Eli	6: 27	Landon
Perley	8: 190	Poore
Perry, Edgar A.	1: 463	Poe
Persia, Apostle of	10: 45	Perkins
Pete, Old	4: 263	Longstreet
Peter Coffin	5: 393	Parsons
Peter Grievous, Esq.	5: 460	Hopkinson
Peter Parley	5: 355	Goodrich
Peter Pepperbox	7: 260	Fessenden
Peter Periwinkle	7: 260	Fessenden
Peter Pilgrim	7: 183	Bird
Peter Quince, Esq.	13: 193	Story
Petroleum Vesuvius Nasby	6: 152	Locke
Pfaal, Hans	1: 463	Poe
Pharmacy, Father of American	5: 347	Procter
Phenomenal Presiding Elder	7: 135	Wilson
Phil, Fighting	4: 260	Kearny
Phil, One-armed	4: 260	Kearny
Philadelphia, Samuel Adams of	14: 135	Chamberlain
Philalethus	4: 232	Mather
Philemon Perch	1: 440	Johnston
Philenia	8: 370	Morton
Philetus Dodds	10: 494	Wayland
Phileunomos	2: 352	Sherman
Philip Hamilton	15: 361	Hubert
Philip Paxton	22: 389	Hammett
Philip Quilibet	10: 39	Pond
Philip, Uncle	7: 90	Hawks
Philo-Cato	5: 514	Davis
Philo Pacificus	1: 185	Worcester
Philomath	1: 328	Franklin
Philonius, Sampfilius	1: 434	Woodworth
Philopolis	2: 40	Marsh
Philorthos	6: 478	Poole
Philotheorus	2: 6	Dexter
Phocion	1: 395	Curtis
Phocion	2: 36	Hartley
Phocion	12: 338	Smith
Phocion, T. C.	1: 395	Curtis
Phœnix, John	5: 241	Derby
Physiography, Father of	B: 93	Davis
Piano, Father of the American	6: 190	Chickering
Picayune Butler	5: 297	Butler
Picturesque Explorer	3: 444	Lanman
Pie-crust Palmer	4: 554	Palmer

Pierrepont	8: 224	Church
Pig Iron Kelley	4: 140	Kelley
Pilgrim, Peter	7: 183	Bird
Pilliber, S. P.	6: 32	Shillaber
Pindar Cockloft	9: 383	Irving
Pindar, Jonathan	7: 136	Tucker
Pindar Puff	5: 405	Verplanck
Pingree, Potato	7: 119	Pingree
Pink of the Press	3: 108	Willis
Pinto, Fernando Mendez	9: 254	Briggs
Pipsissiway Pobbs	5: 540	Rice
Piscator	13: 131	Elliott
Piso, Lucius M.	7: 139	Cranch
Pitcher, Molly	6: 399	Corbin
Plate-glass Industry, Father of the	13: 505	Ford
Plautus	9: 348	Wilder
Plow-boy, Delaware	11: 536	Biggs
Plumed Knight	1: 137	Blaine
Plumed Knight	9: 255	Ingersoll
Pobbs, Pipsissiway	5: 540	Rice
Pocahontas of the Pacific	13: 419	Sacajawea
Poet, Blind	11: 150	Heady
Poet of the Commonplace	2: 160	Longfellow
Poet of the Golden Gate	11: 266	Kirchhoff
Poet, Good Gray	1: 255	Whitman
Poet, Hoosier	6: 31	Riley
Poet-Laureate of the Army	13: 183	Patten
Poet of Low Hampton	6: 542	Miller
Poet, Mad	6: 406	Clarke
Poet Naturalist	2: 300	Thoreau
Poet Priest	13: 249	Tabb
Poet of the Rockies	15: 285	Warman
Poet Scout	8: 175	Crawford
Poet Sportsman	6: 19	McLellan
Political Savior of Virginia	5: 453	Walker
Poliuto	1: 156	Wilkie
Pomeroy, Subsidy	12: 69	Pomeroy
Poor Man's Counsellor	3: 302	Clark
Poor Richard	1: 328	Franklin
Poplica, Valerius	1: 104	Adams
Popularity Sumner	3: 300	Sumner
Porte Crayon	9: 365	Strother
Portia	2: 5	Adams
Potato Pingree	7: 119	Pingree
Potiphar, Paul	3: 96	Curtis
Potter, Paul	3: 458	Congdon
Preacher, Blind	7: 137	Milburn
Preacher, Boy	6: 217	Lipscomb
Preacher, Boy	12: 292	Furman
Preacher, Boy	12: 536	Stover
Presbyterianism in Virginia, Father of	5: 516	Morris
Prescott, Dorothy	19: 133	Poor
Presiding Elder, Phenomenal	7: 135	Wilson
Press, Bayard of the	7: 545	Pleasants
Press, Pink of the	3: 108	Willis
Preston, Paul	13: 185	Picton
Primus, Botheration	5: 374	Niles
Prince John	3: 386	Van Buren
Prince of Parliamentarians	9: 181	Mell
Prince of Pulpit Orators	6: 463	Mason
Prince of Schaghticoke	3: 466	Knickerbacker
Prince of Showmen	3: 258	Barnum
Pringle, Seth	8: 232	Barnard
Probability, Old	4: 216	Myer
Probability, Old	8: 264	Abbe
Prodigy, Mathematical	7: 74	Colburn
Prof. Strongfellow	2: 160	Longfellow
Prohibition in Colorado, Father of	2: 61	Fowler
Prolix, Peregrine	4: 346	Nicklin
Prudentius, Aurelius	6: 412	Mather
Public Functionary, Old	5: 1	Buchanan
Public School System in Alabama, Father of	11: 165	Meek
Public School System in Connecticut, Father of	10: 331	Treadwell
Public School System in New Jersey, Father of	7: 152	Cutler
Public School System in Ohio, Father of	13: 81	Rice
Public School System in Pennsylvania, Father of	2: 286	Wolf
Publican, Sammy the	1: 104	Adams
Publicola	5: 73	Adams
Publius	1: 9	Hamilton
Puff, Pindar	5: 405	Verplanck
Pulpit Orators, Prince of	6: 463	Mason
Puritan Captain	5: 417	Standish
Puritan, College	7: 75	Sherman
Puritan Pepys	5: 339	Sewall
Pussyfoot Johnson	A: 502	Johnson
Put, Old	1: 87	Putnam
Putnam, Eleanor	8: 12	Bates, H. L.
Pylodet, F.	7: 491	Leypoldt
Pym, Arthur Gordon	1: 463	Poe

Q.

Quad, M.	6: 30	Lewis
Quaker, Fighting	10: 12	Wanton
Quaker, Fighting	10: 13	Wanton
Quaker Meadows Joe	2: 173	McDowell
Quaker Poet	1: 407	Whittier
Quakers, King of the	5: 514	Pemberton
Quarles	1: 463	Poe
Queen of the American Stage	6: 60	Duff
Queen Mellen	12: 8	Palmer
Querist	13: 153	Blennerhassett
Querno, Camillo	9: 123	Boucher
Quid Rides	10: 84	Evans
Quiet Man	8: 233	Thayer
Quilibet, Philip	10: 39	Pond
Quilp	16: 138	Phelps
Quince, Peter, Esq.	13: 193	Story
Quinn, Dan	25: 261	Lewis
Quod, John	9: 220	Irving
Quoero	3: 235	Wilmer

R.

Race, G.	12: 399	Pool
Raconteur	8: 190	Poore
Ragged Lawyer	11: 272	Grover
Rail-splitter, The	2: 65	Lincoln
Railway King, The	7: 218	Gould, J.
Raimond, C. E.	10: 377	Pennell
Rains, Padre of	23: 70	Ricard
Randolph of Roanoke	5: 97	Randolph
Randolph of Roanoke	13: 137	Barton
Ranger, Old	11: 44	Reynolds
Raymond, Eugene	11: 363	Hewitt
Raymond, John T.	10: 264	O'Brien
Raymond Westbrook	8: 54	Bishop
Ready-money Spencer	5: 221	Spencer
Rebecca Ann Latimer	13: 410	Felton
Reclamation, Father of	15: 243	Wisner
Recluse	7: 236	Botta
Red Fox of Middlesex	13: 358	Montague
Redeemed Captive, The	1: 258	Williams
Reden, Karl	8: 449	Converse
Rediven	8: 479	Day
Reeks, Austin John	23: 300	Dawson
Refalo, Hon. John Philip	11: 360	Dunlop
Refugitta	4: 320	Harrison
Reginald Reverie	7: 245	Mellen
Register, Seeley	4: 522	Victor
Reid, Christian	20: 293	Tiernan
Reliable, Old	4: 48	Thomas

S.

T.

Thanet, Octave	10:163	French
The Benicia Boy	3:370	Leslie
The Dauphin	1: 68	Williams
The Delicious	1:425	Browne
The Duke	1:396	Stockton
The Howitts of America	8:119	Smith
The Idler	8: 57	Gregory
The Keats of Landscape	4:468	Ochtman
The Late Henry Ellen, Esq.	7:241	Hope
The Lay-preacher	7:204	Dennie
The Ohio Gong	3:142	Allen
The Pathfinder	4:270	Fremont
The Rail-splitter	2: 65	Lincoln
The Railway King	7:218	Gould, J.
The Redeemed Captive	1:258	Williams
The Sachem	2: 9	Hillhouse
The Silent Senator	11: 83	Sturgeon
The Ten Pin Boy	21:216	Smith
The Traveler	13:193	Story
The Wagon Boy	6:399	Corwin
The Worcester Spectator	7:501	Fiske
Thelka	4:525	Mason
Theodore de la Guard	7: 64	Ward
Theodore Tinker	5:509	Woodworth
Theophilus Americanus	3:512	Evans
Thermopylæ of the Civil War	4:103	Hill
Thickneck, Geoffrey	10:255	Niles
Thirteen, Immortal	7:309	Jones
Thistle, Timothy	1: 22	Ellsworth
Thomas, Caroline	6: 56	Dorr
Thomas, Pa	4: 48	Thomas
Thompson, Wolf	9: 56	Seton
Thorn Whyte, Mr.	13:465	Elliott
Thorp, Kamba	12:269	Bellamy
Three Star, Old	4: 1	Grant
Thumb, Tom	10:422	Stratton
Thunder, Little	12:520	Ridge
Thunderbolt of the Revolution	1: 84	Morgan
Thundering Jimmy	10:442	Jenkins
Thurlow Weed, Second	11:426	Marseilles
Thurston, Oliver	11:114	Flanders
Tige, Old	3:308	Smith
Tige, Old	13:247	Anderson
Times, Alden of the	6:326	Alden
Timon, John	6: 97	Mitchell
Timothy Peacock	6:233	Thompson
Timothy Thistle	1: 22	Ellsworth
Timothy Titcomb	1:311	Holland
Timsol, Robert	11:197	Bird
Tinker, Theodore	5:509	Woodworth
Tinto, Dick	13:404	Goodrich
Tip, Old	3: 33	Hamilton
Titcomb, Timothy	1:311	Holland
Titian, American	5:383	Allston
Tobias Guarnerius	10:176	Dimitry, A.
Tobias Guarnerius, Jr.	10:176	Dimitry, C. P.
Toby Candor	5:367	Whitman
Todd, Laurie	7:350	Thorburn
Todkill, Amos	7:330	Cooke
Tolstoi of Texas	13:139	Sjolander
Tom, Blind	10:198	Wiggins
Tom Folio	19:404	Babson
Tom, Long	3: 1	Jefferson
Tom Pepper	9:254	Briggs
Tom Reed of Minn.	7: 96	Paige
Tom Thumb	10:422	Stratton
Tom White	13:465	Elliott
Tono Cheeki	6:201	Freneau
Tony Pastor	9:145	Halsey
Tornado	1: 55	Wayne
Town Oracle	1:470	Bradford
Trask, Katrina	11:444	Trask
Traveler, Genevese	5:514	Davis
Traveler, The	13:193	Story
Traverse Oldfield	3:152	Samson
Treasury, Cerberus of the	1: 22	Ellsworth
Treasury, Watch-dog of the	3: 9	Gallatin
Treasury, Watch-dog of the	4: 14	Washburne
Treasury, Watch-dog of the	22: 4	Cannon
Trebor	6:273	Davis
Tree Surgery, Father of	22: 70	Davey
Trenchard, Asa	1:403	Watterson
Tribulation Periwinkle	1:204	Alcott
Trinity, Golden Gate	13:512	Coolbrith
Trumbull	2:394	Webster
Trusta, H.	9:367	Phelps
Truth, Man of	2:131	Thomson
Truth-teller	2:131	Thomson
Tubal Cain	11:508	Holley
Tubal Cain of America	13:387	Spotswood, A.
Tupper, American	1:311	Holland
Tuscarora John	11: 32	Barnwell
Twain, Mark	6: 24	Clemens

U.

Una	2: 32	Lowell
Una Savin	4:320	Hepworth
Uncle Dick	11: 48	Oglesby
Uncle Esek	4: 28	Shaw
Uncle Frank	5:509	Woodworth
Uncle Fred	6:140	Thomson
Uncle Ike	14: 51	Stephenson
Uncle Jeff	18:379	Rhoads
Uncle Joe	22: 4	Cannon
Uncle Philip	7: 90	Hawks
Uncle Remus	1:410	Harris
Uncle Robert	3:165	Lee
Underhill, Dr. Updike	7: 39	Tyler
Union, Belle of the	6:440	Levert
Union Party of California, Father of the	8:158	Van Dyke
Unitarianism, Father of American	7:403	Gay
Universal Friend	8: 81	Wilkinson
Universalism, American, Father of	13:175	Murray
University of Minnesota, Father of the	10: 65	Pillsbury
University of Missouri, Father of the	8:182	Rollins
Updike, Underhill	7: 39	Tyler
Uri, Barclay of	6:378	Barclay

V.

Vagabondia	1:439	Burnett
Valerius Poplicola	1:104	Adams
Vance, Honest Old Joe	8:340	Shannon
Vandegrift, Margaret	12:460	Janvier
Van Dine, S. S.	C:482	Wright
Van Dyke, Brown	13:373	Cook
Van Dyne, Edith	18:331	Baum
Van Tromp	4:231	Sargent
Van Wert, Rupert	9:501	Eddy
Varley, John Philip	4:522	Mitchell
Vaughan, Mrs. Marion	10:363	Gilman
Venator	13:131	Elliott
Veni Vidi	6:499	Croly
Veritas	11:124	Plumer
Vermont Bar, Member of the	6:233	Thompson
Vernon, Di	2:425	Keith
Vernon, Max	A:203	Vernon
Verus	1: 12	Pickering
Veteran Observer	11:206	Mansfield
Veto Governor	10:431	Winston
Victor	8:154	Smith, M. R.
Victor St. Clair	12: 92	Browne
Vieux Moustache	19:332	Gordon
Vincent, John	13:525	Huntington
Vindex	1:104	Adams

W.

X.

Y.

Z.

Commanders of the United States Army and Navy In Times of War

Revolutionary War

The Army

Commander in Chief

Name	Reference
Washington, George	1: 1

Generals

Name	Reference
Arnold, Benedict	1: 53
Gates, Horatio	1: 47
Greene, Nathanael	1: 39
Kosciuszko, Thaddeus	1: 54
Lafayette, Marquis de	1: 63
Lee, Charles	8:238
Lincoln, Benjamin	1: 62
Montgomery, Richard	1:100
Schuyler, Philip J.	1: 97
Steuben, Frederick W. A.	1: 57
Sullivan, John	1: 56
Wayne, Anthony	1: 55

The Navy

Commander in Chief

Name	Reference
Hopkins, Esek	2: 18

Commanders

Name	Reference
Biddle, Nicholas	5:486
Conyngham, Gustavus	4:266
Jones, John Paul	2: 14
Manly, John	5:163
Nicholson, Samuel	4: 89
Saltonstall, Dudley	7:243
Whipple, Abraham	2: 16
Wickes, Lambert	2: 18

War with Tripoli

The Navy

Commanders

Name	Reference
Barron, Samuel	4:417
Dale, Richard	2: 17
Morris, Richard V.	3:352
Preble, Edward	8: 92
Rodgers, John	5:261

War of 1812

The Army

Commanders

Name	Reference
Brown, Jacob	5:400
Croghan, George	4:256
Dearborn, Henry	1: 93
Harrison, William H.	3: 33
Izard, George	10:183
Jackson, Andrew	5:289
Macomb, Alexander	2:241
Ripley, Eleazar W.	3:263
Scott, Winfield	3:502
Wilkinson, James	1: 56

The Navy

Commanders

Name	Reference
Chauncey, Isaac	8: 95
Macdonough, Thomas	7: 28
Perry, Oliver H.	4:288
Porter, David	2: 98

Mexican War

The Army

General in Chief

Name	Reference
Scott, Winfield	3:502

Commanders

First Division

Name	Reference
Kearny, Stephen W.	13:140

Second Division

Name	Reference
Wool, John Ellis	4:282

Third Division

Name	Reference
Taylor, Zachary	4:367

Generals

Name	Reference
Butler, William O.	6:183
Doniphan, Alexander W.	11:389
Frémont, John C.	4:270
Sloat, John D.	6:176
Stockton, Robert F.	4:205
Twiggs, David E.	4:102
Worth, William J.	4:506

The Navy

Commander

Name	Reference
Conner, David	10:121

Civil War

(For the Confederate Forces see pages 304-305)

The Army

General Commanders

Date	Name	Reference
	Scott, Winfield—until Nov. 6, 1861	3:502
Nov. 6, 1861	McClellan, George B.	4:140
July 11, 1862	Halleck, Henry W.	4:257
Mar. 12, 1864	Grant, Ulysses S.	4: 1

Commanders

Army of the Potomac

Date	Name	Reference
July 27, 1861	McClellan, George B.	4:140
Nov. 5, 1862	Burnside, Ambrose E.	4: 53
Jan. 25, 1863	Hooker, Joseph	4:176
June 27, 1863	Meade, George G.	4: 66

Army of Virginia

Date	Name	Reference
Aug. 12, 1862	Pope, John	4:282

Army of the Ohio

Nov. 9, 1861	Buell, Don Carlos	4:263
Oct. 30, 1862	Rosecrans, William S.	4:162
1863	Wright, Horatio G.	4:273
Apr. 26, 1863	Burnside, Ambrose E.	4: 53
Dec. 12, 1863	Foster, John G.	10:134
Jan. 28, 1864	Schofield, John M.	4:259

Army of the Cumberland

Oct. 24, 1862	Rosecrans, William S.	4:162
Oct. 30, 1863	Thomas, George H.	4: 48

Army of the Tennessee

Jan. 1862	Halleck, Henry W.	4:257
Oct. 16, 1862	Grant, Ulysses S.	4: 1
Oct. 27, 1863	Sherman, William T.	4: 32
Mar. 12, 1864	McPherson, James B.	4:203
July 30, 1864	Howard, Oliver O.	4:103
May 19, 1865	Logan, John A.	4:298

Army of the James

Dec. 1863	Butler, Benjamin F.	1:121

First Army Corps

Aug. 12, 1862	Frémont, John C.	4:270
Apr. 15, 1863	Reynolds, John F.	4:224
Nov. 28, 1864	Hancock, Winfield S.	4:134

Second Army Corps

Aug. 12, 1862	Banks, Nathaniel P.	4:222

Third Army Corps

Aug. 12, 1862	McDowell, Irvin	4: 50

Known as the Twelfth after Sept. 12, 1862.

Fourth Army Corps

Sept. 28, 1863	Granger, Gordon	4:559

Fifth Army Corps

July 22, 1862	Porter, Fitz-John	4:261

Sixth Army Corps

July 22, 1862	Franklin, William Buel	4:133

Seventh Army Corps

July 22, 1862	Dix, John A.	5: 6
Jan. 6, 1864	Steele, Frederick	4: 51

Eighth Army Corps

July 22, 1862	Wool, John Ellis	4:282
Mar. 12, 1863	Wallace, Lew	4:363
July 11, 1864	Ord, Edward O. C.	4:281
July 28, 1864	Wallace, Lew	4:363

Ninth Army Corps

July 22, 1862	Burnside, Ambrose E.	4: 53

Tenth Army Corps

Sept. 3, 1862	Mitchel, Ormsby M.	3:440
Mar. 27, 1865	Terry, Alfred H.	4: 69

Eleventh Army Corps

Sept. 12, 1862	Banks, Nathaniel P.	4:222
Apr. 4, 1864	Consolidated with the Twelfth to form the Twentieth Army Corps	

Twelfth Army Corps

Sept. 12, 1862	McDowell, Irvin	4: 50
Apr. 4, 1864	Consolidated with the Eleventh to form the Twentieth Army Corps	

Thirteenth Army Corps

Oct. 24, 1862	Grant, Ulysses S.	4: 1
Dec. 18, 1862	McClernand, John A.	4:137
Feb. 18, 1865	Granger, Gordon	4:559

Fourteenth Army Corps

Oct. 24, 1862	Rosecrans, William S.	4:162
Jan. 9, 1863	Thomas, George H.	4: 48

Fifteenth Army Corps

Dec. 18, 1862	Sherman, William T.	4: 32

Sixteenth Army Corps

Dec. 18, 1862	Hurlbut, Stephen A.	4:218
Feb. 18, 1865	Smith, Andrew J.	11:471

Seventeenth Army Corps

Dec. 18, 1862	McPherson, James B.	4:203

Eighteenth Army Corps

Dec. 24, 1862	Foster, John G.	10:134
Aug. 1, 1863	Seventh Army Corps transferred to this corps	
July 17, 1864	Smith, William F.	7:518

Nineteenth Army Corps

Jan. 5, 1863	Banks, Nathaniel P.	4:222
July 11, 1864	Gillmore, Quincy A.	4: 54
July 13, 1864	Emory, William H. (in command of portion of corps)	4:336
Nov. 7, 1864	Emory, William H. (appointed to command)	4:336

Twentieth Army Corps

Jan. 9, 1863	McCook, Alexander McD.	4:130
Sept. 28, 1863	Consolidated with the Twenty-first to form the Fourth Army Corps	
Apr. 4, 1864	Hooker, Joseph	4:176

Twenty-first Army Corps

Jan. 9, 1863	Crittenden, Thomas L.	2:169
Sept. 28, 1863	Consolidated with the Twentieth to form the Fourth Army Corps	

Twenty-second Army Corps

Feb. 2, 1863	Heintzelman, Samuel P.	12:287

Twenty-third Army Corps

Apr. 27, 1863	Hartsuff, George Lucas	5:331
Jan. 28, 1864	Stoneman, George	4:112
Apr. 4, 1864	Schofield, John M.	4:259
Mar. 27, 1865	Cox, Jacob D.	22:231

Twenty-fourth Army Corps

Dec. 3, 1864	Ord, Edward O. C.	4:281

Twenty-fifth Army Corps

Dec. 3, 1864	Weitzel, Godfrey	11: 86

Cavalry Corps of the Potomac

Apr. 15, 1863	Stoneman, George	4:112
Apr. 4, 1864	Sheridan, Philip H.	4: 63

The Navy

Commanders

West India (Flying) Squadron

1861-62	Pendergrast, Garrett J.	
1862-63	Wilkes, Charles	2:105
1863-64	Lardner, James L.	4:470

Potomac Flotilla

1861	Ward, James H.	
1861	Craven, Tunis A. McD.	12:371
1861-62	Wyman, Robert H.	4:164
1862-63	Harwood, Andrew A.	4:418
1863-65	Parker, Foxhall A.	5:368

Atlantic Blockading Squadron

1861	Stringham, Silas H.	2:101
1861	Goldsborough, Louis M.	2:107

North Atlantic Blockading Squadron

1861-62	Goldsborough, Louis M.	2:107
1862-64	Lee, Samuel P.	11: 55
1864-65	Porter, David D.	2: 97
1865	Radford, William	4:294

James River Squadron

1862	Wilkes, Charles	2:105

South Atlantic Blockading Squadron

1861-63	DuPont, Samuel F.	5: 50
1863-65	Dahlgren, John A.	9:377

Gulf Blockading Squadron

1861	Mervine, William	
1861-63	McKean, William W.	

East Gulf Blockading Squadron

1862	McKean, William W.	
1862	Lardner, James L.	4:470
1862-64	Bailey, Theodorus	2:106
1864	Greene, Theodore P.	5:330
1864-65	Stribling, John M.	

West Gulf Blockading Squadron

1862-63	Farragut, David G.	2: 45
1863	Bell, Charles H. (*ad. int.*)	2:104
1864	Farragut, David G.	2: 45
1864	Palmer, James S.	4:554
1865	Thatcher, Henry K.	5: 44

Mortar Flotilla

1862	Porter, David D.	2: 97

Naval Forces on Western Waters

1861	Rodgers, George W.	4:222
1861-62	Foote, Andrew H.	5: 10
1862	Davis, Charles H.	4:166

Mississippi Squadron

1862-64	Porter, David D.	2: 97
1864-65	Lee, Samuel P.	11: 55

War with Spain

The Army

Commanders

Santiago Campaign

Shafter, William R. 9: 18

Manila Campaign

Merritt, Wesley 9: 28

Puerto Rico Campaign

Miles, Nelson A. 9: 26

The Navy

Commanders

Asiatic Squadron

Dewey, George 9: 3

Atlantic Squadron

Sampson, William T. 9: 9

Flying Squadron

Schley, Winfield S. 9: 8

World War
American Expeditionary Forces

General Headquarters—Command and Staff

Commander in Chief

May 26, 1917	Pershing, John J.	A:434

Chiefs of Staff

May 26, 1917	Harbord, James G.	A:281
May 6, 1918	McAndrew, James W.	
May 27, 1919	Harbord, James G.	A:281
Aug. 12, 1919	Conner, Fox	

Deputy Chief of Staff

May 1, 1918	Eltinge, LeRoy	

Assistant Chiefs of Staff—Administration

July 5, 1917	Logan, James A., Jr.	
Aug. 19, 1918	Andrews, Avery D.	-B:268
Apr. 23, 1919	Lincoln, Charles S.	

Assistant Chiefs of Staff—Intelligence

July 5, 1917	Nolan, Dennis E.	
July 6, 1919	Moreno, Aristides	

Assistant Chiefs of Staff—Operations

July 5, 1917	Palmer, John McA.	A:191
Aug. 28, 1917	Walker, Kirby (*acting*)	
Oct. 29, 1917	Eltinge, LeRoy (*acting*)	
Nov. 5, 1917	Palmer, John McA.	A:191
Nov. 8, 1917	Conner, Fox	
Feb. 3, 1919	Birnie, Upton (*acting*)	
Mar. 10, 1919	Conner, Fox	
Mar. 12, 1919	Birnie, Upton (*acting*)	
Mar. 26, 1919	Conner, Fox	
Aug. 12, 1919	Kuegle, Albert S.	

Assistant Chiefs of Staff—Supply

Aug. 11, 1917	Connor, William D.	
Apr. 30, 1918	Mosely, George V. H.	

Assistant Chiefs of Staff—Training

Aug. 11, 1917	Malone, Paul B.	
Feb. 14, 1918	Fiske, Harold B.	

Adjutants General

May 26, 1917	Alvord, Benjamin	
Nov. 2, 1917	Davis, Robert C. (*acting*)	
Jan. 22, 1918	Alvord, Benjamin	
May 1, 1918	Davis, Robert C.	

Judge Advocate

May 26, 1917	Bethel, A. Walter	

Inspector General

May 26, 1917	Brewster, André W.	

Chief Quartermasters

May 26, 1917 McCarthy, Daniel E.
Aug. 13, 1917 Rogers, Harry L. 24:411
This office transferred to the Services of Supply on Mar. 11, 1918.

Chief Surgeon

May 26, 1917 Bradley, Alfred E. 19:315
This office transferred to the Services of Supply on Mar. 21, 1918.

Chief Ordnance Officer

May 26, 1917 Williams, Clarence C.
This office transferred to the Services of Supply on Mar. 18, 1918.

Chief Engineer Officer

May 26, 1917 Taylor, Harry 23:141
This office transferred to the Services of Supply on Mar. 19, 1918.

Chief Signal Officer

May 26, 1917 Russel, Edgar 20: 31
This office transferred to the Services of Supply on Mar. 19, 1918.

Chief of Artillery

Apr. 29, 1918 Hinds, Ernest

Chief of Tank Corps

Dec. 23, 1917 Rockenbach, Samuel D.

Chiefs of Air Service

May 26, 1917 Dodd, Townsend F.
June 30, 1917 Mitchell, William 26: 21
Aug. 26, 1917 Kenly, William L.
Nov. 27, 1917 Foulois, Benjamin D.
This office transferred to the Services of Supply on Feb. 19, 1918.

Provost Marshals General

July 20, 1917 Ely, Hanson E.
Aug. 26, 1917 Allaire, William H.
This office transferred to the Services of Supply on Mar. 7, 1918.

General Purchasing Agent

Aug. 30, 1917 Dawes, Charles G. A:508
This office transferred to the Services of Supply on Feb. 19, 1918.

Chief of Chemical Warfare Service

Sept. 3, 1917 Fries, Amos A. B:363
This office transferred to the Services of Supply on Feb. 17, 1918.

Director General of Transportation

Sept. 14, 1917 Atterbury, William W. 24: 40
This office transferred to the Services of Supply on Feb. 17, 1918.

Director of Motor Transportation

Dec. 8, 1917 Pope, Francis H.
This office transferred to the Services of Supply on Mar. 25, 1918.

Headquarters Commandants

Sept. 13, 1917 Bacon, Robert
Jan. 7, 1918 Babcock, Conrad S.
Feb. 28, 1918 Ralston, Francis W.

Services of Supply

Commanders

July 5, 1917 Stanley, David S. (*ad. int.*)
July 25, 1917 Blatchford, Richard M. 25:227
Nov. 2, 1917 Patrick, Mason M. (*ad. int.*) C:276
Nov. 28, 1917 Kernan, Francis J. B: 94
July 29, 1918 Harbord, James G. A:281
May 27, 1919 Connor, William D.

Chiefs of Staff

July 28, 1917 McAdams, John P. (*acting*)
Aug. 27, 1917 Langfitt, William C.
Sept. 28, 1917 McAdams, John P.
Dec. 2, 1917 Hagood, Johnson A:474
Nov. 13, 1918 Connor, William D.
May 27, 1919 Drum, Hugh A. A:523
June 19, 1919 Booth, Ewing E.

Deputy Chief of Staff

Feb. 16, 1918 McAdams, John P.

Assistant Chiefs of Staff—Administration

Feb. 23, 1918 Barber, Alvin B.
June 4, 1918 Kutz, Charles W.
July 23, 1918 Cavanaugh, James B.
Jan. 14, 1919 Booth, Ewing E.
June 19, 1919 Tebbetts, Harry H.

Assistant Chiefs of Staff—Intelligence

Feb. 16, 1918 Gilmore, John C., Jr.
Mar. 10, 1918 Ward, Cabot

Assistant Chiefs of Staff—Operations

Feb. 19, 1918 Winans, Edwin B.
Mar. 30, 1918 Wright, John W.
Office discontinued on July 12, 1918.

Assistant Chiefs of Staff—Supply

Feb. 17, 1918 Smither, Henry C. C:174
Feb. 23, 1919 Rhea, James C.
Aug. 15, 1919 Wills, Van L.

Adjutants General

July 25, 1917 Rafferty, William A. (*acting*)
Aug. 28, 1917 Wolfe, Orrin R.
Nov. 30, 1917 Wilcox, Frank A.
Feb. 10, 1918 Leonori, Clifford U. (*acting*)
Feb. 14, 1918 Bash, Louis H.
July 27, 1919 Hall, Harrison

Judge Advocates

Sept. 1, 1917 Bayne, Hugh A.
Oct. 25, 1917 Howell, Willey
Dec. 26, 1917 Bayne, Hugh A. (*acting*)
Feb. 26, 1918 Hull, John A.
Nov. 27, 1918 Winship, Blanton

Inspectors General

Nov. 2, 1917 Kinnison, Henry L. (*acting*)
Nov. 30, 1917 Alexander, Robert (*acting*)
Feb. 2, 1918 Winn, John S.
Sept. 10, 1918 Donaldson, Thomas Q. 24:225
June 17, 1919 Hughes, John H.
July 27, 1919 Lauber, Philip J. (*acting*)
July 31, 1919 Reed, Walter L.

Provost Marshals General

Sept. 1, 1917 Allaire, William H.
Jan. 21, 1918 Isbell, Ernest L.
Mar. 6, 1918 Allaire, William H.
June 29, 1918 Groome, John C. (*acting*)
Sept. 25, 1918 Bandholtz, Harry H. 19:434

Directors Army Service Corps

Aug. 14, 1918 Settle, Douglas
June 2, 1919 Estes, Frank E.

Directors General of Transportation

Feb. 17, 1918 Atterbury, William W. 24: 40
May 16, 1919 McCoy, Frank R.
Aug. 4, 1919 Cheney, Sherwood A.

Directors Motor Transport Corps

Mar. 25, 1918 Pope, Francis H.
July 9, 1918 Walker, Meriwether L.
Aug. 13, 1919 Stayer, Edgar S.

Chief Surgeons

July 18, 1917 Winter, Francis A.
Feb. 17, 1918 Kean, Jefferson R. A: 86
Mar. 21, 1918 Bradley, Alfred E. 19:315
May 1, 1918 Ireland, Merritte W. A:220
Oct. 10, 1918 McCaw, Walter D. A: 89
July 16, 1919 Manly, Clarence J.

Chief Engineers

Aug. 14, 1917 Kutz, Charles W.
Aug. 26, 1917 McKinstry, Charles H.
Sept. 17, 1917 Patrick, Mason M. C:276
Mar. 19, 1918 Taylor, Harry 23:141
July 11, 1918 Langfitt, William C.
July 16, 1919 Jackson, Thomas H.

Chiefs of Chemical Warfare Service

Nov. 22, 1917 Crawford, Robert W.
Jan. 26, 1918 Joly, Charles L.
Feb. 17, 1918 Fries, Amos A.
Nov. 29, 1918 Johnston, Edward N. (*acting*)

Chiefs of Air Service—Supply and Personnel

Aug. 20, 1917 Gorrell, Edgar S. A:525
Jan. 17, 1918 Day, Clarence R.
Feb. 19, 1918 Foulois, Benjamin D.
May 29, 1918 Patrick, Mason M. C:276
July 9, 1919 Lippincott, Aubrey (*acting*)

Chief Signal Officers

Aug. 21, 1917 Russel, Edgar 20: 31
Sept. 1, 1917 Hickerson, Joseph B. L. (*acting*)
Oct. 6, 1917 Wallace, Charles S.
Mar. 19, 1918 Russel, Edgar 20: 31
July 11, 1919 Coles, Roy H.

Chief Quartermasters

July 5, 1917 Stanly, David S.
Dec. 14, 1917 Carson, John M.
Mar. 11, 1918 Rogers, Harry L. 24:411
Jan. 22, 1919 Carson, John M. (*acting*)
Apr. 10, 1919 Knight, John T.

Chief Ordnance Officers

Aug. 21, 1917 Williams, Clarence C.
Oct. 24, 1917 Jordan, Harry B.
Mar. 18, 1918 Williams, Clarence C.
Apr. 5, 1918 Jordan, Harry B. (*acting*)
May 5, 1918 Wheeler, Charles B.
Oct. 9, 1918 Rice, John H. B:117
Aug. 13, 1919 Bricker, Edwin D.

Chiefs War Risk Section

Jan. 7, 1918 Straight, Willard D.
Feb. 16, 1918 Lindsley, Henry D.
Nov. 11, 1918 Cholmeley-Jones, Richard G. (*acting*)
Jan. 20, 1919 Triplett, George V., Jr.

General Purchasing Agent

Feb. 19, 1918 Dawes, Charles G. A:508

Renting, Requisition and Claims Service

Apr. 22, 1918 Hull, John A.
Nov. 27, 1918 Winship, Blanton

Directors Construction and Forestry

Mar. 19, 1918 Patrick, Mason M. C:276
May 19, 1918 Jadwin, Edgar A:521

Director Light Railways

Mar. 19, 1918 Jadwin, Edgar A:521
May 19, 1918 Deakyne, Herbert
July 27, 1918 McKinstry, Charles H.
Nov. 21, 1918 Markham, Edward M. (*acting*)
Dec. 27, 1918 Perkins, Albert T. A:465

Directors Military Engineering and Engineer Supplies

July 11, 1918 Taylor, Harry 23:141
Sept. 11, 1918 Boggs, Frank C. (*acting*)
Oct. 15, 1918 McIndoe, James F.

Headquarters Commandants

Mar. 11, 1918 Burnside, William A.
May 13, 1918 Edwards, Lynn S.
Oct. 26, 1918 Van Orden, George
July 19, 1919 Giddings, Paul

First Army

Command and Staff

Commanders

Aug. 10, 1918 Pershing, John J. A:434
Oct. 16, 1918 Liggett, Hunter A:498

Chiefs of Staff

Aug. 10, 1918 Drum, Hugh A. A:523
Dec. 22, 1918 Wills, Van L. (*acting*)
Jan. 5, 1919 Drum, Hugh A. A:523
Apr. 17, 1919 Wills, Van L. (*acting*)

Chiefs of Artillery

Aug. 10, 1918 McGlachlin, Edward F., Jr. A:403
Nov. 20, 1918 McNair, William S. A:379

Chiefs of Air Service

Aug. 10, 1918 Mitchell, William 26: 21
Oct. 22, 1918 Milling, Thomas DeW. A:448
Jan. 25, 1919 Johnson, Davenport (*acting*)
Feb. 8, 1919 FitzGerald, Shepler W.

Chief Engineers

Aug. 10, 1918 Morrow, Jay J.
Oct. 24, 1918 Spalding, George R.
Nov. 24, 1918 Peek, Ernest D.
Jan. 6, 1919 Jones, DeWitt C. (*acting*)
Jan. 13, 1919 Hoffman, George M.

Chief Signal Officer

Aug. 10, 1918 Hitt, Parker

Chief Surgeons

Aug. 10, 1918 Stark, Alexander N.
Dec. 3, 1918 Rhoads, Thomas L.

Chief of Tank Corps

Aug. 21, 1918 Rockenbach, Samuel D.

Chiefs of Chemical Warfare Service

Aug. 10, 1918 Ardery, Edward D. (*acting*)
Sept. 1, 1918 Schulz, John W. N.
Feb. 5, 1919 Robbe, Louis E.
Feb. 27, 1919 Schulz, John W. N.

Second Army

Command and Staff

Commander

Oct. 12, 1918 Bullard, Robert L. A:294

Chief of Staff

Oct. 12, 1918 Heintzelman, Stuart

Chiefs of Artillery

Oct. 14, 1918 Lassiter, William A:115
Nov. 18, 1918 Vacant
Nov. 30, 1918 Aultman, Dwight E.

Chief Engineer

Oct. 12, 1918 Deakyne, Herbert

Chiefs of Air Service

Oct. 12, 1918 Milling, Thomas DeW. A:448
Oct. 14, 1918 Lahm, Frank P. ....

Chief Signal Officer

Oct. 12, 1918 Black, Hanson B. ....

Chief Surgeon

Oct. 12, 1918 Reynolds, Charles R. ....

Chiefs of Chemical Warfare Service

Oct. 20, 1918 Goss, Byron C. ....
Nov. 22, 1918 Mackall, Colin M. ....
Feb. 24, 1919 Miller, Rolla W. (*acting*) ....
Mar. 29, 1919 Robbe, Louis E. ....

Third Army

Command and Staff

Commanders

Nov. 15, 1918 Dickman, Joseph T. 20: 11
Apr. 29, 1919 McGlachlin, Edward F., Jr. (*ad. int.*) A:403
May 2, 1919 Liggett, Hunter A:498

Chief of Staff

Nov. 15, 1918 Craig, Malin ....

Chief of Artillery

Apr. 23, 1919 Lassiter, William A:115

Chiefs of Air Service

Nov. 15, 1918 Mitchell, William 26: 21
Jan. 15, 1919 Paegelow, John A. (*acting*) ....
Jan. 21, 1919 Fowler, Harold ....

Chief Engineers

Nov. 15, 1918 Barden, William J. ....
Nov. 25, 1918 Spalding, George R. ....
Jan. 10, 1919 Markham, Edward M. ....
Jan. 22, 1919 Wooten, William P. ....

Chief Signal Officers

Nov. 15, 1918 Voris, Alvin C. ....
Feb. 13, 1919 Carr, Irving J. ....
Apr. 22, 1919 Hitt, Parker ....
June 21, 1919 Hemphill, John E. ....

Chief Surgeon

Nov. 15, 1918 Grissinger, Jay W. ....

Chief of Chemical Warfare Service

Nov. 21, 1918 Rockwell, Charles K. ....

I Army Corps

Command and Staff

Corps Commanders

Jan. 20, 1918 Liggett, Hunter ....
Oct. 12, 1918 Dickman, Joseph T. 20: 11
Nov. 13, 1918 Wright, William M. A:440
Feb. 28, 1919 Sturgis, Samuel D. (*ad. int.*) A:287
Mar. 14, 1919 Wright, William M. A:440

Chiefs of Staff

Jan. 20, 1918 Craig, Malin ....
Nov. 12, 1918 Grant, Walter S. ....
Dec. 31, 1918 Beebe, Royden E. (*acting*) ....
Jan. 5, 1919 Fassett, William M. ....

Chiefs of Artillery

Jan. 29, 1918 Hinds, Ernest ....
Mar. 24, 1918 McGlachlin, Edward F., Jr. A:403
May 17, 1918 Lassiter, William A:115
Aug. 22, 1918 French officers acted in this capacity
Nov. 7, 1918 McNair, William S. A:379
Nov. 20, 1918 Vacant ....
Jan. 5, 1919 Cruikshank, William M. .... A: 90

II Army Corps

Command and Staff

Corps Commanders

Feb. 24, 1918 Chief of Staff acted for Gen. Pershing
June 15, 1918 Read, George W. A:536

Chiefs of Staff

Feb. 24, 1918 Simonds, George S. ....
Feb. 1, 1919 Buchan, Fred E. ....

III Army Corps

Command and Staff

Corps Commander

Mar. 30, 1918 Chief of Staff acted for Gen. Pershing
June 17, 1918 Wright, William M. A:440
July 12, 1918 McMahon, John E. (*ad. int.*) ....
July 14, 1918 Bullard, Robert L. A:294
Oct. 12, 1918 Hines, John L. ....
Feb. 19, 1919 McGlachlin, Edward F., Jr. (*ad. int.*) A:403
Mar. 5, 1919 Hines, John L. ....
Apr. 29, 1919 McGlachlin, Edward F., Jr. (*ad. int.*) A:403
May 11, 1919 Hines, John L. ....

Chiefs of Staff

Mar. 30, 1918 Bjornstad, Alfred W. 25:285
Oct. 23, 1918 King, Campbell ....
Mar. 25, 1919 Shallenberger, Martin C. (*acting*)
Apr. 1, 1919 King, Campbell ....

Chiefs of Artillery

Aug. 2, 1918 Gatchell, George W. ....
Oct. 11, 1918 Flagler, Clement A. F. ....
Nov. 26, 1918 Vacant ....

IV Army Corps

Command and Staff

Corps Commanders

June 19, 1918 Chief of staff acted for Gen. Pershing
Aug. 18, 1918 Dickman, Joseph T. 20: 11
Oct. 12, 1918 Muir, Charles H. .... A: 92
Apr. 14, 1919 Howze, Robert L. (*ad. int.*) 23:139
May 2, 1919 Summerall, Charles P. A:150

Chiefs of Staff

June 19, 1918 Heintzelman, Stuart ....
Sept. 20, 1918 Brown, Preston A:516
Oct. 17, 1918 Wells, Briant H. ....
May 11, 1919 Krueger, Walter (*acting*) ....

Chiefs of Artillery

Aug. 22, 1918 Lassiter, William A:115
Oct. 14, 1918 Donnelly, Edward T. (*acting*) ....
Oct. 30, 1918 Cruikshank, William M. .... A: 90

V Army Corps

Command and Staff

Corps Commanders

July 12, 1918 Wright, William M. A:440
Aug. 21, 1918 Cameron, George H. .... A: 99
Oct. 12, 1918 Summerall, Charles P. A:150

Chiefs of Staff

July 12, 1918	Burtt, Wilson B.	
Dec. 12, 1918	Emerson, Thomas H. (*acting*)	
Dec. 27, 1918	Burtt, Wilson B.	
Feb. 10, 1919	Foreman, Albert W. (*acting*)	

Chiefs of Artillery

Aug. 19, 1918	Alexandre, René (*French army*)	
Oct. 21, 1918	Aultman, Dwight E.	
Nov. 30, 1918	Shepherd, William E., Jr. (*acting*)	

VI Army Corps

Command and Staff

Corps Commanders

Aug. 1, 1918	No corps commander	
Aug. 26, 1918	Bundy, Omar	A:523
Sept. 13, 1918	Chief of Staff acted as corps commander	
Oct. 23, 1918	Ballou, Charles C.	
Nov. 10, 1918	Menoher, Charles T.	
Dec. 17, 1918	Martin, Charles H.	
Dec. 20, 1918	Bell, George, Jr.	25:410
Dec. 24, 1918	Bullard, Robert L. (*ad. int.*)	A:294
Jan. 13, 1919	Cronkhite, Adelbert	
Feb. 3, 1919	Bell, George, Jr. (*ad. int.*)	25:410
Feb. 18, 1919	Cronkhite, Adelbert	
Mar. 25, 1919	Bell, George, Jr. (*ad. int.*)	25:410
Mar. 27, 1919	Cronkhite, Adelbert	
Apr. 10, 1919	Bell, George, Jr.	25:410

Chiefs of Staff

July 30, 1918	Wells, Briant H.	
Oct. 17, 1918	Baltzell, George F. (*acting*)	
Oct. 22, 1918	Collins, Edgar T.	

Chief of Artillery

Nov. 7, 1918	Bowley, Albert J.	

VII Army Corps

Command and Staff

Corps Commanders

Aug. 19, 1918	Wright, William M.	A:440
Sept. 6, 1918	Chief of Staff acted for Gen. Pershing	
Sept. 13, 1918	Bundy, Omar	A:523
Oct. 25, 1918	Chief of Staff acted as corps commander	
Nov. 21, 1918	Haan, William G.	22:423
Apr. 23, 1919	Martin, Charles H. (*ad. int.*)	
May 8, 1919	Allen, Henry T.	

Chiefs of Staff

Aug. 20, 1918	Gerhardt, Charles H. (*acting*)	
Aug. 24, 1918	Johnston, Gordon (*acting*)	
Sept. 26, 1918	King, Campbell	
Oct. 23, 1918	Chaffee, Adna R. (*acting*)	
Oct. 27, 1918	Brees, Herbert J.	

Chief of Artillery

May 9, 1919	Margetts, Nelson E.	

VIII Army Corps

Command and Staff

Corps Commanders

Nov. 26, 1918	Allen, Henry T.	
Apr. 15, 1919	Gordon, Walter H.	21:300

Chiefs of Staff

Nov. 26, 1918	Marshall, George C., Jr.	
Jan. 15, 1919	Erickson, Hjalmer	

Chief of Artillery

Feb. 24, 1919	Margetts, Nelson E. (*acting*)	

IX Army Corps

Command and Staff

Corps Commanders

Nov. 26, 1918	Cronkhite, Adelbert	
Jan. 13, 1919	Bullard, Robert L. (*ad. int.*)	A:294
Jan. 18, 1919	Kuhn, Joseph E. (*ad. int.*)	A: 63
Jan. 26, 1919	Weigel, William (*ad. int.*)	26:300
Jan. 31, 1919	Kuhn, Joseph E. (*ad. int.*)	A: 63
Feb. 28, 1919	Summerall, Charles P.	A:150
Apr. 16, 1919	Allen, Henry T.	
Apr. 21, 1919	Weigel, William (*ad. int.*)	26:300
Apr. 25, 1919	Bailey, Charles J. (*ad. int.*)	A:292
Apr. 28, 1919	Allen, Henry T.	

Chiefs of Staff

Nov. 26, 1918	Naylor, William K.	
Jan. 26, 1919	Barnes, John B. (*acting*)	
Jan. 31, 1919	Naylor, William K.	

Chief of Artillery

Nov. 28, 1918	Davis, Richmond P.	

Confederate States of America

The following southern states seceded from the Union:

State	Date	State	Date
South Carolina	Dec. 20, 1860	Texas	Feb. 1, 1861
Mississippi	Jan. 9, 1861	Virginia	Apr. 17, 1861
Florida	Jan. 10, 1861	Arkansas	May 6, 1861
Alabama	Jan. 11, 1861	North Carolina	May 21, 1861
Georgia	Jan. 19, 1861	Tennessee	June 8, 1861
Louisiana	Jan. 26, 1861		

Missouri, Kentucky, Maryland and Delaware declared themselves neutral, but did not pass ordinances of secession.

Convention at Montgomery, Alabama, February 4, 1861

President—Cobb, Howell, of Georgia 1:226

Secretary—Hooper, Johnson J., of Alabama 11:264

Delegates

South Carolina

Rhett, Robert B. 4:303
Chestnut, James 5: 54
Miles, William P. 11: 35
Withers, T. J. ....
Barnwell, Robert W. 11: 32
Memminger, Christopher G. 4:200
Reitt, L. M. ....
Boyce, W. W. ....

Georgia

Toombs, Robert 4:392
Cobb, Howell 1:226
Hill, Benjamin H. 10:194
Stephens, Alexander H. 3:420
Barton, Frank S. ....
Crawford, Martin J. 2:244
Nisbet, Eugenius A. 5:255
Wright, August R. ....
Cobb, Thomas R. R. 6:533
Kenan, August ....

Alabama

Walker, Richard W. ....
Smith, Robert H. 8:498
McRae, Colin J. ....
Shorter, John G. 10:432
Hale, S. L. ....
Lewis, David P. 10:435
Fearn, Thomas M. ....
Curry, Jabez L. M. 4:357
Chilton, William P. 4:153
Hooper, Johnson J. 11:264

Mississippi

Harris, Wiley P. 4:553
Brooks, Walker ....
Clayton, A. M. ....
Barry, William T. 5:296
Harrison, James T. 12:184
Campbell, Josiah A. P. 7:531
Wilson, W. T. ....

Louisiana

Perkins, John, Jr. ....
Kenner, Duncan F. ....
Conrad, Charles M. 6:181
Sparrow, Edward ....
Marshall, Henry ....
DeCluet, A. ....

Florida

Morton, Jackson 5:259
Anderson, J. P. ....
Owens, James B. ....

On February 9, 1861, a Provisional Constitution for the Confederate States of America was adopted, and officers elected as follows:

President—Davis, Jefferson, of Mississippi 4:148
Vice-President—Stephens, Alexander, of Georgia 3:420

President Davis was inaugurated February 18, 1861.

A permanent government was organized at Richmond, Virginia, on February 22, 1862, with Jefferson Davis as president and Alexander H. Stephens as vice-president.

Senate of the First Congress

Vice-President—Stephens, Alexander H. 3:420

President pro tem—Hunter, Robert M. T. 9:158

Name	Ref.
Baker, James M. (Florida)	5: 88
Barnwell, Robert W. (South Carolina)	11: 32
Brown, Albert G. (Mississippi)	13:488
Burnett, Henry C. (Kentucky)	
Clark, John B. (Missouri)	
Clay, Clement C. (Alabama)	4:198
Davis, George (North Carolina)	3:526
Dortch, William T. (North Carolina)	
Haynes, Landon C. (Tennessee)	
Henry, Gustavus A. (Tennessee)	13:131
Hill, Benjamin H. (Georgia)	10:194
Hunter, Robert M. T. (Virginia)	9:158
Johnson, Robert W. (Arkansas)	5:252
Lewis, John W. (Georgia)	
Maxwell, Augustus A. (Florida)	7:487
Mitchell, Charles B. (Arkansas)	4: 63
Oldham, Williamson S. (Texas)	
Peyton, Robert L. Y. (Missouri)	5:158
Preston, William B. (Virginia)	4:371
Semmes, Thomas J. (Louisiana)	10: 86
Simms, William E. (Kentucky)	
Sparrow, Edward (Louisiana)	
Wigfall, Louis T. (Texas)	5:262
Yancey, William L. (Alabama)	4:319
Orr, James L. (South Carolina)	12:175

Cabinet Officers

Secretaries of State

Term	Name	Ref.
Feb. 21, 1861 to July 25, 1861	Toombs, Robert	4:392
July 25, 1861 to Mar. 18, 1862	Hunter, Robert M. T.	9:158
Mar. 18, 1862 to the end of the war	Benjamin, Judah P.	4:285

Attorneys General

Term	Name	Ref.
Feb. 25, 1861 to Sept. 17, 1861	Benjamin, Judah P.	4:285
Nov. 21, 1861 to Mar. 18, 1862	Bragg, Thomas	4:427
Mar. 18, 1862 to Jan. 1, 1864	Watts, Thomas N.	10:432
Jan. 2, 1864 to the end of the war	Davis, George	3:526

Secretaries of the Treasury

Term	Name	Ref.
Feb. 21, 1861 to July 18, 1864	Memminger, Christopher G.	4:200
July 18, 1864 to the end of the war	Trenholm, George A.	4:382

Secretaries of War

Term	Name	Ref.
Feb. 21, 1861 to Sept. 17, 1861	Walker, LeRoy P.	5:288
Sept. 17, 1861 to Mar. 17, 1862	Benjamin, Judah P.	4:285
Mar. 18, 1862 to Nov. 17, 1862	Randolph, George W.	10:159
Mar. 18, 1862 to Nov. 17, 1862	Smith, Gustavus W. (*acting*)	7:515
Nov. 18, 1862 to Feb. 6, 1865	Seddon, James A.	6:219
Feb. 6, 1865 to the end of the war	Breckinridge, John C.	5: 3

Secretary of the Navy

Term	Name	Ref.
Mar. 1, 1861 to the end of the war	Mallory, Stephen R.	4:364

Postmasters General

Term	Name	Ref.
Feb. 25, 1861 to Mar. 5, 1861	Ellett, Henry T.	10:132
Mar. 6, 1861 to the end of the war	Reagan, John H.	1:292

Officers of the Confederate States Army

Commander in Chief

Date	Name	Reference
Jan. 31, 1865	Lee, Robert E.	4: 95

Generals

Date	Name	Reference
May 16, 1861	Cooper, Samuel	11: 54
May 30, 1861	Johnston, Albert S.	1:388
July 21, 1861	Beauregard, Pierre T. G.	4:178
Aug. 13, 1861	Johnston, Joseph E.	5:328
Apr. 12, 1862	Bragg, Braxton	11:218
Feb. 19, 1864	Smith, E. Kirby	8:132
July 18, 1864	Hood, John B.	4:264

Lieutenant-Generals

Date	Name	Reference
Oct. 9, 1862	Longstreet, James	4:263
Oct. 10, 1862	Polk, Leonidas	11:341
Oct. 10, 1862	Jackson, Thomas J.	4:125
Oct. 10, 1862	Hardee, William J.	4:101
Oct. 10, 1862	Holmes, Theophilus H.	10:116
Oct. 10, 1862	Pemberton, John C.	10:241
May 23, 1863	Ewell, Richard S.	4: 55
May 24, 1863	Hill, Ambrose P.	4:101
July 11, 1863	Hill, Daniel H.	4:102
Apr. 8, 1864	Taylor, Richard	4:331
May 31, 1864	Early, Jubal A.	4:137
May 31, 1864	Anderson, Richard H.	4:295
June 23, 1864	Lee, Stephen D.	5:414
June 23, 1864	Stewart, Alexander P.	4:502
Sept. 20, 1864	Buckner, Simon B.	16:341
Feb. 14, 1865	Hampton, Wade	12:177
Feb. 28, 1865	Forrest, Nathan B.	10: 36
Feb. 28, 1865	Wheeler, Joseph	9: 19
Feb. 28, 1865	Gordon, John B.	1:231

Major-Generals

Date	Name	Reference
May 22, 1862	Twiggs, David E.	4:102
Sept. 19, 1861	Van Dorn, Earl	4:208
Sept. 19, 1861	Smith, Gustavus W.	7:515
Oct. 7, 1861	Hager, Benjamin	
Oct. 7, 1861	Magruder, John B.	4:294
Oct. 7, 1861	Lovell, Mansfield	4:352
Nov. 9, 1861	Crittenden, George B.	4:501
Feb. 15, 1862	Loring, William W.	4:364
Mar. 10, 1862	Cheatham, Benjamin F.	11: 90
Mar. 10, 1862	McCown, John P.	
Mar. 16, 1862	Price, Sterling	12:304
Apr. 6, 1862	Withers, Jones M.	11:207
Apr. 14, 1862	Hindman, Thomas C.	22:130
Apr. 14, 1862	Breckinridge, John C.	5: 3
May 10, 1862	Jones, Samuel	4:466
May 23, 1862	McLaws, Lafayette	4:317
July 25, 1862	Stuart, J. E. B.	4: 51
Aug. 31, 1862	French, S. G.	
Oct. 10, 1862	Stevenson, Carter L.	
Oct. 10, 1862	Pickett, George E.	5: 49
Oct. 11, 1862	Jones, David R.	
Oct. 17, 1862	Forney, William H.	3:521
Nov. 4, 1862	Mowry, Dabney H.	
Nov. 4, 1862	Smith, Martin L.	5: 96
Nov. 8, 1862	Walker, John G.	11:524
Dec. 4, 1862	Elzy, Arnold	6:217
Dec. 13, 1862	Gardner, Franklin K.	4:222
Dec. 13, 1862	Cleburne, Patrick R.	8: 54
Jan. 17, 1863	Trimble, Isaac R.	4:342
Jan. 17, 1863	Donelson, Daniel S.	
Feb. 28, 1863	Whiting, William H. C.	4:488
Feb. 28, 1863	Johnson, Edward	12:442
May 23, 1863	Rodes, Robert E.	5:363
May 23, 1863	Walker, William H. T.	13: 16
May 24, 1863	Heth, Henry	4:464
May 25, 1863	Bowen, John S.	12:270
May 26, 1863	Ransom, Robert, Jr.	
May 27, 1863	Pender, William D.	9:268
Aug. 3, 1863	Wilcox, Cadmus M.	11:512
Aug. 3, 1863	Lee, Fitz-Hugh	9: 1
Aug. 20, 1863	Gilmer, J. F.	
Aug. 20, 1863	Smith, William	4:459
Sept. 9, 1863	Cobb, Howell	1:226
Nov. 10, 1863	Wharton, John A.	15:238
Nov. 10, 1863	Martin, Will T.	
Feb. 12, 1864	Field, Charles W.	
Feb. 17, 1864	Anderson, J. Patten	4:129
Feb. 23, 1864	Bate, William B.	7:213
Apr. 8, 1864	DePolignac, C. T.	
Apr. 18, 1864	Maxey, Samuel B.	4: 50
Apr. 20, 1864	Hoke, Robert F.	12:122
Apr. 23, 1864	Lee, William H. F.	4:280
May 14, 1864	Gordon, John B.	1:231
May 18, 1864	Kershaw, Joseph B.	12:261
May 21, 1864	Johnson, Bushrod R.	
June 1, 1864	Ramseur, Stephen D.	4:473
June 6, 1864	Walthall, Edward C.	1:389
July 7, 1864	Clayton, N. D.	
July 30, 1864	Mahone, William	5: 12
Aug. 4, 1864	Brown, John C.	7:211
Aug. 10, 1864	Lomax, Lunsford L.	6: 16
Sept. 19, 1864	Allen, Henry W.	4: 38
Sept. 19, 1864	Kemper, James L.	5:454
Sept. 19, 1864	Butler, Matthew C.	1:298
Oct. 20, 1864	Lee, George W. C.	3:166
Nov. 1, 1864	Rosser, Thomas L.	3:277
Nov. 26, 1864	Wright, Ambrose R.	12:108
Nov. 26, 1864	Pegram, John	5: 52
Dec. 30, 1864	Young, Pierce M. B.	2:382
Jan. 1, 1865	Preston, William	9:433
Jan. 1, 1865	Taliaferro, William B.	5:216
Feb. 15, 1865	Grimes, Bryan	6:173
Mar. 17, 1865	Marmaduke, John S.	12:308
Mar. 17, 1865	Allen, William W.	19:321
Mar. 17, 1865	Churchill, Thomas J.	10:190
Mar. 17, 1865	Humes, W. Y. C.	10:190
Apr. 9, 1865	Hays, Harry B.	16:347
Apr. 9, 1865	Law, E. M.	
Apr. 9, 1865	Gary, Martin W.	22:379
Apr. 9, 1865	Ransom, Matthew W.	10:251

Commanders of the Confederate States Navy

Naval Defenses of Virginia and North Carolina

1861	Barron, Samuel	4:367
1863-64	Lynch, William F.	13:172

James River Squadron

1861	Buchanan, Franklin	4: 38
1862	Tattnall, Josiah	5:488
1863-64	Forrest, French	
1864	Maury, John S.	
1864-65	Mitchell, John K.	
1865	Semmes, Raphael	4:340

Naval Defenses Cape Fear River

1863-64	Lynch, William F.	13:172
1864	Pinkney, Robert F.	

Naval Defenses South Carolina and Georgia

1862	Tattnall, Josiah	5:488

Naval Defenses of Charleston Harbor, S. C.

1861-62	Ingraham, Duncan N.	8:336
1862-65	Tucker, John R.	4:334

Naval Defenses of Savannah, Ga.

1862-63	Tattnall, Josiah	5:488
1863-64	Hunter, William W.	

Mississippi River Defenses

1862	Hollins, George N.	11:252

Lower Mississippi River Defenses

1862	Mitchell, John K.	

Mobile Defenses

1862-64	Randolph, Victor M.	
1864	Buchanan, Franklin	4: 38
1864-65	Farrand, Ebenezer	

Mississippi River Defense Fleet

1862	Montgomery, J. E.	

Naval Forces in Europe

1862-64	Barron, Samuel	4:367

Naval Defenses Coast of Texas

1861-63	Hunter, William W.	

Americans Preëminent in Literature, the Arts and Sciences, and the Professions

(Date to left of column is approximate year in which career was begun.)

Actors and Actresses

1752..Hallam, Lewis 10: 259
1772..Bernard, John 21: 159
1787..Fennell, James 6: 59
1790..Darley, John 2: 334
1792..Hodgkinson, John 3: 343
1792..Rowson, Susanna 9: 317
1792..Rowson, William 9: 317
1794..Cooper, Thomas A. 10: 260
1798..Wood, William B. 1: 322
1805..Wheatley, Sarah R. 1: 160
1807..Wallack, James W. 4: 439
1809..Duff, Mary A. D. 6: 60
1809..Payne, John H. 2: 347
1811..Finn, Henry J. 8: 462
1811..Gilfert, Agnes H. 2: 441
1813..Booth, Junius B. 3: 180
1813..Conway, William A. 7: 200
1815..Power, Tyrone 13: 577
1816..Woodhull, Jacob 5: 426
1817..Fisher, Clara 10: 471
1817..Vernon, Jane M. F. 10: 453
1819..Hamblin, Thomas S. 3: 120
1819..Smith, Sol 26: 386
1820..Forrest Edwin 5: 86
1820..Holland, George 3: 148
1821..Hadaway, Thomas H. 10: 455
1821..Johnston, David C. 5: 519
1821..Richings, Peter 7: 449
1821..Stone, John A. 8: 88
1822..Barrett, George H. 4: 447
1823..Blake, William R. 4: 144
1823..Dockstader, Lew 23: 237
1823..Placide, Coraline 4: 144
1823..Placide, Henry 8: 57
1823..Placide, Thomas 8: 58
1826..Hackett, James H. 3: 74
1826..Hill, George H. 1: 401
1826..Wheatley, William 1: 190
1827..Drew, Mrs. John 8: 217
1828..Gilbert, John G. 1: 261
1829..Bannister, Nathaniel H. ..22: 445
1829..Kemble, Frances Anne ... 3: 414
1829..Murdoch, James E. 6: 71
1829..Scott, John R. 13: 237
1830..Burton, William Evans .. 2: 351
1830..Davidge, William P. 11: 516
1830..Winslow, Kate R. 1: 181
1831..Clifton, Josephine 6: 517
1832..Gannon, Mary 11: 515
1832..Warren, William 5: 439
1833..Eaton, Charles H. 6: 153
1834..Cushman, Charlotte S. ... 4: 40
1834..De Bar, Benedict 3: 60
1834..Vincent, Mary A. F. 10: 257
1835..Logan, Cornelius A. 12: 189
1836..Davenport, Edward L. ... 9: 319
1836..Mitchell, William 8: 69
1837..Burke, Charles St. T. 8: 124
1837..Cushman, Susan W. 23: 356
1837..Proctor, Joseph 15: 47
1838..Couldock, Charles W. 2: 346
1838..Harrison, Gabriel 5: 218
1838..Jefferson, Joseph 1: 522
1839..Christy, George N. 7: 297
1839..Rice, Thomas D. 11: 207
1839..Vandenhoff, George 1: 427
1839..Walcot, Charles M. 11: 514
1840..Conway, Frederick B. 7: 265
1840..Fechter, Charles A. 5: 130
1840..Ritchie, Anna C. M. 3: 227
1841..Boucicault, Dion 2: 375
1841..Eddy, Edward 6: 291
1842..Brougham, John 9: 448
1842..Christy, Edwin P. 23: 305
1842..Drew, John, Sr. 3: 531
1842..Pray, Isaac C. 13: 420
1843..Field, Joseph M. 13: 140
1843..McVicker, James H. 6: 281
1843..Williams, Maria P. 5: 440
1844..Lander, Jean M. D. 8: 127
1845..Dean, Julia 3: 299
1845..Stoddart, James H. 6: 502
1846..Bowers, Elizabeth 11: 360
1846..Fox, Charles K. 26: 443
1846..Owens, John 5: 191
1846..Pastor, Tony 16: 30
1846..Wallack, Lester 4: 440
1846..Williams, Barney 5: 440
1848..Chanfrau, Frank 7: 323
1848..Janauschek, Francesca R. 10: 70
1848..Pope, Charles R. 8: 138
1848..Smith, Marcus 26: 387
1849..Booth, Edwin 3: 180
1849..Crocker, Sarah G. 11: 360
1849..Florence, William J. 2: 381
1849..Gilbert, Mrs. George H. .. 1: 285
1849..Manchester, Albertine 9: 209
1850..Buchanan, McKean 11: 283
1850..Herne, James A. 5: 83
1850..Waller, Emma 11: 224
1850..Winslow, Catherine M. R. 23: 258
1851..Clarke, John S. 7: 475
1851..Heron, Matilda A. 8: 263
1851..Mitchell, Maggie 25: 222
1852..Booth, Junius B., Jr. 3: 180
1852..Keene, Laura 8: 65
1852..LeMoyne, William J. 5: 389
1852..Robson, Stuart 2: 411
1852..Sothern, Edward A. 5: 490
1852..Thompson, Denman 8: 46
1852..Vezin, Herman 5: 172
1853..Barrett, Lawrence 1: 379
1853..Raymond, John T. 10: 264
1854..Aldrich, Louis 13: 331
1854..Backus, Charles 12: 440
1854..Baker, Henrietta 7: 323
1854..Logan, Olive 6: 528
1855..Albaugh, John W. 2: 167
1855..McEthenrey, Jane 6: 247
1856..Mayo, Frank M. 23: 369
1857..Hosmer, Jean 4: 435
1857..Lewis, James 1: 286
1857..McCullough, John 9: 141
1857..Ward, Genevieve, ... 9: 196
1858..Crabtree, Lotta M. 9: 547
1858..France, Rachel A. N. 20: 309
1858..Maeder, Frederick G. 6: 14
1858..Menken, Adah I. 5: 435
1858..Walcott, Charles M. 11: 514
1860..Adams, Edwin 5: 110
1860..Bateman, Kate J. 10: 456
1860..Booth, Agnes 1: 465
1860..Booth, John Wilkes 3: 182
1861..Herrmann, Alexander 9: 327
1861..Mann, Henry J. 11: 513
1861..Modjeska, Helena 10: 447
1861..Sheridan, William E. 2: 142
1862..Coghlan, Charles 13: 397
1862..Davenport, Fanny L. G. . 4: 57
1862..Morris, Clara 11: 506
1862..Russell, Sol Smith 10: 412
1863..Crane, William H. 2: 153
1863..Keene, Thomas W. 8: 384
1863..Mackay, Frank F. 17: 333
1863..Morris, Felix 11: 160
1864..James, Louis 16: 138
1864..Wilson, Francis 2: 134
1865..Barnabee, Henry C. 8: 35
1865..Oates, Alice 6: 297
1865..Salsbury, Nathan 8: 166
1865..Weathersby, Eliza 5: 435
1866..Coghlan, Rose 13: 397
1866..Emmet, Joseph K. 5: 144
1866..Holland, Edmund M. 11: 438
1866..Richardson, Abby S. 5: 553
1867..Dixey, Henry E. 10: 112
1867..Harrigan, Edward 11: 442
1867..O'Neill, James 11: 185
1867..Warde, Frederick B. 11: 105
1869..Claxton, Kate 22: 189
1869..Evans, Charles E. 11: 396
1869..Russell, Annie 13: 498
1870..Reed, Roland 13: 323
1872..Jewett, Sara 11: 284
1872..Sothern, Edward L. 5: 490
1873..Conried, Heinrich 11: 384
1873..Drew, John 3: 531
1874..Burgess, Neil 2: 170
1874..Rehan, Ada 1: 287
1874..Riddle, George P. 13: 305
1875..Anderson, Mary 1: 243
1875..Martinot, Sadie 12: 556
1876..Dickinson, Anna E. 3: 109
1876..Gillette, William 2: 249
1876..Goodwin, Nathaniel C. ... 6: 291
1876..Mantell, Robert B. 14: 290
1877..Rohlfs, Charles 9: 257
1877..Skinner, Otis 11: 220
1878..Fields, Lew 14: 317
1878..Hopper, De Wolf 10: 450
1878..Mansfield, Richard 9: 117
1878..Mason, John 15: 50
1878..Mather, Margaret 9: 446
1878..Olcott, Chauncey 11: 519
1879..Davis, Jesse B. 8: 62
1879..Sothern, Edward H. 5: 490
1880..Cayvan, Georgia Eva 2: 453
1880..Jewett, Henry 22: 303
1880..Lackaye, Wilton 3: 516
1880..LeMoyne, Sarah C. 13: 303
1880..Olcott, Chauncey 11: 519
1880..Parker, Lottie B. 10: 316
1880..Welch, Joseph 18: 76
1881..Arthur, Julia 10: 455
1881..Fiske, Minnie Maddern ... A: 87
1881..Marlowe, Julia 13: 217
1882..Arden, Edwin H. P. 20: 61
1883..Allen, Viola 13: 332
1883..Cody, William F. 5: 483
1884..Buchanan, Virginia E. ...11: 283
1884..Burroughs, Marie 13: 432
1884..Sully, Daniel 12: 110
1885..Ditrichstein, Leo 22: 270
1885..Harrison, Richard B. 26: 364
1885..Osbourne, George 17: 105
1885..Wilder, Marshall P. 6: 31
1886..Bonstelle, Jessie 25: 178
1886..Hilliard, Robert C. 22: 117
1886..Warfield, David 14: 82
1887..Walsh, Blanche 12: 372
1888..Adams, Maude 13: 497
1889..Burbank, Alfred P. 6: 28
1890..Bacon, Frank 20: 77
1890..Blinn, Holbrook 21: 220
1890..Elliott, Maxine 14: 87
1890..Glendinning, John 18: 223
1892..Hackett, James K. 23: 86
1892..Mannering, Mary .... D: 226
1892..Smith, Winchell 24: 37
1893..Barrymore, Ethel .... B: 496
1893..Bingham, Amelia 21: 120
1894..Hodge, William T. 14: 384
1896..Chaplin, Charles .... A: 531
1898..Manners, J. Hartley 25: 152
1900..Fairbanks, Douglas ...... A: 91
1901..Collier, William 17: 379
1901..Hampden, Walter .... B: 12
1903..Barrymore, John .... B: 497
1903..Gilpin, Charles Sidney 23: 314
1905..Rogers, Will .... B: 67
1906..Janis, Elsie .... A: 549
1908..Pickford, Mary .... A: 92
1909..Cowl, Jane .... B: 202
1915..Lunt, Alfred .... D: 318
1916..Fontanne, Lynn .... D: 317
1916..Le Gallienne, Eva .... C: 385
1917..Cornell, Katharine .... D: 437
1919..Barry, Philip .... C: 516

Aëronautic Engineers

1898..Manly, Charles M. 21: 321
1903..Wright, Orville 14: 57
1903..Wright, Wilbur 14: 56
1907..Curtiss, Glenn H. 22: 195
1907..MacMechen, Rutherford ..16: 292
1907..Squier, George O. 24: 320
1909..Martin, Glenn L. .... A: 324
1911..Loening, Grover .... B: 283
1912..Lawrance, Charles L. .... D: 194
1915..Clark, Virginius E. ...... C: 261
1915..Durand, William F. ...... D: 260
1915..Hammond, John Hays, Jr. D: 391
1917..Gorrell, Edgar S. .... A: 525
1917..Sperry, Elmer A. 23: 78

Anatomists

1732..Chovet, Abraham 21: 419
1762..Shippen, William, Jr. 10: 384
1763..Morgan, John 10: 267
1780..Warren, John 10: 288
1792..Wistar, Caspar 1: 273
1793..Davidge, John B. 22: 330
1806..Warren, John C. 6: 426
1807..Dorsey, John Syng 10: 279
1812..Pattison, Granville S. 6: 69
1815..Horner, William E. 6: 383
1818..Godman, John D. 7: 284
1819..Physick, Philip S. 6: 391
1820..Morton, Samuel G. 10: 265
1825..March, Alden 2: 445
1828..Pancoast, Joseph 10: 274
1829..Miller, Thomas 2: 146
1835..Goddard, Paul B. 23: 384
1837..Wyman, Jeffries 2: 254
1839..Holmes, Oliver W. 2: 336
1844..Leidy, Joseph 5: 220
1854..Thomas, Amos R. 3: 481
1862..Wilder, Burt G. 4: 481
1865..Allen, Harrison 9: 359
1865..Weisse, Faneuil D. 5: 17
1869..Gerrish, Frederic H. 12: 233
1872..Dwight, Thomas 12: 101
1872..McClellan, George 15: 223
1872..Souchon, Edmond 9: 132
1876..Bernays, Augustus C. 6: 233
1878..Gage, Simon H. 4: 483
1878..Osborn, Henry Fairfield ..26: 18
1880..Baker, Frank 19: 260
1880..Huber, G. Carl .... D: 274
1883..Mall, Franklin P. 14: 309
1883..Minot, Charles S. 6: 112
1886..Huntington, George S. ...12: 236
1889..Keiller, William 22: 373
1890..Gallaudet, Bern B. 26: 189
1890..Hamann, Carl A. 21: 453
1891..McClure, Charles F. W. ..15: 227
1892..Donaldson, Henry H. 11: 56
1894..Barker, Lewellys F. ...... A: 265
1896..Harrison, Ross G. 15: 172
1896..Hrdlicka, Ales .... C: 90
1899..De Witt, Lydia M. .... B: 457
1900..Jackson, Clarence M. .... B: 209
1900..Sabin, Florence R. .... C: 288
1901..Streeter, George L. ...... D: 124
1902..Schulte, Hermann von W. 23: 373
1904..Spitzka, Edward A. 19: 450
1905..Phillips, William F. R. ... A: 395

Anthropologists and Ethnologists

1829..Lapham, Increase A. 8: 34
1837..Wyman, Jeffries 2: 254
1851..Gillman, Henry 7: 359
1851..Morgan, Lewis H. 6: 192
1856..Putnam, Frederic W. 23: 257
1857..Meigs, James A. 8: 218
1866..Powell, John W. 3: 340
1867..Brinton, Daniel G. 9: 265
1868..Brigham, William T. 16: 294
1869..Thomas, Cyrus 13: 528
1870..Fletcher, Alice C. 5: 182
1870..Grinnell, George Bird .... B: 478
1871..Bourke, John G. 13: 67
1871..Rathbun, Richard 13: 526
1872..Gatschet, Albert S. 21: 19
1873..Holmes, William H. 16: 441
1874..Zahm, John A. 9: 274
1875..McGee, W J 10: 349
1875..Mooney, James 25: 43
1875..Pilling, James C. 15: 55
1877..Bandelier, Adolphe F. A. .26: 240
1877..Osborn, Henry Fairfield ..26: 18
1879..Stevenson, Matilda C.....20: 53
1880..Fewkes, Jesse W. 15: 32
1880..Matthews, Washington ..13: 54
1881..Talbot, Eugene S. 13: 147
1881..Wilson, Thomas 11: 516
1882..Boas, Franz 12: 509
1882..Starr, Frederick 13: 115
1884..Mason, Otis T. 10: 174
1885..Mercer, Henry C. 21: 479
1886..Hodge, Frederick W. 10: 51
1886..Hough, Walter 25: 277
1890..Culin, Robert S. 13: 216
1890..Dorsey, George A. 22: 200
1890..Garner, Richard L. 13: 314
1892..McGee, Anita N. 10: 350
1894..Breasted, James H. ...... B: 377
1894..Hrdlicka, Ales .... C: 90
1895..Ferris, Harry B. .... A: 339
1896..Heye, George G. .... C: 182
1896..McClintock, Walter ...... C: 134
1897..Barrows, David P. ...... B: 157
1897..Russell, Frank 12: 457
1898..MacCurdy, George G. ..... C: 98
1899..Gregory, William K. ..... A: 105
1899..Pearl, Raymond 15: 382
1899..Wissler, Clark .... B: 257
1900..James, George W. 19: 68
1900..Jones, William 24: 283
1900..Kroeber, Alfred L. 14: 120
1900..Swanton, John R. .... A: 26
1901..Dixon, Roland B. 14: 353
1901..Goddard, Pliny E. 17: 419
1902..Davenport, Charles B. 15: 397
1902..Wissler, Clark .... B: 257
1903..Farabee, William C. 24: 207
1903..Farrand, Livingston 12: 458
1903..Parker, Arthur C. .... C: 175
1904..Stefansson, Vilhjalmur ... A: 230
1906..Alexander, Hartley B. ..... A: 174
1906..Andrews, Roy Chapman .. A: 302
1906..Bingham, Hiram .... A: 28
1906..Hewett, Edgar L. .... C: 31
1913..Hyde, B. T. Babbitt 26: 196
1914..Sullivan, Louis R. 20: 270

Archaeologists

1820..Schoolcraft, Henry R. ... 5: 145
1829..Lapham, Increase A. 8: 34
1835..Thomson, William M. 11: 57
1836..Davis, Edwin H. 13: 319
1836..Haldeman, Samuel S. 9: 246
1837..Robinson, Edward 2: 242
1839..Stephens, John L. 5: 424
1846..Morais, Sabato 10: 170
1849..Squier, Ephraim G. 4: 79
1851..Gillman, Henry 7: 359
1851..Morgan, Lewis H. 6: 192
1852..Thompson, Joseph P. 10: 132
1856..Putnam, Frederic W. 23: 257
1858..Warren, William F. 11: 177
1860..Sommerville, Maxwell 12: 251
1860..Ward, William H. 8: 147
1862..Beauchamp, William M. ..20: 150
1863..Rau, Charles 2: 228
1867..Cesnola, Luigi P. di 1: 422
1867..Paine, John A. 13: 456
1869..Perkins, George H. 10: 309
1870..Goodyear, William H. 19: 455
1872..Cushing, Frank H. 11: 26
1872..Seymour, Thomas D. 12: 365
1872..Winchell, Newton H. 7: 451
1873..Haynes, Henry W. 8: 154
1873..Holmes, William H. 16: 441
1873..Mitchell, Lucy M. W. 6: 147
1874..Barber, Edwin A. 22: 267
1874..Curtiss, Samuel I. 13: 395
1874..Merrill, Selah 13: 218
1874..Thomas, Cyrus 13: 528
1875..Hall, Isaac H. 12: 143
1875..Wright, George F. 7: 66
1876..Abbott, Charles C. 10: 318
1877..Manatt, James I. 8: 361
1878..Waldstein, Charles 11: 249
1880..Bandelier, Adolphe F. A. .26: 240
1880..Merriam, Augustus C. 8: 397
1880..Winslow, William C. 4: 83
1881..White, John W. 12: 352
1881..Wilson, Thomas 11: 516
1882..Fowke, Gerard 23: 275
1882..Moorehead, Warren K. ...10: 217
1882..Starr, Frederick 13: 115
1883..Frothingham, Arthur L. ..23: 138
1883..Hilprecht, Hermann V. ..10: 380
1883..Packard, Lewis R. 4: 550
1884..Brinton, Daniel G. 9: 265
1885..Barton, George A. .... D: 441
1885..Bennett, Robert R. 24: 119
1885..Mercer, Henry C. 21: 479
1885..Moldenke, Charles E. 24: 54
1885..Rood, Ogden N. 13: 507
1886..Hodge, Frederick W. 10: 51
1886..Jastrow, Morris 11: 372
1887..Gates, William .... D: 254
1888..Adler, Cyrus 11: 371
1888..Bowditch, Charles P. 20: 290
1888..Peters, John P. 13: 555
1889..Stevenson, Sara Y. 13: 83
1890..Culin, Robert S. 13: 216
1891..Dorsey, George A. 12: 141
1892..Clay, Albert T. 22: 130
1894..Breasted, James H. ...... B: 377
1895..Borton, Francis 22: 84
1896..Hrdlicka, Ales .... C: 90
1896..Pepper, George H. 24: 376
1897..Butler, Howard C. 20: 56
1897..Shipley, Frederick W. 17: 410
1898..MacCurdy, George G. ..... C: 98
1898..Nies, James B. 20: 256
1899..Carroll, Mitchell 24: 76
1899..Kelsey, Francis W. 14: 484
1902..Mills, William C. 22: 121
1903..Hewett, Edgar L. .... C: 31
1904..Parker, Arthur C. .... C: 175
1905..Robinson, David M. ...... A: 221
1905..Upham, Warren 7: 127
1908..Sanborn, Cyrus A. R. .... A: 404
1909..Fowler, Harold N. .... A: 494
1912..Chiera, Edward 24: 152
1912..De Booy, Theodoor 17: 313
1913..Hyde, B. T. Babbitt 26: 196
1915..Cummings, Byron .... B: 296
1926..Russell, James T., Jr. ... D: 152

Architects

See also Landscape Architects and City Planners

1657..Joy, Thomas 7: 479
1745..Harrison, Peter 23: 396
1780..Thornton, William 13: 470
1784..L'Enfant, Pierre C. 16: 209
1785..Hoban, James 24: 85
1786..Bulfinch, Charles 13: 555
1795..Hadfield, George 23: 115
1795..Hoadley, David 25: 240
1795..Mangin, Joseph F. 25: 289
1797..Hooker, Philip 24: 91
1803..Latrobe, Benjamin H. 9: 425
1807..Godefroy, Maximilian 23: 189
1810..Strickland, William 20: 71
1816..Haviland, John 11: 375
1824..Kneass, Samuel H. 25: 142
1825..Willard, Solomon 4: 431
1826..Davis, Alexander J. 22: 174
1830..Walter, Thomas U. 9: 333
1833..Upjohn, Richard 2: 182
1834..Greenough, Henry 20: 292
1836..Renwick, James 11: 102
1837..Austin, Henry 22: 319
1842..Le Brun, Napoleon 9: 330
1844..Gilman, Arthur E. 23: 161
1848..Emery, Matthew G. 5: 299
1849..Downing, Andrew J. 11: 114
1850..Auchmuty, Richard T. ... 9: 102
1851..Clark, Edward 11: 223
1851..Vaux, Calvert 9: 332
1852..Scott, Frank J. 13: 201
1852..Withers, Frederick C. 2: 165
1853..Mould, Jacob W. 3: 415
1853..Upjohn, Richard M. 2: 245
1855..Cummings, Charles A. ...20: 102
1855..Hunt, Richard M. 6: 430
1856..Mix, Edward T. 2: 233
1856..Stone, Alfred 11: 326
1860..Ware, William R. 8: 440
1861..Longfellow, William P. P. 23: 239
1862..Frederick, George A. 9: 334
1862..Wight, Peter B. 21: 369
1863..VanBrunt, Henry 11: 324
1865..Kendall, Edward H. 12: 247
1865..Post, George B. 15: 250
1865..Sturgis, Russell 9: 330
1866..Earle, Stephen C. 11: 147
1867..Himpler, Francis G. 18: 43
1867..Jenney, William Le B. ...10: 218
1867..Pelz, Paul J. 25: 424
1867..Scofield, Levi T. 12: 321
1868..Loring, George F. 11: 328
1868..Taylor, Isaac S. 12: 23
1868..Thomas, John R. 9: 329
1869..Adler, Dankmar 11: 173
1869..Price, Bruce 13: 303
1869..Richardson, Henry H. 6: 21
1870..Broome, Lewis H. 5: 243

1870..Hardenbergh, Henry J. ..11: 329
1870..Marshall, Henry R. 11: 328
1870..Mead, William R. 23: 91
1870..Peabody, Robert S. 12: 200
1870..Rousseau, Charles M. 19: 378
1870..Yost, Joseph W. 13: 495
1871..Wagner, Albert 6: 461
1872..Atwood, Charles B. 22: 110
1872..Buffington, Leroy S. 22: 364
1872..Codman, Richard 22: 132
1872..Harney, George E. 1: 371
1873..Beebe, Milton E. 3: 395
1873..Bethune, Robert A. 12: 8
1873..Burnham, Daniel H. 9: 335
1873..Kramer, George W. 9: 331
1873..Link, Theodore C. 12: 104
1873..Morgan, Octavius 16: 364
1873..Roeschlaub, Robert S. 12: 494
1873..Root, John W. 8: 114
1875..Bruce, Alexander C. 3: 361
1875..Hammond, George F. 12: 524
1875..Robertson, Robert H. 6: 280
1876..Bethune, Louise B. 12: 9
1876..Wilson, Joseph M. 7: 492
1877..Brush, Charles E. 11: 460
1877..Marean, Willis A. 12: 322
1878..Cook, Walter 14: 344
1878..McKim, Charles F. 23: 89
1878..Mason, George D. .... C: 102
1879..Beman, Solon S. 14: 304
1879..Kellogg, Thomas M. 26: 261
1879..Pond, Irving K. .... C: 127
1879..Spofford, John C. 12: 458
1880..Avery, Henry O. 1: 157
1880..Holabird, William 24: 231
1880..Rotch, Arthur 11: 454
1881..Cobb, Henry I. 11: 488
1881..Eyre, Wilson 11: 328
1881..Frost, Charles S. 26: 144
1881..Gibson, Robert W. 11: 324
1881..Kendall, William M. ..... A: 551
1881..Stead, Robert 9: 332
1881..Sully, Thomas 9: 334
1881..Walsh, Thomas F. 12: 531
1881..White, Stanford 23: 92
1882..Carrere, John M. 11: 325
1882..Hamlin, Alfred D. F. 22: 315
1882..Taylor, Eugene H. 20: 264
1882..Thompson, George K. 6: 88
1882..Young, Thomas C. .... B: 98
1883..Gilbert, Cass 26: 20
1883..Grylls, Humphrey J. M. .. C: 140
1883..Johnston, Clarence H. 9: 334
1884..Eames, William S. 13: 216
1884..Hastings, Thomas 11: 326
1884..Shepley, George F. 22: 99
1884..Widmann, Frederick 21: 378
1885..Bacon, Henry 20: 339
1885..Parkinson, John 26: 482
1885..Wallis, Frank E. 22: 208
1886..Coolidge, Charles A. ..... C: 521
1886..Day, Frank M. 14: 311
1886..Pond, Allen B. 21: 111
1887..Sturgis, R. Clipston ...... A: 368
1888..Carpenter, James E. R. ..24: 271
1888..Cary, George .... C: 396
1888..Ittner, William B. .... C: 286
1888..Waid, Dan E. .... B: 28
1889..Cram, Ralph A. .... B: 228
1889..Lord, Austin W. 11: 330
1890..Conable, George W. 16: 367
1890..Coolidge, J. Randolph 26: 213
1890..Jackson, Arthur C. ...... C: 107
1890..Kahn, Albert .... C: 126
1890..Milburn, Frank P. 12: 103
1890..Stevens, Edward F. ...... B: 244
1890..White, James McL. 24: 123
1891..Flagg, Ernest .... B: 333
1891..Goodhue, Bertram G. 19: 402
1891..Hutchings, John B. 17: 114
1891..Kimball, Thomas R. 25: 364
1891..Magonigle, Harold VanB. . C: 506
1891..Tilton, Edward L. .... A: 319
1892..Audsley, George A. 24: 344
1892..Hill, George 10: 485
1892..Medary, Milton B. 24: 424
1893..Granger, Alfred H. ...... A: 138
1893..Hewlett, James M. 11: 330
1893..Shaw, Howard V. 20: 159
1894..Smith, Henry A. .... C: 184
1894..Woltersdorf, Arthur F. .. C: 112
1895..Hall, Emery S. 17: 9
1895..Matteson, Victor A. ..... C: 157
1895..Platt, Charles A. 11: 306
1895..Wright, Frank L. .... D: 278
1896..Smith, Fred L. .... C: 345
1898..Barber, Donn 25: 368
1898..Butler, Charles .... A: 374
1898..Starrett, Goldwin 24: 42
1898..Weeks, Charles P. 21: 383
1898..White, Howard J. 26: 384
1899..Hornbostel, Henry F. .... C: 324
1899..Luther, Mark L. .... A: 263
1900..Corbett, Harvey W. ...... B: 409
1900..Ford, George B. 25: 369
1900..Lowell, Guy 21: 47
1900..Sheblessy, John F. .... D: 364
1900..Upjohn, Hobart B. .... C: 400
1901..Emerson, William .... A: 362
1901..Murphy, Henry K. .... C: 124
1901..Starrett, William A. 24: 42
1902..Steinback, Gustave E. .... B: 369
1902..Walker, Frank R. .... D: 291
1903..Smith, Wilson L. 23: 155
1905..Bakewell, John, Jr. ...... D: 389
1905..Gardner, Robert W. ...... B: 359
1905..Stimson, George L. ...... C: 447
1906..McCornack, Walter R. ... C: 280
1907..Nyden, John A. 24: 392
1907..Walker, Ralph T. .... B: 496
1908..Ludlow, Thomas W. 21: 397
1909..Irvin, Richard .... D: 372
1910..Brown, Edwin H. 24: 338
1911..Kahn, Ely J. .... D: 160
1911..Urban, Joseph 25: 366
1912..Harris, Albert L. 24: 165
1913..Howe, George .... D: 246
1914..Baum, Dwight J. .... C: 162
1914..Bowman, Lewis .... D: 339
1914..Shepley, Henry R. .... C: 518
1916..Crandall, Norris I. ...... D: 68
1918..White, Lawrence G. ..... C: 191

Artists

See also Engravers and Sculptors

1728..Smybert, John 5: 325
1746..Feke, Robert 8: 425
1760..Copley, John S. 6: 467
1763..West, Benjamin 5: 322
1771..Earle, Ralph 11: 146
1776..Peale, Charles W. 6: 358
1780..Stuart, Gilbert C. 5: 324
1783..Dunlap, William 6: 501
1787..Trumbull, John 3: 334
1790..Ames, Ezra 22: 408
1790..Sargent, Henry 5: 319
1793..Saint-Mémin, Fevret de ..18: 143
1799..Sully, Thomas 5: 215
1800..Allston, Washington 5: 383
1800..Ingham, Charles C. 5: 317
1801..Malbone, Edward G. 9: 255
1801..Vanderlyn, John 1: 414
1804..Peale, Rembrandt 5: 320
1807..Birch, Thomas 12: 269
1807..Foster, Ben. 11: 303
1807..Wilson, Alexander 7: 440
1812..Audubon, John J. 6: 75
1813..Bush, Joseph 6: 505
1814..Fisher, Alvan 11: 309
1817..Evers, John 5: 322
1818..Fraser, Charles 4: 303
1818..Neagle, John 5: 326
1820..Goodridge Sarah 23: 375
1820..Hall, Anne 10: 375
1820..Jouett, Matthew H. 6: 467
1821..Leslie, Charles R. 5: 321
1821..Peale, Titian R. 21: 170
1822..Inman, Henry 9: 247
1823..Catlin, George 3: 270
1824..Weir, Robert W. 11: 295
1825..Cole, Thomas 7: 462
1827..Edmonds, Francis W. 11: 298
1828..Newton, Gilbert S. 5: 424
1830..Cummings, Thomas S. 6: 246
1830..Havell, Robert 22: 91
1830..Sartain, John 6: 472
1831..Healy, George P. A. 15: 317
1832..De Veaux, James 8: 427
1832..Thorpe, Thomas B. 6: 230
1833..Cheney, Seth W. 9: 170
1835..Casilear, John W. 12: 271
1835..Durand, Asher B. 4: 408
1835..Willis, Edmund A. 11: 293
1836..Flagg, George W. 7: 460
1836..Page, William 11: 289
1837..Huntington, Daniel 5: 323
1837..Spencer, Frederick R. 5: 326
1837..Stanley, James M. 6: 467
1839..Le Clear, Thomas 8: 429
1840..Ames, Joseph 7: 460
1840..Banvard, John 5: 326
1840..Brown, George L. 7: 466
1840..Elliott, Charles L. 11: 311
1840..Leutze, Emanuel 12: 360
1841..Hart, William 7: 503
1841..Read, Thomas B. 6: 474
1841..Richards, T. Addison 8: 425
1841..Rossiter, Thomas P. 4: 60
1845..Carpenter, Francis B. 11: 309
1845..Cropsey, Jasper F. 1: 372
1845..Johnson, Eastman 9: 52
1845..Kensett, John F. 7: 560
1846..Baker, George A. 5: 504
1846..Beard, James H. 5: 420
1846..Beard, William H. 11: 294
1847..Church, Frederic E. 20: 33
1847..Lanman, Charles 3: 444
1847..Rothermel, Peter F. 4: 546
1848..Chapman, John G. 7: 460
1848..Darley, Felix O. C. 2: 334
1849..Colyer, Vincent 7: 541
1849..Flagg, Jared B. 7: 549
1849..Rosenthal, Max 20: 86
1849..Stillman, William J. 10: 25
1850..Colman, Samuel 7: 546
1850..Gifford, Sanford R. 2: 443
1850..Guy, Seymour J. 11: 301
1850..Hays, William J. 4: 186
1850..Inman, John O'B. 9: 248
1850..Reinhart, Benjamin F. ...11: 310
1851..Miller, Eleazer H. 5: 319
1851..Oertel, Johannes A. 7: 466
1852..Baumgras, Peter 10: 365
1852..Brandt, Carl L. 8: 423
1852..Meeker, Joseph R. 12: 52
1852..Wood, Thomas W. 3: 345
1853..Bush, Norton 12: 338
1853..McEntee, Jervis 5: 510
1853..Nichols, Edward W. 5: 323
1853..Wight, Moses 12: 324
1854..Cobb, Darius 4: 45
1854..Lawrie, Alexander 25: 315
1854..Smillie, James D. 10: 367
1855..Hoppin, Augustus 9: 483
1855..Hunt, William M. 3: 288
1855..Lamb, Frederick S. 11: 307
1855..Lewis, Edmond D. 26: 438
1855..Robinson, Thomas 5: 316
1856..Vedder, Elihu 6: 328
1857..Bierstadt, Albert 11: 288
1857..Fuller, George 6: 475
1857..Johnson, Samuel F. 7: 471
1857..Martin, Homer D. 9: 53
1857..Ryder, Platt P. 11: 293
1858..Moran, Thomas 22: 24
1858..Sellstedt, Lars G. 8: 428
1859..Bricher, Alfred T. 13: 453
1859..DeHaas, Mauritz F. H. ... 9: 52
1859..Lamb, Joseph 11: 307
1859..Loop, Henry A. 13: 239
1859..Richards, William T. 12: 362
1859..Stephens, Henry L. 5: 411
1859..Whistler, J. McNeill 9: 49
1859..Whittredge, Worthington . 7: 458
1860..Brown, John G. 10: 373
1860..Deakin, Edwin 22: 278
1860..Inness, George 2: 490
1860..Marschall, Nicola 17: 51
1860..Marshall, William E. 7: 460
1860..Miller, Charles H. 8: 423
1860..Moran, Edward 11: 302
1860..Nast, Thomas 7: 461
1860..Smith, Francis H. 5: 326
1861..Bellows, Albert F. 7: 464
1861..Haseltine, William S. 12: 441
1861..LaFarge, John 9: 59
1861..Wyant, Alexander H. 10: 370
1862..Moran, Mary N. 22: 25
1862..Moran, Thomas 22: 24
1862..Parton, Arthur 13: 72
1862..Smillie, George H. 6: 426
1863..Henry, Edward L. 5: 315
1863..Homer, Winslow 11: 304
1863..Weir, John F. 6: 429
1864..Forbes, Edwin 5: 549
1864..Moran, Peter 11: 303
1864..Neal, David D. 9: 53
1864..Robbins, Horace W. 13: 23
1864..Wiles, Lemuel M. 12: 443
1865..Diamant, David S. 16: 222
1865..Eakins, Thomas 5: 421
1865..Fisher, Mark 19: 92
1865..Heaton, Augustus G. 5: 315
1865..Howland, Alfred C. 7: 470
1865..Van Elten, Hendrik D. K. 7: 468
1866..Brandegee, Robert B. 20: 210
1866..Fitch, John L. 7: 559
1866..Sartain, Emily 13: 326
1866..Woodward, John D. 20: 346
1867..Bridgman, Frederick A. .. 2: 110
1868..Duveneck, Frank 20: 87
1868..Herter, Christian 5: 320
1868..Nicoll, James C. 7: 466
1868..Ream, Carducius P. 17: 252

1868..Rosenthal, Toby E. 13: 258
1868..Sartain, William 13: 326
1869..Dolph, John H. 10: 369
1869..Ives, Halsey C. 24: 55
1869..Tatnall, Henry L. 13: 186
1869..Thayer, Abbott H. 6: 471
1869..Tiffany, Louis C. 7: 465
1870..Benjamin, Samuel G. W... 7: 26
1870..Bunce, Gedney 18: 399
1870..Champney, James W. 11: 308
1870..Church, Frederick S. 11: 304
1870..Fenn, Harry 6: 368
1870..Foote, Mary Hallock 6: 472
1870..Gibson, William H. 7: 463
1870..Hartley, J. Scott 7: 459
1870..Hopkin, Robert 17: 365
1870..Knight, Daniel R. 13: 158
1870..Laux, August 7: 472
1870..Merrill, Frank T. 6: 476
1870..Morgan, Matthew S....... 5: 325
1870..Newman, Robert L. 13: 179
1870..Reinhart, Charles S. 7: 465
1870..Shurtleff, Roswell M. 10: 379
1870..Tillinghast, Mary E. 19: 361
1870..Wiggins, Carleton 11: 309
1870..Wilmarth, Lemuel E. 8: 424
1871..Keith, William 13: 168
1871..Rehn, Frank K. M. 9: 55
1872..Frost, Arthur B. 11: 289
1872..Gaul, William G. 12: 366
1872..Inness, George, Jr. 22: 181
1872..Low, Will H. 6: 473
1872..Minor, Robert C. 12: 354
1872..Paris, Walter 7: 511
1872..Tait, John R. 13: 277
1873..Gutherz, Carl 19: 338
1873..Herzog, George 8: 496
1873..Lathrop, Francis 11: 292
1873..Quartley, Arthur 11: 308
1873..:Thompson, Wordsworth .. 8: 430
1874..Blashfield, Edwin H. .... D: 80
1874..Eaton, Wyatt 8: 427
1874..Maynard, George W......11: 287
1874..Shirlaw, Walter 11: 298
1874..Trenchard, Edward 10: 127
1875..Beard, Daniel C. 5: 317
1875..DeLongpre, Paul 16: 273
1875..Enneking, John J. 5: 319
1875..Kelly, James E. 25: 434
1875..Loop, Jeannette S. 13: 239
1875..Norton, William E. 6: 432
1875..Satterlee, Walter 13: 557
1875..Sheppard, Warren W.....13: 224
1875..Travis, William De L. T. .17: 5
1875..Volk, Douglas .... C: 138
1875..Weir, J. Alden 22: 296
1876..Allen, Thomas 24: 92
1876..Briscoe, Franklin D. 10: 368
1876..Coman, Charlotte B. 22: 454
1876..Cox, Palmer 7: 459
1876..Dielman, Frederick 7: 471
1876..Jenks, Phoebe P. 12: 195
1876..Keppler, Joseph 2: 225
1876..Pearce, Charles S. 11: 286
1876..Pyle, Howard 9: 56
1876..Scott, Emily M. S.........11: 415
1877..Andrews, Eliphalet F. ... 8: 432
1877..Creifelds, Richard .... B: 445
1877..Gifford, R. Swain 2: 482
1877..Millar, Addison T. 11: 309
1877..Millet, Francis D. 15: 201
1877..Opper, Frederick B. 6: 475
1877..Steele, Thomas S. 8: 490
1877..Wolf, Henry 10: 376
1878..Armstrong, David M. 19: 69
1878..Beckwith, J. Carroll 7: 470
1878..Chase, William M. 13: 28
1878..Dewey, Charles M. 11: 294
1878..Fowler, Frank 7: 468
1878..Outcault, Richard F. 22: 447
1878..Sargent, John S. 11: 291
1878..Vinton, Frederic P 5: 317
1879..Coffin, William A. 6: 368
1879..Crane, Robert B. 11: 310
1879..Gillam, Bernhard 8: 296
1879..Hart, James McD. 7: 469
1879..Juengling, Frederick 11: 195
1879..Lippincott, William H. ... 6: 474
1879..Marr, Carl 11: 293
1879..Potthast, Edward H. 22: 339
1879..Stark, Otto 20: 358
1879..Story, Julian 19: 86
1880..Abbatt, Agnes D. 8: 431
1880..Daingerfield, Elliott 13: 111
1880..Closson, William B. P. ... 8: 431
1880..Evans, Joe 11: 298
1880..Grover, Oliver D. 11: 305
1880..Harrison, Alexander 11: 300
1880..Janvier, Catherine A. ...12: 460
1880..Jones, H. Bolton 13: 126
1880..Lander, Benjamin 9: 54
1880..Moran, Leon 11: 302
1880..Mosler, Henry 9: 50
1880..Naegele, Charles F. 12: 81
1880..Picknell, William L. 10: 365
1880..Rosenthal, Albert .... B: 25
1880..Walker, Henry O. 22: 401
1880..Wheeler, Dora 1: 405
1881..Alexander, John W. 11: 297
1881..Blum, Robert F. 10: 365
1881..Dean, Walter L. 10: 371
1881..Macy, William S. 3: 423
1881..Palmer, Walter L. 7: 458
1881..Pennell, Joseph 10: 376
1881..Remington, Frederic 22: 244
1881..Sammann, Detlef 10: 372
1881..Seton, Ernest T. .... C: 392
1881..Sharp, Joseph H. 18: 188
1881..Stetson, Charles W. 9: 57
1881..Tryon, Dwight M. 8: 423
1881..Twachtman, John H. 13: 530
1882..Dannat, William T. 12: 380
1882..Earle, James 11: 147
1882..Harrison, Birge 26: 162
1882..Melchers, Gari .... B: 120
1882..Pierce, Heman W. 12: 392
1882..Ryder, Albert P. 10: 508
1882..Sandham, Henry 6: 475
1882..Smedley, William T. 10: 378
1882..Turner, Charles Y. 6: 469
1882..Ulrich, Charles F. 1: 202
1883..Abbey, Edwin A. 15: 280
1883..Beaux, Cecilia 11: 299
1883..Bell, Edward A. 7: 23
1883..Caliga, Isaac H. 12: 65
1883..Cox, Kenyon 5: 321
1883..Curran, Charles C. 13: 364
1883..Dunsmore, John W. 10: 366
1883..Edwards, George W. 11: 414
1883..Vonnoh, Robert W. 7: 462
1884..Baer, William J. 5: 469
1884..Birch, Reginald B. 11: 307
1884..Cornoyer, Paul 24: 353
1884..Nicholls, Rhoda H. 7: 463
1884..Platt, Charles A. 11: 306
1884..Sheppard, Warren W. ...13: 224
1884..Watrous, Harry W. 13: 369
1884..Wiles, Irving R. 6: 468
1885..Benson, Frank W. 13: 413
1885..Brewer, Nicholas R. 12: 469
1885..Clinedinst, Benjamin W. .22: 73
1885..Graves, Abbott F. 17: 458
1885..Howe, William H. 13: 430
1885..Mowbray, H. Siddons 23: 188
1885..Needham, Charles A. 6: 368
1885..Poore, Henry R. .... D: 376
1885..Reid, Robert 6: 476
1885..Weeks, Edwin L. 12: 505
1886..Ball, Thomas W. 26: 121
1886..Brooks, Maria 8: 432
1886..Chapman, Carlton T. 22: 249
1886..Davis, Charles H. 8: 431
1886..Deming, Edwin W. .... D: 91
1886..Ferris, Jean L. G. 23: 385
1886..Keller, Arthur I. 11: 286
1886..Munsell, Albert H. 12: 316
1886..Nourse, Elizabeth 11: 304
1886..Ochtman, Leonard 26: 491
1886..Pope, Alexander 10: 378
1886..Stephens, Alice B. 23: 278
1886..Tarbell, Edmund C....... B: 151
1887..Bailey, Henry T. 23: 306
1887..Browne, Charles Francis .16: 40
1887..Cox, Louise H. K. 11: 301
1887..Foster, Ben. 11: 303
1887..Fuchs, Emil .... B: 513
1887..Gibson, Charles D. 11: 290
1887..Muller-Ury, Adolph 6: 470
1887..Roseland, Harry 11: 286
1888..Butler, Howard R. ...... B: 60
1888..Grant, Charles H. .... A: 439
1888..Mielatz, Charles F. W. ...25: 363
1888..Taylor, William Ladd 12: 64
1889..Hallwig, Paul 6: 465
1889..Hassam, Childe 10: 374
1889..Kendall, William S. 13: 208
1889..Klepper, Max Francis 12: 339
1889..Koehler, Robert 17: 304
1889..Perry, Lilla C. 26: 272
1889..Schreyvogel, Charles 13: 411
1890..Anderson, Abraham A. .. C: 358
1890..Bohm, Max 21: 156
1890..Burbank, Elbridge A. ...11: 292
1890..Burroughs, Bryson ...... A: 131
1890..Conable, George W. 16: 367
1890..Eggleston, Benjamin O. .. 8: 424
1890..Gill, Rosalie L. 7: 462
1890..Kingsley, Elbridge 13: 112
1890..Koopman, Augustus 24: 434
1890..Lockwood, Wilton 24: 275
1890..Maurer, Alfred H. 25: 153
1890..Paulus, Francis P. 17: 210
1890..Waldeck, Carl G. 13: 41
1890..Wenzell, Albert B. 23: 106
1891..Couse, E. Irving 13: 539
1891..Hauser, John 16: 79
1891..Sterner, Albert E. 11: 290
1892..Bailey, Vernon H. ...... D: 426
1892..Chambers, Robert W. .... C: 402
1892..Garnsey, Elmer E. 11: 151
1892..Gutmann, Bernhard 26: 165
1892..Hawthorne, Charles W. ..22: 452
1892..Johnson, Clifton 11: 413
1892..Phillips, Jay C. 13: 288
1892..Tack, Augustus V. ...... C: 395
1893..Detwiller, Frederick K.... B: 219
1893..Ives, Percy 11: 287
1893..Simmons, Edward E. 13: 601
1894..Abrams, Lucien .... C: 255
1894..Parrish, Maxfield 12: 487
1894..Sharp, Joseph H. 11: 188
1894..Yohn, Frederick C. 24: 181
1895..Christy, Howard Chandler 11: 299
1895..Gonzales, Boyer 24: 90
1895..Hill, Arthur T. 25: 229
1896..Congdon, Thomas R. 11: 311
1896..Fuertes, Louis A. 21: 69
1898..Cushing, Howard G. 24: 165
1898..Haskell, Ernest 23: 155
1898..Olinsky, Ivan G. .... B: 159
1899..Fiske, Gertrude H. ...... B: 286
1899..Lie, Jonas .... D: 248
1899..Miller, Richard E. .... A: 270
1900..Ferris, Jean L. G. 23: 385
1901..Singer, William H., Jr. .. B: 320
1901..Williams, Frederick B. ...17: 349
1903..Schmitt, Albert F. ...... A: 481
1903..Schofield, Walter E....... D: 166
1904..Genth, Lillian .... D: 281
1904..Kent, Rockwell .... D: 98
1906..Bellows, George W. 20: 77
1906..King, Paul B. .... D: 380
1907..Roerich, Nicholas K...... C: 146
1908..Seyffert, Leopold .... B: 388
1909..Adams, Wayman .... B: 37
1909..Bosley, Frederick A....... C: 423
1909..Garber, Daniel .... C: 442
1910..Baker, Burtis .... B: 373
1910..Costigan, John E. ...... B: 304
1910..Crosby, Percy L. .... D: 294
1911..Grabach, John R. .... B: 165
1912..Poole, Abram .... C: 271
1912..Speicher, Eugene .... B: 453
1914..Goossens, John .... C: 300
1914..Gross, Juliet M. W. ...... B: 492
1914..Plowman, George T. 23: 110
1914..Rummell, John .... C: 503
1916..Meière, Hildreth .... D: 337
1918..Macrae, Emma F. .... B: 310
1918..Winter, Ezra A. .... D: 97
1919..Heintzelman, Arthur W... C: 123
1921..Stone, Seymour M. .... C: 484
1923..Phillips, Marjorie A. ..... B: 477

Astronomers

1702..Taylor, Jacob 10: 255
1724..Ames, Nathaniel 8: 45
1740..Winthrop, John 7: 165
1761..Cutler, Manasseh 3: 70
1761..Mason, Charles 10: 54
1763..West, Benjamin 8: 31
1769..Brown, Joseph 8: 28
1769..Rittenhouse, David 1: 346
1770..Leeds, John 25: 187
1785..Williams, Samuel 1: 257
1806..Bond, William C. 8: 381
1810..Holcombe, Amasa 3: 311
1812..Mitchell, William 11: 420
1813..Greenleaf, Benjamin 8: 141
1825..Anderson, Henry J. 6: 389
1829..Bowditch, Nathaniel 6: 377
1829..Wilbur, Hervey 10: 450
1830..Loomis, Elias 7: 233
1831..Norton, William A. 9: 187
1831..Smith, Augustus W. 9: 430
1833..Olmsted, Denison 8: 121
1833..Twining, Alexander C. ...19: 17
1834..Hopkins, Albert 6: 240
1836..Mitchel, Ormsby M. 3: 440
1837..Walker, Sears C. 8: 81
1839..Chase, Pliny E. 6: 53
1840..Alexander, Stephen 11: 422
1840..Rutherford, Lewis M. 6: 376
1842..Bond, George P. 5: 503
1842..Chauvenet, William 11: 210

1842..Peirce, Benjamin 8: 152
1843..Herrick, Edward C. 11: 170
1844..Clark, Alvan 6: 440
1845..Davidson, George 7: 227
1845..Hubbard, Joseph S. 9: 238
1846..Mattison, Hiram 12: 127
1847..Mitchell, Maria 5: 236
1849..Gould, Benjamin A. 5: 108
1849..Kirkwood, Daniel 4: 349
1850..Ferrel, William 9: 241
1853..Peters, Christian H. F. ...13: 317
1853..Stockwell, John N. 9: 373
1854..Brunnow, Franz F. E. ...13: 78
1855..Newton, Hubert A. 9: 219
1855..Swift, Lewis 4: 302
1857..Bouvier, Hannah M. 8: 99
1857..Draper, Henry 6: 171
1857..Hall, Asaph 22: 287
1857..Langley, Samuel P. 3: 338
1857..Watson, James C. 7: 70
1857..Winlock, Joseph 9: 266
1857..Young, Charles A. 6: 325
1858..Vaughan, Daniel 13: 171
1859..Clark, Alvan G. 5: 386
1859..Hough, George W. 8: 337
1860..Newcomb, Simon 7: 17
1860..Peirce, Charles S. 8: 409
1861..Hill, George W. 13: 442
1862..Eastman, John R. 13: 554
1863..Harkness, William 8: 395
1863..Safford, Truman H. 13: 359
1864..Coffin, Selden J. 11: 245
1865..Pickering, Edward C. 6: 424
1866..Blake, Francis 22: 25
1866..Garland, Landon C. 8: 226
1867..Abbe, Cleveland 8: 264
1867..Lovering, Joseph 6: 425
1868..Searle, Arthur 19: 34
1870..Holden, Edward S. 7: 229
1870..Skinner, Aaron N. 20: 140
1870..Stone, Ormond 6: 194
1871..Colbert, Elias 13: 359
1871..Lyman, Chester S. 25: 427
1872..Boss, Lewis 13: 251
1872..Paul, Henry M. 10: 403
1873..Bigelow, Frank H. 10: 410
1874..Brashear, John A. 4: 552
1874..Brooks, William R. 5: 197
1875..Doolittle, Charles L. 20: 340
1875..Porter, Jermain G. 13: 73
1875..Rogers, William A. 9: 530
1875..Sawyer, Edwin F. 8: 481
1875..Todd, David P. 7: 203
1876..Burnham, Sherburne W. ..11: 71
1876..Rees, John K. 11: 513
1876..Schaeberle, John M. 26: 392
1877..Harrington, Mark W. 10: 448
1878..Flint, Albert S. 10: 257
1878..Keeler, James E. 10: 498
1878..Pritchett, Henry S. ...... C: 498
1878..Very, Frank W. 12: 49
1879..Comstock, George C. 12: 454
1879..Fleming, Williamina P. .. 7: 29
1879..Tucker, Richard H. 18: 233
1880..Chandler, Seth C. 9: 538
1880..Elkin, William L. 24: 117
1880..Larkin, Edgar L. 20: 251
1880..Winlock, William C. 9: 267
1881..Howe, Herbert A. 20: 10
1882..Leavenworth, Francis P. . 8: 66
1882..Serviss, Garrett P. 11: 349
1882..Woodward, Robert S. 13: 108
1883..Howe, Charles S. 15: 259
1884..Barnes, Willis L. 20: 274
1886..Campbell, William W. ...11: 278
1886..Metcalf, Joel H. 25: 268
1886..Proctor, Mary 9: 282
1887..Pickering, William H. .... B: 325
1887..Updegraff, Milton 15: 145
1887..Upton, Winslow 12: 238
1888..Jacoby, Harold 23: 132
1889..Barnard, Edward E. 7: 44
1889..Douglass, Andrew E. .... D: 439
1889..Hussey, William J. 21: 95
1889..Perrine, Charles D. 13: 556
1890..Klumpke, Dorothea 13: 377
1890..Todd, Mabel L. 9: 142
1892..Frost, Edwin B. 25: 316
1892..Leavitt, Henrietta S. 25: 163
1892..Poor, Charles L. 14: 224
1892..See, Thomas J. J. 13: 234
1893..Brown, Ernest W. 15: 24
1894..Hale, George Ellery ...... C: 45
1894..Lowell, Percival 8: 309
1895..Abbot, Charles G. .... A: 366
1895..Bauer, Louis A. 23: 166
1895..Boothroyd, Samuel L. .... D: 101
1895..Parkhurst, John A. 20: 149
1895..Seares, Frederick H. ...... A: 232
1896..Doolittle, Eric 19: 300
1898..Brown, Stimson J. 13: 121
1898..Cannon, Annie J. .... B: 482
1898..Eichelberger, William S. . C: 75
1898..Poor, John M. 25: 358
1899..Schlesinger, Frank .... C: 497
1899..Wadsworth, Frank L. O. .26: 376
1901..Adams, Walter A. .... B: 171
1901..Curtiss, Ralph H. 21: 259
1903..Fox, Philip .... C: 528
1903..Russell, Henry N. .... A: 346
1903..Stebbins, Joel .... B: 342
1906..Albrecht, Sebastian ...... A: 190
1908..St. John, Charles E. 26: 332
1914..Shapley, Harlow .... C: 95

Authors

See also Poets and Playwrights

1608..Smith, John 13: 378
1624..Winslow, Edward 7: 369
1640..Bradstreet, Anne D. 7: 10
1640..Eliot, John 2: 419
1646..Bulkley, Peter 7: 486
1648..Norton, John 7: 36
1672..Josselyn, John 7: 214
1686..Leeds, Daniel 18: 370
1698..Calef, Robert 8: 164
1713..Stone, William L. 7: 205
1721..Rawle, Francis 6: 186
1725..Franklin, Benjamin 1: 328
1729..Ralph, James 8: 338
1746..Ferguson, Elizabeth G. .. 7: 164
1747..Lennox, Charlotte R. 6: 51
1750..Bellamy, Joseph 7: 78
1758..Fiske, Nathan 7: 501
1760..Bland, Richard 7: 133
1765..Beveridge, John 7: 343
1765..Coombe, Thomas 7: 196
1773..Warren, Mercy 7: 177
1774..De Crevecoeur, Jean H. S. 8: 253
1776..Brackenridge, Hugh H. ... 8: 49
1776..Freneau, Philip 6: 201
1776..Jefferson, Thomas 3: 1
1776..Paine, Thomas 5: 412
1784..Adams, Hannah 5: 459
1784..Webster, Noah 2: 394
1785..Stiles, Ezra 1: 167
1786..Rowson, Susanna 9: 317
1786..Tyler, Royall 7: 39
1787..Bingham, Caleb 8: 19
1789..Williams, John 1: 179
1790..Boudinot, Elias 2: 296
1790..Davis, Matthew L. 5: 514
1790..Morton, Sarah W. A..... 8: 370
1790..Weems, Mason L. 5: 392
1791..Alsop, Richard 4: 437
1791..Harris, Thaddeus M. 8: 194
1792..Story, Isaac 13: 193
1794..Paine, Robert T. 4: 554
1795..Dennie, Joseph 7: 204
1795..Duane, William 8: 180
1796..Fessenden, Thomas G. ... 7: 260
1797..Linn, John B. 13: 542
1797..Peale, Charles W. 6: 358
1800..Brown, Charles B. 7: 59
1801..Austin, William 4: 527
1801..Key, Francis Scott 5: 498
1802..Bristed, John 7: 446
1802..Custis, George W. P. 7: 537
1802..Paulding, James K. 7: 193
1803..Channing, William Ellery . 5: 458
1803..Miller, Samuel 7: 152
1803..Wirt, William 6: 86
1804..Moore, Clement C. 7: 362
1806..Irving, Washington 3: 17
1807..Sargent, Lucius M. 4: 231
1808..Barker, James N. 12: 276
1808..Mayo, Robert 10: 284
1809..Halleck, Fitz-Greene 3: 226
1809..Walsh, Robert 5: 357
1810..Gilman, Caroline H. 6: 259
1810..Shaw, John 8: 368
1811..Hillhouse, James A. 7: 131
1812..Brackenridge, Henry M. .. 9: 468
1812..Woodworth, Samuel 1: 434
1813..Allston, Washington 5: 383
1813..Stone, William L. 7: 205
1813..Verplanck, Gulian C. 5: 405
1814..Beecher, Lyman 3: 126
1814..Everett, Alexander H. 9: 256
1814..Willard, Emma 1: 244
1815..Dana, Richard H. 7: 182
1815..Jay, William 8: 74
1815..Robbins, Thomas 2: 222
1815..Sigourney, Lydia H. 1: 154
1816..Holbrook, Silas P. 7: 289
1816..Withington, Leonard 5: 512
1817..Frisbie, Levi 7: 132
1817..Greene, Nathaniel 11: 228
1817..Hoffman, David 7: 129
1817..Sands, Robert C. 8: 354
1817..Swett, Samuel 13: 146
1817..Thacher, James 7: 401
1818..Hall, Sarah E. 11: 478
1818..Kennedy, John P. 6: 181
1818..Nott, Henry J. 11: 31
1819..Allen, Paul 5: 128
1819..Dearborn, Henry A. S.... 9: 323
1819..Littell, Eliakim 24: 408
1819..Schoolcraft, Henry R. ... 5: 145
1819..Tudor, William 8: 351
1820..Goodrich, Charles A. 23: 241
1820..Gould, Benjamin Apthorp . 3: 515
1820..Longfellow, Henry W. .. 2: 160
1820..Sparks, Jared 5: 433
1820..Woods, Leonard 9: 121
1821..Cooper, J. Fenimore 1: 398
1821..Neal, John 11: 346
1822..Lawson, James 25: 169
1822..Sedgwick, Catherine M. .. 1: 446
1822..Sprague, William B. 5: 239
1823..Hale, Sarah J. 22: 39
1823..Mitchell, John 5: 514
1823..Morris, George P. 5: 434
1824..Dwight, Theodore 11: 216
1824..Knapp, Samuel L. 7: 472
1824..Warfield, Catharine A. ... 5: 306
1824..Wilcox, Carlos 1: 184
1825..Anderson, Rufus 24: 153
1825..Dunlop, James 11: 360
1825..French, Benjamin F. 3: 522
1825..Hawes, Joel 11: 186
1825..Hawes, William P. 11: 355
1825..Janney, Samuel M. 7: 485
1825..Leggett, William 6: 275
1825..Longstreet, Augustus B... 1: 517
1825..Quincy, Josiah 6: 417
1825..Robinson, Therese 2: 242
1825..Simms, W. Gilmore 6: 204
1825..Tucker, George 7: 521
1826..Bacon, Leonard 1: 176
1826..Child, L. Maria 2: 324
1826..Drake, Benjamin 7: 146
1826..Flint, Timothy 6: 364
1826..Hawthorne, Nathaniel ... 3: 64
1826..McLellan, Isaac 6: 19
1826..Sanderson, John 6: 194
1826..Schmucker, Samuel S..... 5: 100
1827..Hentz, Caroline L. 6: 261
1827..Leslie, Eliza 7: 138
1827..Poe, Edgar Allan 1: 463
1827..Rush, James 6: 273
1827..Upham, Thomas C. 13: 171
1827..Willis, Nathaniel P....... 3: 108
1828..Bradford, Alden 8: 57
1828..Embury, Emma C. 9: 211
1828..Fay, Theodore S. 7: 475
1828..Hall, Baynard R. 3: 518
1828..Leeser, Isaac 10: 393
1828..Sealsfield, Charles 2: 193
1828..Upham, Charles W. 8: 398
1829..Blackwell, Antoinette Brown 9: 124
1829..Burton, Warren 7: 516
1829..Holmes, Oliver Wendell .. 2: 336
1829..Lieber, Francis 5: 116
1829..Phelps, Almira H. L. ...11: 359
1829..Pike, Albert 1: 527
1830..Audubon, John J. 6: 75
1830..Brown, David P. 3: 520
1830..Deering, Nathaniel 10: 250
1830..Hoffman, Fenno 8: 379
1830..Hosmer, William H. C. .. 8: 200
1830..Murdock, James 7: 80
1830..Snelling, William J. 2: 126
1831..Bacon, Delia S. 1: 477
1831..Carpenter, William H. ..11: 518
1831..Follen, Charles 7: 289
1831..Neal, Joseph C. 6: 29
1831..Winslow, Hubbard 1: 178
1832..Baird, Robert 8: 171
1832..Colton, Calvin 8: 38
1832..Drake, Samuel G. 7: 61
1832..Hall, James 7: 198
1832..Hildreth, Richard 10: 460
1832..Lee, Hannah F. 25: 129
1832..Paine, Martyn 11: 551
1832..Smith, Samuel F. 6: 51
1833..Clark, L. Gaylord 8: 454
1833..Hayward, John 10: 46
1833..Judson, Emily C. 3: 93
1833..Lee, Mary E. 6: 438
1833..Sleeper, John S. 13: 206
1833..Smith, Seba 8: 118
1833..Smith, William R. 12: 294

1833..Wayland, Francis 8: 22
1834..Abbott, Jacob 6: 136
1834..Bird, Robert M. 7: 183
1834..Colwell, Stephen, ... 4: 524
1834..Hazard, Rowland G. 9: 442
1834..Mansfield, Edward D. 11: 206
1834..Prentiss, Elizabeth P. 7: 106
1834..Stone, William L. 7: 205
1834..Sunderland, LeRoy 5: 354
1834..Woolsey, Theodore D. 1: 170
1835..Adams, Charles F. 8: 351
1835..Benjamin, Park 7: 166
1835..Colton, Walter 4: 305
1835..Ellet, Elizabeth F. 11: 37
1835..Hooker, Herman 7: 99
1835..Locke, Richard A. 13: 151
1835..Peabody, William B. O... 8: 63
1835..Stephens, Ann S. W......10: 20
1835..Thompson, Daniel P...... 6: 233
1835..Todd, John 8: 125
1836..Alcott, A. Bronson 2: 218
1836..Brownson, Orestes A. 7: 197
1836..Clarke, James F. 2: 186
1836..Dupuy, Eliza A 6: 200
1836..Durivage, Francis A. 8: 237
1836..Emerson, Ralph W. 3: 416
1836..Hawks, Francis L. 7: 90
1836..Sargent, Epes 7: 243
1836..Ware, William 5: 358
1837..Brooks, Charles T. 8: 306
1837..Brooks, Nathan C. 4: 557
1837..Coxe, A. Cleveland 3: 474
1837..Farrar, Eliza W. 13: 317
1837..Goodrich, Samuel G. 5: 355
1837..Robbins, Royal 2: 195
1837..Shelton, Frederick W. 9: 253
1837..Thatcher, Benjamin B. ...13: 404
1837..Thoreau, Henry D. 2: 300
1838..Ballou, Maturin M. 7: 307
1838..Claiborne, John F. H....11: 391
1838..Flagg, Edmund 13: 55
1838..Gardner, Samuel J. 13: 405
1838..Haliburton, Thomas C. ... 5: 353
1838..Judson, Edward Z. C.....13: 194
1838..Marsh, George P. 2: 380
1838..Smith, Elizabeth O. P.... 9: 171
1838..Thompson, William T. 9: 335
1838..Tuckerman, Henry T..... 7: 234
1839..Briggs, Charles F. 9: 254
1839..Conant, Thomas J. 12: 288
1839..Dana, Richard H., Jr. 7: 182
1839..Gould, Edward S. 4: 527
1839..Hague, William 3: 225
1839..Herbert, Henry W. 3: 534
1839..Jones, William A. 12: 194
1839..Lowell, James Russell 2: 32
1839..Lunt, George 6: 536
1839..Mayo, Sarah C. E. 2: 437
1840..Bethune, George W. 8: 166
1840..Carter, Robert 8: 41
1840..Cary, Alice 1: 535
1840..Clapp, Henry 9: 121
1840..Congdon, Charles T....... 3: 458
1840..Cranch, Christopher P. .. 7: 140
1840..Earle, Pliny 11: 146
1840..Elwyn, Alfred L. 23: 135
1840..Flagg, Wilson 19: 431
1840..Judd, Sylvester 9: 273
1840..Kirkland, Caroline M. S... 5: 356
1840..Longfellow, Samuel 8: 275
1840..Lossing, Benson J. 4: 324
1840..Peters, Hugh 8: 338
1840..Scoville, Joseph A. 5: 433
1840..Tucker, Nathaniel B. 7: 520
1840..Turnbull, Robert 10: 499
1840..Wise, Daniel 13: 191
1841..Greene, William B. 7: 526
1841..Griswold, Rufus W. 4: 74
1841..Mathews, William 11: 118
1841..Porter, Noah 1: 171
1841..Richards, T. Addison 8: 425
1841..Simonds, William 5: 120
1841..Taylor, Bayard 3: 454
1842..Cary, Phoebe 1: 535
1842..Daveiss, Maria T. 3: 97
1842..Duyckinck, Evert A. 1: 431
1842..Farnham, Thomas J. 4: 355
1842..Homes, Henry A. 13: 42
1842..Lee, Eliza B. 25: 343
1842..Mathews, Cornelius 13: 542
1842..Morris, Edward J. 13: 25
1842..Sherwood, Mary E. W.... 5: 522
1842..Story, William W. 5: 417
1842..Street, Alfred B. 11: 103
1843..Duganne, Augustine J. H. 4: 315
1843..English, Thomas D. 4: 322
1843..Huntington, Jedediah V...13: 525
1843..Jarves, James J. 11: 490
1843..Jeffrey, Rosa V. G. 11: 405
1843..Latimer, Mary E. W. 9: 271
1843..Miller, Stephen F. 9: 263
1844..Abbott, John S. C........ 6: 145
1844..Cooke, Rose T. 6: 300
1844..Ellis, George E. 8: 18
1844..Godwin, Parke 11: 117
1844..Headley, Joel T. 3: 458
1844..Lewis, Estelle A. B. R. ...10: 449
1844..Mayer, Brantz 10: 32
1844..Mitchell, Donald G. 6: 97
1844..Peabody, Oliver W. B. .. 8: 63
1844..Putnam, Mary T. S. 12: 328
1844..Saltus, Edgar E. 19: 201
1844..Thompson, Joseph P. 10: 132
1845..Bledsoe, Albert T. 8: 272
1845..Botta, Anne C. L. 7: 236
1845..Burritt, Elihu 6: 133
1845..Gillett, Ezra H. 5: 530
1845..Lanman, Charles 3: 444
1845..Lester, Charles E. 13: 111
1845..Mackie, John M. 12: 111
1845..Slenker, Elmina D. 7: 488
1845..Stebbins, Mary E. 13: 364
1845..Taylor, Benjamin F. 11: 159
1845..Thorpe, Thomas B. 6: 230
1846..Barnes, Albert 7: 360
1846..Browne, John R. 8: 117
1846..Codman, John 13: 584
1846..Derby, George H. 5: 241
1846..Fiske, Nathan W. 7: 245
1846..Haven, Alice B. 5:386
1846..Larcom, Lucy 1: 406
1846..Littell, John S. 5: 355
1846..Melville, Herman 4: 59
1846..Victor, Metta V. F. 4: 522
1846..Whitcher, Frances M. 6: 30
1847..Boker, George H. 6: 73
1847..Brownell, Henry H. 5: 357
1847..Cozzens, Frederick S. 6: 29
1847..Dorsey, Anna H. 11: 361
1847..Halpine, Charles G. 6: 26
1847..Hough, Franklin B. 13: 340
1847..Palfrey, John G. 7: 199
1847..Parkman, Francis 1: 431
1847..Shillaber, Benjamin P. ... 6: 32
1847..Southworth, E. D. E. N... 1: 432
1847..Stevens, Abel 8: 112
1847..Tyler, William S. 10: 347
1848..Dexter, Henry M. 1: 177
1848..Duyckinck, George L. 10: 502
1848..Elliott, Charles W. 13: 465
1848..Farnham, Eliza W. 4: 355
1848..Hammett, Samuel A. 22: 389
1848..Hudson, Henry N. 9: 490
1848..McCord, Louisa S. C. ... 9: 169
1848..Myers, Peter H. 10: 485
1848..Prime, William C. 13: 254
1848..Schmucker, Samuel M. ... 5: 101
1848..Webber, Charles W. 4: 354
1848..Whipple, Edwin P. 1: 197
1848..Wilson, Augusta E. 4: 457
1848..Wood, Ann T. W. 10: 450
1848..Wood, George 8: 376
1849..Adams, William T. 1: 203
1849..Cheever, Henry T. 13: 483
1849..Coffin, Robert B. 6: 525
1849..Deane, Charles 3: 520
1849..Giles, Henry 2: 448
1849..Leland, Charles G. 5: 356
1849..Stoddard, Richard H. 3: 297
1849..Ticknor, George 6: 477
1849..Warner, Susan 5: 354
1849..Wise, Henry A. 13: 589
1850..Bigelow, John 26: 25
1850..Bristed, Charles A. 6: 366
1850..Bushnell, William H. 1: 431
1850..Chesebrough, Caroline 23: 330
1850..Clarke, Richard H. 1: 257
1850..Cobb, Joseph B. 10: 382
1850..Coffin, Charles C. 1: 438
1850..Cooper, Susan Fenimore .. 6: 301
1850..Croly, Jennie C. 6: 499
1850..Curtis, George William ... 3: 96
1850..Davis, Andrew J. 8: 442
1850..Field, Henry M. 5: 360
1850..Headley, Phineas C. 11: 236
1850..Kimball, Richard B. 10: 32
1850..Kip, Leonard 11: 439
1850..Lippincott, Sara J. 4: 536
1850..Phelps, Elizabeth 9: 367
1850..Roe, Azel S. 4: 544
1850..Roe, Edward P. 7: 15
1850..Savage, John 11: 509
1850..Strother, David H. 9: 365
1850..Tefft, Benjamin F. 13: 575
1850..Trowbridge, John T. 3: 374
1850..Wilson, John 9: 321
1850..Woodworth, Francis C. ... 5: 509
1850..Youmans, Edward L. 2: 466
1851..Brace, Charles L. 10: 166
1851..Brooks, Noah 7: 57
1851..Coggeshall, George 23: 308
1851..Osgood, Samuel 9: 236
1851..Parton, Sara P. 1: 392
1851..Stowe, Harriet Beecher .. 1: 423
1851..Victor, Frances A. F. ...13: 432
1852..Alden, Isabella M. 10: 405
1852..Allibone, Samuel A. 6: 227
1852..Arthur, Timothy S. 8: 480
1852..Baldwin, James 14: 134
1852..Bunce, Oliver B. 2: 512
1852..Guernsey, Lucy E. 6: 168
1852..Hale, Edward Everett 1: 199
1852..Locke, David R. 6: 152
1852..Ward, James W. 10: 247
1853..Bagby, George W. 24: 102
1853..Bowen, Francis 11: 452
1853..DeForest, John W. 4: 293
1853..Hanaford, Phebe A. 13: 307
1853..Hittell, John S. 22: 41
1853..Moulton, Louise C. 3: 365
1853..Robinson, Annie D. 3: 238
1853..Saunders, Frederick 2: 379
1853..Wallace, Susan A. E. 10: 359
1853..Walworth, Mansfield T. .. 5: 359
1853..Warner, Anna B. 4: 530
1853..Warner, Charles Dudley .. 2: 116
1853..White, Richard G. 1: 197
1854..Alcott, Louisa M. 1: 204
1854..Blackburn, William M. ... 9: 441
1854..Cooke, John E. 7: 330
1854..Cummins, Maria S. 6: 135
1854..Finley, Martha 11: 267
1854..Freedley, Edwin T. 10: 124
1854..Gage, Frances D. 2: 321
1854..Goodrich, Frank B. 13: 404
1854..Hallock, Charles 9: 507
1854..Holmes, Mary J. 8: 421
1854..Hoppin, James M. 1: 245
1854..Howe, Julia Ward 1: 402
1854..Peyton, John L. 4: 89
1854..Quincy, Edmund 6: 93
1854..Terhune, Mary V. H. 2: 122
1854..Winter, William 4: 83
1855..Aldrich, Thomas Bailey .. 1: 283
1855..Allen, Elizabeth Akers ... 6: 133
1855..Barrow, Frances E. 4: 556
1855..Brooks, Charles 12: 287
1855..Carpenter, Esther B. 2: 449
1855..Davis, Rebecca H. 8: 176
1855..Fish, Henry C. 3: 523
1855..Halsey, Harlan P. 9: 145
1855..LeVert, Octavia W. 6: 440
1855..Norton, Charles Eliot 6: 425
1855..Sangster, Margaret E. ... 6: 169
1855..Sargent, Winthrop 7: 248
1855..Winthrop, Theodore 1: 130
1856..Cowley, Charles 23: 277
1856..Nordhoff, Charles 11: 226
1856..O'Brien, Fitz-James 6: 79
1856..Parsons, Theophilus 5: 393
1856..Seelye, Julius H. 6: 157
1856..Taylor, William 10: 496
1856..Whedon, Daniel D. 8: 442
1856..Whitman, William E. S. .. 5: 367
1857..Coppee, Henry 7: 111
1857..Ellsworth, Mary W. J. ..11: 492
1857..Ford, Sallie R. 12: 429
1857..Hassard, John R. G. 3: 459
1857..Hitchcock, Ethan A. 11: 196
1857..Richardson, Abby S. 5: 553
1857..Train, George F. 9: 264
1857..Whitney, Adeline D. T. .. 2: 29
1858..Bates, Charlotte F. 13: 111
1858..Browne, Charles F. 1: 425
1858..Conway, Moncure D. 1: 206
1858..Crane, Anne M. 6: 400
1858..Griswold, A. Miner 6: 29
1858..Guild, Reuben A. 3: 460
1858..Halsey, LeRoy J. 3: 517
1858..Harris, George W. 4: 557
1858..Holland, Josiah G. 1: 311
1858..Johnson, Sarah B. 11: 189
1858..Moore, George H. 4: 555
1858..Rice, Rosella 5: 540
1858..Shaw, Henry W. 6: 28
1858..Spofford, Harriet Prescott 4: 308
1858..Warren, Israel P. 4: 235
1859..Arnold, George 9: 432
1859..Blake, Lillie D. 11: 61
1859..Booth, Mary L. 7: 321
1859..Dahlgren, Sarah M. V. ..22: 411
1859..Gibbons, James S. 9: 84
1859..Redpath, James 13: 118
1859..Schieffelin, Samuel B. 4: 521
1859..Stiles, Henry R. 13: 41
1859..Taylor, George B. 11: 399
1859..Townsend, Virginia F. ..13: 165

1859..Winsor, Justin 1:150
1860..Alger, Horatio, Jr. 11:543
1860..Austin, Jane G. 6: 62
1860..Bellaw, Americus W. 5:549
1860..Cheney, Ednah D. 9:170
1860..Clarke, Rebecca S. 8:339
1860..Dodge, Mary A. 9:227
1860..Ford, Emily E. 13:105
1860..Harris, Miriam C. 11:515
1860..Howells, William Dean ... 1:281
1860..Mathews, Albert 8: 50
1860..Peebles, James M. 11:423
1860..Scoville, Joseph A. 5:433
1860..Ticknor, Howard M. 15:172
1861..Beers, Ethelinda E. 8:358
1861..Benjamin, Samuel G. W.. 7: 26
1861..Cooke, George W. 8: 68
1861..Newell, Robert H. 11:528
1861..Pollard, Edward A. 11:339
1861..Seymour, Mary H. B. 4:404
1861..Smith, Charles H. 3:308
1861..Wheeler, Andrew C. 25:375
1862..Botta, Vincenzo 7:235
1862..Clemens, Samuel L. 6: 24
1862..Del Mar, Alexander 4:189
1862..Gilmore, James R. 10:249
1862..Miller, Emily H. 10:305
1862..Scudder, Horace E. 1:284
1862..Wilson, James G. 11:412
1863..Alden, Henry M. 1:153
1863..Bolton, Sarah K. 1:212
1863..Bunner, Henry C. 7:303
1863..Frémont, Jessie B. 4:399
1863..Frothingham, Octavius B. 2:423
1863..Guernsey, Alfred H. 12:233
1863..Heady, Morrison 11:150
1863..Kirk, John F. 1:535
1863..Murray, William H. H. ..10:230
1863..Raymond, Rossiter W. 8: 44
1863..Salter, William M. 24:395
1863..Sanborn, Franklin B. 8:466
1863..Stoddard, Elizabeth D. ... 8:375
1863..Stone, William L. 11:387
1863..Webb, Charles H. 10: 42
1863..Wormeley, Katharine P. .. 8:366
1864..Campbell, Helen S. 9:126
1864..Hooper, Lucy H. 8:171
1864..Hoppin, Augustus 9:483
1864..Johnston, Richard M. ... 1:440
1864..Kirchhoff, Theodor 11:266
1864..Lanier, Sidney 2:438
1864..Logan, Olive 6:528
1864..Mayo, William S. 8:483
1864..Parton, James 1:391
1864..Pond, George E. 10: 39
1864..Pool, Maria L. 6:320
1864..Searing, Laura C. 9:497
1864..Stevens, John A. 13:139
1864..Trumbull, Henry C. 9:383
1864..Weiss, John 10: 61
1865..Ames, Mary Clemmer 7:233
1865..Avery, Rosa M. 6:271
1865..Dimitry, Charles P. 10:176
1865..Downing, Fanny M. 7:497
1865..Eggleston, Edward 6: 57
1865..Garrison, Wendell P. 1:197
1865..Godkin, Edwin L. 8:455
1865..Hinsdale, Grace W. H. ... 9: 96
1865..Jackson, Helen Hunt 1:433
1865..Kellogg, Elijah 2:497
1865..Mitchell, S. Weir 9:346
1865..Perkins, Charles C. 4:524
1865..Richardson, Albert D. 8:465
1865..Rolfe, William J. 4: 86
1865..Thayer, Alexander W. 8:233
1865..Tilton, Theodore 8:100
1865..Townsend, George A. 1:154
1866..Bradley, Warren I. 4:260
1866..Browne, William H. 11:233
1866..Carleton, Will 2:505
1866..Douglas, Amanda M. 2:374
1866..Hale, Lucretia P. 5:353
1866..Hubner, Charles W. 2:142
1866..Lamb, Martha J. R. N. .. 1:443
1866..Lazarus, Emma 3: 25
1866..Meline, James F. 6:353
1866..Mulford, Prentice 1:433
1866..Mullany, Patrick F. 7:525
1866..Proctor, Edna D. 7:250
1866..Putnam, Sarah A. B. 10:381
1866..Wharton, Anne H. 13:366
1867..Alger, William R. 6: 34
1867..Baylor, Frances C. 1:366
1867..Bellamy, Elizabeth W. 12:269
1867..Burnett, Frances Hodgson 20:423
1867..Dall, Caroline Healey 9:159
1867..Davis, Mary E. M. 10: 21
1867..Fiske, John 3: 23
1867..Reeves, Marian C. L. 4:377
1867..Russell, Addison P. 6: 19
1867..Stoddard, Charles W. 7:116
1867..Swinton, William 11:488
1867..Tourgee, Albion W. 7:324
1868..Abbott, Lyman 1:473
1868..Bowker, Richard R. 24: 66
1868..Brent, Henry J. 13:207
1868..Diaz, Abby M. 11:169
1868..Eyster, Nellie B. 10:392
1868..Holt, John S. 6:277
1868..Keenan, Henry F. 6:144
1868..Poole, Hester M. H. 11:208
1868..Reed, Elizabeth A. 15:229
1868..Tyler, Moses C. 4:483
1868..Wilkinson, William C. 11: 72
1868..Young, Egerton R. 14:160
1869..Abbott, Edward 8:179
1869..Barnard, Charles 13: 64
1869..Cable, George W. 1:533
1869..Davidson, James W. 9:100
1869..De Leon, Thomas C. 19:242
1869..Evans, Edward P. 9:433
1869..Gilman, Arthur 6:162
1869..Lewis, Charles B. 6: 30
1869..Page, Thomas N. 19:405
1869..Preston, Harriet W. 8: 32
1869..Sanborn, Kate 9: 94
1869..Stephens, Charles A. 23:122
1869..Stoddard, William O. 8:121
1869..Townsend, Luther T. 10:316
1869..Woodberry, George E. 23:186
1869..Woolson, Constance F. ... 1:369
1870..Bacon, Edwin M. 13:421
1870..Branch, Mary L. 21:397
1870..Buel, James W. 7: 75
1870..Davis, Charles Henry S. ..25: 68
1870..DeVere, Mary A. 8:440
1870..Dodge, Mary Mapes 1:314
1870..Fawcett, Edgar 7:191
1870..Johnson, Virginia W. 13:107
1870..Keith, Eliza D. 2:425
1870..Landon, Melville D. 6: 27
1870..Perry, Nora 15:116
1870..Porter, Rose 10:307
1870..Thorpe, Rose A. H. 10:252
1870..Tiernan, Frances C. F. ..20:293
1870..Venable, William H. 19:364
1870..Walworth, Jeannette H. .. 8: 48
1870..Phelps, Elizabeth Stuart .. 9:368
1871..Browne, Irving 11:322
1871..Burroughs, John 1:247
1871..Eggleston, George C. 1:213
1871..Fuller, Edwin W. 10:397
1871..Furness, Horace H. 8:396
1871..George, Henry 4:325
1871..Greey, Edward 8:119
1871..Hay, John 11: 12
1871..Hinsdale, Burke A. 10:471
1871..Knortz, Karl 10:358
1871..Richmond, Euphemia J. .. 4:468
1871..Stapleton, Patience T. ... 8:151
1871..Woolsey, Sarah C. 11:352
1872..Anderson, Rasmus B. 9:320
1872..Barr, Amelia E. 4:485
1872..Burdette, Robert J. 24:356
1872..Harte, Bret 1:404
1872..Hutton, Laurence 7: 64
1872..Larned, Augusta 13:462
1872..Morgan, Appleton 9:452
1872..Reifsnider, Anna C. E. ...23:414
1872..Roe, Edward P. 7: 15
1872..Sparhawk, Frances C. ...10: 47
1872..Stockton, Frank R. 1:396
1872..Thaxter, Celia L. 1:305
1872..Thompson, Daniel G. 8:386
1872..Tincker, Mary A. 8:413
1872..Wilcox, Ella Wheeler 11:278
1873..Adams, Henry 11:475
1873..Bailey, James M. 6: 28
1873..Champlin, John D. 8:357
1873..Dawson, Sarah M. 23:300
1873..Dodge, Nathaniel S. 11:233
1873..Donnelly, Eleanor C. 2:369
1873..Hawthorne, Julian 25: 45
1873..Holley, Marietta 9:278
1873..Jackson, Edward P. 11:548
1873..Johnson, Rossiter 2: 63
1873..Matthews, Brander 26: 16
1873..Moore, Clara J. 9:473
1873..O'Reilly, John B. 1:428
1873..Prescott, Mary N. 8:364
1873..Riddle, Albert G. 2:371
1873..Wall, Annie C. 5: 70
1873..Wallace, Lew 4:363
1874..Appleton, Thomas G. 8:391
1874..Bascom, John 8:196
1874..Boyesen, Hjalmar H. 1:367
1874..Bryan, Mary E. 8:374
1874..Cox, Palmer 7:459
1874..Griffis, William E. 21:118
1874..Griswold, Hattie T. 10:203
1874..House, Edward H. 13:458
1874..Lathbury, Mary A. 10:179
1874..Nicolay, John G. 8:170
1874..Parsons, George F. 8: 90
1874..Stillman, William J. 10: 25
1874..White, Eliza O. 13:495
1875..Felton, Rebecca L. 13:410
1875..Hearn, Lafcadio 1:409
1875..James, Henry 1:410
1875..Lathrop, George P. 9:193
1875..Nadal, Ehrman S. 11:540
1876..Allmond, Marcus B. 13: 29
1876..Bishop, William H. 8: 54
1876..Didier, Eugene L. 13:153
1876..Dodge, Richard I. 11:512
1876..Habberton, John 4:217
1876..Harper, Olive 5:215
1876..Harrison, Constance C. .. 4:320
1876..Kirk, Ellen Olney 1:373
1876..Larned, Josephus N. 16:344
1876..Lothrop, Harriet M. 8:383
1876..McDowell, Katherine S. B. 11:496
1876..Morse, John T. 12:438
1876..Raymond, George L. 8:458
1876..Schuyler, Eugene 8:339
1876..Sullivan, Thomas R. 16:175
1876..Tenney, Edward P. 7:530
1876..Towle, George M. 8: 83
1877..Alden, William L. 6:326
1877..Bynner, Edwin L. 7:486
1877..Champney, Elizabeth W. .11:308
1877..Dorsey, Sarah A. 3:213
1877..Egan, Maurice F. 11:111
1877..Fletcher, Julia C. 13:458
1877..Harris, Joel Chandler 1:410
1877..Howard, Blanche W. 1:304
1877..Jewett, Sarah O. 1:374
1877..Munkittrick, Richard K... 9:412
1877..Proudfit, David L. 8: 33
1878..Beers, Henry A. 7:297
1878..Bellamy, Edward 1:263
1878..Carleton, Henry G. 13:111
1878..Eastman, Elaine G. 8:139
1878..Elson, Louis C. 8:449
1878..Green, Anna Katharine .. 9:257
1878..Higginson, Thomas W. ... 1:394
1878..Loughead, Flora H. 11:224
1878..Mowry, William A. 25:172
1878..Rand, Edward A. 13:412
1878..Read, Opie P. 1:353
1878..Richardson, Charles F. ... 9: 95
1878..Rollins, Alice M. 8:414
1878..Thompson, Maurice 11:521
1878..Wiggin, Kate Douglas 6:207
1879..Brooks, Elbridge S. 7:156
1879..Bryce, Lloyd 1:252
1879..Cook, Joseph 2:260
1879..Elliott, Sarah B. 21: 65
1879..French, Alice 25:296
1879..Grant, Robert C:431
1879..Hewett, Waterman T. ... 8:419
1879..Hitchcock, Ripley 18:173
1879..Ingersoll, Ernest 9:240
1879..Jackson, George A. 12:529
1879..Miller, Harriet M. 9:208
1879..Munroe, Kirk 11:523
1879..Ober, Frederick A. 13:311
1879..Raymond, George L. 8:457
1879..Smith, Jane L. D. 2:190
1879..Sweet, Alexander E. 6: 69
1880..Adams, Oscar Fay 19: 45
1880..Boutelle, Clarence M. 11:473
1880..Clarke, Mary H. G. 6:235
1880..Coates, Florence E. 18:307
1880..Dole, Nathan H. 13:554
1880..Fields, Annie A. 1:282
1880..Greene, Sarah P. 13:463
1880..Halsey, Francis W. 9:155
1880..Kaler, James Otis 13:475
1880..King, Charles 25:148
1880..Miller, James R. 10: 19
1880..Moore, John T. 13:138
1880..Otis, James 13:475
1880..Page, Thomas N. 19:405
1880..Paine, Albert B. 13: 99
1880..Roberts, Charles G. D. ...11:398
1880..Wells, Carolyn 13:213
1880..Williams, Alfred M. 4:153
1880..Williams, Francis H. 10: 49
1881..Albee, John 15:143
1881..Bates, Arlo 8: 12
1881..Bates, Charlotte F. 13:111
1881..Bates, Katharine Lee 9:314
1881..Burnham, Clara L. 21:151
1881..Catherwood, Mary H. 9:215
1881..Craigie, Pearl M. T. 10:506
1881..Hardy, Arthur S. 2:303

1881..Janvier, Margaret T. 12: 460
1881..Lloyd, John Uri .... D: 106
1881..Montgomery, David H 24: 171
1881..Nye, Edgar W. 6: 25
1881..Pennell, Elizabeth R. 10: 377
1881..Seton, Ernest T. .... C: 392
1882..Adams, Herbert B. 8: 270
1882..Baxter, James P. 9: 422
1882..Crawford, F. Marion 2: 502
1882..De Leon, Edwin 4: 94
1882..Donnelly, Ignatius 1: 397
1882..Hamilton, Kate W. 4: 296
1882..Kobbe, Gustav 10: 410
1882..Litchfield, Grace D. 12: 313
1882..Mabie, Hamilton W. 10: 43
1882..Malone, Walter 13: 173
1882..Martin, Edward S. .... B: 450
1882..Mason, Mary A. 4: 525
1882..Pullen, Elizabeth J. C. ... 8: 373
1882..Spears, John R. 9: 162
1882..Stockton, Louise 8: 336
1882..Taylor, Bert L. 24: 346
1882..Wister, Owen .... C: 459
1883..Foote, Mary Hallock 6: 472
1883..King, Charles 25: 148
1883..Ludlow, James M. 8: 59
1883..Palmer, Anna C. 22: 127
1883..Pyle, Howard 9: 56
1883..Stanwood, Edward 9: 475
1883..Stringer, George A. 13: 198
1883..Williams, George W. 10: 511
1884..Bacheller, Irving .... C: 411
1884..Bradford, Gamaliel 23: 65
1884..Deming, Clarence 12: 437
1884..Hibbard, George 3: 524
1884..Masson, Thomas L. 17: 398
1884..Murfree, Mary N. 2: 363
1884..Parker, Jane M. 10: 22
1884..Scollard, Clinton 23: 160
1884..Shorey, Paul .... C: 36
1884..Thayer, William R. 12: 530
1884..Van Dyke, Henry 25: 10
1885..Bates, Harriet L. V. 8: 12
1885..Bourne, Edward G. 10: 461
1885..Cleveland, Rose E. 2: 238
1885..Deming, Philander 8: 248
1885..Dey, Frederic M. van R. ..26: 178
1885..Gardener, Helen H. 9: 451
1885..Jacobs, Joseph 24: 437
1885..Janvier, Thomas A. 12: 460
1885..Kirkland, Joseph 5: 481
1885..McClelland, Mary G. 2: 485
1885..Magruder, Julia 8: 10
1885..Mitchell, Langdon E. 4: 522
1885..Osborne, Samuel D. 10: 383
1885..Stratemeyer, Edward 16: 37
1885..Thompson, Vance 20: 241
1885..Tooker, Frank 20: 146
1885..Torrey, Bradford 10: 134
1885..Wendell, Barrett 9: 207
1885..Wilson, Woodrow 19: 1
1886..Abbot, Willis J. 11: 103
1886..Deland, Margaret 3: 476
1886..Dromgoole, Will Allen 8: 258
1886..Farmer, Lydia H. 8: 305
1886..Gilder, Jeannette L. 8: 441
1886..Henderson, Isaac 5: 426
1886..Herrick, Christine T. 8: 453
1886..King, Grace E. 2: 344
1886..Peck, Harry T. 11: 528
1886..Pierson, Arthur T. 13: 408
1886..Rexford, Eben E. 10: 55
1886..Van Zile, Edward S. 25: 278
1886..Wilkins, Mary E. 9: 229
1887..Allen, Willis B. 10: 182
1887..Bangs, John K. 9: 323
1887..Bolton, Charles K. ...... B: 113
1887..Boner, John H. 2: 497
1887..Bowen, John E. 6: 159
1887..Edgerly, Webster 20: 444
1887..Ford, Sewell 14: 140
1887..Foster, David S. 25: 241
1887..Gillilan, Strickland W. ... A: 424
1887..Hall, Florence M. H. 19: 88
1887..Jenks, Tudor 24: 284
1887..Lockhart, Arthur J. 8: 420
1887..Meriwether, Lee 10: 128
1887..Speed, John G. 10: 294
1887..Stevens, Benjamin F. 11: 319
1887..Wolfe, Theodore F. 16: 227
1888..Atherton, Gertrude .... D: 378
1888..Cahan, Abraham 11: 171
1888..Edwards, Harry S. 8: 86
1888..Gilman, Nicholas P. 8: 120
1888..Gordon, Armistead C. 8: 137
1888..Pellew, George 4: 356
1888..Pendleton, Louis 10: 145
1888..Perry, Bliss .... C: 451
1888..Repplier, Agnes .... C: 368
1888..Rives, Amélie .... B: 293
1888..Stearns, Frank P. 8: 231
1888..Tomlinson, Everett T. ...25: 435
1888..Troubetzkoy, Amélie Rives B: 293
1888..Whitney, Caspar 25: 284
1889..Bailey, Florence M. .... A: 257
1889..Bok, Edward W. 23: 41
1889..DeKoven, Anna F. 16: 290
1889..Dickinson, Charles M. 11: 91
1889..Ellwanger, George H. 13: 134
1889..Flower, Benjamin O. 9: 228
1889..Ford, Paul Leicester 13: 105
1889..Grinnell, George Bird .... B: 478
1889..Harben, Will N. 10: 310
1889..Learned, Walter 8: 189
1889..Mason, Caroline A. 4: 525
1889..Poulsson, Emilie 10: 463
1889..Wood, John S. 11: 167
1890..Ade, George .... C: 386
1890..Dixon, Thomas, Jr. 13: 189
1890..Earle, Alice M. 13: 574
1890..Finn, Francis J. 22: 418
1890..Fuller, Henry B. 23: 406
1890..James, George W. 19: 68
1890..Lewis, Alfred H. 25: 261
1890..Lloyd, Henry D. 12: 375
1890..McConaughy, James 25: 410
1890..Mead, Theodore H. 25: 386
1890..Mifflin, Lloyd 18: 296
1890..Moore, Alice R. 16: 425
1890..Rutherford, Mildred L. ...10: 416
1890..Shackleton, Robert 19: 346
1890..Trask, Katrina N. 11: 444
1890..Wallace, Charles W. 23: 160
1890..White, Greenough 11: 271
1890..White, William Allen ..... B: 433
1890..Wilder, Marshall P. 6: 33
1891..Allen, James L. 8: 241
1891..Biddle, Anthony J. D. 7: 446
1891..Bigelow, Poultney 9: 143
1891..Brewster, Henry P. 13: 288
1891..Chatfield-Taylor, Hobart C. C: 359
1891..Crane, Stephen 10: 113
1891..Davis, Richard Harding .. 8: 176
1891..Edgerton, James A. ...... B: 197
1891..Garland, Hamlin .... B: 4
1891..Hubbard, Elbert 16: 415
1891..Lummis, Charles F. 11: 227
1891..Pattee, Fred L. .... A: 228
1891..Robinson, Jonah L. 13: 173
1891..Sears, Joseph H. 13: 363
1891..Smith, Nora A. 26: 400
1891..Stoddard, Charles A. 9: 127
1891..Wells, Amos R. 25: 163
1891..Wharton, Edith .... B: 32
1892..Andrews, William L. 13: 347
1892..Dodge, Walter P. 11: 393
1892..Dreiser, Theodore .... C: 93
1892..Gilman, Charlotte P. 13: 212
1892..Grant, Robert .... C: 431
1892..King, Basil 21: 437
1892..Kester, Vaughan 25: 285
1892..Macdermott, William A. ..11: 119
1892..Steffens, Lincoln 14: 455
1893..Boyle, Virginia 13: 406
1893..Carryl, Guy W. 13: 121
1893..Edwards, George W. 11: 414
1893..Henry, Stuart 9: 145
1893..Herrick, Robert .... C: 378
1893..Johnson, Clifton 11: 413
1893..Johnston, Annie F. 13: 441
1893..Owen, Mary A. 13: 188
1893..Paine, Albert B. 13: 99
1893..Stuart, Ruth McE. 4: 522
1893..Zimmerman, Leander M. . A: 192
1894..Doubleday, Neltje B. D. ..13: 400
1894..Elliot, Henry R. 9: 215
1894..Kingsley, Florence M. 11: 272
1894..Moffett, Cleveland 24: 43
1894..More, Paul E. .... C: 296
1894..Muir, John 9: 449
1894..Neilson, Francis .... C: 340
1894..Paine, Ralph D. 25: 408
1894..Santayana, George ...... B: 343
1894..Stevenson, Burton E. 13: 143
1894..Storey, Moorfield 12: 218
1894..Winslow, Helen M. .... B: 188
1895..Baker, George P. 25: 28
1895..Bjerregaard, Carl H. A. .13: 47
1895..Chambers, Robert W. .... C: 402
1895..Churchill, Winston 10: 178
1895..Dresser, Horatio W. 11: 110
1895..Fisher, Sydney G. 13: 343
1895..Harland, Henry 13: 235
1895..Hough, Emerson 19: 60
1895..Howe, Daniel W. 13: 289
1895..Inman, Henry 9: 248
1895..Remington, Frederic 22: 244
1895..Wright, Mabel O. 12: 545
1896..Alden, Raymond M. 20: 118
1896..Altsheler, Joseph A. 11: 205
1896..Baskett, James N. 13: 346
1896..Hillis, Newell D. 21: 280
1896..Rice, Wallace 13: 199
1896..Stimson, Frederick J. 10: 361
1896..Terhune, Albert Payson .. C: 442
1896..Wood, Charles S. 13: 345
1897..Baum, L. Frank 18: 331
1897..Booth, William S. 20: 261
1897..Chapple, Joe M. .... C: 529
1897..Cross, Wilbur L. .... C: 451
1897..Glasgow, Ellen .... C: 348
1897..Lynde, Francis 13: 347
1897..Peabody, Josephine P. 19: 95
1897..Stephens, Kate .... B: 100
1898..Adler, Cyrus 11: 371
1898..Brady, Cyrus T. 10: 477
1898..Bryan, Ella H. 13: 312
1898..Callahan, James M. 11: 546
1898..Cobb, Irvin S. 18: 375
1898..Doubleday, Russell 13: 401
1898..Faris, John I. .... D: 275
1898..Kennard, Joseph S. ...... A: 552
1898..Major, Charles 13: 135
1898..Robins, Edward 13: 342
1898..Schelling, Felix E. ...... A: 426
1898..Sedgwick, Anne Douglas . C: 287
1899..Cook, George Cram 22: 11
1899..Crane, Frank 22: 281
1899..Dixon, Susan B. 13: 20
1899..Harris, Corra M. W. 26: 380
1899..Long, William J. .... D: 354
1899..Lorimer, George H. 13: 423
1899..Tarkington, Booth .... A: 84
1899..Webster, Henry K. .... A: 386
1899..Willard, Josiah F. 13: 366
1900..Baker, Ray S. .... C: 415
1900..Bunn, Henry W. 26: 282
1900..Converse, Florence 13: 144
1900..Dye, Eva Emery 13: 346
1900..Griggs, Edward H. ...... B: 299
1900..Grosvenor, Gilbert H. .... A: 309
1900..Kauffman, Reginald W. ..13: 406
1900..Kelly, Myra 24: 149
1900..London, Jack 13: 133
1900..Nicholson, Meredith ...... A: 512
1900..Pidgin, Charles F. 13: 479
1900..Quick, Herbert 25: 137
1900..White, Stewart Edward ..13: 313
1901..O'Higgins, Harvey J. 25: 296
1901..Porter, Eleanor H. 18: 382
1901..Porter, William Sidney ...15: 170
1901..Pound, Louise .... B: 51
1901..Williams, Francis C. 13: 143
1902..Cabell, James Branch .... A: 245
1902..Hughes, Rupert .... C: 314
1902..Irwin, William H. .... C: 256
1902..Johnston, Mary .... C: 430
1902..Lincoln, Joseph C. .... C: 449
1902..O'Brien, Frederick ...... C: 525
1902..Patchin, Frank G. 22: 365
1902..Poole, Ernest 18: 420
1902..Russell, Charles E. .... A: 106
1902..Whitlock, Brand .... A: 544
1903..Bullard, Arthur 21: 392
1903..Cather, Willa S. .... A: 537
1903..Erskine, John .... B: 59
1903..Miller, Alice Duer .... A: 378
1903..Reeve, Arthur B. 26: 276
1903..Sinclair, Upton .... C: 114
1903..Stein, Gertrude .... D: 397
1903..Towne, Elizabeth L. ...... A: 205
1903..Wright, Harold Bell ...... D: 382
1904..Fisher, Dorothy Canfield ..18: 63
1904..Grey, Zane .... B: 114
1904..Lewisohn, Ludwig .... C: 431
1904..Mencken, Henry L. .... A: 388
1904..Spingarn, Joel E. 17: 438
1904..Spivey, Thomas S. ...... B: 276
1904..Van Vechten, Carl ...... D: 433
1905..Johnson, Burges .... A: 243
1905..Lindsay, Vachel 23: 229
1905..Scott, Leroy 26: 243
1906..Ball, Eustace H. 24: 266
1906..Dawson, Coningsby W. .. A: 394
1906..Gale, Zona .... B: 301
1906..Leonard, William E. ..... C: 199
1906..Walcott, Earle A. .... A: 120
1906..Watts, Mary S. .... C: 412
1906..Wilson, William R. A. ...16: 224
1907..Barton, Bruce .... C: 326
1907..Macy, John A. 23: 108
1907..Marks, Jeannette .... B: 129
1907..Neihardt, John G. .... A: 543
1907..Teasdale, Sara .... A: 218
1908..Brooks, Van Wyck .... D: 436
1908..Burt, Maxwell Struthers .. D: 387

1908..Nathan, George Jean ..... C: 108
1908..Parrington, Vernon L. 25: 248
1908..Rinehart, Mary Roberts .. C: 486
1908..Street, Julian .... C: 260
1908..Train, Arthur C. 14: 427
1909..Dewing, Elizabeth B. .... C: 317
1909..Eaton, Walter Prichard .. A: 517
1909..Glaspell, Susan .... C: 505
1909..Hellman, George S. ...... A: 149
1909..Oppenheim, James .... A: 427
1909..Singmaster, Elsie ....C: 130
1910..Crosby, Percy L. .... D: 294
1910..Glass, Montague M. ...... C: 398
1910..Norris, Kathleen .... C: 366
1910..Skinner, Constance L. ... B: 266
1911..Bjorkman, Edwin .... B: 138
1911..Burroughs, Edgar Rice ... D: 331
1911..Donn-Byrne, Brian 22: 295
1911..Ferber, Edna .... C: 298
1911..Van Doren, Carl .... D: 47
1911..Wheelock, John H. ...... C: 286
1912..Antin, Mary .... C: 375
1912..Davis, Elmer .... D: 310
1912..Johnson, James W. ...... C: 488
1912..Morley, Christopher ...... A: 186
1912..Powell, E. Alexander ..... D: 168
1912..Widdemer, Margaret ..... A: 217
1913..Pitkin, Walter B. .... D: 42
1913..Porter, Harold E. .... A: 259
1913..Van Loon, Hendrick W. . B: 44
1914..Aiken, Conrad P. .... C: 393
1914..Dawson, Warrington ..... C: 476
1914..Frank, Waldo D. .... A: 398
1914..Hergesheimer, Joseph .. B: 56
1914..Hurst, Fannie .... B: 287
1914..Lewis, Sinclair .... B: 202
1914..Wright, Willard H. ...... C: 481
1915..Benét, Stephen Vincent .. A: 215
1915..Lardner, Ring .... C: 30
1915..Norris, Charles G. .... C: 366
1915..Wilde, Percival .... D: 440
1916..Anderson, Sherwood ..... A: 68
1916..Monahan, Michael .... A: 415
1918..Anderson, Robert G. ...... A: 180
1918..Scott, Evelyn D. .... C: 52
1918..Spicer, Anne H. .... C: 538
1919..Auslander, Joseph .... D: 45
1919..Fitzgerald, F. Scott ...... B: 472
1919..Mumford, Lewis .... D: 260
1920..Boyd, Thomas A. 26: 361
1920..Farrington, Harry W. ...23: 71
1920..Rogers, Will .... B: 67
1920..Van Doren, Mark .... D: 48
1921..Bromfield, Louis .... C: 295
1921..Montgomery, Roselle M. ..24: 47
1922..Peterkin, Julia .... C: 75
1922..Tully, Jim .... C: 472
1923..Parrish, Anne .... D: 141
1924..Beals, Carleton .... D: 442
1924..Looms, George 21: 402
1924..Ostenso, Martha .... C: 469
1925..Boyd, James .... C: 381
1925..Halliburton, Richard ..... D: 407
1925..Phillips, Marie T. .... C: 539
1925..Rascoe, Burton .... D: 340

Bacteriologists

1868..Burritt, Thomas J. 18: 187
1876..Vaughan, Victor C. 12: 207
1878..Sedgwick, William T. 13: 290
1878..Welch, William H. 26: 6
1879..Prudden, T. Mitchell 9: 347
1879..Sternberg, George M. 4: 388
1880..Linsley, John H. 15: 370
1882..Ernst, Harold C. 20: 89
1883..Smith, Theobold .... D: 133
1884..Conn, Herbert W. 20: 409
1886..Smith, Erwin F. 20: 273
1887..Paquin, Paul 6: 379
1890..Hektoen, Ludvig 18: 146
1890..Kinyoun, Joseph J. 23: 360
1890..Moore, Veranus A. 22: 366
1890..Russell, Harry L. 16: 417
1891..Novy, Frederick G. 16: 93
1891..Thayer, William S. 24: 409
1892..Flexner, Simon .... B: 19
1892..Schneider, Albert 13: 373
1893..Gorham, Frederic P. 23: 168
1893..Marshall, Charles E. 23: 191
1894..Ohlmacher, Albert P. 26: 222
1894..O'Malley, Austin 23: 149
1894..Prescott, Samuel C. ...... C: 389
1894..Trudeau, Edward L. 13: 564
1895..Hiss, Philip H., Jr. 16: 235
1895..Park, William H. .... C: 314
1895..Westbrook, Frank F. 14: 472
1896..Landsteiner, Karl .... D: 403
1900..Kellerman, Karl F. 26: 160
1900..Winslow, Charles-Edward A. .... D: 443
1901..Gay, Frederick P. .... B: 268
1901..Lipman, Jacob G. .... B: 212
1902..Castellani, Aldo .... C: 535
1904..Rosenow, Edward C. ..... A: 332
1907..Manwaring, Wilfred H. .. C: 110
1908..Nichols, Henry J. 23: 270
1908..Walbach, Simon B. .... D: 197
1911..Zingher, Abraham 26: 31
1913..Breed, Robert S. .... A: 288
1914..Bayne-Jones, Stanhope .. D: 276
1915..Opie, Eugene L. .... D: 242
1917..Jamieson, Walter A. ..... D: 228
1917..Stiles, Charles W. .... D: 62

Biologists

1841..Meehan, Thomas 11: 220
1863..Coues, Elliott 5: 240
1868..Riley, Charles V. 9: 443
1869..Dall, William H. 10: 454
1870..Forbes, Stephen A. .... B: 233
1870..Ward, Richard H. 13: 149
1872..Merriam, C. Hart 13: 264
1873..Eisen, Gustavus A. .... B: 484
1873..Tyler, John Mason 21: 373
1874..Peckham, George W. 12: 346
1874..Ward, Lester F. 13: 112
1876..Clarke, Samuel F. 21: 151
1876..Martin, Henry N. 12: 113
1876..Ryder, John A. 16: 396
1876..Shufeldt, Robert W. 6: 242
1877..Arthur, Joseph C. 12: 350
1877..Gage, Simon H. 4: 483
1877..Hargitt, Charles W. 5: 301
1877..Nelson, Edward W. 26: 434
1878..Howard, Leland O. 12: 356
1879..Osborn, Herbert 13: 202
1879..Sewall, Henry 26: 323
1880..Goode, G. Brown 3: 408
1880..Turck, Fenton B. 25: 175
1880..Whitman, Charles O. 11: 73
1882..Chaney, Lucian W. ...... A: 94
1882..Lucas, Frederic A. 13: 529
1882..Purinton, George D. 8: 189
1882..Stejneger, Leonhard 14: 130
1883..Donaldson, Henry H. 11: 56
1883..Jayne, Horace F. 13: 299
1883..Minot, Charles S. 6: 112
1883..Sedgwick, William T. 13: 290
1884..Atkinson, George F. 13: 478
1884..Bumpus, Hermon C. 13: 110
1884..Conn, Herbert W. 20: 409
1884..Gardiner, Edward G. 14: 204
1884..Gill, Theodore N. 12: 376
1884..Sternberg, George M. 4: 388
1886..Ayres, Howard 18: 398
1886..Evermann, Barton W. ...13: 570
1886..Lee, Thomas G. 26: 165
1886..Patten, William 24: 121
1886..White, David 18: 60
1886..Wilson, Edmund B. 13: 59
1887..Andrews, Ethan A. ...... B: 226
1887..Knowlton, Frank H. 10: 410
1888..Coville, Frederick V. 12: 349
1888..Eigenmann, Carl H. 21: 47
1888..Herrick, Francis H. ...... C: 381
1888..Nelson, Julius 18: 232
1888..Stephens, Charles A. 23: 122
1889..Cobb, Nathan A. 23: 87
1889..Hitchcock, Albert S. 26: 41
1889..Schneider, Albert 13: 373
1890..Edwards, Charles L. 13: 440
1890..Galloway, Thomas W. 22: 63
1890..Kellogg, Vernon L. ...... A: 203
1891..Loeb, Jacques 11: 72
1891..Morgan, Thomas H. ..... D: 44
1892..Flexner, Simon .... B: 19
1892..Mayor, Alfred G. 19: 121
1893..Hough, Theodore 23: 260
1893..Mendel, Lafayette B. 26: 424
1893..Metcalf, Maynard M. ..... B: 20
1894..Claypole, Edith J. 13: 259
1894..Davison, Alvin 18: 381
1894..Dyar, Harrison G. 14: 97
1894..Harrison, Ross G. 15: 172
1894..Howard, Leland O. 12: 356
1894..Mann, Albert 25: 360
1894..Needham, James G. ...... B: 289
1894..Prescott, Samuel C. ...... C: 389
1894..White, Charles A. 6: 231
1896..Moore, George T. 13: 285
1896..Palmer, Theodore S. ..... A: 474
1898..Hollister, Ned 20: 82
1899..Pearl, Raymond 15: 382
1901..Strong, Richard P. .... A: 93
1904..Harris, J. Arthur 22: 32
1905..East, Edward M. .... D: 196
1907..McCollum, Elmer V. ..... C: 477
1907..Riddle, Oscar .... C: 120
1908..Kofoid, Charles A. .... A: 280
1909..Myers, Victor C. .... C: 238
1910..Laughlin, Harry H. ...... D: 238
1912..Hawk, Philip B. .... C: 216
1912..Key, Wilhelmine E. ...... B: 103
1912..Muller, Hermann J. ...... C: 331
1913..Goldsmith, William M. .... C: 291
1913..Hood, J. Douglas .... D: 387
1913..Little, Clarence C. .... B: 205
1915..Sherwin, Carl P. .... C: 220
1916..Killian, John A. .... D: 102
1917..Jamieson, Walter A. ..... D: 228
1919..Roe, Joseph H. .... D: 175

Bishops

See pages 220-240

Botanists

1680..Banister, John 7: 504
1708..Colden, Cadwalader 2: 270
1720..Bartram, John 7: 153
1739..Clayton, John 19: 179
1739..Turner, Albert E. 19: 179
1764..Garden, Alexander 23: 361
1768..Kuhn, Adam 21: 289
1771..Bartram, William 7: 154
1774..Muhlenberg, Gotthilf H. E. 9: 439
1780..Marshall, Moses 20: 455
1786..Wistar, Caspar 1: 273
1791..Hosack, David 9: 354
1798..LeConte, Lewis 11: 105
1801..Drowne, Solomon 8: 31
1804..Darlington, William 10: 271
1805..Rafinesque, Constantine S. 8: 472
1806..McBride, James 11: 203
1808..Dewey, Chester 6: 328
1808..Nuttall, Thomas 8: 374
1810..Kirtland, Jared P. 11: 347
1812..Von Schweinitz, Lewis D. 8: 380
1814..Bigelow, Jacob 4: 526
1815..Baldwin, William 10: 275
1815..Barton, William P. C. 13: 279
1815..Eaton, Amos 5: 312
1817..Michener, Ezra 15: 247
1820..McWilliams, Alexander ..15: 149
1820..Oliver, Daniel 9: 92
1820..Torrey, John 6: 361
1821..Elliott, Stephen 4: 510
1821..Greene, Benjamin D. 7: 509
1824..Beck, Lewis C. 5: 542
1825..Griffith, Robert E. 12: 552
1825..Short, Charles W. 4: 509
1828..Houghton, Douglas 5: 512
1829..Phelps, Almira H. L. 11: 359
1832..Ravenel, Henry W. 10: 47
1834..Bailey, Jacob W. 10: 157
1834..Curtis, Moses A. 5: 244
1834..Gray, Asa 3: 407
1835..Bridges, Robert 5: 346
1835..Engelmann, George 6: 87
1836..Lapham, Increase A. 8: 34
1836..Riddell, John L. 21: 175
1838..Pickering, Charles 13: 176
1840..Lindheimer, Ferdinand J. 24: 369
1840..Meehan, Thomas 11: 220
1840..Olney, Stephen T. 13: 35
1840..Sullivant, William S. 8: 149
1842..Bradford, George P. 7: 494
1842..Buckley, Samuel B. 5: 23
1844..Atkinson, George F. 13: 478
1844..Lesquereux, Leo 9: 438
1845..Kellogg, Albert 25: 205
1845..Mohr, Charles T. 26: 406
1847..Watson, Sereno 6: 111
1848..Earle, John M. 11: 145
1848..Parry, Charles C. 13: 228
1851..Ward, James W. 10: 247
1851..Willey, Henry 10: 40
1852..Clark, William S. 5: 310
1855..Newberry, John S. 9: 235
1858..Tuckerman, Edward 5: 312
1859..Emerson, George B. 11: 526
1859..Peck, Charles H. 13: 49
1860..Chapman, Alvan W. 13: 464
1860..Everhart, Benjamin M. ..10: 470
1860..Goodale, George L. 6: 427
1860..Pringle, Cyrus G. 23: 175
1860..Wolle, Francis 1: 320
1861..Hasse, Hermann E. 16: 167
1862..Brigham, William T. 16: 294
1863..Prentiss, Albert N. 4: 484

1864..Eaton, Daniel C. 11: 461
1865..Allen, Timothy Feld 7: 282
1865..Paine, John A. 13: 456
1866..Clark, Henry J. 9: 197
1866..Gattinger, Augustin 15: 91
1866..Porter, Thomas C. 11: 247
1867..Bailey, William W. 10: 157
1867..Barton, Benjamin S. 8: 377
1868..Beal, William J. 11: 467
1868..Brainerd, Ezra 12: 107
1868..Burrill, Thomas J. 18: 187
1868..Post, George E. 13: 416
1868..Rothrock, Joseph T. 19: 180
1868..Sargent, Charles S. 13: 398
1868..Wood, Alphonso 14: 278
1869..Ward, Richard H. 13: 149
1870..Bessey, Charles E. 8: 361
1870..Brandegee, Townsend S. ..23: 366
1870..Martin, George 15: 371
1870..Sargent, Charles S. 26: 78
1870..Youmans, Eliza A. 5: 539
1871..Farlow, William G. 22: 207
1871..Seaman, William H. 14: 231
1871..Tracy, Samuel M. 18: 45
1872..Coulter, John M. 11: 68
1872..Eckfeldt, John W. 25: 308
1872..Hitchcock, Romyn 19: 42
1872..Ward, Lester F. 13: 112
1873..Dudley, William R. 22: 336
1873..Spalding, Volney M. 10: 56
1874..Bastin, Edson S. 5: 351
1874..Lazenby, William P. 10: 17
1874..Penhallow, David P. 20: 216
1875..Ridgway, Robert 8: 460
1876..Rusby, Henry H. .... A: 172
1877..Merriam, C. Hart 13: 264
1879..Barnes, Charles R. 13: 118
1879..Britton, Elizabeth G. K. ..25: 89
1879..Britton, Nathaniel L. 25: 88
1879..Halsted, Byron D. 10: 123
1879..Kinnicutt, Leonard P. 25: 160
1879..Lloyd, Curtis G. 25: 172
1880..Cutler, Manasseh 3: 70
1880..Macdougal, Daniel T. 13: 125
1880..Macfarlane, John M. .... D: 307
1880..Trelease, William 11: 212
1880..Underwood, Lucien M. ...12: 238
1881..Kellerman, William A. ...26: 160
1882..Bartholomew, Elam 26: 293
1882..Burgess, Edward S. 21: 124
1882..Campbell, Douglas H. .... A: 284
1883..Bailey, Liberty H. 10: 145
1883..Galloway, Beverly T. 12: 504
1884..Arthur, Joseph C. 12: 350
1884..Knowlton, Frank H. 10: 410
1884..MacBride, Thomas H. 11: 473
1885..Atkinson, George F. 13: 478
1885..Greene, Edward L. 19: 332
1885..Pammel, Louis H. 10: 206
1886..Earle, Franklin S. 14: 468
1886..Smith, Erwin F. 20: 273
1887..Coville, Frederick V. 12: 349
1887..Ganong, William F. 14: 483
1887..Millspaugh, Charles F. ...25: 120
1889..Hitchcock, Albert S. 26: 41
1889..Jones, Lewis R. .... A: 456
1889..Pound, Roscoe .... B: 51
1890..Boyer, Charles S. 21: 165
1890..Dewey, Lyster H. 13: 294
1890..Moldenke, Charles E. 24: 54
1890..Robinson, Benjamin L. ..12: 138
1890..Woods, Albert F. .... B: 467
1891..Chesnut, Victor K. 13: 295
1891..Harper, Robert A. .... A: 401
1891..Howe, Marshall A. ...... A: 463
1892..Harshberger, John W. ... B: 139
1892..Mottier, David M. 15: 191
1892..Schneider, Albert 13: 373
1893..Webber, Herbert J. 17: 387
1895..Davis, Bradley M. .... C: 167
1895..Kraemer, Henry 26: 451
1895..Meyer, Frank N. 20: 306
1896..Fairchild, David G. ...... C: 253
1896..Moore, George T. 13: 285
1898..Johnson, Duncan S. ...... A: 237
1898..Rydberg, Per A. 26: 43
1901..Harris, J. Arthur 22: 32
1902..Crocker, William .... D: 330
1902..Kaufman, Calvin H. 22: 299
1902..Safford, William E. 20: 133
1902..Shull, George H. .... A: 126
1905..Heald, Frederick DeF. ... B: 175
1912..Farr, Clifford H. 21: 354
1916..Zimmerman, Percy W. ... D: 91

Chemists

1759..Ewing, John 1: 341
1769..Rush, Benjamin 3: 333
1773..Madison, James 7: 216
1773..Tenney, Samuel 5: 175
1774..Priestley, Joseph 6: 148
1783..Macneven, William J. 9: 364
1784..Wells, William C. 12: 60
1789..Thompson, Benjamin
(Count Rumford) 5: 410
1792..Mitchill, Samuel L. 4: 409
1793..Harrison, John 13: 189
1795..Cooper, Thomas 11: 31
1801..Hare, Robert 5: 398
1802..Rogers, Patrick K. 7: 410
1803..Bruce, Archibald 9: 356
1803..Cleaveland, Parker 13: 56
1805..Silliman, Benjamin 2: 385
1806..Griscom, John 10: 510
1809..Gorham, John 12: 355
1810..Dewey, Chester 6: 328
1817..Dana, James F. 10: 390
1817..Olmsted, Denison 8: 121
1818..Green, Jacob 13: 552
1819..Bache, Franklin 5: 346
1819..Dana, Samuel L. 8: 167
1819..Vanuxem, Lardner 8: 385
1820..Keating William H. 24: 260
1820..Renwick, James 11: 101
1824..Bridges, Robert 5: 346
1824..Torrey, John 6: 361
1825..Bowen, George T. 12: 108
1825..Rogers, James B. 8: 151
1826..Payne, George F. 20: 169
1827..Jackson, Charles T. 3: 97
1827..Rogers, William B. 7: 410
1828..Adams, Charles B. 6: 191
1828..Bache, Alexander D. 3: 348
1828..Hayes, Augustus A. 11: 56
1829..Mather, William W. 8: 146
1830..Beck, Lewis C. 5: 542
1830..Ellet, William H. 11: 37
1830..Guthrie, Samuel 11: 406
1830..Henry, Joseph 3: 405
1830..Peter, Robert 4: 517
1833..Booth, James C. 13: 245
1833..Metcalfe, Samuel L. 5: 518
1833..Mitchell, John K. 9: 346
1834..Chace, George I. 8: 25
1834..Weightman, William 14: 146
1835..Shepard, Charles U. 5: 311
1836..Frazer, John F. 1: 348
1836..Silliman, Benjamin, Jr. .. 2: 386
1837..Burnett, Joseph 26: 359
1837..Green, Traill 11: 243
1838..Means, Alexander 1: 518
1838..Thrall, Homer L. 8: 143
1839..Draper, John W. 3: 406
1839..Johnson, Walter R. 12: 260
1840..Horsford, Eben N. 6: 155
1840..Rogers, Robert E. 7: 518
1842..LeConte, John 7: 228
1843..Parrish, Edward 5: 348
1844..Norton, John P. 8: 255
1844..Ravenel, St. Julian 10: 272
1844..Smith, J. Lawrence 6: 54
1845..Antisell, Thomas 19: 448
1845..French, Howard B. 5: 345
1845..Nichols, James R. 5: 200
1845..Ordway, John M. 7: 259
1845..Squibb, Edward R. 19: 56
1845..Whitney, Josiah D. 9: 120
1846..Gross, Magnus 8: 259
1846..Youmans, Edward L. 2: 466
1847..Hunt, T. Sterry 3: 254
1847..Joy, Charles A. 5: 552
1848..Doremus, Robert O. 12: 190
1848..Douglas, Silas H. 11: 513
1848..Litton, Abram 10: 508
1849..Atwood, Luther 13: 260
1849..Barnard, Frederick A. P. . 6: 345
1849..Cooke, Josiah P. 6: 12
1849..Gibbs, Wolcott 10: 469
1849..Wetherill, Charles M. 13: 257
1850..Brush, George J. 10: 298
1850..Genth, Frederick A. 7: 493
1850..Lea, Mathew C. 10: 114
1850..Vaughan, Daniel 13: 171
1850..Wormley, Theodore G. .. 13: 104
1851..Atwood, William 13: 260
1851..Storer, Francis H. 11: 337
1851..Tweddle, Herbert W. C. ..12: 463
1852..Blake, William P. 25: 202
1852..Goessmann, Charles A. ..11: 350
1852..Steiner, Lewis H. 11: 348
1853..Mallet, John W. 13: 55
1853..Merrill, Joshua 13: 258
1853..Wurtz, Henry 7: 519
1854..Hedrick, Benjamin S. 9: 127
1854..Hill, Nathaniel P. 6: 38
1854..Lupton, Nathaniel T. ...12: 294
1855..Hilgard, Eugene W. 10: 308
1855..Johnson, Samuel W. 6: 262
1856..Peirce, John 10: 406
1856..Pugh, Evan 11: 320
1856..Warner, William R. 2: 167
1857..Barker, George F. 4: 532
1857..Draper, John C. 6: 171
1857..Eliot, Charles W. 6: 421
1857..Manross, Newton S. 11: 63
1858..Keyser, Peter D. 4: 292
1859..Maisch, John M. 5: 348
1859..Peirce, Charles S. 8: 409
1860..Draper, Henry 6: 171
1860..Kimball, James P. 11: 91
1860..Lattimore, Samuel A. 12: 244
1860..Mapes, Charles V. 3: 178
1860..Morton, Henry 24: 374
1860..Nason, Henry B. 2: 157
1860..Warren, Cyrus M. 10: 313
1860..Wharton, Joseph 13: 82
1861..Barker, George F. 4: 532
1861..Crafts, James M. 13: 474
1861..Hinrichs, Gustavus D. 21: 390
1861..Langley, John W. 15: 8
1862..Babcock, James F. 10: 445
1863..Brewer, William H. 13: 561
1863..Hale, Albert C. 10: 454
1863..Kedzie, Robert C. 10: 162
1864..Bailey, Jacob W. 10: 157
1864..Caldwell, George C. 26: 142
1864..Chandler, Charles F. 13: 57
1865..Hiscox, David 1: 472
1865..Hyatt, John W. 12: 148
1865..Lyons, Albert B. 16: 400
1865..Peckham, Stephen F. 9: 214
1865..Prescott, Albert B. 13: 53
1865..Raymond, Rossiter W. ... 8: 44
1865..Schaeffer, Charles A. 26: 426
1866..Levy, Louis E. 13: 589
1867..Bloede, Victor G. .... D: 445
1867..Collier, Peter 8: 356
1867..Jackson, Charles L. 11: 416
1868..Bolton, Henry C. 10: 404
1868..Chauvenet, Regis 7: 446
1868..Richards, Robert H. 12: 347
1869..Herreshoff, J. B. Francis .24: 96
1869..Hill, Henry B. 6: 420
1869..Leffmann, Henry 25: 158
1869..Morley, Edward W. 4: 520
1869..Weber, Henry A. 19: 277
1870..Chandler, William H. 23: 46
1870..Chester, Albert H. 11: 422
1870..Drown, Thomas M. 7: 112
1870..Frazer, Persifor 4: 286
1870..Gulick, John T. 11: 463
1870..Hague, Arnold 3: 225
1870..Jordan, Lyman G. 20: 168
1870..Koenig, George A. 17: 240
1870..Remsen, Ira 9: 240
1870..Taylor, William Henry ...18: 279
1870..White, Henry Clay 9: 184
1871..Atwater, Wilbur O. 6: 262
1871..Dolbear, Amos E. 9: 414
1871..Lloyd, John Uri .... D: 106
1871..McMurtrie, William 12: 206
1871..Munroe, Charles E. 9: 234
1871..Nichols, William H. 24: 285
1871..Sadtler, Samuel P. 5: 350
1871..Seaman, William H. 14: 231
1871..Simon, William 17: 218
1871..Waller, Elwyn 13: 344
1872..Blair, Andrew A. 25: 131
1872..Gooch, Frank A. 12: 329
1872..Hitchcock, Romyn 19: 42
1872..Rising, Willard B. 25: 38
1872..Stubbs, William C. 24: 208
1873..Cabot, Samuel 23: 247
1873..Clarke, Frank W. 26: 80
1873..Doremus, Charles A. 10: 514
1873..Frasch, Herman 19: 347
1873..Grasselli, Caesar A. 21: 193
1873..Hinds, John I. D. 26: 241
1873..Johnson, Otis C. 14: 94
1873..Norton, Sidney A. 12: 123
1873..Richards, Ellen H. 7: 343
1873..Stillman, Thomas B. 16: 191
1873..Wiley, Harvey W. 21: 72
1874..Bartley, Elias H. 8: 212
1874..Cooley, Le Roy C. 11: 263
1874..Hart, Edward 11: 246
1874..Mabery, Charles F. 10: 411
1874..Phillips, Francis C. 18: 262
1875..Babcock, Stephen M. 22: 16
1875..Chittenden, Russell H. ...10: 181
1875..Dubbs, Jesse A. 22: 124
1875..Dudley, Charles B. 12: 348
1875..Hill, Walter N. 12: 359
1875..Jewett, Frank F. 20: 422
1875..Newton, Henry J. 7: 23
1875..Scovell, Melville A. 15: 242

1875..Witthaus, Rudolph A. 11: 60
1875..Young, Andrew H. 22: 17
1876..Andrews, Launcelot W. .. A: 396
1876..Austen, Peter T. 13: 92
1876..Morse, Harmon N. 19: 279
1876..Stillman, John M. 20: 145
1877..Armsby, Henry P. 22: 421
1877..Hutchinson, James 11: 237
1877..Jenkins, Edward H. 24: 424
1878..Norton, Thomas H. 13: 478
1878..Pemberton, Henry 15: 69
1878..Vaughan, Victor C. 12: 207
1880..Acheson, Edward G. 23: 136
1880..Case, Willard E. 19: 112
1880..Dabney, Charles W. ...... B: 239
1880..Dudley, William L. 8: 227
1880..Hillebrand, William F. ...14: 132
1880..Long, John H. 19: 31
1880..Noyes, William A. .... B: 314
1880..Roberts, Charlotte F. 19: 63
1880..Stockbridge, Horace E. ...14: 368
1880..Venable, Frank P. 10: 362
1881..Bradley, Charles S. 15: 82
1881..Kent, Walter H. 7: 536
1881..Mott, Henry A. 3: 171
1881..Newberry, Spencer B. 20: 71
1881..Smith, Edgar F. 21: 53
1881..Voorhees, Edward B. 13: 587
1882..Benjamin, Marcus 10: 347
1882..Downs, William F., Jr. ..20: 347
1882..Hill, Herbert M. 20: 178
1882..Palmer, Chase 21: 406
1882..Pond, George G. 20: 328
1882..Richards, Edgar 11: 54
1883..Abel, John J. .... A: 392
1883..Allen, William Humphries 22: 407
1883..Howe, James L. 9: 520
1883..Wiechmann, Ferdinand G. 14: 343
1884..Ladd, Edwin F. 19: 432
1884..Langenbeck, Karl .... A: 522
1884..Orton, Edward, Jr. 24: 107
1884..Pennock, John D. 19: 211
1884..Richards, Ellen H. 7: 343
1884..Ross, Bennett B. 26: 55
1885..Eccles, Robert G. 10: 238
1885..Hendrick, Elwood 22: 233
1885..Moulton, Charles W. 20: 95
1885..Parr, Samuel W. .... C: 153
1886..Dougherty, George T. .... C: 273
1886..Hall, Charles M. 13: 94
1886..Henius, Max .... C: 363
1886..Little, Arthur D. 15: 64
1886..Nef, John U. 21: 368
1886..Osborne, Thomas B. 21: 356
1886..Richards, Joseph W. 13: 509
1886..Smith, Albert W. 24: 386
1886..Wilke, William .... B: 225
1887..Adamson, George P. 26: 121
1887..Dennis, Louis M. 15: 207
1887..Ferguson, William C. 23: 322
1887..Freer, Paul C. 19: 423
1887..Noyes, Arthur A. 13: 286
1887..Snyder, Harry 21: 148
1888..Dow, Herbert 24: 12
1888..Herty, Charles H. 18: 85
1888..Kastle, Joseph H. 15: 413
1888..Loeb, Morris 26: 10
1888..Parsons, Charles L. 14: 280
1888..Thompson, Gustave W. ...17: 21
1889..Burton, William M. ...... C: 243
1889..Franklin, Edward C. ..... A: 411
1889..Hobbs, Perry L. 16: 65
1889..Randall, Wyatt W. .... A: 181
1889..Richards, Theodore W. ...12: 362
1890..Gomberg, Moses 16: 109
1890..Miles, George W. .... A: 276
1890..Mulliken, Samuel P. 25: 73
1890..Smith, Alexander 20: 421
1890..Teller, George L. .... C: 374
1890..Walker, William H. ...... A: 167
1890..Whitney, Willis R. 15: 393
1891..Baskerville, Charles 13: 300
1891..Cushman, Allerton S. 26: 86
1891..Dohme, Alfred R. L. .... C: 118
1891..Linton, Laura A. 12: 62
1892..Boltwood, Bertram B. 15: 138
1892..Browne, Charles A. ...... B: 143
1892..Duncan, Robert K. 21: 331
1892..Francis, John Miller 20: 327
1892..Holton, Edward C. ...... D: 111
1892..Hulett, George A. .... A: 224
1892..Miller, Edmund H. 20: 253
1892..Steiglitz, Julius .... C: 401
1893..Browne, Arthur Lee 25: 287
1893..Jones, Jesse L. 21: 431
1893..Lenher, Victor 21: 340
1893..Mendel, Lafayette B. 26: 424
1893..Ogden, Jay B. 20: 365
1893..Sherman, Henry C. ...... D: 65
1893..Tassin, Wirt deV. 16: 170
1893..Wynkoop, Gillett 23: 261
1894..Bogert, Marston T. 14: 207
1894..MacDowell, Charles H. ... A: 121
1894..Noyes, Arthur A. 13: 284
1894..Prescott, Samuel C. ...... C: 389
1894..Shannon, Hugh S. 24: 263
1895..Bancroft, Wilder D. 14: 206
1895..Burgess, Charles F. ...... C: 420
1895..Harms, Herman 25: 109
1895..Mathews, John A. 16: 73
1895..Olsen, John C. .... D: 137
1896..Arny, Henry V. .... B: 206
1896..Norris, James F. .... A: 190
1896..Smalley, Frank N. 19: 414
1896..Willard, Julius T. .... C: 503
1897..Easley, Charles W. 20: 44
1897..Freas, Thomas B. 22: 60
1897..Jackson, Daniel D. .... C: 154
1897..Schreiner, Oswald .... B: 74
1898..Drysdale, George A. 20: 409
1898..Folin, Otto K. O. 25: 197
1898..Hawk, Philip B. .... C: 216
1898..Lipman, Jacob G. .... B: 212
1898..Rosanoff, Martin A. ...... C: 285
1898..Shepard, James H. 17: 218
1898..Tower, Olin F. .... C: 315
1898..Wiley, Samuel W. 23: 259
1899..Byers, Horace G. .... A: 287
1899..Gray, Thomas T. 24: 156
1899..Hazard, John G. 23: 122
1899..Teeple, John E. .... B: 417
1900..Leach, Albert E. 19: 449
1900..Patterson, Charles A. 19: 393
1900..Rogers, Allen .... D: 281
1900..Underhill, Frank P. 25: 23
1901..Harris, Isaac F. .... D: 154
1902..Block, D. Julian .... C: 121
1902..Lewis, Winford L. .... A: 369
1902..Murke, Franz 20: 294
1902..Silverman, Alexander .... D: 250
1903..Hill, Edwin A. 22: 349
1904..Bacon, Raymond F. .... B: 460
1904..Nieuwland, Julius A. 26: 357
1905..Fink, Colin G. .... B: 79
1905..Hechenbleikner, Ingenuin 24: 238
1905..James, Charles 26: 47
1905..Mott, William R. 22: 86
1906..Hopkins, B. Smith ...... B: 438
1906..Langmuir, Irving .... C: 29
1906..Sperr, Frederick W. ..... A: 264
1907..Berry, Edward R. 26: 385
1907..Borrowman, George ...... C: 301
1907..Creighton, Henry J. M. .. B: 227
1907..Cusick, James T. .... B: 367
1907..Grosvenor, William M. ... C: 494
1907..McCollum, Elmer V. ...... C: 477
1907..Stine, Charles M. A. ..... B: 46
1908..Alsop, William K. 26: 454
1908..Hale, William J. .... C: 383
1908..Jacobson, Carl A. .... A: 301
1908..Morris, James L. 20: 438
1909..Harper, Robert B. .... C: 149
1909..Jordan, Stroud .... D: 181
1909..McKee, Ralph H. .... C: 213
1909..Myers, Victor C. .... C: 238
1910..Eckman, James R. 21: 377
1910..Redman, Lawrence V. ... D: 148
1911..Bishop, Oakley M. 24: 401
1911..Janney, Nelson W. 26: 74
1912..Chaney, Newcomb K. .... A: 95
1912..Hawk, Philip B. .... C: 216
1912..Peirce, George 24: 259
1914..Curme, George O., Jr. ... D: 54
1914..Field, Crosby .... B: 224
1914..Leaming, Thomas H. 20: 305
1915..Sherwin, Carl P. .... C: 220
1916..Conant, James B. .... D: 48
1916..Killian, John A. .... D: 102
1916..Weidlein, Edward R. .... C: 82
1916..Wilson, John A. .... C: 207
1917..Gordon, Neil E. .... C: 344
1919..Roe, Joseph H. .... D: 175

City Planners

See also Landscape Architects

1784..L'Enfant, Pierre C. 16: 209
1790..Ellicott, Andrew 13: 470
1790..Ellicott, Joseph 13: 471
1850..Vaux, Calvert 9: 332
1853..Cleveland, Horace W. S. . 5: 539
1857..Olmsted, Frederick Law .. 2: 298
1875..McMillan, James 2: 227
1880..Webster, George S. 25: 382
1882..Kessler, George E. 20: 296
1884..Eliot, Charles 13: 108
1885..Carrere, John M. 11: 325
1885..DeForest, Robert W. ..... B: 61
1890..Burnham, Daniel H. 9: 335
1891..Bogue, Virgil G. 13: 472
1891..Robinson, Charles M. 21: 352
1895..Gilbert, Cass 26: 20
1895..McKim, Charles F. 23: 89
1896..Manning, Warren H. .... B: 291
1897..Leavitt, Charles W. 24: 37
1898..Goodrich, Ernest P. ...... C: 262
1899..Dealey, George B. .... A: 200
1900..Arnold, Bion J. .... B: 456
1900..Ford, George B. 25: 369
1902..McFarland, J. Horace ... A: 196
1903..Corbett, Harvey W. ..... B: 409
1905..Bing, Alexander M. ...... B: 440
1905..Merriam, Charles E. ..... D: 435
1905..Nolen, John .... B: 62
1906..Moody, Walter D. 18: 414
1906..Norton, Charles D. 6: 489
1908..Knowles, Morris 26: 342
1909..Wacker, Charles H. 24: 72
1910..Hare, Sid J. .... D: 207
1913..Cutter, Victor M. .... C: 74
1913..Hubbard, Theodora K. ... C: 505
1915..Draper, Earle S. .... D: 36
1917..Mumford, Lewis .... D: 260
1920..Delano, Frederic A. ...... A: 410
1929..Hubbard, Henry Vincent . C: 504

Civil Engineers

1770..Erskine, Robert 24: 403
1772..Colles, Christopher 9: 271
1774..Romans, Bernard 7: 176
1775..Baldwin, Loammi 10: 302
1785..Ellicott, Andrew 13: 470
1786..Latrobe, Benjamin H. ... 9: 425
1791..Roberdeau, Isaac 2: 14
1793..Fulton, Robert 3: 104
1794..Freeman, Thomas 24: 122
1796..Johnson, John 17: 290
1797..Ellicott, Joseph 13: 471
1797..Graff, Frederic 25: 383
1802..Henry, Philip W. 15: 109
1802..Swift, Joseph G. 10: 17
1807..Baldwin, Loammi, Jr. 10: 302
1808..Geddes, James 10: 264
1813..Douglass, David B. 7: 3
1814..Abert, John J. 4: 380
1814..Long, Stephen H. 11: 365
1814..Renwick, James 11: 101
1815..Haviland, John 11: 375
1816..White, Canvass 12: 258
1816..Wright, Benjamin 1: 239
1817..Bates, David S. 18: 171
1817..Jervis, John B. 9: 46
1817..McNeill, William G. 9: 47
1818..Adams, Jonathan 6: 80
1818..Robinson, Moncure 8: 456
1818..Talcott, Andrew 13: 405
1819..Baldwin, George R. 10: 303
1819..Turnbull, William 12: 514
1819..Whistler, George W. 9: 48
1821..Farnam, Henry 11: 517
1821..Kirkwood, James P. 9: 36
1823..Wright, Benjamin H. 1: 160
1824..Allen, Horatio 8: 233
1824..Law, George 3: 94
1825..Craven, Alfred W. 9: 37
1825..Johnson, Edwin F. 17: 291
1825..Mahan, Dennis H. 10: 440
1825..Ransom, Truman B. 18: 323
1825..Roberts, William M. 13: 254
1826..Bryant, Gridley 11: 502
1826..Roebling, John A. 4: 404
1827..Baldwin, James F. 10: 303
1827..Kneass, Samuel H. 25: 142
1827..McAlpine, William J. 10: 507
1827..Redfield, William C. 7: 354
1827..Totten, George M. 18: 109
1827..Welch, Ashbel 9: 36
1828..Borden, Simeon 24: 216
1828..Chesbrough, Ellis S. 9: 35
1828..Knight, Jonathan 11: 486
1828..McKay, Gordon 10: 397
1828..Wilson, W. Hasell 14: 506
1829..Francis, James B. 9: 46
1829..Moore, James 18: 183
1829..Whipple, Squire 9: 35
1830..Dearborn, William L. 9: 41
1830..Geddes, George 10: 170
1830..Pratt, Thomas W. 22: 275
1830..Thomas, J. Edgar 13: 334
1831..Latrobe, Benjamin H. ... 9: 426
1831..Ranney, Henry J. 17: 106
1831..Trautwine, John C. 5: 196
1832..Adams, Julius W. 9: 33

1832..Storrow, Charles S. 21: 93
1833..Laurie, James 9: 38
1834..Tracy, Edward H. 9: 127
1835..Renwick, Henry B. 11: 101
1836..Brown, Thompson S. 4: 441
1836..Childe, John 16: 359
1836..Cresson, John C. 12: 466
1836..Evans, Anthony W. W. ..10: 84
1836..Greene, George S. 1: 320
1836..Haswell, Charles H. 9: 486
1836..Hoadley, John C. 23: 404
1836..Judson, William P. 12: 381
1837..Brevoort, James C. 9: 193
1837..Davies, Thomas A. 3: 26
1837..Talcott, William H. 9: 43
1837..Woodbury, Daniel P. 1: 470
1838..Keefer, Thomas C. 12: 227
1838..Worthen, William E. 12: 206
1839..Benham, Henry W. 6: 277
1839..Eads, James B. 5: 134
1840..Childs, Orville W. 3: 79
1840..Haupt, Herman 10: 224
1840..Sargent, John H. 16: 237
1840..Sayre, Robert H. 5: 106
1840..Whistler, George W. 9: 49
1841..Ellet, Charles 4: 360
1841..Morris, Thomas A. 10: 124
1843..Hilgard, Julius E. 10: 118
1843..Winans, Thomas DeK. 1: 239
1844..Lander, Frederick W. 8: 127
1844..Plympton, George W. 9: 40
1845..Gillespie, William M. 23: 184
1845..Hunt, Edward B. 11: 440
1845..Lane, Moses 9: 34
1845..McNeill, Edwin 18: 163
1845..Paine, Charles 12: 269
1845..Whiton, Augustus S. 1: 198
1846..Guthrie, Alfred 11: 407
1846..Linsley, Daniel C. 16: 233
1847..Barnes, Oliver W. 12: 546
1847..Colburn, Warren 11: 457
1847..Du Barry, Joseph N. 7: 157
1847..Milner, John T. 19: 194
1848..Bacon, John W. 6: 174
1848..Becker, Max J. 12: 231
1848..Chanute, Octave 10: 212
1848..Duane, James C. 10: 85
1848..Sawyer, Edward 12: 320
1848..Stevens, Walter H. 12: 258
1849..Clarke, Thomas C. 7: 500
1849..Doane, Thomas 25: 93
1849..Fink, Albert 9: 489
1849..Flad, Henry 12: 290
1849..Wormeley, James P. 9: 39
1850..Gardner, George C. 13: 282
1850..Latrobe, Charles H. 9: 427
1850..Requa, Isaac L. 6: 248
1850..Viele, Egbert L. 2: 195
1851..Church, George E. 13: 250
1851..Cohen, Mendes 13: 136
1851..Dodge, Grenville M. 16: 191
1851..Foster, Wilbur F. 8: 47
1852..Flint, Edward A. 20: 126
1852..Greenwood, William H. ...16: 364
1852..Hallidie, Andrew S. 7: 191
1852..Manross, Newton S. 11: 63
1852..Shinn, William P. 11: 344
1853..Africa, John S. 8: 461
1853..Brooks, Thomas B. 3: 510
1853..Carll, John F. 12: 361
1853..Craighill, William P. 12: 223
1853..Durfee, William F. 6: 248
1853..Eddy, Luther D. 3: 85
1853..Hermany, Charles 13: 299
1853..Tweeddale, William 5: 484
1853..Whittemore, Don J. 13: 248
1853..Wimmer, Sebastian 12: 365
1854..Abbot, Henry L. 11: 194
1854..Ainsworth, James E. 20: 141
1854..Hudson, Charles H. 10: 174
1854..Katte, Walter 16: 434
1854..Rives, Alfred L. 20: 472
1855..Albert, John S. 9: 230
1855..Collingwood, Francis 13: 230
1855..Holley, Alexander L. 11: 508
1855..Rogers, Fairman 11: 60
1855..Smith, Charles S. 3: 525
1856..Cogswell, William B. 13: 107
1856..Croes, John J. R. 6: 46
1856..Davis, Joseph P. 25: 51
1856..Harrod, Benjamin M. 12: 328
1856..Keeney, Abner 1: 266
1856..Lincoln, William S. 5: 67
1856..Mills, Hiram F. 12: 71
1856..Smedley, Samuel L. 3: 331
1857..Graham, Charles K. 12: 299
1857..Macdonald, Charles 11: 475
1857..Martin, Charles C. 14: 49
1857..Roebling, Washington A. .26: 122
1857..Smith, William S. 4: 498
1857..Towle, Stevenson 11: 321
1858..Alexander, Edward P. 8: 271
1858..Cooper, Theodore 19: 261
1858..Davis, Joseph P. 25: 51
1858..Knap, Joseph M. 10: 351
1858..Moore, Robert 12: 202
1859..Cassatt, Alexander J. 13: 336
1859..McMath, Robert E. 26: 53
1859..Merrill, William E. 10: 223
1859..Pitzman, Julius 22: 449
1860..Ambrose, John W. 24: 132
1860..Babcock, George H. 5: 304
1860..Dahlgren, Charles B. 9: 380
1860..De Lacy, Walter W. 3: 223
1860..Dodge, Joseph T. 17: 378
1860..Goodfellow, Edward 3: 212
1860..Greene, George S. 1: 278
1860..Shedd, J. Herbert 13: 44
1860..Van Buren, John D. 10: 236
1860..Vinton, Francis L. 7: 441
1861..Boller, Alfred P. 9: 43
1861..Clevenger, Shobal V. 5: 267
1861..Emery, Charles E. 9: 34
1861..Newton, Isaac 4: 190
1861..Stanton, John 14: 359
1862..Fanning, John T. 9: 38
1863..Bolton, Channing M. 2: 519
1863..Church, Benjamin S. 3: 332
1863..Curtis, Fayette S. 23: 120
1863..Menocal, Aniceto G. 14: 354
1863..Scofield, Levi T. 12: 321
1863..Watson, William 12: 124
1864..Bowers, Alphonzo B. 12: 527
1864..Ernst, Oswald H. 4: 36
1864..Herschel, Clemens 22: 342
1864..Rothwell, Richard P. 10: 229
1864..Van Buren, Robert 10: 237
1865..Bonzano, Adolphus 16: 312
1865..Bryan, Edward P. 11: 283
1865..De Varona, Ignatius M. ..10: 87
1865..Coxe, Eckley B. 11: 559
1865..Dudley, Plimmon H. 19: 281
1865..Flynn, Patrick J. 4: 203
1865..Fteley, Alphonse 13: 561
1865..Lewis, Eugene C. 8: 417
1865..Ludlow, William 9: 23
1865..Metcalf, William 12: 232
1865..Stone, Charles P. 11: 215
1865..Thacher, Edwin 7: 522
1865..Wellington, Arthur M. ..11: 167
1866..Egleston, Thomas 3: 244
1866..Staley, Cady 11: 154
1866..Stauffer, David McN. 9: 45
1867..Beardsley, Arthur 10: 512
1867..Benzenberg, George H. ...14: 205
1867..Bond, Edward A. 12: 395
1867..Corthell, Elmer L. 9: 42
1867..FitzGerald, Desmond 9: 44
1867..Hood, William 20: 12
1867..McClellan, Carswell 4: 140
1867..Mahan, Frederick A. 10: 441
1867..Morison, George S. 10: 129
1867..Schneider, Charles C. 18: 91
1868..Brush, Charles B. 9: 33
1868..Buck, Leffert L. 10: 115
1868..Endicott, Mordecai T. 15: 237
1868..Felton, Samuel M. .... B: 507
1868..Marshall, William L. 11: 467
1868..Nichols, Othniel F. 9: 45
1868..Peirce, Benjamin M. 10: 449
1868..Randolph, Isham 19: 385
1868..Whinery, Samuel 10: 460
1868..Woodford, Ethelbert G. ..20: 262
1868..Young, David 7: 353
1869..Bogue, Virgil G. 13: 472
1869..Davis, Joseph B. 18: 44
1869..Haupt, Lewis M. 13: 233
1869..Kimball, George A. 15: 132
1869..Noble, Alfred 9: 44
1869..Rodd, Thomas 12: 315
1869..Stearns, Irving A. 11: 392
1869..Yonge, Samuel H. .... B: 330
1870..Chenoweth, Alexander C. .12: 332
1870..Fletcher, Robert 26: 484
1870..Greene, Charles E. 26: 172
1870..Johnson, Warren S. 3: 292
1870..Landreth, Olin H. 9: 37
1870..Rice, George S. 12: 82
1870..Richards, Joseph T. 14: 372
1871..Bullock, William D. 20: 269
1871..Fuertes, Estevan A. 4: 483
1871..Graham, John 20: 173
1871..Kerr, Frank M. 20: 135
1871..Maclay, William W. 13: 75
1871..Mundy, Joseph S. 2: 497
1871..Rea, Samuel 15: 289
1871..Waring, George E., Jr. ... 6: 157
1871..Wegmann, Edward 25: 341
1872..Chaplin, Winfield S. 11: 211
1872..Craven, Henry S. 12: 371
1872..Donovan, Cornelius 20: 293
1872..Earle, Frank H. 14: 418
1872..Greene, Francis V. 23: 23
1872..Merriman, Mansfield 23: 70
1872..Stearns, Frederic P. 14: 306
1872..Woodward, Robert S. 13: 108
1873..Aldrich, William F. 5: 65
1873..Bates, Onward 15: 208
1873..Bixby, William H. 21: 337
1873..Church, Irving P. 22: 381
1873..Darling, John H. 16: 187
1873..Hering, Rudolph 10: 226
1873..Kuichling, Emil 16: 66
1873..Long, Thomas J. 10: 453
1873..Ockerson, John A. 25: 381
1873..Richardson, Thomas F. ..19: 360
1873..Schuyler, James D. 18: 317
1874..Cooley, Lyman E. 9: 41
1874..Crandall, Charles L. 6: 481
1874..DuBois, Augustus J. 15: 406
1874..Gillham, Robert 3: 352
1874..Lindenthal, Gustav 16: 117
1874..Risse, Louis A. 4: 197
1875..Bigelow, Edward M. 20: 398
1875..Burr, William H. .... D: 220
1875..Edes, William C. 6: 516
1875..Ricketts, Palmer C. 26: 236
1875..Webster, George S. 25: 382
1876..Amweg, Frederick J. 16: 43
1876..Carter, Edward C. 22: 19
1876..Gillette, Lewis S. 20: 62
1876..Hunt, Charles W. 13: 144
1876..Kielland, S. Munch 12: 239
1876..Nostrand, Peter E. 12: 201
1876..Rice, Walter P. .... B: 167
1876..Stevens, John F. .... D: 213
1876..Wallace, John F. 10: 168
1876..Wilson, Joseph M. 7: 492
1877..Grunsky, Carl E. 13: 224
1877..Jacoby, Henry S. .... D: 108
1877..Kittredge, George W. 15: 73
1877..Pegram, George H. 9: 40
1877..Rafter, George W. 12: 234
1878..Churchill, Charles S. ..... A: 211
1878..Jarvis, Charles M. 11: 476
1878..Johnson, John B. 11: 217
1878..Purdy, Corydon T. .... C: 485
1878..Shankland, Edward C. ...13: 403
1878..Slater, Willis A. .... B: 353
1879..Campbell, John T. 12: 397
1879..Davis, John W. 4: 306
1879..Hammond, John H. 10: 152
1879..Hoff, Olaf 14: 419
1879..McDonald, Hunter ...... C: 185
1879..Olcott, Eben E. 5: 265
1879..Talcott, Harry R. 7: 109
1880..Cappelen, Frederick W. ..19: 88
1880..Ericson, John E. 16: 91
1880..Henry, Philip W 15: 109
1880..Kiersted, Wynkoop 25: 411
1880..Osborn, Frank C. 14: 174
1880..Ricker, George A. 12: 271
1880..Stevens, Edwin A. 5: 342
1880..Swain, George F. 12: 276
1881..Eidlitz, Otto M. 16: 412
1881..Francis, George B. 16: 276
1881..Giaver, Joachim G. 21: 181
1881..Hendrick, Calvin W. 12: 506
1881..Kirchhoff, Charles 10: 227
1881..Landreth, William B. 12: 97
1881..Parson, William B. 14: 217
1882..Davis, Arthur P. 24: 116
1882..Donovan, John J. 16: 42
1882..Goethals, George W. 24: 6
1882..Ingersoll, Colin M. ...... D: 54
1882..Keith, Herbert C. .... A: 340
1882..Waddell, John A. L. ...... D: 86
1882..Ward, George C. 24: 36
1883..Bassett, Carrol P. 5: 283
1883..Kinnear, Wilson S. ...... D: 393
1883..McHenry, Edwin H. 24: 18
1883..Mead, Elwood 26: 44
1884..Bensel, John A. 11: 239
1884..Bryan, Charles W. 21: 411
1884..Catt, George W. 10: 234
1884..Hutchinson, George H. .. C: 160
1884..Lundie, John 24: 348
1884..Seaman, Henry B. .... C: 248
1885..Adams, Henry S. 21: 200
1885..Bates, Lindon W. 15: 81
1885..Conger, Frank 11: 476
1885..Greiner, John E. .... D: 298
1885..Modjeski, Ralph 15: 68
1885..Nettleton, William A. ...20: 474
1885..O'Shaughnessy, Michael M. 24: 52
1885..Wilgus, William J. 11: 115
1885..Williamson, Sydney B. ... A: 450

1886..Fortier, Samuel .... C: 457
1886..Freeman, John R. .... C: 397
1886..Hamlin, Homer 19: 307
1886..Moore, Charles H. .... D: 423
1886..Moran, Daniel E. .... D: 390
1886..Walker, Robert M. 18: 346
1887..Angier, Walter E. 21: 354
1887..Kay, Edgar B. 22: 310
1887..Ledoux, John W. 23: 93
1887..Norton, George H. 22: 252
1887..Smith, J. Waldo 24: 108
1887..White, James G. 15: 157
1888..Cory, Harry T. 18: 421
1888..Davies, John V. 14: 209
1888..Davis, Arthur P. 24: 116
1888..Howe, Malverd A. 17: 439
1888..Miller, Charles H. 20: 255
1888..Newell, Frederick H. 13: 283
1889..Hayford, John F. 14: 371
1889..Jacobs, Charles M. 14: 208
1890..Armstrong, William C. ..20: 68
1890..Connett, Albert N. ...... C: 419
1890..Sanford, Harry C. 21: 187
1890..Skinner, John F. .... D: 159
1890..Turneaure, Frederick E. . A: 215
1890..Waite, Henry M. .... D: 30
1891..Allen, Andrews .... B: 269
1891..Cooper, Hugh L. .... C: 254
1891..Leavitt, Charles W. 24: 37
1891..Maitland, Alexander 20: 447
1891..Wason, Leonard C. ...... B: 130
1892..Kearny, Clinton H. 23: 381
1892..Strauss, Joseph B. .... B: 332
1893..Ferris, George W. G. 13: 39
1893..Horton, George T. .... B: 33
1893..Waller, Osmar L. 26: 39
1894..Bolton, Reginald P. 13: 462
1894..Riggs, Thomas .... C: 275
1894..Sabin, Louis C. .... D: 405
1895..Fay, Frederic H. .... C: 292
1895..Ten Eyck, Peter G. 18: 179
1896..Swensson, Emil 14: 277
1897..Baxter, John C. 24: 426
1897..Starrett, William A. 24: 42
1898..Beardsley, James W. ..... C: 488
1898..Godfrey, Hollis .... A: 283
1898..Hammond, Alonzo J. .... D: 199
1898..LaBach, Paul M. .... B: 473
1899..Hughes, Hector J. 21: 42
1900..Barnes, Mortimer G. 22: 357
1900..Colpitts, Walter W. ...... C: 335
1900..Hosmer, George L. 25: 433
1900..Howard, Ernest E. ...... B: 433
1900..Hoyt, Warren A. 25: 233
1900..Kelly, William .... D: 300
1901..Goodrich, Ernest P. ...... C: 262
1901..Hayden, Arthur G. ...... D: 57
1901..McDaniel, Allen B. ...... B: 73
1901..Starrett, Theodore 24: 41
1901..Watson, Wilbur J. .... D: 132
1902..Cornish, Lorenzo D. ..... C: 387
1902..Ellsworth, Lincoln .... B: 38
1902..Morgan, Arthur E. .... B: 15
1903..Schanck, Francis R. ...... B: 340
1904..Ammann, Othmar H. .... D: 320
1904..Hidinger, Leroy L. .... C: 192
1905..Henny, David C. 26: 68
1905..Herlihy, Francis J. ...... C: 445
1905..Miller, Harlan D. 21: 352
1906..Baylis, John R. .... C: 401
1906..Crowe, Francis T. .... D: 369
1906..Harza, Leroy F. .... B: 401
1906..Holland, Clifford M. 19: 381
1906..Spooner, Charles W. ..... C: 359
1906..Wheeler, Walter H. ...... B: 241
1907..Burpee, George W. ...... C: 178
1907..Olds, Thomas Hartman ..24: 159
1907..Tefft, William W. 23: 89
1908..Harrington, John L. ..... A: 459
1909..Desmond, Thomas C. ..... B: 133
1909..MacElwee, Roy S. .... D: 315
1909..Siems, V. Bernard .... C: 242
1910..Bechtel, Warren A. 24: 224
1910..Chase, Clement E. 24: 185
1910..Jacoby, Hurlbut S. ...... D: 108
1911..King, Everett E. .... B: 248
1915..Proctor, Carlton S. ...... C: 305

Clergymen

1616..Whiting, Samuel 10: 133
1618..Hooker, Thomas 6: 279
1624..Davenport, John 1: 161
1627..Shepard, Thomas 7: 33
1629..Williams, Roger 10: 4
1630..Wilson, John 20: 98
1633..Stone, Samuel 7: 202
1634..Norton, John 7: 36
1634..Sherman, John 7: 75
1637..Clarke, John 7: 346
1638..Ward, Nathaniel 7: 64
1642..Gorton, Samuel 7: 178
1657..Mather, Increase 6: 412
1657..Wigglesworth, Michael ... 8: 382
1672..Stoddard, Solomon 7: 84
1681..Thatcher, Peter 6: 507
1681..Thatcher, Samuel C. 5: 88
1683..Willard, Samuel 6: 413
1684..Mather, Cotton 4: 232
1685..Blair, James 3: 231
1686..Williams, John 1: 258
1699..Colman, Benjamin 7: 153
1702..Niles, Samuel 8: 370
1708..Dickinson, Jonathan 5: 463
1710..Phillips, Samuel 10: 93
1716..Barnard, John 7: 305
1717..Appleton, Nathaniel 7: 181
1717..Frelinghuysen, Theodorus J. 12: 329
1720..Beissel, Johann C. 7: 497
1721..Chauncy, Charles 5: 168
1722..Edwards, Jonathan, 1st .. 5: 464
1722..Wigglesworth, Edward .. 9: 237
1726..Tennent, Gilbert 8: 73
1733..Byles, Mather 7: 145
1736..Whitefield, George 5: 384
1737..Mayhew, Jonathan 7: 71
1742..Muhlenberg, Henry M. .. 5: 499
1742..Seidel, Nathaniel 2: 19
1743..Hopkins, Samuel, 1st 7: 154
1745..Leaming, Jeremiah 25: 374
1747..Davies, Samuel 5: 465
1747..Langdon, Samuel 6: 416
1747..Witherspoon, John 5: 466
1749..Otterbein, Philip W. 10: 504
1750..Mansfield, Richard 12: 6
1755..Barnard, Thomas 7: 163
1758..Dana, James 23: 309
1764..Deane, Samuel 23: 298
1764..Parker, Thomas 12: 249
1764..Sandeman, Robert 13: 547
1767..Andrews, John 1: 342
1767..Belknap, Jeremy 7: 204
1767..Priestly, Joseph 6: 148
1768..Bacon, John 22: 216
1769..Edwards, Jonathan, 2d ... 7: 169
1770..Livingston, John H. 3: 400
1770..Thatcher, Peter 7: 308
1771..Furman, Richard 12: 292
1771..Kunze, John C. 6: 105
1772..Dwight, Timothy 1: 168
1772..White, William 3: 470
1773..Backus, Charles 12: 429
1773..Emmons, Nathanael 5: 141
1775..Randall, Benjamin 4: 345
1775..Smith, Samuel S. 2: 21
1775..Spring, Samuel 5: 212
1782..Bancroft, Aaron 4: 306
1782..Freeman, James 7: 447
1784..Austin, Samuel 2: 39
1785..Holmes, Abiel 7: 148
1787..Ware, Henry 5: 174
1787..Worcester, Noah 1: 185
1790..Mason, John M. 6: 462
1791..Alexander, Archibald 2: 22
1791..Backus, Azel 7: 405
1791..Worcester, Thomas 1: 203
1792..Ballou, Hosea 5: 487
1792..Miller, Samuel 7: 152
1793..Griffin, Edward D. 6: 237
1793..Hoge, Moses 2: 23
1794..Dana, Daniel 9: 87
1794..Milledoler, Philip 3: 401
1794..Nott, Eliphalet 7: 170
1795..Abbot, Abiel 7: 457
1795..Creath, Jacob 22: 214
1795..Hicks, Elias 11: 464
1796..Albright, Jacob 11: 114
1796..Dow, Lorenzo 10: 472
1796..Porter, Ebenezer 10: 99
1797..Appleton, Jesse 1: 417
1797..Baxter, George A. 2: 24
1797..Beecher, Lyman 3: 126
1797..Jenks, William 24: 299
1798..Woods, Leonard 9: 121
1799..Hobart, John H. 1: 514
1801..Beasley, Frederic 1: 342
1801..Kneeland, Abner 24: 186
1802..Bangs, Nathan 9: 429
1802..Wilson, Joshua L. 12: 94
1803..Channing, William Ellery. 5: 458
1803..Rice, John H. 2: 27
1804..Brownell, Thomas C. 3: 495
1804..Buckminster, Joseph S. .. 7: 141
1805..Prime, Nathaniel S. 7: 237
1806..Benedict, David 9: 468
1807..Humphrey, Heman 5: 308
1807..Tyler, Bennett 9: 87
1808..Brownlee, William C. 11: 494
1808..Smith, John 17: 89
1809..Brown, Francis 9: 86
1809..Nichols, Ichabod 10: 456
1809..Sanders, Daniel C. 2: 39
1810..Campbell, Alexander 4: 161
1810..Herr, John 7: 496
1812..Skinner, Thomas H. 7: 318
1812..Taylor, Nathaniel W. 7: 187
1813..Bascom, Henry B. 4: 515
1814..Brown, John 6: 141
1814..Cone, Spencer H. 22: 187
1815..Bedell, Gregory Townsend 11: 229
1815..Hewit, Nathaniel 11: 357
1815..Knox, John 6: 218
1815..Kurtz, Benjamin 24: 99
1816..Dempster, John 11: 177
1816..Dwight, Sereno E. 7: 406
1817..Cox, Samuel H. 7: 557
1817..Ware, Henry 5: 358
1819..Fisk, Wilbur 3: 177
1819..Sprague, William B. 5: 239
1819..Walker, James 6: 419
1820..Brooks, Charles 12: 287
1820..Hodge, Charles 10: 245
1820..McCalla, William L. 24: 61
1820..Patton, William 10: 164
1820..Schmucker, Samuel S. ... 5: 100
1820..Winebrenner, John 1: 180
1821..Dewey, Orville 5: 47
1821..Hitchcock, Edward 5: 308
1821..Kenrick, Francis P. 1: 485
1821..Muhlenberg, William A. .. 9: 199
1821..Tyng, Stephen H. 2: 187
1822..Eastburn, Manton 6: 15
1822..Scott, Orange 2: 315
1822..Whittemore, Thomas 1: 276
1824..Church, Pharcellus 8: 224
1824..Finney, Charles G. 2: 462
1824..Gannett, Ezra S. 10: 149
1825..Alexander, James W. 6: 490
1825..Barnes, Albert 7: 360
1825..Beecher, Edward 3: 128
1825..Bethune, George W. 8: 166
1825..Chambers, John 15: 298
1825..Dagg, John L. 6: 497
1825..Furness, William H. 2: 316
1825..Wood, James 2: 124
1826..Nevin, John W. 5: 256
1827..Coit, Thomas W. 4: 514
1827..Hawks, Francis L. 7: 90
1827..Plumer, William S. 9: 261
1828..Shepard, George 10: 125
1828..Tappan, Henry P. 1: 249
1828..Winslow, Hubbard 1: 178
1828..Yeomans, John W. 11: 241
1829..Hedge, Frederic H. 8: 271
1829..Leeser, Isaac 10: 393
1829..Murray, Nicholas 7: 98
1830..Hare, George E. 6: 441
1830..Hopkins, Mark 6: 237
1830..Stowe, Calvin E. 10: 140
1831..Adams, William 7: 317
1831..Bellows, Henry W. 3: 261
1831..Bush, George 6: 515
1831..Hopkins, John H. 11: 496
1831..Park, Edward A. 9: 202
1831..Stearns, Oliver 9: 191
1832..Breckinridge, Robert J. .. 9: 242
1832..McClure, Alexander W. ..11: 217
1832..McIlvaine, Charles P. 7: 2
1832..Williams, William R. 10: 149
1833..Anderson, Henry T. 22: 166
1833..Boardman, Henry A. 13: 345
1833..Bushnell, Horace 8: 303
1833..Clarke, James F. 2: 186
1833..Fuller, Richard 23: 291
1833..McAuley, Thomas 7: 316
1833..May, Samuel 19: 244
1833..Pattison, Robert E. 8: 405
1833..Peabody, Andrew P. 3: 357
1833..Prime, S. Irenæus 7: 237
1833..Rice, Nathan L. 3: 77
1833..Sproull, Thomas 7: 119
1834..Adams, Nehemiah 2: 318
1834..Burgess, George 4: 380
1835..Baird, Robert 8: 171
1835..Barrows, Elijah P. 10: 102
1835..Bartol, Cyrus A. 4: 94
1835..Dale, James W. 10: 235
1835..Mattison, Hiram 12: 127
1835..Nast, William 10: 223
1835..Scott, William A. 2: 487
1835..Thornwell, James H. 11: 33
1836..Clark, Thomas M. 1: 445
1836..Dowling, John 9: 216

1836..McClintock, John 6: 466
1836..Parker, Theodore 2: 377
1836..Schaeffer, Charles W. 7: 512
1837..Foster, Randolph S. 13: 62
1837..Hitchcock, Henry L. 7: 224
1837..Merrill, George R. 6: 44
1837..Stebbins, Rufus P. 12: 249
1837..Wise, Daniel 13: 191
1838..Armitage, Thomas 9: 199
1838..Butler, Clement M. 10: 34
1838..Chambers, Talbot W. 9: 258
1838..Dowse, Edmund 18: 346
1838..Gordon, William R. 5: 523
1838..Randall, David 10: 72
1838..Simmons, George F. 7: 499
1839..Beecher, Henry Ward 3: 129
1839..Channing, William H. ...13: 595
1839..Deems, Charles F. 9: 164
1839..Everts, William W. 11: 64
1839..Fisher, Ebenezer 10: 201
1839..Hasselquist, Tufve N. 24: 367
1839..Jacobus, Melancthon W. .. 3: 344
1839..James, Henry 13: 66
1839..Miller, William 6: 542
1839..Tefft, Benjamin F. 13: 575
1840..Duffield, William H. 6: 505
1840..Green, William H. 6: 128
1840..Haskins, Samuel M. 10: 312
1840..Moore, Thomas V. 19: 362
1840..Odenheimer, William H. . 3: 473
1840..Phelps, Austin 9: 366
1840..Thompson, Joseph P. ...10: 132
1840..Vincent, George C. 13: 350
1841..Clark, Rufus W. 10: 359
1841..Curry, Daniel 7: 382
1841..Harris, Samuel 1: 418
1841..Krauth, Charles P. 1: 349
1841..Robinson, Stuart 1: 371
1841..Rockwell, Joel E. 9: 253
1841..Shipp, Albert M. 9: 264
1841..Ward, James T. 1: 206
1841..Woodbridge, Samuel M. ..12: 237
1842..Ballou, Adin 7: 558
1842..Coxe, Arthur C. 3: 474
1842..Fairchild, James H. 2: 464
1842..Hale, Edward Everett ... 1: 199
1842..Huntington, Frederic D. . 3: 363
1842..Seiss, Joseph A. 7: 234
1842..Smith, Henry B. 5: 311
1842..Warren, Israel P. 4: 235
1843..Allen, Joseph H. 9: 286
1843..Bartlett, Samuel C. 9: 89
1843..Fairbairn, Robert B. 5: 65
1843..Harbaugh, Henry 12: 272
1843..Hoge, Moses D. 10: 464
1843..Huidekoper, Frederic 9: 531
1843..Lindsay, John W. 11: 179
1843..McCosh, James 5: 468
1843..Miller, John 10: 173
1843..Samson, George W. 3: 152
1843..Shedd, William G. T. 7: 318
1843..Wise, Isaac M. 10: 116
1843..Wylie, Theodore W. J. ...10: 249
1844..Dexter, Henry M. 1: 177
1844..Gammon, Elijah H. 23: 178
1844..Gillett, Ezra H. 5: 530
1844..Hitchcock, Roswell D. 2: 256
1844..Johnson, Samuel 2: 312
1844..Manly, Basil 25: 122
1845..Bailey, Gilbert S. 22: 110
1845..Craig, Austin 13: 91
1845..Fee, John G. 24: 301
1845..Hall, Charles H. 10: 398
1845..Mahan, Milo 10: 439
1845..Prentiss, George L. 7: 319
1845..Washburn, Edward A. ... 9: 498
1846..Ames, Charles G. 23: 317
1846..Crooks, George R. 22: 147
1846..Cuyler, Theodore L. 5: 246
1846..Dabney, Robert L. 2: 26
1846..Darling, Henry 7: 408
1847..Alger, William R. 6: 34
1847..Butler, James D. 9: 190
1847..Cummins, George D. 9: 274
1847..Frothingham, Octavius B. 2: 423
1847..Hodge, Archibald A. 10: 245
1847..Swett, Josiah 18: 325
1847..Weaver, Jonathan 11: 485
1847..Weston, Sullivan H. 9: 171
1848..Girardeau, John L. 23: 354
1848..Hoffman, Eugene A. 6: 397
1848..Lay, Henry C. 13: 425
1848..McClintock, John 6: 466
1848..Neill, Edward D. 9: 411
1848..Paxton, William Miller ...12: 192
1848..Shields, Charles W. 13: 174
1849..Hovey, Alvah 8: 154
1849..Loy, Matthias 12: 191
1849..Ormiston, William 13: 45
1849..Ridgaway, Henry Bascom . 9: 287
1849..Smith, John C. 8: 120
1850..Craven, Elijah R. 2: 217
1850..Finney, Thomas M. 7: 25
1850..Steele, Daniel 12: 490
1851..Broadus, John A. 18: 430
1851..Morais, Sabato 10: 170
1851..Rankine, James 12: 551
1851..Stebbins, Horatio 24: 200
1851..Wellman, Joshua W. 14: 108
1852..Hastings, Thomas S. 7: 317
1852..Valentine, Milton 10: 389
1853..Apple, Thomas G. 12: 444
1853..Boardman, George N. 6: 537
1853..Fulton, Justin D. 9: 201
1853..Giles, Chauncey 9: 257
1853..Hodge, Caspar W. 10: 245
1853..Hoffman, Eugene A. 6: 397
1853..Ryan, Patrick J. 6: 285
1853..Taylor, William M. 2: 189
1853..Wingfield, John H. D. ... 3: 468
1854..Blackburn, William M. ... 9: 441
1854..Dix, Morgan 23: 130
1854..Fisher, George P. 10: 424
1854..Smyth, Egbert C. 10: 101
1855..Boardman, George D., 2d .12: 479
1855..Boardman, Samuel W. 26: 225
1855..Clark, George W. 11: 279
1855..Kalisch, Isidor 3: 63
1855..Robinson, Charles S. 9: 482
1855..Vincent, John H. 9: 144
1855..Wasson, David A. 9: 99
1855..Whiton, James M. 8: 417
1856..Anderson, Galusha 1: 303
1856..Corwin, Edward T. 23: 115
1856..Doane, William C. 4: 489
1856..Garrett, Alexander C. 13: 501
1856..Munger, Theodore T. 1: 533
1856..Thompson, Hugh M. 9: 326
1857..Appleton, Samuel E. 14: 176
1857..Ewer, Ferdinand C. 9: 165
1857..Larsen, Laur 25: 304
1857..MacCracken, Henry M. .. 6: 324
1857..Osgood, Howard 24: 310
1857..Shipman, Jacob S. 18: 72
1857..Woodrow, James 11: 35
1858..Buckley, James M. 12: 191
1858..Buttz, Henry A. 13: 110
1858..Edwards, Arthur 9: 172
1858..Hurst, John F. 9: 122
1858..Potter, Henry C. 14: 35
1859..Atwood, Isaac M. 10: 202
1859..Bedell, Gregory Thurston. 7: 456
1859..Brooks, Phillips 2: 304
1859..Gotwald, Luther A. 10: 478
1859..Lambert, Louis A. 24: 111
1860..Abbott, Lyman 1: 473
1860..Brastow, Lewis O. 8: 159
1860..Gladden, Washington 10: 256
1860..Johnson, Herrick 10: 352
1860..McLaren, William E. 11: 331
1860..Newton, R. Heber 3: 304
1860..Parker, Edwin P. 25: 386
1861..Crosby, Howard 4: 193
1861..Ireland, John 9: 226
1861..Johnson, Franklin 16: 274
1861..Latimer, James E. 11: 178
1861..Noble, Frederick A. 12: 48
1861..Strong, Augustus H. 12: 514
1861..Swallow, Silas C. 24: 398
1861..Tyng, Stephen H. 2: 187
1862..Gray, George Z. 12: 254
1862..King, Henry M. 25: 273
1862..Schultze, Augustus 8: 365
1862..Vincent, Marvin R. 9: 107
1862..Wright, George F. 7: 66
1863..Brown, Olympia 20: 110
1863..Lyman, Albert J. 25: 318
1864..Abbot, Francis E. 24: 113
1864..Beecher, Willis J. 16: 305
1864..Chadwick, John W. 7: 77
1864..Clarke, William N. 22: 264
1864..Gabriels, Henry 4: 266
1864..Hartranft, Chester D. 6: 42
1864..Pentecost, George F. 20: 73
1864..Savage, Minot J. 1: 351
1864..Van Meter, John B. 26: 70
1865..Abbott, Edward 8: 179
1865..Behrends, Adolphus J. 8: 16
1865..Hamilton, John W. .... B: 365
1865..Hurlbut, Jesse L. 11: 392
1865..John, John P. D. 7: 384
1865..Mann, Newton 20: 115
1865..Sanford, Elias B. 24: 256
1866..Dike, Samuel W. 22: 301
1866..Radcliffe, Wallace 22: 441
1866..Swing, David 3: 16
1866..Worden, James A. 20: 153
1867..Douthit, Jasper L. 14: 510
1867..Miller, James R. 10: 19
1867..Slicer, Thomas R. 14: 126
1867..Smyth, Samuel P. N. 13: 139
1867..Storrs, Henry M. 9: 447
1867..Young, Egerton R. 14: 160
1868..Gannett, William C. 22: 36
1868..Haydn, Hiram C. 7: 225
1868..Reed, Myron W. 18: 392
1868..Wilson, John A. B. 7: 135
1869..Churchill, John W. 10: 98
1869..Goucher, John F. 24: 174
1869..Harris, George 10: 101
1869..Hart, Samuel 13: 48
1869..Jacobs, Henry E. 11: 419
1869..Kelley, William V. 9: 256
1869..Stimson, Henry A. 13: 531
1869..Sweeney, Zachary T. 20: 279
1869..Wendte, Charles W. 14: 453
1870..Alexander, George 23: 227
1870..Barrows, John H. 8: 116
1870..Bixby, James T. 11: 236
1870..Bradford, Amory H. 7: 174
1870..Briggs, Charles A. 7: 318
1870..Burrell, David J. 12: 482
1870..Chapman, Ervin 19: 229
1870..Edwards, Thomas C. 22: 280
1870..Gregg, David 6: 257
1870..Hincks, Edward Y. 10: 103
1870..Hodge, George W. 22: 201
1870..Jones, Jenkin L. 14: 161
1870..Leavell, William H. ...... C: 332
1870..MacArthur, Robert S. 5: 226
1871..Hall, Arthur C. A. 11: 496
1871..Moore, Walter H. 18: 43
1871..Moxom, Philip S. 19: 57
1871..Strong, Josiah 9: 416
1871..Taylor, Elbert O. 20: 220
1871..Wright, George F. 7: 66
1872..Adams, John C. 11: 91
1872..Clutz, Jacob A. 20: 45
1872..Crafts, Wilbur F. 14: 172
1872..Crapsey, Algernon S. 14: 174
1872..Dole, Charles F. 20: 355
1872..Huntington, William E. ..11: 179
1872..McConnell, Samuel D. ...10: 360
1873..Gailor, Thomas F. 12: 86
1873..Mendes, Frederick deS. ..21: 455
1873..Rainsford, William S. ... 1: 385
1873..Russell, Charles Taze 12: 317
1874..Hall, Charles C. 6: 186
1874..Hunter, Robert 6: 300
1874..North, Frank M. 26: 62
1875..Chadwick, John W. 7: 77
1875..Good, James I. 5: 360
1875..Judson, Edward 12: 480
1875..Lee, Jesse 13: 187
1875..McConaughy, James 25: 410
1875..Smith, Henry P. 23: 174
1876..Christian, John T. 20: 449
1876..Clark, Francis E. 13: 51
1876..Hirsch, Emil G. 2: 112
1876..Lawrence, William .... C: 479
1876..Matthew, Winfield S. 24: 240
1876..May, Joseph 17: 253
1876..Van Dyke, Henry 25: 10
1877..Coe, Edward B. 12: 482
1877..Crothers, Samuel McC. ...22: 384
1877..Day, Charles O. 13: 434
1877..Gordon, George A. 22: 307
1877..Horr, George E. 24: 67
1877..Knox, George W. 23: 245
1877..Sheer, George A. 20: 429
1878..Clark, William W. 24: 272
1878..Engelhardt, Zephyrin 24: 134
1878..Torrey, Reuben A. 21: 428
1879..Bushnell, Samuel C. 22: 383
1879..Gailor, Thomas F. .... C: 338
1879..Gunsaulus, Frank W. 7: 42
1879..Mitchell, Hinckley G. 11: 183
1879..Nassau, Charles W. 11: 241
1879..Reinke, Jonathan 22: 265
1880..Crockett, Stuart 18: 107
1881..Hodges, George 22: 79
1881..Noyes, Charles L. 20: 272
1881..Ward, Seth 26: 93
1882..Babcock, Maltbie B. 14: 109
1882..Bliss, William D. P. 20: 91
1882..Braislin, Gibbs .... A: 195
1882..Burton, Ernest DeW. 11: 68
1883..Berkowitz, Henry 22: 55
1883..Brown, William M. ...... C: 485
1883..Faber, William F. .... C: 421
1883..Faulkner, John A. 22: 368
1883..Philipson, David .... B: 302
1883..Pickard, William L. ...... B: 415
1884..Bacon, Benjamin W. 23: 273

1884..Dowie, John A. 13: 252
1884..Faunce, William H. P. ...10: 306
1884..McCormick, John N. .... C: 55
1885..Hamill, Howard M. 16: 35
1885..Long, Simon P. 22: 402
1885..Scarritt, William R. 23: 389
1886..Braislin, Gibbs .... A: 195
1886..Brewster, Benjamin ...... D: 339
1886..Dixon, Thomas, Jr. 13: 189
1886..Hanna, Edward J. .... D: 280
1886..Ottman, Ford C. 22: 211
1887..Hillis, Newell D. 21: 280
1887..Moore, John M. .... C: 368
1887..Mosessohn, Nehemiah 20: 399
1887..Thomas, Jesse B. 17: 74
1887..Weiskotten, Samuel G. ...20: 316
1887..Zimmerman, Leander M. . A: 192
1888..Burdette, Robert J. 24: 356
1888..Cannon, James .... C: 318
1888..Jenks, Edwin H. 22: 158
1888..Miller, Daniel L. 19: 32
1888..Robertson, Archibald T. ..25: 402
1888..Tyler, J. Poyntz 24: 163
1888..Weeden, Charles F. 21: 427
1889..Cadman, S. Parkes ...... B: 121
1889..Jett, Robert C. .... A: 297
1889..Levy, Joseph L. 14: 423
1889..Manning, William T. .... A: 507
1890..Borton, Francis 22: 84
1891..Ainslie, Peter .... A: 341
1891..Barbour, Clarence A. .... A: 283
1891..Cope, Henry F. 20: 239
1891..Johnson, Irving P. ...... C: 409
1892..Briggs, Charles A. 7: 318
1892..Forbush, William B. 23: 346
1892..Mitchell, Charles B. ..... C: 256
1892..Schuyler, Hamilton 24: 179
1892..Stires, Ernest M. .... C: 53
1893..Barton, William E. 17: 380
1893..Beauchamp, William B. ..23: 173
1893..Burk, W. Herbert 24: 214
1893..Hamilton, Franklin E. E..14: 435
1893..Hite, Lewis F. .... A: 169
1893..Murphy, Edgar G. 25: 258
1893..Taylor, William M. ...... C: 441
1893..Wise, Stephen S. .... B: 25
1894..Burleson, Hugh L. .... C: 523
1894..Corrothers, James D. 23: 414
1894..Freeman, James E. 12: 327
1894..Howden, Frederick B. ... A: 299
1894..Longley, Harry S. .... C: 31
1895..Lockrow, David M. 20: 109
1895..Moore, John M. .... D: 125
1895..Simons, Minot .... D: 367
1896..Brooks, Raymond C. ..... A: 256
1896..Davis, Ozora S. 24: 358
1896..Hulse, Hiram R. .... C: 483
1896..Knubel, Frederick H. .... B: 450
1896..Reid, William J., Jr. .... D: 307
1896..Richardson, Ernest G. .... C: 357
1897..Brown, John E. .... B: 470
1897..Johnson, Frederick F. .... C: 405
1897..Reese, Theodore I. .... C: 50
1898..Bates, H. Boswell 18: 424
1898..Faris, John T. .... D: 275
1898..Mikell, Henry J. .... B: 366
1898..Norwood, Robert W. 25: 208
1899..Claiborne, William S. .... B: 63
1899..De Blois, Austen K. ..... B: 348
1899..Green, William M. .... C: 431
1899..Richardson, Ernest G. .... C: 357
1899..Ward, John C. .... C: 423
1900..Beardsley, Frank G. ..... C: 346
1900..Coffin, Henry S. .... B: 36
1900..Ewers, John R. .... C: 171
1900..Gallup, Clarence M. ...... C: 165
1900..Stelzle, Charles .... C: 160
1900..Van Schaick, John, Jr. .. A: 164
1900..Wiers, Edgar S. 23: 276
1901..Dieffenbach, Albert C. ... B: 512
1901..Saunderson, Henry H. ... C: 212
1902..Cook, Philip .... D: 131
1902..Paine, George L. .... C: 124
1902..Ryan, John A. .... C: 190
1902..Ward, John C. .... C: 423
1903..Fosdick, Harry E. .... B: 194
1903..Robbins, Howard C. ..... D: 103
1903..Strayer, Paul Moore 21: 433
1904..Dobbs, Hoyt McW. .... B: 169
1904..Hobbs, James R. .... A: 256
1905..Dietrich, John H. .... C: 279
1905..Faber, William F. .... C: 421
1905..Kretzmann, Paul E. ...... C: 113
1905..Mann, Rowena M. .... B: 258
1905..Remington, William P. .. C: 457
1906..Jones, Paul .... B: 88
1907..Holmes, John H. .... C: 461
1908..Beaven, Albert W. .... C: 299
1908..Jennings, Asa K. 23: 229
1908..Marsh, Daniel L. .... A: 133
1908..Molloy, Thomas E. .... B: 200
1908..Potter, Charles F. .... C: 89
1910..Benson, Samuel C. .... B: 100
1911..Farrington, Harry W. ...23: 71
1911..Rogers, Warren L. ...... C: 128
1911..Sterrett, Frank W. ...... C: 288
1919..Mann, Louis L. .... D: 319
1922..Slaten, Arthur W. .... B: 372

Composers

See Musicians and Composers

Dentists

1804..Hayden, Horace H. 13: 525
1831..Harris, Chapin A. 22: 432
1833..Allen, John 2: 427
1836..Maynard, Edward 11: 339
1836..Wells, Horace 6: 438
1842..Morton, William T. G. ... 8: 332
1845..Evans, Thomas W. 9: 150
1848..Morgan, William H. 8: 228
1850..Kingsley, Norman W. 25: 167
1854..Bonwill, William G. A. ... 5: 177
1855..Truman, James 25: 299
1858..Turner, Vines E. 14: 180
1859..Stockton, Charles S. 15: 204
1860..Fillebrown, Thomas 13: 479
1862..Jenkins, Newell S. 19: 111
1863..Jarvie, William 12: 509
1865..Low, James E. 2: 435
1865..Younger, William J. 20: 250
1866..Abbott, Frank P. 2: 359
1868..Land, Charles H. 14: 331
1869..Garretson, James E. 3: 212
1870..Talbot, Eugene S. 13: 147
1871..Meeker, Charles A. 15: 221
1875..Angle, Edward H. 22: 376
1875..Brophy, Truman W. 12: 374
1876..Morgan, Henry W. 8: 229
1877..Black, Green V. 13: 537
1877..Cryer, Matthew H. 17: 432
1877..Harper, John G. 5: 229
1879..Baker, Henry A. 15: 109
1879..Jackson, Victor H. 22: 112
1880..Smith, B. Holly 8: 219
1880..Weeks, Thomas E. 6: 117
1884..Noyes, Edmund 16: 136
1886..Boardman, Waldo E. 14: 338
1888..Meisburger, Louis 25: 234
1888..Williams, James L. 24: 232
1891..Hinman, Thomas P. 25: 393
1892..Hunt, George E. 15: 63
1893..Hawley, Charles A. 22: 181
1893..Orton, Forrest H. 26: 267
1900..White, Oliver W. 16: 376
1903..Hayden, Gillette 24: 239

Dermatologists

1832..Bulkley, Henry D. 25: 182
1864..Damon, Howard F. 3: 98
1869..Fox, George H. 11: 284
1870..Duhring, Louis A. 20: 351
1871..White, James C. 19: 358
1872..Bulkley, L. Duncan 25: 182
1874..Morrow, Prince A. 21: 184
1875..Shoemaker, John V. 13: 223
1875..Stelwagon, Henry W. 19: 376
1878..Rankin, Egbert 12: 502
1880..Jackson, George T. 11: 561
1881..Swarts, Gardner T. 20: 346
1883..Corlett, William T. 14: 345
1885..Dearborn, Henry M. 9: 350
1887..Wende, Ernest 4: 381
1888..Fordyce, John A. 20: 165
1889..Cutler, Condict W. 22: 168
1893..Ravogli, Augustus 12: 476
1894..Trimble, William B. 26: 338
1905..Clark, A. Schuyler 24: 122

Diplomats

See pages 24-31

Economists

1721..Rawle, Francis 6: 186
1762..Du Pont, Pierre S. de N. . 6: 454
1774..Hamilton, Alexander 1: 9
1776..Webster, Pelatiah 7: 226
1778..Franklin, Benjamin 1: 328
1780..Gallatin, Albert 3: 9
1787..Coxe, Tench 6: 14
1790..Cooper, Thomas 11: 31
1802..Carey, Matthew 6: 278
1814..Biddle, Clement C. 5: 504
1825..McVickar, John 6: 346
1826..Dew, Thomas 3: 235
1828..Phillips, Willard 7: 541
1832..Colwell, Stephen 4: 524
1835..Carey, Henry C. 5: 34
1835..Newman, Samuel P. 10: 123
1837..Wayland, Francis 8: 22
1840..Kellogg, Edward 24: 350
1842..Walker, Amasa 11: 438
1845..Bigelow, Erastus B. 3: 20
1853..Perry, Arthur L. 10: 215
1853..Smith, Erasmus P. 13: 195
1854..Sherman, John 3: 198
1855..Linderman, Henry R. 4: 120
1856..Bowen, Francis 11: 452
1857..Baird, Henry C. 5: 314
1859..Grosvenor, William M. ...20: 254
1861..Atkinson, Edward 9: 416
1861..Conant, Charles A. 14: 227
1862..Del Mar, Alexander 4: 189
1864..Wells, David A. 10: 363
1865..Newcomb, Simon 7: 17
1866..Eaton, Dorman B. 21: 200
1868..Champlin, James T. 8: 406
1868..Dugdale, Richard L. 11: 344
1868..Ward, C. Osborne 13: 112
1869..Burgess, John W. 23: 39
1869..Folwell, William W. 13: 328
1870..Mason, David H. 10: 228
1870..Thompson, Robert E. 10: 18
1871..Dunbar, Charles F. 9: 209
1871..George, Henry 4: 325
1872..Sumner, William G. 25: 8
1873..Walker, Francis A. 5: 401
1873..Wright, Carroll D. 19: 421
1874..Gunton, George 10: 146
1876..Horton, Samuel D. 5: 558
1876..Morse, Anson D. 13: 352
1877..Clark, John B. 13: 48
1877..James, Edmund J. 11: 67
1878..Laughlin, J. Laurence 24: 14
1879..Ely, Richard T. .... B: 201
1879..Taylor, Fred M. 25: 37
1880..Adams, Henry C. 12: 219
1880..Bowker, Richard R. 24: 66
1880..Farnam, Henry W. 24: 254
1880..Lewis, Burwell B. 12: 295
1880..Shearman, Thomas G. 2: 498
1881..Post, Louis F. 18: 150
1881..Shaw, Albert 9: 469
1883..Hadley, Arthur T. 9: 267
1884..Warner, John DeW. 9: 114
1885..Franklin, Fabian .... C: 497
1885..Patten, Simon N. 11: 230
1885..Seligman, Edwin R. A. ..10: 49
1886..Dewey, Davis R. 13: 371
1886..Taussig, Frank W. .... A: 457
1887..Bascom, John 8: 196
1887..Gilman, Nicholas P. 8: 120
1887..Gould, Elgin R. L. 23: 193
1887..Warner, Adoniram J. ...10: 446
1888..Andrews, Elisha B. 8: 26
1888..Blackmar, Frank W. 9: 495
1888..Macfarlane, Charles W. ..22: 361
1888..Willoughby, William F. .. A: 212
1889..Eaton, J. Shirley 25: 263
1889..Jenks, Jeremiah W. ..... B: 140
1889..Warner, Amos G. 13: 446
1890..Commons, John R. .... A: 423
1891..Brooks, John G. 13: 534
1891..Fisher, Irving .... C: 51
1891..Howe, Frederic C. .... D: 84
1891..Veblen, Thorstein B. 21: 73
1892..Houston, David F. .... A: 38
1892..Judson, Harry P. 20: 24
1892..Kinley, David .... B: 76
1892..Plehn, Carl C. .... A: 314
1892..Willcox, Walter F. .... A: 345
1892..Wright, Philip G. 25: 106
1893..Maltbie, Milo R. .... A: 445
1893..Rosewater, Victor 13: 324
1894..Carver, Thomas N. ...... A: 349
1894..Hollander, Jacob H. 13: 372
1894..Hoxie, Robert F. 23: 415
1894..Lindsay, Samuel McC. 12: 374
1894..Parsons, Frank 11: 182
1894..Seager, Henry R. 22: 180
1895..Bullock, Charles J. ...... C: 104
1895..Callender, Guy S. 23: 395
1895..Fetter, Frank A. .... B: 339
1895..LeRossignol, James E. ...13: 304
1895..Rowe, Leo S. 18: 316
1895..Warbasse, James P. ..... C: 330
1895..Willoughby, Westel W. ..13: 435
1896..Emery, Henry C. 21: 101

1896..McVey, Frank LeR. 13:316
1897..Cleveland, Frederick A. ..13:433
1898..Schwab, John C. 26:333
1899..Taylor, Alonzo E. C:222
1899..Teele, Ray P. 20: 38
1900..Andrew, Piatt, Jr. D:205
1900..Sprague, Oliver M. W. ..D: 27
1901..Taylor, Henry C. B:328
1902..Davenport, Herbert J. 26:232
1903..Kemmerer, Edwin W. ...B:126
1903..McCrea, Roswell C. C:513
1904..Meeker, Royal A:535
1905..Wildman, Murray S. 25:330
1906..Warne, Frank J. A:229
1906..Warren, George F. ......D: 27
1907..Agger, Eugene E. ....D: 79
1907..McPherson, Logan G. 25:280
1907..Manly, Basil M. A:444
1907..Robinson, Frederick B. ..C:115
1908..Mitchell, Wesley C. C:511
1908..Patterson, Ernest M. D:298
1909..Nearing, Scott ....D: 53
1911..Shaw, Archibald W. A:354
1912..Young, Arthur N. ....C: 84
1913..Parker, Carleton H. 19:321
1913..Westerfield, Ray B. ......D: 31
1915..Tugwell, Rexford G. .....D: 25
1915..Wolman, Leo ....D: 25
1916..Baruch, Bernard M. ......A: 57
1919..Juchhoff, Frederick ......D: 69
1919..Viner, Jacob ....D: 35
1919..Young, Owen D. ....A: 81
1920..Collings, Harry T. 25: 83
1928..Dalton, John E. D:319

Editors

See Journalists and Editors

Educators

1630..Eliot, John 2:419
1637..Cheever, Ezekiel 12:439
1693..Blair, James 3:231
1698..Pierson, Abraham 1:164
1704..Berkeley, George 6:255
1720..Johnson, Samuel 6:341
1721..Wigglesworth, Edward ...9:237
1723..Edwards, Jonathan 5:464
1729..Lovell, John 12:428
1749..Stiles, Ezra 1:167
1754..Wheelock, Eleazer 9: 85
1762..Cooper, Myles 6:341
1764..Manning, James 8: 20
1766..Willard, Joseph 6:416
1769..Dwight, Timothy 1:168
1769..Smith, Samuel S. 2: 21
1771..Phillips, Samuel 10: 93
1772..Wheelock, John 9: 86
1773..Graham, William 3:163
1776..Alexander, Archibald 2: 22
1778..Pearson, Eliphalet 10: 94
1779..Fitch, Ebenezer 6:237
1779..Smith, John B. 2: 21
1780..Jefferson, Thomas 3: 1
1782..Bingham, Caleb 8: 19
1782..Dod, Thaddeus 7:536
1784..Waddell, Moses 9:179
1788..Abbot, Benjamin 10:104
1789..Maxey, Jonathan 8: 21
1789..Wistar, Caspar 1:273
1790..Griffin, Edward D. 6:237
1790..Nott, Eliphalet 7:170
1790..Quincy, Josiah 6:417
1790..Sanders, Daniel C. 2: 39
1791..Harris, William 6:344
1791..Messer, Asa 8: 21
1792..Adams, Ebenezer 9: 91
1792..Kent, James 3: 55
1793..Griscom, John 10:510
1793..Moore, Zephaniah S. 5:307
1796..Davis, Henry 7:405
1796..Day, Jeremiah 1:169
1797..Kirkland, Samuel 7:404
1797..Knox, Samuel 24:155
1799..Bangs, Nathan 9:429
1799..Chaplin, Jeremiah 8:404
1799..Chase, Philander 7: 1
1799..Kingsley, James L. 10:121
1804..Mason, John M. 6:462
1804..Willard, Emma 1:244
1805..Brown, Francis 9: 86
1807..Clements, Samuel 1:444
1807..Greenleaf, Benjamin 8:141
1807..Lindsley, Philip 8:131
1808..Dewey, Chester 6:328
1808..Gallaudet, Thomas H. 9:138
1809..Lord, Nathan 9: 88
1810..Brown, Goold 8:265
1810..Hawley, Gedeon 13:443
1810..Kirkland, John T. 6:417
1810..Wylie, Andrew 13:116
1812..Cooper, Thomas 11: 31
1812..Guilford, Nathan 12:385
1812..Porter, Ebenezer 10: 99
1812..Strong, Theodore 9:288
1813..Woodbridge, William C. ..11:214
1814..Emerson, George B. 11:526
1815..Beck, Theoderic R. 9:350
1815..Clerc, Laurent 22:253
1815..Hall, Samuel R. 3:504
1815..Hitchcock, Edward 5:308
1816..Davies, Charles 3: 26
1817..Coleman, Lyman 11:247
1817..Eaton, Amos 5:312
1817..McDonogh, John 9:465
1817..Staughton, William 3:151
1817..Wayland, Francis 8: 22
1818..Maclean, John 5:467
1818..Soule, Gideon L. 10:105
1819..Bailey, Ebenezer 4:345
1819..Haddock, Charles B. 9: 96
1819..Johnson, Walter R. 12:260
1819..Mann, Horace 3: 78
1819..Sherwin, Thomas 11:350
1819..Ticknor, George 6:477
1820..Alcott, William A. 12: 59
1820..Anthon, Charles 6:345
1820..Carter, James G. 10:507
1820..Olin, Stephen 9:429
1820..Thayer, Gideon F. 7:532
1821..Benedict, Erastus C. 5:415
1821..Fowle, William B. 10:220
1822..Beecher, Catherine E. ...3:128
1822..Peabody, Elizabeth P. 12:350
1822..Sanders, Charles W. 2:257
1823..Abbott, Jacob 6:136
1823..Humphrey, Heman 5:308
1823..Lieber, Francis 5:116
1823..Swain, David L. 4:424
1823..Woolsey, Theodore D. 1:170
1824..Hopkins, Mark 6:237
1825..Alcott, A. Bronson 2:218
1825..Copland, Patrick 3:231
1825..Fisk, Wilbur 3:177
1825..Smith, Augustus W. 9:430
1826..Kingsbury, John 9:417
1826..Larrabee, William C. 25:308
1826..McGuffey, William H. 4:443
1827..Crosby, Alpheus 9: 97
1827..North, Simeon 7:407
1827..Stearns, William A. 5:309
1828..Allen, George 9:474
1828..Bache, Alexander D. 3:348
1828..Barnard, Frederick A. P. 6:347
1828..Junkin, George 11:240
1828..Lyon, Mary 4:462
1829..Duer, William A. 6:344
1829..Greene, Samuel S. 8:349
1829..Lathrop, John H. 5:178
1829..Porter, Samuel 25:355
1829..Sears, Barnas 8: 24
1830..Dimitry, Alexander 10:176
1830..Hart, John S. 9:263
1830..Miner, Myrtilla 12:185
1830..Pattison, Robert E. 8:405
1831..Abbot, Gorham D. 10:355
1831..Atwater, Lyman H. 12:429
1831..Junkin, David F. 11:240
1831..Porter, Noah 1:171
1832..Howe, Samuel G. 8:372
1832..Mortimer, Mary 7:529
1832..Porter, Sarah 10:292
1832..Stewart, Philo P. 2:460
1832..Tappan, Henry P. 1:249
1832..Taylor, Samuel H. 10: 96
1832..West, Charles E. 8:235
1834..Fisher, Ebenezer 10:201
1834..Stone, Lucinda H. 13:198
1835..Alden, Joseph 5:406
1835..Burrowes, Thomas H. 25:439
1835..Champlin, James T. 8:406
1835..Lord, Asa D. 12:313
1835..Mahan, Asa 2:461
1836..Bartlett, Samuel C. 9: 89
1836..May, Samuel J. 2:313
1836..Pruyn, John V. L. 3:364
1837..Chapin, Aaron L. 3:184
1837..Graves, Zuinglius C. 24:333
1837..Gunn, Frederick W. 13:349
1837..Randall, Samuel S. 18:184
1838..Dwight, Francis 12:268
1838..Hamlin, Cyrus 10:491
1838..Kendall, Ezra O. 2:415
1838..Leach, Daniel 8:467
1838..Raymond, John H. 5:234
1839..Brooks, Nathan C. 4:557
1839..Mayo, Amory D. 25:330
1840..Barnard, Henry 1:505
1840..Calkins, Norman A. 10: 86
1840..Cummings, Joseph 9:430
1840..Green, Lewis W. 2: 25
1841..Anderson, Martin B. 12:243
1841..Emerson, Joseph 11:526
1841..Newell, McFadden A. 12:512
1842..Burroughs, John C. 11: 65
1842..Dwight, Theodore W. 6:346
1842..Hadley, James 1:175
1842..Haldeman, Samuel S. 9:246
1842..Packard, Silas S. 3: 72
1842..Philbrick, John D. 12:242
1843..Ballard, Addison 3:345
1843..Colburn, Dana P. 12:267
1843..Eckard, James R. 11:245
1843..Hill, Thomas 6:420
1843..Harkness, Albert 6: 23
1843..Kiddle, Henry 2:512
1843..North, Edward 4:212
1843..Sheldon, David N. 8:406
1843..Watson, James M. 10:194
1844..Allen, Nathaniel T. 20:212
1844..Fraser, John 9:493
1844..Kraus, John 13:466
1844..Pickard, Joshua L. 12:512
1844..Rickoff, Andrew J. 4:556
1845..Butler, James D. 9:190
1845..Eberhart, John F. 9:508
1845..Mills, Susan L. 19:438
1845..Percival, Chester S. 2:232
1845..Phelps, William F. 12:480
1845..Upson, Anson J. 4:489
1845..Williston, Samuel 5:313
1846..Durant, Henry 7:228
1846..Le Conte, John 7:228
1847..Andrews, Lorin 7: 6
1847..Fetter, George W. 5:249
1847..King, Joseph E. 1:252
1847..Love, Samuel G. 12:130
1847..McCauley, James A. 6:464
1847..Quackenbos, George P. ...13:301
1847..Vincent, John H. 9:144
1848..Chadbourne, Paul A. 6:238
1848..Farrand, Samuel A. 23:368
1848..Olney, Charles F. 6:512
1848..Orton, Edward 7:416
1848..Sheldon, Edward A. 7: 67
1849..Brooks, Edward 2:294
1849..Peet, Isaac L. 13:145
1849..Sill, John M. B. 10:353
1850..Agassiz, Elizabeth C. 12: 46
1850..Boyden, Albert G. 14:256
1850..Camp, David N. 2:520
1850..Campbell, Francis J. 11:374
1850..Hovey, Harriette S. 6:352
1850..Hunter, Thomas 22:244
1850..Merrill, Catharine 19:297
1850..Smith, Luther M. 1:519
1851..Cochran, David H. 3:397
1851..Fisk, Franklin W. 11: 97
1851..Gaines, Absalom G. 10:199
1852..Bascom, John 8:196
1852..Davis, Noah K. 4: 76
1852..Gregory, John M. 12:497
1852..Lyon, Franklin S. 1:181
1852..McCosh, James 5:468
1852..Patterson, James W. 11:364
1852..Robinson, Ezekiel G. 8: 26
1852..White, Emerson E. 13: 40
1852..Williams, Samuel G. 8:418
1853..Dodge, Ebenezer 5:428
1853..Dowd, Charles F. 18:180
1853..Eliot, Charles W. 6:421
1853..Fairbairn, Robert B. 5: 65
1853..Hancock, John 5:553
1853..Pitman, Benn 4: 87
1853..Seelye, Julius H. 6:157
1853..Sheldon, William E. 5:542
1853..Whitford, William C. 6:119
1854..Angell, James B. 1:251
1854..Bicknell, Thomas W. 1:421
1854..Eaton, John 8:390
1854..Payne, William H. 8:134
1854..Warren, Samuel E. 4:199
1854..Wickersham, James P. ...12:239
1855..Folwell, William W. 13:328
1855..Gallaudet, Edward M. 18:128
1855..Gove, Aaron 12:531
1855..Himes, Charles F. 4:144
1855..Hinsdale, Burke A. 10:471
1855..Niles, William H. 12:481
1856..Bryant, John C. 18:395
1856..Gildersleeve, Basil L. 10:469
1856..Gilman, Daniel C. 5:170
1856..Goodwin, William W. 6:428
1856..Hale, Horace M. 6:492

1856..Hartranft, Chester D. 6: 42
1856..Sprague, Homer B. 24: 65
1856..Taylor, Jonathan K. 17: 47
1857..Collar, William C. 21: 253
1857..Edgar, George M. 26: 247
1857..Harris, William T. 15: 1
1857..Howland, Emily 25: 306
1857..Hyatt, Jonathan D. 13: 566
1857..MacCracken, Henry M. ... 6: 324
1857..McPhail, George W. 11: 242
1857..Northrop, Birdsey G. 10: 225
1857..Tappan, Eli T. 7: 7
1857..White, Andrew D. 4: 476
1858..Bartholomew, George K. ..16: 36
1858..Belfield, Henry H. 20: 174
1858..Buehrle, Robert K. 5: 132
1858..Coffin, Seldon J. 11: 245
1858..Comfort, George F. 3: 162
1858..Cooley, LeRoy C. 11: 263
1858..Lane, Albert G. 12: 510
1858..McClellan, Henry B. 4: 140
1858..Seelye, Julius H. 6: 157
1858..Wilkinson, Warring 18: 264
1859..Greenwood, James M. 13: 62
1859..MacVicar, Malcolm 4: 57
1859..Powell, William B. 13: 120
1859..Smart, James H. 6: 106
1859..Thompson, Samuel R. 7: 517
1859..White, Samuel H. 13: 101
1860..Avery, Elroy M. 26: 57
1860..Bancroft, Cecil F. P. 10: 97
1860..Goodale, George L. 6: 427
1860..Jones, Augustine 6: 203
1860..Kraus-Bolté, Maria 13: 467
1860..Morton, Henry 24: 374
1860..Skinner, Charles R. 10: 388
1860..Toy, Crawford H. 6: 94
1860..Tutwiler, Julia S. 15: 101
1860..Woodward, Calvin M. 9: 469
1861..Brooks, William M. ...... A: 255
1861..Fuller, Gardner 15: 54
1861..Marble, Albert P. 13: 581
1861..Morgan, Thomas J. 2: 54
1861..Soulé, George 1: 510
1862..Fay, Edward A. 20: 62
1862..Hill, Frank A. 23: 292
1862..Wilkinson, William C. ...11: 72
1862..Young, Ella F. 19: 26
1863..Atherton, George W. 20: 486
1863..Ely, Charles W. 15: 117
1863..Lewis, Dio 10: 381
1863..Northrop, Cyrus 13: 328
1863..Wait, William B. 2: 451
1864..Andrews, Newton L. 5: 429
1864..Cady, Sarah L. 9: 373
1864..Gilman, Stella S. 10: 363
1864..Goodell, Henry H. 8: 116
1864..King, Charles F. 20: 225
1864..MacAlister, James 13: 79
1864..Mowry, William A. 25: 172
1864..Palmer, George H. 6: 427
1864..Soldan, Frank L. 12: 516
1864..Thayer, Joseph H. 6: 428
1864..Willard, Horace M. 15: 68
1865..Baldwin, James 14: 134
1865..Cook, John W. 5: 550
1865..Corson, Hiram 1: 440
1865..Curry, Jabez L. M. 4: 357
1865..Heald, Edward P. 6: 142
1865..Mitchell, Maria 5: 236
1865..Moss, Lemuel 11: 65
1865..Peirce, Thomas May 5: 26
1865..Pepper, George D. B. 8: 407
1865..Seelye, L. Clark 7: 121
1865..Storer, Francis H. 11: 337
1865..Thurston, Robert H. 4: 479
1866..Chamberlin, Thomas C. ..19: 25
1866..Draper, Andrew S. 12: 498
1866..Garrett, William R. 12: 560
1866..Holst, Hermann E. von ..11: 69
1866..Howison, George H. 23: 179
1866..Lehr, Henry S. 20: 129
1866..Moore, James W. 11: 246
1866..Orton, James 11: 280
1866..Silliman, Justus M. 11: 245
1866..Stillé, Charles J. 1: 344
1866..Sumner, William G. 25: 8
1866..Webb, Alexander S. 3: 31
1867..Coates, Charles T. 19: 51
1867..Backus, Truman J. 5: 375
1867..Butts, Annice Bradford ...11: 74
1867..Hyatt, Alpheus 3: 101
1867..Staley, Cady 11: 154
1867..Williams, Job 16: 37
1868..Crane, Thomas F. 23: 146
1868..Eddy, Henry T. 15: 331
1868..Hart, James M. 9: 263
1868..Lyte, Eliphalet O. 5: 227
1868..Reese, William M. 1: 521
1868..Sloane, William M. 21: 95
1868..Stowell, Thomas B. 21: 429
1868..Thompson, Robert E. 10: 18
1868..Whitman, Charles O. 11: 73
1869..Cook, Ezekiel H. 13: 579
1869..Currier, Enoch Henry ...18: 210
1869..Dougherty, Newton C. 13: 532
1869..Goucher, John F. 8: 250
1869..Humphreys, Milton W. ... B: 53
1869..Torbet, David 18: 402
1870..Cady, Calvin B. 21: 425
1870..Clarke, Francis D. 22: 155
1870..Coulter, John Merle 11: 68
1870..Gates, Merrill E. 5: 309
1870..Green, James M. 13: 516
1870..Griffis, William E. 21: 118
1870..Jordan, David Starr 22: 68
1870..Judson, Harry P. 20: 24
1870..Langdell, Christopher C. . 6: 423
1870..Low, Seth 6: 348
1870..Lowber, James W. 6: 108
1870..Munroe, Wilfred H. ...... B: 335
1870..Salisbury, Albert 11: 384
1870..White, John S. 2: 335
1870..Wilson, James O. 13: 58
1870..Wilson, Luella M. 10: 209
1871..Boyden, Arthur C. 25: 276
1871..Gobble, Aaron E. 5: 19
1871..Owen, William Baxter ...11: 246
1871..Patrick, Mary M. .... A: 482
1871..Patton, Francis L. 5: 468
1872..Fairchild, Edward T. 19: 38
1872..Fosdick, Frank S. 12: 194
1872..Hall, G. Stanley 9: 203
1872..McMaster, John B. 11: 445
1872..Maxwell, William H. 13: 218
1872..Poulsson, Emilie 10: 463
1873..Baker, James H. 6: 493
1873..Butler, Nathaniel 8: 409
1873..Chase, George 20: 233
1873..Clark, Addison, ... 6: 107
1873..De Garmo, Charles 6: 354
1873..Laughlin, J. Laurence 24: 14
1873..Olds, George D. 24: 384
1873..Powers, James K. 15: 362
1874..Boutelle, Clarence M. 11: 473
1874..Brinsmade, John C. 22: 156
1874..Frissell, Hollis B. 18: 387
1874..Hale, William G. 12: 80
1874..Hart, Edward 11: 246
1874..Hart, William R. .... B: 252
1874..Hill, David J. 12: 244
1874..Holgate, Thomas F. ..... B: 184
1874..Howe, Edward G. 24: 366
1874..Painter, Franklin V. N. ..10: 59
1874..Palmer, Alice E. Freeman 7: 328
1874..Pattengill, Henry R. 19: 257
1874..Thomas, Calvin 16: 220
1875..Capen, Elmer H. 6: 241
1875..Corson, Oscar T. 12: 510
1875..Glenn, Gustavus R. 13: 96
1875..Harper, William R. 11: 65
1875..Ricketts, Palmer C. 26: 236
1875..Schaeffer, Nathan C. 22: 454
1875..Smith, William H. 1: 235
1876..Adler, Felix 23: 98
1876..Anagnos, Michael 13: 257
1876..Andrews, Elisha B. 8: 26
1876..Boone, Richard G. 20: 107
1876..Burton, Ernest De W. 11: 68
1876..Fowler, Edwin 7: 188
1876..Hull, John 19: 390
1876..Mace, William H. 4: 407
1876..Payne, William M. 11: 222
1876..Sexton, Pliny T. 20: 66
1877..Ames, James B. 18: 141
1877..Canfield, James H. 7: 417
1877..Dabney, Charles W. ...... B: 239
1877..Gilman, Arthur 6: 162
1877..Hooper, Franklin W. ... 13: 46
1877..James, Edmund J. 11: 67
1877..Murlin, Lemuel H. 26: 285
1878..Amen, Harlan P. 10: 107
1878..Brown, Elmer E. 14: 252
1878..Cooley, Edwin G. 14: 136
1878..Edson, Andrew W. 20: 235
1878..Gayley, Charles M. 23: 128
1878..Knight, George W. 24: 410
1878..Poteat, William L. .... A: 244
1879..Burdett, Charles A. 22: 313
1879..Campbell, Prince L. 21: 231
1879..Cummings, Byron .... B: 296
1879..Ely, Richard T. .... B: 201
1879..Hadley, Arthur T. 9: 267
1879..Harrison, Elizabeth 21: 135
1879..Howe, Charles S. 15: 259
1879..Morgan, James H. .... B: 355
1880..Dix, J. Augustus 5: 306
1880..Hurst, S. Grant 24: 238
1880..Keyes, Charles H. 20: 386
1880..McCormick, Samuel B. ...24: 141
1880..Minot, Charles S. 6: 112
1880..Morrissey, Andrew 13: 327
1880..Redway, Jacques W. 4: 235
1880..Schurman, Jacob G. 4: 478
1880..Sutton, William S. 21: 436
1880..Tucker, William J. 24: 242
1881..Beardshear, William M. ..12: 291
1881..Cooley, Mortimer E. ..... A: 511
1881..Evans, Lawton B. .... B: 326
1881..Forbes, George M. 26: 65
1881..Hulbert, Eri B. 11: 67
1881..Joyner, James Y. .... A: 307
1881..McIver, Charles D. 25: 113
1881..Palmer, Thomas W. 20: 136
1881..Small, Albion W. 25: 242
1881..Smith, Henry L. 15: 141
1881..Spence, Clara B. 20: 336
1881..Stewart, William M. 20: 363
1881..Thach, Charles C. 26: 263
1882..Alderman, Edwin A. 23: 38
1882..Claxton, Philander P. 15: 270
1882..Clement, Arthur G. 21: 380
1882..Curme, George O. ...... D: 53
1882..Kincannon, Andrew A. ...15: 326
1882..Larson, Lars Moore 3: 67
1882..Miller, John H. 22: 271
1882..VanHoose, Azor W. 19: 159
1883..Adams, Herbert B. 8: 270
1883..Goodnow, Frank J. .... C: 19
1883..Hart, Albert B. 11: 394
1883..Kieran, James M. 26: 14
1883..Knox, James H. Mason ..11: 243
1884..Collitz, Hermann .... D: 284
1884..Crane, William I. 13: 434
1884..Dewey, John .... A: 547
1884..Kinley, David .... B: 76
1884..McGlothin, William J. ... A: 349
1884..Peabody, Endicott ...... A: 308
1884..Smith, David E. .... B: 21
1885..Allen, Edward E. .... A: 130
1885..Bishop, John R. 7: 187
1885..Bruner, James D. .... A: 402
1885..Butler, Nicholas Murray .. B: 186
1885..Cross, Wilbur L. .... C: 451
1885..Gamage, Frederick L. ...14: 162
1885..Jacoby, Henry S. .... D: 108
1885..Jastrow, Morris 11: 372
1885..Matas, Rudolph .... D: 399
1885..Nollen, John S. .... A: 414
1885..Pratt, Richard H. 13: 89
1885..Shorey, Paul .... C: 36
1885..Sneath, E. Hershey 26: 336
1885..Tufts, James H. 11: 75
1885..VanMeter, John B. 26: 70
1885..Wilson, Woodrow 19: 1
1886..Condon, Randall J. 23: 62
1886..Davidson, William M. 22: 369
1886..Dunning, William A. 19: 27
1886..Eggleston, Joseph D. ..... B: 293
1886..Hatfield, James T. .... A: 226
1886..Schelling, Felix E. .... A: 426
1886..Taussig, Frank W. .... A: 457
1887..Button, Frank C. 25: 389
1887..Capps, Edward .... A: 416
1887..Dabney, Charles W. ..... B: 239
1887..Eastman, Frederick C. ...18: 433
1887..Farrand, Wilson 18: 69
1887..Owen, William Bishop ..23: 66
1888..Baker, George P. 25: 28
1888..Blakely, Gilbert S. 20: 360
1888..Brittain, Marion L. ...... B: 126
1888..Carpenter, George R. 23: 328
1888..Houston, David F. .... A: 38
1888..Lange, Alexis F. 25: 329
1888..Lowes, John L. .... D: 96
1888..Merriam, John C. .... A: 485
1888..Pendleton, Ellen Fitz .... A: 190
1888..Rusby, Henry H. .... A: 172
1888..Warfield, Ethelbert D. 11: 243
1889..Case, Charles O. 24: 25
1889..Crabbe, John G. 19: 43
1889..Finegan, Thomas E. 23: 268
1889..Hewett, Edgar L. .... C: 31
1889..Huber, G. Carl .... D: 274
1889..Kirchwey, George W. ..... B: 466
1890..Barnes, Jasper C. .... A: 484
1890..Benton, Guy P. 15: 171
1890..Bradford, Mary C. C. ... B: 207
1890..Heatwole, Cornelius J. ... A: 489
1890..Mead, William E. 16: 292
1890..Monroe, Paul .... B: 206
1890..Olsen, John C. .... D: 137
1890..Peirce, William F. 8: 138
1890..Roberts, Arthur J. 21: 329
1890..Stagg, Amos A. 18: 199
1890..Trotter, Frank B. .... A: 234
1890..Turneaure, Frederick E. .. A: 215

1890..Wayland, John W. ...... A: 394
1891..Adams, Comfort A. ...... A: 421
1891..Chandler, Julian A. C. ...24: 73
1891..Dinwiddie, Albert B. .... D: 268
1891..Graves, Frank P. .... A: 277
1891..Hibben, John G. 15: 199
1891..Johnson, Franklin W. .... D: 200
1891..Merrifield, Webster 17: 278
1891..Miller, Edwin L. 25: 54
1891..Neilson, William A. ...... A: 286
1891..Newbold, William R. 22: 251
1891..Pattee, Fred L. .... A: 228
1891..Phelps, William Lyon .... A: 375
1891..Priest, Arthur R. .... A: 413
1891..Robinson, James Harvey . C: 28
1891..Rose, Wickliffe .... A: 265
1891..Russell, Claude C. 25: 43
1891..Shipley, Katharine M. ...23: 318
1891..Siebert, Wilbur H. ...... D: 124
1892..Bailey, Edward L. 25: 389
1892..Copeland, Charles T. .... C: 22
1892..Garfield, Harry A. .... A: 102
1892..Henderson, Charles Richmond 11: 75
1892..Hulett, George A. .... A: 224
1892..Johnson, Allen 21: 34
1892..Judson, Harry P. 20: 24
1892..Keppel, Mark 22: 344
1892..Mendel, Lafayette B. 26: 424
1892..Mezes, Sidney E. 15: 206
1892..Osborne, Oliver T. .... D: 447
1892..Penniman, Josiah H. .... D: 104
1892..Richards, Charles R. ..... B: 393
1892..Richardson, Charles H. ...26: 64
1892..Stryker, M. Woolsey 26: 142
1892..Wulling, Frederick J. .... B: 498
1893..Angell, James R. .... B: 5
1893..Farrand, Livingston ..... A: 117
1893..Gill, Wilson L. 4: 90
1893..Lamkin, Nina B. 18: 103
1893..Lindley, Ernest H. .... B: 345
1893..Norlin, George .... A: 320
1893..Pepper, George Wharton . A: 469
1893..Rice, Joseph M. 12: 203
1893..Tucker, William J. 24: 242
1893..Wier, Jeanne E. .... A: 466
1893..Woolman, Mary Schenck . A: 543
1894..Carver, Thomas N. ...... A: 349
1894..Mathews, Edward B. .... A: 365
1894..Pound, Louise .... B: 51
1894..Quinn, Arthur H. .... D: 307
1894..Woodbridge, Frederick J. E. .... D: 301
1895..Baker, Thomas S. .... C: 507
1895..Colvin, George 21: 404
1895..Dodd, William E. .... D: 34
1895..Elliott, Edward C. .... B: 361
1895..Hinitt, Frederick W. 22: 237
1895..Jones, Adam L. 24: 28
1895..Wilson, Harry B. .... A: 160
1895..Wirt, William A. .... A: 138
1896..Abbott, Mather A. 24: 21
1896..Fess, Simeon D. 27:340.. C: 283
1896..Few, William P. 15: 196
1896..Galloway, Lee .... D: 426
1896..Judd, Charles H. .... A: 252
1896..Pearson, Alfred J. .... A: 188
1897..Armstrong, Edward C. ... B: 274
1897..Bacon, Caroline T. 22: 101
1897..Barrows, David P. .... B: 157
1897..Brackett, Byron B. ...... B: 208
1897..French, Calvin H. 25: 298
1897..Fulton, Charles H. .... B: 474
1897..Hopkins, B. Smith .... B: 438
1897..Lowell, A. Lawrence ..... D: 46
1897..MacKenzie, Alexander C. .17: 265
1897..Meiklejohn, Alexander ... A: 406
1897..Murphree, Albert A. ..... C: 144
1897..Perry, Louis C. 22: 345
1897..Spaulding, Frank E. ..... D: 264
1897..Strong, Frank .... B: 217
1897..Suzzallo, Henry 24: 39
1898..Benedict, Harry Y. ...... D: 389
1898..Breasted, James H. ...... B: 377
1898..Carter, Jesse B. 23: 225
1898..Godfrey, Hollis .... A: 283
1898..Kimball, Dexter S. ...... D: 343
1898..Kingsley, Clarence D. 20: 93
1898..Moore, Clifford H. 24: 102
1898..Opie, Eugene L. .... D: 242
1898..Williams, Blanche C. .... B: 183
1899..Bolton, Herbert E. .... A: 204
1899..Comstock, Ada L. .... C: 21
1899..Harper, William A. ...... A: 217
1899..Hazard, Caroline .... C: 501
1899..MacCracken John H. 15: 205
1899..Perry, Lewis .... D: 41
1899..Pound, Roscoe .... B: 51
1899..Snowden, Albert A. 22: 403
1899..Wilbur, Ray Lyman ...... C: 12
1900..Canby, Henry S. .... A: 126
1900..Jackson, Clarence M. .... B: 209
1900..Lylburn, William H. C. ..24: 362
1900..Merriam, Charles E. ..... D: 435
1900..Sieg, Lee P. .... D: 38
1900..Van Dyke, Henry 25: 10
1900..Winslow, Charles-Edward A. .... D: 443
1900..Woolley, Mary E. .... D: 58
1901..Bagley, William C. ...... A: 322
1901..Bestor, Arthur E. .... A: 336
1901..Bogue, Benjamin N. ..... B: 201
1901..Davis, Harvey N. .... A: 348
1901..Gault, Franklin B. 18: 200
1901..Hitchcock, Embury A. ... D: 271
1901..Munro, William B. .... D: 404
1901..Ostrander, Le Roy F. 22: 332
1901..Snavely, Guy E. .... B: 305
1902..Berry, Martha M. .... C: 49
1902..Buttrick, Wallace 22: 419
1902..Hullihen, Walter .... D: 434
1902..Inglis, Alexander J. 23: 54
1902..Long, Joseph R. .... A: 464
1902..Park, Marion E. .... A: 224
1902..Peters, Iva .... A: 549
1902..Reed, Anna Y. .... D: 381
1902..Vinson, Robert E. .... D: 370
1903..Blaisdell, James A. .... A: 213
1903..Blunt, Katharine .... B: 385
1903..Erskine, John .... B: 59
1903..Gates, Caleb F. .... C: 167
1903..Jones, Gilbert H. .... D: 201
1903..Maddox. William A. 25: 291
1903..Mason, Max .... B: 485
1903..Woods, George B. .... B: 137
1904..Burris, Benjamin J. 21: 418
1904..Coffin, Henry S. .... B: 36
1904..Franklin, Lucy J. .... D: 123
1904..Ganfield, William A. ..... B: 176
1904..Hocking, William E. ..... D: 452
1904..Kingsley, Clarence D. 20: 93
1904..Leonard, Robert J. 25: 251
1904..Robinson, David M. ...... A: 221
1904..Rogers, Ernest A. .... A: 195
1905..Chase, Harry W. .... A: 298
1905..Koch, Frederick H. ...... A: 361
1905..Myers, Garry C. .... D: 146
1905..Patterson, Ernest M. .... D: 298
1905..Strayer, George D. .... A: 337
1905..Wolbach, Simon B. ...... D: 197
1906..Archer, Gleason L. 16: 289
1906..Frankfurter, Felix .... D: 28
1906..Holloway, Emory .... A: 363
1906..Pease, Arthur S. .... A: 463
1906..Splawn, Walter M. W. ... B: 365
1907..Coffman, Lotus D. .... C: 241
1907..Graves, Marion C. .... D: 353
1907..Mendell, Clarence W. .... D: 94
1907..Reilly, Marion 26: 404
1907..Robinson, Frederick B. ... C: 115
1907..Tigert, John J. .... D: 428
1908..Chapman, Charles E. .... A: 128
1908..Currier, Richard D. ...... B: 335
1908..Flexner, Abraham .... D: 61
1908..Good, John W. .... A: 441
1908..Hetzel, Ralph D. .... B: 349
1908..MacCracken, Henry N. .. D: 238
1908..Merriam, Harold G. ..... D: 272
1908..Mierow, Charles C. ...... D: 442
1909..Bender, Harold H. ...... D: 309
1909..Foster, William T. 15: 300
1909..Irwin, Robert B. .... D: 400
1909..Jacobson, Carl Alfred .... A: 301
1909..McConaughy, James L. .. B: 424
1909..Seymour, Charles .... D: 431
1910..Cutten, George B. .... D: 263
1910..Woods, Albert F. .... B: 467
1911..Gildersleeve, Virginia C. . A: 181
1911..Graham, Frank P. .... D: 409
1911..Harvey, Samuel C. .... D: 395
1911..Shenton, Herbert N. ..... D: 412
1912..Brown, Philip M. .... A: 222
1912..James, Herman G. .... D: 287
1912..Thurber, Clarence H. .... D: 258
1913..Little, Clarence C. .... B: 205
1913..Weaver, Rufus W. .... A: 453
1914..Dodds, Harold W. .... D: 59
1914..Gaines, Francis P. ...... D: 302
1915..Barbour, Clarence A. .... A: 283
1915..Bayne-Jones, Stanhope .. D: 276
1915..Blodgett, Frank D. ...... D: 252
1915..Haas, Francis J. .... D: 34
1915..Marvin, Cloyd H. .... D: 377
1916..Conant, James B. .... D: 48
1916..Hopkins, Ernest M. ...... A: 119
1916..Norton, Arthur H. .... C: 108
1918..Lawrence, Russell E. 25: 307
1918..Rees, Robert I. .... A: 300
1919..Clark, Charles E. .... D: 424
1919..Day, Frank P. .... C: 37
1919..Frank, Glenn .... C: 454
1919..Sykes, Richard E. .... A: 250
1920..Hutchins, William J. .... D: 368
1920..Morgan, Arthur E. ...... B: 15
1921..Howe, Henry V. .... D: 398
1921..Kefauver, Grayson, N. .. D: 299
1923..Clothier, Robert C. ...... D: 427
1923..Dennett, Tyler .... D: 429
1925..Chace, S. Howard 25: 93
1925..Hutchins, Robert M. ...... C: 54
1926..Marsh, Daniel L. .... A: 133
1927..Holt, Hamilton .... D: 273
1927..Oxnam, G. Bromley ...... A: 452

Electrical Engineers

1731..Franklin, Benjamin 1: 328
1740..Hopkinson, Thomas 7: 249
1746..Kinnersley, Ebenezer 1: 532
1801..Hare, Robert 5: 398
1811..Morse, Samuel F. B. 4: 449
1817..Dana, James F. 10: 390
1826..Henry, Joseph 3: 405
1831..Saxton, Joseph 9: 220
1832..Jackson, Charles T. 3: 97
1836..Vail, Alfred 4: 450
1839..Lillie, John H. 9: 512
1840..Locke, John 15: 264
1840..Page, Charles G. 5: 255
1841..Stager, Anson 4: 454
1844..House, Royal E. 12: 279
1844..Rogers, Henry J. 4: 453
1846..Lane, Jonathan H. 3: 275
1847..Farmer, Moses G. 7: 361
1847..Prescott, George B. 5: 279
1850..Phelps, George M. 7: 505
1852..Tinker, Charles A. 2: 144
1854..Field, Cyrus W. 4: 451
1854..Green, Norvin 11: 550
1857..Pope, Franklin L. 7: 414
1860..Brown, Joseph 8: 28
1864..Loomis, Mahlon 25: 80
1865..Gray, Elisha 4: 453
1865..Houston, Edwin J. 13: 359
1865..Ward, George G. 14: 370
1866..Brush, Charles F. 21: 1
1867..Dolbear, Amos E. 9: 414
1869..Carhart, Henry S. 4: 455
1869..Trowbridge, John 23: 53
1869..Westinghouse, George 15: 41
1870..Cross, Charles R. 11: 183
1870..Johnson, Edward H. 6: 258
1870..Mayer, Alfred M. 13: 164
1870..Wright, Arthur W. 13: 348
1871..Avery, Elroy M. 26: 57
1871..Thomson, Elihu .... B: 106
1872..Anthony, William A. 11: 389
1872..Jones, Francis W. 4: 84
1872..Moore, James W. 11: 246
1872..Weston, Edward 5: 176
1873..Tesla, Nikola 6: 500
1874..Bell, Alexander Graham .. 6: 220
1874..Nipher, Francis E. 22: 55
1875..Lockwood, Thomas D. 22: 439
1875..Peckham, William C. 11: 516
1875..Van De Poele, Charles J. .13: 246
1876..Gower, Frederick A. 9: 216
1876..Kennelly, Arthur E. 13: 452
1876..Rowland, Henry A. 11: 25
1876..Scribner, Charles E. 13: 192
1876..Short, Sidney H. 13: 247
1877..Baker, William E. 19: 346
1877..Berliner, Emile 21: 6
1877..Rogers, James H. 21: 464
1877..Stanley, William 24: 394
1878..Sprague, Frank J. 24: 15
1879..Brown, Harold P. .... B: 329
1879..Carty, John J. 23: 36
1879..Case, Willard E. 19: 112
1879..Hammer, William J. 15: 218
1879..Martin, Thomas C. 13: 582
1880..Byllesby, Henry M. 15: 310
1880..Colby, Edward A. 26: 184
1880..Lieb, John W. 13: 284
1880..Pearson, Frederick S. ...18: 123
1881..Acheson, Edward G. 23: 136
1881..Barker, George F. 4: 532
1881..Bradley, Charles S. 15: 82
1881..Crocker, Francis B. 12: 424
1881..Howell, John W. .... B: 503
1881..Hunter, Rudolph M. 25: 22
1881..Soden, Francis H. 16: 100
1882..Hodgkinson, Francis ..... B: 18
1882..Wheeler, Schuyler S. 10: 162
1883..Chamberlain, Jacob C. ...24: 88
1883..Rice, E. Wilbur, Jr. 26: 10

1884..Duncan, Louis 14:145
1884..Hering, Carl 12:349
1884..Mendenhall, Thomas C. ...10:117
1885..Mailloux, Cyprien O. 26:428
1885..Perrine, Frederic A. C. ..19:388
1885..Sargent, Frederick 22:147
1885..Shaver, George F. 4:231
1885..Sheldon, Samuel 14:208
1885..Stott, Henry G. 14:240
1886..Bristol, William H. 26: 26
1886..Fessenden, Reginald A. ..15: 21
1886..Lloyd, Robert McA. 18: 83
1886..Stillwell, Lewis B. 14:520
1887..Jackson, Dugald C. B:357
1887..Scott, Charles F..........13:207
1887..Townley, Calvert 24:340
1887..White, James G. 15:157
1888..Blake, Henry W. 22: 75
1888..Blood, William H. 26: 14
1888..Emmet, William Le R. .. D:413
1888..Ferguson, Louis A. 14:526
1888..Hunting, Fred S. B:403
1888..Keller, Emil E. D:406
1888..Lamme, Benjamin G. ....20: .36
1889..Arnold, Bion J. B:456
1889..Farrand, Dudley 24:160
1889..Hale, Irving 6:174
1889..Langley, John W. 15: 8
1889..Leonard, H. Ward 15: 3
1890..Adams, Comfort A. A:421
1890..Comstock, Louis K. 14:129
1890..Marks, Louis B. 15: 72
1890..Mershon, Ralph D. 15:225
1890..Stone, John S. 14:106
1891..Alexander, Harry 23:176
1891..Davis, Harry P. 25: 17
1891..Dunn, Gano S. 18:105
1891..Jenks, John S. 24:188
1892..Berresford, Arthur W. ... A:378
1892..Caldwell, Eugene W. 18:197
1892..Doane, Samuel E. 16:324
1892..Gotshall, William C. 26: 38
1892..Munger, Edwin T. 16:403
1892..Rohrer, Albert L. D:240
1892..Sinclair, Henry H. 15:257
1892..Steinmetz, Charles P. 23: 94
1893..Codman, John S. A:382
1893..Moody, Walter S. C:325
1893..Russel, Edgar 20: 31
1894..Pupin, Michael 26: 5
1895..Junkersfeld, Peter 22:348
1895..Lincoln, Paul M. B:280
1895..Swain, George R. C:371
1896..Baldwin, George P. 25: 13
1896..Bond, Charles O. 19:237
1897..Brackett, Byron B. B:208
1897..Deeds, Edward A. A:327
1897..Harper, John L. 20:395
1897..James, Henry D. D:364
1898..Barclay, John C. 26:178
1898..Hewitt, Peter C. 14:470
1898..Rice, Calvin W. 25: 35
1899..Clark, Walter G. 14:261
1899..DeForest, Lee .... A: 18
1899..Eveleth, Charles E. 24:105
1899..Lunn, Ernest C:430
1899..Magnusson, C. Edward ... C:353
1900..Curtis, Augustus D. 23: 15
1900..Squier, George O. 24:320
1900..Therrell, Daniel M. B:422
1900..Underhill, Charles R. A:135
1901..Alexanderson, Ernst F. W. A: 30
1901..Sharp, Clayton H. C:299
1902..Faccioli, Giuseppe 24: 81
1902..Jewett, Frank B. C:272
1903..Cherry, Louis B. C:446
1903..Kintner, Samuel M. D:374
1905..Lee, William S. 24:155
1905..Peek, Frank W. 24:289
1906..Kelly, William D:300
1907..Weagant, Roy A. C:349
1908..Karapetoff, Vladimir N. .. D:176
1908..Nexsen, Randolph H. D:139
1908..Shepherd, Claude H. B:350
1909..Doherty, Robert E. B:271
1910..Leland, George H. D:120
1910..Lincoln, Edwin S. D:225
1911..Chaffee, E. Leon B:376
1911..McAllister, Addams S. ...15: 75
1911..Sarnoff, David B:162
1911..Schuchardt, Rudolph F. ..25:118
1912..Condon, Edward J. B:338
1913..Garland, Claude M. A:224
1913..Longoria, Antonio .... D: 96
1914..Field, Crosby B:224
1918..Fuller, Leonard F. B:216

Engineers

See also Aëronautic, Civil, Electrical, Hydraulic, Mechanical, Military, Mining and Metallurgical, and Marine Engineers.

Engravers

1670..Foster, John 22:345
1730..Pelham, Peter 6:467
1750..Copley, John S. 6:467
1774..Peale, Charles W. 6:358
1775..Doolittle, Amos 11:146
1780..Rollinson, William 7:523
1787..Dunlap, William 6:501
1796..Earle, James 11:147
1796..Saint-Memin, Fevert de ..18:143
1798..Anderson, Alexander 6:259
1800..Birch, Thomas 12:269
1800..Birch, William 12:269
1800..Trenchard, Edward 10:127
1804..Kneass, William 25:141
1805..Charles, William 22:241
1806..Kearny, Francis 24:240
1811..Childs, Cephas G. 22:232
1812..Durand, Asher B. 4:408
1812..Maverick, Peter 4:408
1814..Perkins, Jacob 10:123
1816..Gobrecht, Christian 12:145
1816..Hill, John 23:299
1817..Goodman, Charles 23:305
1817..Jocelyn, Nathaniel 25:419
1818..Neagle, John 5:326
1818..Otis, Bass 21:216
1819..Barber, John W. 3:215
1820..Longacre, James B. 25:365
1821..Danforth, Moseley I. 22:356
1823..Andrews, Joseph 11: 77
1827..Sartain, John 6:472
1829..Clay, Edward W. 22:173
1829..Smillie, James 2:368
1830..Johnston, David C. 5:519
1830..Smillie, William C. 2:377
1832..Casilear, John W. 12:271
1832..Cheney, John 19:359
1832..Cheney, Seth W. 9:170
1832..Edson, Tracy R. 19:394
1836..Burt, Charles 12:386
1836..Chapman, John G. 7:460
1837..Lossing, Benson J. 4:324
1840..Jones, Alfred 12:386
1840..Kensett, John F. 7:560
1840..Leslie, Frank 3:370
1843..Avery, Samuel P. 1:157
1843..Orr, Nathaniel 11:426
1847..Linton, William J. 8: 13
1848..Darley, Felix O. C. 2:334
1848..Marshall, William E. 7:460
1851..Oertel, Johannes A. 7:466
1852..Smillie William M. 2:155
1853..Smillie, James D. 10:367
1858..Goodall, Albert G. 18:388
1859..Keith, William 13:168
1860..Whitehouse, James H. 4:169
1864..Kruell, Gustav 11:144
1865..Drake, Alexander W. 6: 10
1866..Juengling, Frederick 11:195
1866..Kingsley, Elbridge 13:112
1866..Sartain, Emily 13:326
1867..Foote, Mary Hallock 6:471
1868..Sartain, William 13:326
1869..Barber, Charles E. 16:182
1869..Tiffany, Louis C. 7:465
1870..French, Frank 11:301
1871..Wolf, Henry 10:376
1872..French, Edwin D. 14: 44
1873..Kelly, James Edward 11:494
1873..Lee, Homer 5:439
1875..Cole, Timothy .... C. 329
1875..Moran, Peter 11:303
1880..Barnard, William S. 12:434
1880..Closson, William B. P. ... 8:431
1881..Sandham, Henry 6:475
1882..Lander, Benjamin 9: 54
1890..Comstock, Anna B. 22: 11
1894..Rosenthal, Max 20: 86

Entomologists

1808..Kirtland, Jared P. 11:347
1815..Rafinesque, Constantine S. 8:472
1821..Hentz, Nicholas M. 9:428
1835..Fitch, Asa 7:252
1837..Haldeman, Samuel S. 9:246
1841..Herrick, Edward C. 11:170
1845..Le Conte, John L. 11:106
1848..Lintner, Joseph A. 5:260
1853..Glover, Townend 23:209
1853..Taylor, Charlotte 2:164
1858..Cresson, Ezra Townesnd 23:225
1860..Horn, George H. 7:502
1860..Strecker, Herman 10:317
1862..Bassett, Homer F. 6:481
1864..Riley, Charles V. 9:443
1866..Snow, Francis H. 9:494
1867..Hagen, Hermann A. 5:225
1867..Verrill, Addison E. 21: 52
1868..Robinson, Coleman T. 21:189
1869..Emerton, James H. 22: 90
1869..Kellicott, David S. 13:299
1869..Packard, Alpheus S. 3:102
1869..Thomas, Cyrus 13:528
1870..Grote, Augustus R. 22: 74
1870..Smith, John B. 15: 71
1871..Fernald, Charles H. 9:232
1873..McCook, Henry C. 4:131
1874..Comstock, John H. 22: 10
1875..Webster, Francis M. 13:603
1876..Uhler, Philip R. 8:250
1878..Howard, Leland O. 12:356
1879..Ashmead, William H. 20:113
1879..Comstock, Anna B. 22: 11
1879..Osborn, Herbert 13:202
1879..Trelease, William 11:212
1880..Barnard, William S. 12:434
1880..Bruner, Lawrence 13:232
1880..Dury, Charles 24:339
1881..Chittenden, Frank H. 24:384
1882..Emerton, James H. 22: 90
1882..Forbes, Stephen A. 22:291
1885..Good, Adolphus C. 23: 61
1885..Knab, Frederick 24:188
1886..Marlatt, Charles L. 13:186
1886..Perkins, George H. 10:309
1886..Scudder, Samuel H. 24:180
1887..Gillette, Clarence P. 13:407
1887..Peckham, George W. 12:346
1889..Holland, William J. 13:141
1890..Fernald, Henry T. 18:362
1890..Hopkins, Andrew D. 13:185
1890..Kellogg, Vernon L. A:208
1890..Slingerland, Mark V. 13:315
1891..Felt, Ephraim P. 12:330
1891..Kunze, Richard E. 3:504
1893..Aldrich, John M. A:254
1893..Calvert, Philip P. 12:335
1894..Skinner, Henry 21:139
1895..Ball, Elmer D. 18:263
1896..Hunter, Walter D. 21:155
1897..Dyar, Harrison G. 14: 97
1898..Parrott, Percival J. A:309
1898..Sanderson, Dwight A:251
1901..Britton, Wilton E. A:260
1904..Patch, Edith M. 18:408
1912..McColloch, James W. ...23:389
1913..Gunder, Jeane D. C:290
1913..Hood, J. Douglas D:387

Ethnologists

See Anthropologists and Ethnologists

Explorers and Pioneers

1492..Columbus, Christopher ... 3:436
1497..Cabot, Sebastian 7: 62
1499..Vespucius, Americus 3:149
1510..Balboa, Vasco N. de 5:431
1513..Ponce de Leon, Juan 11:335
1519..Magellan, Ferdinand 6:249
1527..Cabeza De Vaca, Alvar N. 25:438
1539..De Soto, Fernando 5:126
1565..Menendez, Pedro 11:164
1567..Drake, Sir Francis 9:284
1584..Raleigh, Sir Walter 7:221
1585..Hariot, Thomas 7:162
1602..Gosnold, Bartholomew 12:186
1606..Gorges, Sir Ferdinando .. 5:166
1607..Hudson, Henry 9:453
1607..Smith, John 13:378
1609..De La Warr, Lord 13:380
1610..Strachey, William 8:194
1614..Block, Adriæn 10:295
1619..Blackstone, William 8:197
1619..Pory, John 8:416
1620..Alden, John 10:295
1620..Bradford, William 7:368
1620..Brewster, William 7: 30
1620..Carver, John 7:367
1620..Standish, Miles 5:417
1620..Winslow, Edward 7:369
1622..Morton, Thomas 7:350
1623..Conant, Roger R. 11:362

1623..Maverick, Samuel 8:414
1625..Claiborne, William 11:421
1625..Minuit, Peter 12:208
1629..Waterman, Richard 8:198
1629..Willett, Thomas 8: 38
1630..Clap, Roger 8: 76
1630..Coddington, William 10: 1
1630..Colby, Anthony 11:129
1630..Conyers, Edward 8:144
1630..Hawthorne, William 8:422
1630..Johnson, Isaac 12:334
1630..Pynchon, William 7:355
1630..Underhill, John 1:415
1630..Van Curler, Arendt 4:507
1630..Winthrop, John 6:201
1631..Almy, William 9:194
1631..Spencer, William 5:405
1631..Williams, Roger 10: 4
1632..Coggeshall, John 10: 2
1633..Calvert, Cecil 7:331
1633..Calvert, Leonard 7:332
1633..Herman, Augustin 4:509
1633..Parker, Thomas 12:249
1633..Wilbur, Samuel 12:384
1634..Cudworth, James 9:449
1634..Easton, Nicholas 10: 3
1634..Hutchinson, William 10: 1
1634..Scott, Richard 11:206
1635..Bulkley, Peter 7:486
1635..Mason, John 4:136
1635..Poole, Edward 7:257
1635..Sedgwick, Robert 2:181
1635..Whitney, John 10:154
1636..Hooker, Thomas 6:279
1636..Wheelwright, John 1:232
1637..Eaton, Theophilus 6:121
1637..Hopkins, Edward 10:319
1637..Pole, Elizabeth 4:549
1638..Newman, Samuel 8: 10
1638..Verplank, Gulian 11:345
1638..Wentworth, William 5:149
1639..Jackson, John 11:323
1639..Treat, Robert 10:323
1640..Ward, John 12:204
1641..Melyn, Cornelis 10:221
1641..Van Der Donck, Adriaen .12:205
1642..Coffin, Tristram 6:258
1643..Keen, George 11:367
1649..Stone, William 7:333
1651..Fitch, Thomas 10:327
1655..Vanderheyden, Dirk 12:204
1656..Zadkin, Daniel 2: 58
1658..Alsop, George 8:202
1658..Bourne, Richard 12:345
1665..Yeamans, Sir John 12:151
1668..Marquette, Jacques 12:220
1669..Jolliet, Louis 5:121
1669..West, Joseph 12:151
1670..La Salle, Robert, Sieur de 5:125
1671..Culpepper, John 12:223
1678..DuLuth, Daniel De G. 4: 62
1681..Penn, John 2:276
1681..Penn, Richard 2:276
1681..Penn, William 2:274
1682..Pusey, Cabel 10:447
1682..Trent, William 12:150
1683..Pastorius, Francis D. 11:352
1699..Byrd, William 7:247
1699..Le Moyne, Jean Baptist .. 5:491
1699..Le Moyne, Peter 5:121
1702..Cadillac, Antoine de la M. 5:172
1707..Haywood, John 4:324
1709..DeGraffenried, Christopher 13:363
1713..Moore, Maurice 10:452
1716..Shute, Samuel 7:374
1718..Lynch, Charles 11:231
1725..Read, John 6:185
1725..Shipley, William 12:371
1730..Brickell, John 7:278
1733..Oglethorpe, James 1:490
1734..Cosby, William 12: 5
1735..Neisser, George 5:441
1735..Sergeant, John 1:479
1736..Nitschmann, David 5:199
1736..Robinson, Samuel 1:473
1740..Faneuil, Peter 1:441
1750..Borden, Joseph 13:428
1753..Sharpe, Horatio 7:337
1753..Von Stiegel, Henrich W. .11:197
1754..Stevenson, John 12:374
1760..Cooper, William 4:545
1760..Marschall, Frederic W. von 2:447
1762..Harris, John 12:556
1763..Chouteau, Pierre 13:469
1763..Liguest, Pierre L. 13:468
1766..Carver, Jonathan 1:476
1768..Filson, John 10:314
1769..Boone, Daniel 3:110
1769..Durkee, John 12:234
1769..Serra, Junipero 12:134
1769..Zane, Ebenezer 11: 90
1770..Girty, Simon 2:437
1770..Robertson, Charlotte R. .. 2:221
1772..Maclay, William 5:143
1772..Sevier, John 3:430
1773..Harrod, James 12:283
1773..McAfee, James 3:521
1773..Painter, Gamaliel 12:105
1775..Martin, Joseph 7:239
1775..Patterson, Robert 10:469
1776..Clark, George Rogers 1: 82
1777..Kenton, Simon 3:527
1778..Ledyard, John 5:122
1780..Allen, John 6:253
1780..Ballard, Bland W. 5:124
1781..Lockwood, James B. 3:286
1781..Martin, William 7:240
1783..Lyon, Matthew 2:426
1783..Winchester, James 4: 60
1785..Bigelow, Timothy 5:422
1785..Dubuque, Julien 8:459
1786..Webster, Ephraim 4:348
1787..Leonard, Joseph 12:257
1787..Symmes, John C. 11:452
1787..White, James 11:556
1788..Gray, Robert 5:121
1789..Ellicott, Andrew 13:470
1789..Ellicott, Joseph 13:471
1789..Hendy, John 12:236
1790..Reed, Seth 13:473
1794..Thibodaux, Henry S. 10: 75
1795..Atwater, Amzi 6: 21
1795..Juneau, Solomon 6: 18
1795..Massie, Nathaniel 2:439
1796..Carter, Lorenzo 3:298
1796..Cleveland, Moses 6:257
1796..Kingsbury, James 5:181
1797..Hillman, James 11:523
1798..Perkins, Simon 10: 56
1799..Cass, Lewis 5: 3
1799..Demint, James 12:232
1800..Rochester, Nathaniel 9:485
1802..Kilbourne, James 5:123
1803..Longworth, Nicholas 11:339
1803..Rapp, George 4:353
1804..Clark, William 12:301
1804..Lewis, Meriwether 5:122
1804..McNair, Alexander 12:302
1805..Pike, Zebulon M. 2:516
1805..Sibley, George C. 2: 28
1809..Robidoux, James 12:215
1815..Bowie, James 4:210
1815..Coquillard, Alexis 11: 76
1815..Wright, Benjamin 1:182
1816..Flower, George 6:153
1816..Plumb, Joseph 12:454
1818..Lane, Joseph 8: 2
1818..Long, Stephen H. 11:365
1819..Palmer, Nathaniel B. 25: 79
1820..Austin, Moses 5:157
1820..Conway, James S. 10:184
1820..Doty, James D. 12: 72
1820..Ralston, Alexander 12:216
1820..Schoolcraft, Henry R. 5:145
1821..De Smet, Peter J. 11:453
1821..McLoughlin, John 6:390
1823..Sealsfield, Charles 2:193
1825..Royce, J. B. 4:509
1825..Smith, Erastus 2:108
1826..Comstock, Addison J. 1:201
1830..Campbell, Sidney S. 12:348
1830..McCarver, Morton 4:548
1830..Shipherd, John J. 2:459
1831..Bonneville, Benjamin L.E.12:264
1831..Sherman, Sidney 2:130
1832..Bridger, James 13:428
1832..Walker, Joseph R. 5:425
1832..Wyeth, Nathaniel J. 6: 73
1833..Cobb, Silas B. 4:547
1833..Le Claire, Antoine 12:554
1834..Blake, Thatcher 11: 77
1834..Parker, Samuel 7:246
1834..Sutter, John A. 4:191
1835..Horner, John S. 5:271
1835..Whitman, Marcus 11:112
1836..Crockett, David 4: 85
1836..Green, Thomas J. 11:510
1836..Reed, Harrison 11:380
1837..Hebard, Alfred 12:221
1837..Robinson, Edward 2:242
1838..Allen, Samuel Louis 9:428
1838..Frémont, John C. 4:270
1838..Radcliff, Jacob 13:471
1838..Rudd, Anson 1:478
1839..Scranton, George W. 9:138
1839..Stephens, John L. 5:424
1839..Wilkes, Charles 2:105
1840..Lovejoy, Asa Lawrence ..12: 99
1841..Bidwell, John 3:531
1841..Weber, Charles M. 7:455
1842..Castro, Henry 3:268
1842..Kane, Elisha K. 3:288
1843..Hart, Ossian B. 11:380
1844..Marshall, James W. 5:146
1846..Jones, Alfred D. 12:421
1848..Burnett, Peter H. 4:105
1849..Bigler, John 4:106
1849..Broderick, David C. 4:185
1849..Coleman, William T. 8:336
1849..Conness, John 11:369
1849..Downey, John G. 4:108
1849..Fair, James G. 11:189
1849..Haggin, James B. A. 19:213
1849..Haun, Henry P. 11:369
1849..Hearst, George F. 1:315
1849..Hopkins, Mark 20: 49
1849..Huntington, Collis P. 15: 15
1849..McDougall, John 4:106
1849..Phelan, James 8:478
1849..Rogers, John 6:496
1849..Stevens, John H. 12:361
1849..Tevis, Lloyd 8: 66
1849..Williams, William 12:498
1850..Hall, Charles F. 3:281
1850..Hayes, Isaac I. 3:280
1852..Byers, William N. 13:514
1852..Stanford, Leland 2:128
1852..Stuart, Granville 12:123
1853..Lander, Frederick W. 8:127
1854..Anthony, Daniel R. 6:365
1855..Montgomery, James 8:301
1855..Muir, John 9:449
1856..Stevenson, James 12:556
1859..Kennicott, Robert 24:406
1863..Pumpelly, Raphael 6:359
1865..De Long, George W. 3:282
1867..Butler, James D. 9:190
1867..Greely, Adolphus W. 3:285
1867..Orton, James 11:280
1867..Powell. John W. 3:340
1868..Stanley, Henry M. 4:233
1869..Pavy, Octave P. 7:534
1870..Ober, Frederick A. 13:311
1870..Thomas, William W. 2:132
1871..Nindemann, William F. C. 3:284
1873..Glover, James N. 7:292
1873..Melville, George W. 3:283
1874..Chaillé-Long, Charles 10: 28
1876..Glazier, Willard 5:284
1878..Danenhower, John W. ... 3:284
1878..Gilder, William H. 3:287
1878..Schwatka, Frederick 3:285
1881..Brainard, David L. 3:286
1886..Heilprin, Angelo 12:381
1886..Peary, Robert E. 14: 60
1890..Davis, Henry G. 10:468
1891..Bryant, Henry G. 25:359
1891..Cook, Frederick A. 13:338
1895..Smith, A. Donaldson 13:608
1898..Birch, Stephen 15:393
1901..Ellsworth, Lincoln .... B: 38
1901..Huntington, Ellsworth ... A:510
1904..Stefansson, Vilhjalmur ... A:230
1905..Akeley, Carl E. 26:130
1906..Bingham, Hiram .... A: 28
1908..MacMillan, Donald B. B:476
1909..Andrews, Roy Chapman .. A:302
1910..Rainey, Paul J. 19:411
1914..Roosevelt, Theodore 14: 1
1917..Griscom, Ludlow B:300
1923..McDonald, Eugene F. ... D:202
1925..Byrd, Richard E., Jr. B:431
1925..Roosevelt, Theodore, Jr. .. D: 64

Foresters

1860..Minier, George W. 12:186
1870..Sargent, Charles S. 26: 78
1873..Appleton, Francis H. 12:231
1873..Davey, John 22: 70
1873..Hough, Franklin B. 13:340
1873..Warder, John A. 4:536
1876..Northrop, Birdsey G. 10:225
1878..Pack, Charles L. A:408
1882..Egleston, Nathaniel H. ...13:340
1883..Fernow, Bernhard E. 19:166
1886..Sudworth, George B. 14:195
1887..Roth, Filibert 21:146
1889..Vanderbilt, George W. ... 6:213
1890..Pettigrew, Richard F. 2:202
1891..Pinchot, Gifford 14: 30
1893..Rothrock, Joseph T. 19:180
1896..Graves, Henry S. A:479
1897..Lukens, Theodore P. 18:282
1899..Allen, Edward Tyson 18: 27
1899..Schwarz, George F. 22:394

1901..Pettis, Clifford R. 20: 364
1903..Woolsey, T. Salisbury 26: 340
1904..Dunlap, Frederick .... A: 493
1906..Stuart, Robert Y. 25: 156
1907..Dana, Samuel T. .... C: 163
1908..Moore, Barrington 18: 17

Geographers and Hydrographers

1749..Evans, Lewis 11: 427
1770..Hutchins, Thomas 9: 267
1777..De Witt, Simeon 3: 215
1777..Erskine, Robert 24: 404
1784..Morse, Jedidiah 13: 353
1817..Worcester, Joseph E. 6: 50
1839..Guyot, Arnold 4: 448
1841..Robinson, Edward 2: 242
1850..Paine, William H. 21: 242
1863..Davidson, George 7: 227
1869..Haupt, Lewis M. 13: 233
1871..Gannett, Henry 19: 207
1872..Russell, Israel C. 10: 306
1873..Baker, Marcus 11: 251
1879..Welker, Philip A. 21: 325
1880..Adams, Cyrus C. .... D: 288
1882..Stejneger, Leonhard 14: 130
1883..Newell, Frederick H. 13: 283
1885..Davis, William M. 24: 32
1888..Keith, Arthur .... C: 475
1889..Goode, John P. 23: 386
1890..Dodge, Richard E. 13: 549
1890..Ward, Robert De C. 24: 190
1891..Bryant, Henry G. 25: 359
1892..Brigham, Albert P. 24: 281
1896..Semple, Ellen C. .... A: 389
1896..Tarr, Ralph S. 10: 311
1897..Huntington, Ellsworth ... A: 510
1898..Brooks, Alfred H. 22: 298
1899..Gregory, Herbert E. ..... A: 395
1899..Grosvenor, Gilbert H. ..... A: 309
1901..Johnson, Douglas .... D: 177
1902..Adams, Charles C. .... A: 448
1903..Wissler, Clark .... B: 257
1904..Stefansson, Vilhjalmur ... A: 230
1906..Bingham, Hiram .... A: 28
1907..Fenneman, Nevin M. .... D: 304
1908..Dryer, Charles R. 23: 107
1908..Ruthven, Alexander G. ... C: 95
1914..Jones, E. Lester 26: 24
1915..Carney, Frank .... C: 388

Geologists

1769..Robertson, James 2: 221
1806..Silliman, Benjamin 2: 385
1809..Maclure, William 13: 368
1810..Troost, Gerard 7: 349
1815..Emerson, Benjamin K. ...12: 316
1815..Lea, Isaac 6: 23
1815..VanRensselaer, Jeremiah . 7: 525
1817..Eaton, Amos 5: 312
1819..Cooper, Thomas 11: 31
1819..Vanuxem, Lardner 8: 385
1821..Hitchcock, Edward 5: 308
1826..Emmons, Ebenezer 8: 477
1826..Mitchell, Elisha 7: 30
1827..Gibbes, Robert W. 11: 36
1827..Jackson, Charles T. 3: 97
1827..Lapham, Increase A. 8: 34
1827..Owen, David D. 8: 113
1828..Houghton, Douglas 5: 512
1828..Rogers, William B. 7: 410
1829..Mather, William W. 8: 146
1830..Rogers, Henry D. 7: 543
1830..Taylor, Richard C. 9: 265
1831..Metcalfe, Samuel L. 5: 518
1832..Agassiz, Louis 2: 360
1833..Dana, James D. 6: 206
1834..Alexander, John H. 9: 192
1834..Bailey, Jacob W. 10: 157
1834..Ducatel, Julius T. 4: 544
1834..Percival, James G. 8: 306
1835..Clingman, Thomas L. 7: 199
1836..Adams, Charles B. 5: 311
1836..Haldeman, Samuel S. 9: 246
1836..Hall, James 3: 280
1836..Hodge, James T. 4: 548
1836..Johnson, Walter R. 12: 260
1836..Worthen, Amos H. 6: 20
1837..Foster, John W. 10: 169
1837..Kirtland, Jared P. 11: 347
1840..Boynton, John F. 4: 91
1840..Buckley, Samuel B. 5: 23
1840..Condon, Thomas 13: 280
1840..Tuomey, Michael 13: 95
1840..Whitney, Josiah D. 9: 120
1841..Shumard, Benjamin F. .. 8: 256
1842..Cox, Edward T. 12: 328
1843..Hilgard, Julius E. 10: 118
1845..Marcou, Jules 25: 74
1845..Thompson, Zadoc 6: 188
1847..Hunt, T. Sterry 3: 254
1848..Lesquereux, Leo 9: 438
1848..Meek, Fielding B. 11: 284
1848..Safford, James M. 8: 228
1848..Winchell, Alexander 16: 119
1850..Davidson, George 7: 227
1850..LeConte, Joseph 7: 231
1851..Lieber, Oscar M. 13: 170
1851..Newberry, John S. 9: 235
1852..Blake, William P. 25: 202
1852..Dyer, Charles B. 4: 528
1852..Hanks, Henry G. 13: 129
1853..Cook, George H. 6: 304
1853..Hayden, Ferdinand V. ...11: 97
1853..Ruffner, William H. 12: 526
1854..Cutting, Hiram A. 10: 204
1854..Hovey, Horace C. 15: 545
1856..Lesley, J. Peter 8: 79
1856..Orton, James 11: 280
1856..Whitfield, Robert P. 5: 92
1856..Young, Augustus 3: 506
1857..Broadhead, Garland C. ..13: 225
1857..Hager, Albert D. 3: 224
1857..Hitchcock, Charles H. 12: 342
1858..Hilgard, Eugene W. 10: 308
1858..Kimball, James P. 11: 91
1858..Lyman, Benjamin S. 9: 217
1859..Hague, James D. 23: 164
1859..Powell, John W. 3: 340
1860..Hartt, Charles F. 11: 260
1860..Julien, Alexis A. 18: 40
1861..Packard, Alpheus S. 3: 102
1862..Brigham, William T. 16: 294
1863..Dall, William H. 10: 454
1863..King, Clarence 13: 248
1863..Pumpelly, Raphael 6: 359
1863..Smock, John C. 11: 560
1863..Uhler, Philip R. 8: 250
1864..Carll, John F. 12: 361
1864..Kerr, Washington C. 7: 450
1864..Rice, William N. 12: 264
1864..Shaler, Nathaniel S. 9: 315
1865..Dwight, William B. 10: 491
1866..Brooks, Thomas B. 3: 510
1866..Davis, William Jonathan .13: 22
1866..Marsh, Othniel C. 9: 318
1866..White, Charles A. 6: 231
1867..Emmons, Samuel F. 10: 448
1867..Hague, Arnold 3: 225
1867..Hyatt, Alpheus 23: 362
1868..Muir, John 9: 449
1869..Frazer, Persifor 4: 286
1869..Newton, Henry 4: 190
1869..Stevenson, John J. 7: 137
1869..Winchell, Newton H. 7: 451
1870..Campbell, John T. 12: 397
1870..Cope, Edward D. 7: 474
1870..Derby, Orville A. 10: 460
1870..Perkins, George H. 10: 309
1870..Wright, George F. 7: 66
1871..Chapin, James H. 10: 202
1871..Gilbert, Grove K. 13: 46
1871..Niles, William H. 12: 481
1873..Chamberlin, Thomas C. ..19: 25
1873..Holmes, William H. 16: 441
1873..Orton, Edward 24: 106
1873..Wadsworth, Marshman E. 13: 538
1874..Ashburner, Charles A. 11: 54
1874..Bastin, Edson S. 5: 351
1874..Branner, John C. 24: 278
1874..Calvin, Samuel 13: 182
1874..Fairchild, Herman Leroy .13: 527
1874..Killebrew, Joseph B. 8: 308
1874..Platt, Franklin 5: 181
1874..Spencer, Joseph W. W. ..14: 282
1874..Upham, Warren 7: 127
1875..Becker, George F. 20: 272
1875..Brownell, Walter A. 2: 111
1875..Comstock, Theodore B. ...13: 450
1875..Crump, Malcolm H. 2: 183
1875..Dutton, Clarence E. 13: 297
1875..McGee, W J 10: 349
1875..Russell, Israel C. 10: 306
1875..White, Israel C. 18: 164
1876..Bailey, Gilbert E. 22: 110
1876..Crosby, William O. 22: 328
1876..Davis, William M. 24: 32
1876..Hay, Oliver P. 22: 31
1876..Walcott, Charles D. 22: 135
1877..Lewis, Henry C. 5: 181
1877..Shepard, Edward M. 12: 395
1878..Hall, Christopher W. 9: 502
1879..Diller, Joseph S. 3: 514
1879..Hollick, Charles A. 24: 373
1879..Smith, Erminnie A. 13: 183
1879..Smith, Eugene A. 6: 185
1880..Clarke, John M. 19: 456
1880..Cross, Whitman 15: 214
1880..Dumble, Edwin T. 21: 421
1880..Heilprin, Angelo 12: 381
1880..Iddings, Joseph P. 15: 391
1880..Leverett, Frank 10: 473
1880..Merrill, George P. 8: 35
1880..Williams, Henry S. 21: 327
1880..Woodrow, James 11: 35
1881..Claypole, Edward W. 13: 259
1881..Salisbury, Rollin D. 11: 73
1881..Todd, James E. 10: 117
1881..Ward, Lester F. 13: 112
1881..Williams, Edward H., Jr. 24: 22
1881..Yeates, William S. 13: 60
1882..Starr, Frederick 13: 115
1882..Turner, Henry W. 18: 320
1883..Branner, John C. 24: 278
1883..Pearson, Herbert W. 18: 257
1883..Prosser, Charles S. 12: 544
1883..Weed, Walter H. 13: 457
1884..Beecher, Charles E. 13: 564
1884..Herrick, Clarence L. 26: 198
1884..Kemp, James F. 21: 5
1884..Orton, Edward, Jr. 24: 107
1884..Talmadge, James E. 16: 19
1885..Cushing, Henry P. 19: 249
1885..Merrill, Frederick J. H. .13: 293
1886..Grant, Ulysses Sherman ..13: 534
1886..White, David 18: 60
1887..Clark, William Bullock ...18: 191
1887..Hovey, Edmund O. 22: 375
1887..Tarr, Ralph S. 10: 311
1888..Hill, Robert T. 14: 267
1888..Lane, Alfred C. 13: 395
1888..Oldroyd, Tom S. 24: 279
1888..Penrose, Richard A. F.,Jr. 26: 378
1889..Babcock, Earle J. 25: 55
1889..Keyes, Charles R. 13: 144
1889..Pirsson, Louis V. 10: 248
1889..Van Ingen, Gilbert 22: 36
1889..Willard, Daniel E. 13: 343
1889..Winchell, Horace V. 20: 200
1890..Armstrong, Edwin J. 20: 218
1890..Dodge, Richard E. 13: 549
1891..Holmes, Joseph A. 23: 104
1891..Kümmel, Henry B. 14: 280
1891..Mathews, Edward B. ...... A: 365
1892..Fenneman, Nevin M. .... D: 304
1892..Van Hise, Charles R. 19: 19
1893..Woodworth, Jay B. 20: 232
1894..Brooks, Alfred H. 22: 298
1894..Douglass, Earl 26: 126
1894..Weidman, Samuel 13: 220
1895..Jagger, Thomas A. .... C: 150
1895..Keith, Arthur .... C: 475
1895..Richardson, Charles H. ...26: 64
1896..Smith, George O. 14: 130
1897..Berkey, Charles P. .... B: 154
1897..Bickley, Francis D. T. ...20: 483
1897..Buckley, Ernest R. 19: 443
1897..Pratt, Joseph H. .... C: 373
1897..Ransome, Frederick L. ...26: 408
1899..Irving, John D. 23: 267
1900..Day, Arthur L. .... A: 147
1900..Howe, Ernest 25: 246
1900..Wright, Frederick E. ..... A: 550
1901..Cleland, Herdman F. 26: 116
1901..Johnson, Douglas .... D: 178
1901..Louderback, George D. ...17: 426
1901..VanOrstrand, Charles E. . D: 102
1904..Gregory, Herbert E. ..... A: 395
1906..Merwin, Herbert E. ...... D: 360
1907..Lupton, Charles T. 26: 101
1909..Carney, Frank .... C: 388
1910..Fenner, Clarence N. ..... D: 115
1910..Robinson, J. French ..... A: 211
1911..De Golyer, Everette L. ... D: 356
1912..Washington, Henry S. ... C: 520
1915..Jillson, Willard R. .... A: 178
1916..Powers, Sidney 25: 16
1920..Morse, Paul F. 22: 73
1921..Howe, Henry V. .... D: 398
1930..Fuller, Richard E. .... D: 407

Gynecologists and Obstetricians

1803..James, Thomas C. 11: 184
1817..Meigs, Charles D. 6: 390
1820..Atlee, John L. 11: 25
1835..Miller, Henry 12: 229
1835..White, James P. 7: 277
1836..Bedford, Gunning S. 9: 361
1839..Taylor, Isaac E. 9: 353
1840..Byford, William H. 2: 13

1841..Peaslee, Edmund R. 10: 289
1842..Campbell, Henry F. 12: 68
1844..Howard, William T. 12: 316
1845..Barker, Fordyce 4: 157
1848..Bozeman, Nathan 21: 246
1848..Seymour, William P. 4: 210
1849..Cole, Richard B. 7: 288
1849..Sims, J. Marion 2: 356
1851..King, John 15: 258
1852..Reynolds, John P. 12: 216
1852..Thomas, T. Gaillard 26: 49
1853..Atlee, Washington L. 11: 25
1853..Penrose, Richard A. F. 2: 443
1854..Reamy, Thaddeus A. 12: 474
1855..Emmet, Thomas Addis ...10: 286
1855..Gordon, Seth C. 12: 66
1855..Jenks, Edward W. 4: 216
1855..Storer, Horatio R. 11: 337
1856..Smith, Albert H. 25: 62
1857..Battey, Robert 9: 349
1857..Wilson, Henry P. C. 6: 340
1860..Duer, Edward L. 25: 297
1860..Taylor, William H. 5: 330
1860..Wait, Phebe J. B. 2: 451
1861..Hanks, Horace T. 2: 175
1861..Opie, Thomas 12: 188
1862..Clarke, Augustus P. 6: 234
1862..Palmer, Chauncey D. 24: 25
1865..Lusk, William S. 9: 337
1865..Maury, Richard B. 14: 240
1865..Meacham, John G. 16: 132
1865..Seymour, William Pierce . 4: 210
1865..Skene, Alexander J. C. ... 5: 436
1865..Storer, Horatio R. 11: 337
1865..VanDeWarker, Edward E. 12: 187
1866..Hyde, Joel W. 3: 150
1866..Marcy, Henry O. 6: 510
1866..Mundé, Paul F. 12: 272
1866..Sell, Edward H. M. 3: 224
1867..Richardson, William L. ..22: 61
1868..Betts, B. Frank 3: 482
1868..Browne, Bennet B. 19: 79
1868..Johnson, Joseph T. 12: 143
1869..Polk, William M. 26: 256
1870..Dearborn, Brainerd W. ...16: 306
1870..Jackson, Abraham R. 7: 510
1870..Simons, Manning 16: 402
1870..Wylie, W. Gill 1: 471
1871..Chadwick, James R. 12: 368
1871..Engelmann, George J. ...11: 157
1872..Cleveland, Clement 14: 427
1872..Dunning, Lehman H. 14: 279
1872..Hanks, Horace T. 2: 175
1872..Janvrin, Joseph E. 4: 269
1872..Parvin, Theophilus 4: 305
1873..Lewis, Ernest S. 11: 509
1873..Mitchell, J. Nicholas 3: 485
1873..Ostrom, Homer I. 6: 215
1874..Baker, William H. 15: 35
1874..Doering, Edmond J. 16: 111
1874..Reed, Charles A. L. 24: 325
1875..Dudley, Emilius L. 13: 109
1875..Ill, Edward J. 13: 237
1875..Partridge, Edward L. 21: 109
1877..Byford, Henry T. 2: 154
1877..McNutt, Sarah J. 15: 264
1877..Wiggin, Frederick H. 12: 397
1878..Eastman, Joseph 7: 46
1878..Montgomery, Edward E. ..13: 238
1879..Jenks, Edward W. 4: 216
1879..Mann, Matthew D. 10: 34
1879..Rhett, Robert B. 12: 444
1880..Dickinson, Gordon K. 22: 191
1880..Hypes, Benjamin M. 12: 93
1880..Jewett, Charles 13: 238
1880..Newman, Henry P. 16: 76
1881..Carstens, J. Henry 16: 333
1881..Dudley, Augustus P. 2: 205
1881..Green, Charles M. .... A: 316
1881..Reed, Charles A. L. 12: 478
1882..Boldt, Hermann J. .... C: 285
1882..Martin, Franklin H. ..... C: 372
1883..Kelly, Howard A. 15: 210
1883..Miller, Aaron B. 20: 192
1884..Bacon, Charles S. .... C: 178
1884..Mitchell, Giles S. 13: 294
1884..Penrose, Charles B. 20: 459
1885..Baldy, John M. 14: 144
1885..Bovee, John W. 22: 257
1885..Gilliam, David T. 17: 60
1885..Reder, Francis LeS. ..... B: 289
1885..Reynolds, Edward 9: 556
1886..Bonifield, Charles L. 24: 135
1886..Robertson, Samuel E. 6: 372
1886..Sturmdorf, Arnold 25: 228
1887..McGannon, Matthew C. .. 9: 175
1887..Rees, Charles M. 16: 247
1888..Cragin, Edwin B. 15: 189
1888..Williams, J. Whitredge ...25: 187
1890..McMurtry, Lewis S. 13: 280
1891..Clark, John G. 21: 63
1893..Polak, John Osborn 25: 33
1895..Peterson, Reuben .... B: 190
1898..Davis, Edward P. .... A: 440
1899..Hall, Rufus B. 13: 457
1900..Graves, William P. ...... A: 141
1909..Curtis, Arthur H. .... D: 244
1911..Huntington, James L. ... A: 486
1915..DuBose, Francis G. ...... B: 358
1917..Bartholomew, Rudolph A. . B: 151

Historians

1629..Smith, John 13: 378
1650..Bradford, William 7: 368
1669..Morton, Nathaniel 7: 38
1677..Hubbard, William 11: 529
1695..Penhallow, Samuel 8: 349
1727..Colden, Cadwalader 2: 270
1727..Prince, Thomas 7: 144
1738..Callender, John 7: 40
1745..Niles, Samuel 8: 370
1750..Stith, William 3: 232
1757..Smith, William 11: 275
1764..Hutchinson, Thomas 7: 376
1784..Filson, John 10: 314
1785..Ramsay, David 7: 285
1786..Minot, George R. 7: 133
1792..Belknap, Jeremy 7: 204
1797..Trumbull, Benjamin 11: 321
1798..Holmes, Abiel 7: 148
1800..Tucker, George 7: 521
1805..Beverly, Robert 7: 308
1805..Otis, Mercy 7: 177
1811..Bozman, John L. 20: 479
1812..Marshall, Humphrey 2: 368
1820..Watson, John F. 7: 157
1824..Bancroft, George 3: 160
1824..Lee, Henry 25: 303
1826..Willard, Joseph 4: 431
1827..Barber, John W. 3: 215
1829..Field, David D. 4: 236
1830..Logan, Deborah N. 25: 86
1831..Campbell, William W. 11: 445
1832..Hawks, Francis L. 7: 90
1832..Williamson, William D. .. 6: 305
1837..Hildreth, Richard 10: 460
1839..Howe, Henry 3: 344
1840..Hildreth, Samuel P. 9: 554
1841..Thompson, Zadock 6: 188
1842..Schaff, Philip 3: 76
1843..Prescott, William H. 6: 66
1844..Ellis, George E. 8: 18
1845..Ingersoll, Charles J. 7: 141
1845..Motley, John L. 5: 213
1845..Stevens, Henry 11: 318
1845..Willson, Marcius 10: 39
1846..Gayarré, Charles E. A. .. 6: 253
1847..Eliot, Samuel 3: 496
1847..Hoffman, David 7: 129
1847..Lea, Henry C. 23: 17
1847..Parkman, Francis 1: 431
1847..Sabine, Lorenzo 5: 120
1848..Frothingham, Richard ...11: 398
1848..Grigsby, Hugh B. 19: 379
1848..Kirk, John F. 1: 535
1849..Moore, George H. 4: 555
1850..Bowen, Francis 11: 452
1850..Greene, George W. 7: 309
1850..Trumbull, J. Hammond .. 9: 422
1851..Pickett, Albert J. 9: 388
1851..Wheeler, John H. 6: 485
1853..Brodhead, John R. 12: 66
1853..Gibbes, Robert W. 11: 36
1853..Hough, Franklin B. 13: 340
1854..Kapp, Friedrich 24: 143
1855..Abbott, John S. C. 6: 145
1857..Del Mar, Alexander 4: 189
1857..Draper, Lyman C. 9: 390
1857..White, Andrew D. 4: 476
1858..Bronson, Henry 22: 266
1858..Neill, Edward D. 9: 411
1858..Palfrey, John G. 7: 199
1859..Bancroft, Hubert H. 5: 112
1860..Claiborne, John F. H. 11: 391
1861..Victor, Orville J. 11: 575
1863..Dean, Amos 22: 116
1863..Draper, John W. 3: 406
1864..Adams, Charles K. 4: 477
1864..Jordan, John W. 11: 158
1865..Stone, William L. 11: 387
1866..Stillé, Charles J. 1: 344
1867..Drake, Francis S. 4: 101
1867..Stephens, Alexander H. .. 3: 420
1868..DeCosta, Benjamin F. 22: 355
1870..Fiske, John 3: 23
1870..Swank, James M. 20: 312
1872..Sloane, William M. 21: 95
1873..Burgess, John W. 23: 39
1873..Grosvenor, Edwin A. 10: 493
1873..Henry, William W. 9: 272
1873..Holst, Hermann E. Von ..11: 69
1873..Jones, Charles C. 5: 159
1874..Adams, Charles Francis .. 8: 353
1874..Ridpath, John C. 6: 485
1874..Scharf, J. Thomas 7: 196
1875..Carrington, Henry B. 22: 253
1875..Sheldon, George 17: 174
1876..Adams, Henry 11: 475
1876..Adams, Herbert B. 8: 270
1876..Battle, Kemp P. 13: 243
1876..Egle, William H. 8: 198
1876..Griffis, William E. 21: 118
1876..Moses, Bernard 26: 120
1876..Schuyler, Eugene 8: 339
1877..Adams, George B. 14: 253
1877..Dexter, Franklin B. 19: 344
1877..Johnston, Henry P. 11: 169
1878..Jordan, John W. 11: 158
1878..Morse, Anson D. 13: 352
1879..Baird, Henry M. 8: 171
1879..Johnston, Alexander 24: 369
1880..Lambing, Andrew A. 6: 338
1880..Lowell, Edward J. 26: 336
1881..Bandelier, Adolphe F. A. .26: 240
1881..Lodge, Henry C. 19: 52
1881..Ropes, John C. 11: 404
1882..Jameson, John F. 10: 442
1883..Hart, Albert B. 11: 394
1883..McMaster, John B. 11: 445
1883..Mahan, Alfred T. 10: 440
1883..Tuttle, Herbert 10: 217
1883..Wilson, Woodrow 19: 1
1884..Browne, William H. 11: 233
1884..Channing, Edward 13: 432
1884..Gross, Charles 22: 410
1885..Jacobs, Joseph 24: 437
1885..Maclay, Edgar S. 10: 111
1885..Perkins, James B. 13: 38
1886..Brown, Alexander 19: 171
1886..Dunning, William A. 19: 27
1886..Severance, Frank H. 26: 40
1886..Stephens, H. Morse 13: 463
1887..Good, James I. 5: 360
1887..McLaughlin, Andrew C. ..13: 217
1888..Fortier, Alcée 9: 135
1888..Thwaites, Reuben G. 10: 35
1889..Bruce, Philip A. 18: 47
1889..Myers, Philip Van N. 12: 149
1889..Haskins, Charles H. ...... C: 378
1890..Johnston, Robert M. 23: 158
1890..Robinson, James Harvey . C: 28
1890..Sparks, Edwin E. 20: 350
1890..Turner, Frederick J. 13: 174
1891..Adams, Ephraim D. 22: 144
1891..Siebert, Wilbur H. .... D: 124
1892..Johnson, Allen 21: 34
1892..Rhodes, James F. 7: 92
1892..Steiner, Bernard C. 26: 311
1893..Greene, Evarts B. .... C: 278
1893..Munro, Dana C. 23: 81
1894..Beer, George L. 19: 167
1894..Leach, Josiah G. 19: 268
1894..Weeks, Stephen B. 10: 89
1895..Bourne, Edward G. 10: 461
1895..Burnett, Edmund C. ..... A: 299
1895..Chittenden, Hiram M. 17: 404
1895..Garrett, William R. 12: 560
1895..Howe, Daniel W. 13: 289
1895..Latané, John H. 23: 394
1895..Sachse, Julius F. 25: 361
1896..Fisher, Sydney G. 13: 343
1896..Ford, Paul Leicester 13: 105
1896..Severance, Allen D. 21: 394
1896..Wayland, John W. ...... A: 394
1897..Callahan, James M. 11: 546
1897..Gordy, Wilbur F. .... B: 480
1897..Riley, Franklin L. 24: 289
1897..Sullivan, James 24: 392
1898..Dow, George F. 26: 239
1898..Jones, Henry F. 21: 14
1899..Bolton, Herbert E. .... A: 204
1899..Smith, Justin H. .... B: 471
1900..Dodd, William E. .... D: 34
1900..Shotwell, James T. .... B: 16
1901..Lowery, Woodbury 18: 186
1902..Rowland, Dunbar .... B: 274
1902..Van Tyne, Claude H. 26: 268
1903..White, Melvin J. 23: 42
1904..Beard, Charles A. .... D: 231
1905..Breasted, James H. ...... B: 377
1905..Upham, Warren 7: 127
1906..Alexander, DeAlva S. 20: 159
1907..Moehlman, Conrad Henry . C: 38
1907..Paltsits, Victor H. 17: 198
1908..Chapman, Charles E. .... A: 128

1908..Folwell, William W. 13: 328
1908..Golder, Frank A. 23: 204
1908..Kerner, Robert J. .... A: 293
1909..Hunt, Gaillard 19: 81
1910..Gibbons, Herbert A. ..... A: 492
1911..Seymour, Charles .... D: 431
1912..Adams, James Truslow ... D: 56
1912..Parrington, Vernon L. ...25: 248
1913..Penniman, James H. 22: 263
1913..Van Loon, Hendrick W. .. B: 44
1916..Barnes, Harry E. .... C: 35
1918..Dennett, Tyler .... D: 429
1919..Jones, Leonard C. 25: 125

Homeopaths

1826..Hering, Constantine 3: 477
1828..Detwiller, Henry 5: 25
1832..Bute, George H. 3: 478
1832..Jeanes, Jacob 3: 480
1836..Williamson, Walter 3: 478
1837..Kitchen, James 3: 479
1837..Neidhard, Charles 3: 480
1840..Hallock, Lewis 9: 356
1842..Small, Alvin E. 3: 480
1844..Guernsey, Henry N. 3: 479
1847..Holcombe, William H. ... 3: 312
1848..Sanders, John C. 12: 320
1850..Guernsey, Egbert 2: 484
1851..Dake, Jabez P. 11: 442
1851..Raue, Charles G. 3: 477
1852..Dunham, Carroll 3: 224
1852..Hale, Edwin M. 11: 190
1852..Helmuth, William Tod ...12: 471
1852..Humphreys, Frederick ... 7: 282
1852..Ludlam, Reuben 12: 102
1853..Talbot, Israel T. 11: 179
1854..Watson, William H. 7: 449
1855..Thomas, Amos R. 3: 481
1856..McClatchey, Robert J. ... 3: 479
1857..Angell, Henry C. 11: 183
1857..Franklin, Edward C. 7: 56
1857..Gause, Owen B. 3: 481
1857..James, Bushrod W. 3: 492
1857..Wesselhoeft, Conrad 11: 180
1859..Wesselhoeft, Walter 18: 359
1863..Boothby, Alonzo 14: 203
1864..Fiske, William M. L. 3: 534
1864..Grosvenor, Lemuel C. 7: 270
1865..Jones, Gaius J. 11: 315
1867..Allen, Timothy F. 7: 282
1867..James, John E. 3: 483
1868..Farrington, Ernest E. ... 3: 480
1868..Korndoerfer, Augustus ... 3: 491
1869..Bradford, Thomas L. 3: 492
1869..Campbell, James A. 7: 287
1869..Cowperthwaite, Allen C...11: 251
1870..Betts, B. Frank 3: 482
1870..Goodno, William C. 3: 484
1871..Bigler, William H. 3: 485
1871..Dudley, Pemberton 3: 482
1871..Keim, William H. 3: 490
1871..Runnels, Orange S. 14: 283
1872..Guernsey, Joseph C. 3: 490
1872..Terry, Marshall O. 16: 60
1873..Mitchell, J. Nicholas 3: 485
1873..Pratt, Edwin H. 11: 552
1874..Obetz, Henry L. 16: 307
1874..Thomas, Charles M. 3: 483
1875..Hamer, James H. 3: 485
1875..Harris, W. John 7: 273
1875..Mohr, Charles 3: 484
1877..Carleton, Bukk G. 7: 48
1877..Howard, Erving M. 3: 486
1878..Rankin, Egbert G. 2: 340
1879..Bartlett, Clarence 3: 488
1879..Ivins, Horace F. 3: 486
1880..Dearborn, Henry M. 9: 350
1880..Forster, William A. 5: 327
1880..Gramm, Edward M. 3: 488
1880..Smedley, Isaac G. 3: 489
1880..Van Baun, William W. .. 3: 489
1880..Van Lennep, William B. . 3: 487
1881..Martin, George H. 7: 286
1881..Mercer, Edward W. 3: 489
1882..Haines, Oliver S. 3: 488
1882..Norton, Arthur B. 18: 262
1883..Ward, James W. 7: 269
1884..Snader, Edward R. 3: 487
1885..Messervé, Frederic W. ... 3: 488
1887..Helmuth, William T. 12: 472
1887..Lee, John M. 20: 455
1887..Vischer, Carl V. 3: 489
1888..Boger, Cyrus M. 17: 138
1890..Hobson, Sarah M. .... A: 477
1905..Coffin, Mary E. .... D: 276

Horticulturists

1720..Bartram, John 7: 153
1767..Bartram, William 7: 154
1777..Deane, Samuel 23: 298
1803..Chapman, John 11: 98
1807..Thorburn, Grant 7: 350
1813..Dearborn, Henry A. S. .. 9: 323
1815..Kirtland, Jared P. 11: 347
1815..Prince, William R. 20: 427
1819..Longworth, Nicholas 11: 339
1822..Fessenden, Thomas G. ... 7: 260
1823..Downing, Charles 11: 114
1823..Wilder, Marshall P. 1: 358
1830..Downing, Andrew J. 11: 114
1831..Tucker, Luther 24: 40
1835..Hovey, Charles M. 26: 383
1837..Hunnewell, Horatio H. ...25: 132
1840..Barry, Patrick 13: 135
1843..Henderson, Peter 6: 143
1845..Olmsted, Frederick L. ... 2: 298
1845..Saunders, William 10: 409
1848..Stark, Washington 16: 378
1848..Vick, James 4: 469
1850..Warder, John A. 4: 536
1851..Shaw, Henry 9: 233
1853..Meehan, Thomas 11: 220
1853..Wellhouse, Frederick 15: 153
1854..Colman, Norman J. 16: 69
1854..Meyer, Christian F. G. ...12: 30
1860..Earle, Parker 16: 236
1860..Pringle, Cyrus G. 23: 175
1861..Pennock, Abraham L. 18: 29
1861..Riehl, Emil A. 20: 399
1863..Harris, John S. 4: 528
1865..Garey, Thomas A. 23: 131
1867..Hart, Edmund H. 24: 219
1869..Jones, Albert N. 22: 331
1870..Burrill, Thomas J. 18: 187
1870..Gale, Elbridge 23: 271
1871..Egan, William C. 22: 103
1871..Munson, Thomas V. 18: 265
1872..Ellwanger, George H. ...13: 134
1874..Childs, John L. 24: 245
1874..Green, Charles A. 20: 332
1878..Burbank, Luther 11: 374
1878..Burpee, Washington A. ..16: 286
1878..Chase, Howard A. 22: 292
1879..Wickson, Edward J. 18: 270
1880..Eisen, Gustavus A. ...... B: 484
1880..Logan, James H. 21: 163
1882..Eliot, Charles 13: 108
1882..Goff, Emmett S. 23: 278
1882..Melbane, Alexander D. ...20: 195
1883..Galloway, Beverly T. 12: 504
1884..Bailey, Liberty H. 10: 145
1885..Hansen, George 22: 243
1886..Earle, Franklin S. 14: 468
1893..Woods, Albert F. .... B: 467
1896..Powell, G. Harold 20: 477
1897..Emerson, Rollins A. ..... D: 361
1906..Lewis, Claude I. 20: 339
1912..Ward, Aaron 18: 373
1915..Burpee, David 16: 286

Hydraulic Engineers

1835..Storrow, Charles S. 21: 93
1837..Francis, James B. 9: 46
1837..Talcott, William H. 9: 43
1838..Worthen, William E. 12: 206
1840..Eads, James B. 5: 134
1840..Keefer, Thomas C. 12: 227
1846..Chesbrough, Ellis S. 9: 35
1848..Sawyer, Edward 12: 320
1849..Craven, Alfred W. 9: 37
1855..Kirkwood, James P. 9: 36
1856..Harrod, Benjamin M. 12: 328
1856..Lane, Moses 9: 34
1856..Mills, Hiram F. 12: 71
1857..Frizell, Joseph P. 23: 221
1857..Hermany, Charles 13: 299
1860..Shedd, J. Herbert 13: 44
1863..Menocal, Aniceto G. 14: 354
1865..Gray, Samuel M. 19: 175
1866..Merrill, William E. 10: 223
1868..Kuichling, Emil 16: 66
1869..Brush, Charles B. 9: 33
1869..Judson, William P. 12: 381
1870..Williams, Benezette 16: 71
1871..Kerr, Frank M. 20: 135
1872..Fanning, John T. 9: 38
1872..Stearns, Frederic P. 14: 306
1873..FitzGerald, Desmond 9: 44
1873..Flynn, Patrick J. 4: 203
1874..Holman, Minard L. 14: 419
1874..Rafter, George W. 12: 234
1878..Donovan, Cornelius 20: 293
1878..Vermeule, Cornelius C. ...14: 105
1881..Landreth, William B. 12: 97
1882..Alvord, John W. 16: 48
1882..Ericson, John E. 16: 91
1883..Herschel, Clemens 22: 342
1884..Schuyler, James D. 18: 317
1885..Bates, Lindon W. 15: 81
1886..Bassett, George B. .... A: 182
1887..Gaillard, David D. 15: 318
1888..Ledoux, John W. 23: 93
1890..Smith, J. Waldo 24: 108
1891..Sabin, Louis C. .... D: 405
1892..Hill, Nicholas S., Jr. 16: 28
1896..Chittenden, Hiram M. 17: 404
1902..Newell, Frederick H. 23: 162
1902..Perkins, Edmund T. 17: 329
1905..Miller, Charles H. 20: 255
1907..Goethals, George 14: 40
1908..Tefft, William W. 23: 89

Hydrographers

See Geographers and Hydrographers

Indians

1607..Pocahontas 7: 102
1607..Powhatan 10: 413
1622..Canonicus 11: 319
1632..Miantonomo 10: 407
1638..Uncas 12: 461
1642..Hiacoomes 11: 156
1647..Ninigret 9: 218
1662..King Philip 10: 50
1665..Madockawando 9: 484
1674..Canonchet 10: 402
1735..Skenando 9: 277
1746..Pontiac 10: 415
1751..Hendrick 10: 304
1752..Brant, Joseph 9: 142
1755..Logan, John 10: 204
1778..McGillivray, Alexander ...18: 371
1790..Little Turtle 10: 60
1795..Tecumseh 11: 363
1804..Black Hawk 9: 477
1804..Sacajawea 13: 419
1807..Red Jacket 13: 422
1812..Keokuk 9: 221
1812..McIntosh, William 9: 273
1813..Weatherford, William 18: 339
1826..Guess, George 5: 510
1828..Ross, John 11: 224
1835..Osceola 9: 211
1838..Mayes, Joel B. 25: 94
1849..Black Beaver 19: 235
1850..Parker, Ely S. 5: 330
1858..Geronimo 23: 351
1861..Black Kettle 19: 308
1862..Sitting Bull 13: 454
1885..Pushmatah 8: 154

Inventors

1646..Jenks, Joseph 22: 58
1730..Godfrey, Thomas 23: 368
1731..Franklin, Benjamin 1: 328
1746..Kinnersley, Ebenezer 1: 532
1753..Orr, Hugh 2: 54
1763..Rittenhouse, David 1: 346
1765..Wilkinson, Jeremiah 8: 74
1768..Henry, William 11: 521
1770..Clymer, George 8: 78
1770..Niles, Nathaniel 5: 374
1776..Bushnell, David 9: 244
1776..Wheeler, Samuel 8: 250
1779..Prince, John 7: 345
1780..Evans, Oliver 6: 65
1780..Morey, Samuel 11: 168
1781..Perkins, Jacob 10: 123
1782..Blodget, Samuel 13: 348
1783..Whitney, Eli 4: 495
1783..Whittemore, Amos 7: 527
1784..Rumsey, James 5: 130
1785..Fitch, John 6: 63
1788..Longstreet, William 9: 434
1789..Read, Nathan 4: 558
1790..Cochran, James 7: 536
1790..Earle, Pliny 11: 145
1792..Brown, Sylvanus 24: 322
1792..Stevens, John 11: 21
1792..Thornton, William 13: 470
1793..Fulton, Robert 3: 104
1797..Roosevelt, Nicholas 12: 127
1797..Wilkinson, David 8: 302

1798..Borden, Simeon 24: 216
1800..Moody, Paul 25: 209
1801..Blanchard, Thomas 6: 186
1801..Hare, Robert 5: 398
1804..Ames, Oliver 14: 201
1804..Kimball, Increase 4: 293
1804..Nott, Eliphalet 7: 170
1805..Wheeler, Dexter 12: 98
1807..Terry, Eli 6: 258
1809..Alger, Cyrus 6: 113
1809..Norton, Lewis M. 4: 301
1810..Crane, Zenas 13: 69
1810..Dod, Daniel 24: 359
1810..Pratt, Zadock 9: 164
1811..Cooper, Peter 3: 114
1811..Treadwell, Daniel 10: 165
1812..Arnold, Asa 13: 255
1812..Bomford, George 7: 405
1812..Bruce, George 11: 274
1812..Francis, Joseph 10: 88
1812..Rollinson, William 7: 523
1813..Ogden, Francis B. 11: 369
1814..Wood, Jethro 11: 360
1815..Allen, Zachariah 8: 263
1815..Jerome, Chauncey 7: 246
1816..Horstman, William H. ...13: 325
1816..McCormick, Robert 24: 139
1816..McCormick, Stephen 25: 161
1816..Shreve, Henry M. 2: 185
1817..Edwards, William 11: 225
1818..Boyden, Seth 11: 87
1818..Hinkley, Holmes 5: 534
1818..Morse, Samuel F. B. 4: 449
1818..Stevens, Robert L. 11: 21
1819..Baldwin, Matthias W. 9: 476
1819..Saxton, Joseph 9: 220
1819..Scarbrough, William 2: 237
1820..Bogardus, James 8: 193
1820..Brown, James S. 11: 351
1820..Burden, Henry 2: 333
1820..Porter, Rufus 7: 184
1821..Gobrecht, Christian 12: 145
1822..Silver, Thomas 6: 191
1823..Bryant, Gridley 11: 502
1823..Renwick, James 11: 101
1823..Stevens, Edwin A. 11: 22
1824..Babbitt, Isaac 13: 442
1824..Norcross, Leonard 13: 422
1824..Winans, Ross 11: 358
1825..Danforth, Charles 13: 208
1825..Ericsson, John 4: 46
1825..Gedney, Jonathan H. 5: 532
1825..Poole, Daniel 7: 258
1826..Blake, Eli W. 9: 215
1826..Guthrie, Samuel 11: 406
1826..Hallock, Homan 11: 193
1826..Henry, Joseph 3: 405
1826..Hunt, Walter 19: 245
1827..Dixon, Joseph 22: 346
1828..Adams, Isaac 9: 224
1828..Buckland, Cyrus 11: 493
1828..Conner, James 5: 480
1828..Howe, John I. 4: 373
1829..Allen, Horatio 8: 233
1829..Camp, Hiram 8: 155
1829..Simpson, Michael H. 10: 387
1830..Chickering, Jonas 6: 190
1830..Gill, John L. 4: 89
1830..Pitts, Hiram A. 13: 251
1830..Talcott, Andrew 13: 405
1831..Ames, John 13: 69
1831..Fairbanks, Thaddeus 10: 300
1831..Geissenhainer, Frederick W. 11: 175
1831..Goodyear, Charles 3: 86
1831..McCormick, Cyrus H. 21: 78
1831..Metcalf, Mason J. 12: 500
1831..Washburn, Ichabod 10: 448
1832..Batchelder, Samuel 5: 16
1832..Bigelow, Erastus B. 3: 20
1832..Harvey, Thomas W. 12: 418
1832..Hoe, Richard M. 7: 320
1832..Jackson, Charles T. 3: 97
1832..Mason, William 10: 386
1833..Burt, William A. 18: 367
1833..Cochran, John W. 11: 269
1833..Davenport, Thomas 3: 339
1833..Hussey, Obed 11: 361
1833..Osgood, Jason C. 6: 175
1834..Long, Stephen H. 11: 365
1835..Babbitt, Benjamin T. 8: 9
1835..Ball, Ephraim 11: 275
1835..Coleman, Obed M. 7: 557
1835..Colt, Samuel 6: 175
1835..Rutherfurd, Lewis M. 6: 376
1835..Tuck, Joseph H. 7: 528
1836..Angell, William G. 2: 392
1836..Barstow, Amos C. 3: 305
1836..Griffiths, John W. 8: 70
1836..Maynard, Edward 11: 339
1836..Parrott, Robert P. 5: 366
1837..Crompton, William 10: 160
1837..Haswell, Charles H. 9: 486
1837..Pitts, John A. 13: 252
1837..Rogers, Thomas 19: 174
1838..Corliss, George H. 10: 394
1838..Hayden, Hiram W. 25: 19
1838..Hayes, Augustus A. 11: 56
1838..Hayward, Nathaniel 12: 120
1838..Slocum, Samuel 7: 529
1838..Vail, Alfred 4: 450
1839..Coes, Loring 13: 68
1839..Eads, James B. 5: 134
1839..Gatling, Richard 4: 158
1839..Lillie, John H. 9: 512
1839..Morse, Jedidiah 13: 353
1840..Cottrell, Calvert B. 3: 397
1840..Davison, Darius 2: 198
1840..Howe, William 7: 507
1840..Knowles, Lucius J. 5: 256
1840..Locke, John 15: 264
1840..Pond, Theron T. 8: 82
1840..Sharps, Christian 5: 517
1840..Tatham, William P. 13: 250
1840..Wells, Horace 6: 438
1840..Whipple, Squire 9: 35
1841..Herring, Silas C. 9: 238
1841..Heywood, Levi 10: 307
1841..Hubbard, Henry G. 10: 402
1841..Nason, Joseph 24: 150
1841..Timby, Theodore R. 9: 116
1841..Worthington, Henry R. .. 6: 303
1842..Campbell, Andrew 9: 154
1842..Douglas, Benjamin 8: 437
1842..Goulding, Francis R. 7: 174
1842..Kingsford, Thomas 5: 221
1843..Allen, John 2: 427
1843..Cornell, Ezra 4: 475
1844..Andrews, William D. 13: 146
1844..Boyden, Uriah A. 11: 88
1844..Clark, Alvan 6: 440
1844..Cutting, James A. 13: 101
1844..House, Royal E. 12: 279
1844..Howe, Elias 4: 432
1844..Kellogg, George 7: 494
1844..Pratt, Thomas W. 22: 275
1844..Rogers, Henry J. 4: 453
1845..Booth, James C. 13: 245
1845..Carhart, Jeremiah 5: 183
1845..Dodge, Thomas H. 2: 520
1845..Harrison, Joseph 12: 495
1845..Lake, Jesse S. 20: 228
1845..Morton, William T. G. ... 8: 332
1845..Needham, Elias P. 5: 183
1845..Otis, Elisha G. 11: 119
1845..Sawyer, Sylvanus 4: 318
1846..Alden, Timothy 12: 276
1846..Batchelder, John P. 9: 351
1846..Beach, Alfred E. 8: 122
1846..Wagner, Webster 9: 208
1847..Bachelder, John 12: 549
1847..Craven, John J. 23: 60
1847..Farmer, Moses G. 7: 361
1847..Hunt, William P. 10: 210
1847..Kelly, William 13: 196
1847..Smyth, David M. 7: 323
1847..Wilson, Allen B. 9: 460
1848..Baker, George W. 21: 349
1848..Mitchel, Ormsby M. 3: 440
1848..Renwick, Edward S. 11: 102
1848..Spencer, Charles A. 13: 255
1848..Whipple, John A. 7: 525
1848..Young, McClintock 10: 221
1849..Barney, Nathan 12: 375
1849..Mapes, James J. 3: 178
1849..Plimpton, James L. 7: 512
1849..Root, Elisha K. 18: 313
1849..Sellers, Coleman 11: 53
1849..Singer, Isaac M. 5: 557
1849..Washburn, Nathan 10: 18
1850..Channing, William F. ...23: 284
1850..Conant, Hezekiah 22: 57
1850..Cutter, Ephraim 3: 188
1850..Eliot, Ezekiel B. 2: 255
1850..Emerson, James E. 12: 343
1850..Gaylord, Edward L. 22: 162
1850..Gorrie, John 15: 345
1850..Hamlin, Emmons 23: 378
1850..Hobbs, Alfred C. 23: 336
1850..Laidley, Theodore T. S. .. 7: 24
1850..Lawrence, Richard S. 24: 142
1850..Malcolm, William 13: 423
1850..Mayall, Thomas J. 5: 506
1850..Skinner, Halcyon 5: 300
1850..Twining, Alexander C. ...19: 17
1850..West, Jonathan B. 10: 400
1850..Winans, Thomas De K. .. 1: 239
1851..Atwood, Luther 13: 260
1851..Brittan, Nathan 5: 22
1851..Brooke, John M. 22: 29
1851..Burt, William A. 18: 367
1851..Gordon, George P. 5: 405
1851..Manny, John H. 11: 486
1851..Riddell, John L. 21: 175
1851..Shaffner, Taliaferro P. ..10: 482
1851..Smith, John L. 6: 54
1851..Wood, Walter D. 12: 326
1851..Yale, Linus, Jr. 11: 188
1852..Bollman, Wendell 11: 233
1852..Brown, Joseph R. 10: 395
1852..Bullock, William A. 9: 538
1852..Jones, Evan W. 25: 133
1852..Latta, Alexander B. 13: 418
1852..McKay, Gordon 10: 397
1852..Miller, Ezra 7: 116
1852..Prescott, George B. 5: 279
1852..Rees, James 23: 218
1852..Sargent, James 3: 433
1852..Smith, Horace 10: 476
1852..Wetherill, Samuel 7: 506
1852..Wolle, Francis 1: 320
1852..Wood, Walter A. 6: 398
1853..Borden, Gail 7: 306
1853..Bowers, Alphonzo B. 12: 527
1853..Dahlgren, John A. 9: 377
1853..Klapp, Lyman 13: 204
1853..Rowland, Thomas F. 12: 346
1853..Stevens, Enos 11: 318
1853..Wales, Thomas C. 10: 406
1853..Wesson, Daniel B. 10: 476
1853..Wheeler, Cyrenus, Jr. 12: 98
1853..Zentmayer, Joseph 13: 215
1854..Babcock, George H. 5: 304
1854..Babcock, James F. 10: 445
1854..Baird, Matthew 6: 123
1854..Bonwill, William G. A. ... 5: 177
1854..Bradley, David 11: 148
1854..Cornell, John B. 13: 156
1854..Eickemeyer, Rudolf 1: 184
1854..Ellet, Charles 4: 360
1854..Haskell, James R. 13: 106
1854..Keen, Morris L. 11: 367
1854..Marks, Amasa A. 11: 386
1854..Neff, Peter 13: 253
1854..Orr, William 3: 74
1854..Porter, Charles T. 20: 494
1854..Sergeant, Henry C. 15: 155
1854..Spencer, Christopher M. ..22: 63
1855..Birdsell, John C. 11: 345
1855..Boynton, John F. 4: 91
1855..Crane, Richard T. 26: 450
1855..Gibbs, James E. A. 19: 255
1855..Gill, John L. 4: 89
1855..Hallidie, Andrew S. 7: 191
1855..Miller, Lewis 6: 216
1855..Myer, Albert J. 24: 196
1855..Oliver, James 12: 522
1855..Warren, Cyrus M. 10: 313
1856..Atkins, Elias C. 16: 139
1856..Baldwin, Frank S. 16: 281
1856..Beach, Moses S. 13: 329
1856..Brown, Martin B. 8: 453
1856..Campbell, John T. B. 12: 397
1856..Hotchkiss, Benjamin B. .. 6: 431
1856..Hudson, William S. 24: 242
1856..Jones, Joshua W. 10: 128
1856..Larned, Joseph G. E. 24: 176
1856..Lowe, Thaddeus S. C. 9: 542
1856..Merrill, Joshua 13: 258
1856..Stoddard, Joshua C. 7: 530
1856..Waters, Daniel H. 10: 207
1857..Appleby, John F. 11: 268
1857..Brown, John H. 4: 381
1857..Crompton, George 10: 161
1857..Doane, William H. 7: 556
1857..Hunt, Edward B. 11: 440
1857..Keely, John E. W. 9: 137
1857..Johnston, Samuel 24: 75
1857..Morgan, Charles H. 23: 197
1857..Tolles, Robert B. 13: 256
1857..Westlake, William 2: 416
1858..Blake, Ira G. 13: 306
1858..Boynton, Nathaniel A. 12: 487
1858..Goddu, Louis 13: 77
1858..Haupt, Herman 10: 224
1858..Lyman, Benjamin S. 9: 217
1858..Marsh, Charles W. 11: 268
1858..Shaw, Thomas 15: 355
1858..Spaulding, Nathan W. ...13: 163
1859..Essick, Samuel 3: 323
1859..Firm, Joseph L. 7: 356
1859..Harroun, Gilbert K. 11: 559
1859..Henszey, William P. 24: 142
1859..Holly, Birdsall 26: 108

1859..James, Charles T. 3: 324
1859..Lamb, Isaac W. 7: 554
1859..Perkins, Charles H. 2: 271
1859..Pullman, George M. 11: 279
1859..Stone, Ebenezer W. 4: 390
1859..Tweddle, Herbert W. C. ..12: 463
1860..Clark, Alvan 6: 440
1860..Clark, James J. 19: 265
1860..House, Henry A. 23: 84
1860..Hough, George W. 8: 337
1860..Moss, John C. 11: 426
1860..Mowbray, George M. 23: 376
1860..Rodman, Thomas J. 4: 396
1860..Stiles, Norman C. 10: 151
1860..Wiard, Harry 22: 145
1860..Wyman, Horace 13: 212
1861..Benton, James G. 4: 138
1861..Blake, George F. 12: 521
1861..Bliss, Delos 10: 218
1861..Brown, Frederick H. 13: 326
1861..Hyatt, John W. 12: 148
1861..Lyall, James 7: 496
1861..Otis, Charles R. 11: 120
1861..Westinghouse, George 15: 41
1862..Allen, Richard N. 9: 211
1862..Corliss, William 4: 171
1862..Davis, William A. 16: 78
1862..Dederick, Peter K. 19: 131
1862..Doremus, Robert O. 12: 190
1862..Durfee, William F. 6: 248
1862..Herreshoff, James B. 12: 352
1862..Maury, Mathew F. 6: 35
1862..Peirce, John 10: 406
1862..Williams, John I. 11: 316
1863..Butterick, Ebenezer 13: 231
1863..Coldwell, Thomas 8: 65
1863..Harkness, William 8: 395
1863..Holley, Alexander H. 11: 508
1863..Huntington, John 9: 102
1863..Mann, William D. 11: 444
1863..Mills, Anson 10: 453
1863..Nicholson, William T. 8: 262
1863..Ravenel, St. Julian 10: 272
1863..Rice, Vietts L. 1: 512
1863..Robinson, Stillman W. ...10: 232
1863..Rowland, Henry A. 11: 25
1863..Shock, William H. 6: 200
1863..Smith, Oberlin 12: 461
1863..Sweet, John E. 13: 54
1864..Barney, Everett H. 3: 89
1864..Bolthoff, Henry 20: 352
1864..Brooke, Homer 20: 19
1864..Carll, John F. 12: 361
1864..Davidson, Alexander 3: 320
1864..Flad, Henry 12: 290
1864..French, Aaron 24: 267
1864..Herschel, Clemens 22: 342
1864..Ketcham, Isaac A. 6: 142
1864..Lay, John L. 7: 528
1864..Pope, Franklin L. 7: 414
1864..Pratt, John 3: 315
1864..Sellers, William 7: 185
1865..Abbott, Henry L. 11: 194
1865..Balbach, Edward 7: 249
1865..Ballantine, Alexander T. . 7: 540
1865..Bowles, Thomas H. 2: 478
1865..Brooks, William R. 5: 197
1865..Crowell, Luther C. 13: 604
1865..Dodge, William C. 10: 476
1865..Emery, Albert H. 21: 343
1865..Fuller, Robert M. 12: 265
1865..Hammerstein, Oscar 17: 40
1865..Harvey, Hayward A. 13: 63
1865..Hilgard, Eugene W. 10: 308
1865..Holloway, Josephus F. ...12: 116
1865..Holmes, Hector A. 10: 479
1865..Merritt, Israel J. 5: 131
1865..Sackett, Augustine 16: 334
1865..Sternbergh, James H. 10: 22
1866..Arkell, James 1: 367
1866..Barron, Walter J. 3: 318
1866..Blake, Francis 22: 25
1866..Chase, Denison 4: 494
1866..Delany, Patrick B. 13: 590
1866..Edison, Thomas A. 25: 1
1866..Fuller, Levi K. 8: 330
1866..Giles, David 13: 169
1866..Libbey, Hosea W. 12: 515
1866..Steinway, C. F. Theodore 2: 513
1867..Albright, Andrew 4: 446
1867..Davol, William C., Jr. ...20: 259
1867..Densmore, Amos 3: 317
1867..Dolbear, Amos E. 9: 414
1867..Gray, Elisha 4: 453
1867..Gilbert, Rufus H. 11: 388
1867..Hadley, Horace W. 19: 446
1867..Hall, Thomas 3: 323
1867..Landis, Franklin F. 25: 24
1867..Merriam, Henry C. 13: 338
1867..Oliver, Paul A. 5: 40
1867..Sholes, Christopher L. ... 3: 315
1867..Webb, Charles H. 10: 42
1868..Allen, Samuel L. 17: 222
1868..Bonzano, Adolphus 16: 312
1868..Cooley, Leroy C. 11: 263
1868..Filbert, Ludwig S. 4: 487
1868..Kidder, Wellington P. 3: 435
1868..McCollum, Fenelson 20: 378
1868..Sander, Enno 13: 306
1868..Starrett, Laroy S. 18: 428
1868..Tapley, Jesse F. 13: 360
1869..Draper, Daniel 6: 172
1869..Fairbanks, Henry 10: 300
1869..Fell, George E. 12: 340
1869..Gally, Merritt 4: 215
1869..Good, John 2: 516
1869..Grant, George B. 24: 378
1869..King, James W. 13: 186
1869..Levy, Louis E. 13: 589
1869..Roosevelt, Hilborne L. 26: 143
1869..Selden, George B. 20: 222
1869..Somers, Daniel M. 16: 428
1869..Taylor, Warren H. 17: 238
1869..Wright, Elizur 2: 317
1870..Billings, Charles E. 5: 408
1870..Chesebrough, Robert A. ..25: 311
1870..Ingersoll, Oliver R. 23: 357
1870..Johnson, Warren S. 3: 292
1870..Langley, Samuel P. 15: 7
1870..Marvil, Joshua H. 11: 537
1870..Masury, John W. 5: 155
1870..Olsen, Tinius 23: 74
1870..Porteous, James 20: 139
1870..Prescott, George B. 5: 279
1870..Richards, Francis H. 7: 420
1870..Roberts, Benjamin O. 5: 55
1870..Smead, Isaac D. 3: 335
1870..Swasey, Ambrose .... B: 274
1870..Uhlig, Richard W. 13: 418
1870..Van De Poele, Charles J. 13: 246
1870..Wellman, Samuel T. 13: 37
1870..Weston, Edward 5: 176
1871..Robinson, John K. 24: 169
1871..Rose, Rufus E. .... A: 176
1871..Silliman, Justus M. 11: 245
1871..Wait, William B. 2: 451
1872..Draper, Henry 6: 171
1872..Fitch, Ezra C. 13: 465
1872..Kruesi, John 26: 100
1872..Leavitt, Erasmus D. 24: 324
1872..Otis, Fessenden N. 10: 280
1872..Rand, Addison C. 11: 265
1872..Rogers, James H. 21: 464
1872..Schneller, George O. 8: 246
1872..Smyth, William H. 18: 251
1872..Thurston, Robert H. 4: 479
1872..Wood, DeVolson 13: 351
1873..Acheson, Edward G. 23: 136
1873..Bissell, Melville R. 7: 163
1873..Boies, Henry M. 5: 118
1873..Brooks, Edward J. 7: 526
1873..Everhart, James M. 5: 60
1873..Haish, Jacob 5: 476
1873..Hickley, Arthur S. 7: 118
1873..Johnson, Tom L. 14: 148
1873..Mundy, Joseph S. 2: 497
1873..Rothwell, Richard P. 10: 229
1873..Seaton, Charles W. 12: 217
1873..Yost, George W. N. 3: 317
1874..Barnard, William S. 12: 434
1874..Baren, Ernest R. 3: 318
1874..Brooks, Byron A. 3: 319
1874..Burton, George D. 12: 467
1874..Crandall, Lucian S. 3: 322
1874..Gillham, Robert 3: 352
1874..Glidden, Joseph F. 23: 350
1874..Herreshoff, John B. F. ...12: 354
1874..Richards, Robert H. 12: 347
1874..Stanley, Francis E. 18: 429
1874..Wright, Arthur W. 13: 348
1875..Adams, S. Jarvis 24: 365
1875..Campbell, Andrew C. 25: 70
1875..Herreshoff, Nathaniel G. ..12: 353
1875..Hill, Walter N. 12: 359
1875..Jeffers, William N. 4: 281
1875..Jones, Francis W. 4: 84
1875..Knox, Thomas W. 7: 89
1875..Morse, Everett F. 24: 342
1875..Newton, Henry J. 7: 23
1875..Pidgin, Charles F. 13: 479
1875..Schoen, Charles T. 25: 389
1875..Shaver, George F. 4: 231
1875..Willcox, Charles H. 19: 67
1876..Bell, Alexander Graham .. 6: 220
1876..Borton, Stockton 18: 339
1876..Burden, James A. 1: 511
1876..Cahill, LeRoy 5: 117
1876..Capewell, George J. 16: 396
1876..Dodge, James M. 12: 490
1876..Ford, Thomas P. 14: 141
1876..Fox, Oscar C. 1: 310
1876..Green, Charles H. 3: 156
1876..Hamachek, Frank 18: 108
1876..Hammond, James B. 3: 321
1876..Laufman, Philip H. 11: 445
1876..Leavitt, Frank M. 15: 20
1876..Mergenthaler, Ottmar 9: 490
1876..Scribner, Charles E. 13: 192
1876..Thomson, Elihu .... B: 106
1877..Berliner, Emile 21: 6
1877..Brush, Charles F. 21: 1
1877..Lufkin, Richard H. 20: 484
1877..Maxim, Hiram S. 6: 36
1877..Nash, Lewis H. 20: 276
1877..Reynolds, Edwin 2: 524
1877..Royle, Vernon 12: 399
1877..Sherman, John A. 13: 23
1877..Spencer, Herbert R. 13: 256
1878..Bettendorf, William P. ...21: 260
1878..Blake, Francis 22: 25
1878..DeLaVergne, John C. 2: 210
1878..Dwight, William B. 9: 491
1878..Ferguson, Thomas B. 13: 343
1878..Gates, Elmer 10: 354
1878..Gower, Frederick A. 9: 216
1878..Hunter, Rudolph M. 25: 22
1878..Ives, Frederic E. 15: 77
1878..Munger. Robert S. 25: 407
1878..Nickerson, William E. 24: 74
1878..Partridge, Charles S. 18: 414
1878..Sargent, George F. 11: 440
1878..Todd, David P. 7: 203
1878..Wellington, Arthur M. ...11: 167
1878..Yaryan, Homer T. 13: 171
1879..Bartholomew, Miles M. .. 3: 323
1879..Clark, William 5: 161
1879..Fearey, Frederick T. 5: 539
1879..MacDonald, Marshall 13: 321
1879..See, Horace 2: 220
1879..Snowden, Archibald L. ...12: 119
1880..Browning, John M. 20: 8
1880..Brunton, David W. 23: 99
1880..Burridge, Lee S. 16: 63
1880..Eastman, George 26: 32
1880..Ford, John B. 13: 505
1880..Hooper, Francis X. 17: 248
1880..Jacobs. Arthur I. 16: 41
1880..Pelton, Lester A. 13: 602
1880..Perkins, Charles G. 4: 290
1880..Rood, Ogden N. 13: 507
1880..Short, Sidney H. 13: 247
1880..Sperry, Elmer A. 23: 78
1880..Walkup, Liberty 4: 56
1880..Wight, Peter B. 21: 369
1881..Beard, Andrew 4: 438
1881..Bogert, John L. 16: 29
1881..Bradley, Charles S. 15: 82
1881..Briggs, Thomas A. 24: 80
1881..Colburn, Irving W. 24: 379
1881..Crocker, Francis B. 12: 424
1881..Haynes, Elwood 25: 12
1881..Leggett, Joseph P. 20: 379
1882..Benton, Linn B. .... A: 89
1882..Church, Duane H. 12: 117
1882..DesJardins, Benjamin M. .12: 536
1882..Fenner, George P. 16: 237
1882..Gaskill, Harvey F. 23: 187
1882..Schieren, Charles A. 3: 189
1882..Smead, Isaac D. 3: 335
1882..Stanley, William 24: 394
1882..Thacher, Edwin 7: 522
1882..Veeder, Curtis H. .... C: 373
1882..Wilson, Theodore D. 7: 508
1883..Daniels, Fred H. 22: 306
1883..Edwards, Victor E. 24: 383
1883..Jackson, Dugald C. ...... B: 357
1883..Jenney, William LeB. 10: 218
1883..McMillan, John L. .... C: 531
1883..Rice, E. Wilbur, Jr. 26: 10
1883..Waterman, Lewis E. 1: 372
1883..Woodbury, Charles J. H. .12: 81
1883..Zalinski, Edmund L. 7: 248
1884..Blake, Lucien I. 18: 210
1884..Brown, Joseph C. 21: 381
1884..Buffington, Adelbert R. ... 5: 329
1884..Douglas, James 12: 8
1884..Duryea, Charles E. .... D: 78
1884..Houston, Edwin J. 13: 359
1884..Hunt, William P. 10: 210
1884..Mercer, Alfred C. 12: 211
1884..Saunders, William L. 26: 81
1884..Sprague, Frank J. 24: 15
1884..Totten, Charles A. L. 10: 237
1885..Gayley, James 14: 70

1885..Lanston, Tolbert 13: 573
1885..Lewis, Isaac N. 16: 213
1885..Long, Thomas J. 10: 453
1885..Lorimer, John H. 19: 69
1885..Maxim, Hudson 13: 520
1885..Mergenthaler, Ottmar 9: 490
1885..Williston, Benjamin F. ...20: 125
1886..Adams, Frederick U. 14: 458
1886..Gates, William H. 20: 180
1886..Hall, Charles M. 13: 94
1886..Pasko, Wesley W. 2: 60
1886..Rice, John V. 15: 366
1887..Felt, Dorr E. 11: 441
1887..Goodwin, Hannibal W. ...23: 377
1887..Humphrey, Seth K. 23: 288
1887..Minot, Charles S. 6: 112
1887..Noyes, La Verne 17: 156
1887..Player, John 11: 323
1888..Bennett, John H. 18: 370
1888..Bristol, William A. 26: 26
1888..Dennis, Adolphus 13: 537
1888..Herschel, Clemens 22: 342
1888..Kennedy, Julian 24: 135
1888..Leonard, H. Ward 15: 3
1888..Leyner, J. George 25: 207
1888..Ludlum, Albert C. .... B: 37
1888..Munson, James E. 12: 497
1888..Rogers, John R. .... C: 270
1888..Tesla, Nikola 6: 500
1888..Wheeler, Schuyler S. 10: 162
1889..Austin, John T. 18: 129
1889..Chamberlain, Rufus N. ...22: 334
1889..Coppage, Benjamin D. ...22: 93
1889..Jaeger, Herman J. 24: 47
1889..Lamme, Benjamin G. 20: 36
1889..Packard, James W. 20: 15
1889..Powers, William P. ...... B: 28
1889..Pupin, Michael I. 26: 5
1889..Shuman, Frank 19: 253
1889..Stobaeus, John B. 6: 102
1889..Vauclain, Samuel M. ..... B: 318
1890..Du Pont, Alfred I. 25: 25
1890..Ferris, George W. G. 13: 39
1890..Fiske, Bradley A. .... B: 57
1890..Glass, Perly R. 16: 240
1890..Lewis, Isaac N. 16: 213
1890..Skinner, Le Grand 19: 369
1891..Dodge, Philip T. 24: 198
1891..Dunn, Gano S. 18: 105
1891..Howell, John A. 6: 43
1891..Junggren, Oscar F. 26: 22
1891..King, Charles B. .... D: 157
1891..Stearns, Edward C. 11: 558
1891..Winton, Alexander ...... C: 79
1892..Blackham, George E. 13: 15
1892..Graydon, James W. 13: 43
1892..Heisler, Charles L. 25: 399
1892..Owens, Michael J. 13: 504
1893..Astor, John Jacob, 3d 8: 104
1893..Christensen, Niels A. .... D: 308
1893..Edgar, Charles 19: 333
1893..Eickemeyer, Carl 11: 149
1893..Jones, Samuel M. 10: 414
1893..Mitchell, George 13: 362
1893..Newcomb, Charles L. 22: 90
1893..Scripture, Edward W. ...10: 310
1894..Jenkins, Charles F. ...... B: 246
1895..Curtiss, Glenn H. 22: 195
1895..Holland, John P. 15: 4
1895..Ohmer, Wilfred I. .... A: 350
1895..Squier, George O. 24: 320
1896..Crozier, William 12: 267
1896..Davis, Harry P. 25: 17
1896..Goding, Frederick W. 12: 500
1896..Lloyd, Marshall B. 25: 121
1896..McClean, Samuel N. 26: 37
1896..Urban, Charles .... A: 487
1897..Hoxie, William D. 24: 250
1897..Ray, Albert H. 23: 358
1897..Wadsworth, Frank L. O. .26: 376
1897..Wappler, Reinhold 26: 125
1898..Andrews, Launcelot W. .. A: 396
1898..Hewitt, Peter C. 14: 470
1898..Hubert, Conrad 24: 341
1898..Seiberling, Frank A. ..... C: 33
1899..Bruce, William M., Jr. ..22: 236
1899..Caldwell, Eugene W. 18: 197
1899..Mercer, Henry C. 21: 479
1899..Todd, Libanus McL. 26: 112
1899..White, Rollin H. .... D: 128
1900..Acker, Charles E. 13: 573
1900..Black, Lee J. 25: 396
1900..De Zeng, Henry L. 24: 350
1900..Furlow, Floyd C. 20: 240
1900..Willoughby, Hugh deL. ..17: 17
1901..Lincoln, Paul M. .... B: 280
1901..Parr, Samuel W. .... C: 153
1901..Staude, Edwin G. 16: 45
1901..Underhill, Charles R. .... A: 135
1902..DeForest, Lee .... A: 18
1902..Minkler, Chester T. ...... B: 361
1902..Pickard, Greenleaf W. .... B: 294
1903..Best, William N. 21: 138
1903..Craft, Edward B. 22: 256
1903..Herr, Herbert T. .... B: 68
1903..Manly, Charles M. 21: 321
1904..Jewett, Frank B. .... C: 272
1904..Kebler, Leonard .... B: 475
1904..Moore, James L. 22: 183
1905..Duesenberg, Fred S. 16: 295
1905..Kettering, Charles F. ..... B: 260
1905..Lawrance, Charles L. .... D: 194
1906..Alexanderson, Ernst F. W. A: 30
1906..Campbell, Ben J. 24: 34
1906..Comstock, Daniel F. ..... D: 325
1907..Garland, Claude M. ...... A: 224
1907..Howell, Albert S. .... D: 255
1908..Bunn, Benjamin H. ...... C: 106
1908..Castle, Samuel N. .... A: 412
1908..Ives, Herbert E. .... C: 39
1908..Lucke, Charles E. .... B: 64
1908..Whaley, William .... B: 455
1909..Langmuir, Irving .... C: 29
1909..Spitz, Samuel .... B: 259
1911..Arnold, Harold DeF. 25: 184
1912..Hammond, John H., Jr. .. D: 391
1913..Brown, Harold P. .... B: 329
1913..Burton, William M. ...... C: 243
1913..Dubbs, Carbon P. .... D: 299
1913..Longoria, Antonio .... D: 96
1914..Austin, Basil G. .... A: 363
1914..Field, Crosby .... B: 224
1914..Sperr, Frederick W., Jr. . A: 264
1915..Hicks, Thomas W. .... C: 223
1915..Morse, Robert V. .... D: 288
1916..Naumburg, Robert E. .... C: 394
1917..Ferdon, William S. .... A: 78
1918..Case, Theodore W. .... D: 416

Journalists and Editors

1681..Green, Samuel 20: 28
1719..Bradford, Andrew 19: 276
1721..Franklin, Benjamin 1: 328
1721..Franklin, James 8: 17
1727..Parks, William 20: 280
1733..Zenger, John P. 23: 147
1743..Fowle, Daniel 23: 288
1745..Green, Jonas 24: 368
1751..Miller, John H. 24: 432
1755..Davis, James 7: 379
1755..Edes, Benjamin 11: 230
1760..Holt, John 23: 280
1764..Green, Thomas 17: 251
1771..Dunlap, John 19: 363
1771..Thomas, Isaiah 6: 264
1773..Greenleaf, Thomas 23: 255
1779..Kollock, Shepard 10: 158
1780..Spooner, Judah 19: 41
1783..Claypoole, David C. 20: 253
1783..Haswell, Anthony 8: 261
1784..Duane, William 8: 180
1786..Bradford, John 1: 470
1787..Davis, Matthew L. 5: 514
1787..Gales, Joseph 9: 482
1788..Andrews, Loring 20: 84
1789..Fenno, John 19: 326
1790..Bache, Benjamin F. 19: 28
1792..Southwick, Solomon 4: 304
1793..Webster, Noah 2: 394
1795..Dennie, Joseph 7: 204
1795..Dwight, Theodore 11: 216
1796..Smith, Samuel H. 20: 295
1799..Miner, Charles 5: 525
1800..Coleman, William 11: 350
1800..Lewis, Zachariah 11: 352
1803..Willis, Nathaniel 14: 264
1804..Ritchie, Thomas 7: 544
1805..Buckingham, Joseph T. .. 7: 326
1805..Niles, Hezekiah 10: 255
1807..Seaton, William W. 2: 226
1808..Charless, Joseph 21: 211
1809..Hill, Isaac 11: 127
1810..Thomas, Ebenezer S. 5: 393
1810..Walton, Ezekiel P. 16: 445
1811..Hale, Nathan 11: 107
1811..Walsh, Robert 5: 357
1812..Greene, Nathaniel 11: 228
1813..Hammond, Charles 22: 115
1813..Stone, William L. 7: 205
1814..Osborn, John W. 18: 293
1816..Kendall, Amos 5: 296
1816..Weed, Thurlow 3: 12
1819..Littell, Eliakim 24: 408
1819..Locke, Richard A. 13: 151
1819..Noah, Mordecai M. 9: 200
1819..Skinner, John S. 2: 150
1819..Woodruff, William E. 8: 463
1820..Bennett, James G., Sr. ... 7: 241
1820..Hale, David 11: 194
1820..Kinney, William B. 13: 156
1821..Greene, Charles G. 4: 445
1821..Reed, David 12: 64
1822..Bartlett, John S. 22: 185
1822..Simpson, Stephen 5: 543
1823..Earle, John M. 11: 145
1823..Green, Duff 1: 233
1823..Morse, Sidney E. 13: 353
1824..Bowles, Samuel, 1st 1: 317
1824..Croswell, Edwin 10: 31
1824..Hale, Sarah J. 22: 39
1824..Hallock, Gerard 11: 193
1824..Pleasants, John H. 7: 545
1825..Bryant, William Cullen ... 4: 79
1825..Prentice, George D. 3: 121
1825..Robinson, Solon 3: 454
1825..Severance, Luther 13: 473
1826..Greeley, Horace 3: 448
1826..McMichael, Morton 2: 211
1826..Stanton, Henry B. 2: 331
1826..Tucker, Luther 24: 40
1827..Bond, Thomas E. 11: 161
1827..Webb, J. Watson 3: 30
1827..Willis, Nathaniel P. 3: 108
1828..Gallagher, William D. 9: 250
1828..Holmes, Ezekiel 24: 234
1828..Hunt, Freeman 24: 352
1828..Inman, John 9: 248
1828..Leggett, William 6: 275
1828..Smith, Vivus W. 5: 301
1829..Harding, Jesper 22: 18
1830..Harper, Fletcher 1: 152
1830..Ripley, George 3: 453
1830..Rives, John C. 3: 177
1830..Sargent, Nathan 13: 320
1831..Brooks, James 6: 47
1831..Dawson, George 2: 204
1832..Cowardin, James A. 2: 51
1832..Holloway, David P. 7: 499
1833..Sleeper, John S. 13: 206
1833..Walton, Eliakim P. 20: 69
1834..Knapp, George 19: 210
1834..Zollicoffer, Felix K. 11: 230
1835..Arnold, Samuel G. 9: 226
1835..Beach, Moses Y. 1: 307
1835..Benjamin, Park 7: 166
1835..Brooks, Erastus 6: 47
1835..Clapp, Almon M. 1: 359
1835..Jones, George 21: 36
1836..Abell, Arunah S. 21: 8
1836..Bailey, Gamaliel 2: 417
1836..Burr, Alfred E. 1: 243
1836..Donahoe, Patrick 13: 591
1836..Foote, Thomas M. 7: 533
1836..Goodhue, James M. 24: 329
1836..Greeley, Horace 3: 448
1836..Hudson, Frederick 11: 163
1837..Brigham, Charles D. 9: 280
1837..Godwin, Parke 11: 117
1837..Kendall, George W. 12: 289
1837..Lunsden, Francis A. 13: 449
1837..Wentworth, John 10: 482
1838..Anthony, Henry B. 9: 398
1838..Ballou, Maturin M. 7: 307
1838..Canonge, L. Placide 22: 73
1838..Flagg, Edmund 13: 55
1838..Langdon, Charles C. 18: 149
1838..Poore, Ben P. 8: 190
1838..Robinson, William S. 3: 464
1838..Rogers, Nathaniel P. 2: 320
1838..Thompson, William T. 9: 335
1839..Baldwin, Henry E. 19: 91
1839..Fitzgerald, Thomas 1: 375
1839..Sheppard, George 13: 109
1839..Speer, John 7: 50
1839..Waggoner, Clark 14: 243
1840..Cassidy, William 22: 258
1840..Forney, John W. 3: 267
1840..Haldeman, Walter N. 18: 239
1840..Hooper, Johnson J. 11: 264
1840..Piatt, Donn 13: 157
1840..Swain, James B. 6: 274
1841..Forsyth, John 8: 471
1841..Gobright, Lawrence A. ... 5: 355
1841..McElrath, Thomas 3: 456
1841..Raymond, Henry J. 8: 482
1842..Baldwin, John D. 6: 275
1842..Congdon, Charles T. 3: 458
1842..Gray, Joseph W. 22: 320
1842..Hale, Nathan 11: 107
1843..Burleigh, William H. 2: 378
1843..Cramer, William E. 1: 267

1843..Dana, Charles A. 1: 307
1843..Forrest, Joseph K. C. 7: 487
1843..Francis, John M. 1: 242
1844..Bonner, Robert 10: 298
1844..Bowles, Samuel, 2d 1: 317
1844..Debow, James D. B. 8: 161
1844..Gay, Sydney H. 2: 494
1844..Geist, Jacob M. W. 5: 392
1844..Lomax, Joseph 14: 326
1845..Beach, Moses S. 13: 329
1845..Butts, Isaac 21: 140
1845..Kinney, Thomas T. 6: 135
1845..Russell, Addison P. 6: 19
1845..Winser, Henry J. 10: 394
1846..Beach, Alfred E. 1: 428
1846..Cowles, Edwin 23: 50
1846..Ford, Daniel S. 5: 257
1846..McClure, Alexander K. ... 1: 466
1846..Pickering, Loring 25: 107
1847..Clapp, William W. 2: 237
1847..Daniel, John M. 10: 33
1847..Guild, Curtis 9: 502
1847..Holland, Josiah G. 1: 311
1847..Thompson, John R. 6: 49
1847..Watterson, Harvey M. ... 1: 403
1848..Bigelow, John 26: 25
1848..Bowen, Henry C. 1: 205
1848..Cauldwell, William 1: 237
1848..Dyer, Oliver 3: 95
1848..Elwell, Edward H. 9: 259
1848..Heinzen, Karl P. 12: 247
1848..Scripps, John L. 7: 558
1848..Wales, Salem H. 3: 310
1849..Anneke, Mathilde F. 4: 556
1849..DeLand, Charles V. 6: 264
1849..Leland, Charles G. 5: 356
1849..Mason, David H. 10: 228
1849..Stone, David M. 1: 265
1849..Taggart, John H. 5: 402
1850..Aldrich, Charles 9: 317
1850..Childs, George W. 2: 272
1850..Curtis, George W. 3: 96
1850..Hughes, Robert W. 7: 551
1850..McKean, William V. 8: 52
1850..Picton, Thomas 13: 185
1850..Savage, John 11: 509
1850..Spalding, James R. 5: 359
1850..Trousdale, Leonidas 8: 310
1851..Brooks, Noah 7: 57
1851..Browne, Junius H. 13: 357
1851..Godkin, Edwin L. 8: 455
1851..Halstead, Murat 1: 270
1851..Hester, William 19: 231
1851..Marling, John L. 13: 372
1851..Pease, Albert S. 16: 303
1851..Plimpton, Florus B. 5: 510
1851..Ray, Charles H. 7: 551
1852..Abbott, Joseph C. 5: 48
1852..Bonner, John 12: 246
1852..Bross, William 23: 374
1852..Locke, David R. 6: 152
1852..Medill, Joseph 1: 131
1852..Meginness, John F. 10: 381
1852..Purcell, William 1: 209
1852..Rublee, Horace 1: 213
1852..Wheeler, Andrew C. 25: 375
1853..Bailey, E. Prentiss 16: 171
1853..Balsley, Alfred H. 2: 478
1853..Church, William C. 8: 224
1853..Judd, Orange 8: 350
1853..Morwitz, Edward 8: 16
1853..Richardson, Albert D. 8: 465
1853..Stockdale, John M. 17: 161
1853..Villard, Henry 3: 498
1854..Armstrong, William W. ..24: 352
1854..Blaine, James G. 1: 137
1854..Croly, David G. 11: 234
1854..House, Edward H. 13: 458
1854..Kauffmann, Samuel H. ...13: 177
1854..Knapp, John 12: 112
1854..Pomeroy, Mark M. 2: 502
1854..Smith, William H. 19: 442
1855..Ford, Patrick 22: 317
1855..Noyes, Crosby S. 5: 286
1855..Redpath, James 13: 118
1855..Sylvester, Richard H. 3: 325
1855..Stevens, John L. 2: 172
1855..Van Horn, Robert T. ... 3: 250
1855..Whitman, William E. S. .. 5: 367
1856..Avery, Benjamin P. 1: 319
1856..Avery, Isaac W. 3: 238
1856..Hester, William 19: 231
1856..Hutchins, Stilson 1: 234
1856..McKnight, Charles 22: 297
1856..Rich, Jacob 15: 130
1856..Scruggs, William L. 2: 165
1856..Troup, Alexander 17: 27
1856..Upton, George P. 18: 392
1856..Wheelock, Joseph A. 13: 168
1856..Young, John R. 2: 214
1857..Adams, John M. 1: 214
1857..Barrett, Joseph H. 13: 167
1857..Gray, David 9: 500
1857..Hassard, John R. G. 3: 459
1857..Hurlbut, William H. 5: 505
1857..Scripps, James E. 15: 28
1857..Swinton, John 8: 251
1857..Wilkie, Franc B. 1: 156
1858..Alden, William L. 6: 326
1858..Bittinger, John L. 1: 187
1858..Lukens, Henry C. 13: 347
1858..Reid, Whitelaw 22: 1
1858..Seals, John H. 2: 151
1859..Bromley, Isaac H. 12: 336
1859..Grosvenor, William M. ...20: 254
1859..Harding, William W. 22: 19
1859..McCullagh, Joseph B. 1: 465
1859..Murray, Bredett C. 6: 103
1859..Newell, Robert H. 11: 528
1859..Sherwood, Katherine M. B. 2: 201
1859..Smith, Charles E. 11: 17
1859..Stowell, Henry 17: 294
1860..Adams, George W. 15: 371
1860..Bennett, James G., Jr. ... 7: 242
1860..Bryan, Mary E. 8: 374
1860..Foltz, Moses A. 16: 249
1860..Howard, Joseph, Jr. 4: 213
1860..Metcalf, Lorettus S. 1: 353
1860..Pittock, Henry L. 16: 27
1860..Smithee, James N. 7: 94
1860..Townsend, George A. 1: 154
1861..Anthony, Daniel R. 6: 365
1861..Beadle, John H. 18: 344
1861..Finch, William R. 15: 400
1861..Kinsella, Thomas 9: 560
1861..O'Brien, Frank P. 1: 207
1861..Otis, Eliza A. W. 14: 331
1861..Prime, William C. 13: 254
1861..Quinby, William E. 1: 254
1862..Clarkson, James S. 2: 118
1862..Houser, Daniel M. 12: 11
1862..Jenkins, Howard M. 25: 57
1862..Kincaid, Harrison R. 7: 132
1862..Shanks, William F. G. 3: 459
1862..Smalley, George W. 3: 454
1862..Stanwood, Edward 9: 475
1863..Alden, Henry M. 1: 153
1863..Bacon, Edwin M. 13: 421
1863..Baker, Lewis 1: 246
1863..Burr, Willie O. 19: 431
1863..Goodale, George P. 18: 27
1863..Howe, Edgar W. 10: 138
1863..Mulford, Prentice 1: 433
1864..Clement, Edward H. 22: 148
1864..Cochran, Thomas B. 6: 274
1864..Dennett, John R. 8: 169
1864..Edwards, Arthur 9: 172
1864..Irish, John P. 12: 477
1864..Peters, Bernard 1: 157
1864..Phillips, Morris 9: 197
1864..Pond, George E. 10: 39
1864..Stone, Melville E. 21: 24
1864..Warburton, Charles E. ...11: 437
1865..Bayles, James C. 13: 437
1865..Belo, Alfred H. 1: 205
1865..Bridgman, Herbert L. ...22: 51
1865..Cary, Edward 25: 406
1865..Cockerill, John A. 1: 153
1865..Dawson, Francis W. 23: 300
1865..DeYoung, Meichel H. 1: 269
1865..Finerty, John F. 13: 324
1865..Hatton, Frank 4: 252
1865..Jones, Charles H. 1: 386
1865..Kaler, James Otis 13: 475
1865..McMichael, Clayton 2: 211
1865..Mann, William D. 11: 444
1865..Marden, George A. 6: 284
1865..Miller, George La F. 19: 135
1865..Mott, Edward H. 18: 308
1865..Otis, Harrison G. 12: 187
1865..Richardson, Beale H. 4: 493
1865..Russell, Martin J. 10: 115
1865..Scott, Harvey W. 16: 151
1865..Sherman, Loren A. 16: 327
1865..Sleicher, John A. 13: 429
1865..Smith, Charles E. 11: 17
1865..Stevens, Morris H. 19: 68
1865..Taylor, Charles H. 2: 192
1865..Todd, Sereno E. 9: 272
1865..Woodrow, James 11: 35
1866..Bierce, Ambrose 14: 180
1866..Bundy, Jonas M. 1: 202
1866..Dunning, Silas W. 20: 129
1866..Freeman, Frederick K. ...24: 323
1866..Greenhow, William H. 18: 133
1866..Haldeman, William B. ...18: 240
1866..Hearn, John T. 1: 451
1866..Longwell, William H. 19: 236
1866..Marseilles, Charles 11: 425
1866..Phillips, Walter P. 19: 43
1866..Schuyler, Montgomery ...15: 27
1866..Spears, John R. 11: 162
1866..Weightman, Richard C. ..16: 445
1867..De Leon, Thomas C. 19: 242
1867..Handy, Moses P. 16: 254
1867..Hicks, John 12: 141
1867..Howell, Evan P. 1: 236
1867..Leach, DeWitt C. 17: 302
1867..McKelway, St. Clair 17: 383
1867..Mann, William D. 11: 444
1867..Meeker, Ralph 19: 93
1867..Metcalf, Henry H. 22: 455
1867..Munford, Morrison 6: 272
1867..Naar, Joseph L. 13: 93
1867..Nevins, Winfield S. 19: 248
1867..O'Neill, Eugene M. 5: 393
1867..Pulitzer, Joseph 1: 375
1868..Baker, Page M. 13: 565
1868..Beadle, John H. 18: 344
1868..Biddle, Charles J. 25: 444
1868..Bowker, Richard R. 24: 66
1868..Chamberlin, Joseph E. ...25: 71
1868..Covert, John C. 18: 35
1868..King, Henry 24: 184
1868..Knapp, Charles W. 18: 227
1868..McLean, Andrew 13: 552
1868..Nixon, William P. 9: 176
1868..Poor, Henry W. 16: 33
1868..Puffer, Charles C. 17: 248
1868..Rolfe, William J. 4: 86
1868..Whiting, Charles G. 9: 365
1869..Browne, Francis F. 10: 364
1869..Fiske, Amos K. 20: 70
1869..Foord, John 13: 416
1869..Lewis, Charles B. 6: 30
1869..Waite, John L. 16: 142
1869..Young, John P. 17: 449
1870..Chambers, Julius 14: 444
1870..Clarkson, James S. 2: 118
1870..Davis, Robert S. 6: 273
1870..Eggleston, George C. 1: 213
1870..Goodrich, Charles T. 16: 107
1870..Grady, Henry W. 1: 526
1870..Griffin, Solomon B. 21: 482
1870..Hood, Horace 20: 256
1870..Kelly, Robert M. 11: 416
1870..Lanigan, George T. 8: 90
1870..Lawson, Victor F. 13: 51
1870..Lord, Chester S. 25: 11
1870..MacGahan, Janarius A. .. 6: 187
1870..Riis, Jacob A. 13: 114
1870..Schenck, Leopold 4: 557
1870..Woodward, Clement J. ...22: 117
1871..Brownell, William C. 22: 6
1871..Burlingame, Edward L. .. 8: 56
1871..Capdevielle, Armand 10: 462
1871..Clark, Charles H. 25: 6
1871..Dunlop, Joseph R. 1: 216
1871..Garrison, James H. 18: 276
1871..Hart, Charles B. 13: 470
1871..Linn, William A. 26: 218
1871..Mitchell, Edward P. 4: 524
1871..Morss, Samuel E. 1: 261
1871..Ralph, Julian 1: 149
1871..Rosewater, Edward 13: 323
1871..Wright, George E. 9: 506
1872..Barrett, John E. 4: 93
1872..Brickell, William D. 1: 259
1872..Brooks, Louis J. 9: 105
1872..Curtis, William E. 5: 43
1872..Deming, Clarence 12: 437
1872..Griffin, Solomon B. 21: 482
1872..Hemphill, James C. 2: 29
1872..Jenkins, Arthur 25: 337
1872..Macgowan, John E. 1: 428
1872..Madden, George A. 5: 380
1872..Matthews, George E. 12: 281
1872..Miller, Charles R. 1: 210
1872..O'Connor, Joseph 13: 189
1872..Patterson, Robert W. 12: 53
1872..Ralph, Julian 1: 149
1872..Roe, George M. 4: 86
1872..Scott, James W. 2: 55
1872..Seymour, Horatio W. 10: 229
1872..Somers, Frederic M. 22: 397
1872..Smith, Brainard G. 22: 289
1872..Thompson, David D. 13: 447
1872..Wayland, Heman L. 10: 494
1872..Weeks, Joseph D. 13: 27
1872..Youmans, William J. 2: 466
1873..Bowles, Samuel, 3d 1: 318
1873..Carroll, Howard 3: 309
1873..Field, Eugene 1: 158
1873..Gordon, Laura deF. 2: 235

1873..Halsey, Francis W. 9:155
1873..Hawthorne, Julian 25: 45
1873..Johnson, Frederick C. ...11:253
1873..Johnson, Robert U. C:519
1873..Leupp, Francis E. 15:413
1873..McLean, John R. 1:444
1873..Powell, Joseph C. 13:357
1873..Read, Opie P. 1:353
1873..Sperry, Watson R. 1:416
1873..Stevens, Walter B. 12: 11
1873..Williams, Talcott 15:306
1874..Field, Kate 6:275
1874..Frost, George H. 18:110
1874..Keith, Adelphus B. 12:536
1874..Murphy, Bernard 18: 52
1874..Nicholson, Eliza J. 1:306
1874..Richardson, Francis H. ..13:114
1874..Scott, James F. 22:248
1874..Walker, John B. 9:195
1874..Yost, Robert M. 16:240
1875..Barron, Clarence W. 21:183
1875..Baskette, Gideon H. 8:475
1875..Bonsall, Henry L. 4:230
1875..Flickinger, Samuel J. 2:445
1875..Harper, Ida H. 25: 61
1875..Potts, James H. 10:317
1875..Taft, Charles P. 23: 7
1875..Warren, Orris H. 3: 87
1876..Carroll, John F. 18: 97
1876..Hallock, Joseph N. 11:572
1876..Lawson, Victor F. 26:177
1876..Rice, Allen T. 3:259
1876..Speed, John G. 10:294
1877..Creelman, James 14:236
1877..Edmonds, Richard H. 2:149
1877..Faulkes, Fred W. 16:196
1877..Heath, Perry S. 16:204
1877..Holman, Alfred 24:297
1877..Jenkins, Arthur 25:337
1877..Jewell, Marshall H. 11:156
1877..Luby, James 6: 49
1877..Maclennan, Frank P. 11:400
1877..Manning, James H. 1:365
1877..Ochs, Adolph S. .... A: 76
1877..Schroers, John 12: 21
1877..Singerly, William M. 1:198
1877..Smythe, William E. 17:443
1878..Arkins, John 1:268
1878..Craighead, Erwin 24:228
1878..Mack, Norman E. 26: 43
1878..Patterson, Raymond A. ...25: 48
1878..Ridder, Herman 22: 72
1878..Thompson, George 3:168
1878..Tichenor, Henry M. 20: 82
1879..Carroll, John F. 18: 97
1879..Cotnam, Perry 18:138
1879..Ferrill, William C. 18:350
1879..Fiske, Harrison G. 10:252
1879..Hudson, Joseph K. 1:208
1879..McRae, Milton A. 16:148
1879..Merrill, William B. 1:211
1879..Rice, Edwin W. 3:410
1879..Shaw, Albert 9:469
1879..Wheeler, Edward J. 18:132
1879..Windsor, Henry H. 15: 55
1880..Bailey, Edwin N. 21:103
1880..Blethen, Alden J. 17:364
1880..Daniels, Josephus .... A: 46
1880..Glass, Carter .... A: 36
1880..Glass, Franklin P. C:528
1880..Grasty, Charles H. 22:334
1880..Graves, John T. 2: 63
1880..Hepworth, George H. 4:320
1880..Keeran, Thomas J. 5: 38
1880..Markbreit, Leopold 12:467
1880..Nelson, William R. 4:170
1880..Nieman, L. W. 1:264
1880..Osborn, Norris G. 25:418
1880..Page, Walter H. 19: 13
1880..Pennypacker, Isaac R. ...13:410
1880..Porter, John A. 9:244
1880..Shuman, Edwin L. 15:275
1880..Stanley, Hiram A. 13:148
1880..Twining, Kinsley 13:450
1880..Wilson, George 8:297
1881..Bixby, Ammi L. 13:324
1881..Brown, Hilton U. 18:206
1881..Hills, William H. 4: 73
1881..Murphy, Richard J. 3:367
1881..Pepper, Charles M. 22:133
1881..Pond, Frederick E. 10:208
1881..Russell, Charles E. A:106
1881..Weiss, Anton C. 16:446
1882..Allen, George M. 5: 40
1882..Barrett, William E. 14:172
1882..Benjamin, Marcus 10:347
1882..Bok, Edward W. 23: 41
1882..Dresser, Horatio W. 11:110
1882..Heaton, John L. 11:156
1882..Jordan, James J. 4:200
1882..Kennedy, Jacob M. 14:528
1882..Munsey, Frank A. 20: 47
1882..Murphy, William J. 20:215
1882..Myrick, Herbert 25:128
1882..Norris, True L. 20:365
1882..VanNess, Joseph 18:332
1883..Brisbane, Arthur 14:156
1883..Chapple, Joe M. C:529
1883..Coolidge, Louis A. 15:198
1883..Mitchell, John A. 1:405
1883..White, Howard 5: 39
1884..Avirett, John W. 16:114
1884..Ball, Norman C. 23:185
1884..Bixby, Tams 19:222
1884..Forman, Allan 1:212
1884..Hershman, Oliver S. 21:143
1884..Howell, Clark 1:473
1884..Johnson, William E. A:502
1884..Keenan, Thomas J. 5: 38
1884..Older, Fremont C:183
1884..Owen, Sidney M. 14:381
1884..Parry, Will H. 18:116
1884..Pindell, Henry M. 18: 40
1884..Preetorius, Edward L. ...16:401
1884..Robinson, Jonah L. 13:173
1884..Walcott, Earle A. A:120
1884..Whitney, Caspar 25:284
1884..Williams, Walter C:522
1885..Bailey, George M. 5:354
1885..Bigelow, Poultney 9:143
1885..Grozier, Edwin A. 19:435
1885..Harvey, George 13:604
1885..Hitchcock, Gilbert M. ...25:100
1885..Morgan, William Y. 23:157
1885..Olcott, Ralph T. 25:232
1885..Robert, Dent H. 17:179
1885..Schermerhorn, James B:285
1885..Winship, Albert E. 2:119
1885..Wright, John E. 20: 59
1886..Babize, August C. 18:336
1886..Barr, Albert J. 5:484
1886..Cohen, John S. D:106
1886..Crothers, Robert A. D:324
1886..Dingley, Edward N. 21:167
1886..Golding, Louis T. B:156
1886..Hawthorne, Frank W. ... 6:223
1886..Lamont, Hammond 25:177
1886..Mayhall, William E. 18:126
1886..Phelps, Sheffield 11:334
1886..Phillips, John S. A:478
1886..Rathom, John R. 20:314
1886..Rowley, Frank E. 16: 99
1886..Seibold, Louis B:120
1886..Stovall, Wallace F. 12:324
1886..Tammen, Harry H. 20:321
1886..White, William Allen B:433
1886..Young, Edward S. 16:130
1887..Baker, Charles W. 16:103
1887..Beach, Charles F. 1:428
1887..Bill, Edward L. 12:525
1887..Burleigh, Clarence B. 14:377
1887..Cochrane, Elizabeth 1:241
1887..Edgerton, James A. B:197
1887..Farmer, William L. 16:424
1887..McMurchy, Wilton G. 6:356
1887..Moffett, Cleveland 14:381
1887..Stockton, Thomas T. 5:267
1887..Summers, Iverson B. 20:121
1888..Alexander, Robert C. 6: 48
1888..Booth, George G. C:187
1888..Bryce, Lloyd 1:252
1888..Cuningham, Alan 6:515
1888..Hinman, George W. 11:318
1888..Mooney, Charles P. J. 23:262
1888..Richardson, William W. ..18:335
1888..Roberts, Samuel J. 17:317
1889..Daly, Thomas A. A:218
1889..Flower, Benjamin O. 9:228
1889..Hamm, Margherita A. 9:155
1889..Mandell, George S. 25: 75
1889..Wilkins, Beriah 6:528
1890..Cobb, Frank I. 22:128
1890..Dunning, Albert E. 13:432
1890..Ellis, Bertram 18:293
1890..Finley, John H. 13:503
1890..Patterson, Thomas M. 12:555
1890..Smith, Delavan 19:442
1890..Wright, Nathaniel C. 20: 83
1891..Koenigsberg, Moses B:311
1891..Kohlsaat, Herman H. 19: 65
1891..O'Brien, Robert L. B:435
1891..Porterfield, William H. ...21:162
1891..Sears, Joseph 13:363
1891..Wiley, Franklin B. B:435
1891..Wooster, Charles 20:217
1892..Cruikshank, John M. 15:125
1892..Steffens, Lincoln 14:455
1893..Capper, Arthur .... C: 58
1893..Ellis, Bertram 18:293
1893..Moses, George H. .... C: 71
1893..Osborn, John W. 18:293
1893..Ottley, James H. 24: 64
1893..Wheelock, Webster 13:169
1894..Booth, Ralph H. C:188
1894..Cattell, J. McKeen .... D: 94
1894..Cox, James M. D:269
1894..Milton, George F. 10:293
1895..Bass, John F. 23:407
1895..Coleman, Harry H. 17:425
1895..De Graffenreid, Claude C. 18:213
1895..Harriman, Karl E. 13:357
1895..Lorimer, George H. 13:423
1895..Rosewater, Victor 13:324
1896..Auld, Robert C. 15:396
1896..Griffith, William C:532
1896..Knight, Charles L. 18:292
1896..Smith, Delavan 19:442
1896..Villard, Oswald G. D:247
1897..Ferrin, Augustin W. 15: 62
1897..Holt, Hamilton D:273
1897..Pugh, Leonard E. 22: 54
1897..Rice, Joseph M. 12:203
1898..Baker, Elbert H. C:514
1898..Congdon, Charles H. 26:208
1898..McVeigh, Thomas M. 26: 13
1898..Towne, Elizabeth L. A:205
1899..Grosvenor, Gilbert H. A:309
1899..Johnson, Burges A:243
1899..Mencken, Henry L. A:388
1899..Siddall, John M. 19: 97
1900..Bernstein, Herman C:116
1900..Bryan, John S. D:380
1900..Gibbons, Herbert A. A:492
1900..Gray, James R. 12:115
1900..Hale, William B. 15:182
1900..Hopwood, Erie C. 20:445
1900..Lee, James M. 23: 20
1900..McCormick, Medill 19: 94
1900..Stevens, Isaac N. 11:269
1901..Foster, Marcellus E. A:210
1902..Marcosson, Isaac F. D:189
1903..Banning, Kendall D:262
1903..Bullard, Arthur 21:392
1904..May, Walter W. R. D:222
1904..Silverman, Sime 24: 44
1905..Nathan, George Jean C:108
1906..Van Loon, Hendrik W. ... B: 44
1907..Bickel, Karl A. C:463
1908..Kelly, John H. 26:139
1908..Rascoe, Burton D:340
1908..Scripps, James G. 22:312
1909..Crowell, Merle C:126
1909..McCormick, Robert R. ... D: 80
1909..Mellett, Donald R. 20:362
1911..Canby, Henry S. A:126
1911..Lippmann, Walter .... D: 69
1911..Sullivan, Walter B. 19: 87
1912..Buder, Gustavus A. C:135
1912..Dealey, Walter A. 26:186
1912..Leach, Henry G. .... C: 68
1914..Crane, Frank 22:281
1914..Nye, Gerald P. C:360
1915..Kirkwood, Irwin R. 22:282
1915..Lawrence, David C:468
1915..Pickering, Loring 25:107
1919..Durkin, Martin T. 23:105
1919..Van Doren, Carl .... D: 47

Judges

See Lawyers and Judges

Jurists

1630..Ludlow, Roger 12: 60
1686..Lloyd, David 16:112
1692..Sewall, Samuel 5:339
1700..Reed, John 19:135
1702..Finney, Samuel 17:187
1725..De Lancey, James 4:550
1745..Sherman, Roger 2:352
1749..Coleman, William 17:166
1750..Shippen, Edward 10:385
1760..Cushing, William 12:548
1765..Rutledge, John 1: 21
1770..Bassett, Richard 11:530
1772..Innes, Harry 10:409
1774..Johnson, Thomas 9:289
1774..Wilson, James 1: 22
1775..Ellsworth, Oliver 1: 22
1776..Blair, John 1: 23
1776..Evans, John 17:189
1776..Jay, John 1: 20

1777..Iredell, James 1: 23
1780..Lowell, John 7: 62
1780..Marshall, John 1: 25
1787..Paterson, William 1: 24
1788..Chase, Samuel 1: 24
1789..Washington, Bushrod 1: 231
1790..Hitchcock, Samuel 11: 195
1790..Smith, Jeremiah 11: 123
1792..Trimble, Robert 2: 469
1793..Tilghman, Richard 6: 194
1795..Rutledge, John 1: 21
1796..Bourne, Benjamin 12: 345
1796..Davis, John 22: 349
1800..Potter, Henry 11: 259
1805..Story, Joseph 2: 468
1811..Taney, Roger B. 1: 27
1815..Catron, John 2: 261
1815..Turner, Squire 19: 110
1818..Bouvier, John 16: 34
1820..Jessup, William 10: 143
1820..Lumpkin, Joseph H. 10: 23
1822..Baldwin, Henry 2: 257
1823..Nelson, Samuel 2: 470
1824..Potter, Platt 10: 301
1825..Barbour, Philip P. 2: 259
1825..Hoar, Ebenezer R. 4: 20
1827..McAllister, Matthew H. ..11: 474
1828..Field, David D. 4: 236
1828..Hillyer, Junius 10: 210
1828..Parker, Amasa J. 2: 175
1830..Cowen, Benjamin S. 12: 58
1831..Sharswood, George 2: 169
1831..Swayne, Noah H. 4: 156
1834..Gaston, William 3: 513
1836..Daniel, Peter V. 2: 174
1837..Fowler, Asa 5: 192
1840..Bradley, Joseph P. 1: 33
1842..Rex, George 12: 65
1842..Thayer, Martin R. 10: 148
1845..Semmes, Thomas J. 10: 86
1846..Carpenter, Elisha 5: 243
1846..Johnson, Alexander S. ... 5: 507
1848..Allen, William J. 20: 441
1848..Davis, David 2: 474
1848..Earl, Robert 12: 59
1849..Andrews, Charles 12: 56
1850..Drummond, Thomas 20: 111
1850..Field, Stephen J. 1: 32
1850..Miller, Samuel F. 2: 473
1850..Waite, Morrison R. 1: 30
1851..Estes, Bedford M. 10: 132
1852..Blatchford, Samuel 1: 36
1854..Choate, William G. 22: 309
1854..Drake, Charles D. 3: 427
1855..Richardson, William A. .. 4: 17
1857..Strong, William 21: 4
1858..Dillon, John F. 1: 268
1858..Fuller, Melville W. 1: 31
1858..Rogers, Horatio 10: 239
1858..Stone, Wilbur F. 19: 335
1858..Valentine, Daniel M. 5: 175
1858..Van Brunt, Charles H. ..10: 141
1861..Brewer, David J. 1: 37
1862..Jackson, Howell E. 8: 243
1863..Harlan, John M. 1: 34
1863..Shipman, Nathaniel 19: 234
1864..Caldwell, Henry C. 11: 478
1864..Gray, Horace 1: 35
1865..Farman, Elbert E. 6: 508
1865..Hunt, Ward 2: 475
1865..Jenkins, James G. 19: 188
1865..Lowell, John 11: 550
1865..Nott, Charles C. 12: 357
1865..Putnam, William LeB. ...19: 278
1865..Root, Elihu 26: 1
1865..Simonton, Charles H. 12: 436
1866..McCrary, George W. 3: 201
1866..Martin, David 12: 63
1866..Whitehouse, William P. ..10: 20
1867..Lamar, Lucius Q. C. 1: 37
1868..Barringer, Victor C. 13: 351
1868..Hosea, Lewis M. 19: 360
1868..Pardee, Don A. 18: 253
1869..Davis, J. C. Bancroft 11: 115
1869..Meldrim, Peter W. 24: 9
1870..Holmes, Oliver W. 12: 349
1873..Clements, James M. 19: 356
1873..Parker, Alton B. 10: 122
1873..Ward, Henry G. 23: 25
1874..Shafer, John D. 20: 448
1875..Brown, Henry B. 1: 38
1875..Lawson, John D. 22: 287
1875..Lurton, Horace H. 8: 235
1876..Peelle, Stanton J. 14: 96
1876..Thayer, Amos M. 10: 504
1877..Butler, Fred M. 25: 138
1877..Dodge, Frederic 22: 413
1877..Fell, D. Newlin 17: 124
1877..Loring, William C. 22: 283
1878..Adams, Elmer B. 5: 385
1878..White, Edward D. 21: 3
1879..Colt, Le Baron B. 15: 408
1880..Howry, Charles B. 22: 55
1880..Richards, John K. 13: 227
1880..Sanborn, Walter H. 12: 526
1880..Stanton, Zed S. 19: 120
1881..Hall, Harry A. 18: 30
1881..Morrow, William W. ..... B: 308
1881..Townsend, William K. ...20: 239
1882..Brandeis, Louis D. .... C: 432
1882..McCall, John E. 19: 229
1882..Tuck, Somerville P. 12: 369
1882..Wallace, William J. 17: 316
1882..Ward, Henry G. 23: 25
1883..Peckham, Rufus William .11: 410
1883..Wheeler, George W. 24: 136
1884..Van De Graaff, Adrian S. 19: 416
1885..Lamar, Joseph R. 15: 414
1885..Smyth, Constantine J. ...19: 99
1886..Day, William R. 11: 11
1887..Burdick, Francis M. 26: 219
1887..Taft, William H. 23: 1
1888..Hosmer, George S. 19: 21
1889..Van Devanter, Willis .... D: 82
1889..Wigmore, John H. .... A: 79
1890..Marshall, Louis 26: 115
1890..Moody, William H. 14: 21
1891..Hughes, Charles E. ...... A: 6
1891..Moore, John Bassett ..... A: 72
1892..Gilbert, William B. ...... C: 470
1892..McKenna, Joseph 11: 18
1893..Siddons, Frederick L. 23: 119
1894..Hough, Charles M. 20: 190
1895..Minor, Raleigh C. 26: 144
1895..Mullan, George V. 24: 268
1895..Noyes, Walter C. 20: 318
1898..Gray, George 26: 17
1898..Kavanagh, Marcus .... C: 415
1898..Lowell, Francis C. 21: 320
1898..Peaslee, Robert J. .... C: 109
1899..Evans, Walter 17: 112
1899..Pound, Roscoe .... B: 51
1900..Kenyon, William S. 24: 60
1900..Rogers, Henry Wade 26: 50
1901..Long, Joseph R. .... A: 464
1901..Mayer, Julius M. 20: 371
1901..Pitney, Mahlon 15: 61
1901..Ricks, James B. 17: 171
1901..Roberts, Owen J. .... A: 88
1902..Bingham, George H. ..... C: 424
1902..Lobingier, Charles S. .... C: 64
1902..McCarty, William M. 19: 301
1903..Cardozo, Benjamin N. ... D: 50
1903..Hinton, Edward W. 26: 369
1903..McReynolds, James C. ... A: 42
1904..Costigan, George P. 26: 150
1906..Graves, Waller W. 26: 324
1906..Rugg, Arthur P. 17: 243
1907..Sanford, Edward T. 21: 92
1907..Sater, John E. .... D: 335
1908..Hoyt, Franklin C. .... A: 233
1908..Musser, George W. 19: 235
1909..Butler, Pierce .... A: 136
1909..Thomas, William H. ...... A: 21
1909..Von Moschzisker, Robert . A: 54
1910..Stone, Harlan F. .... A: 11
1912..Isaacs, Nathan .... B: 378
1912..Meyer, Carl L. W. .... B: 317
1913..Allen, Florence E. .... C: 111
1913..Anderson, George W. .... A: 412
1913..Davis, John W. .... A: 25
1914..Frankfurter, Felix .... D: 28
1920..Marshall, Carrington T. .. C: 335
1921..Faville, Frederick F. ..... D: 79
1921..McCormick, Paul J. ...... C: 459
1927..Clark, Charles E. .... D: 424

Landscape Architects

1791..L'Enfant, Pierre C. 16: 209
1830..Lamb, Joseph 11: 307
1841..Downing, Andrew J. 11: 114
1841..Mitchell, Donald G. 6: 97
1843..Pilat Ignaz A. 15: 307
1848..Saunders, William 10: 409
1850..Vaux, Calvert 9: 332
1853..Cleveland, Horace W. S. . 5: 539
1857..Olmsted, Frederick Law .. 2: 298
1859..Bushnell, Horace 8: 303
1875..Olmsted, John C. 13: 460
1878..Simonds, Ossian C. 22: 91
1879..Parsons, Samuel 26: 308
1881..Eliot, Charles 13: 108
1881..Hare, Sid J. .... D: 207
1882..Kessler, George E. 20: 296
1885..Hansen, George 22: 243
1886..Manning, Warren H. .... B: 291
1886..Platt, Charles A. 11: 306
1899..Lowell, Guy 15: 33
1901..Caparn, Harold A. ...... D: 340
1901..Hubbard, Henry Vincent . C: 504
1902..Brinckerhoff, Arthur F. .. B: 453
1905..Davis, Edward G. 26: 411
1905..Nolen, John .... B: 62
1907..Blossom, Harold H. ...... D: 269
1909..Morell, Anthony U. 20: 323
1915..Draper, Earle S. .... D: 36
1918..Hubbard, Theodora Kimball C: 505

Laryngologists, Rhinologists and Otologists

1830..Green, Horace 26: 91
1836..Dix, John H. 11: 456
1860..Solis-Cohen, Jacob daS. ..10: 92
1863..Roosa, D. B. St. John ... 9: 349
1865..Allen, Harrison 9: 359
1866..Knight, Frederick I. 14: 188
1866..Powers, George H. 15: 329
1867..Roberts, Nathan S. 2: 390
1868..Jones, Samuel J. 10: 276
1868..Lincoln, Rufus P. 15: 200
1868..Spencer, Horatio N. 5: 35
1869..Burnett, Charles H. 25: 294
1869..Calhoun, Abner W. 16: 303
1869..Campbell, James A. 7: 287
1869..Ehrhardt, Julius G. 5: 113
1869..Wagner, Clinton 1: 209
1870..Buck, Albert H. 9: 358
1870..Lefferts, George M. 23: 34
1870..Strawbridge, George 15: 143
1871..Gruening, Emil 19: 47
1871..Pomeroy, Oren D. 20: 331
1872..Robinson, Beverly 21: 125
1876..Bishop, Seth S. 21: 272
1876..Brown, Moreau R. 16: 331
1876..Burnett, Swan M. 1: 439
1876..Douglas, Orlando B. 6: 286
1876..Hyndman, James G. 14: 517
1876..Oppenheimer, Henry S. .. 2: 226
1877..Delavan, D. Bryson ..... D: 155
1877..Mayer, Emil 25: 131
1877..Swinburne, Ralph E. 2: 506
1878..Daly, William H. 10: 268
1878..Sajous, Charles E. 9: 351
1878..Shurly, Ernest L. 21: 401
1878..Thomas, Charles M. 3: 483
1880..Randall, B. Alexander ...25: 91
1881..Schadle, Jacob E. 12: 528
1881..Shapleigh, John B. 16: 105
1881..Thrasher, Allen B. 23: 279
1882..Curtis, H. Holbrook 14: 376
1882..Mackenzie, John N. 25: 343
1882..Phillips, Wendell C. 25: 186
1883..Barclay, Robert 6: 378
1883..Berens, Conrad 26: 377
1883..Casselberry, William E. ..17: 127
1884..Claiborne, John H. 3: 219
1884..Miller, Frank E. 26: 472
1884..Newcomb, James E. 23: 335
1885..Pynchon, Edward 20: 307
1885..Schadle, Jacob E. 12: 528
1885..Thorner, Max 13: 19
1886..Glasgow, William C. 5: 99
1886..Richards, George L. 24: 19
1886..Richardson, Charles W. ..22: 446
1886..Smith, S. MacCuen .... C: 162
1887..DeRoaldes, Arthur W. 7: 54
1887..Stucky, Joseph A. 25: 295
1888..Bryant, William S. .... B: 501
1888..Fitzpatrick, Thomas V. ..17: 204
1888..Holmes, Christian R. 18: 361
1888..Knight, Charles H. 25: 109
1888..Scheppegrell, William ...11: 547
1889..Makuen, G. Hudson 19: 30
1890..Loeb, Hanau W. 25: 217
1891..Brown, Richard H. 18: 397
1892..MacKenty, John E. 23: 254
1894..Kyle, D. Braden 26: 289
1896..Cullom, Marvin M. .... C: 231
1896..Johnston, Richard H. 20: 242
1898..Coakley, Cornelius G. 26: 87
1898..Smith, Harmon 26: 92
1899..Todd, Frank C. 18: 278
1900..Eagleton, Wells P. ...... D: 394
1900..Iglauer, Samuel .... D: 229
1900..Skillern, Ross H. .... B: 295
1901..Metzenbaum, Myron ..... D: 97
1902..Chamberlin, William B. .. C: 165
1904..Kopetzky, Samuel J. ..... C: 279
1907..Bigelow, Frederick N. ...20: 311
1907..Lynch, Robert C. 24: 292
1908..Wilson, John G. 17: 308
1909..Mullin, William V. 26: 84
1915..Muncie, Curtis H. .... A: 517

Lawyers and Judges

1679..Clark, William 16: 374
1682..Simcock, John 16: 443
1685..Trott, Nicholas 12: 240
1686..Lloyd, David 16: 112
1692..Sewall, Samuel 5: 339
1702..Dudley, Paul 7: 175
1710..Bull, Henry 9: 427
1715..Kinsey, John 16: 297
1724..Smith, William 11: 20
1737..Pratt, Benjamin 7: 147
1743..Bourne, Shearjashub 12: 345
1748..Livingston, William 5: 201
1752..Paine, Robert T. 5: 429
1755..Cushing, William 12: 548
1755..L'Hommedieu, Ezra 12: 417
1758..Atlee, William A. 16: 140
1760..Clinton, George 3: 41
1761..Gardiner, John 23: 296
1763..Peters, Richard 12: 235
1764..Mathews, John 12: 160
1770..Johnson, Thomas 9: 289
1771..Morris, Gouverneur 2: 526
1771..Varnum, James M. 6: 158
1773..Lewis, William 16: 410
1777..Bourne, Benjamin 12: 345
1778..Sewall, Samuel 6: 189
1781..Duncan, Thomas 16: 298
1782..Dane, Nathan 9: 196
1783..Greenup, Christopher 13: 2
1783..Rawle, William 7: 442
1785..Dallas, Alexander J. 5: 372
1785..Graham, John A. 24: 381
1785..Harper, Robert G. 5: 374
1785..Kirkpatrick, Andrew 12: 241
1785..Livingston, Edward 5: 293
1785..Van Vechten, Abraham .. 9: 162
1786..Jones, John R. 16: 268
1786..Pinkney, William 5: 373
1787..Gibbons, Thomas 24: 364
1789..Taylor, John L. 9: 285
1790..Cranch, William 7: 139
1792..Ross, John 16: 293
1792..Thompson, Smith 6: 86
1792..Wirt, William 6: 86
1794..Huston, Charles 16: 245
1795..Daviess, Joseph H. 6: 401
1796..Bell, Samuel 11: 125
1798..Grundy, Felix 6: 436
1798..Kennedy, John 16: 382
1798..Throop, Enos T. 3: 46
1800..Berrien, John M. 5: 298
1800..Binney, Horace 10: 444
1800..Clay, Henry 5: 77
1800..Kilty, William 24: 265
1800..Parke, Benjamin 16: 268
1800..Rush, Richard 5: 80
1800..Tod, John 16: 283
1801..Wilkins, William 6: 9
1802..Forsyth, John 6: 435
1802..Murphey, Archibald D. .. 7: 168
1804..Burnside, Thomas 16: 241
1804..Dearborn, Henry A. S. .. 9: 323
1804..Emmet, Thomas A. 5: 63
1804..Frelinghuysen, Theodore . 3: 401
1804..Webster, Daniel 3: 36
1805..Anthon, John 12: 548
1805..Austin, James T. 22: 209
1805..Whittlesey, Elisha 14: 523
1806..Hardin, Benjamin 12: 146
1807..Calhoun, John C. 6: 83
1807..Hamilton, James, Jr. 12: 166
1808..Crittenden, John J. 13: 6
1809..Betts, Samuel R. 22: 30
1809..Case, Leonard 11: 152
1809..Fessenden, Samuel 10: 452
1809..Parris, Albion K. 6: 306
1809..Pettibone, Rufus 16: 409
1809..Reed, John 16: 154
1809..Ruffin, Thomas 6: 289
1809..Speer, Emory 6: 161
1809..Wickliffe, Charles A. 6: 8
1810..Hubbard, Gardiner G. 5: 162
1810..Kelley, Alfred 15: 225
1810..Upshur, Abel P. 6: 8
1811..Miller, Stephen D. 12: 166
1811..Rogers, Molton C. 16: 38
1812..Coxe, Richard S. 19: 354
1812..Hayne, Robert Y. 12: 166
1812..Hoffman, Murray 11: 84
1812..Smith, Samuel E. 6: 307
1814..Baldwin, Roger S. 10: 336
1814..Dallas, George M. 6: 268
1814..McDuffie, George 12: 167
1814..O'Neall, John B. 6: 170
1814..Rawle, William H. 10: 90
1815..Badger, George E. 3: 305
1815..Booth, John B. 18: 167
1815..Loring, Charles G. 22: 284
1815..Ruggles, John 12: 230
1816..Dewey, Charles 16: 416
1816..Gerard, James W. 11: 333
1816..Marcy, William L. 6: 269
1817..Butler, Benjamin F. 5: 297
1817..Nelson, Samuel 2: 470
1817..Pennington, William 5: 206
1817..Simpson, James 12: 48
1817..Storer, Bellamy 11: 338
1818..Hall, James 7: 198
1818..Judah, Samuel 24: 361
1818..Morehead, James T. 13: 5
1819..Doty, James D. 12: 72
1819..Howard, Tilghman A. 18: 56
1819..Kinney, Amory 18: 10
1819..Mason, John Y. 6: 7
1820..Conyngham, John N. 9: 282
1820..Edmonds, John W. 10: 231
1820..Jones, Joel 7: 13
1820..Legaré, Hugh S. 6: 5
1820..Sewall, Samuel E. 10: 466
1820..Stevens, Thaddeus 4: 30
1821..Choate, Rufus 6: 17
1821..McMahon, John VanL. 11: 186
1821..Robinson, James F. 13: 9
1821..Walker, Robert J. 6: 269
1822..Cushing, Caleb 4: 151
1822..Gilpin, Henry D. 6: 437
1822..Helm, John La R. 13: 7
1822..Miller, Andrew G. 16: 230
1822..Pearson, John J. 14: 335
1823..Haines, Daniel 5: 207
1823..Hise, Elijah 12: 54
1823..Hoffman, Ogden 11: 84
1823..Mitchell, William 10: 238
1823..Moore, Bartholomew F. .. 9: 457
1825..Andrews, Sherlock J. 6: 11
1825..Ashmun, George 6: 430
1825..Cadwalader, John 15: 305
1825..Inglis, William 9: 223
1825..Kent, Edward 6: 308
1825..Latrobe, John H. B. 9: 426
1824..Laurence, William D. 9: 399
1826..Pearson, Richmond M. 11: 89
1826..Rice, Harvey 13: 81
1827..Birchard, Matthew 15: 53
1827..Fessenden, William P. 2: 90
1827..Green, William 22: 242
1827..Williams, Thomas 15: 329
1828..Dean, Amos 22: 116
1829..Black, Jeremiah S. 5: 5
1829..Cilley, Jonathan 10: 109
1829..Prentiss, Seargent S. 7: 477
1829..Rantoul, Robert, Jr. 11: 232
1829..Silliman, Benjamin D. 6: 54
1830..Williams, Joseph 12: 342
1831..Bradley, Robert McA. 7: 539
1831..Butler, Charles E. 18: 121
1832..Cony, Samuel 6: 314
1832..Davis, David 2: 474
1833..Sargent, John O. 9: 432
1833..Willey, Waitman T. 12: 455
1834..Douglas, Stephen A. 2: 428
1834..Merrick, Edwin T. 10: 147
1834..Spooner, Lysander 18: 419
1835..Hosmer, Hezekiah L. 13: 237
1835..Joy, James F. 18: 120
1835..Reade, Edwin G. 11: 459
1835..Scammon, Jonathan Y. .. 7: 527
1835..Stevenson, John W. 13: 9
1835..Upham, Don Alonzo J. 10: 168
1836..Arnold, Isaac N. 11: 375
1836..Calvin, Samuel 12: 544
1836..Lockwood, Rufus A. 18: 161
1836..Shafter, Oscar L. 15: 309
1836..Tower, Charlemagne 5: 188
1836..Williams, Othniel S. 7: 267
1837..Bushnell, Nehemiah 16: 34
1837..Chandler, Peleg W. 15: 350
1837..Fowler, Asa 5: 192
1837..Glover, Samuel T. 25: 370
1837..Morrill, Lot M. 6: 313
1837..Roberts, Oran M. 9: 73
1838..Hamilton, Peter 12: 550
1838..Pruyn, Isaac 7: 160
1838..Seddon, James A. 6: 219
1838..Taft, Alphonso 4: 24
1839..Curtin, Andrew G. 24: 412
1839..English, Elbert H. 12: 507
1839..Frelinghuysen, Frederick T. 4: 250
1839..Hall, Benjamin F. 13: 24
1839..Parker, Cortlandt 12: 268
1839..Russell, Charles Theodore .11: 181
1840..Bingham, John A. 9: 375
1840..Dana, Richard H. 24: 178
1840..Doyle, John T. 7: 454
1840..King, Rufus 23: 364
1840..MacArthur, Arthur 13: 477
1840..Upton, William W. 12: 44
1841..Broadhead, James O. 5: 68
1841..Davis, Noah 11: 236
1841..Fisher, George P. 22: 346
1841..Lawrence, William 24: 246
1841..Robertson, William J. 19: 383
1841..Stites, Henry J. 12: 110
1842..Aldrich, James T. 12: 138
1842..Bashford, Coles 12: 74
1842..Cobb, Thomas R. R. 6: 533
1842..Currey, John 12: 418
1842..Estabrook, Experience 14: 286
1842..Lawton, Alexander R. 2: 148
1842..Miller, Elihu S. 10: 172
1843..Butler, William A. 7: 315
1843..Cooke, William M. 16: 302
1843..Ingersoll, Robert G. 9: 255
1843..Nash, Stephen P. 11: 470
1843..Phelps, Edward J. 5: 411
1843..Sanger, George P. 11: 412
1844..Bullitt, Joshua F. 13: 19
1844..Campbell, James V. 9: 145
1844..Crawford, Samuel 17: 8
1844..Lothrop, George Van N. . 5: 160
1845..Barnes, William 1: 469
1845..Bullitt, John C. 22: 422
1845..Hill, Benjamin H. 10: 194
1845..Lewis, James T. 12: 75
1845..Miller, William E. 12: 70
1845..Southmayd, Charles F. 15: 39
1846..Bingham, Harry 13: 151
1846..Carpenter, Elisha 5: 243
1846..Coffey, Titian J. 5: 135
1846..Cooley, Thomas McI. 9: 522
1846..Fish, Asa I. 16: 61
1846..Gerard, James W., Jr. 11: 333
1846..Gibson, Charles 5: 114
1846..Jewett, Freeborn G. 12: 65
1846..Richardson, William A. .. 4: 17
1846..Seevers, William H. 12: 70
1846..Vanderpoel, Aaron J. 21: 419
1846..Wood, Daniel P. 2: 248
1847..Bell, Charles H. 11: 137
1847..Carpenter, Matthew H. .. 4: 22
1847..Carrington, Henry B. 22: 253
1847..Carroll, David W. 5: 115
1847..Deady, Matthew P. 19: 50
1847..Dougherty, Daniel 5: 477
1847..McCagg, Ezra B. 20: 235
1847..MacKinstry, Elisha W. 16: 57
1847..Terry, David S. 12: 104
1848..Allen, William J. 20: 441
1848..Alvey, Richard H. 12: 238
1848..Betts, George F. 22: 31
1848..Durfee, Thomas 12: 251
1848..Earl, Robert 12: 59
1848..Goudy, William C. 16: 311
1848..Pike, Robert G. 24: 100
1848..Stark, Joshua 2: 138
1848..Van Alstyne, Thomas J. .. 9: 325
1849..Calvin, Delano C. 5: 151
1849..Cobb, Amasa 6: 191
1849..Du Pont, Victor 21: 408
1849..Fassett, Newton P. 5: 173
1849..Hittell, Theodore H. 22: 42
1849..Pryor, Roger A. 9: 147
1849..Sullivan, Algernon S. 24: 380
1850..Andrews, Christopher C. .11: 393
1850..Bangs, Francis H. 11: 370
1850..Bingham, Edward F. 11: 463
1850..Eaton, Dorman B. 21: 200
1850..Gilfillan, James 16: 311
1850..Heard, Franklin F. 23: 320
1850..McAllister, Ward 6: 169
1850..Paxon, Edward 5: 382
1850..Shipman, William D. 11: 262
1851..Bruce, Horatio W. 11: 212
1851..Caswell, Lucien B. 16: 397
1851..Converse, George L. 5: 338
1851..Harding, George F. 19: 129
1851..Hindman, Thomas C. 22: 130
1851..Hitchcock, Henry 11: 196
1851..Keyes, Elisha W. 10: 152
1851..Middlebrook, Louis N. 16: 384
1851..Miller, Benjamin K. 16: 230
1851..Nott, Charles C. 12: 357
1851..Parsons, Richard C. 6: 251
1851..Simonton, Charles H. 12: 436
1851..Taussig, James 16: 382
1851..Walker, James M. 15: 381
1852..Abbott, Austin 2: 342
1852..Abbott, Benjamin V. 5: 107
1852..Buist, Henry 2: 108
1852..Caldwell, Henry C. 11: 478
1852..Choate, Charles F. 14: 253
1852..Duncombe, John F. 24: 60

1852..Edgerton, Alonzo J. 12: 54
1852..Gordon, Jonathan W. 18: 264
1852..Knott, J. Proctor 13: 11
1852..Ireland, John 9: 74
1852..Magee, Christopher 14: 185
1852..Vest, George G. 2: 297
1853..Bedle, Joseph D. 5: 210
1853..Bell, Clarke 13: 204
1853..Carter, James C. 22: 26
1853..Cheever, Henry M. 5: 93
1853..Corson, Dighton 16: 405
1853..Coudert, Frederic R. 6: 59
1853..French, Asa 14: 257
1853..Garland, Augustus H. ... 2: 409
1853..Green, Robert S. 5: 212
1853..Henry, William W. 9: 272
1853..Hitchcock, Thomas 17: 185
1853..Kean, Robert G. H. 12: 549
1853..Lothrop, Thornton K. ... D: 144
1853..Moore, William A. 9: 107
1853..Ordronaux, John 12: 331
1853..Penrose, Clement B. 16: 428
1853..Richardson, George F. ...15: 168
1853..Rose, U. M. 7: 126
1853..Smith, Nelson 6: 76
1853..Tunnicliff, Damon G. 18: 194
1854..Arnold, Reuben 16: 234
1854..Choate, William G. 22: 309
1854..Gresham, Walter Q. 24: 330
1854..Langdell, Christopher C. .. 6: 423
1854..Walker, Edwin 10: 474
1855..Carter, Walter S. 23: 178
1855..Choate, Joseph H. 9: 159
1855..Ewing, Thomas 25: 15
1855..Fenner, Charles E. 16: 224
1855..Jenkins, James G. 19: 188
1855..Judson, Stiles 16: 325
1855..Otis, Alfred G. 11: 95
1855..Salomon, Edward 12: 75
1855..Tenney, Daniel K. 16: 329
1855..Tree, Lambert 6: 161
1855..Vanderburgh, Charles E. . 6: 131
1855..Woerner, J. Gabriel 5: 48
1856..Cowley, Charles 23: 277
1856..Dent, Thomas 17: 278
1856..Guffy, Bayless L. D. 12: 454
1856..Magie, William J. 12: 424
1856..O'Connor, Charles 3: 387
1856..Rhodes, Augustus L. 12: 97
1856..Thayer, James B. 9: 436
1856..Weaver, James B. 16: 146
1857..Black, George R. 16: 229
1857..Clark, Greenleaf 22: 305
1857..Dittenhoefer, Abram J. ..14: 362
1857..Kimball, Eben W. 7: 254
1857..Knott, A. Leo 11: 545
1857..Wade, Decius S. 12: 71
1857..Willie, Asa H. 11: 435
1857..Zane, Charles S. 12: 128
1858..Battle, Burrill B. 6: 21
1858..Brewster, Lyman D. 6: 114
1858..Dodd, Samuel C. T. 24: 264
1858..Dwight, Theodore W. 6: 346
1858..Ellis, Thomas C. W. 11: 83
1858..Griffin, Levi T. 20: 99
1858..Hallett, Moses 12: 339
1858..Hazeltine, George C. 5: 194
1858..Isham, Edward S. 7: 107
1858..McCullough, John G. 14: 322
1858..Riggs, Samuel A. 11: 250
1858..Shope, Simeon P. 12: 69
1858..Spaulding, Oliver L. 20: 75
1858..Wallace, William J. 17: 316
1859..Box, Henry W. 2: 37
1859..Butler, John M. 2: 355
1859..Eder, Phanor J. .... B: 111
1859..Guernsey, Rocellus S. 12: 275
1859..Howe, William F. 22: 49
1859..Olney, Richard 7: 143
1859..Somerville, Henderson M. 18: 220
1859..Woods, Thomas H. 12: 453
1860..Candler, Flamen B. 16: 96
1860..Dickinson, Don M. 2: 410
1860..Fairchild, Lucius 12: 76
1860..Gardiner, Asa Bird 14: 332
1860..Gilfillan, John B. 21: 390
1860..Granger, Charles T. 12: 69
1860..Horton, Albert H. 6: 129
1860..Loew, Frederick W. 7: 309
1860..Sims, William H. 6: 113
1861..Applegate, John S. 15: 412
1861..Bispham, George T. 19: 123
1861..Gibson, Charles 5: 114
1861..Lore, Charles B. 7: 553
1861..Shapley, Rufus E. 2: 190
1861..Springer, William McK. ..11: 85
1861..Teller, Henry M. 15: 228
1861..Wheeler, Everett P. 12: 53
1862..Gordon, Laura de F. 2: 235
1862..Gray, John C. 16: 206
1862..Hamilton, Samuel K. 14: 235
1862..Schouler, James 11: 181
1862..Stillman, Thomas E. 15: 103
1862..Tourgee, Albion W. 7: 324
1863..Cooke, Martin W. 5: 31
1863..Davis, Lowndes H. 19: 244
1863..Gray, George 26: 17
1863..Hadlock, Harvey D. 1: 237
1863..Horton, Oliver H. 16: 86
1863..Hyde, E. Francis 24: 124
1863..James, Edward C. 9: 370
1863..Johnson, John G. 16: 421
1863..Miller, Richard T. 5: 305
1863..Phelps, William W. 7: 451
1863..Platt, Henry C. 5: 501
1863..Symonds, Joseph W. 15: 346
1864..Baer, George F. 14: 37
1864..Cadwalader, John 15: 305
1864..Gazzam, Joseph M. 15: 40
1864..Hill, Lysander 16: 136
1864..Lincoln, Solomon 14: 295
1864..Page, Samuel D. 15: 352
1864..Uhl, Edwin F. 15: 100
1865..Barton, Robert T. 7: 519
1865..Bradley, William O'C. ...13: 12
1865..Bristow, Benjamin H. ... 4: 23
1865..Conrad, Holmes 16: 399
1865..Delmas, Delphin M. 24: 387
1865..Doyle, John H. 19: 80
1865..Greene, Richard H. 24: 306
1865..Hamilton, James K. 18: 380
1865..Harris, Addison C. 17: 191
1865..Hungerford, Frank L. ...16: 143
1865..Jones, William M. 5: 46
1865..Kibbee, Charles C. 7: 51
1865..Lewis, Charlton T. 11: 62
1865..Mead, Warren H. 6: 490
1865..Miller, William H. H. 18: 189
1865..O'Brien, Thomas J. 25: 420
1865..Rogers, John I. 14: 230
1865..Sulzberger, Mayer 15: 283
1865..Vann, Irving G. 6: 220
1866..Betts, Frederic H. 2: 38
1866..Bunn, Henry G. 9: 446
1866..Cox, Rowland 15: 76
1866..Dolph, Cyrus A. 16: 56
1866..Douglas, William W. 14: 241
1866..Gross, Judson N. 6: 322
1866..Hagerman, James 16: 169
1866..Hanna, Septimus J. 19: 119
1866..Howard, Timothy E. 16: 441
1866..Lauterback, Edward 26: 227
1866..Payne, Sereno E. 10: 398
1866..Pennypacker, Samuel W. . 9: 487
1866..Robb, John S. 5: 338
1866..Taylor, Robert S. 17: 414
1866..Williamson, Samuel E. ...12: 420
1866..Wood, Horatio D. 16: 373
1867..Beaman, Charles C. 15: 167
1867..Beekman, Henry R. 12: 469
1867..Black, John C. 12: 101
1867..Christian, George L. 20: 321
1867..Duncan, John S. 16: 314
1867..Emery, Woodward 14: 225
1867..Fenn, Augustus H. 16: 374
1867..Hines, Thomas H. 12: 453
1867..Howe, Daniel W. 13: 289
1867..Monroe, Frank A. 12: 103
1867..Packard, Samuel W. 10: 177
1867..Parsons, Henry C. 14: 497
1867..Peelle, Stanton J. 14: 96
1867..Spooner, John C. 14: 33
1867..Sterling, John W. 19: 36
1867..Taggart, Moses 16: 306
1867..Taylor, Henry C. 17: 230
1868..Boyle, Wilbur F. 12: 35
1868..Dayton, Charles W. 11: 491
1868..De Witt, George G. 12: 341
1868..Fletcher, Thomas 12: 325
1868..Fuller, Paul 16: 380
1868..Hart, William H. H. 9: 382
1868..Hershfield, Abraham 24: 54
1868..Hosea, Lewis M. 19: 360
1868..Kinne, La Vega G. 12: 446
1868..Pugsley, Isaac P. 16: 189
1868..Remley, Milton 16: 294
1868..Root, Elihu 26: 1
1868..Smith, John P. 18: 105
1868..Sprague, Henry H. 14: 195
1868..Thorndike, John L. 20: 260
1868..Truax, Charles H. 12: 261
1868..Vanamee, William 16: 50
1868..Wright, Luke E. 26: 94
1869..Ayer, Benjamin F. 9: 521
1869..Bartlett, Willard 15: 412
1869..Bates, Clement 23: 68
1869..Case, Nelson 19: 103
1869..Kneeland, Stillman F. ... 7: 312
1869..Lewis, Lunsford L. 12: 96
1869..Meldrim, Peter W. 24: 9
1869..Morrow, William W. ..... B: 308
1869..Plumley, Frank 26: 206
1869..Rabe, Rudolph F. 5: 231
1869..Springer, Frank 20: 23
1869..Stanley, Charles H. 16: 301
1869..Stone, Carlos M. 15: 136
1869..Thompson, Seymour D. ..19: 28
1869..Thurston, John M. 5: 105
1869..Tompkins, Henry C. 7: 339
1870..Bowers, John M. 24: 38
1870..Eaton, Sherburne B. 7: 130
1870..Hall, John M. 15: 227
1870..Harriman, Hiram P. 14: 273
1870..Hummel, Abraham H. ...25: 440
1870..McBride, Thomas A. ..... B: 325
1870..Miller, John S. .... B: 464
1870..Shields, Albert S. L. 18: 218
1870..Toole, Joseph K. 11: 82
1870..Weeks, William R. 10: 358
1870..Wright, Luke E. 14: 20
1871..Alexander, Robert 10: 292
1871..Allen, Joseph S. 18: 51
1871..Beatty, Robert M. 7: 99
1871..Boyd, A. Hunter 15: 86
1871..Chambers, William L. 25: 62
1871..Chester, Alden 24: 96
1871..Clearwater, Alphonso T. .18: 417
1871..Couzins, Phoebe 15: 348
1871..Fall, Charles G. 23: 63
1871..Frank, Nathan .... C: 293
1871..Gaynor, William J. 16: 353
1871..Grady, John C. 5: 33
1871..Gregory, Stephen S. 18: 273
1871..Ide, Henry C. 23: 29
1871..Johnson, Frank A. 18: 407
1871..Jones, William M. 5: 46
1871..McClain, Emlin 16: 253
1871..Peck, George R. 10: 317
1871..Rawle, Francis 17: 388
1871..Russell, Talcott H. 25: 397
1871..Soley, James R. 16: 136
1871..Trude, Alfred S. 14: 132
1872..Alexander, Charles B. 15: 83
1872..Barclay, Shepard 12: 455
1872..DeForest, Robert W. ..... B: 61
1872..Elam, John B. 18: 193
1872..Farrar, Edgar H. 19: 346
1872..Gregory, Charles N. 16: 239
1872..Griggs, John W. 11: 19
1872..Gross, Charles E. 20: 470
1872..Holcomb, Marcus H. 23: 381
1872..Huey, Samuel B. 3: 67
1872..Joline, Adrian H. 15: 392
1872..Leventritt, David 14: 310
1872..Lexow, Clarence 5: 496
1872..Lilienthal, Jesse 20: 207
1872..Lindley, Curtis H. 25: 166
1872..McClellan, Thomas N. 12: 549
1872..Moore, William H. 23: 72
1872..Newton, Henry G. 16: 155
1872..Notman, John 15: 103
1872..Parker, Ralzemond A. 15: 271
1872..Shelby, John T. 19: 100
1873..Backus, Henry C. 6: 164
1873..Birney, Arthur A. 21: 434
1873..Graves, Charles A. 22: 197
1873..Harrity, William F. 25: 393
1873..Ivins, William M. 12: 378
1873..Judson, Frederick N. 7: 284
1873..Keasbey, Edward Q. 18: 95
1873..Lord, Franklin B. 14: 491
1873..Martin, William L. 7: 399
1873..Nagel, Charles .... D: 266
1873..Nevius, Henry M. 14: 433
1873..Peters, George S. 21: 380
1873..Philipp, M. Bernard 26: 190
1873..Pierce, Henry D. 22: 326
1873..Reid, Harry M. 7: 364
1873..Simpson, John W. 25: 182
1873..Ward, Henry G. 23: 25
1873..Wegg, David S. 18: 231
1873..Wilson, Floyd B. 25: 194
1873..Woolley, John G. 20: 359
1874..Bonaparte, Charles J. 14: 22
1874..Brooke, D. Tucker 16: 405
1874..Burford, John H. 14: 432
1874..Carson, Hampton L. 3: 264
1874..Curtis, Leonard E. 20: 238
1874..Dickinson, Jacob M. 14: 410
1874..Dougherty, John H. 20: 124
1874..Fairbanks, Charles W. ...14: 10
1874..Grosscup, Peter S. 15: 253
1874..Gulliver, William C. 16: 332
1874..Hemingway, Wilson E. ..18: 354

1874..Judkins, J. Byron 16: 51
1874..Knight, Clarence A. 15: 132
1874..Loesch, Frank J. .... C: 18
1874..Noyes, George H. 17: 20
1874..O'Brien, Morgan J. ..... D: 235
1874..Richards, Franklin S. ...18: 151
1874..Russell, Charles H. 26: 85
1874..Squire, Andrew .... C: 284
1874..Stevens, Hiram F. 16: 335
1874..Sullivan, Jeremiah F. 20: 28
1874..Sutro, Theodore 3: 14
1874..Thornton, Charles S. 10: 219
1875..Allen, John M. 17: 269
1875..Atkinson, George W. 12: 432
1875..Beckley, John N. 5: 278
1875..Bulkeley, Alpheus T. 24: 176
1875..Burton, Theodore E. 21: 50
1875..Calhoun, William J. 14: 429
1875..Chickering, William H. ...24: 218
1875..Cotter, James E. 14: 313
1875..Darlington, Joseph J. 19: 272
1875..Dunn, Frank K. .... D: 431
1875..Edwards, Samuel 15: 97
1875..Elder, Samuel J. 21: 457
1875..Estabrook, Henry D. 14: 286
1875..Haight, George W. 15: 308
1875..Hays, Daniel P. 24: 53
1875..Jennings, Frederick B. ...14: 503
1875..King, Alexander C. 22: 431
1875..Knox, Philander C. 24: 7
1875..Ledyard, Lewis C. 22: 28
1875..Maxwell, Lawrence 23: 204
1875..Mynderse, Wilhelmus 15: 104
1875..Powers, Samuel L. 24: 309
1875..Prentice, Samuel O. 16: 182
1875..Snow, Zerubbabel L. 19: 447
1875..Somers, Peter J. 2: 184
1875..Taggart, Rush 14: 75
1875..Thacher, Thomas 24: 229
1875..Vaile, Joel F. 17: 331
1875..Wade, Levi C. 15: 212
1876..Barker, Forrest E. 16: 387
1876..Belmont, Perry .... D: 349
1876..Clark, Champ 14: 171
1876..Downing, Henry H. 18: 427
1876..Eastman, Sidney C. 22: 278
1876..Fish, Frederick P. 26: 202
1876..Goff, John W. 15: 254
1876..Harrison, Robert L. ...... C: 221
1876..Johnes, Edward R. 3: 269
1876..Kendrick, Edmund P. 20: 120
1876..Krauthoff, Louis C. 18: 165
1876..McKenney, William R. ...16: 26
1876..Mays, Franklin P. 25: 240
1876..Metcalf, Victor H. 14: 25
1876..Moot, Adelbert 24: 94
1876..Nicoll, DeLancey 14: 297
1876..Parker, Bowdoin S. 15: 267
1876..Payne, John B. .... D: 348
1876..Rogers, Henry W. 26: 50
1876..Ryan, Daniel J. 19: 301
1876..Shaw, Leslie M. 23: 118
1876..Shields, John K. 26: 109
1875..Steele, John N. 14: 77
1876..Townsend, James M. 14: 490
1876..Walker, Robert F. 26: 107
1876..Warner, John DeW. 9: 114
1877..Brandeis, Louis D. .... C: 432
1877..Bryan, John P. K. 11: 151
1877..Bunn, Charles W. .... C: 368
1877..Courtnay, Dominic G. 16: 401
1877..Dana, Richard H. 24: 178
1877..Dunne, Edward F. 16: 122
1877..Eustis, John E. 25: 327
1877..Goebel, William 13: 13
1877..Hurlburt, Henry F. 20: 241
1877..Kellogg, Frank B. .... A: 8
1877..Kelly, Edmond 14: 222
1877..Lines, George 22: 292
1877..Noel, Edmund F. 14: 518
1877..Sheldon, Theodore 15: 296
1877..Southard, Louis C. 16: 384
1877..Streeter, Frank S. 16: 293
1877..Turner, Wilbur R. .... A: 132
1877..Watson, John H. 21: 409
1878..Andrews, James O. 19: 373
1878..Bonner, Wilkerson A. 18: 208
1878..Bullitt, William C. 15: 343
1878..Butler, Fred M. 25: 138
1878..Campbell, Henry M. 15: 328
1878..Campbell, Thomas M. 14: 43
1878..Carpenter, William L. ...14: 364
1878..Clarke, John H. .... A: 248
1878..Darrow, Clarence .... B: 222
1878..Dawley, Frank F. 16: 394
1878..DeForest, Henry W. ..... D: 217
1878..Denégre, George 24: 375
1878..Dill, James B. 6: 443
1878..Elliott, George F. 10: 291
1878..Hiscock, Frank H. .... A: 10
1878..Macfarlane, Hugh C. 11: 212
1878..Marshall, Louis 26: 115
1878..Moody, William H. 14: 21
1878..Sanger, William C. 20: 84
1878..Sears, Nathaniel C. 16: 74
1878..Stanchfield, John B. 14: 360
1878..Untermyer, Samuel 17: 396
1878..Wilcox, Ansley 21: 201
1879..Bartlett, David 18: 226
1879..Beauchamp, James K. ... A: 325
1879..Black, Frank S. 16: 255
1879..Buchanan, Arthur S. 18: 22
1879..Chamberlain, George E. ..14: 135
1879..Chilton, William E. 15: 343
1879..Cutting, Charles S. 26: 415
1879..Houghton, Frank W. 24: 233
1879..Larner, John B. 22: 378
1879..Mechem, Floyd R. 23: 361
1879..Miller, John H. 26: 334
1879..O'Donnell, Thomas J. 16: 229
1879..Redding, William A. ..... C: 426
1879..Sackett, Henry W. 7: 134
1879..Whitridge, Frederick W. .15: 74
1880..Bancroft, Edgar A. 14: 373
1880..Benedict Alfred B. 25: 197
1880..Bowers, Lloyd W. 22: 148
1880..Buckingham, Charles L. .. 2: 499
1880..Bullitt, Joshua F. 18: 224
1880..Cabell, James A. 22: 273
1880..Curtiss, George B. 18: 436
1880..Davison, Charles S. ...... C: 257
1880..Dayton, Alston G. 17: 77
1880..Defrees, Joseph H. 25: 26
1880..Foster, Roger S. B. 23: 355
1880..Godman, Melvin M. 16: 195
1880..Guthrie, William D. 15: 96
1880..Holls, Frederick W. 11: 38
1880..Johnson, James M. 25: 359
1880..La Follette, Robert M. ...19: 425
1880..Lyon, Frank A. 19: 258
1880..O'Doherty, Mathew 22: 71
1880..Paul, Amasa C. 16: 200
1880..Sherman, James S. 14: 406
1880..Steele, Charles 14: 78
1880..Steele, Isaac N. 14: 77
1880..Villere, Omer 18: 193
1880..Wickersham, George W. .. C: 16
1880..Wickersham, James ...... D: 279
1880..Williams, Mornay 21: 334
1881..Beale, William G. 20: 289
1881..Burroughs, Ambrose H. ..25: 247
1881..Dixon, N. Walter 6: 141
1881..Fearons, George H. 14: 74
1881..Guy, Charles L. 24: 349
1881..Hall, Harry A. 18: 30
1881..Hanks, Charles S. 14: 247
1881..Harlan, Henry D. 9: 116
1881..Kleberg, Robert J. .... C: 267
1881..Mayer, Levy 6: 531
1881..Morawetz, Victor .... D: 193
1881..Moss, Frank 9: 328
1881..Olcott, Jacob Van V. 14: 210
1881..Payne, John Barton ..... D: 348
1881..Sheehan, William F. 18: 144
1881..Sherwood, Carl G. .... B: 413
1881..Smith, Edwin W. .... C: 426
1881..Sweetland, William H. ... B: 249
1881..Titus, Harry L. 18: 352
1881..Van Devanter, Willis .... D: 82
1881..Wood, Fremont .... A: 524
1881..Woodward, John 6: 162
1882..Arnold, William H. .... B: 154
1882..Baylies, Edmund L. 18: 320
1882..Bruce, William C. 18: 47
1882..Cotton, William W. 18: 213
1882..Crawford, Corie I. 14: 200
1882..Ewing, Presley K. 17: 213
1882..Gerber, David 14: 363
1882..Goodnow, Frank J. .... C: 19
1882..Lamberton, James M. 16: 379
1882..Loring, Victor J. 15: 119
1882..McCall, John E. 19: 229
1882..McCarter, Robert H. ..... D: 233
1882..Magoon, Charles E. 14: 32
1882..Marshall, Charles C. ...... C: 496
1882..Merrick, Edwin T. 26: 354
1882..Miller, George P. 23: 126
1882..Morrow, Thomas R. 19: 387
1882..Page, George T. .... A: 366
1882..Pitney, Mahlon 15: 61
1882..Remick, James W. .... A: 77
1882..Rowe, William V. 22: 139
1882..Russell, William H. 15: 323
1882..Taft, Edgar S. 21: 370
1882..Van Rensselaer, Courtlandt S. 23: 256
1882..Ward, Herbert H. 22: 224
1882..Webster, Thayer 26: 412
1882..Wellman, Arthur H. 14: 108
1883..Benneson, Cora A. 17: 398
1883..Bissell, Herbert P. 22: 137
1883..Bradford, Ernest W. 16: 227
1883..Brownell, George F. 24: 82
1883..Carey, Charles H. 16: 284
1883..Gaston, William A. 15: 399
1883..Gillett, Emma M. 17: 180
1883..Lee, Blair .... C: 453
1883..MacVeagh, Charles 23: 17
1883..Moore, John Bassett ..... A: 72
1883..Oakley, Horace S. 22: 257
1883..Packer, Gibson D. 22: 240
1883..Paton, Thomas B. 16: 59
1883..Penrose, Boies 2: 444
1883..Pettit, Horace 25: 280
1883..Place, Ira A. 21: 218
1883..Roberts, David E. 16: 327
1883..Russell, Charles W. 15: 358
1883..Smith, Burton .... D: 313
1883..Speer, Emory 6: 161
1883..Welling, Richard W. G. .. C: 145
1883..Wheeler, George W. 24: 136
1883..Williams, Nathan W. 22: 288
1883..Wiltsie, Charles H. 25: 57
1884..Atwood, John H. 18: 434
1884..Bacon, Selden .... D: 72
1884..Bartlett, Philip G. .... B: 246
1884..Brown, Albert O. .... A: 50
1884..Burrage, Albert C. 12: 551
1884..Carter, Orrin N. 24: 335
1884..Elliott, Charles B. 15: 104
1884..Evans, Beverly D. 6: 142
1884..Felder, Thomas B. 20: 307
1884..Gresham, Otto .... D: 204
1884..Hughes, Charles E. .... A: 6
1884..Jerome, William T. 26: 149
1884..Kelley, Hermon A. 15: 226
1884..Leaming, Thomas 15: 137
1884..Lothrop, George Van N. . 5: 160
1884..Lum, Charles M. .... C: 339
1884..McGown, Floyd 6: 524
1884..McReynolds, James C. .... A: 42
1884..Merrill, Joseph H. 17: 14
1884..Preston, Byron W. ...... D: 124
1884..Rackham, Horace H. 24: 235
1884..Sater, John E. .... D: 335
1884..Schofield, William 15: 138
1884..Scovel, Henry S. 17: 263
1884..Trask, Walter J. 16: 330
1884..Vickery, Willis .... A: 209
1884..Whipple, Sherman L. 26: 432
1884..Woodbury, Egburt E. 18: 309
1885..Abbott, Howard S. 16: 47
1885..Anderson, Jefferson R. ...16: 31
1885..Babb, James E. 26: 55
1885..Bates, John L. 10: 133
1885..Dittenhoefer, Irving M. ..14: 363
1885..Gregory, Thomas W. ..... A: 43
1885..Grubb, William I. .... C: 478
1885..Haff, Delbert J. 16: 133
1885..Ingersoll, George P. 24: 216
1885..Keeler, Harvey R. 16: 203
1885..Long, Chester I. .... C: 56
1885..McAdoo, William G. ..... A: 34
1885..Mathewson, Charles F. ...14: 193
1885..Melville, Henry 16: 49
1885..Pou, James H. 26: 34
1885..Rand, John L. .... B: 178
1885..Rector, Edward 24: 419
1885..Reed, James A. 15: 99
1885..Settle, Thomas 18: 400
1885..Sharpe, Nelson 26: 26
1885..Short, Frank H. 19: 330
1885..Smyth, Constantine J. ...19: 99
1885..Wise, Edmond E. 24: 397
1885..Wyman, Henry A. 26: 83
1886..Ballinger, Richard A. 14: 413
1886..Boston, Charles A. 16: 108
1886..Cope, Walter B. 15: 278
1886..Cravath, Paul D. .... C: 110
1886..Crissinger, Daniel R. .... C: 244
1886..Curtis, James B. 25: 422
1886..Evans, Victor J. 16: 424
1886..Garrison, Lindley M. ..... A: 39
1886..Hardon, Henry W. 25: 254
1886..Ogden, Howard N. 16: 131
1886..Page, William H. 17: 195
1886..Pam, Max 14: 394
1886..Pomerene, Atlee .... C: 341
1886..Pound, Cuthbert W. 25: 5
1886..Powers, George McC. 17: 334
1886..Shipman, Andrew J. 15: 209
1887..Beach, Edward S. .... B: 284
1887..Cunningham, Donnell LaF. D: 325
1887..Depew, Ganson .... C: 258

1887..Dowling, Victor J. .... C: 347
1887..Esch, John J. .... A: 530
1887..Gould, Frank H. 20: 227
1887..Jackson, Percy .... C: 305
1887..Lowden, Frank O. .... B: 35
1887..Minor, Benjamin S. ...... C: 193
1887..O'Brien, Thomas D. 21: 396
1887..Ramsey, Robert 25: 200
1887..Trask, James E. 16: 333
1887..Wiest, Howard .... D: 304
1888..Allis, Wallace S. 26: 238
1888..Betts, Samuel R. 22: 30
1888..Bordwell, Walter 16: 184
1888..Boyden, Roland W. 23: 57
1888..Bradley, Thomas E. D. ... C: 287
1888..Butler, Pierce .... A: 136
1888..Cochran, George I. 16: 369
1888..Craig, Charles C. .... D: 241
1888..Elkus, Abram I. .... D: 366
1888..Fisher, Walter L. 17: 406
1888..Frost, Thomas G. 14: 431
1888..Garfield, James R. 14: 27
1888..Jerome, William T. 14: 234
1888..Johnson, Hiram W. 15: 133
1888..Lane, Franklin K. 19: 101
1888..Parker, Chauncey G. ..... A: 251
1888..Weil, A. Leo .... C: 306
1888..Williams, William 14: 369
1889..Cox, Charles E. 26: 322
1889..Fitzhugh, Guston T. 18: 347
1889..Greeley, William B. 16: 72
1889..Lansing, Robert 20: 1
1889..Manahan, James 23: 330
1889..Pepper, George W. ...... A: 469
1889..Quarles, James .... B: 155
1889..Shea, Joseph H. 22: 31
1889..Speer, Peter M. 24: 128
1889..Strawn, Silas H. .... C: 44
1889..Tracy, Howard C. 15: 336
1889..Waterman, Charles W. ...24: 258
1890..Anderson, George W. .... A: 412
1890..Battle, George Gordon .... C: 195
1890..Borah, William E. .... B: 115
1890..Brown, Charles A. .... B: 480
1890..Ewing, Thomas 25: 15
1890..Garner, John N. .... D: 9
1890..Gates, John H. 18: 418
1890..Hill, John W. 16: 135
1890..Hill, William A. 26: 343
1890..Hughes, William L. 19: 48
1890..Kenyon, William S. 24: 60
1890..Kirby, William F. .... C: 191
1890..Sargent, John G. .... A: 12
1890..Van Wyck, Sidney McM. .23: 338
1890..Wilbur, Curtis D. .... A: 13
1890..Woodman, Albert S. 25: 433
1891..Barker, James M. 14: 494
1891..Brandon, William W. .... C: 295
1891..Brown, James E. 25: 176
1891..Butler, Charles C. .... C: 227
1891..Cardozo, Benjamin N. ... D: 50
1891..Crocker, Henry G. 23: 224
1891..Duane, Russell 4: 415
1891..Goff, Guy D. 24: 24
1891..Landis, Kenesaw M. ...... A: 22
1891..McCarter, Thomas N. .... D: 84
1891..Olson, Harry .... B: 118
1891..Stimson, Henry L. .... C: 8
1891..Taylor, Walter F. 20: 430
1891..Thayer, Ezra R. 16: 185
1891..Thompson, William H. ...15: 57
1892..Bentley, Franklin R. 16: 288
1892..Brock, Charles R. 24: 335
1892..Buder, Gustavus A. ...... C: 135
1892..Budge, Alfred .... D: 185
1892..Colby, Bainbridge .... A: 32
1892..Dyer, Frank L. .... D : 71
1892..Fryberger, Harrison E. ... D: 328
1892..Gerard, James W. .... A: 168
1892..Green, Theodore F. 18: 211
1892..Gunnison, Frederic E. ...19: 122
1892..Hudnall, George B. M. ... C: 225
1892..King, James G. 23: 154
1892..Kronshage, Theodore 24: 75
1892..Lobingier, Charles S. ..... C: 64
1892..Marshall, Carrington T. .. C: 335
1892..Rogers, William P. 20: 79
1892..Shaw, Ralph M. .... D: 243
1892..Sumner, Edward A. 16: 106
1892..Williams, Robert L. 14: 496
1892..Woodbridge, Freeman .... C: 161
1893..Abbott, William T. 14: 157
1893..Bailey, William D. 22: 382
1893..Bayard, Thomas F. ...... C: 152
1893..Bulow, William J. .... C: 63
1893..Butterfield, Ora E. 16: 416
1893..Conley, William G. ...... C: 453
1893..Cummings, Homer S. .... D: 13
1893..Dunscomb, Samuel W. ...18: 234
1893..Estes, William L. 23: 227
1893..Gore, Thomas P. 14: 323
1893..Hinebaugh, William H. ... C: 354
1893..Hines, Walker D. 24: 30
1893..Kohler, Max J. .... B: 180
1893..McCulloch, Edgar A. 15: 360
1893..Miller, Nathan L. .... D: 70
1893..Murray, John P. 24: 71
1893..Mussey, Ellen S. .... A: 402
1893..Myers, Louis W. .... B: 134
1893..Palmer, A. Mitchell .... A: 44
1893..Pattangall, William R. ... D: 121
1893..Sanders, Jared Y. 14: 104
1893..Siddons, Frederick L. 23: 119
1893..Terry, Charles T. 12: 534
1893..Vahey, James H. 14: 199
1893..Warren, Charles B. 26: 15
1893..Watkins, Thomas D. 18: 130
1893..Whitehouse, Robert T. ...20: 267
1894..Baldwin, Samuel P. ...... C: 148
1894..Biggs, J. Crawford ...... D: 24
1894..Brown, Walter F. .... C: 10
1894..Early, Marion C. .... B: 46
1894..Gary, Hampson .... A: 432
1894..Gould, William H. G. 25: 42
1894..Hayne, Daniel H. 16: 59
1894..Lindsey, Benjamin B. 15: 183
1894..Menken, S. Stanwood .... A: 417
1894..Newton, James T. .... A: 453
1894..Rabbino, Bernhard 24: 49
1894..Sampson, Flem D. .... A: 326
1894..Seabury, Samuel .... D: 76
1894..Smith, William B. 20: 361
1894..Waste, William H. .... D: 161
1894..Whitman, Charles S. 15: 207
1894..Woodruff, John S. 21: 382
1895..Cooke, George A. .... B: 298
1895..Davis, John W. .... A: 25
1895..Franklin, Alfred .... D: 159
1895..Mullan, George V. 24: 268
1895..Newcomb, Harry T. ..... C: 232
1895..Noel, James W. 16: 271
1895..Parsons, Herbert 14: 458
1895..Price, William J. .... D: 100
1895..Scott, Joseph 16: 32
1895..Wilson, Samuel B. .... B: 492
1896..Blair, James T. .... B: 159
1896..Bond, Carroll T. .... B: 198
1896..Burke, Haslett P. .... D: 109
1896..Calhoun, Clarence C. ..... A: 158
1896..Crothers, George E. ..... D: 270
1896..Hiscock, Frank H. .... A: 10
1896..Logan, Marvel M. .... D: 231
1896..Mitchell, William D. ...... C: 10
1896..Ogden, Hugh W. .... A: 438
1896..Platt, Samuel .... A: 445
1896..Saner, Robert E. L. ...... B: 152
1896..Von Moschzisker, Robert . A: 54
1896..Young, Owen D. .... A: 81
1897..Atwood, Harry 25: 214
1897..Baker, Newton D. .... A: 40
1897..Bingham, Robert W. ..... D: 32
1897..Carusi, Charles F. 22: 288
1897..Chandler, Walter M. 14: 515
1897..Cohen, Julius H. .... B: 135
1897..Doyle, Michael F. .... A: 524
1897..Flattery, Maurice D. 16: 291
1897..Goodwin, Clarence N. .... B: 412
1897..Hawes, Harry B. .... C: 65
1897..Hoyne, Maclay 18: 61
1897..Long, Joseph R. .... A: 464
1897..Main, John F. .... B: 139
1897..Matson, Roderick N. ..... B: 509
1897..Meyers, Sidney S. 15: 100
1897..Milroy, Charles M. 16: 449
1897..Otts, Cornelius 17: 24
1897..Morley, Clarence J. ...... B: 321
1897..Pleasant, Ruffin G. ...... C: 405
1897..Polk, Frank L. .... A: 417
1897..Riter, William D. 20: 450
1897..Sims, Henry U. .... A: 192
1897..Stoll, Richard C. .... B: 234
1898..Anderson, Henry W. ..... C: 19
1898..Brown, John A. 14: 392
1898..Creed, Wigginton E. 22: 448
1898..Dodge, Walter P. 11: 393
1898..Emery, Dean .... D: 118
1898..Evans, Victor J. .... B: 172
1898..Hamlin, Elbert B. 26: 36
1898..Harrison, Francis B. ..... C: 204
1898..Kagey, Charles L. .... C: 316
1898..Lothrop, Thornton K. .... D: 144
1898..Milbank, Albert G. .... D: 204
1898..Millis, Wade .... B: 70
1898..Morrow, Dwight W. 23: 10
1898..Offutt, Thiemann S. ..... B: 290
1898..Oxtoby, Walter E. .... C: 396
1898..Ritchie, Albert C. .... A: 75
1898..Roberts, Owen J. .... A: 88
1898..Stone, Harlan F. .... A: 11
1898..Westengard, Jens I. 18: 202
1899..Blair, David E. .... B: 169
1899..Catherwood, Robert ...... B: 374
1899..Colladay, Edward F. ..... C: 115
1899..Harper, Samuel A. ...... C: 137
1899..McNeill, Neal E. .... B: 238
1899..Mooney, Henry 21: 446
1899..Patterson, Frank M. ..... B: 221
1899..Phillips, Harold M. ...... D: 172
1899..Scott, James B. .... C: 69
1899..Wilfley, Xenophon P. 25: 84
1900..Cotton, Joseph P. 23: 151
1900..Cox, Archibald 15: 77
1900..Denison, Robert F. ...... D: 192
1900..Hyde, Arthur M. .... C: 13
1900..Keller, Herbert P. 15: 56
1900..Kelly, Harry E. 26: 486
1900..Mackintosh, Kenneth ..... C: 79
1900..Peters, Andrew J. .... C: 229
1900..Rosenberg, Louis J. ...... C: 215
1900..Smith, Leon R. 18: 107
1900..Stout, W. Frank 16: 226
1900..Throckmorton, Archibald H. .... C: 205
1900..Todd, Hiram C. .... C: 441
1900..Wagner, Robert F. ...... D: 39
1901..Baldwin, Arthur D. ...... C: 301
1901..Bensinger, Arthur B. 26: 338
1901..Burcham, James T. 21: 487
1901..Davies, Joseph E. .... C: 456
1901..Friebolin, Carl D. .... C: 340
1901..Garvan, Francis P. ...... C: 156
1901..George, Walter F. .... A: 521
1901..Martin, Clarence E. ...... D: 278
1901..Means, Rice W. .... C: 177
1901..Morris, Dave H. .... D: 107
1901..Payer, Harry F. .... C: 492
1901..Robinson, Beverley R. .... D: 212
1901..Roper, Daniel C. .... D: 18
1901..Swan, Frank H. .... D: 105
1901..Thorne, Clifford 17: 197
1901..Woolsey, John M. .... C: 311
1902..Badger, William O. 17: 3
1902..Becker, Alfred L. 17: 361
1902..Burkhalter, Robert P. 18: 407
1902..Calfee, Robert M. .... D: 197
1902..Chamberlain, Joseph P. .. D: 313
1902..Levine, Manuel .... D: 340
1902..McAlister, Archibald G. .. B: 370
1902..Thomas, William H. ..... A: 21
1902..Wilson, Joseph R. 16: 409
1903..Ellis, George W. 17: 400
1903..Fitzpatrick, John T. 24: 112
1903..Garrigues, James E. ..... A: 134
1903..Grosvenor, Edwin P. 21: 400
1903..Hill, John P. .... D: 114
1903..Lecher, Louis A. .... C: 208
1903..Marble, John H. 16: 250
1903..Small, Charles H. .... A: 431
1903..Sullivan, Mark A. 16: 216
1903..Tate, Hugh McC. .... D: 201
1903..Taylor, Amos L. .... D: 179
1904..Low, Benjamin R. C. .... C: 523
1904..Poor, Henry V. 25: 144
1904..Richberg, Donald R. ..... D: 23
1904..Schall, Thomas D. .... C: 337
1904..Taplin, Charles F. .... C: 347
1905..Avery, Coleman .... C: 158
1905..Hills, Arthur S. .... D: 85
1905..McCarren, Patrick A. .... D: 214
1905..Maltbie, William M. ..... D: 212
1905..Monroe, John D. .... C: 307
1905..Oberlin, John F. .... D: 182
1906..Bates, Sanford .... C: 331
1906..Bulkley, Robert J. .... D: 244
1906..Clark, J. Reuben, Jr. .... D: 290
1906..Cooke, Levi 25: 44
1906..Frankfurter, Felix ...... D: 28
1906..Miller, Robert N. .... C: 265
1907..Bracelen, Charles M. ..... C: 142
1907..Gibbs, Louis DeW. .... B :421
1907..Ickes, Harold L. .... D: 16
1907..Monnette, Orra E. .... C: 281
1907..Pierce, Henry H. .... C: 412
1907..Roosevelt, Franklin D. ... D: 1
1907..Stone, John H. 25: 78
1907..Thacher, Thomas D. ..... D: 252
1907..Zoller, J. Frank .... C: 153
1908..Aron, Harold G. .... D: 297
1908..Hilkey, Charles J. .... B: 235
1908..Holliday, Wallace T. ..... C: 125
1908..Hopkins, Albert L. .... C: 236
1908..Hurley, Patrick J. .... C: 9
1908..Leavenworth, Ellis W. ... D: 419
1908..Louderback, Harold ...... B: 362

1908..Overton, Winston 25: 372
1908..Quarles, Louis .... C: 180
1908..Rogers, James G. .... C: 205
1909..Alburn, Cary R. .... C: 179
1909..Kavanagh, Francis B. .... D: 392
1909..Loomis, Homer L. .... B: 391
1909..Minot, William .... C: 247
1909..Norris, Jean H. .... C: 163
1909..Quarles, Charles B. ..... D: 268
1910..Crandall, Samuel B. ...... B: 264
1910..Hudson, Manley O. .... C: 348
1910..Isaacs, Nathan .... B: 378
1910..Robertson, Andrew W. ... C: 328
1911..Peaslee, Amos J. .... B: 304
1911..Sapiro, Aaron .... C: 120
1911..Wickser, Philip J. .... D: 451
1912..Adams, Annette A. .... A: 370
1912..Donovan, William J. ..... C: 141
1912..Gregory, Tappan .... C: 171
1912..Hughes, Charles E., Jr. .. C: 61
1912..McCarthy, Charles P. .... D: 289
1913..Allen, Florence E. .... C: 111
1913..Clark, Charles E. .... D: 424
1913..Cochran, Herbert G. ..... A: 397
1913..Sunderland, Edwin S. S. . D: 296
1914..Clarke, John H. .... A: 248
1915..Willebrandt, Mabel W. ... B: 211
1916..Berle, Adolf A., Jr. ..... D: 26
1917..McLaughlin, Agnes W. ... C: 122
1917..Olson, Floyd B. .... D: 176
1917..Traxler, Dean L. .... C: 399
1918..Fraser, Leon .... D: 36
1919..Brucker, Wilber M. ...... D: 126
1919..Jackson, Raymond T. .... D: 75
1919..Page, George T. .... A: 366
1921..Faville, Frederick F. ..... D: 79
1921..Glenn, Otis F. .... A: 20
1923..Ingalls, David S. .... C: 309
1925..Hutchins, Robert M. ..... C: 54

Librarians

1779..Smith, John 9: 95
1815..Watterston, George 7: 501
1821..Cogswell, Joseph G. 11: 462
1825..Sibley, John L. 11: 278
1826..Peirce, Benjamin 10: 180
1829..Meehan, John S. 13: 170
1832..Kingsley, James L. 10: 121
1837..Jewett, Charles C. 5: 356
1837..Moore, Nathaniel F. 6: 345
1838..Parvin, Theodore S. 8: 150
1841..Moore, George H. 4: 555
1843..Herrick, Edward C. 11: 170
1845..Edmands, John 12: 460
1847..Guild, Reuben A. 3: 460
1848..Street, Alfred B. 11: 103
1849..Poole, William F. 6: 478
1850..Spofford, Ainsworth R. ... 6: 477
1852..Capen, Edward 6: 482
1852..Fiske, Daniel W. 25: 279
1853..Homes, Henry A. 13: 42
1854..Draper, Lyman C. 9: 390
1855..Nelson, Charles A. 24: 211
1856..Durrie, Daniel S. 11: 271
1856..Poole, Fitch 6: 483
1856..Vinton, Frederic 6: 483
1859..Saunders, Frederick 2: 379
1860..Cutter, Charles A. 13: 180
1861..Fletcher, William I. 12: 379
1861..Rice, William 6: 479
1862..Uhler, Philip R. 8: 250
1865..Van Name, Addison 19: 122
1867..Williams, John F. 4: 467
1867..Winsor, Justin 1: 150
1870..Bassett, Homer F. 6: 481
1870..Folwell, William W. 13: 328
1871..Green, Samuel A. 2: 28
1871..Green, Samuel S. 6: 484
1872..Howell, George R. 3: 512
1872..Winters, William H. 11: 417
1873..Taylor, Barton S. 5: 475
1874..Coolbrith Ina D. 13: 512
1874..Dewey, Melvil 23: 14
1874..Elmendorf, Theresa West .23: 28
1875..Chadwick, James R. 12: 368
1875..Hewins, Caroline Maria ..21: 159
1875..Ward, James W. 10: 247
1877..Crunden, Frederick M. ... 6: 483
1877..Flint, Weston 11: 198
1877..Larned, Josephus N. 16: 344
1877..Stone, Frederick D. 9: 389
1877..Van Dyke, John C. ...... C: 489
1878..Burr, George L. 4: 479
1879..Allibone, Samuel A. 6: 227
1879..Billings, John S. 4: 78
1879..Bjerregaard, Carl H. A. .13: 47
1879..Holden, Edward S. 7: 229
1880..Browning, Eliza G. 6: 482
1880..Griswold, William McC. ..23: 330
1881..Hill, Frank P. 2: 149
1881..Koopman, Harry L. 11: 543
1883..Andrews, Clement W. 14: 340
1883..Baker, George H. 6: 349
1883..Gay, Frank B. 25: 192
1883..Richardson, Ernest C. ...13: 461
1884..Brett, William H. 6: 480
1884..Fairchild, Salome C. 20: 263
1884..Montgomery, Thomas L. .24: 396
1884..Putnam, Herbert .... D: 52
1884..Steiner, Lewis H. 11: 348
1885..Eames, Wilberforce 9: 275
1885..Jordan, John W. 11: 158
1885..Utley, Henry M. 17: 213
1886..Carr, Henry J. 12: 368
1886..Roden, Carl B. .... C: 479
1886..Thwaites, Reuben G. 10: 35
1887..Cheney, John V. 6: 289
1887..Cole, George W. .... D: 42
1887..Keen, Gregory B. 11: 367
1887..Lane, William Coolidge ...12: 261
1887..Root, Azariah S. 22: 112
1888..Adler, Cyrus 11: 371
1888..Ballard, Harlan H. 9: 488
1888..Dana, John Cotton 22: 321
1888..Jones, Gardner M. 6: 483
1888..Paltsits, Victor H. 17: 198
1888..Patten, Frank C. 24: 357
1888..Plummer, Mary W. 21: 107
1889..Ahern, Mary E. .... A: 538
1889..Browne, Nina E. .... A: 23
1889..Jennings, Judson T. ..... D: 282
1890..Beer, William 12: 442
1890..Bolton, Charles K. .... B: 113
1890..Kephart, Horace 6: 322
1890..Orr, Charles S. 13: 37
1891..Elmendorf, Henry L. 21: 139
1892..Anderson, Edwin H. ..... D: 56
1892..Hosmer, James K. 6: 481
1892..Steiner, Bernard C. 26: 311
1893..Rathbone, Josephine A. .. D: 411
1894..Hodges, Nathaniel D. C. .12: 262
1894..King, James L. 6: 481
1894..Wellman, Hiller C. ...... A: 293
1895..Belden, Charles 23: 53
1895..Bostwick, Arthur E. 14: 339
1895..Eastman, Linda A. ...... C: 465
1895..Hamilton, Morris R. 1: 322
1896..Galbreath, Charles B. 25: 112
1896..Hume, Jessie F. .... A: 447
1896..Peckham, George W. 12: 346
1896..Wyer, James I. .... D: 44
1897..Brown, Walter L. 24: 107
1897..Flagg, Charles A. 19: 247
1897..Foote, Elizabeth L. ...... C: 443
1897..Henry, William E. 26: 158
1898..Brigham, Johnson 14: 375
1898..Jastrow, Morris 11: 372
1898..Rosenthal, Herman 11: 192
1899..Canfield, James H. 7: 417
1899..Keogh, Andrew .... D: 267
1899..Stevenson, Burton E. 13: 143
1899..Utley, George B. .... A: 481
1900..Parker, Henry W. 15: 31
1901..McCarthy, Charles 19: 251
1902..Bishop, William W. ..... D: 312
1902..Meyer, Herman H. B. .... D: 92
1902..Sonneck, Oscar G. T. 25: 283
1902..Wadlin, Horace G. 16: 435
1902..Wing, George W. 17: 139
1903..Dickinson, Asa D. .... B: 72
1904..Bogle, Sarah C. N. .... C: 504
1904..Legler, Henry E. 24: 296
1904..Whitmore, Frank H. ..... C: 155
1905..Hadley, Chalmers .... A: 258
1905..Schwab, John C. 26: 333
1909..Wilson, Florence .... C: 420
1912..Shearer, Augustus H. .... D: 347
1913..Skinner, Charles R. 10: 388
1914..Norlie, Olaf M. .... C: 391

Marine Engineers

See Naval Architects and Marine Engineers

Mathematicians

1579..Hariot, Thomas 7: 162
1634..Sherman, John 7: 75
1702..Taylor, Jacob 10: 255
1707..Berkeley, George 6: 255
1716..Jones, Hugh 24: 156
1724..Ames, Nathaniel 8: 45
1727..Franklin, Benjamin 1: 328
1732..Godfrey, Thomas 23: 368
1738..Winthrop, John 7: 165
1753..West, Benjamin 8: 31
1760..Rittenhouse, David 1: 346
1770..Daboll, Nathan 23: 403
1773..Banneker, Benjamin 5: 36
1773..Pike, Nicholas 20: 362
1779..Patterson, Robert 26: 59
1781..Meigs, Josiah 9: 178
1784..Ellicott, Andrew 13: 470
1791..Ewing, John 1: 341
1794..Leavitt, Dudley 25: 112
1796..Caldwell, Joseph 13: 241
1801..Hassler, Ferdinand R. 3: 413
1802..Bowditch, Nathaniel 6: 377
1802..Mansfield, Jared 3: 214
1805..Gummere, John 23: 409
1808..Adams, Ebenezer 9: 91
1810..Adrain, Robert 1: 347
1810..Colburn, Zerah 7: 74
1813..Greenleaf, Benjamin 8: 141
1816..Davies, Charles 3: 26
1816..Nicholson, James W. 13: 236
1824..Courteney, Edward H. ... 5: 519
1825..Anderson, Henry J. 6: 389
1825..Olmsted, Denison 8: 121
1825..Robinson, Horatio N. 2: 190
1825..Walker, Sears C. 8: 81
1827..Snell, Ebenezer S. 5: 311
1827..Strong, Theodore 9: 288
1828..Barnard, Frederick A. P. . 6: 347
1828..Smyth, William 10: 474
1829..Coffin, James H. 8: 12
1829..Wright, Elizur 2: 317
1831..Buckingham, Catherinus P.13: 47
1831..Smith, Augustus W. 9: 430
1832..Bonnycastle, Charles 13: 180
1833..Loomis, Elias 7: 233
1834..Alexander, Stephen 11: 422
1834..Ray, Joseph 1: 349
1836..Coffin, John H. C. 5: 530
1836..Jackman, Alonzo 16: 373
1838..Kirkwood, Daniel 4: 349
1840..Chauvenet, William 11: 210
1841..Hudson, William W. 8: 183
1842..Peirce, Benjamin 8: 152
1842..Venable, Charles S. 10: 386
1844..Clark, Alvan 6: 440
1845..Winlock, Joseph 9: 266
1846..Lane, Jonathan H. 3: 275
1846..Peck, William G. 5: 520
1849..Colburn, Warren 11: 457
1849..Oliver, James E. 14: 342
1849..Runkle, John D. 6: 350
1850..Hitchcock, Henry E. 8: 361
1850..Safford, Truman H. 13: 359
1851..Gillespie, William M. 23: 184
1852..Bull, Richard H. 9: 472
1852..Newton, Hubert A. 9: 219
1852..Young, Augustus 3: 506
1853..Barr, Samuel D. 5: 474
1854..Newcomb, Simon 7: 17
1859..Peirce, Charles S. 8: 409
1859..Tappan, Eli T. 7: 7
1859..Wentworth, George A. ...10: 106
1860..Van Amringe, John Howard 13: 241
1860..Watson, James C. 7: 70
1861..Hill, George W. 13: 442
1862..Johnson, William W. 23: 237
1862..Clarke, Benjamin F. 10: 308
1863..Hall, Asaph 22: 287
1863..Quackenbos, George P. ...13: 301
1864..Cain, William .... A: 290
1864..Martin, Artemas 2: 180
1865..Eastman, John R. 13: 554
1866..Bayma, Joseph 17: 107
1866..Rockwood, Charles G. 16: 188
1867..Greenwood, James M. 13: 62
1867..McClintock, Emory 12: 202
1867..Miller, Bloomfield J. 12: 95
1868..Bowser, Edward A. 19: 415
1869..Eddy, Henry T. 15: 331
1869..Ladd-Franklin, Christine .26: 422
1869..Peirce, James M. 10: 25
1870..Sherman, Frank A. 9: 92
1870..Soulé, George 1: 510
1871..Gibbs, Josiah W. 4: 543
1872..Paul, Henry M. 10: 403
1872..Wood, De Volson 13: 351
1872..Woodward, Robert S. 13: 108
1874..Smith, William B. 9: 133
1875..Halsted, George B. 3: 518
1875..Story, William E. 24: 371
1878..Gore, James H. 12: 514
1880..Franklin, Fabian .... C: 497
1880..Peirce, Benjamin O. 20: 366
1881..Fine, Henry B. 14: 499
1881..Hardy, Arthur S. 2: 303
1881..Sloan, Benjamin 13: 116
1882..Wells, Webster 17: 124

1883..Brown, Stimson J. 13: 121
1883..Lowell, Percival 8: 309
1884..Davis, Ellery W. 8: 363
1884..Smith, David E. .... B: 21
1884..Van Vleck, Edward B. ... A: 338
1884..White, Henry S. 14: 382
1885..Cole, Frank N. 21: 74
1885..Crawley, Edwin S. 24: 436
1887..Francis, William A. 10: 107
1887..Miller, George A. 16: 388
1887..Moore, Eliakim H. 12: 447
1887..Morley, Frank 15: 147
1888..Nixon, Henry B. 17: 244
1890..Fiske, Thomas S. 12: 489
1890..Harris, Rollin A. 22: 388
1890..Osgood, William F. 13: 524
1890..Steinmetz, Charles P. 23: 94
1891..Bocher, Maxime 18: 302
1891..Brown, Ernest W. 15: 24
1892..See, Thomas J. J. 13: 234
1893..Holgate, Thomas F. .... B: 184
1896..Pierpont, James 16: 108
1897..Dickson, Leonard E. 18: 411
1900..Bliss, Gilbert A. .... A: 371
1900..Hancock, Harris 16: 70
1900..Kasner, Edward 16: 61
1903..Kellogg, Oliver D. 23: 183
1903..Mason, Max .... B: 485
1903..Young, John W. 23: 279
1904..Richardson, Roland G. D. . C: 302
1907..Wilson, Edwin B. .... D: 271
1908..Frary, Hobart D. 23: 391
1912..Fischer, Charles A. 20: 62

Mechanical Engineers

1745..Hornblower, Josiah 6: 169
1772..Colles, Christopher 9: 271
1791..Roberdeau, Isaac 2: 14
1792..Whitney, Eli 4: 495
1793..Fulton, Robert 3: 104
1814..Abert, John J. 4: 380
1814..Long, Stephen H. 11: 365
1814..Renwick, Henry B. 11: 101
1817..Ericsson, John 4: 46
1818..Robinson, Moncure 8: 456
1820..Childs, Orville W. 3: 79
1824..Allen, Horatio 8: 233
1824..Mahan, Dennis H. 10: 440
1825..Baldwin, Matthias W. 9: 476
1825..Boyden, Uriah A. 11: 88
1825..Brown, Thompson S. 4: 441
1826..Roebling, John A. 4: 404
1829..Francis, James B. 9: 46
1830..Ward, Lebbeus B. 1: 246
1832..Turnbull, William 12: 514
1834..Geddes, George 10: 170
1834..Harrison, Joseph 12: 495
1835..Hobbs, Alfred C. 23: 336
1835..Hudson, William S. 24: 242
1836..Haswell, Charles H. 9: 486
1837..Benham, Henry W. 4: 277
1837..Howe, Elias 4: 432
1837..Woodbury, Daniel P. 1: 470
1838..Towne, John H. 24: 431
1838..Worthen, William E. 12: 206
1839..Eads, James B. 5: 134
1840..Tatham, William P. 13: 250
1841..Worthington, Henry R. .. 6: 303
1843..Cornell, Ezra 4: 475
1843..Winans, Thomas DeK. ... 1: 239
1844..Hoadley, John C. 23: 404
1844..Isherwood, Benjamin F. ..12: 199
1845..Wood, William W. W. ...12: 198
1846..Guthrie, Alfred 11: 407
1846..Holloway, Josephus F. ...12: 116
1847..Colburn, Zerah 12: 137
1848..Trowbridge, William P. .. 4: 529
1849..Fritz, John 13: 74
1850..Babcock, George H. 5: 304
1850..Reynolds, Edwin 2: 524
1851..Loring, Charles H. 12: 502
1851..Richards, Charles B. 25: 50
1852..Stanton, John 14: 359
1853..Durfee, William F. 6: 248
1853..Holley, Alexander L. 11: 508
1853..Tweedale, William 5: 484
1854..Porter, Charles T. 20: 494
1854..Smith, William S. 4: 498
1855..Leavitt, Erasmus D. 24: 324
1855..Morgan, Charles H. 23: 197
1856..Forney, Matthias N. 22: 78
1856..Sellers, Coleman 11: 53
1856..Smedley, Samuel L. 3: 331
1857..Graham, Charles K. 12: 299
1857..Newton, Isaac 4: 190
1857..Roebling, Washington A. . 4: 405
1857..Waring, George E., Jr. .. 6: 157
1857..Wood, De Volson 13: 351
1858..Young, Alexander 12: 419
1860..Babcock, George H. 5: 304
1860..Ellet, Charles 4: 360
1860..Viele, Egbert L. 2: 195
1860..Vinton, Francis L. 7: 441
1861..Albert, John S. 9: 230
1861..Emery, Charles E. 9: 34
1861..Foster, Wilbur F. 8: 47
1861..Melville, George W. 3: 283
1861..Thurston, Robert H. 4: 479
1862..Billings, Charles E. 5: 408
1862..Billings, George H. 11: 549
1862..Gillespie, George L. 12: 184
1862..Meier, Edward D. 23: 103
1863..Doane, Thomas 25: 93
1863..Smith, Oberlin 12: 461
1864..Birkinbine, John 12: 199
1864..Ernst, Oswald H. 4: 36
1864..Sweet, John E. 13: 54
1865..Bolton, Channing M. 2: 519
1865..Coxe, Eckley B. 11: 559
1865..Hunt, Robert W. 19: 17
1865..Jones, Evan W. 25: 133
1865..See, Horace 2: 220
1865..Stone, Charles P. 11: 215
1865..Towne, Henry R. 21: 384
1865..Whiting, Stephen B. 17: 177
1866..Davis, Ezekiel F. C. 12: 323
1866..Lewis, Eugene C. 8: 417
1866..Robinson, Stillman W. ...10: 232
1866..Westinghouse, George 15: 41
1867..Wellman, Samuel T. 13: 37
1868..Alden, George I. 20: 380
1868..Johnson, Warren S. 3: 292
1868..Marshall, William L. 11: 467
1868..Risse, Louis A. 4: 197
1868..Skinner, Le Grand 19: 369
1869..Eddy, Henry T. 15: 331
1869..Mundy, Joseph S. 2: 497
1870..Brashear, John A. 4: 552
1870..Rice, Vietts L. 1: 512
1870..Stirling, Allan 21: 204
1870..Swasey, Ambrose .... B: 274
1871..Rand, Addison C. 11: 265
1871..Reynolds, Edwin 2: 524
1872..Dodge, James M. 12: 490
1872..Humphreys, Alexander C. 13: 203
1872..Mahan, Frederick A. 10: 441
1872..Smith, Jesse M. 22: 165
1873..Grant, George B. 26: 474
1873..Hunt, Charles W. 13: 455
1873..Klein, Joseph F. 18: 156
1874..Forsyth, William 20: 237
1874..Gillham, Robert 3: 352
1874..Hewitt, William 19: 89
1874..Holman, Minard L. 14: 419
1874..Hunter, Rudolph M. 25: 22
1874..Keely, John W. 9: 137
1875..Kennedy, Julian 24: 135
1876..Church, Irving P. 22: 381
1876..Hutton, Frederick R. 16: 439
1876..Leavitt, Frank McD. 15: 20
1876..Trautwein, Alfred P. 18: 276
1877..Wilke, William .... B: 225
1878..Bolton, Reginald P. 13: 462
1878..Carpenter, Rolla C. 4: 480
1878..Hollis, Ira N. 22: 21
1878..Porter, Holbrook F. J. ... B: 336
1878..Stevens, Edwin A. 5: 342
1878..Woodbury, Charles J. H. .12: 81
1879..Goss, William F. M. 20: 16
1879..Main, Charles T. 15: 327
1879..Sperry, Elmer A. 23: 78
1880..Halsey, Frederick A. 26: 451
1880..Jones, Edward C. 24: 128
1880..Newcomb, Charles L. 22: 90
1881..Bogert, John L. 16: 29
1881..Cooley, Mortimer E. ..... A: 511
1881..Warner, Worcester R. ...21: 70
1882..Lieb, John W. 13: 606
1882..Saunders, William L. 14: 190
1882..Tyler, Charles C. .... C: 389
1882..Veeder, Curtis H. .... C: 373
1882..Williston, Benjamin F. ...20: 125
1883..Sague, James E. 26: 133
1883..Taylor, Frederick W. 23: 47
1884..Cogswell, William B. 13: 107
1884..Herr, Edwin M. 23: 243
1884..Jacobus, David S. .... C: 112
1884..Keep, William J. 18: 207
1884..Lundie, John 24: 348
1884..Orton, Edward, Jr. 24: 107
1884..Parker, John C. .... C: 429
1884..Riker, Andrew L. 22: 61
1886..Freeman, John R. .... C: 397
1886..Miller, Edward F. 24: 195
1887..Brown, Harold P. .... B: 329
1887..Durand, William F. ...... D: 260
1888..Bristol, William H. 26: 26
1888..Cobb, Edward S. 5: 524
1888..Doty, Paul 16: 95
1888..Goodnow, George F. ..... B: 406
1888..Low, Frederick R. .... C: 337
1888..Weil, Charles L. 19: 311
1889..Christensen, Niels A. .... D: 308
1889..Churchill, William W. 18: 96
1889..Coppage, Benjamin D. ...22: 93
1889..Hartness, James 15: 294
1889..Hoxie, William D. 24: 250
1889..Piez, Charles 24: 17
1890..Flather, John J. 22: 125
1890..Heisler, Charles L. 25: 399
1890..Hitchcock, Embury A. ... D: 271
1890..Rice, Calvin W. 25: 35
1891..Beutner, Victor 12: 197
1891..Bliss, Collins P. .... C: 519
1891..King, Charles B. .... D: 157
1891..Norris, Henry McC. 20: 331
1892..Allen, John R. 19: 296
1892..Hutton, Frederick R. 16: 439
1892..Munger, Edwin T. 16: 403
1892..Wadsworth, Frank L. O. .26: 376
1893..Graydon, James W. 13: 43
1894..Barthel, Oliver E. 16: 160
1894..Keller, Emil E. .... D: 406
1895..Harrington, John L. ..... A: 459
1896..Alford, Leon Pratt .... A: 183
1896..Davis, Harry P. 25: 17
1896..James, Henry D. .... D: 364
1897..Duesenberg, Fred S. 16: 295
1898..Harper, John L. 20: 395
1898..Kimball, Dexter S. .... D: 343
1898..Manly, Charles M. 21: 321
1898..Richards, John R. .... B: 393
1899..Carman, Edwin S. .... C: 406
1900..Moyle, Edward H. 16: 399
1900..Peck, Eugene C. .... D: 165
1900..Zimmerman, Oliver B. ... A: 491
1901..Junggren, Oscar F. 26: 22
1902..Hall, Elbert J. .... A: 110
1902..Waddell, Joseph A., 2d ...25: 338
1903..Viall, Ethan .... C: 177
1904..Vincent, Jesse G. .... A: 111
1904..Wright, Roy V. .... D: 296
1905..Castle, Samuel N. .... A: 412
1905..Garland, Claude M. ...... A: 224
1905..Lawrance, Charles L. .... D: 194
1905..Whaley, William .... B: 455
1906..Dunbar, Frank H. .... D: 333
1906..Hitchcock, Halbert K. ...24: 90
1906..Kommers, Jesse B. .... B: 150
1906..Lucke, Charles E. .... B: 64
1908..Seward, Herbert Lee ..... D: 363
1910..Fast, Gustave .... C: 351
1912..Eddison, William B. ..... B: 320
1913..Schieren, George A. ...... D: 345
1915..Emmons, Walter T. .... A: 321
1916..Naumburg, Robert E. .... C: 394
1918..Fuller, Leonard F. ...... B: 216
1919..Davis, Harvey N. .... A: 348

Meteorologists

1810..Dewey, Chester 6: 328
1828..Caswell, Alexis 8: 25
1835..Loomis, Elias 7: 233
1835..Maury, Matthew F. 6: 35
1836..Coffin, James H. 8: 12
1836..Espy, James P. 6: 205
1836..Lapham, Increase A. 8: 34
1840..Capen, Francis L. 5: 303
1842..Brocklesby, John 12: 287
1843..Herrick, Edward C. 11: 170
1847..Horr, Asa 13: 123
1848..Winchell, Alexander 16: 119
1851..Blodget, Lorin 4: 530
1852..Newton, Hubert A. 9: 219
1856..Ferrel, William 9: 241
1856..Lowe, Thaddeus S. C. 9: 542
1860..Abbe, Cleveland 8: 264
1864..Chase, Pliny E. 6: 53
1865..Myer, Albert J. 24: 196
1868..Greeley, Adolphus W. 3: 285
1869..Draper, Daniel 6: 172
1870..Harrington, Mark W. 10: 448
1870..Mallery, Garrick 7: 506
1873..Bigelow, Frank H. 10: 410
1873..Dunn, Elias B. 6: 153
1875..Hazen, Henry A. 8: 114
1877..Nipher, Francis E. 22: 55
1878..Drum, Richard C. 12: 359
1879..Campbell, John T. 12: 397
1880..Beals, Edward A. 24: 233
1880..Hazen, William B. 3: 408

1880..Moore, Willis L. 21: 84
1880..Upton, Winslow 12: 238
1882..Cline, Isaac M. 16: 126
1884..Cox, Henry J. 24: 307
1884..Libbey, William 10: 401
1884..Marvin, Charles F. 16: 47
1884..Rotch, A. Lawrence 15: 2
1886..Hayden, Edward E. 8: 112
1894..Ward, Robert De C. 24: 190
1902..Milham, Willis I. 14: 430
1906..Abbe, Cleveland, Jr. 26: 157

Microscopists

1834..Bailey, Jacob W. 10: 157
1838..Spencer, Charles A. 13: 255
1848..Leidy, Joseph 5: 220
1848..Salisbury, James H. 8: 469
1850..Brocklesby, John 12: 287
1850..Cutter, Ephraim 3: 188
1853..Smith, Hamilton L. 12: 466
1853..Woodward, Joseph J. 11: 518
1854..Zentmayer, Joseph 13: 215
1856..Clark, Henry J. 9: 197
1856..Lieber, Oscar M. 13: 170
1858..Tolles, Robert B. 13: 256
1862..Peirce, John 10: 406
1866..Hyatt, Jonathan D. 13: 566
1867..Kempster, Walter 5: 21
1868..Burrill, Thomas J. 18: 187
1868..White, Charles B. 13: 50
1869..Ward, Richard H. 13: 149
1870..Bessey, Charles E. 8: 361
1870..Hanks, Henry G. 13: 129
1870..Rogers, William A. 9: 530
1871..Curtis, Lester 24: 51
1871..Kellicott, David S. 13: 299
1872..Hitchcock, Romyn 19: 42
1872..Levy, Louis E. 13: 589
1873..Fox, Oscar C. 1: 310
1873..Spencer, Herbert R. 13: 256
1875..Cox, Jacob D. 22: 231
1875..Ward, James W. 10: 247
1877..Gage, Simon H. 4: 483
1877..Mark, Edward L. 9: 271
1878..Blackham, George E. 13: 15
1878..Jameson, Henry 10: 459
1879..Osborn, Herbert 13: 202
1880..Birge, Edward A. 12: 290
1880..Bleile, Albert M. 24: 78
1880..Mercer, A. Clifford 12: 211
1880..Rafter, George W. 12: 234
1881..Claypole, Edward W. 13: 259
1881..Cobb, Nathan A. 23: 87
1881..McCalla, Albert 13: 313
1882..Lewis, William J. 13: 17
1883..Minot, Charles S. 6: 112
1884..Wolle, Francis 1: 320
1885..Fell, George E. 12: 340
1886..Ewell, Marshall D. 12: 375
1886..Smith, Frank .... D: 93
1887..Galloway, Thomas W. ...22: 63
1887..James, Frank L. 12: 226
1887..Kingsley, John S. 12: 119
1887..Whitman, Charles O. 11: 73
1893..Kraus, William C. 12: 210
1894..Kofoid, Charles A. .... A: 280
1895..Eigenmann, Carl H. 21: 47
1896..Brookover, Charles 20: 69
1896..Heald, Frederick D. ..... B: 175
1898..Guyer, Michael F. .... A: 357
1898..Ward, Henry B. 13: 150
1902..Hertzler, Arthur E. ...... C: 189
1907..Wellman, Creighton ...... D: 302

Military Engineers

1630..Gardiner, Lion 23: 181
1776..Duportail, Louis L. 9: 417
1776..Kosciuszko, Thaddeus 1: 54
1791..Roberdeau, Isaac 2: 14
1794..Williams, Jonathan 3: 239
1796..Bernard, Simon 24: 243
1802..Swift, Joseph G. 10: 17
1803..Armistead, Walter K. ... 5: 507
1805..Godefroy, Maximilian 23: 189
1805..Macomb, Alexander 2: 241
1805..Totten, Joseph G. 4: 164
1806..Gratiot, Charles 12: 323
1808..Thayer, Sylvanus 7: 37
1812..DeRussy, Rene E. 4: 555
1813..Douglass, David B. 7: 3
1813..Partridge, Alden 18: 322
1814..Abert, John J. 4: 380
1814..Long, Stephen H. 11: 365
1818..Delafield, Richard 11: 29
1822..Mansfield, Joseph K. F. .. 4: 179
1824..Mahan, Dennis H. 10: 440
1829..Lee, Robert E. 4: 95
1831..Humphreys, Andrew A. .. 7: 34
1833..Cullum, George W. 4: 258
1836..Woodbury, Daniel P. 1: 470
1837..Benham, Henry W. 4: 277
1838..Gunnison, John W. 23: 326
1841..Wright, Horatio G. 4: 273
1842..Newton, John 4: 312
1844..Smith, Gustavus W. 7: 515
1845..Hunt, Edward B. 11: 440
1848..Duane, James C. 10: 85
1849..Gillmore, Quincy A. 4: 54
1850..Warren, Gouverneur K. .. 4: 68
1851..McClellan, George B. 4: 140
1853..Craighill, William P. 12: 223
1853..McPherson, James B. 4: 203
1854..Abbot, Henry L. 11: 194
1855..Comstock, Cyrus B. 22: 437
1857..Robert, Henry M. 10: 142
1859..Casey, Thomas L. 4: 279
1859..Merrill, William E. 10: 223
1862..Gillespie, George L. 12: 184
1862..Haupt, Herman 10: 224
1862..Wilson, John M. 4: 538
1864..Mackenzie, Alexander 14: 250
1867..Mahan, Frederick A. 10: 441
1868..Marshall, William L. 11: 467
1873..Bixby, William H. 21: 337
1874..Symons, Thomas W. 19: 37
1877..Black, William M. .... A: 489
1880..Goethals, George W. 24: 6
1881..Biddle, John 26: 301
1884..Chittenden, Hiram M. ...17: 404
1884..Gaillard, David DuB. 15: 318
1884..Taylor, Harry 23: 141
1886..Patrick, Mason M. .... C: 276
1890..Jadwin, Edgar .... A: 521
1890..Keller, Charles .... B: 220
1898..Fries, Amos A. .... B: 363
1899..Kelly, William .... D: 300
1909..Dunwoody, Halsey .... D: 535

Military Surgeons

1754..Craik, James 7: 494
1755..Cochran, John 8: 410
1760..Jackson, Hall 16: 386
1774..Hutchinson, James 11: 237
1775..Morgan, John 10: 267
1776..Shippen, William, Jr. ...10: 384
1776..Thacher, James 7: 401
1777..Tilton, James 3: 515
1811..Lawson, Thomas 4: 186
1812..Beaumont, William 18: 291
1812..Lovell, Joseph 4: 181
1818..Finley, Clement A. 4: 180
1818..Satterlee, Richard S. 11: 162
1831..Foltz, Jonathan M. 5: 150
1834..Palmer, James C. 8: 222
1840..Barnes, Joseph K. 4: 359
1842..Swift, Ebenezer 5: 177
1847..Crane, Charles H. 4: 174
1849..Edgar, William F. 12: 82
1849..Hammond, William A. ...26: 468
1849..Letterman, Jonathan 18: 338
1852..Sutherland, Charles 4: 473
1853..Moore, John 12: 209
1854..Myer, Albert J. 24: 196
1855..Gihon, Albert L. 9: 154
1861..Baxter, Jedediah H. 4: 180
1861..Billings, John S. 4: 78
1861..Forwood, William H. 15: 148
1861..Sternberg, George M. 4: 388
1863..Coues, Elliott 5: 240
1865..O'Reilly, Robert M. 18: 261
1867..Powell, Junius L. 20: 135
1872..Bransford, John F. 16: 308
1874..Hamilton, John B. 23: 245
1874..Hoff, John Van R. 21: 483
1875..Reed, Walter 13: 284
1875..Beyer, Henry G. 14: 250
1876..Wyman, Walter 12: 508
1879..Gorgas, William C. 14: 528
1880..Carter, Henry R. 25: 346
1883..Devine, William H. 6: 57
1883..Kean, Jefferson R. .... A: 86
1884..McCaw, Walter D. .... A: 89
1885..Wood, Leonard 9: 20
1891..Garrison, Fielding H. 26: 51
1891..Ireland, Merritte W. ..... A: 220
1892..Kennedy, James M. 22: 308
1893..Munson, Edward L. ...... D: 115
1897..Ashford, Bailey K. .... A: 29
1898..Gilchrist, Harry L. ...... A: 464
1898..Hutton, Paul C. .... B: 117
1898..Seaman, Louis L. 5: 521
1906..Nicholas, Henry J. 23: 270
1913..Bainbridge, William
Seaman .... D: 190
1917..Albee, Fred A. .... C: 129

Mineralogists

1800..Bruce, Archibald 9: 356
1810..Gibbs, George 12: 131
1812..Troost, Gerard 7: 349
1815..Lea, Isaac 6: 23
1816..Cleaveland, Parker 13: 56
1821..Delafield, Joseph 11: 28
1826..Shepard, Charles U. 5: 311
1827..Hale, Benjamin 13: 39
1828..Houghton, Douglas 5: 512
1829..Mather, William W. 8: 146
1834..Alexander, John H. 9: 192
1834..Dana, James D. 6: 206
1837..Haldeman, Samuel S. 9: 246
1840..Silliman, Benjamin, Jr. .. 2: 386
1841..Jefferis, William W. 15: 372
1842..Smith, J. Laurence 6: 54
1846..Boynton, John F. 4: 91
1847..Hunt, T. Sterry 3: 254
1848..Genth, Frederick A. 7: 493
1848..Thomas, William S. 10: 129
1849..Fritz, John 13: 74
1850..Newberry, John S. 9: 235
1852..Manross, Newton S. 11: 63
1855..Brush, George J. 10: 298
1856..Young, Augustus 3: 506
1862..Blake, William P. 25: 202
1863..Drown, Thomas M. 7: 112
1865..Metcalf, William 12: 232
1866..Marsh, Othniel C. 9: 317
1868..Koenig, George A. 17: 240
1868..Smith, Eugene A. 6: 185
1869..Frazer, Persifor 4: 286
1870..Chester, Albert H. 11: 422
1872..Howe, Henry M. 13: 78
1873..Canfield, Frederick A. ...20: 175
1874..Dana, Edward S. 6: 537
1874..Kirchhoff, Charles 10: 227
1876..Kunz, George F. 4: 433
1885..Wadsworth, Marshman E. 13: 538
1887..Luquer, Lea McI. 23: 195
1887..Richards, Joseph W. 13: 509
1891..Mathews, Edward B. ..... A: 365
1892..Van Horn, Frank R. 24: 225
1893..Weeks, Joseph D. 13: 27
1895..Washington, Henry S. ... C: 520
1901..Kraus, Edward H. .... B: 232
1901..Louderback, George D. ...17: 426
1903..Cross, Whitman 15: 214
1907..Merwin, Herbert E. ...... D: 360

Mining and Metallurgical Engineers

1832..Clemson, Thomas G. 13: 43
1850..Balback, Edward 7: 249
1850..Wharton, Joseph 13: 82
1852..Blake, William P. 25: 202
1852..Stanton, John 14: 359
1855..Brush, George J. 10: 298
1857..Del Mar, Alexander 4: 189
1857..Hegeler, Edward C. 23: 60
1858..Hague, James D. 23: 164
1859..Agassiz, Alexander 3: 98
1860..Coxe, Eckley B. 11: 559
1860..Strong, Charles L. 17: 35
1860..Vinton, Francis L. 7: 441
1861..Egleston, Thomas 3: 244
1861..Janin, Louis 18: 11
1862..Eilers, Anton F. 14: 222
1862..King, Clarence 13: 248
1862..Lyman, Benjamin Smith . 9: 217
1862..Spilsbury, Edmund G. 13: 546
1863..Holley, Alexander L. 11: 508
1863..Raymond, Rossiter W. ... 8: 44
1864..Douglas, James 23: 22
1864..Rothwell, Richard P. 10: 229
1865..Pearse, John B. S. 26: 418
1866..Brooks, Thomas B. 3: 510
1866..Hunt, Robert W. 19: 17
1867..Emmons, Samuel F. 10: 448
1867..Hill, Nathaniel P. 6: 38
1868..Newton, Henry 4: 190
1868..Stearns, Irving A. 11: 392
1870..Williams, Gardner F. 9: 528
1871..Davenport, Russell W. ...25: 126
1871..Howe, Henry M. 13: 78
1871..James, William F. 18: 432
1873..Meyer, August R. 16: 172

1874..Christy, Samuel B. 20: 147
1874..Olcott, Eben E. 5: 265
1875..Brunton, David W. 23: 99
1876..Gayley, James 14: 70
1876..Grant, James B. 6: 450
1876..Hunt, Alfred E. 25: 38
1876..Lathrop, William A. 18: 358
1876..Williams, Edward H., Jr. 24: 22
1877..Jennings, Hennen 18: 89
1877..Kirchhoff, Charles 10: 227
1878..Devereux, Walter B. 25: 255
1878..D'Invilliers, Edward V. ..22: 372
1878..Saunders, William L. 26: 81
1878..Schneider, Albert F. 24: 70
1879..Cogswell, William B. 13: 107
1880..Goetz, George W. 24: 402
1880..Hammond, John Hays ...26: 45
1882..Cowles, Alfred H. 22: 44
1882..Cowles, Eugene H. 23: 51
1882..Wilfley, Arthur R. 21: 369
1883..Sperr, Frank W. 21: 43
1883..Yeatman, Pope 18: 176
1884..Hand, Carlton H. 20: 126
1885..Manning, Vannoy H. .... A: 316
1885..Thayer, Benjamin B. 5: 66
1886..Bilharz, Oscar M. 21: 468
1886..Dougherty, George T. .... C: 273
1886..Ingalls, Walter R. 16: 127
1886..Kemp, James F. 21: 5
1886..Richards, Joseph W. 13: 509
1887..Jennings, Sidney J. 26: 326
1888..Holden, Albert F. 22: 230
1888..Mitchell, George 13: 362
1888..Sully, John M. 26: 174
1889..Dwight, Arthur S. .... C: 228
1889..Ludlow, Edwin 23: 151
1889..Ludlum, Albert C. .... B: 37
1889..Wilkens, Henry A. J. 15: 399
1890..Bradford, Robert H. 23: 374
1890..Breitung, Edward N. 20: 425
1890..Moldenke, Richard G. G. ..21: 202
1890..Sauveur, Albert .... D: 104
1891..Browne, David H. 23: 93
1891..Merrill, Charles W. 15: 102
1893..Barringer, Daniel M. 22: 317
1893..Jones, Jesse L. 21: 431
1893..Tone, Frank J. .... D: 420
1893..Winchell, Horace V. 20: 200
1894..Carnahan, Robert B., Jr. .17: 206
1895..Bassett, William H. 26: 156
1895..Eavenson, Howard N. ... A: 364
1895..Hoover, Herbert C. ...... C: 1
1895..Rohn, Oscar 20: 237
1896..Jackling, Daniel C. ...... D: 245
1897..Fulton, Charles H. ...... B: 474
1897..Mathewson, Edward P. .. C: 41
1898..Birch, Stephen 15: 393
1898..Drysdale, George A. 20: 409
1898..Loring, William J. .... A: 538
1900..Beatty, Alfred C. 14: 238
1900..Lyon, Frank R. 24: 405
1900..Moyle, Edward H. 16: 399
1901..Boynton, Henry C. ...... D: 292
1901..Dern, George H. 26: 9
1901..Hepburn, Arthur E. ..... C: 377
1902..Becket, Frederick M. .... B: 163
1902..Mathews, John A. 16: 73
1903..Elliott, George K. 25: 239
1903..Holmes, Joseph A. 23: 104
1904..Outerbridge, Alexander E. 13: 118
1904..Riddell, Guy C. .... D: 422
1905..Black, Robert M. .... D: 222
1908..Colburn, Clare L. .... B: 71
1910..Jeffries, Zay .... A: 155
1910..Robinson, J. French ..... A: 211
1918..Feild, Alexander L. ...... C: 221

Missionaries

1635..Eliot, John 2: 419
1646..Mayhew, Thomas 7: 146
1646..Mayhew, Thomas 7: 147
1658..Bourne, Richard 12: 345
1666..Marquette, Jacques 12: 220
1698..Mayhew, Experience 5: 515
1702..Talbot, John 3: 460
1735..Sergeant, John 1: 479
1740..Pyrlaus, John C. 6: 38
1741..Jungmann, John G. 6: 150
1742..Brainerd, David 2: 253
1745..Zeisberger, David 2: 250
1746..Grube, Bernhard A. 6: 120
1749..Post, Christian F. 25: 315
1750..Junipero, Miguel J. S. ...12: 134
1757..McAden, Hugh 9: 275
1762..Heckewelder, John G. E. . 9: 258
1766..Kirkland, Samuel 7: 404
1772..Taylor, John 9: 283
1775..Sergeant, John 1: 464
1800..Badger, Joseph 6: 123
1809..Parker, Samuel 7: 246
1811..Judson, Adoniram 3: 92
1812..Hall, Gordon 10: 246
1812..Jessup, Samuel 10: 144
1812..Judson, Ann H. 3: 93
1812..Mills, Samuel J. 13: 187
1815..Scudder, John 2: 62
1817..McCoy, Isaac 18: 229
1819..Byington, Cyrus 8: 211
1820..Andrews, Lorrin 9: 209
1820..Williams, Eleazer 1: 68
1820..Worcester, Samuel A. 1: 271
1821..DeSmet, Peter J. 11: 453
1822..Ashmun, Jehudi 6: 195
1822..Goodell, William 5: 198
1822..Richards, William 4: 533
1822..Ricksecker, Peter 5: 480
1824..Nitschmann, David 5: 199
1825..Judson, Sarah H. B. 3: 93
1826..Smith, Eli 8: 15
1827..Allen, David O. 6: 56
1827..Judd, Gerritt P. 25: 193
1830..Brewer, Josiah 2: 228
1830..Dwight, Harrison G. O. ..10: 490
1830..Hill, John H. 24: 206
1830..Mazzuchelli, Samuel C. ...25: 328
1831..Baraga, Frederic 12: 415
1831..Schauffler, William G. 18: 280
1832..Riggs, Elias 3: 120
1833..Coan, Titus 2: 339
1833..Eckard, James R. 11: 245
1833..Hoisington, Henry R. 24: 244
1833..Perkins, Justin 10: 45
1833..Thomson, William McC. ..11: 57
1833..Wilson, John L. 21: 226
1834..Lee, Jason 25: 309
1834..Parker, Peter 10: 284
1835..Grant, Asahel 4: 457
1835..Whitman, Marcus 11: 112
1836..Spalding, Henry H. 2: 20
1837..Homes, Henry A. 13: 42
1837..Riggs, Stephen R. 3: 119
1838..Brown, Samuel R. 8: 453
1838..Labaree, Benjamin 12: 106
1839..Winslow, Miron 1: 183
1840..VanDyck, Cornelius V. ... 5: 560
1842..Loughridge, Robert M. ...19: 127
1843..Fiske, Fidelia 3: 525
1843..McCartee, Divie B. 24: 159
1843..Stoddard, David T. 4: 292
1843..Taylor, Edward T. 13: 464
1844..Happer, Andrew P. 22: 401
1844..Ravalli, Anthony 3: 507
1846..Atkinson, George H. 6: 496
1847..Hodge, Archibald A. 10: 245
1847..Menetry, Joseph 6: 459
1847..Yates, Mathew T. 10: 110
1849..Taylor, William 10: 496
1850..Ashmore, William 25: 76
1850..Vassar, John E. 5: 252
1851..Fletcher, James C. 13: 130
1851..Gulick, Luther H. 26: 370
1853..Nevius, John L. 10: 293
1855..Bliss, Daniel 19: 176
1855..Jessup, Henry H. 10: 144
1856..Bingham, Hiram 14: 98
1856..Butler, William 12: 61
1857..Dwight, Henry O. 10: 490
1858..Allen, Young J. 21: 483
1858..Andrus, Alpheus N. 18: 24
1858..Washburn, George 10: 492
1859..Parker, Edwin W. 5: 514
1860..Schereschewsky, Samuel I. 13: 429
1863..Parker, Henry H. 22: 403
1864..Gulick, John T. 11: 463
1864..Seghers, Charles J. 13: 32
1865..Hart, Virgil 22: 285
1867..Brondel, John B. 13: 327
1867..Cushing, Joshua N. 12: 384
1867..Tracy, Charles C. 11: 103
1868..Dennis, James S. 22: 320
1868..Young, Edgerton R. 14: 160
1869..Greene, Daniel C. 23: 324
1869..Jackson, Sheldon 9: 251
1870..Buck, Philo M. 22: 22
1872..Harpster, John H. 15: 153
1872..McAuley, Jerry 11: 525
1873..Harris, Merriman C. 14: 122
1874..Hume, Robert A. 26: 358
1878..Jones, John P. 23: 137
1878..Marty, Martin 12: 416
1879..Chambers, Robert 17: 269
1879..Reinke, Jonathan 22: 265
1882..Anderson, David L. 23: 310
1882..Booth, Eugene S. 23: 411
1883..Bergen, Paul D. 16: 200
1883..Leavitt, Mary C. 5: 152
1885..Appenzeller, Henry G. ...23: 290
1886..Lambuth, Walter R. 19: 264
1886..Stanford, Arthur W. 19: 58
1887..Jones, George H. 18: 263
1888..Moseley, Hartwell R. 20: 44
1888..Mott, John R. .... A: 235
1888..Newton, John C. C. 23: 271
1891..Fiske, Pliny 3: 525
1899..Williams, John E. 21: 122
1901..Cowman, Charles E. 19: 295
1902..Kumm, Herman K. W. ..23: 323

Musicians and Composers

1720..Beissel, Johann C. 7: 497
1767..Law, Andrew 25: 146
1770..Billings, William 5: 421
1777..Holyoke, Samuel 13: 177
1778..Read, Daniel 7: 243
1792..Holden, Oliver 13: 178
1802..Hastings, Thomas 7: 431
1804..Gould, Nathaniel D. 7: 426
1809..Horn, Charles E. 6: 146
1810..Gilfert, Charles 9: 374
1810..Oliver, Henry K. 13: 424
1816..Jones, John 11: 356
1819..Jones, Sissieretta 13: 424
1822..Hill, Ureli C. 22: 38
1822..Mason, Lowell 7: 422
1830..Wallace, William V. 5: 140
1831..Bishop, Anna 3: 289
1831..Bull, Ole 4: 234
1833..Russell, Henry 5: 249
1834..Heinrich, Anthony P. 8: 447
1835..Fry, William H. 8: 443
1836..Bristow, George F. 23: 194
1836..Nau, Maria D. B. J. 5: 441
1837..Baker, Benjamin F. 7: 429
1838..Lind, Jenny 3: 255
1839..Greatorex, Henry W. 6: 245
1839..Hutchinson, Abby J. 10: 27
1839..Hutchinson, Adoniram J. J.10: 27
1839..Hutchinson, Asa 10: 26
1839..Hutchinson, John W. 10: 27
1839..Hutchinson, Judson 10: 27
1839..Maretzek, Max 8: 448
1840..Bradbury, William B. 5: 140
1840..Phillips, Adelaide 6: 149
1840..Tuckerman, Samuel P. ...12: 260
1842..Ansorge, Charles 5: 260
1842..Eichberg, Julius 13: 320
1842..Ryan, Thomas 10: 197
1843..Foster, Stephen C. 7: 439
1843..Webster, Joseph P. 19: 428
1844..Root, George F. 9: 384
1845..Cheney, Simeon P. 6: 288
1845..Dodge, Ossian E. 4: 384
1846..Thomas, Theodore 2: 139
1846..Warren, George W. 4: 553
1847..Richings, Caroline M. 9: 189
1848..Bergmann, Charles 5: 416
1849..Balatka, Hans 10: 197
1849..Brandeis, Frederick 7: 433
1849..Hoffman, Richard 26: 395
1849..Thomas, John Rogers 8: 445
1849..Wels, Charles 7: 424
1850..Klauser, Karl 7: 427
1850..Lloyd, Thomas S. 22: 367
1850..Mathews, William S. B. ..10: 356
1850..Winner, Septimus 1: 310
1852..Dwight, John S. 8: 444
1852..Ritter, Frederick L. 7: 426
1853..Emerson, Luther O. 7: 432
1853..Foote, John H. 4: 184
1853..Mollenhauer, Henry 13: 484
1853..Penfield, Smith N. 11: 493
1854..Mason, William 7: 423
1854..Muller, Carl C. 7: 435
1854..Parker, James C. D. 5: 199
1854..Perkins, William O. 9: 386
1854..Zerrahn, Charles 1: 327
1855..Auer, Leopold 22: 384
1855..Danks, Hart P. 8: 447
1856..Damrosch, Leopold 2: 147
1856..Millard, Harrison 7: 425
1856..Paine, John K. 7: 436
1856..Runcie, Constance F. 7: 238
1856..Woolf, Benjamin E. 1: 411
1857..Gilder, John F. 7: 438
1857..Hays, William S. 3: 178
1858..Boise, Otis B. 26: 213
1858..Cappa, Carlo A. 9: 387
1858..Fairlamb, James R. 10: 466
1858..Lang, Benjamin J. 7: 430
1858..Whitney, Myron W. 2: 143

Naturalists

See also the various departments of Natural Science

1882..Evermann, Barton W. 13: 570
1882..Lucas, Frederick A. 13: 529
1882..Simpson, Charles T. 23: 255
1883..Minot, Charles S. 6: 112
1884..Akeley, Carl E. 26: 130
1885..Harris, Charles M. 17: 279
1886..Good, Adolphus C. 23: 61
1887..Holland, William J. 13: 141
1889..Mills, Enos A. 20: 165
1890..Edwards, Charles L. 13: 440
1890..Kellogg, Vernon L. ...... A: 203
1892..Jennings, Herbert S. ...... A: 278
1894..Needham, James G. ...... B: 289
1895..Castle, William E. 16: 297
1895..Rotzell, Willett E. 12: 144
1895..Wright, Mabel O. 12: 545
1899..Beebe, William .... B: 337
1902..Gudger, Eugene W. ...... D: 417

Naval Architects and Marine Engineers

1785..Fitch, John 6: 63
1789..Stevens, John 11: 21
1790..Morey, Samuel 11: 168
1793..Fulton, Robert 3: 104
1793..Lenthall, John 26: 387
1796..Eckford, Henry 1: 350
1808..Stevens, Robert L. 11: 21
1817..Ogden, Francis B. 11: 369
1820..Newton, Isaac 5: 195
1825..Francis, Joseph 10: 88
1828..Griffiths, John W. 8: 70
1830..Cramp, William 5: 253
1836..Haswell, Charles H. 9: 486
1836..Webb, William H. 2: 263
1837..Englis, John 9: 478
1840..Davison, Darius 2: 198
1840..Roach, John 3: 157
1844..Clyde, William P. 20: 57
1844..Corliss, George H. 10: 394
1844..Isherwood, Benjamin F. ..12: 199
1844..King, James W. 13: 186
1845..McKay, Donald 2: 249
1845..Rees, James 23: 218
1845..Shock, William H. 6: 200
1845..Steers, George 1: 148
1845..Wood, William W. W. ...12: 198
1848..Cramp, Charles H. 5: 254
1850..Holloway, Josephus F. 12: 116
1851..Loring, Charles H. 12: 502
1854..Silver, Thomas 6: 191
1856..Herreshoff, Charles F. 12: 352
1858..Sergeant, Henry C. 15: 155
1861..Melville, George W. 3: 283
1864..Herreshoff, John B. 12: 353
1864..Taylor, Stevenson 23: 116
1865..See, Horace 2: 220
1866..Wilson, Theodore D. 7: 508
1868..Rae, Charles W. 15: 355
1869..Herreshoff, Nathaniel G. .12: 353
1871..Roach, John B. 15: 286
1872..Baird, George W. .... B: 245
1873..Herreshoff, James B. 12: 352
1875..Hanley, Charles C. 26: 149
1878..Grogan, Frank W. .... A: 458
1879..Bowles, Francis T. 20: 39
1882..Nixon, Lewis 13: 42
1883..Burgess, Edward 1: 449
1883..Dickie, George W. 22: 326
1885..Amory, John J. 14: 239
1885..Peck, Robert J. 22: 414
1885..Taylor, David W. 15: 87
1886..Capps, Washington L. 26: 42
1888..Chesebrough, Albert S. ...17: 127
1890..Patterson, William H. 15: 221
1891..Durand, William F. ...... D: 260
1891..Paterson, James V. 17: 171
1892..Macalpine, John H. 20: 419
1894..Ferguson, Homer L. 17: 166
1894..Palen, Frederick P. 16: 196
1895..Nock, Frederic S. 17: 141
1897..Magoun, Henry A. 26: 103
1900..Palmer, William F. 16: 423
1903..Pillsbury, Albert F. .... C: 237
1907..Donnelly, William T. 26: 426
1911..Emmet, William Le R. .... D: 413

Neurologists

1851..Miles, Francis T. 20: 437
1861..Mitchell, S. Weir 9: 346
1866..Hammond, William A. ... 9: 338
1866..Hughes, Charles H. 5: 64
1866..Wilder, Burt G. 4: 481
1868..Beard, George M. 8: 206
1868..Brower, Daniel R. 9: 363
1868..Emerson, Justin E. 12: 378
1869..Putnam, James J. 18: 36
1870..Hamilton, Allan McL. ... 9: 349
1871..Lyman, Henry M. 12: 298
1872..Ott, Isaac 20: 188
1874..Bartholow, Roberts 22: 212
1874..Mills, Charles K. .... B: 331
1876..Spitzka, Edward C. 19: 450
1877..Dercum, Francis X. 22: 143
1878..Kellogg, Theodore H. .... B: 229
1879..Clevenger, Shobal V. 5: 267
1879..Jelly, George F. 15: 92
1879..Morton, William J. 8: 333
1879..Zenner, Philip .... D: 129
1880..Bullard, William N. 26: 75
1880..Corning, James L. 17: 177
1880..Gray, Landon C. 5: 380
1881..Hammond, Graeme M. ...15: 199
1881..Prince, Morton 25: 313
1882..Hun, Henry 19: 285
1883..Dana, Charles L. 13: 528
1883..Hinsdale, Guy .... A: 493
1883..Knapp, Philip C. 24: 181
1883..Starr, Moses A. 16: 102
1884..Peterson, Frederick 16: 175
1885..Thomas, Henry M. 20: 163
1886..Edes, Robert T. 8: 212
1887..Potts, Charles S. 26: 181
1889..Donaldson, Henry H. 11: 56
1889..Hoppe, Herman H. 22: 386
1892..Bailey, Pearce 24: 192
1892..Crafts, Leo M. 15: 57
1894..Fritz, William W. 16: 206
1894..Patrick, Hugh .... D: 453
1895..Hall, Herbert J. 20: 322
1896..Cushing, Harvey .... C: 36
1896..Taylor, Edward W. 25: 157
1896..Timme, Walter .... C: 141
1898..Heym, Albrecht .... D: 283
1898..Hughes, Marc R. 12: 468
1899..Barker, Lewellys F. ...... A: 265
1899..Schlapp, Max G. 15: 76
1907..Swift, Walter B. .... D: 112
1907..Wolfsohn, Julian M. ..... D: 301
1909..Dowman, Charles E. 23: 173
1910..Kennedy, Foster .... B: 248
1913..Dandy, Walter E. .... D: 344
1913..Eckel, John L. 26: 46
1914..Orton, Samuel T. .... D: 117
1916..Kraus, Walter M. .... D: 323
1919..Favill, John .... C: 131

Obstetricians

See Gynecologists and Obstetricians

Ophthalmologists

1820..Hays, Isaac 11: 256
1821..Delafield, Edward 10: 278
1836..Dix, John H. 11: 456
1849..Williams, Henry W. 3: 223
1855..Angell, Henry C. 11: 183
1857..Hinton, John H. 2: 177
1859..Agnew, Cornelius R. 8: 205
1859..Jeffries, Benjamin 24: 253
1860..Friedenwald, Aaron 23: 270
1861..Norris, William F. 18: 175
1862..Carmalt, William H. 14: 207
1862..Derby, Hasket 17: 422
1863..Roosa, D. B. St. John 9: 349
1865..Keyser, Peter D. 4: 292
1865..Stevens, George T. 1: 214
1865..Wadsworth, Oliver F. 20: 389
1866..Green, John 14: 268
1867..Gruening, Emil 19: 47
1867..Theobald, Samuel 24: 74
1868..Jones, Samuel J. 10: 276
1869..Pooley, Thomas R. 25: 442
1870..Holmes, Christian R. 18: 361
1870..Risley, Samuel D. 7: 513
1870..Strawbridge, George 15: 143
1871..Bull, Charles S. 9: 336
1871..Pomeroy, Oren D. 20: 331
1872..Gray, Clifton S. 12: 453
1873..Campbell, James A. 7: 287
1873..DeRosset, Moses J. 11: 202
1873..Turnbull, Charles S. 8: 209
1874..Gradle, Henry 24: 193
1874..Lippincott, James A. 10: 506
1875..Connor, Leartus 12: 456
1875..Ehrhardt, Julius G. 5: 113
1875..Harlan, George C. 24: 129
1875..Kalish, Richard 21: 67
1876..Burnett, Swan M. 1: 439
1876..Howe, Lucien 23: 218
1878..Carvelle, Henry D. 20: 73
1878..Post, Martin H. 19: 31
1878..Stucky, Joseph A. 25: 295
1878..Thomas, Charles M. 3: 483
1878..Valk, Francis 2: 197
1879..Standish, Myles 23: 168
1880..Fulton, John F. 25: 234
1881..Dennis, David N. 22: 62
1881..De Schweinitz, George E. . C: 144
1882..Norton, Arthur B. 18: 262
1883..Culver, Charles M. 12: 493
1883..Ewing, Arthur E. 22: 16
1883..Randall, B. Alexander 25: 91
1883..Schneideman, Theodore B. 24: 260
1884..Claiborne, John H., Jr. ... 3: 219
1885..Coleman, William F. 16: 138
1885..Ring, G. Oram 24: 292
1885..Wolfner, Henry L. 26: 375
1885..Wood, Hilliard 25: 52
1886..Gifford, Harold 22: 227
1886..Lambert, Walter E. 24: 389
1887..Duane, Alexander 26: 306
1887..May, Charles H. 14: 206
1888..Gould, George M. 10: 509
1888..Jackson, Edward 12: 446
1889..Shastid, Thomas H. ...... C: 214
1889..Thorington, James .... C: 535
1889..Wilmer, William H. ...... C: 78
1889..Wood, Casey A. 10: 284
1891..Ball, James M. 21: 377
1891..Reese, Robert G. 20: 479
1892..Suker, George F. 25: 267
1893..Masters, John L. 17: 153
1893..Pyle, Walter L. 19: 130
1894..Wescott, Cassius D. ...... C: 226
1895..Thomson, Edgar S. 22: 141
1896..Cullom, Marvin M. .... C: 231
1896..Lichtenberg, Joseph S. ...24: 73
1897..Denig, Rudolph 14: 491
1899..Kress, George H. 16: 126
1899..Todd, Frank C. 18: 278
1899..Verhoeff, Frederick H. .... B: 265
1900..Eagleton, Wells P. ...... D: 394
1901..Warbrick, John C. 16: 388
1902..Hollis, William A. 20: 180
1903..Breitenbach, Oscar C. 22: 385
1903..Slocum, George 24: 180
1905..Smyth, P. Somers 26: 94
1911..Berens, Conrad .... D: 418

Orientalists

1755..Stiles, Ezra 1: 167
1813..Stuart, Moses 6: 244
1821..Robinson, Edward 2: 242
1826..Pickering, John 7: 294
1826..Smith, Eli 8: 15
1833..Dwight, Harrison G. O. ..10: 490
1835..Williams, Samuel W. 1: 422
1837..Homes, Henry A. 13: 42
1838..Alexander, Joseph A. 1: 242
1838..Day, George E. 13: 574
1838..Turner, William W. 9: 198
1849..Salisbury, Edward E. 11: 448
1851..Green, William H. 6: 128
1852..Cotheal, Alexander I. 1: 322
1852..Hall, Fitzedward 11: 448
1853..Thompson, Joseph P. 10: 132
1856..Whitney, William D. 2: 340
1860..Schereschewsky, Samuel I. J. 13: 429
1860..Ward, William H. 8: 147
1864..Thayer, Joseph H. 6: 428
1865..Van Name, Addison 19: 122
1868..Jastrow, Marcus 11: 372
1872..Gilman, Daniel C. 5: 170
1874..Merrill, Selah 13: 218
1875..Hall, Isaac H. 12: 143
1876..Lanman, Charles R. 11: 96
1878..Davis, Charles H. S. 25: 68
1880..Harper, William R. 11: 65
1880..Haupt, Paul 22: 157
1880..Toy, Crawford H. 6: 94
1880..Winslow, William C. 4: 83
1881..Bigelow, William S. 20: 177
1881..Bloomfield, Maurice 10: 400
1881..Hopkins, Edward W. 14: 476
1881..Rockhill, William W. 8: 129
1883..Hilprecht, Hermann V. ..10: 380
1883..Moore, George F. 10: 101
1884..Peters, John P. 13: 555
1884..Price, Ira M. 4: 508
1884..Schechter, Solomon 13: 414
1885..Jastrow, Morris 11: 372
1886..Harper, Robert F. 22: 98
1887..Jackson, Abraham V. W. 13: 550
1888..Adler, Cyrus 11: 371
1889..Stevenson, Sara Y. 13: 83
1890..Müller, Wilhelm M. 21: 413
1891..Gottheil, Richard J. H. ...14: 276
1892..Barton, George A. .... D: 441

1892..Clay, Albert T. 22: 130
1893..Rogers, Robert W. 23: 95
1894..Breasted, James H. .... B: 377
1895..Bjerregaard, Carl H. A. ..13: 47
1896..Newbold, William R. 22: 251
1898..Margolis, Max L. 23: 383
1901..Nies, James B. 20: 256

Ornithologists

1804..Wilson, Alexander 7: 440
1808..Audubon, John J. 6: 75
1809..Nuttall, Thomas 8: 374
1813..Ord, George 13: 356
1818..Kirtland, Jared P. 11: 347
1832..Wilson, Thomas B. 13: 165
1833..Cassin, John 22: 240
1837..Brewer, Thomas M. 22: 59
1837..Linsley, James H. 4: 540
1842..Lawrence, George N. 2: 203
1855..Elliot, Daniel G. 16: 196
1860..Baird, Spencer F. 3: 405
1864..Coues, Elliott 5: 240
1864..Shufeldt, Robert W. 6: 242
1867..Ridgway, Robert 8: 460
1868..Sage, John H. 21: 177
1869..Lewis, Graceanna 9: 447
1870..Allen, Joel A. 3: 100
1871..Ober, Frederick A. 13: 311
1872..Merriam, C. Hart 13: 264
1873..Forbes, Stephen A. 22: 291
1873..Ingersoll, Ernest 9: 240
1874..Merrill, James C. 15: 246
1874..Sennett, George B. 14: 281
1875..Baskett, James N. 13: 346
1875..Scott, William E. D. 13: 291
1878..Forbush, Edward H. 21: 316
1880..Brewster, William........22: 140
1880..Bruner, Lawrence 13: 232
1880..Cory, Charles B. 13: 225
1880..Frost, Albert H. 15: 70
1881..Cooke, Wells W. 21: 379
1881..Mearns, Edgar A. 25: 124
1881..Nutting, Charles C. 21: 467
1881..Stejneger, Leonhard 14: 130
1885..Fisher, Albert K. .... A: 377
1885..Torrey, Bradford 10: 134
1887..Chapman, Frank M. ..... C: 188
1889..Richmond, Charles W. ...23: 62
1890..Palmer, Theodore S. ..... A: 474
1893..Wright, Mabel O. 12: 545
1894..Abbott, Charles C. 10: 318
1894..Bailey, Florence M. ...... A: 257
1894..Baldwin, Samuel P. ...... C: 148
1895..Rotzell, Willett E. 12: 144
1900..Dwight, Jonathan 22: 353
1901..Swales, Bradshaw H. 23: 250
1902..Pearson, T. Gilbert ...... D: 334
1913..Griscom, Ludlow .... B: 300
1916..Beebe, William .... B: 337

Orthopædic Surgeons

1818..Barton, John R. 22: 175
1842..Sayre, Lewis A. 2: 31
1850..Hudson, Erasmus D. 2: 393
1853..Bauer, Louis 5: 482
1856..Taylor, Charles F. 9: 362
1858..Lee, Benjamin 11: 99
1867..Allis, Oscar H. 24: 341
1867..Shaffer, Newton M. 3: 392
1868..Steele, Aaron J. 20: 298
1871..Gibney, Virgil P. 21: 46
1873..Moore, James E. 6: 388
1873..Phelps, Abel M. 12: 233
1875..Judson, Adoniram B. 20: 384
1875..Ketch, Samuel 22: 387
1876..Barton, Bernard 21: 388
1878..Willard, De Forest 15: 86
1880..Ridlon, John 17: 368
1880..Townsend, Wisner R. 20: 475
1882..Taylor, Henry H. 24: 296
1884..Elliott, George R. 26: 248
1885..Myers, T. Halsted 21: 432
1885..Sherman, Harry M. 21: 334
1886..Lovett, Robert W. 20: 398
1886..Sayre, Reginald H. 21: 161
1887..Cook, Ansel G. 24: 413
1887..Gillette, Arthur J. 19: 227
1890..McCurdy, Stewart L. 12: 483
1893..Lord, John P. 16: 68
1894..Freiberg, Albert H. ...... D: 294
1896..Test, Frederick C. .... A: 209
1900..Fassett, Fred J. 20: 381
1902..Ogilvy, Charles .... D: 277
1902..Soutter, Robert 24: 363

1902..Watkins, James T. 24: 83
1903..Albee, Fred H. .... C: 129
1904..Allison, Nathaniel 26: 200
1906..Osgood, Robert B. .... D: 60
1908..Rich, Edward A. 24: 241
1909..Swaim, Loring T. .... D: 63
1917..Moffat, Barclay W. ...... B: 312
1925..Gratz, Charles M. .... C: 422

Otologists

See Laryngologists, Rhinologists and Otologists

Paleontologists

1818..Green, Jacob 13: 552
1819..Agassiz, Louis 2: 360
1821..Hitchcock, Edward 5: 308
1826..Emmons, Ebenezer 8: 477
1827..Lea, Isaac 6: 23
1831..Conrad, Timothy A. 8: 466
1834..Morton, Samuel G.........10: 265
1836..Haldeman, Samuel S. 9: 246
1836..Hall, James 3: 280
1837..Owen, David D. 8: 113
1844..Leidy, Joseph 5: 220
1846..Shumard, Benjamin F. ... 8: 256
1847..Yandell, Lunsford P. 4: 301
1848..Lesquereux, Leo 9: 438
1848..Whitfield, Robert P. 5: 92
1851..Newberry, John S. 9: 235
1852..Dyer, Charles B. 4: 528
1852..Meek, Fielding B. 11: 284
1853..Hayden, Ferdinand V. 11: 97
1855..Wachsmuth, Charles 7: 159
1862..Gabb, William M. 4: 376
1862..Hyatt, Alpheus 23: 362
1862..Marcy, Oliver 13: 536
1862..Marsh, Othniel C. 9: 317
1864..Shaler, Nathaniel S. 9: 315
1866..White, Charles A. 6: 231
1869..Springer, Frank 20: 23
1869..Winchell, Alexander 16: 119
1870..Cope, Edward D. 7: 474
1871..Williams, Henry S. 21: 327
1873..Fontaine, William M. 19: 187
1876..Walcott, Charles D. 22: 135
1877..Osborn, Henry Fairfield ..26: 18
1879..Davis, William J. 13: 22
1879..Heilprin, Angelo 12: 381
1879..Hollick, Charles A. 24: 373
1880..Scott, William B. 13: 214
1881..Claypole, Edward W. 13: 259
1882..Barbour, Erwin H. 14: 278
1884..Hay, Oliver P. 22: 31
1884..Knowlton, Frank H. 10: 410
1885..Clarke, John M. 19: 456
1885..Dall, William H. 10: 454
1885..Prosser, Charles S. 12: 544
1885..Scudder, Samuel H. 24: 180
1885..Ward, Lester F. 13: 112
1886..White, David 18: 60
1887..Holland, William J. 13: 141
1888..Beecher, Charles E. 13: 564
1888..Clark, William Bullock ...18: 191
1890..Armstrong, Edwin J. 20: 218
1890..Eyerman, John 9: 204
1890..Keyes, Charles R. 13: 144
1891..Schuchert, Charles 15: 122
1893..Merriam, John C. .... A: 485
1893..Patten, William 24: 121
1894..Douglass, Earl 26: 126
1894..Lull, Richard S. .... A: 419
1899..Gidley, James W. 24: 331
1899..Gregory, William K. ...... A: 105
1901..Dean, Bashford 21: 29
1901..Lucas, Frederic A. 13: 529

Pathologists

1814..Horner, William E. 6: 383
1836..Stillé, Alfred 9: 358
1862..Keen, William W. 11: 367
1863..Delafield, Francis 10: 278
1865..Tyson, James 9: 356
1867..Satterthwaite, Thomas E. 12: 298
1871..Fitz, Reginald H. 10: 456
1871..Janeway, Edward G. 13: 499
1873..Fenger, Christian 17: 279
1875..Welch, William H. 26: 6
1879..Prudden, Theophil M. 9: 347
1880..Councilman, William T. .. 5: 550
1881..Ernst, Harold C. 20: 89
1883..Smith, Theobald .... D: 133
1885..Biggs, Hermann M. 19: 219

1886..Kinyoun, Joseph J. 23: 360
1886..Smith, Allen J. 20: 104
1886..Smith, Erwin F. 20: 273
1887..Paquin, Paul 6: 379
1888..Dock, George .... C: 360
1890..Hektoen, Ludvig 18: 146
1890..Schroeder, Ernest C. ..... B: 277
1891..Warthin, Aldred S. 25: 367
1892..Flexner, Simon .... B: 19
1892..Turck, Fenton B. 25: 175
1893..Ewing, James 18: 209
1893..Gaylord, Harvey R. 20: 285
1894..Ohlmacher, Albert P. 26: 222
1895..Moore, Veranus A. 22: 366
1897..Opie, Eugene L. .... D: 242
1897..Orton, William A. 21: 60
1897..Wood, Francis C. 18: 288
1898..Anderson, John F. .... B: 102
1898..MacCallum, William G. ...15: 287
1899..Taylor, Alonzo E. .... C: 222
1900..Christian, Henry A. 18: 17
1900..Thayer, William S. 24: 409
1900..Westbrook, Frank F. 14: 472
1901..Gay, Frederick P. .... B: 268
1902..Pearce, Richard M., Jr. ..15: 204
1903..Darling, Samuel T. 19: 417
1903..Schultz, Oscar T. 16: 211
1903..Turley, Louis A. .... C: 128
1903..Wolbach, Simon B. .... D: 197
1904..Manwaring, Wilfred H. .. C: 110
1904..Rosenow, Edward C. ..... A: 332
1909..Rivas, Damaso de .... C: 333
1910..DeWitt, Lydia M. .... B: 457
1910..Murphy, James B. .... B: 119
1911..Brem, Walter V., Jr. ..... A: 26

Pediatricians

1853..Jacobi, Abraham 9: 345
1853..Smith, J. Lewis 2: 201
1856..Reynolds, James B. 14: 482
1864..Grosvenor, Lemuel C. 7: 270
1869..Putnam, Charles P. 16: 374
1872..Love, Isaac N. 6: 375
1873..Winters, Joseph E. 2: 501
1874..Buckingham, Edward M. .20: 271
1874..Osler, William 12: 201
1875..Forchheimer, Frederick ..16: 388
1876..Rotch, Thomas M. 19: 350
1877..McNutt, Sarah J. 15: 264
1878..Cotton, Alfred C. 16: 150
1878..Saunders, Edward W. 21: 215
1879..Fruitnight, John H. 3: 257
1881..Holt, L. Emmett 20: 46
1884..Crandall, Floyd M. 15: 384
1885..Watson, William P. 19: 444
1887..Coit, Henry L. 22: 102
1894..Abt, Isaac A. .... D: 223
1900..Ladd, Maynard .... D: 122
1901..Howland, John 21: 392
1904..Scott, George D. .... D: 446
1905..Dennett, Roger H. .... D: 282
1907..Talbot, Fritz B. .... A: 341
1908..McLean, Stafford 24: 356
1909..Fleishner, E. Charles 24: 422
1913..Retan, George M. .... D: 302
1916..Gelston, Clain F. .... D: 387
1925..Kugelmass, I. Newton ... D: 130

Pharmacists

1819..Smith, Daniel B. 5: 343
1825..Milhau, John 2: 225
1826..Ellis, Charles 5: 344
1843..Parrish, Edward 5: 348
1844..Procter, William 5: 347
1847..Bullock, Charles 5: 344
1851..Maisch, John M. 5: 348
1851..Squibb, Edward R. 19: 56
1853..Sander, Enno 13: 306
1854..Shinn, James T. 25: 231
1856..Simpson, William 24: 167
1860..Searby, William M. 20: 51
1861..Dohme, Charles E. 23: 191
1865..Oldberg, Oscar 20: 429
1865..Prescott, Albert B. 13: 53
1866..Remington, Joseph P. 5: 349
1866..Sayre, Lucius E. 22: 100
1867..Davis, George S. 18: 48
1869..Patch, Edgar L. 25: 339
1873..Frasch, Herman 19: 347
1874..Godding, John G. 22: 425
1875..Hurty, John N. 22: 370
1876..Payne, George F. 20: 169
1877..Hynson, Henry P. 19: 367
1877..Lloyd, John Uri .... D: 106

1878..Fuller, Robert M. 12: 265
1879..Alpers, William C. 22: 76
1879..Jacobs, Joseph 7: 415
1883..Rusby, Henry H. .... A: 172
1883..Whelpley, Henry M. 20: 488
1887..Kauffman, George B. 19: 33
1887..Mayo, Caswell A. 22: 52
1887..Wulling, Frederick J. .... B: 498
1893..Abel, John J. .... A: 392
1897..Arny, Henry V. .... B: 206
1902..Linton, Arthur W. 19: 433

Philanthropists

1638..Harvard, John 6: 408
1701..Stoughton, William 7: 373
1703..Coram, Thomas 6: 17
1715..Yale, Elihu 1: 163
1728..Oglethorpe, James 1: 490
1740..Faneuil, Peter 1: 441
1740..Pemberton, Israel 5: 514
1744..Franklin, Benjamin 1: 328
1750..Brown, Nicholas 8: 27
1753..Abbott, Samuel 5: 503
1755..Williams, Ephraim 6: 236
1760..Brown, Joseph 8: 28
1770..Phillips, John 10: 103
1771..Randall, Robert R. 11: 253
1774..Brown, Moses 2: 327
1774..Girard, Stephen 7: 11
1774..Graham, Isabella 4: 375
1776..Treadwell, John 10: 331
1777..Phillips, Samuel 10: 93
1784..Thompson, Benjamin 5: 410
1785..Phillips, William 10: 94
1786..Astor, John Jacob 8: 102
1786..Brown, Nicholas, 2d 8: 27
1789..Pintard, John 3: 461
1792..Rawle, William 7: 442
1793..Combs, Moses N. 23: 339
1794..Appleton, Samuel 5: 127
1794..Bowdoin, James 1: 419
1794..Eddy, Thomas 3: 512
1795..Dexter, Ebenezer K. 8: 420
1796..Hopper, Isaac T. 2: 330
1801..Gratz, Rebecca 10: 130
1802..Rutgers, Henry 3: 400
1802..Touro, Judah 6: 444
1805..Clinton, DeWitt 3: 43
1806..Bartlet, William 10: 99
1806..Farrar, Samuel 10: 99
1807..Mercer, Jesse 6: 497
1808..Dodge, David L. 20: 171
1808..Mercer, Charles F. 13: 222
1808..Norris, John 6: 396
1809..Seton, Elizabeth A. 2: 436
1810..Birney, James G. 2: 312
1812..Boudinot, Elias 2: 296
1812..Maclure, William 13: 368
1812..Tuckerman, Joseph 6: 230
1813..Coffin, Levi 12: 124
1813..Crosby, William B. 10: 60
1815..Augustus, John 6: 59
1817..Gallaudet, Thomas H. 9: 138
1817..McDonogh, John 9: 465
1818..Vaux, Roberts 15: 210
1820..Dane, Nathan 9: 196
1823..Clark, Sheldon 22: 221
1823..Gerard, James W. 11: 333
1824..Baldwin, Matthias W. 9: 476
1824..Smith, Daniel B. 5: 343
1826..Perkins, Thomas H. 5: 245
1826..Woodward, William 5: 251
1827..Howe, Samuel G. 8: 372
1828..Brown, John Carter 11: 402
1828..Doremus, Sarah P. 6: 166
1828..Field, Moses 23: 212
1828..Ladd, William 13: 187
1828..Packer, Asa 7: 110
1829..Lawrence, Amos 3: 62
1829..Smithson, James 3: 405
1830..Minturn, Robert B. 9: 114
1830..Pepper, George S. 7: 487
1832..Hall, Edward B. 8: 467
1832..Lowell, John 7: 195
1833..Gibbons, Abigail H. 7: 313
1834..Barnard, Charles F. 8: 232
1834..Lyon, Mary 4: 462
1835..Butler, Charles 23: 356
1835..Stuart, Mary McC. 7: 150
1836..Gray, Francis C. 1: 443
1837..Reed, William 11: 399
1837..Williston, Samuel 5: 313
1838..Griffing, Josephine S. W. . 6: 88
1839..Lenox, James 3: 413
1839..Marquand, Frederick 19: 399
1841..Barton, Clara 15: 314
1841..Hazard, Rowland G. 9: 442
1841..Newberry, Walter L. 24: 223
1842..Bussey, Benjamin 4: 171
1842..Fairbanks, Thaddeus 10: 300
1842..Lawrence, William 5: 462
1843..Muhlenberg, William A. .. 9: 199
1843..Stearns, George L. 8: 231
1844..Farmer, Hannah T. S. ... 7: 362
1844..Field, Benjamin H. 3: 464
1844..Robbins, Thomas 2: 222
1845..Astor, John Jacob, 3d 8: 104
1845..Eliot, Samuel 3: 496
1846..Durant, Henry F. 7: 327
1847..Crozer, John P. 10: 171
1847..Lawrence, Abbott 3: 62
1847..Smith, Gerrit 2: 322
1847..Williams, Mary A. 7: 17
1848..Hitchcock, Samuel A. 5: 313
1848..Stewart, Alexander T. ... 7: 352
1849..Bromfield, John 6: 155
1849..Sinton, David 13: 42
1850..Bottome, Margaret M. 13: 48
1850..Cobb, George T. 6: 228
1850..Colgate, William 13: 159
1850..Gaffney, Margaret 2: 373
1850..Grinnell, Henry 3: 281
1850..Peabody, George 5: 335
1850..Plankinton, John 1: 248
1850..Shattuck, George C. 12: 197
1850..Shields, Mary 3: 374
1850..Wittenmyer, Anna T. 12: 363
1851..Camp, Hiram 8: 155
1851..Miner, Myrtilla 12: 185
1851..Stuart, Robert L. 10: 24
1852..Bates, Joshua 5: 195
1852..Brace, Charles L. 10: 166
1852..Coburn, Abner 6: 313
1853..Cooper, Peter 3: 114
1853..Hewitt, Abram S. 3: 294
1853..Phelps, Anson G. 12: 491
1854..Corcoran, William W. ... 3: 153
1854..Culver, Helen 17: 178
1854..Jesup, Morris K. 11: 93
1854..Sanborn, Franklin B. 8: 466
1855..Claflin, Lee 11: 176
1855..Colby, Gardner 8: 404
1855..Lunt, Orrington 2: 213
1855..Sleeper, Jacob 11: 176
1855..Vassar, Matthew 5: 233
1855..Wagner, William 6: 280
1856..Rich, Isaac 11: 175
1857..Hazard, Roland 12: 221
1858..Shaw, Henry 11: 233
1859..McCormick, Cyrus H. 21: 78
1859..Ottendorfer, Anna B. 8: 194
1859..Ottendorfer, Oswald 3: 411
1859..Robert, Christopher R. ...10: 492
1859..Smith, Sophia 7: 121
1860..Griffith, Goldsborough S. .. 2: 418
1860..Helmuth, Fannie I. 12: 472
1860..Kennedy, John S. 15: 150
1860..Morgan, Edwin B. 13: 218
1860..Seligman, Jesse 4: 226
1860..Sheffield, Joseph E. 11: 515
1860..Welsh, John 3: 412
1861..Battels, Sarah M. E. 1: 380
1861..McCormick, Leander J. .. 1: 361
1861..Schuyler, Louisa Lee 20: 19
1861..Townsend, James M. 4: 196
1861..Vassar, John G. 5: 233
1861..Vassar, Matthew 5: 233
1861..Ward, Marcus L. 5: 209
1862..Bergh, Henry 3: 106
1862..Cornell, Ezra 4: 475
1862..Freeman, Julia S. W. 7: 505
1862..Wheelock, Julia S. 7: 505
1863..Converse, Elisha S. 10: 120
1863..Roosevelt, James H. 12: 6
1864..Farnam, Henry 11: 517
1864..Pardee, Ario 11: 240
1865..Stone, Amasa 11: 522
1866..Anagnos, Michael 13: 257
1866..Drew, Daniel 11: 502
1866..Miller, Lewis 6: 216
1866..Rouss, Charles B. 8: 433
1866..Still, William 2: 318
1867..Childs, George W. 2: 272
1867..Hopkins, Johns 5: 169
1868..Angell, George T. 7: 477
1868..Blair, John I. 7: 21
1868..Sage, Henry W. 4: 478
1868..Stevens, Edwin A. 11: 22
1868..Thomas, George C. 15: 193
1869..Cooper, Sarah B. 3: 132
1869..Jermain, James B. 16: 245
1869..Marquand, Henry G. 8: 390
1869..Pratt, Charles 26: 72
1869..Thompson, Elizabeth 5: 405
1870..Battell, Robbins 14: 254
1870..Cogswell, Henry D. 8: 500
1870..Colgate, James B. 24: 329
1870..Evans, Thomas W. 9: 150
1870..Ford, Daniel S. 5: 257
1870..Gammon, Elijah H. 23: 178
1870..Gerry, Elbridge T. 8: 242
1870..Green, John C. 11: 336
1870..Paine, Robert T. 26: 13
1870..Peck, Ferdinand W. 3: 355
1870..Thaw, William 17: 298
1870..Todd, William C. 9: 276
1871..Buchtel, John R. 2: 496
1871..Champion, Aristarchus ...13: 592
1871..Drumgoole, John C. 13: 211
1871..Langdon, Woodbury G. ... 2: 153
1871..Morgan, J. Pierpont 14: 66
1871..Pepper, William 1: 345
1872..Emery, Mary M. H. 24: 127
1872..Emery, Thomas J. 24: 27
1872..Sage, Margaret O. 16: 422
1872..White, Alfred T. 23: 301
1872..Wolfe, Catharine L. 10: 411
1873..Biddle, Clement M. 22: 107
1873..Converse, John H. 9: 419
1873..Hardin, Charles H. 12: 307
1873..Letchworth, William P. ..15: 324
1873..Towne, John H. 24: 431
1874..Colgate, Samuel 13: 159
1875..Burke, John M. 20: 79
1875..Harrison, Albert M. 17: 439
1875..Hersey, Samuel F. 11: 248
1875..Moore, Clara J. 9: 473
1875..Richards, Ellen 7: 343
1876..Case, Leonard 11: 153
1876..Dodge, Grace H. 18: 310
1876..Drexel, Joseph W. 2: 366
1876..Lick, James 3: 350
1876..Lowell, Josephine S. 8: 142
1876..Mills, Darius O. 18: 133
1876..Riis, Jacob A. 13: 114
1877..Munro, George 7: 114
1878..Hand, Daniel 3: 494
1878..Hearst, Phoebe A. 25: 322
1878..Holden, Erastus F. 13: 127
1879..Carnegie, Andrew 9: 151
1879..Sutro, Adolph 21: 126
1880..Auchmuty, Richard T. ... 9: 102
1880..Drexel, Anthony J. 2: 273
1880..Freer, Charles L. 15: 416
1880..Higinbotham, Harlow N. .18: 389
1880..Magee, Christopher L. 5: 179
1880..Neilson, James 26: 436
1880..Peabody, George H. 3: 423
1880..Skinner, William 23: 110
1881..Drake, Francis M. 11: 434
1881..Heilprin, Michael 8: 168
1881..Morton, Henry 11: 23
1881..Washington, Booker T. ... 7: 363
1882..Aldrich, Josephine C. 5: 66
1882..Billings, Frederick 25: 361
1882..DeForest, Robert W. ..... B: 61
1882..Osborn, William H. 11: 104
1882..Slater, John F. 12: 148
1882..Stewart, William R. 22: 22
1882..Tulane, Paul 9: 130
1883..Chamberlin, Humphrey B. 1: 460
1883..Dutton, Ira B. 22: 17
1883..Hackley, Charles H. 9: 82
1883..Pearsons, Daniel K. 24: 417
1883..Vanderbilt, Cornelius 6: 211
1884..DePauw, Washington C. .. 7: 380
1884..Goucher, John F. 24: 174
1884..Trudeau, Edward L. 13: 564
1884..Widener, Peter A. B. 15: 11
1885..Mulry, Thomas M. 25: 32
1885..Rindge, Frederick H. 16: 342
1885..Stanford, Jane L. 24: 81
1885..Stanford, Leland 2: 128
1885..Stetson, John B. 11: 57
1886..Cheney, Benjamin P. 10: 213
1886..Crerar, John 22: 62
1886..Pratt, Enoch 2: 379
1887..Clark, Jonas G. 9: 203
1887..Skinner, Belle 23: 110
1888..Booth, Ballington 14: 54
1888..Booth, Maud C. 14: 54
1888..Creighton, John A. 11: 369
1888..Gates, Frederick T. 23: 250
1888..Rosenberg, Henry 9: 523
1888..Vanderbilt, George W. ... 6: 213
1888..Williamson, Isaiah V. 5: 261
1889..Butler, Charles 23: 356
1889..Howard, Charles T. 9: 173
1889..Howard, Frank T. 9: 173
1889..Huntington, John 9: 102
1889..Rockefeller, John D., Sr. .11: 63
1889..Simmons, Zalmon G. 15: 136

1890..Dwight, John 24: 310
1890..Fayerweather, Daniel B. ..23: 128
1890..George, William R. ...... C: 467
1890..Harbison, Samuel P. 14: 228
1890..Healy, A. Augustus 19: 134
1890..Ogden, Robert C. 14: 415
1890..Schiff, Jacob H. 13: 533
1890..Wright, Sophie B. 10: 51
1891..Bartlett, Herschel 6: 541
1891..Warner, Lucien C. 9: 537
1892..Duke, Benjamin N. 21: 11
1892..Macy, V. Everit 22: 35
1892..Straus, Lina G. 22: 47
1892..Straus, Nathan 22: 46
1895..Babbott, Frank L. 25: 273
1895..Brookings, Robert S. ..... A: 179
1895..Cupples, Samuel 19: 169
1895..Gould, Helen M. 13: 523
1895..Morgan, Anne T. .... B: 88
1895..Taft, Anna S. 23: 8
1895..Taft, Charles P. 23: 7
1896..Alden, Cynthia Westover .22: 52
1896..Anderson, Elizabeth M. ..23: 49
1896..Flattery, Maurice D. 16: 291
1896..Gould, William J. 22: 218
1896..Inman, Samuel M. 2: 422
1896..Lathrop, Rose H. 9: 194
1896..Severance, Louis H. 15: 357
1898..Jones, Frank S. 25: 149
1900..Baker, George F. 23: 75
1900..Eastman, George 26: 32
1900..Frick, Henry C. 23: 31
1900..Gratwick, William H. 24: 131
1900..Harkness, William L. 25: 438
1900..Hepburn, A. Barton 23: 100
1900..McCormick, Harriet H. ...21: 81
1900..Maloney, Martin 23: 292
1900..Poulson, Niels 14: 299
1900..Rockefeller, John D., Jr. . B: 21
1900..Rosenwald, Julius 26: 110
1900..Shedd, John G. 17: 1
1900..Sprunt, James 20: 214
1900..Sterling, John W. 19: 36
1901..Buhl, Frank H. 24: 433
1901..Libbey, Edward D. 13: 503
1901..Logan, Frank G. .... B: 452
1902..Berry, Martha M. .... C: 49
1902..Dodge, Arthur M. 15: 277
1902..McCormick, Edith R. .... C: 149
1902..Morgan, J. Pierpont, Jr. . C: 418
1902..Tuck, Edward 16: 38
1903..Mather, Samuel .... C: 96
1903..Scribner, Lucy S. 23: 144
1903..Sloan, Earl S. 20: 406
1904..Huntington, Archer M. ..15: 19
1905..Bloede, Victor G. .... D: 445
1905..Pitcairn, John 16: 376
1906..Arbuckle, John 15: 24
1906..Harris, Norman W. 17: 323
1906..Loeb, Morris 26: 10
1906..Stoeckel, Carl 17: 323
1907..Candler, Asa G. 7: 142
1907..Craig, John M. 19: 323
1907..Presser, Theodore 20: 8
1908..Ladd, Kate Macy .... D: 137
1909..Ginn, Edwin 10: 481
1909..Harriman, Mary W. 23: 187
1909..Hershey, Milton S. ...... D: 352
1909..Juilliard, Augustus D. 14: 521
1910..Grasselli, Caesar A. 21: 393
1910..Loose, Jacob L. 19: 34
1910..Robinson, William O. 21: 346
1911..Treat, Milo C. 24: 50
1912..Brady, James B. 19: 412
1912..Erwin, William A. 24: 432
1912..Falk, Maurice .... D: 272
1912..Gray, Philip H. 23: 346
1913..Altman, Benjamin 15: 188
1913..Ley, Harold A. .... D: 105
1913..Mellon, Andrew W. ...... A: 16
1914..Rector, Edward 24: 419
1914..Swasey, Ambrose B: 274
1914..Thompson, William B. ...22: 123
1916..Fels, Mary H. .... A: 430
1917..Guggenheim, Simon ...... C: 50
1918..Noyes, LaVerne 17: 156
1919..Gould, Edwin 24: 274
1919..McLean, William L. 23: 148
1919..Strong, Hattie M. 24: 61
1919..Tiffany, Louis C. 7: 465
1920..DuPont, Alfred I. 25: 25
1920..DuPont, Pierre S. .... A: 97
1921..Campbell, Eleanor A. .... D: 198
1921..Heckscher, August 14: 177
1922..Filene, Edward A. .... A: 319
1923..Ball, William C. 19: 23
1924..Duke, James B. 17: 382
1924..Rackham, Horace H. 24: 235
1925..Conners, William J. 21: 153
1925..Guggenheim, Daniel 22: 7
1925..Penney, James C. .... A: 317
1925..Schepp, Leopold 20: 487
1926..Guinsburg, Henry A. .... B: 164
1926..Prevost, Henry C. 23: 393
1928..Falk, Leon 23: 182
1930..Propp, Morris 24: 189
1931..Folger, William L. 23: 9
1932..Curtis, Cyrus H. K. 24: 26
1937..Sloan, Alfred P. .... B: 493

Philologists

1772..Smith, John 9: 95
1784..Webster, Noah 2: 394
1789..Wilson, Peter 6: 276
1790..Duponceau, Peter S. 7: 510
1799..Pickering, John 7: 294
1808..Ord, George 13: 356
1816..Robinson, Therese A. L. .. 2: 242
1820..Anthon, Charles 6: 345
1822..Andrews, Ethan A. 13: 416
1824..Turner, Samuel H. 7: 192
1825..Conant, Thomas J. 12: 288
1828..Worcester, Joseph E. 6: 50
1831..Robinson, Edward 2: 242
1831..Woolsey, Theodore D. 1: 170
1832..Kendrick, Asahel C. 12: 245
1833..Crosby, Alpheus 9: 97
1833..Sims, Edward D. 7: 131
1835..Thacher, Thomas A. 9: 260
1838..Turner, William W. 9: 198
1839..Sophocles, Evangelinus A. 5: 239
1843..Drisler, Henry 4: 254
1846..Green, William H. 6: 128
1846..Morais, Sabato 10: 170
1847..Short, Charles 7: 7
1848..Hadley, James 1: 175
1849..Lewis, Tayler 10: 131
1850..Hall, Fitzedward 11: 448
1851..Child, Francis 8: 256
1851..Crosby, Howard 4: 193
1851..Harkness, Albert 6: 23
1852..Butler, James D. 9: 190
1854..Dimitry, Alexander 10: 176
1855..Goodwin, William W. 6: 428
1855..March, Francis A. 11: 244
1856..Bingham, Hiram 14: 98
1856..Gildersleeve, Basil L. 10: 469
1856..Whitney, William D. 2: 340
1857..Haldeman, Samuel S. 9: 246
1857..Harris, William T. 15: 1
1857..McIlvaine, Joshua H. 5: 456
1859..Price, Thomas R. 12: 248
1860..Davis, Charles H. S. 25: 68
1861..Taylor, Samuel H. 10: 96
1863..Packard, Lewis R. 4: 550
1865..Beecher, Willis J. 16: 305
1865..Kohut, Alexander 4: 533
1865..Lounsbury, Thomas R. 8: 101
1865..Rolfe, William J. 4: 86
1865..Sewall, Jotham B. 12: 259
1866..Allen, Frederick deF. 12: 225
1867..Allen, William F. 6: 160
1867..D'Ooge, Martin L. 12: 207
1867..Garnett, James M. 1: 506
1868..Elliott, Aaron M. 14: 229
1868..Hart, James M. 9: 263
1868..Jastrow, Marcus 11: 372
1868..Matthews, Washington ...13: 54
1868..Merriam, Augustus C. 8: 397
1868..Toy, Crawford H. 6: 94
1868..White, John W. 12: 352
1869..Humphreys, Milton W. ... B: 53
1869..Smith, Clement L. 7: 163
1870..Pike, Albert 1: 527
1870..Poland, William C. 22: 356
1870..Trumbull, James H. 9: 422
1871..Peck, Tracy 12: 214
1871..Sherman, Lucius A. 24: 141
1871..VanName, Addison 19: 122
1872..Burton, Henry F. 12: 245
1872..Gummere, Francis B. 18: 9
1872..Sachs, Julius 13: 560
1872..Seymour, Thomas D. 12: 365
1872..Warren, Minton 12: 443
1873..Manatt, James I. 8: 361
1873..Wright, John H. 8: 48
1874..Hale, William G. 23: 80
1874..Thomas, Calvin 16: 220
1875..Hall, Isaac H. 12: 143
1875..Harper, William R. 11: 65
1875..Montague, Andrew P. 25: 232
1875..Scarborough, William S. .12: 55
1875..Smith, Charles F. 12: 368
1876..Lanman, Charles R. 11: 96
1877..Sheldon, Edward S. 6: 189
1878..Wright, John Henry 8: 48
1879..Blackwell, James S. 8: 187
1879..Carroll, John J. 7: 251
1879..Collitz, Hermann .... D: 284
1879..Francke, Kuno 10: 512
1879..Goodrich, Ralph L. 7: 363
1879..Morris, Edward P. ...... A: 223
1879..Price, Ira M. 4: 508
1880..Allinson, Francis G. 23: 192
1880..Fortier, Alcée 9: 135
1880..Hale, William G. 23: 80
1880..Kelsey, Francis W. 14: 484
1880..Learned, Marion D. 4: 538
1880..Sprague-Smith, Charles ..24: 148
1880..Todd, Henry A. 24: 33
1881..Bloomfield, Maurice 10: 400
1881..Carpenter, William H. ... 8: 496
1881..Cook, Albert S. 9: 167
1881..Perrin, Bernadotte 12: 243
1882..Bright, James W. 20: 189
1882..Curme, George O. .... D: 53
1882..Merrill, Elmer T. 14: 312
1882..Rolfe, John C. .... A: 341
1883..Fairclough, Henry R. .... C: 59
1883..Harkness, Albert G. 19: 413
1883..Hart, Samuel 13: 48
1883..Haupt, Paul 22: 157
1883..Hewett, Waterman T. ... 8: 419
1883..Smyth, Herbert W. 13: 539
1883..West, Andrew F. 12: 209
1884..Abbott, Frank F. 19: 430
1884..Hatfield, James T. .... A: 226
1885..Bruner, James D. .... A: 402
1885..Fowler, Harold N. .... A: 494
1885..Jastrow, Morris 11: 372
1885..Platner, Samuel B. 12: 214
1885..Safford, William E. 20: 133
1885..Shorey, Paul .... C: 36
1886..Brinton, Daniel G. 9: 265
1886..Kirkland, James H. 8: 227
1886..Leach, Abby 12: 257
1886..Schilling, Hugo K. 23: 353
1886..Wheeler, Benjamin I. de . 4: 480
1887..Adler, Cyrus 11: 371
1887..Capps, Edward .... A: 416
1887..Goodell, Thomas D. 19: 146
1887..Jackson, Abraham V. W..13: 550
1888..Kittredge, George L. 13: 96
1888..Wilson, Charles B. 13: 192
1889..Hohlfeld, Rudolph A. .... A: 302
1889..Kelsey, Francis W. 26: 46
1890..Fay, Edwin W. 24: 328
1890..Knapp, Charles .... A: 194
1890..Peck, Harry T. 11: 528
1890..Rennert, Hugo A. 22: 185
1890..Tolman, Herbert C. 26: 193
1891..Bailey, Mark 12: 371
1891..Emerson, Oliver F. 24: 35
1891..Margolis, Max L. 23: 383
1892..Buck, Carl D. .... A: 278
1893..Graves, Frank P. .... A: 277
1893..Hempl, George 13: 365
1893..Prince, John D. .... C: 43
1894..Bruce, J. Douglas 21: 115
1896..Alden, Raymond M. 20: 118
1897..Armstrong, Edward C. .. B: 274
1897..Greenlaw, Edwin 22: 5
1897..Greenough, Robert B. 26: 379
1897..Parrington, Vernon L. ...25: 248
1898..Moore, Clifford H. 24: 102
1901..Frank, Tenney 19: 236
1904..Buffum, Douglas L. .... A: 102
1906..Pease, Arthur S. .... A: 463
1907..Mendell, Clarence W. .... D: 94
1909..Bender, Harold H. .... D: 309

Philosophers

1720..Edwards, Jonathan 5: 464
1732..Franklin, Benjamin 1: 328
1755..Alison, Francis 1: 346
1775..Paine, Thomas 5: 412
1779..Smith, Samuel S. 2: 221
1782..Stiles, Ezra 1: 167
1784..Gross, John D. 12: 555
1785..Jefferson, Thomas 3: 1
1785..Wheelock, John 9: 86

1790..Rittenhouse, David 1:346
1805..Frisbie, Levi 7:132
1813..Beasley, Frederic 1:342
1817..McVickar, John 6:346
1821..Wayland, Francis 8: 22
1823..Tucker, George 7:521
1824..Nott, Henry J. 11: 31
1825..Upham, Thomas C. 13:171
1826..Marsh, James 2: 40
1827..Hopkins, Mark 6:237
1829..Lathrop, John H. 5:178
1830..Vethake, Henry 1:344
1832..Tappan, Henry P. 1:249
1834..Alcott, A. Bronson 2:218
1834..McCosh, James 5:468
1834..Smith, Asa D. 9: 89
1834..Wylie, Samuel B. 1:348
1836..Emerson, Ralph W. 3:416
1836..Hickok, Laurens P. 7:171
1836..Rauch, Friedrich A. 11: 62
1837..Thoreau, Henry D. 2:300
1839..Brown, Samuel G. 7:408
1840..Bowen, Francis 11:452
1846..Bartlett, Samuel C. 9: 89
1846..Porter, Noah 1:171
1847..Smith, Henry B. 5:311
1848..March, Francis A. 11:244
1848..Stallo, John B. 11:259
1849..Ormiston, William 13: 45
1850..Wilson, William D. 12:510
1852..Battle, Archibald J. 6:498
1852..LeConte, Joseph 7:231
1852..Robinson, Ezekiel G. 8: 26
1853..Andrews, Stephen Pearl .. 6:442
1854..Atwater, Lyman H. 12:429
1855..Ballou, Hosea 6:241
1855..Bascom, John 8:196
1856..Mullany, Patrick F. 8:525
1857..Harris, William T. 15: 1
1859..Peirce, Charles S. 8:409
1863..Draper, John W. 3:406
1865..Davidson, Thomas 23:311
1866..Abbot, Theophilus C. 9:483
1866..Howison, George H. 23:179
1867..Chace, George Ide 8: 25
1869..Fiske, John 3: 23
1869..James, William 18: 81
1870..Wright, Chauncey 1:420
1871..Hall, G. Stanley 9:203
1873..Davis, Noah K. 4: 76
1873..Palmer, George H. 6:427
1873..Raymond, Bradford P. ... 9:431
1875..Capen, Elmer H. 6:241
1876..Adler, Felix 23: 98
1876..Blackwell, Antoinette Brown 9:124
1876..Bowne, Borden P. 11:180
1876..Carus, Paul H. 14:476
1878..Hall, Alexander W. 3: 87
1878..Royce, Josiah 25:356
1879..Ladd, George T. 13: 81
1880..Salter, William M. 24:395
1881..Abbot, Francis E. 24:113
1881..Garman, Charles E. 23:112
1883..Fullerton, George S. 12: 57
1883..Hill, David J. 12:244
1884..Dewey, John A:547
1884..Gardiner, Harry N. 21: 81
1885..Sneath, E. Hershey 26:336
1886..Mulford, Prentice 1:433
1886..Schurman, Jacob G. 4:478
1888..Hyslop, James H. 26: 54
1888..Münsterberg, Hugo 13: 85
1889..Baldwin, J. Mark 25: 89
1889..Curtis, Mattoon M. 12:109
1889..Santayana, George B:343
1889..Tufts, James H. 11: 75
1891..Creighton, James E. 23:220
1891..Griggs, Edward H. B:299
1891..Hibben, John G. 15:199
1891..Lloyd, Alfred H. 23: 88
1891..Newbold, William R. 22:251
1892..Foster, George B. 18:250
1892..Hughes, Edwin H. 13:417
1892..Le Rossignol, James E. ..13:304
1893..Sunderland, Eliza R. 10:219
1894..Mezes, Sidney E. 15:206
1894..Woodbridge, Frederick J. E. D:301
1895..Bjerregard, Carl H. A. ...13: 47
1897..Calkins, Mary W. 13: 75
1897..Meiklejohn, Alexander ... A:406
1904..Hocking, William E. D:452
1908..Alexander, Hartley B. A:174
1912..Babbitt, Irving 23: 19
1917..Durant, Will C:473

Physicians and Surgeons

*See also **Anatomists, Bacteriologists, Biologists, Dermatologists, Gynecologists and Obstetricians, Homeopaths, Laryngologists, Rhinologists and Otologists, Military Surgeons, Neurologists, Ophthalmologists, Orthopædic Surgeons, Pathologists, Pediatricians, Physiologists, Psychiatrists, Public Health and Roentgenologists.***

1635..Clark, John 20:148
1710..Boylston, Zabdiel 7:270
1710..Brickell, John 7:278
1718..Douglass, William 3: 80
1732..Chovet, Abraham 21:419
1734..Bond, Thomas 13:431
1735..Shippen, William 10:384
1739..Bond, Phineas 13:431
1745..Gardiner, Sylvester 8:207
1749..Holyoke, Edward A. 7:488
1754..Craik, James 7:494
1756..Munson, Æneas 13:420
1757..Morgan, John 10:267
1760..Church, Benjamin 7:167
1762..Arnold, Jonathan 13:146
1762..Shippen, William, Jr. 10:384
1767..Bard, Samuel 8:209
1767..Galt, John M. 20:325
1767..Jones, John 5:149
1768..Archer, John 22:105
1768..Aspinwall, William 11:282
1768..Rush, Benjamin 3:333
1770..Hayward, Lemuel 11:484
1770..Sergeant, Erastus 2:193
1771..Potts, Jonathan 12:254
1772..Bayley, Richard 8:206
1772..McClurg, James 3:413
1773..Ramsey, David 7:285
1773..Warren, John 10:288
1775..Crosby, Ebenezer 10: 60
1775..Holbrook, Amos 13:184
1775..McKnight, Charles 9:352
1776..Binney, Barnabas 10:443
1776..Drowne, Solomon 8: 31
1777..Hutchinson, James 11:237
1779..Wells, William C. 12: 60
1783..Waterhouse, Benjamin ... 9:254
1785..Cogswell, Mason F. 8:207
1785..Dick, Elisha C. 23:405
1785..Smith, Nathan 3:153
1787..Post, Wright 9:341
1788..Harris, Charles 7:303
1788..Physick, Philip S. 6:391
1788..Wistar, Caspar 1:273
1789..Miller, Edward 10:172
1790..Thomson, Samuel 6: 70
1791..Hosack, David 9:354
1792..Smith, Elihu H. 9:270
1793..Caldwell, Charles 7:276
1793..Davidge, John B. 22:330
1794..Coxe, John R. 22:151
1796..McDowell, Ephraim 5:148
1796..Potter, Nathaniel 5:526
1797..Spalding, Lyman 2:194
1798..Gallup, Joseph A. 5:250
1799..Brown, Samuel 4:348
1800..Jackson, James 5:401
1801..Ives, Eli 12:253
1802..Dorsey, John S. 10:279
1804..Chapman, Nathaniel 3:294
1804..Darlington, William 10:271
1805..Cock, Thomas 11:353
1805..Macneven, William J. 9:364
1805..Parrish, Joseph 12:486
1806..Childs, Henry H. 20: 39
1806..Dudley, Benjamin W. 11: 60
1806..Warren, John C. 6:426
1807..Baldwin, William 10:275
1807..Mott, Valentine 6:281
1809..Gorham, John 12:355
1809..Lawson, Thomas 4:186
1809..McCreery, Charles 3:214
1809..Mettauer, John P. 15:315
1809..Mussey, Reuben D. 9: 91
1810..Adams, Frederick W. 9:229
1810..Fort, Tomlinson 2:200
1810..Francis, John W. 1:393
1810..Gibson, William 2:440
1810..Oliver, Daniel 9: 92
1810..Shelby, John 2:151
1811..Beck, Theodoric R. 9:350
1811..Stevens, Alexander H. ... 9:355
1812..Lovell, Joseph 4:181
1812..Moultrie, James 12:229
1812..Parsons, Usher 8:204
1812..Shattuck, George C. 12:197
1813..Jameson, Horatio G. 15: 36
1814..Dickson, Samuel H. 10:285
1814..Hayward, George 11:484
1814..Perry, William 11:213
1815..Batchelder, John P. 9:351
1815..Smith, Joseph M. 6:390
1815..Williams, Stephen W. 1:182
1816..Beaumont, William 18:291
1816..Delafield, Edward 10:278
1816..Paine, Martyn 11:551
1816..Wood, Isaac 20:265
1817..Beck, John B. 20:336
1817..Drake, Daniel 5:110
1817..McClellan, George 4:139
1817..Meigs, Charles D. 6:390
1817..Randolph, Jacob 10:282
1818..Barton, John 22:175
1818..Brigham, Amariah 10:270
1818..Satterlee, Richard S. 11:162
1818..Wood, George B. 5:346
1819..Mauran, Joseph 10:275
1820..Atlee, John L. 11: 25
1820..Griffith, Robert E. 12:552
1820..March, Alden 2:445
1820..Spencer, Thomas 5:245
1822..Mitchell, John K. 9:346
1822..Pitcher, Zina 12:214
1823..McClellan, Samuel 4:140
1824..Crosby, Dixi 9: 97
1824..Dunglison, Robley 10:270
1824..Morton, Samuel G. 10:265
1824..Smith, Nathan R. 3:154
1825..Beach, Wooster 23:318
1825..Monette, John W. 15: 4
1825..Storer, David H. 11:336
1826..Bell, Luther V. 22:160
1826..La Borde, Maximilian 11: 34
1826..Ruschenberger, William F. W. 13:369
1827..Bartlett, Elisha 12: 70
1827..Bronson, Henry 22:266
1827..Cooke, John E. 4:518
1827..Dickson, James H. 9:363
1827..Kimball, Gilman 5:200
1827..Post, Alfred C. 9:342
1827..Wellford, Beverly R. 12:201
1827..Wixom, Isaac 1:188
1828..Eve, Paul F. 10: 30
1828..Gross, Samuel D. 8:216
1828..Lindsley, Harvey 12:205
1828..Logan, Thomas M. 12:235
1828..Pancoast, Joseph 10:274
1829..Atlee, Washington L. 11: 25
1829..Gibbons, Henry 7:287
1829..Miller, Thomas 2:146
1830..Arnold, Richard D. 22:424
1830..Buck, Gurdon 11:512
1830..Gerhard, William W. 23:340
1830..Parker, Willard 9:337
1831..Stone, Warren 5: 22
1832..Parrish, Isaac 12:486
1833..Awl, William M. 22:133
1833..Bush, James M. 13:468
1833..Longshore, Joseph S. 5:243
1834..Brainard, Daniel 20:309
1834..Cabell, James L. 12:452
1834..Garlick, Theodatus 24:354
1834..Outten, Warren B. 7:279
1834..Parker, Peter 10:284
1834..Wood, James R. 9:357
1835..Bush, Lewis P. 12:398
1835..Hamilton, Frank H. 9:358
1835..McCready, Benjamin W. .. 9:364
1835..Mendenhall, George 12:230
1835..Selden, William 10:424
1835..Sims, J. Marion 2:356
1835..White, James P. 7:277
1835..Woolsey, Elliott H. 7:272
1836..Bowditch, Henry I. 8:214
1836..Bowling, William K. 12:225
1836..Carnochan, John M. 9:362
1836..Clark, Alonzo 1:354
1836..Flint, Austin 8:311
1836..Hall, William W. 11:437
1836..Stillé, Alfred 9:358
1836..Wolcott, Erastus B. 16: 24
1837..Cox, Christopher C. 10:497
1837..Davis, Nathan S. 10:266
1838..Barnes, Joseph K. 4:359
1838..Bauer, Louis 5:482
1838..King, John 15:258
1838..Meigs, John F. 25:180
1838..Moore, Edward M. 12: 55
1839..Cabot, Samuel 25:262
1839..Long, Crawford W. 13:210
1839..Reese, John J. 6:387
1839..Taylor, Isaac E. 9:353

1839..Wood, Thomas 18: 255
1840..Bolton, James 2: 518
1840..Goldsmith, Middleton 23: 344
1840..Hibberd, James F. 12: 236
1840..Smith, Francis G. 10: 446
1840..Van Buren, William H. ..10: 287
1841..Cooper, Elias S. 22: 128
1841..Crosby, Thomas R. 9: 97
1841..Garnett, Alexander Y. P. 12: 230
1841..Ludlow, John L. 3: 499
1841..Markoe, Thomas M. 11: 30
1841..Peaslee, Edmund R. 10: 289
1841..Pope, Charles A. 12: 217
1842..Buchanan, Joseph R. 10: 277
1842..Campbell, Henry F. 12: 68
1842..Jones, William P. 11: 368
1842..Sayre, Lewis A. 2: 31
1842..Swift, Ebenezer 5: 177
1843..Joynes, Levin S. 11: 149
1843..Oliver, Fitch E. 25: 417
1844..Bemiss, Samuel M. 9: 464
1844..McClellan, John H. B. ... 4: 140
1844..Minot, Francis 12: 211
1845..Bigelow, Henry J. 7: 37
1845..Hartshorne, Henry 8: 202
1845..Michel, William M. 24: 78
1846..Agnew, D. Hayes 8: 203
1846..Clarke, Edward H. 8: 213
1846..Douglas, George 6: 387
1846..Ely, James W. C. 10: 252
1846..Gaston, James McF. 12: 290
1846..Gunn, Moses 12: 423
1846..Hunter, Robert 7: 281
1846..Ketchum, George A. 8: 211
1846..Swinburne, John 7: 33
1847..Bell, Agrippa N. 8: 210
1847..Dalton, John C. 10: 500
1847..Hupp, John C. 10: 418
1847..Miner, Julius F. 16: 104
1847..Yandell, David W. 12: 219
1848..Bemis, Merrick 12: 95
1848..Bentley, Edwin 6: 374
1848..Comegys, Cornelius G. ...16: 279
1848..Hamomnd, William A. ... 9: 338
1848..Hayes, P. Harold 12: 293
1848..Hodgen, John T. 8: 204
1848..Levick, James J. 9: 344
1848..Kinloch, Robert A. 15: 139
1848..White, Octavius A. 3: 22
1849..Cole, Richard B. 7: 288
1849..Edgar, William F. 12: 83
1849..Finnell, Thomas C. 5: 440
1849..Glisan, Rodney 9: 532
1849..Gregory, Elisha H. 10: 504
1849..Jameson, Patrick H. 9: 340
1849..Lente, Frederick D. 7: 507
1849..Mastin, Claudius H. 10: 279
1849..Mott, Alexander B. 9: 360
1849..Rauch, John H. 12: 452
1849..Seymour, William P. 4: 210
1849..Steiner, Lewis H. 11: 348
1850..Briggs, William T. 12: 56
1850..Brodie, William 12: 224
1850..Claiborne, John H. 10: 483
1850..Janes, Edward H. 8: 214
1850..Mitchell, S. Weir 9: 346
1850..Morton, William T. G. ... 8: 332
1850..Smith, Stephen 2: 207
1850..Toner, Joseph M. 7: 539
1851..Barber, Isaac H. 9: 344
1851..Blackwell, Elizabeth 9: 123
1851..Blodget, Lorin 4: 530
1851..Lane, Levi C. 14: 341
1851..Longshore, Hannah E. ... 5: 244
1851..Meigs, James A. 8: 218
1851..Thebaud, Julius S. 9: 353
1851..Todd, Robert N. 11: 204
1852..Hunt, Ezra M. 12: 129
1852..Lincoln, Nathan S. 3: 154
1852..Lindsley, Charles A. 8: 309
1852..Otis, George A. 10: 208
1852..Parvin, Theophilus 4: 305
1852..Preston, Ann 10: 467
1852..Salisbury, James H. 8: 469
1852..Taylor, George H. 5: 494
1853..Dawson, William W. 12: 250
1853..Jacobi, Abraham 9: 345
1853..Johnson, Hosmer A. 12: 490
1853..Loomis, Alfred L. 8: 223
1853..Lozier, Clemence S. 25: 281
1853..Maddin, Thomas L. 8: 136
1853..Marks, Solon 2: 139
1853..Packard, John H. 6: 373
1853..Reeve, John C. 20: 202
1853..Storer, Horatio R. 11: 337
1853..Woodward, Joseph J. 11: 518
1854..Agnew, Cornelius R. 8: 205
1854..Chancellor, Charles W. ...10: 271
1854..DaCosta, Jacob M. 9: 342
1854..Gaillard, Edwin S. 24: 312
1854..Hinton, John H. 2: 177
1854..Mayo, William W. 19: 241
1854..Sands, Henry B. 9: 361
1855..Blackwell, Emily 9: 124
1855..Howe, Andrew J. 9: 339
1855..Jones, Joseph 10: 285
1855..Lee, Benjamin 11: 99
1855..LeHardy, Julius-Cæsar ...10: 265
1856..Crosby, Alpheus B. 9: 98
1856..Pancoast, William H. 10: 274
1856..Simmons, Gustavus L. 7: 269
1857..Bloodgood, Delavan 4: 333
1857..Cochran, Jerome 5: 225
1857..Flint, Austin, 2d 9: 360
1857..Formento, Felix 12: 228
1857..Henry, Morris H. 2: 485
1857..Sim, F. L. 2: 499
1858..Callender, John H. 8: 135
1858..Dalton, Edward B. 10: 501
1858..Draper, William 7: 490
1858..Hodge, Hugh L. 10: 244
1858..Shrady, George F. 7: 271
1858..Smith, Andrew H. 5: 523
1858..Wall, John P. 4: 94
1859..Buist, John R. 8: 215
1859..DeRosset, Moses J. 11: 202
1859..Thomson, William H. 23: 321
1859..Weir, Robert F. 12: 377
1860..Billings, John S. 4: 78
1860..Foote, Edward B. 3: 68
1860..Francis, Samuel W. 4: 528
1860..Hadden, Alexander 2: 228
1860..Lyster, Henry F. L. 16: 308
1860..McGuire, Hunter H. 5: 163
1860..Pallen, Montrose A. 5: 188
1860..Reed, Richard C. S. 12: 477
1861..Allen, Harrison 9: 359
1861..Allen, Timothy F. 7: 282
1861..Comstock, Thomas G. 7: 279
1861..Conner, Phineas S. 12: 68
1861..Curtis, Edward 25: 169
1861..Damon, Howard F. 3: 98
1861..Edes, Robert T. 8: 212
1861..Graham, Neil F. 1: 369
1861..Jarvis, George C. 5: 221
1861..Lyman, Henry M. 12: 298
1861..McNutt, William F. 7: 276
1861..Pooley, James H. 10: 277
1861..Robbins, Henry A. 5: 72
1861..Shrady, John 4: 195
1861..Smith, Alan P. 3: 154
1861..Sternberg, George M. 4: 388
1861..Wagner, Clinton 1: 209
1862..Baruch, Simon 18: 72
1862..Bramble, David D. 22: 368
1862..Caswell, Edward T. 12: 333
1862..Curry, Walker 2: 217
1862..Foster, Frank P. 22: 314
1862..Keen, William W. 11: 367
1862..Owens, John E. 24: 168
1862..Speir, Samuel F. 4: 173
1862..Walcott, Henry P. 12: 445
1862..Wood, Horatio C. 13: 569
1863..Delafield, Francis 10: 278
1863..Gibbons, Henry, Jr. 7: 271
1863..McGraw, Theodore A. 20: 176
1863..Marcy, Henry O. 6: 510
1863..Skene, Alexander J. C. ... 5: 436
1863..Tyson, James 9: 356
1863..Vander Veer, Albert 16: 359
1864..Holbrook, Martin L. 12: 334
1864..Janeway, Edward G. 13: 499
1864..Leale, Charles A. 2: 52
1864..Otis, Fessenden N. 10: 280
1864..Weisse, Faneuil D. 5: 17
1865..Beard, George M. 8: 206
1865..Book, James B. 18: 81
1865..Garretson, James E. 3: 212
1865..Prentiss, Daniel W. 3: 367
1865..Shurly, Ernest L. 21: 401
1865..Stevens, George T. 1: 214
1865..Sturgis, Frederic R. 4: 197
1865..Ward, Samuel B. 1: 245
1866..Bailey, William 13: 45
1866..Crothers, Thomas D. 17: 430
1866..Curtin, Roland G. 3: 348
1866..Fuller, Robert M. 12: 265
1866..Hooper, Philo O. 7: 452
1866..Kornitzer, Joseph 7: 51
1866..Walker, Henry O. 9: 527
1866..Wynkoop, Gerardus H. ...10: 288
1867..Duhring, Louis A. 20: 351
1867..Fitz, Reginald H. 10: 456
1867..Gavin, Michael F. 15: 303
1867..Keyes, Edward L. 9: 343
1867..Mathews, Joseph M. 13: 18
1867..Satterthwaite, Thomas E. .12: 298
1867..Souchon, Edmond 9: 132
1868..Beach, Henry H. A. 15: 164
1868..Bridge, Norman 22: 50
1868..Bryant, Joseph D. 23: 81
1868..Bryson, John P. 5: 267
1868..Geiger, Jacob 16: 257
1868..Grant, William W. 12: 513
1868..Johnson, Laurence 16: 322
1868..Klotz, Herman G. 22: 426
1868..Kunze, Richard E. 3: 504
1868..Nichol, William L. 8: 136
1868..Satterlee, F. Le Roy 7: 232
1868..Senn, Nicholas 6: 371
1868..Tiffany, Louis McL. 24: 358
1868..Weed, Frank J. 3: 373
1868..Woolsey, Elliott H. 7: 272
1869..Boise, Eugene 22: 218
1869..Dearborn, Henry M. 9: 350
1869..Gerrish, Frederic H. 12: 233
1869..Halley, George 4: 535
1869..Hamilton, John B. 23: 245
1869..Weaver, Rufus B. 3: 486
1870..Collings, Samuel P. 8: 220
1870..Curtis, Frederic C. 2: 168
1870..DeNancrede, Charles B. G. 14: 370
1870..Hechelman, Herman W. ..12: 133
1870..Jelks, James T. 7: 548
1870..Lay, John C., Jr. 6: 370
1870..McBurney, Charles 26: 48
1870..McClellan, George 15: 223
1870..Simons, Manning 16: 402
1870..Thomas, Joseph D. 6: 149
1870..Tuholske, Herman 5: 242
1871..Denison, Charles 17: 281
1871..Fowler, George B. 4: 214
1871..Fowler, George R. 4: 194
1871..Gere, George G. 7: 365
1871..Griffith, Jefferson D. 11: 255
1871..Jacobi, Mary P. 8: 219
1871..Jameson, Henry 10: 459
1871..Jonas, Augustus F. ...... B: 322
1871..Kinnicutt, Francis P. ...15: 255
1871..Lemen, Lewis E. 6: 494
1871..Lewis, Richard H. .... A: 467
1871..McCollom, John H. 16: 134
1871..Meigs, Arthur V. 15: 217
1871..Trudeau, Edward L. 13: 564
1871..Wylie, W. Gill 1: 471
1872..Bulkley, L. Duncan 25: 182
1872..Bull, William T. 9: 345
1872..Foster, Eugene 6: 393
1872..Gerster, Arpad G. 26: 427
1872..Glasgow, William C. 5: 99
1872..Love, Isaac N. 6: 375
1872..Russell, Linus E. 16: 246
1872..Shaw, William C. 6: 372
1872..Stamm, Martin 21: 325
1873..French, Pinckney 11: 105
1873..Guiteras, Juan 22: 408
1873..Keating, John M. 25: 377
1873..Moore, James E. 6: 388
1873..Ostrom, Homer I. 6: 215
1873..Phelps, Abel M. 12: 233
1873..Potter, Thompson E. 19: 386
1873..Pratt, Edwin H. 11: 552
1873..Shattuck, Frederick C. ...12: 272
1873..Wyeth, John A. 6: 74
1874..Funkhouser, Robert N. ... 7: 286
1874..Gray, Clifton S. 12: 453
1874..Mastin, William McD. ...25: 113
1874..Osler, William 12: 201
1874..Reed, Charles A. L. 24: 325
1874..Shoemaker, John V. 13: 223
1874..White, John B. 3: 22
1875..Lindley, Walter 21: 263
1875..McIntire, Charles 12: 128
1875..Mosher, Eliza M. 15: 304
1875..Prudden, Theophil M. ... 9: 347
1875..Steele, Daniel A. K. 22: 301
1875..Stelwagon, Henry W. 19: 376
1875..Welch, William H. 26: 6
1875..Wingate, Uranus O. B. ...23: 384
1876..Briggs, Waldo 12: 126
1876..Cabot, Arthur T. 15: 46
1876..Cole, Charles K. 8: 99
1876..Huntington, Thomas W. .22: 292
1876..Lutz, Frank J. 12: 454
1876..Park, Roswell 8: 220
1876..Patton, G. Farrar 24: 76
1876..Richardson, Maurice H. ..18: 425
1876..Rohé, George H. 7: 275
1876..Wilson, James C. 25: 365
1877..Abbe, Robert 21: 197
1877..Benjamin, Dowling 5: 90
1877..Carleton, Bukk G. 7: 48
1877..Dickinson, Gordon K. 22: 191
1877..Fenger, Christian 17: 279

1877..Halsted, William S. 20: 209
1877..McGuire, Frank A. 5: 385
1877..Wheaton, Charles A. 6: 384
1878..Babcock, Robert H. 18: 90
1878..Bemiss, John H. 9: 132
1878..Bernays, Augustus C. 6: 233
1878..Councilman, William T. .. 5: 550
1878..Deaver, John B. 22: 7
1878..Ewing, William G. 8: 137
1878..Harte, Richard H. 22: 441
1878..Jamison, Alcinous B. 6: 383
1878..Pynchon, Edwin 20: 307
1878..Rankin, Egbert G. 2: 340
1878..Rockey, Alpha E. 21: 364
1878..Streett, David 2: 187
1878..Taylor, John M. 18: 53
1878..Vaughn, Victor C. 12: 207
1879..Beates, Henry 11: 479
1879..Burrell, Herbert L. 14: 506
1879..Christie, William H. 13: 77
1879..Clevenger, Shobal V. 5: 267
1879..Matas, Rudolph .... D: 399
1879..Parham, Frederick W. ...10: 281
1879..Sajous, Charles E. 9: 351
1879..Smith, William T. 9: 92
1879..Stickler, Joseph W. 7: 23
1879..Von Ruck, Karl 20: 374
1880..Allen, Dudley P. 16: 165
1880..Brill, Nathan E. 20: 267
1880..Chancellor, Eustathius .... C: 265
1880..Crook, James K. 8: 218
1880..Darlington, Thomas ...... D: 117
1880..Dunn, James H. 6: 125
1880..Elliot, John W. 22: 424
1880..Eve, Paul F., Jr. 10: 30
1880..Fisk, Samuel A. 6: 375
1880..Jennings, Charles G. 26: 351
1880..Kammerer, Frederick 23: 210
1880..Mercer, Alfred C. 12: 211
1880..Meyer, Willy .... C: 480
1880..Mooney, Fletcher D. 8: 212
1880..Ohmann-Dumesnil, Amant H. 12: 502
1880..Ravogli, Augustus 12: 476
1880..Roosevelt, J. West 24: 34
1880..Sherman, Harry M. 21: 334
1880..Vaughan, George T. 18: 300
1881..Billings, Frank 23: 315
1881..Fordyce, John A. 20: 165
1881..Lydston, G. Frank 24: 123
1881..Lewis, Daniel 7: 277
1881..Mudd, Harvey G. 24: 273
1881..Prince, Morton 25: 313
1883..Powers, Charles A. 30: 60
1881..Wilcox, Reynold W. 23: 207
1881..Williams, Howard J. 18: 75
1882..Abrams, Albert 19: 386
1882..Archinard, Paul E. 9: 134
1882..Barber, Calvin F. 25: 61
1882..Beck, Carl 10: 287
1882..Cutler, Condict W. 22: 168
1882..Ferguson, Alexander H. ..16: 109
1882..Fitzgibbon, Thomas 10: 272
1882..Hall, Josiah N. .... A: 206
1882..Hun, Henry 19: 285
1882..Lord, John P. 16: 68
1882..Sewall, Henry .... A: 199
1883..Bevan, Arthur D. .... D: 90
1883..Bissell, Joseph B. 16: 159
1883..Hinsdale, Guy .... A: 493
1883..Long, John W. 21: 399
1883..Mayfield, William H. 12: 500
1883..Mayo, William J. .... A: 330
1883..Meltzer, Samuel J. 15: 354
1883..Ott, Charles H. 19: 38
1883..Wood, Leonard 9: 20
1884..Davis, Byron B. 25: 119
1884..Davis, Nathan S. 13: 301
1884..Davis, William E. B. 13: 514
1884..Hare, Hobart A. 13: 584
1884..Hartley, Frank 15: 224
1884..Hawley, Donly C. 14: 424
1884..Hemmeter, John C. ...... B: 481
1884..Hill, Luther L. 8: 485
1884..Hutchinson, Woods 21: 376
1884..Pryor, John H. 20: 325
1884..Reder, Francis LeS. ...... B: 289
1884..Rusby, Henry H. .... A: 172
1885..Abbott, Wallace C. 24: 124
1885..Biggs, Hermann M. 19: 219
1885..Favill, Henry B. 10: 497
1885..Fell, George E. 12: 340
1885..Guiteras, Ramon 20: 244
1885..McRae, Floyd W. 19: 283
1885..Morgan, James D. 22: 427
1885..Shober, John B. 24: 129
1886..Babcock, James W. 22: 222
1886..Bunts, Frank E. 21: 415
1886..Holmes, Bayard T. 10: 479
1886..James, Walter B. 21: 26
1886..Martin, Frank 19: 373
1886..Ochsner, Albert J. 20: 439
1886..Osborne, Oliver T. .... D: 447
1886..Paquin, Paul 6: 379
1886..Robertson, Samuel E. 6: 372
1887..Crile, George W. .... C: 72
1887..Davison, Charles .... C: 201
1887..Van Rensselaer, Howard . 3: 187
1888..Bullard, Frank E. 13: 442
1888..Dock, George .... C: 360
1888..Einhorn, Max .... C: 237
1888..Fisk, Eugene L. 25: 425
1888..Gould, George M. 10: 509
1888..Lambert, Alexander ...... D: 219
1888..Le Conte, Robert G. 20: 162
1888..Maher, Stephen J. .... D: 171
1888..Mayo, Charles H. .... A: 331
1888..Minor, Charles L. 24: 343
1888..Sawyer, John P. .... C: 32
1888..Schumpert, Thomas E. ...11: 557
1888..Sherrill, J. Garland ...... B: 226
1889..Gaertner, Frederick 22: 228
1889..Krauss, James 18: 126
1889..Kunitzer, Robert 15: 205
1889..Lilienthal, Howard ...... C: 223
1889..McBrayer, Lewis B. ...... A: 296
1889..Stewart, George D. 23: 30
1889..Thayer, William S. 24: 409
1890..Barker, Lewellys F. ...... A: 265
1890..Dennis, Andrew J. L. 20: 53
1890..Hobson, Sarah M. .... A: 477
1890..Horton, George M. 21: 374
1890..McArthur, William T. 24: 355
1890..White, James W. 17: 135
1891..Baldwin, Edward R. ...... B: 99
1891..Bloodgood, Joseph C. 26: 210
1891..Dunham, Theodore .... C: 462
1891..Eitel, George G. 21: 119
1891..Greene, Charles L. 12: 40
1891..Lower, William E. .... C: 244
1891..McGuire, Stuart .... A: 124
1891..Martin, Edmund D. 24: 79
1891..Trimble, William B. 26: 338
1892..Beck, Carl .... C: 211
1892..Cabot, Richard C. .... A: 223
1892..Coffey, Robert C. 25: 380
1892..Martin, Walton .... C: 139
1892..Nietert, Herman L. 12: 519
1892..Vietor, Agnes C. .... C: 238
1892..Walker, Frank B. 16: 40
1892..Yenney, Robert C. 19: 303
1893..Bainbridge, William Seaman .... D: 190
1893..DuBose, Francis G. ...... B: 358
1893..Furbush, C. Lincoln 20: 222
1893..Walker, John B. 15: 168
1894..Detwiler, Augustus K. 21: 75
1894..Hertzler, Arthur E. ...... C: 189
1894..Illoway, Henry .... A: 144
1894..Morgan, William G. ...... C: 94
1894..Turck, Fenton B. 25: 175
1894..Wesener, John A. 20: 448
1895..Brooks, Harlow .... D: 370
1895..Bryant, Frank A. 11: 185
1895..Connors, John F. 26: 165
1895..Cushing, Harvey .... C: 36
1895..Gardner, James A. 21: 90
1895..Jordan, William M. ...... B: 178
1895..Pottenger, Francis M. .... D: 122
1895..Robinson, Frank N. 18: 125
1895..Warbasse, James P. ..... C: 330
1895..Wright, Hamilton 22: 430
1896..Goodman, Charles .... D: 424
1896..Helmer, George J. 10: 234
1896..Janeway, Theodore C. ...17: 214
1896..Potter, Nathaniel B. 26: 79
1897..Clarke, Lee B. 20: 421
1897..Goldberger, Joseph 21: 83
1897..Griess, Walter .... D: 144
1897..Morton, Blanche R. S. ... C: 268
1897..Strong, Richard P. ...... A: 93
1898..Janeway, Henry H. 26: 90
1898..Matheny, Albert R. 19: 86
1898..Wellman, Creighton ..... D: 302
1899..Abbe, Truman .... D: 166
1899..Brickner, Walter M. 25: 305
1899..Moorehead, Frederick B. . C: 384
1899..Norris, George W. .... B: 86
1899..Scott, Richard J. E. 25: 138
1899..Wilbur, Ray Lyman ...... C: 12
1900..Christian, Henry A. 18: 17
1900..McCoy, George W. .... C: 87
1900..Reinhardt, George F. 15: 135
1900..Smyth, John 26: 37
1901..Allison, Nathaniel 26: 200
1901..Metzenbaum, Myron ..... D: 97
1901..Solis-Cohen, Myer .... C: 365
1901..Von Ruck, Silvio H. 18: 62
1902..Emerson, Kendall .... D: 312
1902..Graham, Archie J. .... D: 165
1902..Hare, Arley Munson ..... B: 393
1902..Hoag, Ernest B. 19: 462
1902..Mills, Ralph W. 20: 401
1902..Robinson, Edward P. ..... B: 487
1904..Beer, Edwin .... C: 495
1904..Coffin, Mary E. .... D: 276
1904..Ransohoff, Joseph L. ..... D: 157
1905..Carrel, Alexis 15: 301
1905..Dowman, Charles E. 23: 173
1905..Ehrenfried, Albert 18: 333
1905..Holden, William B. ...... D: 189
1905..Matson, Ralph C. .... D: 386
1905..Ordway, Thomas .... A: 367
1905..Sloan, Edwin P. 26: 316
1905..Smith, S. Calvin .... B: 137
1906..Caulk, John R. .... D: 261
1906..Janney, Nelson W. 26: 74
1906..Penhallow, Dunlap P. .... D: 187
1906..Verbrycke, J. Russell, Jr. D: 202
1907..Ferrell, John A. .... B: 346
1907..Wyeth, George A. .... D: 88
1908..Cannaday, John E. .... C: 527
1908..Hayhurst, Emery R. ..... D: 329
1908..Heuer, George J. .... D: 143
1908..Lahey, Frank H. .... B: 465
1908..Snyder, R. Garfield ...... C: 353
1908..Swift, Homer F. .... B: 310
1909..Balfour, Donald C. .... B: 330
1910..Gilcreest, Edgar L. ...... D: 408
1910..McAlpin, Kenneth R. .... C: 199
1910..Neal, Josephine B. .... B: 160
1910..Palmer, Walter W. .... B: 447
1911..Harvey, Samuel C. .... D: 395
1912..Moore, John W. .... D: 75
1913..Dandy, Walter E. .... D: 344
1913..Hedblom, Carl A. .... C: 429
1913..Johnson, T. Arthur ...... C: 453
1914..Gatewood, Doctor .... C: 343
1914..Hutton, James H. .... D: 171
1914..Joyce, Thomas M. .... D: 253
1914..Lisser, Hans .... D: 127
1914..Millet, John A. P. .... D: 385
1914..Reid, Mont R. .... D: 119
1916..Bigelow, George H. 25: 72
1917..Montague, Joseph F. ..... C: 325
1919..Barach, Alvan L. .... D: 67
1919..Shepardson, H. Clare .... D: 198
1920..Collings, Clyde W. .... C: 161
1921..Beck, Claude S. .... D: 305
1921..Short, James J. .... C: 401
1923..Wakeman, A. Maurice ...25: 115
1925..Osgood, Edwin E. .... D: 385

Physicists

1738..Winthrop, John 7: 165
1779..Thompson, Benjamin (Count Rumford) 5: 410
1817..Olmsted, Denison 8: 121
1820..Draper, Henry 6: 171
1822..Allen, Zachariah 8: 263
1826..Henry, Joseph 3: 405
1828..Bache, Alexander D. 3: 348
1832..Shepard, Charles U. 5: 311
1835..Rutherfurd, Lewis M. 6: 376
1836..Draper, John W. 3: 406
1837..Lyman, Chester S. 25: 427
1838..Thrall, Homer L. 8: 143
1840..Locke, John 15: 264
1842..Le Conte, John 7: 228
1856..Mayer, Alfred M. 13: 164
1858..Norton, Sidney A. 12: 123
1858..Rood, Ogden N. 13: 507
1859..Peirce, Charles S. 8: 409
1860..Cooley, Le Roy C. 9: 263
1860..Morton, Henry 24: 374
1861..Barker, George F. 4: 532
1862..Peirce, John 10: 406
1865..Bell, Alexander Graham .. 6: 220
1866..Bayma, Joseph 17: 107
1866..Blake, Francis 22: 25
1866..Edison, Thomas A. 25: 1
1866..Trowbridge, John 23: 53
1867..Anthony, William A. 11: 389
1868..Dolbear, Amos E. 9: 414
1868..Pickering, Edward C. 6: 424
1869..Brush, Charles F. 21: 1
1869..Wright, Arthur W. 13: 348
1870..Cross, Charles R. 11: 183
1870..Langley, Samuel P. 3: 338
1870..Peckham, William C. 11: 516
1870..Swasey, Ambrose .... B: 274

1871..Gibbs, Josiah W. 4: 543
1872..Carhart, Henry S. 4: 543
1872..Rowland, Henry A. 11: 25
1872..Zahm, John A. 9: 274
1873..Chute, Horatio N. 11: 469
1873..Mendenhall, Thomas C. ...10: 117
1873..Very, Frank W. 12: 49
1874..Dana, Edward S. 6: 537
1874..Nipher, Francis E. 22: 55
1875..Michelson, Albert A. ..... C: 42
1875..Rogers, William A. 9: 530
1876..Peirce, Benjamin O. 20: 366
1878..Morley, Edward W. 4: 520
1878..Nicholas, Edward L. 4: 482
1879..Becker, George F. 20: 272
1879..Magie, William F. 12: 425
1880..Ayres, Brown 18: 372
1880..Barus, Carl 26: 8
1883..Blake, Lucien I. 18: 210
1883..Loomis, Elmer H. 25: 246
1884..Goodspeed, Arthur W. 15: 30
1884..Marvin, Charles F. 16: 47
1885..St. John, Charles E. 26: 332
1885..Stratton, Samuel W. 13: 142
1885..Webster, Arthur G. 13: 532
1886..Fessenden, Reginald A. ...15: 21
1887..Crew, Henry 15: 60
1888..Ames, Joseph S. .... A: 342
1888..Sheldon, Samuel 14: 208
1889..Daniel, John .... A: 67
1889..Merritt, Ernest G. 15: 195
1889..Pupin, Michael I. 26: 5
1889..Sabine, Wallace C. 15: 411
1890..Bliss, William J. A. ...... A: 198
1890..Parker, Herschel C. 14: 260
1891..Bumstead, Henry A. 21: 77
1891..Lewis, Exum P. 22: 411
1891..Nichols, Ernest F. 21: 68
1891..Rosa, Edward B. 26: 312
1892..Franklin, William S. 22: 140
1892..Guthe, Karl E. 22: 348
1892..Trowbridge, Charles C. ...18: 314
1892..Wadsworth, Frank L. O. .26: 376
1893..Austin, Louis W. 24: 118
1893..Ives, James E. .... A: 500
1893..Miller, Dayton C. .... C: 515
1893..Taylor, Samuel N. .... A: 267
1894..Boltwood, Bertram B. 15: 138
1896..Millikan, Robert A. ...... A: 268
1897..Duane, William .... A: 345
1897..McClenahan, Howard 26: 464
1897..Wood, Robert W. 14: 457
1898..Child, Clement D. .... A: 304
1898..Kilby, Clinton M. .... A: 154
1898..Maclaurin, Richard 14: 483
1900..Burgess, George K. 24: 312
1900..Sieg, Lee P. .... D: 38
1902..Jewett, Frank B. .... C: 272
1903..Davis, Harvey N. .... A: 348
1903..Nutting, Perley G. .... D: 218
1903..Squier, George O. 24: 320
1903..Trowbridge, Augustus ... C: 470
1904..Kovarik, Alois F. .... D: 444
1905..Comstock, Daniel F. ..... D: 325
1907..Sheard, Charles .... B: 273
1908..Rentschler, Harvey C. ... D: 384
1909..Hersey, Mayo D. .... A: 175
1909..Langmuir, Irving .... C: 29
1910..Fulcher, Gordon S. .... C: 101
1910..Kingsbury, Edwin F. .... C: 119
1910..Richtmyer, Floyd K. ..... B: 174
1910..Webster, David L. .... A: 363
1911..Arnold, Harold DeF. 25: 184
1911..Chaffee, E. Leon .... B: 376
1911..Davisson, Clinton J. ...... C: 233
1912..Goddard, Robert H. ...... A: 154
1912..Ives, Herbert E. .... C: 39
1913..Chapman, James C. 20: 341
1913..Compton, Karl T. .... C: 81
1913..Crandall, Irving B. 22: 278
1917..Compton, Arthur H. ..... C: 34
1921..Wilkins, T. Russell ...... D: 446

Physiologists

1743..Lining, John 25: 445
1822..Beaumont, William 18: 291
1824..Dunglison, Robley 10: 270
1824..Mitchell, John K. 9: 346
1836..Draper, John W. 3: 406
1842..Smith, Francis G. 10: 446
1850..Seguin, Edouard 15: 151
1851..Dalton, John Call 10: 500
1857..Flint, Austin, 2d 9: 360
1860..Mitchell, S. Weir 9: 346
1861..Hitchcock, Edward 13: 95
1865..Wood, Horatio C. 13: 569
1871..Bowditch, Henry P. 12: 252
1872..Minot, Charles S. 6: 112
1873..Keyt, Alonzo T. 15: 240
1875..Chittenden, Russell H. ...10: 181
1876..Beyer, Henry G. 14: 250
1877..Gage, Simon H. 4: 483
1879..Clevenger, Shobal V., 2d . 5: 267
1879..Reichert, Edward T. 23: 206
1882..Sewall, Henry .... A: 199
1883..Martin, Henry N. 12: 113
1883..Meltzer, Samuel J. 15: 354
1884..Loeb, Jacques 11: 72
1886..Hough, Theodore 23: 260
1886..Lee, Frederic S. .... B: 262
1886..Mall, Franklin P. 14: 309
1887..Porter, William T. 15: 288
1887..Stewart, George N. 23: 402
1890..Fish, Pierre A. 23: 359
1890..Webber, Herbert J. 17: 387
1890..Woods, Albert F. .... B: 467
1891..Lusk, Graham 15: 88
1895..Hall, Winfield S. .... C: 193
1895..Ott, Isaac 20: 188
1897..Hemmeter, John C. ...... B: 481
1897..Hyde, Ida H. .... B: 146
1897..Woodworth, Robert S. .... A: 24
1898..Henderson, Yandell ...... D: 86
1898..MacCallum, William G. ...15: 287
1899..Franz, Shepherd I. ...... A: 477
1899..Riddle, Oscar .... C: 120
1900..Cannon, Walter B. 15: 287
1900..MacCallum, John B. 15: 288
1901..Carlson, Anton J. 18: 396
1905..Carrel, Alexis 15: 301
1911..Van Duyne, Sarah E. .... B: 408

Playwrights

1759..Godfrey, Thomas 8: 36
1766..Rogers, Robert 7: 450
1773..Warren, Mercy 7: 177
1776..Brackenridge, Hugh H. .. 8: 49
1786..Tyler, Royall 7: 39
1789..Dunlap, William 6: 501
1807..Barker, James N. 12: 276
1807..Noah, Mordecai M. 9: 200
1810..Woodworth, Samuel 1: 434
1813..Payne, John Howard 2: 347
1821..Stone, John A. 8: 88
1825..Bird, Robert M. 7: 183
1830..Brown, David P. 3: 520
1834..Logan, Cornelius A. 12: 189
1835..Brougham, John 9: 448
1836..Pray, Isaac C. 13: 420
1836..Sargent, Epes 7: 243
1836..Willis, Nathaniel P. 3: 108
1839..Walcot, Charles M. 11: 514
1840..Canonge, L. Placide 22: 73
1841..Boucicault, Dion 2: 375
1844..Bannister, Nathaniel H. ..22: 445
1844..Miles, George H. 6: 439
1848..Boker, George H. 6: 73
1848..Bunce, Oliver B. 2: 512
1858..Gayler, Charles 24: 360
1867..Gordon, Archibald D. 3: 528
1870..Howard, Bronson 3: 75
1870..MacKaye, Steele 14: 158
1871..Campbell, Bartley 9: 517
1871..Young, William 20: 258
1876..Sullivan, Thomas R. 16: 175
1877..Harrigan, Edward 11: 442
1878..Herne, James A. 5: 83
1879..Belasco, David 14: 83
1880..Dickinson, Anna E. 3: 109
1880..Baum, L. Frank 18: 331
1881..Burnett, Frances Hodgson 20: 423
1883..Carter, Lincoln J. 20: 402
1884..Gillette, William 2: 249
1886..Fitch, Clyde 15: 192
1887..Thomas, Augustus .... C: 438
1889..Gordin, Jacob 23: 286
1890..Isham, Frederic S. 20: 64
1890..Klein, Charles 24: 216
1890..Mitchell, Langdon E....... 4: 522
1893..Crothers, Rachel .... C: 83
1894..Neilson, Francis .... C: 340
1895..Parker, Lottie Blair 10: 316
1897..MacKaye, Percy W. 14: 159
1899..Cohan, George M. 15: 285
1899..Mapes, Victor .... A: 479
1899..Tully, Richard W. 16: 93
1900..Ade, George .... C: 386
1900..Peabody, Josephine P. ...19: 95
1900..Pollock, Channing .... A: 163
1900..Wolf, Rennold 19: 258
1902..Manners, J. Hartley 25: 152
1903..Armstrong, Paul 18: 383
1903..Megrue, Roi C. 20: 407
1904..Davis, Richard Harding .. 8: 176
1906..Moody, William Vaughan .11: 69
1906..Moore, Carlyle 20: 384
1906..Smith, Winchell 24: 37
1906..Tarkington, Booth .... A: 84
1907..Bynner, Witter .... A: 175
1907..Koch, Frederick H. .... A: 361
1907..Rinehart, Mary Roberts .. C: 486
1908..Smith, Harry J. 18: 77
1913..Glass, Montague .... C: 398
1913..O'Higgins, Harvey J. 25: 296
1913..O'Neill, Eugene .... A: 443
1914..Rice, Elmer L. .... A: 534
1915..Glaspell, Susan .... C: 505
1915..Wilde, Percival .... D: 440
1916..Dreiser, Theodore .... C: 93
1917..Cook, George Cram 22: 11
1917..Williams, Jesse L. 21: 26
1918..Gale, Zona .... B: 301
1919..Bacon, Frank 20: 77
1919..Barry, Philip .... C: 516

Poets

1640..Bradstreet, Anne D. 7: 10
1662..Wigglesworth, Michael ... 8: 382
1670..Tompson, Benjamin 8: 82
1718..Rose, Aquila 8: 78
1770..Bleecker, Ann E. 8: 457
1772..Dwight, Timothy 1: 168
1772..Trumbull, John 7: 351
1773..Warren, Mercy 7: 177
1778..Barlow, Joel 3: 186
1778..Sewall, Jonathan M. 2: 30
1780..Morton, Sarah W. A. 8: 370
1781..Freneau, Philip 6: 201
1784..Hopkins, Lemuel 7: 282
1784..Ladd, Joseph B. 7: 501
1790..Humphreys, David 1: 71
1790..Johnson, William M. 9: 90
1792..Story, Isaac 13: 193
1795..Linn, John B. 13: 542
1800..Dinsmoor, Robert 7: 160
1801..Key, Francis Scott 5: 498
1805..Brooks, Maria G. 8: 169
1805..Payne, John Howard 2: 347
1807..Bryant, William Cullen ... 4: 79
1809..Halleck, Fitz-Greene 3: 226
1815..Percival, James G. 8: 305
1815..Sigourney, Lydia H. 1: 154
1816..Pierpont, John 6: 155
1817..Cooke, Philip P. 7: 330
1817..Greene, Nathaniel 11: 228
1817..Sands, Robert C. 8: 354
1817..Woodworth, Samuel 1: 434
1818..Brainard, John G. C. 8: 274
1819..Drake, J. Rodman 5: 420
1819..Tappan, William B. 5: 241
1820..Clarke, McDonald 6: 406
1820..Longfellow, Henry W. 2: 160
1820..Sprague, Charles 6: 229
1823..Morris, George P. 5: 434
1824..Gallagher, William D. 9: 250
1824..Wilcox, Carlos 1: 184
1825..Hewitt, John H. 11: 363
1825..Holmes, Oliver Wendell ... 2: 336
1825..Pinkney, Edward C. 6: 443
1825..Simms, William G. 6: 204
1825..Whittier, John G. 1: 407
1826..Mellen, Grenville 7: 245
1826..Willis, Nathaniel P. 3: 108
1827..Dana, Richard H. 7: 182
1827..Poe, Edgar A. 1: 463
1828..Prentice, George D. 3: 121
1830..Dawes, Rufus 10: 412
1831..Bolton, Sarah T. 10: 172
1831..Osgood, Frances S. 2: 196
1831..Street, Alfred B. 11: 103
1831..Whitman, Walt 1: 255
1832..Benjamin, Park 7: 166
1832..Gould, Hannah F. 8: 269
1832..Greene, Albert G. 9: 501
1832..Judson, Emily C. 3: 93
1832..Smith, Samuel F. 6: 51
1833..Sargent, Epes 7: 243
1833..Whitman, Sarah Helen ... 8: 145
1834..Clark, Willis G. 8: 454
1835..Channing, William Ellery 13: 431
1835..Emerson, Ralph Waldo ... 3: 416
1836..Howe, Julia Ward 1: 402
1836..Hoyt, Ralph 7: 453
1836..Parsons, Thomas W. 5: 359
1836..Wallace, William R. 8: 375
1837..Thoreau, Henry D. 2: 300
1837..Tuckerman, Henry T. 7: 234
1837..Welby, Amelia B. C. 6: 503

1839..Lowell, James Russell 2: 32
1839..Very, Jones 6:276
1840..Aldrich, James 9:474
1840..Bethune, George W. 8:166
1840..Story, William W. 5:417
1841..Davidson, Margaret M. ... 7:476
1841..Taylor, Bayard 3:454
1842..Brooks, Charles T. 8:306
1842..Cary, Phoebe 1:535
1842..Fenner, Cornelius G. 8: 43
1842..Hoffman, Fenno 8:379
1842..Read, T. Buchanan 6:474
1843..Hill, Thomas 6:420
1843..Jeffrey, Rosa V. G. 11:405
1843..Lippincott, Sara J. 4:536
1844..Clarke, James Freeman .. 2:186
1844..Cranch, Christopher P. .. 7:140
1844..Moore, Clement C. 7:362
1844..Van Alstyne, Frances J. . 7: 65
1845..Botta, Anne C. Lynch 7:236
1845..Cutter, George W. 22:146
1845..Hirst, Henry B. 13:160
1845..Lord, William W. 3:516
1845..Stoddard, Richard H. 3:297
1845..Timrod, Henry 7:473
1846..Larcom, Lucy 1:406
1846..Saxe, John Godfrey 1:438
1847..Beers, Ethel Lynn 8:358
1847..Cozzens, Frederick S. 6: 29
1847..Dorr, Julia C. R. 6: 56
1847..Finch, Francis M. 11:356
1848..Boker, George H. 6: 73
1848..Eastman, Charles G. 9:252
1849..Burleigh, George S. 8:190
1849..Halpine, Charles G. 6: 26
1849..Kinney, Coates 7:302
1849..Leland, Charles G. 5:356
1850..Aldrich, James T. 12:138
1850..Cary, Alice 1:535
1850..Cooke, Rose Terry 6:300
1850..Drinker, Anne 11:502
1850..Hayne, Paul Hamilton ... 4:307
1850..Holland, Josiah G. 1:311
1850..Jackson, Henry R. 3:369
1851..Benton, Joel 8:200
1853..Moulton, Louise C. 3:365
1853..Taylor, Benjamin F. 11:159
1854..Mace, Frances L. 10:233
1854..Realf, Richard 8: 60
1855..Aldrich, Thomas Bailey ... 1:283
1855..Howarth, Ellen C. 7:487
1855..Sangster, Margaret 6:169
1856..Cooper, George 8:245
1856..Gray, David 9:500
1856..Stedman, Edmund C. 3:136
1857..Piatt, John J. 8:260
1857..Shanly, Charles D. 8:371
1857..Whitney, Adeline Train .. 2: 29
1858..Hay, John 11: 12
1858..Ludlow, Fitz Hugh 13:463
1858..Spofford, Harriet Prescott 4:308
1859..Clemmer, Mary 7:233
1859..Hope, James B. 7:241
1859..Lowe, Martha P. 10: 52
1859..Lowell, Robert T. S. 8:416
1859..Townsend, Mary A. 11:527
1860..Dickinson, Emily 23: 82
1860..Lucas, Daniel B. 6:534
1861..Palmer, John W. 8:222
1861..Preston, Margaret J. 7:147
1861..Randall, James R. 8:166
1861..Randolph, Anson D. F. ... 8:460
1861..Ticknor, Francis O. 11:311
1861..Willson, Forceythe 7:292
1862..Dickinson, Charles M. 11: 91
1863..Trowbridge, John T. 3:374
1864..Bolton, Sarah K. 1:212
1865..Coolbrith, Ina D. 13:512
1865..Jackson, Helen Hunt 1:443
1865..Lukens, Henry C. 13:347
1865..Sill, Edward R. 7:249
1866..Miller, Joaquin 7: 69
1866..Proctor, Edna D. 7:250
1866..Weeks, Robert K. 8: 11
1867..Kimball, Harriet McE. ...11:158
1867..Lazarus, Emma 3: 25
1867..Thaxter, Celia 1:305
1868..Carleton, Will 2:505
1870..Adams, Charles Follen ... 1:279
1870..Bloede, Gertrude 10:379
1870..Branch, Mary L. B. 21:397
1870..DeVere, Mary A. 8:440
1871..Piatt, Sarah Morgan 8:260
1872..Fields, James T. 1:283
1872..Venable, William H. 19:364
1872..Wilcox, Ella Wheeler 11:278
1873..Moore, Clara J. 9:473
1873..Riley, James Whitcomb .. 6: 31
1874..Dodge, Mary Mapes 1:314
1874..Lanier, Sidney 2:438
1875..Chadwick, John W. 7: 77
1875..Gilder, Richard W. 1:312
1875..Green, Anna Katharine .. 9:257
1875..Tabb, John B. 13:249
1876..Palmer, Ray 8: 8
1876..Powers, Horatio N. 10: 56
1876..Russell, Irwin 4:153
1878..Cooke, Edmund V. 23:101
1878..Day, Richard E. 8:479
1878..De Kay, Charles 9:206
1878..Peck, Samuel Minturn 7:474
1879..Bates, Katharine L. 9:314
1880..Bates, Arlo 8: 12
1880..Clarke, Mary H. Gray 6:235
1880..Ryan, Abram J. 5:411
1880..Woolsey, Sarah C. 11:352
1881..Johnson, Robert U. C:519
1882..Mitchell, S. Weir 9:346
1882..Moore, Charles L. 11:387
1883..Boner, John H. 2:497
1883..Koopman, Harry L. 11:543
1883..Woodberry, George E. 23:186
1884..Guiney, Louise Imogen ... 9:483
1884..Hovey, Richard 6:352
1884..Scollard, Clinton 23:160
1885..Reese, Lizette W. C:447
1885..Rogers, Robert C. 15:281
1885..Thomas, Edith M. 9:456
1886..Morse, James H. 10:306
1887..Cawein, Madison J. 8:231
1887..Sherman, Frank D. 7:190
1887..Stanton, Frank L. 11:497
1889..Edgerton, James A. B:197
1890..Carman, Bliss 21:429
1890..Field, Eugene 1:158
1891..Stephens, Herbert T. 22:165
1892..Foss, Sam Walter 9: 32
1893..Dunbar, Paul Lawrence .. 9:276
1893..Lacy, Ernest 20:101
1893..Lodge, George C. 24:386
1893..Loveman, Robert 13:479
1894..Lytle, William H. 4:338
1894..Santayana, George B:343
1895..Knowles, Frederic L. 18:243
1895..Neihardt, John G. A:543
1896..Brown, Alice 15:283
1896..Robinson, Edwin Arlington B: 15
1897..Mifflin, Lloyd 18:296
1897..Van Dyke, Henry 25: 10
1898..Church, Samuel H. 9:518
1898..Coates, Florence E. 18:307
1898..Griffith, William C:532
1898..Masters, Edgar Lee A:387
1898..Peabody, Josephine P. 19: 95
1898..Rice, Cale Young C:375
1898..Van Noppen, Leonard C. .26: 40
1899..Markham, Edwin 9:157
1900..Branch, Anna H. C:541
1900..Hulley, Lincoln 24: 35
1900..Moody, William Vaughan .11: 69
1900..Widdemer, Margaret A:217
1902..Lowell, Amy 19:407
1903..Bynner, Witter A:175
1903..Erskine, John .... B: 59
1904..Dargan, Oliver T. C:435
1904..Kreymborg, Alfred .... C: 70
1905..Lindsay, Vachel 23:229
1905..Wilkinson, Marguerite O. B. 21: 30
1906..Daly, Thomas A. A:218
1907..Benét, William Rose A:214
1907..Ficke, Arthur D. B:158
1907..Jeffers, Robinson .... C: 37
1907..Teasdale, Sara A:218
1908..Eaton, Walter P. A:517
1908..Pound, Ezra .... C: 80
1908..Stork, Charles W. A:467
1908..Wheelock, John H. C:286
1909..Guiterman, Arthur A:299
1909..Oppenheim, James A:427
1910..Eliot, Thomas S. .... C: 99
1910..Seeger, Alan 20: 68
1910..Untermeyer, Louis A:381
1911..Kilmer, Joyce 19:290
1911..Low, Benjamin R. C. C:523
1912..Millay, Edna St. Vincent . B:176
1912..Robertson, Margaret C. ... B:315
1913..Fletcher, John G. .... C: 94
1913..Frost, Robert A:540
1914..Aldington, Hilda D. C:329
1914..Sandburg, Carl A:258
1915..Benét, Stephen Vincent .. A:215
1915..Dresbach, Glenn W. D:246
1916..Hall, Hazel 22:364
1917..Hillyer, Robert S. D:332
1917..Piper, Edwin F. .... A: 74
1917..Reed, John 19:282
1918..Sarett, Lew A:424
1919..Auslander, Joseph .... D: 45
1920..Wylie, Elinor 21: 14

Political Scientists

1744..Franklin, Benjamin 1:328
1774..Hamilton, Alexander 1: 9
1826..Dew, Thomas R. 3:235
1827..Lieber, Francis 5:116
1859..Bascom, John 8:196
1868..Champlin, James T. 8:406
1869..Burgess, John W. 13:410
1871..Baldwin, Simeon 21: 86
1873..Foster, John W. 3:268
1876..Moses, Bernard 26:120
1876..Tucker, Benjamin R. 13:403
1877..James, Edmund J. 11: 67
1880..Smith, Monroe 11:100
1881..Shaw, Albert 9:469
1883..Macy, Jesse 21: 18
1883..Wilson, Woodrow 19: 1
1885..Dunning, William A. 19: 27
1885..Hill, David J. 12:244
1888..Blackmar, Frank W. 9:495
1888..Willoughby, William F. .. A:212
1890..Hart, Albert B. 11:394
1891..Jenks, Jeremiah W. B:140
1892..Judson, Harry P. 11: 67
1893..Root, Elihu 26: 1
1894..Freund, Ernst 26: 98
1895..Dealy, James Q. A:201
1895..Garfield, Harry A. A:102
1895..Rowe, Leo S. 12:148
1895..Willoughby, Westel W. ..13:435
1896..Duggan, Stephen P. ..... C: 61
1898..Ford, Henry J. 21: 14
1898..Moore, John Bassett .... A: 72
1899..Jordan, David Starr 22: 68
1899..Reinsch, Paul S. 19:285
1900..Lowell, A. Lawrence .... D: 46
1900..Merriam, Charles E. D:435
1900..Munro, William B. D:404
1901..McCarthy, Charles 19:251
1903..Goodnow, Frank J. ...... C: 19
1903..Parsons, Frank 11:182
1904..Beard, Charles A. D:231
1907..Butler, Nicholas Murray .. B:186
1910..Lien, Arnold J. B:233
1910..Lowrie, Selden G. B:252
1911..Hornbeck, Stanley K. D:131
1911..James, Herman G. D:287
1914..Fenwick, Charles G. B:224
1916..Conover, Milton D:411
1916..Moley, Raymond C. ...... D: 21
1919..Dodds, Harold W. .... D: 59

Psychiatrists

1784..Rush, Benjamin 3:333
1793..Galt, John M. 20:325
1811..Beck, Theodoric R. 9:350
1832..Kirkbride, Thomas S. 6:388
1837..Bell, Luther V. 22:160
1838..Awl, William M. 22:133
1840..Brigham, Amariah 10:270
1840..Earle, Pliny 11:146
1842..Jarvis, Edward 12:116
1848..Bemis, Merrick 12: 95
1848..Wilbur, Hervey B. 10:450
1850..Gray, John P. 7:273
1858..Grissom, Eugene 22: 98
1858..Kerlin, Isaac N. 4:229
1859..Godding, William W. 23:247
1861..Mitchell, S. Weir 9:346
1862..Hughes, Charles H. 5: 64
1862..Powell, Theophilus O. 2:484
1864..Kempster, Walter 5: 21
1865..Kellogg, Theodore H. B:229
1869..MacDonald, Carlos F. 20: 7
1870..Callender, John H. 8:135
1870..Hurd, Henry M. 12:112
1872..Channing, Walter 19:124
1874..Hill, Gershom H. 20:258
1874..Stearns, Henry P. 22: 87
1878..Bancroft, Charles P. 20: 29
1878..Brush, Edward N. 24:297
1878..Tuttle, George T. 20:455
1879..Blumer, G. Adler D:322
1879..Cowles, Edward 19:250
1879..Jelly, George F. 15: 92
1881..Lawton, Shailer E. 20:164
1882..Pilgrim, Charles W. 25:391
1884..Eyman, Henry C. 21:186

1884..Wagner, Charles G. 24: 143
1885..Burr, Colonel B. .... B: 311
1885..Evans, Britton D. 9: 523
1891..Babcock, James W. 22: 222
1893..Hutchings, Richard H. ... D: 288
1895..Hoch, August 23: 281
1896..Hall, Herbert J. 20: 322
1896..Haviland, Clarence F. 24: 31
1896..Work, Hubert .... A: 14
1898..Wallace, George L. 26: 102
1899..Kirby, George H. 26: 35
1900..Cotton, Henry A. 24: 388
1901..Southard, Elmer E. 19: 113
1903..Salmon, Thomas W. 21: 39
1905..Hamilton, Samuel W. .... D: 293
1910..Kempf, Edward J. .... D: 153
1911..Adler, Herman M. 26: 455
1911..Farnell, Frederic J. ...... A: 160
1911..Gesell, Arnold .... D: 418
1914..Orton, Samuel T. .... D: 117

Psychologists

1836..Hickok, Laurens P. 7: 171
1842..Buchanan, Joseph R. 10: 277
1850..McCosh, James 5: 468
1850..Wilson, William D. 12: 510
1855..Bascom, John 8: 196
1859..Peirce, Charles S. 8: 409
1862..LeConte, Joseph 7: 231
1864..Hammond, William A. ...26: 468
1867..Harris, William T. 15: 1
1869..James, William 18: 31
1869..Welch, Adonijah S. 12: 291
1876..Thompson, Daniel G. 8: 386
1878..Gates, Elmer 10: 354
1878..Royce, Josiah 25: 356
1879..Ladd-Franklin, Christine .26: 422
1880..Schurman, Jacob Gould ... 4: 478
1881..Hall, G. Stanley 9: 203
1882..Chittenden, Russell H. ...10: 181
1882..Prince, Morton 25: 313
1883..Abel, John J. .... A: 392
1883..Coues, Elliott 5: 240
1883..Fullerton, George S. 12: 57
1883..Starr, M. Allen 16: 102
1884..Clevenger, Shobal V., 2d . 5: 267
1886..Dewey, John .... A: 547
1887..Bryan, William L. 13: 464
1887..Cattell, J. McKeen .... D: 94
1887..Ladd, George T. 13: 81
1888..Hyslop, James H. 26: 54
1888..Jastrow, Joseph 11: 373
1888..Münsterberg, Hugo 13: 85
1888..Sanford, Edmund C. 12: 272
1889..Baldwin, J. Mark 25: 89
1889..Tufts, James H. 11: 75
1889..Wolfe, Harry K. 18: 252
1890..Peirce, William F. 8: 138
1890..Warren, Howard C. 25: 344
1891..Gardiner, Harry N. 21: 81
1891..Newbold, William R. 22: 251
1891..Thorndike, Edward L. ...15: 205
1892..Scripture, Edward W. 10: 310
1892..Titchener, Edward B. 22: 94
1893..Farrand, Livingston ..... A: 117
1894..Angell, James R. .... B: 5
1894..Creighton, James E. 23: 220
1894..Marshall, Henry R. 11: 328
1894..Stratton George M. 13: 551
1895..Pillsbury, Walter B. 15: 416
1895..Seashore, Carl E. .... A: 227
1896..Sidis, Boris 24: 68
1897..Calkins, Mary W. 13: 75
1897..Scott, Colin A. 26: 431
1898..Dodge, Raymond .... B: 324
1898..Judd, Charles H. .... A: 251
1898..Lindley, Ernest H. .... B: 345
1898..Martin, Lillien J. 16: 153
1899..Goddard, Henry H. 15: 236
1901..Barnes, Jasper C. .... A: 484
1902..Baird, John W. 22: 213
1902..Yerkes, Robert M. .... A: 109
1903..Watson, John B. .... A: 86
1903..Woodworth, Robert S. ..... A: 24
1904..Franz, Shepherd I. ...... A: 477
1905..Gault, Robert H. .... C: 155
1910..Miles, Walter R. .... D: 146
1911..Gesell, Arnold L. .... D: 418
1912..Davis, Herbert B. 22: 114
1912..Myers, Garry C. .... D: 146
1913..Root, William T., Jr. .... C: 139
1915..Prince, Walter F. 24: 29
1916..Grumbine, Harvey C. .... A: 189
1920..Kempf, Edward J. .... D: 153

Public Health

1720..Boylston, Zabdiel 7: 270
1770..Revere, Paul 1: 83
1791..Hosack, David 9: 354
1800..Waterhouse, Benjamin ... 9: 254
1816..Bigelow, Jacob 4: 526
1842..Bartlett, Elisha 12: 70
1847..Holmes, Oliver Wendell .. 2: 336
1850..Snow, Edwin M. 13: 285
1852..Campbell, Henry F. 12: 68
1852..Flint, Austin 8: 311
1854..Arnold, Richard D. 22: 424
1855..Harris, Elisha 9: 352
1855..Kirkwood, James P. 9: 36
1858..Cabell, James L. 12: 452
1860..Gibbs, Wolcott 10: 469
1860..Jacobi, Abraham 9: 345
1860..Jarvis, Edward 12: 116
1861..Barton, Clara 15: 314
1861..Gihon, Albert L. 9: 154
1861..Mitchell, S. Weir 9: 346
1863..Dalton, Edward B. 10: 501
1864..Abbott, Samuel W. 20: 350
1864..Hunt, Ezra M. 12: 129
1864..Swinburne, John 7: 33
1865..Billings, John S. 4: 78
1865..Smith, Stephen 2: 207
1865..Wood, Thomas F. 9: 276
1866..Chandler, Charles F. 23: 46
1866..Eaton, Dorman B. 21: 200
1866..Snow, Francis H. 9: 494
1866..Worthen, William E. 12: 206
1867..Durgin, Samuel H. 13: 574
1867..Rauch, John H. 12: 452
1867..Sternberg, George M. 4: 388
1867..Sturgis, Frederic R. 4: 197
1869..Bailey, William 13: 45
1869..Cox, Christopher C. 10: 497
1869..Walker, Francis A. 5: 401
1870..Cochran, Jerome 5: 225
1870..Folsom, Charles F. 19: 375
1872..Toner, Joseph M. 7: 539
1873..Reed, Walter 13: 284
1874..Lindsley, Charles A. 26: 409
1875..Draper, Frank W. 17: 182
1875..Hering, Rudolph 10: 226
1876..Bowditch, Henry I. 8: 214
1876..Wyman, Walter 12: 508
1877..Kedzie, Robert C. 8: 488
1877..Rotch, Thomas M. 19: 350
1878..Howard, Leland O. 12: 356
1878..Robinson, Franklin C. ...14: 181
1878..Vaughan, Victor C. 12: 207
1878..Welch, William H. 26: 6
1878..Wiley, Harvey W. 21: 72
1879..Guiteras, Juan 22: 408
1881..Walcott, Henry P. 12: 445
1882..Atwater, Wilbur O. 6: 262
1882..Babcock, Stephen M. 22: 16
1882..Morrow, Prince A. 21: 184
1883..Smith, Theobald .... D: 133
1884..Ernst, Harold C. 20: 89
1884..Richards, Ellen H. 7: 343
1884..Trudeau, Edward L. 13: 564
1885..Biggs, Hermann M. 19: 219
1886..Gulick, Luther H. 26: 371
1886..Hutchinson, Woods 21: 376
1886..Mills, Hiram F. 12: 71
1886..Sedgwick, William T. 13: 290
1887..Conn, Herbert W. 20: 409
1887..Drown, Thomas M. 7: 112
1887..Howe, Lucien 23: 218
1888..Carter, Henry R. 25: 346
1888..Delano, Jane A. 19: 131
1888..Dixon, Samuel G. 13: 562
1888..Heg, Elmer E. 20: 72
1888..Kastle, Joseph H. 15: 413
1888..Swarts, Gardner T. 20: 346
1889..Holt, L. Emmett 20: 46
1889..Wesener, John A. 20: 448
1889..Whipple, George C. 24: 104
1889..Worcester, Dean C. 20: 246
1890..Coit, Henry L. 22: 102
1890..Prudden, Theophil M. ... 9: 347
1890..Wright, John W. 20: 381
1891..Stiles, Charles W. .... D: 62
1892..Flexner, Simon .... B: 19
1892..Harrington, Thomas F. ..22: 394
1892..Lewis, Richard H. .... A: 467
1892..Straus, Nathan 22: 46
1893..Blue, Rupert 15: 129
1893..Furbush, C. Lincoln 20: 222
1895..Fisher, Irving .... C: 51
1895..Park, William H. .... C: 314
1895..Prescott, Samuel C. ...... C: 389
1896..Hurty, John N. 22: 370
1896..Westbrook, Frank F. 14: 472
1898..Anderson, John F. ...... B: 102
1898..Ashford, Bailey K. ...... A: 29
1898..Currie, Donald H. 20: 154
1898..Fisk, Eugene L. 25: 425
1898..Fronczak, Francis E. .... C: 277
1898..Gorgas, William C. 14: 528
1898..Sherman, Henry C. ...... D: 65
1898..Wood, Leonard 9: 20
1899..Barker, Lewellys F. ..... A: 265
1899..Goldberger, Joseph 21: 83
1899..Gorham, Frederic P. 23: 168
1899..Lusk, Graham 15: 88
1899..Strong, Richard P. ...... A: 93
1899..Winslow, Charles-Edward A. .... D: 443
1900..Lazear, Jesse W. 15: 60
1900..McCoy, George W. .... C: 87
1903..Gay, Frederick P. .... B: 268
1903..Salmon, Thomas W. 21: 39
1904..Darlington, Thomas, Jr. .. 2: 179
1904..Opie, Eugene L. .... D: 242
1904..Perkins, Roger G. 26: 448
1905..Cabot, Richard C. .... A: 223
1905..Pearl, Raymond 15: 382
1906..Darling, Samuel T. 19: 417
1906..Goddard, Henry H. 15: 236
1907..Willcox, Walter F. ...... A: 345
1908..Farrand, Livingston ..... A: 117
1909..Ferrell, John A. .... B: 346
1909..Frankel, Lee K. 23: 208
1909..Rose, Wickliffe .... A: 265
1910..Burnham, Athel C. 24: 343
1911..Dublin, Louis I. .... D: 101
1911..Zingher, Abraham 26: 31
1912..Lathrop, Julia C. 24: 298
1914..Parker, Valeria H. ...... A: 234
1915..Mitchell, Harold H. ..... B: 125
1916..Campbell, Eleanor A. .... D: 198
1917..Baylis, John R. .... C: 401
1917..Kofoid, Charles A. ...... A: 280
1917..McCollum, Elmer V. ..... C: 477
1917..Vincent, George E. ...... B: 6
1919..Bigelow, George H. 25: 72
1919..Emerson, Kendall .... D: 312
1919..Powers, Charles A. 20: 60
1919..Wilbur, Ray Lyman ..... C: 12
1920..Hayhurst, Emery R. ..... D: 329
1922..Wilson, Edwin B. .... D: 271

Reformers

1782..Benezet, Anthony 5: 419
1790..Eddy, Thomas 3: 512
1803..Channing, William Ellery . 5: 458
1803..Rantoul, Robert 11: 232
1808..Mercer, Charles F. 13: 222
1815..Jay, William 8: 74
1815..Murphey, Archibald D. ... 7: 168
1816..Owen, Robert 6: 521
1820..Mott, Lucretia 2: 310
1821..Wright, Fanny 2: 319
1823..Ballou, Adin 7: 558
1823..Gerard, James W. 11: 333
1824..Greeley, Horace 3: 448
1824..Howe, Samuel G. 8: 372
1825..Birney, James G. 2: 312
1825..Brown, John 2: 307
1825..Owen, Robert D. 9: 222
1827..Scott, Walter 2: 342
1828..Delavan, Edward C. 11: 207
1828..Garrison, William Lloyd .. 2: 305
1830..Dow, Neal 5: 432
1830..Evans, Frederick W. 11: 255
1830..Grimké, Thomas S. 2: 326
1830..Quincy, Edmund 6: 93
1831..Lay, Benjamin 25: 168
1831..Leavitt, Joshua 2: 528
1832..May, Samuel J. 2: 313
1833..Crandall, Prudence 2: 307
1833..Davis, Paulina K. W. 22: 327
1833..Green, Beriah 2: 326
1833..Mott, James 6: 158
1833..Wright, Elizur 2: 317
1834..Alcott, A. Bronson 2: 218
1834..Stanton, Henry B. 2: 331
1835..Andrews, Stephen P. 6: 442
1835..Chapman, Maria W. 2: 315
1835..Hastings, Samuel D. 10: 142
1835..Phillips, Wendell 2: 314
1836..Burleigh, William H. 2: 378
1836..Child, L. Maria 2: 324
1837..Mann, Horace 3: 78
1838..Emerson, Ralph W. 3: 416
1838..Pierpont, John 6: 155
1838..Thoreau, Henry D. 2: 300

1839..Beecher, Henry Ward 3:129
1839..Field, David D. 4:236
1840..Anthony, Susan B. 4:403
1840..Cheever, George B. 7: 82
1840..Dorr, Thomas W. 8:234
1840..Noyes, John H. 11:238
1840..Pillsbury, Parker 2:330
1840..Whittier, John G. 1:407
1841..Burritt, Elihu 6:133
1841..Channing, William H. ...13:595
1841..Dix, Dorothea L. 3:438
1841..Parker, Theodore 2:377
1841..Ripley, George 3:453
1842..Hale, Edward Everett 1:199
1842..Huntington, Frederic D. .. 3:363
1842..Swisshelm, Jane G. 2:316
1843..Hunt, Harriot K. 9:259
1845..Still, William 2:313
1846..Burleigh, George S. 8:190
1846..Loomis, Arphaxad 25:219
1846..Stanton, Elizabeth C. 3: 84
1847..Smith, Gerrit 2:322
1847..Stone, Lucy 2:316
1848..Brockway, Zebulon R. 19:160
1848..Cabet, Etienne 9:550
1849..Griffing, Josephine S. W. . 6: 88
1850..Higginson, Thomas W. ... 1:394
1850..Stowe, Harriet Beecher ... 1:423
1851..Bloomer, Amelia J. 8:173
1852..Brace, Charles L. 10:166
1853..Blackwell, Henry B. 20:294
1854..Dall, Caroline H. 9:159
1856..Sanborn, Franklin B. 8:466
1857..Howland, Emily 25:306
1857..Swinton, John 8:251
1858..Harris, Thomas L. 3:289
1859..Blackwell, Elizabeth 9:123
1860..Stephens, Uriah S. 1:262
1861..Corson, Robert R. 9:458
1861..Stearns, Sarah B. 10:230
1861..Stewart, Eliza D. 7: 37
1862..Cheney, Ednah D. 9:170
1862..Livermore, Mary A. 3: 82
1863..Brown, Olympia 20:110
1864..Angell, George T. 7:477
1864..Gompers, Samuel 11:539
1866..Eaton, Doremus B. 7:413
1866..Love, Alfred H. 16:203
1866..Pingree, Hazen S. 7:119
1869..Blake, Lillie D. 11: 61
1869..Howe, Julia Ward 1:402
1869..Smiley, Albert K. 15: 38
1870..Hunt, Mary H. H. 9:156
1870..Powderly, Terence V. 8:181
1870..Willard, Frances E. 1:376
1871..George, Henry 4:325
1872..Comstock, Anthony 15:241
1872..Swallow, Silas C. 24:398
1872..White, Alfred T. 23:301
1873..Gordon, Anna A. A:295
1873..Letchworth, William P. ..15:324
1875..Riis, Jacob A. 13:114
1876..Adler, Felix 23: 98
1876..Spencer, Anna C. .... B: 41
1876..Stryker, M. Woolsey 26:142
1879..Ogden, Robert C. 14:415
1879..Rambaut, Mary L. B. 6:100
1880..Debs, Eugene V. 12:340
1880..Parkhurst, Charles H. 4:402
1880..Shaw, Anna H. 14:456
1881..Dike, Samuel W. 22:301
1881..Lathrop, Julia C. 24:298
1881..Nathan, Maude 15: 52
1881..Small, Albion W. 25:242
1881..Tutwiler, Julia S. 15:101
1882..Welsh, Herbert 3:412
1883..Banks, Louis A. 13:103
1884..Altgeld, John P. 11: 51
1885..Bliss, William D. P. 20: 91
1885..Ivins, William M. 12:378
1886..Boole, Ella A. B:492
1886..McGlynn, Edward 9:242
1887..Bailey, Hannah J. 10:421
1887..Crosby, Ernest H. 10: 61
1887..Moses, Frank 9:328
1888..Matthews, Nathan 25:323
1889..Flower, Benjamin O. 9:228
1889..Richmond, Mary E. 21:383
1890..Bacon, Albion F. D:365
1890..Fels, Joseph 20:419
1890..Folks, Homer A:459
1890..Gilman, Charlotte P. 13:212
1890..Gould, Elgin R. I. 23:193
1890..Russell, Howard H. 13:330
1890..Sewall, May Wright 19:108
1891..Gill, Wilson L. 4: 90
1892..Johnson, William F. A:502
1893..Coleman, George W. C:455
1893..Wheeler, Wayne B. ...... B: 14
1894..Baker, Harvey H. 21: 74
1895..Jones, Samuel M. 10:414
1895..Tolman, William H. 14:218
1896..MacVicar, John 15: 37
1896..Scott, Colin A. 26:431
1897..Seabury, Samuel .... D: 76
1899..Schoff, Hannah K. 18: 99
1901..McBride, Francis S. ..... A: 65
1904..Barnard, Kate 5:110
1904..Poling, Daniel A. .... B: 33
1912..Boissevain, Inez M. 16:216

Rhinologists

See Laryngologists, Rhinologists and Otologists

Roentgenologists

1877..Garratt, John M. 18:311
1889..Goodspeed, Arthur W. ...15: 30
1896..Dodd, Walter J. 17: 37
1896..Sandborn, Manly J. 20:345
1897..Gray, Alfred L. 23:223
1898..Titterington, Miles B. ...20:221
1901..Baetjer, Frederick H. ...25:128
1901..Caldwell, Eugene W. 18:197
1901..Hickey, Preston M. 26:348
1902..Childs, Samuel B. C:231
1903..Carman, Russell D. 20:330
1903..Mills, Ralph W. 20:401
1905..Jennings, Curtis H. 26:154
1905..Leix, Frederick 19:284
1907..Duane, William A:345
1909..Osmond, John D. D:218
1916..Belden, Webster W. 23:228

Scientists

See also special scientific groups, such as Anthropologists and Ethnologists, Archæologists, Astronomers, Bacteriologists, Biologists, Botanists, Entomologists, Geologists, Meteorologists, Microscopists, Mineralogists, Naturalists, Ornithologists, Paleontologists, Physicists and Zoölogists.

1708..Colden, Cadwallader 2:270
1738..Winthrop, John 7:165
1751..Bowdoin, James 2:488
1767..Priestley, Joseph 6:148
1780..DeWitt, Simeon 3:215
1792..Churchman, John 9:287
1792..Mitchill, Samuel L. 4:409
1805..Seybert, Adam 4:237
1805..Silliman, Benjamin 2:385
1810..Dewey, Chester 6:328
1812..Renwick, James 11:101
1815..Lea, Isaac 6: 23
1817..Dana, James F. 10:390
1817..Hassler, Ferdinand R. ... 3:413
1817..Olmsted, Denison 8:121
1821..Hitchcock, Edward 5:308
1821..Redfield, William C. 7:354
1822..Rogers, William B. 7:410
1825..Carpenter, George W. ...10:235
1825..Morton, Samuel G. 10:265
1825..Shepard, Charles U. 5:311
1825..Snell, Ebenezer S. 5:311
1826..Henry, Joseph 3:405
1827..Gibbes, Robert W. 11: 36
1828..Bache, Alexander D. 3:348
1828..Barnard, Frederick A. P. . 6:347
1828..Caswell, Alexis 8: 25
1831..Jackson, Charles T. 3: 97
1833..Loomis, Elias 7:233
1834..Bailey, Jacob W. 10:157
1835..Green, Traill 11:243
1835..Maury, Matthew F. 6: 35
1836..Blake, Eli W. 9:215
1836..Draper, John W. 3:406
1836..Frazer, John F. 1:348
1836..Johnson, Walter R. 12:260
1839..Smith, Hamilton L. 12:466
1840..Lovering, Joseph 6:425
1841..Chauvenet, William 11:210
1842..LeConte, John 7:228
1842..Smith, J. Lawrence 6: 54
1843..Herrick, Edward C. 11:170
1845..Hilgard, Julius E. 10:118
1846..Lane, Jonathan H. 3:275
1847..Horr, Asa 13:123
1847..Hunt, T. Sterry 3:254
1847..Winchell, Alexander 16:119
1851..Brooke, John M. 22: 29
1851..Gillman, Henry 7:359
1851..Jones, William L. 9:184
1852..LeConte, Joseph 7:231
1852..Orton, Edward 24:106
1856..Himes, Charles F. 4:144
1857..Brown, John J. 2:141
1857..Kerr, Washington C. 7:450
1858..Davidson, George 7:227
1858..Gill, Theodore N. 12:376
1858..Newcomb, Simon 7: 17
1859..Agassiz, Alexander 3: 98
1859..Peirce, Charles S. 8:409
1862..Gabb, William M. 4:376
1862..Verrill, Addison E. 21: 52
1863..Dall, William H. 10:454
1864..Niles, William H. 12:481
1867..Cutting, Hiram A. 10:204
1869..Coues, Elliott 5:240
1869..Frazer, Persifor 4:286
1869..Ladd-Franklin, Christine .26:422
1872..Merriam, C. Hart 13:264
1872..Minot, Charles S. 6:112
1872..Woodward, Robert S. 13:108
1872..Zahm, John A. 9:274
1873..Mendenhall, Thomas C. ..10:117
1876..Wright, George F. 7: 66
1879..Barus, Carl 26: 8
1879..Campbell, John T. 12:397
1879..Davis, William Jonathan .13: 22
1880..Libbey, William 10:401
1888..Brookover, Charles 20: 69
1895..Bauer, Louis A. 23:166

Sculptors

See also Artists

1770..Wright, Patience L. 8:278
1785..Houdon, Jean A. 8:292
1789..Dixey, John 9: 77
1789..Rush, William 8:287
1809..Willard, Solomon 4:431
1815..Augur, Hezekiah 8:284
1824..Frazee, John 8:289
1825..Greenough, Horatio 6:232
1826..Hughes, Robert B. 24:380
1835..Hart, Joel T. 6:514
1835..Powers, Hiram 3:421
1836..King, John C. 8:291
1837..Dexter, Henry 8:288
1839..Brackett, Edward A. 13:583
1839..Crawford, Thomas 8:292
1840..Clevenger, Shobal V. 8:280
1840..MacDonald, James W. A. 25:390
1840..Stephenson, Peter 8:455
1842..Hawkins, Benjamin W. ..11:169
1843..Barbee, William R. 18:423
1843..Brown, Henry K. 1:511
1844..Greenough, Richard S. ...23:252
1845..Mosier, Joseph 8:481
1845..Rinehart, William H. 2:345
1846..Mills, Clark 5:160
1846..Palmer, Erastus D. 5:416
1847..Bartholomew, Edwards S. 8:290
1848..Foley, Margaret E. 9:121
1848..Story, William W. 5:417
1848..Volk, Leonard W. 7:469
1850..Akers, Paul 6:130
1850..Rogers, Randolph 8:286
1850..Stebbins, Emma 8:292
1852..Ball, Thomas 5:199
1852..Hosmer, Harriet G. 8:284
1852..Mundy, Johnson M. 8:282
1852..Walcutt, William 13: 87
1857..Mead, Larkin G. 1:278
1857..Ward, John Q. A. 2:364
1859..Jackson, John A. 8:291
1860..Barbee, Herbert 18:424
1860..Rimmer, William 4:375
1860..Rogers, John 8:277
1863..Baerer, Henry 12: 98
1863..Milmore, Joseph 8:291
1863..Milmore, Martin 8:291
1864..Simmons, Franklin 11:316
1865..Cobb, Cyrus 4: 44
1865..Lewis, Edmonia 5:173
1865..Ney, Elizabet 13:371
1865..O'Donovan, William R. ..20:467
1865..Valentine, Edward V. ...10:377
1865..Whitney, Anne 7: 72
1866..Gould, Thomas R. 8:281
1868..Calder, Milne 20: 97
1868..Hoxie, Vinnie Ream 1:442
1869..Turner, William G. 17:211
1870..Connelly, Pierce F. 23:313
1870..Ellicott, Henry J. 12:122

1870..Ezekiel, Moses J. 18: 217
1870..French, Daniel C. .... A: 460
1870..Hartley, J. Scott 7: 459
1870..Noble, W. Clark .... A: 454
1873..Warner, Olin L. 8: 282
1874..Saint-Gaudens, Augustus . 8: 287
1875..Couper, William .... C: 219
1876..Bissell, George E. 8: 278
1876..Gelert, Johannes S. 9: 58
1878..Boyle, John J. 13: 73
1878..Doyle, Alexander 10: 371
1878..Kemeys, Edward 8: 279
1878..Thompson, Launt 8: 283
1879..Kelly, James E. 25: 434
1880..Cohen, Katherine M. 10: 369
1880..Grafly, Charles 22: 40
1880..Niehaus, Charles H. 9: 57
1881..Buberl, Caspar 11: 405
1881..Elwell, Francis E. 10: 368
1881..Partridge, William Ordway 23: 12
1883..Dallin, Cyrus E. 14: 478
1883..Kitson, Henry H. 12: 398
1883..Martiny, Philip 24: 86
1883..Zolnay, George J. 10: 372
1884..Weir, John F. 6: 429
1885..Remington, Frederic 22: 244
1886..Brooks, Richard E. 22: 229
1886..Clarke, Thomas S. 10: 372
1886..MacMonnies, Frederick ... 8: 289
1886..Mears, Helen F. 25: 287
1886..Taft, Lorado .... A: 461
1887..Barnard, George .... A: 67
1887..Bartlett, Paul W. 12: 553
1887..Fuchs, Emil .... B: 513
1887..Tilden, Douglas 24: 489
1888..Haag, Charles O. 25: 195
1889..Bitter, Karl 24: 385
1889..Potter, Edward C. 26: 272
1889..Weinert, Albert 10: 370
1889..Yandell, Enid 13: 210
1890..Adams, Herbert 13: 510
1890..Quinn, Edmond T. 26: 163
1890..Rankin, Ellen H. 8: 286
1891..Borglum, Gutzon 14: 80
1891..Mulligan, Charles J. 26: 287
1892..MacNeil, Hermon A. 13: 480
1892..Mayer, Caspar 10: 374
1892..Pratt, Bela L. 14: 378
1892..Vonnoh, Bessie P. 11: 164
1893..Bush-Brown, Henry K. 10: 374
1894..Harvey, Eli 12: 522
1894..Perry, R. Hinton 9: 54
1894..Scofield, Levi T. 12: 321
1895..Lenz, Oscar L. 17: 390
1895..Pike, Charles J. 24: 101
1896..Aitken, Robert I. 15: 215
1898..Borglum, Solon H. 13: 214
1898..Fraser, James E. .... C: 468
1899..Keck, Charles .... D: 179
1899..Potter, Louis McC. 26: 194
1900..Lawrie, Lee .... D: 49
1900..Longman, Evelyn B. ...... B: 313
1901..Lukeman, Augustus .... B: 437
1901..Rumsey, Charles C. 25: 26
1901..Shrady, Henry M. 13: 393
1902..Frishmuth, Harriet W. .... B: 242
1902..McKenzie, Robert T. ...... C: 357
1904..Abbate, Paolo .... B: 91
1905..Patigian, Haig 18: 44
1906..Lachaise, Gaston .... D: 388
1908..Nadelman, Elie .... B: 159
1908..Whitney, Gertrude V. ..... B: 54
1909..Akeley, Carl E. 26: 130
1909..Manship, Paul .... C: 312
1910..Baker, Percy B. .... D: 109
1910..Sterling, Lindsey M. ...... C: 107
1912..Putnam, Brenda .... B: 398
1915..Fraser, Laura G. .... C: 469
1915..Novani, Guilio C. .... B: 351
1918..Garrison, Robert E. .... D: 338
1920..Walter, Valerie H. .... C: 385
1922..Vagis, Polygnotos G. ..... B: 323

Social Workers

1816..Owen, Robert 6: 521
1824..Howe, Samuel G. 8: 372
1828..Doremus, Sarah P. 6: 166
1859..Blackwell, Elizabeth 9: 123
1860..Trott, Eli 19: 254
1861..Barton, Clara 15: 314
1861..Corson, Robert R. 9: 458
1863..Griffing, Josephine S. W. . 6: 88
1864..Lowell, Josephine Shaw .. 8: 142
1865..Howe, Mary A. 8: 159
1871..Schuyler, Louisa L. 20: 19
1875..McDowell, Mary E. .... B: 355
1876..Dodge, Grace H. 18: 310
1879..Ogden, Robert C. 14: 415
1881..Lathrop, Julia C. 24: 298
1881..Tutwiler, Julia S. 15: 101
1882..Addams, Jane .... C: 83
1882..DeForest, Robert W. ...... B: 61
1884..Spencer, Anna C. G. ...... B: 41
1885..Wright, Sophie B. 10: 51
1888..Booth, Ballington 14: 54
1888..Booth, Maud C. 14: 54
1888..Scudder, Vida D. 4: 468
1889..Richmond, Mary E. 21: 383
1890..Bacon, Albion F. .... D: 365
1890..Crane, Caroline B. 15: 64
1890..Folks, Homer .... A: 459
1891..Kelley, Florence 23: 111
1891..Zueblin, Charles 14: 454
1893..Bicknell, Ernest P. 25: 46
1894..Reynolds, James B. 10: 235
1896..Alden, Cynthia Westover .22: 52
1896..Devine, Edward T. 18: 214
1896..Gould, William J. 22: 218
1896..Hunter, Robert 14: 253
1899..Frankel, Lee K. 23: 208
1899..Schoff, Hannah K. 18: 99
1901..Kellar, Francis A. 15: 248
1904..Barnard, Kate 15: 110
1905..Cratty, Mabel 22: 183
1905..Lewis, Orlando F. 25: 349
1906..Baldwin, Roger N. .... D: 170
1908..Abbott, Grace .... C: 25
1909..Thomas, Norman .... C: 259
1910..Loeb, Sophie I. 24: 205
1910..Perkins, Frances .... D: 19
1915..Berry, Gordon L. 23: 324

Sociologists

1776..Paine, Thomas 5: 412
1816..Owen, Robert 6: 521
1820..Warren, Josiah 5: 179
1835..Andrews, Stephen 6: 442
1840..Brisbane, Albert 4: 560
1852..Brace, Charles L. 10: 166
1854..Fitzhugh, George 9: 383
1857..Swinton, John 8: 251
1859..Blackwell, Elizabeth 9: 123
1860..Atkinson, Edward 9: 416
1867..Ward, Cyrenus O. 13: 112
1868..Dugdale, Richard L. 11: 344
1870..Gronlund, Laurence 11: 199
1870..Lloyd, Henry D. 12: 375
1871..George, Henry 4: 325
1872..Gilman, Nicholas P. 8: 120
1872..Sumner, William G. 25: 8
1873..Burgess, John W. 23: 39
1873..Wright, Carroll D. 19: 421
1876..Adler, Felix 23: 98
1876..Tucker, Benjamin R. 13: 403
1878..Bellamy, Edward 1: 263
1880..Gunton, George 10: 146
1881..Dike, Samuel W. 22: 301
1881..Post, Louis F. 18: 150
1882..Addams, Jane .... C: 83
1883..Ely, Richard T. .... B: 204
1883..Ward, Lester F. 13: 112
1884..Shaw, Albert 9: 469
1885..Bliss, William D. P. 20: 91
1885..Giddings, Franklin H. 15: 9
1885..Gould, Elgin R. L. 23: 193
1886..Dewey, Davis R. 13: 371
1886..Vincent, George E. .... B: 6
1888..Small, Albion W. 25: 242
1888..Warner, Amos G. 13: 446
1889..Blackmar, Frank W. 9: 495
1890..Albertson, Ralph 15: 367
1890..Weber, Gustavus A. 16: 289
1891..Brooks, J. Graham 13: 534
1891..Devine, Edward T. 18: 214
1891..Kelley, Florence 23: 111
1891..Ross, Edward A. 18: 98
1892..Commons, John R. .... A: 423
1892..Gray, John H. 15: 29
1892..Henderson, Charles R. 11: 75
1892..Herron, George D. 9: 277
1892..Veblen, Thorstein 21: 73
1893..Coleman, George W. ...... C: 455
1893..Lindsay, Samuel McC. 12: 374
1894..Hollander, Jacob H. 13: 372
1895..Dealey, James Q. .... A: 201
1896..Hunter, Robert 14: 353
1897..Vail, Charles H. 11: 507
1898..Koren, John 19: 397
1899..Parsons, Frank 6: 182
1900..Veditz, Charles W. A. 23: 33
1901..Davis, Katharine B. .... A: 263
1901..Eaves, Lucile .... A: 506
1901..LeRossignol, James E. 13: 304
1902..Dewey, John .... A: 547
1902..Ellis, George W. 17: 400
1904..Howard, George E. 23: 246
1905..Gillin, John L. .... A: 163
1906..Williams, James M. .... D: 184
1908..Abbott, Grace .... C: 25
1909..Thomas, Norman .... C: 259
1910..Laidler, Harry W. .... D: 346
1910..Sanderson, Dwight .... A: 251
1910..Shenton, Herbert N. ...... D: 412
1911..Nasmyth, George W. 18: 246
1912..Peters, Iva .... A: 549
1913..Haas, Francis J. .... D: 34
1914..Lapp, John A. .... D: 155
1914..Nearing, Scott .... D: 53

Statisticians

1812..Shattuck, George C. 12: 197
1819..Fletcher, Richard 12: 92
1837..Jarvis, Edward 12: 116
1844..DeBow, James D. B. 8: 161
1849..Kennedy, Joseph C. G. 16: 444
1854..Delmar, Alexander 4: 189
1859..Dun, Robert G. 2: 523
1866..Brock, Sidney G. 1: 364
1868..Maxwell, Sidney D. 7: 179
1869..Walker, Francis A. 5: 401
1870..Baker, Henry B. 12: 136
1870..Seaton, Charles W. 12: 217
1872..Swank, James M. 20: 312
1872..Weeks, Joseph D. 13: 27
1873..Leech, Edward O. 13: 87
1873..Pidgin, Charles F. 13: 479
1873..Wright, Carroll D. 19: 421
1875..Jenney, Charles A. 11: 208
1876..Porter, Robert P. 12: 216
1877..Smiley, Charles W. 2: 371
1880..Adams, Henry C. 12: 219
1880..North, Simon N. D. 13: 62
1881..Austin, Oscar P. 24: 157
1885..Ford, Worthington C. 12: 105
1886..Dewey, Davis R. 13: 371
1888..Peabody, James T. W. 16: 380
1890..Weber, Gustavus A. 16: 289
1892..Willcox, Walter F. .... A: 345
1898..Babson, Roger W. .... A: 475
1898..Koren, John 19: 397
1899..Mitchell, Wesley C. .... C: 511
1900..Durand, Edward D. .... C: 450
1900..Mathewson, Park, 2d 23: 202
1900..Rossiter, William S. 23: 333
1900..Steuart, William M. .... A: 19
1903..McPherson, Logan G. 25: 280
1905..Robinson, Leland R. ...... A: 144
1908..Ayres, Leonard P. .... A: 148
1909..Dublin, Louis I. .... D: 101
1912..Warne, Frank J. .... A: 229
1913..Meeker, Royal .... A: 535
1920..Fisher, Irving .... C: 51
1922..Wilson, Edwin B. .... D: 271

Theologians

1612..Cotton, John 7: 27
1618..Hooker, Thomas 6: 279
1681..Thacher, Peter 6: 507
1708..Dickinson, Jonathan 5: 463
1722..Edwards, Jonathan 5: 464
1722..Wigglesworth, Edward ... 9: 237
1742..Bellamy, Joseph 7: 78
1743..Hopkins, Samuel, 1st 7: 154
1764..Parker, Thomas 12: 249
1767..Priestly, Joseph 6: 148
1769..Edwards, Jonathan, 2d .. 7: 169
1773..Emmons, Nathaniel 5: 141
1791..Alexander, Archibald 2: 22
1792..Miller, Samuel 7: 152
1793..Hoge, Moses 2: 23
1798..Woods, Leonard 9: 121
1801..Beasley, Frederic 1: 342
1802..Bangs, Nathan 9: 429
1803..Channing, William Ellery 5: 458
1804..David, John B. M. 12: 149
1806..Stuart, Moses 6: 244
1807..Tyler, Bennett 9: 87
1810..Bruté, Simon G. 12: 413
1811..Thacher, Samuel G. 5: 88
1812..Taylor, Nathaniel W. 7: 187
1813..Skinner, Thomas H. 7: 318
1817..Ware, Henry 5: 358
1818..Norton, Andrews 7: 63
1818..Turner, Samuel H. 7: 192
1819..Murdock, James 7: 80
1820..Hodge, Charles 10: 245
1820..Schmucker, Samuel S. 5: 100
1821..Kenrick, Francis P. 1: 485

Zoölogists

1895..Castle, William E. 16: 297
1895..Guyer, Michael F. .... A: 357
1896..Lefevre, George 20: 268
1898..Jennings, Herbert S. .... A: 278
1899..Beebe, William .... B: 337
1899..Riddle, Oscar .... C: 120
1901..Carpenter, Frederic W. ..20: 322
1903..Adams, Charles C. .... A: 448
1906..Andrews, Roy Chapman . A: 302
1906..Ruthven, Alexander G. ... C: 95
1907..Metcalf, Maynard M. ..... B: 20
1907..Petrunkevitch, Alexander . A: 449
1910..Kofoid, Charles A. .... A: 280
1912..Muller, Hermann J. ...... C: 331
1919..Struthers, Parke H. ..... D: 398

Miscellaneous

Compact Signed on Board the Mayflower

"In ye name of God. Amen. We whose names are underwritten, the loyall subjects of our dread soveraigne Lord, King James, by ye grace of God, of Great Britaine, France & Ireland king, defender of ye faith, &c., haveing undertaken, for ye glorie of God, and advancemente of ye Christian faith, and honour of our king & countrie, a voyage to plant ye first colonie in ye Northerne part of Virginia, doe by these presents solemnly & mutualy in ye presence of God, and one of another, covenant & combine our selves togeather into a civill body politick, for our better ordering & preservation & furtherance of ye ends aforesaid; and by vertue hereof to enacte, constitute, and frame such just & equall lawes, ordinances, acts, constitutions & offices, from time to time, as shall be thought most meete & convenient for ye generall good of ye Colonie, unto which we promise all due submission and obedience. In witness whereof we have hereunder subscribed our names at Cap-Codd ye 11 of December, in ye year of ye raigne of our soveraigne lord, King James, of England, France & Ireland ye eighteenth, and of Scotland ye fiftie fourth Ano: Dom. 1620."

Carver, John
Bradford, William
Winslow, Edward
Brewster, William
Allerton, Isaac
Standish, Myles
Alden, John
Fuller, Samuel
Martin, Christopher
Mullins, William
White, William
Warren, Richard
Howland, John
Hopkins, Stephen
Tilley, Edward
Tilley, John
Lister, Edward
Cooke, Francis
Rogers, Thomas
Tinker, Thomas
Gardiner, Richard
Allerton, John
English, Thomas
Doty, Edward
Fuller, Edward
Turner, John
Eaton, Francis
Chilton, James
Brown, Peter
Britteridge, Richard
Soule, George
Clarke, Richard
Crackston, John
Billington, John
Fletcher, Moses
Goodman, John
Priest, Degory
Williams, Thomas
Winslow, Gilbert
Margeson, Edmund
Ridgedale, John

Passengers on the Mayflower

Arrived at Plymouth

December 21, 1620 (New Style Calendar)

Alden, John
Allerton, Isaac
Allerton, Mary (Mrs. Isaac)
Allerton, Bartholomew
Allerton, John
Allerton, Mary
Allerton, Remember
Billington, John
Billington, Ellen (Mrs. John)
Billington, John, Jr.
Billington, Francis
Brewster, William
Brewster, Mary (Mrs. William)
Brewster, Love
Brewster, Wrasling (or Wrastled)
Bradford, William
Bradford, Dorothy (Mrs. William)
Britteridge (or Bitteridge), Richard
Browne, Peter
Carter, Robert
Carver, John
Carver, Catherine (Mrs. John)
Mrs. Carver's maid
Chilton, James
Chilton, Mrs. James
Chilton, Mary
Clarke, Richard
Cooke, Francis
Cooke, John
Cooper, Humility
Crackston (or Crackstone, Craxton, Croxton), John
Crackston, John, Jr.
Doty (or Doten, Dovey), Edward
Eaton, Francis
Eaton, Sarah (Mrs. Francis)
Eaton, Samuel
Ely, ———
English (or Enlish), Thomas
Fletcher, Moses
Fuller, Edward
Fuller, Mrs. Edward
Fuller, Samuel
Fuller, Samuel, Jr.
Gardiner (or Gardner), Richard
Goodman, John
Heale, Giles
Holbeck, William
Hooke, John
Hopkins, Stephen (or Steven)
Hopkins, Elizabeth (Mrs. Stephen)
Hopkins, Constanta (or Constance)
Hopkins, Damaris
Hopkins, Giles
Hopkins, Oceanus
Howland, John
Langemore, John
Latham, William
Lister (or Leicester, Listler), Edward
Margeson (or Morgeson), Edmund
Martin, Christopher
Martin, Mrs. Christopher
Minter, Desire
More, Ellen
More, Jasper
More, Richard
More, ———
Mullins (or Mollines, Molines), William
Mullins, Mrs. William
Mullins, Joseph
Mullins, Priscilla
Priest, Degory (or Digerie)
Prower, Solomon
Ridgedale (or Rigdale, Ridgsdale), John
Ridgedale, Alice (Mrs. John)
Rogers, Joseph
Rogers, Thomas
Samson (or Sampson), Henry
Soule (or Sowle, Sole, Soul), George
Standish, Myles
Standish, Rose (Mrs. Myles)
Story, Elias
Thomson (or Thompson, Tomson), Edward
Tilley (or Tilly, Tillie), Edward
Tilley, Ann (Mrs. Edward)
Tilley, Elizabeth
Tilley, John
Tilley, Bridget (Mrs. John)
Tinker, Thomas
Tinker, Mrs. Thomas
Tinker, ———
Trevore (or Trevour), William
Turner, John
Turner, ———
Turner, ———
Warren, Richard
White, William
White, Susanna (Mrs. William)
White, Resolved
Wilder, Roger
Williams, Thomas
Winslow, Edward
Winslow, Elizabeth (Mrs. Edward)
Winslow, Gilbert

Passengers on the Welcome

Arrived at Delaware

October, 1682

Barber, John
Barber, Elizabeth
Bradford, William
Buckman, William
Buckman, Mary (Mrs. William)
Buckman, Mary
Buckman, Sarah
Carver, John
Carver, Mary (Mrs. John)
Chambers, Benjamin
Cowgill, Ellen, and family
Croasdale, Thomas, and six children
Croasdale, Agnes (Mrs. Thomas)
Fisher, John
Fisher, Margaret
Fisher, John, Jr.
Fitzwater, Thomas
Fitzwater, Mary (Mrs. Thomas; died on the passage)
Fitzwater, George
Fitzwater, Josiah
Fitzwater, Mary
Fitzwater, Thomas, Jr.
Gillett, Thomas
Green, Bartholomew
Harrison, Nathaniel
Hayhurst, Cuthbert, wife and family
Herriott, Thomas
Hey, John
Ingelo, Richard
Ingham, Isaac
Jones, Thomas
Knight, Giles
Knight, Mary (Mrs. Giles)
Knight, Joseph
Lushington, William
Matthews, Jean
Mogdridge, Hannah
Morris, Joshua
Ogden, David
Oliver, David
Oliver, Elizabeth
Oliver, Evan
Oliver, Evan, Jr.
Oliver, Hannah
Oliver, Jean
Oliver, John
Oliver, Mary
Oliver, Seaborn
Pearson, Thomas
Penn, William
Rochford, Dennis
Rochford, Mary
Rochford, Grace (died at sea)
Rochford, Mary (died at sea)
Rowland, John
Rowland, Priscilla
Rowland, Thomas
Sharples, Jan, and family
Smith, William
Songhurst, John
Stackhouse, John
Stackhouse, Margery (Mrs. John)
Thompson, George
Townsend, Anne
Townsend, Hannah
Townsend, James
Townsend, Richard
Wade, William
Walmsley, Thomas
Walmsley, Elizabeth
Walmsley, Henry
Walmsley, Thomas
Waln, Nicholas, wife and three children
Woodroofe, Joseph
Wrightsworth, Thomas
Wrightworth, Mrs. Thomas
Wynne, Thomas

The American Company of Revisers of the Bible

OLD TESTAMENT CO.

Green, William H. *(Chairman)* . 6: 128
Day, George E. *(Secretary)* 13: 574
Aiken, Charles A. 7: 171
Chambers, Talbot W. 9: 258
Conant, Thomas J. 12: 288
De Witt, John 7: 261
Green, William H. 6: 128
Hare, George E. 6: 441
Krauth, Charles P. 1: 349
Lewis, Tayler 10: 131
Mead, Charles M. 10: 103
Osgood, Howard 24: 310
Packard, Joseph 9: 556
Stowe, Calvin E. 10: 140
Strong, James 13: 360
Van Dyck, Cornelius Van A. ... 5: 560

NEW TESTAMENT CO.

Schaff, Philip *(President)* 3: 76
Woolsey, Theodore D. *(Chairman)* 1: 170
Thayer, Joseph A. *(Secretary)*.. 6: 428
Abbot, Ezra 4: 384
Chase, Thomas 9: 554
Crosby, Howard 4: 193
Dwight, Timothy 1: 173
Hackett, Horatio B. 5: 72
Hadley, James 1: 175
Hodge, Charles 10: 245
Kendrick, Asahel C. 12: 245
Lee, Alfred 11: 99
Riddle, Matthew B. 13: 600
Short, Charles 7: 7
Smith, Henry B. 5: 311
Washburn, Edward A. 9: 498

Commission which met at Newport, R. I., to Inquire into the Destruction of the Gaspee, June 9, 1772

Auchmuty, Robert (Mass.) 9: 102
Horsmanden, Daniel (N. Y.) ... 7: 560
Oliver, Peter (Mass.) 4: 344
Smyth, Frederick (N. J.) 12: 377
Wanton, Joseph (R. I.) 10: 15

Board of War and Ordnance

ORIGINAL MEMBERS

Adams, John 2: 1
Harrison, Benjamin 10: 153
Peters, Richard *(Secretary)* 12: 235
Rutledge, Edward 12: 162
Sherman, Roger 2: 352
Wilson, James 1: 22

Commanders of the U. S. Frigate Constitution

1798–99..Nicholson, Samuel 4: 89
1799–1801Talbot, Silas 3: 501
1803–04..Preble, Edward 8: 92
1804 ..Barron, James 5: 502
1804 ..Decatur, Stephen 4: 56
1804–06..Rodgers, John 5: 261
1806–07..Campbell, Hugh G. 4: 555
1809–10..Rodgers, John 5: 261
1810–12..Hull, Isaac 13: 426
1812–13..Bainbridge, William ... 8: 93
1813–15..Stewart, Charles 8: 156
1821–23..Jones, Jacob 2: 233
1827–28..Patterson, Daniel T. ..
1833 ..Hull, Isaac 13: 426
1835–39..Elliott, Jesse D. 7: 39
1839–41..Turner, Daniel 4: 551
1843–46..Percival, John 20: 437
1847–49..Gwinn, John ....
1849–51..Conover, Thomas A. .. 4: 551
1853–55..Rudd, John ....

Delegates to the Peace Convention, Washington, D.C., February 4, 1861

Adams, Henry J. (Kans.) 13: 586
Alden, Charles S. (N. J.) ......
Alexander, William C. (N. J.) .13: 541
Allen, Charles (Mass.) 9: 186
Ames, Samuel (R. I.) 10: 304
Anderson, Josiah M. (Tenn.) ...
Arnold, Samuel G. (R. I.) 13: 148
Backus, Franklin T. (Ohio) 13: 520
Baldwin, Roger S. (Conn.) 10: 336
Barringer, Daniel M. (N. C.) ..11: 505
Bates, Daniel M. (Del.) 13: 476
Battell, Robbins (Conn.) 14: 254
Baxter, H. Henry (Vt.) ....
Bell, Joshua F. (Ky.) 13: 581
Boutwell, George S. (Mass.) 4: 382
Bradford, Augustus W. (Md.) .. 9: 307
Brockenbrough, J. W. (Va.) ...
Bronson, Greene C. (N. Y.) 3: 387
Browne, George H. (R. I.) 13: 588
Buckner, Aylett H. (Mo.) 13: 584
Butler, William O. (Ky.) 6: 183
Cannon, William (Del.) 11: 535
Caruthers, Robert (Tenn.) .....
Chamberlain, Levi (N. H.) .....
Chandler, Theophilus P. (Mass.)
Chase, Salmon P. (Ohio) 1: 28
Chittenden, Lucius E. (Vt.) 13: 553
Clay, James B. (Ky.) 13: 319
Cleveland, Chauncey F. (Conn.) .10: 335
Coalter, John D. (Mo.) ....
Coburn, Stephen (Mo.) ....
Conway, Martin F. (Kans.) 8: 55
Cook, Burton C. (Ill.) 13: 592
Crisfield, John W. (Md.) 13: 542
Crowninshield, Francis B. (Mass.)
Cullom, Alvin (Tenn.) ....
Curtis, Samuel R. (Iowa) 4: 300
Davis, George (N. C.) 3: 526
Dent, John F. (Md.) ....
Dodge, William E. (N. Y.) 3: 174
Duncan, Alexander (R. I.) 9: 559
Ellis, Erastus W. H. (Ind.) .....
Ewing, Thomas (Ohio) 25: 14
Ewing, Thomas, Jr. (Kans.) ...14: 101
Fessenden, William P. (Maine) . 2: 90
Field, David D. (N. Y.) 4: 236
Forbes, John M. (Mass.) ....
Foster, Stephen C. (Maine) ....
Fowler, Asa (N. H.) 5: 192
Franklin, Thomas E. (Pa.) ....
Frelinghuysen, Frederick T. (N. J.) 4: 250
French, Ezra B. (Maine) ......
Goldsborough, William T. (Md.)
Goodrich, John Z. (Mass.) 9: 557
Granger, Francis (N. Y.) 6: 7
Grimes, James W. (Iowa) 11: 430
Groesbeck, William S. (Ohio) ..13: 150
Guthrie, James (Ky.) 4: 147
Hackleman, Pleasant A. (Ind.) .12: 273
Hall, Hiland (Vt.) 8: 322
Harlan, James (Iowa) 2: 457
Harris, Broughton D. (Vt.) 4: 534
Hawkins, Isaac R. (Tenn.) 13: 542
Hickerson, William P. (Tenn.)..
Hitchcock, Reuben (Ohio) 13: 592
Hoppin, William W. (R. I.) 9: 400
Horton, Valentine B. (Ohio) ...13: 592
Hough, Harrison (Mo.) ....
Houston, John W. (Del.) ....
Howard, Benjamin C. (Md.) ... 6: 136
James, Amaziah B. (N. Y.) ....
Johnson, Reverdy (Md.) 4: 371
Johnson, Waldo P. (Mo.) 12: 392
Jones, George W. (Tenn.) ......
King, John A. (N. Y.) 3: 50
Logan, Stephen T. (Ill.) 7: 492
Loomis, A. W. (Pa.) ....
McCurdy, Charles J. (Conn.) ... 4: 376
McKennan, William (Pa.) 9: 553
McKinney, Robert J. (Tenn.) .. 5: 552
Martin, Thomas (Tenn.) ....
Meredith, William M. (Pa.) 4: 370
Milligan, Samuel (Tenn.) 5: 193
Morehead, Charles S. (Ky.) 13: 8
Morehead, John M. (N. C.) 4: 425
Morrill, Lot M. (Maine) 6: 313
Morse, Freeman H. (Maine) ...
Noyes, William C. (N. Y.) 18: 94
Orth, Godlove S. (Ind.) 5: 128
Palmer, John M. (Ill.) 11: 49
Perry, John J. (Maine) 13: 568
Pollock, James (Pa.) 2: 289
Pratt, J. T. (Conn.) ....
Price, Rodman M. (N. J.) 5: 207
Randolph, Joseph F. (N. J.) ...
Reid, David S. (N. C.) 4: 427
Ridgley, Henry (Del.) ....
Rives, William C. (Va.) 6: 486
Rodney, George B. (Del.) 13: 542
Roman, J. Dixon (Md.) ....
Ruffin, Thomas (N. C.) 7: 366
Seddon, James A. (Va.) 6: 219
Slaughter, Thomas C. (Ind.) ...
Smith, Caleb B. (Ind.) 2: 88
Smith, J. C. (N. Y.) ....
Somes, Daniel E. (Maine) ......
Stephens, William H. (Tenn.) ..
Stockton, Robert F. (N. J.) 4: 205
Stone, J. C. (Kans.) ....
Stryker, Thomas J. (N. J.) ....
Summers, George W. (Va.) 13: 580
Totten, A. W. O. (Tenn.) ......
Treat, Amos S. (Conn.) ....
Tuck, Amos (N. H.) 13: 518
Turner, Thomas J. (Ill.) ....
Tyler, John (Va.) 6: 1
Underwood, Levi (Vt.) ....
Vandever, William (Iowa) 4: 366
Vroom, Peter D. (N. J.) 5: 205
Wadsworth, James S. (N. Y.) .. 5: 13
Waters, Richard P. (Mass.) ....
White, Thomas (Pa.) ....
Wickliffe, Charles A. (Ky.) 6: 8
Williamson, Benjamin (N. J.) ..12: 337
Wilmot, David (Pa.) 3: 419
Wolcott, C. P. (Ohio) ....
Wood, John (Ill.) 11: 47

Peace Commissioners of 1864

Campbell, John A. 2: 472
Hunter, Robert M. T. 9: 158
Stephens, Alexander H. 3: 420

Joint Congressional Committee on Reconstruction, Appointed December 4, 1865

THE HOUSE

Stevens, Thaddeus *(Chairman)* .. 4: 30
Bingham, John A. 9: 375
Blow, Henry T. 4: 291
Boutwell, George S. 4: 382
Conkling, Roscoe 3: 220
Grider, Henry 7: 499
Morrill, Justin S. 1: 377
Rogers, Andrew J. 7: 48
Washburne, Elihu B. 4: 14

THE SENATE

Fessenden, William P. 2: 90
Grimes, James W. 11: 430
Harris, Ira 2: 96
Howard, Jacob M. 4: 472
Johnson, Reverdy 4: 371
Williams, George H. 4: 21

Electoral Commission

Created by Congress in 1877 to decide on the validity of the disputed electoral votes of 1876 from Louisiana, Florida, South Carolina and Oregon.

Abbott, Josiah G. 8: 175
Bayard, Thomas F. 2: 404
Bradley, Joseph P. 1: 33
Clifford, Nathan 2: 473
Edmunds, George F. 2: 384
Field, Stephen J. 1: 32
Frelinghuysen, Frederick T. 4: 250
Garfield, James A. 4: 238
Hoar, George F. 1: 453
Hunton, Eppa 13: 459
Kernan, Francis *(Substituted for Thurman, who had become ill)* 8: 368
Miller, Samuel F. 2: 473
Morton, Oliver P. 13: 271
Payne, Henry B. 1: 427
Strong, William 1: 33
Thurman, Allen G. 3: 144

International Monetary Conference held in Paris, August 10-28, 1878

U. S. DELEGATES

Fenton, Reuben E. *(Chairman)* . 3: 51
Groesbeck, William S. 13: 150
Horton, Samuel Dana 5: 558
Walker, Francis A. 5: 401

International Monetary Conference held in Paris, April 19 to May 19, 1881

U. S. DELEGATES

Evarts, William M. 3: 197
Horton, Samuel Dana 5: 558
Howe, Timothy O. 4: 252
Thurman, Allen G. 3: 144

International Monetary Congress held at Washington, 1891-92

U. S. DELEGATES

Blaine, James G. 1: 137
Hill, Nathaniel P. 6: 38
Tree, Lambert 6: 161

International Monetary Conference held at Brussels, Belgium, November 22 to December 17, 1892

U. S. DELEGATES

Allison, William B. 1: 296
Andrews, E. Benjamin 8: 26
Cannon, Henry W. 1: 158
Jones, John P. 1: 300
McCreary, James B. 13: 10
Terrell, Edwin H. 1: 387

Special Commission sent by President McKinley to Negotiate a Monetary Agreement with the Leading Countries of Europe in 1897

Paine, Charles J. 1: 448
Stevenson, Adlai E. 2: 487
Wolcott, Edward O. 8: 397

World Monetary and Economic Conference held in London, June 12 to July 27, 1933

U. S. DELEGATES

Hull, Cordell .... D: 10
Cox, James M. .... D: 269
Pittman, Key .... B: 375
Couzens, James .... A: 216
MacReynolds, Sam D. ....
Morrison, Ralph W. ....

Members of the War Inquiry Commission

Appointed by President McKinley, in September, 1898, in response to a widespread public demand for an inquiry into the management of the quartermaster's, subsistance, and medical bureaus of the war department during the War with Spain.

Beaver, James A. 2: 293
Conner, Phineas S. 12: 68
Denby, Charles 8: 276
Dodge, Grenville M. 16: 191
Howell, Evan P. 1: 236
McCook, Alexander McD. 4: 130
Sexton, James A. 12: 109
Wilson, John M. 4: 538
Woodbury, Urban A. 8: 330

American Anti-Slavery Society

Presidents

1833..Tappan, Arthur 2: 320
1840..Coates, Lindley 5: 559
1843..Garrison, William Lloyd .. 2: 305
1865..Phillips, Wendell 2: 314

Daughters of the American Revolution

Presidents-General

1890..Fairbanks, Mrs. Charles W.
1905..McLean, Mrs. Donald ....
1909..Scott, Mrs. Julia G. 20: 306
1913..Story, Mrs. William C. 26: 291
1919..Guernsey, Mrs. G. T. .....
1920..Minor, Mrs. George M. ...
1923..Cook, Mrs. Anthony Wayne
1926..Brosseau, Grace Lincoln Hall .... D: 181
1929..Hobart, Mrs. Lowell Fletcher ....
1932..Magna, Mrs. Russell W. ..
1935..Becker, Mrs. William A. ..

Huguenot Society of America

Presidents

1883..Jay, John 7: 347
1894..Marquand, Henry G. 8: 390
1896..DePeyster, Frederic J. ... 2: 528
1905..Jay, William 24: 197
1915..Mitchell, William ....
1921..Partridge, Edward L. 21: 109
1922..Schieffelin, William J. ....

Society of the Cincinnati

Presidents-General

1783..Washington, George 1: 1
1800..Hamilton, Alexander 1: 9
1805..Pinckney, Charles C. 2: 302
1825..Pinckney, Thomas 12: 160
1829..Ogden, Aaron 5: 208
1839..Lewis, Morgan ....
1844..Popham, William 4: 237
1848..Dearborn, Henry A. S. ... 9: 323
1854..Fish, Hamilton 4: 15
1896..Wayne, William 4: 304
1901..Vacant
1902..Warren, Winslow 12: 292
1930..Daves, John Collins ......

Sons of the American Revolution

Presidents-General

1889..Webb, William S. 1: 532
1901..Logan, Walter S. 2: 417
1902..Warfield, Edwin 13: 205
1903..Greeley, Edwin S. ....
1904..Hancock, James D. 23: 117
1905..Appleton, Francis H. 12: 231
1906..Pugsley, Cornelius A. 26: 490
1907..McClary, Nelson A. ......
1908..Stockbridge, Henry ......
1909..Beardsley, Morris B. 26: 75
1910..Marble, William A. 15: 127
1911..Parker, Moses G. ....
1912..Richardson, James M. ....
1913..Thruston, Rogers C. B. ...16: 328
1915..Woodworth, Newell B. ...
1916..Wentworth, Elmer M. ....
1919..Jenks, L. ....
1921..McCamant, W. ....
1922..Adams, Washington I. L. .10: 521
1923..Sumner, A. P. ....
1924..Lewis, Marvin H. ....
1925..Remington, Harvey F. ...
1926..Barret, Wilbert H. ....
1927..Rogers, Ernest E. ....
1928..Depew, Ganson .... C: 258
1929..Rowley, Howard C. ......
1930..Van Orsdel, Josiah A. ....
1931..Johnson, Benjamin N. ...24: 276
1932..Van Orsdel, Josiah A. ...
1933..Millspaugh, Frederick M. .
1934..McCrillis, Arthur M. .....
1935..Baker, Henry F. ....
1936..Kendall, Messmore .... B: 239

French Legion of Honor

Grand Cross

1907..McCormick, Robert S. 13: 375
1914..Herrick, Myron T. 13: 68
1918..Pershing, John J. ....A: 434
1919..Benson, William S. 23: 388
1919..Bliss, Tasker H. 21: 86
1919..Sharp, William G. 19: 299
1921..Wallace, Hugh C. .... B: 147
1928..Hyde, James H. ....
1929..Kellogg, Frank B. ....A: 8
1929..Tuck, Edward 16: 38
1936..Cromwell, William N. ....
1937..Butler, Nicholas Murray .. B: 186

Grand Officer

1902..Tower, Charlemagne 26: 124
1904..Francis, David R. 24: 322
1904..Loomis, Francis B. 12: 195
1913..Peary, Robert E. 14: 60
1917..Whitlock, Brand ....A: 544
1918..Wood, Leonard 9: 20
1919..March, Peyton C. ....A: 541
1919..Mayo, Henry T. 15: 44
1919..Morgenthau, Henry 15: 363
1919..Sims, William S. ....A: 192
1919..Wilson, Henry B. .... B: 350
1920..Allen, Henry T. ....
1920..Elkus, Abram I. .... D: 366
1921..Butler, Nicholas Murray .. B: 186
1922..Gerard, James W. ....A: 168
1922..Hill, David J. 12: 244
1922..Johnson, Robert U. ...... C: 519
1923..Boyden, Roland W. 23: 57
1926..Lowell, A. Lawrence ..... D: 46
1926..Perkins, Thomas N. ......
1926..Polk, Frank L. ....A: 417
1927..Cooke, Walter P. 23: 143
1928..Guthrie, William D. 15: 96
1928..Strong, Benjamin ....
1929..Cutcheon, Franklin W. M.
1930..Gilbert, S. Parker ....

Anniversary Calendar

NOTEWORTHY EVENTS AND BIRTHDAYS IN AMERICAN HISTORY AND BIOGRAPHY

JANUARY 1.

New Year's Day

1717 Hugh Orr, inventor of cotton spinning machinery, born 2: 54
1735 John Lamb, soldier, born 1: 44
1735 Paul Revere, silversmith and patriot, born 1: 83
1745 Anthony Wayne, soldier, born 1: 55
1750 Frederick A. C. Muhlenberg, clergyman and congressman, born 1: 149
1752 Betsy Ross, said to have made the first American flag, born 12: 438
1773 Isaac Lewis, clergyman and author / Zachariah Lewis, journalist } twins, born 11: 353
1776 American troops attacked Quebec, Canada 1: 85
1776 The first flag bearing thirteen red and white stripes raised at Cambridge, Mass. 13: 180
1778 Charles A. Lesueur, zoologist and artist, born 8: 475
1790 Claudius Crozet, engineer and educator, born 18: 393
1799 Opening of Transylvania university, Kentucky 4: 513
1800 Thomas Whittemore, clergyman, author and journalist, born 1: 276
1800 Constantine Hering, "the Father of Homeopathy in America," born 3: 477
1810 Charles Ellet, military engineer, who designed the first wire suspension bridge in America, born 4: 360
1815 First attack of the British upon New Orleans 5: 291
1819 Philip Schaff, theologian and historian, born 3: 76
1822 The first United States settlers arrived in Texas 6: 71
1825 Stephen V. Ryan, R. C. bishop, born 12: 484
1827 The first school of Hanover college opened 2: 123
1827 John Ireland, jurist, soldier and governor of Texas, born 9: 74
1830 Paul Hamilton Hayne, poet, born 4: 307
1831 Garrison's "Liberator" first issued 2: 305
1831 First issue of the "Country Gentleman" 24: 40
1838 Thomas R. Lounsbury, philologist and author, born 8: 101
1839 James R. Randall, song writer, born 8: 166
1840 Patrick Walsh, U. S. senator and journalist, born 2: 50
1848 Girard college opened 7: 13
1848 John William Goff, jurist, born 15: 254
1850 Charles Spiro, inventor of music-box, watch making machinery, typewriter, etc., born 3: 322
1853 Harry A. Richardson, U. S. senator, born 14: 310
1853 "Una," woman suffrage periodical, first issued 22: 327
1856 Frank Gunsaulus, clergyman and poet, born 7: 42
1859 Michael J. Owens, inventor of a glass-blowing machine, born 13: 504
1862 Mason and Slidell, Confederate envoys, released from prison on demand of England 2: 93
1863 Lincoln's Emancipation Proclamation went into effect 2: 70
1863 Galveston, Tex., recaptured by Confederates 4: 294
1867 Dr. Eugene L. Fisk, founder of the Life Extension Institute, born 25: 425
1870 Agnes M. Claypoole, biologist / Edith J. Claypoole, biologist } twins, born 13: 259
1876 The Chicago "Daily News" first issued 13: 51
1913 Parcel post system inaugurated ..... A: 46
1915 International treaty restricting the sale of opium became effective 22: 431
1934 The Federal bank deposit insurance act went into effect ..... D: 394

JANUARY 2.

1647 Nathaniel Bacon, Jr., colonist, leader of Bacon's rebellion, born 5: 337
1752 Philip Freneau, "Poet of the Revolution," born 6: 201
1771 James Fenner, Rhode Island governor and senator, born 9: 394
1794 William G. Goddard, educator and author, born 8: 225
1797 Hugh S. Legaré, statesman, born 6: 5
1797 Eliakim Littell, editor and author, born 24: 408
1820 Isaac Errett, clergyman, editor and author, born 6: 272
1830 Henry M. Flagler, capitalist, born 15: 10
1831 Justin Winsor, librarian and historian, born 1: 150
1832 Thomas T. Crittenden, governor of Missouri, born 12: 307
1833 William Forbes Adams, P. E. bishop, born 12: 87
1849 Francis E. Leupp, editor and author, born 15: 413
1853 George A. Gordon, theologian, born 22: 307
1856 Edward S. Martin, journalist and author, born . 10: 359
1857 William K. Bixby, president of the American Car & Foundry Co., born 12: 43
1860 William C. Mills, archæologist, born 22: 121
1861 North Carolina took formal possession of Fort Macon, Wilmington and Fayetteville 4: 427
1863 Battle of Murfreesboro or Stone river, Tenn. 4: 163
1863 Raymond Weeks, philologist and inventor of instruments to study organs of speech, born 18: 428
1865 William Lyon Phelps, author, professor of English literature at Yale, born ..... A: 375
1870 Augustus Trowbridge, physicist, born ..... C: 470

JANUARY 3.

1711 Richard Gridley, soldier, born 6: 65
1776 Thomas Morris, U. S. senator, born 11: 39
1777 Battle of Princeton, N. J. 10: 171
1788 John A. King, governor of New York, born 3: 50
1793 Lucretia Mott, reformer and woman suffragist, born 2: 310
1812 Elisha M. Pease, lawyer and governor of Texas, born 9: 68
1815 James R. Doolittle, U. S. senator, born 4: 382
1816 Samuel C. Pomeroy, Kansas free state advocate and U. S. senator, born 12: 69
1819 Thomas H. Watts, lawyer and governor of Alabama, born 10: 432
1821 George R. Balch, naval officer, born 5: 30
1823 Edward S. Renwick, inventor of a self-binding reaping machine, born 11: 102
1828 Frank Frick, Baltimore merchant, born 1: 252
1835 Larkin G. Mead, sculptor, born 1: 278
1837 Charles H. Hackley, capitalist and philanthropist, born 9: 82
1837 James L. Coker, manufacturer and philanthropist, born 17: 21
1840 Henry Holt, New York publisher, born 9: 486
1855 James A. Tawney, congressman, born 18: 12
1867 Harry M. Adams, traffic expert, born ..... A: 23
1883 "Life," a humorous magazine, first issued 1: 406
1883 Patrick J. Hurley, secretary of war under Franklin D. Roosevelt, born ..... C: 9
1885 Harry E. Widener, bibliophile, born 15: 12

JANUARY 4.

1679 Roger Wolcott, soldier, judge and author, born 10: 326
1716 Aaron Burr, clergyman, and president of Princeton, born 5: 463
1752 Harry Innes, Kentucky patriot and jurist, born 10: 409
1772 Caesar A. Rodney, statesman, attorney-general under Jefferson, born 3: 11
1780 Horace Binney, lawyer, a director and defender of the United States Bank, born 10: 444
1789 Benjamin Lundy, abolitionist, born 2: 308
1793 Roger S. Baldwin, governor of Connecticut, jurist, born 10: 336
1798 Robley Dunglison, physician, "father of American physiology," born 10: 270
1801 David L. Swain, governor of North Carolina, president of University of North Carolina, born 4: 424
1804 Samuel M. Isaacs, clergyman, born 11: 523
1811 Walter Williamson, physician, born 3: 478
1821 John W. Hutchinson, of a famous family of singers, born 10: 27
1822 Washington C. DePauw, glass manufacturer and philanthropist, born 7: 380
1830 John Stewart Kennedy, New York financier and philanthropist, born 15: 150
1831 Edward P. Dutton, publisher, born 6: 60
1831 Howard Osgood, theologian, born 24: 310
1838 Charles S. Stratton (Tom Thumb), dwarf, born 10: 422
1852 Juan Guiteras, physician and hygienist, born 22: 408
1856 William Goebel, governor of Kentucky, born 13: 13
1858 Carter Glass, financier and statesman, born ..... A: 36

1864	The Philadelphia "Evening Telegraph" first published	11: 437
1870	Patents issued for a new method of knitting stockings	23: 84
1873	Blanche Walsh, actress, born	12: 372
1874	George K. Burgess, physicist, who established a new absolute standard of light, born	24: 312
1896	Utah admitted to the Union	7: 552

JANUARY 5.

1608	Capt. John Smith captured by the Indians	13: 378
1771	David Wilkinson, inventor, born	8: 302
1778	"Battle of the Kegs"	9: 245
1779	Zebulon M. Pike, explorer, for whom Pike's Peak was named, born	2: 516
1779	Stephen Decatur, naval officer, born	4: 56
1781	Richmond, Va., burned by the British	1: 53
1783	Robert Henley, naval officer, born	13: 52
1809	Daniel Agnew, jurist, born	4: 28
1811	Cyrus Hamlin, president of Robert college in Turkey, born	10: 491
1818	George Hammell Cook, scientist, born	6: 304
1821	Joseph D. Bedle, New Jersey lawyer, jurist and governor, born	5: 210
1829	George F. Seymour, P. E. bishop, born	10: 357
1831	William P. Johnston, first president of Tulane university, born	9: 130
1833	Eugene W. Hilgard, agricultural chemist, born	10: 308
1835	Olympia Brown, first woman minister ordained in America, born	20: 110
1838	John C. Moss, inventor of the process of photo-engraving, born	11: 426
1844	Albert E. Dunning, clergyman and author, born	13: 432
1852	Arthur T. Cabot, physician and surgeon, born	15: 46
1854	George Inness, Jr., artist, born	22: 181
1857	David S. Bispham, singer, born	11: 424
1871	Frederick S. Converse, composer, born	B: 196
1877	Henry Sloane Coffin, president of Union theological seminary, born	B: 36
1887	The first library school in the United States opened at Columbia university	23: 14

JANUARY 6.

Twelfth Day, or Twelfth Tide

1730	Thomas Chittenden, Vermont statesman and governor, born	8: 312
1770	Edward D. Griffin, president of several colleges, including Williams, born	6: 237
1793	James M. Porter, Pennsylvania lawyer and a founder of Lafayette college, born	6: 9
1794	Rebecca W. Lukens, iron manufacturer, born	15: 375
1801	Daniel Haines, governor of New Jersey, born	5: 207
1807	Joseph Holt, statesman and judge-advocate general in the Civil War, born	1: 354
1811	Charles Sumner, U. S. senator, born	3: 300
1824	Thomas McI. Cooley, teacher of law and political science, born	9: 522
1828	William J. Stillman, journalist and author, born	10: 25
1832	First anti-slavery society founded	2: 320
1833	James A. Burden, iron manufacturer, born	1: 511
1836	Truman H. Safford, astronomer and mathematician, born	13: 359
1838	The first telegraph instrument completed	4: 450
1839	William F. Norris, ophthalmologist, born	18: 175
1842	Clarence King, geologist, founder of the U. S. geological survey, born	13: 248
1843	John C. Spooner, U. S. senator, born	14: 33
1858	Albert H. Munsell, artist and inventor, born	12: 316
1859	Henry E. Dixey, actor, born	10: 112
1861	U. S. arsenal at Apalachicola, Fla., seized by state troops	11: 379
1861	A. Lawrence Rotch, meteorologist, born	15: 2
1864	Ward B. Holloway, merchant, born	15: 393
1878	Carl Sandburg, poet, born	A: 258
1914	The first office of public defender established	A: 207
1912	New Mexico admitted to the Union	19: 245
1927	U. S. marines and war vessels ordered to Nicaragua to protect American interests	21: 4

JANUARY 7.

1699	A treaty of peace made with Indians in Massachusetts	8: 145
1718	Israel Putnam, soldier, born	1: 87
1776	George Gibbs, mineralogist, born	12: 131
1786	William C. Bouck, governor of New York, born	3: 46
1789	The first national election held	1: 5
1799	Daniel Tyler, iron manufacturer and Federal soldier, born	4: 393
1800	Millard Filmore, President of the United States, born	6: 177
1818	Thomas Hill, president of Antioch and Harvard colleges, born	6: 420
1820	Austin Phelps, clergyman and author, born	9: 366
1826	Oliver H. Kelley, founder of the Patrons of Husbandry, born	23: 117
1829	James B. Angell, president of the University of Michigan, born	1: 251
1830	Albert Bierstadt, artist, born	11: 288
1832	T. DeWitt Talmage, Presbyterian clergyman, born	4: 26
1847	William Henry Bishop, author, born	8: 54
1851	Bernhard E. Fernow, forester, born	19: 166
1851	M. Woolsey Stryker, author and president of Hamilton college, born	26: 142
1856	Charles H. Davis, artist, born	8: 431
1861	Louise Imogen Guiney, author and poet, born	9: 483
1861	A secession convention met in Jackson, Miss.	13: 491
1862	Mary E. Wilkins, author, born	9: 229
1862	Robert Cameron Rogers, editor and poet, born	15: 281
1863	Battle of Springfield, Mo.	12: 308
1873	Adolph Zukor, motion picture producer, born	C: 263
1875	Act renewing specie payments passed by Congress	4: 9

JANUARY 8.

Jackson Day—Holiday in Louisiana

1681	Jonathan Belcher, governor of Massachusetts, New Hampshire and New Jersey, born	6: 301
1735	John Carroll, R. C. archbishop of Baltimore, born	1: 480
1769	Nathan Smith, lawyer and U. S. senator, born	5: 516
1777	Bird Wilson, jurist and theologian, born	2: 207
1786	Nicholas Biddle, president of the United States Bank, born	6: 163
1788	John Canfield Spencer, statesman, born	6: 6
1791	Jacob Collamer, postmaster general under Taylor, born	4: 371
1792	Lowell Mason, musician and composer, born	7: 422
1802	Edward Kent, governor of Maine, born	6: 308
1811	Wreck of the "Revenge" off Watch Hill, R. I.	4: 267
1815	Battle of New Orleans, La.	5: 291
1821	James Longstreet, engineer and soldier, born	4: 263
1829	David H. Mason, editor and author, born	10: 228
1830	Gouverneur K. Warren, Federal soldier and engineer, born	4: 68
1831	The capital of Louisiana was transferred from Donaldsville to New Orleans	10: 76
1831	Charles H. Morgan, mechanical engineer, born	23: 197
1838	Charles A. Tinker, electrical engineer, born	2: 144
1839	William A. Clark, U. S. senator, born	21: 10
1840	Isaac W. Lamb, inventor of a knitting machine, born	7: 554
1846	William W. Gilchrist, composer, born	10: 350
1852	Jermain G. Porter, astronomer, born	13: 73
1853	Edmund Noble, journalist and author, born	12: 460
1857	Augustus Thomas, playwright, born	C: 438
1861	George Hamilton Cameron, soldier, born	A: 99
1862	Frank N. Doubleday, publisher, born	13: 400
1863	First ground broken for the Central Pacific railway	15: 16
1873	Harvey Wiley Corbett, architect, born	B: 409
1884	Gordon L. Berry, director-general of the League of Red Cross Societies, born	23: 324
1892	United States Daughters of 1812 Society founded	19: 139
1918	President Wilson outlined to congress the famous "fourteen points" that became the basis of settlement of the World war	19: 9

JANUARY 9.

1738	Joseph Willard, president of Harvard college, born	6: 416
1745	Caleb Strong, governor of Massachusetts, born	1: 110
1781	Lemuel Shaw, Massachusetts jurist and senator, born	5: 415
1805	Charles E. A. Gayarre, Southern historian, born	6: 253
1806	Augustus W. Bradford, governor of Maryland, born	9: 307
1808	Henry A. Boardman, clergyman and author, born	13: 345
1816	John P. Usher, lawyer and secretary of the interior under Lincoln, born	2: 88
1817	Nathan S. Davis, founder of the Chicago medical college, born	10: 266
1828	Alexander K. McClure, journalist, born	1: 466
1839	John K. Paine, musician and composer, born	7: 436
1840	John Torrey Morse, Jr., author, born	12: 438
1847	Mexicans defeated at La Mesa, Calif.	4: 205
1851	William A. Babcock, jurist, born	16: 448
1852	William Henry Nichols, chemist, head of the General Chemical Co., born	24: 285
1856	Lizette W. Reese, poet, born	1: 387
1856	James F. Bell, soldier, born	22: 276
1857	Henry B. Fuller, author, born	23: 406

1859 Carrie Chapman Catt, suffragist, born 15: 341
1861 Mississippi seceded from the Union 2: 67
1861 The Federal ship "Star of the West" fired upon 12: 179
1863 George Clinton Ward, engineer, associated with Henry E. Huntington in southern California projects, born 24: 36
1866 Fisk university opened 22: 300
1868 Edward Howard Griggs, lecturer and author, born .... B: 299
1892 University of Missouri buildings destroyed by fire 8: 189
1900 Richard Halliburton, traveller and author, born D: 407

JANUARY 10.

1737 Ethan Allen, soldier, born 1: 45
1742 John Cadwalader, soldier, born 1: 89
1762 Julien Dubuque, pioneer, for whom Julien and Dubuque, Iowa, were named, born 8: 459
1766 Elias H. Derby, Boston merchant, born 4: 545
1804 Oakes Ames, shovel manufacturer, and a builder of the Union Pacific railroad, born 2: 199
1805 South Carolina college opened 11: 30
1810 Jeremiah S. Black, attorney-general and secretary of state under Buchanan, born 5: 5
1813 Daniel Wise, author, better known as Francis Forrester and Lawrence Lancewood, born 13: 191
1817 Enoch L. Fancher, first judge of the court of arbitration, New York, born 7: 505
1818 Louisa Lane Drew, actress, born 8: 217
1822 Theodore L. Cuyler, Presbyterian clergyman, born 5: 246
1828 John T. Hoffman, governor of New York, born . 3: 52
1830 Edward R. Welles, P. E. bishop of Wisconsin, born 11: 58
1838 John W. Ambrose, engineer, for whom Ambrose channel, New York harbor, was named, born 24: 132
1841 George W. Melville, naval engineer, prominent in Arctic exploration, born 3: 283
1841 John Pitcairn, industrialist, founder of the Pittsburgh Plate Glass Co., born 16: 376
1843 Carroll S. Page, governor of Vermont, born ... 8: 329
1844 Elisha B. Andrews, president of Nebraska and Brown universities, born 8: 26
1846 Waterman T. Hewett, educator and author, born 8: 419
1847 Jacob H. Schiff, financier, born 13: 533
1850 John W. Root, Chicago architect, born 8: 114
1859 Herbert W. Conn, bacteriologist, founder of a new science of dairy bacteriology, born 20: 409
1861 Florida adopted an ordinance of secession 11: 379
1862 Battle of Middle Creek, Ky. 4: 239
1862 Reed Smoot, U. S. senator, born 13: 197
1867 John Archer Lejeune, soldier, born .... A: 375
1873 Howard G. Christy, artist, born 11: 299
1884 Chester W. Cuthell, lawyer, general counsel for the Emergency Fleet Corporation in the World war, born .... A: 143
1885 Walter Sherman Gifford, president of the American Telephone and Telegraph Co., born ..... B: 101
1887 Robinson Jeffers, poet, born .... C: 37
1888 Harvey process of making armor plate invented 13: 63
1902 Carnegie institute incorporated 13: 108

JANUARY 11.

1665 Clarendon (Carolina) colony established 12: 151
1757 Alexander Hamilton, statesman and first secretary of the treasury, born 1: 9
1760 Oliver Wolcott, Jr., financier and governor of Connecticut, born 10: 333
1784 Francis Brown, president of Dartmouth college, born 9: 86
1785 William W. Seaton, journalist, born 2: 226
1792 Robert Patterson, Federal soldier and manufacturer, born 10: 250
1793 Cave Johnson, judge and banker, born 6: 270
1801 Samuel M. Janney, Quaker minister and author, born 7: 485
1804 Isaac Knapp, abolitionist, born 2: 321
1805 Territory of Michigan created 3: 34
1807 Ezra Cornell, founder of Cornell university, born 4: 475
1813 Tunis A. McD. Craven, "the Sidney of the American navy," born 12: 371
1816 Fitz Henry Warren, soldier, born 12: 228
1822 John A. Kasson, congressman and diplomat, born 4: 379
1824 Robert Ogden Doremus, chemist, born 12: 190
1825 Bayard Taylor, journalist and author, born 3: 454
1857 George Q. Cannon, U. S. senator, born 12: 511
1835 Sidney A. Norton, educator, born 12: 123
1835 William S. Haseltine, artist, born 12: 441
1836 Alexander H. Wyant, artist, born 10: 370
1839 Franklin Simmons, sculptor, born 11: 316
1842 William James, psychologist and philosopher, born 18: 31
1849 Richard G. Davenport, naval officer, born 20: 119
1850 Joseph C. Arthur, botanist, born 12: 350

1859 Victor J. Loring, lawyer, born 15: 119
1861 Alabama seceded from the Union 10: 432
1863 Federal forces captured Arkansas Post 4: 137
1863 The "Alabama" sank the U. S. Steamer "Hatteras" 4: 340
1864 Thomas Dixon, Jr., clergyman and author, born 13: 189
1867 Edward B. Titchener, psychologist, born 22: 94
1873 Dwight W. Morrow, financier and statesman, born 23: 10
1899 Eva Le Gallienne, actress and producer, born .. C: 385

JANUARY 12.

1588 John Winthrop, first colonial governor of Massachusetts, born 6: 201
1723 Samuel Langdon, president of Harvard college, born 6: 416
1737 John Hancock, first signer of the Declaration of Independence, born 1: 103
1788 Alexander Thomson, judge, born 12: 425
1814 Willis A. Gorman, governor of Minnesota and Federal soldier, born 10: 62
1820 Caroline M. Severance, reformer, born 8: 107
1821 William Travis Howard, Minnesota physician, born 12: 316
1825 Francis H. Underwood, author, born 5: 379
1834 Martin Marty, R. C. bishop, born 12: 416
1837 Thomas Moran, artist, born 22: 24
1841 James T. Harahan, railroad president, born 15: 162
1841 Edward L. Henry, artist, born 5: 315
1846 Rasmus B. Anderson, author and diplomat, born 9: 320
1848 Battle of San Blas, Mexico 2: 106
1849 Henry A. Hazen, meteorologist, born 8: 114
1850 Two hundred shipwreck passengers saved in the first practical demonstration of the Francis life-car 10: 88
1850 Wilbur F. Crafts, clergyman, founder of the American Sabbath Union, born 14: 172
1851 John J. Boyle, sculptor, born 13: 73
1853 Robert Underwood Johnson, editor and author, born .... C: 519
1856 John S. Sargent, portrait artist, born 11: 291
1861 Florida seceded from the Union 11: 379
1861 Confederates seized forts and barracks at Pensacola, Fla. 11: 379
1861 James Mark Baldwin, psychologist, born 25: 89
1876 Jack London, author, born 13: 133

JANUARY 13.

1733 English colonists arrived at Charleston, S. C., to settle Georgia 1: 490
1781 British forces at Georgetown, S. C., attacked by Americans 1: 61
1785 Samuel Woodworth, author of "The Old Oaken Bucket," born 1: 434
1787 John Davis, Massachusetts governor and U. S. senator, born 1: 115
1793 John P. Crozer, manufacturer and founder of Crozer theological seminary, born 10: 171
1806 Alfred C. Post, physician and surgeon, born ... 9: 342
1806 Ralph Cheney, silk manufacturer, born 19: 72
1808 Salmon P. Chase, chief justice of the U. S. supreme court, born 1: 28
1812 Humphrey Marshall, congressman and Confederate soldier, born 6: 65
1813 Nathaniel H. Bannister, actor and author of more than 100 plays, born 22: 445
1827 Ethelinda E. Beers (Ethel Lynn), poet, born .. 8: 358
1827 Curtis Guild, journalist and editor, born 9: 502
1832 Horatio Alger, Jr., author of the "Ragged Dick" stories for boys, born 11: 543
1840 William C. Winslow, archæologist, born 4: 83
1840 The S. S. "Lexington" burned on Long Island sound 8: 462
1863 Naval engagement at Charleston, S. C. 4: 392
1865 Bombardment and assault of Fort Fisher, N. C. 2: 98
1865 Alexander Legge, president of the International Harvester Co. and chairman of the Federal farm board, born 26: 466
1870 Ross G. Harrison, anatomist, born 15: 172
1885 Alfred C. Fuller, brush manufacturer, born .... A: 351
1886 Order of the King's Daughters founded 13: 48
1890 Elmer Davis, author, born .... D: 310

JANUARY 14.

1639 A constitution adopted at Hartford, Conn. 12: 61
1697 Judge Sewall of Boston publicly confessed his error in the witchcraft trials 5: 340
1730 William Whipple, New Hampshire soldier and patriot, born 4: 437
1741 Benedict Arnold, traitor, born 1: 53
1749 James Garrard, governor of Kentucky, born 13: 2

1777 Congress ordered the British "union" to be replaced by thirteen stars for an American flag 13: 180
1779 Joseph Kent, Maryland physician and governor, born 9: 301
1780 Henry Baldwin, justice of the U. S. supreme court, born 2: 257
1782 Thomas Sergeant, Philadelphia jurist, said to have never been reversed, born 2: 157
1802 Hubbard H. Kavanaugh, M. E. bishop, born 9: 246
1806 Matthew F. Maury, meteorologist, born 6: 35
1807 Morton McCarver, founder of Burlington, Iowa, and Tacoma, Wash., born 4: 548
1816 Francis Kernan, U. S. senator, born 8: 368
1820 Robert W. Steele, governor of "Jefferson territory" (Colorado), born 11: 174
1824 William A. Phillips, Kansas soldier and congressman, born 8: 257
1832 John L. Lay, inventor of the Lay submarine torpedo, born 7: 528
1834 John R. Tait, artist, born 13: 277
1836 Hugh J. Kilpatrick, soldier, born 4: 273
1837 George F. Shrady, surgeon, and editor of the "Medical Record," born 7: 271
1840 John A. Paine, archæologist, born 13: 456
1842 Joseph C. Breckinridge, soldier, born 9: 23
1845 Robert M. O'Reilly, surgeon general, born 18: 261
1873 Two governors of Louisiana inaugurated 10: 81
1882 Hendrik van Loon, journalist and author, born B: 44
1885 Frederic J. Farnell, psychiatrist, born A: 160
1894 Polygnotos George Vagis, sculptor, born B: 323

JANUARY 15.

1716 Philip Livingston, signer of the Declaration of Independence, born 3: 306
1751 The first colonial assembly of Georgia met 1: 491
1777 Vermont passed a Declaration of Independence 4: 29
1780 Parker Cleaveland, educator and mineralogist, born 13: 56
1782 Thomas Wildey, founder of the Odd Fellows Society in the United States, born 11: 363
1791 Noah Noble, governor of Indiana, born 13: 267
1796 William Wagner, founder of the Wagner free institute of science, born 6: 280
1800 Moses Y. Beach, journalist, born 1: 307
1802 Charles Butler, lawyer and philanthropist, born 23: 356
1803 William S. Sullivant, botanist, born 8: 149
1811 Abby Kelly Foster, reformer, born 2: 323
1815 Naval battle between the "Endymion" and the "President" 4: 56
1821 Lafayette McLaws, Confederate soldier, born 4: 317
1821 Marshall Lefferts, electrician, president of the first American telegraph company, born 10: 243
1824 Cyrus M. Warren, chemist, born 10: 313
1830 Charter for Randolph-Macon college granted 13: 407
1833 George B. Roberts, railroad president, born 13: 335
1836 Constance F. Runcie, composer, founder of the first woman's club in the United States 7: 238
1836 Frances L. Mace, poet, born 10: 233
1841 Charles A. Briggs, theologian, tried for heresy, born 7: 318
1845 Ella Flagg Young, superintendent of public schools, born 19: 26
1854 John A. L. Waddell, civil engineer, born 12: 468
1859 Nathaniel L. Britton, botanist and director of the New York botanical garden, born 25: 88
1860 Benjamin W. Bacon, clergyman, distinguished for his Bible interpretations, born 23: 273
1861 Otis elevator patented 11: 120
1865 Ft. Fisher captured by the Federals 4: 69
1865 Ralph S. Tarr, geologist, born 10: 311
1866 Horatio W. Dresser, metaphysician, born 11: 110
1870 Pierre Samuel du Pont, of the famous family of explosives makers, born A: 97
1881 "Critic" magazine founded 8: 441
1881 John Rodgers, naval officer, who made the first flight to Hawaiian Islands, born 20: 425
1886 Presidential succession law passed 8: 245

JANUARY 16.

1713 Meshech Weare, first president of New Hampshire, born 13: 344
1752 George Cabot, merchant, senator and secretary of the navy under John Adams, born 2: 5
1782 Nicholas Longworth, pioneer of Cincinnati, Ohio, born 11: 339
1794 Isaac Newton, naval architect, born 5: 195
1800 William Henry Sparks, poet, born 5: 393
1807 Charles H. Davis, Federal naval officer, born 4: 166
1809 John H. Clifford, governor of Massachusetts, born 1: 116
1815 Henry W. Halleck, Federal soldier, born 4: 257
1822 George Fuller, artist, born 6: 475
1824 Peirce Crosby, Federal naval officer, born 10: 52
1824 Seymour J. Guy, artist, born 11: 301
1826 National Academy of Design organized 6: 246
1831 Edward Brooks, educator, born 2: 294
1833 James D. Smillie, engraver and painter, born 10: 367
1834 Henry Wood, "Emerson of the new metaphysical thought," born 19: 284
1836 Charles S. Smith, bridge engineer, born 3: 525
1839 William M. Gabb, paleontologist, born 4: 376
1845 Charles D. Sigsbee, naval officer, born 9: 2
1858 Henry W. Ranger, artist, born 15: 269
1858 Elwood Mead, irrigation engineer, born A: 528
1859 William Roscoe Thayer, poet and author, born 12: 530
1864 Frank Bacon, actor, born 20: 77
1868 Alvin Davison, biologist and bacteriologist, born 18: 381
1869 Alice Fischer, actress, born 13: 345
1879 William M. Jardine, secretary of agriculture under Coolidge, born A: 14
1928 President Coolidge opened the Pan-American conference in Havana 24: 5

JANUARY 17.

Thrift Week Begins on Franklin's birthday

1706 Benjamin Franklin, statesman and scientist, born 1: 328
1718 Israel Putnam, soldier, born 1: 87
1768 Smith Thompson, justice of the U. S. supreme court, born 6: 86
1771 Charles Brockden Brown, novelist, born 7: 59
1781 Battle of Cowpens, S. C. 1: 86
1781 Robert Hare, scientist, inventor of the calorimeter, born 5: 398
1796 Thaddeus Fairbanks, inventor of the platform scales, born 10: 300
1800 Anna M. T. Redfield, educator and author, born 2: 448
1800 Caleb Cushing, jurist and diplomat, born 4: 151
1803 Christopher G. Memminger, Confederate statesman and educator, born 4: 200
1811 George S. Houston, governor of Alabama and U. S. senator, born 10: 436
1814 James M. Stanley, artist, born 6: 467
1818 William R. Barbee, sculptor, born 18: 423
1820 James M. Hoppin, educator and clergyman, born 1: 245
1821 Ossian B. Hart, Florida jurist and governor, born 11: 380
1824 Hayward A. Harvey, inventor of a process of making steel, born 13: 63
1827 Samuel H. Pook, naval architect, early advocate of ironclads, born 4: 532
1832 Henry M. Baird, author and educator, born 8: 171
1834 Cyrus D. Foss, M. E. bishop and president of Wesleyan university, born 9: 430
1837 Richard H. Ward, microscopist, born 13: 149
1845 John A. Mitchell, editor and author, born 1: 405
1846 Don McD. Dickinson, postmaster-general under Cleveland, born 2: 410
1851 Arthur B. Frost, artist and illustrator, born 11: 289
1853 Alexander Harrison, artist, born 11: 300
1857 Marcus Benjamin, editor, born 10: 347
1865 Monitor "Patapsco" destroyed by a torpedo 4: 62
1886 Glenn L. Martin, aircraft manufacturer, born A: 324
1899 Robert M. Hutchins, president of the University of Chicago, born C: 54
1903 Department of commerce and labor created 13: 302
1917 The Danish West Indies passed to the sovereignty of the United States 20: 2

JANUARY 18.

1782 Daniel Webster, statesman and orator, born 3: 36
1789 Richard C. Taylor, geologist and mining engineer, born 9: 265
1799 Charles P. McIlvaine, P. E. bishop, born 7: 2
1799 Joseph Dixon, inventor of graphite lead pencils, born 22: 346
1802 Detroit (Mich.) incorporated as a city 5: 172
1813 George R. Graham, publisher, born 6: 277
1815 Richard Yates, congressman and governor of Illinois, born 11: 48
1816 Aaron D. Farmer, type founder, born 3: 309
1820 John R. Buchtel, manufacturer, and founder of Buchtel college, born 2: 496
1826 Charles T. Porter, engineer and inventor of the Porter steam governor, born 20: 494
1836 Union theological seminary organized 7: 316
1837 The "gag law" adopted by congress 6: 266
1844 Isaac L. Nicholson, P. E. bishop, born 11: 59
1844 Walter Satterlee, artist, born 13: 557
1849 James W. Graydon, engineer and inventor, born 13: 43
1850 Seth Low, president of Columbia university, and mayor of New York, born 6: 348
1852 Paul Carus, philosopher, born 14: 476
1856 John Hyatt Brewer, organist and composer, born 15: 364
1856 Willis L. Moore, meteorologist of the U. S. weather bureau, born 21: 84

1859 Frank J. Goodnow, president of Johns Hopkins university, born .... C: 19
1919 The peace conference after the World war convened at Paris 19: 9

JANUARY 19.

Holiday in Florida, Georgia, North Carolina, South Carolina and Virginia

1749 Isaiah Thomas, journalist and patriot, born 6: 264
1788 Albion K. Parris, Maine judge, senator, and governor, born 6: 306
1789 Pierre Chouteau, Missouri pioneer, born 13: 469
1795 William C. Bloss, abolitionist, born 12: 517
1799 Howard Malcolm, educator, born 12: 300
1803 Sarah Helen Whitman, poet, born 8: 145
1804 Matthew Richard, jurist, born 15: 53
1806 Ball Hughes, sculptor, born 8: 290
1807 Robert E. Lee, Confederate general, born 4: 95
1808 Nathaniel Hayward, rubber manufacturer and inventor, born 12: 120
1808 Lysander Spooner, lawyer and political economist, born 18: 419
1809 Edgar Allan Poe, poet, born 1: 463
1809 Duel between Humphrey Marshall and Henry Clay 2: 369
1823 Thomas R. Pynchon, president of Trinity college, born 3: 497
1834 William Watson, scientist and engineer, born .. 12: 124
1839 James M. Guffey, Pennsylvania oil merchant and capitalist, born 14: 243
1840 Lieut. Wilkes discovered the Antarctic continent 2: 105
1841 Samuel V. Essick, inventor of a printing telegraph, born 3: 323
1842 George Trumbull Ladd, psychologist, born 13: 81
1847 Rev. Josiah Strong, author and philosopher, born 9: 416
1848 Minor C. Keith, founder of the United Fruit Company's banana industry, born 22: 275
1851 David Starr Jordan, naturalist and president of Stanford university, born 22: 68
1853 Stephen M. White, California lawyer and senator, born 12: 509
1861 Georgia seceded from the Union 2: 67
1862 Battle of Mill Springs (Logan's Crossroads), Ky. 4: 48
1880 James G. Scrugham, governor of Nevada, born B: 423
1892 Patent issued for the modern trolley car system 13: 246

JANUARY 20.

1657 The Pettaquamscot (R. I.) purchase from the Indians 12: 384
1730 Alexander Garden, physician and naturalist, for whom the Gardenia flower was named, born 23: 361
1732 Richard Henry Lee, statesman, born 3: 159
1734 Robert Morris, financier, "Superintendent of Finance" during the Revolutionary war, born 2: 411
1776 The Georgia provincial congress organized 1: 219
1777 British troops defeated near Summit, N. J. 7: 517
1783 Armistice with Great Britain signed at Versailles 2: 3
1785 Treaty with Indians in Northwest Territory signed at Ft. Mackintosh 5: 430
1798 Anson Jones, Texas patriot and president of the republic, born 9: 67
1806 Nathaniel P. Willis, poet and journalist, born .. 3: 108
1812 Edouard Seguin, physician, born 15: 151
1814 David Wilmot, U. S. senator and author of the famous "Wilmot Proviso," born 3: 419
1815 Jedediah V. Huntington, author and clergyman, born 13: 525
1830 Henry A. Coit, clergyman and schoolmaster, born 9: 531
1834 George D. Robinson, Massachusetts congressman and governor, born 1: 124
1848 Frances Courtenay Baylor, author, born 1: 366
1850 Frank H. Peavey, capitalist, born 6: 44
1854 Thomas D. Boyd, educator, born 13: 236
1869 William S. Kendall, artist, born 13: 208
1882 Karl August Bickel, journalist, born .... C: 463
1884 Charles W. Whittlesey, lawyer, commanded the "Lost Battalion" in the World war, born 20: 396

JANUARY 21.

1736 Charles Nisbet, first president of Dickinson college, born 6: 462
1743 John Fitch, an inventor of the steamboat, born 6: 63
1745 Loammi Baldwin, civil engineer, born 10: 302
1757 Elijah Paine, jurist, born 8: 174
1786 Roberts Vaux, penologist, born 15: 210
1802 Francis E. Spinner, congressman and financier, born 12: 388
1806 Baltimore merchants presented a resolution to congress which led to the Embargo Act 9: 296
1809 Horace Binney, Jr., lawyer, born 10: 445
1813 John C. Fremont, soldier, called "The Pathfinder," born 4: 270
1815 Horace Wells, dentist, one of several discoverers of anaesthesia, born 6: 438
1815 Daniel C. McCallum, military engineer, born .. 7: 553
1815 John A. Bingham, jurist and legislator, born .. 9: 375
1821 John C. Breckinridge, vice-president of the United States, born 5: 3
1821 Mexico conceded the right to found an American colony in Texas 5: 157
1824 Thomas J. (Stonewall) Jackson, Confederate soldier, born 4: 125
1827 Thomas C. Fletcher, governor of Missouri, born 12: 306
1827 John Austin Stevens, author, born 13: 139
1828 James E. Rhoads, first president of Bryn Mawr college, born 13: 84
1839 Harry Wiard, inventor, born 22: 145
1842 James V. Blake, clergyman, poet and playwright, born 20: 283
1843 Edward Ford, a founder of the Pittsburgh Plate Glass Co., born 18: 312
1850 Jerome S. Ricard, meteorologist who discovered the relation of sun-spots to terrestrial weather, born 23: 69
1853 Helen H. Gardener, author, born 9: 451
1854 Erwin Frink Smith, botanist, a student of the pathology of plants, born 20: 273
1857 James Henry Morgan, president of Dickinson college, born .... B: 355
1857 Samuel W. Parr, metallurgist and chemist, born C: 153
1861 Southern members withdrew from congress 7: 200
1863 Gen. Fitz-John Porter dismissed from the army 4: 261
1865 Theodore Starrett, engineer in building construction, born 24: 41
1930 A world conference on naval armaments convened in London 23: 11

JANUARY 22.

1743 Timothy Dexter, Massachusetts merchant, born 6: 226
1758 Elkanah Watson, promoter of public works, born 5: 249
1786 John Delafield, New York banker, born 11: 28
1788 Cyrus Griffin, president of congress, born 5: 228
1791 Charles S. Todd, soldier and diplomat, born ... 1: 409
1798 Charles Davies, mathematician, born 3: 26
1799 John H. Lathrop, founder of the University of Missouri, born 5: 178
1802 Richard Upjohn, architect, born 2: 182
1804 Charles O'Conor, New York lawyer, born 3: 387
1813 The Raisin river massacre occurred 4: 61
1814 Edmund R. Peaslee, physician, born 10: 289
1816 Enos Stevens, meteorologist and inventor, born 11: 318
1821 John H. Taggart, founder of "Taggart's Times," born 5: 402
1832 Alonzo B. Cornell, governor of New York, born 3: 54
1832 George E. Belknap, naval officer; originator of new methods of deep sea soundings, born 4: 206
1838 George F. Wright, theologian and geologist, born 7: 66
1842 George F. Jelly, physician, born 15: 92
1843 Francis L. Patton, president of Princeton college, born 5: 468
1849 Terence V. Powderly, head of the Knights of Labor, born 8: 181
1852 Joshua W. Alexander, secretary of commerce under Wilson, born .... A: 51
1856 Walter Gay, artist, born 11: 296
1867 Benjamin O. Eggleston, artist, born 8: 424
1867 Forerunner of the caterpillar tractor patented .. 20: 229
1874 Leonard E. Dickson, mathematician, born 18: 411
1874 George P. Baldwin, electrical engineer, born ... 25: 13
1895 National Association of Manufacturers organized 12: 530
1903 The Panama canal treaty between the United States and Colombia signed 14: 5
1917 President Wilson proposed a League of Nations to the U. S. senate 19: 7
1932 Reconstruction Finance Corporation created ... C: 6

JANUARY 23.

1730 Joseph Hewes, signer of the Declaration of Independence, born 10: 139
1744 Josiah Quincy, lawyer and patriot, born 1: 19
1754 Amos Holbrook, physician, born 13: 184
1761 Richard Alsop, poet, born 4: 437
1765 Thomas Todd, Kentucky jurist, one of the "Hartford Wits," born 2: 467
1790 Samuel H. Turner, Hebraist, born 7: 192
1811 William Page, artist, born 11: 289
1812 Silas B. Cobb, pioneer capitalist, founder of Cobb Hall, University of Chicago, born 4: 547
1823 Stephen P. Quackenbush, naval officer, born ... 4: 62
1827 Charles L. Scott, diplomat, born 12: 210
1845 Thomas S. Perry, author and essayist, born ... 21: 91

1854 The Kansas-Nebraska bill introduced in the U. S. senate 2:430
1855 John M. Browning, inventor of firearms, born 20: 8
1862 Frank Shuman, inventor of wire-glass and "Safetee" glass, born 19:253
1865 Gen. Hood relieved of his command at his own request 4:265
1869 Josiah F. Willard (Josiah Flynt), author, born 13:366
1872 Holbrook Blinn, actor, born 21:220

JANUARY 24.

1733 Benjamin Lincoln, soldier, born 1: 62
1754 Andrew Ellicott, civil engineer, who surveyed and laid out Washington, D. C., born 13:470
1806 William Quarter, R. C. bishop, born 9: 78
1811 Henry Barnard, president of St. John's college, born 1:505
1820 Henry J. Raymond, founder of the New York "Times," born 8:482
1824 Catharine Merrill, Indiana educator, born 19:297
1828 Indiana college established 13:116
1829 William Mason, musician, born 7:423
1832 Joseph H. Choate, New York lawyer, born 9:159
1833 Joseph W. Drexel, Philadelphia banker and philanthropist, born 2:366
1834 Charles Henry Webb (John Paul), author, born 10: 42
1835 Charles Kendall Adams, educator, born 4:477
1836 Hugh S. Thompson, soldier and governor of South Carolina, born 12:179
1838 First demonstration of electric telegraph 4:449
1839 William W. Newell, scholar, born 21:163
1848 Gold discovered in California 5:146
1850 Mary N. Murfree (Charles Egbert Craddock), author, born 2:363
1851 George A. Gates, president of Iowa college, born 13: 80
1852 Max W. C. Vogrich, pianist and composer, born 8:448
1852 Robert Grant, judge and author, born C:431
1855 Charles H. Niehaus, sculptor, born 9: 57
1862 Edith Wharton, author, born ..... B: 32
1865 Paul W. Bartlett, sculptor, born 12:553
1865 Horace Howard Furness, Jr., Shakespearean scholar, born 23:205
1925 Total eclipse of the sun over Canada and northeastern United States 20:149

JANUARY 25.

St. Paul's Day

1614 Ezekiel Cheever, educator, born 12:439
1783 William Colgate, soap manufacturer, born 13:159
1785 First issue of the "Pennsylvania Herald" 6:278
1787 Springfield (Mass.) arsenal attacked in Shays's Rebellion 2:138
1795 Joel Parker, judge, born 12:113
1811 James E. Murdoch, actor, born 6: 71
1813 J. Marion Sims, physician and gynecologist, born 2:356
1819 University of Virginia established 5:446
1825 George E. Pickett, Confederate soldier, born 5: 49
1830 Robert Y. Hayne addressed congress in defense of state's rights 3:103
1830 Thomas W. Palmer, senator and diplomat, born 11:362
1835 Theodore F. Seward, musician, born 11:450
1837 First number of New Orleans "Picayune" appeared 12:289
1839 Selden Connor, Maine soldier and governor, born 6:316
1840 William C. De Witt, lawyer, born 11:331
1852 William M. Taggart, editor and proprietor of "Taggart's Times," born 5:403
1855 S. Newton Cutler, merchant, born 15:262
1859 Frank J. Cannon, U. S. senator, born 16:442
1860 Charles Curtis, vice-president of the United States, born ..... C: 7
1861 Louisiana passed an ordinance of secession 10: 78
1863 Gen. Burnside relieved by Gen. Hooker 4:177
1878 Ernst F. W. Alexanderson, electrical engineer and inventor, born ..... A: 30
1890 Louis Leopold Mann, clergyman, born D:319
1891 William C. Bullitt, ambassador to Russia, born.. D: 35
1909 White House conference on care of dependent children 22: 43
1915 New York-San Francisco telephone line opened to public 23: 36

JANUARY 26.

1782 Cornelius P. Van Ness, governor of Vermont, born 8:316
1790 William Capers, M. E. bishop, born 13:100
1799 Samuel G. Morton, physician and ethnologist, born 10:265
1810 Joseph R. Brown, inventor and manufacturer of sewing machines, born 10:395
1815 Arthur MacArthur, jurist and author, born 13:477
1818 Nicholas Pike, naturalist who brought the English sparrows to the United States, born 24:100
1824 Horace C. Wilcox, manufacturer, born 9:207
1826 Charles A. White, geologist, born 6:231
1832 George Shires, justice of the U. S. supreme court, born 2:477
1832 Rufus H. Gilbert, physician and originator of New York's elevated roads, born 11:388
1833 Grenville D. Wilson, composer, born 8:447
1833 Cornelius N. Bliss, merchant and secretary of the interior under McKinley, born 11: 15
1836 Lucius F. Hubbard, soldier and governor of Minnesota, born 10: 66
1837 Michigan admitted to the Union 5:271
1837 Daniel S. Tuttle, P. E. bishop, born 6: 58
1838 Joseph Cook, author and lecturer, born 2:260
1840 Hattie Tyng Griswold, author and poet, born .. 10:203
1846 Benjamin F. Keith, theatre proprietor, born 15:297
1847 John B. Clark, political economist, born 13: 48
1847 Paul Fuller, New York lawyer, born 16:380
1848 George T. Oliver, steel manufacturer, newspaper publisher and U. S. senator, born 22:286
1854 George F. Atkinson, botanist, born 13:478
1855 John Barton Payne, secretary of the interior under Wilson, and head of the American National Red Cross, born D:348
1859 Mabel O. Wright, author of nature books, born 12:545
1860 Harry M. Daugherty, attorney-general under Harding, born ..... A: 27
1861 Louisiana seceded from the Union 10: 78
1861 Frank O. Lowden, governor of Illinois, born 10:483
1862 Eliakim H. Moore, educator, born 12:447
1865 Louis A. Bauer, magnetician and authority on terrestrial magnetism, born 23:166
1869 Holley converter for making Bessemer steel patented 11:508
1877 Charles W. Sutton, consulting engineer to the Peruvian government, born 18:316
1880 Douglas MacArthur, soldier, born C:407
1884 Roy Chapman Andrews, zoologist and explorer, born A:302

JANUARY 27.

1738 Robert Yates, Revolutionary patriot and judge, born 5:260
1778 New Providence, Bahamas, attacked by American troops 8: 42
1785 Charter granted to the University of Georgia .. 9:178
1795 Eli Whitney Blake, inventor of the Blake stone-crusher, born 9:215
1800 James H. Otey, P. E. bishop, born 5:486
1811 Theodore Sedgwick, lawyer, diplomat, author, born 2:335
1824 David McK. Key, postmaster-general under Hayes, born 3:203
1824 First number of the Richmond "Virginia Whig" issued 7:545
1825 William Henry Green, Hebrew scholar, born .. 6:128
1826 Richard Taylor, soldier, born 4:331
1827 Charles F. Chickering, piano manufacturer and inventor, born 10: 48
1828 Cornelius C. Beekman, pioneer expressman and banker, born 17:192
1830 Webster delivered his famous speech in reply to Hayne 3: 36
1834 Lorenzo Crounze, governor of Nebraska, born.. 12: 3
1840 Rossiter Johnson, editor and author, born 2: 63
1847 Ella M. Glynes, actress, author and president of Sorosis, born 13: 68
1850 Samuel Gompers, president of the American Federation of Labor, born 11:539
1863 Ft. McAllister, Ga., bombarded in the Civil war 4:284
1868 First issue of the New York "Sun" under Charles A. Dana 1:308
1876 William Crocker, botanist and director of the Boyce Thompson institute for plant research, born D:330
1880 Edison received a patent for his incandescent lamp 25: 2

JANUARY 28.

1671 William Stephens, governor of Georgia, born .. 1:490
1754 John Wheelock, president of Dartmouth college, born 9: 86
1760 Mathew Carey, Philadelphia publisher, born ... 6:278
1779 William Tudor, author and editor of the "North American Review," born 8:351
1804 Elisha H. Allen, jurist and statesman, born 9: 32
1809 Richard V. Whelan, R. C. bishop, born 10:156
1811 Charles S. Boggs, Federal naval officer, born ... 2:106
1814 Henry N. Hudson, P. E. clergyman and author, born 9:490

1817 Alfred S. Barnes, publisher, born 4:378
1818 George S. Boutwell, Massachusetts governor and congressman, born 4:382
1820 Jersey City incorporated under its present name 13:471
1823 Robert C. Kedzie, chemist, born 10:162
1825 Amos Densmore, typewriter inventor, born 3:317
1826 Charles T. Porter, engineer who developed a high speed engine, born 20:494
1827 Coleman Sellers, engineer and inventor, born... 11: 53
1833 Horace C. Hovey, clergyman, author and geologist, born 12:545
1836 Joseph J. Lawrence, physician, born 12: 32
1838 Edward W. Morley, chemist, born 4:520
1838 James C. Watson, astronomer, born 7: 70
1841 Henry M. Stanley, explorer, born 4:253
1841 Edward Rosewater, journalist, born 13:323
1842 David S. Kellicott, entomologist, born 13:299
1843 Henry Carrington Bolton, chemist, born 10:404
1855 The Panama railroad was completed and the first locomotive ran from ocean to ocean 18:110
1857 Alexander Doyle, sculptor, born 10:371
1858 Herbert Adams, sculptor, born 13:510
1861 Senator Iverson of Georgia withdrew from the senate 4:438
1861 Daniel Willard, president of the Baltimore and Ohio railway, born 18: 8
1866 John M. Aldrich, entomologist, born A:254
1872 Augustus Lukeman, sculptor, born B:437
1915 First American ship sunk by Germany in the World war 21: 65

JANUARY 29.

1717 Jeffrey Amherst, governor of Virginia, born ... 1:101
1737 Thomas Paine, a free-thinker outlawed by England, born 5:412
1750 Joseph B. Varnum, soldier and statesman, born 1: 70
1754 Moses Cleveland, founder of Cleveland, Ohio, born 6:257
1756 Henry Lee (Light Horse Harry), soldier, born 3: 25
1761 Albert Gallatin, statesman and financier, born.. 3: 9
1792 Lemuel H. Arnold, governor of Rhode Island, born 9:395
1798 Basil Manly, educator, born 12:293
1799 Alexis Caswell, educator, born 8: 25
1801 Bartholomew F. Moore, lawyer and legislator, born 9:457
1802 Nathaniel J. Wyeth, explorer, born 6: 73
1817 William Ferrel, meteorologist and inventor of a tide prediction machine, born 9:241
1829 Frederick D. Tappen, financier, born 12:450
1834 James K. Hosmer, author and librarian, born .. 6:481
1834 John D. Champlin, author, born 8:357
1840 Henry H. Rogers, executive of the Standard Oil Co. and founder and president of the Amalgamated Copper Co., born 22: 66
1843 William McKinley, 25th president of the United States, born 11: 1
1845 Charles F. Crisp, congressman and speaker of the house, born 1:385
1845 Sarah C. Woolsey, author, born 11:352
1861 Kansas admitted to the Union 8:343
1863 Alfred C. Lane, geologist, born 13:395
1867 Sheridan Ford, art critic and journalist, born .. 19:451
1871 Philip P. Calvert, entomologist, born 12:335
1874 John D. Rockefeller, Jr., financier and philanthropist, born .... B: 21
1877 Congress appointed an electoral commission to decide the Hayes-Tilden presidential contest .. 3:194
1891 International League of Press Clubs organized 5: 38

JANUARY 30.

1744 Oziel Wilkinson, manufacturer, born 8:302
1754 John Lansing, chancellor of New York, born .. 4:254
1783 Treaty of Peace with Great Britain proclaimed by congress 1: 4
1792 John H. Hopkins, P. E. bishop, born 11:496
1797 Edwin V. Sumner, soldier, born 4:183
1797 John Fairfield, congressman, senator and four times governor of Maine, born 6:309
1799 Thomas C. Upham, metaphysician, born 13:171
1804 Henry Bronson, physician, who had the largest practice in New England in his day, born ... 22:266
1816 Nathaniel P. Banks, Federal soldier, Massachusetts governor and congressman, born 4:222
1818 William Butler, Methodist missionary, born 12: 61
1831 John M. Maisch, pharmacist, born 5:348
1836 Joseph W. Keifer, Federal soldier and congressman, born 4:389
1839 Samuel C. Armstrong, soldier and founder of Hampton (Va.) institute, born 1:436
1841 George A. Townsend (Gath), author and war correspondent, born 1:154
1847 The name Yerba Buena officially changed to that of San Francisco 13: 53
1851 Jacob McG. Dickinson, lawyer, secretary of state under Taft, born 14:410
1853 William M. Salter, Ethical Culture lecturer and philosopher, born 24:395
1862 The ironclad "Monitor' launched 4:181
1862 Walter Damrosch, musician; director of the Oratorio and Symphony societies, born ...... C: 57
1863 Joseph Jastrow, psychologist, born 11:373
1864 Ernst Freund, legal scholar and educator, born .. 26: 98
1865 Gen. Pope took command of the Department of the Missouri 4:282
1866 Gelett Burgess, author, born 14:144
1882 Franklin D. Roosevelt, President of the United States, born .... D: 1
1900 Governor Goebel of Kentucky assassinated 13: 13
1934 Gold reserve act signed by the President .... D: 6

JANUARY 31.

1585 Peter Bulkley, clergyman and founder of Concord, Mass. 7:486
1640 Samuel Willard, clergyman and president of Harvard, born 6:413
1734 Robert Morris, financier, born 2:411
1752 Gouverneur Morris, statesman, born 2:526
1774 Thomas W. Veazey, governor of Maryland, born 9:303
1793 Hamilton Oneida academy (later Hamilton college) chartered 7:404
1796 Nathaniel Jocelyn, artist, engraver, and a founder of the American Bank Note Co., born 25:419
1812 John R. Tucker, Confederate naval officer, born 4:334
1812 William H. Russell, founder of the Pony Express, born 20:451
1814 Henry W. Sage, philanthropist, born 4:478
1820 William B. Washburn, governor of Massachusetts and congressman, born 1:120
1826 Daniel F. Appleton, founder of the Waltham Watch Company, born 11:417
1830 James G. Blaine, statesman, born 1:137
1831 Rudolph Wurlitzer, manufacturer of musical instruments, born 16:423
1835 Jeremiah E. Tracy, New York lawyer, born .. 21:192
1843 Edward Kemeys, sculptor, born 8:279
1845 John H. Boner, poet, born 2:497
1848 Nathan Straus, merchant, philanthropist, and a partner in R. H. Macy & Company, born 22: 46
1849 Francis D. Clarke, teacher of the deaf, born ... 22:155
1854 William H. Sherwood, pianist and composer, born 9:385
1855 William A. Coffin, artist, born 6:368
1857 Charles B. Cory, ornithologist, born 13:225
1857 George B. Francis, civil engineer, born 16:276
1860 James G. Huneker, musician, author, critic, born 14: 44
1862 Companion of Sirius discovered by Alvan Clark, Jr. 5:386
1862 Curtis H. Veeder, mechanical engineer and inventor, born C:373
1862 George W. Perkins, financier, born 15: 33
1866 William W. Atterbury, railway expert in charge of transportation during the World war, born 26:105
1868 Theodore W. Richards, chemist and Nobel prize winner, born 12:362
1869 Irving L. Lenroot, U. S. senator, born B:184
1872 Zane Grey, author, born B:114
1872 Rupert Hughes, author, born C:314
1889 Hans F. Schoenfeld, diplomat, born A:129
1893 Mt. Holyoke seminary became a college 4:463
1924 The U. S. senate instructed President Coolidge to bring court action to cancel Doheny and Sinclair oil land leases in California and Wyoming 24: 2

FEBRUARY 1.

1733 English colonists under Oglethorpe settled in Georgia 1:490
1780 David Porter, naval officer, born 2: 98
1781 Battle of Cowan's Ford, N. C. 1: 80
1800 Naval battle between the "Constellation" and "La Vengeance" 2:432
1801 Titus Coan, missionary to Hawaii, born 2:339
1801 Thomas Cole, artist, a painter of historical landscapes, born 7:462
1808 Edmund Quincy, abolitionist, born 6: 93
1815 Jonas G. Clark, merchant and founder of Clark university, born 9:203
1820 George H. Houghton, clergyman, born 6: 16
1820 Horace C. Johnson, artist, born 12:183
1822 Homer C. Blake, naval officer, born 4:208
1825 Francis J. Child, philologist, born 8:256
1828 George F. Edmunds, U. S. senator, born 2:384
1830 James F. Cox, underwriter and originator of a system of individual underwriting, born ... 4: 95
1838 Joseph Keppler, artist and caricaturist, one of the founders of the magazine "Puck," born 2:225
1839 James A. Herne, actor and playwright, born .. 5: 83

1844 G. Stanley Hall, psychologist and first president of Clark university, born 9:203
1844 Frederick A. Smith, jurist, born 19: 49
1859 Oregon admitted to the Union 8: 4
1859 Victor Herbert, violoncellist and composer, born 22: 23
1861 Texas seceded from the Union 2: 67
1869 William J. Homer, penologist, born 18: 49
1872 George L. Wallace, mental hygienist, born 26:102
1894 Gardner Hale, author, born 23: 80
1899 Rear-Adm. Taussig took possession of Guam in the name of the United States 24: 25

FEBRUARY 2.

Candlemas Day

1651 Sir William Phips, colonial governor of Massachusetts, born 6: 97
1794 William A. Otis, Ohio financier, born 26:107
1802 Moncure Robinson, civil engineer, born 8:456
1803 Albert Sidney Johnston, Confederate soldier, born 1:388
1809 George Engelmann, physician and botanist, born 6: 87
1811 Delia S. Bacon, author, born 1:477
1814 George Loring Brown, artist, born 7:466
1825 John C. Dalton, physiologist, born 10:500
1843 Knute Nelson, Minnesota governor, congressman and senator, born 19: 18
1848 Treaty of Guadaloupe Hidalgo between the United States and Mexico signed 6:267
1850 Isaac L. Rice, editor of "Forum," and chess expert, born 11:447
1854 Philadelphia obtained a new charter enlarging her boundaries 10:413
1858 A patent issued for Arctic gaiters 10:406
1860 Curtis Guild, Jr., governor of Massachusetts, born 14:454
1861 Josiah D. Dort, carriage manufacturer and founder of the Dort automobile business, born 17:232
1865 Stephen B. Weeks, historian and bibliographer, born 10: 89
1869 Smith W. Brookhart, U. S. senator, born B:276
1861 Solomon R. Guggenheim, industrialist, born ... 12: 85
1870 Walker D. Hines, director-general of railroads in the World war, born 24: 30
1881 The Christian Endeavor Society organized 13: 52
1886 William Rose Benét, poet, born A:214

FEBRUARY 3.

1717 Nicholas Cooke, first state governor of Rhode Island, born 9:391
1779 British defeated on Port Royal island, S. C. 1: 96
1799 Capt. Barry sank the "Amour de la Patrie" .. 4:189
1799 Francis Thomas, Maryland congressman and governor, born 9:304
1802 William G. Harrison, president of the B. & O. railroad, born 18: 2
1807 Joseph E. Johnston, Confederate soldier, born 5:328
1807 Joseph C. Neal, humorist, born 6: 29
1809 Territory of Illinois created 11: 42
1811 Horace Greeley, journalist, born 3:448
1815 Hiram Orcutt, educator, born 7:129
1819 Amelia B. C. Welby, poet, born 6:503
1820 Elisha Kent Kane, scientist and explorer, born 3:288
1821 Elizabeth Blackwell, pioneer woman physician and woman suffrage advocate, born 9:123
1823 Spencer F. Baird, naturalist, born 3:405
1823 Timothy Alden, inventor, born 12:276
1824 George T. Anderson, Confederate soldier, born .. 13:247
1830 Randolph-Macon college founded 13:407
1831 Ogden N. Rood, scientist and inventor, born .. 13:507
1842 Sidney Lanier, Southern poet, born 2:438
1844 Tolbert Lanston, inventor of a type-setting machine, born 13:573
1846 Judson Harmon, U. S. attorney-general under Cleveland and governor of Ohio, born 13:279
1851 Charles A. L. Totten, soldier and author, born . 10:237
1853 Hudson Maxim, inventor of explosives, born .. 13:520
1863 Battle of Ft. Donelson, Tenn. 4:486
1865 Battle of Salkahatchie, S. C. 1:147
1865 Peace Conference met at Hampton Roads, Va.. 2: 74
1870 Joseph H. Pratt, geologist, born C:373
1872 Alexander Meiklejohn, president of Amherst college, born A:406
1873 John Howland, physician, born 21:392
1900 International Sunshine Society incorporated ... 22: 52
1917 Diplomatic relations with Germany severed 19: 7

FEBRUARY 4.

1697 James Franklin, printer, brother of Benjamin Franklin, born 8: 17
1755 John Lacey, soldier, born 1:128
1770 William Jarvis, merchant and diplomat, born .. 12: 64
1792 James G. Birney, statesman, born 2:312
1772 Josiah Quincy, orator, statesman and president of Harvard college, born 6:417
1802 Mark Hopkins, president of Williams college, born 6:237
1828 Frederick C. Withers, architect, born 2:165
1831 Oliver Ames, manufacturer and governor of Massachusetts, born 1:124
1833 George H. Hepworth, clergyman and journalist, born 4:320
1834 Thomas Hall, typewriter inventor, born 3:323
1840 John H. Galey, pioneer oil producer, born 18: 18
1847 Charles H. Hart, art critic and expert on historical portraits, born 18:148
1848 Francis W. Ayer, advertising expert, born 20:154
1852 John Henry Wright, philologist, born 8: 48
1861 A peace congress met in Washington 3:526
1861 Southern Confederacy formed at Montgomery, Ala. 4:149
1870 John Mitchell, president of the United Mine Workers of America, born 24:334
1884 Chicago manual training school opened 20:174
1887 Inter-state commerce commission established .. 11: 50
1899 Insurrection in the Philippine islands began .. 9: 30
1902 Charles A. Lindbergh, aviator, born .... B: 34

FEBRUARY 5.

1725 James Otis, orator and statesman, born 1: 17
1782 William Miller, founder of the Adventists, or "Millerites," born 6:542
1785 William Taylor Barry, postmaster-general under Jackson, born 5:296
1807 Frederick C. Havemeyer, sugar manufacturer, born 13:451
1810 Ole B. Bull, violinist, born 4:234
1824 The Franklin institute of Pennsylvania organized 12:507
1830 John Henry Harjes, head of Morgan, Harjes & Co., American bankers in Paris, born 19:262
1833 George D. B. Pepper, educator, born 8:407
1837 The hot blast first successfully used in iron making 3:360
1837 Dwight L. Moody, evangelist, born 7:244
1837 Leffert L. Buck, civil engineer, born 10:115
1837 Edward E. Poor, banker, born 14:224
1837 Edward M. Gallaudet, founder of the first college for deaf-mutes in the world, born 18:128
1838 Abraham J. Ryan, R. C. clergyman and poet, born 5:411
1840 Hiram S. Maxim, inventor of improvements in electric lamps, a machine gun, smokeless powder and an aeroplane, born 6: 36
1840 Simeon E. Baldwin, Connecticut lawyer, judge and governor, born 21: 86
1843 Charles B. Calvert, legislator, born 16:232
1844 Samuel I. Curtiss, theologian, born 13:395
1847 Samuel T. Wellman, mechanical engineer, born 13: 37
1850 Famous Compromise bill introduced in congress 5: 80
1862 Jesse D. Bright of Indiana expelled from the senate 3:428
1865 Harvey W. Loomis, composer of nearly 1000 songs, born 22: 83
1866 Rossetter G. Cole, musician, born 18:281
1872 Lafayette B. Mendel, chemist, discoverer of Vitamin A, born 26:424
1873 Maxine Elliot, actress, born 14: 87

FEBRUARY 6.

1682 La Salle began his descent of the Mississippi river 5:125
1733 James Duane, mayor of New York city, born .. 2:489
1752 James Winchester, soldier and founder of Memphis, Tenn., born 4: 60
1756 Aaron Burr, vice-president of the United States, born 3: 5
1778 Treaty of alliance made with France 12:357
1799 Henry J. Anderson, educator, born 6:389
1806 Sailor's Snug Harbor, Staten Island, incorporated 11:253
1807 Hiram Sibley, financier, first president of the Western Union Telegraph Co., born 4:454
1813 Joseph R. Anderson, Confederate officer and iron manufacturer, born 12:423
1814 Henry T. Cheever, clergyman and author, born 13:483
1818 William M. Evarts, lawyer and statesman, born 3:197
1819 Duel between Senator Mason and John McCarty 4:550
1826 Joseph Winlock, astronomer, born 9:266
1826 Thomas Durfee, jurist, born 12:251
1832 John B. Gordon, soldier, U. S. senator, governor of Georgia, born 1:231
1833 James E. B. Stuart, Confederate general, born 4: 51
1837 Thomas O. Selfridge, Jr., naval officer, born .. 7:552
1841 Arthur Amory, New York merchant, born 12:451

1842	Frank Beard, artist, originator of "chalk talks," born	13:245
1844	Daniel O'Day, manufacturer, born	14:175
1847	Henry J. Hardenbergh, architect, born	11:329
1857	Ernest Flagg, architect, born	B:333
1858	Jonathan P. Dolliver, lawyer and U. S. senator, born	12:392
1862	Capture of Ft. Henry, Tenn., by Federal gunboats	5: 11
1864	George J. Gould, financier and railroad president, born	13:522
1865	Charles W. Wallace, Shakespearean scholar, born	23:160
1868	George A. Dorsey, anthropologist, born	22:200
1878	Walter B. Pitkin, psychologist, a founder of the "New Realism," born	D: 42
1895	Robert M. LaFollette, Jr., U. S. senator, born	C:351

FEBRUARY 7.

1746	Benjamin Ogle, governor of Maryland, born	9:295
1749	Benjamin Randall, Baptist clergyman, born	4:345
1752	Samuel Phillips, Massachusetts judge and legislator, founder of Phillips academy at Andover, born	10: 93
1763	St. John Honeywood, lawyer and poet, born	9:156
1777	John Pickering, linguist and philologist, born	7:294
1779	Eli Ives, physician, born	12:253
1782	William J. Lowndes, congressman, born	13:195
1794	John W. Osborn, journalist and temperance reformer, born	18:293
1804	John Deere, plow inventor and manufacturer, born	20: 63
1806	Charles Fenno Hoffman, author and poet, born	8:379
1811	Abiel Abbot Low, New York merchant, born	1:500
1814	George P. Putnam, publisher, born	2:388
1815	Noadiah M. Hill, linguist, master of fifty languages and dialects, born	1:397
1820	John J. Brown, educator, born	2:141
1820	First provisional legislature of Arkansas met	10:183
1821	John B. Cornell, manufacturer and inventor, born	13:156
1827	Richard W. Johnson, Federal soldier, born	15:391
1833	Jacob M. Da Costa, physician, born	9:342
1837	Duel between Felix Huston and Gen. Johnston	1:388
1841	Meeting of western pioneers to organize a territorial government in Oregon	25:310
1850	J. B. Francis Herreshoff, chemist, born	24: 96
1854	Francis Wilson, actor, born	2:134
1854	Robert B. Mantell, actor, born	14:290
1874	Louis A. Fuertes, artist and naturalist, born	21: 69
1885	Sinclair Lewis, author, born	B:202
1911	Arizona constitution ratified by the people	C: 41

FEBRUARY 8.

1690	Schenectady, N. Y. burned, and the inhabitants massacred by French and Indians	5:121
1754	Isaac Tichenor, Vermont jurist and governor, born	8:313
1791	First United States Bank incorporated	10:512
1802	James W. Webb, journalist and diplomat, born	3: 30
1811	Edwin D. Morgan, merchant and governor of New York, born	3: 51
1813	Andrew G. Magrath, governor of South Carolina, born	12:174
1817	John M. Wieting, physician, born	2:417
1817	Richard S. Ewell, Confederate soldier, born	4: 55
1818	Austin Blair, governor of Michigan, born	5:273
1819	Leander J. McCormick, manufacturer, born	1:361
1820	William T. Sherman, Federal soldier, born	4: 32
1822	Thomas Pattison, naval officer, first American officer to enter Tokio, born	4:155
1822	Joseph Albert Lintner, entomologist, born	5:260
1827	James M. Watson, author of textbooks, born	10:194
1828	Oliver Bell Bunce, author, born	2:512
1831	Joseph A. Wheelock, journalist, born	13:168
1833	Launt Thompson, sculptor, born	8:283
1844	Richard Watson Gilder, author and editor, born	1:312
1844	Samuel Parsons, landscape architect, born	26:308
1860	Rush Rhees, president of the University of Rochester, born	12:245
1861	Arkansas troops seized Ft. Smith and the United States arsenal at Little Rock	4:386
1861	Ward Leonard, electrical engineer and inventor, born	15: 3
1862	Roanoke island taken by Federals	4: 53
1865	John M. Schofield placed in command of the department of North Carolina	4:260
1867	Peabody Education Fund created	5:336
1880	Patent issued to Hammond for a typewriter	3:321
1898	Patent issued for the universal envelope machine	13: 23

FEBRUARY 9.

1739	William Bartram, botanist and ornithologist, born	7:154
1748	Luther Martin, Maryland lawyer, born	3:431
1768	William King, first governor of Maine, born	6:305
1769	Samuel Thomson, originator of the Thomsonian system of medicine, born	6: 70
1773	William H. Harrison, 9th President of the United States, born	3: 33
1796	First bank in Delaware incorporated	11:530
1799	"L'Insurgent" captured by the frigate "Constellation"	2:432
1814	Samuel J. Tilden, governor of New York, born	3: 53
1815	Richard H. Rousseau, lawyer and diplomat, born	12:185
1820	Moses G. Farmer, electrician and inventor, born	7:361
1822	James Parton, author and biographer, born	1:391
1826	Samuel Bowles, journalist, founder of the "Springfield (Mass.) Republican," born	1:317
1826	John A. Logan, Federal soldier and U. S. senator, born	4:298
1827	William D. Whitney, philologist, born	2:340
1835	Samuel Johnston, inventor of improved reaping machines, born	13:132
1836	Franklin B. Gowen, lawyer and railroad president, born	13:375
1839	Addison E. Verrill, zoologist, born	21: 52
1840	William T. Sampson, naval officer, born	9: 9
1843	Nathan Goff, Jr., secretary of the navy under Hayes, born	3:202
1849	William G. Hale, educator, whose fame as a Latanist was international, born	23: 80
1851	Daniel S. Lamont, journalist, born	3: 58
1854	Charles A. Ashburner, geologist, born	11: 54
1861	Arthur P. Davis, irrigation engineer, the first to propose the Boulder Dam, born	24:116
1864	Famous escape of federal prisoners from Libby prison	4:466
1865	Robert E. Lee made commander-in-chief of Confederate forces	4:100
1866	George Ade, author and journalist, born	C:386
1870	U. S. weather bureau established	4:216
1874	Amy Lowell, poet and critic, born	19:407

FEBRUARY 10.

1676	Mrs. Rowlandson captured by Indians	8:371
1676	Lancaster, Mass., attacked by King Philip	10: 50
1763	Treaty of Paris signed, ceding Canada, Louisianna (east of the Mississippi) and West Florida to England	10: 73
1766	Benjamin S. Barton, physician and botanist, born	8:377
1769	Thomas Worthington, governor of Ohio, born	3:138
1802	Albert G. Greene, jurist and poet, born	9:501
1807	Theodore S. Fay, author and minister to Switzerland, born	7:475
1808	John E. Thomson, president of the Pennsylvania railroad, born	13:334
1810	Joel T. Hart, sculptor, born	6:514
1810	Buffalo, N. Y., incorporated by the legislature	13:471
1817	Henry N. Guernsey, a pioneer homeopathic physician, born	3:479
1818	Isham G. Harris, Tennessee senator and governor, born	2:209
1819	Frederick B. Conway, actor, born	7:265
1824	John C. Bullitt, lawyer, "father of Greater Philadelphia," born	22:422
1827	Edward Atkinson, economist, born	9:416
1836	Augustus P. Cooke, naval officer, born	6:379
1837	Harrison G. Otis, soldier and journalist, born	12:187
1846	Ira Remsen, chemist and president of Johns Hopkins university, born	9:240
1858	W. Clark Noble, sculptor, born	A:454
1861	Frederic M. Dey, author, who continued the famous "Nick Carter" stories, born	26:178
1862	Naval battle off the coast of North Carolina	2:101
1863	Hugh Campbell Wallace, financier, ambassador to France, born	B:147
1868	William Allen White, author and editor, born	B:433
1880	Jesse G. Vincent, mechanical engineer, co-designer of the Liberty motor for aircraft, born	A:112

FEBRUARY 11.

1735	Daniel Boone, Kentucky pioneer, born	3:110
1753	Jonas Galusha, governor of Vermont, born	8:314
1776	Governor Wright, of Georgia, escaped from the patriots	1:492
1802	Lydia M. Child, author and philanthropist, born	2:324
1802	James B. Rogers, chemist, born	8:151
1811	Benjamin F. Sands, Federal naval officer, born	4:295
1812	Alexander H. Stephens, statesman, vice-president of the southern Confederacy, born	3:420

1812 Joseh P. B. Wilmer, P. E. bishop, born 11: 342
1821 John Ross Browne, author and diplomat, born 8: 117
1822 Theodore O'Hara, Louisiana soldier and poet, born 4: 362
1824 William H. Ruffner, geologist and educator, born 12: 526
1831 John M. Walden, M. E. bishop, born 12: 496
1833 Melville W. Fuller, chief-justice of the U. S. supreme court, born 1: 31
1836 Washington Gladden, clergyman and author, born 10: 256
1839 Josiah W. Gibbs, chemist, born 4: 543
1840 Samuel D. Greene, naval officer, born 2: 107
1844 Alexander Herrmann, prestidigitator, born 9: 327
1844 Frederick A. Smith, Chicago jurist, born 19: 49
1845 Alexander M. Dockery, governor of Missouri, born 20: 44
1847 Thomas A. Edison, inventor, born 25: 1
1851 Franklin W. Hooper, director of the Brooklyn Institute of Arts and Sciences, born 13: 46
1854 Benjamin O. Peirce, mathematician and physicist, born 20: 366
1899 The American flag raised at Iloilo, P. I. 9: 31
1903 The Alaska boundary treaty ratified by the United States 14: 7

FEBRUARY 12.

Lincoln's birthday celebrated

1606 John Winthrop, governor of Connecticut, born .. 10: 321
1663 Cotton Mather, clergyman, born 4: 232
1746 Thaddeus Kosciuszko, Polish general, and aide-de-camp to Washington, born 1: 54
1765 John C. Smith, congressman and governor of Connecticut, born 10: 332
1785 Alden Partridge, founder of several military schools including Norwich university, born .. 18: 322
1791 Peter Cooper, merchant and philanthropist, born 3: 114
1796 Henry Dutton, jurist and professor of law at Yale, born 10: 338
1804 Elizur Wright, reformer and mathematician, born 2: 317
1804 William F. Havemeyer, sugar manufacturer, born 17: 28
1809 Abraham Lincoln, 16th president of the United States, born 2: 65
1810 William M. Roberts, civil engineer, born 13: 254
1813 Benson J. Lossing, author, artist and historian, born 4: 324
1813 James Dwight Dana, geologist and mineralogist, born 6: 206
1815 Martin B. Anderson, president of Rochester university, born 12: 243
1816 Alexander G. Cattell, U. S. senator, born 2: 35
1819 William W. Story, sculptor and poet, born 5: 417
1831 Myra Bradwell, pioneer woman lawyer, born 2: 137
1833 Henry Clay introduced his compromise tariff bill in congress 5: 79
1838 Alfred C. Howland, artist, born 7: 470
1850 William M. Davis, physiographer, world authority on physical geography, born 24: 32
1852 Frank W. Very, astronomer, born 12: 49
1855 George Cary Comstock, astronomer, born 12: 454

FEBRUARY 13.

1760 Samuel W. Dana, lawyer and U. S. senator, born 2: 10
1776 James Wilson proposed separation from Great Britain 1: 23
1776 Battle of Moore's Creek, N. C. 10: 246
1780 Lewis D. von Schweinitz, botanist, an early student of American fungi, born 8: 380
1795 University of North Carolina opened 13: 242
1799 Henry Grinnell, merchant, born 3: 281
1800 Orange Scott, clergyman, organizer of the Wesleyan Methodist church in the United States, born 2: 315
1805 David Dudley Field, jurist and author, born .. 4: 236
1812 Samuel P. Lee, Federal naval officer, born 11: 55
1825 Julia C. R. Dorr, poet and author, born 6: 56
1827 Benjamin S. Hedrick, anti-slavery leader, born 9: 127
1831 John A. Rawlins, soldier and secretary of war under Grant, born 4: 218
1838 Charles Barnard, author and dramatist, born .. 13: 64
1840 Alexis A. Julien, geologist, born 18: 40
1849 Frederick A. Ober, author and traveller, born .. 13: 311
1850 Isaac Henderson, author, born 5: 426
1851 George Brown Goode, ichthyologist, born 3: 408
1851 Act establishing the University of Minnesota passed 13: 328
1861 Charles C. Curran, artist, born 13: 364
1862 Assault on Ft. Donelson, Tenn., began 4: 3
1863 Rodman Wanamaker, merchant, born 21: 27
1864 Edwin H. P. Arden, actor, born 20: 61
1865 Dugald C. Jackson, electrical engineer, born .. B: 357
1870 Joseph C. Lincoln, author, born .... C: 449
1883 Robert Y. Stuart, chief of the U. S. forest service, born 25: 156

FEBRUARY 14.

St. Valentine's Day

1693 William and Mary-college chartered 3: 231
1748 Samuel Osgood, first postmaster general, born .. 1: 18
1754 James Thacher, physician and author, born .. 7: 401
1766 Louis G. V. Dubourg, R. C. bishop, born 4: 435
1766 William Coleman, journalist, born 11: 350
1778 United States flag first seen in foreign lands and saluted 2: 15
1779 Battle of Kettle Creek, Ga. 1: 70
1786 James Appleton, "father of Prohibition," born 11: 417
1791 Primogeniture abolished in South Carolina 12: 162
1792 William Goodell, missionary, born 5: 198
1798 Henry S. Potter, financier, born 12: 396
1800 Emory Washburn, governor of Massachusetts, born 1: 116
1809 George Geddes, engineer, born 10: 170
1811 Cyrus Wakefield, manufacturer, born 12: 125
1812 Columbus became the capital of Ohio 12: 440
1819 Christopher L. Sholes, "father of the Typewriter," born 3: 315
1820 James M. Walker, president of the Chicago, Burlington and Quincy railroad, born 15: 381
1822 James H. McVicker, theatrical manager, born .. 6: 281
1824 Winfield S. Hancock, Federal soldier, born 4: 134
1833 William W. Folwell, educator, born 13: 328
1838 Edwin Ginn, Boston publisher, born 10: 481
1839 Julia G. Scott, president of the Daughters of the American Revolution, born 20: 306
1842 Juliet Corson, originator of cooking schools, born 8: 453
1847 Anna Howard Shaw, reformer, born 14: 456
1858 Carl Marr, artist, born 11: 293
1859 Oregon admitted to the Union 8: 4
1859 George W. G. Ferris, engineer who built the Ferris wheel at the World's Columbian exposition, born 13: 39
1864 Gainesville, Fla., captured by Federals 4: 55
1876 Elisha Gray and Alexander Graham Bell both patented a speaking telephone ... 4: 454 and 6: 221
1882 George Jean Nathan, editor, author and critic, born .... C: 108
1912 Arizona admitted to the Union 26: 96

FEBRUARY 15.

1726 Abraham Clark, signer of the Declaration of Independence, born 3: 302
1764 St. Louis, Mo., founded by the French 13: 468
1797 Henry E. Steinway, piano manufacturer, born 2: 513
1797 John Bell, secretary of war under Harrison, born 3: 39
1802 Charles Butler, New York philanthropist, born 23: 356
1809 Cyrus Hall McCormick, manufacturer of reaping machines, born 21: 78
1812 Charles L. Tiffany, jeweller, born 2: 57
1812 Stephen T. Olney, botanist, born 13: 35
1814 Joseph H. Williams, lawyer, abolitionist and governor of Maine, born 6: 312
1815 Rufus W. Griswold, editor and author, born 4: 74
1820 Susan B. Anthony, reformer, born 4: 403
1822 Henry B. Whipple, P. E. bishop, born 4: 58
1822 William F. Phelps, educator, born 12: 480
1825 Carter H. Harrison, mayor of Chicago, born .. 10: 144
1829 S. Weir Mitchell, physician and author, born .. 9: 346
1832 Nelson Dingley, Jr., governor of Maine and U. S. senator, born 6: 315
1832 William E. Dodge, merchant, born 13: 352
1837 Knox college chartered 24: 26
1842 Russel H. Conwell, clergyman, founder of Temple college, born 3: 29
1845 Elihu Root, lawyer and statesman, born 26: 1
1848 Americans clashed with Mexicans at San José .. 5: 50
1848 Charles B. Brush, civil engineer, born 9: 33
1852 Peter S. Grosscup, judge, born 15: 253
1858 John J. Montgomery, scientist and inventor, co-experimenter with the Wright brothers in aviation, born 15: 338
1858 Marcella Sembrich, singer, born 25: 69
1858 William Henry Pickering, astronomer, born .... B: 325
1863 James A. Farrell, president of the United States Steel Corporation, born .... D: 66
1880 Joseph Hergesheimer, author, born .... B: 56
1882 John Barrymore, actor, born .... B: 497
1898 Battleship "Maine" destroyed by an explosion in Havana harbor, 260 lives lost 9: 2

FEBRUARY 16.

1621 Samoset, Indian chief, visited the Plymouth colony with the greeting "Welcome, Englishmen" 7: 367
1724 Christopher Gadsden, merchant and revolutionary patriot, born 1: 76
1729 Edward Shippen, Pennsylvania jurist, born 10: 385
1746 Isaac Collins, printer and publisher, born 19: 190
1799 Chauncey F. Cleveland, governor of Connecticut, born 10: 335
1802 Phineas P. Quimby, pioneer practicioner of mental science, born 11: 539
1804 The "Philadelphia" destroyed in Tripoli harbor 4: 56
1809 John J. Gilchrist, jurist, born 7: 508
1812 Henry Wilson, vice-president of the United States, born 4: 13
1820 Franklin W. Fisk, theologian and educator, born 11: 97
1829 Sarah A. Dorsey, author, born 3: 213
1838 Henry Adams, educator and historian, born 11: 475
1838 Robert F. Weir, New York surgeon, born 12: 377
1839 George E. Bissell, sculptor, born 8: 278
1840 Henry Watterson, editor of the Louisville "Courier-Journal," born 1: 468
1843 Rudolph Blankenburg, reform mayor of Philadelphia, born 17: 226
1845 George Kennan, journalist and author, born 1: 393
1856 Charles T. Main, engineer and architect, born 15: 327
1858 Worthington C. Ford, statistician, born 13: 105
1858 Charles E. Scribner, electrical inventor, born 13: 192
1860 Carl Venth, composer, born 18: 175
1861 Thomas S. Foster, merchant, born 15: 395
1862 Surrender of Ft. Donelson, Tenn. 6: 38
1887 American Newspaper Publishers' Association organized 22: 51
1898 Katharine Cornell, actress, born D: 437

FEBRUARY 17.

1718 Matthew Tilgham, patriot, born 1: 523
1740 John Sullivan, soldier, born 1: 56
1755 Thomas Truxtun, naval officer, born 2: 431
1756 Andrew Kirkpatrick, New Jersey jurist, born 12: 241
1770 David Stone, governor of North Carolina and U. S. senator, born 4: 421
1804 Uriah A. Boyden, engineer and inventor, born 11: 88
1806 Enoch C. Wines, penologist, born 1: 180
1807 William L. Dayton, U. S. senator and minister to France, born 4: 325
1816 Timothy O. Howe, U. S. senator and postmaster general under President Arthur, born 4: 252
1824 William F. Smith, Federal soldier and engineer, born 7: 518
1827 Rose Terry Cooke, author, born 6: 300
1828 Franklin Farrel, inventor and manufacturer, born 24: 97
1833 John Englis, Jr., New York steamboat builder, born 16: 347
1839 John N. Galleher, P. E. bishop, born 11: 342
1844 Montgomery Ward, mail order merchant, born 13: 38
1845 Charles McBurney, surgeon, born 14: 315
1855 Hubert Vos, artist, born 25: 52
1856 Frederic E. Ives, inventor of the half-tone plate and the photochromoscope system of color photography, born 15: 77
1857 Samuel S. McClure, organizer of the first newspaper syndicate, born 12: 45
1863 Gen. E. Kirby Smith assumed command of the Trans-Mississippi department 8: 133
1865 Surrender of Columbia, S. C. 4: 34
1865 Gen. Hardee burned and evacuated Charleston 4: 102
1866 David F. Houston, secretary of the treasury and of agriculture under Wilson, born A: 38
1870 William S. Bainbridge, surgeon, born D: 190
1876 Henry A. Christian, physician, born 18: 17
1879 Dorothy Canfield Fisher, author, born 18: 63
1887 First issue of "The Open Court" 23: 60

FEBRUARY 18.

1729 William Fleming, Virginia colonist, scholar and soldier, born 22: 427
1773 Grant Thorburn, pioneer seed merchant, born 7: 350
1775 William H. Winder, soldier, born 10: 487
1783 James Biddle, naval officer, born 6: 55
1795 George Peabody, Boston merchant and philanthropist, born 5: 335
1804 Thomas G. Pratt, Maryland lawyer, senator and governor, born 9: 305
1805 Louis M. Goldsborough, naval officer, born 2: 107
1817 Walter P. Lane, Federal soldier, born 8: 77
1822 Philip H. Laufman, "father of the tin plate industry," born 11: 445
1823 Jasper F. Cropsey, artist, born 1: 372
1824 Earl English, naval officer, born 5: 394
1832 Octave Chanute, civil engineer, born 10: 212
1841 Samuel P. Warren, organist, born 9: 377
1841 Samuel W. Shattuck, Federal soldier and president of Norwich university, born 18: 324
1842 Charles B. Lewis (M. Quad), journalist and humorist, born 6: 30
1842 Charles Emory Smith, postmaster general under Harrison, born 11: 17
1848 Louis G. Tiffany, artist, born 7: 465
1851 Ida Husted Harper, author, born 25: 61
1856 Russell H. Chittenden, educator, born 10: 181
1861 Jefferson Davis inaugurated as provisional president of the Confederate States 4: 149
1862 Charles M. Schwab, president of the Bethlehem Steel Co., born A: 238
1870 Edwin Denby, secretary of the navy under Harding, born 21: 486

FEBRUARY 19.

1766 Wright Post, physician and surgeon, born 9: 341
1784 Marcus Morton, judge and governor of Massachusetts, born 1: 115
1792 John Locke, physicist who made discoveries in electricity, optics and terrestrial magnetism, born 15: 264
1793 Sidney Rigdon, Mormon elder and leader, born 16: 15
1802 Leonard Bacon, clergyman, "the Nestor of Congregationalism," born 1: 176
1806 Nehemiah Adams, clergyman and author, born 2: 318
1808 George Ide Chace, educator, born 8: 25
1821 Francis P. Blair, 2d, Federal soldier and U. S. senator, born 4: 223
1823 Stephen Smith, surgeon, pioneer in public health, born 2: 207
1824 Orlando W. Wight, surgeon and author, born 7: 547
1835 Jeremiah Murphy, lawyer, born 12: 518
1836 James L. Little, surgeon, born 13: 404
1837 Benjamin M. Harrod, engineer, born 12: 328
1839 Alpheus S. Packard, naturalist, born 3: 102
1840 Andrew R. McGill, governor of Minnesota, born 10: 67
1843 Adelina Patti, soprano, born 7: 480
1844 Lewis G. Janes, sociologist, born 12: 114
1847 Sara Y. Stevenson, archæologist, born 13: 83
1848 Richard L. Garner, naturalist, who studied the languages of the apes, born 13: 314
1849 Edward T. Bedford, founder and head of the Corn Products Refining Co., born 22: 67
1853 Wellington P. Kidder, printing press inventor, born 3: 435
1855 William Crozier, soldier and inventor, born 12: 267
1856 Carl Barus, physicist, born 26: 8
1861 Surrender of U. S. troops and property in Texas 4: 282
1864 First lodge of the Knights of Pythias formed 2: 170
1865 Evacuation of Fort Anderson, N. C., by Confederates 4: 260
1866 Thomas J. J. See, astronomer, born 13: 234
1868 The Society of Patrons of Husbandry (the Grange) formally organized 23: 118
1878 Phonograph patented by Edison 25: 2
1934 The United States cancelled all air-mail contracts, delegating the task of carrying the air mail to the army D: 15

FEBRUARY 20.

1726 William Prescott, soldier, commander of the Americans at the battle of Bunker Hill, born 1: 91
1754 Stephen R. Bradley, U. S. senator and jurist, born 2: 432
1772 Isaac Chauncey, naval officer, born 8: 95
1781 Robert Morris appointed superintendent of finance by congress 2: 412
1783 Phillips academy, Exeter, opened 10: 104
1784 John E. Wool, soldier, born 4: 282
1794 Carlton Chase, P. E. bishop, born 11: 226
1803 Henry Stanbery, lawyer and attorney-general under Johnson, born 2: 458
1805 Angelina E. Grimke, reformer, born 2: 325
1811 Henry H. Sibley, Minnesota author, soldier and governor, born 10: 63
1815 The British vessels "Cyane" and "Levant" captured by the "Constitution" 8: 157
1816 William Rimmer, sculptor, born 4: 375
1820 Hiram W. Hayden, inventor of machines for manufacturing brass, born 25: 19
1822 Henry F. Durant, founder of Wellesley college, born 7: 327
1825 William Allen Butler, admiralty lawyer, born 7: 315
1829 Joseph Jefferson, actor, born 1: 522
1831 Patrick J. Ryan, R. C. archbishop, born 6: 285
1836 Samuel C. T. Dodd, lawyer, born 24: 264
1841 Nathaniel S. Shaler, geologist, born 9: 315
1844 Benjamin Lander, artist, born 9: 54
1848 Edward H. Harriman, railroad executive, born 14: 196
1852 American debut of Theodore Thomas as a boy violinist 23: 195

1858 Samuel M. Roosevelt, artist, born 12:128
1858 Howard A. Kelly, physician, born 15:210
1862 Winton, N. C., destroyed for using a white flag as a decoy 4: 62
1864 Battle of Olustee, Fla. 8:301
1871 Raymond Dodge, psychologist, born B:324
1872 Herbert S. Hadley, governor of Missouri, born .. 14:475
1907 The U. S. senate voted to admit Reed Smoot to his seat, notwithstanding the opposition of the anti-Mormons 13:197
1917 The United States purchased the Danish West Indies 20: 2

FEBRUARY 21.

1676 Medfield, Mass., attacked by Indians 10: 50
1752 Nathaniel Rochester, founder of Rochester, N. Y. born 9:485
1783 Benjamin Ruggles, U. S. senator, born 13:162
1805 David Tod, lawyer and governor of Ohio, born 3:141
1816 Ebenezer R. Hoar, attorney-general under Grant, born 4: 20
1821 Elizabeth Thompson, philanthropist, born 5:405
1821 Charles Scribner, publisher, born 6:366
1822 Robert W. Shufeldt, Federal naval officer, born .. 4:293
1822 Oliver W. Gibbs, chemist, born 10:469
1825 Jean Baptist Salpointe, R. C. archbishop, born 12: 50
1837 John Meredith Read, diplomat, born 2:223
1845 Lloyd Lowndes, governor of Maryland, born .. 9:313
1845 Emma C. Thursby, singer, born 22:358
1852 Hampton L. Carson, lawyer and author, born .. 3:264
1852 Henry Lloyd, Maryland lawyer, governor and jurist, born 9:312
1852 John N. Hurty, physician, born 22:370
1855 Alice E. F. Palmer, president of Wellesley college, born 7:328
1855 George L. Tracy, composer, born 8:446
1855 Elizabeth R. Pennell, author, born 10:377
1862 Battle of Valverdo, N. Mex. 2:365
1863 Augustus O. Thomas, president of the World Federation of Education Associations, born . C:499
1865 Gen. Cook captured at Cumberland, Md. 4: 70
1865 James S. Alexander, New York banker, born .. 24:204
1866 Ezra R. Thayer, dean of the Harvard law school, born 16:185
1867 Otto H. Kahn, New York banker, born .... B: 41
1868 Secretary Stanton discharged from the cabinet 2: 85
1871 District of Columbia given a territorial government 13: 81
1927 "Warfield Day" in St. Petersburg, Fla. .... B: 10

FEBRUARY 22.

Washington's birthday celebrated

1732 George Washington, "the First American," born 1: 1
1764 Comfort Tyler, soldier, born 2:449
1765 Robert Waln, congressman and merchant, born 10:361
1770 Jacob Burnet, Ohio jurist, born 11:155
1778 Rembrandt Peale, artist, born 5:320
1794 Joseph Duncan, Illinois soldier and governor, born 11: 45
1808 Washington L. Atlee, physician and surgeon, born 11: 25
1818 William Henry Morgan, dentist, born 8:228
1818 Carroll Spence, diplomat, born 12:318
1819 James Russell Lowell, poet, born 2: 32
1819 Florida ceded to the United States by Spain .. 4:180
1821 Joshua F. Bullitt, jurist, born 13: 19
1822 Frances E. Barrow (Aunt Fanny), author of children's stories, born 4:556
1826 Samuel J. R. McMillan, Minnesota senator and jurist, born 4:469
1831 William N. Byers, Western pioneer journalist, born 13:514
1832 Alpheus B. Crosby, surgeon, born 9: 98
1833 Rebecca S. Clarke (Sophie May), author, born.. 8:339
1838 Margaret E. Sangster, author and poet, born . 6:169
1847 Battle of Buena Vista began 4:282
1850 Isaac L. Rice, founder of "Forum" magazine, born 11:447
1851 William J. Gaynor, New York judge and mayor, born 16:353
1857 Frank L. Stanton, journalist and poet, born .. 11:497
1858 Charles Mills Gayley, educator and author, born 23:128
1861 Great Union war meeting in San Francisco 4:109
1862 Confederate government organized at Richmond, Va. 4:427
1863 Ground broken for the Central Pacific railroad .. 2:129
1863 Lee Christmas, soldier of fortune, born 6:380
1863 Charles L. Heisler, inventor of locomotive improvements, born 25:399
1865 Wilmington, N. C., captured by Federals 4:260
1866 Herman L. Nietert, surgeon, born 12:519
1873 Samuel Seabury, lawyer and reformer, born .... D: 76
1876 The Society of the Sons of the Revolution organized 13:140
1888 Ralph O. Brewster, governor of Maine, born .. B: 24
1892 Edna St. Vincent Millay, author, born B:176
1914 U. S. senate ratified an arbitration treaty with Japan 18: 20

FEBRUARY 23.

1680 Jean Baptiste Le Moyne (Sieur de Bienville), founder of New Orleans, born 5:491
1751 Henry Dearborn, soldier and minister to Portugal, born 1: 93
1764 William Eaton, soldier and adventurer, born ... 11:505
1787 Mrs. Emma Willard, founder of the Willard school, born 1:244
1809 Charles E. West, president of the Vanderbilt railroad lines, born 8:235
1823 James G. Batterson, founder and first president of the Travelers Insurance Co., born 6: 9
1823 Henry J. Newton, chemist, born 7: 23
1832 John H. Vincent, M. E. bishop and founder of the Chautauqua movement, born 24:378
1836 Siege of the Alamo, in Texas, opened by the Mexicans 4:211
1836 Lucy Randall Comfort, novelist, born 18:184
1839 William R. Jones, pioneer Pittsburgh steel manufacturer, born 15: 45
1840 Alfred P. Boller, civil engineer and bridge builder, born 9: 43
1844 James F. Babcock, chemist and inventor of a fire extinguisher, born 10:445
1851 Frederick B. Warde, tragedian, born 11:105
1855 Maurice Bloomfield, philologist, born 10:400
1856 Douglas Volk, artist, born C:138
1857 Margaret Deland, author, born 3:476
1861 Frederick R. Burton, composer and a student of Indian music, born 7:202
1862 Ernest P. Bicknell, a director of the American Red Cross, born 25: 46
1868 William E. B. DuBois, famous Negro educator, born 13:307
1869 George S. Addams, pioneer of the juvenile court in Ohio, born 24:370
1870 Hiram R. Revels, the first negro to become a U. S. senator, took his oath of office 11:406
1871 George T. Moore, scentist, born 13:285
1884 Percy White Zimmerman, botanist who devised a new method of root development, born .... D: 91
1889 John G. Winant, governor of New Hampshire, born B:471
1892 Louisiana lottery received a permanent charter from Nicaragua 4:138
1903 George B. Cortelyou appointed first secretary of commerce and labor 14: 6
1905 First Rotary club meeting A:503
1917 Federal board for vocational education created 20: 36

FEBRUARY 24.

1715 Ephraim Williams, soldier and founder of Williams college, born 6:236
1742 Samuel Provoost, P. E. bishop, born 1:513
1750 Theophilus Parsons, Massachusetts jurist, born . 5:441
1772 William Harris Crawford, statesman, born 5: 82
1792 Jonathan M. Wainwright, P. E. bishop, born .. 1:515
1800 Stephen T. Logan, lawyer (partner of Lincoln) and judge, born 7:492
1802 Wilson Shannon, governor of Ohio and Kansas, born 8:340
1808 John Wise, aëronaut and inventor, born 1:178
1811 Edward D. Baker, U. S. senator and soldier, born 2: 92
1811 Henry S. Lane, U. S. senator and governor of Indiana, born 13:270
1812 Nathan A. Farwell, Maine legislator, born 10: 89
1813 Battle between the "Hornet" and the "Peacock" 8: 92
1814 Henry Kirke Brown, sculptor, born 1:511
1824 George William Curtis, author, born 3: 96
1833 Walter S. Carter, New York lawyer, born 23:178
1836 Winslow Homer, artist, born 11:304
1838 Duel between William J. Graves and Jonathan Cilley 10:110
1841 Levi K. Fuller, organ manufacturer and inventor, and governor of Vermont, born 8:330
1842 John Habberton, author, born 4:217
1842 John P. Holland, inventor of the submarine, born 15: 4
1849 John H. Comstock, entomologist, born 22: 10
1855 The court of claims established at Washington 7:508
1860 Frank W. Rollins, governor of New Hampshire, originator of "Old Home Week," born . 11:141
1863 Arizona organized as a territory 24:338
1864 Kentucky university burned 4:516

1868 Bill to impeach President Johnson introduced .. 2:456
1933 Minnesota banned mortgage foreclosures on farms and homes D:176

FEBRUARY 25.

1639 First popular assembly met in Maryland 7:333
1676 Weymouth, Mass., attacked by Indians 10: 50
1746 Charles Cotesworth Pinckney, soldier and statesman, born 2:302
1754 Benjamin Tallmadge, soldier, born 1: 90
1779 British post at Vincennes, Ind., captured by George R. Clark 1: 82
1791 The Girard Bank of Philadelphia chartered 21:440
1801 Samuel Medary, journalist, and governor of Kansas, born 8:342
1809 George W. Cullum, Federal soldier, born 4:258
1816 George Henry Preble, Federal naval officer, born 8: 95
1816 Parke Godwin, author, and editor of the New York "Evening Post," born 11:117
1819 Talbot W. Chambers, clergyman, born 9:258
1821 William L. Lee, jurist, born 12:383
1831 Jane Goodwin Austin, author, born 6: 62
1833 John P. St. John, governor of Kansas, born .. 8:346
1834 Charlton T. Lewis, lawyer and author, born 11: 62
1836 First patent to Colt for a revolver 6:175
1841 Ida Lewis, heroine, the "Grace Darling of America," born 5:247
1845 Franklin F. Landis, inventor of agricultural machines, born 25: 24
1846 Duel between John H. Pleasants and Thomas Ritchie, Jr. 7:545
1848 Edward H. Harriman, financier and railroad president, born 14:196
1856 Charles L. Freer, manufacturer of railway cars, and founder of the Freer Gallery of Art in Washington, born 15:416
1858 Charles B. Galbreath, librarian and author, born 25:112
1862 The greenback or legal tender act passed by congress 6:356
1863 An act to establish a national banking system passed by congress 1: 30
1866 Edwin Gould, financier and railroad president, born 24:274

FEBRUARY 26.

1643 Indians of Hoboken, N. J., massacred by the Dutch 6: 92
1770 Tristam Burges, congressman and orator, born 8: 32
1775 Troops sent to Salem, Mass., to seize cannon .. 7:378
1800 John B. Purcell, archbishop of Cincinnati, born 5:186
1821 Robert C. Kirk, diplomat, born 12:440
1823 Joseph LeConte, scientist, born 7:231
1825 William A. Tower, banker, born 15: 98
1826 Oswald Ottendorfer, editor of the New York "Staats-Zeitung," born 3:411
1832 John G. Nicolay, Lincoln's private secretary, and later his biographer, born 8:170
1834 Thomas E. Osmun (Alfred Ayres), author, born 9:125
1836 Elihu Vedder, artist, born 6:328
1840 Eugene Schuyler, author and diplomat, born .. 8:339
1844 Horace H. Lurton, justice of the U. S. supreme court, born 8:235
1845 William F. Cody (Buffalo Bill), frontiersman and scout, born 5:483
1847 Rudolph Hering, civil engineer, born 10:226
1849 Katherine S. McDowell, author, born 11:496
1849 Edward T. Stotesbury, Philadelphia financier and philanthropist, born B:104
1856 Costa Rica declared war against Walker, the filibuster 11: 24
1858 William J. Hammer, electrical engineer and inventor, born 15:218
1861 Jefferson territory (Colorado) created by congress 6:445
1866 Herbert H. Dow, manufacturing chemist, born 24: 12
1869 The 15th amendment, giving suffrage to the negroes, passed by congress 13: 50
1883 Coningsby Dawson, author, born A:394
1895 Patent granted for a machine for blowing glass 13:504

FEBRUARY 27.

1733 Thomas Conway, soldier, of "Conway Cabal" notoriety, born 1: 50
1760 Indians attacked Fort Dobbs, N. C. 9:472
1776 Battle of Moore's Creek Bridge, N. C. 10:246
1784 William Maxwell, lawyer, and president of Hampden-Sidney college, born 2: 24
1787 Jacob Bigelow, physician and scientist, born .. 4:526
1807 Henry W. Longfellow, poet, born 2:160
1810 John G. Gilbert, actor, born 1:261
1811 Samuel Cony, lawyer and governor of Maine, born 6:314
1823 William B. Franklin, Federal soldier, born 4:133
1826 Howard Crosby, clergyman and author, and chancellor of the University of the City of New York, born 4:193
1828 James E. Jouett, Federal naval officer, born ... 4:501
1830 Arthur L. Perry, political economist, born 10:215
1830 Horatio R. Storer, Boston surgeon, born 11:337
1835 Abraham Lansing, lawyer, born 17:126
1836 Russell A. Alger, soldier, governor and secretary of war under McKinley, born 5:276
1850 Henry E. Huntington, vice-president of the Southern Pacific railroad system and owner and operator of vast electric light and power and traction properties on the Pacific coast born 15: 17
1850 Laura E. Richards, author, born 15:176
1853 Kate Stephens, author, born B:100
1860 Edward Wisner, the "Father of Reclamation," born 15:243
1865 Sheridan's raid in Virginia begun 4:275
1866 Hermon A. MacNeil, sculptor, born 13:480
1867 Irving Fisher, economist, born .... C: 51
1870 Louis Adolphe Coerne, composer, born 26:249
1873 Congressman James Brooks and Oakes Ames censured by the house for connection with the "Credit Mobilier" 6: 47
1878 Alvan T. Fuller, governor of Massachusetts, born B: 30
1882 Burton K. Wheeler, U. S. senator, born A:153
1886 Hugo L. Black, U. S. senator and associate justice of the supreme court, born C:502
1891 David Sarnoff, electrical engineer, head of the Radio Corporation of America, born B:162
1902 Organization of the General Education Board .. 23:250

FEBRUARY 28.

1609 Lord De La Warr appointed governor of Virginia for life 10:399
1747 John Tyler, Virginia jurist and statesman, born 5:444
1752 William Washington, soldier, born 2:492
1788 Ezekiel F. Chambers, Maryland jurist, born 7:307
1791 Cornelius V. W. Lawrence, merchant, financier and mayor of New York, born 8: 85
1795 Benjamin Kurtz, Lutheran clergyman, born ... 24: 99
1797 Mary Lyon, educator, founder of Mt. Holyoke seminary, born 4:462
1799 Samuel S. Schmucker, theologian, born 5:100
1804 Henry S. Foote, statesman and governor of Mississippi, born 13:490
1806 Augustus A. Hayes, chemist, born 11: 56
1809 Jefferson's embargo act repealed 12: 56
1816 William D. Wilson, educator, born 12:510
1825 Quincy Adams Gillmore, Federal soldier, born . 4: 54
1827 Charter for the Baltimore and Ohio railroad granted 18: 1
1838 Jacob da S. Solis-Cohen, laryngologist, born ... 10: 92
1838 Edward O. Guerrant, evangelist, founder of the Society of Soul Winners, born 18:426
1844 An explosion on the S.S. "Princeton" killed several members of Mr. Tyler's cabinet 6: 8
1847 Battle of Sacramento, Mexico 11:389
1849 William S. Barnard, naturalist, born 12:434
1851 Samuel W. McCall, Masachusetts congressman and governor, born 20:303
1859 Basil King, author, born 21:437
1860 Ruth Stuart, author, born 4:522
1863 The Confederate privateer "Nashville" destroyed by the "Montauk" 4:284
1865 Transylvania university consolidated with Kentucky university 4:515
1876 John Alden Carpenter, composer, born A:380
1878 The Bland-Allison silver bill passed over President Hayes's veto 10:160
1882 Geraldine Farrar, singer, born 16:263
1882 William W. Tefft, hydro-electric engineer, born B:112
1893 Patent granted on a process for making carborundum 23:136

FEBRUARY 29.

Leap year — every four years

1704 Deerfield, Mass., attacked by Indians and French 1:258
1736 Ann Lee, founder of the Shakers in America, born 5:132
1784 Ben Hardin, lawyer and congressman, born .. 12:146
1804 Sidney S. Campbell, Michigan pioneer, born .. 12:348
1820 Lewis A. Sayre, orthopedic surgeon, born 2: 31
1820 Lewis Swift, astronomer, born 4:302
1824 William T. Coleman, California merchant, and head of the San Francisco vigilantes, born .. 8:336
1828 Evan Pugh, chemist, born 11:320
1828 Henry A. Tupper, Baptist clergyman, born 1:272

1836 Battle with Indians on the Withlacoochee river, Florida ... 9:372
1836 Philadelphia "Public Ledger" founded ... 3:263
1844 French E. Chadwick, naval officer, born ... 9: 16
1856 John W. Dunsmore, artist, born ... 10:366
1856 Herbert W. Bowen, author, diplomat, born ... 20: 46

MARCH 1.

1732 William Cushing, jurist, born ... 12:548
1749 Otho H. Williams, Revolutionary soldier, born ... 1: 91
1769 John L. Taylor, North Carolina jurist, born ... 9:285
1780 First bank in the United States chartered ... 2:411
1785 John Sevier became governor of the state of Franklin (Tennessee) ... 3:430
1793 Warren Colburn, mathematician and educator, born ... 10:445
1794 William J. Worth, soldier, born ... 4:506
1800 Stephen H. Tyng, P. E. clergyman and author, born ... 2:187
1807 Wilford Woodruff, 4th president of the Mormon church, born ... 16: 6
1809 Territory of Illinois organized ... 11: 42
1815 Georgetown college (later Georgetown university) incorporated ... 12:132
1815 Thomas B. Thorpe, author and war correspondent, born ... 6:230
1816 John B. Kerfoot, P. E. bishop and president of Trinity college, born ... 3:497
1823 Charles C. Perkins, author and critic, born ... 4:524
1826 First public appearance of James H. Hackett ... 3: 74
1833 George Washburn, president of Robert college, Constantinople, born ... 26:102
1835 John James Platt, poet and journalist, born ... 8:260
1837 William Dean Howells, author and poet, born ... 1:281
1839 Albert S. Bickmore, naturalist, born ... 8:268
1841 Blanche K. Bruce, U. S. senator, born ... 11:394
1842 Job Williams, pioneer teacher of the deaf and dumb, born ... 16: 37
1844 Lillian M. N. Stevens, reformer, born ... 13:264
1845 Texas annexed to the United States ... 6:266
1847 Chihuahua, Mexico, occupied by Americans ... 11:389
1848 Augustus St. Gaudens, sculptor, born ... 8:287
1853 Richard H. Jesse, educator, born ... 8:188
1859 Charles F. Lummis, author and explorer, born ... 11:227
1861 Henry Harland (Sidney Luska), author, born ... 13:235
1867 Nebraska admitted to the Union ... 12: 1
1904 Smith patented his process for the manufacture of chloroform ... 24:386
1920 Railroads returned to their owners on the dissolution of the U. S. railroad administration A: 49

MARCH 2.

1710 David Wooster, Revolutionary soldier, born ... 1: 82
1769 DeWitt Clinton, New York statesman, born ... 3: 43
1779 Joel R. Poinsett, secretary of war under Van Buren, born ... 6:435
1779 Simon Gabriel Bruté, R. C. bishop, born ... 12:413
1791 Stephen Olin, president of Randolph-Macon and Wesleyan colleges, born ... 9:429
1793 Sam Houston, Texas statesman and soldier, born 9: 63
1815 Alexander H. Bullock, Massachusetts lawyer, editor and governor, born ... 1:118
1819 Arkansas territory formed from Missouri ... 10:183
1819 Preston H. Leslie, governor of Kentucky and Montana, born ... 11: 81
1820 "Missouri Compromise" Bill passed ... 12:302
1829 William B. Allison, U. S. senator, born ... 1:296
1829 Carl Schurz, leader of the "Mugwump" movement, born ... 3:202
1831 Alexander E. Orr, merchant, "Father of the New York Subway," born ... 23: 40
1832 William C. Doane, P. E. bishop, born ... 4:489
1833 Charlotte B. Wilbur, philanthropist, born ... 13:370
1836 John W. Foster, diplomat, secretary of state under Harrison, born ... 3:268
1836 Declaration of Independence of Texas signed ... 4:350
1836 Charles E. Warburton, Philadelphia journalist, born ... 11:437
1847 Samuel Spencer, railroad president, born ... 14:420
1848 Henry M. Howe, metallurgist, born ... 13: 78
1849 John A. McCall, president of the New York Life Insurance Company, born ... 11: 88
1853 Washington territory organized ... 12:137
1861 Dakota territory organized ... 2:455
1861 Clifford S. Walton, lawyer and author, born ... 15:375
1864 Ulysses S. Grant's nomination as lieutenant-general confirmed by senate ... 4: 6
1865 Battle of Waynesboro, Va. (Sheridan's raid) ... 4:138
1865 William C. Carl, organist, born ... 8:448
1867 Reconstruction bills passed by congress over President Johnson's veto ... 2:456
1867 Department of education established ... 4:240
1886 Fundamental patent for storage battery issued... 21: 2

MARCH 3.

1513 Ponce de Leon sailed from Puerto Rico to find the "Fountain of Youth" ... 11:335
1675 Thomas Chalkley, Quaker preacher, the subject of Whittier's "Chalkley Hall," born ... 11: 92
1776 Americans bombarded British troops in Boston 1: 3
1779 Battle of Briar Creek, Ga. ... 6:438
1783 Francis B. Ogden, inventor of a steam engine, born ... 11:369
1791 The District of Columbia organized ... 1: 5
1791 An excise law on distilled liquors passed, causing the "Whiskey Rebellion" in Pennsylvania ... 2:283
1796 Theodore Dwight, author and one of the "Hartford Wits," born ... 11:216
1803 Moses H. Grinnell, merchant and shipowner, born 1:499
1805 Territory of Louisiana created ... 12:301
1815 War declared against Algiers ... 4: 56
1817 Alabama territory formed ... 10:425
1826 Joseph Wharton, metallurgist, born ... 13: 82
1831 George M. Pullman, sleeping-car manufacturer, born ... 11:279
1837 Independence of Texas recognized by the United States ... 4:168
1843 Congress appropriated $30,000 to build Morse's experimental telegraph line ... 4:449
1845 Florida admitted to the Union ... 11:378
1846 Fire at Brook Farm broke out resulting in the collapse of the undertaking ... 1:307
1847 Alexander Graham Bell, telephone inventor, born 6:220
1848 James Lane Allen, novelist, born ... 8:241
1849 Department of the interior established ... 3: 39
1849 Minnesota territory created ... 10: 62
1856 Frank McD. Leavitt, inventor, born ... 15: 20
1862 Fernandina, Fla., captured by Federals ... 5:366
1863 Idaho territory formed ... 2:456
1863 Bombardment of Ft. McAllister, Ga. ... 4:219
1863 Congress authorized the suspension of the writ of habeas corpus ... 4:500
1865 Freedmen's bureau established ... 4:104
1870 William Green, president of the American Federation of Labor, born ... B: 45
1874 Richard Mills Pearce, Jr., pathologist, born ... 15:204
1887 Monroe Curtis, lawyer, born ... B:142
1899 George Dewey made the third admiral of the U. S. navy ... 9: 6
1901 National bureau of standards established by congress ... 13:142
1904 Isthmian canal commission appointed ... 13:368
1905 American Academy in Rome chartered by congress (a post graduate school for American architects) ... 23: 90
1913 Bill creating the department of labor signed by President Taft ... A: 52

MARCH 4.

Inauguration Day (prior to 1937)

1681 William Penn received a grant of land which became Pennsylvania ... 2:275
1748 Casimir Pulaski, Polish general in the Revolutionary war, born ... 1: 69
1754 Benjamin Waterhouse, one of the first American physicians to practice vaccination, born ... 9:254
1774 Joseph H. Daveiss, Kentucky lawyer, born ... 6:401
1776 New Providence, West Indies, captured from the British ... 2: 18
1777 Fourth Congress met at Philadelphia ... 1:103
1781 Rebecca Gratz, philanthropist, the original of Scott's heroine in "Ivanhoe," born ... 10:130
1789 First congress under the Constitution met ... 1: 5
1791 Vermont admitted to the Union ... 8:313
1792 Isaac Lea, naturalist, born ... 6: 23
1792 Samuel Slocum, inventor of a pen-making machine, born ... 7:529
1793 Second Federal Congress met in Philadelphia, George Washington, president ... 1: 5
1815 John W. Foster, geologist, born ... 10:169
1817 Edwards Pierrepont, statesman, born ... 4: 21
1818 James B. Colgate, New York banker and patron of Colgate university, born ... 24:329
1821 William W. Hubbell, inventor of firearms and ammunition, born ... 16:447
1832 Samuel Colman, artist, born ... 7:546
1832 Seneca D. Kimbark, merchant, born ... 15:300
1836 The Bank of the United States ceased to be a government institution ... 5:292
1842 Peter Moran, artist, born ... 11:303
1845 Henry C. Taylor, naval officer, born ... 9: 15
1845 Alexander McDowell, banker, born ... 15:380
1847 Charles F. Brooker, industrialist, founder and president of the American Brass Co., born ... 18: 42
1848 Carleton Wiggins, artist, born ... 11:309
1849 David R. Atchison, statesman, born ... 10:223
1855 Luther E. Holt, pediatrician, born ... 20: 46

1857 Gustav Kobbé, author and critic, born 10: 410
1864 Col. Ulric Dahlgren killed in his attempt to rescue Federal prisoners 9: 380
1869 Brand Whitlock, author and diplomat, born .... A: 544
1864 David W. Taylor, naval constructor, born 15: 87
1873 Guy Wetmore Carryl, humorist, born 13: 121
1877 Thomas W. Ferry became ex-officio president of the United States 9: 169
1880 Channing Pollock, dramatist, born .... A: 163

MARCH 5.

1770 The Boston massacre occurred 1: 19
1777 Thomas Wharton inaugurated president of Pennsylvania 2: 280
1794 Robert C. Grier, justice of the U. S. supreme court, born 2: 472
1802 George C. De Kay, naval officer, born 9: 205
1815 "Long" John Wentworth, journalist and congressman, born 10: 482
1820 Alvah Hovey, clergyman and president of Newton theological institute, born 8: 154
1825 James P. Wickersham, educator, born 12: 239
1827 Henry P. C. Wilson, physician, born 6: 340
1830 Theodore T. Munger, clergyman and author, born 1: 533
1832 Isaac I. Hayes, Arctic explorer, born 3: 280
1836 Hans Balatka, musician, born 10: 197
1843 George W. Maynard, mural artist, born 11: 287
1849 Zachary Taylor inaugurated president of the United States 4: 369
1851 Herman Ridder, journalist, born 22: 72
1852 William Henry Maxwell, educator, born 13: 218
1853 Arthur Foote, composer, born 7: 435
1853 Howard Pyle, artist and author, born 9: 56
1853 Richard K. Munkittrick, author, born 9: 412
1861 Peter Cooper Hewitt, electrician and inventor, born 14: 470
1861 Frederick W. Abbott, physician of the eclectic school, born 18: 14
1862 Peter Newell, author and illustrator, born 20: 77
1862 Frederick H. Newell, irrigation engineer and director of the U. S. reclamation service, born 23: 162
1863 Engagement at Thompson's Station, Tenn. 10: 36
1868 Impeachment court convened to try President Johnson 4: 31
1877 Rutherford B. Hayes inaugurated president of the United States 3: 194
1903 Association of Licensed Automobile Manufacturers organized 20: 223
1917 Woodrow Wilson inaugurated president of the United States 19: 1
1933 President Franklin D. Roosevelt proclaimed a nation-wide "bank holiday" to prevent further withdrawals of deposits .... D: 3

MARCH 6.

1648 Samuel Green, Colonial printer and publisher, born 20: 28
1724 Henry Laurens, statesman, born 3: 426
1760 Thomas L. Winthrop, merchant and antiquarian, born 7: 504
1797 Gerrit Smith, philanthropist, born 2: 322
1798 George R. Noyes, Unitarian clergyman and Orientalist, born 18: 307
1802 Thomas Purse, merchant and originator of railroad time schedules, born 2: 194
1815 George Hammond, merchant and chess player, born 12: 524
1818 William Claflin, governor of Massachusetts, born 1: 119
1820 Horatio G. Wright, soldier and engineer, born .. 4: 273
1824 Halcyon Skinner, inventor of carpet-making machines, born 5: 300
1828 Johnson N. Camden, U. S. senator, born 21: 327
1831 Philip H. Sheridan, Federal soldier, born 4: 63
1832 James M. Comly, journalist and diplomat, born 12: 465
1833 Isaac H. Bromley, journalist and author, born .. 12: 336
1836 Massacre of the Alamo 4: 211
1837 Arthur Pierson, clergyman and author, born .. 13: 408
1838 Stillman W. Robinson, inventor of a shoe-nailing machine, born 10: 232
1847 Henry S. Williams, geologist, born 21: 327
1853 Albert S. Cook, editor and educator, born 9: 167
1857 The famous Dred Scott decision rendered 1: 27
1858 Decree organizing the Paulist Fathers issued .. 9: 167
1862 Battle of Pea Ridge, Ark. 4: 300
1871 Leland L. Summers, consulting engineer, famous for his World war services, born 20: 464
1885 Ring Lardner, author, born .... C: 30

MARCH 7.

1638 The Portsmouth (R. I.) covenant signed 12: 384
1707 Stephen Hopkins, signer of the Declaration of Independence, born 10: 13
1737 William Heath, Revolutionary soldier and jurist, born 1: 68
1740 Thaddeus Dod, clergyman and founder of Washington college, born 7: 536
1778 Engagement between the "Randolph" and "Yarmouth" 5: 486
1789 Francis Jackson, reformer, president of the Anti-Slavery Society, born 2: 318
1791 Goold Brown, grammarian, born 8: 265
1811 Increase A. Lapham, Wisconsin botanist and geologist, born 8: 34
1817 John Bachelder, inventor, born 12: 549
1820 Francis Wharton, lawyer, clergyman and author, born 11: 184
1825 University of Virginia opened to matriculates .. 3: 4
1826 John W. Davis, politician and governor of Rhode Island, born 9: 407
1827 Henry D. Clayton, educator, born 12: 296
1828 Richard M. Upjohn, architect, born 2: 245
1832 Galusha Anderson, president of Chicago and Denison universities, born 1: 303
1835 Daniel G. Elliot, zoologist, born 16: 196
1836 James M. Thoburn, M. E. bishop, born 10: 294
1837 Henry Draper, scientist, who discovered oxygen in the sun by photography, born 6: 171
1838 Edward P. Roe, clergyman and novelist, born 7: 15
1841 Touro Robertson, printer and inventor, born .. 7: 538
1844 Anthony Comstock, reformer, born 15: 241
1845 Daniel D. Palmer, founder of the chiropractic treatment of disease, born 18: 301
1849 Luther Burbank, "The Wizard of Horticulture," born 11: 374
1850 Webster made his famous speech to conciliate the South 3: 36
1850 Champ Clark, speaker of the house, born 14: 171
1851 Archer Brown, merchant, born 15: 163
1867 Resolution introduced in Congress to impeach President Johnson 11: 79
1868 Sewell Ford, author, born 14: 140
1872 Howard Crosby Butler, archæologist, born 20: 56
1876 First patent for Bell's telephone issued 6: 221
1886 Mark A. Carleton, botanist, an authority on diseases of food plants, born 23: 344
1919 Pioneer post of the American Legion organized 26: 24

MARCH 8.

1665 "The Duke's Laws" promulgated in New York 8: 51
1765 Stamp Act passed by British House of Lords .. 1: 104
1785 Gen. Henry Knox elected secretary of war by Continental congress 1: 16
1799 Simon Cameron, secretary of war under Lincoln, born 2: 79
1799 George P. Upshur, naval officer, born 4: 198
1800 Robert J. Breckinridge, Presbyterian clergyman and author, born 9: 242
1804 Alvan Clark, optician, builder of the largest telescope of his day, born 6: 440
1807 Samuel Downer, merchant and manufacturer, born 11: 208
1813 Christopher P. Cranch, artist and poet, born .. 7: 140
1819 Edwin P. Whipple, critic and essayist, born ... 1: 197
1822 Richard M. Johnston, author, born 1: 440
1827 John Crerar, Chicago merchant and banker, born 22: 62
1828 Catherine Lorillard Wolfe, philanthropist, born . 10: 411
1832 John Huntington, pioneer oil dealer, born 9: 102
1839 James M. Crafts, chemist and president of the Massachusetts institute of technology, born .. 13: 474
1841 Oliver Wendell Holmes, justice of the U. S. supreme court, born 12: 349
1847 Eugene Solomon Talbot, dentist, born 13: 147
1850 Warren Upham, geologist, born 7: 127
1853 Frank S. Black, governor of New York, born .. 16: 255
1855 Niagara suspension bridge opened 4: 405
1856 Mary W. Plummer, librarian and teacher of library practice, born 21: 107
1857 Spirit Lake massacre occurred 12: 499
1862 Leesburg, Va., captured by Federals 2: 291
1862 "Merrimac" sank the "Cumberland" at Hampton Roads 4: 278
1862 The "Monitor" arrived at Hampton Roads to oppose the "Merrimac" 4: 284
1863 Albert E. Sterner, artist, born 11: 290
1865 Kinston, N. C., captured by Federals 4: 260
1867 Homer C. Davenport, cartoonist, born 11: 257
1872 Ira L. Reeves, soldier, inventor and president of Norwich university, born 18: 329
1881 The Blake transmitter for telephones patented .. 22: 26
1888 Knute Rockne, football coach, born 25: 416

MARCH 9.

1451 Americus Vespucius, explorer, born 3:419
1759 William Jackson, statesman and soldier, born .. 3:274
1773 Isaac Hull, naval officer, a commander of the "Constitution," born 13:426
1778 The "Alfred" captured by the "Ariadne" and "Ceres" 11:356
1783 Battle between the "Alliance" and three British frigates 4:189
1806 Edwin Forrest, actor, born 5: 86
1812 Plot to destroy the Union revealed to the senate by President Madison 5: 81
1814 John Evans, physician and governor of Colorado, born 6:445
1815 David Davis, justice of the U. S. supreme court, born 2:474
1820 Samuel Blatchford, justice of the U. S. supreme court, born 1: 36
1824 Leland Stanford, California pioneer and founder of Stanford university, born 2:128
1829 The postmaster general is made a member of the president's cabinet 5:296
1829 James W. Davidson, author and journalist, born 9:100
1829 Edward Orton, scientist and president of Ohio state university, born 24:106
1834 Henry A. Ward, scientist, born 3:410
1839 Guy V. Henry, soldier, governor-general of Puerto Rico, born 9: 27
1847 Gen. Winfield Scott landed at Vera Cruz, Mexico 3:503
1856 Edward G. Acheson, first to make carborundum, born 23:136
1861 J. Waldo Smith, engineer, builder of the Catskill water supply system for New York, born 24:108
1862 Battle between the Federal "Monitor" and the Confederate "Merrimac" 4:284
1863 Carl H. Eigenmann, zoologist, born 21: 47
1916 Massacre of Americans by Mexicans at Columbus, N. Mex. A:435
1933 The Emergency Banking Act passed .... D: 4

MARCH 10.

1702 Jeremiah Gridley, Boston lawyer, born 6: 65
1704 Josias Lyndon, Colonial governor of Rhode Island, born 10: 15
1741 John Greaton, soldier, born 1: 82
1783 First of the Newburg addresses issued 1: 48
1809 William D. Porter, naval officer, born 2:100
1810 Nathan K. Hall, postmaster general under Fillmore, born 6:183
1812 Henry A. Homes, librarian and author, born ... 13: 42
1817 Patrick N. Lynch, R. C. bishop, born 12:410
1821 Donald M. Fairfax, naval officer, born 4:459
1832 Henry R. Stiles, New York physician and author, born 13: 41
1839 Robert Hoe, manufacturer of printing presses, born 3: 16
1839 Dudley Buck, organist and composer, born 7:434
1839 John A. Martin, journalist, soldier and governor of Kansas, born 8:347
1840 Everett P. Wheeler, New York lawyer, born 12: 53
1843 James D. Richardson, congressman and Masonic leader, born 17:383
1846 Charles E. Fay, educator, mountain climber, born 22:274
1851 William McMurtrie, chemist, born 12:206
1854 Henry E. Krehbiel, music critic and author, born 12:546
1856 William A. Keener, dean of the Columbia law school, born 9:148
1870 Archer M. Huntington, author and founder of the Hispanic Society of America, born 15: 19

MARCH 11.

1731 Robert Treat Paine, signer of the Declaration of Independence, born 5:429
1753 Solomon Drowne, physician, botanist and educator, born 8: 31
1781 Anthony P. Heinrich, composer, born 8:447
1785 John McLean, postmaster general under Monroe and Adams, and justice of the U. S. supreme court, born 2:469
1785 James Thomas, Maryland lawyer, soldier and governor, born 9:303
1792 Thomas Ewbank, scientist and author, born 7:559
1796 Francis Wayland, president of Brown university, born 8: 22
1812 James Speed, attorney-general under Lincoln, born 2: 89
1818 Henry J. Bigelow, surgeon and educator, born .. 7: 37
1818 Thomas LeClear, portrait painter, born 8:429
1820 John Plankinton, Milwaukee capitalist, born .. 1:248
1822 James H. Spotts, Federal naval officer, born ... 4:279
1832 Twenty-one pioneers left Boston for Oregon .. 6: 73
1839 Arthur P. Gorman, U. S. senator, born 1:296
1844 Henry E. Alvord, pioneer dairy expert, born .. 2:184
1859 Edward J. Wheeler, author, poet and magazine editor, born 18:132
1860 Thomas Hastings, architect of the famous firm of Carrere & Hastings, born 11:326
1862 Gen. Henry W. Halleck given command of the Department of the Mississippi 4:257
1865 Capture of Fayetteville, N. C. 4: 32
1868 Georgia ratified a new constitution 1:229
1890 H. C. Witwer, author, born 21:290
1904 First successful tunnel under Hudson river finished .... A: 35

MARCH 12.

1612 Third patent for Virginia granted 13:380
1640 Newport and Portsmouth (R. I.) colonies united 10: 2
1684 George Berkeley, clergyman and philosopher, born 6:255
1758 Jesse Lee, Methodist clergyman, born 13:187
1770 Fevret de Saint-Mémin, artist, famed for his profile portraits of early American notables, born 18:143
1775 Henry Eckford, naval architect, born 1:350
1781 Anson G. Phelps, merchant, born 12:491
1788 Samuel E. Smith, jurist and governor of Maine, born 6:307
1796 Thomas Reynolds, governor of Missouri, born .. 12:303
1801 Joseph Francis, inventor of the Francis life-car, born 10: 88
1805 Justin Perkins, missionary, "Apostle of Persia," born 10: 45
1812 Joseph H. Tuck, inventor of a dredging machine and a rotary engine, born 7:528
1818 John L. Worden, naval officer, born 4:284
1822 Chester S. Percival, author and poet, born 2:232
1822 Thomas B. Read, artist and poet, born 6:474
1822 Daniel B. Fayerweather, merchant and philanthropist, born 23:128
1824 Louis Prang, art lithographer, originator of the "chromo" print, born 11:159
1825 Ludwig S. Filbert, physician and inventor, born 4:487
1825 John H. Brunner, educator, born 12:312
1830 Thomas E. Rose, soldier, born 4:464
1831 Clement Studebaker, wagon manufacturer, born 11:109
1832 Clarke Bell, lawyer, born 13:204
1834 Hilary A. Herbert, secretary of the navy under Cleveland, born 7:544
1835 Simon Newcomb, astronomer and mathematician, born 7: 17
1858 Adolph S. Ochs, journalist who developed the New York "Times," born .... A: 76
1862 Jacksonville, Fla., occupied by Federal forces .. 5: 50
1862 Jane A. Delano, director of Red Cross nurses during World war, born 19:131
1864 Gen. Sherman took command of the Department of the Mississippi 4: 33
1866 Harry L. Russell, bacteriologist, born 16:417
1870 Henry A. Bumstead, physicist and educator, born 21: 77
1873 Stewart E. White, author, born 13:318
1874 Edward A. Deeds, electrical engineer, one of the founders of the Delco-light industry, born A:327
1907 The Russell Sage Foundation created 16:423
1914 Alaskan engineering commission created 6:517

MARCH 13.

1698 First service held in Trinity Church, New York 1:516
1758 Major Rogers defeated by the French and Indians 7:450
1785 Abel Cushing, jurist, born 18:156
1797 George Bacon Wood, physician and author, born 5:346
1808 William Orr, inventor and manufacturer of paper mill machinery, born 3: 74
1814 William W. Everts, theologian and author, born 11: 64
1820 Levi Stockbridge, agriculturist, born 5:508
1828 Benjamin Rose, capitalist, born 12:287
1829 Richard Coke, Texas lawyer, governor and U. S. senator, born 9: 72
1830 John Shrady, physician and surgeon, born 4:195
1832 John T. Gulick, missionary, scientist and author, born 11:463
1833 William F. Warren, president of Boston university, born 11:177
1834 Charles Hallock, naturalist and author, born ... 9:507
1840 William C. Gannett, clergyman, born 22: 36
1841 Joseph K. Emmet, actor, born 5:144
1846 Camillus P. Maes, R. C. bishop, born 12: 51
1852 Ernest Ingersoll, author and lecturer on scientific topics, born 9:240
1854 Henry A. Todd, philologist, born 24: 33
1855 Percival Lowell, astronomer, born 8:309
1862 Francis P. Paulus, artist, born 17:210
1865 Engagement at Silver Run, Fayetteville, N. C. .. 4:273

1865 Franklin S. Spalding, P. E. bishop, born 15: 374
1866 Dayton C. Miller, physicist, born ..... C: 515
1868 New constitution ratified by Arkansas 10: 188
1872 Oswald G. Villard, author and editor of the New York "Evening Post" and "The Nation," born D: 247
1875 Philadelphia "Times" first issued 1: 467
1883 Clifford M. Holland, civil engineer, born 19: 381
1884 System of standard time established 4: 249
1888 Severe blizzard in New York 16: 407

MARCH 14.

1644 Charter granted Rhode Island, uniting it with the Providence Plantations 10: 5
1676 Northampton, Mass., attacked by Indians 10: 50
1774 Boston port bill introduced in English parliament 1: 108
1781 Jonathan G. Hunton, lawyer and governor of Maine, born 6: 307
1782 Thomas H. Benton, U. S. senator, born 4: 399
1788 William Gibson, internationally famed surgeon, born 2: 441
1789 Joseph M. Smith, physician, born 6: 390
1794 Cotton gin patented by Eli Whitney 4: 495
1800 James Bogardus, inventor of cotton machinery, an engraving machine and the first dry gas meter, born 8: 193
1808 Francis Dwight, educator, born 12: 268
1813 Joseph P. Bradley, justice of the U. S. supreme court, born 1: 33
1819 William E. Worthen, civil engineer, born 12: 206
1833 John S. Marmaduke, soldier and governor of Missouri, born 12: 308
1837 Charles A. Cutter, librarian, born 13: 180
1839 Charles Wright Ely, educator, born 15: 117
1850 Holyoke, Mass., incorporated as a town 12: 341
1854 Thomas R. Marshall, vice-president of the United States, born 19: 137
1859 William G. Sharp, manufacturer, congressman and diplomat, born 12: 299
1862 Battle of New Berne, N. C. 4: 53
1862 New Madrid, Mo., captured by Federal troops .. 4: 282
1863 Admiral Farragut passed Port Hudson on the Mississippi river 2: 50
1864 A constitution ratified by Arkansas (unrecognized by congress) 10: 188
1867 William B. Walker, manufacturer of thermos bottles, born 15: 108
1876 Wallace Irwin, author, born 14: 184
1886 Basil M. Manly, economist, born ..... A: 444
1895 First printed telegraph letters transmitted 21: 464

MARCH 15.

1697 Haverhill, Mass., attacked by Indians 6: 102
1744 Outbreak of the French and Indian war 3: 330
1752 William Dorrel, founder of the sect of "Dorrelites," born 4: 63
1763 James Wilson, first American globe maker, born 17: 102
1767 Andrew Jackson, 7th president of the United States, born 5: 289
1781 Battle of Guilford Court House, Va. 1: 43
1800 James H. Hackett, actor, born 3: 74
1801 George P. Marsh, philologist and diplomat, born 2: 380
1812 James H. Adams, governor of South Carolina, born 12: 172
1815 James D. Butler, clergyman and author of books of travel, born 9: 190
1816 Richard H. Wilmer, P. E. bishop, born 3: 465
1820 Maine admitted to the Union 6: 305
1827 Michael C. Kerr, congressman, born 8: 462
1831 Thomas F. Rowland, iron manufacturer, born .. 12: 346
1841 Clement A. Griscom, head of the International Navigation Company, born 4: 186
1844 George C. Chase, president of Bates college, born 8: 395
1845 St. Clair McKelway, journalist, born 17: 383
1846 Wesley M. Stanford, bishop of the United Evangelical church, born 13: 559
1848 Toby E. Rosenthal, artist, born 13: 258
1852 Julian Kennedy, mechanical engineer and inventor of improvements in the blast furnace, born 24: 135
1861 William Patten, biologist, a life-long student of evolution, born 24: 121
1865 Credit Mobilier of America incorporated 4: 240
1869 John H. Bartlett, governor of New Hampshire, born ..... B: 119
1874 Harold L. Ickes, secretary of the interior under Franklin Roosevelt, born ..... D: 16
1879 Bishop McCloskey made the first American cardinal 1: 195
1889 Great hurricane at Samoa 10: 181
1916 Pershing's punitive expedition crossed into Mexico ..... A: 435

MARCH 16.

1618 Lord De la Warr started on his last voyage to Virginia 13: 381
1674 William Byrd, founder of Richmond, Va., born .. 7: 247
1695 William Greene, colonial governor of Rhode Island, born 10: 12
1739 George Clymer, signer of the Declaration of Independence, born 3: 272
1748 John Delafield, a New York "merchant prince," born 11: 28
1750 Samuel S. Smith, founder and first president of Hampton-Sidney college, born 2: 21
1751 James Madison, fourth president of the United States, born 5: 369
1774 Jethro Wood, inventor of a cast-iron plow, born 11: 360
1777 Jacob Osgood, founder of the sect of "Osgoodites," born 4: 375
1789 Henry U. Onderdonk, P. E. bishop, born 3: 470
1789 Charles King, president of Columbia college, born 6: 345
1792 Thomas Rogers, manufacturer, born 19: 174
1794 Lawrence Brainerd, philanthropist and U. S. senator, born 8: 474
1802 West Point military academy established 3: 239
1806 John C. Cresson, civil engineer, born 12: 466
1821 George W. Brooks, jurist, born 8: 167
1822 John Pope, soldier, born 4: 282
1823 Henry Hartshorne, physician and author, born 8: 202
1824 Edmund Kirby Smith, Confederate soldier and chancellor of the University of Nashville, born 8: 132
1830 Samuel A. Green, physician, soldier and author, born 2: 28
1831 Charles B. Lore, chief justice of Delaware, born 7: 553
1836 Andrew S. Hallidie, engineer and inventor of the cable railroad, born 7: 191
1838 Charles H. Fernald, naturalist and educator, born 9: 232
1844 John R. Proctor, civil service commissioner, born 13: 216
1856 Charles W. Russell, lawyer and diplomat, born 15: 358
1861 Ethelbert Warfield, president of Miami university and Lafayette college, born 11: 243
1865 Battle of Averysboro, N. C. 4: 34
1865 Daniel T. Macdougal, botanist, born 13: 125
1867 George Wharton Pepper, lawyer, educator and U. S. senator, born ..... A: 469
1873 Lilian Blauvelt, singer, born 12: 459
1875 Percy MacKaye, poet and dramatist, born 14: 159
1893 Elsie Janis, actress, born ..... A: 549
1904 First flight of Montgomery's aeroplane 15: 339

MARCH 17.

St. Patrick's Day

Also Evacuation Day in Boston

1725 Lachlan McIntosh, soldier, born 1: 72
1764 William Pinkney, U. S. attorney-general under Madison, born 5: 373
1776 Evacuation of British troops from Boston 1: 40
1777 Roger B. Taney, chief justice of the U. S. supreme court, born 1: 27
1805 William A. Stearns, president of Amherst college, born 5: 309
1819 Sarah C. E. Mayo, author, born 2: 437
1823 Charles P. Krauth, clergyman and educator, born 1: 349
1824 Josiah L. Pickard, educator, born 12: 512
1828 Patrick R. Cleburne, soldier, "Stonewall of the West," born 8: 54
1828 Albert K. Smiley, educator and reformer, born 15: 38
1832 Moncure D. Conway, author and clergyman, born 1: 206
1832 Walter Q. Gresham, secretary of state under Cleveland, born 24: 330
1833 Charles E. Wilbour, author and Egyptologist, born 13: 370
1836 Constitution of the Texas republic adopted 4: 351
1840 John A. Howell, naval officer and torpedo inventor, born 6: 43
1841 Emily Sartain, artist, born 13: 326
1843 Henry W. Lawton, soldier, born 10: 290
1847 George W. Macfarlane, financier and statesman, born 12: 554
1848 Clara Morris, actress and author, born 11: 506
1849 Charles F. Brush, electrician who adapted the arc lamp to commercial use, born 21: 1
1850 Theodore C. Link, architect, born 12: 104
1858 William E. Chilton, U. S. senator, born 15: 343
1862 First bombardment of Island No. 10, Mississippi river 6: 247
1864 Gen. Grant took command of all Federal armies 2: 73
1866 Pierce Butler, justice of the U. S. supreme court, born ..... A: 135
1874 Stephen S. Wise, rabbi, born ..... B: 25
1885 Patent granted to Yost for Caligraph typewriter 3: 317
1902 "Bobby" Jones, golf champion, born ..... A: 326

MARCH 18.

1673 West Jersey bought by the Friends 2:276
1747 William Duer, New York statesman, born 7:503
1766 The Stamp Act repealed by the British parliament 1:105
1782 John C. Calhoun, secretary of war under Monroe, vice president and secretary of state under Tyler, born 6: 83
1785 James M. Mathews, first chancellor of the University of the City of New York, born 6:323
1800 Francis Lieber, educator and publicist, born 5:116
1800 Gerard Hallock, journalist, editor of the New York "Journal of Commerce," born 11:193
1810 Samuel Hunt, clergyman and author, born 13: 41
1813 Joshua B. Lippincott, founder of a famous publishing house, born 26:182
1823 Joseph A. Seiss, clergyman and author, born ... 7:234
1834 James B. Herreshoff, shipbuilder, born 12:352
1837 Grover Cleveland, 22d and 24th president of the United States, born 2:400
1848 Nathaniel G. Herreshoff, sailboat designer, born 12:353
1850 Chester S. Lord, managing editor of the New York "Sun" for many years, born 25: 11
1852 Haley Fiske, president of the Metropolitan Life Insurance Company, born 21: 71
1856 Susa Young Gates, author, born B:445
1860 Edwin J. Marshall, financier and ranch owner, born 15:369
1872 Richard P. Strong, authority on tropical medicine, born .... A: 93

MARCH 19.

1639 John Winthrop, colonial governor of Connecticut, born 10:324
1687 La Salle treacherously murdered 5:126
1734 Thomas McKean, signer of the Declaration of Independence, president of the state of Delaware and governor of Pennsylvania, born 2:284
1742 Isaac Huger, Revolutionary soldier, born 7:514
1748 Elias Hicks, clergyman of the Society of Friends, born 11:464
1770 John M. Mason, clergyman and president of Dickinson college, born 6:462
1790 Alexander H. Everett, diplomat and author, born 9:256
1800 Erastus C. Benedict, educator and lawyer, born 5:415
1811 Andrew P. Peabody, clergyman and educator, born 3:357
1817 Seth Green, pisciculturist, born 6:199
1828 John J. Knox, comptroller of the currency under Grant and Hayes, born 3: 15
1830 Hubert A. Newton, mathematician and astronomer, born 9:219
1833 Philip Sidney Post, soldier and congressman, born 4:315
1833 William Penn Nixon, Chicago journalist, born 9:176
1835 James E. Scripps, newspaper publisher, born .. 15: 28
1836 Battle near Goliad, Tex., between Mexicans and Texans 4:138
1837 Joseph L. Firm, inventor of printing presses and a folding machine, born 7:356
1839 Frank M. Mayo, actor who played "Davy Crockett" 2000 times, born 23:369
1842 Thomas M. Drown, president of Lehigh university, born 7:112
1845 Moorfield Storey, lawyer, author and publicist, born 12:218
1847 Albert P. Ryder, artist, born 10:508
1847 William W. Taylor, manufacturer, born 13:458
1850 Alice French (Octave Thanet), author, born ... 25:296
1855 David P. Todd, astronomer, born 7:203
1856 Herbert Osborn, naturalist, born 13:202
1859 Peter J. Hamilton, lawyer and author, born 13:397
1860 William Jennings Bryan, politician, orator and secretary of state under Wilson, born 19:453
1865 Battle of Bentonville, N. C. 5:328
1868 Charles E. Acker, manufacturer and inventor in the field of electro-chemistry, born 13:573

MARCH 20.

1776 Joshua Bates, president of Middlebury college, born 12:106
1777 Edmund P. Gaines, soldier, born 9:372
1804 Neal Dow, reformer, author of the Maine (prohibition) Law, born 5:432
1804 Jersey City, N. J., founded 13:471
1810 John McCloskey, first American cardinal of the Roman Catholic church, born 1:195
1830 Eugene A. Carr, Federal soldier, born 12:199
1830 Francis A. Jackson, educator, born 12:445
1834 Charles William Eliot, president of Harvard, born 6:421
1835 John G. Walker, naval officer, born 11:524
1836 Col. Fannin surrendered to the Mexicans with 500 men, who were massacred a week later .. 4:133
1839 James Schouler, lawyer, educator and historian, born 11:181
1840 James Russell Miller, author and clergyman, born 10: 19
1841 Theodore C. Search, manufacturer, born 12:393
1844 David H. Greer, P. E. bishop, born 8:272
1845 Lucy M. W. Mitchell, archæologist, born 6:147
1849 Mrs. Bellamy Storer, originator of the famous Rookwood pottery, born 11:338
1856 Frederick W. Taylor, metallurgist and efficiency engineer, born 23: 47
1857 Lewis L. Dyche, naturalist, born 21:101

MARCH 21.

Vernal Equinox

1752 Peter Thacher, Congregational clergyman, born 6:507
1763 William J. Macneven, physician and Irish patriot, born 9:364
1786 Joseph Vance, soldier, congressman and governor of Ohio, born 3:139
1790 David B. Douglass, engineer and president of Kenyon college, born 7: 3
1791 Bank of New York incorporated 11:345
1817 Cyrenus Wheeler, inventor who made valuable improvements in the reaping machine, born .. 12: 98
1825 Fitzedward Hall, philologist, born 11:448
1826 Thomas Meehan, scientist and horticulturist, born 11:220
1829 Edward Sanderson, Wisconsin manufacturer and political leader, born 1:248
1829 Eugene A. Hoffman, clergyman, and dean of the General theological seminary, born 6:397
1833 Mary Abigail Dodge, author, born 9:227
1836 Henry B. Brown, justice of the U. S. supreme court, born 1: 38
1837 Theodore N. Gill, naturalist, born 12:376
1844 Lewis M. Haupt, civil engineer, born 13:233
1854 Henry Hun, neurologist, born 19:285
1857 Hunter Liggett, soldier, born A:498
1859 Henry R. Poore, artist, born 5:316
1863 Battle of Somerset, Ky. 4: 55
1864 George Edgar Vincent, president of the Rockefeller Foundation, born .... B: 6
1865 Gen. George O. Squier, inventor of valuable improvements in telegraph and wireless communication, born 24:320
1868 Sorosis Club (for women) organized 13:370
1881 Morning edition of Chicago "Daily News" first issued as the "Morning News" 13: 51

MARCH 22.

1765 The British Stamp Act became a law 1:333
1790 Thomas Jefferson became the first secretary of state 3: 3
1799 Joseph Saxton, a mechanician and inventor with the U. S. mint and coast survey, born 9:220
1803 Abner Coburn, governor of Maine, born 6:313
1811 Nathaniel M. Crawford, president of Mercer university and Georgetown (Ky.) college, born 6:497
1812 Stephen P. Andrews, philosopher, born 6:442
1814 Thomas Crawford, sculptor, born 8:292
1814 August M. L. Gemunder, violin maker, born ... 23:287
1816 John F. Kensett, artist, born 7:560
1817 Braxton Bragg, Confederate soldier, born 11:218
1818 Charles E. Butler, New York lawyer, born 18:121
1819 Joseph P. Webster, composer, born 19:428
1820 Duel between Commodores Decatur and Barron.. 4: 56
1823 George H. Williams, U. S. senator and attorney-general under Grant, born 4: 21
1834 William T. Nicholson, inventor of file cutting machinery, born 8:262
1834 Charles W. Marsh, inventor of improvements in reaping machines, born 11:268
1837 Henry Baerer, sculptor, born 12: 98
1840 Oberlin Smith, mechanical engineer, born 12:461
1845 Frederick S. Gibbs, legislator, born 12:533
1845 John B. Tabb, poet and priest, born 13:249
1846 Elwyn Waller, chemist, born 13:344
1846 Frederick Keppel, art connoisseur, born 22:386
1847 Bombardment of Vera Cruz, Mexico, begun 3:503
1853 Herman H. Kohlsaat, Chicago journalist, born 19: 65
1860 Richard O. Campbell, mine operator, born 15:175
1862 Laura Jean Libbey, author, born 19:141
1865 Wilson's raid from Chickasaw, Ala., to Macon, Ga., begun 2:525
1865 First "variety house" in America opened by Tony Pastor 16: 31
1868 Robert A. Millikan, physicist, winner of the Nobel prize, born A:268
1871 Governor Holden, of North Carolina, impeached and removed from office 4:428
1876 Richard E. Miller, artist, born A:270

1904 Patent issued for a method of inoculating the soil 13:285
1929 The U. S. coast guard vessel "Dexter" sank the schooner "I'm Alone," creating an international incident .... D: 83

MARCH 23.

1699 John Bartram, botanist, born 7:153
1736 Arthur St. Clair, soldier, governor of Northwest territory, born 1: 94
1755 Samuel Hitchcock, Vermont jurist, born 11:195
1775 Patrick Henry made his famous speech urging resistance to England 1:338
1787 Robert M. Patterson, scientist, director of the mint, born 26: 59
1790 Benjamin Franklin petitioned congress to abolish slavery 1:337
1802 Christopher R. Robert, philanthropist, patron of schools and colleges, and founder of Robert college, Turkey, born 10:492
1805 George Keim, Pennsylvania congressman, born 3:508
1812 Stephen R. Riggs, missionary to the Indians, born 3:119
1815 Ezekiel G. Robinson, president of Brown university, born 8: 26
1818 Don Carlos Buell, Federal soldier, born 4:263
1823 Schuyler Colfax, vice-president under Grant, born 4: 12
1829 George Crompton, inventor of cotton looms, born 10:161
1831 Edwin Reynolds, engineer and inventor, born .. 2:524
1831 James Phinney Baxter, Maine merchant and author, born 9:422
1836 Crawford H. Toy, Biblical scholar and philologist, born 6: 94
1837 Thomas E. Stillman, New York lawyer, born .. 15:103
1839 William J. Davis, Confederate soldier, author and scientist, born 13: 22
1842 Clemens Herschel, civil engineer and inventor, born 22:342
1843 James A. Mount, governor of Indiana, born 13:276
1843 Homer Laughlin, pottery manufacturer, born .. 16:251
1845 George W. Peckham, biologist, born 12:346
1846 DeForest Willard, orthopædist, born 15: 86
1849 Charles G. Perkins, electrician and inventor, born 4:290
1851 Samuel G. Dixon, bacteriologist, born 13:562
1855 Franklin H. Giddings, sociologist, born 15: 9
1857 Fannie M. Farmer, cooking expert, head of the Boston cooking school, born 22:206
1862 Battle of Kernstown, Va. 4:127
1865 Armies of Sherman, Terry and Schofield united at Goldsboro, N. C. 4: 34
1865 Madison J. Cawein, "Poet of Nature," born 8:231
1865 Paul Leicester Ford, author, born 13:105
1901 Aguinaldo, the Philippine leader, captured 11: 41

MARCH 24.

1638 Rhode Island purchased from the Indians for forty fathoms of beads 10:407
1725 Thomas Cushing, statesman, born 7:113
1733 Joseph Priestley, scientist and clergyman, born 6:148
1747 Alexander Scammell, soldier, born 2:261
1754 Joel Barlow, diplomat and poet, one of the "Hartford Wits," born 3:186
1755 Rufus King, U. S. senator and diplomat, born 6:301
1805 Charles W. Sanders, educator, born 2:257
1811 Horace P. Biddle, lawyer, poet and scientist, born 11:348
1814 George F. Simmons, clergyman, noted for his opposition to slavery, born 7:499
1815 The U. S. "Hornet" captured the British "Penguin" 6: 56
1818 William E. LeRoy, naval officer, born 4:413
1820 Frances Jane Van Alstyne (Fanny J. Crosby), poet and hymn writer, born 7: 65
1826 Matilda J. Gage, reformer, born 2:244
1828 Horace Gray, justice of the U. S. supreme court, born 1: 35
1828 Joseph J. Couch, inventor, born 15:256
1829 George Francis Train, author and financier, born 9:264
1832 Treaty of Cusseta with the Creek Indians 10:427
1834 John W. Powell, geologist and explorer, born 3:340
1837 George H. Mackenzie, chess champion, born 4:152
1841 Augustine Sackett, inventor and manufacturer of plaster board sheathing paper, born 16:334
1845 David McN. Stauffer, civil engineer and Federal soldier and naval officer, born 9: 45
1851 James S. Hogg, governor of Texas, born 9: 75
1851 Garrett P. Serviss, astronomer and author, born 11:349
1852 Edward P. Mitchell, journalist, born 4:524
1855 Andrew W. Mellon, Pittsburgh banker, and secretary of the treasury under Hoover, born A: 16
1860 Charles S. Prosser, geologist, born 12:544
1862 Frank W. Benson, artist, born 13:413
1865 Hobart C. Chatfield-Taylor, author, born C:359

1869 Claude Kitchin, lawyer and congressman, born 15: 66
1886 Frank J. Coleman, judge, born 25:103
1900 Work on the New York underground rapid transit system begun 13: 71
1934 President Franklin Roosevelt signed the Philippine independence act, granting independence to the islands after a ten-year period .... D: 7

MARCH 25.

Annunciation Day

Celebrated as Maryland day in that state in commemoration of the landing of Lord Baltimore's first colonists

1602 Gosnold set sail for America with twenty colonists 12:186
1634 Lord Baltimore's first colonists landed in Maryland 7:332
1655 Battle at Annapolis, Md., between Puritans and Royalists 7:333
1714 Matthew Griswold, jurist and governor of Connecticut, born 10:329
1753 Richard Varick, recording secretary on Washington's staff, born 13:471
1758 Richard D. Spaight, statesman and governor of North Carolina, born 4:420
1789 William C. Redfield, scientist and engineer, born 7:354
1797 John Winebrenner, founder of "The Church of God," born 1:180
1800 Stephen Colwell, financier and author, born ... 4:524
1809 Charles S. Storrow, civil engineer, builder of the dam at Lawrence, Mass., born 21: 93
1811 Jonathan Bourne, leader in the whaling industry, born 19:451
1818 Isaac I. Stevens, soldier and territorial governor of Washington, born 12:137
1827 Stephen B. Luce, naval officer, born 4:410
1831 Robert S. Green, New Jersey lawyer, congressman and governor, born 5:212
1836 First issue of the Philadelphia "Public Ledger" 21: 8
1838 Elwell S. Otis, Federal soldier, born 9: 29
1839 William B. Wait, educator of the blind, born .. 2:451
1846 John S. Kountz, Federal soldier and commander-in-chief of the Grand Army of the Republic, born 4:332
1848 William Keith Brooks, zoölogist, born 23: 83
1849 Jerome Daugherty, president of Georgetown university, born 12:131
1854 John Lind, congressman and governor of Minnesota, born 10: 69
1862 Louis Duncan, electrical engineer, born 14:145
1863 General Burnside took command of the Department of the Ohio 4: 53
1863 Brentwood, Tenn., captured by the Confederates 10: 36
1863 Simon Flexner, bacteriologist and pathologist, born .... B: 19
1865 Ft. Stedman, Va., captured by the Confederates 4:100
1867 Gutzon Borglum, sculptor, born 14: 80
1872 Chicago "Inter-Ocean" first issued 7:527
1880 Harry T. Collings, economist, born 25: 83

MARCH 26.

1676 Marlborough, Mass., destroyed by Indians 10: 50
1706 Mather Byles, clergyman, born 7:145
1738 Benjamin Cleveland, soldier, "hero of King's Mountain," born 1:508
1742 Moses Robinson, jurist, U. S. senator and governor of Vermont, born 8:313
1749 William Blount, territorial governor of Tennessee, born 7:206
1753 Benjamin Thompson (Count Rumford), statesman and scientist, born 5:410
1773 Nathaniel Bowditch, mathematician, born 6:377
1776 South Carolina declared her independence of the British crown 12:159
1779 Heman Humphrey, clergyman and president of Amherst college, born 5:308
1780 Moses Stuart "father of Biblical learning in America," born 6:244
1781 Nathaniel D. Gould, musician, born 7:426
1794 First embargo in history of the United States .. 12: 56
1796 Bellamy Storer, lawyer, born 11:338
1799 Thomas Sherwin, head master of the famous English high school, Boston, born 11:350
1804 David H. Storer, physician and naturalist, born 11:336
1804 Louisiana Purchase divided into the territory of Orleans and the district of Louisiana 12:301
1814 Brigadier-General Hull court-martialed 1: 67
1817 Herman Haupt, chief of the U. S. military railroads in the Civil war, born 10:224
1823 George H. Williams, attorney-general under Grant, born 4: 12
1823 Margaret M. Davidson, poet, born 7:476

1829 John R. Thomas, composer and singer, born 8:445

1842 Arthur Parton, landscape artist, born 13: 72

1843 Thomas E. Satterthwaite, physician, born 12:298

1847 Joseph P. Remington, educator and pharmacist, born 5:349

1848 Edward O. Wolcott, U. S. senator, born 8:397

1850 Edward Bellamy, author, born 1:263

1851 George F. Loring, Boston architect, born 11:328

1852 David McLean Parry, manufacturer, born 12:462

1858 William T. Smedley, artist and illustrator, born 10:378

1859 Elliott Daingerfield, artist, born 13:111

1864 Paducah, Ky., captured by the Confederates 10: 37

1874 Condé Nast, publisher, born 15: 80

1875 Robert Frost, poet, born A:540

1879 Othmar H. Ammann, engineer, designer of George Washington bridge across the Hudson, born D:320

1893 James B. Conant, chemist and president of Harvard, born D: 48

MARCH 27.

1513 Florida discovered by Ponce de Leon 11:335

1634 St. Mary's, first settlement in Maryland, founded 7:332

1666 Gurdon Saltonstall, governor of Connecticut, born 1:163

1794 Origin of the new U. S. navy under the Constitution 4:189

1802 Tayler Lewis, educator, born 10:131

1812 Governor of New York prorogued the legislature, a privilege used for the first time 6: 83

1813 Nathaniel Currier, publisher of the Currier and Ives prints, born 21:173

1814 Creeks defeated in battle of Horseshoe Bend (Tohopeka) 9:273

1815 William R. Smith, congressman and president of the University of Alabama, born 12:294

1817 George S. Coe, financier, born 7:488

1819 Sidney Perham, congressman and governor of Maine, born 6:315

1822 Charles S. Burke, actor, born 8:124

1823 Nathaniel C. Bryant, naval officer, born 3:167

1826 James P. Wormeley, civil engineer, born 9: 39

1826 Joseph Zentmayer, optician, born 13:215

1832 Francis H. Storer, chemist, born 11:337

1833 John Davis Washburn, diplomat, born 12:464

1836 Massacre at Goliad, Tex. 4:133

1838 Geneviève Ward (Countess de Guerbel), actress, born 9:196

1840 George F. Baker, New York banker and philanthropist, born 23: 75

1842 Horace L. Hotchkiss, financier, born 23:163

1844 Adolphus W. Greely, Arctic explorer and chief signal officer of the U. S. army, born 3:285

1844 Henry S. Carhart, physicist, born 4:455

1845 Edwin Norton, inventor of machines for making cans, and president of the American Tin Can Co., born 26:167

1847 Surrender of General Morales to General Scott at Vera Cruz 3:503

1855 Charles W. Pilgrim, psychiatrist, born A:329

1860 Frank F. Abbott, classical scholar, born 19:430

1866 President Johnson vetoed the Civil Rights bill 2:456

1901 The Chicago "Record" merged with the "Times-Herald" under the name of the Chicago "Record-Herald" 13: 51

MARCH 28.

1638 Wilhelm Kieft, governor of New Netherlands, arrived to take office 6: 91

1652 Samuel Sewall, jurist famous in the Witchcraft trials, born 5:339

1706 Andrew Oliver, Colonial statesman, born 7:498

1779 British privateer "Gregson" captured by the "General Arnold" 9:546

1787 Theodore Frelinghuysen, lawyer, U. S. senator and president of Rutgers college, born 3:401

1793 Henry R. Schoolcraft, ethnologist, born 5:145

1796 Elijah Iles, pioneer settler of Springfield, Ill., born 12:205

1802 John J. Shipherd, founder of Oberlin college, born 2:459

1814 Surrender of U. S. frigate "Essex" to the British 2: 99

1818 Wade Hampton, soldier and governor of South Carolina, born 12:177

1830 Treaty with Denmark signed 1:274

1831 Cyrus F. Knight, P. E. bishop, born 11: 58

1834 Rufus B. Bullock, reconstruction governor of Georgia, born 1:229

1834 The senate resolved that President Jackson had exceeded his authority when he removed the public deposits from the U. S. Bank 5: 79

1836 Austin Flint, physician, born 9:360

1837 Jacob H. Gallinger, U. S. senator, born 2:247

1837 Charles H. Deere, manufacturer of plows, born 3:272

1841 Alexander E. Sweet, humorist, born 6: 69

1844 William R. O'Donovan, sculptor, born 20:467

1848 Daniel R. Brown, hardware merchant and governor of Rhode Island, born 9:409

1861 Alfred B. Kittredge, U. S. senator, born 16:125

1892 James K. Hackett made his stage debut 23: 86

MARCH 29.

1676 Providence, R. I., attacked by King Philip and nearly destroyed 10: 7

1770 David Everett, journalist and poet, born 7:226

1779 William Baldwin, physician and botanist, born 10:275

1790 John Tyler, tenth president of the United States, born 6: 1

1813 Robert E. Rogers, chemist, born 7:518

1819 Isaac M. Wise, president of Hebrew Union college, born 10:116

1819 Edwin L. Drake, who drilled the first oil well, in 1859, born 26:458

1821 Frank Leslie, founder of "Frank Leslie's Illustrated Newspaper," born 3:370

1829 Edward L. Pierce, lawyer and author, born 4:522

1831 Amelia E. Barr, novelist, born 4:485

1834 Henry Mason Matthews, governor of West Virginia, born 12:431

1838 Charles H. Emery, civil engineer, born 9: 34

1841 Pierce F. Connelly, sculptor, born 23:313

1844 The Springfield "Republican" first issued 1:317

1850 Henry White, diplomat, born 14:171

1853 Elihu Thomson, electrical engineer and inventor with the General Electric Co., born B:106

1860 Carl Hering, electrical engineer, born 12:349

1860 Richard H. Dabney, educator, born 13:348

1866 George W. Wilder, head of the Butterick Co., dress pattern makers and publishers of the "Delineator," born 22: 43

1869 Ales Hrdlicka, anthropologist, born C: 90

1885 Walter R. Miles, psychologist, specialist in the psychology of reading and of music, born D:146

1887 Albert C. Read, aviator who made the first flight across the Atlantic, born A:496

1892 Behring sea arbitration treaty with Great Britain ratified by senate 5:411

MARCH 30.

Celebrated as Seward day in Alaska

1719 John Wentworth, New Hampshire jurist, born 4:350

1790 Joseph Smith, naval officer, born 4:381

1810 John C. Trautwine, engineer, born 5:196

1821 James Hadley, educator and scholar, born 1:175

1822 Territorial government established in Florida 11:376

1825 Samuel B. Maxey, soldier and U. S. senator, born 4: 50

1829 Roswell Smith, publisher, founder of the "Century Magazine," born 1:311

1832 Roger Q. Mills, U. S. senator, born 8:403

1833 Charles H. Peck, botanist, born 13: 49

1842 John Fiske, historian and philosopher, born 3: 23

1842 Ether first used as an anæsthetic 13:210

1851 Alexander C. Humphreys, president of Stevens institute of technology, born 13:203

1856 Charles Waldstein, archæologist, born 11:249

1857 Romeyn B. Hough, naturalist and author, born 20:170

1858 DeWolf Hopper, actor, born 10:450

1863 Archer Alexander, a fugitive slave, captured 12:422

1866 Free academy became the College of the City of New York 19:320

1867 Alaska purchased from Russia for $7,200,000 2: 79

1870 Texas readmitted into the Union 9: 71

1870 Fifteenth Amendment to the U. S. Constitution went into force 13: 50

1880 James L. Huntington, obstetrician, born A:486

MARCH 31.

1770 Jacob Crowninshield, statesman, born 3: 7

1774 Boston Port Bill passed by Parliament 1:108

1782 Samuel Prentiss, jurist and U. S. senator, born 8:402

1806 John Parker Hale, U. S. senator and minister to Spain, born 3:120

1809 James P. Henderson, Texas statesman and governor, born 1:442

1810 James Alden, naval officer, born 2:104

1812 Thomas Gold Appleton, author, born 8:391

1823 William Hart, artist, born 7:503

1826 Alexander B. Mott, surgeon, born 9:360

1829 Charles S. Robinson, clergyman and author, born 9:482

1835 John C. Draper, physician and scientist, born 6:171

1835 Stephen Salisbury, banker and antiquarian, born 7:554

1835 John La Farge, artist, born 9: 59

1837 Burke A. Hinsdale, educator, editor and author, born 10: 471
1839 Charles H. Willcox, inventor of the "lock stitch" device for sewing machines, born 19: 67
1848 William Waldorf Astor, capitalist and author, born 8: 105
1850 Charles D. Walcott, paleontologist and geologist, born 22: 135
1853 Angelo Heilprin, scientist, born 12: 381
1854 Treaty between the United States and Japan signed 4: 43
1855 William G. Gaul, artist, born 12: 366
1855 Alfred B. Hunt, metallurgist, born 25: 38
1855 John Hays Hammond, mining engineer, born .. 26: 45
1856 Franklin H. Sargent, founder of the Lyceum school of acting, born 6: 330
1862 Union City, Ky., captured 4: 220
1933 The unemployment relief act authorizing the establishment of the Civilian Conservation Corps signed .... D: 13

APRIL 1.

All Fools' Day

1684 William Joseph appointed president of the regency of Maryland 7: 334
1742 Samuel Bard, physician and educator, born 8: 209
1743 William Hindman, U. S. senator, born 2: 133
1743 Richard Butler, soldier, born 8: 83
1745 Jonathan Potts, surgeon, born 12: 254
1781 Robert Lucas, soldier, governor of Ohio and territorial governor of Iowa, born 11: 428
1788 Oliver Phelps and Nathaniel Gorham purchased from the Commonwealth of Massachusetts a large tract in what is now New York state 7: 40
1805 John Cadwalader, jurist, born 15: 305
1806 Charles B. Dyer, geologist, born 4: 528
1811 James McCosh, theologian and president of Princeton college, born 5: 468
1815 Henry B. Anthony, R. I. statesman and governor, born 9: 398
1823 Simon B. Buckner, Confederate soldier and governor of Kentucky, born 16: 341
1826 Edward A. Sothern, actor, born 5: 490
1826 Construction of the first railroad in Massachusetts begun 11: 502
1826 Theodore G. Wormley, chemist and toxicologist, born 13: 104
1834 James Fisk, spectacular financier, largely responsible for "Black Friday" panic, born 22: 170
1836 Horace J. Wickham, inventor of envelope-making machines, born 26: 76
1840 Organization of the "Liberty" party 1: 29
1844 George Harris, president of Amherst college, born 10: 101
1848 Charles H. Clark, publisher and editor of the Hartford "Courant," born 25: 6
1852 Edwin A. Abbey, artist, born 15: 280
1854 William W. Rockhill, orientalist and diplomat, born 8: 129
1855 Eugene H. Cowles, inventor of the electric smelter, born 23: 51
1858 Agnes Repplier, essayist, born .... C: 368
1864 Battle of Fitzhugh's Woods, Ark. 11: 394
1865 Battle of Five Forks, Va. 4: 68
1869 John N. Latané, historian and head of the school of international relations at Johns Hopkins university, born 23: 394
1882 Charles E. Dowman, neurologist, born 23: 173

APRIL 2.

1689 Arthur Dobbs, governor of North Carolina, born 5: 543
1743 Thomas Jefferson, 3d president of the United States, born 3: 1
1745 Richard Bassett, Delaware statesman and governor, born 11: 530
1749 David Ramsay, physician and historian, born .. 7: 285
1781 The "Alliance" captured two British privateers 4: 188
1791 David Henshaw, merchant and congressman, born 6: 7
1792 The United States mint established 1: 347
1802 Dennis H. Mahan, civil engineer and dean of the United States military academy, born 10: 440
1807 Alexander H. H. Stuart, secretary of the interior under Fillmore, born 6: 182
1814 Erastus B. Bigelow, inventor of machines for weaving carpets, born 3: 20
1817 Erastus D. Palmer, sculptor, born 5: 416
1826 Henry Howard, manufacturer and governor of Rhode Island, born 9: 404
1829 Alfred H. Littlefield, manufacturer and governor of Rhode Island, born 9: 406
1833 Thomas H. Ruger, Federal soldier and governor of Georgia, born 1: 229
1841 Daniel Draper, meteorologist, designer of self-recording instruments, born 6: 172
1844 George H. Putnam, publisher, born 2: 389
1847 Alvarado, Mexico, surrendered to Americans .. 9: 186
1851 Thomas F. Walsh, mine operator, born 15: 191
1854 Frank Billings, famed for his work in the advancement of medicine, born 23: 315
1857 George B. Foster, theologian and philosopher, born 18: 250
1862 William B. Wilson, first secretary of labor, born A: 52
1862 Nicholas Murray Butler, president of Columbia university, born .... B: 186
1864 Frank H. Vizetelly, lexicographer, born .... C: 105
1865 Confederates evacuated Richmond, Va. 2: 98
1865 Selma, Ark., captured by Confederates 10: 37
1875 Walter P. Chrysler, automobile designer and manufacturer, born .... D: 89
1878 Edward Kasner, mathematician, born 16: 61
1889 Patent issued for aluminum refining process .. 13: 94
1917 President Wilson appealed to Congress to declare a state of war with Germany—"The world must be made safe for democracy" 19: 7

APRIL 3.

1639 Sir Ferdinando Gorges made lord proprietary of Maine 5: 167
1755 Simon Kenton, soldier and Indian fighter, born 3: 527
1779 John Percival (Mad Jack), naval officer, one of the commanders of the "Constitution," born 20: 437
1782 Alexander Macomb, soldier, born 2: 241
1783 Washington Irving, author, born 3: 17
1798 Charles Wilkes, naval officer, born 2: 105
1799 John P. King, U. S. senator and railroad president, born 2: 178
1814 Lorenzo Snow, fifth president of the Mormon church, born 16: 7
1816 Charter of the United States Bank renewed ... 5: 372
1822 Edward Everett Hale, clergyman and author, born 1: 199
1822 Henry Martyn Field, clergyman, editor and author, born 5: 360
1823 George H. Derby (John Phoenix), humorist, born 5: 241
1828 Elias J. (Lucky) Baldwin, California pioneer and miner, born 22: 381
1833 Samuel H. Elbert, Colorado jurist and governor, born 6: 449
1835 Harriet Prescott Spofford, author and poet, born 4: 308
1836 John H. Van Amringe, mathematician, born .. 13: 241
1837 John Burroughs, author, born 1: 247
1844 George L. Osgood, composer, born 7: 436
1856 St. Lawrence university chartered by New York legislature 10: 199
1858 Albert J. Ochsner, surgeon, who made many notable contributions to the science of surgery, born 20: 439
1860 The "Pony Express" from Missouri to California officially inaugurated 20: 451
1861 Reginald de Koven, composer, born 26: 254
1865 Petersburg and Richmond, Va., occupied by the Federals 4: 7
1866 William J. Long, clergyman and author, born .. D: 354

APRIL 4.

1609 Henry Hudson sailed from Holland on his third exploratory voyage 9: 453
1707 Samuel Robinson, pioneer settler of Bennington, Vt., born 1: 473
1746 John Andrews, provost of the University of Pennsylvania, born 1: 342
1748 William White, P. E. bishop, born 3: 470
1769 Cadwallader D. Colden, New York lawyer, mayor and congressman, born 7: 504
1769 Nicholas Brown, Rhode Island merchant and philanthropist, born 8: 27
1788 David G. Burnet, Texas statesman and patriot, provisional president of the republic of Texas, born 5: 147
1792 Thaddeus Stevens, Pennsylvania lawyer and congressman, born 4: 30
1799 David Wallace, Indiana congressman and governor, born 13: 267
1802 Dorothea L. Dix, philanthropist, born 3: 438
1804 Samuel Morrill, ink manufacturer, born 24: 327
1809 Benjamin Peirce, mathematician and astronomer, born 8: 152
1810 James Freeman Clarke, clergyman and author, born 2: 186
1819 William B. Greene, author and reformer, born 7: 526
1820 Charles Devens, attorney-general under Hayes, born 3: 203
1821 Linus Yale, Jr., inventor of locks, safes and vaults, born 9: 188

1825 Charles W. Shields, clergyman and educator, born 13:174
1828 Thomson Kingsford, manufacturer, born 5:222
1834 Edwin B. Harvey, Massachusetts physician and legislator, born 15:276
1838 Lawrence Barrett, actor, born 1:379
1840 Henry P. Bowditch, physician and educator, born 12:252
1841 President Harrison died and was succeeded by Tyler 6: 3
1841 John G. Johnson, lawyer, "King of the American Bar," born 16:421
1844 James B. Oliver, steel manufacturer, born 16:110
1850 William S. Bigelow, physician and orientalist, born 20:177
1856 Washington I. Chambers, naval officer, noted for designing ordnance improvements, born 25:442
1866 George Pierce Baker, professor of dramatic art, born 25: 28
1876 Claude W. Kress, merchant, born D:267
1879 Public electric lighting permanently installed .. 21: 2
1882 Repeating shotgun patented 22: 63
1917 Resolution declaring a state of war against Germany passed by the U. S. senate 19: 8
1933 Rear-Adm. Moffett and 73 of his crew killed in the "Akron" disaster 25:404

APRIL 5.

1739 Philemon Dickinson, soldier and U. S. senator, born 7:517
1768 New York chamber of commerce established ... 1:495
1798 Jonas Chickering, piano manufacturer, born ... 6:190
1808 Mark A. D. Howe, P. E. bishop, born 13:278
1816 Samuel F. Miller, justice of the U. S. supreme court, born 2:473
1819 William H. Van Buren, surgeon, born 10:287
1822 Theodore R. Timby, inventor, born 9:116
1822 Ebenezer W. Peirce, Federal soldier and author, born 13:106
1826 Algernon S. Sullivan, lawyer and philanthropist, born 24:380
1832 John Henry Devereux, railroad president, born 12:274
1834 Frank R. Stockton, author and humorist, born 1:396
1834 Prentice Mulford, journalist and proponent of the White Cross system of occult thought, born 1:433
1835 Francis M. Ramsay, naval officer, born 15:122
1836 John O'Brien (John T. Raymond), comedian, born 10:264
1837 Henry G. Thomas, soldier, born 12:249
1837 Edward A. Rand, clergyman and author, born 13:412
1838 Elmer H. Capen, president of Tufts college, born 6:241
1838 Thomas Shaw, inventor of the Shaw gas tester and numerous other devices, born 15:355
1838 Alpheus Hyatt, paleontologist, born 23:362
1839 Robert Smalls, Federal soldier and congressman, born 12:425
1844 Robert E. Thompson, educator and economist, born 10: 18
1856 Booker T. Washington, educator, born 7:363
1862 Siege of Yorktown, Va., by Federals commenced 4:141
1865 First national Unitarian convention held in New York 1:118
1871 Winchell Smith, actor and dramatist, one of the most skilled directors of the American stage, born 24: 37
1933 United States ordered the return of gold coin, bullion and certificates to the Federal Reserve banks .... D: 4

APRIL 6.

Confederate Memorial Day

1709 Thomas Hopkinson, lawyer and electrician, born 7:249
1756 Anthony Haswell, journalist and ballad writer, born 8:261
1776 Engagement between the British "Glasgow" and the American squadron 2: 18
1785 John Pierpont, poet and clergyman, born 6:155
1786 William R. King, statesman, born 4:147
1787 Duncan L. Clinch, soldier and congressman, born 12: 63
1788 Isaac Hill, New Hampshire statesman and governor, born 11:127
1789 Washington chosen president of the United States by the electors 1: 5
1802 Thomas W. Gilmer, statesman, governor of Virginia and secretary of the navy under Tyler, born 5:449
1803 Alexander S. Mackenzie, naval officer, born 4:527
1805 Alexander E. Hosack, surgeon, born 9:355
1810 Edmund H. Sears, clergyman and author, born .. 8:378
1813 Lewiston, Del., bombarded by the British 11:531
1814 Edward E. Salisbury, philologist, born 11:448
1823 Joseph Medill, journalist, born 1:131
1830 First Mormon church organized 7:387
1834 Hart Pease Danks, composer, born 8:447
1841 Cornerstone of the Mormon temple at Nauvoo, Ill., laid 7:387
1848 Merrill E. Gates, president of Rutgers and Amherst colleges, born 5:309
1849 Thomas Earley, financier, born 16:232
1852 Timothy Cole, wood engraver, born C:329
1858 John J. Riker, merchant, born 8:294
1862 Battle of Shiloh (or Pittsburg Landing), Tenn. 4: 32
1865 Battle of Sailor's Creek, Va. 4:100
1866 First post of the Grand Army of the Republic organized 14:111
1869 American Museum of Natural History incorporated 8:268
1872 Samuel Taylor Darling, pathologist, born 19:417
1874 Edwin Greenlaw, scholar, born 22: 5
1874 Harry Houdini, prestidigitator, born 22: 79
1909 Peary reached the north pole 14: 62
1917 Resolution declaring a state of war against Germany passed by the house and signed by President Wilson 19: 8
1926 Announcement of the discovery of illinium B:438

APRIL 7.

1775 Francis C. Lowell, cotton manufacturer, born 7:151
1780 William Ellery Channing, clergyman, born 5:458
1788 Marietta, Ohio, settled by the Ohio Company .. 3: 70
1793 Beverley Kennon, naval officer, born 4:552
1798 Territory of Mississippi organized by Congress .. 13:485
1801 Henry Eagle, naval officer, born 3:278
1807 Henry W. Herbert (Frank Forester), author, born 3:534
1808 Charles F. Barnard, philanthropist, born 8:232
1809 William H. Talcott, civil engineer, born 9: 43
1819 Alfred Jones, artist, born 12:386
1825 John H. Gear, governor of Iowa, born 11:433
1840 George H. Horn, entomologist, born 7:502
1858 E. Campion Acheson, P. E. bishop, born 26: 66
1859 Jacques Loeb, physiologist, born 11: 72
1859 Walter C. Camp, famous Yale athlete and manufacturer, born 21:293
1861 Lewis Nixon, naval architect, born 13: 42
1862 Island No. 10 captured by the Federals 4:282
1863 Fort Sumter, S. C., attacked in an unsuccessful attempt to take Charleston 5: 51
1865 Grant requested Lee to surrender the army of northern Virginia 4:100
1914 Treaty between Colombia and the United States signed 19: 4

APRIL 8.

1513 Ponce de Leon first landed in Florida 11:335
1731 William Williams, signer of the Declaration of Independence, born 10:392
1732 David Rittenhouse, astronomer, born 1:346
1782 Naval battle between the "Hyder Ali" and the "General Monk" 4:167
1798 Pliny Freeman, underwriter, born 11:219
1811 George W. Greene, author, born 7:309
1814 Israel P. Warren, author and clergyman, born 4:235
1817 Walter Harriman, Federal soldier and governor of New Hampshire, born 11:133
1820 John Taylor Johnston, organizer and president of the Central R. R. of New Jersey and first president of the Metropolitan museum of art, born 23:156
1826 Duel between Henry Clay and John Randolph .. 5: 78
1832 Howell E. Jackson, U. S. senator and justice of the U. S. supreme court, born 8:243
1833 James B. Reynolds, physician, born 14:482
1836 William E. Hale, promoter of the hydraulic elevator, born 26:117
1847 Harry B. Hutchins, president of Cornell university, born 16:371
1850 William H. Welch, pathologist and bacteriologist, born 26: 6
1853 Laura A. Linton, chemist and physician, born 12: 62
1856 Frederick E. Pond (Will Wildwood), journalist, born 10:208
1861 Irving R. Wiles, artist, born 6:468
1861 James E. Creighton, philosopher, born 23:220
1864 Battle of Sabine Cross Roads, La. 4:223
1865 Albion F. Bacon, social reformer, born D:365
1869 Harvey Cushing, surgeon, born .... C: 36
1881 Remsen B. Ogilby, president of Trinity college, born .... A: 94
1882 Elbert J. Hall, mechanical engineer, co-designer of the Liberty motor for aircraft, born A:111
1893 Mary Pickford, actress, born .... A: 92

APRIL 9.

1676 Canonchet, sachem, captured 10:402
1682 La Salle reached the mouth of the Mississippi river and took possession of Louisiana 5:125
1738 Rufus Putnam, soldier, born 1:128
1758 Fisher Ames, statesman and orator, born 2:382
1766 John Overton, jurist and one of the founders of Memphis, Tenn., born 4: 60
1793 Alonzo Church, president of the University of Georgia, born 9:180
1811 Hiram Camp, inventor and philanthropist, born 8:155
1812 Randolph B. Marcy, soldier, born 4:330
1815 James T. Brady, criminal lawyer, born 3:387
1816 African Methodist Episcopal church organized .. 13:201
1823 Andrew Garrett, conchologist, born 2:162
1826 Chatham R. Wheat, soldier, born 9:168
1826 Hugh McLaughlin, politician, born 14:516
1827 Maria S. Cummins, author, born 6:135
1828 Samuel A. King, aëronaut, born 24:137
1830 Eadweard James Muybridge, photographer, born 19:152
1838 Samuel Fleet Speir, physician, born 4:173
1839 Joseph T. Rothrock, botanist, "Father of Forestry in Pennsylvania," born 19:180
1842 William F. Draper, manufacturer, born 6: 98
1843 Samuel W. Pennypacker, Pennsylvania jurist and governor, born 9:487
1844 Olin Levi Warner, sculptor, born 8:282
1844 Stella S. Gilman, founder of Radcliff college, born 10:363
1847 Robert Garrett, president of the Baltimore & Ohio railroad, born 18: 4
1862 Charles H. Brent, P. E. bishop, born 26:482
1864 Battle of Pleasant Hill, La. 4:223
1864 Henry Hudson Kitson, sculptor, born 12:398
1865 Gen. Lee surrendered to Gen. Grant 4:100
1865 Fort Blakeley, Mobile, Ala., captured by the Federals 13:338
1865 Charles P. Steinmetz, electrical engineer and inventor, born 23: 94
1866 Civil Rights bill passed over President Johnson's veto 2:456
1880 Herbert A. Gibbons, historian, born A:492
1906 San Francisco earthquake and fire 8:478
1912 U. S. children's bureau established; Julia C. Lathrop its first chief 24:298
1918 Bill establishing the War Finance Corporation adopted B:271

APRIL 10.

1606 King James I issued two land patents for "the First and Second colonies" in North America 5:166
1778 The "Ranger," under John Paul Jones, sailed from Brest on a cruise that terrorized the English coast 2: 15
1792 Newtown (Elmira), N. Y., settlement organized 12:236
1794 Edward Robinson, Biblical scholar and explorer, born 2:242
1806 Horatio Gates, Revolutionary soldier, died 1: 48
1806 Leonidas Polk, P. E. bishop and Confederate soldier, born 11:341
1810 Benjamin H. Day, founder of the New York "Sun," born 13:307
1817 John C. Robinson, soldier, born 4:460
1820 Slave traders captured by the "Cyane" 10:126
1823 Thomas R. R. Cobb, lawyer and Confederate soldier, born 6:533
1827 Lew Wallace, Federal soldier and author, born 4:363
1832 John N. Stockwell, astronomer, born 9:373
1833 David McM. Gregg, soldier, born 4:330
1835 Louise Chandler Moulton, short story writer and poet, born 3:365
1835 Henry Villard, railway promoter, financier, born 3:498
1837 Alphonse Fteley, civil engineer, specializing in water works, dams and sewerage, born 13:561
1837 Harriette Charlotte Keatinge, pioneer woman physician of the gulf states, born 18:129
1838 Frank Stephen Baldwin, inventor of calculating machines, born 16:281
1839 Alfred T. Bricher, artist, born 13:453
1841 The New York "Tribune" first issued 3:450
1847 Joseph Pulitzer, proprietor and editor of the New York "World," born 1:375
1850 Fanny Davenport, actress, born 4: 57
1862 Federal forces opened siege on Fort Pulaski, Ga. 4:310
1863 Battle of Franklin, Tenn. 4:559
1865 Joseph H. Sears, editor and author, born 13:363
1866 Society for the Prevention of Cruelty to Animals chartered 3:106
1870 Charles B. Warren, attorney-general and diplomat, born 26: 15
1877 John A. Macy, literary critic, born 23:108
1885 Frances Perkins, secretary of labor under Roosevelt, the first woman to hold a cabinet portfolio, born .... D: 19

APRIL 11.

1639 John Haynes became governor of Connecticut .. 7:371
1639 First election held under the constitution of Connecticut 10:320
1789 John Emory, M. E. bishop, born 10:353
1794 Edward Everett, Massachusetts statesman and governor, born 6:179
1798 Pierce Mason Butler, governor of South Carolina, born 12:168
1800 Samuel B. Ruggles, New York lawyer, born ... 13:419
1807 Augustus E. Silliman, financier and author, born 6:231
1815 Charles W. Couldock, actor, born 2:346
1816 The first bishop of the African Methodist Episcopal church consecrated 13:201
1819 Henry Gurdon Marquand, banker and art patron, born 8:390
1837 Elmer E. Ellsworth, soldier, born 4:166
1838 Monticello (Ill.) seminary opened 6: 39
1848 Illinois and Michigan canal completed 11: 47
1852 James B. Forgan, president of the First National Bank of Chicago, born 18:176
1859 Enoch Herbert Crowder, soldier, born A:455
1860 John Wingate Weeks, U.S. senator and secretary of war under Harding and Coolidge, born 20: 4
1861 William Ordway Partridge, sculptor, born 23: 12
1862 Fort Pulaski, Ga., surrendered to Federals 4: 54
1862 William W. Campbell, astronomer, born 11:278
1862 Charles Evans Hughes, chief justice of the U. S. supreme court, born .... A: 6
1864 Robert Loveman, poet, born 13:479
1865 Forts Huger and Tracy, Ala., captured by Federal navy, opening the way to Mobile 5: 44
1869 Harvey H. Baker, first judge of the Boston juvenile court, born 21: 74
1873 Death of Gen. Canby through treachery of Indians 5:333
1883 Chicago manual training school incorporated ... 20:174
1883 Harry Woodburn Chase, president of the University of North Carolina, born A:298
1895 Duel between Governor John Sanford and William Goebel 13: 13
1917 Conference of railroad representatives signed an agreement to operate under one management for the duration of the war 18: 9

APRIL 12.

1770 All duties revoked by Great Britain, except on tea 1: 8
1777 Henry Clay, statesman and orator, born 5: 77
1782 Naval battle between the fleets of Lord Rodney and Count de Grasse 11:271
1789 Andrew Wylie, president of Washington and Indiana colleges, born 13:116
1791 Francis P. Blair, journalist, born 4:268
1795 Richard Borden, manufacturer, born 10:309
1805 Theodorus Bailey, naval officer, born 2:106
1805 John Thomas, founder of the sect of Christadelphians, born 4: 61
1811 Daniel R. Goodwin, provost of the University of Pennsylvania, born 1:344
1811 Trading post of Astoria established on the Pacific coast 8:103
1816 Benjamin Douglass, founder of the mercantile credit reporting agency which became R. G. Dun & Co., born 24:317
1818 Michael Heiss, R. C. archbishop, born 12:411
1821 Adonijah S. Welch, president of Iowa State agricultural college, born 12:291
1822 Donald Grant Mitchell (Ik Marvel), author, born 6: 97
1828 Charles Foster, governor of Ohio and secretary of the treasury under Harrison, born 1:139
1831 Alva Woods inaugurated first president of the University of Alabama 12:293
1831 Grenville M. Dodge, soldier, engineer, railroad president, born 16:191
1832 George G. Rockwood, photographer, born 13:208
1838 John S. Billings, physician and author, born ... 4: 78
1839 William R. Garrett, soldier and educator, born 12:560
1841 Richard Channing Jones, president of the University of Alabama, born 12:296
1844 Treaty to annex Texas signed by the secretary of state 6:266
1848 Frank K. M. Rehn, artist, born 9: 55
1856 Benjamin Tappan, naval officer, born 18:377
1859 Frank E. Miller, laryngologist, born 26:472
1861 Bombardment of Fort Sumter, S. C. 5:261
1862 Attempt to destroy the Georgia State railroad .. 9:471
1864 Battle of Coushatta, La. 8:275
1864 The Fort Pillow (Tenn.) massacre occurred ... 10: 37
1865 Mobile, Ala., surrendered to the Federals 5: 44
1880 Daniel L. Marsh, clergyman and president of Boston university, born A:133
1884 Paolo Abbate, sculptor and evangelist, born .... B: 91
1916 Skirmish between American and Mexican troops A:435

APRIL 13.

Year	Event	Ref.
1772	Eli Terry, inventor and manufacturer, born	6:258
1777	Battle of Bound Brook, N. J.	7:543
1788	The "doctors' mob" in New York	8:206
1795	James Harper, publisher, born	1:151
1796	George N. Briggs, governor of Massachusetts, born	1:115
1813	John H. Lillie, inventor, born	9:512
1818	The U. S. flag, as finally adopted, first raised	8: 98
1823	Sabato Morais, clergyman and educator, born	10:170
1825	William H. Beard, artist, born	11:294
1827	Peter Neff, photographer and inventor, born	13:253
1830	Denison Chase, inventor, born	4:494
1833	Milo M. Belding, silk manufacturer, born	1:437
1837	Samuel H. Scudder, entomologist, born	24:180
1840	William H. S. Wood, founder of William Wood & Co., medical publishers, and president of the Bowery Savings Bank of New York City, born	24:389
1842	Anson R. Graves, P. E. bishop, born	4:286
1846	Pennsylvania Railroad Co. organized	13:333
1851	William Q. Judge, theosophist, born	15:337
1851	Robert Abbe, surgeon, born	21:197
1852	Frank W. Woolworth, merchant, originator of the five and ten cent store, born	23: 16
1854	Richard T. Ely, economist, born	B:204
1863	Albert Schneider, botanist, born	13:373
1865	Raleigh, N. C., surrendered to the Federals	4: 34
1869	George Westinghouse received his first airbrake patent	15: 42
1870	Metropolitan Museum of Art incorporated	1:157
1872	Benjamin D. Coppage, inventor, born	22: 93
1873	John W. Davis, lawyer and diplomat, born	A: 25
1875	Ray Lyman Wilbur, president of Stanford university and secretary of the interior under Hoover, born	C: 12
1877	Mary Garden, singer, born	15:209
1879	Redfield Proctor, governor of Vermont, born	B:432
1888	John Hays Hammond, Jr., inventor, born	D:391
1895	First professional appearance of Isadora Duncan	22:159

APRIL 14.

Year	Event	Ref.
1775	The first abolition society organized	1:336
1780	Battle of Monk's Corner, S. C.	7:514
1785	Town of Louisbourg (afterwards Harrisburg), Pa., incorporated	12:556
1800	John C. Green, merchant, born	11:336
1801	Henry D. Gilpin, attorney-general under Van Buren, born	6:437
1801	John P. Richardson, governor of South Carolina, born	12:168
1802	Horace Bushnell, clergyman, born	8:303
1802	The law preventing the natives of an enemy's country from becoming citizens of the United States repealed	13:182
1808	William Marvin, judge, and provisional governor of Florida, born	11:379
1810	Justin S. Morrill, U. S. senator, born	1:377
1813	Junius S. Morgan, banker, born	14: 66
1814	Fourth embargo act repealed	12: 56
1820	Maturin M. Ballou, journalist and author, born	7:307
1820	Daniel K. Pearsons, Chicago philanthropist, born	24:417
1822	Theodore T. S. Laidley, soldier and inventor, born	7: 24
1831	John Pratt, journalist and inventor, born	3:315
1839	Charles A. Nelson, librarian, born	24:211
1842	Adna R. Chaffee, soldier, born	10:493
1842	Congress authorizes construction of the "Stevens" battery	11: 22
1844	Delphin M. Delmas, New York lawyer, born	24:387
1846	Elbridge S. Brooks, author, born	7:156
1847	Moses P. Handy, news correspondent, born	16:254
1849	Elijah E. Hoss, M. E. bishop, the "foreign minister of southern Methodism," born	25: 58
1850	Rose Coghlan, actress, born	13:397
1853	Harlan P. Amen, principal of Phillips Exeter academy, born	10:107
1857	Edgar S. Kelley, composer, born	11:388
1858	Edward E. Hayden, naval officer and meteorologist, born	8:112
1861	Fort Sumter evacuated by Federal forces	4:179
1861	John Joseph Carty, electrical engineer, a pioneer in long-distance telephone service, born	23: 36
1863	Destruction of the Confederate "Queen of the West"	6:444
1865	President Lincoln assassinated	3:182
1879	James Branch Cabell, author, born	A:245
1905	The remains of John Paul Jones discovered in Paris by Gen. Horace Porter	2: 16

APRIL 15.

Arbor Day in Utah

Year	Event	Ref.
1638	English settlers arrived at New Haven, Conn.	6:121
1689	Richard Ward, colonial governor of Rhode Island, born	10: 12
1728	John Montgomerie, governor of New York and New Jersey, assumed office	13:453
1741	Charles W. Peale, artist, born	6:358
1757	Caleb Bingham, pioneer Boston educator, and author of the first text book on geography in use in America, born	8: 19
1767	Philip Van Rensselaer, mayor of Albany, born	7:525
1814	John Lothrop Motley, historian and diplomat, born	5:213
1817	Hartford (Conn.) school for the deaf opened	9:139
1821	Joseph E. Brown, lawyer and governor of Georgia, born	1:227
1822	Sylvanus Sawyer, inventor, born	4:318
1829	James Kelly, bibliographer, born	5:460
1831	George W. N. Yost, inventor, born	3:317
1837	Horace Porter, soldier and diplomat, born	4:310
1843	Henry James, author, born	1:410
1850	John M. Longyear, mine operator, born	15:295
1859	Abbott F. Graves, artist, born	7:458
1861	President Lincoln called for 75,000 troops	2: 68
1861	Bliss Carman, poet, born	21:429
1862	General Sherman began the siege of Corinth, Mass.	4: 32
1865	Death of President Lincoln; Andrew Johnson took the oath of office	2: 74
1912	S.S. "Titanic" sank in Atlantic ocean	8:107
1924	Japanese barred from admission to the United States in violation of the "gentleman's agreement"	A: 2

APRIL 16.

Year	Event	Ref.
1684	Francis Howard (Lord Effingham) assumed the office of governor of Virginia	13:386
1760	William Bull became governor of South Carolina	12:158
1794	George Bass Holmes, manufacturer, born	12:282
1808	Caleb B. Smith, secretary of the interior under Lincoln, born	2: 88
1818	Charles J. Folger, judge and secretary of the treasury under Arthur, born	4:250
1819	Edward A. Washburn, P. E. clergyman, born	9:498
1823	Orlando B. Wilcox, soldier, born	4:220
1839	Frederick W. Putnam, anthropologist, born	23:257
1850	Herbert B. Adams, historian, born	8:270
1851	William H. Hubbard, clergyman, born	15:121
1853	Charles R. Williams, editor-in-chief of the Indianapolis "News" and author and poet, born	21:288
1857	Henry S. Pritchett, president of the Carnegie Foundation for the Advancement of Teaching, born	C:498
1859	William L. Dudley, chemist and educator, born	8:227
1862	Slavery abolished in the District of Columbia	2: 69
1863	Federal fleet of gunboats and three transports ran the Confederate batteries at Vicksburg	2: 98
1865	Battle of Columbus, Ga.	4:276
1865	Franz P. Kaltenborn, musician, born	10:198
1867	Wilbur Wright, airplane inventor, born	14: 56
1868	Alfred G. Mayor, zoologist, born	19:121
1889	Charles Chaplin, actor and motion picture producer, born	A:531

APRIL 17.

Year	Event	Ref.
1492	Agreement between Ferdinand and Isabella and Columbus signed	3:437
1741	Samuel Chase, signer of the Declaration of Independence, born	1: 24
1744	John Page, governor of Virginia, born	3:219
1770	Mahlon Dickerson, secretary of the navy under Jackson, and governor of New Jersey, born	5:295
1776	Battle between the "Lexington" and the "Edward"	4:188
1786	Walter Forward, secretary of the treasury under Tyler, born	6: 5
1787	George Brown, banker, born	1:474
1795	George E. Badger, secretary of the navy under Harrison, and U. S. senator, born	3:305
1806	William Gilmore Simms, novelist and poet, born	6:204
1813	Susan Fenimore Cooper, author, born	6:301
1816	Samuel A. Allibone, author, born	6:227
1826	William Lee, publisher, born	11:454
1827	George Nichols, acting president of Norwich university, born	18:327
1835	Jonas M. Bundy, editor and author, born	1:202
1837	J. Pierpont Morgan, financier, born	14: 66
1837	Elizabeth W. Bellamy, author, born	12:269
1841	Dr. Harrison Allen, physician and scientist, born	9:359
1842	Charles H. Parkhurst, clergyman and reformer, born	4:402
1848	Louis Charles Elson, musician and author, born	8:449
1849	William R. Day, secretary of state under McKinley, and justice of the U. S. supreme court, born	11: 11
1851	James Taylor Du Bois, diplomat, born	18:363
1852	William Potter, lawyer, diplomat and president of Jefferson medical college, born	13:469

1853 W J McGee, anthropologist and geologist, born 10: 349
1854 Edward D. Libbey, manufacturer of glassware, born 13: 503
1856 John Addison Porter, editor and author, born .. 9: 244
1859 Willis Van Devanter, associate justice of the U. S. supreme court, born D: 82
1861 Virginia seceded from the Union 4: 96
1861 Willard Saulsbury, U. S. senator, born 15: 105
1863 Vance Thompson, author and playwright, born 20: 241
1865 West Point, Miss., captured by the Federals 6: 448
1870 Ray Stannard Baker (David Grayson), author, born C: 415
1888 Patent for Venturi (water pressure) meter issued 22: 342

APRIL 18.

1644 Indian massacre in Virginia 13: 383
1689 The royal governor of New England overthrown 6: 90
1728 Ebenezer Larned, soldier, born 1: 78
1743 William Stephens became president of the colony of Georgia 1: 490
1775 Paul Revere's famous ride 1: 83
1799 John Young Mason, secretary of the navy under Tyler and U. S. attorney-general under Polk, born 6: 7
1805 Henry P. Tappan, president of the University of Michigan, born 1: 249
1806 Ralph Hoyt, P. E. clergyman and poet, born .. 7: 453
1815 Sanford E. Church, jurist, born 11: 267
1815 Beriah Magoffin, governor of Kentucky, born .. 13: 8
1815 David Palmer, financier, born 18: 139
1835 John Henry Dolph, artist, born 10: 369
1842 Rhode Island suffragists held an election 8: 234
1846 William A. Stone, governor of Pennsylvania, born 24: 388
1847 Battle of Cerro Gordo, Mexico 3: 503
1856 Wilton Lloyd-Smith, Presbyterian clergyman and missionary / Walter Lloyd-Smith, jurist } twins, born 21: 121
1857 Clarence Darrow, lawyer, born B: 222
1860 George N. Stewart, physiologist, born 23: 402
1861 First volunteer troops reached Washington, D. C. 2: 290
1861 Harper's Ferry evacuated by Gen. Johnston 4: 127
1863 Rollin A. Harris, oceanographer, born 22: 388
1864 Richard Harding Davis, journalist and author, born 8: 176
1864 Isaac Murphy inaugurated governor of Arkansas 10: 188
1866 Charles Austin Bates, financier, born 15: 74
1868 Louisiana ratified a new constitution 10: 81
1877 Martin E. Trapp, governor of Oklahoma, born B: 196
1881 Robert G. Anderson, author, born A: 180

APRIL 19.

Patriots' Day

(*Holiday in Maine and Massachusetts.*)

1619 George Yeardley assumed office as governor of Virginia 13: 381
1672 Sir John Yeamans proclaimed governor of South Carolina 12: 151
1721 Roger Sherman, statesman, born 2: 352
1759 Amos Whittemore, inventor, born 7: 527
1775 Battle of Lexington, Mass. 1: 96
1782 Holland recognized the independence of the colonies 2: 3
1799 Edward W. Clay, caricaturist and engraver, born 22: 173
1812 James S. Rollins, "father of the University of Missouri," born 8: 182
1812 Duel between Charles S. Mitchell and Thomas Marshall 12: 54
1831 Mary L. Booth, author, born 7: 321
1833 Oberlin, Ohio, founded 2: 461
1833 Wayne MacVeagh, U. S. attorney-general under Garfield, born 4: 246
1836 Augustus D. Juilliard, New York merchant and patron of music, born 14: 521
1839 Eliza Sunderland, reformer, lecturer, educator, born 10: 219
1842 Indians defeated at Palaklaklaha, Fla. 4: 506
1844 Leo Rassieur, lawyer and soldier, born 4: 343
1847 Jalapa, Mexico, captured 3: 503
1849 John Uri Lloyd, chemist and author, born D: 106
1850 The Clayton-Bulwer treaty concluded 6: 179
1861 Federal troops attacked in Baltimore, Md. — first blood shed in the Civil war 2: 68
1862 Thomas R. Kimball, architect who designed St. Cecilia's cathedral, Omaha, born 25: 364
1870 Harry H. Rousseau, naval engineer, born 26: 169
1933 The United States abandoned the gold standard D: 6

APRIL 20.

1676 "Bacon's Rebellion" broke out 5: 337
1689 Provisional government established in Massachusetts, with Simon Bradstreet as governor .. 7: 372
1718 David Brainerd, missionary, born 2: 253
1723 Cornelius Harnett, patriot, born 7: 403
1764 Jacob Radcliff, a founder of Jersey City, born 13: 471
1775 Siege of Boston begun 1: 67
1775 First council of war at Cambridge, Mass. 10: 154
1775 Governor Dunsmore of Virginia removed the powder from the Williamsburg (Va.) arsenal 13: 391
1777 Constitution of the state of New York adopted 3: 41
1791 Henry Burden, inventor, born 2: 333
1792 William L. Stone, author and journalist, born .. 7: 205
1797 Andrew Talcott, civil engineer, born 13: 405
1801 "Sol" F. Smith, actor, lawyer and author, born 2: 197
1802 William H. Furness, clergyman, born 2: 316
1807 John Milton, governor of Florida, born 11: 378
1813 Henry T. Tuckerman, critic, essayist and poet, born 7: 234
1818 Benjamin M. Everhart, mycologist, born 10: 470
1824 Albert G. Porter, Indiana statesman and governor, born 13: 274
1837 Massachusetts board of education established ... 3: 78
1841 Ohio C. Barber, president of the Diamond Match Co., born 2: 523
1841 John A. Mead, governor of Vermont and president of the Howe Scale Co., born 19: 61
1842 John M. Farley, R. C. cardinal, born 13: 394
1850 Daniel Chester French, sculptor, born A: 460
1861 Great mass meeting in Union Square, New York, at the beginning of the Civil War 2: 92
1861 Robert E. Lee resigned his commission in the U. S. army 4: 96
1861 Governor Ellis of North Carolina seized the U. S. mint at Charlotte 4: 427
1861 Warships and naval stores in the Portsmouth navy yard destroyed to prevent their falling into the hands of Confederates 5: 12
1861 James D. Phelan, San Francisco mayor and U. S. senator, born 8: 478
1863 Capture of Opelousas, La., by Federal troops .. 4: 223
1863 President Lincoln proclaimed West Virginia's admission to the Union 12: 430
1864 Confederates captured Plymouth, N. C. 12: 241

APRIL 21.

Anniversary of the battle of San Jacinto in Texas

1773 Joseph Caldwell, president of the University of North Carolina, born 13: 241
1775 Alexander Anderson, "Father of wood engraving in the United States," born 6: 259
1778 Phillips academy, Andover, Mass., founded 10: 93
1783 Samuel J. Mills, missionary, born 13: 187
1794 Henry Ware, Jr., clergyman, born 5: 358
1809 Robert M. T. Hunter, statesman, one of the "Southern Triumvirate," born 9: 158
1810 George P. Gordon, printer and inventor, born .. 5: 405
1816 Louis T. Wigfall, Confederate soldier and member of both the Confederate and U. S. senates, born 5: 262
1818 Henry W. Shaw (Josh Billings), humorist, born 6: 28
1821 James R. Kendrick, clergyman, and president of Vassar college, born 5: 235
1821 Edward T. Cox, geologist, born 12: 328
1830 James Orton, clergyman and naturalist, born .. 11: 280
1838 John Muir, naturalist and geologist, born 9: 449
1842 Charles Follen Adams, author, born 1: 279
1846 Charles S. Bull, physician, born 9: 336
1846 William Henry Goodyear, archæologist, born 19: 455
1850 John R. Spears, journalist and author, born ... 9: 162
1856 Battle of San Jacinto, Texas 9: 65
1856 John Charles Van Dyke, art educator and author, born C: 489
1857 Henry K. Bush-Brown, sculptor, born 10: 374
1857 Roger S. B. Foster, lawyer, born 23: 355
1867 Clarence A. Barbour, president of Brown university, born A: 283
1868 Alfred Henry Maurer, artist, exponent of "modern" and "cubist" art, born 25: 153
1896 Powers patented his system of temperature control 20: 35
1898 The United States requested withdrawal of Spanish authority and government from Cuba 11: 3

APRIL 22.

Arbor Day in Nebraska

1688 Jonathan Dickinson, clergyman and first president of the College of New Jersey, born 5: 463
1711 Eleazer Wheelock, founder and first president of Dartmouth college, born 9: 85

1744 James Sullivan, governor of Massachusetts, born ... 1:110
1759 James Freeman, Unitarian clergyman, born ... 7:447
1766 Alexander V. Griswold, P. E. bishop, born ... 4: 78
1771 Thomas G. Fessenden, journalist and poet, born 7:260
1786 Amos Lawrence, merchant and philanthropist, born ... 3: 62
1793 Washington issued a proclamation of neutrality 1: 6
1806 Moody Currier, governor of New Hampshire, born ... 11: 38
1812 Loring Coes, manufacturer and inventor, born 13: 68
1816 Nathan Washburn, manufacturer and inventor, born ... 10: 18
1818 Cadwallader C. Washburn, governor of Wisconsin, born ... 12: 77
1822 John J. Williams, R. C. archbishop, born ... 4:415
1831 Alexander McD. McCook, soldier, born ... 4:130
1831 Zoheth S. Durfee, steel manufacturer, born ... 6:189
1832 J. Sterling Morton, secretary of agriculture under Cleveland, and founder of Arbor Day, born 6:487
1843 George W. Baird, naval engineer and inventor, born ... B:245
1846 Bradford P. Raymond, president of Lawrence and Wesleyan universities, born ... 9:431
1851 William Mills Ivins, lawyer, born ... 12:378
1853 Samuel Richards, artist, born ... 6:367
1859 First issue of Colorado's first newspaper, the "Rocky Mountain News" ... 13:515
1859 John Elliott, painter, born ... 21: 61
1859 Charles C. Kilgen, organ builder, born ... 24:103
1860 Ada Rehan, actress, born ... 1:287
1861 Robert E. Lee nominated commander of the Virginia troops ... 4: 96
1865 Guy Eastman Tripp, chairman of the board of the Westinghouse Electric & Manufacturing Co., born ... 20:326
1873 Oliver M. W. Sprague, economist, adviser to the Bank of England, the Bank for International Settlements and the Roosevelt administration, born ... D: 27
1874 Ellen Glasgow, author, born ... C:348
1889 Oklahoma opened for settlement ... 1:135
1930 Treaty of London signed ... 23: 11

APRIL 23.

1607 Hudson sailed on his first voyage of discovery 9:453
1662 Connecticut's famous charter granted ... 10:322
1737 Josiah Martin, governor of North Carolina, born 13:439
1775 "Republic" of Transylvania organized at Boonesboro, Ky. ... 8:304
1779 Samuel Parker, pioneer missionary, born ... 7:246
1781 Fort Watson, S. C., captured from the British 1: 61
1791 James Buchanan, 15th president of the United States, born ... 5: 1
1803 Adin Ballou, clergyman, and founder of the Hopedale Community, born ... 7:558
1805 Augustus A. Gould, conchologist, born ... 3:515
1813 Stephen A. Douglas, statesman, born ... 2:428
1817 Andrew G. Curtin, war governor of Pennsylvania, born ... 24:412
1821 James Phelan, California pioneer and banker, born ... 8:478
1821 William Ormiston, clergyman, born ... 13: 45
1823 John M. Ordway, chemist, born ... 7:259
1825 Thomas T. Eckert, president of the Western Union Telegraph Co., born ... 12:121
1827 Organization of the Baltimore & Ohio R. R. Co., first railroad company in America ... 18: 21
1831 William Patterson Jones, founder of Northwestern female college (later absorbed by Northwestern university), born ... 24:115
1833 William Swinton, journalist and author, born .. 11:488
1834 Chauncey M. Depew, railroad president and U. S. senator, born ... 23: 96
1838 First vessel crossed the Atlantic under steam power ... 19:312
1839 James B. Hammond, inventor of the Hammond typewriter, born ... 3:321
1840 Henry A. House, inventor of nearly 300 useful machines and devices, born ... 23: 84
1844 Sanford B. Dole, provisional president and first governor of the territory of Hawaii, born ... 12:419
1848 George Willis Cooke, author, born ... 8: 68
1852 Edwin Markham, educator and poet, born ... 9:157
1852 Edward N. Brush, psychiatrist, head of the Enoch Pratt hospital, born ... 24:297
1853 Winthrop M. Crane, paper manufacturer, governor of Massachusetts and U. S. senator, born ... 13: 69
1853 Thomas Nelson Page, author and diplomat, born 19:405
1855 Harry Stillwell Edwards, author and journalist, born ... 8: 86
1856 Arthur T. Hadley, president of Yale university, born ... 9:267
1857 Andrew S. Rowan, soldier, famous as the hero of Hubbard's "Message to Garcia," born ... D:228
1858 Lenor F. Loree, president of the Baltimore & Ohio railroad, born ... C:274
1863 Walter F. Prince, psychologist, student of telepathy and psychic phenomena, born ... 24: 29
1881 Charles Gilman Norris, author, born ... C:366

APRIL 24.

1704 Boston "News-Letter," first permanent newspaper of the New World, issued ... 7:549
1750 John Trumbull, poet and lawyer, born ... 7:351
1750 Nathan Daboll, mathematician, publisher of the "Connecticut Almanack," born ... 23:403
1764 Thomas Addis Emmet, lawyer, born ... 5: 63
1802 Georgia ceded her western territory to the United States ... 1:221
1804 Thomas O. Selfridge, Sr., naval officer, born .. 7:552
1807 Charles F. Smith, soldier, born ... 11:390
1807 John F. H. Claiborne, congressman, editor and historian, born ... 11:391
1808 First R. C. bishop of New York consecrated .. 1:191
1809 Joseph A. Alexander, orientalist and linguist, born ... 1:242
1827 Formal organization of the B. & O. railroad .. 9:301
1837 Timothy F. Allen, physician and author, born .. 7:282
1841 John B. Herreshoff, shipbuilder, born ... 12:353
1841 Charles S. Sargent, dendrologist, born ... 26: 78
1843 Charles C. Schneider, engineer specializing in bridge building, born ... 18: 91
1845 China issued edict permitting foreigners to teach Christian religion ... 5: 16
1847 Susan Dimock, physician and founder of the first training school for nurses in America, born .. 19: 30
1847 John Howard Harris, president of Bucknell university, born ... 22:134
1858 Edward H. Forbush, naturalist, born ... 21:316
1862 Farragut passed the forts below New Orleans .. 2: 49
1864 Battle of Cane River Ferry ... 4:223
1876 Charles M. Manly, engineer, born ... 21:321
1879 Orris P. Van Sweringen, railroad operator, born A:539
1898 Col. Rowan set forth to carry the message to Garcia ... D:229
1930 Josiah Macy, Jr., Foundation established for the prevention and cure of disease ... D:137

APRIL 25.

1635 Fight between William Claiborne and Maryland colonists ... 7:332
1697 Joseph Blake became governor of South Carolina 12:153
1716 Robert Daniel became governor of South Carolina 12:155
1775 Governor Wanton of Rhode Island protested against the levying of troops ... 10: 16
1781 Battle of Hobkirk's Hill, near Camden, S. C. .. 1: 43
1787 Justin Edwards, Jr., clergyman, reformer, and president of Andover theological seminary, born ... 10:100
1791 David Hale, journalist, born ... 11:194
1808 James S. T. Stranahan, financier, "first citizen of Brooklyn," born ... 3:433
1812 Isaac E. Taylor, physician, born ... 9:353
1816 Eliza D. Stewart, philanthropist, born ... 7: 37
1825 Charles Ferdinand Dowd, originator of the present system of standard time, born ... 18:180
1826 William Deering, manufacturer of harvesters, born ... 11:268
1836 Leroy S. Starrett, inventor and manufacturer of a meat chopper, and other tools, born ... 18:428
1837 Edward Gay, artist, born ... 10:375
1839 Thomas J. Burrill, botanist, born ... 18:187
1840 Charles C. Coleman, artist, born ... 21:233
1845 Felix Morris, actor, born ... 11:160
1846 First engagement of Mexican war at La Rosia 4:279
1846 Constance C. (Mrs. Burton) Harrison, author, born ... 4:320
1848 Robert W. DeForest, lawyer, born ... B: 61
1853 John F. Stevens, chief engineer of the Isthmian canal commission, born ... D:213
1859 Spencer Miller, engineer and inventor, born ... 15: 31
1860 Thomas S. Clarke, sculptor and painter, born 10:372
1861 Edwin R. A. Seligman, political economist, born 10: 49
1862 Confederate forces withdrawn from New Orleans 4:352
1869 Paul Armstrong, playwright, born ... 18:383
1898 War declared against Spain ... 11: 4

APRIL 26.

Confederate Memorial Day in Alabama, Georgia, Florida and Mississippi. Also War Memorial Day in Georgia.

1607 Landing of English settlers at Cape Henry, Va. 8:197
1635 Sir Fernando Gorges appointed governor-general of New England ... 5:167
1636 First court of magistrates convened in Connecticut ... 12: 61

1718 Esek Hopkins, naval officer, born 2: 18
1773 Ebenezer K. Dexter, philanthropist, born 8: 240
1813 Edward Maynard, dental surgeon and inventor, born 11: 339
1814 James H. Strong, naval officer, born 11: 96
1819 First lodge of Odd Fellows organized 11: 363
1820 Alice Cary, author and poet, born 1: 535
1822 Frederick Law Olmsted, landscape architect, born 2: 298
1828 Martha Finley, author, born 11: 267
1830 Benjamin F. Tracy, secretary of the navy under Harrison, born 1: 145
1831 Harvey Fisk, financier, born 11: 261
1834 Charles F. Browne (Artemus Ward), humorist, born 1: 425
1834 Horatio R. Palmer, editor and composer, born .. 7: 429
1836 Erminnie A. Smith, geologist and ethnologist, born 13: 183
1836 Thomas H. White, manufacturer of sewing machines, bicycles and automobiles, born 21: 350
1840 John C. Ridpath, historian, born 6: 485
1860 Charles Henderson, governor of Alabama, born B: 254
1861 Woman's Central Relief Association organized 9: 124
1865 J. Wilkes Booth, assassin of Lincoln, killed 3: 182
1865 Gen. Johnston surrendered to Gen. Sherman 4: 34
1866 Confederate memorial day appointed by a woman 7: 17
1868 Robert Herrick, author, born .... C: 378
1871 Jonathan McM. Davis, governor of Kansas, born B: 43

APRIL 27.

1521 Magellan, the explorer, killed in the Philippines 6: 249
1648 John Usher, lieutenant-governor of New Hampshire, born 13: 454
1686 New York charter granted by Governor Dongan 10: 241
1763 Indian council, resulting in war with the Ottawa and other Indian tribes 10: 415
1777 Danbury, Conn., attacked by the British 7: 514
1778 Gideon Lee, leather merchant, born 5: 423
1791 Samuel F. B. Morse, inventor of an electromagnetic telegraph system, born 4: 449
1795 Edward Kavanagh, Maine statesman and governor, born 6: 309
1805 Derne, Tripoli, captured 4: 417
1813 Capture of York (Toronto), Canada 2: 517
1818 Amasa Stone, financier and philanthropist, born 11: 522
1821 Walter N. Haldeman, founder of the Louisville "Courier," born 18: 239
1822 Ulysses S. Grant, 18th president of the United States, born 4: 1
1840 Rossiter W. Raymond, mining engineer and author, born 8: 44
1843 Ira B. Dutton (Brother Joseph), philanthropist, successor of Father Damien at Leper colony in Hawaii, born 22: 17
1846 Charles J. Van De Poele, inventor of the overhead trolley car, born 13: 246
1852 Richard Edwin Day, poet, born 8: 479
1853 Alice Morse Earle, author, born 13: 574
1853 Charles Sprague-Smith, founder of the Peoples Institute, born 24: 148
1855 Benjamin N. Duke, leader in the tobacco industry in North Carolina, and patron of Duke university, born 21: 11
1860 Charles Townsend Copeland, educator, born .... C: 22
1862 Farragut's fleet anchored before New Orleans, La. 1: 123
1866 A. Donaldson Smith, explorer, born 13: 608
1883 Newcomb K. Chaney, chemist, born .... A: 95
1892 Cornerstone of Grant's tomb laid 4: 12
1893 Norman Bel Geddes, theatrical and industrial designer, born .... D: 188
1934 The United States signed the Argentine anti-war pact at Buenos Aires .... D: 11

APRIL 28.

1635 Governor Harvey of Virginia deposed by the colonial assembly 13: 383
1758 James Monroe, 5th president of the United States, born 6: 81
1759 William Rawle, jurist, born 7: 442
1815 Andrew J. Smith, soldier, born 11: 471
1817 Lewis E. Parsons, provincial governor of Alabama, born 10: 433
1819 Ezra Abbott, Biblical scholar, born 4: 384
1824 Robert Bonner, publisher, born 10: 298
1826 Silas S. Packard, educator, born 3: 72
1827 Joseph Bailey, Federal soldier, born 5: 394
1830 The Boston Society of Natural History founded 7: 509
1832 James Grant Wilson, author and editor, born .. 11: 412
1836 John C. Ropes, lawyer and historian, born 11: 404
1840 Palmer Cox, artist and author, born 7: 459
1846 Frank Hatton, postmaster-general under Arthur, born 4: 252
1848 William H. Gelshenen, banker, born 12: 209
1849 First issue of the Minnesota "Pioneer" 13: 168
1862 Fort St. Philip surrendered to Farragut 4: 186
1863 General Hooker's army crossed the Rappahannock 4: 177
1865 Hugh Lincoln Cooper, hydro-electric engineer, born .... C: 254
1869 Bertram Grosvenor Goodhue, architect, born ... 19: 402
1869 Walter P. Cooke, lawyer and statesman, president of the Hague arbitral tribunal and member of the reparations commission, born 23: 143
1900 Pillsbury played twenty games of blindfold chess simultaneously, creating a new record 13: 49

APRIL 29.

1697 Escape of Hannah Dustin from her Indian captors 6: 102
1718 Robert Sandeman, religionist, founder of the sect known as Sandemanians, born 13: 547
1745 Oliver Ellsworth, chief-justice of the U. S. supreme court, born 1: 22
1752 Theodore Foster, U. S. senator and antiquarian, born 2: 9
1765 William Harris, clergyman and president of Columbia university, born 6: 344
1779 Myron Holley, reformer, born 2: 332
1792 Matthew Vassar, founder of Vassar college, born 5: 233
1811 Jacob W. Bailey, microscopist, born 10: 157
1814 Naval battle between the "Peacock" and the "Epervier" 6: 232
1814 Homer V. M. Miller, U. S. senator, born 12: 344
1820 Henry W. Allen, governor of Louisiana, born .. 10: 78
1830 Adolph H. J. Sutro, mining engineer, builder of the famous Sutro tunnel, and mayor of San Francisco, born 21: 126
1831 William J. Le Moyne, actor, born 5: 389
1832 Hiram W. Thomas, clergyman, born 9: 316
1835 Charles R. Otis, inventor and manufacturer of the Otis elevator, born 11: 120
1836 William Henry Venable, author and educator, born 19: 364
1838 Willis J. Beecher, theologian, born 16: 305
1841 Edward R. Sill, educator and poet, born 7: 249
1846 Henry Schradieck, musician, born 20: 207
1853 George B. Cox, Ohio politician, born 17: 298
1855 William L. Elkin, astronomer, born 24: 117
1856 Ira M. Price, philologist, born 4: 508
1860 Lorado Taft, sculptor, born .... A: 461
1861 Maryland house of delegates rejected an ordinance of secession 9: 307
1863 Bombardment of Grand Gulf, Miss. 2: 98
1880 Mary Mannering, actress, born .... D: 226
1880 Jonas Lie, artist, famous for his emotional interpretation of nature, born .... D: 248
1925 First woman elected a member of the National Academy of Arts and Sciences .... C: 289

APRIL 30.

1652 Governor Berkeley of Virginia deposed 13: 384
1694 William Pitkin, governor of Connecticut, born 10: 327
1717 Robert Johnson commissioned governor of South Carolina 12: 155
1731 Thomas Jones, jurist and loyalist, born 9: 250
1771 Hosea Ballou, Universalist clergyman, born 5: 487
1774 John Logan's family murdered 10: 204
1778 Chain stretched across the Hudson river in the Revolutionary war 8: 249
1778 Phillips academy, Andover, Mass., opened 10: 93
1781 George W. P. Custis, author and painter, born 7: 537
1785 Spencer H. Cone, clergyman, born 22: 187
1789 Washington inaugurated first president of the United States 1: 5
1798 Navy department formally created 5: 32
1801 William Leggett, editor and author, born 6: 275
1803 Signing of the treaty under which Louisiana was purchased from France for $15,000,000 .. 2: 396
1812 Louisiana admitted to the Union 10: 74
1813 Cyrus A. Bartol, clergyman, born 4: 94
1814 William B. Hyman, jurist, born 12: 253
1822 Hannibal W. Goodwin, clergyman, and inventor of the celluloid film for photographic negatives, born 23: 377
1823 Henry O. Houghton, publisher, born 1: 281
1825 Joseph M. Toner, physician, born 7: 539
1825 Jesse S. Lake, inventor of a caterpillar tractor, born 20: 228
1829 Samuel H. Kauffmann, journalist, born 13: 177
1839 Robert C. Minor, artist, born 12: 354
1842 Charles S. Fairchild, lawyer and secretary of the treasury under Cleveland, born 2: 406
1845 William H. Crane, actor, born 2: 153
1869 Charles M. Robinson, city planner, born 2: 352
1870 Homer S. Cummings, attorney-general under Franklin Roosevelt, born .... D: 13
1873 Rescue of nineteen men who had been cast away on an ice floe for six months 3: 282
1921 Port Authority created by New York and New Jersey .... B: 136

MAY 1.
May Day

1689 Charter government resumed in Rhode Island .. 10: 7
1751 Ira Allen, Vermont statesman, born 4: 29
1753 Winthrop Sargent, soldier and territorial governor of Mississippi, born 13: 485
1759 Jacob Albright, clergyman, born 11: 114
1764 Benjamin H. Latrobe, architect and engineer, born 9: 425
1776 Archibald Bulloch became governor of Georgia .. 1: 492
1783 Dedication of Phillips Exeter academy 10: 104
1786 Samuel Ward, banker, born 4: 435
1792 Rufus Porter, inventor and founder of the "Scientific American," born 7: 184
1796 Junius Brutus Booth, actor, born 3: 180
1813 Siege of Fort Meigs, Ohio, begun 3: 35
1825 George Inness, artist, born 2: 490
1829 Robert Clarke, publisher, born 10: 481
1829 Maxwell Sommerville, glyptologist, born 12: 251
1830 Mary H. Jones (Mother Jones), advocate of labor reform, born 23: 72
1834 James M. Peirce, mathematician, born 10: 25
1837 Richard P. Rothwell, mining engineer, organizer and president of the American Institute of Mining Engineers, born 10: 229
1844 National Whig convention nominated Henry Clay for president 5: 80
1845 Methodist Episcopal church, South, organized .. 10: 261
1846 Wharton Barker, financier, born 1: 368
1847 Henry D. Lloyd, journalist, born 12: 375
1852 Simon N. Patten, economist, born 11: 230
1853 Jacob Gordin, playwright, "Shakespeare of the Ghetto," born 23: 286
1862 Gen. Butler took possession of New Orleans, La. 1: 123
1862 Walter H. Weed, geologist, born 13: 457
1863 Confederates defeated at Port Gibson 4: 5
1863 Battle of Chancellorsville begun 4: 98
1867 William S. Corby, pioneer in the modern quantity-baking industry, born 25: 9
1872 Convention of Liberal Republicans which nominated Horace Greeley for president met 3: 452
1878 First elevated trains operated in New York city 11: 389
1878 Walter C. Teagle, president of the Standard Oil Co. of New Jersey, born .... A: 325
1898 Spanish fleet destroyed in the battle of Manilla bay 9: 5
1901 Pan-American exposition opened 2: 271
1904 Opening of the Louisiana Purchase exposition .. 12: 10

MAY 2.

1740 Elias Boudinot, first president of the American Bible Society, born 2: 296
1778 Nathan Bangs, president of Wesleyan university, born 9: 429
1787 Federal convention assembled in Philadelphia to adopt a national constitution 1: 5
1794 Charles G. Loring, lawyer, born 22: 284
1796 John G. Palfrey, congressman and author, born 7: 199
1806 Edwin B. Morgan, philanthropist, born 13: 218
1814 Benjamin H. Field, merchant and philanthropist, born 3: 464
1816 Lawrence A. Gobright, journalist, born 5: 355
1818 Fordyce Barker, physician, born 4: 157
1821 William Taylor, M.E. missionary bishop, born 10: 496
1832 William L. Elkins, financier, born 9: 324
1834 Wilbur F. Sanders, Montana lawyer and senator, born 1: 457
1837 Selah Merrill, clergyman and archæologist, born 13: 218
1837 Henry M. Robert, military engineer, born 10: 142
1838 Albion W. Tourgee, author and jurist, born 7: 324
1842 Gen. Fremont set forth on his first expedition to explore the western territories 4: 270
1847 Hugh J. Chisholm, financier, born 15: 154
1851 Franklin B. Gault, pioneer Western educator, born 18: 200
1856 Reginald B. Birch, artist and illustrator, born .. 11: 307
1863 "Stonewall" Jackson shot by his own troops .. 4: 128
1865 Clyde Fitch, dramatist, born 15: 192

MAY 3.

1765 The first medical school in America founded 1: 340
1768 Daniel C. Sanders, first president of the University of Vermont, born 2: 39
1793 Ogden Hoffman, lawyer and congressman, born 11: 84
1794 James O. Andrew, M. E. bishop, born 1: 521
1813 Lot M. Morrill, governor of Maine, U. S. senator and secretary of the treasury under Grant, born 6: 313
1816 Montgomery C. Meigs, soldier, born 4: 69
1817 William Procter, pharmacopœcist, born 5: 347
1833 Reuben W. Millsaps, banker, and founder of Millsaps college, born 18: 422
1836 John Dymond, sugar planter and inventor, born 25: 350
1837 Leighton Coleman, P. E. bishop, born 11: 100
1842 Governments of two opposing parties organized in Newport, R. I., resulting in Dorr's rebellion 8: 234
1843 William L. Wilson, congressman, postmaster general under Cleveland and president of Washington and Lee university, born 8: 162
1843 Edmond F. Prendergast, R. C. archbishop, born 15: 222
1844 Wilbur O. Atwater, chemist, born 6: 262
1844 Charles C. Harrison, provost of the University of Pennsylvania, born 13: 393
1849 Jacob A. Riis, reformer, born 13: 114
1850 Thomas Thacher, corporation lawyer, born 24: 229
1860 Edwin Musser Herr, mechanical engineer, born 23: 243
1862 Confederate evacuation of Yorktown, Va., begun after a month's siege 4: 141
1863 Col. Streight's Federal raiders overtaken and captured in Georgia 10: 36
1869 Julia Arthur, actress, born 10: 455
1871 Henry S. Graves, forester, born .... A: 479

MAY 4.

1626 Peter Minuit, first governor of New Netherlands, arrived to take office 12: 208
1765 First church of the Sandemanian sect established 13: 547
1775 Patrick Henry led Virginians in their first act of physical resistance to the crown 1: 338
1776 Rhode Island issued a declaration of independence 4: 356
1777 Capture of the British brig "Joseph" by the "Surprise" 4: 266
1780 John J. Audubon, ornithologist, born 6: 75
1793 William C. Rives, Virginia statesman and senator, born 6: 486
1796 Horace Mann, educator, born 3: 78
1796 William Pennington, governor of New Jersey, born 5: 206
1799 Amasa Walker, political economist, born 11: 438
1801 Samuel V. Merrick, first president of the Pennsylvania Railroad Co., born 13: 333
1802 Charles W. Upham, author, born 8: 398
1806 Cornelius A. Logan, dramatist and actor, born.. 12: 189
1807 Gurdon Buck, surgeon, born 11: 512
1812 John W. Stevenson, Kentucky governor and senator, born 13: 9
1820 John Whiteaker, governor of Oregon, born 8: 4
1821 Gordon McKay, inventor and manufacturer, born 10: 397
1825 Henry B. Blackwell, reformer, an advocate of woman's suffrage, born 20: 294
1826 Frederick E. Church, landscape artist, born 20: 33
1827 Lewis H. Steiner, physician and librarian, born 11: 348
1831 Mendes Cohen, civil engineer, born 13: 136
1840 George Gray, jurist, member of the Permanent Court of International Arbitration, born 26: 17
1844 Lucien S. Crandall, inventor, born 3: 322
1852 Roswell Park, 5th, physician and surgeon, born 8: 220
1862 Confederate troops evacuated Yorktown, Va. ... 4: 96
1862 August M. Gemunder, violin maker, born 21: 277
1864 Army of the Potomac crossed the Rapidan 4: 99
1864 Richard Hovey, poet and author, born 6: 352
1865 Gen. Taylor surrendered to Gen. Canby 4: 331
1865 Confederate naval forces at Mobile surrendered 5: 44
1872 A. Mitchell Palmer, attorney-general under Wilson, born .... A: 44
1875 John J. Blaine, Wisconsin governor and U. S. senator, born 26: 280
1886 Haymarket riot in Chicago occurred 11: 51

MAY 5.

1738 John Frost, soldier, born 1: 72
1772 Jacob Hays, head of the New York constabulary for nearly half a century, born 12: 354
1777 Dexter Wheeler, inventor and manufacturer, born 12: 98
1779 Delaware ratified the articles of confederation .. 4: 398
1806 Robert Bridges, physician and pharmacist, born 5: 346
1809 Frederick A. P. Barnard, president of Columbia college, born 6: 347
1811 John W. Draper, scientist and philosopher, born 3: 406
1813 Charles W. Schaeffer, theologian, born 7: 512
1817 George W. Julian, abolitionist, born 5: 502
1824 Robert W. Furnas, Nebraska agriculturist and governor, born 12: 1
1830 John B. Stetson, hat manufacturer and philanthropist, born 11: 57
1832 Hubert Howe Bancroft, historian, born 5: 112
1834 Sixty pioneers under Wyeth left Missouri for Oregon 6: 73
1840 Democratic national convention nominated Martin Van Buren for president 6: 434
1841 Samuel L. Allen, inventor and manufacturer of "Planet Jr." farm implements, born 17: 222

1856 Governor Robinson of Kansas indicted for high treason ... 8:343
1860 James A. O'Gorman, U. S. senator, born ... 15: 13
1862 Hermon C. Bumpus, biologist, born ... 13:110
1862 Battle of Williamsburg, Va. ... 4:176
1863 Clement L. Vallandigham arrested for "disloyal utterances" ... 3:145
1863 Martin J. Caton, educator, born ... 12:147
1864 Battle of the Wilderness (Va.) begun ... 4: 6
1864 Attack on Confederate ram "Albermarle" by the "Sassacus" and six other vessels ... 9:375
1880 Harlan D. Miller, civil engineer, born ... 21:352
1884 Indiana Asbury university became De Pauw university ... 7:381
1890 Christopher Morley, author, born ... A:186

MAY 6.

1606 John Norton, clergyman, born ... 7: 36
1646 First patent granted in American colonies ... 22: 58
1704 South Carolina Church Act signed ... 12:240
1740 John Penn, signer of the Declaration of Independence, born ... 7: 58
1748 Peleg Wadsworth, congressman and soldier, born 2:191
1769 William Emerson, clergyman, born ... 13:405
1777 Joseph C. Hornblower, lawyer, born ... 13:155
1801 George S. Greene, Federal soldier and engineer, born ... 1:320
1803 John H. B. Latrobe, Baltimore lawyer, born .. 9:426
1806 Chapin A. Harris, dental surgeon, born ... 22:432
1808 William Strong, justice of the U. S. supreme court, born ... 21: 4
1813 Alonzo Garcelon, governor of Maine, born ... 6:316
1823 Elizabeth D. B. Stoddard, author, born ... 8:375
1829 Phoebe A. Hanaford, author and Congregational minister, born ... 13:307
1830 Abraham Jacobi, physician, born ... 9:345
1830 Henry Fairbanks, clergyman and inventor, born 10:300
1831 Samuel I. J. Schereschewsky, P. E. missionary bishop, born ... 13:429
1835 New York "Herald" founded by James G. Bennett 7:241
1839 Mary C. Ames (Hudson), journalist and author, born ... 7:233
1843 Grove K. Gilbert, geologist, born ... 13: 46
1849 Wyatt Eaton, artist, born ... 8:427
1851 Dr. John Gorrie patented an ice-making machine 15:345
1853 Philander C. Knox, lawyer, U. S. senator and secretary of state under Taft, born ... 24: 7
1854 Hennen Jennings, mining engineer, born ... 18: 89
1856 Robert E. Peary, discoverer of the North Pole, born ... 14: 60
1858 Hugo A. Rennert, Hispanist, born ... 22:185
1858 Samuel B. McCormick, president of Coe college and chancellor of the University of Pittsburgh, born ... 24:141
1859 Elmer Gates, inventor and scientist, born ... 10:354
1860 Frank Dempster Sherman, educator and poet, born ... 7:190
1860 Ward Foster, founder of the "Ask Mr. Foster" travel service, born ... B:249
1861 Arkansas seceded from the Union ... 10:187
1862 Oscar W. Underwood, U. S. senator, born ... 21: 22
1864 Sherman began his march to the sea ... 4: 33
1867 Edward T. Devine, social economist and humanitarian, born ... 18:214
1896 Langley's model aerodrome flew successfully ... 15: 7

MAY 7.

1643 Stephanus Van Cortlandt, statesman, born ... 5:532
1763 Massacre of Detroit, planned for this day, betrayed by an Indian girl ... 10:415
1774 William Bainbridge, naval officer, born ... 8: 93
1777 Capture of the British "Prince of Orange" by the "Surprise" ... 4:266
1802 Luther Tucker, editor and publisher of the "Country Gentleman," born ... 24: 40
1816 Joseph Proctor, actor, born ... 15: 47
1833 James S. Boynton, governor of Georgia, born .. 1:230
1836 Joseph G. Cannon, speaker of the house, born 22: 4
1838 George E. Lounsbury, governor of Connecticut, born ... 12:283
1840 Charles C. Beaman, New York lawyer, born .. 15:167
1848 Edwin Warfield, governor of Maryland, born ... 13:205
1849 Attack on Macready, the actor, resulting in a riot three days later ... 5: 87
1850 Anton Seidl, musician, born ... 8:450
1854 Albert Mills, soldier, born ... 11:555
1857 Tudor Jenks, author of children's books, born .. 24:284
1862 Battle of West Point, Va. ... 4:488
1869 Howard Shaw, architect, born ... 20:159
1870 Marcus Loew, pioneer in the motion picture business, born ... 23: 68
1885 Walker R. Young, construction engineer of Boulder dam, born ... D:374
1915 Passenger steamship "Lusitania" sunk by a German submarine ... 19: 5

MAY 8.

1676 Bridgewater, Mass., attacked by Indians ... 10: 50
1725 Battle with the Indians at Pigwacket, Maine .. 10:398
1776 Opening of the Maryland convention that relieved Governor Eden of his office ... 11:110
1779 Gen. Pulaski fortified Charleston, S. C. ... 1: 69
1786 James Hamilton, Jr., statesman and governor of South Carolina, born ... 12:166
1816 American Bible Society founded ... 2:296
1821 William H. Vanderbilt, financier, born ... 6:209
1824 William Walker, filibuster, born ... 11: 24
1828 American Peace Society founded ... 13:187
1835 Augusta E. Wilson, author, born ... 4:457
1839 George Miller Beard, physician, born ... 8:206
1846 Battle of Palo Alto, beginning of the Mexican war ... 7: 69
1848 Oscar Hammerstein, inventor, operatic impresario and theatrical producer, born ... 17: 40
1857 Charles F. Naegele, artist, born ... 12: 81
1862 Battle of McDowell, Va. ... 4:127
1863 President Lincoln issued a proclamation relative to drafting aliens ... 2: 72
1864 Battle of Spottsylvania begun ... 4: 6
1869 James Rowland Angell, president of Yale university, born ... B: 5
1871 A treaty providing for the adjustment of the Alabama Claims concluded ... 4: 16
1878 Robert I. Aitken, sculptor, born ... 15:215
1879 Application for a patent on an automobile motor filed by George B. Selden ... 20:223

MAY 9.

Second Sunday in May is observed as Mother's Day

1502 Columbus sailed on his fourth voyage ... 3:438
1689 Charter government resumed in Connecticut ... 10:324
1746 Theodore Sedgwick, judge and U. S. senator, born ... 2: 8
1775 Jacob Brown, general-in-chief of the U. S. army, born ... 5:400
1777 Zenas Crane, founder of the Crane Paper Mills in Massachusetts, born ... 13: 69
1780 William J. Duane, secretary of the treasury under Jackson, born ... 5:294
1781 The Spaniards captured Pensacola, Fla. ... 9:121
1785 James P. Espy, meteorologist, the "Storm King," born ... 6:205
1797 Walter Colton, journalist and author, born ... 4:305
1798 Fast day appointed by President Adams ... 2: 2
1800 John Brown, "of Osawatomie," abolitionist, born ... 2:307
1804 The Richmond "Enquirer" established ... 7:544
1810 John Brougham, actor and playwright, born ... 9:448
1811 James Laurie, railroad engineer and bridge builder, born ... 9: 38
1813 Siege of Fort Meigs, Ohio, abandoned ... 3: 35
1825 George Davidson, geodesist and astronomer, born 7:227
1828 Charles H. Cramp, shipbuilder, born ... 5:254
1829 Fire partially destroyed Transylvania university, Kentucky ... 4:514
1831 William W. Goodwin, Eliot professor of Greek at Harvard, born ... 6:428
1832 Lafayette college opened ... 11:240
1843 Belle Boyd, Confederate spy, born ... 23:363
1846 Battle of Resaca de la Palma ... 4:368
1846 Rev. Charles T. Torrey, abolitionist, died in Maryland state prison ... 6:200
1850 Edward Weston, electrician and inventor, born 5:176
1854 Lewis S. Gillette, civil engineer, pioneer in constructing skeleton steel buildings, born ... 20: 62
1858 Frederic W. Goding, diplomat and inventor, born 12:500
1860 Constitutional Union party nominated John Bell for President ... 3: 40
1862 Gen. Hunter issued his famous emancipation order ... 4:264
1864 Sheridan began his famous raid ... 4: 64
1901 Panic in Wall Street ... 13:355
1926 Admiral Byrd flew over the North Pole ... B:431

MAY 10.

Confederate Memorial Day in North and South Carolina

1501 Americus Vespucius sailed on his second voyage to America ... 3:419
1637 The General Court of Connecticut declared war against the Pequot Indians ... 12: 61
1639 Peleg Sanford, colonial governor of Rhode Island, born ... 10: 8
1720 Francis Nash, Revolutionary soldier, born ... 1: 54
1730 George Ross, judge, signer of the Declaration of Independence, born ... 10:119
1740 Clement Biddle, Revolutionary soldier, born ... 14:134

1770 First town meeting held to resist British aggression 7:257
1775 Ft. Ticonderoga and Crown Point, N. Y., captured 1: 45
1775 Second continental congress met in Philadelphia, Peyton Randolph, president 2:115
1775 A mob threatened President Cooper of King's college for his Tory principles 6:342
1778 William Ladd, philanthropist, born 13:187
1781 Camden, S. C., evacuated by the British 1: 43
1789 Jared Sparks, historian, born 5:433
1797 The frigate "United States" launched 4:189
1800 Timothy Pickering, secretary of state, removed by President Adams 1: 13
1801 Paul Tulane, philanthropist, born 9:130
1802 Horatio Allen, civil engineer, born 8:233
1802 James D. Westcott, U. S. senator, born 12:464
1808 Elisha K. Root, inventor and manufacturer of firearms, born 18:313
1812 Montgomery Blair, postmaster general under Lincoln, born 2: 88
1823 Orlando B. Potter, lawyer, manufacturer and congressman, born 1:186
1823 John Sherman, U. S. senator and secretary of the treasury under Hayes, born 3:198
1827 William Windom, senator, secretary of the treasury under Harrison, born 1:148
1832 William R. Grace, merchant, and mayor of New York, born 1:288
1841 James Gordon Bennett, Jr., journalist, born ... 7:242
1843 Francis A. Cook, naval officer, born 9: 17
1843 Kaufman Kohler, rabbi, born 13:396
1849 Astor place opera house riot in New York 5: 87
1861 Capture of Camp Jackson, Mo. 4:202
1862 Naval engagement on the Mississippi 4:166
1864 Battle of Cloyd's Mountain, W. Va. 4: 70
1864 William H. Hunt, banker and merchant, pioneer in extending the banking facilities of the United States to foreign countries, born 18:317
1865 Jefferson Davis captured at Irwinville, Ga. 4:503
1867 Curtis D. Wilbur, secretary of the navy under Coolidge, born .... A: 13
1869 Samuel McC. Lindsay, educator, born 12:374
1869 The tracks of the Union Pacific and the Central Pacific railroads joined 15: 16
1892 Arthur E. Nelson, lawyer, born A:344

MAY 11.

1647 Peter Stuyvesant arrived in New Amsterdam .. 5:138
1690 Surrender of Port Royal 6: 98
1751 Ralph Earle, artist, born 11:146
1777 British "Fox" captured by the "Hancock" 5:163
1781 British force captured at Orangeburg, S. C. 1: 79
1786 Henry M. Brackenridge, jurist and historian, born 9:468
1792 Columbia river discovered 5:121
1799 John Lowell, philanthropist, born 7:195
1799 Robert C. Sands, author and poet, born 8:354
1809 Matthew Vassar, philanthropist, born 5:233
1811 George W. Scranton, founder of Scranton, Pa., born 9:138
1813 Chauncey Giles, clergyman and author, born ... 9:257
1817 John Fox Potter, congressman, born 8:236
1818 First ligation of the innominate artery 6:282
1827 Septimus Winner, composer, born 1:310
1836 Josephus N. Larned, librarian and author, famous for his "History for Ready Reference," born 16:344
1840 Theodore D. Wilson, naval architect, born 7:508
1844 Samuel R. Van Sant, governor of Minnesota, born 13:325
1848 James D. Schuyler, engineer, born 18:317
1852 Charles W. Fairbanks, vice-president of the United States, born 14: 10
1854 Ottmar Mergenthaler, inventor, born 9:490
1854 Albion W. Small, sociologist and president of Colby university, born 25:242
1858 Minnesota admitted to the Union 10: 63
1862 Confederate forces evacuated Norfolk, Va. 5:488
1862 The "Merrimac" burned by the Confederates to prevent capture 5:588
1866 Henry C. Wallace, secretary of agriculture under Harding, born 19: 14
1871 Frank Schlesinger, astronomer, born C:497
1891 Henry Morgenthau, Jr., secretary of the treasury under Franklin D. Roosevelt, born .... D: 11
1894 Strike at Pullman, Ill., begun 12:341
1898 Attack on the torpedo-boat "Winslow" at Cardenas, Cuba 9:495
1912 Sherwood dollar-a-day pension law passed 2:153

MAY 12.

1621 First marriage in Plymouth colony, Edward Winslow to Susanna White 7:369
1638 Act excluding religious dissenters from Massachusetts colony passed 12:384
1678 Treaty of peace made with Sagamore Indians 5:376
1736 David Jones, clergyman and soldier, born 8:273
1780 Charleston captured by the British 1: 63
1789 Tammany Society founded 3:376
1803 William Howe, sewing machine inventor, born 7:507
1809 Robert C. Winthrop, congressman, U. S. senator and orator, born 6:217
1812 Ezra Miller, inventor, born 7:116
1816 George L. Prentiss, theologian, born 7:319
1822 James L. Orr, governor of South Carolina, born 12:175
1824 Edward P. Allis, manufacturer, born 7:546
1824 Matthew P. Deady, jurist, called "Oregon's greatest citizen," born 19: 50
1829 George W. Childs, publisher and philanthropist, born 2:272
1835 James E. Munson, phonographer and author, born 12:497
1840 Alexander Cochrane, chemical manufacturer, born 14:493
1844 John W. Sterling, lawyer, a generous benefactor of Yale university, born 19: 36
1849 Duane H. Church, inventor, born 12:117
1850 Henry Cabot Lodge, U. S. senator and historian, born 19: 52
1851 Joseph K. Toole, lawyer and governor of Montana, born 11: 82
1855 George E. Woodberry, author and poet, long the most popular professor at Columbia, born 23:186
1861 Frank Crane, clergyman and author, born 22:281
1862 Natchez, Miss., surrendered 2: 70
1863 Battle of Raymond, Miss. 4:204
1863 Attack on Warrenton, Miss. 13:240
1863 William H. S. Demarest, president of Rutgers college, born 15: 35
1864 Cavalry battle at Yellow Tavern, Va. 14: 53
1864 Alfred I. Dupont, manufacturer, inventor and philanthropist, born 25: 25
1865 Thomas S. Fiske, mathematician, born 12:489
1866 Harry Roseland, artist, born 11:286
1866 William T. Manning, P. E. bishop, born A:507
1870 Wendell C. Neville, soldier, born 22:277
1880 Lincoln Ellsworth, civil engineer and explorer, born .... B: 38
1898 San Juan, Puerto Rico, bombarded by Americans 9: 10
1926 The "Norge" the first airship to fly over the North Pole .... B: 38
1933 Creation of the agricultural adjustment administration, known as the AAA .... D: 4

MAY 13.

1607 Wingfield elected first president of first council of first permanent English colony in America 13:377
1729 Henry W. von Stiegel, Pennsylvania ironmaster and glass maker, born 11:197
1742 Manasseh Cutler, clergyman and pioneer, born.. 3: 70
1781 Benedict Arnold became commander-in-chief of British forces in Virginia 1: 53
1783 Society of the Cincinnati organized 1: 16
1795 Joshua R. Sands, naval officer, born 4:416
1813 John Sullivan Dwight, music critic, born 8:444
1825 John L. LeConte, naturalist, born 11:106
1832 Johnson M. Mundy, sculptor, born 8:282
1839 Otho S. A. Sprague, Chicago merchant and philanthropist, born 15:244
1846 War against Mexico declared 6:267
1850 Arthur Rotch, architect, born 11:454
1851 William B. Hornblower, judge, born 7:398
1854 Edward P. Meany, New York lawyer, born 14:467
1856 John Lewis Childs, horticulturist, born 24:245
1860 Percy Stickney Grant, clergyman, born 15:261
1861 Baltimore occupied by Federal troops 1:122
1862 Capture of the Confederate dispatch boat "Planter" by a negro slave 12:425
1864 Battle of Drury's Bluff, Va. 4: 55
1864 John F. Monnot, metallurgist and mining engineer, born 14:342
1867 Jefferson Davis admitted to bail 4:149
1869 William Boyce Thompson, financier and founder of Boyce Thompson Botanical Foundation, born 22:123
1915 Germany warned that the United States would protect the rights of its citizens on the high seas 19: 6

MAY 14.

1602 Bartholomew Gosnold, explorer, landed near York harbor, Maine 12:186
1692 Sir William Phips, governor of Massachusetts, arrived with a new charter 6: 98
1737 Samuel H. Parsons, soldier, born 1: 73
1739 Paine Wingate, U. S. senator and judge, born .. 12:558
1752 Timothy Dwight, clergyman, and president of Yale college, born 1:168

1761 Samuel Dexter, jurist and secretary of war and secretary of the treasury under John Adams, born 2: 6
1770 Cornerstone of Brown university laid 8: 20
1771 Robert Owen, reformer, born 6: 521
1784 John Anthony, jurist, born 12: 548
1787 Convention assembled to draft Constitution for the United States 4: 398
1796 William H. Prescott, historian, born 6: 66
1804 Lewis and Clarke started up the Missouri river to explore the Western country 5: 122
1808 Edwin D. Sanborn, educator, born 9: 93
1812 Daniel Brainard, surgeon, born 20: 309
1823 David A. Wasson, clergyman and author, born .. 9: 99
1833 James D. Cameron, secretary of war under Grant, and U. S. senator, born 4: 25
1834 George Soulé, mathematician, born 1: 510
1840 George Cooper, poet, born 8: 245
1843 Henry O. Walker, artist, born 22: 401
1850 George A. Kimball, civil engineer, born 15: 132
1852 Alton Brooks Parker, judge, born 10: 122
1861 Gen. George B. McClellan became commander of the Department of the Ohio 4: 141
1863 Capture of Jackson, Miss. 4: 33
1868 Theodore S. Henderson, M. E. bishop, leader in evangelistic work, born 25: 302

MAY 15.

1687 Thomas Prince, clergyman and author, born ... 7: 144
1749 Levi Lincoln, Massachusetts statesman and governor, and attorney-general under Jefferson, born 1: 111
1777 Duel between Gen. McIntosh and Governor Gwinnett 1: 493
1788 James Gadsden, who negotiated the Gadsden purchase from Mexico, born 12: 68
1802 Isaac R. Trimble, Confederate soldier, born ... 4: 342
1810 Jacob Thompson, secretary of the interior under Buchanan, born 5: 8
1819 Thomas L. Crittenden, soldier, born 2: 169
1823 Thomas Lake Harris, founder of the society of the "Brotherhood of the New Life," born 3: 289
1830 Noah K. Davis, educator, born 4: 76
1832 Richard T. Crane, founder of the Crane Co., manufacturer of pipe and fittings, born 26: 450
1841 Clarence E. Dutton, soldier and geologist, born .. 13: 297
1842 William A. Hemphill, founder of the Atlanta "Constitution," born 1: 277
1847 American army occupied Puebla, Mexico 3: 503
1853 Reuben G. Thwaites, librarian and editor, born 10: 35
1854 Edward M. Shepard, geologist, born 12: 395
1856 Second vigilance committee organized in San Francisco 4: 107
1856 L. Frank Baum, author and playwright, born .. 18: 331
1857 Williamina P. Fleming, astronomer, born 7: 29
1859 William Murdock McCarty, judge, born 19: 301
1860 Ellen Louise A. Wilson, wife of President Wilson, born 19: 12
1861 Edwin A. Alderman, president of Tulane university and the universities of North Carolina and Virginia, born 23: 38
1861 William S. Bryant, oto-laryngologist, born ..... B: 501
1867 Charles W. Stiles, bacteriologist, who made valuable contributions to the advancement of public health, born .... D: 62
1873 Joseph Welch, comedian, born 18: 76
1873 Edgar S. Wiers, Unitarian clergyman, founder of Unity Institute, born 23: 276
1876 The New York Society for Ethical Culture organized by Felix Adler 23: 98
1911 The Supreme Court of the United States ordered the Standard Oil Co. dissolved 21: 114
1918 The first regular aeroplane mail service inaugurated .... A: 46

MAY 16.

1639 Newport, R. I., founded 10: 1
1691 Jacob Leisler executed in New York on charges of high treason 13: 449
1771 Governor Tryon defeated the Regulators at Alamance Creek, N. C. 13: 193
1773 Adam Seybert, scientist and congressman, born 4: 237
1780 Loammi Baldwin, Jr., engineer, born 10: 302
1799 Ebenezer Emmons, geologist, born 8: 477
1801 William H. Seward, governor of New York, U. S. senator and secretary of state under Lincoln, born 2: 77
1804 Elizabeth P. Peabody, educator and author, born 12: 350
1811 Battle between American frigate "President" and British sloop-of-war "Little Belt" 5: 262
1824 Levi P. Morton, vice-president of the United States, born 1: 136
1824 Edmund Kirby Smith, soldier and chancellor of the University of Nashville, born 8: 132
1827 Norman J. Colman, first secretary of agriculture, appointed by Cleveland, born 16: 69
1832 Philip D. Armour, founder of Armour & Co., Chicago packers, born 7: 443
1834 Edward P. Bacon, merchant, prominent in the movement to secure national legislation for the regulation of railway rates, born 2: 234
1837 Richard W. Jones, president of four colleges, born 19: 21
1843 Charles M. Lamson, clergyman, born 7: 488
1844 Charles S. Reinhart, artist, born 7: 465
1846 Worcester R. Warner, of Warner & Swasey, who designed and constructed some of the world's largest telescopes, born 21: 70
1850 First tract of land located for Oakland, Calif. .. 12: 451
1854 Moses Allen Starr, neurologist, born 16: 102
1855 William H. Smyth, engineer and inventor, the first to suggest "technocracy," born 18: 251
1858 Frank Lynes, composer, born 8: 447
1860 Robert Herman Foerderer, leather manufacturer, originator of "Vici kid," born 18: 78
1861 Gen. Benjamin F. Butler became commander of the Department of Eastern Virginia 1: 222
1862 Elwood Worcester, clergyman, born 14: 84
1863 Battle of Champion Hills or Baker's Creek, Miss. 4: 5
1864 William Sullivan Peirce, ordnance expert in command of Springfield arsenal during the World war, born 19: 239
1869 John Turnell Austin, inventor of improvements for organs and maker of some of the largest modern organs, born 18: 129
1888 Lew Sarett, naturalist and poet, born .... A: 424
1919 First aeroplane to cross the Atlantic left Nova Scotia .... A: 496

MAY 17.

1672 Jolliet and Marquette set out to explore the Mississippi valley 5: 121
1690 Casco, Maine, captured by French and Indians .. 7: 149
1743 Seth Warner, Revolutionary soldier, born 1: 86
1759 John F. Mercer, soldier, and governor of Maryland, born 9: 295
1760 William Duane, journalist, born 8: 180
1774 Gen. Thomas Gage sworn into office as last royal governor of Massachusetts 7: 377
1776 Amos Eaton, botanist and geologist, born 5: 312
1794 Edward Delafield, physician, born 10: 278
1797 Theophilus Parsons, author, born 5: 393
1820 Frederick A. Genth, chemist and mineralogist, born 7: 493
1832 Grace W. Hinsdale, author, born 9: 96
1836 Joseph G. Cannon, speaker of the U. S. house of representatives, born 22: 4
1837 First number of the Baltimore "Sun" issued ... 21: 8
1840 Francis W. Dawson, editor, born 23: 300
1842 James S. Clarkson, editor and railroad president, born 2: 118
1842 Mary Edwards Bryan, author and editor, born . 8: 374
1845 Charles F. Dole, clergyman, author and peace advocate, born 20: 355
1859 Corydon T. Purdy, civil engineer, born .... C: 485
1860 Schuyler S. Wheeler, electrical engineer, born .. 10: 162
1861 Gen. McDowell placed in command of the Department of Northeastern Virginia 4: 50
1861 California legislature pledged the state to the Union 4: 109
1862 J. Randolph Coolidge, Boston architect, born .. 26: 213
1866 John W. Abercrombie, president of the University of Alabama, born 12: 297
1868 Horace E. Dodge, automobile manufacturer, born 19: 267
1877 Gen. Grant started on his journey around the world 4: 9
1883 First appearance of Cody's "Wild West Show" 5: 483
1884 Alaska, by act of Congress, created a civil and judicial district with the same laws as Oregon 12: 355
1904 Gaylord patented a method of molding amber .. 22: 163
1929 Terms of Tacna-Arica settlement by Chile and Peru announced as a result of the mediatory offices of the United States government ...... A: 9

MAY 18.

1675 Death of Father Marquette 12: 221
1705 John Leeds, mathematician and astronomer, born 25: 187
1759 John Pintard, philanthropist and antiquary, born 3: 461
1786 Sereno E. Dwight, clergyman and president of Hamilton college, born 7: 406
1798 Ethan A. Hitchcock, soldier, born 11: 196
1802 Le Roy Sunderland, clergyman and author, born 5: 354
1812 Peter H. Bell, governor of Texas, born 9: 67
1815 James B. Francis, civil engineer, born 9: 46
1824 Edson Adams, founder of Oakland, Calif., born 12: 451
1824 Leonard Norcross patented a machine for making iron nails 13: 422

1834 Sheldon Jackson, Presbyterian missionary, born 9: 251
1835 Charles N. Sims, clergyman and author, born .. 13: 206
1837 William Steinitz, world champion in chess, born 10: 457
1838 James McMillan, manufacturer, railroad builder, and U. S. senator, born 2: 227
1838 William H. Niles, geologist, born 12: 481
1845 John B. Allen, U. S. senator, born 11: 561
1846 Matamoros, Mexico, capitulated 4: 506
1849 William T. Bull, physician and surgeon, born .. 9: 345
1849 Charles B. Atwood, architect, born 22: 110
1850 James C. Hemphill, journalist, born 2: 29
1853 Isaac H. Platt, physician, born 15: 113
1856 Samuel M. Vauclain, president of the Baldwin Locomotive Works, born .... B: 318
1862 Josephus Daniels, secretary of the navy under Wilson, born .... A: 46
1863 Siege of Vicksburg, Miss., began 4: 5
1864 A bogus proclamation for more troops issued .. 4: 213
1864 Federal works at Petersburg, Va., captured 5: 49
1866 Edward L. White, author and educator, born .. 18: 297
1899 International Peace Conference met at The Hague 11: 38
1917 Selective service act passed for the World war A: 41
1933 The Muscle Shoals bill, authorizing public development of the Tennessee river valley, signed D: 4

MAY 19.

1643 The colonies of New Haven, Massachusetts and Connecticut formed a confederation 22: 47
1647 Newport, Portsmouth, Providence and Warwick, R. I., confederated 10: 2
1729 William Henry, congressman and inventor of the screw auger, born 11: 521
1772 First recorded town meeting in Vermont 8: 401
1780 The "Dark Day" in New England 11: 235
1795 Johns Hopkins, Baltimore merchant and philanthropist, founder of the university bearing his name, born 5: 169
1800 George W. Whistler, engineer, who built the railroad between St. Petersburg and Moscow, born 9: 48
1812 Felix K. Zollicoffer, journalist, congressman and Confederate soldier, born 11: 230
1814 Henry W. Ravenel, botanist, whose name has been given to more than 50 plants, born 10: 47
1819 James O. Broadhead, lawyer and diplomat, born 5: 68
1824 Henry Brewster, carriage manufacturer, born . 13: 122
1827 Richard I. Dodge, soldier and author, born 11: 512
1856 Senator Sumner began his famous speech on "The Crime against Kansas" in the senate .. 3: 300
1857 Horace E. Stockbridge, agricultural chemist and editor, born 14: 368
1857 A patent issued for an automatic fire-alarm telegraph system 23: 285
1857 John Jacob Abel, pharmacologist and physiological chemist, born .... A: 392
1861 Federals attacked Confederate battery at Sewall's Point, Va. 5: 248
1864 Carl Akeley, taxidermist, African explorer and sculptor, born 26: 130
1872 Sime Silverman, editor and publisher, creator of "Variety," a radical departure in theatrical journalism, born 24: 44
1872 John W. Garrett, diplomat and banker, born .. A: 335
1879 Arthur F. Bestor, president of Chautauqua Institution, born .... A: 336
1898 Spanish fleet under Cervera arrived at Santiago, Cuba 9: 2
1921 An act became effective limiting the number of immigrants of any nationality to three per cent of the number of that nationality resident in the United States in 1910 .... 19: 271
1924 The soldiers' bonus bill passed over the president's veto 24: 5

MAY 20.

1499 Americus Vespucius sailed for the West Indies 3: 419
1506 Columbus died at Valladolid, Spain 3: 438
1706 Seth Pomeroy, soldier, born 1: 54
1751 William Lenoir, soldier and North Carolina statesman, born 7: 65
1775 Artemas Ward commissioned first commander-in-chief of Colonial forces, the post afterwards held by Washington 23: 24
1779 The "Gen. Arnold" captured the privateer "Nanny" 9: 547
1781 David Dudley Field, clergyman and author, born 4: 236
1808 Thomas D. Rice, actor, born 11: 207
1813 Elijah Kellogg, clergyman and author, born ... 2: 497
1818 William G. Fargo, founder of the American and the Wells-Fargo express companies, born ... 12: 44
1819 George F. Blake, inventor and manufacturer of water meters and steam pumps, born 12: 521
1820 John Swinburne, physician, creator of the quarantine station in New York harbor, born ... 7: 33
1822 Dabney H. Maury, soldier, born 4: 35
1825 Antoinette L. B. Blackwell, minister and author, born 9: 124
1826 Potter Palmer, Chicago merchant, born 12: 541
1834 Richard McIlwaine, president of Hampden-Sidney college, born 2: 26
1835 National Democratic convention, which nominated Martin Van Buren for president, met 6: 433
1838 Gustav Cramer, photographer, born 5: 157
1843 Col. Albert A. Pope, bicycle manufacturer, born 1: 446
1845 Henry Mottet, clergyman, whose church in New York was the first free-pew P. E. church in America, born 23: 61
1846 Desmond Fitz Gerald, civil engineer, born 9: 44
1847 Oscar G. Murray, president of the Baltimore & Ohio railroad, born 18: 7
1851 Rose H. Lathrop, author and philanthropist, born 9: 194
1851 Emile Berliner, inventor of the carbon microphone transmitter and the "gramaphone," born 21: 6
1861 North Carolina seceded from the Union 4: 428
1862 Homestead act approved by President Lincoln .. 3: 300
1863 Marion Butler, U. S. senator, instrumental in establishing the free rural mail delivery system, born 13: 19
1872 John A. Mathews, pioneer producer of vanadium steel, born 16: 73
1879 St. Patrick's cathedral, New York, dedicated .. 1: 195
1927 Charles Lindbergh took off from New York on his solo flight to Paris .... B: 34
1929 Appointment of the national law enforcement commission, with George W. Wickersham as chairman .... C: 17
1930 Bank for International Settlements began to function .... C: 297
1932 Amelia Earhart took off from Newfoundland on her solo flight across the Atlantic .... D: 395

MAY 21.

1755 Alfred Moore, Revolutionary soldier and justice of the U. S. supreme court, born 2: 467
1762 Roger Griswold, governor of Connecticut, born 10: 331
1773 Samuel B. Wylie, clergyman and educator, born 1: 348
1780 Johnstown, N. Y., burned by Tories 8: 156
1796 Reverdy Johnson, attorney-general under Tyler and Fillmore, born 4: 371
1797 Nathan R. Smith, surgeon, born 3: 154
1806 Isaac McLellan, poet, born 6: 19
1812 Nelson Sizer, phrenologist, born 3: 246
1817 Edgar P. Wadhams, R. C. bishop, born 12: 50
1830 Rosa Miller Avery, philanthropist, born 6: 271
1832 First national Democratic convention met in Baltimore and nominated Andrew Jackson for president 5: 289
1833 John TenBrook Campbell, author and civil engineer, born 12: 397
1835 Newton M. Curtis, Federal soldier, born 4: 328
1836 Anna C. Brackett, head of a famous school for girls in New York city, born 21: 264
1843 Plimmon H. Dudley, engineer, inventor of the recording dynamometer, born 19: 281
1845 Charles Edwin Bessey, botanist, and acting chancellor of the University of Nebraska, born 8: 361
1850 Gustav Lindenthal, engineer who built the Hell Gate bridge, born 16: 117
1855 Edmund J. James, economist, born 11: 67
1856 Grace H. Dodge, founder of the Travelers' Aid Society, and active in Y.W.C.A. work, born .. 18: 310
1864 Battle of Spottsylvania ended indecisively, with heavy losses on both sides 4: 6
1864 Edward W. Scripture, psychologist, born 10: 310
1870 W. Cameron Forbes, banker, born .... C: 509
1878 Glenn H. Curtiss, airplane inventor and inventor of the hydroplane, born 22: 195
1881 American Red Cross organized with Clara Barton as president 15: 314
1888 Head of the department of agriculture made a member of the president's cabinet 5: 164
1915 First large steamship passed through the Cape Cod canal 25: 39
1925 The Amundsen-Ellsworth expedition took off from Spitzbergen to explore the polar basin ...... B: 38

MAY 22.

1743 Gamaliel Painter, judge, born 12: 105
1755 Tench Coxe, political economist, born 6: 14
1786 Arthur Tappan, reformer, born 2: 320
1807 Aaron Burr's trial for treason begun 3: 7
1808 William Henry Brown, silhouettist, born 20: 38
1809 Charles H. Haswell, engineer in chief of the U. S. navy, born 9: 486

1814 Sydney H. Gay, editor and author, born 2:494
1819 The "Savannah," the first steamship to cross the ocean, sailed for Europe 2:237
1820 Worthington Whittredge, artist, born 7:458
1826 Christopher C. Langdell, educator, born 6:423
1826 Ferdinand C. Ewer, clergyman, born 9:165
1838 Thomas H. Tibbles, journalist, and champion of the Indians, born 21: 76
1845 Mary Cassatt, artist, born 13:337
1853 Henry Trimble, chemist, born 5:350
1853 Nathaniel Butler, president of Colby university, born 8:409
1854 Jacob G. Schurman, president of Cornell university, born 4:478
1856 Preston S. Brooks assaulted Charles Sumner in the senate chamber 3:300
1862 Battle of Lewisburg, W. Va. 4: 70
1863 Attack on Confederate outworks at Vicksburg, Miss. 4: 5
1863 Federal ironclad "Cincinnati" sunk 13:192
1865 President Johnson proclaimed Southern ports open to foreign commerce 2:456
1865 Last bloodshed of Civil war 4:112
1868 First train robbery in the United States 13:272
1870 Frederick H. Knubel, president of the United Lutheran church in America, born B:450

MAY 23.

1609 Second Company of Virginia incorporated 13:379
1740 John Gibson, territorial governor of Indiana, born 13:265
1772 Dudley Leavitt, almanac compiler, born 25:112
1780 Charles E. Dudley, U. S. senator, born 4:353
1786 Samuel W. King, governor of Rhode Island, born 9:396
1788 Lewis Tappan, merchant and philanthropist, born 2:321
1794 Charles B. Storrs, reformer, president of Western Reserve university, born 2:326
1796 Zadoc Thompson, Vermont naturalist and historian, born 6:188
1803 Edwin F. Johnson, civil engineer, early advocate of steam transportation, who projected some of the first steam railroads, born 17:291
1810 Martin J. Spalding, R. C. archbishop of Baltimore, born 1:486
1818 William D. Andrews, inventor of pumps and pump engines, born 13:146
1820 William T. Walters, Baltimore merchant and philanthropist, born 1:155
1820 James B. Eads, engineer, who built the first ironclads for the Federal government in the Civil war, as well as the steel-arched bridge over the Mississippi at St. Louis, born 5:134
1821 Richard Grant White, author and critic, born .. 1:197
1824 Ambrose E. Burnside, Federal soldier, U. S. senator and governor of Rhode Island, born . 4: 53
1828 Edward Hitchcock, scientist, born 13: 95
1830 Henry M. Teller, U. S. senator and secretary of the interior under Arthur, born 15:228
1831 William O. Perkins, musician, born 9:386
1838 William T. Lusk, New York physician and educator, born 9:337
1840 George W. Marston, musician, born 7:432
1840 John F. Appleby, inventor, born 11:268
1852 Weldon B. Heyburn, U. S. senator, born 13:101
1854 Edgar Fahs Smith, chemist, provost of the University of Pennsylvania, born 21: 53
1858 Francis W. Kelsey, philologist and archæologist, born 26:461
1862 Battle at Port Royal, Va. 6:144
1875 Alfred P. Sloan, Jr., president of the General Motors Corp., born B:493
1883 Douglas Fairbanks, actor, born ..... A: 91
1889 Mabel Walker Willebrandt, lawyer, born B:212
1911 The New York public library opened 26: 25

MAY 24.

1701 William Kidd, pirate, executed 7:373
1750 Stephen Girard, philanthropist, born 7: 11
1764 Boston protested against English taxation 1:105
1775 John Hancock, president of the Continental congress, signer of the Declaration of Independence, and first governor of the commonwealth of Massachusetts, born 1:103
1777 General Meigs captured British garrison at Sag Harbor, Long Island 1: 83
1793 Edward Hitchcock, geologist, and president of Amherst college, born 5:308
1795 Silas Wright, U. S. senator and governor of New York, born 3: 47
1804 William Williams Mather, geologist, born 8:146
1810 Melancton Smith, Federal naval officer, born .. 5: 52
1816 Emanuel Leutze, artist, born 12:360
1818 Gen. Jackson captured Pensacola, Fla. 6: 82
1820 William Chauvenet, chancellor of Washington university, born 11:210
1820 Morris L. Keen, inventor of a process of making paper from wood, born 11:367
1829 John N. Stearns, founder of the National Temperance Society and Publication House, born 6:154
1844 Morse sent his famous telegraph message from Washington to Baltimore 4:450
1845 Carl H. A. Bjerregaard, author and librarian, born 13: 47
1850 Henry W. Grady, editor of the Atlanta "Constitution," born 1:526
1850 Grinnell expedition started in search of Franklin 3:281
1852 Maurice F. Egan, educator and author, born .. 11:111
1853 Willis A. Marean, architect, born 12:322
1857 Richard Mansfield, actor, born 9:117
1861 Col. Ellsworth was shot at Alexandria, Va. .. 4:166
1861 Federal troops occupied Arlington Heights at Alexandria, Va. 11:215
1861 Henry Milton Whelpley, pharmacologist, born .. 20:488
1862 Clara B. Spence, educator, head of a New York girls' school, born 20:336
1863 Austin, Miss., burned by Federals 4:360
1863 George G. G. Barnard, sculptor, born ..... A: 67
1865 Sherman's army reviewed at Washington 4: 34
1869 Exploration of the Colorado canyon commenced 3:340
1870 Benjamin N. Cardozo, justice of U. S. supreme court, born ..... D: 50
1878 Harry Emerson Fosdick, clergyman, born B:194
1882 James Oppenheim, author, born A:427
1883 Brooklyn bridge opened 26:123
1898 Battleship "Oregon" completed her remarkable trip of 14,500 miles around Cape Horn 9: 12
1929 Joseph P. Cotton appointed first under-secretary of state by President Hoover 23:152

MAY 25.

1539 De Soto landed in Florida in search of gold 5:126
1781 Siege of Ninety-six, S. C., begun 1: 43
1783 Philip P. Barbour, statesman and jurist, born .. 2:259
1787 A national constitutional convention met in Philadelphia 9:178
1790 Tennessee territory established 7:206
1803 Ralph Waldo Emerson, poet and philosopher, born 3:416
1809 Frederick A. P. Barnard, president of Columbia college, born 6:347
1810 William H. Channing, clergyman, born 13:595
1814 William Henry C. Hosmer, author and poet, born 8:200
1816 Henry H. Sibley, soldier, born 2:365
1823 Lorin Blodget, climatologist, born 4:530
1828 William P. Trowbridge, engineer, born 4:529
1835 Henry C. Potter, P. E. bishop, born 14: 35
1845 John J. McCook, New York lawyer, born 4:131
1847 John Alexander Dowie, "Divine Healer," and founder of the Christian Catholic church, born 13:252
1854 David P. Penhallow, botanist, authority on the organization of extinct conifers, born 20:216
1854 Clara Louise Burnham, novelist, born 21:151
1856 Brown Ayres, president of the University of Tennessee, born 18:372
1860 Price Collier, essayist, born 15:232
1860 J. McKeen Cattell, psychologist, born ..... D: 94
1862 Second battle of Winchester 4:223
1863 Repulse of Federals at Port Hudson, La. 4:223
1864 Battle near Dallas, Ga. 4:177
1865 John R. Mott, evangelist, born A:235
1869 John A. Ryan, theologian, born C:190
1887 Yale college became a university 1:173
1920 Gray patented his process for eliminating the "knock" in gasoline motors 24:156

MAY 26.

1637 Battle of Mystic, Conn., terminated the Pequot war 23:181
1668 First general assembly of New Jersey held at Elizabeth Town 19:263
1745 Jonathan Edwards, Jr., clergyman, and president of Union college, born 7:169
1748 William Barton, the Revolutionary soldier who captured Gen. Prescott, born 1: 74
1750 Jonathan Williams, soldier, and first superintendent of the U. S. military academy, born 3:239
1778 John Treat Irving, judge and author, born 9:220
1801 John Kingsbury, educator, born 9:417
1806 Henry K. Thatcher, naval officer, born 5: 44
1812 Hamilton college chartered 7:405
1828 Samuel W. Allerton, capitalist, born 17: 71
1837 Washington A. Roebling, civil engineer and builder of the Brooklyn bridge, born 26:122
1845 John A. Wyeth, New York surgeon, born 6: 74
1847 Edgar Fawcett, author and poet, born 7:191

1847 Sara Jewett, actress, born 11: 284
1857 Dred Scott and family emancipated in St. Louis 2: 307
1861 Federal troops occupied Parkersburg, W. Va. 4: 141
1863 Shailer Mathews, educator, born 11: 74
1864 Montana territory organized 11: 78
1865 Gen. Kirby Smith surrendered in Texas — end of the Civil war 4: 7
1865 Robert W. Chambers, author and artist, born .. C: 402
1866 Harry A. Wheeler, banker and first president of the Chamber of Commerce of the United States, born .... B: 281
1867 Julius Stieglitz, chemist, born .... C: 401
1868 The court of impeachment abandoned the case against President Johnson 2: 456
1871 Treaty of Washington (with Great Britain) ratified 4: 20
1872 Russell Doubleday, publisher, born 13: 401
1872 Joseph Urban, architect and scenic artist, distinguished for his stage settings and theatrical designs, born 25: 366
1882 Frank C. Emerson, governor of Wyoming, born 25: 423

MAY 27.

1725 Samuel Ward, colonial governor of Rhode Island, born 10: 14
1794 Cornelius Vanderbilt, financier, born 6: 208
1807 James P. Kirkwood, civil engineer, born 9: 36
1813 Ft. George, Canada, captured by Americans .. 11: 533
1818 John D. Philbrick, educator, born 12: 242
1819 Julia Ward Howe, author, born 1: 402
1819 Thomas H. Stevens, naval officer, born 4: 313
1821 Samuel Wetherill, inventor and the first in this country to produce metallic zinc commercially, born 7: 506
1828 Robert Parr Whitfield, paleontologist, born 5: 92
1832 William R. Ware, founder of the first American school of architecture, born 8: 440
1835 Charles Francis Adams, historian and president of the Union Pacific Railroad, born 8: 353
1836 Jay Gould, leading financier of his day, born ... 7: 218
1840 Wordsworth Thompson, artist, born 8: 430
1844 National Democratic convention nominated James K. Polk for president 6: 265
1844 John A. Watterson, R. C. bishop, born 9: 413
1844 May Wright Sewall, educator and reformer, born 19: 108
1849 Franklin C. Woodward, president of South Carolina college, born 11: 36
1850 Francis G. du Pont, who developed smokeless gunpowder, born 23: 233
1853 Julian Ralph, editor and author, born 1: 149
1861 Gen. McDowell placed in command of the Army of the Potomac 4: 50
1861 Border states convention began at Frankfort, Ky. 13: 7
1862 Battle of Hanover Court House, Va. 4: 262
1862 John Kendrick Bangs, editor and author, born 9: 323
1863 Siege of Port Hudson, La., began 4: 222
1864 Battle of Pickett's Mill 9: 19
1868 William H. Woodin, industrialist, and secretary of the treasury under Franklin D. Roosevelt, born 25: 4
1878 Isadora Duncan, dancer, born 22: 159
1889 Nathan Straus, Jr., New York merchant, journalist and legislator, born .... B: 146
1919 Commander Albert C. Read reached Portugal on the first flight of an airplane across the Atlantic .... A: 496
1933 Opening of the Century of Progress exposition in Chicago .... D: 403

MAY 28.

1748 Thomas Butler, soldier, born 8: 84
1764 Edward Livingston, jurist, secretary of state under Jackson, and minister to France, born 5: 293
1776 Louis McLane, secretary of the treasury and secretary of state under Jackson, born 5: 293
1780 Nathaniel Chapman, physician and educator, born 3: 294
1803 Cornerstone of New York city hall laid 25: 289
1804 Frederick Fraley, financier, born 7: 513
1804 William A. Buckingham, governor of Connecticut, born 10: 339
1807 Louis Agassiz, naturalist, born 2: 360
1809 George M. Totten, builder of the Panama railroad, born 18: 109
1816 Albert G. Riddle, lawyer and author, born 2: 371
1818 Pierre G. T. Beauregard, soldier, born 4: 178
1818 Amelia J. Bloomer, dress reformer, born 8: 173
1825 Richard C. Drum, soldier, born 12: 359
1826 B. Gratz Brown, lawyer, editor and governor of Missouri, born 20: 318
1829 Daniel L. Braine, naval officer, born 5: 248
1833 Charles A. Stoddard, clergyman, editor and author, born 9: 127
1840 Tony Pastor, actor and pioneer in vaudeville entertainment, born 16: 30
1846 Alfred T. White, pioneer in housing reform, born 23: 301
1855 Abby Leach, educator, born 12: 257
1857 Robert C. Hilliard, actor, born 22: 117
1864 Michael M. O'Shaughnessy, engineer, builder of the Morena dam and the Hetch-Hetchy water system, born 24: 52
1890 Willard Rouse Jillson, Kentucky geologist, born A: 178
1914 Glenn H. Curtiss flew with Langley's flying machine at Hammondsport, N. Y. 15: 7
1918 First independent action of American troops in World war .... A: 436

MAY 29.

1676 Nathaniel Bacon denounced as a traitor by by Governor Berkeley 5: 337
1736 Patrick Henry, statesman and orator, born ... 1: 337
1741 Lord Charles Greville Montagu, royal governor of South Carolina, born 12: 158
1766 First issue of the New York "Journal" 23: 280
1790 Rhode Island ratified the Constitution, the last state to do so 9: 393
1806 James J. Mapes, agricultural chemist, born .. 3: 178
1810 Erasmus D. Keyes, Federal soldier, born 4: 398
1813 Battle of Sackett's Harbor, N. Y. 5: 400
1819 Charles W. Webber, author, born 4: 354
1826 Ebenezer Butterick, originator of paper patterns for dresses, born 13: 231
1828 Thomas A. Emmet, New York physician, born 10: 286
1829 Work on the Chesapeake and Ohio canal begun 9: 302
1831 Joseph Killebrew, agriculturist, born 8: 308
1832 Joel Benton, author, essayist and poet, born .. 8: 200
1836 Wisconsin territory organized 12: 72
1841 Eugene F. Ware, lawyer and commissioner of pensions, born 9: 202
1844 Stephen A. Forbes, naturalist, born 22: 291
1848 Wisconsin admitted to the Union 12: 73
1851 Charles F. Richardson, educator and author, born 9: 95
1857 Charles R. Van Hise, geologist, and president of the University of Wisconsin, born 19: 19
1858 Thomas Leaming, lawyer, born 15: 137
1858 Marcus Klaw, theatrical producer, born .... A: 428
1860 The Hall expedition left New London, Conn., in search of Franklin 3: 281
1862 Confederates evacuated Corinth, Miss. 4: 179
1865 President Johnson issued a general amnesty for those who participated in the rebellion 2: 455
1874 Henry W. Bunn, author, born 26: 282
1883 George A. Parks, governor of Alaska, born .... B: 236
1901 Reginald A. Fessenden obtained a patent for improvement in wireless telegraphy 15: 22
1910 Glenn H. Curtiss made flight from Albany to New York winning New York "World" prize of $10,000 .... 22: 196
1911 The Supreme Court of the United States ordered the American Tobacco Co. dissolved 15: 291
1934 In a treaty of relations signed with Cuba the United States renounced the right of armed intervention in Cuban affairs .... D: 7

MAY 30.

Memorial or Decoration Day

1498 Columbus sailed on his third voyage 3: 438
1632 William Stoughton, chief justice of the superior court during the witchcraft trials, and acting governor of Massachusetts, born 7: 373
1743 Robert Patterson, mathematician, director of the mint, born 26: 59
1746 John Henry Livingston, clergyman and president of Queen's (later Rutgers) college, born 3: 400
1765 The famous "Virginia resolutions" passed 1: 338
1790 James Renwick, chemist and inventor, born 11: 101
1806 Duel between Andrew Jackson and Charles Dickinson 5: 291
1812 John A. McClernand, lawyer and Federal soldier, born 4: 137
1823 William L. Crittenden, soldier, born 4: 500
1828 James Woodrow, clergyman and president of South Carolina college, born 11: 35
1831 Samuel Merrill, publisher (Bobbs-Merrill & Co.), born 24: 366
1836 William McK. Springer, congressman and judge, born 11: 85
1843 Augustus C. Merriam, archæologist, born 8: 397
1844 Herbert L. Bridgman, journalist and explorer, for whom Cape Bridgman, Greenland, was named, born 22: 51
1847 Edward L. Mark, zoologist, born 9: 271
1848 Edward L. Burlingame, editor, born 8: 56
1850 Frederick D. Grant, soldier and U. S. minister to Austria, born 15: 93

1850 William Lawrence, P. E. bishop, born .... C: 479
1851 Gustav H. Schwab, American representative of the North German Lloyd Steamship Co., born 11: 90
1853 Katrina Trask, author, born 11: 444
1854 Kansas-Nebraska bill became a law 2: 430
1867 Rupert Blue, sanitarian, born 15: 129
1874 Josephine Preston Peabody, poet and dramatist, born 19: 95
1880 League of American Wheelmen organized 11: 523
1888 James A. Farley, postmaster general under Franklin D. Roosevelt, born .... D: 14
1901 The Hall of Fame at New York university formally opened 13: 523

MAY 31.

1607 First colonists sailed from Plymouth, England .. 5: 166
1752 John Brooks, governor of Massachusetts, born 1: 112
1769 Asa Messer, president of Brown university, born 8: 21
1775 Charles Jackson, Massachusetts jurist, born ... 5: 401
1775 Mecklenburg Declaration of Independence adopted 11: 341
1778 Horatio Seymour, judge and U. S. senator, born 8: 473
1791 John B. Francis, Rhode Island governor and U. S. senator, born 9: 396
1802 Ira Harris, U. S. senator, born 2: 96
1809 Don Alonzo J. Upham, Wisconsin lawyer, born 10: 168
1810 Horatio Seymour, twice governor of New York, born 3: 48
1813 Albert G. Brown, U. S. senator and governor of Mississippi, born 13: 488
1818 John A. Andrew, abolitionist and governor of Massachusetts, born 1: 118
1819 Walt Whitman, poet, born 1: 255
1819 William W. Mayo, physician and surgeon, born 19: 241
1821 Baltimore R. C. Cathedral dedicated 1: 483
1824 Jessie Benton Frémont, author, born 4: 399
1828 Samuel A. Lattimore, chemist, born 12: 244
1834 Joel H. Shedd, civil and hydraulic engineer, born 13: 44
1841 William Rockefeller, president of the Standard Oil Co. of New York, born 11: 63
1843 Wesleyan Methodist church organized 2: 316
1847 James Jeffrey Roche, author and poet, born .. 8: 265
1853 Elisha K. Kane set forth on his second expedition to the Arctic seas 3: 288
1853 Will H. Low, artist, born 6: 473
1854 George P. Merrill, geologist, born 8: 35
1861 Cynthia M. W. Alden, journalist and founder of the Sunshine Society, born 22: 52
1862 Battle of Fair Oaks, or Seven Pines, Va. 4: 141
1864 Radical convention at Cleveland, Ohio, nominated John C. Frémont for president 4: 272
1869 Walter Folger Brown, postmaster general under Hoover, born .... C: 10
1889 The Johnstown (Pa.) flood 5: 27
1926 The Sesquicentennial exposition opened in Philadelphia .... A: 343

JUNE 1.

1637 Jacques Marquette, explorer and missionary, born 12: 220
1660 Mary Dyer, Quaker martyr, hanged in Boston .. 11: 438
1774 Boston Port Bill became operative, closing the harbor against commerce; the day observed with fasting and mourning 1: 108
1790 Levi W. Leonard, clergyman and founder of the first public library in America, born 26: 228
1791 John Nelson, attorney-general under Tyler, born 6: 8
1792 Kentucky admitted to the Union 13: 2
1796 Tennessee admitted to the Union 7: 206
1800 Caroline Lee Hentz, Southern author and poet, born 6: 261
1801 Brigham Young, second president of the Mormon Church, born 16: 3
1806 John B. Floyd, governor of Virginia and secretary of war under Buchanan, born 5: 7
1813 Capt. Lawrence mortally wounded in the battle between the "Chesapeake" and the "Shannon" 8: 92
1816 Charles G. Eastman, poet, the "Burns of the Green Mountains," born 9: 252
1826 John H. Morgan, Confederate soldier, born 4: 317
1826 Thomas W. Ferry, statesman, born 9: 169
1826 William P. Blake, geologist and mining engineer, born 25: 202
1828 William J. Stillman, editor and author, born ... 10: 25
1829 Cullen A. Battle, lawyer and Confederate soldier, born 12: 351
1829 First issue of the "Pennsylvania Inquirer" 22: 18
1831 Redfield Proctor, governor of Vermont, secretary of war under Harrison and U. S. senator, born 1: 141
1831 John B. Hood, Confederate soldier, born 4: 264
1832 DeVolson Wood, educator and inventor, born ... 13: 351
1833 John M. Harlan, justice of the U. S. supreme court, born 1: 34
1834 Eben Tourjee, musician and founder of the New England conservatory of music, born 7: 234
1835 Edward W. Claypole, naturalist, born 13: 259
1842 Joseph C. Hartzell, M. E. bishop, born 13: 128
1849 Minnesota territory organized 10: 62
1849 Francis E. Stanley, inventor of a machine for coating dry-plates and a steam motor car, born 18: 429
1855 Edward H. Angle, orthodontist, born 22: 376
1856 Rolla Wells, capitalist, born .... C: 203
1862 Gen. Lee succeeded Gen. Johnston in command of the Army of Northern Virginia 4: 96
1865 National fast day for death of President Lincoln 2: 74
1866 Fenian raid into Canada 4: 8
1866 Charles B. Davenport, biologist and authority on eugenics, born 15: 397
1869 Ernest Fox Nichols, physicist, and president of Dartmouth college and the Massachusetts institute of technology, born 21: 68
1914 Col. House presented his plan to avert war to the emperor of Germany .... A: 56

JUNE 2.

1689 The Leisler insurrection broke out in New York 13: 448
1773 John Randolph "of Roanoke," congressman and U. S. senator, distinguished for his eloquence and wit, born 5: 97
1780 Naval battle between the "Trumbull" and the "Watt" 2: 231
1783 Reuel Williams, U. S. senator, born 10: 254
1794 William A. Hallock, editor, prominent in the development of the American Tract Society, born 10: 489
1800 Nicholas P. Trist, lawyer, who negotiated the treaty of Guadalupe Hidalgo with Mexico, born 7: 505
1815 Philip Kearny, soldier, born 4: 260
1816 John G. Saxe, poet, born 1: 438
1817 George H. Corliss, inventor of an improved steam engine, born 10: 394
1820 George L. Curry, governor of Oregon, born 8: 4
1820 Willard Saulsbury, Delaware statesman, born .. 11: 471
1833 George W. Smalley, journalist, born 3: 454
1838 Charles F. Himes, educator and pioneer in amateur photography, born 4: 144
1840 John L. Spalding, R. C. bishop, born 10: 44
1845 Arthur MacArthur, soldier, famous for his exploits in the Civil and Spanish-American wars and numerous Indian campaigns, born 14: 151
1851 Maine prohibition law enacted 5: 438
1861 Confederate privateer "Savannah" escaped from Charleston harbor 4: 156
1864 Occupation of Bermuda Hundred, Va., by the Federals 4: 69
1865 Occupation of Galveston, Tex., the last Confederate city to surrender to the Federals ... 4: 295
1866 William Brewster, carriage manufacturer, born 13: 128
1919 Nation-wide bomb plot uncovered, following an attempt to blow up Atty. Gen. Palmer's home A: 45

JUNE 3.

Holiday in Florida, Georgia and Virginia

1705 William Tennent, Presbyterian clergyman, born 8: 73
1712 Thomas Bond, physician, born 13: 431
1769 The Transit of Venus observed and valuable astronomical data obtained 1: 346
1803 William Knabe, piano manufacturer, born 11: 340
1805 Treaty of peace between the United States and Tripoli signed 5: 262
1807 Oliver Stearns, Unitarian clergyman and theologian, born 9: 191
1808 Jefferson Davis, president of the Confederate states, born 4: 148
1811 Henry James, theologian, born 13: 66
1819 Thomas Ball, sculptor, born 5: 199
1820 Sereno E. Todd, author and editor, born 9: 272
1821 Edward L. Youmans, scientist and editor, founder of the "Popular Science Monthly," born 2: 466
1830 George U. Morris, naval officer, born 4: 278
1833 Joseph Howard, Jr., journalist and lecturer, author of the "Bogus Proclamation," born 4: 218
1842 William J. Keep, engineer, born 18: 207
1844 Garret A. Hobart, vice-president of the United States, born 11: 10
1844 First issue of the "Morning Courier," Louisville, Ky., appeared 18: 239
1857 Charles H. Steinway, piano manufacturer, born 18: 266
1861 Capture of the "Savannah," the first Confederate privateer taken during the Civil war 4: 156
1864 Assault on Cold Harbor, Va., resulted in heavy Federal losses 4: 99
1866 James Brown Scott, authority on international law, born .... C: 69
1867 Governor James M. Wells, of Louisiana, removed from office 10: 79

1879 Raymond Pearl, biologist, born 15:382
1887 Roland Hayes, singer, born A:529
1898 The collier "Merrimac" sunk to block the entrance to Santiago harbor 9: 10
1929 Through the offices of the United States the Tacna-Arica boundary dispute was concluded with a treaty between Chile and Peru .... A: 9

JUNE 4.

1744 Jeremy Belknap, clergyman and author, born 7:204
1752 John Eager Howard, Revolutionary soldier, and governor of Maryland, born 9:292
1776 The British fleet arrived in Charleston harbor to begin a campaign in the South 8:239
1838 George C. Lorimer, clergyman, born 11:358
1839 Eckley B. Coxe, mining engineer, born 11:559
1840 Wendell P. Garrison, author and literary editor of the "Nation," born 1:197
1842 Samuel B. Whitney, organist and composer, born 9:388
1843 Charles C. Abbott, naturalist and author, born 10:318
1845 Mexico declared war against the United States.. 6:267
1849 Obediah C. Auringer, clergyman, poet and author, born 7:177
1854 Walter L. Dean, artist, born 10:371
1859 Paul E. Archinard, physician specializing in the treatment of nervous diseases, born 9:134
1862 Henry Jewett, actor, founder of the first civic repertory theatre in the United States, born .. 22:303
1893 Ohio Anti-Saloon League organized 13:330
1903 The James Millikin university buildings dedicated 18:117
1928 Contents of the Philadelphia "Bulletin's" issue for this day published in book form, under the title "One Day" 23:149

JUNE 5.

1762 Bushrod Washington, justice of the U. S. supreme court and founder and first president of the American Colonization Society, born .. 2:231
1769 Sir Robert Eden, last proprietary governor of Maryland, took office 7:337
1773 William Sprague, manufacturer who introduced calico printing, born 8: 19
1775 Lyman Spalding, physician, an early advocate of vaccination against smallpox, born 2:194
1780 Melancthon T. Woolsey, naval officer, born 8: 98
1781 Augusta, Ga., surrendered to the Americans 8: 25
1782 Battle near Sandusky, Ohio, with the Indians .. 9:283
1783 Bennington (Vt.) "Gazette" first issued 8:261
1784 Ichabod Nichols, clergyman, born 10:456
1804 Maximilian LaBorde, physician, legislator and educator, born 11: 34
1806 William Tyler, R. C. bishop, born 10:136
1809 Columbus Delano, congressman and secretary of the interior under Grant, born 4: 18
1823 George T. Angell, a founder and president of the Massachusetts Society for the Prevention of Cruelty to Animals, born 7:477
1825 Jabez L. M. Curry, soldier, educator and diplomat, born 4:357
1826 John C. Reeve, physician and surgeon, a pioneer in medical thermometry and anaesthesia, born 20:202
1828 Henry Wurtz, chemist, devised new methods of preparation and manufacture of chemicals, born 7:519
1829 Marcus Jastrow, clergyman and lexicographer, born 11:372
1849 Samuel Garman, naturalist, born 10:294
1851 First chapter of "Uncle Tom's Cabin" published 1:424
1861 Frank K. Sanders, Biblical scholar, born 25: 48
1864 Battle of Piedmont, Va. 4:264
1870 Richard C. Maclaurin, president of Massachusetts institute of technology, born 14:483

JUNE 6.

1755 Nathan Hale, Revolutionary soldier, hanged for a spy by the British, born 1: 51
1756 John Trumbull, soldier, and a famous painter of historical subjects, born 3:334
1775 Governor John Murray, of Virginia, took refuge on board a British man-of-war 13:391
1778 Charles F. Mercer, congressman, born 13:222
1786 Nathaniel Gorham commenced his term as president of the Continental congress 2:525
1797 Samuel P. Newman, clergyman and educator, born 10:123
1804 Louis A. Godey, publisher, whose "Lady's Book" was the most popular magazine of its day, born 22: 39
1806 Daniel Leach, promoter of education in Rhode Island, born 8:467
1809 Timothy S. Arthur, author of moral tales, and founder and editor of Arthur's "Home Magazine," born 8:480
1813 Israel Washburn, governor of Maine, born 5:400
1813 Battle of Stony Creek, Canada 10:487
1816 Catherine A. Warfield, poet and novelist, born .. 5:306
1841 Henry Mosler, artist, born 9: 50
1842 Steele MacKaye, actor and playwright, born 14:158
1846 John Davey, "father of tree surgery," born 22: 70
1847 Thomas L. Bradford, physician and bibliographer, born 3:492
1850 James A. McFaul, R. C. bishop, born 12:347
1852 John A. Sherman, inventor and manufacturer, born 13: 23
1859 George Hempl, philologist, born 13:365
1860 Charles MacVeagh, noted New York lawyer, and ambassador to Japan, born 23: 17
1862 The Federal Fleet took possession of Memphis, Tenn. 4:166
1871 Alfred E. Stearns, educator, born 13: 63
1881 Harvey N. Davis, president of Stevens institute of technology, born A:348
1891 Peary left New York for Greenland with a party of scientists 14: 60
1902 Reginald A. Fessenden received a patent for the high-frequency arc in wireless telegraphy 15: 22

JUNE 7.

1610 Remnant of the English colony in Virginia embarked for England 13:380
1714 Edward Winslow, loyalist, born 1:188
1745 Lindley Murray, grammarian, born 7:178
1758 Francis Fauquier became governor of Virginia 13:390
1776 The resolution for the declaration of independence introduced in congress 3:159
1780 Elijah Hedding, M. E. bishop, born 10:207
1798 Treaties with France abrogated 4:189
1804 William Scott, judge, born 12:188
1817 James Birney, lawyer and diplomat, born 12:224
1824 Alfred Pleasanton, Federal soldier, and railroad president, born 4:164
1835 John A. Darling, soldier who, under the name of "August Mignon," also distinguished himself as a composer, born 8:359
1839 John Satterfield, Pennsylvania oil operator, born 5: 34
1840 Thomas B. Wheeler, Texas lawyer and pioneer, born 15:118
1843 Susan E. Blow, pioneer kindergartner, born ... 4:291
1845 Leopold Auer, violinist, born 22:384
1845 John F. Goucher, clergyman, a founder and president of Goucher college, Baltimore, born . 24:174
1848 The Whig national convention nominated Zachary Taylor for president 4:369
1857 Samuel McC. Crothers, clergyman and author, born 22:384
1862 James J. Andrews, a Federal spy, hanged 9:471
1863 Albert Sidney Burleson, postmaster general under Wilson, born .... A: 45
1876 R. S. Reynolds Hitt, diplomat, born 14:477
1887 First patent for the monotype machine issued .. 13:573
1913 Mt. McKinley, Alaska, first climbed to the summit 23:267

JUNE 8.

1595 Thomas Parker, clergyman, born 12:249
1610 The Virginia colonists' abandonment of Jamestown forestalled by the approach of Lord De la Warr 13:380
1754 Henry Burbeck, soldier, born 1: 71
1780 Robert McCormick, inventor of a hemp brake, a grist mill and other farming machines, born 24:139
1783 Thomas Sully, artist, born 5:215
1784 Samuel Batchelder, inventor of the dynamometer, born 5: 16
1786 Samuel R. Betts, maritime jurist, born 22: 30
1788 Charles A. Wickliffe, governor of Kentucky, and postmaster general under Tyler, born 6: 8
1797 Samuel Bowles, founder of the Springfield "Republican," born 1:317
1797 Hector Humphreys, president of St. John's college, Annapolis, born 1:504
1799 William M. Meredith, secretary of the treasury under Taylor, born 4:370
1806 Gideon J. Pillow, soldier, born 9:279
1811 Abija Hunt killed in duel with George Poindexter 13:486
1812 Richard Soule, author, born 2:115
1813 David D. Porter, second admiral of the U. S. navy, born 2: 97
1822 Duel between George McDuffie and Col. William Cumming 12:167
1830 Henry M. Hoyt, governor of Pennsylvania, born 2:292
1830 Henry C. Trumbull, editor and author, born 9:383
1838 George M. Sternberg, army surgeon and author, born 4:388

1842 John Q. A. Brackett, governor of Massachusetts, born ... 1:125
1848 Franklin H. King, authority on agricultural physics, creator of the science of rural engineering, born ... 19:292
1850 Charles M. Jacobs, engineer who built the first tunnel under the East river, born ... 14:208
1854 John F. Shafroth, Colorado governor and U. S. senator, born ... 14:502
1861 Tennessee seceded from the Union ... 7:210
1861 Texas proclaimed a state of war against the Federal government ... 9: 69
1861 Central Pacific Railroad Co. of California organized ... 15: 16
1862 Battle of Cross Keys, Va. ... 3:206
1869 Frank Lloyd Wright, architect, the "father of modern architecture," born ... D:278
1877 Robert F. Wagner, judge and U. S. senator, author of important constructive legislation, born ... D: 39

JUNE 9.

1738 Samuel Holten, Massachusetts physician and patriot, born ... 13:154
1768 Samuel Slater, pioneer cotton manufacturer, born 24:220
1785 Sylvanus Thayer, "father of the U. S. military academy," born ... 7: 37
1787 Samuel L. Southard, secretary of the navy under Monroe and Adams, and governor of New Jersey, born ... 6: 85
1791 John Howard Payne, actor and poet, author of "Home Sweet Home," born ... 2:347
1794 George H. Barrett, actor, born ... 4:447
1808 Frederick W. Evans, Shaker elder and reformer, born ... 11:255
1809 Richard W. Thompson, secretary of the navy under Hayes, born ... 3:202
1811 James T. Champlin, president of Waterville college and its successor, Colby university, born 8:406
1820 Edmund Randolph, lawyer and pioneer settler of California, born ... 1:445
1822 Peter Henderson, horticulturist, born ... 6:143
1827 Francis M. Finch, jurist and poet, author of "The Blue and the Gray," born ... 11:356
1836 Eugene Hale, U. S. senator, born ... 20:220
1844 Henry T. Eddy, mathematician, born ... 15:331
1846 Vernon Royle, inventor and manufacturer, born 12:399
1849 William F. Nichols, P. E. bishop, born ... 12: 86
1849 Thomas Clinton Pears, inventor and manufacturer, prominent in the Pittsburgh glass industry, born ... 22:179
1850 James Stillman, financier, born ... 15: 28
1851 Vigilance committee in San Francisco formed .. 4:106
1851 Charles J. Bonaparte, statesman, born ... 14: 22
1852 Elam Bartholomew, mycologist, born ... 26:293
1857 Wendell C. Phillips, physician, who did much to ameliorate the condition of the deaf, born .. 25:186
1862 Battle of Port Republic, Va. ... 8: 2
1863 Engagements at Beverly Ford and Brandy Station, Va. ... 11:469

JUNE 10.

1610 Lord De la Warr arrived at Jamestown, Va., with supplies for the colonists ... 13:380
1676 Bacon tried as a rebel and acquitted ... 5:337
1691 French and Indians attacked the garrison at Wells, Maine ... 8:144
1735 John Morgan, physician, a founder of the first medical school in America, born ... 10:267
1753 William Eustis, secretary of war under Jefferson and Madison and Massachusetts governor, born 5:372
1761 Battle of Etchoee with Cherokee Indians ... 7:532
1762 Joseph Bartlett, lawyer, whose wit gained him wide notoriety, born ... 13:161
1772 British schooner "Gaspé" destroyed ... 2: 16
1772 David L. Morril, New Hampshire governor and U. S. senator, born ... 11:125
1775 James Barbour, governor of Virginia, secretary of war under John Q. Adams, and minister to England, born ... 5:446
1777 David S. Bates, civil engineer, an expert on canal construction, born ... 18:171
1798 Francis L. Hawks, P. E. clergyman and historian, born ... 7: 90
1801 Tripoli declared war against the United States 4: 56
1803 Anson P. Morrill, governor of Maine, born ... 6:312
1810 Robert T. Conrad, lawyer and author, born ... 11:551
1822 John Jacob Astor (3d), capitalist, born ... 8:104
1822 William J. Demorest, publisher and reformer, born ... 10:311
1833 John S. Brown, pioneer Denver merchant and banker, born ... 15:353
1833 Pauline Cushman, actress and Civil war spy, born ... 23:151
1841 Minot J. Savage, clergyman, born ... 1:351
1846 Iowa college founded ... 13: 80
1847 The Chicago "Tribune" first issued as a daily .. 7:558
1849 David Lubin, merchant, born ... 19:440
1850 David Jayne Hill, president of Bucknell university and the University of Rochester, and author and lecturer, born ... 12:244
1851 First trial and execution by the vigilance committee in San Francisco, Calif. ... 4:106
1856 Caroline Hazard, president of Wellesley college, born ... C:501
1858 Second attempt to lay the Atlantic cable begun 4:452
1861 Engagement at Big Bethel, Va. ... 1:122
1864 Engagement at Petersburg, Va. ... 4: 99
1864 Battle at Brice's Cross Roads, Miss. ... 10: 37
1869 Paul S. Reinsch, political economist, authority on international politics, American minister to China, born ... 19:285
1869 William S. Kenyon, jurist and U. S. senator, born ... 24: 60
1887 Harry F. Byrd, governor of Virginia and U. S. senator, born ... B:430
1921 U. S. bureau of the budget created ... A:509

JUNE 11.

1741 Joseph Warren, physician and patriot, born .. 1: 57
1752 Eliphalet Pearson, first principal of Phillips academy at Andover, born ... 10: 94
1775 Patriots seized the powder in the arsenal at Savannah, Ga. ... 1: 18
1782 Death by torture of Col. William Crawford ... 9:283
1814 Henry W. Bellows, clergyman, who organized the sanitary commission in the Civil war, born 3:261
1819 Eli Thayer, educator, congressman and inventor, born ... 11:414
1821 Platt P. Ryder, artist, born ... 11:293
1821 Alexander B. Latta, inventor of a steam fire engine, born ... 13:418
1824 Orson D. Munn, publisher of the "Scientific American," born ... 7: 83
1832 Augustus H. Garland, governor of Arkansas, U. S. senator and attorney-general under Cleveland, born ... 2:409
1835 Eliphalet F. Andrews, artist, born ... 8:432
1839 Sarah Gertrude Banks, a pioneer woman physician, born ... 18:101
1840 William H. Conley, manufacturer, born ... 14: 72
1844 William Robert Brooks, astronomer and inventor, born ... 5:197
1845 Arthur Brooks, clergyman, born ... 8:465
1846 William L. Marshall, engineer and inventor, born 11:467
1849 Edwin Noyes Bailey (Bailey of Britt), editor and publisher, born ... 21:103
1849 David W. Brunton, mining engineer and inventor, who built the famous Cowenhoven tunnel, born ... 23: 99
1857 Leland O. Howard, entomologist, born ... 12:356
1857 Nicholas R. Brewer, artist, born ... 12:469
1864 Engagement at Trevilian Station, Va. ... 5: 65
1871 Adm. Rodgers bombarded Korean forts in retaliation for an attack on his party ... 5: 14
1871 John E. Williams, missionary to China, born .. 21:122

JUNE 12.

1630 John Winthrop arrived at Salem, Mass., with the Massachusetts colony charter ... 6:202
1665 English municipal government formally established in New York ... 13:448
1676 Hadley, Mass., attacked by Indians ... 11:459
1756 John Blair Smith, president of Hampden-Sidney college, born ... 2: 21
1758 The Newport (R. I.) "Mercury" first issued ... 8: 18
1775 Proclamation of Governor Gage, declaring the patriots rebels, and offering pardon to all save Hancock and Adams ... 7:378
1775 First naval battle of the Revolution occurred off Machias, Maine ... 11:113
1776 Declaration of Rights adopted by the Virginia committee ... 3:337
1789 John Farmer, antiquarian and author, born... 12:553
1794 Chauncey Brooks, president of the Baltimore and Ohio R. R., born ... 18: 2
1796 George Bush, theologian, born ... 6:515
1802 John Young, congressman and governor of New York, born ... 3: 48
1806 John A. Roebling, bridge builder, born ... 4:404
1823 William H. Hunt, judge, diplomat, secretary of the navy under Garfield, born ... 4:244
1830 John McL. Keating, sanitarian, rendered valuable service to Memphis during yellow fever epidemics, born ... 23:185

1838 Iowa territory formed 3:510
1844 Janarius A. McGahan, editor and author, born.. 6:187
1847 Alice M. W. Rollins, author, born 8:414
1848 A public funeral held in New York in memory of officers lost in the Mexican war 9:112
1850 Francis S. Saltus, poet and author, born 6:188
1860 Hunter McDonald, civil engineer, born C:185
1862 Gen. J. E. B. Stuart started on raid to pass around Gen. McClellan's army 4: 52
1864 Grant's army withdrew across the James river 4: 99
1864 Frank M. Chapman, ornithologist, born C:188
1867 Howard C. Warren, psychologist, founder of the "Journal of Experimental Psychology," and bibliographer and lexicographer, born 25:344
1869 Duel between William E. Cameron and Robert W. Hughes 7:551
1879 James Oliver Curwood, author, born 21:127
1883 Roi Cooper Megrue, playwright, born 20:407
1893 Leland R. Robinson, investment banker, born .. A:144
1898 First American troops sailed for Cuba 9: 18

JUNE 13.

1743 Francis Dana, statesman and jurist, born 3:240
1782 William B. Johnson, clergyman, born 12:323
1784 Isaac McCoy, missionary to the Indians, born 18:229
1786 Winfield Scott, soldier, born 3:502
1789 George W. Freeman, P. E. bishop, born 13:452
1792 John P. K. Henshaw, P. E. bishop, born 11:107
1792 William A. Burt, inventor of a solar compass and the "typographer," the precursor of the typewriter, born 18:367
1803 George A. Carrell, first archbishop of Covington, Ky., born 12: 51
1809 P. St. George Cooke, soldier, born 4:189
1813 Ebenezer D. Draper, manufacturer of textile machinery, and president of The Hopedale Community, born 23: 54
1820 John H. Stevens, pioneer, born 12:361
1821 Gustavus V. Fox, naval officer, born 8:355
1822 David D. Acker, merchant, born 1:179
1822 Fitz-John Porter, soldier in the Mexican and Civil wars, born 4:261
1824 Julius Eichberg, composer, born 13:320
1830 Everett Peabody, soldier, born 4:155
1839 Treaty of "peace, friendship, navigation and commerce" with Ecuador concluded 13:159
1846 Frederic W. Root, composer, born 9:384
1854 Bradley A. Fiske, naval officer and inventor, born .... B: 57
1856 Launcelot W. Andrews, chemist, and inventor of processes for manufacturing chemicals, born A:396
1858 A treaty with China signed at Tientsin 1:422
1863 Battle of Winchester, Va. 4:219
1863 Federals repulsed at Port Hudson, La. 7:223
1867 Henry P. Davison, banker, born 20: 88
1875 Miriam A. Ferguson, governor of Texas, the second woman governor in the United States, born A:428
1894 Mark Van Doren, teacher and critic of English literature, born .... D: 48
1917 Gen. Pershing and staff arrived in Paris, in advance of the American troops, for the World war A:436

JUNE 14.
Flag Day

1662 Sir Henry Vane, governor of Massachusetts colony, beheaded 7:372
1748 Henry Allen, founder of the religious sect of Allenites, born 7:492
1757 David C. Claypoole, publisher of the "Pennsylvania Packet," which became the first daily newspaper in the United States, born 20:253
1759 Kensey Johns, U. S. senator and chancellor of Delaware, born 5:196
1774 David Low Dodge, merchant and philanthropist, born 20:171
1777 Flag of stars and stripes adopted by Congress 12:438
1805 Robert Anderson, soldier, born 4:179
1810 Ward Hunt, justice of the U. S. supreme court, born 2:475
1811 Harriet Beecher Stowe, author, born 1:423
1818 Daniel W. Powers, Rochester banker and philanthropist, born 10: 57
1819 Henry Joseph Gardner, governor of Massachusetts, born 1:117
1819 Charles Lanman, author and editor, born 3:444
1820 John Bartlett, compiler of "Familiar Quotations," born 11:235
1821 Andrew Campbell, inventor of improvements in printing presses, born 9:154

1826 Robert Hunter, physician, born 7:281
1826 William Orton, president of the Western Union Telegraph Co., born 7:502
1834 Richard Realf, poet, born 8: 60
1834 The diving suit patented 13:422
1837 Margaret J. (Maggie) Mitchell, actress, born 25:222
1838 Roswell M. Shurtleff, artist, born 10:379
1851 John A. Zahm, scientist and educator, born 9:274
1854 Wilbur F. Gordy, educator, author of history text books, born 21: 85
1855 Robert La Follette, governor of Wisconsin and U. S. senator, born 19:425
1862 John J. Glennon, archbishop of St. Louis, born 13: 31
1867 Livingston Farrand, anthropologist and president of Cornell university, born A:117
1877 William A. Starrett, engineer, architect and builder, born 24: 42
1881 Steamship "Jeanette" sunk in Arctic ocean 3:283
1901 First juvenile court in Pennsylvania held at Philadelphia 18: 99
1907 Flag day inaugurated by Mary R. Day of Tennessee 22:235

JUNE 15.

1752 Franklin drew electricity from the clouds and proved its identity with lightning 1:332
1775 George Washington elected commander-in-chief of the Continental army 1: 3
1789 Josiah Henson, Negro preacher, the supposed original of Harriet Beecher Stowe's "Uncle Tom," born 22:383
1805 John M. Henni, first archbishop of Milwaukee, born 7:516
1805 William B. Ogden, pioneer Chicago merchant and president of the Union Pacific R. R., born 13:283
1807 William Nast, clergyman and editor, the founder of "German Methodism," born 10:223
1811 John Guy Vassar, philanthropist, born 5:233
1821 William Henry Shock, engineer-in-chief, U. S. navy, born 6:200
1823 Henry S. Sanford, diplomat, born 7:140
1826 Charles H. Smith (Bill Arp), humorist, born .. 3:308
1835 Adah I. Menken, actress, born 5:435
1835 Edward M. McCook, soldier and governor of Colorado, born 6:448
1836 Arkansas admitted to the Union 10:184
1836 George L. Shoup, governor of Idaho and U. S. senator, born 12:491
1844 Patent issued to Goodyear for making rubber ... 3: 86
1846 Treaty with England, establishing boundary west of the Rocky mountains, signed 8: 1
1848 Sol Smith Russell, actor, born 10:412
1848 First submarine cable laid between New York and Jersey City 23: 60
1856 Edward Channing, historian, born 13:432
1858 Francis E. Elwell, sculptor, born 10:368
1859 William H. P. Faunce, clergyman, and president of Brown university, born 10:306
1863 Battle of Winchester ended 4:219
1864 Operations against Petersburg, Va., began ... 7:518
1869 Musical festival held in Boston, Mass. 3:292
1872 Johanna Gadski-Tauscher, opera singer, born .. B:186
1889 Harry Elmer Barnes, educator and historian, born .... C: 35
1929 Enactment of a farm relief bill creating a federal farm board to advance loans to farm organizations .... C: 6

JUNE 16.

1710 John Lovell, educator, born 12:428
1751 Thomas Melvill, soldier, inspiration of Holmes's "The Last Leaf," born 11:364
1775 Fortifications erected on Breed's hill, Charlestown, Mass. 1:113
1778 Harry Croswell, New Haven (Conn.) journalist and clergyman, born 10: 31
1780 Battle of Camden, N. J. 7:543
1789 William Jay, jurist and author, born 8: 74
1804 Alvin Adams, founder of the Adams Express Co., born 7:494
1816 Luke P. Blackburn, Kentucky physician and governor, born 13: 10
1820 Jared B. Flagg, clergyman and artist, born 7:549
1830 Charles Denby, lawyer, soldier and diplomat, born 8:276
1833 Thomas W. Walker, soldier and president of Norwich university, born 18:325
1836 Wesley Merritt, military governor of the Philippines, born 9: 28
1838 Cushman K. Davis, U. S. senator and governor of Minnesota, born 10: 65

1844 James W. Nicholson, president of the Louisiana state university and agricultural and mechanical college, born 13:236
1844 Henry William Poor, financier, publisher of Poor's manuals, born 16: 33
1845 Texas congress approved terms of annexation .. 6:267
1847 Tobasco, Mexico, stormed by Americans 4:527
1861 George D. Widener, Philadelphia financier, born 15: 12
1862 Federals defeated at Secessionville, S. C. 4:277
1864 Lynchburg, Va., invaded by Gen. Hunter 4: 70
1867 Francis Hodgkinson, engineer and inventor of improvements in turbine construction, born . B: 18
1869 Frederick O'Brien, author, born C:525
1872 Jesse B. Carter, philologist, and director of the American academy in Rome, born 23:225
1883 Walter M. W. Splawn, president of the University of Texas, born B:365
1933 National Recovery Administration (NRA) created by act of congress ..... D: 20

JUNE 17.

Holiday in Boston

1579 Sir Francis Drake landed on the coast of California 9:284
1673 Marquette and Jolliet reached the Mississippi river 5:121
1703 John Wesley, founder of Methodism, born 5: 57
1742 William Hooper, a signer of the Declaration of Independence, born 5:457
1743 John Lowell, Massachusetts jurist, born 7: 62
1745 Louisburg, Nova Scotia, captured by the English 3:330
1746 Joseph Winston, soldier, born 6: 12
1751 Joshua Humphreys, shipbuilder, "the father of the American navy," born 5:110
1775 Battle of Bunker Hill 1: 91
1790 Abel Parker Upshur, secretary of the navy and of state under Tyler, born 6: 8
1795 Samuel Williston, philanthropist, born 5:313
1813 Thomas Silver, inventor of the marine governor, born 6:191
1815 Algerian vessel "Mashanda" captured in first engagement of war with Algiers 4: 56
1817 Emanuel V. Gerhart, president of Franklin and Marshall college, born 12:443
1825 Luther S. Dixon, judge, born 12:513
1828 David Ames Wells, financier and economist, born 10:363
1830 Jeremiah McL. Rusk, governor of Wisconsin and secretary of agriculture under Harrison, born 1: 47
1832 George H. Babcock, inventor of a printing press and a safety tubular boiler, born 5:304
1843 Bunker Hill monument dedicated 4:431
1847 Francis H. Appleton, agriculturist, born 12:231
1848 Frank Springer, lawyer and paleontologist, born 20: 23
1852 Indiana college became a state university 13:117
1853 Charles Spencer Francis, diplomat, born 12:117
1858 Eben S. Draper, Massachusetts manufacturer and governor, born 23: 55
1860 Charles Frohman, theatrical manager, born ... 11:441
1861 Battle of Booneville, Mo. 4:202
1863 Capture of the Confederate "Atlanta" by the "Weehawken" 5: 14
1872 International peace jubilee opened in Boston ... 3:292
1876 Battle of Rose Bud Creek, Mont., with Sioux Indians 9: 28
1880 Carl Van Vechten, novelist and music critic, born D:433
1887 Hazen ascended in a balloon to 16,000 feet 8:115
1902 The national irrigation law passed by congress 13:283
1928 Amelia Earhart took off from Newfoundland, the first woman to fly across the Atlantic D:396

JUNE 18.

1621 First duel fought in America 7:532
1684 Charter of Massachusetts Bay Colony forfeited 8:474
1717 John Collins, Rhode Island patriot and governor, born 9:392
1775 Lord William Campbell, last royal governor of South Carolina, took office 12:159
1776 Canada evacuated by Americans 1: 53
1778 British evacuated Philadelphia 1: 4
1781 Benjamin W. Leigh, lawyer and U. S. senator, born 11:312
1787 Amasa Holcombe, scientist, designer and manufacturer of reflecting telescopes, born 3:311
1791 Denison Olmsted, astronomer, born 8:121
1798 McDonald Clarke, "The Mad Poet," born 6:406
1798 The first of the alien laws, excluding natives of enemy countries from citizenship in the United States, passed 13:182
1798 Leonard Norcross, inventor of the diving suit, born 13:422
1802 Henry Durant, first president of the University of California, born 7:228
1803 Robert W. Weir, artist, born 11:295
1811 Frances S. Osgood, poet and author, born 2:196
1812 War against England declared 5:370
1818 Joseph R. Bodwell, quarryman and governor of Maine, born 6:318
1819 Samuel Longfellow, clergyman, born 8:275
1824 George T. Anthony, governor of Kansas, born .. 8:345
1832 Battle of Rock River, Wis., with Indians 9:477
1838 Edward S. Morse, zoologist, ethnologist and archæologist, born 24:407
1841 Lester F. Ward, botanist and paleontologist, born 13:112
1848 John R. Thomas, New York architect, born 9:329
1850 Cyrus H. K. Curtis, publisher, founder of the "Ladies Home Journal" and the "Saturday Evening Post," born 24: 26
1851 Neil Burgess, actor, born 2:170
1852 Roland Reed, actor, born 13:323
1853 Allen Thorndike Rice, editor, born 3:259
1856 William C. Bullitt, lawyer and industrialist, born 15:343
1857 Henry C. Folger, president of the Standard Oil Co. of New York, and founder of the Shakespearian library in Washington, born 23: 9
1858 William Cox Redfield, secretary of commerce under Wilson, born ..... A: 50
1864 Battle of Lynchburg, Va., ended 4:264
1869 Carolyn Wells, author, born 13:213
1870 Charles Baskerville, chemist, born 13:300
1896 Philip Barry, dramatist, born C:516
1910 Passage of the Mann-Elkins law clothing the interstate commerce commission with authority to fix railroad rates 1:142

JUNE 19.

1700 Peter Faneuil, Boston merchant, born 1:441
1750 Lemuel Hopkins, Connecticut physician and poet, born 7:282
1754 Congress of seven colonies met at Albany to discuss union for defense 13:344
1774 Samuel L. Knapp, author, born 7:472
1778 Benedict Arnold put in command of Philadelphia 1: 53
1793 Joseph E. Sheffield, merchant and benefactor of the Sheffield scientific school at Yale, born .. 11:515
1799 Grenville Mellen, poet, born 7:245
1812 George Kellogg, inventor, born 7:494
1815 Algerian vessel "Estido" captured by the Americans 11: 76
1816 William Henry Webb, New York ship-builder, born 2:263
1819 The "Savannah," the first steamship to cross the Atlantic ocean, arrived in Liverpool 4: 88
1819 Maine separated from Massachusetts 6:305
1826 Charles Loring Brace, New York philanthropist, born 10:166
1829 Charles C. Everett, clergyman and author, born 9:253
1841 Hermann E. von Holst, historian, born 11: 69
1843 William E. Coleman, author, born 5: 20
1851 Samuel Macauley Jackson, Presbyterian clergyman, born 9:434
1855 Charles W. Dabney, president of the universities of Tennessee and Cincinnati, born B:239
1856 Elbert Hubbard, author and publisher, born .. 16:415
1858 Sam Walter Foss, poet, born 9: 32
1860 Charles Clinton Marshall, lawyer and author, born C:496
1861 Convention at Wheeling met to form the new state of West Virginia 12:430
1864 Battle between the "Kearsarge" and the Confederate privateer, the "Alabama" 2:103
1871 The Omaha "Bee" first issued 13:323
1878 Lieut. Schwatka started for the Arctic in search of Franklin relics 3:285
1912 Organization of the Progressive party 19: 94

JUNE 20.

1542 Death of DeSoto; he was buried in the river he discovered 5:127
1632 Maryland granted to Lord Baltimore 7:331
1759 William R. Davie, soldier, governor of North Carolina, and a founder of the University of North Carolina, born 1: 77
1767 British parliament levied taxes on the American colonies 1:334
1774 Citizens of Philadelphia declared the Boston Port Bill to be unconstitutional 2:282
1774 Frederick, Md., protested against Great Britain's oppression 10:312
1777 Congress established an invalid regiment for Revolutionary war wounded 6:399
1779 Battle at Stone Ferry, S. C. 7:514
1796 Daniel Saunders, manufacturer and founder of Lawrence, Mass., born 11:526
1798 Daniel McCook, lawyer and soldier, born 4:130
1812 Louis W. Wyeth, Alabama judge, born 6: 74

1815 Allegheny college organized 13:291
1823 Jesse L. Reno, soldier in the Mexican and Civil wars, born 4:103
1824 John T. Morgan, U. S. senator, born 1:295
1832 Benjamin H. Bristow, soldier, and secretary of the treasury under Grant, born 4: 23
1833 Christopher M. Spencer, inventor and manufacturer of firearms and an automatic turret machine, born 22: 63
1837 David J. Brewer, justice of the U. S. supreme court, born 1: 37
1838 Joseph M. Wilson, architect and civil engineer, born 7:492
1844 Francis E. Warren, U. S. senator, first citizen of Wyoming, born 23:220
1854 Charles F. Millspaugh, botanist and curator of the Field museum, Chicago, born 25:120
1856 Rudolph M. Hunter, engineer, inventor and patent expert, born 25: 22
1860 Alexander Winton, inventor and manufacturer of the Winton motor carriage, born .... C: 79
1863 West Virginia admitted to the Union 12:430
1864 Cuthbert W. Pound, jurist, born 25: 5
1867 Russia ceded Alaska to the United States for $7,200,000 .... 2: 79
1868 Helen M. Gould, founder of the Hall of Fame at New York university, born 13:523
1878 Arthur E. Morgan, civil engineer and president of Antioch college, born .... B: 15
1893 The American Railway Union founded 12:341

JUNE 21.

Summer Solstice

1639 Increase Mather, clergyman, and president of Harvard college, born 6:412
1681 William Penn arrived in New York 2:276
1736 Enoch Poor, soldier, born 1: 76
1746 Egbert Benson, judge and a founder and first president of the New York Historical Society, born 3:461
1759 Alexander J. Dallas, secretary of the treasury under Madison, born 5:372
1768 First medical degree (Bachelor of Medicine) conferred by any college in America 22:105
1774 Daniel D. Tompkins, vice-president of the United States and governor of New York, born 6: 83
1776 A convention in Maryland met and declared "the united colonies free and independent states" 11:110
1777 British driven from New Brunswick, N. J. 1: 41
1794 Walter Rogers Johnson, scientist, born 12:260
1801 Samuel Eccleston, archbishop of Baltimore, born 1:484
1803 Timothy A. Conrad, paleontologist, born 8:466
1805 Charles T. Jackson, scientist, considered to be the discoverer of the anaesthetic properties of ether, born 3: 97
1811 Horatio King, postmaster general under Buchanan, born 5: 8
1811 Matthew Simpson, first president of Indiana Asbury university, and M. E. bishop, born .. 7:381
1811 Samuel H. Treat, judge, born 12:374
1820 William G. T. Shedd, Presbyterian clergyman and author, born 7:318
1825 William P. Blake, geologist and mining engineer, born 10: 40
1830 Morris K. Jesup, New York merchant and philanthropist, one of the founders of the Y.M.C.A., born 11: 93
1831 Patent issued to Fairbanks for the platform-scale 10:300
1834 McCormick obtained his first patent for a reaping machine 5:250
1836 Sanford F. Bennett, physician and hymn writer, born 7:525
1848 Andrew S. Draper, president of the University of Illinois, born 12:498
1850 Daniel C. Beard, artist and illustrator, born .. 5:317
1852 Dietrich E. Loewe, hat manufacturer, who established the principle that labor unions were responsible for losses from boycott, born ... 15:373
1855 Henry Guy Carleton, author and playwright, born 13:111
1862 Henry Holden Huss, pianist and composer, born 8:448
1864 Martha Van Rensselaer, a founder of the department of home economics at Cornell university, born 23:370
1872 New York convention of Liberal Republicans nominated William S. Groesbeck for president 13:150
1881 Daniel D. Luckenbill, Assyriologist, born 21:224
1882 Rockwell Kent, artist, author and illustrator, born .... D: 98
1898 First American troops arrived in Cuba 9: 18
1929 Congress authorized the Boulder canyon dam project, "the greatest engineering work ever undertaken in the United States" D:374

JUNE 22.

1732 John Ewing, Presbyterian clergyman, and provost of the University of Pennsylvania, born 1:341
1766 Samuel Appleton, Boston merchant, born 5:127
1793 A charter for Williams college granted 6:236
1803 Luther S. Cushing, jurist, born 13:318
1807 The British "Leopard" fired upon the "Chesapeake" and took off four men as deserters .. 5:502
1812 Printing office of the Balitmore "Federal Republican" destroyed by a mob 12:235
1814 James H. Lane, soldier, and U. S. senator, born 4:278
1822 Caroline Healey Dall, reformer and author, born 9:159
1823 William Leighton, author, born 1:273
1826 Henry J. Clark, naturalist, born 9:197
1831 Henry B. Nason, chemist, born 2:157
1831 Topographical bureau made part of the war department 4:380
1837 Arthur Gilman, educator and author, born 6:162
1837 Paul C. Morphy, chess player, born 13: 37
1838 Edmond J. Lindsay, manufacturer, born 2:374
1843 Mayer Sulzberger, lawyer and humanitarian, born 15:283
1844 Octave P. Pavy, naturalist, born 7:534
1846 James B. Ames, dean of the Harvard law school, born 18:141
1846 Julian Hawthorne, author and newspaper correspondent, born 25: 45
1847 Walter Learned, financier and poet, born 8:189
1849 Francis Lathrop, artist, born 11:292
1870 U. S. department of justice organized 4: 20
1884 Survivors of the Greely expedition rescued 9: 8
1888 Alan Seeger, poet, famous for his "Ode in Memory of the American Volunteers Fallen for France," born 20: 68
1892 Frederick Beck Patterson, president of the National Cash Register Co., born B:479
1898 U.S.S. "St. Paul" attacked off Puerto Rico by the Spanish "Isabel II" and "Terror" 9: 2
1898 Santiago, Chile, forts bombarded 9: 15
1933 Illinois ship canal, linking the Great Lakes and the Gulf of Mexico, officially opened D:338

JUNE 23.

1683 William Penn made his famous treaty with the Indians 2:275
1722 Charleston, S. C., incorporated 12:156
1744 A treaty with the Iroquois Indians signed 7:540
1777 Frederick Bates, governor of Missouri, born .. 12:302
1780 British defeated at Springfield, N. J. 1: 44
1780 Reuben D. Mussey, physician, and founder of Miami medical college, born 9: 91
1785 Pelatiah Perit, New York merchant, born 1:499
1786 Nathaniel W. Taylor, theologian, born 7:187
1812 First naval encounter of the War of 1812 .... 5:262
1815 Robert M. McLane, governor of Maryland and diplomat, born 9:311
1817 John Jay, abolitionist, advocate of civil service reform and diplomat, born 7:347
1819 Henry P. Gray, artist, born 5: 32
1822 Felix O. C. Darley, artist and illustrator, born 2:334
1831 Andrew Albright, inventor, born 4:446
1834 Samuel Pasco, lawyer and U. S. senator, born 1:293
1835 Daniel H. Chamberlain, governor of South Carolina, born 12:176
1837 Henry O. Marcy, who introduced antiseptic surgery in the United States, born 6:510
1843 Charles Y. Wheeler, steel manufacturer, who developed the "Wheeler-Sterling" projectiles, born 18: 11
1847 Henry J. Ellicott, sculptor, born 12:122
1851 Clarence Eddy, organist, born 7:427
1857 William Kelly patented his "air-boiling" process for making steel 13:196
1860 Northern Democrats nominated Stephen A. Douglas for president 2:431
1860 Southern Democrats nominated John C. Breckinridge for president 5: 3
1864 William S. Thayer, physician, born 24:409
1869 Patent granted to Sholes for a typewriter 3:315
1876 Irvin S. Cobb, author and journalist, born 18:375

JUNE 24.

Midsummer Day

1497 John and Sebastian Cabot sighted Cape Breton on their first voyage to America 7: 62
1726 Robert Monckton, governor of New York and commander-in-chief of the province, born ... 13:117
1753 William Hull, Revolutionary general, born 1: 66
1771 Eleuthere Irénée Du Pont, manufacturer of gunpowder, born 6:456
1782 Battle with Creek Indians 1: 55

1785 Alexander Porter, judge and U. S. senator, born 13:158
1788 Thomas Blanchard, inventor, born 6:186
1794 A charter granted to Bowdoin college 1:417
1795 John Jay's treaty with England ratified by the senate 1: 6
1797 John Hughes, archbishop of New York, born 1:193
1805 Daniel Read, president of the University of the State of Missouri, born 8:185
1807 David Dale Owen, geologist, born 8:113
1811 John A. Campbell, justice of the United States supreme court and Confederate statesman, born 2:472
1813 Henry Ward Beecher, Congregational clergyman, distinguished as an orator and editor, born 3:129
1816 Theodore F. Randolph, R. R. president, U. S. senator and governor of New Jersey, born 5:210
1828 Edward Sawyer, civil engineer, born 12:320
1831 Rebecca Harding Davis, author, born 8:176
1834 George Arnold, author, born 9:432
1842 Ambrose Bierce, editor and author, born 14:180
1848 Brooks Adams, lawyer and historian, born 10:397
1851 Stuyvesant Fish, railroad executive and banker, born 19: 15
1856 Henry C. Mercer, archæologist, born 21:479
1856 Hermann J. Boldt, physician, and inventor of surgical instruments, born C:285
1858 George Von L. Meyer, U. S. minister to Italy and Russia, postmaster general under Theodore Roosevelt, and secretary of the navy under Taft, born 14:413
1863 Confederate army under Lee crossed the Potomac 4: 98
1863 Gen. Rosecrans began to drive the Confederates back to Chattanooga 4:163
1879 George B. Ford, city planning engineer, born 25:369

JUNE 25.

1689 Edward Holyoke, clergyman and president of Harvard college, born 6:415
1741 John Langdon, New Hampshire statesman and governor, born 11:123
1759 William Plumer, governor of New Hampshire, born 11:124
1773 Eliphalet Nott, clergyman and president of Union college, born 7:170
1791 Nathaniel Deering, author and playwright, born 10:250
1798 The second of the alien laws, providing for deportation of dangerous aliens, passed 13:182
1803 Sumner Fairfield, poet, born 12:283
1811 John W. Casilear, landscape painter, born 12:271
1825 William M. Baker, Presbyterian clergyman and author, born 8:392
1831 Olive Thorne Miller, author, born 9:208
1835 William H. Ward, clergyman and editor, born 8:147
1836 McClintock Young, inventor of machines for manufacturing matches, brushes and hinges, and of a self-rake used on the McCormick reaper, born 10:221
1837 Charles T. Yerkes, capitalist, organizer of street railroads, born 9:462
1842 Dorr's rebellion broke out 9:397
1846 LeBaron Bradford Colt, judge and U. S. senator, born 15:408
1859 Americans assisted the British in an engagement with the Chinese 5:488
1862 Battle of Oak Grove, near Fair Oaks, Va. 4:141
1863 Mine exploded at Vicksburg, Miss. 4: 5
1868 South Carolina readmitted to the Union 12:175
1876 Battle of Big Horn, in which Gen. Custer and his men were massacred by Sioux Indians 13:455
1910 President Taft signed the bill creating the postal savings banks system 23: 4

JUNE 26.

1700 Richard Dana, jurist and patriot, born 10:389
1703 Thomas Clap, president of Yale college, born 1:166
1721 First vaccination for small-pox, by Zabdiel Boylston 7:270
1742 Arthur Middleton, South Carolina patriot and a signer of the Declaration of Independence, born 5:197
1781 George Bruce, pioneer type founder, born 11:274
1783 Solomon Willard, architect, designer and builder of Bunker Hill monument, born 4:431
1812 John H. Alexander, scientist, born 9:192
1816 George W. Flagg, artist, born 7:460
1819 Abner Doubleday, Federal soldier, born 4:185
1832 Battle of Velasco, Tex. 4:438
1835 Thomas W. Knox, author, traveler and inventor, born 7: 89
1843 Sereno E. Payne, New York lawyer and congressman, born 10:398
1843 George J. Capewell, inventor of an automatic machine for manufacturing nails, born 16:396
1846 John S. Huyler, candy manufacturer and philanthropist, born 15: 96
1848 William Frank Powell, diplomat, born 12:195
1849 James W. Scott, journalist, founder of the Chicago "Herald" and Chicago "Evening Post," born 2: 55
1850 A. Augustus Healy, leather merchant, and a founder of the Brooklyn institute of arts and sciences, born 19:134
1862 Battle of Mechanicsville, Va. 4:142
1862 The Army of Virginia formed 4:272
1863 Battle of Shelbyville, Tenn. 4:163
1878 William M. Bruce, Jr., inventor of the Bruce mercury contact cable relay, born 22:236
1886 Duncan Phillips, art critic, born B:476
1917 First contingent of the American expeditionary force arrived in France B: 47
1919 First issue of the New York "Daily News," a pictorial tabloid D: 81
1920 Annette Adams became the first woman assistant attorney general A:370

JUNE 27.

1689 Andros, the governor of New England, impeached before a Colonial council 6: 90
1696 Sir William Pepperrell, soldier, acting governor of Massachusetts, born 3:330
1776 San Francisco founded 12:134
1805 Henry B. Stanton, editor and abolitionist, born 2:331
1806 Paul F. Eve, surgeon, born 10: 30
1818 Cortlandt Parker, New Jersey lawyer, born 12:268
1820 Leonard Case, founder of the Case school of applied science, born 11:153
1820 Ignaz A. Pilat, landscape gardener, born 15:307
1823 Dorman B. Eaton, lawyer and civil service reformer, born 21:200
1844 Joseph and Hyrum Smith, Mormon leaders, killed by a mob at Carthage jail 16: 2
1846 Henry E. Abbey, theatrical and operatic manager, born 7:141
1850 Lafcadio Hearn, author, born 1:409
1850 Francis Vinton Greene, soldier, engineer and historian, born 23: 23
1863 Maj. Gen. Hooker superseded by Maj. Gen. George G. Meade 4:177
1864 Battle of Kenesaw Mountain, Ga. 4: 34
1864 Varina Anne Jefferson Davis, author, born 23:165
1872 Paul Laurence Dunbar, poet and author, born 9:276
1873 David P. Barrows, president of the University of California, born B:157
1880 Helen A. Keller, blind deaf-mute, born 15:177

JUNE 28.

1742 James Robertson, founder of Nashville, Tenn., born 2:221
1776 Attack on Fort Moultrie, Charleston harbor, S. C. 1: 96
1778 Battle of Monmouth, N. J. 8:240
1781 Fort Ninety-six evacuated by the British 1: 43
1805 Richmond M. Pearson, North Carolina jurist, born 11: 89
1807 Richard Hildreth, author and editor, born 10:460
1814 U. S. sloop-of-war "Wasp" captured the British sloop-of-war "Reindeer" 5:440
1821 Thomas W. Waterman, jurist, born 4:523
1828 Samson Talbot, president of Denison university, born 1:302
1834 Hosea W. Libbey, physician and inventor, born 12:515
1835 John Y. Brown, Kentucky statesman and governor, born 13: 12
1836 Lyman J. Gage, Chicago financier and secretary of the treasury under McKinley and Theodore Roosevelt, born 11: 14
1844 John Boyle O'Reilly, author and poet, born 1:428
1857 Emerson Hough, journalist and author, born 19: 60
1857 Everett Fleet Morse, inventor of the "Rocker-joint" chain, born 24:342
1858 Otis Skinner, actor, born 11:220
1860 Steamship "Great Eastern," largest vessel of its day, arrived in New York 2: 71
1863 Action at Donaldsonville, La. 13:226
1864 Columbia Institution's department for the higher education of the deaf, later known as the National deaf mute college, organized 9:140
1873 Alexis Carrel, surgeon and physiologist, born 15:301
1902 The United States purchased the French franchises in the Panama canal 14: 5
1919 Treaty of Versailles signed 19: 11
1934 National housing act signed by the president D: 32

JUNE 29.

1752 St. George Tucker, judge and poet, born 7:136
1767 The king approved taxes imposed upon tea, glass, paper, etc., by parliament 1:105

1776 Virginia state constitution adopted and Patrick Henry made governor 1: 339
1794 Pioneer negro church dedicated in Philadelphia 13: 200
1804 Charles U. Shepard, mineralogist, born 5: 311
1811 James C. Palmer, surgeon-general of the U. S. navy, born 8: 222
1819 Thomas Dunn English, editor and poet, the author of "Ben Bolt," born 4: 322
1819 Donn Piatt, editor and publisher, born 13: 157
1830 John Q. A. Ward, sculptor, born 2: 364
1836 Celia Thaxter, author, born 1: 305
1840 Francis H. Snow, entomologist, and chancellor of the University of Kansas, born 9: 494
1841 J. Harvey Mathes, soldier and editor, born 12: 313
1841 William B. Clark, president of the Aetna Insurance Co., born 18: 217
1845 George W. Atkinson, congressman, and governor of West Virginia, born 12: 432
1846 Andrew W. Preston, head of the United Fruit Co., born 26: 302
1847 Patrick F. Mullany, educator and author, one of the founders of the Catholic Chautauqua, born 7: 525
1847 Lewis Pyle Mercer, clergyman, born 12: 82
1852 John Bach McMaster, historian, born 11: 445
1852 Rufus Hildreth Thayer, judge of the U. S. court in Shanghai, China, born 18: 55
1855 Walker repulsed at Rivas, Nicaragua 11: 24
1858 George W. Goethals, military engineer, builder of the Panama canal, born 24: 6
1858 Julia C. Lathrop, leader in child welfare work, born 24: 298
1861 William J. Mayo, surgeon, born .... A: 330
1862 Battle of Savage's Station, Va. 4: 142
1863 James Harvey Robinson, historian, born .... C: 28
1865 William E. Borah, U. S. senator, born .... B: 115
1868 George E. Hale, astronomer, born .... C: 45
1871 Capt. Charles F. Hall's arctic expedition sailed from New York 3: 281
1873 Charles McCarthy, librarian and political economist, who developed the legislative reference library, born 19: 251
1875 Edwin W. Kemmerer, economist, born .... B: 126
1906 The bill regulating railway rates became a law 2: 234
1927 Comr. Byrd took off from New York on his transatlantic flight 21: 28

JUNE 30.

1675 Attack on Swansea, Mass., by the Indians marked the beginning of King Philip's war 10: 50
1744 Treaty between Maryland and the Six Nations 7: 337
1775 First New York regiment formed 11: 542
1780 The sect of Free-Will Baptists established 4: 345
1783 Eighth Continental congress met at Princeton with Elias Boudinot as president 2: 296
1800 Benjamin Fitzpatrick, U. S. senator and governor of Alabama, born 10: 429
1803 Lewis Hallock, New York physician, born 9: 356
1806 William B. Reed, Pennsylvania lawyer, diplomat and author, born 7: 533
1815 Treaty of peace with Algiers signed 4: 56
1815 Naval battle between the "Peacock" and the "Nautilus" 6: 232
1819 William A. Wheeler, vice-president of the United States, born 3: 196
1819 Harriet Sewall, poet, born 10: 347
1828 Frederick F. Low, California banker, governor and diplomat, born 4: 109
1837 William E. Marshall, artist and engraver, born 7: 460
1840 The independent treasury system established .. 6: 434
1841 James H. Smart, president of Purdue university, and of the National Education Association, born 6: 106
1848 Edward Burgess, designer of yachts to defend America's cup, born 1: 449
1851 Thomas H. Norton, chemist, born 13: 478
1852 Charles Foster Smith, philologist, born 12: 368
1852 James M. Dodge, engineer, born 12: 490
1853 Albert Mann, diatomist, born 25: 360
1862 Battle of White Oak Swamp, Va. 4: 97
1862 Battle of Frazier's Farm, Va. 4: 142
1862 A new and brilliant comet discovered by Swift 4: 302
1864 Salmon P. Chase resigned from Lincoln's cabinet 1: 30
1876 Ernest Haskell, painter, etcher and lithographer, born 23: 155
1879 Walter Hampden, actor, born .... B: 12
1886 John Gibbons made second cardinal of the Roman Catholic church in the United States 1: 489
1906 Passage of the pure food and drugs act 21: 72
1921 President Taft appointed chief justice of the U. S. supreme court, the first person to hold the two highest governmental offices 23: 5

JULY 1.

Designated as the beginning of the fiscal year, by law of August 28, 1842

1725 Jean Baptiste Rochambeau, French soldier, born 1: 68
1781 James B. Finley, missionary, born 12: 557
1793 Cornerstone of Hamilton college laid 7: 404
1802 Gideon Welles, editor, and secretary of the navy under Lincoln, born 2: 86
1804 Charles G. Greene, journalist, born 4: 445
1811 William J. Boone, P. E. bishop, born 5: 16
1823 Charles B. Farwell, U. S. senator, born 6: 394
1827 George B. Markle, coal operator and banker, born 24: 138
1832 Aaron Ward Weaver, naval officer, born 13: 226
1833 Alfred T. A. Torbert, soldier, born 4: 537
1833 William P. Craighill, civil engineer, born 12: 223
1833 Erastus M. Cravath, a founder and first president of Fisk university, born 22: 300
1836 Bequest for Smithsonian Institution accepted by Congress 3: 405
1840 Charles M. Walcot, actor, born 11: 514
1846 William H. Brett, librarian, born 6: 480
1850 David R. Francis, governor of Missouri, president of the Louisiana Purchase Exposition Co., and ambassador to Russia, born 24: 322
1854 Albert B. Hart, historian, born 11: 394
1856 Battle with the Comanche Indians 4: 208
1858 Alice Barber Stephens, artist and illustrator, born 23: 278
1860 Harry L. Koopman, poet and librarian, born ... 11: 543
1861 The Confederate "Sumter" ran the blockade of the Mississippi river 4: 340
1862 Battle of Malvern Hill, Va. 4: 143
1862 David White, geologist and paleobotanist, born 18: 60
1862 Engagement at Booneville, Mo. 4: 64
1863 Battle of Gettysburg, Pa., began 4: 67
1864 Charles F. Hall set forth on his second expedition in search of Franklin 3: 281
1882 Susan Glaspell, author, born .... C: 505
1890 Idaho admitted to the Union 12: 491
1893 A secret operation performed on President Cleveland 23: 31
1898 Battle of San Juan, Cuba 9: 21
1898 Battle of El Caney, Cuba 9: 23
1924 First through flight of the transcontinental air mail service .... C: 186

JULY 2.

1728 Jacob Bailey, soldier and statesman, born 8: 242
1759 Nathan Read, inventor, one of the first in this country to receive a patent on a steamboat, born 4: 558
1776 In the Continental congress, delegates of all the colonies, except New York, voted to adopt the Declaration of Independence 1: 23
1776 New Jersey adopted a declaration of independence 7: 517
1778 Seventh Continental congress met in Philadelphia 3: 426
1802 Jonathan Cilley, lawyer, born 10: 109
1807 George Fitzhugh, sociologist, born 9: 383
1810 Robert Toombs, Confederate secretary of State, born 4: 392
1814 Nathaniel Holmes, jurist, born 3: 409
1819 Lucius J. Knowles, inventor, born 5: 256
1820 George L. Curry, governor of Oregon, born 8: 4
1823 James W. Patterson, educator and U. S. senator, born 11: 364
1825 Richard H. Stoddard, poet, born 3: 297
1832 Green Clay Smith, soldier and governor of Montana, born 11: 78
1833 First public trial of Hussey's reaping machine 11: 361
1840 Francis A. Walker, statistician and economist, born 5: 401
1842 Charles Chaille-Long, soldier, explorer and diplomat, born 10: 28
1850 Robert Ridgway, ornithologist, born 8: 460
1853 Frederick T. Gates, clergyman, financial adviser to John D. Rockefeller, and projector of the Rockefeller Institute for Medical Research and the Rockefeller Foundation, born 23: 250
1854 Waldo Briggs, physician and surgeon, born 12: 126
1855 Clarence W. Barron, publisher, the pioneer organizer of financial journalism in America, born 21: 183
1859 Oliver S. Hershman, journalist, born 21: 143
1861 Battle of Falling Waters, Va. 4: 48
1861 Charles A. Conant, economist, born 14: 227
1863 Federals seized Little Round Top on the field at Gettysburg 4: 67
1881 President Garfield assassinated 4: 242
1888 James Boyd, author, born .... C: 381

1894 Lewis W. Douglas, director of the budget under Franklin D. Roosevelt, born .... D: 22
1921 President Harding signed a joint resolution declaring peace with Germany and Austria 19:270

JULY 3.

1728 Duel between Benjamin Woodbridge and Henry Phillips in Boston 12:237
1731 Samuel Huntington, Connecticut jurist and governor, and a signer of the Declaration of Independence, born 10:329
1737 John Singleton Copley, artist, born 6:467
1775 Washington took command of the army at Cambridge 1: 3
1812 Francis H. Jenks, founder of the safe deposit business in the United States, born 18:115
1814 Fort Erie, Canada, captured by Americans 5:400
1827 Richard H. Clarke, author and lawyer, born 1:257
1829 Henry Hitchcock, lawyer, born 11:196
1830 Samuel W. Johnson, a founder and director of the first agricultural experiment station in the United States, born 6:262
1833 David McC. Smyth, inventor, born 7:323
1844 First treaty between United States and China signed, permitting trade and residence in certain ports 4:151
1848 Theodore Presser, music publisher, founder of the "Etude," born 20: 8
1852 Branch of the U. S. mint established by Congress at San Francisco 4:107
1857 Ripley Hitchcock, author, editor and art critic, born 18:173
1860 Charlotte P. Gilman, author and lecturer, born 13:212
1860 Hubert Work, postmaster general under Harding, and secretary of the interior under Harding and Coolidge, born .... A: 14
1861 Frederick S. Pearson, electrical engineer, builder of electric power plants and railways, born .. 18:123
1863 Gen. Pemberton agreed to surrender to Gen. Grant at Vicksburg 4: 5
1863 Gen. Pickett led his famous charge on the last day at Gettysburg 4: 67
1863 Helena, Ark., attacked by Confederates 5:363
1879 A. Harry Moore, governor of New Jersey and U. S. senator, born B:178
1890 Idaho admitted to the Union 1:455
1898 Cervera's fleet destroyed off Santiago harbor, Cuba, in the war with Spain 9: 10

JULY 4.
Independence Day

1754 Washington surrendered Ft. Necessity to the French 1: 2
1754 Benjamin Franklin proposed a union of all the colonies for a common defense against French encroachment 13:344
1756 William Rush, sculptor, born 8:287
1766 Ethan Allen Brown, U. S. senator and governor of Ohio, born 8:138
1775 A provisional congress met in Georgia, in defiance of the governor, to elect delegates to the Continental congress 1:492
1776 The Declaration of Independence adopted by the Continental congress 3: 2
1778 Duel between Generals Cadwallader and Conway 1: 90
1778 The Wyoming (Pa.) massacre occurred 1: 52
1800 Government of Indiana territory organized 3: 34
1801 Elijah Hise, lawyer and congressman, born 12: 54
1802 Bela B. Edwards, clergyman, editor and author, born 10:102
1802 John La R. Helm, Kentucky lawyer and governor, born 13: 7
1804 Nathaniel Hawthorne, author, born 3: 64
1804 Charles G. Atherton, U. S. senator, author of the "Atherton gag," born 10:383
1809 John Stephenson, manufacturer, who designed and constructed the first street railway car, born 7:364
1817 Work on the Erie canal commenced 3: 45
1817 John M. Carnochan, surgeon, born 9:362
1819 Reuben E. Fenton, U. S. senator and governor of New York, born 3: 51
1819 Edward R. Squibb, manufacturing chemist, born 19: 56
1826 Two ex-presidents, John Adams and Thomas Jefferson, died 2: 5
1826 Stephen C. Foster, composer, born 7:439
1826 Process of making malleable castings devised ... 11: 87
1828 Corner-stone of the Baltimore and Ohio railroad laid 9:301
1831 An agreement signed by France and the United States with reference to the French spoliation claims 13:376
1832 Matthew Henry Buckham, president of the University of Vermont, born 2: 42
1832 Andrew C. Wheeler (Nym Crinkle), journalist and author, born 25:375
1833 George E. Waring, Jr., sanitary expert, born .. 6:157
1836 Origin of the U. S. patent bureau 12:230
1839 Felix Agnus, soldier and publisher, born 1:200
1839 Helen Campbell, author and educator, born 9:126
1845 Texas ratified the act of annexation 6:267
1848 Cornerstone of the Washington monument laid 5:299
1850 John C. Branner, geologist and president of Stanford university, born 24:278
1853 Lucy Skidmore Scribner, founder of Skidmore college, born 23:144
1860 Joseph Pennell, artist and author, born 10:376
1861 Francis Bacon Crocker, electrical engineer and inventor, born 12:424
1861 Lawrence D. Tyson, U. S. senator, lawyer, financier and soldier, born 21:487
1863 Ulysses S. Grant, appointed a major-general in the regular army 4: 5
1863 Vicksburg, Miss., evacuated by the Confederates 4: 5
1866 Oliver F. Winchester patented a rifle 11:455
1868 Opening of the national Democratic convention which nominated Horatio Winslow for president 3: 50
1868 John R. Rathom, news correspondent and editor, who unmasked the activities of the German propaganda service in America during the World war, born 20:314
1868 Henrietta S. Leavitt, astronomer who measured the magnitude of stars, born 25:163
1872 Calvin Coolidge, 30th president of the United States, born 24: 1
1874 Opening of Eads bridge across the Mississippi at St. Louis, Mo. 5:134
1878 George M. Cohan, actor and playwright, born .. 15:285
1883 Bartholdi's Statue of Liberty Enlightening the World presented to the United States in Paris 1:136
1894 First trial of the Haynes automobile 25: 13

JULY 5.

1779 New Haven, Conn., plundered by the British ... 7:514
1795 Sylvester Graham, dietician, originator of graham bread, born 5:416
1796 Isaac Hays, physician, born 11:256
1801 David G. Farragut, first admiral of the U. S. navy, born 2: 45
1810 Phineas T. Barnum, showman, born 3:258
1810 Henry C. Murphy, lawyer, born 10: 33
1811 Jesse Applegate, Oregon pioneer, born 20: 30
1812 Horatio Southgate, first P. E. bishop of Constantinople, born 13:417
1814 Battle of Chippewa, Canada 3:502
1817 Frank Cheney, silk manufacturer, born 19: 73
1841 William C. Whitney, lawyer and secretary of the navy under Cleveland, born 2:407
1841 Mass meeting in Providence, R. I., in the interest of extended suffrage 8:234
1841 Frank Thomson, president of the Pennsylvania railroad, born 13:335
1846 Joseph B. Foraker, governor of Ohio, born 3:144
1851 William Brewster, ornithologist, an organizer of the first Audubon society, born 22:140
1858 Will N. Harben, author, born 10:310
1860 Robert Bacon, a partner of J. P. Morgan & Co., secretary of state under Theodore Roosevelt and Taft, and ambassador to France, born 14: 16
1861 Battle of Carthage, Mo. 4:136
1867 Andrew E. Douglass, astronomer, notable for his studies of the planet Mars, born D:439
1868 John M. Sully, mining engineer, who developed the Chino copper mines in New Mexico, born . 26:174
1879 Dwight F. Davis, secretary of war under Coolidge, born .... A: 10

JULY 6.

1730 James Wadsworth, soldier, born 1: 55
1747 Paul Jones, naval officer, born 2: 14
1757 William McKendree, M. E. bishop, born 10:224
1759 Joshua Barney, naval officer, born 4:167
1762 Ashbel Green, president of the College of New Jersey, born 5:467
1766 Alexander Wilson, ornithologist, and pioneer in American nature literature, born 7:440
1774 Non-importation resolutions adopted at "the great meeting in the fields" in New York 11:542
1776 Maryland adopted a declaration of independence 13:496
1777 Americans evacuated Ft. Ticonderoga, N. Y. .. 1: 95
1781 Engagement at Green Springs, Va. 1: 55
1798 The third of the alien laws, providing that citizens of a hostile nation may be apprehended in time of war, passed 13:182

1800 Alonzo Potter, P. E. bishop and educator, born.. 3:470
1813 Ellis S. Chesbrough, civil engineer, born 9: 35
1822 John M. Gregory, president of Kalamazoo college and the University of Illinois, born 12:497
1824 John L. Beveridge, U. S. senator and governor of Illinois, born 11: 50
1825 Randolph Rogers, sculptor, born 8:286
1831 Daniel Colt Gilman, president of the University of California and Johns Hopkins university and of Carnegie institution, born 5:170
1837 Minister plenipotentiary from Texas received at Washington 10:388
1846 Comr. Sloat occupied Monterey, Calif. 6:176
1852 Katherine W. Tingley, theosophist, born 15:337
1854 The Republican party formally organized 4:472
1864 Thomas A. Sperry, merchant, who originated coupon premiums for customers, born 15:360
1876 Lillian Genth, artist, famous for her studies of the nude, born D:281
1880 Kathleen Norris, author, born C:366
1883 Continuous performance entertainment inaugurated 15:297
1892 Steel mill strikers and Pinkerton detectives clashed at Homestead, Pa. 23: 32
1928 First all-talking motion pictures presented D:230

JULY 7.

1586 Thomas Hooker, clergyman and founder of Hartford, Conn., born 6:279
1750 Anthony W. White, soldier, born 1: 69
1768 Philip S. Physick, "the father of American surgery," born 6:391
1777 Battle of Hubbardton, Vt. 1: 85
1779 Fairfield, Conn., burned by the British 7:514
1810 George Sharswood, jurist, born 2:168
1811 Jephtha H. Wade, who built the first telegraph line west of Buffalo, and was first president of the Pacific and Western Union telegraph companies, born 1:213
1811 Henry Meiggs, builder of South American railroads, born 13:138
1826 Samuel D. Barr, educator, born 5:474
1828 William F. Howe, New York lawyer, called the "father of the criminal bar," born 22: 49
1834 Miriam Harris, author, born 11:515
1837 Burwell B. Lewis, congressman, and president of the University of Alabama, born 12:295
1849 Theophil M. Prudden, physician, born 9:347
1850 William E. Mason, U. S. senator, born 12:445
1852 Abraham F. Huston, head of the Lukens Iron and Steel Co., born 15:376
1858 Program of rules for the Paulist Fathers approved by Archbishop Hughes 9:167
1858 Davis Sessums, P. E. bishop, born 11:343
1862 President Lincoln visited the army on the Potomac 2: 71
1865 Execution of persons implicated in the murder of Lincoln 4:347
1898 President McKinley signed the bill annexing the Hawaiian islands 11: 3
1930 Construction work on Boulder Dam begun 24:116

JULY 8.

1663 The liberal Royal charter granted to Rhode Island 10: 5
1721 Death of Elihu Yale, patron of Yale college 1:164
1758 Battle of Ticonderoga, N. Y. 1:102
1790 Fitz-Greene Halleck, poet, born 3:226
1790 William Howard Allen, naval officer, born 6:515
1795 Washington college (Tennessee) chartered 7:340
1797 William Blount expelled from the U. S. senate 7:206
1805 Samuel D. Gross, surgeon, born 8:216
1809 Robert W. Gibbes, scientist and historian, born 11: 36
1812 John F. Frazer, scientist, born 1:348
1819 Alexander Hays, Federal soldier, born 4:313
1821 Maria Lowell, poet, born 8: 18
1826 Robert K. Scott, soldier and governor of South Carolina, born 12:175
1829 David Turpie, U. S. senator, born 1:218
1830 Frederick W. Seward, journalist and diplomat, born 11:445
1839 John D. Rockefeller, capitalist, born 11: 63
1849 Henry Wood, philologist, born 13:585
1850 Charles R. Lanman, Orientalist, born 11: 96
1856 Charles L. Huston, mechanical engineer and manufacturer, born 15:377
1862 Two patents for revolving towers discharging guns by electricity granted to Timby 9:116
1863 Battle of Boonesboro, Md. 5:276
1869 William V. Moody, educator, poet and playwright, born 11: 69
1878 Famous Sutro tunnel of the Comstock mines completed 21:126
1879 The "Jeanette" expedition sailed from San Francisco 3:282
1881 Mantis J. Van Sweringen, railroad operator, born A:539

JULY 9.

1577 Thomas West, Lord De La Warr, colonial governor, born 13:380
1750 Thomas Posey, soldier and governor of Indiana territory, born 13:265
1755 Gen. Braddock defeated at Monongahela, Pa. .. 2: 59
1758 William Polk, patriot, born 11:341
1766 Jacob Perkins, inventor, who made improvements in banknote engraving and in the detection of counterfeits, born 10:123
1776 Battle of Gwynn's Island, Va. 6:323
1778 Articles of Confederation signed by eight states 4:398
1780 Naval battle between the American "Protector" and the British "Admiral Duff" 4:152
1799 The twins, Oliver W. B. Peabody, lawyer and editor, and William B. O. Peabody, clergyman and author, born 8: 63
1802 Thomas Davenport, inventor, pioneer in the design of electric motors, born 3:339
1802 Charles Downing, horticulturist, born 11:114
1811 Sara P. Parton (Fanny Fern), author, born .. 1:392
1815 Oran Milo Roberts, soldier, jurist and governor of Texas, born 9: 73
1819 Elias Howe, inventor of sewing machines, born 4:432
1825 Isaac M. Ridge, physician and surgeon, born ... 12:520
1830 Stanford E. Chaillé, physician who distinguished himself in the war on yellow fever, born 9:131
1838 Philip P. Bliss, composer and singer, born 8:443
1838 George H. Frost, engineer, founder of the "Engineering News," born 18:110
1840 William F. Vilas, lawyer, postmaster general and secretary of the interior under Cleveland, and U. S. senator, born 2:409
1842 Clara Louise Kellogg, singer, born 2:446
1844 Edwin J. Houston, electrician and inventor, a founder of the Thomson-Houston Electric Co., born 13:359
1847 Frederick L. Goss, who founded and developed the Goss Printing Press Co., born 18:182
1850 Millard Fillmore became president of the United States on the death of Zachary Taylor 6:178
1853 William T. Dannat, artist, born 12:380
1856 Daniel Guggenheim, industrialist, head of the American Smelting & Refining Co., whose philanthropies included the Daniel and Florence Guggenheim Foundation and the Daniel Guggenheim Fund for the Promotion of Aeronautics, born 22: 7
1857 Robert F. Blum, artist, born 10:365
1858 Franz Boas, anthropologist, born 12:509
1858 Richard A. Ballinger, lawyer, secretary of the interior under Taft, born 14:413
1861 James M. Beck, lawyer, born B:463
1863 Port Hudson, La., surrendered by the Confederates 4:222
1864 Battle of Monocacy river, Md. 4:138
1882 George William Nasmyth, sociologist, a promoter of international good will through student centers and organizations, born 18:246

JULY 10.

1752 David Humphreys, soldier and diplomat, one of the "Hartford wits," born 1: 71
1776 Declaration of Independence received in New York; King George's statue destroyed 10:330
1777 Maj. Gen. Prescott, of the British army, captured 1: 74
1792 George M. Dallas, vice-president of the United States and minister to Russia and England, born 6:268
1805 Jacob M. Howard, U. S. senator; author of the platform of the Republican party, born 4:472
1809 Robert M. Patton, governor of Alabama, born .. 10:434
1818 Stephen D. Trenchard, naval officer, born 10:126
1820 James D. B. De Bow, journalist, born 8:161
1823 Sanford R. Gifford, landscape painter, born 2:443
1825 Paul Akers, sculptor, born 6:132
1832 President Jackson vetoed the bill re-chartering the U. S. Bank 5: 79
1832 Alvan G. Clark, optician and astronomer, born .. 5:386
1834 James A. McN. Whistler, artist, born 9: 49
1846 Col. Fremont became governor of California 4:271
1848 George H. Ellwanger, author and horticulturist, born 13:134
1849 John W. Griggs, governor of New Jersey and attorney-general under McKinley, born 11: 19
1856 Isaac N. Seligman, New York banker, born ... 3:343
1857 Marion D. Learned, philologist, born 4:538

1859 William LeRoy Emmet, electrical engineer, who improved the steam turbine and developed the mercury vapor process, born ... D: 413
1861 Albert Bigelow Paine, author and editor, born .. 13: 99
1863 Gen. Gillmore occupied part of Morris island, the first step in the reduction of Ft. Wagner 4: 55
1867 Finley Peter Dunne, humorist, famous for his "Mr. Dooley" letters, born ... 14: 53
1871 Hugh Manson Dorsey, governor of Georgia, born 18: 356
1872 National Democratic convention nominated Horace Greeley for president ... 3: 452
1881 Donald R. Richberg, lawyer, general counsel of the National Recovery Administration, born .. D: 23
1890 Wyoming admitted to the Union ... 1: 135
1891 Rexford G. Tugwell, economist, first under secretary of agriculture, born ... D: 25

JULY 11.

1744 Pierce Butler, U. S. senator, born ... 2: 162
1767 John Quincy Adams, 6th president of the United States, born ... 5: 73
1771 John Rodgers, naval officer, born ... 5: 261
1779 Norwalk, Conn., burned by the British ... 7: 514
1780 Timothy Flint, author, born ... 6: 364
1782 Savannah, Ga., evacuated by the British ... 1: 492
1795 Samuel L. Dana, chemist, who devised new methods of bleaching and printing cotton, born .. 8: 167
1800 Daniel Boone appointed commander of the Femme Osage district ... 3: 110
1801 John H. Hewitt, poet, born ... 11: 363
1804 Duel between Alexander Hamilton and Aaron Burr ... 3: 6
1808 Henry Reed, author and educator, born ... 2: 349
1811 Joseph Lanman, naval officer, born ... 4: 312
1819 Susan Warner, novelist, born ... 5: 354
1822 Edward J. Phelps, U. S. minister to Great Britain, born ... 5: 411
1827 Austin Corbin, railroad president, born ... 5: 430
1838 John Wanamaker, merchant and postmaster general under Harrison, born ... 1: 143
1839 Kate Sanborn, author, born ... 9: 94
1842 Henry Abbey, poet, born ... 7: 403
1847 John H. Barrows, clergyman, and president of Oberlin college, born ... 8: 116
1861 The U. S. senate expelled ten Southern members 2: 87
1861 Battle of Rich Mountain, W. Va. ... 4: 162
1861 George W. Norris, U. S. senator, champion of agricultural interests, born ... B: 171
1862 Gen. Halleck appointed commander-in-chief of the army ... 4: 258
1863 The "Hatteras" sunk by the "Alabama" ... 4: 208
1863 Drafting of soldiers in New York City precipitated a week of rioting ... 3: 50
1864 Confederate troops threatened Washington, D. C. ... 4: 138
1867 John Washington Hoffman, president of Ohio Weslyan university, born ... B: 215

JULY 12.

1743 Jeremiah Wadsworth, soldier and congressman, born ... 1: 78
1755 Alexander Murray, naval officer, born ... 2: 18
1762 James Ross, U. S. senator, born ... 5: 438
1780 Battle of Catawba river ... 1: 79
1807 Silas Casey, soldier, born ... 4: 279
1807 Andrew H. Reeder, first governor of Kansas territory, born ... 8: 340
1808 First issue of the "Missouri Gazette and Louisiana Advertiser," the first newspaper west of the Mississippi and the forerunner of the "St. Louis Republic" ... 21: 212
1814 Benjamin P. Shillaber, humorist, born ... 6: 32
1817 Henry D. Thoreau, author, poet and naturalist, born ... 2: 300
1817 Nathan C. Meeker, author, editor and colonizer, born ... 8: 387
1817 Alvin Saunders, governor of Nebraska territory, and U. S. senator, born ... 13: 221
1821 Daniel H. Hill, soldier and author, born ... 4: 102
1823 Nathaniel A. Boynton, inventor and manufacturer, born ... 12: 487
1832 James M. Swank, statistician, born ... 20: 312
1840 Benjamin Altman, New York merchant and philanthropist, born ... 15: 188
1849 William Osler, physician, born ... 12: 201
1850 George Urban, Jr., merchant miller, born ... 21: 387
1854 George Eastman, founder of the Kodak industry, whose inventions have done much to simplify and cheapen the process of photography, born ... 13: 132
1864 Engagement near Ft. Stevens, Washington, D.C. 4: 138
1869 Irving T. Bush, builder of the Bush terminal in Brooklyn, born ... 14: 102
1871 Riots in Jersey City and New York on the anniversary of the battle of the Boyne ... 5: 210
1877 Arthur Mastick Hyde, governor of Missouri, and secretary of agriculture under Hoover, born .. C: 13
1889 Hugh Ferriss, architectural designer and artist, born ... B: 97

JULY 13.

1753 College of Philadelphia (later the University of Pennsylvania) chartered ... 1: 340
1787 Famous "Ordinance of 1787" passed by congress for the government of the Northwest territory 9: 197
1815 William B. Stevens, P. E. bishop, born ... 3: 471
1815 James A. Seddon, lawyer, member of Jefferson Davis's cabinet, born ... 6: 219
1821 Junius Brutus Booth made his first appearance in America ... 3: 180
1821 Nathan B. Forrest, Confederate soldier, born .. 10: 36
1824 James I. Waddell, Confederate naval officer, born 5: 364
1832 Source of the Mississippi discovered ... 5: 145
1839 William J. Tucker, president of Dartmouth college, born ... 24: 242
1846 Charles A. Meeker, dentist, founder of the American Academy of Dental Surgery, born . 15: 221
1847 Roger Wolcott, governor of Massachusetts, born 1: 127
1850 James H. Rogers, inventor of a method of telegraphic printing and the Rogers system of underground and undersea wireless telegraphy, born ... 21: 464
1854 Com. Hollins bombarded San Juan de Nicaragua 11: 252
1861 Battle of Carrick's Ford, W. Va. ... 4: 141
1862 Battle of Murfreesboro, Tenn. ... 10: 36
1863 Battle of La Fourche, La. ... 8: 78
1863 Capture of Yazoo City, Miss., by Federal troops 11: 524
1863 Mary E. Woolley, president of Mt. Holyoke college, born ... D: 58
1864 John Jacob Astor, 4th, author, inventor and capitalist, born ... 8: 106
1865 William Marvin appointed provisional governor of Florida ... 11: 379
1866 The "Great Eastern" started to lay the third Atlantic cable ... 4: 453
1877 Carl E. Milliken, governor of Maine, born ... B: 82

JULY 14.

1675 Mendon, Mass., attacked by Indians ... 10: 50
1729 John Penn, lieutenant-governor of Pennsylvania, born ... 2: 276
1750 Matthew Lyon, journalist and congressman, born 2: 426
1779 Sir James Wright returned to Georgia as royal governor ... 1: 492
1782 Jesse D. Elliott, naval officer, born ... 7: 39
1798 The sedition law, forbidding persons to combine or conspire against the government, passed .. 13: 182
1807 Albert Hopkins, astronomer, born ... 6: 240
1810 James Aldrich, poet and editor, born ... 9: 474
1811 Clara (Fisher) Maeder, actress, born ... 10: 471
1818 Nathaniel Lyon, soldier, born ... 4: 201
1824 Austin Craig, clergyman, and president of Antioch college, born ... 13: 91
1825 James C. Welling, president of St. John's college, born ... 1: 505
1835 George F. Barker, chemist and toxicologist, born 4: 532
1837 Amanda M. Douglas, author, born ... 2: 374
1839 John C. Gray, lawyer and educator, born ... 16: 206
1851 Hollis B. Frissell, educator of the Negro and Indian, born ... 18: 387
1851 William H. Burr, civil engineer, born ... D: 220
1853 Commodore Perry secured an interview with the Mikado which eventually resulted in the abandonment of the Japanese non-intercourse policy 4: 43
1853 Second World's Fair opened in New York city.. 4: 146
1860 Owen Wister, novelist, born ... C: 459
1864 Battle of Harrisburg, Miss. ... 10: 37
1865 Arthur Capper, journalist, governor of Kansas, and U. S. senator, born ... C: 58
1866 Edwin B. Frost, astronomer, who developed the stellar spectograph and discovered the asteroid, Frostia, born ... 25: 316
1870 Act to authorize refunding of the national debt passed ... 4: 383

JULY 15.

1765 Charles Goldsborough, governor of Maryland, born ... 9: 299
1779 Clement C. Moore, educator, author of "The Night Before Christmas," born ... 7: 362
1779 Capture of Stony Point, N. Y. ... 1: 55
1791 Benjamin T. Onderdonk, P. E. bishop, born .. 1: 515

1800 Sidney Breese, judge and U. S. senator, born ... 8: 122
1813 George P. A. Healy, artist, born 15: 317
1817 Henry T. Blow, industrialist, congressman and diplomat, born 4: 291
1817 Thomas Bowman, president of Indiana Asbury (later De Pauw) university, and M. E. bishop, born 7: 383
1830 Treaty with western tribes at Prairie du Chien made 9: 477
1831 Richard T. Auchmuty, philanthropist, founder of the New York trade-schools, born 9: 102
1833 Thomas C. Platt, U. S. senator, and political leader in New York state, born 11: 509
1836 William Winter, author and dramatic critic, born 4: 83
1841 Edward Abbott, clergyman and author, born .. 8: 179
1842 Bartlett Tripp, jurist and diplomat, born 8: 100
1848 William A. Leonard, P. E. bishop, born 24: 326
1851 Thomas Fell, president of St. John's college, born 1: 507
1853 William Henry Carpenter, philologist, born .. 8: 496
1854 Benjamin Ide Wheeler, president of the University of California, born 4: 480
1856 Preston S. Brooks, congressman from South Carolina, resigned his seat following the Sumner-Brooks incident 4: 339
1859 Stewart LeR. McCurdy, physician, born 12: 483
1862 Battle between Confederate ram "Arkansas" and Federal vessels 6: 247
1863 President Lincoln appointed a day of thanksgiving 2: 73
1864 Franklin K. Lane, chairman of the interstate commerce commission, and secretary of the interior under Wilson, born 19: 101
1870 Richmond P. Hobson, naval officer, born 9: 10
1874 Joseph Goldberger, hygienist, U. S. public health surgeon who established the cause of pellagra and a method of controlling it, born 21: 83
1918 American troops turned back the Germans in their final attempt to cross the Marne 20: 11

JULY 16.

1661 Pierre LeMoyne (Sieur d'Iberville), who explored the mouth of the Mississippi and fortified and colonized Mobile, Ala., born 5: 121
1696 The French and Indians captured a fort at Pemaquid, Maine 5: 121
1769 First mission in California founded at San Diego 12: 134
1790 District of Columbia established 9: 294
1798 Marine hospital service created by act of Congress 15: 129
1801 Daniel Hand, philanthropist, donor of the Daniel Hand Educational Fund for Colored People, born 3: 494
1821 Mary Baker Eddy, founder of Christian Science, born 3: 80
1829 Robert B. Potter, Federal soldier, born 4: 392
1838 Arthur W. Soper, founder of the Safety Car Heating and Lighting Co., born 12: 189
1841 Eri B. Hulbert, clergyman and educator, born .. 11: 67
1843 J. Wells Champney (Champ), artist, born 11: 308
1848 Eben E. Rexford, author of magazine articles and much verse that has been set to music, including "Silver Threads Among the Gold," born 10: 55
1849 First territorial legislature of Oregon met 8: 2
1849 Thomas A. Janvier, author, born 12: 460
1849 Benjamin F. Riley, educator, born 9: 183
1851 Charles M. Dewey, landscape painter, born 11: 294
1856 Lawrence M. Keitt, congressman, resigned his seat following the Sumner-Brooks incident .. 3: 300
1862 The rank of rear-admiral created by congress to honor Farragut 2: 50
1863 Jackson, Miss., evacuated by the Confederates .. 4: 5
1863 Battle of Honey Springs, Indian territory 9: 443
1863 Battle with the Japanese in the straits of Shimonoseki 13: 130
1863 Fanny Bloomfield Zeisler, pianist, born 14: 192
1898 Santiago, Cuba, surrendered to American forces 9: 18

JULY 17.

1744 Elbridge Gerry, vice-president of the United States and governor of Massachusetts, born .. 5: 371
1745 Timothy Pickering, secretary of war and secretary of state under Washington, born 1: 12
1749 Peter Gansevoort, soldier, the "hero of Ft. Stanwix," born 1: 382
1754 King's college (now Columbia) opened 6: 341
1763 John J. Astor, merchant, founder of a famous American family, born 8: 102
1769 William Cranch, jurist, born 7: 139
1774 A congress of colonies and a non-intercourse policy towards Great Britain proposed at a meeting of patriots in Fairfax county, Virginia 3: 337
1774 John Wilbur, Quaker preacher and author, born 10: 139
1777 Convention to frame a constitution for Vermont met 8: 242
1784 Bass Otis, painter, engraver and pioneer lithographer, born 21: 216
1812 Ft. Mackinaw surrendered to the British 13: 110
1812 The "Constitution" fell in with the British blockading squadron, making its famous escape three days later 13: 427
1813 British repelled at Ft. George, Canada 7: 379
1814 Alexander B. Meek, poet and lawyer, "father of the public schools of Alabama," born 11: 164
1835 Horace See, naval architect and engineer, born 2: 220
1842 Horatio N. Spencer, otologist, born 5: 35
1843 Washington Matthews, ethnologist, born 13: 54
1850 The first successful experiment in stellar photography made 7: 525
1851 Henry F. Burton, educator, born 12: 245
1861 Confederate troops routed at Fulton, Mo. 5: 216
1864 Gen. Joseph E. Johnston (Confederate army) superseded by Gen. Hood 5: 328
1882 Indian battle of Big Dry Wash, Ariz. 10: 493
1884 Sanford Bates, lawyer and penologist, born .... C: 331

JULY 18.

1710 John Cruger, mayor of New York city and first president of its chamber of commerce, born .. 1: 495
1757 Royall Tyler, jurist and author, born 7: 39
1817 Birdsey G. Northrop, educator, born 10: 225
1819 Benjamin F. Taylor, author and poet, born 11: 159
1822 Theodore W. Dwight, founder of the school of law at Columbia, born 6: 346
1830 Paul A. Oliver, soldier, inventor and manufacturer, born 5: 40
1839 James A. Scrymser, founder of the All-America cable system, born 18: 314
1842 Matthew C. D. Borden, cotton manufacturer, born 11: 441
1847 Samuel P. Sadtler, chemist, born 5: 350
1850 Rose Hartwick Thorpe, author, born 10: 252
1854 Tom L. Johnson, Ohio manufacturer and reformer, born 14: 148
1860 Charles Henry Muir, soldier, born .... A: 92
1861 Samuel Wesley Stratton, physicist, first director of the national bureau of standards, born 13: 142
1863 Federals repulsed in an unsuccessful attack on Ft. Wagner, S. C. 4: 55
1864 Conference at Niagara Falls between Horace Greeley and Confederate commissioners 3: 452
1864 Charles L. Bernheimer, New York merchant, born .... B: 307
1867 Joseph M. Flannery, industrialist, who introduced Vanadium steel commercially and who obtained the first American radium, born 23: 231
1871 Alfred H. Brooks, geologist, for whom the Brooks range in Alaska was named, born ... 22: 298
1882 Hermann Hagedorn, author, born .... A: 247
1918 American troops participated in the launching of the Aisne-Marne offensive .... A: 150
1932 The Canadian-American treaty for the joint development of the St. Lawrence waterway was signed at Washington .... C: 255

JULY 19.

1753 Felix Walker, soldier and Kentucky pioneer, born 7: 304
1767 Gideon Granger, postmaster general under Jefferson and Madison, born 5: 391
1769 The British armed sloop "Liberty" scuttled by the citizens of Newport 10: 15
1785 Mordecai M. Noah, journalist, born 9: 200
1792 Henry Delafield, New York shipping merchant, born 11: 29
1801 Robert J. Walker, U. S. senator, secretary of the treasury under Polk, and territorial governor of Kansas, born 6: 269
1806 Alexander D. Bache, scientist, superintendent of the U. S. coast survey, born 3: 348
1814 Samuel Colt, inventor of the Colt revolver and other firearms, born 6: 175
1814 Patrick H. Mell, Baptist clergyman and chancellor of Mercer university, born 9: 181
1817 Mary Ann Bickerdyke, Civil war nurse and humanitarian, born 21: 131
1820 Missouri adopted a state constitution 12: 302
1825 Malcolm Douglass, clergyman and president of Norwich university, born 18: 325
1827 Orville H. Platt, U. S. senator, author of the Platt amendment, born 2: 339
1828 Roger A. Pryor, congressman and judge, born.. 9: 147
1829 Morrison Heady, poet and author, born 11: 150
1837 William S. Hays, song writer, born 3: 178
1838 Joel A. Allen, ornithologist and mammalogist, born 3: 100
1842 Frederic T. Greenhalge, governor of Massachusetts, born 1: 126

1846 Edward Charles Pickering, director of the Harvard astronomical observatory, born 6:424
1846 John Graham Brooks, sociologist, born 13:534
1847 John J. Hennessy, R. C. bishop, born 12:405
1848 First Woman's Rights convention opened 3: 84
1865 Charles Horace Mayo, surgeon, who, with his brother, endowed the Mayo Foundation for Medical Education and Research, at Rochester, Minn., born A:331
1879 John P. Mitchel, who instituted many civic reforms as mayor of New York city, born 18:289

JULY 20.

1744 Joshua Clayton, Delaware physician and governor, and U. S. senator, born 11:530
1765 William Tryon became governor of North Carolina 7:514
1775 Day of fasting and humiliation observed throughout the colonies 5:457
1777 Treaty of the Long island of the Holston made with the Indians 7:239
1793 John Ireland Howe, inventor of pin-making machines, born 4:373
1795 Hiland Hall, governor of Vermont, born 8:322
1807 Roger S. Howard, clergyman and president of Norwich university, born 18:325
1811 Elisha Dyer, manufacturer, and governor of Rhode Island, born 9:400
1818 James C. Derby, New York publisher, born ... 11:497
1822 Franklin B. Hough, author, born 13:340
1829 Alfred Owen, president of Denison university, born 1:303
1832 Alexander L. Holley, metallurgist, who built the first Bessemer steel plant in this country and made many contributions to the development of the steel industry, born 11:508
1838 Augustin Daly, dramatist and theatrical manager, born 1:285
1849 Robert A. Van Wyck, judge and first mayor of Greater New York, born 13:261
1849 Talcott Williams, director of the school of journalism of Columbia university, born 15:306
1850 Richard J. Reynolds, president of the Reynolds Tobacco Co., born 18:349
1855 Frederic J. Stimson (J. S. of Dale), lawyer and author, born 10:361
1861 The Confederate congress met at Richmond 2: 69
1863 Gates White McGarrah, president of the Bank for International Settlements, born C:297
1864 Confederate troops repulsed in the first of the three battles in defense of Atlanta 4: 33
1868 Josiah H. Penniman, provost of the University of Pennsylvania, born D:104
1933 The NRA blanket code to shorten hours and raise wages decreed by President Franklin D. Roosevelt .... D: 5

JULY 21.

1690 Rhode Island sailors defeated a French fleet 10: 10
1700 Ebenezer Prime, clergyman and Revolutionary patriot, born 7:236
1775 Franklin submitted to the Continental congress a plan for the union of the colonies 1:335
1797 John M. Read, jurist, born 4:500
1801 Theron Baldwin, missionary, the "father of western colleges," born 6: 39
1802 David Hunter, Federal soldier, born 4:264
1818 Charles Robinson, first state governor of Kansas, born 8:342
1823 First issue of the "Western Register and Terre Haute Advertiser" 18:293
1824 Stanley Matthews, justice of the U. S. supreme court, born 2:476
1826 Robert Barry Coffin, author, born 6:525
1826 Mahlon Loomis, inventor, who patented a wireless telegraph device in 1872, born 25: 80
1838 John R. Brooke, governor-general of Puerto Rico and Cuba, born 9: 24
1847 Blanche W. Howard, author, born 1:304
1849 Robert S. Woodward, scientist, president of Carnegie Institution, born 13:108
1859 Chauncey Olcott, actor, a clever delineator of Irish characters, born 11:519
1861 First battle of Bull Run, Va. 4: 50
1870 Henry R. Seager, economist, active in labor reform movements, born 22:180
1925 John T. Scopes found guilty of having taught evolution in defiance of Tennessee laws B:222

JULY 22.

1620 A number of Pilgrims sailed for America from Holland in the "Speedwell" but were compelled to abandon that vessel in favor of the "Mayflower" 7:367
1708 Nathaniel Ames, mathematician, born 8: 45
1763 James Geddes, civil engineer, born 10:264
1779 Edward Lloyd, Maryland governor and U. S. senator, born 9:297
1795 Thomas W. Harvey, inventor of machines for manufacturing screws, nails, rivets, etc., born 12:418
1796 Moses Cleveland selected the site for Cleveland, Ohio 6:257
1798 Maiden voyage of the frigate "Constitution" begun 4: 89
1814 Treaty with the Michigan Indians concluded 5: 4
1824 John D. G. Shea, historian, born 6:162
1830 Julia Dean, actress, born 8:299
1830 William Sooy Smith, Federal soldier and civil engineer, born 4:498
1839 David H. Moffat, railroad and bank president, and builder of the Moffat tunnel, born 6:349
1849 Emma Lazarus, author, an ardent champion of the Jews, born 3: 25
1852 Henry R. Marshall, architect and author, born 11:328
1853 Hugh L. Scott, soldier, whose services in the Philippines and in Cuba were notable, born .. 26:171
1857 Frank H. Cushing, archæologist and ethnologist, born 11: 26
1859 Sarah Le Moyne, actress, born 13:303
1861 John C. Kilgo, president of Trinity (N. C.) college, born 13: 97
1862 Battle between the "Essex" and the Confederate ram "Arkansas" 2:100
1864 Second battle of Atlanta, Ga., which cost the life of the Federal general, James B. McPherson.. 4: 34
1864 The Confederate general, William H. T. Walker, killed in action at Atlanta 13: 16
1875 Joseph P. Cotton, under secretary of state, who introduced a method of diplomacy unique in international relations, born 23:151
1889 Morris Fishbein, editor of the "Journal of the American Medical Association," born C:466
1898 Stephen Vincent Benét, author, born A:215

JULY 23.

1792 Lardner Vanuxem, geologist, born 8:385
1810 Henry G. Reed, founder of Reed & Barton, silversmiths, born 10: 55
1813 Sylvester Judd, clergyman and author, born 9:273
1813 Fletcher Webster, lawyer, born 13:169
1816 Charlotte S. Cushman, actress, born 4: 40
1819 William R. Travers, New York broker, born ... 8: 86
1821 Joseph W. Fabens, U. S. consul and author, born 7:178
1823 James C. Lane, Federal soldier, and engineer, born 4:294
1828 Samuel Fiske (Dunn Browne), soldier and author, born 11:438
1829 Patent for a "typographer," the precursor of the modern typewriter, issued to William A. Burt 18:367
1831 William Westlake, inventor of car heaters, oil stoves and railroad lanterns, born 2:416
1834 James Gibbons, R. C. prelate, born 1:488
1837 Oliver R. Ingersoll, boat builder and inventor of marine life-saving devices, born 23:357
1846 Walter Cook, architect, born 14:344
1850 Edward M. Shepard, lawyer, born 17:365
1856 Arthur Bird, composer, born 9:387
1857 Albert Shaw, editor of the "American Review of Reviews," born 9:469
1861 Gen. William S. Rosecrans took command of the Department of the Ohio 4:162
1862 John L. Whitman, penologist, born 15:365
1865 The S. S. "Great Eastern" started to lay the second Atlantic cable 4:452
1865 Edward T. Sanford, justice of the U. S. supreme court, born 21: 92
1871 Jacob H. Hollander, economist, born 13:372
1877 Montague M. Glass, author and playwright, born C:398
1883 The "Proteus" wrecked in Kane sea, Arctic ocean 9: 8

JULY 24.

Pioneer Day in Utah

1621 A written constitution granted to the Virginia colony by the London Company 13:381
1696 Benning Wentworth, governor of New Hampshire, born 6:303
1701 Cadillac established the first settlement at Detroit 5:172
1796 John M. Clayton, secretary of state under Taylor, and U. S. senator, born 6:179
1798 John Adams Dix, secretary of the treasury under Buchanan, and governor of New York, born 5: 6
1803 Alexander J. Davis, architect, born 22:174

1819 Josiah G. Holland, author and editor, born 1:311
1822 Benn Pitman, phonographer, born 4: 87
1823 Arthur I. Boreman, governor of West Virginia, born 12:430
1829 Lewis Miller, inventor of labor-saving machines, and a founder of the Chautauqua movement, born 6:216
1831 Edwin W. Rice, clergyman, born 3:410
1833 Alexander Hadden, physician, born 2:228
1844 Persifor Frazer, scientist, born 4:286
1846 Alonzo B. Hepburn, president of the Chase National Bank, and an internationally recognized authority in financial matters, born 23:100
1847 Brigham Young led the Mormons into the valley of the Great Salt Lake 16: 4
1851 William Gillette, actor and playwright, born .. 2:249
1857 Eugene A. Philbin, lawyer, born 12:236
1858 Willy Meyer, surgeon, born C:480
1864 Battle of Kearnstown, near Winchester, Va. 4:138
1897 The Dingley tariff act passed 11: 5
1898 Amelia Earhart, aviator, first woman to accomplish a solo flight across the Atlantic, born D:395
1929 President Hoover announced ratification of the Kellogg-Briand treaty, renouncing war as an instrument of national policy .... C: 6

JULY 25.

1689 Protestant Associators seized the government in Maryland 7:335
1750 Henry Knox, soldier, secretary of war under Washington, and founder of the Society of the Cincinnati, born 1: 14
1779 British fort at the mouth of the Penobscot attacked by the Massachusetts fleet 4:152
1796 Gideon L. Soule, principal of Phillips Exeter academy, born 10:105
1797 Nicholas M. Hentz, entomologist and educator, born 9:428
1802 William S. Plummer, clergyman, born 9:261
1803 Samuel A. Maverick, Texas patriot, born 6:466
1805 William Clark and Meriwether Lewis discovered the three forks of the Missouri river 5:122
1814 Battle of Lundy's Lane, Canada 3:503
1824 Richard Oglesby, U. S. senator and governor of Illinois, born 11: 48
1840 Flora A. Darling, founder of the Daughters of the American Revolution, born 19:138
1840 Carroll D. Wright, economist and statistician, born 19:421
1844 Thomas Eakins, artist, born 5:421
1848 Charles de Kay, poet, born 9:206
1851 Frederick A. Gower, inventor of the Gower telephone, born 9:216
1854 James B. Dill, New Jersey lawyer and judge, born 6:443
1855 John B. Deaver, surgeon, born 22: 7
1857 Nat C. Goodwin, actor, born 6:291
1857 Frank J. Sprague, electrician and inventor, born 24: 15
1859 David Belasco, playwright and theatrical producer, born 14: 83
1866 Farragut first to receive the title of permanent admiral of the navy 2: 50
1868 Wyoming territory formed from Dakota, Utah and Idaho 2:455
1870 Maxfield Parrish, artist and illustrator, born ... 12:487
1873 Anne T. Morgan, philanthropist, born .... B: 88
1880 The Egyptian obelisk arrived in New York ... 6:439
1898 American troops landed at Puerto de Guanica in the Spanish-American war 9: 25

JULY 26.

1739 George Clinton, vice-president of the U. S., and governor of New York, born 3: 41
1758 Gen. Amherst captured Louisburg, Nova Scotia, from the French 1:101
1766 Arthur Livermore, judge and congressman, born 12:436
1775 Franklin appointed colonial postmaster general 1:335
1781 John D. Sloat, naval officer, born 6:176
1784 Charles Morris, naval officer, born 9:118
1790 Theodore Strong, mathematician, born 9:288
1796 George Catlin, painter, born 3:270
1799 Isaac Babbitt, manufacturer and inventor, producer of "Babbitt metal," born 13:442
1805 Julian M. Sturtevant, president of Illinois college, born 13:601
1809 Charles F. Herreshoff, shipbuilder, born 12:352
1822 Orange Judd, publisher of the "Orange-Judd Farmer," born 8:350
1823 Charles C. Coffin, newspaper correspondent, born 1:438
1831 William J. Florence, actor, born 2:381
1833 Otto Singer, conductor and composer, born 7:438
1836 Francis M. Kirkham, clergyman and editor, born 18:152
1847 Moses G. Farmer exhibited his electro-magnetic locomotive 7:361
1848 John D. Archbold, capitalist, who succeeded John D. Rockefeller as president of the Standard Oil Co. of New Jersey, born 21:114
1849 William R. Merriam, governor of Minnesota, born 10: 68
1849 Robert S. McCormick, diplomat, born 13:375
1856 William R. Harper, Hebraist, and president of Chicago university, born 11: 65
1858 Edward M. House, statesman, born .... A: 55
1861 James K. Vardaman, Mississippi governor and U. S. senator, born 13:495
1862 George R. Cortelyou, secretary of commerce and labor, postmaster general and secretary of the treasury under Theodore Roosevelt, born 14: 18
1863 The Confederate raider Morgan, and the remnant of his army, captured near New Lisbon, Ohio 4:317
1866 George B. McCutcheon, novelist, born 14:264
1869 Eric Doolittle, astronomer, born 19:300
1927 Leon H. Barnett patented his chemical process for producing precious gems D:209

JULY 27.

1660 Goffe and Whalley, the regicides, arrived in Boston 11:458
1748 Alexander Macomb, New York merchant, born 2:241
1752 Samuel Smith, soldier, U. S. senator, and acting secretary of the navy, born 1: 73
1753 John Warren, Boston physician and surgeon, born 10:288
1759 Ticonderoga captured from the French 1:101
1774 The first secession meeting in Georgia held at Tondees tavern, Savannah 1:219
1782 Herman Knickerbocker, lawyer, born 11:188
1787 Thomas Say, naturalist, born 6:107
1806 Friedrich A. Rauch, first president of Marshall college, born 11: 62
1812 Thomas L. Clingman, soldier, U. S. senator and scientist, born 7:199
1812 Jonathan Young Scammon, Chicago lawyer, and founder of a number of the city's most important banking, journalistic and educational institutions, born 7:527
1818 Eben N. Horsford, chemist, born 6:155
1825 Cyrus Thomas, scientist, born 13:528
1831 Charles Henry Hersey, inventor of a rotary pump, a sugar granulator, a water meter, a steam drier, and various devices for manufacturing soap, born 17:311
1838 Albert M. Palmer, theatrical manager, born .. 1:128
1846 William B. Haldeman, editor of the Louisville "Courier-Journal" and the Louisville "Times," born 18:240
1849 Theodore B. Comstock, geologist, founder and director of the School of Mines of Arizona, and president of the University of Arizona, born.. 13:450
1852 George Foster Peabody, financier, born 15:140
1853 Henry M. Dunham, composer and organist, born 21:239
1855 John Ripley Freeman, engineer, designer of the Hetch-Hetchy water supply and power system, born C:397
1861 Gen. George B. McClellan took command of the Department of Washington and Northeastern Virginia 4:141
1866 The laying of the third Atlantic cable completed 4:453
1868 Alaska territory organized 4:366

JULY 28.

1729 Nicholas Brown (1st), merchant and benefactor of Brown university, born 8: 27
1751 Joseph Habersham, postmaster general under Washington, John Adams and Jefferson, born 1: 18
1767 James A. Bayard, U. S. senator, born 7:300
1778 Charles Stewart, naval officer, born 8:156
1809 Ormsby McKnight Mitchel, astronomer and soldier, born 3:440
1810 James C. Booth, chemist and geologist, born 13:245
1812 Second attack on the Baltimore "Federalist" office 12:235
1820 Elisha S. Converse, manufacturer and financier, born 10:120
1824 Holland N. McTyeire, M. E. bishop, and first president of Vanderbilt university, born 8:226
1824 James J. Levick, Philadelphia physician, born.. 9:344
1837 John H. Brown, inventor of the segmental tube wire-wound gun, and the diamond quilting machine, born 4:381
1840 Edward Drinker Cope, scientist, born 7:474
1852 S.S. "Henry Clay" burned on the Hudson river.. 11:114
1859 Mary Anderson, actress, noted for her rare beauty and talent, born 1:243

1859 Hermann V. Hilprecht, archaeologist, born 10: 380
1859 Ballington Booth, founder of the Volunteers of America, born 14: 54
1864 Third battle of Atlanta, Ga. 4: 34
1868 Fourteenth Amendment to the Constitution ratified 2: 456
1868 Burlingame treaty with China signed in Washington 8: 56
1874 Alice Duer Miller, author and poet, born ..... A: 378
1917 War industries board organized ..... A: 58

JULY 29.

1721 Johann de Kalb, soldier, born 1: 73
1742 Isabella Graham, philanthropist, born 4: 375
1775 George Clymer and Michael Hillegas appointed first Continental treasurers 3: 272
1778 The French fleet under D'Estaing arrived in Narragansett bay 1: 56
1786 Leonard Case, lawyer and land agent, born 11: 152
1794 Thomas Corwin, U. S. senator, secretary of the treasury under Fillmore and governor of Ohio, born 6: 180
1795 Edwin A. Stevens, inventor, and founder of Stevens institute of technology, born 11: 22
1796 Walter Hunt, who invented a lock-stitch sewing machine before Howe, born 19: 245
1797 Daniel Drew, capitalist, and founder of Drew theological seminary, born 11: 502
1805 Hiram Powers, sculptor, born 3: 421
1820 Clement L. Vallandigham, congressman, whose pro-slavery and pacifist sentiments caused his deportation from the Union, born 3: 145
1824 Eastman Johnson, artist, born 9: 52
1825 John V. Farwell, Chicago dry goods merchant, born 14: 228
1828 John S. Pillsbury, Minnesota governor and industrialist, born 10: 65
1840 Simon Baruch, physician and surgeon, born 18: 72
1845 Othniel F. Nichols, civil engineer, born 9: 45
1858 Second treaty with Japan signed 5: 493
1862 Percy Moran, artist, born 10: 367
1863 Robert Reid, mural and portrait painter, born..... 6: 476
1869 Booth Tarkington, author, playwright, born ..... A: 84
1877 William Beebe, naturalist, born ..... B: 337

JULY 30.

1602 Samuel Stone, clergyman and a founder of Hartford, Conn., born 7: 202
1619 First representative assembly in America met at Jamestown, Va. 13: 381
1802 Duel between John Swartout and De Witt Clinton 7: 536
1815 Thomas J. Rodman, soldier, born 4: 396
1822 William T. Adams (Oliver Optic), author, born 1: 203
1838 Henry A. Du Pont, soldier and U. S. senator, born 6: 457
1841 George W. Melville, naval engineer, born 3: 283
1842 James D. McCabe, author, born 7: 511
1844 Robert J. (Bob) Burdette, humorist and clergyman, born 24: 356
1844 John S. Runnels, president of the Pullman Co., born ..... B: 109
1849 Lettie S. Bigelow, poet and author, born 6: 273
1854 John S. Williams, congressman and U. S. senator, born 13: 396
1855 James E. Kelly, engraver and sculptor, born 25: 434
1856 Harriet L. V. Bates (Eleanor James), author, born 8: 12
1857 Thorstein B. Veblen, a pioneer in economic thought, born 21: 73
1858 Frederick C. Pierce, historian and genealogist, born 10: 470
1863 Henry Ford, industrialist, born ..... B: 1
1864 Chambersburg, Pa., burned by Confederates 4: 138
1867 Governor Throckmorton removed from office 9: 71
1867 Rufus C. Dawes, Chicago financier, head of the "Century of Progress" exposition, born ..... D: 402
1872 A patent issued to Mahlon Loomis for wireless telegraphy 25: 80
1880 Robert R. McCormick, head of the Chicago "Tribune," born ..... D: 80

JULY 31.

1740 Marinus Willett, soldier and mayor of New York, born 3: 378
1763 James Kent, jurist, born 3: 55
1779 William D. Williamson, governor of Maine and historian, born 6: 305
1802 George W. Carpenter, merchant and scientist, born 10: 235
1803 John Ericsson, inventor of the screw propellor, born 4: 46
1809 Thomas S. Kirkbride, alienist, born 6: 388
1816 George H. Thomas, soldier, born 4: 48
1817 Philip Cook, soldier, born 4: 182
1820 John W. Garrett, Baltimore banker and president of the Baltimore & Ohio R. R., born 18: 3
1822 Abram S. Hewitt, iron manufacturer, congressman, and mayor of New York, born 3: 294
1824 George Henry Miles, poet and author, born 6: 439
1826 George Hoadley, governor of Ohio, born 3: 143
1826 William S. Clark, educator, born 5: 310
1829 John Hall, clergyman, and chancellor of the University of the City of New York, born 6: 323
1831 Helena P. H. Blavatsky, one of the founders of the Theosophical Society, born 15: 336
1841 Robert S. MacArthur, clergyman, born 5: 226
1842 Edward H. Kendall, architect, born 12: 247
1850 Robert L. Taylor, U. S. senator and governor of Tennessee, born 8: 365
1852 Ben Foster, artist, born 11: 303
1859 Theobald Smith, pathologist, whose studies of the comparative etiology, pathology and immunology of infectious diseases won him international fame, born ..... D: 133
1864 Edward N. Hurley, manufacturer of electric machinery for domestic uses, and chairman of the U. S. shipping board, born ..... A: 60
1868 Harry P. Davis, electrical engineer, pioneer in commercializing radio, born 25: 17
1882 Herbert E. Ives, scientist and inventor, pioneer in the development of television, born ..... C: 39
1918 Postmaster General Burleson, as federal supervisor, assumed control of communications systems for the duration of the World war ..... A: 46

AUGUST 1.

1502 Columbus first landed on American continent at Honduras 3: 437
1749 Samuel Doak, Tennessee educator, born 7: 340
1767 Benjamin Bakewell, "Father of the Flint Glass Industry in the United States," born 22: 217
1770 William Clark, soldier, explorer and governor of Missouri territory, born 12: 301
1778 John C. Warren, Boston surgeon and educator, born 6: 426
1779 Francis Scott Key, author of "The Star Spangled Banner," born 5: 498
1781 Joshua Soule, M. E. bishop, born 5: 85
1791 George Ticknor, author and educator, born 6: 477
1801 Robert W. Barnwell, U. S. senator and president of South Carolina college, born 11: 32
1808 Henry D. Rogers, geologist, born 7: 543
1815 Richard Henry Dana, 2d, jurist and author, born 7: 182
1818 Maria Mitchell, astronomer, the first woman member of the American Academy of Arts and Sciences, born 5: 236
1819 Herman Melville, author, born 4: 59
1820 John L. Stevens, diplomat, born 2: 172
1829 James E. A. Gibbs, inventor of the Wilcox & Gibbs sewing machine, born 19: 255
1829 Treaty with Indian tribes in Wisconsin made 22: 417
1832 Gilbert C. Walker, governor of Virginia, born 5: 453
1833 Sailors' Snug Harbor, New York, dedicated 11: 253
1838 Peter B. Wight, architect and inventor of a fire-proofing process, born 21: 369
1843 Robert T. Lincoln, lawyer, diplomat and president of the Pullman Co., born 21: 59
1844 David J. Burrell, clergyman, born 12: 482
1845 Francis M. Burdick, educator, born 12: 262
1847 Thomas J. Conaty, R. C. bishop, born 12: 407
1854 Walter L. Palmer, artist, born 7: 458
1861 Office of assistant secretary of war created 13: 335
1873 First cable car line in the world began functioning in San Francisco 7: 192
1876 Colorado admitted into the Union 6: 450
1895 First conduit electric traction railway system began operating 23: 34
1933 The "Blue Eagle," emblem of the NRA, made its official appearance throughout the United States ..... D: 21

AUGUST 2.

1675 Battle with Indians at Brookfield, Mass. (King Philip's war) 9: 517
1684 Treaty of peace concluded at Albany between the Colonies and the Iroquois 10: 241
1754 Pierre Charles L'Enfant, architect, who laid out the plan for Washington, D. C., born 16: 209
1779 David Campbell, soldier and governor of Virginia, born 5: 449
1798 Ignatius A. Reynolds, R. C. bishop, born 12: 410
1807 Robert McClelland, governor of Michigan and secretary of the interior under Pierce, born 4: 150

1810 Amos Tuck, congressman, born 13:518
1812 The "Constitution" sailed from Boston on her famous cruise 13:427
1813 Fort Stephenson, Ohio, attacked by the British .. 11: 45
1819 Thomas Armitage, clergyman, born 9:199
1826 John P. Stockton, U. S. senator and jurist, born 13: 86
1827 James Millikin, banker and founder of Millikin university, born 18:117
1832 Henry S. Olcott, a founder and president of the Theosophical Society, born 8:464
1832 Battle of Bad Axe river, Wis. 11: 44
1835 Elisha Gray, inventor of a telegraph, telephone and telautograph, born 4:453
1835 Moses Coit Tyler, author and educator, born ... 4:483
1846 Melville M. Bigelow, lawyer, born 11:184
1847 Treaty made with Ojibway Indians 12:213
1852 Duel between Gen. James W. Denver and Edward Gilbert 5:523
1854 F. Marion Crawford, author, born 2:502
1856 Eliza Orne White, author, born 13:495
1861 Battle of Dug Spring, Mo. 4:336
1861 David Kinley, economist and president of the University of Illinois, born .... B: 76
1865 Irving Babbitt, scholar and critic, born 23: 19
1866 Charles Francis Adams, secretary of the navy under Hoover, born .... C: 11
1867 Frank A. Perret, inventor and volcanologist, born 15:334
1867 Hamilton Wright, physician, public health expert, and father of the movement regulating the sale of opium, born 22:430
1923 President Warren G. Harding died in office 19:271

AUGUST 3.

1492 Columbus sailed on his first voyage from Palos 3:437
1681 First council in Pennsylvania appointed 5:545
1729 Richard Caswell, soldier and governor of North Carolina, born 4:419
1755 Nicholas Gilman, U. S. senator and one of the framers of the Constitution, born 2:447
1773 Jeremiah Day, president of Yale, born 1:169
1777 Attack on Fort Schuyler (Fort Stanwix), N. Y. 1:382
1795 Treaty of Greenville, Ohio, with the Indians signed 10: 60
1808 Hamilton Fish, governor of New York and secretary of state under Grant, born 4: 15
1811 Elisha G. Otis, elevator inventor, born 11:119
1816 John E. Smith, soldier, born 12:248
1820 Luther O. Emerson, composer, born 7:432
1820 Agrippa N. Bell, physician and sanitary reformer, born 8:210
1821 Uriah S. Stephens, founder of the Knights of Labor, born 1:262
1821 Graceanna Lewis, philanthropist and naturalist, born 9:447
1824 William B. Woods, justice of the U. S. supreme court, born 2:476
1835 Artemas Martin, mathematician, born 2:180
1836 Augustus H. Strong, educator, born 12:514
1839 John E. Hudson, lawyer and promoter, born ... 5: 83
1839 George L. Goodale, botanist, born 6:427
1841 Francis Delafield, New York physician, born ... 10:278
1846 Samuel M. Jones, Ohio manufacturer and reformer, born 10:414
1852 Henry Wolf, engraver, born 10:376
1852 Jared S. Torrance, financier, founder of the industrial city of Torrance, Calif., born 19:238
1855 Henry C. Bunner, author and editor of "Puck," born 7:303
1857 Paul Shorey, classicist, born 11: 75
1857 William B. Landreth, civil engineer, born 12: 97
1861 Pope Yeatman, mining engineer, born 18:176
1871 Vernon L. Parrington, whose history of American literature won the Pulitzer prize, born ... 25:248
1907 The Standard Oil Co. was fined $29,240,000 for accepting rebates 14: 7
1923 Calvin Coolidge sworn in as president of the United States 24: 2

AUGUST 4.

1718 Scotch immigrants arrived to settle the town of Londonderry, N. H. 3:448
1743 Jedidiah Huntington, soldier, born 1: 77
1759 Crown Point, N. Y., captured from the French 1:101
1781 Isaac Hayne hanged by the British 1:441
1782 Lewis Le Conte, naturalist, born 11:105
1794 The Christian church organized 13:283
1808 Henry W. Hilliard, diplomat and author, born .. 2:114
1810 Robert Purvis, abolitionist, president of the "Underground Railway," born 1:413
1812 Peter H. Myers, lawyer and author, born 10:485
1814 Siege of Fort Erie, Canada, begun 9:372
1816 Russell Sage, New York financier, born 10:135
1817 Frederick T. Frelinghuysen, U. S. senator and secretary of state under Arthur, born 4:250
1818 Lovell H. Rousseau, Kentucky soldier and lawyer, born 4:366
1823 Oliver H. P. Morton, statesman and governor of Indiana, born 13:271
1826 John Cotton Smith, clergyman, born 8:120
1829 Frederic S. Hill, naval officer and author, born 15: 38
1838 Louis Wagner, soldier and banker, born 4:304
1846 Silas G. Pratt, composer, born 10:196
1853 John H. Twachtman, artist, born 13:530
1863 Patent issued for a button-hole sewing machine 23: 84
1869 John F. Mowbray-Clarke, artist, born 15:366
1869 John E. MacKenty, surgeon, who developed an artificial larynx for patients whose larynges had been removed because of cancer, born 23:254
1874 A wire weaving machine patented by Wickwire 19:127

AUGUST 5.

1749 Thomas Lynch, a signer of the Declaration of Independence, born 10:135
1763 Indian battle of Bushy Run, Mich., began 10:415
1790 Edward R. McCall, naval officer, born 12:497
1795 Byron Diman, R. I. politician and governor, born 9:397
1802 Edward K. Collins, who established the first steamship line between New York and England, born 23:126
1811 Washington Hunt, governor of New York, born 3: 48
1811 William G. Eliot, clergyman and chancellor of Washington university, born 11:210
1814 James Dixon, U. S. senator and judge, born ... 4:447
1819 John Bidwell, Californa pioneer and congressman, born 3:531
1837 Charles H. Lewis, soldier and president of Norwich university, born 18:326
1842 Edwin L. Bynner, author, born 7:486
1843 John Trowbridge, physicist, born 23: 53
1848 James M. Taylor, president of Vassar college, born 5:235
1851 Charles F. Holder, author, born 7:402
1853 Frank S. Streeter, lawyer, born 16:293
1858 Completion of Atlantic telegraph cable 4:452
1858 H. Siddons Mowbray, artist, born 23:188
1859 Frank Strong, educator, born 13:440
1859 Thomas B. Osborne, chemist, born 21:356
1862 Battle of Baton Rouge, La. 5: 3
1864 Battle of Mobile bay, Ala. 2: 50
1869 John C. W. Beckham, governor of Kentucky, born 13: 14
1875 Clare A. Briggs, cartoonist, born 23:317
1880 Arthur J. Morris, financier, born .... B: 12
1882 Hugh S. Johnson, soldier and first administrator of the National Recovery Act, born .... D: 20
1886 Bruce Barton, author and advertising agent, born C:326
1909 Payne-Aldrich tariff bill passed by the senate and signed by President Taft 23: 4

AUGUST 6.

1774 Solomon Van Rensselaer, Revolutionary soldier and congressman, born 11:285
1777 Battle of Oriskany, N. Y. 1: 70
1780 Battle of Hanging Rock, S. C. 1: 79
1786 Gulian C. Verplanck, New York author and politician, born 5:405
1788 James Brewster, manufacturer of wagons and carriages, born 13:122
1806 John H. Wheeler, historian of North Carolina, born 6:485
1810 William D. Ticknor, publisher, born 5:142
1811 Judah P. Benjamin, U. S. senator and secretary of state of the Southern confederacy, born ... 4:285
1817 Zerelda G. Wallace, reformer, born 5:404
1819 Samuel P. Carter, naval and army officer in both Mexican and Civil wars, born 2:104
1825 John P. Gray, physician, born 7:273
1828 Andrew T. Still, founder of osteopathy, born 26:245
1834 Cyrus Cobb, sculptor, born 4: 44
1834 Darius Cobb, artist, born 4: 45
1838 Walter Shirlaw, artist, born 11:298
1846 Independent treasury system reënacted 6:434
1861 Act of confiscation of enemy property, including slaves, passed by Congress 2: 69
1862 Confederate ram "Arkansas" destroyed 2:101
1863 A Thanksgiving observed for Federal victories in the Civil war 2: 73
1870 Guy Lowell, architect, born 21: 47
1874 James T. Shotwell, historian, born .... B: 16
1890 First legal execution by electricity 7:272

AUGUST 7.

1727 James Bowdoin, statesman and scientist, for whom Bowdoin college was named, born 2:488
1742 Nathanael Greene, soldier, born 1: 39
1781 Naval battle between the "Trumbull" and "Iris" 2:231
1789 The war department of the United States government organized 1: 16

1795 Joseph Rodman Drake, poet, born 5:420
1804 Second bombardment of Tripoli by an American fleet 8:412
1811 Elias Loomis, scientist and author of textbooks, born 7:233
1814 Commissioners from England and the United States met at Ghent to arrange a treaty of peace 5: 75
1819 Joseph P. Thompson, Egyptologist, the "Fiery American," born 10:132
1826 Robert G. Dun, mercantile credit expert, born .. 2:523
1829 Robert B. Roosevelt, New York statesman and author, born 3:415
1829 Thomas Ewing, soldier, judge and congressman, born 25: 15
1833 Powell Clayton, Arkansas soldier, statesman, and governor, born 16:262
1835 Roswell P. Flower, New York governor, born ... 2:344
1839 John F. Dryden, U. S. senator and president of the Prudential Insurance Co., born 9:415
1843 Charles W. Stoddard, author and poet, born ... 7:116
1844 Alfred Noble, civil engineer, born 9: 44
1844 George P. Mains, clergyman, born 12:474
1846 Francis Rawle, lawyer, born 17:388
1858 George A. Clapp (Lew Dockstader), actor, born 23:237
1865 Edgar Jadwin, military engineer in charge of construction work for the American troops in France, born A:521
1933 The United States-Haiti pact signed at Port-au-Prince .... D: 11

AUGUST 8.

1607 First settlers (from Plymouth, England) landed in Maine 5:166
1716 Abner Nash, patriot and governor of North Carolina, born 4:419
1779 Benjamin Silliman, Sr., scientist, "The Nestor of American Science," born 2:385
1794 Cornerstone of the first Methodist church in Boston laid 13:187
1812 John Rodgers, naval officer, born 5: 14
1819 Charles A. Dana, proprietor and editor of the New York "Sun," born 1:307
1822 George Stoneman, soldier and governor of California, born 4:112
1822 Birdsall Holly, originator of steam heating of buildings, born 26:108
1824 Benjamin F. Jones, manufacturer, born 13:222
1829 The "Stourbridge Lion," the first locomotive to run in the United States, tried at Honesdale, Pa. 8:233
1830 Cornelius R. Agnew, physician, born 8:205
1833 Dexter M. Ferry, seed merchant, born 21:308
1839 Nelson A. Miles, soldier, the "Indian Fighter," born 9: 26
1843 Laurence Hutton, author and critic, born 7: 64
1846 The Wilmot Proviso introduced in congress by Hannibal Hamlin 3:419
1852 Frederick W. Whitridge, lawyer, born 15: 74
1854 Smith & Wesson patented metallic cartridges with center fire 10:476
1857 Henry F. Osborn, paleontologist, born 26: 18
1862 Writ of habeas corpus suspended by President Lincoln 2: 72
1863 Florence Merriam Bailey, ornithologist and author, born 13:263
1863 Jean Leon Gerome Ferris, artist, born 23:385
1870 First yacht race to regain the America's cup ... 1:447
1884 Sara Teasdale, poet, born A:218
1894 President Cleveland formally recognized the Hawaiian republic 12:419

AUGUST 9.

1642 The first commencement of Harvard college held 6:409
1736 James Clinton, soldier, born 1:305
1737 Sir John Wentworth, last royal governor of New Hampshire, born 5:194
1757 Fort William Henry, N. Y., captured by Montcalm 1: 87
1784 Thomas L. L. Brent, diplomat, born 12:337
1788 Adoniram Judson, Baptist missionary, born 3: 92
1793 Laurent S. Juneau, founder of Milwaukee, born 6: 18
1805 Pike's expedition left St. Louis, Mo., to trace the source of the Mississippi 2:517
1808 Henry I. Bowditch, physician, born 8:214
1812 Egbert P. Judson, manufacturer of an improved form of dynamite, born 24:108
1819 Jonathan H. Lane, scientist and inventor, born 3:275
1819 William T. G. Morton, dentist, who first used sulphuric ether professionally as an anesthetic, born 8:332
1827 William M. Stewart, U. S. senator, born 1:325
1836 Alexander Del Mar, political economist, born ... 4:189
1837 Marvin Hughitt, president of the Chicago & North Western railroad, born 20: 22
1840 John Henry Stiness, jurist, born 12:248
1842 Ashburton treaty concluded in Washington 3: 38
1848 Free Soil national convention nominated Martin Van Buren for president 8:352
1849 Charles Nagel, secretary of commerce and labor under Taft, born D:266
1861 Arthur Dean Bevan, surgeon, born .... D: 90
1862 Battle of Culpepper Court House (or Cedar Mountain), Va. 4:223
1862 David Philipson, rabbi, born 13:339
1878 Norman H. Davis, diplomat, born A:314

AUGUST 10.

1519 Magellan sailed on his famous voyage of exploration 6:249
1622 New Hampshire granted to Sir Ferdinando Gorges 5:167
1753 Edmund Randolph, statesman, born 1: 12
1781 William Gibbons, scientist and author, born 13:181
1787 John McVickar, clergyman and professor of moral philosophy at Columbia for nearly fifty years, born 6:346
1790 George McDuffie, governor of South Carolina, born 12:167
1799 Samuel D. Hubbard, postmaster general under Fillmore, born 6:183
1799 Paul Dillingham, governor of Vermont, born ... 8:324
1799 Cyrus Buckland, inventor of fire-arms and machines for their manufacture, born 11:493
1806 Arunah S. Abell, journalist and founder of the Philadelphia "Public Ledger" and Baltimore "Sun," born 21: 8
1814 William L. Yancey, congressman, born 4:319
1814 John C. Pemberton, soldier in the Mexican and Civil wars, born 10:241
1815 William Henry Fry, composer, born 8:443
1820 Enoch L. Lowe, governor of Maryland, born ... 9:305
1821 Jay Cooke, financier, the "Robert Morris of the Civil War," born 1:253
1821 Missouri admitted to the Union 12:302
1826 Thomas J. Mayall, inventor of a cylinder press, fire-arms and a self-acting drawbridge, born 5:506
1830 Charles C. Van Zandt, governor of Rhode Island, born 9:405
1830 Thomas S. Lloyd, musician, and composer of church music, born 22:367
1834 Horace White, journalist and author, born 10:246
1843 Joseph McKenna, attorney-general under McKinley and justice of the U. S. supreme court, born 11: 18
1843 Charles Edgar Clark, naval officer, born 25:116
1845 Gertrude Bloede (Stuart Sterne), poet, born 10:379
1846 The Smithsonian Institution established 3:405
1847 Howard M. Hamill, Methodist clergyman, born .. 16: 35
1856 Francis X. Dercum, neurologist, born 22:143
1862 An extraordinary shower of shooting stars occurred 4:302
1862 William J. Hussey, astronomer, who specialized in the study of double stars, born 21: 95
1868 Paul Warburg, New York banker, born 26:151
1874 Herbert Hoover, thirty-first president of the United States, born .... C: 1
1881 Witter Bynner, author and poet, born A:175
1898 Battle of Hormigueros, Puerto Rico 9: 25
1917 U. S. food administration established .... C: 3

AUGUST 11.

1738 John Bayard, Maryland patriot, born 1: 71
1798 Ichabod Washburn, inventor and wire manufacturer, born 10:448
1807 Fulton's steamboat "Clermont" made her first trip up the Hudson river 3:105
1807 David R. Atchison, U. S. senator and president of the United States for one day, born 10:223
1814 Jeffries Wyman, scientist, born 2:254
1827 Jesse Seligman, banker and philanthropist, born 4:226
1827 Henry M. Knight, physician, born 15:234
1833 Robert G. Ingersoll, lawyer and orator, born 9:255
1836 George W. Armstrong, expressman, born 2:152
1836 Sarah M. B. Piatt, poet, born 8:260
1837 Archibald L. Snowden, diplomat, born 12:119
1839 Battle of Plum creek, Texas, with Indians 9: 66
1841 Burt Green Wilder, scientist, born 4:481
1841 Henry H. Gorringe, naval officer, born 6:439
1847 Benjamin R. Tillman, governor of South Carolina, and U. S. senator, born 12:180
1847 Abraham A. Anderson, artist, born C:358
1857 The first submarine cable broke 4:452
1860 Gari Melchers, artist, born B:120
1865 Gifford Pinchot, forester and governor of Pennsylvania, born 14: 80
1868 The "positive motion shuttle" patented by James Lyall 7:496

AUGUST 12.

1676 Death of King Philip, ending his war on the colonists 10: 51
1762 William Branch Giles, statesman, born 5: 447
1769 Benjamin F. Bache, printer and journalist, grandson of Benjamin Franklin, born 19: 28
1778 Gen. Charles Lee suspended from the army 8: 240
1781 Robert Mills, architect, designed the Washington and Bunker Hill monuments, born 18: 415
1798 Abraham Rencher, congressman and territorial governor of New Mexico, born 12: 337
1804 Alexander H. Holley, cutlery manufacturer and governor of Connecticut, born 10: 338
1812 Samuel S. Haldeman, scientist, born 9: 246
1812 Ephraim Ball, inventor of a stove, plow and mowing and reaping machine, born 11: 275
1815 Benjamin P. Cheney, pioneer expressman, born . 10: 218
1816 Charles C. Jewett, bibliographer, born 5: 356
1817 Duel between Charles Lucas and Thomas H. Benton 13: 322
1822 Frederic Robie, governor of Maine, born 6: 318
1826 Harris' hemp dressing machine patented 10: 300
1829 Alpha J. Kynett, clergyman, born 4: 346
1835 Lillie Devereux Blake, reformer and author, born 11: 61
1843 George P. Goodale, journalist, called the "dean of dramatic critics," born 18: 27
1844 Edward Lauterbach, New York lawyer, born ... 26: 227
1849 Abbott H. Thayer, artist, born 6: 471
1851 Second filibustering expedition from the United States landed in Cuba 4: 500
1851 Patents on a sewing machine issued to both Isaac M. Singer and Allen B. Wilson 9: 461
1854 Edith M. Thomas, poet, born 9: 456
1862 Julius Rosenwald, merchant and philanthropist, born 26: 110
1867 President Johnson removed Secretary of War Stanton from his cabinet 2: 85
1867 Ulysses S. Grant appointed sercetary of war *ad interim* 4: 8
1876 Mary Roberts Rinehart, novelist, born .... C: 486
1882 George W. Bellows, artist, born 20: 77
1898 Hawaiian islands formally annexed by the United States 11: 3
1898 Peace protocol signed ending hostilities between Spain and the United States 11: 4

AUGUST 13.

1730 Montgomerie charter for New York City granted 13: 453
1778 Duel between Robert Howe and Christopher Gadsden 6: 79
1779 Loss of the American fleet on the Penobscot river 7: 243
1805 Ashbel Smith, Texas statesman and soldier, born 10: 160
1805 Robert Rantoul, Jr., legislator, born 11: 232
1812 U. S. frigate "Essex" captured the brig "Alert" 2: 99
1818 Lucy Stone, reformer, born 2: 316
1821 Henry M. Dexter, clergyman and author, born .. 1: 177
1822 James M. Safford, geologist, born 8: 228
1823 John H. B. McClellan, surgeon, born 4: 140
1828 George William Bagby (Moses Adams), editor, author and lecturer, born 7: 542
1831 Henry L. Abbot, military engineer, who improved the defense against submarine mines, born .. 11: 194
1834 Philip Phillips, singing evangelist, born 7: 530
1846 Los Angeles, Calif., captured by the Americans 4: 205
1847 Arthur S. Hardy, mathematician, author and diplomat, born 2: 303
1849 Dwight William Tryon, artist, born 8: 423
1851 Felix Adler, founder of the Ethical Culture movement, born 23: 98
1852 Arthur S. Hickley, inventor of a telephone, fire-alarm and electric lamp, born 7: 118
1858 Arthur I. Jacobs, inventor and manufacturer of book-making machines, born 16: 41
1861 Morris Jastrow, philologist, born 11: 372
1861 Elmer Apperson, pioneer automobile builder, manufacturer of the Haynes-Apperson auto, born 24: 117
1863 Sidney J. Jennings, engineer, born 26: 326
1867 Emma Eames, opera singer, born 5: 404
1867 Lee K. Frankel, promoter of public health service, born 23: 208
1877 Charles Foster Kent, theologian, and professor of Biblical literature at Yale, born 24: 28
1883 Walter A. Strong, publisher of the Chicago "Daily News," born 24: 285
1898 Manila, Philippine islands, surrendered to the Americans 11: 4

AUGUST 14.

1734 Thomas Sumter, soldier, U. S. senator and diplomat, born 1: 79
1756 Fort Oswego captured by the French under Montcalm 1: 97
1773 Peter B. Porter, soldier and secretary of war under John Quincy Adams, born 5: 81
1779 Paul Jones in the "Bon Homme Richard" sailed from France on his second depredatory cruise around the British Isles 2: 16
1780 Patrick T. Jackson, pioneer cotton manufacturer, born 5: 401
1786 John Tipton, U. S. senator, born 11: 314
1807 Frederick Saunders, librarian and author, born 2: 379
1809 Park Benjamin, journalist, poet and lecturer, born 7: 166
1813 The British sloop "Pelican" captured the brig "Argus" 8: 15
1814 Josiah Swett, clergyman, and acting president of Norwich university, born 18: 325
1817 Arrival in Philadelphia of a party of Separatists from Germany 13: 147
1822 James Strong, Biblical scholar, born 13: 360
1841 Edwin F. Uhl, lawyer and diplomat, born 15: 100
1842 George K. Nash, lawyer and governor of Ohio, born 5: 337
1842 End of the Seminole war in Florida proclaimed 6: 4
1848 Oregon territory organized 8: 1
1859 James F. Kemp, geologist, born 21: 5
1860 Ernest Thompson Seton, artist and author, born C: 392
1861 Bion J. Arnold, electrical engineer, born .... B: 456
1872 Indian battle at Pryor Creek, Indian territory .. 4: 137
1889 Ex-judge Terry killed in California while attempting to assassinate Justice Field of the U. S. supreme court 1: 33
1891 G. Bromley Oxnam, president of De Pauw university, born .... A: 452
1935 Social Security Act approved .... D: 5

AUGUST 15.

1688 Joseph Sewall, clergyman, "The Weeping Prophet," born 2: 37
1730 Richard Morris, New York jurist, born 12: 508
1754 Benjamin Hawkins, soldier and U. S. senator, born 4: 59
1761 Edward Preble, naval officer, born 8: 92
1766 William Irving, New York merchant and author, eldest brother of Washington Irving, born 9: 383
1782 Charles Lowell, clergyman, born 11: 355
1790 John Carroll consecrated as first Roman Catholic bishop in the United States 1: 481
1791 Duff Green, diplomat, born 1: 233
1795 Aaron V. Brown, congressman, governor of Tennessee, and postmaster general under Buchanan, born 5: 8
1796 John Torrey, botanist, born 6: 361
1798 Charles H. Bell, naval officer, born 2: 104
1801 Samuel Wells, Maine jurist and governor, born .. 6: 312
1810 John B. Magruder, Confederate soldier, born 4: 294
1814 Fort Erie, Canada, attacked unsuccessfully 9: 372
1823 Orris S. Ferry, congressman and U. S. senator, born 2: 95
1824 Charles G. Leland (Hans Breitmann), author, born 5: 356
1826 Charles Lyman Strong, mining engineer and originator of the cyanide process of silver mining, born 17: 35
1835 Committee of fifteen appointed to consider the independence of Texas 9: 62
1838 Merritt Gally, inventor of the Universal press, a multiple telegraph system, an organ and a typesetter, born 4: 215
1838 Mary S. C. Logan, editor and author, born 4: 299
1844 William M. Polk, physician, born 2: 109
1852 Alfred Harding, P. E. bishop, born 15: 258
1855 Walter H. Page, editor and ambassador to the Court of St. James, born 19: 13
1860 Elgin R. L. Gould, social economist, born 23: 193
1861 Gen. Robert Anderson took command of the Department of the Cumberland 4: 179
1879 Ethel Barrymore, actress, born .... B: 496
1887 Edna Ferber, author, born .... C: 298
1900 Foreign legations at Pekin rescued by a relief expedition in the Boxer rebellion 11: 5
1914 Panama canal officially opened 24: 7

AUGUST 16.

Anniversary of the Battle of Bennington celebrated in Vermont

1647 Ship "Princess" sailed from New Amsterdam for Holland with Governor Kieft 6: 92
1705 Joseph Wanton, last colonial governor of Rhode Island, born 10: 15
1731 William Greene, Rhode Island statesman and governor, born 9: 392
1739 Elias Hasket Derby, Boston merchant, "Father of American Commerce with India," born 5: 32

1763 Henry W. de Saussure, South Carolina jurist, born 13:154
1771 Jonathan Roberts, U. S. senator, born 4:508
1777 Battle of Bennington, Vt. 1: 81
1780 Gen. Gates defeated at Camden, S. C. 1: 47
1784 Nathan Hale, journalist and author, born 11:107
1789 Amos Kendall, postmaster general under Jackson, born 5:296
1794 James Walker, president of Harvard college, born 6:419
1798 Mirabeau B. Lamar, soldier, statesman and president of Texas, born 9: 66
1811 George Jones, journalist, a founder of the New York "Times," born 21: 36
1812 Detroit, Mich., surrendered to the British 1: 67
1813 Sarah Porter, head of a famous school for girls in Connecticut, born 10:292
1823 Mathew Carey Lea, chemist, born 10:114
1829 Rowland Hazard, philanthropist, born 12:221
1831 Daniel Manning, secretary of the treasury under Cleveland, born 2:405
1831 Hiram Bingham, missionary to the Gilbert islands, born 14: 98
1836 John Peirce, scientist, inventor of the Peirce microscope cell, born 10:406
1841 President Tyler first vetoed the Fiscal Bank bill 6: 3
1848 William Jacob Holland, naturalist, born 13:141
1851 William L. Crittenden shot by Spanish authorities for filibustering in Cuba 4:500
1858 The first message sent by Atlantic cable from Queen Victoria to President Buchanan 4:452
1862 Amos A. Stagg, physical director, famous football coach, born 18: 99

AUGUST 17.

Discovery Day in Alaska

1721 The "New England Courant" first issued 8: 17
1728 Jonathan Sewall, colonial lawyer and loyalist during the Revolution, born 2: 59
1765 Treaty of peace made with the Indians at Detroit 10:416
1770 John T. Kirkland, president of Harvard college, born 6:417
1786 David Crockett, pioneer and soldier, who was executed after the surrender of the Texas Alamo, born 4: 85
1794 Robert P. Dunlap, Maine politician and governor, born 6:308
1807 Asahel Grant, missionary, born 4:457
1818 Sidney Edgerton, congressman and governor of Montana territory, born 11: 78
1828 George W. Warren, organist and composer, born 4:553
1834 John F. Hurst, M. E. bishop, born 9:122
1835 Peter Collier, scientist, organized what was probably the first farmers' institute, born 8:356
1838 Laura de Force Gordon, lawyer and journalist, born 2:235
1839 Michael A. Corrigan, archbishop of New York, born 1:196
1839 Thomas J. Morgan, soldier, educator and commissioner of Indian affairs, born 2: 54
1851 Frank O. Briggs, U. S. senator, born 14:305
1855 Oscar Fay Adams, author, born 19: 45
1858 Harry B. Thayer, president of the American Telephone & Telegraph Co., born 15:123
1861 Dorothea Klumpke, astronomer, born 13:377
1862 Outbreak of the Sioux Indians 10: 64
1863 Bombardment of Fort Sumter, S. C., begun 4: 55
1864 Edward W. Eberle, naval officer, born 21:328
1870 Julia Marlowe, actress, born 13:217
1871 Jesse Lynch Williams, author and playwright, born 21: 26
1872 Bessie Potter Vonnoh, sculptor, born 11:164
1896 Discovery of gold in the Klondike valley in Alaska 19:437

AUGUST 18.

1769 Alexander O'Reilly, governor of Louisiana, arrived in New Orleans 10: 73
1774 Meriweather Lewis, who with William Clark explored the Northwest, born 5:122
1780 Battle of Fishing Creek, S. C. 1: 79
1785 Seth Thomas, manufacturer, born 3:118
1788 Usher Parsons, physician, born 8:204
1803 Nathan Clifford, attorney-general under Polk and associate justice of the U. S. supreme court, born 2:473
1807 Charles Francis Adams, statesman, born 8:351
1808 Augustus J. Pleasonton, soldier, born 10:480
1812 John H. Means, governor of South Carolina, born 12:171
1819 Thomas W. Parsons, dentist and poet, born 5:359
1820 Pliny E. Chase, astronomer, born 6: 53
1824 Warren Colburn, civil engineer, born 11:457
1828 The Wilkes expedition left Norfolk, Va., to explore the South Pacific 2:105
1828 George D. Boardman, clergyman, born 12:479
1834 George C. Gardner, civil engineer, born 13:282
1835 Marshall Field, Chicago merchant, born 6:104
1844 Marshall D. Ewell, lawyer, physician and educator, born 12:375
1846 Santa Fé, N. Mex., taken by Gen. Kearney .. 13:141
1847 Robley D. Evans (Fighting Bob), naval officer, born 9: 13
1848 Mark W. Harrington, astronomer, born 10:448
1850 First appearance in America of Fred B. Conway, actor 7:265
1852 Morton F. Plant, financier and philanthropist, who assisted in founding Connecticut college for women, born 18:287
1854 James H. Hyslop, psychologist and educator, born 26: 54
1856 Frank W. Higgins, governor of New York, born 13:551
1859 George S. Fullerton, psychologist, born 12: 57
1862 Sioux massacre began in Minnesota 10: 63
1864 Gen. Warren seized the Weldon railroad and repulsed the first Confederate attack 4: 99

AUGUST 19.

1779 Paulus Hook, N. J., captured by "Light Horse Harry" Lee 3: 25
1782 Battle of Blue Lick, Ky. 2:437
1793 Samuel G. Goodrich (Peter Parley), author, born 5:355
1793 Elisha Mitchell, educator and geologist, for whom Mitchell's Peak, N. C., was named, born 7: 30
1793 James Hall, Illinois judge, editor and author, born 7:198
1800 James Lenox, New York philanthropist, founder of the Lenox library, born 3:413
1803 Henry J. Whitehouse, P. E. bishop, born 11:331
1812 Naval battle between the "Constitution" and the "Guerriere" 13:427
1814 British landed in Chesapeake bay for an advance on Washington, D. C. 5:371
1829 Edward Moran, artist, born 11:302
1831 William C. Langdon, clergyman who devoted his life to the cause of church unity, born 8: 76
1835 Richard P. Bland, congressman, born 10:160
1846 Walter Clark, North Carolina chief-justice and historian, born 8: 63
1847 John J. P. Odell, banker, born 13: 16
1855 Wilson G. Smith, pianist and composer, born 11:554
1856 Harold Frederic, journalist and author, born 5:358
1856 John Cotton Dana, librarian, born 22:321
1857 George Evan Roberts, financier, born 12:365
1859 Henry I. Cobb, Chicago architect, born 11:488
1865 Lillian Bell, author, born 14:393
1867 Mark Bailey, philologist, born 12:371
1870 Bernard M. Baruch, financier, head of the War Industries Board during the World war, born A: 57
1872 Hamilton Holt, editor and educator, who as president of Rollins college gave that institution a national reputation, born D:273
1893 Alfred Lunt, actor, born D:318

AUGUST 20.

1737 John Wentworth, last royal governor of New Hampshire, born 4:350
1745 Francis Asbury, pioneer M. E. bishop in America, born 6:293
1746 Ft. Massachusetts captured by the French and Indians 9:435
1764 Samuel L. Mitchill, scientist, born 4:409
1780 William Woodbridge, Michigan governor and U. S. senator, born 5:272
1785 Oliver H. Perry, naval officer, born 4:288
1785 Valentine Mott, New York surgeon, whose fame was world wide, born 6:281
1787 John M. Niles, U. S. senator and postmaster general under Van Buren, born 6:436
1792 Nathaniel S. Wheaton, clergyman, and president of Trinity college, born 3:495
1794 Battle with Indians at Fallen Timbers, Ohio .. 10: 60
1795 Robert F. Stockton, naval officer, active in securing California for the United States, born 4:205
1825 Paul A. Smith, Adirondack guide, born 18: 75
1832 Thaddeus S. C. Lowe, meteorologist, born 9:542
1833 Benjamin Harrison, 23d president of the United States, born 1:133
1846 William R. Mead, New York architect of the firm of McKim, Mead & White, born 23: 91
1847 Battles of Churubusco and Contreras, Mexico 11:390
1852 Paul Dana, journalist, editor of the New York "Sun," born 8:258
1853 Edward C. Butler, diplomat and author, born .. 8:476
1857 Andrew D. Hopkins, entomologist, born 13:185
1860 Herbert Myrick, editor and publisher of "Farm and Home," "Good Housekeeping," and the "Orange Judd Farmer," and a leader in the promotion of scientific agriculture, born 25:128

1862 Gen. Stuart raided the Federal camp at Catlett Station, Va. 4: 52
1881 Frank W. Peek, electrical engineer, specialist in high voltage engineering, born 24: 289
1898 Naval review in New York harbor on return of the fleet from the Spanish American war .. 9: 13

AUGUST 21.

1757 Josiah Meigs, president of the University of Georgia, born 9: 178
1784 Enos T. Throop, New York governor, born ... 3: 46
1808 William D. Gallagher, poet and journalist, born 9: 250
1810 Justin Loomis, educator, born 12: 300
1811 William Kelly, inventor of the air-boiling process in steel manufacture, antedating Bessemer's process, born 13: 196
1821 Calvert B. Cottrell, inventor and manufacturer of printing presses, born 3: 397
1821 Richard S. Storrs, clergyman, born 8: 110
1822 John Fritz, mechanical engineer, born 13: 74
1831 The Nat Turner insurrection of slaves in Virginia began 5: 448
1832 Daniel Seelye Gregory, who as president of Lake Forest university established the standards of collegiate education in the West, born 19: 251
1843 William Pepper, physician and provost of the University of Pennsylvania, born 1: 345
1845 William H. Dall, naturalist, born 10: 454
1854 Frank A. Munsey, editor and publisher, born .. 20: 47
1862 Edward N. Dingley, political economist, born .. 21: 167
1864 Federals surprised at Memphis, Tenn., by Gen. Forrest 10: 37
1875 John Francis O'Ryan, lawyer and soldier, who commanded the 27th, the famous "Rainbow," division in the World war, born .... A: 61

AUGUST 22.

1744 Richard Peters, patriot and judge, born 12: 235
1778 James K. Paulding, author, born 7: 193
1779 The Six Nations punished for the Wyoming and Cherry Valley massacres 1: 56
1787 Trial trip of John Fitch's steamboat on the Delaware river 6: 64
1790 Joseph Delafield, scientist, born 11: 28
1798 William G. Schauffler, missionary, born 18: 280
1802 John I. Blair, financier, born 7: 21
1802 Gurdon S. Hubbard, pioneer and fur trader, born 25: 300
1809 Albert Brisbane, social reformer, born 4: 560
1809 George W. Kendall, journalist, born 12: 289
1817 Emily C. Judson (Fanny Forrester), author, born 3: 93
1817 John B. Gough, temperance lecturer, born 3: 336
1824 Daniel R. Anthony, Kansas pioneer, born 6: 365
1841 Willard Glazier, soldier and explorer of the source of the Mississippi river, born 5: 284
1841 Frank Baker, anatomist, educator and author, born 19: 260
1844 George W. DeLong, Arctic explorer, born 3: 282
1845 William L. Douglas, Massachusetts governor and shoe manufacturer, born 25: 216
1848 Melville E. Stone, journalist, born 21: 24
1851 The yacht "America" won the "Cup of All Nations" at the international regatta, Cowes, England 1: 447
1854 Charles Fillmore, founder of "Unity" and the Unity school, born .... B: 58
1864 The Treaty of Geneva for the relief of sick and wounded soldiers signed by twelve governments 15: 315
1867 Fisk university, Tenn., chartered 1: 310
1867 Charles Francis Jenkins, inventor, born .... B: 246
1868 Maud Powell, violinist, born 13: 120
1868 Willis R. Whitney, chemist, born 15: 393
1875 Henry Suzzalo, president of the University of Washington, born 24: 39

AUGUST 23.

1761 Jedidiah Morse, clergyman, "Father of American Geography," born 13: 353
1781 John M. Berrien, U. S. senator and attorney-general under Jackson, born 5: 298
1784 State of Franklin, afterwards Tennessee, formed 3: 430
1788 Joseph G. Totten, military engineer, born 4: 164
1811 George F. Emmons, naval officer, born 4: 182
1813 Jones Very, poet, born 6: 276
1814 James R. Bayley, R. C. archbishop, born 1: 487
1820 Rufus Ingalls, soldier, born 12: 240
1825 Henry L. Pierce, manufacturer of Baker's chocolate, born 4: 308
1826 Francis Wayland, lawyer, educator and penologist, born 12: 221
1829 Israel J. Merritt, of Merritt's Wrecking Organization, born 5: 131
1830 Oscar C. Fox, inventor, born 1: 310
1830 David Swing, clergyman, born 3: 16
1833 Theodore Lyman, zoölogist, born 24: 347
1835 Thomas Robinson, artist, born 5: 316
1836 Charles Henry Hitchcock, geologist, born 12: 342
1839 George C. Perkins, California shipping merchant and governor, born 4: 111
1840 Charles F. Hartt, geologist, born 11: 260
1855 Barrett Wendell, educator and author, born ... 9: 207
1863 Amélie Rives Troubetzkoy, author, born .... B: 293
1864 Fort Morgan, Ala., surrendered to the Federals 4: 559
1869 Edgar Lee Masters, poet, born .... A: 387
1884 Ogden L. Mills, secretary of the treasury under Coolidge, born .... D: 77

AUGUST 24.

1694 Elisha Williams, president of Yale and judge, born 1: 65
1747 John Dickins, clergyman and founder of the Methodist Book Concern, born 3: 507
1784 Joseph E. Worcester, lexicographer, born 6: 50
1795 James W. Wallack, actor, born 4: 439
1810 Theodore Parker, clergyman, pioneer in liberal religious thought, born 2: 377
1814 Washington, D. C., attacked by the British and the Capitol burned 5: 370
1814 Gen. Winder defeated at Bladensburg, Md. 10: 487
1819 Henry Stevens, bibliographer, born 11: 318
1823 John Newton, soldier and civil engineer, born .. 4: 312
1834 Samuel Pierpont Langley, scientist and secretary of the Smithsonian Institution, born 15: 7
1839 William Walter Phelps, congressman and diplomat, born 7: 451
1842 John C. Watson, naval officer, born 9: 7
1846 Henry Gannett, geographer, born 19: 207
1847 Charles F. McKim, architect, of the famous firm of McKim, Mead & White; a leading spirit in founding the American Academy at Rome, born 23: 89
1848 Kate Claxton, actress, famous in "The Two Orphans," born 22: 189
1851 William C. Loring, jurist, born 22: 283
1867 Johns Hopkins university incorporated 5: 170
1897 Patent issued to Ira G. Blake for a time lock system 13: 306

AUGUST 25.

1588 Elizabeth Pole, a founder of Taunton, Mass., born 4: 549
1662 John Leverett, president of Harvard, born 6: 413
1664 The British fleet arrived at Gravesend and demanded the surrender of New Amsterdam 13: 447
1718 French immigrants arrived in Louisiana and founded New Orleans 5: 491
1774 First independent assembly in North Carolina held 13: 439
1783 Samuel Chester Reid, naval officer, born 8: 97
1793 John Neal, editor and author, born 11: 346
1796 James Lick, philanthropist, born 3: 350
1800 Andrew J. Donelson, lawyer and diplomat, born 7: 489
1818 Frederick A. Muhlenberg, educator, born 5: 499
1819 Allan Pinkerton, detective, born 3: 208
1822 Gardiner Greene Hubbard, lawyer, born 5: 162
1825 Samuel R. Franklin, naval officer, born 4: 391
1835 "Moon Hoax" published in the New York "Sun" 13: 152
1836 Bushrod W. James, physician, a specialist in ophthalmology, born 3: 492
1839 Bret Harte, author, born 1: 404
1842 Edward Tuck, financier and philanthropist, who founded Tuck school of finance at Dartmouth, born 16: 38
1850 Edgar Wilson Nye (Bill Nye), humorist, born 6: 25
1851 George P. Lathrop, author, born 9: 193
1851 Henry J. Ford, editor, publicist and historian, born 21: 14
1852 Henry R. Carter, sanitarian and epidemiologist, born 25: 346
1857 Fenton B. Turck, pathologist and biologist, author of the theory of the physical character of shock, born 25: 175
1862 Confederates captured supplies at Manassas Junction 4: 128
1862 William C. Procter, soap manufacturer and philanthropist, born 25: 384
1864 Engagement at Ream's Station, Va. 7: 145
1889 Waldo Frank, author, born .... A: 398
1921 Treaty ending the technical state of war with Germany signed .... A: 7

AUGUST 26.

1791 The first patents for steamboats issued simultaneously to Fitch, Read, Rumsey and Stevens 4:558
1804 Thomas S. Cummings, artist, born 6:246
1808 Benjamin G. Humphreys, governor of Mississippi, born 13:492
1813 James L. Cabell, physician, born 12:452
1814 Joshua C. Stoddard, inventor of a steam calliope, horse rake and hay tedder, born 7:530
1818 Illinois adopted a constitution 11: 43
1820 James Harlan, U. S. senator and secretary of the interior under Johnson, born 2:457
1821 Stephen P. Nash, New York lawyer, born 11:470
1822 James W. King, engineer, born 13:186
1826 Emily E. Ford, author, born 13:105
1827 Annie Turner Wittenmyer, philanthropist, born 12:363
1831 T. Jefferson Coolidge, merchant, financier and diplomat, born 12: 58
1833 Charles J. Paine, soldier and yachtsman, born 1:448
1839 William W. Thomas, American minister to Sweden, born 2:132
1840 John W. Philip, naval officer, born 9: 13
1844 John William Burgess, historian, preëminent as a teacher of history and political science, born 23: 39
1861 The Hatteras expedition sailed from Fortress Monroe 1:122
1868 Frank Russell, anthropologist, born 12:457
1872 Joseph T. Robinson, U. S. senator and governor of Arkansas, born B:193
1873 Lee de Forest, inventor, improved wireless telegraphy, born 17: 11
1874 Zona Gale, author, born B:301
1920 The 19th amendment, granting suffrage to women, became effective 20:111

AUGUST 27.

1741 Joseph Reed, patriot and soldier, born 1: 74
1749 James Madison, first P. E. bishop of Virginia, and president of William and Mary college, born 7:216
1776 Battle of Long Island, N. Y. 1: 3
1782 Skirmish on the Combahee River, S. C., last battle of the Revolution 1: 68
1790 Gridley Bryant, engineer, inventor of the portable derrick, born 11:502
1793 Jasper Adams, president of Hobart college, born 12:520
1796 Sophia Smith, founder of Smith college, born 7:121
1800 William S. Harney, soldier, born 5:288
1809 Hannibal Hamlin, statesman and vice-president of the United States, born 2: 76
1822 William H. English, congressman, born 9:376
1825 John H. Starin, New York merchant, born 2: 19
1830 Charles H. Perkins, inventor and manufacturer, born 2:271
1839 Emory Upton, soldier, born 4:276
1840 Ralph L. Goodrich, lawyer and philologist, born 7:363
1841 Patrick W. Riordan, R. C. archbishop, born 15:248
1843 The steam frigate "Missouri" burned at Gibraltar 4:151
1845 Anti-rent insurrection in Delaware county, N.Y. 3: 47
1846 Bernard Moses, political scientist and diplomat, born 26:120
1859 Oil came in at Titusville, Pa., from the first well drilled in the United States 26:458
1862 Battle of Kettle Run, Warren's Junction, Va. 4:176
1865 Charles G. Dawes, banker and vice-president of the United States, born A:508
1865 James H. Breasted, Egyptologist, born B:377
1871 Theodore Dreiser, author, born C: 93
1928 The Kellogg-Briand treaty renouncing war signed by fifteen nations in Paris A: 10

AUGUST 28.

St. Augustine's Day

1565 Menendez arrived at St. Augustine, Fla. 11:164
1609 Henry Hudson entered Delaware bay 9:454
1728 John Stark, soldier, born 1: 80
1749 Francois L. T. de Fleury, soldier, born 13: 57
1774 Elizabeth A. Seton, founder of the Sisters of Charity, born 2:436
1778 James L. Kingsley, educator, born 10:121
1781 Timothy Alden, clergyman and president of Allegheny college, born 13:291
1788 Nathaniel Hewit, clergyman and temperance reformer, born 11:357
1823 James Oliver, inventor and manufacturer, born 12:522
1823 Charles C. Parry, botanist, born 13:228
1828 William A. Hammond, surgeon-general of the U. S. army, and neurologist, born 26:468
1829 Patrick A. Feehan, R. C. archbishop of Chicago, born 9: 80
1840 Ira D. Sankey, evangelist and author, born 7:244
1841 John F. Weir, artist, born 6:429
1842 Placide L. Chapelle, R. C. archbishop, born 7:554
1843 Edward L. Keyes, New York surgeon, born 9:343
1844 Henry R. Towne, engineer, head of the Yale & Towne Manufacturing Co., makers of locks, born 21:384
1847 Bellamy Storer, lawyer and diplomat, born 11:338
1848 Francis G. Newlands, U. S. senator, born 13:219
1851 Frank H. Bigelow, meteorologist, born 10:410
1862 Battle of Warrenton Turnpike, Va. 4: 97
1871 Ralph D. Paine, author and sportsman, born 25:408

AUGUST 29.

1778 Battle of Portsmouth, R. I. 8: 51
1779 Battle with Tories and Indians at Tioga, N. Y. 1: 56
1780 Richard Rush, secretary of the treasury under John Quincy Adams, born 5: 80
1792 Charles G. Finney, clergyman and president of Oberlin college, born 2:462
1805 William G. Brownlow, clergyman and governor of Tennessee, born 7:210
1809 Oliver Wendell Holmes, physician, author and poet, born 2:336
1809 Francis Vinton, soldier and clergyman, born 7:537
1815 Anna Ella Carroll, strategist, born 5:193
1819 Joseph E. McDonald (Old Saddle Bags), U. S. senator, born 11:504
1824 Eliza Allen Starr, artist and author, born 13:564
1826 George F. Hoar, U. S. senator, born 1:453
1829 Abby Hutchinson, of the famous Hutchinson family of singers, born 10: 27
1829 Benjamin F. Reinhart, artist, born 11:310
1830 J. Proctor Knott, legislator and governor of Kentucky, born 13: 11
1831 Duel between Thomas Biddle and Spencer Pettis 7:533
1835 George W. McCrary, U. S. senator and secretary of war under Hayes, born 3:201
1843 David B. Hill, New York governor and U. S. senator, born 1:453
1845 Carlos F. MacDonald, psychiatrist, born 20: 7
1846 Luke E. Wright, governor-general of the Philippines and secretary of war under Theodore Roosevelt, born 14: 20
1861 Federal forces captured Forts Hatteras and Clark, N. C. 2:102
1862 Battle of Groveton, Manassas, or Second Bull Run 4:142
1863 Army of the Cumberland began to pursue Gen. Bragg across the Tennessee 3:218
1871 The "Polaris" reached the farthest point north 3:282
1876 Albert Cabell Ritchie, governor of Maryland, born A: 75
1876 Charles Franklin Kettering, manufacturer and inventor, born B:260
1881 Byron Patton Harrison, U. S. senator, born A:174

AUGUST 30.

1734 Ezra L'Hommedieu, legislator, born 12:417
1752 Jonathan Mason, U. S. senator, born 2: 7
1768 Joseph Dennie, journalist, born 7:204
1776 Long Island evacuated by the Americans 1: 3
1784 Robert Walsh, journalist and litterateur, born 5:357
1794 Stephen W. Kearny, soldier, who took possession of New Mexico and California for the United States, born 13:140
1797 Charles Danforth, inventor, born 13:208
1812 Samuel Osgood, clergyman and author, born 9:236
1813 Massacre at Fort Mimms, Ala., by Creek Indians 5:291
1817 John Williams, P. E. bishop and president of Trinity college, Hartford, born 3:496
1818 Alexander H. Rice, governor of Massachusetts, born 1:120
1820 George F. Root, composer, born 9:384
1830 Philip G. Hubert, New York architect, specializing in apartment houses, born 15:361
1840 Hazen S. Pingree, governor of Michigan, born 7:119
1841 George W. Brown, industrialist, born 15:198
1845 Edwin A. Grosvenor, author, born 10:493
1846 Rudolph A. Witthaus, toxicologist, born 11: 60
1851 William C. Brownell, author and literary critic, born 22: 6
1852 Julian Alden Weir, artist, a founder of the "Ten American Painters," born 22:296
1861 Charles S. Hamlin, financier, born 15:265
1886 Mayo D. Hersey, physicist, born A:175
1893 Huey P. Long, governor of Louisiana and U. S. senator, born D:409
1924 The Allies and Germany signed an agreement to accept the Dawes reparation plan A:510

AUGUST 31.

1739 George Mathews, Georgia soldier, congressman and governor, born 1: 219
1744 John Houston, governor of Georgia, born 1: 493
1769 David Hosack, physician and scientist, born .. 9: 354
1792 Wilbur Fisk, clergyman and president of Wesleyan university, born 3: 177
1798 Ebenezer Thresher, clergyman and manufacturer, born 12: 464
1801 Pierre Soule, U. S. senator and minister to Spain, born 3: 117
1807 The Theological seminary at Andover organized 10: 99
1810 Jacob Brinkerhoff, congressman and chief justice of Ohio, born 13: 152
1820 Edward Creighton, pioneer telegraph builder and banker, born 22: 169
1822 Fitz-John Porter, Federal soldier, born 4: 261
1823 Galusha A. Grow, congressman, born 2: 91
1828 George L. Andrews, Federal soldier, born 16: 419
1834 Anson Mills, soldier and inventor, born 10: 453
1841 Edward G. Janeway, physician and pathologist, born 13: 499
1842 Mary Putnam Jacobi, physician and author, born 8: 219
1844 Elizabeth Stuart Phelps, author, born 9: 368
1852 Nathan Haskell Dole, author, born 13: 554
1853 William E. Meehan, pisciculturist, born 16: 355
1861 Gen. Fremont issued an order freeing slaves in Missouri 4: 271
1864 Battle of Jonesboro, Ga. 4: 34
1874 Edward L. Thorndike, psychologist, born 15: 205
1886 Severe earthquake occurred at Charleston, S. C. 12: 441
1925 Commander Rodgers started on the first flight to the Hawaiian islands 20: 426

SEPTEMBER 1.

First Monday in September Celebrated as Labor Day

1675 Deerfield, Mass., burned by Indians 10: 50
1675 Hadley, Mass., attacked by Indians 11: 459
1730 John Cochran, surgeon in the Revolutionary army, born 8: 410
1785 Peter Cartwright, clergyman, born 6: 61
1785 Philip Allen, manufacturer, and governor of Rhode Island, born 9: 399
1791 Lydia H. Sigourney, author, born 1: 154
1798 Richard Delafield, soldier and engineer, born ... 11: 29
1799 John A. Quitman, soldier and governor of Mississippi, born 13: 489
1804 Zerah Colburn, mathematical prodigy, who, from the age of six, had extraordinary powers of computation, born 7: 74
1806 Stephen Alexander, astronomer, born 11: 422
1807 William W. Hoppin, governor of Rhode Island, born 9: 400
1812 James Campbell, postmaster general under Pierce, born 4: 152
1813 Mark Hopkins, California pioneer, born 20: 49
1814 Naval Engagement between the "Wasp" and "Avon" 5: 440
1826 Alfred Ely Beach, editor and inventor of an improved typewriter, born 8: 122
1827 The New York "Journal of Commerce" first issued 2: 320
1843 William Ziegler, manufacturer of baking powder, who sponsored an expedition to discover the North Pole, born 16: 44
1849 Elizabeth Harrison, a pioneer kindergarten educator, born 21: 135
1854 Whitman Cross, geologist, born 15: 214
1854 Anna B. Comstock, naturalist and wood-engraver, born 22: 11
1857 Maine state seminary opened 8: 394
1861 Gen. Ulysses S. Grant took command of the district of southeastern Missouri 4: 2
1862 Battle of Chantilly, Va. 4: 261
1869 National Prohibition party organized at a convention in Chicago 19: 217
1872 First training school for nurses in America opened at the New England hospital for women and children 19: 30
1877 Rex Beach, author and playwright, born 14: 58
1877 Raynal C. Bolling, lawyer and soldier, organizer of the aviation service of the A.E.F. in the World war, born 19: 242
1885 First electric street railway in the United States opened in Baltimore 3: 179
1885 Stanley patented his electrical transformer, which made possible the alternating current system of long distance light and power 24: 394
1907 First night court in the world opened in New York city 15: 208
1916 The Keating-Owen bill, for the limitation of child labor, became a law 19: 6
1932 James J. Walker resigned as mayor of New York city ..... D: 2

SEPTEMBER 2.

1609 Henry Hudson entered New York bay 9: 454
1615 Richard Waldron, colonial governor of New Hampshire, born 13: 434
1768 Jonathan Maxcy, president of Brown university born 8: 21
1779 Joseph Parrish, physician, born 12: 486
1781 John B. White, artist, born 3: 21
1798 Thomas H. Hicks, governor of Maryland, and U. S. senator, born 9: 306
1800 Willard Parker, surgeon, born 9: 337
1807 Jacob H. Vanderbilt, transportation executive, born 6: 211
1808 William Mason, inventor and manufacturer, born 10: 386
1820 Lucretia Peabody Hale, author, born 5: 353
1821 Anne Whitney, sculptor, born 7: 72
1829 Murat Halstead, journalist, born 1: 270
1831 William P. Frye, U. S. senator, born 1: 290
1834 Sumner I. Kimball, first superintendent of the United States life-saving service, born 2: 348
1837 James H. Wilson, soldier, engineer and author, born 2: 205
1838 Frederick Douglass escaped from slavery 2: 309
1839 Henry George, political economist, born 4: 325
1843 Allan D. Brown, naval officer and president of Norwich university, born 18: 327
1850 Eugene Field, journalist and poet, born 1: 158
1850 Albert G. Spalding, sportsman, merchant, born .. 3: 394
1855 Hoke Smith, Georgia governor and statesman, born 1: 183
1856 Jeremiah W. Jenks, economist, born ..... B: 140
1858 Frederick Starr, anthropologist, born 13: 115
1858 Newell D. Hillis, clergyman, born 21: 280
1860 Frank H. Knowlton, paleontologist and botanist, born 10: 410
1861 Caspar Whitney, sportsman and author, active in the development of amateur sports, born 25: 284
1864 Atlanta, Ga., occupied by the Federals 4: 34

SEPTEMBER 3.

1757 John Hendy, pioneer and soldier, born 12: 236
1763 Detroit, Mich., relieved from siege by Indians ... 10: 415
1783 Definitive Treaty of peace with Great Britain signed at Paris 1: 336
1789 Hannah F. Gould, poet, born 8: 269
1793 John Scudder, missionary to India, born 2: 62
1795 Francis H. Blanchet, missionary and first archbishop of Oregon, born 13: 32
1803 Prudence Crandall, abolitionist, pioneer teacher of Negro women, born 2: 307
1807 Gorham D. Abbot, clergyman and a founder of a famous school for girls in New York city, born 10: 355
1810 Gardner Colby, philanthropist, for whom Colby college was named, born 8: 404
1811 John H. Noyes, founder of the Oneida community, born 11: 238
814 John Armstrong, secretary of war under Madison, resigned from the cabinet 1: 48
1814 The "Adams" driven into Penobscot river and scuttled to avoid capture by British 9: 119
1818 Williams Rutherford, educator and author, born 9: 183
1820 George F. Hearst, U. S. senator, born 1: 315
1827 John Drew, Sr., actor, born 3: 531
1827 John E. W. Keely, inventor, born 9: 137
1833 Joseph Simms, physician and physiognomist, born 7: 124
1833 John S. Clarke, actor and theatrical manager, born 7: 475
1833 The New York "Sun" first issued 13: 307
1835 Stewart L. Woodford, Federal soldier and diplomat, born 9: 2
1839 George L. Raymond, educator and author, born .. 8: 457
1849 Sarah Orne Jewett (Alice Eliot), author, born .. 1: 374
1855 Battle with Sioux Indians at Sand Hills 5: 288
1860 Edward A. Filene, Boston merchant, born ..... A: 319
1864 Jonathan D. Maxwell, pioneer automobile manufacturer, born 25: 28
1872 National convention of Radical Democrats nominated Charles O'Conor for president 3: 387
1872 Ernest R. Buckley, geologist, born 19: 443
1883 Harold DeF. Arnold, physicist, who perfected vacuum tubes making possible the transmission of a trans-Atlantic speech by radio, born 25: 184
1901 First stake driven for the Louisiana purchase exposition in St. Louis 12: 10
1925 Fatal crash of the U. S. airship "Shenandoah" .. 25: 404

SEPTEMBER 4.

1580 George Percy, colonial governor of Virginia, born 13: 379
1757 Levin Winder, governor of Maryland, born 9: 298
1789 Alexander H. Stevens, surgeon, born 9: 355
1792 Seba Smith (Jack Downing), editor and author, born 8: 118

1793	Edward Bates, lawyer, congressman and attorney-general under Lincoln, born	2: 89
1796	Charles T. C. Follen, educator, born	7: 289
1799	William B. Kinney, journalist, born	13: 156
1802	Marcus Whitman, pioneer missionary to Oregon, born	11: 112
1804	The "Intrepid" blown up in Tripoli harbor	8: 413
1804	Thomas U. Walter, architect, born	9: 333
1805	William E. Dodge, New York merchant, congressman and philanthropist, born	3: 174
1815	Lyman C. Draper, historian, born	9: 390
1824	Phoebe Cary, poet, born	1: 535
1826	Willard Warner, Federal soldier and U. S. senator, born	10: 396
1826	George P. Quackenbos, educator and author of textbooks, born	13: 301
1828	John H. Rauch, physician, born	12: 452
1838	David Hastings Moore, M. E. bishop, born	19: 20
1842	Thomas W. Goodspeed, clergyman, instrumental in founding the new University of Chicago, born	22: 269
1846	Daniel H. Burnham, chief architect of the Columbia exposition at Chicago, born	9: 335
1848	Richard R. Bowker, publisher and political economist, born	24: 66
1855	William Montgomery Brown, P. E. bishop, born	C: 485
1859	David Du Bose Gaillard, military engineer, born	15: 318
1862	Confederate forces under Gen. Lee invaded Maryland	4: 97
1862	The Confederate "Oreto" ran the blockade of Mobile	8: 95
1864	Battle of Greenville, Tenn., at which Morgan, the Confederate raider, was killed	4: 317
1866	Simon Lake, submarine inventor, born	15: 5
1882	First central station for electric lighting in the United States opened by the New York Edison Co.	15: 218
1886	Apache Indians, under Geronimo, surrendered to Gen. Nelson A. Miles at Ft. Bowie	23: 351
1918	Franco-American troops crossed the Vesle river	A: 294

SEPTEMBER 5.

1749	Thomas Lee became governor of Virginia	13: 389
1758	Thomas Eddy, reformer, born	3: 512
1763	Indian battle of Bloody Bridge, Mich.	10: 415
1774	First Continental congress, with 56 delegates representing 11 colonies, met in Philadelphia	2: 115
1795	Treaty, buying off the pirates with annual tribute, signed with Algiers	1: 71
1802	Duel between Governor Spaight of North Carolina and John Stanly	4: 421
1804	William Alexander Graham, U. S. senator, governor of North Carolina and secretary of the navy under Fillmore, born	4: 426
1809	Hannah O'Brien Conant, author and translator, born	22: 93
1810	The American Board of Commissioners for Foreign Missions formed	10: 246
1812	Ft. Hamilton, Ind., attacked by Indians	4: 367
1813	Naval battle in which the "Enterprise" captured the British "Boxer"	7: 72
1817	William A. Newell, congressman and governor of New Jersey, born	5: 208
1825	Darius O. Mills, California financier and philanthropist, born	18: 133
1826	Thomas Sterry Hunt, scientist specializing in chemistry and mineralogy, born	3: 254
1830	George H. Doane, clergyman, born	8: 88
1832	Henry Van Brunt, architect, born	11: 324
1835	John G. Carlisle, speaker of the house and U. S. senator, born	1: 461
1836	Edward H. House, author and journalist, born	13: 458
1848	George W. Guthrie, Pittsburgh reformer and American ambassador to Japan, born	18: 19
1852	Stockton Borton, early inventor of sewing machines, born	18: 339
1862	Confederates under Gen. Bragg invaded Kentucky	11: 218
1867	Amy Marcy Cheney Beach, pianist and composer, born	C: 526
1879	Frank Baldwin Jewett, electrical engineer, born	C: 272
1905	Through the offices of President Theodore Roosevelt, the Russo-Japanese war was concluded by a treaty signed at Portsmouth, N. H.	14: 7

SEPTEMBER 6.

Lafayette Day

1620	The "Mayflower" sailed from England for America	7: 367
1711	Henry M. Muhlenberg, clergyman, organizer of the Lutheran churches in America, born	5: 499
1738	Moses Brown, Rhode Island merchant, a benefactor of Brown university, born	2: 327
1757	Marquis de Lafayette, French champion of the cause of the American revolution, born	1: 63
1781	New London plundered and burned by Benedict Arnold	1: 54
1781	Ft. Griswold, Conn., captured by the British	5: 175
1795	Fanny Wright, reformer, born	2: 319
1804	Rhode Island college became Brown university	8: 22
1805	Horatio Greenough, sculptor, born	6: 232
1806	James Henry Coffin, meteorologist, born	8: 12
1811	James M. Gilliss, astronomer, born	9: 230
1812	Samuel D. Burchard, clergyman, who coined the slogan "Rum, Romanism and Rebellion," born	11: 473
1813	John Cassin, ornithologist, born	22: 240
1819	William S. Rosecrans, Federal soldier, born	4: 162
1821	Alvin P. Hovey, Federal soldier and governor of Indiana, born	13: 274
1824	William T. Coggeshall, journalist and author, born	12: 57
1830	William E. Armitage, P. E. bishop, born	11: 58
1836	Myron W. Whitney, singer, born	2: 143
1840	John C. De La Vergne, inventor of refrigeration machinery, born	2: 210
1840	William H. H. Miller, attorney-general under Harrison, born	18: 189
1857	William Eustis Russell, governor of Massachusetts, born	1: 125
1857	John B. Kendrick, governor of Wyoming, and U. S. senator, born	25: 108
1859	Irving Bacheller, author, born	C: 411
1860	Jane Addams, sociologist, born	C: 83
1861	Gen. Grant took possession of Paducah, Ky.	4: 3
1869	James K. Hackett, actor, born	23: 86
1873	Howard E. Coffin, engineer and designer of automobiles, born	16: 53
1881	President Garfield removed to Elberon, N. J., in hope of saving his life. Day observed by fasting and prayer	4: 242
1901	President McKinley shot while attending the Pan-American exposition	11: 8

SEPTEMBER 7.

1630	Boston, Mass., settled	12: 334
1727	William Smith, historian and first provost of the College of Philadelphia, born	1: 340
1782	Clark Bissell, jurist and governor of Connecticut, born	10: 336
1795	James G. Carter, educator, first to develop the normal school idea, born	10: 507
1803	Silas C. Herring, inventor of fire-proof safes, born	9: 238
1811	"Niles Register," Baltimore weekly newspaper, first issued	10: 255
1815	Howell Cobb, governor of Georgia, secretary of the treasury under Buchanan, and president of the Confederate congress, born	1: 226
1818	Thomas Talbot, manufacturer and governor of Massachusetts, born	1: 121
1819	Thomas A. Hendricks, vice-president of the United States, born	2: 403
1820	Nathaniel Wheeler, manufacturer of sewing machines, born	9: 460
1823	Joseph S. Hubbard, noted astronomer, born	9: 238
1824	McFadden A. Newell, educator, born	12: 512
1829	Ferdinand V. Hayden, geologist, born	11: 97
1838	William H. Forwood, surgeon general, U.S. army, born	15: 148
1839	Melville D. Landon (Eli Perkins), humorist, born	6: 27
1840	Luther C. Crowell, inventor of bag printing machinery and newspaper folders, born	13: 604
1846	Paul F. Mundé, physician, born	12: 272
1848	Edmund M. Holland, actor, born	11: 438
1849	Jacob G. Schmidlapp, Cincinnati philanthropist, who established funds to educate working girls and to build model homes for negroes, born	19: 315
1858	Charles R. Barnes, botanist, born	13: 118
1863	Ft. Wagner, S. C., evacuated by the Confederates after a long siege	4: 55
1867	J. Pierpont Morgan, Jr., financier, born	C: 418
1868	Edwin B. Parker, jurist, prominent in World war activities, born	21: 12
1875	Henry Kitchell Webster, author of stories dealing with industry and modern business, born	A: 386
1885	Elinor Wylie, poet and author, born	21: 14
1916	U.S. employees' compensation commission created	19: 6

SEPTEMBER 8.

1565	St. Augustine, Fla., founded	11: 164
1685	Thomas Fleet, colonial printer, born	20: 481
1727	Naphtali Daggett, president of Yale, born	1: 166
1738	Dudley Saltonstall, naval officer, born	7: 243
1755	Battle of Lake George, N. Y., in which the French were defeated	5: 103
1760	Montreal surrendered and all Canada passed into the hands of the British	1: 101
1780	George M. Troup, U. S. senator and governor of Georgia, born	1: 223

1780 William A. Duer, judge and president of Columbia college, born ... 6:344
1781 The British defeated in the battle of Eutaw Springs, S. C. ... 1: 43
1790 Canvass White, civil engineer, born ... 12:258
1794 Joshua Leavitt, reformer, born ... 2:528
1799 Henry Placide, actor, born ... 8: 57
1811 Francis Bowen, editor, author and educator, born 11:452
1815 Alexander Ramsey, governor of Minnesota, born 10: 62
1816 Severn T. Wallis, Maryland lawyer and author, born ... 9:136
1826 Addison P. Russell, editor and author, born ... 6: 19
1828 George Crook, famous Indian fighter, born ... 4: 70
1828 Clarence C. Cook, art critic, born ... 10:167
1828 Margaret O. Sage, philanthropist, born ... 16:422
1830 Oscar M. Lieber, geologist, born ... 13:170
1836 Arthur W. Wright, physicist and inventor, born 13:348
1837 Raphael Pumpelly, geologist and author, born .. 6:359
1838 Robert C. Clowry, president of the Western Union Telegraph Co., born ... 13:119
1847 Battle of Molino Del Rey, Mexico ... 4: 1
1847 William Barbour, thread manufacturer, born ... 15: 79
1851 William St.J. Harper, artist, born ... 13:533
1852 Wallack's theatre, New York city, opened ... 4:440
1853 Emilie Poulsson, author of books on kindergartening, born ... 10:463
1857 Julian Story, portrait painter, born ... 19: 86
1862 Gaillard Hunt, historian and chief of the bureau of manuscripts of the Library of Congress, born 19: 81
1869 Bryson Burroughs, artist, particularly a painter of mythological subjects, born ... A:131
1872 George Henry Dern, governor of Utah and secretary of war under Franklin D. Roosevelt, born 26: 9
1900 A hurricane struck Galveston, Tex. ... 23:174
1906 President Palma appealed to the United States for intervention in Cuba ... 23: 3
1916 U. S. tariff commission created ... 19:372

SEPTEMBER 9.

Holiday in California

1708 "Saybrook Platform" formed as the ecclesiastical constitution of Connecticut ... 1:163
1711 Thomas Hutchinson, colonial governor of Massachusetts, born ... 7:376
1721 Edmund Pendleton, colonial patriot and statesman, born ... 10:240
1753 George Logan, U. S. senator, born ... 8:255
1755 Benjamin Bourne, congressman and judge, born . 12:345
1773 Richard Riker, lawyer and politician, born ... 3:385
1776 Calvin Pease, chief justice of Ohio, born ... 7:557
1789 William C. Bond, astronomer, born ... 8:381
1807 Alfred Lee, first P. E. bishop of Delaware, born 11: 99
1812 Richard H. Stanton, congressman and judge, born ... 10: 38
1815 George W. Eastman, expert penman, founder of the first of numerous business schools, and father of the Kodak inventor, born ... 13:132
1816 John G. Fee, clergyman and founder of Berea (Ky.) college, born ... 24:301
1823 Joseph Leidy, physician and naturalist, born ... 5:220
1837 William L. Andrews, merchant and author, born 13:347
1840 Arthur H. Nichols, physician, founder of the Boston Guild of Bell Ringers, born ... 20:121
1842 Elliott Coues, biologist and zoologist, born ... 5:240
1844 Maurice Thompson, author, born ... 11:521
1847 Henry Leffmann, chemist and author of many books on a variety of subjects, born ... 25:158
1850 Henry Clay's compromise bill, admitting California to the Union as a free state, passed ... 5: 80
1850 Utah territory organized ... 7:389
1850 Victor F. Lawson, Chicago editor and publisher, and "Father of Postal Savings Banks in the United States," born ... 26:177
1851 Walter H. Graves, irrigation engineer, U. S. superintendent of irrigation, born ... 18: 46
1861 William S. Rossiter, publisher, born ... 23:333
1874 William DeWitt Mitchell, attorney-general under Hoover, born ... C: 10
1892 Fifth moon of Jupiter discovered by Edward E. Barnard ... 7: 44
1919 Boston police went on strike ... 24: 2

SEPTEMBER 10.

1736 Carter Braxton, Virginia statesman and signer of the Declaration of Independence, born ... 7:302
1750 Nicholas Biddle, naval officer, born ... 5:486
1755 The Acadians exiled from Nova Scotia ... 1:182
1787 John J. Crittenden, U. S. senator, attorney-general under Harrison and governor of Kentucky, born ... 13: 6
1801 Garrett Davis, U. S. senator from Kentucky who opposed secession, born ... 2:225
1806 William Crompton, inventor of power looms, born 10:160
1813 Americans under Perry defeated the British in the naval battle of Lake Erie ... 4:288
1813 Frank H. Hamilton, New York surgeon, born .. 9:358
1818 Noah Davis, New York judge, born ... 11:236
1820 Erection of Ft. Snelling, Mich. begun ... 2:159
1822 John A. Whipple, inventor, born ... 7:525
1822 Edwin McNeill, civil engineer, born ... 18:163
1825 Henry C. Baird, publisher and political economist, born ... 5:314
1825 Henry Mollenhauer, violoncellist, born ... 13:484
1835 William T. Harris, philosopher, author and U. S. commissioner of education, born ... 15: 1
1836 Joseph Wheeler, Confederate soldier and congressman, born ... 9: 19
1838 Emory college, Georgia, opened ... 1:517
1839 Charles Peirce, scientist and philosopher, born .. 8:409
1844 Chester Griswold, iron and steel manufacturer, born ... 15:374
1846 Elias Howe obtained a patent for his sewing machine ... 4:432
1847 John B. Walker, editor and author, born ... 9:195
1852 William I. Buchanan, diplomat, who represented the United States at several Pan-American conferences, born ... 2:271
1852 John F. Wallace, civil engineer, born ... 10:168
1852 Peter T. Austen, chemist, born ... 13: 92
1855 Poultney Bigelow, journalist and author, born .. 9:143
1857 James E. Keeler, astronomer, born ... 10:498
1861 Battle of Carnifex Ferry, Va. ... 4:162
1862 The "Barbara Fritchie" incident occurred in Frederick, Md. ... 10:113
1863 Little Rock, Ark., captured by the Federals ... 4: 51
1865 Convention in Alabama met to abolish slavery and nullify the secession ordinance ... 10:433
1885 Carl Van Doren, author, critic of English literature and a co-founder of the Literary Guild of America, born ... D: 47
1886 Hilda Doolittle Aldington (H. D.), poet, born .. C:329
1892 Arthur Holly Compton, physicist, who specialized in X-ray and radioactivity, born ... C: 34

SEPTEMBER 11.

1731 Josiah Whitney, soldier, born ... 10:154
1744 Sarah Bache, philanthropist, born ... 7: 60
1763 Isaac Roberdeau, civil engineer, born ... 2: 14
1766 James Brown, U. S. senator and judge, born ... 4:376
1777 Battle of Brandywine, Pa. ... 1: 41
1777 Felix Grundy, Kentucky statesman, attorney-general under Van Buren, born ... 6:436
1789 Alexander Hamilton became the first secretary of the treasury ... 1: 11
1800 Daniel S. Dickinson, U. S. senator and attorney-general of New York state, born ... 5:388
1810 James Pollock, governor of Pennsylvania and congressman, born ... 2:289
1813 Henry C. Bowen, merchant and founder of the New York "Independent," born ... 1:205
1814 Battle of Plattsburg, N. Y. ... 2:241
1821 Erastus F. Beadle, publisher, originator of the "dime novel," born ... 19:125
1826 William Morgan abducted by the Freemasons because of threats to expose the rites of the fraternity ... 3: 12
1833 George D. Ruggles, soldier, born ... 12:559
1838 John Ireland, R. C. bishop, born ... 9:226
1840 Frederick G. Maeder, actor and playwright, born 6: 14
1841 All members, excepting Daniel Webster, resigned from Tyler's cabinet because of conflict over the national bank bill ... 6: 3
1841 Silas Casey, naval officer, born ... 21: 57
1842 Franklin B. Dexter, librarian and historian, born 19:344
1852 Thomas B. Mosher, publisher and editor, born .. 20:247
1853 Henry B. Endicott, shoe manufacturer, born ... 19:294
1854 William S. Macy, artist, born ... 3:423
1854 William Holabird, architect, a pioneer in the use of iron skeleton construction, born ... 24:231
1861 Gen. Fremont's confiscation proclamation modified by President Lincoln ... 2: 69
1862 William S. Porter (O. Henry), author, famous for his short stories, born ... 15:170
1865 Alexander Smith, chemist and author of textbooks, born ... 20:421

SEPTEMBER 12.

1609 Henry Hudson entered the river named for him 9:454
1654 The Rhode Island towns united ... 10: 3
1687 John Alden, Plymouth colonist, died ... 10:296
1777 President McKinly of Delaware captured by the British ... 5:544
1781 Governor Burke, of North Carolina, captured by Tories under the notorious David Fanning ... 7:264
1788 John T. Shubrick, naval officer, born ... 8: 98
1797 Samuel J. May, abolitionist, born ... 2:313
1797 George B. Emerson, educator, born ... 11:526

1806 Andrew Hull Foote, naval officer, born 5: 10
1810 Philip Francis Thomas, governor of Maryland and secretary of the treasury under Buchanan, born 5: 6
1811 James Hall, paleontologist, born 3: 280
1812 Elias P. Needham, inventor, born 5: 183
1812 Richard M. Hoe, inventor, born 7: 320
1814 The "Wasp" captured the "Three Brothers" 5: 440
1818 Richard J. Gatling, inventor of the machine gun, born 4: 158
1825 Ainsworth R. Spofford, librarian-in-chief of the Library of Congress, born 6: 477
1829 Charles Dudley Warner, editor and author, born 2: 116
1829 Alexander Stewart, lumberman and congressman, born 15: 190
1830 William Sprague, manufacturer, and governor of Rhode Island, born 9: 402
1832 William H. Rhawn, banker, born 12: 532
1839 John J. Keane, R. C. archbishop, born 6: 285
1842 Charles W. Super, president of Ohio university, born 4: 444
1851 Hannis Taylor, lawyer and author, born 8: 118
1851 Francis E. Clark, clergyman and founder of the Christian Endeavor Society, born 13: 51
1853 Lucien I. Blake, submarine signal inventor, born 18: 210
1857 Loss of S.S. "Central America" en route from Havana 4: 201
1859 Florence Kelley, social worker at Hull house, Chicago, and the Henry street settlement, New York, born 23: 111
1860 Walker, the filibuster, court-martialed and shot by the Honduras government 11: 24
1861 Battle of Cheat Mountain, W. Va. 9: 231
1866 Kansas state university opened 8: 343
1872 Warren A. Bechtel, engineer and constructor, built many western engineering projects including Boulder dam and the San Francisco bridge, born 24: 224
1877 Frederick Henry Koch, educator, dramatist and author, born .... A: 361
1880 Henry L. Mencken, author and editor, born .... A: 388
1918 American troops participated in the launching of the St. Mihiel offensive .... A: 151

SEPTEMBER 13.

1759 Battle of the Plains of Abraham, Quebec, Canada 1: 102
1761 Caspar Wistar, physician, born 1: 273
1791 Thomas De Witt, clergyman, born 2: 434
1813 John Sedgwick, soldier, born 4: 132
1813 Charles A. Spencer, optical and microscopic lens maker, born 13: 255
1817 John M. Palmer, soldier, U. S. senator and governor of Illinois, born 11: 49
1819 Thomas A. Markoe, New York surgeon, born 11: 30
1825 William Henry Rinehart, sculptor, born 2: 345
1826 Anthony J. Drexel, Philadelphia banker and financier, born 2: 273
1826 Leonard Kip, attorney and author, born 11: 439
1828 Alice B. Haven, author, born 5: 386
1829 Charles Wachsmuth, scientist, an associate of Agassiz, born 7: 159
1831 Samuel Cupples, St. Louis merchant and benefactor of Washington university, born 19: 169
1835 Edward C. Hegeler, metallurgist, pioneer zinc smelter and inventor of metallurgical furnaces, born 23: 60
1836 James Lyall, inventor and manufacturer of cotton looms and shuttles, born 7: 496
1851 Walter Reed, physician who gave his life to the study and cure of yellow fever, born 13: 284
1857 Milton S. Hershey, chocolate manufacturer and philanthropist, born .... D: 352
1859 Duel between Judge Terry and Senator Broderick of California 4: 108
1860 John J. Pershing, soldier, commander of the American expeditionary forces during the World war, born .... A: 434
1863 George M. Bowers, U. S. commissioner of fish and fisheries, born 13: 301
1876 Sherwood Anderson, author, born .... A: 68
1880 Jesse L. Lasky, theatrical manager, motion picture producer and financier, born 18: 168
1881 Nelson W. Janney, chemist, specialist in endocrinology, born 26: 74
1887 Theodore Roosevelt, Jr., civil governor of Puerto Rico and the Philippine islands, born .... D: 64
1898 Patent issued to Hannibal W. Goodwin for a sensitized film for photography 23: 378

SEPTEMBER 14.

1638 John Harvard died bequeathing his library and half of his estate for a college 6: 408
1742 James Wilson, one of the original justices of the U. S. supreme court, born 1: 22
1755 William Bradford, attorney-general under Washington, born 1: 14
1775 John H. Hobart, P. E. bishop, born 1: 514
1809 Sterling Price, soldier and governor of Missouri, born 12: 304
1814 Francis Scott Key composed "The Star Spangled Banner" 5: 498
1816 James R. Wood, New York physician, born 9: 357
1818 Solomon Juneau settled on the site of Milwaukee, Wis. 6: 18
1823 Benjamin H. Hill, member of the U. S. and Confederate senates, born 10: 194
1824 Julius H. Seelye, president of Amherst college, born 6: 157
1828 John Hitz, educator of deaf-mutes, born 12: 62
1828 William H. Brewer, chemist and geologist, born 13: 561
1832 Henry Steers, ship builder, born 25: 55
1837 Harry Fenn, artist and illustrator, born 6: 368
1843 George E. Whiting, organist and composer, born 8: 446
1844 Martin Milmore, sculptor, born 8: 291
1846 George Baldwin Selden, lawyer and inventor of the first internal combustion engine for automobiles, born 20: 222
1847 Mexico City captured by the Americans after the battle of Chapultepec 3: 503
1850 Lewis S. McMurtry, Louisville physician, born 13: 280
1852 John C. Olmstead, landscape architect, born 13: 460
1854 Julia Magruder, author, born 8: 10
1860 Hamlin Garland, author, born .... B: 4
1861 Confederate privateer "Judah" captured by Lieut. Russell 5: 15
1862 Battle of South Mountain, Md. 4: 176
1867 Charles Dana Gibson, illustrator, creator of the "Gibson Girl," born 11: 290
1872 The Alabama claims settled, Great Britain agreed to pay the United States $15,500,000 .... 8: 353
1887 Karl T. Compton, president of the Massachusetts institute of technology, born .... C: 81
1897 Patent issued to Corby for a machine for making bread in bulk 25: 9
1901 President McKinley died; Theodore Roosevelt took the oath of office 11: 10

SEPTEMBER 15.

1679 Council with Indian chiefs at Lake Superior, first friendly meeting with Sioux and other tribes .. 4: 62
1771 Henry Davis, president of Hamilton college, born 7: 405
1776 British under Howe entered New York city 7: 151
1778 Richard Somers, naval officer, born 8: 412
1783 Luther Bradish, lawyer and legislator, born 3: 463
1783 Levi Frisbie, educator, born 7: 132
1789 James Fenimore Cooper, novelist, born 1: 398
1795 Zachariah Allen, engineer and inventor of the automatic cut-off valve, born 8: 263
1795 James Gates Percival, geologist and poet, born 8: 305
1801 Eli Smith, missionary to Asia Minor, born 8: 15
1805 Conway Robinson, lawyer and author, born 1: 475
1809 James Y. Smith, manufacturer, and governor of Rhode Island, born 9: 403
1816 Joseph C. Talbot, P. E. bishop, born 3: 466
1818 Connecticut adopted a new state constitution 10: 333
1820 James G. Benton, soldier and inventor of ordnance improvements, born 4: 138
1824 Adeline D. T. Whitney, poet and author, born .. 2: 29
1830 Sylvester Waterhouse, author and educator, born 8: 147
1832 Treaty concluded with Black Hawk, Indian chief 13: 56
1835 Richard Olney, secretary of state under Cleveland, born 7: 143
1841 Sarah Knowles Bolton, author and biographer, born 1: 212
1842 Henry C. Corbin, soldier, born 12: 278
1844 Milton W. Humphreys, educator and soldier, born 13: 481
1846 Lloyd Mifflin, author and poet, born 18: 296
1856 Kirk Munroe, author, born 11: 523
1857 Brigham Young proclaimed martial law in Utah 16: 8
1857 William Howard Taft, president of the United States and chief justice of the supreme court, born 23: 1
1862 Harper's Ferry, Va., surrendered to Confederates 2: 72
1863 President Lincoln suspended the writ of habeas corpus and proclaimed martial law 2: 72
1863 The Lamb knitting machine first patented 7: 554
1863 Exum P. Lewis, physicist, who made important contributions to spectroscopy, born 22: 411
1879 Leonard P. Ayres, statistician, born .... A: 148

SEPTEMBER 16.

1733 Abraham Whipple, naval officer, born 2: 16
1776 Battle of Harlem Heights, N. Y. 2: 299
1796 William A. Muhlenberg, clergyman and founder of St. Johnland, Long Island, N. Y., a social project, born 9: 199
1799 Moses Norris, U. S. senator, born 12: 394
1802 John M. Botts, congressman, born 8: 156

1803 Orestes A. Brownson, author and clergyman, born 7:197
1804 Squire Whipple, civil engineer, called "the Father of American Bridge Building," born 9: 35
1823 Francis Parkman, author and historian, born 1:431
1825 Stephen M. Merrill, M. E. bishop, born 5:518
1827 Charles C. Nott, chief justice of the U. S. court of claims, born 12:357
1830 George B. Prescott, electrical engineer and inventor, born 5:279
1830 Henry Mitchell, hydraulic engineer, born 8:488
1834 Asa S. Bushnell, manufacturer and governor of Ohio, born 8: 43
1834 Alfred M. Waddell, congressman and author, born 8:124
1835 John G. McCullough, governor of Vermont and president of the Panama and other railroads, born 14:322
1838 James J. Hill, financier, who built and developed the Northern Pacific and Great Northern railroads, born 13:354
1841 Edward Stanwood, editor of the "Youth's Companion" and author, born 9:475
1847 Albert Ross Parsons, musician and composer, born 2:495
1848 Hyperion, the 7th satellite of Saturn, discovered by William C. Bond 8:381
1861 Charles Battell Loomis, humorist, born 14:476
1862 Battle of Antietam, Md., began 4:176
1876 Ellsworth Huntington, geographer and explorer, born A:510

SEPTEMBER 17.

1683 Nicholas Spencer became acting governor of Virginia 13:386
1720 William Burnet arrived in New York to become governor of New York and New Jersey 7:374
1721 Samuel Hopkins, clergyman and theologian, born 7:154
1762 Benjamin Abbot, the first principal of Phillips Exeter academy, born 10:104
1776 Americans under John Brown captured important outposts of Ft. Ticonderoga 1: 45
1776 Langdon Cheves, congressman and president of the U. S. Bank, born 10: 19
1787 The United States Constitution completed and signed by the convention 1: 5
1788 John James Abert, military engineer, born 4:380
1811 John Brough, governor of Ohio and founder of the Cincinnati "Enquirer," born 3:142
1818 Moses D. Hoge, clergyman, born 10:464
1819 J. Peter Lesley, geologist, educator and engineer, born 8: 79
1820 Earl Van Dorn, Confederate soldier, born 4:208
1825 Lucius Q. C. Lamar, U. S. senator and secretary of the interior under Cleveland, born 1: 37
1825 James R. Haskell, inventor of firearms, born 13:106
1841 Addison C. Rand, manufacturer of rockdrills and air compressing machinery, born 11:265
1843 William E. Griffis, educator, clergyman and author, born 21:118
1845 Calvin S. Brice, U. S. senator, born 2:425
1857 Harry W. Watrous, artist, called the "American Meissonier," born 13:369
1858 Robert W. Vonnoh, artist, born 7:462
1862 Gen. Bragg captured Mumfordville, Ky. 11:218
1871 Leo S. Rowe, educator, prominent in Puerto Rico affairs and director-general of the Pan-American Union, born 18:316
1900 Martha Ostenso, author, born C:469

SEPTEMBER 18.

1733 George Read, a signer of the Declaration of Independence, born 3:297
1765 Oliver Holden, musician, composer and music publisher, born 13:178
1770 Benjamin Hazard, legislator in the Rhode Island assembly for thirty-one years, born 8: 17
1779 Joseph Story, justice of the U. S. supreme court and twice acting chief justice, born 2:468
1781 John Herr, a founder of the Reformed Mennonite church, born 7:498
1798 Rufus Babcock, president of Waterville (later Colby) college, born 8:405
1804 Walter L. Newberry, Chicago merchant and realtor, left a trust fund to establish the Newberry library, born 24:223
1805 John S. C. Abbott, clergyman and author, born 6:145
1812 Herschel V. Johnson, U. S. senator and governor of Georgia, born 1:226
1818 Mary A. F. Vincent, actress, born 10:257
1827 John T. Trowbridge, author, born 3:374
1836 William J. Palmer, railroad builder, founder and president of the Denver & Rio Grande, born 23:399
1842 Battle of Salado, Tex. 2:241
1843 Charles V. Riley, entomologist, born 9:443
1844 Spencer Trask, New York banker and broker, born 11:444
1851 First issue of the New York "Times" 8:483
1857 John H. Clarke, railroad attorney, justice of the U. S. supreme court, and founder and president of the League of Nations Non-Partisan Association, born A:248
1858 Henry C. King, president of Oberlin college, born 13:296
1860 Otto M. Eidlitz, construction engineer, president of the U. S. Housing Corporation, born 16:412
1860 Carlton T. Chapman, artist, born 22:249
1860 Clinton Scollard, poet, author and educator, born 23:160
1861 Battle of Lexington, Mo., began 5:329
1862 Lee's army retreated across the Potomac after the battle of Antietam 4:176
1867 Maryland ratified a new constitution 9:309
1868 Ellen Beach Yaw, singer, born 13:246

SEPTEMBER 19.

1692 Giles Corey crushed to death for contempt of court during a witchcraft trial at Salem 12:507
1739 Andrew Pickens, Revolutionary soldier and congressman, born 1: 70
1752 William Popham, Revolutionary soldier and lawyer, born 4:237
1765 Jared Ingersoll, royal stamp master for New England, forced to resign because of popular indignation over the Stamp Act 2:439
1777 Battle of Saratoga, N. Y., where Burgoyne surrendered to the Americans 1: 47
1777 Battle of Paoli, Pa. 1: 55
1778 William Gaston, North Carolina jurist, born 3:513
1792 William B. Astor, merchant and capitalist, born 8:104
1796 Washington's "Farewell Address" issued 1: 7
1813 Christian H. F. Peters, astronomer, born 13:317
1815 Edgar Cowan, lawyer and U. S. senator, born 2: 94
1821 Opening of Amherst college 5:307
1821 Gilbert Haven, M. E. bishop, born 13:261
1824 William Sellers, iron and steel manufacturer, born 7:185
1825 Henry Charles Lea, historian, born 23: 17
1825 Edwin Cowles, owner and editor of the Cleveland "Leader," born 23: 50
1831 James De Koven, clergyman and educator, born 11:199
1835 Ethan Allen Hitchcock, secretary of the interior under McKinley and Theodore Roosevelt, born 11: 16
1838 Samuel Q. Brown, oil operator, born 15:239
1839 John S. Crosby, soldier and governor of Montana, born 24:217
1840 Gedney Bunce, landscape painter, known as the "painter of Venice," born 18:399
1841 Richard C. Morse, general secretary of the Y.M.C.A. for 46 years, born 21:102
1858 George W. Wickersham, attorney-general under Taft, and chairman of Hoover's national commission on law observance, born C: 16
1859 Marshall P. Wilder, humorist, born 6: 33
1862 Battle of Iuka, Miss. 8:370
1863 Battle of Chickamauga, Tenn. 4:163
1863 Ernest Lacy, poet and dramatist, born 20:101
1864 Battle of Winchester, Va. 4: 65
1864 Confederate guerillas seized and robbed steamers on Lake Ontario 4:445
1881 President Garfield died in office 4:242
1887 Harold E. Porter (Holworthy Hall), author, born A:259

SEPTEMBER 20.

1565 Spaniards massacred the French at Port Caroline, Fla. 11:164
1737 Charles Carroll, of Carrollton, Maryland patriot and signer of the Declaration of Independence, born 7:441
1743 George Clinton arrived in New York city to become governor of the province 5:541
1790 Job Durfee, chief justice of Rhode Island, born. 7:414
1795 Alden March, surgeon, founder of the Albany medical college, born 2:445
1810 Joseph Harrison, locomotive designer and builder, born 12:495
1811 John F. Boynton, mineralogist and inventor, born 4: 91
1815 Charles M. Walcot, actor and playwright, born. 11:514
1820 George W. Morgan, soldier and congressman, born 4: 71
1820 American literary, scientific and military academy (later Norwich university), opened 18:322
1821 Thomas Doane, civil engineer, who built the Hoosac tunnel and several railroads, and founded Doane college, Lincoln, Nebr., born 25: 93
1827 Albert J. Myer, soldier, inventor of the wig-wagging system of communication, and founder of the U. S. weather bureau, born 24:196
1833 David R. Locke, humorist, born 6:152
1837 L. Clark Seelye, first president of Smith college, born 7:121
1838 Wilburn B. Hall, Confederate naval officer, born 8:269
1848 First meeting of the American Association for the Advancement of Science held at Philadelphia 8:220

1849 George Bird Grinnell, ethnologist and author, born . . . . B: 478
1851 Lloyd Bryce, author and editor of the "North American Review," born 1: 252
1861 Capture of Lexington, Mo., by the Confederates 5: 329
1861 Herbert Putnam, librarian of the Library of Congress, born . . . . D: 52
1862 Revolving gun turret, first used on the "Monitor," patented by Theodore R. Timby 9: 116
1868 George John Hamlin, concert and opera singer, born 19: 59
1878 Upton Sinclair, author, born . . . . C: 114
1881 Chester A. Arthur took the oath of office as president of the United States 4: 247
1893 Charles Francis Brush, Jr., scientist, founder of the Brush laboratories, born 20: 21

SEPTEMBER 21.

1638 Peace treaty made between the Narragansett and Pequot Indians 10: 407
1645 Louis Jolliet, explorer of the Mississippi valley, born 5: 121
1757 James Jackson, soldier, U. S. senator and governor of Georgia, born 1: 220
1758 Christopher Gore, governor of Massachusetts and U. S. senator, born 1: 112
1779 English fort at Baton Rouge captured by Galvez for Spain 10: 74
1793 Gideon F. Thayer, educator, founder of Chauncey Hall school, Boston, born 7: 532
1800 Samuel McClellan, surgeon, a founder of Jefferson medical college, born 4: 140
1809 Douglas Houghton, geologist and educator, born 5: 512
1820 Abraham H. Cassel, antiquarian and bibliophile, born 3: 276
1820 John F. Reynolds, Federal soldier, born 4: 224
1827 Michael Corcoran, Federal soldier who organized the "Corcoran Legion," born 4: 54
1831 Wesleyan university opened at Middletown, Conn. 3: 177
1834 Edward B. Dalton, physician, originated the ambulance system, born 10: 501
1836 Pembroke D. Gwaltney, founder of the peanut industry in the South, born 17: 113
1846 Battle of Monterey, Mexico, began 4: 148
1853 Henry P. Armsby, agricultural chemist, a pioneer in animal nutrition and head of various state experimental stations, born 22: 421
1855 Samuel Rea, president of the Pennsylvania railroad, born 15: 289
1863 Clark Howell, Georgia legislator and editor of the Atlanta "Constitution," born 1: 473
1864 Frederic F. Bullard, composer, born 13: 228
1866 Marie Burroughs (Lillie Arrington), actress, born 13: 432
1867 Henry L. Stimson, secretary of state under Hoover, born . . . . C: 8
1869 U.S. hospital ship "Idaho" wrecked by a typhoon at Nagasaki, Japan 9: 155
1873 John Lyell Harper, electrical engineer, developed the hydro-electic power plants at Niagara Falls, born 20: 395
1877 George A. Wyeth, surgeon, cancer specialist, born D: 88

SEPTEMBER 22.

Emancipation Day

1752 James Bowdoin, statesman and benefactor of Bowdoin college, born 1: 419
1774 Joshua Lacy Wilson, clergyman and author, born 12: 94
1776 Nathan Hale hanged as a spy by the British . . . 1: 52
1780 Gen. Benedict Arnold met Major Andre and arranged to betray West Point to the British . . . 1: 49
1790 Augustus B. Longstreet, judge, educator and author, president of three Southern colleges, born 1: 517
1798 Marshall P. Wilder, Boston merchant and pomologist, born 1: 358
1800 Richard A. Locke, journalist, perpetrator of the famous "moon" and "lost manuscript" hoaxes, born 13: 151
1803 Thomas H. Clay, Kentucky legislator and U. S. minister to Honduras, born 13: 51
1809 Parker Pillsbury, clergyman and abolitionist, born 2: 330
1812 Samuel Wells Williams, authority on and editor of Chinese literature, who held the first lectureship in this subject at Yale, born 1: 422
1819 Joseph Seligman, New York banker, born 3: 342
1827 Peter Turney, governor and chief justice of Tennessee, born 7: 213
1827 John G. Parke, civil engineer and soldier, born 12: 242
1829 William W. Belknap, lawyer, and secretary of war under Grant until forced to resign, born. 4: 23
1833 Stephen D. Lee, Confederate soldier, born 5: 414
1834 Settlement of Portland, Oreg., by Americans under Nathaniel Wyeth 6: 73
1834 William B. Cogswell, civil engineer, born 13: 107
1840 Samuel D. Page, lawyer and banker, born 15: 352
1851 George P. Riddle, elocutionist, born 13: 305
1854 Henry T. Finck, music critic, born 14: 153
1862 Lincoln's first Emancipation Proclamation issued 2: 70
1862 Meeting of loyal governors held at Altoona, Pa. 12: 75
1862 Wilson Farrand, educator, an organizer of the college entrance examination board, born 18: 69
1864 Battle of Fisher's Hill, Va., in which Sheridan defeated the Confederates under Gen. Early . . 4: 138

SEPTEMBER 23.

Autumnal Equinox

1647 Joseph Dudley, colonial governor of Massachusetts, born 7: 372
1692 Martha Corey hanged for a witch 12: 507
1745 Isaac Hayne, patriot, hanged by the British at Charleston, S. C., born 1: 440
1745 John Sevier, pioneer and governor of Tennessee, born 3: 430
1779 Naval battle between the "Bon Homme Richard" and "Serapis" 2: 15
1780 Major Andre captured by three American soldiers 1: 49
1786 John England, R. C. bishop, born 5: 28
1793 James F. Dana, scientist, born 10: 390
1800 William Holmes McGuffey, author of the McGuffey readers and spelling books, and president of Ohio university, born 4: 443
1816 Elihu B. Washburne, secretary of state under Grant and minister to France, born 4: 14
1819 Charles J. Stillé, provost of the University of Pennsylvania, born 1: 344
1820 Thomas Kilby Smith, Federal soldier, born 8: 275
1823 Sara Clarke Lippincott (Grace Greenwood), author and editor, born 4: 536
1826 Alexander Davidson, inventor, who standardized the typewriter keyboard, born 3: 320
1833 William J. Duane, secretary of the treasury under Jackson, removed from office 5: 294
1838 Robert T. Edes, physician and educator, born . . 8: 212
1839 Indiana Asbury (De Pauw) university opened . . 7: 381
1840 Paul J. Sorg, tobacco manufacturer and congressman, born 18: 161
1842 George F. Pentecost, evangelist, born 20: 73
1845 J. Scott Hartley, sculptor, born 7: 459
1848 Hjalmar H. Boyesen, educator and author, born 1: 367
1852 J. Carroll Beckwith, artist, born 7: 470
1856 S.S. "Pacific" of the Collins line left Liverpool for New York and was never heard from 23: 127
1858 William De Witt Hyde, president of Bowdoin college, born 1: 419
1859 Thomas Mott Osborne, manufacturer, warden of Sing Sing prison and a noted prison reformer, born 21: 90
1860 Eli Harvey, sculptor and painter, born 12: 522
1862 Battle with Sioux Indians at Wood Lake, Minn. 10: 63
1862 Kirke LaShelle, author and theatrical manager, born 12: 185
1889 Walter Lippmann, journalist and author, born . . D: 69

SEPTEMBER 24.

1664 Fort Orange (Albany), N. Y., taken over by the English 2: 483
1743 Andrew Porter, Revolutionary soldier, born 1: 77
1755 John Marshall, chief justice of the United States, born 1: 25
1768 Treaty of Ft. Stanwix with the Indians 5: 104
1785 John C. Stevens, yachtsman, born 1: 447
1789 Richard H. Wilde, congressman and scholar, born 1: 357
1804 William E. Burton, actor, born 2: 351
1811 Charles Steedman, naval officer, born 4: 357
1827 Henry W. Slocum, lawyer, soldier and congressman, born 24: 305
1829 Nathan W. Spaulding, inventor of improvements in the lumber industry, born 13: 163
1832 William P. Henszey, inventor and locomotive designer, born 24: 142
1833 Henry A. Barnum, soldier, born 4: 36
1833 Augustus P. Clarke, Boston physician and surgeon, born 6: 234
1835 William O. Stoddard, journalist, author and secretary to President Lincoln, born 8: 121
1837 Mark Hanna, Cleveland merchant and U. S. senator, born 22: 13
1846 Monterey, Mexico, surrendered to the U.S. troops 4: 148
1858 Thomas Darlington, physician, pioneer in public health and child welfare work, born 2: 179
1862 William T. Porter, physiologist, born 15: 288
1864 Surrender of Athens, Ga., to the Confederates . . 10: 37
1866 James W. Good, congressman who instigated the national budget system, and secretary of war under Hoover, born 21: 94
1869 "Black Friday" financial panic 22: 171
1876 Hallett's reef dynamited to enlarge Hell Gate channel in New York harbor 4: 313
1896 F. Scott Fitzgerald, author, born . . . . B: 472

SEPTEMBER 25.

1513 Balboa discovered the Pacific Ocean 5:431
1690 First and only issue of "Publick Occurrences," the first attempt at a newspaper in America.. 25:260
1728 Mercy Warren, colonial playwright and author, born 7:177
1775 Unsuccessful attack on Montreal, Canada....... 1: 46
1780 Benedict Arnold escaped to the British ship "Vulture" after attempting to betray West Point 1: 54
1794 John S. Sleeper, author and journalist, born.... 13:206
1807 Alfred Vail, inventor, a co-worker with Morse in developing the telegraph, born 4:450
1823 Thomas J. Wood, soldier, born 4:259
1830 Alphonzo B. Bowers, civil engineer, inventor of the hydraulic dredge, born 12:527
1832 William LeB. Jenney, architect, originator of the steel skeleton for large buildings, born 10:218
1842 James M. Bailey, humorist, known as the "Danbury News Man," born 6: 28
1843 Thomas C. Chamberlin, geologist and president of the University of Wisconsin, born 19: 25
1844 George H. Perkins, entomologist and educator, born 10:309
1847 Vinnie Ream Hoxie, sculptor, born 1:442
1855 William S. Benson, naval officer, first chief of naval operations, born 23:388
1861 Star theatre, New York, opened 4:440
1870 Isaac A. Mekeel, publisher of trade journals, born 15: 83
1883 Barrington Moore, forester, president of the Ecological Society of America and editor of "Ecology," born 18: 17

SEPTEMBER 26.

1651 Francis D. Pastorius, founder of Germantown, Pa., born 11:352
1721 Christopher Sower, clergyman and Bible publisher, born 13:346
1756 Ebenezer Fitch, first president of Williams college, born 6:237
1777 British troops under Cornwallis entered Philadelphia 7:543
1785 Gideon Hawley, lawyer, born 13:443
1786 Thomas S. Grimké, lawyer and peace advocate, born 2:326
1789 James A. Hillhouse, poet, born 7:131
1797 James W. Eastburn, poet, born 9:237
1816 David H. Strother (Porte Crayon), author, artist and Federal soldier, born 9:365
1822 William S. Holman, congressman, called the "Great Objector," born 5:457
1823 William Henry Milburn, the "Blind Preacher," born 7:137
1827 American debut of Louisa Lane Drew 8:217
1839 Willard B. Rising, chemist, born 12:341
1840 Samuel Pollock Harbison, brick manufacturer, born 14:229
1841 Stephen B. Elkins, lawyer and secretary of war under Benjamin Harrison, born 1:142
1843 Thomas V. Munson, viticulturist, who propagated many new varieties of grapes, born 18:265
1855 Channing F. Meek, industrialist, born 15:153
1859 Irving Bacheller, editor and author, born.......... C:411
1862 Arthur B. Davies, artist, born 14:453
1862 Charles H. Richardson, geologist, born 26: 64
1863 Charles L. Marlatt, entomologist, born 13:186
1875 Eleanor Gates, author, born 15:263
1881 A day of general mourning for President Garfield 4:248
1888 Thomas Stearns (T. S.) Eliot, poet and critic, born .... C: 99
1914 Federal trade commission created to prevent unfair business practices 19: 3
1918 Launching of the Argonne-Meuse offensive in the World war .... A: 90

SEPTEMBER 27.

1647 Wreck off Wales of the vessel from New Amsterdam with Governor Kieft, Pastor Bogardus and others on board 9:288
1722 Samuel Adams, Massachusetts statesman, "Father of the Revolution," born 1:104
1722 Hugh Drysdale became governor of Virginia.... 13:388
1732 The "Rhode Island Gazette" first issued........ 8: 17
1767 Isaac H. Williamson, governor and chancellor of New Jersey, born 5:204
1774 John Griscom, chemist, born 10:510
1786 Joseph G. Cogswell, book collector and librarian of the Astor library, born 11:462
1792 Benjamin S. Cowen, legislator and judge, born.. 12: 58
1803 Samuel Francis du Pont, naval officer, born..... 5: 50
1809 Raphael Semmes, naval officer, born 4:340
1809 David S. McDougal, naval officer, born 13:130
1813 Epes Sargent, journalist and author, born 7:243
1814 Daniel Kirkwood, mathematician, born 4:349
1814 Naval engagement between the "General Armstrong" and three British vessels.......... 8: 97
1817 Charles Lucas killed in a duel with Thomas H. Benton 13:322
1823 Thomas H. Dodge, patent lawyer, and inventor, born 2:520
1823 Frederick Billings, lawyer and president of the Northern Pacific railroad, born 25:361
1824 Benjamin Apthorp Gould, astronomer, born 5:108
1830 William B. Hazen, chief signal officer of the U. S. army, born 3:408
1830 Treaty of Dancing Rabbit Creek whereby the Choctaw Indians ceded their lands to the United States 10:426
1837 Edward McGlynn, R. C. clergyman, born 9:242
1839 William D. Mann, soldier, manufacturer and editor, born 11:444
1840 Thomas Nast, caricaturist, born 7:461
1840 Alfred T. Mahan, naval officer and author, born 10:440
1840 Cyrus A. Dolph, lawyer, born 16: 56
1854 The S.S. "Arctic" sank with a loss of 300 lives. 2:349
1855 Kuno Francke, historian and philologist, born .. 10:512
1860 Charles W. Kent, educator, author and editor, born 18:143
1864 Battle of Ft. Davidson, Pilot Knob, Mo. 7:400
1869 Francis M. Pottenger, physician, tuberculosis specialist, born 16:363
1874 Myrtle Reed McCullough, author, born 15:229
1874 Nicholas K. Roerich, artist, born C:146
1878 F. Warrington Dawson, author and foreign correspondent, born C:476
1886 Raymond Moley, political scientist, leader of the "brains trust," which served President Franklin D. Roosevelt in an advisory capacity, born .... D: 21

SEPTEMBER 28.

1565 Massacre of ship-wrecked Frenchmen by the Spaniards at Matanzas, Fla. 11:164
1721 Eliphalet Dyer, Connecticut judge and member of the first Continental Congress, born 11:172
1755 William Edmond, Connecticut judge and congressman, born 2:530
1770 Henry Middleton, governor of South Carolina and minister to Russia, born 12:163
1776 The first state constitution of Pennsylvania adopted 7:522
1781 The siege of Yorktown began 1: 4
1795 David Paul Brown, lawyer and dramatist, born. 3:520
1797 John H. W. Hawkins, temperance advocate, born 11:370
1807 Arnold Guyot, geographer, born 4:448
1810 Francis R. Goulding, clergyman and author, born 7:174
1813 Naval battle of Lake Ontario 8: 99
1817 Richard H. Bull, mathematician who introduced the duodecimal system of calculation, born.... 9:472
1824 The Springfield (Mass.) "Republican" first issued 1:317
1828 Theodore Winthrop, author, born 1:130
1838 Arthur B. Farquhar, machinery manufacturer, born 2:209
1839 Frances E. Willard, president of the National and World Women's Christian Temperance unions, born 1:376
1840 Henry M. MacCracken, chancellor of the University of the City of New York, born 6:324
1845 William Wright Baldwin, railroad official, born. B: 80
1855 George deForest Brush, artist, born 13:578
1856 Kate Douglas Wiggin, author, born 6:207
1862 Philander P. Claxton, U. S. commissioner of education, born 15:270
1863 Frederick MacMonnies, sculptor, born 8:289
1864 George Mitchell, metallurgist, born 13:362
1879 John Wise left St. Louis, Mo., on a fatal balloon trip 1:178
1892 Elmer Rice, playwright, Pulitzer prize winner, born A:534

SEPTEMBER 29.

Michaelmas Day

1699 Charles Calvert, 5th Lord Baltimore, born...... 7:336
1773 Daniel Adams, mathematician, author of "Scholars' Arithmetic," born 20:438
1799 Thomas Kingsford, starch manufacturer, born... 5:221
1807 Thomas H. Seymour, soldier, governor of Connecticut and minister to Russia, born 10:337
1813 Jesse Hutchinson, one of the famous Hutchinson family of singers, born 10: 26
1818 Thomas P. Rossiter, artist, born 4: 60
1831 John M. Schofield, soldier and secretary of war under Johnson and Grant, born 4:259
1835 Edward P. Tenney, author, born 7:530
1838 Henry H. Richardson, noted architect who designed Trinity Church, Boston, born 6: 21

1839 James K. Jones, U. S. senator, born 1: 293
1844 Buenos Aires squadron captured off Montevideo.. 4: 311
1844 Christopher C. Shayne, fur merchant, born...... 7: 550
1849 Frederick Schwatka, Arctic explorer, born 3: 285
1856 George Frederick Kunz, mineralogist and gem expert, born 4: 433
1859 Philip R. Alger, naval officer, born 15: 118
1862 Gen. Jefferson C. Davis quarreled with and killed Gen. William Nelson in Louisville, Ky. 5: 366
1864 Federals attacked Newmarket, Va. 1: 449
1864 Ft. Harrison, Va., captured by the Federals..... 4: 7
1867 Edwin C. Dinwiddie, temperance advocate, born 26: 234
1879 The Ute massacre at White River agency occurred 8: 388
1906 Secretary Taft proclaimed U. S. intervention in Cuba, with himself as provisional governor ... 23: 3
1918 American troops broke the Hindenburg line at St. Quentin in the World war .... A: 62

SEPTEMBER 30.

1762 Nathan Smith, physician, founder of the medical departments at Dartmouth, Yale and Bowdoin colleges, born 3: 153
1775 Robert Adrain, mathematician, born 1: 347
1791 The College of Philadelphia became the University of Pennsylvania 1: 341
1800 A convention signed with France as a temporary treaty 1: 77
1800 Bradford R. Wood, lawyer and minister to Denmark, born 12: 504
1802 Truman B. Ransom, soldier and president of Norwich university, born 18: 323
1805 Samuel P. Heintzelman, soldier, born 12: 287
1808 Seargent S. Prentiss, lawyer and orator, born... 7: 477
1808 William Leighton, pioneer glass maker, born 26: 476
1813 William Weightman, manufacturing chemist, the first to introduce quinine in the United States, born 14: 146
1814 Jacob Estey, organ manufacturer, born 1: 215
1814 Lucinda Hinsdale Stone, educator, born 13: 198
1824 Samuel S. (Sunset) Cox, editor and politician, born 6: 363
1824 Vincent Colyer, artist and originator of the U.S. Christian commissions during the Civil war, born 7: 541
1824 Charles P. Stone, soldier in the American and Egyptian armies, born 11: 215
1827 Ellis H. Roberts, journalist and congressman, born 11: 507
1833 Mathew S. Quay, U. S. senator, born 1: 459
1834 Cyrus Northrop, president of the University of Minnesota, born 13: 328
1836 Montgomery Sicard, naval officer, born 10: 485
1837 John W. Albaugh, actor and theatrical manager, born 2: 167
1837 Franklin Carter, president of Williams college, born 6: 239
1840 Elmer L. Corthell, civil engineer, born......... 9: 42
1842 Charles Pickering Bowditch, archæologist, an authority on the Mayan civilization, born...... 20: 290
1847 James P. Taliaferro, U. S. senator, born 10: 175
1849 Meichel De Young, editor of the San Francisco "Chronicle," born 1: 269
1849 John W. Danenhower, Arctic explorer, a survivor of the ill-fated "Jeannette" expedition, born.. 3: 284
1851 Louis Dyer, classical scholar and author, born... 22: 190
1862 Wilton Lackaye, actor, born 3: 516
1870 Thomas W. Lamont, banker, a partner of J. P. Morgan & Co., born .... A: 20
1875 John Henry MacCracken, president of Lafayette college, born 15: 205
1882 Charles L. Lawrance, aeronautic engineer, designer of the "Whirlwind" motor, born ..... D: 194
1889 Margaret Widdemer, author and poet, born ..... A: 217

OCTOBER 1.

First Friday in October Observed as Health Day in the Boston Schools

1664 Fort Casimir, Del., surrendered to the English .. 9: 451
1723 Richard Mansfield, clergyman, born 12: 6
1730 Richard Stockton, signer of the Declaration of Independence, born 12: 218
1735 Simeon Olcott, judge and U. S. senator, born .. 1: 363
1746 John P. G. Muhlenberg, clergyman, soldier and U. S. senator, born 1: 149
1767 Victor M. DuPont, manufacturer and diplomat, born 6: 455
1768 Thomas M. Randolph, Virginia governor and congressman, born 5: 446
1781 James Lawrence, naval officer, born 8: 92
1795 Daniel Pierce Thompson, novelist, born 6: 233
1799 Rufus Choate, lawyer and statesman, born 6: 17
1802 Edward Coate Pinkney, author and poet, born 6: 443
1807 Roswell Park, clergyman, author, and founder and first president of Racine (Wis.) college, born 8: 220
1826 Benjamin B. Hotchkiss, inventor of firearms, born 6: 431
1832 Henry Clay Work, composer, well known for his "Marching through Georgia," born 1: 182
1834 Augustus O. Bourn, governor of Rhode Island, born 9: 406
1838 Kate Field, actress, author and journalist, born 6: 275
1839 James Lewis, comedian, born 1: 286
1850 David R. Francis, Missouri merchant and governor, secretary of the interior under Cleveland, and U. S. ambassador to Russia, born .. 24: 322
1856 George Dana Purinton, scientist, born 8: 189
1861 Frederic Remington, artist, author and illustrator, born 22: 244
1866 Dean C. Worcester, scientist, and secretary of the interior of the Philippine insular government, who founded the island's sanitary and agricultural services and developed its industries, born 20: 246
1881 Stuart P. Sherman, educator and literary critic, born 21: 88
1884 The Lyceum school of acting, the first of its kind in America, founded by Franklin H. Sargent 6: 330
1887 Glenn Frank, president of the University of Wisconsin, born .... C: 454
1890 McKinley tariff bill became a law 11: 2
1891 Opening of the Leland Stanford Junior university 22: 68
1910 The Los Angeles "Times" building dynamited by labor agitators 15: 50

OCTOBER 2.

1737 Francis Hopkinson, lawyer, musician and author, a signer of the Declaration of Independence, born 5: 460
1774 Henry Middleton of South Carolina elected president of the Continental congress 5: 367
1775 Lyman Beecher, theologian, born 3: 126
1780 Major André hanged as a spy 1: 49
1780 Junius Smith, lawyer and merchant, a pioneer in steam navigation, born 19: 311
1817 Webster Wagner, inventor and manufacturer of railway car equipment, born 9: 208
1828 Charles Aldrich, editor and legislator, born 9: 317
1830 Charles Pratt, oil merchant and philanthropist, born 26: 72
1831 Edwin L. Godkin, journalist, born 8: 455
1833 An anti-slavery society founded in New York .. 2: 320
1835 Theodore Tilton, editor and author, born 8: 100
1846 Appleton Morgan, editor, author, and Shakespearean commentator, born 9: 452
1846 Eliza M. Mosher, physician, born 15: 304
1852 James W. Bright, philologist, born 20: 189
1865 Gen. Robert E. Lee became president of Washington college (Washington and Lee university) 4: 100
1871 Cordell Hull, U. S. senator and secretary of state under Franklin D. Roosevelt, born .... D: 10
1885 Ruth Bryan Owen, congressman and diplomat, the first woman to serve as an American minister, born .... A: 368
1889 First Pan-American congress opened in Washington 1: 134
1918 The "Lost Battalion" became separated from its division in the Argonne forest, France 20: 396

OCTOBER 3.

1775 Benjamin Church convicted of treason 7: 167
1782 Charles Jared Ingersoll, congressman and historian, born 7: 141
1782 David Johnson, South Carolina jurist and governor, born 12: 170
800 George Bancroft, historian, secretary of the navy under Polk, and American minister to Great Britain and Germany, born 3: 160
1801 William G. McNeill, civil engineer, born 9: 47
1802 George Ripley, editor and literary critic, born .. 3: 453
1804 Townsend Harris, merchant and diplomat, born 5: 493
1807 Seth Padelford, governor of Rhode Island, born 9: 404
1807 Samuel H. Taylor, principal of Phillip Andover academy, born 10: 96
1820 William Gaston, Massachusetts lawyer and governor, born 1: 120
1820 Edward H. Janes, physician, born 8: 214
1823 Benjamin F. Stephenson, physician, founder of the Grand Army of the Republic, born 14: 111
1826 Amos R. Thomas, physician and dean of Hahnemann medical college, born 3: 481
1828 Charles Gordon Ames, clergyman and editor, born 23: 317
1832 Edward F. Noyes, soldier, governor of Ohio and American minister to France, born 3: 142

1836 Cornerstone of Mt. Holyoke seminary laid 4:462

1837 John H. Whittemore, industrialist, born 15: 70

1842 Louis James, actor, born 16:438

1846 Charles W. Dayton, New York lawyer and political leader, born 11:491

1847 John I. Sabin, founder of the first telephone company on the Pacific coast and president of the Chicago Bell Telephone Co., born 21:136

1849 Jeannette L. Gilder, editor and author, born .. 8:441

1855 Lilian Whiting, author, editor and poet, born .. 9:261

1861 Battle at Greenbrier river, W. Va. 9:232

1862 Battle of Corinth, Miss., began 4:162

1862 Andrew J. Montague, governor of Virginia, born 13:358

1863 President Lincoln instituted a permanent national festival, setting apart the last Thursday in November to be observed as a day of national thanksgiving 2: 73

1864 Mark V. Slingerland, entomologist, born 13:315

1873 International conference of the Evangelical Alliance met in New York city 3: 76

1877 William L. Harding, governor of Iowa, born ... B: 98

OCTOBER 4.

1765 Samuel Huntington, Ohio judge and governor, born 3:137

1777 Battle of Germantown, Pa. 1: 41

1780 Phillips academy at Andover incorporated 10: 93

1798 Louis C. Beck, scientist, born 5:542

1809 Robert C. Schenck, congressman, soldier and diplomat, born 3:206

1812 Battle of Ogdensburg, N. Y. 5:400

1814 William Gilpin, governor of Colorado, born 6:445

1816 Frederick William Gunn, founder of the Gunnery school, Washington, Conn., born 13:349

1822 Rutherford B. Hayes, president of the United States, born 3:191

1823 Edward A. Sheldon, educator, a pioneer in the objective system of teaching, born 7: 67

1823 Francis A. Roe, naval officer, born 12:547

1828 James E. Garretson, surgeon, born 3:212

1829 First Roman Catholic provincial council met in Baltimore 1:484

1835 Charles A. Curtis, Federal soldier and author, and president of Norwich university, born ... 18:326

1841 John J. Enneking, artist, born 5:319

1841 A convention met in Rhode Island to frame an amended state constitution, resulting in Dorr's rebellion 8:234

1841 Thomas C. Mendenhall, physicist, interested in gravity research and electrical phenomena, born 10:117

1846 Agnes Booth, actress, born 1:465

1858 Michael I. Pupin, inventor and physicist, born .. 26: 5

1863 William G. Haan, soldier, commander of the 32d division, known as "Les Terribles" in the World war, born 22:423

1861 Walter Rauschenbusch, theologian, born 19:193

1861 Edward B. Rosa, physicist, born 26:312

1862 Edward Stratemeyer, author, born 16: 37

1864 Leon Moran, artist, born 11:302

OCTOBER 5.

1675 Springfield, Mass., attacked by Indians 10: 50

1703 Jonathan Edwards, theologian and president of the College of New Jersey (Princeton), born 5:464

1750 James Iredell, justice of the U. S. supreme court, born 1: 23

1804 Robert P. Parrott, soldier, inventor and manufacturer of rifled cannon and projectiles, born 5:366

1822 Moses S. Beach, journalist, and inventor of printing and stereotyping appliances, born 13:329

1830 Chester A. Arthur, president of the United States, born 4:247

1834 David F. Boyd, Confederate soldier, and president of Louisiana state university and Alabama state college, born 13:235

1842 Thomas Evans, glass manufacturer, born 13:504

1846 First constitutional convention in Wisconsin .. 10:168

1848 Edward L. Trudeau, physician, founder of the Adirondack cottage sanitarium and the Saranac laboratory for the study of tuberculosis, born 13:564

1850 William Hamilton Gibson, artist, naturalist and author, born 7:463

1851 Thomas P. Anshutz, artist, born 15:279

1862 Gen. Price defeated at Big Hatchie river, Miss. 12:304

1870 Charles F. D. Belden, librarian, director of the Boston public library, and a pioneer in the development of library science, born 23: 53

1879 John Erskine, educator and author, born ..... B: 59

1881 The International cotton exposition, the first world's fair in the South, opened in Atlanta by Bishop Elliott 13:502

1882 Robert H. Goddard, physicist, born A:154

OCTOBER 6.

German Day in Pennsylvania

1683 The first German immigrants arrived in Philadelphia 11:352

1690 Seth Sothell usurped the government of South Carolina 12:152

1759 William Longstreet, inventor, who applied steam power to cotton gins, sawmills and riverboats, born 9:434

1770 Ferdinand R. Hassler, scientist, first superintendent of the U. S. coast survey, born 3:413

1777 Fts. Clinton and Montgomery captured from Gen. James Clinton by Sir Henry Clinton ... 1:305

1779 Nathan Appleton, cotton manufacturer and congressman, born 11:110

1780 John Chambers, congressman, and governor of Iowa, born 11:428

1785 William Burrows, naval officer, born 7: 71

1795 Joshua R. Giddings, abolitionist, born 2:329

1798 Robert Baird, author and clergyman, born 8:171

1809 John W. Griffiths, naval architect, born 8: 70

1812 Lazarus W. Powell, Kentucky governor and U. S. senator, born 13: 7

1816 William B. Bradbury, piano manufacturer and hymnologist, born 5:140

1820 Andrew H. Green, lawyer and civic leader, "the Father of Greater New York," born 13: 70

1822 Albert Harkness, philologist, born 6: 23

1823 George H. Boker, poet, playwright and diplomat, born 6: 73

1824 William N. Jeffers, Federal naval officer, inventor of a system of breech-loading guns, born 4:281

1828 Joshua Merrill, manufacturing chemist, who improved on processes for refining oil, born 13:258

1837 Trial trip of the "Sandusky" locomotive 19:175

1844 Samuel Davis, Confederate spy, "the Nathan Hale of the South," born 8:334

1844 Margaret H. Bates, author, born 10: 61

1846 George Westinghouse, air brake inventor and manufacturer, born 15: 41

1848 Allan McL. Hamilton, physician, a pioneer in the use of galvano-cautery and electrolysis, born 9:349

1848 Mary D. Hall, president of Sorosis, born 12:111

1857 Joseph T. Dickman, soldier, born 20: 11

1859 Frank A. Seiberling, founder of the Goodyear Tire and Rubber Co., born .... C: 33

1862 Albert J. Beveridge, U. S. senator, born 13: 26

1863 Joseph W. Bailey, U. S. senator, born 13:587

1867 George H. Lorimer, author, editor of the "Saturday Evening Post," born 13:423

1871 Enid Yandell, sculptor, born 13:210

1873 Oscar G. T. Sonneck, musicologist, born 25:283

1877 Charles E. Mitchell, head of the National City Bank of New York, born A:315

1888 Clarence Cook Little, president of the University of Michigan, born B:205

OCTOBER 7.

"Riley Day" in Indiana

1727 William S. Johnson, president of Columbia college, born 6:342

1728 Caesar Rodney, Delaware statesman, signer of the Declaration of Independence, born 5:173

1745 Henry Rutgers, patriot, and patron of Rutgers college, born 3:400

1746 William Billings, composer, born 5:421

1747 Ebenezer Zane, a founder of Zanesville, Ohio, born 11: 90

1756 First issue of the "New Hampshire Gazette" .. 23:288

1757 Robert Dinsmoor, poet, born 7:160

1765 Anti-Stamp Act Congress met in New York, nine colonies represented 1: 18

1769 Solomon Sibley, pioneer and judge, first mayor of Detroit, born 2:174

1775 Bristol, R. I., bombarded by the British 2:373

1776 Walter Jones, Virginia lawyer, born 1:365

1777 Battle of Saratoga (Bemis Heights), N. Y. ... 1: 53

1780 Battle of King's Mountain, N. C. 1:508

1821 Richard H. Anderson, Confederate soldier, born 4:295

1824 Pliny H. Hayes, physician, born 12:293

1827 William Barr, merchant and philanthropist, born 14:522

1832 Charles C. Converse, composer, born 8:449

1842 Bronson Howard, dramatist, born 3: 75

1842 Regis Chauvenet, chemist, president of the Colorado state school of mines, born 7:446

1842 Kate J. Bateman, actress, born 10:456

1850 George D. Ladd, physician, born 9:525

1853 James Whitcomb Riley, poet and humorist, born 6: 31

1856 John W. Alexander, artist, born 11:297

1857 George P. McLean, governor of Connecticut and U. S. senator, born B:395

1858 Charles F. Marvin, meteorologist, born 16: 47

1858 Francis Tiffany Bowles, chief constructor of the U. S. navy, and president of the Fore River Shipbuilding Co., born 20: 39
1864 Confederate S.S. "Florida" captured at Bahia, Brazil 4: 413
1873 George Cram Cook, founder and director of the Provincetown Players, born 22: 11
1888 Henry A. Wallace, editor of "Wallace's Farmer" and secretary of agriculture under Franklin D. Roosevelt, born ..... D: 17
1918 Rescue of the "Lost Battalion" after five days of enemy fire 20: 397

OCTOBER 8.

1609 John Clarke, one of the founders of Rhode Island, born 7: 346
1697 William Smith, colonial judge, born 11: 20
1720 Jonathan Mayhew, clergyman, born 7: 71
1753 William Jones, governor of Rhode Island, born 9: 394
1764 Harman Blennerhassett, political adventurer, born 13: 153
1765 Harrison Gray Otis, congressman and U. S. senator, born 7: 66
1789 John Ruggles, U. S. senator, born 12: 230
1797 William H. DeLancey, P. E. bishop, and provost of the University of Pennsylvania, born 1: 342
1807 George Abernethy, pioneer and governor of Oregon, born 8: 1
1810 James W. Marshall, discoverer of gold in California, born 5: 146
1812 Capture of the "Detroit" and the "Caledonia" on Lake Erie 7: 39
1816 Robert T. S. Lowell, clergyman, author and poet, born 8: 416
1818 John H. Reagan, postmaster general of the Confederacy, congressman and U. S. senator, born 1: 292
1833 Edmund Clarence Stedman, poet, critic and lecturer, born 3: 136
1838 John Hay, author and statesman, secretary of state under McKinley and Theodore Roosevelt, born 11: 12
1840 The self-acting "mule" for cotton machines patented 10: 386
1844 Alfred Arthur, composer, born 12: 273
1846 George H. Fox, physician, born 11: 284
1846 Elbert H. Gary, chairman of the U. S. Steel Corp., born 14: 69
1857 Edward F. Albee, theatrical manager, born 22: 53
1858 Sidney H. Short, electrical engineer and inventor, born 13: 247
1858 Edgar E. Saltus, author, born 19: 201
1861 Confederate attack on Fort Pickens, Fla. 4: 297
1862 Battle of Perrysville or Chaplain's Hill, Ky. 4: 263
1863 Edward Orton, Jr., ceramist and geologist, born 24: 107
1868 Coleman L. Blease, governor of South Carolina, born 15: 276
1869 Ex-President Franklin Pierce died 4: 146
1871 Great fire in Chicago broke out 11: 49
1871 Albert Edward Wiggam, author, born ..... C: 240
1918 Corporal York, with sixteen men, captured 132 German prisoners during the battle of the Argonne ..... A: 393

OCTOBER 9.

1779 Unsuccessful attack on the British at Savannah, Ga. 1: 69
1782 Lewis Cass, Michigan statesman and soldier, born 5: 3
1798 Matthew Lyon convicted under the Sedition law 2: 427
1798 Isaac Ferris, clergyman, and chancellor of the University of the City of New York, born 6: 323
1800 John Todd, clergyman and author, born 8: 125
1800 William Turnbull, engineer, born 12: 514
1801 Rowland G. Hazard, author and economist, born 9: 442
1805 William McK. Gwin, U. S. senator, born 5: 145
1818 Henry Lippitt, cotton manufacturer, and governor of Rhode Island, born 9: 405
1822 George Sykes, Federal soldier, born 4: 280
1827 John Dobson, woolen textiles manufacturer, a pioneer in the American carpet industry, born 17: 120
1830 Harriet Hosmer, sculptor, born 8: 284
1832 Elizabeth Akers Allen, poet, born 6: 133
1832 Francis J. Campbell, instructor of the blind, born 11: 374
1835 Charles T. Granger, judge, born 12: 69
1837 William L. Alden, journalist, born 6: 326
1838 Thomas H. Hines, judge, born 12: 453
1839 Winfield Scott Schley, naval officer, born 9: 8
1841 Samuel H. Buck, cotton merchant, born 12: 499
1843 Bradford Torrey, author and editor, born 10: 134
1846 William F. Allen, railroad expert, founder of standard time regulation, born 23: 230
1847 Battle of Huamantla, Mexico 8: 2
1848 Frank Duveneck, artist, born 20: 87
1852 James B. Lockwood, Arctic explorer, born 3: 286
1854 Myron T. Herrick, governor of Ohio, born 13: 68
1860 Leonard Wood, soldier and governor-general of the Philippine islands, born 9: 20
1861 Attack on Santa Rosa island, Fla. 4: 297
1862 Gen. Stuart started his raid on Chambersburg, Pa. 4: 52
1863 Edwin W. Bok, journalist and philanthropist, born 23: 41
1863 Gamaliel Bradford, poet and biographer, born .. 23: 65
1867 Alaska formally transferred to the United States 4: 366
1894 First presentation of motion picture plays in New York ..... B: 469

OCTOBER 10.

1738 Benjamin West, artist, born 5: 322
1758 Pierre Chouteau, pioneer trader, born 13: 469
1770 Benjamin Wright, chief engineer of the Erie Canal, born 1: 239
1774 Battle with Shawnee Indians at Point Pleasant, W. Va. 3: 430
1775 The last colonial governor of Massachusetts sailed for England 7: 378
1777 Hezekiah Niles, editor and author, born 10: 255
1788 Joshua Bates, banker and philanthropist, born .. 5: 195
1791 Daniel Treadwell, inventor of rope-making machinery, born 10: 165
1796 Ichabod Goodwin, governor of New Hampshire, born 11: 131
1802 George P. Morris, poet, editor and song writer, born 5: 434
1815 William J. Hardee, Confederate soldier, born .. 4: 101
1828 Samuel J. Randall, speaker of the house of representatives, born 3: 57
1831 Henry Mason, piano manufacturer, born 13: 437
1832 John W. Mallet, chemist, born 13: 55
1836 William D. Hoard, Wisconsin dairyman and governor, born 16: 398
1837 Robert Gould Shaw, Federal soldier, born 8: 142
1838 Edna Dean Proctor, poet, born 7: 250
1838 Harlow N. Higinbotham, merchant, and president of the World's Columbian exposition in Chicago, born 18: 389
1839 William Everett, congressman and author, born 9: 222
1841 John J. Stevenson, geologist, born 7: 137
1844 Louis McL. Tiffany, surgeon, pioneer advocate of antiseptic surgery, born 24: 358
1845 The U. S. naval academy formally opened with Franklin Buchanan as first superintendent.... 4: 38
1852 John Wheelock Elliot, surgeon, one of the first to perform a successful appendectomy, born .. 22: 424
1853 Henry Wade Rogers, president of Northwestern university, born 26: 50
1858 Benjamin M. Des Jardins, inventor of an automatic type-setter, an adding-machine and a cryptograph, born 12: 536
1860 Henry Platt Cushing, geologist, an authority on pre-Cambrian formations in northern New York, born 19: 249
1861 George Brand Duncan, soldier, born ..... A: 64
1862 Galveston, Tex., captured by Comr. Renshaw .. 12: 66
1863 Alanson B. Houghton, industrialist and diplomat, born ..... B: 7
1864 John D. Ryan, industrialist, president of the Anaconda Copper Mining Co., born 23: 248
1873 George Cabot Lodge, poet, born 24: 386

OCTOBER 11.

1759 Mason L. Weems, Episcopal clergyman, biographer, originator of the George Washington hatchet story, born 5: 392
1764 Prentiss Mellen, judge and U. S. senator, born .. 11: 335
1776 Benedict Arnold, in command of a small fleet on Lake Champlain, engaged in battle with the British 1: 53
1798 Samuel G. Drake, antiquarian, born 7: 61
1802 Levi Scott, M. E. bishop, born 9: 529
1806 Henry Dexter, sculptor, born 8: 288
1811 First steam ferry in the world established between New York city and Hoboken, N. J. .. 11: 21
1816 Henry Howe, historian and publisher, born 3: 344
1816 Richard B. Kimball, author, lawyer and traveler, born 10: 32
1822 John D. Runkle, mathematician, and a founder and president of the Massachusetts institute of technology, born 6: 350
1835 Theodore Thomas, musician, born 2: 139
1835 Hunter H. McGuire, surgeon, born 5: 163
1842 Treaty with the Sac and Fox Indians 12: 221
1844 Henry J. Heinz, head of the Heinz pickling and preserving industry, born 5: 270
1853 New York clearing house, first in America, began its operations 2: 504

1855 James Gayley, metallurgist, born 14: 70
1863 Harry Augustus Garfield, president of Williams college, born .... A: 102
1872 Harlan F. Stone, justice of the U. S. supreme court, born .... A: 11
1890 Daughters of the American Revolution founded in Washington, D. C. 19: 138
1897 Joseph Auslander, author, an outstanding critic of poetry, born .... D: 45

OCTOBER 12.

Columbus Day

1492 Columbus discovered America 3: 438
1710 Jonathan Trumbull (Brother Jonathan), governor of Connecticut, born 10: 328
1743 John F. Williams, naval officer, born 4: 152
1753 John Pratt, soldier, born 12: 470
1793 Cornerstone of the University of North Carolina laid 13: 241
1803 Alexander T. Stewart, New York merchant, born 7: 352
1808 Frances D. Gage (Aunt Fanny), author and reformer, born 2: 321
1812 Charles Loring Elliott, artist, born 11: 311
1813 Lyman Trumbull, U. S. senator, born 12: 342
1818 William Thaw, an officer of the Pennsylvania Railroad Co. and a founder of the Red Star steamship line, born 17: 298
1827 Josiah P. Cooke, chemist, born 6: 12
1837 Preston B. Plumb, U. S. senator, born 2: 529
1844 George W. Cable, author, born 1: 533
1844 Helena Modjeska, actress, born 10: 447
1844 Charles King, soldier and author, born 25: 148
1846 Louis E. Levy, inventor, born 13: 589
1848 Alvina Valleria, singer, born 1: 426
1852 George T. Winston, president of the University of North Carolina, born 13: 243
1853 Winslow Upton, astronomer, born 12: 238
1858 Isaac N. Lewis, soldier and inventor of the Lewis machine gun, born 16: 213
1860 Elmer A. Sperry, inventor of the gyro-compass, gyro stabilizers for ships and airplanes, a high intensity searchlight, etc., born 23: 78
1860 William L. Sibert, soldier, born .... B: 47
1861 Confederate commissioners to France and England ran the blockade 2: 93
1861 The ram "Manassas" attacked the Federal fleet 11: 252
1861 Charles D. Armstrong, manufacturer of linoleum, born 25: 87
1877 Howard M. Gore, secretary of agriculture under Coolidge, and governor of West Virginia, born B: 45
1892 First comet discovered by photography 7: 44
1915 The first trans-Atlantic speech by radio 25: 184

OCTOBER 13.

1701 Isaac Norris, statesman, born 5: 88
1727 William Gooch became governor of Virginia 13: 388
1744 Molly Pitcher, heroine of the battle of Monmouth, born 9: 262
1765 Azel Backus, first president of Hamilton college, born 7: 405
1769 Horace H. Hayden, founder and first president of the Baltimore college of dental surgery, born 13: 525
1799 John Baldwin, originator of the grindstone industry in Berea, Ohio, and founder of Baldwin university, born 21: 142
1810 Alpheus Crosby, educator, born 9: 97
1812 Battle of Queenstown Heights, Canada 11: 285
1813 Amos H. Worthen, geologist, born 6: 20
1816 Benjamin H. Brewster, attorney-general under Arthur, born 4: 253
1822 Eben D. Jordan, founder of Jordan Marsh & Co., Boston merchants, born 2: 393
1823 James H. Salisbury, physician, born 8: 469
1827 James H. Stoddart, actor, born 6: 502
1831 John W. Hoyt, governor of Wyoming, and first president of the University of Wyoming, born 13: 158
1841 Charles W. Hunt, mechanical engineer, inventor of the Hunt automatic railway, born 13: 455
1845 Texas ratified a state constitution 5: 165
1845 Charles H. Stockton, naval officer and president of George Washington university, born 25: 214
1848 William B. P. Closson, artist, born 8: 431
1851 Charles S. Pearce, artist, born 11: 286
1854 Augustus C. Bernays, St. Louis surgeon, born .. 6: 233
1862 John R. Commons, economist, born .... A: 423

OCTOBER 14.

1644 William Penn, founder of Pennsylvania, born.. 2: 274
1696 Samuel Johnson, clergyman and first president of Kings (Columbia) college, born 6: 341
1734 Francis L. Lee, signer of the Declaration of Independence, born 5: 252
1780 Gen. Nathanael Greene appointed commander of the Southern army 1: 42
1806 Preston King, U. S. senator, born 2: 93
1816 Daniel Huntington, artist, born 5: 323
1827 James C. Carter, lawyer, born 22: 26
1833 Junius Henry Browne, journalist, born 13: 357
1837 Abby Sage Richardson, author, born 5: 553
1841 Henry D. Coffinberry, a founder of the fresh-water ship-building industry in Cleveland, born 15: 277
1846 Willard Bartlett, jurist and editor, born 15: 412
1847 James O'Neill, actor, born 11: 185
1857 Joseph R. Lamar, justice of the U. S. supreme court, born 15: 414
1857 Elwood Haynes, metallurgist, and designer and manufacturer of one of the earliest successful gasoline motor cars, born 25: 12
1859 Benjamin W. Clinedinst, artist, born 22: 73
1863 Battle of Bristoe's Station, Va. 4: 68
1866 Charles Frederick Hughes, naval officer, born.. 25: 117
1913 Langmuir applied for a patent on his high vacuum tube .... C: 30

OCTOBER 15.

1746 Leonard Neale, archbishop of Baltimore, and president of Georgetown college, born 1: 482
1762 Samuel Holyoke, musician, born 13: 177
1770 William Nelson became acting governor of Virginia 13: 391
1775 John Vanderlyn, artist, born 1: 414
1784 Thomas Hastings, composer and editor, born ... 7: 431
1801 Seabury Ford, governor of Ohio, born 3: 140
1818 Irwin McDowell, Federal soldier, born 4: 50
1826 Daniel Dougherty, lawyer and orator, born 5: 477
1829 Asaph Hall, mathematical astronomer, born 22: 287
1831 Horace Austin, Minnesota governor and jurist, born 10: 64
1833 Denman Thompson, actor, born 8: 46
1843 Herbert W. Ladd, merchant, philanthropist and governor of Rhode Island, born 18: 137
1847 Ralph A. Blakelock, landscape artist, born 15: 406
1848 Charles H. Colton, R. C. bishop, born 12: 485
1851 Samuel Bowles, 3d, editor and publisher of the Springfield (Mass.) "Republican," born 1: 318
1854 James E. Quigley, archbishop of Chicago, born .. 12: 484
1857 Andrew J. Shipman, New York lawyer, born 15: 209
1858 Frank Van Der Stucken, musician, born 11: 39
1858 William S. Sims, naval officer, commander of U. S. naval forces operating in European waters in the World war, born .... A: 192
1866 Max L. Margolis, philologist, an eminent student of and authority on the Hebrew Bible, born 23: 383
1872 Ben Wilson Olcott, governor of Oregon, born .. B: 442
1880 Arthur B. Reeve, author, born 26: 276
1884 Opening of the Groton (Mass.) school for boys A: 308
1888 Willard Huntington Wright, author, editor and critic, born .... C: 481
1914 Passage of the Clayton anti-trust act 19: 3

OCTOBER 16.

1660 Hugh Peters, clergyman of Massachusetts Bay Colony, beheaded in London 8: 338
1690 Sir Francis Nicholson assumed the government of Virginia 13: 386
1701 Yale college granted a charter by the Connecticut assembly 1: 164
1725 First newspaper in New York city issued by William Bradford 19: 276
1754 Morgan Lewis, soldier, and governor of New York, born 3: 43
1758 Noah Webster, lexicographer, born 2: 394
1758 John Paulding, revolutionary soldier, who participated in the apprehension of Major André, born 13: 318
1759 Bland W. Ballard, Kentucky pioneer, born 5: 124
1760 Jonathan Dayton, speaker of the house and U. S. senator, born 1: 306
1762 Paul Hamilton, governor of South Carolina and secretary of the navy under Madison, born .. 5: 373
1777 Lorenzo Dow, clergyman, born 10: 472
1795 William B. Sprague, clergyman, author and editor, born 5: 239
1806 William P. Fessenden, U. S. senator and secretary of the treasury under Lincoln, born 2: 90
1807 Mason J. Metcalf, inventor, born 12: 500
1815 Francis R. Lubbock, governor of Texas, and Confederate soldier, born 9: 69
1816 William Preston, Confederate soldier, and diplomat, born 9: 433
1824 John B. Bowman, founder of Kentucky university, born 4: 516

1831 Alfred L. Loomis, physician, born 8: 223
1835 Augustine Jones, lawyer and educator, principal of the Friends' school in Providence, R. I., born 6: 203
1835 William R. Shafter, soldier, born 9: 18
1835 William H. Pancoast, surgeon, born 10: 274
1836 Russell Sturgis, architect, born 9: 330
1838 Horace E. Scudder, author, and editor of the "Atlantic Monthly," born 1: 284
1840 Frederick L. Hosmer, clergyman and hymn writer, born 21: 31
1846 The first public demonstration of ether as an anaesthetic 8: 332
1847 Beloit college, Wisconsin, opened 3: 184
1847 Samuel P. Jones, evangelist, born 13: 438
1850 Charles Arthur Mallory, hat manufacturer, born 15: 403
1859 John Brown's insurrection at Harper's Ferry .. 2: 308
1863 Gen. Grant appointed to command the Division of the Mississippi 4: 6
1863 Beverly T. Galloway, scientist, born 12: 504
1869 Claude H. Van Tyne, historian, born 26: 268
1875 Henry Clapp Sherman, chemist, specialist in the chemistry of foods and study of vitamins, born D: 65
1888 Eugene O'Neill, playwright, winner of the 1936 Nobel prize for literature, born .... A: 443

OCTOBER 17.

1683 Representative government, "Dongan's charter of Liberties and Privileges," adopted in New York 10: 241
1775 Burning of Falmouth (Portland), Maine, by the British 5: 441
1777 Burgoyne surrendered to the Americans at Saratoga 1: 47
1781 Richard M. Johnson, vice-president of the United States, born 6: 434
1796 Ross Winans, mechanic and inventor, born 11: 358
1813 Alfred Hitchcock, surgeon, born 4: 27
1823 George L. Duyckinck, editor and biographer, born 10: 502
1825 William P. Seymour, gynecologist, born 4: 210
1825 William R. Marshall, Federal soldier and governor of Minnesota, born 10: 64
1836 Society for the Diffusion of Useful Knowledge incorporated 10: 356
1837 Lorettus S. Metcalf, founder and editor of "The Forum," born 1: 353
1845 Peter Bourgade, archbishop of Santa Fé, born . 12: 50
1857 Bruce Crane, artist, born 11: 310
1859 Childe Hassam, artist, born 10: 374
1864 Robert Lansing, secretary of state under Wilson, born 20: 1
1867 Harold Van Buren Magonigle, architect, born.. C: 506
1911 Mail carried in a hydro-aeroplane down the Mississippi river from Minneapolis to Rock Island (314 miles) 15: 401

OCTOBER 18.

1540 Encounter between Spaniards and Indians in Alabama 5: 126
1635 Roger Williams tried for heresy 10: 5
1675 Treaty signed with the Narragansett Indians .. 10: 403
1787 Robert L. Stevens, boat-builder and inventor, born 11: 21
1796 Hosea Ballou, 2d, first president of Tufts college, born 6: 241
1802 Homer L. Thrall, physicist, born 8: 143
1803 Amos Binney, zoologist, specializing in mollusks, born 7: 510
1809 Thomas H. Chivers, author and poet, who claimed to have given Poe the inspiration for "The Raven," born 21: 223
1811 Waitman T. Willey, U. S. senator, born 12: 455
1812 The "Wasp" captured the English brig "Frolic," but both ships were taken by the British later on the same day 6: 56
1812 Julius W. Adams, civil engineer, born 9: 33
1818 Edward O. C. Ord, Federal soldier, born 4: 281
1820 Anson D. F. Randolph, publisher and poet, born 8: 460
1823 Thomas Hicks, artist, born 5: 509
1824 Allen B. Wilson, inventor of a sewing-machine, born 9: 460
1824 John Lowell, Massachusetts judge and statesman, born 11: 550
1828 Isaac P. Gray, governor of Indiana and minister to Mexico, born 13: 273
1831 Helen Hunt Jackson (H. H.), author, born ... 1: 433
1835 Marshall MacDonald, icthyologist, born 13: 321
1836 Frederick A. O. Schwarz, New York toy merchant, born 11: 249
1839 Thomas B. Reed, congressman, born 2: 383
1844 Harvey W. Wiley, chemist and pure food expert, born 21: 72
1846 Frederick Juengling, wood engraver, etcher and painter, born 11: 195
1849 Sarah T. H. Rorer, domestic economist, born .. 16: 232
1854 "Ostend Manifesto" signed by Soulé, Buchanan and Mason 3: 117
1859 John Brown captured by U. S. troops 2: 307
1863 Roland W. Boyden, lawyer and student of international affairs, who represented the United States in the reparations commission, the permanent court of arbitration at The Hague, and various economic conferences sponsored by the League of Nations, born 23: 57
1870 Gano S. Dunn, electrician and inventor, born .. 18: 105
1878 James Truslow Adams, historian, Pulitzer prize winner, born .... D: 56
1882 Struthers Burt, author, born .... D: 387
1892 Long distance telephone service opened between Chicago and New York 5: 83
1898 U. S. troops took formal possession of Puerto Rico 11: 4

OCTOBER 19.

1595 Edward Winslow, a "Mayflower" passenger, and governor of the Plymouth colony, born 7: 369
1635 Roger Williams ordered to leave the Massachusetts colony 10: 5
1673 Benjamin Colman, Boston clergyman and author, born 7: 153
1720 John Woolman, Quaker leader and abolitionist, born 1: 288
1744 John Brown, soldier, born 1: 44
1765 A secretly met provincial congress adopted a declaration of rights and grievances 5: 534
1770 James Kilbourne, explorer and pioneer settler of Ohio, born 5: 123
1779 Thomas C. Brownell, P. E. bishop and president of Trinity college, born 3: 495
1781 Cornwallis surrendered at Yorktown, Va. 1: 4
1784 John McLoughlin, factor of the Hudson Bay colony, born 6: 390
1794 Charles R. Leslie, painter and author, born 5: 321
1810 Cassius M. Clay, abolitionist and ambassador, born 2: 311
1821 William W. Patton, clergyman, president of Howard university, born 10: 165
1831 Thomas Hunter, founder and first president of Hunter college, born 22: 244
1833 William C. Wilkinson, educator and author, born 11: 72
1834 Francis C. Barlow, soldier, born 8: 333
1835 Amanda Theodosia Jones, author, editor and inventor, born 7: 547
1840 John W. Chadwick, clergyman, author and poet, born 7: 77
1842 John L. Mitchell, U. S. senator, born 2: 341
1849 Thomas Allen, artist, born 24: 92
1850 Baltimore "Daily Dispatch" first issued 2: 51
1855 George Smedley Webster, civil engineer, born... 25: 382
1856 Edmund B. Wilson, biologist, born 13: 59
1861 William J. Burns, detective, born 24: 209
1863 John H. Finley, editor and lecturer, president of Knox college, born 13: 503
1864 Battle of Cedar Creek, Va. 4: 138
1869 George Taylor Plowman, etcher, born 23: 110
1871 Donn Barber, architect, designer of the Broadway Temple, New York city, and originator of the "atelier" idea in the United States, born 25: 368
1871 Walter B. Cannon, physiologist, discoverer of a new hormone in the human system, born ..... D: 72
1889 Fannie Hurst, author, born .... B: 287
1919 William O. Jenkins, American consular agent at Puebla, Mexico, was kidnapped, precipitating an international incident 20: 2

OCTOBER 20.

1674 James Logan, president of the executive council of Pennsylvania, born 2: 278
1711 Timothy Ruggles, Massachusetts judge and soldier, born 2: 57
1774 Articles of Association signed 13: 540
1801 John Cheney, engraver, born 19: 359
1806 George N. Lawrence, ornithologist, born 2: 203
1810 Alfred W. Craven, civil engineer, born 9: 37
1811 Oliver Ditson, music publisher, born 7: 358
1812 Austin Flint, physician, a founder of Buffalo medical college, born 8: 311
1816 James W. Grimes, Iowa governor and U. S. senator, born 11: 430
1818 Treaty respecting boundaries, fisheries and the restoration of slaves, concluded between England and the United States 5: 81
1820 Benjamin F. Cheatham, Confederate soldier, the "Ney of the Confederacy," born 11: 90

1822 Mansfield Lovell, Confederate soldier, born 4:352
1825 Marshall Jewell, governor of Connecticut, diplomat, and postmaster general under Grant, born 4: 20
1825 Daniel E. Sickles, Federal soldier and minister to Spain, born 12:450
1838 David D. Neal, artist, born 9: 53
1839 Oliver McClintock, merchant and political reformer, born 12: 7
1843 Alexander T. McGill, jurist, born 12:364
1845 John E. Trowbridge, composer, born 7:438
1847 Guaymas, Mexico, captured by Comr. Montgomery 10: 31
1848 Hugh Bolton Jones, artist, born 13:126
1850 Francis H. Richards, inventor of the Richards envelope machine and an automatic weighing machine, born 7:420
1850 Octavius Morgan, architect, born 16:364
1859 John Dewey, educator and philosopher, born .. A:547
1862 Maud Nathan, reformer, born 15: 52
1862 Benjamin B. Thayer, mining engineer, born 15: 66
1867 Thomas N. McCarter, lawyer, and organizer and president of the Public Service Corp. of New Jersey, born ..... D: 84
1869 John C. Merriam, paleontologist, president of the Carnegie Institution of Washington, D. C., born A:485
1890 Henry John Doermann, president of the University of the City of Toledo, born 25:347

OCTOBER 21.

1520 Magellan entered the strait that bears his name 6:249
1681 William Gooch, governor of Virginia, born 13:388
1736 William Shippen, Jr., physician, born 10:384
1754 James Hillhouse, U. S. senator, born 2: 9
1776 George Izard, Arkansas soldier and governor, born 10:183
1784 William Henry Allen, naval officer, born 8: 15
1785 Henry M. Shreve, inventor, who improved on Fulton's steamboat, born 2:185
1796 John G. C. Brainard, poet and editor, born 8:274
1797 Frigate "Constitution" launched at Boston 25:198
1804 Jabez Coney, pioneer in New England in building mills, water wheels, iron vessels and marine engines, born 23:164
1808 Samuel F. Smith, clergyman and author, who wrote the words of the national hymn, "America," born 6: 51
1812 Thomas H. Vail, P. E. bishop, born 12: 89
1821 Mrs. George H. Gilbert, actress, born 1:285
1823 Paul A. Chadbourne, president of the University of Wisconsin and of Williams college, born .. 6:238
1826 Lemuel M. Wiles, artist, born 12:443
1832 John E. Sweet, inventor and manufacturer of the straight-line high-speed engine, born 13: 54
1835 Pro-slavery demonstration in Boston 2:314
1835 State anti-slavery convention met at Utica, N. Y. 2:332
1837 James A. Beaver, Federal soldier, and governor of Pennsylvania, born 2:293
1837 Arthur Searle, essayist and astronomer, famous for his studies of zodiacal light, born 19: 34
1842 Horace W. Robbins, artist, born 13: 23
1845 Will Carleton, poet and lecturer, born 2:505
1847 Charles A. Stephens, scientist, author and editor, born 23:122
1855 Howard H. Russell, clergyman and reformer, born 13:330
1859 Margaret Mather, actress, born 9:446
1861 Battle of Ball's Bluff, Va. 11:215
1869 William E. Dodd, historian and U. S. ambassador to Germany, born ..... D: 34
1878 Melvin Alvah Traylor, Chicago banker, one of the committe which organized the Bank for International Settlements, born 25:137
1879 First practical incandescent light produced by Edison 25: 2
1887 James L. McConaughy, president of Wesleyan university, born B:424
1915 U. S. note to Great Britain condemned the British blockade of Germany 20: 1
1915 First telephone message sent across the Atlantic 23: 36
1917 First American division in the trenches in the World War D:436

OCTOBER 22.

1738 James Manning, clergyman, founder and president of Rhode Island college (Brown university), born 8: 20
1759 Thomas Cooper, scientist, economist, and president of South Carolina college, born 11: 31
1773 Constantine S. Rafinesque, botanist, born 8:472
1774 Henry Middleton elected president of the Continental congress 5:367
1777 British unsuccessfully attacked Fort Mercer, N.J. 8:298
1779 William Tryon attainted by act of congress because of his cruelty in the Revolution 7:514
1780 John Forsyth, U. S. senator, governor of Georgia and secretary of state under Jackson and Van Buren, born 6:435
1812 Shobal V. Clevenger, sculptor, born 8:280
1817 Alexander W. Thayer, author, born 8:233
1832 Leopold Damrosch, musician, born 2:147
1833 Emily Huntington Miller, author and editor, born 10:305
1833 James A. Gary, postmaster general under McKinley, born 11: 16
1842 Annie Louise Cary, singer, born 1:426
1843 Charles Dole, president of Norwich university, born 18:327
1843 Stephen M. Babcock, agricultural chemist, originator of the Babcock test for determining the butter-fat content of milk, born 22: 16
1844 Day predicted for the end of the world by Miller, the Adventist 6:273
1862 Engagement at Old Fort Wayne, Ark. 9:443
1868 Andrew L. Riker, electrical and mechanical engineer, designer of high-speed electric cars and of the Locomobile, born 22: 61
1883 Opening of the Metropolitan opera house, New York 2:147
1901 Beginning of the second Pan-American congress in Mexico City 13:240
1914 Commission for relief in Belgium organized A:166

OCTOBER 23.

1750 Thomas Pinckney, governor of South Carolina and diplomat, born 12:160
1762 Samuel Morey, steamboat inventor, born 11:168
1783 George Watterston, author and librarian of congress, born 7:501
1790 Chauncey A. Goodrich, lexicographer, born 4:511
1800 William B. Laurence, diplomat and expert on international law, born 9:399
1801 Benjamin W. Raymond, merchant, born 12:449
1805 John R. Bartlett, historian, ethnologist, and acting governor of Rhode Island, born 9:402
1806 Myron H. Clark, governor of New York, born.. 3: 50
1810 William W. Turner, philologist, born 9:198
1812 William C. Kenyon, founder and president of Alfred university, born 5:231
1815 Walter Abbott Wood, inventor of reaping machines, born 6:398
1817 James W. Denver, Western pioneer and governor of Kansas territory, in whose honor the city of Denver was named, born 8:341
1819 Isaac B. Woodbury, musician and composer, born 2:121
1823 John R. Thompson, poet and editor, born 6: 49
1829 William M. Taylor, clergyman, born 2:189
1835 Adlai E. Stevenson, vice-president of the United States, born 2:487
1837 Harlan P. Halsey (Old Sleuth), author, born . 9:145
1838 Francis Hopkinson Smith, engineer, author and artist, born 5:326
1845 George A. Stringer, author, born 13:198
1847 Henry P. Smith, clergyman, born 23:174
1852 William Burt, M. E. bishop, born 26:475
1853 Wallace Buttrick, president of the General Education Board endowed by John D. Rockefeller, born 22:419
1861 Herbert Quick, lawyer and editor, born 25:137
1902 The Pennsylvania coal strike, involving 145,000 anthracite miners, settled 14: 13

OCTOBER 24.

1683 Germantown, Pa., laid out 11:352
1788 Sarah J. Hale, author and editor of the "Ladies Magazine," born 22: 39
1791 Joseph R. Underwood, U. S. senator, born 3:428
1801 Isaac Rich, philanthropist, born 11:175
1803 Albert S. White, U. S. senator, born 3:507
1808 John Sartain, artist and engraver, born 6:472
1809 Daniel Clark, U. S. senator, born 2: 87
1810 Thomas G. Turner, governor of Rhode Island, born 9:401
1819 Erie canal opened between Rome and Utica, N.Y. 3: 45
1825 John M. Daniel, editor of the Richmond "Examiner," born 10: 33
1830 Belva A. B. Lockwood, lawyer, who secured the passage of a bill admitting women lawyers to the U. S. supreme court, and was the first woman admitted under it, born 2: 61
1830 Noah Brooks, editor and author, born 7: 57
1836 George W. Hough, astronomer, born 8:337
1848 William F. Apthorp, music critic, born 21:130
1861 The first transcontinental telegraph line completed 22:170
1866 Peabody Institute, Baltimore, inaugurated 5:336

1867 Frank L. O. Wadsworth, scientist and engineer, inventor of improvements in astronomical instruments, methods of manufacturing glass, steel and electrical apparatus, etc., born ..... D: 203
1871 Henry M. Shrady, sculptor, born 13: 393
1883 Marcella Sembrich made her début at the Metropolitan opera house 25: 69
1916 Joy patented his process for producing motion pictures in natural color .... A: 488
1931 George Washington bridge officially opened to traffic .... D: 321

OCTOBER 25.

1754 Richard Howell, governor of New Jersey, born 5: 202
1775 Governor Murray attacked Hampton, Va., and was defeated by the colonists 13: 391
1782 Levi Lincoln, 2d, Massachusetts judge and governor, born 1: 114
1784 Chester Dewey, scientist, born 6: 328
1792 Franklin Bache, chemist, born 5: 346
1795 John P. Kennedy, author, and secretary of the navy under Fillmore, born 6: 181
1806 George Law, steamship and railroad executive, born 3: 94
1810 William A. Norton, scientist, born 9: 187
1811 Carl F. W. Walther, theologian, born 26: 118
1812 The frigate "Macedonian" captured by the frigate "United States" 8: 15
1813 William L. Herndon, naval officer, born 4: 201
1819 First general assembly of Alabama met 10: 425
1825 Francis A. March, philologist, born 11: 244
1834 George P. Upton, editor, author and music critic, born 18: 392
1839 Robert H. Thurston, mechanical engineer, born 4: 479
1840 Thomas Davidson, philosopher, reputed to be one of the twelve most learned men in the world, born 23: 311
1847 Archibald Clavering Gunter, author, born 15: 247
1848 William Henry Moore, corporation lawyer and financier, born 23: 72
1862 Grant took command of the Department of the Tennessee 4: 4
1863 George R. Carpenter, author and editor, best known for his contributions to the Dante bibliography, born 23: 328
1864 John F. Dodge, automobile manufacturer, born 19: 266
1865 Walter R. Ingalls, mining and metallurgical engineer, born 16: 127
1866 Thomas J. Garland, P. E. bishop, born 22: 311
1888 Richard E. Byrd, Jr., aviator and explorer, first to fly to the North and South poles, born B: 431

OCTOBER 26.

1757 Ashur Robbins, Rhode Island lawyer and U. S. senator, born 1: 452
1757 Charles Pinckney, South Carolina statesman, born 12: 161
1777 Increase Kimball, inventor of a nail-manufacturing machine, born 4: 293
1789 Reuben H. Walworth, chancellor of New York, born 3: 56
1791 Charles Sprague, poet, "the American Pope," born 6: 229
1804 Lorenzo Thomas, soldier, born 11: 352
1816 Philip P. Cooke, poet, born 7: 330
1818 James R. M. Mullany, naval officer, born 4: 37
1818 Elizabeth Prentiss, author, born 7: 106
1821 Benjamin Chew Tilghman, inventor of the sand blast, born 15: 263
1824 Joseph B. Holder, naturalist, born 7: 402
1825 Erie canal opened to traffic 3: 45
1831 John W. Noble, lawyer, secretary of the interior under Harrison, born 1: 146
1833 Adelaide Phillips, prima donna, born 6: 149
1836 Thomas A. Osborn, lawyer, governor of Kansas, diplomat, born 8: 345
1839 Thomas P. Ochiltree, congressman, born 2: 193
1839 Henry C. Hasbrouck, soldier, born 15: 356
1840 Thomas Wallace Keene, actor, born 8: 384
1842 Founders of the Amana Society landed in America 13: 39
1843 Daniel C. Heath, textbook publisher, born 10: 466
1845 Edward Harrigan, actor, born 11: 442
1846 Lewis Boss, astronomer, born 13: 251
1854 Charles W. Post, originator of "Postum" and other prepared foods, born 25: 40
1855 George D. Burton, inventor of an electrical welding process, born 12: 467
1860 Will Allen Dromgoole, author, born 8: 258
1862 Gen. McClelland advanced into Maryland 4: 143
1868 George Gordon Battle, New York lawyer, born.. C: 195
1877 Max Mason, president of the University of Chicago, born .... B: 485
1915 Eva Le Gallienne's début on the American stage C: 385

OCTOBER 27.

1682 The "Welcome," with a hundred Friends aboard, arrived at New Castle, Del. 2: 276
1763 William Maclure, geologist, born 13: 368
1795 Treaty of San Lorenzo with Spain signed, defining the boundaries of Spanish possessions in North America 4: 530
1811 Isaac M. Singer, sewing machine inventor, born 5: 557
1814 John McClintock, clergyman, and president of Drew theological seminary, born 6: 466
1819 Henry B. Plant, railroad builder, "the King of Florida," born 18: 286
1823 William D. Simpson, South Carolina lawyer and governor, born 12: 178
1827 Albert Fink, civil engineer, born 9: 489
1828 Jacob D. Cox, Federal soldier, governor of Ohio and secretary of the interior under Grant, born 22: 231
1829 Christopher C. Andrews, lawyer, Federal soldier and minister to Norway and Sweden, born ... 11: 393
1836 Erasmus D. Leavitt, mechanical engineer, inventor of high-duty pumps, born 24: 324
1837 Whitelaw Reid, journalist and diplomat, born .. 22: 1
1838 John D. Long, governor of Massachusetts and secretary of the navy under McKinley, born.. 11: 15
1841 Eugene A. Smith, geologist, born 6: 185
1856 Kenyon Cox, artist and illustrator, born 5: 321
1858 Theodore Roosevelt, president of the United States, born 14: 1
1858 John L. Bogert, mechanical engineer and inventor, designer of the Bogert unsinkable freight-ship and submarine destroyers, born 16: 29
1861 Edward M. Grout, lawyer, born 8: 39
1863 Capture of Brown's Ferry, Tenn., by the Federals 7: 518
1864 Confederate ram "Albemarle" destroyed by a torpedo 9: 374
1870 Roscoe Pound, lawyer and dean of the Harvard law school, born .... B: 51
1873 James J. Davis, secretary of labor under Harding, Coolidge and Hoover, born .... A: 17
1874 Janet Scudder, sculptor, born 15: 346
1874 Owen D. Young, chairman of the board of the General Electric Co. and the Radio Corporation of America, and author of the Young plan for the settlement of the World war reparations problem, born .... A: 81
1904 New York subway opened to the public 12: 548

OCTOBER 28.

1586 Francis West, governor of Virginia, born 13: 382
1636 Harvard college founded by the general court of the Massachusetts bay colony 6: 408
1646 John Eliot preached his first sermon in the Indian language 2: 420
1664 Part of New Jersey purchased from the Indians 19: 263
1765 James Blythe, clergyman and first president of Hanover college, born 2: 123
1771 First copy of the "Pennsylvania Packet" issued 19: 363
1776 Battle of White Plains, N. Y. 9: 292
1792 Erastus Fairbanks, governor of Vermont and manufacturer of the platform scale, born 8: 320
1798 Levi Coffin, leader in the operation of the "underground railway," born 12: 124
1801 Henry Inman, portrait and genre painter, born 9: 247
1808 Horace Smith, inventor and manufacturer of firearms, born 10: 476
1821 Collis P. Huntington, railroad builder, born 15: 15
1831 Cornelius Hedges, lawyer, born 12: 250
1832 Hiram Rich, banker and poet, born 9: 390
1835 Battle of Concepcion, Tex. 4: 211
1835 Robert Treat Paine, Boston lawyer and philanthropist, born 26: 13
1836 Homer D. Martin, artist, born 9: 53
1842 Anna E. Dickinson, lecturer and author, born .. 3: 109
1844 John K. Cowen, president of the Baltimore & Ohio railroad, born 18: 6
1844 Moses J. Ezekiel, sculptor, born 18: 217
1847 J. Walter Thompson, pioneer advertising director, first to exploit magazine advertising, born 21: 132
1854 Calvin Thomas, philologist, authority on Germanic languages and literature, born 16: 220
1854 Birge Harrison, artist, born 26: 162
1859 John Mason, actor, born 15: 50
1862 Earl Douglass, paleontologist, who discovered valuable fossils in Utah, born 26: 126
1864 Battle of Newtonia, Mo. 9: 443
1865 Florida repealed the ordinance of secession 11: 379
1867 Bashford Dean, zoologist, born 21: 29
1869 Joseph W. Folk, Missouri governor and reformer, born 22: 171
1885 Charles Francis Potter, founder of the First Humanist Society of New York city, born .. C: 89
1886 Statue of Liberty in New York bay unveiled 11: 216
1934 The Hetch Hetchy system for supplying water to the city of San Francisco began functioning .. 24: 52

OCTOBER 29.

1754 John Reynolds assumed the office of governor of Georgia ... 1:491
1764 Hartford "Courant" first issued ... 1:457
1782 William H. Wilmer, clergyman, and president of William and Mary college, born ... 3:235
1784 Robert Hoe, printing press manufacturer, born . 7:320
1794 William B. Tappan, poet, born ... 5:241
1801 Edward Bourns, president of Norwich university, born ... 18:324
1802 Ephraim G. Peyton, Mississippi jurist, born .. 7:294
1808 Josue M. Young, R. C. bishop, born ... 13:460
1814 The "Robert Fulton," the first steam war vessel, launched ... 1:350
1815 Daniel D. Emmett, song writer, famous for his "Dixie," born ... 21:156
1817 John E. Gavit, president of the American Bank Note Co., and a patron of the arts and sciences, born ... 17:319
1821 Capture of the piratical schooner "Moscow" by the sloop-of-war "Hornet" ... 13: 52
1828 Thomas F. Bayard, U. S. senator, secretary of state under Cleveland, and ambassador to Great Britain, born ... 2:404
1831 Samuel E. Warren, educator, born ... 4:199
1831 Othniel C. Marsh, paleontologist, born ... 9:317
1832 Wyeth's party of eastern colonists arrived in Oregon ... 6: 73
1839 Justus H. Rathbone, founder of the Knights of Pythias, born ... 2:170
1845 George A. MacBeth, glass manufacturer, born.. 13:505
1855 John F. Hill, governor of Maine, born ... 13:314
1857 Joe Evans, landscape artist, born ... 11:298
1866 Dora Reade Goodale, poet, born ... 8:266
1869 T. Rutherford MacMechen, aeronautical engineer, born ... 16:292
1872 Julian A. C. Chandler, president of the College of William and Mary, born ... B:439
1893 Assassination of Mayor Harrison of Chicago ... 10:145
1902 "Mitchell day" celebrated annually by the miners of Pennsylvania ... 24:335

OCTOBER 30.

1706 Samuel Mather, clergyman, born ... 6:407
1716 John Jones, surveyor, the inspiration for Mrs. Stowe's "Sheriff Jones," born ... 5: 29
1735 John Adams, 2d President of the United States, born ... 2: 1
1768 First Methodist church in America dedicated .. 6:293
1773 Hugh L. White, Tennessee judge and congressman, born ... 11:395
1790 Zadock Pratt, manufacturer and congressman, born ... 9:164
1795 Charles Brooks, clergyman and educator, born.. 12:287
1800 David Meriwether, U. S. senator and governor of New Mexico territory, born ... 12:219
1807 James S. Wadsworth, Federal soldier, born ... 5: 13
1811 Abiel A. Livermore, Unitarian clergyman, born 15:255
1815 Andrew J. Downing, landscape gardener, born . 11:114
1829 Roscoe Conkling, lawyer, congressman and U. S. senator, born ... 3:220
1829 John Rogers, sculptor, born ... 8:277
1833 William Tod Helmuth, organizer and dean of the St. Louis college of homeopathic physicians and surgeons, born ... 12:471
1840 Albert W. Kelsey, political and industrial economist, born ... 18: 46
1840 William G. Sumner, political and social economist, trail-blazer in scientific sociology, born ... 25: 8
1844 Charles A. Needham, artist, born ... 6:503
1845 Edward Payson Ripley, president of the Atchison, Topeka & Santa Fé railroad, born 18:313
1848 Jesse M. Smith, mechanical engineer, born ... 22:165
1850 William S. Rainsford, clergyman, born ... 1:385
1851 John DeWitt Warner, lawyer, political reformer and congressman, born ... 9:114
1854 Thomas H. Carter, lawyer and U. S. senator, born ... 13:199
1857 Gertrude F. Atherton, author, born ... D:378
1862 Gen. Don Carlos Buell superseded by Gen. Rosecrans ... 4:263
1867 Louis W. Austin, radio engineer, born ... 24:118
1881 Death of Capt. DeLong, the explorer, in the Arctic region ... 3:283
1885 Ezra Pound, poet, born ... C: 80
1894 The silver purchasing clause of the Sherman act repealed ... 2:402

OCTOBER 31.

Hallowe'en — Founders Day for Girl Scouts

1687 Connecticut's charter allegedly concealed in an oak ... 10:324
1737 James Lovell, educator, born ... 12:428
1740 William Paca, Maryland statesman and signer of the Declaration of Independence, born ... 9:291
1766 Sons of Liberty organized ... 1: 71
1788 David R. Porter, governor of Pennsylvania, born 2:287
1790 William B. Shubrick, Federal naval officer, born 2:237
1800 The "National Intelligencer" first issued in Washington, D. C. ... 20:296
1801 Theodore D. Woolsey, president of Yale college, born ... 1:170
1803 Frigate "Philadelphia" ran aground off Tripoli and its entire crew captured ... 8: 94
1816 Charles P. Daly, New York judge and author, born ... 3:158
1816 Philo Remington, manufacturer, born ... 9:129
1819 Alexander W. Randall, governor of Wisconsin and postmaster general under Johnson, born.. 2:458
1819 Alexander Burgess, P. E. bishop, born ... 11:468
1820 Ashbel P. Willard, governor of Indiana, born .. 13:270
1821 Alexander C. Rhind, Federal naval officer, born 4:316
1825 William C. Prime, author and editor of the "Journal of Commerce," born ... 13:254
1826 Joseph R. Hawley, journalist, Federal soldier and U. S. senator, born ... 1:457
1826 Albert G. Goodall, engraver, who introduced American methods in foreign countries, born 18:388
1828 Richard M. Hunt, architect, born ... 6:430
1831 Daniel Butterfield, Federal soldier, born ... 4:128
1835 Adelbert Ames, Federal soldier and governor of Mississippi, born ... 13:492
1840 R. Heber Newton, clergyman, born ... 3:304
1844 Nicholas Senn, Chicago surgeon, born ... 6:371
1846 Charles Henry Truax, judge, born ... 12:261
1860 Juliette M. Low, founder of the Girl Scouts, born 24:172
1863 William Gibbs McAdoo, secretary of the treasury under Wilson, born ... A: 34
1864 Nevada admitted to the Union ... 11:200
1867 David Graham Phillips, journalist and author, born ... 14: 47
1872 Frederic W. Thompson, promoter of spectacular amusement enterprises, including "Luna Park" and the "Hippodrome," in New York, born . 19:105
1873 Capture of the "Virginius" by the Spaniards .. 12: 64

NOVEMBER 1.

All Saint's Day — Holiday in Louisiana

1747 Samuel Tucker, naval officer, born ... 12:347
1760 Joseph Ellicott, engineer, who laid out the towns of Batavia and Buffalo, N. Y., born ... 13:471
1764 Stephen Van Rensselaer, last of the patrons, and founder of Rensselaer polytechnic institute, born 2:397
1765 The Stamp Act became effective ... 1:333
1777 The "Ranger," the first war vessel to fly the stars and stripes, sailed from Portsmouth, N. H., in search of British vessels ... 2: 15
1800 Charter granted for Middlebury (Vt.) college... 12:105
1806 William H. Ellet, chemist, born ... 11: 37
1808 John Taylor, president of the Mormon church, born ... 16: 5
1811 Frances M. Whitcher, humorist, author of the "Widow Bedott" papers, born ... 6: 30
1815 Crawford W. Long, physician, one of the discoverers of anaesthesia, born ... 13:210
1827 Morgan Dix, New York clergyman, born ... 23:130
1833 William Hanna Thomson, physician, and student of religion, born ... 23:321
1835 Godfrey Weitzel, Federal soldier and engineer, born ... 11: 86
1836 George E. Spencer, Federal soldier and U. S. senator, born ... 13: 72
1848 Israel C. White, geologist, born ... 18:164
1849 William M. Chase, artist, born... 13: 28
1849 Herbert R. Spencer, optician, born ... 13:256
1849 James N. Baskett, naturalist and author, born.. 13:346
1850 University of Rochester formally opened... 12:243
1851 Indiana's new constitution became operative... 13:269
1856 William L. Saunders, mechanical engineer, president of the Ingersoll-Sargent Drill Co., born .. 26: 81
1859 Charles Eliot, landscape architect, born ... 13:108
1861 Gen. George B. McClellan took command of the U. S. armies ... 4:141
1865 Horace V. Winchell, geologist and mining engineer, born ... 20:200
1867 Joseph C. Bloodgood, surgeon and cancer specialist, born ... 26:210
1868 Robert K. Duncan, chemist, born ... 21:331
1870 First weather bulletins issued by the U. S. government ... 24:196
1871 Stephen Crane, author, born ... 10:113
1874 William Hodge, actor, born ... 14:384
1918 Franco-American troops began the advance on Sedan ... A:380

NOVEMBER 2.

All Souls' Day

1691 Philip Ludwell became governor of South Carolina ... 12:153
1734 Issues of Zenger's "Weekly Journal" ordered seized and destroyed, resulting in a famous trial to establish the "freedom of the press"... 23:147
1775 St. John, New Brunswick, captured by the Americans ... 1:100
1778 Frances Slocum captured by Indians ... 10:225
1783 Washington made his farewell address to the army ... 1: 4
1788 James Iredell, Jr., lawyer, U. S. senator and governor of North Carolina, born ... 4:423
1795 James K. Polk, 11th president of the United States, born ... 6:265
1807 Robert Carter, New York publisher, born ... 8: 41
1810 Andrew A. Humphreys, Federal soldier, born... 7: 34
1818 Thomas A. Jenckes, congressman, the "father of civil service reform," born ... 8:436
1820 Ben P. Poore, journalist and author, born... 8:190
1821 William A. Richardson, secretary of the treasury under Grant, born ... 4: 17
1822 Thomas S. Phelps, Federal naval officer, born... 4:341
1826 William H. Lytle, Federal soldier and poet, born 4:338
1827 Edward Yorke McCauley, Federal naval officer, born ... 13:131
1828 Harris M. Plaisted, soldier, lawyer and governor of Maine, born ... 6:317
1831 Indians attacked Bowie's party on the San Saba river in Texas ... 4:210
1833 Horace H. Furness, Shakespearean scholar, born 8:396
1843 John Cudahy, meat packer, born ... 11:385
1846 Nicholas M. Bell, merchant, noted for his achievements as superintendent of foreign mails, born 12: 22
1848 Leslie M. Shaw, governor of Iowa and secretary of the treasury under Theodore Roosevelt, born 23:118
1852 Albert Reid Ledoux, mining engineer, born... 12:449
1855 Richard Barthold, congressman and president of the Interparliamentary Union for Promotion of Arbitration, born ... 25:120
1861 Gen. David Hunter took command of the Western department ... 4:264
1865 Warren G. Harding, 29th president of the United States, born ... 19:268
1881 Herbert N. Strauss, New York merchant, born .. 24:160
1885 Harlow Shapley, astronomer, born ... C: 95
1885 Winthrop W. Aldrich, president of the Chase National Bank, New York city, largest bank in the world, born ... D: 74
1889 North and South Dakota admitted to the Union 2:202
1920 First broadcast of election returns by radio.... A: 74

NOVEMBER 3.

1723 Samuel Davies, clergyman and president of the College of New Jersey (Princeton), born ... 5:465
1741 William Irvine, Revolutionary patriot and soldier, born ... 1: 90
1757 Robert Smith, secretary of the navy and U. S. attorney-general under Jefferson and secretary of state under Madison, born ... 3: 11
1762 Treaty of Paris, by which France ceded Western Louisiana to Spain and Eastern Louisiana (New Orleans excepted) to England ... 10: 73
1770 James Whitfield, archbishop, born ... 1:483
1776 "Declaration of Rights" adopted by Maryland.. 11:110
1782 Lewis Warrington, naval officer, born ... 6:232
1783 Revolutionary army disbanded ... 1: 66
1793 Stephen F. Austin, Texas pioneer and statesman, born ... 6: 70
1794 David Thomas, iron manufacturer, born ... 3:360
1794 William Cullen Bryant, poet and editor, born.... 4: 79
1798 James M. Mason, U. S. senator and Confederate statesman, born ... 2: 93
1813 Battle of Tallasahatchee, Ala. ... 7:208
1816 Jubal A. Early, Confederate soldier, born ... 4:137
1818 James Renwick, architect, who designed St. Patrick's cathedral in New York city, born ... 11:102
1830 John Esten Cooke, Confederate soldier and author, born ... 7:330
1831 Ignatius Donnelly, Minnesota statesman and author, born ... 1:397
1834 Charles Fleischmann, originator of compressed yeast, born ... 22: 88
1841 Isabella Alden (Pansy), author, born ... 10:405
1845 Edward D. White, U. S. senator, and chief justice of the supreme court, born ... 21: 3
1846 Francis D. Millet, artist, born ... 15:201
1860 Denis J. Stafford, clergyman and lecturer, born 12:437
1867 Pearl M. T. Craigie (John Oliver Hobbes), author and playwright, born ... 10:506

NOVEMBER 4.

1732 Thomas Johnson, Maryland statesman and governor, born ... 9:289
1782 Elias Boudinot elected president of the Continental congress ... 2:296
1782 John Branch, U. S. senator, governor of Florida and North Carolina, and secretary of the navy under Jackson, born ... 5:295
1788 Asa Arnold, inventor, born ... 13:255
1791 Governor St. Clair routed by Indians in the Northwest territory ... 1: 95
1795 Dayton, Ohio, founded ... 11:362
1796 John Neagle, artist, born ... 5:326
1809 Benjamin R. Curtis, justice of the U. S. supreme court, born ... 2:472
1809 John McGill, R. C. bishop, born ... 10:156
1810 Lucius Robinson, governor of New York, born .. 3: 54
1811 Abner Jackson, president of Trinity college, Hartford, born ... 3:497
1812 Richard M. Bishop, Ohio merchant and governor, born ... 3:143
1812 Samuel I. Prime, clergyman and editor, born... 7:237
1816 Stephen J. Field, justice of the U. S. supreme court, born ... 1: 32
1816 James L. Alcorn, Mississippi statesman and governor, born ... 13:493
1821 Thomas C. Keefer, civil engineer, born ... 12:227
1822 Jehu Baker, congressman, diplomat and author, born ... 12:427
1834 Allen D. Candler, congressman and governor of Georgia, born ... 2:121
1837 James Douglas, mining engineer who specialized in copper, born ... 23: 22
1840 Thomas M. Patterson, journalist and U. S. senator, born ... 12:555
1850 Caesar A. Grasselli, manufacturing chemist, born 21:393
1854 Samuel M. Peck, poet, born ... 7:474
1855 George F. Shaver, inventor of a duplex telephone, born ... 4:231
1856 Ernest H. Crosby, lawyer, reformer and author, born ... 10: 61
1862 Patent granted to Richard J. Gatling for a rapid-fire gun known as the Gatling gun ... 4:158
1863 Charles N. Winship, manufacturer of knit goods, born ... 15:386
1864 Anita N. McGee, physician, in charge of army nurses during the Spanish-American war, born 10:350
1865 Herbert C. Tolman, philologist, born ... 26:198
1868 Calvin W. Rice, civil engineer, twenty-eight years secretary of the American Society of Mechanical Engineers and founder of that society's "Journal" and its famous "Engineering Index," born ... 25: 35
1872 Lloyd C. Griscom, diplomat, born ... 12:196
1876 James E. Fraser, sculptor, designer of medals and coins, including the "Buffalo nickel," born C: 468
1879 Edison received a patent for the incandescent lamp ... 25: 2
1879 Will Rogers, stage and screen comedian and author, born ... B: 67

NOVEMBER 5.

1605 Thomas Shepard, clergyman, born ... 7: 33
1732 John Glover, soldier, born ... 8:223
1733 First issue of the New York "Weekly Journal" 23:147
1748 Judah Spooner, publisher of the first newspaper in Vermont, born ... 19: 41
1749 Charles Backus, clergyman and educator, born .. 12:429
1769 Enoch Parsons, banker, born ... 1: 74
1777 Nathan Sanford, U. S. senator, born ... 3:383
1779 Washington Allston, painter, "the American Titian," born ... 5:383
1781 John Hanson elected "president of the United States in congress assembled" ... 10:312
1795 Lewis F. Linn, U. S. senator, born ... 4:551
1799 Jesper Harding, publisher of the Pennsylvania "Inquirer," born ... 22: 18
1805 Thomas W. Dorr, reformer, leader of the rebellion in Rhode Island, born ... 8:234
1807 Oliver Ames, shovel manufacturer, and president of the Union Pacific railroad, born ... 14:201
1810 John F. Winslow, iron and steel manufacturer, who built the "Monitor" for the Federal government, born ... 4:181
1814 Alphonso Taft, secretary of war and attorney-general under Grant, born ... 4: 24
1816 Rodman McCauley Price, governor of New Jersey, born ... 5:207
1818 Benjamin F. Butler, lawyer, soldier and governor of Massachusetts, born ... 1:121
1818 Thomas R. Gould, sculptor, born ... 8:281
1818 Hamilton L. Smith, scientist, born ... 12:466
1827 James Rankine, clergyman, and president of Hobart college, born ... 12:551

1835 William Corliss, inventor and manufacturer of a burglar-proof safe, born 4: 171
1844 Norman B. Ream, Chicago financier, leader of the "Big Four" of the Chicago board of trade, born 16: 357
1846 Edward S. Holden, astronomer, and president of the University of California, born 7: 229
1850 Ella Wheeler Wilcox, poet, born 11: 278
1853 Arthur Foote, composer, born 7: 435
1855 Eugene V. Debs, labor leader, born 12: 340
1857 Ida M. Tarbell, author, born 14: 111
1862 Gen. McClellan superseded by Gen. Burnside.... 4: 143
1862 Alfred C. Bedford, president of the Standard Oil Co., born 23: 13
1863 James W. Packard, designer and manufacturer of the Packard motor car, born 20: 15
1869 Nicholas Longworth, speaker of the house of representatives, born 23: 70
1871 Frederick W. Loring, journalist, killed by Indians 8: 359
1871 Clarence E. Whitehill, singer, born 14: 505
1879 Will H. Hays, postmaster-general under Harding, and policy director of the motion picture industry, born .... A: 354
1880 Treaty regulating Chinese immigration adopted by congress 3: 196
1885 Will Durant, philosopher whose writings humanized philosophy for "the man in the street," born .... C: 473
1894 Philip G. Johnson, manufacturer of airplanes, and head of the United Aircraft & Transport Corp., born .... D: 120
1895 Selden patented his three cylinder automobile engine 20: 223

NOVEMBER 6.

1637 Rev. John Wheelwright dismissed from the church at Boston 1: 232
1756 Richard Dale, naval officer, born 2: 17
1795 William Robert Prince, horticulturist, born 20: 427
1807 Cornelius C. Felton, Greek scholar and president of Harvard college, born 6: 419
1828 Hiram Corson, educator, born 1: 440
1834 Charles H. Morgan, Federal soldier, born 5: 14
1836 Francis E. Abbot, clergyman and philosopher, born 24: 113
1841 Nelson W. Aldrich, U. S. senator and an authority on finance, whose national monetary commission was the forerunner of the Federal reserve system, born 25: 20
1842 Ellen Olney Kirk (Henry Hayes), author, born 1: 373
1847 First American missionary church organized in China 10: 110
1854 John P. Sousa, bandmaster and composer, born. 9: 386
1855 Daniel Sully, actor and playwright, born 12: 110
1857 William A. Noyes, chemist, born .... B: 314
1859 Madison C. Peters, clergyman and author, born 2: 501
1861 Thomas Watt Gregory, attorney-general under Wilson, born .... A: 43

NOVEMBER 7.

1775 Joseph Wanton deposed as governor of Rhode Island 10: 16
1798 Silas H. Stringham, naval officer, born 2: 101
1800 Platt R. Spencer, educator, originator of the Spencerian system of penmanship, born 8: 11
1811 Battle of Tippecanoe, Ind. 3: 35
1811 William R. Taylor, naval officer, born 4: 155
1817 Peter Hamilton, lawyer, born 12: 550
1823 The inclined plane for the Morris canal patented 11: 101
1826 Luther Atwood, chemist, born 13: 260
1828 Leonard W. Volk, sculptor, born 7: 469
1829 George H. Morrill, manufacturer of printer's ink, born 24: 327
1832 Andrew D. White, first president of Cornell university, born 4: 476
1835 Texas resolved to organize as a state of Mexico.. 4: 169
1837 Fatal anti-slavery riot occurred at Alton, Ill. 2: 328
1837 Michael Anagnos, director of the Perkins institute for the training of the blind, born.... 13: 257
1837 Louis Janin, mining engineer and metallurgist, born 18: 11
1838 Rufus W. Peckham, justice of the U. S. supreme court, born 11: 410
1847 Lotta Crabtree, actress, born 9: 547
1850 William M. Beardshear, president of Iowa state college of agricultural and mechanical arts, born 12: 291
1858 Horace M. DuBose, M. E. bishop and author, born 18: 301
1860 George F. Shepley, architect, born 22: 99
1860 Warren Henry Manning, landscape designer and regional planner, born .... B: 291
1861 Battle of Belmont, Mo. 4: 137
1861 Expedition against Confederate vessels in Galveston bay, Texas 4: 502
1861 Port Royal forts, N. C., taken by Federals 5: 50
1873 Capt. Fry and crew of thirty of the "Virginius" shot by Spaniards 12: 64
1874 Samuel A. Baker, educator, and governor of Missouri, born .... B: 216

NOVEMBER 8.

1732 John Dickinson, statesman, born 2: 281
1735 George Plater, governor of Maryland, born.... 9: 293
1772 William Wirt, orator, author, and attorney-general under Monroe, born 6: 86
1780 Samuel A. Foote, U. S. senator and governor of Connecticut, born 10: 334
1780 Gen. Sumter defeated Maj. Wemyss at Fish Dam 12: 165
1780 John B. Gibson, jurist, born 14: 338
1811 David Bradley, manufacturer, born 11: 148
1813 Battle of Talladega, Ala. 5: 291
1817 George B. Loring, congressman and diplomat, a student of agricultural science, born 15: 349
1823 Charles Burt, engraver, born 12: 386
1829 William Henry Watson, physician, born 7: 449
1829 Samuel W. Crawford, Federal soldier, born 12: 232
1830 Oliver O. Howard, Federal soldier, born 4: 103
1836 Maria Kraus-Boelté, a pioneer in the development of the kindergarten in America, born 13: 467
1840 George F. Seward, diplomat, born 7: 91
1851 Charles O. Day, clergyman, president of Andover theological seminary, born 13: 434
1860 James H. Penniman, historian and philanthropist, born 22: 263
1861 Confederate commissioners, Mason and Slidell, taken from the British steamer "Trent" 2: 93
1868 First number of the Louisville "Courier-Journal" published 1: 468
1871 Robert W. Bingham, judge and diplomat, born . D: 32
1887 Patent on the gramaphone issued to Berliner... 10: 441
1889 Montana admitted to the Union 13: 199

NOVEMBER 9.

1731 Benjamin Banneker, mathematician, born 5: 36
1768 Joseph C. Yates, New York jurist and governor, born 3: 45
1795 Josiah Tattnall, naval officer, born 5: 488
1796 Ira Allen captured on the vessel "Olive Branch" 4: 29
1799 Samuel E. Sewall, reformer, born 10: 466
1799 Ira Perley, judge, born 12: 435
1800 Asa Mahan, first president of Oberlin college, born 2: 461
1800 Robert Dale Owen, reformer, born 9: 222
1801 Gail Borden, originator and manufacturer of "Eagle Brand" condensed milk, born 7: 306
1802 Elijah P. Lovejoy, abolitionist, born 2: 328
1803 Henry Farnam, civil engineer, born 11: 517
1810 Thomas Bragg, U. S. senator and governor of North Carolina, afterwards a member of the Confederate cabinet, born 4: 427
1811 Benjamin H. Throop, capitalist, a pioneer settler in Scranton, Pa., born 15: 261
1812 Marcus L. Ward, governor of New Jersey, born 5: 209
1825 Ambrose P. Hill, Confederate soldier, born 4: 101
1831 Boston "Post" first issued 4: 445
1835 Frost Johnson, artist, born 7: 471
1843 Cornerstone of the Cincinnati observatory laid.. 3: 440
1848 Julia J. Irvine, president of Wellesley college, born 12: 221
1852 Robert Simon, silk manufacturer, born 14: 215
1853 Charles F. Thwing, president of Western Reserve university, born 7: 226
1853 Stanford White, architect, born 23: 92
1858 John M. Carrere, member of the firm of Carrere and Hastings, architects, who designed the New York public library and the Cathedral of St. John the Divine, born 11: 325
1865 Frederick Funston, soldier, born 11: 40
1871 Florence R. Sabin, anatomist, born .... C: 288

NOVEMBER 10.

1755 Aaron Bancroft, clergyman, born 4: 306
1773 Charles Lee arrived in America 8: 238
1775 Hampden Sidney college opened 2: 21
1777 British attack on Ft. Mifflin, Pa., began 1: 41
1791 Henry L. Ellsworth, commissioner of patents, born 7: 516
1791 William W. Ellsworth, Connecticut jurist and governor, born 10: 335
1791 Robert Y. Hayne, U. S. senator and governor of South Carolina, born 12: 166
1792 Samuel Nelson, justice of the U. S. supreme court, born 2: 470
1793 Jared P. Kirtland, physician and naturalist, born 11: 347

1800 James H. Roosevelt, philanthropist, born 12: 6
1801 Samuel G. Howe, founder of the Perkins institution for the blind, born 8: 372
1805 Thomas C. Wales, manufacturer and inventor, born 10: 406
1805 Charles Pickering, physician and naturalist, born 13: 176
1810 Charles C. Burleigh, abolitionist, born 2: 320
1813 Charles Deane, historian, born 3: 520
1827 Alfred H. Terry, Federal soldier, born 4: 69
1832 Bancroft Gherardi, Federal naval officer, born... 12: 489
1834 Wager Swayne, Federal soldier and lawyer, born 4: 156
1837 Amos E. Dolbear, physicist and inventor, born.. 9: 414
1841 Cincinnatus H. Miller (Joaquin Miller), poet, born 7: 69
1847 Frederic A. Bridgman, artist, born 2: 110
1852 Edward C. Spitzka, neurologist, born 19: 450
1852 Henry Van Dyke, clergyman and author, born 25: 10
1859 Wallace Rice, author and critic, born 13: 199
1869 Wayne B. Wheeler, prohibitionist, general counsel of the Anti-Saloon League of America, born.. 20: 13
1871 Winston Churchill, author, born 10: 178
1874 Donald B. McMillan, explorer, born ...... B: 476
1879 Vachel Lindsay, poet and author, born 23: 229
1919 Congressman Berger excluded from the house of representatives as a protest against his pacifism in the World war 22: 163

NOVEMBER 11.

Armistice Day — Martinmas

1733 Philip J. Schuyler, soldier and statesman, born . 1: 97
1771 Ephraim McDowell, physician, born 5: 148
1778 Tories and Indians descended on Cherry Valley, N. Y. 9: 142
1782 Cyrus Alger, iron manufacturer and inventor, born 6: 113
1789 St. John's college opened 1: 503
1789 William Meade, P. E. bishop, born 7: 216
1798 Edward Cross, Arkansas judge and congressman, born 22: 104
1811 Ben McCulloch, Confederate soldier, born...... 4: 104
1813 Battle of Chrysler's field, Canada 9: 372
1813 Battle of Williamsburg, Canada 10: 135
1814 Henry Clapp, humorist, born 9: 121
1815 Anne C. Botta, author, born 7: 236
1826 William Morgan kidnapped — an incident that gave rise to the Anti-Masonic party 7: 526
1831 John G. Brown, artist, born 10: 373
1831 Nat Turner, insurgent, hanged 13: 597
1835 Lemuel E. Wilmarth, artist, born 8: 424
1836 Henry M. Alden, editor and author, born...... 1: 153
1836 Thomas B. Aldrich, poet and novelist, born.... 1: 283
1844 Charles F. Pidgin, author, statistician and inventor, born 13: 479
1846 Anna Katherine Green, author, born 9: 257
1847 Com. Shubrick captured Mazatlan, Mexico...... 5: 50
1863 J. Ogden Armour, Chicago meat packer, born.. 23: 57
1864 George W Crile, surgeon, born ...... C: 72
1872 Maud Adams, actress, born 13: 497
1889 Washington admitted to the Union 1: 135
1891 Society of the Daughters of the Revolution founded 19: 139
1918 Signing of the armistice which ended the World war 19: 9
1919 First successful flight of a helicopter 21: 7
1921 Limitation of armaments conference met in Washington 19: 271

NOVEMBER 12.

1655 Francis Nicholson, governor of Virginia, born .. 13: 386
1751 Margaret Corbin, revolutionary heroine, born... 6: 399
1770 Joseph Hopkinson, jurist, born 7: 158
1775 Montreal surrendered to the Americans 1: 100
1780 Battle of Broad River, N. C. 1: 70
1808 Ray Palmer, clergyman and author, born...... 8: 8
1813 Canoe fight with Indians on the Alabama river. 11: 270
1815 Elizabeth Cady Stanton, reformer, born 3: 84
1823 Thomas W. Wood, artist, born 3: 345
1825 George Munro, publisher, born 7: 114
1835 Provisional governor of Texas elected 9: 62
1838 Edward V. Valentine, sculptor, born 10: 377
1840 George M. Bache, naval officer, born 13: 192
1841 Lewis Sells, showman, organizer of the famous Sells Brothers' circus, born 16: 208
1843 Charles L. Doolittle, astronomer, born 20: 340
1850 Patent issued to Allen B. Wilson for an improved sewing machine 9: 460
1850 William M. Sloane, historian, born 21: 95
1855 Louis A. Banks, clergyman, born 13: 103
1856 Francis Lynde, author, born 13: 347
1888 Anne Parrish, author, born ...... D: 141

NOVEMBER 13.

1809 John A. Dahlgren, naval officer, whose inventions revolutionized the system of naval ordnance, born 9: 377
1813 Allen G. Thurman, U. S. senator, born 3: 144
1814 Joseph Hooker (Fighting Joe), Federal soldier, born 4: 176
1824 Philip L. Moen, wire manufacturer, born 6: 205
1829 Sam Patch jumped the Genesee falls, N. Y., and was killed 5: 521
1833 Edwin Booth, tragedian, born 3: 180
1833 Remarkable display of meteor stars visible over North America 8: 121
1834 Peter A. B. Widener, who reorganized the street railroads and other public utilities in the principal cities of the United States, born 15: 11
1836 Alfred M. Mayer, physicist, born 13: 164
1837 Henry C. Merriam, soldier, born 13: 338
1838 Joseph F. Smith, president of the Mormon church, born 16: 9
1841 Lucius F. C. Garvin, governor of Rhode Island, born 26: 109
1849 California adopted a state constitution 4: 105
1852 First train operated on the Pacific railroad.... 21: 20
1854 John Drew, Jr., actor, born 3: 531
1854 George W. Chadwick, composer, born...... 7: 326
1856 Louis D. Brandeis, justice of the U. S. supreme court, born ...... C: 432
1864 James Cannon, Jr., M. E. bishop, born ...... C: 318
1866 Abraham Flexner, outstanding authority on educational standards, born ...... D: 61
1890 George H. Bigelow, physician, a student of communicable diseases, born 25: 72
1916 Katherine Cornell's first stage appearance ...... D: 437
1927 Official opening of the Holland tunnel between New York and New Jersey 19: 381
1932 The course of the Colorado river diverted to facilitate the construction of Boulder dam ...... D: 370

NOVEMBER 14.

1627 Francis West became governor of Virginia.... 13: 382
1750 Lewis Burwell became acting governor of Virginia 13: 389
1765 Robert Fulton, inventor of a steamboat, born .. 3: 104
1775 American troops under Benedict Arnold reached Quebec, Canada 1: 53
1777 Nathaniel H. Claiborne, congressman, born 12: 558
1784 Samuel Seabury consecrated the first P. E. bishop in the United States 3: 475
1789 John Carroll appointed first R. C. bishop in the United States 2: 481
1795 Charles Hudson, clergyman and author, born ... 24: 168
1803 John G. Morris, clergyman, born 3: 61
1803 Jacob Abbott, clergyman, author and educator, born 6: 136
1803 Duel between Richard Riker and Robert Swartwout 7: 536
1810 James M. McKim, abolitionist, born 2: 529
1814 Stuart Robinson, clergyman, born 1: 371
1819 Christopher R. P. Rodgers, Federal naval officer, born 4: 222
1820 Anson Burlingame, congressman and diplomat, born 8: 55
1827 Isaac J. Wistar, Federal soldier and lawyer, born 12: 359
1828 James B. McPherson, Federal soldier, born 4: 203
1829 Kruseman Van Elten, artist, born 7: 468
1832 Charles Carroll, of Carrollton, last surviving signer of the Declaration of Independence, died 7: 441
1832 John McCullough, tragedian, born 9: 141
1833 Henry Clay Barnabee, comedian, born 8: 35
1833 William T. Richards, artist, born 12: 362
1840 William K. Van Reypen, naval officer, born.... 13: 215
1846 Americans captured Tampico, Mexico 4: 155
1850 Jesse W. Fewkes, ethnologist, born 15: 32
1854 Frank Parsons, economist, born 11: 182
1861 The U. S. Christian commission organized 7: 541
1863 Leo H. Baekeland, chemist, inventor of Bakelite, born 15: 330
1876 Harvey O'Higgins, author, born 25: 296

NOVEMBER 15.

1730 Frederick William A. Steuben, Prussian nobleman, who fought in the Revolutionary war, born 1: 57
1752 Nathaniel Chipman, jurist and U. S. senator, born 2: 10
1763 Mason and Dixon arrived from England to survey the boundary line between Pennsylvania and Maryland 10: 54
1775 James Carnahan, president of the College of New Jersey (Princeton), born 5: 467

1777 Articles of Confederation drafted by the Continental congress ... 4: 398
1787 Richard Henry Dana, poet and author, born ... 7: 182
1791 George Croghan, soldier, born ... 4: 256
1797 Thurlow Weed, journalist and political organizer, born ... 3: 12
1799 James A. Bayard, U. S. senator, born ... 13: 206
1802 Solomon Foot, U. S. senator, born ... 2: 91
1806 Pike's peak discovered ... 2: 517
1807 Peter H. Burnett, first state governor of California, born ... 4: 105
1807 James H. Hammond, U. S. senator and governor of South Carolina, born ... 12: 169
1809 Michael H. Simpson, manufacturer and inventor, born ... 10: 387
1815 Edward L. Davenport, actor, born ... 9: 319
1829 Benjamin Szold, rabbi and author, born ... 13: 65
1833 William F. Durfee, engineer and inventor, born 6: 248
1837 Richard R. Donnelley, Chicago printer and publisher, born ... 22: 154
1849 Louis F. Post, editor and economist, born ... 18: 150
1850 Saturn's dusky rings discovered ... 5: 503
1864 Gen. Sherman ordered Confederate stores and supplies in Atlanta destroyed by fire... 4: 34
1884 Charles L. O'Donnell, president of the University of Notre Dame, born ... 25: 86

NOVEMBER 16.

1753 James McHenry, secretary of war under Washington, born ... 1: 13
1757 Daniel Read, composer, born ... 7: 243
1776 Ft. Washington, N. Y., captured by the British 1: 41
1777 Ft. Mifflin captured by the British ... 1: 41
1792 Isaac Toucey, attorney-general under Polk and secretary of the navy under Buchanan, born... 5: 7
1798 Persifer Smith, soldier, born ... 7: 522
1801 First issue of the New York "Evening Post" ... 11: 350
1804 Jason C. Osgood, inventor, born ... 6: 175
1805 Robert B. Minturn, merchant, born ... 9: 114
1823 Henry G. Davis, U. S. senator, born ... 10: 468
1826 John B. Henderson, lawyer and U. S. senator, born ... 13: 49
1827 Charles Eliot Norton, educator, author and editor, born ... 6: 425
1828 Timothy Dwight, president of Yale university, born ... 1: 173
1833 Henry Gillman, anthropologist and archæologist, born ... 7: 359
1834 Homer Eaton, clergyman, born ... 12: 474
1846 James C. Pilling, ethnologist, born ... 15: 55
1847 Martin Stamm, Swiss-American surgeon, who introduced many new operative methods, born.. 21: 325
1849 Edward S. Dana, mineralogist, born ... 6: 537
1853 Minnie Hauk, opera singer, born ... 8: 296
1856 Annie F. Loud, composer and organist, born... 8: 444
1864 Gen. Sherman commenced his march from Atlanta to the sea ... 4: 34

NOVEMBER 17.

1741 Adam Kuhn, physician and botanist, a founder and president of the College of Physicians of Philadelphia, born ... 21: 289
1753 Gotthilf H. E. Muhlenberg, clergyman and botanist, born ... 9: 439
1764 Alexander Brown, banker, founder of the Baltimore banking house of Alexander Brown & Sons, born ... 1: 474
1786 William P. C. Barton, botanist and physician, born ... 13: 279
1787 Thomas Ruffin, North Carolina jurist, born ... 6: 289
1788 Seth Boyden, first to manufacture patent leather in America, and inventor and manufacturer of steam locomotives, harness fittings, nails, etc., born ... 11: 87
1789 Stephen Champlin, naval officer, born ... 4: 543
1794 John B. Montgomery, naval officer, born ... 10: 31
1809 Stephen S. Foster, abolitionist, born ... 2: 328
1811 John B. Ford, manufacturer, "father of the plate glass industry in America," born ... 13: 505
1812 William Warren, actor, born ... 5: 439
1835 Frederick Leypoldt, publisher and bibliographer, one of the founders of the American Library Association, born ... 7: 491
1835 William A. Anthony, electrical engineer, born.. 11: 389
1856 Francis P. Venable, chemist, and president of the University of North Carolina, born ... 13: 245
1856 Thomas Taggart, U. S. senator and leader of the Democratic party, born ... 22: 430
1864 Frank A. Vanderlip, financier, born ... 15: 29
1874 John A. Cousens, merchant and banker, president of Tufts college, born ... B: 360
1875 Theosophical Society founded in New York ... 8: 464
1876 Homer Lea, author, and general in the Chinese army, born ... 2: 500
1878 Grace Abbott, chief of the U. S. children's bureau, born ... C: 25
1880 Treaty between United States and China regulating immigration ratified ... 3: 196

NOVEMBER 18.

1752 Benjamin Austin, political writer, born ... 12: 429
1755 New England shaken by an earthquake ... 7: 166
1787 Eliza Leslie, author, born ... 7: 138
1787 James Freeman, refused ordination by the bishop of his church, was ordained by his own congregation in a ceremony that marked the beginning of the Unitarian church in America 7: 447
1801 John Butterfield, expressman and financier, born 22: 61
1802 Jonathan Worth, governor of North Carolina, born ... 4: 428
1806 Leo Lesquereux, botanist, born ... 9: 438
1808 James J. Walworth, who intoduced ventilating, steam heat and hot water systems in the United States, born ... 18: 374
1810 Asa Gray, botanist, born ... 3: 407
1820 James W. Abert, Federal soldier, born ... 4: 395
1820 Henry Cordis Brown, Denver pioneer and builder, born ... 16: 417
1824 Franz Sigel, Federal soldier, born ... 4: 136
1827 George W. Plympton, civil engineer, born ... 9: 40
1828 John A. J. Creswell, U. S. senator, and postmaster general under Grant, born ... 4: 19
1861 Gen. Halleck took command of the Western department ... 4: 257
1871 Jessie Bonstelle, actress and theatrical producer, founder of a civic theatre in Detroit, born... 25: 178
1872 Susan B. Anthony and fifteen other women arrested for attempting to vote ... 4: 403
1883 Standard time for railroads introduced by the American Railway Association ... 23: 231
1903 In a treaty with Panama the United States recognized the independence of that nation and and secured the right to construct a ship canal through Panama, to acquire necessary territory and to exercise the authority in the canal zone 14: 5

NOVEMBER 19.

1752 George R. Clark, soldier, born ... 1: 82
1791 Lee Claflin, philanthropist, a founder of Boston and Claflin universities, born ... 11: 176
1794 Jay's treaty with England concluded in London 1: 21
1794 Harvey P. Peet, author and educator, who devoted himself to the instruction of deaf-mutes, born ... 12: 550
1797 Charles Anthon, classical scholar, born ... 6: 345
1802 Barnas Sears, president of Brown university, born ... 8: 24
1810 Elias Riggs, missionary, born ... 3: 120
1810 Ario Pardee, merchant, manufacturer, and patron of Lafayette college, born ... 11: 240
1811 John A. Winslow, Federal naval officer, born... 2: 102
1822 John Cleves Symmes petitioned congress for aid in making a voyage to the interior of the globe ... 11: 452
1824 Nathan Babcock, manufacturer of printing machinery, born ... 16: 238
1826 William C. Endicott, secretary of war under Cleveland, born ... 2: 406
1827 Martin F. Conway, congressman, born ... 8: 55
1831 James A. Garfield, president of the United States, born ... 4: 238
1832 Nullification convention met at Columbia, S. C. 12: 166
1835 Fitzhugh Lee, soldier and governor of Virginia, born ... 9: 1
1847 Mary Hallock Foote, author and illustrator, born 6: 472
1856 William E. Ritter, zoologist, born ... 16: 43
1862 William Ashley (Billy) Sunday, evangelist, born A: 123
1862 Wickliffe Rose, hygienist, director of the International Health Board, born ... A: 265
1863 Lincoln delivered his famous address at the dedication of the battle field at Gettysburg... 2: 73
1873 William M. (Boss) Tweed convicted of fraud... 3: 389
1874 National Woman's Christian Temperance Union organized ... 13: 264
1875 Hiram Bingham, explorer, governor of Connecticut and U. S. senator, born ... A: 28
1883 Standard time went into effect in the United States ... 18: 181

NOVEMBER 20.

1726 Oliver Wolcott, soldier, signer of the Declaration of Independence and governor of Connecticut, born ... 10: 330
1751 Robert Dinwiddie became governor of Virginia 13: 389
1774 Jacob J. Janeway, clergyman, born ... 13: 498
1780 Battle of Blackstock Hill, N. C. ... 1: 79

1781 Joshua Collett, judge, born 12:342
1804 New York Historical Society organized......... 3:461
1805 Benjamin F. Perry, governor of South Carolina, born 12:174
1817 Benjamin Champney, artist, born 4:289
1827 Emily Howland, educator and humanitarian, born 25:306
1829 Charles G. Halpine, Federal soldier and journalist, born 6: 26
1841 John Russell Young, journalist and diplomat, born 2:214
1848 William Dudley Foulke, lawyer, reformer and author, born 8:191
1851 John M. Coulter, botanist, president of the University of Indiana and Lake Forest university, born 11: 68
1851 Robert McIntyre, M. E. bishop, born 16: 92
1855 Josiah Royce, philosopher, born 25:356
1863 Donald Sage Mackay, clergyman, born 12:482
1865 William R. Newbold, philosopher, born 22:251
1866 Kenesaw M. Landis, jurist and baseball commissioner, born .... A: 22
1867 Patrick Joseph Hayes, R. C. cardinal, born C:246
1871 Arthur Guiterman, poet, born A:299
1873 Daniel Gregory Mason, musician and author, born 15:166
1874 Walter E. Edge, governor of New Jersey and U. S. senator, born B:279
1884 Norman Thomas, Socialist candidate for president of the United States, born C:259
1889 Brian Donn-Byrne, author, born 22:295

NOVEMBER 21.

1620 Famous "Mayflower" compact signed 7:367
1661 Christopher Graffenried, pioneer, founder of Newbern, N. C., born 13:363
1729 Josiah Bartlett, signer of the Declaration of Independence and governor of New Hampshire, born 11:121
1785 William Beaumont, pioneer American physiologist, noted for his original studies of the digestive process, born 18:291
1789 George Howard, governor of Maryland, born 9:302
1802 Jacob Sleeper, merchant, philanthropist, and a founder of Boston university, born 11:176
1811 William G. Angell, inventor and manufacturer, born 2:392
1815 Henry B. Smith, clergyman and educator, born 5:311
1818 Lewis Henry Morgan, anthropologist, born 6:192
1822 Josiah Pickett, soldier, born 12:229
1831 Theodore G. Thomas, physician, born 3:307
1831 John F. Miller, U. S. senator, born 8: 91
1835 Hetty Green, financier, born 15:128
1836 George W. Smith, president of Trinity college, born 3:498
1838 George B. Cluett, collar manufacturer, born 3:307
1839 William Keith, painter, born 13:168
1842 Rhode Island ratified a new state constitution .. 9:397
1845 William N. Rice, geologist, born 12:264
1858 John B. Smith, entomologist, born 15: 71
1858 Allen B. Pond, architect, born 21:111
1859 Albert C. Burrage, lawyer and financier, born .. 12:551
1862 Benaiah L. Whitman, president of Colby university (Colby college), born 8:408
1864 Battle of Spring Hill, Tenn. 10: 36
1867 Frederic C. Howe, economist, organizer of the federal employment service and a member of the Paris peace conference, born .... D: 84
1870 Mary Johnston, novelist, born C:430

NOVEMBER 22.

1633 Ships "Ark" and "Dove" sailed from Cowes with 200 persons to found a colony in Maryland ... 7:332
1643 La Salle, the French explorer, born 5:125
1682 George Jaffrey, jurist, born 12:315
1754 Abraham Baldwin, statesman, founder and first president of the University of Georgia, born .. 9:178
1800 James F. D. Lanier, banker, whose firm, Winslow, Lanier & Co., was the first in this country to negotiate railroad securities and sell railroad bonds to the public, born 23:199
1803 Harrison G. O. Dwight, missionary, born 10:490
1806 La Fayette S. Foster, U. S. senator and acting vice-president of the United States, born 2: 95
1806 Francis W. Edmonds, artist, born 11:298
1815 James W. Beekman, capitalist, born 12: 58
1829 Shelby M. Cullom, U. S. senator and governor of Illinois, born 11: 50
1832 Samuel C. Lawrence, Federal soldier, manufacturer and railroad president, born 16:436
1846 James C. Nicoll, artist, born 7:466
1847 Matamoras, Mexico, captured by Gen. Lane 8: 2
1854 William H. Elson, author of text-books, born ... 26:367
1856 Heber J. Grant, president of the Mormon church, born 18: 26
1856 John C. Winston, Philadelphia publisher, active in political reforms, born 19:293
1858 Herbert A. Howe, astronomer, born 20: 10
1858 William Stanley, electrical engineer, inventor of transformers, generators and motors, born 24:394
1864 Battle of Griswoldville, Ga. 6: 37
1866 James Peter Warbasse, surgeon and economist, born C:330
1868 John N. Garner, vice-president of the United States, born .... D: 9
1870 Howard Brockway, pianist and composer, born .. 13:366
1872 Arthur A. Hamerschlag, first president of the Carnegie institute of technology, born 23: 52
1873 Steamer "Ville du Havre" lost at sea 11:410

NOVEMBER 23.

1732 Samuel Locke, president of Harvard college, born 6:416
1744 Abigail Adams, wife of President John Adams, born 2: 5
1745 John Treadwell, judge and governor of Connecticut, born 10:331
1749 Edward Rutledge, signer of the Declaration of Independence, and governor of South Carolina, born 12:162
1778 Robert Rantoul, reformer, born 11:232
1795 Hezekiah G. Leigh, clergyman, one of the founders of Randolph Macon college, born 13:407
1797 Benjamin Hale, clergyman, author and president of Geneva (Hobart) college, born 13: 39
1801 Duel between Philip Hamilton and George L. Eacker 12:274
1803 Theodore D. Weld, abolitionist, born 2:318
1804 Franklin Pierce, 14th president of the United States, born 4:145
1805 Joseph Pancoast, surgeon, born 10:274
1807 James Smillie, engraver, born 2:368
1810 George M. Randall, P. E. bishop, born 8: 44
1815 William Dennison, governor of Ohio and postmaster general under Lincoln, born 3:141
1816 Evert A. Duyckinck, editor and author, born 1:431
1818 James Vick, horticulturist, born 4:469
1819 Josiah D. Whitney, geologist, born 9:120
1820 John W. Ellis, governor of North Carolina, born 4:427
1830 William S. Wyman, president of the University of Alabama, born 12:297
1832 Grand public trial of the first Baldwin locomotive 9:476
1837 The Crompton power-loom patented 10:160
1855 Frank Friday Fletcher, naval officer, born 15:144
1861 Unsuccessful attack made in Ft. Pickens, Fla., by the Confederates 4:225
1862 The gunboat "Ellis" attacked Jacksonville, Fla. . 9:374
1864 Henry B. Joy, president of the Packard Motor Car Co., born B:327
1865 George B. McClellan, congressman, born 4:144
1872 B. T. Babbitt Hyde, manufacturer and archæologist, born 26:196
1876 William Edwin Rudge, printer and publisher, born C:323
1921 The Sheppard-Towner Act, providing for research in maternity and infancy problems, became a law .... C: 25

NOVEMBER 24.

Last Thursday in the Month is Thanksgiving Day

1637 New Haven purchased from the Indians 6:121
1713 Father Junipero Serra, missionary, born 12:134
1740 Samuel A. Otis, congressman, born 2:500
1758 The French abandoned Ft. Duquesne at the approach of the English forces 1: 3
1783 Allen Trimble, governor of Ohio, born 3:138
1784 Zachary Taylor, 12th president of the United States, born 4:367
1800 Henry K. Oliver, musician, born 13:424
1807 Leonard Woods, president of Bowdoin college, born 1:418
1816 Joel Parker, governor of New Jersey, born 5:209
1818 William Woods Holden, journalist, and governor of North Carolina, born 4:427
1818 D. Hayes Agnew, surgeon, born 8:203
1820 Benjamin F. Shumard, physician and geologist, born 8:256
1822 James M. Ashley, congressman and governor of Montana, born 11: 79
1826 Coates Kinney, poet, born 7:302
1828 Henry Lomb, partner in the Bausch & Lomb Optical Co., one of the world's largest manufacturers of optical instruments, born 23:343
1829 Cyrus C. Carpenter, congressman and governor of Iowa, born 11:432
1830 Louisville "Journal" first issued 3:121
1832 South Carolina adopted the famous nullification resolution, declaring the tariff laws of 1828 and 1832 null and void 12:166

1833	William Wirt Howe, jurist, born	13: 161
1840	John A. Brashear, scientist, maker of astronomical instruments, born	4: 552
1842	William E. Simonds, lawyer and author, born	1: 363
1842	William B. Cushing, naval officer, born	9: 374
1843	Richard Croker, politician, born	13: 202
1844	Charles V. Gridley, naval officer, born	9: 6
1849	Frances Hodgson Burnett, author, born	20: 423
1854	Walter G. Smith, Philadelphia lawyer, born	21: 43
1856	Harry Thurston Peck, educator and author, born	11: 528
1857	Clayton Johns, musician and composer, born	13: 421
1863	Battle of Lookout Mountain, Tenn.	4: 177
1879	Alexander J. Inglis, educator, who did much to promote secondary education in the United States, born	23: 54
1880	Paul Jones, P. E. bishop, born	B: 88
1888	Dale Carnegie, lecturer and author, born	D: 402

NOVEMBER 25.

1757	Henry B. Livingston, justice of the U. S. supreme court, born	2: 467
1758	John Armstrong, Jr., soldier, U. S. senator and diplomat, secretary of war under Madison, born	1: 48
1758	Noah Worcester, clergyman, founder of the Massachusetts Peace Society, born	1: 185
1758	The English under Washington, Forbes and Armstrong captured Ft. Duquesne (renamed Pittsburgh)	25: 315
1770	Henry Sargent, artist and soldier, born	5: 319
1783	The British evacuated New York city	1: 4
1796	Jacob Randolph, surgeon, born	10: 282
1805	William B. Preston, secretary of the navy under Taylor, born	4: 371
1808	John Englis, shipbuilder, born	9: 478
1809	Adolph E. Borie, merchant and financier, secretary of the navy under Grant, born	4: 25
1816	Lewis M. Rutherford, astronomer, who originated the photographic method of observation, born	6: 376
1817	John Bigelow, journalist, diplomat and author, born	7: 348
1827	Hayden W. Wheeler, manufacturer of watch cases, born	12: 433
1835	Andrew Carnegie, industrialist, and philanthropist, born	9: 151
1835	Arthur Sewall, shipbuilder, bank president and leader of the Democratic party, born	10: 502
1835	Sidney E. Morse, publisher, born	13: 353
1839	Cecil F. P. Bancroft, principal of Phillips academy at Andover, born	24: 311
1847	Benjamin F. Trueblood, president of Wilmington (Ohio) and Penn colleges, and peace advocate, born	18: 25
1850	St. Francis Xavier college opened	4: 115
1850	Chauncey Y. Turner, artist, born	6: 469
1857	William Walker, filibuster, invaded Nicaragua for the third time	11: 24
1858	Paul Haupt, Orientalist, a world-famous Biblical scholar, born	22: 157
1860	Bliss Perry, author and editor, born	C: 451
1862	Ethelbert Nevin, composer, born	7: 437
1863	Battle of Chattanooga (or Missionary ridge), Tenn.	4: 33
1863	William E. B. Davis, physician, born	13: 514
1869	Ben B. Lindsey, jurist and reformer, "the father of the juvenile court," born	15: 183

NOVEMBER 26.

1727	Artemas Ward, soldier and statesman, first commander-in-chief of the revolutionary army, born	23: 24
1774	William Hunter, U. S. senator and diplomat, born	9: 269
1792	Sarah Moore Grimké, reformer, born	2: 325
1800	Matthew H. McAllister, judge, born	11: 474
1803	Balie Peyton, lawyer, soldier and diplomat, born	7: 176
1807	William D. Mount, painter, born	14: 457
1810	Seth W. Cheney, engraver and crayon artist, born	9: 170
1816	William H. T. Walker, Confederate soldier, born	13: 16
1822	Octavius B. Frothingham, theologian and biographer, the founder of the Independent Liberal Society, born	2: 423
1823	Leonard E. Wales, jurist, born	11: 354
1832	First street railway car exhibited and operated	7: 364
1832	Mary E. Walker, physician and reformer, born	13: 99
1835	Col. Bowie led the Texans in the Grass fight	4: 211
1839	George Cary Eggleston, author and editor, born	1: 213
1844	Thomas G. Jones, lawyer and governor of Alabama, born	10: 437
1857	Edward C. Potter, sculptor, born	26: 272
1859	Willis Vickery, jurist and author, born	A: 209
1863	Battle of Ringgold, Ga.	8: 54
1867	Solomon C. Mead, secretary of the Merchants' Association of New York, born	A: 142

NOVEMBER 27.

1703	James De Lancey, jurist, born	4: 550
1746	Increase Sumner, governor of Massachusetts, born	1: 109
1746	Robert R. Livingston, signer of the Declaration of Independence, chancellor of New York, and diplomat, born	2: 396
1783	William P. Preble, judge and diplomat, born	13: 220
1785	Henry Wheaton, lawyer and diplomat, born	1: 274
1805	Ralph P. Lowe, governor of Iowa and jurist, born	11: 431
1809	Fanny Kemble, actress and author, born	3: 414
1820	Edwin Forrest made his first appearance on the American stage	5: 86
1820	Augustine F. Hewit, R.C. clergyman, born	11: 358
1824	Charles F. Southmayd, lawyer, born	15: 39
1827	Horace Wyman, inventor, born	13: 212
1829	Harrison Millard, singer and composer, born	7: 425
1829	Albert F. Bellows, artist, born	7: 464
1842	Alvey A. Adee, diplomat, and second assistant secretary of state for thirty-six years, born	12: 459
1843	Cornelius Vanderbilt, financier and railroad president, born	6: 211
1843	William Ludlow, military and civil governor of Havana, born	9: 23
1848	Henry A. Rowland, physicist, born	11: 25
1850	Edward Wegmann, civil engineer, born	25: 341
1863	Samuel Davis hanged as a spy	8: 335
1863	Escape of the Confederate prisoners, Capt. Hines and Gen. Morgan, from the Ohio penitentiary	12: 453
1864	William Henry Todd, head of the Todd shipyards in Brooklyn, N. Y., and Tacoma, Wash.	25: 268
1867	Margaret R. Lang, composer, born	7: 430
1868	Custer defeated the Cheyennes in the battle of the Wachita	4: 275
1873	Hoosac tunnel in Massachusetts opened to traffic	25: 93
1875	Début of Mary Anderson, actress	1: 243
1889	Leon Fraser, financier, second American president of the Bank for International Settlements, born	D: 36

NOVEMBER 28.

1520	Magellan entered the Pacific ocean in his circumnavigation of the world	6: 249
1765	The landing of revenue stamps at Brunswick, N. C., resisted	9: 473
1777	John H. Rice, clergyman, born	2: 27
1785	Treaty of Hopewell with the Cherokee Indians	7: 239
1792	Nathan Lord, clergyman, president of Dartmouth college, born	9: 88
1805	John L. Stephens, traveler and author, born	5: 424
1812	George Ticknor Curtis, jurist and author, born	1: 395
1815	Benjamin F. Angel, diplomat, born	10: 478
1825	John H. Manny, inventor of a reaping machine, born	11: 486
1831	John W. Mackay, mine operator, banker, founder of a transatlantic cable system, born	4: 487
1837	John W. Hyatt, who originated and developed the manufacture of celluloid in the United States, born	12: 148
1837	Berthold Fernow, historian, born	23: 371
1859	Cass Gilbert, architect, born	C: 464
1863	Arthur G. Webster, physicist, born	13: 352
1864	Lindley Miller Garrison, secretary of war under Wilson, born	A: 39
1866	Henry Bacon, architect, designer of the Lincoln memorial in Washington, D. C., born	20: 339
1866	John Barrett, diplomat, director-general of the Pan American Union, born	D: 450
1874	Suzanne Adams, singer, born	13: 402
1895	First automobile race run in America	D: 78

NOVEMBER 29.

1693	Governor Ludwell of South Carolina removed from office, Thomas Smith succeeding him	12: 153
1722	Benjamin Chew, jurist, born	5: 84
1727	Ezra Stiles, clergyman, scholar, and president of Yale college, born	1: 167
1729	Charles Thomson, author, patriot and secretary of the Continental congress, born	2: 131
1752	Jemima Wilkinson, religionist, born	8: 81
1759	Jeremiah Smith, jurist, and governor of New Hampshire, born	11: 123
1760	Detroit surrendered to the British	7: 450
1773	"Sons of Liberty" reorganized in New York	1: 44
1798	Hamilton R. Gamble, Missouri judge and governor, born	12: 305
1799	A. Bronson Alcott, author, born	2: 218
1811	Wendell Phillips, orator and reformer, born	2: 314
1813	Battle of Autossie, Ala.	9: 273
1816	Morrison R. Waite, chief justice of the U. S. supreme court, born	1: 30
1817	Henry M. Rice, an original proprietor of St. Paul, expert on Indian affairs, and U. S. senator, born	21: 273

1818	William Ellery Channing, poet, biographer and essayist, born	13: 431
1823	La Fayette Grover, governor of Oregon, born	8: 5
1831	Frederick T. Ward, general in the Chinese army, born	2: 55
1832	Louisa M. Alcott, author, born	1: 204
1834	Thomas E. G. Ransom, Federal soldier, born	16: 104
1839	Elisha Dyer, governor of Rhode Island, born	9: 410
1847	Dr. and Mrs. Marcus Whitman and fourteen others massacred by the Indians	11: 112
1849	Simon N. D. North, statistician, born	13: 62
1851	Grace E. King, author, born	2: 344
1864	Massacre of the Cheyenne Indians at Sand Creek	19: 308
1876	George D. Strayer, educator, an authority on school administration, and president of the National Education Association, born	A: 337
1879	John Haynes Holmes, clergyman, born	C: 461
1912	First trial before a jury of women	20: 122
1917	The Allied Conference opened in Paris, with Col. House as chairman of the American war mission	A: 56
1929	Comr. Byrd flew over the South Pole	B: 432

NOVEMBER 30.

1711	Ebenezer Kinnersley, physicist, born	1: 532
1723	William Livingston, governor of New Jersey, born	5: 201
1725	Martin Boehm, clergyman, a founder of the United Brethren in Christ, born	21: 137
1729	Samuel Seabury, P. E. bishop, born	3: 475
1740	Thomas Knowlton, soldier, born	2: 299
1782	Provisional articles of peace with Great Britain signed at Paris	2: 3
1789	Lawrence Kearny, naval officer, born	21: 335
1800	Luther Lee, clergyman and abolitionst, born	25: 101
1819	Cyrus W. Field, who laid the first transatlantic telegraph cables, born	4: 451
1835	William C. Oates, soldier, congressman and governor of Alabama, born	2: 243
1835	Samuel L. Clemens (Mark Twain), humorist and author, born	6: 24
1837	Henry Hopkins, president of Williams college, born	13: 96
1843	Charles H. Craven, naval officer, born	12: 370
1858	Charles A. Coolidge, architect, born	C: 521
1864	Battle of Franklin, Tenn.	4: 260
1864	Battle of Honey Hill, S. C.	12: 400
1878	Douglas Johnson, geologist and topographer, born	D: 177
1883	Brotherhood of St. Andrew founded	15: 238
1884	Daniel Alfred Poling, clergyman and president of the United Society of Christian Endeavor, born	B: 33

DECEMBER 1.

1741	Samuel Kirkland, missionary, and founder of Hamilton college, born	7: 404
1789	William Carr Lane, soldier, physician and territorial governor of New Mexico, born	5: 98
1792	Francis Granger, postmaster general under William Harrison, born	6: 7
1795	James Whitcomb, U. S. senator and governor of Indiana, born	13: 268
1798	Albert Barnes, clergyman, born	7: 360
1803	Josiah Scott, judge, born	12: 222
1815	Clark Mills, sculptor, born	5: 160
1824	James Sargent, inventor of time-locks, born	3: 433
1826	William Mahone, Confederate soldier (hero of the Crater) and U. S. senator, born	5: 12
1826	Sereno Watson, botanist, born	6: 111
1830	Matilda Heron, actress, born	8: 263
1841	Edmond Souchon, anatomist, surgeon and sanitarian, born	9: 132
1842	Frederick S. Church, artist, born	11: 304
1847	Christine Ladd-Franklin, scientist, born	26: 422
1850	Robert Wilson Shufeldt, naturalist and physician, born	6: 242
1860	George W. Wheeler, jurist, born	24: 136
1863	Patent granted for utilizing sponge rubber in the manufacture of artificial feet and hands	11: 386
1863	Edward I. Edwards, banker, governor of New Jersey and U. S. senator, born	24: 256
1866	Patent for a typewriter issued to John Pratt	3: 315
1867	Vernon L. Kellogg, zoölogist and entomologist, born	A: 203
1867	Robert P. Lamont, industrialist, secretary of commerce under Hoover, born	C: 13
1917	First session of the supreme war council at Versailles	A: 275
1918	The American army of occupation established headquarters at Coblenz, Germany	20: 12

DECEMBER 2.

1694	William Shirley, governor of Massachusetts, born	7: 375
1736	Richard Montgomery, soldier, born	1: 100
1760	John Breckenridge, U. S. senator and attorney-general under Jefferson, born	3: 9
1780	Gen. Nathanael Greene took command of the Southern army	1: 42
1810	James F. Joy, lawyer, and president of the Michigan Central railroad, born	18: 120
1814	Gen. Jackson arrived in New Orleans to defend the city against the British	5: 291
1816	Mary Mortimer, a founder and head of the Milwaukee female college, born	7: 529
1822	Erastus Wells, congressman, and pioneer business man of St. Louis, born	5: 438
1823	President Monroe's message to congress enunciated the famous "Monroe Doctrine"	6: 82
1840	Franklin L. Pope, electrical engineer and inventor, born	7: 414
1840	John H. Converse, locomotive manufacturer, born	9: 419
1852	Frederick E. Farnsworth, banker, born	15: 322
1859	John Brown, abolitionist, hanged	2: 308
1863	First ground broken at Omaha for the Union Pacific railroad	9: 264
1868	Frederick L. Ransome, geologist, born	26: 408
1873	The Reformed Episcopal church organized	7: 57

DECEMBER 3.

1733	Joseph Brown, scientist, born	8: 28
1741	Jonathan Arnold, physician and legislator, born	13: 146
1751	George Cabot, U. S. senator and first secretary of the navy (under John Adams), born	2: 5
1755	Gilbert C. Stuart, portrait painter, born	5: 324
1756	Aaron Ogden, soldier and governor of New Jersey, born	5: 203
1766	Barbara Fritchie, the heroine of Whittier's poem, born	10: 113
1771	Isaac T. Hopper, humanitarian, born	2: 330
1787	Members of the Ohio company left Ipswich, Mass., to establish a settlement at Marietta	3: 70
1789	George W. Gale, founder of Galesburg, Ill., and Knox college, born	24: 26
1796	Francis P. Kenrick, archbishop of Baltimore, born	1: 485
1806	Henry A. Wise, congressman, diplomat, governor of Virginia and Confederate soldier, born	5: 452
1810	Mary T. S. Putnam, author, born	12: 328
1818	Illinois admitted to the Union	11: 42
1820	T. Addison Richards, author and artist, born	8: 425
1826	George B. McClellan, Federal soldier, and governor of New Jersey, born	4: 140
1827	Anne Drinker (Edith May), poet, born	11: 502
1831	James G. Fair, financier, who acquired a fortune in silver mining and furthered silver legislation as a member of the U. S. senate, born	11: 189
1833	Oberlin college opened	2: 461
1838	Cleveland Abbe (Old Probabilities), meteorologist, who published the first daily weather forecast bulletins in America, born	8: 264
1842	Ellen H. Richards, chemist and sanitarian, born	7: 343
1842	Phoebe A. Hearst, philanthropist, benefactor of the University of California, born	25: 322
1844	The law "gagging" the discussion of slavery rescinded by congress	5: 76
1844	Joseph C. Root, capitalist, and founder of the Modern Woodmen of America, born	15: 271
1860	John Bassett Moore, judge of the Permanent Court of International Justice, born	A: 72
1862	Charles Grafly, sculptor, born	22: 40
1863	Siege of Knoxville, Tenn., abandoned by the Confederate troops	4: 33
1864	Battle of Tullafumy river, S. C.	12: 400
1870	Eugene W. Caldwell, scientist and physician, a pioneer in the development of X-ray treatment, born	18: 197
1871	Newton D. Baker, secretary of war under Wilson, born	A: 40

DECEMBER 4.

1585	John Cotton, clergyman and author, born	7: 27
1682	The first general assembly in Pennsylvania convened at Chester	2: 275
1727	Archibald Laidlie, clergyman, born	13: 399
1736	Thomas Godfrey, poet, author of the first American drama, born	8: 36
1783	Washington bade farewell to his officers at Fraunces tavern, New York city	1: 4
1809	Ashbel Welch, civil engineer, born	9: 36
1816	Benjamin Silliman, Jr., chemist, one of the organizers of the Sheffield scientific school at Yale, born	2: 386
1818	William W. Loring, soldier, born	4: 364

1818 John LeConte, physicist, and president of the University of California, born ... 7:228
1820 Charles F. Deems, clergyman, and educator, born 9:164
1824 Isaac L. Peet, noted instructor of deaf-mutes, born ... 13:145
1833 American Anti-Slavery Society organized in Philadelphia ... 1:413
1843 Edgar M. Cullen, jurist, born ... 13:444
1861 Lillian Russell, singer, "the American beauty," born ... 4:345
1861 John C. Breckenridge of Kentucky expelled from the senate ... 5: 3
1865 James M. Kennedy, surgeon, born ... 22:308
1866 Albert T. Clay, archæologist, an authority on the sources of the Old Testament, born ... 22:130
1867 Charles H. Herty, chemist, born ... 18: 85
1915 Henry Ford's "peace ship" sailed for Europe ... B: 3
1918 President Wilson sailed for France, the first American president to visit a foreign country while in office ... 19: 9

DECEMBER 5.

1735 Hugh Williamson, surgeon, author, member of the Continental congress, born ... 2:492
1762 Abraham Van Vechten, jurist, born ... 9:162
1770 James Gould, jurist and author, head of the Litchfield law school, the first of its kind in America, born ... 19: 23
1782 Martin Van Buren, 8th president of the United States, born ... 6:433
1783 Simon Greenleaf, lawyer, author and educator, born ... 7:360
1792 James Guthrie, secretary of the treasury under Pierce, born ... 4:147
1800 Thomas Ford, Illinois judge and governor, born 11: 46
1802 Thomas R. Dew, economist, president of William and Mary college, born ... 3:235
1803 Thomas J. Rusk, Texas statesman, born ... 3:113
1811 David Van Nostrand, publisher, born ... 9:123
1816 William Wheatley, actor and manager, born ... 1:190
1822 Elizabeth C. Agassiz, author and educator, first president of Radcliffe college, born ... 12: 46
1823 John H. Upshur, naval officer, born ... 4:316
1826 John B. Sanborn, Federal soldier, born ... 5:287
1829 John Eaton, college president and organizer of the U. S. bureau of education, born ... 8:390
1830 Adolphus Bonzano, founder of the Phoenix Bridge Co., and inventor of the Bonzano rail joint, born ... 16:312
1835 Charles E. Billings, inventor. founder of Billings & Spencer, tool manufacturers, born ... 5:408
1839 George A. Custer, soldier, hero of the battle of the Little Big Horn, born ... 4:274
1850 Lyman E. Cooley, civil and sanitary engineer, born ... 9: 41
1855 C. Hart Merriam, biologist, born ... 13:264
1857 Alice Brown, author, born ... 15:283
1872 Harry N. Pillsbury, chess champion, born ... 13: 49
1933 The 18th (Prohibition) Amendment to the Constitution repealed ... D: 7

DECEMBER 6.

1637 Sir Edmund Andros, colonial governor of New England, born ... 6: 90
1752 Gabriel Duval, associate justice of the U. S. supreme court, born ... 2:468
1762 Charles C. Ridgely, governor of Maryland, born . 9:299
1791 George Holland, actor, born ... 3:148
1796 William Williams, pioneer settler of Fort Dodge, Iowa, born ... 12:498
1815 Jane G. Swisshelm, reformer, born ... 2:316
1816 Curtis Hooks Brogden, legislator and governor of North Carolina, born ... 4:428
1820 Thomas De K. Winans, engineer and inventor, born ... 1:239
1822 Eberhard Faber, pencil manufacturer, born ... 14:267
1830 George G. Vest, U. S. senator, born ... 2:297
1830 Don Juan Whittemore, civil engineer, born ... 13:248
1833 John S. Mosby, Confederate soldier, born ... 4:326
1834 Henry W. Blair, U. S. senator, born ... 1:458
1835 William Joyce Sewell, U. S. senator and Federal soldier, born ... 12:217
1836 Charles F. Chandler, chemist and sanitarian, and dean of Columbia university for thirty-three years, born ... 23: 46
1840 Richard H. Pratt, founder and first superintendent of the Indian school at Carlisle, Pa., born 13: 89
1849 William Henry Lippincott, artist and illustrator, born ... 6:474
1858 Mount Vernon sold to The Ladies' Mount Vernon Association of the Union ... 21:225
1859 Edward H. Sothern, actor, born ... 5:490
1860 Howard Elliott, president of the Northern Pacific and the New York, New Haven and Hartford railroads, born ... 20: 5
1863 Sherman relieved Knoxville, Tenn., which had been besieged by Longstreet ... 4: 33
1863 Charles M. Hall, inventor of a process for producing aluminum on a commercial scale, born 13: 94
1867 Karl Bitter, sculptor, director of sculpture at the Buffalo Pan-American and St. Louis expositions, born ... 24:385
1877 Fred S. Duesenberg, inventor of improved motors for boats, automobiles and airplanes, born ... 16:295
1886 Joyce Kilmer, poet, born ... 19:290

DECEMBER 7.

1757 Dwight Foster, U. S. senator and judge, born .. 2: 6
1796 Washington delivered his last address to Congress 1: 7
1801 Abigail Hopper Gibbons, humanitarian, born ... 7:313
1804 Noah H. Swayne, justice of the U. S. supreme court, born ... 4:156
1804 William B. Rogers, physicist and geologist, born 7:410
1805 George Opdyke, merchant, banker and mayor of New York, born ... 11:464
1808 Hugh McCulloch, secretary of the treasury under three presidents, born ... 4:251
1809 Asahel Clark Kendrick, philologist, born ... 12:245
1812 William J. Linton, engraver and poet, born ... 8: 13
1815 Elizabeth H. Whittier, poet, born ... 8:109
1817 Edward Tuckerman, botanist, born ... 5:312
1822 William Saunders, horticulturist, who introduced seedless oranges in the United States, born ... 10:409
1826 Edmund G. Ross, journalist, U. S. senator and governor of New Mexico, born ... 13:232
1828 James D. Porter, Confederate soldier and governor of Tennessee, born ... 7:211
1835 Everett H. Barney, inventor and manufacturer, born ... 3: 89
1835 George E. Church, civil engineer, soldier and author, born ... 13:250
1835 George A. Hearn, New York merchant, born ... 16:316
1841 Michael Cudahy, meat packer, born ... 11:385
1843 Henry D. Perky, cereal manufacturer, originator of "Shredded Wheat," and founder and president of the Oread institute, born ... 24:349
1850 Solomon Schecter, Hebraist, born ... 13:414
1857 Alice R. Moore, author, born ... 16:425
1858 Carl Stoeckel, patron of the arts, born ... 17:323
1862 Battle of Prairie Grove, Ark. ... 9:443
1872 Cale Young Rice, poet and novelist, born ... C:375
1876 Willa Cather, author, born ... A:537
1885 Marshall L. Mertins, clergyman, lecturer and author, born ... A:150
1891 Ralph A. O'Neill, aviation executive, born ... C:467

DECEMBER 8.

1765 Eli Whitney, inventor of the cotton gin, born .. 4:495
1770 Nicholas Van Dyke, U. S. senator, born ... 4:346
1804 Gilman Kimball, surgeon, born ... 5:200
1810 Elihu Burritt (the Learned Blacksmith), reformer, born ... 6:133
1813 Marcius Willson, historian, born ... 10: 39
1816 August Belmont, banker and U. S. minister to Holland, born ... 11:499
1820 James M. Brown, head of the house of Alexander Brown & Sons, and a founder and president of the Society for the Prevention of Cruelty to Animals, born ... 8: 14
1823 Robert Collyer, clergyman, born ... 1:369
1828 Clinton B. Fisk, soldier, banker and reformer, founder of the Fisk School of Freedmen (Fisk university), born ... 6:244
1829 Henry Timrod, poet, born ... 7:473
1831 William P. Kellogg, U. S. senator and governor of Louisiana, born ... 10: 82
1833 Edward P. Evans, author and educator, born ... 9:433
1837 Wendell Phillips made his first public speech ... 2:314
1839 Alexander J. Cassatt, president of the Pennsylvania railroad, born ... 13:336
1841 James H. Logan, jurist and horticulturist, originator of the loganberry industry in Oregon, born ... 21:163
1847 John B. White, lumberman, born ... 15:380
1856 Henry T. Mayo, naval officer, born ... 15: 44
1858 Alfred H. Cowles, metallurgist, who perfected an electric furnace for the reduction of refractory ores, born ... 22: 44
1859 William Henry O'Connell, R. C. cardinal, born .. 15:294
1879 Arthur Bullard (Albert Edwards), newspaper correspondent and author, born ... 21:392
1891 Percy L. Crosby, artist and author, born ... D:294
1920 Inauguration of the first regular nightly concerts broadcast by radio ... 25: 18

DECEMBER 9.

1773 Robert T. Paine, Jr., poet and author, born 4: 554
1775 Battle of Great Bridge, Va. 6: 301
1790 Henry S. Geyer, lawyer and U. S. senator, born 4: 61
1791 Augustus L. Hillhouse, hymnologist, born 4: 559
1812 James H. Thornwell, clergyman, and president of South Carolina college, born 11: 33
1816 Samuel P. Brown, shipbuilder and banker, born 15: 124
1830 Christian F. G. Meyer, merchant, born 12: 30
1832 Thomas Egleston, mining engineer, born 3: 244
1832 William J. Magie, jurist, born 12: 424
1832 Joseph T. Duryea, clergyman, born 12: 451
1834 Carlo A. Cappa, musician, born 9: 387
1838 Robert W. Hunt, metallurgist and engineer, born 19: 17
1839 Amos I. Root, apiculturist, born 25: 253
1844 Charles T. Schoen, inventor and manufacturer of pressed steel cars, born 25: 389
1848 Joel Chandler Harris, author, creator of the "Uncle Remus" folk-lore, born 1: 410
1849 Emma Abbott Wetherell, opera singer, born 3: 258
1849 Thomas Morgan Rotch, physician, born 19: 350
1850 Edward O. Leech, statistician, director of the U. S. mint, born 13: 87
1851 George W. Rafter, civil engineer, born 12: 234
1866 Meredith Nicholson, author, born .... A: 512
1872 Thomas W. Hardwick, U. S. senator and governor of Georgia, born .... B: 296
1879 Karl F. Kellerman, bacteriologist, born 26: 160

DECEMBER 10.

1641 The Massachusetts "Body of Liberties" adopted 7: 64
1664 John Williams, "The Redeemed Captive," clergyman, born 1: 258
1741 John Murray, "father of Universalism in America," born 13: 175
1778 John Jay elected president of the Continental congress 1: 20
1785 Daniel Appleton, publisher, born 2: 509
1787 Thomas H. Gallaudet, founder of the first school for deaf-mutes in America, born 9: 138
1795 Matthias W. Baldwin, pioneer locomotive builder, born 9: 476
1800 Levi Heywood, chair manufacturer and inventor, born 10: 307
1805 William Lloyd Garrison, abolitionist, born 2: 305
1810 George Goldthwaite, U. S. senator and jurist, born 4: 350
1813 Zachariah Chandler, U. S. senator and secretary of the interior under Grant, born 4: 18
1816 Oren B. Cheney, first president of Bates college, born 8: 394
1817 Fielding B. Meek, paleontologist, born 11: 284
1817 Mississippi admitted to the Union 13: 485
1827 William J. Rolfe, Shakespearean scholar, born .. 4: 86
1830 Emily E. Dickinson, poet, born 23: 82
1832 President Jackson issued his famous proclamation against nullifiers 5: 293
1835 San Antonio captured by the Texan patriot army 4: 211
1837 Edward Eggleston, clergyman, editor and author, born 6: 57
1847 Francis E. Nipher, physicist, born 22: 55
1850 Jennie A. Brownscombe, artist, born 16: 425
1851 Melvil Dewey, educator and librarian, founder of the first library school and leader of the simplified spelling movement, born 23: 14
1852 Israel C. Russell, geologist, born 10: 306
1860 Howell Cobb, secretary of the treasury under Buchanan, resigned and allied himself with the Georgia secessionists 1: 226
1863 Edward M. Lewis, soldier, born .... B: 96
1898 Treaty of peace concluded between United States and Spain 11: 11

DECEMBER 11.

1660 Philip Calvert became governor of Maryland 7: 334
1750 Isaac Shelby, soldier and governor of Kentucky, born 13: 1
1757 Samuel Sewall, Massachusetts jurist, born 6: 189
1777 Washington went into winter quarters at Valley Forge 1: 4
1797 Hiram Paulding, naval officer, born 4: 135
1811 Thornton A. Jenkins, Federal naval officer, born 4: 311
1816 Indiana admitted to the Union 13: 266
1822 George David Cummins, founder of the Reformed Episcopal church, born 7: 57
1823 Sarah H. Palfrey (E. Foxton), author, born 7: 530
1835 Benjamin S. Lyman, geologist, born 9: 217
1836 Henry Morton, scientist, first president of Stevens institute of technology, born 24: 374
1838 Atherton introduced the infamous "gag law" on the slavery issue 10: 383
1862 Gen. Burnside crossed the Rappahannock before Fredericksburg, Va. 4: 98
1862 William M. Reedy, journalist, born 19: 140
1863 Coleman du Pont, head of the Dupont gunpowder industry, U. S. senator and builder of the Dupont highway in Delaware, born 22: 3
1863 Annie J. Cannon, astronomer, born .... B: 482
1867 Bela L. Pratt, sculptor, born 14: 378
1872 Fusion legislature of Louisiana impeached and suspended Governor Warmoth 10: 80

DECEMBER 12.

1745 John Jay, statesman and first chief justice of the U. S. supreme court, born 1: 20
1757 Joseph Peabody, New England merchant, born . 5: 403
1786 William Learned Marcy, governor of New York, secretary of war under Polk and secretary of state under Pierce, born 6: 269
1790 Edward T. Channing, educator and editor, born 13: 150
1791 Peter D. Vroom, governor of New Jersey, congressman and diplomat, born 5: 205
1805 Frederic H. Hedge, clergyman and author, born 8: 271
1806 Isaac Leeser, clergyman, editor and author, born 10: 393
1810 James Shields, soldier, U. S. senator and first territorial governor of Oregon, born 8: 2
1815 Anna H. Dorsey, author, born 11: 361
1818 Mary Todd Lincoln, wife of Abraham Lincoln, born 2: 75
1830 John Swinton, journalist, born 8: 251
1831 National Republican party nominated Henry Clay for president 5: 79
1831 Edward H. Cole, manufacturer, born 12: 525
1832 Mauritz F. H. de Haas, marine painter, born ... 9: 52
1832 Albert B. Prescott, chemist, born 13: 53
1836 Sarah B. Cooper, pioneer kindergarten teacher, born 3: 132
1837 Isaac H. Hall, Orientalist, born 12: 143
1838 Sherburne W. Burnham, astronomer, who discovered more than 1000 new stars, born 11: 71
1840 Cady Staley, president of the Case school of applied science, born 11: 154
1843 William P. Dillingham, governor of Vermont and U. S. senator, born 8: 411
1845 Byron A. Brooks, author and typewriter inventor, born 3: 319
1845 Bruce Price, architect, born 13: 303
1849 William K. Vanderbilt, financier, born 6: 212
1849 Peter F. Collier, publisher, born 10: 226
1853 William F. Hillebrand, chemist, born 14: 132
1859 Lillian Nordica Döme (Mme. Nordica), singer, born 9: 217
1860 Lewis Cass, secretary of state under Buchanan, resigned 5: 5
1864 Paul Elmer More, editor and author, a leader in humanist thought, born .... C: 296
1870 First negro member of Congress (Joseph H. Rainey) admitted 11: 398
1878 Rachel Crothers, playwright, born .... C: 83
1881 Harry M. Warner, talking picture producer, born D: 230
1882 William N. Doak, labor leader, secretary of labor under Hoover, born 25: 29
1888 Theodore Willard Case, scientist, specializing in photo-electricity and radiation, who invented many devices for talking pictures, born ...... D: 416

DECEMBER 13.

1621 A Thanksgiving day appointed by Governor Bradford 7: 368
1654 Robert Livingston, colonist, born 24: 57
1664 Last general court of the New Haven colony convened 10: 322
1765 Ambrose Spencer, jurist and congressman, born 3: 423
1769 Charter granted for Dartmouth college 9: 85
1776 Gen. Charles Lee captured by the British 8: 240
1793 John Ludlow, provost of the University of Pennsylvania, born 1: 343
1802 Thomas J. Conant, Biblical scholar, born 12: 288
1816 Clement C. Clay, lawyer, U. S. senator and Confederate agent, born 4: 198
1823 George Schneider, journalist and banker, born .. 10: 403
1827 Hervey C. Parke, drug manufacturer, founder of Parke, Davis & Co., born 24: 167
1828 John Savage, dramatist, journalist and poet, born 11: 509
1831 William E. McLaren, P. E. bishop and educator, born 11: 331
1835 Phillips Brooks, P. E. bishop, born 2: 304
1835 Samuel Fallows, bishop of the Reformed Episcopal church, born 9: 223
1836 Robert H. Newell (Orpheus C. Kerr), journalist, author and poet, born 11: 528
1844 John H. Patterson, founder of the National Cash Register Co., born 20: 337
1845 Hamilton Wright Mabie, essayist, born 10: 43
1849 Edmund L. Zalinski, inventor of the pneumatic dynamite torpedo gun, born 7: 248
1849 George Thomas Marye, Jr., diplomat, born ..... A: 139

1851 Lee Mantle, U. S. senator, born 11:313
1852 Charles E. Sajous, physician, editor and author of a cyclopedia of practical medicine, born ... 9:351
1856 A. Lawrence Lowell, president of Harvard university, born .... D: 46
1859 Edwin Fremont Ladd, chemist, president of the North Dakota agricultural college and U. S. senator, born 19:432
1862 Battle of Fredericksburg, Va. 4: 98
1864 Gen. Hazen captured Ft. McAllister, Ga. 3:408
1890 J. French Robinson, geologist and engineer, born A:211

DECEMBER 14.

1590 John West, colonial governor of Virginia, born 13:383
1719 First number of the Boston "Gazette" issued ... 8: 17
1774 Ft. William and Mary seized by New Hampshire patriots 2:261
1775 Philander Chase, P. E. bishop and founder and first president of Kenyon college, born 7: 1
1780 "Vermont Gazette," first newspaper in the state, issued 19: 41
1782 Charleston, S. C., evacuated by the British 1: 43
1794 Erastus Corning, manufacturer and railroad promoter, born 9:533
1795 John B. Jervis, civil engineer, born 9: 46
1799 George Washington died at Mount Vernon 1: 7
1801 Joseph Lane, "the Marion of the Mexican army," and territorial governor of Oregon, born 8: 2
1805 James A. Pearce, U. S. senator, born 10:249
1811 Noah Porter, president of Yale college, born 1:171
1819 Alabama admitted to the Union 10:425
1822 First issue of the "Farmers & Mechanics Journal" in Indiana 18:293
1829 John Mercer Langston, congressman, educator and diplomat, born 3:328
1832 Thomas L. Young, Federal soldier and governor of Ohio, born 3:143
1842 Charles O. Whitman, biologist, born 11: 73
1845 Claude Matthews, governor of Indiana, born 13:275
1851 Hastings H. Hart, penologist, founder of the Child Welfare League of America, born 23:170
1856 Louis Marshall, New York lawyer and philanthropist, born 26:115
1872 Marion Dorset, biochemist, born 26:300
1880 Henry V. Poor, lawyer, born 25:144
1886 Francis Little, clergyman, born 25:275
1890 Sitting Bull, Indian chief, killed 13:455
1890 Jane Cowl, actress, born B:202
1894 Eugene V. Debs sentenced to prison as a result of his leadership of the Pullman strike 12:341

DECEMBER 15.

1727 Ezra Stiles, president of Yale college, born 1:167
1733 Samuel Johnston, governor of North Carolina, born 4:420
1757 Thomas Gibbons, lawyer, who instituted the suit that broke Fulton's steamboat monopoly, born 24:364
1764 Thomas H. Perkins, founder of Perkins institute, born 5:245
1764 Theodore Dwight, journalist, born 11:216
1786 Edward Coles, governor of Illinois, born 11: 43
1787 Edward Bishop Dudley, governor of North Carolina, born 4:425
1790 The first lecture on law delivered "in the presence of Washington and his cabinet, both houses of congress and the state legislature" 1:341
1793 Henry Charles Carey, political economist, born 5: 34
1797 Antoine Le Claire, pioneer, founder of the city of Davenport, Iowa, born 12:554
1798 Edward Burleson, Texas soldier and legislator, born 18: 13
1814 The Hartford convention of New England Federalists met 3:511
1815 Fabius Stanly, Federal naval officer, born 4:470
1823 Bernard J. McQuaid, R. C. bishop, born 12:141
1831 Franklin B. Sanborn, editor and educator, a staunch abolitionist and advocate of social reforms, born 8:466
1831 George J. Brush, mineralogist, born 10:298
1834 Charles A. Young, astronomer, born 6:325
1837 George B. Post, New York architect, born 15:250
1841 August Dreier, planter, born 12:267
1845 Anne H. Wharton, author, born 13:366
1845 Robert E. Jennings, industrialist, a founder of the Crucible Steel Co. of America, born 23:339
1846 John E. Pillsbury, naval officer, whose investigations of the Gulf stream currents have proved most useful to mariners, born 20:287
1848 Edwin H. Blashfield, artist and illustrator, born D: 80
1851 John R. Coryell, author, creator of "Nick Carter," born 21:279
1858 John Markle, coal operator and philanthropist, born C:525
1860 William Bullock Clark, geologist, born 18:191
1861 Charles E. Duryea, pioneer automobile builder, born .... D: 78
1864 Battle of Nashville, Tenn., begun 4: 48
1871 An arbitration tribunal met at Geneva to settle the Alabama claims 4: 21

DECEMBER 16.

1714 George Whitefield, evangelist, born 5:384
1752 John F. Grimké, lawyer, born 2:325
1769 Jesse Mercer, pioneer preacher and philanthropist, for whom Mercer university was named, born 6:497
1773 The Boston "tea party" occurred 1:108
1783 Mordecai Bartley, governor of Ohio, born 3:140
1792 Abbott Lawrence, merchant and diplomat, born.. 3: 62
1818 J. Lawrence Smith, physician and scientist, born 6: 54
1823 Gordon L. Ford, railroad president, born 13:104
1830 John F. Hartranft, Federal soldier and governor of Pennsylvania, born 2:291
1834 Charles B. Manville, inventor and manufacturer of asbestos products, founder of the Johns-Manville Co., born 24: 20
1835 A great fire occurred in New York city 10: 17
1839 Stephen H. Thayer, banker and poet, born 9:453
1843 Joseph V. Quarles, lawyer and U. S. senator, born 13: 17
1847 Mary H. Catherwood, author, born 9:215
1848 Isaac Sharpless, Quaker leader and president of Haverford college, born 21:105
1850 Arlo Bates, poet, editor and author, born 8: 12
1852 John P. Peters, clergyman and archæologist, born 13:555
1853 Joseph Fels, soap manufacturer and social reformer, born 20:419
1857 Edward E. Barnard, astronomer, especially noted as a comet observer, born 7: 44
1863 Ralph A. Cram, architect, born B:228
1863 George Santayana, poet and philosopher, born .. B:343
1864 Battle of Nashville, Tenn., ended 4: 48
1905 First issue of "Variety" established a new policy in theatrical publications 24: 44
1922 First woman elected associate justice of a state supreme court C:111

DECEMBER 17.

1734 Return J. Meigs, soldier, born 1: 83
1734 William Floyd, a signer of the Declaration of Independence, born 4: 75
1757 Nathanial Macon, speaker of the house and presiding officer of the U. S. senate, born 5:176
1760 Deborah Sampson, Revolutionary heroine, born .. 8:331
1762 Pliny Earle, inventor, born 11:145
1765 Andrew Oliver took oath not to enforce the Stamp Act 10:390
1773 John Harrison, manufacturing chemist, born 13:189
1774 Littleton W. Tazewell, U. S. senator and governor of Virginia, born 5:448
1779 Jacob Barker, merchant and financier, born ... 11: 41
1789 Clement C. Clay, Alabama lawyer and governor, and U. S. senator, born 10:427
1795 Benjamin F. Butler, attorney general under Jackson and Van Buren and secretary of war under Jackson, born 5:297
1799 Joseph Henry, scientist, born 3:405
1807 John Greenleaf Whittier, poet, born 1:407
1817 Francis Wolle, botanist and inventor, born 1:320
1817 Henry R. Worthington, pump manufacturer and inventor, born 6:303
1822 Frederick W. Lander, soldier, engineer and explorer, born 8:127
1818 J. Lawrence Smith, chemist, born 6: 54
1824 Thomas Starr King, clergyman, born 4:472
1824 Lewis Gerstle, pioneer in the sealing industry in Alaska, born 13:245
1835 Alexander Agassiz, scientist, born 3: 98
1836 Charles S. Stockton, dentist, born 15:204
1837 William Harkness, astronomer, born 8:395
1837 Byron Wilson, Federal naval officer, born 13:240
1839 Newton H. Winchell, geologist, born 7:451
1844 Ezra Brainerd, president of Middlebury college, born 12:107
1844 William G. Farlow, a leading authority on phytopathology and cryptogamic botany, born 22:207
1844 Frank Plumley, umpire of the Venezuela mixed claims commissions, born 26:206
1851 John P. Haines, president of the American Society for the Prevention of Cruelty to Animals, born 13:142
1855 Julian Edwards, composer, born 7:424
1860 James H. McGraw, publisher of trade journals, born B:105
1861 Arthur E. Kennelly, electrical engineer and inventor, born 13:452
1903 First successful flight of a flying machine made by the Wright brothers 14: 56

DECEMBER 18.

1688 John Blackwell became deputy governor of Pennsylvania ... 5: 545
1794 William C. Woodbridge, educator, born ... 11: 214
1795 Henry Detwiller, pioneer homeopathist in Pennsylvania, born ... 5: 25
1796 Welcome Farnum, textile manufacturer, born ... 12: 472
1801 South Carolina college established ... 12: 163
1802 George D. Prentice, journalist, born ... 3: 121
1811 Horace B. Claflin, dry goods merchant, born ... 3: 228
1811 Alfred B. Street, librarian and poet, born ... 11: 103
1815 Sarah T. Bolton, poet, born ... 10: 172
1819 Isaac T. Hecker, R. C. clergyman, founder of the Paulist Fathers, born ... 9: 166
1821 University of Alabama incorporated ... 12: 293
1831 Austin Abbott, lawyer and author of textbooks on law, born ... 2: 342
1833 Albert C. Perkins, educator, born ... 10: 106
1835 Lyman Abbott, theologian, born ... 1: 473
1840 Donald Mackay, financier, born ... 16: 429
1848 Frederick G. Gleason, composer, born ... 7: 433
1850 Charles Edward Garman, philosopher, born ... 23: 112
1860 John J. Crittenden introduced in the senate his measure to renew the Missouri line of 36°30′ .. 13: 7
1861 Edward MacDowell, pianist and composer, born 11: 446
1864 S. Parkes Cadman, clergyman and author, born B: 121
1865 The 13th Amendment to the Constitution, abolishing slavery, went into force ... 13: 50
1873 Francis B. Harrison, governor-general of the Philippine islands, born ... C: 204
1874 Lyman A. Cotten, naval officer, credited with keeping the German submarines out of the English channel during the World war, born .. 20: 284
1893 Amelia Bingham made her first appearance on the New York stage ... 21: 120

DECEMBER 19.

1606 The first English settlers left London for Virginia ... 13: 377
1675 The Narragansett Indians defeated at South Kingston, R. I. ... 10: 50
1686 Sir Edmund Andros arrived in Boston with a commission as governor of New England ... 6: 90
1714 John Winthrop, scientist, born ... 7: 165
1731 Thomas Willing, merchant and banker, first president of the Bank of the United States, born . 10: 512
1735 Benjamin Trumbull, clergyman and historian, born ... 11: 321
1743 James Glen assumed the duties of governor of South Carolina ... 12: 157
1753 John T. Gilman, governor of New Hampshire, born ... 11: 122
1807 Benjamin H. Latrobe, chief engineer of the Baltimore and Ohio railroad, born ... 9: 426
1814 Edwin M. Stanton, secretary of war under Lincoln, born ... 2: 83
1815 Henry E. Baldwin, editor and cartoonist, born .. 19: 91
1816 Richard Vaux, lawyer, congressman and penologist, born ... 3: 111
1819 St. Julien Ravenel, physician and chemist and designer of the "Little David," the Confederate torpedo boat, born ... 10: 272
1821 Mary A. Livermore, reformer, born ... 3: 82
1825 Basil Manly, clergyman and educator, born ... 25: 122
1828 South Carolina legislature protested against the tariff ... 12: 166
1830 Nathaniel T. Lupton, president of the University of Alabama, born ... 12: 294
1831 Jennie C. Croly (Jenny June), journalist and author, founder and first president of the Sorosis Club of New York city, born ... 6: 499
1831 Kemp P. Battle, president of the University of North Carolina, born ... 13: 243
1833 Samuel A. Drake, historian, born ... 25: 71
1842 George S. Morison, civil engineer, born ... 10: 129
1846 George E. Merrill, clergyman, and president of Colgate university, born ... 13: 226
1846 Ambrose Swasey, engineer and telescope builder, born ... B: 274
1849 Henry Clay Frick, industrialist, born ... 23: 31
1852 Albert Abraham Michelson, physicist, born ... C: 42
1861 Sadie Martinot, actress, born ... 12: 556
1865 Minnie Maddern Fiske, actress, born ... A: 87
1868 Eleanor H. Porter, author, the creator of "Pollyanna," born ... 18: 382
1899 Gen. Henry W. Lawton killed in action in the Philippines ... 10: 290

DECEMBER 20.

1779 William Wilkins, judge, diplomat, secretary of war under Tyler, born ... 6: 9
1790 First cotton yarn successfully manufactured in America ... 24: 220
1794 John D. Godman, physician and naturalist, born 7: 284
1798 John Wood, Federal soldier and governor of Illinois, born ... 11: 47
1813 Samuel J. Kirkwood, governor of Iowa, U. S. senator and secretary of the interior under Garfield, born ... 4: 245
1824 Calvert Vaux, landscape architect, born ... 9: 332
1825 Romeyn B. Ayres, Federal soldier, born ... 4: 255
1847 Arthur M. Wellington, civil engineer, born ... 11: 167
1849 Harry Pratt Judson, author and educator, president of the University of Chicago, born ... 20: 24
1851 Theodore E. Burton, U. S. senator and peace advocate, born ... 21: 50
1860 South Carolina seceded from the Union ... 5: 2
1861 Battle of Dranesville, Va. ... 4: 52
1861 Cyrus Townsend Brady, clergyman and author, born ... 10: 477
1862 Holly Springs, Miss., captured by the Confederates ... 9: 212
1862 Trenton, Tenn., captured by the Confederates .. 10: 36
1864 The Confederates evacuated Savannah, Ga. ... 4: 36
1868 Harvey S. Firestone, tire and rubber manufacturer, born ... C: 66
1870 Governor Holden of North Carolina impeached .. 4: 428
1874 Henry Hadley, composer and conductor, born .. D: 200

DECEMBER 21.

Forefathers' Day

1615 Benedict Arnold, president of Providence Plantations and governor of Rhode Island, born .. 10: 6
1620 Landing of the Pilgrims at Plymouth Rock ... 7: 367
1719 Revolution in South Carolina, James Moore chosen governor ... 12: 156
1740 Arthur Lee, diplomat, born ... 8: 298
1764 John P. Boyd, soldier, born ... 10: 135
1776 Benjamin Franklin reached Paris as envoy to France ... 1: 335
1786 Philip Lindsley, clergyman and president of the University of Nashville, born ... 8: 131
1790 First cotton mill in Rhode Island started ... 4: 121
1798 The Virginia resolutions denouncing the Alien and Sedition laws, passed ... 9: 509
1821 John C. Bryant, co-founder of the Bryant and Stratton business colleges, born ... 18: 395
1829 Laura D. Bridgman, blind deaf-mute educator, born ... 2: 424
1830 Mary Virginia Terhune (Marion Harland), author, born ... 2: 122
1843 Charles P. Taft, Cincinnati journalist and philanthropist, born ... 23: 7
1846 Carl Faelten, director of the New England conservatory of music, born ... 7: 325
1846 Lorenzo D. Lewelling, governor of Kansas, born 8: 347
1847 Howard Van Epps, jurist and editor, born ... 10: 473
1849 James Lane Allen, author, born ... 8: 241
1854 Henry Frank, rationalist, founder of the Peoples' Liberal church, born ... 23: 196
1854 Morton H. Prince, neurologist, a leading experimentalist in abnormal psychology, born ... 25: 313
1856 David L. Brainard, Arctic explorer, member of the ill-fated Greeley expedition, born ... 3: 286
1858 Lon V. Stephens, governor of Missouri, born ... 12: 309
1864 Gen. Sherman occupied Savannah ... 4: 34
1864 Frederick P. Gutelius, railway engineer, born ... A: 208
1870 Charles H. Haskins, historian, born ... C: 378
1872 Albert Payson Terhune, author, born ... C: 442
1874 Lynn J. Frazier, U. S. senator and governor of North Dakota, born ... B: 189
1877 Frank P. Underhill, chemist, born ... 25: 23
1880 David A. Reed, lawyer and U. S. senator, born.. B: 384

DECEMBER 22.

1696 James E. Oglethorpe, founder and first governor of Georgia, born ... 1: 490
1719 Publication of the "American Weekly Mercury," first newspaper in Pennsylvania, begun ... 19: 276
1727 William Ellery, signer of the Declaration of Independence, born ... 8: 59
1758 George R. Minot, historian and orator, born ... 7: 133
1761 Thomas Boone assumed the office of governor of South Carolina ... 12: 158
1789 Levi Woodbury, governor of New Hampshire, U. S. senator, cabinet member and justice of the U. S. supreme court, born ... 2: 471
1789 Ann Hasseltine Judson, missionary, born ... 3: 93
1796 George McClellan, physician and surgeon, founder of Jefferson medical college, born ... 4: 139
1798 George W. Crawford, governor of Georgia and secretary of war under Taylor, born ... 4: 370
1803 Joseph K. F. Mansfield, Federal soldier, born ... 4: 179
1803 The United States took possession of Louisiana 10: 74
1807 Embargo Act, prohibiting foreign commerce, passed ... 5: 409

1810 Alexander Stuart, merchant, born 10: 24
1814 John S. Phelps, congressman and governor of Missouri, born 12: 307
1821 Josiah B. Grinnell, congressman, and founder of Grinnell university (later Grinnell college), born 8: 399
1822 John S. Newberry, paleontologist, born 9: 235
1823 Thomas Wentworth Higginson, author and abolitionist, born 1: 394
1824 Matthew Hale Carpenter, U. S. senator, born .. 4: 22
1839 Hezekiah Butterworth, poet, editor and author, born 2: 111
1848 Alfred Dolge, felt manufacturer, born 1: 309
1852 Opie P. Read, journalist and author, founder of the "Arkansas Traveler," born 1: 353
1856 Frank B. Kellogg, U. S. senator, diplomat and secretary of state under Coolidge, born .... A: 8
1865 Gen. Thomas issued an order suspending the Episcopal clergy of Alabama 4: 49
1868 Solon H. Borglum, sculptor, born 13: 214
1869 Bainbridge Colby, secretary of state under Wilson, born .... A: 32
1869 Edwin Arlington Robinson, poet, born .... B: 15
1885 Deems Taylor, composer and musical critic, born B: 8

DECEMBER 23.

1657 Hannah Dustin, colonial heroine, born 6: 102
1783 Thomas Macdonough, naval officer, born 7: 28
1783 Washington resigned his commission in the army 9: 291
1783 John Syng Dorsey, physician and surgeon, born 10: 279
1788 Maryland voted to cede a district 10 miles square for the seat of the national government 9: 293
1799 Joseph H. Lumpkin, Georgia jurist, born 10: 23
1802 James S. Brown, inventor and manufacturer, born 11: 351
1805 Joseph Smith, founder and first president of the Mormon church, born 16: 1
1814 Jackson attacked the British below New Orleans, La. 5: 291
1815 Henry H. Garnet, negro clergyman, and U. S. minister to Liberia, born 2: 414
1816 Peace treaty made with the Dey of Algeria 8: 96
1817 David M. Stone, editor-in-chief of the New York "Journal of Commerce," born 1: 265
1823 Thomas W. Evans, dentist, born 9: 150
1832 Hiram A. Cutting, scientist and physician, born 10: 204
1840 R. Swain Gifford, painter, born 2: 482
1850 Oscar S. Straus, lawyer, diplomat, author, born . 10: 42
1852 Charles S. Minot, biologist, born 6: 112
1856 James B. Duke, tobacco manufacturer, born 17: 382
1862 President Davis proclaimed Gen. Butler an outlaw and a felon following the latter's issuance of his "Order No. 28" 1: 123
1862 Amos R. Wells, author and for 42 years editor of the "Christian Endeavor World," born 25: 163
1864 Powder boat "Louisiana" blown up to destroy Ft. Fisher, N. C. 4: 317
1913 The Glass-Owen bill, creating the Federal Reserve Bank, became a law 19: 3

DECEMBER 24.

1737 Silas Deane, diplomat, born 12: 357
1763 Abiel Holmes, clergyman, born 7: 148
1780 Willard Hall, Delaware jurist and congressman, born 11: 500
1784 Opening of the Christmas conference in Baltimore for the purpose of organizing the Methodist Episcopal church in the United States ... 6: 294
1789 Jackson Kemper, P. E. bishop, born 11: 57
1800 Robert B. Rhett, U. S. senator and an ardent secessionist, born 4: 303
1808 Henry Walke, Federal naval officer, born 6: 247
1809 Christopher (Kit) Carson, trapper and Indian agent, born 3: 273
1814 Treaty of peace with Great Britain signed at Ghent 5: 75
1815 Orrington Lunt, Chicago grain merchant and philanthropist, born 2: 213
1815 Henry Russell, composer, born 5: 249
1821 William Frederick Poole, librarian, originator of "Poole's Index," born 6: 478
1823 John R. Tucker, lawyer and congressman, born 7: 487
1825 Frederick B. Doolittle, agriculturist and pioneer Iowa citizen, born 15: 165
1839 Kinahan Cornwallis, journalist and author, born 22: 260
1840 James Stevenson, ethnologist and geologist, born 12: 556
1851 A fire in the national capital destroyed a large part of the Library of Congress 13: 170
1860 R. Clipston Sturgis, architect, born .... A: 368
1863 James Henry McRae, soldier, born .... B: 83
1864 Bombardment of Ft. Fisher, N. C., by the Federal fleet 2: 98
1881 Charles Wakefield Cadman, composer, born ..... B: 210

DECEMBER 25.

Christmas Day

1756 Simeon De Witt, scientist, chief geographer and surveyor-general to the United States, born .. 3: 215
1776 Washington crossed the Delaware and attacked Trenton, N. J. 1: 4
1776 John Slater, cotton manufacturer, born 8: 270
1778 Caleb Atwater, historian, born 22: 416
1779 Nashville, Tenn., founded 2: 221
1782 Nathaniel F. Moore, president of Columbia college, born 6: 345
1784 David Hoffman, jurist and historian, born 7: 129
1784 Christian Gobrecht, engraver for the U. S. mint, born 12: 145
1793 Edward T. Taylor, clergyman, born 13: 464
1808 Stephen C. Rowan, naval officer, born 2: 101
1810 Lorenzo L. Langstroth, the "father of American apiculture," who invented an improved bee hive, born 24: 399
1811 Gen. James Wilkinson, acquitted of scheming with Aaron Burr to found a southwestern empire 1: 57
1811 Eber B. Ward, manufacturer, lumberman and miner, born 13: 125
1813 Joseph Lovering, physicist, born 6: 425
1813 Milledge L. Bonham, Confederate soldier and governor of South Carolina, born 12: 173
1818 William H. Herndon, Lincoln's law partner and biographer, born 23: 29
1819 Eliza Greatorex, artist and illustrator, born 5: 521
1819 Nathan Barney, inventor and manufacturer of the automatic dumping boat, born 12: 375
1821 Clara Barton, humanitarian, first president of the American Association of the Red Cross, born.. 15: 314
1825 Newton Booth, U. S. senator and governor of California, born 4: 110
1828 Theodore L. De Vinne, printer, born 7: 67
1829 Patrick S. Gilmore, band leader and composer, born 3: 292
1831 John F. Dillon, jurist, born 1: 268
1837 Battle of Okechobee, Fla., with the Seminole Indians 4: 368
1837 Elbridge T. Gerry, lawyer and humanitarian, founder of the New York Society for the Prevention of Cruelty to Children, born 8: 242
1842 Battle of Mier, Mexico 11: 510
1846 Battle of Bracito river, Mexico 11: 389
1847 Frederick Dielman, artist, born 7: 471
1848 Charles N. Flagg, portrait painter, born 21: 142
1850 Herbert W. Pearson, geologist, born 18: 257
1850 Francis Blake, astronomer, and inventor of the Blake transmitter and other improvements on the telephone, born 22: 25
1851 Herman Frasch, chemist, founder of the sulphur industry in America, born 19: 347
1865 Evangeline Booth, for thirty years commander of the Salvation Army in America, born .... B: 127
1885 Paul Manship, sculptor, born .... C: 312
1888 David Lawrence, journalist and author, founder of the "United States Daily," born .... C: 468

DECEMBER 26.

1613 John Sherman, mathematician and clergyman, born 7: 75
1738 Thomas Nelson, Jr., a signer of the Declaration of Independence, born 7: 253
1778 Joseph C. Cabell, "the De Witt Clinton of Virginia," and, with Jefferson, a founder of the University of Virginia, born 22: 139
1803 Charles Cheney, silk manufacturer, born 19: 71
1804 William J. Snelling, author, editor of the Boston "Herald," born 2: 126
1811 Thomas A. Morris, engineer, born 10: 124
1819 Emma D. E. N. Southworth, author, born 1: 432
1822 Dion Boucicault, actor and playwright, born 2: 375
1828 Charles H. Loring, marine engineer, born 12: 502
1836 Charles H. Van Brunt, New York jurist, born .. 10: 141
1837 George Dewey, naval officer, hero of Manila bay, born 9: 3
1837 Morgan G. Bulkeley, governor of Connecticut, born 10: 345
1854 Eva March Tappan, author, born 22: 161
1856 John H. Long, chemist, born 19: 31
1860 Maj. Robert Anderson abandoned Ft. Moultrie and occupied Ft. Sumter, from which he was subsequently driven by Confederate forces 4: 179
1861 Capture of Tybee island by the Federals 5: 30
1861 Battle of Sacramento, Ky. 10: 36
1875 Edward T. Allen, specialist in forest protection and timber economy, forester for the Western Forestry and Conservation Association, born .. 18: 27
1917 Secretary of the Treasury McAdoo became director-general of the railroads for the duration of the war 19: 8

DECEMBER 27.

1719 John Phillips, founder of Phillips Exeter academy, born 10: 103
1767 Nicholas Roosevelt, who was associated with Robert Fulton in introducing the steamboat, born 12: 127
1771 William Johnson, associate justice of the U. S. supreme court, born 2: 467
1773 Jeremiah Atwater, president of Middlebury and Dickinson colleges, born 12: 105
1784 Lyne Starling, pioneer merchant of Columbus, Ohio, and founder of Starling medical college, born 12: 439
1794 William C. Preston, lawyer, U. S. senator and president of the College of South Carolina, born 11: 33
1798 William W. Corcoran, banker and philanthropist, born 3: 153
1809 Oliver Johnson, abolitionist, born 2: 319
1810 Roger N. Stembel, naval officer, born 5: 367
1831 Lucius Fairchild, Federal soldier, governor of Wisconsin and diplomat, born 12: 76
1844 Edward Judson, clergyman, founder of the Judson Memorial Church, New York city, born .. 12: 480
1846 John S. Wise, lawyer and author, born 11: 319
1862 Federal forces failed to capture Vicksburg 4: 32
1862 First Union League organized in Philadelphia .. 10: 206
1862 Julia Seton, founder of the New Thought movement, born 16: 295
1864 Peyton C. March, soldier, born .... A: 541
1882 Pendleton civil service bill passed 4: 248
1885 Frederick W. Sperr, chemist and inventor, dealing principally with coke and its by-products, born .... A: 264
1896 Louis Bromfield, author, born .... C: 295

DECEMBER 28.

1715 Samuel Curwen, loyalist, born 8: 163
1763 Nathaniel Massie, Ohio pioneer, born 2: 439
1788 Enoch Lincoln, lawyer and governor of Maine, born 6: 306
1789 Catharine M. Sedgwick, author, born 1: 446
1789 Thomas Ewing, U. S. senator, secretary of the treasury under Harrison and secretary of the interior under Taylor, born 25: 14
1810 Machine for making wrought-iron nails patented 11: 87
1814 Jeremiah Clemens, lawyer, author and U. S. senator, born 7: 234
1816 American Colonization Society organized 9: 179
1822 William R. Alger, author and clergyman, born .. 6: 34
1824 Thomas A. Scott, president of the Pennsylvania, the Union Pacific and the Texas Pacific railroads, born 13: 334
1827 Ward McAllister, lawyer and social leader, born 6: 169
1832 Ira G. Blake, inventor and manufacturer, born 13: 306
1835 William E. Chandler, secretary of the navy under McArthur, and U. S. senator, born 4: 252
1835 The Dade massacre occurred 12: 197
1837 Benjamin J. Lang, musician and composer, born 7: 430
1846 Homer N. Bartlett, musician and composer, born 7: 495
1846 Iowa admitted to the Union 11: 429
1849 Virginia W. Johnson (Cousin Virginia), author, born 13: 107
1856 Woodrow Wilson, 28th president of the United States, born 19: 1
1859 Frank W. Taussig, economist, born .... A: 457
1861 Confederates routed at Mount Zion, Mo. 5: 363
1862 Capture of Ft. Van Buren, Ark., by the Federals 9: 443
1871 Frank B. Willis, governor of Ohio and U. S. senator, born 21: 445
1888 Merle Crowell, editor, born .... C: 126
1917 U. S. government assumed control of the railroads as a war measure 20: 5

DECEMBER 29.

1752 Nathan Dane, author of the famous Ordinance of 1787, born 9: 196
1778 Savannah, Ga., taken by the British 6: 79
1779 John McDonogh, philanthropist, born 9: 465
1798 Laurens P. Hickok, clergyman and philosopher, president of Union college, born 7: 171
1800 Charles Goodyear, inventor of a process for vulcanizing rubber, born 3: 86
1804 John L. Sibley, librarian and author, born 11: 278
1805 Asa Packer, builder and president of the Lehigh Valley railroad and founder of Lehigh university, born 7: 110
1808 Andrew Johnson, 17th president of the United States, born 2: 454
1808 Edwards A. Park, theologian, born 9: 202
1809 Albert Pike, lawyer and poet, who became the highest Masonic dignitary in the United States, born 1: 527
1812 British "Java" destroyed by the "Constitution" .. 8: 94
1822 J. C. Bancroft Davis, lawyer and minister to Germany, born 11: 115
1827 Margaret Bottome, founder of the Order of the King's Daughters, born 13: 48
1831 Adam Badeau, soldier and author, born 6: 396
1833 John J. Ingalls, U. S. senator, born 8: 415
1835 Treaty of New Echota, in which the Cherokee Indians ceded their lands in Alabama, signed .. 10: 428
1840 George H. Smillie, landscape painter, born 8: 426
1845 Texas admitted to the Union 6: 267
1848 John Vance Cheney, poet and author, born 6: 289
1853 Horace Chilton, U. S. senator, born 2: 241
1855 George H. Pegram, civil engineer, born 9: 40
1855 William T. Sedgwick, biologist, born 13: 290
1862 Drumgoold's Bluff on the Yazoo river attacked by the Federals 13: 425
1865 Salmon Oliver Levinson, publicist and lawyer, born .... C: 510
1901 The "Pillar of Fire" church founded by Bishop Alma White .... B: 208

DECEMBER 30.

1678 Henry Chicheley became deputy governor of Virginia 13: 385
1722 Nathaniel Woodhull, soldier, born 5: 423
1784 Stephen H. Long, engineer, born 11: 365
1799 Hiram A. and John A. Pitts (twins), inventors of threshing machines, born 13: 251
1808 Thomas T. Craven, Federal naval officer, born .. 12: 370
1813 Joel T. Headley, author, born 3: 458
1819 John W. Geary, Federal soldier and governor of Kansas and Pennsylvania, born 2: 291
1822 Cornelius G. Fenner, poet, born 8: 43
1828 Charter granted for Hanover college 2: 123
1830 Francis M. Drake, Federal soldier and governor of Iowa, born 11: 434
1833 Andrew M. Davis, antiquarian, born 22: 453
1844 Charles A. Coffin, founder and president of the General Electric Co., born 20: 20
1853 The Gadsden purchase negotiated by the United States 12: 69
1861 The greenback or legal tender bill introduced in Congress 6: 356
1862 Battle at Parker's Cross-Roads, Tenn. 10: 36
1863 William Hallock Park, bacteriologist, who produced the first diphtheria anti-toxin in America, born .... C: 314
1873 Alfred E. Smith, governor of New York, born .. A: 404
1905 The murder of ex-Governor Steunenberg climaxed the Idaho mine labor troubles 21: 7

DECEMBER 31.

1744 Edward Hand, soldier, born 1: 75
1775 American forces repulsed at Quebec; Gen. Montgomery killed 1: 101
1780 Nehemiah R. Knight, U. S. senator and governor of Rhode Island, born 9: 394
1783 Joseph G. Swift, soldier and engineer, born 10: 17
1786 Andrews Norton, theologian and author, born .. 7: 63
1803 George Lunt, author and poet, born 6: 536
1806 William McC. Thomson, clergyman, born 11: 57
1809 Pliny Earle, physician, born 11: 146
1815 George G. Meade, soldier, born 4: 66
1817 James T. Fields, publisher and author, born 1: 283
1824 Theodore M. Pomeroy, congressman, born 12: 255
1824 Alexander Winchell, geologist, chancellor of Syracuse university, born 16: 119
1831 The Granville literary and theological institute (Denison university) formally opened 1: 301
1833 Hussey's mowing and reaping machine patented (antedating McCormick's) 11: 361
1835 Battle of the Ouithlacoochee, Fla. 9: 211
1837 John R. Sweney, composer, born 4: 350
1837 John T. Fanning, civil engineer and inventor, born 9: 38
1839 First of the Lowell institution lectures delivered 7: 195
1844 John B. Smithman, pioneer oil promoter, born .. 25: 400
1847 Wilson S. Bissell, postmaster general under Cleveland, born 13: 117
1850 James I. Good, clergyman and historian, born .. 5: 360
1851 Henry C. Adams, political economist and statistician, born 12: 219
1853 Tasker H. Bliss, army officer and a member of the supreme war council of the World war, born 21: 86
1858 Harry S. New, U. S. senator and postmaster general under Harding, born .... A: 13
1861 Federal naval force captured Biloxi, Miss. 5: 52
1862 Battle of Murfreesboro or Stone River, Tenn., began 4: 163
1862 The iron-clad "Monitor" foundered at sea 5: 366
1923 First complete radio program broadcast to Europe 25: 18
1890 Ellis island immigration depot opened 11: 329

INDEX

A

B

C

D

E

F

G

H

I

J

K

L

M

N

O

P

T

U

V

W

Y

Z

ATTENTION REFERENCE LIBRARIAN

IMPORTANT REFERENCE MATERIAL

The following list refers to names already appearing in WHITE'S CONSPECTUS OF AMERICAN BIOGRAPHY whose biographies have just been published in Volume XXVIII of THE NATIONAL CYCLOPEDIA OF AMERICAN BIOGRAPHY. They represent:

1. Biographies which appeared in previous volumes prior to death and which have been republished in Volume XXVIII in final form
2. Biographies published for the first time in the Cyclopedia.

Our suggestion is that a member of your staff make the necessary insertions and alterations in your copy of WHITE'S CONSPECTUS in order that your readers may have access to the latest biographies.

JAMES T. WHITE & COMPANY, Publishers
70 Fifth Avenue, New York, N.Y.

* *

CONSPECTUS PAGE NO.	GROUP	SUBJECT	Vol. XXVIII PAGE NO.
5	Secretaries of State (1925)	Kellogg, Frank B.	28:3
6	Secretaries of Treasury (1921)	Mellon, Andrew W.	28:336
9	Postmasters-General (1913)	Burleson, Albert S.	28:386
17	Comptrollers of the Currency (1886)	Trenholm, William L.	28:376
17	Treasurers of the U.S. (1887)	Hyatt, James W.	28:282
17	Treasurers of the U.S. (1893)	Morgan, Daniel N.	28:21
17	Commissioners of Internal Revenue (1896)	Forman, William St. J.	28:312
17	Chiefs of Staff (1910)	Wood, Leonard	28:107
17	Judge Advocate Generals (1901)	Barr, Thomas F.	28:178
18	Quartermaster Generals (1896)	Sawtelle, Charles G.	28:360
19	Chiefs of the Bureau of Construction and Repair (1910)	Watt, Richard M.	28:19
19	Chiefs of the Bureau of Medicine and Surgery (1893)	Tryon, J. Rufus	28:102
19	Commissioners of Education (1906)	Brown, Elmer E.	28:323
19	Commissioners of Education (1929)	Cooper, William J.	28:371
19	Pension Commissioners (1897)	Evans, Henry C.	28:128
19	Pension Commissioners (1913)	Saltzgaber, Gaylord M.	28:414
20	Commissioners of Patents (1869)	Fisher, Samuel S.	28:91
20	Chairmen, Interstate Commerce Commission (1915 & 1921)	McChord, Charles C.	28:398
20	Chairmen, Board of Governors, Federal Reserve (1914)	Hamlin, Charles S.	28:448
20	" " " (1916)	Harding, Warren P.G.	28:315
20	" " " (1933)	Black, Eugene R.	28:383
20	Chairmen, Federal Trade Com. (1918)	Colver, William B.	28:278
22	Fourth Circuit (1922-27)	Rose, John C.	28:302
22	Fifth Circuit (1914-36)	Walker, Richard W.	28:425
22	Sixth Circuit (1910-30)	Knappen, Loyal E.	28:241
22	Sixth Circuit (1919-28)	Donahue, Maurice H.	28:293
22	Seventh Circuit (1905-18)	Kohlsaat, Christian C.	28:442
23	Court of Claims-Chief Justices (1896)	Nott, Charles C.	28:10
23	Court of Claims–Associate (1865)	Nott, Charles C.	28:10
23	Court of Claims–Associate (1906)	Barney, Samuel S.	28:86
23	Permanent Court of International Justice (1930)	Kellogg, Frank B.	28:3
24	Belgium (1911)	Anderson, Larz	28:274
25	Canada (1933)	Robbins, Warren D.	28:110
25	Cuba (1913)	Gonzales, William E.	28:277
25	Cuba (1927)	Judah, Nobel B.	28:142
26	El Salvador (1928)	Robbins, Warren D.	28:110
27	France (1897)	Porter, Horace	28:285
27	Great Britain (1923)	Kellogg, Frank B.	28:3
27	Great Britain (1932)	Mellon, Andrew W.	28:336
27	Guatemala (1908)	Heimke, William	28:462
27	Guatemala (1910)	Hitt, Robert S.R.	28:103
28	Japanese Empire (1912)	Anderson, Larz	28:274
28	Korea (1890)	Heard, Augustine	28:327
28	Korea (1897)	Allen, Horace N.	28:282
29	Netherlands (1921)	Ramer, John E.	28:316
29	Panama (1909)	Hitt, Robert S.R.	28:103
30	Peru (1919)	Gonzales, William E.	28:277
30	Poland (1930)	Willys, John N.	28:42
44-45	50th through 55th Congresses	Faulkner, Charles J.	28:346
47-52	60th through 74th Congresses	Borah, William E.	28:1
47	60th and 61st Congresses	Frazier, James B.	28:106
48-50	62nd through 67th Congresses	Pomerene, Atlee	28:129
48-49	63rd through 65th Congresses	Lewis, J. Hamilton	28:38
49-50	65th through 67th Congresses	Kellogg, Frank B.	28:3
49-50	65th through 67th Congresses	Wolcott, Josiah O.	28:45
51	72nd Congress	Cohen, John S.	28:259

CONSPECTUS PAGE NO.	GROUP	SUBJECT	Vol. XXVIII PAGE NO.
51-52	72nd through 74th Congresses	Carey, Robert D.	28:30
52	72nd through 74th Congresses	Lewis, J. Hamilton	28:38
111	Arizona - Governors (1933)	Moeur, Benjamin B.	28:422
117	Delaware - U.S. Senators (1917)	Wolcott, Josiah O.	28:45
120	Georgia - U.S. Senators (1932)	Cohen, John S.	28:259
121	Idaho - U.S. Senators (1907)	Borah, William E.	28:1
122	Illinois - U.S. Senators (1913)	Lewis, J. Hamilton	28:38
122	Illinois - U.S. Senators (1931)	Lewis, J. Hamilton	28:38
124	Iowa - Governors (1913)	Clarke, George W.	28:410
124	Iowa - Governors (1917)	Harding, William L.	28:41
124	Iowa - Chief Justices (1909)	Evans, William D.	28:330
124	Iowa - Chief Justices (1916)	Evans, William D.	28:330
124	Iowa - Chief Justices (1921)	Evans, William D.	28:330
125	Iowa - Chief Justices (1927)	Evans, William D.	28:330
128	Louisiana - Governors (1932)	Allen, Oscar K.	28:435
135	Michigan - Governors (1927)	Green, Fred W.	28:471
136	Minnesota - U.S. Senators (1917)	Kellogg, Frank B.	28:3
141	Nevada - Chief Justices (1919)	Coleman, Benjamin W.	28:340
150	North Dakota - Chief Justices (1917)	Bruce, Andrew A.	28:445
152	Ohio - U.S. Senators (1911)	Pomerene, Atlee	28:129
155	Pennsylvania - Chief Justices (1930)	Frazer, Robert S.	28:229
160	South Carolina - Governors (1931)	Blackwood, Ibra C.	28:220
161	Tennessee - Governors (1903)	Frazier, James B.	28:106
161	Tennessee - U.S. Senators (1905)	Frazier, James B.	28:106
168	West Virginia - U.S. Senators (1887)	Faulkner, Charles J.	28:346
169	Wyoming - Governors (1919)	Carey, Robert D.	28:30
169	Wyoming - U.S. Senators (1931)	Carey, Robert D.	28:30
170	Amherst College Observatory (1881)	Todd, David P.	28:35
171	Atlanta University (1929)	Hope, John	28:344
174	Howard University (1906)	Thirkield, Wilbur P.	28:393
175	Iowa State Agricultural College (1883)	Knapp, Seaman A.	28:401
175	Iowa State Agricultural College (1886)	Chamberlain, William I.	28:426
176	University of Maryland (1894)	Carter, Bernard	28:61
176	University of Missouri (1922)	Jones, John C.	28:337
176	University of Missouri (1930)	Williams, Walter	28:137
177	New York University (1911)	Brown, Elmer E.	28:323
177	University of North Carolina (1900)	Venable, Francis P.	28:427
177	University of Oregon (1876)	Johnson, John W.	28:8
179	Swarthmore College (1889)	Appleton, William H.	28:290
179	Tulane University (1918)	Dinwiddie, Albert B.	28:124
180	University of Utah (1897)	Kingsbury, Joseph T.	28:348
181	West Virginia University (1901)	Purinton, Daniel B.	28:354
182	Amn. Anthropological Assn. (1927)	Saville, Marshall H.	28:468
182	Amn. Assn. for Advancement of Science (1881)	Brush, George J.	28:198
183	Amn. Assn. for Advancement of Science (1933)	Abel, John J.	28:23
184	American Bar Association (1912)	Kellogg, Frank B.	28:3
184	American Chemical Society (1905)	Venable, Francis P.	28:427
184	American College of Surgeons (1931)	Kanavel, Allen B.	28:17
185	American Fine Arts Society (1889)	Butler, Howard R.	28:176
185	American Forestry Association (1916)	Pack, Charles L.	28:125
185	American Gynecological Society (1915)	Watkins, Thomas J.	28:275
186	American Historical Association (1918)	Thayer, William R.	28:427
186	American Historical Association (1922)	Haskins, Charles H.	28:183
186	Amn. Inst. Consulting Engineers (1926)	Parsons, Harry de B.	28:82
186	Amn. Inst. Electrical Engineers (1923)	Ryan, Harris J.	28:421
186	Amn. Inst. Mining and Metallurgical Engineers (1924)	Kelly, William	28:102
186	" " (1929)	Bradley, Frederick W.	28:133
186	" " (1931)	Tally, Robert E.	28:216
188	Amn. Neurological Assn. (1899)	Lloyd, James H.	28:446
188	Amn. Neurological Assn. (1903)	Putnam, James W.	28:328
188	Amn. Neurological Assn. (1929)	Frazier, Charles H.	28:397
188	Amn. Ophthalmological Society (1879)	Noyes, Henry D.	28:122
188	Amn. Ophthalmological Society (1920)	Woods, Hiram	28:90
188	Amn. Orthopaedic Assn. (1898)	Lovett, Robert W.	28:470
188	Amn. Orthopaedic Assn. (1924)	Baer, William S.	28:14
189	Amn. Philological Assn. (1904)	Smyth, Herbert W.	28:215
189	Amn. Philological Assn. (1914)	Morris, Edward P.	28:56
189	Amn. Philological Assn. (1923)	Bassett, Samuel E.	28:218
189	Amn. Philological Assn. (1925)	Fairclough, Henry R.	28:413
191	Amn. Soc. Biological Chemists (1908)	Abel, John J.	28:24
191	Amn. Soc. of Civil Engineers (1917)	Pegram, George H.	28:296
191	Amn. Soc. of Civil Engineers (1934)	Eddy, Harrison P.	28:266
192	Amn. Society of Zoologists (1911)	Wilson, Henry V.	28:321
192	Amn. Surgical Assn. (1933)	Jones, Daniel F.	28:31
193	Chamber of Commerce of U.S. (1928)	Butterworth, William	28:253
194	Franklin Institute (1907)	Clark, Walton	28:101
196	National Tuberculosis Assn. (1922)	Brown, Lawrason	28:130
196	Soc. American Bacteriologists (1915)	Bergey, David H.	28:338
198	Architectural League of N.Y. (1917)	Pope, John Russell	28:120
198	Architectural League of N.Y. (1926)	Hood, Raymond M.	28:389
200	Chemists Medal (1931)	Mellon, Andrew W.	28:336
204	Edison Medal (1918)	Lamme, Benjamin G.	28:271
205	Willard Gibbs Medal (1927)	Abel, John J.	28:23
208	George M. Kober Medal (1934)	Abel, John J.	28:23
208	Laetare Medal (1901)	Cockran, William B.	28:385
208	Laetare Medal (1920)	Flick, Lawrence F.	28:435

CONSPECTUS PAGE NO.	GROUP	SUBJECT	Vol. XXVIII PAGE NO.
209	Edward Longstreth Medal (1894)	Johnston, Andrew L.	28:368
209	Edward Longstreth Medal (1909)	Crisfield, J.A.P.	28:153
211	Nat. Inst. of Arts & Letters Gold Medal (1918)	Thayer, William R.	28:427
211	" " " " " " (1931)	Gillette, William	28:362
212	Nat. Inst. of Social Sciences Gold Medal (1926)	Cadman, S. Parkes	28:193
212	Alfred B. Nobel Prize in Peace (1929)	Kellogg, Frank B.	28:3
213	Norman Medal (1915)	Hazen, Allen M.	28:342
213	Norman Medal (1925)	Eddy, Harrison P.	28:266
215	Pulitzer Prize for American Play (1925)	Howard, Sidney C.	28:469
215	Roosevelt Medal (1923)	Wood, Leonard	28:109
216	Thomas Fitch Rowland Prize (1900)	Hazen, Allen	28:342
216	Thomas Fitch Rowland Prize (1925)	Parsons, Harry de B.	28:82
217	William Lawrence Saunders Medal (1932)	Bradley, Frederick W.	28:134
217	Spingarn Medal (1936)	Hope, John	28:344
223	American Episcopates (1899)	Kinsolving, Lucien L.	28:160
231	" " (Southern Brazil-1907)	Kinsolving, Lucien L.	28:160
240	Methodist Episcopal Bishops (1912)	Thirkield, Wilbur P.	28:393
240	Methodist Episcopal Bishops (1920)	Fisher, Fred B.	28:149
241	Amn. Museum of Natural History (1924)	Sherwood, George H.	28:205
246	Conventions Signed Oct. 19, 1907	Porter, Horace	28:285
248	Fifth Intl. Conference in 1923	Kellogg, Frank B.	28:3
248	Fifth Intl. Conference in 1923	Pomerene, Atlee	28:129
249	Conventions Signed Feb. 20, 1928	Judah, Noble B.	28:142
249	Conventions Signed Feb. 20, 1928	O'Brien, Morgan J.	28:95
249	Pact of Paris	Kellogg, Frank B.	28:3
249	Inter-American Arbitration Treaty	Kellogg, Frank B.	28:3
249	Conv. of Inter-American Conciliation	Kellogg, Frank B.	28:3
306	Actors and Actresses (1876)	Gillette, William	28:362
309	Artists (1888)	Butler, Howard R.	28:176
310	Astronomers (1875)	Todd, David	28:35
315	Chemists (1848)	Doremus, Robert O.	28:275
316	Chemists (1880)	Venable, Frank P.	28:427
316	Chemists (1883)	Abel, John J.	28:23
317	Civil Engineers (1877)	Pegram, George H.	28:296
319	Clergymen (1843)	Allen, Joseph H.	28:443
320	Clergymen (1889)	Cadman, S. Parkes	28:192
322	Educators (1878)	Brown, Elmer E.	28:323
323	Educators (1891)	Dinwiddie, Albert B.	28:124
324	Electrical Engineers (1888)	Lamme, Benjamin G.	28:270
324	Entomologists (1890)	Kellogg, Vernon L.	28:354
325	Foresters (1878)	Pack, Charles L.	28:125
326	Geologists (1899)	Pirsson, Louis V.	28:199
327	Historians (1889)	Haskins, Charles H.	28:183
332	Journalists (1848)	Noyes, Crosby S.	28:363
332	Journalists (1857)	Scripps, James E.	28:164
333	Journalists (1884)	Williams, Walter	28:187
333	Journalists (1886)	Cohen, John S.	28:258
334	Jurists (1865)	Nott, Charles C.	28:10
335	Lawyers and Judges (1851)	Nott, Charles C.	28:10
335	Lawyers and Judges (1820)	Conyngham, John N.	28:383
337	Lawyers and Judges (1874)	O'Brien, Morgan J.	28:95
337	Lawyers and Judges (1881)	Morawetz, Victor	28:11
337	Lawyers and Judges (1886)	Pomerene, Atlee	28:129
340	Mathematicians (1887)	Morley, Frank	28:330
340	Mechanical Engineers (1841)	Worthington, Henry R.	28:206
341	Military Surgeons (1885)	Wood, Leonard	28:107
341	Mineralogists (1855)	Brush, George J.	28:197
341	Mining & Metallurgical Engineers (1855)	Brush, George J.	28:197
343	Naturalists (1854)	Ward, Henry A.	28:169
344	Neurologists (1889)	Donaldson, Henry H.	28:374
344	Ophthalmologists (1883)	Culver, Charles M.	28:104
345	Orthopaedic Surgeons (1886)	Lovett, Robert W.	28:470
347	Philanthropists (1913)	Mellon, Andrew W.	28:336
347	Philologists (1879)	Morris, Edward P.	28:56
347	Philologists (1883)	Fairclough, Henry R.	28:413
347	Philologists (1883)	Smyth, Herbert W.	28:215
351	Playwrights (1884)	Gillette, William	28:362
356	Theologians (1890)	Cadman, S. Parkes	28:192
356	Zoologists (1890)	Kellogg, Vernon L.	28:354
360	French Legion of Honor-Grand Cross (1929)	Kellogg, Frank B.	28:3
360	French Legion of Honor-Grand Officer (1930)	Gilbert, S. Parker	28:331
363	January 11, 1824	Robert Ogden Doremus	28:275
376	March 9, 1834	Henry A. Ward	28:169
378	March 19, 1835	James E. Scripps	28:164
378	March 19, 1855	David P. Todd	28:35
392	May 19, 1857	John Jacob Abel	28:23
396	June 7, 1876	R.S. Reynolds Hitt	28:103
400	June 23, 1857	William Kelly	28:102
402	June 29, 1865	William E. Borah	28:1
407	July 19, 1846	John Graham Brooks	28:449
408	July 24, 1851	William Gillette	28:362
415	August 30, 1861	Charles S. Hamlin	28:448
420	September 16, 1827	Charles C. Nott	28:10
424	October 3, 1877	William L. Harding	28:44
425	October 9, 1860	Leonard Wood	28:107
434	November 17, 1856	Francis P. Venable	28:427

CONSPECTUS PAGE NO.	GROUP	SUBJECT	Vol. XXVIII PAGE NO.
440	December 15, 1831	George J. Brush	28:197
441	December 21, 1870	Charles H. Haskins	28:183
442	December 22, 1856	Frank B. Kellogg	28:3